Occupational Outlook Handbook

2016–2017

U.S. Department of Labor
Thomas E. Perez, Secretary

Bureau of Labor Statistics
Erica L. Groshen, Commissioner

Bulletin 2700

Exclusive to JIST Career Solutions' *OOH*:

- **"The Personality-Career Quiz: Match Your Personality to *OOH* Jobs"**
- **"How Educators, Counselors, Librarians, and Business Professionals Can Best Use the *OOH*"**
- **"Best 100 Jobs in the *Occupational Outlook Handbook*"**

Introduction

The *Occupational Outlook Handbook* is a nationally recognized source of career information, designed to provide valuable assistance to individuals making decisions about their future work lives. Revised every two years, the *Handbook* describes what workers do on the job, working conditions, the training and education needed, earnings, and expected job prospects in a wide range of occupations.

Employment in the hundreds of occupations discussed in detail in the 2016–2017 *Handbook* accounts for 8 of every 10 jobs in the economy. Combined with the updated special features of the *Handbook*, the occupational information presented in this new edition provides invaluable assistance to individuals making decisions about their future work lives.

CAREER SOLUTIONS
JIST

St. Paul

Senior Vice President Linda Hein
Editor in Chief Christine Hurney
Contributing Editor and Indexer Laurence Shatkin, PhD.
Assistant Developmental Editor Katie Werdick
Director of Production Timothy W. Larson
Production Editor Shannon Kottke
Cover Designer Jack Ross
Production Specialist Kristin Goble
Proofreader Margaret Trejo
Product Manager Selena Hicks

About career materials published by JIST. Our materials encourage people to be self-directed and to take control of their destinies. We work hard to provide excellent content, solid advice, current labor market information, and techniques that get results. Visit www.jist.com for information on JIST, free job search information, tables of contents, sample pages, and ordering information on our many products.

Minor differences exist between this edition and the web-based *Occupational Outlook Handbook*, as released by the U.S. Department of Labor in December 2015. Most of these differences occur in the photographic images. JIST has also added useful bonus content to this edition.

Important Note

Many trade associations, professional societies, unions, industrial organizations, and government agencies provide career information that is valuable to counselors and jobseekers. For the convenience of *Occupational Outlook Handbook (OOH)* users, some of these organizations and their Internet addresses are listed at the end of each occupational profile. Although these references were carefully compiled, the Bureau of Labor Statistics has neither the authority nor the facilities for investigating the organizations or the information or publications that may be sent to the Bureau in response to a request. As a result, the Bureau cannot guarantee the accuracy of such information and the listing of an organization does not constitute in any way an endorsement or recommendation by the Bureau, either of the organization and its activities or of the information it may supply. Each organization has sole responsibility for whatever information it may issue.

The *OOH* describes the job outlook over a projected 10-year period for occupations across the nation; consequently, short-term labor market fluctuations and regional differences in job outlook generally are not discussed. Similarly, the *OOH* provides a general, composite description of jobs and cannot be expected to reflect work situations in specific establishments or localities. The *OOH*, therefore, is not intended, and should never be used, for any legal purpose. For example, the *OOH* should not be used as a guide for determining wages, hours of work, the right of a particular union to represent workers, appropriate bargaining units, or formal job evaluation systems. Nor should wage data in the *OOH* be used to compute the future loss of earnings in adjudication proceedings involving work injuries or accidental deaths.

The Bureau of Labor Statistics has no role in establishing educational, licensing, or practicing standards for any occupation; any such standards are established by national accrediting organizations and are merely reported by the Bureau in the *OOH*. The education information provided by the *OOH* pertains to the typical requirements for entry into the given occupation and does not describe the education and training of those individuals already employed in the occupation. In addition, education requirements for occupations may change over time and often vary by employer or state. Therefore, the information in the *OOH* should not be used to determine if an applicant is qualified to enter a specific job in an occupation.

All text, charts, and tables presented are in the public domain, and, with appropriate credit, may be reproduced without permission. Most photographs and illustrations are protected by copyright. Comments about the contents of this publication and suggestions for improving it are welcome. Address all comments to Chief, Division of Occupational Employment Projections, Office of Occupational Statistics and Employment Projections, Bureau of Labor Statistics, U.S. Department of Labor, 2 Massachusetts Ave. NE, Room 2135, Washington, DC 20212. Phone: (202) 691-5700. Fax: (202) 691-5745. Additional information is available at www.bls.gov/ooh/. Information in the *OOH* is available upon request to individuals with sensory impairments. Voice phone: (202) 691-5200; Federal Relay Service: (800) 877-8339.

ISBN 978-0-7638-7213-7 (digital)
ISBN 978-1-6333-2139-7 (softcover)
ISBN 978-1-6333-2138-0 (hardcover)

875 Montreal Way
St. Paul, MN 55102
E-mail: info@jist.com
Website: www.jist.com

Printed in the United States of America
21 20 19 18 17 16 1 2 3 4 5 6

Contents

Special Features

Occupational Coverage

Acknowledgments

The Bureau of Labor Statistics produces the *Occupational Outlook Handbook* under the general guidance and direction of Rebecca Rust, Assistant Commissioner for Occupational Statistics and Employment Projections, and Kristina J. Bartsch, former Division Chief of Occupational Employment Projections. Roger J. Moncarz, Teresa L. Morisi, and Francisco Velez Jr., Branch Chiefs of Occupational Outlook Studies, provided planning and day-to-day direction.

Technical leads reviewing the research and preparation of material were Andrew J. Hogan, Stanislava Ilic-Godfrey, Henry T. Kasper, T. Alan Lacey, Andrew G. O'Bar, Emily Richards, and Craig Stalzer. Occupational analysts who contributed material were Vidalina Alpuerto-Abadam, Domingo Angeles, Jennifer Chi, Christopher Harper, Erin Lane, William Lawhorn, Sean Martin, Kevin M. McCarron, Michael J. Rieley, Patricia Tate, Jeffrey Wilkins, and Alan Zilberman.

Editorial work was provided by staff in the Office of Publications: Edith S. Baker, Peter C. Fisk, John C. Roach, and Maureen E. Soyars, under the supervision of Leslie Brown Joyner, Branch Chief of Special Publications, Terry L. Schau, Monthly Labor Review Branch Chief, and Emily Liddel, Division Chief of Publishing. Data-processing and technical support were provided by C. Brett Lockard, Brian Roberts, D. Terkanian, and Dalton B. Terrell, under the supervision of Michael Wolf. Technical and computer-programming support was provided by Kristyn Jeschelnik, Jerie Refugia, Dinara Sagatova, Roopa Sengupta, Connie Sielaff, and Reginald Simmons, all of the Office of Technology and Survey Processing, under the supervision of Jo-Ann Yu, Branch Chief, and Amrit Kohli, Division Chief of Enterprise Web Systems.

The majority of photographs used in this edition of the *OOH* are in the public domain; however, JIST Career Solutions wishes to express its appreciation to the organizations that contributed photographs. Situations portrayed in the photographs may not be free of every possible safety or health hazard. The depiction of a company or trade name in no way constitutes endorsement by the U.S. Department of Labor.

Many of the public-domain photographs were created by the New Jersey Department of Labor.

The photograph used for Industrial Engineers was obtained from the U.S. Department of Energy.

The photograph used for Mining and Geological Engineers was taken by William C. Haneberg, PhD, and is used with the permission of GeoTek Solutions.

The photograph used for Industrial Designers is used with the permission of Beyond Design, Inc., which holds the copyright (2015).

The photograph used for Health Educators was taken by Dawn Arlotta and is used with the permission of the Centers for Disease Control and Prevention.

The photograph used for Ironworkers is used with the permission of the Washington State Department of Transportation.

The photograph used for Medical Transcriptionists is used with the permission of Des Moines Area Community College.

The photograph used for Nursing Aides, Orderlies, and Attendants was taken by Rhoda Baer and is used with the permission of the National Cancer Institute (http://www.cancer.gov).

The photograph used for Occupational Therapy Assistants and Aides was taken by Amanda Mills and is used with the permission of the Centers for Disease Control and Prevention.

The photograph used for Psychiatric Technicians and Aides was taken by the Mathews Media Group and is used with the permission of the National Cancer Institute (http://www.cancer.gov).

The photograph used for Medical Equipment Repairers is used with the permission of Ardus Medical, Inc.

The photograph used for Anthropologists and Archeologists is used with the permission of the Kentucky Archaeological Survey.

The photograph used for Environmental Science and Protection Technicians was taken by Ron Nichols and is used with the permission of the USDA Natural Resources Conservation Service.

The photograph used for Forensic Science Technicians was taken by Airman 1st Class Melissa Rodrigues and is used with the permission of the United States Air Force Office of Special Investigations.

The photograph used for Librarians is under copyright © by Garrett Brown and used with the permission of the UC Santa Barbara Library.

The photograph used for Medical Scientists was taken by Scott Bauer and is used with the permission of the U.S. Department of Agriculture, Agricultural Research Service.

The photograph used for Microbiologists is used with the permission of the Centers for Disease Control and Prevention.

The photograph used for Wildlife Biologists is used with the permission of the National Parks Service.

The photograph used for Computer Network Architects was taken by Maggie Bartlett and is used with the permission of the National Human Genome Research Institute (www.genome.gov).

The photograph used for Web Developers is used with the permission of the Centers for Disease Control and Prevention.

The photograph used for Butchers was taken by Mo Riza and is licensed under the Creative Commons Attribution 2.0 Generic license. It was originally posted at www.flickr.com/photos/moriza/62054214/sizes/l/.

The photograph used for Emergency Management Directors was taken by Jocelyn Augustino and is used with the permission of the Federal Emergency Management Administration.

The photograph used for Genetic Counselors is used with the permission of the Centers for Disease Control and Prevention.

The photograph used for Nurse Anesthetists, Nurse Midwives, and Nurse Practitioners is used with the permission of the Department of Nurse Anesthesia Education, University of Kansas.

The photograph used for Phlebotomists is used with the permission of the U.S. Department of Veterans Affairs.

The photograph used for Public Relations Specialists was taken by Jocelyn Augustino and is used with the permission of the Federal Emergency Management Administration.

The photograph used for School Career Counselors, "Marines see their shadow on Groundhog Day job tour" by Lance Cpl. Glen Santy, is licensed under public domain.

The photograph used for Social Workers, "Exodus Transitional Community 1" by David Shankbone, is licensed under CC BY 3.0.

The photograph used for Software Developers, "Programmer writing code with Unit Tests" by Joonspoon, is licensed under CC BY-SA 4.0.

The photograph used for Surveying and Mapping Technicians, "Chicago surveyor" by Daniel Schwen, is licensed under CC BY-SA 4.0.

The photograph used for Water Transportation Workers, "ZSG–Bachtel 2010-08-31 18-51-22" by Roland zh, is licensed under CC BY-SA 3.0.

The photograph used for Web Developers, "CSIRO ScienceImage 8131 The computer lab on RV Southern Surveyor" by James Porteous of CSIRO, is licensed under CC BY 3.0.

The photograph used for Exercise Physiologists, taken from the YouTube video "HIT–The benefits of high-intensity workouts" by SBS World News and The Conversation, is licensed under CC BY.

The Personality-Career Quiz: Match Your Personality to *OOH* Jobs

With so many occupations to choose from, you might appreciate some help narrowing down your options. That's what this chapter is for. In the following pages, you'll gain some insights into the work-related aspects of your personality and learn which careers in the *OOH* best suit your personality. Of course, personality is not the only factor you should consider when you make a career choice. But it's a good place to start because it provides a big-picture view of the world of work.

In the early 1950s, John L. Holland developed the most widely used personality theory about careers. The theory says that people tend to be happier and more successful in jobs in which they feel comfortable with the work tasks, the physical environment, and their coworkers. Holland identified six personality types that describe basic aspects of work situations:

- Realistic
- Investigative
- Artistic
- Social
- Enterprising
- Conventional

The initials spell RIASEC, so that acronym is often used to refer to the personality types.

Holland argued that most people can be described by one of the RIASEC personality types—and that likewise each of the various occupations that make up our economy can be described as having work situations and settings compatible with one of these personality types. Therefore, if you understand your dominant personality type, jobs consistent with that type will suit you best.

Holland recognized that many people and jobs also tend toward a second or third personality type—for example, someone might be described primarily as Social and secondarily as Enterprising. That person would fit best in a job with the "SE" code, such as Health Educators. People like this should also consider jobs coded "ES," and they might find satisfaction in many jobs with a variety of Holland codes beginning with either S or E.

This exercise helps you clarify your main personality type or types. Keep in mind that personality measurement is not an exact science and this checklist is not scientific. Use common sense to combine your results with other information about yourself and your work options.

The exercise is easy—just follow the directions. This is not a test, so there are no right or wrong answers and no time limit.

If someone else will be using this book, write your responses on a separate sheet of paper.

Step 1: Respond to the Statements

Carefully read each work activity (items 1 through 120). If you think you would LIKE to do the activity, circle the number of the activity. Don't consider whether you have the education or training needed for it or how much money you might earn if it were part of your job. Simply decide whether you would *like* the activity. If you know you would dislike the activity or you're not sure, leave the number unmarked.

After you respond to all 120 activities, score your responses in Step 2.

Circle the numbers of the activities you would LIKE to do.

1. Build kitchen cabinets
2. Guard money in an armored car
3. Operate a dairy farm
4. Lay brick or tile
5. Monitor a machine on an assembly line
6. Repair household appliances
7. Drive a taxicab
8. Assemble electronic parts
9. Drive a truck to deliver packages to offices and homes
10. Paint houses
11. Enforce fish and game laws
12. Work on an offshore oil-drilling rig
13. Perform lawn care services
14. Catch fish as a member of a fishing crew
15. Refinish furniture
16. Fix a broken faucet
17. Do cleaning or maintenance work
18. Test the quality of parts before shipment
19. Operate a motorboat to carry passengers
20. Put out forest fires

__________ **Total Score for R**

Circle the numbers of the activities you would LIKE to do.

21. Study the history of past civilizations
22. Study animal behavior
23. Develop a new medicine
24. Study ways to reduce water pollution
25. Determine the infection rate of a new disease
26. Study rocks and minerals
27. Diagnose and treat sick animals
28. Study the personalities of world leaders
29. Study whales and other types of marine life
30. Investigate crimes
31. Study the movement of planets
32. Examine blood samples by using a microscope
33. Investigate the cause of a fire
34. Develop psychological profiles of criminals
35. Invent a replacement for sugar
36. Study genetics
37. Study the governments of different countries
38. Do research on plants or animals
39. Do laboratory tests to identify diseases
40. Study weather conditions

__________ **Total Score for I**

41. Direct a play
42. Create dance routines for a show
43. Write books or plays
44. Play a musical instrument
45. Write reviews of books or plays
46. Compose or arrange music
47. Act in a movie
48. Dance in a Broadway show
49. Draw pictures
50. Create special effects for movies
51. Conduct a musical choir
52. Audition singers and musicians for a musical show
53. Design sets for plays
54. Announce a radio show
55. Write a song
56. Perform jazz or tap dance
57. Direct a movie
58. Sing in a band
59. Design artwork for magazines
60. Pose for a photographer

__________ **Total Score for A**

Circle the numbers of the activities you would LIKE to do.

61. Perform nursing duties in a hospital
62. Give CPR to someone who has stopped breathing
63. Help people with personal or emotional problems
64. Teach children how to read
65. Work with children with developmental disabilities
66. Teach an elementary school class
67. Give career guidance to people
68. Supervise the activities of children at a camp
69. Help people with family-related problems
70. Perform rehabilitation therapy
71. Help elderly people with their daily activities
72. Teach children how to play sports
73. Teach sign language to people with hearing disabilities
74. Help people who have problems with drugs or alcohol
75. Help families care for ill relatives
76. Provide massage therapy to people
77. Plan exercises for disabled students
78. Organize activities at a recreational facility
79. Take care of children at a day care center
80. Teach a high school class

__________ **Total Score for S**

81. Buy and sell stocks and bonds
82. Manage a retail store
83. Operate a beauty salon or barbershop
84. Sell merchandise over the telephone
85. Run a stand that sells newspapers and magazines
86. Give a presentation about a product you are selling
87. Sell furniture at a home furnishings store
88. Manage the operations of a hotel
89. Sell houses
90. Manage a supermarket
91. Sell a soft drink product line to stores and restaurants
92. Sell refreshments at a movie theater
93. Sell hair-care products to stores and salons
94. Start your own business
95. Negotiate business contracts
96. Represent a client in a lawsuit
97. Negotiate contracts for professional athletes
98. Market a new line of clothing
99. Sell automobiles
100. Sell computer equipment in a store

__________ **Total Score for E**

Circle the numbers of the activities you would LIKE to do.

101. Develop a spreadsheet using computer software
102. Proofread records or forms
103. Use a computer program to generate customer bills
104. Schedule conferences for an organization
105. Keep accounts payable/receivable for an office
106. Load computer software into a large computer network
107. Organize and schedule office meetings
108. Use a word processor to edit and format documents
109. Direct or transfer phone calls for a large organization
110. Perform office filing tasks
111. Compute and record statistical and other numerical data
112. Take notes during a meeting
113. Calculate the wages of employees
114. Assist senior-level accountants in performing bookkeeping tasks
115. Inventory supplies by using a handheld computer
116. Keep records of financial transactions for an organization
117. Record information from customers applying for charge accounts
118. Photocopy letters and reports
119. Stamp, sort, and distribute mail for an organization
120. Handle customers' bank transactions

__________ **Total Score for C**

Step 2: Score Your Responses

Here's how to score your responses:

1. **Score the responses in each column.** In each column of responses, go from top to bottom and count how many numbers are circled. Then write that total on the "Total Score" line at the bottom of the column. Go to the next column and do the same there.

2. **Determine your primary interest area.** Which Total Score is your highest: R, I, A, S, E, or C? Enter the letter for that personality type on the following line.

   My Primary Personality Type: __________

You will use your Primary Personality Type *first* to explore careers. (If two Total Scores are tied for the highest score or are within 4 points of each other, use both of them for your Primary Personality Type. You are equally divided between two types.)

R = Realistic. Realistic personalities like work activities that include practical, hands-on problems and solutions. They enjoy dealing with plants and animals and real-world materials such as wood, tools, and machinery. They enjoy outside work. Often they do not like occupations that mainly involve doing paperwork or working closely with others.

I = Investigative. Investigative personalities like work activities that have to do with ideas and thinking more than with physical activity. They like to search for facts and figure out problems mentally rather than persuade or lead people.

A = Artistic. Artistic personalities like work activities that deal with the artistic side of things, such as forms, designs, and patterns. They like self-expression in their work. They prefer settings in which work can be done without following a clear set of rules.

S = Social. Social personalities like work activities that assist others and promote learning and personal development. They prefer to communicate more than to work with objects, machines, or data. They like to teach, give advice, help, or otherwise be of service to people.

E = Enterprising. Enterprising personalities like work activities involving starting up and carrying out projects, especially business ventures. They like persuading and leading people and making decisions. They like taking risks for profit. These personalities prefer action rather than thought.

C = Conventional. Conventional personalities like work activities that follow set procedures and routines. They prefer working with data and details rather than with ideas. They prefer work in which there are precise standards rather than work in which they have to judge things by themselves. These personalities like working where the lines of authority are clear.

3. **Determine your secondary interest areas.** Which Total Score is the next highest? Which is your third-highest score? Enter the letters for those areas on the following lines.

   My Secondary Personality Types: _______ _______

(If you do not find many occupations that you like by using your Primary Personality Type, you can use your Secondary Personality Types to look at more career options.)

Step 3: Find Jobs That Suit Your Personality Type

Start with your Primary Personality Type, and find matching jobs in the following table, which is organized according to the six personality types ("RIASEC"). When you find a job that interests you, turn to the index to find the page where the job is described. Don't rule out a job just because the title is not familiar to you.

If you want to find jobs that combine your Primary Personality Type and a Secondary Personality Type, look in the following table for RIASEC codes that match the two codes. For example, if your Primary Personality Type is Enterprising and your Secondary Personality Type is Conventional, you would look for jobs in the table coded EC; and you'd find 15, such as Administrative Services Managers. In addition, some relevant occupations may be coded EC_, such as Human Resources Specialists (coded ECS). You also may want to consider reversing the codes you're looking for. In the current example, you might look for jobs coded CE, such as Cashiers, or CE_, such as Accountants and Auditors (coded CEI). But you need to keep in mind that these jobs may not be quite as satisfying because your Primary Personality Type, though represented, does not dominate.

The following table omits Military Careers. The Department of Labor does not provide personality-type information for these jobs, but that does not mean you should rule them out.

Occupation Name	*RIASEC Code(s)*
Agricultural Workers	R
Automotive Body and Glass Repairers	R
Fishing and Hunting Workers	R
Sheet Metal Workers	R
Automotive Service Technicians and Mechanics	RI
Mechanical Engineers	RI
Veterinary Technologists and Technicians	RI
Conservation Scientists and Foresters	RIE
Aerospace Engineering and Operations Technicians	RIC
Agricultural and Food Science Technicians	RIC
Biological Technicians	RIC
Civil Engineers	RIC
Dental and Ophthalmic Laboratory Technicians and Medical Appliance Technicians	RIC
Electrical and Electronics Engineering Technicians	RIC
Electrical and Electronics Installers and Repairers	RIC
Electro-Mechanical Technicians	RIC
Elevator Installers and Repairers	RIC
Environmental Engineering Technicians	RIC
Geological and Petroleum Technicians	RIC
Mechanical Engineering Technicians	RIC
Medical Equipment Repairers	RIC
Stationary Engineers and Boiler Operators	RIC
Telecommunications Equipment Installers and Repairers, except Line Installers	RIC
Jewelers and Precious Stone and Metal Workers	RA
Firefighters	RS
Radiologic and MRI Technologists	RS
Veterinary Assistants and Laboratory Animal Caretakers	RSI
Surgical Technologists	RSC
Athletes and Sports Competitors	RE
Taxi Drivers and Chauffeurs	RE
Correctional Officers and Bailiffs	REC
Manicurists and Pedicurists	REC
Water Transportation Workers	REC
Animal Care and Service Workers	RC
Bakers	RC
Boilermakers	RC
Bus Drivers	RC
Construction Equipment Operators	RC
Construction Laborers and Helpers	RC
Diesel Service Technicians and Mechanics	RC
Drywall and Ceiling Tile Installers, and Tapers	RC
Flooring Installers and Tile and Marble Setters	RC
Food and Tobacco Processing Workers	RC
Food Preparation Workers	RC
Glaziers	RC
Grounds Maintenance Workers	RC
Hand Laborers and Material Movers	RC
Hazardous Materials Removal Workers	RC
Heating, Air Conditioning, and Refrigeration Mechanics and Installers	RC
Heavy and Tractor-Trailer Truck Drivers	RC
Insulation Workers	RC
Janitors and Building Cleaners	RC
Masonry Workers	RC
Material Moving Machine Operators	RC
Metal and Plastic Machine Workers	RC
Painters, Construction and Maintenance	RC
Painting and Coating Workers	RC
Pest Control Workers	RC
Plumbers, Pipefitters, and Steamfitters	RC
Power Plant Operators, Distributors, and Dispatchers	RC
Roofers	RC
Small Engine Mechanics	RC
Solar Photovoltaic Installers	RC
Water and Wastewater Treatment Plant and System Operators	RC
Welders, Cutters, Solderers, and Brazers	RC
Wind Turbine Technicians	RC
Woodworkers	RC
Aircraft and Avionics Equipment Mechanics and Technicians	RCI
Airline and Commercial Pilots	RCI
Broadcast and Sound Engineering Technicians	RCI
Carpenters	RCI
Cartographers and Photogrammetrists	RCI
Civil Engineering Technicians	RCI
Computer Support Specialists	RCI
Construction and Building Inspectors	RCI
Drafters	RCI
Electricians	RCI
Fire Inspectors	RCI
Forest and Conservation Workers	RCI
General Maintenance and Repair Workers	RCI
Heavy Vehicle and Mobile Equipment Service Technicians	RCI
Industrial Machinery Mechanics and Maintenance Workers and Millwrights	RCI
Ironworkers	RCI
Line Installers and Repairers	RCI
Logging Workers	RCI
Machinists and Tool and Die Makers	RCI
Nuclear Technicians	RCI
Surveyors	RCI
Assemblers and Fabricators	RCE
Butchers	RCE
Cooks	RCE
Delivery Truck Drivers and Driver/Sales Workers	RCE
Railroad Workers	RCE

Occupation Name	*RIASEC Code(s)*
Security Guards and Gaming Surveillance Officers	RCE
Historians	I
Aerospace Engineers	IR
Agricultural and Food Scientists	IR
Atmospheric Scientists, including Meteorologists	IR
Biomedical Engineers	IR
Chemical Engineers	IR
Chemists and Materials Scientists	IR
Electrical and Electronics Engineers	IR
Environmental Engineers	IR
Geoscientists	IR
Hydrologists	IR
Industrial Engineers	IR
Marine Engineers and Naval Architects	IR
Microbiologists	IR
Physicists and Astronomers	IR
Veterinarians	IR
Zoologists and Wildlife Biologists	IR
Geographers	IRA
Medical Scientists	IRA
Dentists	IRS
Nuclear Medicine Technologists	IRS
Agricultural Engineers	IRE
Materials Engineers	IRE
Mining and Geological Engineers	IRE
Chemical Technicians	IRC
Computer and Information Research Scientists	IRC
Computer Hardware Engineers	IRC
Environmental Science and Protection Technicians	IRC
Forensic Science Technicians	IRC
Health and Safety Engineers	IRC
Industrial Engineering Technicians	IRC
Medical and Clinical Laboratory Technologists and Technicians	IRC
Network and Computer Systems Administrators	IRC
Nuclear Engineers	IRC
Petroleum Engineers	IRC
Anthropologists and Archeologists	IA
Biochemists and Biophysicists	IAR
Political Scientists	IAS
Sociologists	IAS
Audiologists	IS
Dietitians and Nutritionists	IS
Epidemiologists	IS
Diagnostic Medical Sonographers and Cardiovascular Technologists and Technicians, including Vascular Technologists	ISR
Nurse Anesthetists, Nurse Midwives, and Nurse Practitioners	ISR
Optometrists	ISR
Physicians and Surgeons	ISR
Podiatrists	ISR
Psychologists	ISA
Environmental Scientists and Specialists	IER
Urban and Regional Planners	IEA
Management Analysts	IEC
Market Research Analysts	IEC
Computer Programmers	IC
Computer Systems Analysts	IC
Occupational Health and Safety Specialists	IC
Software Developers	ICR
Mathematicians	ICA
Pharmacists	ICS
Economists	ICE
Operations Research Analysts	ICE

Occupation Name	*RIASEC Code(s)*
Survey Researchers	ICE
Film and Video Editors and Camera Operators	AR
Photographers	AR
Dancers and Choreographers	ARS
Craft and Fine Artists	ARE
Architects	AI
Multimedia Artists and Animators	AI
Landscape Architects	AIR
Desktop Publishers	AIC
Technical Writers	AIC
Interpreters and Translators	AS
Actors	AE
Art Directors	AE
Interior Designers	AE
Music Directors and Composers	AE
Musicians and Singers	AE
Fashion Designers	AER
Floral Designers	AER
Graphic Designers	AER
Industrial Designers	AER
Models	AER
Reporters, Correspondents, and Broadcast News Analysts	AEI
Writers and Authors	AEI
Barbers, Hairdressers, and Cosmetologists	AES
Editors	AEC
School and Career Counselors	S
Career/Technical Education Teachers	SR
Home Health Aides	SR
Licensed Practical and Licensed Vocational Nurses	SR
Massage Therapists	SR
Occupational Therapy Assistants and Aides	SR
Physical Therapist Assistants and Aides	SR
Psychiatric Technicians and Aides	SR
Athletic Trainers	SRI
Orthotists and Prosthetists	SRI
Fitness Trainers and Instructors	SRE
Dental Hygienists	SRC
Personal Care Aides	SRC
Radiation Therapists	SRC
Exercise Physiologists	SI
Occupational Therapists	SI
Registered Nurses	SI
Rehabilitation Counselors	SI
Social Workers	SI
Chiropractors	SIR
EMTs and Paramedics	SIR
Physical Therapists	SIR
Physician Assistants	SIR
Respiratory Therapists	SIR
Genetic Counselors	SIA
Mental Health Counselors and Marriage and Family Therapists	SIA
Postsecondary Teachers	SIA
Speech-Language Pathologists	SIA
Childcare Workers	SA
Middle School Teachers	SA
Preschool Teachers	SA
Special Education Teachers	SA
Recreational Therapists	SAI
Substance Abuse and Behavioral Disorder Counselors	SAI
Adult Literacy and High School Equivalency Diploma Teachers	SAE
High School Teachers	SAE
Kindergarten and Elementary School Teachers	SAC

Occupation Name	*RIASEC Code(s)*
Training and Development Specialists	SAC
Arbitrators, Mediators, and Conciliators	SE
Emergency Management Directors	SE
Health Educators and Community Health Workers	SE
Coaches and Scouts	SER
Instructional Coordinators	SEI
Recreation Workers	SEA
Customer Service Representatives	SEC
Preschool and Childcare Center Directors	SEC
Probation Officers and Correctional Treatment Specialists	SEC
Waiters and Waitresses	SEC
Teacher Assistants	SC
Medical Assistants	SCR
Nursing Assistants and Orderlies	SCR
Sales Engineers	ERI
Chefs and Head Cooks	ERA
Police and Detectives	ERS
Computer Network Architects	ERC
Construction Managers	ERC
Farmers, Ranchers, and Other Agricultural Managers	ERC
Umpires, Referees, and Other Sports Officials	ERC
Architectural and Engineering Managers	EI
Lawyers	EI
Natural Sciences Managers	EIC
Public Relations and Fundraising Managers	EA
Announcers	EAS
Public Relations Specialists	EAS
Producers and Directors	EAC
Social and Community Service Managers	ES
Training and Development Managers	ES
Skincare Specialists	ESR
Judges and Hearing Officers	ESI
Elementary, Middle, and High School Principals	ESC
Flight Attendants	ESC
Funeral Service Workers	ESC
Human Resources Managers	ESC
Medical and Health Services Managers	ESC
Administrative Services Managers	EC
Air Traffic Controllers	EC
Buyers and Purchasing Agents	EC
Cost Estimators	EC
Financial Examiners	EC
Financial Managers	EC
Private Detectives and Investigators	EC
Property, Real Estate, and Community Association Managers	EC
Purchasing Managers	EC
Real Estate Brokers and Sales Agents	EC
Retail Sales Workers	EC
Sales Managers	EC
Securities, Commodities, and Financial Services Sales Agents	EC
Travel Agents	EC
Wholesale and Manufacturing Sales Representatives	EC
Food Service Managers	ECR
Industrial Production Managers	ECR
Opticians, Dispensing	ECR
Computer and Information Systems Managers	ECI
Advertising, Promotions, and Marketing Managers	ECA
Advertising Sales Agents	ECA
Fundraisers	ECA
Compensation and Benefits Managers	ECS
Human Resources Specialists	ECS
Insurance Sales Agents	ECS
Labor Relations Specialists	ECS
Lodging Managers	ECS
Meeting, Convention, and Event Planners	ECS
Personal Financial Advisors	ECS
Postsecondary Education Administrators	ECS
Top Executives	ECS
Medical Transcriptionists	CR
Occupational Health and Safety Technicians	CR
Pharmacy Technicians	CR
Postal Service Workers	CR
Quality Control Inspectors	CR
Surveying and Mapping Technicians	CR
Dental Assistants	CRS
Phlebotomists	CRS
Food and Beverage Serving and Related Workers	CRE
Material Recording Clerks	CRE
Police, Fire, and Ambulance Dispatchers	CRE
Database Administrators	CI
Statisticians	CI
Information Security Analysts	CIR
Web Developers	CIR
Actuaries	CIE
Financial Analysts	CIE
Paralegals and Legal Assistants	CIE
Library Technicians and Assistants	CSR
Librarians	CSE
Social and Human Service Assistants	CSE
Appraisers and Assessors of Real Estate	CE
Bill and Account Collectors	CE
Bookkeeping, Accounting, and Auditing Clerks	CE
Cashiers	CE
Claims Adjusters, Appraisers, Examiners, and Investigators	CE
Compensation, Benefits, and Job Analysis Specialists	CE
Court Reporters	CE
Financial Clerks	CE
Medical Records and Health Information Technicians	CE
Secretaries and Administrative Assistants	CE
Tax Examiners and Collectors, and Revenue Agents	CE
Tellers	CE
Bartenders	CER
Gaming Services Workers	CER
General Office Clerks	CER
Accountants and Auditors	CEI
Archivists, Curators, and Museum Workers	CEI
Budget Analysts	CEI
Insurance Underwriters	CEI
Logisticians	CEI
Information Clerks	CES
Loan Officers	CES
Receptionists	CES

How Educators, Counselors, Librarians, and Business Professionals Can Best Use the *OOH*

The *OOH* is the best-selling career information resource of all time, and it is so popular because it has such a wide range of information and is designed to appeal to many kinds of career explorers. One drawback of this format is that people who are in the early stages of career exploration may not know where in this thick volume to get started. On the other hand, people with highly specific career information needs may require help to apply the general statements in the *OOH* to their particular situations.

If you are a professional who works with career decision makers, this chapter can suggest ways to help your clients get the most out of *OOH*. It also has suggestions for how to use the *OOH* in classroom activities for academic subjects. The *OOH* published by the Department of Labor does not include a chapter like this, but the career experts at JIST Career Solutions thought you would benefit from practical suggestions for using the various components of the *OOH* with your clients and students. If you have had success with any strategies not mentioned here, please contact the editors at JIST and share your ideas so we can include them in a future edition.

Identifying Occupations to Consider

Many of your clients may want to use the *OOH* to discover interesting occupations they previously had not thought about. Some may enjoy browsing randomly through the pages and looking at the photos and the opening tables of key facts to identify occupations that seem promising. You may save these clients time, however, by showing them the table of contents and encouraging them to focus their browsing on the major occupational group or groups that are of greatest interest to them—e.g., Sales, Construction, or Transportation. The table of contents can be especially useful for these kinds of clients:

- People who are transitioning from one occupation to another and want to find work in a similar field
- Students who want to identify occupations related to their program of study
- Career explorers who have a rough idea of their interests

Note that, with one exception (Military Careers), the table of contents uses a two-tiered organization to help clients zoom in from major occupational groups to specific occupations. For example, the section on Farming, Fishing, and Forestry Occupations contains four specific occupations: Agricultural Workers, Fishing and Hunting Workers, Forest and Conservation Workers, and Logging Workers. This organization helps clients narrow down their thinking.

Looking for a Specific Occupation

If a client already has a specific occupation in mind, you can find the page number quickly in the index. The index also includes alternative titles so that, for example, a client who looks for CAD operators is directed to look under Drafters, which is the name of the *OOH* article. If a client is unable to make clear to you what occupation he or she is trying to find or you cannot find a good match in the index, use the table of contents, where the general-to-specific structure can help you locate the occupation that the client has in mind or one reasonably close to it.

Occasionally a client may be looking for an occupation that is so specialized that the *OOH* does not cover it. In such cases you can often locate information about the specialized occupation by finding the most closely related *OOH* occupation and consulting resources identified in the section of the article called "Contacts for More Information." For example, the occupation underwater welders does not appear in the index or table of contents and is not even referred to in the *OOH* article about Welders, Cutters, Solderers, and Brazers. Nevertheless, this article refers to the website of the American Welding Society, which, in fact, has information about underwater welders.

Getting the Most from an *OOH* Article

You can easily locate the information you want in the *OOH* because every article is organized according to the same format, with nine sections that are described below.

Significant Points

The bulleted items at the beginning of each article highlight key facts for each occupation: the 2014 median pay (usually, but not always, in terms of both annual pay and hourly pay); the typical entry-level education; the usual requirement (if any) for work experience in a related occupation; the usual requirement (if any) for on-the-job training; the number of jobs held in 2014; the job outlook for the years 2014–2024, expressed as both a percentage of growth (or shrinkage), with a verbal tag that indicates how this change compares to the average across occupations; and the change in absolute number of jobs for the years 2014–2024.

For more detailed explanations of how to interpret these facts, see the following discussions of the sections that amplify on these brief facts.

What They Do

This section discusses what workers do on the job, what tools and equipment they use, and how closely they are supervised. You should point out to your clients that this is an overview of a diverse collection of workers, and that, in fact, few workers perform the full set of tasks itemized here. The duties for an individual worker often vary by industry or employer, and beginning workers often perform a limited number of routine tasks under close supervision until they are trained for more varied tasks and can take greater responsibility.

In many cases the work force covered by the article is so diverse that it actually divides into several occupational specialties. For example, the article on Accountants and Auditors discusses a few specialties, such as public accountants, management accountants, and internal auditors. Although the skills and knowledge required for the occupation usually are discussed in a later section, this section sometimes mentions them, particularly the unique requirements of occupational specializations. For example, the article on Secretaries and Administrative Assistants notes, "Medical secretaries need to be familiar with medical terminology and codes, medical records, and hospital or laboratory procedures." Specialties and alternative occupational titles are easy to find in the text because they are italicized. Some articles—such as the one for Advertising, Promotions, and Marketing Managers—discuss titles or specialties for which separate articles are available elsewhere in the *OOH*. If a client asks about a reference such as "See the profiles sales managers, public relations and fundraising managers, public relations specialists, and market research analysts," you should explain that "profile" means an article and help the client find that article.

Your clients will find this section useful for several reasons:

- If you have discussed or assessed your clients' interests, this section gives your clients an idea of what kinds of problems, materials, and tools they will encounter on the job so that they can decide whether these are a good match for their interests. Remind them to make these comparisons.
- If you have discussed some of the intrinsic rewards of work, this section can suggest some of these aspects of the occupation. However, because such matters usually require inference, your clients may need your help in drawing a connection between the work tasks and their values. For example, this section of the article on Real Estate Brokers and Sales Agents begins, "Because of the complexity of buying or selling a home or commercial property, people often seek help from real estate brokers and sales agents." For a client who values helping other people, you may need to point out explicitly that this occupation offers opportunities for that kind of fulfillment.
- Clients who want to change careers may want to read this section of the article about their *current* occupation. The description of tasks and tools may suggest experiences that they can mention in their résumés. It can also provide fodder for a discussion with you about what aspects of the current job are interesting and rewarding—or uninteresting and discouraging. Some clients may find occupational specialties that are promising alternatives to what they are doing now.

Work Environment

This section identifies how many people work in the occupation, the proportion who are self-employed, the typical hours worked, the workplace environment (both physical and psychological), physical activities and susceptibility to injury, special equipment, and the extent of travel required. If conditions vary between the occupational specialties, that is mentioned here.

Here are some of the ways this section may be valuable to your clients:

- Clients who want to move into or remain in a specific industry should pay attention to this section because it indicates which industries provide most of the employment for the occupation. This knowledge also can help your clients target their job-hunting efforts. The industries that are mentioned here are, of course, not the only industries where your clients may find jobs.
- If you know a client is interested in self-employment or part-time work, you should direct the client to look for relevant information in this section.
- Clients with disabilities will want to take note of the physical requirements that are mentioned here and consider whether they can meet these requirements with or without suitable accommodations.
- Clients who are sensitive to conditions such as heights, stress, or a cramped workspace should be told to pay attention to this section.
- If clients have pressing family responsibilities, you should remind them to be sure either that the occupation has conventional work hours and requires little travel or that they have a plan for coping with the problems that would result from an unconventional work schedule or a lot of travel. Conversely, clients who are looking for opportunities for travel or unusual work hours should be encouraged to look at this section.
- As with the first section, you may want to have your clients read this section of the article about their current occupation. Encourage them to discuss which aspects of their present working conditions please and displease them.
- If an otherwise promising occupation has a working condition that a client wants to avoid, check the wording of the section to see whether this is an inevitable attribute of the occupation or whether it only *may* apply. Even if the wording implies that the condition is typical of the occupation, encourage the client to explore the occupation using other sources, especially personal contacts with workers or educators, to learn whether it is possible to carve out a niche in this occupation that avoids the unappealing working condition.

Education/Training

This is the section where your clients can learn how to prepare for the occupation and how to advance in it. It identifies the significant entry routes—those that are most popular and that are preferred by employers. These entry routes may be informal methods such as hobbies or work experience; they may be formal training programs such as apprenticeship, military, and other on-the-job programs; or they may be educational programs such as vocational school, a postsecondary certification program, a college major, or an advanced degree program. If licensure or certification is necessary for entry or advancement, this section mentions this requirement and how to qualify for it. This section also identifies the particular skills, aptitudes, and work habits ("Important Qualities") that employers value.

Your clients may benefit from this section in several ways:

- Clients who are considering entering an occupation can learn what hurdles they must overcome to enter it. You can help them by comparing the requirements to their backgrounds and to the educational and training opportunities that are available to them, perhaps locally. Be sure to consider nontraditional and informal entry routes as well as the formal routes.
- Suggest that clients try to leverage their previous education, training, and work experience rather than abandoning it. As they read the educational and skill requirements in this section they should look for specifics already on their résumés—educational accomplishments, skills, work habits—that will meet employers' expectations and thus make a career transition easier. These considerations should be part of the career decision.
- Clients who are decided on an occupation and ready to apply for a job in it should be encouraged to pay attention to what this section says about relevant skills and personal attributes. This information can help these clients slant their résumés and focus their interview statements in ways that make them stronger job candidates.
- Clients may also find it useful to read what this section says about their current occupation. It may suggest an advancement route

that they have not yet considered. More likely they are already aware of the common advancement routes, and a discussion of why they are *not* considering these options may be fruitful. For example, it may uncover negative perceptions clients have about themselves, about the occupation, or about change, and it may lead to ideas for other occupations they might explore. Similarly, this section may suggest transferable skills that should be included in the client's résumé or may highlight skills that the client does *not* want to use in future jobs.

- If certification with a professional organization is required or recommended, contact information for the organization is usually listed at the end of the article among the "Contacts for More Information," so your clients can easily find where to learn the details about certification prerequisites and procedures.

Pay

This section discusses typical earnings for the occupation and identifies the most common ways workers are compensated—for example, with an hourly wage, a commission, tips, and so forth. If the occupation is divided into specialties, the differing wages are listed separately, usually in a table. If earnings vary widely among different industries, these differences may also be shown in a table. Additional factors that cause wage variations may be identified. Standard benefits usually are not mentioned, but uncommon benefits such as summers off or discounted merchandise may be mentioned.

Most of the wage figures are derived from the Occupational Employment Survey and are two years old when the *OOH* goes to press. Occasionally figures from other salary surveys are also included.

Your clients are likely to be very interested in this section, and here are some suggestions for how to help them use this information:

- Remind your clients to note the date of the wage figures and to be aware that, although most of the figures are comparable with one another, they may lag behind current wage levels. The good news is that wage inflation is currently at a low rate, so the figures remain generally relevant for several years.
- Also remind your clients that the wage figures are national averages. This is particularly important for clients to understand if they look at the wages that the *OOH* lists for their current occupation. If actual wages in your geographic region are considerably higher or lower, tell your clients what the trend is. In addition, you may want to point out that an average figure means that half of the workers earn more, half less, and the actual salary any one worker earns can vary greatly from that average.
- Your clients may find the information in this section helps them choose an occupation that meets or exceeds their wage aspirations or a specialty that pays better than other specialties. However, you can help your clients by getting a sense of whether they have considered *other* potential job satisfactions and work conditions and are putting the wages into a realistic context. Be sure they are making a choice based on the whole occupation, not just the paycheck.
- If your clients are young or do not have much work experience, they may not have a realistic understanding of the relationship between wages and lifestyles. That is, the wage figures given in this section may not have concrete meaning for them in terms of what kind of neighborhood they might live in, what kind of car they might drive, and so forth. You can help them by preparing descriptions of fictional people (perhaps familiar characters on television) in various lifestyles, together with the wage levels that would correspond.

Job Outlook

This section gives the *OOH* its name. It describes the economic forces that will affect future employment in the occupation: the growth or decline of industries that employ workers; factors such as technology, business practices, or changes in the law that impact demand for workers; and demographic issues such as the impending retirement of large numbers of workers. It sometimes mentions how the supply of workers compares to the demand for workers. The subsection on "Job Prospects" explains how these economic forces create advantages and disadvantages for various kinds of jobseekers and niches within the occupation.

Here are some of the ways you can use this section to your clients' advantage:

- Some of the wording in this section is shorthand that avoids statistics or complex statements about economic conditions. Your clients generally will be able to apply the wording to their own situations, but if someone asks what exactly is meant by (for example) "much faster than average employment growth," tell the client to turn to the introductory chapter called "Occupational Information Included in the *OOH*" and note the table at the end of the chapter.
- The information in this section can help your clients identify occupations with a good job outlook so that they have better-than-average chances of finding work. You should tell them to be alert for any mention of an advantage that they may have over other job-seekers (e.g., a college degree) or any other factor, such as geographic location or type of employer, that can improve job opportunities or, conversely, might lead to keen competition.
- If a client is highly motivated and highly qualified for a particular occupation, do not let a bad employment outlook discourage the client. Job openings occur even in shrinking or overcrowded occupations, and people with (for example) exceptional talent or good personal connections may go on to great success.
- Keep in mind that although these projections are the most definitive ones available, they are not foolproof and apply only to a ten-year time span. Help your clients understand that no matter what occupation they choose, they will need to be flexible and adapt to future changes in the economy.
- Clients should consult this section of the article about their present occupation. If the outlook is not good, the information may convince them to consider preparing for work in another field. Alternatively, with knowledge of the forces that are threatening the occupation they may be able to devise a counterstrategy—for example, moving into a specialization where jobs will remain plentiful. If the outlook is good, they may learn how to take advantage of the best opportunities.

Similar Occupations

This section identifies occupations that are similar to the occupation that is featured in the article in terms of work tasks, interests, skills, education, or training. Your clients may find the information useful in the following ways:

- If a client is interested in an occupation but is not strongly committed to pursuing it, this section may suggest another occupation with similar rewards that may turn out to be a better fit. Advise the client to read the *OOH* articles on the related occupations. If you know some specific shortcomings the client perceives in the occupation at hand (e.g., a lot of weekend work), you may know which related occupations are most likely to be more satisfying.

- Clients who are considering a career change may want to consult this section in the article about their current occupation. Some of the related occupations listed here may be good routes for career transition.
- You may be able to use occupations listed here to inspire clients whose aspirations fall short of their full potential. For example, you could point out that only a little more education in the same field would open the door to certain highly rewarding occupations.
- Conversely, you may use this section to suggest realistic alternatives to a client whose aspirations seem unrealistic. Try to do so in a manner that does not disrespect the client's dreams—encourage the client to select one of these alternative occupational choices as an achievable plan-B goal if the original goal should turn out to be unattainable. For example, if a client is unlikely to be able to get into or complete law school, you could point to paralegal or title examiner as occupations that work in the same field but require less education.

Contacts for More Information

Although information-packed, the *OOH* has limited space to describe the occupations it includes. This section lists several sources and resources your clients can turn to for more information about the occupation. Here are some suggestions for advising your clients about using these references:

- Encourage your clients to consult these sources. The *OOH* should be only the beginning of their career decision-making process. They need more detailed information from several viewpoints to make an informed decision. Ask some probing questions to be sure that your clients know how to locate the additional resources. If possible, help their further research efforts by providing such aids as web access, a college directory, or a local business directory.
- Many people, especially young people, regard the World Wide Web as the font of all knowledge and may not explore beyond the websites listed here. Remind your clients that, like politics, all jobs are local. Your clients need to talk to and observe individual workers to learn what the workdays are like, what the workers enjoy and dislike about the job, how they got hired, and what effects the job has had on other aspects of their lives. Your clients may make contact with local workers through the local chapter of an organization listed here.
- If licensure or certification is mentioned as a requirement in the section on "Education/Training," one of the sources listed here may have detailed information about the procedures that apply to your clients' jurisdiction. Be sure your clients investigate these matters so they understand all the hurdles that stand between them and job entry and can plan an appropriate course of action.
- Remind your clients that these sources may provide detailed information about occupational specialties that are not described or that are described only briefly, in the *OOH* article. If a client perceives certain minor drawbacks in an otherwise appealing occupation, these sources may point out niche jobs that avoid these problems—for example, the high-paying specialties in an occupation that generally pays a moderate salary.
- One of these sources may provide information that contradicts what the *OOH* says. Such situations are rare but might occur because the information in the *OOH* has gone out of date or because local conditions are very different from national norms. Try to help your client identify the reason for the inconsistency in light of what will be most helpful in making a career decision. For example, if local job conditions are unique but the client intends to relocate elsewhere, advise the client to base the career decision on the national averages reported in the *OOH*.

Using the *OOH* for Class Assignments

The paragraphs above explain how to use the *OOH* to help people make career decisions and plans. The *OOH* is also useful as the focus of many kinds of class activities that can teach important academic skills and concepts while simultaneously making young people better informed about careers. Here are some examples:

For a Mathematics Class

- The "Work Environment" section of some articles about diverse occupations (e.g., Food and Beverage Serving and Related Workers) includes a table that lists the distribution of workers among the specialized occupations. Have students use such a table to create a pie chart.
- The "Pay" section of some articles includes a table that lists the earnings of workers in different industries. Have students use the data to create a bar chart showing the comparisons.
- The "Pay" section of some articles (e.g., Police and Detectives) lists the median 2014 earnings for each specialization within the large occupation that is the subject of the article. In these articles, the "Outlook" section also includes an "Employment Projections Data" table that shows the 2014 employment for each of these specializations. Use the figures in these two tables to show how to compute a *weighted average* for the earnings of the titular occupation. This figure should match the figure for the titular occupation in the earnings graph.
- The "Pay" section of many articles identifies the median earnings of all workers, plus the earnings of the middle 50 percent of workers and the lowest and highest 10 percent. Have students make a graph on which the x-axis shows dollar figures in increments of $5,000 or $10,000 (or 50 cents if hourly earnings are shown). Have them mark the locations of the five data points mentioned above and then superimpose a normal curve over the graph with the highest point above the median figure. Ask students to comment on whether the curve accurately describes the distribution of earnings. For example, are the high and low 10 percent figures equidistant from the median? For a particularly lopsided distribution, choose the article on Real Estate Brokers and Sales Agents.

For an English Class

- Have students write an essay comparing and contrasting two occupations. (It may be useful to ask the students to choose two that belong to the same occupational group.)
- Have students write an essay on what they consider the best (or worst) occupation in the *OOH*. Tell them to specify facts about the occupation that make it outstanding and relate these to their own likes or dislikes.

- Have students write an essay comparing and contrasting the work experiences of a contemporary fictional character with the facts reported in the *OOH* article on the equivalent occupation. The thesis of the essay should be a judgment of how realistic the portrayal is.
- Have students write an article in the *OOH* format describing the occupation of a fictional character from a work they have read. Tell them that every fact must be based on evidence from the fictional work (you may even require them to cite page numbers), rather than on facts gleaned from the *OOH* itself.

For a Social Studies Class

- The "Job Outlook" section of many articles mentions economic forces that are causing the occupation to grow or shrink. Have students look at several articles and identify one economic trend that is having an impact on several occupations (examples: aging baby boomers; increased use of automation; increased interest in energy conservation). Have them research the trend using other current resources and prepare a poster identifying the trend, defining it briefly, and listing some occupations that are affected.
- The "Education/Training" section of many articles mentions that certification or licensure is required by law for the occupation. Have students choose one such occupation and prepare a brief report on why the regulation exists, what requirements are imposed on workers (e.g., passing an exam), and which level and branch of government is involved. The "Contacts for More Information" section usually tells where to find this information.
- Have students research and write an article in the *OOH* format describing an occupation that no longer exists (or is held by only a few craftsworkers), such as alchemist, bowmaker, saddler, scrivener, or wheelwright.

Best 100 Jobs in the *Occupational Outlook Handbook*

By the Editors at JIST

The *Occupational Outlook Handbook (OOH)* covers so many jobs that you may be looking for a quick way to narrow down your choices. The Personality-Career Quiz in Chapter 1 is one way to do this, and this chapter offers another: It identifies the 100 jobs with the best economic rewards.

The procedure we used to create this chapter is the same one we use in many popular JIST books, such as *Best Jobs for the 21st Century, 50 Best Jobs for Your Personality*, and *150 Best Jobs for Your Skills*. We determined the best 100 jobs in the *OOH* by focusing on three economic criteria: earnings, projected job growth, and projected job openings.

Why these three criteria? First, everybody agrees that these three are very important. Many other characteristics of jobs are matters of individual preference. One person may be looking for a job that offers opportunities for leadership; somebody else may be looking for a great variety of work tasks; still another person may be looking for work that contributes to society. But everybody wants to get paid, and almost everybody agrees that more pay is better.

It's also important for you to get hired. After all, if you're not hired, you won't get any of the satisfactions of work. So job growth and job openings are both very important. Understand that these are not two ways of saying the same thing. You need to know both. Consider the occupation Biomedical Engineers, which is projected to grow at the impressive rate of 23 percent. There should be lots of opportunities in such a fast-growing job, right? Not exactly. This is a small occupation, with only about 22,000 people currently employed. So, even though the workforce is growing rapidly, the occupation will not create many new jobs (about 1,000 per year). Now consider Elementary, Middle, and High School Principals. This occupation is projected to grow only slightly, by 6 percent. Nevertheless, this is a very large occupation that employs more than 200,000 workers. So, even though the workforce size will not grow at a rapid pace, the occupation is expected to take on about 8,000 new workers each year, many through job turnover. That's why we base our selection of the best jobs on *both* of these economic indicators and why you should pay attention to both when you scan the list of the 100 best jobs.

Another important reason we use these three criteria is that accurate and objective information about them is available. People might disagree about which occupations offer the most opportunities for creativity or freedom from stress. But the U.S. Department of Labor gets universal respect for the figures it publishes on earnings, projected job growth, and projected job openings. These concepts are numerical and therefore are easy to compare objectively.

Here's how we made the comparisons: We started with the 329 civilian occupations that the *OOH* describes with full profiles and eliminated 3 occupations (Actors; Military Careers; and Musicians and Singers) because annual earnings data was not available. We sorted the remaining 326 occupations three times, from highest to lowest, in terms of earnings, growth rate through 2024, and average number of annual openings. Each time, we assigned a number to their relative position on the list. We then combined the job-position numbers of the three lists, putting the job with the best total score at the top, followed by the job with next-best total score, on down the list.

Some jobs have the same scores for one or more data elements. For example, Actuaries and Information Security Analysts are both projected to grow at the rate of 17.9 percent. In such cases, we ordered the jobs alphabetically, and their order in relation to each other has no other significance. Avoiding these ties was impossible, so understand that the difference of several positions on a list may not mean as much as it seems.

We're not suggesting that the 100 jobs with the best overall scores for earnings, growth, and number of openings are all good ones for you to consider—some will not be. Read the job descriptions, and use some of the resources listed there for getting additional information. As you narrow down your choices, talk to people in the career and people in the educational or training programs. Do some on-site career exploration. If you do your homework, you probably can identify a career that has good economic rewards and many other features that will suit you.

Best 100 Jobs in the *Occupational Outlook Handbook*

Job	Annual Earnings	Percent Growth	Annual Openings
1. Physicians and Surgeons	$187,200	14.0%	29,000
2. Nurse Anesthetists, Nurse Midwives, and Nurse Practitioners	$108,460	31.4%	9,360
3. Software Developers	$98,150	16.8%	18,660
4. Physical Therapists	$82,390	34.0%	12,830
5. Computer Systems Analysts	$82,710	20.9%	19,160
6. Personal Financial Advisors	$81,060	29.6%	13,640
7. Computer and Information Systems Managers	$127,640	15.4%	9,480
8. Medical and Health Services Managers	$92,810	16.9%	14,050
9. Registered Nurses	$66,640	16.0%	108,840

Job	Annual Earnings	Percent Growth	Annual Openings
10. Management Analysts	$80,880	13.6%	20,850
11. Dentists	$154,640	17.6%	5,760
12. Physician Assistants	$95,820	30.5%	5,000
13. Postsecondary Teachers	$63,010	11.7%	55,060
14. Accountants and Auditors	$65,940	10.7%	49,800
15. Occupational Therapists	$78,810	26.6%	5,260
16. Financial Managers	$115,320	6.8%	16,930
17. Market Research Analysts	$61,290	18.6%	15,140
18. Operations Research Analysts	$76,660	30.2%	4,390
19. Top Executives	$100,910	5.8%	76,000
20. Optometrists	$101,410	27.1%	2,550
21. Financial Analysts	$78,620	11.7%	8,940
22. Dental Hygienists	$71,520	18.7%	7,030
23. Speech-Language Pathologists	$71,550	21.3%	6,310
24. Psychologists	$70,700	18.7%	6,980
25. Web Developers	$63,490	26.6%	5,860
26. Lawyers	$114,970	5.6%	15,770
27. Information Security Analysts	$88,890	17.9%	2,550
28. Civil Engineers	$82,050	8.4%	10,670
29. Securities, Commodities, and Financial Services Sales Agents	$72,070	9.5%	9,140
30. Electricians	$51,110	13.7%	18,180
31. Human Resources Managers	$102,780	8.8%	4,660
32. Postsecondary Education Administrators	$88,390	8.7%	6,610
33. Administrative Services Managers	$83,790	8.2%	7,720
34. Industrial Machinery Mechanics, Machinery Maintenance Workers, and Millwrights	$47,570	15.8%	18,250
35. Database Administrators	$80,280	11.2%	3,920
36. Licensed Practical and Licensed Vocational Nurses	$42,490	16.3%	32,220
37. Medical and Clinical Laboratory Technologists and Technicians	$49,310	15.9%	13,050
38. Computer Support Specialists	$50,380	11.6%	18,740
39. Sales Managers	$110,660	5.0%	10,800
40. Statisticians	$79,990	33.7%	1,540
41. Diagnostic Medical Sonographers and Cardiovascular Technologists and Technicians, Including Vascular Technologists	$61,450	24.4%	2,760
42. Physical Therapist Assistants and Aides	$41,640	40.0%	8,870
43. Network and Computer Systems Administrators	$75,790	7.9%	7,940
44. Environmental Engineers	$83,360	12.5%	2,240
45. Computer Network Architects	$98,430	8.7%	3,150
46. Social Workers	$45,500	11.5%	23,120
47. Actuaries	$96,700	17.9%	1,170
48. Biomedical Engineers	$86,950	23.1%	1,090
49. Environmental Scientists and Specialists	$66,250	10.8%	3,930
50. Plumbers, Pipefitters, and Steamfitters	$50,660	11.6%	10,520
51. Mechanical Engineers	$83,060	5.3%	10,250
52. Medical Scientists	$78,920	8.3%	4,450
53. Producers and Directors	$69,100	9.1%	5,050
54. Home Health Aides	$21,380	38.1%	55,480
55. Advertising, Promotions, and Marketing Managers	$122,960	8.7%	1,970
56. Occupational Therapy Assistants and Aides	$52,300	40.1%	2,890
57. Medical Assistants	$29,960	23.5%	26,210
58. Petroleum Engineers	$130,050	9.7%	1,300

Job	Annual Earnings	Percent Growth	Annual Openings
59. Social and Community Service Managers	$62,740	9.5%	4,980
60. Cost Estimators	$60,050	8.8%	7,950
61. Public Relations and Fundraising Managers	$101,510	7.1%	2,710
62. Personal Care Aides	$20,440	25.9%	60,110
63. Pharmacists	$120,950	3.1%	7,840
64. Respiratory Therapists	$56,730	12.3%	4,330
65. Insurance Sales Agents	$47,860	9.3%	16,580
66. Loan Officers	$62,620	8.1%	7,500
67. Dental Assistants	$35,390	18.4%	13,750
68. High School Teachers	$56,310	5.8%	28,400
69. Heating, Air Conditioning, and Refrigeration Mechanics and Installers	$44,630	13.6%	8,420
70. Police and Detectives	$60,130	4.1%	94,830
71. Nursing Assistants and Orderlies	$25,080	17.3%	61,680
72. Geoscientists	$89,910	10.4%	1,500
73. Kindergarten and Elementary School Teachers	$53,750	5.8%	43,480
74. Wholesale and Manufacturing Sales Representatives	$58,920	6.5%	11,720
75. Chiropractors	$66,720	17.5%	1,600
76. Audiologists	$73,060	28.0%	680
77. Podiatrists	$120,700	14.6%	330
78. Mental Health Counselors and Marriage and Family Therapists	$42,290	18.7%	6,660
79. Sales Engineers	$96,340	7.2%	2,300
80. Mathematicians	$103,720	20.0%	130
81. EMTs and Paramedics	$31,700	24.2%	9,800
82. Training and Development Specialists	$57,340	7.5%	8,040
83. Construction Managers	$85,630	4.8%	7,010
84. Customer Service Representatives	$31,200	9.8%	88,870
85. Veterinarians	$87,590	8.8%	1,900
86. Architectural and Engineering Managers	$130,620	2.0%	5,950
87. Middle School Teachers	$54,940	5.8%	17,550
88. Special Education Teachers	$55,890	6.3%	12,350
89. Construction Equipment Operators	$42,900	10.1%	11,820
90. Computer and Information Research Scientists	$108,360	10.5%	600
91. Property, Real Estate, and Community Association Managers	$54,270	8.1%	7,990
92. Line Installers and Repairers	$61,740	5.8%	8,250
93. Construction Laborers and Helpers	$30,350	13.0%	18,010
94. Interpreters and Translators	$43,590	28.7%	2,720
95. Architects	$74,520	6.7%	3,130
96. Cartographers and Photogrammetrists	$60,930	29.3%	740
97. Technical Writers	$69,030	10.2%	1,720
98. Substance Abuse and Behavioral Disorder Counselors	$39,270	22.4%	4,110
99. Radiation Therapists	$80,090	13.9%	620
100. Massage Therapists	$37,180	21.6%	4,900

Occupational Information Included in the *OOH*

The *Occupational Outlook Handbook (OOH)* is a career resource offering information on the hundreds of occupations that provide the overwhelming majority of jobs in the United States. Each occupational profile describes the duties required by the occupation, the work environment of that occupation, the typical education and training needed to enter the occupation, the median pay for workers in the occupation, and the job outlook into the next 10 years for that occupation. Each profile is in a standard format that makes it easy to compare occupations.

Sections of Occupational Profiles

- Summary
- What They Do
- Work Environment
- Education/Training
- Pay
- Job Outlook
- Similar Occupations
- Contacts for More Information

Summary

All profiles have a "Significant Points" table that gives information on the following topics:

- **2014 Median Pay:** The wage at which half of the workers in the occupation earned more than that amount and half earned less. Median wage data are from the Bureau of Labor Statistics (BLS) Occupational Employment Statistics (OES) survey. In May 2014, the median annual wage for all workers was $35,540.
- **Typical Entry-Level Education:** The typical level of education that most workers need to enter the occupation.
- **Work Experience in a Related Occupation:** Work experience that is commonly considered necessary by employers or is a commonly accepted substitute for more formal types of training or education.
- **On-the-job Training:** Postemployment training necessary to attain competency in the skills needed in the occupation. The training is occupation-specific rather than job specific, in that the skills learned can be transferred to another job in the same occupation.
- **Number of Jobs, 2014:** The employment, or size, of the occupation in 2014, the base year of the 2014–2024 employment projections.
- **Job Outlook, 2014–24:** The projected percent change in employment from 2014 to 2024. The average growth rate for all occupations is 7 percent.
- **Employment Change, 2014–24:** The projected numeric change in employment from 2014 to 2024.

The summary section briefly describes all of the sections included in each occupational profile.

What They Do

This section describes the main work of people in the occupation.

All occupations have a list of duties or typical tasks performed by these workers. The list includes daily responsibilities, such as answering phone calls or taking a patient's medical history.

This section also may describe the equipment, tools, software, or other items that people in the occupation typically use. For example, medical records and health information technicians frequently use electronic health records to document a patient's medical information. The section also may describe those with whom workers in the occupation interact, such as clients, patients, and coworkers.

Some profiles discuss specialties, alternate job titles, or types of occupations within a given occupation. This subsection includes a brief explanation of each specialty's job duties and how specialties differ from one another. For example, the profile on dentists includes several specialties, such as orthodontists, oral and maxillofacial surgeons, and pediatric dentists.

Work Environment

Job seekers and career planners should learn an occupation's working conditions, including the typical workplace, expected level of physical activity, and typical hours.

The section typically begins by noting the employment size of the occupation in 2014 and often includes a table of the industries, or settings, which employed the most workers in the occupation that year. The section also notes whether employees sometimes need to travel, and if so, how frequently. The section describes the workplace and discusses whether employees work in a safe work environment (such as an office) or a potentially hazardous one (such as a commercial fishing boat). If the workplace is hazardous, the section lists the type of equipment an employee must wear, such as a hardhat or protective goggles, to guard against accidents or exposure to harmful conditions. A subsection on Injuries and Illnesses may appear if this information is notable.

Work Schedules

Information on the typical schedule for workers in an occupation is included in this section, noting whether the majority of workers are employed full time or part time. Full-time workers typically work 35 or more hours in a week, whereas part-time employees work less than 35 hours. For some occupations, the profile also might include the time of day an employee is expected to begin work and for how long. Registered nurses, for example, may work all hours of the day and on weekends because medical facilities are open around the clock. A discussion of work schedules for occupations in which work may be seasonal, such as agricultural workers, also is in this section.

Education/Training

Knowing the typical paths for entry into an occupation gives job seekers and students an idea of how to become a doctor, flight attendant, or wind turbine technician, for example. All profiles have subsections on education and important qualities of workers in the occupation. Optional subsections include information on work experience; training; other experience, such as volunteering or internships; licenses, certifications, and registrations; and advancement.

Education

This subsection describes the education that most workers typically need to enter an occupation. Some occupations require no formal education, whereas others may require, for example, a doctoral or professional degree. In some occupations, such as computer support specialists, workers can enter with different educational backgrounds. In these cases, the profile discusses all of the typical paths for entry into the occupation.

This subsection also may include information on the college majors and subjects that people study in preparation for the occupation, as well as a list of typical courses that may aid a high school student in preparing for an occupation. For example, high school students interested in applying to respiratory therapy programs should take courses in health, biology, math, chemistry, and physics.

Work Experience in a Related Occupation

This subsection describes whether employers require work experience in a related occupation. Many managerial occupations rely on work experience in a related occupation. For example, architectural and engineering managers typically have previous work experience as an architect or engineer.

Training

Here, information includes typical on-the-job training necessary to attain competency in an occupation, including both practical and classroom training that workers receive after being hired. For example, firefighters must complete training at a fire academy or at an institution with a similar program before they are considered prepared to combat fires.

Apprenticeships, internships, and residency programs are also discussed this subsection. For example, the profile on physicians and surgeons includes information on residency programs and the architects profile has information on internships that architects complete as part of a training program to become licensed.

Other Experience

Other types of experience may be helpful or essential in getting a job in the occupation, such as experience gained through volunteering or student internships completed while one is in school. Students and job seekers may find this section helpful as it may provide additional content for their résumés.

Licenses, Certifications, and Registrations

This subsection describes whether credentials such as licenses, certifications, and registrations typically are needed for an occupation and, if so, how workers can earn the credentials.

States issue licenses to workers to signify that they have met specific legal requirements to practice in certain occupations. To become licensed, workers usually need to pass an exam and comply with eligibility requirements, such as possessing a minimum level of education, work experience, or training; or completing an internship, a residency, or a formal apprenticeship. States have their own regulatory boards that set standards for practicing a licensed occupation, so rules and eligibility criteria, including recertification requirements, may vary from state to state, even for the same occupation.

Some occupations have certifications available that typically are voluntary. For example, fitness trainers and instructors are encouraged, but not required, to become certified before entering the occupation. Some employers will allow a trainer or instructor to become certified after being hired. Certification requires demonstrated competency in a skill or a set of skills and commonly requires passing an exam or having a certain amount and type of work experience or training. For some certification programs, the candidate must have a certain level of education before becoming eligible for certification.

This subsection explains any prerequisites for certification, licensure, or registration, as well as how a person would complete them—such as by passing an exam, performing a certain type of work, or receiving certain training or education. If states require workers to be certified before they can be licensed, this section also notes that information.

Certification should not be confused with certificates from an educational institution. A certificate awarded by a postsecondary educational institution is a postsecondary nondegree award and is discussed in the subsection on education.

Registrations typically are required and issued by state or local governments. Workers seeking registration may need to be licensed or certified. In most cases, workers must pay fees to receive or maintain their registration.

Important Qualities

What does it take to be an engineer or teacher? This subsection describes important characteristics of workers in the occupation and includes an explanation of why those characteristics are useful.

The qualities may include skills, aptitudes, and personal characteristics. For example, an emergency medical technician must be physically strong, and a web developer needs creativity and customer-service skills.

Advancement

This subsection often explains the requirements for advancement, such as certification or additional formal education.

Opportunities for advancement can come from within the occupation, such as a promotion to a supervisory or managerial level; from advancement into another occupation, such as moving from a computer support specialist to a network and computer systems administrator; or by becoming self-employed, such as a dentist opening up his or her own practice.

Pay

Almost all occupational profiles in the *OOH* show median wage data for wage and salary workers in the occupation. The data are from the Bureau of Labor Statistics (BLS) Occupational Employment Statistics (OES) program. The median wage is the wage at which half of the workers in an occupation earned more and half earned less. A chart that compares the median wage of workers in the occupation to the median wage of workers across all occupations accompanies the wage data.

Profiles typically include median wages and the wages earned by the top 10 percent and bottom 10 percent of workers in the occupation. Many profiles also include wages earned by workers in selected industries—those in which most of an occupation's workers are employed. The wage data by industry also are from the OES survey.

Some occupational profiles may cite wage data from sources other than the BLS. For example, the Medical Group Management Association provides wage data for physicians and surgeons. Unless otherwise noted, the source of pay data for occupations in the *OOH* is the OES survey.

Job Outlook

How is employment projected to grow or decline between 2014 and 2024? This section has a chart that compares the rate of growth or decline for the occupation(s) covered in the profile to the rate for all occupations. In addition to presenting the projections, the section discusses the major factors expected to affect the outlook for employment in the occupation. Some of the factors are changes in technology, in business practices, and in demographics.

The outlook section sometimes includes a Job Prospects subsection, which provides a qualitative discussion of the relative ease or difficulty experienced by those who seek to enter the occupation.

Similar Occupations

Some occupations have similar job duties or similar required skills. This section identifies and provides key facts about those occupations.

Contacts for More Information

This section includes external links to associations, organizations, and other institutions that provide readers with additional information.

The section also includes links to the Occupational Information Network (O*NET) system for the occupation or occupations included in the profile. State employment service offices use O*NET to classify applicants and job openings. For each occupation, O*NET lists a number of descriptors, including common tasks, necessary knowledge and skills, and frequently used technology.

Key Phrases in the *OOH*

The following tables explain how to interpret the key phrases used to describe projected changes in employment:

Changing employment between 2014 and 2024

If the statement reads:	*Employment is projected to:*
Grow much faster than average	increase 14 percent or more
Grow faster than average	increase 9 to 13 percent
Grow about as fast as average	increase 5 to 8 percent
Grow more slowly than average	increase 2 to 4 percent
Little or no change	decrease 1 percent to increase 1 percent
Decline	decrease 2 percent or more

Sources of Career Information

This chapter identifies some major sources of information on careers. These sources are meant to be used in addition to those listed in the "Contacts for More Information" section of each profile.

How to use this information best. The sources mentioned in this chapter offer different types of information. For example, people you know may provide highly specific information because they have knowledge of you, your abilities and interests, and your qualifications. Other sources, such as those found in the state sources listed, provide information on occupations in each state. Gathering information from a wide range of sources is the best way to determine what occupations may be appropriate for you and in what geographic regions these occupations are found. The sources of information discussed in this chapter are not exhaustive, and other sources could prove equally valuable in your career search.

Career Information

Like any major decision, selecting a career involves a lot of fact finding. Fortunately, some of the best informational resources are easily accessible. You should assess career guidance materials carefully. Information that seems out of date or glamorizes an occupation—overstates its earnings or exaggerates the demand for workers, for example—should be evaluated with skepticism. Gathering as much information as possible will help you make a more informed decision.

People you know. One of the best resources can be your friends and family. They may answer some questions about a particular occupation or put you in touch with someone who has some experience in the field. This personal networking can be invaluable in evaluating an occupation or an employer. People you know will be able to tell you about their specific duties and training, as well as what they did or did not like about a job. People who have worked in an occupation locally also may be able to give you a recommendation and get you in touch with specific employers.

Employers. These are the primary source of information on specific jobs. Employers may post lists of job openings and application requirements, including the exact training and experience required, starting wages and benefits, and advancement opportunities and career paths.

Informational interviews. People already working in a particular field often are willing to speak with people interested in joining their field. An informational interview will allow you to get good information from experts in a specific career without the pressure of undergoing a job interview. These interviews allow you to determine how a certain career may appeal to you while helping you build a network of personal contacts.

Professional societies, trade groups, and labor unions. These sources have information on an occupation or various related occupations with which they are associated or that they actively represent. This information may cover training requirements and earnings, and may provide listings of local employers. These sources may train members or potential members themselves, or they may be able to put you in contact with organizations or individuals who perform such training.

Each occupational profile in the *Handbook* concludes with a "Contacts for More Information" section, which lists organizations that may be contacted for additional information.

Guidance counselors and career counselors. Counselors can help you make choices about which careers might suit you best. They can help you establish which occupations fit your skills by testing your aptitude for various types of work and determining your strengths and interests. Counselors can help you evaluate your options and search for a job in your field or help you select a new field altogether. They also can help you determine which educational or training institutions best fit your goals and then assist you in finding ways to finance your education or training. Some counselors offer other services, such as interview coaching, résumé building, and help in filling out various forms. Counselors in secondary schools and postsecondary institutions may arrange guest speakers, field trips, or job fairs.

You can find guidance and career counselors at

- High school guidance offices
- College career planning and placement offices
- Placement offices in private vocational or technical schools and institutions
- Vocational rehabilitation agencies
- Counseling services offered by community organizations
- Private counseling agencies and private practices
- State employment service offices

When using a private counselor, check to see that the counselor is experienced. One way to do so is to ask people who have used the counselor's services in the past. The National Board of Certified Counselors is an institution that accredits career counselors. To verify the credentials of a career counselor and to find a career counselor in your area, visit www.nbcc.org/.

Postsecondary institutions. Colleges, universities, and other postsecondary institutions typically put a lot of effort into helping place their graduates in good jobs, because the success of their graduates reflects the quality of their institution and may affect the institution's ability to attract new students. Postsecondary institutions commonly have career centers with information on different careers, listings of related jobs, and alumni contacts in various professions. Career centers frequently employ career counselors who generally provide their services only to their students and alumni. Career centers can help you build your résumé, find internships and co-ops—which can lead to full-time positions—and tailor your course selection or program to make you a more marketable job applicant.

Local libraries. Libraries can be a valuable source of information. Because most areas have libraries, they can be a convenient place to look for information. Also, many libraries provide access to the Internet and email.

Libraries may have information on job openings, locally and nationally; potential contacts within occupations or industries; colleges and financial aid; vocational training; individual businesses or careers; and writing résumés. Libraries frequently have subscriptions to various trade magazines that can provide information on occupations and industries. Your local library also may have video materials. These sources often have references to organizations that can provide additional information about training and employment opportunities.

If you need help getting started or finding a resource, ask your librarian for assistance.

Internet resources. A wide variety of career information is easily accessible on the Internet. Online resources include job listings, résumé posting services, and information on job fairs, training, and local wages. Many of the resources listed elsewhere in this chapter have Internet sites that include valuable information on potential careers. No single source contains all of the information on an occupation, field, or employer; therefore, you will likely need to use a variety of sources.

When using Internet resources, be sure that the organization is a credible, established source of information on the particular occupation you are interested in. Individual companies may include job listings on their websites, as well as information about required credentials, wages and benefits, and the job's location. Contact information, such as whom to call or where to send a résumé, is usually included.

Some sources exist primarily as a web service. These sources often have information on specific jobs and can greatly aid in the job-hunting process. Some commercial sites offer web services, as do federal, state, and some local governments.

Online Sources from the Department of Labor. A free major resource in the U.S. Department of Labor's Labor Market Information System is the CareerOneStop site (www.careeronestop.org). This site includes links to the following sources:

- State job banks allow you to search job openings listed with state employment agencies.
- America's Career InfoNet provides data on employment growth and wages by occupation; the knowledge, skills, and abilities required by an occupation; and links to employers.
- America's Service Locator is a comprehensive database of career centers and information on unemployment benefits, job training, and educational opportunities.
- O*NET Online provides occupational information, including descriptors on hundreds of occupations.

For more information on specific occupations, you can also visit the Department of Labor's Bureau of Labor Statistics (BLS). BLS publishes a wide range of labor market information, from regional wages for specific occupations to statistics on national, state, and area employment. For more information, visit www.bls.gov, especially the section on occupational wage data.

For information on training, workers' rights, and job listings, visit the Employment and Training Administration website (www.doleta.gov).

Career Outlook is a career magazine published by the BLS. The magazine includes many articles about finding, applying for, and choosing jobs. See, for example, the following Career Outlook articles:

- "Job search in the age of Internet: Six jobseekers in search of employers," online at www.bls.gov/careeroutlook/2003/summer/art01.pdf
- "Focused jobseeking: A measured approach to looking for work," online at www.bls.gov/careeroutlook/2011/spring/art01.pdf
- "Résumés, applications, and cover letters," online at www.bls.gov/careeroutlook/2009/summer/art03.pdf
- "Informational interviewing: Get the inside scoop on careers," online at www.bls.gov/careeroutlook/2002/summer/art03.pdf
- "Getting back to work: Returning to the labor force after an absence," online at www.bls.gov/careeroutlook/2004/winter/art03.pdf

Organizations for specific groups. Some organizations provide information designed to help specific groups of people. Consult directories in your library's reference center or in a career guidance office for information on additional organizations associated with specific groups.

Workers with disabilities:
Information on employment opportunities, transportation, and other considerations for people with a wide variety of disabilities is available from the following sources:

- National Organization on Disability, 5 East 86th Street, New York, NY 10028. Telephone: (646) 505-1191
- Job Accommodation Network (JAN), Telephone: (800) 526-7234 TTY: (877) 781-9403
- A comprehensive federal Web site of disability-related resources, accessible at www.disability.gov

Workers with vision problems:
Information on the free national reference and referral service for the blind can be obtained by contacting

- National Federation of the Blind, 200 East Wells Street, Baltimore, MD 21230. Telephone: (410) 659-9314

Older workers:

- National Council on Aging, 1901 L St. NW, 4th Floor, Washington, DC 20036. Telephone: (202) 479-1200
- National Caucus and Center on Black Aged, Inc., 1220 L St. NW, Suite 800, Washington, DC 20005. Telephone: (202) 637-8400

Veterans:
Contact the nearest regional office of the U.S. Department of Labor's Veterans Employment and Training Service or

- Credentialing Opportunities Online (COOL), which explains how military personnel can meet civilian certification and license requirements related to their Military Occupational Specialty (MOS).

Women:

- Department of Labor, Women's Bureau. Telephone: (800) 827-5335

Federal laws, executive orders, and selected federal grant programs bar employment discrimination based on race, color, religion, sex, national origin, age, and handicap. Information on how to file a charge of discrimination is available from U.S. Equal Employment Opportunity Commission offices around the country. Their addresses and telephone numbers are listed in telephone directories under U.S. Government, EEOC. Telephone: (800) 669-4000 TTY: (800) 669-6820

Office of Personnel Management. Information on obtaining civilian positions within the federal government is available from the U.S. Office of Personnel Management through USAJobs.gov, the federal government's official employment information system.

Military. The military employs people in, and has information on, hundreds of occupations. Information is available on tuition assistance programs, which provide money for school and other educational debt repayments. Information on military service can be provided by your local recruiting office, or visit the *Handbook* profile on military careers. You can also find more information on careers in the military at Today's Military (www.todaysmilitary.com).

Architecture and Engineering

Aerospace Engineering and Operations Technicians

- **2014 Median Pay** .... $63,780 per year
  $30.66 per hour
- **Typical Entry-Level Education** .... Associate's degree
- **Work Experience in a Related Occupation** .... None
- **On-the-job Training** .... None
- **Number of Jobs, 2014** 11,400
- **Job Outlook, 2014–24** .... 4% (Slower than average)
- **Employment Change, 2014–24** 400

What Aerospace Engineering and Operations Technicians Do

Aerospace engineering and operations technicians operate and maintain equipment used in testing new aircraft and spacecraft. Increasingly, these workers are being required to program and run computer simulations that test new designs. Their work is critical in preventing the failure of key parts of new aircraft, spacecraft, and missiles. They also help in the quality assurance, testing, and operation of advanced technology equipment used in producing aircraft and the systems that go into the aircraft.

Duties. Aerospace engineering and operations technicians typically do the following:

- Meet with aerospace engineers to discuss details and implications of test procedures
- Build and maintain test facilities for aircraft systems
- Make and install parts and systems to be tested in test equipment
- Operate and calibrate computer systems so that they comply with test requirements
- Ensure that test procedures are performed smoothly and safely
- Record data from test parts and assemblies
- Install instruments in aircraft and spacecraft
- Monitor and ensure quality in producing systems that go into the aircraft

New aircraft designs undergo years of testing before they are put into service, because the failure of key parts during flight can be fatal. As part of the job, technicians often calibrate test equipment, such as wind tunnels, and determine the causes of equipment malfunctions. They also may program and run computer simulations that test the new designs.

Some aerospace engineering and operations technicians are beginning to specialize in three-dimensional printing, or additive manufacturing, as this technology becomes more common in the work they do.

Work Environment

Aerospace engineering and operations technicians held about 11,400 jobs in 2014. The industries that employed the most aerospace engineering and operations technicians were as follows:

Aerospace engineering and operations technicians work to prevent the failure of key parts of new aircraft, spacecraft, or missiles.

Aerospace product and parts manufacturing	33%
Engineering services	18
Computer and electronic product manufacturing	17
Testing laboratories	16
Research and development in the physical, engineering, and life sciences	5

They usually work in manufacturing or industrial plants, laboratories, and offices. Aerospace engineering and operations technicians who work in manufacturing or industrial plants are frequently directly involved in assembling aircraft, missiles, and spacecraft. Many are exposed to hazards from equipment or from toxic materials, but incidents are rare as long as proper procedures are followed.

Work Schedules. Aerospace engineering and operations technicians have opportunities for employment throughout the private sector, with large and small manufacturing organizations, as well as with engineering services firms. Schedules worked tend to parallel those of the other engineering and operations staff members, and most work full time.

Median Annual Wages, May 2014

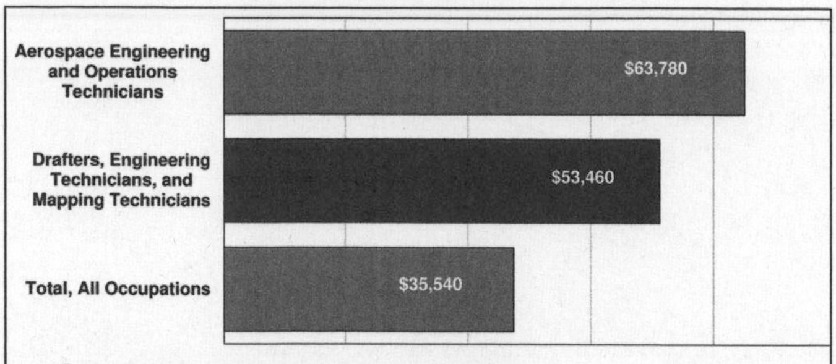

Note: All Occupations includes all occupations in the U.S. Economy.
Source: U.S. Bureau of Labor Statistics, Occupational Employment Statistics

Percent Change in Employment, Projected 2014–2024

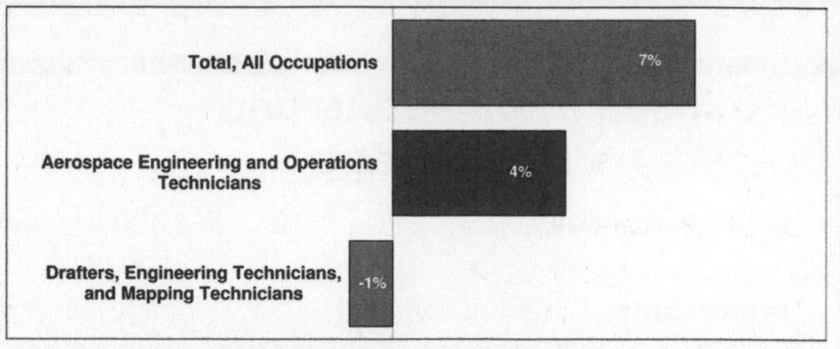

Note: All Occupations includes all occupations in the U.S. Economy.
Source: U.S. Bureau of Labor Statistics, Office of Occupational Statistics and Employment Projections

Education/Training

Many employers prefer to hire aerospace engineering and operations technicians who have earned an associate's degree in engineering technology. Prospective technicians also may earn certificates or diplomas offered by vocational or technical schools. Some aerospace engineering and operations technicians must have security clearances to work on projects related to national defense. U.S. citizenship may be required for certain types and levels of clearances.

Education. High school students interested in becoming aerospace engineering and operations technicians should take classes in math, science, and, if available, drafting and computer skills. Courses that help students develop skills working with their hands also are valuable, because these technicians build what aerospace engineers design. In addition, technicians should have a basic understanding of computers and programs in order to model or simulate products.

Aerospace engineering and operations technicians typically need to earn an associate's degree or a graduate certificate from a community college or vocational-technical school. Community colleges offer programs similar to those in technical institutes but include more theory-based and liberal arts coursework and programs. Community colleges typically award an associate's degree. Vocational-technical schools include postsecondary public institutions that emphasize training needed by local employers. Students who complete these programs typically receive a diploma or certificate.

The Engineering Technology Accreditation Commission of ABET accredits programs that include at least college algebra, trigonometry, and basic science courses.

Many vocational and community colleges offer cooperative programs with work experience built into the curriculum.

Important Qualities

Communication skills. Aerospace engineering and operations technicians receive instructions from aerospace engineers. Therefore, they must be able to understand and follow those instructions, as well as communicate any problems to their supervisors.

Critical-thinking skills. Aerospace engineering and operations technicians must be able to help aerospace engineers troubleshoot particular design issues. They must be able to help evaluate system capabilities, identify problems, formulate the right question, and then find the right answer.

Detail oriented. Aerospace engineering and operations technicians make and keep precise measurements needed by aerospace engineers. Consequently, they must make correct measurements and keep accurate records.

Interpersonal skills. Aerospace engineering and operations technicians must be able to take instructions and offer advice. The ability to work well with supervising engineers, other technicians, and mechanics is essential because technicians interact with people from other divisions, businesses, and governments.

Math skills. Aerospace engineering and operations technicians use the principles of mathematics for analysis, design, and troubleshooting tasks in their work.

Mechanical skills. Aerospace engineering and operations technicians must be able to assist aerospace engineers by building what the engineers design. Mechanical skills are needed to help with the processes and directions required to move from design to production.

Licenses, Certifications, and Registrations. Although not required for the job, certification is offered by the Federal Aviation Administration (FAA). Certification may be beneficial because it shows employers that a technician can carry out the theoretical designs of aerospace engineers.

Both companies and the FAA seek to ensure the highest standards for the safety of the aircraft. SpaceTEC, the National Science Foundation's Center for Aerospace Technical Education, coordinates a nationwide program through community and technical colleges to help students prepare for certification.

Pay

The median annual wage for aerospace engineering and operations technicians was $63,780 in May 2014. The median wage is the wage at which half the workers in an occupation earned more than that amount and half earned less. The lowest 10 percent

Employment Projections Data for Aerospace Engineering and Operations Technicians

Occupational Title	SOC Code	Employment, 2014	Projected Employment, 2024	Change, 2014–2024 Percent	Change, 2014–2024 Numeric
Aerospace engineering and operations technicians	17-3021	11,400	11,800	4	400

Source: U.S. Bureau of Labor Statistics, Employment Projections Program

Similar Occupations. This table shows a list of occupations with job duties that are similar to those of aerospace engineering and operations technicians.

Occupations	Entry-level Education	2014 Median Pay	Projected Job Growth	Average Annual Openings
Aerospace Engineers	Bachelor's degree	$105,380	-2%	-160
Drafters	Associate's degree	$51,940	-3%	-620
Electro-mechanical Technicians	Associate's degree	$53,070	1%	10
Industrial Engineering Technicians	Associate's degree	$53,370	-5%	-300
Mechanical Engineering Technicians	Associate's degree	$53,530	2%	90

earned less than $38,440, and the highest 10 percent earned more than $93,330.

In May 2014, the median annual wages for aerospace engineering and operations technicians in the top industries in which they worked were as follows:

Aerospace product and parts manufacturing.................... $69,400
Computer and electronic product manufacturing............... 67,180
Research and development in the physical, engineering, and life sciences.. 60,440
Engineering services.. 59,550
Testing laboratories... 56,350

Job Outlook

Employment of aerospace engineering and operations technicians is projected to grow 4 percent from 2014 to 2024, slower than the average for all occupations. Aerospace engineering and operations technicians work on many projects related to national defense and therefore require security clearances. This restriction will help to keep jobs in the United States. In addition, aircraft are being redesigned to cut down on noise pollution and to raise fuel efficiency. Need for such redesigns should raise demand for research and development, particularly in support of air transportation.

Aerospace engineering and operations technicians work mainly in national defense–related projects or in constructing civilian aircraft. These technicians also are employed in the rising market for pilotless aerial vehicles. Successful research and development projects, ranging from more efficient propulsion systems to new air transport concepts, will result in new product lines and create demand for these workers.

Those who work on engines or propulsion will be increasingly needed as design and production emphasis shifts to rebuilding existing aircraft so that they give off less noise while using less fuel. Opportunities for employment with civilian space companies should increase as spaceflight shifts to the civilian market from government agencies.

However, aerospace engineering and operations technicians also are working to improve productivity through the use of automation and robotics, and the increased productivity likely will reduce low-end production employment in this occupation. Another factor that may slow growth in the occupation is the continuing adoption of computational fluid dynamics software. This technology has lowered testing costs and has replaced more traditional testing. As a result, these technicians will see a shift toward more high-end technology tasks.

Contacts for More Information

For more information about accredited programs, visit
➤ ABET (www.abet.org)

For more information about careers in engineering, visit
➤ Technology Student Association (www.tsaweb.org)

For more information about certification, visit
➤ Federal Aviation Administration (www.faa.gov)
➤ SpaceTEC (http://spacetec.us/wordpress11)

O*NET

➤ Aerospace Engineering and Operations Technicians (17-3021.00)

Aerospace Engineers

- **2014 Median Pay** .... $105,380 per year
  $50.66 per hour
- **Typical Entry-Level Education** .... Bachelor's degree
- **Work Experience in a Related Occupation** .... None
- **On-the-job Training** .... None
- **Number of Jobs, 2014** 72,500
- **Job Outlook, 2014–24** .... -2% (Decline)
- **Employment Change, 2014–24** .... -1,600

What Aerospace Engineers Do

Aerospace engineers design primarily aircraft, spacecraft, satellites, and missiles. In addition, they test prototypes to make sure that they function according to design.

Duties. Aerospace engineers typically do the following:

- Direct and coordinate the design, manufacture, and testing of aircraft and aerospace products
- Assess proposals for projects to determine if they are technically and financially feasible
- Determine if proposed projects will result in safe aircraft and parts
- Evaluate designs to see that the products meet engineering principles, customer requirements, and environmental challenges
- Develop acceptance criteria for design methods, quality standards, sustainment after delivery, and completion dates
- Ensure that projects meet quality standards
- Inspect malfunctioning or damaged products to identify sources of problems and possible solutions

Aerospace engineers may develop new technologies for use in aviation, defense systems, and spacecraft. They often specialize in areas such as aerodynamic fluid flow; structural design; guidance, navigation, and control; instrumentation and communication; robotics; and propulsion and combustion.

Aerospace engineers can specialize in designing different types of aerospace products, such as commercial and military airplanes and helicopters; remotely piloted aircraft and rotorcraft;

spacecraft, including launch vehicles and satellites; and military missiles and rockets.

Aerospace engineers often become experts in one or more related fields: aerodynamics, thermodynamics, celestial mechanics, flight mechanics, propulsion, acoustics, and guidance and control systems.

Aerospace engineers typically specialize in one of two types of engineering: aeronautical or astronautical.

Aeronautical engineers work with aircraft. They are involved primarily in designing aircraft and propulsion systems and in studying the aerodynamic performance of aircraft and construction materials. They work with the theory, technology, and practice of flight within Earth's atmosphere.

Astronautical engineers work with the science and technology of spacecraft and how they perform inside and outside Earth's atmosphere.

Aeronautical and astronautical engineers face different environmental and operational issues in designing aircraft and spacecraft. However, the two fields overlap a great deal because they both depend on the basic principles of physics.

Work Environment

Aerospace engineers held about 72,500 jobs in 2014. The industries that employed the most aerospace engineers were as follows:

Aerospace product and parts manufacturing	38%
Engineering services	14
Federal government, excluding postal service	13
Research and development in the physical, engineering, and life sciences	12
Navigational, measuring, electromedical, and control instruments manufacturing	5

They are employed in industries where workers design or build aircraft, missiles, systems for national defense, or spacecraft. Aerospace engineers work primarily for firms that engage in manufacturing, analysis and design, research and development, and for the federal government.

Aerospace engineers now spend more of their time in an office environment than they have in the past, because modern aircraft design requires the use of sophisticated computer equipment and software design tools, modeling, and simulations for tests, evaluation, and training.

Aerospace engineers study the necessary physics for designing aircraft that will fly.

Aerospace engineers work with other professionals involved in designing and building aircraft, spacecraft, and their components. Therefore, they must be able to communicate well, divide work into manageable tasks, and work with others toward a common goal.

Work Schedules. Aerospace engineers typically work full time. Engineers who direct projects must often work extra hours to monitor progress, to ensure that the design meets requirements, to determine how to measure aircraft performance, to see that production meets design standards, and to ensure that deadlines are met.

Education/Training

Aerospace engineers must have a bachelor's degree in aerospace engineering or another field of engineering or science related to aerospace systems. Aerospace engineers who work on projects that are related to national defense may need a security clearance. U.S. citizenship may be required for certain types and levels of clearances.

Education. Entry-level aerospace engineers usually need a bachelor's degree. High school students interested in studying aerospace engineering should take courses in chemistry, physics, and math, including algebra, trigonometry, and calculus.

Bachelor's degree programs include classroom, laboratory, and field studies in subjects such as general engineering principles, propulsion, stability and control, structures, mechanics, and aerodynamics, which is the study of how air interacts with moving objects.

Some colleges and universities offer cooperative programs in partnership with regional businesses, which give students practical experience while they complete their education. Cooperative programs and internships enable students to gain valuable experience and to finance part of their education.

At some universities, a student can enroll in a 5-year program that leads to both a bachelor's degree and a master's degree upon completion. A graduate degree will allow an engineer to work as an instructor at a university or to do research and development. Programs in aerospace engineering are accredited by ABET.

Important Qualities

Analytical skills. Aerospace engineers must be able to identify design elements that may not meet requirements and then must formulate alternatives to improve the performance of those elements.

Business skills. Much of the work done by aerospace engineers involves meeting federal government standards. Meeting these standards often requires knowledge of standard business practices, as well as knowledge of commercial law.

Critical-thinking skills. Aerospace engineers must be able to translate a set of issues into requirements and to figure out why a particular design does not work. They must be able to ask the right question, then find an acceptable answer.

Math skills. Aerospace engineers use the principles of calculus, trigonometry, and other advanced topics in math for analysis, design, and troubleshooting in their work.

Problem-solving skills. Aerospace engineers use their education and experience to upgrade designs and troubleshoot problems when meeting new demands for aircraft, such as increased fuel efficiency or improved safety.

Writing skills. Aerospace engineers must be able both to write papers that explain their designs clearly and to create documentation for future reference.

Licenses, Certifications, and Registrations. Licensure is not required for entry-level positions as an aerospace engineer. A

Median Annual Wages, May 2014

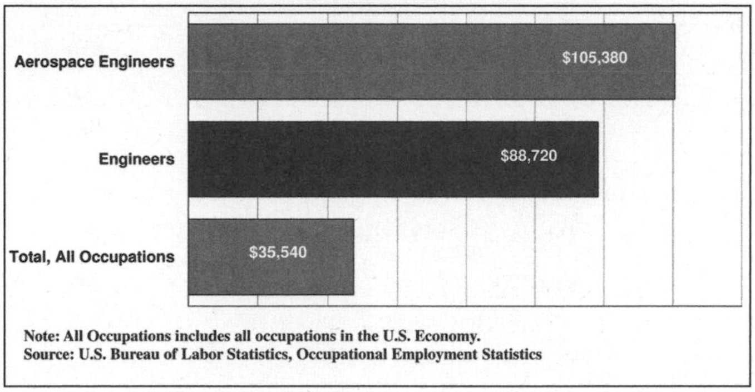

Percent Change in Employment, Projected 2014–2024

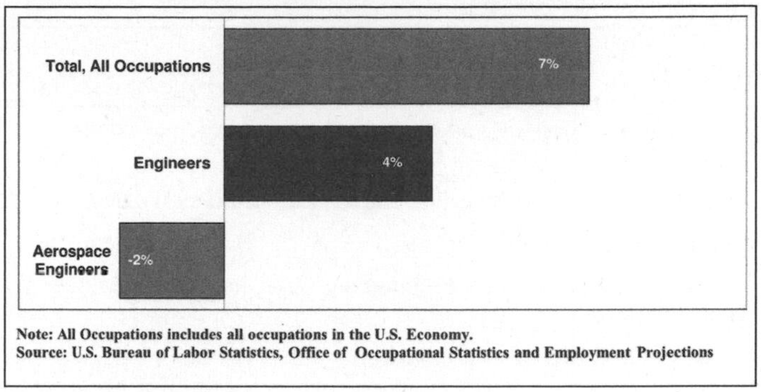

Professional Engineer (PE) license, which allows for higher levels of leadership and independence, can be acquired later in one's career. Licensed engineers are called professional engineers (PEs). A PE can oversee the work of other engineers, sign off on projects, and provide services directly to the public. State licensure generally requires:

- A degree from an ABET-accredited engineering program
- A passing score on the Fundamentals of Engineering (FE) exam
- Relevant work experience, typically at least 4 years
- A passing score on the Principles and Practice of Engineering (PE) exam

The initial FE exam can be taken after one earns a bachelor's degree. Engineers who pass this exam are commonly called engineers in training (EITs) or engineer interns (EIs). After meeting work experience requirements, EITs and EIs can take the second exam, called Principles and Practice of Engineering.

Advancement. Eventually, aerospace engineers may advance to become technical specialists or to supervise a team of engineers and technicians. Some may even become engineering managers or move into executive positions, such as program managers.

Pay

The median annual wage for aerospace engineers was $105,380 in May 2014. The median wage is the wage at which half the workers in an occupation earned more than that amount and half earned less. The lowest 10 percent earned less than $66,110, and the highest 10 percent earned more than $155,240.

In May 2014, the median annual wages for aerospace engineers in the top industries in which they worked were as follows:

Federal government, excluding postal service	$113,550
Navigational, measuring, electromedical, and control instruments manufacturing	111,660
Research and development in the physical, engineering, and life sciences	107,490
Engineering services	103,450
Aerospace product and parts manufacturing	102,430

Job Outlook

Employment of aerospace engineers is projected to decline 2 percent from 2014 to 2024. Aircraft are being redesigned to cut down on noise pollution and to raise fuel efficiency, which will help sustain demand for research and development. However, growth will be tempered because many of these engineers are employed in manufacturing industries that are projected to grow slowly or even decline.

Most of the work of aerospace engineers involves national defense–related projects or the design of civilian aircraft. Research-and-development projects, such as those related to improving the safety, efficiency, and environmental soundness of aircraft, should sustain demand for workers in this occupation.

Aerospace engineers who work on engines or propulsion will continue to be needed as the emphasis in design and production shifts to rebuilding existing aircraft so that they are less noisy and more fuel efficient.

In addition, as governments refocus their space efforts, new companies are emerging to provide access to space beyond the access afforded by standard space agencies. The efforts of these companies will include low-orbit and beyond-earth-orbit capabilities for human and robotic space travel. Unmanned aerial vehicles will create some opportunities for aerospace engineers as authorities find domestic uses for them, such as finding missing persons lost in large tracts of forest or helping to put out forest fires.

Job Prospects. Aerospace engineers who know how to use collaborative engineering tools and processes and who are familiar with modeling, simulation, and robotics should have good opportunities. Employment opportunities also should be favorable for those trained in computational fluid dynamics software, which has enabled companies to test designs in a digital environment, thereby lowering testing costs. Finally, the aging of workers in this occupation should help to create openings in it over the next decade.

Contacts for More Information

For information about general engineering education and career resources, visit

- ➤ American Society for Engineering Education (www.asee.org)
- ➤ Technology Student Association (www.tsaweb.org)

Employment Projections Data for Aerospace Engineers

Occupational Title	SOC Code	Employment, 2014	Projected Employment, 2024	Change, 2014–2024 Percent	Change, 2014–2024 Numeric
Aerospace engineers	17-2011	72,500	70,800	-2	-1,600

Source: U.S. Bureau of Labor Statistics, Employment Projections Program

Similar Occupations. This table shows a list of occupations with job duties that are similar to those of aerospace engineers.

Occupations	Entry-level Education	2014 Median Pay	Projected Job Growth	Average Annual Openings
Aerospace Engineering and Operations Technicians	Associate's degree	$63,780	4%	40
Architectural and Engineering Managers	Bachelor's degree	$130,620	2%	370
Computer Hardware Engineers	Bachelor's degree	$108,430	3%	240
Electrical and Electronics Engineering Technicians	Associate's degree	$59,820	-2%	-280
Electrical and Electronics Engineers	Bachelor's degree	$93,260	0%	-10
Industrial Engineers	Bachelor's degree	$81,490	1%	210
Materials Engineers	Bachelor's degree	$87,690	1%	30
Mechanical Engineers	Bachelor's degree	$83,060	5%	1,460

For more information about licensure as an aerospace engineer, visit

➤ National Council of Examiners for Engineering and Surveying (www.ncees.org)

➤ National Society of Professional Engineers (www.nspe.org/index.html)

For information about accredited engineering programs, visit

➤ ABET (www.abet.org)

For information about current developments in aeronautics, visit

➤ American Institute of Aeronautics and Astronautics (www.aiaa.org)

O*NET

➤ Aerospace Engineers (17-2011.00)

Agricultural Engineers

- **2014 Median Pay** .... $71,730 per year $34.48 per hour
- **Typical Entry-Level Education** .... Bachelor's degree
- **Work Experience in a Related Occupation** .... None
- **On-the-job Training** .... None
- **Number of Jobs, 2014** 2,900
- **Job Outlook, 2014–24** .... 4% (Slower than average)
- **Employment Change, 2014–24** 100

What Agricultural Engineers Do

Agricultural engineers attempt to solve agricultural problems concerning power supplies, the efficiency of machinery, the use of structures and facilities, pollution and environmental issues, and the storage and processing of agricultural products.

Duties. Agricultural engineers typically do the following:

- Use computer software to design equipment, systems, or structures
- Modify environmental factors that affect animal or crop production, such as airflow in a barn or runoff patterns on a field
- Test equipment to ensure its safety and reliability
- Oversee construction and production operations
- Plan and work together with clients, contractors, consultants, and other engineers to ensure effective and desirable outcomes

Agricultural engineers work in farming, including aquaculture (farming of seafood), forestry, and food processing. They work on a wide variety of projects. For example, some agricultural engineers work to develop climate control systems that increase the comfort and productivity of livestock whereas others work to increase the storage capacity and efficiency of refrigeration. Many agricultural engineers attempt to develop better solutions for animal waste disposal. Those with computer programing skills work to integrate artificial intelligence and geospatial systems into agriculture. For example, they work to improve efficiency in fertilizer application or to automate harvesting systems.

Work Environment

Agricultural engineers held about 2,900 jobs in 2014. The industries that employed the most agricultural engineers were as follows:

Engineering services	14%
Federal government, excluding postal service	13
Food manufacturing	10
Colleges, universities, and professional schools; state	10
State and local government, excluding education and hospitals	10

Agricultural engineers work in a variety of industries. Some work for the federal government, and others provide engineering contracting or consultation services or work for agricultural machinery manufacturers.

Agricultural engineers typically work in offices, but may spend time at a variety of worksites, both indoors and outdoors. They may travel to agricultural settings to see that equipment and machinery are functioning according to both the manufacturers' specifications and federal and state regulations. Some agricultural engineers occasionally work in laboratories to test the quality of processing equipment. They may work onsite when they supervise livestock facility upgrades or water resource management projects.

Agricultural engineers work with others in designing solutions to problems or applying technological advances. They work with people from a variety of backgrounds, such as business, agronomy, animal sciences, and public policy.

Work Schedules. Agricultural engineers typically work full time. Schedules may vary because of weather conditions or other complications. When working on outdoor projects, agricultural engineers may work more hours to take advantage of good weather or fewer hours in case of bad weather.

Agricultural engineering includes designing farming equipment and processes.

In addition, agricultural engineers may need to be available outside of normal work hours to address unexpected problems that come up in manufacturing operations or rural construction projects.

Education/Training

Agricultural engineers must have a bachelor's degree, preferably in agricultural engineering or biological engineering.

Education. Students who are interested in studying agricultural engineering will benefit from taking high school courses in mathematics and sciences. University students take courses in advanced calculus, physics, biology, and chemistry. They also may take courses in business, public policy, and economics.

Entry-level jobs in agricultural engineering require a bachelor's degree. Bachelor's degree programs in agricultural engineering or biological engineering typically include significant hands-on components in areas such as science, mathematics, and engineering principles. Most colleges and universities encourage students to gain practical experience through projects such as participating in engineering competitions in which teams of students design equipment and attempt to solve real problems.

ABET accredits programs in agricultural engineering.

Important Qualities

Analytical skills. Agricultural engineers may design systems that are part of a larger agricultural or environmental system. They must be able to analyze the needs of complex systems that involve workers, machinery and equipment, and the environment.

Communication skills. Agricultural engineers must understand the needs of clients, workers, and others working on a project. Furthermore, they must be able to communicate their thoughts about systems and about solutions to any problems they have been working on.

Math skills. Agricultural engineers use calculus, trigonometry, and other advanced mathematical disciplines for analysis, design, and troubleshooting.

Problem-solving skills. Agricultural engineers' main role is to solve problems found in agricultural production. Goals may include designing safer equipment for food processing or reducing erosion. To solve these problems, agricultural engineers must be able to creatively apply the principles of engineering.

Licenses, Certifications, and Registrations. Licensure is not required for entry-level positions as an agricultural engineer. A Professional Engineer (PE) license, which allows for higher levels of leadership and independence, can be acquired later in one's career. Licensed engineers are called professional engineers (PEs). A PE can oversee the work of other engineers, sign off on projects, and provide services directly to the public. State licensure generally requires

- A degree from an ABET-accredited engineering program
- A passing score on the Fundamentals of Engineering (FE) exam
- Relevant work experience, typically at least 4 years
- A passing score on the Principles and Practice of Engineering (PE) exam

The initial FE exam can be taken after earning a bachelor's degree. Engineers who pass this exam commonly are called engineers in training (EITs) or engineer interns (EIs). After meeting work experience requirements, EITs and EIs can take the second exam, called Principles and Practice of Engineering.

Each state issues its own licenses. Most states recognize licensure from other states, as long as the licensing state's requirements meet or exceed their own licensure requirements. Several states require continuing education for engineers to keep their licenses.

Advancement. New engineers usually work under the supervision of experienced engineers. As they gain knowledge and experience, beginning engineers move to more difficult projects and increase their independence in developing designs, solving problems, and making decisions.

With experience, agricultural engineers may advance to supervise a team of engineers and technicians. Some advance to become engineering managers. Agricultural engineers who go into sales use their engineering background to discuss a product's technical aspects with potential buyers and to help in product planning, installation, and use. For more information, see the profiles on architectural and engineering managers and sales engineers.

Engineers who have a master's degree or a Ph.D. are more likely to be involved in research and development activities and may become postsecondary teachers.

Pay

The median annual wage for agricultural engineers was $71,730 in May 2014. The median wage is the wage at which half the workers in an occupation earned more than that amount and half earned less. The lowest 10 percent earned less than $45,940, and the highest 10 percent earned more than $112,700.

In May 2014, the median annual wages for agricultural engineers in the top industries in which they worked were as follows:

Federal government, excluding postal service	$81,080
Engineering services	76,440
Food manufacturing	73,180
State and local government, excluding education and hospitals	59,930
Colleges, universities, and professional schools; state	51,930

Job Outlook

Employment of agricultural engineers is projected to grow 4 percent from 2014 to 2024, slower than the average for all occupations. The need to increase the efficiency of agricultural production systems and to reduce environmental damage should maintain demand for these workers.

Agricultural engineers have been expanding the range of projects they work on. Some of these new project areas that will drive demand for this occupation are alternative energies and biofuels;

Median Annual Wages, May 2014

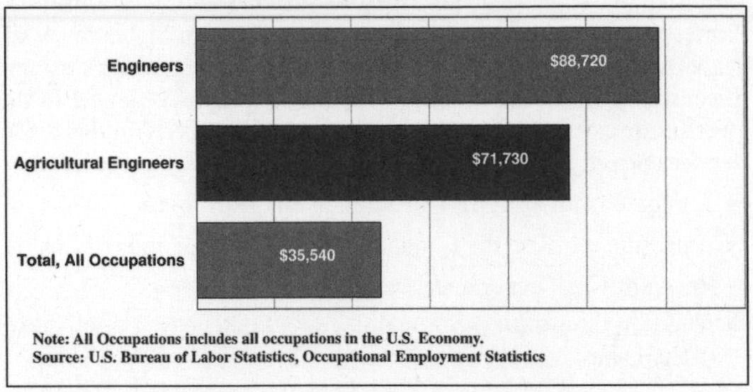

Percent Change in Employment, Projected 2014–2024

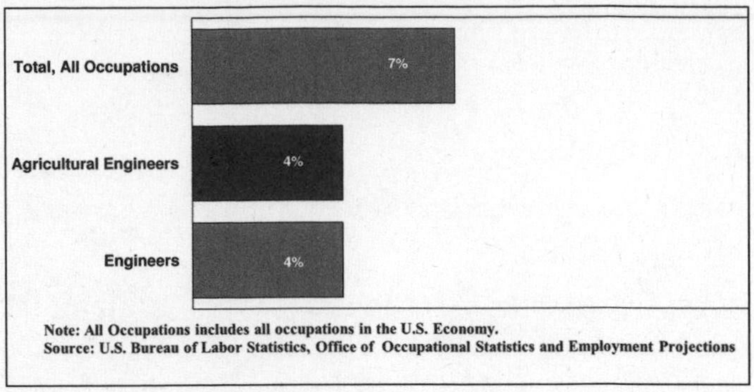

precision and automated farming technologies for irrigation, spraying, and harvesting; and, even more cutting edge, how to grow food in space to support future exploration.

New, more efficient designs for traditional agricultural engineering projects such as irrigation, storage, and worker safety systems will also maintain demand for these workers. Growing populations and stronger global competition will continue to pressure farmers to find more efficient means of production, and toward this end, they will need agricultural engineers.

Job Prospects. Typically, graduates of engineering programs have good job prospects and can often enter related engineering fields in addition to the field in which they have earned their degree. Agricultural engineering offers good opportunities, but it is a small occupation, and engineers trained in other fields, such as civil or mechanical engineering, also may compete for these jobs. Graduates of biological and agricultural engineering programs may have some advantage when applying for agricultural engineering jobs, but some may find good prospects outside of the agricultural sector.

Contacts for More Information

For more information about agricultural engineers, visit

- American Society of Agricultural and Biological Engineers (www.asabe.org)

For information about general engineering education and career resources, visit

- American Society for Engineering Education (www.asee.org)
- Technology Student Association (www.tsaweb.org)

For more information about licensure for agricultural engineers, visit

- National Council of Examiners for Engineering and Surveying (http://ncees.org)
- National Society of Professional Engineers (www.nspe.org)

For information about accredited engineering programs, visit

- ABET (www.abet.org)

Employment Projections Data for Agricultural Engineers

Occupational Title	SOC Code	Employment, 2014	Projected Employment, 2024	Change, 2014–2024 Percent	Change, 2014–2024 Numeric
Agricultural engineers	17-2021	2,900	3,000	4	100

Source: U.S. Bureau of Labor Statistics, Employment Projections Program

Similar Occupations. This table shows a list of occupations with job duties that are similar to those of agricultural engineers.

Occupations	Entry-level Education	2014 Median Pay	Projected Job Growth	Average Annual Openings
Agricultural and Food Science Technicians	Associate's degree	$35,140	5%	160
Agricultural and Food Scientists	Bachelor's degree	$60,690	5%	190
Biomedical Engineers	Bachelor's degree	$86,950	23%	510
Civil Engineers	Bachelor's degree	$82,050	8%	2,360
Conservation Scientists and Foresters	Bachelor's degree	$60,360	7%	270
Environmental Engineers	Bachelor's degree	$83,360	12%	680
Farmers, Ranchers, and Other Agricultural Managers	High school diploma or equivalent	$68,050	-2%	-1,810
Hydrologists	Bachelor's degree	$78,370	7%	50
Industrial Engineers	Bachelor's degree	$81,490	1%	210
Mechanical Engineers	Bachelor's degree	$83,060	5%	1,460

For a variety of information concerning agriculture, grants, and government initiatives, visit

➤ U.S. Department of Agriculture's National Institute of Food and Agriculture (http://nifa.usda.gov/grants)

O*NET

➤ Agricultural Engineers (17-2021.00)

Architects

- **2014 Median Pay** .... $74,520 per year $35.83 per hour
- **Typical Entry-Level Education** .... Bachelor's degree
- **Work Experience in a Related Occupation** .... None
- **On-the-job Training** .... Internship/residency
- **Number of Jobs, 2014** 112,600
- **Job Outlook, 2014–24** .... 7% (As fast as average)
- **Employment Change, 2014–24** 7,800

What Architects Do

Architects plan and design houses, factories, office buildings, and other structures.

Duties. Architects typically do the following:

- Meet with clients to determine objectives and requirements for structures
- Give preliminary estimates on cost and construction time
- Prepare structure specifications
- Direct workers who prepare drawings and documents
- Prepare scaled drawings, either with computer software or by hand
- Prepare contract documents for building contractors
- Manage construction contracts
- Visit worksites to ensure that construction adheres to architectural plans
- Seek new work by marketing and giving presentations

People need places to live, work, play, learn, shop, and eat. Architects are responsible for designing these places. They work on public or private projects and design both indoor and outdoor spaces. Architects can be commissioned to design anything from a single room to an entire complex of buildings.

Architects discuss the objectives, requirements, and budget of a project with clients. In some cases, architects provide various predesign services, such as feasibility and environmental impact studies, site selection, cost analyses, and design requirements.

Architects develop final construction plans after discussing and agreeing on the initial proposal with clients. These plans show the building's appearance and details of its construction. Accompanying these plans are drawings of the structural system; air-conditioning, heating, and ventilating systems; electrical systems; communications systems; and plumbing. Sometimes, landscape plans are included as well. In developing designs, architects must follow state and local building codes, zoning laws, fire regulations, and other ordinances, such as those requiring easy access to buildings for people who are disabled.

Computer-aided design and drafting (CADD) and building information modeling (BIM) have replaced traditional drafting paper and pencil as the most common methods for creating designs and construction drawings. However, hand-drawing skills are still required, especially during the conceptual stages of a project and when an architect is at a construction site.

As construction continues, architects may visit building sites to ensure that contractors follow the design, adhere to the schedule, use the specified materials, and meet work-quality standards. The job is not complete until all construction is finished, required tests are conducted, and construction costs are paid.

Architects may also help clients get construction bids, select contractors, and negotiate construction contracts.

Architects often collaborate with workers in related occupations, such as civil engineers, urban and regional planners, drafters, interior designers, and landscape architects.

Work Environment

Architects held about 112,600 jobs in 2014, with 69 percent employed in architectural, engineering, and related services. About 1 in 5 were self-employed.

Architects spend much of their time in offices, where they meet with clients, develop reports and drawings, and work with other architects and engineers. They also visit construction sites to ensure clients' objectives are met and to review the progress of projects. Some architects work from home offices.

Work Schedules. Most architects work full time and many work additional hours, especially when facing deadlines. Self-employed architects may have more flexible work schedules.

Education/Training

There are typically three main steps to becoming a licensed architect: completing a professional degree in architecture, gaining relevant experience through a paid internship, and passing the Architect Registration Examination.

Education. In all states, earning a professional degree in architecture is typically the first step to becoming an architect. Most architects earn their professional degree through a 5-year Bachelor of Architecture degree program, intended for students with no previous architectural training. Many earn a master's degree in architecture, which can take 1 to 5 years in addition to the time spent earning a bachelor's degree. The amount of time required depends on the extent of the student's previous education and training in architecture.

It takes many years of education and experience to become a licensed architect.

A typical bachelor's degree program includes courses in architectural history and theory, building design with an emphasis on computer-aided design and drafting (CADD), structures, construction methods, professional practices, math, physical sciences, and liberal arts. Central to most architectural programs is the design studio, where students apply the skills and concepts learned in the classroom to create drawings and three-dimensional models of their designs.

Currently, 34 states require that architects hold a professional degree in architecture from one of the 123 schools of architecture accredited by the National Architectural Accrediting Board (NAAB). State licensing requirements can be found at the National Council of Architectural Registration Boards (NCARB). In the states that do not have that requirement, applicants can become licensed with 8 to 13 years of related work experience in addition to a high school diploma. However, most architects in these states still obtain a professional degree in architecture.

Training. All state architectural registration boards require architecture graduates to complete a lengthy paid internship—generally 3 years of experience—before they may sit for the Architect Registration Examination. Most new graduates complete their training period by working at architectural firms through the Intern Development Program (IDP), a program run by NCARB that guides students through the internship process. Some states allow a portion of the training to occur in the offices of employers in related careers, such as engineers and general contractors. Architecture students who complete internships while still in school can count some of that time toward the 3-year training period.

Interns in architectural firms may help design part of a project. They may help prepare architectural documents and drawings, build models, and prepare construction drawings on CADD. Interns may also research building codes and write specifications for building materials, installation criteria, the quality of finishes, and other related details. Licensed architects will take the documents that interns produce, make edits to them, finalize plans, and then sign and seal the documents.

Licenses, Certifications, and Registrations. All states and the District of Columbia require architects to be licensed. Licensing requirements typically include completing a professional degree in architecture, gaining relevant experience through a paid internship, and passing the Architect Registration Examination.

Most states also require some form of continuing education to keep a license, and some additional states are expected to adopt mandatory continuing education. Requirements vary by state but usually involve additional education through workshops, university classes, conferences, self-study courses, or other sources.

A growing number of architects voluntarily seek certification from NCARB. This certification makes it easier to become licensed across states, because it is the primary requirement for reciprocity of licensing among state boards that are NCARB members. In 2014, approximately one-third of all licensed architects had the certification.

Advancement. After many years of work experience, some architects advance to become architectural and engineering managers. These managers typically coordinate the activities of employees and may work on larger construction projects.

Important Qualities

Analytical skills. Architects must understand the content of designs and the context in which they were created. For example, architects must understand the locations of mechanical systems and how those systems affect building operations.

Communication skills. Architects share their ideas, both in oral presentations and in writing, with clients, other architects, and workers who help prepare drawings. Many also give presentations to explain their ideas and designs.

Creativity. Architects design the overall look of houses, buildings, and other structures. Therefore, the final product should be attractive and functional.

Organizational skills. Architects often manage contracts. Therefore, they must keep records related to the details of a project, including total cost, materials used, and progress.

Technical skills. Architects need to use CADD technology to create plans as part of building information modeling (BIM).

Visualization skills. Architects must be able to see how the parts of a structure relate to each other. They also must be able to visualize how the overall building will look once completed.

Pay

The median annual wage for architects was $74,520 in May 2014. The median wage is the wage at which half the workers in an occupation earned more than that amount and half earned less. The lowest 10 percent earned less than $44,940, and the highest 10 percent earned more than $121,910.

Some firms pay tuition and fees toward continuing education requirements for their employees.

Job Outlook

Employment of architects is projected to grow 7 percent from 2014 to 2024, about as fast as the average for all occupations.

Architects will be needed to make plans and designs for the construction and renovation of homes, offices, retail stores, and other structures. Many school districts and universities are expected to build new facilities or renovate existing ones. In addition, demand is expected for more healthcare facilities as the baby-boomer population ages and as more individuals use healthcare services.

Median Annual Wages, May 2014

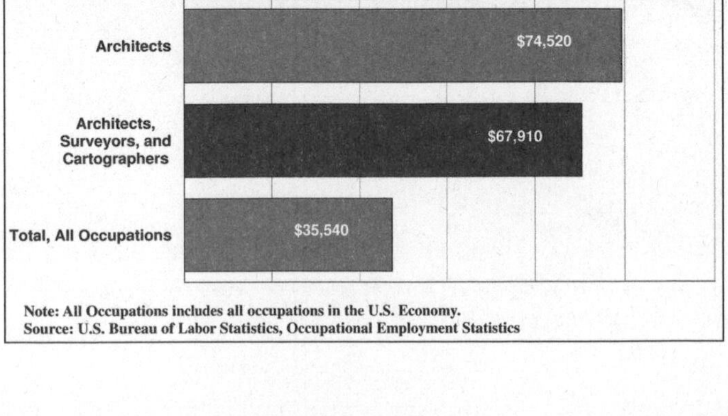

Percent Change in Employment, Projected 2014–2024

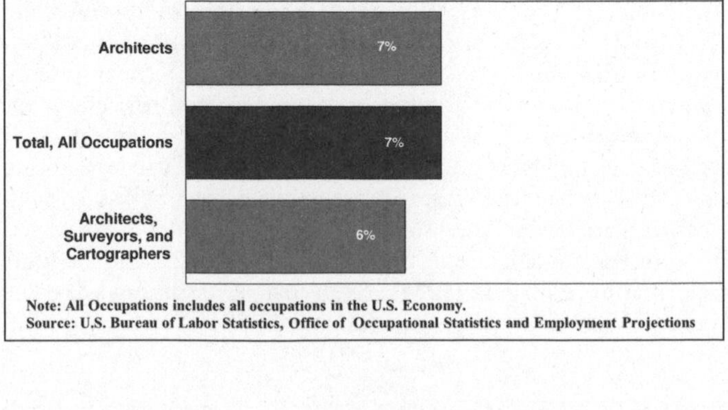

Employment Projections Data for Architects

Occupational Title	SOC Code	Employment, 2014	Projected Employment, 2024	Change, 2014–2024 Percent	Change, 2014–2024 Numeric
Architects, except landscape and naval	17-1011	112,600	120,400	7	7,800

Source: U.S. Bureau of Labor Statistics, Employment Projections Program

Similar Occupations. This table shows a list of occupations with job duties that are similar to those of architects.

Occupations	Entry-level Education	2014 Median Pay	Projected Job Growth	Average Annual Openings
Civil Engineers	Bachelor's degree	$82,050	8%	2,360
Construction Managers	Bachelor's degree	$85,630	5%	1,780
Drafters	Associate's degree	$51,940	-3%	-620
Graphic Designers	Bachelor's degree	$45,900	1%	360
Industrial Designers	Bachelor's degree	$64,620	2%	80
Interior Designers	Bachelor's degree	$48,400	4%	220
Landscape Architects	Bachelor's degree	$64,570	5%	120
Urban and Regional Planners	Master's degree	$66,940	6%	240

The construction of new retail establishments may also require more architects.

Demand is projected for architects with knowledge of "green design," also called sustainable design. Sustainable design emphasizes the efficient use of resources, such as energy and water conservation; waste and pollution reduction; and environmentally friendly design, specifications, and materials. Rising energy costs and increased concern about the environment have led to many new buildings being built with more sustainable designs.

The use of CADD and, more recently, BIM has made architects more productive. These technologies have allowed architects to do more work without the help of drafters while making it easier to share the work with engineers, contractors, and clients.

Job Prospects. With a high number of students graduating with degrees in architecture, very strong competition for internships and jobs is expected. Competition for jobs will be especially strong at the most prestigious architectural firms. Those with up-to-date technical skills—including a strong grasp of CADD and BIM—and experience in sustainable design will have an advantage.

Employment of architects is strongly tied to the activity of the construction industry. Therefore, these workers may experience periods of unemployment when there is a slowdown in requests for new projects or when the overall level of construction falls.

Contacts for More Information

For information about careers in architecture, visit

- American Institute of Architects (www.aia.org)
- National Architectural Accrediting Board (www.naab.org)
- National Council of Architectural Registration Boards (www.ncarb.org)

O*NET

- Architects, Except Landscape and Naval (17-1011.00)

Biomedical Engineers

- **2014 Median Pay** .... $86,950 per year
  $41.81 per hour
- **Typical Entry-Level Education** .... Bachelor's degree
- **Work Experience in a Related Occupation** .... None
- **On-the-job Training** .... None
- **Number of Jobs, 2014** 22,100
- **Job Outlook, 2014–24** .... 23% (Much faster than average)
- **Employment Change, 2014–24** 5,100

Biomedical engineers combine the work of science and engineering to build new replacement parts for the human body.

What Biomedical Engineers Do

Biomedical engineers combine engineering principles with medical and biological sciences to design and create equipment, devices, computer systems, and software used in healthcare.

Duties. Biomedical engineers typically do the following:

- Design equipment and devices, such as artificial internal organs, replacements for body parts, and machines for diagnosing medical problems
- Install, adjust, maintain, repair, or provide technical support for biomedical equipment
- Evaluate the safety, efficiency, and effectiveness of biomedical equipment
- Train clinicians and other personnel on the proper use of equipment
- Work with life scientists, chemists, and medical scientists to research the engineering aspects of the biological systems of humans and animals
- Prepare procedures, write technical reports, publish research papers, and make recommendations based on their research findings
- Present research findings to scientists, nonscientist executives, clinicians, hospital management, engineers, other colleagues, and the public

Biomedical engineers design instruments, devices, and software used in healthcare; bring together knowledge from many technical sources to develop new procedures; or conduct research needed to solve clinical problems.

They often serve a coordinating function, using their background in both engineering and medicine. For example, they may create products for which an in-depth understanding of living systems and technology is essential. They frequently work in research and development or in quality assurance.

Biomedical engineers design electrical circuits, software to run medical equipment, or computer simulations to test new drug therapies. In addition, they design and build artificial body parts, such as hip and knee joints. In some cases, they develop the materials needed to make the replacement body parts. They also design rehabilitative exercise equipment.

The work of these engineers spans many professional fields. For example, although their expertise is based in engineering and biology, they often design computer software to run complicated instruments, such as three-dimensional X-ray machines. Alternatively, many of these engineers use their knowledge of chemistry and biology to develop new drug therapies. Others draw heavily on mathematics and statistics to build models to understand the signals transmitted by the brain or heart.

The following are examples of specialty areas within the field of biomedical engineering:

Bioinstrumentation uses electronics, computer science, and measurement principles to develop devices used in the diagnosis and treatment of disease.

Biomaterials is the study of naturally occurring or laboratory-designed materials that are used in medical devices or as implantation materials.

Biomechanics involves the study of mechanics, such as thermodynamics, to solve biological or medical problems.

Clinical engineering applies medical technology to optimize healthcare delivery.

Rehabilitation engineering is the study of engineering and computer science to develop devices that assist individuals with physical and cognitive impairments.

Systems physiology uses engineering tools to understand how systems within living organisms, from bacteria to humans, function and respond to changes in their environment.

Some people with training in biomedical engineering become professors. For more information, see the profile on postsecondary teachers.

Work Environment

Biomedical engineers held about 22,100 jobs in 2014. The industries that employed the most biomedical engineers were as follows:

Medical equipment and supplies manufacturing	23%
Research and development in the physical, engineering, and life sciences	16
Pharmaceutical and medicine manufacturing	12
Navigational, measuring, electromedical, and control instruments manufacturing	8
Hospitals; state, local, and private	8

Biomedical engineers work in a variety of settings. Some work in hospitals, where therapy occurs, and others work in laboratories, doing research. Still others work in manufacturing settings, where they design biomedical engineering products. Yet other biomedical engineers work in commercial offices, where they make or support business decisions.

Biomedical engineers work in teams with scientists, healthcare workers, or other engineers. Where and how they work depends on the project. For example, a biomedical engineer who has developed a new device designed to help a person with a disability to walk again might have to spend hours in a hospital to determine whether the device works as planned. If the engineer finds a way to improve the device, he or she might have to return to the

Median Annual Wages, May 2014

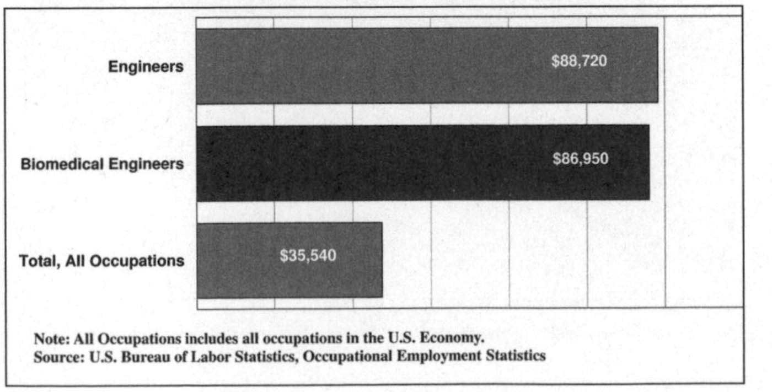

Percent Change in Employment, Projected 2014–2024

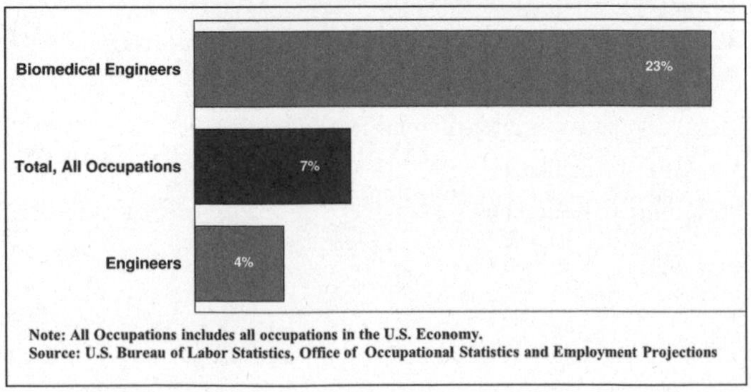

Employment Projections Data for Biomedical Engineers

Occupational Title	SOC Code	Employment, 2014	Projected Employment, 2024	Change, 2014–2024 Percent	Change, 2014–2024 Numeric
Biomedical engineers	17-2031	22,100	27,200	23	5,100

Source: U.S. Bureau of Labor Statistics, Employment Projections Program

manufacturer to help alter the manufacturing process in order to improve the design.

Work Schedules. Biomedical engineers usually work full time on a normal schedule. However, as with employees in almost any engineering occupation, biomedical engineers occasionally may have to work additional hours to meet the needs of patients, managers, colleagues, and clients.

Education/Training

Biomedical engineers typically need a bachelor's degree in biomedical engineering or bioengineering from an accredited program in order to enter the occupation. Alternatively, they can get a bachelor's degree in a different field of engineering and then either choose biological science electives or get a graduate degree in biomedical engineering.

Education. Prospective biomedical engineering or bioengineering students should take high school science courses, such as chemistry, physics, and biology. They should also take math courses, including algebra, geometry, trigonometry, and calculus. Courses in drafting or mechanical drawing and in computer programming are also useful.

Bachelor's degree programs in biomedical engineering and bioengineering focus on engineering and biological sciences. Programs include laboratory-based courses, in addition to classroom-based courses, in subjects such as fluid and solid mechanics, computer programming, circuit design, and biomaterials. Other required courses may include biological sciences, such as physiology.

Accredited programs also include substantial training in engineering design. Many programs include co-ops or internships, often with hospitals and medical device and pharmaceutical manufacturing companies, to provide students with practical applications as part of their study. Biomedical engineering and bioengineering programs are accredited by ABET.

Important Qualities

Analytical skills. Biomedical engineers must be able to analyze the needs of patients and customers to design appropriate solutions.

Communication skills. Because biomedical engineers sometimes work with patients and frequently work on teams, they must be able to express themselves clearly. They must seek others' ideas and incorporate those ideas into the problem-solving process.

Creativity. Biomedical engineers must be creative to come up with innovative and integrative advances in healthcare equipment and devices.

Math skills. Biomedical engineers use the principles of calculus and other advanced topics in mathematics, as well as statistics, for analysis, design, and troubleshooting in their work.

Problem-solving skills. Biomedical engineers typically deal with and solve problems in complex biological systems.

Advancement. Biomedical engineers typically receive greater responsibility through experience and more education. To lead a research team, a biomedical engineer generally needs a graduate degree. Some biomedical engineers attend medical or dental school to specialize in applications at the forefront of patient care, such as using electric impulses in new ways to get muscles moving again. Some earn law degrees and work as patent attorneys. Others pursue a master's degree in business administration (MBA) and move into managerial positions. For more information, see the profiles on lawyers and architectural and engineering managers.

Pay

The median annual wage for biomedical engineers was $86,950 in May 2014. The median wage is the wage at which half the workers in an occupation earned more than that amount and half earned less. The lowest 10 percent earned less than $52,680, and the highest 10 percent earned more than $139,350.

In May 2014, the median annual wages for biomedical engineers in the top industries in which they worked were as follows:

Similar Occupations. This table shows a list of occupations with job duties that are similar to those of biomedical engineers.

Occupations	Entry-level Education	2014 Median Pay	Projected Job Growth	Average Annual Openings
Architectural and Engineering Managers	Bachelor's degree	$130,620	2%	370
Biochemists and Biophysicists	Doctoral or professional degree	$84,940	8%	280
Chemical Engineers	Bachelor's degree	$96,940	2%	60
Electrical and Electronics Engineers	Bachelor's degree	$93,260	0%	-10
Mechanical Engineers	Bachelor's degree	$83,060	5%	1,460
Physicians and Surgeons	Doctoral or professional degree	This wage is equal to or greater than $187,200.	14%	9,930
Sales Engineers	Bachelor's degree	$96,340	7%	490

Research and development in the physical, engineering, and life sciences ... $97,160
Navigational, measuring, electromedical, and control instruments manufacturing ... 91,480
Medical equipment and supplies manufacturing ... 91,010
Pharmaceutical and medicine manufacturing ... 79,670
Hospitals; state, local, and private ... 72,060

Job Outlook

Employment of biomedical engineers is projected to grow 23 percent from 2014 to 2024, much faster than the average for all occupations.

Biomedical engineers likely will see more demand because of growing technology and its application to medical equipment and devices. Smartphone technology and three-dimensional printing are examples of technology being applied to biomedical advances.

As the aging baby-boom generation lives longer and stays active, the demand for biomedical devices and procedures, such as hip and knee replacements is expected to increase. In addition, as the public has become more aware of medical advances, increasing numbers of people are seeking biomedical solutions to their health problems from their physicians.

Biomedical engineers work with scientists, other medical researchers, and manufacturers to address a wide range of injuries and physical disabilities. Their ability to work in different activities with workers from other fields is enlarging the range of applications for biomedical engineering products and services.

Job Prospects. Rapid advances in technology will continue to change what biomedical engineers do and continue to create new areas for them to work in. Thus, the expanding range of activities in which biomedical engineers are engaged should translate into very favorable job prospects. In addition, the aging of the population and retirement of a substantial percentage of biomedical engineers is likely to help create job openings between 2014 and 2024.

Contacts for More Information

For information about general engineering education and biomedical engineering career resources, visit

➤ American Institute for Medical and Biological Engineering (http://aimbe.org)
➤ American Society for Engineering Education (www.asee.org)
➤ Biomedical Engineering Society (http://bmes.org)
➤ IEEE Engineering in Medicine and Biology Society (http://embs.org)
➤ Technology Student Association (www.tsaweb.org)

For information about accredited engineering programs, visit

➤ ABET (www.abet.org)

O*NET

➤ Biomedical Engineers (17-2031.00)

Cartographers and Photogrammetrists

- **2014 Median Pay** ... $60,930 per year
  $29.29 per hour
- **Typical Entry-Level Education** ... Bachelor's degree
- **Work Experience in a Related Occupation** ... None
- **On-the-job Training** ... None
- **Number of Jobs, 2014** ... 12,300
- **Job Outlook, 2014–24** ... 29% (Much faster than average)
- **Employment Change, 2014–24** ... 3,600

What Cartographers and Photogrammetrists Do

Cartographers and photogrammetrists collect, measure, and interpret geographic information in order to create and update maps and charts for regional planning, education, and other purposes.

Cartographers are mapmakers who design user-friendly maps. Photogrammetrists are specialized mapmakers who use aerial photographs, satellite images, and light-imaging detection and ranging (LIDAR) technology to build models of Earth's surface and its features for the purpose of creating maps.

Duties. Cartographers typically do the following:

- Collect geographic data
- Create visual representations of data, such as annual precipitation patterns
- Examine and compile data from ground surveys, reports, aerial photographs, and satellite images
- Prepare maps in digital or graphic form for environmental and educational purposes
- Update and revise existing maps and charts

Photogrammetrists typically do the following:

- Plan aerial and satellite surveys to ensure complete coverage of the area in question
- Collect and analyze spatial data, such as elevation and distance
- Develop base maps that allow geographic information system (GIS) data to be layered on top

Cartographers and photogrammetrists use information from geodetic surveys (land surveys that account for the curvature of Earth's surface) and remote-sensing systems, including aerial cameras and satellites. Some also use light-imaging detection and ranging (LIDAR) technology. LIDAR systems use lasers attached to planes or cars to digitally map the topography of Earth. Because LIDAR is often more accurate than traditional surveying methods, it can also be used to collect other forms of data, such as the location and density of forest canopies.

Cartographers and photogrammetrists increasingly work on online and mobile maps. Interactive maps are growing in popularity, and cartographers and photogrammetrists collect data and design these maps for mobile phones and navigation systems.

Cartographers and photogrammetrists also create maps and perform aerial surveys for governments to aid in urban and regional planning. Such maps may include information on population density and demographic characteristics. Some cartographers and photogrammetrists help build maps for government agencies for work involving national security and public safety. Accurate and updated maps help emergency responders provide assistance as quickly as possible.

A cartographer who uses GIS technology to create maps is often known as a *geographic information specialist.* GIS technology is typically used to assemble, integrate, analyze, and present spatial information in a digital format. Maps created with GIS technology combine spatial graphic features with nongraphic information. These maps are used to provide support for decisions involving environmental studies, geology, engineering, land-use planning, and business marketing.

Work Environment

Cartographers and photogrammetrists held about 12,300 jobs in 2014. The industries that employed the most cartographers and photogrammetrists were as follows:

Cartographers and photogrammetrists are employed at firms in architectural and engineering services, and also in local and federal government agencies.

Architectural, engineering, and related services	33%
Local government, excluding education and hospitals	26
Management, scientific, and technical consulting services	12

Although cartographers and photogrammetrists spend much of their time in offices, certain jobs require extensive fieldwork to acquire data and verify results. For example, cartographers may travel to the physical locations that they are mapping to better understand the topography of the region. Similarly, photogrammetrists may do fieldwork to plan ground control for an aerial survey and to validate interpretations.

Work Schedules. Most cartographers and photogrammetrists work full time. Those who do fieldwork may have longer workdays.

Education/Training

A bachelor's degree in cartography, geography, geomatics, surveying, or a related field is the most common path of entry into this occupation. Some states require cartographers and photogrammetrists to be licensed as surveyors, and some states have specific licenses for photogrammetrists.

Education. Cartographers and photogrammetrists usually have a bachelor's degree in cartography, geography, geomatics, or surveying. (Geomatics combines the science, engineering, math, and art of collecting and managing geographically referenced information.) Although it is not as common, some have a bachelor's degree in engineering, forestry, or computer science.

Growing use of geographic information system (GIS) technology has resulted in cartographers and photogrammetrists needing more courses in computer programming, engineering, math, GIS technology, surveying, and geography.

Cartographers must also be familiar with web-based mapping technologies, including newer modes of compiling data that incorporate the positioning capabilities of mobile phones and in-car navigation systems.

Photogrammetrists must be familiar with remote sensing, image processing, and light-imaging detection and ranging (LIDAR) technology, and they must be knowledgeable about using the software that is necessary with these tools.

Many aspiring cartographers and photogrammetrists benefit from internships while in school.

High school students interested in becoming a cartographer or photogrammetrist should take courses in algebra, geometry, trigonometry, drafting, and computer science.

Licenses, Certifications, and Registrations. Licensing requirements for cartographers and photogrammetrists vary by state. A number of states require cartographers and photogrammetrists to be licensed as surveyors, and some states have specific licenses for photogrammetrists. Although licensing requirements vary by state, candidates must have a minimum of a high school diploma and pass a test.

Cartographers and photogrammetrists may also receive certification from the American Society for Photogrammetry and Remote Sensing (ASPRS). Candidates must meet experience and education requirements and must pass an exam. Although certification is not required, it can demonstrate competence and may help candidates get a job.

Important Qualities

Computer skills. Both cartographers and photogrammetrists must have experience working with computer data and coding. Because maps are created digitally, knowing how to edit them on a computer is essential.

Critical-thinking skills. Cartographers may work from existing maps, surveys, and other records, and they must be able to determine the accuracy of each feature being mapped.

Decision-making skills. Both cartographers and photogrammetrists must make decisions about the accuracy and readability of a map. They must decide what information they require in order to meet the client's needs.

Detail oriented. Cartographers must focus on details when conceiving a map and deciding what features to include. Photogrammetrists must pay close attention to detail when interpreting aerial photographs and remotely sensed data.

Problem-solving skills. Cartographers and photogrammetrists must be able to reconcile differences between aerial photographs, land surveys, and satellite images.

Median Annual Wages, May 2014

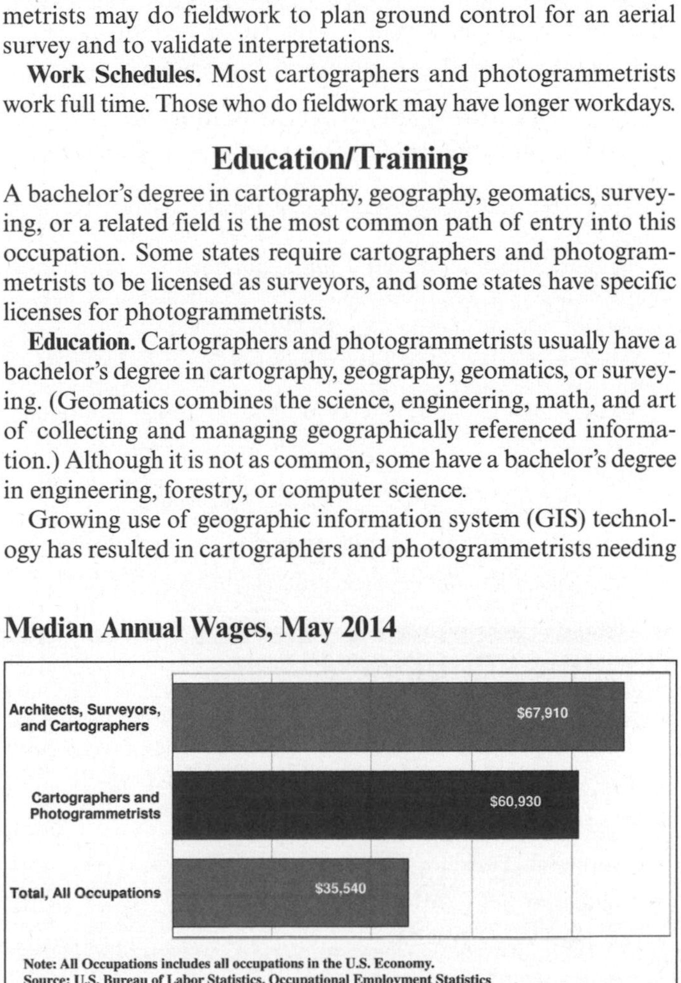

Percent Change in Employment, Projected 2014–2024

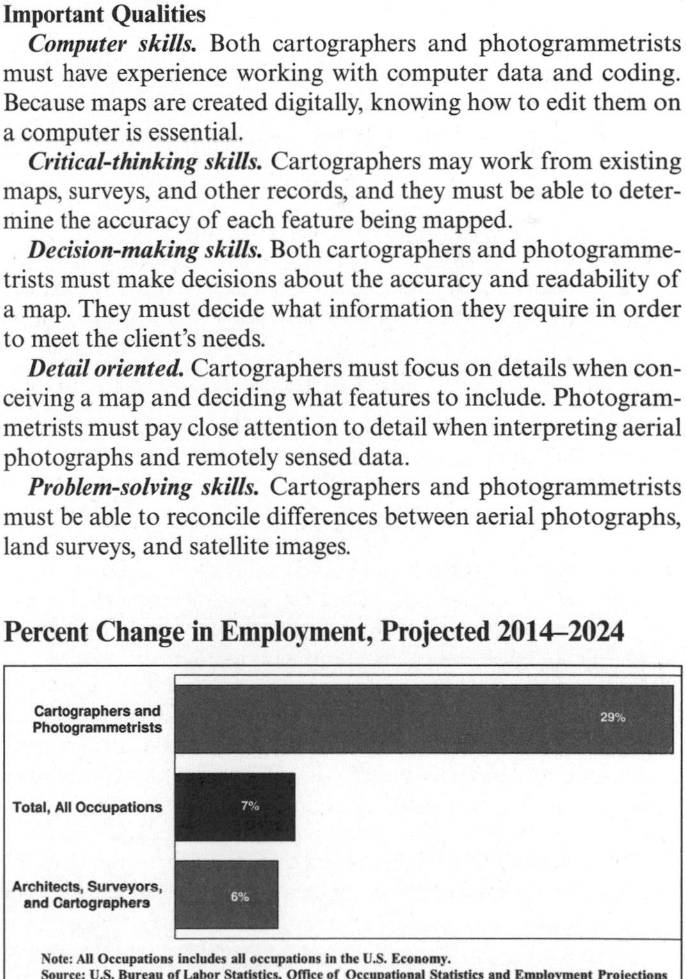

Employment Projections Data for Cartographers and Photogrammetrists

Occupational Title	SOC Code	Employment, 2014	Projected Employment, 2024	Change, 2014–2024	
				Percent	Numeric
Cartographers and photogrammetrists	17-1021	12,300	15,900	29	3,600

Source: U.S. Bureau of Labor Statistics, Employment Projections Program

Similar Occupations. This table shows a list of occupations with job duties that are similar to those of cartographers and photogrammetrists.

Occupations	Entry-level Education	2014 Median Pay	Projected Job Growth	Average Annual Openings
Civil Engineers	Bachelor's degree	$82,050	8%	2,360
Environmental Scientists and Specialists	Bachelor's degree	$66,250	11%	1,020
Forest and Conservation Workers	High school diploma or equivalent	$27,160	4%	60
Geographers	Bachelor's degree	$76,420	-2%	0
Landscape Architects	Bachelor's degree	$64,570	5%	120
Surveying and Mapping Technicians	High school diploma or equivalent	$40,770	-8%	-430
Surveyors	Bachelor's degree	$57,050	-2%	-90
Urban and Regional Planners	Master's degree	$66,940	6%	240

Pay

The median annual wage for cartographers and photogrammetrists was $60,930 in May 2014. The median wage is the wage at which half the workers in an occupation earned more than that amount and half earned less. The lowest 10 percent earned less than $38,610, and the highest 10 percent earned more than $97,570.

In May 2014, the median annual wages for cartographers and photogrammetrists in the top industries in which they worked were as follows:

Management, scientific, and technical consulting services $64,000
Local government, excluding education and hospitals 59,000
Architectural, engineering, and related services 58,700

Job Outlook

Employment of cartographers and photogrammetrists is projected to grow 29 percent from 2014 to 2024, much faster than the average for all occupations. However, because it is a small occupation, the fast growth will result in only about 3,600 new jobs over the 10-year period.

Cartographers and photogrammetrists are likely to be in demand to ensure the reliability and accuracy of maps produced and updated. The increasing use of maps for government planning should fuel employment growth. In addition, the growing number of mobile and web-based map products should result in new jobs for cartographers and photogrammetrists.

The management of forests, waterways, and other natural resources will require constant updating of maps. Cartographers and photogrammetrists will be needed to operate geographic information systems (GIS), which are increasingly being used to map and locate areas that are in need during natural disasters.

Photogrammetrists will be needed to manage the aerial, satellite, and light-imaging detection and ranging (LIDAR) images that are now common.

Cartographers will also be needed to visualize spatial information and design the final presentation of information for clients. Their design skills help data become more accessible to users.

Job Prospects. Cartographers and photogrammetrists are expected to have excellent job opportunities. There has been a large increase in the amount of GIS and mapping data available and cartographers and photogrammetrists will be needed to interpret, refine, and create mapping products using these data.

Contacts for More Information

For more information about cartographers and photogrammetrists, visit

➤ Cartography and Geographic Information Society (www.cartogis.org)

For more information about photogrammetrists, photogrammetric technicians, remote-sensing scientists, image-based cartographers, or GIS specialists' careers, visit

➤ American Society for Photogrammetry and Remote Sensing (www.asprs.org)

For information about careers in remote sensing, photogrammetry, surveying, GIS analysis, and other geography-related disciplines, visit

➤ Association of American Geographers (www.aag.org)

O*NET

➤ Cartographers and Photogrammetrists (17-1021.00)

Chemical Engineers

- **2014 Median Pay** .... $96,940 per year
  $46.60 per hour
- **Typical Entry-Level Education** .... Bachelor's degree
- **Work Experience in a Related Occupation** .... None
- **On-the-job Training** .... None
- **Number of Jobs, 2014** 34,300
- **Job Outlook, 2014–24** .... 2% (Slower than average)
- **Employment Change, 2014–24** 600

What Chemical Engineers Do

Chemical engineers apply the principles of chemistry, biology, physics, and mathematics to solve problems that involve the production or use of chemicals, fuel, drugs, food, and many other products. They design processes and equipment for large-scale manufacturing, plan and test production methods and byproducts treatment, and direct facility operations.

Duties. Chemical engineers typically do the following:

- Conduct research to develop new and improved manufacturing processes
- Develop safety procedures for those working with dangerous chemicals
- Develop processes for separating components of liquids and gases, or for generating electrical currents, by using controlled chemical processes
- Design and plan the layout of equipment
- Conduct tests and monitor the performance of processes throughout production
- Troubleshoot problems with manufacturing processes
- Evaluate equipment and processes to ensure compliance with safety and environmental regulations
- Estimate production costs for management

Some chemical engineers specialize in a particular process, such as oxidation (a reaction of oxygen with chemicals to make other chemicals) or polymerization (making plastics and resins). Others specialize in a particular field, such as nanomaterials (extremely small substances) or biological engineering. Still others specialize in developing specific products.

In addition, chemical engineers work in the production of energy, electronics, food, clothing, and paper. They must understand how the manufacturing process affects the environment and the safety of workers and consumers.

Chemical engineers also conduct research in the life sciences, biotechnology, and business services.

Work Environment

Chemical engineers held about 34,300 jobs in 2014. The industries that employed the most chemical engineers were as follows:

Engineering services	16%
Basic chemical manufacturing	14
Research and development in the physical, engineering, and life sciences	10
Petroleum and coal products manufacturing	7
Resin, synthetic rubber, and artificial synthetic fibers and filaments manufacturing	7

Chemical engineers generally work in a laboratory setting, although sometimes they must work in an industrial setting to oversee production.

Chemical engineers work mostly in offices or laboratories. They may spend time at industrial plants, refineries, and other locations, where they monitor or direct operations or solve onsite problems. Chemical engineers must be able to work with those who design other systems and with the technicians and mechanics who put the designs into practice.

Some engineers travel extensively to plants or worksites, both domestically and abroad.

Injuries and Illnesses. Chemical engineers can be exposed to health or safety hazards when handling certain chemicals and plant equipment, but such exposure can be avoided if proper procedures are followed.

Work Schedules. Nearly all chemical engineers work full time. Occasionally, they may have to work additional hours to meet production targets and design standards or to troubleshoot problems with manufacturing processes.

Education/Training

Chemical engineers must have a bachelor's degree in chemical engineering. Employers also value practical experience, so internships and cooperative engineering programs, in which students earn college credit and experience, can be helpful.

Education. Chemical engineers must have a bachelor's degree in chemical engineering. Programs usually take 4 years to complete and include classroom, laboratory, and field studies. High school

Median Annual Wages, May 2014

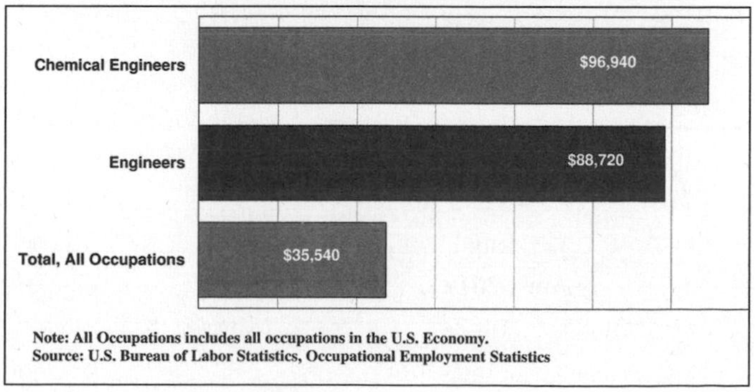

Percent Change in Employment, Projected 2014–2024

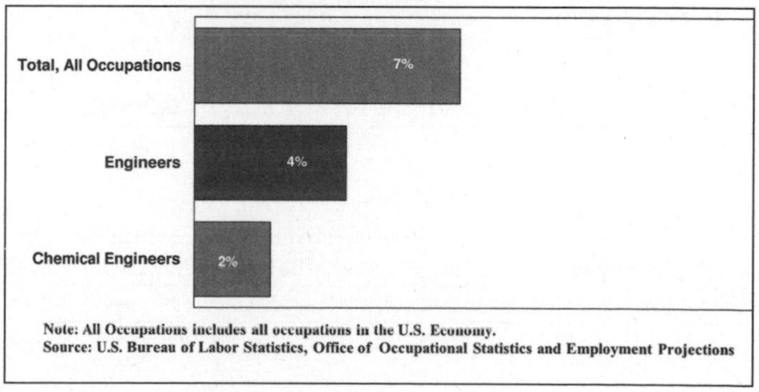

students interested in studying chemical engineering will benefit from taking science courses, such as chemistry, physics, and biology. They also should take math courses, including algebra, trigonometry, and calculus.

At some universities, students can opt to enroll in 5-year programs that lead to both a bachelor's degree and a master's degree. A graduate degree, which may include a degree up to the Ph.D. level, allows an engineer to work in research and development or as a postsecondary teacher.

Some colleges and universities offer internships and cooperative programs in partnership with industry. In these programs, students gain practical experience while completing their education.

ABET accredits engineering programs. ABET-accredited programs in chemical engineering include courses in chemistry, physics, and biology. These programs also include applying the sciences to the design, analysis, and control of chemical, physical, and biological processes.

Important Qualities

Analytical skills. Chemical engineers must be able to troubleshoot designs that do not work as planned. They must be able to ask the right questions and then find answers that work.

Creativity. Chemical engineers must be able to explore new ways of applying engineering principles. They work to invent new materials, advanced manufacturing techniques, and new applications in chemical and biomedical engineering.

Ingenuity. Chemical engineers learn the broad concepts of chemical engineering, but their work requires them to apply those concepts to specific production problems.

Interpersonal skills. Because their role is to put scientific principles into practice in manufacturing industries, chemical engineers must develop good working relationships with other workers involved in production processes.

Math skills. Chemical engineers use the principles of calculus and other advanced topics in mathematics for analysis, design, and troubleshooting in their work.

Problem-solving skills. In designing equipment and processes for manufacturing, these engineers must be able to anticipate and identify problems, including such issues as workers' safety and problems related to manufacturing and environmental protection.

Licenses, Certifications, and Registrations. Licensure for chemical engineers is not as common as it is for other engineering occupations, nor is it required for entry-level positions. A Professional Engineer (PE) license, which allows for higher levels of leadership and independence, can be acquired later in one's career. Licensed engineers are called professional engineers (PEs). A PE can oversee the work of other engineers, sign off on projects, and provide services directly to the public. State licensure generally requires

- A degree from an ABET-accredited engineering program
- A passing score on the Fundamentals of Engineering (FE) exam
- Relevant work experience, typically at least 4 years
- A passing score on the Principles and Practice of Engineering (PE) exam

The initial FE exam can be taken after one earns a bachelor's degree. Engineers who pass this exam commonly are called engineers in training (EITs) or engineer interns (EIs). After meeting work experience requirements, EITs and EIs can take the second exam, called the "Principles and Practice of Engineering."

Several states require engineers to take continuing education to keep their license. Most states recognize licensure from other states if the licensing state's requirements meet or exceed their own licensure requirements.

Advancement. Entry-level engineers usually work under the supervision of experienced engineers. In large companies, new engineers also may receive formal training in classrooms or seminars. As junior engineers gain knowledge and experience, they move to more difficult projects with greater independence to develop designs, solve problems, and make decisions.

Eventually, chemical engineers may advance to supervise a team of engineers and technicians. Some may become architectural and engineering managers. However, preparing for management positions usually requires working under the guidance of a more experienced chemical engineer.

An engineering background enables chemical engineers to discuss a product's technical aspects and assist in product planning and use. For more information, see the profile on sales engineers.

Pay

The median annual wage for chemical engineers was $96,940 in May 2014. The median wage is the wage at which half the workers in an occupation earned more than that amount and half earned less. The lowest 10 percent earned less than $59,480, and the highest 10 percent earned more than $156,980.

In May 2014, the median annual wages for chemical engineers in the top industries in which they worked were as follows:

Petroleum and coal products manufacturing	$112,670
Basic chemical manufacturing	100,530
Resin, synthetic rubber, and artificial synthetic fibers and filaments manufacturing	100,040
Research and development in the physical, engineering, and life sciences	98,860
Engineering services	96,950

A 2015 survey report by the American Institute of Chemical Engineers indicated that the median yearly salary of those with no supervisory responsibility was $106,300.

Job Outlook

Employment of chemical engineers is projected to grow 2 percent from 2014 to 2024, slower than the average for all occupations. Demand for chemical engineers' services depends largely on demand for the products of various manufacturing industries. The

Employment Projections Data for Chemical Engineers

Occupational Title	SOC Code	Employment, 2014	Projected Employment, 2024	Change, 2014–2024 Percent	Change, 2014–2024 Numeric
Chemical engineers	17-2041	34,300	34,900	2	600

Source: U.S. Bureau of Labor Statistics, Employment Projections Program

Similar Occupations. This table shows a list of occupations with job duties that are similar to those of chemical engineers.

Occupations	Entry-level Education	2014 Median Pay	Projected Job Growth	Average Annual Openings
Architectural and Engineering Managers	Bachelor's degree	$130,620	2%	370
Biomedical Engineers	Bachelor's degree	$86,950	23%	510
Chemical Technicians	Associate's degree	$44,180	2%	120
Chemists and Materials Scientists	Bachelor's degree	$74,720	3%	260
Nuclear Engineers	Bachelor's degree	$100,470	-4%	-70
Occupational Health and Safety Specialists	Bachelor's degree	$69,210	4%	280

ability of these engineers to stay on the forefront of new emerging technologies will sustain employment growth.

Many chemical engineers work in industries that have output sought by many manufacturing firms. For instance, they work for firms that manufacture plastic resins, used to increase fuel efficiency in automobiles. Increased availability of domestically produced natural gas should increase manufacturing potential in the industries employing these engineers.

In addition, chemical engineering is migrating into new fields, such as nanotechnology, alternative energies, and biotechnology, thereby helping to sustain demand for engineering services in many manufacturing industries.

However, overall growth of employment will be tempered by a decline in employment in manufacturing sectors, including chemical manufacturing.

Job Prospects. The need to find alternative fuels to meet increasing energy demand while maintaining environmental sustainability will continue to require the expertise of chemical engineers in oil- and gas-related industries. In addition, the integration of chemical and biological sciences and rapid advances in innovation will create new areas in biotechnology and in medical and pharmaceutical fields for them to work in. Thus, those with a background in biology will have better chances to gain employment. Chemical engineers should have favorable job prospects as many workers in the occupation reach retirement age from 2014 to 2024.

Contacts for More Information

For more information on becoming a chemical engineer, visit

➤ American Institute of Chemical Engineers (www.aiche.org)

For information about general engineering education and career resources, visit

➤ American Society for Engineering Education (www.asee.org)

➤ Technology Student Association (www.tsaweb.org)

For more information about licensure as a professional engineer, visit

➤ National Council of Examiners for Engineering and Surveying (http://ncees.org)

➤ National Society of Professional Engineers (www.nspe.org)

For information about accredited engineering programs, visit

➤ ABET (www.abet.org)

O*NET

➤ Chemical Engineers (17-2041.00)

Civil Engineering Technicians

- **2014 Median Pay** .... $48,340 per year
  $23.24 per hour
- **Typical Entry-Level Education** ....Associate's degree
- **Work Experience in a Related Occupation**.............. None
- **On-the-job Training** .... None
- **Number of Jobs, 2014** 74,000
- **Job Outlook, 2014–24** .... 5% (As fast as average)
- **Employment Change, 2014–24** 3,500

What Civil Engineering Technicians Do

Civil engineering technicians help civil engineers to plan, design, and build the highways, bridges, utilities, and other infrastructure projects. They also help to plan, design, and build commercial, industrial, residential, and land development projects.

Duties. Civil engineering technicians typically do the following:

- Read and review project drawings and plans to determine the sizes of structures
- Confer with engineers about preparing plans
- Use computer aided design software under the charge of engineers
- Evaluate pre-construction field conditions
- Observe project sites and evaluate contractors' work to detect problems with a design
- Test construction materials and soil samples in laboratories
- Help to ensure that project construction conforms to design specifications and applicable codes
- Develop plans and estimate costs for constructing systems and operating facilities
- Prepare reports and document project activities and data
- Collect data and prepare analyses
- Set up and help maintain project files and records

Civil engineering technicians typically work under the charge of licensed civil engineers. These technicians generally help civil engineers, performing some of the same tasks as the engineers. However, because they are not licensed, civil engineering technicians cannot approve designs or supervise the overall project.

Civil engineering technicians assume varied duties on the job. They sometimes estimate construction costs and develop specifications. Other times, they prepare drawings or survey land. They also may set up and monitor various instruments for traffic studies. These technicians' duties often require familiarity with and

Civil engineering technicians read and review project blueprints to determine dimensions of structures.

use of various computer programs to design projects, collect and analyze data, prepare correspondence and reports, and manage file systems.

Work Environment

Civil engineering technicians held about 74,000 jobs in 2014. The industries that employed the most civil engineering technicians were as follows:

Engineering services	40%
State government, excluding education and hospitals	28
Local government, excluding education and hospitals	18
Construction	4

Civil engineering technicians work in offices, where they help civil engineers plan and design projects. Civil engineering technicians sometimes visit the jobsite where a construction project is taking place, to collect or test materials or observe the project.

When civil engineering technicians visit the jobsite where a construction project is taking place, they may test materials, assist in surveying, or perform field observations in order to help ensure that the designs approved by licensed civil engineers are being built correctly and in a timely manner. Civil engineering technicians also may work at several sites, using cars or trucks as a mobile office.

Work Schedules. When civil engineering technicians work at construction sites, their schedules may be subject to factors that affect construction, such as bad weather. In addition, their schedules vary with the length and completion of construction projects. Those who work mostly in laboratories to test construction materials have more stable work schedules, but are still subject to schedule variations related to construction.

Education/Training

Although not always required, an associate's degree in civil engineering technology is preferred for employment as a civil engineering technician.

Education. To prepare for programs in engineering technology after high school, prospective civil engineering technicians should take science and math courses, such as chemistry, geometry, and calculus. They should also have basic knowledge of the use of computers.

Employers generally prefer engineering technicians to have an associate's degree from a program accredited by ABET, although a degree is not always required. Engineering technology programs are also available at technical or vocational schools that award a postgraduate certificate or diploma.

Courses at technical or vocational schools may include engineering, design, and computer software. To complete an associate's degree, students also usually need to take other courses in liberal arts and the sciences.

Important Qualities

Critical-thinking skills. As assistants to civil engineers, civil engineering technicians must be able to help the engineers identify and solve problems to develop infrastructure plans and to help agencies avoid wasting time, effort, and funds.

Decision-making skills. Pressures from deadlines mean that technicians must be able to quickly discern which types of information are most important for the work at hand, and which plan of action will help keep the project on schedule.

Math skills. Civil engineering technicians use math for analysis, design, and troubleshooting in their work.

Observational skills. Civil engineering technicians sometimes have to go to jobsites and assess a project for the engineer. Therefore, they must know what to look for and how best to report back to the engineer who is overseeing the project.

Problem-solving skills. Like civil engineers, civil engineering technicians help design projects to solve a particular problem. Technicians must be able to understand and work with all the related systems involved in building a project.

Reading skills. Civil engineering technicians carry out plans and designs for projects that a civil engineer has approved. Thus, they must be able to understand all the reports, plans, and documents describing these designs.

Writing skills. Civil engineering technicians often are asked to relay their findings in writing. They must be able to write reports that are well organized and clearly written.

Median Annual Wages, May 2014

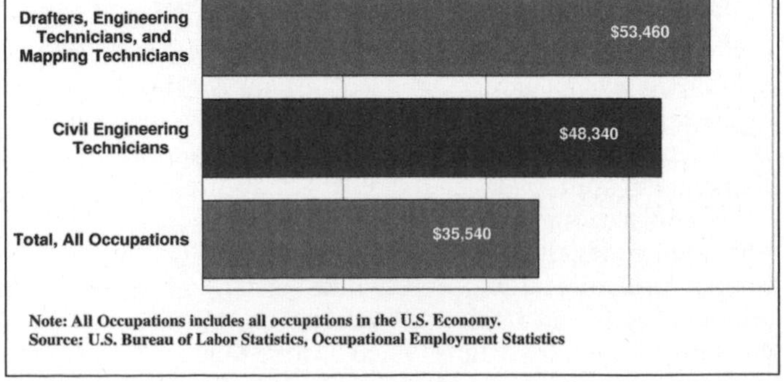

Percent Change in Employment, Projected 2014–2024

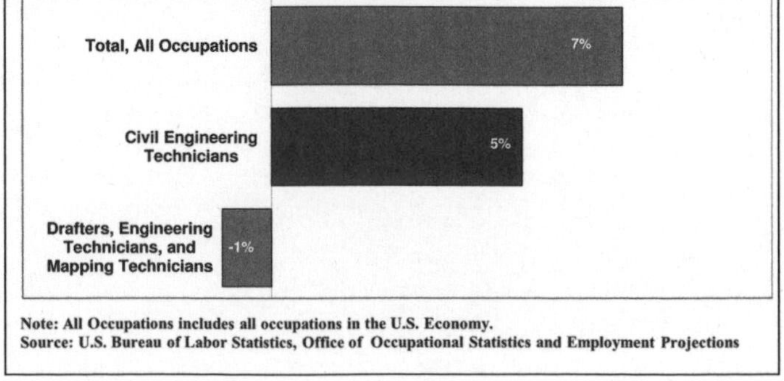

Employment Projections Data for Civil Engineering Technicians

Occupational Title	SOC Code	Employment, 2014	Projected Employment, 2024	Change, 2014–2024 Percent	Change, 2014–2024 Numeric
Civil engineering technicians	17-3022	74,000	77,600	5	3,500

Source: U.S. Bureau of Labor Statistics, Employment Projections Program

Similar Occupations. This table shows a list of occupations with job duties that are similar to those of civil engineering technicians.

Occupations	Entry-level Education	2014 Median Pay	Projected Job Growth	Average Annual Openings
Civil Engineers	Bachelor's degree	$82,050	8%	2,360
Drafters	Associate's degree	$51,940	-3%	-620
Surveying and Mapping Technicians	High school diploma or equivalent	$40,770	-8%	-430
Surveyors	Bachelor's degree	$57,050	-2%	-90

Work Experience in a Related Occupation. Although an associate's degree is preferred by most employers, prospective civil engineering technicians may enter the occupation after gaining work experience in a related occupation, particularly as a drafter or CAD operator. A worker who begins as a drafter or CAD operator for an engineering firm may advance to a civil engineering technician position as his or her knowledge of design and construction improves.

Licenses, Certifications, and Registrations. Certification is not needed to enter this occupation, but it can help technicians advance their careers. The National Institute for Certification in Engineering Technologies (NICET) is one of the primary organizations overseeing certification for civil engineering technicians.

Certification as a technician requires passing an exam and providing documentation, including a work history, recommendations, and, for most programs, supervisor confirmation of specific experience. NICET requires technicians to update their skills and knowledge through a recertification process that encourages continuing professional development.

Advancement. Civil engineering technicians can advance in their careers by learning to design systems for a variety of projects, such as storm sewers and sanitary systems. It is also useful for civil engineering technicians to become skilled at reading plans and profiles—the graphical depiction of proposed projects.

Civil engineering technicians can also benefit with increasing knowledge of computer systems and application, in particular familiarity with word processing and spreadsheet programs, as well as geographic information systems (GIS) and global positioning systems (GPS).

Pay

The median annual wage for civil engineering technicians was $48,340 in May 2014. The median wage is the wage at which half the workers in an occupation earned more than that amount and half earned less. The lowest 10 percent earned less than $31,060, and the highest 10 percent earned more than $73,860.

In May 2014, the median annual wages for civil engineering technicians in the top industries in which they worked were as follows:

Local government, excluding education and hospitals	$55,160
Construction	53,860
Engineering services	47,860
State government, excluding education and hospitals	44,200

Job Outlook

Employment of civil engineering technicians is projected to grow 5 percent from 2014 to 2024, about as fast as the average for all occupations.

The need to preserve, repair, upgrade, and enhance the country's infrastructure continues to increase. Bridges, roads, levees, airports, and dams will need to be rebuilt, maintained, and upgraded. Also, a growing population means that water systems must be maintained to reduce or eliminate loss of drinkable water. In addition, more waste treatment plants will be needed to help clean the nation's waterways. Civil engineers must plan, design, and oversee this work, and civil engineering technicians will be needed to assist the engineers in these projects.

Civil engineering technicians also will find work assisting civil engineers with renewable-energy projects. With regard to wind energy, these engineering technicians may assist in the development of a wind farm to minimize costs while also accommodating the unique dimensions and weight of wind turbines. For installation of solar power, these engineering technicians make sure that civil engineers' designs for foundations to hold up solar arrays are implemented correctly.

States, however, continue to face financial challenges and may have difficulty funding all the projects that need attention.

Job Prospects. Civil engineering technicians learn to use design software that civil engineers might not learn in their college curriculum. Thus, those civil engineering technicians who master that software, keep their skills current, and stay abreast of new software will improve their chances for employment.

Contacts for More Information

For more information about summer apprenticeships in civil engineering, visit

- Pathways to Science (www.pathwaystoscience.org)

For more information about accredited programs, visit

- ABET (www.abet.org)

For more information about certification, visit

- American Society of Certified Engineering Technicians (www.ascet.org)

➤ National Institute for Certification in Engineering Technologies (http://tinyurl.com/j3uw575) (NICET)

O*NET

➤ Civil Engineering Technicians (17-3022.00)

Civil Engineers

- **2014 Median Pay** .... $82,050 per year $39.45 per hour
- **Typical Entry-Level Education** .... Bachelor's degree
- **Work Experience in a Related Occupation**.............. None
- **On-the-job Training** .... None
- **Number of Jobs, 2014** 281,400
- **Job Outlook, 2014–24** .... 8% (As fast as average)
- **Employment Change, 2014–24** 23,600

What Civil Engineers Do

Civil engineers design, build, supervise, operate, and maintain construction projects and systems in the public and private sector, including roads, buildings, airports, tunnels, dams, bridges, and systems for water supply and sewage treatment. Many civil engineers work in design, construction, research, and education.

Duties. Civil engineers typically do the following:

- Analyze long range plans, survey reports, maps, and other data in order to plan projects
- Consider construction costs, government regulations, potential environmental hazards, and other factors in planning the stages of, and risk analysis for, a project
- Compile and submit permit applications to local, state, and federal agencies, verifying that projects comply with various regulations
- Perform or oversee soil testing to determine the adequacy and strength of foundations
- Test building materials, such as concrete, asphalt, or steel, for use in particular projects
- Provide cost estimates for materials, equipment, or labor to determine a project's economic feasibility
- Use design software to plan and design transportation systems, hydraulic systems, and structures in line with industry and government standards
- Perform or oversee surveying operations in order to establish reference points, grades, and elevations to guide construction
- Present their findings to the public on topics such as bid proposals, environmental impact statements, or descriptions of property
- Manage the repair, maintenance, and replacement of public and private infrastructure

Civil engineers inspect projects to insure regulatory compliance. In addition, they are tasked with ensuring that safe work practices are followed at construction sites.

Many civil engineers hold supervisory or administrative positions ranging from supervisor of a construction site to city engineer, public works director, and city manager. Others work in design, construction, research, and teaching. Civil engineers work with others on projects and may be assisted by civil engineering technicians.

Civil engineers prepare permit documents for work on projects in renewable energy. They verify that the projects will comply with federal, state, and local requirements. With regard to solar energy, these engineers conduct structural analyses for large-scale photovoltaic projects. They also evaluate the ability of solar array support structures and buildings to tolerate stresses from wind, seismic activity, and other sources. For large-scale wind projects, civil engineers often prepare roadbeds to handle large trucks that haul in the turbines. In addition, they prepare the sites on the shore or offshore to make sure that the foundations for the turbines will safely keep them upright in expected environmental conditions.

Civil engineers work on complex projects, so they usually specialize in one of several areas.

Construction engineers manage construction projects, ensuring that they are scheduled and built in accordance with plans and specifications. These engineers typically are responsible for the design and safety of temporary structures used during construction.

Geotechnical engineers work to make sure that foundations are solid. They focus on how structures built by civil engineers, such as buildings and tunnels, interact with earth (including soil and rock). In addition, they design and plan for slopes, retaining walls, and tunnels.

Structural engineers design and assess major projects, such as buildings, bridges, or dams, to ensure their strength and durability.

Transportation engineers plan, design, operate, and maintain everyday systems, such as streets and highways, but they also plan larger projects, such as airports, ship ports, mass transit systems, and harbors.

The work of civil engineers is closely related to the work of environmental engineers.

Work Environment

Civil engineers held about 281,400 jobs in 2014. The industries that employed the most civil engineers were as follows:

Engineering services	46%
State government, excluding education and hospitals	13
Local government, excluding education and hospitals	11
Nonresidential building construction	5
Federal government, excluding postal service	4

Civil engineers work in a variety of locations and conditions. When working on designs, civil engineers may spend most of

Civil engineers design major transportation projects.

their time indoors in offices. However, construction engineers may spend much of their time outdoors at construction sites monitoring operations or solving onsite problems. Some jobs may require frequent relocation to different areas and offices in job site trailers.

Civil engineers who function as project managers may work from cars or trucks as they move from site to site. Many civil engineers work for governments agencies in government office buildings or facilities. Occasionally, civil engineers travel abroad to work on large engineering projects in other countries.

Work Schedules. Civil engineers typically work full time, and about 1 in 4 worked more than 40 hours per week in 2014. Engineers who direct projects may need to work extra hours to monitor progress on the projects, to ensure that designs meet requirements, and to guarantee that deadlines are met.

Education/Training

Civil engineers need a bachelor's degree. They typically need a graduate degree and licensure for promotion to senior positions. Although licensure requirements vary within the United States, civil engineers usually must be licensed in the locations where they provide services directly to the public.

Education. Civil engineers need a bachelor's degree in civil engineering, in one of its specialties, or in civil engineering technology. Programs in civil engineering and civil engineering technology include coursework in math, statistics, engineering mechanics and systems, and fluid dynamics, among other courses, depending on the specialty. Courses include a mix of traditional classroom learning, work in laboratories, and fieldwork.

A degree from a program accredited by the ABET is needed in order to earn the Professional Engineer (PE) license. In many states, a bachelor's degree in civil engineering technology also will suffice as an academic requirement for obtaining a license.

About 1 in 4 civil engineers have a master's degree. Further education after the bachelor's degree, along with the PE license and previous experience, is helpful in getting a job as a manager. For more information on engineering managers, see the profile on architectural and engineering managers.

Important Qualities

Decision-making skills. Civil engineers often balance multiple and frequently conflicting objectives, such as determining the feasibility of plans with regard to financial costs and safety concerns. Urban and regional planners often look to civil engineers for advice on these issues. Civil engineers must be able to make good decisions based on best practices, their own technical knowledge, and their own experience.

Leadership skills. Civil engineers take ultimate responsibility for the projects that they manage or research that they perform. Therefore, they must be able to lead planners, surveyors, construction managers, civil engineering technicians, civil engineering technologists, and others in implementing their project plan.

Math skills. Civil engineers use the principles of calculus, trigonometry, and other advanced topics in mathematics for analysis, design, and troubleshooting in their work.

Organizational skills. Only licensed civil engineers can sign the design documents for infrastructure projects. This requirement makes it imperative that civil engineers be able to monitor and evaluate the work at the jobsite as a project progresses. That way, they can ensure compliance with the design documents. Civil engineers also often manage several projects at the same time, and thus must be able to balance time needs and to effectively allocate resources.

Problem-solving skills. Civil engineers work at the highest level of the planning, design, construction, and operation of multifaceted projects or research. The many variables involved require that they possess the ability to identify and evaluate complex problems. They must be able to then utilize their skill and training to develop cost-effective, safe, and efficient solutions.

Speaking skills. Civil engineers must present reports and plans to audiences of people with a wide range of backgrounds and technical knowledge. This requires the ability to speak clearly and to converse with people in various settings, and to translate engineering and scientific information into easy to understand concepts.

Writing skills. Civil engineers must be able to communicate with others, such as architects, landscape architects, and urban and regional planners. They also must be able to explain projects to elected officials and citizens. This means that civil engineers must be able to write reports that are clear, concise, and understandable to those with little or no technical or scientific background.

Licenses, Certifications, and Registrations. Licensure is not required for entry-level positions as a civil engineer. A Professional Engineer (PE) license, which allows for higher levels of leadership and independence, can be acquired later in one's career. Licensed engineers are called professional engineers (PEs). A PE can oversee the work of other engineers, approve design plans, sign off on projects, and provide services directly to the public. State licensure generally requires

- A degree from an ABET-accredited engineering program
- A passing score on the Fundamentals of Engineering (FE) exam
- Relevant work experience, typically at least 4 years working under a licensed engineer
- A passing score on the Principles and Practice of Engineering (PE) exam

Median Annual Wages, May 2014

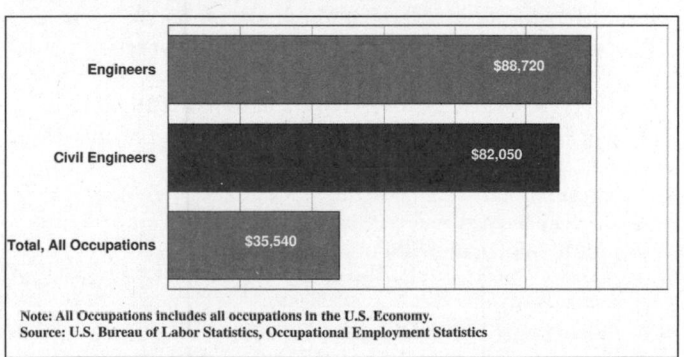

Note: All Occupations includes all occupations in the U.S. Economy.
Source: U.S. Bureau of Labor Statistics, Occupational Employment Statistics

Percent Change in Employment, Projected 2014–2024

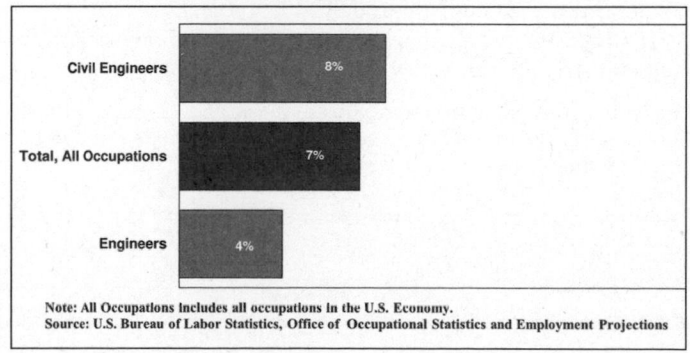

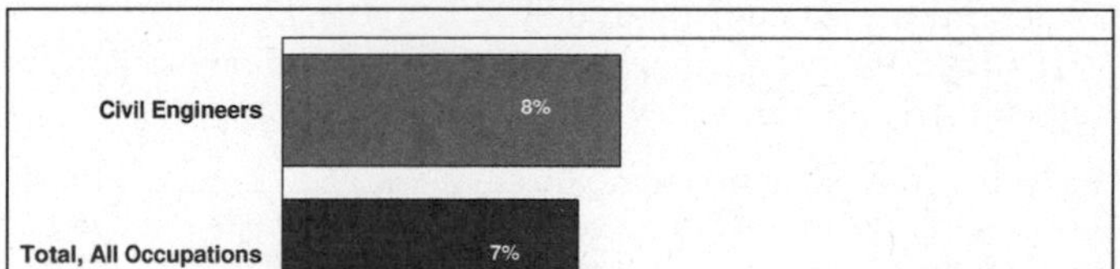

Note: All Occupations includes all occupations in the U.S. Economy.
Source: U.S. Bureau of Labor Statistics, Office of Occupational Statistics and Employment Projections

Employment Projections Data for Civil Engineers

Occupational Title	SOC Code	Employment, 2014	Projected Employment, 2024	Change, 2014–2024 Percent	Change, 2014–2024 Numeric
Civil engineers	17-2051	281,400	305,000	8	23,600

Source: U.S. Bureau of Labor Statistics, Employment Projections Program

Similar Occupations. This table shows a list of occupations with job duties that are similar to those of civil engineers.

Occupations	Entry-level Education	2014 Median Pay	Projected Job Growth	Average Annual Openings
Architects	Bachelor's degree	$74,520	7%	780
Civil Engineering Technicians	Associate's degree	$48,340	5%	350
Construction Managers	Bachelor's degree	$85,630	5%	1,780
Environmental Engineers	Bachelor's degree	$83,360	12%	680
Landscape Architects	Bachelor's degree	$64,570	5%	120
Mechanical Engineers	Bachelor's degree	$83,060	5%	1,460
Surveyors	Bachelor's degree	$57,050	-2%	-90
Urban and Regional Planners	Master's degree	$66,940	6%	240

The initial FE exam can be taken after earning a bachelor's degree. Engineers who pass this exam commonly are called engineers in training (EITs) or engineer interns (EIs). After meeting work experience requirements, EITs and EIs can take the second exam, called the Principles and Practice of Engineering.

Each state issues its own licenses. Most states recognize licensure from other states, as long as the licensing state's requirements meet or exceed their own licensure requirements. Several states require continuing education for engineers to keep their licenses.

Advancement. Civil engineers with ample experience may move into senior positions, such as project managers or functional managers of design, construction, operation, or maintenance. However, they would first need to obtain the Professional Engineer (PE) license, because only licensed engineers can assume responsibilities for public projects.

After gaining licensure, a professional engineer may seek credentialing that attests to his or her expertise in a civil engineering specialty. Such a credential may be of help for advancement to senior technical or even managerial positions.

Pay

The median annual wage for civil engineers was $82,050 in May 2014. The median wage is the wage at which half the workers in an occupation earned more than that amount and half earned less. The lowest 10 percent earned less than $52,570, and the highest 10 percent earned more than $128,110.

In May 2014, the median annual wages for civil engineers in the top industries in which they worked were as follows:

Federal government, excluding postal service	$90,340
Local government, excluding education and hospitals	85,820
Engineering services	81,830
State government, excluding education and hospitals	78,330
Nonresidential building construction	74,030

Job Outlook

Employment of civil engineers is projected to grow 8 percent from 2014 to 2024, about as fast as the average for all occupations. As infrastructure continues to age, civil engineers will be needed to manage projects to rebuild bridges, repair roads, and upgrade levees and dams as well as airports and buildings.

A growing population leading to increasing urbanization means that new water systems will be required while, at the same time, existing water systems must be maintained to reduce or eliminate leaks as they age. In addition, more waste treatment plants will be needed to help clean the nation's waterways. Civil engineers will continue to play a key part in all of this work.

The work of civil engineers will be needed for renewable-energy projects. Often, getting permits for many of these projects takes years, and civil engineers play a key part in the process. Thus, as these new projects gain approval, civil engineers will be further involved in overseeing the construction of structures such as wind farms and solar arrays.

Although states continue to face financial challenges and may have difficulty funding all of their projects that need attention, some of the projects that have been delayed will ultimately have to be completed in order to build and maintain critical infrastructure, and to protect the public and the environment.

Job Prospects. Applicants who gain experience by participating in a co-op program while in college will have the best opportunities. In addition, new standards known collectively as the Body of Knowledge are growing in importance within civil engineering, and this development is likely to result in a heightened need for a graduate education. Therefore those who enter the occupation with a graduate degree will likely have better prospects.

Contacts for More Information

For information about general engineering education and career resources, visit

- American Society for Engineering Education (www.asee.org)
- Technology Student Association (www.tsaweb.org)

For more information about licensure, visit

- National Council of Examiners for Engineering and Surveying (http://ncees.org)
- National Society of Professional Engineers (www.nspe.org/index.html)

For information about accredited programs in civil engineering and civil engineering technology, visit

➤ ABET (www.abet.org)

For more information about civil engineers, visit

➤ American Society of Civil Engineers (www.asce.org)

O*NET

➤ Civil Engineers (17-2051.00)

➤ Transportation Engineers (17-2051.01)

Computer Hardware Engineers

- **2014 Median Pay** .... $108,430 per year
  $52.13 per hour
- **Typical Entry-Level Education** .... Bachelor's degree
- **Work Experience in a Related Occupation** .... None
- **On-the-job Training** .... None
- **Number of Jobs, 2014** 77,700
- **Job Outlook, 2014–24** .... 3% (Slower than average)
- **Employment Change, 2014–24** 2,400

What Computer Hardware Engineers Do

Computer hardware engineers research, design, develop, and test computer systems and components such as processors, circuit boards, memory devices, networks, and routers. These engineers discover new directions in computer hardware, which generate rapid advances in computer technology.

Duties. Computer hardware engineers typically do the following:

- Design new computer hardware, creating schematics of computer equipment to be built
- Test the completed models of the computer hardware they design
- Analyze the test results and modify the design as needed
- Update existing computer equipment so that it will work with new software
- Oversee the manufacturing process for computer hardware
- Maintain knowledge of computer engineering trends and new technology

Many hardware engineers design noncomputer devices that incorporate processors and other computer components and connect to the Internet. For example, many car parts have computer systems embedded in them. Computer hardware engineers also are designing a growing number of medical devices with a computer system and the ability to connect to the Internet.

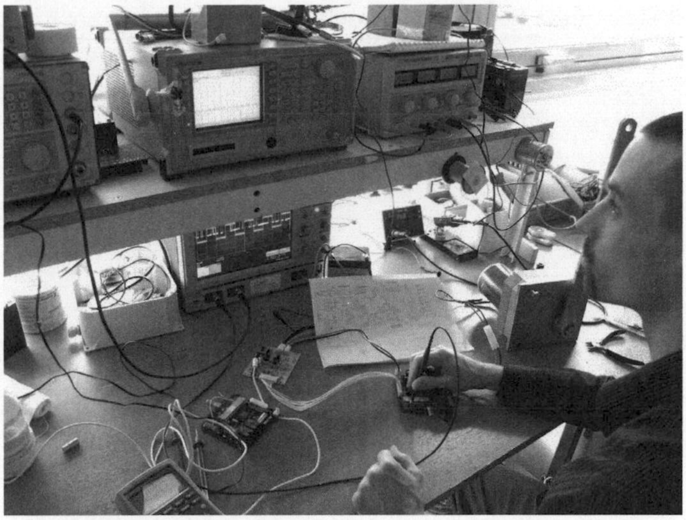

Computer hardware engineers solve problems that arise in complex computer systems.

Computer hardware engineers ensure that computer hardware components work together with the latest software. Therefore, hardware engineers often work with software developers. For example, the hardware and software for a mobile phone frequently are developed jointly. Hardware engineers also may perform some computer programming in a hardware description language (HDL), which describes the digital circuits in hardware. Using this language, computer hardware engineers can simulate how the hardware design would work, test for errors, and then fix the design.

Work Environment

Computer hardware engineers held about 77,700 jobs in 2014. The industries that employed the most computer hardware engineers were as follows:

Computer systems design and related services	22%
Computer and peripheral equipment manufacturing	16
Semiconductor and other electronic component manufacturing	15
Research and development in the physical, engineering, and life sciences	7
Government	6

Computer hardware engineers usually work in research laboratories that build and test various types of computer models. Most work in high-tech manufacturing firms.

Median Annual Wages, May 2014

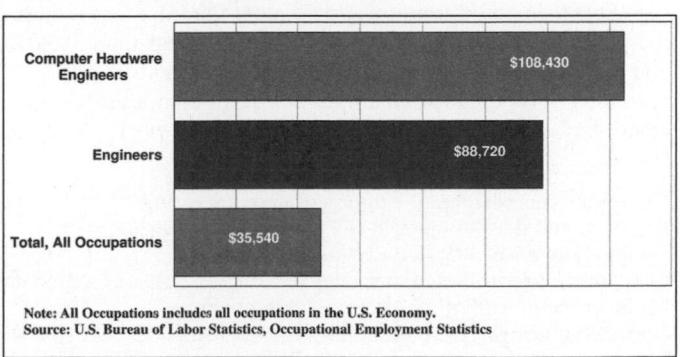

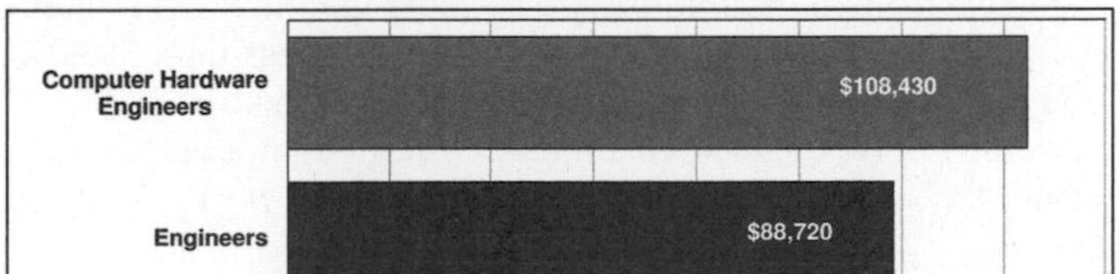

Percent Change in Employment, Projected 2014–2024

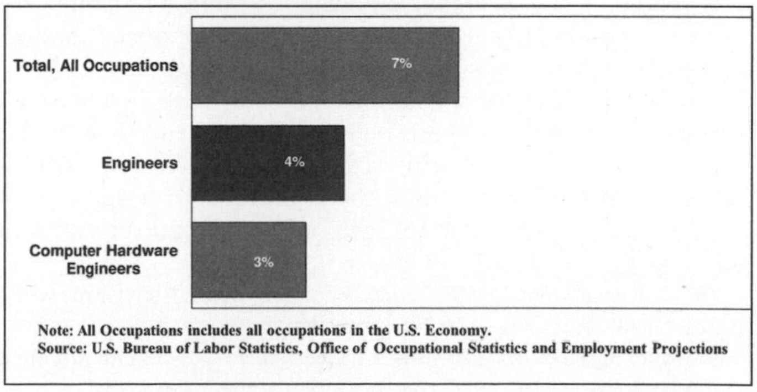

Employment Projections Data for Computer Hardware Engineers

Occupational Title	SOC Code	Employment, 2014	Projected Employment, 2024	Change, 2014–2024 Percent	Change, 2014–2024 Numeric
Computer hardware engineers	17-2061	77,700	80,100	3	2,400

Source: U.S. Bureau of Labor Statistics, Employment Projections Program

Similar Occupations. This table shows a list of occupations with job duties that are similar to those of computer hardware engineers.

Occupations	Entry-level Education	2014 Median Pay	Projected Job Growth	Average Annual Openings
Aerospace Engineers	Bachelor's degree	$105,380	-2%	-160
Computer and Information Research Scientists	Doctoral or professional degree	$108,360	11%	270
Computer and Information Systems Managers	Bachelor's degree	$127,640	15%	5,370
Computer Network Architects	Bachelor's degree	$98,430	9%	1,270
Computer Programmers	Bachelor's degree	$77,550	-8%	-2,650
Electrical and Electronics Engineers	Bachelor's degree	$93,260	0%	-10
Information Security Analysts	Bachelor's degree	$88,890	18%	1,480
Mathematicians	Master's degree	$103,720	21%	70
Mechanical Engineers	Bachelor's degree	$83,060	5%	1,460
Software Developers	Bachelor's degree	$97,990	17%	18,660

Work Schedules. Most computer hardware engineers work full time. About 1 in 4 worked more than 40 hours per week in 2014.

Education/Training

Most computer hardware engineers need a bachelor's degree from an accredited computer engineering program.

Education. Most entry-level computer hardware engineers have a bachelor's degree in computer engineering, although a degree in electrical engineering or computer science also is generally acceptable. A computer engineering major is similar to a major in electrical engineering but with a heavy emphasis on computer science.

Many engineering programs are accredited by ABET (formerly the Accreditation Board for Engineering and Technology). Employers may prefer students from an accredited program. To prepare for a major in computer or electrical engineering, students should have a solid background in math and science.

Because hardware engineers commonly work with computer software systems, a familiarity with computer programming usually is expected. This background may be obtained through computer science courses.

Some large firms or specialized jobs may require a master's degree in computer engineering. Some experienced engineers obtain a master's degree in business administration (MBA). All engineers must continue their learning over the course of their careers in order to keep up with rapid advances in technology.

Other Experience. Some students participate in internships while in school so that they can gain practical experience.

Advancement. Some computer hardware engineers can advance to become computer and information systems managers.

Important Qualities

Analytical skills. Computer hardware engineers use computer programming tools to analyze the digital circuits in hardware to determine the best design.

Creativity. Computer hardware engineers design new types of information technology devices.

Critical-thinking skills. These engineers use logic and reasoning to clarify goals, examine assumptions, and identify the strengths and weaknesses of alternative solutions to problems.

Problem-solving skills. Computer hardware engineers identify complex problems in computer hardware, develop and evaluate possible solutions, and figure out the best way to implement them.

Speaking skills. Engineers often work on teams and must be able to communicate with other types of engineers as well as with nontechnical team members.

Pay

The median annual wage for computer hardware engineers was $108,430 in May 2014. The median wage is the wage at which half the workers in an occupation earned more than that amount and half earned less. The lowest 10 percent earned less than $66,070, and the highest 10 percent earned more than $160,610.

In May 2014, the median annual wages for computer hardware engineers in the top industries in which they worked were as follows:

Computer and peripheral equipment manufacturing	$113,900
Research and development in the physical, engineering, and life sciences	110,770
Computer systems design and related services	109,080
Semiconductor and other electronic component manufacturing	108,040
Government	107,420

Job Outlook

Employment of computer hardware engineers is projected to grow 3 percent from 2014 to 2024, slower than the average for all occupations. A limited number of engineers will be needed to meet the demand for new computer hardware because more technological innovation takes place with software than with hardware. However, demand may grow for hardware engineers as more industries outside of the computer and electronic product manufacturing industry begin to research and develop their own electronic devices. Thus, although declining employment in the manufacturing industries that employ many of these workers will impede the growth of this occupation, computer hardware engineers should be less affected than production occupations because firms are less likely to outsource their type of work.

An increase in hardware startup firms and the ongoing increase in devices with computer chips embedded in them, such as household appliances, medical devices, and automobiles, may lead to some job growth for computer hardware engineers.

Job Prospects. Engineers who have a higher-level degree, as well as knowledge or experience with computer software, will have the best job prospects. Job applicants with a computer engineering degree from an ABET-accredited program will have better chances of landing a job.

Contacts for More Information

For more information about computer hardware engineers, visit

➤ Association for Computing Machinery (www.acm.org)

➤ IEEE Computer Society (www.computer.org)

For more information about ABET-accredited college and university programs in applied science, computing, engineering, and technology, visit

➤ ABET (www.abet.org)

O*NET

➤ Computer Hardware Engineers (17-2061.00)

Drafters

- **2014 Median Pay** .... $51,940 per year
$24.97 per hour
- **Typical Entry-Level Education** .... Associate's degree
- **Work Experience in a Related Occupation** .... None
- **On-the-job Training** .... None
- **Number of Jobs, 2014** 204,400
- **Job Outlook, 2014–24** .... -3% (Decline)
- **Employment Change, 2014–24** .... -6,200

What Drafters Do

Drafters use software to convert the designs of architects and engineers into technical drawings. Most workers specialize in architectural, civil, electrical, or mechanical drafting and use technical drawings to help design everything from microchips to skyscrapers.

Duties. Drafters typically do the following:

- Design plans using computer-aided design (CAD) software
- Work from rough sketches and specifications created by engineers and architects
- Design products with engineering and manufacturing techniques
- Add details to architectural plans from their knowledge of building techniques
- Specify dimensions, materials, and procedures for new products
- Work under the supervision of engineers or architects

Many drafters are referred to as *CAD operators*. Using CAD systems, drafters create and store technical drawings digitally. These drawings contain information on how to build a structure or machine, the dimensions of the project, and what materials are needed to complete the project.

Drafters work with CAD so they can create schematics that can be viewed, printed, or programmed directly into building information modeling (BIM) systems. These systems allow drafters, architects, construction managers, and engineers to create and collaborate on digital models of physical buildings and machines. Through three-dimensional rendering, BIM software allows designers and engineers to see how different elements in their projects work together.

Architectural drafters draw architectural and structural features of buildings for construction projects. These workers may specialize in a type of building, such as residential or commercial. They may also specialize by the materials used, such as steel, wood, or reinforced concrete.

Civil drafters prepare topographical maps used in construction and civil engineering projects, such as highways, bridges, and flood-control projects.

Electrical drafters prepare wiring diagrams that other construction workers use to install and repair electrical equipment and wiring in power plants, electrical distribution systems, and residential and commercial buildings.

Electronics drafters produce wiring diagrams, assembly diagrams for circuit boards, and layout drawings used in manufacturing and in installing and repairing electronic devices and components.

Most drafters use computer-aided design and drafting software.

Median Annual Wages, May 2014

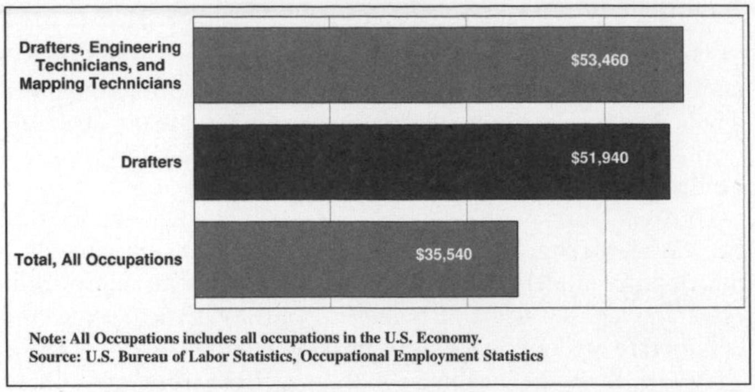

Percent Change in Employment, Projected 2014–2024

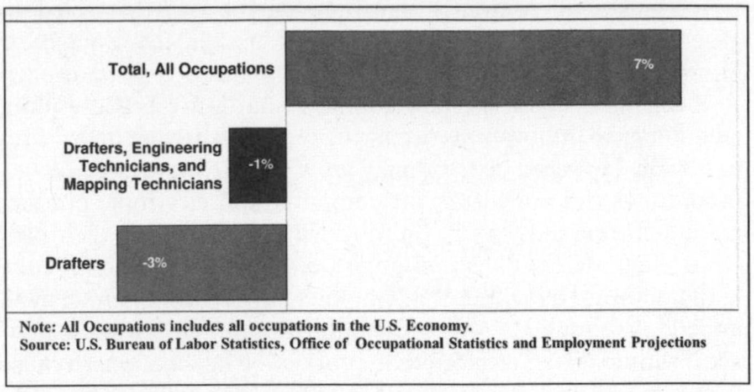

Mechanical drafters prepare layouts that show the details for a wide variety of machinery and mechanical tools and devices, such as medical equipment. These layouts indicate dimensions, fastening methods, and other requirements needed for assembly. Mechanical drafters sometimes create production molds.

Work Environment

Drafters held about 204,400 jobs in 2014. The industries that employed the most drafters were as follows:

Architectural, engineering, and related services	49%
Manufacturing	26
Construction	9

Although drafters spend much of their time working on computers in an office, some may visit jobsites in order to collaborate with architects and engineers.

Work Schedules. Most drafters work full time.

Education/Training

Drafters typically need specialized training, which can be accomplished through a technical program that leads to a certificate or an associate's degree in drafting.

Education. Drafters generally need to complete postsecondary education in drafting. This is typically done through a 2-year associate's degree from a technical institute or community college.

Technical institutes offer instruction in design fundamentals, sketching, and CAD (computer-aided design) software, and they award certificates or diplomas upon completion. Programs vary in length but are generally 2 years of full-time education. The types of courses offered will also vary by institution. Some institutions may specialize in only one type of drafting, such as mechanical or architectural drafting.

Community colleges offer programs similar to those in technical institutes that lead to an associate of applied science in drafting or related degree. After completing an associate's degree program, graduates may get jobs as drafters or continue their education in a related field at a 4-year college. Most 4-year colleges do not offer training in drafting, but they do offer classes in engineering, architecture, and mathematics.

To prepare for postsecondary education, high school students who take courses in mathematics, science, computer technology, design, computer graphics, and where available, drafting, may find such classes useful.

Licenses, Certifications, and Registrations. The American Design Drafting Association (ADDA) offers certification for drafters. Although not mandatory, certification demonstrates competence and knowledge of nationally recognized practices. Certifications are offered for several specialties, including architectural, civil, and mechanical drafting.

Important Qualities

Creativity. Drafters must be able to turn plans and ideas into technical drawings that will guide the creation of real buildings, tools, and systems.

Detail oriented. Drafters must pay close attention to details so that the plans they convert are technically accurate according to the outlined specifications.

Interpersonal skills. Drafters work closely with architects, engineers, and other designers to make sure that final plans are accurate. This requires the ability to take advice and constructive criticism, as well as to offer it.

Math skills. Drafters work on technical drawings. They may be required to solve mathematical calculations involving factors such as angles, weights, and costs.

Technical skills. Drafters in all specialties must be able to use computer software, such as CAD, and work with database tools, such as BIM (building information modeling).

Time-management skills. Drafters often work under strict deadlines. As a result, they must work efficiently in order to produce the required output according to set schedules.

Employment Projections Data for Drafters

Occupational Title	SOC Code	Employment, 2014	Projected Employment, 2024	Change, 2014–2024 Percent	Change, 2014–2024 Numeric
Drafters	17-3010	204,400	198,300	-3	-6,200
Architectural and civil drafters	17-3011	94,000	91,200	-3	-2,800
Electrical and electronics drafters	17-3012	30,100	31,700	5	1,600
Mechanical drafters	17-3013	65,700	61,200	-7	-4,500
Drafters, all other	17-3019	14,700	14,200	-3	-500

Source: U.S. Bureau of Labor Statistics, Employment Projections Program

Similar Occupations. This table shows a list of occupations with job duties that are similar to those of drafters.

Occupations	Entry-level Education	2014 Median Pay	Projected Job Growth	Average Annual Openings
Architects	Bachelor's degree	$74,520	7%	780
Civil Engineering Technicians	Associate's degree	$48,340	5%	350
Electrical and Electronics Engineering Technicians	Associate's degree	$59,820	-2%	-280
Electrical and Electronics Engineers	Bachelor's degree	$93,260	0%	-10
Electrical and Electronics Installers and Repairers	Postsecondary nondegree award	$53,900	-4%	-540
Electro-mechanical Technicians	Associate's degree	$53,070	1%	10
Industrial Designers	Bachelor's degree	$64,620	2%	80
Landscape Architects	Bachelor's degree	$64,570	5%	120
Mechanical Engineering Technicians	Associate's degree	$53,530	2%	90
Mechanical Engineers	Bachelor's degree	$83,060	5%	1,460
Surveying and Mapping Technicians	High school diploma or equivalent	$40,770	-8%	-430
Surveyors	Bachelor's degree	$57,050	-2%	-90

Pay

The median annual wage for drafters was $51,940 in May 2014. The median wage is the wage at which half the workers in an occupation earned more than that amount and half earned less. The lowest 10 percent earned less than $33,230, and the highest 10 percent earned more than $81,240.

Median annual wages for drafters in May 2014 were as follows:

Electrical and electronics drafters $58,790
Mechanical drafters 52,200
Drafters, all other 49,990
Architectural and civil drafters 49,970

Job Outlook

Employment of drafters is projected to decline 3 percent from 2014 to 2024. Employment growth will vary by specialty.

Computer-aided design (CAD) and building information modeling (BIM) technologies allow engineers and architects to perform many tasks that used to be done by drafters, which may curb demand for all drafters. However, CAD and BIM software both require someone to build and maintain large databases, and drafters experienced with this software will be needed to work with these databases.

Employment of mechanical drafters is projected to decline 7 percent from 2014 to 2024. Although some mechanical drafters will be needed to aid in designing machines, vehicles, and medical equipment, increased use of CAD by related engineers will reduce the need for these workers compared with what would have been required without the use of these technologies by engineers.

Employment of architectural and civil drafters is projected to decline 3 percent from 2014 to 2024. Although construction projects will likely result in some demand for architectural and civil drafters, other related occupations, such as architects and engineers, are using CAD and BIM more frequently. This will reduce the need for these types of drafters, compared with what would have been required without the use of these technologies by architects and engineers.

Employment of electrical and electronics drafters is projected to grow 5 percent from 2014 to 2024, about as fast as the average for all occupations. Electrical and electronics drafters will continue to be needed to work on the electrical system designs in buildings, cars, and devices that have electrical systems.

Job Prospects. Overall competition for jobs is expected to be strong.

Specifically, architectural and civil drafters may experience more competition for jobs than mechanical or electrical drafters due to the relatively high number of students graduating in those drafting specialties. Typically, the number of graduates in architectural and civil programs greatly exceeds the number of available positions.

Demand for particular drafting specialties varies across the country because jobs depend on the needs of local industries. Job prospects for mechanical drafters should be best in large manufacturing hubs.

Because many drafting jobs are in construction and manufacturing, job opportunities for drafters will be sensitive to fluctuations in the overall economy.

Candidates proficient in CAD and BIM are likely to have better job opportunities.

Contacts for More Information

For more information on schools offering programs in drafting and related fields, visit

- Accrediting Commission of Career Schools and Colleges (www.accsc.org)

For more information on certification, visit

- American Design Drafting Association (www.adda.org)

O*NET

- Architectural and Civil Drafters (17-3011.00)
- Architectural Drafters (17-3011.01)
- Civil Drafters (17-3011.02)
- Electrical and Electronics Drafters (17-3012.00)
- Electronic Drafters (17-3012.01)
- Electrical Drafters (17-3012.02)
- Mechanical Drafters (17-3013.00)
- Drafters, All Other (17-3019.00)

Electrical and Electronics Engineering Technicians

- **2014 Median Pay** .... $59,820 per year
  $28.76 per hour
- **Typical Entry-Level Education** .... Associate's degree
- **Work Experience in a Related Occupation** .... None
- **On-the-job Training** .... None
- **Number of Jobs, 2014** 139,400
- **Job Outlook, 2014–24** .... -2% (Decline)
- **Employment Change, 2014–24** .... -2,800

Engineering technicians assist engineers in designing and testing new products.

What Electrical and Electronics Engineering Technicians Do

Electrical and electronics engineering technicians help engineers design and develop computers, communications equipment, medical monitoring devices, navigational equipment, and other electrical and electronic equipment. They often work in product evaluation and testing, using measuring and diagnostic devices to adjust, test, and repair equipment. They are also involved in the manufacture and deployment of equipment for automation.

Duties. Electrical engineering technicians typically do the following:

- Put together electrical and electronic systems and prototypes
- Build, calibrate, and repair electrical instruments or testing equipment
- Visit construction sites to observe conditions affecting design
- Identify solutions to technical design problems that arise during the construction of electrical systems
- Inspect designs for quality control, report findings, and make recommendations
- Draw diagrams and write specifications to clarify design details of experimental electronics units

Electrical engineering technicians install and maintain electrical control systems and equipment, and modify electrical prototypes, parts, and assemblies to correct problems. When testing systems, they set up test equipment and evaluate the performance of developmental parts, assemblies, or systems under simulated conditions. They then analyze test information to resolve design-related problems.

Electronics engineering technicians typically do the following:

- Design basic circuitry and draft sketches to clarify details of design documentation, under engineers' direction
- Build prototypes from rough sketches or plans
- Assemble, test, and maintain circuitry or electronic components according to engineering instructions, technical manuals, and knowledge of electronics
- Adjust and replace defective circuitry and electronic components
- Make parts, such as coils and terminal boards, by using bench lathes, drills, or other machine tools

Electronics engineering technicians identify and resolve equipment malfunctions and then work with manufacturers to get replacement parts. They also calibrate and perform preventative maintenance on equipment and systems.

These technicians often need to read blueprints, schematic drawings, and engineering instructions for assembling electronic units. They also write reports and record data on testing techniques, laboratory equipment, and specifications.

Work Environment

Electrical and electronics engineering technicians held about 139,400 jobs in 2014. The industries that employed the most electrical and electronics engineering technicians were as follows:

Computer and electronic product manufacturing	27%
Engineering services	12
Federal government	10
Utilities	5
Scientific research and development services	4

Median Annual Wages, May 2014

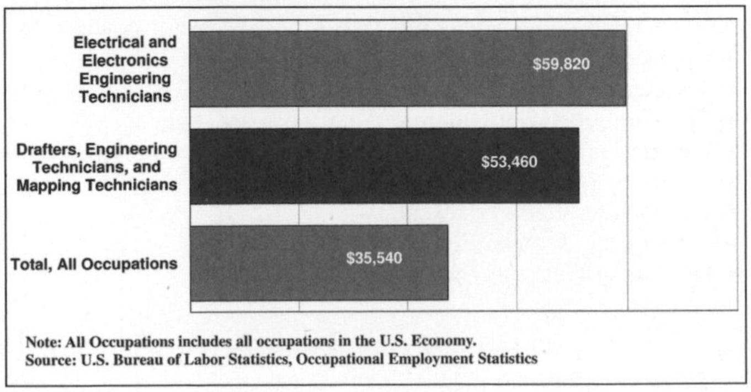

Percent Change in Employment, Projected 2014–2024

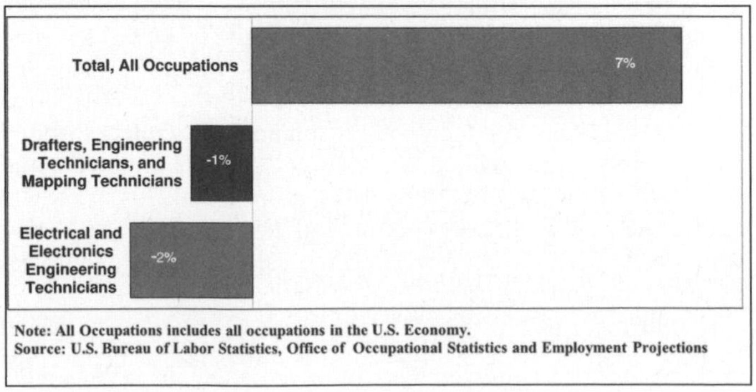

Employment Projections Data for Electrical and Electronics Engineering Technicians

Occupational Title	SOC Code	Employment, 2014	Projected Employment, 2024	Change, 2014–2024 Percent	Change, 2014–2024 Numeric
Electrical and electronics engineering technicians	17-3023	139,400	136,600	-2	-2,800

Source: U.S. Bureau of Labor Statistics, Employment Projections Program

Electrical and electronics engineering technicians work closely with electrical and electronics engineers. For this reason, teamwork is an important part of the job. They work in offices, laboratories, and factories because their job tasks involve both engineering theory and assembly-line production.

Electrical and electronics engineering technicians may be exposed to hazards from equipment or toxic materials, but incidents are rare if proper procedures are followed.

Work Schedules. Electrical and electronics engineering technicians work schedules common to production workers in the industries in which they are employed. In the federal government, their schedules tend to follow a standard workweek. In manufacturing industries and laboratories, these technicians also most commonly work a standard workweek, except for particular periods when overtime might be required.

Education/Training

Education. Programs for electrical and electronics engineering technicians usually lead to an associate's degree in electrical or electronics engineering technology. Vocational-technical schools include postsecondary institutions that serve local students and emphasize training needed by local employers.

Community colleges offer programs similar to those in technical institutes but include more theory-based and liberal arts coursework. Some of these colleges allow students to concentrate in computer electronics, industrial electronics, or communications electronics.

Prospective electrical and electronics engineering technicians usually take courses in ANSI C, C++ programming, Java programming, physics, microprocessors, and circuitry. The Technology Accreditation Commission of ABET accredits programs that include at least college algebra, trigonometry, and basic science courses.

Important Qualities

Logical-thinking skills. Electrical and electronics engineering technicians must isolate and then identify problems for the engineering staff to work on. They need good reasoning skills to identify and fix problems. Technicians must also be able to follow a logical sequence or specific set of rules to carry out engineers' designs, inspect designs for quality control, and put together prototypes.

Math skills. Electrical and electronics engineering technicians use math for analysis, design, and troubleshooting in their work.

Mechanical skills. Electronics engineering technicians in particular must be able to use hand tools and soldering irons on small circuitry and electronic parts to create detailed electronic components by hand.

Observational skills. Electrical engineering technicians sometimes visit construction sites to make sure that electrical engineers' designs are being carried out correctly. They are responsible for evaluating projects onsite and reporting problems to engineers.

Problem-solving skills. Electrical and electronics engineering technicians create what engineers have designed and often test the designs to make sure that they work. Technicians help to resolve any problems that come up in carrying out the engineers' designs.

Writing skills. These technicians must write reports about onsite construction, the results of testing, or problems they find when carrying out designs. Their writing must be clear and well organized so that the engineers they work with can understand the reports.

Licenses, Certifications, and Registrations. The National Institute for Certification in Engineering Technologies (NICET) offers certification in electrical power testing. This certification would benefit those technicians working in the electric power generation, transmission, and distribution industry.

ETA International also offers certifications in several fields, including basic electronics, biomedical, and renewable energy.

The International Society of Automation offers certification as a Control Systems Technician. To gain such certification, technicians must demonstrate skills in pneumatic, mechanical, and electronic instrumentation. In addition, they must demonstrate an understanding of process control loops and process control systems.

Pay

The median annual wage for electrical and electronics engineering technicians was $59,820 in May 2014. The median wage is the wage at which half the workers in an occupation earned more than that amount and half earned less. The lowest 10 percent earned less than $35,880, and the highest 10 percent earned more than $87,840.

In May 2014, the median annual wages for electrical and electronics engineering technicians in the top industries in which they worked were as follows:

Utilities	$68,310
Federal government	63,650
Scientific research and development services	63,050
Engineering services	57,110
Computer and electronic product manufacturing	56,130

Electrical and electronics engineering technicians work schedules common to production workers in the industries in which they are employed. In the federal government, their schedules tend to follow a standard workweek.

Job Outlook

Employment of electrical and electronics engineering technicians is projected to decline 2 percent from 2014 to 2024.

Some of these technicians work in traditional manufacturing industries, many of which are declining or growing slowly. In addition, employment of these technicians in the federal government is projected to decline. However, employment growth for electrical and electronics engineering technicians will likely occur in engineering services firms as companies seek to contract out these services as a way to lower costs.

Electrical and electronics engineering technicians also work closely with electrical and electronics engineers and computer hardware engineers in the computer systems design services

Similar Occupations. This table shows a list of occupations with job duties that are similar to those of electrical and electronics engineering technicians.

Occupations	Entry-level Education	2014 Median Pay	Projected Job Growth	Average Annual Openings
Electrical and Electronics Engineers	Bachelor's degree	$93,260	0%	-10
Electrical and Electronics Installers and Repairers	Postsecondary nondegree award	$53,900	-4%	-540
Electro-mechanical Technicians	Associate's degree	$53,070	1%	10
Mechanical Engineering Technicians	Associate's degree	$53,530	2%	90

industry. Demand for these technicians overall is expected to be sustained by demand for workers in this industry because of the continuing integration of computer and electronics systems. For example, computer, cellular phone, and global positioning system (GPS) technologies are being included in automobiles and various portable and household electronics systems.

Contacts for More Information

For information about general engineering education and career resources, visit

- American Society for Engineering Education (www.asee.org)
- Technology Student Association (www.tsaweb.org)

For information about accredited programs, visit

- ABET (www.abet.org)

For information about certification, visit

- ETA International (www.eta-i.org)
- International Society of Automation (http://tinyurl.com/hn32pdz)
- International Society of Certified Electronics Technicians (www.iscet.org)
- National Institute for Certification in Engineering Technologies (NICET) (http://tinyurl.com/gpjtxa2)

O*NET

- Electrical and Electronic Engineering Technicians (17-3023.00)
- Electronics Engineering Technicians (17-3023.01)
- Electrical Engineering Technicians (17-3023.03)

Electrical and Electronics Engineers

- **2014 Median Pay** .... $93,260 per year
  $44.84 per hour
- **Typical Entry-Level Education** .... Bachelor's degree
- **Work Experience in a Related Occupation** .... None
- **On-the-job Training** .... None
- **Number of Jobs, 2014** 315,900
- **Job Outlook, 2014–24** .... 0% (Little or no change)
- **Employment Change, 2014–24** .... -100

What Electrical and Electronics Engineers Do

Electrical engineers design, develop, test, and supervise the manufacturing of electrical equipment, such as electric motors, radar and navigation systems, communications systems, or power generation equipment. Electrical engineers also design the electrical systems of automobiles and aircraft.

Electronics engineers design and develop electronic equipment, such as broadcast and communications systems, from portable music players to global positioning systems (GPSs). Many also work in areas closely related to computer hardware.

Duties. Electrical engineers typically do the following:

- Design new ways to use electrical power to develop or improve products
- Perform detailed calculations to develop manufacturing, construction, and installation standards and specifications
- Direct the manufacture, installation, and testing of electrical equipment to ensure that products meet specifications and codes
- Investigate complaints from customers or the public, evaluate problems, and recommend solutions
- Work with project managers on production efforts to ensure that projects are completed satisfactorily, on time, and within budget

Electronics engineers typically do the following:

- Design electronic components, software, products, or systems for commercial, industrial, medical, military, or scientific applications
- Analyze customer needs and determine the requirements, capacity, and cost for developing an electrical system plan
- Develop maintenance and testing procedures for electronic components and equipment
- Evaluate systems and recommend design modifications or equipment repair
- Inspect electronic equipment, instruments, and systems to make sure that they meet safety standards and applicable regulations
- Plan and develop applications and modifications for electronic properties used in parts and systems in order to improve technical performance

Electrical engineers design tests for new products.

Electronics engineers who work for the federal government research, develop, and evaluate electronic devices used in a variety of areas, such as aviation, computing, transportation, and manufacturing. They work on federal electronic devices and systems, including satellites, flight systems, radar and sonar systems, and communications systems.

The work of electrical engineers and electronics engineers is often similar. Both use engineering and design software and equipment to do engineering tasks. Both types of engineers also must work with other engineers to discuss existing products and possibilities for engineering projects.

Engineers whose work is related exclusively to computer hardware are considered computer hardware engineers.

Work Environment

Electrical and electronics engineers held about 315,900 jobs in 2014. The industries that employed the most electrical engineers in 2014 were as follows:

Engineering services.. 22%
Electric power generation, transmission and distribution....... 10
Semiconductor and other electronic component manufacturing.. 7
Navigational, measuring, electromedical, and control instruments manufacturing 7
Research and development in the physical, engineering, and life sciences.. 6

The industries that employed the most electronics engineers in 2014 were as follows:

Telecommunications 18%
Federal government, excluding postal service 13
Engineering services... 11
Semiconductor and other electronic component manufacturing.. 9
Navigational, measuring, electromedical, and control instruments manufacturing 7

Electrical and electronics engineers generally work indoors in offices. However, they may visit sites to observe a problem or a piece of complex equipment.

Work Schedules. Most electrical and electronics engineers work full time.

Education/Training

Electrical and electronics engineers must have a bachelor's degree. Employers also value practical experience, such as participation in cooperative engineering programs, in which students earn academic credit for structured work experience. Having a Professional Engineer (PE) license may improve an engineer's chances of finding employment.

Education. High school students interested in studying electrical or electronics engineering benefit from taking courses in physics and mathematics, including algebra, trigonometry, and calculus. Courses in drafting are also helpful, because electrical and electronics engineers often are required to prepare technical drawings.

In order to enter the occupation, prospective electrical and electronics engineers need a bachelor's degree in electrical engineering, electronics engineering, or electrical engineering technology. Programs include classroom, laboratory, and field studies. Courses include digital systems design, differential equations, and electrical circuit theory. Programs in electrical engineering, electronics engineering, or electrical engineering technology should be accredited by ABET.

Some colleges and universities offer cooperative programs in which students gain practical experience while completing their education. Cooperative programs combine classroom study with practical work. Internships provide similar experience and are growing in number.

At some universities, students can enroll in a 5-year program that leads to both a bachelor's degree and a master's degree. A graduate degree allows an engineer to work as an instructor at some universities, or in research and development.

Important Qualities

Concentration. Electrical and electronics engineers design and develop complex electrical systems and electronic components and products. They must be able to keep track of multiple design elements and technical characteristics when performing these tasks.

Initiative. Electrical and electronics engineers must be able to apply their knowledge to new tasks in every project they undertake. In addition, they must engage in continuing education to keep up with changes in technology.

Interpersonal skills. Electrical and electronics engineers must be able to work with others during the manufacturing process to ensure that their plans are implemented correctly. This collaboration includes monitoring technicians and devising remedies to problems as they arise.

Math skills. Electrical and electronics engineers must be able to use the principles of calculus and other advanced math in order to analyze, design, and troubleshoot equipment.

Speaking skills. Electrical and electronics engineers work closely with other engineers and technicians. They must be able to explain their designs and reasoning clearly and to relay instructions during product development and production. They also may need to explain complex issues to customers who have little or no technical expertise.

Median Annual Wages, May 2014

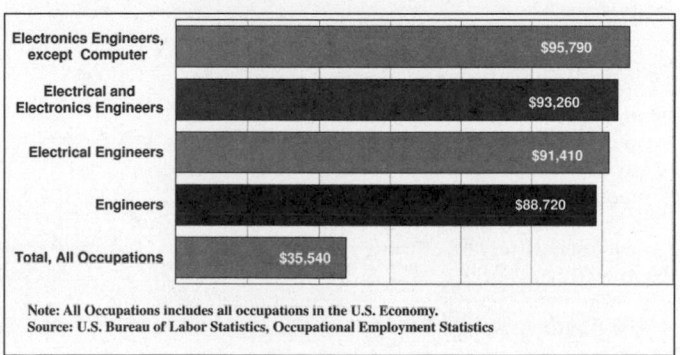

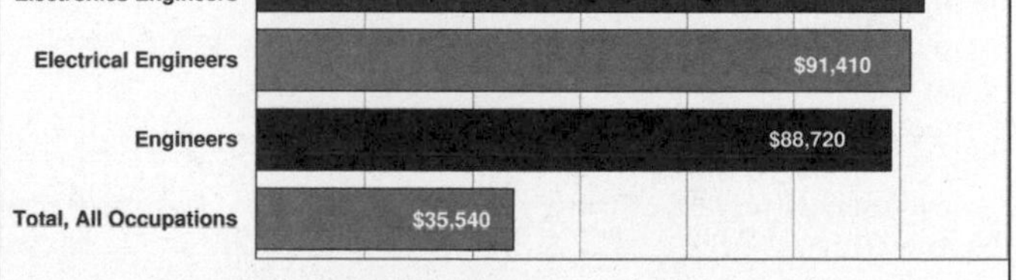

Note: All Occupations includes all occupations in the U.S. Economy.
Source: U.S. Bureau of Labor Statistics, Occupational Employment Statistics

Percent Change in Employment, Projected 2014–2024

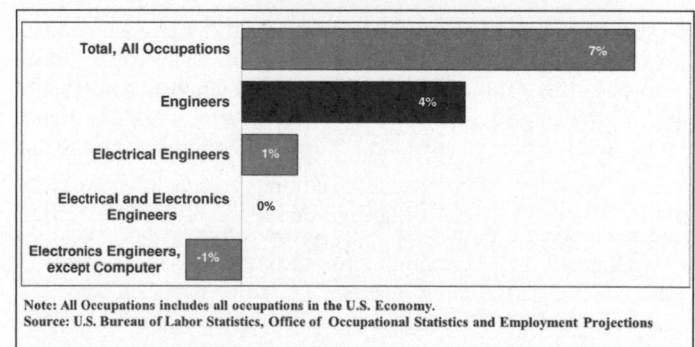

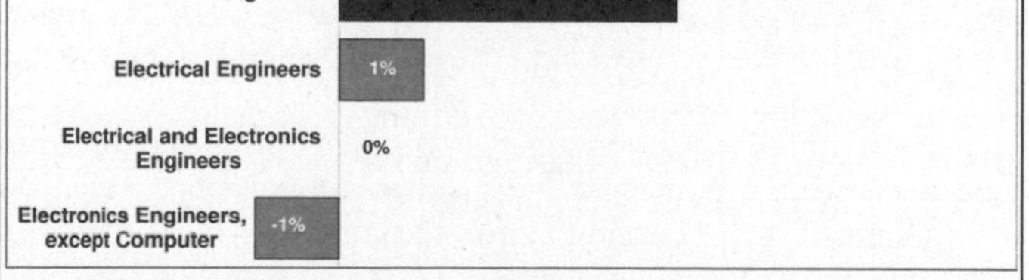

Note: All Occupations includes all occupations in the U.S. Economy.
Source: U.S. Bureau of Labor Statistics, Office of Occupational Statistics and Employment Projections

Employment Projections Data for Electrical and Electronics Engineers

Occupational Title	SOC Code	Employment, 2014	Projected Employment, 2024	Change, 2014–2024 Percent	Change, 2014–2024 Numeric
Electrical and electronics engineers	17-2070	315,900	315,700	0	-100
Electrical engineers	17-2071	178,400	180,200	1	1,800
Electronics engineers, except computer	17-2072	137,400	135,500	-1	-1,900

Source: U.S. Bureau of Labor Statistics, Employment Projections Program

Similar Occupations. This table shows a list of occupations with job duties that are similar to those of electrical and electronics engineers.

Occupations	Entry-level Education	2014 Median Pay	Projected Job Growth	Average Annual Openings
Aerospace Engineers	Bachelor's degree	$105,380	-2%	-160
Architectural and Engineering Managers	Bachelor's degree	$130,620	2%	370
Biomedical Engineers	Bachelor's degree	$86,950	23%	510
Computer Hardware Engineers	Bachelor's degree	$108,430	3%	240
Electrical and Electronics Engineering Technicians	Associate's degree	$59,820	-2%	-280
Electrical and Electronics Installers and Repairers	Postsecondary nondegree award	$53,900	-4%	-540
Electricians	High school diploma or equivalent	$51,110	14%	8,590
Electro-mechanical Technicians	Associate's degree	$53,070	1%	10
Sales Engineers	Bachelor's degree	$96,340	7%	490

Writing skills. Electrical and electronics engineers develop technical publications related to equipment they develop, including maintenance manuals, operation manuals, parts lists, product proposals, and design methods documents.

Licenses, Certifications, and Registrations. Licensure is not required for entry-level positions as electrical and electronics engineers. A Professional Engineer (PE) license, which allows for higher levels of leadership and independence, can be acquired later in one's career. Licensed engineers are called professional engineers (PEs). A PE can oversee the work of other engineers, sign off on projects, and provide services directly to the public. State licensure generally requires

- A degree from an ABET-accredited engineering program
- A passing score on the Fundamentals of Engineering (FE) exam
- Relevant work experience
- A passing score on the Principles and Practice of Engineering (PE) exam

The initial Fundamentals of Engineering (FE) exam can be taken right after graduation from a college or university. Engineers who pass this exam commonly are called engineers in training (EITs) or engineer interns (EIs). After getting work experience, EITs can take the second exam, called the Principles and Practice of Engineering exam.

Several states require engineers to take continuing education courses to keep their license. Most states recognize licensure from other states if the licensing state's requirements meet or exceed their own licensure requirements.

Advancement. Electrical and electronic engineers may advance to supervisory positions in which they lead a team of engineers and technicians. Some may move to management positions, working as engineering or program managers. Preparation for managerial positions usually requires working under the guidance of a more experienced engineer. For more information, see the profile on architectural and engineering managers.

For sales work, an engineering background enables engineers to discuss a product's technical aspects and assist in product planning and use. For more information, see the profile on sales engineers.

Pay

The median annual wage for electrical engineers was $91,410 in May 2014. The median wage is the wage at which half the workers in an occupation earned more than that amount and half earned less. The lowest 10 percent earned less than $59,140, and the highest 10 percent earned more than $143,200.

The median annual wage for electronics engineers, except computer was $95,790 in May 2014. The lowest 10 percent earned less than $61,780, and the highest 10 percent earned more than $147,570.

In May 2014, the median annual wages for electrical engineers in the top industries in which they worked were as follows:

Semiconductor and other electronic component manufacturing	$105,200
Research and development in the physical, engineering, and life sciences	104,820
Navigational, measuring, electromedical, and control instruments manufacturing	92,530
Engineering services	89,960
Electric power generation, transmission and distribution	88,790

In May 2014, the median annual wages for electronics engineers in the top industries in which they worked were as follows:

Federal government, excluding postal service	$104,830
Navigational, measuring, electromedical, and control instruments manufacturing	102,560
Semiconductor and other electronic component manufacturing	100,070
Engineering services	95,250
Telecommunications	87,200

Job Outlook

Employment of electrical and electronics engineers is projected to show little or no change from 2014 to 2024. Change in employment is expected to be tempered by slow growth or decline in most manufacturing sectors in which electrical and electronics engineers are employed.

Job growth for electrical and electronics engineers will occur largely in engineering services firms, because more companies are expected to cut costs by contracting their engineering services rather than directly employing engineers. These engineers also will be in demand to develop sophisticated consumer electronics.

The rapid pace of technological innovation and development will likely drive demand for electrical and electronics engineers in research and development, an area in which engineering expertise will be needed to develop distribution systems related to new technologies. These engineers will play key roles in new developments having to do with solar arrays, semiconductors, and communications technologies.

Contacts for More Information

For information about general engineering education and career resources, visit

➤ American Society for Engineering Education (www.asee.org)
➤ Technology Student Association (www.tsaweb.org)

For more information about licensure as an electrical or electronics engineer, visit

➤ National Council of Examiners for Engineering and Surveying (http://ncees.org)
➤ National Society of Professional Engineers (www.nspe.org/index.html)

For information about accredited engineering programs, visit

➤ ABET (www.abet.org)

O*NET

➤ Electrical Engineers (17-2071.00)
➤ Electronics Engineers, Except Computer (17-2072.00)
➤ Radio Frequency Identification Device Specialists (17-2072.01)

Electro-mechanical Technicians

- **2014 Median Pay** .... $53,070 per year, $25.52 per hour
- **Typical Entry-Level Education** .... Associate's degree
- **Work Experience in a Related Occupation** .... None
- **On-the-job Training** .... None
- **Number of Jobs, 2014** 14,700
- **Job Outlook, 2014–24** .... 1% (Little or no change)
- **Employment Change, 2014–24** 100

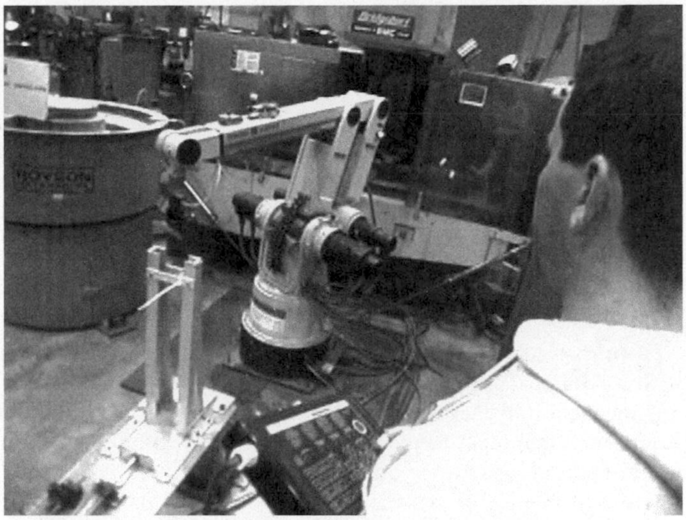

Electro-mechanical technicians install, repair, upgrade, and test electronic and computer-controlled mechanical systems.

What Electro-mechanical Technicians Do

Electro-mechanical technicians combine knowledge of mechanical technology with knowledge of electrical and electronic circuits. They operate, test, and maintain unmanned, automated, robotic, or electromechanical equipment.

Duties. Electro-mechanical technicians typically do the following:

- Read blueprints, schematics, and diagrams to determine the method and sequence of assembly of a part, machine, or piece of equipment
- Verify dimensions of parts, using precision measuring instruments, to ensure that specifications are met
- Operate metalworking machines to make housings, fittings, and fixtures
- Inspect parts for surface defects
- Repair and calibrate hydraulic and pneumatic assemblies
- Test the performance of electro-mechanical assemblies, using test instruments
- Install electronic parts and hardware, using soldering equipment and hand tools
- Operate, test, or maintain robotic equipment
- Analyze and record test results, and prepare written documentation

Electro-mechanical technicians test and operate machines in factories and other worksites. They also analyze and record test results, and prepare written documentation to describe the tests they did and what the test results were.

Electro-mechanical technicians install, maintain, and repair automated machinery and equipment in industrial settings. This kind of work requires knowledge and training in the application of photonics, the science of light. The technological aspects of the work have to do with the generating, controlling, and detecting of the light waves so that the automated processes can proceed as designed by the engineers.

Electro-mechanical technicians also test, operate, or maintain robotic equipment at worksites. This equipment may include unmanned submarines, aircraft, or similar types of equipment for uses including oil drilling, deep-ocean exploration, or hazardous-waste removal.

Work Environment

Electro-mechanical technicians held about 14,700 jobs in 2014. The industries that employed the most electro-mechanical technicians were as follows:

Navigational, measuring, electromedical, and control instruments manufacturing	13%
Semiconductor and other electronic component manufacturing	9
Support activities for mining	8
Engineering services	7
Machinery manufacturing	7

Electro-mechanical technicians work closely with electrical and mechanical engineers. They work in many industrial environments, including energy, plastics, computer, and communications equipment manufacturing, and aerospace. They often work both at production sites and in offices.

Because their job involves manual work with many machines and types of equipment, electro-mechanical technicians are sometimes exposed to hazards from equipment or toxic materials. However, incidents are rare as long as they follow proper safety procedures.

Work Schedules. Electro-mechanical technicians often work for larger companies in manufacturing or for engineering firms. Like others at these firms, these technicians tend to work regular shifts. However, sometimes they must work longer hours to make repairs so that manufacturing operations can continue.

Education/Training

Education. Associate's degree programs and postsecondary certificates for electro-mechanical technicians are offered at vocational-technical schools and community colleges. Vocational-technical schools include postsecondary public institutions that serve local students and emphasize teaching the skills needed by local employers. Community colleges offer programs similar to those in technical institutes, but they may include more theory-based and liberal arts coursework.

ABET accredits associate's and higher degree programs. Most associate's degree programs that are accredited by ABET include at least college algebra and trigonometry, as well as basic science courses.

ABET-accredited programs offer training in engineering technology specialties. In community college programs, prospective electro-mechanical technicians can concentrate in fields such as the following:

- Electro-mechanics
- Industrial maintenance
- Computer-integrated manufacturing
- Mechatronics

Earning an associate's degree in electronic or mechanical technology facilitates entry into a bachelor's degree programs in electrical engineering and mechanical engineering. For more information, see the profiles on electrical and electronics engineers and mechanical engineers.

Training in mechatronics provides an understanding of four key systems on which this occupation works: mechanical systems, electronic systems, control systems, and computer systems.

Important Qualities

Detail oriented. Electro-mechanical technicians must make and keep the precise, accurate measurements that mechanical engineers need.

Dexterity. Electro-mechanical technicians must be able to use hand tools and soldering irons on small circuitry and electronic parts to create detailed electronic components by hand.

Interpersonal skills. Electro-mechanical technicians must be able to take instruction and offer advice when needed. In addition, they often need to coordinate their work with that of others.

Logical-thinking skills. To carry out engineers' designs, inspect designs for quality control, and assemble prototypes, electro-mechanical technicians must be able to read instructions and follow a logical sequence or a specific set of rules.

Math skills. Electro-mechanical technicians use mathematics for analysis, design, and troubleshooting in their work.

Mechanical skills. Electro-mechanical technicians must be able to apply the theory and instructions of engineers by creating or building new components for industrial machinery or equipment. They must be adept at operating machinery, including drill presses, grinders, and engine lathes.

Writing skills. Electro-mechanical technicians must write reports that cover onsite construction, the results of testing, or problems they find when carrying out designs. Their writing must be clear and well-organized so that the engineers they work with can understand the reports.

Licenses, Certifications, and Registrations. Electro-mechanical technicians can gain certification as a way to demonstrate professional competence.

The International Society of Automation offers certification as a Certified Control Systems Technician. This requires, at a minimum, 5 years of experience on the job, or 3 years of work experience if the technician has completed 2 years of postsecondary education.

Median Annual Wages, May 2014

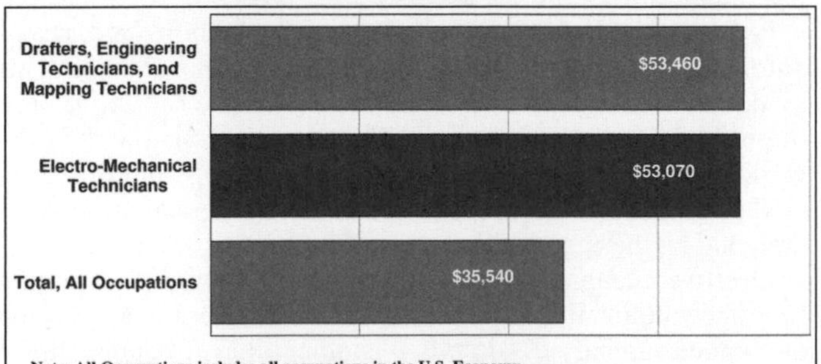

Note: All Occupations includes all occupations in the U.S. Economy.
Source: U.S. Bureau of Labor Statistics, Occupational Employment Statistics

Percent Change in Employment, Projected 2014–2024

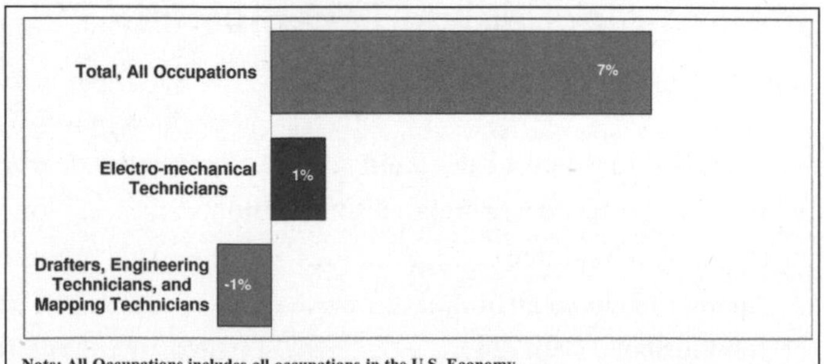

Note: All Occupations includes all occupations in the U.S. Economy.
Source: U.S. Bureau of Labor Statistics, Office of Occupational Statistics and Employment Projections

Employment Projections Data for Electro-mechanical Technicians

Occupational Title	SOC Code	Employment, 2014	Projected Employment, 2024	Change, 2014–2024 Percent	Change, 2014–2024 Numeric
Electro-mechanical technicians	17-3024	14,700	14,800	1	100

Source: U.S. Bureau of Labor Statistics, Employment Projections Program

Similar Occupations. This table shows a list of occupations with job duties that are similar to those of electro-mechanical technicians.

Occupations	Entry-level Education	2014 Median Pay	Projected Job Growth	Average Annual Openings
Drafters	Associate's degree	$51,940	-3%	-620
Electrical and Electronics Engineering Technicians	Associate's degree	$59,820	-2%	-280
Electrical and Electronics Engineers	Bachelor's degree	$93,260	0%	-10
Electrical and Electronics Installers and Repairers	Postsecondary nondegree award	$53,900	-4%	-540
Machinists and Tool and Die Makers	High school diploma or equivalent	$41,510	6%	2,900
Mechanical Engineering Technicians	Associate's degree	$53,530	2%	90
Mechanical Engineers	Bachelor's degree	$83,060	5%	1,460

The National Institute for Certification in Engineering Technologies (NICET) offers certification in electrical power testing, industrial instrumentation, and other specialties.

Pay

The median annual wage for electro-mechanical technicians was $53,070 in May 2014. The median wage is the wage at which half the workers in an occupation earned more than that amount and half earned less. The lowest 10 percent earned less than $33,260, and the highest 10 percent earned more than $82,700.

In May 2014, the median annual wages for electro-mechanical technicians in the top industries in which they worked were as follows:

Machinery manufacturing	$57,130
Engineering services	56,800
Semiconductor and other electronic component manufacturing	51,950
Navigational, measuring, electromedical, and control instruments manufacturing	50,210
Support activities for mining	39,840

Job Outlook

Employment of electro-mechanical technicians is projected to show little or no change from 2014 to 2024. Many of these technicians are employed in manufacturing industries that are projected to experience employment declines.

Electro-mechanical technicians are generalists in technology, and their broad skill set will help sustain employment. This is especially the case as their skills working with machines wired to computer control systems grow in importance in the manufacturing sector.

There should be demand for electro-mechanical technicians as demand increases for engineers to design and build new equipment in various fields. Consequently, employers will likely seek out electro-mechanical technicians with knowledge of photonics to help implement and maintain automated processes.

Increasing adoption of renewable energies, such as solar power and wind turbines, may also contribute to increased demand for electro-mechanical technicians.

Contacts for More Information

For information about general engineering education and career resources, visit

- American Society for Engineering Education (www.asee.org)
- IEEE (www.ieee.org/index.html)
- Technology Student Association (www.tsaweb.org)

For information on accredited programs, visit

- ABET (www.abet.org)

For more information about certification, visit

- International Society of Automation (http://tinyurl.com/yh2hkhr)
- National Institute for Certification in Engineering Technologies (www.nicet.org) (NICET)

For information about working in automation, visit

- Automation Federation (http://tinyurl.com/j82qhk9)

O*NET

- Electro-Mechanical Technicians (17-3024.00)
- Robotics Technicians (17-3024.01)

Environmental Engineering Technicians

- **2014 Median Pay** .... $48,170 per year, $23.16 per hour
- **Typical Entry-Level Education** .... Associate's degree
- **Work Experience in a Related Occupation** .... None
- **On-the-job Training** .... None
- **Number of Jobs, 2014** 18,600
- **Job Outlook, 2014–24** .... 10% (Faster than average)
- **Employment Change, 2014–24** 1,900

Environmental engineering technicians must wear protective gear when they are working outdoors on environmental remediation.

What Environmental Engineering Technicians Do

Environmental engineering technicians carry out the plans that environmental engineers develop.

Duties. Environmental engineering technicians typically do the following:

- Set up, test, operate, and modify equipment used to prevent or clean up environmental pollution
- Maintain project records and computer program files
- Conduct pollution surveys, for which they collect and analyze samples such as air and groundwater
- Perform indoor and outdoor work on environmental quality
- Work to mitigate sources of environmental pollution
- Review technical documents to ensure their completeness and conformance to requirements
- Review work plans to schedule activities
- Arrange for the disposal of lead, asbestos, and other hazardous materials

In laboratories, environmental engineering technicians record observations, test results, and document photographs. To keep laboratories supplied, they also may gather product information, identify vendors and suppliers, and order materials and equipment.

Environmental engineering technicians help environmental engineers develop devices used to clean up environmental pollution. They also inspect facilities for compliance with the regulations that govern substances such as asbestos, lead, and wastewater.

Work Environment

Environmental engineering technicians held about 18,600 jobs in 2014. The industries that employed the most environmental engineering technicians were as follows:

Engineering services	23%
Management, scientific, and technical consulting services	23
Local government, excluding education and hospitals	12
Waste management and remediation services	9
Testing laboratories	7

Environmental engineering technicians work under the direction of engineers and as part of a team with other technicians. They must be able to work well with both supervisors and peers.

Environment engineering technicians typically work indoors, usually in laboratories, and often have regular working hours. They also work outdoors, sometimes in remote locations.

Because environmental engineering technicians help out in environmental cleanup, they can be exposed to hazards from equipment, chemicals, or toxic materials. For this reason, they must follow proper safety procedures, such as wearing hazmat suits and sometimes respirators, even in warm weather. When they work in wet areas, environmental engineering technicians wear heavy rubber boots to keep their legs and feet dry.

Work Schedules. Most environmental engineering technicians work full time and typically have regular hours. However, they must sometimes work irregular hours in order to monitor operations or contain a major environmental threat.

Education/Training

Environmental engineering technicians typically need an associate's degree in environmental engineering technology or a related field.

Education. Environmental engineering technicians typically need an associate's degree in environmental engineering technology or a related field. Programs in environmental engineering technology generally include courses in mathematics, chemistry, hazardous waste management, and environmental assessment, among others.

Programs can be found in vocational-technical schools and community colleges. Community colleges offer programs similar to those in vocational-technical schools but include more theory-based and liberal arts coursework. Some environmental engineering technicians enter the occupation with a bachelor's degree in a natural science, such as biology or chemistry.

Median Annual Wages, May 2014

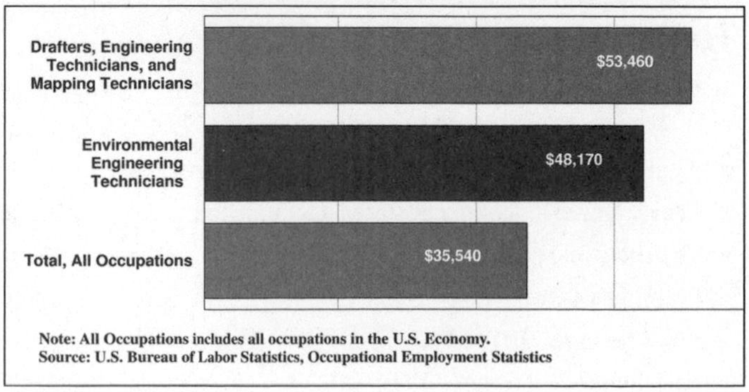

Percent Change in Employment, Projected 2014–2024

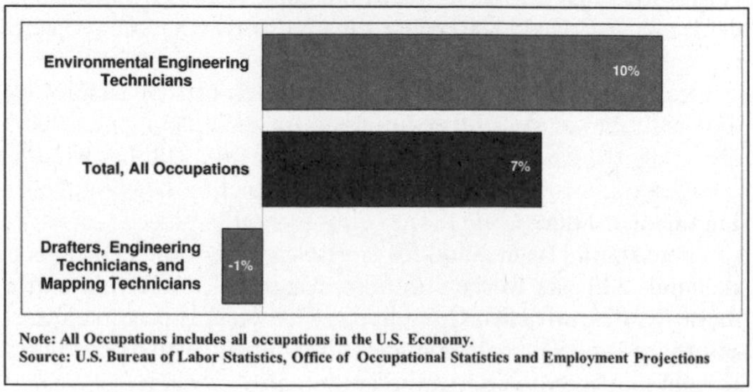

Employment Projections Data for Environmental Engineering Technicians

Occupational Title	SOC Code	Employment, 2014	Projected Employment, 2024	Change, 2014–2024 Percent	Change, 2014–2024 Numeric
Environmental engineering technicians	17-3025	18,600	20,400	10	1,900

Source: U.S. Bureau of Labor Statistics, Employment Projections Program

Similar Occupations. This table shows a list of occupations with job duties that are similar to those of environmental engineering technicians.

Occupations	Entry-level Education	2014 Median Pay	Projected Job Growth	Average Annual Openings
Environmental Engineers	Bachelor's degree	$83,360	12%	680
Environmental Science and Protection Technicians	Associate's degree	$42,190	9%	340
Environmental Scientists and Specialists	Bachelor's degree	$66,250	11%	1,020
Hazardous Materials Removal Workers	High school diploma or equivalent	$38,520	7%	330

ABET accredits engineering and engineering technology programs at the associate's level and above.

Prospective engineering technicians should take as many high school science and math courses as possible to prepare for programs in engineering technology after high school.

Important Qualities

Communication skills. When working on teams, environmental engineering technicians must be able to listen well and report back to their group or team leader.

Critical-thinking skills. Environmental engineers rely on environmental engineering technicians to help identify problems and solutions and to implement the engineers' plans. To do these tasks, technicians must be able to think critically and logically.

Observational skills. Environmental engineering technicians are the eyes and ears of environmental engineers and must assume responsibility for properly evaluating situations onsite. These technicians must be able to recognize problems so that the environmental engineers are informed as quickly as possible.

Reading skills. Environmental engineering technicians must be able to read and understand legal and technical documents in order to ensure that regulatory requirements are being met.

Advancement. Environmental engineering technicians usually begin work as trainees in entry-level positions supervised by an environmental engineer or a more experienced technician. As they gain experience, technicians take on more responsibility and carry out assignments under general supervision. Some eventually enter positions as senior environmental technicians or lead environmental technicians, who function as supervisors when onsite.

Technicians with a bachelor's degree often are able to advance to become environmental engineers.

Pay

The median annual wage for environmental engineering technicians was $48,170 in May 2014. The median wage is the wage at which half the workers in an occupation earned more than that amount and half earned less. The lowest 10 percent earned less than $30,250, and the highest 10 percent earned more than $77,030.

In May 2014, the median annual wages for environmental engineering technicians in the top industries in which they worked were as follows:

Local government, excluding education and hospitals	$54,860
Engineering services	50,370
Waste management and remediation services	45,460
Management, scientific, and technical consulting services	44,990
Testing laboratories	39,890

Job Outlook

Employment of environmental engineering technicians is projected to grow 10 percent from 2014 to 2024, faster than the average for all occupations.

Employment in this occupation is typically tied to projects created by environmental engineers. State and local governments are expected to focus their efforts and resources on efficient water use, storm water management, and wastewater treatment over the next decade. These areas of emphasis should serve to increase demand for environmental engineering technicians. There will also be demand for environmental technicians working in consulting firms as governments and larger firms look to reduce costs.

The increasing call to clean up contaminated sites, as mandated by Congress and directed by the Environmental Protection Agency (EPA), is expected to help sustain demand for environmental engineering technicians' services. Recently, the EPA expanded its purview under the Clean Water Act to cover tributaries. Environmental engineering technicians are expected to be needed to help utilities and water treatment plants comply with new federal or state environmental regulations.

Contacts for More Information

For more information about accredited programs, visit

➤ ABET (www.abet.org)

For more information about general engineering education and career resources, visit

➤ Technology Student Association (www.tsaweb.org)

O*NET

➤ Environmental Engineering Technicians (17-3025.00)

Environmental Engineers

- **2014 Median Pay** .... $83,360 per year
  $40.08 per hour
- **Typical Entry-Level Education** .... Bachelor's degree
- **Work Experience in a Related Occupation** .... None
- **On-the-job Training** .... None
- **Number of Jobs, 2014** 55,100
- **Job Outlook, 2014–24** .... 12% (Faster than average)
- **Employment Change, 2014–24** 6,800

Environmental engineers design systems for managing and cleaning municipal water supplies.

What Environmental Engineers Do

Environmental engineers use the principles of engineering, soil science, biology, and chemistry to develop solutions to environmental problems. They are involved in efforts to improve recycling, waste disposal, public health, and water and air pollution control. They also address global issues, such as unsafe drinking water, climate change, and environmental sustainability.

Duties. Environmental engineers typically do the following:

- Prepare, review, and update environmental investigation reports
- Design projects that lead to environmental protection, such as water reclamation facilities, air pollution control systems, and operations that convert waste to energy
- Obtain, update, and maintain plans, permits, and standard operating procedures
- Provide technical support for environmental remediation projects and for legal actions
- Analyze scientific data and do quality-control checks
- Monitor the progress of environmental improvement programs
- Inspect industrial and municipal facilities and programs in order to ensure compliance with environmental regulations
- Advise corporations and government agencies about procedures for cleaning up contaminated sites

Environmental engineers conduct hazardous-waste management studies in which they evaluate the significance of a hazard and advise on treating and containing it. They also design systems for municipal and industrial water supplies and industrial wastewater treatment, and research the environmental impact of proposed construction projects. Environmental engineers in government develop regulations to prevent mishaps.

Some environmental engineers study ways to minimize the effects of acid rain, climate change, automobile emissions, and ozone depletion. They also collaborate with environmental scientists, planners, hazardous waste technicians, and other engineers, as well as with specialists such as experts in law and business, to address environmental problems and environmental sustainability. For more information, see the job profiles on environmental scientists and specialists, hazardous materials removal workers, lawyers, and urban and regional planners.

Work Environment

Environmental engineers held about 55,100 jobs in 2014. The industries that employed the most environmental engineers were as follows:

Engineering services	28%
Management, scientific, and technical consulting services	20
State government, excluding education and hospitals	15
Local government, excluding education and hospitals	7
Federal government, excluding postal service	6

They work in a variety of settings because of the nature of the tasks they do:

- When they are working with other engineers and with urban and regional planners, environmental engineers are likely to be in offices.
- When they are working with businesspeople and lawyers, environmental engineers are likely to be at seminars, where they present information and answer questions.
- When they are working with hazardous waste technicians and environmental scientists, environmental engineers work at specific sites outdoors.

Work Schedules. Most environmental engineers work full time. Those who manage projects often work more than 40 hours per week to monitor the project's progress, ensure deadlines are met, and recommend corrective action when needed. About 1 out of 5 worked more than 40 hours per week in 2014.

Education/Training

Environmental engineers must have a bachelor's degree in environmental engineering or a related field, such as civil, chemical, or general engineering. Employers also value practical experience. Therefore, cooperative engineering programs, in which college credit is awarded for structured job experience, are valuable as well.

Education. Entry-level environmental engineering jobs require a bachelor's degree. Programs include classroom, laboratory, and field studies. Some colleges and universities offer cooperative programs in which students gain practical experience while completing their education.

At some colleges and universities, a student can enroll in a 5-year program that leads to both a bachelor's and a master's degree. A graduate degree allows an engineer to work as an instructor at some colleges and universities or to do research and development, and some employers prefer candidates to have a master's degree.

Students interested in becoming an environmental engineer should take high school courses in chemistry, biology, physics, and math, including algebra, trigonometry, and calculus.

Many engineering programs are accredited by ABET. Some employers prefer to hire candidates who have graduated from an

Median Annual Wages, May 2014

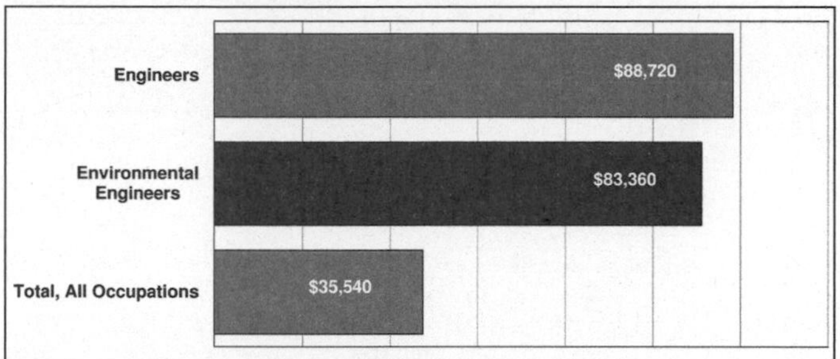

Note: All Occupations includes all occupations in the U.S. Economy.
Source: U.S. Bureau of Labor Statistics, Occupational Employment Statistics

Percent Change in Employment, Projected 2014–2024

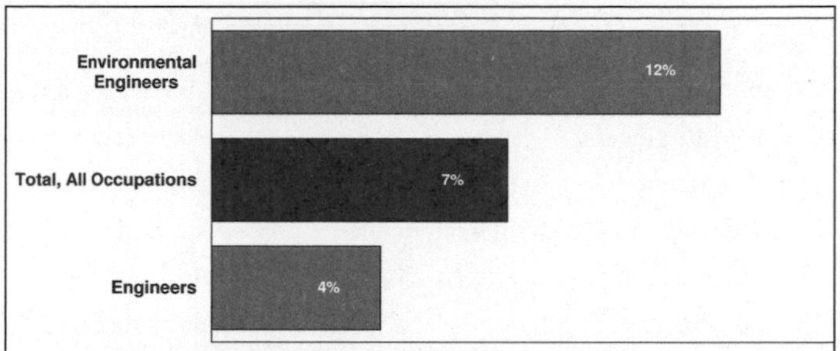

Note: All Occupations includes all occupations in the U.S. Economy.
Source: U.S. Bureau of Labor Statistics, Office of Occupational Statistics and Employment Projections

accredited program. A degree from an ABET-accredited program is usually necessary for a person to become a licensed professional engineer.

Important Qualities

Imagination. Environmental engineers sometimes have to design systems that will be part of larger ones. They must be able to foresee how the proposed designs will interact with other components of the larger system, including the workers, machinery, and equipment, as well as with the environment.

Interpersonal skills. Environmental engineers must be able to work with others toward a common goal. They usually work with engineers and scientists who design other systems and with the technicians and mechanics who put the designs into practice.

Problem-solving skills. When designing facilities and processes, environmental engineers strive to solve several issues at once, from workers' safety to environmental protection. They must be able to identify and anticipate problems in order to prevent losses for their employers, safeguard workers' health, and mitigate environmental damage.

Reading skills. Environmental engineers often work with businesspeople, lawyers, and other professionals outside their field. They frequently are required to read and understand documents with topics outside their scope of training.

Writing skills. Environmental engineers must be able to write clearly so that others without their specific training can understand their plans, proposals, specifications, findings, and other documents.

Licenses, Certifications, and Registrations. Licensure is not required for entry-level positions as an environmental engineer. A Professional Engineering (PE) license, which allows for higher levels of leadership and independence, can be acquired later in one's career. Licensed engineers are called professional engineers (PEs). A PE can oversee the work of other engineers, sign off on projects, and provide services directly to the public. State licensure generally requires

- A degree from an ABET-accredited engineering program
- A passing score on the Fundamentals of Engineer (FE) exam
- Relevant work experience
- A passing score on the Principles and Practice of Engineering (PE) exam

The initial FE exam can be taken after one earns a bachelor's degree. Engineers who pass this exam are commonly called engineers in training (EITs) or engineer interns (EIs). After meeting work experience requirements, EITs and EIs can take the second exam, called Principles and Practice of Engineering.

Several states require continuing education in order for engineers to keep their licenses. Most states recognize licensure from other states if the licensing state's requirements meet or exceed their own requirements.

After licensing, environmental engineers can earn board certification from the American Academy of Environmental Engineers and Scientists. This certification shows that an environmental engineer has expertise in one or more areas of specialization.

Advancement. As beginning engineers gain knowledge and experience, they move on to more difficult projects and they have greater independence to develop designs, solve problems, and make decisions. Eventually, environmental engineers may advance to become technical specialists or to supervise a team of engineers and technicians.

Some may even become engineering managers or move into executive positions, such as program managers. However, before assuming a managerial position, an engineer most often works under the supervision of a more experienced engineer. For more information, see the profile on architectural and engineering managers.

Pay

The median annual wage for environmental engineers was $83,360 in May 2014. The median wage is the wage at which half the workers in an occupation earned more than that amount and half earned less. The lowest 10 percent earned less than $50,120, and the highest 10 percent earned more than $125,380.

In May 2014, the median annual wages for environmental engineers in the top industries in which they worked were as follows:

Federal government, excluding postal service	$100,520
Engineering services	84,690

Employment Projections Data for Environmental Engineers

Occupational Title	SOC Code	Employment, 2014	Projected Employment, 2024	Change, 2014–2024 Percent	Change, 2014–2024 Numeric
Environmental engineers	17-2081	55,100	62,000	12	6,800

Source: U.S. Bureau of Labor Statistics, Employment Projections Program

Similar Occupations. This table shows a list of occupations with job duties that are similar to those of environmental engineers.

Occupations	Entry-level Education	2014 Median Pay	Projected Job Growth	Average Annual Openings
Chemical Engineers	Bachelor's degree	$96,940	2%	60
Civil Engineers	Bachelor's degree	$82,050	8%	2,360
Environmental Engineering Technicians	Associate's degree	$48,170	10%	190
Environmental Scientists and Specialists	Bachelor's degree	$66,250	11%	1,020
Hydrologists	Bachelor's degree	$78,370	7%	50
Natural Sciences Managers	Bachelor's degree	$120,050	3%	180

Local government, excluding education and hospitals....... $78,620
Management, scientific, and technical consulting services.......... 78,590
State government, excluding education and hospitals.......... 74,670

Job Outlook

Employment of environmental engineers is projected to grow 12 percent from 2014 to 2024, faster than the average for all occupations.

State and local governments' concerns about water are leading to efforts to increase the efficiency of water use. Such a focus differs from that of wastewater treatment, for which this occupation is traditionally known. Most employment growth is projected to be in professional, scientific, and technical services, as governments at the state, county, and local levels draw on this industry to help address these water concerns.

The requirement by the federal government to clean up contaminated sites is expected to help sustain demand for these engineers' services. In addition, wastewater treatment is becoming a larger concern in areas of the country where new methods of drilling for shale gas require the use and disposal of massive volumes of water.

Environmental engineers should continue to be needed to help utilities and water treatment plants comply with any new federal or state environmental regulations, such as regulations regarding emissions from coal-fired power plants.

Job Prospects. Job prospects should be favorable because this occupation may experience a wave of retirements. Also, a person can improve his or her job prospects by obtaining a master's degree in environmental engineering, an advanced degree that many employers prefer.

Contacts for More Information

For more information about environmental engineers, visit

➤ American Academy of Environmental Engineers and Scientists (www.aaees.org)

For more information about education for engineers, visit

➤ American Society for Engineering Education (www.asee.org)

For more information about accredited engineering programs, visit

➤ ABET (www.abet.org)

For more information about becoming licensed as a professional engineer, visit

➤ National Council of Examiners for Engineering and Surveying (http://ncees.org)

➤ National Society of Professional Engineers (www.nspe.org/index.html)

O*NET

➤ Environmental Engineers (17-2081.00)

➤ Water/Wastewater Engineers (17-2081.01)

Health and Safety Engineers

- **2014 Median Pay** .... $81,830 per year; $39.34 per hour
- **Typical Entry-Level Education** ....Bachelor's degree
- **Work Experience in a Related Occupation**.............. None
- **On-the-job Training** .... None
- **Number of Jobs, 2014** 25,200
- **Job Outlook, 2014–24**................. 6% (As fast as average)
- **Employment Change, 2014–24** 1,600

What Health and Safety Engineers Do

Health and safety engineers develop procedures and design systems to prevent people from getting sick or injured and to keep property from being damaged. They combine knowledge of systems engineering and of health or safety to make sure that chemicals, machinery, software, furniture, and other consumer products will not cause harm to people or damage to buildings.

Duties. Health and safety engineers typically do the following:

- Review plans and specifications for new machinery and equipment to make sure they meet safety requirements
- Identify and correct potential hazards by inspecting facilities, machinery, and safety equipment
- Evaluate the effectiveness of various industrial control mechanisms
- Ensure that buildings or products comply with health and safety regulations, especially after an inspection that required changes
- Install safety devices on machinery or direct the installation of these devices
- Review employee safety programs and recommend improvements
- Maintain and apply knowledge of current policies, regulations, and industrial processes

Health and safety engineers also investigate industrial accidents, injuries, or occupational diseases to determine their causes and to determine whether the incidents could have been or can be prevented in the future. They interview employers and employees to learn about work environments and incidents that lead to accidents or injuries. They also evaluate the corrections that were made to remedy violations found during health inspections.

Health and safety engineers are also active in two related fields: industrial hygiene and occupational hygiene. In industrial hygiene,

Health and safety engineers apply their knowledge of the sciences, such as chemistry, to promote safety on the job.

they focus on the effects of chemical, physical, and biological agents. They recognize, evaluate, and control these agents to keep people from becoming sick or injured. For example, they might anticipate that a particular manufacturing process will give off a potentially harmful chemical and recommend either a change to the process or a way to contain and control the chemical.

In occupational hygiene, health and safety engineers investigate the environment in which people work, and then use science and engineering to recommend changes to keep workers from being exposed to sickness or injuries. They help employers and employees understand risks, and improve working conditions and practices. For example, they might observe that the noise level in a factory is likely to cause harm to workers' hearing and recommend ways to reduce the noise level through changes to the building or reducing exposure time, or by having workers wear proper hearing protection.

Health and safety engineering is a broad field covering many activities. The following are examples of types of health and safety engineers:

Aerospace safety engineers work on missiles, radars, and satellites to make sure that they function safely as designed.

Fire prevention and protection engineers design fire prevention systems for all kinds of buildings. They often work for architects during the design phase of new buildings or renovations. They must be licensed and must keep up with changes in fire codes and regulations.

Product safety engineers investigate the causes of accidents or injuries that might have resulted from the use or misuse of a product. They create solutions that reduce or eliminate safety issues associated with products. They also help design new products to prevent injuries, illnesses, or property damage.

Systems safety engineers work in many fields, including aerospace, and are moving into new fields, such as software safety, medical safety, and environmental safety. These engineers take a systemic approach to identify hazards so that accidents and injuries can be avoided.

For information on health and safety engineers who work in mines, see the profile on mining and geological engineers.

Work Environment

Health and safety engineers held about 25,200 jobs in 2014. The industries that employed the most health and safety engineers were as follows:

Manufacturing	26%
Construction	21
State and local government, excluding education and hospitals	10
Engineering services	8
Management, scientific, and technical consulting services	4

Health and safety engineers typically work in offices. However, they also must spend time at worksites when necessary, which sometimes requires travel.

Work Schedules. Most health and safety engineers work full time.

Education/Training

Health and safety engineers must have a bachelor's degree, typically in an engineering discipline such as electrical, chemical, mechanical, industrial, or systems engineering. Another acceptable field of study is occupational or industrial hygiene. Employers value practical experience, so cooperative-education engineering programs at universities are valuable as well.

Education. High school students interested in becoming health and safety engineers will benefit from taking high school courses in math and science, such as algebra, trigonometry, calculus, biology, chemistry, and physics.

Entry-level jobs as a health and safety engineer require a bachelor's degree. Bachelor's degree programs typically are 4-year programs and include classroom, laboratory, and field studies in applied engineering. Students interested in becoming a health and safety engineer should seek out coursework in occupational safety and health, industrial hygiene, ergonomics, or environmental safety. In addition to programs in mechanical, electrical, and industrial engineering, programs in systems engineering and fire protection engineering constitute good preparation for this occupation. ABET accredits programs in engineering.

Students interested in entering the relatively new field of software safety engineering may pursue a degree in computer science.

Many colleges and universities offer cooperative-education programs, which allow students to gain practical experience while completing their education.

A few colleges and universities offer 5-year accelerated programs through which students graduate with both a bachelor's and a master's degree. A master's degree allows engineers to enter the occupation at a higher level, where they can develop and implement safety systems.

Important Qualities

Creativity. Health and safety engineers produce designs showing potential problems and remedies for them. They must be creative to deal with situations unique to a project.

Critical-thinking skills. Health and safety engineers must be able to identify hazards to humans and property in the workplace or in the home before they cause material damage or become a health threat.

Observational skills. Health and safety engineers must observe and learn how operations function so that they can identify risks to people and property. This requires the ability to think in terms of overall processes within an organization. Health and safety engineers can then recommend systemic changes to minimize risks.

Median Annual Wages, May 2014

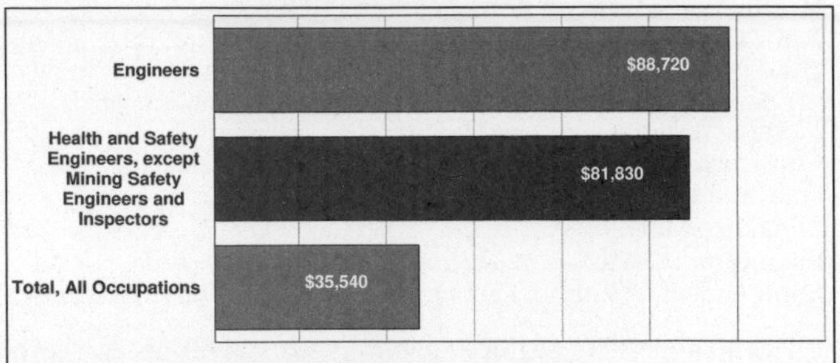

Percent Change in Employment, Projected 2014–2024

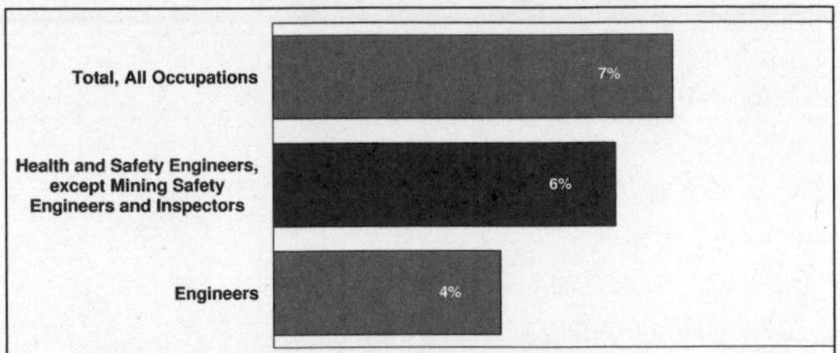

Problem-solving skills. In designing solutions for entire organizational operations, health and safety engineers must take into account processes from more than one system at the same time. In addition, they must try to anticipate a range of human reactions to the changes they recommend.

Reading skills. Health and safety engineers must be able to interpret federal and state regulations and their intent so that they can propose proper designs for specific work environments.

Licenses, Certifications, and Registrations. Licensure is not required for entry-level positions as a health and safety engineer. A Professional Engineer (PE) license, which allows for higher levels of leadership and independence, can be acquired later in one's career. Licensed engineers are called professional engineers (PEs). A PE can oversee the work of other engineers, sign off on projects, and provide services directly to the public. State licensure generally requires

- A degree from an ABET-accredited engineering program
- A passing score on the Fundamentals of Engineering (FE) exam
- Relevant work experience
- A passing score on the Principles and Practice of Engineering (PE) exam

The initial FE exam can be taken after one earns a bachelor's degree. Engineers who pass this exam are commonly called engineers in training (EITs) or engineer interns (EIs). After meeting work experience requirements, EITs and EIs can take the second exam, called Principles and Practice of Engineering.

Only a few states require health and safety engineers to be licensed. Licensure is generally advised for those opting for a career in systems safety engineering. States requiring licensure usually require continuing education for engineers in order to keep their license. Most states recognize licensure from other states, if the licensing state's requirements meet or exceed their own licensure requirements.

Health and safety engineers typically have professional certification. Certifications include the following:

The Board of Certified Safety Professionals offers the Certified Safety Professional (CSP) certification, the Occupational Health and Safety Technologist (OHST), and a new certification called the Associate Safety Professional (ASP)

The American Board of Industrial Hygiene awards a certification known as a Certified Industrial Hygienist (CIH)

The American Society of Safety Engineers offers a Certificate in Safety Management (CSM)

The International Council on Systems Engineering offers a program leading to a designation as a Certified Systems Engineering Professional (CSEP)

Certification is generally needed to advance into management positions.

Advancement. New health and safety engineers usually work under the supervision of experienced engineers. To move to more difficult projects with greater independence, a graduate degree is generally required, such as a master's degree in engineering or a Master of Public Health (MPH) degree.

An advanced degree allows an engineer to develop and implement safety programs. Certification as a safety professional or as an industrial hygienist is generally required for entry into management positions. For more information, see the profile on architectural and engineering managers.

Pay

The median annual wage for health and safety engineers was $81,830 in May 2014. The median wage is the wage at which half the workers in an occupation earned more than that amount and half earned less. The lowest 10 percent earned less than $48,260, and the highest 10 percent earned more than $126,850.

In May 2014, the median annual wages for health and safety engineers in the top industries in which they worked were as follows:

Engineering services	$84,590
Manufacturing	82,980

Employment Projections Data for Health and Safety Engineers

Occupational Title	SOC Code	Employment, 2014	Projected Employment, 2024	Change, 2014–2024 Percent	Change, 2014–2024 Numeric
Health and safety engineers, except mining safety engineers and inspectors	17-2111	25,200	26,800	6	1,600

Source: U.S. Bureau of Labor Statistics, Employment Projections Program

Similar Occupations. This table shows a list of occupations with job duties that are similar to those of health and safety engineers.

Occupations	Entry-level Education	2014 Median Pay	Projected Job Growth	Average Annual Openings
Construction and Building Inspectors	High school diploma or equivalent	$56,040	8%	810
Fire Inspectors	See Education/Training	$54,020	6%	90
Industrial Engineers	Bachelor's degree	$81,490	1%	210
Mining and Geological Engineers	Bachelor's degree	$90,160	6%	50
Occupational Health and Safety Specialists	Bachelor's degree	$69,210	4%	280
Occupational Health and Safety Technicians	High school diploma or equivalent	$48,120	9%	140

State and local government, excluding education and hospitals........76,140
Management, scientific, and technical consulting services........74,960
Construction........74,640

Job Outlook

Employment of health and safety engineers is projected to grow 6 percent from 2014 to 2024, about as fast as the average for all occupations.

Health and safety engineers have long been employed in manufacturing industries to cut costs, save lives, and produce safe consumer products. The same principles are being applied in new areas, such as healthcare. Recent studies have documented the high costs of accidents in hospitals. Accident prevention, particularly with regard to radiation safety, is likely to become increasingly important for the healthcare industry as a way of cutting costs. As a result, strong demand is expected for health and safety engineers in consulting firms. Demand is also expected to be strong in construction.

The emerging field of software safety engineering is likely to help drive employment as well. Software must work exactly as intended, especially when it controls, for example, elevators or automobiles, where a glitch in the software could cause serious injury to people and damage to equipment. The need to apply the principles of systems safety engineering to software is likely to grow as more machines and mechanical devices are controlled by software.

Contacts for More Information

For information about general engineering education and career resources, visit

➤ American Society for Engineering Education (www.asee.org)
➤ Technology Student Association (www.tsaweb.org)

For more information about accredited engineering programs, visit

➤ ABET (www.abet.org)
➤ American Society of Safety Engineers (www.asse.org)

For more information about the Professional Engineer license, visit

➤ National Council of Examiners for Engineering and Surveying (http://ncees.org)
➤ National Society of Professional Engineers (www.nspe.org/index.html)

For information about protecting worker health, visit

➤ American Industrial Hygiene Association (www.aiha.org/Pages/default.aspx)

For information about certification, visit

➤ American Board of Industrial Hygiene (www.abih.org)
➤ American Society of Safety Engineers (www.asse.org/education/cert-prog)
➤ Board of Certified Safety Professionals (www.bcsp.org)
➤ International Council on Systems Engineering (www.incose.org)

O*NET

➤ Health and Safety Engineers, Except Mining Safety Engineers and Inspectors (17-2111.00)
➤ Industrial Safety and Health Engineers (17-2111.01)
➤ Fire-Prevention and Protection Engineers (17-2111.02)
➤ Product Safety Engineers (17-2111.03)

Industrial Engineering Technicians

- **2014 Median Pay**........$53,370 per year
  $25.66 per hour
- **Typical Entry-Level Education**........Associate's degree
- **Work Experience in a Related Occupation**........None
- **On-the-job Training**........None
- **Number of Jobs, 2014**........66,500
- **Job Outlook, 2014–24**........-5% (Decline)
- **Employment Change, 2014–24**........-3,000

What Industrial Engineering Technicians Do

Industrial engineering technicians help industrial engineers implement designs to use personnel, materials, and machines effectively. They prepare machinery and equipment layouts, plan workflows, conduct statistical production studies, and analyze production costs.

Duties. Industrial engineering technicians typically do the following:

- Suggest revisions to methods of operation, material handling, or equipment layout
- Interpret engineering drawings, schematic diagrams, and formulas
- Confer with management or engineering staff to determine quality and reliability standards

Industrial engineering technicians help develop plans for use of machinery and for efficient workflow.

- Recommend changes to production standards in order to achieve the best quality within the limits of the capabilities of the equipment
- Help plan work assignments, taking into account workers' performance, the capabilities of machines, and production schedules
- Prepare charts, graphs, and diagrams to illustrate workflow, routing, floor layouts, how materials are handled, and how machines are used
- Collect data to assist in process improvement activities

Industrial engineering technicians study the time and steps workers take to do a task (time and motion studies). To set reasonable production rates, they consider how workers perform operations such as maintenance, production, and service.

They also observe workers to make sure that equipment is being used and maintained according to quality assurance standards. They then evaluate the resulting data to recommend or justify changes to the operations or to the standards for improving quality and efficiency.

Industrial engineering technicians' versatility allows them to be useful in a variety of projects. For example, they work in supply chain management to help businesses minimize inventory costs, in quality assurance to help businesses keep their customers satisfied, and in the growing field of project management to control costs and maximize efficiencies.

Industrial engineering technicians generally work in teams under the supervision of industrial engineers.

Work Environment

Industrial engineering technicians held about 66,500 jobs in 2014. The industries that employed the most industrial engineering technicians were as follows:

Semiconductor and other electronic component manufacturing	17%
Transportation equipment manufacturing	15
Machinery manufacturing	8
Chemical manufacturing	7
Plastics and rubber products manufacturing	6

Industrial engineers usually ask industrial engineering technicians to help carry out certain studies and make specific observations. Consequently, these technicians typically work at the location where products are manufactured or where services are delivered.

Work Schedules. Industrial engineering technicians usually work standard schedules. Most work full time.

Education/Training

Industrial engineering technicians typically need an associate's degree or a postsecondary certificate. Community colleges and technical institutes generally offer associate's degree programs, and vocational-technical schools offer certificate programs.

Education. High school students interested in becoming industrial engineering technicians should take courses in math, science, and drafting, where available. Courses that help students develop computer skills are helpful when the students later need to learn computer-aided design/computer-aided manufacturing software, known as CAD/CAM.

Postsecondary programs in industrial engineering are offered at vocational-technical schools, technical institutes, and community colleges. Vocational-technical schools and technical institutes serve local students and emphasize training needed by local employers. These programs generally award a certificate. Community colleges offer programs similar to those in technical institutes, but usually include more theory-based and liberal arts courses. Students who complete these programs earn associate's degrees.

ABET accredits engineering and engineering technology programs.

Generally, prospective industrial engineering technicians should major in applied science, industrial technology, or industrial engineering technology.

Median Annual Wages, May 2014

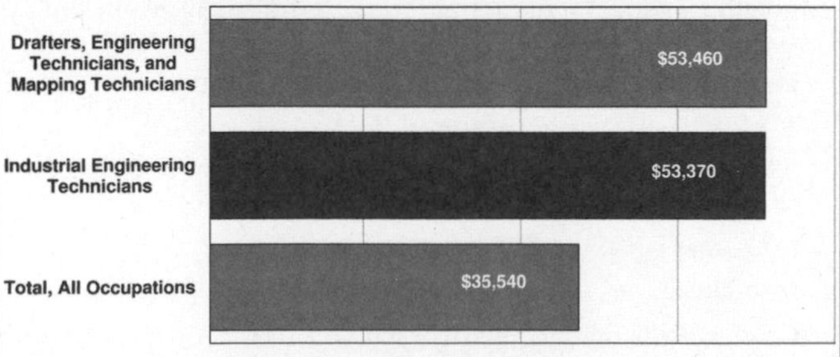

Note: All Occupations includes all occupations in the U.S. Economy.
Source: U.S. Bureau of Labor Statistics, Occupational Employment Statistics

Percent Change in Employment, Projected 2014–2024

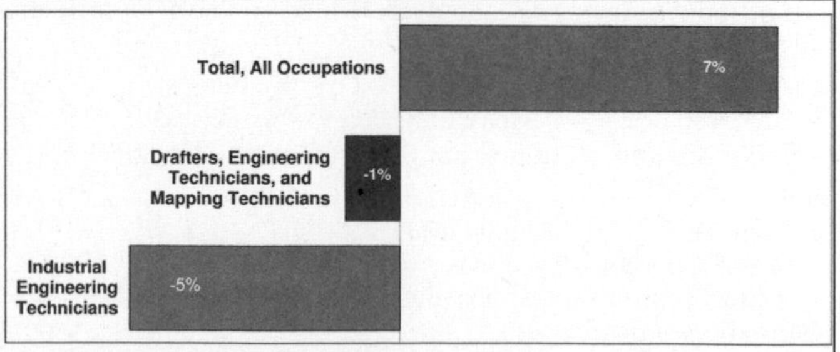

Note: All Occupations includes all occupations in the U.S. Economy.
Source: U.S. Bureau of Labor Statistics, Office of Occupational Statistics and Employment Projections

Employment Projections Data for Industrial Engineering Technicians

Occupational Title	SOC Code	Employment, 2014	Projected Employment, 2024	Change, 2014–2024 Percent	Change, 2014–2024 Numeric
Industrial engineering technicians	17-3026	66,500	63,500	-5	-3,000

Source: U.S. Bureau of Labor Statistics, Employment Projections Program

Similar Occupations. This table shows a list of occupations with job duties that are similar to those of industrial engineering technicians.

Occupations	Entry-level Education	2014 Median Pay	Projected Job Growth	Average Annual Openings
Cost Estimators	Bachelor's degree	$60,050	9%	1,870
Health and Safety Engineers	Bachelor's degree	$81,830	6%	160
Industrial Engineers	Bachelor's degree	$81,490	1%	210
Logisticians	Bachelor's degree	$73,870	2%	250
Quality Control Inspectors	High school diploma or equivalent	$35,330	0%	-110

Important Qualities

Analytical skills. Industrial engineering technicians must be able to help industrial engineers figure out how systems should work and how changes in conditions, operations, and the environment will affect outcomes.

Communication skills. Industrial engineering technicians receive instructions from industrial engineers. They must be able to clearly understand and follow instructions and communicate problems to their supervisors.

Critical-thinking skills. Industrial engineering technicians must be able to help industrial engineers figure out why certain processes or operations are not working as well as they might. They must ask the right questions to identify and correct weaknesses.

Detail oriented. Industrial engineering technicians must gather and record measurements and observations needed by industrial engineers.

Math skills. Industrial engineering technicians use the principles of mathematics for analysis, design, and troubleshooting in their work.

Observational skills. These technicians spend much of their time evaluating the performance of other people or organizations and then make suggestions for improvements or corrective action. They must gather and record information without interfering with workers in their environments.

Pay

The median annual wage for industrial engineering technicians was $53,370 in May 2014. The median wage is the wage at which half the workers in an occupation earned more than that amount and half earned less. The lowest 10 percent earned less than $34,180, and the highest 10 percent earned more than $80,730.

In May 2014, the median annual wages for industrial engineering technicians in the top industries in which they worked were as follows:

Transportation equipment manufacturing	$59,150
Chemical manufacturing	55,860
Semiconductor and other electronic component manufacturing	55,050
Machinery manufacturing	51,150
Plastics and rubber products manufacturing	47,410

Job Outlook

Employment of industrial engineering technicians is projected to decline 5 percent from 2014 to 2024.

The growing emphasis on cost control through increased efficiency is expected to sustain demand somewhat for industrial engineering technicians' services.

However, this occupation's employment is expected to decline, in large part because of the projected decline in the manufacturing industries that employ them, such as semiconductor and other electronic components, transportation equipment, and plastics and rubber products.

Contacts for More Information

For more information about industrial engineering, visit

➤ Institute of Industrial Engineers (www.iienet2.org/Default.aspx)

For information on general engineering education and career resources, visit

➤ American Society for Engineering Education (www.asee.org)

➤ Technology Student Association (www.tsaweb.org)

For more information about accredited programs, visit

➤ ABET (www.abet.org)

O*NET

➤ Industrial Engineering Technicians (17-3026.00)

Industrial Engineers

- **2014 Median Pay** .... $81,490 per year, $39.18 per hour
- **Typical Entry-Level Education** .... Bachelor's degree
- **Work Experience in a Related Occupation** .... None
- **On-the-job Training** .... None
- **Number of Jobs, 2014** 241,100
- **Job Outlook, 2014–24** .... 1% (Little or no change)
- **Employment Change, 2014–24** 2,100

What Industrial Engineers Do

Industrial engineers find ways to eliminate wastefulness in production processes. They devise efficient systems that integrate workers, machines, materials, information, and energy to make a product or provide a service.

Duties. Industrial engineers typically do the following:

- Review production schedules, engineering specifications, process flows, and other information to understand methods that are applied and activities that take place in manufacturing and services
- Figure out how to manufacture parts or products, or deliver services, with maximum efficiency
- Develop management control systems to make financial planning and cost analysis more efficient
- Enact quality control procedures to resolve production problems or minimize costs
- Design control systems to coordinate activities and production planning in order to ensure that products meet quality standards
- Confer with clients about product specifications, vendors about purchases, management personnel about manufacturing capabilities, and staff about the status of projects

Industrial engineers apply their skills to many different situations, from manufacturing to healthcare systems to business administration. For example, they design systems for

- Moving heavy parts within manufacturing plants
- Delivering goods from a company to customers, including finding the most profitable places to locate manufacturing or processing plants
- Evaluating job performance
- Paying workers

Industrial engineers focus on how to get the work done most efficiently, balancing many factors, such as time, number of workers needed, available technology, actions workers need to take, achieving the end product with no errors, workers' safety, environmental concerns, and cost.

To find ways to reduce waste and improve performance, industrial engineers study product requirements carefully. Then they use mathematical methods and models to design manufacturing and information systems to meet those requirements most efficiently.

Industrial engineers devise ways to most effectively use all resources in a production process.

Their versatility allows industrial engineers to engage in activities that are useful to a variety of businesses, governments, and nonprofits. For example, industrial engineers engage in supply chain management to help businesses minimize inventory costs, conduct quality assurance activities to help businesses keep their customer bases satisfied, and work in the growing field of project management as industries across the economy seek to control costs and maximize efficiencies.

Work Environment

Industrial engineers held about 241,100 jobs in 2014. The industries that employed the most industrial engineers were as follows:

Computer and electronic product manufacturing	13%
Machinery manufacturing	9
Aerospace product and parts manufacturing	8
Motor vehicle parts manufacturing	6
Engineering services	5

Depending on their tasks, industrial engineers work either in offices or in the settings they are trying to improve. For example, when observing problems, they may watch workers assembling parts in a factory. When solving problems, industrial engineers may be in an office at a computer where they analyze data that they or others have collected.

Industrial engineers may need to travel to observe processes and make assessments in various work settings.

Work Schedules. Most industrial engineers work full time. Depending upon the projects in which these engineers are engaged, and the industries in which the projects are taking place, hours may vary.

Education/Training

Industrial engineers must have a bachelor's degree. Employers also value experience, so cooperative education engineering programs at universities are also valuable.

Education. Industrial engineers need a bachelor's degree, typically in industrial engineering. However, many industrial engineers have degrees in mechanical engineering, electrical engineering, manufacturing engineering, industrial engineering technology, or general engineering. Students interested in studying industrial engineering should take high school courses in mathematics, such as algebra, trigonometry, and calculus; computer science; and sciences such as chemistry and physics.

Bachelor's degree programs include lectures in classrooms and practice in laboratories. Courses include statistics, production systems planning, and manufacturing systems design, among others. Many colleges and universities offer cooperative education programs in which students gain practical experience while completing their education.

A few colleges and universities offer 5-year degree programs in industrial engineering that lead to a bachelor's and master's degree upon completion, and several more offer similar programs in mechanical engineering. A graduate degree allows an engineer to work as a professor at a college or university or to engage in research and development. Some 5-year or even 6-year cooperative education plans combine classroom study with practical work, permitting students to gain experience and to finance part of their education.

Programs in industrial engineering are accredited by ABET.

Median Annual Wages, May 2014

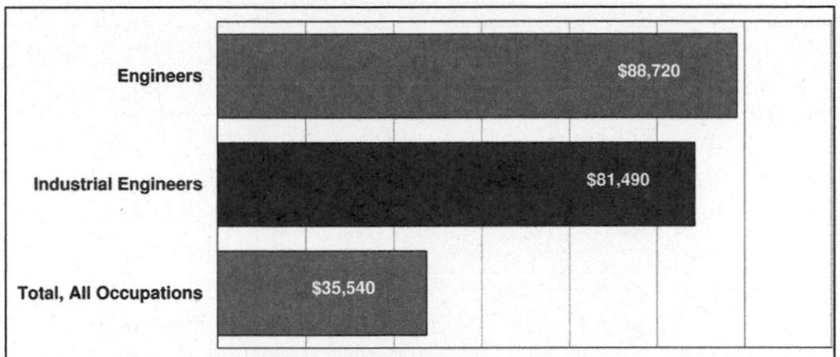

Note: All Occupations includes all occupations in the U.S. Economy.
Source: U.S. Bureau of Labor Statistics, Occupational Employment Statistics

Percent Change in Employment, Projected 2014–2024

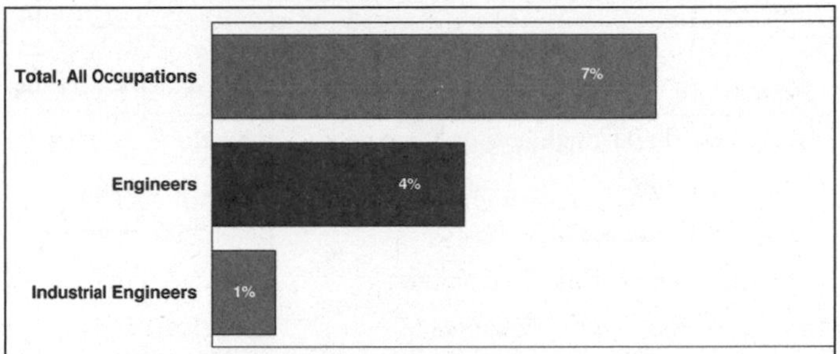

Note: All Occupations includes all occupations in the U.S. Economy.
Source: U.S. Bureau of Labor Statistics, Office of Occupational Statistics and Employment Projections

Important Qualities

Creativity. Industrial engineers use creativity and ingenuity to design new production processes in many kinds of settings in order to reduce the use of material resources, time, or labor while accomplishing the same goal.

Critical-thinking skills. Industrial engineers create new systems to solve problems related to waste and inefficiency. Solving these problems requires logic and reasoning to identify strengths and weaknesses of alternative solutions, conclusions, or approaches to the problems.

Listening skills. These engineers often operate in teams, but they also must solicit feedback from customers, vendors, and production staff. They must listen to customers and clients in order to fully grasp ideas and problems the first time.

Math skills. Industrial engineers use the principles of calculus, trigonometry, and other advanced topics in mathematics for analysis, design, and troubleshooting in their work.

Problem-solving skills. In designing facilities for manufacturing and processes for providing services, these engineers deal with several issues at once, from workers' safety to quality assurance.

Speaking skills. Industrial engineers sometimes have to explain their instructions to production staff or technicians before they can make written instructions available. Being able to explain concepts clearly and quickly is crucial to preventing costly mistakes and loss of time.

Writing skills. Industrial engineers must prepare documentation for other engineers or scientists, or for future reference. The documentation must be coherent and explain their thinking clearly so that the others can understand the information.

Licenses, Certifications, and Registrations. Licensure is not required for entry-level positions as an industrial engineer. A Professional Engineer (PE) license, which allows for higher levels of leadership and independence, can be acquired later in one's career. Licensed engineers are called professional engineers (PEs). A PE can oversee the work of other engineers, sign off on projects, and provide services directly to the public. State licensure generally requires

- A degree from an ABET-accredited engineering program
- A passing score on the Fundamentals of Engineering (FE) exam
- Relevant work experience
- A passing score on the Principles and Practice of Engineering (PE) exam

The initial FE exam can be taken after one earns a bachelor's degree. Engineers who pass this exam are commonly called engineers in training (EITs) or engineer interns (EIs). After meeting work experience requirements, EITs and EIs can take the second exam, called Principles and Practice of Engineering.

Several states require engineers to take continuing education in order to keep their licenses. Most states recognize licenses from other states, as long as the other state's licensing requirements meet or exceed their own licensing requirements.

Advancement. Beginning industrial engineers usually work under the supervision of experienced engineers. In large companies, new engineers also may receive formal training in classes or seminars. As beginning engineers gain knowledge and experience, they move on to more difficult projects with greater independence to develop designs, solve problems, and make decisions.

Eventually, industrial engineers may advance to become technical specialists, such as quality engineers or facility planners. In that role, they supervise a team of engineers and technicians. Obtaining a master's degree facilitates such specialization and thus advancement.

Many industrial engineers move into management positions because the work they do is closely related to the work of managers. For more information, see the profile on architectural and engineering managers.

Pay

The median annual wage for industrial engineers was $81,490 in May 2014. The median wage is the wage at which half the workers in an occupation earned more than that amount and half earned less. The lowest 10 percent earned less than $52,510, and the highest 10 percent earned more than $123,400.

In May 2014, the median annual wages for industrial engineers in the top industries in which they worked were as follows:

Aerospace product and parts manufacturing..................... $90,280
Computer and electronic product manufacturing................ 88,610

Employment Projections Data for Industrial Engineers

Occupational Title	SOC Code	Employment, 2014	Projected Employment, 2024	Change, 2014–2024 Percent	Change, 2014–2024 Numeric
Industrial engineers	17-2112	241,100	243,200	1	2,100

Source: U.S. Bureau of Labor Statistics, Employment Projections Program

Similar Occupations. This table shows a list of occupations with job duties that are similar to those of industrial engineers.

Occupations	Entry-level Education	2014 Median Pay	Projected Job Growth	Average Annual Openings
Architectural and Engineering Managers	Bachelor's degree	$130,620	2%	370
Cost Estimators	Bachelor's degree	$60,050	9%	1,870
Health and Safety Engineers	Bachelor's degree	$81,830	6%	160
Industrial Engineering Technicians	Associate's degree	$53,370	-5%	-300
Industrial Production Managers	Bachelor's degree	$92,470	-4%	-630
Logisticians	Bachelor's degree	$73,870	2%	250
Management Analysts	Bachelor's degree	$80,880	14%	10,340
Materials Engineers	Bachelor's degree	$87,690	1%	30
Occupational Health and Safety Specialists	Bachelor's degree	$69,210	4%	280
Quality Control Inspectors	High school diploma or equivalent	$35,330	0%	-110

Engineering services.. $86,030
Machinery manufacturing 77,310
Motor vehicle parts manufacturing 73,900

Job Outlook

Employment of industrial engineers is projected to show little or no change from 2014 to 2024. This occupation is versatile both in the nature of the work it does and in the industries in which its expertise can be put to use.

Because they are not as specialized as other engineers, industrial engineers are employed in a wide range of industries, including major manufacturing industries, consulting and engineering services, research and development firms, and wholesale trade. This versatility arises from the fact that these engineers' expertise focuses on reducing internal costs, making their work valuable for many industries. For example, their work is important for manufacturing industries that are considering relocating from overseas to domestic sites. In addition, growth in healthcare and changes in how healthcare is delivered will create demand for industrial engineers in firms in professional, scientific, and consulting services. Projected declines in employment in some manufacturing sectors will temper growth for industrial engineers overall.

Job Prospects. Likely retirements over the next decade will create more openings within the occupation and therefore more employment opportunities for aspiring industrial engineers.

Contacts for More Information

For more information about industrial engineers, visit

➤ Institute of Industrial Engineers (www.iienet2.org/Default.aspx)

For information about general engineering education and career resources, visit

➤ American Society for Engineering Education (www.asee.org)

➤ Technology Student Association (www.tsaweb.org)

For more information about licensure as an industrial engineer, visit

➤ National Council of Examiners for Engineering and Surveying (http://ncees.org)

➤ National Society of Professional Engineers (www.nspe.org/index.html)

For information about accredited engineering programs, visit

➤ ABET (www.abet.org)

O*NET

➤ Industrial Engineers (17-2112.00)

➤ Human Factors Engineers and Ergonomists (17-2112.01)

Landscape Architects

- **2014 Median Pay** .... $64,570 per year
  $31.04 per hour
- **Typical Entry-Level Education** .... Bachelor's degree
- **Work Experience in a Related Occupation**.............. None
- **On-the-job Training** .... Internship/residency
- **Number of Jobs, 2014** 22,500
- **Job Outlook, 2014–24** .... 5% (As fast as average)
- **Employment Change, 2014–24** 1,200

What Landscape Architects Do

Landscape architects design parks and the outdoor spaces of campuses, recreational facilities, private homes, and other open spaces.

Duties. Landscape architects typically do the following:

- Meet with clients, engineers, and building architects to understand the requirements of a project
- Prepare site plans, specifications, and cost estimates
- Coordinate the arrangement of existing and proposed land features and structures
- Prepare graphic representations of plans using computer-aided design and drafting (CADD) software
- Select appropriate materials for use in landscape designs
- Analyze environmental reports on land conditions, such as drainage and energy usage
- Inspect landscape project progress to ensure that it adheres to plans
- Seek new work through marketing activities or by giving presentations

Landscape architects design attractive and functional public parks, gardens, playgrounds, residential areas, college campuses, and public spaces. They also plan the locations of buildings, roads, walkways, flowers, shrubs, and trees within these environments.

Landscape architects are involved in a wide variety of construction projects.

Landscape architects design these areas so that they are not only easy to use but also harmonious with the natural environment.

Landscape architects use several different technologies in their work. For example, using computer-aided design and drafting (CADD) software, landscape architects prepare models of their proposed work. They present these models to clients for feedback and then prepare the final look of the project. Many landscape architects also use geographic information systems (GIS) which offer GPS coordinates of different geographical features. This helps landscape architects design different environments by giving them clues on where to start planning and how to anticipate future effects of the landscape, such as rainfall running into a valley.

The goals of landscape architects are to enhance the natural beauty of a space and provide environmental benefits. They may plan the restoration of natural places that were changed by humans or nature, such as wetlands, streams, and mined areas. They may also design "green roofs" or rooftop gardens that can retain storm water, absorb air pollution, and cool buildings while also providing pleasant scenery. Landscape architects also play a role in preserving and restoring historic landscapes. Landscape architects and architects sometimes work together to create historic memorials, such as the World War II memorial in Washington, D.C.

Landscape architects who work for government agencies design sites and landscapes for government buildings, parks, and other public lands, as well as plan for landscapes and recreation areas in national parks and forests. In addition, they prepare environmental impact assessments based on proposed construction.

Work Environment

Landscape architects held about 22,500 jobs in 2014. Of this total, about 49 percent were employed in the architectural, engineering, and related services industry, and another 15 percent were employed in the landscaping services industry. About 1 in 5 were self-employed in 2014.

Landscape architects spend much of their time in offices, creating plans and designs, preparing models and preliminary cost estimates, doing research, and attending meetings with clients and workers involved in designing or planning a project. They spend the rest of their time at jobsites.

Work Schedules. Most landscape architects work full time.

Education/Training

All states except for Illinois, Massachusetts, Maine, and Washington, D.C. require landscape architects to have a license. In addition, all 50 states (but not Washington, D.C.) require applicants to be licensed before they can use the title "landscape architect" while soliciting business. Licensing requirements vary among states, but usually include a degree in landscape architecture from an accredited school, internship experience, and passing the Landscape Architect Registration Examination.

Education. A bachelor's or master's degree in landscape architecture usually is necessary for entry into the profession. There are two undergraduate landscape architect professional degrees: a Bachelor of Landscape Architecture (BLA) and a Bachelor of Science in Landscape Architecture (BSLA). These programs usually require 4 to 5 years of study.

Accredited programs are approved by the Landscape Architectural Accreditation Board (LAAB). Those with an undergraduate degree in a field other than landscape architecture may enroll in a Master of Landscape Architecture (MLA) graduate degree program, which typically takes 3 years of full-time study.

Courses typically include surveying, landscape design and construction, landscape ecology, site design, and urban and regional planning. Other relevant coursework may include history of landscape architecture, plant and soil science, geology, professional practice, and general management.

The design studio is a key component of any curriculum. Whenever possible, students are assigned real projects, providing them with valuable hands-on experience. While working on these projects, students become proficient in the use of computer-aided design and drafting (CADD), model building, and other design software.

Median Annual Wages, May 2014

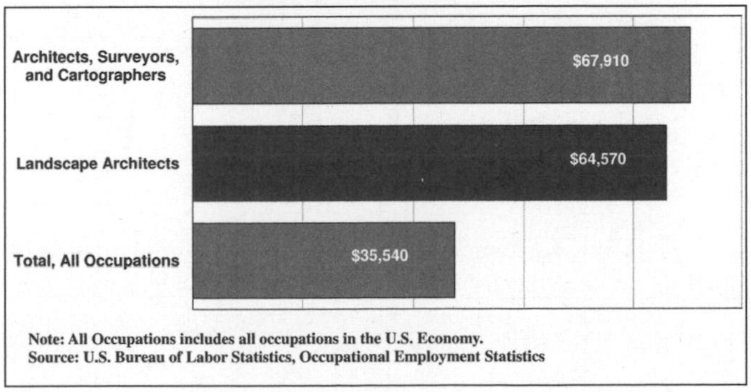

Percent Change in Employment, Projected 2014–2024

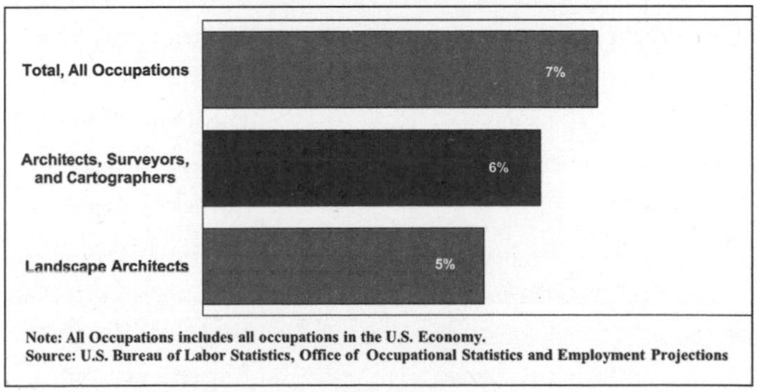

Training. In order to become licensed, candidates must meet experience requirements determined by each state. A list of training requirements can be found at the Council of Landscape Architectural Registration Boards.

New hires are called intern landscape architects until they become licensed. Although duties vary with the type and size of the employing firm, interns typically must work under the supervision of a licensed landscape architect for the experience to count toward licensure. In addition, all drawings and specifications must be signed and sealed by the licensed landscape architect.

Potential prospects may benefit by completing an internship with a landscape architecture firm during educational studies. Interns may improve their technical skills and gain an understanding of the day-to-day operations of the business, including learning how to recruit clients, generate fees, and work within a budget.

Licenses, Certifications, and Registrations. Candidates become licensed by passing the Landscape Architect Registration Examination (LARE), which is sponsored by the Council of Landscape Architectural Registration Boards.

Candidates who are interested in taking the exam usually need a degree from an accredited school and several years of work experience under the supervision of a licensed landscape architect, although standards vary by state. For those without an accredited landscape architecture degree, many states provide alternative paths to qualify to take the LARE, which usually require more work experience.

In addition to the LARE, some states have their own registration exam to test for competency on state-specific issues, such as earthquakes in California or hurricanes in Florida. State-specific exams may focus on laws, environmental regulations, plants, soils, climate, and other characteristics unique to the state.

Because requirements for licensure vary, landscape architects may find it difficult to transfer their registration from one state to another. Common requirements include graduating from an accredited program, completing several years of an internship under the supervision of a licensed landscape architect, and passing the LARE. By meeting national requirements, a landscape architect may also obtain certification from the Council of Landscape Architectural Registration Boards, which may be useful in getting a license in another state.

Important Qualities

Analytical skills. Landscape architects must understand the content of designs. When designing a building's drainage system, for example, landscape architects must understand how the building's location and surrounding land affect each other.

Communication skills. Landscape architects share their ideas, both orally and in writing, with clients, other architects, and workers who help prepare drawings. Effective communication is essential to ensuring that the vision for a project gets translated into reality.

Creativity. Landscape architects create the overall look of gardens, parks, and other outdoor areas. Their designs should be both pleasing to the eye and functional.

Problem-solving skills. When designing outdoor spaces, landscape architects must be able to provide solutions to unanticipated challenges. These solutions often involve looking at challenges from different perspectives and providing the best recommendations.

Technical skills. Landscape architects use computer-aided design and drafting (CADD) programs to create representations of their projects. Some also must use geographic information systems (GIS) for their designs.

Visualization skills. Landscape architects must be able to imagine how an overall outdoor space will look once completed.

Pay

The median annual wage for landscape architects was $64,570 in May 2014. The median wage is the wage at which half the workers in an occupation earned more than that amount and half earned

Employment Projections Data for Landscape Architects

Occupational Title	SOC Code	Employment, 2014	Projected Employment, 2024	Change, 2014–2024 Percent	Change, 2014–2024 Numeric
Landscape architects	17-1012	22,500	23,700	5	1,200

Source: U.S. Bureau of Labor Statistics, Employment Projections Program

Similar Occupations. This table shows a list of occupations with job duties that are similar to those of landscape architects.

Occupations	Entry-level Education	2014 Median Pay	Projected Job Growth	Average Annual Openings
Architects	Bachelor's degree	$74,520	7%	780
Cartographers and Photogrammetrists	Bachelor's degree	$60,930	29%	360
Civil Engineers	Bachelor's degree	$82,050	8%	2,360
Construction Managers	Bachelor's degree	$85,630	5%	1,780
Environmental Scientists and Specialists	Bachelor's degree	$66,250	11%	1,020
Geoscientists	Bachelor's degree	$89,910	10%	380
Hydrologists	Bachelor's degree	$78,370	7%	50
Surveying and Mapping Technicians	High school diploma or equivalent	$40,770	-8%	-430
Surveyors	Bachelor's degree	$57,050	-2%	-90
Urban and Regional Planners	Master's degree	$66,940	6%	240

less. The lowest 10 percent earned less than $40,690, and the highest 10 percent earned more than $106,120.

Job Outlook

Employment of landscape architects is projected to grow 5 percent from 2014 to 2024, about as fast as the average for all occupations.

Planning and developing landscapes for new and existing commercial, industrial, and residential construction projects will drive employment growth. The public's desire for beautiful and functional spaces will continue to require good site planning and landscape design.

In addition, environmental concerns and increased demand for sustainably designed buildings and open spaces will spur demand for the services of landscape architects. For example, landscape architects are involved in the design of green roofs, which are covered with vegetation and help reduce air and water pollution, as well as reduce the costs of heating and cooling a building.

Landscape architects will also be needed to design plans to manage storm-water runoff in order to conserve water resources and avoid polluting waterways. This is especially useful in areas prone to drought.

Job Prospects. Decent job opportunities are expected overall. However, competition for jobs in the largest and most prestigious landscape architecture firms is expected to be strong.

Many employers prefer to hire entry-level landscape architects who already have internship experience. Having experience significantly reduces the amount of on-the-job training required.

Job opportunities will be best for candidates with strong technical and communication skills and thorough knowledge of environmental codes and regulations. Familiarity with geographic information systems (GIS) may also be helpful.

Contacts for More Information

For more information, including a list of colleges and universities offering accredited programs in landscape architecture, visit

➤ American Society of Landscape Architects (www.asla.org)

For information on registration or licensing requirements, visit

➤ Council of Landscape Architectural Registration Boards (www.clarb.org)

O*NET

➤ Landscape Architects (17-1012.00)

Marine Engineers and Naval Architects

- **2014 Median Pay** .... $92,930 per year
  $44.68 per hour
- **Typical Entry-Level Education** .... Bachelor's degree
- **Work Experience in a Related Occupation** .... None
- **On-the-job Training** .... None
- **Number of Jobs, 2014** 8,300
- **Job Outlook, 2014–24** .... 9% (Faster than average)
- **Employment Change, 2014–24** 700

What Marine Engineers and Naval Architects Do

Marine engineers and naval architects design, build, and maintain ships from aircraft carriers to submarines, from sailboats to tankers. Marine engineers are also known as marine design engineers or marine mechanical engineers, and are primarily responsible for the internal systems of a ship, such as propulsion, electrical, refrigeration, and steering. Naval architects are primarily responsible for ship design, including the form, structure, and stability of hulls.

Duties. Marine engineers typically do the following:

- Prepare system layouts and detailed drawings and schematics
- Inspect marine equipment and machinery, and draw up work requests and job specifications
- Conduct environmental, operational, or performance tests on marine machinery and equipment
- Design and oversee the testing, installation, and repair of marine equipment
- Investigate and test machinery and equipment to ensure compliance with standards
- Coordinate activities with regulatory bodies to ensure that repairs and alterations are done safely and at minimal cost
- Prepare technical reports for use by engineers, managers, or sales personnel
- Prepare cost estimates, contract specifications, and design and construction schedules
- Maintain contact with contractors to be sure that the work is being done correctly, on schedule, and within budget

Naval architects typically do the following:

- Study design proposals and specifications to establish basic characteristics of a ship, such as its size, weight, and speed
- Develop sectional and waterline curves of the ship's hull to establish the center of gravity, ideal hull form, and data on buoyancy and stability
- Design entire ship hulls and superstructures, following safety and regulatory standards
- Design the complete layout of ships' interiors, including spaces for machinery and auxiliary equipment, passenger compartments, cargo space, ladder wells, and elevators
- Confer with marine engineers to design the layout of boiler room equipment, heating and ventilation systems, refrigeration equipment, electrical distribution systems, safety systems, steering, and propulsion machinery
- Lead teams from a variety of specialties to oversee building and testing prototypes

Marine engineers and naval architects design and supervise the construction of ships.

- Evaluate how ships perform during trials, both in the dock and at sea, and change designs as needed to make sure that national and international standards are met

Marine engineers and naval architects apply knowledge from a range of engineering fields to the entire water vehicles' design and production processes. Marine engineers also design and maintain offshore oil rigs and may work on alternative energy projects, such as wind turbines located offshore and tidal power.

Marine engineers and naval architects who work for ship and boat building firms design large ships such as passenger ships and cargo ships, as well as small craft such as inflatable boats and rowboats. Those who work in the federal government may design or test the designs of ships or systems for the Army, Navy, or Coast Guard.

Ship engineers, who are sometimes called marine engineers, operate or supervise the operation of the machinery on a ship. Their work differs from that of the marine engineers discussed in this profile. For more information on ship engineers, see the profile on water transportation workers.

Work Environment

Marine engineers and naval architects held about 8,300 jobs in 2014. The industries that employed the most marine engineers and naval architects were as follows:

Engineering services	23%
Ship and boat building	13
Federal government, excluding postal service	12
Water transportation	9
Mining, quarrying, and oil and gas extraction	7

They typically work in offices, where they have access to computer software and other tools necessary for analyzing projects and designing solutions. Sometimes, they must go to sea on ships to test or maintain the ships that they have designed or built.

Marine engineers and naval architects who work on power generation projects, such as offshore wind turbines and tidal power, work along the coast—both offshore and on land. They also sometimes work on oil rigs, where they oversee the repair or maintenance of systems that they may have designed.

Naval architects often lead teams to create feasible designs, and they must effectively use the skills that each person brings to the design process.

Work Schedules. Marine engineers and naval architects work full time, and about 1 in 3 worked more than 40 hours per week in 2014. Marine engineers who work at sea will work a schedule tied to the operations of their particular ship. Those who work on shore will have somewhat more regular work schedules. Because naval architects are primarily designers, they are much more likely to work a regular schedule in an office or at a shipyard.

Education/Training

Marine engineers typically need a bachelor's degree in marine engineering, marine systems engineering, or marine engineering technology, and naval architects typically need a bachelor's degree in naval architecture. Employers also value practical experience, so cooperative education programs, which provide college credit and job experience, are valuable.

Education. Marine engineers typically need a bachelor's degree in marine engineering, marine systems engineering, or marine engineering technology, and naval architects typically need a bachelor's degree in naval architecture. Programs typically include courses in calculus, physics, and computer-aided design. Some programs are offered at one of the six state maritime academies. Courses specific to marine engineering and naval architecture include fluid mechanics, ship hull strength, and mechanics of materials. Some marine engineers have bachelor's degrees in mechanical or electrical engineering.

Students studying marine engineering and naval architecture at the maritime academies spend time at sea, usually during the summer, to gain onboard operating experience.

Programs in marine engineering, naval architecture, marine systems engineering, and marine engineering technology are accredited by ABET.

Students interested in preparing for this occupation benefit from taking high school courses in math, such as algebra, trigonometry, and calculus; and science, such as chemistry and physics. For aspiring naval architects, drafting courses are helpful.

Important Qualities

Communication skills. Marine engineers and naval architects must be able to give clear instructions and explain complex concepts when leading teams of professionals on projects.

Ingenuity. Marine engineers and naval architects must use operations analysis to create a design that will most likely perform the ship's functions. They then employ skills of critical thinking to anticipate and correct any deficiencies before the ship is built or set to sea.

Interpersonal skills. Marine engineers and naval architects meet with clients to analyze their needs for ship systems. Engineers must be able to discuss progress with clients to keep redesign options open before the project is too far along.

Math skills. Marine engineers and naval architects use the principles of calculus, trigonometry, and other advanced topics in math for analysis, design, and troubleshooting in their work.

Median Annual Wages, May 2014

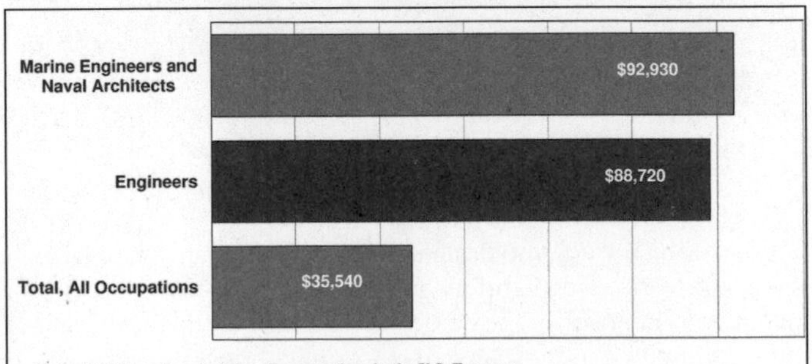

Note: All Occupations includes all occupations in the U.S. Economy.
Source: U.S. Bureau of Labor Statistics, Occupational Employment Statistics

Percent Change in Employment, Projected 2014–2024

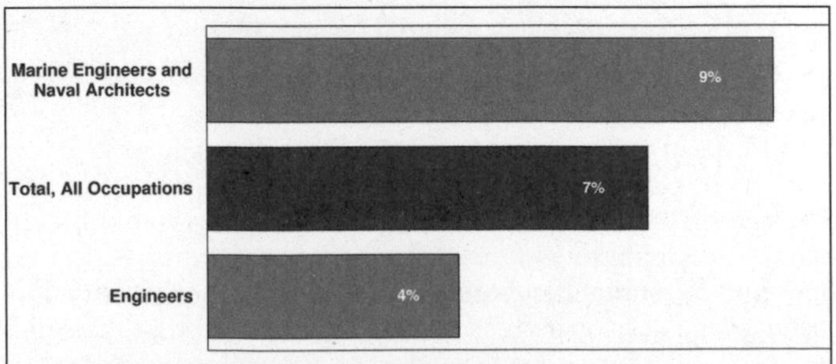

Note: All Occupations includes all occupations in the U.S. Economy.
Source: U.S. Bureau of Labor Statistics, Office of Occupational Statistics and Employment Projections

Employment Projections Data for Marine Engineers and Naval Architects

Occupational Title	SOC Code	Employment, 2014	Projected Employment, 2024	Change, 2014–2024 Percent	Change, 2014–2024 Numeric
Marine engineers and naval architects	17-2121	8,300	9,000	9	700

Source: U.S. Bureau of Labor Statistics, Employment Projections Program

Similar Occupations. This table shows a list of occupations with job duties that are similar to those of marine engineers and naval architects.

Occupations	Entry-level Education	2014 Median Pay	Projected Job Growth	Average Annual Openings
Aerospace Engineers	Bachelor's degree	$105,380	-2%	-160
Electrical and Electronics Engineers	Bachelor's degree	$93,260	0%	-10
Mechanical Engineers	Bachelor's degree	$83,060	5%	1,460
Petroleum Engineers	Bachelor's degree	$130,050	10%	340

Problem-solving skills. Marine engineers must design several systems that work well together in ships. Naval architects and marine engineers are expected to solve problems for their clients. They must draw on their knowledge and experience to make effective decisions.

Licenses, Certifications, and Registrations. Along with earning a bachelor's degree, students at states' maritime academies take an exam for a U.S. Merchant Mariner's license from the U.S. Coast Guard. The first stage of the license is known as the 3rd Assistant Engineer's License. With experience and further testing, a marine engineer may get a 2nd and then a 1st Assistant Engineer's License. The highest level of licensure is known as Chief Engineer. Higher grades of licensing usually are accompanied by higher pay and more responsibilities.

Licensure is not required for entry-level positions as an engineer. A Professional Engineer (PE) license, which allows for higher levels of leadership and independence, can be acquired later in one's career. Licensed engineers are called professional engineers (PEs). A PE can oversee the work of other engineers, sign off on projects, and provide services directly to the public. State licensure generally requires all of the following:

- A degree from an ABET-accredited engineering program
- A passing score on the Fundamentals of Engineering (FE) exam
- Relevant work experience
- A passing score on the Principles and Practice of Engineering (PE) exam

The initial FE exam can be taken after one earns a bachelor's degree. Engineers who pass this exam are commonly called engineers in training (EITs) or engineer interns (EIs). After meeting work experience requirements, EITs and EIs can take the second exam, called Principles and Practice of Engineering.

Advancement. Beginning marine engineers usually work under the supervision of experienced engineers. In larger companies, new engineers also may receive formal training in classrooms or seminars. As beginning engineers gain knowledge and experience, they move on to more difficult projects where they have greater independence to develop designs, solve problems, and make decisions.

Eventually, marine engineers may advance to become technical specialists or to supervise a team of engineers and technicians. Some may even become engineering managers or move into other managerial positions or sales work. In sales, an engineering background enables them to discuss technical aspects of certain kinds of engineering projects. Such knowledge is also useful in assisting clients in project planning, installation, and use. For more information, see the profiles on architectural and engineering managers and sales managers.

Pay

The median annual wage for marine engineers and naval architects was $92,930 in May 2014. The median wage is the wage at which half the workers in an occupation earned more than that amount and half earned less. The lowest 10 percent earned less than $59,110, and the highest 10 percent earned more than $146,840.

In May 2014, the median annual wages for marine engineers and naval architects in the top industries in which they worked were as follows:

Mining, quarrying, and oil and gas extraction	$116,830
Federal government, excluding postal service	98,570
Engineering services	91,470
Water transportation	89,890
Ship and boat building	87,830

Union Membership. Compared with workers in all occupations, marine engineers and naval architects had a higher percentage of workers who belonged to a union in 2014.

Job Outlook

Employment of marine engineers and naval architects is projected to grow 9 percent from 2014 to 2024, faster than the average for all occupations.

The need to design ships and systems to transport energy products, such as liquefied natural gas, across the globe will help to spur employment growth for this occupation. Employment of marine engineers and naval architects also will be supported by the need to modify existing ships and their systems because of new emissions and pollution regulations on cargo shipping.

Marine engineers who design and maintain offshore oil rigs are expected to be in demand as more companies seek and drill for oil and gas deposits in the ocean floor. In addition, an increase in international overseas transportation of liquefied natural gas is expected to lead to demand for marine engineers to work on ship crews, although sometimes on ships sailing under foreign flags.

Demand for marine engineers and naval architects also will come from the desire to have cargo ships that pollute less. The technology to produce less pollution is becoming more cost effective, and the United States and other countries are focusing more on reducing pollution. This task will include the adoption of new and alternative energy sources, such as offshore wind turbines and tidal power generators.

Contacts for More Information

For more information about marine engineers and naval architects, visit

- Marine Engineers' Beneficial Association (http://mebaunion.org/MEBA)
- American Society of Naval Engineers (www.navalengineers.org/Pages/default.aspx)

For more information about general engineering education and career resources, visit

- American Society for Engineering Education (www.asee.org)
- Technology Student Association (www.tsaweb.org)

For more information about accredited engineering programs, visit

- ABET (www.abet.org)

O*NET

- Marine Engineers and Naval Architects (17-2121.00)
- Marine Engineers (17-2121.01)
- Marine Architects (17-2121.02)

Materials Engineers

- **2014 Median Pay** .... $87,690 per year $42.16 per hour
- **Typical Entry-Level Education** .... Bachelor's degree
- **Work Experience in a Related Occupation** .... None
- **On-the-job Training** .... None
- **Number of Jobs, 2014** 25,300
- **Job Outlook, 2014–24** .... 1% (Little or no change)
- **Employment Change, 2014–24** 300

What Materials Engineers Do

Materials engineers develop, process, and test materials used to create a range of products, from computer chips and aircraft wings to golf clubs and biomedical devices. They study the properties and structures of metals, ceramics, plastics, composites, nanomaterials (extremely small substances), and other substances to create new materials that meet certain mechanical, electrical, and chemical requirements. They also help select materials for specific products, develop new ways to use existing materials, and develop new materials.

Duties. Materials engineers typically do the following:

- Plan and evaluate new projects, consulting with other engineers and managers as necessary
- Prepare proposals and budgets, analyze labor costs, write reports, and perform other managerial tasks
- Supervise the work of technologists, technicians, and other engineers and scientists
- Design and direct the testing of processing procedures
- Monitor how materials perform and evaluate how they deteriorate

Materials engineers develop, process, and test a wide variety of materials used in all kinds of products.

- Determine causes of product failure and develop ways of overcoming such failure
- Evaluate technical specifications and economic factors relating to the design objectives of processes or products

Materials engineers create and study materials at an atomic level. They use computers to replicate the characteristics of materials and their components. They solve problems in a number of engineering fields, such as mechanical, chemical, electrical, civil, nuclear, and aerospace.

Materials engineers may specialize in understanding specific types of materials. The following are examples of types of materials engineers:

Ceramic engineers develop ceramic materials and the processes for making them into useful products, from high-temperature rocket nozzles to glass for LCD flat-panel displays.

Composites engineers develop materials with special, engineered properties for applications in aircraft, automobiles, and related products.

Metallurgical engineers specialize in metals, such as steel and aluminum, usually in alloyed form with additions of other elements to provide specific properties.

Plastics engineers develop and test new plastics, known as polymers, for new applications.

Semiconductor processing engineers apply materials science and engineering principles to develop new microelectronic materials for computing, sensing, and related applications.

Work Environment

Materials engineers held about 25,300 jobs in 2014. The industries that employed the most materials engineers were as follows:

Aerospace product and parts manufacturing	13%
Engineering services	11
Primary metal manufacturing	10
Computer and electronic product manufacturing	10
Research and development in the physical, engineering, and life sciences	8

They often work in offices where they have access to computers and design equipment. Others work in factories or research and development laboratories. Materials engineers may work in teams with scientists and engineers from other backgrounds.

Work Schedules. Materials engineers generally work full time. About 1 out of 3 materials engineers worked more than 40 hours per week in 2014.

Education/Training

Materials engineers must have a bachelor's degree in materials science and engineering or in a related engineering field. Completing internships and cooperative engineering programs while in school can be helpful in getting a position as a materials engineer.

Education. Students interested in studying materials engineering should take high school courses in mathematics, such as algebra, trigonometry, and calculus; in science, such as biology, chemistry, and physics; and in computer programming.

Entry-level jobs as a materials engineer require a bachelor's degree. Bachelor's degree programs include classroom and laboratory work focusing on engineering principles.

Some colleges and universities offer a 5-year program leading to both a bachelor's and master's degree. A graduate degree, which may be at the Ph.D. level, allows an engineer to work as a postsecondary teacher or to do research and development.

Many colleges and universities offer internships and cooperative programs in partnership with industry. In these programs, students gain practical experience while completing their education.

Many engineering programs are accredited by ABET. Some employers prefer to hire candidates who have graduated from an accredited program. A degree from an ABET-accredited program is usually necessary to become a licensed professional engineer.

Important Qualities

Analytical skills. Materials engineers often work on projects related to other fields of engineering. They must determine how materials will be used and how they must be structured to withstand different conditions.

Math skills. Materials engineers use the principals of calculus and other advanced topics in math for analysis, design, and troubleshooting in their work.

Problem-solving skills. Materials engineers must understand the relationship between materials' structures, their properties, how they are made, and how these factors affect the products they are used to make. They must also figure out why a product might have failed, design a solution, and then conduct tests to make sure that the product does not fail again. These skills involve being able to identify root causes when many factors could be at fault.

Speaking skills. While working with technicians, technologists, and other engineers, materials engineers must state concepts and directions clearly. When speaking with managers, these engineers must also be able to communicate engineering concepts to people who may not have an engineering background.

Writing skills. Materials engineers must write plans and reports clearly so that people without a materials engineering background can understand the concepts.

Licenses, Certifications, and Registrations. Licensure for materials engineers is not as common as it is for other engineering occupations, nor it is required for entry-level positions. A Professional Engineer (PE) license, which allows for higher levels of leadership and independence, can be acquired later in one's career. Licensed engineers are called professional engineers (PEs). A PE can oversee the work of other engineers, sign off on projects, and provide services directly to the public. State licensure generally requires

- A degree from an ABET-accredited engineering program
- A passing score on the Fundamentals of Engineering (FE) exam
- Relevant work experience
- A passing score on the Principles and Practice of Engineering (PE) exam

The initial Fundamentals of Engineering (FE) exam can be taken after graduation from college. Engineers who pass this exam are commonly called engineers in training (EITs) or engineer interns (EIs). After meeting work experience requirements, EITs and EIs can take the second exam, called Principles and Practice of Engineering.

Several states require continuing education for engineers to keep their license. Most states recognize licensure from other states if the licensing state's requirements meet or exceed their own requirements.

Certification in the field of metallography, the science and art of dealing with the structure of metals and alloys, is available through ASM International and other materials science organizations.

Additional training in fields directly related to metallurgy and materials' properties, such as corrosion or failure analysis, is available through ASM International.

Advancement. Junior materials engineers usually work under the supervision of experienced engineers. In large companies, new engineers may receive formal training in classrooms or seminars. As engineers gain knowledge and experience, they move on to more difficult projects where they have greater independence to develop designs, solve problems, and make decisions.

Eventually, materials engineers may advance to become technical specialists or to supervise a team of engineers and technicians. Many become engineering managers or move into other

Median Annual Wages, May 2014

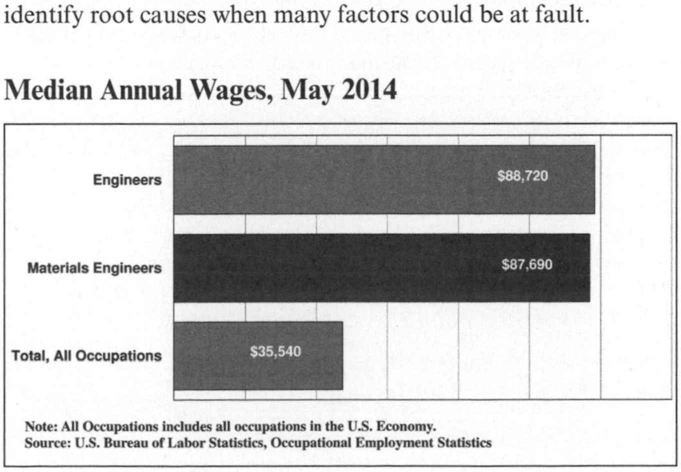

Percent Change in Employment, Projected 2014–2024

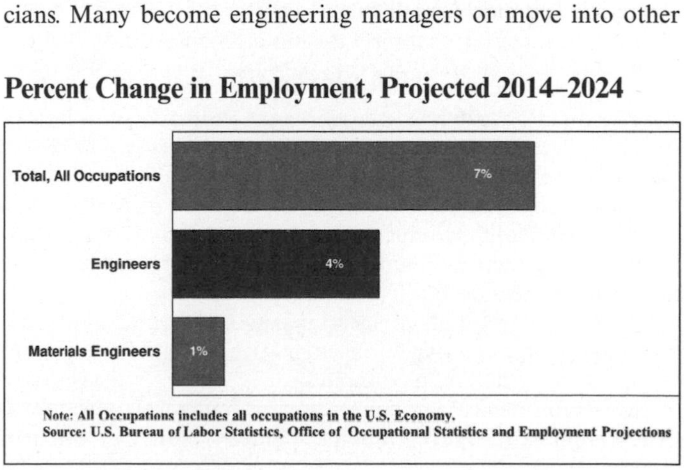

Employment Projections Data for Materials Engineers

Occupational Title	SOC Code	Employment, 2014	Projected Employment, 2024	Change, 2014–2024 Percent	Change, 2014–2024 Numeric
Materials engineers	17-2131	25,300	25,600	1	300

Source: U.S. Bureau of Labor Statistics, Employment Projections Program

Similar Occupations. This table shows a list of occupations with job duties that are similar to those of materials engineers.

Occupations	Entry-level Education	2014 Median Pay	Projected Job Growth	Average Annual Openings
Aerospace Engineers	Bachelor's degree	$105,380	-2%	-160
Architectural and Engineering Managers	Bachelor's degree	$130,620	2%	370
Biomedical Engineers	Bachelor's degree	$86,950	23%	510
Chemical Engineers	Bachelor's degree	$96,940	2%	60
Chemists and Materials Scientists	Bachelor's degree	$74,720	3%	260
Electrical and Electronics Engineers	Bachelor's degree	$93,260	0%	-10
Mechanical Engineers	Bachelor's degree	$83,060	5%	1,460
Physicists and Astronomers	Doctoral or professional degree	$109,290	7%	150
Sales Engineers	Bachelor's degree	$96,340	7%	490

managerial positions or sales work. An engineering background is useful in sales because it enables sales engineers to discuss a product's technical aspects and assist in product planning, installation, and use. For more information, see the profiles on architectural and engineering managers and sales engineers.

Pay

The median annual wage for materials engineers was $87,690 in May 2014. The median wage is the wage at which half the workers in an occupation earned more than that amount and half earned less. The lowest 10 percent earned less than $53,290, and the highest 10 percent earned more than $138,450.

In May 2014, the median annual wages for materials engineers in the top industries in which they worked were as follows:

Aerospace product and parts manufacturing	$104,310
Computer and electronic product manufacturing	90,700
Research and development in the physical, engineering, and life sciences	90,210
Engineering services	85,360
Primary metal manufacturing	74,830

Job Outlook

Employment of materials engineers is projected to show little or no change from 2014 to 2024. Materials engineers will be needed to design uses for new materials both in traditional industries, such as aerospace manufacturing, and in industries focused on new medical or scientific products. However, most materials engineers work in manufacturing industries, which are expected to experience employment declines.

Demand for materials engineers is expected to come from growing fields, such as biomedical engineering. Material engineers' expertise is crucial in helping biomedical engineers develop new materials for medical implants. Research and development firms will continue to employ materials engineers as they explore new uses for materials technology in consumer products, industrial processes, and medicine.

Job Prospects. Prospects should be best for applicants who gain experience by participating in internships or co-op programs while in college.

Computer modeling and simulations, rather than extensive and costly laboratory testing, are increasingly being used to predict the performance of new materials. Thus, those with a background in computer modeling should have better employment opportunities.

Contacts for More Information

For information about materials engineering career resources, visit

- American Ceramic Society (http://ceramics.org)
- American Institute of Mining, Metallurgical, and Petroleum Engineers (www.aimehq.org)
- Materials Research Society (www.mrs.org/home)
- The Minerals, Metals and Materials Society (www.tms.org/TMSHome.aspx)

For information about general engineering career resources, visit

- American Society for Engineering Education (www.asee.org)
- Technology Student Association (www.tsaweb.org)

For more information about licensure as a professional engineer, visit

- National Council of Examiners for Engineering and Surveying (http://ncees.org)
- National Society of Professional Engineers (www.nspe.org)

For more information about certification, visit

- ASM International (www.asminternational.org/home)

For information about accredited engineering programs, visit

- ABET (www.abet.org)

O*NET

- Materials Engineers (17-2131.00)

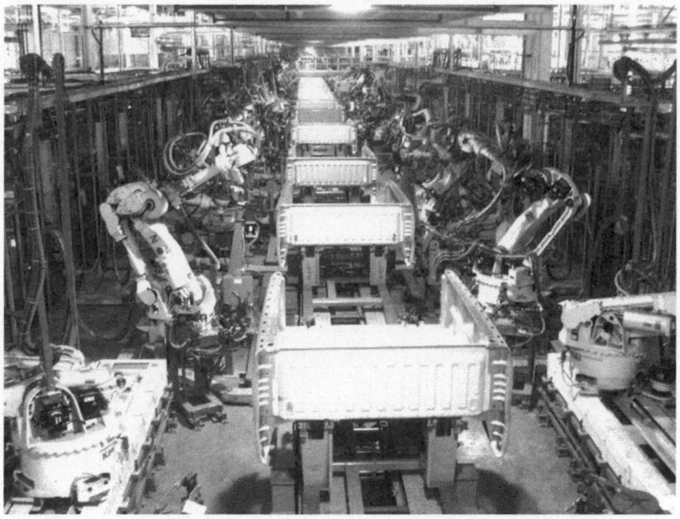

Mechanical engineering technicians plan the assembly process to be used in industrial settings.

Mechanical Engineering Technicians

- **2014 Median Pay** .... $53,530 per year
  $25.74 per hour
- **Typical Entry-Level Education** .... Associate's degree
- **Work Experience in a Related Occupation** .... None
- **On-the-job Training** .... None
- **Number of Jobs, 2014** 48,400
- **Job Outlook, 2014–24** .... 2% (Slower than average)
- **Employment Change, 2014–24** 900

What Mechanical Engineering Technicians Do

Mechanical engineering technicians help mechanical engineers design, develop, test, and manufacture mechanical devices, including tools, engines, and machines. They may make sketches and rough layouts, record and analyze data, make calculations and estimates, and report their findings.

Duties. Mechanical engineering technicians typically do the following:

- Evaluate design drawings for new or changed tools by measuring dimensions on the drawings and comparing them with the original specifications
- Prepare layouts and drawings of parts to be made and of the process for putting the parts together, often using three-dimensional design software
- Discuss changes with coworkers—for example, in the design of a part and in the way it will be made and assembled
- Review instructions and blueprints for projects in order to ensure that test specifications and procedures are followed and objectives are met
- Plan, produce, and assemble new or changed mechanical parts for products, such as industrial machinery or equipment
- Set up and conduct tests of complete units and parts and record results
- Compare test results with design specifications and with test objectives and make recommendations for changes in products or in test methods
- Estimate labor costs, equipment life, and plant space

Some mechanical engineering technicians test and inspect machines and equipment, or work with engineers to eliminate production problems. They may assist in testing products by, for example, setting up instrumentation for vehicle crash tests.

Work Environment

Mechanical engineering technicians held about 48,400 jobs in 2014. The industries that employed the most mechanical engineering technicians were as follows:

Engineering services	18%
Machinery manufacturing	14
Transportation equipment manufacturing	12
Computer and electronic product manufacturing	10
Research and development in the physical, engineering, and life sciences	7

Some mechanical engineering technicians may be exposed to hazards from equipment, chemicals, or toxic materials, but injuries are rare as long as proper procedures are followed.

Work Schedules. Most mechanical engineering technicians work full time.

Education/Training

Most employers prefer to hire candidates with associate's degrees or other postsecondary training in mechanical engineering technology. Prospective engineering technicians should take as many science and math courses as possible while in high school.

Education. Mechanical engineering technicians typically need an associate's degree or a certificate from a community college or vocational-technical school. Community colleges offer programs

Median Annual Wages, May 2014

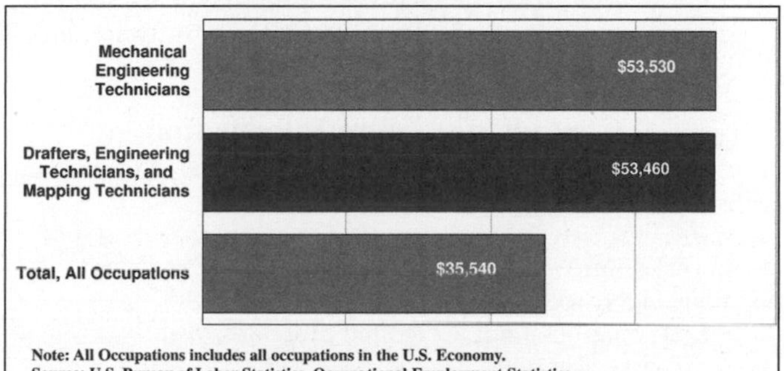

Note: All Occupations includes all occupations in the U.S. Economy.
Source: U.S. Bureau of Labor Statistics, Occupational Employment Statistics

Percent Change in Employment, Projected 2014–2024

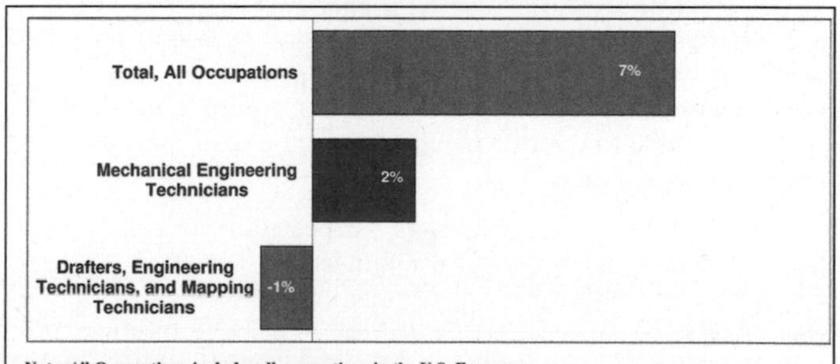

Note: All Occupations includes all occupations in the U.S. Economy.
Source: U.S. Bureau of Labor Statistics, Office of Occupational Statistics and Employment Projections

Employment Projections Data for Mechanical Engineering Technicians

Occupational Title	SOC Code	Employment, 2014	Projected Employment, 2024	Change, 2014–2024	
				Percent	Numeric
Mechanical engineering technicians	17-3027	48,400	49,300	2	900

Source: U.S. Bureau of Labor Statistics, Employment Projections Program

Similar Occupations. This table shows a list of occupations with job duties that are similar to those of mechanical engineering technicians.

Occupations	Entry-level Education	2014 Median Pay	Projected Job Growth	Average Annual Openings
Drafters	Associate's degree	$51,940	-3%	-620
Environmental Engineering Technicians	Associate's degree	$48,170	10%	190
Industrial Engineering Technicians	Associate's degree	$53,370	-5%	-300
Machinists and Tool and Die Makers	High school diploma or equivalent	$41,510	6%	2,900

similar to those in technical institutes but include more theory-based and liberal arts coursework and programs. Community colleges typically award an associate's degree. Vocational-technical schools include postsecondary public institutions that emphasize training needed by local employers. Students who complete these programs typically receive a diploma or certificate.

ABET accredits associate's programs in relevant fields of study, such as mechanical engineering technology.

Completing an associate's degree in mechanical engineering technology opens the way to studying for a bachelor's degree.

High school students interested in becoming mechanical engineering technicians should take classes in math, science, and computer skills. Courses that help students develop skills working with their hands also are valuable, because these technicians build what mechanical engineers design.

Important Qualities

Communication skills. Mechanical engineering technicians must be able to clearly understand and follow instructions or, if they do not understand, ask their supervisors to explain. They must be able to clearly explain, both orally and in writing, the need for changes in designs or test procedures.

Creativity. Mechanical engineering technicians help mechanical engineers bring their plans and designs to life. Doing so often requires helping the engineer to overcome problems that might not have been anticipated.

Detail oriented. Mechanical engineering technicians must make precise measurements and keep accurate records for mechanical engineers.

Math skills. Mechanical engineering technicians use mathematics for analysis, design, and troubleshooting in their work.

Mechanical skills. Mechanical engineering technicians must apply theory and instructions from engineers by making new components for industrial machinery or equipment. They may need to be able to operate machinery such as drill presses, grinders, and engine lathes.

Pay

The median annual wage for mechanical engineering technicians was $53,530 in May 2014. The median wage is the wage at which half the workers in an occupation earned more than that amount and half earned less. The lowest 10 percent earned less than $33,920, and the highest 10 percent earned more than $79,670.

In May 2014, the median annual wages for mechanical engineering technicians in the top industries in which they worked were as follows:

Research and development in the physical, engineering, and life sciences	$56,810
Computer and electronic product manufacturing	55,220
Transportation equipment manufacturing	54,570
Engineering services	53,970
Machinery manufacturing	51,590

Job Outlook

Employment of mechanical engineering technicians is projected to grow 2 percent from 2014 to 2024, slower than the average for all occupations. Employment in this occupation is projected to decline in manufacturing.

Mechanical engineering technicians also work for firms in engineering services and in research and development, both of which provide contract services to manufacturing and other industries. Contracting for this work allows firms to hire these services at a lower cost than employing in-house technicians. Employment of mechanical engineering technicians in engineering services is projected to grow 12 percent from 2014 to 2024.

Mechanical engineering technicians find work as assistants to mechanical engineers and thus work in emerging fields, such as automation, remanufacturing, three-dimensional printing, robotics, and alternative energies.

Job Prospects. Mastering new technology and software will likely become more important for workers in this occupation. Those who gain skills to help deploy the latest technological developments, such as three-dimensional design software, should have the best job prospects.

Contacts for More Information

For more information about general engineering education and career resources, visit

- American Society for Engineering Education (www.asee.org)
- American Society of Mechanical Engineers (www.asme.org)
- Technology Student Association (www.tsaweb.org)

For information about accredited programs, visit

- ABET (www.abet.org)

O*NET

- ➤ Mechanical Engineering Technicians (17-3027.00)
- ➤ Automotive Engineering Technicians (17-3027.01)

Mechanical Engineers

- **2014 Median Pay** .... $83,060 per year
  $39.93 per hour
- **Typical Entry-Level Education** .... Bachelor's degree
- **Work Experience in a Related Occupation**.............. None
- **On-the-job Training** .... None
- **Number of Jobs, 2014** 277,500
- **Job Outlook, 2014–24** .... 5% (As fast as average)
- **Employment Change, 2014–24** 14,600

Mechanical engineers develop and build mechanical devices for use in industrial processes.

What Mechanical Engineers Do

Mechanical engineering is one of the broadest engineering disciplines. Mechanical engineers research, design, develop, build, and test mechanical and thermal sensors and devices, including tools, engines, and machines.

Duties. Mechanical engineers typically do the following:

- Analyze problems to see how mechanical and thermal devices might help solve a particular problem
- Design or redesign mechanical and thermal devices or subsystems, using analysis and computer-aided design
- Develop and test prototypes of devices they design
- Analyze the test results and change the design or system as needed
- Oversee the manufacturing process for the device

Mechanical engineers design and oversee the manufacture of many products ranging from medical devices to new batteries.

Mechanical engineers design power-producing machines, such as electric generators, internal combustion engines, and steam and gas turbines, as well as power-using machines, such as refrigeration and air-conditioning systems.

Mechanical engineers design other machines inside buildings, such as elevators and escalators. They also design material-handling systems, such as conveyor systems and automated transfer stations.

Like other engineers, mechanical engineers use computers extensively. Mechanical engineers are routinely responsible for the integration of sensors, controllers, and machinery. Computer technology helps mechanical engineers create and analyze designs, run simulations and test how a machine is likely to work, interact with connected systems, and generate specifications for parts.

Work Environment

Mechanical engineers held about 277,500 jobs in 2014. The industries that employed the most mechanical engineers were as follows:

Engineering services	19%
Machinery manufacturing	15
Computer and electronic product manufacturing	7
Research and development in the physical, engineering, and life sciences	6
Aerospace product and parts manufacturing	6

Mechanical engineers generally work in offices. They may occasionally visit worksites where a problem or piece of equipment needs their personal attention. In most settings, they work with other engineers, engineering technicians, and other professionals as part of a team.

Work Schedules. Most mechanical engineers work full time, and about 1 in 3 worked more than 40 hours a week in 2014.

Education/Training

Mechanical engineers typically need a bachelor's degree in mechanical engineering or mechanical engineering technology. Mechanical engineers who sell services publicly must be licensed in all states and the District of Columbia.

Education. Mechanical engineering programs usually include courses in mathematics and life and physical sciences, as well as engineering and design courses. Mechanical engineering

Median Annual Wages, May 2014

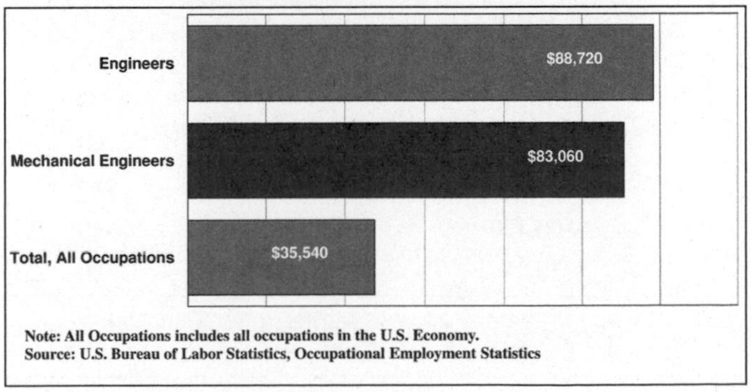

Percent Change in Employment, Projected 2014–2024

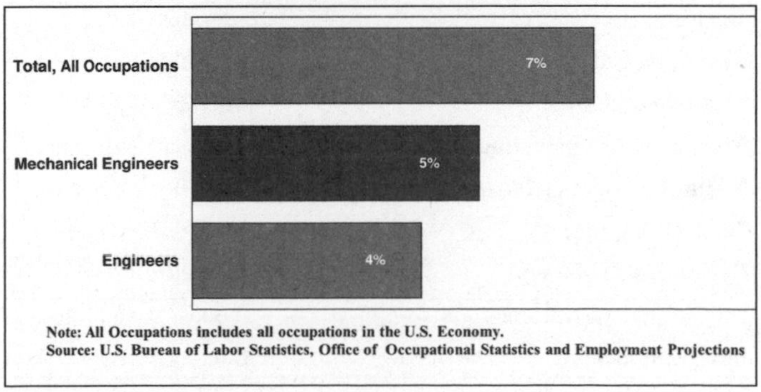

Employment Projections Data for Mechanical Engineers

Occupational Title	SOC Code	Employment, 2014	Projected Employment, 2024	Change, 2014–2024	
				Percent	Numeric
Mechanical engineers	17-2141	277,500	292,100	5	14,600

Source: U.S. Bureau of Labor Statistics, Employment Projections Program

technology programs focus less on theory and more on the practical application of engineering principles. They may emphasize internships and co-ops to prepare students for work in industry.

Some colleges and universities offer 5-year programs that allow students to obtain both a bachelor's and a master's degree. Some 5-year or even 6-year cooperative plans combine classroom study with practical work, enabling students to gain valuable experience and earn money to finance part of their education.

ABET accredits programs in engineering and engineering technology. Most employers prefer to hire students from an accredited program. A degree from an ABET-accredited program is usually necessary to become a licensed professional engineer.

Important Qualities

Creativity. Mechanical engineers design and build complex pieces of equipment and machinery. A creative mind is essential for this kind of work.

Listening skills. Mechanical engineers often work on projects with others, such as architects and computer scientists. They must listen to and analyze different approaches made by other experts to complete the task at hand.

Math skills. Mechanical engineers use the principles of calculus, statistics, and other advanced subjects in math for analysis, design, and troubleshooting in their work.

Mechanical skills. Mechanical skills allow engineers to apply basic engineering concepts and mechanical processes to the design of new devices and systems.

Problem-solving skills. Mechanical engineers need good problem-solving skills to take scientific discoveries and use them to design and build useful products.

Licenses, Certifications, and Registrations. Licensure is not required for entry-level positions as a mechanical engineer. A Professional Engineer (PE) license, which allows for higher levels of leadership and independence, can be acquired later in one's career. Licensed engineers are called professional engineers (PEs). A PE can oversee the work of other engineers, sign off on projects, and provide services directly to the public. State licensure generally requires

- A degree from an ABET-accredited engineering program
- A passing score on the Fundamentals of Engineering (FE) exam
- Relevant work experience
- A passing score on the Principles and Practice of Engineering (PE) exam

The initial FE exam can be taken after one earns a bachelor's degree. Engineers who pass this exam are commonly called engineers in training (EITs) or engineer interns (EIs). After meeting work experience requirements, EITs and EIs can take the second exam, called Principles and Practice of Engineering.

Several states require engineers to take continuing education to renew their licenses every year. Most states recognize licensure from other states, as long as the other state's licensing requirements meet or exceed their own licensing requirements.

Several professional organizations offer a variety of certification programs for engineers to demonstrate competency in specific fields of mechanical engineering.

Advancement. A Ph.D. is essential for engineering faculty positions in higher education, as well as for some research and development programs. Mechanical engineers may earn graduate degrees in engineering or business administration to learn new technology, broaden their education, and enhance their project management skills. Mechanical engineers may become administrators or managers after obtaining the requisite experience.

Pay

The median annual wage for mechanical engineers was $83,060 in May 2014. The median wage is the wage at which half the workers in an occupation earned more than that amount and half earned

Similar Occupations. This table shows a list of occupations with job duties that are similar to those of mechanical engineers.

Occupations	Entry-level Education	2014 Median Pay	Projected Job Growth	Average Annual Openings
Architectural and Engineering Managers	Bachelor's degree	$130,620	2%	370
Drafters	Associate's degree	$51,940	-3%	-620
Materials Engineers	Bachelor's degree	$87,690	1%	30
Mathematicians	Master's degree	$103,720	21%	70
Mechanical Engineering Technicians	Associate's degree	$53,530	2%	90
Natural Sciences Managers	Bachelor's degree	$120,050	3%	180
Nuclear Engineers	Bachelor's degree	$100,470	-4%	-70
Petroleum Engineers	Bachelor's degree	$130,050	10%	340
Physicists and Astronomers	Doctoral or professional degree	$109,290	7%	150
Sales Engineers	Bachelor's degree	$96,340	7%	490

less. The lowest 10 percent earned less than $53,210, and the highest 10 percent earned more than $126,430.

In May 2014, the median annual wages for mechanical engineers in the top industries in which they worked were as follows:

Research and development in the physical, engineering, and life sciences	$94,640
Aerospace product and parts manufacturing	89,600
Computer and electronic product manufacturing	87,530
Engineering services	84,580
Machinery manufacturing	76,190

Job Outlook

Employment of mechanical engineers is projected to grow 5 percent from 2014 to 2024, about as fast as the average for all occupations. Mechanical engineers can work in many industries and on many types of projects. As a result, their growth rate will differ by the industries that employ them. Job prospects may be best for those who stay informed regarding the most recent advances in technology.

Mechanical engineers are projected to experience much faster than average growth in engineering services as companies continue to contract work from these firms. Mechanical engineers will also remain involved in various manufacturing industries, particularly transportation equipment. They will be needed to design the next generations of vehicles and vehicle systems, such as hybrid-electric cars and clean diesel automobiles.

Mechanical engineers often work on the newest industrial pursuits. The fields of alternative energies, remanufacturing, and nanotechnology may offer new opportunities for occupational growth. Remanufacturing—rebuilding goods for a new use after they have worn out or become nonfunctional—holds promise because it reduces the cost of waste disposal.

Nanotechnology, which involves manipulating matter at the tiniest levels, may affect the employment of mechanical engineers because they will be needed to design production projects on the basis of that technology. Nanotechnology will be useful in areas such as healthcare and designing more powerful computer chips.

Job Prospects. Prospects for mechanical engineers overall are expected to be good. They will be best for those with training in the latest software tools, particularly for computational design and simulation. Such tools allow engineers and designers to take a project from the conceptual phase directly to a finished product, eliminating the need for prototypes.

Engineers who have experience or training in three-dimensional printing also will have better job prospects.

Contacts for More Information

For more information about general engineering education and mechanical engineering career resources, visit

- American Society of Mechanical Engineers (www.asme.org)
- American Society for Engineering Education (www.asee.org)
- Technology Student Association (www.tsaweb.org)

For more information about accredited engineering programs, visit

- ABET (www.abet.org)

For more information about licensure as a mechanical engineer, visit

- National Council of Examiners for Engineering and Surveying (http://ncees.org)
- National Society of Professional Engineers (www.nspe.org/index.html)

O*NET

- Mechanical Engineers (17-2141.00)
- Fuel Cell Engineers (17-2141.01)
- Automotive Engineers (17-2141.02)

Mining and Geological Engineers

- **2014 Median Pay** .... $90,160 per year $43.34 per hour
- **Typical Entry-Level Education** .... Bachelor's degree
- **Work Experience in a Related Occupation** .... None
- **On-the-job Training** .... None
- **Number of Jobs, 2014** 8,300
- **Job Outlook, 2014–24** .... 6% (As fast as average)
- **Employment Change, 2014–24** 500

What Mining and Geological Engineers Do

Mining and geological engineers design mines to safely and efficiently remove minerals such as coal and metals for use in manufacturing and utilities.

Duties. Mining and geological engineers typically do the following:

- Design open-pit and underground mines
- Supervise the construction of mine shafts and tunnels
- Devise methods for transporting minerals to processing plants

Mining and geological engineers often work outdoors to collect samples and take measurements.

Median Annual Wages, May 2014

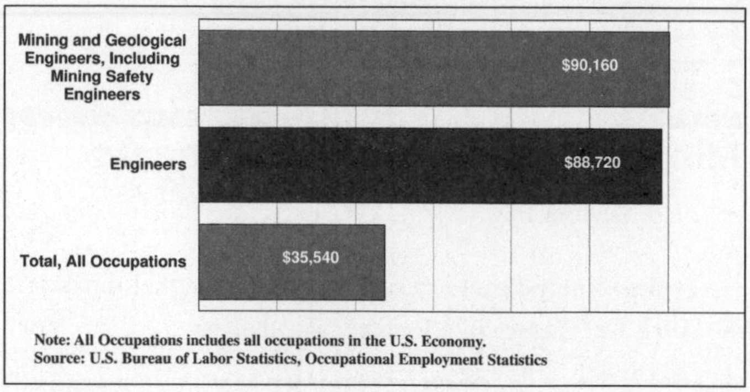

Percent Change in Employment, Projected 2014–2024

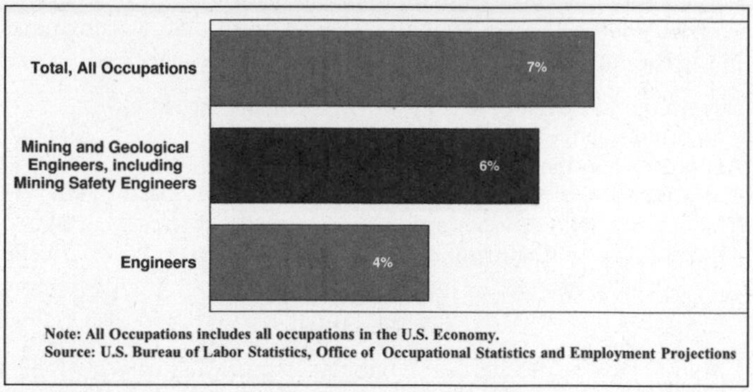

- Prepare technical reports for miners, engineers, and managers
- Monitor mine production to assess the effectiveness of operations
- Provide solutions to problems related to land reclamation, water and air pollution, and sustainability
- Ensure that mines are operated in safe and environmentally sound ways

Geological engineers search for mineral deposits and evaluate possible sites. Once a site is identified, they plan how the metals or minerals will be extracted in efficient and environmentally sound ways.

Mining engineers often specialize in one particular mineral or metal, such as coal or gold. They typically design and develop mines and determine the best way to extract metal or minerals to get the most out of deposits.

Some mining engineers work with geoscientists and metallurgical engineers to find and evaluate ore deposits. Other mining engineers develop new equipment or direct mineral-processing operations to separate minerals from dirt, rock, and other materials.

Mining safety engineers use best practices and their knowledge of mine design to ensure workers' safety and to maintain compliance with state and federal safety regulations. They inspect mines' walls and roofs, monitor the air quality, and examine mining equipment for possible hazards.

Engineers who hold a master's or a doctoral degree frequently teach engineering at colleges and universities. For more information, see the profile on postsecondary teachers.

Work Environment

Mining and geological engineers held about 8,300 jobs in 2014. The industries that employed the most mining and geological engineers were as follows:

Engineering services	24%
Metal ore mining	15
Support activities for mining	11
Oil and gas extraction	11
Coal mining	10

Many work at mining operations in remote locations; some work in sand-and-gravel operations that are located near large cities; and some engineers work in offices of mining firms or consulting companies, which are generally in large urban areas.

Work Schedules. Most mining and geological engineers work full time, and more than 2 in 5 worked more than 40 hours a week in 2014. The remoteness of some of the locations gives rise to variable schedules and weeks during which they work more hours than usual.

Education/Training

A bachelor's degree from an accredited engineering program is required to become a mining or geological engineer, including a mining safety engineer. Requirements for licensure vary by state but most states require applicants to pass two exams.

Education. High school students interested in entering mining engineering programs in college should take courses in mathematics and science.

Relatively few schools offer mining engineering programs. Typical bachelor's degree programs in mining engineering include courses in geology, physics, thermodynamics, mine design and safety, and mathematics. Programs also include laboratory and field work, as well as traditional classroom study.

Programs in mining and geological engineering are accredited by ABET, whose accreditation is based on a program's faculty, curriculum, facilities, and other factors.

Master's degree programs in mining and geological engineering typically are 2-year programs and include coursework in specialized subjects, such as mineral resource development and mining regulations. Some programs require a written thesis for graduation.

Important Qualities

Analytical skills. Mining and geological engineers must consider the wider implications of their immediate work to plan for restoring environmental health. They must be able to consider several competing, but interconnected, issues at the same time.

Employment Projections Data for Mining and Geological Engineers

Occupational Title	SOC Code	Employment, 2014	Projected Employment, 2024	Change, 2014–2024 Percent	Change, 2014–2024 Numeric
Mining and geological engineers, including mining safety engineers	17-2151	8,300	8,800	6	500

Source: U.S. Bureau of Labor Statistics, Employment Projections Program

Decision-making skills. These engineers make decisions that influence many critical outcomes—from worker safety to company profits. The ability to anticipate problems and deal with them immediately is crucial.

Logical-thinking skills. In planning mines' operations, mineral processing, and environmental reclamation, these engineers have to put work plans into a coherent, logical sequence.

Math skills. Mining and geological engineers use the principles of calculus, trigonometry, and other advanced topics in math for analysis, design, and troubleshooting in their work.

Problem-solving skills. Mining and geological engineers must explore for mines, plan their operations and mineral processing, and design environmental reclamation projects. These are all complex projects requiring an ability to identify and work toward goals, while solving problems along the way.

Writing skills. Mining and geological engineers must prepare reports and instructions for other workers. Therefore, they must be able to write clearly so that others can easily understand their ideas and plans.

Licenses, Certifications, and Registrations. Licensure is not required for entry-level positions as a mining or geological engineer. A Professional Engineer (PE) license, which allows for higher levels of leadership and independence, can be acquired later in one's career. Licensed engineers are called professional engineers (PEs). A PE can oversee the work of other engineers, sign off on projects, and provide services directly to the public. State licensure generally requires

- A degree from an ABET-accredited engineering program
- A passing score on the Fundamentals of Engineering (FE) exam
- Relevant work experience
- A passing score on the Principles and Practice of Engineering (PE) exam

The initial FE exam can be taken after one earns a bachelor's degree. Engineers who pass this exam are commonly called engineers in training (EITs) or engineer interns (EIs). After meeting work experience requirements, EITs and EIs can take the second exam, called Principles and Practice of Engineering.

In several states, engineers must earn continuing education credits to keep their licenses. Most states recognize licenses from other states, provided that licensure requirements in the other states meet or exceed the first state's own requirements.

Advancement. Beginning mining and geological engineers usually work under the supervision of experienced engineers. In large companies, new engineers also may receive formal classroom or seminar-type training. As engineers gain knowledge and experience, they are assigned more difficult projects and they are given greater independence to develop designs, solve problems, and make decisions.

Engineers may advance to become technical specialists or to supervise a staff or team of engineers and technicians. Some eventually become engineering managers or enter other managerial or sales jobs. In sales, an engineering background enables them to discuss a product's technical aspects and to assist in product planning, installation, and use. For more information, see the profiles on architectural and engineering managers and sales engineers.

Pay

The median annual wage for mining and geological engineers was $90,160 in May 2014. The median wage is the wage at which half the workers in an occupation earned more than that amount and half earned less. The lowest 10 percent earned less than $52,780, and the highest 10 percent earned more than $159,010.

In May 2014, the median annual wages for mining and geological engineers in the top industries in which they worked were as follows:

Oil and gas extraction	$115,860
Support activities for mining	103,590
Metal ore mining	85,530
Coal mining	83,390
Engineering services	78,560

Job Outlook

Employment of mining and geological engineers is projected to grow 6 percent from 2014 to 2024, about as fast as the average for all occupations.

Employment growth for mining and geological engineers will depend upon demand for mining operations. Growth will be affected by recent changes in federal policy concerning clean air policy. Coal with low sulfur content is found on federal lands and is the most environmentally friendly, and mining such coal presents the best possibility for continued operations. The feasibility studies and proposals needed to gain access to these and other mineral deposits will help spur demand for these engineers.

Similar Occupations. This table shows a list of occupations with job duties that are similar to those of mining and geological engineers.

Occupations	Entry-level Education	2014 Median Pay	Projected Job Growth	Average Annual Openings
Architectural and Engineering Managers	Bachelor's degree	$130,620	2%	370
Civil Engineers	Bachelor's degree	$82,050	8%	2,360
Environmental Scientists and Specialists	Bachelor's degree	$66,250	11%	1,020
Geological and Petroleum Technicians	Associate's degree	$54,810	12%	190
Geoscientists	Bachelor's degree	$89,910	10%	380
Hydrologists	Bachelor's degree	$78,370	7%	50
Mechanical Engineers	Bachelor's degree	$83,060	5%	1,460
Natural Sciences Managers	Bachelor's degree	$120,050	3%	180
Petroleum Engineers	Bachelor's degree	$130,050	10%	340
Sales Engineers	Bachelor's degree	$96,340	7%	490

Other countries may restrict exports of certain minerals known as "rare earths," which are used in the manufacture of many high-tech products and military equipment. This could help encourage exploration and further development of mines in the United States that yield these minerals.

Employment growth also will be driven by demand for engineering services. As companies look for ways to cut costs, they are expected to contract more engineering services with these firms, rather than employ engineers directly.

Job Prospects. Job prospects should be favorable for those entering the occupation, because many of these engineers will be reaching retirement age by 2024. In addition, the education and licensing required to enter this occupation will limit the supply of engineers competing for these positions.

Contacts for More Information

For more information about mining and geological engineers, visit

➤ Society for Mining, Metallurgy, and Exploration (www.smenet.org)

For information about general engineering education and career resources, visit

➤ American Society for Engineering Education (www.asee.org)

➤ Technology Student Association (www.tsaweb.org)

For more information about licensure as a mining or geological engineer, visit

➤ National Council of Examiners for Engineering and Surveying (http://ncees.org)

➤ National Society of Professional Engineers (www.nspe.org/index.html)

For information about accredited engineering programs, visit

➤ ABET (www.abet.org)

O*NET

➤ Mining and Geological Engineers, Including Mining Safety Engineers (17-2151.00)

Nuclear Engineers

- **2014 Median Pay** .... $100,470 per year, $48.30 per hour
- **Typical Entry-Level Education** .... Bachelor's degree
- **Work Experience in a Related Occupation** .... None
- **On-the-job Training** .... None
- **Number of Jobs, 2014** 16,800
- **Job Outlook, 2014–24** .... -4% (Decline)
- **Employment Change, 2014–24** .... -700

What Nuclear Engineers Do

Nuclear engineers research and develop the processes, instruments, and systems used to derive benefits from nuclear energy and radiation. Many of these engineers find industrial and medical uses for radioactive materials—for example, in equipment used in medical diagnosis and treatment. Many others specialize in the development of nuclear power sources for ships or spacecraft.

Duties. Nuclear engineers typically do the following:

- Design or develop nuclear equipment, such as reactor cores, radiation shielding, and associated instrumentation
- Direct operating or maintenance activities of operational nuclear power plants to ensure that they meet safety standards

A principal job of nuclear engineers is to design and operate nuclear power plants.

- Write operational instructions to be used in nuclear plant operation or in handling and disposing of nuclear waste
- Monitor nuclear facility operations to identify any design, construction, or operation practices that violate safety regulations and laws
- Perform experiments to test whether methods of using nuclear material, reclaiming nuclear fuel, or disposing of nuclear waste are acceptable
- Take corrective actions or order plant shutdowns in emergencies
- Examine nuclear accidents and gather data that can be used to design preventive measures

In addition, nuclear engineers are at the forefront of developing uses of nuclear material for medical imaging devices, such as positron emission tomography (PET) scanners. They also may develop or design cyclotrons, which produce a high-energy beam that the healthcare industry uses to treat cancerous tumors.

Work Environment

Nuclear engineers held about 16,800 jobs in 2014. The industries that employed the most nuclear engineers were as follows:

Electric power generation, transmission, and distribution	41%
Federal government, excluding postal service	17
Research and development in the physical, engineering, and life sciences	16
Engineering services	9
Manufacturing	6

They typically work in offices. However, their work setting varies with the industry in which they are employed. For example, those employed in power generation and supply work in power plants. Many also work for the federal government and for consulting firms.

Nuclear engineers work with others, including mechanical engineers and electrical engineers, and they must be able to incorporate systems designed by these engineers into their own designs.

Work Schedules. The majority of nuclear engineers work full time, and about 1 in 3 worked more than 40 hours per week in 2014. Their schedules may vary with the industries in which they work.

Education/Training

Nuclear engineers must have a bachelor's degree in nuclear engineering. Employers also value experience, and this can be gained through cooperative-education engineering programs.

Education. Entry-level nuclear engineering jobs in private industry require a bachelor's degree. Some entry-level nuclear engineering jobs may require at least a master's degree, or even a Ph.D.

Students interested in studying nuclear engineering should take high school courses in mathematics, such as algebra, trigonometry, and calculus; and science, such as biology, chemistry, and physics.

Bachelor's degree programs consist of classroom, laboratory, and field studies in areas that include mathematics and engineering principles. Most colleges and universities offer cooperative-education programs in which students gain experience while completing their education.

Some universities offer 5-year programs leading to both a bachelor's and a master's degree. A graduate degree allows an engineer to work as an instructor at a university or engage in research and development. Some 5-year or even 6-year cooperative-education plans combine classroom study with work, permitting students to gain experience and to finance part of their education.

Master's and Ph.D. programs consist of classroom, laboratory, and research efforts in areas of advanced mathematics and engineering principles. These programs require successful completion of a research study usually conducted in conjunction with a professor on a government or private research grant.

Programs in nuclear engineering are accredited by ABET.

Important Qualities

Analytical skills. Nuclear engineers must be able to identify design elements in order to help build facilities and equipment that produce material needed by various industries.

Communication skills. Nuclear engineers' work depends heavily on their ability to work with other engineers and technicians. They need to be able to communicate effectively, both in writing and in person.

Detail oriented. Nuclear engineers supervise the operation of nuclear facilities. They must pay close attention to what is happening at all times and ensure that operations comply with all regulations and laws pertaining to the safety of workers and the environment.

Logical-thinking skills. Nuclear engineers design complex systems. Therefore, they must be able to order information logically and clearly so that others can follow their written information and instructions.

Math skills. Nuclear engineers use the principles of calculus, trigonometry, and other advanced topics in math for analysis, design, and troubleshooting in their work.

Problem-solving skills. Because of the hazard posed by nuclear materials and by accidents at facilities, nuclear engineers must be able to anticipate problems before they occur and safeguard against them.

Training. A newly hired nuclear engineer at a nuclear power plant must usually complete training onsite, in such areas as safety procedures, safety practices, and regulations, before being allowed to work independently. Training lasts from 6 weeks to 3 months. In addition, these engineers must undergo continuous training every year to keep their knowledge, skills, and abilities current with laws, regulations, and safety procedures.

Licenses, Certifications, and Registrations. Licensure is not required for entry-level positions as a nuclear engineer. A Professional Engineer (PE) license, which allows for higher levels of leadership and independence, can be acquired later in one's career. Licensed engineers are called professional engineers (PEs). A PE can oversee the work of other engineers, sign off on projects, and provide services directly to the public. State licensure generally requires

- A degree from an ABET-accredited engineering program
- A passing score on the Fundamentals of Engineering (FE) exam
- Relevant work experience
- A passing score on the Principles and Practice of Engineering (PE) exam

The initial FE exam can be taken after one earns a bachelor's degree. Engineers who pass this exam are commonly called engineers in training (EITs) or engineer interns (EIs). After meeting work experience requirements, EITs and EIs can take the second exam, called Principles and Practice of Engineering.

Nuclear engineers can obtain licensing as a Senior Reactor Operator, a designation that is granted after an intensive, 2-year, site-specific program. The credential, granted by the Nuclear Regulatory Commission, asserts that the engineer can operate a nuclear power plant within federal government requirements.

Advancement. New nuclear engineers usually work under the supervision of experienced engineers. In large companies, new engineers may receive formal training in classrooms or seminars. As beginning engineers gain knowledge and experience, they move to more difficult projects with greater independence to develop designs, solve problems, and make decisions.

Eventually, nuclear engineers may advance to become technical specialists or to supervise a team of engineers and technicians. Some may become engineering managers or move into sales work. For more information, see the profiles on architectural and engineering managers and sales engineers.

Median Annual Wages, May 2014

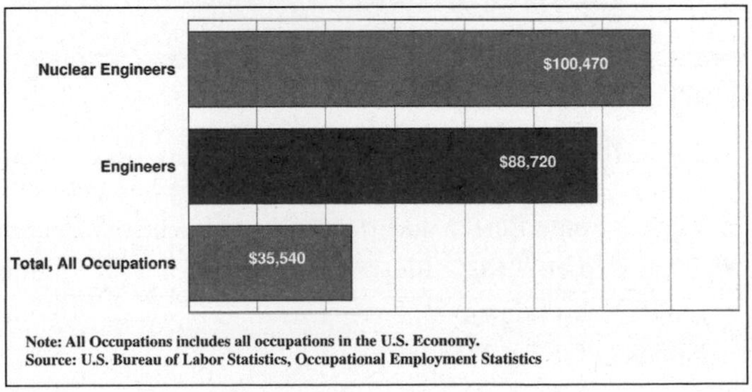

Percent Change in Employment, Projected 2014–2024

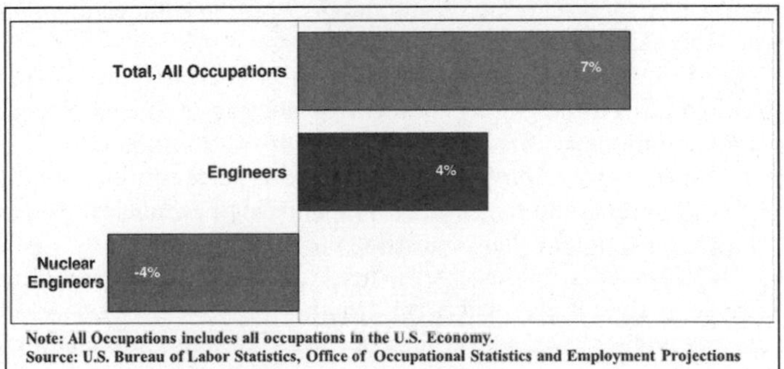

Employment Projections Data for Nuclear Engineers

Occupational Title	SOC Code	Employment, 2014	Projected Employment, 2024	Change, 2014–2024 Percent	Change, 2014–2024 Numeric
Nuclear engineers	17-2161	16,800	16,200	-4	-700

Source: U.S. Bureau of Labor Statistics, Employment Projections Program

Similar Occupations. This table shows a list of occupations with job duties that are similar to those of nuclear engineers.

Occupations	Entry-level Education	2014 Median Pay	Projected Job Growth	Average Annual Openings
Civil Engineers	Bachelor's degree	$82,050	8%	2,360
Electrical and Electronics Engineering Technicians	Associate's degree	$59,820	-2%	-280
Electrical and Electronics Engineers	Bachelor's degree	$93,260	0%	-10
Health and Safety Engineers	Bachelor's degree	$81,830	6%	160
Mechanical Engineers	Bachelor's degree	$83,060	5%	1,460
Physicists and Astronomers	Doctoral or professional degree	$109,290	7%	150

Nuclear engineers also can become medical physicists. A master's degree in medical or health physics or a related field is necessary for someone to enter this field.

Pay

The median annual wage for nuclear engineers was $100,470 in May 2014. The median wage is the wage at which half the workers in an occupation earned more than that amount and half earned less. The lowest 10 percent earned less than $66,890, and the highest 10 percent earned more than $151,710.

In May 2014, the median annual wages for nuclear engineers in the top industries in which they worked were as follows:

Research and development in the physical, engineering, and life sciences	$108,490
Engineering services	103,330
Electric power generation, transmission and distribution	101,390
Manufacturing	95,380
Federal government, excluding postal service	91,440

Union Membership. Compared with workers in all occupations, nuclear engineers had a higher percentage of workers who belonged to a union in 2014.

Job Outlook

Employment of nuclear engineers is projected to decline 4 percent from 2014 to 2024. Employment in several of the industries that employ nuclear engineers is projected to decline, including electric power distribution, research and development in engineering, and the federal government.

Traditionally, utilities that own or build nuclear power plants have employed the greatest number of nuclear engineers. Recent events might cause the Nuclear Regulatory Commission to issue guidelines for upgrading safety protocols at nuclear utility plants. The upgrades could raise the cost of building new nuclear power plants, limiting new plant construction.

Developments in nuclear medicine, diagnostic imaging, and cancer treatment also will drive demand for nuclear engineers in engineering services, who will be needed to develop new methods for treatment.

Job Prospects. Job prospects are expected to be relatively limited; however, there will be job openings due to retirements. Openings also will stem from operating extensions being granted to older nuclear power plants. Those with training in developing fields, such as nuclear medicine, should have better prospects.

Contacts for More Information

For more information about general engineering education and career resources, visit

- American Nuclear Society (www.ans.org/pi/matters/careers)
- American Society for Engineering Education (www.asee.org)
- Center for Nuclear Science and Technology Information (http://tinyurl.com/qejwuqz)
- Health Physics Society (http://hps.org)
- Technology Student Association (www.tsaweb.org)

For more information about licensure as a nuclear engineer, visit

- National Council of Examiners for Engineering and Surveying (http://ncees.org)
- National Society of Professional Engineers (www.nspe.org/index.html)

For more information about accredited engineering programs, visit

- ABET (www.abet.org)

For more information about federal government education requirements for nuclear engineer positions, visit

- U.S. Office of Personnel Management (http://tinyurl.com/zpvt9mv)

O*NET

- Nuclear Engineers (17-2161.00)

Petroleum Engineers

- **2014 Median Pay** .... $130,050 per year, $62.53 per hour
- **Typical Entry-Level Education** .... Bachelor's degree
- **Work Experience in a Related Occupation** .... None
- **On-the-job Training** .... None
- **Number of Jobs, 2014** 35,100

- **Job Outlook, 2014–24**............ 10% (Faster than average)
- **Employment Change, 2014–24** 3,400

What Petroleum Engineers Do

Petroleum engineers design and develop methods for extracting oil and gas from deposits below Earth's surface. Petroleum engineers also find new ways to extract oil and gas from older wells.

Duties. Petroleum engineers typically do the following:

- Design equipment to extract oil and gas in the most profitable way
- Develop ways to inject water, chemicals, gases, or steam into an oil reserve to force out more oil
- Develop plans to drill in oil and gas fields, and then to recover the oil and gas
- Evaluate the production of wells through testing and surveys
- Use computer-controlled drilling or fracturing to connect a larger area of an oil and gas deposit to a single well
- Make sure that oil field equipment is installed, operated, and maintained properly

Oil and gas deposits, or reservoirs, are located deep in rock formations underground. These reservoirs can only be accessed by drilling wells, either on land or at sea from offshore oil rigs.

Once oil and gas are discovered, petroleum engineers work with geoscientists and other specialists to understand the geologic formation of the rock containing the reservoir. They then determine the drilling methods, design the drilling equipment, implement the drilling plan, and monitor operations.

The best techniques currently being used recover only a portion of the oil and gas in a reservoir, so petroleum engineers also research and develop new ways to recover more of the oil and gas. This helps to lower the cost of drilling and production.

The following are examples of types of petroleum engineers:

Completions engineers decide the best way to finish building wells so that oil or gas will flow up from underground. They oversee work to complete the building of wells, which might involve the use of tubing, hydraulic fracturing, or pressure-control techniques.

Drilling engineers determine the best way to drill oil or gas wells, taking into account a number of factors, including cost. They also ensure that the drilling process is safe, efficient, and minimally disruptive to the environment.

Petroleum engineers often travel to the oil rigs and pumping stations to oversee operations first-hand.

Production engineers take over wells after drilling is completed. They typically monitor wells' oil and gas production. If wells are not producing as much as expected, production engineers figure out ways to increase the amount being extracted.

Reservoir engineers estimate how much oil or gas can be recovered from underground deposits, known as reservoirs. They study reservoirs' characteristics and determine which methods will get the most oil or gas out of them. They also monitor operations to ensure that the optimal levels of these resources are being recovered.

Work Environment

Petroleum engineers held about 35,100 jobs in 2014. The industries that employed the most petroleum engineers were as follows:

Oil and gas extraction	45%
Support activities for mining	16
Management of companies and enterprises	9
Petroleum and coal products manufacturing	9
Engineering services	4

Petroleum engineers generally work in offices or in research laboratories. However, they also must spend time at drilling sites, often for long periods of time. This means they must travel, sometimes with little notice.

Petroleum engineers work around the world; in fact, the best employment opportunities may include some work in other countries. Petroleum engineers also must be able to work with people from a wide variety of backgrounds, including other oil and gas workers who will carry out the engineers' drilling plans.

Work Schedules. Petroleum engineers typically work full time. However, about 2 in 5 worked more than 40 hours a week in 2014. Overtime may be necessary when traveling to and from drilling sites to help in their operation or respond to problems when they arise. When they are at a drilling site, it is common for these engineers to work in a rotation: on duty for 84 hours and then off duty for 84 hours.

Education/Training

However, a bachelor's degree in mechanical or chemical engineering may also meet employer requirements. Employers also value work experience, so college cooperative-education programs, in which students earn academic credit and job experience, are valuable as well.

Education. Students interested in studying petroleum engineering will benefit from taking high school courses in math, such as algebra, trigonometry, and calculus; and in science, such as biology, chemistry, and physics.

Entry-level petroleum engineering jobs require a bachelor's degree. Bachelor's degree programs include classes, laboratory work, and field studies in areas such as engineering principles, geology, and thermodynamics. Most colleges and universities offer cooperative programs in which students gain practical experience while completing their education.

Some colleges and universities offer 5-year programs in chemical or mechanical engineering that lead to both a bachelor's degree and a master's degree. Some employers may prefer applicants who have earned a graduate degree. A graduate degree also allows an engineer to work as an instructor at some universities or in research and development.

ABET accredits programs in petroleum engineering.

Median Annual Wages, May 2014

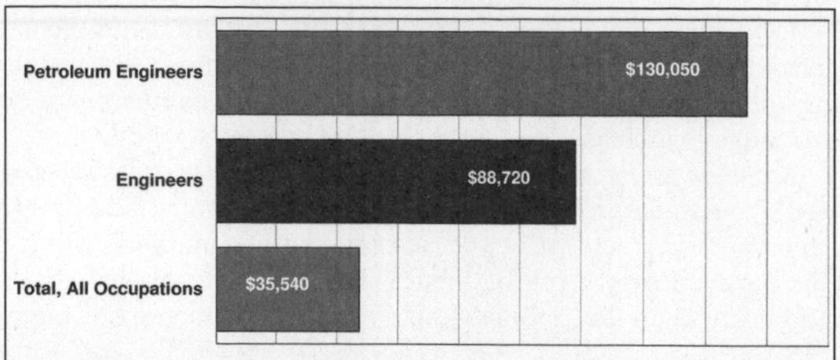

Note: All Occupations includes all occupations in the U.S. Economy.
Source: U.S. Bureau of Labor Statistics, Occupational Employment Statistics

Percent Change in Employment, Projected 2014–2024

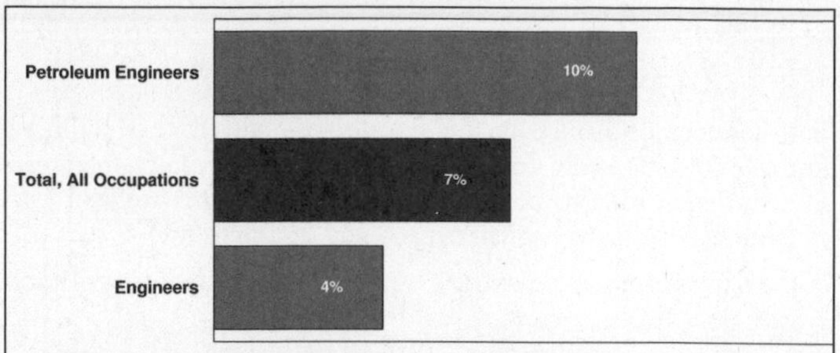

Note: All Occupations includes all occupations in the U.S. Economy.
Source: U.S. Bureau of Labor Statistics, Office of Occupational Statistics and Employment Projections

Important Qualities

Analytical skills. Petroleum engineers must be able to assess complex plans for drilling and anticipate possible flaws or complications before the company commits money and people to a project.

Creativity. Petroleum engineers must come up with new ways to extract oil and gas because each new drill site presents challenges. They must know how to ask the necessary questions to find possible deposits of oil and gas.

Interpersonal skills. Petroleum engineers must work with others on projects that require highly expensive machinery, equipment, and infrastructure. Communicating and working well with others is crucial to protecting and preserving firms' huge capital investments.

Math skills. Petroleum engineers use the principles of calculus and other advanced topics in math for analysis, design, and troubleshooting in their work.

Problem-solving skills. Identifying problems in drilling plans is critical for petroleum engineers because drilling operations can be costly. They must be careful not to overlook any potential issues and quickly address problems that do occur.

Licenses, Certifications, and Registrations. Licensure is not required for entry-level positions as a petroleum engineer. A Professional Engineer (PE) license, which allows for higher levels of leadership and independence, can be acquired later in one's career. Licensed engineers are called professional engineers (PEs). A PE can oversee the work of other engineers, sign off on projects, and provide services directly to the public. State licensure generally requires

- A degree from an ABET-accredited engineering program
- A passing score on the Fundamentals of Engineering (FE) exam
- Relevant work experience
- A passing score on the Principles and Practice of Engineering (PE) exam

The initial FE exam can be taken after one earns a bachelor's degree. Engineers who pass this exam are commonly called engineers in training (EITs) or engineer interns (EIs). After meeting work experience requirements, EITs and EIs can take the second exam, called Principles and Practice of Engineering.

Several states require engineers to take continuing education courses in order to keep their licenses. Most states recognize licensure from other states if the licensing state's requirements meet or exceed their own licensure requirements.

The Society of Petroleum Engineers offers certification. To be certified, petroleum engineers must be members of the Society, pass an exam, and meet other qualifications.

Advancement. Entry-level engineers usually work under the supervision of experienced engineers. In large companies, new engineers also may receive formal training. As engineers gain knowledge and experience, they move to more difficult projects where they have greater independence to develop designs, solve problems, and make decisions.

Eventually, petroleum engineers may advance to supervise a team of engineers and technicians. Some become engineering managers or move into other managerial positions. For more information, see the profile on architectural and engineering managers.

Petroleum engineers also may go into sales and use their engineering background to inform the discussion of a product's technical aspects with potential buyers and help in product planning, installation, and use. For more information, see the profile on sales engineers.

Pay

The median annual wage for petroleum engineers was $130,050 in May 2014. The median wage is the wage at which half the workers in an occupation earned more than that amount and half earned less. The lowest 10 percent earned less than $73,990, and the highest 10 percent earned more than $187,200.

In May 2014, the median annual wages for petroleum engineers in the top industries in which they worked were as follows:

Management of companies and enterprises	$154,410
Engineering services	143,940
Oil and gas extraction	142,620
Petroleum and coal products manufacturing	118,190
Support activities for mining	102,370

Employment Projections Data for Petroleum Engineers

Occupational Title	SOC Code	Employment, 2014	Projected Employment, 2024	Change, 2014–2024 Percent	Change, 2014–2024 Numeric
Petroleum engineers	17-2171	35,100	38,500	10	3,400

Source: U.S. Bureau of Labor Statistics, Employment Projections Program

Similar Occupations. This table shows a list of occupations with job duties that are similar to those of petroleum engineers.

Occupations	Entry-level Education	2014 Median Pay	Projected Job Growth	Average Annual Openings
Aerospace Engineers	Bachelor's degree	$105,380	-2%	-160
Architectural and Engineering Managers	Bachelor's degree	$130,620	2%	370
Chemists and Materials Scientists	Bachelor's degree	$74,720	3%	260
Geoscientists	Bachelor's degree	$89,910	10%	380
Industrial Engineering Technicians	Associate's degree	$53,370	-5%	-300
Industrial Engineers	Bachelor's degree	$81,490	1%	210
Materials Engineers	Bachelor's degree	$87,690	1%	30
Mechanical Engineering Technicians	Associate's degree	$53,530	2%	90
Mechanical Engineers	Bachelor's degree	$83,060	5%	1,460
Sales Engineers	Bachelor's degree	$96,340	7%	490

Job Outlook

Employment of petroleum engineers is projected to grow 10 percent from 2014 to 2024, faster than the average for all occupations. Job prospects should be favorable because many engineers are expected to retire.

Oil prices will be a major determinant of employment growth. Because many petroleum engineers work in oil and gas extraction, any changes in oil prices will likely affect employment levels. Higher prices can cause oil and gas companies to drill in deeper waters and in less hospitable places and return to existing wells to try new extraction methods. This means that oil drilling operations will likely become more complex and will require more engineers to work on each drilling operation.

Demand for petroleum engineers in support activities for mining should also be strong, as oil and gas companies find it convenient and cost-effective to seek their services on an as-needed basis.

Job Prospects. Job prospects are expected to be favorable because of projected growth and because many petroleum engineers may retire or leave the occupation for other reasons over the next decade.

Contacts for More Information

For information about general engineering education and career resources, visit

- American Society for Engineering Education (www.asee.org)
- Technology Student Association (www.tsaweb.org)

For information about the Professional Engineer license, visit

- National Council of Examiners for Engineering and Surveying (http://ncees.org)
- National Society of Professional Engineers (www.nspe.org/index.html)

For information about accredited engineering programs, visit

- ABET (www.abet.org)

For information about certification, visit

- Society of Petroleum Engineers (www.spe.org/index.php)

O*NET

- Petroleum Engineers (17-2171.00)

Surveying and Mapping Technicians

- **2014 Median Pay** .... $40,770 per year $19.60 per hour
- **Typical Entry-Level Education** .... High school diploma or equivalent
- **Work Experience in a Related Occupation** .... None
- **On-the-job Training** .... Moderate-term on-the-job training
- **Number of Jobs, 2014** 57,300
- **Job Outlook, 2014–24** .... -8% (Decline)
- **Employment Change, 2014–24** .... -4,300

What Surveying and Mapping Technicians Do

Surveying and mapping technicians collect data and make maps of Earth's surface. Surveying technicians visit sites to take measurements of the land. Mapping technicians use geographic data to create maps. They both assist surveyors, cartographers, and photogrammetrists.

Duties. Surveying technicians typically do the following:

- Visit sites to record survey measurements and other descriptive data
- Operate surveying instruments, such as electronic distance-measuring equipment (robotic total stations), to collect data on a location
- Set out stakes and marks to conduct a survey
- Search for previous survey points, such as old stone markers
- Enter the data from surveying instruments into computers, either in the field or in an office

Surveying technicians help surveyors in the field on teams known as survey parties. A typical survey party has a party chief and one or more surveying technicians. The party chief, either a surveyor or a senior surveying technician, leads day-to-day work activities. After data is collected by the survey party, surveying technicians help to process the data by entering the data into computers.

Mapping technicians typically do the following:

- Select needed information from databases to create maps
- Edit and process images that have been collected in the field

Surveying and mapping technicians do field work but also represent measurements in graphic form.

- Produce maps showing boundaries, water locations, elevation, and other features of the terrain
- Update maps to ensure accuracy
- Assist photogrammetrists by laying out aerial photographs in sequence to identify areas not captured by aerial photography

Mapping technicians help cartographers and photogrammetrists produce and upgrade maps. They do this work on computers, combining data from different sources.

Geographic Information System (GIS) technicians use GIS technology to assemble, integrate, and display data about a particular location in a digital format. They also use GIS technology to compile information from a variety of sources. GIS technicians also maintain and update databases for GIS devices.

Work Environment

Surveying and mapping technicians held about 57,300 jobs in 2014. Most surveying and mapping technicians work for firms that provide engineering, surveying, and mapping services on a contractual basis. Local governments also employ these workers in highway and planning departments.

Surveying technicians work outside extensively and can be exposed to all types of weather. They often stand for long periods, walk considerable distances, and may have to climb hills with heavy packs of surveying instruments. Traveling is sometimes part of the job, and surveying technicians may commute long distances, stay away from home overnight, or temporarily relocate near a survey site.

Mapping technicians work primarily on computers in office environments. However, mapping technicians must sometimes conduct research by using resources such as survey maps and legal documents to verify property lines and to obtain information needed for mapping. This task may require traveling to storage sites, such as county courthouses or lawyers' offices, that house these legal documents.

Work Schedules. Surveying and mapping technicians typically work full time but may work additional hours during the summer, when weather and light conditions are most suitable for fieldwork. Construction-related work may be limited during times of harsh weather.

Mapping technicians who develop and maintain Geographic Information System (GIS) databases generally work normal business hours.

Education/Training

Surveying technicians usually need a high school diploma. However, mapping technicians often need formal education after high school to study technology applications, such as Geographic Information Systems (GIS).

Education. Surveying technicians generally need a high school diploma, but some have postsecondary training in survey technology. Postsecondary training is more common among mapping technicians where an associate's degree or bachelor's degree in a relevant field, such as geomatics, is beneficial.

High school students interested in working as a surveying or mapping technician should take courses in algebra, geometry, trigonometry, drafting, mechanical drawing, and computer science. Knowledge of these subjects will help in finding a job and in advancing.

Training. Surveying technicians learn their job duties under the supervision of a surveyor or a surveying party chief. Initially, surveying technicians handle simple tasks, such as placing markers on land and entering data into computers. With experience, they help to decide where and how to measure the land.

Mapping technicians receive on-the-job training under the supervision of a lead mapper. During training, technicians learn how maps are created and stored in databases.

Licenses, Certifications, and Registrations. The growing need to make sure that data are useful to other professionals has caused certification to become more common. The American Society for Photogrammetry and Remote Sensing (ASPRS) offers certification for photogrammetric technologists, remote-sensing technologists, and Geographic Information System/Land Information System (GIS/LIS) technologists. The National Society of Professional Surveyors offers the Certified Survey Technician credential.

Median Annual Wages, May 2014

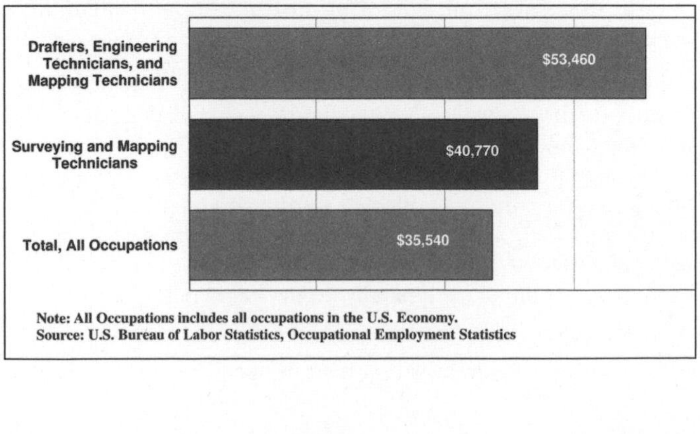

Percent Change in Employment, Projected 2014–2024

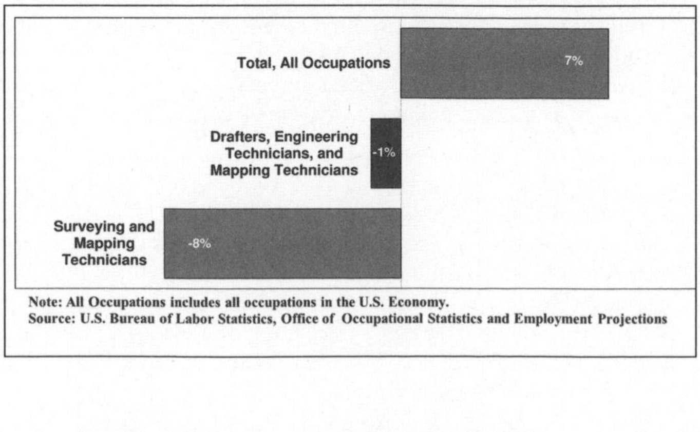

Employment Projections Data for Surveying and Mapping Technicians

Occupational Title	SOC Code	Employment, 2014	Projected Employment, 2024	Change, 2014–2024	
				Percent	Numeric
Surveying and mapping technicians	17-3031	57,300	52,900	-8	-4,300

Source: U.S. Bureau of Labor Statistics, Employment Projections Program

Similar Occupations. This table shows a list of occupations with job duties that are similar to those of surveying and mapping technicians.

Occupations	Entry-level Education	2014 Median Pay	Projected Job Growth	Average Annual Openings
Architects	Bachelor's degree	$74,520	7%	780
Cartographers and Photogrammetrists	Bachelor's degree	$60,930	29%	360
Drafters	Associate's degree	$51,940	-3%	-620
Landscape Architects	Bachelor's degree	$64,570	5%	120
Surveyors	Bachelor's degree	$57,050	-2%	-90

Advancement. With many years of experience and formal training in surveying, surveying technicians may advance to senior survey technician, then to party chief. Depending on state licensing requirements, they may be able to become licensed surveyors.

Important Qualities

Concentration. Surveying and mapping technicians must be precise and accurate in their work. Their results are often entered into legal records.

Decision-making skills. Surveying technicians must be able to exercise some independent judgment in the field because they may not always be able to communicate with team members.

Listening skills. Surveying technicians work outdoors and must communicate with party chiefs and other team members across distances. Following spoken instructions from the party chief is crucial for saving time and preventing errors.

Physical stamina. Surveying technicians usually work outdoors, often in rugged terrain. Physical fitness is necessary to carry equipment and to stand most of the day.

Problem-solving skills. Surveying and mapping technicians must be able to identify and fix problems with their equipment. They also must note potential problems with the day's work plan.

Pay

The median annual wage for surveying and mapping technicians was $40,770 in May 2014. The median wage is the wage at which half the workers in an occupation earned more than that amount and half earned less. The lowest 10 percent earned less than $25,270, and the highest 10 percent earned more than $67,320.

Job Outlook

Employment of surveying and mapping technicians is projected to decline 8 percent from 2014 to 2024. Advancements in surveying technology, such as robotic total stations, let surveyors and surveying technicians complete more work in less time, reducing the demand for surveying technicians.

Job Prospects. Some job openings will result from the need to replace workers who leave the occupation. Demand for surveying services is closely tied to construction activity, and job opportunities will vary by geographic region, often depending on local economic conditions. When real estate sales and construction activity slow down, surveying technicians may face greater competition for jobs. However, because surveying technicians can work on many different types of projects, they may have steadier work than others when construction slows.

Prospects should be best for those who are trained in Geographic Information Systems (GIS).

Contacts for More Information

For more information about certification in Geographic Information Systems (GIS), visit

➤ GIS Certification Institute (www.gisci.org)

For information about career opportunities and the surveying technician certification program, visit

➤ National Society of Professional Surveyors (www.acsm.net)

For more information about photogrammetric technicians and GIS specialists, visit

➤ American Society for Photogrammetry and Remote Sensing (www.asprs.org)

O*NET

➤ Surveying and Mapping Technicians (17-3031.00)

➤ Surveying Technicians (17-3031.01)

➤ Mapping Technicians (17-3031.02)

Surveyors

- **2014 Median Pay** .... $57,050 per year, $27.43 per hour
- **Typical Entry-Level Education** .... Bachelor's degree
- **Work Experience in a Related Occupation** .... Less than 5 years
- **On-the-job Training** .... None
- **Number of Jobs, 2014** 44,300
- **Job Outlook, 2014–24** .... -2% (Decline)
- **Employment Change, 2014–24** .... -900

What Surveyors Do

Surveyors make precise measurements to determine property boundaries. They provide data relevant to the shape and contour of Earth's surface for engineering, mapmaking, and construction projects.

Duties. Surveyors typically do the following:

- Measure distances and angles between points on, above, and below Earth's surface
- Travel to locations and use known reference points to determine the exact location of important features
- Research land records, survey records, and land titles
- Look for evidence of previous boundaries to determine where boundary lines are located
- Record the results of surveying and verify the accuracy of data
- Prepare plots, maps, and reports
- Present findings to clients and government agencies
- Establish official land and water boundaries for deeds, leases, and other legal documents and testify in court regarding survey work

Surveyors provide documentation of legal property lines and help determine the exact locations of real estate and construction projects. For example, when a house or commercial building is bought or sold, it may need to be surveyed to prevent boundary disputes. During construction, surveyors determine the precise location of roads or buildings and proper depths for building foundations. The survey also shows changes to the property line and indicates potential restrictions on the property, such as what can be built on it and how large the structure can be.

When taking measurements in the field, surveyors make use of the Global Positioning System (GPS), a system of satellites that locates reference points with a high degree of precision. Surveyors use handheld GPS units and robotic total stations to collect relevant information about the terrain they are surveying. (Robotic total stations use laser systems and GPS to automatically calculate distances between boundaries and geological features of the survey area.) Data is then loaded into a computer, where surveyors interpret and verify the results.

Surveyors also use Geographic Information Systems (GIS)—technology that allows surveyors to present spatial information visually as maps, reports, and charts. For example, a surveyor can overlay aerial or satellite images with GIS data, such as tree density in a given region, and create digital maps. They then use the results to advise governments and businesses on where to plan homes, roads, and landfills.

Although advances in surveying technology now allow many jobs to be performed by just one surveyor, they also may work with the help of a crew. The crew may consist of a licensed surveyor and trained survey technicians. The person in charge of the crew, known as the *party chief*, may be either a surveyor or a senior surveying technician. The party chief leads day-to-day work activities.

Surveyors may be involved in settling boundary disputes. When property is sold or new construction takes place, such as the building of a fence, issues may arise because of outdated records or the misinterpretation of available records. A surveyor can be called in to settle the dispute, and may provide testimony in court if the involved parties do not come to an agreement.

Surveyors also work with civil engineers, landscape architects, and urban and regional planners to develop comprehensive design documents.

Land surveyors frequently take measurements in the field.

Some surveyors work in specialty fields to survey particular characteristics of Earth.

The following are two types of surveyors:

Geodetic surveyors use high-accuracy technology, including aerial and satellite observations, to measure large areas of Earth's surface.

Marine or hydrographic surveyors survey harbors, rivers, and other bodies of water to determine shorelines, the topography of the floor, water depth, and other features.

Work Environment

Surveyors held about 44,300 jobs in 2014. The industries that employed the most surveyors were as follows:

Architectural, engineering, and related services	70%
Government	11
Construction	8

Most surveyors work for private surveying or engineering firms. Some also work in construction and for state and local governments.

Depending on the specific job duties, surveying involves both fieldwork and office work. Fieldwork involves working outdoors in all types of weather, walking long distances, and standing for extended periods while measurements are taken. Surveyors sometimes climb hills with heavy packs of surveying instruments. When working near hazards such as traffic, surveyors generally wear brightly colored or reflective vests so they may be seen more easily.

Traveling is often part of the job, and surveyors may commute long distances or stay at a project location for an extended period of time. Those who work on resource extraction projects may work in remote areas and spend long periods away from home.

Work Schedules. Surveyors usually work full time. When construction activity is high, they may work more hours than usual.

Median Annual Wages, May 2014

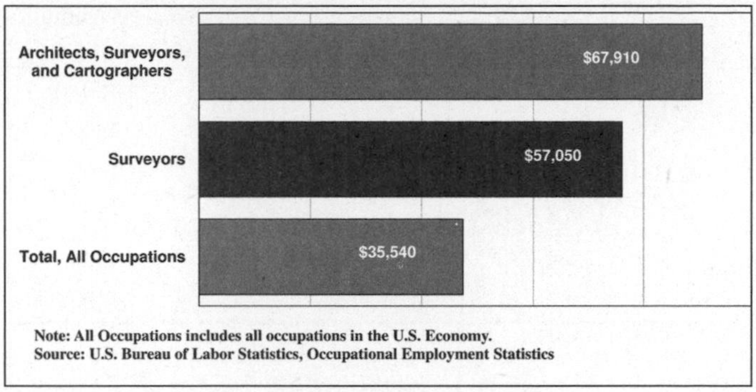

Percent Change in Employment, Projected 2014–2024

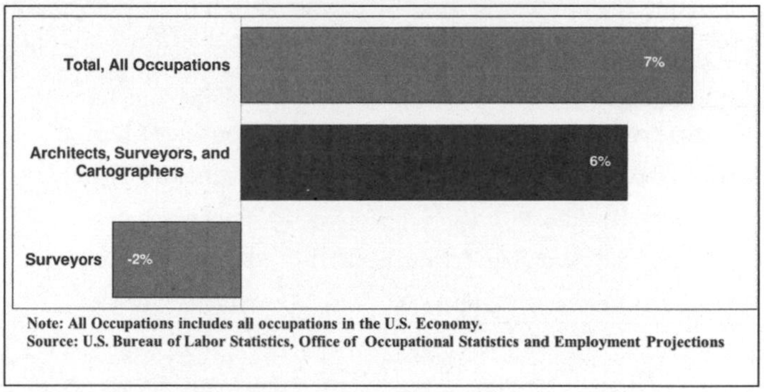

Education/Training

Surveyors typically need a bachelor's degree. They must be licensed before they can certify legal documents and provide surveying services to the public.

Education. Some colleges and universities offer bachelor's degree programs specifically designed to prepare students to become licensed surveyors. A bachelor's degree in a closely related field, such as civil engineering or forestry, is sometimes acceptable as well.

Many states require individuals who want to become licensed surveyors to have a bachelor's degree from a school accredited by ABET and approximately 4 years of work experience under a licensed surveyor. In other states, an associate's degree in surveying, coupled with more years of work experience under a licensed surveyor, may be sufficient. Most states also have continuing education requirements.

Work Experience in a Related Occupation. Candidates with significant work experience as a survey technician can become licensed surveyors. To receive credit for this experience, candidates must work under a licensed surveyor. Many surveying technicians become licensed surveyors after working for as many as 10 years in the field of surveying. The amount of work experience required varies by state.

Licenses, Certifications, and Registrations. All 50 states and the District of Columbia require surveyors to be licensed before they can certify legal documents that show property lines or determine proper markings on construction projects. Candidates with a bachelor's degree must usually work for several years under the direction of a licensed surveyor in order to qualify for licensure.

Although the process of obtaining a license varies by state, the National Council of Examiners for Engineering and Surveying has a generalized process of four steps:

- Complete the level of education required in your state
- Pass the Fundamentals of Surveying (FS) exam
- Gain sufficient work experience under a licensed surveyor
- Pass the Principles and Practice of Surveying (PS) exam

Important Qualities

Communication skills. Surveyors must provide clear instructions to team members, clients, and government officials. They also must be able to receive instructions from architects and construction managers, and explain the job's progress to developers, lawyers, financiers, and government authorities.

Detail oriented. Surveyors must work with precision and accuracy because they produce legally binding documents.

Physical stamina. Surveyors traditionally work outdoors, often in rugged terrain. They must be able to walk long distances for long periods.

Problem-solving skills. Surveyors must figure out discrepancies between documents showing property lines and current conditions on the land. If there were changes in previous years, they must discover the reason behind them and reestablish property lines.

Time-management skills. Surveyors must be able to effectively plan their time and their team members' time on the job. This is critical when pressing deadlines exist or while working outside during winter months when daylight hours are short.

Visualization skills. Surveyors must be able to envision new buildings and altered terrain.

Pay

The median annual wage for surveyors was $57,050 in May 2014. The median wage is the wage at which half the workers in an occupation earned more than that amount and half earned less. The lowest 10 percent earned less than $32,740, and the highest 10 percent earned more than $93,370.

In May 2014, the median annual wages for surveyors in the top industries in which they worked were as follows:

Government	$65,790
Construction	59,570
Architectural, engineering, and related services	55,310

Job Outlook

Employment of surveyors is projected to decline 2 percent from 2014 to 2024. Advancements in surveying technology, such as robotic total stations, let surveyors complete more work in less

Employment Projections Data for Surveyors

Occupational Title	SOC Code	Employment, 2014	Projected Employment, 2024	Change, 2014–2024	
				Percent	Numeric
Surveyors	17-1022	44,300	43,400	-2	-900

Source: U.S. Bureau of Labor Statistics, Employment Projections Program

Similar Occupations. This table shows a list of occupations with job duties that are similar to those of surveyors.

Occupations	Entry-level Education	2014 Median Pay	Projected Job Growth	Average Annual Openings
Architects	Bachelor's degree	$74,520	7%	780
Cartographers and Photogrammetrists	Bachelor's degree	$60,930	29%	360
Civil Engineers	Bachelor's degree	$82,050	8%	2,360
Landscape Architects	Bachelor's degree	$64,570	5%	120
Surveying and Mapping Technicians	High school diploma or equivalent	$40,770	-8%	-430
Urban and Regional Planners	Master's degree	$66,940	6%	240

time, reducing the demand for surveyors. However, some surveyors will continue to be needed to certify boundary lines, work on resource extraction projects, and review sites for construction.

Job Prospects. Job opportunities for those with a bachelor's degree in surveying or a related field are expected to be good. Increased use of sophisticated technology and math has resulted in higher education requirements. As a result, those with the right combination of skills and a bachelor's degree from a school accredited by ABET will have the best job opportunities.

Demand for traditional surveying services is closely tied to construction activity, therefore job opportunities will vary by geographic region, and often depend on local economic conditions. When real estate sales and construction activity slow down, surveyors may face greater competition for jobs. However, because surveyors can work on many different types of projects, they may have steadier work than others in the industry when construction slows.

Contacts for More Information

For information about surveying, career opportunities, and licensure requirements, visit

- National Society of Professional Surveyors (www.nspsmo.org)
- National Council of Examiners for Engineering and Surveying (www.ncees.org)

For information about a career as a geodetic surveyor, visit

- American Association for Geodetic Surveying (www.aagsmo.org)

For a list of schools offering accredited programs, visit

- ABET (www.abet.org)

O*NET

- Surveyors (17-1022.00)
- Geodetic Surveyors (17-1022.01)

Arts and Design

Art Directors

- **2014 Median Pay** .... $85,610 per year
  $41.16 per hour
- **Typical Entry-Level Education** .... Bachelor's degree
- **Work Experience in a Related Occupation**............ 5 years or more
- **On-the-job Training** .... None
- **Number of Jobs, 2014** 74,600
- **Job Outlook, 2014–24** .... 2% (Slower than average)
- **Employment Change, 2014–24** 1,800

What Art Directors Do

Art directors are responsible for the visual style and images in magazines, newspapers, product packaging, and movie and television productions. They create the overall design and direct others who develop artwork or layouts.

Duties. Art directors typically do the following:

- Determine how best to represent a concept visually
- Determine which photographs, art, or other design elements to use
- Develop the overall look or style of a publication, an advertising campaign, or a theater, television, or film set
- Lead graphic designers, set and exhibit designers, or other design staff
- Review and approve designs, artwork, photography, and graphics developed by other staff members
- Talk to clients to develop an artistic approach and style
- Coordinate activities with other artistic and creative departments
- Develop detailed budgets and timelines
- Present designs to clients for approval

Art directors typically oversee the work of other designers and artists who produce images for television, film, live performances, advertisements, or video games. They determine the overall style in which a message is communicated visually to its audience. For each project, they articulate their vision to artists. The artists then create images, such as illustrations, graphics, photographs, or charts and graphs, or design stage and movie sets, according to the art director's vision.

Art directors work with art and design staffs in advertising agencies, public relations firms, and book, magazine, or newspaper publishers to create designs and layouts. They also work with producers and directors of theater, television, or movie productions to oversee set designs. Their work requires them to understand the design elements of projects, inspire other creative workers, and keep projects on budget and on time. Sometimes they are responsible for developing budgets and timelines.

The following are some specifics of what art directors do in different industries:

In publishing, art directors typically oversee the page layout of catalogs, newspapers, or magazines. They also choose the cover art for books and periodicals. Often, this work includes publications for the Internet, so art directors oversee production of the websites used for publication.

Art directors determine which photographs, art, or other design elements to use.

In advertising and public relations, art directors ensure that their clients' desired message and image are conveyed to consumers. Art directors are responsible for the overall visual aspects of an advertising or media campaign and coordinate the work of other artistic or design staff, such as graphic designers.

In movie production, art directors collaborate with directors to determine what sets will be needed for the film and what style or look the sets should have. They hire and supervise a staff of assistant art directors or set designers to complete designs.

Work Environment

Art directors held about 74,600 jobs in 2014. The industries that employed the most art directors were as follows:

Advertising, public relations, and related services	15%
Newspaper, periodical, book, and directory publishers	5
Specialized design services	4
Motion picture and video industries	3
Retail trade, except motor vehicle and parts dealers, food and beverage stores, and general merchandise stores	2

About half of art directors were self-employed in 2014. Even though the majority of art directors are self-employed, they must still collaborate with designers or other staff on visual effects or marketing teams. Art directors usually work in a fast-paced office environment, and they often work under pressure to meet strict deadlines.

Work Schedules. Most art directors worked full time in 2014.

Education/Training

Art directors need at least a bachelor's degree in an art or design subject and previous work experience. Depending on the industry, they may have worked as graphic designers, fine artists, editors, or photographers, or in another art or design occupation before becoming art directors.

Median Annual Wages, May 2014

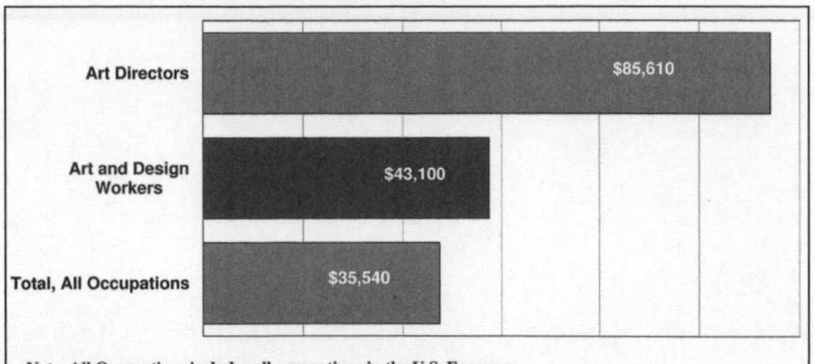

Note: All Occupations includes all occupations in the U.S. Economy.
Source: U.S. Bureau of Labor Statistics, Occupational Employment Statistics

Percent Change in Employment, Projected 2014–2024

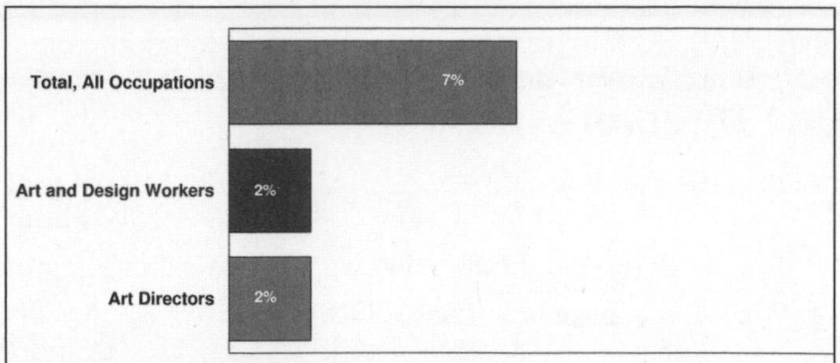

Note: All Occupations includes all occupations in the U.S. Economy.
Source: U.S. Bureau of Labor Statistics, Office of Occupational Statistics and Employment Projections

Education. Many art directors start out in another art-related occupation, such as fine artists or photographers. Work experience in art or design occupations develops an art director's ability to visually communicate to a specific audience creatively and effectively. They gain the appropriate education for that occupation, usually by earning a Bachelor of Arts or Bachelor of Fine Arts degree.

To supplement their work experience in those occupations and show their ability to take on a more creative or a more managerial role, some complete a Master of Fine Arts (MFA) degree.

Work Experience in a Related Occupation. Most art directors work 5 years or more in another occupation before becoming art directors. Depending upon the industry, they may work as graphic designers, fine artists, editors, photographers, or in another art or design occupation before becoming art directors.

For many artists, including art directors, developing a portfolio—a collection of an artist's work that demonstrates his or her styles and abilities—is essential. Managers, clients, and others look at artists' portfolios when they are deciding whether to hire an employee or contract for an art project.

Important Qualities

Communication skills. Art directors must be able to listen to and speak with staff and clients to ensure that they understand employees' ideas and clients' desires for advertisements, publications, or movie sets.

Creativity. Art directors must be able to come up with interesting and innovative ideas to develop advertising campaigns, set designs, or layout options.

Leadership skills. Art directors must be able to organize, direct, and motivate other artists. They need to articulate their visions to artists and oversee the work as it progresses.

Resourcefulness. Art directors must be able to adapt their latest designs to the changing technology used in their industry.

Time-management skills. Balancing competing priorities and multiple projects while meeting strict deadlines is critical for art directors.

Pay

The median annual wage for art directors was $85,610 in May 2014. The median wage is the wage at which half the workers in an occupation earned more than that amount and half earned less. The lowest 10 percent earned less than $45,060, and the highest 10 percent earned more than $168,040.

In May 2014, the median annual wages for art directors in the top industries in which they worked were as follows:

Motion picture and video industries	$101,080
Specialized design services	93,590
Advertising, public relations, and related services	89,060
Newspaper, periodical, book, and directory publishers	69,340
Retail trade, except motor vehicle and parts dealers, food and beverage stores, and general merchandise stores	65,320

Job Outlook

Employment of art directors is projected to grow 2 percent from 2014 to 2024, slower than the average for all occupations. Art directors will continue to be needed to oversee the work of graphic designers, illustrators, photographers, and others engaged in artwork or layout design.

Employment of art directors is projected to decline in the publishing industry from 2014 to 2024. Growth may decline as traditional print publications lose ground to other media forms, although some growth may occur as the number of electronic magazines and Internet-based publications increases. Rather than focusing on the print layout of images and text, art directors for newspapers and magazines will increasingly design for web and mobile platforms.

Job Prospects. Strong competition for jobs is expected as many talented designers and artists seek to move into art director positions. Prospective art directors with a strong understanding of creating designs that are intuitive to the user will have better prospects working with interactive digital platforms. Workers with a good portfolio, which demonstrates strong visual design and conceptual work across all multimedia platforms, will have the best prospects.

Employment Projections Data for Art Directors

Occupational Title	SOC Code	Employment, 2014	Projected Employment, 2024	Change, 2014–2024 Percent	Change, 2014–2024 Numeric
Art directors	27-1011	74,600	76,400	2	1,800

Source: U.S. Bureau of Labor Statistics, Employment Projections Program

Similar Occupations. This table shows a list of occupations with job duties that are similar to those of art directors.

Occupations	Entry-level Education	2014 Median Pay	Projected Job Growth	Average Annual Openings
Craft and Fine Artists	See Education/Training	$44,400	2%	90
Fashion Designers	Bachelor's degree	$64,030	3%	70
Graphic Designers	Bachelor's degree	$45,900	1%	360
Industrial Designers	Bachelor's degree	$64,620	2%	80
Multimedia Artists and Animators	Bachelor's degree	$63,630	6%	390
Photographers	High school diploma or equivalent	$30,490	3%	390
Writers and Authors	Bachelor's degree	$58,850	2%	310

Contacts for More Information

For more information about art directors in advertising, public relations, or publishing, visit

➤ Art Directors Club (www.adcglobal.org)

For more information about art directors in film and television, visit

➤ Art Directors Guild (www.adg.org)

O*NET

➤ Art Directors (27-1011.00)

Craft and Fine Artists

- **2014 Median Pay** .... $44,400 per year $21.35 per hour
- **Typical Entry-Level Education** .... See Education/Training
- **Work Experience in a Related Occupation** .... None
- **On-the-job Training** .... Long-term on-the-job training
- **Number of Jobs, 2014** 50,300
- **Job Outlook, 2014–24** .... 2% (Slower than average)
- **Employment Change, 2014–24** 900

What Craft and Fine Artists Do

Craft artists create handmade objects, such as pottery, glassware, textiles, and other objects that are designed to be functional. Fine artists, including painters, sculptors, and illustrators, create original works of art for their aesthetic value, rather than for a functional one.

Duties. Craft and fine artists typically do the following:

- Use techniques such as knitting, weaving, glassblowing, painting, drawing, and sculpting
- Develop creative ideas or new methods for making art
- Create sketches, templates, or models to guide their work
- Select which materials to use on the basis of color, texture, strength, and other qualities
- Shape, join, or cut materials for a final product
- Use visual techniques, such as composition, color, space, and perspective, to produce desired artistic effects
- Develop portfolios highlighting their artistic styles and abilities to show to gallery owners and others interested in their work
- Display their work at auctions, craft fairs, galleries, museums, and online marketplaces
- Complete grant proposal and applications to obtain financial support for projects

Artists create objects that are beautiful, thought provoking, and sometimes shocking. They often strive to communicate ideas or feelings through their art.

Craft artists work with many different materials, including ceramics, glass, textiles, wood, metal, and paper, to create unique pieces of art, such as pottery, quilts, stained glass, furniture, jewelry, and clothing. Many craft artists also use fine-art techniques—for example, painting, sketching, and printing—to add finishing touches to their products.

Fine artists typically display their work in museums, in commercial or nonprofit art galleries, at craft fairs, in corporate collections, on the Internet, and in private homes. Some of their artwork may be commissioned (requested by a client), but most is sold by the artist or through private art galleries or dealers. The artist, gallery, and dealer together decide in advance how much of the proceeds from the sale each will keep.

Most craft and fine artists spend their time and effort selling their artwork to potential customers and building a reputation. In addition to selling their artwork, many artists have at least one other job to support their craft or art careers.

Some artists work in museums or art galleries as art directors or as archivists, curators, or museum workers, planning and setting up exhibits. Others teach craft or art classes or conduct workshops in schools or in their own studios. For more information on workers who teach art classes, see the profiles on kindergarten and elementary school teachers, middle school teachers, high school teachers, and postsecondary teachers.

Craft and fine artists specialize in one or more types of art. The following are examples of types of craft and fine artists:

Cartoonists draw political, advertising, comic, and sports cartoons. Some cartoonists work with others who create the idea or story and write captions. Some create plots and write captions themselves. Most cartoonists have comic, critical, or dramatic talents, in addition to drawing skills.

Ceramic artists shape, form, and mold artworks out of clay, often using a potter's wheel and other tools. They glaze and fire pieces in kilns, which are large, special furnaces that dry and harden the clay.

Fiber artists use fabric, yarn, or other natural and synthetic fibers to weave, knit, crochet, or sew textile art. They may use a loom to weave fabric, needles to knit or crochet yarn, or a sewing machine to join pieces of fabric for quilts or other handicrafts.

Fine-art painters paint landscapes, portraits, and other subjects in a variety of styles, ranging from realistic to abstract. They may use one or more media, such as watercolors, oil paints, or acrylics.

Furniture makers cut, sand, join, and finish wood and other materials to make handcrafted furniture. For information about other workers who assemble wood furniture, see the profile on woodworkers.

Glass artists process glass in a variety of ways—such as by blowing, shaping, or joining it—to create artistic pieces. Specific processes used include glassblowing, lampworking, and staining glass. Some of these processes require the use of kilns, ovens, and other equipment and tools that bend glass at high temperatures. These workers also decorate glass objects, such as by etching or painting.

Illustrators create pictures for books, magazines, and other publications and for commercial products, such as textiles, wrapping paper, stationery, greeting cards, and calendars. Increasingly, illustrators are using computers in their work. They might draw in pen and pencil and then scan the image into a computer program to be colored in, or they might use a special pen to draw images directly onto the computer.

Jewelry artists use metals, stones, beads, and other materials to make objects for personal adornment, such as earrings or necklaces. For more information about other workers who create jewelry, see the profile on jewelers and precious stone and metal workers.

Medical and scientific illustrators combine drawing skills with knowledge of biology or other sciences. Medical illustrators work with computers or with pen and paper to create images of human anatomy and surgical procedures, as well as three-dimensional models and animations. Scientific illustrators draw animal and plant life, atomic and molecular structures, and geologic and planetary formations. These illustrations are used in medical and scientific publications and in audiovisual presentations for teaching purposes. Some medical and scientific illustrators work for lawyers, producing exhibits for court cases.

Public artists create large paintings, sculptures, and installations that are meant to be seen in public spaces. These works are typically displayed in parks, museum grounds, train stations, and other public areas.

Printmakers create images on a silk screen, woodblock, lithography stone, metal etching plate, or other types of matrices. A printing press or hand press then creates the final work of art, inking and transferring the matrix to a piece of paper.

Sculptors design and shape three-dimensional works of art, either by molding and joining materials such as clay, glass, plastic, and metal or by cutting and carving forms from a block of plaster, wood, or stone. Some sculptors combine various materials to create mixed-media installations. For example, some incorporate light, sound, and motion into their works.

Sketch artists, who are a particular type of illustrator, often create likenesses of subjects with pencil, charcoal, or pastels. Their sketches are used by law enforcement agencies to help identify suspects, by the news media to show courtroom scenes, and by individual customers for their own enjoyment.

Tattoo artists use stencils and draw by hand to create original images and text on the skin of their clients. With specialized needles, these artists use a variety of styles and colors based on their clients' preferences.

Video artists shoot and record experimental video that is typically shown in a recurring loop in art galleries, museums, or performance spaces. These artists sometimes use multiple monitors or create unusual spaces for the video to be shown.

Many artists receive formal training in their specialty.

Work Environment

Craft and fine artists held about 50,300 jobs in 2014.

About half of craft and fine artists were self-employed in 2014; others were employed in various industries.

Some artists work for companies that manufacture glass or clay products or for museums, historical sites, or similar institutions. Some fine artists are employed by motion picture and video production companies, by schools, or by publishers of periodicals. Other types of artists and related workers work for the federal government or for advertising and public relations firms.

Many artists work in fine-art or commercial art studios located in office buildings, warehouses, or lofts. Others work in private studios in their homes. Some artists share studio space, where they also may exhibit their work.

Studios are usually well lit and ventilated. However, artists may be exposed to fumes from glue, paint, ink, and other materials. They may also have to deal with dust or other residue from filings, splattered paint, or spilled cleaning and other fluids. Artists often wear protective gear, such as breathing masks and goggles, in order to remain safe from exposure to harmful materials. Ceramic and glass artists must use caution when they operate equipment and tools that can get very hot, such as kilns.

Work Schedules. Most craft and fine artists work full time, although part-time and variable work schedules are also common. Many hold another job in addition to their work as an artist. During busy periods, artists may work additional hours to meet deadlines. Self-employed artists can set their own hours.

Education/Training

Most fine artists earn a bachelor's or master's degree in fine arts in order to improve their skills and job prospects. A formal educational credential is typically not needed for craft artists. Craft and fine artists improve their skills through practice and repetition.

Education. Most fine artists pursue postsecondary education to earn degrees that can improve their skills and job prospects. A formal educational credential is typically not needed for craft artists. However, it is difficult to gain adequate artistic skills without some formal education. High school classes such as art, shop, and home economics can teach prospective craft artists some of the basic skills they will need, such as drawing, woodworking, and sewing.

A large number of colleges and universities offer bachelor's and master's degrees in fine arts. In addition to offering studio art and art history, postsecondary programs may include core subjects, such as English, marketing, social science, and natural science. Independent schools of art and design also offer postsecondary education programs, which can lead to a certificate in an art-related specialty or to an associate's, bachelor's, or master's degree in fine arts.

In 2014, the National Association of Schools of Art and Design (NASAD) accredited approximately 320 postsecondary institutions with programs in art and design. Most of these schools award a degree in art.

Medical illustrators must have a demonstrated artistic ability and a detailed knowledge of human and animal anatomy, living organisms, and surgical and medical procedures. They usually need a bachelor's degree that combines art and premedical courses. Medical illustrators may choose to get a master's degree in medical illustration. Three accredited schools offer this degree in the United States.

Portfolios are essential, because art directors, clients, and others look at them in deciding whether to hire an artist or to buy the artist's work. In addition to compiling a physical portfolio, many artists choose to create a portfolio online so that potential buyers and clients can view their work on the Internet.

Bachelor's or higher degrees in fine arts or arts administration are usually necessary for management or administrative positions in government, management positions in private foundations, and teaching positions in colleges and universities. Those who teach fine arts at public elementary or secondary schools usually have a teaching certificate in addition to a bachelor's degree. For more information on workers who teach art classes, see the profiles on kindergarten and elementary school teachers, middle school teachers, high school teachers, and postsecondary teachers.

Training. Craft and fine artists improve their skills through practice and repetition. They can train in several ways other than—or in addition to—formal schooling. Craft and fine artists can train with simpler projects before attempting something more ambitious.

Some artists learn on the job from more experienced artists. Others attend noncredit classes or workshops or take private lessons, which may be offered in artists' studios or at community colleges, art centers, galleries, museums, or other art-related institutions.

Still other artists work closely with other artists or assist them on either a formal or an informal basis. Formal arrangements may include internships or apprenticeship programs. Artists hired by firms often start with relatively routine work. While doing this work, they may observe other artists and practice their own skills.

Important Qualities

Artistic ability. Craft and fine artists create artwork and other objects that are visually appealing or thought provoking. This endeavor usually requires significant skill and attention to detail in one or more art forms.

Business skills. Craft and fine artists must promote themselves and their art to build a reputation and to sell their art. They often study the market for their crafts or artwork to increase their understanding of what potential customers might want. Many craft and fine artists sell their work on the Internet, so developing an online presence is an important part of their art sales.

Creativity. Artists must have active imaginations to develop new and original ideas for their work.

Customer-service skills. Craft and fine artists, especially those who sell their work themselves, must be good at dealing with customers and potential buyers.

Dexterity. Most artists work with their hands and must be good at manipulating tools and materials to create their art.

Interpersonal skills. Artists often must interact with many people, including coworkers, gallery owners, and the public.

Advancement. Craft and fine artists advance professionally as their work circulates and as they establish a reputation for their particular style. Many of the most successful artists continually develop new ideas, and their work often evolves over time.

Many artists do freelance work while continuing to hold a full-time job until they are established as professional artists. Others freelance part time while still in school, to develop experience and to build a portfolio of published work.

Freelance artists try to develop a set of clients who regularly contract for work. Some freelance artists are widely recognized for their skill in a specialty, such as illustrating children's books or cartooning. These artists may earn high incomes and can choose the type of project they undertake.

Pay

The median annual wage for craft and fine artists was $44,400 in May 2014. The median wage is the wage at which half the workers in an occupation earned more than that amount and half earned

Median Annual Wages, May 2014

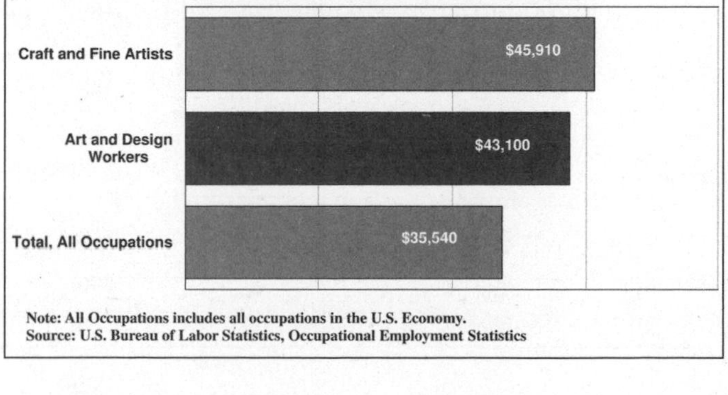

Note: All Occupations includes all occupations in the U.S. Economy.
Source: U.S. Bureau of Labor Statistics, Occupational Employment Statistics

Percent Change in Employment, Projected 2014–2024

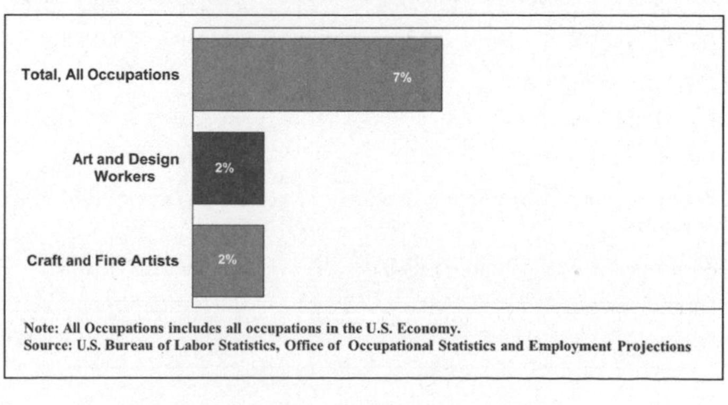

Note: All Occupations includes all occupations in the U.S. Economy.
Source: U.S. Bureau of Labor Statistics, Office of Occupational Statistics and Employment Projections

Employment Projections Data for Craft and Fine Artists

Occupational Title	SOC Code	Employment, 2014	Projected Employment, 2024	Change, 2014–2024 Percent	Change, 2014–2024 Numeric
Craft and fine artists	—	50,300	51,200	2	900
Craft artists	27-1012	10,600	10,600	1	100
Fine artists, including painters, sculptors, and illustrators	27-1013	26,300	27,100	3	800
Artists and related workers, all other	27-1019	13,400	13,500	0	100

Source: U.S. Bureau of Labor Statistics, Employment Projections Program

less. The lowest 10 percent earned less than $18,850, and the highest 10 percent earned more than $93,260.

Median annual wages for craft and fine artists in May 2014 were as follows:

Artists and related workers, all other	$58,250
Fine artists, including painters, sculptors, and illustrators	43,890
Craft artists	31,080

Job Outlook

Employment of craft and fine artists is projected to grow 2 percent from 2014 to 2024, slower than the average for all occupations.

Employment growth of artists depends in large part on the overall state of the economy, because people usually make art purchases when they can afford to spend the money. During good economic times, more people and businesses are interested in buying artwork; during economic downturns, they generally buy less. However, there is always some demand for art by private collectors and museums.

Job growth for craft artists may be limited by the sale of inexpensive, mass-produced items designed to look like handmade American crafts. A continued interest in locally made products and crafted goods will likely offset some of these employment losses.

Demand for illustrators who work on a computer is likely to increase as media companies use more detailed images and backgrounds in their designs. Illustrators and cartoonists who work in publishing may see their job opportunities decline as traditional print publications lose ground to other media forms. However, new opportunities are expected to arise as the number of electronic magazines and Internet-based publications continues to grow.

Job Prospects. Competition for jobs as craft and fine artists is expected to be strong because there are more qualified candidates than available jobs. Competition is likely to grow among independent artists given that many of them sell their work in the same online marketplaces. In addition, competition among artists for the privilege of having their work shown in galleries is expected to remain intense.

Because the demand for artwork depends on consumers having extra income to spend, many of these artists will find that their income changes as does the overall economy. Only the most successful craft and fine artists receive major commissions for their work.

Despite the competition, studios, galleries, and individual clients are always on the lookout for artists who display outstanding talent, creativity, and style. Talented individuals who have developed a mastery of artistic techniques and marketing skills are likely to have the best job prospects.

Contacts for More Information

For more about art and design and a list of accredited college-level programs, visit

➤ National Association of Schools of Art and Design (http://nasad.arts-accredit.org)

For more information on careers in the craft arts and for a list of schools and workshops, visit

➤ American Craft Council (www.craftcouncil.org)

For more information on careers in the arts, visit

➤ New York Foundation for the Arts (www.nyfa.org)

For more information on careers in illustration, visit

➤ Society of Illustrators (www.societyillustrators.org)

➤ For more information on careers in medical illustration, visit the Association of Medical Illustrators (www.ami.org)

Similar Occupations. This table shows a list of occupations with job duties that are similar to those of craft and fine artists.

Occupations	Entry-level Education	2014 Median Pay	Projected Job Growth	Average Annual Openings
Archivists, Curators, and Museum Workers	See Education/Training	$46,300	7%	210
Art Directors	Bachelor's degree	$85,610	2%	180
Fashion Designers	Bachelor's degree	$64,030	3%	70
Graphic Designers	Bachelor's degree	$45,900	1%	360
Industrial Designers	Bachelor's degree	$64,620	2%	80
Jewelers and Precious Stone and Metal Workers	High school diploma or equivalent	$36,870	-11%	-450
Multimedia Artists and Animators	Bachelor's degree	$63,630	6%	390
Photographers	High school diploma or equivalent	$30,490	3%	390
Woodworkers	High school diploma or equivalent	$28,900	-1%	-140

- For information on grant-funding programs and other local resources for artists, contact your state arts agency. A list of these agencies is available from the National Assembly of State Arts Agencies (www.nasaa-arts.org)

For more information on how the federal government awards grants for art, visit

- National Endowment for the Arts (http://arts.gov)

O*NET

- Craft Artists (27-1012.00)
- Fine Artists, Including Painters, Sculptors, and Illustrators (27-1013.00)
- Artists and Related Workers, All Other (27-1019.00)

Fashion Designers

- **2014 Median Pay** .... $64,030 per year $30.78 per hour
- **Typical Entry-Level Education** .... Bachelor's degree
- **Work Experience in a Related Occupation** .... None
- **On-the-job Training** .... None
- **Number of Jobs, 2014** 23,100
- **Job Outlook, 2014–24** .... 3% (Slower than average)
- **Employment Change, 2014–24** 700

What Fashion Designers Do

Fashion designers create original clothing, accessories, and footwear. They sketch designs, select fabrics and patterns, and give instructions on how to make the products they designed.

Duties. Fashion designers typically do the following:

- Study fashion trends and anticipate designs that will appeal to consumers
- Decide on a theme for a collection
- Use computer-aided design (CAD) programs to create designs
- Visit manufacturers or trade shows to get samples of fabric
- Select fabrics, embellishments, colors, or a style for each garment or accessory
- Work with other designers or team members to create prototype designs
- Present design ideas to the creative director or showcase them in fashion or trade shows
- Market designs to clothing retailers or directly to consumers
- Oversee the final production of their designs

Larger apparel companies typically employ a team of designers headed by a creative designer. Some fashion designers specialize in clothing, footwear, or accessory design; others create designs in all three fashion categories.

For some fashion designers, the first step in creating a new design is researching current fashion and making predictions about future trends using trend reports published by fashion industry trade groups. Other fashion designers create collections from inspirations they get from their regular surroundings, from the cultures they have experienced and places they have visited, or from various art media that inspire them.

After they have an initial idea, fashion designers try out various fabrics and produce a prototype, often with less expensive material than will be used in the final product. They work with models to see how the design will look and adjust the designs as needed.

Although most designers first sketch their designs by hand, many now also sketch their ideas digitally with computer-aided design (CAD) programs. CAD allows designers to see their work on virtual models. They can try out different colors, design, and shapes while making adjustments more easily than they can when working with real fabric on real people.

Designers produce samples with the actual materials that will be used in manufacturing. Samples that get good responses from editors or trade and fashion shows are then manufactured and sold to consumers.

Although the design process may vary by specialty, in general it takes 6 months from initial design concept to final production, when either the spring or fall collection is released. Some companies may release new designs as frequently as every month, in addition to releasing designs during the spring and fall.

The Internet and e-commerce allow fashion designers to offer their products outside of traditional brick-and-mortar stores. These designers can ship directly to the consumer, without having to invest in a physical shop to showcase their product lines.

The following are examples of types of fashion designers:

Clothing designers create and help produce men's, women's, and children's apparel, including casual wear, suits, sportswear, evening wear, outerwear, maternity clothing, and intimate apparel.

Footwear designers create and help produce different styles of shoes and boots. As new materials, such as lightweight synthetic materials used in shoe soles, become available, footwear designers produce new designs that combine comfort, form, and function.

Accessory designers design and produce items such as handbags, suitcases, belts, scarves, hats, hosiery, and eyewear.

Costume designers design costumes for the performing arts and for motion picture and television productions. They research the styles worn during the period in which the performance takes place, or they work with directors to select and create appropriate attire. They also must stay within the costume budget for the particular production.

Work Environment

Fashion designers held about 23,100 jobs in 2014. The industries that employed the most fashion designers were as follows:

Fashion designers study trends and design clothing and accessories for consumers.

Apparel, piece goods, and notions merchant wholesalers	32%
Apparel manufacturing	13
Management of companies and enterprises	10
Specialized design services	6

More fashion designers work for wholesalers or manufacturers than in any other industries. These wholesalers and manufacturers sell lines of apparel and accessories to retailers or other marketers for distribution to individual stores, catalog companies, or online retailers. Many establishments employ in-house designers. Although the brands may be familiar to many consumers, the individual designers are largely unknown.

About 1 in 4 fashion designers were self-employed in 2014. They typically design high-fashion garments and one-of-a-kind apparel on an individualized or custom basis. Self-employed fashion designers who are able to set up their own independent clothing lines often already have experience and a strong understanding of the industry. In some cases, a self-employed fashion designer may have a clothing line that bears his or her name.

Most designers travel several times a year to trade and fashion shows to learn about the latest fashion trends. Designers also sometimes travel to other countries to meet suppliers of materials and manufacturers who produce the final products.

Most fashion designers work in New York and California.

Work Schedules. Most fashion designers work full time. Occasionally, fashion designers work many hours to meet production deadlines or prepare for fashion shows. Designers who freelance generally work under a contract and tend to work longer hours and adjust their workday to their clients' schedules and deadlines.

Education/Training

Most fashion designers have a bachelor's degree in a related field, such as fashion design or fashion merchandising. Employers usually seek applicants with creativity, as well as a good technical understanding of the production process for clothing, accessories, or footwear.

Education. Most fashion designers have a bachelor's degree in fashion design or fashion merchandising. In these programs, they learn about textiles and fabrics and how to use computer-aided design (CAD) technology. They also are able to work on projects that can be added to their portfolio, which showcases their designs.

For many artists, including fashion designers, developing a portfolio—a collection of design ideas that demonstrates their styles and abilities—is essential because employers rely heavily on a designer's portfolio in deciding whether to hire the individual. For employers, it is an opportunity to gauge talent and creativity. Students studying fashion design often have opportunities to enter their designs in student or amateur contests, helping them to develop their portfolios.

The National Association of Schools of Art and Design accredits approximately 320 postsecondary institutions with programs in art and design, and many of these schools award degrees in fashion design. Many schools require students to have completed basic art and design courses before they enter a program. Applicants usually have to submit sketches and other examples of their artistic ability.

Other Experience. Fashion designers often gain their initial experience in the fashion industry through internships or by working as an assistant designer. Internships provide aspiring fashion designers an opportunity to experience the design process, building their knowledge of textiles and colors and how the industry works.

Advancement. Experienced designers may advance to chief designer, design department head, creative director, or another supervisory position in which they oversee certain fashion lines or company brands.

Some experienced designers may start their own design company or sell their designs in their own retail stores. A few of the most successful designers work for high-fashion design houses that offer personalized design services to their clients.

Important Qualities

Artistic ability. Fashion designers sketch their initial design ideas, which are used later to create prototypes. Designers must be able to express their vision for the design through illustration.

Communication skills. Fashion designers often work in teams throughout the design process and therefore must be effective in communicating with their team members. For example, they may need to give instructions to sewers regarding how a garment should be constructed.

Computer skills. Fashion designers use technology to design. They must be able to use computer-aided design (CAD) programs and be familiar with graphics editing software.

Creativity. Fashion designers work with a variety of fabrics, shapes, and colors. Their ideas must be unique, functional, and stylish.

Decision-making skills. Because they often work in teams, fashion designers are exposed to many ideas. They must be able to decide which ideas to incorporate into their designs.

Detail oriented. Fashion designers must have a good eye for small differences in color and other details that can make a design successful.

Pay

The median annual wage for fashion designers was $64,030 in May 2014. The median wage is the wage at which half the workers in an

Median Annual Wages, May 2014

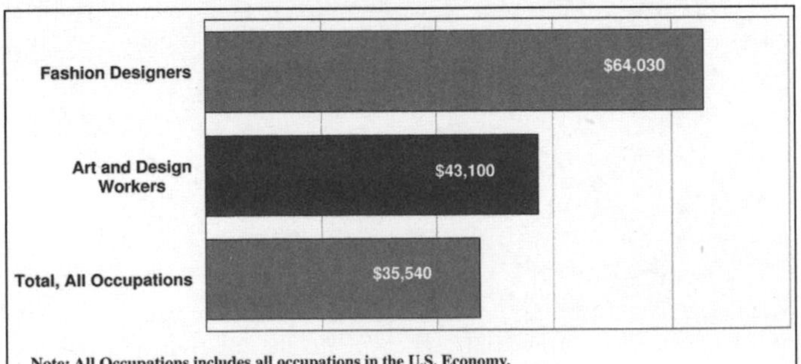

Note: All Occupations includes all occupations in the U.S. Economy.
Source: U.S. Bureau of Labor Statistics, Occupational Employment Statistics

Percent Change in Employment, Projected 2014–2024

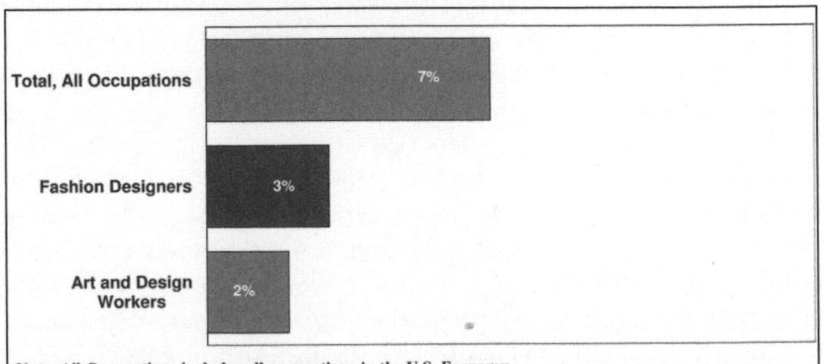

Note: All Occupations includes all occupations in the U.S. Economy.
Source: U.S. Bureau of Labor Statistics, Office of Occupational Statistics and Employment Projections

Employment Projections Data for Fashion Designers

Occupational Title	SOC Code	Employment, 2014	Projected Employment, 2024	Change, 2014–2024 Percent	Change, 2014–2024 Numeric
Fashion designers	27-1022	23,100	23,800	3	700

Source: U.S. Bureau of Labor Statistics, Employment Projections Program

Similar Occupations. This table shows a list of occupations with job duties that are similar to those of fashion designers.

Occupations	Entry-level Education	2014 Median Pay	Projected Job Growth	Average Annual Openings
Art Directors	Bachelor's degree	$85,610	2%	180
Buyers and Purchasing Agents	Bachelor's degree	$58,520	2%	720
Floral Designers	High school diploma or equivalent	$24,750	-3%	-200
Graphic Designers	Bachelor's degree	$45,900	1%	360
Industrial Designers	Bachelor's degree	$64,620	2%	80
Jewelers and Precious Stone and Metal Workers	High school diploma or equivalent	$36,870	-11%	-450
Models	No formal educational credential	$19,970	0%	0

occupation earned more than that amount and half earned less. The lowest 10 percent earned less than $33,260, and the highest 10 percent earned more than $129,380.

In May 2014, the median annual wages for fashion designers in the top industries in which they worked were as follows:

Management of companies and enterprises $80,470
Apparel manufacturing 67,080
Apparel, piece goods, and notions merchant wholesalers 62,120
Specialized design services 57,020

Earnings in this occupation can vary widely with experience, the employer, and the designer's reputation. Starting salaries in fashion design tend to be very low. Salaried fashion designers usually earn higher and more stable incomes than self-employed, freelance designers. However, a few of the most successful self-employed fashion designers earn many times the salary of the highest paid salaried designers.

Job Outlook

Employment of fashion designers is projected to grow 3 percent from 2014 to 2024, slower than the average for all occupations.

Most apparel continues to be produced internationally. As a result, employment of fashion designers in the apparel manufacturing industry is projected to decline 47 percent over the projection period. Declining employment in the apparel manufacturing industry is slowing the overall employment growth of fashion designers.

However, employment of fashion designers in the wholesale apparel industry is projected to increase 17 percent over the projection period. Retailers are selling more fashion-inspired clothing which increases the demand for fashion designers to design clothing and accessories for the mass market and everyday wear.

Job Prospects. Those with formal education in fashion design, excellent portfolios, and industry experience will have the best job prospects. However, strong competition for jobs is expected because of the large number of people who seek employment as fashion designers and the relatively few positions available.

In addition, it may be necessary for some fashion designers to relocate because employment opportunities for fashion designers are concentrated in New York and California.

Contacts for More Information

For more information about careers in fashion design, visit

➤ Council of Fashion Designers of America (www.cfda.com)

For more information about educational programs in fashion design, visit

➤ National Association of Schools of Art and Design (http://nasad.arts-accredit.org)

O*NET

➤ Fashion Designers (27-1022.00)

Floral Designers

- **2014 Median Pay** .... $24,750 per year $11.90 per hour
- **Typical Entry-Level Education** .... High school diploma or equivalent
- **Work Experience in a Related Occupation** .... None
- **On-the-job Training** ..... Moderate-term on-the-job training
- **Number of Jobs, 2014** 58,700
- **Job Outlook, 2014–24** .... -3% (Decline)
- **Employment Change, 2014–24** .... -2,000

What Floral Designers Do

Floral designers, also called florists, cut and arrange live, dried, and silk flowers and greenery to make decorative displays. They also help customers select flowers, containers, ribbons, and other accessories.

Duties. Floral designers typically do the following:

- Grow flowers or order them from wholesalers, to ensure an adequate supply to meet customers' needs

- Determine the type of arrangement desired, the occasion, and the date, time, and location for delivery
- Recommend flowers and greenery for each arrangement in accordance with the customer's budget
- Design floral displays that evoke a particular sentiment or style
- Answer telephones, take orders, and wrap arrangements

Floral designers may create a single arrangement for a special occasion or design floral displays for rooms and open spaces for large-scale functions, such as weddings, funerals, or banquets. They use their sense of artistry and their knowledge of different types of flowers to choose the appropriate flowers for each occasion. Floral designers may also create single arrangements to serve a customer's emotional needs, helping the customers to relax. Floral designers need to know what flowers are in season and when they will be available.

Floral designers also need to know the properties of each flower. Some flowers, such as carnations, can last for many hours outside of water. Other flowers are more delicate and wilt more quickly. Some plants are poisonous to certain types of animals. For example, lilies are toxic to cats.

Floral designers must know the color varieties of each flower and the average size of each type of flower. They may calculate the number of flowers that will fit into a particular vase or how many rose petals are needed to cover a carpet.

Floral designers use their knowledge to recommend flowers and designs to customers. After the customer selects the flowers, the designer arranges them in a visually appealing display. The designer may include items such as stuffed animals or balloons or may use decorative vases when designing a floral arrangement.

Although more complex displays must be ordered in advance, designers often will create small bouquets or arrangements while customers wait. When they are responsible for floral arrangements for a special occasion, such as a wedding or banquet, floral designers usually set up the floral decorations just before the event, then tear them down afterwards. Some designers work with event planners on a contract basis when creating arrangements for events such as weddings.

Floral designers also give customers instructions on how to care for flowers, including what the ideal temperature is and how often the water should be changed. For cut flowers, floral designers often will provide flower food to the customer.

Floral designers also order new flowers from suppliers. They process newly arrived flowers by stripping leaves that would be below the water line. They cut new flowers, mix flower food solutions, fill floral containers with the food solutions, and sanitize workspaces. They keep most flowers in cool display cases so that the flowers stay fresh and live longer.

Some designers have long-term agreements with hotels and restaurants or the owners of office buildings and private homes to replace old flowers with new flower arrangements on a recurring schedule—usually daily, weekly, or monthly—to keep areas looking fresh and appealing. Some work with interior designers in creating displays.

Floral designers who are self-employed or have their own shop also must do business tasks. They must keep track of income, expenses, and taxes. Some hire and supervise staff to help with those tasks.

Work Environment

Floral designers held about 58,700 jobs in 2014. The industries that employed the most floral designers were as follows:

Most floral designers work in small independent floral shops.

Florists	49%
Grocery stores	13
Miscellaneous nondurable goods merchant wholesalers	2
Sporting goods, hobby, and musical instrument stores	2
Lawn and garden equipment and supplies stores	2

Floral designers in retail businesses can expect walk-in customers, as well as customer orders placed over the telephone or over the Internet, or transmitted electronically by other florists. Some floral designers who work on a contract basis when creating arrangements for events such as weddings have to travel to the various locations of the events.

About 1 in 4 floral designers were self-employed in 2014.

Work Schedules. Many floral designers work full time, although their hours may vary with the work setting.

Independent shops in downtown areas or business districts typically are open during business hours. Floral departments inside grocery stores or other stores in suburban locations and shopping malls may stay open longer.

Floral designers are busier at certain times of the year, such as holidays, than at other times. Because freshly cut flowers are perishable, most orders cannot be completed too far in advance. Therefore, designers often work additional hours just before and during holidays. In addition, many part-time and seasonal opportunities can be found around certain holidays, such as Christmas, Valentine's Day, and Mother's Day.

Education/Training

Most floral designers have a high school diploma or the equivalent and learn their skills on the job over the course of a few months.

Education. Most floral designers have a high school diploma or the equivalent. There are postsecondary programs that are useful for florists who want to start their own businesses. Programs in floral design and caring techniques for flowers are available through private floral schools, vocational schools, and community colleges. Most offer a certificate or diploma. Classes in flower and plant identification, floral design concepts, and advertising, as well as other business courses, plus experience working in a greenhouse are part of many certificate and diploma programs.

Some community colleges and universities offer associate's or bachelor's degree programs in floral design.

Training. New floral designers typically get hands-on experience working with an experienced floral designer. They may start by preparing simple flower arrangements and practicing the basics of

Median Annual Wages, May 2014

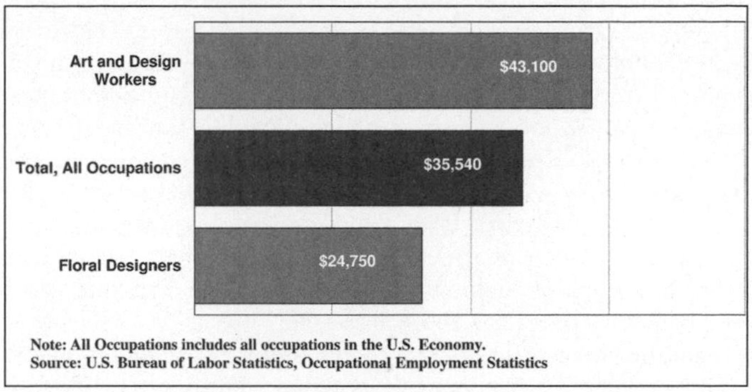

Percent Change in Employment, Projected 2014–2024

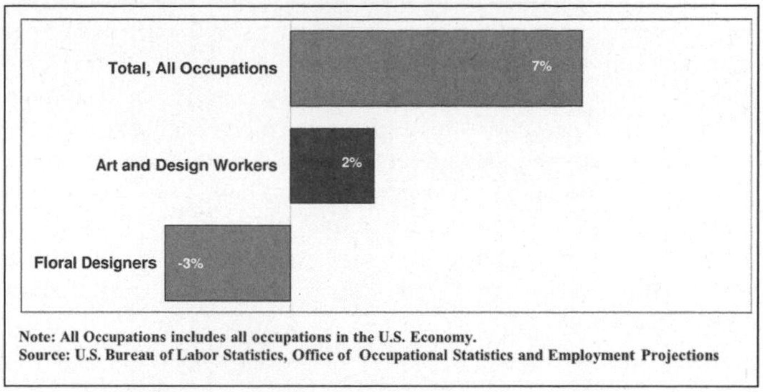

tying bows and ribbons, cutting stems to appropriate lengths, and learning about the proper handling and care of flowers. They also learn about the different types of flowers, their growth properties, and how to use them in more complex floral designs.

Licenses, Certifications, and Registrations. The American Institute of Floral Designers offers the Certified Floral Designer credential. Although certification in floral design is voluntary, it indicates a measure of achievement and expertise. To become certified, a floral designer must demonstrate a grasp of floral design knowledge gained through work experience or education.

Advancement. Taking formal floral design training can help people who are interested in opening their own business or in becoming a chief floral designer or supervisor.

Important Qualities

Artistic ability. Designers use their sense of style to develop aesthetically pleasing designs.

Creativity. Floral designers use their artistic abilities and knowledge of design to develop appropriate designs for different occasions. They also must be open to new ideas, because trends in floral design change quickly.

Customer-service skills. Floral designers spend a substantial part of their day interacting with customers and suppliers. They must be able to understand what a customer is looking for, explain options, and provide high-quality flowers and service.

Organizational skills. Floral designers need to be well organized, to keep the business operating smoothly and to ensure that orders are completed on time.

Pay

The median annual wage for floral designers was $24,750 in May 2014. The median wage is the wage at which half the workers in an occupation earned more than that amount and half earned less. The lowest 10 percent earned less than $17,920, and the highest 10 percent earned more than $37,660.

In May 2014, the median annual wages for floral designers in the top industries in which they worked were as follows:

Lawn and garden equipment and supplies stores	$27,140
Grocery stores	25,860
Sporting goods, hobby, and musical instrument stores	24,780
Florists	24,460
Miscellaneous nondurable goods merchant wholesalers	22,830

Job Outlook

Employment of floral designers is projected to decline 3 percent from 2014 to 2024. Many floral designers are employed in the florist industry, in which overall industry employment is projected to decline over the projection period.

Although demand for floral arrangements for events such as weddings, funerals, and anniversaries will continue, the need for floral designers is expected to decline with the number of florist

Employment Projections Data for Floral Designers

Occupational Title	SOC Code	Employment, 2014	Projected Employment, 2024	Change, 2014–2024 Percent	Change, 2014–2024 Numeric
Floral designers	27-1023	58,700	56,700	-3	-2,000

Source: U.S. Bureau of Labor Statistics, Employment Projections Program

Similar Occupations. This table shows a list of occupations with job duties that are similar to those of floral designers.

Occupations	Entry-level Education	2014 Median Pay	Projected Job Growth	Average Annual Openings
Craft and Fine Artists	See Education/Training	$44,400	2%	90
Fashion Designers	Bachelor's degree	$64,030	3%	70
Graphic Designers	Bachelor's degree	$45,900	1%	360
Interior Designers	Bachelor's degree	$48,400	4%	220
Meeting, Convention, and Event Planners	Bachelor's degree	$46,490	10%	990

shops in the industry. Orders made online from flower delivery services often are fulfilled by local florist shops. This arrangement can increase the number of orders florist shops receive but can also dampen the demand for additional floral shops as each florist shop becomes increasingly able to serve a wider area of customers.

In addition, grocery stores and general merchandise stores offer floral decorations and loose cut flowers. These stores can make it more convenient for customers to purchase the flowers, thus decreasing the number of trips people make to florist shops for floral decorations. As a result, employment of floral designers is projected to decline 11 percent in florist shops and grow 5 percent in grocery stores.

Job Prospects. Those with formal education in floral design will have better prospects.

Source: U.S. Bureau of Labor Statistics, Employment Projections Program

Contacts for More Information

For more information about becoming a Certified Floral Designer, visit

➤ American Institute of Floral Designers (www.aifd.org)

For more information about careers in floral design, visit

➤ Society of American Florists (www.safnow.org)

O*NET

➤ Floral Designers (27-1023.00)

Graphic Designers

- **2014 Median Pay** .... $45,900 per year
  $22.07 per hour
- **Typical Entry-Level Education** .... Bachelor's degree
- **Work Experience in a Related Occupation** .... None
- **On-the-job Training** .... None
- **Number of Jobs, 2014** 261,600
- **Job Outlook, 2014–24** .... 1% (Little or no change)
- **Employment Change, 2014–24** 3,600

What Graphic Designers Do

Graphic designers create visual concepts, using computer software or by hand, to communicate ideas that inspire, inform, and captivate consumers. They develop the overall layout and production design for various applications such as for advertisements, brochures, magazines, and corporate reports.

Duties. Graphic designers typically do the following:

- Meet with clients or the art director to determine the scope of a project
- Use digital illustration, photo-editing software, and layout software to create designs
- Create visual elements such as logos, original images, and illustrations that help deliver a desired message
- Design layouts and select colors, images, and typefaces to use
- Present design concepts to clients or art directors
- Incorporate changes recommended by clients or art directors into final designs
- Review designs for errors before printing or publishing them

Graphic designers combine art and technology to communicate ideas through images and the layout of websites and printed pages. They may use a variety of design elements to achieve artistic or decorative effects.

Graphic designers work with both text and images. They often select the type, font, size, color, and line length of headlines, headings, and text. Graphic designers also decide how images and text will go together on a print or webpage, including how much space each will have. When using text in layouts, graphic designers collaborate closely with writers who choose the words and decide whether the words will be put into paragraphs, lists, or tables. Through the use of images, text, and color, graphic designers can transform statistical data into visual graphics and diagrams, which can make complex ideas more accessible.

Graphic design is important to marketing and selling products, and is a critical component of brochures and logos. Therefore, graphic designers, also referred to as graphic artists or communication designers, often work closely with people in advertising and promotions, public relations, and marketing.

Frequently, designers specialize in a particular category or type of client. For example, some create the graphics used on retail products packaging, still others may work on the visual designs used on book jackets.

Graphic designers need to keep up to date with the latest software and computer technologies to remain competitive.

Some individuals with a background in graphic design teach in design schools, colleges, and universities. For more information, see the profile on postsecondary teachers.

Work Environment

Graphic designers held about 261,600 jobs in 2014. The industries that employed the most graphic designers were as follows:

Specialized design services	10%
Advertising, public relations, and related services	8
Newspaper, periodical, book, and directory publishers	7
Printing and related support activities	7
Wholesale trade	6

Graphic designers generally work in studios where they have access to drafting tables, computers, and the software necessary to create their designs. Although many graphic designers work independently, those who work for specialized graphic design firms often work as part of a design team. Many graphic designers collaborate with colleagues or work with clients on projects.

Work Schedules. Most graphic designers work full time, but schedules can vary depending on workloads and deadlines.

Graphic designers must be familiar with computer graphics and design software.

In 2014, about 1 in 5 graphic designers were self-employed. Graphic designers who are self-employed may need to adjust their workday to meet with clients in the evenings or on weekends. In addition, they may spend some of their time looking for new projects or competing with other designers for contracts.

Education/Training

Graphic designers usually need a bachelor's degree in graphic design or a related field. Candidates for graphic design positions should demonstrate their creativity and originality through a professional portfolio that features their best designs.

Education. A bachelor's degree in graphic design or a related field is usually required. However, those with a bachelor's degree in another field may pursue technical training in graphic design to meet most hiring qualifications.

The National Association of Schools of Art and Design accredits about 320 postsecondary colleges, universities, and independent institutes with programs in art and design. Most schools include studio art, principles of design, computerized design, commercial graphics production, printing techniques, and website design. In addition, students should consider courses in writing, marketing, and business, all of which are useful in helping designers work effectively on project teams.

High school students interested in graphic design should take basic art and design courses in high school, if the courses are available. Many bachelor's degree programs require students to complete a year of basic art and design courses before being admitted to a formal degree program. Some schools require applicants to submit sketches and other examples of their artistic ability.

Many programs provide students with the opportunity to build a professional portfolio of their designs. For many artists, including graphic designers, developing a portfolio—a collection of design ideas that demonstrates their styles and abilities—is essential because employers rely heavily on a designer's portfolio in deciding whether to hire the individual.

Graphic designers must keep up with new and updated computer graphics and design software, either on their own or through formal software training programs. Professional associations that specialize in graphic design, such as AIGA, offer courses intended to keep the skills of their members up to date.

Other Experience. Graphic designers often gain their initial experience through internships. It provides aspiring graphic designers an opportunity to work with designers and experience the design process from concept to completion while completing a design program.

Licenses, Certifications, and Registrations. Certification programs are generally available through software product vendors. Certification in graphic design software can demonstrate a level of competence and may provide a jobseeker with a competitive advantage.

Advancement. Experienced graphic designers may advance to chief designer, art director, or other supervisory positions.

Important Qualities

Analytical skills. Graphic designers must be able to look at their work from the point of view of their consumers and examine how the designs they develop will be perceived by consumers to ensure they convey the client's desired message.

Artistic ability. Graphic designers must be able to create designs that are artistically interesting and appealing to clients and consumers. They produce rough illustrations of design ideas, either by hand sketching or by using computer programs.

Communication skills. Graphic designers must communicate with clients, customers, and other designers to ensure that their designs accurately reflect the desired message and effectively express information.

Computer skills. Most graphic designers use specialized graphic design software to prepare their designs.

Creativity. Graphic designers must be able to think of new approaches to communicating ideas to consumers. They develop unique designs that convey a recognizable meaning on behalf of their clients.

Time-management skills. Graphic designers often work on multiple projects at the same time, each with a different deadline.

Pay

The median annual wage for graphic designers was $45,900 in May 2014. The median wage is the wage at which half the workers in an occupation earned more than that amount and half earned less. The lowest 10 percent earned less than $27,100, and the highest 10 percent earned more than $80,570.

In May 2014, the median annual wages for graphic designers in the top industries in which they worked were as follows:

Specialized design services	$48,240
Advertising, public relations, and related services	45,920
Wholesale trade	44,080
Newspaper, periodical, book, and directory publishers	40,720
Printing and related support activities	37,720

Job Outlook

Employment of graphic designers is projected to show little or no change from 2014 to 2024. The work of graphic designers will continue to be important in the marketing of products throughout the economy.

The change in employment of graphic designers from 2014 to 2024 is projected to vary by industry. Employment of graphic

Median Annual Wages, May 2014

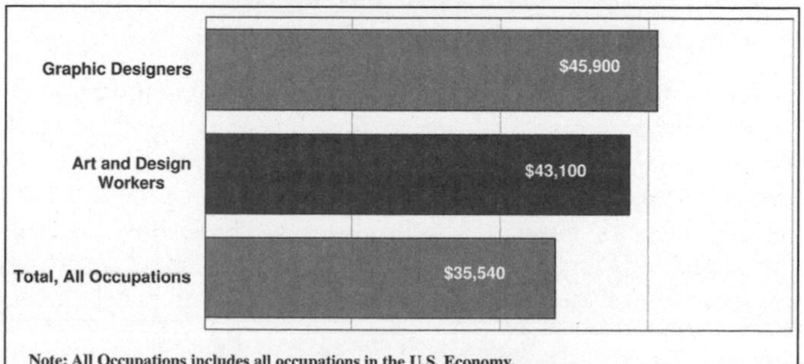

Note: All Occupations includes all occupations in the U.S. Economy.
Source: U.S. Bureau of Labor Statistics, Occupational Employment Statistics

Percent Change in Employment, Projected 2014–2024

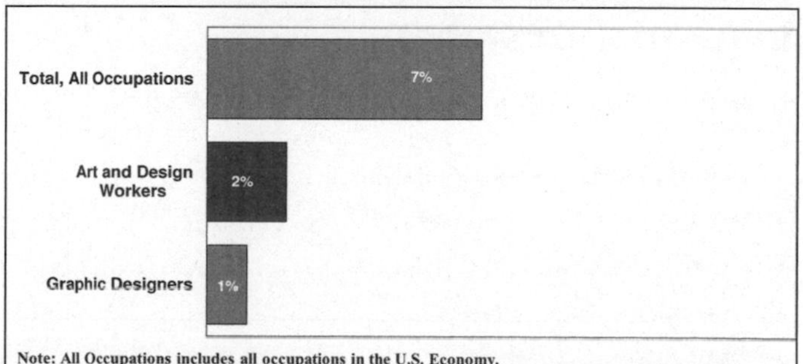

Note: All Occupations includes all occupations in the U.S. Economy.
Source: U.S. Bureau of Labor Statistics, Office of Occupational Statistics and Employment Projections

Employment Projections Data for Graphic Designers

Occupational Title	SOC Code	Employment, 2014	Projected Employment, 2024	Change, 2014–2024	
				Percent	Numeric
Graphic designers	27-1024	261,600	265,200	1	3,600

Source: U.S. Bureau of Labor Statistics, Employment Projections Program

Similar Occupations. This table shows a list of occupations with job duties that are similar to those of graphic designers.

Occupations	Entry-level Education	2014 Median Pay	Projected Job Growth	Average Annual Openings
Art Directors	Bachelor's degree	$85,610	2%	180
Craft and Fine Artists	See Education/Training	$44,400	2%	90
Desktop Publishers	Associate's degree	$38,200	-21%	-310
Drafters	Associate's degree	$51,940	-3%	-620
Industrial Designers	Bachelor's degree	$64,620	2%	80
Multimedia Artists and Animators	Bachelor's degree	$63,630	6%	390
Technical Writers	Bachelor's degree	$69,030	10%	530
Web Developers	Associate's degree	$63,490	27%	3,950

designers in newspaper, periodical, book, and directory publishers is projected to decline 35 percent from 2014 to 2024. However, employment of graphic designers in computer systems design and related services is projected to grow 21 percent over the same period. With the increasing use of the Internet, companies are increasing their digital presence and graphic designers will be needed to help create visually appealing and effective layouts of websites.

Job Prospects. Graphic designers are expected to face strong competition for available positions. Many talented individuals are attracted to careers as graphic designers. Prospects will be better for applicants who work with various types of media, such as websites and print publications.

Contacts for More Information

For more information about graphic design, visit

➤ AIGA (www.aiga.org)

➤ Graphic Artists Guild (www.graphicartistsguild.org)

For more information about art and design and a list of accredited college-level programs, visit

➤ National Association of Schools of Art and Design (http://nasad.arts-accredit.org)

O*NET

➤ Graphic Designers (27-1024.00)

Industrial Designers

- **2014 Median Pay** .... $64,620 per year $31.07 per hour
- **Typical Entry-Level Education** .... Bachelor's degree
- **Work Experience in a Related Occupation** .... None
- **On-the-job Training** .... None
- **Number of Jobs, 2014** 38,400
- **Job Outlook, 2014–24** .... 2% (Slower than average)
- **Employment Change, 2014–24** 800

What Industrial Designers Do

Industrial designers develop the concepts for manufactured products, such as cars, home appliances, and toys. They combine art, business, and engineering to make products that people use every day. Industrial designers consider the function, aesthetics, production costs, and the usability of products when developing new product concepts.

Duties. Industrial designers typically do the following:

- Consult with clients to determine requirements for designs
- Research the various ways a particular product might be used, and who will use it
- Sketch out ideas or create renderings, which are images on paper or on a computer that provide a better visual of design ideas
- Use computer software to develop virtual models of different designs
- Create physical prototypes of their designs
- Examine materials and manufacturing requirements to determine production costs
- Work with other specialists such as mechanical engineers or manufacturers to evaluate whether their design concepts will fill needs at a reasonable cost
- Evaluate product safety, appearance, and function to determine if a design is practical
- Present designs and demonstrate prototypes to clients for approval

Some industrial designers focus on a particular product category. For example, some design medical equipment, or work on consumer electronics products, such as computers and smart phones. Other designers develop ideas for other products such as new bicycles, furniture, housewares, and snowboards. Self-employed designers have more flexibility in the product categories they work on. Designers who work for manufacturers help create the look and feel of a brand through their designs.

Industrial designers imagine how consumers might use a product and test different designs with consumers to see how each

Industrial designers often use computers to create renderings: images that provide a better visual of design ideas.

design looks and works. Industrial designers often work with engineers, production experts, and market research analysts to find out if their designs are feasible. They apply the input from their colleagues' professional expertise to further develop their designs. For example, industrial designers may work with market research analysts to develop plans to market new product designs to consumers.

Computers are a major tool for industrial designers. They use two-dimensional computer-aided design (CAD) software to sketch ideas, because computers make it easy to make changes and show alternatives. Three-dimensional CAD software is increasingly being used by industrial designers as a tool to transform their two-dimensional designs into models with the help of three-dimensional printers. If they work for manufacturers, they also may use computer-aided industrial design (CAID) software to create specific machine-readable instructions that tell other machines exactly how to build the product.

Work Environment

Industrial designers held about 38,400 jobs in 2014. The industries that employed the most industrial designers were as follows:

Manufacturing	32%
Specialized design services	11
Architectural, engineering, and related services	8
Wholesale trade	8

About 1 in 4 were self-employed in 2014.

Work spaces for industrial designers often include work tables for sketching designs, meeting rooms with whiteboards for brainstorming with colleagues, and computers and other office equipment for preparing designs and communicating with clients. Although industrial designers work primarily in offices, they may travel to testing facilities, design centers, clients' exhibit sites, users' homes or workplaces, and places where the product is manufactured.

Work Schedules. Most industrial designers work full time.

Industrial designers who are self-employed or work for firms that hire them out to other organizations may need to frequently adjust their workdays to meet with clients in the evenings or on weekends. In addition, they may spend some of their time looking for new projects or competing with other designers for contracts.

Education/Training

A bachelor's degree is usually required for entry-level industrial design jobs. It is also important for industrial designers to have an electronic portfolio with examples of their best design projects.

Education. Most industrial design programs include courses that industrial designers need in design: drawing, computer-aided design and drafting (CADD), and three-dimensional modeling. Most programs will also include courses in business, industrial materials and processes, and manufacturing methods that industrial designers need when developing their design.

The National Association of Schools of Art and Design accredits approximately 320 postsecondary colleges, universities, and independent institutes with programs in art and design. Many schools require successful completion of some basic art and design courses before entry into a bachelor's degree program. Applicants also may need to submit sketches and other examples of their artistic ability.

Many programs provide students with the opportunity to build a professional portfolio of their designs by collecting examples of their designs from classroom projects, internships, or other experiences. Students can use these examples of their work to demonstrate their design skills when applying for jobs and bidding on contracts for work.

Some designers have a Master of Business Administration (MBA) degree which helps further develop a designer's business skills. These skills help designers understand how to fit their designs to meet the cost limitations a firm may have for the production of a given product.

Important Qualities

Analytical skills. Industrial designers use logic or reasoning skills to study consumers and recognize the need for new products.

Artistic ability. Industrial designers sketch their initial design ideas, which are used later to create prototypes. As such, designers must be able to express their design through illustration.

Computer skills. Industrial designers use computer-aided design software to develop their designs and create prototypes.

Creativity. Industrial designers must be innovative in their designs and the ways in which they integrate existing technologies into their new product.

Interpersonal skills. Industrial designers must develop cooperative working relationships with clients and colleagues who specialize in related disciplines.

Mechanical skills. Industrial designers must understand how products are engineered, at least for the types of products that they design.

Problem-solving skills. Industrial designers identify complex design problems such as the need, size, and cost of a product, anticipate production issues, develop alternatives, evaluate options, and implement solutions.

Advancement. Experienced designers in large firms may advance to chief designer, design department head, or other supervisory positions. Some designers become teachers in design schools or in colleges and universities. For more information, see the profile on postsecondary teachers. Many teachers continue to consult privately or operate small design studios in addition to teaching. Some experienced designers open their own design firms.

Median Annual Wages, May 2014

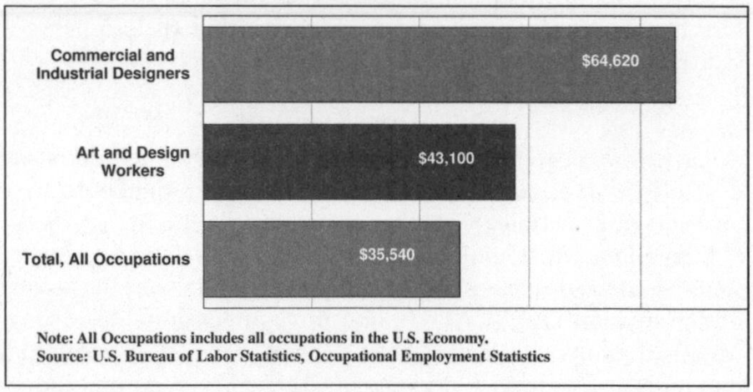

Percent Change in Employment, Projected 2014–2024

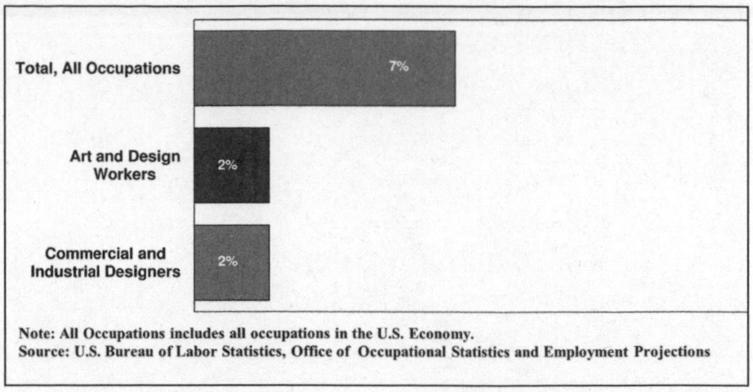

Pay

The median annual wage for industrial designers was $64,620 in May 2014. The median wage is the wage at which half the workers in an occupation earned more than that amount and half earned less. The lowest 10 percent earned less than $37,030, and the highest 10 percent earned more than $100,070.

In May 2014, the median annual wages for industrial designers in the top industries in which they worked were as follows:

Architectural, engineering, and related services	$68,970
Manufacturing	62,330
Specialized design services	61,460
Wholesale trade	57,970

Job Outlook

Employment of industrial designers is projected to grow 2 percent from 2014 to 2024, slower than the average for all occupations. Consumer demand for innovative products and new product styles will sustain the demand for industrial designers. Employment in the manufacturing industry is projected to experience a slight decline over the projection period, contributing to slower than the average growth for industrial designers overall.

Employment of industrial designers who design precision instruments and medical equipment is likely to continue to grow. Both areas require a high degree of technical ability and design sophistication. Products in these areas also require detailed specifications and precise equipment manufacturing because of the delicate uses of the finished product.

Job Prospects. Prospects are best for job applicants with a strong background in two- and three-dimensional computer-aided design (CAD) and computer-aided industrial design (CAID). The increasing trend toward the use of sustainable resources is likely to improve prospects for applicants with the knowledge to work with sustainable resources.

Contacts for More Information

For more information about industrial designers, visit

➤ Industrial Designers Society of America (www.idsa.org)

For more information about accredited college-level programs in art and design, visit

➤ National Association of Schools of Art and Design (http://nasad.arts-accredit.org)

O*NET

➤ Commercial and Industrial Designers (27-1021.00)

Employment Projections Data for Industrial Designers

Occupational Title	SOC Code	Employment, 2014	Projected Employment, 2024	Change, 2014–2024	
				Percent	Numeric
Commercial and industrial designers	27-1021	38,400	39,200	2	800

Source: U.S. Bureau of Labor Statistics, Employment Projections Program

Similar Occupations. This table shows a list of occupations with job duties that are similar to those of industrial designers.

Occupations	Entry-level Education	2014 Median Pay	Projected Job Growth	Average Annual Openings
Architects	Bachelor's degree	$74,520	7%	780
Art Directors	Bachelor's degree	$85,610	2%	180
Desktop Publishers	Associate's degree	$38,200	-21%	-310
Drafters	Associate's degree	$51,940	-3%	-620
Fashion Designers	Bachelor's degree	$64,030	3%	70
Graphic Designers	Bachelor's degree	$45,900	1%	360
Industrial Engineers	Bachelor's degree	$81,490	1%	210
Interior Designers	Bachelor's degree	$48,400	4%	220

Interior Designers

- **2014 Median Pay** .... $48,400 per year
$23.27 per hour
- **Typical Entry-Level Education** .... Bachelor's degree
- **Work Experience in a Related Occupation** .... None
- **On-the-job Training** .... None
- **Number of Jobs, 2014** 58,900
- **Job Outlook, 2014–24** .... 4% (Slower than average)
- **Employment Change, 2014–24** 2,200

What Interior Designers Do

Interior designers make interior spaces functional, safe, and beautiful by determining space requirements and selecting decorative items, such as colors, lighting, and materials. They read blueprints and must be aware of building codes and inspection regulations, as well as universal accessibility standards.

Duties. Interior designers typically do the following:

- Search for and bid on new projects
- Determine the client's goals and requirements for the project
- Consider how the space will be used and how people will move through the space
- Sketch preliminary design plans, including electrical and partition layouts
- Specify materials and furnishings, such as lighting, furniture, wall finishes, flooring, and plumbing fixtures
- Create a timeline for the interior design project and estimate project costs
- Place orders for materials and oversee the installation of the design elements
- Conduct the construction administration of the project and coordinate with general building contractors to implement the plans and specifications to build the project
- Visit the site after the project is complete, to ensure that the client is satisfied

Interior designers work closely with architects, structural engineers, mechanical engineers, and builders to determine how interior spaces will function, look, and be furnished. Interior designers read blueprints and must be aware of building codes and inspection regulations. For more information on structural engineers, see the profile on civil engineers. For more information on builders, see the profile on construction laborers and helpers.

Although some sketches or drawings may be freehand, most interior designers use computer-aided design (CAD) software for the majority of their drawings. Throughout the design process, interior designers often will use building information modeling (BIM) software to create three-dimensional visualizations that include construction elements such as walls or roofs.

Many designers specialize in a particular type of building, such as homes, hospitals, or hotels; a specific room, such as bathrooms or kitchens; or a specific style. Some designers work for home-furnishings stores, providing design services to help customers choose materials and furnishings.

Some interior designers produce designs, plans, and drawings for construction and installation. These may include construction and demolition plans, electrical layouts, and plans needed for building permits. Interior designers may draft the preliminary design into documents that could be as simple as sketches or as inclusive as construction documents, with schedules and attachments.

The following are examples of types of interior designers:

Healthcare designers use the evidence-design process in designing and renovating healthcare centers, clinics, doctors' offices, hospitals, and residential care facilities. They specialize in making design decisions based on credible research to achieve the best possible outcomes for patients, residents, and the facility.

Sustainable designers use strategies to improve energy and water efficiencies and indoor air quality, and they specify environmentally preferable products, such as bamboo and cork for floors. They may obtain certification in Leadership in Energy and Environmental Design (LEED) from the U.S. Green Building Council. Such certification indicates that a building and its interior space were designed with the use of sustainable concepts.

Universal designers renovate spaces in order to make them more accessible. Often, these designs are used to renovate spaces for elderly people and people with special needs; however, universal designs can benefit anyone. For example, an entranceway without steps may be necessary for someone in a wheelchair, but it is also helpful for someone pushing a baby stroller.

Kitchen and bath designers specialize in kitchens and bathrooms and have expert knowledge of the variety of cabinets, fixtures, appliances, plumbing, and electrical solutions for these rooms.

Corporate designers create interior designs for professional workplaces from small office settings to large-scale corporations within high-rise buildings. They focus on creating spaces that are efficient, functional, and safe for employees. They may incorporate design elements that reflect a company's brand in their designs.

Work Environment

Interior designers held about 58,900 jobs in 2014. The industries that employed the most interior designers were as follows:

Specialized design services	30%
Architectural, engineering, and related services	15
Furniture stores	8
Wholesale trade	6
Residential building construction	4

Most interior designers work in clean, comfortable offices. About 1 in 4 interior designers were self-employed in 2014. Technology has changed the way many designers work. For example,

An increasing number of interior designers are involved with architectural detailing.

rather than using drafting tables, interior designers now use complex software to create two-dimensional or three-dimensional images.

Work Schedules. Most interior designers work full time. They may need to adjust their workday to suit their clients' schedules and deadlines, meeting with clients during evening and weekend hours when necessary. Interior designers also travel to the clients' design sites.

Education/Training

Interior designers usually need a bachelor's degree with a focus on interior design.

Education. A bachelor's degree is usually required, as are classes in interior design, drawing, and computer-aided design (CAD). A bachelor's degree in any field is acceptable, and interior design programs are available at the associate's, bachelor's, and master's degree levels.

The National Association of Schools of Art and Design accredits about 320 postsecondary colleges, universities, and independent institutes with programs in art and design. The Council for Interior Design Accreditation accredits more than 180 professional-level (bachelor's or master's degrees) interior design programs.

The National Kitchen & Bath Association accredits kitchen and bath design specialty programs (certificate, associate's, and bachelor's degree levels) in 45 colleges and universities.

Applicants may be required to submit sketches and other examples of their artistic ability for admission to interior design programs.

Licenses, Certifications, and Registrations. Licensure requirements vary by state. In some states, only licensed designers may do interior design work. In other states, both licensed and unlicensed designers may do such work; however, only licensed designers may use the title "interior designer." In still other states, both licensed and unlicensed designers may call themselves interior designers and do interior design work.

In states where laws restrict the use of the title "interior designer," only those who pass their state-approved exam, most commonly the National Council for Interior Design Qualification (NCIDQ) exam, may call themselves registered interior designers. Qualifications for eligibility to take the NCIDQ exam include a combination of education and experience. For example, applicants must have at least a bachelor's degree in interior design and 2 years of experience.

California requires a different exam, administered by the California Council for Interior Design Certification (CCIDC). Qualifications for eligibility to take the CCIDC exam include a combination of education and experience.

Voluntary certification in an interior design specialty, such as healthcare interior design, allows designers to demonstrate expertise in a particular area of the occupation. Interior designers often specialize to distinguish the type of design work they do and to promote their expertise. Certifications usually are available through professional and trade associations and are independent from the NCIDQ licensing examination.

Important Qualities

Artistic ability. Interior designers use their sense of style to develop designs that are aesthetically pleasing.

Creativity. Interior designers need to be imaginative in selecting furnishings and fabrics and in creating spaces that serve the client's needs and fit the client's lifestyle.

Detail oriented. Interior designers need to be precise in measuring interior spaces and creating drawings, so that it can be used by other workers such as engineers or other designers.

Interpersonal skills. Interior designers need to be able to communicate effectively with clients and others. Much of their time is spent soliciting new clients and new work and collaborating with other designers, engineers, and general building contractors on ongoing projects.

Problem-solving skills. Interior designers must address challenges, such as construction delays and the high cost or sudden unavailability of certain materials, while keeping the project on time and within budget.

Visualization. Interior designers need a strong sense of proportion and visual awareness in order to understand how pieces of a design will fit together to create the intended interior environment.

Pay

The median annual wage for interior designers was $48,400 in May 2014. The median wage is the wage at which half the workers in an occupation earned more than that amount and half earned less. The lowest 10 percent earned less than $27,170, and the highest 10 percent earned more than $89,700.

In May 2014, the median annual wages for interior designers in the top industries in which they worked were as follows:

Architectural, engineering, and related services	$55,710
Wholesale trade	50,470
Residential building construction	48,890
Specialized design services	46,470
Furniture stores	44,100

Job Outlook

Employment of interior designers is projected to grow 4 percent from 2014 to 2024, slower than the average for all occupations.

Median Annual Wages, May 2014

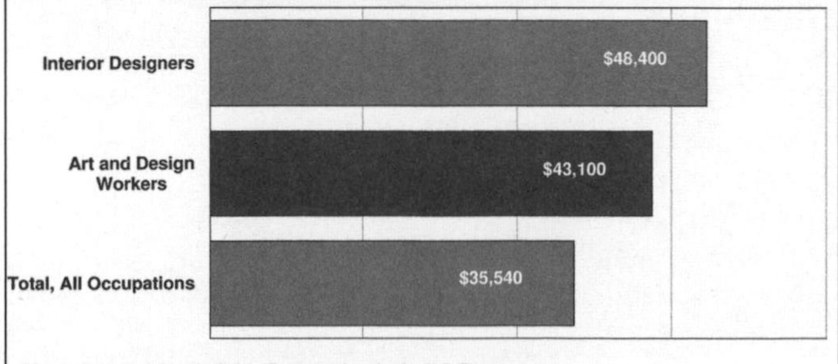

Note: All Occupations includes all occupations in the U.S. Economy.
Source: U.S. Bureau of Labor Statistics, Occupational Employment Statistics

Percent Change in Employment, Projected 2014–2024

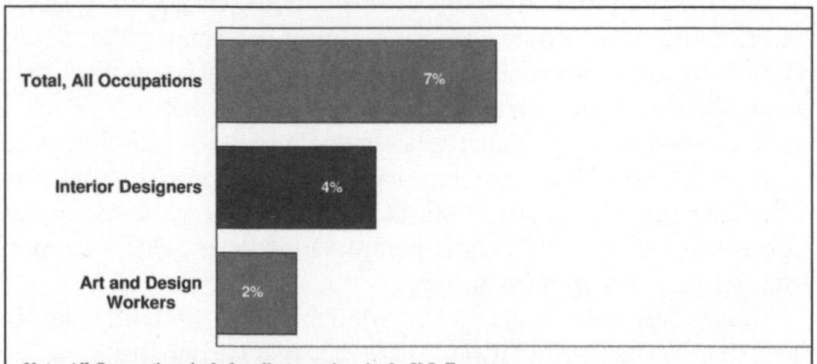

Note: All Occupations includes all occupations in the U.S. Economy.
Source: U.S. Bureau of Labor Statistics, Office of Occupational Statistics and Employment Projections

Employment Projections Data for Interior Designers

Occupational Title	SOC Code	Employment, 2014	Projected Employment, 2024	Change, 2014–2024 Percent	Change, 2014–2024 Numeric
Interior designers	27-1025	58,900	61,100	4	2,200

Source: U.S. Bureau of Labor Statistics, Employment Projections Program

Similar Occupations. This table shows a list of occupations with job duties that are similar to those of interior designers.

Occupations	Entry-level Education	2014 Median Pay	Projected Job Growth	Average Annual Openings
Architects	Bachelor's degree	$74,520	7%	780
Art Directors	Bachelor's degree	$85,610	2%	180
Craft and Fine Artists	See Education/Training	$44,400	2%	90
Fashion Designers	Bachelor's degree	$64,030	3%	70
Floral Designers	High school diploma or equivalent	$24,750	-3%	-200
Graphic Designers	Bachelor's degree	$45,900	1%	360
Industrial Designers	Bachelor's degree	$64,620	2%	80
Landscape Architects	Bachelor's degree	$64,570	5%	120

Designers will be needed to respond to consumer expectations that the interiors of structures such as residential homes or office spaces meet certain conditions, such as being environmentally friendly and more easily accessible.

Although only about 5 percent of interior designers are directly employed in the construction industry, many interior designers are heavily dependent on that industry to generate new construction and renovation projects for them to work on. Overall employment in the construction industry is projected to grow over the projection period.

Long-term funding plans help ensure demand for interior designs. Remodeling of large public spaces and facilities, such as hospitals, hotels, and schools, often is funded as part of a long-term project. Companies typically budget money over many years, so that they can afford remodeling efforts when necessary, regardless of economic conditions. In addition, as part of creating their corporate image, more companies are expected to take advantage of opportunities to use new furnishing and design concepts, to make their interior space easily identifiable.

Employment of interior designers in specialized design services firms is projected to grow 8 percent from 2014 to 2024. As interior designers focus on increasingly specialized design areas such as hospitality, healthcare, and commercial and corporate design, there will be a greater need for them to collaborate with other designers and in other design-related fields.

Job Prospects. Job prospects should be better in high-income areas, because wealthy clients are more likely than others to engage in remodeling and renovating their spaces. Keeping up to date with the newest design tools, such as three-dimensional computer-aided design (CAD) software, also will improve one's job prospects.

Interior designers who specialize, such as those who design kitchens, may benefit by becoming an expert in their particular area. By specializing in a unique area of design, interior designers can use their knowledge of products to better fulfill customer requests.

Contacts for More Information

For more information about interior designers, visit

➤ American Society of Interior Designers (www.asid.org)

➤ International Interior Design Association (www.iida.org)

For more information on accredited college degree programs in interior design, visit

➤ National Association of Schools of Art and Design (http://nasad.arts-accredit.org)

➤ Council for Interior Design Accreditation (www.accredit-id.org)

For more information on the national licensure qualifying exam, visit

➤ National Council for Interior Design Qualification (www.ncidq.org)

For more information on accredited kitchen and bath specialty programs in colleges and universities and voluntary certification programs in residential kitchen and bath design, visit

➤ National Kitchen & Bath Association (www.nkba.org)

O*NET

➤ Interior Designers (27-1025.00)

Multimedia Artists and Animators

- **2014 Median Pay** .... $63,630 per year
  $30.59 per hour
- **Typical Entry-Level Education** ....Bachelor's degree
- **Work Experience in a Related Occupation**............... None
- **On-the-job Training**..... Moderate-term on-the-job training
- **Number of Jobs, 2014** 64,400
- **Job Outlook, 2014–24** .... 6% (As fast as average)
- **Employment Change, 2014–24** 3,900

What Multimedia Artists and Animators Do

Multimedia artists and animators create two- and three-dimensional models, animation, and visual effects for television, movies, video games, and other forms of media.

Duties. Multimedia artists and animators typically do the following:

- Use computer programs and illustrations to create graphics and animation
- Work with a team of animators and artists to create a movie, game, or visual effect
- Research upcoming projects to help create realistic designs or animations
- Develop storyboards that map out key scenes in animations
- Edit animations and effects on the basis of feedback from directors, other animators, game designers, or clients
- Meet with clients, other animators, games designers, directors, and other staff (which may include actors) to review deadlines and development time lines

Multimedia artists and animators often work in a specific medium. Some focus on creating animated movies or video games. Others create visual effects for movies and television shows. Creating computer-generated images (known as CGI) may include taking images of an actor's movements and then animating them into three-dimensional characters. Other animators design scenery or backgrounds for locations.

Artists and animators can further specialize within these fields. Within animated movies and video games, artists often specialize in characters or in scenery and background design. Video game artists may focus on level design: creating the look, feel, and layout for the levels of a video game.

Animators work in teams to develop a movie, a visual effect, or an electronic game. Each animator works on a portion of the project, and then the pieces are put together to create one cohesive animation.

Some multimedia artists and animators create their work primarily by using computer software or by writing their own computer code. Many animation companies have their own computer animation software that artists must learn to use. Video game designers also work in a wide variety of platforms, including mobile gaming and online social networks.

Other artists and animators prefer to work by drawing and painting by hand and then translating the resulting images into computer programs. Some multimedia artists use storyboards or "animatics," which look like a comic strip, to help visualize the final product during the design process.

Many multimedia artists and animators put their creative work on the Internet. If the images become popular, these artists can gain more recognition, which can lead to future employment or freelance work.

Work Environment

Multimedia artists and animators held about 64,400 jobs in 2014. The industries that employed the most multimedia artists and animators were as follows:

Motion picture and video industries	12%
Computer systems design and related services	6
Software publishers	5
Advertising, public relations, and related services	5

In 2014, a little more than half of workers were self-employed. Many artists and animators work in offices; others work from home.

Work Schedules. Most multimedia artists and animators work a regular work schedule; however, when deadlines are approaching, they may need to work nights and weekends.

Multimedia artists and animators create two- and three-dimensional models and animation.

Education/Training

Most multimedia artists and animators need a bachelor's degree in computer graphics, art, or a related field to develop both an impressive portfolio of work and the strong technical skills that many employers prefer.

Education. Employers typically require a bachelor's degree, and they look for workers who have a good portfolio of work and strong technical skills. Multimedia artists and animators typically have a bachelor's degree in fine art, computer graphics, animation, or a related field. Programs in computer graphics often include courses in computer science in addition to art courses.

Bachelor's degree programs in art include courses in painting, drawing, and sculpture. Degrees in animation often require classes in drawing, animation, and film. Many schools have specialized degrees in topics such as interactive media or game design.

Training. Some animation studios have their own software and computer applications that they use to create films, and they often provide on-the-job training so that workers can use the specific software and computer applications.

Important Qualities

Artistic talent. Animators and artists should have artistic ability and a good understanding of color, texture, and light. However, they may be able to compensate for artistic shortcomings with better technical skills.

Communication skills. Multimedia artists and animators need to work as part of a complex team and respond well to criticism and feedback.

Computer skills. Many multimedia artists and animators use computer programs or write programming code to do most of their work.

Creativity. Artists and animators must be able to think creatively to develop original ideas and make them come to life.

Time-management skills. The hours required by most studio and game design companies can be long, particularly when there are tight deadlines. Artists and animators need to be able to manage their time effectively when a deadline approaches.

Pay

The median annual wage for multimedia artists and animators was $63,630 in May 2014. The median wage is the wage at which half the workers in an occupation earned more than that amount and half earned less. The lowest 10 percent earned less than $35,510, and the highest 10 percent earned more than $112,030.

Median Annual Wages, May 2014

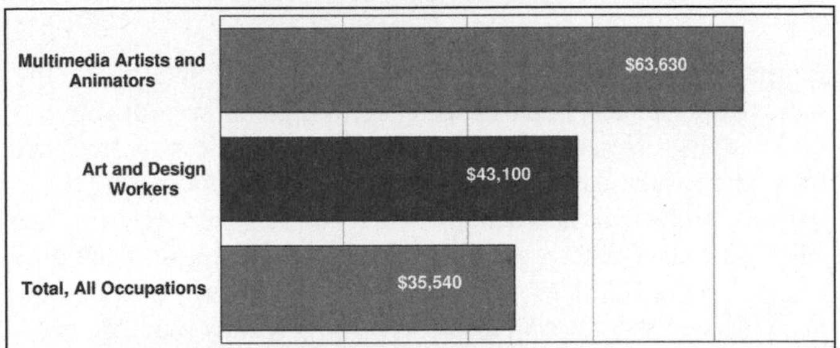

Note: All Occupations includes all occupations in the U.S. Economy.
Source: U.S. Bureau of Labor Statistics, Occupational Employment Statistics

Percent Change in Employment, Projected 2014–2024

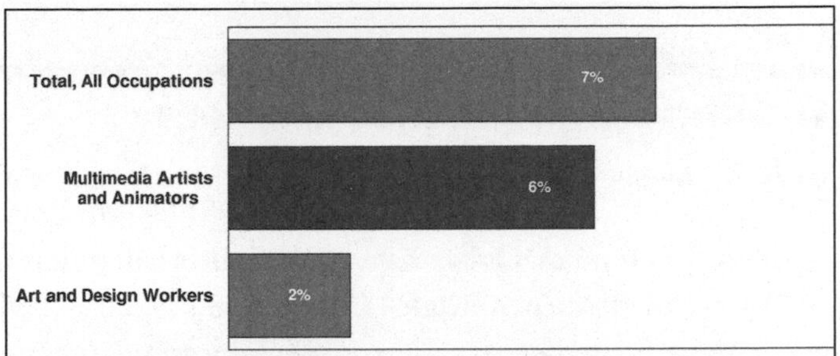

Note: All Occupations includes all occupations in the U.S. Economy.
Source: U.S. Bureau of Labor Statistics, Office of Occupational Statistics and Employment Projections

In May 2014, the median annual wages for multimedia artists and animators in the top industries in which they worked were as follows:

Software publishers...$72,960
Computer systems design and related services.....................68,080
Motion picture and video industries...................................65,330
Advertising, public relations, and related services...............59,600

Most multimedia artists and animators work a regular work schedule; however, when deadlines are approaching, they may need to work nights and weekends.

Job Outlook

Employment of multimedia artists and animators is projected to grow 6 percent from 2014 to 2024, about as fast as the average for all occupations. Projected growth will be due to increased demand for animation and visual effects in video games, movies, and television. Job growth may be slowed, however, by companies hiring animators and artists who work overseas. Studios may save money on animation by using lower paid workers outside of the United States.

Consumers will continue to demand more realistic video games, movie and television special effects, and three-dimensional movies. They will also demand newer computer hardware, which adds to the complexity of the games themselves. Video game studios will require additional multimedia artists and animators to meet this increased demand.

Further, an increased demand for computer graphics for mobile devices, such as smart phones, will lead to more job opportunities. Multimedia artists will be needed to create animation for games and applications for mobile devices.

Job Prospects. Despite positive job growth, there will be competition for job openings because many recent graduates are interested in entering the occupation. Opportunities should be best for those who specialize in a specific type of animation or in a specific skill, such as drawing or computer programming.

Contacts for More Information

For information on accredited schools of art and design, visit

- National Association of Schools of Art and Design (http://nasad.arts-accredit.org)

For additional information about careers in video game design, visit

- Game Career Guide (www.gamecareerguide.com)

Related BLS Article

For more information about careers in video game design, read the *Occupational Outlook Quarterly* article titled "Work for Play: Careers in Video Game Development" (http://tinyurl.com/jjat3c9)

O*NET

- Multimedia Artists and Animators (27-1014.00)

Employment Projections Data for Multimedia Artists and Animators

Occupational Title	SOC Code	Employment, 2014	Projected Employment, 2024	Change, 2014–2024 Percent	Change, 2014–2024 Numeric
Multimedia artists and animators	27-1014	64,400	68,300	6	3,900

Source: U.S. Bureau of Labor Statistics, Employment Projections Program

Similar Occupations. This table shows a list of occupations with job duties that are similar to those of multimedia artists and animators.

Occupations	Entry-level Education	2014 Median Pay	Projected Job Growth	Average Annual Openings
Art Directors	Bachelor's degree	$85,610	2%	180
Computer Programmers	Bachelor's degree	$77,550	-8%	-2,650
Craft and Fine Artists	See Education/Training	$44,400	2%	90
Graphic Designers	Bachelor's degree	$45,900	1%	360
Web Developers	Associate's degree	$63,490	27%	3,950

Building and Grounds Cleaning

Grounds Maintenance Workers

- **2014 Median Pay** .... $24,810 per year
  $11.93 per hour
- **Typical Entry-Level Education** .... See Education/Training
- **Work Experience in a Related Occupation**............... None
- **On-the-job Training** .... See Education/Training
- **Number of Jobs, 2014** 1,282,000
- **Job Outlook, 2014–24** .... 6% (As fast as average)
- **Employment Change, 2014–24** 77,600

What Grounds Maintenance Workers Do

Grounds maintenance workers ensure that the grounds of houses, businesses, and parks are attractive, orderly, and healthy in order to provide a pleasant outdoor environment.

Duties. Grounds maintenance workers typically do the following:

- Mow, edge, and fertilize lawns
- Weed and mulch landscape beds
- Trim hedges, shrubs, and small trees
- Remove dead, damaged, or unwanted trees
- Plant flowers, trees, and shrubs
- Water lawns, landscapes, and gardens
- Monitor and maintain plant health

Grounds maintenance workers are generally under the direction of a professional grounds manager and perform a variety of tasks to achieve a pleasant and functional outdoor environment. They also care for indoor gardens and plantings in commercial and public facilities, such as malls, hotels, and botanical gardens.

The following are examples of types of grounds maintenance workers:

Landscaping workers plant trees, flowers, and shrubs to create new outdoor spaces or upgrade existing ones. They also trim, fertilize, mulch, and water plants. Some grade and install lawns or construct hardscapes such as walkways, patios, and decks. Others help install lighting or sprinkler systems. Landscaping workers are employed in a variety of residential and commercial settings, such as homes, apartment buildings, office buildings, shopping malls, and hotels and motels.

Groundskeeping workers, also called *groundskeepers*, maintain grounds. They care for plants and trees, rake and mulch leaves, and clear snow from walkways. They work on athletic fields, golf courses, cemeteries, university campuses, and parks, as well as in many of the same settings that landscaping workers work. They also see to the proper upkeep of sidewalks, parking lots, fountains, fences, planters, and benches, as well as groundskeeping equipment.

Groundskeeping workers who care for athletic fields keep natural and artificial turf in top condition, mark out boundaries, and paint turf with team logos and names before events. They mow, water, fertilize, and aerate the fields regularly. They must ensure that the underlying soil on fields with natural turf has the composition required to allow proper drainage and to support the grass used on the field. In sports venues, they vacuum and disinfect synthetic turf to prevent the growth of harmful bacteria and they remove the turf and replace the cushioning pad periodically.

Groundskeepers in parks and recreation facilities care for lawns, trees, and shrubs; maintain playgrounds; clean buildings; and keep parking lots, picnic areas, and other public spaces free of litter. They also may erect and dismantle snow fences and maintain swimming pools. These workers inspect buildings and equipment, make needed repairs, and keep everything freshly painted.

Some groundskeepers specialize in caring for cemeteries and memorial gardens. They dig graves to specified depths, generally using a backhoe. They mow grass regularly, apply fertilizers and other chemicals, prune shrubs and trees, plant flowers, and remove debris from graves.

Greenskeepers maintain golf courses. Their work is similar to that of groundskeepers, but they also periodically relocate holes on putting greens and maintain benches and tee markers along the course and provide more intense turf maintenance. In addition, greenskeepers keep canopies, benches, and tee markers repaired and freshly painted.

Pesticide handlers, sprayers, and applicators apply herbicides, fungicides, and insecticides on plants or the soil to prevent or control weeds, insects, and diseases. Those who work for chemical lawn or tree service firms are more specialized, inspecting lawns for problems and applying fertilizers, pesticides, and other chemicals to stimulate growth and prevent or control weeds, diseases, or insect infestations.

Tree trimmers and pruners, also called *arborists,* cut away dead or excess branches from trees or shrubs to clear utility lines, roads, and sidewalks. Although many of these workers strive to improve

Grounds maintenance workers mow lawns and trim hedges and trees.

the appearance and health of trees and plants, some specialize in diagnosing and treating tree diseases. Others specialize in pruning, trimming, and shaping ornamental trees and shrubs. Tree trimmers and pruners use chain saws, chippers, and stump grinders while on the job. When trimming near power lines, they usually work on truck-mounted lifts and use power pruners.

Work Environment

Grounds maintenance workers held about 1.3 million jobs in 2014. The industries that employed the most grounds maintenance workers were as follows:

Services to buildings and dwellings	41%
State and local government, excluding education and hospitals	8
Other amusement and recreation industries	7
Educational services; state, local, and private	4

Employment in the detailed occupations that make up grounds maintenance workers was distributed as follows:

Landscaping and groundskeeping workers	1,167,800
Tree trimmers and pruners	53,200
Pesticide handlers, sprayers, and applicators, vegetation	36,400
Grounds maintenance workers, all other	24,500

Grounds maintenance work is done outdoors in all kinds of weather. The work can be repetitive and physically demanding, requiring frequent bending, lifting, and shoveling.

Injuries and Illnesses. Grounds maintenance workers have a rate of injuries and illnesses that is higher than the national average. Workers who use dangerous equipment, such as lawnmowers and chain saws, must wear protective clothing, eyewear, and earplugs.

Those who apply chemicals such as pesticides or fertilizers must wear protective gear, including appropriate clothing, gloves, goggles, and sometimes respirators.

Tree trimmers and pruners, who often work at great heights, must always use fall protection gear in addition to wearing hardhats and eye protection for most activities.

Work Schedules. Many grounds maintenance jobs are seasonal. Jobs are most common in the spring, summer, and fall, when planting, mowing, and trimming are most frequent. However, many also provide other seasonal services, such as snow removal and installation and removal of holiday décor.

Education/Training

Most grounds maintenance workers need no formal education and are trained on the job. Most states require licensing for workers who apply pesticides and fertilizers.

Education. Although most grounds maintenance jobs have no education requirements, some employers may require formal education or certification in areas such as landscape design, horticulture, or arboriculture.

Licenses, Certifications, and Registrations. Most states require workers who apply pesticides and fertilizers to be licensed. Obtaining a license usually involves passing a test on the proper use and disposal of insecticides, herbicides, and fungicides.

The National Association of Landscape Professionals offers seven certifications in landscaping and grounds maintenance for workers at various experience levels.

The Tree Care Industry Association offers certification for tree care safety professionals.

The International Society of Arboriculture offers six certifications for workers at various experience levels.

The Professional Grounds Management Society offers certification for workers at various experience levels.

Training. A short period of on-the-job training is usually enough to teach new hires the skills they need, which often include how to plant and maintain areas and how to use mowers, trimmers, leaf blowers, small tractors, and other equipment. Large institutional employers such as golf courses, university campuses, or municipalities may supplement on-the-job training with coursework in horticulture or small-engine repair.

Advancement. Grounds maintenance workers who have good communication skills may become crew leaders or advance into other supervisory positions. Becoming a manager or a landscape contractor may require some formal education and several years of related work experience. Some workers use their experience to start their own landscaping companies.

Important Qualities

Physical stamina. Grounds maintenance workers must be capable of doing physically strenuous labor for long hours, occasionally in extreme heat or cold.

Self-motivated. Because they often work with little supervision, grounds maintenance workers must be able to do their job independently.

Pay

The median hourly wage for grounds maintenance workers was $11.93 in May 2014. The median wage is the wage at which half the workers in an occupation earned more than that amount and half earned less. The lowest 10 percent earned less than $8.62, and the highest 10 percent earned more than $19.38.

Median hourly wages for grounds maintenance workers in May 2014 were as follows:

Median Hourly Wages, May 2014

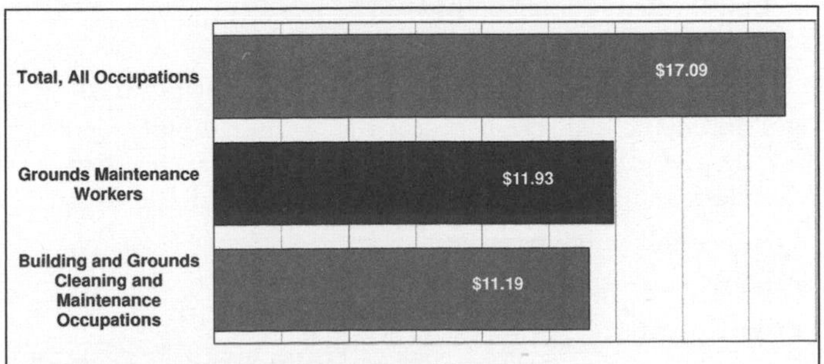

Note: All Occupations includes all occupations in the U.S. Economy.
Source: U.S. Bureau of Labor Statistics, Occupational Employment Statistics

Percent Change in Employment, Projected 2014–2024

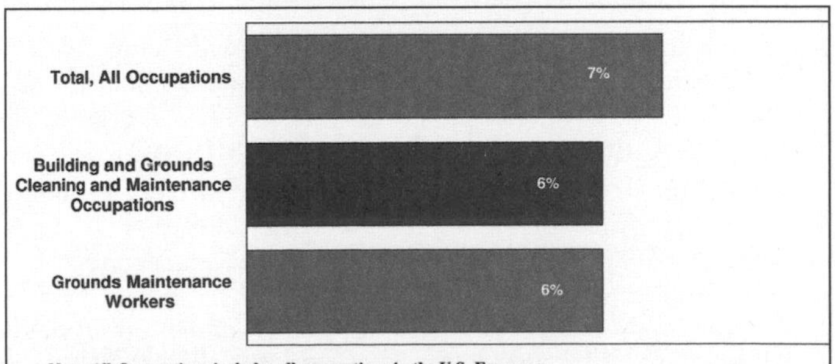

Note: All Occupations includes all occupations in the U.S. Economy.
Source: U.S. Bureau of Labor Statistics, Office of Occupational Statistics and Employment Projections

Employment Projections Data for Grounds Maintenance Workers

Occupational Title	SOC Code	Employment, 2014	Projected Employment, 2024	Change, 2014–2024 Percent	Change, 2014–2024 Numeric
Grounds maintenance workers	37-3000	1,282,000	1,359,600	6	77,600
Landscaping and groundskeeping workers	37-3011	1,167,800	1,239,600	6	71,700
Pesticide handlers, sprayers, and applicators, vegetation	37-3012	36,400	37,800	4	1,400
Tree trimmers and pruners	37-3013	53,200	56,200	6	3,000
Grounds maintenance workers, all other	37-3019	24,500	26,100	6	1,600

Source: U.S. Bureau of Labor Statistics, Employment Projections Program

Similar Occupations. This table shows a list of occupations with job duties that are similar to those of grounds maintenance workers.

Occupations	Entry-level Education	2014 Median Pay	Projected Job Growth	Average Annual Openings
Agricultural Workers	See Education/Training	$19,330	-6%	-4,750
Farmers, Ranchers, and Other Agricultural Managers	High school diploma or equivalent	$68,050	-2%	-1,810
Forest and Conservation Workers	High school diploma or equivalent	$27,160	4%	60
Landscape Architects	Bachelor's degree	$64,570	5%	120
Logging Workers	High school diploma or equivalent	$35,160	-4%	-200

Tree trimmers and pruners $15.85
Pesticide handlers, sprayers, and applicators, vegetation 15.02
Grounds maintenance workers, all other 13.85
Landscaping and groundskeeping workers 11.68

Job Outlook

Overall employment of grounds maintenance workers is projected to grow 6 percent from 2014 to 2024, about as fast as the average for all occupations. Employment growth will vary by specialty.

Employment of landscaping and groundskeeping workers—the largest specialty—is projected to grow 6 percent from 2014 to 2024, about as fast as the average for all occupations. More workers will be needed to keep up with increasing demand for lawn care and landscaping services from large institutions, including universities and corporate campuses. Many aging or busy homeowners also may need lawn care services to help maintain their yards.

Employment of tree trimmers and pruners is projected to grow 6 percent from 2014 to 2024. Many municipalities are planting more trees in urban areas, likely increasing the demand for these workers.

Job Prospects. Overall job opportunities are expected to be very good. Job opportunities will stem from employment growth and from the need to replace workers who leave the occupation each year.

Job opportunities should be best in areas with temperate climates, where more landscaping services are required year round.

Contacts for More Information

For more information about tree trimmers and pruners, including certification, visit

- International Society of Arboriculture (www.isa-arbor.com)
- Tree Care Industry Association (www.tcia.org)

For information about landscaping and groundskeeping workers, visit

- Professional Grounds Management Society (http://pgms.org)
- National Association of Landscape Professionals (www.landscapeprofessionals.org)

For information about becoming a licensed pesticide applicator, contact your state's licensing official.

O*NET

- Landscaping and Groundskeeping Workers (37-3011.00)
- Pesticide Handlers, Sprayers, and Applicators, Vegetation (37-3012.00)
- Tree Trimmers and Pruners (37-3013.00)
- Grounds Maintenance Workers, All Other (37-3019.00)

Janitors and Building Cleaners

- **2014 Median Pay** .... $22,840 per year, $10.98 per hour
- **Typical Entry-Level Education** .... No formal educational credential
- **Work Experience in a Related Occupation** .... None
- **On-the-job Training** .... Short-term on-the-job training
- **Number of Jobs, 2014** 2,360,600
- **Job Outlook, 2014–24** .... 6% (As fast as average)
- **Employment Change, 2014–24** 136,300

What Janitors and Building Cleaners Do

Janitors and building cleaners keep many types of buildings clean, orderly, and in good condition.

Duties. Janitors and building cleaners typically do the following:

- Gather and empty trash
- Sweep, mop, or vacuum building floors
- Clean restrooms and stock them with supplies
- Lock doors to secure buildings
- Clean spills and other hazards with appropriate equipment
- Wash windows, walls, and glass

- Order cleaning supplies
- Make minor building repairs
- Notify managers when a building needs major repairs

Janitors and building cleaners keep office buildings, schools, hospitals, retail stores, hotels, and other places clean, sanitary, and in good condition. Some only clean, while others have a wide range of duties.

In addition to keeping the inside of buildings clean and orderly, some janitors and building cleaners work outdoors, mowing lawns, sweeping walkways, and removing snow. Some workers also monitor the building's heating and cooling system, ensuring that it functions properly.

Janitors and building cleaners use many tools and equipment. Simple cleaning tools may include mops, brooms, rakes, and shovels. Other tools may include snowblowers, floor buffers, and carpet extraction equipment.

Some janitors are responsible for repairing minor electrical or plumbing problems, such as leaky faucets.

The following are examples of types of janitors and building cleaners:

Building superintendents are responsible for maintaining residential buildings, such as apartments and condominiums. Although their duties are similar to those of other janitors, some building superintendents also help collect rent and show vacancies to potential tenants.

Custodians are janitors or cleaning workers who typically maintain institutional facilities, such as public schools and hospitals.

Work Environment

Janitors and building cleaners held about 2.4 million jobs in 2014. The industries that employed the most janitors and building cleaners were as follows:

Services to buildings and dwellings	35%
Elementary and secondary schools; state, local, and private	13
Healthcare and social assistance	7
Religious, grantmaking, civic, professional, and similar organizations	6

Most janitors and building cleaners work indoors, but some work outdoors part of the time, sweeping walkways, mowing lawns, and shoveling snow. They spend most of the day walking, standing, or bending while cleaning. Sometimes they must move or lift heavy supplies and equipment. As a result, the work may be strenuous on the back, arms, and legs. Some tasks, such as cleaning restrooms and trash areas, can be dirty and unpleasant.

Injuries and Illnesses. Janitors and building cleaners have a higher rate of injuries and illnesses than the national average.

Building cleaning workers are employed in hospitals, office buildings, and other settings.

Workers suffer minor cuts, bruises, and burns from machines, tools, and chemicals. As a result, workers are increasingly required to take safety training and ergonomics instruction.

Work Schedules. Most janitors and building cleaners work full time, but some work part time. Because office buildings often are cleaned while they are empty, many cleaners work evening hours. Janitors in schools, however, usually work during the day.

When there is a need for 24-hour maintenance, as there often is in hospitals and hotels, janitors work in shifts.

Education/Training

Most janitors and building cleaners learn on the job. Formal education is not required.

Education. Janitors and building cleaners do not need any formal educational credential. However, high school courses in shop can be helpful for jobs involving repair work.

Training. Most janitors and building cleaners learn on the job. Beginners typically work with a more experienced janitor, learning how to use and maintain equipment such as vacuums, floor buffers, and other tools. On the job, they also learn how to repair minor electrical and plumbing problems.

Licenses, Certifications, and Registrations. Although not required, certification is available through the Building Service Contractors Association International, the International Executive Housekeepers Association, and ISSA—The International Sanitary Supply Association. Certification can demonstrate competence and may make applicants more appealing to employers.

Median Hourly Wages, May 2014

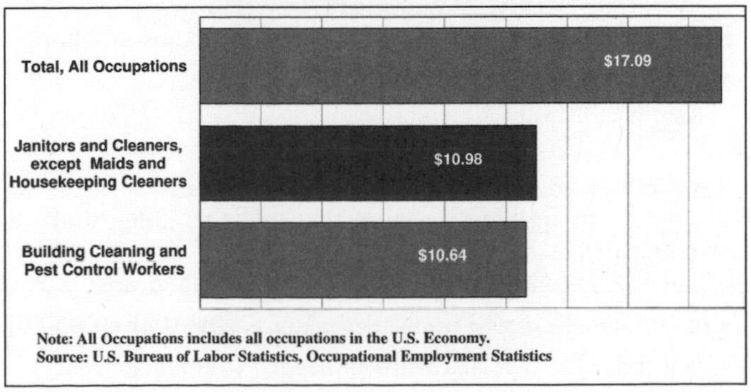

Percent Change in Employment, Projected 2014–2024

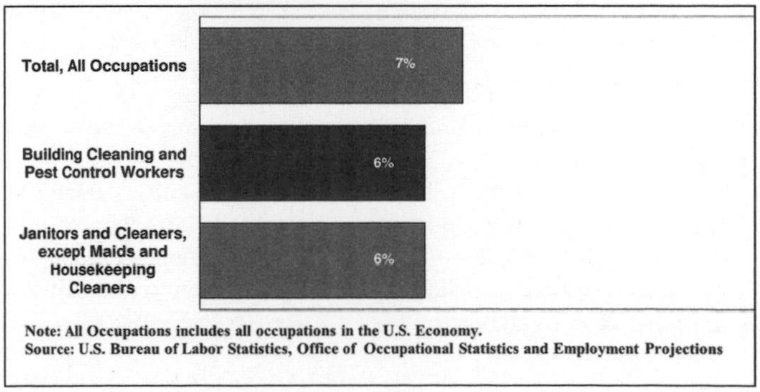

Employment Projections Data for Janitors and Building Cleaners

Occupational Title	SOC Code	Employment, 2014	Projected Employment, 2024	Change, 2014–2024 Percent	Change, 2014–2024 Numeric
Janitors and cleaners, except maids and housekeeping cleaners	37-2011	2,360,600	2,496,900	6	136,300

Source: U.S. Bureau of Labor Statistics, Employment Projections Program

Similar Occupations. This table shows a list of occupations with job duties that are similar to those of janitors and building cleaners.

Occupations	Entry-level Education	2014 Median Pay	Projected Job Growth	Average Annual Openings
Grounds Maintenance Workers	See Education/Training	$24,810	6%	7,760
Pest Control Workers	High school diploma or equivalent	$30,660	-1%	-90

Important Qualities

Interpersonal skills. Janitors and building cleaners should get along well with their supervisors, other cleaners, and the people who live or work in the buildings they clean.

Mechanical skills. Janitors and building cleaners should understand general building operations. They should be able to make routine repairs, such as repairing leaky faucets.

Physical stamina. Janitors and building cleaners spend most of their workday on their feet, operating cleaning equipment and lifting and moving supplies or tools. As a result, they should have good physical stamina.

Physical strength. Janitors and building cleaners often must lift and move cleaning materials and heavy equipment. Cases of liquid cleaner and trash receptacles, for example, can be very heavy, so workers should be strong enough to lift them without injuring their back.

Time-management skills. Janitors and building cleaners should be able to plan and complete tasks in a timely manner.

Pay

The median hourly wage for janitors and building cleaners was $10.98 in May 2014. The median wage is the wage at which half the workers in an occupation earned more than that amount and half earned less. The lowest 10 percent earned less than $8.23, and the highest 10 percent earned more than $18.46.

In May 2014, the median hourly wages for janitors and building cleaners in the top industries in which they worked were as follows:

Elementary and secondary schools; state, local, and private	$13.19
Healthcare and social assistance	11.23
Religious, grantmaking, civic, professional, and similar organizations	10.69
Services to buildings and dwellings	9.91

Job Outlook

Employment of janitors and building cleaners is projected to grow 6 percent from 2014 to 2024, about as fast as the average for all occupations. Many new jobs are expected in facilities related to healthcare, an industry that is expected to grow rapidly.

In addition, as more companies outsource their cleaning services, cleaning or janitorial contractors are likely to benefit and experience employment growth.

Job Prospects. Overall job prospects are expected to be favorable. Those with related work experience and training should have the best job opportunities. Most job openings will come from the need to replace the many workers who leave or retire from this very large occupation.

Contacts for More Information

For more information about janitors and building cleaners, visit

➤ Association of Residential Cleaning Services International (www.arcsi.org)

➤ Building Service Contractors Association International (www.bscai.org)

➤ IEHA (www.ieha.org)
(formerly International Executive Housekeepers Association)

➤ ISSA-The Worldwide Cleaning Industry Association (www.issa.com)

Information about janitorial and building cleaning jobs is available from state employment service offices.

O*NET

➤ Janitors and Cleaners, Except Maids and Housekeeping Cleaners (37-2011.00)

Pest Control Workers

- **2014 Median Pay** .... $30,660 per year
$14.74 per hour
- **Typical Entry-Level Education** .... High school diploma or equivalent
- **Work Experience in a Related Occupation** .... None
- **On-the-job Training** .... Moderate-term on-the-job training
- **Number of Jobs, 2014** 74,100
- **Job Outlook, 2014–24** ....-1% (Little or no change)
- **Employment Change, 2014–24** .... -900

What Pest Control Workers Do

Pest control workers remove unwanted creatures, such as roaches, rats, ants, bedbugs, and termites that infest buildings and surrounding areas.

Duties. Pest control workers typically do the following:

- Inspect buildings and premises for signs of pests or infestation
- Determine the type of treatment needed to eliminate pests

Pest control workers help to keep buildings free of insects, rodents, and other animals.

- Measure the dimensions of the area needing treatment
- Estimate the cost of their services
- Use baits and set traps to remove or kill pests
- Apply pesticides in and around buildings and other structures
- Design and carry out pest management plans
- Drive trucks equipped with power spraying equipment
- Create barriers to prevent pests from entering a building

Unwanted pests that infest buildings and surrounding areas can pose serious risks to the health and safety of occupants. Pest control workers control, manage, and remove these creatures from homes, apartments, offices, and other structures to protect people and to maintain the structural integrity of buildings.

To design and carry out integrated pest management plans, pest control workers must know the identity and biology of a wide range of pests. They must also know the best ways to control and remove the pests.

Although roaches, rats, ants, bedbugs, and termites are the most common pests, some pest control workers also remove irritant birds and other wildlife.

Pest control workers' position titles and job duties often vary by state.

The following are examples of types of pest control workers:

Pest control technicians identify potential and actual pest problems, conduct inspections, and design control strategies. They work directly with customers and, as entry-level workers, use only a limited range of pesticides.

Applicators use a wide range of pesticides and may specialize in a particular area of pest control:

- Termite control technicians use chemicals and modify structures to eliminate termites and prevent future infestations. Some also repair structural damage caused by termites and build barriers to separate pests from their food source.
- Fumigators use gases, called fumigants, to treat specific kinds of pests or large-scale infestations. Fumigators seal infested buildings before using hoses to fill the structure with fumigants. Warning signs are posted to keep people from going into fumigated buildings, and fumigators monitor buildings closely to detect and stop leaks.

Work Environment

Pest control workers held about 74,100 jobs in 2014. About 88 percent worked in the services to buildings and dwellings industry.

Pest control workers must travel to clients' sites. They work both indoors and outdoors, in all types of weather. To inspect and treat sites, workers must often kneel, bend, and crawl in tight spaces.

When working with pesticides, pest control workers must wear protective gear, including gloves, goggles, and when required, respirators.

Work Schedules. Most pest control workers are employed full time. Working evenings and weekends is common. About 1 in 4 pest control workers worked more than 40 hours per week in 2014.

Injuries and Illnesses. Pest control chemicals are toxic and can be harmful to humans, so care should be taken to use such chemicals properly. Workers are trained and licensed for pesticide usage and wear protective equipment. However, some injuries and illnesses from pesticide exposure may still occur. Pest control workers are also susceptible to strains and sprains because workers must often kneel, bend, and crawl in tight spaces.

Education/Training

Most workers need a high school diploma and receive on-the-job training, usually lasting less than 3 months.

Many pest control companies require that employees have good driving records.

Education. A high school diploma or equivalent is typically the minimum qualification for most pest control jobs.

Training. Most pest control workers begin as technicians, receiving both formal technical instruction and moderate-term on-the-job training from employers. They often study specialties such as rodent control, termite control, and fumigation. Technicians also must complete general training in pesticide use and safety. Pest control training can usually be completed in less than 3 months.

After completing the required training, workers are qualified to provide pest control services. Because pest control methods change, workers often attend continuing education classes.

Licenses, Certifications, and Registrations. Pest control workers must be licensed. Licensure requirements vary by state, but workers usually must complete training and pass an exam. Some states have additional requirements, such as having a high school diploma or equivalent, completing an apprenticeship, and passing a background check. States may have additional requirements for applicators.

Advancement. Pest control workers typically advance as they gain experience. Applicators with several years of experience often become supervisors. Some experienced workers start their own pest management company.

Median Annual Wages, May 2014

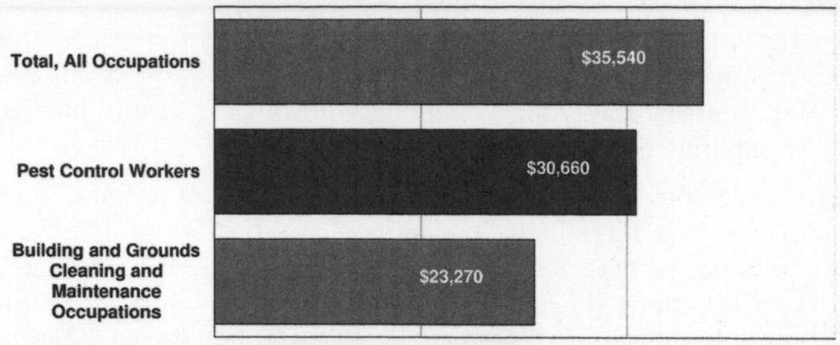

Note: All Occupations includes all occupations in the U.S. Economy.
Source: U.S. Bureau of Labor Statistics, Occupational Employment Statistics

Percent Change in Employment, Projected 2014–2024

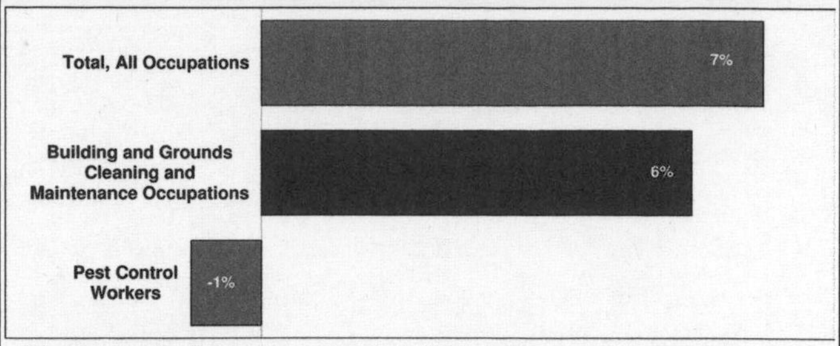

Note: All Occupations includes all occupations in the U.S. Economy.
Source: U.S. Bureau of Labor Statistics, Office of Occupational Statistics and Employment Projections

Important Qualities

Bookkeeping skills. Pest control workers must keep accurate records of the hours they work, chemicals they use, and payments they collect. Self-employed workers, in particular, need these skills in order to run their business.

Customer-service skills. Pest control workers should be friendly and polite when they interact with customers at their homes or businesses.

Detail oriented. Because pest control workers apply pesticides, they need to be able to follow instructions carefully in order to prevent harm to residents, pets, the environment, and themselves.

Physical stamina. Pest control workers may spend hours on their feet, often crouching, kneeling, and crawling. They also must be able to withstand uncomfortable conditions, such as heat when they climb into attics in the summertime and cold when they enter crawl spaces during winter.

Pay

The median annual wage for pest control workers was $30,660 in May 2014. The median wage is the wage at which half the workers in an occupation earned more than that amount and half earned less. The lowest 10 percent earned less than $20,100, and the highest 10 percent earned more than $48,600.

Job Outlook

Employment of pest control workers is projected to show little or no change from 2014 to 2024.

Some people may choose to control pests themselves rather than pay for professional pest control services. However, the growing number of invasive species, such as stink bugs, may increase demand for pest control services.

Job Prospects. Job opportunities are expected to be good. The limited number of people seeking work in pest control and the need to replace workers who leave this occupation should result in many job openings.

Contacts for More Information

For information about state licensing requirements, contact state licensing officials.

For information on pest control officials, visit

➤ Association of Structural Pest Control Regulatory Officials (www.aspcro.org/?q=control-officials)

O*NET

➤ Pest Control Workers (37-2021.00)

Employment Projections Data for Pest Control Workers

Occupational Title	SOC Code	Employment, 2014	Projected Employment, 2024	Change, 2014–2024 Percent	Change, 2014–2024 Numeric
Pest control workers	37-2021	74,100	73,200	-1	-900

Source: U.S. Bureau of Labor Statistics, Employment Projections Program

Similar Occupations. This table shows a list of occupations with job duties that are similar to those of pest control workers.

Occupations	Entry-level Education	2014 Median Pay	Projected Job Growth	Average Annual Openings
Construction Laborers and Helpers	See Education/Training	$30,190	13%	18,010
Grounds Maintenance Workers	See Education/Training	$24,810	6%	7,760
Janitors and Building Cleaners	No formal educational credential	$22,840	6%	13,630

Business and Financial

Accountants and Auditors

- **2014 Median Pay** .... $65,940 per year
  $31.70 per hour
- **Typical Entry-Level Education** .... Bachelor's degree
- **Work Experience in a Related Occupation**.............. None
- **On-the-job Training** .... None
- **Number of Jobs, 2014** 1,332,700
- **Job Outlook, 2014–24**............ 11% (Faster than average)
- **Employment Change, 2014–24** 142,400

What Accountants and Auditors Do

Accountants and auditors prepare and examine financial records. They ensure that financial records are accurate and that taxes are paid properly and on time. Accountants and auditors assess financial operations and work to help ensure that organizations run efficiently.

Duties. Accountants and auditors typically do the following:

- Examine financial statements to ensure that they are accurate and comply with laws and regulations
- Compute taxes owed, prepare tax returns, and ensure that taxes are paid properly and on time
- Inspect account books and accounting systems for efficiency and use of accepted accounting procedures
- Organize and maintain financial records
- Assess financial operations and make best-practices recommendations to management
- Suggest ways to reduce costs, enhance revenues, and improve profits

In addition to examining and preparing financial documentation, accountants and auditors must explain their findings. This includes preparing written reports and meeting face-to-face with organization managers and individual clients.

Many accountants and auditors specialize, depending on the particular organization that they work for. Some work for organizations that specialize in assurance services (improving the quality or context of information for decision-makers) or risk management (determining the probability of a misstatement on financial documentation). Other organizations specialize in specific industries, such as healthcare.

Some workers with a background in accounting and auditing teach in colleges and universities. For more information, see the profile on postsecondary teachers.

The following are examples of types of accountants and auditors:

Public accountants perform a broad range of accounting, auditing, tax, and consulting tasks. Their clients include corporations, governments, and individuals.

Public accountants work with financial documents that clients are required by law to disclose. These include tax forms and balance sheet statements that corporations must provide potential investors. For example, some public accountants concentrate on tax matters, advising corporations about the tax advantages of certain business decisions or preparing individual income tax returns.

Public accountants, many of whom are Certified Public Accountants (CPAs), generally have their own businesses or work for public accounting firms. Publicly traded companies are required to have CPAs sign documents they submit to the Securities and Exchange Commission (SEC), including annual and quarterly reports.

Some public accountants specialize in forensic accounting, investigating financial crimes such as securities fraud and embezzlement, bankruptcies and contract disputes, and other complex and possibly criminal financial transactions. Forensic accountants combine their knowledge of accounting and finance with law and investigative techniques to determine if an activity is illegal. Many forensic accountants work closely with law enforcement personnel and lawyers during investigations and often appear as expert witnesses during trials.

Management accountants, also called *cost*, *managerial*, *industrial*, *corporate*, or *private accountants*, record and analyze the financial information of the organizations for which they work. The information that management accountants prepare is intended for internal use by business managers, not by the general public.

Management accountants often work on budgeting and performance evaluation. They also may help organizations plan the cost of doing business. Some may work with financial managers on

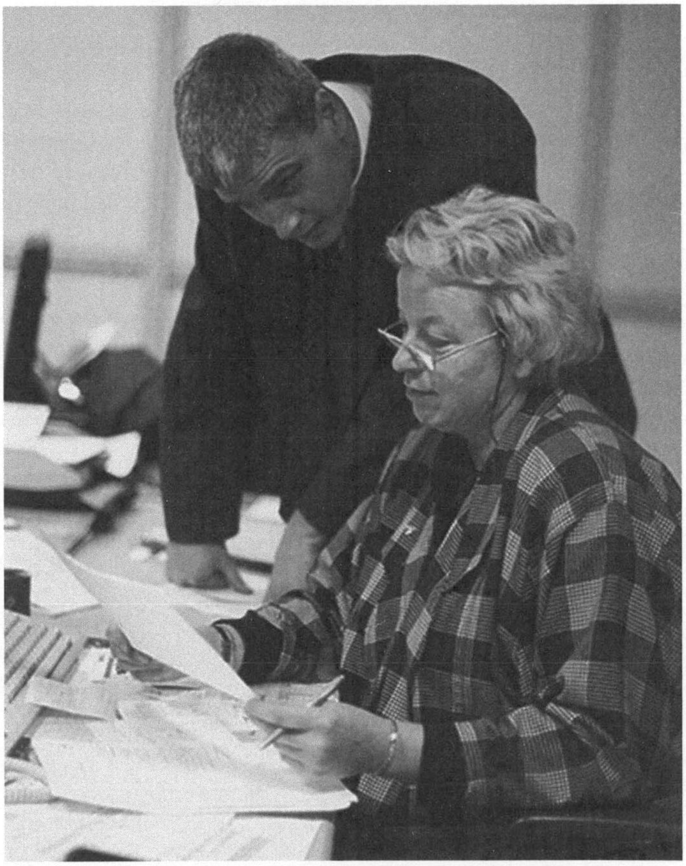

Accountants and auditors analyze and interpret financial information.

asset management, which involves planning and selecting financial investments such as stocks, bonds, and real estate.

Government accountants maintain and examine the records of government agencies and audit private businesses and individuals whose activities are subject to government regulations or taxation. Accountants employed by federal, state, and local governments ensure that revenues are received and spent in accordance with laws and regulations.

Internal auditors check for mismanagement of an organization's funds. They identify ways to improve the processes for finding and eliminating waste and fraud. The practice of internal auditing is not regulated, but The Institute of Internal Auditors (IIA) provides generally accepted standards.

External auditors perform similar duties as internal auditors, but are employed by an outside organization, rather than the one they are auditing. They review clients' financial statements and inform investors and authorities that the statements have been correctly prepared and reported.

Information technology auditors are internal auditors who review controls for their organization's computer systems, to ensure that the financial data comes from a reliable source.

Work Environment

Accountants and auditors held about 1.3 million jobs in 2014. The industries that employed the most accountants and auditors were as follows:

Accounting, tax preparation, bookkeeping, and payroll services	26%
Government	8
Finance and insurance	8
Management of companies and enterprises	7
Manufacturing	6

Most accountants and auditors work in offices, although some work from home. The work tends to be fast-paced and can be stressful. Although they complete much of their work alone, they sometimes work in teams with other accountants and auditors. Accountants and auditors may travel to their clients' places of business.

Work Schedules. Most accountants and auditors work full time. In 2014, about 1 in 5 worked more than 40 hours per week. Longer periods of work are typical at certain times of the year, such as at the end of the budget year or during tax season.

Education/Training

Certification within a specific field of accounting improves job prospects. For example, many accountants become Certified Public Accountants (CPAs).

Education. Most accountant and auditor positions require at least a bachelor's degree in accounting or a related field. Some employers prefer to hire applicants who have a master's degree, either in accounting or in business administration with a concentration in accounting.

A few universities and colleges offer specialized programs, such as a bachelor's degree in internal auditing. In some cases, those with associate's degrees, as well as bookkeepers and accounting clerks who meet the education and experience requirements set by their employers, get junior accounting positions and advance to accountant positions by showing their accounting skills on the job.

Many colleges help students gain practical experience through summer or part-time internships with public accounting or business firms.

Licenses, Certifications, and Registrations. Every accountant filing a report with the Securities and Exchange Commission (SEC) is required by law to be a Certified Public Accountant (CPA). Many other accountants choose to become a CPA to enhance their job prospects or to gain clients. Many employers will often pay the costs associated with the CPA exam.

CPAs are licensed by their state's Board of Accountancy. Becoming a CPA requires passing a national exam and meeting other state requirements. Almost all states require CPA candidates to complete 150 semester hours of college coursework to be certified, which is 30 hours more than the usual 4-year bachelor's degree. Many schools offer a 5-year combined bachelor's and master's degree to meet the 150-hour requirement, but a master's degree is not required.

A few states allow a number of years of public accounting experience to substitute for a college degree.

All states use the four-part Uniform CPA Examination from the American Institute of Certified Public Accountants (AICPA). Candidates do not have to pass all four parts at once, but most states require that they pass all four parts within 18 months of passing their first part.

Almost all states require CPAs to take continuing education to keep their license.

Certification provides an advantage in the job market because it shows professional competence in a specialized field of accounting and auditing. Accountants and auditors seek certifications from a variety of professional societies. Some of the most common certifications are listed below:

The Institute of Management Accountants offers the Certified Management Accountant (CMA) to applicants who complete a bachelor's degree. Applicants must have worked at least 2 years in management accounting, pass a two-part exam, agree to meet continuing education requirements, and comply with standards of professional conduct. The exam covers areas such as financial statement analysis, working-capital policy, capital structure, valuation issues, and risk management.

The Institute of Internal Auditors (IIA) offers the Certified Internal Auditor (CIA) to graduates from accredited colleges and universities who have worked for 2 years as internal auditors and have passed a four-part exam. The IIA also offers the Certified in Control Self-Assessment (CCSA), Certified Government Auditing Professional (CGAP), Certified Financial Services Auditor (CFSA), and Certification in Risk Management Assurance (CRMA) to those who pass the exams and meet educational and experience requirements.

ISACA offers the Certified Information Systems Auditor (CISA) to candidates who pass an exam and have 5 years of experience auditing information systems. Information systems experience, financial or operational auditing experience, or related college credit hours can be substituted for up to 3 years of experience in information systems auditing, control, or security.

For accountants with a CPA, the AICPA offers the option to receive any or all of the Accredited in Business Valuation (ABV), Certified Information Technology Professional (CITP), or Personal Financial Specialist (PFS) certifications. The ABV requires a written exam, completion of at least six business valuation projects, and 75 hours of continuing education. The CITP requires 1,000 hours of business technology experience and 75 hours of continuing education. Candidates for the PFS also must complete a certain amount of work experience and continuing education, and pass a written exam.

Advancement. Some top executives and financial managers have a background in accounting, internal auditing, or finance.

Median Annual Wages, May 2014

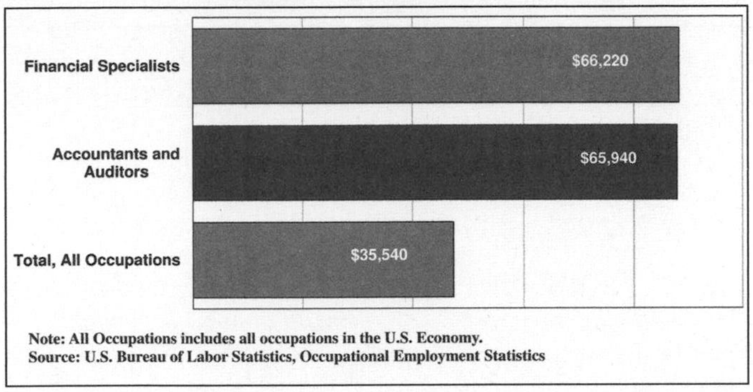

Percent Change in Employment, Projected 2014–2024

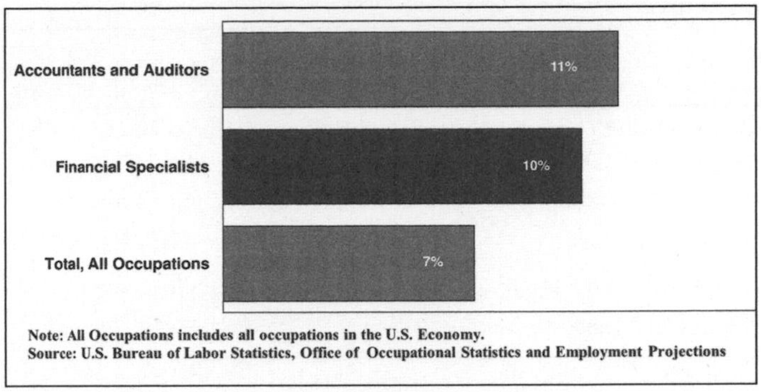

Beginning public accountants often advance to positions with more responsibility in 1 or 2 years and to senior positions within another few years. Those who excel may become supervisors, managers, or partners; open their own public accounting firm; or transfer to executive positions in management accounting or internal auditing in private firms.

Management accountants often start as cost accountants, junior internal auditors, or trainees for other accounting positions. As they rise through the organization, they may advance to accounting manager, chief cost accountant, budget director, or manager of internal auditing. Some become controllers, treasurers, financial vice presidents, chief financial officers, or corporation presidents.

Public accountants, management accountants, and internal auditors can move from one aspect of accounting and auditing to another. Public accountants often move into management accounting or internal auditing. Management accountants may become internal auditors, and internal auditors may become management accountants. However, it is less common for management accountants or internal auditors to move into public accounting.

Important Qualities

Analytical skills. Accountants and auditors must be able to identify issues in documentation and suggest solutions. For example, public accountants use analytical skills in their work to minimize tax liability, and internal auditors use these skills to detect fraudulent use of funds.

Communication skills. Accountants and auditors must be able to listen carefully to facts and concerns from clients, managers, and others. They must also be able to discuss the results of their work in both meetings and written reports.

Detail oriented. Accountants and auditors must pay attention to detail when compiling and examining documentation.

Math skills. Accountants and auditors must be able to analyze, compare, and interpret facts and figures, although complex math skills are not necessary.

Organizational skills. Strong organizational skills are important for accountants and auditors who often work with a range of financial documents for a variety of clients.

Pay

The median annual wage for accountants and auditors was $65,940 in May 2014. The median wage is the wage at which half the workers in an occupation earned more than that amount and half earned less. The lowest 10 percent earned less than $40,850, and the highest 10 percent earned more than $115,950.

In May 2014, the median annual wages for accountants and auditors in the top industries in which they worked were as follows:

Finance and insurance	$69,350
Management of companies and enterprises	68,370
Manufacturing	67,460
Accounting, tax preparation, bookkeeping, and payroll services	66,020
Government	63,770

Job Outlook

Employment of accountants and auditors is projected to grow 11 percent from 2014 to 2024, faster than the average for all occupations. Globalization, a growing overall economy, and an increasingly complex tax and regulatory environment are expected to lead to strong demand for accountants and auditors.

In general, employment growth of accountants and auditors is expected to be closely tied to the health of the overall economy. As the economy grows, these workers will continue to be needed to prepare and examine financial records. In addition, as more companies go public, there will be greater need for public accountants to handle the legally required financial documentation.

Stricter laws and regulations, particularly in the financial sector, will likely increase the demand for accounting services as organizations seek to comply with new standards. In addition, tighter lending standards are expected to increase the importance of audits, as this is a key way for organizations to demonstrate their creditworthiness.

The continued globalization of business may lead to increased demand for accounting expertise and services related to international trade and international mergers and acquisitions.

Job Prospects. Accountants and auditors who have earned professional recognition, especially as Certified Public Accountants

Employment Projections Data for Accountants and Auditors

Occupational Title	SOC Code	Employment, 2014	Projected Employment, 2024	Change, 2014–2024 Percent	Change, 2014–2024 Numeric
Accountants and auditors	13-2011	1,332,700	1,475,100	11	142,400

Source: U.S. Bureau of Labor Statistics, Employment Projections Program

Similar Occupations. This table shows a list of occupations with job duties that are similar to those of accountants and auditors.

Occupations	Entry-level Education	2014 Median Pay	Projected Job Growth	Average Annual Openings
Bookkeeping, Accounting, and Auditing Clerks	Some college, no degree	$36,430	-8%	-14,870
Budget Analysts	Bachelor's degree	$71,220	3%	150
Cost Estimators	Bachelor's degree	$60,050	9%	1,870
Financial Analysts	Bachelor's degree	$78,620	12%	3,230
Financial Managers	Bachelor's degree	$115,320	7%	3,770
Management Analysts	Bachelor's degree	$80,880	14%	10,340
Personal Financial Advisors	Bachelor's degree	$81,060	30%	7,390
Postsecondary Teachers	See Education/Training	$70,790	13%	17,700
Tax Examiners and Collectors, and Revenue Agents	Bachelor's degree	$51,120	-6%	-420
Top Executives	Bachelor's degree	$102,750	6%	14,700

(CPAs), should have the best prospects. Job applicants who have a master's degree in accounting or a master's degree in business with a concentration in accounting also may have an advantage.

Strong demand for accountants may lead to good prospects for entry-level positions. However, competition will be stronger for jobs with the most prestigious accounting and business firms.

Contacts for More Information

For more information about accredited accounting programs, visit

➤ AACSB International—Association to Advance Collegiate Schools of Business (www.aacsb.edu)

For more information about the Certified Public Accountant (CPA) designation, visit

➤ American Institute of Certified Public Accountants (AICPA) (www.aicpa.org)

For more information about management accounting and the Certified Management Accountant (CMA) designation, visit

➤ Institute of Management Accountants (www.imanet.org)

For more information about internal auditing and the Certified Internal Auditor (CIA) designation, visit

➤ The Institute of Internal Auditors (www.theiia.org)

For more information about information systems auditing and the Certified Information Systems Auditor (CISA) designation, visit

➤ ISACA (www.isaca.org)

O*NET

➤ Accountants and Auditors (13-2011.00)

➤ Accountants (13-2011.01)

➤ Auditors (13-2011.02)

Appraisers and Assessors of Real Estate

- **2014 Median Pay** .... $52,570 per year
  $25.27 per hour
- **Typical Entry-Level Education** .... Bachelor's degree
- **Work Experience in a Related Occupation** .... None
- **On-the-job Training** .... Long-term on-the-job training
- **Number of Jobs, 2014** 85,800
- **Job Outlook, 2014–24** .... 8% (As fast as average)
- **Employment Change, 2014–24** 6,800

What Appraisers and Assessors of Real Estate Do

Appraisers and assessors of real estate provide an estimate of the value of land and the buildings on the land usually before it is sold, mortgaged, taxed, insured, or developed.

Duties. Appraisers and assessors of real estate typically do the following:

- Verify legal descriptions of real estate properties in public records
- Inspect new and existing properties, noting the characteristics
- Photograph the interior and exterior of properties
- Analyze "comparables," or similar nearby properties, to help provide values
- Prepare written reports on the property values
- Prepare and maintain current data on each real estate property

Appraisers and assessors work in localities that they are familiar with so that they know any environmental or other concerns that may affect the property's value.

Appraisers typically value one property at a time, and they often specialize in a certain type of real estate:

- *Commercial appraisers* specialize in income-producing property, such as office buildings, stores, and hotels.
- *Residential appraisers* focus on appraising property in which people live, such as single family homes and condominiums. They only appraise properties that house one to four units.

When evaluating a property's value, appraisers note the characteristics of the property and surrounding area, such as a view or noisy highway nearby. They also consider the overall condition of a building, including its foundation and roof or any renovations that may have been done. Appraisers photograph the outside of the building and some of the interior features to document its condition. After visiting the property, the appraiser analyzes the property relative to comparable home sales, including lease records, location, view, previous appraisals, and income potential. During the entire process, appraisers record their research, observations, and methods used in providing an estimate of the property's value.

Assessors value properties for property tax assessments. Most work for local governments. Unlike appraisers, who generally focus on one property at a time, assessors often value an entire neighborhood of homes at once by using mass appraisal techniques and computer-assisted appraisal systems.

Assessors must be up to date on tax assessment procedures. Taxpayers sometimes challenge the assessed value because they feel they are being charged too much for property tax. Assessors must be able to defend the accuracy of their property assessments, either to the owner directly or at a public hearing.

Assessors also keep a database of every property in their jurisdiction, identifying the property owner, assessment history, and characteristics of the property, as well as property maps detailing the property distribution of the jurisdiction.

Work Environment

Appraisers and assessors of real estate held about 85,800 jobs in 2014. The industries that employed the most appraisers and assessors of real estate were as follows:

Local government, excluding education and hospitals	30%
Activities related to real estate	29
Depository credit intermediation	2

About 1 in 4 appraisers and assessors of real estate were self-employed.

Although appraisers and assessors of real estate work in offices, they may spend a large part of their time conducting site visits to assess properties. Time spent away from the office depends on the specialty. For example, residential appraisers tend to spend less time on office work than commercial appraisers, who might spend up to several weeks analyzing information and writing reports on one property. Appraisers who work for banks and mortgage companies generally spend most of their time inside the office, making site visits only when necessary.

Work Schedules. Appraisers and assessors of real estate typically work full time during regular business hours. However, self-employed appraisers, often called *independent fee appraisers*, usually work more than a standard 40-hour workweek, because they must often write reports during evenings and on weekends.

Appraisers play an important role in the purchasing and selling of real estate.

Education/Training

The requirements to become a fully qualified appraiser or assessor of real estate are complex and vary by state and, sometimes, by the value or type of property. Most appraisers of residential or commercial property must have at least a bachelor's degree to obtain the entry-level state license category. Check with your state's licensing board for specific requirements for both assessors and appraisers.

Education. Although requirements may vary by state, appraisers of residential or commercial property usually must have at least a bachelor's degree.

College courses in subjects such as economics, finance, mathematics, computer science, English, and business or real estate law can be useful for prospective appraisers and assessors.

Most states set education and experience requirements that assessors must meet in order to practice. A few states have no statewide requirements; instead, each locality sets the standards. In some localities, candidates may qualify with a high school diploma.

Training. Employers generally require candidates to take basic appraisal courses, complete long-term on-the-job training, and work enough hours to meet the requirements for licenses or certificates.

Licenses, Certifications, and Registrations. Federal law requires appraisers to have a state license or certification when working on federally related transactions, such as appraisals for loans made by federally insured banks and financial institutions. The Appraisal Foundation (TAF) offers information on appraisal licensing. There is no such federal requirement for assessors, although some states require certification. For state specific requirements, applicants should contact their state board.

Real property appraisers usually value one property at a time, while assessors value many at once, but both occupations use similar methods and techniques. As a result, assessors and appraisers tend to take the same courses for certification. In addition to passing a statewide examination, candidates must usually complete a set number of on-the-job hours.

The credential level determines what type of property a person may appraise. The four federal appraiser classifications are as follows:

- Licensed Trainee Real Property Appraiser
- Licensed Residential Real Property Appraiser
- Certified Residential Real Property Appraiser
- Certified General Real Property Appraiser

Many states offer a Licensed Trainee Real Property Appraiser credential to candidates working toward licensure or certification. Training programs vary by state, but they usually require candidates to take at least 75 hours of specified appraiser education before applying for a job as a trainee.

Many states offer the Licensed Residential Real Property Appraiser. With this license, a qualified person may appraise noncomplex one-to-four unit residences with a value of less than $1 million and complex one-to-four unit residences with a value of less than $250,000. A candidate must have the following qualifications to get this certificate:

- 30 semester hours of college-level education
- 150 hours of appraiser-qualifying education
- 2,000 hours of on-the-job training completed over at least 1 year

Being a Certified Residential Real Property Appraiser is the minimum requirement to appraise a residential property with a

Median Annual Wages, May 2014

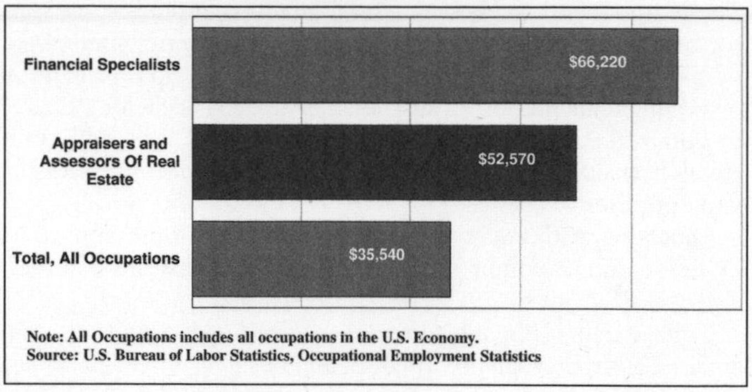

Percent Change in Employment, Projected 2014–2024

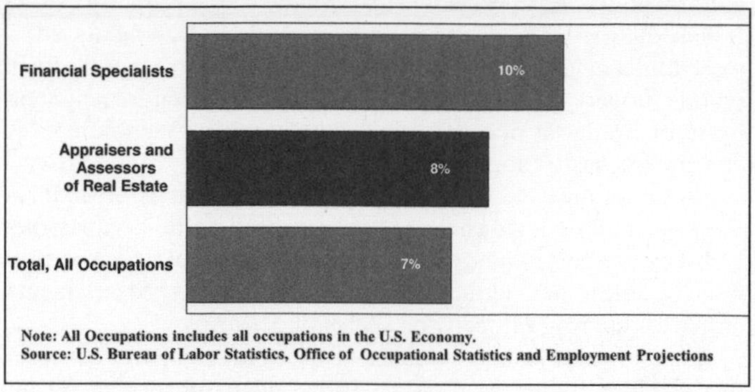

loan amount over $250,000 or any other type of residential property even if the loan amount is less than $250,000. A candidate must have the following qualifications to get this certificate:

- Bachelor's degree
- 200 hours of appraiser-specific qualifying education
- 2,500 hours of work experience completed over at least 2 years

Being a Certified General Real Property Appraiser permits a person to appraise real property of any type and any value. A candidate must have the following qualifications to get this certificate:

- Bachelor's degree
- 300 hours of appraiser-specific qualifying education
- 3,000 hours of work experience completed over at least 2½ years

For all of these credentials, except the Trainee License credential, candidates must have the following qualifications:

- Have 15 hours of classroom instruction on the Uniform Standards of Professional Appraisal Practice
- Pass an exam

Unlike appraisers, assessors have no federal requirement for certification. In states that mandate certification for assessors, the requirements are usually similar to those for appraisers. For example, the International Association of Assessing Officers (IAAO) offers the Certified Assessment Evaluator (CAE). This designation covers topics that include property valuation for tax purposes, property tax administration, and property tax policy. Applicants are required to have a bachelor's degree prior to obtaining the designation.

For those states that do not require certification for assessors, the hiring office usually requires the candidate to take basic appraisal courses, complete on-the-job training, and meet the work-hours requirements for appraisal licenses or certificates. Many assessors also have a state appraiser license or credential.

Assessors tend to start working in an assessor's office that provides on-the-job training; smaller municipalities are often unable to provide this work experience. An alternate source of experience for aspiring assessors is through a revaluation firm.

Both appraisers and assessors must take continuing education courses to keep the license or certification. Exact requirements vary by state and certification.

Important Qualities

Analytical skills. Appraisers and assessors of real estate use many sources of data when valuing a property. As a result, they must carefully research and analyze all factors before estimating a value and producing a final written report.

Customer-service skills. Because appraisers must regularly interact with clients, being polite and friendly is important. In addition, these characteristics may help expand future business opportunities.

Math skills. Accurately analyzing real estate data includes such steps as calculating square footage of land and building space, so workers must have good math skills.

Organizational skills. To successfully accomplish all the tasks related to appraising and assessing a property, appraisers and assessors of real estate need good organizational skills.

Problem-solving skills. Appraising or assessing a property's value may involve unexpected problems. The ability to develop and apply an alternative solution is crucial to successfully completing the appraisal and report on time.

Time-management skills. Appraisers and assessors of real estate often work under time constraints, sometimes appraising many properties in a single day. As a result, managing time and meeting deadlines are important.

Pay

The median annual wage for appraisers and assessors of real estate was $52,570 in May 2014. The median wage is the wage at which half the workers in an occupation earned more than that amount and half earned less. The lowest 10 percent earned less than $26,980, and the highest 10 percent earned more than $95,020.

In May 2014, the median annual wages for appraisers and assessors of real estate in the top industries in which they worked were as follows:

Depository credit intermediation	$72,190
Activities related to real estate	52,560
Local government, excluding education and hospitals	47,310

Employment Projections Data for Appraisers and Assessors of Real Estate

Occupational Title	SOC Code	Employment, 2014	Projected Employment, 2024	Change, 2014–2024 Percent	Change, 2014–2024 Numeric
Appraisers and assessors of real estate	13-2021	85,800	92,500	8	6,800

Source: U.S. Bureau of Labor Statistics, Employment Projections Program

Similar Occupations. This table shows a list of occupations with job duties that are similar to those of appraisers and assessors of real estate.

Occupations	Entry-level Education	2014 Median Pay	Projected Job Growth	Average Annual Openings
Claims Adjusters, Appraisers, Examiners, and Investigators	See Education/Training	$62,300	3%	960
Construction and Building Inspectors	High school diploma or equivalent	$56,040	8%	810
Real Estate Brokers and Sales Agents	High school diploma or equivalent	$43,430	3%	1,090

Earnings for independent fee appraisers can vary significantly because they are paid fees on the basis of each appraisal.

Job Outlook

Employment of appraisers and assessors of real estate is projected to grow 8 percent from 2014 to 2024, about as fast as the average for all occupations.

Demand for appraisal services is linked to the real estate market, which can fluctuate in the short term. Over the long term, employment growth will be driven by economic expansion and population increases—factors that generate demand for property.

Greater use of mobile technology, which allows workers to appraise and assess properties more efficiently, will increase productivity and may slow future employment growth. In addition, the increased use of alternate valuation products, such as automated valuation models to aid in the appraisal of property for mortgages, might also increase productivity, reducing demand for additional appraisers.

Job Prospects. Overall job opportunities are expected to be highly competitive. Employment opportunities should be best in areas with active real estate markets. However, the cyclical nature of the real estate market will directly affect demand, especially for those who appraise residential properties. As a result, job opportunities should be best for those who are able to switch specialties and appraise different types of properties.

Contacts for More Information

For more information about appraisers of real estate, visit

➤ American Society of Appraisers (www.appraisers.org)
➤ Appraisal Institute (www.appraisalinstitute.org)

For more information about assessors of real estate, visit

➤ International Association of Assessing Officers (www.iaao.org)

For more information about licensure requirements for appraisers and assessors of real estate, visit

➤ The Appraisal Foundation (www.appraisalfoundation.org)

O*NET

➤ Appraisers and Assessors of Real Estate (13-2021.00)
➤ Assessors (13-2021.01)
➤ Appraisers, Real Estate (13-2021.02)

Budget Analysts

- **2014 Median Pay** .... $71,220 per year $34.24 per hour
- **Typical Entry-Level Education** .... Bachelor's degree
- **Work Experience in a Related Occupation**.............. None
- **On-the-job Training** .... None
- **Number of Jobs, 2014** 60,800
- **Job Outlook, 2014–24**............. 3% (Slower than average)
- **Employment Change, 2014–24** 1,500

What Budget Analysts Do

Budget analysts help public and private institutions organize their finances. They prepare budget reports and monitor institutional spending.

Duties. Budget analysts typically do the following:

- Work with program and project managers to develop the organization's budget
- Review managers' budget proposals for completeness, accuracy, and compliance with laws and other regulations
- Combine all the program and department budgets together into a consolidated organizational budget and review all funding requests for merit
- Explain their recommendations for funding requests to others in the organization, legislators, and the public
- Help the chief operations officer, agency head, or other top managers analyze proposed plans and find alternatives if the projected results are unsatisfactory
- Monitor organizational spending to ensure that it is within budget
- Inform program managers of the status and availability of funds
- Estimate future financial needs

Budget analysts advise various institutions—including governments, universities, and businesses—on how to organize their finances. They prepare annual and special reports and evaluate budget proposals. They analyze data to determine the costs and benefits of various programs and recommend funding levels based on their findings. Although elected officials (in government) or top executives (in a private company) usually make the final decision on an organization's budget, they rely on the work of budget analysts to prepare the information for that decision.

Sometimes, budget analysts use cost-benefit analyses to review financial requests, assess program tradeoffs, and explore alternative funding methods. Budget analysts also may examine past budgets and research economic and financial developments that affect the organization's income and expenditures. Budget analysts may recommend program spending cuts or redistributing extra funds.

Throughout the year, budget analysts oversee spending to ensure compliance with the budget and determine whether changes to funding levels are needed for certain programs. Analysts also evaluate programs to determine whether they are producing the desired results.

In addition to providing technical analysis, budget analysts must effectively communicate their recommendations to officials within the organization. For example, if there is a difference between the approved budget and actual spending, budget analysts may write a report explaining the variations and recommend changes to reconcile the differences.

Budget analysts working in government attend committee hearings to explain their recommendations to legislators. Occasionally, budget analysts may evaluate how well a program is doing, provide policy analysis, and draft budget-related legislation.

Work Environment

Budget analysts held about 60,800 jobs in 2014. The industries that employed the most budget analysts were as follows:

Federal government	20%
Educational services; state, local, and private	15
State government, excluding education and hospitals	13
Professional, scientific, and technical services	10
Local government, excluding education and hospitals	10

Although budget analysts usually work in offices, some may travel to get budget details firsthand or to verify funding allocations.

Budget analysts spend most of their time analyzing data and preparing budget proposals. In nonprofit and government organizations, analysts try to find the most efficient way to distribute funds and other resources among various departments and programs. In private firms, a budget analyst's main responsibility is to review the budget and seek new ways to improve efficiency and increase profits.

Work Schedules. Most budget analysts work full time, and overtime is sometimes required during final reviews of budgets. The pressures of deadlines and tight work schedules can be stressful.

Education/Training

A bachelor's degree is typically required to become a budget analyst, although some employers prefer candidates with a master's degree.

Education. Employers generally require budget analysts to have at least a bachelor's degree. However, some employers may require candidates to have a master's degree. Because developing a budget requires strong numerical and analytical skills, courses in statistics or accounting are helpful. Federal, state, and local governments have varying requirements, but usually require a bachelor's degree in one of many areas, such as accounting, finance, business, public administration, economics, statistics, political science, or sociology.

Sometimes, budget-related or finance-related work experience can be substituted for formal education.

Licenses, Certifications, and Registrations. Government budget analysts may earn the Certified Government Financial Manager credential from the Association of Government Accountants. To earn this certification, candidates must have a minimum of a bachelor's degree, 24 credit hours of study in financial management, 2 years of professional-level experience in governmental financial management, and they must pass a series of exams. To keep the certification, budget analysts must take 80 hours of continuing education every 2 years.

Budget analysts help organizations determine the best use of financial resources.

Advancement. Entry-level budget analysts begin with limited responsibilities, but advancement is common. As analysts gain experience, they have the opportunity to advance to intermediate and senior budget analyst positions.

Important Qualities

Analytical skills. Budget analysts must be able to process a variety of information, evaluate costs and benefits, and solve complex problems.

Communication skills. Budget analysts need strong communication skills because they often have to explain and defend their analyses and recommendations in meetings and legislative committee hearings.

Detail oriented. Creating an efficient budget requires careful analysis of each budget item.

Median Annual Wages, May 2014

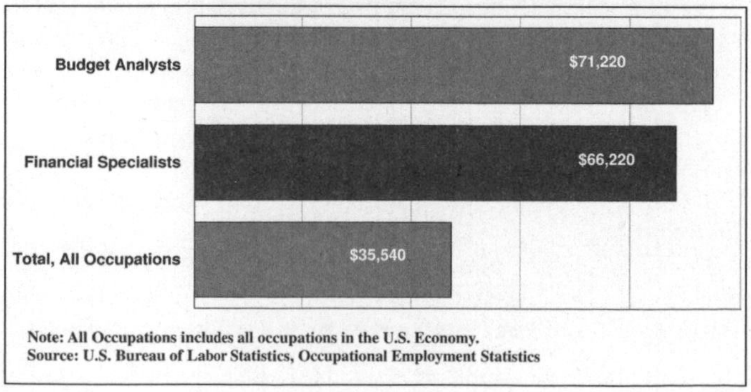

Percent Change in Employment, Projected 2014–2024

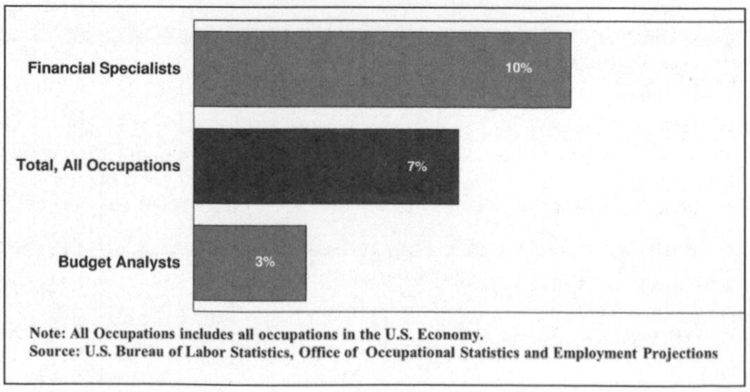

Employment Projections Data for Budget Analysts

Occupational Title	SOC Code	Employment, 2014	Projected Employment, 2024	Change, 2014–2024 Percent	Change, 2014–2024 Numeric
Budget analysts	13-2031	60,800	62,300	3	1,500

Source: U.S. Bureau of Labor Statistics, Employment Projections Program

Similar Occupations. This table shows a list of occupations with job duties that are similar to those of budget analysts.

Occupations	Entry-level Education	2014 Median Pay	Projected Job Growth	Average Annual Openings
Accountants and Auditors	Bachelor's degree	$65,940	11%	14,240
Cost Estimators	Bachelor's degree	$60,050	9%	1,870
Economists	Master's degree	$95,710	6%	120
Financial Analysts	Bachelor's degree	$78,620	12%	3,230
Financial Managers	Bachelor's degree	$115,320	7%	3,770
Management Analysts	Bachelor's degree	$80,880	14%	10,340
Tax Examiners and Collectors, and Revenue Agents	Bachelor's degree	$51,120	-6%	-420

Math skills. Most budget analysts need math skills and should be able to use certain software, including spreadsheets, database functions, and financial analysis programs.

Writing skills. Budget analysts must present technical information in writing that is understandable for the intended audience.

Pay

The median annual wage for budget analysts was $71,220 in May 2014. The median wage is the wage at which half the workers in an occupation earned more than that amount and half earned less. The lowest 10 percent earned less than $46,230, and the highest 10 percent earned more than $107,230.

In May 2014, the median annual wages for budget analysts in the top industries in which they worked were as follows:

Professional, scientific, and technical services	$79,440
Federal government	76,860
Local government, excluding education and hospitals	66,910
State government, excluding education and hospitals	62,840
Educational services; state, local, and private	60,620

Job Outlook

Employment of budget analysts is projected to grow 3 percent from 2014 to 2024, slower than the average for all occupations.

Efficient use of public funds is increasingly expected at the federal, state, and local levels. Budget analysts should be in demand for their ability to manage the allocation of public funds. Many state and local governments, which previously had hiring freezes due to revenue shortfalls, are now seeing growth in revenue and spending. This should allow for increased hiring of budget analysts, as these governments fill positions that were previously left vacant. Budget analysts working in state government are projected to grow 2 percent, while those working in local government are projected to grow 6 percent.

However, recent slowdowns in federal spending and employment have limited overall employment growth at the federal level. Because of this, budget analysts working in the federal government are projected to decline 10 percent.

Job Prospects. This occupation has fairly steady turnover, as budget analysts often leave the occupation to pursue opportunities to work in similar areas. These opportunities include positions as higher-level budget analysts at other organizations and positions in related business and financial occupations, such as financial analysts. For this reason, job prospects are expected to be good for entry-level budget analysts.

Contacts for More Information

For information about the Government Financial Manager certification, visit

➤ Association of Government Accountants (www.agacgfm.org)

O*NET

➤ Budget Analysts (13-2031.00)

Buyers and Purchasing Agents

- **2014 Median Pay** .... $58,520 per year
  $28.14 per hour
- **Typical Entry-Level Education** .... Bachelor's degree
- **Work Experience in a Related Occupation** .... None
- **On-the-job Training** .... Long-term on-the-job training
- **Number of Jobs, 2014** 443,200
- **Job Outlook, 2014–24** .... 2% (Slower than average)
- **Employment Change, 2014–24** 7,200

What Buyers and Purchasing Agents Do

Buyers and purchasing agents buy products and services for organizations to use or resell. They evaluate suppliers, negotiate contracts, and review the quality of products.

Duties. Buyers and purchasing agents typically do the following:

- Evaluate suppliers on the basis of the price, quality, and speed of delivery of their products and services

- Interview vendors and visit suppliers' plants and distribution centers to examine and learn about products, services, and prices
- Attend meetings, trade shows, and conferences to learn about new industry trends and make contacts with suppliers
- Analyze price proposals, financial reports, and other information to determine reasonable prices
- Negotiate contracts on behalf of their organization
- Work out agreements with suppliers, such as when products will be delivered
- Meet with staff and vendors to discuss defective or unacceptable goods or services and determine corrective action
- Evaluate and monitor contracts to be sure that vendors and supplies comply with the terms and conditions of the contract and to determine the need for changes
- Maintain and review records of items bought, costs, deliveries, product performance, and inventories

Buyers and purchasing agents buy farm products, durable and nondurable goods, and services for organizations and institutions. They try to get the best deal for their organization: the highest quality goods and services at the lowest cost. They do this by studying sales records and inventory levels of current stock, identifying foreign and domestic suppliers, and keeping up to date with changes affecting both the supply of, and demand for, products and materials.

To be effective, purchasing agents and buyers must have a working technical knowledge of the goods or services they are purchasing.

Evaluating suppliers is one of the most critical functions of a buyer or purchasing agent. Many organizations run on a lean manufacturing schedule and use just-in-time inventories, so any delays in the supply chain can shut down production and cause the organization to lose customers.

Buyers and purchasing agents use many resources to find out all they can about potential suppliers. They attend meetings, trade shows, and conferences to learn about new industry trends and make contacts with suppliers.

They often interview prospective suppliers and visit their plants and distribution centers to assess their capabilities. For example, they may discuss the design of products with design engineers, quality concerns with production supervisors, or shipping issues with managers in the receiving department.

Buyers and purchasing agents must make certain that the supplier can deliver the desired goods or services on time, in the correct quantities, and without sacrificing quality. Once they have gathered information on suppliers, they sign contracts with suppliers who meet the organization's needs and they place orders.

Buyers who purchase items to resell to customers may determine which products their organization will sell. They need to be able to predict what will appeal to their customers. If they are wrong, they could jeopardize the profits and reputation of their organization.

Buyers who work for large organizations often specialize in purchasing one or two categories of products or services. Buyers who work for smaller businesses or government agencies may be responsible for making a greater variety of purchases.

Wholesale and retail buyers purchase goods for resale to consumers. Examples of these goods are clothing and electronics. Purchasing specialists who buy finished goods for resale are commonly known as *buyers* or *merchandise managers*.

Buyers and purchasing agents evaluate suppliers, negotiate contracts, and review product quality.

Purchasing agents and buyers of farm products buy agricultural products for further processing or resale. Examples of these products are grain, cotton, and tobacco.

Purchasing agents, except wholesale, retail, and farm products buy items for the operation of an organization. Examples of these items are chemicals and industrial equipment needed for a manufacturing establishment, and office supplies.

Work Environment

Buyers and purchasing agents held about 443,200 jobs in 2014. The industries that employed the most buyers and purchasing agents were as follows:

Manufacturing	23%
Wholesale trade	15
Retail trade	9
Management of companies and enterprises	9
Federal government	8

Most buyers and purchasing agents work in comfortable offices. Travel is sometimes necessary, and purchasers for global organizations may need to travel outside the United States.

Work Schedules. Most buyers and purchasing agents work full time. Overtime is common in these occupations. About 1 in 5 worked more than 40 hours per week in 2014.

Education/Training

Although a high school diploma may be sufficient for some positions, many employers require buyers and purchasing agents to have a bachelor's degree. Most entry-level positions require some form of on-the-job training.

Education. Educational requirements usually vary with the size of the organization. Although a high school diploma may be enough at some organizations, many businesses require applicants to have a bachelor's degree. For many positions, a degree in business, finance, or supply management is sufficient.

For those interested in a career as a buyer or purchasing agent of farm products, a degree in agriculture, agriculture production, or animal science is often beneficial.

Training. Buyers and purchasing agents typically get on-the-job training for more than 1 year. During this time, they learn how to perform their basic duties, including monitoring inventory levels and negotiating with suppliers.

Median Annual Wages, May 2014

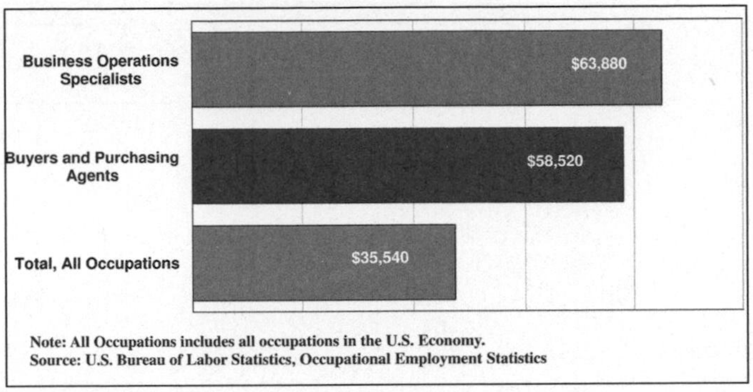

Percent Change in Employment, Projected 2014–2024

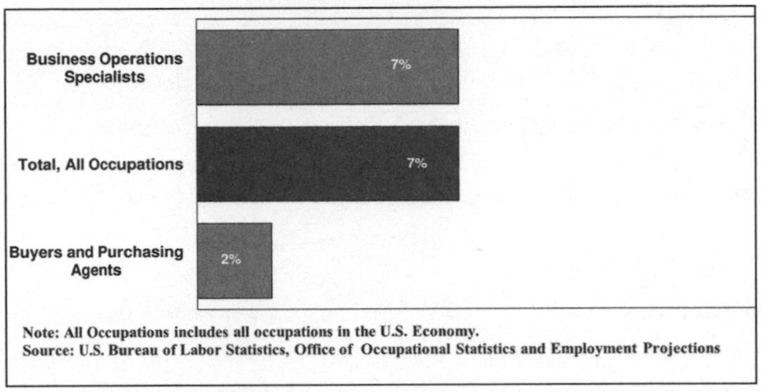

Licenses, Certifications, and Registrations. There are several certifications available for buyers and purchasing agents. Although some employers require certification, many do not.

Most of these certifications involve oral or written exams and have education and work experience requirements.

The Institute for Supply Management offers the Certified Professional in Supply Management (CPSM) credential, which covers a wide scope of purchasing professional duties. To receive the CPSM credential, candidates must pass three exams and those with a bachelor's degree must possess at least 3 years of relevant work experience while those without a bachelor's degree must have at least 5 years of relevant work experience.

The American Purchasing Society offers the Certified Purchasing Professional (CPP) certification. The CPP certification is valid for 5 years. Candidates must earn a certain number of professional development "points" to renew their certification. Candidates initially become eligible and can renew their certification through a combination of purchasing-related experience, education, and professional contributions (such as published articles or delivered speeches).

APICS offers the Certified Supply Chain Professional (CSCP) credential. Applicants must have 3 years of relevant business experience or a bachelor's degree in order to be eligible for the CSCP credential. The credential is valid for 5 years. Candidates must also earn a certain number of professional development points to renew their certification.

The Next Level Purchasing Association offers the Senior Professional in Supply Management (SPSM) Certification. Although there are no education or work experience requirements, applicants must complete six online courses and pass an SPSM exam. Certification is valid for 4 years. Candidates must complete 32 continuing education hours in procurement-related topics to recertify for an additional four-year period.

The Universal Public Procurement Certification Council (UPPCC) offers two certifications for workers in federal, state, and local government. The Certified Professional Public Buyer (CPPB) credential requires applicants to have earned at least an associate's degree, possess at least 3 years of public procurement experience, and complete relevant training courses. The Certified Public Purchasing Officer (CPPO) requires applicants to have earned a bachelor's degree, possess at least 5 years of public procurement experience, and complete additional training courses.

Those with the CPPB or the CPPO designation must renew their certification every 5 years by completing continuing education courses or attending procurement-related conferences or events.

The National Institute of Government Purchasing (NIGP), Institute for Public Procurement offers preparation courses for the UPPCC certification exams.

Advancement. An experienced purchasing agent or buyer may become an assistant purchasing manager before advancing to purchasing manager, supply manager, or director of materials management. Buyers and purchasing agents with extensive work experience can also advance to become the Chief Procurement Officer (CPO) for an organization.

Important Qualities

Analytical skills. When evaluating suppliers, buyers and purchasing agents must analyze their options and choose a supplier with the best combination of price, quality, delivery, or service.

Decision-making skills. Buyers and purchasing agents must have the ability to make informed and timely decisions, choosing products that they think will sell.

Math skills. Buyers and purchasing agents must possess basic math skills. They must be able to compare prices from different suppliers to ensure that their organization is getting the best deal.

Negotiating skills. Buyers and purchasing agents often must negotiate the terms of a contract with a supplier. Interpersonal skills and self-confidence, in addition to knowledge of the product, can help lead to successful negotiations.

Employment Projections Data for Buyers and Purchasing Agents

Occupational Title	SOC Code	Employment, 2014	Projected Employment, 2024	Change, 2014–2024 Percent	Change, 2014–2024 Numeric
Buyers and purchasing agents	13-1020	443,200	450,300	2	7,200
Buyers and purchasing agents, farm products	13-1021	12,900	13,500	5	600
Wholesale and retail buyers, except farm products	13-1022	129,500	137,500	6	8,100
Purchasing agents, except wholesale, retail, and farm products	13-1023	300,800	299,300	0	-1,500

Source: U.S. Bureau of Labor Statistics, Employment Projections Program

Similar Occupations. This table shows a list of occupations with job duties that are similar to those of buyers and purchasing agents.

Occupations	Entry-level Education	2014 Median Pay	Projected Job Growth	Average Annual Openings
Advertising, Promotions, and Marketing Managers	Bachelor's degree	$123,450	9%	1,970
Bookkeeping, Accounting, and Auditing Clerks	Some college, no degree	$36,430	-8%	-14,870
Financial Clerks	High school diploma or equivalent	$36,260	6%	8,930
Financial Managers	Bachelor's degree	$115,320	7%	3,770
Food Service Managers	High school diploma or equivalent	$48,560	5%	1,570
Lodging Managers	High school diploma or equivalent	$47,680	8%	370
Logisticians	Bachelor's degree	$73,870	2%	250
Purchasing Managers	Bachelor's degree	$106,090	1%	70
Wholesale and Manufacturing Sales Representatives	See Education/Training	$58,380	7%	11,720

Pay

The median annual wage for buyers and purchasing agents was $58,520 in May 2014. The median wage is the wage at which half the workers in an occupation earned more than that amount and half earned less. The lowest 10 percent earned less than $34,370, and the highest 10 percent earned more than $97,070.

Median annual wages for buyers and purchasing agents in May 2014 were as follows:

Purchasing agents, except wholesale, retail, and farm products $60,980
Buyers and purchasing agents, farm products 55,080
Wholesale and retail buyers, except farm products 52,270

Job Outlook

Employment of buyers and purchasing agents is projected to grow 2 percent from 2014 to 2024, slower than the average for all occupations.

These workers will continue to be needed to buy goods and services for business operations or for resale to customers. In addition, buyers and purchasing agents often play an important role in controlling costs for an organization.

However, growth may be negatively affected due to more outsourcing of less complex procurement functions like processing purchase orders or making one-time purchases of items. Some organizations also may rely on third parties to handle other tasks, such as performing market research or supplier risk assessments. Organizations may outsource these functions in order to focus on more complex or core procurement tasks and to reduce costs.

In the public sector, employment demand may be negatively impacted by the increasing use of cooperative purchasing agreements. These agreements allow state, local, and municipal governments to share resources in order to buy supplies and make other general purchases. Because the same standard contracts can be used multiple times by multiple government agencies, the rise of purchasing cooperatives may limit the need to hire additional procurement officers.

The projected decline in the manufacturing industry may also limit the demand for buyers and purchasing agents employed within this industry.

Job Prospects. Job prospects for those interested in becoming a buyer or purchasing agent should be good. Candidates with a bachelor's degree, in addition to strong negotiating, communication, and interpersonal skills, are likely to have the best prospects.

Contacts for More Information

For more information about buyers and purchasing agents, including information on education, training, employment, and certification, visit

- American Purchasing Society (www.american-purchasing.com)
- APICS (www.apics.org)
- Institute for Supply Management (www.instituteforsupplymanagement.org)
- Next Level Purchasing Association (www.nextlevelpurchasing.com/index.html)
- The National Institute of Government Purchasing (NIGP), Institute for Public Procurement (www.nigp.org/eweb/StartPage.aspx)
- Universal Public Procurement Certification Council (www.uppcc.org)

O*NET

- Buyers and Purchasing Agents, Farm Products (13-1021.00)
- Wholesale and Retail Buyers, Except Farm Products (13-1022.00)
- Purchasing Agents, Except Wholesale, Retail, and Farm Products (13-1023.00)

Claims Adjusters, Appraisers, Examiners, and Investigators

- **2014 Median Pay** .... $62,300 per year; $29.95 per hour
- **Typical Entry-Level Education** .... See Education/Training
- **Work Experience in a Related Occupation** .... None
- **On-the-job Training** .... See Education/Training
- **Number of Jobs, 2014** 315,300
- **Job Outlook, 2014–24** .... 3% (Slower than average)
- **Employment Change, 2014–24** 9,600

What Claims Adjusters, Appraisers, Examiners, and Investigators Do

Claims adjusters, appraisers, examiners, and investigators evaluate insurance claims. They decide whether an insurance company must pay a claim and, if so, how much.

Duties. Claims adjusters, appraisers, examiners, and investigators typically do the following:

- Investigate, evaluate, and settle insurance claims
- Determine whether the insurance policy covers the loss claimed
- Decide the appropriate amount the insurance company should pay
- Ensure that claims are not fraudulent
- Contact claimants' doctors or employers to get additional information on questionable claims
- Confer with legal counsel on claims when needed
- Negotiate settlements
- Authorize payments

Claims adjusters, appraisers, examiners, and investigators have varying duties, depending on the type of insurance company they work for. They must know a lot about what their company insures. For example, workers in property and casualty insurance must know housing and construction costs to properly evaluate damage from floods or fires. Workers in health insurance must be able to determine which types of treatments are medically necessary and which are questionable.

Adjusters inspect property damage to determine how much the insurance company should pay for the loss. They might inspect a home, a business, or an automobile.

Adjusters interview the claimant and witnesses, inspect the property, and do additional research, such as look at police reports. They may consult with other workers, such as accountants, architects, construction workers, engineers, lawyers, and physicians, who can offer a more expert evaluation of a claim.

Adjusters gather information—including photographs and statements, either written or recorded on audio or video—and put together a report for claims examiners to evaluate. When the examiner approves the claim, the adjuster negotiates with the policyholder and settles the claim.

If the claimant contests the outcome of the claim or the settlement, adjusters work with attorneys and expert witnesses to defend the insurer's position.

Some claims adjusters work as self-employed *public adjusters*. Often, they are hired by claimants who prefer not to rely on the insurance company's adjuster. The goal of adjusters working for insurance companies is to save as much money for the company as possible. The goal of a public adjuster working for a claimant is to get the highest possible amount paid to the claimant. They are paid a percentage of the settled claim.

Sometimes, self-employed adjusters are hired by insurance companies in place of hiring adjusters as regular employees. In this case, the self-employed adjusters work in the interest of the insurance company.

Appraisers estimate the cost or value of an insured item. Most appraisers who work for insurance companies and independent adjusting firms are *auto damage appraisers*. They inspect damaged vehicles after an accident and estimate the cost of repairs. This information then goes to the adjuster, who puts the estimated cost of repairs into the settlement.

Claims examiners review claims after they are submitted to ensure claimants and adjusters followed proper guidelines. They may assist adjusters with complicated claims or when, for example, a natural disaster occurs and the volume of claims increases.

Most claims examiners work for life or health insurance companies. Examiners who work for health insurance companies review health-related claims to see whether the costs are reasonable, given the diagnosis. After they review the claim, they authorize appropriate payment, deny the claim, or refer the claim to an investigator.

Examiners who work for life insurance companies review the causes of death and pay particular attention to accidents, because most life insurance companies pay additional benefits if a death is accidental. Examiners also may review new applications for life insurance policies, to make sure that the applicants have no serious illnesses that would make them a high risk to insure.

Insurance investigators handle claims in which the company suspects fraudulent or criminal activity such as arson, staged accidents, or unnecessary medical treatments. The severity of insurance fraud cases varies, from overstated claims of damage to vehicles to complicated fraud rings. Investigators often do surveillance work. For example, in the case of a fraudulent workers' compensation claim, an investigator may covertly watch the claimant to see if he or she does anything that would be ruled out by injuries stated in the claim.

Work Environment

Claims adjusters, appraisers, examiners, and investigators held about 315,300 jobs in 2014. The industries that employed the most claims adjusters, appraisers, examiners, and investigators were as follows:

Insurance carriers	49%
Agencies, brokerages, and other insurance related activities	24
Federal government	15
State and local government, excluding education and hospitals	4
Management of companies and enterprises	3

Claims adjusters and examiners spend time in offices, reviewing documents and conducting research; they work outside when examining damaged property. Appraisers and investigators work outside more often, inspecting damaged buildings and

Workers who inspect damaged buildings must be wary of potential hazards, such as collapsed roofs and floors, as well as weakened structures.

automobiles and conducting surveillance. Auto damage appraisers spend much of their time at automotive body shops, estimating vehicle damage costs.

Work Schedules. Most claims adjusters, appraisers, examiners, and investigators work full time. However, their work schedules vary.

Adjusters often arrange their work schedules to accommodate evening and weekend appointments with clients. This requirement sometimes results in adjusters working irregular schedules, especially when they have a lot of claims to review.

In contrast, auto damage appraisers typically work regular hours and rarely work on weekends, although they frequently spend much of their time at automotive body shops, estimating vehicle damage costs.

Insurance investigators often work irregular schedules because of the need to conduct surveillance and contact people who are not available during normal business hours. Early morning, evening, and weekend work is common.

Education/Training

A high school diploma or equivalent is typically required for a person to work as an entry-level claims adjuster, examiner, or investigator. Higher level positions may require a bachelor's degree or some insurance-related work experience. Auto damage appraisers typically have either a postsecondary nondegree award or work experience in identifying and estimating the cost of automotive repair.

Education. A high school diploma or equivalent is typically required for a person to work as an entry-level claims adjuster, examiner, or investigator. However, employers sometimes prefer to hire applicants who have a bachelor's degree or some insurance-related work experience or vocational training. Auto damage appraisers typically have either a postsecondary nondegree award or experience working in an auto repair shop, identifying and estimating the cost of automotive repair.

The varying types of work in these occupations can require different backgrounds or different college coursework. For example, a business or an accounting background might be best for someone who wishes to specialize in claims of financial loss due to strikes, equipment breakdowns, or merchandise damage. College training in architecture or engineering is helpful for adjusting industrial claims, such as those involving damage from fires or other accidents. A legal background is beneficial to someone handling workers' compensation and product liability cases. A medical background is useful for examiners working on medical and life insurance claims.

Although auto damage appraisers are not required to have a college education, most companies prefer to hire people who have the formal training, experience, or knowledge and technical skills to identify and estimate the cost of automotive repair. Many vocational schools and some community colleges offer programs in auto body repair and teach students how to estimate the cost of repairing damaged vehicles.

For investigator jobs, a high school diploma or equivalent is the typical education requirement. Most insurance companies prefer to hire people trained as law enforcement officers, private investigators, claims adjusters, or examiners, because these workers have good interviewing and interrogation skills.

Training. At the beginning of their careers, claims adjusters, examiners, and investigators work on small claims, under the supervision of an experienced worker. As they learn more about claims investigation and settlement, they are assigned larger, more complex claims.

Auto damage appraisers typically get on-the-job training, which may last several months. This training usually involves working under the supervision of a more experienced appraiser while estimating damage costs, until the employer decides that the trainee is ready to do estimates on his or her own.

Licenses, Certifications, and Registrations. Licensing requirements for claims adjusters, appraisers, examiners, and investigators vary by state. Some states have few requirements; others require either completing pre-licensing education or receiving a satisfactory score on a licensing exam (or both).

In some states, claims adjusters employed by insurance companies do not have to become licensed themselves because they can work under the company license.

Public adjusters may need to meet separate or additional requirements.

Some states that require licensing also require a certain number of continuing education credits per year to renew the license. Federal and state laws and court decisions affect how claims must be handled and what insurance policies can and must cover. Examiners working on life and health claims must stay up to date on new medical procedures and the latest prescription drugs. Examiners working on auto claims must be familiar with new car models and the most recent repair techniques. In order to fulfill their continuing education requirements, workers can attend classes or workshops, write articles for claims publications, or give lectures and presentations.

Important Qualities

Analytical skills. Adjusters and examiners must both evaluate whether the insurance company is obligated to pay a claim and determine the amount to pay. Adjusters must carefully consider various pieces of information to reach a decision.

Communication skills. Claims adjusters and investigators must get information from a wide range of people, including claimants,

Median Annual Wages, May 2014

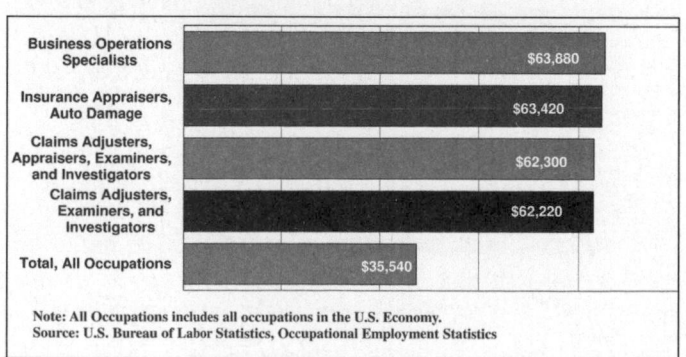

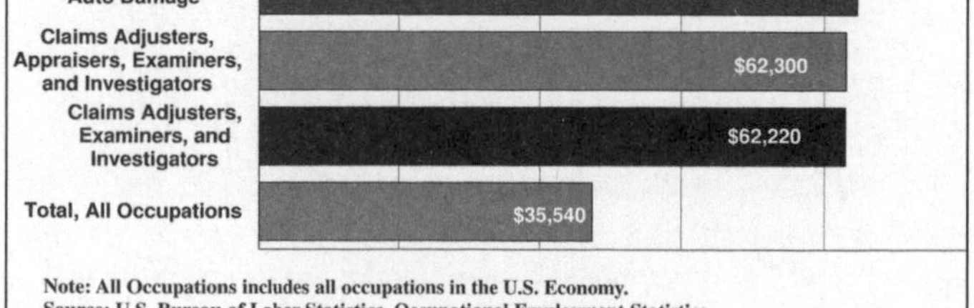

Note: All Occupations includes all occupations in the U.S. Economy.
Source: U.S. Bureau of Labor Statistics, Occupational Employment Statistics

Percent Change in Employment, Projected 2014–2024

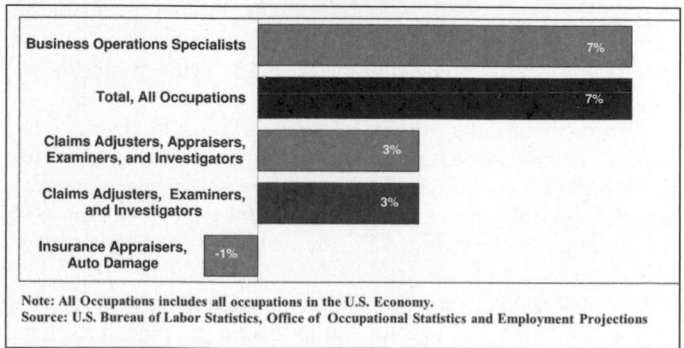

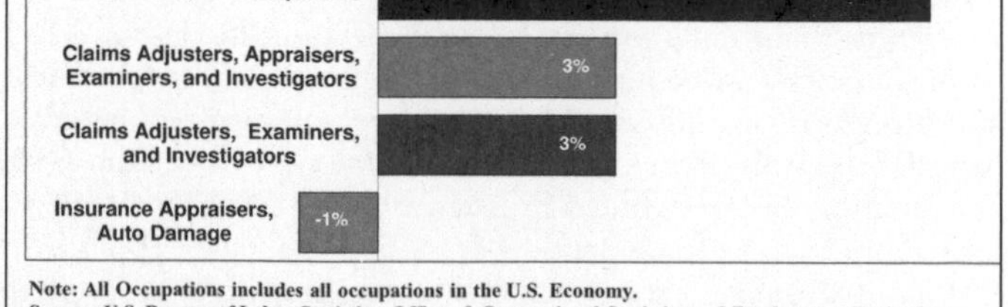

Note: All Occupations includes all occupations in the U.S. Economy.
Source: U.S. Bureau of Labor Statistics, Office of Occupational Statistics and Employment Projections

Employment Projections Data for Claims Adjusters, Appraisers, Examiners, and Investigators

Occupational Title	SOC Code	Employment, 2014	Projected Employment, 2024	Change, 2014–2024 Percent	Change, 2014–2024 Numeric
Claims adjusters, appraisers, examiners, and investigators	13-1030	315,300	324,900	3	9,600
Claims adjusters, examiners, and investigators	13-1031	299,700	309,500	3	9,800
Insurance appraisers, auto damage	13-1032	15,500	15,400	-1	-200

Source: U.S. Bureau of Labor Statistics, Employment Projections Program

Similar Occupations. This table shows a list of occupations with job duties that are similar to those of claims adjusters, appraisers, examiners, and investigators.

Occupations	Entry-level Education	2014 Median Pay	Projected Job Growth	Average Annual Openings
Appraisers and Assessors of Real Estate	Bachelor's degree	$52,570	8%	680
Automotive Body and Glass Repairers	High school diploma or equivalent	$39,260	9%	1,530
Automotive Service Technicians and Mechanics	Postsecondary nondegree award	$37,120	5%	3,910
Construction and Building Inspectors	High school diploma or equivalent	$56,040	8%	810
Cost Estimators	Bachelor's degree	$60,050	9%	1,870
Fire Inspectors	See Education/Training	$54,020	6%	90

witnesses, and medical experts. They must know the right questions to ask in order to gather the information they need.

Detail oriented. Adjusters, appraisers, examiners, and investigators must carefully review documents and damaged property, because small details can have large financial consequences.

Interpersonal skills. Adjusters, examiners, and investigators often meet with claimants and others who may be upset by the situation that requires a claim or by the settlement the company is offering. These workers must be understanding, yet firm with their company's policies.

Math skills. Appraisers must be able to calculate property damage.

Pay

The median annual wage for claims adjusters, examiners, and investigators was $62,220 in May 2014. The median wage is the wage at which half the workers in an occupation earned more than that amount and half earned less. The lowest 10 percent earned less than $37,580, and the highest 10 percent earned more than $92,620.

The median annual wage for insurance appraisers, auto damage, was $63,420 in May 2014. The lowest 10 percent earned less than $43,510, and the highest 10 percent earned more than $90,840.

In May 2014, the median annual wages for claims adjusters, appraisers, examiners, and investigators in the top industries in which they worked were as follows:

Federal government	$69,740
Management of companies and enterprises	61,500
Insurance carriers	60,910
Agencies, brokerages, and other insurance related activities	58,940
State and local government, excluding education and hospitals	58,310

Job Outlook

Employment of claims adjusters, appraisers, examiners, and investigators is projected to grow 3 percent from 2014 to 2024, slower than the average for all occupations.

Employment of claims adjusters, examiners, and investigators is projected to grow 3 percent from 2014 to 2024, slower than the average for all occupations. Employment growth should stem primarily from the growth of the health insurance industry. Federal legislation mandating individual coverage may increase the number of health insurance customers, including high-risk individuals who are more likely to file claims. Any such increase is expected, in turn, to increase the demand for claims adjusters to determine which treatments are approved and how much the company will pay.

In addition, rising medical costs may result in a greater need for claims examiners to carefully review a growing number of medical claims. An increase in the number of claims being made by a growing elderly population also should spur demand for health insurance claims adjusters and examiners.

The number of natural disasters, such as floods and fires, influences demand for claims adjusters in property and casualty insurance. Future increases in the number of natural disasters could result in strong employment growth for claims adjusters in the field.

All of the preceding factors will be somewhat offset by automation. Technology allows less complex claims to be processed automatically, freeing adjusters to work on more complex claims. As a result, fewer adjusters are needed per claim, reducing the number of adjusters required on staff.

Employment of auto damage appraisers is projected to decline 1 percent from 2014 to 2024. In recent years, the number of automobile accidents relative to the population has declined. As automobiles become safer, the number of traffic accidents is expected to decline as well, leading to decreased demand for the services of auto damage appraisers.

Job Prospects. Job opportunities for claims adjusters and examiners should be best in the health insurance industry as the number of health insurance customers expands. In addition, prospects for claims adjusters in property and casualty insurance will likely be best in areas susceptible to natural disasters. These areas include the Gulf Coast, which can have a large number of hurricanes, and the West Coast, which is vulnerable to wildfires.

Contacts for More Information

For more information about insurance, visit

- ➤ The Institutes (www.theinstitutes.org)
- ➤ International Claim Association (www.claim.org/index.cfm)
- ➤ National Association of Public Insurance Adjusters (www.napia.com)

O*NET

- ➤ Claims Adjusters, Examiners, and Investigators (13-1031.00)
- ➤ Claims Examiners, Property and Casualty Insurance (13-1031.01)
- ➤ Insurance Adjusters, Examiners, and Investigators (13-1031.02)
- ➤ Insurance Appraisers, Auto Damage (13-1032.00)

Compensation, Benefits, and Job Analysis Specialists

- **2014 Median Pay** .... $60,600 per year $29.13 per hour
- **Typical Entry-Level Education** .... Bachelor's degree
- **Work Experience in a Related Occupation** .... Less than 5 years
- **On-the-job Training** .... None
- **Number of Jobs, 2014** 84,700
- **Job Outlook, 2014–24** .... 4% (Slower than average)
- **Employment Change, 2014–24** 3,400

What Compensation, Benefits, and Job Analysis Specialists Do

Compensation, benefits, and job analysis specialists conduct an organization's compensation and benefits programs. They also evaluate position descriptions to determine details such as a person's classification and salary.

Duties. Compensation, benefits, and job analysis specialists typically do the following:

- Research compensation and benefits policies and plans to ensure the organization's offerings are current, cost effective, and competitive
- Use data and cost analyses to compare compensation and benefits plans
- Evaluate position descriptions to determine a person's classification and salary
- Ensure that the company complies with federal and state laws
- Collaborate with outside partners, such as benefits vendors, insurance brokers, and investment managers
- Design and prepare reports summarizing research and analysis
- Present recommendations to other human resources managers

Some specialists perform tasks within all areas of compensation, benefits, and job analysis. Others specialize in a specific area.

Compensation specialists assess the organization's pay structure. They research compensation trends and review surveys to determine how their organization's pay compares with that of other organizations in a particular industry and region. They often perform complex data or cost analyses to evaluate compensation policies. For example, they may research and analyze the cost of different pay-for-performance strategies, which offer rewards such as bonuses, paid leave, and other incentives.

Compensation specialists also must ensure that the organization's pay practices comply with federal and state laws and regulations, such as workers' compensation, minimum wage, overtime, and equal pay laws.

Benefits specialists administer the organization's benefits programs, which include retirement plans, leave policies, wellness programs, and insurance policies, such as health, life, and disability insurance. They research and analyze benefits plans, policies, and programs, and make recommendations based on their analysis. They must frequently monitor government regulations, legislation, and benefits trends to ensure that their programs are current, legal, and competitive.

Benefits specialists also work closely with insurance brokers and benefits carriers and manage the enrollment, renewal, and delivery of benefits to the organization's employees.

Job analysis specialists, also known as *position classifiers*, evaluate positions by writing or assigning job descriptions, determining position classifications, and preparing salary scales. When an organization introduces a new job or reviews existing jobs, specialists must research and make recommendations to managers on the status, description, classification, and salary of those jobs.

Work Environment

Compensation, benefits, and job analysis specialists held about 84,700 jobs in 2014 and worked in nearly every industry. Many specialists work for large firms, such as those found in the finance, insurance, and healthcare industries. Many also work for government or educational institutions.

Compensation, benefits, and job analysis specialists typically work in offices.

Work Schedules. Most compensation, benefits, and job analysis specialists work full time during regular business hours.

Compensation, benefits, and job analysis specialists analyze employees' pay, fringe benefits, and other forms of compensation.

Median Annual Wages, May 2014

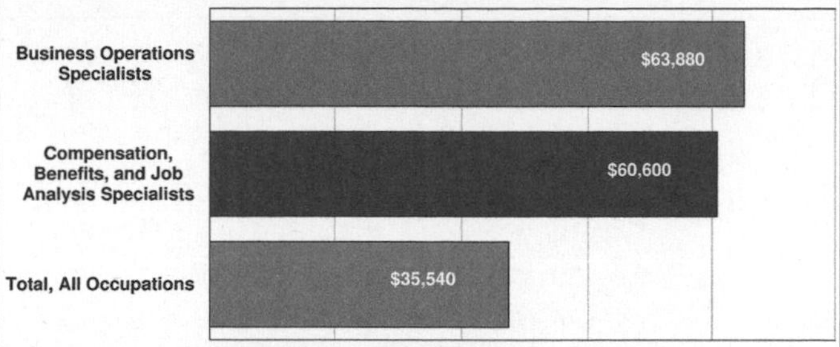

Note: All Occupations includes all occupations in the U.S. Economy.
Source: U.S. Bureau of Labor Statistics, Occupational Employment Statistics

Percent Change in Employment, Projected 2014–2024

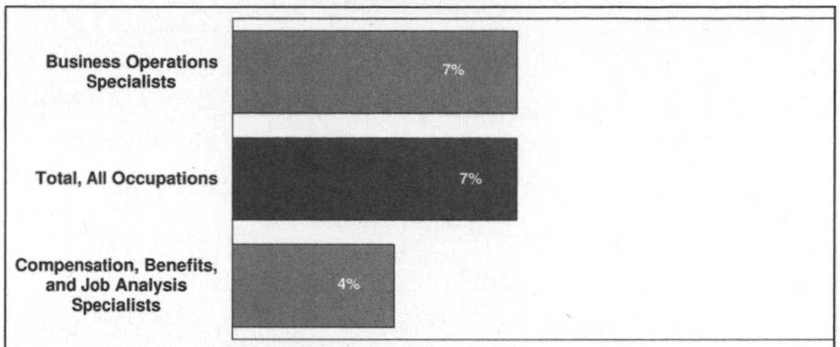

Note: All Occupations includes all occupations in the U.S. Economy.
Source: U.S. Bureau of Labor Statistics, Office of Occupational Statistics and Employment Projections

Education/Training

Compensation, benefits, and job analysis specialists typically need a bachelor's degree, and some specialists need related work experience.

Education. Most employers require that compensation, benefits, and job analysis specialists have a bachelor's degree. Many specialists have a degree in human resources, business administration, finance, communication, or a related field. Some employers may accept previous work experience in lieu of a formal degree.

Not all colleges and universities offer an undergraduate degree in human resources, but many offer courses in human resources management, compensation analysis, and benefits administration. Students with a background in other disciplines may benefit from taking courses in business, management, finance, and accounting.

Work Experience in a Related Occupation. For many jobs, compensation, benefits, and job analysis specialists must have previous work experience. Employers commonly require that the previous experience includes performing compensation analysis, benefits administration, or general human resources work. Experience in related fields, such as finance, insurance, or business administration, also may be beneficial.

Jobseekers without a degree in human resources must have relevant work experience. Some workers may gain this experience through internships. However, most gain experience from working in human resources.

Licenses, Certifications, and Registrations. Although certification is not required, it can demonstrate professional expertise. Some employers prefer to hire certified candidates, but many employers will have their employees become certified after they are already working. Certification programs for management positions often require several years of related work experience in order to qualify for the credential.

Many associations for human resources workers offer classes to enhance the skills of their members. Some associations, including the International Foundation of Employee Benefit Plans and WorldatWork, offer certification programs that specialize in compensation and benefits. Others, including the HR Certification Institute and the Society for Human Resource Management, offer general human resources credentials.

Advancement. Compensation, benefits, and job analysis specialists may advance to a position as compensation and benefits manager or a human resources manager. Specialists typically need several years of work experience to advance.

Important Qualities

Analytical skills. Many specialists perform data or cost analyses to form logical conclusions. For example, they may analyze the cost of choosing a particular salary scale for a class of workers.

Business acumen. Specialists must understand basic finance and accounting.

Communication skills. Specialists often work with employees throughout their organization to provide information on compensation and benefits. They may give presentations or advise managers or employees about compensation policies or benefit plans.

Critical-thinking skills. Specialists must think critically when evaluating job positions, salary scales, promotion practices, and other compensation and benefits policies.

Detail oriented. Specialists must pay attention to detail, especially when ensuring that the organization is compliant with federal and state laws.

Pay

The median annual wage for compensation, benefits, and job analysis specialists was $60,600 in May 2014. The median wage is the wage at which half the workers in an occupation earned more than that amount and half earned less. The lowest 10 percent earned less than $38,540, and the highest 10 percent earned more than $96,360.

Job Outlook

Employment of compensation, benefits, and job analysis specialists is projected to grow 4 percent from 2014 to 2024, slower than the average for all occupations. As compensation and benefits plans become increasingly complex and costly, many companies are outsourcing the administration of these plans to external providers in order to reduce costs while also staying compliant in a highly regulated field.

For example, to reduce administrative costs, organizations commonly use outside vendors for processing payroll and insurance

Employment Projections Data for Compensation, Benefits, and Job Analysis Specialists

Occupational Title	SOC Code	Employment, 2014	Projected Employment, 2024	Change, 2014–2024	
				Percent	Numeric
Compensation, benefits, and job analysis specialists	13-1141	84,700	88,100	4	3,400

Source: U.S. Bureau of Labor Statistics, Employment Projections Program

Similar Occupations. This table shows a list of occupations with job duties that are similar to those of compensation, benefits, and job analysis specialists.

Occupations	Entry-level Education	2014 Median Pay	Projected Job Growth	Average Annual Openings
Buyers and Purchasing Agents	Bachelor's degree	$58,520	2%	720
Compensation and Benefits Managers	Bachelor's degree	$108,070	6%	110
Human Resources Managers	Bachelor's degree	$102,780	9%	1,080
Human Resources Specialists	Bachelor's degree	$57,420	5%	2,200
Insurance Sales Agents	High school diploma or equivalent	$47,860	9%	4,350
Training and Development Managers	Bachelor's degree	$101,930	7%	230
Training and Development Specialists	Bachelor's degree	$57,340	7%	1,890

claims. These outside vendors are able to administer compensation and benefits plans and operate call centers more efficiently, reducing the need for as many specialists.

Organizations will continue to hire benefits specialists to analyze, select, and update their benefits policies. Employee wellness programs are also becoming increasingly popular as a way to reduce healthcare costs. Organizations will need benefits specialists to design, analyze, or administer these programs.

In addition, organizations must offer competitive compensation packages to attract and keep highly qualified workers. To allocate their limited compensation funds effectively, many organizations are using strategies such as pay-for-performance plans, which may include bonuses, paid leave, or other incentives as part of the compensation package. Organizations will need specialists to analyze these compensation policies and plans and to ensure that they are both competitive and cost effective.

Job Prospects. Job prospects should be best for those with previous work experience performing compensation analysis or benefits administration, and related human resources work.

Contacts for More Information

For more information about compensation, benefits, and job analysis specialists, including certification, visit

➤ International Foundation of Employee Benefit Plans (www.ifebp.org)

➤ WorldatWork (www.worldatwork.org)

For information about human resources careers, visit

➤ Society for Human Resource Management (www.shrm.org)

For more information about human resources certifications, visit

➤ HR Certification Institute (www.hrci.org)

O*NET

➤ Compensation, Benefits, and Job Analysis Specialists (13-1141.00)

Cost Estimators

- **2014 Median Pay** .... $60,050 per year $28.87 per hour
- **Typical Entry-Level Education** .... Bachelor's degree
- **Work Experience in a Related Occupation** .... None
- **On-the-job Training** .... None
- **Number of Jobs, 2014** 213,500
- **Job Outlook, 2014–24** .... 9% (Faster than average)
- **Employment Change, 2014–24** 18,700

What Cost Estimators Do

Cost estimators collect and analyze data in order to estimate the time, money, materials, and labor required to manufacture a product, construct a building, or provide a service. They generally specialize in a particular product or industry.

Duties. Cost estimators typically do the following:

- Identify factors affecting costs, such as production time, materials, and labor
- Read blueprints and technical documents in order to prepare estimates
- Collaborate with engineers, architects, clients, and contractors
- Calculate, analyze, and adjust estimates
- Recommend ways to reduce costs
- Work with sales teams to prepare estimates and bids for clients
- Maintain records of estimated and actual costs

Accurately estimating the costs of construction and manufacturing projects is vital to the survival of businesses. Cost estimators provide managers with the information they need in order to submit competitive contract bids or price products appropriately.

Estimators analyze production processes to determine how much time, money, and labor a project needs. Their estimates account for many factors, including allowances for wasted material, bad weather, shipping delays, and other variables that can increase costs and lower profitability.

In building construction, cost estimators use software to simulate the construction process and evaluate the effects of design choices. They often consult databases to compare the costs of similar projects.

The following are examples of types of cost estimators:

Construction cost estimators prepare estimates for a building project. They may calculate the total cost of building a bridge or commercial shopping center, or they may calculate the cost of just one component, such as the foundation. They identify costs of elements such as raw materials and labor, and they may set a timeline for how long they expect the project to take. Although many work directly for construction firms, some work for contractors and engineering firms.

Manufacturing cost estimators calculate the costs of developing, producing, or redesigning a company's goods or services. For example, a cost estimator working for a home appliance manufacturer may determine a new dishwasher's production costs, allowing managers to make production decisions.

Some manufacturing cost estimators work in software development. Many high-technology products require a considerable

Cost estimators develop information that business owners and managers need to determine the potential profitability of a new project or product.

amount of computer programming, and calculating the costs of software development requires great expertise.

Other workers, such as operations research analysts and construction managers, may also estimate costs in the course of their usual duties.

Work Environment

Cost estimators held about 213,500 jobs in 2014. The industries that employed the most cost estimators were as follows:

Construction of buildings	17%
Building equipment contractors	16
Manufacturing	13
Building finishing contractors	8

Cost estimators work mostly in offices, and some estimators visit construction sites and factory floors during the course of their work.

Work Schedules. Cost estimators usually work full time, and some may work overtime in order to meet deadlines.

Education/Training

A bachelor's degree is generally required to become a cost estimator, although some highly experienced construction workers may qualify without a bachelor's degree.

Education. Employers generally prefer candidates who have a bachelor's degree. A strong background in mathematics is essential.

Construction cost estimators typically need a bachelor's degree in an industry-related field, such as construction management, building science, or engineering.

Those interested in estimating manufacturing costs typically need a bachelor's degree in engineering, business, or finance.

Training. Some newly hired cost estimators may receive on-the-job training, depending on their experience. Training may include learning a company's cost-estimating software and techniques.

Work Experience in a Related Occupation. Some employers prefer that construction cost estimators, particularly those without a bachelor's degree, have previous work experience in the construction industry. For example, experienced electricians and plumbers can become construction cost estimators if they have the necessary construction knowledge and math skills.

Candidates interested in becoming cost estimators can also gain experience through internships and cooperative education programs.

Licenses, Certifications, and Registrations. Voluntary certification can show competence and experience in the field. In some instances, employers may require professional certification before hiring.

The following organizations offer a variety of certifications:

- American Society of Professional Estimators
- Association for the Advancement of Cost Estimating International
- International Cost Estimating and Analysis Association

Estimators must generally have at least 2 years of estimating experience and must pass a written exam to become certified.

Important Qualities

Analytical skills. Cost estimators consider and evaluate different construction and manufacturing methods and options to determine the most cost-effective solution that meets the required specifications.

Detail oriented. Cost estimators must pay attention to details, as minor changes can significantly affect the overall cost of a project or product.

Math skills. Cost estimators calculate labor, material, and equipment cost estimates for construction projects. They use software, such as spreadsheets and databases, and they need excellent math skills to accurately calculate these estimates.

Time-management skills. Cost estimators often work on fixed deadlines, so they must plan their work in advance and work efficiently and accurately.

Writing skills. Cost estimators write comprehensive reports, which often help managers make production decisions.

Median Annual Wages, May 2014

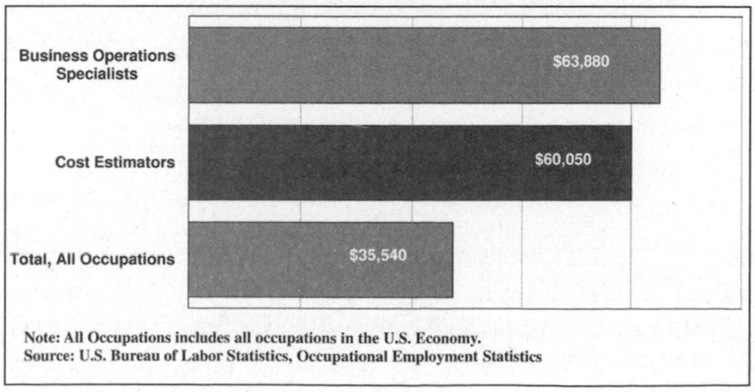

Percent Change in Employment, Projected 2014–2024

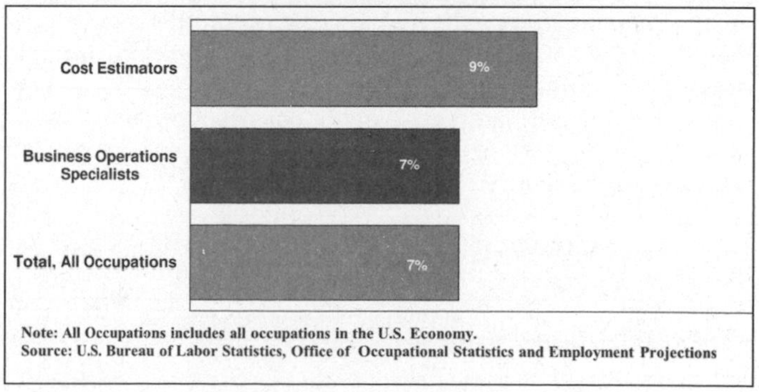

Employment Projections Data for Cost Estimators

Occupational Title	SOC Code	Employment, 2014	Projected Employment, 2024	Change, 2014–2024 Percent	Change, 2014–2024 Numeric
Cost estimators	13-1051	213,500	232,300	9	18,700

Source: U.S. Bureau of Labor Statistics, Employment Projections Program

Similar Occupations. This table shows a list of occupations with job duties that are similar to those of cost estimators.

Occupations	Entry-level Education	2014 Median Pay	Projected Job Growth	Average Annual Openings
Accountants and Auditors	Bachelor's degree	$65,940	11%	14,240
Budget Analysts	Bachelor's degree	$71,220	3%	150
Claims Adjusters, Appraisers, Examiners, and Investigators	See Education/Training	$62,300	3%	960
Construction Managers	Bachelor's degree	$85,630	5%	1,780
Financial Analysts	Bachelor's degree	$78,620	12%	3,230
Financial Managers	Bachelor's degree	$115,320	7%	3,770
Industrial Production Managers	Bachelor's degree	$92,470	-4%	-630
Operations Research Analysts	Bachelor's degree	$76,660	30%	2,760

Pay

The median annual wage for cost estimators was $60,050 in May 2014. The median wage is the wage at which half the workers in an occupation earned more than that amount and half earned less. The lowest 10 percent earned less than $34,450, and the highest 10 percent earned more than $99,370.

In May 2014, the median annual wages for cost estimators in the top industries in which they worked were as follows:

Building equipment contractors	$63,390
Construction of buildings	62,200
Building finishing contractors	57,120
Manufacturing	57,100

Job Outlook

Employment of cost estimators is projected to grow 9 percent from 2014 to 2024, faster than the average for all occupations.

Demand for cost estimators is expected to continue because companies need accurate cost projections to ensure that their products and services are profitable.

Growth in the construction industry is expected to create the majority of new jobs for cost estimators, particularly in the specialty trade contractors industries.

Job Prospects. Overall job prospects should be good. Those with a bachelor's degree, industry work experience, and excellent math skills should have the best job opportunities. Knowledge of building information modeling (BIM) software is helpful for those seeking employment in construction.

Jobs of cost estimators working in construction, like those of workers in many other trades in the construction industry, are sensitive to changing economic conditions.

Contacts for More Information

For more information about cost estimators, visit

➤ Association for the Advancement of Cost Engineering International (AACE International) (www.aacei.org)

➤ American Society of Professional Estimators (www.aspenational.org)

➤ International Cost Estimating and Analysis Association (www.iceaaonline.com)

O*NET

➤ Cost Estimators (13-1051.00)

Financial Analysts

- **2014 Median Pay** .... $78,620 per year, $37.80 per hour
- **Typical Entry-Level Education** .... Bachelor's degree
- **Work Experience in a Related Occupation** .... None
- **On-the-job Training** .... None
- **Number of Jobs, 2014** 277,600
- **Job Outlook, 2014–24** .... 12% (Faster than average)
- **Employment Change, 2014–24** 32,300

What Financial Analysts Do

Financial analysts provide guidance to businesses and individuals making investment decisions. They assess the performance of stocks, bonds, and other types of investments.

Duties. Financial analysts typically do the following:

- Recommend individual investments and collections of investments, which are known as portfolios
- Evaluate current and historical financial data
- Study economic and business trends
- Examine a company's financial statements to determine its value
- Meet with company officials to gain better insight into the company's prospects
- Assess the strength of the management team
- Prepare written reports

Financial analysts evaluate investment opportunities. They work in banks, pension funds, mutual funds, securities firms, insurance companies, and other businesses. Financial analysts are also called *securities analysts* and *investment analysts*.

Financial analysts can be divided into two categories: buy-side analysts and sell-side analysts.

- Buy-side analysts develop investment strategies for companies that have a lot of money to invest. These companies, called institutional investors, include mutual funds, hedge funds, insurance companies, independent money managers, and nonprofit organizations with large endowments, such as some universities.
- Sell-side analysts advise financial services sales agents who sell stocks, bonds, and other investments.

Some analysts work for the business media or other research houses, which are independent from the buy and sell side.

Financial analysts generally focus on trends affecting a specific industry, geographical region, or type of product. For example, an analyst may focus on a subject area such as the energy industry, a world region such as Eastern Europe, or the foreign exchange market. They must understand how new regulations, policies, and political and economic trends may affect investments.

Investing is becoming more global, and some financial analysts specialize in a particular country or region. Companies want those financial analysts to understand the language, culture, business environment, and political conditions in the country or region that they cover.

The following are examples of types of financial analysts:

Portfolio managers select the mix of products, industries, and regions for their company's investment portfolio. These managers are responsible for the overall performance of the portfolio. They are also expected to explain investment decisions and strategies in meetings with stakeholders.

Fund managers work exclusively with hedge funds or mutual funds. Both fund and portfolio managers frequently make buy or sell decisions in reaction to quickly changing market conditions.

Ratings analysts evaluate the ability of companies or governments to pay their debts, including bonds. On the basis of their evaluation, a management team rates the risk of a company or government not being able to repay its bonds.

Risk analysts evaluate the risk in investment decisions and determine how to manage unpredictability and limit potential losses. This job is carried out by making investment decisions such as selecting dissimilar stocks or having a combination of stocks, bonds, and mutual funds in a portfolio.

Financial analysts research and analyze financial data, helping managers make sound decisions.

Work Environment

Financial analysts held about 277,600 jobs in 2014. The industries that employed the most financial analysts were as follows:

Securities, commodity contracts, and other financial investments and related activities	24%
Management of companies and enterprises	14
Credit intermediation and related activities	13
Professional, scientific, and technical services	12
Insurance carriers and related activities	8

Financial analysts work primarily in offices, but travel frequently to visit companies or clients.

Work Schedules. Most financial analysts work full time, and about 1 in 3 worked more than 40 hours per week in 2014. Much of their research must be done after office hours because their days are filled with telephone calls and meetings.

Median Annual Wages, May 2014

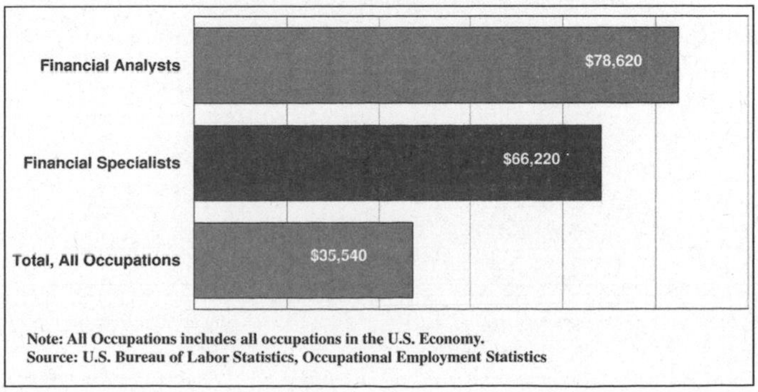

Percent Change in Employment, Projected 2014–2024

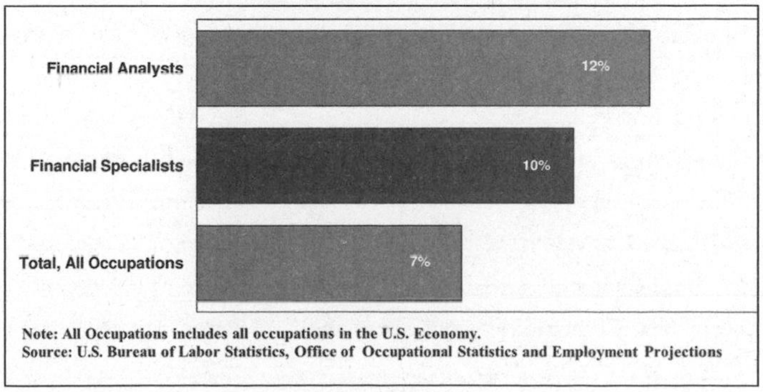

Employment Projections Data for Financial Analysts

Occupational Title	SOC Code	Employment, 2014	Projected Employment, 2024	Change, 2014–2024 Percent	Change, 2014–2024 Numeric
Financial analysts	13-2051	277,600	310,000	12	32,300

Source: U.S. Bureau of Labor Statistics, Employment Projections Program

Education/Training

Financial analysts typically must have a bachelor's degree, but a master's degree is often required for advanced positions.

Education. Most positions require a bachelor's degree. A number of fields of study provide appropriate preparation, including accounting, economics, finance, statistics, and mathematics. For advanced positions, employers often require a master's degree in business administration (MBA) or a master's degree in finance. Knowledge of options pricing, bond valuation, and risk management are important.

Licenses, Certifications, and Registrations. The Financial Industry Regulatory Authority (FINRA) is the main licensing organization for the securities industry. It requires licenses for many financial analyst positions. Most of the licenses require sponsorship by an employer, so companies do not expect individuals to have these licenses before starting a job.

Certification is often recommended by employers and can improve the chances for advancement. An example is the Chartered Financial Analyst (CFA) certification from the CFA Institute. Financial analysts can become CFA certified if they have a bachelor's degree, 4 years of qualified work experience, and pass three exams. Financial analysts can also become certified in their field of specialty.

Advancement. Financial analysts typically start by specializing in a specific investment field. As they gain experience, they can become portfolio managers, who select the mix of investments for a company's portfolio. They can also become fund managers, who manage large investment portfolios for individual investors. A master's degree in finance or business administration can improve an analyst's chances of advancing to one of these positions.

Important Qualities

Analytical skills. Financial analysts must process a range of information in finding profitable investments.

Communication skills. Financial analysts must explain their recommendations to clients in clear language that clients can easily understand.

Computer skills. Financial analysts must be adept at using software packages to analyze financial data, see trends, create portfolios, and make forecasts.

Decision-making skills. Financial analysts must provide a recommendation to buy, hold, or sell a security.

Detail oriented. Financial analysts must pay attention to details when reviewing possible investments, as small issues may have large implications for the health of an investment.

Math skills. Financial analysts use mathematical skills when estimating the value of financial securities.

To be successful, financial analysts must be motivated to seek out obscure information that may be important to the investment. Many work independently and must have self-confidence in their judgment.

Pay

The median annual wage for financial analysts was $78,620 in May 2014. The median wage is the wage at which half the workers in an occupation earned more than that amount and half earned less. The lowest 10 percent earned less than $48,170, and the highest 10 percent earned more than $154,680.

In May 2014, the median annual wages for financial analysts in the top industries in which they worked were as follows:

Securities, commodity contracts, and other financial investments and related activities	$90,550
Professional, scientific, and technical services	80,720
Management of companies and enterprises	77,070
Credit intermediation and related activities	76,050
Insurance carriers and related activities	73,790

Fund managers are typically compensated by fees, usually structured as a percentage of assets under management and a percentage of the fund's annual return.

Job Outlook

Employment of financial analysts is projected to grow 12 percent from 2014 to 2024, faster than the average for all occupations. A growing range of financial products and the need for in-depth knowledge of geographic regions are expected to lead to strong employment growth.

Investment portfolios are becoming more complex, and there are more financial products available for trade. In addition, emerging markets throughout the world are providing new investment opportunities, which require expertise in geographic regions where those markets are located.

Similar Occupations. This table shows a list of occupations with job duties that are similar to those of financial analysts.

Occupations	Entry-level Education	2014 Median Pay	Projected Job Growth	Average Annual Openings
Budget Analysts	Bachelor's degree	$71,220	3%	150
Financial Managers	Bachelor's degree	$115,320	7%	3,770
Insurance Underwriters	Bachelor's degree	$64,220	-11%	-1,170
Personal Financial Advisors	Bachelor's degree	$81,060	30%	7,390
Securities, Commodities, and Financial Services Sales Agents	Bachelor's degree	$72,070	10%	3,250

The continued implementation of financial regulatory reform could constrict growth in the industry, as rulemaking bodies place a greater emphasis on stability. Restrictions on trading by banks may shift employment of financial analysts from investment banks to hedge funds and private equity groups.

Job Prospects. Despite employment growth, strong competition is expected for financial analyst positions. Growth in financial services is projected to create new positions, but there are still far more people who would like to enter the occupation than there are jobs in the occupation. Having certifications and a graduate degree can significantly improve an applicant's prospects.

Contacts for More Information

For more information about licensure for financial analysts, visit

➤ Financial Industry Regulatory Authority (FINRA) (www.finra.org)

For more information about training and certification, visit

➤ Global Academy of Finance and Management (http://gafm.com)

➤ CFA Institute (www.cfainstitute.org)

O*NET

➤ Financial Analysts (13-2051.00)

Financial Examiners

- **2014 Median Pay** .... $76,310 per year, $36.69 per hour
- **Typical Entry-Level Education** .... Bachelor's degree
- **Work Experience in a Related Occupation** .... None
- **On-the-job Training** .... Moderate-term on-the-job training
- **Number of Jobs, 2014** 38,200
- **Job Outlook, 2014–24** .... 10% (Faster than average)
- **Employment Change, 2014–24** 3,700

What Financial Examiners Do

Financial examiners ensure compliance with laws governing financial institutions and transactions. They review balance sheets, evaluate the risk level of loans, and assess bank management.

Duties. Financial examiners typically do the following:

- Monitor the financial condition of banks and other financial institutions
- Review balance sheets, operating income and expense accounts, and loan documentation to confirm institution assets and liabilities
- Prepare reports that detail an institution's safety and soundness

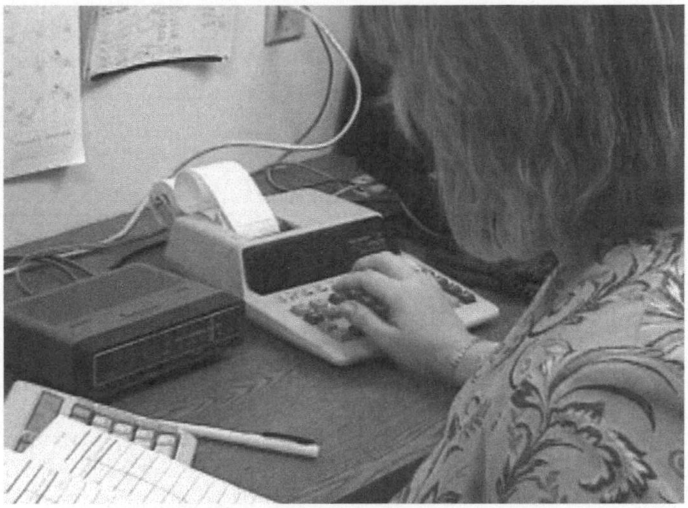

Financial examiners review balance sheets, evaluate the risk level of loans, and assess bank management.

- Examine the minutes of meetings of managers and directors
- Train other examiners in the financial examination process
- Review and analyze new regulations and policies to determine their impact on the organization
- Establish guidelines for procedures and policies that comply with new and revised regulations

Financial examiners typically work in one of two main areas: risk scoping or consumer compliance.

Those working in risk scoping evaluate the health of financial institutions. Their role is to ensure that banks and other financial institutions offer safe loans and that they have enough cash on hand to handle unexpected losses. These procedures help ensure that the financial system as a whole remains stable. These examiners also evaluate the performance of bank managers.

They ensure that banks extend loans that borrowers are likely to be able to pay back. They help borrowers avoid "predatory loans"—loans that may generate profit for banks through high interest payments but may be costly to borrowers and damage their credit scores. Examiners also ensure that banks do not discriminate against borrowers based on ethnicity or other characteristics.

Work Environment

Financial examiners held about 38,200 jobs in 2014. The industries that employed the most financial examiners were as follows:

Federal government	19%
Depository credit intermediation	18

Median Annual Wages, May 2014

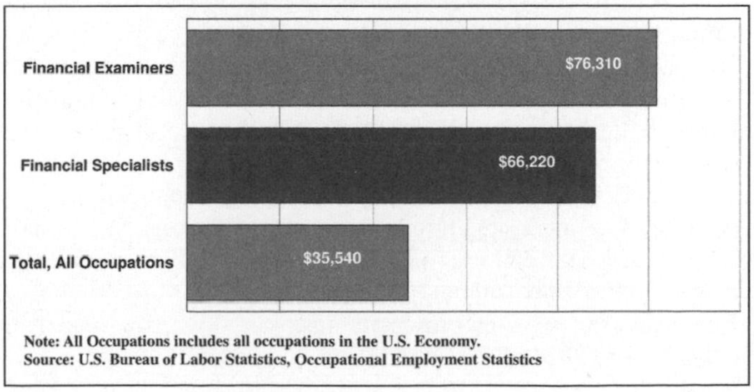

Percent Change in Employment, Projected 2014–2024

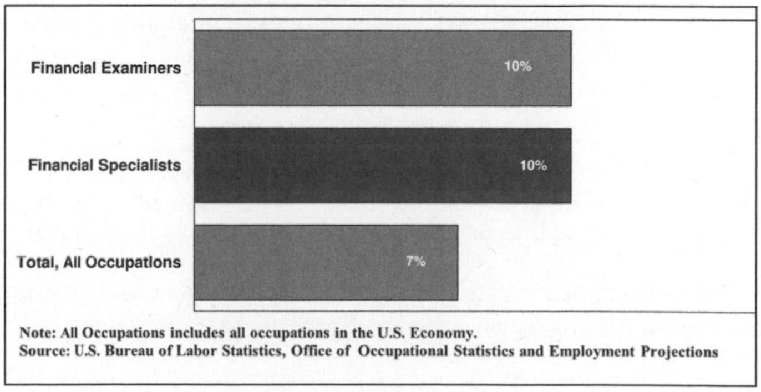

Employment Projections Data for Financial Examiners

Occupational Title	SOC Code	Employment, 2014	Projected Employment, 2024	Change, 2014–2024	
				Percent	Numeric
Financial examiners	13-2061	38,200	42,000	10	3,700

Source: U.S. Bureau of Labor Statistics, Employment Projections Program

Similar Occupations. This table shows a list of occupations with job duties that are similar to those of financial examiners.

Occupations	Entry-level Education	2014 Median Pay	Projected Job Growth	Average Annual Openings
Accountants and Auditors	Bachelor's degree	$65,940	11%	14,240
Budget Analysts	Bachelor's degree	$71,220	3%	150
Financial Analysts	Bachelor's degree	$78,620	12%	3,230
Loan Officers	Bachelor's degree	$62,620	8%	2,450
Management Analysts	Bachelor's degree	$80,880	14%	10,340
Personal Financial Advisors	Bachelor's degree	$81,060	30%	7,390
Tax Examiners and Collectors, and Revenue Agents	Bachelor's degree	$51,120	-6%	-420

State government, excluding education and hospitals............ 13%
Securities, commodity contracts, and other financial investments and related activities 12
Management of companies and enterprises.......................... 11

Financial examiners typically work in offices. They frequently have to travel to inspect a bank onsite.

Work Schedules. Most financial examiners worked full time in 2014.

Education/Training

Financial examiners typically need a bachelor's degree that includes some coursework in accounting. Entry-level examiners are trained on the job by senior examiners.

Education. Specific requirements for financial examiners vary between federal and state governments. However, all financial examiners typically need a bachelor's degree that includes some coursework in accounting, finance, economics, or a related field. Examiners working for the Federal Deposit Insurance Corporation (FDIC) must have at least 6 semester hours in accounting.

Training. Once hired, financial examiners receive on-the-job training. Entry-level workers begin under the supervision of senior examiners, as they learn their job duties.

Advancement. After a few years of experience, financial examiners can advance to a senior examiner position. Requirements for these positions vary by employer but often require a master's degree in either accounting or business or becoming a Certified Public Accountant (CPA).

Important Qualities

Analytical skills. Financial examiners need strong analytical skills to evaluate how well the managers of financial institutions are handling risk and whether the individual loans the institution makes are safe.

Detail oriented. Financial examiners must pay close attention to details when reviewing balance sheets to identify risky assets.

Math skills. Financial examiners need good math skills to monitor balance sheets and see if the bank's or other financial institution's available cash is dangerously low.

Writing skills. Financial examiners regularly write reports on the safety and soundness of financial institutions. They must be able to explain technical information clearly.

Pay

The median annual wage for financial examiners was $76,310 in May 2014. The median wage is the wage at which half the workers in an occupation earned more than that amount and half earned less. The lowest 10 percent earned less than $44,660, and the highest 10 percent earned more than $146,190.

In May 2014, the median annual wages for financial examiners in the top industries in which they worked were as follows:

Federal government $110,920
Securities, commodity contracts, and other financial investments and related activities 82,090
Management of companies and enterprises........................ 75,540
State government, excluding education and hospitals.......... 65,840
Depository credit intermediation....................................... 65,530

Job Outlook

Employment of financial examiners is projected to grow 10 percent from 2014 to 2024, faster than the average for all occupations. Employment growth for financial examiners will vary by industry group. Implementation of new financial regulations is expected to create a need for more examiners among financial institutions. However, declining overall employment in the federal government will slow growth for these workers.

Demand for these workers has risen in the financial industry because of an increasing number of new regulations. More financial institutions are hiring financial examiners to help navigate the new regulatory environment, and reduce the cost of compliance. Financial examiners' employment is projected to grow 16 percent from 2014 to 2024 in the finance and insurance industry.

At the federal level, the creation of the Consumer Financial Protection Bureau (CFPB) has increased employment of financial examiners in recent years. As this agency continues to grow, more financial examiner positions will be added. However, overall budget constraints in the federal government may limit employment growth. Employment of financial examiners in the federal government is projected to grow 1 percent from 2014 to 2024.

Employment of financial examiners tends to increase during periods of financial instability. As bank losses and failures become more prevalent during economic downturns, more examiners are needed to enforce regulation. However, during normal economic times, employment tends to be steady.

Job Prospects. Financial examiners should face strong competition for jobs. Those with previous work experience in banking should have the best prospects.

Contacts for More Information

For more information about financial examiners, visit

➤ Federal Deposit Insurance Corporation (www.fdic.gov)

➤ Consumer Financial Protection Bureau (www.consumerfinance.gov)

O*NET

➤ Financial Examiners (13-2061.00)

Fundraisers

- **2014 Median Pay** .... $52,430 per year
  $25.21 per hour
- **Typical Entry-Level Education** .... Bachelor's degree
- **Work Experience in a Related Occupation** .... None
- **On-the-job Training** .... None
- **Number of Jobs, 2014** 73,400
- **Job Outlook, 2014–24** .... 9% (Faster than average)
- **Employment Change, 2014–24** 6,900

What Fundraisers Do

Fundraisers organize events and campaigns to raise money and other donations for an organization. They may design promotional materials and increase awareness of an organization's work, goals, and financial needs.

Duties. Fundraisers typically do the following:

- Research prospective donors
- Create a strong fundraising message that appeals to potential donors

Fundraisers identify and contact potential donors and apply for grants.

- Identify and contact potential donors
- Use online platforms, such as crowdsourcing, to raise donations
- Organize a campaign or event to solicit donations
- Maintain records of donor information
- Evaluate the success of previous fundraising events
- Train volunteers in fundraising procedures and practices
- Ensure that all legal reporting requirements are satisfied

Fundraisers plan and oversee campaigns and events to raise money and other kinds of donations for an organization. They ensure that campaigns are effective by researching potential donors ahead of time and examining records of those who have given in the past. Many of the organizations that employ fundraisers rely heavily on donations to run their operations.

Many states require "charitable soliciting organizations" to register with a state agency. The National Association of State Charity Officials provides advice to charities, as well as links to each state's charity office. Professional fundraisers who work as private consultants need to register with the state in which they do business. Fundraisers who work for an organization that engages in fundraising activity will not have to register individually as long as their organization is already registered.

Fundraisers who work for political campaigns must be knowledgeable about campaign finance laws, such as the contribution limits of an individual giving to a specific candidate. More information on federal campaign finance laws can be found at

Median Annual Wages, May 2014

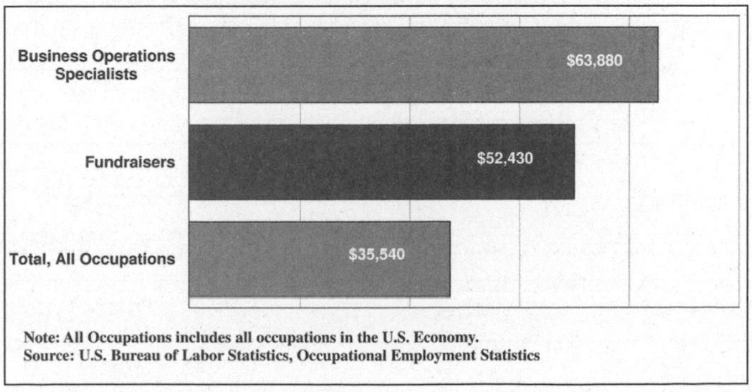

Percent Change in Employment, Projected 2014–2024

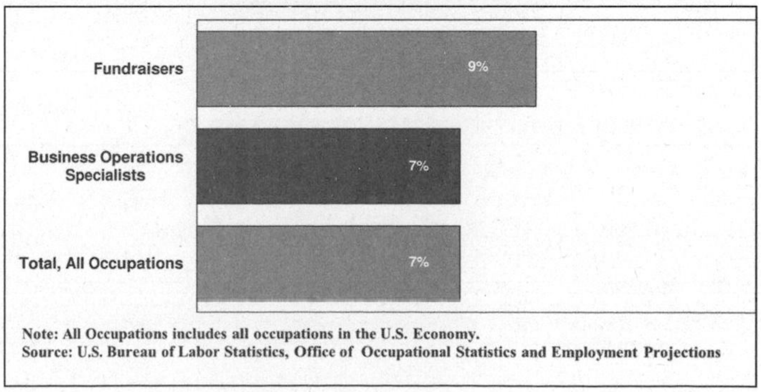

the Federal Election Commission. State laws can be found at the National Conference of State Legislatures.

The following are examples of types of fundraisers:

Major-gifts fundraisers specialize in face-to-face interaction with donors who can give large amounts.

Planned-giving fundraisers solicit donations from those who are looking to pledge money at a future date or in installments over time. These fundraisers must have specialized training in taxes regarding gifts of stocks, bonds, charitable annuities, and real estate bequests in a will.

Direct-mailing fundraisers send out requests for donations to large numbers of people through the mail, over the phone, and online.

Events fundraisers obtain donations through charity events, including dinners, auctions, galas, and charity races such as 10Ks.

Annual campaign fundraisers solicit donations once a year for their organization. Many nonprofit organizations have annual giving campaigns.

Capital campaign fundraisers raise money for a specific project, such as the construction of a new building at a university. Capital campaigns also raise money for renovations and the creation or expansion of an endowment.

Work Environment

Fundraisers held about 73,400 jobs in 2014. The industries that employed the most fundraisers were as follows:

Religious, grantmaking, civic, professional, and similar organizations	50%
Educational services; state, local, and private	22
Social assistance	9

Fundraisers work primarily for nonprofit charitable organizations, including educational institutions, religious organizations, healthcare foundations, social services organizations, and political campaigns.

Most fundraisers are employed by the organization for which they raise funds. Some fundraisers work for consulting firms that have many clients.

Fundraisers spend much of their time communicating with other employees and potential donors, either in person, on the phone, or through email.

Some fundraisers may need to travel to locations where fundraising events are held. Events may include charity runs, walks, galas, and dinners.

Work Schedules. Most fundraisers work full time during regular business hours. Some, however, work under pressure of deadlines and tight schedules, possibly requiring additional hours. Nearly 1 in 5 worked part time in 2014.

Education/Training

Fundraisers typically need a bachelor's degree and strong communication and organizational skills. Employers generally prefer candidates who have studied public relations, journalism, communications, English, or business.

Education. Fundraisers have a variety of academic backgrounds. However, some employers prefer candidates with bachelor's degrees in public relations, journalism, communications, English, or business, but degrees in other subjects also may be acceptable.

Several schools offer master's degree programs in philanthropic studies or fundraising. Requirements for entering these programs generally are based on work or volunteer experience at a nonprofit or grantmaking foundation. Students may take courses in annual campaigns, planned giving, major gifts, grant proposals, and marketing.

In addition to taking relevant coursework, students can gain experience by volunteering at local charities or participating in student-led organizations.

Other Experience. Internships and previous work experience are important in obtaining a paid position as a fundraiser. Many fundraising campaigns rely on volunteers having face-to-face or over-the-phone interaction with potential donors. It is important that the fundraiser who organizes the campaign have experience with this type of work.

Licenses, Certifications, and Registrations. Certification is voluntary, but fundraisers may obtain it to demonstrate a level of professional competency. CFRE International offers the Certified Fund Raising Executive designation for fundraisers. Candidates are required to have 5 years of work experience in fundraising, as well as 80 hours of continuing education through attendance at conferences and classroom instruction. To keep their certification valid, fundraisers must apply for renewal every 3 years.

Advancement. Fundraisers can advance to fundraising manager positions. However, some manager positions may require a master's degree, in addition to years of work experience as a fundraiser.

Important Qualities

Communication skills. Fundraisers need strong communication skills to clearly explain the message and goals of their organization so that people will make donations.

Detail oriented. Fundraisers must be detail oriented because they deal with large volumes of data, including lists of people's names and phone numbers, and must comply with state and federal regulations. Failing to do so may result in penalties.

Leadership. Many fundraisers manage large teams of volunteers and must be able to lead them without having the usual incentive of pay at their disposal.

Organizational skills. Fundraisers manage large campaigns and events. They must have strong planning and organizational skills in order to succeed.

Pay

The median annual wage for fundraisers was $52,430 in May 2014. The median wage is the wage at which half the workers in an occupation earned more than that amount and half earned less.

Employment Projections Data for Fundraisers

Occupational Title	SOC Code	Employment, 2014	Projected Employment, 2024	Change, 2014–2024 Percent	Change, 2014–2024 Numeric
Fundraisers	13-1131	73,400	80,300	9	6,900

Source: U.S. Bureau of Labor Statistics, Employment Projections Program

Similar Occupations. This table shows a list of occupations with job duties that are similar to those of fundraisers.

Occupations	Entry-level Education	2014 Median Pay	Projected Job Growth	Average Annual Openings
Advertising, Promotions, and Marketing Managers	Bachelor's degree	$123,450	9%	1,970
Meeting, Convention, and Event Planners	Bachelor's degree	$46,490	10%	990
Public Relations and Fundraising Managers	Bachelor's degree	$101,510	7%	470
Public Relations Specialists	Bachelor's degree	$55,680	6%	1,490

The lowest 10 percent earned less than $31,190, and the highest 10 percent earned more than $90,160.

In May 2014, the median annual wages for fundraisers in the top industries in which they worked were as follows:

Educational services; state, local, and private $57,280
Religious, grantmaking, civic, professional, and similar organizations 51,990
Social assistance.. 46,560

Job Outlook

Employment of fundraisers is projected to grow 9 percent from 2014 to 2024, faster than the average for all occupations. Employment growth will be driven by the continued need of nonprofit organizations to collect donations in order to run their operations.

Organizations that will receive less financial support than in the past, such as colleges and universities, will need fundraisers to solicit donations to make up for shortfalls. Political campaigns also will continue to hire fundraisers.

More nonprofit organizations are focusing on cultivating an online presence and are increasingly using social media for fundraising activities. As a result, social media have created a new avenue for fundraisers to connect with potential donors and to spread their organization's message.

Job Prospects. Job prospects for fundraisers are expected to be good because organizations are always looking to raise more donations. Although candidates with different backgrounds are often eligible to become fundraisers, those with experience in nonprofit and grantmaking industries will have better job opportunities.

Contacts for More Information

For more information about fundraising certification, visit

➤ CFRE International (http://cfre.org)

O*NET

➤ Fundraisers (13-1131.00)

Human Resources Specialists

- **2014 Median Pay** .... $57,420 per year
  $27.60 per hour
- **Typical Entry-Level Education** ....Bachelor's degree
- **Work Experience in a Related Occupation**............... None
- **On-the-job Training** .... None
- **Number of Jobs, 2014** 482,000
- **Job Outlook, 2014–24**................. 5% (As fast as average)
- **Employment Change, 2014–24** 22,000

What Human Resources Specialists Do

Human resources specialists recruit, screen, interview, and place workers. They often handle tasks related to employee relations, compensation and benefits, and training.

Duties. Human resources specialists typically do the following:

- Consult with employers to identify employment needs
- Interview applicants about their experience, education, and skills
- Contact references and perform background checks on job applicants
- Inform applicants about job details, such as duties, benefits, and working conditions
- Hire or refer qualified candidates for employers
- Conduct or help with new employee orientation
- Keep employment records and process paperwork

Human resources specialists are often trained in all human resources disciplines and perform tasks throughout all areas of the department. In addition to recruiting and placing workers, human resources specialists help guide employees through all human resources procedures and answer questions about policies. They sometimes administer benefits, process payroll, and handle any associated questions or problems, although many specialists may focus more on strategic planning and hiring instead of administrative duties. They also ensure that all human resources functions comply with federal, state, and local regulations.

Employment interviewers speak with applicants and ask them questions before referring them to appropriate jobs.

The following are examples of types of human resources specialists:

Human resources generalists handle all aspects of human resources work. They may have duties in all areas of human resources including recruitment, employee relations, compensation, benefits, training, as well as the administration of human resources policies, procedures, and programs.

Placement specialists match employers with qualified job seekers. They search for candidates who have the skills, education, and work experience needed for jobs, and they try to place those candidates with employers. They also may help set up interviews.

Recruitment specialists, sometimes known as *personnel recruiters* or "*head hunters*," find, screen, and interview applicants for job openings in an organization. They search for applicants by posting listings, attending job fairs, and visiting college campuses. They also may test applicants, contact references, and extend job offers.

Work Environment

Human resources specialists held about 482,000 jobs in 2014. The industries that employed the most human resources specialists were as follows:

Employment services	16%
Government	14
Professional, scientific, and technical services	12
Healthcare and social assistance	11
Manufacturing	7

Because hiring needs may vary throughout the year, many organizations contract recruitment and placement work to outside human resources firms rather than keep permanent human resources specialists on staff.

Work Schedules. Human resources specialists generally work in offices. Some, particularly recruitment specialists, travel extensively to attend job fairs, visit college campuses, and meet with applicants.

Most specialists work full time during regular business hours.

Education/Training

Human resources specialists must usually have a bachelor's degree.

Education. Applicants seeking positions as a human resources specialist must usually have a bachelor's degree in human resources, business, or a related field.

Coursework typically includes business, industrial relations, psychology, professional writing, human resource management, and accounting.

Work Experience in a Related Occupation. Some positions, particularly human resources generalists, may require previous work experience. Candidates can gain experience as human resources assistants, in customer service positions, or in other related jobs.

Licenses, Certifications, and Registrations. Many professional associations that specialize in human resources offer courses intended to enhance the skills of their members, and some offer certification programs. For example, the Society for Human Resource Management (SHRM) offers the SHRM Certified Professional (SHRM-CP) and SHRM Senior Certified Professional (SHRM-SCP).

Although certification is usually voluntary, some employers may prefer or require it. Human resources generalists, in particular, can benefit from certification because it shows knowledge and professional competence across all human resources areas.

Advancement. Human resources specialists who possess a thorough knowledge of their organization, as well as an understanding of regulatory compliance needs, can advance to become human resources managers. Specialists can increase their chance of advancement by completing voluntary certification programs.

Important Qualities

Decision-making skills. Human resources specialists use decision-making skills when reviewing candidates' qualifications or when working to resolve disputes.

Detail oriented. Specialists must be detail oriented when evaluating applicants' qualifications, performing background checks, maintaining records of an employee grievance, and ensuring that a workplace is in compliance with labor standards.

Interpersonal skills. Specialists continually interact with new people and must be able to converse and connect with people from different backgrounds.

Listening skills. Listening skills are essential for human resources specialists. When interviewing job applicants, for example, specialists must pay careful attention to candidates' responses, understand the points they are making, and ask relevant follow-up questions.

Speaking skills. All specialists need strong speaking skills to be effective at their job. They often give presentations and must be able to clearly convey information about their organizations and jobs within them.

Pay

The median annual wage for human resources specialists was $57,420 in May 2014. The median wage is the wage at which half the workers in an occupation earned more than that amount and half earned less. The lowest 10 percent earned less than $33,630, and the highest 10 percent earned more than $98,130.

In May 2014, the median annual wages for human resources specialists in the top industries in which they worked were as follows:

Professional, scientific, and technical services	$63,310
Government	62,200
Manufacturing	61,060

Median Annual Wages, May 2014

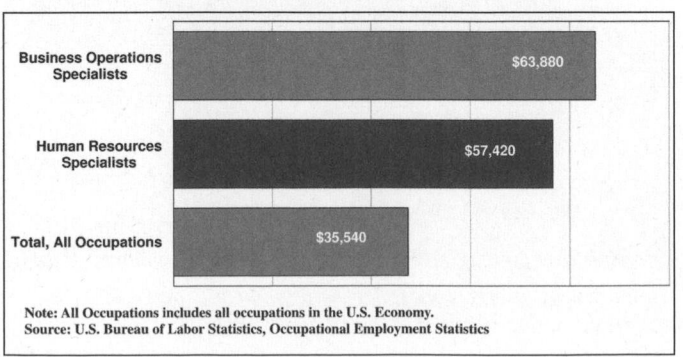

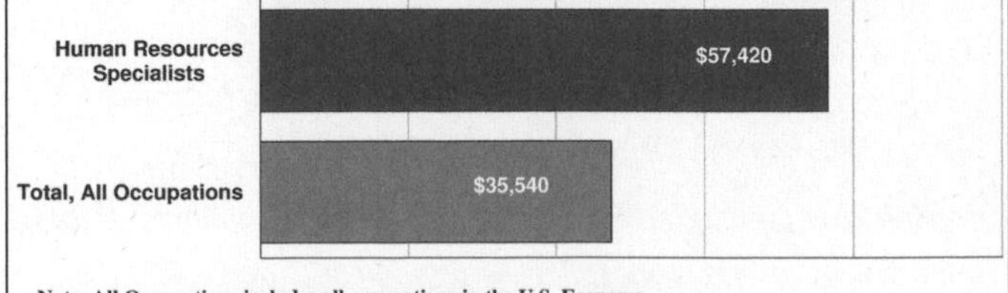

Note: All Occupations includes all occupations in the U.S. Economy.
Source: U.S. Bureau of Labor Statistics, Occupational Employment Statistics

Percent Change in Employment, Projected 2014–2024

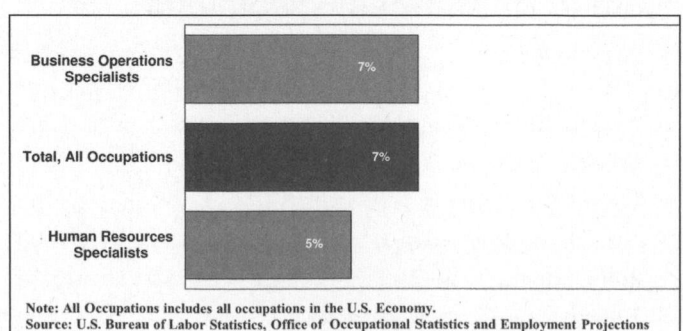

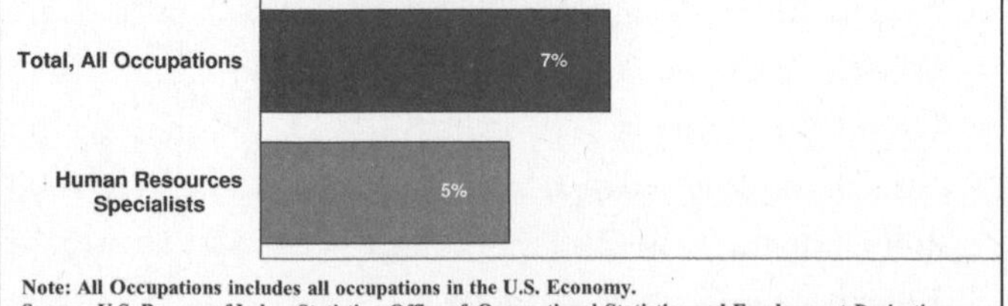

Note: All Occupations includes all occupations in the U.S. Economy.
Source: U.S. Bureau of Labor Statistics, Office of Occupational Statistics and Employment Projections

Employment Projections Data for Human Resources Specialists

Occupational Title	SOC Code	Employment, 2014	Projected Employment, 2024	Change, 2014–2024 Percent	Change, 2014–2024 Numeric
Human resources specialists	13-1071	482,000	503,900	5	22,000

Source: U.S. Bureau of Labor Statistics, Employment Projections Program

Similar Occupations. This table shows a list of occupations with job duties that are similar to those of human resources specialists.

Occupations	Entry-level Education	2014 Median Pay	Projected Job Growth	Average Annual Openings
Compensation and Benefits Managers	Bachelor's degree	$108,070	6%	110
Customer Service Representatives	High school diploma or equivalent	$31,200	10%	25,290
Human Resources Managers	Bachelor's degree	$102,780	9%	1,080
Insurance Sales Agents	High school diploma or equivalent	$47,860	9%	4,350
Labor Relations Specialists	Bachelor's degree	$56,950	-8%	-640
Public Relations Specialists	Bachelor's degree	$55,680	6%	1,490
Social and Human Service Assistants	High school diploma or equivalent	$29,790	11%	4,420
Tax Examiners and Collectors, and Revenue Agents	Bachelor's degree	$51,120	-6%	-420
Training and Development Managers	Bachelor's degree	$101,930	7%	230
Training and Development Specialists	Bachelor's degree	$57,340	7%	1,890

Healthcare and social assistance 49,420
Employment services 48,170

Many human resources specialists, particularly recruiters, travel extensively to attend job fairs, visit college campuses, and meet with applicants.

Job Outlook

Employment of human resources specialists is projected to grow 5 percent from 2014 to 2024, about as fast as the average for all occupations.

About 16 percent of human resources specialists work in the employment services industry, which includes employment placement agencies, temporary help services, and professional employer organizations. Employment growth in employment services is projected to be faster than the average as organizations continue to outsource human resources functions to professional employer organizations—companies that provide human resources services to client businesses.

Companies will need human resources specialists to find replacements for workers leaving the workforce. Organizations will likely need more human resources generalists to handle increasingly complex employment laws and healthcare coverage options.

However, employment of human resources specialists will be tempered as companies make better use of available technologies. Rather than sending recruiters to colleges and job fairs, for example, some employers are increasingly conducting their entire recruiting process online. In addition, administrative tasks are more efficient with software that allows workers to quickly manage, process, or update human resources information.

Job Prospects. Job prospects for human resources specialists are expected to be favorable. Specifically, job opportunities should be good in the employment services industry, as companies continue to outsource portions of their human resources functions to other firms.

Overall, candidates with a bachelor's degree and professional certification should have the best job prospects.

Contacts for More Information

For more information about human resources careers and certification, visit

- Society for Human Resource Management (www.shrm.org/pages/default.aspx)
- Human Resource Certification Institute (www.hrci.org)
- WorldatWork (www.worldatwork.org)

O*NET

- Human Resources Specialists (13-1071.00)

Insurance Underwriters

- **2014 Median Pay** .... $64,220 per year
  $30.88 per hour
- **Typical Entry-Level Education** .... Bachelor's degree
- **Work Experience in a Related Occupation** .... None
- **On-the-job Training** ..... Moderate-term on-the-job training
- **Number of Jobs, 2014** 103,400
- **Job Outlook, 2014–24** .... -11% (Decline)
- **Employment Change, 2014–24** .... -11,700

What Insurance Underwriters Do

Insurance underwriters decide whether to provide insurance and under what terms. They evaluate insurance applications and determine coverage amounts and premiums.

Duties. Insurance underwriters typically do the following:

- Analyze information stated on insurance applications
- Determine the risk involved in insuring a client
- Screen applicants on the basis of set criteria
- Evaluate recommendations from underwriting software
- Contact field representatives, medical personnel, and others to obtain further information
- Decide whether to offer insurance
- Determine appropriate premiums and amounts of coverage

Underwriters are the main link between an insurance company and an insurance agent. Insurance underwriters use computer software programs to determine whether to approve an applicant. They take specific information about a client and enter it into a program. The program then provides recommendations on coverage and premiums. Underwriters evaluate these recommendations and decide whether to approve or reject the application. If a decision is difficult, they may consult additional sources, such as medical documents and credit scores.

Underwriters analyze the risk factors appearing on an application. For instance, if an applicant reports a previous bankruptcy, the underwriter must determine whether that information is relevant to the current policy. The underwriter would consider how far in the past the bankruptcy occurred and how the applicant's financial situation has changed since the applicant filed for bankruptcy.

Insurance underwriters must achieve a balance between risky and cautious decisions. If underwriters allow too much risk, the insurance company will pay out too many claims. But if they don't approve enough applications, the company will not make enough money from premiums.

Most insurance underwriters specialize in one of three broad fields: life, health, and property and casualty. Although the job duties in each field are similar, the criteria that underwriters use vary. For example, for someone seeking life insurance, underwriters consider age and financial history. For someone applying for car insurance (a form of property and casualty insurance), underwriters consider the person's driving record.

Within the broad field of property and casualty, underwriters may specialize even further, into commercial (business) insurance or personal insurance. They may also specialize by the type of policy, such as insuring automobiles, boats (marine insurance), or homes (homeowners' insurance).

Insurance underwriters review insurance applications and determine the appropriate premium to charge a customer.

Work Environment

Insurance underwriters held about 103,400 jobs in 2014. The industries that employed the most insurance underwriters were as follows:

Direct insurance (except life, health, and medical) carriers	47%
Insurance agencies and brokerages	14
Direct health and medical insurance carriers	7
Other insurance-related activities	5
Management of companies and enterprises	4

Underwriters work indoors in offices. Some property and casualty underwriters may visit properties to assess them in person.

Work Schedules. Most underwriters work full time.

Median Annual Wages, May 2014

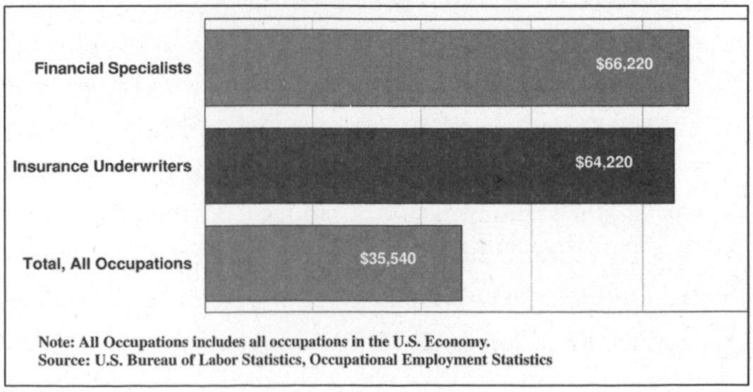

Percent Change in Employment, Projected 2014–2024

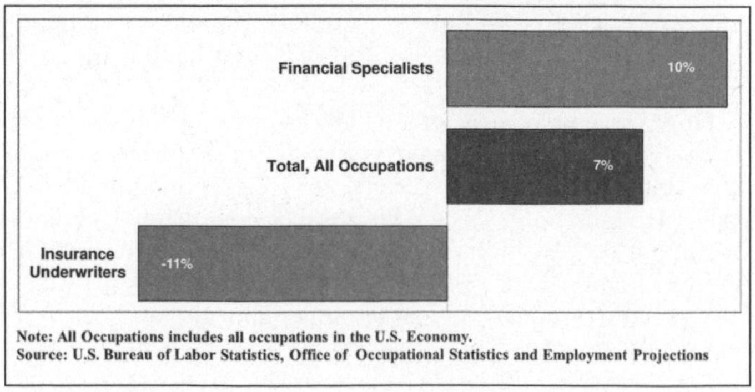

Employment Projections Data for Insurance Underwriters

Occupational Title	SOC Code	Employment, 2014	Projected Employment, 2024	Change, 2014–2024 Percent	Change, 2014–2024 Numeric
Insurance underwriters	13-2053	103,400	91,600	-11	-11,700

Source: U.S. Bureau of Labor Statistics, Employment Projections Program

Similar Occupations. This table shows a list of occupations with job duties that are similar to those of insurance underwriters.

Occupations	Entry-level Education	2014 Median Pay	Projected Job Growth	Average Annual Openings
Actuaries	Bachelor's degree	$96,700	18%	440
Budget Analysts	Bachelor's degree	$71,220	3%	150
Claims Adjusters, Appraisers, Examiners, and Investigators	See Education/Training	$62,300	3%	960
Cost Estimators	Bachelor's degree	$60,050	9%	1,870
Insurance Sales Agents	High school diploma or equivalent	$47,860	9%	4,350
Loan Officers	Bachelor's degree	$62,620	8%	2,450

Education/Training

Employers prefer to hire candidates who have a bachelor's degree. However, insurance-related work experience and strong computer skills may be enough. Certification is generally necessary for advancement to senior underwriter and underwriter manager positions.

Education. Most firms prefer to hire applicants who have a bachelor's degree. Courses in business, finance, economics, and mathematics are particularly helpful.

Training. Beginning underwriters usually work as trainees under the supervision of senior underwriters. Trainees work on basic applications and learn the most common risk factors. As they gain experience, they become responsible for more complex applications and work independently.

Licenses, Certifications, and Registrations. Employers often expect underwriters to become certified through coursework. Courses are important for keeping current with new insurance policies and for adjusting to new technology and changes in state and federal regulations. Certification is often necessary for advancement to senior underwriter and underwriter management positions. Many certification options are available.

For underwriters with at least 3 years of insurance experience, The Institutes offer the Chartered Property and Casualty Underwriter (CPCU) designation. For beginning underwriters, The Institutes offer a training program.

The Institutes also offer two special designations: Associate in Commercial Underwriting (AU) and Associate in Personal Insurance (API). To earn either the AU or API designation, underwriters complete a series of courses and exams that generally take 1 to 2 years.

The National Association of Insurance and Financial Advisors offers an introductory course in basic insurance concepts: the Life Underwriter Training Council Fellow (LUTCF). The American College of Financial Services offers the Chartered Life Underwriter (CLU) certification.

Important Qualities

Analytical skills. Underwriters must be able to evaluate information from a variety of sources and solve complex problems.

Decision-making skills. Underwriters must consider the costs and benefits of various decisions and choose the appropriate one.

Detail oriented. Underwriters must pay attention to detail, because each individual item on an insurance application can affect the coverage decision.

Interpersonal skills. Underwriters need good communication and interpersonal skills because much of their work involves dealing with other people, such as insurance agents.

Math skills. Determining the probability of losses on an insurance policy and calculating appropriate premiums require mathematical ability.

Pay

The median annual wage for insurance underwriters was $64,220 in May 2014. The median wage is the wage at which half the workers in an occupation earned more than that amount and half earned less. The lowest 10 percent earned less than $39,260, and the highest 10 percent earned more than $113,010.

In May 2014, the median annual wages for insurance underwriters in the top industries in which they worked were as follows:

Direct health and medical insurance carriers	$64,290
Other insurance related activities	64,160
Direct insurance (except life, health, and medical) carriers	63,700
Management of companies and enterprises	62,130
Insurance agencies and brokerages	61,680

Job Outlook

Employment of insurance underwriters is projected to decline 11 percent from 2014 to 2024. Automated underwriting software allows workers to process applications more quickly than before, reducing the need for underwriters. As this technology improves, more underwriting decisions can be made automatically. However, there still will be a need for underwriters to evaluate automated recommendations, particularly in complex or specific fields, such as marine insurance.

Job Prospects. Job opportunities should be best for those with a background in finance and strong computer and analytical skills.

Contacts for More Information

For more information about property and casualty insurance, visit

➤ Insurance Information Institute (www.iii.org)

For more information about certifications, visit

➤ The Institutes (www.theinstitutes.org)

➤ The American College of Financial Services (www.theamerican college.edu)

➤ National Association of Insurance and Financial Advisors (www .naifa.org)

O*NET

➤ Insurance Underwriters (13-2053.00)

Labor Relations Specialists

- **2014 Median Pay** .... $56,950 per year $27.38 per hour
- **Typical Entry-Level Education** .... Bachelor's degree
- **Work Experience in a Related Occupation**......... Less than 5 years
- **On-the-job Training** .... None
- **Number of Jobs, 2014** 82,100
- **Job Outlook, 2014–24**............................... -8% (Decline)
- **Employment Change, 2014–24** .... -6,400

Human resources specialists consult with managers to identify employment needs and preferred qualifications.

What Labor Relations Specialists Do

Labor relations specialists interpret and administer labor contracts regarding issues such as wages and salaries, healthcare, pensions, and union and management practices.

Duties. Labor relations specialists typically do the following:

- Advise management on contracts, worker grievances, and disciplinary procedures
- Lead meetings between management and labor
- Meet with union representatives
- Draft proposals and rules or regulations
- Ensure that human resources policies are consistent with union agreements
- Interpret formal communications between management and labor
- Investigate validity of labor grievances
- Train management on labor relations

Labor relations specialists work with representatives in a labor union and a company's management. In addition to leading meetings between the two groups, these specialists draft formal language as part of the collective bargaining process. These contracts are called collective bargaining agreements (CBAs), and they serve as a legal and procedural guide for employee/management relations.

Labor relations specialists also address specific grievances a worker might have, and ensure that all labor and management solutions comply within the relevant agreement.

Work Environment

Labor relations specialists held about 82,100 jobs in 2014. About 76 percent of labor relations specialists worked in labor unions and similar labor organizations in 2014.

The work of labor relations specialists can be stressful because negotiating contracts and resolving labor grievances can be tense.

Work Schedules. Most labor relations specialists work full time during regular business hours. Some specialists work longer periods when preparing for meetings or settling disputes.

Education/Training

Applicants usually have a bachelor's degree in labor relations, human resources, industrial relations, business, or a related field. However, the level of education and experience required to become a labor relations specialist varies by position and employer.

Median Annual Wages, May 2014

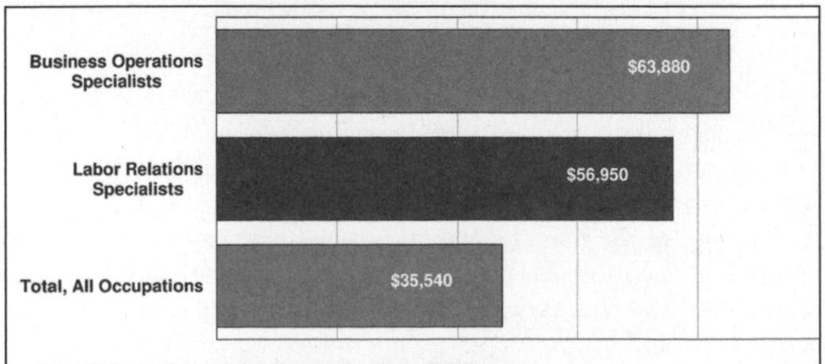

Note: All Occupations includes all occupations in the U.S. Economy.
Source: U.S. Bureau of Labor Statistics, Occupational Employment Statistics

Percent Change in Employment, Projected 2014–2024

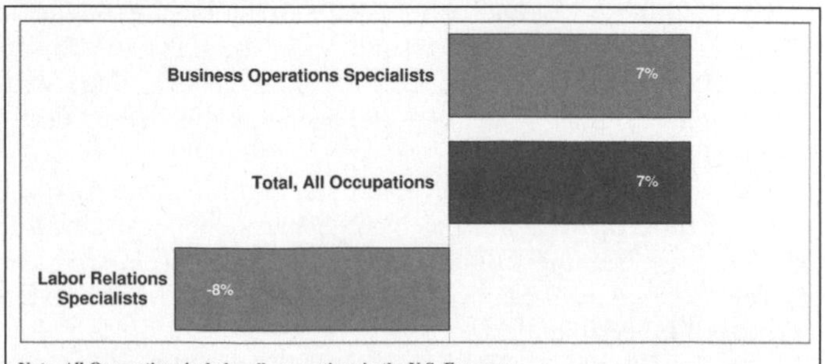

Note: All Occupations includes all occupations in the U.S. Economy.
Source: U.S. Bureau of Labor Statistics, Office of Occupational Statistics and Employment Projections

Employment Projections Data for Labor Relations Specialists

Occupational Title	SOC Code	Employment, 2014	Projected Employment, 2024	Change, 2014–2024	
				Percent	Numeric
Labor relations specialists..	13-1075	82,100	75,600	-8	-6,400

Source: U.S. Bureau of Labor Statistics, Employment Projections Program

Similar Occupations. This table shows a list of occupations with job duties that are similar to those of labor relations specialists.

Occupations	Entry-level Education	2014 Median Pay	Projected Job Growth	Average Annual Openings
Compensation, Benefits, and Job Analysis Specialists	Bachelor's degree	$60,600	4%	340
Human Resources Managers	Bachelor's degree	$102,780	9%	1,080
Human Resources Specialists	Bachelor's degree	$57,420	5%	2,200
Public Relations Specialists	Bachelor's degree	$55,680	6%	1,490
Social and Human Service Assistants	High school diploma or equivalent	$29,790	11%	4,420
Training and Development Managers	Bachelor's degree	$101,930	7%	230
Training and Development Specialists	Bachelor's degree	$57,340	7%	1,890

Education. Labor relations specialists usually have a bachelor's degree. Some schools offer a bachelor's degree in labor or employment relations. These programs focus on labor-specific topics such as employment law and contract negotiation.

Candidates also may qualify for labor relations specialist positions with a bachelor's degree in human resources, industrial relations, business, or a related field. Coursework typically includes business, professional writing, human resource management, and accounting.

Work Experience in a Related Occupation. Many positions require previous work experience. Candidates can gain experience as human resources specialists or generalists before specializing in labor relations.

Licenses, Certifications, and Registrations. Some colleges and universities offer labor relations certificates to specialists who prefer greater specialization in certain topics, such as mediation. These certificates give participants a better understanding of labor law, the collective bargaining process, and worker grievance procedures.

Important Qualities

Decision-making skills. Labor relations specialists use decision-making skills to help management and labor agree on decisions when resolving grievances or other disputes.

Detail oriented. Specialists must be detail oriented when evaluating labor laws and maintaining records of an employee grievance.

Interpersonal skills. Interpersonal skills are essential for labor relations specialists. When mediating between labor and management, specialists must be able to converse and connect with people from different backgrounds.

Listening skills. Listening skills are essential for labor relations specialists. When evaluating grievances, for example, they must pay careful attention to workers' responses, understand the points they are making, and ask relevant follow-up questions.

Writing skills. All labor relations specialists need strong writing skills to be effective at their job. They often draft proposals and must be able to convey complex information to both workers and management.

Pay

The median annual wage for labor relations specialists was $56,950 in May 2014. The median wage is the wage at which half the workers in an occupation earned more than that amount and half earned less. The lowest 10 percent earned less than $17,940, and the highest 10 percent earned more than $107,780.

Job Outlook

Employment of labor relations specialists is projected to decline 8 percent from 2014 to 2024. The number of workers represented by unions has declined. About 12.3 percent of employed wage and salary workers were represented by unions in 2014. This rate fell steadily from 23.3 percent in 1983, and the decline is likely to continue. This means there is less demand for the services of labor relations specialists.

Job Prospects. Job prospects for labor relations specialists are expected to be less than favorable because there will be less demand for their work. Overall, candidates with a bachelor's degree and related work experience should have the best job prospects.

Contacts for More Information

For more information about labor relations careers and certification, visit

- Society for Human Resource Management (www.shrm.org/pages/default.aspx)

Related BLS Article

For more information about union membership, read the Bureau of Labor Statistics' Union Membership Annual News Release (www.bls.gov/news.release/union2.htm).

O*NET

- Labor Relations Specialists (13-1075.00)

Loan Officers

- **2014 Median Pay** .... $62,620 per year $30.11 per hour
- **Typical Entry-Level Education** .... Bachelor's degree
- **Work Experience in a Related Occupation** .... None
- **On-the-job Training** ..... Moderate-term on-the-job training
- **Number of Jobs, 2014** 303,200
- **Job Outlook, 2014–24** .... 8% (As fast as average)
- **Employment Change, 2014–24** 24,500

What Loan Officers Do

Loan officers evaluate, authorize, or recommend approval of loan applications for people and businesses.

Duties. Loan officers typically do the following:

- Contact companies or people to ask if they need a loan
- Meet with loan applicants to gather personal information and answer questions
- Explain different types of loans and the terms of each one to applicants
- Obtain, verify, and analyze the applicant's financial information, such as the credit rating and income level
- Review loan agreements to ensure that they comply with federal and state regulations
- Approve loan applications or refer them to management for a decision

Loan officers use a process called underwriting to assess whether applicants qualify for loans. After collecting and verifying all the required financial documents, the loan officer evaluates the information they obtain to determine the applicant's need for a loan and ability to pay back the loan. Most firms use underwriting software, which produces a recommendation for the loan based on the applicant's financial status. After the underwriting software produces a recommendation, loan officers review the output of the software and consider any additional information to make a final decision.

The work of loan officers has sizable customer-service and sales components. Loan officers often answer questions and guide customers through the application process. In addition, many loan officers must market the products and services of their lending institution and actively solicit new business.

The following are common types of loan officers:

Commercial loan officers specialize in loans to businesses, which often use the loans to buy supplies and upgrade or expand operations. Commercial loans frequently are larger and more complicated than other types of loans. Because companies have such complex financial situations and statements, commercial loans usually require human judgment in addition to the analysis by underwriting software. Furthermore, some commercial loans are so large that no single bank will provide the entire amount requested. In such cases, loan officers may have to work with multiple banks to put together a package of loans.

Consumer loan officers specialize in loans to people. Consumers take out loans for many reasons, such as buying a car or paying college tuition. For some simple consumer loans, the underwriting process is fully automated. However, the loan officer is still needed to guide applicants through the process and to handle cases with unusual circumstances. Some institutions—usually small banks and credit unions—do not use underwriting software and instead rely on loan officers to complete the underwriting process manually.

Mortgage loan officers specialize in loans used to buy real estate (property and buildings), which are called mortgage loans. Mortgage loan officers work on loans for both residential and commercial properties. Often, mortgage loan officers must seek out clients, which requires developing relationships with real estate companies and other sources that can refer prospective applicants.

Within these three fields, some loan officers specialize in a particular part of the loan process:

Loan collection officers contact borrowers who fail to make their loan payments on time. They work with borrowers to help them find a way to keep paying off the loan. If the borrower continues to miss payments, loan officers start the process of taking away what the borrower used to secure the loan (called "collateral")—often a home or car—and selling it to repay the loan.

Loan underwriters specialize in evaluating whether a client is creditworthy. They collect, verify, and evaluate the client's financial information provided on their loan applications and then use loan underwriting software to produce recommendations.

Work Environment

Loan officers held about 303,200 jobs in 2014, of which 83 percent were in the credit intermediation and related activities industry. This industry includes commercial banks, credit unions, mortgage companies, and other financial institutions.

Loan officers who specialize in consumer loans usually work in offices. Mortgage and commercial loan officers often work outside the office and meet with clients at their homes or businesses.

Work Schedules. Most loan officers work full time.

Education/Training

Most loan officers need a bachelor's degree and receive on-the-job training. Mortgage loan officers must be licensed.

Loan officers guide clients through the loan application process.

Median Annual Wages, May 2014

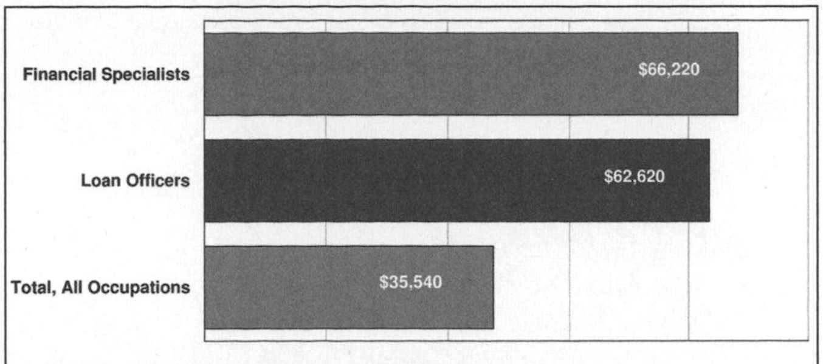

Note: All Occupations includes all occupations in the U.S. Economy.
Source: U.S. Bureau of Labor Statistics, Occupational Employment Statistics

Percent Change in Employment, Projected 2014–2024

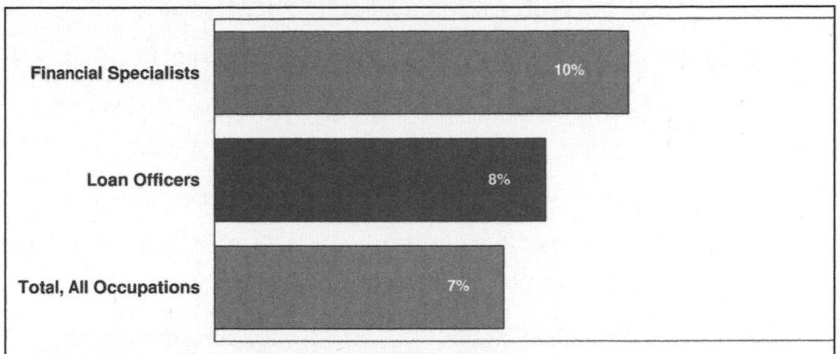

Note: All Occupations includes all occupations in the U.S. Economy.
Source: U.S. Bureau of Labor Statistics, Office of Occupational Statistics and Employment Projections

Education. Loan officers typically need a bachelor's degree, usually in a field such as business or finance. Because commercial loan officers analyze the finances of businesses applying for credit, they need to understand general business accounting, including how to read financial statements.

Some loan officers may be able to enter the occupation without a bachelor's degree if they have related work experience, such as experience in sales, customer service, or banking.

Training. Once hired, loan officers usually receive some on-the-job training. This may be a combination of formal, company-sponsored training and informal training during the first few months on the job.

Licenses, Certifications, and Registrations. Mortgage loan officers must have a Mortgage Loan Originator (MLO) license. To become licensed, they must complete at least 20 hours of coursework, pass an exam, and submit to background and credit checks. Licenses must be renewed annually, and individual states may have additional requirements.

Several banking associations, including the American Bankers Association and the Mortgage Bankers Association, as well as a number of schools, offer courses, training programs, or certifications for loan officers. Although not required, certification shows dedication and expertise and thus may enhance a candidate's employment opportunities.

Important Qualities

Decision-making skills. Loan officers must assess an applicant's financial information and decide whether to award the applicant a loan.

Detail oriented. Each piece of information on an application can have a major effect on the profitability of a loan, meaning that loan officers must pay attention to detail.

Initiative. Loan officers need to seek out new clients. They often act as salespeople, promoting their lending institution and contacting firms to determine their need for a loan.

Interpersonal skills. Because loan officers work with people, they must be able to guide customers through the application process and answer their questions.

Pay

The median annual wage for loan officers was $62,620 in May 2014. The median wage is the wage at which half the workers in an occupation earned more than that amount and half earned less. The lowest 10 percent earned less than $33,050, and the highest 10 percent earned more than $128,390.

The form of compensation varies widely by employer. Some loan officers are paid a flat salary; others are paid on commission. Those on commission usually are paid a base salary plus a commission for the loans they originate. Loan officers also may receive extra commission or bonuses based on the number of loans they originate or how well the loans perform.

Job Outlook

Employment of loan officers is projected to grow 8 percent from 2014 to 2024, about as fast as the average for all occupations. The need for loan officers fluctuates with the economy, generally increasing in times of economic growth, low interest rates, and population growth—all of which create demand for loans.

After a period of decreased lending resulting from the recent recession, banks and other lending institutions are granting an increasing number of loans to people and businesses. Because lending activity is sensitive to fluctuations in the economy, consumer and mortgage loans are expected to increase as the economy recovers. Similarly, many businesses postponed borrowing funds for maintenance, improvement, and expansion during the recession, so commercial loans should increase as businesses become more willing to borrow and banks more willing to lend.

The need for regulatory compliance also should create demand for loan officers. In the wake of the housing and financial crisis, loan applications are undergoing more scrutiny. Loan officers must ensure that the loans they originate are in accordance with state and federal laws, including recently enacted consumer financial protection laws. A stricter regulatory environment means a more labor-intensive loan approval process and a greater need for loan officers.

However, growth in the number of jobs could be somewhat tempered by the expanded use of loan underwriting software,

Employment Projections Data for Loan Officers

Occupational Title	SOC Code	Employment, 2014	Projected Employment, 2024	Change, 2014–2024 Percent	Change, 2014–2024 Numeric
Loan officers	13-2072	303,200	327,700	8	24,500

Source: U.S. Bureau of Labor Statistics, Employment Projections Program

Similar Occupations. This table shows a list of occupations with job duties that are similar to those of loan officers.

Occupations	Entry-level Education	2014 Median Pay	Projected Job Growth	Average Annual Openings
Financial Analysts	Bachelor's degree	$78,620	12%	3,230
Financial Examiners	Bachelor's degree	$76,310	10%	370
Financial Managers	Bachelor's degree	$115,320	7%	3,770
Insurance Sales Agents	High school diploma or equivalent	$47,860	9%	4,350
Insurance Underwriters	Bachelor's degree	$64,220	-11%	-1,170
Personal Financial Advisors	Bachelor's degree	$81,060	30%	7,390
Real Estate Brokers and Sales Agents	High school diploma or equivalent	$43,430	3%	1,090
Securities, Commodities, and Financial Services Sales Agents	Bachelor's degree	$72,070	10%	3,250
Tax Examiners and Collectors, and Revenue Agents	Bachelor's degree	$51,120	-6%	-420
Tellers	High school diploma or equivalent	$25,760	-8%	-4,000

which has made the loan application process much faster. Some loan applications can be completed online and underwritten automatically, allowing loan officers to process more applications in a much shorter period of time.

Job Prospects. Prospects for loan officers should improve over the coming decade as lending activity rebounds from the recent recession. Job opportunities should be good for those with lending, banking, or sales experience. In addition, some firms require loan officers to find their own clients, so candidates with established contacts and a referral network should have the best job opportunities.

Contacts for More Information

For more information about certification and training for loan officers, visit

➤ American Bankers Association (www.aba.com)

For more information about a career as a mortgage loan officer, visit

➤ Mortgage Bankers Association (www.mba.org)

For more information about licensing for mortgage loan officers, visit

➤ Nationwide Mortgage Licensing System & Registry Resource Center (http://mortgage.nationwidelicensingsystem.org/Pages/default.aspx)

State bankers associations have specific information about job opportunities in their state. Also, individual banks can supply information about job openings and the activities, responsibilities, and preferred qualifications of their loan officers.

O*NET

➤ Loan Officers (13-2072.00)

Logisticians

- **2014 Median Pay** .... $73,870 per year; $35.51 per hour
- **Typical Entry-Level Education** .... Bachelor's degree
- **Work Experience in a Related Occupation** .... None
- **On-the-job Training** .... None
- **Number of Jobs, 2014** 130,400
- **Job Outlook, 2014–24** .... 2% (Slower than average)
- **Employment Change, 2014–24** 2,500

What Logisticians Do

Logisticians analyze and coordinate an organization's supply chain—the system that moves a product from supplier to consumer. They manage the entire life cycle of a product, which includes how a product is acquired, distributed, allocated, and delivered.

Duties. Logisticians typically do the following:

- Manage the logistical aspects of a product's life cycle from design to disposal
- Direct the allocation of materials, supplies, and products
- Develop business relationships with suppliers and clients
- Understand clients' needs and know how to meet them
- Design strategies to minimize the cost or time required to transport goods
- Review logistical functions and identify areas for improvement
- Propose improvements to management and customers

Logisticians oversee activities that include purchasing, transportation, inventory, and warehousing. They may direct the movement of a range of goods, people, or supplies, from common consumer goods to military supplies and personnel.

Logisticians use software systems to plan and track the movement of products. They operate software programs designed specifically to manage logistical functions, such as procurement, inventory management, and other supply chain planning and management systems.

Work Environment

Logisticians held about 130,400 jobs in 2014. The industries that employed the most logisticians were as follows:

Manufacturing	26%
Federal government	22
Professional, scientific, and technical services	17
Management of companies and enterprises	9
Wholesale trade	7

Although logisticians work in nearly every industry, nearly half of them are employed in manufacturing and the federal government. About 26 percent of logisticians worked in manufacturing, and about 22 percent worked in the federal government. Some logisticians work in the logistical department of a company, and

When problems arise, logisticians must respond quickly and devise solutions.

others work for firms that specialize in logistical work, such as freight-shipping companies.

The job can be stressful because logistical work is fast-paced. Logisticians must ensure that operations stay on schedule, and they must work quickly to solve any problems that arise. Some logisticians travel to manufacturing plants or distribution centers.

Work Schedules. Most logisticians work full time during regular business hours. However, they sometimes work overtime to ensure that operations stay on schedule. Nearly one-fourth of these workers worked more than 40 hours per week in 2014.

Education/Training

Industry certification and work experience in a related field is helpful for job seekers.

Education. Logisticians may qualify for some positions with an associate's degree. However, as logistics becomes increasingly complex, more companies prefer to hire workers who have at least a bachelor's degree. Many logisticians have a bachelor's degree in business, systems engineering, or supply chain management.

Bachelor's degree programs often include coursework in operations and database management, and system dynamics. In addition, most programs offer courses that train students on software and technologies commonly used by logisticians, such as radio-frequency identification (RFID).

Licenses, Certifications, and Registrations. Although not required, certification can demonstrate professional competence and a broad knowledge of logistics. Logisticians can obtain certification through APICS or the International Society of Logistics (SOLE). To become certified, a logistician typically needs to have a certain amount of education and work experience and to pass an exam.

Work Experience in a Related Occupation. Prospective logisticians can benefit from previous work experience in a field related to logistics or business. Others gain work experience while serving in the military. Experience allows a worker to learn about products and supply chain processes. Some employers allow applicants to substitute several years of work experience for a degree.

Important Qualities

Communication skills. Logisticians need strong communication skills in order to collaborate with colleagues and do business with suppliers and customers.

Critical-thinking skills. Logisticians must develop, adjust, and carry out logistical plans. They often must find ways to reduce costs and improve efficiency.

Organizational skills. Logisticians must be able to perform several tasks at one time, keep detailed records, and simultaneously manage several projects in a fast-paced environment.

Problem-solving skills. Logisticians must handle unforeseen issues, such as delivery problems, and adjust plans as needed to resolve the issues.

Pay

The median annual wage for logisticians was $73,870 in May 2014. The median wage is the wage at which half the workers in an occupation earned more than that amount and half earned less. The lowest 10 percent earned less than $45,880, and the highest 10 percent earned more than $113,940.

In May 2014, the median annual wages for logisticians in the top industries in which they worked were as follows:

Federal government	$80,430
Manufacturing	73,900
Professional, scientific, and technical services	72,930
Management of companies and enterprises	72,390
Wholesale trade	65,810

Job Outlook

Employment of logisticians is projected to grow 2 percent from 2014 to 2024, slower than the average for all occupations. Employment growth will be driven by the need for logistics in the transportation of goods in a global economy. Growth will be moderated, however, because this occupation is concentrated in government and manufacturing, both of which are projected to decline from 2014 to 2024.

Median Annual Wages, May 2014

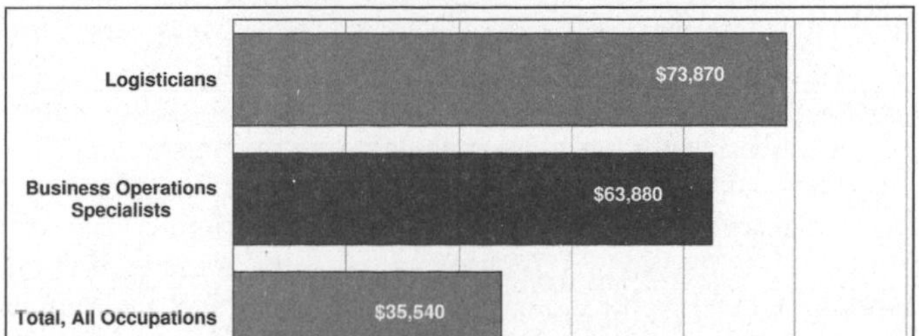

Percent Change in Employment, Projected 2014–2024

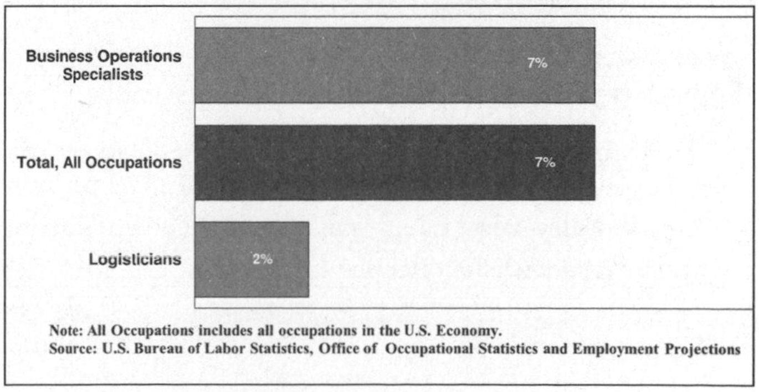

Employment Projections Data for Logisticians

Occupational Title	SOC Code	Employment, 2014	Projected Employment, 2024	Change, 2014–2024 Percent	Change, 2014–2024 Numeric
Logisticians	13-1081	130,400	132,900	2	2,500

Source: U.S. Bureau of Labor Statistics, Employment Projections Program

Similar Occupations. This table shows a list of occupations with job duties that are similar to those of logisticians.

Occupations	Entry-level Education	2014 Median Pay	Projected Job Growth	Average Annual Openings
Cost Estimators	Bachelor's degree	$60,050	9%	1,870
Industrial Engineering Technicians	Associate's degree	$53,370	-5%	-300
Industrial Engineers	Bachelor's degree	$81,490	1%	210
Industrial Production Managers	Bachelor's degree	$92,470	-4%	-630
Management Analysts	Bachelor's degree	$80,880	14%	10,340
Operations Research Analysts	Bachelor's degree	$76,660	30%	2,760
Quality Control Inspectors	High school diploma or equivalent	$35,330	0%	-110

The performance of the logistical and supply chain process is an important factor in a company's profitability. Companies rely on logisticians to manage the movement of their products and supplies. Supply and distribution systems have become increasingly complex as they continue to try to gain more efficiencies at minimal cost. Therefore, employment is expected to grow as companies need more logisticians to move products more efficiently, solve problems, and identify areas for improvement.

Governments and the military also rely on logisticians. Planning for and moving military supplies and personnel require an enormous amount of logistical work. Employment of logisticians in contracting firms should continue to grow to meet the needs of the military.

Job Prospects. Overall job opportunities should be good because many logisticians are expected to retire or otherwise leave the occupation by 2024. Prospects should be best for candidates who have previous experience using logistical software or doing logistical work for the military.

Contacts for More Information

For more information about logisticians, including certification, visit

➤ APICS (www.apics.org)
➤ International Society of Logistics (www.sole.org)

O*NET

➤ Logisticians (13-1081.00)
➤ Logistics Engineers (13-1081.01)

Management Analysts

- **2014 Median Pay** .... $80,880 per year
  $38.89 per hour
- **Typical Entry-Level Education** .... Bachelor's degree
- **Work Experience in a Related Occupation**......... Less than 5 years
- **On-the-job Training** .... None
- **Number of Jobs, 2014** 758,000
- **Job Outlook, 2014–24**.... 14% (Much faster than average)
- **Employment Change, 2014–24** 103,400

What Management Analysts Do

Management analysts, often called *management consultants*, propose ways to improve an organization's efficiency. They advise managers on how to make organizations more profitable through reduced costs and increased revenues.

Duties. Management analysts typically do the following:

- Gather and organize information about the problem to be solved or the procedure to be improved
- Interview personnel and conduct onsite observations to determine the methods, equipment, and personnel that will be needed
- Analyze financial and other data, including revenue, expenditure, and employment reports
- Develop solutions or alternative practices
- Recommend new systems, procedures, or organizational changes
- Make recommendations to management through presentations or written reports
- Confer with managers to ensure changes are working

Although some management analysts work for the organization that they analyze, most work as consultants on a contractual basis.

Whether they are self-employed or part of a large consulting company, the work of a management analyst may vary from project to project. Some projects require a team of consultants, each specializing in one area. In other projects, consultants work independently with the client organization's managers.

Management analysts often specialize in certain areas, such as inventory management or reorganizing corporate structures to eliminate duplicate and nonessential jobs. Some consultants specialize in a specific industry, such as healthcare or telecommunications. In government, management analysts usually specialize by type of agency.

Management analysts collect and analyze information in order to make recommendations to managers.

Organizations hire consultants to develop strategies for entering and remaining competitive in today's marketplace.

Management analysts who work on contract may write proposals and bid for jobs. Typically, an organization that needs the help of a management analyst solicits proposals from a number of consultants and consulting companies that specialize in the needed work. Those who want the work must then submit a proposal by the deadline that explains how the consultant will do the work, who will do the work, why they are the best consultants to do the work, what the schedule will be, and how much it will cost. The organization that needs the consultants then selects the proposal that best meets its needs and budget.

Work Environment

Management analysts held about 758,000 jobs in 2014. The industries that employed the most management analysts were as follows:

Management, scientific, and technical consulting services	22%
Finance and insurance	10
Federal government	8
State and local government, excluding education and hospitals	7
Management of companies and enterprises	5

Management analysts usually divide their time between their offices and the client's site. Because they must spend a significant amount of time with clients, analysts travel frequently. Analysts may experience stress when trying to meet a client's demands, often on a tight schedule.

In 2014, about 1 in 5 management analysts were self-employed. Self-employed analysts can decide how much, when, and where to work. However, self-employed analysts often are under more pressure than those who are wage and salary employees, because their livelihood depends on their ability to maintain and expand their client base.

Work Schedules. Analysts often work many hours under tight deadlines. In 2014, about 3 in 10 worked more than 40 hours per week.

Education/Training

Most management analysts have at least a bachelor's degree. The Certified Management Consultant (CMC) designation may improve job prospects.

Education. A bachelor's degree is the typical entry-level requirement for management analysts. However, some employers prefer to hire candidates who have a master's degree in business administration (MBA).

Few colleges and universities offer formal programs in management consulting. However, many fields of study provide a suitable education because of the range of areas that management analysts address. Common fields of study include business, management, economics, political science and government, accounting, finance, marketing, psychology, computer and information science, and English.

Analysts also routinely attend conferences to stay up to date on current developments in their field.

Licenses, Certifications, and Registrations. The Institute of Management Consultants USA (IMC USA) offers the Certified Management Consultant (CMC) designation to those who meet minimum levels of education and experience, submit client reviews, and pass an interview and exam covering the IMC USA's code of ethics. Management consultants with a CMC designation must be recertified every 3 years. Management analysts are not required to get certification, but it may give job seekers a competitive advantage.

Work Experience in a Related Occupation. Many analysts enter the occupation with several years of work experience. Organizations that specialize in certain fields typically try to hire candidates who have experience in those areas. Typical work backgrounds include experience in management, human resources, and information technology.

Advancement. As consultants gain experience, they often take on more responsibility. At the senior level, consultants may supervise teams working on more complex projects and become more involved in seeking out new business. Those with exceptional skills may eventually become partners in their consulting organization and focus on attracting new clients and bringing in revenue. Senior consultants who leave their consulting company often move to senior management positions at nonconsulting organizations.

Median Annual Wages, May 2014

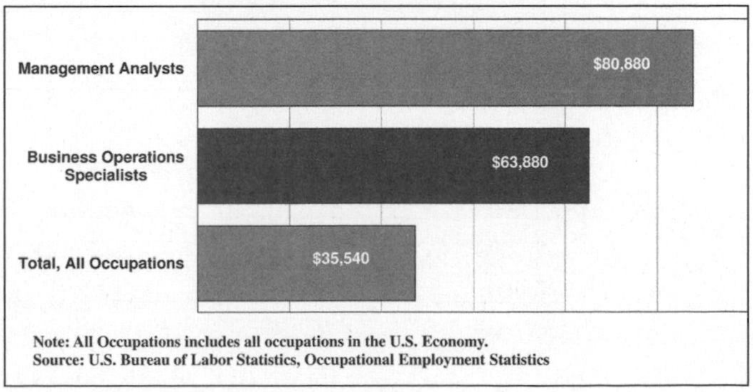

Percent Change in Employment, Projected 2014–2024

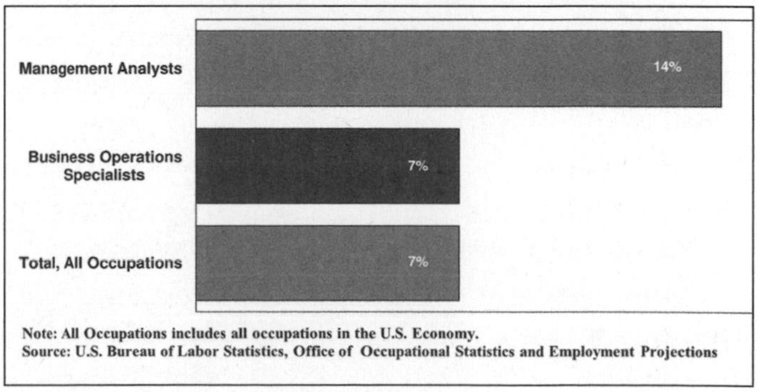

Employment Projections Data for Management Analysts

Occupational Title	SOC Code	Employment, 2014	Projected Employment, 2024	Change, 2014–2024	
				Percent	Numeric
Management analysts	13-1111	758,000	861,400	14	103,400

Source: U.S. Bureau of Labor Statistics, Employment Projections Program

Important Qualities

Analytical skills. Management analysts must be able to interpret a wide range of information and use their findings to make proposals.

Communication skills. Management analysts must be able to communicate clearly and precisely in both writing and speaking. Successful analysts also need good listening skills to understand the organization's problems and propose appropriate solutions.

Interpersonal skills. Management analysts must work with managers and other employees of the organizations where they provide consulting services. They should work as a team toward achieving the organization's goals.

Problem-solving skills. Management analysts must be able to think creatively to solve clients' problems. Although some aspects of different clients' problems may be similar, each situation is likely to present unique challenges for the analyst to solve.

Time-management skills. Management analysts often work under tight deadlines and must use their time efficiently to complete projects on time.

Pay

The median annual wage for management analysts was $80,880 in May 2014. The median wage is the wage at which half the workers in an occupation earned more than that amount and half earned less. The lowest 10 percent earned less than $45,360, and the highest 10 percent earned more than $148,110.

In May 2014, the median annual wages for management analysts in the top industries in which they worked were as follows:

Federal government	$86,220
Management, scientific, and technical consulting services	85,710
Management of companies and enterprises	81,080
Finance and insurance	78,640
State and local government, excluding education and hospitals	62,350

Management analysts working for consulting firms are usually paid a base salary in addition to a year-end bonus. Self-employed analysts are paid directly by their clients, typically either by the hour, or per project.

Job Outlook

Employment of management analysts is projected to grow 14 percent from 2014 to 2024, much faster than the average for all occupations. Demand for consulting services is expected to grow as organizations seek ways to improve efficiency and control costs. As markets become more competitive, firms will need to use resources more efficiently.

Demand for management analysts is expected to be strong in healthcare. This industry segment is experiencing higher costs in part because of an aging population. In addition, federal health care reform has mandated changes to business practices for healthcare providers and insurance companies. More management analysts may be needed to help navigate these changes.

Growth will be particularly strong in smaller consulting companies that specialize in specific industries or types of business function, such as information technology or human resources. Government agencies will also seek the services of management analysts as they look for ways to reduce spending and improve efficiency.

Growth of international business will also contribute to an expected increase in demand for management analysts. As U.S. organizations expand their business abroad, many will hire management analysts to help them form the right strategy for entering the foreign market.

Job Prospects. Jobseekers may face strong competition for management analyst positions because the high earning potential

Similar Occupations. This table shows a list of occupations with job duties that are similar to those of management analysts.

Occupations	Entry-level Education	2014 Median Pay	Projected Job Growth	Average Annual Openings
Accountants and Auditors	Bachelor's degree	$65,940	11%	14,240
Administrative Services Managers	Bachelor's degree	$83,790	8%	2,350
Budget Analysts	Bachelor's degree	$71,220	3%	150
Cost Estimators	Bachelor's degree	$60,050	9%	1,870
Economists	Master's degree	$95,710	6%	120
Financial Analysts	Bachelor's degree	$78,620	12%	3,230
Financial Managers	Bachelor's degree	$115,320	7%	3,770
Market Research Analysts	Bachelor's degree	$61,290	19%	9,230
Operations Research Analysts	Bachelor's degree	$76,660	30%	2,760
Survey Researchers	Master's degree	$49,760	12%	190
Top Executives	Bachelor's degree	$102,750	6%	14,700

in this occupation makes it attractive to many job seekers. Job opportunities are expected to be best for those who have a graduate degree or a certification, specialized expertise, fluency in a foreign language, or a talent for sales and public relations.

Contacts for More Information

For more information about the Certified Management Consultant designation, visit

➤ Institute of Management Consultants USA (www.imcusa.org)

O*NET

➤ Management Analysts (13-1111.00)

Market Research Analysts

- **2014 Median Pay** .... $61,290 per year
  $29.47 per hour
- **Typical Entry-Level Education** .... Bachelor's degree
- **Work Experience in a Related Occupation** .... None
- **On-the-job Training** .... None
- **Number of Jobs, 2014** 495,500
- **Job Outlook, 2014–24** .... 19% (Much faster than average)
- **Employment Change, 2014–24** 92,300

What Market Research Analysts Do

Market research analysts study market conditions to examine potential sales of a product or service. They help companies understand what products people want, who will buy them, and at what price.

Duties. Market research analysts typically do the following:

- Monitor and forecast marketing and sales trends
- Measure the effectiveness of marketing programs and strategies
- Devise and evaluate methods for collecting data, such as surveys, questionnaires, and opinion polls
- Gather data on consumers, competitors, and market conditions
- Analyze data using statistical software
- Convert complex data and findings into understandable tables, graphs, and written reports
- Prepare reports and present results to clients and management

Market research analysts research and gather data to help a company market its products or services. They gather data on consumer demographics, preferences, needs, and buying habits. They collect data and information using a variety of methods, such as

Market research analysts may give presentations to clients.

interviews, questionnaires, focus groups, market analysis surveys, public opinion polls, and literature reviews.

Analysts help determine a company's position in the marketplace by researching their competitors and analyzing their prices, sales, and marketing methods. Using this information, they may determine potential markets, product demand, and pricing. Their knowledge of the targeted consumer enables them to develop advertising brochures and commercials, sales plans, and product promotions.

Market research analysts evaluate data using statistical techniques and software. They must interpret what the data mean for their client, and they may forecast future trends. They often make charts, graphs, infographics, and other visual aids to present the results of their research.

Workers who design and conduct surveys are known as survey researchers.

Work Environment

Market research analysts held about 495,500 jobs in 2014. The industries that employed the most market research analysts were as follows:

Management, scientific, and technical consulting services	10%
Wholesale trade	10
Finance and insurance	10
Management of companies and enterprises	8
Manufacturing	8

Because most industries use market research, these analysts are employed throughout the economy.

Median Annual Wages, May 2014

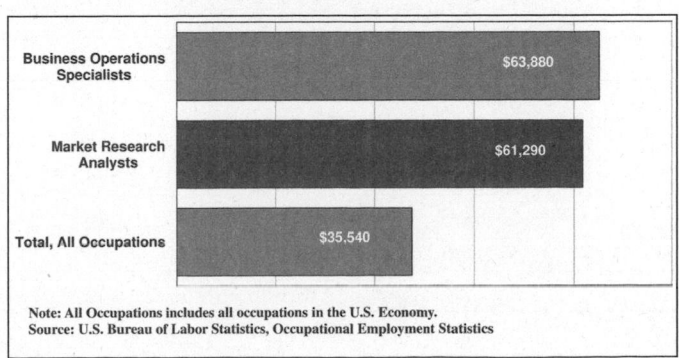

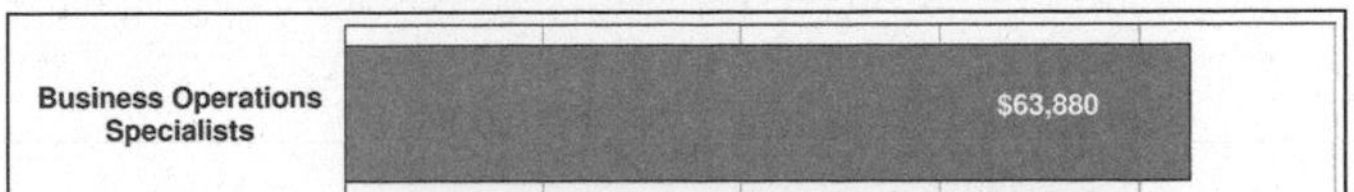

Note: All Occupations includes all occupations in the U.S. Economy.
Source: U.S. Bureau of Labor Statistics, Occupational Employment Statistics

Percent Change in Employment, Projected 2014–2024

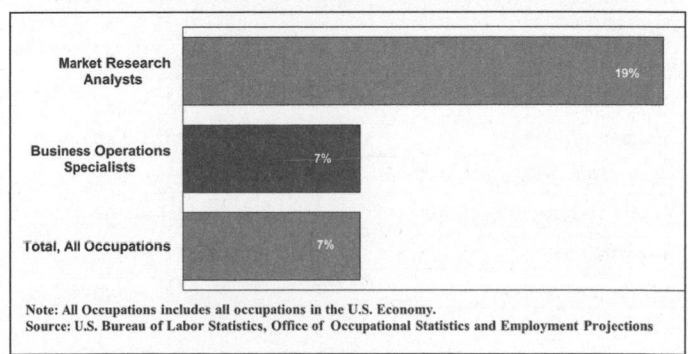

Note: All Occupations includes all occupations in the U.S. Economy.
Source: U.S. Bureau of Labor Statistics, Office of Occupational Statistics and Employment Projections

Employment Projections Data for Market Research Analysts

Occupational Title	SOC Code	Employment, 2014	Projected Employment, 2024	Change, 2014–2024 Percent	Change, 2014–2024 Numeric
Market research analysts and marketing specialists	13-1161	495,500	587,800	19	92,300

Source: U.S. Bureau of Labor Statistics, Employment Projections Program

Some market research analysts study trends for the company for which they work. Others work for consulting firms that do market research for many different clients.

Market research analysts can work individually or as part of a team, collecting, analyzing, and presenting data. For example, some analysts may work with graphic designers and artists to create charts, graphs, and infographics summarizing the research and findings.

Work Schedules. Most market research analysts work full time during regular business hours. Some, however, work under pressure of deadlines and tight schedules, which may require additional hours of work.

Education/Training

Most market research analysts need at least a bachelor's degree. Top research positions may require a master's degree. Strong math and analytical skills are essential.

Education. Market research analysts typically need a bachelor's degree in market research or a related field. Many have degrees in fields such as statistics, math, and computer science. Others have backgrounds in business administration, the social sciences, or communications.

Courses in statistics, research methods, and marketing are essential for these workers. Courses in communications and social sciences, such as economics or consumer behavior, are also important.

Some market research analyst jobs require a master's degree. Several schools offer graduate programs in marketing research, but many analysts complete degrees in other fields, such as statistics and marketing, and/or earn a master's degree in business administration (MBA). A master's degree is often required for leadership positions or positions that perform more technical research.

Licenses, Certifications, and Registrations. Certification is voluntary, but analysts may pursue certification to demonstrate a level of professional competency. The Marketing Research Association offers the Professional Researcher Certification (PRC) for market research analysts. Candidates qualify based on experience and knowledge; they must pass an exam, be a member of a professional organization, and have at least 3 years working in opinion and marketing research. Individuals must complete 20 hours of industry-related continuing education courses every 2 years to renew their certification.

Important Qualities

Analytical skills. Market research analysts must be able to understand large amounts of data and information.

Communication skills. Market research analysts need strong communication skills when gathering information, interpreting data, and presenting results to clients.

Critical-thinking skills. To determine what marketing strategy would work best for a company, market research analysts must assess all available information.

Detail oriented. Market research analysts must be detail oriented because they often do precise data analysis.

Pay

The median annual wage for market research analysts was $61,290 in May 2014. The median wage is the wage at which half the workers in an occupation earned more than that amount and half earned less. The lowest 10 percent earned less than $33,460, and the highest 10 percent earned more than $116,740.

In May 2014, the median annual wages for market research analysts in the top industries in which they worked were as follows:

Management of companies and enterprises	$69,420
Manufacturing	68,650
Finance and insurance	67,750
Wholesale trade	58,830
Management, scientific, and technical consulting services	57,560

Similar Occupations. This table shows a list of occupations with job duties that are similar to those of market research analysts.

Occupations	Entry-level Education	2014 Median Pay	Projected Job Growth	Average Annual Openings
Advertising, Promotions, and Marketing Managers	Bachelor's degree	$123,450	9%	1,970
Cost Estimators	Bachelor's degree	$60,050	9%	1,870
Economists	Master's degree	$95,710	6%	120
Mathematicians	Master's degree	$103,720	21%	70
Operations Research Analysts	Bachelor's degree	$76,660	30%	2,760
Public Relations Specialists	Bachelor's degree	$55,680	6%	1,490
Statisticians	Master's degree	$79,990	34%	1,010
Survey Researchers	Master's degree	$49,760	12%	190

Job Outlook

Employment of market research analysts is projected to grow 19 percent from 2014 to 2024, much faster than the average for all occupations.

Employment growth will be driven by an increasing use of data and market research across all industries—to understand the needs and wants of customers and to measure the effectiveness of marketing and business strategies.

In addition, market research provides companies and organizations with an opportunity to increase sales and cut costs. Companies increasingly use research on consumer behavior to develop improved marketing strategies. By doing so, companies are better able to market directly to their target population.

Market research also lets companies monitor customer satisfaction and gather feedback about how to improve products or services, allowing companies to build an advantage over their competitors. They may use research to decide the location of stores, placement of products, and services offered. As more companies use research to develop marketing strategies, competing companies will likely engage in similar market research.

Job Prospects. Job prospects should be best for those with a master's degree in market research, marketing, statistics, or business administration.

Those with a strong quantitative background in statistical and data analysis or related work experience will have better job opportunities than those without it.

Contacts for More Information

For more information about market research analysts, visit

- Council of American Survey Research Organizations (www.casro.org)
- Marketing Research Association (www.marketingresearch.org)

O*NET

- Market Research Analysts and Marketing Specialists (13-1161.00)

Meeting, Convention, and Event Planners

- **2014 Median Pay** .... $46,490 per year $22.35 per hour
- **Typical Entry-Level Education** .... Bachelor's degree
- **Work Experience in a Related Occupation** .... None
- **On-the-job Training** .... None
- **Number of Jobs, 2014** 100,000
- **Job Outlook, 2014–24** .... 10% (Faster than average)
- **Employment Change, 2014–24** 9,900

What Meeting, Convention, and Event Planners Do

Meeting, convention, and event planners coordinate all aspects of events and professional meetings. They arrange meeting locations, transportation, and other details.

Duties. Meeting, convention, and event planners typically do the following:

- Meet with clients to understand the purpose of the meeting or event
- Plan the scope of the event, including time, location, and cost
- Solicit bids from venues and service providers
- Inspect venues to ensure that they meet the client's requirements
- Coordinate event services such as rooms, transportation, and food service
- Monitor event activities to ensure the client and event attendees are satisfied
- Review event bills and approve payments

There are millions of meetings and events held each year. Meeting, convention, and event planners organize a variety of these events including weddings, educational conferences, and business conventions. They coordinate every detail of these events, including finances. Before a meeting event, for example, planners will meet with clients to estimate attendance and determine the meeting's purpose. During the event, they handle logistics, such as registering guests and organizing audio/visual equipment. After the meeting, they make sure all vendors are paid and may survey attendees to obtain feedback on the event.

Meeting, convention, and event planners search for potential meeting sites, such as hotels and convention centers. They consider the lodging and services that the facility can provide, how easy it will be for people to get there, and the attractions that the surrounding area has to offer. Planners may also consider whether an online meeting can achieve the same objectives as one that requires attendees to meet in a physical location.

Once a location is selected, planners arrange the meeting space and support services, such as catering and interpreters. They negotiate contracts with suppliers and coordinate plans with the venue's staff, and they may also organize speakers, entertainment, and activities.

The following are examples of types of meeting, convention, and event planners:

Association planners organize annual conferences and trade shows for professional associations. Because member attendance is usually voluntary, it is important for associations to emphasize the meeting's value and location; for some association planners, marketing is an important aspect of their work.

Convention service managers work for hotels and convention centers. They act as liaisons between the meeting facility and the planners who work for associations, businesses, and governments. They present food service options to outside planners, coordinate

Meeting planners work with clients to determine the scope and purpose of a meeting.

special requests, and suggest hotel services that work within a planner's budget.

Corporate planners organize internal business meetings and meetings between businesses. These events may be in person or online, held either within corporate facilities or offsite to include more people.

Event planners arrange the details of a variety of events. *Wedding planners* are the most well-known, but event planners also coordinate celebrations such as anniversaries, reunions, and other large social events, as well as corporate events including product launches, galas, and award ceremonies.

Government meeting planners organize meetings for government officials and agencies. Familiarity with government regulations, such as procedures for buying materials and booking hotels, is essential to their work.

Healthcare meeting planners specialize in organizing meetings and conferences for allied healthcare professionals. Healthcare meetings have to meet strict standards in order for the meeting to count as continuing education and to comply with government regulations.

Nonprofit event planners plan large events with the goal of raising donations for a charity or advocacy organization. Events may include banquets, charity races, and food drives.

Work Environment

Meeting, convention, and event planners held about 100,000 jobs in 2014. Although most worked for private companies across a wide range of industries, about 20 percent worked for religious, grantmaking, civic, professional, and similar organizations, and another 14 percent worked in accommodation and food service organizations. About 1 in 10 were self-employed.

Meeting, convention, and event planners spend time in their offices and onsite at hotels or convention centers. They may travel regularly to attend the events they organize and to visit prospective meeting sites, sometimes in exotic locations around the world. Planners regularly collaborate with clients, hospitality workers, and meeting attendees.

The work of meeting, convention, and event planners can be fast-paced and demanding. Planners oversee many aspects of an event at the same time and face numerous deadlines. They may also coordinate multiple meetings or events at the same time.

Work Schedules. Most meeting, convention, and event planners work full time. As major events approach, they often work many additional hours to finalize preparations. During meetings or conventions, planners may work on weekends and for more hours than they usually work in a day.

Education/Training

Applicants usually need a bachelor's degree and some experience related to event planning.

Education. Many employers prefer applicants who have a bachelor's degree and some work experience in hotels or planning. The proportion of planners with a bachelor's degree is increasing because work responsibilities have become more complex. Although some colleges offer degree programs in meeting and event management, other common fields of study include hospitality and tourism management. If an applicant's degree is not related to these fields, employers are likely to require at least 1 to 2 years of related hospitality or planning experience.

Planners who have studied meeting and event management or hospitality management may start out with greater responsibilities than those from other academic disciplines. Some colleges offer continuing education courses in meeting and event planning.

Licenses, Certifications, and Registrations. The Convention Industry Council offers the Certified Meeting Professional (CMP) credential, a voluntary certification for meeting and convention planners. Although the CMP is not required, it is widely recognized in the industry and may help in career advancement. To qualify, candidates must have a minimum of 36 months of meeting management experience, recent employment in a meeting management job, and proof of continuing education credits. Those who qualify must then pass an exam that covers topics such as strategic planning, financial and risk management, facility operations and services, and logistics.

In 2014, the Convention Industry Council created the Certified Meeting Professional-Healthcare (CMP-HC) certification, a CMP specialization related to healthcare industry meeting planners. Planners who want to earn CMP-HC certification must first hold CMP certification and also meet the work and planning requirements specifically in healthcare industry meeting planning.

The Society of Government Meeting Professionals (SGMP) offers the Certified Government Meeting Professional (CGMP) designation for meeting planners who work for, or contract with, federal, state, or local government. This certification is not required to work as a government meeting planner; however, it may be helpful for those who want to show that they know government purchasing policies and travel regulations. To qualify, candidates must have worked as a meeting planner for at least 1 year and have been a member of SGMP for 6 months. To become a certified planner, members must take a 3-day course and pass an exam.

Some organizations offer voluntary certifications in wedding planning, including the American Association of Certified Wedding Planners and the Association of Certified Professional

Median Annual Wages, May 2014

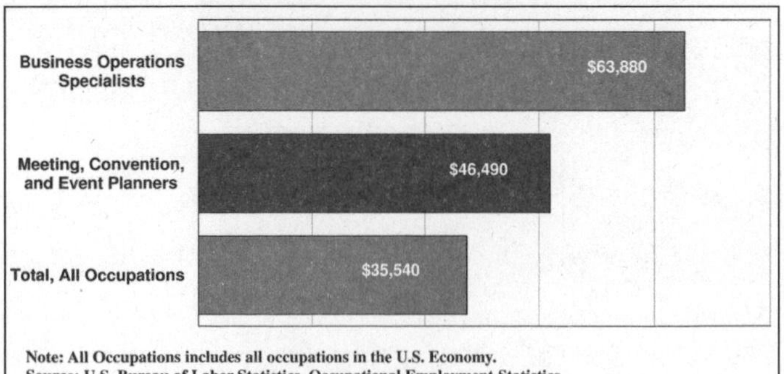

Note: All Occupations includes all occupations in the U.S. Economy.
Source: U.S. Bureau of Labor Statistics, Occupational Employment Statistics

Percent Change in Employment, Projected 2014–2024

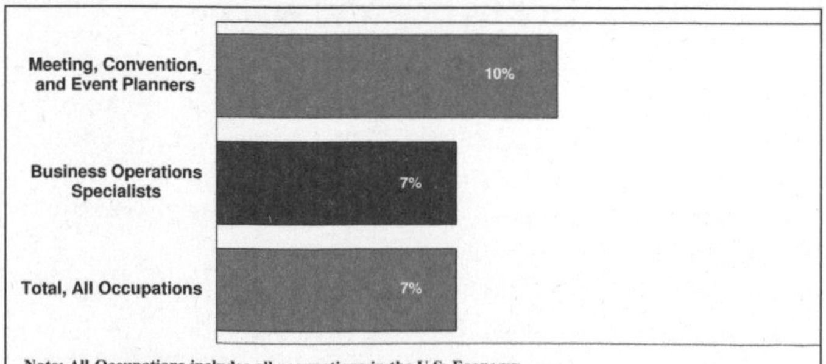

Note: All Occupations includes all occupations in the U.S. Economy.
Source: U.S. Bureau of Labor Statistics, Office of Occupational Statistics and Employment Projections

Employment Projections Data for Meeting, Convention, and Event Planners

Occupational Title	SOC Code	Employment, 2014	Projected Employment, 2024	Change, 2014–2024 Percent	Change, 2014–2024 Numeric
Meeting, convention, and event planners	13-1121	100,000	109,900	10	9,900

Source: U.S. Bureau of Labor Statistics, Employment Projections Program

Similar Occupations. This table shows a list of occupations with job duties that are similar to those of meeting, convention, and event planners.

Occupations	Entry-level Education	2014 Median Pay	Projected Job Growth	Average Annual Openings
Administrative Services Managers	Bachelor's degree	$83,790	8%	2,350
Food Service Managers	High school diploma or equivalent	$48,560	5%	1,570
Fundraisers	Bachelor's degree	$52,430	9%	690
Lodging Managers	High school diploma or equivalent	$47,680	8%	370
Travel Agents	High school diploma or equivalent	$34,800	-12%	-870

Wedding Consultants. Although not required, the certifications can be helpful in attracting clients and proving knowledge.

Other Experience. It is beneficial for new meeting, convention, and event planners to have experience in hospitality industry jobs. Working in a variety of positions at hotels, convention centers, and convention bureaus provides knowledge of how the hospitality industry operates. Other beneficial work experiences include coordinating university or volunteer events and shadowing professionals.

Important Qualities

Communication skills. Meeting, convention, and event planners communicate with clients, suppliers, and event staff. They must have excellent written and oral communication skills to convey the needs of their clients effectively.

Composure. Meeting, convention, and event planners often work in a fast-paced environment and must be able to make quick decisions while remaining calm under pressure. When necessary materials do not arrive on schedule, they make alternative arrangements calmly and swiftly.

Interpersonal skills. Meeting, convention, and event planners must establish and maintain positive relationships with clients and suppliers. There are often a limited number of vendors in an area which can be used, and they will likely need them for future events.

Negotiation skills. Meeting, convention, and event planners must be able to negotiate service contracts events. They need to secure quality products and services at reasonable prices for their clients.

Organizational skills. Meeting, convention, and event planners must multitask, pay attention to details, and meet tight deadlines in order to provide high-quality meetings. Many meetings are planned more than a year in advance, so long-term thinking is vital.

Problem-solving skills. Meeting, convention, and event planners must be able to develop creative solutions that satisfy clients. They must be able to recognize potential problems and identify solutions in advance.

Pay

The median annual wage for meeting, convention, and event planners was $46,490 in May 2014. The median wage is the wage at which half the workers in an occupation earned more than that amount and half earned less. The lowest 10 percent earned less than $25,940, and the highest 10 percent earned more than $82,060.

Job Outlook

Employment of meeting, convention, and event planners is projected to grow 10 percent from 2014 to 2024, faster than the average for all occupations. As businesses and organizations become more global in scope, meetings and conventions are expected to become even more important.

For organizations with geographically separate offices and members, meetings are the only time they can bring everyone together. Despite the spread of online communication, face-to-face interaction continues to be preferred by many people.

Job Prospects. Candidates with a bachelor's degree in meeting and event management, hospitality, or tourism management should have the best job opportunities. A Certified Meeting Professional (CMP) credential is also viewed favorably by potential employers. Those who have experience in the hospitality industry or with virtual meeting software and social media outlets should also have an advantage.

Job opportunities for corporate planners fluctuate with economic activity. When the economy is in a downturn, companies often cut budgets for meetings. Planners who work for the healthcare industry are least likely to experience cutbacks during a recession because attendance at healthcare meetings and conventions is often required for medical professionals to maintain their license.

Contacts for More Information

For more information about meeting, convention, and event planners, including information about certification and industry trends, visit

- Convention Industry Council (www.conventionindustry.org)
- Meeting Professionals International (www.mpiweb.org)
- Professional Convention Management Association (www.pcma.org)
- Society of Government Meeting Professionals (www.sgmp.org)

For more information about wedding planners including information about certification, visit

- American Association of Certified Wedding Planners (http://aacwp.org)

- ➤ Association for Wedding Professionals International (http://afwpi.com)
- ➤ Association of Bridal Consultants (www.bridalassn.com)
- ➤ Association of Certified Professional Wedding Consultants (www.acpwc.com)

O*NET

- ➤ Meeting, Convention, and Event Planners (13-1121.00)

Personal Financial Advisors

- **2014 Median Pay** .... $81,060 per year, $38.97 per hour
- **Typical Entry-Level Education** .... Bachelor's degree
- **Work Experience in a Related Occupation** .... None
- **On-the-job Training** .... Long-term on-the-job training
- **Number of Jobs, 2014** 249,400
- **Job Outlook, 2014–24** .... 30% (Much faster than average)
- **Employment Change, 2014–24** 73,900

What Personal Financial Advisors Do

Personal financial advisors provide advice on investments, insurance, mortgages, college savings, estate planning, taxes, and retirement to help individuals manage their finances.

Duties. Personal financial advisors typically do the following:

- Meet with clients in person to discuss their financial goals
- Explain the types of financial services they provide to potential clients
- Educate clients and answer questions about investment options and potential risks
- Recommend investments to clients or select investments on their behalf
- Help clients plan for specific circumstances, such as education expenses or retirement
- Monitor clients' accounts and determine if changes are needed to improve the performance or to accommodate life changes, such as getting married or having children
- Research investment opportunities

Personal financial advisors assess the financial needs of individuals and help them with decisions on investments (such as stocks and bonds), tax laws, and insurance. Advisors help clients plan for short- and long-term goals, such as meeting education expenses and saving for retirement through investments. They invest clients' money based on the clients' decisions. Many advisors also provide tax advice or sell insurance.

Although most planners offer advice on a wide range of topics, some specialize in areas such as retirement or risk management (evaluating how willing the investor is to take chances and adjusting investments accordingly).

Many personal financial advisors spend a lot of time marketing their services, and they meet potential clients by giving seminars or through business and social networking. Networking is the process of meeting and exchanging information with people, or groups of people, who have similar interests.

After financial advisors have invested funds for a client, they and the client receive regular investment reports. Advisors monitor the client's investments and usually meet with each client at least once a year to update the client on potential investments and to adjust

Personal financial advisors usually work with many clients and often must find their own customers.

the financial plan based on the client's circumstances or because investment options may have changed.

Many personal financial advisors are licensed to directly buy and sell financial products, such as stocks, bonds, annuities, and insurance. Depending on the agreement they have with their clients, personal financial advisors may have the client's permission to make decisions about buying and selling stocks and bonds.

Private bankers or *wealth managers* are personal financial advisors who work for people who have a lot of money to invest. These clients are similar to institutional investors (commonly, companies or organizations), and they approach investing differently than the general public does. Private bankers manage a collection of investments, called a portfolio, for these clients by using the resources of the bank, including teams of financial analysts, accountants, and other professionals.

Work Environment

Personal financial advisors held about 249,400 jobs in 2014. The industries that employed the most personal financial advisors were as follows:

Other financial investment activities	29%
Securities and commodity contracts intermediation and brokerage	23
Credit intermediation and related activities	16
Management of companies and enterprises	3
Professional, scientific, and technical services	3

In 2014, about 1 in 5 personal financial advisors were self-employed.

Personal financial advisors typically work in offices. Some also travel to attend conferences or teach finance classes in the evening to bring in more clients. The work of personal financial advisors tends to be less stressful than other financial occupations.

Work Schedules. Most personal financial advisors work full time, and about 3 in 10 worked more than 40 hours per week in 2014. They often go to meetings on evenings and weekends to meet with existing clients or to try to bring in new ones.

Median Annual Wages, May 2014

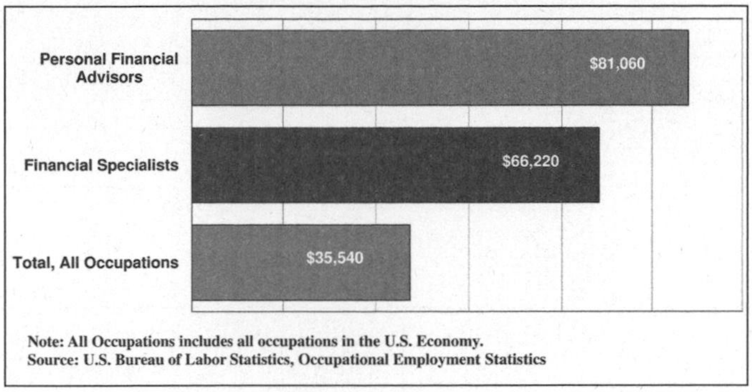

Percent Change in Employment, Projected 2014–2024

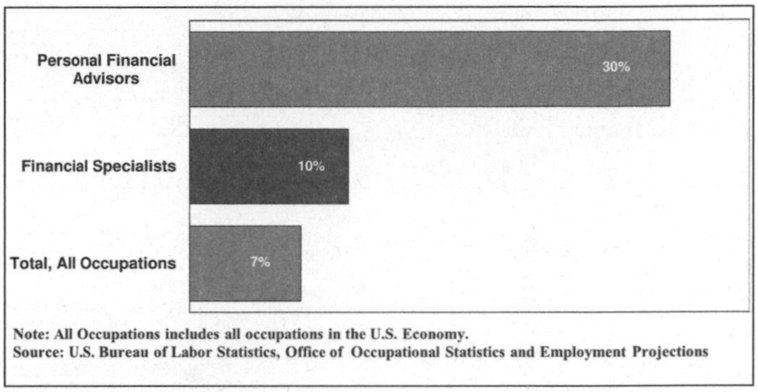

Education/Training

Personal financial advisors typically need a bachelor's degree. A master's degree and certification can improve one's chances for advancement in the occupation.

Education. Personal financial advisors typically need a bachelor's degree. Although employers usually do not require personal financial advisors to have completed a specific course of study, a degree in finance, economics, accounting, business, mathematics, or law is good preparation for this occupation. Courses in investments, taxes, estate planning, and risk management are also helpful. Programs in financial planning are becoming more available in colleges and universities.

Training. Once they are hired, personal financial advisors often enter an on-the-job training period. During this time, new advisors work under the supervision of senior advisors and learn how to perform their duties, including building a client network and developing investment portfolios. This training usually lasts for more than a year.

Licenses, Certifications, and Registrations. Personal financial advisors who directly buy or sell stocks, bonds, or insurance policies, or who provide specific investment advice, need a combination of licenses that varies with the products they sell. In addition to being required to have those licenses, advisors in smaller firms that manage clients' investments must be registered with state regulators and those in larger firms must be registered with the Securities and Exchange Commission. Personal financial advisors who choose to sell insurance need licenses issued by state boards. Information on state licensing board requirements for registered investment advisors is available from the North American Securities Administrators Association.

Certifications can enhance a personal financial advisor's reputation and can help bring in new clients. The Certified Financial Planner Board of Standards offers the Certified Financial Planner (CFP) certification. For this certification, advisors must have a bachelor's degree, complete at least 3 years of relevant work experience, pass an exam, and agree to adhere to a code of ethics. The exam covers the financial planning process, insurance and risk management, employee benefits planning, taxes and retirement planning, investment and real estate planning, debt management, planning liability, emergency fund reserves, and statistical modeling.

Advancement. A master's degree in an area such as finance or business administration can improve a personal financial advisor's chances of moving into a management position and attracting new clients.

Important Qualities

Analytical skills. In determining an investment portfolio for a client, personal financial advisors must be able to take into account a range of information, including economic trends, regulatory changes, and the client's comfort with risky decisions.

Interpersonal skills. A major part of a personal financial advisor's job is making clients feel comfortable. Advisors must establish trust with clients and respond well to their questions and concerns.

Math skills. Personal financial advisors should be good at mathematics because they constantly work with numbers. They determine the amount invested, how that amount has grown or decreased over time, and how a portfolio is distributed among different investments.

Sales skills. To expand their base of clients, personal financial advisors must be convincing and persistent in selling their services.

Speaking skills. Personal financial advisors interact with clients every day. They must explain complex financial concepts in understandable language.

Pay

The median annual wage for personal financial advisors was $81,060 in May 2014. The median wage is the wage at which half the workers in an occupation earned more than that amount and half earned less. The lowest 10 percent earned less than $35,500, and the highest 10 percent earned more than $187,200.

In May 2014, the median annual wages for personal financial advisors in the top industries in which they worked were as follows:

Other financial investment activities	$91,740
Securities and commodity contracts intermediation and brokerage	89,880
Management of companies and enterprises	80,270
Professional, scientific, and technical services	75,890
Credit intermediation and related activities	60,710

Wages of self-employed advisors are not included in the earnings reported here.

Personal financial advisors who work for financial services firms are often paid a salary plus bonuses. Bonuses are not included in the wage data here.

Advisors who work for financial investment firms or financial planning firms, or who are self-employed, typically earn their money by charging a percentage of the clients' assets that they manage. They also may earn money by charging an hourly fee or by getting fees on stock and insurance purchases. In addition to their fees, advisors generally get commissions for financial products that they sell.

Employment Projections Data for Personal Financial Advisors

Occupational Title	SOC Code	Employment, 2014	Projected Employment, 2024	Change, 2014–2024	
				Percent	Numeric
Personal financial advisors	13-2052	249,400	323,200	30	73,900

Source: U.S. Bureau of Labor Statistics, Employment Projections Program

Similar Occupations. This table shows a list of occupations with job duties that are similar to those of personal financial advisors.

Occupations	Entry-level Education	2014 Median Pay	Projected Job Growth	Average Annual Openings
Budget Analysts	Bachelor's degree	$71,220	3%	150
Financial Analysts	Bachelor's degree	$78,620	12%	3,230
Financial Managers	Bachelor's degree	$115,320	7%	3,770
Insurance Sales Agents	High school diploma or equivalent	$47,860	9%	4,350
Insurance Underwriters	Bachelor's degree	$64,220	-11%	-1,170
Real Estate Brokers and Sales Agents	High school diploma or equivalent	$43,430	3%	1,090
Securities, Commodities, and Financial Services Sales Agents	Bachelor's degree	$72,070	10%	3,250

Job Outlook

Employment of personal financial advisors is projected to grow 30 percent from 2014 to 2024, much faster than the average for all occupations.

The primary driver of employment growth will be the aging population. As large numbers of baby boomers approach retirement, they will seek planning advice from personal financial advisors. Also, longer lifespans will lead to longer retirement periods, further increasing demand for financial planning services.

In addition, the replacement of traditional pension plans with individual retirement accounts is expected to continue. Many people used to receive defined pension payments in retirement, but most companies no longer offer these plans. Therefore, individuals must save and invest for their own retirement, increasing the demand for personal financial advisors.

Job Prospects. Job prospects for personal financial advisors should be relatively favorable compared with prospects in other financial sector occupations. Those who obtain certification will likely have the best prospects.

Contacts for More Information

For more information about personal financial advisors, visit

➤ Global Academy of Finance and Management (http://gafm.com)

For more information about regulation and licensure of personal financial advisors, visit

➤ Financial Industry Regulatory Authority (FINRA) (www.finra.org)

➤ North American Securities Administrators Association (www.nasaa.org)

➤ U.S. Securities and Exchange Commission (SEC) (www.sec.gov)

➤ Certified Financial Planner Board of Standards (www.cfp.net)

O*NET

➤ Personal Financial Advisors (13-2052.00)

Purchasing Managers

- **2014 Median Pay** .... $106,090 per year
  $51.01 per hour
- **Typical Entry-Level Education** .... Bachelor's degree
- **Work Experience in a Related Occupation**............ 5 years or more
- **On-the-job Training** .... None
- **Number of Jobs, 2014** 73,000
- **Job Outlook, 2014–24** ....1% (Little or no change)
- **Employment Change, 2014–24** 700

What Purchasing Managers Do

Purchasing managers plan, direct, and coordinate the buying of materials, products, or services for wholesalers, retailers, or organizations. They oversee the work of procurement-related occupations including buyers and purchasing agents.

Duties. Purchasing managers typically do the following:

- Coordinate the activities of buyers and purchasing agents engaged in buying materials, equipment, or supplies for the organization
- Supervise, hire, and train staff
- Evaluate potential suppliers on the basis of price, quality, and speed of delivery
- Interview vendors and visit suppliers' plants and distribution centers to examine and learn about products, services, and prices
- Attend meetings, trade shows, and conferences to learn about new industry trends and make contacts with suppliers
- Analyze price proposals, financial reports, and other information to determine reasonable prices
- Negotiate contracts on behalf of their organization

- Work out agreements with suppliers, such as when products will be delivered
- Meet with staff and vendors to discuss defective or unacceptable goods or services and determine corrective action
- Ensure that vendors and suppliers comply with the terms and conditions of the contract and, if they don't, determine the need for changes

Purchasing managers plan and coordinate the work of buyers and purchasing agents and hire and train new staff.

Purchasing managers, sometimes known as *contract managers*, are also responsible for developing their organization's procurement policies and procedures. These policies help ensure that procurement professionals are meeting ethical standards to avoid potential conflicts of interest or inappropriate supplier and customer relations.

Besides establishing procurement standards, purchasing managers set guidelines on how often their department will get price quotes for items, how many bids to accept, and which vendors to consider.

In addition to carrying out their managerial and administrative responsibilities, purchasing managers buy goods and services for their organization or institution. Like buyers and purchasing agents, purchasing managers negotiate contracts and consider price, quality, availability, reliability, and technical support when identifying and choosing suppliers and merchandise. Their negotiations and contracts are typically more complex than those carried out by buyers and purchasing agents.

Purchasing managers must study their organization's sales records and inventory levels of current stock, identify foreign and domestic suppliers, and keep up to date with changes affecting both the supply of, and demand for, products and materials.

Purchasing managers use many resources to find out all they can about potential suppliers. They attend meetings, trade shows, and conferences to learn about new industry trends and to make contacts with suppliers.

Before signing a contract and placing an order, purchasing managers must make certain that the supplier can deliver the desired goods or services on time, in the correct quantities, and without sacrificing quality. Purchasing managers monitor the terms of the contracts in order to ensure that the supplier is complying with its terms and conditions and resolve any supplier-related issues that arise.

Work Environment

Purchasing managers held about 73,000 jobs in 2014. The industries that employed the most purchasing managers were as follows:

Manufacturing	30%
Management of companies and enterprises	16
Wholesale trade	12
Professional, scientific, and technical services	8
Federal government	8

Most purchasing managers work in offices. Travel is sometimes necessary, and purchasers for global organizations may need to travel outside the United States.

Work Schedules. Most purchasing managers work full time. Overtime is common in this occupation.

Education/Training

Purchasing managers need a bachelor's degree and work experience as a buyer or purchasing agent.

Education. Purchasing managers usually have at least a bachelor's degree and some work experience in procurement. A master's degree may be required for advancement to some top-level purchasing manager jobs.

Purchasing professionals use many resources to gather information about potential suppliers.

Work Experience in a Related Occupation. Purchasing managers typically must have at least 5 years of experience as a buyer or purchasing agent. At the top levels, purchasing manager duties may overlap with other management functions, such as production, planning, logistics, and marketing.

Licenses, Certifications, and Registrations. There are several certifications available for purchasing managers and others employed in a procurement-related field. Although some employers require certification, many do not.

Most of the certifications involve oral or written exams and have education and work experience requirements.

The Institute for Supply Management offers the Certified Professional in Supply Management (CPSM) credential, which covers a wide scope of purchasing professional duties. To receive the CPSM credential, candidates must pass three exams and possess at least 3 years of relevant work experience for those with a bachelor's degree or 5 years of relevant work experience for those without a bachelor's degree.

The American Purchasing Society offers the Certified Purchasing Professional (CPP) and the Certified Professional Purchasing Manager (CPPM) credentials. Certification is valid for 5 years. Candidates must earn a certain number of professional development "points" to renew their certification. Candidates initially become eligible, and can renew their certification, through a combination of purchasing-related experience, education, and professional contributions (such as articles published or speeches delivered).

APICS, founded as the American Production and Inventory Control Society, offers the Certified Supply Chain Professional (CSCP) credential. Applicants must have 3 years of related business experience or a bachelor's degree in order to be eligible for the CSCP credential, which is valid for 5 years. Candidates must also earn a certain number of professional development points to renew their certification.

The Next Level Purchasing Association offers the Senior Professional in Supply Management (SPSM) certification. Although there are no education or work experience requirements, applicants must complete six online courses and pass an SPSM exam. Certification is valid for 4 years. Candidates must complete 32 continuing education hours in procurement-related topics to recertify for an additional 4-year period.

Median Annual Wages, May 2014

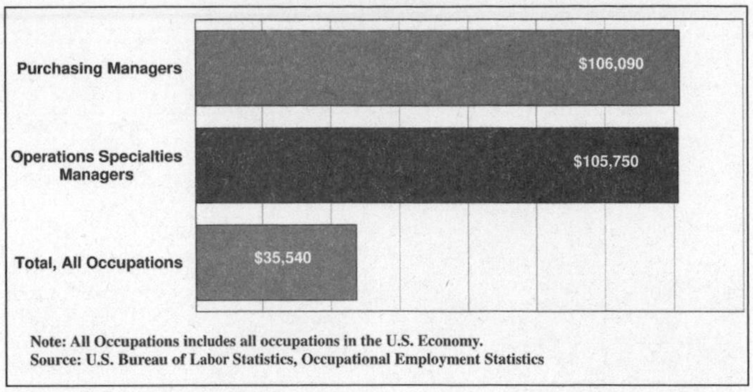

Percent Change in Employment, Projected 2014–2024

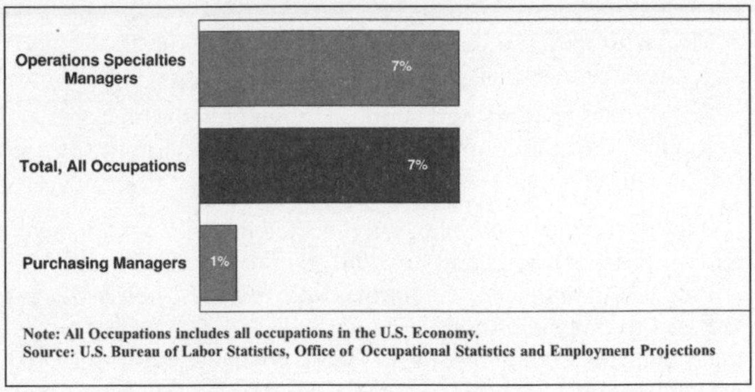

The Universal Public Procurement Certification Council (UPPCC) offers two certifications for workers in federal, state, and local government. The Certified Professional Public Buyer (CPPB) credential requires applicants to have earned at least an associate's degree, to have at least 3 years of public procurement experience, and to complete relevant training courses. The Certified Public Purchasing Officer (CPPO) requires applicants to have earned a bachelor's degree, to have at least 5 years of public procurement experience, and to complete additional training courses.

Those with the CPPB or the CPPO designation must renew their certification every 5 years by completing continuing education courses or attending procurement-related conferences or events.

The National Institute of Government Purchasing's (NIGP's) Institute for Public Procurement offers preparation courses for the UPPCC certification exams.

Advancement. An experienced and qualified purchasing manager may advance to become the chief procurement officer for a business or organization.

Important Qualities

Analytical skills. When evaluating suppliers, purchasing managers must analyze their options and choose a supplier with the best combination of price, quality, delivery, service, or other criteria.

Decision-making skills. Purchasing managers must have the ability to make informed and timely decisions, choosing products that they think will sell.

Math skills. Purchasing managers must possess basic math skills. They must be able to compare prices from different suppliers to ensure that their organization is getting the best deal.

Negotiating skills. Purchasing managers often must negotiate the terms of a contract with a supplier. Interpersonal skills and self-confidence, in addition to knowledge of the product, can help lead to successful negotiation.

Pay

The median annual wage for purchasing managers was $106,090 in May 2014. The median wage is the wage at which half the workers in an occupation earned more than that amount and half earned less. The lowest 10 percent earned less than $60,840, and the highest 10 percent earned more than $169,000.

In May 2014, the median annual wages for purchasing managers in the top industries in which they worked were as follows:

Federal government	$123,980
Professional, scientific, and technical services	122,750
Management of companies and enterprises	116,380
Manufacturing	96,520
Wholesale trade	94,170

Job Outlook

Employment of purchasing managers is projected to show little or no change from 2014 to 2024.

These workers will continue to be needed to oversee the purchase of goods and services for business operations or for resale to customers. In addition, purchasing managers often play an important role in controlling costs for an organization.

However, some organizations may increasingly rely on third parties to handle some of the tasks previously performed by purchasing managers, such as business strategy development and contract management.

In the public sector, employment demand may be negatively impacted by the increasing use of cooperative purchasing agreements. These agreements allow state, local, and municipal governments to share resources in order to buy supplies and make other general purchases. Because the same standard contracts can be used multiple times by multiple government agencies, the rise of purchasing cooperatives will likely limit the need to hire additional procurement officers and managers.

The projected decline in the manufacturing industry should also limit the demand for purchasing managers employed within that industry.

Job Prospects. As with many other managerial positions, competition for jobs is expected to be strong. Candidates for purchasing manager positions may improve their prospects by obtaining a master's degree in business or supply management.

Employment Projections Data for Purchasing Managers

Occupational Title	SOC Code	Employment, 2014	Projected Employment, 2024	Change, 2014–2024 Percent	Change, 2014–2024 Numeric
Purchasing managers	11-3061	73,000	73,700	1	700

Source: U.S. Bureau of Labor Statistics, Employment Projections Program

Similar Occupations. This table shows a list of occupations with job duties that are similar to those of purchasing managers.

Occupations	Entry-level Education	2014 Median Pay	Projected Job Growth	Average Annual Openings
Administrative Services Managers	Bachelor's degree	$83,790	8%	2,350
Advertising, Promotions, and Marketing Managers	Bachelor's degree	$123,450	9%	1,970
Bookkeeping, Accounting, and Auditing Clerks	Some college, no degree	$36,430	-8%	-14,870
Buyers and Purchasing Agents	Bachelor's degree	$58,520	2%	720
Financial Clerks	High school diploma or equivalent	$36,260	6%	8,930
Financial Managers	Bachelor's degree	$115,320	7%	3,770
Food Service Managers	High school diploma or equivalent	$48,560	5%	1,570
Industrial Production Managers	Bachelor's degree	$92,470	-4%	-630
Lodging Managers	High school diploma or equivalent	$47,680	8%	370
Logisticians	Bachelor's degree	$73,870	2%	250
Sales Managers	Bachelor's degree	$110,660	5%	1,900
Wholesale and Manufacturing Sales Representatives	See Education/Training	$58,380	7%	11,720

Contacts for More Information

For more information about purchasing managers, including education, training, employment, and certification, visit

- American Purchasing Society (www.american-purchasing.com)
- APICS (www.apics.org)
- Institute for Supply Management (www.ism.ws)
- Next Level Purchasing (www.nextlevelpurchasing.com/index.html)
- NIGP: The Institute for Public Procurement (www.nigp.org)
- Universal Public Procurement Certification Council (www.uppcc.org)
- National Contract Management Association (www.ncmahq.org/ncma-home)

O*NET

- Purchasing Managers (11-3061.00)

Tax Examiners and Collectors, and Revenue Agents

- **2014 Median Pay** .... $51,120 per year $24.58 per hour
- **Typical Entry-Level Education** .... Bachelor's degree
- **Work Experience in a Related Occupation** .... None
- **On-the-job Training** ..... Moderate-term on-the-job training
- **Number of Jobs, 2014** 67,900
- **Job Outlook, 2014–24** .... -6% (Decline)
- **Employment Change, 2014–24** .... -4,200

What Tax Examiners and Collectors, and Revenue Agents Do

Tax examiners and collectors, and revenue agents ensure that federal, state, and local governments get their tax money from businesses and citizens. They review tax returns, conduct audits, identify taxes owed, and collect overdue tax payments.

Duties. Tax examiners and collectors, and revenue agents typically do the following:

- Review filed tax returns to determine whether credits and deductions claimed are allowed by law
- Contact taxpayers to address problems and to request supporting documentation
- Conduct field audits and investigations of income tax returns to verify information or to update tax liabilities
- Evaluate financial information, using their familiarity with accounting procedures and knowledge of changes to tax laws and regulations
- Keep records on each case they deal with, including contacts, telephone numbers, and actions taken
- Notify taxpayers of any overpayment or underpayment and either issue a refund or request additional payment

In addition to verifying that tax returns are filed properly, they follow up with taxpayers whose returns are questionable or who owe more money.

Different levels of government collect different types of taxes. The federal government deals primarily with personal and business income taxes. State governments collect income and sales taxes. Local governments collect sales and property taxes.

Because many states assess individual income taxes based on the taxpayer's reported federal income, tax examiners working for the federal government report to the states any adjustments or corrections they make. State tax examiners then determine whether the adjustments affect how much the taxpayer owes the state.

Tax examiners and collectors, and revenue agents have different duties and responsibilities:

Tax examiners usually deal with the simplest tax returns—those filed by individual taxpayers who claim few deductions and those filed by small businesses. At the entry level, many tax examiners do clerical tasks, such as reviewing tax returns and entering them into a computer system for processing. Tax examiners also may contact individual taxpayers in order to resolve any outstanding problems with their returns.

Tax examiners and collectors, and revenue agents work for federal, state, and local governments.

Much of a tax examiner's job involves making sure that tax credits and deductions claimed by taxpayers are lawful. If a taxpayer owes additional taxes, tax examiners adjust the total amount by assessing fees, interest, and penalties and then notify the taxpayer of the total amount owed.

Revenue agents specialize in tax-related accounting for the U.S. Internal Revenue Service (IRS) and for equivalent agencies in state and local governments. Like tax examiners, they review returns for accuracy. However, revenue agents handle complicated tax returns of large businesses and corporations.

Many experienced revenue agents specialize in a particular area. For example, they may focus exclusively on multinational businesses. Regardless of their specialty, revenue agents must keep up to date with changes in the lengthy and complex tax laws and regulations.

Collectors, also called *revenue officers* in the IRS, deal with overdue accounts. The process of collecting an overdue payment starts with the revenue agent or tax examiner sending a report to the taxpayer. If the taxpayer makes no effort to pay, the case is assigned to a collector.

When a collector takes a case, he or she first sends a notice to the taxpayer. The collector then works with the taxpayer to settle the debt. Settlement may involve setting up a plan in which the amount owed is paid back in small amounts over time.

When delinquent taxpayers claim that they cannot pay their taxes, collectors investigate and verify these claims. Collectors research information on taxpayer mortgages or financial statements and locate taxpayer-owned items of value through third parties, such as neighbors or local departments of motor vehicles. Ultimately, collectors must decide whether the IRS should take a lien—a claim on an asset such as a bank account, real estate, or an automobile—to settle a debt. Collectors also have the authority to garnish wages—that is, take a portion of earned wages—to collect taxes owed.

Work Environment

Tax examiners and collectors, and revenue agents held about 67,900 jobs in 2014. The industries that employed the most tax examiners and collectors, and revenue agents were as follows:

Federal government	42%
State government, excluding education and hospitals	38
Local government, excluding education and hospitals	20

Many work primarily in an office environment; others spend most of their time conducting field audits in taxpayers' homes or places of business.

Work Schedules. Most tax examiners, collectors, and revenue agents work full time.

Education/Training

Most tax examiners, collectors, and revenue agents need a bachelor's degree in accounting or a related field. However, the required level of education and experience varies by position and employer.

Education. Tax examiners need a bachelor's degree in accounting or a related field, or a combination of relevant education and specialized experience in accounting, auditing, or tax compliance work. Candidates for tax examiner positions at the Internal Revenue Service (IRS) must have a bachelor's degree or 1 year of full-time specialized experience.

Revenue agents need a bachelor's degree in accounting, business administration, economics, or a related discipline. A combination of relevant education and full-time experience in business administration, accounting, or auditing is also qualifying. Revenue agents with the IRS must have either a bachelor's degree or 30 semester hours of accounting coursework, along with specialized experience. Specialized experience includes work in accounting, bookkeeping, or tax analysis.

Collectors usually must have some combination of relevant college education and specialized experience. Specialized experience may include previous work as a loan officer or credit manager, or a background in collections, management, customer service, or tax compliance. A bachelor's degree is needed for employment as a collector with the IRS; no additional experience is required, and experience may not be substituted for the degree. Employers desire degrees in business, finance, accounting, and criminal justice.

Median Annual Wages, May 2014

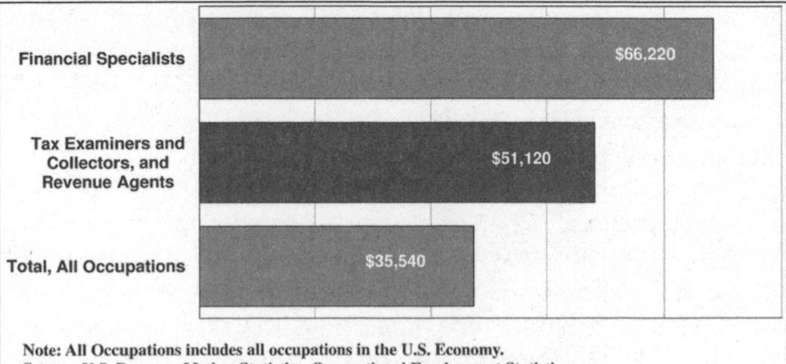

Note: All Occupations includes all occupations in the U.S. Economy.
Source: U.S. Bureau of Labor Statistics, Occupational Employment Statistics

Percent Change in Employment, Projected 2014–2024

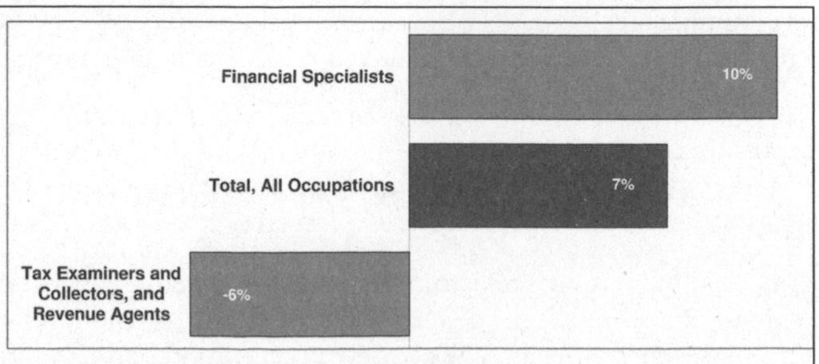

Note: All Occupations includes all occupations in the U.S. Economy.
Source: U.S. Bureau of Labor Statistics, Office of Occupational Statistics and Employment Projections

Employment Projections Data for Tax Examiners and Collectors, and Revenue Agents

Occupational Title	SOC Code	Employment, 2014	Projected Employment, 2024	Change, 2014–2024	
				Percent	Numeric
Tax examiners and collectors, and revenue agents	13-2081	67,900	63,700	-6	-4,200

Source: U.S. Bureau of Labor Statistics, Employment Projections Program

Similar Occupations. This table shows a list of occupations with job duties that are similar to those of tax examiners and collectors, and revenue agents.

Occupations	Entry-level Education	2014 Median Pay	Projected Job Growth	Average Annual Openings
Accountants and Auditors	Bachelor's degree	$65,940	11%	14,240
Bookkeeping, Accounting, and Auditing Clerks	Some college, no degree	$36,430	-8%	-14,870
Budget Analysts	Bachelor's degree	$71,220	3%	150
Cost Estimators	Bachelor's degree	$60,050	9%	1,870
Financial Analysts	Bachelor's degree	$78,620	12%	3,230
Financial Managers	Bachelor's degree	$115,320	7%	3,770
Loan Officers	Bachelor's degree	$62,620	8%	2,450
Personal Financial Advisors	Bachelor's degree	$81,060	30%	7,390

At the state and local levels, a bachelor's degree is not always required, although related work experience is desired.

Training. Newly hired tax examiners get some formal training, which typically lasts between 1 month and 1 year. All tax examiners must keep current with changes in the tax code and enforcement procedures.

Entry-level collectors get both formal training and on-the-job training under an instructor's guidance before working independently. Collectors also are encouraged to continue their professional education by attending meetings to exchange information about how modifications to tax laws affect collection methods.

Other Experience. Some state and local governments accept work experience as a substitute for education. In these cases, employers may hire tax examiners and revenue agents who have work experience in accounting, bookkeeping, or tax analysis. Employers may also hire collectors who have work experience in related areas, such as collections, customer service, or credit checking.

Advancement. Tax examiners, revenue agents, and collectors have different opportunities for career advancement. Tax examiners who review individual tax returns may advance to revenue agent positions, working on more complex business returns. Those with experience in supervisory or managerial roles may move to jobs that involve supervision of other examiners and revenue agents. Collectors who demonstrate leadership skills and a thorough knowledge of tax collection activities may advance to supervisory or managerial collector positions.

Important Qualities

Analytical skills. Tax examiners and revenue agents must be able to identify questionable claims for credits and deductions. Ultimately, they must be able to determine, on further review of financial documentation, if the credits or deductions are lawful.

Computer skills. Tax examiners and revenue agents must be comfortable using a variety of computer programs. These programs include tax preparation and bookkeeping software used by individuals and businesses.

Detail oriented. Tax examiners and revenue agents verify the accuracy of each entry on the tax returns they review. Therefore, it is important that they pay attention to detail.

Interpersonal skills. Collectors must be comfortable dealing with people, including speaking with them during confrontational situations. When pursuing overdue accounts, collectors should be firm and composed.

Organizational skills. Tax examiners and revenue agents often work with multiple returns and a variety of financial documents. Keeping the various pieces of information organized is essential.

Pay

The median annual wage for tax examiners and collectors, and revenue agents was $51,120 in May 2014. The median wage is the wage at which half the workers in an occupation earned more than that amount and half earned less. The lowest 10 percent earned less than $31,410, and the highest 10 percent earned more than $94,350.

In May 2014, the median annual wages for tax examiners and collectors, and revenue agents in the top industries in which they worked were as follows:

Federal government	$60,840
State government, excluding education and hospitals	48,370
Local government, excluding education and hospitals	40,940

Union Membership. Compared with workers in all occupations, tax examiners and collectors, and revenue agents had a higher percentage of workers who belonged to a union in 2014.

Job Outlook

Employment of tax examiners and collectors, and revenue agents is projected to decline 6 percent from 2014 to 2024. Employment change will depend primarily on future changes to federal, state, and local government budgets. Budget reductions in recent years have resulted in decreased hiring for the agencies that employ these workers.

Within the federal government, the primary employer of these workers is the Internal Revenue Service (IRS), which has experienced more severe budget cuts than other federal agencies. Further employment declines for these workers in the federal government may occur if the IRS continues to operate with budget cuts. Overall employment in federal government, excluding postal service, is projected to decline 19 percent.

At the state and local level, funding for these workers' departments has been more stable. Therefore, employment of these workers in state and local government is expected to grow in line with overall state and local government employment.

Contacts for More Information

For more information about tax examiner and collector, and revenue agent careers at the Internal Revenue Service (IRS), visit

➤ Internal Revenue Service (http://jobs.irs.gov)

For more information about requirements for federal government positions as an internal revenue officer, visit

➤ U.S. Office of Personnel Management (www.opm.gov/policy-data-oversight/classification-qualifications/general-schedule-qualification-standards/1100/internal-revenue-officer-series-1169)

For more information about requirements for federal government positions as a tax specialist, visit

➤ U.S. Office of Personnel Management (www.opm.gov/policy-data-oversight/classification-qualifications/general-schedule-qualification-standards/0500/tax-specialist-series-0526)

For more information about requirements for federal government positions as an internal revenue agent, visit

➤ U.S. Office of Personnel Management (www.opm.gov/policy-data-oversight/classification-qualifications/general-schedule-qualification-standards/0500/internal-revenue-agent-series-0512)

O*NET

➤ Tax Examiners and Collectors, and Revenue Agents (13-2081.00)

Training and Development Specialists

- **2014 Median Pay** .... $57,340 per year, $27.57 per hour
- **Typical Entry-Level Education** .... Bachelor's degree
- **Work Experience in a Related Occupation** .... Less than 5 years
- **On-the-job Training** .... None
- **Number of Jobs, 2014** 252,600
- **Job Outlook, 2014–24** .... 7% (As fast as average)
- **Employment Change, 2014–24** 18,900

What Training and Development Specialists Do

Training and development specialists help plan, conduct, and administer programs that train employees and improve their skills and knowledge.

Duties. Training and development specialists typically do the following:

- Assess training needs through surveys, interviews with employees, or consultations with managers or instructors
- Design and create training manuals, online learning modules, and course materials
- Review training materials from a variety of vendors and choose appropriate materials
- Deliver training to employees using a variety of instructional techniques
- Monitor and evaluate training programs to ensure they are current and effective
- Select and assign instructors or vendors to conduct training
- Perform administrative tasks such as monitoring costs, scheduling classes, setting up systems and equipment, and coordinating enrollment

Training and development specialists create, administer, and deliver training programs for businesses and organizations. To do this, they must first assess the needs of an organization. Once those needs are determined, specialists develop custom training programs that take place in classrooms or training facilities. Training programs are increasingly delivered through computers, tablets, or other hand-held electronic devices.

Training and development specialists organize or deliver training sessions using lectures, group discussions, team exercises, hands-on examples, and other formats. Training can be in the form of a video, self-guided instructional manual, or online application. Training also may be collaborative, which allows employees to connect informally with experts, mentors, and colleagues, often through the use of technology.

Training and development specialists may monitor instructors, guide employees through media-based programs, or facilitate informal or collaborative learning programs.

Work Environment

Training and development specialists held about 252,600 jobs in 2014. The industries that employed the most training and development specialists were as follows:

Professional, scientific, and technical services	14%
Healthcare and social assistance	13
Finance and insurance	11
Educational services; state, local, and private	11
Manufacturing	7

They spend much of their time working with people, giving presentations, and leading training activities.

Work Schedules. Most training and development specialists work full time during regular business hours. About one-fifth worked more than 40 hours per week in 2014.

Education/Training

Training and development specialists need a bachelor's degree, and most need related work experience.

Education. Training and development specialists need a bachelor's degree. Specialists may have a variety of education backgrounds, but many have a bachelor's degree in training and development, human resources, education, or instructional design. Others may have a degree in business administration or a social science, such as educational or organizational psychology.

In addition, as technology continues to play a larger role in training and development, a growing number of organizations seek candidates who have a background in information technology or computer science.

Work Experience in a Related Occupation. Related work experience is important for most training and development specialists. Many positions require work experience in areas such as training

Training and development specialists often develop visual aids to convey complex ideas.

and development or instructional design, or in related occupations, such as human resources specialists or even teachers.

Employers may prefer to hire candidates with previous work experience in the industry in which the company operates. However, some employers may hire candidates with a master's degree in lieu of work experience. Increasingly, employers prefer candidates with experience in information technology, as organizations introduce more e-learning, mobile training, and technology-based tools.

Licenses, Certifications, and Registrations. Many human resources associations offer classes to enhance the skills of their members. Some associations, including the Association for Talent Development and International Society for Performance Improvement, specialize in training and development and offer certification programs. Although not required, certification can show professional expertise and credibility. Some employers prefer to hire certified candidates, and some positions may require certification.

Advancement. Training and development specialists may advance to training and development manager or human resources manager positions. Workers typically need several years of experience to advance. Some employers require managers to have a master's degree in a related area.

Important Qualities

Analytical skills. Training and development specialists must evaluate training programs, methods, and materials, and choose those that best fit each situation.

Creativity. Specialists should be creative when developing training materials. They may need to think of and implement new approaches, such as new technology, when evaluating existing training methods.

Instructional skills. Training and development specialists often deliver training programs to employees. They use a variety of teaching techniques and sometimes must adapt their methods to meet the needs of particular groups.

Interpersonal skills. Specialists need strong interpersonal skills because delivering training programs requires collaboration with instructors, trainees, and subject-matter experts. They accomplish much of their work through teams.

Speaking skills. Speaking skills are essential for training and development specialists because they often give presentations. Specialists must communicate information clearly and facilitate learning by diverse audiences.

Pay

The median annual wage for training and development specialists was $57,340 in May 2014. The median wage is the wage at which half the workers in an occupation earned more than that amount and half earned less. The lowest 10 percent earned less than $31,980, and the highest 10 percent earned more than $97,660.

In May 2014, the median annual wages for training and development specialists in the top industries in which they worked were as follows:

Professional, scientific, and technical services	$65,460
Finance and insurance	59,930
Educational services; state, local, and private	58,480
Manufacturing	58,290
Healthcare and social assistance	51,760

Job Outlook

Employment of training and development specialists is projected to grow 7 percent from 2014 to 2024, about as fast as the average for all occupations. Employees in many occupations are required to take continuing education and skill development courses throughout their careers, creating demand for workers who lead training activities.

Employment of training and development specialists is expected to grow across most industries as companies develop and introduce new media and technology into their training programs. Innovations in training methods and learning technology should continue throughout the next decade. For example, organizations increasingly use social media, visual simulations, and mobile learning in their training programs. Training and development specialists will need to modify their programs to fit a new generation of workers for whom technology is a part of daily life and work.

Median Annual Wages, May 2014

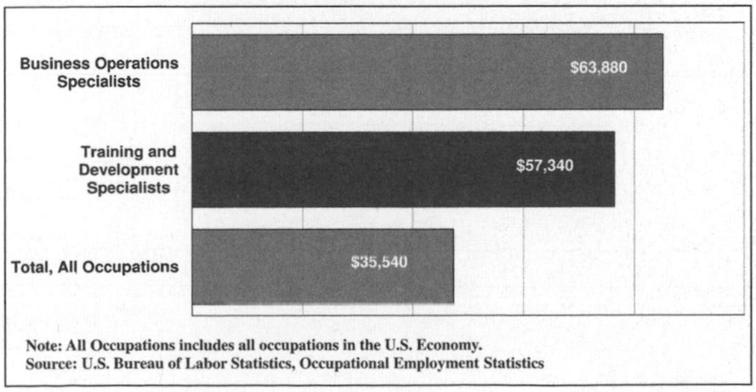

Percent Change in Employment, Projected 2014–2024

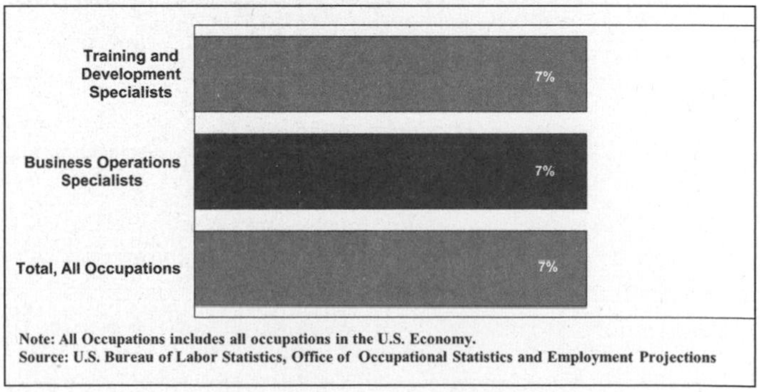

Employment Projections Data for Training and Development Specialists

Occupational Title	SOC Code	Employment, 2014	Projected Employment, 2024	Change, 2014–2024 Percent	Change, 2014–2024 Numeric
Training and development specialists	13-1151	252,600	271,500	7	18,900

Source: U.S. Bureau of Labor Statistics, Employment Projections Program

Similar Occupations. This table shows a list of occupations with job duties that are similar to those of training and development specialists.

Occupations	Entry-level Education	2014 Median Pay	Projected Job Growth	Average Annual Openings
Career and Technical Education Teachers	Bachelor's degree	$51,830	4%	1,020
Compensation and Benefits Managers	Bachelor's degree	$108,070	6%	110
Compensation, Benefits, and Job Analysis Specialists	Bachelor's degree	$60,600	4%	340
Human Resources Managers	Bachelor's degree	$102,780	9%	1,080
Human Resources Specialists	Bachelor's degree	$57,420	5%	2,200
Instructional Coordinators	Master's degree	$61,550	7%	1,050
Labor Relations Specialists	Bachelor's degree	$56,950	-8%	-640
Psychologists	See How to Become One	$70,700	19%	3,250
School and Career Counselors	Master's degree	$53,370	8%	2,250
Training and Development Managers	Bachelor's degree	$101,930	7%	230

Since training and development contracting firms may have greater access to technology and technical expertise to produce new training initiatives, some organizations outsource specific training efforts when internal staff or resources are not able to meet the training needs of the organization.

Additionally, as baby boomers reach retirement age and begin to leave the workforce, organizations will need capable training and development staff to train their replacements. The need to replace a large workforce of highly skilled and knowledgeable employees should result in organizations increasing their training staff, or contracting out services, to sustain a workforce of high quality employees and maintain a competitive edge.

Job Prospects. Overall, job opportunities should be good. Candidates with a bachelor's degree in training and development, education, human resources, computer science, or instructional design, and with experience in training and development, particularly online and mobile training and development programs, will have the best prospects.

Contacts for More Information

For more information about training and development specialists, visit

- Association for Talent Development (www.td.org)
- International Society for Performance Improvement (www.ispi.org)

For more information about human resources management careers and certification, visit

- Society for Human Resource Management (www.shrm.org)

O*NET

- Training and Development Specialists (13-1151.00)

Community and Social Service

Health Educators and Community Health Workers

- **2014 Median Pay** .... $42,450 per year $20.41 per hour
- **Typical Entry-Level Education** .... See Education/Training
- **Work Experience in a Related Occupation** .... None
- **On-the-job Training** .... See Education/Training
- **Number of Jobs, 2014** 115,700
- **Job Outlook, 2014–24** .... 13% (Faster than average)
- **Employment Change, 2014–24** 15,600

What Health Educators and Community Health Workers Do

Health educators teach people about behaviors that promote wellness. They develop and implement strategies to improve the health of individuals and communities. Community health workers provide a link between the community, health educators, and other healthcare and social service professionals. They develop and implement strategies to improve the health of individuals and communities. They collect data and discuss health concerns with members of specific populations or communities. Although the two occupations often work together, responsibilities of health educators and community health workers are distinct.

Duties. Health educators typically do the following:

- Assess the health needs of the people and communities they serve
- Develop programs and events to teach people about health topics
- Teach people how to manage existing health conditions
- Evaluate the effectiveness of programs and educational materials
- Help people find health services or information
- Provide training programs for community health workers or other health professionals
- Supervise staff who implement health education programs
- Collect and analyze data to learn about a particular community and improve programs and services
- Advocate for improved health resources and policies that promote health

Community health workers typically do the following:

- Discuss health concerns with community members
- Educate people about the importance and availability of healthcare services, such as cancer screenings
- Collect data
- Report findings to health educators and other healthcare providers
- Provide informal counseling and social support
- Conduct outreach programs
- Facilitate access to the healthcare services
- Advocate for individual and community needs

The duties of health educators, also known as *health education specialists*, vary with their work settings. Most work in healthcare facilities, colleges, public health departments, nonprofits, and private businesses. Those who teach health classes in middle and high schools are considered teachers. For more information, see the profiles on middle school teachers and high school teachers.

In *healthcare facilities*, health educators may work one-on-one with patients or with their families. They teach patients about their diagnoses and about any necessary treatments or procedures. They may be called *patient navigators* because they help consumers find out about their health insurance options and direct people to outside resources, such as support groups or home health agencies. They lead hospital efforts in developing and administering surveys to identify major health issues and concerns of the surrounding communities and developing programs to meet those needs. Health educators also help organize health screenings, such as blood pressure checks, and health classes on topics such as installing a car seat correctly. They also create programs to train medical staff to interact more effectively with patients. For example, they may teach doctors how to explain complicated procedures to patients in simple language.

In *colleges*, health educators create programs and materials on topics that affect young adults, such as smoking and alcohol use. They may train students to be peer educators and supervise the students' delivery of health information in person or through social media. Health educators also advocate for campus-wide policies to promote health.

In *public health departments*, health educators administer public health campaigns on topics such as emergency preparedness, immunizations, proper nutrition, or stress management. They develop materials to be used by other public health officials. During emergencies, they may provide safety information to the public and the media. Some health educators work with other professionals to create public policies that support healthy behaviors and environments. They may also oversee grants and grant-funded programs to improve the health of the public. Some participate in statewide and local committees dealing with topics such as aging.

In *nonprofits* (including community health organizations), health educators create programs and materials about health issues faced by the community that they serve. They help organizations obtain funding and other resources. They may educate policymakers about ways to improve public health and work on securing grant funding for programs to promote health and disease awareness. Many nonprofits focus on a particular disease or audience, so health educators in these organizations limit programs to that specific topic or audience. For example, a health educator may design a program to teach people with diabetes how to better manage their condition or a program for teen mothers on how to care for their newborns.

In *private businesses*, health educators identify common health problems among employees and create programs to improve health. They work with management to develop incentives for employees to adopt healthy behaviors, such as losing weight or controlling cholesterol. Health educators recommend changes in the workplace to improve employee health, such as creating smoke-free areas.

Health educators attempt to prevent illnesses by informing and educating individuals and communities about health-related topics.

Community health workers have an in-depth knowledge of the communities they serve. Within their community, they identify health-related issues, collect data, and discuss health concerns with the people they serve. For example, they may help eligible residents of a neighborhood enroll in programs such as Medicaid or Medicare and explain the benefits that these programs offer. Community health workers address any barriers to care and provide referrals for such needs as food, housing, education, and mental health services.

Community health workers share information with health educators and healthcare providers so that health educators can create new programs or adjust existing programs or events to better suit the needs of the community. Community health workers also advocate for the health needs of community members. In addition, they conduct outreach to engage community residents, assist residents with health system navigation, and to improve care coordination.

Work Environment

Health educators held about 61,400 jobs in 2014. Community health workers held about 54,300 jobs in 2014.

The industries that employed the most health educators in 2014 were as follows:

Government	22%
Hospitals; state, local, and private	21
Ambulatory health care services	16
Religious, grantmaking, civic, professional, and similar organizations	10
Social assistance	10

The industries that employed the most community health workers in 2014 were as follows:

Individual and family services	21%
Ambulatory health care services	19
State and local government, excluding education and hospitals	16
Religious, grantmaking, civic, professional, and similar organizations	15
Hospitals; state, local, and private	8

Although most health educators work in an office, they may spend a lot of time away from the office to carry out programs or attend meetings. Community health workers may spend much of their time in the field, communicating with community members, holding events, and collecting data.

Work Schedules. Most health educators and community health workers work full time. They may need to work nights and weekends to attend programs or meetings.

Education/Training

Some employers may require the Certified Health Education Specialist (CHES) credential. Community health workers typically have at least a high school diploma and must complete a brief period of on-the-job training. Some states have certification programs for community health workers.

Education. Health educators need at least a bachelor's degree in health education or health promotion. Students learn theories and methods of health behavior and health education and gain the knowledge and skills they will need to develop health education materials and programs. Most programs include an internship.

Some health educator positions require a master's or doctoral degree. Graduate programs are commonly in community health education, school health education, public health education, or health promotion. A variety of undergraduate majors may be acceptable for entry to a master's degree program.

Community health workers typically have a high school diploma, although some jobs may require postsecondary education. Education programs may lead to a 1-year certificate or a 2-year associate's degree and cover topics such as wellness, ethics, and cultural awareness, among others.

Training. Community health workers typically complete a brief period of on-the-job training. Training often covers core competencies, such as communication or outreach skills, and information about the specific health topics that they will be focusing on. For example, community health workers who work with Alzheimer's patients may learn about how to communicate effectively with patients dealing with dementia.

Other Experience. Community health workers usually have some knowledge of a specific community, population, medical condition, or disability. The ability to speak a foreign language may be helpful.

Licenses, Certifications, and Registrations. Some employers require health educators to obtain the Certified Health Education Specialist (CHES) credential, which is offered by the National Commission for Health Education Credentialing, Inc. To obtain certification, candidates must pass an exam that is aimed at entry-level health educators who have completed at least a bachelor's degree. To maintain their certification, they must complete 75 hours of continuing education every 5 years. There is also the Master Certified Health Education Specialist (MCHES) credential for health educators with advanced education and experience.

Most states do not require community health workers to become certified, however voluntary certification exists or is being considered or developed in a number of states. Requirements vary but may include completing an approved training program. For more information, contact your state's board of health, nursing, or human services.

Important Qualities

Analytical skills. Health educators collect and analyze data in order to evaluate programs and to determine the needs of the people they serve.

Instructional skills. Health educators and community health workers should be comfortable with public speaking so that they can lead programs, teach classes, and facilitate discussion with clients and families.

Median Annual Wages, May 2014

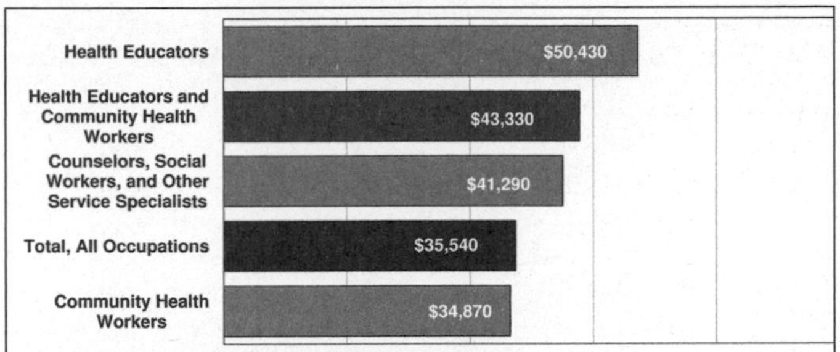

Note: All Occupations includes all occupations in the U.S. Economy.
Source: U.S. Bureau of Labor Statistics, Occupational Employment Statistics

Percent Change in Employment, Projected 2014–2024

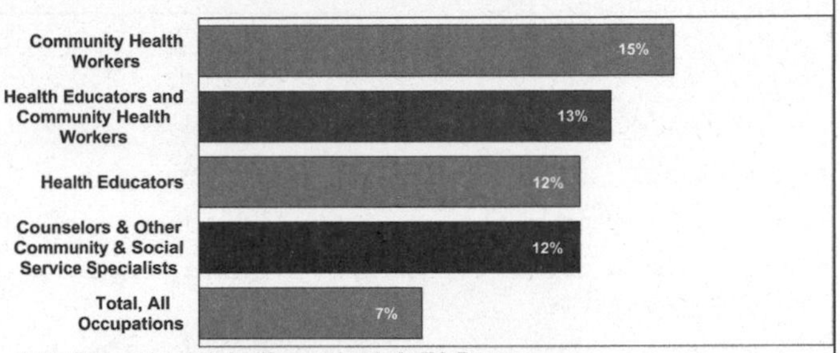

Note: All Occupations includes all occupations in the U.S. Economy.
Source: U.S. Bureau of Labor Statistics, Office of Occupational Statistics and Employment Projections

Interpersonal skills. Health educators and community health workers interact with many people from a variety of backgrounds. They must be good listeners and be culturally sensitive to respond to the needs of the people they serve.

Problem-solving skills. Health educators and community health workers must think creatively about how to improve the health of the community through health education programs. In addition, they may need to solve problems that arise in planning programs, such as changes to their budget or resistance from the community they are serving.

Writing skills. Health educators and community health workers develop written materials to convey health-related information. Health educators also write proposals to develop programs and apply for funding.

Pay

The median annual wage for health educators was $50,430 in May 2014. The median wage is the wage at which half the workers in an occupation earned more than that amount and half earned less. The lowest 10 percent earned less than $29,650, and the highest 10 percent earned more than $90,260.

The median annual wage for community health workers was $34,870 in May 2014. The lowest 10 percent earned less than $20,790, and the highest 10 percent earned more than $60,360.

In May 2014, the median annual wages for health educators in the top industries in which they worked were as follows:

Hospitals; state, local, and private	$60,720
Government	52,550
Ambulatory health care services	49,180
Religious, grantmaking, civic, professional, and similar organizations	46,820
Social assistance	38,810

In May 2014, the median annual wages for community health workers in the top industries in which they worked were as follows:

Hospitals; state, local, and private	$41,310
Religious, grantmaking, civic, professional, and similar organizations	38,470
State and local government, excluding education and hospitals	37,890
Ambulatory health care services	34,450
Individual and family services	30,730

Job Outlook

Employment of health educators and community health workers is projected to grow 13 percent from 2014 to 2024, faster than the average for all occupations. Growth will be driven by efforts to improve health outcomes and to reduce healthcare costs by teaching people healthy habits and behaviors and explaining how to use available healthcare services.

Insurance companies, employers, and governments are trying to find ways to improve the quality of care and health outcomes, while reducing costs. They hire health educators and community health workers to teach people about how to live healthy lives, obtain screenings, and how to avoid costly diseases and medical procedures. They explain how lifestyle changes can reduce the probability of contracting illnesses such as lung cancer, HIV, heart disease, and skin cancer. Health educators and community health workers also help people understand how to manage their condition and avoid unnecessary trips to the emergency room. Health educators and community health workers help people understand how their actions affect their health.

For many illnesses, such as breast cancer and testicular cancer, finding the disease early greatly increases the likelihood that treatment will be successful. Therefore, it is important for people to know how to identify potential health problems and when to seek medical help. The need to get this information to the public is expected to increase demand for health educators and community health workers.

The number of individuals who have access to health insurance is expected to continue to increase because of federal health insurance reform. Health educators and community health workers would be needed to show patients how to get access to healthcare services, such as preventive screenings. In addition, health educators and community health workers might take part in state and

Employment Projections Data for Health Educators and Community Health Workers

Occupational Title	SOC Code	Employment, 2014	Projected Employment, 2024	Change, 2014–2024 Percent	Change, 2014–2024 Numeric
Health educators and community health workers	—	115,700	131,300	13	15,600
Health educators	21-1091	61,400	68,900	12	7,500
Community health workers	21-1094	54,300	62,400	15	8,100

Source: U.S. Bureau of Labor Statistics, Employment Projections Program

Similar Occupations. This table shows a list of occupations with job duties that are similar to those of health educators and community health workers.

Occupations	Entry-level Education	2014 Median Pay	Projected Job Growth	Average Annual Openings
Dietitians and Nutritionists	Bachelor's degree	$56,950	16%	1,100
Epidemiologists	Master's degree	$67,420	6%	40
High School Teachers	Bachelor's degree	$56,310	6%	5,590
Mental Health Counselors and Marriage and Family Therapists	Master's degree	$42,250	19%	3,140
Middle School Teachers	Bachelor's degree	$54,940	6%	3,680
Postsecondary Teachers	See Education/Training	$70,790	13%	17,700
School and Career Counselors	Master's degree	$53,370	8%	2,250
Social and Human Service Assistants	High school diploma or equivalent	$29,790	11%	4,420
Social Workers	See Education/Training	$45,500	12%	7,480
Substance Abuse and Behavioral Disorder Counselors	Bachelor's degree	$39,270	22%	2,120

local programs designed to treat and prevent conditions such as diabetes and obesity.

Job Prospects. Community health workers who have completed a formal education program and those who have experience working with a specific population may have favorable job prospects. In addition, opportunities may be better for candidates who speak a foreign language.

Contacts for More Information

For more information about health educators and community health workers, visit

➤ Society for Public Health Education (www.sophe.org)

➤ American Public Health Association (www.apha.org)

For more information about the Certified Health Education Specialist (CHES) credential, visit

➤ National Commission for Health Education Credentialing, Inc. (www.nchec.org)

O*NET

➤ Health Educators (21-1091.00)

➤ Community Health Workers (21-1094.00)

Mental Health Counselors and Marriage and Family Therapists

- **2014 Median Pay** .... $42,250 per year $20.31 per hour
- **Typical Entry-Level Education** ....Master's degree
- **Work Experience in a Related Occupation**.............. None
- **On-the-job Training** .... Internship/residency
- **Number of Jobs, 2014** 168,200
- **Job Outlook, 2014–24**.... 19% (Much faster than average)
- **Employment Change, 2014–24** 31,400

What Mental Health Counselors and Marriage and Family Therapists Do

Mental health counselors and marriage and family therapists help people manage and overcome mental and emotional disorders and problems with their family and other relationships. They listen to clients and ask questions to help the clients understand their problems and develop strategies to improve their lives.

Duties. Mental health counselors and marriage and family therapists typically do the following:

- Diagnose and treat mental and emotional disorders, such as anxiety and depression
- Encourage clients to discuss their emotions and experiences
- Help clients process their reactions and adjust to difficult changes in their life, such as divorce and layoffs
- Guide clients through the process of making decisions about their future
- Help clients develop strategies and skills to change their behavior and to cope with difficult situations
- Refer clients to other resources or services in the community, such as support groups or inpatient treatment facilities

Mental health counselors and marriage and family therapists use a variety of techniques and tools to help their clients. Many apply cognitive behavioral therapy, a goal-oriented approach that helps clients understand harmful thoughts, feelings, and beliefs and teaches how to replace them with positive, life-enhancing ones. Furthermore, mental health counselors use cognitive behavioral therapy to teach clients to eliminate unwanted and damaging behaviors and to replace them with more productive ones.

Although some disorders can be overcome, others need to be managed. With the latter, mental health counselors and marriage and family therapists help the client develop strategies and skills to minimize the effects of their disorders or illnesses.

Many mental health counselors and marriage and family therapists work in private practice. They must spend time marketing their practice to prospective clients and working with insurance companies and clients to get payment for their services.

Mental health counselors provide treatment to individuals, families, couples, and groups. Some work with specific populations, such as the elderly, college students, or children. Mental health counselors deal with a variety of issues, including anxiety, depression, grief, low self-esteem, stress, and suicidal impulses. They also help with mental and emotional health issues and relationship problems.

Counselors work in diverse community settings designed to provide a variety of counseling, rehabilitation, and support services.

Marriage and family therapists work with individuals, couples, and families. Unlike other types of mental health professionals, they bring a family-centered perspective to treatment, even when treating individuals. They evaluate family roles and development, to understand how clients' families affect their mental health. They treat the clients' relationships, not just the clients themselves. They address issues, such as low self-esteem, stress, addiction, and substance abuse.

Mental health counselors and marriage and family therapists coordinate patient treatment with other professionals, such as psychiatrists and social workers.

Work Environment

Mental health counselors held about 134,500 jobs in 2014.The industries that employed the most mental health counselors in 2014 were as follows:

Individual and family services	21%
Outpatient mental health and substance abuse centers	17
Residential intellectual and developmental disability, mental health, and substance abuse facilities	12
Hospitals; state, local, and private	11
State and local government, excluding education and hospitals	9

Marriage and family therapists held about 33,700 jobs in 2014. The industries that employed the most marriage and family therapists in 2014 were as follows:

Individual and family services	30%
State and local government, excluding education and hospitals	23
Outpatient care centers	15
Offices of other health practitioners	8
Nursing and residential care facilities	6

Mental health counselors and marriage and family therapists work in a variety of settings, such as mental health centers, substance abuse treatment centers, hospitals, and colleges. They also work in private practice and in Employee Assistance Programs (EAPs), which are mental health programs that some employers provide, to help employees deal with personal problems.

Working with and assisting clients with a variety of emotional and mental problems may be stressful.

Mental health counselors and marriage and family therapists occasionally may travel to meet clients and patients.

Work Schedules. Mental health counselors and marriage and family therapists generally work full time. Some counselors and therapists work evenings and weekends in order to accommodate their clients' schedules.

Education/Training

Mental health counselors and marriage and family therapists are typically required to have a master's degree and a license to practice.

Education. To become a mental health counselor or a marriage and family therapist, applicants typically need a master's degree in psychology, clinical mental health counseling, marriage and family therapy, or a related mental health field. A bachelor's degree in most fields is acceptable to enter a master's program.

Counseling programs prepare students to recognize symptoms of mental and emotional disorders and to use effective counseling strategies. Marriage and family therapy programs teach students about how marriages, families, and relationships function and how these relationships can affect mental and emotional disorders.

Many employers prefer to hire counselors who have graduated from programs accredited by the Council for Accreditation of Counseling & Related Educational Programs.

Training. Candidates gain hands-on experience through postdegree supervised clinical work, sometimes referred to as an internship or residency. In training, they learn to provide family therapy, group therapy, psychotherapy, and other therapeutic interventions, under the supervision of a licensed counselor.

Licenses. All states require mental health counselors and marriage and family therapists to be licensed in the state in which they practice. Licensure requires a master's degree and 2,000 to 4,000 hours of postdegree supervised clinical experience, sometimes referred to as an internship or residency. In addition, counsclors and therapists must pass a state-recognized exam and complete annual continuing education classes.

Contact information for state boards regulating mental health counselors is available through the National Board for Certified Counselors.

Contact and licensing information for marriage and family therapists is available through the Association of Marital and Family Therapy Regulatory Boards.

Important Qualities

Compassion. Counselors and therapists often work with people who are dealing with stressful and difficult situations, so they must be compassionate and empathize with their clients.

Interpersonal skills. Being able to work with different types of people is essential for counselors and therapists. They spend most of their time working directly with clients and other professionals and must be able to encourage good relationships.

Listening skills. Good listening skills are essential for mental health counselors and marriage and family therapists, both of whom need to give their full attention to their clients to understand their problems, values, and goals.

Organizational skills. Good organizational skills are especially important for counselors and therapists in private practice, who must keep track of payments and work with insurance companies.

Speaking skills. Mental health counselors and marriage and family therapists need to be able to communicate with clients effectively. They must express ideas and information in a way that clients can understand easily.

Median Annual Wages, May 2014

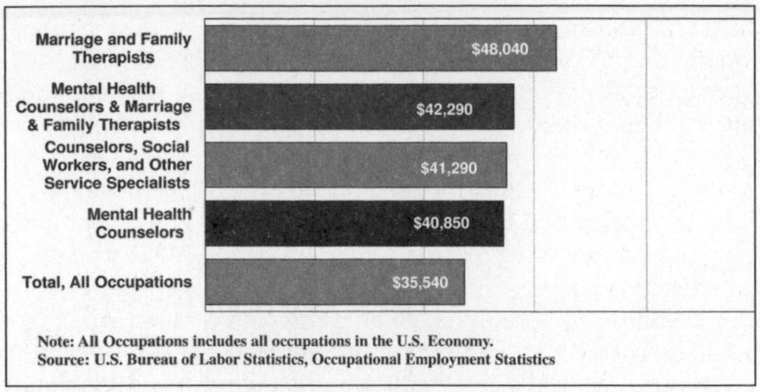

Percent Change in Employment, Projected 2014–2024

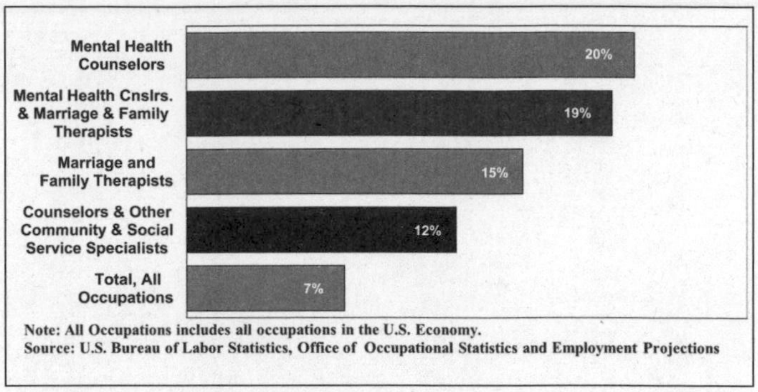

Pay

The median annual wage for marriage and family therapists was $48,040 in May 2014. The median wage is the wage at which half the workers in an occupation earned more than that amount and half earned less. The lowest 10 percent earned less than $30,510, and the highest 10 percent earned more than $78,920.

The median annual wage for mental health counselors was $40,850 in May 2014. The lowest 10 percent earned less than $26,030, and the highest 10 percent earned more than $66,930.

In May 2014, the median annual wages for marriage and family therapists in the top industries in which they worked were as follows:

State and local government, excluding education and hospitals	$63,960
Offices of other health practitioners	47,910
Outpatient care centers	46,640
Individual and family services	42,580
Nursing and residential care facilities	42,430

In May 2014, the median annual wages for mental health counselors in the top industries in which they worked were as follows:

State and local government, excluding education and hospitals	$47,610
Hospitals; state, local, and private	45,080
Outpatient mental health and substance abuse centers	40,670
Individual and family services	39,310
Residential intellectual and developmental disability, mental health, and substance abuse facilities	34,590

Job Outlook

Employment of mental health counselors and marriage and family therapists is projected to grow 19 percent from 2014 to 2024, much faster than the average for all occupations.

Employment of mental health counselors is projected to grow 20 percent from 2014 to 2024, much faster than the average for all occupations. Employment of marriage and family therapists is projected to grow 15 percent from 2014 to 2024, much faster than the average for all occupations. Growth is expected in both occupations as more people have mental health counseling services covered by their insurance policies.

The number of individuals who have access to health insurance is expected to continue to increase because of federal health insurance reform. The law requires insurance plans to cover treatment for mental health issues in the same way as other chronic diseases. This will increase access to prevention and treatment services to more people who were previously uninsured, did not have these services covered, or found treatment to be cost-prohibitive. Mental health centers and other treatment and counseling facilities will need to hire more mental health counselors and marriage and family therapists to meet this increased demand.

In addition, the number of military veterans needing and seeking mental health treatment is expected to increase over the next decade. The federal government, community clinics, and local hospitals will need to expand their mental health counseling staff to provide timely and effective treatment for veterans and active duty personnel.

Job Prospects. Job prospects are expected to be good for mental health counselors and marriage and family therapists, particularly in rural areas or other communities that are underserved by mental health practitioners.

Contacts for More Information

For more information about mental health counselors, visit

- American Mental Health Counselors Association (www.amhca.org)

For more information about accredited mental health counselor programs, visit

- Council for Accreditation of Counseling & Related Educational Programs (www.cacrep.org)

For more information about marriage and family therapists, visit

- American Association for Marriage and Family Therapy (www.aamft.org)
- Association of Marital and Family Therapy Regulatory Boards (www.amftrb.org)

Employment Projections Data for Mental Health Counselors and Marriage and Family Therapists

Occupational Title	SOC Code	Employment, 2014	Projected Employment, 2024	Change, 2014–2024 Percent	Numeric
Mental health counselors and marriage and family therapists	—	168,200	199,600	19	31,400
Mental health counselors	21-1014	134,500	160,900	20	26,400
Marriage and family therapists	21-1013	33,700	38,700	15	5,000

Source: U.S. Bureau of Labor Statistics, Employment Projections Program

Similar Occupations. This table shows a list of occupations with job duties that are similar to those of mental health counselors and marriage and family therapists.

Occupations	Entry-level Education	2014 Median Pay	Projected Job Growth	Average Annual Openings
Physicians and Surgeons	Doctoral or professional degree	This wage is equal to or greater than $187,200.	14%	9,930
Psychologists	See Education/Training	$70,700	19%	3,250
Rehabilitation Counselors	Master's degree	$34,380	9%	1,080
School and Career Counselors	Master's degree	$53,370	8%	2,250
Social and Community Service Managers	Bachelor's degree	$62,740	10%	1,320
Social and Human Service Assistants	High school diploma or equivalent	$29,790	11%	4,420
Social Workers	See Education/Training	$45,500	12%	7,480
Substance Abuse and Behavioral Disorder Counselors	Bachelor's degree	$39,270	22%	2,120

For more information about counseling and for information about counseling specialties, visit

➤ American Counseling Association (www.counseling.org)

For information about contacting state regulating boards, visit

➤ National Board for Certified Counselors (www.nbcc.org)

O*NET

➤ Marriage and Family Therapists (21-1013.00)

➤ Mental Health Counselors (21-1014.00)

Probation Officers and Correctional Treatment Specialists

- **2014 Median Pay** .... $49,060 per year
  $23.59 per hour
- **Typical Entry-Level Education** .... Bachelor's degree
- **Work Experience in a Related Occupation** .... None
- **On-the-job Training** .... Short-term on-the-job training
- **Number of Jobs, 2014** 91,700
- **Job Outlook, 2014–24** .... 4% (Slower than average)
- **Employment Change, 2014–24** 3,300

What Probation Officers and Correctional Treatment Specialists Do

Probation officers and correctional treatment specialists monitor and work with probationers to prevent them from committing new crimes.

Duties. Probation officers and correctional treatment specialists typically do the following:

- Meet with probationers in an office or at the probationer's residence
- Evaluate probationers to determine the best course of rehabilitation
- Provide probationers with resources, such as job training
- Test probationers for drugs and offer substance abuse counseling
- Monitor probationers' contact with law enforcement
- Conduct meetings with probationers and their family and friends
- Write reports and maintain case files on probationers

Probation officers and correctional treatment specialists work with probationers who are given probation instead of jail time, who are still in prison, or who have been released from prison.

The following are examples of types of probation officers and correctional treatment specialists:

Probation officers, who are sometimes referred to as *community supervision officers*, supervise people who have been placed on probation instead of sent to prison. They work to ensure that the probationer is not a danger to the community and to help in their rehabilitation through frequent visits with the probationer. Probation officers write reports that detail each probationer's treatment plan and their progress since being put on probation. Most work exclusively with either adults or juveniles.

Parole officers work with people who have been released from jail and are serving parole, helping them re-enter society. Parole officers monitor post-release parolees and provide them with information on various resources, such as substance abuse counseling or job training, to aid in their rehabilitation. By doing so, the officers try to change the parolee's behavior and thus reduce the risk of that person committing another crime and having to return to prison.

Both probation and parole officers supervise those under community supervision through personal contact with the probationers and their families. Probation and parole officers require regularly scheduled contact with supervisees by telephone or through office visits, and they also check on them at their homes or places of work. When making home visits, probation and parole officers take into account the safety of the neighborhood in which the probationers and parolees live and any mental health considerations that may be pertinent. Probation and parole officers also oversee drug testing and electronic monitoring of those under supervision. In some states, officers do the jobs of both probation and parole officers.

Pretrial services officers investigate a pretrial defendant's background to determine if the defendant can be safely allowed back into the community before his or her trial date. Officers must assess the risk and make a recommendation to a judge, who decides on the appropriate sentencing or bond amount. When pretrial defendants are allowed back into the community, pretrial officers supervise them to make sure that they stay within the terms of their release and appear at their trials.

Correctional treatment specialists, also known as *case managers* or *correctional counselors*, advise probationers and develop rehabilitation plans for them to follow when they are no longer in prison or on parole. They may evaluate inmates using questionnaires and psychological tests. They also work with inmates, probation officers, and staff of other agencies to develop parole and release plans. For example, they may plan education and training programs to improve probationers' job skills.

Correctional treatment specialists write case reports that cover the inmate's history and the likelihood that he or she will commit another crime. When inmates are eligible for release, the case reports are given to the appropriate parole board. The specialist may help set up counseling for the parolees and their families, find substance abuse or mental health treatment options, aid in job placement, and find housing. Correctional treatment specialists also explain the terms and conditions of the prisoner's release and keep detailed written accounts of each parolee's progress.

The number of cases a probation officer or correctional treatment specialist handles at one time depends on the needs of individuals under supervision and the risks associated with each individual. Higher risk probationers usually command more of an officer's time and resources. Caseload size also varies by agency.

Technological advancements—such as improved tests for drug screening and electronic devices to monitor clients—help probation officers and correctional treatment specialists supervise and counsel probationers.

Probation and parole officers supervise offenders on probation or parole through personal contact with the offenders and their families.

Work Environment

Probation officers and correctional treatment specialists held about 91,700 jobs in 2014. Nearly all worked for state or local governments.

Probation officers and correctional treatment specialists work with probationers and parolees, some of whom may be dangerous. While supervising individuals, they may interact with others, such as family members and friends of their clients, who may be upset or difficult to work with. Workers may be assigned to fieldwork in high-crime areas or in institutions where there is a risk of violence or communicable disease.

Many officers travel to perform home and employment checks and property searches. Because of the hostile environments they may encounter, some may carry a firearm or pepper spray for protection.

All of these factors, in addition to the frustration some officers experience in dealing with probationers and parolees who violate the terms of their release, contribute to a stressful work environment. Although the high stress levels can make the job difficult at times, this work can also be rewarding. Many officers and specialists receive personal satisfaction from counseling members of their community and helping them become productive citizens.

Work Schedules. Although many officers and specialists work full time, the demands of the job often lead to working overtime. For example, many agencies rotate an on-call officer position. When these workers are on-call, they must respond to any issues with probationers or law enforcement 24 hours a day. Extensive travel and paperwork can also contribute to more hours of work.

Education/Training

Probation officers and correctional treatment specialists usually need a bachelor's degree. In addition, most employers require candidates to pass competency exams, drug testing, and a criminal background check.

A valid driver's license is often required, and most agencies require applicants to be at least 21 years old.

Education. A bachelor's degree in social work, criminal justice, behavioral sciences, or a related field is usually required. Some employers require a master's degree in a related field. Exact requirements will vary by jurisdiction.

Training. Most probation officers and correctional treatment specialists must complete a training program sponsored by their state government or the federal government, after which they may have to pass a certification test. In addition, they may be required to work as trainees for up to 1 year before being offered a permanent position.

Median Annual Wages, May 2014

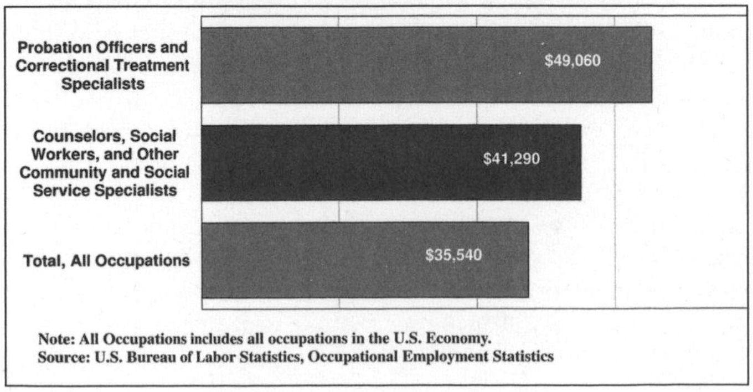

Percent Change in Employment, Projected 2014–2024

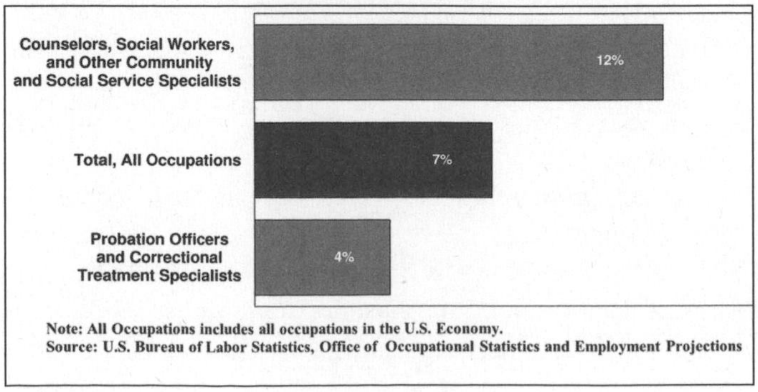

Employment Projections Data for Probation Officers and Correctional Treatment Specialists

Occupational Title	SOC Code	Employment, 2014	Projected Employment, 2024	Change, 2014–2024 Percent	Change, 2014–2024 Numeric
Probation officers and correctional treatment specialists.......	21-1092	91,700	95,000	4	3,300

Source: U.S. Bureau of Labor Statistics, Employment Projections Program

Similar Occupations. This table shows a list of occupations with job duties that are similar to those of probation officers and correctional treatment specialists.

Occupations	Entry-level Education	2014 Median Pay	Projected Job Growth	Average Annual Openings
Correctional Officers and Bailiffs	High school diploma or equivalent	$39,700	4%	1,790
Police and Detectives	See Education/Training	$58,630	4%	3,310
Social and Human Service Assistants	High school diploma or equivalent	$29,790	11%	4,420
Social Workers	See Education/Training	$45,500	12%	7,100
Substance Abuse and Behavioral Disorder Counselors	Bachelor's degree	$39,270	22%	2,120

Some probation officers and correctional treatment specialists specialize in a certain type of casework. For example, an officer may work only with domestic violence probationers or deal only with substance abuse cases. Some may work only cases involving juvenile offenders. Officers receive the appropriate specific training so that they are better prepared to help that type of probationer. Training may include site visits to probationers' homes under the watch of a probation officer supervisor.

Other Experience. Although job requirements vary, previous work experience in probation, pretrial services, parole, corrections, criminal investigations, substance abuse treatment, social work, or counseling can be helpful in the hiring process.

Previous experience working in courthouses or with probationers in the criminal justice field can also be useful for some positions.

Advancement. Advancement to supervisory positions is primarily based on experience and performance. A master's degree in criminal justice, social work, or psychology may be required for advancement.

Important Qualities

Communication skills. Probation officers and correctional treatment specialists must be able to effectively interact with many different people, such as probationers and their family members, lawyers, judges, treatment providers, and law enforcement.

Critical-thinking skills. Workers must be able to assess the needs of individual probationers before determining the best resources for helping them.

Decision-making skills. Probation officers and correctional treatment specialists must consider the relative costs and benefits of potential actions and be able to choose appropriately.

Emotional stability. Workers must cope with hostile individuals or otherwise upsetting circumstances on the job.

Organizational skills. Probation officers and correctional treatment specialists must be able to manage multiple cases at the same time.

Pay

The median annual wage for probation officers and correctional treatment specialists was $49,060 in May 2014. The median wage is the wage at which half the workers in an occupation earned more than that amount and half earned less. The lowest 10 percent earned less than $32,810, and the highest 10 percent earned more than $83,920.

Union Membership. Compared with workers in all occupations, probation officers and correctional treatment specialists had a higher percentage of workers who belonged to a union in 2014.

Job Outlook

Employment of probation officers and correctional treatment specialists is projected to grow 4 percent from 2014 to 2024, slower than the average for all occupations.

Employment growth depends primarily on the amount of state and local government funding for corrections, especially the amount allocated to probation and parole systems.

However, because community corrections is viewed as an economically viable alternative to incarceration in some cases, demand for probation officers and correctional treatment specialists should continue. Parole officers will continue to be needed to supervise individuals who will be released from prison in the future.

Job Prospects. Many job openings will result from the need to replace those who leave the occupation each year due to the heavy workloads and high job-related stress. Job opportunities should be plentiful for those who qualify.

Contacts for More Information

For more information about probation officers and correctional treatment specialists, visit

- American Probation and Parole Association (www.appa-net.org/eweb)
- Discover Corrections (www.discovercorrections.com)

For more information about criminal justice job opportunities in your area, contact the departments of corrections, criminal justice, or probation for individual states.

O*NET

- Probation Officers and Correctional Treatment Specialists (21-1092.00)

Rehabilitation Counselors

- **2014 Median Pay** .... $34,380 per year
$16.53 per hour
- **Typical Entry-Level Education** ....Master's degree
- **Work Experience in a Related Occupation**.............. None
- **On-the-job Training** .... None
- **Number of Jobs, 2014** 120,100
- **Job Outlook, 2014–24**.............. 9% (Faster than average)
- **Employment Change, 2014–24** 10,800

Rehabilitation counselors evaluate clients' abilities, interests, experience, skills, health, and education.

What Rehabilitation Counselors Do

Rehabilitation counselors help people with physical, mental, developmental, and emotional disabilities live independently. They work with clients to overcome or manage the personal, social, or psychological effects of disabilities on employment or independent living.

Duties. Rehabilitation counselors typically do the following:

- Provide individual and group counseling to help clients adjust to their disability
- Evaluate clients' abilities, interests, experiences, skills, health, and education
- Develop a treatment plan for clients in consultation with other professionals, such as doctors, therapists, and psychologists
- Arrange for clients to obtain services, such as medical care or career training
- Help employers understand the needs and abilities of people with disabilities, as well as laws and resources that affect people with disabilities
- Help clients develop their strengths and adjust to their limitations
- Locate resources, such as wheelchairs or computer programs, that help clients live and work more independently
- Maintain client records and monitor clients' progress, adjusting the rehabilitation or treatment plan as necessary
- Advocate for the rights of people with disabilities to live in a community and work in the job of their choice

Rehabilitation counselors help people with disabilities at various stages in their lives. Some work with students to develop strategies to live with their disability and move from school to work. Others help veterans cope with the mental or physical effects of their military service. Still others help elderly people adapt to disabilities developed later in life from illness or injury. Some may provide expert testimony or assessments during personal injury or workers' compensation cases.

Some rehabilitation counselors deal specifically with employment issues. These counselors, sometimes called *vocational rehabilitation counselors*, typically work with older students and adults.

Rehabilitation counselors who work in private practice must spend time marketing their practice to prospective clients and working with insurance companies and clients to get paid for their services.

Work Environment

Rehabilitation counselors held about 120,100 jobs in 2014. The industries that employed the most rehabilitation counselors were as follows:

Vocational rehabilitation services	26%
State and local government, excluding education and hospitals	20
Individual and family services	20
Nursing and residential care facilities	13

They work in a variety of settings, such as community rehabilitation centers, senior citizen centers, youth guidance organizations, and state and federal rehabilitation agencies. They also work in private practice and in state, private, and nonprofit rehabilitation agencies.

Work Schedules. Most rehabilitation counselors work full time. Depending on where they work, they may work evenings or weekends.

Education/Training

Rehabilitation counselors typically need a master's degree in rehabilitation counseling or a related field. Some positions require certification or a license.

Education. Most employers require a master's degree in rehabilitation counseling or a related field. A bachelor's degree in most fields is acceptable to enter a master's degree program. Master's degree programs teach students the theories, skills, and techniques that will enable them to provide effective mental health counseling. These programs also train students in evaluating clients' needs, formulating and implementing job placement strategies, and understanding the medical and psychological aspects of a disability. They typically require a period of supervised clinical experience, such as an internship.

Although some employers hire workers with a bachelor's degree in rehabilitation and disability studies, these workers typically cannot offer the full range of services that a rehabilitation counselor with a master's degree can provide. Students in bachelor's degree programs learn about issues that people with disabilities face and about the process of providing rehabilitation services. Some universities offer dual-degree programs in rehabilitation counseling, in which students can earn a bachelor's and master's degree in 5 years.

Licenses, Certifications, and Registrations. Licensing requirements for rehabilitation counselors differ by state and by type of services provided. Those providing counseling services to clients and patients must attain a license through their state licensing board. Other services provided by rehabilitation counselors, however, may be exempt from state licensing requirements. For example, rehabilitation counselors who provide only vocational rehabilitation services or job placement assistance may not need a license.

Licensure typically requires a master's degree and 2,000 to 4,000 hours of supervised clinical experience. In addition, counselors must pass a state-recognized exam. To maintain their licensure, counselors must complete annual continuing education credits.

Applicants should contact their state licensing board for information on what services or counseling positions require licensure. Contact information for these state licensing boards can be found through the Commission on Rehabilitation Counselor Certification.

Some employers prefer or require rehabilitation counselors to be certified. The Commission on Rehabilitation Counselor Certification offers the Certified Rehabilitation Counselor (CRC) certification. Applicants must meet advanced education, work experience, and clinical supervision requirements and pass a test. Certification must be renewed every 5 years. Counselors must complete continuing education requirements or pass a reexamination to renew their certification.

Important Qualities

Communication skills. Rehabilitation counselors need to be able to effectively communicate with clients. They must express ideas and information in a way that is easy to understand.

Compassion. Counselors often work with people who are dealing with stressful and difficult situations. They must be compassionate and empathize with their clients.

Critical-thinking skills. Counselors must be able to develop a treatment plan to help clients reach their goals by considering each client's abilities and interests.

Interpersonal skills. Being able to work with different types of people is essential for rehabilitation counselors, who spend most of their time working directly with clients, families, employers, or other professionals. They must be able to develop and maintain good working relationships.

Listening skills. Good listening skills are essential for rehabilitation counselors. They need to give their full attention in sessions in order to understand clients' problems, concerns, and values.

Patience. To help people learn new skills and strategies, rehabilitation counselors must have patience as clients struggle to learn about and address their disabilities.

Pay

The median annual wage for rehabilitation counselors was $34,380 in May 2014. The median wage is the wage at which half the workers in an occupation earned more than that amount and half earned less. The lowest 10 percent earned less than $21,200, and the highest 10 percent earned more than $59,810.

In May 2014, the median annual wages for rehabilitation counselors in the top industries in which they worked were as follows:

State and local government, excluding education and hospitals	$44,180
Individual and family services	32,890
Vocational rehabilitation services	30,280
Nursing and residential care facilities	29,550

Job Outlook

Employment of rehabilitation counselors is projected to grow 9 percent from 2014 to 2024, faster than the average for all occupations. Demand for rehabilitation counselors is expected to grow with the increase in the elderly population and with the continued rehabilitation needs of other groups, such as veterans and people with disabilities.

Older adults are more likely than other age groups to become disabled or injured. Rehabilitation counselors will be needed to help the elderly learn to adapt to any new limitations and learn strategies to live independently.

In addition, there will be a continued need for rehabilitation counselors to work with veterans who were disabled during their military service. They will also be needed to work with other groups, such as people who have learning disabilities, autism spectrum disorders, or substance abuse problems.

Contacts for More Information

For more information about counseling and information about counseling specialties, visit

- American Counseling Association (www.counseling.org)
- American Rehabilitation Counseling Association (www.arcaweb.org)

For more information about accredited degree programs in rehabilitation counseling, visit

- Council on Rehabilitation Education (www.core-rehab.org)

For more information about the Certified Rehabilitation Counselors certification and state licensing boards, visit

- Commission on Rehabilitation Counselor Certification (www.crccertification.com)

O*NET

- Rehabilitation Counselors (21-1015.00)

Median Annual Wages, May 2014

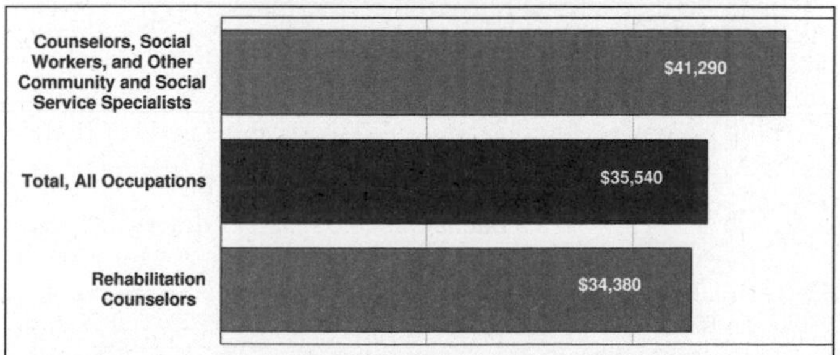

Note: All Occupations includes all occupations in the U.S. Economy.
Source: U.S. Bureau of Labor Statistics, Occupational Employment Statistics

Percent Change in Employment, Projected 2014–2024

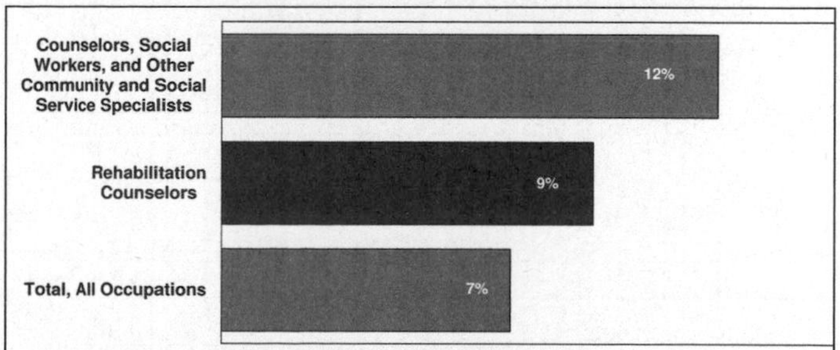

Note: All Occupations includes all occupations in the U.S. Economy.
Source: U.S. Bureau of Labor Statistics, Office of Occupational Statistics and Employment Projections

Employment Projections Data for Rehabilitation Counselors

Occupational Title	SOC Code	Employment, 2014	Projected Employment, 2024	Change, 2014–2024 Percent	Change, 2014–2024 Numeric
Rehabilitation counselors	21-1015	120,100	130,900	9	10,800

Source: U.S. Bureau of Labor Statistics, Employment Projections Program

Similar Occupations. This table shows a list of occupations with job duties that are similar to those of rehabilitation counselors.

Occupations	Entry-level Education	2014 Median Pay	Projected Job Growth	Average Annual Openings
Mental Health Counselors and Marriage and Family Therapists	Master's degree	$42,250	19%	3,140
Occupational Therapists	Master's degree	$78,810	27%	3,040
Occupational Therapy Assistants and Aides	See Education/Training	$52,300	40%	1,680
Psychologists	See Education/Training	$70,700	19%	3,250
School and Career Counselors	Master's degree	$53,370	8%	2,250
Social and Human Service Assistants	High school diploma or equivalent	$29,790	11%	4,420
Special Education Teachers	Bachelor's degree	$55,980	6%	2,810
Substance Abuse and Behavioral Disorder Counselors	Bachelor's degree	$39,270	22%	2,120

School and Career Counselors

- **2014 Median Pay** .... $53,370 per year $25.66 per hour
- **Typical Entry-Level Education** .... Master's degree
- **Work Experience in a Related Occupation** .... None
- **On-the-job Training** .... None
- **Number of Jobs, 2014** 273,400
- **Job Outlook, 2014–24** .... 8% (As fast as average)
- **Employment Change, 2014–24** 22,500

What School and Career Counselors Do

School counselors help students develop academic and social skills and succeed in school. Career counselors assist people with the process of making career decisions by helping them develop skills or choose a career or educational program.

Duties. School counselors typically do the following:

- Evaluate students' abilities and interests through aptitude assessments, interviews, and individual planning
- Identify issues that impact school performance, such as poor classroom attendance rates
- Help students understand and overcome social or behavioral problems through classroom guidance lessons and counseling
- Counsel individuals and small groups on the basis of student and school needs
- Work with students to develop skills, such as organizational and time management abilities and effective study habits
- Help students create a plan to achieve academic and career goals
- Collaborate with teachers, administrators, and parents to help students succeed
- Teach students and school staff about certain topics, such as bullying, drug abuse, and planning for college or careers after graduation
- Report possible cases of neglect or abuse and refer students and parents to resources outside the school for additional support

The specific duties of school counselors vary with the ages of their students.

Elementary school counselors focus on helping students develop certain skills, such as those used in decision making and studying, that they need in order to be successful in their social and academic lives. They meet with parents or guardians to discuss their child's strengths and weaknesses, and any possible special needs and behavioral issues. School counselors also work with teachers and administrators to ensure that the curriculum addresses both the developmental and academic needs of students.

Middle school counselors work with school staff, parents and the community to create a caring, supportive climate and atmosphere for students to achieve academic success. They help the students develop the skills and strategies necessary to succeed academically and socially.

High school counselors advise students in making academic and career plans. Many help students overcome personal issues that interfere with their academic development. They help students choose classes and plan for their lives after graduation. Counselors provide information about choosing and applying for colleges, training programs, financial aid, and internships and apprenticeships. They may present career workshops to help students search and apply for jobs, write résumés, and improve their interviewing skills.

Career counselors typically do the following:

- Use aptitude and achievement assessments to help clients evaluate their interests, skills, and abilities
- Evaluate clients' background, education, and training, to help them develop realistic goals

Career counselors assist people with the process of making career decisions.

- Guide clients through making decisions about their careers, such as choosing a new profession and the type of degree to pursue
- Help clients learn job search skills, such as interviewing and networking
- Assist clients in locating and applying for jobs, by teaching them strategies to find openings and how to write a resume
- Advise clients on how to resolve problems in the workplace, such as conflicts with bosses or coworkers
- Help clients select and apply for educational programs, to obtain the necessary degrees, credentials, and skills

Career counselors work with clients at various stages of their careers. Some work in colleges. They may help students choose a major or help students determine what jobs they are qualified for with their degrees.

Career counselors also work with people who have already entered the workforce. These counselors develop plans to improve their client's current career. They also provide advice about entering a new profession.

Some career counselors work in outplacement firms and assist laid-off workers with transitioning into new jobs or careers. Others work in corporate career centers to assist employees in making decisions about their career path within the company.

Career counselors who work in private practice must spend time marketing their practice to prospective clients and working with clients to receive payments for their services.

Work Environment

School and career counselors held about 273,400 jobs in 2014. The industries that employed the most school and career counselors were as follows:

Elementary and secondary schools; state, local, and private	45%
Junior colleges, colleges, universities, and professional schools; state, local, and private	33
Community and vocational rehabilitation services	5
State and local government, excluding education and hospitals	3

School counselors work in private and public schools. They often have private offices so that they can have confidential conversations with students. Career counselors work in colleges, businesses, government agencies, and career centers.

Work Schedules. Both school and career counselors generally work full time. Some school counselors do not work during the summer when school is not in session.

Education/Training

Most school counselors must have a master's degree in school counseling or a related field and have a state-issued credential. Some employers prefer that career counselors have a master's degree. Career counselors who work in private practices may also need a license.

Education. Most states require school counselors to have a master's degree in school counseling or a related field. Programs in school counseling teach students about fostering academic development; conducting group and individual counseling; working with parents, school staff, and community organizations; and using data to develop, implement, and evaluate comprehensive school counseling programs for all students. These programs often require students to gain experience through an internship or practicum.

Some employers prefer that career counselors have a master's degree in counseling with a focus on career development. Career counseling programs prepare students to assess clients' skills and interests and to teach career development techniques. Many programs require students to have a period of supervised experience, such as an internship.

Licenses, Certifications, and Registrations. Public school counselors must have a state-issued credential to practice. This credential can be called a certification, a license, or an endorsement, depending on the state. Licensure or certification typically requires a master's degree in school counseling and an internship or practicum completed under the supervision of a licensed professional school counselor.

Median Annual Wages, May 2014

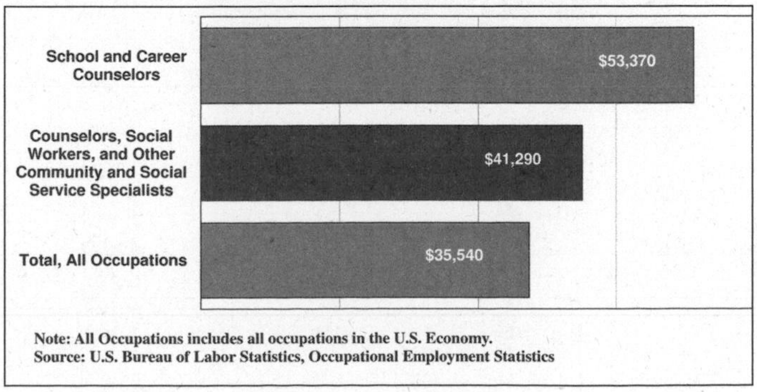

Percent Change in Employment, Projected 2014–2024

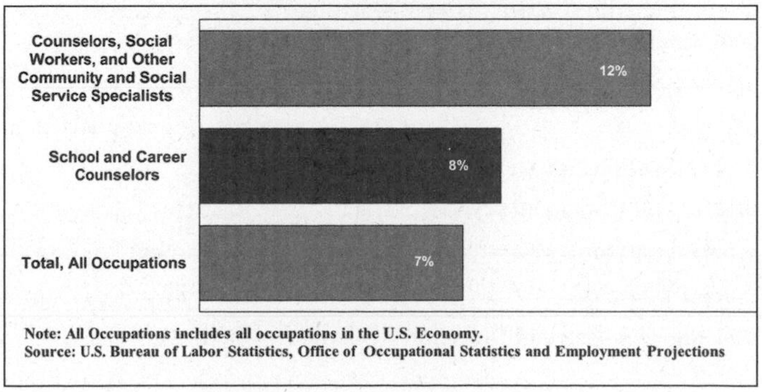

Employment Projections Data for School and Career Counselors

Occupational Title	SOC Code	Employment, 2014	Projected Employment, 2024	Change, 2014–2024 Percent	Change, 2014–2024 Numeric
Educational, guidance, school, and vocational counselors	21-1012	273,400	295,900	8	22,500

Source: U.S. Bureau of Labor Statistics, Employment Projections Program

Some states require applicants to have 1 to 2 years of classroom teaching experience, or to hold a teaching license, prior to being certified. Most states require a criminal background check as part of the credentialing process. Information about requirements for each state is available from the American School Counselor Association.

Although some employers prefer to hire licensed career counselors, licensure is not required by all states. Contact information for state regulating boards is available from the National Board for Certified Counselors.

Work Experience in a Related Occupation. Although most states do not require work experience in a related occupation, some states require school counselors to have 1 to 2 years of classroom teaching experience, or to hold a teaching license, prior to being certified. Please see the Similar Occupations table for more information on teaching occupations.

Important Qualities

Compassion. School and career counselors often work with people who are dealing with stressful and difficult situations, so they must be compassionate and empathize with their clients and students.

Interpersonal skills. School and career counselors must be able to work with different types of people. They spend most of their time working directly with clients, students, or other professionals and need to form and maintain good working relationships.

Listening skills. Good listening skills are essential for school and career counselors. They need to give their full attention to students and clients in order to understand their problems.

Speaking skills. School and career counselors must communicate effectively with clients and students. They should express ideas and information in a way that their clients and students understand easily.

Pay

The median annual wage for school and career counselors was $53,370 in May 2014. The median wage is the wage at which half the workers in an occupation earned more than that amount and half earned less. The lowest 10 percent earned less than $31,960, and the highest 10 percent earned more than $86,610.

In May 2014, the median annual wages for school and career counselors in the top industries in which they worked were as follows:

Elementary and secondary schools; state, local, and private	$60,660
State and local government, excluding education and hospitals	49,860
Junior colleges, colleges, universities, and professional schools; state, local, and private	46,850
Community and vocational rehabilitation services	35,870

Job Outlook

Employment of school and career counselors is projected to grow 8 percent from 2014 to 2024, about as fast as the average for all occupations.

Rising student enrollments in elementary, middle, and high schools, as well as colleges and universities, may increase demand for school counselors. As enrollments grow, schools will require more counselors to respond to the developmental and academic needs of their students. Colleges will need to hire additional

Similar Occupations. This table shows a list of occupations with job duties that are similar to those of school and career counselors.

Occupations	Entry-level Education	2014 Median Pay	Projected Job Growth	Average Annual Openings
High School Teachers	Bachelor's degree	$56,310	6%	5,590
Human Resources Specialists	Bachelor's degree	$57,420	5%	2,200
Kindergarten and Elementary School Teachers	Bachelor's degree	$53,760	6%	8,780
Mental Health Counselors and Marriage and Family Therapists	Master's degree	$42,250	19%	3,140
Middle School Teachers	Bachelor's degree	$54,940	6%	3,680
Psychologists	See Education/Training	$70,700	19%	3,250
Rehabilitation Counselors	Master's degree	$34,380	9%	1,080
Social and Community Service Managers	Bachelor's degree	$62,740	10%	1,320
Social and Human Service Assistants	High school diploma or equivalent	$29,790	11%	4,420
Social Workers	See Education/Training	$45,500	12%	7,480
Substance Abuse and Behavioral Disorder Counselors	Bachelor's degree	$39,270	22%	2,120

counselors to meet the demand for career counseling services from their students.

However, any employment growth may be tempered by strained state and local government budgets. When governments experience budget deficits, they may lay off employees, including counselors.

Demand for career counseling is projected to increase in universities as an increasing number of campuses open onsite career centers to help students develop skills and prepare for transition to the workforce.

Career counselors also will be needed in vocational rehabilitation services to assist those who change careers, to help laid-off workers find employment, and to help military personnel transition into the civilian job market.

Contacts for More Information

For more information about counseling and information about counseling specialties, visit

➤ American Counseling Association (www.counseling.org)

For more information about school counselors, visit

➤ American School Counselor Association (http://schoolcounselor.org)

For more information about career counselors, visit

➤ National Career Development Association (www.ncda.org)

For more information about state credentialing, visit

➤ National Board for Certified Counselors (www.nbcc.org)

O*NET

➤ Educational, Guidance, School, and Vocational Counselors (21-1012.00)

Social and Human Service Assistants

- **2014 Median Pay** .... $29,790 per year $14.32 per hour
- **Typical Entry-Level Education** .... High school diploma or equivalent
- **Work Experience in a Related Occupation**............... None
- **On-the-job Training** ....Short-term on-the-job training
- **Number of Jobs, 2014** 386,600
- **Job Outlook, 2014–24**............. 11% (Faster than average)
- **Employment Change, 2014–24** 44,200

What Social and Human Service Assistants Do

Social and human service assistants provide client services, including support for families, in a wide variety of fields, such as psychology, rehabilitation, and social work. They assist other workers, such as social workers, and they help clients find benefits or community services.

Duties. Social and human service assistants typically do the following:

- Help determine what type of aid their clients need
- Work with clients and other professionals, such as social workers, to develop a treatment plan
- Help clients find assistance with daily activities, such as eating and bathing
- Research services, such as food stamps and Medicaid, that are available to their clients in their communities
- Coordinate services provided to clients
- Help clients complete paperwork to apply for assistance programs
- Transport clients—for example, by driving them to appointments or to services within their community
- Check in with clients to ensure that services are provided appropriately

Social and human service assistants have many job titles, including *case work aide, clinical social work aide, family service assistant, social work assistant, addictions counselor assistant*, and *human service worker*.

Social and human service assistants help clients to identify and obtain benefits and services. In addition to initially connecting clients with benefits or services, social and human service assistants may follow up with clients to ensure that they are receiving the intended services and that the services are meeting their needs. They work under the direction of social workers, psychologists, or other social and human service workers.

With *children and families*, social and human service assistants ensure that the children live in safe homes. They help parents get the resources, such as food stamps or childcare, they need to care for their children.

With the *elderly*, these workers help clients stay in their own homes and live under their own care whenever possible. Social and human service assistants may coordinate meal deliveries or find personal care aides to help with the clients' day-to-day needs, such as running errands and bathing. In some cases, human service workers help look for residential care facilities, such as nursing homes.

For *people with disabilities*, social and human service assistants help find rehabilitation services that aid their clients. They may work with employers to make a job more accessible to people with disabilities. Some workers find personal care services to help clients with daily living activities, such as bathing and making meals.

For *people with addictions*, human service assistants find rehabilitation centers that meet their clients' needs. They also may find support groups for people who are dependent on alcohol, drugs, gambling, or other substances or behaviors.

With *veterans*, assistants help people who have been discharged from the military adjust to civilian life. They help with practical needs, such as locating housing and finding ways to apply skills gained in the military to civilian jobs. They may also help their clients navigate the overwhelming number of services available to veterans.

For *people with mental illnesses*, social and human service assistants help clients find the appropriate resources to help them cope with their illness. They find self-help and support groups to provide their clients with an assistance network. In addition, they may find personal care services or group housing to help those with more severe mental illnesses care for themselves.

With *immigrants*, workers help clients adjust to living in a new country. They help the clients locate jobs and housing. They also may help them find programs that teach English, or they may find legal assistance to help immigrants get various kinds of administrative paperwork in order.

With *former prison inmates*, human service assistants find job training or placement programs to help clients reenter society. Human service assistants help former inmates find housing and connect with programs that help them start a new life for themselves.

With *homeless people*, assistants help clients meet their basic needs. They find temporary or permanent housing for their clients and locate places, such as soup kitchens, that provide

Social and human service assistants help social workers, healthcare workers, and other professionals to provide services to people.

meals. Human service assistants also may help homeless people find resources to address other problems they may have, such as joblessness.

Work Environment

Social and human service assistants held about 386,600 jobs in 2014. The industries that employed the most social and human service assistants were as follows:

Individual and family services	28%
State and local government, excluding education and hospitals	20
Nursing and residential care facilities	16
Community and vocational rehabilitation services	11
Religious, grantmaking, civic, professional, and similar organizations	8

They work for nonprofit organizations, private for-profit social service agencies, and state and local government. They may work in offices, clinics, hospitals, group homes, and shelters. Some travel around their communities to see clients.

Work Schedules. Most social and human service assistants work full time. About 1 in 6 worked part time in 2014. Some work nights and weekends.

Education/Training

Requirements for social and human service assistants vary, although they typically have at least a high school diploma and must complete a brief period of on-the-job training. Some employers prefer to hire workers who have additional education or experience.

Education. Although a high school diploma is typically required, some employers prefer to hire workers who have relevant work experience or education beyond high school. A certificate or an associate's degree in a subject such as human services, gerontology (working with older adults), or social or behavioral science is common for workers entering this occupation.

Human service degree programs train students to observe and interview patients, carry out treatment plans, and handle people who are undergoing a crisis. Many programs include fieldwork to give students hands-on experience.

The level of education that social and human service assistants have completed often determines the responsibilities they are given. Those with a high school diploma are likely to do lower level work, such as helping clients fill out paperwork. Assistants with some college education may coordinate program activities or manage a group home.

Although postsecondary education is important, some employers may prefer or allow for applicants who have related work experience. In some cases, candidates may substitute such experience in place of postsecondary education.

Training. Many social and human service assistants, particularly those without any postsecondary education, undergo a period of on-the-job training. Because such workers often are dealing with multiple clients from a wide variety of backgrounds, on-the-job training in case management helps prepare them to respond appropriately to the different needs and situations of their clients.

Advancement. For social and human service assistants, additional education is almost always necessary for advancement. In general, advancement to case management or social work jobs requires a bachelor's or master's degree in human services, counseling, rehabilitation, social work, or a related field.

Important Qualities

Communication skills. Social and human service assistants talk with clients about the challenges in their lives and assist them in getting help. These workers must be able to listen to their clients and to communicate the clients' needs to organizations that can help them.

Compassion. Social and human service assistants often work with people who are in stressful and difficult situations. To develop strong relationships, they must have compassion and empathy for their clients.

Median Hourly Wages, May 2014

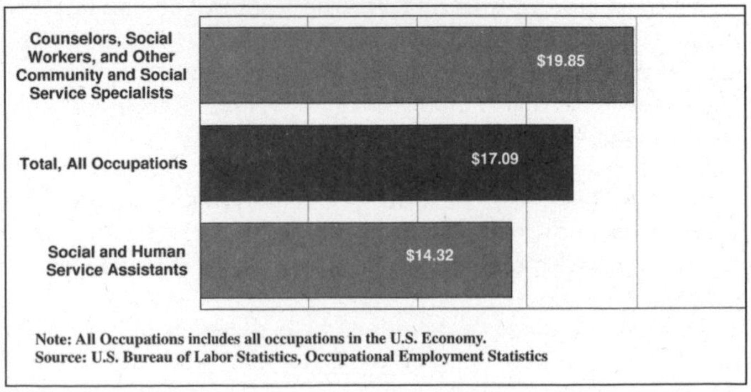

Percent Change in Employment, Projected 2014–2024

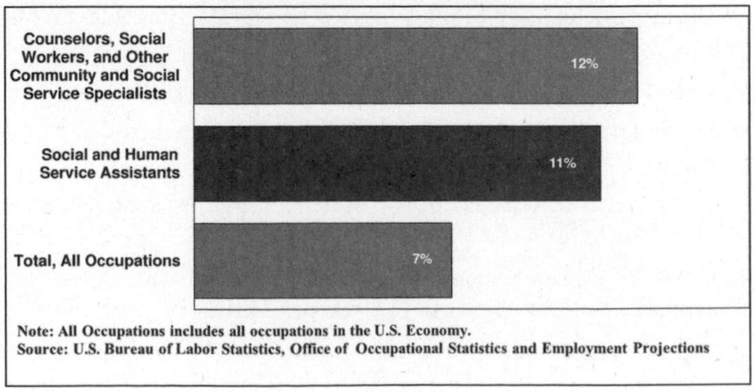

Employment Projections Data for Social and Human Service Assistants

Occupational Title	SOC Code	Employment, 2014	Projected Employment, 2024	Change, 2014–2024 Percent	Change, 2014–2024 Numeric
Social and human service assistants	21-1093	386,600	430,800	11	44,200

Source: U.S. Bureau of Labor Statistics, Employment Projections Program

Interpersonal skills. Social and human service assistants must make their clients feel comfortable discussing sensitive issues. Assistants also need to build relationships with other service providers to become familiar with all of the resources that are available in their communities.

Organizational skills. Social and human service assistants often must complete lots of paperwork and work with many different clients. They must be organized in order to ensure that the paperwork is filed properly and that clients are getting the help they need.

Problem-solving skills. Social and human service assistants help clients find solutions to their problems. They must be able to listen carefully to their clients' needs and offer practical solutions.

Time-management skills. Social and human service assistants often work with many clients. They must manage their time effectively to ensure that their clients are getting the attention they need.

Some employers require a criminal background check. In some settings, workers need a valid driver's license.

Pay

The median hourly wage for social and human service assistants was $14.32 in May 2014. The median wage is the wage at which half the workers in an occupation earned more than that amount and half earned less. The lowest 10 percent earned less than $9.55, and the highest 10 percent earned more than $22.85.

In May 2014, the median hourly wages for social and human service assistants in the top industries in which they worked were as follows:

State and local government, excluding education and hospitals	$17.07
Religious, grantmaking, civic, professional, and similar organizations	15.15
Individual and family services	14.04
Community and vocational rehabilitation services	12.84
Nursing and residential care facilities	12.65

Job Outlook

Employment of social and human service assistants is projected to grow 11 percent from 2014 to 2024, faster than the average for all occupations. Growth is projected due to a growing elderly population and rising demand for healthcare and social services.

The number of individuals who have access to health insurance is expected to continue to increase because of federal health insurance reform. An increase in the number of older adults is expected to result in growing demand for social services. The elderly population often needs services such as delivery of meals and adult daycare. Social and human service assistants, who help find and provide these services, will be needed to meet this increased demand.

In addition, growth is expected as more people seek treatment for their addictions and more drug offenders are sent to treatment programs rather than to jail. These phenomena should increase demand for social and human service assistants who work in treatment programs or work with people with addictions.

Social and human service assistants will continue to be needed to work in group homes, which are residences where individuals with

Similar Occupations. This table shows a list of occupations with job duties that are similar to those of social and human service assistants.

Occupations	Entry-level Education	2014 Median Pay	Projected Job Growth	Average Annual Openings
Childcare Workers	High school diploma or equivalent	$19,730	5%	6,930
Health Educators and Community Health Workers	See Education/Training	$42,450	13%	1,560
Home Health Aides	No formal educational credential	$21,380	38%	34,840
Mental Health Counselors and Marriage and Family Therapists	Master's degree	$42,250	19%	3,140
Personal Care Aides	No formal educational credential	$20,440	26%	45,810
Probation Officers and Correctional Treatment Specialists	Bachelor's degree	$49,060	4%	330
Rehabilitation Counselors	Master's degree	$34,380	9%	1,080
School and Career Counselors	Master's degree	$53,370	8%	2,250
Social and Community Service Managers	Bachelor's degree	$62,740	10%	1,320
Social Workers	See Education/Training	$45,500	12%	7,480
Substance Abuse and Behavioral Disorder Counselors	Bachelor's degree	$39,270	22%	2,120

particular needs can live and receive treatment. For example, there are group homes specifically for women or children of domestic abuse.

There also will be continued demand for child and family social and human service assistants. These workers will be needed to help others, such as social workers, investigate child abuse cases, as well as to place children in foster care and with adoptive families.

Job Prospects. Job prospects will be good overall but will be best for those with a degree in healthcare from an accredited college. Low pay and heavy workloads cause many workers to leave this occupation, creating opportunities for new workers entering the field.

Contacts for More Information

For more information about social and human service assistants, visit

- National Organization for Human Services (www.nationalhumanservices.org)

O*NET

- Social and Human Service Assistants (21-1093.00)

Social Workers

- **2014 Median Pay** .... $45,500 per year $21.88 per hour
- **Typical Entry-Level Education**.... See Education/Training
- **Work Experience in a Related Occupation**.............. None
- **On-the-job Training** .... None
- **Number of Jobs, 2014** 649,300
- **Job Outlook, 2014–24**............ 12% (Faster than average)
- **Employment Change, 2014–24** 74,800

What Social Workers Do

Social workers help people solve and cope with problems in their everyday lives. One group of social workers—clinical social workers—also diagnose and treat mental, behavioral, and emotional issues.

Duties. Social workers typically do the following:

- Identify people and communities in need of help
- Assess clients' needs, situations, strengths, and support networks to determine their goals
- Help clients adjust to changes and challenges in their lives, such as illness, divorce, or unemployment
- Research, refer, and advocate for community resources, such as food stamps, childcare, and healthcare to assist and improve a client's well-being.
- Respond to crisis situations such as child abuse and mental health emergencies
- Follow up with clients to ensure that their situations have improved
- Evaluate services provided to ensure that they are effective
- Develop and evaluate programs and services to ensure that basic client needs are met
- Provide psychotherapy services

Social workers help people cope with challenges in their lives. They help with a wide range of situations, such as adopting a child or being diagnosed with a terminal illness.

Social workers may work with children, people with disabilities, and people with serious illnesses and addictions. Their work varies based on the type of client they are working with.

Some social workers work with groups, community organizations, and policymakers to develop or improve programs, services, policies, and social conditions. This focus of work is referred to as macro social work.

Advocacy is an important aspect of social work. Social workers advocate or raise awareness with and on behalf of their clients and the social work profession on local, state, and national levels.

The following are examples of types of social workers:

Child and family social workers protect vulnerable children and help families in need of assistance. They help families find housing or services, such as childcare, or apply for benefits, such as food stamps. They intervene when children are in danger of neglect or abuse. Some help arrange adoptions, locate foster families, or work to reunite families.

Clinical social workers—also called *licensed clinical social workers*—diagnose and treat mental, behavioral, and emotional disorders, including anxiety and depression. They provide individual, group, family, and couples therapy; they work with clients to develop strategies to change behavior or cope with difficult situations; and they refer clients to other resources or services, such as support groups or other mental health professionals. Clinical social workers can develop treatment plans with the client, doctors, and other healthcare professionals and may adjust the treatment plan if necessary based on their client's progress. They may also provide mental healthcare to help children and families cope with changes in their lives, such as divorce or other family problems.

Many clinical social workers work in private practice. In these settings, clinical social workers also perform administrative and recordkeeping tasks, such as working with insurance companies in order to receive payment for their services. Some work in a group practice with other social workers or mental health professionals.

School social workers work with teachers, parents, and school administrators to develop plans and strategies to improve students' academic performance and social development. Students and their families are often referred to social workers to deal with problems such as aggressive behavior, bullying, or frequent absences from school.

Healthcare social workers help patients understand their diagnosis and make the necessary adjustments to their lifestyle, housing, or healthcare. For example, they may help people make the transition from the hospital back to their homes and communities. In addition, they may provide information on services, such as home healthcare or support groups, to help patients manage their illness or disease. Social workers help doctors and other healthcare professionals understand the effects that diseases and illnesses have on patients' mental and emotional health.

Some healthcare social workers specialize in geriatric social work, hospice and palliative care, or medical social work:

- *Geriatric social workers* help senior citizens and their families. They help clients find services, such as programs that provide older adults with meals or with home healthcare. They may provide information about assisted living facilities or nursing homes, or work with older adults in those settings. They help clients and their families make plans for possible health complications or for where clients will live if they can no longer care for themselves.
- *Hospice and palliative care social workers* help patients adjust to serious, chronic, or terminal illnesses. Palliative care focuses on relieving or preventing pain and other symptoms associated

with serious illness. Hospice is a type of palliative care for people who are dying. Social workers in this setting provide and find services, such as support groups or grief counselors, to help patients and their families cope with the illness or disease.

- *Medical social workers* in hospitals help patients and their families by linking patients with resources in the hospital and in their own community. They may work with medical staff to create discharge plans, make referrals to community agencies, facilitate support groups, or conduct follow-up visits with patients once they have been discharged.

Mental health and substance abuse social workers help clients with mental illnesses or addictions. They provide information on services, such as support groups and 12-step programs, to help clients cope with their illness. Many clinical social workers function in these roles as well.

Work Environment

Social workers held about 649,300 jobs in 2014. The industries that employed the most social workers were as follows:

State and local government, excluding education and hospitals	29%
Individual and family services	18
Ambulatory healthcare services	13
Hospitals; state, local, and private	11
Nursing and residential care facilities	9

They work in the following settings:

- Hospitals, primary care settings, and clinics, including veterans' clinics
- Senior centers and long-term care facilities
- Settlement houses and community centers
- Mental health clinics
- Private practices
- State and local governments
- Schools, colleges, and universities
- Substance abuse clinics
- Military bases and hospitals
- Correctional facilities
- Child welfare agencies
- Employee assistance programs

Although most social workers work in an office, they may spend time visiting clients. School social workers may be assigned to multiple schools and travel around the school district to see students. Understaffing and large caseloads may cause the work to be stressful.

Social workers may work remotely through distance counseling, using videoconferencing or mobile technology to meet with clients and organize support and advocacy groups. Distance counseling can be effective for clients with paranoia or social anxiety and for clients who live in rural areas.

Work Schedules. Social workers generally work full time. They sometimes work evenings, weekends, and holidays to see clients or attend meetings.

Education/Training

Although most social workers need a bachelor's degree in social work, clinical social workers must have a master's degree and 2 years of post-master's experience in a supervised clinical setting.

Social workers help people to cope with challenges in their lives by listening to and understanding their clients' needs.

Clinical social workers must also be licensed in the state in which they practice.

Education. A bachelor's degree in social work (BSW) is the most common requirement for entry-level positions. However, some employers may hire workers who have a bachelor's degree in a related field, such as psychology or sociology.

A BSW prepares students for direct-service positions such as caseworker or mental health assistant. These programs teach students about diverse populations, human behavior, social welfare policy, and ethics in social work. All programs require students to complete supervised fieldwork or an internship.

Some positions require a master's degree in social work (MSW), which generally takes 2 years to complete. Master's degree programs in social work prepare students for work in their chosen specialty by developing clinical assessment and management skills. All programs require students to complete a supervised practicum or an internship.

A bachelor's degree in social work is not required in order to enter a master's degree program in social work. Although a degree in almost any major is acceptable, courses in psychology, sociology, economics, and political science are recommended. Some programs allow graduates with a bachelor's degree in social work to earn their master's degree in 1 year.

In 2015, there were more than 500 bachelor's degree programs and more than 200 master's degree programs accredited by the Council on Social Work Education.

Some universities offer doctoral programs in social work, where students can earn a Doctorate of Social Work (DSW) or a Ph.D. Most doctoral programs in social work require students to have a master's in social work and experience in the field. Many doctor's students go on to work as postsecondary teachers.

Licenses, Certifications, and Registrations. Most states have licensure or certification requirements for nonclinical social workers. Requirements vary by state.

All states require clinical social workers to be licensed. However, some states provide exemptions for clinical social workers who work in government agencies. Becoming a licensed clinical social worker requires a master's degree in social work and a minimum of 2 years of supervised clinical experience after graduation. After

Median Annual Wages, May 2014

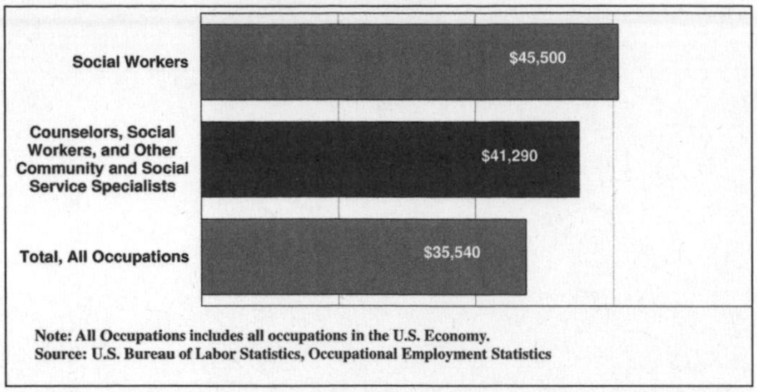

Percent Change in Employment, Projected 2014–2024

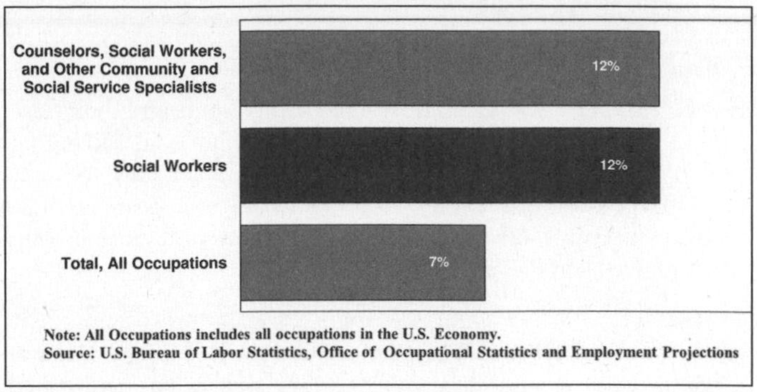

completing their supervised experience, clinical social workers must pass a clinical exam to be licensed.

Because licensing requirements vary by state, those interested should contact their state board. For more information about regulatory licensure boards by state, contact the Association of Social Work Boards.

Important Qualities

Communication skills. Clients talk to social workers about challenges in their lives. To effectively help, social workers must be able to listen to and understand their clients' needs.

Empathy. Social workers often work with people who are in stressful and difficult situations. To develop strong relationships, they must have compassion and empathy for their clients.

Interpersonal skills. Being able to work with different groups of people is essential for social workers. They need strong people skills to foster healthy and productive relationships with their clients and colleagues.

Organizational skills. Social workers must help and manage multiple clients, often assisting with their paperwork or documenting their treatment.

Problem-solving skills. Social workers need to develop practical and innovative solutions to their clients' problems.

Time-management skills. Social workers often have many clients and administrative responsibilities. They must effectively manage their time to provide adequate service to all of their clients.

Pay

The median annual wage for social workers was $45,500 in May 2014. The median wage is the wage at which half the workers in an occupation earned more than that amount and half earned less. The lowest 10 percent earned less than $28,240, and the highest 10 percent earned more than $75,850.

Median annual wages for social workers in May 2014 were as follows:

Social workers, all other	$59,100
Healthcare social workers	51,930
Child, family, and school social workers	42,120
Mental health and substance abuse social workers	41,380

Job Outlook

Overall employment of social workers is projected to grow 12 percent from 2014 to 2024, faster than the average for all occupations. Employment growth will be driven by increased demand for healthcare and social services, but will vary by social worker specialty.

Employment of child, family, and school social workers is projected to grow 6 percent from 2014 to 2024, about as fast as the average for all occupations. Child and family social workers will be needed to work with families to strengthen parenting skills, prevent child abuse, and identify alternative homes for children who are unable to live with their biological families. In schools, more social workers will be needed due to rising student enrollments. However, employment growth of child, family, and school social workers may be limited by federal, state, and local budget constraints.

Employment of healthcare social workers is projected to grow 19 percent from 2014 to 2024, much faster than the average for all occupations. Healthcare social workers will continue to be needed to help aging populations and their families adjust to new treatments, medications, and lifestyles.

Employment of mental health and substance abuse social workers is projected to grow 19 percent from 2014 to 2024, much faster than the average for all occupations. Employment will grow as more people seek treatment for mental illness and substance abuse. In addition, drug offenders are increasingly being sent to treatment programs, which are staffed by these social workers, rather than being sent to jail.

Job Prospects. Overall, job prospects should be good, particularly so for candidates with a master's degree and licensure.

Employment Projections Data for Social Workers

Occupational Title	SOC Code	Employment, 2014	Projected Employment, 2024	Change, 2014–2024 Percent	Change, 2014–2024 Numeric
Social workers	21-1020	649,300	724,100	12	74,800
Child, family, and school social workers	21-1021	305,200	324,200	6	19,000
Healthcare social workers	21-1022	160,100	191,000	19	30,900
Mental health and substance abuse social workers	21-1023	117,800	140,000	19	22,300
Social workers, all other	21-1029	66,400	68,900	4	2,500

Source: U.S. Bureau of Labor Statistics, Employment Projections Program

Similar Occupations. This table shows a list of occupations with job duties that are similar to those of social workers.

Occupations	Entry-level Education	2014 Median Pay	Projected Job Growth	Average Annual Openings
Health Educators and Community Health Workers	See Education/Training	$42,450	13%	1,560
Mental Health Counselors and Marriage and Family Therapists	Master's degree	$42,250	19%	3,140
Probation Officers and Correctional Treatment Specialists	Bachelor's degree	$49,060	4%	330
Psychologists	See Education/Training	$70,700	19%	3,250
Rehabilitation Counselors	Master's degree	$34,380	9%	1,080
School and Career Counselors	Master's degree	$53,370	8%	2,250
Social and Community Service Managers	Bachelor's degree	$62,740	10%	1,320
Social and Human Service Assistants	High school diploma or equivalent	$29,790	11%	4,420
Substance Abuse and Behavioral Disorder Counselors	Bachelor's degree	$39,270	22%	2,120

Contacts for More Information

For more information about social workers and clinical social workers, visit

- American Board of Examiners in Clinical Social Work (www.abecsw.org)
- Association for Community Organization and Social Administration (www.acosa.org)
- National Association of Social Workers (www.socialworkers.org)

For more information about accredited social work degree programs, visit

- Council on Social Work Education (www.cswe.org)
- MSW Guide (www.mswguide.org)
- Online MSW Programs (www.onlinemswprograms.com)

For more information about licensure requirements, visit

- Association of Social Work Boards (www.aswb.org)

O*NET

- Child, Family, and School Social Workers (21-1021.00)
- Healthcare Social Workers (21-1022.00)
- Mental Health and Substance Abuse Social Workers (21-1023.00)
- Social Workers, All Other (21-1029.00)

Substance Abuse and Behavioral Disorder Counselors

- **2014 Median Pay** .... $39,270 per year $18.88 per hour
- **Typical Entry-Level Education** .... Bachelor's degree
- **Work Experience in a Related Occupation** .... None
- **On-the-job Training** .... None
- **Number of Jobs, 2014** 94,900
- **Job Outlook, 2014–24** .... 22% (Much faster than average)
- **Employment Change, 2014–24** 21,200

What Substance Abuse and Behavioral Disorder Counselors Do

Substance abuse and behavioral disorder counselors advise people who suffer from alcoholism, drug addiction, eating disorders, or other behavioral problems. They provide treatment and support to help the client recover from addiction or modify problem behaviors.

Duties. Substance abuse and behavioral disorder counselors typically do the following:

- Evaluate clients' mental and physical health, addiction, or problem behavior and assess their readiness for treatment
- Help clients develop treatment goals and plans
- Review and recommend treatment options with clients and their families
- Help clients develop skills and behaviors necessary to recover from their addiction or modify their behavior
- Work with clients to identify behaviors or situations that interfere with their recovery
- Teach families about addiction or behavior disorders and help them develop strategies to cope with those problems
- Refer clients to other resources and services, such as job placement services and support groups
- Conduct outreach programs to help people identify the signs of addiction and other destructive behavior, as well as steps to take to avoid such behavior

Substance abuse and behavioral disorder counselors, also called *addiction counselors*, work with clients individually and in group sessions. Many incorporate the principles of 12-step programs, such as Alcoholics Anonymous (AA) to guide their practice. They teach clients how to cope with stress and life's problems in ways that help them recover. Furthermore, they help clients rebuild professional relationships and, if necessary, reestablish their career. They also help clients improve their personal relationships and find ways to discuss their addiction or other problems with family and friends.

Some addiction counselors work in facilities that employ many types of healthcare and mental health professionals. Addiction counselors may work with psychiatrists, social workers, physicians, and registered nurses to develop treatment plans and coordinate care for patients.

Some counselors work with clients who have been ordered by a judge to receive treatment for addiction. Others work with specific populations, such as teenagers, veterans, or people with disabilities. Some specialize in crisis intervention; these counselors step

Substance abuse and behavioral disorder counselors work with clients both one-on-one and in group counseling sessions.

in when someone is endangering his or her own life or the lives of others. Other counselors specialize in noncrisis interventions, which encourage a person with addictions or other issues to get help. Noncrisis interventions often are performed at the request of friends and family.

Some substance abuse and behavioral disorder counselors work in private practice, where they work alone or with a group of counselors or other professionals. These counselors manage their practice as a business. This includes working with clients and insurance companies to receive payment for their services. In addition, they market their practice to bring in new clients.

Work Environment

Substance abuse and behavioral disorder counselors held about 94,900 jobs in 2014. The industries that employed the most substance abuse and behavioral disorder counselors were as follows:

Outpatient care centers	22%
Residential intellectual and developmental disability, mental health, and substance abuse facilities	20
Individual and family services	14
Hospitals; state, local, and private	11
State and local government, excluding education and hospitals	10

They also work in halfway houses, detox centers, or in employee assistance programs (EAPs). EAPs are mental health programs provided by some employers to help employees deal with personal problems.

Some addiction counselors work in residential treatment centers, where clients live in the facility for a fixed period of time. Others work with clients in outpatient treatment centers. Some counselors work in private practice, where they may work alone or with a group of counselors or other professionals.

Although rewarding, the work of substance abuse and behavioral disorder counselors is often stressful. Many counselors have to deal with large workloads. They do not always have enough resources to meet the demand for their services. Also, they may have to intervene in crisis situations or work with agitated clients, which can be difficult.

Work Schedules. Most substance abuse and behavioral disorder counselors work full time. In some settings, such as inpatient facilities, they may need to work evenings, nights, or weekends.

Education/Training

Most positions require a bachelor's degree. Although most employers require a bachelor's degree, some positions require more or less education

Education. Most positions require a bachelor's degree. However, depending on the employer, educational requirements can vary from a high school diploma and certification to a master's degree. Workers with more education are able to provide more services to their clients, such as private one-on-one counseling sessions, and they require less supervision than those with less education. Those interested should research their state's educational requirements.

Licenses, Certifications, and Registrations. Substance abuse and behavioral disorder counselors in private practice must be licensed. Licensing requirements vary by state, but all states require a master's degree and 2,000 to 4,000 hours of supervised clinical experience. In addition, counselors must pass a state-issued exam and complete continuing education every year. Contact information for your state's regulating board can be found through the National Board for Certified Counselors.

The licensure or certification criteria for substance abuse and behavioral disorder counselors outside of private practice vary from state to state. For example, not all states require a specific degree, but many require applicants to pass an exam. Contact information for your state's licensing board can be found through the Addiction Technology Transfer Center Network.

Important Qualities

Compassion. Substance abuse and behavioral disorder counselors often work with people who are dealing with stressful and

Median Annual Wages, May 2014

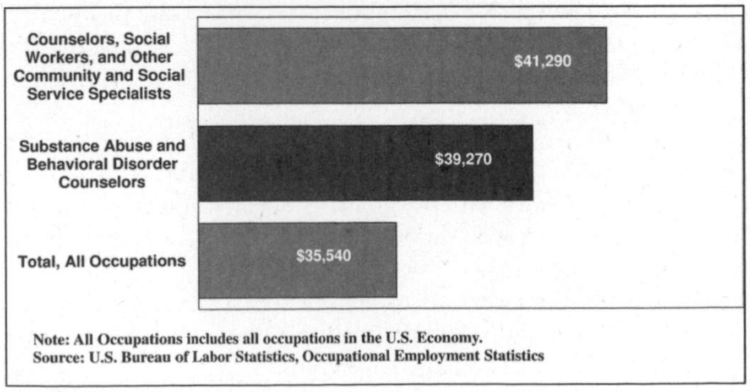

Percent Change in Employment, Projected 2014–2024

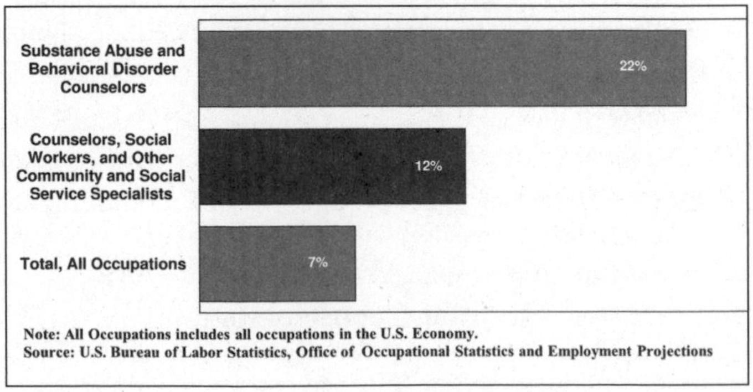

Employment Projections Data for Substance Abuse and Behavioral Disorder Counselors

Occupational Title	SOC Code	Employment, 2014	Projected Employment, 2024	Change, 2014–2024 Percent	Change, 2014–2024 Numeric
Substance abuse and behavioral disorder counselors	21-1011	94,900	116,200	22	21,200

Source: U.S. Bureau of Labor Statistics, Employment Projections Program

difficult situations, so they must be compassionate and empathize with their clients.

Interpersonal skills. They spend most of their time working directly with clients or other professionals and must be able to develop and nurture good relationships.

Listening skills. Good listening skills are essential for substance abuse and behavioral disorder counselors. They need to give their full attention to a client to be able to understand that client's problems and values.

Patience. Substance abuse and behavioral disorder counselors must be able to remain calm when working with all types of clients, including those who may be distressed or angry.

Speaking skills. Substance abuse and behavioral disorder counselors need to be able to effectively communicate with clients. They must express ideas and information in a way that their clients easily understand.

Pay

The median annual wage for substance abuse and behavioral disorder counselors was $39,270 in May 2014. The median wage is the wage at which half the workers in an occupation earned more than that amount and half earned less. The lowest 10 percent earned less than $25,310, and the highest 10 percent earned more than $61,420.

In May 2014, the median annual wages for substance abuse and behavioral disorder counselors in the top industries in which they worked were as follows:

Hospitals; state, local, and private	$45,870
State and local government, excluding education and hospitals	44,290
Outpatient care centers	38,630
Individual and family services	38,350
Residential intellectual and developmental disability, mental health, and substance abuse facilities	35,390

Job Outlook

Employment of substance abuse and behavioral disorder counselors is projected to grow 22 percent from 2014 to 2024, much faster than the average for all occupations. Growth is expected as addiction and mental health counseling services are increasingly covered by insurance policies.

The number of individuals who have access to health insurance is expected to continue to increase because of federal health insurance reform. The law requires insurance plans to cover treatment for mental health disorders in the same way as other chronic diseases. This will increase access to prevention and treatment services to those who were previously uninsured, did not have these services covered, or found treatment to be cost-prohibitive. Mental health centers, hospitals, and other treatment and counseling facilities will need to hire more counselors in order to meet this increased demand.

Demand for substance abuse and behavioral disorder counselors is also expected to increase as states seek treatment and counseling services for drug offenders rather than jail time. In recent years, the criminal justice system has recognized that drug and other substance abuse addicts are less likely to offend again if they get treatment for their addiction. As a result, sentences often require drug offenders to attend treatment and counseling programs. In addition, some research suggests that these programs are more cost effective than incarceration and may be increasingly used by states to deal with both budget cuts and overcrowded prisons.

Similar Occupations. This table shows a list of occupations with job duties that are similar to those of substance abuse and behavioral disorder counselors.

Occupations	Entry-level Education	2014 Median Pay	Projected Job Growth	Average Annual Openings
Mental Health Counselors and Marriage and Family Therapists	Master's degree	$42,250	19%	3,140
Physicians and Surgeons	Doctoral or professional degree	This wage is equal to or greater than $187,200.	14%	9,930
Psychologists	See Education/Training	$70,700	19%	3,250
Registered Nurses	Bachelor's degree	$66,640	16%	43,930
Rehabilitation Counselors	Master's degree	$34,380	9%	1,080
School and Career Counselors	Master's degree	$53,370	8%	2,250
Social and Community Service Managers	Bachelor's degree	$62,740	10%	1,320
Social and Human Service Assistants	High school diploma or equivalent	$29,790	11%	4,420
Social Workers	See Education/Training	$45,500	12%	7,480

Job Prospects. Job prospects are expected to be good for substance abuse and behavioral disorder counselors, particularly for those with a bachelor's or master's degree. In addition, many workers leave the field after a few years and need to be replaced. As result, those interested in entering this field should find favorable prospects.

Contacts for More Information

For more information about addiction counselors, visit

- Addiction Technology Transfer Center Network (www.nattc.org)
- NAADAC, The Association for Addiction Professionals (www.naadac.org)

For more information about counseling and counseling specialties, visit

- American Counseling Association (www.counseling.org)

For contact information for state regulating boards, visit

- National Board for Certified Counselors (www.nbcc.org)

O*NET

- Substance Abuse and Behavioral Disorder Counselors (21-1011.00)

Computer and Information Technology

Computer and Information Research Scientists

- **2014 Median Pay** .... $108,360 per year $52.09 per hour
- **Typical Entry-Level Education** .... Doctoral or professional degree
- **Work Experience in a Related Occupation** .... None
- **On-the-job Training** .... None
- **Number of Jobs, 2014** 25,600
- **Job Outlook, 2014–24** .... 11% (Faster than average)
- **Employment Change, 2014–24** 2,700

What Computer and Information Research Scientists Do

Computer and information research scientists invent and design new approaches to computing technology and find innovative uses for existing technology. They study and solve complex problems in computing for business, science, medicine, and other fields.

Duties. Computer and information research scientists typically do the following:

- Explore fundamental issues in computing and develop theories and models to address those issues
- Help scientists and engineers solve complex computing problems
- Invent new computing languages, tools, and methods to improve the way in which people work with computers
- Develop and improve the software systems that form the basis of the modern computing experience
- Design experiments to test the operation of these software systems
- Analyze the results of their experiments
- Publish their findings in academic journals and present their findings at conferences

Computer and information research scientists create and improve computer software and hardware.

Creating and improving software involves working with algorithms, which are sets of instructions that tell a computer what to do. Some computer tasks are very difficult and require complex algorithms. Computer and information research scientists try to simplify these algorithms to make computer systems as efficient as possible. The algorithms allow advancements in many types of technology, such as machine learning systems and cloud computing.

Computer and information research scientists design new computer architecture that improves the performance and efficiency of computer hardware. Their work often leads to technological advancements and efficiencies, such as better networking technology, faster computing speeds, and improved information security. In general, computer and information research scientists work at a more theoretical level than do other computer professionals.

Many people with a computer and information research science background become postsecondary teachers. In general, researchers in an academic setting focus on computer theory, although those working for businesses or scientific organizations usually focus on projects that may produce profits.

Some computer scientists work with electrical engineers, computer hardware engineers, and other specialists on multidisciplinary projects. The following are examples of types of specialties for computer and information research scientists:

Data mining. Computer and information research scientists write algorithms that are used to detect and analyze patterns in very large datasets. They improve ways to sort, manage, and display data. Computer scientists build algorithms into software packages that make the data easier for analysts to use. For example, they may create an algorithm to analyze a very large set of medical data in order to find new ways to treat diseases. They may also look for patterns in traffic data to help clear accidents faster.

Robotics. Some computer and information research scientists study how to improve robots. Robotics explores how a machine can interact with the physical world. Computer and information research scientists create the programs that control the robots. They work closely with engineers who focus on the hardware design of robots. Together, these workers test how well the robots do the tasks they were created to do, such as assemble cars and collect data on other planets.

Programming. Computer and information research scientists design new programming languages that are used to write software. The new languages make software writing more efficient by improving an existing language, such as Java, or by making a specific aspect of programming, such as image processing, easier.

Computer scientists develop theories that lead to technological innovation.

Work Environment

Computer and information research scientists held about 25,600 jobs in 2014. The industries that employed the most computer and information research scientists were as follows:

Federal government, excluding postal service	28%
Computer systems design and related services	18
Information	14
Research and development in the physical, engineering, and life sciences	12
Colleges, universities, and professional schools; state, local, and private	11

Most computer scientists employed by the federal government work for the Department of Defense.

Work Schedules. Most computer and information research scientists work full time. About 1 in 10 worked more than 40 hours per week in 2014.

Education/Training

The Ph.D. degree is the most common career-entry route for computer and information research scientists. In the federal government, a bachelor's degree may be sufficient for some jobs.

Education. Most computer and information research scientists need a Ph.D. in computer science or a related field, such as computer engineering. A Ph.D. usually requires 4 to 5 years of study after earning a bachelor's degree, typically in a computer-related field, such as computer science or information systems. During their first 2 years in a Ph.D. program, students take a variety of computer science classes. They then choose a specialty and spend the remaining years in the program doing research within that specialty.

Computer scientists who work in a specialized field may need knowledge of that field. For example, those working on biomedical applications may have to take some biology classes.

Advancement. Some computer scientists may become computer and information systems managers.

Important Qualities

Analytical skills. Computer and information research scientists must be organized in their thinking and analyze the results of their research to formulate conclusions.

Communication skills. Computer and information research scientists must communicate well with programmers and managers and be able to clearly explain their conclusions to people with no technical background. They often present their research at conferences.

Critical-thinking skills. Computer and information research scientists work on many complex problems.

Detail oriented. Computer and information research scientists must pay close attention to their work, because a small programming error can cause an entire project to fail.

Ingenuity. Computer and information research scientists must continually come up with innovative ways to solve problems, particularly when their ideas do not initially work as intended.

Logical thinking. Computer algorithms rely on logic. Computer and information research scientists must have a talent for reasoning.

Math skills. Computer and information research scientists must have knowledge of advanced math and other technical topics that are critical in computing.

Pay

The median annual wage for computer and information research scientists was $108,360 in May 2014. The median wage is the wage at which half the workers in an occupation earned more than that amount and half earned less. The lowest 10 percent earned less than $66,030, and the highest 10 percent earned more than $165,600.

In May 2014, the median annual wages for computer and information research scientists in the top industries in which they worked were as follows:

Computer systems design and related services	$117,480
Research and development in the physical, engineering, and life sciences	115,300
Information	112,590
Federal government, excluding postal service	104,390
Colleges, universities, and professional schools; state, local, and private	97,280

Job Outlook

Employment of computer and information research scientists is projected to grow 11 percent from 2014 to 2024, faster than the average for all occupations.

The research and development work of computer and information research scientists turns ideas into industry-leading technology. As demand for new and better technology grows, demand for computer scientists will grow as well.

Rapid growth in data collection by businesses will lead to an increased need for data-mining services. Computer scientists will be needed to write algorithms that help businesses make sense of very large amounts of data. With this information, businesses understand their consumers better, making the work of computer and information research scientists increasingly vital.

Median Annual Wages, May 2014

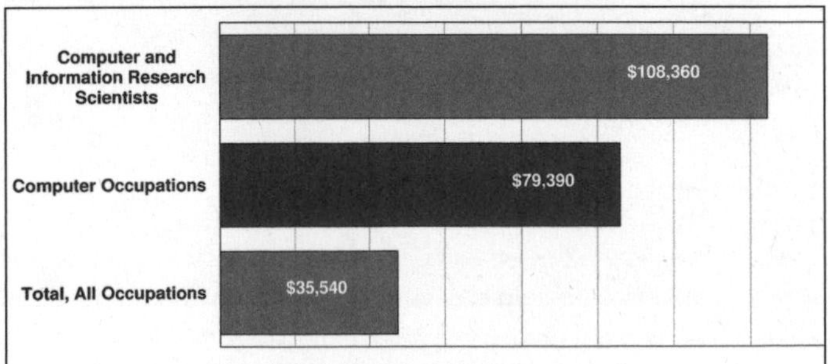

Note: All Occupations includes all occupations in the U.S. Economy.
Source: U.S. Bureau of Labor Statistics, Occupational Employment Statistics

Percent Change in Employment, Projected 2014–2024

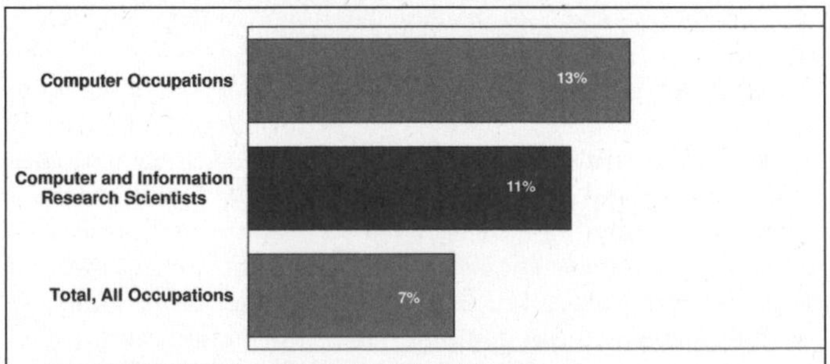

Note: All Occupations includes all occupations in the U.S. Economy.
Source: U.S. Bureau of Labor Statistics, Office of Occupational Statistics and Employment Projections

Employment Projections Data for Computer and Information Research Scientists

Occupational Title	SOC Code	Employment, 2014	Projected Employment, 2024	Change, 2014–2024 Percent	Change, 2014–2024 Numeric
Computer and information research scientists	15-1111	25,600	28,300	11	2,700

Source: U.S. Bureau of Labor Statistics, Employment Projections Program

Similar Occupations. This table shows a list of occupations with job duties that are similar to those of computer and information research scientists.

Occupations	Entry-level Education	2014 Median Pay	Projected Job Growth	Average Annual Openings
Computer and Information Systems Managers	Bachelor's degree	$127,640	15%	5,370
Computer Hardware Engineers	Bachelor's degree	$108,430	3%	240
Computer Programmers	Bachelor's degree	$77,550	-8%	-2,650
Database Administrators	Bachelor's degree	$80,280	11%	1,340
Mechanical Engineers	Bachelor's degree	$83,060	5%	1,460
Postsecondary Teachers	See Education/Training	$70,790	13%	17,700
Software Developers	Bachelor's degree	$97,990	17%	18,660

A growing emphasis on cybersecurity also should lead to new jobs, because computer scientists will be needed to find innovative ways to prevent cyberattacks.

In addition, an increase in demand for software may increase the need for computer scientists who create new programming languages to make software writing more efficient.

Job Prospects. Computer and information research scientists are likely to have excellent job prospects. There are a limited number of Ph.D. graduates each year. As a result, many companies report difficulties finding these highly skilled workers. Later in the decade, prospects will be even better, as older computer and information research scientists retire.

For applicants seeking employment in a specialized field, such as finance or biology, knowledge of that field, along with a computer science degree, may be helpful in getting a job.

Contacts for More Information

For more information about computer and information research scientists, visit

- Association for Computing Machinery (www.acm.org)
- IEEE Computer Society (www.computer.org)

For information about opportunities for women pursuing information technology careers, visit

- National Center for Women & Information Technology (www.ncwit.org)

O*NET

- Computer and Information Research Scientists (15-1111.00)

Computer Network Architects

- **2014 Median Pay** .... $98,430 per year $47.32 per hour
- **Typical Entry-Level Education** .... Bachelor's degree
- **Work Experience in a Related Occupation** .... 5 years or more
- **On-the-job Training** .... None
- **Number of Jobs, 2014** 146,200
- **Job Outlook, 2014–24** .... 9% (Faster than average)
- **Employment Change, 2014–24** 12,700

What Computer Network Architects Do

Computer network architects design and build data communication networks, including local area networks (LANs), wide area networks (WANs), and intranets. These networks range from small connections between two offices to next-generation networking capabilities such as a cloud infrastructure that serves multiple customers. Network architects must have extensive knowledge of an organization's business plan to design a network that can help the organization achieve its goals.

Duties. Computer network architects typically do the following:

- Create plans and layouts for data communication networks
- Present plans to management and explain why they are in the organization's best interest to pursue them
- Consider information security when designing networks
- Upgrade hardware, such as routers or adaptors, and software, such as network drivers, as needed to support computer networks
- Research new networking technologies to determine what would best support their organization in the future

Computer network architects, or *network engineers*, often work with their organization's chief technology officer (CTO) to predict where the organization will most need new networks. They spend most of their time planning these new networks. Some computer network architects work with engineers such as computer hardware engineers who help build the network a network architect has designed. Network architects are often experienced staff and have 5 to 10 years of experience working in network administration or with other information technology (IT) systems.

Computer network architects also create models to predict future network needs by analyzing current data traffic and estimating how growth will affect the network. They also keep up to date on new hardware and software technology and test how it can improve network performance. In addition, computer network architects have to keep security in mind and when network vulnerabilities arise, implement security patches or other countermeasures.

Work Environment

Computer network architects held about 146,200 jobs in 2014. The industries that employed the most computer network architects were as follows:

Computer systems design and related services	26%
Finance and insurance	11
Wired telecommunications carriers	9
Management of companies and enterprises	7
Government	6

Computer network architects spend most of their time in offices, but they occasionally work in server rooms, where they have access to the hardware that makes up an organization's computer and information network.

Work Schedules. Most computer network architects work full time. About 1 in 4 worked more than 40 hours per week in 2014.

Education/Training

Most computer network architects have a bachelor's degree in a computer-related field and experience in a related occupation, such as network and computer systems administrators.

Education. Computer network architects usually need at least a bachelor's degree in computer science, information systems, engineering, or a related field. Degree programs in a computer-related field give network architects hands-on laboratory work in classes such as network security or database design. These programs prepare network architects to be able to work with the wide array of technologies used in networks.

Employers of network architects sometimes prefer applicants to have a Master of Business Administration (MBA) in information systems. MBA programs generally require 2 years of study beyond the undergraduate level and include both business and computer-related courses.

Work Experience in a Related Occupation. Network architects generally need to have at least 5 to 10 years of experience working with information technology (IT) systems. They often have experience as a network and computer system administrator but also may come from other computer-related occupations such as database administrator or computer systems analyst.

Network architects design LANs, WANs, and intranets.

Certification. Certification programs are generally offered by product vendors or software firms. Vendor-specific certification verifies a set of skills to ensure network architects are able to work in specific networking environments. Companies may require their network architects to be certified in the products they use.

Advancement. Some network architects advance to become computer and information systems managers.

Important Qualities

Analytical skills. Computer network architects have to examine data networks and decide how to best connect the networks based on the needs and resources of the organization.

Detail oriented. Computer network architects create comprehensive plans of the networks they are creating with precise information describing how the network parts will work together.

Interpersonal skills. These workers must be able to work with different types of employees to successfully design and implement computer and information networks.

Leadership skills. Many computer network architects direct teams of engineers who build the networks they have designed, such as computer hardware engineers.

Organizational skills. Computer network architects who work for large firms must coordinate many different types of communication networks and make sure they work well together.

Pay

The median annual wage for computer network architects was $98,430 in May 2014. The median wage is the wage at which half the workers in an occupation earned more than that amount and

Median Annual Wages, May 2014

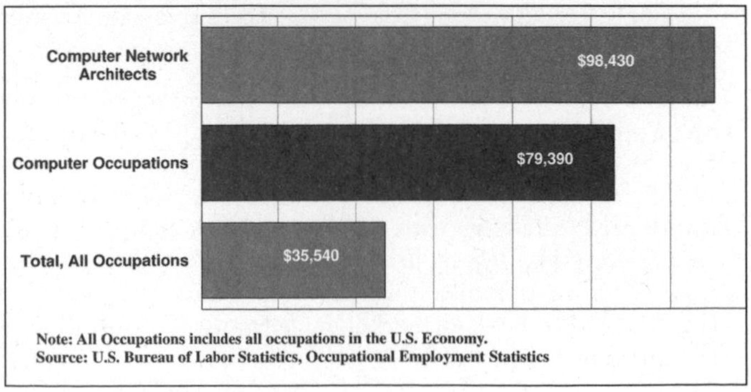

Percent Change in Employment, Projected 2014–2024

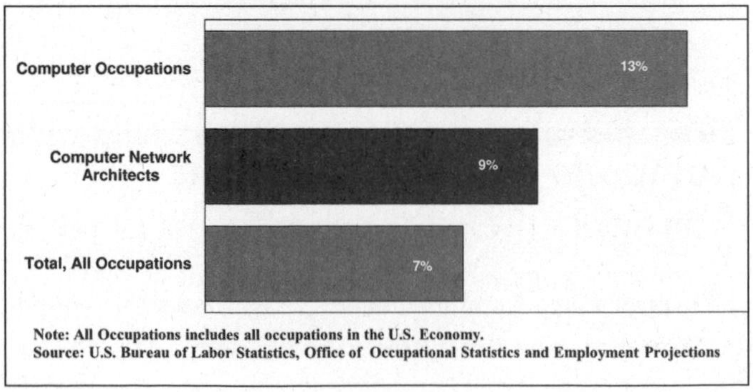

Employment Projections Data for Computer Network Architects

Occupational Title	SOC Code	Employment, 2014	Projected Employment, 2024	Change, 2014–2024 Percent	Change, 2014–2024 Numeric
Computer network architects	15-1143	146,200	158,900	9	12,700

Source: U.S. Bureau of Labor Statistics, Employment Projections Program

Similar Occupations. This table shows a list of occupations with job duties that are similar to those of computer network architects.

Occupations	Entry-level Education	2014 Median Pay	Projected Job Growth	Average Annual Openings
Computer and Information Research Scientists	Doctoral or professional degree	$108,360	11%	270
Computer and Information Systems Managers	Bachelor's degree	$127,640	15%	5,370
Computer Hardware Engineers	Bachelor's degree	$108,430	3%	240
Computer Programmers	Bachelor's degree	$77,550	-8%	-2,650
Computer Support Specialists	See Education/Training	$50,380	12%	8,880
Computer Systems Analysts	Bachelor's degree	$82,710	21%	11,860
Database Administrators	Bachelor's degree	$80,280	11%	1,340
Information Security Analysts	Bachelor's degree	$88,890	18%	1,480
Network and Computer Systems Administrators	Bachelor's degree	$75,790	8%	3,020
Software Developers	Bachelor's degree	$97,990	17%	18,660

half earned less. The lowest 10 percent earned less than $55,160, and the highest 10 percent earned more than $150,460.

In May 2014, the median annual wages for computer network architects in the top industries in which they worked were as follows:

Finance and insurance	$107,010
Wired telecommunications carriers	104,320
Computer systems design and related services	99,030
Management of companies and enterprises	97,460
Government	71,990

Job Outlook

Employment of computer network architects is projected to grow 9 percent from 2014 to 2024, faster than the average for all occupations.

Demand for computer network architects will increase as firms continue to expand their information technology (IT) networks. Designing and building these new networks, as well as upgrading existing ones, will create opportunities for computer network architects. The expansion of healthcare information technology will also contribute to employment growth.

Adoption of cloud computing, which allows users to access storage, software, and other computer services over the Internet, is likely to dampen the demand for computer network architects. Organizations will no longer have to design and build networks in-house; instead, firms that provide cloud services will do this. Smaller firms with minimal IT requirements will find it more cost effective to outsource their reliance on IT to cloud service providers. However, because architects at cloud providers can work on more than one organization's network, these providers will not have to employ as many architects as individual organizations do for the same amount of work.

Job Prospects. Applicants with relevant certification should have better prospects for positions where specific hardware or software knowledge and expertise is preferred.

Contacts for More Information

For more information about computer careers, visit

- Association for Computing Machinery (www.acm.org)
- IEEE Computer Society (www.computer.org)
- Computing Research Association (www.cra.org)
- CompTIA (www.comptia.org)

For information about opportunities for women pursuing information technology careers, visit

- National Center for Women & Information Technology (www.ncwit.org)

O*NET

- Computer Network Architects (15-1143.00)
- Telecommunications Engineering Specialists (15-1143.01)

Computer Programmers

- **2014 Median Pay** .... $77,550 per year $37.28 per hour
- **Typical Entry-Level Education** .... Bachelor's degree
- **Work Experience in a Related Occupation** .... None
- **On-the-job Training** .... None
- **Number of Jobs, 2014** 328,600
- **Job Outlook, 2014–24** .... -8% (Decline)
- **Employment Change, 2014–24** .... -26,500

What Computer Programmers Do

Computer programmers write and test code that allows computer applications and software programs to function properly. They turn the program designs created by software developers and engineers into instructions that a computer can follow. In addition, programmers test newly created applications and programs to ensure that they produce the expected results. If they do not work correctly, computer programmers check the code for mistakes and fix them.

Duties. Computer programmers typically do the following:

- Write programs in a variety of computer languages, such as C++ and Java
- Update and expand existing programs
- Test programs for errors and fix the faulty lines of computer code responsible
- Create and test code in an integrated development environment (IDE)
- Use code libraries, which are collections of independent lines of code, to simplify the writing

Programmers work closely with software developers, and in some businesses their duties overlap. When such overlap occurs, programmers can do work that is typical of developers, such as designing the program. Program design entails planning the software initially, creating models and flowcharts detailing how the code is to be written, writing and debugging code, and designing an application or systems interface. Programmers often use an IDE, which allows them to create, edit, and test code.

A program's purpose determines the complexity of its computer code. For example, a weather application for a mobile device will require less programming than a social-networking application. Simpler programs can be written in less time. Complex programs, such as computer operating systems, can take a year or more to complete.

Software-as-a-service (SaaS), which consists of applications provided through the Internet, is a growing field. Although programmers typically need to rewrite their programs to work on different system platforms, such as Windows or OS X, applications created with SaaS work on all platforms. Accordingly, programmers writing SaaS applications may not have to rewrite as much code as other programmers do and can instead spend more time writing new programs.

Work Environment

Computer programmers held about 328,600 jobs in 2014. The industries that employed the most computer programmers were as follows:

Programmers write instructions that a computer can follow, allowing it to perform specific tasks.

Computer systems design and related services	38%
Software publishers	7
Finance and insurance	7
Manufacturing	5
Administrative and support services	5

Programmers normally work alone, but sometimes work with other computer specialists on large projects. Because writing code can be done anywhere, many programmers telecommute.

Work Schedules. Most computer programmers work full time.

Education/Training

Most computer programmers have a bachelor's degree in computer science or a related subject; however, some employers hire workers with an associate's degree. Most programmers specialize in a few programming languages.

Education. Most computer programmers have a bachelor's degree; however, some employers hire workers who have an associate's degree. Most programmers get a degree in computer science

Median Annual Wages, May 2014

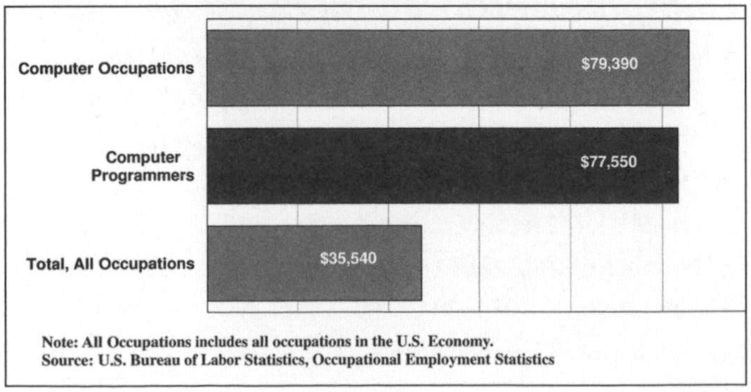

Percent Change in Employment, Projected 2014–2024

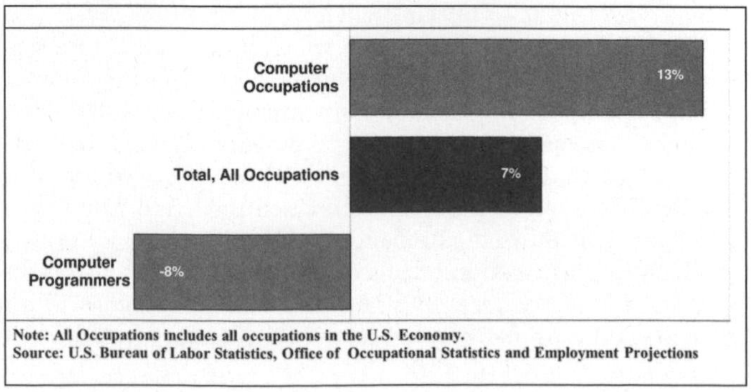

Employment Projections Data for Computer Programmers

Occupational Title	SOC Code	Employment, 2014	Projected Employment, 2024	Change, 2014–2024 Percent	Change, 2014–2024 Numeric
Computer programmers	15-1131	328,600	302,200	-8	-26,500

Source: U.S. Bureau of Labor Statistics, Employment Projections Program

or a related subject. Programmers who work in specific fields, such as healthcare or accounting, may take classes in that field to supplement their degree in computer programming. In addition, employers value experience, which many students gain through internships.

Most programmers learn a few computer languages while in school. However, a computer science degree gives students the skills needed to learn new computer languages easily. During their classes, students receive hands-on experience writing code, testing programs, fixing errors, and doing many other tasks that they will perform on the job.

To keep up with changing technology, computer programmers may take continuing education and professional development seminars to learn new programming languages or about upgrades to programming languages they already know.

Licenses, Certifications, and Registrations. Programmers can become certified in specific programming languages or for vendor-specific programming products. Some companies require their computer programmers to be certified in the products they use.

Other Experience. Many students gain experience in computer programming by completing an internship at a software company while in college.

Advancement. Programmers who have general business experience may become computer systems analysts. With experience, some programmers may become software developers. They may also be promoted to managerial positions. For more information, see the profiles on computer systems analysts, software developers, and computer and information systems managers.

Important Qualities

Analytical skills. Computer programmers must understand complex instructions in order to create computer code.

Concentration. Programmers must be able to work at a computer, writing lines of code for long periods.

Detail oriented. Computer programmers must closely examine the code they write because a small mistake can affect the entire computer program.

Troubleshooting skills. An important part of a programmer's job is to check the code for errors and fix any they find.

Pay

The median annual wage for computer programmers was $77,550 in May 2014. The median wage is the wage at which half the workers in an occupation earned more than that amount and half earned less. The lowest 10 percent earned less than $44,140, and the highest 10 percent earned more than $127,640.

In May 2014, the median annual wages for computer programmers in the top industries in which they worked were as follows:

Software publishers	$99,580
Finance and insurance	84,260
Administrative and support services	79,780
Manufacturing	76,910
Computer systems design and related services	76,240

Job Outlook

Employment of computer programmers is projected to decline 8 percent from 2014 to 2024. Computer programming can be done from anywhere in the world, so companies sometimes hire

Similar Occupations. This table shows a list of occupations with job duties that are similar to those of computer programmers.

Occupations	Entry-level Education	2014 Median Pay	Projected Job Growth	Average Annual Openings
Computer and Information Research Scientists	Doctoral or professional degree	$108,360	11%	270
Computer and Information Systems Managers	Bachelor's degree	$127,640	15%	5,370
Computer Hardware Engineers	Bachelor's degree	$108,430	3%	240
Computer Network Architects	Bachelor's degree	$98,430	9%	1,270
Computer Support Specialists	See Education/Training	$50,380	12%	8,880
Computer Systems Analysts	Bachelor's degree	$82,710	21%	11,860
Database Administrators	Bachelor's degree	$80,280	11%	1,340
Information Security Analysts	Bachelor's degree	$88,890	18%	1,480
Network and Computer Systems Administrators	Bachelor's degree	$75,790	8%	3,020
Software Developers	Bachelor's degree	$97,990	17%	18,660
Web Developers	Associate's degree	$63,490	27%	3,950

programmers in countries where wages are lower. This ongoing trend is projected to limit growth for computer programmers in the United States. However, the high costs associated with managing projects given to overseas programmers sometimes offsets the savings from the lower wages, causing some companies to bring back or keep programming jobs in the United States.

Many computer programmers work in the computer system design and related services industry, which is expected to grow as a result of increasing demand for new computer software. The software publishers industry is also expected to grow as the use of software offered over the Internet increases. This new use of software over the Internet should lower costs for firms and allow users more customization. In addition, new applications will have to be developed for mobile technology and the healthcare industry. An increase in computer systems that are built into electronics and other noncomputer products should result in some job growth for computer programmers and software developers.

Job Prospects. Job prospects will be best for programmers who have a bachelor's degree or higher and knowledge of a variety of programming languages. Keeping up to date with the newest programming tools will also improve job prospects.

Contacts for More Information

For more information about computer programmers, visit

- Association for Computing Machinery (www.acm.org)
- CompTIA (www.techamerica.org)
- IEEE Computer Society (www.computer.org)

For information about opportunities for women pursuing information technology careers, visit

- National Center for Women & Information Technology (www.ncwit.org)

O*NET

- Computer Programmers (15-1131.00)

Computer Support Specialists

- **2014 Median Pay** .... $50,380 per year, $24.22 per hour
- **Typical Entry-Level Education** .... See Education/Training
- **Work Experience in a Related Occupation** .... None
- **On-the-job Training** .... None
- **Number of Jobs, 2014** 766,900
- **Job Outlook, 2014–24** .... 12% (Faster than average)
- **Employment Change, 2014–24** 88,800

What Computer Support Specialists Do

Computer support specialists provide help and advice to people and organizations using computer software or equipment. Some, called computer network support specialists, support information technology (IT) employees within their organization. Others, called computer user support specialists, assist non-IT users who are having computer problems.

Duties. *Computer network support specialists* typically do the following:

- Test and evaluate existing network systems
- Perform regular maintenance to ensure that networks operate correctly
- Troubleshoot local area networks (LANs), wide area networks (WANs), and Internet systems

Computer network support specialists, also called *technical support specialists*, usually work in their organization's IT department. They help IT staff analyze, troubleshoot, and evaluate computer network problems. They play an important role in the routine maintenance of their organization's networks such as performing file backups on the network. Maintenance can be performed daily, weekly, or monthly and is important to an organization's disaster recovery efforts. Solving an IT problem promptly is important because organizations depend on their network systems. Network support specialists may assist the organization's computer users through phone, email, or in-person visits. They often work under network and computer systems administrators, who handle more complex tasks.

Computer user support specialists typically do the following:

- Pay attention to customers' descriptions of their computer problems
- Ask customers questions to properly diagnose the problem
- Walk customers through the recommended problem-solving steps
- Set up or repair computer equipment and related devices
- Train users to work with new computer hardware or software, such as printers, word-processing software, and email
- Provide other team members and managers in the organization with information about what gives customers the most trouble and about other concerns customers have

Computer user support specialists, also called *help-desk technicians*, usually provide technical help to non-IT computer users. They respond to phone and email requests for help. They can usually help users remotely, but they also may make site visits so that they can solve a problem in person.

Help-desk technicians may solve a range of problems that vary with the industry and the particular firm. Some technicians work for large software companies or for support service firms and must give instructions to business customers on how to use business-specific programs such as an electronic health records program used in hospitals or physicians' offices. Sometimes they work with other technicians to resolve problems.

Other help-desk technicians work in call centers, answering simpler questions from non-business customers. They may walk customers through basic steps in re-establishing an Internet connection or troubleshooting household IT products such as a Wi-Fi router.

Work Environment

Computer support specialists held about 766,900 jobs in 2014. They work in many different industries, including information technology (IT), education, finance, healthcare, and telecommunication. Many help-desk technicians work for outside support service firms on a contract basis and provide help to a range of businesses and consumers.

The industries that employed the most computer user support specialists in 2014 were as follows:

Computer systems design and related services	20%
Educational services; state, local, and private	13
Information	11
Administrative and support services	9
Wholesale trade	7

Computer support specialists work for a variety of industries.

The industries that employed the most computer network support specialists in 2014 were as follows:

Computer systems design and related services	20%
Wired telecommunications carriers	10
Finance and insurance	9
Educational services; state, local, and private	8
Wholesale trade	6

Faster computer networks are making it possible for some support specialists, particularly help-desk technicians, to work from a home office. However, a few specialized help-desk technicians may have to travel to a client's location to solve a problem.

Work Schedules. Most computer support specialists have full-time work schedules; however, many do not work typical 9-to-5 jobs. Because computer support is important for businesses, support specialists must be available 24 hours a day. As a result, many support specialists must work nights or weekends.

Education/Training

Because of the wide range of skills used in different computer support jobs, there are many paths into the occupation. A bachelor's degree is required for some computer support specialist positions, but an associate's degree or postsecondary classes may be enough for others.

Education. Education requirements for computer support specialists vary. Computer user support specialist jobs require some computer knowledge, but not necessarily a postsecondary degree. Applicants who have taken some computer-related classes are often qualified. For computer network support specialists, many employers accept applicants with an associate's degree, although some prefer applicants to have a bachelor's degree.

Large software companies that provide support to business users who buy their products or services often require a bachelor's degree. Positions that are more technical are likely to require a degree in a field such as computer science, engineering, or information science, but for others, the applicant's field of study is less important.

To keep up with changes in technology, many computer support specialists continue their education throughout their careers.

Certification. Certification programs are generally offered by vendors or from vendor-neutral certification providers. Certification validates the knowledge of and best practices required by computer support specialists. Companies may require their computer support specialists to hold certifications in the products the companies use.

Advancement. Many computer support specialists advance to other information technology positions, such as network and computer systems administrators and software developers. Some become managers in the computer support services department. Some organizations provide paths for support specialists to move into other parts of the organization, such as sales. For more information, see the profiles on network and computer systems administrators and software developers.

Important Qualities

Customer-service skills. Computer support specialists must be patient and sympathetic. They must often help people who are frustrated with the software or hardware they are trying to use.

Listening skills. Support workers must be able to understand the problems that their customers are describing and know when to ask questions to clarify the situation.

Problem-solving skills. Support workers must identify both simple and complex computer problems, analyze them, and solve them.

Median Annual Wages, May 2014

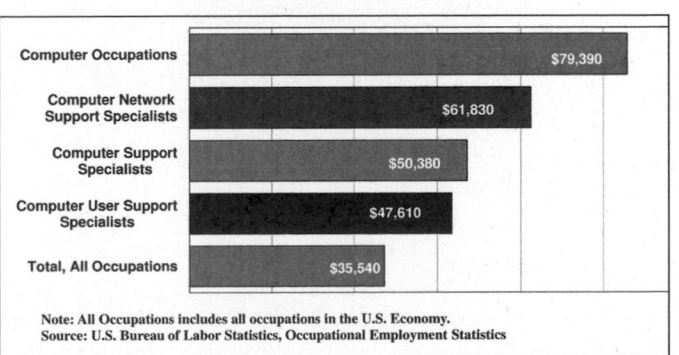

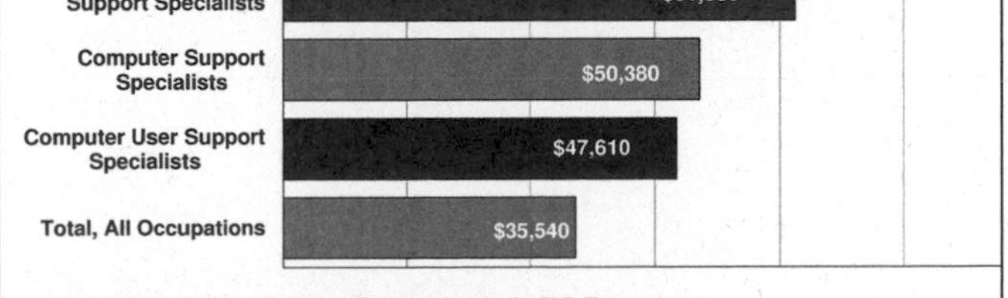

Note: All Occupations includes all occupations in the U.S. Economy.
Source: U.S. Bureau of Labor Statistics, Occupational Employment Statistics

Percent Change in Employment, Projected 2014–2024

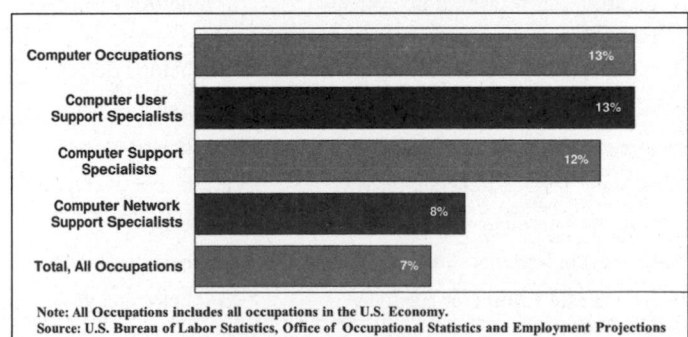

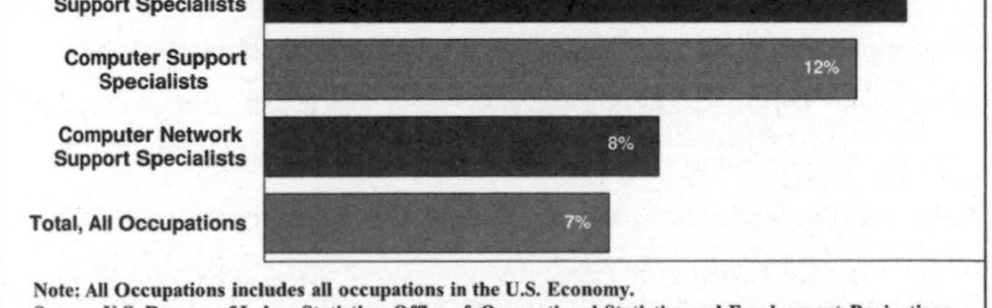

Note: All Occupations includes all occupations in the U.S. Economy.
Source: U.S. Bureau of Labor Statistics, Office of Occupational Statistics and Employment Projections

Employment Projections Data for Computer Support Specialists

Occupational Title	SOC Code	Employment, 2014	Projected Employment, 2024	Change, 2014–2024 Percent	Change, 2014–2024 Numeric
Computer support specialists	15-1150	766,900	855,700	12	88,800
Computer user support specialists	15-1151	585,900	661,000	13	75,100
Computer network support specialists	15-1152	181,000	194,600	8	13,600

Source: U.S. Bureau of Labor Statistics, Employment Projections Program

Speaking skills. Support workers must describe the solutions to computer problems in a way that a nontechnical person can understand.

Writing skills. Strong writing skills are useful for preparing instructions and email responses for employees and customers, as well as real-time web chat interactions.

Pay

The median annual wage for computer user support specialists was $47,610 in May 2014. The median wage is the wage at which half the workers in an occupation earned more than that amount and half earned less. The lowest 10 percent earned less than $28,280, and the highest 10 percent earned more than $80,180.

The median annual wage for computer network support specialists was $61,830 in May 2014. The lowest 10 percent earned less than $35,870, and the highest 10 percent earned more than $104,010.

In May 2014, the median annual wages for computer user support specialists in the top industries in which they worked were as follows:

Wholesale trade	$50,730
Information	49,050
Computer systems design and related services	47,940
Educational services; state, local, and private	44,670
Administrative and support services	43,780

In May 2014, median annual wages for computer network support specialists in the top industries in which they worked were as follows:

Wired telecommunications carriers	$71,950
Finance and insurance	67,260
Wholesale trade	63,460
Computer systems design and related services	63,200
Educational services; state, local, and private	51,940

Job Outlook

Employment of computer support specialists is projected to grow 12 percent from 2014 to 2024, faster than the average for all occupations. More support services will be needed as organizations upgrade their computer equipment and software. Computer support staff will be needed to respond to the installation and repair requirements of increasingly complex computer equipment and software. However, a rise in cloud computing could increase the productivity of computer support specialists, slowing their growth at many firms. Smaller businesses that do not have information technology (IT) departments will contract services from IT consulting firms and increase the demand for computer support specialists in those firms. Employment of support specialists in computer systems design and related firms is projected to grow 31 percent from 2014 to 2024.

Employment growth may also come from increasing demand for IT support services from healthcare industries. This field is expected to greatly increase its use of IT, and support services will be crucial to keep everything running properly.

Some lower level tech support jobs, commonly found in call centers, may be sent to countries that have lower wage rates. However, a recent trend to move jobs to lower cost regions of the United States may offset some loss of jobs to other countries.

Job Prospects. Job prospects should be favorable. There are usually clear advancement possibilities for computer support specialists, creating new job openings. Applicants with a bachelor's degree and a strong technical background should have the best job opportunities.

Similar Occupations. This table shows a list of occupations with job duties that are similar to those of computer support specialists.

Occupations	Entry-level Education	2014 Median Pay	Projected Job Growth	Average Annual Openings
Computer and Information Systems Managers	Bachelor's degree	$127,640	15%	5,370
Computer Network Architects	Bachelor's degree	$98,430	9%	1,270
Computer Programmers	Bachelor's degree	$77,550	-8%	-2,650
Computer Systems Analysts	Bachelor's degree	$82,710	21%	11,860
Customer Service Representatives	High school diploma or equivalent	$31,200	10%	25,290
Database Administrators	Bachelor's degree	$80,280	11%	1,340
Information Security Analysts	Bachelor's degree	$88,890	18%	1,480
Network and Computer Systems Administrators	Bachelor's degree	$75,790	8%	3,020
Software Developers	Bachelor's degree	$97,990	17%	18,660
Web Developers	Associate's degree	$63,490	27%	3,950

Contacts for More Information

For more information about computer support specialists, visit
- Technology Services Industry Association (www.tsia.com)
- Help Desk Institute (HDI) (www.thinkhdi.com)
- Association of Support Professionals (http://asponline.com)

For more information about computer careers, visit
- Association for Computing Machinery (www.acm.org)
- IEEE Computer Society (www.computer.org)
- Computing Research Association (www.cra.org)

For information about opportunities for women pursuing information technology careers, visit
- National Center for Women & Information Technology (www.ncwit.org)

O*NET

- Computer User Support Specialists (15-1151.00)
- Computer Network Support Specialists (15-1152.00)

Computer Systems Analysts

- **2014 Median Pay** .... $82,710 per year
  $39.76 per hour
- **Typical Entry-Level Education** .... Bachelor's degree
- **Work Experience in a Related Occupation**.............. None
- **On-the-job Training** .... None
- **Number of Jobs, 2014** 567,800
- **Job Outlook, 2014–24**.... 21% (Much faster than average)
- **Employment Change, 2014–24** 118,600

What Computer Systems Analysts Do

Computer systems analysts study an organization's current computer systems and procedures and design information systems solutions to help the organization operate more efficiently and effectively. They bring business and information technology (IT) together by understanding the needs and limitations of both.

Duties. Computer systems analysts typically do the following:

- Consult with managers to determine the role of IT systems in an organization
- Research emerging technologies to decide if installing them can increase the organization's efficiency and effectiveness
- Prepare an analysis of costs and benefits so that management can decide if IT systems and computing infrastructure upgrades are financially worthwhile
- Devise ways to add new functionality to existing computer systems
- Design and implement new systems by choosing and configuring hardware and software
- Oversee the installation and configuration of new systems to customize them for the organization
- Conduct testing to ensure that the systems work as expected
- Train the systems' end users and write instruction manuals

Computer systems analysts use a variety of techniques such as data modeling to design computer systems. Data modeling allows analysts to view the processes and data flows even before programs have been written.

Once programs have been written, analysts conduct in-depth tests and analyze information and trends in the data to increase a system's performance and efficiency.

Analysts calculate requirements for how much memory and speed the computer system needs. They prepare flowcharts or other kinds of diagrams for programmers or engineers to use when building the system. Analysts also work with these people to solve problems that arise after the initial system is set up. Most analysts do some programming in the course of their work.

Most computer systems analysts specialize in certain types of computer systems that are specific to the organization they work with. For example, an analyst might work predominantly with financial computer systems or engineering computer systems.

Systems analysts help other IT team members understand how computer systems can best serve an organization by working closely with the organization's business leaders.

In some cases, analysts who supervise the initial installation or upgrade of IT systems from start to finish may be called IT project managers. They monitor a project's progress to ensure that deadlines, standards, and cost targets are met. IT project managers who plan and direct an organization's IT department or IT policies are included in the profile on computer and information systems managers.

Many computer systems analysts are general-purpose analysts who develop new systems or fine-tune existing ones; however, there are some specialized systems analysts. The following are examples of types of computer systems analysts:

Systems designers or *systems architects* specialize in helping organizations choose specific types of hardware and software systems. They translate the long-term business goals of an organization into technical solutions. Analysts develop a plan for the computer systems that will be able to reach those goals. They work with management to ensure that systems and the IT infrastructure are set up to best serve the organization's mission.

Software quality assurance (QA) analysts do in-depth testing and diagnose problems of the systems they design in order to make sure that critical requirements are met. They also write reports to management recommending ways to improve the systems.

Programmer analysts design and update their system's software and create applications tailored to their organization's needs. They do more coding and debugging than other types of analysts, although they still work extensively with management and business

Computer systems analysts use information technology to help organizations operate more effectively.

analysts to determine what business needs the applications are meant to address. Other occupations that do programming are computer programmers and software developers.

Work Environment

Computer systems analysts held about 567,800 jobs in 2014. The industries that employed the most computer systems analysts were as follows:

Computer systems design and related services	27%
Finance and insurance	13
Management of companies and enterprises	8
Information	8
State and local government, excluding education and hospitals	7

Computer systems analysts can work directly for an organization or as consultants. Consultants usually work for an information technology firm. The projects that computer systems analysts work on usually require them to collaborate and coordinate with others.

Although technological advances have made telecommuting more common, consultants still need to travel to see their clients. The length of an assignment can vary with the complexity of the job.

Work Schedules. Most systems analysts work full time. About 1 in 5 worked more than 40 hours per week in 2014.

Education/Training

A bachelor's degree in a computer or information science field is common, although not always a requirement. Some firms hire analysts with business or liberal arts degrees who have skills in information technology or computer programming.

Education. Because these analysts also are heavily involved in the business side of a company, it may be helpful to take business courses or major in management information systems.

Some employers prefer applicants who have a master's degree in business administration (MBA) with a concentration in information systems. For more technically complex jobs, a master's degree in computer science may be more appropriate.

Although many computer systems analysts have technical degrees, such a degree is not always a requirement. Many analysts have liberal arts degrees and have gained programming or technical expertise elsewhere.

Many systems analysts continue to take classes throughout their careers so they can learn about new and innovative technologies. Technological advances come so rapidly in the computer field that continual study is necessary to remain competitive.

Systems analysts must understand the business field they are working in. For example, a hospital may want an analyst with a thorough understanding of health plans and programs such as Medicare and Medicaid, and an analyst working for a bank may need to understand finance. Systems analysts who know their industry can better communicate with managers to determine the role of the information technology (IT) systems in an organization.

Advancement. With experience, a systems analyst can advance to project manager and lead a team of analysts. Some can eventually become IT directors or chief technology officers. For more information, see the profile on computer and information systems managers.

Important Qualities

Analytical skills. Analysts must interpret complex information from various sources and be able to decide the best way to move forward on a project. They must also be able to figure out how changes may affect the project.

Communication skills. Analysts work as a go-between with management and the IT department and must be able to explain complex issues in a way that both will understand.

Creativity. Because analysts are tasked with finding innovative solutions to computer problems, an ability to "think outside the box" is important.

Pay

The median annual wage for computer systems analysts was $82,710 in May 2014. The median wage is the wage at which half the workers in an occupation earned more than that amount and half earned less. The lowest 10 percent earned less than $50,780, and the highest 10 percent earned more than $129,980.

In May 2014, the median annual wages for computer systems analysts in the top industries in which they worked were as follows:

Computer systems design and related services	$85,070
Management of companies and enterprises	84,760
Information	83,860
Finance and insurance	83,390
State and local government, excluding education and hospitals	73,620

Job Outlook

Employment of computer systems analysts is projected to grow 21 percent from 2014 to 2024, much faster than the average for all occupations.

As organizations across the economy increase their reliance on information technology (IT), analysts will be hired to design and install new computer systems. Smaller firms with minimal IT

Median Annual Wages, May 2014

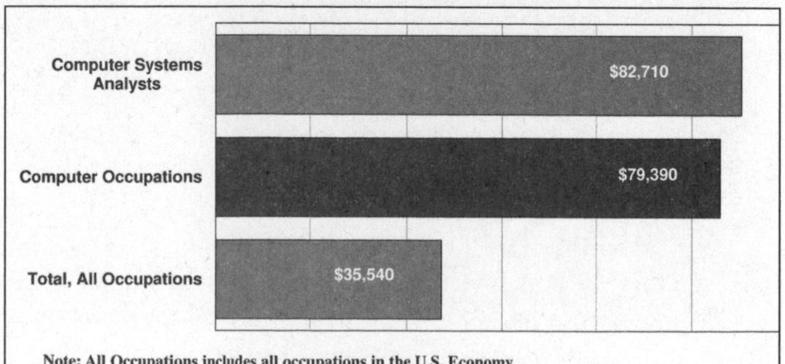

Percent Change in Employment, Projected 2014–2024

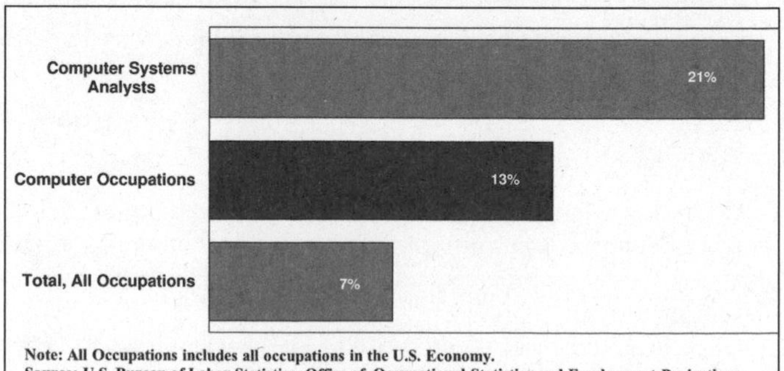

Employment Projections Data for Computer Systems Analysts

Occupational Title	SOC Code	Employment, 2014	Projected Employment, 2024	Change, 2014–2024	
				Percent	Numeric
Computer systems analysts	15-1121	567,800	686,300	21	118,600

Source: U.S. Bureau of Labor Statistics, Employment Projections Program

Similar Occupations. This table shows a list of occupations with job duties that are similar to those of computer systems analysts.

Occupations	Entry-level Education	2014 Median Pay	Projected Job Growth	Average Annual Openings
Actuaries	Bachelor's degree	$96,700	18%	440
Computer and Information Research Scientists	Doctoral or professional degree	$108,360	11%	270
Computer and Information Systems Managers	Bachelor's degree	$127,640	15%	5,370
Computer Network Architects	Bachelor's degree	$98,430	9%	1,270
Computer Programmers	Bachelor's degree	$77,550	-8%	-2,650
Database Administrators	Bachelor's degree	$80,280	11%	1,340
Information Security Analysts	Bachelor's degree	$88,890	18%	1,480
Management Analysts	Bachelor's degree	$80,880	14%	10,340
Network and Computer Systems Administrators	Bachelor's degree	$75,790	8%	3,020
Operations Research Analysts	Bachelor's degree	$76,660	30%	2,760
Software Developers	Bachelor's degree	$97,990	17%	18,660

requirements will find it more cost effective to outsource to cloud service providers or to industries that employ expert IT service providers. This will create additional job growth in the data processing, hosting, and related services industry and the computer systems design and related services industry, respectively.

Analysts who work in the computer systems design and related services industry move from one project to the next as they complete work for clients. As more small- and medium-sized firms demand advanced systems, the practice of analysts moving between businesses is expected to increase. Employment of systems analysts is projected to grow 33 percent in the computer systems design and related services industry from 2014 to 2024.

Additional job growth is expected in healthcare fields. Computer systems analysts will be needed to accommodate the anticipated increase in use and implementation of electronic health records, e-prescribing, and other forms of healthcare IT.

Job Prospects. Job applicants with a background in business may have better prospects because jobs for computer systems analysts often require knowledge of an organization's business needs. An understanding of the specific field an analyst is working in is also helpful. For example, a hospital may desire an analyst with a background or coursework in health management.

Contacts for More Information

For more information about computer systems analysts, visit

- ➤ Association for Computing Machinery (www.acm.org)
- ➤ IEEE Computer Society (www.computer.org)
- ➤ Computing Research Association (www.cra.org)

For information about opportunities for women pursuing information technology careers, visit

- ➤ National Center for Women & Information Technology (www.ncwit.org)

O*NET

- ➤ Computer Systems Analysts (15-1121.00)
- ➤ Informatics Nurse Specialists (15-1121.01)

Database Administrators

- **2014 Median Pay** .... $80,280 per year $38.60 per hour
- **Typical Entry-Level Education** .... Bachelor's degree
- **Work Experience in a Related Occupation** .... Less than 5 years
- **On-the-job Training** .... None
- **Number of Jobs, 2014** 120,000
- **Job Outlook, 2014–24** .... 11% (Faster than average)
- **Employment Change, 2014–24** 13,400

What Database Administrators Do

Database administrators use specialized software to store and organize data, such as financial information and customer shipping records. They make sure that data are available to users and are secure from unauthorized access.

Duties. Database administrators typically do the following:

- Ensure that organizational data is secure
- Back up and restore data to prevent data loss
- Identify user needs to create and administer databases
- Ensure that the database operates efficiently and without error
- Make and test modifications to the database structure when needed
- Maintain the database and update permissions
- Merge old databases into new ones

Database administrators, often called DBAs, make sure that data analysts can easily use the database to find the information they need and that the system performs as it should. DBAs sometimes work with an organization's management to understand the company's data needs and to plan the goals of the database. They also may work with computer and information systems managers to provide database solutions. Database administrators are responsible for backing up systems to prevent data loss in case of a power outage or other disaster. They also ensure the integrity of the database, guaranteeing that the data stored in it come from reliable sources.

Some DBAs oversee the development of new databases. They have to determine what the needs of the database are and who will be using it. They often monitor database performance and conduct performance-tuning support. Database administrators often plan security measures, making sure that data are secure from unauthorized access. Many databases contain personal or financial information, making security important.

Many database administrators are general-purpose DBAs and have all these duties. However, some DBAs specialize in certain tasks that vary with an organization and its needs. Two common specialties are as follows:

System DBAs are responsible for the physical and technical aspects of a database, such as installing upgrades and patches to fix program bugs. They typically have a background in system architecture and ensure that the firm's database management systems work properly.

Application DBAs support a database that has been designed for a specific application or a set of applications, such as customer-service software. Using complex programming languages, they may write or debug programs and must be able to manage the applications that work with the database. They also do all the tasks of a general DBA, but only for their particular application.

Work Environment

Database administrators held about 120,000 jobs in 2014. The industries that employed the most database administrators were as follows:

Database administrators usually need a bachelor's degree in a computer- or information-related subject.

Computer systems design and related services	15%
Information	12
Educational services; state, local, and private	11
Management of companies and enterprises	7
Insurance carriers and related activities	7

The largest number work for firms in the computer systems design and related services industry, such as data hosting and data processing firms. Other DBAs are employed by firms with large databases, such as insurance companies and banks, both of which keep track of vast amounts of personal and financial data for their clients. Some DBAs administer databases for retail companies that keep track of their buyers' credit card and shipping information; others work for healthcare firms and manage patients' medical records.

Work Schedules. Almost all database administrators work full time. About 1 in 5 worked more than 40 hours per week in 2014.

Education/Training

Database administrators (DBAs) usually have a bachelor's degree in an information- or computer-related subject such as computer science. Before becoming an administrator, these workers typically get work experience in a related field.

Education. Firms with large databases may prefer applicants who have a master's degree focusing on data or database management, typically either in computer science, information systems, or information technology.

Database administrators need an understanding of database languages, the most common of which is Structured Query

Median Annual Wages, May 2014

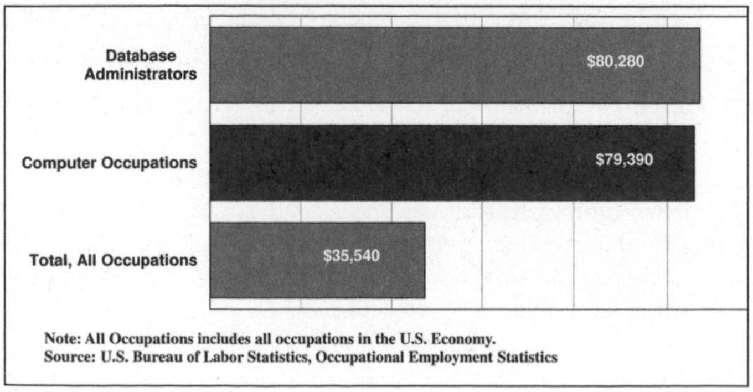

Percent Change in Employment, Projected 2014–2024

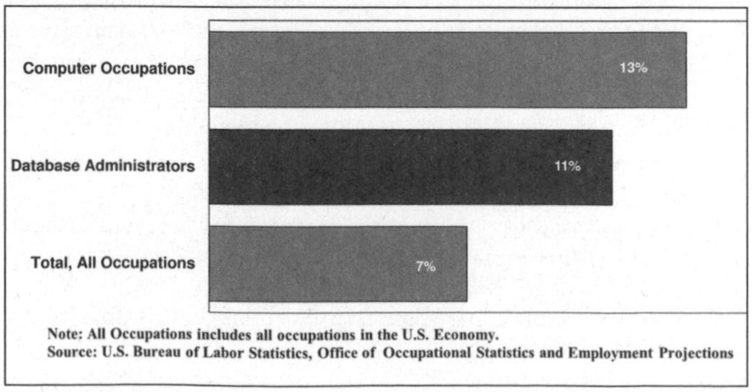

Employment Projections Data for Database Administrators

Occupational Title	SOC Code	Employment, 2014	Projected Employment, 2024	Change, 2014–2024 Percent	Change, 2014–2024 Numeric
Database administrators	15-1141	120,000	133,400	11	13,400

Source: U.S. Bureau of Labor Statistics, Employment Projections Program

Language, commonly called SQL. Most database systems use some variation of SQL, and a DBA will need to become familiar with whichever programming language the firm uses.

Licenses, Certifications, and Registrations. Certification is generally offered directly from software vendors or from vendor-neutral certification providers. Certification validates the knowledge and best practices required from DBAs. Companies may require their database administrators to be certified in the products they use.

Work Experience in a Related Occupation. Most do not begin their careers as database administrators. Many first work as database developers or data analysts. A database developer is a type of software developer who specializes in creating databases. The job of a data analyst is to interpret the information stored in a database in a way the firm can use. Depending on their specialty, data analysts can have different job titles, including financial analyst, market research analyst, and operations research analyst. After mastering one of these fields, they may become a database administrator. For more information, see the profiles on software developers, financial analysts, market research analysts, and operations research analysts.

Advancement. Database administrators can advance to become computer and information systems managers.

Important Qualities

Analytical skills. DBAs must be able to monitor a database system's performance to determine when action is needed. They must be able to evaluate complex information that comes from a variety of sources.

Communication skills. Most database administrators work on teams and must be able to communicate effectively with developers, managers, and other workers.

Detail oriented. Working with databases requires an understanding of complex systems, in which a minor error can cause major problems. For example, mixing up customers' credit card information can cause someone to be charged for a purchase he or she didn't make.

Logical thinking. Database administrators must make sense of data and organize it in a meaningful pattern so that it is easily retrievable.

Problem-solving skills. When problems with a database arise, administrators must be able to troubleshoot and correct the problems.

Pay

The median annual wage for database administrators was $80,280 in May 2014. The median wage is the wage at which half the workers in an occupation earned more than that amount and half earned less. The lowest 10 percent earned less than $44,470, and the highest 10 percent earned more than $123,780.

In May 2014, the median annual wages for database administrators in the top industries in which they worked were as follows:

Computer systems design and related services	$89,200
Management of companies and enterprises	87,910
Insurance carriers and related activities	85,200
Information	84,570
Educational services; state, local, and private	64,940

Job Outlook

Employment of database administrators (DBAs) is projected to grow 11 percent from 2014 to 2024, faster than the average for

Similar Occupations. This table shows a list of occupations with job duties that are similar to those of database administrators.

Occupations	Entry-level Education	2014 Median Pay	Projected Job Growth	Average Annual Openings
Computer and Information Systems Managers	Bachelor's degree	$127,640	15%	5,370
Computer Network Architects	Bachelor's degree	$98,430	9%	1,270
Computer Programmers	Bachelor's degree	$77,550	-8%	-2,650
Computer Support Specialists	See Education/Training	$50,380	12%	8,880
Computer Systems Analysts	Bachelor's degree	$82,710	21%	11,860
Financial Analysts	Bachelor's degree	$78,620	12%	3,230
Information Security Analysts	Bachelor's degree	$88,890	18%	1,480
Market Research Analysts	Bachelor's degree	$61,290	19%	9,230
Network and Computer Systems Administrators	Bachelor's degree	$75,790	8%	3,020
Operations Research Analysts	Bachelor's degree	$76,660	30%	2,760
Software Developers	Bachelor's degree	$97,990	17%	18,660
Web Developers	Associate's degree	$63,490	27%	3,950

all occupations. Growth in this occupation will be driven by the increased data needs of companies in all sectors of the economy. Database administrators will be needed to organize and present data in a way that makes it easy for analysts and other stakeholders to understand.

The increasing popularity of database-as-a-service, which allows database administration to be done by a third party over the Internet, could increase the employment of DBAs at cloud computing firms in the data processing, hosting, and related services industry. Employment of DBAs is projected to grow 26 percent in this industry from 2014 to 2024.

Employment of DBAs is projected to grow 26 percent in computer systems design and related services from 2014 to 2024. The increasing adoption of cloud services by small and medium-sized businesses that do not have their own dedicated information technology (IT) departments could increase the employment of DBAs in establishments in this industry.

Employment of DBAs is projected to grow 7 percent in general medical and surgical hospitals from 2014 to 2024. As the use of electronic medical records increases, more databases will be needed to keep track of patient information.

Job Prospects. Job prospects should be favorable. Database administrators are in high demand, and firms sometimes have difficulty finding qualified workers. Applicants who have experience with the latest technology should have the best prospects.

Contacts for More Information

For more information about database administrators, visit

➤ Association for Computing Machinery (www.acm.org)
➤ IEEE Computer Society (www.computer.org)
➤ Computing Research Association (www.cra.org)

For more information about opportunities for women pursuing information technology careers, visit

➤ National Center for Women & Information Technology (www.ncwit.org)

O*NET

➤ Database Administrators (15-1141.00)

Information Security Analysts

- **2014 Median Pay** .... $88,890 per year, $42.74 per hour
- **Typical Entry-Level Education** .... Bachelor's degree
- **Work Experience in a Related Occupation** .... Less than 5 years
- **On-the-job Training** .... None
- **Number of Jobs, 2014** 82,900
- **Job Outlook, 2014–24** .... 18% (Much faster than average)
- **Employment Change, 2014–24** 14,800

What Information Security Analysts Do

Information security analysts plan and carry out security measures to protect an organization's computer networks and systems. Their responsibilities are continually expanding as the number of cyberattacks increases.

Duties. Information security analysts typically do the following:

- Monitor their organization's networks for security breaches and investigate a violation when one occurs
- Install and use software, such as firewalls and data encryption programs, to protect sensitive information
- Prepare reports that document security breaches and the extent of the damage caused by the breaches
- Conduct penetration testing, which is when analysts simulate attacks to look for vulnerabilities in their systems before they can be exploited
- Research the latest information technology (IT) security trends
- Help plan and carry out an organization's way of handling security
- Develop security standards and best practices for their organization
- Recommend security enhancements to management or senior IT staff
- Help computer users when they need to install or learn about new security products and procedures

Information security analysts must continually adapt to stay a step ahead of cyberattackers. They must stay up to date on the latest methods attackers are using to infiltrate computer systems and on IT security. Analysts need to research new security technology to decide what will most effectively protect their organization. This may involve attending cybersecurity conferences to hear firsthand accounts of other professionals who have experienced new types of attacks.

IT security analysts are heavily involved with creating their organization's disaster recovery plan, a procedure that IT employees follow in case of emergency. These plans allow for the continued operation of an organization's IT department. It includes preventive measures such as regularly copying and transferring data to an offsite location. It also involves plans to restore proper IT functioning after a disaster. Analysts continually test the steps in their recovery plans.

Because information security is important, these workers usually report directly to upper management. Many information security analysts work with an organization's computer and information systems manager or chief technology officer (CTO) to design security or disaster recovery systems.

Work Environment

Information security analysts held about 82,900 jobs in 2014. The industries that employed the most information security analysts were as follows:

Computer systems design and related services	26%
Information	10
Management of companies and enterprises	8
Depository credit intermediation	7
Management, scientific, and technical consulting services	5

Many information security analysts work with other members of an information technology department, such as network administrators or computer systems analysts.

Work Schedules. Most information security analysts work full time. Information security analysts sometimes have to be on call outside of normal business hours in case of an emergency at their organization. About 1 in 4 worked more than 40 hours per week in 2014.

Education/Training

Most information security analyst positions require a bachelor's degree in a computer-related field. Employers usually prefer analysts to have experience in a related occupation.

Information security analysts install and use software, such as firewalls and data encryption programs, to protect sensitive information.

Education. Information security analysts usually need at least a bachelor's degree in computer science, programming, or a related field. As information security continues to develop as a career field, many schools are responding with information security programs for prospective job seekers. These programs may become a common path for entry into the occupation. Currently, a well-rounded computer education is preferred.

Employers of information security analysts sometimes prefer applicants who have a Master of Business Administration (MBA) in information systems. Programs offering the MBA in information systems generally require 2 years of study beyond the undergraduate level and include both business and computer-related courses.

Work Experience in a Related Occupation. Information security analysts generally need to have previous experience in a related occupation. Many analysts have experience in an information technology department, often as a network or systems administrator. Some employers look for people who have already worked in fields related to the one in which they are hiring. For example, if the job opening is in database security, they may look for a database administrator. If they are hiring in systems security, a computer systems analyst may be an ideal candidate.

Licenses, Certifications, and Registrations. There are a number of information security certifications available, and many employers prefer job candidates to have one. Certification validates the knowledge and best practices required from information security analysts. Some are general information security certificates, such as the Certified Information Systems Security Professional, and others have a narrow focus, such as penetration testing or systems auditing.

Advancement. Information security analysts can advance to become chief security officers or another type of computer and information systems manager.

Important Qualities

Analytical skills. Information security analysts must carefully study computer systems and networks and assess risks to determine how security policies and protocols can be improved.

Detail oriented. Because cyberattacks can be difficult to detect, information security analysts pay careful attention to their computer systems and watch for minor changes in performance.

Ingenuity. Information security analysts anticipate information security risks and implement new ways to protect their organizations' computer systems and networks.

Problem-solving skills. Information security analysts respond to security alerts and uncover and fix flaws in computer systems and networks.

Pay

The median annual wage for information security analysts was $88,890 in May 2014. The median wage is the wage at which half the workers in an occupation earned more than that amount and half earned less. The lowest 10 percent earned less than $50,300, and the highest 10 percent earned more than $140,460.

In May 2014, the median annual wages for information security analysts in the top industries in which they worked were as follows:

Management, scientific, and technical consulting services	$95,530
Information	94,000
Depository credit intermediation	92,930
Computer systems design and related services	88,680
Management of companies and enterprises	85,720

Job Outlook

Employment of information security analysts is projected to grow 18 percent from 2014 to 2024, much faster than the average for all occupations.

Demand for information security analysts is expected to be very high. Cyberattacks have grown in frequency, and analysts will be needed to come up with innovative solutions to prevent hackers from stealing critical information or creating problems for computer networks.

The federal government is expected to greatly increase its use of information security analysts to protect the nation's critical information technology (IT) systems. In addition, as the healthcare

Median Annual Wages, May 2014

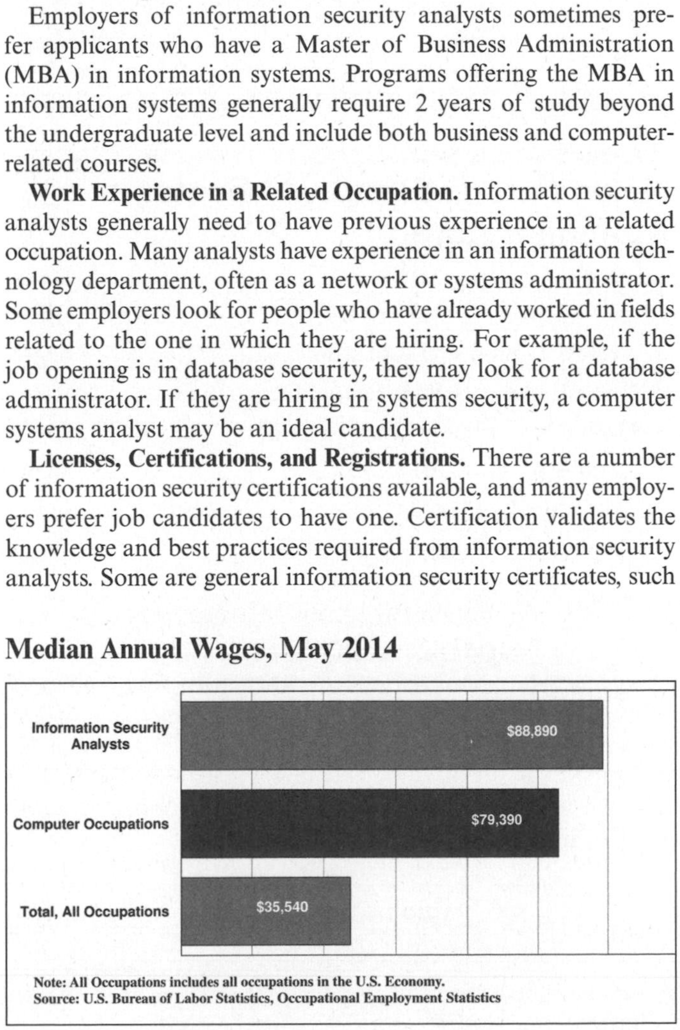

Percent Change in Employment, Projected 2014–2024

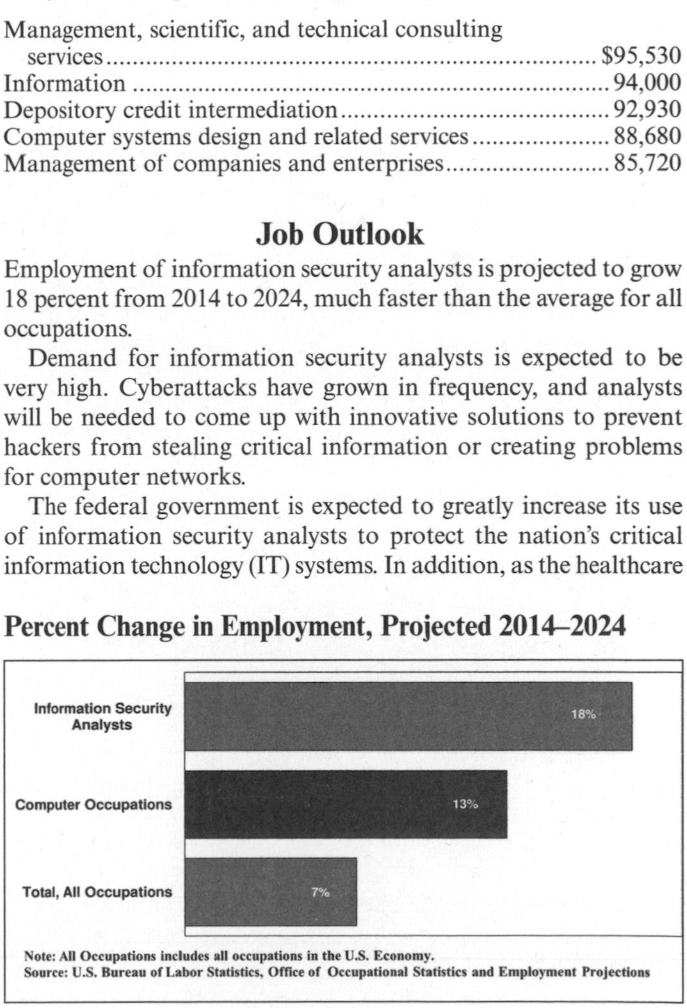

Employment Projections Data for Information Security Analysts

Occupational Title	SOC Code	Employment, 2014	Projected Employment, 2024	Change, 2014–2024 Percent	Change, 2014–2024 Numeric
Information security analysts	15-1122	82,900	97,700	18	14,800

Source: U.S. Bureau of Labor Statistics, Employment Projections Program

Similar Occupations. This table shows a list of occupations with job duties that are similar to those of information security analysts.

Occupations	Entry-level Education	2014 Median Pay	Projected Job Growth	Average Annual Openings
Computer and Information Research Scientists	Doctoral or professional degree	$108,360	11%	270
Computer and Information Systems Managers	Bachelor's degree	$127,640	15%	5,370
Computer Network Architects	Bachelor's degree	$98,430	9%	1,270
Computer Programmers	Bachelor's degree	$77,550	-8%	-2,650
Computer Support Specialists	See Education/Training	$50,380	12%	8,880
Computer Systems Analysts	Bachelor's degree	$82,710	21%	11,860
Database Administrators	Bachelor's degree	$80,280	11%	1,340
Information Security Analysts	Bachelor's degree	$88,890	18%	1,480
Network and Computer Systems Administrators	Bachelor's degree	$75,790	8%	3,020
Software Developers	Bachelor's degree	$97,990	17%	18,660
Web Developers	Associate's degree	$63,490	27%	3,950

industry expands its use of electronic medical records, ensuring patients' privacy and protecting personal data are becoming more important. More information security analysts are likely to be needed to create the safeguards that will satisfy patients' concerns.

Employment of information security analysts is projected to grow 36 percent in computer systems design and related services from 2014 to 2024. The increasing adoption of cloud services by small- and medium-sized businesses that do not have their own dedicated IT departments could increase the employment of information security analysts in those establishments.

Job Prospects. Job prospects for information security analysts should be good. Information security analysts with related work experience will have the best prospects. For example, an applicant with experience as a database administrator would have better prospects in database security than someone without that experience.

Contacts for More Information

For more information about computer careers, visit

- Association for Computing Machinery (www.acm.org)
- IEEE Computer Society (www.computer.org)
- Computing Research Association (www.cra.org)

For information about opportunities for women pursuing information technology careers, visit

- National Center for Women & Information Technology (www.ncwit.org)

O*NET

- Information Security Analysts (15-1122.00)

Network and Computer Systems Administrators

- **2014 Median Pay** .... $75,790 per year
  $36.44 per hour
- **Typical Entry-Level Education** .... Bachelor's degree
- **Work Experience in a Related Occupation** .... None
- **On-the-job Training** .... None
- **Number of Jobs, 2014** 382,600
- **Job Outlook, 2014–24** .... 8% (As fast as average)
- **Employment Change, 2014–24** 30,200

What Network and Computer Systems Administrators Do

Computer networks are critical parts of almost every organization. Network and computer systems administrators are responsible for the day-to-day operation of these networks. They organize, install, and support an organization's computer systems, including local area networks (LANs), wide area networks (WANs), network segments, intranets, and other data communication systems.

Duties. Network and computer systems administrators typically do the following:

- Determine an organization's network and computer system needs before setting one up
- Install all network hardware and software and make needed upgrades and repairs

Administrators need strong computer skills.

- Maintain network and computer system security and ensure that all systems are operating correctly
- Collect data in order to evaluate and optimize network or system performance
- Add users to a network and assign and update security permissions on the network
- Train users in the proper use of hardware and software
- Interpret and solve problems when a user or an automated monitoring system alerts them that one exists

Administrators manage an organization's servers and desktop and mobile equipment. They ensure that email and data storage networks work properly. They also make sure that employees' workstations are working efficiently and stay connected to the central computer network. Some administrators manage telecommunication networks.

In some cases, administrators help network architects design and analyze network models. They also participate in decisions about buying future hardware or software to upgrade their organization's network. Some administrators provide technical support to computer users, and they also may supervise computer support specialists who help solve users' problems.

Work Environment

Network and computer systems administrators held about 382,600 jobs in 2014. The industries that employed the most network and computer systems administrators were as follows:

Computer systems design and related services	16%
Information	11
Educational services; state, local, and private	10
Finance and insurance	8
Administrative and support services	7

Network and computer systems administrators work with many types of workers, including information technology (IT) workers, such as computer network architects and computer and information systems managers, and non-IT staff.

Work Schedules. In 2014, most network and computer systems administrators worked full time. Most organizations depend on their computer networks, so many administrators must work overtime to ensure that the networks are operating properly. About 1 in 4 of these administrators worked more than 40 hours per week in 2014.

Education/Training

Most employers require network and computer systems administrators to have a bachelor's degree in a field related to computer or information science. Others may require only a postsecondary certificate.

Education. Although some employers require only a postsecondary certificate, most require a bachelor's degree in a field related to computer or information science. There are degree programs that focus on computer network and system administration. However, because administrators work with computer hardware and equipment, a degree in computer engineering or electrical engineering usually is acceptable as well. Programs in these fields usually include classes in computer programming, networking, or systems design.

Because network technology is continually changing, administrators need to keep up with the latest developments. Many continue to take courses throughout their careers and attend information technology (IT) conferences to keep up with the latest technology. Some businesses require that an administrator get a master's degree.

Licenses, Certifications, and Registrations. Certification programs are generally offered directly from vendors or from vendor-neutral certification providers. Certification validates knowledge and best practices required from network and computer systems administrators. Companies may require their network and computer systems administrators to be certified in the product they use. Microsoft and Cisco offer some of the most common certifications.

Other Experience. To gain practical experience, many network administrators participate in internship programs while in school.

Advancement. Network administrators can advance to become computer network architects. They can also advance to managerial

Median Annual Wages, May 2014

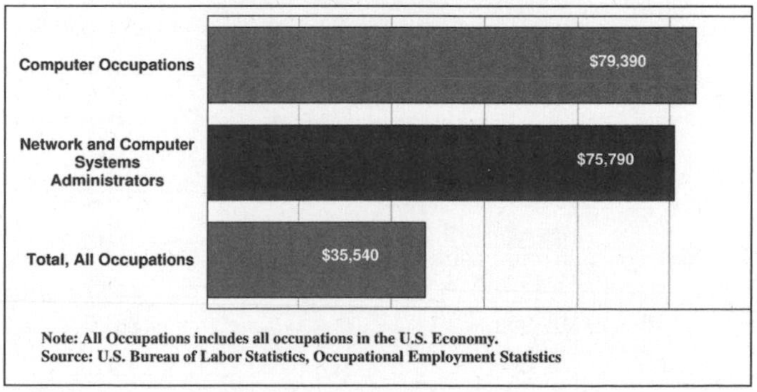

Note: All Occupations includes all occupations in the U.S. Economy.
Source: U.S. Bureau of Labor Statistics, Occupational Employment Statistics

Percent Change in Employment, Projected 2014–2024

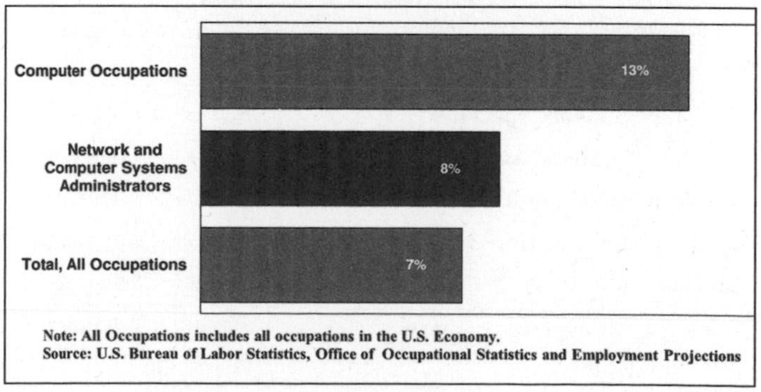

Note: All Occupations includes all occupations in the U.S. Economy.
Source: U.S. Bureau of Labor Statistics, Office of Occupational Statistics and Employment Projections

Employment Projections Data for Network and Computer Systems Administrators

Occupational Title	SOC Code	Employment, 2014	Projected Employment, 2024	Change, 2014–2024	
				Percent	Numeric
Network and computer systems administrators	15-1142	382,600	412,800	8	30,200

Source: U.S. Bureau of Labor Statistics, Employment Projections Program

jobs in information technology (IT) departments, such as computer and information systems managers.

Important Qualities

Analytical skills. Administrators need analytical skills to evaluate network and system performance and determine how changes in the environment will affect them.

Communication skills. Administrators must be able to describe problems and their solutions to non-IT workers.

Computer skills. Administrators oversee the connections of many different types of computer equipment and must ensure that they all work together properly.

Multitasking skills. Administrators may have to work on many problems and tasks at the same time.

Problem-solving skills. Administrators must be able to quickly resolve any problems that arise with computer networks.

Pay

The median annual wage for network and computer systems administrators was $75,790 in May 2014. The median wage is the wage at which half the workers in an occupation earned more than that amount and half earned less. The lowest 10 percent earned less than $46,220, and the highest 10 percent earned more than $120,000.

In May 2014, the median annual wages for network and computer systems administrators in the top industries in which they worked were as follows:

Information	$81,160
Computer systems design and related services	80,080
Finance and insurance	79,710
Administrative and support services	75,860
Educational services; state, local, and private	64,840

Job Outlook

Employment of network and computer systems administrators is projected to grow 8 percent from 2014 to 2024, about as fast as the average for all occupations. Demand for information technology workers is high and should continue to grow as firms invest in newer, faster technology and mobile networks. Growth is also expected in healthcare industries as their use of information technology increases. More administrators will be required to manage the growing systems and networks found at hospitals and other healthcare institutions. However, an increase in cloud computing could raise the productivity of network administrators, slowing their growth across many industries.

Employment of network administrators in the computer systems design and related services industry is projected to grow 31 percent from 2014 to 2024. The increasing adoption of cloud services by small and medium-sized businesses that do not have their own dedicated information technology (IT) departments could increase the demand for network and computer systems administrators in establishments within this industry.

Job Prospects. Job opportunities should be favorable in this occupation. Prospects should be best for applicants who have a bachelor's degree in computer network and system administration or computer science and who are up to date on the latest technology, especially cloud computing.

Contacts for More Information

For more information about computer careers, visit

➤ Association for Computing Machinery (www.acm.org)

➤ IEEE Computer Society (www.computer.org)

➤ CompTIA (www.techamerica.org)

Similar Occupations. This table shows a list of occupations with job duties that are similar to those of network and computer systems administrators.

Occupations	Entry-level Education	2014 Median Pay	Projected Job Growth	Average Annual Openings
Computer and Information Systems Managers	Bachelor's degree	$127,640	15%	5,370
Computer Hardware Engineers	Bachelor's degree	$108,430	3%	240
Computer Network Architects	Bachelor's degree	$98,430	9%	1,270
Computer Programmers	Bachelor's degree	$77,550	-8%	-2,650
Computer Support Specialists	See Education/Training	$50,380	12%	8,880
Computer Systems Analysts	Bachelor's degree	$82,710	21%	11,860
Database Administrators	Bachelor's degree	$80,280	11%	1,340
Electrical and Electronics Engineers	Bachelor's degree	$93,260	0%	-10
Information Security Analysts	Bachelor's degree	$88,890	18%	1,480
Software Developers	Bachelor's degree	$97,990	17%	18,660
Web Developers	Associate's degree	$63,490	27%	3,950

For information about opportunities for women pursuing information technology careers, visit

➤ National Center for Women & Information Technology (www.ncwit.org)

O*NET

➤ Network and Computer Systems Administrators (15-1142.00)

Software Developers

- **2014 Median Pay** .... $97,990 per year
  $47.11 per hour
- **Typical Entry-Level Education** .... Bachelor's degree
- **Work Experience in a Related Occupation** .... None
- **On-the-job Training** .... None
- **Number of Jobs, 2014** 1,114,000
- **Job Outlook, 2014–24** .... 17% (Much faster than average)
- **Employment Change, 2014–24** 186,600

What Software Developers Do

Software developers are the creative minds behind computer programs. Some develop the applications that allow people to do specific tasks on a computer or another device. Others develop the underlying systems that run the devices or that control networks.

Duties. Software developers typically do the following:

- Analyze users' needs and then design, test, and develop software to meet those needs
- Recommend software upgrades for customers' existing programs and systems
- Design each piece of an application or a system and plan how the pieces will work together
- Create a variety of models and diagrams (such as flowcharts) that instruct programmers how to write software code
- Ensure that a program continues to function normally through software maintenance and testing
- Document every aspect of an application or a system as a reference for future maintenance and upgrades
- Collaborate with other computer specialists to create optimum software

Software developers are in charge of the entire development process for a software program. They may begin by asking how the customer plans to use the software. They must identify the core functionality that users need from software programs. Software developers must also determine user requirements that are unrelated to the functionality of software, such as the level of security and performance needs. They design the program and then give instructions to programmers, who write computer code and test it.

If the program does not work as expected or if testers find it too difficult to use, software developers go back to the design process to fix the problems or improve the program. After the program is released to the customer, a developer may perform upgrades and maintenance.

Developers usually work closely with computer programmers. However, in some companies, developers write code themselves instead of giving instructions to the programmers.

Developers who supervise a software project from the planning stages through implementation sometimes are called information technology (IT) project managers. These workers monitor the project's progress to ensure that it meets deadlines, standards, and cost targets. IT project managers who plan and direct an organization's IT department or IT policies are included in the profile on computer and information systems managers.

Software developers design computer programs.

The following are examples of types of software developers:

Applications software developers design computer applications, such as word processors and games, for consumers. They may create custom software for a specific customer or commercial software to be sold to the general public. Some applications software developers create complex databases for organizations. They also create programs that people use over the Internet and within a company's intranet.

Systems software developers create the systems that keep computers functioning properly. These could be operating systems for computers that the general public buys or systems built specifically for an organization. Often, systems software developers also build the system's interface, which is what allows users to interact with the computer. Systems software developers are creating the operating systems that control most of the consumer electronics in use today, including the systems in phones or cars.

Work Environment

Software developers held about 1.1 million jobs in 2014. The industries that employed the most software developers were as follows:

Computer systems design and related services	33%
Software publishers	8
Finance and insurance	8
Computer and electronic product manufacturing	8
Management of companies and enterprises	4

Many software developers work for firms that deal in computer systems design and related services firms or for software publishers. Some systems developers work in computer- and electronic product–manufacturing industries. Applications developers work in office environments, such as offices of insurance carriers or corporate headquarters.

In general, software development is a collaborative process, and developers work on teams with others who also contribute to designing, developing, and programming successful software. However, some developers telecommute (work away from the office).

Work Schedules. Most software developers work full time, and long hours are common.

Median Annual Wages, May 2014

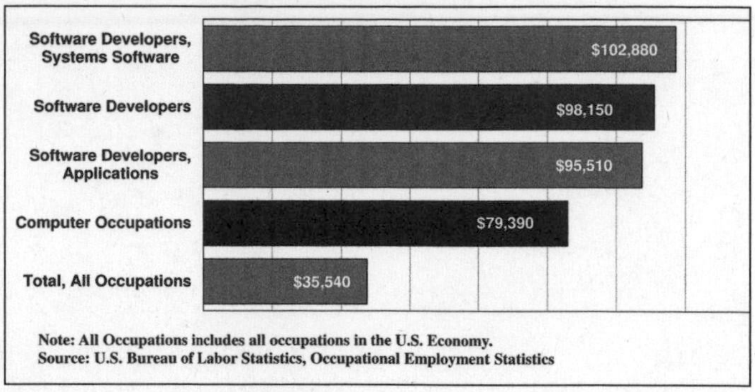

Percent Change in Employment, Projected 2014–2024

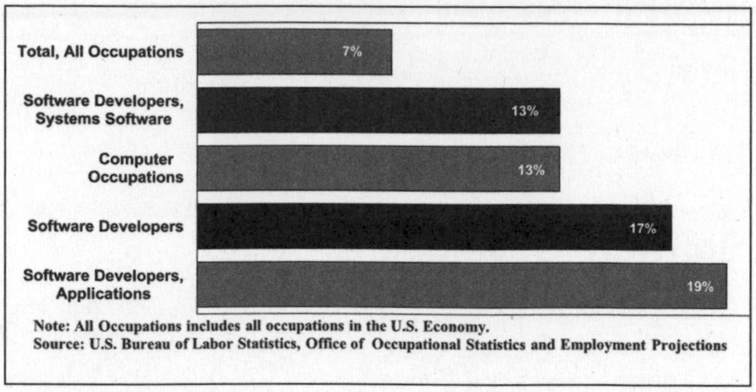

Education/Training

Software developers usually have a bachelor's degree in computer science and strong computer programming skills.

Education. Software developers usually have a bachelor's degree, typically in computer science, software engineering, or a related field. A degree in mathematics is also acceptable. Computer science degree programs are the most common, because they tend to cover a broad range of topics. Students should focus on classes related to building software in order to better prepare themselves for work in the occupation. For some positions, employers may prefer a master's degree.

Although writing code is not their first priority, developers must have a strong background in computer programming. They usually gain this experience in school. Throughout their career, developers must keep up to date on new tools and computer languages.

Software developers also need skills related to the industry in which they work. Developers working in a bank, for example, should have knowledge of finance so that they can understand a bank's computing needs.

Other Experience. Many students gain experience in software development by completing an internship at a software company while in college.

Some software developers first work as computer programmers and then are given more responsibility as they gain experience. Eventually, they become developers.

Advancement. Software developers can advance to become information technology (IT) project managers, also called computer and information systems managers, a position in which they oversee the software development process.

Important Qualities

Analytical skills. Developers must analyze users' needs and then design software to meet those needs.

Communication skills. Developers must be able to give clear instructions to others working on a project. They must also explain to their customers how the software works and answer any questions that arise.

Computer skills. Developers must understand computer capabilities and programming languages in order to design effective software.

Creativity. Developers are the creative minds behind new computer software.

Detail oriented. Developers often work on many parts of an application or system at the same time and must therefore be able to concentrate and pay attention to detail.

Interpersonal skills. Software developers must be able to work well with others who contribute to designing, developing, and programming successful software.

Problem-solving skills. Because developers are in charge of software from beginning to end, they must be able to solve problems that arise throughout the design process.

Pay

The median annual wage for software developers, applications was $95,510 in May 2014. The median wage is the wage at which half the workers in an occupation earned more than that amount and half earned less. The lowest 10 percent earned less than $56,310, and the highest 10 percent earned more than $149,480.

The median annual wage for software developers, systems software was $102,880 in May 2014. The lowest 10 percent earned less than $63,250, and the highest 10 percent earned more than $154,800.

In May 2014, the median annual wages for software developers in the top industries in which they worked were as follows:

Computer and electronic product manufacturing	$109,810
Software publishers	106,580
Finance and insurance	98,060
Computer systems design and related services	95,270
Management of companies and enterprises	94,890

Employment Projections Data for Software Developers

Occupational Title	SOC Code	Employment, 2014	Projected Employment, 2024	Change, 2014–2024 Percent	Change, 2014–2024 Numeric
Software developers	—	1,114,000	1,300,600	17	186,600
Software developers, applications	15-1132	718,400	853,700	19	135,300
Software developers, systems software	15-1133	395,600	447,000	13	51,300

Source: U.S. Bureau of Labor Statistics, Employment Projections Program

Similar Occupations. This table shows a list of occupations with job duties that are similar to those of software developers.

Occupations	Entry-level Education	2014 Median Pay	Projected Job Growth	Average Annual Openings
Computer and Information Research Scientists	Doctoral or professional degree	$108,360	11%	270
Computer and Information Systems Managers	Bachelor's degree	$127,640	15%	5,370
Computer Hardware Engineers	Bachelor's degree	$108,430	3%	240
Computer Network Architects	Bachelor's degree	$98,430	9%	1,270
Computer Programmers	Bachelor's degree	$77,550	-8%	-2,650
Computer Support Specialists	See Education/Training	$50,380	12%	8,880
Computer Systems Analysts	Bachelor's degree	$82,710	21%	11,860
Database Administrators	Bachelor's degree	$80,280	11%	1,340
Information Security Analysts	Bachelor's degree	$88,890	18%	1,480
Mathematicians	Master's degree	$103,720	21%	70
Postsecondary Teachers	See Education/Training	$70,790	13%	17,700
Web Developers	Associate's degree	$63,490	27%	3,950

Job Outlook

Employment of software developers is projected to grow 17 percent from 2014 to 2024, much faster than the average for all occupations. Employment of applications developers is projected to grow 19 percent, and employment of systems developers is projected to grow 13 percent. The main reason for the rapid growth in both applications developers and systems developers is a large increase in the demand for computer software.

The need for new applications on mobile devices and tablets will help increase the demand for application software developers.

The health and medical insurance and reinsurance carriers industry will need innovative software to manage new healthcare policy enrollments and administer existing policies digitally. As the number of people who use this digital platform increases over time, demand for software developers will grow.

Systems developers are likely to see new opportunities because of an increase in the number of products that use software. For example, more computer systems are being built into consumer electronics and other products, such as cell phones and appliances.

Concerns over threats to computer security could result in more investment in security software to protect computer networks and electronic infrastructure. In addition, an increase in software offered over the Internet should lower costs and allow more customization for businesses, also increasing demand for software developers.

Some outsourcing to foreign countries that offer lower wages may occur. However, because software developers should be close to their customers, the offshoring of this occupation is expected to be limited.

Job Prospects. Job prospects will be best for applicants with knowledge of the most up-to-date programming tools and for those who are proficient in one or more programming languages.

Contacts for More Information

For more information about software developers, visit

➤ Association for Computing Machinery (www.acm.org)
➤ IEEE Computer Society (www.ieee.org/index.html)
➤ Computing Research Association (www.cra.org)
➤ CompTIA (www.techamerica.org)

For information about opportunities for women pursuing information technology careers, visit

➤ National Center for Women & Information Technology (www.ncwit.org)

O*NET

➤ Software Developers, Applications (15-1132.00)
➤ Software Developers, Systems Software (15-1133.00)

Web Developers

- **2014 Median Pay** .... $63,490 per year
  $30.52 per hour
- **Typical Entry-Level Education** .... Associate's degree
- **Work Experience in a Related Occupation** .... None
- **On-the-job Training** .... None
- **Number of Jobs, 2014** 148,500
- **Job Outlook, 2014–24** .... 27% (Much faster than average)
- **Employment Change, 2014–24** 39,500

What Web Developers Do

Web developers design and create websites. They are responsible for the look of the site. They are also responsible for the site's technical aspects, such as its performance and capacity, which are measures of a website's speed and how much traffic the site can handle. In addition, web developers may create content for the site.

Duties. Web developers typically do the following:

- Meet with clients or management to discuss the needs and design of a website
- Create and test applications for a website
- Write code for websites, using programming languages such as HTML or XML
- Work with other team members to determine what information the site will contain

Developers build websites for all types of businesses.

- Work with graphics and other designers to determine the website's layout
- Integrate graphics, audio, and video into the website
- Monitor website traffic

When creating a website, developers have to make their client's vision a reality. They build particular types of websites, such as ecommerce, news, or gaming sites, to fit clients' needs. Different types of websites may require different applications to work right. For example, a gaming site should be able to handle advanced graphics, whereas an ecommerce site needs a payment-processing application. The developer decides which applications and designs will best fit the site.

Some developers handle all aspects of a website's construction, and others specialize in a certain aspect of it. The following are examples of types of specialized web developers:

Back-end web developers are responsible for the overall technical construction of the website. They create the basic framework of the site and ensure that it works as expected. Back-end web developers also establish procedures for allowing others to add new pages to the website and meet with management to discuss major changes to the site.

Front-end web developers are responsible for how a website looks. They create the site's layout and integrate graphics, applications (such as a retail checkout tool), and other content. They also write web-design programs in a variety of computer languages, such as HTML or JavaScript.

Webmasters maintain websites and keep them updated. They ensure that websites operate correctly, and they test for errors such as broken links. Many webmasters respond to user comments as well.

Work Environment

Web developers held about 148,500 jobs in 2014. The industries that employed the most web developers were as follows:

Computer systems design and related services	20%
Educational services; state, local, and private	7
Religious, grantmaking, civic, professional, and similar organizations	5
Publishing industries (except Internet)	5
Other information services	5

About 1 in 7 of web developers were self-employed in 2014.

Work Schedules. Most web developers work full time.

Education/Training

The typical education needed to become a web developer is an associate's degree in web design or a related field. Web developers need knowledge of both programming and graphic design.

Education. Educational requirements for web developers vary with the setting they work in and the type of work they do. Requirements range from a high school diploma to a bachelor's degree. An associate's degree in web design or related field is the most common requirement.

However, for more technical developer positions, such as back-end web developers, some employers prefer workers who have at least a bachelor's degree in computer science, programming, or a related field.

Web developers need to have a thorough understanding of HTML programming. The most recent version, HTML5, contains new features that web developers need to understand. Many employers also want developers to understand other programming languages, such as JavaScript or SQL, as well as have some knowledge of multimedia publishing tools, such as Flash. Throughout their careers, web developers must keep up to date on new tools and computer languages.

Some employers prefer web developers who have both a computer degree and coursework in graphic design, especially if the developer will be heavily involved in the website's visual appearance.

Advancement. Web developers who have a bachelor's degree can advance to become project managers. For more information, see the profile on computer and information systems managers.

Median Annual Wages, May 2014

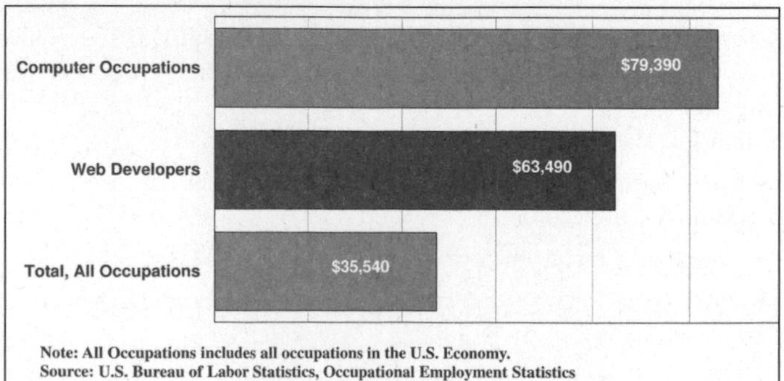

Percent Change in Employment, Projected 2014–2024

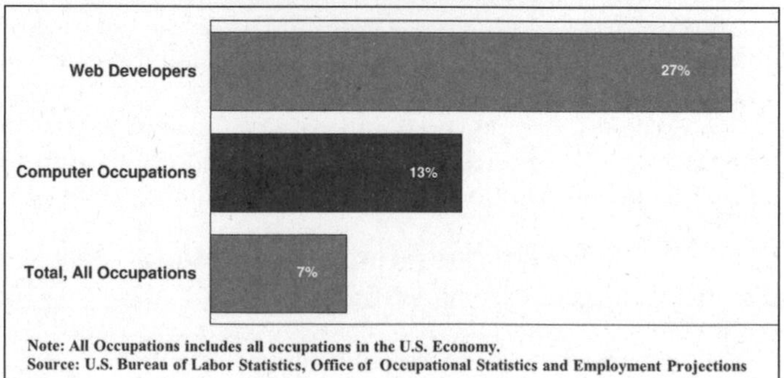

Employment Projections Data for Web Developers

Occupational Title	SOC Code	Employment, 2014	Projected Employment, 2024	Change, 2014–2024 Percent	Change, 2014–2024 Numeric
Web developers	15-1134	148,500	188,000	27	39,500

Source: U.S. Bureau of Labor Statistics, Employment Projections Program

Similar Occupations. This table shows a list of occupations with job duties that are similar to those of web developers.

Occupations	Entry-level Education	2014 Median Pay	Projected Job Growth	Average Annual Openings
Computer and Information Systems Managers	Bachelor's degree	$127,640	15%	5,370
Computer Programmers	Bachelor's degree	$77,550	-8%	-2,650
Computer Support Specialists	See Education/Training	$50,380	12%	8,880
Computer Systems Analysts	Bachelor's degree	$82,710	21%	11,860
Database Administrators	Bachelor's degree	$80,280	11%	1,340
Graphic Designers	Bachelor's degree	$45,900	1%	360
Information Security Analysts	Bachelor's degree	$88,890	18%	1,480
Multimedia Artists and Animators	Bachelor's degree	$63,630	6%	390
Software Developers	Bachelor's degree	$97,990	17%	18,660

Important Qualities

Concentration. Web developers must sit at a computer and write detailed code for long periods.

Creativity. Web developers often are involved in designing the appearance of a website and must make sure that it looks innovative and up to date.

Customer-service skills. Webmasters have to respond politely and correctly to user questions and requests.

Detail oriented. When web developers write in HTML, a minor error could cause an entire webpage to stop working.

Pay

The median annual wage for web developers was $63,490 in May 2014. The median wage is the wage at which half the workers in an occupation earned more than that amount and half earned less. The lowest 10 percent earned less than $33,790, and the highest 10 percent earned more than $112,680.

In May 2014, the median annual wages for web developers in the top industries in which they worked were as follows:

Other information services	$67,270
Publishing industries (except Internet)	66,380
Computer systems design and related services	64,850
Religious, grantmaking, civic, professional, and similar organizations	59,170
Educational services; state, local, and private	58,930

Job Outlook

Employment of web developers is projected to grow 27 percent from 2014 to 2024, much faster than the average for all occupations.

Employment of web developers is projected to grow as ecommerce continues to expand. Online purchasing is expected to grow faster than the overall retail industry. As retail firms expand their online offerings, demand for web developers will increase. In addition, an increase in the use of mobile devices to search the web will lead to an increase in employment of web developers. Instead of designing a website for a desktop computer, developers will have to create sites that work on mobile devices with many different screen sizes, leading to more work.

Because websites can be built from anywhere in the world, some web developer jobs may be moved to countries with lower wages, decreasing employment growth. However, this practice may decline because the cost of managing web developers in multiple countries can offset the savings to businesses. Furthermore, web developers must understand cultural nuances that allow webpages to communicate effectively with users, and domestic web developers are better equipped for this task, curtailing the work that may be moved to other countries.

Job Prospects. Job opportunities for web developers are expected to be good. Those with knowledge of multiple programming languages and digital multimedia tools, such as Flash and Photoshop, will have the best opportunities.

Contacts for More Information

For more information about web developers, visit

- World Organization of Webmasters (http://webprofessionals.org)

For more information about computer careers, visit

- Association for Computing Machinery (www.acm.org)
- IEEE Computer Society (www.computer.org)
- Computing Research Association (www.cra.org)

For information about opportunities for women pursuing information technology careers, visit

- National Center for Women & Information Technology (www.ncwit.org)

O*NET

- Web Developers (15-1134.00)

Construction and Extraction

Boilermakers

- **2014 Median Pay** .... $59,860 per year
  $28.78 per hour
- **Typical Entry-Level Education** .... High school diploma or equivalent
- **Work Experience in a Related Occupation** .... None
- **On-the-job Training** .... Apprenticeship
- **Number of Jobs, 2014** 17,400
- **Job Outlook, 2014–24** .... 9% (Faster than average)
- **Employment Change, 2014–24** 1,500

What Boilermakers Do

Boilermakers assemble, install, and repair boilers, closed vats, and other large vessels or containers that hold liquids and gases.

Duties. Boilermakers typically do the following:

- Use blueprints to determine locations, positions, or dimensions of parts
- Install small premade boilers into buildings and manufacturing facilities
- Lay out prefabricated parts of larger boilers before assembling them
- Assemble boiler tanks, often using robotic or automatic welders
- Test and inspect boiler systems for leaks or defects
- Clean vats, using scrapers, wire brushes, and cleaning solvents
- Replace or repair broken valves, pipes, or joints, using hand and power tools, gas torches, and welding equipment

Boilers, tanks, and vats are used in many buildings, factories, and ships. Boilers heat water or other fluids under extreme pressure to generate electric power and to provide heat. Large tanks and vats are used to process and store chemicals, oil, beer, and hundreds of other products.

Boilers are made out of steel, iron, copper, or stainless steel. Manufacturers are increasingly automating the production of boilers to improve the quality of these vessels. However, boilermakers still use many tools to assemble or repair boilers. For example, they often use hand and power tools or flame-cutting torches to align, cut, and shape pieces for a boiler. Boilermakers also may use plumb bobs, levels, wedges, and turnbuckles to align pieces accurately.

If the plate sections are very large, cranes lift the parts into place. Once boilermakers have the parts lined up, they use metalworking machinery and other tools to remove irregular edges so that the parts fit together properly. They then join the parts by bolting, welding, or riveting them together.

In addition to installing and maintaining boilers and other vessels, boilermakers help erect and repair air pollution abatement equipment, blast furnaces, water treatment plants, storage and process tanks, and smokestacks. Boilermakers also install refractory brick and other heat-resistant materials in fireboxes or pressure vessels. Some install and maintain the huge pipes used in dams to send water to and from hydroelectric power generation turbines.

Because boilers last a long time—sometimes 50 years or more—boilermakers must maintain them regularly by upgrading parts. As a result, they frequently inspect fittings, feed pumps, safety and check valves, water and pressure gauges, and boiler controls.

Work Environment

Boilermakers held about 17,400 jobs in 2014. The industries that employed the most boilermakers were as follows:

Building equipment contractors	30%
Utility system construction	12
Fabricated metal product manufacturing	11

Boilermakers perform physically demanding and dangerous work. They often work outdoors in all types of weather, including extreme heat and cold.

Because dams, boilers, storage tanks, and pressure vessels are large, boilermakers frequently work at great heights. When working on a dam, for example, they may be hundreds of feet above the ground.

Boilermakers also work in cramped quarters inside boilers, vats, or tanks that are often dark, damp, noisy, and poorly ventilated.

Injuries and Illnesses. Although boilermakers often use dangerous equipment, they have lower rates of injuries and illnesses than many other construction occupations. Still, common injuries include burns from acetylene torches, cuts from power grinders, muscle strains from lifting heavy parts and tools, and bruises or broken bones from falling off ladders or large vessels.

Boilermakers weld sections of the boiler together.

Median Annual Wages, May 2014

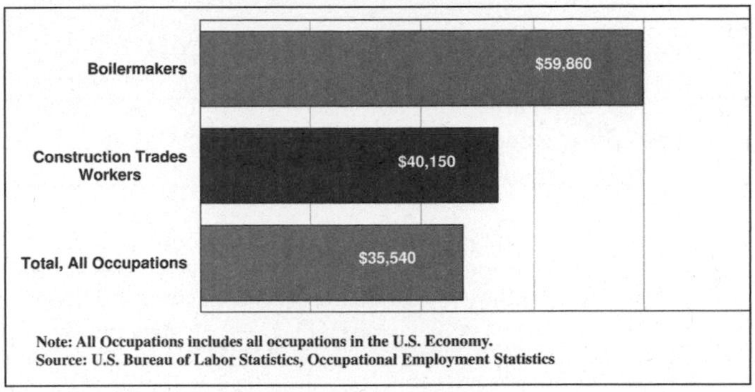

Percent Change in Employment, Projected 2014–2024

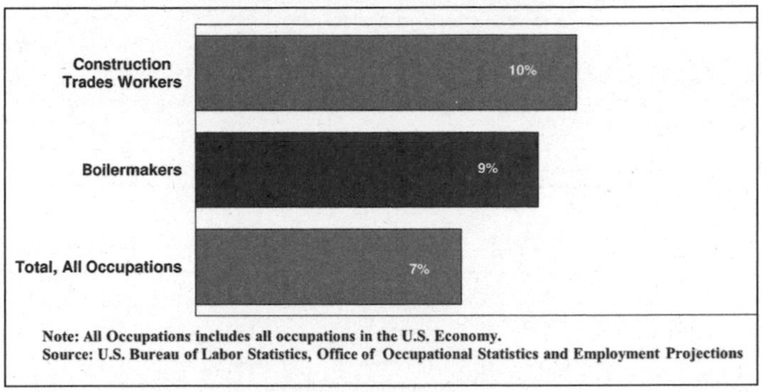

To reduce the chance of injuries, boilermakers often wear hardhats, harnesses, protective clothing, earplugs, and safety glasses. In addition, when working inside enclosed spaces, boilermakers frequently wear a respirator.

Work Schedules. Nearly all boilermakers work full time and may experience extended periods of overtime when equipment is shut down for maintenance. Overtime work also may be necessary to meet construction or production deadlines, especially during the spring and fall seasons, when many power plants receive routine maintenance. In contrast, because most field construction and repair work is contract work, there may be periods of unemployment when a contract is complete. There may be periods of unemployment during the winter and summer, when major maintenance is complete.

Many boilermakers must travel to worksites and live away from home for long periods.

Education/Training

Most boilermakers learn their trade through an apprenticeship program. Candidates are more likely to be accepted into training programs if they already have welding experience and certification.

Education. A high school diploma or equivalent is generally required. High school courses in math and welding are considered useful.

Training. Most boilermakers learn their trade through a 4- or 5-year apprenticeship. Each year, apprentices must have at least 144 hours of related technical training and 2,000 hours of paid on-the-job training. During technical training, apprentices learn about metals and installation techniques, as well as basic mathematics, blueprint reading and sketching, general construction techniques, safety practices, and first aid. On the job, apprentices learn how to signal crane operators and use the tools and equipment of the trade. Those who already have welding experience complete training sooner than those without it.

A few groups, including unions and contractor associations, sponsor apprenticeship programs. The basic qualifications for entering an apprenticeship program are as follows:

- Minimum age of 18
- High school education or equivalent
- Physically able to do the work

In addition to satisfying these qualifications, candidates with certified or documented welding experience usually have priority over applicants without experience. Some apprenticeship programs have preferred entry for veterans.

When they finish the apprenticeship program, boilermakers are considered to be journey workers, performing tasks under the guidance of experienced workers.

Some boilermakers enter the trade through training in similar occupations, such as pipefitters, millwrights, sheet metal workers, or welders. Much of the core training of those occupations is similar to that of boilermakers.

Important Qualities

Mechanical skills. Boilermakers use and maintain a large variety of equipment, such as hoists and welding machines.

Physical stamina. Boilermakers must have high endurance because they spend many hours on their feet while lifting heavy boiler components.

Physical strength. Boilermakers must be strong enough to move heavy vat components into place.

Unafraid of confined spaces. Boilermakers often work inside boilers and vats, so they cannot be claustrophobic.

Unafraid of heights. Some boilermakers must work at great heights. While installing water storage tanks, for example, workers may need to weld tanks several stories above the ground.

Pay

The median annual wage for boilermakers was $59,860 in May 2014. The median wage is the wage at which half the workers in an occupation earned more than that amount and half earned less. The lowest 10 percent earned less than $36,000, and the highest 10 percent earned more than $87,320.

In May 2014, the median annual wages for boilermakers in the top industries in which they worked were as follows:

Building equipment contractors	$66,280
Utility system construction	63,090
Fabricated metal product manufacturing	47,690

Apprentices usually start at about 60 percent of the rate paid to fully trained boilermakers. They receive pay increases as they learn to do more tasks.

Union Membership. Compared with workers in all occupations, boilermakers had a higher percentage of workers who belonged to a union in 2014. Although there is no single union that covers all boilermakers, the largest organizer of these workers is the International Brotherhood of Boilermakers, Iron Ship Builders, Blacksmiths, Forgers, and Helpers.

Job Outlook

Employment of boilermakers is projected to grow 9 percent from 2014 to 2024, faster than the average for all occupations.

While boilers typically last more than 50 years, the need to replace parts, such as boiler tubes, heating elements, and ductwork, is an ongoing process that will require the work of boilermakers.

The installation of new boilers and pressure vessels, air pollution abatement equipment, water treatment plants, storage and process

Employment Projections Data for Boilermakers

Occupational Title	SOC Code	Employment, 2014	Projected Employment, 2024	Change, 2014–2024 Percent	Change, 2014–2024 Numeric
Boilermakers	47-2011	17,400	19,000	9	1,500

Source: U.S. Bureau of Labor Statistics, Employment Projections Program

Similar Occupations. This table shows a list of occupations with job duties that are similar to those of boilermakers.

Occupations	Entry-level Education	2014 Median Pay	Projected Job Growth	Average Annual Openings
Assemblers and Fabricators	High school diploma or equivalent	$29,280	-1%	-970
Industrial Machinery Mechanics, Machinery Maintenance Workers, and Millwrights	High school diploma or equivalent	$47,450	16%	7,340
Insulation Workers	See Education/Training	$37,790	13%	740
Machinists and Tool and Die Makers	High school diploma or equivalent	$41,510	6%	2,900
Plumbers, Pipefitters, and Steamfitters	High school diploma or equivalent	$50,660	12%	4,910
Sheet Metal Workers	High school diploma or equivalent	$45,070	7%	940
Stationary Engineers and Boiler Operators	High school diploma or equivalent	$56,330	1%	60
Welders, Cutters, Solderers, and Brazers	High school diploma or equivalent	$37,420	4%	1,440

tanks, electrostatic precipitators, and stacks and liners will spur some demand for boilermakers, although to a lesser extent than repairs and upgrades will.

Additionally, the demand for boilermakers is linked to the cost of coal relative to that of natural gas. Coal-fired power plants require more boilermakers for installation and maintenance. As a result, if natural-gas prices continue to remain low relative to the cost of coal, fewer boilermakers will be needed.

Job Prospects. Overall job prospects should be favorable because the work of a boilermaker remains difficult and physically demanding, leading some qualified applicants to seek other types of work. Although employment growth will generate some job openings, the majority of positions will stem from the need to replace the large number of boilermakers expected to retire in the coming decade.

People who have welding training or a welding certificate should have the best opportunities to be selected for boilermaker apprenticeship programs. In addition, workers with military service experience are viewed favorably during initial selection.

As with many other construction workers, employment of boilermakers is sensitive to fluctuations of the economy. On the one hand, workers may experience periods of unemployment when the overall level of construction falls. On the other hand, shortages of workers may occur in some areas during peak periods of building activity.

Nonetheless, maintenance and repair of boilers must continue even during economic downturns, so boilermaker mechanics in manufacturing and other industries generally have more stable employment than those in construction.

The spring and fall seasons are the busiest times for boilermakers.

Contacts for More Information

For information about apprenticeships or job opportunities as a boilermaker, contact local boiler construction contractors; a local chapter of the International Brotherhood of Boilermakers, Iron Ship Builders, Blacksmiths, Forgers, and Helpers; a local joint union–management apprenticeship committee; or the nearest office of your state employment service or apprenticeship agency. Apprenticeship information is available from the U.S. Department of Labor's ApprenticeshipUSA program (www.dol.gov/apprenticeship) online or by phone at 877-872-5627.

For more information about apprenticeship and training, visit

- International Brotherhood of Boilermakers, Iron Ship Builders, Blacksmiths, Forgers, and Helpers (www.boilermakers.org)
- NCCER (www.nccer.org/boilermaking?pID=105)

For information about welding certification, visit

- American Welding Society (www.aws.org)

O*NET

- Boilermakers (47-2011.00)

Carpenters

- **2014 Median Pay** .... $40,820 per year $19.63 per hour
- **Typical Entry-Level Education** .... High school diploma or equivalent
- **Work Experience in a Related Occupation**.............. None
- **On-the-job Training** .... Apprenticeship
- **Number of Jobs, 2014** 945,400
- **Job Outlook, 2014–24**................. 6% (As fast as average)
- **Employment Change, 2014–24** 60,400

What Carpenters Do

Carpenters construct and repair building frameworks and structures—such as stairways, doorframes, partitions, rafters, and bridge supports—made from wood and other materials. They also may install kitchen cabinets, siding, and drywall.

Duties. Carpenters typically do the following:

- Follow blueprints and building plans to meet the needs of clients

- Install structures and fixtures, such as windows and molding
- Measure, cut, and shape wood, plastic, and other materials
- Construct building frameworks, including walls, floors, and doorframes
- Erect, level, and install building framework with the aid of rigging hardware and cranes
- Inspect and replace damaged framework or other structures and fixtures
- Instruct and direct laborers and other construction helpers

Carpenters are one of the most versatile construction occupations, with workers usually doing many different tasks. For example, some carpenters primarily insulate office buildings and others install drywall or kitchen cabinets in homes. Those who help construct tall buildings or bridges often install the wooden concrete forms for cement footings or pillars and are commonly referred to as *rough carpenters*. Other carpenters erect shoring and scaffolding for buildings.

Carpenters use many different hand and power tools to cut and shape wood, plastic, fiberglass, or drywall. They commonly use hand tools, including squares, levels, and chisels, as well as many power tools, such as sanders, circular saws, nail guns, and welding machines. Carpenters fasten materials together with nails, screws, staples, and adhesives, and do a final check of their work to ensure that it is completed according to specifications. They use a tape measure on nearly every project to make sure that the pieces being cut are the proper size, which reduces waste and saves time. Many employers require applicants to supply their own tools.

The following are examples of types of carpenters:

Residential carpenters typically specialize in single-family, townhome, and condominium building and remodeling. As part of a single job, they might build and set forms for footings, walls, and slabs, and frame and finish exterior walls, roofs, and decks. They also frame interior walls, build stairs, and install drywall, crown molding, doors, and cabinets. In addition, residential carpenters may tile floors and lay wood floors and carpet. Fully trained carpenters can easily switch from new homebuilding to remodeling.

Commercial carpenters typically build and remodel commercial office buildings, hospitals, hotels, schools, and shopping malls. Some specialize in working with light-gauge and load-bearing steel framing for interior partitions, exterior framing, and curtain wall construction. Others specialize in working with concrete forming systems and finishing interior and exterior walls, partitions, and ceilings. Most commercial carpenters perform many of the same tasks as residential carpenters.

Industrial carpenters typically work on civil engineering projects and in industrial settings, where they build scaffolding and create and set forms for pouring concrete. Some industrial carpenters build tunnel bracing or partitions in underground passageways and mines to control the circulation of air to worksites. Others build concrete forms for tunnels, bridges, dams, power plants, or sewers.

Work Environment

Carpenters held about 945,400 jobs in 2014. The industries that employed the most carpenters were as follows:

Residential building construction	20%
Nonresidential building construction	12
Building finishing contractors	11

About 1 in 3 carpenters were self-employed in 2014. Most carpenters work in the construction industry, where they account for the largest share of the building trades occupations.

A carpenter uses a pneumatic gun for hammering nails.

Because carpenters are involved in many types of construction, from building highways and bridges to installing kitchen cabinets, they work both indoors and outdoors.

Carpenters may work in cramped spaces. They frequently shift between lifting, standing, and kneeling, the result of which can be tiring. Those who work outdoors are subject to variable weather conditions, which may limit a carpenter's ability to work.

Injuries and Illnesses. Carpenters have one of the highest rates of injuries and illnesses of all occupations. Although a few types of accidents are potentially fatal, the most common injuries include muscle strains from lifting heavy materials, falls from ladders, and cuts from sharp objects and tools.

Work Schedules. Nearly all carpenters work full time, which may include working evenings and weekends. Overtime is common in order to meet deadlines. Extreme temperatures or inclement weather may cause delays and limit the number of hours of work.

About 1 in 3 carpenters were self-employed in 2014. Self-employed workers often work in residential construction and may be able to set their own schedule.

Education/Training

Although most carpenters learn their trade through an apprenticeship, some learn on the job, starting as a helper.

Education. A high school diploma or equivalent is required. High school courses in mathematics, mechanical drawing, and general vocational technical training are considered useful.

Training. Most carpenters learn their trade through a 3- or 4-year apprenticeship program. For each year of a typical program, apprentices must complete at least 144 hours of technical training and 2,000 hours of paid on-the-job training. In the technical training, apprentices learn carpentry basics, blueprint reading, mathematics, building code requirements, and safety and first-aid practices. They also may receive specialized training in creating and setting concrete forms, rigging, welding, scaffold building, working within confined workspaces, and fall protection. All carpenters must pass the Occupational Safety and Health Administration (OSHA) 10- and 30-hour safety courses.

After finishing an apprenticeship, carpenters are considered to be journey workers and may perform tasks on their own.

Several groups, including unions and contractor associations, sponsor apprenticeship programs. Some apprenticeship programs have preferred entry for veterans. The basic qualifications for a person to enter an apprenticeship program are as follows:

Median Annual Wages, May 2014

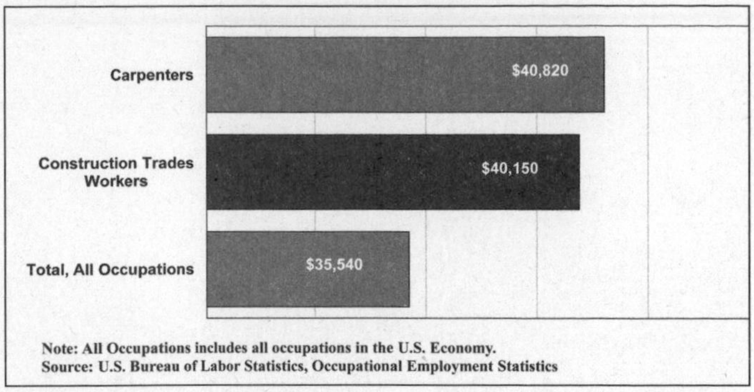

Percent Change in Employment, Projected 2014–2024

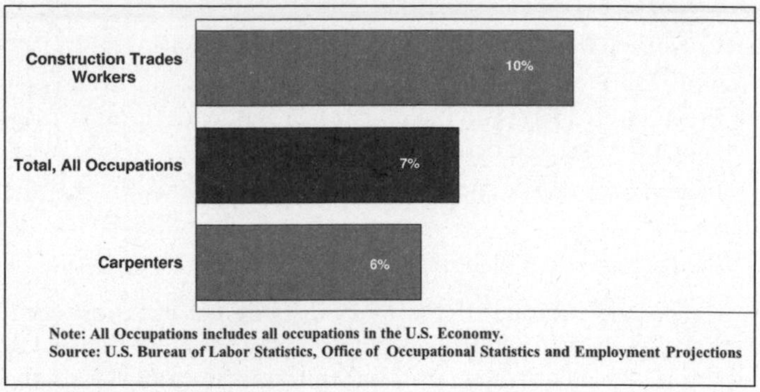

- Minimum age of 18
- High school education or equivalent
- Physically able to do the work
- U.S. citizen or proof of legal residency
- Pass substance abuse screening

Some contractors have their own carpenter training program, which may be an accredited apprenticeship program.

Although many workers enter apprenticeships directly, some carpenters start out as helpers.

Some workers can earn certificates before entering an apprenticeship. The National Association of Home Builders offers Pre-Apprenticeship Certificate Training (PACT) through the Home Builders Institute. PACT is available for several different groups, from youths to veterans, and covers information for eight construction trades, including painting.

Workers typically learn the proper use of hand and power tools on the job. They often start by working with more experienced carpenters and are given more complex tasks as they prove that they can handle simpler tasks, such as measuring and cutting wooden and metal studs.

A number of 2-year technical schools offer carpentry degrees that are affiliated with unions or contractor organizations. Credits earned as part of an apprenticeship program usually count toward an associate's degree.

Advancement. Because they are involved in all phases of construction, carpenters usually have more opportunities than other construction workers to become first-line supervisors, independent contractors, or general construction supervisors.

Carpenters seeking advancement often take additional training provided by associations, unions, or employers. Communication in both English and Spanish also is helpful for relaying instructions to workers.

Important Qualities

Business skills. Self-employed carpenters must be able to bid on new jobs, track inventory, and plan work assignments.

Detail oriented. Carpenters perform many tasks that are important in the overall building process. Making precise measurements, for example, may reduce gaps between windows and frames, limiting any leaks around the window.

Dexterity. Carpenters use many tools and need hand-eye coordination to avoid injury or damaging materials. Striking the head of a nail, for example, is crucial to not damaging wood or injuring oneself.

Math skills. Carpenters use basic math skills every day to calculate volume and measure materials to be cut.

Physical stamina. Carpenters need physical endurance. They frequently stand, climb, or bend for long periods.

Physical strength. Carpenters use tools and materials that are heavy. For example, plywood sheets can weigh 50 to 100 pounds.

Problem-solving skills. Because construction jobs vary, carpenters must adjust project plans accordingly. For example, if a prefabricated window arrives at the worksite slightly oversized, carpenters must shave framework to make the window fit.

Pay

The median annual wage for carpenters was $40,820 in May 2014. The median wage is the wage at which half the workers in an occupation earned more than that amount and half earned less. The lowest 10 percent earned less than $25,640, and the highest 10 percent earned more than $74,750.

In May 2014, the median annual wages for carpenters in the top industries in which they worked were as follows:

Nonresidential building construction	$45,620
Building finishing contractors	41,100
Residential building construction	38,990

The starting pay for apprentices usually is between 30 percent and 50 percent of what fully trained carpenters make. As apprentices learn to do more, they receive pay increases.

Job Outlook

Employment of carpenters is projected to grow 6 percent from 2014 to 2024, about as fast as the average for all occupations.

Employment Projections Data for Carpenters

Occupational Title	SOC Code	Employment, 2014	Projected Employment, 2024	Change, 2014–2024 Percent	Change, 2014–2024 Numeric
Carpenters	47-2031	945,400	1,005,800	6	60,400

Source: U.S. Bureau of Labor Statistics, Employment Projections Program

Similar Occupations. This table shows a list of occupations with job duties that are similar to those of carpenters.

Occupations	Entry-level Education	2014 Median Pay	Projected Job Growth	Average Annual Openings
Construction Laborers and Helpers	See Education/Training	$30,190	13%	18,010
Drywall and Ceiling Tile Installers, and Tapers	No formal educational credential	$38,970	5%	660
Flooring Installers and Tile and Marble Setters	No formal educational credential	$37,380	5%	590
Industrial Machinery Mechanics, Machinery Maintenance Workers, and Millwrights	High school diploma or equivalent	$47,450	16%	7,340
Insulation Workers	See Education/Training	$37,790	13%	740
Masonry Workers	See Education/Training	$38,720	15%	3,730

Population growth should result in more new-home construction—the largest segment employing carpenters—which will stimulate the need for many new workers. Home remodeling needs should also spur demand for carpenters.

In addition, the need to repair and replace roads and bridges should increase employment of carpenters. Much of this growth, however, depends on spending by federal and state governments as they attempt to upgrade existing infrastructure.

The construction of factories and power plants also may result in some new jobs.

However, moderating some of the growth will be the increasing use of modular and prefabricated components. Roof assemblies, walls, stairs, and complete bathrooms are just a few of the prefabricated components that can be manufactured in a separate facility and then assembled onsite by carpenters. Installing prefabricated components replaces the most labor-intensive and time-consuming onsite building activities.

Job Prospects. Overall job prospects for carpenters should be good over the coming decade as construction activity continues to grow. There remains a need to replace many carpenters who left the occupation since 2006. Prospective carpenters with a basic set of carpentry tools will have better prospects.

The number of job openings is expected to vary by geographic area. Because construction activity parallels the movement of people and businesses, areas of the country with the largest population increases will require the most carpenters.

Employment of carpenters, like that of many other construction workers, is sensitive to fluctuations in the economy. On the one hand, workers in these trades may experience periods of unemployment when the overall level of construction falls. On the other hand, peak periods of building activity may produce shortages of carpenters.

Contacts for More Information

For details about apprenticeships or other work opportunities in this trade, contact the offices of the state employment service, the state apprenticeship agency, local contractors or firms that employ carpenters, or local union–management carpenter apprenticeship committees. Apprenticeship information is available from the U.S. Department of Labor's ApprenticeshipUSA program (www.dol.gov/apprenticeship) online or by phone at 877-872-5627.

For more information about carpenters, including training opportunities, visit

- ➤ Associated Builders and Contractors (www.abc.org)
- ➤ Associated General Contractors of America (www.agc.org)
- ➤ Home Builders Institute (www.hbi.org)
- ➤ NCCER (www.nccer.org/carpentry?pID=105)
- ➤ United Brotherhood of Carpenters and Joiners of America (www.carpenters.org/Home.aspx)

O*NET

- ➤ Carpenters (47-2031.00)
- ➤ Construction Carpenters (47-2031.01)
- ➤ Rough Carpenters (47-2031.02)

Construction and Building Inspectors

- **2014 Median Pay** .... $56,040 per year $26.94 per hour
- **Typical Entry-Level Education** .... High school diploma or equivalent
- **Work Experience in a Related Occupation**............ 5 years or more
- **On-the-job Training**....... Moderate-term on-the-job training
- **Number of Jobs, 2014** 101,200
- **Job Outlook, 2014–24**................. 8% (As fast as average)
- **Employment Change, 2014–24** 8,100

What Construction and Building Inspectors Do

Construction and building inspectors ensure that construction meets local and national building codes and ordinances, zoning regulations, and contract specifications.

Duties. Construction and building inspectors typically do the following:

- Review plans to ensure they meet building codes, local ordinances, zoning regulations, and contract specifications
- Approve building plans that are satisfactory
- Monitor construction sites periodically to ensure overall compliance
- Use survey instruments, metering devices, and test equipment to perform inspections
- Inspect plumbing, electrical, and other systems to ensure that they meet code
- Verify alignment, level, and elevation of structures to ensure building meets specifications
- Issue violation notices and stop-work orders until building is compliant

- Keep daily logs, including photographs taken during inspections
- Provide written documentation of findings

People want to live and work in safe places, and construction and building inspectors ensure that construction meets codified requirements. Construction and building inspectors examine buildings, highways and streets, sewer and water systems, dams, bridges, and other structures. They also inspect electrical; heating, ventilation, air-conditioning, and refrigeration (HVACR); and plumbing systems. Although no two inspections are alike, inspectors perform an initial check during the first phase of construction and follow-up inspections throughout the construction project. When the project is finished, they perform a final, comprehensive inspection and provide written and oral feedback related to their findings.

The following are examples of types of construction and building inspectors:

Building inspectors check the structural quality and general safety of buildings. Some specialize further, inspecting only structural steel or reinforced-concrete structures, for example.

Coating inspectors examine the exterior paint and coating on bridges, pipelines, and large holding tanks. Inspectors perform checks at various stages of the painting process to ensure proper coating.

Electrical inspectors examine the installed electrical systems to ensure they function properly and comply with electrical codes and standards. The inspectors visit worksites to inspect new and existing sound and security systems, wiring, lighting, motors, photovoltaic systems, and generating equipment. They also inspect the installed electrical wiring for HVACR systems and appliances.

Elevator inspectors examine lifting and conveying devices, such as elevators, escalators, moving sidewalks, lifts and hoists, inclined railways, ski lifts, and amusement rides. The inspections include both the mechanical and electrical control systems.

Home inspectors typically inspect newly built or previously owned homes, condominiums, townhomes, and other dwellings. Prospective home buyers often hire home inspectors to check and report on a home's structure and overall condition. Sometimes, homeowners hire a home inspector to evaluate their home's condition before placing it on the market.

In addition to examining structural quality, home inspectors examine all home systems and features, including the roof, exterior walls, attached garage or carport, foundation, interior, plumbing, electrical, and HVACR systems. They look for violations of building codes, but home inspectors do not have the power to enforce compliance with the codes.

Mechanical inspectors examine the installation of HVACR systems and equipment to ensure that they are installed and function properly. They may also inspect commercial kitchen equipment, gas-fired appliances, and boilers. Mechanical inspectors should not be confused with quality control inspectors, who inspect goods at manufacturing plants.

Plan examiners determine whether the plans for a building or other structure comply with building codes. They also determine whether the structure is suited to the engineering and environmental demands of the building site.

Plumbing inspectors examine the installation of systems that ensure the safety and health of drinking water, the sanitary disposal of waste, and the safety of industrial piping.

Public works inspectors ensure that the construction of federal, state, and local government water and sewer systems, highways, streets, bridges, and dams conforms to detailed contract specifications. Workers inspect excavation and fill operations, the placement of forms for concrete, concrete mixing and pouring, asphalt paving, and grading operations. Public works inspectors may specialize in highways, structural steel, reinforced concrete, or ditches. Others may specialize in dredging operations required for bridges, dams, or harbors.

Although inspections are primarily visual, inspectors may use tape measures, survey instruments, and metering devices.

Specification inspectors ensure that construction work is performed according to design specifications. Specification inspectors represent the owner's interests, not those of the general public. Insurance companies and financial institutions also may use their services.

Some building inspectors are concerned with fire prevention safety. Fire inspectors and investigators ensure that buildings meet fire codes.

Work Environment

Construction and building inspectors held about 101,200 jobs in 2014. About 48 percent were employed in government, with most working for local governments. An additional 28 percent were employed in the architectural, engineering, and related services industries. About 1 in 10 were self-employed in 2014.

Although construction and building inspectors spend most of their time inspecting worksites, they also spend time in a field office reviewing blueprints, writing reports, and scheduling inspections.

Some inspectors may have to climb ladders or crawl in tight spaces to complete their inspections.

Inspectors typically work alone. However, some inspectors may work as part of a team on large, complex projects, particularly because inspectors usually specialize in different areas of construction.

Work Schedules. Most inspectors work full time during regular business hours. However, some may work additional hours during periods of heavy construction activity. Also, if an accident occurs at a construction site, inspectors must respond immediately and

Median Annual Wages, May 2014

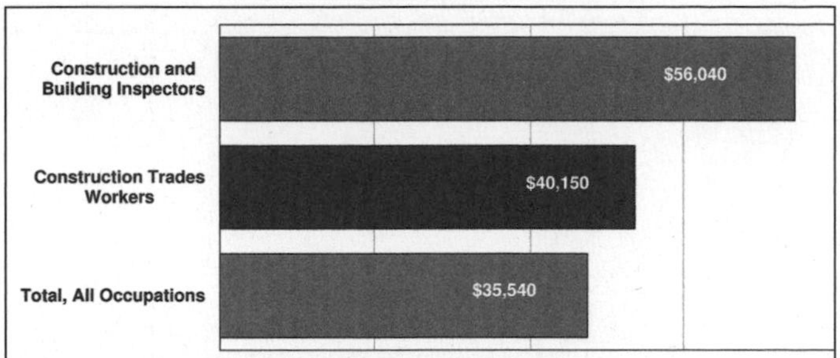

Note: All Occupations includes all occupations in the U.S. Economy.
Source: U.S. Bureau of Labor Statistics, Occupational Employment Statistics

Percent Change in Employment, Projected 2014–2024

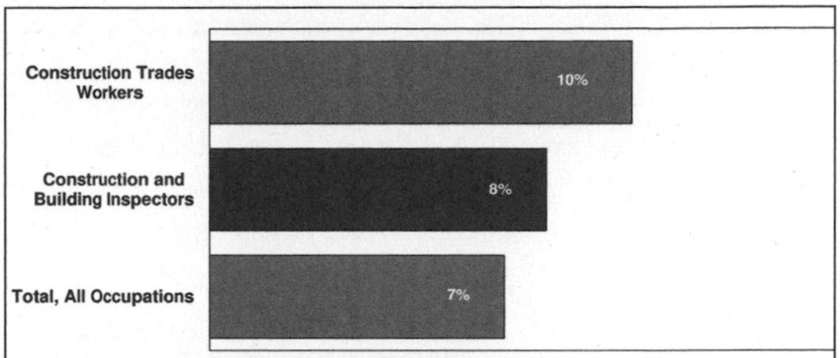

Note: All Occupations includes all occupations in the U.S. Economy.
Source: U.S. Bureau of Labor Statistics, Office of Occupational Statistics and Employment Projections

may work additional hours to complete their report. Nongovernment inspectors—especially those who are self-employed—may have to work evenings and weekends. This is particularly true of home inspectors, who typically inspect homes during the day and write reports in the evening.

Education/Training

Most employers require construction and building inspectors to have at least a high school diploma and considerable knowledge of construction trades. Inspectors typically learn on the job. Many states and local jurisdictions require some type of license or certification.

Education. Most employers require inspectors to have at least a high school diploma, even for workers who have considerable related work experience.

Employers also seek candidates who have studied engineering or architecture or who have a certificate or an associate's degree that includes courses in building inspection, home inspection, construction technology, and drafting. Many community colleges offer programs in building inspection technology. Courses in blueprint reading, vocational subjects, algebra, geometry, and writing are also useful. Courses in business management are helpful for those who plan to run their own inspection business.

A growing number of construction and building inspectors are entering the occupation with a bachelor's degree, which can often substitute for related work experience.

Training. Training requirements vary by state, locality, and type of inspector. In general, construction and building inspectors receive much of their training on the job, although they must learn building codes and standards on their own. Working with an experienced inspector, they learn about inspection techniques; codes, ordinances, and regulations; contract specifications; and recordkeeping and reporting duties. Training also may include supervised onsite inspections.

Work Experience in a Related Occupation. Because inspectors must possess the right mix of technical knowledge, work experience, and education, employers prefer applicants who have both training and experience in a construction trade. For example, many inspectors have experience working as carpenters, electricians, or plumbers. Many home inspectors combine knowledge of multiple specialties, so many of them enter the occupation having a combination of certifications and previous experience in various construction trades.

Licenses, Certifications, and Registrations. Most states and local jurisdictions require construction and building inspectors to have a license or certification. Some states have individual licensing programs for construction and building inspectors. Others may require certification by associations such as the International Code Council, the International Association of Plumbing and Mechanical Officials, the International Association of Electrical Inspectors, and the National Fire Protection Association.

Similarly, most states require home inspectors to follow defined trade practices or obtain a state-issued license or certification. Currently, 36 states have policies regulating the conduct of home inspectors; a few states are considering adding licensure or certification requirements for home inspectors.

Home inspector license or certification requirements vary by state but may require that inspectors do the following:

- Achieve a specified level of education
- Possess experience with inspections
- Maintain liability insurance
- Pass an exam

The exam is often based on the American Society of Home Inspectors and National Association of Home Inspectors certification exams. Most inspectors must renew their license periodically and take continuing education courses.

Inspectors must have a valid driver's license because they must travel to inspection sites.

Important Qualities

Communication skills. Inspectors must have good communication skills in order to explain any problems they find and to help people understand what is needed to fix the problems. In addition, they need to provide a written report of their findings.

Craft experience. Inspectors perform checks and inspections throughout the construction project. Experience in a related

Employment Projections Data for Construction and Building Inspectors

Occupational Title	SOC Code	Employment, 2014	Projected Employment, 2024	Change, 2014–2024	
				Percent	Numeric
Construction and building inspectors	47-4011	101,200	109,200	8	8,100

Source: U.S. Bureau of Labor Statistics, Employment Projections Program

Similar Occupations. This table shows a list of occupations with job duties that are similar to those of construction and building inspectors.

Occupations	Entry-level Education	2014 Median Pay	Projected Job Growth	Average Annual Openings
Appraisers and Assessors of Real Estate	Bachelor's degree	$52,570	8%	680
Architects	Bachelor's degree	$74,520	7%	780
Carpenters	High school diploma or equivalent	$40,820	6%	6,040
Civil Engineers	Bachelor's degree	$82,050	8%	2,360
Construction Managers	Bachelor's degree	$85,630	5%	1,780
Cost Estimators	Bachelor's degree	$60,050	9%	1,870
Electrical and Electronics Engineering Technicians	Associate's degree	$59,820	-2%	-280
Electrical and Electronics Engineers	Bachelor's degree	$93,260	0%	-10
Electricians	High school diploma or equivalent	$51,110	14%	8,590
Plumbers, Pipefitters, and Steamfitters	High school diploma or equivalent	$50,660	12%	4,910
Surveying and Mapping Technicians	High school diploma or equivalent	$40,770	-8%	-430
Surveyors	Bachelor's degree	$57,050	-2%	-90

construction occupation provides inspectors with the necessary background to become certified.

Detail oriented. Inspectors must thoroughly examine many different construction activities, often at the same time. Therefore, they must pay close attention to detail so as to not overlook any items that need to be checked.

Mechanical knowledge. Inspectors use a variety of testing equipment as they check complex systems. In order to perform tests properly, they also must have detailed knowledge of how the systems operate.

Physical stamina. Inspectors are constantly on their feet and often must crawl through attics and other tight spaces. As a result, they should be somewhat physically fit.

Pay

The median annual wage for construction and building inspectors was $56,040 in May 2014. The median wage is the wage at which half the workers in an occupation earned more than that amount and half earned less. The lowest 10 percent earned less than $33,970, and the highest 10 percent earned more than $88,830.

Union Membership. Compared with workers in all occupations, construction and building inspectors had a higher percentage of workers who belonged to a union in 2014.

Job Outlook

Employment of construction and building inspectors is projected to grow 8 percent from 2014 to 2024, about as fast as the average for all occupations. Public interest in safety and the desire to improve the quality of construction are factors that may continue to create demand for inspectors. Employment growth for inspectors is expected to be strongest in government and in firms specializing in architectural, engineering, and related services.

Although employment of home inspectors should continue to grow, some states limit entry into the field to those with related work experience or who are certified. Furthermore, due to shrinking budgets, some state and local jurisdictions may prefer to hire only those who have certification in multiple specialties.

Job Prospects. Certified construction and building inspectors who can perform a variety of inspections should have the best job opportunities. Inspectors with construction-related work experience or training in engineering, architecture, construction technology, or related fields are also likely to have better job prospects.

Larger jurisdictions usually hire specialized inspectors with knowledge in a particular area of construction, such as electrical or plumbing. Conversely, due to limited budgets, smaller jurisdictions typically prefer to hire combination inspectors with broad knowledge of multiple disciplines.

Those who are self-employed, such as home inspectors, are more likely to be affected by economic downturns or fluctuations in the real estate market.

Contacts for More Information

For more information about building codes, certification, and a career as a construction or building inspector, visit

- International Code Council (www.iccsafe.org)
- National Fire Protection Association (www.nfpa.org)

For more information about coating inspectors, visit

- NACE International (www.nace.org)

For more information about construction inspectors, visit

- Association of Construction Inspectors (www.aci-assoc.org)

For more information about electrical inspectors, visit

- International Association of Electrical Inspectors (www.iaei.org)

For more information about elevator inspectors, visit

- National Association of Elevator Safety Authorities International (www.naesai.org)

For more information about education and training for mechanical and plumbing inspectors, visit

- International Association of Plumbing and Mechanical Officials (www.iapmo.org)

For information about becoming a home inspector, visit

- American Society of Home Inspectors (www.ashi.org)
- International Association of Certified Home Inspectors (InterNACHI) (www.nachi.org)
- The National Association of Home Inspectors, Inc. (www.nahi.org)

O*NET

- Construction and Building Inspectors (47-4011.00)

Construction Equipment Operators

- **2014 Median Pay** .... $42,900 per year $20.62 per hour
- **Entry-Level Education** .... High school diploma or equivalent
- **Work Experience in a Related Occupation**.............. None
- **On-the-Job Training**.....Moderate-term on-the-job training
- **Number of Jobs 2014** 424,800
- **Job Outlook, 2014–24**............ 10% (Faster than average)
- **Employment Change, 2014–24** 43,200

What Construction Equipment Operators Do

Construction equipment operators drive, maneuver, or control the heavy machinery used to construct roads, bridges, buildings, and other structures.

Duties. Construction equipment operators typically do the following:

- Clean and maintain equipment, making basic repairs as necessary
- Report malfunctioning equipment to supervisors
- Move levers, push pedals, or turn valves to control equipment
- Drive and maneuver equipment
- Coordinate machine actions with crew members using hand or audio signals
- Ensure that safety standards are met

Construction equipment operators use machinery to move construction materials, earth, and other heavy materials at construction sites and mines. They operate equipment that clears and grades land to prepare it for the construction of roads, bridges, and buildings, as well as runways, power generation facilities, dams, levees, and other structures.

Operating engineers and other construction equipment operators work with one or several types of power construction equipment. They may operate excavation and loading machines equipped with scoops, shovels, or buckets that dig sand, gravel, earth, or similar materials. In addition to operating bulldozers, they operate trench excavators, road graders, and similar equipment. Sometimes, they may drive and control industrial trucks or tractors equipped with forklifts or booms for lifting materials. They may also operate and maintain air compressors, pumps, and other power equipment at construction sites.

Paving and surfacing equipment operators control the machines that spread and level asphalt or spread and smooth concrete for roadways or other structures.

- *Asphalt spreader operators* turn valves to regulate the temperature and flow of asphalt being applied to the roadbed. They must ensure a constant flow of asphalt into the hopper and that the machine distributes the paving material evenly.
- *Concrete paving machine operators* control levers and turn handwheels to move attachments that spread, vibrate, and level wet concrete. They must watch the surface of the concrete carefully to identify low spots that need additional concrete.
- *Tamping equipment operators* use machines that compact earth and other fill materials for roadbeds, railroads, or other construction sites. They may also operate machines with interchangeable hammers to cut or break up old pavement and drive guardrail posts into the ground.

Pile-driver operators use large machines mounted on skids, barges, or cranes to hammer piles into the ground. Piles are long, heavy beams of concrete, wood, or steel driven into the ground to support retaining walls, bridges, piers, or building foundations. Some pile-driver operators work on offshore oil rigs.

Work Environment

Construction equipment operators held about 424,800 jobs in 2014.

The employment levels of construction equipment operators in 2014 were as follows:

Operating engineers and other construction equipment operators	363,400
Paving, surfacing, and tamping equipment operators	57,700
Pile-driver operators	3,700

Construction equipment operators work in nearly every weather condition, although rain or extremely cold weather can stop some types of construction. Workers often get dirty, greasy, muddy, or dusty. Some operators work in remote locations on large construction projects, such as highways and dams, or in factories or mines.

Injuries and Illnesses. Operating engineers and other construction equipment operators have a higher rate of injuries and illnesses than the national average. Slips, falls, and transportation incidents can generally be avoided by observing proper operating procedures and safety practices. Bulldozers, scrapers, and especially pile-drivers, are noisy and shake or jolt the operator, which may lead to repetitive stress injuries.

Work Schedules. Construction equipment operators may have irregular hours because work on construction projects must sometimes continue around the clock or be done late at night. The vast majority of construction equipment operators work full time.

Education/Training

Many workers learn equipment operation on the job after earning a high school diploma or equivalent, while others learn through an apprenticeship or by attending vocational schools.

Education. A high school diploma or equivalent is required for most jobs. Vocational training and math courses are useful, and a course in auto mechanics can be helpful because workers often perform maintenance on their equipment.

Construction equipment operators level the surface of a construction site.

Median Annual Wages, May 2014

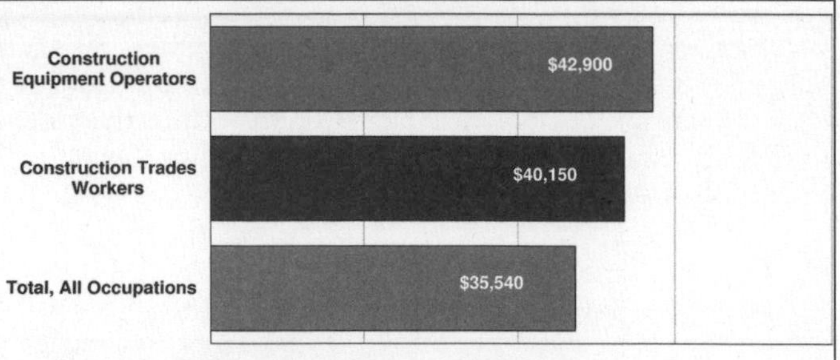

Note: All Occupations includes all occupations in the U.S. Economy.
Source: U.S. Bureau of Labor Statistics, Occupational Employment Statistics

Percent Change in Employment, Projected 2014–2024

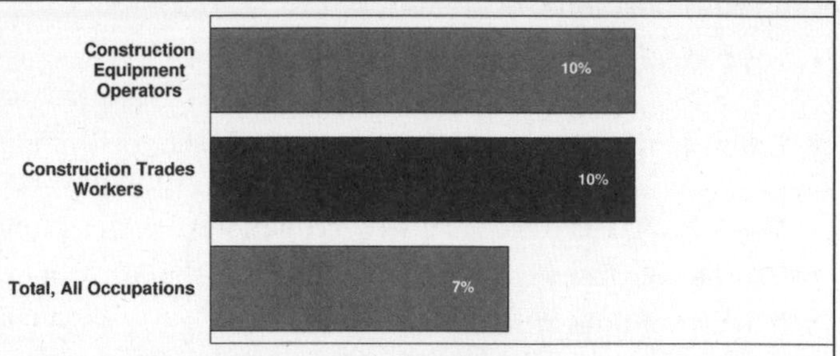

Note: All Occupations includes all occupations in the U.S. Economy.
Source: U.S. Bureau of Labor Statistics, Office of Occupational Statistics and Employment Projections

Education at a private vocational school may be beneficial in finding a job, and the variety of construction equipment that is taught varies from school to school. However, people considering this kind of training should check the school's reputation among employers in the area and find out if the school offers the opportunity to train on actual machines in realistic situations.

Many training facilities incorporate sophisticated simulators into their training, allowing beginners to familiarize themselves with the equipment in a virtual environment before operating real machines.

Training. Many workers learn their jobs by operating light equipment under the guidance of an experienced operator. Later, they may operate heavier equipment, such as bulldozers. Technologically advanced construction equipment with computerized controls requires greater skill to operate. Operators of such equipment may need more training and some understanding of electronics.

Other workers learn their trade through a 3- or 4-year apprenticeship. For each year of the program, apprentices must have at least 144 hours of technical instruction and 2,000 hours of paid on-the-job training. On the job, apprentices learn to maintain equipment, operate machinery, and use special technology, such as a global positioning system (GPS). In the classroom, apprentices learn operating procedures for special equipment, safety practices, and first aid, as well as how to read grading plans. Because apprentices learn to operate a wider variety of machines than do other beginners, they usually have better job opportunities.

A few groups, including unions and contractor associations, sponsor apprenticeship programs. Some apprenticeship programs have preferred entry for veterans. The basic qualifications for entering an apprenticeship program are as follows:

- Minimum age of 18
- High school education or equivalent
- Physically able to do the work
- Valid driver's license

After completing an apprenticeship program, apprentices are considered journey workers and perform tasks with less guidance.

Licenses, Certifications, and Registrations. Construction equipment operators often need a commercial driver's license (CDL) to haul their equipment to various jobsites. State laws governing CDLs vary.

A few states have special licenses for operators of backhoes, loaders, and bulldozers.

Currently, 17 states require pile-driver operators to have a crane license because similar operational concerns apply to both pile-drivers and cranes. In addition, the cities of Chicago, New Orleans, New York, Omaha, Philadelphia, and Washington, DC require special crane licensure.

Important Qualities

Hand-eye-foot coordination. Construction equipment operators should have steady hands and feet to guide and control heavy machinery precisely, sometimes in tight spaces.

Mechanical skills. Construction equipment operators often perform basic maintenance on the equipment they operate. As a result, they should be familiar with hand and power tools and standard equipment care.

Physical strength. Construction equipment operators may be required to lift more than 50 pounds as part of their duties.

Unafraid of heights. Construction equipment operators may work at great heights. For example, pile-driver operators may need to service the pulleys located at the top of the pile-driver's tower, which may be several stories tall.

Pay

The median annual wage for construction equipment operators was $42,900 in May 2014. The median wage is the wage at which half the workers in an occupation earned more than that amount and half earned less. The lowest 10 percent earned less than $27,600, and the highest 10 percent earned more than $74,890.

Employment Projections Data for Construction Equipment Operators

Occupational Title	SOC Code	Employment, 2014	Projected Employment, 2024	Change, 2014–2024 Percent	Change, 2014–2024 Numeric
Construction equipment operators	47-2070	424,800	467,900	10	43,200
Paving, surfacing, and tamping equipment operators	47-2071	57,700	63,000	9	5,300
Pile-driver operators	47-2072	3,700	4,300	17	600
Operating engineers and other construction equipment operators	47-2073	363,400	400,600	10	37,200

Source: U.S. Bureau of Labor Statistics, Employment Projections Program

Similar Occupations. This table shows a list of occupations with job duties that are similar to those of construction equipment operators.

Occupations	Entry-level Education	2014 Median Pay	Projected Job Growth	Average Annual Openings
Agricultural Workers	See Education/Training	$19,330	-6%	-4,750
Farmers, Ranchers, and Other Agricultural Managers	High school diploma or equivalent	$68,050	-2%	-1,810
Heavy and Tractor-trailer Truck Drivers	Postsecondary nondegree award	$39,520	5%	9,880
Material Moving Machine Operators	See Education/Training	$32,890	3%	1,950

Median annual wages for construction equipment operators in May 2014 were as follows:

Pile-driver operators $51,510
Operating engineers and other construction equipment operators 43,510
Paving, surfacing, and tamping equipment operators 38,660

The starting pay for apprentices is usually between 60 percent and 70 percent of what fully trained operators make. They receive pay increases as they learn to operate more complex equipment.

Union Membership. Compared with workers in all occupations, construction equipment operators had a higher percentage of workers who belonged to a union in 2014. Although no single union covers all operators, the largest organizer of these workers is the International Union of Operating Engineers.

Job Outlook

Employment of construction equipment operators is projected to grow 10 percent from 2014 to 2024, faster than the average for all occupations. Employment growth is expected to vary across the construction equipment operator occupations (see the Employment Projections table). Spending on infrastructure is expected to increase, resulting in many new positions over the next ten years. Across the country, many roads, bridges, and water and sewer systems are in great need of repair. In addition, population growth will require new infrastructure projects such as roads and sewer lines, which are also expected to generate jobs.

Pile-driver operators, the smallest of the three occupations in this profile, is projected to grow 17 percent from 2014 to 2024, much faster than the average for all occupations. However, because it is a small occupation, the fast growth will result in only about 600 new jobs over the 10-year period.

Job Prospects. Workers with the ability to operate multiple types of equipment should have the best job opportunities, and veterans are viewed favorably during initial hiring. In addition, employment opportunities should be best in metropolitan areas, where most large commercial and residential buildings are constructed, and in states that undertake large transportation-related projects.

As with many other types of construction worker jobs, employment of construction equipment operators is sensitive to fluctuations of the economy. On the one hand, workers may experience periods of unemployment when the overall level of construction falls. On the other hand, shortages of workers may occur in some areas during peak periods of building activity.

Contacts for More Information

For information about apprenticeships or job opportunities as a construction equipment operator, contact local cement or highway construction contractors, a local joint union–management apprenticeship committee, or the nearest office of your state employment service or apprenticeship agency. Apprenticeship information is available from the U.S. Department of Labor's Apprenticeship-USA program (www.dol.gov/apprenticeship) online or by phone at 877-872-5627.

For more information about construction equipment operators, visit

➤ The Associated General Contractors of America (www.agc.org/craft-programs/search)
➤ Pile Driving Contractors Association (www.piledrivers.org)

For more information about training of construction equipment operators, visit

➤ International Union of Operating Engineers (www.iuoe.org/training)
➤ NCCER (www.nccer.org/heavy-equipment-operations?pID=105)

For more information about crane certification and licensure, visit

➤ National Commission for the Certification of Crane Operators (www.nccco.org)

O*NET

➤ Paving, Surfacing, and Tamping Equipment Operators (47-2071.00)
➤ Pile-Driver Operators (47-2072.00)
➤ Operating Engineers and Other Construction Equipment Operators (47-2073.00)

Construction Laborers and Helpers

- **2014 Median Pay** .... $30,190 per year $14.51 per hour
- **Typical Entry-Level Education** .... See Education/Training
- **Work Experience in a Related Occupation**............... None
- **On-the-job Training** ....Short-term on-the-job training
- **Number of Jobs, 2014** 1,386,400
- **Job Outlook, 2014–24** .... 13% (Faster than average)
- **Employment Change, 2014–24** 180,100

What Construction Laborers and Helpers Do

Construction laborers and helpers perform many tasks that require physical labor on construction sites.

Duties. Construction laborers and helpers typically do the following:

- Clean and prepare construction sites by removing debris and possible hazards
- Load or unload building materials to be used in construction
- Build or take apart bracing, scaffolding, and temporary structures
- Dig trenches, backfill holes, or compact earth to prepare for construction

- Operate or tend equipment and machines used in construction
- Follow construction plans and instructions from supervisors or more experienced workers
- Assist craftworkers with their duties

Construction laborers and helpers work on almost all construction sites, performing a wide range of tasks varying in complexity from very easy to extremely difficult and hazardous. Although many of the tasks they perform require some training and experience, most tasks can be learned quickly.

Construction laborers, are also referred to as *construction craft laborers*, perform a wide variety of construction-related activities during all phases of construction. Many laborers spend their time preparing and cleaning up construction sites, using tools such as shovels and brooms. Other workers, for example, those on road crews, may specialize and learn to control traffic patterns and operate pavement breakers, jackhammers, earth tampers, or surveying equipment.

With special training, laborers may help transport and use explosives or run hydraulic boring machines to dig out tunnels. They may learn to use lasers to place pipes and to use computers to control robotic pipe cutters. They may become certified to remove asbestos, lead, or chemicals.

Helpers assist construction craftworkers, such as electricians and carpenters, with a variety of tasks. They may carry tools and materials or help set up equipment. For example, many helpers work with cement masons to move and set the forms that determine the shape of poured concrete. Many other helpers assist with taking apart equipment, cleaning up sites, and disposing of waste, as well as helping with any other needs of craftworkers.

Many construction trades have helpers who assist craftworkers. The following trades have associated helpers:

- Brickmasons, blockmasons, and stonemasons, and tile and marble setters
- Carpenters
- Electricians
- Painters, paperhangers, plasterers, and stucco masons
- Pipelayers, plumbers, pipefitters, and steamfitters
- Roofers

Work Environment

Construction laborers and helpers held about 1.4 million jobs in 2014.

Construction laborers held about 1.2 million jobs in 2014, of which 60 percent were employed in the construction industry. About 1 in 4 construction laborers were self-employed in 2014.

Construction helpers held about 227,300 jobs in 2014. The employment levels of construction helper occupations in 2014 were as follows:

Helpers—electricians	69,000
Helpers—pipelayers, plumbers, pipefitters, and steamfitters	52,400
Helpers—carpenters	39,700
Helpers—brickmasons, blockmasons, stonemasons, and tile and marble setters	23,500
Helpers—construction trades, all other	19,500
Helpers—painters, paperhangers, plasterers, and stucco masons	11,900
Helpers—roofers	11,300

Most construction laborers and helpers perform physically demanding work. Some work at great heights or outdoors in all weather conditions; others may be required to work in tunnels. They must use earplugs around loud equipment and wear gloves, safety glasses, and other protective gear.

Construction laborers often work building homes and businesses.

Injuries and Illnesses. Construction laborers have one of the highest rates of injuries and illnesses of all occupations. Workers may experience cuts from materials and tools, fatal and nonfatal falls from ladders and scaffolding, and burns from chemicals or equipment. Some jobs expose workers to harmful materials, fumes, or odors, or to dangerous machinery. Workers may also experience muscle fatigue and injuries related to lifting and carrying heavy materials.

Although they face similar hazards to construction laborers, some construction helpers experience a rate of injuries and illnesses that is closer to the national average. The helpers of carpenters, electricians, and pipelayers, plumbers, pipefitters and steamfitters, however, have a higher rate of injuries and illnesses than the national average.

Work Schedules. Like many construction workers, most laborers and helpers work full time. Although they must sometimes stop work because of bad weather, they often work overtime to meet deadlines. Laborers and helpers on highway and bridge projects may need to work overnight to avoid causing major traffic disruptions. In some parts of the country, construction laborers and helpers may work only during certain seasons. For example, in northern climates, cold weather frequently disrupts construction activity in the winter.

About 1 in 4 construction laborers were self-employed in 2014. Self-employed construction laborers may be able to set their own schedule. In contrast, very few helpers were self-employed.

Education/Training

Construction laborers and helpers learn their trade through on-the-job training (OJT). The length of training depends on the employer and the specialization. Formal education is not typically required.

Education. Although formal education is not typically required, high school classes in mathematics, blueprint reading, welding, and other vocational subjects can be helpful.

To receive further education, some workers attend a trade school or community college.

Training. Construction laborers and helpers learn through OJT after being hired by a construction contractor. Workers typically

Median Annual Wages, May 2014

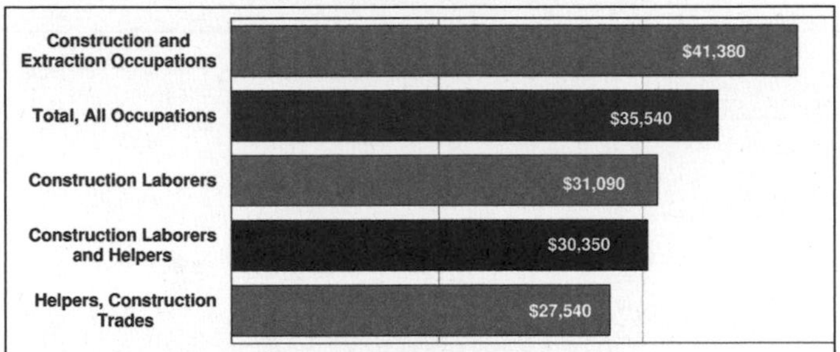

Note: All Occupations includes all occupations in the U.S. Economy.
Source: U.S. Bureau of Labor Statistics, Occupational Employment Statistics

Percent Change in Employment, Projected 2014–2024

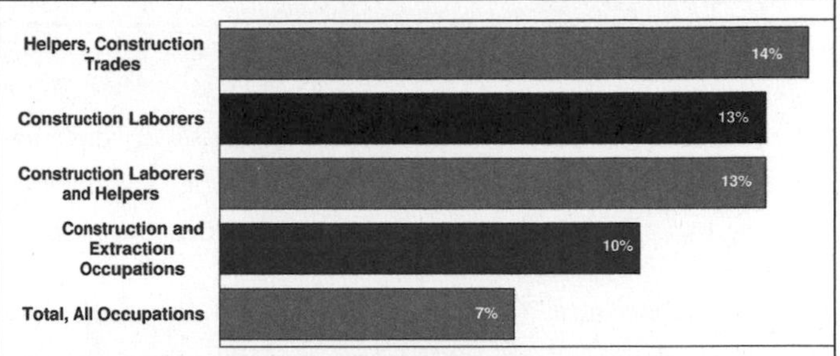

Note: All Occupations includes all occupations in the U.S. Economy.
Source: U.S. Bureau of Labor Statistics, Office of Occupational Statistics and Employment Projections

gain experience by performing tasks under the guidance of experienced workers.

Although the majority of construction laborers and helpers learn by assisting experienced workers, some construction laborers opt for apprenticeship programs. Programs generally include 2 to 4 years of technical instruction and OJT. The Laborers' International Union of North America (LIUNA) requires a minimum of 4,000 hours of OJT, accompanied by 300 hours of related instruction in such areas as signaling, blueprint reading, using proper tools and equipment, and following health and safety procedures. The remainder of the curriculum consists of specialized training in one of these eight areas:

- Building construction
- Demolition and deconstruction
- Environmental remediation
- Road and utility construction
- Tunneling
- Masonry
- Landscaping
- Pipeline construction

Several groups, including unions and contractor associations, sponsor apprenticeship programs, which usually have only a basic age qualification—age 18 or older—for entrance. Apprentices must obtain a high school diploma or equivalent before completing their apprenticeship. Some apprenticeship programs have preferred entry for veterans.

Licenses, Certifications, and Registrations. Laborers who remove hazardous materials (hazmat) must meet the federal and state requirements for hazardous materials removal workers.

Depending on the work they do, laborers may need specific certifications, which may be attained through LIUNA. Rigging and scaffold building are commonly attained certifications. Certification can help workers prove that they have the knowledge to perform more complex tasks.

Advancement. Through experience and training, construction laborers and helpers can advance into positions that involve more complex tasks. For example, laborers may earn certifications in welding, erecting scaffolding, or finishing concrete, and then spend more time performing those activities. Similarly, helpers sometimes move into construction craft occupations after gaining experience in the field. For example, experience as an electrician's helper may lead to becoming an apprentice electrician.

Important Qualities

Color vision. Construction laborers and helpers may need to be able to distinguish colors to do their job. For example, an electrician's helper must be able to distinguish different colors of wire to help the lead electrician.

Math skills. Construction laborers and some helpers need to perform basic math calculations while measuring on jobsites or assisting a surveying crew.

Mechanical skills. Construction laborers are frequently required to operate and maintain equipment, such as jackhammers.

Physical stamina. Construction laborers and helpers must have the endurance to perform strenuous tasks throughout the day.

Employment Projections Data for Construction Laborers and Helpers

Occupational Title	SOC Code	Employment, 2014	Projected Employment, 2024	Change, 2014–2024 Percent	Change, 2014–2024 Numeric
Construction laborers and helpers	—	1,386,400	1,566,500	13	180,100
Construction laborers	47-2061	1,159,100	1,306,500	13	147,400
Helpers—brickmasons, blockmasons, stonemasons, and tile and marble setters	47-3011	23,500	28,800	22	5,300
Helpers—carpenters	47-3012	39,700	42,700	7	3,000
Helpers—electricians	47-3013	69,000	81,500	18	12,500
Helpers—painters, paperhangers, plasterers, and stucco masons	47-3014	11,900	13,100	11	1,200
Helpers—pipelayers, plumbers, pipefitters, and steamfitters	47-3015	52,400	59,400	13	7,000
Helpers—roofers	47-3016	11,300	13,000	15	1,700
Helpers, construction trades, all other	47-3019	19,500	21,500	10	2,000

Source: U.S. Bureau of Labor Statistics, Employment Projections Program

Similar Occupations. This table shows a list of occupations with job duties that are similar to those of construction laborers and helpers.

Occupations	Entry-level Education	2014 Median Pay	Projected Job Growth	Average Annual Openings
Carpenters	High school diploma or equivalent	$40,820	6%	6,040
Electricians	High school diploma or equivalent	$51,110	14%	8,590
Flooring Installers and Tile and Marble Setters	No formal educational credential	$37,380	5%	590
Grounds Maintenance Workers	See Education/Training	$24,810	6%	7,760
Hazardous Materials Removal Workers	High school diploma or equivalent	$38,520	7%	330
Masonry Workers	See Education/Training	$38,720	15%	3,730
Material Moving Machine Operators	See Education/Training	$32,890	3%	1,950
Painters, Construction and Maintenance	No formal educational credential	$35,950	7%	2,650
Plumbers, Pipefitters, and Steamfitters	High school diploma or equivalent	$50,660	12%	4,910

Highway laborers, for example, spend hours on their feet—often in hot temperatures—with few breaks.

Physical strength. Construction laborers and helpers must often lift heavy materials or equipment. For example, cement mason helpers must move cinder blocks, which typically weigh more than 40 pounds each.

Pay

The median annual wage for construction laborers and helpers was $30,190 in May 2014. The median wage is the wage at which half the workers in an occupation earned more than that amount and half earned less. The lowest 10 percent earned less than $19,940, and the highest 10 percent earned more than $56,790.

Median annual wages for construction laborers and helpers in May 2014 were as follows:

Construction laborers	$31,090
Helpers—brickmasons, blockmasons, stonemasons, and tile and marble setters	28,830
Helpers, construction trades, all other	28,010
Helpers—electricians	27,940
Helpers—pipelayers, plumbers, pipefitters, and steamfitters	27,710
Helpers—carpenters	26,600
Helpers—roofers	26,060
Helpers—painters, paperhangers, plasterers, and stucco masons	25,910

Job Outlook

Employment of construction laborers and helpers is projected to grow 13 percent from 2014 to 2024, faster than the average for all occupations.

Employment of construction laborers is projected to grow 13 percent from 2014 to 2024, faster than the average for all occupations. Laborers work in all fields of construction, and demand for laborers will mirror the level of overall construction activity. Repairing and replacing the nation's infrastructure, such as roads, bridges, and water lines, should result in steady demand for laborers.

Although employment growth of specific types of helpers is expected to vary (see Employment Projections table), overall demand for helpers will be driven by the construction of homes, schools, office buildings, factories, and power plants. Remodeling activity will also result in some new jobs. Roofer, electrician, and brickmason, blockmason, stonemason, and tile and marble setter helpers are all projected to grow much faster than the average for all occupations. However, because roofer helpers is a small occupation, the fast growth will result in only about 1,700 new jobs over the 10-year period.

Job Prospects. Construction laborers who are able to perform a wide range of tasks should have the best job opportunities. Job opportunities for helpers will vary by occupation; for example, electrician's helpers should have the best job prospects, while helpers for roofers will likely find fewer job openings. In addition, veterans are viewed favorably during initial hiring.

Employment of construction laborers and helpers is especially sensitive to the fluctuations of the economy. On the one hand, workers in these trades may experience periods of unemployment when the overall level of construction falls. On the other hand, shortages of these workers may occur in some areas during peak periods of building activity.

Contacts for More Information

For details about apprenticeships or other work opportunities for construction laborers and helpers, contact the offices of the state employment service, the state apprenticeship agency, local construction contractors or firms that employ laborers, or local union–management apprenticeship committees. Apprenticeship information is available from the U.S. Department of Labor's ApprenticeshipUSA program (www.dol.gov/apprenticeship) online or by phone at 877-872-5627.

For more information about education programs for laborers, visit

- Laborers' International Union of North America (www.liuna.org/home)
- NCCER (www.nccer.org/construction-craft-laborer?pID=105)

O*NET

- Construction Laborers (47-2061.00)
- Helpers—Brickmasons, Blockmasons, Stonemasons, and Tile and Marble Setters (47-3011.00)
- Helpers—Carpenters (47-3012.00)
- Helpers—Electricians (47-3013.00)
- Helpers—Painters, Paperhangers, Plasterers, and Stucco Masons (47-3014.00)
- Helpers—Pipelayers, Plumbers, Pipefitters, and Steamfitters (47-3015.00)
- Helpers—Roofers (47-3016.00)
- Helpers, Construction Trades, All Other (47-3019.00)

Drywall and Ceiling Tile Installers, and Tapers

- **2014 Median Pay** .... $38,970 per year
  $18.73 per hour
- **Entry-Level Education** .... No formal educational credential
- **Work Experience in a Related Occupation** .... None
- **On-the-Job Training** .... Moderate-term on-the-job training
- **Number of Jobs 2014** 127,000
- **Job Outlook, 2014–24** .... 5% (As fast as average)
- **Employment Change, 2014–24** 6,600

What Drywall and Ceiling Tile Installers, and Tapers Do

Drywall and ceiling tile installers hang wallboard and install ceiling tile inside buildings. Tapers prepare the wallboard for painting, using tape and other materials. Many workers both install and tape wallboard.

Duties. Drywall and ceiling tile installers, and tapers, typically do the following:

- Review design plans to minimize the number of cuts and waste of wallboard
- Determine the precise locations of electrical outlets, plumbing, and windows
- Cut drywall or ceiling tiles to the right size, using utility knives and power saws
- Fasten panels and tiles, using cement adhesive, nails, screws, or clips
- Patch, trim, and smooth rough spots and edges
- Apply tape and sealing compound to cover joints between wallboards
- Add coats of sealing compound to create an even surface
- Sand all joints and holes to a smooth, seamless finish

Drywall is the most commonly used interior wall covering. It owes its popularity to its ability to take a wide variety of finishes when it is properly prepared, as well as its low installation costs. In addition to covering insulation, electrical wires, and plumbing pipes, drywall dampens sound and provides fire resistance.

To hang and prepare ceilings, workers may use mechanical lifts or stand on stilts, ladders, or scaffolds. Once wallboards are hung, workers use progressively wider trowels to spread multiple coats of sealing compound over cracks, indentations, and any remaining imperfections. Some workers may use a mechanical applicator, a tool that spreads sealing compound on the wall joint while dispensing and setting tape at the same time.

Drywall installers are also called *drywallers* or *hangers*. They cut and hang the panels of wallboard.

Ceiling tile installers hang ceiling tiles and create suspended ceilings. Tiles may be applied directly to the ceiling, attached to furring strips, or suspended on runners that are connected by wire to the ceiling. Workers are sometimes called *acoustical carpenters*, because they also install tiles that block sound.

Tapers are also called *finishers*, because they prepare the drywall for covering by plaster, paint, and wallpaper. Tapers apply paper or fiberglass mesh tape to cover drywall seams.

Drywall and ceiling tile installers and tapers learn their trade through informal training programs or through apprenticeships.

In addition to performing new installations, many installers and tapers make repairs such as fixing damaged drywall and replacing ceiling tiles. The wall coverings applied to the finished drywall are installed by painters, plasterers, and paperhangers.

Work Environment

Drywall and ceiling tile installers, and tapers, held about 127,000 jobs in 2014, of which 66 percent worked in the drywall and insulation contractors industry. About 1 in 5 were self-employed in 2014.

Drywall and ceiling tile installers, and tapers, work indoors. As in many other construction trades, the work is physically demanding. Workers spend most of the day standing, bending, or reaching, and they must often lift and maneuver heavy, oversized wallboard.

Because the work creates a lot of dust, which irritates the skin, eyes, and lungs, workers may wear protective masks, goggles, and gloves. Common injuries falls from ladders or stilts, cuts from sharp tools, and muscle strains from lifting heavy materials.

Work Schedules. Most drywall and ceiling tile installers, and tapers, work full time.

About 1 in 5 were self-employed in 2014. Self-employed installers and tapers may be able to set their own schedule.

Education/Training

Most drywall and ceiling tile installers, and tapers, learn their trade on the job. A formal educational credential is typically not required to enter the occupation.

Education. Although there are no education requirements for becoming a drywall and ceiling tile installers, or taper, high school math and vocational technical courses are considered useful.

Median Annual Wages, May 2014

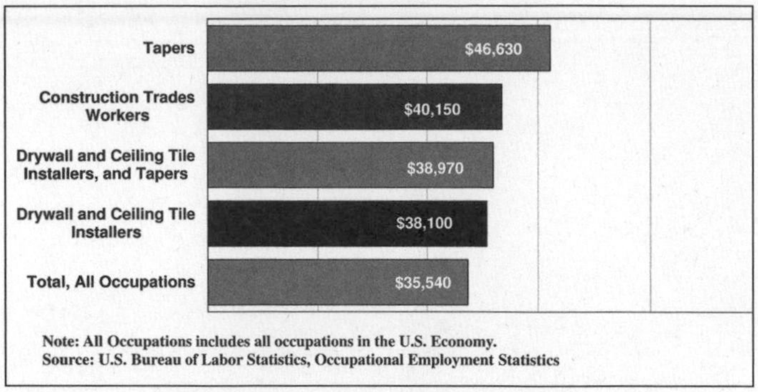

Percent Change in Employment, Projected 2014–2024

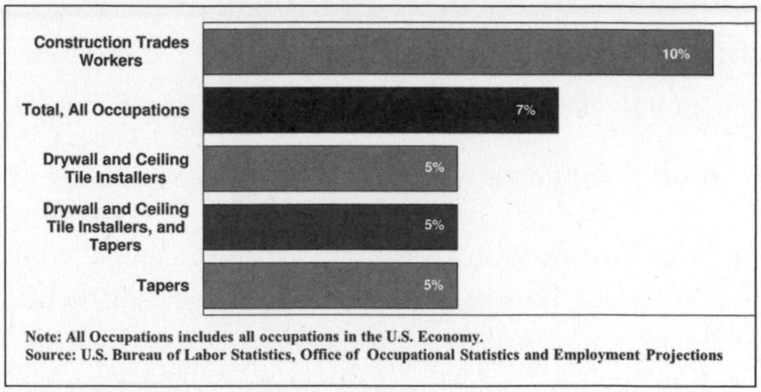

Training. Most drywall and ceiling tile installers, and tapers, learn their trade on the job by helping more experienced workers and gradually being given more duties. They start by carrying materials and cleaning up, and then learn to use the tools of the trade. They also learn to measure, cut, and install or apply materials. Employers usually provide some on-the-job training, lasting up to 12 months.

A few drywall and ceiling tile installers, and tapers, learn their trade through a 3- or 4-year apprenticeship. For each year of the program, apprentices must have at least 144 hours of related technical work and 2,000 hours of paid on-the-job training. During training, apprentices learn construction basics related to blueprint reading, mathematics, building code requirements, and safety and first-aid practices.

A few groups, including the United Brotherhood of Carpenters and contractor associations, sponsor apprenticeship programs. The basic qualifications for entering such a program are as follows:

- Minimum age of 18
- High school education or equivalent
- Physically able to perform the work

After completing an apprenticeship program, they are considered to be journey workers and may perform duties on their own.

Important Qualities

Balance. Drywall and ceiling tile installers, and tapers, often wear stilts. They must be able to move around and use tools overhead without falling.

Math skills. Drywall and ceiling tile installers, and tapers, use math skills for measurement on every job. For example, they must be able to estimate the quantity of materials needed and measure accurately when cutting panels.

Physical stamina. Drywall and ceiling tile installers, and tapers, constantly lift and move heavy materials into place, so workers should be in good physical shape.

Physical strength. Drywall and ceiling tile installers must often lift heavy panels over their heads to secure onto the ceiling.

Pay

The median annual wage for drywall and ceiling tile installers was $38,100 in May 2014. The median wage is the wage at which half the workers in an occupation earned more than that amount and half earned less. The lowest 10 percent earned less than $25,360, and the highest 10 percent earned more than $75,570.

The median annual wage for tapers was $46,630 in May 2014. The lowest 10 percent earned less than $28,750, and the highest 10 percent earned more than $85,500.

The starting wage for apprentices is usually between 40 percent and 50 percent of what fully trained drywall and ceiling tile installers and tapers make. As apprentices learn to do more, they receive pay increases.

Job Outlook

Employment of drywall and ceiling tile installers, and tapers, is projected to grow 5 percent from 2014 to 2024, about as fast as the average for all occupations.

Drywall is, and will continue to be, the most common interior wall covering in nearly every building. As a result, new residential and commercial building construction will drive demand for workers. Home-remodeling projects are also expected to create jobs, because existing homes and other buildings will require improvements.

Job Prospects. Job prospects for drywall and ceiling tile installers, and tapers, are expected to be good as building construction and remodeling activity continue to grow. As with many other construction workers, employment is sensitive to fluctuations of the economy. On the one hand, these workers may experience periods of unemployment when the overall level of construction falls. On the other hand, shortages of workers may occur in some areas during peak periods of building activity.

Drywall and ceiling tile installers, and tapers, with a good employment history and experience in the construction industry should have the best job opportunities.

Employment Projections Data for Drywall and Ceiling Tile Installers, and Tapers

Occupational Title	SOC Code	Employment, 2014	Projected Employment, 2024	Change, 2014–2024 Percent	Change, 2014–2024 Numeric
Drywall installers, ceiling tile installers, and tapers	—	127,000	133,600	5	6,600
Drywall and ceiling tile installers	47-2081	106,000	111,500	5	5,500
Drywall installers, ceiling tile installers, and tapers	—	127,000	133,600	5	6,600
Drywall and ceiling tile installers	47-2081	106,000	111,500	5	5,500

Source: U.S. Bureau of Labor Statistics, Employment Projections Program

Similar Occupations. This table shows a list of occupations with job duties that are similar to those of drywall and ceiling tile installers, and tapers.

Occupations	Entry-level Education	2014 Median Pay	Projected Job Growth	Average Annual Openings
Carpenters	High school diploma or equivalent	$40,820	6%	6,040
Construction Laborers and Helpers	See Education/Training	$30,190	13%	18,010
Flooring Installers and Tile and Marble Setters	No formal educational credential	$37,380	5%	590
Insulation Workers	See Education/Training	$37,790	13%	740
Masonry Workers	See Education/Training	$38,720	15%	3,730
Painters, Construction and Maintenance	No formal educational credential	$35,950	7%	2,650

Contacts for More Information

For details about apprenticeships or other work opportunities in this trade, contact the offices of the state employment service; the state apprenticeship agency; local contractors or firms that employ drywall installers, ceiling tile installers, and tapers; or local union–management finishing trade apprenticeship committees. Apprenticeship information is available from the U.S. Department of Labor's ApprenticeshipUSA program (www.dol.gov/apprenticeship) online or by phone at 877-872-5627.

For more information about drywall and ceiling tile installers and tapers, visit

➤ Associated Builders and Contractors, Inc. (www.abc.org)
➤ Association of the Wall and Ceiling Industry (http://store.awci.org/cgi-bin/awci)
➤ Finishing Trades Institute (www.finishingtradesinstitute.org)
➤ National Association of Home Builders (www.nahb.org)
➤ NCCER (www.nccer.org/drywall)
➤ United Brotherhood of Carpenters (www.carpenters.org/Home.aspx)

O*NET

➤ Drywall and Ceiling Tile Installers (47-2081.00)
➤ Tapers (47-2082.00)

Electricians

- **2014 Median Pay** .... $51,110 per year $24.57 per hour
- **Typical Entry-Level Education** .... High school diploma or equivalent
- **Work Experience in a Related Occupation** .... None
- **On-the-job Training** .... Apprenticeship
- **Number of Jobs, 2014** 628,800
- **Job Outlook, 2014–24** .... 14% (Much faster than average)
- **Employment Change, 2014–24** 85,900

What Electricians Do

Electricians install, maintain, and repair electrical power, communications, lighting, and control systems in homes, businesses, and factories.

Duties. Electricians typically do the following:

- Read blueprints or technical diagrams
- Install and maintain wiring, control, and lighting systems
- Inspect electrical components, such as transformers and circuit breakers
- Identify electrical problems using a variety of testing devices
- Repair or replace wiring, equipment, or fixtures using hand tools and power tools
- Follow state and local building regulations based on the National Electrical Code
- Direct and train workers to install, maintain, or repair electrical wiring or equipment

Almost every building has an electrical power, communications, lighting, and control system that is installed during construction and maintained after that. These systems power the lights, appliances, and equipment that make people's lives and jobs easier and more comfortable.

Installing electrical systems in newly constructed buildings is often less complicated than maintaining equipment in existing buildings because electrical wiring is more easily accessible during construction. Maintaining equipment and systems involves identifying problems and repairing broken equipment that is sometimes difficult to reach. Maintenance work may include fixing or replacing parts, light fixtures, control systems, motors, and other types of electrical equipment.

Electricians read blueprints, which are technical diagrams of electrical systems that show the location of circuits, outlets, and other equipment. They use different types of hand and power tools, such as conduit benders, to run and protect wiring. Other commonly used hand and power tools include screwdrivers, wire strippers, drills, and saws. While troubleshooting, electricians also may use ammeters, voltmeters, thermal scanners, and cable testers to find problems and ensure that components are working properly.

Many electricians work alone, but sometimes they collaborate with others. For example, experienced electricians may work with building engineers and architects to help design electrical systems for new construction. Some electricians may also consult with other construction specialists, such as elevator installers and heating and air conditioning workers, to help install or maintain electrical or power systems. At larger companies, electricians are more likely to work as part of a crew; they may direct helpers and apprentices to complete jobs.

The following are examples of types of electricians:

Inside electricians maintain and repair large motors, equipment, and control systems in businesses and factories. They use their knowledge of electrical systems to help these facilities run safely and efficiently. Some also install the wiring for businesses and

An electrician prepares the wiring for an interior room.

factories that are being built. To minimize equipment failure, inside electricians often perform scheduled maintenance.

Residential electricians install wiring and troubleshoot electrical problems in peoples' homes, which can be either single-family or multi-family dwellings. Those who work in new-home construction install outlets and provide access to power where needed. Those who work in maintenance and remodeling typically repair and replace faulty equipment. For example, if a circuit breaker repeatedly trips after being reset, electricians determine the cause and fix it.

Although *lineman electricians* install distribution and transmission lines to deliver electricity from its source to customers, they are covered in the line installers and repairers profile.

Work Environment

Electricians held about 628,800 jobs in 2014, of which 63 percent were in the electrical contractors and other wiring installation contractors industry. About 1 in 10 electricians were self-employed in 2014.

Electricians work indoors and outdoors, at homes, businesses, factories, and construction sites. Because electricians must travel to different worksites, local or long-distance commuting is often required.

On the jobsite, they occasionally work in cramped spaces. The long periods of standing and kneeling can be tiring. Those who work in factories are often subject to noisy machinery. As a result, hearing protection must be worn to protect workers from excess noise.

Many electricians work alone, but sometimes they collaborate with others. At larger companies, electricians are more likely to work as part of a crew; they may direct helpers and apprentices to complete jobs.

Injuries and Illnesses. Electricians have a higher rate of injuries and illnesses than the national average. Although a few accidents are potentially fatal, common injuries include electrical shocks, falls, burns, and other minor injuries. Workers must therefore wear protective clothing and safety glasses to reduce these risks.

Work Schedules. Almost all electricians work full time, which may include evenings and weekends. However, work schedules may vary during times of inclement weather. During scheduled maintenance, or on construction sites, electricians can expect to work overtime.

About 1 in 10 electricians were self-employed in 2014. Self-employed electricians often work in residential construction and may have the ability to set their own schedule.

Education/Training

Although most electricians learn through an apprenticeship, some start out by attending a technical school. Most states require electricians to be licensed. For more information, contact your local or state electrical licensing board.

Education. A high school diploma or equivalent is required.

Some electricians start out by attending a technical school. Many technical schools offer programs related to circuitry, safety practices, and basic electrical information. Graduates usually receive credit toward their apprenticeship.

After completing their initial training, electricians may be required to take continuing education courses. These courses are usually related to safety practices, changes to the electrical code, and training from manufacturers in specific products.

Training. Most electricians learn their trade in a 4- or 5-year apprenticeship program. For each year of the program, apprentices must complete at least 144 hours of technical training and 2,000 hours of paid on-the-job training.

In the classroom, apprentices learn electrical theory, blueprint reading, mathematics, electrical code requirements, and safety and first-aid practices. They also may receive specialized training related to soldering, communications, fire alarm systems, and elevators.

Median Annual Wages, May 2014

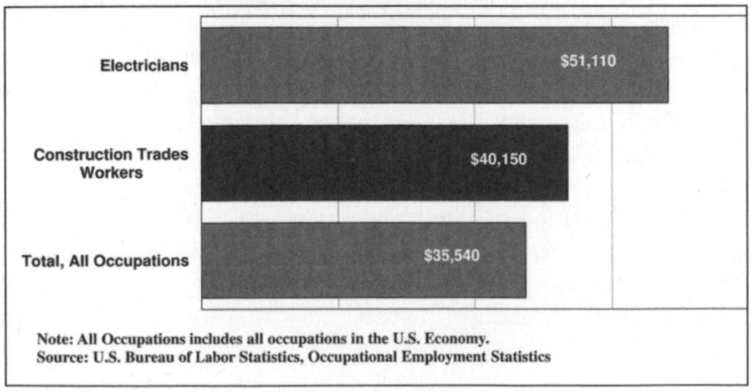

Percent Change in Employment, Projected 2014–2024

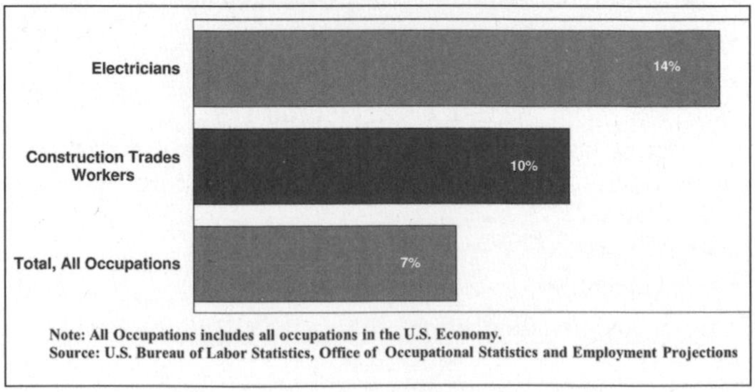

Several groups, including unions and contractor associations, sponsor apprenticeship programs. Many apprenticeship programs have preferred entry for veterans. The basic qualifications to enter an apprenticeship program are as follows:

- Minimum age of 18
- High school education or equivalent
- One year of algebra
- Qualifying score on an aptitude test
- Pass substance abuse screening

Some electrical contractors have their own training programs, which are not recognized apprenticeship programs but include both classroom and on-the-job training. Although most workers enter apprenticeships directly, some electricians enter apprenticeship programs after working as a helper. The Home Builders Institute offers a pre-apprenticeship certificate training (PACT) program for eight construction trades, including electricians.

After completing an apprenticeship program, electricians are considered to be journey workers and may perform duties on their own, subject to any local or state licensing requirements. Because of this comprehensive training, those who complete apprenticeship programs qualify to do both construction and maintenance work.

Some states may require a master electrician to either perform or supervise the work.

Licenses, Certifications, and Registrations. Most states require electricians to pass a test and be licensed. Requirements vary by state. For more information, contact your local or state electrical licensing board. Many of the requirements can be found on the National Electrical Contractors Association's website.

The tests have questions related to the National Electrical Code, and state and local electrical codes, all of which set standards for the safe installation of electrical wiring and equipment.

Important Qualities

Business skills. Self-employed electricians must be able to bid on new jobs, track inventory, and plan payroll and work assignments.

Color vision. Electricians must identify electrical wires by color.

Critical-thinking skills. Electricians perform tests and use the results to diagnose problems. For example, when an outlet is not working, they may use a multimeter to check the voltage, amperage, or resistance to determine the best course of action.

Customer-service skills. Residential electricians work with people on a regular basis. They should be friendly and be able to address customers' questions.

Physical stamina. Electricians often need to move around all day while running wire and connecting fixtures to the wire.

Physical strength. Electricians need to be strong enough to move heavy components, which may weigh up to 50 pounds.

Troubleshooting skills. Electricians find, diagnose, and repair problems. For example, if a motor stops working, they perform tests to determine the cause of its failure and then, depending on the results, fix or replace the motor.

Pay

The median annual wage for electricians was $51,110 in May 2014. The median wage is the wage at which half the workers in an occupation earned more than that amount and half earned less. The lowest 10 percent earned less than $31,170, and the highest 10 percent earned more than $85,590.

The starting pay for apprentices is usually between 40 percent and 50 percent of what fully trained electricians make, receiving pay increases as they learn to do more. Electricians in manufacturing and power generation and transmission typically have higher wages than those in construction.

Union Membership. Compared with workers in all occupations, electricians had a higher percentage of workers who belonged to a union in 2014. Although there is no single union, the largest organizer for electricians is the International Brotherhood of Electrical Workers.

Job Outlook

Employment of electricians is projected to grow 14 percent from 2014 to 2024, much faster than the average for all occupations. As homes and businesses require more wiring, electricians will be needed to install the necessary components. Overall growth of the construction industry and the need to maintain older equipment in manufacturing plants also will require more electricians.

Alternative power generation, such as solar and wind, is an emerging field that should require more electricians for installation. Increasingly, electricians will be needed to link these alternative power sources to homes and power grids over the coming decade. Employment growth stemming from these sources, however, will largely be dependent on government policy.

With greater efficiency and reliability of newer manufacturing plants, demand for electricians in manufacturing should increase as more electricians are needed to install and maintain systems. However, this increase in demand will be partially offset by the closing of older facilities.

Job Prospects. The job prospects for electricians should be very good as many employers report difficulty finding qualified applicants. In addition to job growth, there also are a large number of electricians approaching retirement age, which should produce more job openings in the coming decade.

Employment of electricians fluctuates with the overall economy. On the one hand, there is greater demand for electricians during peak periods of building construction and maintenance. On the other hand, workers may experience periods of unemployment when the overall level of construction and maintenance falls.

Electricians in factories tend to have the most stable employment.

Electricians who can perform many different tasks, such as electronic systems repair, solar photovoltaic installation, and industrial component wiring should have the best job opportunities. In addition, workers with military service experience are viewed favorably during initial hiring.

Employment Projections Data for Electricians

Occupational Title	SOC Code	Employment, 2014	Projected Employment, 2024	Change, 2014–2024	
				Percent	Numeric
Electricians	47-2111	628,800	714,700	14	85,900

Source: U.S. Bureau of Labor Statistics, Employment Projections Program

Similar Occupations. This table shows a list of occupations with job duties that are similar to those of electricians.

Occupations	Entry-level Education	2014 Median Pay	Projected Job Growth	Average Annual Openings
Construction Laborers and Helpers	See Education/Training	$30,190	13%	18,010
Drafters	Associate's degree	$51,940	-3%	-620
Electrical and Electronics Engineering Technicians	Associate's degree	$59,820	-2%	-280
Electrical and Electronics Installers and Repairers	Postsecondary nondegree award	$53,900	-4%	-540
Elevator Installers and Repairers	High school diploma or equivalent	$78,620	13%	270
Heating, Air Conditioning, and Refrigeration Mechanics and Installers	Postsecondary nondegree award	$44,630	14%	3,960
Line Installers and Repairers	High school diploma or equivalent	$61,740	6%	1,370
Solar Photovoltaic Installers	High school diploma or equivalent	$40,020	24%	140
Wind Turbine Technicians	Some college, no degree	$48,800	108%	480

Contacts for More Information

For details about apprenticeships or other work opportunities in this trade, contact the offices of the state employment service, the state apprenticeship agency, local electrical contractors, firms that employ maintenance electricians, or local union–management electrician apprenticeship committees. Apprenticeship information is available from the U.S. Department of Labor's Apprenticeship-USA program (www.dol.gov/apprenticeship) online or by phone at 877-872-5627.

For more information about apprenticeship and training programs for electricians, visit

- ➤ IBEW – NECA Electrical Training Alliance (www.electricaltrainingalliance.org)
- ➤ Associated Builders and Contractors, Inc. (www.abc.org)
- ➤ Home Builders Institute (www.hbi.org/Products-Services/Licensing/PACT)
- ➤ Independent Electrical Contractors, Inc. (www.ieci.org)
- ➤ National Association of Home Builders (www.nahb.org)
- ➤ NCCER (www.nccer.org/electrical?pID=86)

O*NET

- ➤ Electricians (47-2111.00)

Elevator Installers and Repairers

- **2014 Median Pay** .... $78,620 per year $37.80 per hour
- **Typical Entry-Level Education** .... High school diploma or equivalent
- **Work Experience in a Related Occupation**.............. None
- **On-the-job Training** .... Apprenticeship
- **Number of Jobs, 2014** 20,700
- **Job Outlook, 2014–24** .... 13% (Faster than average)
- **Employment Change, 2014–24** 2,700

What Elevator Installers and Repairers Do

Elevator installers and repairers install, fix, and maintain elevators, escalators, moving walkways, and other lifts.

Duties. Elevator installers and repairers typically do the following:

- Read blueprints to determine the equipment needed for installation or repair
- Install or repair elevator doors, cables, motors, and control systems
- Locate malfunctions in brakes, motors, switches, and control systems
- Connect electrical wiring to control panels and electric motors
- Use test equipment, such as ammeters and voltmeters, to diagnose problems
- Adjust counterweights, door mechanisms, and safety controls
- Test newly installed equipment to ensure that it meets specifications
- Ensure elevator compliance with safety regulations and building codes
- Keep service records of all maintenance and repair tasks

Elevator installers and repairers, also called *elevator constructors* or *elevator mechanics*, assemble, install, maintain, and replace elevators, escalators, chairlifts, moving walkways, and similar equipment in buildings.

Elevator installers and repairers usually specialize in installation, maintenance, or repair work. Maintenance and repair workers generally require greater knowledge of electronics, hydraulics, and electricity than do installers because a large part of maintenance and repair work is troubleshooting. Today, most elevators have computerized control systems, resulting in more complex systems and troubleshooting than in the past.

After an elevator is installed, elevator installers and repairers must regularly maintain and service it to keep the elevator working properly. Workers generally perform preventive maintenance, such as oiling and greasing moving parts, replacing worn parts, and adjusting equipment for optimal performance. They also troubleshoot and may be called to perform emergency repairs. Workers who specialize in elevator maintenance typically service many of the same elevators on multiple occasions over time.

A service crew usually handles major repairs—for example, replacing cables, elevator doors, or machine bearings. These tasks may require the use of cutting torches or rigging equipment—tools that an elevator repairer would not normally carry. Service crews also perform major modernization and alteration work, such as replacing electric motors, hydraulic pumps, and control panels.

Employment of elevator installers and repairers is less affected by economic downturns and seasonality than employment in other construction trades.

The following are examples of types of elevator installers and repairers:

Adjusters specialize in fine-tuning all the equipment after installation. They ensure that an elevator operates according to specifications and stops correctly at each floor within a specified time. Adjusters need a thorough knowledge of electronics and computers to ensure that newly installed elevators operate properly.

Assistant mechanics have completed a 4-year apprenticeship program, and although they are fully trained, they typically work under the guidance of a more experienced mechanic.

Work Environment

Elevator installers and repairers held about 20,700 jobs in 2014, of which 89 percent were in the building equipment contractors industry. In contrast to other construction trades, few elevator installers and repairers are self-employed.

Elevator installers and repairers often work in cramped quarters inside crawl spaces and machine rooms, and may be exposed to heights in elevator shafts.

Although installation and major repairs require mechanics to work in teams, workers often work alone when troubleshooting minor problems.

Injuries and Illnesses. Elevator installers and repairers may suffer falls from ladders, burns due to electrical shocks, and muscle strains from lifting and carrying heavy equipment. As a result, workers must take precautions and wear protective equipment such as hard hats, harnesses, and safety glasses.

Work Schedules. Almost all elevator installers and repairers work full time. They often work overtime when emergency repairs need to be made or construction deadlines need to be met. Workers may sometimes be on call 24 hours a day.

Education/Training

Nearly all elevator installers and repairers learn through an apprenticeship. Currently, 35 states require workers to be licensed.

Education. A high school diploma or equivalent is required. High school classes in math, mechanical drawing, and shop may help applicants compete for apprenticeship openings.

Training. Elevator installers and repairers learn their trade through a 4-year apprenticeship. For each year of the program, apprentices must have at least 144 hours of related technical instruction and 2,000 hours of paid on-the-job training. During training, apprentices learn about safety, blueprint reading, elevator and escalator parts, electrical theory, and electronics.

Unions and individual contractors offer apprenticeship programs. The basic qualifications to enter an apprenticeship program are the following:

- Be at least 18 years old
- Possess a high school diploma or equivalent
- Be physically able to do the job
- Pass basic math, reading, and mechanical aptitude tests

When they finish the apprenticeship program, elevator installers and repairers are fully trained and become mechanics or assistant mechanics. Ongoing training is important for elevator installers and repairers in order to keep up with technological developments throughout their careers.

Licenses, Certifications, and Registrations. Currently, 35 states require elevator installers and repairers to be licensed. Check with your state's individual licensing agencies for specific requirements.

Although not required, certification can show competence and proficiency in the field. The National Association of Elevator Contractors offers two certification programs for elevator installers and repairers:

- Certified Elevator Technician
- Certified Accessibility and Private Residence Lift Technician

Advancement. Some installers may receive additional training in specialized areas and advance to become a mechanic-in-charge, adjuster, supervisor, or elevator inspector.

Important Qualities

Detail oriented. Elevator installers must keep accurate records of their service schedules. These records are used to schedule future maintenance, which often helps reduce breakdowns.

Mechanical skills. Elevator installers use a variety of power tools and hand tools to install and repair lifts. Escalators, for

Median Annual Wages, May 2014

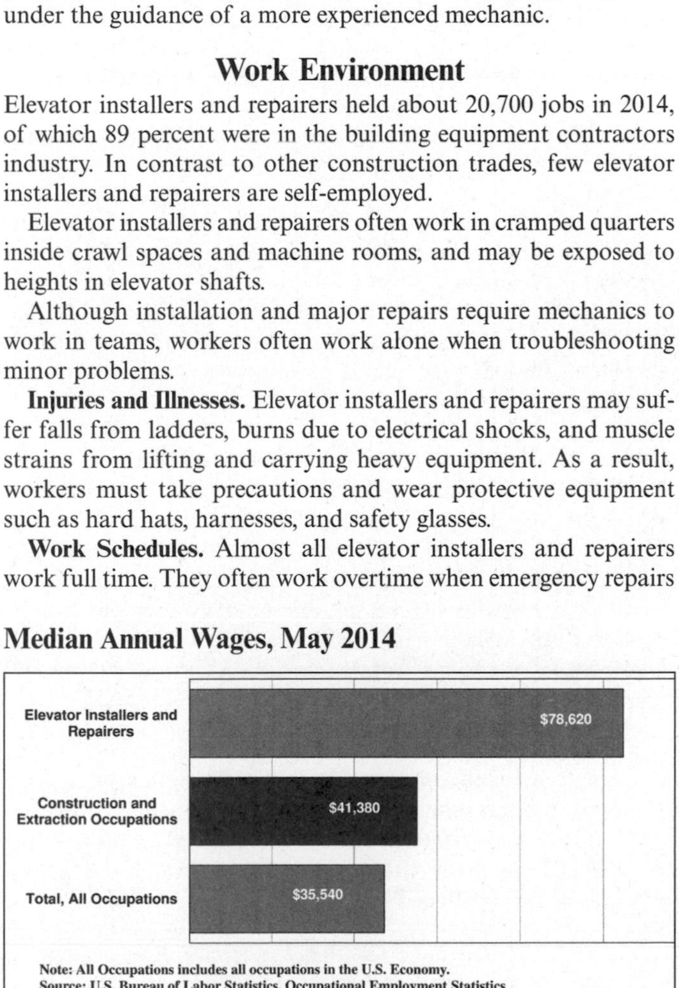

Percent Change in Employment, Projected 2014–2024

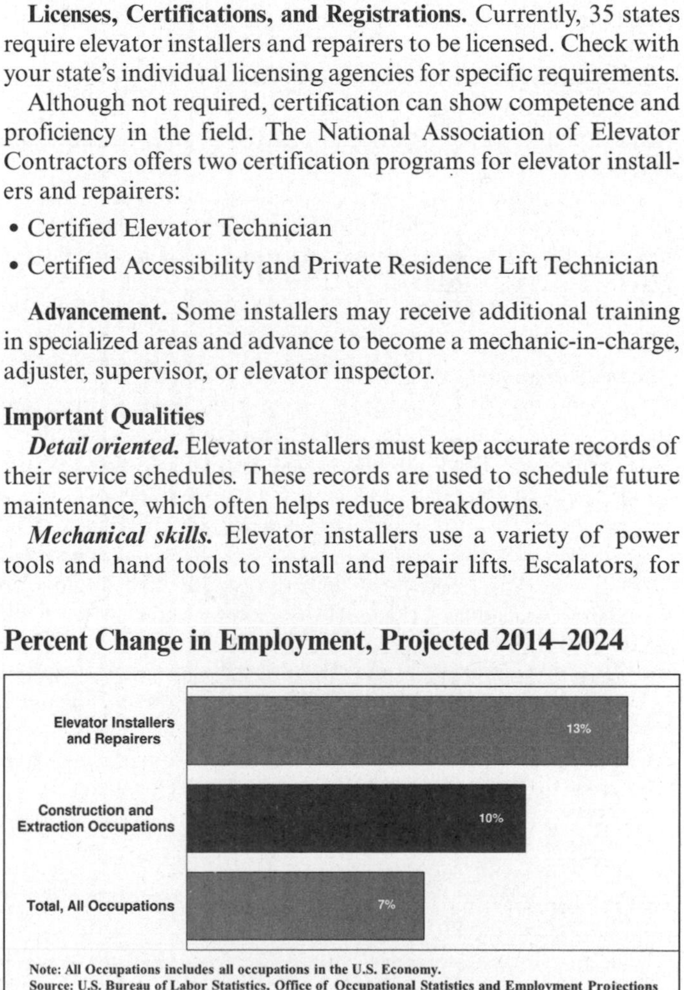

Employment Projections Data for Elevator Installers and Repairers

Occupational Title	SOC Code	Employment, 2014	Projected Employment, 2024	Change, 2014–2024 Percent	Change, 2014–2024 Numeric
Elevator installers and repairers..	47-4021	20,700	23,400	13	2,700

Source: U.S. Bureau of Labor Statistics, Employment Projections Program

Similar Occupations. This table shows a list of occupations with job duties that are similar to those of elevator installers and repairers.

Occupations	Entry-level Education	2014 Median Pay	Projected Job Growth	Average Annual Openings
Boilermakers	High school diploma or equivalent	$59,860	9%	150
Electrical and Electronics Installers and Repairers	Postsecondary nondegree award	$53,900	-4%	-540
Electricians	High school diploma or equivalent	$51,110	14%	8,590
Industrial Machinery Mechanics, Machinery Maintenance Workers, and Millwrights	High school diploma or equivalent	$47,450	16%	7,340
Ironworkers	High school diploma or equivalent	$48,520	9%	710
Sheet Metal Workers	High school diploma or equivalent	$45,070	7%	940

example, run on tracks that must be installed using wrenches and screwdrivers.

Physical stamina. Elevators installers must be able to perform strenuous work, especially in cramped and confined spaces, for long periods.

Physical strength. Elevator installers often lift heavy equipment and parts, including escalator steps, conduit, and metal tracks. Some apprentices must be able to lift 100 pounds to participate in a program.

Troubleshooting skills. Elevator installers and repairers must be able to diagnose and repair problems. When an escalator stops moving, for example, mechanics determine why it stopped and make the necessary repairs.

Pay

The median annual wage for elevator installers and repairers was $78,620 in May 2014. The median wage is the wage at which half the workers in an occupation earned more than that amount and half earned less. The lowest 10 percent earned less than $41,930, and the highest 10 percent earned more than $109,450.

The starting pay for apprentices is usually 50 percent of what fully trained elevator installers and repairers make. They earn pay increases as they progress in their apprenticeship. Apprentices who are also certified welders usually receive higher wages while welding. Assistant mechanics, by contract, receive 80 percent of the rate paid to journey worker elevator installers and repairers.

Union Membership. Most elevator installers and repairers belonged to a union in 2014. Although no single union covers all elevator installers and repairers, the largest organizer of these workers is the International Union of Elevator Constructors.

Job Outlook

Employment of elevator installers and repairers is projected to grow 13 percent from 2014 to 2024, faster than the average for all occupations.

Demand for these workers will depend on growth of nonresidential construction, such as office buildings and stores that have elevators and escalators. This sector of the construction industry is expected to grow rapidly during the next decade as the economy rebounds from the recent recession.

In addition, the need to regularly maintain, update, and repair old equipment; provide access to the disabled; and install increasingly sophisticated equipment and controls will maintain demand for elevator installers and repairers.

Job Prospects. The high wages of elevator installers and repairers will attract many applicants, and job seekers may face strong competition.

Job opportunities for entry-level workers should be best for those who have postsecondary education in electronics or who are military veterans.

Elevators, escalators, lifts, moving walkways, and related equipment need to work year round, so employment of elevator repairers is less affected by economic downturns and seasonality than employment in other construction occupations.

Contacts for More Information

For information about apprenticeships or job opportunities as an elevator mechanic, contact local elevator contractors, a local chapter of the International Union of Elevator Constructors, a local joint union–management apprenticeship committee, or the nearest office of your state employment service or apprenticeship agency. Apprenticeship information is available from the U.S. Department of Labor's ApprenticeshipUSA program (www.dol.gov/apprenticeship) online or by phone at 877-872-5627.

For more information about elevator installers and repairers, visit

➤ International Union of Elevator Constructors (www.iuec.org)

For more information about the NAEC Apprenticeship Program, the Certified Elevator Technician program, or the Certified Accessibility and Private Residence Lift Technician program, visit

➤ National Association of Elevator Contractors (www.naec.org)

O*NET

➤ Elevator Installers and Repairers (47-4021.00)

Flooring Installers and Tile and Marble Setters

- **2014 Median Pay** .... $37,380 per year
  $17.97 per hour
- **Typical Entry-Level Education** .... No formal educational credential
- **Work Experience in a Related Occupation** .... None
- **On-the-job Training** .... See Education/Training
- **Number of Jobs, 2014** 125,400
- **Job Outlook, 2014–24** .... 5% (As fast as average)
- **Employment Change, 2014–24** 5,900

What Flooring Installers and Tile and Marble Setters Do

Flooring installers and tile and marble setters lay and finish carpet, wood, vinyl, and tile.

Duties. Flooring installers and tile and marble setters typically do the following:

- Remove existing flooring or wall covering
- Clean and level the surface to be covered
- Measure the area and cut flooring material to fit
- Arrange flooring according to design plans
- Place flooring, using adhesives, nails, or staples
- Fill joints with filler compound and remove excess compound
- Trim excess carpet or linoleum
- Apply necessary finishes, such as sealants and stains

Nearly every building has a finished floor, and flooring installers and tile and marble setters lay the materials that improve the look and feel of homes, offices, restaurants, and other buildings. Although most of the materials installed by these workers cover only floors, some materials are also installed on walls and countertops or in showers.

A smooth, even base of mortar or plywood is required in order for floors and tile to be installed. The base may be installed by flooring installers and tile and marble setters or by other construction craftworkers. When remodeling, workers may need to remove the old flooring and smooth the surface.

Carpet installers lay lengths of carpet on new floors or over older flooring. They use special tools, including "knee kickers," to position the carpet and power stretchers to pull the carpet snugly against walls. Carpet seams are joined with special heat-activated tape.

Carpet tile installers lay small, modular pieces of carpet that may be glued into place. Carpet tiles allow for easy replacement and design patterns that are not possible with standard carpet.

Floor sanders and finishers perform the final steps in hardwood floor installation. After carpenters install the hardwood floor, workers use power sanders to smooth it. They apply stains and sealants to preserve the wood.

Floor layers, except carpet, wood, and hard tiles, install a wide variety of resilient flooring materials. *Linoleum installers* lay the hard, washable floor material of the same name. The linoleum is cut to size and glued into place. *Vinyl installers* install plastic-based flooring that includes vinyl ester, vinyl sheeting, and luxury vinyl tile. Installers of laminate, manufactured wood, and wood tile floors are included in this category.

Tile and marble setters install ceramic and marble tile. *Tile installers*, sometimes called *tile setters*, cut and place tile. To cut tiles, workers use wet saws, tile scribes, or handheld tile cutters to create even edges. They use trowels of different sizes to spread mortar or a sticky paste, called mastic, evenly on the surface to be tiled. To minimize imperfections and keep rows even, they put spacers between tiles. Spacers keep tiles the same distance from each other until the mortar is dry. *Tile finishers* apply grout between tiles after the tiles are set, using a rubber trowel which is called a float. When the grout dries, they must wipe the tiles for a clean, finished look. *Marble setters* cut marble to a specified size with a wet saw. After fastening the stone, marble setters polish the marble to a high luster, using hand or power sanders.

Work Environment

Flooring installers and tile and marble setters held about 125,400 jobs in 2014. Approximately 41 percent of them were employed in the building finishing contractors industry. About 4 in 10 were self-employed.

Employment in the detailed occupations that make up the occupation of flooring installers and tile and marble setters in 2014 was distributed as follows:

Tile and marble setters	55,100
Carpet installers	45,300
Floor layers, except carpet, wood, and hard tiles	17,100
Floor sanders and finishers	7,900

Flooring and tile are usually installed after most of the construction has been completed, so the work area is typically clean and uncluttered, although some materials and tasks may be messy.

Installing flooring, tile, and marble is physically demanding, with workers spending much of their time reaching, bending, and kneeling. As a result, workers typically wear kneepads for protection. Workers also wear safety goggles when using grinders, saws, and sanders. In enclosed areas with poor access to ventilation, workers often use dust masks or respirator systems to prevent the inhalation of dust. Dust is generated from cutting tiles and from sanding adhesives and mortars.

Tile installers lay floor coverings in homes and other types of buildings.

Work Schedules. Most flooring installers and tile and marble setters work full time. In commercial settings, installers may work evenings and weekends, often for higher wages, to avoid disturbing regular business operations.

About 4 in 10 flooring installers and tile and marble setters were self-employed in 2014. Self-employed workers may have the ability to set their own schedules.

Education/Training

Although some flooring installers and tile and marble setters learn their trade through an apprenticeship, most learn on the job, sometimes starting as a helper.

Education. There are no specific education requirements for someone to become a flooring installer or tile and marble setter. A high school diploma or equivalent is preferred for those entering an apprenticeship program.

High school art, math, and vocational courses are considered helpful for flooring installers and tile and marble setters.

Training. Most contractors have their own training programs for flooring installers and tile and marble setters. New workers typically learn by working with experienced installers. Although workers may enter training directly, many start out as helpers.

New workers usually start by performing simple tasks, such as moving materials. As they gain experience, they are given more complex tasks, such as cutting carpet. Some tile installer helpers become tile finishers before becoming tile installers.

Some flooring installers and tile and marble setters learn their trade through a 2- to 4-year apprenticeship. For each year of the program, apprentices must complete at least 144 hours of related technical training and 2,000 hours of paid on-the-job training. Some of these programs now include online training. Many new workers begin with 12 weeks of pre-apprenticeship instruction at a training center to learn construction basics. This instruction may include mathematics, building code requirements, safety and first-aid practices, and blueprint reading.

Several groups, including unions and contractor associations, sponsor apprenticeship programs. The basic qualifications for entering an apprenticeship program are as follows:

- Minimum age of 18
- High school education or equivalent
- Physically able to do the work

After completing an apprenticeship program, flooring installers and tile and marble setters are considered to be journey workers and may perform duties on their own.

Some flooring manufacturers offer product-specific training for their products. In addition, some installers attend conferences that offer training sessions in various flooring materials.

Certification. The Ceramic Tile Education Foundation (CTEF) offers the Certified Tile Installer (CTI) certification for workers with 2 or more years of experience. Applicants are required to complete a written test and a hands-on performance evaluation.

Several groups, including the Ceramic Tile Education Foundation, the International Masonry Institute (IMI), the International Union of Bricklayers & Allied Craftworkers (IUBAC), the National Tile Contractors Association (NTCA), the Tile Contractors' Association of America (TCAA), and the Tile Council of North America (TCNA) have created the Advanced Certifications for Tile Installers (ACT) program. Certification requirements include passing both an exam and a field test. Workers must also have either completed a qualified apprenticeship program or earned the CTI certification to qualify for testing. The program offers certifications in five specific areas of tile installation:

- Large-format tile and substrate preparation
- Membranes
- Mortar (mud) floors
- Mortar (mud) walls
- Shower receptors

The National Wood Flooring Association (NWFA) has a voluntary certification for floor sanders and finishers. Sanders and finishers must have 2 years of experience and must have completed NWFA-approved training. Applicants are also required to complete written and performance tests.

The International Certified Floorcovering Installers Association (CFI) offers certification for flooring and tile installers. Installers need 2 years of experience before they can take the written test and a hands-on performance evaluation.

The International Standards & Training Alliance (INSTALL) offers a comprehensive flooring certification program for flooring and tile installers. INSTALL certification requires 4 years of classroom and hands-on training, and covers all major types of flooring.

Important Qualities

Color vision. Flooring installers and tile and marble setters often need to determine small color variations. Because tile patterns may include many different colors, workers must be able to distinguish among colors and among patterns for the best-looking finish.

Customer-service skills. Flooring installers and tile and marble setters commonly work in customers' homes. Therefore, workers

Median Annual Wages, May 2014

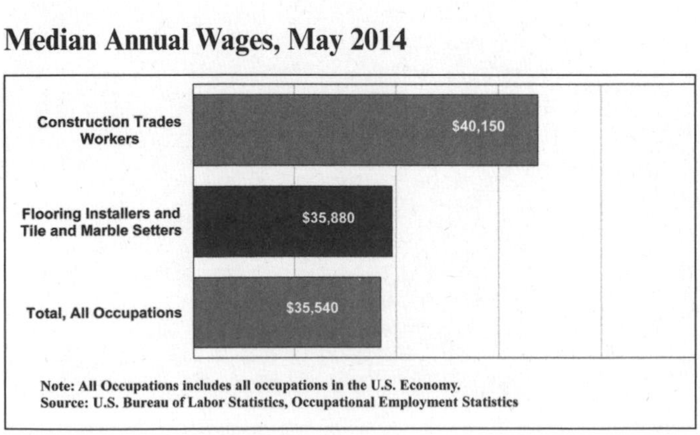

Percent Change in Employment, Projected 2014–2024

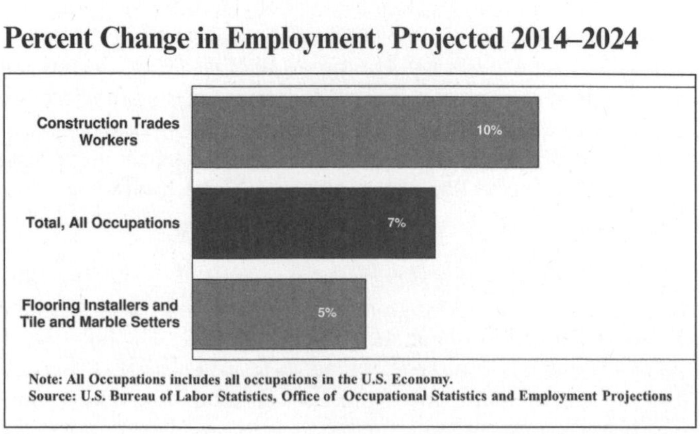

Employment Projections Data for Flooring Installers and Tile and Marble Setters

Occupational Title	SOC Code	Employment, 2014	Projected Employment, 2024	Change, 2014–2024	
				Percent	Numeric
Carpet, floor, and tile installers and finishers	47-2040	125,400	131,300	5	5,900
Carpet installers	47-2041	45,300	45,100	-1	-200
Floor layers, except carpet, wood, and hard tiles	47-2042	17,100	19,200	12	2,100
Floor sanders and finishers	47-2043	7,900	8,400	6	500
Tile and marble setters	47-2044	55,100	58,700	6	3,500

Source: U.S. Bureau of Labor Statistics, Employment Projections Program

must be courteous and considerate of a customer's property while completing tasks.

Detail oriented. Flooring installers and tile and marble setters need to plan and lay out materials. Some carpet patterns can be highly detailed and artistic, so workers must ensure that the patterns are properly and accurately aligned.

Math skills. Flooring installers and tile and marble setters use measurement-related math skills on every job. Besides measuring the area to be covered, workers must calculate the number of carpet tiles needed to cover that area.

Physical stamina. Flooring installers and tile and marble setters must have the endurance to stand or kneel for many hours. Workers need to spread adhesives quickly and place tile on floors before the adhesives harden.

Physical strength. Flooring installers and tile and marble setters need to lift and carry heavy materials. Workers must be strong enough to lift, carry, and set heavy pieces of marble into position.

Pay

The median annual wage for flooring installers and tile and marble setters was $37,380 in May 2014. The median wage is the wage at which half the workers in an occupation earned more than that amount and half earned less. The lowest 10 percent earned less than $21,960, and the highest 10 percent earned more than $71,830.

Median annual wages for flooring installers and tile and marble setters in May 2014 were as follows:

Tile and marble setters	$38,980
Floor layers, except carpet, wood, and hard tiles	36,670
Carpet installers	35,880
Floor sanders and finishers	35,770

Job Outlook

Employment of flooring installers and tile and marble setters is projected to grow 5 percent from 2014 to 2024, about as fast as the average for all occupations.

Employment growth of specific types of flooring and tile and marble installers is expected to vary (see Employment Projections table). The majority of flooring and tile and marble installation work is expected to be in remodeling and replacement. Population and business growth, coupled with the popularity of some new resilient floor material, will be the major source of demand for workers. Although carpet is still the dominant flooring, other products are growing in popularity, which is why the employment of the other flooring installer occupations are projected to grow faster than carpet installers. Tile and marble will continue to be commonly installed in bathrooms, shopping malls, and restaurants, as well as in other commercial and government buildings.

Job Prospects. Overall job prospects should be good over the coming decade as high turnover and new building construction will create job opportunities for flooring installers and tile and marble setters. Experienced workers with a good employment history who are able to install multiple types of floors will have the best employment opportunities.

As with many other types of construction occupations, employment of these workers is sensitive to the fluctuations of the economy. On the one hand, workers may experience periods of unemployment when the overall level of construction falls. On the other hand, shortages of workers may occur in some areas during peak periods of building activity.

Contacts for More Information

For details about apprenticeships, training, or other work opportunities in this trade, contact the offices of the state employment service, the state apprenticeship agency, local contractors or firms that employ flooring installers and tile and marble setters, or

Similar Occupations. This table shows a list of occupations with job duties that are similar to those of flooring installers and tile and marble setters.

Occupations	Entry-level Education	2014 Median Pay	Projected Job Growth	Average Annual Openings
Carpenters	High school diploma or equivalent	$40,820	6%	6,040
Construction Laborers and Helpers	See Education/Training	$30,190	13%	18,010
Drywall and Ceiling Tile Installers, and Tapers	No formal educational credential	$38,970	5%	660
Masonry Workers	See Education/Training	$38,720	15%	3,730
Painters, Construction and Maintenance	No formal educational credential	$35,950	7%	2,650
Roofers	No formal educational credential	$35,760	13%	1,580

local union–management apprenticeship committees. Apprenticeship information is available from the U.S. Department of Labor's ApprenticeshipUSA program (www.dol.gov/apprenticeship) online or by phone at 877-872-5627.

For more information about flooring installers and tile and marble setters, visit

- Ceramic Tile Education Foundation (http://tilecareer.com)
- International Masonry Institute (http://imiweb.org)
- International Union of Bricklayers & Allied Craftworkers (www.bacweb.org)
- Tile Contractors' Association of America (www.tcaainc.org/index.php)
- The Tile Council of North America, Inc. (www.tcnatile.com)
- Home Builders Institute (www.hbi.org)

For more information about training and certification of flooring installers and tile and marble setters, visit

- International Certified Floorcovering Installers Association (www.cfiinstallers.com)
- Finishing Trades Institute International (www.finishingtradesinstitute.org)
- International Standards & Training Alliance (www.installfloors.org) (INSTALL)
- National Tile Contractors Association (www.tile-assn.com)
- National Wood Flooring Association (www.nwfa.org)

O*NET

- Carpet Installers (47-2041.00)
- Floor Layers, Except Carpet, Wood, and Hard Tiles (47-2042.00)
- Floor Sanders and Finishers (47-2043.00)
- Tile and Marble Setters (47-2044.00)

Glaziers

- **2014 Median Pay** .... $38,410 per year $18.47 per hour
- **Entry-Level Education** .... High school diploma or equivalent
- **Work Experience in a Related Occupation**.............. None
- **On-the-Job Training** .... Apprenticeship
- **Number of Jobs 2014** 45,300
- **Job Outlook, 2014–24** .... 4% (Slower than average)
- **Employment Change, 2014–24** 1,900

What Glaziers Do

Glaziers install glass in windows, skylights, and other fixtures in storefronts and buildings.

Duties. Glaziers typically do the following:

- Follow blueprints or specifications
- Remove any old or broken glass before installing replacement glass
- Cut glass to the specified size and shape
- Make or install sashes or moldings for glass installation
- Fasten glass into sashes or frames with clips, moldings, or other types of fasteners
- Add weather seal or putty around pane edges to seal joints

Glass has many uses in everyday life. For example, insulated and specially treated glass keeps in warm or cool air and controls sound and condensation. Tempered and laminated glass makes doors and windows more secure by making them less prone to breaking. The use of large windows, glass doors, and skylights makes buildings bright, airy, and inviting. Glaziers specialize in installing these different glass products.

In homes, glaziers install or replace windows, mirrors, shower doors, and bathtub enclosures. They fit glass for tabletops and display cases. On commercial interior projects, glaziers install items such as heavy, often etched, decorative room dividers or security windows. Glazing projects also may involve exterior work such as replacing storefront windows for supermarkets, auto dealerships, banks, and many other establishments.

For most large-scale construction jobs, glass is precut and mounted into frames at a factory or a contractor's shop. The finished glass arrives at the jobsite ready for glaziers to position and secure into place. Using cranes or hoists with suction cups, workers lift large, heavy pieces of glass for installation. In cases where the glass is not secure inside the frame, glaziers may attach steel and aluminum sashes or frames to the building, and then secure the glass with clips, moldings, or other types of fasteners.

Many windows are now being covered with laminates—a thin film or coating placed over the glass. These coatings provide additional durability, security, and can add color or tint to interior and exterior glass. The laminate also provides safety benefits by making glass less prone to shattering, which makes it ideal for commercial use in areas prone to high winds.

A few glaziers work with plastics, granite, marble, and other materials used as glass substitutes.

Workers who replace and repair glass in motor vehicles are covered in the profile for automotive body and glass repairers.

Work Environment

Glaziers held about 45,300 jobs in 2014, of which 66 percent were in the foundation, structure, and building exterior contractors industry. Another 14 percent of glaziers were employed in the building material and supplies dealers industry in 2014.

As in many other construction trades, the work is physically demanding. Glaziers spend most of the day standing, bending, or reaching, and they often must lift and maneuver heavy, cumbersome materials, such as large glass plates.

When installing glass plates on buildings, glaziers often lead a team of construction workers in guiding and installing the pieces into place.

Injuries and Illnesses. Glaziers have a higher rate of injuries and illnesses than the national average for all occupations. Typical

Glaziers cut class to lengths specified by the customer.

Median Annual Wages, May 2014

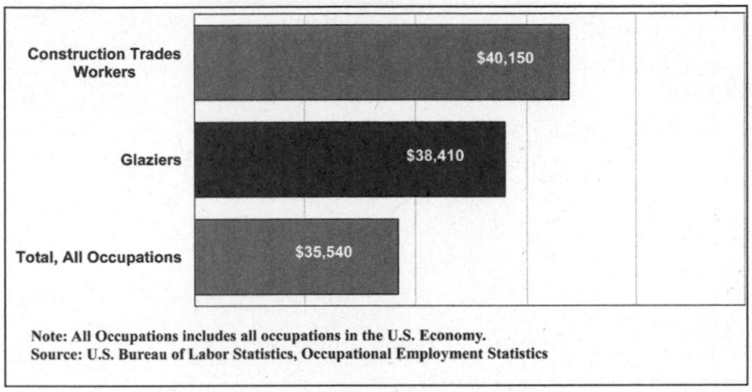

Percent Change in Employment, Projected 2014–2024

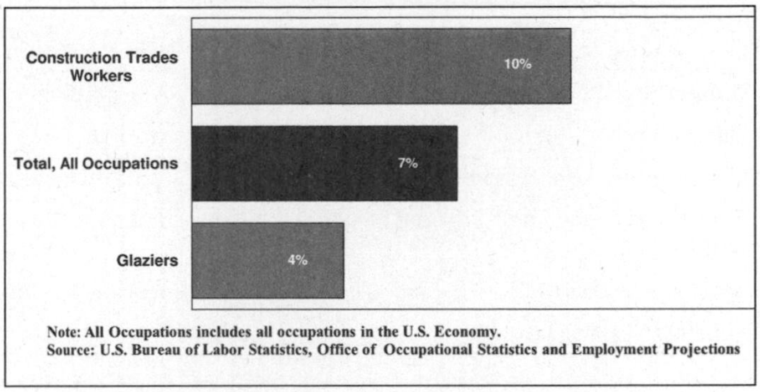

injuries for glaziers include cuts from tools and glass, and falls from ladders and scaffolding.

Work Schedules. Most glaziers work full time.

Education/Training

Glaziers typically enter the occupation with a high school diploma and learn their trade through an apprenticeship.

Education. The typical entry route for glaziers is a high school diploma or equivalent. High school courses in math are considered useful.

Training. The typical training for glaziers is a 4-year apprenticeship. Each year, apprentices must have at least 144 hours of related technical training and 2,000 hours of paid on-the-job training. On the job, they learn to use the tools and equipment of the trade; handle, measure, cut, and install glass and metal framing; cut and fit moldings; and install and balance glass doors. Technical training includes learning different installation techniques, as well as basic mathematics, blueprint reading and sketching, general construction techniques, safety practices, and first aid.

After completing an apprenticeship program, glaziers are considered to be journey workers who may do tasks on their own.

A few groups sponsor apprenticeship programs, including several union and contractor associations. Some apprenticeship programs have preferred entry for veterans. The basic qualifications to enter an apprenticeship program are as follows:

- Minimum age of 18
- High school education or equivalent
- Physically able to perform the work

Licenses, Certifications, and Registrations. Connecticut and Florida are the only two states to require glaziers to have a license. Licensure requirements include passing a test, completing an apprenticeship, and possessing a combination of education and work experience.

Important Qualities

Balance. Glaziers need a good sense of balance while working on ladders and scaffolding to minimize the risk of falling.

Hand-eye coordination. Glaziers must be able to cut glass precisely. As a result, a steady hand is needed to cut the correct size and shape in the field.

Physical stamina. Glaziers must be on their feet and move heavy pieces of glass most of the day. They need to be able to hold glass in place until it can be fully secured.

Physical strength. Glaziers must often lift heavy pieces of glass for hanging. Physical strength, therefore, is important for the occupation.

Pay

The median annual wage for glaziers was $38,410 in May 2014. The median wage is the wage at which half the workers in an occupation earned more than that amount and half earned less. The lowest 10 percent earned less than $24,670, and the highest 10 percent earned more than $76,840.

The starting pay for apprentices is about 40 percent of what fully trained glaziers make, receiving pay increases as they learn to do more. Glaziers who work at great heights may be eligible for hazard-premium pay.

Job Outlook

Employment of glaziers is projected to grow 4 percent from 2014 to 2024, slower than the average for all occupations.

Employment growth is expected as commercial construction increasingly uses glass exteriors. As glass manufacturers continue to improve the energy efficiency of glass windows, architects are designing more buildings with glass exteriors, especially in the South.

In addition, the continuing need to modernize and repair existing structures, including many homes, often involves installing new windows. Furthermore, specialized laminated glass is increasingly being installed in homes and commercial and government buildings.

Nonetheless, the availability of prefabricated windows that carpenters and general contractors can install is expected to moderate employment growth of glaziers.

Employment Projections Data for Glaziers

Occupational Title	SOC Code	Employment, 2014	Projected Employment, 2024	Change, 2014–2024	
				Percent	Numeric
Glaziers	47-2121	45,300	47,200	4	1,900

Source: U.S. Bureau of Labor Statistics, Employment Projections Program

Similar Occupations. This table shows a list of occupations with job duties that are similar to those of glaziers.

Occupations	Entry-level Education	2014 Median Pay	Projected Job Growth	Average Annual Openings
Automotive Body and Glass Repairers	High school diploma or equivalent	$39,260	9%	1,530
Carpenters	High school diploma or equivalent	$40,820	6%	6,040
Construction Laborers and Helpers	See Education/Training	$30,190	13%	18,010
Flooring Installers and Tile and Marble Setters	No formal educational credential	$37,380	5%	590
Masonry Workers	See Education/Training	$38,720	15%	3,730
Sheet Metal Workers	High school diploma or equivalent	$45,070	7%	940

Job Prospects. Good job opportunities are expected from the need to replace glaziers who leave the occupation each year.

Because employers prefer workers who can do many different tasks, glaziers with a wide range of skills will have the best job opportunities. In addition, workers with military service experience are viewed favorably during initial hiring.

Like many other types of construction worker jobs, employment of glaziers is sensitive to the fluctuations of the economy. On the one hand, glaziers may experience periods of unemployment when the overall level of construction falls. On the other hand, shortages of workers may occur in some areas during peak periods of building activity.

Employment opportunities should be best in metropolitan areas where most glazing contractors and glass shops are located.

Contacts for More Information

For details about apprenticeships or other work opportunities in this trade, contact the offices of the state employment service, the state apprenticeship agency, local contractors or firms that employ glaziers, or local union–management finishing trade apprenticeship committees. Apprenticeship information is available from the U.S. Department of Labor's ApprenticeshipUSA program (www.dol.gov/apprenticeship) online or by phone at 877-872-5627.

For more information about glaziers, visit

- ➤ Associated Builders and Contractors, Inc. (www.abc.org)
- ➤ Finishing Trades Institute (www.finishingtradesinstitute.org)
- ➤ International Union of Painters and Allied Trades (www.iupat.org/pages/start-a-career/glazing)
- ➤ National Glass Association (www.glass.org)

O*NET

- ➤ Glaziers (47-2121.00)

Hazardous Materials Removal Workers

- **2014 Median Pay** .... $38,520 per year $18.52 per hour
- **Typical Entry-Level Education** .... High school diploma or equivalent
- **Work Experience in a Related Occupation** .... None
- **On-the-job Training** ..... Moderate-term on-the-job training
- **Number of Jobs, 2014** 43,700
- **Job Outlook, 2014–24** .... 7% (As fast as average)
- **Employment Change, 2014–24** 3,300

What Hazardous Materials Removal Workers Do

Hazardous materials (hazmat) removal workers identify and dispose of asbestos, lead, radioactive waste, and other hazardous materials. They also neutralize and clean up materials that are flammable, corrosive, or toxic.

Duties. Hazmat removal workers typically do the following:

- Follow safety procedures before, during, and after cleanup
- Comply with state and federal laws regarding waste disposal
- Test hazardous materials to determine the proper way to clean up
- Construct scaffolding or build containment areas before cleaning up
- Remove, neutralize, or clean up hazardous materials that are found or spilled
- Clean contaminated equipment for reuse
- Package, transport, or store hazardous materials
- Keep records of cleanup activities

Hazmat removal workers clean up materials that are harmful to people and the environment. They usually work in teams and follow strict instructions and guidelines. The specific duties of hazmat removal workers depend on the substances that are targeted and the location of the cleanup. For example, removing lead and asbestos requires different actions than does cleaning up radiation contamination and toxic spills, and cleaning up a fuel spill from a train derailment is more urgent than removing lead paint from a bridge.

The following are examples of types of hazmat removal workers:

Asbestos abatement workers and *lead abatement workers* remove asbestos and lead, respectively, from buildings and structures, particularly those which are being renovated or demolished. Most of this work is in older buildings that were originally built with asbestos insulation and lead-based paints—both of which are now banned.

Asbestos and lead abatement workers apply chemicals to surfaces, such as walls and ceilings, in order to soften asbestos or remove lead-based paint. Once the chemicals are applied, workers cut out asbestos from the surfaces or strip the walls. They package the residue or paint chips and place them in approved bags or containers for proper disposal. Lead abatement workers operate sandblasters, high-pressure water sprayers, and other tools to remove paint. Asbestos abatement workers also use scrapers or vacuums to remove asbestos from buildings.

Decommissioning and decontamination workers remove and treat radioactive materials generated by nuclear facilities and power plants. They break down contaminated items such as "glove boxes," which are used to process radioactive materials, and they

Some hazardous materials removal workers specialize in radioactive substances.

clean and decontaminate closed or decommissioned (taken out of service) facilities.

Emergency and disaster response workers clean up hazardous materials in response to natural or human-made disasters and accidents, such as those involving trains, trucks, or other vehicles transporting hazardous materials.

Radiation-protection technicians measure, record, and report radiation levels; operate high-pressure cleaning equipment for decontamination; and package radioactive materials for removal or storage.

Treatment, storage, and disposal workers prepare and transport hazardous materials for treatment, storage, or disposal. Proper treatment of materials requires these workers to follow U.S. Environmental Protection Agency (EPA) or Occupational Safety & Health Administration (OSHA) regulations. Using equipment such as forklifts, earthmoving machinery, and trucks, these workers move materials from contaminated sites to incinerators, landfills, or storage facilities. Workers also organize and track the locations of items in these facilities.

Work Environment

Hazardous materials removal workers held about 43,700 jobs in 2014. The industries that employed the most hazardous materials removal workers were as follows:

Waste management and remediation services	74%
Construction	9
Government	4

Working conditions vary with the hazardous material being removed. For example, workers removing lead or asbestos often work in confined spaces or at great heights and bend or stoop to remove the material. Emergency and disaster response workers may work outside in all weather conditions.

Asbestos and lead abatement workers typically work in buildings that are being renovated or torn down. Completing projects often requires night and weekend work to meet deadlines.

Treatment, storage, and disposal workers are usually employed at facilities such as landfills, incinerators, and industrial furnaces.

Decommissioning and decontamination workers and technicians work at nuclear facilities and electric power plants.

Injuries and Illnesses. Cleaning or removing hazardous materials is dangerous, and workers must follow specific safety procedures to avoid injuries and illnesses. They usually work in teams and follow instructions from a team leader or site supervisor.

Workers wear coveralls, gloves, shoe covers, and safety glasses or goggles to reduce their exposure to harmful materials. Some must wear fully closed protective suits, which may be hot and uncomfortable, for several hours at a time. Hazmat removal workers are required to wear respirators to protect themselves from airborne particles or noxious gases in extremely toxic cleanups. Lead abatement workers wear personal air monitors that measure the amount of lead exposure.

Work Schedules. Most hazmat removal workers are employed full time. Overtime and shift work are common, especially for emergency and disaster response workers.

Some hazmat removal workers travel to areas affected by a disaster. During a cleanup, workers may be away from home for several days or weeks until the project is completed.

Hazmat removal workers at nuclear facilities are busiest during periods of refueling and may experience unemployment at other times.

Education/Training

Hazardous materials (hazmat) removal workers receive on-the-job training. They must complete up to 40 hours of training in accordance with Occupational Safety & Health Administration (OSHA) standards.

There are no formal education requirements beyond a high school diploma.

Some hazmat removal workers must be licensed. Positions in nuclear facilities require candidates to be U.S. citizens, pass a security background investigation, and pass drug and alcohol abuse screening.

Education. Hazmat removal workers typically need a high school diploma. Although not required, associate's degree programs related to radiation protection may help candidates seeking positions in nuclear facilities.

Training. Hazmat removal workers receive training on the job. Training generally includes a combination of classroom instruction and fieldwork. In the classroom, they learn safety procedures and the proper use of personal protective equipment. Onsite, they learn about equipment and chemicals, and are supervised by an experienced worker.

As part of this training, workers must complete up to 40 hours of training in accordance with OSHA standards. The length of training depends on the type of hazardous material that workers handle. The training covers health hazards, personal protective equipment and clothing, site safety, recognizing and identifying hazards, and decontamination.

Median Annual Wages, May 2014

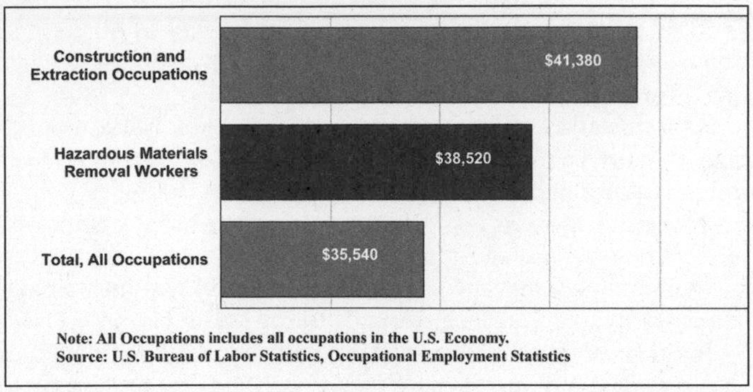

Percent Change in Employment, Projected 2014–2024

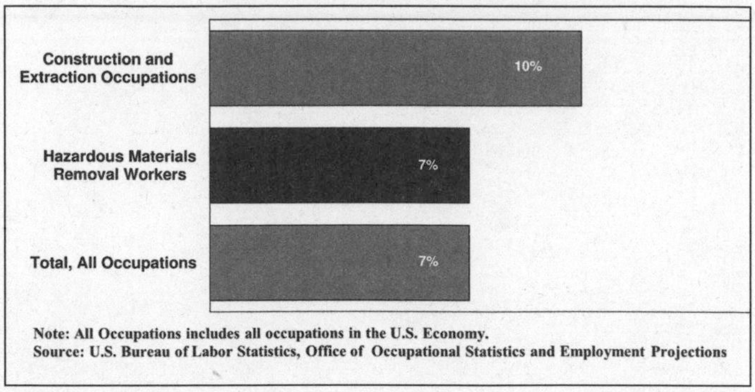

To work with a specific hazardous material, workers must complete training requirements and work requirements set by state or federal agencies on handling that material.

Workers who treat asbestos or lead, the most common contaminants, must complete an employer-sponsored training program that covers technical and safety subjects outlined by OSHA.

Decommissioning and decontamination workers at nuclear facilities receive extensive training. In addition to completing the OSHA-required hazardous waste removal training, workers must take courses on nuclear materials and radiation safety as mandated by the U.S. Nuclear Regulatory Commission. These courses may take up to 3 months to complete, although most are not taken consecutively.

Organizations and companies provide training programs that are approved by the U.S. Environmental Protection Agency, the U.S. Department of Energy, and other regulatory agencies.

Licenses, Certifications, and Registrations. In addition to completing the training required by OSHA, some states mandate permits or licenses, particularly for asbestos and lead removal. Workers who transport hazardous materials may need a state or federal permit.

License requirements vary by state, but candidates typically must meet the following criteria:

- Be at least 18 years old
- Complete training mandated by a state or federal agency
- Pass a written exam

To maintain licensure, workers must take continuing education courses each year. For more information, check with the state's licensing agency.

Work Experience in a Related Occupation. Although previous work experience is not required, some employers prefer candidates with experience in the construction trades, such as construction laborers and helpers.

In addition, some employers at nuclear facilities prefer to hire workers with at least 2 years of related work experience. Experience in nuclear operations in the U.S. Navy as a nuclear technician or power plant operator or experience working as a janitor at a nuclear facility may be helpful.

Important Qualities

Decision-making skills. Hazmat removal workers identify materials in a spill or leak and choose the proper method for cleaning up.

Detail oriented. Hazmat removal workers must follow safety procedures and keep records of their work. For example, workers must track the amount and type of waste disposed, equipment or chemicals used, and number of containers stored.

Math skills. Workers must be able to perform basic mathematical conversions and calculations when mixing solutions that neutralize contaminants.

Mechanical skills. Hazmat removal workers may operate heavy equipment to clean contaminated sites.

Physical stamina. Workers may have to stand and scrub equipment or surfaces for hours at a time to remove toxic materials.

Pay

The median annual wage for hazardous materials removal workers was $38,520 in May 2014. The median wage is the wage at which half the workers in an occupation earned more than that amount and half earned less. The lowest 10 percent earned less than $25,860, and the highest 10 percent earned more than $67,420.

In May 2014, the median annual wages for hazardous materials removal workers in the top industries in which they worked were as follows:

Government	$48,920
Waste management and remediation services	38,470
Construction	34,960

Union Membership. Compared with workers in all occupations, hazardous materials removal workers had a higher percentage of workers who belonged to a union in 2014.

Employment Projections Data for Hazardous Materials Removal Workers

Occupational Title	SOC Code	Employment, 2014	Projected Employment, 2024	Change, 2014–2024 Percent	Change, 2014–2024 Numeric
Hazardous materials removal workers	47-4041	43,700	47,000	7	3,300

Source: U.S. Bureau of Labor Statistics, Employment Projections Program

Similar Occupations. This table shows a list of occupations with job duties that are similar to those of hazardous materials removal workers.

Occupations	Entry-level Education	2014 Median Pay	Projected Job Growth	Average Annual Openings
Construction Laborers and Helpers	See Education/Training	$30,190	13%	18,010
Firefighters	Postsecondary nondegree award	$45,970	5%	1,740
Insulation Workers	See Education/Training	$37,790	13%	740
Painters, Construction and Maintenance	No formal educational credential	$35,950	7%	2,650
Power Plant Operators, Distributors, and Dispatchers	High school diploma or equivalent	$72,910	-6%	-330
Water and Wastewater Treatment Plant and System Operators	High school diploma or equivalent	$44,100	6%	700

Job Outlook

Employment of hazardous materials (hazmat) removal workers is projected to grow 7 percent from 2014 to 2024, about as fast as the average for all occupations.

Employment growth will be driven by the need to safely remove and clean up hazardous materials at sites recognized by the U.S. Environmental Protection Agency. Recycling waste activities should also contribute to some employment growth.

In addition, with nuclear plants continuing to be decommissioned in the next decade, hazmat removal workers will be needed to decontaminate equipment, store waste, and clean up these facilities for safe closure.

Employment growth of some hazmat removal workers often depends on the amount of federal funding for cleanup projects.

Job Prospects. Overall job opportunities for hazmat removal workers should be good because of the need to replace workers who leave the occupation each year. Hazmat removal workers may face competition from those construction laborers and insulation workers who are trained to do hazmat removal or cleanups.

Applicants who have previous work experience with reactors in the U.S. Navy may have better job opportunities at nuclear facilities.

Contacts for More Information

For more information about hazardous materials removal workers in the construction industry, including information on training, visit

➤ Laborers' International Union of North America (www.liuna.org/home)

For more information about working in the nuclear industry, visit

➤ Nuclear Energy Institute (www.nei.org)

For information about training and regulations mandated by federal agencies, visit

➤ Occupational Safety & Health Administration (www.osha.gov/index.html)
➤ U.S. Department of Energy (http://energy.gov)
➤ U.S. Environmental Protection Agency (www.epa.gov)
➤ U.S. Nuclear Regulatory Commission (www.nrc.gov)

O*NET

➤ Hazardous Materials Removal Workers (47-4041.00)

Insulation Workers

- **2014 Median Pay** .... $37,790 per year
  $18.17 per hour
- **Typical Entry-Level Education**.... See Education/Training
- **Work Experience in a Related Occupation**.............. None
- **On-the-job Training** .... See Education/Training
- **Number of Jobs, 2014** 55,600
- **Job Outlook, 2014–24**............ 13% (Faster than average)
- **Employment Change, 2014–24** 7,400

What Insulation Workers Do

Insulation workers install and replace the materials used to insulate buildings and their mechanical systems to help control and maintain the temperatures in buildings. These workers are often referred to as *insulators.*

Duties. Insulation workers typically do the following:

- Remove old insulation and dispose of it properly
- Read blueprints and specifications to determine the requirements of the job
- Determine the amount and type of insulation needed
- Measure and cut insulation to fit into walls and around pipes
- Fasten insulation in place with staples, tape, or screws
- Use compressors to spray insulation into some spaces
- Install plastic barriers to protect insulation from moisture
- Follow safety guidelines

Properly insulated buildings save energy by keeping heat in during the winter and out in the summer. Insulated vats, vessels, boilers, steam pipes, and hot-water pipes also prevent the wasteful loss of heat or cold and prevent burns. In addition, insulation helps reduce noise that passes through walls and ceilings.

When renovating old buildings, insulators often must remove the old insulation. In the past, asbestos—now known to cause cancer—was used extensively to insulate walls, ceilings, pipes, and industrial equipment. Because of this danger, hazardous materials removal workers or specially trained insulators are required to remove asbestos before workers can begin installation.

Insulation workers use common hand tools, such as knives and scissors. They also may use a variety of power tools, including power saws to cut insulating materials, welders to secure clamps, and staple guns to fasten insulation to walls. Some insulators use compressors to spray insulation.

Workers sometimes wrap a cover of aluminum, sheet metal, or vapor barrier (plastic sheeting) over the insulation. Doing so protects the insulation from contact damage and keeps moisture out.

Floor, ceiling, and wall insulators install insulation in attics, under floors, and behind walls in homes and other buildings. Most of these workers unroll, cut, fit, and staple batts of fiberglass insulation between wall studs and ceiling joists. Some workers, however, spray foam insulation with a compressor hose into the space being filled.

Mechanical insulators apply insulation to equipment, pipes, or ductwork in businesses, factories, and many other types of buildings. When insulating a steam pipe, for example, they consider the temperature, thickness, and diameter of the pipe in determining the type of insulation to be used.

Work Environment

Insulators held about 55,600 jobs in 2014. Employment was split about evenly between mechanical insulators and floor, ceiling, and wall insulators.

The majority of floor, ceiling, and wall insulators were employed in the drywall and insulation contractors industry.

About 55 percent of mechanical insulators were employed in the building equipment contractors industry. Another 20 percent were employed in the drywall and insulation contractors industry in 2014.

Insulation workers generally work indoors in residential and commercial settings. Mechanical insulators work both indoors and outdoors. They spend most of their workday standing, bending, or kneeling in confined spaces.

Injuries and Illnesses. Although installing insulation is not inherently dangerous, falls from ladders and cuts from knives are common hazards. In addition, small particles from insulation materials, especially when sprayed, can irritate the eyes, skin, and lungs. To protect themselves, insulators must keep the work area well ventilated and follow product and employer safety recommendations. They may also wear personal protective equipment (PPE), including suits, masks, and respirators, which protects against hazardous fumes or materials.

Mechanical insulators may get burns from the pipes they insulate if the pipes are in service.

Work Schedules. Although most insulators work full time, more than 40 hours a week may be required to meet construction schedules. Those who insulate outdoors may have to stop work when it rains or during very cold weather.

Education/Training

Most floor, ceiling, and wall insulation workers learn their trade on the job since no formal education is typically required. Most mechanical insulation workers complete an apprenticeship program after earning a high school diploma or equivalent.

Education. There are no specific education requirements for floor, ceiling, and wall insulation workers. Mechanical insulation workers should have a high school diploma. High school courses in basic math, woodworking, mechanical drawing, algebra, and general science are considered helpful for all insulation workers.

Training. Most floor, ceiling, and wall insulation workers learn their trade on the job. New workers are provided basic instruction on installation and begin to place insulation immediately. Insulators who install blown or sprayed insulation will work alongside more experienced workers to learn how to operate equipment before being tasked with leading a spray installation job.

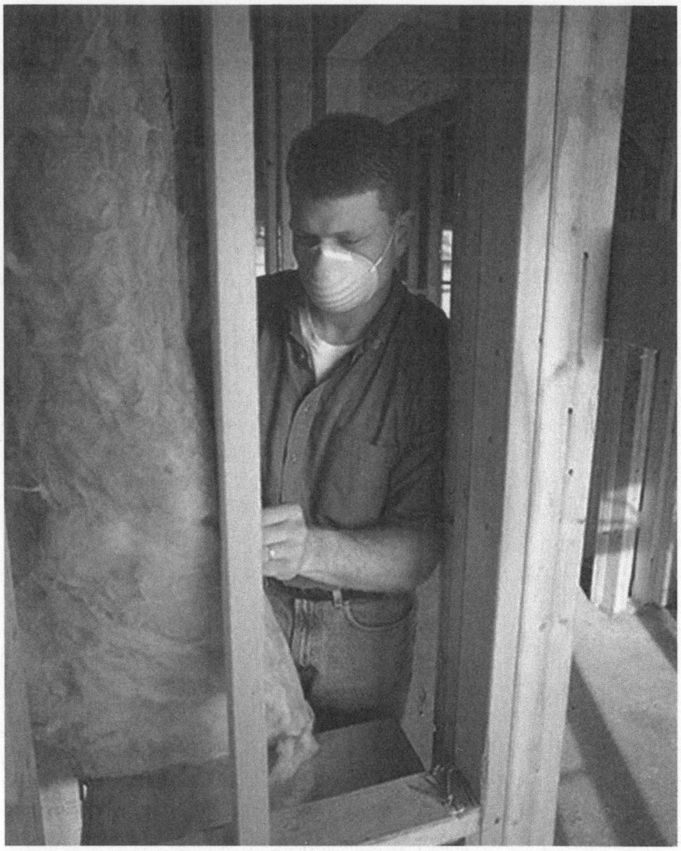

Insulation workers should have excellent job opportunities.

Most mechanical insulation workers learn their trade through a 4-year apprenticeship. Some apprenticeships may last up to 5 years, depending on the program. For each year of a typical program, apprentices must have at least 1,700 to 2,000 hours of paid on-the-job training and a minimum of 144 hours of related technical instruction. Technical instruction includes learning about installation techniques as well as basic mathematics, how to read and draw blueprints, general construction techniques, safety practices, and first aid.

Unions and individual contractors offer apprenticeship programs. Although most new workers start out by entering apprenticeships directly, others begin by working as helpers. Some apprenticeship programs have preferred entry for veterans. The basic qualifications required for entering an apprenticeship program are as follows:

- Being 18 years old
- Being physically able to do the work

Licenses, Certifications, and Registrations. Insulation workers who remove and handle asbestos must be trained through a program accredited by the U.S. Environmental Protection Agency.

Insulation contractor organizations offer voluntary certification to help workers prove their skills and knowledge of residential and industrial insulation.

The National Insulation Association also offers a certification for mechanical insulators who conduct energy appraisals to determine if and how insulation can benefit industrial customers.

Important Qualities

Dexterity. Insulation workers must be able to work in confined spaces while maintaining coordination and control of tools and

Median Annual Wages, May 2014

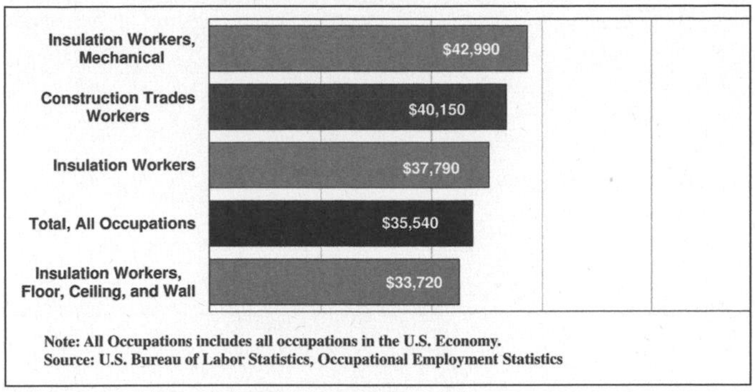

Percent Change in Employment, Projected 2014–2024

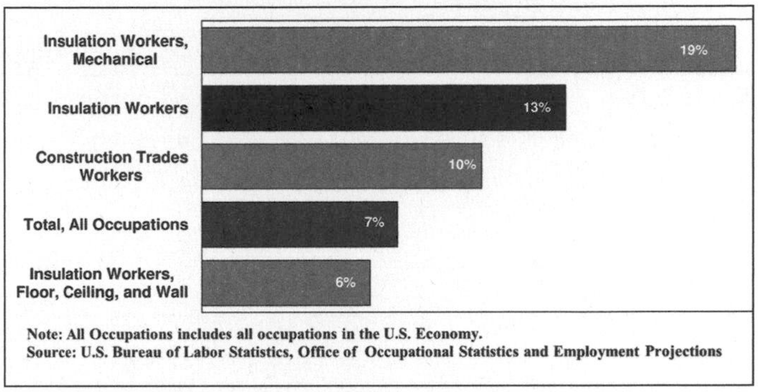

materials. Also, insulators often must reach above their heads to fit and fasten insulation into place.

Math Skills. Mechanical insulators need to measure the size of the equipment or pipe they are insulating. This is especially important when insulation is formed off site so that additional cuts are unnecessary.

Mechanical skills. Insulation workers use a variety of hand and power tools to install insulation. Those who apply foam insulation, for example, must be able to operate and maintain a compressor and sprayer to spread the foam onto walls or across attics.

Physical stamina. Insulators may spend up to 12 hours a day standing, reaching, and bending. Workers should be able to stay physically active without getting tired.

Pay

The median annual wage for insulation workers, floor, ceiling, and wall was $33,720 in May 2014. The median wage is the wage at which half the workers in an occupation earned more than that amount and half earned less. The lowest 10 percent earned less than $22,000, and the highest 10 percent earned more than $61,450.

The median annual wage for insulation workers, mechanical was $42,990 in May 2014. The lowest 10 percent earned less than $27,000, and the highest 10 percent earned more than $87,210.

The starting pay for apprentices is usually near 50 percent of what fully trained insulators make. As apprentices learn to do more, they receive pay increases.

In some areas, workers receive a per diem to offset travel costs.

Union Membership. Compared with workers in all occupations, insulation workers had a higher percentage of workers who belonged to a union in 2014.

Job Outlook

Overall employment of insulation workers is projected to grow 13 percent from 2014 to 2024, faster than the average for all occupations. Growth rates, however, will vary by occupation.

Employment of mechanical insulation workers is projected to grow 19 percent from 2014 to 2024, much faster than the average for all occupations. Demand for mechanical insulators will be spurred by the need to make new and existing buildings more energy efficient. In the past, mechanical insulation had been reduced or cut from building plans as a cost-saving method, but energy analyses show that improved insulation provides a greater return on investment. The anticipated construction of new power plants, which are big users of insulated pipes and equipment, also should result in greater employment demand. In addition, jobs are being created that are related to the extraction and transportation of oil and natural gas.

Employment of floor, ceiling, and wall insulators is projected to grow 6 percent from 2014 to 2024, about as fast as the average for all occupations. Increases in home building will spur employment growth over the coming decade. In addition, insulation will continue to be added into existing buildings to save energy.

Job Prospects. Floor, ceiling, and wall insulators are expected to face competition for jobs as they often compete with other construction trade workers and there are fewer job entry requirements for these insulators. Job openings will continue to arise because the difficult working conditions cause many insulation workers in residential construction to leave the occupation each year.

Mechanical insulation workers who have completed training should have the best job opportunities. In fact, overall opportunities for mechanical insulators should be very good as new construction continues to grow, as the increased focus on maintenance and retrofitting continues, and as government and private businesses strive for more energy efficiency. Workers with military service experience are viewed favorably during initial hiring.

Insulation workers in the construction industry may experience periods of unemployment because of the short duration of many construction projects and the cyclical nature of construction activity. Workers employed to perform industrial plant maintenance generally have more stable employment because maintenance and repair must be done regularly.

Employment Projections Data for Insulation Workers

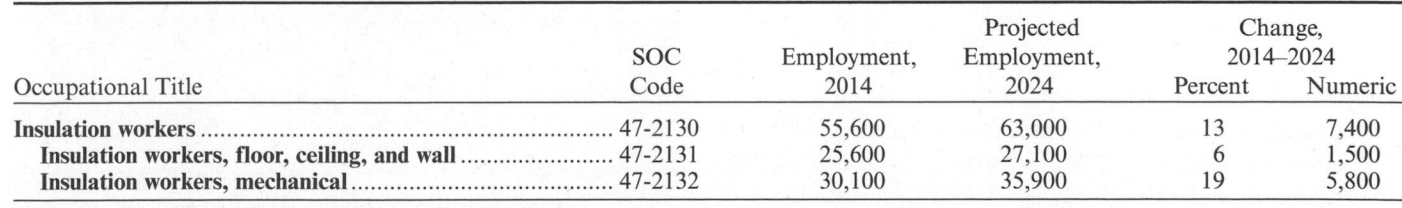

Occupational Title	SOC Code	Employment, 2014	Projected Employment, 2024	Change, 2014–2024	
				Percent	Numeric
Insulation workers	47-2130	55,600	63,000	13	7,400
Insulation workers, floor, ceiling, and wall	47-2131	25,600	27,100	6	1,500
Insulation workers, mechanical	47-2132	30,100	35,900	19	5,800

Source: U.S. Bureau of Labor Statistics, Employment Projections Program

Similar Occupations. This table shows a list of occupations with job duties that are similar to those of insulation workers.

Occupations	Entry-level Education	2014 Median Pay	Projected Job Growth	Average Annual Openings
Carpenters	High school diploma or equivalent	$40,820	6%	6,040
Construction Laborers and Helpers	See Education/Training	$30,190	13%	18,010
Drywall and Ceiling Tile Installers, and Tapers	No formal educational credential	$38,970	5%	660
Roofers	No formal educational credential	$35,760	13%	1,580
Sheet Metal Workers	High school diploma or equivalent	$45,070	76%	940

Contacts for More Information

For details about apprenticeships or other opportunities for insulation workers, contact the offices of the state employment service, the state apprenticeship agency, local insulation contractors or firms that employ insulators, or local union–management apprenticeship committees. Apprenticeship information is available from the U.S. Department of Labor's ApprenticeshipUSA program (www.dol.gov/apprenticeship) online or by phone at 877-872-5627.

For more information about apprenticeship or training for insulation workers, visit

- National Insulation Association (www.insulation.org/index.cfm)
- NCCER (www.nccer.org/insulating?pID=105)
- International Association of Heat and Frost Insulators and Allied Workers (http://tinyurl.com/gtduzz9)

O*NET

- Insulation Workers, Floor, Ceiling, and Wall (47-2131.00)
- Insulation Workers, Mechanical (47-2132.00)

Ironworkers

- **2014 Median Pay** .... $48,520 per year
  $23.33 per hour
- **Typical Entry-Level Education** .... High school diploma or equivalent
- **Work Experience in a Related Occupation** .... None
- **On-the-job Training** .... Apprenticeship
- **Number of Jobs, 2014** 80,100
- **Job Outlook, 2014–24** .... 9% (Faster than average)
- **Employment Change, 2014–24** 7,100

What Ironworkers Do

Ironworkers install structural and reinforcing iron and steel to form and support buildings, bridges, and roads.

Duties. Ironworkers typically do the following:

- Read and follow blueprints, sketches, and other instructions
- Unload and stack prefabricated iron and steel so that it can be lifted with slings
- Signal crane operators who lift and position structural and reinforcing iron and steel
- Use shears, rod-bending machines, and welding equipment to cut, bend, and weld the structural and reinforcing iron and steel
- Align structural and reinforcing iron and steel vertically and horizontally, using tag lines, plumb bobs, lasers, and levels
- Connect iron and steel with bolts, wire, or welds

Structural and reinforcing iron and steel are important components of buildings, bridges, roads, and other structures. Even though the primary metal involved in this work is steel, workers often are known as ironworkers or *erectors*. Although most of the work involves erecting new structures, some ironworkers may also help in the demolition, decommissioning, and rehabilitation of older buildings and bridges.

When building tall structures such as skyscrapers, *structural iron and steel workers* erect steel frames and assemble the cranes and derricks that move materials and equipment around the construction site. Workers connect precut steel columns, beams, and girders, using equipment such as spud wrenches and drift pins. A few ironworkers install precast walls or work with wood or composite materials.

Reinforcing iron and rebar workers use one of three different materials to support concrete:

- Reinforcing steel (rebar) is used to strengthen the concrete that forms highways, buildings, bridges, and other structures. These workers are sometimes called *rod busters*, in reference to rods of rebar.
- Cables are used to reinforce concrete by pre- or post-tensioning. These techniques allow designers to create larger open areas in a building because supports can be placed farther apart. As a result, pre- and post-tensioning are commonly used to construct arenas, concrete bridges, and parking garages.
- Welded wire reinforcing (WWR) is also used to strengthen concrete. This reinforcing is made up of narrow-diameter rods or wire welded into a grid.

Workers use wire ties to connect rebar.

Some ironworkers are assemblers and fabricators. They fabricate metal in shops, which are usually located away from the construction site.

Work Environment

Ironworkers held about 80,100 jobs in 2014. Nearly all ironworkers were employed in the construction industry.

Structural iron and steel workers held about 61,400 jobs in 2014. Approximately 45 percent were employed by foundation, structure, and building exterior contractors, and about 23 percent were employed in nonresidential building construction.

Reinforcing iron and rebar workers held about 18,700 jobs in 2014. Approximately 66 percent were employed by foundation, structure, and building exterior contractors, and about 12 percent were employed in nonresidential building construction.

Ironworkers help build the supporting structures for bridges and for industrial, commercial, and large residential buildings. Structural ironworkers usually work outside in most types of weather, and some work at great heights. In doing so, they perform physically demanding and dangerous work. As a result, workers must wear safety devices, such as harnesses, to reduce the risk of falls. Rod busters must be able to carry, bend, cut, and connect rebar at a rapid pace to keep projects on schedule. They spend much of their time moving, bending, and stooping, also physically demanding work.

Injuries and Illnesses. Structural iron and steel workers experience several work-related deaths each year that are due to falls and contacts with objects and equipment. Ironworkers may experience cuts from sharp metal edges and equipment, as well as muscle strains and other injuries from moving and guiding heavy iron and steel.

Work Schedules. The vast majority of ironworkers work full time, and in contrast to other construction occupations, few are self-employed.

Structural ironworkers who work at great heights do not work during wet, icy, or extremely windy conditions. Reinforcing ironworkers may be limited by any kind of precipitation.

Education/Training

Although most ironworkers learn through an apprenticeship, some learn on the job. Certifications in welding, rigging, and signaling can be helpful for new entrants.

Education. A high school diploma or equivalent is generally required. Courses in math, as well as training in vocational subjects such as blueprint reading and welding, can be particularly useful.

Training. For each year of the program, apprentices must have at least 144 hours of related technical training and 2,000 hours of paid on-the-job training. Nearly all apprenticeship programs teach both reinforcing and structural ironworking. On the job, apprentices learn to use the tools and equipment of the trade; handle, measure, cut, and lay rebar; and construct metal frameworks. In technical training, they are taught mathematics, blueprint reading and sketching, general construction techniques, safety practices, and first aid.

A few groups, including unions and contractor associations, sponsor apprenticeship programs. Some programs have preferred entry for veterans. The basic qualifications required for entering an apprenticeship program are as follows:

- Minimum age of 18
- High school diploma or equivalent
- Physical ability to perform the work
- Pass substance abuse screening

After completing an apprenticeship program, they are considered to be journey workers who perform tasks without direct supervision.

Licenses, Certifications, and Registrations. Certifications in welding, rigging, and crane signaling may increase a worker's usefulness on the jobsite and result in higher pay. Many ironworkers become welders certified by the American Welding Society. Several organizations offer rigging certifications, including the International Association of Bridge, Structural, Ornamental and Reinforcing Iron Workers, and the National Commission for the Certification of Crane Operators (NCCCO).

Important Qualities

Balance. Ironworkers often walk on narrow beams, so a good sense of balance is important to keep them from falling while doing their job.

Depth perception. Ironworkers must be able to judge the distance between objects and themselves in order to work safely. Ironworkers often signal crane operators who move beams and bundles of rebar.

Hand-eye coordination. Ironworkers must be able to tie rebar together quickly and precisely. An experienced worker can tie rebar together in seconds and move on to the next spot; a beginner may take much longer.

Physical stamina. Ironworkers must have physical endurance because they spend many hours performing physically demanding tasks, such as moving rebar, each day.

Physical strength. Ironworkers must be strong enough to guide heavy beams into place and tighten bolts.

Unafraid of heights. Ironworkers must not be afraid to work at great heights. For example, as they erect skyscrapers, workers must

Median Annual Wages, May 2014

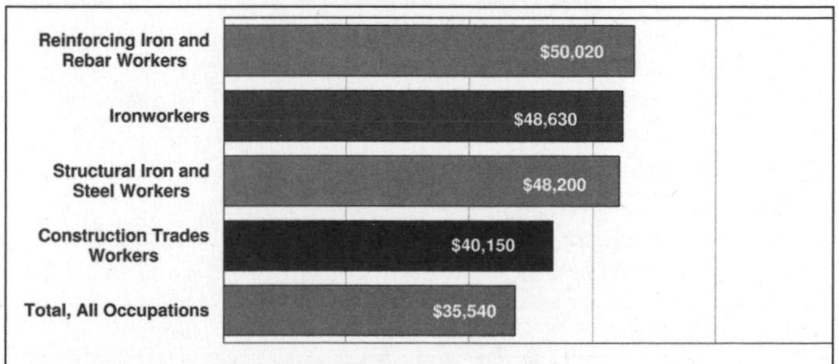

Note: All Occupations includes all occupations in the U.S. Economy.
Source: U.S. Bureau of Labor Statistics, Occupational Employment Statistics

Percent Change in Employment, Projected 2014–2024

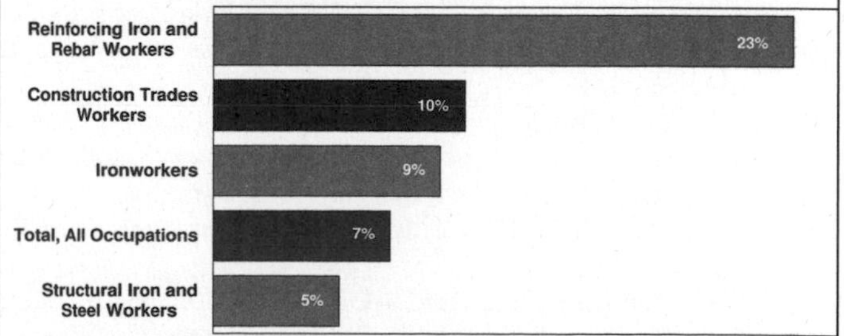

Note: All Occupations includes all occupations in the U.S. Economy.
Source: U.S. Bureau of Labor Statistics, Office of Occupational Statistics and Employment Projections

Employment Projections Data for Ironworkers

Occupational Title	SOC Code	Employment, 2014	Projected Employment, 2024	Change, 2014–2024 Percent	Change, 2014–2024 Numeric
Ironworkers	—	80,100	87,200	9	7,100
Reinforcing iron and rebar workers	47-2171	18,700	23,100	23	4,400
Structural iron and steel workers	47-2221	61,400	64,200	4	2,700

Source: U.S. Bureau of Labor Statistics, Employment Projections Program

Similar Occupations. This table shows a list of occupations with job duties that are similar to those of ironworkers.

Occupations	Entry-level Education	2014 Median Pay	Projected Job Growth	Average Annual Openings
Assemblers and Fabricators	High school diploma or equivalent	$29,280	-1%	-970
Boilermakers	High school diploma or equivalent	$59,860	9%	150
Carpenters	High school diploma or equivalent	$40,820	6%	6,040
Construction Laborers and Helpers	See Education/Training	$30,190	13%	18,010
Masonry Workers	See Education/Training	$38,720	15%	3,730
Welders, Cutters, Solderers, and Brazers	High school diploma or equivalent	$37,420	4%	1,440

walk on narrow beams—sometimes over 50 stories high—while connecting girders.

Pay

The median annual wage for reinforcing iron and rebar workers was $50,020 in May 2014. The median wage is the wage at which half the workers in an occupation earned more than that amount and half earned less. The lowest 10 percent earned less than $27,920, and the highest 10 percent earned more than $91,160.

The median annual wage for structural iron and steel workers was $48,200 in May 2014. The lowest 10 percent earned less than $29,000, and the highest 10 percent earned more than $88,310.

The starting pay for apprentices is usually between 50 percent and 55 percent of what journey worker ironworkers make. They receive pay increases as they learn to do more.

Union Membership. Compared with workers in all occupations, structural iron and steel workers had a higher percentage of workers who belonged to a union in 2014. Although there is no single union that covers all ironworkers, the largest organizer of these workers is the International Association of Bridge, Structural, Ornamental and Reinforcing Iron Workers.

Job Outlook

Employment of ironworkers is projected to grow 9 percent from 2014 to 2024, faster than the average for all occupations. Employment growth will vary by specialty.

Employment of structural iron and steel workers is projected to grow 4 percent from 2014 to 2024, slower than the average for all occupations.

Employment of reinforcing iron and rebar workers is projected to grow 23 percent from 2014 to 2024, much faster than the average for all occupations. However, because it is a small occupation, the fast growth will result in only about 4,400 new jobs over the 10-year period.

Steel and reinforced concrete are an important part of commercial and industrial buildings. Future construction of these structures is anticipated to create demand for ironworkers.

The need to rehabilitate, maintain, or replace an increasing number of older highways and bridges is also expected to lead to some employment growth, particularly because state and federal legislatures will likely fund these infrastructure projects. Growth will be limited if long-term infrastructure plans are not funded.

Job Prospects. Those who are certified in welding, rigging, and crane signaling should have the best job opportunities. Those with prior military service are viewed favorably during initial hiring.

Employment opportunities should be best in metropolitan areas, where most large commercial and industrial buildings are constructed.

As with many other construction workers, employment of ironworkers is sensitive to fluctuations of the economy. On the one hand, workers may experience periods of unemployment when the overall level of construction falls. On the other hand, shortages of workers may occur in some areas during peak periods of building activity.

Contacts for More Information

For information about apprenticeships or job opportunities as an ironworker, contact local structural and reinforcing iron and steel construction contractors, a local joint union–management apprenticeship committee, or the nearest office of your state employment service or apprenticeship agency. Apprenticeship information is available from the U.S. Department of Labor's Apprenticeship-USA program (www.dol.gov/apprenticeship) online or by phone at 877-872-5627.

For ironworker and apprenticeship information, visit

- International Association of Bridge, Structural, Ornamental and Reinforcing Iron Workers (www.ironworkers.org)
- NCCER (www.nccer.org/curriculum?mID=86)

For more information about ironworkers, visit

- Associated Builders and Contractor, Inc. (www.abc.org)
- The Associated General Contractors of America (www.agc.org)

O*NET

- Reinforcing Iron and Rebar Workers (47-2171.00)
- Structural Iron and Steel Workers (47-2221.00)

Masonry Workers

- **2014 Median Pay** .... $38,720 per year $18.61 per hour
- **Typical Entry-Level Education** .... See Education/Training
- **Work Experience in a Related Occupation**.............. None
- **On-the-job Training** .... See Education/Training
- **Number of Jobs, 2014** 252,900
- **Job Outlook, 2014–24**.... 15% (Much faster than average)
- **Employment Change, 2014–24** 37,300

What Masonry Workers Do

Masonry workers, also known as *masons*, use bricks, concrete blocks, concrete, and natural and manmade stones to build walls, walkways, fences, and other masonry structures.

Duties. Masons typically do the following:

- Read blueprints or drawings to calculate materials needed
- Lay out patterns, forms, or foundations according to plans
- Break or cut materials to required size
- Mix mortar or grout and spread it onto a slab or foundation
- Clean excess mortar with trowels and other hand tools
- Construct corners with a corner pole or by building a corner pyramid
- Align structure vertically and horizontally
- Clean and polish surfaces with hand or power tools
- Fill expansion joints with the appropriate caulking materials

Masonry materials are some of the most common and durable materials used in construction. Brick, block, and stone structures can last for hundreds of years. Concrete—a mixture of cement, sand, gravel, and water—is the foundation for everything from decorative patios and floors to huge dams or miles of roadways.

Brickmasons and *blockmasons*—often called *bricklayers*—build and repair walls, floors, partitions, fireplaces, chimneys, and other structures with brick, terra cotta, precast masonry panels, concrete block, and other masonry materials. *Pointing, cleaning, and caulking workers* are brickmasons who repair brickwork, particularly on older structures on which mortar has come loose. *Refractory masons* are brickmasons who specialize in installing firebrick, gunite, castables, and refractory tile in high-temperature boilers, furnaces, cupolas, ladles, and soaking pits in industrial establishments.

Cement masons and concrete finishers place and finish concrete. They may color concrete surfaces, expose aggregate (small stones) in walls and sidewalks, or make concrete beams, columns, and panels. Throughout the process of pouring, leveling, and finishing concrete, cement masons must monitor how the wind, heat, or cold affects the curing of the concrete. They must have a thorough knowledge of the characteristics of concrete so that they can determine what is happening to the concrete and take measures to prevent defects. Some small jobs may require the use of a supportive wire mesh called lath. On larger jobs, reinforcing iron and rebar workers install the reinforcing mesh.

Segmental pavers—also referred to as *patio pavers*—install interlocking masonry walkways, driveways, and patios. Workers need to prepare the site carefully to ensure the masonry units connect properly without gaps or ridges.

A blockmason sets concrete blocks.

Stonemasons build stone walls, as well as set stone exteriors and floors. They work with two types of stone: natural-cut stone, such as marble, granite, and limestone; and artificial stone, made from concrete, marble chips, or other masonry materials. Using a special hammer or a diamond-blade saw, workers cut stone to make various shapes and sizes. Some stonemasons specialize in setting marble, which is similar to setting large pieces of stone.

Terrazzo workers and finishers, also known as *terrazzo masons*, create decorative walkways, floors, patios, and panels. Much of the terrazzo preliminary work of pouring, leveling, and finishing concrete is similar to that of cement masons. Epoxy terrazzo requires less base preparation and is significantly thinner when completed. Terrazzo workers create decorative finishes by blending fine marble chips into the epoxy or cement, which is often colored. Once the terrazzo is thoroughly set, workers correct any depressions or imperfections with a grinder to create a smooth, uniform finish. Terrazzo workers also install decorative toppings and/or polishing compounds to new or existing concrete.

Work Environment

Masonry workers held about 252,900 jobs in 2014.

Employment in the detailed occupations that make up this group in 2014 was distributed as follows:

Cement masons and concrete finishers	155,200
Brickmasons and blockmasons	78,100
Stonemasons	14,900
Terrazzo workers and finishers	3,400
Segmental pavers	1,300

About 66 percent of masonry workers were employed in the specialty trade contractors industry in 2014. About 1 in 10 masons were self-employed in 2014. Although most masons work in residential construction, many also work in nonresidential

Median Annual Wages, May 2014

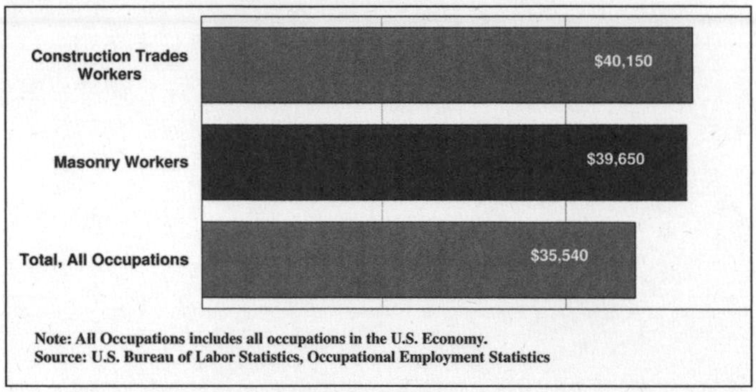

Percent Change in Employment, Projected 2014–2024

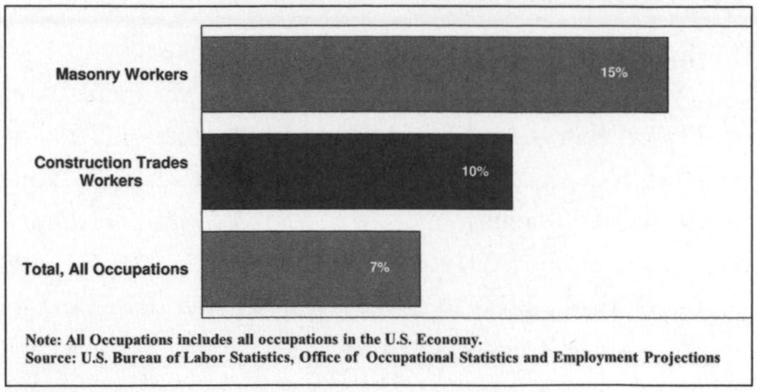

construction because most nonresidential buildings are now built with walls made of some combination of concrete block, brick veneer, stone, granite, marble, tile, and glass.

As with many other construction occupations, the work is fast-paced and strenuous. Masons often lift heavy materials and stand, kneel, and bend for long periods. The work, either indoors or outdoors, may be in areas that are muddy, dusty, or dirty. Poor weather conditions may reduce work activity because masons usually work outdoors.

Injuries and Illnesses. Brickmasons and blockmasons and cement masons and concrete finishers have a higher rate of injuries and illnesses than the national average. Common injuries include muscle strains from lifting heavy materials, as well as cuts from tools and falls from scaffolds. To avoid injuries, many workers wear protective gear, including kneepads, harnesses, and water-repellent boots.

Work Schedules. Although most masons work full time, some work more hours to meet construction deadlines. However, because they primarily work outdoors, masons may have to stop work in extreme cold or rainy weather. Nonetheless, new materials, such as concrete additives that cure at lower temperatures, have been developed that allow masons to work in a greater variety of weather conditions than in the past. Terrazzo masons may need to work at night when businesses are closed.

About 1 in 10 masonry workers were self-employed in 2014. Self-employed workers may be able to set their own schedule.

Education/Training

Most masons have a high school diploma or equivalent and learn either on the job or through an apprenticeship program. Others learn through masonry programs at technical schools.

Education. A high school diploma or equivalent is required for most masons. High school courses in mathematics, mechanical drawing, and vocational education are considered useful.

Many technical schools offer programs in basic masonry. These programs operate both independently and in conjunction with apprenticeship training. The credits earned as part of an apprenticeship program usually count toward an associate's degree. Some people take courses before being hired, and some take them later as part of on-the-job training.

Training. A 3- to 4-year apprenticeship is how most masons learn the trade. For each year of the program, apprentices must complete at least 144 hours of related technical instruction and 2,000 hours of paid on-the-job training. In the future, apprenticeships are expected to focus more on proven competencies than time-in-training and therefore the duration of apprenticeships may decrease.

Apprentices learn construction basics such as blueprint reading; mathematics, including measurement, volume, and mixing proportions; building code requirements; and safety and first-aid practices.

Several groups, including unions and contractor associations, sponsor apprenticeship programs. Some apprenticeship programs have preferred entry for veterans. The basic qualifications for entering an apprenticeship program are as follows:

- Minimum age of 18
- High school education or equivalent
- Physically able to do the work

Some contractors have their own training programs for masons. Although workers may enter apprenticeships directly, some masons start out as construction helpers. The Home Builders Institute and the International Masonry Institute offer pre-apprenticeship training program for eight construction trades, including masonry.

After completing an apprenticeship program, masons are considered journey workers and are able to perform tasks on their own.

Important Qualities

Color vision. Terrazzo workers must be able to distinguish between small variations in color when setting terrazzo patterns in order to produce the best looking finish.

Hand-eye coordination. Workers must be able to apply smooth, even layers of mortar, set bricks, and remove any excess before the mortar hardens.

Math skills. Cement masons use their knowledge of math—including measurement, volume, and mixing proportions—when they mix their own mortar.

Physical stamina. Brickmasons must keep a steady pace while setting bricks all day. Although no individual brick is extremely heavy, the constant lifting can be tiring.

Physical strength. Workers must be strong enough to lift more than 50 pounds. They must also carry heavy tools, equipment, and other materials, such as bags of mortar and grout.

Visualization. Stonemasons must be able to see how stones fit together in order to build attractive and stable structures.

Pay

The median annual wage for masonry workers was $38,720 in May 2014. The median wage is the wage at which half the workers in an occupation earned more than that amount and half earned less. The lowest 10 percent earned less than $25,400, and the highest 10 percent earned more than $70,580.

Employment Projections Data for Masonry Workers

Occupational Title	SOC Code	Employment, 2014	Projected Employment, 2024	Change, 2014–2024 Percent	Change, 2014–2024 Numeric
Masonry workers	—	252,900	290,200	15	37,300
Brickmasons and blockmasons	47-2021	78,100	92,600	19	14,500
Stonemasons	47-2022	14,900	17,100	14	2,100
Cement masons and concrete finishers	47-2051	155,200	175,500	13	20,300
Terrazzo workers and finishers	47-2053	3,400	3,600	7	200
Segmental pavers	47-4091	1,300	1,400	9	100

Source: U.S. Bureau of Labor Statistics, Employment Projections Program

Median annual wages for masonry workers in May 2014 were as follows:

Brickmasons and blockmasons	$47,650
Terrazzo workers and finishers	39,090
Stonemasons	37,880
Cement masons and concrete finishers	36,760
Segmental pavers	32,180

Job Outlook

Employment of masonry workers is projected to grow 15 percent from 2014 to 2024, much faster than the average for all occupations. Although employment growth will vary by occupation, growth will depend on the number of commercial, public, and civil construction projects such as new roads, bridges, and buildings.

Employment of brickmasons and block masons is projected to grow 19 percent from 2014 to 2024, much faster than the average for all occupations. Population growth will result in the construction of more schools, hospitals, apartment buildings, and other structures, many of which are made of brick and block. In addition, masons will be needed to restore a growing number of brick buildings. Although expensive, brick exteriors should remain popular, reflecting a preference for low-maintenance, durable exterior materials.

Employment of cement masons and concrete finishers is projected to grow 13 percent from 2014 to 2024, faster than the average for all occupations. More cement masons will be needed to build and renovate highways, bridges, factories, and residential structures in order to meet the demands of a growing population and to make repairs to aging infrastructure.

The use of concrete for buildings is increasing because its strength is an important asset in areas prone to severe weather. For example, residential construction projects in Florida are using more concrete as building requirements change in reaction to the increased frequency and intensity of hurricanes. The use of concrete is likely to expand into other hurricane-prone areas as the durability of Florida homes built with concrete becomes more established.

Employment of segmental pavers is projected to grow 9 percent from 2014 to 2024, faster than the average for all occupations. Segmental pavers install a wide variety of durable walkway and driveway material options that are in demand.

Employment of stonemasons is projected to grow 14 percent from 2014 to 2024, much faster than the average for all occupations. However, because it is a small occupation, the fast growth will result in only about 2,100 new jobs over the 10-year period. Natural stone is both a durable and popular material. As incomes and the population continue to grow, more homeowners will want natural stone to differentiate their homes from those around them.

Employment of terrazzo workers and finishers is projected to grow 7 percent from 2014 to 2024, about as fast as the average for all occupations. Terrazzo is a durable and attractive flooring option that is often used in schools, government buildings, and hospitals. The construction and renovation of such buildings will spur demand for these workers. However, because polished concrete is similar to terrazzo and usually less expensive, this may limit the need for terrazzo workers.

Job Prospects. Overall job prospects for masons should continue to be favorable as construction activity continues to grow to meet the demand for new buildings and roads. As with many other construction workers, employment of masons is sensitive to the fluctuations of the economy. On the one hand, workers may experience periods of unemployment when the overall level of construction falls. On the other hand, shortages of workers may occur in some areas during peak periods of building activity.

While many masons are expected to retire over the next decade, more job openings will result from employment growth.

Workers with a good job history and with experience in construction should have the best job opportunities. Those who have taken masonry courses in high school or technical college should

Similar Occupations. This table shows a list of occupations with job duties that are similar to those of masonry workers.

Occupations	Entry-level Education	2014 Median Pay	Projected Job Growth	Average Annual Openings
Carpenters	High school diploma or equivalent	$40,820	6%	6,040
Construction Laborers and Helpers	See Education/Training	$30,190	13%	18,010
Drywall and Ceiling Tile Installers, and Tapers	No formal educational credential	$38,970	5%	660
Flooring Installers and Tile and Marble Setters	No formal educational credential	$37,380	5%	590
Insulation Workers	See Education/Training	$37,790	13%	740

have slightly better opportunities. In addition, workers with military service experience are viewed favorably during initial hiring.

Contacts for More Information

For details about apprenticeships or other work opportunities for masonry workers, contact the offices of the state employment service, the state apprenticeship agency, local contractors or firms that employ masons, or local union–management apprenticeship committees. Apprenticeship information is available from the U.S. Department of Labor's ApprenticeshipUSA program (www.dol.gov/apprenticeship) online or by phone at 877-872-5627.

For more information about training for masons, visit

- The Associated General Contractors of America (www.agc.org)
- Associated Builders and Contractors, Inc. (www.abc.org)
- International Masonry Institute (www.imiweb.org)
- Mason Contractors Association of America (www.masoncontractors.org)
- National Association of Home Builders (www.nahb.org)
- The National Terrazzo and Mosaic Association (www.ntma.com)
- Operative Plasterers' and Cement Masons' International Association (www.opcmia.org)

For more information about training, including obtaining a credential in green construction, visit

- NCCER (www.nccer.org)

O*NET

- Brickmasons and Blockmasons (47-2021.00)
- Stonemasons (47-2022.00)
- Cement Masons and Concrete Finishers (47-2051.00)
- Terrazzo Workers and Finishers (47-2053.00)
- Segmental Pavers (47-4091.00)

Painters, Construction and Maintenance

- **2014 Median Pay** .... $35,950 per year $17.29 per hour
- **Typical Entry-Level Education** ..... No formal educational credential
- **Work Experience in a Related Occupation** .... None
- **On-the-Job Training** ...... Moderate-term on-the-job training
- **Number of Jobs 2014** 360,500
- **Job Outlook, 2014–24** .... 7% (As fast as average)
- **Employment Change, 2014–24** 26,500

What Painters, Construction and Maintenance Do

Painters apply paint, stain, and coatings to walls and ceilings, buildings, bridges, and other structures.

Duties. Painters typically do the following:

- Cover floors, furniture, and trim with dropcloths, tarps, and masking tape, to protect surfaces
- Remove and replace pictures and outlet and switch covers
- Fill holes and cracks with putty or plaster
- Prepare surfaces by scraping, wire brushing, or sanding to a smooth finish
- Calculate the area to be painted and the amount of paint needed
- Apply primers or sealers so the paint will adhere
- Install scaffolding and set up ladders
- Apply paint or other finishes, using hand brushes, rollers, or sprayers

Applying paint to interior walls makes surfaces attractive and vibrant. In addition, paints and other sealers protect exterior surfaces from damage caused by weather, sunlight, and pollution.

Because there are several ways to apply paint, workers must be able to choose the proper tool for each job, such as the correct roller, power sprayer, or brush. Choosing the right tool typically depends on the surface to be covered and the characteristics of the material applied.

A few painters—mainly industrial—use special safety equipment. For example, painting in confined spaces, such as the inside of a large storage tank, requires workers to wear self-contained suits to avoid inhaling toxic fumes. On some projects they may operate abrasive blasters to remove old coatings, which may require the use of additional clothing and protective eyewear. When painting bridges, ships, tall buildings, or oil rigs, painters may work from scaffolding, bosun's chairs, and harnesses in order to reach work areas.

The following are examples of types of painters:

Construction painters apply paints, stains, and coatings to interior and exterior walls, new buildings, and other structural surfaces.

Maintenance painters remove old finishes and apply paints, stains, and coatings later in a structure's life. Some painters specialize in painting or coating industrial structures, such as bridges and oil rigs, to prevent corrosion. These workers are sometimes called *industrial painters*.

Artisan painters specialize in creating distinct finishes by using one of many decorative techniques. One such technique is adding glaze for increased depth and texture. Other common techniques include sponging, distressing, rag rolling, color blocking, and faux finishing.

Work Environment

Painters held about 360,500 jobs in 2014, of which 36 percent were employed in the painting and wall covering contractors industry. About 4 in 10 were self-employed in 2014.

Because painters apply finishes to a wide variety of structures—from bridges to the interiors and exteriors of buildings—they typically work both indoors and outdoors.

Painting requires a lot of climbing, bending, kneeling, and reaching. Those who paint bridges or buildings may be exposed to extreme heights and uncomfortable positions; some painters are suspended by ropes or cables as they work.

Injuries and Illnesses. Painters have one of the highest rates of injuries and illnesses of all occupations. Falls from ladders, muscle strains from lifting, and exposure to irritants such as drywall dust are common risks. Maintenance painters who apply industrial coatings may have to go through additional safety training because of concerns related to falls.

Work Schedules. Most painters work full time. About 4 in 10 were self-employed in 2014. Self-employed workers may be able to set their own schedule.

Education/Training

Most painters learn their trade on the job. No formal education is typically required to enter the occupation.

Education. There are no specific education requirements to become a painter, but high school courses in mathematics, shop, and blueprint reading can be useful. Also, some 2-year technical schools offer courses through apprenticeships affiliated with union

Painters must stand for long periods, often working from scaffolding and ladders.

and contractor organizations. Credits earned as part of an apprenticeship program usually count toward an associate's degree.

Training. Most painters learn their trade on the job. They typically begin by doing simple tasks, such as helping carry materials and laying drop cloths, and then move on to more complicated tasks, such as priming surfaces to be finished.

Some painters learn their trade through a 3- or 4-year apprenticeship, although a few local unions have additional time requirements. For each year of the typical program, apprentices must have at least 144 hours of technical instruction and 2,000 hours of paid on-the-job training. Through technical instruction, apprentices learn how to: use and care for tools and equipment, prepare surfaces, mix and match paint, and read blueprints. In addition, they may learn about application techniques, the characteristics of different finishes, including wood finishing, and safety practices.

After completing an apprenticeship program, painters are considered journey workers and may perform tasks on their own.

Unions and contractors sponsor apprenticeship programs. Some apprenticeship programs have preferred entry for veterans. The basic qualifications to enter an apprenticeship program are as follows:

- Minimum age of 18
- High school diploma or equivalent
- Physically able to do the work

Although the vast majority of workers learn their trade on the job or through an apprenticeship, some contractors offer their own training program for new workers. The National Association of Home Builders through the Home Builders Institute offers Pre-Apprenticeship Certificate Training (PACT), which covers information for eight construction trades, including painting.

Licenses, Certifications, and Registrations. Those interested in industrial painting can earn several certifications from NACE International Institute or from the Society for Protective Coatings. The most common certification, from both groups, is called Protective Coating Specialist. Courses range from 1 day to several weeks, depending on the certification program and specialty. Applicants also must meet work experience requirements.

Important Qualities

Color vision. Painters must be able to identify and differentiate between subtle changes in color.

Customer-service skills. Workers who paint the inside and outside of residential homes often interact with clients. They must communicate with the client, listen to what the client wants, and help select colors and application techniques that satisfy the client.

Detail oriented. Painters must be precise when creating or painting edges, because minor flaws can be noticeable.

Physical stamina. Painters should be able to stay physically active for many hours, because they spend most of the day standing with their arms extended while climbing ladders.

Physical strength. Painters must lift and move numerous items during the course of a job. For example, a 5-gallon bucket of paint weighs over 40 pounds.

Pay

The median annual wage for painters, construction and maintenance was $35,950 in May 2014. The median wage is the wage at which half the workers in an occupation earned more than that amount and half earned less. The lowest 10 percent earned less than $23,730, and the highest 10 percent earned more than $62,090.

The starting pay for apprentices is usually between 40 percent and 70 percent of what fully trained painters make. Apprentices receive pay increases as they learn to do more.

Workers who specialize in painting structures, such as bridges, tend to have higher wages.

Median Annual Wages, May 2014

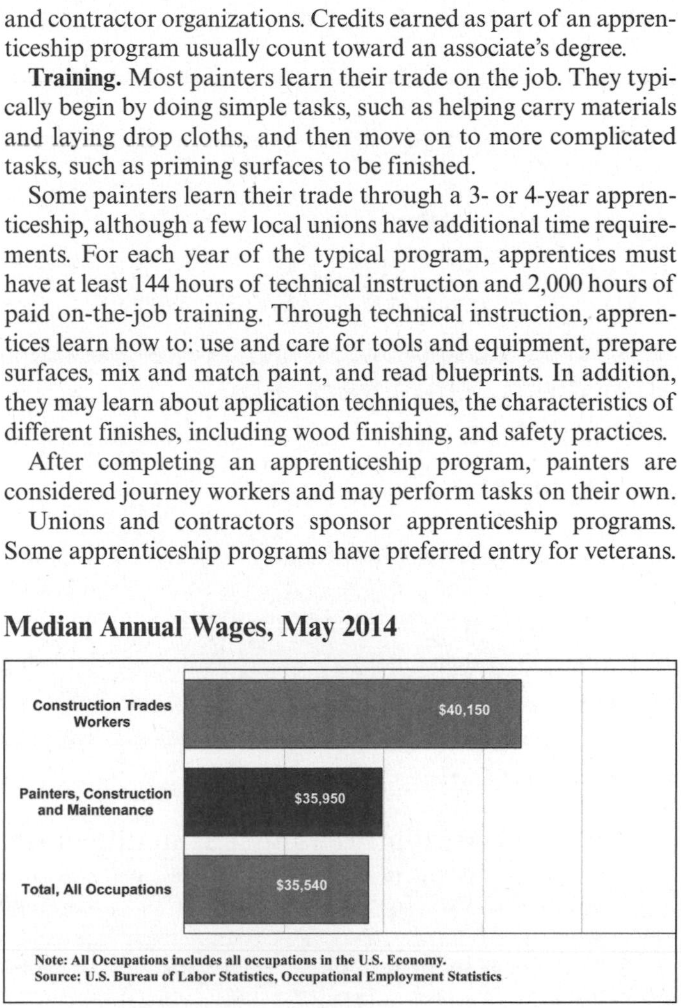

Percent Change in Employment, Projected 2014–2024

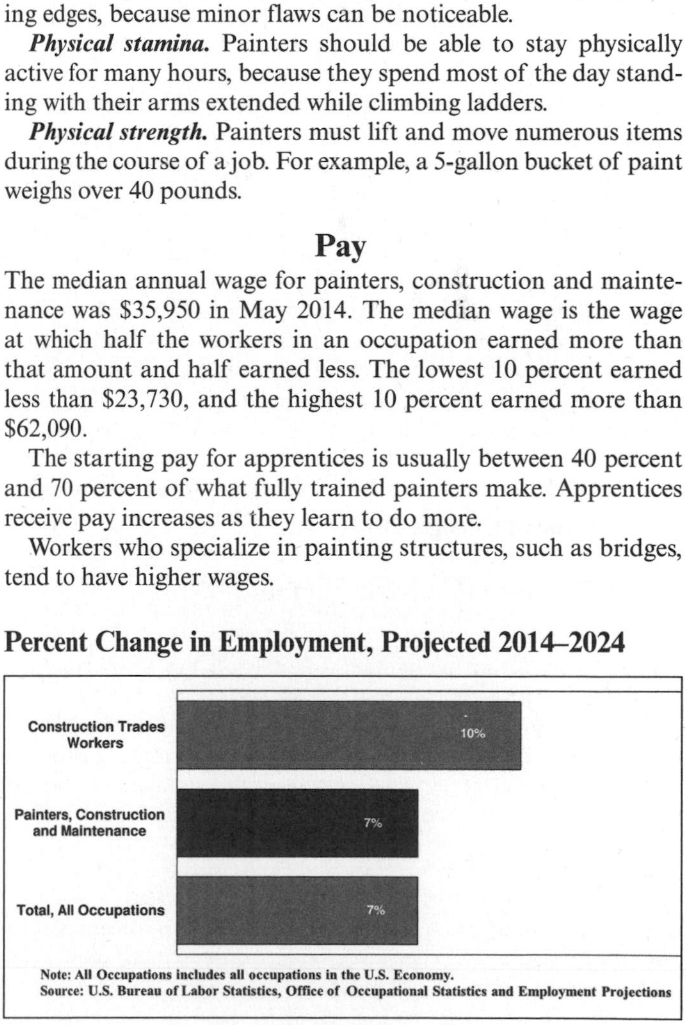

Employment Projections Data for Painters, Construction and Maintenance

Occupational Title	SOC Code	Employment, 2014	Projected Employment, 2024	Change, 2014–2024	
				Percent	Numeric
Painters, construction and maintenance	47-2141	316,200	378,800	20	62,600

Source: U.S. Bureau of Labor Statistics, Employment Projections Program

Similar Occupations. This table shows a list of occupations with job duties that are similar to those of painters, construction and maintenance.

Occupations	Entry-level Education	2014 Median Pay	Projected Job Growth	Average Annual Openings
Carpenters	High school diploma or equivalent	$40,820	6%	6,040
Construction Laborers and Helpers	See Education/Training	$30,190	13%	18,010
Drywall and Ceiling Tile Installers, and Tapers	No formal educational credential	$38,970	5%	660
Painting and Coating Workers	See Education/Training	$33,740	1%	210

Job Outlook

Employment of painters is projected to grow 7 percent from 2014 to 2024, about as fast as the average for all occupations.

The relatively short life of paint on homes, as well as changing trends in color and application, will continue to result in demand for painters. Investors who sell properties or rent them out also will require painters' services. Nonetheless, the ability of many homeowners to do the work themselves will temper employment growth somewhat.

Growing demand for industrial painting will be driven by the need to prevent the corrosion and deterioration of many industrial structures by painting or coating them. Applying a protective coating to the inside and outside of a steel tank, for example, can add years to its life expectancy.

Job Prospects. Overall job prospects should be good because of the need to replace workers who leave the occupation each year. There are no formal education requirements for entry into this job, so many people with limited abilities work as painters for a relatively short time and then move on to other types of work with higher pay or better working conditions.

Job opportunities for industrial painters should be excellent because the number of positions available should be greater than the pool of individuals qualified to fill them. Although industrial structures that require painting are located throughout the nation, the best employment opportunities will likely be in the Gulf Coast region, where strong demand exists. In addition, workers with military experience are viewed favorably during initial hiring.

New painters and those with limited experience should expect some periods of unemployment. In addition, most new construction painting projects last only a short time.

Employment of painters, like that of many other construction workers, is sensitive to fluctuations in the economy. On the one hand, painters may experience periods of unemployment when the overall level of construction falls. On the other hand, peak periods of building activity may produce shortages of painters.

Contacts for More Information

For details about apprenticeships or other work opportunities for painters, contact the offices of the state employment service, the state apprenticeship agency, local contractors or firms that employ painters, or local union–management painter apprenticeship committees. Apprenticeship information is available from the U.S. Department of Labor's ApprenticeshipUSA program (www.dol.gov/apprenticeship) online or by phone at 877-872-5627.

For more information about painters and training opportunities, visit

- ➤ Associated Builders and Contractors, Inc. (www.abc.org)
- ➤ International Union of Painters and Allied Trades (www.iupat.org)
- ➤ Home Builders Institute (www.hbi.org)
- ➤ NCCER (www.nccer.org)
- ➤ Painting and Decorating Contractors of America (www.pdca.org)

For information about the work of industrial painters and about opportunities for training and certification as a protective coating specialist, visit

- ➤ NACE International Institute (www.naceinstitute.org/Certification)
- ➤ Society for Protective Coatings (http://tinyurl.com/gm2j244)

O*NET

- ➤ Painters, Construction and Maintenance (47-2141.00)

Plumbers, Pipefitters, and Steamfitters

- **2014 Median Pay** .... $50,660 per year, $24.36 per hour
- **Typical Entry-Level Education** .... High school diploma or equivalent
- **Work Experience in a Related Occupation** .... None
- **On-the-job Training** .... Apprenticeship
- **Number of Jobs, 2014** 425,000
- **Job Outlook, 2014–24** .... 12% (Faster than average)
- **Employment Change, 2014–24** 49,100

What Plumbers, Pipefitters, and Steamfitters Do

Plumbers, pipefitters, and steamfitters install and repair pipes that carry liquids or gases to, from, and within businesses, homes, and factories.

Duties. Plumbers, pipefitters, and steamfitters typically do the following:

- Install pipes and fixtures
- Study blueprints and follow state and local building codes
- Determine the amount of material and type of equipment needed
- Inspect and test installed pipe systems and pipelines
- Troubleshoot systems that are not working
- Replace worn parts

The movement of liquids and gases through pipes is critical to modern life. In homes, water is needed for both drinking and sanitation. In factories, chemicals are moved to aid in product manufacturing. In power plants, steam is moved to drive turbines that generate electricity. Plumbers, pipefitters, and steamfitters install and repair these pipe systems.

Although plumbers, pipefitters, and steamfitters perform three distinct and specialized roles, their duties are often similar. For example, they all install pipes and fittings that carry water, steam, air, or other liquids or gases. They connect pipes, determine the necessary materials for a job, and perform pressure tests to ensure that a pipe system is airtight and watertight.

Plumbers, pipefitters, and steamfitters install, maintain, and repair many different types of pipe systems. Some of these systems carry water, dispose of waste, supply gas to ovens, or heat and cool buildings. Other systems, such as those in power plants, carry the steam that powers huge turbines. Pipes also are used in manufacturing plants to move acids, gases, and waste byproducts through the production process.

Master plumbers on construction jobs may be involved with developing blueprints that show the placement of all the pipes and fixtures. Their input helps ensure that a structure's plumbing meets building codes, stays within budget, and works well with the location of other features, such as electric wires. Many diagrams are now created digitally using Building Information Modeling (BIM), which allows a building's physical systems to be planned and coordinated across occupations.

Plumbers, pipefitters, and steamfitters may use many different materials and construction techniques, depending on the type of project. Residential water systems, for example, use copper, steel, and plastic pipe that one or two plumbers can install. Power plant water systems, by contrast, are made of large steel pipes that usually take a crew of pipefitters to install. Some workers install stainless steel pipes on dairy farms and in factories, mainly to prevent contamination.

Plumbers and pipefitters sometimes cut holes in walls, ceilings, and floors. With some pipe systems, workers may hang steel supports from ceiling joists to hold the pipe in place. Because pipes are seldom manufactured to exact lengths, plumbers and pipefitters measure and then cut and bend lengths of pipe as needed. Their tools often include saws and pipe cutters.

They then connect the pipes, using methods that vary by type of pipe. For example, copper pipe is joined with solder, whereas steel pipe often is screwed together.

In addition to performing installation and repair work, journey- and master-level plumbers, pipefitters, and steamfitters frequently direct apprentices and helpers.

The following are examples of types of plumbers, pipefitters, and steamfitters:

Plumbers install and repair water, drainage, and gas pipes in homes, businesses, and factories. They install and repair large water lines, such as those which supply water to buildings, and smaller ones, including lines that supply water to refrigerators. Plumbers also install plumbing fixtures—bathtubs, showers, sinks, and toilets—and appliances such as dishwashers, garbage disposals, and water heaters. In addition, they fix plumbing problems. For example, when a pipe is clogged or leaking, plumbers remove the clog or replace the pipe. Some plumbers maintain septic systems—the large, underground holding tanks that collect waste from houses not connected to a city or county's sewer system.

Plumbers commonly solder copper pipes.

Pipefitters, sometimes referred to as just *fitters*, install and maintain pipes that carry chemicals, acids, and gases. These pipes are used mostly in manufacturing, commercial, and industrial settings. Fitters often install and repair pipe systems in power plants, as well as heating and cooling systems in large office buildings. Some pipefitters specialize:

- *Gasfitters* install pipes that provide natural gas to heating and cooling systems and to stoves. They also install pipes that provide clean oxygen to patients in hospitals.
- *Sprinklerfitters* install and repair fire sprinkler systems in businesses, factories, and residential buildings.
- *Steamfitters* install pipe systems that move steam under high pressure. Most steamfitters work at college campuses and natural-gas power plants where heat and electricity are generated, but others work in factories that use high-temperature steam pipes.

Work Environment

Plumbers, pipefitters, and steamfitters held about 425,000 jobs in 2014, of which 61 percent were in the plumbing, heating, and air-conditioning contractors industry. About 1 in 10 were self-employed.

Plumbers, pipefitters, and steamfitters work in factories, homes, businesses, and other places where there are pipes or septic systems.

Plumbers and fitters often must lift heavy materials, climb ladders, and work in tight spaces. Some plumbers travel to a variety of worksites every day. A few work outdoors, even in bad weather.

Injuries and Illnesses. Plumbers, pipefitters, and steamfitters have one of the highest rates of injuries and illnesses of all occupations. Cuts from sharp tools, burns from hot pipes and soldering equipment, and falls from ladders are common injuries.

Work Schedules. The vast majority of plumbers, pipefitters, and steamfitters work full time, including nights and weekends. They are often on call to handle emergencies, and overtime is common.

Median Annual Wages, May 2014

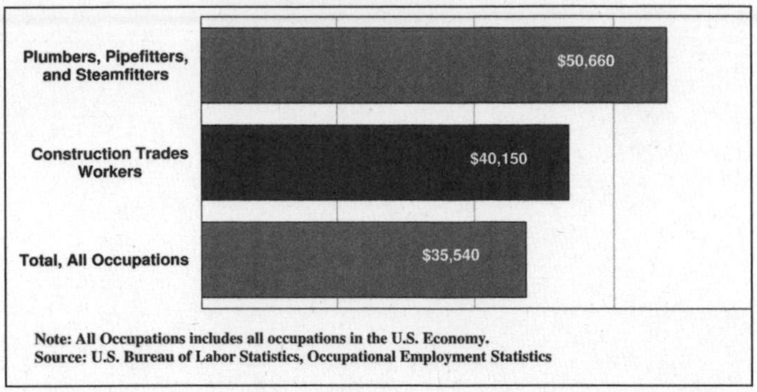

Percent Change in Employment, Projected 2014–2024

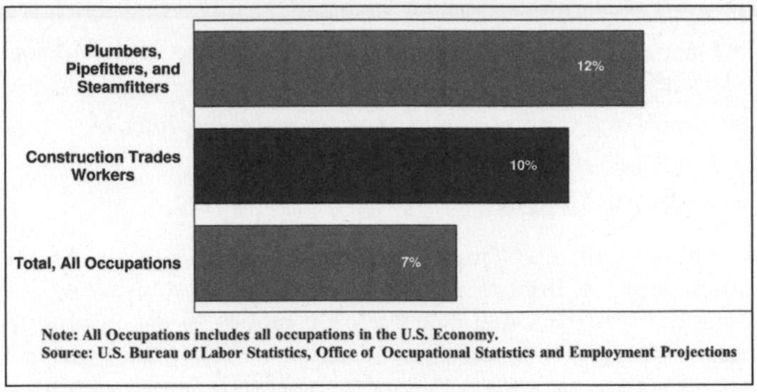

About 1 in 10 plumbers, pipefitters, and steamfitters were self-employed in 2014. Although self-employed plumbers can set their own schedules, they are also more likely to deal with afterhours emergencies.

Education/Training

Although most plumbers, pipefitters, and steamfitters learn on the job through an apprenticeship, some start out by attending a technical school. Most states and localities require plumbers to be licensed.

Education. A high school diploma or equivalent is required.

Technical schools offer courses on pipe system design, safety, and tool use. They also offer welding courses that are considered necessary by some pipefitter and steamfitter apprenticeship training programs.

Training. Most plumbers, pipefitters, and steamfitters learn their trade through a 4- or 5-year apprenticeship. Each year, apprentices must have at least 1,700 to 2,000 hours of paid on-the-job training and a minimum of 246 hours of related technical education.

In the classroom, apprentices learn safety, local plumbing codes and regulations, and blueprint reading. They also study mathematics, applied physics, and chemistry.

Apprenticeship programs are offered by unions and businesses. Although most workers enter apprenticeships directly, some start out as helpers. Some apprenticeship programs have preferred entry for veterans. To enter an apprenticeship program, a trainee must meet the following requirements:

- Be at least 18 years old
- Have a high school diploma or equivalent
- Pass a basic math test
- Pass substance abuse screening
- Know how to use computers

Some plumbers, pipefitters, and steamfitters learn on the job through specific task-oriented training. Employers provide training that enables workers to complete a variety of tasks. The Home Builders Institute offers a pre-apprenticeship training program for eight construction trades, including plumbing.

After completing an apprenticeship program, plumbers, pipefitters, and steamfitters are considered to be journey workers, qualifying them to perform duties on their own.

With additional technical education and several years of plumbing experience, plumbers are eligible to earn master status. Some states require a business to employ a master plumber in order to obtain a plumbing contractor's license.

Licenses, Certifications, and Registrations. Most states and localities require plumbers to be licensed. Although licensing requirements vary, most states and localities require workers to have 2 to 5 years of experience and to pass an exam that shows their knowledge of the trade and of local plumbing codes before they are permitted to work independently.

A few states require pipefitters to be licensed. Several states require a special license to work on gas lines. Obtaining a license requires taking a test, gaining experience through work, or both. For more information, check with your state's licensing board.

Important Qualities

Business skills. Plumbers who own their own business must be able to direct workers, bid on jobs, and plan work schedules.

Customer-service skills. Plumbers work with customers on a regular basis, so they should be polite and courteous.

Mechanical skills. Plumbers, pipefitters, and steamfitters use a variety of tools to assemble and repair pipe systems. Choosing the right tool and successfully installing, repairing, or maintaining a system is crucial to their work.

Physical strength. Plumbers, pipefitters, and steamfitters must be strong enough to lift and move heavy pipe.

Troubleshooting skills. Plumbers, pipefitters, and steamfitters find, diagnose, and repair problems. For example, pipefitters must be able to perform pressure tests to pinpoint the location of a leak.

Pay

The median annual wage for plumbers, pipefitters, and steamfitters was $50,660 in May 2014. The median wage is the wage at which half the workers in an occupation earned more than that amount

Employment Projections Data for Plumbers, Pipefitters, and Steamfitters

Occupational Title	SOC Code	Employment, 2014	Projected Employment, 2024	Change, 2014–2024 Percent	Change, 2014–2024 Numeric
Plumbers, pipefitters, and steamfitters	47-2152	425,000	474,100	12	49,100

Source: U.S. Bureau of Labor Statistics, Employment Projections Program

Similar Occupations. This table shows a list of occupations with job duties that are similar to those of plumbers, pipefitters, and steamfitters.

Occupations	Entry-level Education	2014 Median Pay	Projected Job Growth	Average Annual Openings
Boilermakers	High school diploma or equivalent	$59,860	9%	150
Construction and Building Inspectors	High school diploma or equivalent	$56,040	8%	810
Construction Laborers and Helpers	See Education/Training	$30,190	13%	18,010
Construction Managers	Bachelor's degree	$85,630	5%	1,780
Electricians	High school diploma or equivalent	$51,110	14%	8,590
Heating, Air Conditioning, and Refrigeration Mechanics and Installers	Postsecondary nondegree award	$44,630	14%	3,960

and half earned less. The lowest 10 percent earned less than $29,470, and the highest 10 percent earned more than $88,160.

The starting pay for apprentices usually is between 30 percent and 50 percent of the rate paid to fully trained plumbers, pipefitters, and steamfitters. As they learn to do more, apprentices receive pay increases.

Union Membership. Compared with workers in all occupations, plumbers, pipefitters, and steamfitters had a higher percentage of workers who belonged to a union in 2014. The largest organizer of these workers is the United Association Union of Plumbers, Fitters, Welders, and Service Techs.

Job Outlook

Employment of plumbers, pipefitters, and steamfitters is projected to grow 12 percent from 2014 to 2024, faster than the average for all occupations.

Demand for plumbers will stem from new building construction and stricter efficiency standards for plumbing systems, such as low-flow toilets and water heaters. The construction and retrofitting of power plants and factories should spur demand for pipefitters and steamfitters. Employment of sprinklerfitters is expected to increase as states continue to adopt changes to building codes that require use of fire suppression systems.

Job Prospects. Overall job opportunities are expected to be good, with some employers continuing to report difficulty finding qualified workers. In addition, many plumbers, pipefitters, and steamfitters are expected to retire over the next 10 years, resulting in more job openings. Workers with knowledge of Building Information Modeling (BIM) should have the best job opportunities as integrated building-planning abilities increase in demand. In addition, workers with military service experience are viewed favorably during initial hiring.

As with other construction workers, employment of plumbers, pipefitters, and steamfitters is sensitive to fluctuations in the economy. On the one hand, workers may experience periods of unemployment when the overall level of construction falls. On the other hand, shortages of workers may occur in some areas during peak periods of building activity.

However, maintenance and repair of plumbing and pipe systems must continue even during economic downturns, so plumbers and fitters outside of construction, especially those in manufacturing, tend to have more stable employment.

Contacts for More Information

For details about apprenticeship or other opportunities in this trade, contact the offices of the state employment service; the state apprenticeship agency; local plumbing, heating, and cooling contractors or firms that employ fitters; or local union–management apprenticeship committees. Apprenticeship information is available from the U.S. Department of Labor's ApprenticeshipUSA program (www.dol.gov/apprenticeship) online or by phone at 877-872-5627.

For more information about apprenticeships for plumbers, pipefitters, and steamfitters, visit

➤ United Association Union of Plumbers, Fitters, Welders, and Service Techs (www.ua.org)

For more information about pre-apprenticeship training, visit

➤ Home Builders Institute (http://tinyurl.com/hj3a6rj)

For more information about plumbers and pipefitters, visit

➤ Mechanical Contractors Association of America (www.mcaa.org)
➤ NCCER (www.nccer.org/curriculum?mID=105)
➤ Plumbing-Heating-Cooling Contractors Association (www.phccweb.org)

For information about sprinklerfitters, visit

➤ American Fire Sprinkler Association (www.firesprinkler.org)
➤ National Fire Sprinkler Association (www.nfsa.org)

O*NET

➤ Plumbers, Pipefitters, and Steamfitters (47-2152.00)
➤ Pipe Fitters and Steamfitters (47-2152.01)
➤ Plumbers (47-2152.02)

Roofers

- **2014 Median Pay** .... $35,760 per year $17.19 per hour
- **Typical Entry-Level Education** .... No formal educational credential
- **Work Experience in a Related Occupation**.............. None
- **On-the-job Training** .... Moderate-term on-the-job training
- **Number of Jobs, 2014** 123,400
- **Job Outlook, 2014–24** .... 13% (Faster than average)
- **Employment Change, 2014–24** 15,800

What Roofers Do

Roofers replace, repair, and install the roofs of buildings using a variety of materials, including shingles, bitumen, and metal.

Duties. Roofers typically do the following:

- Inspect problem roofs to determine the best way to repair them
- Measure roofs to calculate the quantities of materials needed
- Replace damaged or rotting joists or plywood
- Install vapor barriers or layers of insulation

- Install shingles, asphalt, metal, or other materials to make the roof weatherproof
- Align roofing materials with edges of the roof
- Cut roofing materials to fit around walls or vents
- Cover exposed nail or screw heads with roofing cement or caulk to prevent leakage

Properly installed roofs keep water from leaking into buildings and damaging the interior, equipment, or furnishings. There are two basic types of roofs: low-slope and steep-slope. Solar and vegetative features are sometimes incorporated into both low- and steep-slope roofs. Roofers may specialize in the installation and replacement of one or more of these roof systems.

Low-slope. Low-slope roofs rise less than 3 inches per horizontal foot and are installed in layers. Low-slope roofs make up nearly three-quarters of all roofs, as most commercial, industrial, and apartment buildings use this type.

Many of today's low-slope roofs are covered with a single-ply membrane of waterproof rubber or thermoplastic compound. Most previously installed low-slope roofs, however, use several layers of roofing materials or felt membranes stuck together with hot bitumen (a tar-like substance).

Steep-slope. Steep-slope roofs rise more than 3 inches per horizontal foot and most commonly use asphalt shingles, which often cost less than other coverings. Steep-slope roofs make up most of the remaining roofs, as most single-family homes use this type.

Although roofers most commonly install asphalt shingles, some also lay tile, solar shingles, metal shingles, or shakes (rough wooden shingles) on steep-slope roofs.

Traditional roofing systems may incorporate plants and landscape materials, and these features are becoming more common. A vegetative roof is typically a waterproof low-slope roof, covered by a root barrier. Soil, plants, and landscaping materials are then placed on the roof.

Solar features are increasingly popular on roofs. These systems include solar reflective, which prevents the absorption of energy; solar thermal, which absorbs energy to heat water; and solar photovoltaic, which converts sunlight into electricity. Roofers install some photovoltaic products such as solar shingles and solar tiles, but solar photovoltaic (PV) installers typically install PV panels. Plumbers and heating, air conditioning, and refrigeration mechanics also may install solar thermal systems.

Work Environment

Roofers held about 123,400 jobs in 2014, of which 72 percent were in the roofing contractors industry. About 1 in 5 roofers were self-employed.

Roofers need good physical condition, strength, and balance.

Roofing work can be physically demanding. It involves heavy lifting, as well as climbing, bending, and kneeling, frequently in very hot weather. Roofers work outdoors in all types of weather, particularly when making repairs. However, they rarely install roofs when it rains or when it is very cold.

Although some roofers work alone, many work as part of a crew.

Injuries and Illnesses. Roofers have a higher rate of injuries and illnesses than the national average. Workers may slip or fall from scaffolds, ladders, or roofs, where they do most of their work. They may also be burned by hot bitumen. Proper safety precautions and equipment can prevent most accidents and fatalities.

Roofs can become extremely hot during the summer, which can cause heat-related illnesses.

Work Schedules. Like many construction workers, most roofers work full time. In northern states, roofing work is limited during the winter months. During the summer, roofers may work overtime to complete jobs quickly, especially before rainfall.

About 1 in 5 roofers were self-employed in 2014. Self-employed workers may be able to set their own schedules.

Education/Training

Although most roofers learn on the job, some learn their trade through an apprenticeship program. There are no specific education requirements for roofers.

Median Annual Wages, May 2014

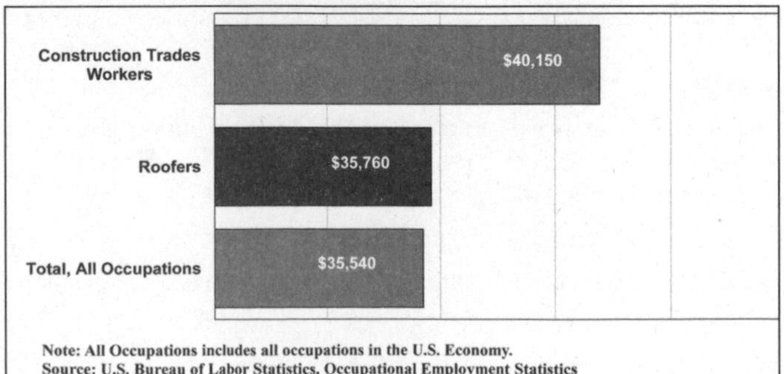

Percent Change in Employment, Projected 2014–2024

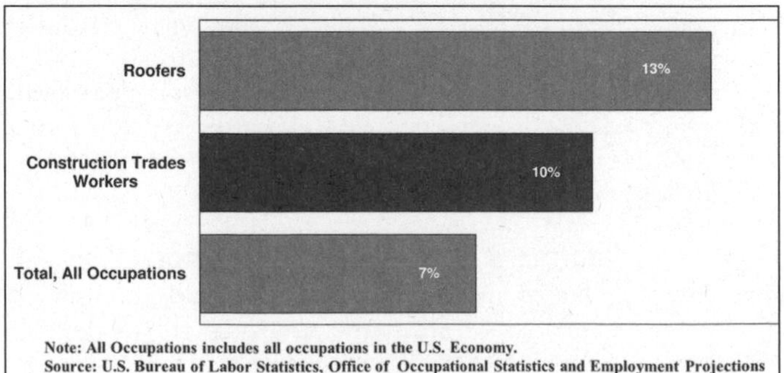

Employment Projections Data for Roofers

Occupational Title	SOC Code	Employment, 2014	Projected Employment, 2024	Change, 2014–2024 Percent	Change, 2014–2024 Numeric
Roofers	47-2181	123,400	139,300	13	15,800

Source: U.S. Bureau of Labor Statistics, Employment Projections Program

Education. Although there are no specific education requirements for roofers, high school courses in math, vocational education, mechanical drawing, and blueprint reading are considered helpful. Technical schools that offer courses related to roofing may be available in a few areas.

Training. Most on-the-job training programs consist of instruction in which experienced workers teach new workers how to use roofing tools, equipment, machines, and materials. Trainees begin with tasks such as carrying equipment and material and erecting scaffolds and hoists. Within 2 or 3 months, they are taught to measure, cut, and fit roofing materials, and later, to lay asphalt or fiberglass shingles. Because some roofing materials, such as solar tiles, are used infrequently, it can take several years to gain experience on all types of roofing. As training progresses, assignments become more complex.

Some roofers learn through a 3-year apprenticeship. For each year of the program, apprentices must have at least 144 hours of related technical training and 2,000 hours of paid on-the-job training. Apprentices learn about roofing and construction basics, such as blueprint reading, mathematics, building code requirements, safety, and first-aid practices.

Several groups sponsor apprenticeship programs, including unions and contractor associations. Some apprenticeship programs have preferred entry for veterans. The basic qualifications to enter an apprenticeship program are as follows:

- Minimum age of 18
- High school diploma or equivalent
- Physically able to do the work

After completing an apprenticeship program, roofers are considered journey workers who can perform tasks on their own.

Important Qualities

Balance. Roofing is often done on steep slopes at significant heights. Because of this, workers should have excellent balance to avoid falling.

Physical stamina. Roofers must have the endurance to perform strenuous duties throughout the day. They may spend hours on their feet, bending and stooping—often in hot temperatures—with few breaks.

Physical strength. Roofers often lift and carry heavy materials. Some roofers, for example, must carry bundles of shingles that weigh 60 pounds or more.

Unafraid of heights. Because work is often done at significant heights, roofers must not fear working far above the ground.

Pay

The median annual wage for roofers was $35,760 in May 2014. The median wage is the wage at which half the workers in an occupation earned more than that amount and half earned less. The lowest 10 percent earned less than $23,410, and the highest 10 percent earned more than $61,240.

The starting pay for apprentices is usually between 50 percent and 60 percent of what fully trained workers earn. They receive pay increases as they learn to do more.

Job Outlook

Employment of roofers is projected to grow 13 percent from 2014 to 2024, faster than the average for all occupations. Replacement and repair of roofs, as well as the installation of new roofs, will create demand for roofers.

Roofs deteriorate more quickly than most other parts of buildings, and as a result, they need to be replaced or repaired more often. Results of a National Roofing Contractors Association survey indicate that about three-quarters of all roofing work is for repair and replacement. In addition to normal deterioration, extreme weather events often damage roofs and require immediate repair or replacement.

In addition to replacement and repair work, the need to install roofs on new buildings may also result in job growth. However, some roofing activities, such as removing old roofs, also may be done by other construction workers, which may slow job growth for traditional roofing contractors.

Similar Occupations. This table shows a list of occupations with job duties that are similar to those of roofers.

Occupations	Entry-level Education	2014 Median Pay	Projected Job Growth	Average Annual Openings
Carpenters	High school diploma or equivalent	$40,820	6%	6,040
Construction Laborers and Helpers	See Education/Training	$30,190	13%	18,010
Drywall and Ceiling Tile Installers, and Tapers	No formal educational credential	$38,970	5%	660
Flooring Installers and Tile and Marble Setters	No formal educational credential	$37,380	5%	590
Masonry Workers	See Education/Training	$38,720	15%	3,730
Sheet Metal Workers	High school diploma or equivalent	$45,070	7%	940
Solar Photovoltaic Installers	High school diploma or equivalent	$40,020	24%	140

Job Prospects. Job opportunities for roofers should be excellent. Most jobs for roofers will stem primarily from the need to replace the many workers who leave the occupation each year, some of whom seek jobs in other construction trades. Jobs are generally easier to find during spring and summer. In addition, workers with military service experience are viewed favorably during initial hiring.

Demand for roofers is less vulnerable to downturns than for other construction trades because much roofing work consists of repair and reroofing, in addition to new construction. Still, workers may experience periods of unemployment when the overall level of new construction falls, and shortages of workers may occur in some areas during peak periods of building activity.

Contacts for More Information

For details about apprenticeships or other work opportunities for roofers, contact the offices of the state employment service, the state apprenticeship agency, local contractors or firms that employ roofers, or local union–management apprenticeship committees. Apprenticeship information is available from the U.S. Department of Labor's ApprenticeshipUSA program (www.dol.gov/apprenticeship) online or by phone at 877-872-5627.

For more information about the work of roofers, visit

- ➤ National Roofing Contractors Association (www.nrca.net)
- ➤ United Union of Roofers, Waterproofers, and Allied Workers (www.unionroofers.com)

O*NET

- ➤ Roofers (47-2181.00)

Sheet Metal Workers

- **2014 Median Pay** .... $45,070 per year $21.67 per hour
- **Typical Entry-Level Education** .... High school diploma or equivalent
- **Work Experience in a Related Occupation** .... None
- **On-the-Job Training** .... Apprenticeship
- **Number of Jobs 2014** 141,000
- **Job Outlook, 2014–24** .... 7% (As fast as average)
- **Employment Change, 2014–24** 9,400

What Sheet Metal Workers Do

Sheet metal workers fabricate or install products that are made from thin metal sheets, such as ducts used in heating and air conditioning systems.

Duties. Sheet metal workers typically do the following:

- Select types of sheet metal according to plans
- Measure and mark dimensions and reference lines on metal sheets
- Drill holes in metal for screws, bolts, and rivets
- Install metal sheets with supportive frameworks
- Fabricate or alter parts at construction sites
- Maneuver and anchor large sheet metal parts
- Fasten seams or joints by welding, bolting, riveting, or soldering

Sheet metal is thin steel, aluminum, or other alloyed metal that is used in both manufacturing and construction. Sheet metal is commonly used to make ducts for heating and air conditioning systems, but it is also used to make products such as rain gutters, outdoor signs, and siding.

In addition to installing sheet metal, some workers install nonmetallic materials such as fiberglass and plastic board.

The following are examples of types of sheet metal workers:

Fabrication sheet metal workers, sometimes called *precision sheet metal workers*, make precision sheet metal parts for a variety of industries, from power generation to medical device manufacturing. Most work in shops and factories, operating tools and equipment. In large-scale manufacturing, the work may be highly automated and repetitive. Many fabrication shops have automated machinery, such as computer-controlled saws, lasers, shears, and presses, which measure, cut, bend, and fasten pieces of sheet metal. Workers often use computer-aided drafting and design (CADD) and building information modeling (BIM) systems to make products. Some of these workers may be responsible for limited programming of the computers controlling their equipment. Workers who primarily program computerized equipment are called metal and plastic machine workers.

Installation sheet metal workers install heating, ventilation, and air conditioning (HVAC) ducts. They also install other sheet metal products, such as metal roofs, siding, and gutters. They typically work on new construction and on renovation projects. Information about workers who install or repair roofing systems can be found in the profile on roofers.

Maintenance sheet metal workers repair and clean ventilation systems so the systems use less energy. Workers remove dust and moisture and fix leaks or breaks in the sheet metal that makes up the ductwork.

Testing and balancing sheet metal specialists ensure that HVAC systems heat and cool rooms properly by adjusting sheet metal ducts to achieve proper airflow. Information on workers who install or repair HVAC systems can be found in the profile on heating, air conditioning, and refrigeration mechanics and installers.

Sheet metal workers use a torch to cut a sheet of metal.

Median Annual Wages, May 2014

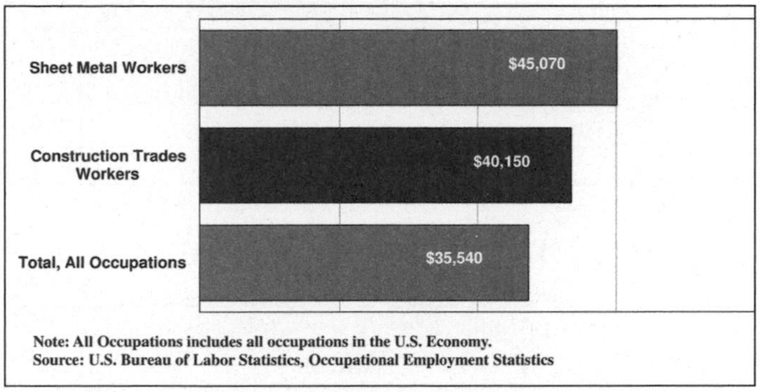

Percent Change in Employment, Projected 2014–2024

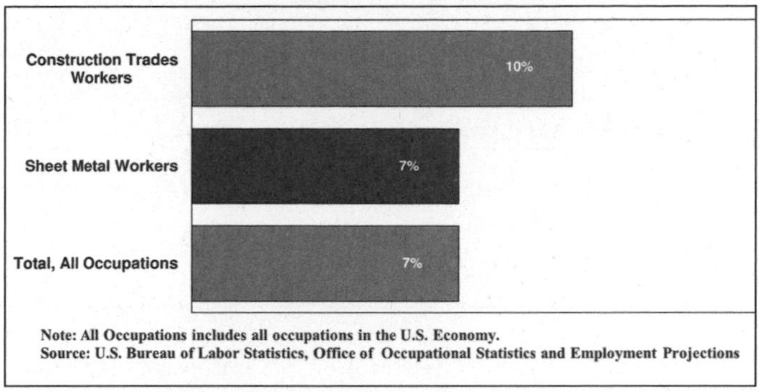

Work Schedules. The vast majority of sheet metal workers are employed full time.

Education/Training

Sheet metal workers who work in construction typically learn their trade through an apprenticeship, while those who work in manufacturing often learn on the job or at a technical school.

Education. Most sheet metal workers have a high school diploma or equivalent. Those interested in becoming a sheet metal worker should take high school classes in algebra, geometry, and general vocational education courses including blueprint reading, mechanical drawing, and welding.

Many technical schools have programs that teach welding and metalworking. These programs help provide the basic welding and sheet metal fabrication knowledge that many workers need to perform their job.

Some manufacturers have partnerships with local technical schools to develop training programs specific to their factories.

Training. Most construction sheet metal workers learn their trade through 4- or 5-year apprenticeships. Each year, apprentices must have 1,700 to 2,000 hours of paid on-the-job training and 144 to 320 hours of related technical instruction, depending on the program. Apprentices learn construction basics such as blueprint reading, math, building code requirements, and safety and first-aid practices. Welding may be included as part of the training.

Although most construction workers enter apprenticeships directly after finishing high school, some start out as helpers before entering apprenticeships.

Apprenticeship programs are offered by unions and businesses. The basic qualifications for entering an apprenticeship program are being 18 years old and having a high school diploma or the equivalent. Some apprenticeship programs have preferred entry for veterans.

After completing an apprenticeship program, sheet metal workers are considered to be journey workers who are qualified to perform tasks on their own.

Licenses, Certifications, and Registrations. Although not required, sheet metal workers can earn certifications for several of the tasks that they perform. For example, some sheet metal workers can become certified in welding from the American Welding Society. In addition, the International Training Institute for the Sheet Metal and Air Conditioning Industry offers certification in building information modeling (BIM), welding, testing and balancing, and other related activities. The Fabricators & Manufacturers Association, International, offers a certification in precision sheet metal work.

Important Qualities

Computer skills. Sheet metal workers use computer-aided drafting and design (CADD) programs and building information modeling (BIM) systems as they design products and cut sheet metal.

Dexterity. Sheet metal workers need good hand-eye coordination and motor control to make precise cuts and bends in metal pieces.

Math skills. Sheet metal workers must calculate the proper sizes and angles of fabricated sheet metal, as it is important to ensure the alignment and fit of ductwork.

Mechanical skills. Sheet metal workers use saws, lasers, shears, and presses to do their job. As a result, they should have good mechanical skills in order to operate and maintain equipment.

Physical stamina. Sheet metal workers in factories may spend many hours standing at their workstation.

Physical strength. Sheet metal workers must be able to lift and move ductwork that is often heavy and cumbersome. Some jobs require workers to be able to lift 50 pounds.

Pay

The median annual wage for sheet metal workers was $45,070 in May 2014. The median wage is the wage at which half the workers in an occupation earned more than that amount and half earned less. The lowest 10 percent earned less than $25,590, and the highest 10 percent earned more than $79,430.

In May 2014, the median annual wages for sheet metal workers in the top industries in which they worked were as follows:

Plumbing, heating, and air-conditioning contractors	$49,310
Architectural and structural metals manufacturing	39,060
Foundation, structure, and building exterior contractors	38,550

Those who work in manufacturing are more likely to participate in profit sharing, work overtime, and receive output incentives to supplement their basic wages.

The starting pay for apprentices usually is between 40 percent and 50 percent of what fully trained sheet metal workers make. As they learn more skills, their pay increases.

Union Membership. Compared with workers in all occupations, sheet metal workers had a higher percentage of workers who belonged to a union in 2014. Although there is no single union, the largest organizer for sheet metal workers is the International Association of Sheet Metal, Air, Rail and Transportation Workers (SMART).

Job Outlook

Employment of sheet metal workers is projected to grow 7 percent from 2014 to 2024, about as fast as the average for all occupations.

Employment Projections Data for Sheet Metal Workers

Occupational Title	SOC Code	Employment, 2014	Projected Employment, 2024	Change, 2014–2024	
				Percent	Numeric
Sheet metal workers	47-2211	141,000	150,500	7	9,400

Source: U.S. Bureau of Labor Statistics, Employment Projections Program

Similar Occupations. This table shows a list of occupations with job duties that are similar to those of sheet metal workers.

Occupations	Entry-level Education	2014 Median Pay	Projected Job Growth	Average Annual Openings
Assemblers and Fabricators	High school diploma or equivalent	$29,280	-1%	-970
Glaziers	High school diploma or equivalent	$38,410	4%	190
Heating, Air Conditioning, and Refrigeration Mechanics and Installers	Postsecondary nondegree award	$44,630	14%	3,960
Machinists and Tool and Die Makers	High school diploma or equivalent	$41,510	6%	2,900
Metal and Plastic Machine Workers	High school diploma or equivalent	$33,550	-13%	-13,390
Roofers	No formal educational credential	$35,760	13%	1,580

Employment growth reflects an expected increase in the number of industrial, commercial, and residential structures that will be built over the coming decade. It also reflects the continuing need to install and maintain energy-efficient air conditioning, heating, and ventilation systems in existing buildings.

Sheet metal workers in architectural and structural metals manufacturing are expected to experience 11 percent employment growth from 2014 to 2024, as domestic manufacturing expands.

Job Prospects. Overall job opportunities should be very good due to job growth and replacement needs. Job prospects should be particularly good for sheet metal workers who complete apprenticeship training or who are certified welders. Workers with military service experience are viewed favorably during initial hiring.

Some manufacturing companies report having difficulty finding qualified applicants. Workers who program equipment, possess multiple welding certifications, and show commitment to their work will have the best job opportunities.

Employment of construction sheet metal workers, like that of many other construction workers, is sensitive to fluctuations in the economy. On the one hand, workers in these trades may experience periods of unemployment when the overall level of construction falls. On the other hand, peak periods of building activity may produce shortages of sheet metal workers.

Contacts for More Information

For more information about apprenticeships or other work opportunities, contact local sheet metal contractors or heating, refrigeration, and air conditioning contractors; a local of the Sheet Metal Workers International Association; a local of the Sheet Metal and Air Conditioning Contractors' National Association; a local joint union–management apprenticeship committee; or the nearest office of your state employment service or apprenticeship agency. Apprenticeship information is available from the U.S. Department of Labor's ApprenticeshipUSA program (www.dol.gov/apprenticeship) online or by phone at 877-872-5627.

For more information about sheet metal workers, visit

- ➤ Fabricators & Manufacturers Association, International (www.fmanet.org)
- ➤ International Association of Sheet Metal, Air, Rail and Transportation Workers (SMART) (http://smart-union.org)
- ➤ NCCER (www.nccer.org/sheet-metal?pID=105)
- ➤ Sheet Metal and Air Conditioning Contractors' National Association (www.smacna.org)

For more information about certification, visit

- ➤ American Welding Society (www.aws.org/certification)
- ➤ International Training Institute for the Sheet Metal and Air Conditioning Industry (www.sheetmetal-iti.org)
- ➤ Sheet Metal Institute (www.sheetmetalinstitute.org)

O*NET

- ➤ Sheet Metal Workers (47-2211.00)

Solar Photovoltaic Installers

- **2014 Median Pay** .... $40,020 per year $19.24 per hour
- **Typical Entry-Level Education** .... High school diploma or equivalent
- **Work Experience in a Related Occupation** .... None
- **On-the-job Training** .... Moderate-term on-the-job training
- **Number of Jobs, 2014** 5,900
- **Job Outlook, 2014–24** .... 24% (Much faster than average)
- **Employment Change, 2014–24** 1,400

What Solar Photovoltaic Installers Do

Solar photovoltaic (PV) installers, often called *PV installers*, assemble, install, or maintain solar panel systems on roofs or other structures.

Duties. PV installers typically do the following:

- Plan PV system configuration based on customer needs and site conditions
- Install solar modules, panels, or support structures in accordance with building codes and standards

Because solar panels typically weigh between 30 and 40 pounds, solar photovoltaic installers must do heavy lifting at times.

- Connect PV panels to the power grid
- Apply weather sealing to equipment being installed
- Activate and test PV systems to verify performance
- Perform routine PV system maintenance

Sunlight is considered an environmentally friendly source of energy. By way of photovoltaic panels, sunlight is transformed into electricity. Recent technological advances have sufficiently reduced the cost of solar panels to make it a viable source of electricity for businesses and homeowners alike. PV installers put these systems in place.

PV installers use a variety of hand and power tools to install photovoltaic panels. They often use wrenches, saws, and screwdrivers to connect panels to frames, wires, and support structures.

Many new workers begin by performing basic tasks, such as installing support structures and placing PV panels or PV shingles on top of them. Once the panels are in place, more experienced installers usually perform more complex duties, such as connecting electrical components.

Depending on the job and state laws, PV installers may connect the solar arrays to the electric grid, although electricians sometimes perform this duty. Once installed, workers check electrical systems for proper wiring, polarity, grounding, and integrity of terminations, and perform maintenance as needed.

Work Environment

Solar photovoltaic installers held about 5,900 jobs in 2014. The industries that employed the most solar photovoltaic installers were as follows:

Plumbing, heating, and air-conditioning contractors	39%
Electrical contractors and other wiring installation contractors	24
Power and communication line and related structures construction	6

Because photovoltaic (PV) panels convert sunlight into electricity, most PV installation is done outdoors. Residential installers work on rooftops and in attics and crawl spaces to connect panels to the electric grid. PV installers who build solar farms work at ground level and need to build structures to hold the PV panel framework.

PV installers may work alone or as part of a team. Installation of a solar array may require the help of roofers and electricians as well as solar photovoltaic installers.

PV installers must travel to job sites. Residential installers are likely to work at a different location every day.

Injuries and Illnesses. Solar photovoltaic installers risk falls from ladders and roofs, electrical shocks, and burns from hot equipment and materials while installing and maintaining PV systems. Those working on roofs must use required fall protection equipment.

Work Schedules. Nearly all solar photovoltaic installers work full time, which may include evening and weekend hours. They may be on call to handle emergencies, meaning they are not formally on duty but are available to work if necessary.

Education/Training

There are multiple paths to becoming a solar photovoltaic (PV) installer, often called PV installers. Some workers need only a high school diploma and receive on-the-job training lasting up to 1 year. Other candidates take a course at a technical school or community college. Some PV installers learn to install panels as part of an apprenticeship.

Education. Some PV installers take courses at local community colleges or trade schools to learn about solar panel installation. Courses range from basic safety and PV knowledge to system design. Although course length varies by state and locality, most usually last a few days to several months.

Some candidates may enter the field by taking online training courses. This is particularly useful for candidates with prior construction experience, such as former electricians.

Training. Some PV installers learn their trade on the job by working with experienced installers. On-the-job training usually

Median Annual Wages, May 2014

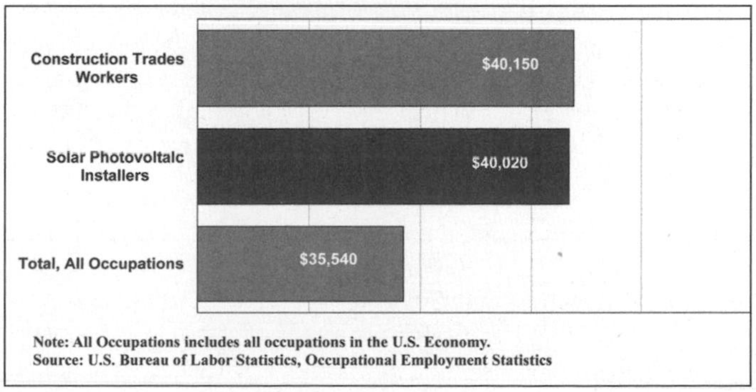

Percent Change in Employment, Projected 2014–2024

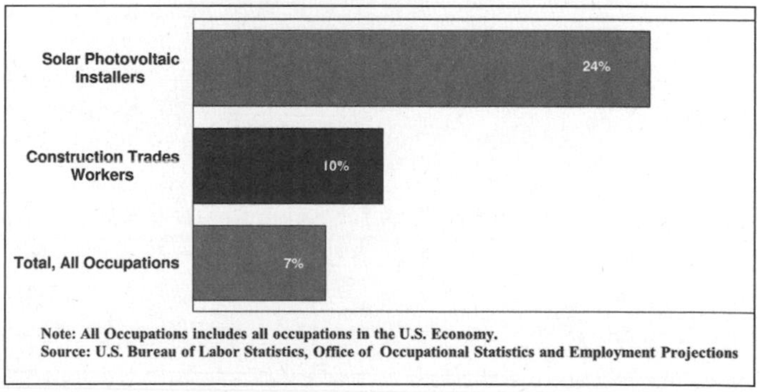

lasts between 1 month and 1 year, during which workers learn about safety, tool use, and PV system installation techniques.

Solar PV system manufacturers may also provide specific training on a product. Such training usually includes a system overview and proper installation techniques of the manufacturer's products.

Some large construction contractors provide training to new employees on their own. Workers learn basic PV safety and are given increasingly complex tasks as they prove their abilities.

The U.S. Department of Energy and the U.S. Department of Defense launched the Solar Ready Vets program in 2014 to connect veterans with jobs in the solar industry.

Although there are currently no apprenticeship programs for solar photovoltaic installers, some learn PV installation through other occupational apprenticeship programs. Electrician and roofing apprentices and journey workers may complete photovoltaic-specific training modules.

In most states, an electrician is fully qualified to connect PV systems to electric grids. They are also able to connect panels to inverters and batteries.

Important Qualities

Customer-service skills. Residential panel installers must work in customers' homes. As a result, workers must maintain professionalism and perform the work in a timely manner.

Detail oriented. PV installers must carefully follow instructions during installation. If they fail to do so, the system may not work properly.

Mechanical skills. PV installers work with complex electrical and mechanical equipment. They must be able to build support structures that hold PV panels in place and properly connect the panels to the electrical system.

Physical stamina. PV installers are often on their feet carrying panels and other heavy equipment. When installing rooftop panels, workers may need to climb ladders many times during the course of the day.

Physical strength. PV installers must often lift heavy equipment, parts, and tools. Workers should be strong enough to lift panels that weigh up to 50 pounds.

Work Experience in a Related Occupation. Experience in construction may shorten a new employee's training time. For example, workers with experience as an electrician, roofer, carpenter, or laborer typically already understand and can perform basic construction duties.

In addition, those with knowledge of electrical work, such as electricians, are highly valued by contractors.

Licenses, Certifications, and Registrations. Although not mandatory, PV installers may obtain certification from the North American Board of Certified Energy Practitioners. Certification can demonstrate professionalism and basic PV knowledge to employers. To qualify, workers must complete at least 58 hours of advanced PV training at an accredited school or organization, as well as a 10-hour construction safety course through Occupational Safety & Health Administration (OSHA). They also need to pass an exam and show documentation of having led three to five PV installation projects, depending on prior experience.

The Electronics Technicians Association, International (ETA) also offers photovoltaic installer certification. Education and training must be taken from an ETA-approved school.

There is also the Certified Solar Roofing Professional (CSRP) credential offered by Roof Integrated Solar Energy (RISE) Inc. In order to qualify, workers need to prove they have 40 hours of education or training related to basic competencies. Additionally, candidates need to have 3 years of roofing or PV installation experience and have completed at least five PV installations. They must also pass a test.

Pay

The median annual wage for solar photovoltaic installers was $40,020 in May 2014. The median wage is the wage at which half the workers in an occupation earned more than that amount and half earned less. The lowest 10 percent earned less than $28,420, and the highest 10 percent earned more than $58,340.

In May 2014, the median annual wages for solar photovoltaic installers in the top industries in which they worked were as follows:

Plumbing, heating, and air-conditioning contractors	$41,520
Power and communication line and related structures construction	38,750
Electrical contractors and other wiring installation contractors	38,570

Job Outlook

Employment of solar photovoltaic (PV) installers, often called *PV installers*, is projected to grow 24 percent from 2014 to 2024, much faster than the average for all occupations. However, because it is a small occupation, the fast growth will result in only about 1,400 new jobs over the 10-year period.

The expansion and adoption of solar panel installation is expected to create new jobs. As the cost of PV panels and shingles continues to fall, more residential households are expected to take advantage of these systems, resulting in greater demand for the workers who install them. The increasing popularity of solar leasing plans—in which homeowners lease rather than purchase systems—should create additional demand, as they no longer bear the upfront costs of installation.

The long-term outlook, however, is heavily dependent on government incentives, cost, and the continued improvement of PV panels. States and localities that provide incentives to reduce the cost of PV systems should experience greater demand for workers. Common incentives include tax rebates, direct subsidies, renewable energy purchase mandates, and net metering.

Job Prospects. PV installers who complete a course in photovoltaic systems at a community college or technical school will have the best job opportunities. Those with apprenticeship or journey electrician experience will also have very good job opportunities. Workers with experience in construction occupations, such as

Employment Projections Data for Solar Photovoltaic Installers

Occupational Title	SOC Code	Employment, 2014	Projected Employment, 2024	Change, 2014–2024 Percent	Change, 2014–2024 Numeric
Solar photovoltaic installers	47-2231	5,900	7,400	24	1,400

Source: U.S. Bureau of Labor Statistics, Employment Projections Program

Similar Occupations. This table shows a list of occupations with job duties that are similar to those of solar photovoltaic installers.

Occupations	Entry-level Education	2014 Median Pay	Projected Job Growth	Average Annual Openings
Carpenters	High school diploma or equivalent	$40,820	6%	6,040
Construction Laborers and Helpers	See Education/Training	$30,190	13%	18,010
Electricians	High school diploma or equivalent	$51,110	14%	8,590
Glaziers	High school diploma or equivalent	$38,410	4%	190
Ironworkers	High school diploma or equivalent	$48,520	9%	710
Masonry Workers	See Education/Training	$38,720	15%	3,730
Plumbers, Pipefitters, and Steamfitters	High school diploma or equivalent	$50,660	12%	4,910
Roofers	No formal educational credential	$35,760	13%	1,580
Sheet Metal Workers	High school diploma or equivalent	$45,070	7%	940

laborers, roofers, and carpenters, will have better job opportunities than those without construction experience.

Employment of PV installers fluctuates with the overall economy. On the one hand, there is great demand for PV installers during peak periods of building activity. On the other hand, workers may experience periods of unemployment when the overall level of construction falls.

Contacts for More Information

For details about apprenticeship or other training opportunities in this trade, contact the offices of the state employment service, technical colleges, the state apprenticeship agency, local photovoltaic contractors, firms that employ PV installers, or local union–management apprenticeship committees. Apprenticeship information is available from the U.S. Department of Labor's ApprenticeshipUSA program (www.dol.gov/apprenticeship) online or by phone at 877-872-5627.

For more information about apprenticeships for solar photovoltaic installers, visit

- IBEW – NECA Electrical Training Alliance (www.electricaltrainingalliance.org)

For more information about accredited training programs, visit

- Electronics Technicians Association, International (ETA) (www.eta-i.org)
- Interstate Renewable Energy Council, Inc. (www.irecusa.org)
- North American Board of Certified Energy Practitioners (www.nabcep.org)
- NCCER (www.nccer.org/solar-photovoltaics?pID=105)

Related BLS Article

For more information on solar photovoltaic installers, see *Green Jobs:* "Careers in Solar Power" (www.bls.gov/green/solar_power).

O*NET

- Solar Photovoltaic Installers (47-2231.00)

Education, Training, and Library

Adult Literacy and High School Equivalency Diploma Teachers

- **2014 Median Pay** .... $49,590 per year
  $23.84 per hour
- **Typical Entry-Level Education** .... Bachelor's degree
- **Work Experience in a Related Occupation** .... None
- **On-the-job Training** .... Internship/residency
- **Number of Jobs, 2014** 77,500
- **Job Outlook, 2014–24** .... 7% (As fast as average)
- **Employment Change, 2014–24** 5,500

What Adult Literacy and High School Equivalency Diploma Teachers Do

Adult literacy and high school equivalency diploma teachers instruct adults in basic skills, such as reading, writing, and speaking English. They also help students earn their high school equivalent diploma.

Duties. Adult literacy and high school equivalency diploma teachers typically do the following:

- Plan and teach lessons to help students gain the knowledge and skills needed to meet their goals, such as learning English or earning their high school equivalent diploma
- Adapt teaching methods based on students' strengths and weaknesses
- Emphasize skills that will help students find jobs, such as learning English words and common phrases used in the workplace
- Assess students for possible learning disabilities
- Monitor students' progress
- Help students develop study skills
- Connect students to other resources in their community, such as mental health services or job placement services

Before students enter these education programs, their educational level and skills are assessed. These assessments are typically performed by another staff member; however, in some programs the teacher may conduct the assessments. Based on the results of the assessment and student's goals, teachers develop an individualized education program.

Teachers must formally evaluate their students periodically to determine their progress and potential to go on to the next level of classes. However, teachers may informally evaluate their students' progress continually.

Adult literacy and high school equivalency diploma teachers often have students of various education levels in their classes. As a result, teachers need to use different teaching strategies and methods that meet all of their students' needs. They may work with students in classes or tutor them one-on-one.

Teachers prepare students for further education and help them to develop skills that they will need in the workplace. For example, they may teach students how to read a contract or how to estimate the cost of materials needed to remodel a kitchen.

There are three basic types of education that adult literacy and high school equivalency diploma teachers provide:

Adult basic education classes teach students the basics of reading, writing, and math. Students who enter these classes usually do not have a high school diploma. They generally are 16 years or older and need to gain proficiency in these skills to improve their job situation.

High school equivalency and adult secondary education classes prepare students to take the test to earn a high school equivalent diploma. Some programs are combined with career preparation programs so that students can earn a high school equivalent diploma and a career-related credential at the same time.

The high school equivalency exam is composed of four subjects: language arts, math, science, and social studies. In addition to teaching these subjects, teachers also help their students improve their skills in communicating, critical thinking, and problem solving—skills they will need to prepare for further education and successful careers.

English as a Second Language (ESL), also called *English for Speakers of Other Languages (ESOL)*, classes teach students to read, write, and speak English. Students in these classes are immigrants to the United States or those whose native language is not English.

ESL teachers often focus on helping their students with practical vocabulary for jobs and daily living. They also may focus on preparing their students to take the citizenship exam.

ESL teachers may have students from many different countries and cultures in their classroom. Because the ESL teacher and the students may not share a common native language, ESL teachers must be creative in fostering communication in the classroom to achieve their education goals.

Work Environment

Adult literacy and high school equivalency diploma teachers held about 77,500 jobs in 2014. The industries that employed the most adult literacy and high school equivalency diploma teachers were as follows:

Adult literacy and GED teachers instruct adults in basic skills, such as reading, writing, and speaking English.

Median Annual Wages, May 2014

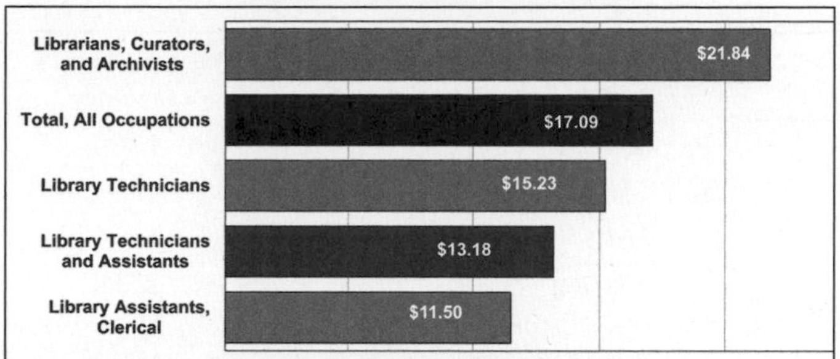

Note: All Occupations includes all occupations in the U.S. Economy.
Source: U.S. Bureau of Labor Statistics, Occupational Employment Statistics

Percent Change in Employment, Projected 2014–2024

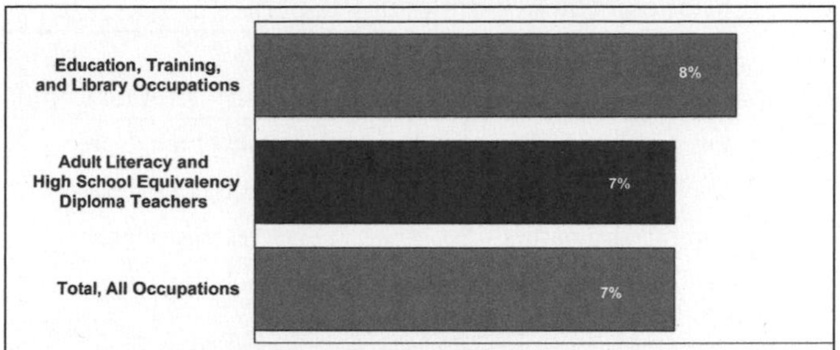

Note: All Occupations includes all occupations in the U.S. Economy.
Source: U.S. Bureau of Labor Statistics, Office of Occupational Statistics and Employment Projections

Elementary and secondary schools; state, local, and private 29%
Junior colleges; state, local, and private 28
Other schools and instruction; state, local, and private 11
Healthcare and social assistance 7
Colleges, universities, and professional schools; state, local, and private 4

Students in adult literacy and high school equivalency programs attend classes by choice. As a result, they are often highly motivated, which can make teaching them rewarding and satisfying.

Work Schedules. Classes are held at times when students are not at work, so many teachers work in the mornings and evenings. Many adult literacy and high school equivalency diploma teachers work part time.

Education/Training

Most adult literacy and high school equivalency diploma teachers must have at least a bachelor's degree. Employers typically prefer workers who have some teaching experience.

Education. Most states require adult literacy and high school equivalency diploma teachers to have at least a bachelor's degree. Some employers, such as community colleges, prefer to hire those with a master's degree or graduate coursework in adult education or English as a Second Language (ESL). Some colleges and universities offer master's degrees or graduate certificates in teaching adult education or ESL.

Programs in adult education prepare prospective teachers to develop adult education programs, to use effective teaching strategies for adult learners, to work with students from a variety of cultures and backgrounds, and to teach adults with learning disabilities. Some programs allow these prospective teachers to specialize in adult basic education, secondary education, or ESL.

Prospective ESL teachers should take courses or training in linguistics and theories of how people learn second languages. Knowledge of a second language is not necessary to teach ESL, but it can be helpful to understand what students are going through.

Many adult literacy and high school equivalency diploma teachers take professional development classes to improve their teaching skills and ensure that they keep up with the latest research in teaching adults.

Licenses, Certifications, and Registrations. Some states require adult literacy and high school equivalency diploma teachers to have a teaching certificate to work in government-run programs. Some states have certificates specifically for adult education. Other states require teachers to have a certificate in elementary or secondary education.

To obtain a license, adult literacy and high school equivalency diploma teachers typically need a bachelor's degree and must complete an approved teacher-training program. For more information, contact the state director of adult education. Contact information can be found from the U.S. Department of Education.

Training. In order to receive certification or licensure, teachers may need to perform fieldwork, commonly referred to as student teaching. During student teaching, they work with a mentor teacher and get experience teaching students in a classroom setting. The amount of student teaching that is required varies by state.

Important Qualities

Communication skills. Adult literacy and high school equivalency teachers must collaborate with other teachers and program administrators. In addition, they talk with students about their progress and goals, and must explain concepts in terms that students can understand.

Cultural sensitivity. Teachers must be able to work with students from a variety of cultural, educational, and economic backgrounds. They must be understanding and respectful of their students' backgrounds and be familiar with their concerns.

Patience. Working with students of different abilities and backgrounds can be difficult. Teachers must be patient when students struggle with material.

Resourcefulness. Adult literacy and high school equivalency diploma teachers must respond appropriately to difficult situations and think on their feet. For example, they need to be able to alter

Employment Projections Data for Adult Literacy and High School Equivalency Diploma Teachers

Occupational Title	SOC Code	Employment, 2014	Projected Employment, 2024	Change, 2014–2024 Percent	Change, 2014–2024 Numeric
Adult basic and secondary education and literacy teachers and instructors	25-3011	77,500	83,000	7	5,500

Source: U.S. Bureau of Labor Statistics, Employment Projections Program

Similar Occupations. This table shows a list of occupations with job duties that are similar to those of adult literacy and high school equivalency diploma teachers.

Occupations	Entry-level Education	2014 Median Pay	Projected Job Growth	Average Annual Openings
Career and Technical Education Teachers	Bachelor's degree	$51,830	4%	1,020
High School Teachers	Bachelor's degree	$56,310	6%	5,590
Instructional Coordinators	Master's degree	$61,550	7%	1,050
Kindergarten and Elementary School Teachers	Bachelor's degree	$53,760	6%	8,780
Librarians	Master's degree	$56,170	2%	270
Middle School Teachers	Bachelor's degree	$54,940	6%	3,680
Postsecondary Teachers	See Education/Training	$70,790	13%	17,700
School and Career Counselors	Master's degree	$53,370	8%	2,250
Social Workers	See Education/Training	$45,500	12%	7,480
Special Education Teachers	Bachelor's degree	$55,980	6%	2,810
Teacher Assistants	Some college, no degree	$24,430	6%	7,860

their teaching methods to meet the needs of each student they teach and find ways to keep students engaged in learning.

Pay

The median annual wage for adult literacy and high school equivalency diploma teachers was $49,590 in May 2014. The median wage is the wage at which half the workers in an occupation earned more than that amount and half earned less. The lowest 10 percent earned less than $28,290, and the highest 10 percent earned more than $81,990.

In May 2014, the median annual wages for adult literacy and high school equivalency diploma teachers in the top industries in which they worked were as follows:

Elementary and secondary schools; state, local, and private	$57,350
Junior colleges; state, local, and private	49,540
Colleges, universities, and professional schools; state, local, and private	47,810
Other schools and instruction; state, local, and private	42,720
Healthcare and social assistance	39,570

Classes are held at times when students are not at work, so many teachers work in the mornings and evenings. Many adult literacy and high school equivalency diploma teachers work part time.

Job Outlook

Employment of adult literacy and high school equivalency diploma teachers is projected to grow 7 percent from 2014 to 2024, about as fast as the average for all occupations.

Employment growth is expected as continued immigration to the United States creates a need for adult literacy and high school equivalency diploma programs. Some immigrants do not speak English and will want to improve their communication skills to help them find jobs in the United States. English as a Second Language (ESL) teachers will be needed to help these students gain the required skills.

In addition, traditional schooling does not always give some adults the literacy or other skills they need to find employment. These students often seek to improve their skills in adult education programs later in life.

However, student enrollments in adult education and ESL programs have declined in recent years. At the same time, high school graduation rates have increased, reducing the need for adults to obtain high school equivalent diplomas. Fewer students will result in less demand for the adult literacy and high school equivalency diploma teachers who teach them.

Enrollment in these programs is often related to the ability of students to pay, either directly or through government-sponsored programs. Changes in government funding for adult education and ESL programs will impact the demand for adult literacy and high school equivalency diploma teachers.

Job Prospects. Many adult literacy and high school equivalency diploma teacher positions are part time, and full-time positions are uncommon and difficult to find. As a result, prospects will be best for workers who are willing and able to take a part-time position. In addition, those with experience teaching will have better prospects.

Contacts for More Information

For more information about adult education in your state, visit

➤ U.S. Department of Education (http://tinyurl.com/j2kayb6)

O*NET

➤ Adult Basic and Secondary Education and Literacy Teachers and Instructors (25-3011.00)

Career and Technical Education Teachers

- **2014 Median Pay** .... $51,830 per year
- **Typical Entry-Level Education** .... Bachelor's degree
- **Work Experience in a Related Occupation** .... Less than 5 years
- **On-the-job Training** .... See Education/Training
- **Number of Jobs, 2014** 231,800
- **Job Outlook, 2014–24** .... 4% (Slower than average)
- **Employment Change, 2014–24** 10,200

What Career and Technical Education Teachers Do

Career and technical education teachers instruct students in various technical and vocational subjects, such as auto repair, healthcare, and culinary arts. They teach academic and technical content to provide students with the skills and knowledge necessary to enter an occupation.

Duties. Career and technical education teachers typically do the following:

- Create lesson plans and assignments
- Instruct students on how to develop certain skills
- Show how to apply classroom knowledge through hands-on activities
- Demonstrate and supervise the safe and proper use of tools and equipment
- Monitor students' progress, assign tasks, and grade assignments
- Discuss students' progress with parents, students, and counselors
- Develop and enforce classroom rules and safety procedures

Career and technical education teachers help students explore and prepare to enter a specific occupation, in fields such as healthcare or information technology. They use a variety of teaching techniques to help students learn and develop skills related to a specific career or field of study. They demonstrate tasks, techniques, and tools used in an occupation. They may assign hands-on tasks, such as replacing brakes on cars, taking blood pressure, or recording vital signs. Teachers typically oversee these tasks in workshops and laboratories in the school.

Some teachers establish relationships with local businesses and nonprofit organizations to provide practical work experience for students. They also serve as advisers to students participating in career and technical student organizations.

The specific duties of career and technical education teachers vary by the grade and subject they teach. In middle schools and high schools, they teach general concepts in a classroom and through practical exercises in workshops and laboratories.

In postsecondary schools, they teach specific career skills that help students earn a certificate, diploma, or an associate's degree, and prepare them for a specific job. For example, welding instructors teach students various welding techniques and essential safety practices. They also monitor the use of tools and equipment, and have students practice procedures until they meet the specific standards required by the trade.

In most states, teachers in middle and high schools instruct one subject within the 16 major career fields, also known as Career Clusters. For example, the career cluster known as *architecture and construction* includes instruction in designing, planning, managing, building, and maintaining structures.

Teachers instructing courses in *agricultural, food, and natural resources* teach topics such as agricultural production; agriculture-related business; veterinary science; and plant, animal, and food systems. For example, they may have students plant and care for crops and tend to animals so that students can apply what they have learned in the classroom.

Career and technical education teachers in *hospitality and tourism* teach students in subjects such as nutrition, culinary arts, or hotel lodging. For example, teachers may instruct and supervise students in creating menus and preparing food.

Some teach the skills necessary to work as technicians and assistants, such as nursing and dental assistants in *health-science occupations*.

Career and technical education teachers assign students hands-on tasks so that they can gain experience.

For information on all 16 major Career Clusters and programs in all other states, visit National Association of State Directors of Career Technical Education Consortium (www.careertech.org).

Work Environment

Career and technical education teachers held about 231,800 jobs in 2014. Most work in public schools, including middle, high, and postsecondary schools, such as 2-year colleges. Others work in technical, trade, and business schools.

Work Schedules. Career and technical education teachers in middle and high schools generally work during school hours. They may meet with parents, students, and school staff before and after classes.

Some career and technical education teachers, especially those in postsecondary schools, instruct courses and develop lesson plans during evening hours and on weekends.

Teachers usually work the traditional 10-month school year and have a 2-month break during the summer. Some teachers work for summer programs.

Teachers in districts with a year-round schedule typically work 8 weeks in a row then have a break for 1 week. They also have a 5-week midwinter break.

Education/Training

Career and technical education teachers must have a bachelor's degree. They also need work experience in the subject they teach. Some teachers, particularly those in public schools, also may be required to have a state-issued certification or license. Requirements for certification vary by state.

Education. Career and technical education teachers in public schools generally need a bachelor's degree in the field they teach, such as agriculture, engineering, or computer science.

Work Experience in a Related Occupation. Many career and technical education teachers need work experience in the field they teach. For example, automotive mechanics, chefs, and nurses typically spend years in their career before moving into teaching.

Training. Some states require prospective career and technical education teachers to complete a period of fieldwork, commonly referred to as student teaching. In some states, this program is a prerequisite for a license to teach in public schools. During student teaching, prospective teachers gain experience in preparing lessons and teaching students under the supervision and guidance of a

Median Annual Wages, May 2014

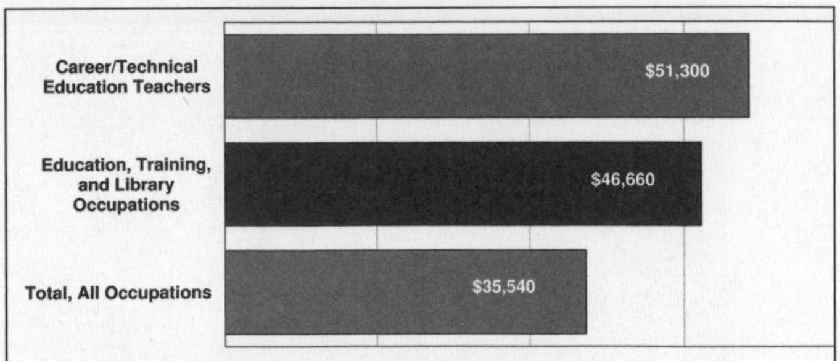

Note: All Occupations includes all occupations in the U.S. Economy.
Source: U.S. Bureau of Labor Statistics, Occupational Employment Statistics

Percent Change in Employment, Projected 2014–2024

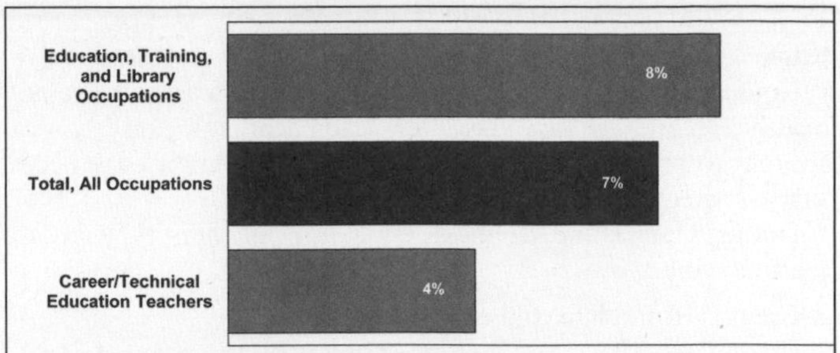

Note: All Occupations includes all occupations in the U.S. Economy.
Source: U.S. Bureau of Labor Statistics, Office of Occupational Statistics and Employment Projections

mentor teacher. The amount of time required for these programs varies by state, but may last from 1 to 2 years.

Licenses, Certifications, and Registrations. States may require career and technical education teachers in public schools to be licensed or certified. Requirements for certification vary by state. Most states require teachers to pass a background check.

Certification typically requires completing a student teaching program and a bachelor's degree. States usually require candidates to pass a general teaching certification test.

Teachers may be required to complete annual professional development courses to maintain their license. For certification requirements in your state, visit Teach.org (www.teach.org).

Some states offer an alternative route to certification for prospective teachers who have a bachelor's degree or work experience in their field, but lack the education courses required for certification. Alternative programs typically cover teaching methods, development of lesson plans, and classroom management.

In addition to teaching certification, career and technical education teachers who prepare students for an occupation that requires a license or certification may need to have and maintain the same credential. For example, career and technical education teachers who instruct welding may need to have certification in welding.

Advancement. Experienced teachers can advance to become mentors and lead teachers, helping less experienced teachers to improve their teaching skills.

Teachers may become school counselors, instructional coordinators, or principals. These positions generally require additional education, an advanced degree, or certification. An advanced degree in education administration or leadership may be helpful.

Important Qualities

Communication skills. Career and technical education teachers must be able to explain technical concepts in terms that students can understand.

Organizational skills. Career and technical education teachers have many students in different classes throughout the day. They must be able to organize their time and teaching materials.

Patience. Working with students of different abilities and backgrounds can be difficult. Teachers must be patient with each student in their classroom and develop a positive learning environment.

Resourcefulness. Teachers need to be able to develop different ways of presenting information and demonstrating tasks so that students can learn.

Pay

The median annual wage for career and technical education teachers was $51,830 in May 2014. The median wage is the wage at which half the workers in an occupation earned more than that amount and half earned less. The lowest 10 percent earned less than $31,780, and the highest 10 percent earned more than $84,400.

Median annual wages for career and technical education teachers in May 2014 were as follows:

Career/technical education teachers, secondary school $55,200
Career/technical education teachers, middle school 54,090
Vocational education teachers, postsecondary 48,360

Job Outlook

Overall employment of career and technical education teachers is projected to grow 4 percent from 2014 to 2024, slower than the average for all occupations. Employment growth will vary by type. (See Employment Projections table.)

Overall demand for career and technical education teachers will be driven by a continued need for programs that prepare students for technical careers.

As middle and high school students continue to be required to take more academic and fewer career and technical classes,

Employment Projections Data for Career and Technical Education Teachers

Occupational Title	SOC Code	Employment, 2014	Projected Employment, 2024	Change, 2014–2024 Percent	Change, 2014–2024 Numeric
Career/technical education teachers	—	231,800	242,000	4	10,200
Vocational education teachers, postsecondary	25-1194	138,500	147,600	7	9,100
Career/technical education teachers, middle school	25-2023	13,700	14,600	6	800
Career/technical education teachers, secondary school	25-2032	79,600	79,900	0	300

Source: U.S. Bureau of Labor Statistics, Employment Projections Program

Similar Occupations. This table shows a list of occupations with job duties that are similar to those of career and technical education teachers.

Occupations	Entry-level Education	2014 Median Pay	Projected Job Growth	Average Annual Openings
Elementary, Middle, and High School Principals	Master's degree	$89,540	6%	1,400
High School Teachers	Bachelor's degree	$56,310	6%	5,590
Instructional Coordinators	Master's degree	$61,550	7%	1,050
Middle School Teachers	Bachelor's degree	$54,940	6%	3,680
Postsecondary Teachers	See Education/Training	$70,790	13%	17,700
School and Career Counselors	Master's degree	$53,370	8%	2,250
Special Education Teachers	Bachelor's degree	$55,980	6%	2,810
Teacher Assistants	Some college, no degree	$24,430	6%	7,860

employment growth of career and education teachers in middle and high schools may be impacted.

In addition, employment growth of teachers, particularly those in public schools, will depend on government funding for career and technical programs.

Postsecondary career and technical education programs have experienced an increase in the number of career and technical institutions and an increase in the number of graduates who have received certificates or diplomas. This will have a positive impact on the demand for career and technical teachers.

Employment growth of career and technical education teachers at the postsecondary level, such as technical, trade, and business schools, often depends on the economy. As jobs become more limited, people seek additional technical skills to help them get a job. Also, changes in technology will drive the demand for people with technical skills. This will result in an increased demand for career and technical teachers at the postsecondary level.

Job Prospects. Most job opportunities will come from the need to replace teachers who leave the occupation. As a result, teachers with work experience in the subject they teach and certifications should have the best job prospects.

Job opportunities also may be better in certain specialties, particularly at the postsecondary level. For example, those with experience in healthcare support occupations, who can teach skills necessary to work as medical or dental assistants, may have better job opportunities.

Contacts for More Information

For more information about career and technical education teachers, visit

- ➤ Association for Career and Technical Education (www.acteonline.org)
- ➤ National Association of State Directors of Career Technical Education Consortium (www.careertech.org/career-clusters)

For more information about teaching and becoming a teacher, visit

- ➤ Teach.org (www.teach.org)

O*NET

- ➤ Career/Technical Education Teachers, Middle School (25-2032.00)
- ➤ Career/Technical Education Teachers, Middle School (25-2023.00)

Archivists, Curators, and Museum Workers

- **2014 Median Pay** .... $46,300 per year
  $22.26 per hour
- **Typical Entry-Level Education** .... See Education/Training
- **Work Experience in a Related Occupation** .... None
- **On-the-job Training** .... None
- **Number of Jobs, 2014** 31,300
- **Job Outlook, 2014–24** .... 7% (As fast as average)
- **Employment Change, 2014–24** 2,100

What Archivists, Curators, and Museum Workers Do

Archivists appraise, process, catalog, and preserve permanent records and historically valuable documents. Curators oversee collections of artwork and historic items, and may conduct public service activities for an institution. Museum technicians and conservators prepare and restore objects and documents in museum collections and exhibits.

Duties. Archivists typically do the following:

- Authenticate and appraise historical documents and archival materials
- Preserve and maintain documents and objects
- Create and manage system to maintain and preserve electronic records
- Organize and classify archival records to make them easy to search through
- Safeguard records by creating film and digital copies
- Direct workers who help arrange, exhibit, and maintain collections
- Set and administer policy guidelines concerning public access to materials
- Provide help to users
- Find and acquire new materials for their archives

Curators, museum technicians, and conservators typically do the following:

- Acquire, store, and exhibit collections
- Select the theme and design of exhibits
- Design, organize, and conduct tours and workshops for the public
- Attend meetings and civic events to promote their institution
- Clean objects such as ancient tools, coins, and statues
- Direct and supervise curatorial, technical, and student staff
- Plan and conduct special research projects

Archivists preserve documents and records for their importance or historical significance. They coordinate educational and public outreach programs, such as tours, workshops, lectures, and classes. They also may work with researchers on topics and items relevant to their collections.

Some archivists specialize in an era of history so they can have a better understanding of the records from that period.

Archivists typically work with specific forms of records, such as manuscripts, electronic records, websites, photographs, maps, motion pictures, and sound recordings.

Curators, also known as *museum directors*, direct the acquisition, storage, and exhibition of collections, including negotiating and authorizing the purchase, sale, exchange, and loan of collections. They may authenticate, evaluate, and categorize the specimens in a collection.

Curators often oversee and help conduct their institution's research projects and related educational programs. They may represent their institution in the media, at public events, at conventions, and at professional conferences.

Some curators who work in large institutions may specialize in a particular field, such as botany, art, or history. For example, a large natural history museum might employ separate curators for its collections of birds, fish, insects, and mammals.

Some curators focus primarily on taking care of their collections, others on researching items in their collections, and still others spend most of their time performing administrative tasks. In small institutions with only one or a few curators, one curator may be responsible for a number of tasks, from taking care of collections to directing the affairs of the museum.

Museum technicians, commonly known as *registrars* or *collections specialists*, concentrate on the care and safeguarding of the objects in museum collections and exhibitions. They oversee the logistics of acquisitions, insurance policies, risk management, and loaning of objects to and from the museum for exhibition or research. They keep detailed records of the conditions and locations of the objects that are on display, in storage, or being transported to another museum. They also maintain and store any documentation associated with the objects.

Museum technicians also may answer questions from the public and help curators and outside scholars use the museum's collections.

Conservators handle, preserve, treat, and keep records of works of art, artifacts, and specimens—work that may require substantial historical, scientific, and archeological research. They document their findings and treat items to minimize deterioration or to restore them to their original state. Conservators usually specialize in a particular material or group of objects, such as documents and books, paintings, decorative arts, textiles, metals, or architectural material.

Some conservators use X-rays, chemical testing, microscopes, special lights, and other laboratory equipment and techniques to examine objects, determine their condition, and decide on the best way to preserve them. They also may participate in outreach programs, research topics in their specialty, and write articles for scholarly journals.

Museum technicians often prepare materials for display.

Work Environment

Archivists, curators, and museum workers held about 31,300 jobs in 2014. The industries that employed the most archivists, curators, and museum workers were as follows:

Museums, historical sites, and similar institutions	37%
Government	23
Educational services; state, local, and private	18

Because most curators work at museums, zoos, aquariums, botanical gardens, nature centers, and historical sites, their working conditions vary. Depending on the size of the institution and the position, they may work at a desk or spend their time working with the public, providing reference assistance and educational services. Museum workers who restore and set up exhibits or work with bulky, heavy record containers may have to lift objects, climb ladders and scaffolding, and stretch to reach items.

Work Schedules. Most archivists, curators, museum technicians, and conservators work full time.

Archivists in government agencies and corporations generally work during regular business hours. Curators in large institutions may travel extensively to evaluate potential additions to the collection, organize exhibits, and conduct research. However, for curators in small institutions, travel may be rare. Museum technicians may need to work evenings and weekends, when institutions are open to the public.

Education/Training

Most archivist, curator, and conservator positions require a master's degree related to the position's field. Museum technicians must have a bachelor's degree. People often gain experience through an internship or by volunteering in archives and museums.

Education. Archivists. Archivists typically need a master's degree in history, library science, archival science, political science, or public administration. Although many colleges and universities have history, library science, or other similar programs, only a few institutions offer master's degrees in archival studies. Students may gain valuable archiving experience through volunteer or internship opportunities.

Curators. Curators typically need a master's degree in art history, history, archaeology, or museum studies. Students with internship experience may have an advantage in the competitive job market.

In small museums, curator positions may be available to applicants with a bachelor's degree. Because they also may have administrative and managerial responsibilities, courses in business administration, public relations, marketing, and fundraising are recommended.

Museum technicians. Museum technicians, commonly known as *registrars*, typically need a bachelor's degree. Because few schools offer a bachelor's degree in museum studies, it is common for registrars to obtain an undergraduate degree in a related field, such as art history, history, or archeology. Some jobs may require candidates to have a master's degree in museum studies. Museums may prefer candidates with knowledge of the museum's specialty, training in museum studies, or previous experience working in museums.

Conservators. Conservators typically need a master's degree in conservation or in a closely related field. Graduate programs last 2 to 4 years, the latter years of which include internship training. Only a few graduate programs in museum conservation techniques are offered in the United States. To qualify for entry into these programs, a student must have a background in chemistry, archeology, studio art, or art history. Completing a conservation internship as an undergraduate can enhance admission prospects.

Licenses, Certifications, and Registrations. At this time, only a few employers require or prefer certification for archivists. However, archivists may choose to earn voluntary certification because it allows them to demonstrate expertise in a particular area.

The Academy of Certified Archivists offers the Certified Archivist credential. To earn certification, candidates must have a master's degree, have professional archival experience, and pass an exam. They must renew their certification periodically by retaking the exam or fulfilling continuing education credits.

Other Experience. To gain marketable experience, candidates may have to work part time, as an intern or as a volunteer, during or after completing their education. Substantial experience in collection management, research, exhibit design, or restoration, as well as database management skills, is necessary for full-time positions.

Advancement. Continuing education is available through meetings, conferences, and workshops sponsored by archival, historical, and museum associations. Some large organizations, such as the U.S. National Archives and Records Administration in Washington, DC, offer in-house training.

Top museum positions are highly sought after and are competitive. Performing unique research and producing published work are important for advancement in large institutions. In addition, a doctoral degree may be needed for some advanced positions.

Museum workers employed in small institutions may have limited opportunities for promotion. They typically advance by transferring to a larger institution that has supervisory positions.

Important Qualities

Analytical skills. Archivists, curators, museum technicians, and conservators need excellent analytical skills to determine the origin, history, and importance of many of the objects they work with.

Computer skills. Archivists and museum technicians should have good computer skills because they use and develop complex databases related to the materials they store and access.

Customer-service skills. Archivists, curators, museum technicians, and conservators work with the general public on a regular basis. They must be courteous and friendly and be able to help users find materials.

Organizational skills. Archivists, curators, museum technicians, and conservators must be able to store and easily retrieve records and documents. They must also develop logical systems of storage for the public to use.

Technical skills. Many historical objects need to be analyzed and preserved. Conservators must use the appropriate chemicals and techniques to preserve different objects, such as documents, paintings, fabrics, and pottery.

Pay

The median annual wage for archivists, curators, and museum workers was $46,300 in May 2014. The median wage is the wage at which half the workers in an occupation earned more than that amount and half earned less. The lowest 10 percent earned less than $26,030, and the highest 10 percent earned more than $82,760.

Median annual wages for archivists, curators, and museum workers in May 2014 were as follows:

Curators	$51,280
Archivists	49,120
Museum technicians and conservators	39,940

Job Outlook

Employment of archivists, curators, and museum workers is projected to grow 7 percent from 2014 to 2024, about as fast as the average for all occupations. Employment growth will vary by specialty.

Employment of archivists is projected to grow 7 percent from 2014 to 2024, about as fast as the average for all occupations. Demand for archivists is expected to increase as public and private organizations require increasing volumes of records and

Median Annual Wages, May 2014

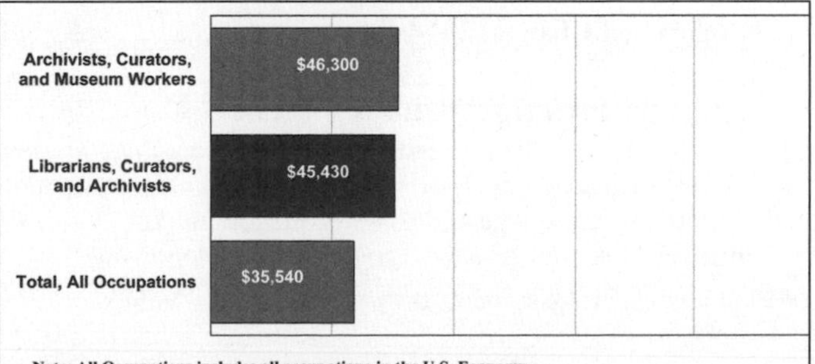

Note: All Occupations includes all occupations in the U.S. Economy.
Source: U.S. Bureau of Labor Statistics, Occupational Employment Statistics

Percent Change in Employment, Projected 2014–2024

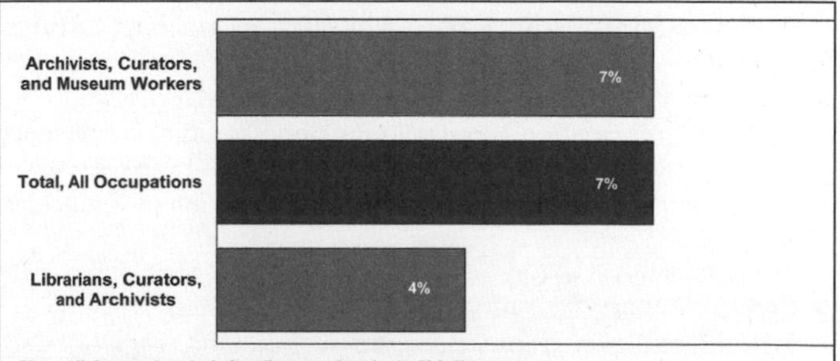

Note: All Occupations includes all occupations in the U.S. Economy.
Source: U.S. Bureau of Labor Statistics, Office of Occupational Statistics and Employment Projections

Employment Projections Data for Archivists, Curators, and Museum Workers

Occupational Title	SOC Code	Employment, 2014	Projected Employment, 2024	Change, 2014–2024 Percent	Change, 2014–2024 Numeric
Archivists, curators, and museum technicians	25-4010	31,300	33,400	7	2,100
Archivists	25-4011	6,900	7,400	7	500
Curators	25-4012	13,100	14,100	8	1,000
Museum technicians and conservators	25-4013	11,300	11,900	5	600

Source: U.S. Bureau of Labor Statistics, Employment Projections Program

Similar Occupations. This table shows a list of occupations with job duties that are similar to those of archivists, curators, and museum workers.

Occupations	Entry-level Education	2014 Median Pay	Projected Job Growth	Average Annual Openings
Anthropologists and Archeologists	Master's degree	$59,280	4%	30
Craft and Fine Artists	See Education/Training	$44,400	2%	90
Historians	Master's degree	$55,870	2%	10
Librarians	Master's degree	$56,170	2%	270

information to be organized and made accessible. The growing use of electronic records may cause demand for archivists who specialize in electronic records and records management.

Employment of curators is projected to grow 8 percent from 2014 to 2024, about as fast as the average for all occupations. Museums receive millions of visitors every year. Continued public interest in these cultural centers will lead to demand for curators and for the collections they manage.

Employment of museum technicians and conservators is projected to grow 5 percent from 2014 to 2024, about as fast as the average for all occupations. Public interest in science, art, history, and technology is expected to spur some demand for museum technicians and conservators.

Archives and museums can be subject to cuts in funding during recessions and periods of budget tightening, reducing demand for these workers.

Job Prospects. Candidates seeking archivist, curator, museum technician, or conservator jobs should expect very strong competition due to the high number of qualified applicants per job opening. Graduates with highly specialized training, a master's degree, and internship or volunteer experience should have the best job prospects.

Contacts for More Information

For information about archivists and about schools offering courses in archival studies, visit

➤ Society of American Archivists (www.archivists.org)

For more information about archivists and archivist certification, visit

➤ Academy of Certified Archivists (www.certifiedarchivists.org)

For more information about training opportunities, conferences, and workshops for museum workers, visit

➤ U.S. National Archives and Records Administration (www.archives.gov)

For information about government archivists, visit

➤ Council of State Archivists (www.statearchivists.org)

For information about museum technicians, registrars, or collections specialists, visit

➤ Association of Registrars and Collections Specialists (www.arcsinfo.org)

For more information about museum careers, including schools offering courses in museum studies for curators and museum technicians, visit

➤ American Alliance of Museums (www.aam-us.org)

For more information about careers and education programs in conservation and preservation for conservators, visit

➤ American Institute for Conservation of Historic and Artistic Works (www.conservation-us.org)

For information about job openings as curators, museum technicians, and conservators with the federal government, visit

➤ USAJobs (www.usajobs.gov)

O*NET

➤ Archivists (25-4011.00)

➤ Curators (25-4012.00)

➤ Museum Technicians and Conservators (25-4013.00)

High School Teachers

- **2014 Median Pay** .... $56,310 per year
- **Typical Entry-Level Education** .... Bachelor's degree
- **Work Experience in a Related Occupation** .... None
- **On-the-job Training** .... Internship/residency
- **Number of Jobs, 2014** 961,600
- **Job Outlook, 2014–24** .... 6% (As fast as average)
- **Employment Change, 2014–24** 55,900

What High School Teachers Do

High school teachers help prepare students for life after graduation. They teach academic lessons and various skills that students will need to attend college and to enter the job market.

Duties. High school teachers typically do the following:

- Plan lessons in the subjects they teach, such as biology or history
- Assess students to evaluate their abilities, strengths, and weaknesses

High school teachers generally specialize in a subject, such as English, math, or science.

- Teach students in full class settings or in small groups
- Adapt lessons to any changes in class size
- Grade students' assignments and exams to monitor progress
- Communicate with parents about students' progress
- Work with individual students to challenge them, to improve their abilities, and to work on their weaknesses
- Prepare students for standardized tests required by the state
- Develop and enforce classroom rules and administrative policies
- Supervise students outside of the classroom—for example, at lunchtime or during detention

High school teachers generally teach students from the 9th through 12th grades. They usually specialize in one subject area, such as math, science, or history. They may teach several different classes within that subject area. For example, a high school math teacher may teach courses in algebra, calculus, and/or geometry.

High school teachers may teach students from different grades throughout the day. For example, in one class they may have students from the 9th grade and then in the next class they may have 12th-grade students. In many schools, students are divided into classes on the basis of their abilities, so teachers need to change their courses to match the students' abilities.

High school teachers see several different classes of students throughout the day. They may teach the same material—for example, world history—to more than one class if the school has many students taking that subject.

Some high school teachers instruct special classes, such as art, music, and physical education.

When they do not have classes, teachers plan lessons, grade assignments, and meet with other teachers and staff.

In some schools, teachers of English as a second language (ESL) and teachers of English for speakers of other languages (ESOL) work exclusively with students who are learning the English language. These students are often referred to as English language learners (ELLs). These teachers work with students individually or in groups to help them improve their English language skills and help them with assignments for other classes.

Students with learning disabilities and emotional or behavioral disorders often are taught in traditional classes. Therefore, high school teachers may work with special education teachers to adapt lessons to these students' needs and to monitor the students' progress.

Some teachers maintain websites to communicate with parents about students' assignments, upcoming events, and grades. For students, teachers may create websites or discussion boards to present information and to expand a lesson taught in class.

Some high school teachers coach sports and advise student clubs and other groups, activities that frequently take place before or after school.

Work Environment

High school teachers held about 961,600 jobs in 2014.

Most high school teachers work in either public or private schools. Some teach in public magnet and charter schools. Others teach in private religious or secular schools.

Most states have tenure laws, which state that, after a certain number of years of satisfactory classroom teaching, teachers may have some job security.

Watching students develop new skills and gain an appreciation for knowledge and learning can be very rewarding.

However, teaching may be stressful. Some schools have large classes and lack important teaching tools, such as computers and up-to-date textbooks. Most teachers are held accountable for their students' performance on standardized tests, a requirement that can be frustrating. Occasionally, teachers must cope with unmotivated or disrespectful students.

Work Schedules. High school teachers generally work school hours, which vary from school to school. However, they often spend time in the evenings and on weekends grading papers and preparing lessons. In addition, they may meet with parents, students, and other teachers before and after school. Plus, teachers who coach sports or advise clubs generally do so before or after school.

Many work the traditional 10-month school year and have a 2-month break during the summer. Although most do not teach during the summer, some may teach in summer programs.

Teachers in districts with a year-round schedule typically work 8 weeks in a row and then have a break for 1 week. They also have a 5-week midwinter break.

Education/Training

High school teachers must have a bachelor's degree. In addition, public school teachers must have a state-issued certification or license.

Education. All states require public high school teachers to have at least a bachelor's degree. Most states require high school teachers to have majored in a subject area, such as science or history. Teachers typically enroll in their institution's teacher preparation program and take classes in education and child psychology as well.

In teacher education programs, prospective high school teachers learn how to present information to students and how to work with students of varying abilities and backgrounds. Programs typically include fieldwork, such as student teaching. For information about teacher preparation programs in your state, visit Teach.org (www.teach.org).

Some states require high school teachers to earn a master's degree after earning their teaching certification.

Teachers in private schools do not need to meet state requirements. However, private schools typically seek high school teachers who have a bachelor's degree and a major in a subject area.

Licenses, Certifications, and Registrations. All states require teachers in public schools to be licensed or certified. Those who

Median Annual Wages, May 2014

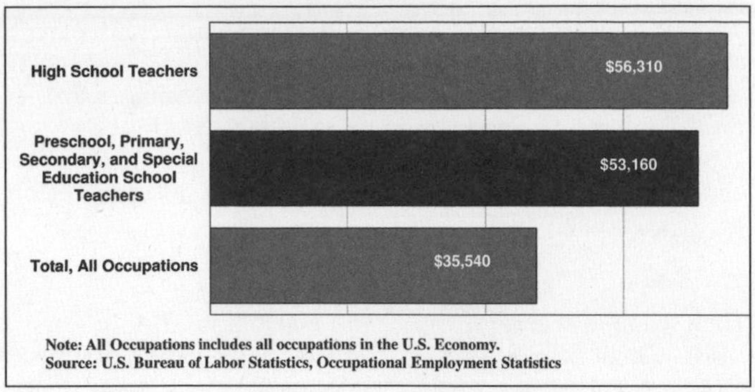

Percent Change in Employment, Projected 2014–2024

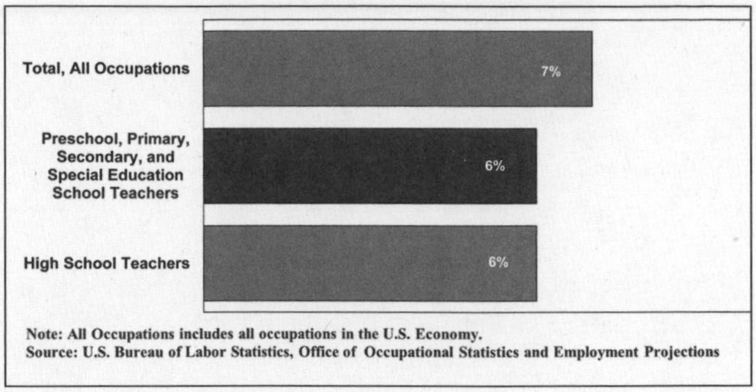

teach in private schools are generally not required to be licensed. Most states require teachers to pass a background check.

High school teachers typically are awarded a secondary or high school certification, which allows them to teach the 7th through the 12th grades.

Requirements for certification vary by state. In addition to requiring a bachelor's degree, states require teachers to complete a teacher preparation program and supervised experience in teaching, typically gained through student teaching. States also typically require candidates to pass a general teaching certification test, as well as a test that demonstrates their knowledge in the subject they will teach. Some states require teachers to have a minimum grade point average as well. For information on certification requirements in your state, visit Teach.org (www.teach.org).

Often, teachers are required to complete annual professional development classes to keep their license. Some states require teachers to complete a master's degree after receiving their certification.

All states offer an alternative route to certification for people who already have a bachelor's degree but lack the education courses required for certification. Some alternative certification programs allow candidates to begin teaching immediately under the supervision of an experienced teacher. These programs cover teaching methods and child development. After they complete the program, candidates are awarded full certification. Other programs require students to take classes in education before they can teach. Students may be awarded a master's degree after completing either type of program.

Training. In order to receive certification, teachers need to undergo a period of fieldwork, commonly referred to as student teaching. During student teaching, they work with a mentor teacher and gain experience teaching students in a classroom setting. The amount of time required varies by state.

Important Qualities

Communication skills. Teachers must collaborate with other teachers and special education teachers. In addition, teachers need to discuss students' needs with parents and administrators.

Patience. Working with students of different abilities and backgrounds can be difficult. High school teachers must be patient when students struggle with material.

Resourcefulness. In addition, they must be able to engage students in learning and adapt lessons to each student's needs.

Advancement. Experienced teachers can advance to be mentors or lead teachers. In these positions, they often work with less experienced teachers to help them improve their teaching skills.

With additional education or certification, teachers may become school counselors, school librarians, or instructional coordinators. Some become assistant principals or principals. Becoming a principal usually requires additional instruction in education administration or leadership. For more information, see the profiles on school and career counselors, librarians, instructional coordinators, and elementary, middle, and high school principals.

Pay

The median annual wage for high school teachers was $56,310 in May 2014. The median wage is the wage at which half the workers in an occupation earned more than that amount and half earned less. The lowest 10 percent earned less than $37,540, and the highest 10 percent earned more than $88,910.

Union Membership. Compared with workers in all occupations, high school teachers had a higher percentage of workers who belonged to a union in 2014.

Job Outlook

Employment of high school teachers is projected to grow 6 percent from 2014 to 2024, about as fast as the average for all occupations. Overall growth is expected to be impacted by larger class sizes and enrollment rate. Employment growth will vary by region.

From 2014 to 2024, the average classroom size is expected to increase, meaning that each teacher is responsible for more students.

Employment growth for public high school teachers will depend on state and local government budgets. If state and local governments experience budget deficits, school boards may lay off

Employment Projections Data for High School Teachers

Occupational Title	SOC Code	Employment, 2014	Projected Employment, 2024	Change, 2014–2024 Percent	Change, 2014–2024 Numeric
Secondary school teachers, except special and career/technical education	25-2031	961,600	1,017,500	6	55,900

Source: U.S. Bureau of Labor Statistics, Employment Projections Program

Similar Occupations. This table shows a list of occupations with job duties that are similar to those of high school teachers.

Occupations	Entry-level Education	2014 Median Pay	Projected Job Growth	Average Annual Openings
Career and Technical Education Teachers	Bachelor's degree	$51,830	4%	1,020
Childcare Workers	High school diploma or equivalent	$19,730	5%	6,930
Elementary, Middle, and High School Principals	Master's degree	$89,540	6%	1,400
Instructional Coordinators	Master's degree	$61,550	7%	1,050
Kindergarten and Elementary School Teachers	Bachelor's degree	$53,760	6%	8,780
Librarians	Master's degree	$56,170	2%	270
Middle School Teachers	Bachelor's degree	$54,940	6%	3,680
Postsecondary Teachers	See Education/Training	$70,790	13%	17,700
Preschool Teachers	Associate's degree	$28,120	7%	2,960
School and Career Counselors	Master's degree	$53,370	8%	2,250
Social Workers	See Education/Training	$45,500	12%	7,480
Special Education Teachers	Bachelor's degree	$55,980	6%	2,810
Teacher Assistants	Some college, no degree	$24,430	6%	7,860

employees, including teachers. As a result, employment growth of high school teachers may be reduced by state and local government budget deficits.

Student enrollment will vary by region or area which will also affect the demand for high school teachers.

Job Prospects. From 2014 to 2024, a significant number of older teachers will reach retirement age. Their retirement will create job openings for new teachers.

Many schools report that they have difficulty filling teaching positions for certain subjects, including math, science (especially chemistry and physics), English as a second language, and special education. As a result, teachers with education in those subjects or certifications to teach those specialties should have better job prospects. For more information about high school special education teachers, see the profile on special education teachers.

There is significant variation by region of the country and school setting. Opportunities are likely to be better in urban and rural school districts than in suburban school districts.

Contacts for More Information

For more information about teaching and becoming a teacher, visit

- Teach.org (www.teach.org)
- American Federation of Teachers (www.aft.org)
- National Education Association (www.nea.org)

For more information about teacher preparation programs, visit

- Council for the Accreditation of Educator Preparation (www.caepsite.org)

O*NET

- Secondary School Teachers, Except Special and Career/Technical Education (25-2031.00)

Instructional Coordinators

- **2014 Median Pay** .... $61,550 per year / $29.59 per hour
- **Typical Entry-Level Education** .... Master's degree
- **Work Experience in a Related Occupation** .... 5 years or more
- **On-the-job Training** .... None
- **Number of Jobs, 2014** 151,100
- **Job Outlook, 2014–24** .... 7% (As fast as average)
- **Employment Change, 2014–24** 10,500

What Instructional Coordinators Do

Instructional coordinators oversee school curriculums and teaching standards. They develop instructional material, coordinate its implementation with teachers and principals, and assess its effectiveness.

Duties. Instructional coordinators typically do the following:

- Develop and coordinate implementation of curriculum
- Plan, organize, and conduct teacher training conferences or workshops
- Analyze student test data
- Assess and discuss implementation of curriculum standards with school staff
- Review and recommend textbooks and other educational materials
- Recommend teaching techniques and the use of different or new technologies
- Develop procedures for teachers to implement curriculum
- Train teachers and other instructional staff in new content or programs
- Mentor or coach teachers to improve their skills

Instructional coordinators evaluate how well a school or training program's curriculum meets students' needs.

Instructional coordinators evaluate the effectiveness of curriculums and teaching techniques established by school boards, states, or federal regulations. They may observe teachers in the classroom, review student test data, and interview school staff and principals about curriculums. Based on their research, they may recommend changes in curriculums to school boards. They may also recommend that teachers use different teaching techniques.

Instructional coordinators may plan and conduct training for teachers related to teaching methods or the use of technology. For example, when a school district introduces new learning standards, instructional coordinators explain the new standards to teachers and demonstrate effective teaching methods to achieve them.

Instructional coordinators, also known as *curriculum specialists*, *instructional coaches*, or *assistant superintendents of instruction*, may specialize in particular grade levels or specific subjects. Those in elementary and secondary schools may also focus on special education or English as a second language programs.

Work Environment

Instructional coordinators held about 151,100 jobs in 2014. The industries that employed the most instructional coordinators were as follows:

Elementary and secondary schools; state, local, and private	39%
Colleges, universities, and professional schools; state, local, and private	16
Government	9
Educational support services; state, local, and private	6

Most instructional coordinators work in an office, but they also may spend part of their time traveling to schools within their school district to teach professional development classes and monitor the implementation of the curriculum.

Work Schedules. Instructional coordinators generally work full time. They typically work year-round and do not have summer breaks, unlike teachers. Coordinators may meet with teachers and other administrators before and after classroom hours.

Education/Training

Instructional coordinators need a master's degree and related work experience, such as teaching or school administration. Coordinators in public schools may be required to have a state-issued license.

Education. Most employers, particularly public schools, require instructional coordinators to have a master's degree in education or curriculum and instruction. Some instructional coordinators have a degree in the field they plan to specialize in, such as math or history.

Master's degree programs in curriculum and instruction teach about curriculum design, instructional theory, and collecting and analyzing data. To enter these programs, candidates usually need a bachelor's degree in teaching.

Licenses, Certifications, and Registrations. Instructional coordinators in public schools may be required to have a license, such as a teaching license or an education administrator license. For information about teaching licenses, see the profile on high school teachers. For information about education administrator licenses, see the profile on elementary, middle, and high school principals. Check with your state's Board of Education for specific license requirements.

Work Experience in a Related Occupation. Most instructional coordinators need several years of related work experience. Experience working as a teacher or as a principal is helpful. For some positions, experience teaching a specific subject or grade level may be required.

Important Qualities

Analytical skills. Instructional coordinators examine student test data and evaluate teaching strategies. Based on their analysis, coordinators recommend improvements in curriculums and teaching.

Communication skills. Instructional coordinators need to clearly explain changes in the curriculum and teaching standards to teachers, principals, and school staff.

Decision-making skills. Instructional coordinators must be able to make sound decisions when recommending changes to curriculums, teaching methods, and textbooks.

Median Annual Wages, May 2014

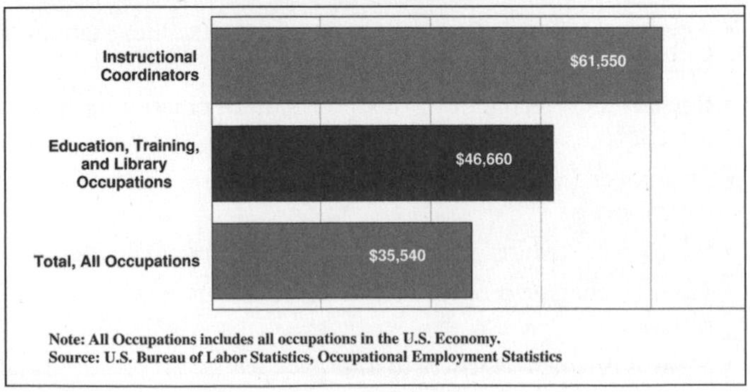

Percent Change in Employment, Projected 2014–2024

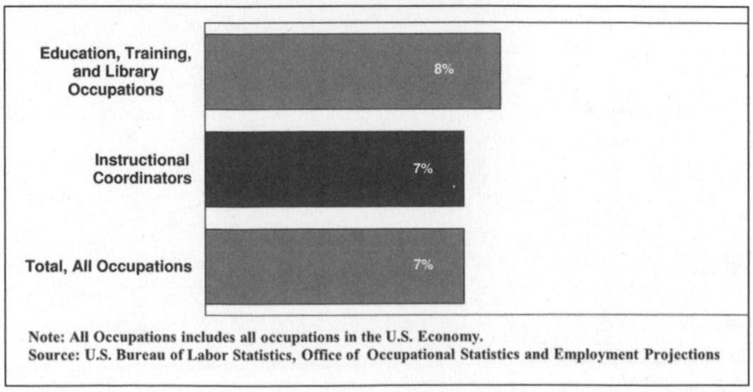

Employment Projections Data for Instructional Coordinators

Occupational Title	SOC Code	Employment, 2014	Projected Employment, 2024	Change, 2014–2024 Percent	Change, 2014–2024 Numeric
Instructional coordinators	25-9031	151,100	161,600	7	10,500

Source: U.S. Bureau of Labor Statistics, Employment Projections Program

Similar Occupations. This table shows a list of occupations with job duties that are similar to those of instructional coordinators.

Occupations	Entry-level Education	2014 Median Pay	Projected Job Growth	Average Annual Openings
Elementary, Middle, and High School Principals	Master's degree	$89,540	6%	1,400
High School Teachers	Bachelor's degree	$56,310	6%	5,590
Kindergarten and Elementary School Teachers	Bachelor's degree	$53,760	6%	8,780
Librarians	Master's degree	$56,170	2%	270
Middle School Teachers	Bachelor's degree	$54,940	6%	3,680
Postsecondary Teachers	See Education/Training	$70,790	13%	17,700
Preschool Teachers	Associate's degree	$28,120	7%	2,960
School and Career Counselors	Master's degree	$53,370	8%	2,250
Special Education Teachers	Bachelor's degree	$55,980	6%	2,810
Teacher Assistants	Some college, no degree	$24,430	6%	7,860

Interpersonal skills. Instructional coordinators need to be able to establish and maintain positive working relationships with teachers, principals, and other administrators.

Leadership skills. Instructional coordinators serve as mentors to teachers. They train teachers in developing useful and effective teaching techniques.

Pay

The median annual wage for instructional coordinators was $61,550 in May 2014. The median wage is the wage at which half the workers in an occupation earned more than that amount and half earned less. The lowest 10 percent earned less than $35,700, and the highest 10 percent earned more than $95,590.

In May 2014, the median annual wages for instructional coordinators in the top industries in which they worked were as follows:

Government	$68,700
Elementary and secondary schools; state, local, and private	67,060
Educational support services; state, local, and private	62,650
Colleges, universities, and professional schools; state, local, and private	54,410

Job Outlook

Employment of instructional coordinators is projected to grow 7 percent from 2014 to 2024, about as fast as the average for all occupations.

Employment growth is expected as schools focus on evaluating and improving curriculums and teachers' effectiveness. Schools are focusing on the teachers' role in improving students' learning. Instructional coordinators can provide training for teachers in curriculum changes and teaching techniques, thereby helping schools to meet standards in student achievement.

There is an increased emphasis on holding states and schools accountable for student achievement. Some states and school districts are using accountability measures, such as test scores and graduation rates, to evaluate their school curriculums. Instructional coordinators will be needed to evaluate and improve curriculums and provide mentoring for teachers. As schools seek additional training for teachers, demand for instructional coordinators is expected to grow.

However, many instructional coordinators are employed by state and local governments. Therefore, employment growth will depend largely on state and local government budgets.

Contacts for More Information

For more information about instructional coordinators, visit

➤ Learning Forward (www.learningforward.org)

O*NET

➤ Instructional Coordinators (25-9031.00)

➤ Instructional Designers and Technologists (25-9031.01)

Kindergarten and Elementary School Teachers

- **2014 Median Pay** .... $53,760 per year
- **Typical Entry-Level Education** .... Bachelor's degree
- **Work Experience in a Related Occupation** .... None
- **On-the-job Training** .... Internship/residency
- **Number of Jobs, 2014** 1,517,400
- **Job Outlook, 2014–24** .... 6% (As fast as average)
- **Employment Change, 2014–24** 87,800

What Kindergarten and Elementary School Teachers Do

Kindergarten and elementary school teachers prepare younger students for future schooling by teaching them basic subjects such as math and reading.

Duties. Kindergarten and elementary school teachers typically do the following:

- Create lesson plans to teach students subjects, such as reading, science, social studies, and math
- Teach students how to study and communicate with others
- Observe students to evaluate their abilities, strengths, and weaknesses
- Teach lessons they have planned to an entire class of students or to smaller groups
- Grade students' assignments to monitor their progress
- Communicate with parents about their child's progress
- Work with students individually to help them overcome specific learning challenges
- Prepare students for standardized tests required by the state
- Develop and enforce classroom rules to teach children proper behavior
- Supervise children outside of the classroom—for example, during lunchtime or recess

Kindergarten and elementary school teachers help students learn and apply important concepts. Many teachers use a hands-on approach to help students understand abstract concepts, solve problems, and develop critical thinking skills. For example, they may demonstrate how to do a science experiment and then have the students conduct the experiment themselves. They may have students work together to learn how to collaborate to solve problems.

Kindergarten and elementary school teachers generally teach kindergarten through 4th or 5th grade. However, in some schools, elementary school teachers may teach 6th, 7th, and 8th grade. They typically teach students several subjects throughout the day.

Some teachers may teach in a multilevel classroom that includes students across two or more grades. They may teach the same group of students for several years.

Kindergarten and elementary school students spend most of their day in one classroom. Teachers may escort students to assemblies; to classes taught by other teachers, such as art or music; or to recess. While students are away from the classroom, teachers plan lessons, grade assignments, or meet with other teachers and staff.

In some schools, teachers may work in subject specialization teams in which they teach one or two specific subjects, either English and social studies or math and science. Generally, students spend half their time with one teacher and half their time with the other.

Some kindergarten and elementary school teachers teach special classes, such as art, music, and physical education.

Some schools employ teachers of English as a second language (ESL) or English for speakers of other languages (ESOL). Both of these types of teachers work exclusively with students who are learning the English language, often referred to as English language learners (ELLs). The teachers work with students individually or in groups to help them improve their English language skills and to help them with assignments from other classes.

Students with learning disabilities or emotional or behavioral disorders are often taught in traditional classes. Kindergarten and elementary teachers work with special education teachers to adapt lesson plans to these students' needs and monitor the students' progress. In some cases, kindergarten and elementary school teachers may co-teach lessons with special education teachers.

Kindergarten and elementary school teachers use a variety of tools, such as computers, to present information to students.

Some teachers maintain websites to communicate with parents about students' assignments, upcoming events, and grades. For students in higher grades, teachers may create websites or discussion boards to present information or to expand on a lesson taught in class.

Work Environment

Kindergarten and elementary school teachers held about 1.5 million jobs in 2014.

Kindergarten and elementary school teachers work in public and private schools.

Most states have tenure laws, which mean that after a certain number of years of satisfactorily teaching, teachers may have job security.

Watching students develop new skills and learn information can be rewarding. However, teaching may be stressful. Some schools have large classes and lack important teaching tools, such as computers and up-to-date textbooks. Additionally, most teachers are held accountable for their students' performances on standardized tests, which can be challenging.

Work Schedules. Kindergarten and elementary school teachers generally work during school hours when students are present. They may meet with parents, students, and other teachers before and after school. They often spend time in the evenings and on weekends grading papers and preparing lessons.

Many kindergarten and elementary school teachers work the traditional 10-month school year and have a 2-month break during the summer. Some teachers may teach summer programs. Teachers in districts with a year-round schedule typically work 8 weeks in a row then have a break for 1 week before starting a new schooling session. They also have a 5-week midwinter break.

Education/Training

Kindergarten and elementary school teachers must have a bachelor's degree. In addition, public school teachers must have a state-issued certification or license.

Education. All states require public kindergarten and elementary school teachers to have at least a bachelor's degree in elementary education. Some states also require kindergarten and elementary school teachers to major in a content area, such as math or science. They typically enroll in their college's teacher preparation program and also take classes in education and child psychology in addition to those required by their major.

In teacher education programs, future teachers learn how to present information to young students and how to work with young students of varying abilities and backgrounds. Programs typically include fieldwork, such as student teaching. For information about teacher preparation programs in your state, visit Teach.org (www.teach.org).

Some states require all teachers to earn a master's degree after receiving their teaching certification.

Private schools typically seek kindergarten and elementary school teachers who have a bachelor's degree in elementary education.

Licenses, Certifications, and Registrations. All states require teachers in public schools to be licensed or certified. Those who teach in private schools are generally not required to be licensed. Most states require teachers to pass a background check.

Kindergarten and elementary school teachers are typically certified to teach early childhood grades, which are usually preschool through 3rd grade, or elementary school grades, which are usually first through 6th grades or 1st through 8th grades.

Requirements for certification vary by state. In addition to earning a bachelor's degree, they are required to complete a teacher preparation program and supervised experience in teaching, typically gained through student teaching. Some states require a minimum grade point average. States often require candidates to pass a general teaching certification test, as well as a test that demonstrates their knowledge of the subject they will teach. Although kindergarten and elementary school teachers typically do not teach only a single subject, they may be required to pass a content area test to earn their certification. For information on certification requirements in your state, visit Teach.org (www.teach.org).

Teachers are frequently required to complete annual professional development classes to keep their license. Some states require teachers to complete a master's degree after receiving their certification.

All states offer an alternative route to certification for people who already have a bachelor's degree but lack the education courses required for certification. Some alternative certification programs allow candidates to begin teaching immediately after graduation, under the supervision of an experienced teacher. These programs cover teaching methods and child development. After they complete the program, candidates are awarded full certification. Other programs require students to take classes in education before they can teach. Students may be awarded a master's degree after completing one of these programs.

Training. In order to receive certification, teachers need to undergo a period of fieldwork, commonly referred to as student teaching. During student teaching, they work with a mentor teacher and get experience teaching students in a classroom setting. The amount of time required varies by state.

Important Qualities

Communication skills. Teachers must collaborate with teacher assistants and special education teachers. In addition, they need to discuss students' needs with parents and administrators.

Creativity. Kindergarten and elementary school teachers must plan lessons that engage young students, adapting the lessons to different learning styles.

Patience. Working with students of different abilities and backgrounds can be difficult. Kindergarten and elementary school teachers must respond with patience when students struggle with material.

Physical stamina. Working with kindergarten and elementary-aged students can be tiring. Teachers need to be able to physically, mentally, and emotionally keep up with the students.

Resourcefulness. Kindergarten and elementary school teachers need to be able to explain difficult concepts in terms that young students can understand. In addition, they must be able to get students engaged in learning and adapt their lessons to meet students' needs.

Advancement. Experienced teachers can advance to serve as mentors to newer teachers or to become lead teachers. In these roles, they help less experienced teachers to improve their teaching skills.

With additional education or certification, teachers may become school counselors, school librarians, or instructional coordinators. Some become assistant principals or principals, both of which generally require additional schooling in education administration or leadership.

Pay

The median annual wage for kindergarten teachers, except special education was $50,600 in May 2014. The median wage is the wage at which half the workers in an occupation earned more than that amount and half earned less. The lowest 10 percent earned less than $33,460, and the highest 10 percent earned more than $78,170.

The median annual wage for elementary school teachers, except special education was $54,120 in May 2014. The lowest 10 percent earned less than $36,040, and the highest 10 percent earned more than $83,910.

Median Annual Wages, May 2014

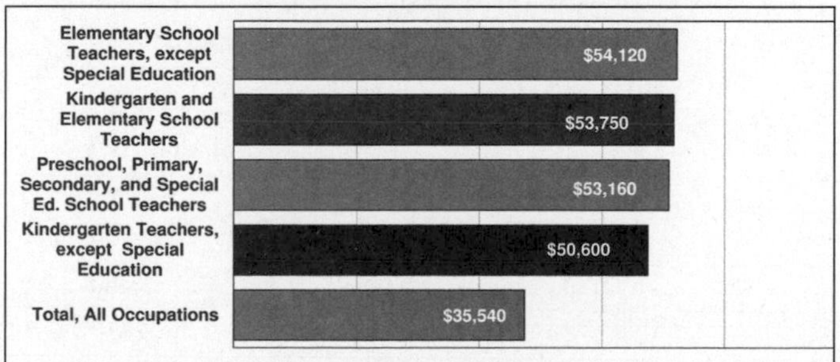

Note: All Occupations includes all occupations in the U.S. Economy.
Source: U.S. Bureau of Labor Statistics, Occupational Employment Statistics

Percent Change in Employment, Projected 2014–2024

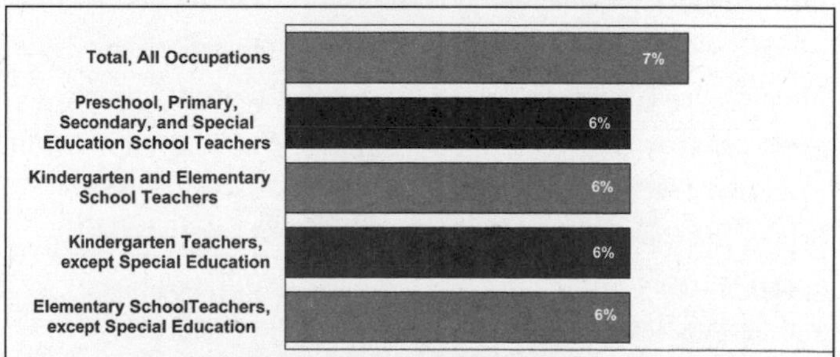

Note: All Occupations includes all occupations in the U.S. Economy.
Source: U.S. Bureau of Labor Statistics, Office of Occupational Statistics and Employment Projections

Employment Projections Data for Kindergarten and Elementary School Teachers

Occupational Title	SOC Code	Employment, 2014	Projected Employment, 2024	Change, 2014–2024 Percent	Change, 2014–2024 Numeric
Kindergarten and elementary school teachers	—	1,517,400	1,605,200	6	87,800
Kindergarten teachers, except special education	25-2012	159,400	168,900	6	9,500
Elementary school teachers, except special education	25-2021	1,358,000	1,436,300	6	78,300

Source: U.S. Bureau of Labor Statistics, Employment Projections Program

Union Membership. Compared with workers in all occupations, kindergarten and elementary school teachers had a higher percentage of workers who belonged to a union in 2014.

Job Outlook

Employment of kindergarten and elementary school teachers is projected to grow 6 percent from 2014 to 2024, about as fast as the average for all occupations. Growth is expected because of projected increases in student enrollment. However, employment growth will vary by region.

The number of students enrolling in kindergarten and elementary schools is expected to increase over the coming decade, and the number of classes needed to accommodate these students will also rise. As a result, more teachers will be required to teach these additional classes of kindergarten and elementary school students. In addition, the average classroom size is growing. This means that each teacher is responsible for more students.

Despite expected increases in enrollment, employment growth for kindergarten and elementary school teachers will depend on state and local government budgets. If state and local governments experience budget deficits, they may lay off employees, including teachers. As a result, employment growth of kindergarten and elementary school teachers may be somewhat reduced by state and local government budget deficits.

Job Prospects. Kindergarten and elementary school teachers with education or certifications should have better job opportunities.

A substantial number of older teachers are expected to reach retirement age between 2014 and 2024. Their retirement will increase the need to replace workers who leave the occupation. However, many areas of the country already have a surplus of teachers who are trained to teach kindergarten and elementary school, making it more difficult for new teachers to find jobs.

Opportunities will vary by region and school setting. There will be better opportunities in urban and rural school districts than in suburban school districts.

Contacts for More Information

For more information about teaching and becoming a teacher, visit

- Teach.org (www.teach.org)
- American Federation of Teachers (www.aft.org)
- National Education Association (www.nea.org)
- Teacher.org (www.teacher.org)

For more information about teacher preparation programs, visit

- Council for the Accreditation of Educator Preparation (http://caepnet.org)

O*NET

- Kindergarten Teachers, Except Special Education (25-2012.00)
- Elementary School Teachers, Except Special Education (25-2021.00)

Similar Occupations. This table shows a list of occupations with job duties that are similar to those of kindergarten and elementary school teachers.

Occupations	Entry-level Education	2014 Median Pay	Projected Job Growth	Average Annual Openings
Career and Technical Education Teachers	Bachelor's degree	$51,830	4%	1,020
Childcare Workers	High school diploma or equivalent	$19,730	5%	6,930
Elementary, Middle, and High School Principals	Master's degree	$89,540	6%	1,400
High School Teachers	Bachelor's degree	$56,310	6%	5,590
Instructional Coordinators	Master's degree	$61,550	7%	1,050
Librarians	Master's degree	$56,170	2%	270
Middle School Teachers	Bachelor's degree	$54,940	6%	3,680
Postsecondary Teachers	See Education/Training	$70,790	13%	17,700
Preschool Teachers	Associate's degree	$28,120	7%	2,960
School and Career Counselors	Master's degree	$53,370	8%	2,250
Social Workers	See Education/Training	$45,500	12%	7,480
Special Education Teachers	Bachelor's degree	$55,980	6%	2,810
Teacher Assistants	Some college, no degree	$24,430	6%	7,860

Librarians

- **2014 Median Pay** .... $56,170 per year
$27.01 per hour
- **Typical Entry-Level Education** .... Master's degree
- **Work Experience in a Related Occupation** .... None
- **On-the-job Training** .... None
- **Number of Jobs, 2014** 143,100
- **Job Outlook, 2014–24** .... 2% (Slower than average)
- **Employment Change, 2014–24** 2,700

What Librarians Do

Librarians help people find information and conduct research for personal and professional use. Their job duties may change based on the type of library they work in, such as public, school, and medical libraries.

Duties. Librarians typically do the following:

- Help library patrons conduct research and find the information they need
- Teach classes about information resources
- Help patrons evaluate search results and reference materials
- Organize library materials so they are easy to find, and maintain collections
- Plan programs for different audiences, such as storytelling for young children
- Develop and use databases of library materials
- Research new books and materials by reading book reviews, publishers' announcements, and catalogs
- Choose new books, audio books, videos, and other materials for the library
- Research and buy new computers and other equipment as needed for the library
- Train and direct library technicians, assistants, other support staff, and volunteers
- Prepare library budgets

In small libraries, librarians are often responsible for many or all aspects of library operations. They may manage a staff of library assistants and technicians.

In larger libraries, librarians usually focus on one aspect of library work, including user services, technical services, or administrative services.

The following are examples of types of librarians:

User services librarians help patrons conduct research using both electronic and print resources. These librarians also teach patrons how to use library resources to find information on their own. This may include familiarizing patrons with catalogs of print materials, helping them access and search digital libraries, or educating them on Internet search techniques. Some user services librarians work with a particular audience, such as children or young adults.

Technical services librarians obtain, prepare, and organize print and electronic library materials. They arrange materials to make it easy for patrons to find information. They are also responsible for ordering new library materials and archiving to preserve older items.

Administrative services librarians manage libraries. They hire and supervise staff, prepare budgets, and negotiate contracts for library materials and equipment. Some conduct public relations or fundraising for the library.

Librarians who work in different settings sometimes have different job duties.

Academic librarians assist students, faculty, and staff in colleges and universities. They help students research topics related to their coursework and teach students how to access information. They also assist faculty and staff in locating resources related to their research projects or studies. Some campuses have multiple libraries, and librarians may specialize in a particular subject.

Public librarians work in their communities to serve all members of the public. They help patrons find books to read for pleasure; conduct research for schoolwork, business, or personal interest; and learn how to access the library's resources. Many public librarians plan programs for patrons, such as story time for children, book clubs, or other educational activities.

School librarians, sometimes called *school media specialists*, work in elementary, middle, and high school libraries, and teach students how to use library resources. They also help teachers develop lesson plans and find materials for classroom instruction.

Special librarians work in settings other than school or public libraries. They are sometimes called *information professionals*. Law firms, hospitals, businesses, museums, government agencies, and many other groups have their own libraries that use special librarians. The main purpose of these libraries and information centers is to serve the information needs of the organization that houses the library. Therefore, special librarians collect and organize materials focused on those subjects. The following are examples of special librarians:

- *Corporate librarians* assist employees in private businesses in conducting research and finding information. They work for a wide range of businesses, including insurance companies, consulting firms, and publishers.
- *Government librarians* provide research services and access to information for government staff and the public.
- *Law librarians* help lawyers, law students, judges, and law clerks locate and organize legal resources. They often work in law firms and law school libraries.
- *Medical librarians*, also called *health science librarians*, help health professionals, patients, and researchers find health and

Librarians help people find information and use it effectively for personal and professional purposes.

science information. They may provide information about new clinical trials and medical treatments and procedures, teach medical students how to locate medical information, or answer consumers' health questions.

Work Environment

Librarians held about 143,100 jobs in 2014. The industries that employed the most librarians were as follows:

Elementary and secondary schools; state, local, and private	36%
Local government, excluding education and hospitals	29
Colleges, universities, and professional schools; state, local, and private	18
Information	5

Most librarians typically work on the floor with patrons, behind the circulation desk, in the offices, or go on site visits. Some librarians have private offices, but those in smaller libraries usually share work space with others.

Work Schedules. Most librarians work full time, although opportunities exist for part-time work. In 2014, about 1 in 5 of librarians worked part time.

Public and academic librarians often work on weekends and evenings, and may work holidays. School librarians usually have the same work and vacation schedules as teachers, including summers off. Special librarians, such as law or corporate librarians, typically work normal business hours, but may need to work more than 40 hours to help meet deadlines.

Education/Training

Most librarians need a master's degree in library science. Some positions have additional requirements, such as a teaching certificate or a degree in another field.

Education. Most employers require librarians to have a master's degree in library science (MLS). Students need a bachelor's degree in any major to enter MLS programs.

MLS programs usually take 1 to 2 years to complete. Coursework typically covers selecting library materials, organizing information, research methods and strategies, online reference systems, and Internet search methods.

A degree from an American Library Association accredited program may lead to better job opportunities. Some colleges and universities have other names for their library science programs, such as Master of Information Studies or Master of Library and Information Studies.

Librarians working in a special library, such as a law, medical, or corporate library, usually supplement a master's degree in library science with knowledge of their specialized field. Some employers require special librarians to have a master's degree, a professional degree, or a Ph.D. in that subject. For example, a law librarian may be required to have a law degree or a librarian in an academic library may need a Ph.D.

Licenses, Certifications, and Registrations. Public school librarians typically need a teacher's certification. Some states require librarians to pass a standardized test, such as the PRAXIS II Library Media Specialist test. A list of requirements by state and contact information for state regulating boards is available from Libraries Unlimited.

Some states also require certification for librarians in public libraries. Requirements vary by state. Contact your state's licensing board for specific requirements.

Important Qualities

Communication skills. Librarians need to be able to explain ideas and information in ways that patrons and users understand.

Initiative. New information, technology, and resources constantly change the details of what librarians do. They must be able and willing to continually update their knowledge on these changes to be effective at their jobs in the varying circumstances.

Interpersonal skills. Librarians must be able to work both as part of a team and with the public or with researchers.

Problem-solving skills. Librarians conduct and assist with research. This requires being able to identify a problem, figure out where to find information, and draw conclusions based on the information found.

Reading skills. Librarians must be excellent readers. Those working in special libraries are expected to continually read the latest literature in their field of specialization.

Technology skills. Librarians use technology to help patrons research topics. They also use computers to classify resources, create databases, and perform administrative duties.

Pay

The median annual wage for librarians was $56,170 in May 2014. The median wage is the wage at which half the workers in an occupation earned more than that amount and half earned less. The lowest 10 percent earned less than $33,680, and the highest 10 percent earned more than $87,060.

In May 2014, the median annual wages for librarians in the top industries in which they worked were as follows:

Colleges, universities, and professional schools; state, local, and private	$59,700
Elementary and secondary schools; state, local, and private	57,820
Information	52,310
Local government, excluding education and hospitals	50,990

Median Annual Wages, May 2014

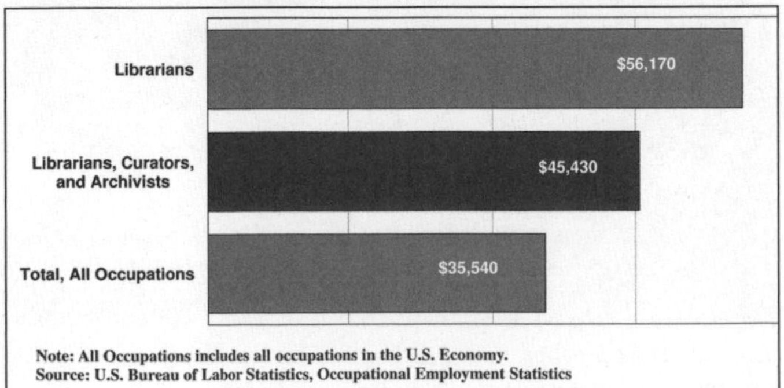

Note: All Occupations includes all occupations in the U.S. Economy.
Source: U.S. Bureau of Labor Statistics, Occupational Employment Statistics

Percent Change in Employment, Projected 2014–2024

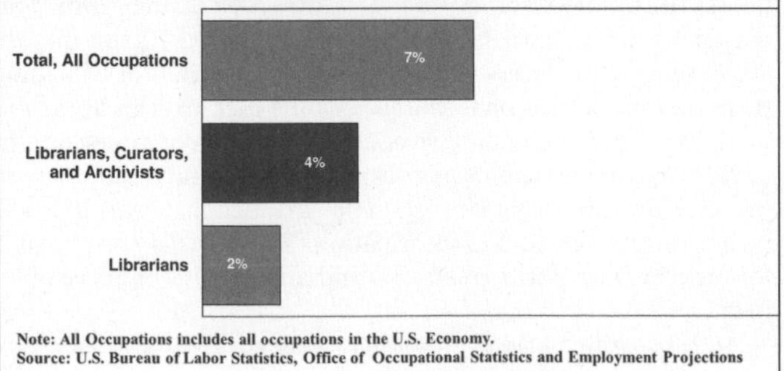

Note: All Occupations includes all occupations in the U.S. Economy.
Source: U.S. Bureau of Labor Statistics, Office of Occupational Statistics and Employment Projections

Employment Projections Data for Librarians

Occupational Title	SOC Code	Employment, 2014	Projected Employment, 2024	Change, 2014–2024 Percent	Change, 2014–2024 Numeric
Librarians	25-4021	143,100	145,700	2	2,700

Source: U.S. Bureau of Labor Statistics, Employment Projections Program

Similar Occupations. This table shows a list of occupations with job duties that are similar to those of librarians.

Occupations	Entry-level Education	2014 Median Pay	Projected Job Growth	Average Annual Openings
Adult Literacy and High School Equivalency Diploma Teachers	Bachelor's degree	$49,590	7%	550
Archivists, Curators, and Museum Workers	See Education/Training	$46,300	7%	210
Health Educators and Community Health Workers	See Education/Training	$42,450	13%	1,560
High School Teachers	Bachelor's degree	$56,310	6%	5,590
Kindergarten and Elementary School Teachers	Bachelor's degree	$53,760	6%	8,780
Library Technicians and Assistants	See Education/Training	$27,420	5%	1,120
Middle School Teachers	Bachelor's degree	$54,940	6%	3,680
Postsecondary Teachers	See Education/Training	$70,790	13%	17,700

Union Membership. Compared with workers in all occupations, librarians had a higher percentage of workers who belonged to a union in 2014.

Job Outlook

Employment of librarians is projected to grow 2 percent from 2014 to 2024, slower than the average for all occupations.

Budget limitations, especially in local government and educational services, may slow demand for librarians. Some libraries may close, reduce the size of their staff, or focus on hiring library technicians and assistants, who can fulfill some librarian duties at a lower cost.

However, there will continue to be a need for librarians to manage libraries and help patrons find information. Parents value the learning opportunities that libraries present for children because libraries are able to provide children with information they often cannot access from home. In addition, the increased availability of electronic information is also expected to increase the demand for librarians in research and special libraries, where patrons will need help sorting through the large amount of digital information.

Job Prospects. Jobseekers may face strong competition, especially early in the 2014–2024 decade, as many people with master's degrees in library science compete for a limited number of available positions. Later in the decade, prospects may improve, as older library workers retire and generate openings.

A degree from an American Library Association accredited program and work experience may lead to better job opportunities. Candidates who are able to adapt with the rapidly changing technology will have better prospects.

Contacts for More Information

For more information about librarians, including accredited library education programs, visit

➤ American Library Association (www.ala.org)

For more information about careers in libraries, visit

➤ LibraryCareers.org (http://librarycareers.drupalgardens.com)

For information about medical librarians, visit

➤ Medical Library Association (www.mlanet.org)

For information about law librarians, visit

➤ American Association of Law Libraries (www.aallnet.org)

For information about many different types of special librarians, visit

➤ Special Libraries Association (www.sla.org)

For more information about school librarians, visit

➤ Libraries Unlimited (www.abc-clio.com/LibrariesUnlimited.aspx)

O*NET

➤ Librarians (25-4021.00)

Library Technicians and Assistants

- **2014 Median Pay** .... $27,420 per year $13.18 per hour
- **Typical Entry-Level Education** .... See Education/Training
- **Work Experience in a Related Occupation** .... None
- **On-the-job Training** .... See Education/Training
- **Number of Jobs, 2014** 210,700
- **Job Outlook, 2014–24** .... 5% (As fast as average)
- **Employment Change, 2014–24** 11,200

What Library Technicians and Assistants Do

Library technicians and assistants help librarians with all aspects of running a library. They assist patrons, organize library materials and information, and perform clerical and administrative tasks.

Duties. Library technicians and assistants typically do the following:

- Loan library materials to patrons and collect returned materials
- Sort and reshelve returned books, periodicals, and other materials
- Catalogue and maintain library materials
- Handle interlibrary loans
- Register new patrons and issue library cards
- Answer routine reference questions
- Teach patrons how to find and use library resources
- Maintain computer databases used to locate library materials
- Answer the phone, organize files, and perform other routine clerical tasks
- Help plan and participate in special programs, such as used-book sales, story times, and outreach programs

A librarian usually supervises library technicians and assistants. Library technicians and assistants usually help patrons find information and organize library materials. However, library technicians typically have more responsibilities than do library assistants, such as administering library programs and overseeing lower level staff.

Library technicians and assistants in smaller libraries have a broader range of duties. In larger libraries, they tend to specialize in a particular area, such as user services or technical services. Technicians and assistants specializing in user services assist library patrons with locating resources and information. Those specializing in technical services research, acquire, catalog, and process materials to be added to the library's collections.

The following are examples of types of library technicians and assistants:

Academic library technicians and assistants help students, faculties, and staff in colleges and universities access resources and information related to coursework or research projects. Some help teach students how to access and use library resources. They may work at service desks for reserve materials, special collections, or computer labs.

Public library technicians and assistants work in community libraries to serve members of the public. They help patrons find books to read for pleasure; assist patrons with their research; and teach patrons how to access the library's resources. Some technicians in public libraries may help plan programs for users, such as story time for children, book clubs for teens or adults, or other educational or recreational activities.

School library technicians and assistants show students how to find and use library resources, maintain textbook collections, and they help teachers develop curriculum materials.

Library technicians sort and reshelve returned books, periodicals, and other materials.

Special library technicians and assistants work in libraries in government agencies, corporations, museums, law firms, and medical centers. They assist users, search library resources, compile bibliographies, and provide information on subjects of interest to the organization.

Work Environment

Library technicians and assistants held about 210,700 jobs in 2014. They work in local public libraries, corporate and specialty libraries, and school and university libraries.

Library technicians and assistants generally work indoors. They spend much of their time at public service desks or at computer terminals. Some spend time in the library stacks reshelving books, a task that may require bending or stretching to reach the shelves.

Work Schedules. More than half of library technicians and assistants worked part time in 2014.

Library technicians and assistants in school libraries work during regular school hours. Those in public or college libraries often work weekends, evenings, and some holidays. In corporate libraries, library technicians and assistants work normal business hours but may be asked to work overtime.

Education/Training

Most library technicians need a postsecondary certificate or an associate's degree. Library assistants typically need a high school degree and usually learn through short-term on-the-job (OTJ) training.

Median Hourly Wages, May 2014

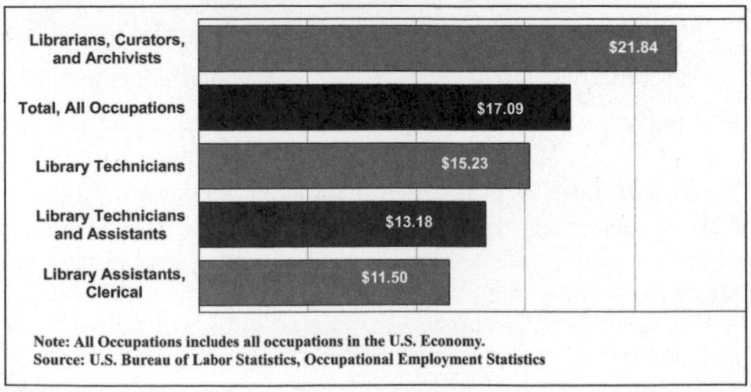

Percent Change in Employment, Projected 2014–2024

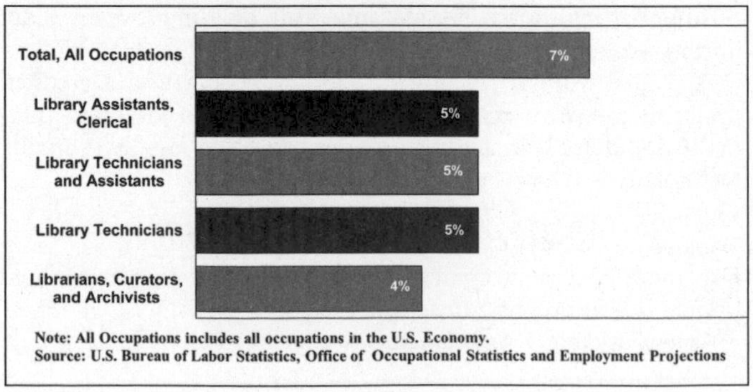

Employment Projections Data for Library Technicians and Assistants

Occupational Title	SOC Code	Employment, 2014	Projected Employment, 2024	Change, 2014–2024 Percent	Change, 2014–2024 Numeric
Library technicians and assistants	—	210,700	221,900	5	11,200
Library technicians	25-4031	101,800	107,100	5	5,300
Library assistants, clerical	43-4121	108,800	114,700	5	5,900

Source: U.S. Bureau of Labor Statistics, Employment Projections Program

Education. Most libraries prefer to hire library technicians who have a postsecondary certificate or an associate's degree. However, some smaller libraries might hire prospective technicians with only a high school diploma. Certificate and associate's degree programs in library technology include coursework in acquisitions, cataloguing, circulation, reference, and automated library systems. In some cases, library technicians who work in public schools must meet the same requirements as teacher assistants.

Most library assistants typically need a high school diploma or equivalent.

Training. Library assistants usually receive some short-term OTJ training to learn about libraries and library resources.

Important Qualities

Communication skills. Library technicians and assistants need to listen to and understand patrons' needs, provide clear answers to questions, and teach them how to use library resources.

Detail oriented. Library technicians and assistants must pay close attention to ensure that library materials and information are organized correctly and according to the library's organizational system. Cataloging and processing library materials also requires attention to detail.

Interpersonal skills. Library technicians and assistants provide customer service to library patrons and work with librarians, teachers, or researchers.

Technology skills. Library technicians and assistants use computers to help patrons research topics. They also use technology to maintain the library's database of collections.

Advancement. Library technicians and assistants can advance as they assume additional responsibilities in other areas of the library. Some eventually become supervisors and oversee daily library operations. To become a librarian, technicians and assistants need to earn a master's degree in library science.

Pay

The median hourly wage for library technicians was $15.23 in May 2014. The median wage is the wage at which half the workers in an occupation earned more than that amount and half earned less. The lowest 10 percent earned less than $9.18, and the highest 10 percent earned more than $24.13.

The median hourly wage for library assistants, clerical was $11.50 in May 2014. The lowest 10 percent earned less than $8.35, and the highest 10 percent earned more than $18.47.

Job Outlook

Employment of library technicians and assistants is projected to grow 5 percent from 2014 to 2024, about as fast as the average for all occupations.

Because of budget constraints, more libraries are hiring technicians and assistants to provide library services instead of traditional librarians. This is because technicians and assistants typically work part time and are cheaper to employ compared to librarians. Therefore, demand for library technicians and assistants should increase.

Job Prospects. Candidates who can adapt to rapidly changing technology will have better prospects as a library technician or assistant. Those who want to become a library technician may have better job prospects if they obtain an associate's degree or a certificate. Those who want to become a library assistant may benefit from obtaining a high school degree.

Contacts for More Information

For more information about library technicians and assistants careers, visit

➤ American Library Association (www.ala.org)

For more information about careers in libraries, visit

➤ LibraryCareers.org (http://librarycareers.drupalgardens.com)

For information about medical libraries, visit

➤ Medical Library Association (www.mlanet.org)

For information about law libraries, visit

➤ American Association of Law Libraries (www.aallnet.org)

For information about many different types of special libraries, visit

➤ Special Libraries Association (www.sla.org)

O*NET

➤ Library Technicians (25-4031.00)

➤ Library Assistants, Clerical (43-4121.00)

Similar Occupations. This table shows a list of occupations with job duties that are similar to those of library technicians and assistants.

Occupations	Entry-level Education	2014 Median Pay	Projected Job Growth	Average Annual Openings
Librarians	Master's degree	$56,170	2%	270
Medical Records and Health Information Technicians	Postsecondary nondegree award	$35,900	15%	2,900
Receptionists	High school diploma or equivalent	$26,760	10%	9,780
Teacher Assistants	Some college, no degree	$24,430	6%	7,860

Middle School Teachers

- **2014 Median Pay** .... $54,940 per year
- **Typical Entry-Level Education** ....Bachelor's degree
- **Work Experience in a Related Occupation**.............. None
- **On-the-job Training** .... Internship/residency
- **Number of Jobs, 2014** 627,500
- **Job Outlook, 2014–24** .... 6% (As fast as average)
- **Employment Change, 2014–24** 36,800

What Middle School Teachers Do

Middle school teachers educate students, typically in 6th through 8th grade. Middle school teachers help students build on the fundamentals taught in elementary school and prepare students for the more difficult curriculum they will face in high school.

Duties. Middle school teachers typically do the following:

- Create lesson plans to teach students a subject, such as biology or history
- Assess students to evaluate their abilities, strengths, and weaknesses
- Teach lessons they have planned to an entire class or to smaller groups
- Grade students' assignments and exams to monitor their progress
- Communicate with parents about their child's progress
- Work with students individually to help them overcome specific learning challenges
- Prepare students for standardized tests required by the state
- Develop and enforce classroom rules
- Supervise students outside of the classroom—for example, at lunchtime or during detention

Middle school teachers generally teach students from 6th to 8th grades. However, in some school districts, they may teach students as early as 4th grade or as late as 9th grade.

In many schools, middle school teachers are responsible for only some of the subjects their students learn. For example, one teacher may be responsible for teaching English and social studies while another may be responsible for teaching math and science. Some middle school instructors teach specialized classes, such as art, music, or physical education.

Students typically change classrooms several times a day to attend lessons in different subjects. As a result, middle school teachers see several different classes of students throughout the day. However, in some middle schools, teachers teach all the subjects for one class of students the entire day. In either type of school, teachers use time during the day when they do not have classes to plan lessons, grade assignments, or meet with other teachers and staff.

Some middle school teachers work in teams that teach the same group of students. These teachers meet to discuss students' progress and to plan future lessons.

In some schools, teachers of English as a second language (ESL) or English for speakers of other languages (ESOL) work exclusively with students who are learning the English language. These students are often referred to as English language learners (ELLs). ESL and ESOL teachers work with students individually or in groups to help them improve their English language skills and to help the students with assignments for their other classes.

Middle school teachers may also work with special education teachers to adapt lessons taught in traditional classes to meet the needs of students with learning disabilities and emotional or behavioral disorders. In some cases, middle school teachers may co-teach lessons with special education teachers.

Some teachers maintain websites to communicate with parents about students' assignments, upcoming events, and grades. For their students, teachers may create websites or discussion boards to present information or to expand a lesson taught in class.

Some middle school teachers coach sports teams and advise student clubs and groups, whose practices and meetings frequently take place before or after school.

Work Environment

Middle school teachers held about 627,500 jobs in 2014. The majority of middle school teachers work in public and private schools.

Most states have tenure laws, which mean that after a certain number of years of satisfactory classroom teaching, teachers may have some job security.

Watching students develop new skills and gain an appreciation for knowledge and learning can be very rewarding. However, teaching may be stressful. Some schools have large classes and lack important teaching tools, such as computers and current textbooks.

Additionally, most teachers are held accountable for their students' performance on standardized tests, which can be frustrating. Working with middle school students also can be challenging because the students are becoming adolescents and teachers need to be able to understand what they are going through.

Work Schedules. Middle school teachers generally work school hours when students are present. They may meet with parents, students, and other teachers before and after school. Teachers who coach sports or advise clubs generally do so before or after school. Teachers often spend time in the evenings and on weekends grading papers and preparing lessons.

Many work the traditional 10-month school year and have a 2-month break during the summer. Some teachers teach summer programs.

Middle school teachers help students build on the fundamentals they learned in elementary schools to prepare them for the more difficult subjects and lessons in high school.

Median Annual Wages, May 2014

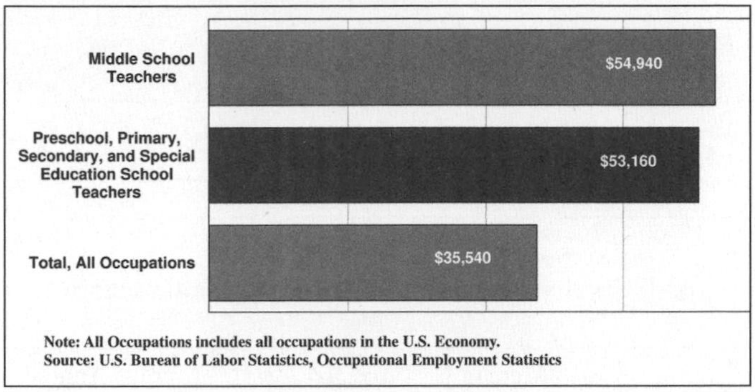

Percent Change in Employment, Projected 2014–2024

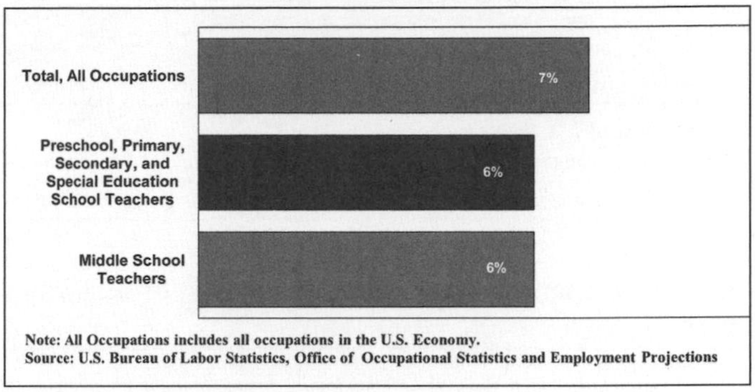

Teachers in districts with a year-round schedule typically work 8 weeks in a row then have a break for 1 week before starting a new school session. They also have a 5-week midwinter break.

Education/Training

Middle school teachers must have a bachelor's degree. In addition, public school teachers must have a state-issued certification or license.

Education. All states require public middle school teachers to have at least a bachelor's degree. Many states require middle school teachers to major in a content area, such as math or science. Other states require middle school teachers to major in elementary education. Middle school teachers typically enroll in their college's teacher preparation program and take classes in education and child psychology in addition to the classes required by their major.

Teacher education programs teach prospective middle school teachers how to present information to students and how to work with students of varying abilities and backgrounds. Programs typically include fieldwork such as student teaching. For information about teacher preparation programs in your state, visit Teach.org (www.teach.org).

Some states require middle school teachers to earn a master's degree after receiving their teaching certification.

Teachers in private schools do not need to meet state requirements. However, private schools typically seek middle school teachers who have a bachelor's degree and a major in elementary education or a content area.

Licenses, Certifications, and Registrations. All states require teachers in public schools to be licensed or certified. Those who teach in private schools are not usually required to be licensed. Most states require teachers to pass a background check.

Certification of middle school teachers varies considerably from state to state. In some states, they are certified to teach elementary school grades, which are typically 1st through 6th grades or 1st through 8th grades. In other states, they are certified to teach middle school grades, which include 6th through 8th grades. Other states provide middle school teachers with a secondary school or high school certification, which often includes 7th through 12th grades.

Requirements for certification also vary by state. In addition to earning a bachelor's degree, they are also required to complete a teacher preparation program and supervised experience in teaching, which is typically gained through student teaching. Some states require a minimum grade point average. States typically require candidates to pass a general teaching certification test, as well as a test that demonstrates their knowledge of the subject they will teach. For information on certification requirements in your state, visit Teach.org (www.teach.org).

Teachers are often required to complete annual professional development classes to keep their license. Some states require teachers to complete a master's degree after receiving their certification.

All states offer an alternative route to certification for people who already have a bachelor's degree but lack the education courses required for certification. Some alternative certification programs allow candidates to begin teaching immediately under the supervision of an experienced teacher. These programs cover teaching methods and child development. After they complete the program, candidates are awarded full certification. Other programs require students to take classes in education before they can teach. Students may be awarded a master's degree after completing either of these programs.

Training. In order to receive certification, teachers need to perform fieldwork, commonly referred to as student teaching. During student teaching, they work with a mentor teacher and get experience teaching students in a classroom setting. The amount of time required varies by state.

Important Qualities

Communication skills. Teachers must collaborate with other teachers and special education teachers. In addition, they need to discuss students' needs with parents and administrators.

Patience. Working with students of different abilities and backgrounds can be difficult. Middle school teachers must be patient when students struggle with material.

Physical stamina. Working with middle school aged students can be tiring. Teachers need to be able to physically, mentally, and emotionally keep up with the students.

Resourcefulness. Middle school teachers need to be able to explain difficult concepts in terms that students can understand. In addition, they need to be able to get students engaged in learning and adapt lessons to each student's needs.

Advancement. Experienced teachers can advance to serve as mentors to newer teachers or to become lead teachers. In these positions, they help less experienced teachers to improve their teaching skills.

With additional education or certification, teachers may become school counselors, school librarians, or instructional coordinators. Some become assistant principals or principals, both of which generally require additional education in education administration or leadership. For more information, see the profiles on school and career counselors, librarians, instructional coordinators, and elementary, middle, and high school principals.

Pay

The median annual wage for middle school teachers was $54,940 in May 2014. The median wage is the wage at which half the workers

Employment Projections Data for Middle School Teachers

Occupational Title	SOC Code	Employment, 2014	Projected Employment, 2024	Change, 2014–2024	
				Percent	Numeric
Middle school teachers, except special and career/technical education	25-2022	627,500	664,200	6	36,800

Source: U.S. Bureau of Labor Statistics, Employment Projections Program

Similar Occupations. This table shows a list of occupations with job duties that are similar to those of middle school teachers.

Occupations	Entry-level Education	2014 Median Pay	Projected Job Growth	Average Annual Openings
Career and Technical Education Teachers	Bachelor's degree	$51,830	4%	1,020
Childcare Workers	High school diploma or equivalent	$19,730	5%	6,930
Elementary, Middle, and High School Principals	Master's degree	$89,540	6%	1,400
High School Teachers	Bachelor's degree	$56,310	6%	5,590
Instructional Coordinators	Master's degree	$61,550	7%	1,050
Librarians	Master's degree	$56,170	2%	270
Postsecondary Teachers	See Education/Training	$70,790	13%	17,700
Preschool Teachers	Associate's degree	$28,120	7%	2,960
School and Career Counselors	Master's degree	$53,370	8%	2,250
Social Workers	See Education/Training	$45,500	12%	7,480
Special Education Teachers	Bachelor's degree	$55,980	6%	2,810
Teacher Assistants	Some college, no degree	$24,430	6%	7,860

in an occupation earned more than that amount and half earned less. The lowest 10 percent earned less than $37,390, and the highest 10 percent earned more than $84,610.

Union Membership. Compared with workers in all occupations, middle school teachers had a higher percentage of workers who belonged to a union in 2014.

Job Outlook

Employment of middle school teachers is projected to grow 6 percent from 2014 to 2024, about as fast as the average for all occupations. Growth is projected because of expected increases in enrollment. However, employment growth will vary by region.

The number of students in middle schools is expected to increase over the coming decade, and the number of classes needed to accommodate these students is projected to rise also. As a result, more teachers will be required to teach the additional classes of middle school students. In addition, the average classroom size is expected to increase. This means that each teacher will be responsible for more students.

Despite expected increases in enrollment, employment growth for middle school teachers will depend on state and local government budgets. If state and local governments experience budget deficits, they may lay off employees, including teachers. As a result, employment growth of middle school teachers may be somewhat reduced by state and local government budget difficulties.

Job Prospects. From 2014 to 2024, a significant number of older teachers are expected to reach retirement age. Their retirement will increase the need to replace workers who leave the occupation.

There is wide variation of job opportunities by region. Opportunities will vary by region and school setting. There may be better opportunities in urban and rural school districts than in suburban school districts.

Contacts for More Information

For more information about teaching and becoming a teacher, visit

- Teach.org (www.teach.org)
- American Federation of Teachers (www.aft.org)
- National Education Association (www.nea.org)

For more information about teacher preparation programs, visit

- Council for the Accreditation of Educator Preparation (www.caepsite.org)

O*NET

- Middle School Teachers, Except Special and Career/Technical Education (25-2022.00)

Postsecondary Teachers

- **2014 Median Pay** .... $70,790 per year
- **Typical Entry-Level Education** .... See Education/Training
- **Work Experience in a Related Occupation** .... See Education/Training
- **On-the-job Training** .... None
- **Number of Jobs, 2014** 1,313,000
- **Job Outlook, 2014–24** .... 13% (Faster than average)
- **Employment Change, 2014–24** 177,000

What Postsecondary Teachers Do

Postsecondary teachers instruct students in a wide variety of academic and career and technical subjects beyond the high school level. They also conduct research and publish scholarly papers and books.

Duties. Postsecondary teachers typically do the following:

- Teach courses in their subject area
- Work with students who are taking classes to improve their knowledge or career skills
- Develop an instructional plan (known as a course outline or syllabus) for the course(s) they teach and ensure that it meets college and department standards
- Plan lessons and assignments
- Work with colleagues to develop or modify the curriculum for a degree or certificate program involving a series of courses
- Assess students' progress by grading assignments, papers, exams, and other work
- Advise students about which classes to take and how to achieve their goals
- Stay informed about changes and innovations in their field
- Conduct research and experiments to advance knowledge in their field
- Supervise graduate students who are working toward doctoral degrees
- Publish original research and analysis in books and academic journals
- Serve on academic and administrative committees that review and recommend policies, make budget decisions, or advise on hiring and promotions within their department

Postsecondary teachers, often referred to as *professors* or *faculty*, specialize in a variety of subjects and fields. Some teach academic subjects, such as English or philosophy. Others focus on career-related subjects, such as law, nursing, or culinary arts.

At colleges and universities, professors are organized into departments that specialize in a subject, such as history, science, business, or music. A professor may teach one or more courses within that department. For example, a mathematics professor may teach calculus, statistics, and a graduate seminar in a very specific area of mathematics.

Postsecondary teachers' duties vary with their positions in a university or college. In large colleges or universities, they may spend their time teaching, conducting research or experiments, applying for grants to fund their research, or supervising graduate teaching assistants who are teaching classes.

Postsecondary teachers who work in small colleges and universities or in community colleges often spend more time teaching classes and working with students. They may spend some time conducting research, but they do not have as much time to devote to it.

Full-time professors, particularly those who have tenure (those who cannot be fired without just cause), often are expected to spend more time on research. They also may be expected to serve on more college and university committees.

Part-time professors, often known as *adjunct professors*, spend most of their time teaching students.

Professors may teach large classes of several hundred students (often with the help of graduate teaching assistants), smaller classes of about 40 to 50 students, seminars with just a few students, or laboratories where students practice the subject matter. They work with an increasingly varied student population as more part-time, older, and culturally diverse students are going to postsecondary schools.

Professors need to keep up with developments in their field by reading scholarly articles, talking with colleagues, and participating in professional conferences. A tenured professor must do original research, such as experiments, document analysis, or critical reviews, and publish their findings.

Some postsecondary teachers work for online universities or teach online classes. They use websites to present lessons and information, to assign and accept students' work, and to participate in course discussions. Online professors communicate with students by email and by phone and might never meet their students in person.

Work Environment

Postsecondary teachers held about 1.3 million jobs in 2014.

In 2014, about 76 percent of postsecondary teachers worked for colleges, universities, and professional schools and about 20 percent worked for junior colleges. Much smaller percentages of postsecondary teachers worked in industries such as career and technical schools, business schools and computer and management training facilities, and hospitals.

Many postsecondary teachers find their jobs rewarding because they are surrounded by others who enjoy their subject. The opportunity to share their expertise with others also is appealing to many.

However, some postsecondary teachers must find a balance between teaching students and doing research and publishing their findings. This can be stressful, especially for beginning teachers seeking advancement in 4-year research universities. At the community college level, professors focus mainly on teaching students and administrative duties.

Classes are generally held during the day, although some are offered in the evenings and weekends to accommodate students who have jobs or family obligations.

Although some postsecondary teachers teach summer courses, many do not and use that time to conduct research, involve themselves in professional development, or travel.

Work Schedules. Many postsecondary teachers work part time. They may work part time at several colleges or universities.

Professors and other postsecondary teachers instruct students in the theory and practice of a variety of subjects.

Postsecondary teachers' schedules generally are flexible. Full-time teachers need to be on campus to teach classes and have office hours. Otherwise, they are free to set their schedule to prepare for classes and grade assignments. They may also spend time carrying out administrative responsibilities such as serving on committees.

Education/Training

Educational requirements vary with the subject taught and the type of educational institution. Most commonly, postsecondary teachers must have a Ph.D. However, a master's degree may be enough for some postsecondary teachers at community colleges. In career and technical schools, work experience may be important for getting a postsecondary teaching job.

Education. Postsecondary teachers who work for 4-year colleges and universities typically need a doctoral degree in their field. Some schools may hire those with a master's degree or those who are doctoral degree candidates for some specialties, such as fine arts, or for some part-time positions.

Doctoral programs generally take multiple years after the completion of a bachelor's degree program. They spend time completing a master's degree and then writing a doctoral dissertation, which is a paper presenting original research in the student's field of study. Candidates usually specialize in a subfield, such as organic chemistry or European history.

Community colleges or career and technical schools also may hire those with a master's degree. However, in some fields, there are more applicants than available positions. In these situations, institutions can be more selective, and they frequently choose applicants who have a Ph.D. over those with a master's degree.

Postsecondary teachers who teach career and technical education courses, such as culinary arts or cosmetology, may not be required to have graduate-level education. At a minimum they must hold the degree of the program in which they are teaching. For example, the teacher must hold an associate's degree if they teach a program that is at the associate's degree level. In addition, work experience or certification may be just as important as education for getting a postsecondary teaching job at a career or technical school.

Other Experience. Some institutions may prefer to hire those with teaching or other work experience, but this is not a requirement for all fields or for all employers.

In health specialties, art, or education fields, hands-on work experience in the industry can be important. Postsecondary teachers in these fields often gain experience by working in an occupation related to their field of expertise.

In fields such as biological science, physics, and chemistry, some postsecondary teachers have postdoctoral research experience. These short-term jobs, sometimes called "post-docs," usually involve working for 2 to 3 years as a research associate or in a similar position, often at a college or university.

Some postsecondary teachers gain teaching experience by working as graduate teaching assistants—students who are enrolled in a graduate program and teach classes in the institution in which they are enrolled.

Some postsecondary teachers, especially adjunct professors, have another job in addition to teaching.

Licenses, Certifications, and Registrations. Postsecondary teachers who prepare students for an occupation that requires a license, certification, or registration, may need to have—or they may benefit from having—the same credential. For example, a postsecondary nursing teacher might need a nursing license or a postsecondary education teacher might need a teaching license.

Advancement. A major goal for postsecondary teachers with a doctoral degree is attaining a tenure—a guarantee that a professor cannot be fired without just cause. It can take up to 7 years of moving up the ranks in tenure-track positions. The ranks are assistant professor, associate professor, and professor. Tenure is granted through a review of the candidate's research, contribution to the institution, and teaching.

Tenure and tenure-track positions are declining as institutions are relying more heavily on part-time faculty.

Some tenured professors advance to administrative positions, such as dean or president. For information on deans and other administrative positions, see the profile on postsecondary education administrators. For more information about college and university presidents, see the profile on top executives.

Important Qualities

Critical-thinking skills. To challenge established theories and beliefs, conduct original research, and design experiments, postsecondary teachers need good critical-thinking skills.

Interpersonal skills. Most postsecondary teachers need to be able to work well with others and must have good communication skills to serve on committees and give lectures.

Resourcefulness. Postsecondary teachers need to be able to present information in a way that students will understand. They need to adapt to the different learning styles of their students and teach students who have little or no experience with the subject.

Speaking skills. Postsecondary teachers need good communication skills to give lectures.

Writing skills. Most postsecondary teachers need to be skilled writers to publish original research and analysis.

Pay

The median annual wage for postsecondary teachers was $70,790 in May 2014. The median wage is the wage at which half the workers in an occupation earned more than that amount and half

Median Annual Wages, May 2014

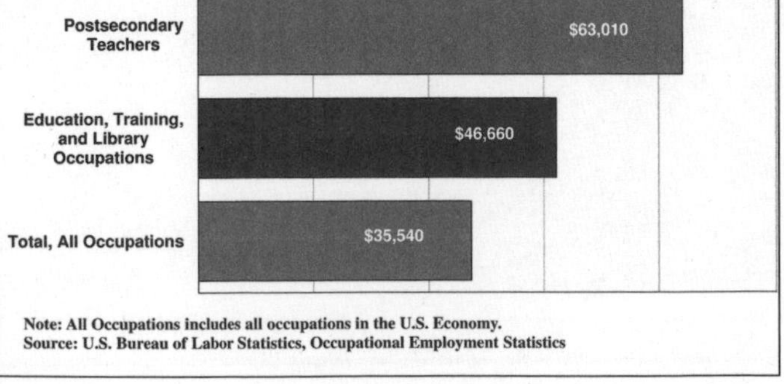

Note: All Occupations includes all occupations in the U.S. Economy.
Source: U.S. Bureau of Labor Statistics, Occupational Employment Statistics

Percent Change in Employment, Projected 2014–2024

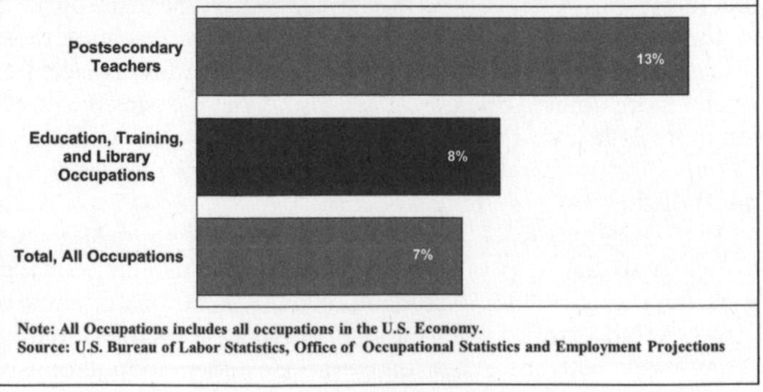

Note: All Occupations includes all occupations in the U.S. Economy.
Source: U.S. Bureau of Labor Statistics, Office of Occupational Statistics and Employment Projections

earned less. The lowest 10 percent earned less than $35,570, and the highest 10 percent earned more than $149,820.

Median annual wages for postsecondary teachers in May 2014 were as follows:

Law teachers, postsecondary	$109,980
Engineering teachers, postsecondary	94,130
Economics teachers, postsecondary	90,870
Health specialties teachers, postsecondary	90,210
Agricultural sciences teachers, postsecondary	86,260
Forestry and conservation science teachers, postsecondary	84,090
Atmospheric, earth, marine, and space sciences teachers, postsecondary	81,780
Physics teachers, postsecondary	80,720
Environmental science teachers, postsecondary	77,470
Anthropology and archeology teachers, postsecondary	74,750
Biological science teachers, postsecondary	74,580
Business teachers, postsecondary	74,090
Political science teachers, postsecondary	73,790
Architecture teachers, postsecondary	73,720
Chemistry teachers, postsecondary	73,080
Computer science teachers, postsecondary	72,010
Geography teachers, postsecondary	71,320
Area, ethnic, and cultural studies teachers, postsecondary	68,950
Psychology teachers, postsecondary	68,690
Sociology teachers, postsecondary	67,880
History teachers, postsecondary	66,840
Library science teachers, postsecondary	66,580
Nursing instructors and teachers, postsecondary	66,100
Social sciences teachers, postsecondary, all other	65,320
Mathematical science teachers, postsecondary	65,190
Art, drama, and music teachers, postsecondary	64,300
Philosophy and religion teachers, postsecondary	63,630
Communications teachers, postsecondary	62,550
Social work teachers, postsecondary	62,440
English language and literature teachers, postsecondary	60,160
Education teachers, postsecondary	59,720
Foreign language and literature teachers, postsecondary	59,490
Criminal justice and law enforcement teachers, postsecondary	57,200

Employment Projections Data for Postsecondary Teachers

Occupational Title	SOC Code	Employment, 2014	Projected Employment, 2024	Change, 2014–2024 Percent	Change, 2014–2024 Numeric
Postsecondary teachers	—	1,313,000	1,490,000	13	177,000
Business teachers, postsecondary	25-1011	106,800	116,200	9	9,400
Computer science teachers, postsecondary	25-1021	43,400	47,200	9	3,800
Mathematical science teachers, postsecondary	25-1022	63,500	73,900	16	10,400
Architecture teachers, postsecondary	25-1031	9,100	9,900	9	800
Engineering teachers, postsecondary	25-1032	46,000	52,000	13	6,000
Agricultural sciences teachers, postsecondary	25-1041	12,100	12,800	6	700
Biological science teachers, postsecondary	25-1042	64,300	74,800	16	10,400
Forestry and conservation science teachers, postsecondary	25-1043	2,300	2,400	7	200
Atmospheric, earth, marine, and space sciences teachers, postsecondary	25-1051	13,200	14,300	9	1,100
Chemistry teachers, postsecondary	25-1052	26,600	30,700	15	4,100
Environmental science teachers, postsecondary	25-1053	6,700	7,300	9	600
Physics teachers, postsecondary	25-1054	17,700	20,400	15	2,700
Anthropology and archeology teachers, postsecondary	25-1061	7,500	8,200	9	700
Area, ethnic, and cultural studies teachers, postsecondary	25-1062	11,600	13,300	15	1,700
Economics teachers, postsecondary	25-1063	17,300	18,900	10	1,700
Geography teachers, postsecondary	25-1064	5,400	5,900	8	400
Political science teachers, postsecondary	25-1065	21,600	23,700	10	2,100
Psychology teachers, postsecondary	25-1066	47,300	54,700	16	7,500
Sociology teachers, postsecondary	25-1067	20,700	23,900	15	3,200
Social sciences teachers, postsecondary, all other	25-1069	12,900	15,100	17	2,200
Health specialties teachers, postsecondary	25-1071	210,400	250,400	19	40,000
Nursing instructors and teachers, postsecondary	25-1072	68,600	81,800	19	13,200
Education teachers, postsecondary	25-1081	75,700	82,500	9	6,900
Library science teachers, postsecondary	25-1082	5,600	6,000	8	400
Criminal justice and law enforcement teachers, postsecondary	25-1111	17,400	21,100	21	3,700
Law teachers, postsecondary	25-1112	21,100	25,700	22	4,600
Social work teachers, postsecondary	25-1113	13,700	15,600	14	1,900
Art, drama, and music teachers, postsecondary	25-1121	120,700	133,700	11	13,000
Communications teachers, postsecondary	25-1122	36,000	39,500	10	3,500
English language and literature teachers, postsecondary	25-1123	90,800	100,200	10	9,400
Foreign language and literature teachers, postsecondary	25-1124	37,200	41,300	11	4,100
History teachers, postsecondary	25-1125	29,200	32,100	10	2,900
Philosophy and religion teachers, postsecondary	25-1126	30,700	34,200	12	3,600

Source: U.S. Bureau of Labor Statistics, Employment Projections Program

Job Outlook

Employment of postsecondary teachers is projected to grow 13 percent from 2014 to 2024, faster than the average for all occupations. Both part-time and full-time postsecondary teachers are included in this projection.

Growth is expected as enrollments at postsecondary institutions continue to rise, although it will be at a slower rate than it has been in the past.

The number of people attending postsecondary institutions is expected to grow from 2014 to 2024. Students will continue to seek higher education to gain the additional education and skills necessary to meet their career goals. As more people enter colleges and universities, more postsecondary teachers will be needed to serve these additional students.

However, despite expected increases in enrollment, employment growth in public colleges and universities will depend on state and local government budgets. When budgets for higher education are reduced, employment growth may be limited.

Enrollment is expected to decrease in online colleges and universities. As a result, there will be less demand for postsecondary teachers in these types of schools.

Overall employment of postsecondary teachers is projected to increase, but it will vary by field. For example, nursing and health specialties teachers are projected to grow much faster than the average. As an aging population increasingly demands healthcare services, many additional postsecondary teachers are expected to be needed to help educate the workers who will provide these services.

In all fields, there is expected to be a limited number of full-time non-tenure and full-time tenure positions. Many colleges and universities are hiring more part-time positions.

Job Prospects. There are expected to be more job opportunities for part-time postsecondary teachers since many institutions are hiring more part-time than full-time positions.

There will be a limited number of full-time tenure track positions and competition is expected to be high.

Some fields, such as health specialties and nursing, will likely experience better job prospects than others, such as those in the humanities.

Community colleges or career and technical schools may hire those with a master's degree. However, there are more applicants than available positions in some fields. In these situations, institutions can be more selective, and they frequently choose applicants who have a Ph.D. over those with a master's degree.

Contacts for More Information

For more information about postsecondary teachers, visit

- Council of Graduate Schools (www.cgsnet.org)
- Association for Career and Technical Education (www.acteonline.org)

O*NET

- Business Teachers, Postsecondary (25-1011.00)
- Computer Science Teachers, Postsecondary (25-1021.00)
- Mathematical Science Teachers, Postsecondary (25-1022.00)
- Architecture Teachers, Postsecondary (25-1031.00)
- Engineering Teachers, Postsecondary (25-1032.00)
- Agricultural Sciences Teachers, Postsecondary (25-1041.00)
- Biological Science Teachers, Postsecondary (25-1042.00)
- Forestry and Conservation Science Teachers, Postsecondary (25-1043.00)
- Atmospheric, Earth, Marine, and Space Sciences Teachers, Postsecondary (25-1051.00)
- Chemistry Teachers, Postsecondary (25-1052.00)
- Environmental Science Teachers, Postsecondary (25-1053.00)
- Physics Teachers, Postsecondary (25-1054.00)
- Anthropology and Archeology Teachers, Postsecondary (25-1061.00)
- Area, Ethnic, and Cultural Studies Teachers, Postsecondary (25-1062.00)
- Economics Teachers, Postsecondary (25-1063.00)
- Geography Teachers, Postsecondary (25-1064.00)
- Political Science Teachers, Postsecondary (25-1065.00)
- Psychology Teachers, Postsecondary (25-1066.00)
- Sociology Teachers, Postsecondary (25-1067.00)
- Social Sciences Teachers, Postsecondary, All Other (25-1069.00)
- Health Specialties Teachers, Postsecondary (25-1071.00)
- Nursing Instructors and Teachers, Postsecondary (25-1072.00)
- Education Teachers, Postsecondary (25-1081.00)
- Library Science Teachers, Postsecondary (25-1082.00)

Similar Occupations. This table shows a list of occupations with job duties that are similar to those of postsecondary teachers.

Occupations	Entry-level Education	2014 Median Pay	Projected Job Growth	Average Annual Openings
Anthropologists and Archeologists	Master's degree	$59,280	4%	30
Biochemists and Biophysicists	Doctoral or professional degree	$84,940	8%	280
Career and Technical Education Teachers	Bachelor's degree	$51,830	4%	1,020
Chemists and Materials Scientists	Bachelor's degree	$74,720	3%	260
Economists	Master's degree	$95,710	6%	120
Geographers	Bachelor's degree	$76,420	-2%	0
Historians	Master's degree	$55,870	2%	10
Microbiologists	Bachelor's degree	$67,790	4%	80
Political Scientists	Master's degree	$104,920	-2%	-10
Postsecondary Education Administrators	Master's degree	$88,390	9%	1,520
Psychologists	See Education/Training	$70,700	19%	3,250
Sociologists	Master's degree	$72,810	-1%	0
Zoologists and Wildlife Biologists	Bachelor's degree	$58,270	4%	80

- ➤ Criminal Justice and Law Enforcement Teachers, Postsecondary (25-1111.00)
- ➤ Law Teachers, Postsecondary (25-1112.00)
- ➤ Social Work Teachers, Postsecondary (25-1113.00)
- ➤ Art, Drama, and Music Teachers, Postsecondary (25-1121.00)
- ➤ Communications Teachers, Postsecondary (25-1122.00)
- ➤ English Language and Literature Teachers, Postsecondary (25-1123.00)
- ➤ Foreign Language and Literature Teachers, Postsecondary (25-1124.00)
- ➤ History Teachers, Postsecondary (25-1125.00)
- ➤ Philosophy and Religion Teachers, Postsecondary (25-1126.00)

Preschool Teachers

- **2014 Median Pay** .... $28,120 per year
  $13.52 per hour
- **Typical Entry-Level Education** .... Associate's degree
- **Work Experience in a Related Occupation** .... None
- **On-the-job Training** .... None
- **Number of Jobs, 2014** 441,000
- **Job Outlook, 2014–24** .... 7% (As fast as average)
- **Employment Change, 2014–24** 29,600

What Preschool Teachers Do

Preschool teachers educate and care for children younger than age 5 who have not yet entered kindergarten. They teach reading, writing, science, and other subjects in a way that young children can understand.

Duties. Preschool teachers typically do the following:

- Teach children basic skills such as color, shape, number, and letter recognition
- Work with children in groups or one on one, depending on the needs of children and the subject matter
- Plan and carry out a curriculum that targets different areas of child development, such as language, motor, and social skills
- Organize activities so children can learn about the world, explore interests, and develop skills
- Develop schedules and routines to ensure children have enough physical activity, rest, and playtime
- Watch for signs of emotional or developmental problems in children and bring them to the attention of the parents
- Keep records of the students' progress, routines, and interests, and inform parents about their child's development

Young children learn from playing, problem solving, questioning, and experimenting. Preschool teachers use play and other instructional techniques to teach children about the world. For example, they use storytelling and rhyming games to teach language and vocabulary. They may help improve children's social skills by having them work together to build a neighborhood in a sandbox or teach math by having children count when building with blocks.

Preschool teachers work with children from different ethnic, racial, and religious backgrounds. Teachers include topics in their lessons to teach children to respect people of different backgrounds and cultures.

Preschool teachers use play to teach children about the world.

Work Environment

Preschool teachers held about 441,000 jobs in 2014. The industries that employed the most preschool teachers were as follows:

Child day care services	55%
Religious, grantmaking, civic, professional, and similar organizations	19
Elementary and secondary schools; state, local, and private	17
Individual and family services	3

Many preschool teachers work in public and private schools or in formal childcare centers that have preschool classrooms. Others work for charitable or religious organizations that have preschool programs or Head Start programs. Head Start programs receive federal funding in order to provide educational courses for low-income families and their children from birth to age 5.

Seeing children develop new skills and gain an appreciation of knowledge and learning can be very rewarding. However, it can also be tiring to work with young, active children all day.

Work Schedules. Preschool teachers in public schools generally work during school hours. Many work the traditional 10-month school year and have a 2-month break during the summer. Some preschool teachers may teach in summer programs.

Teachers in districts with a year-round schedule typically work 8 weeks in a row then have a break for 1 week before starting a new school session. They also have a 5-week midwinter break.

Those working in day care settings may work longer hours and often work the whole year.

Education/Training

Education and training requirements vary based on settings and state regulations. They range from a high school diploma and certification to a college degree.

Education. In childcare centers, preschool teachers generally are required to have a least a high school diploma and a certification in early childhood education. However, employers may prefer to hire workers with at least some postsecondary education in early childhood education.

Preschool teachers in Head Start programs are required to have at least an associate's degree. However, at least 50 percent of all preschool teachers in Head Start programs nationwide must have

Median Annual Wages, May 2014

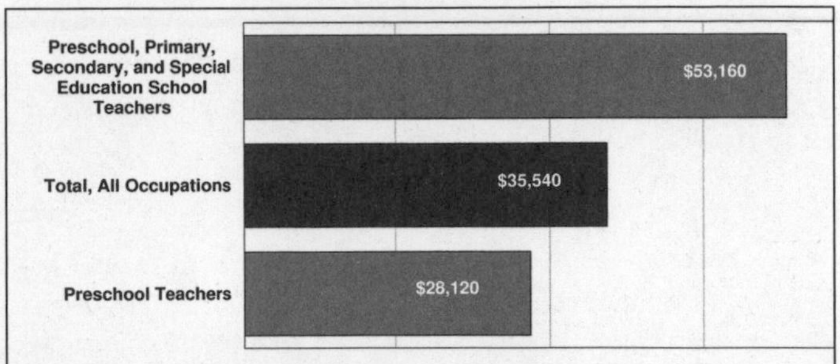

Note: All Occupations includes all occupations in the U.S. Economy.
Source: U.S. Bureau of Labor Statistics, Occupational Employment Statistics

Percent Change in Employment, Projected 2014–2024

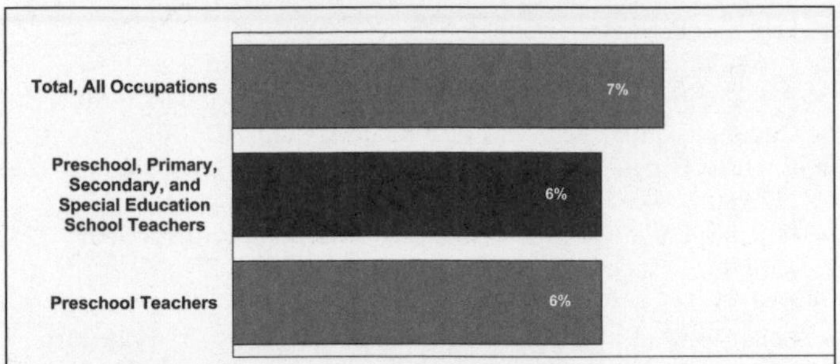

Note: All Occupations includes all occupations in the U.S. Economy.
Source: U.S. Bureau of Labor Statistics, Office of Occupational Statistics and Employment Projections

a bachelor's degree in early childhood education or a related field. Those with a degree in a related field must have experience teaching preschool-age children.

In public schools, preschool teachers are generally required to have at least a bachelor's degree in early childhood education or a related field. Bachelor's degree programs teach students about children's development, strategies to teach young children, and how to observe and document children's progress.

Licenses, Certifications, and Registrations. Some states require preschool teachers to obtain the Child Development Associate (CDA) credential offered by the Council for Professional Recognition. Obtaining the CDA credential requires coursework, experience in the field, a written exam, and observation of the candidate working with children. The CDA credential is valid for three years and requires renewal.

Some states recognize the Certified Childcare Professional (CCP) designation offered by the National Early Childhood Program Accreditation. Some of the requirements needed to obtain the CCP include that the candidate must be 18 years old, have a high school diploma, have experience in the field, take courses in early childhood education, and pass an exam. The CCP accreditation requires renewal every two years through the CCP maintenance process.

In public schools, preschool teachers must be licensed to teach early childhood education, which covers preschool through 3rd grade. Requirements vary by state, but they generally require a bachelor's degree and passing an exam to demonstrate competency. Most states require teachers to complete continuing education credits to maintain their license.

Other Experience. A few states require preschool teachers to have some work experience in a childcare setting. The amount of experience necessary varies by state. In these cases, preschool teachers often start out as childcare workers or teacher assistants.

Important Qualities

Communication skills. Preschool teachers need good communication skills to talk to parents and colleagues about students' progress. They need good writing and speaking skills to convey this information effectively. They must also be able to communicate well with small children.

Creativity. Preschool teachers must plan lessons that engage young students. In addition, they need to adapt their lessons to suit different learning styles.

Interpersonal skills. Preschool teachers must understand children's emotional needs and be able to develop good relationships with parents, children, and colleagues.

Organizational skills. Teachers need to be organized to plan lessons and keep records of their students.

Patience. Working with children can be frustrating, and preschool teachers should be able to respond calmly to overwhelming and difficult situations.

Physical stamina. Working with children can be physically taxing, so preschool teachers should have a lot of energy.

Advancement. Experienced preschool teachers can advance to become the director of a preschool or childcare center or a lead teacher, who may be responsible for the instruction of several classes. Those with a bachelor's degree in early childhood education frequently are qualified to teach kindergarten through grade 3, in addition to preschool. Teaching positions at these higher grades typically pay more. For more information, see the profiles on preschool and childcare center directors and kindergarten and elementary school teachers.

Pay

The median annual wage for preschool teachers was $28,120 in May 2014. The median wage is the wage at which half the workers in an occupation earned more than that amount and half earned less. The lowest 10 percent earned less than $18,680, and the highest 10 percent earned more than $50,880.

In May 2014, the median annual wages for preschool teachers in the top industries in which they worked were as follows:

Elementary and secondary schools; state, local, and private	$42,580
Individual and family services	30,150
Religious, grantmaking, civic, professional, and similar organizations	28,500
Child day care services	25,590

Job Outlook

Employment of preschool teachers is projected to grow 7 percent from 2014 to 2024, about as fast as the average for all occupations.

The number of preschool-aged children is expected to increase; however, their share of the overall population should remain constant.

Early childhood education is important for a child's short- and long-term intellectual and social development. More preschool teachers should be needed as a result of the increasing demand for early childhood education. In addition, some parents are starting to enroll children as young as infants in preschool because of the educational benefit.

Job Prospects. Workers who have postsecondary education, particularly those with a bachelor's degree, should have better job prospects than those with less education. In addition, those with previous experience working with preschool-aged children will have better opportunities finding a job.

Employment Projections Data for Preschool Teachers

Occupational Title	SOC Code	Employment, 2014	Projected Employment, 2024	Change, 2014–2024 Percent	Change, 2014–2024 Numeric
Preschool teachers, except special education	25-2011	441,000	470,600	7	29,600

Source: U.S. Bureau of Labor Statistics, Employment Projections Program

Similar Occupations. This table shows a list of occupations with job duties that are similar to those of preschool teachers.

Occupations	Entry-level Education	2014 Median Pay	Projected Job Growth	Average Annual Openings
Childcare Workers	High school diploma or equivalent	$19,730	5%	6,930
High School Teachers	Bachelor's degree	$56,310	6%	5,590
Kindergarten and Elementary School Teachers	Bachelor's degree	$53,760	6%	8,780
Middle School Teachers	Bachelor's degree	$54,940	6%	3,680
Preschool and Childcare Center Directors	Bachelor's degree	$45,260	7%	420
Special Education Teachers	Bachelor's degree	$55,980	6%	2,810
Teacher Assistants	Some college, no degree	$24,430	6%	7,860

Contacts for More Information

For more information about early childhood education, visit

➤ National Association for the Education of Young Children (www.naeyc.org)

For more information about professional credentials, visit

➤ Council for Professional Recognition (www.cdacouncil.org)

O*NET

➤ Preschool Teachers, Except Special Education (25-2011.00)

Special Education Teachers

- **2014 Median Pay** .... $55,980 per year
- **Typical Entry-Level Education** .... Bachelor's degree
- **Work Experience in a Related Occupation**............... None
- **On-the-job Training** .... Internship/residency
- **Number of Jobs, 2014** 450,700
- **Job Outlook, 2014-24**.................. 6% (As fast as average)
- **Employment Change, 2014–24** 28,100

What Special Education Teachers Do

Special education teachers work with students who have a wide range of learning, mental, emotional, and physical disabilities. They adapt general education lessons and teach various subjects, such as reading, writing, and math, to students with mild and moderate disabilities. They also teach basic skills, such as literacy and communication techniques, to students with severe disabilities.

Duties. Special education teachers typically do the following:

- Assess students' skills to determine their needs and to develop appropriate teaching plans
- Adapt general lessons to meet the needs of students
- Develop Individualized Education Programs (IEPs) for each student
- Plan, organize, and assign activities that are specific to each student's abilities
- Teach and mentor students as a class, in small groups, and one-on-one
- Implement IEPs, assess students' performance, and track their progress
- Update IEPs throughout the school year to reflect students' progress and goals
- Discuss student's progress with parents, teachers, counselors, and administrators
- Supervise and mentor teacher assistants who work with students with disabilities
- Prepare and help students transition from grade to grade and for life after graduation

Special education teachers work with general education teachers, counselors, school superintendents, administrators, and parents. As a team, they develop IEPs specific to each student's needs. IEPs outline the goals and services for each student, such as sessions with the school psychologists, counselors, and special education teachers. Teachers also meet with parents, school administrators, and counselors to discuss updates and changes to the IEPs.

Special education teachers' duties vary by the type of setting they work in, student disabilities, and teacher specialty.

Some special education teachers work in classrooms or resource centers that include only students with disabilities. In these settings, teachers plan, adapt, and present lessons to meet each student's needs. They teach students in small groups or on a one-on-one basis.

In inclusive classrooms, special education teachers teach students with disabilities who are in general education classrooms. They work with general education teachers to present the information in a manner that students with disabilities can more easily understand. They also assist general education teachers to adapt lessons that will meet the needs of the students with disabilities in their classes.

Special education teachers also collaborate with teacher assistants, psychologists, and social workers to accommodate requirements of students with disabilities. For example, they may have a teacher assistant work with them to provide support for a student who needs particular attention.

Special education teachers work with students who have a wide variety of mental, emotional, physical, and learning disabilities. For example, some work with students who need assistance in subject areas, such as reading and math. Others help students develop study skills, such as by using flashcards and text highlighting.

Some special education teachers work with students who have physical and sensory disabilities, such as blindness and deafness, and with students who are wheelchair-bound. They also may work with those who have autism spectrum disorders and emotional disorders, such as anxiety and depression.

Special education teachers work with students from preschool to high school. Some teachers work with students who have severe disabilities until the students are 21 years old.

Special education teachers help students with severe disabilities develop basic life skills, such as how to respond to questions and how to follow directions. Some teach the skills necessary for students with moderate disabilities to live independently, find a job, and manage money and their time. For more information about other workers who help individuals with disabilities develop skills necessary to live independently, see the profiles on occupational therapists and occupational therapy assistants and aides.

Most special education teachers use computers to keep records of their students' performance, prepare lesson plans, and update IEPs. Some teachers also use various assistive technology aids, such as Braille writers and computer software that help them communicate with students.

Work Environment

Special education teachers held about 450,700 jobs in 2014.

Most special education teachers work in public schools. Some teach in magnet, charter, and private schools. Some also work with young children in childcare centers.

A few work with students in residential facilities, hospitals, and students' homes. They may travel to these locations. Some teachers work with infants and toddlers at the child's home. They also teach the child's parents methods and ways to help the child develop skills.

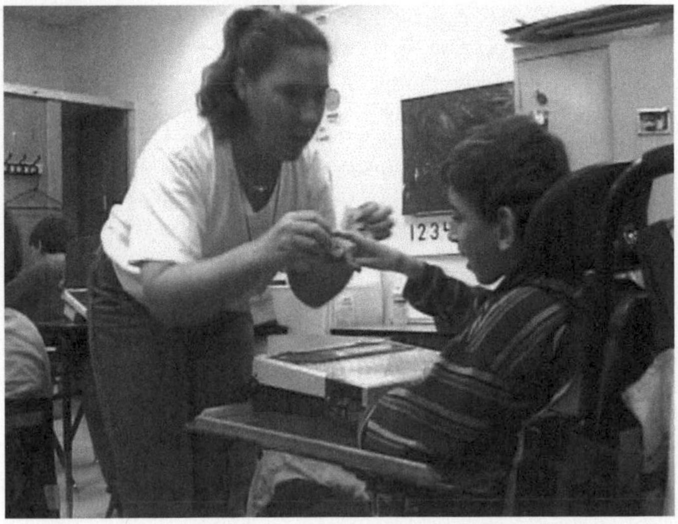

Special education teachers work with students who may have a wide range of learning, mental, emotional, and physical disabilities.

Helping students with disabilities can be highly rewarding. It also can be quite stressful—emotionally demanding and physically draining.

Work Schedules. Special education teachers typically work during school hours. They also use that time to grade papers, update students' records, and prepare lessons. They may meet with parents, students, and other teachers before and after classes.

Many work the traditional 10-month school year and have a 2-month break during the summer. Some teachers may work for summer programs.

Teachers in districts with a year-round schedule typically work 8 weeks in a row then are on break for 1 week. They also have a 5-week midwinter break.

Education/Training

Special education teachers in public schools are required to have at least a bachelor's degree and a state-issued certification or license. Private schools typically require teachers to have a bachelor's degree, but teachers are not required to be licensed or certified. For information about teacher preparation programs and certification requirements, visit Teach.org (www.teach.org) or contact your state's board of education.

Education. All states require special education teachers in public schools to have at least a bachelor's degree. Some earn a degree specifically in special education. Others major in elementary education or a content area, such as math or science, with a minor in special education.

In a program leading to a bachelor's degree in special education, prospective teachers learn about the different types of disabilities and how to present information so that students will understand. These programs typically include fieldwork, such as student teaching. To become fully certified, some states require special education teachers to complete a master's degree in special education.

Teachers in private schools do not need to meet state requirements. However, private schools may prefer to hire teachers who have at least a bachelor's degree in special education.

Licenses, Certifications, and Registrations. All states require teachers in public schools to be licensed. A license is frequently referred to as a certification. Those who teach in private schools are not required to be licensed. Most states require teachers to pass a background check.

Requirements for certification vary by state. In addition to a bachelor's degree, states also require teachers to complete a teacher preparation program and supervised experience in teaching. Some states require a minimum grade point average. Teachers may be required to complete annual professional development classes or a master's degree program to maintain their license.

Many states offer general licenses in special education that allow teachers to work with students with a variety of disabilities. Others offer licenses or endorsements based on a disability-specific category, such as autism or behavior disorders.

Some states allow special education teachers to transfer their licenses from another state. Other states require even an experienced teacher to pass their state's licensing requirements.

All states offer an alternative route to certification for people who already have a bachelor's degree. Some alternative certification programs allow candidates to begin teaching immediately, under the close supervision of an experienced teacher. These alternative programs cover teaching methods and child development. Candidates are awarded full certification after they complete the program. Other programs require prospective teachers to take

Median Annual Wages, May 2014

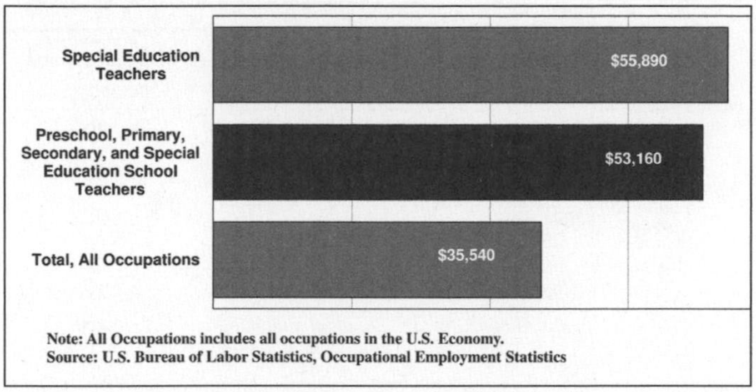

Percent Change in Employment, Projected 2014–2024

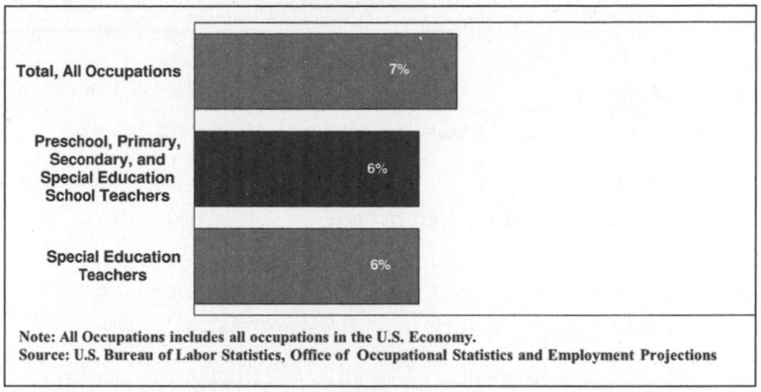

classes in education before they can start to teach. They may be awarded a master's degree after completing either type of program.

Training. Some special education teachers need to complete a period of fieldwork, commonly referred to as student teaching, before they can work as a teacher. In some states, this program is a prerequisite for a license to teach in public schools. During student teaching, they gain experience in preparing lesson plans and teaching students in a classroom setting, under the supervision and guidance of a mentor teacher. The amount of time required for these programs varies by state, but may last from 1 to 2 years. Many universities offer student teaching programs as part of a degree in special education.

Advancement. Experienced teachers can advance to become mentor or lead teachers who help less experienced teachers improve their teaching skills.

Teachers may become school counselors, instructional coordinators, assistant principals, or principals. These positions generally require additional education, an advanced degree, or certification. An advanced degree in education administration or leadership may be helpful.

Important Qualities

Communication skills. Special education teachers discuss students' needs and performances with general education teachers, parents, and administrators. They also explain difficult concepts in terms that students with learning disabilities can understand.

Critical-thinking skills. Special education teachers assess students' progress and use that information to adapt lessons to help them learn.

Interpersonal skills. Special education teachers regularly work with general education teachers, school counselors, administrators, and parents to develop Individualized Education Programs. As a result, they need to be able to build positive working relationships.

Patience. Working with students with special needs and different abilities can be difficult. Special education teachers should be patient with each student, as some may need the instruction given aloud, at a slower pace, or in writing.

Resourcefulness. Special education teachers must develop different ways to present information in a manner that meets the needs of their students. They also help general education teachers adapt their lessons to the needs of students with disabilities.

Pay

The median annual wage for special education teachers was $55,980 in May 2014. The median wage is the wage at which half the workers in an occupation earned more than that amount and half earned less. The lowest 10 percent earned less than $37,110, and the highest 10 percent earned more than $88,080.

Median annual wages for special education teachers in May 2014 were as follows:

Special education teachers, secondary school	$57,810
Special education teachers, middle school	56,760
Special education teachers, kindergarten and elementary school	54,570
Special education teachers, preschool	54,000

Job Outlook

Employment of special education teachers is projected to grow 6 percent from 2014 to 2024, about as fast as the average for all occupations. The employment growth of special education teachers will vary by type. (See Employment Projections table.) However, overall demand will be driven by enrollment, the need for special education services, and the federal budget situation.

Although enrollment in special education programs has slightly decreased, better screening and identification of various disabilities in children are expected to affect the demand for special education services. Children with disabilities are being identified earlier and enrolled into special education programs.

Employment Projections Data for Special Education Teachers

Occupational Title	SOC Code	Employment, 2014	Projected Employment, 2024	Change, 2014–2024 Percent	Change, 2014–2024 Numeric
Special education teachers	—	491,100	522,000	6	31,000
Special education teachers, preschool	25-2051	25,500	27,800	9	2,300
Special education teachers, kindergarten and elementary school	25-2052	198,100	210,600	6	12,500
Special education teachers, middle school	25-2053	93,000	98,500	6	5,500
Special education teachers, secondary school	25-2054	134,000	141,900	6	7,900

Source: U.S. Bureau of Labor Statistics, Employment Projections Program

Similar Occupations. This table shows a list of occupations with job duties that are similar to those of special education teachers.

Occupations	Entry-level Education	2014 Median Pay	Projected Job Growth	Average Annual Openings
Career and Technical Education Teachers	Bachelor's degree	$51,830	4%	1,020
Childcare Workers	High school diploma or equivalent	$19,730	5%	6,930
Elementary, Middle, and High School Principals	Master's degree	$89,540	6%	1,400
High School Teachers	Bachelor's degree	$56,310	6%	5,590
Instructional Coordinators	Master's degree	$61,550	7%	1,050
Kindergarten and Elementary School Teachers	Bachelor's degree	$53,760	6%	8,780
Middle School Teachers	Bachelor's degree	$54,940	6%	3,680
Occupational Therapists	Master's degree	$78,810	27%	3,040
Preschool Teachers	Associate's degree	$28,120	7%	2,960
Recreational Therapists	Bachelor's degree	$44,000	12%	220
Social Workers	See Education/Training	$45,500	12%	7,480
Teacher Assistants	Some college, no degree	$24,430	6%	7,860

Employment growth will also depend on government funding, since laws require free public education for students with disabilities. Every state must maintain the same level of financial support for special education every year.

Job Prospects. Teaching students with disabilities can be quite stressful, emotionally demanding, and physically draining. As a result, many schools have difficulties recruiting and retaining special education teachers. Special education teachers are expected to have good job opportunities, which will stem from the need to replace teachers who leave the occupation each year.

Job opportunities also may be better in certain specialties, such as those requiring experience with early childhood intervention and skills in working with students who have multiple disabilities, severe disabilities, or autism spectrum disorders. Those with experience and knowledge of working with students with learning disabilities and speech or language impairments may have the best job prospects.

Contacts for More Information

For more information about special education teachers, visit

- ➤ Council for Exceptional Children (www.cec.sped.org)
- ➤ Personnel Improvement Center (www.personnelcenter.org)
- ➤ National Association of Special Education Teachers (www.naset.org)

For more information about teaching and becoming a teacher, visit

- ➤ Teach.org (www.teach.org)
- ➤ American Federation of Teachers (www.aft.org)
- ➤ National Education Association (www.nea.org)

O*NET

- ➤ Special Education Teachers, Preschool (25-2051.00)
- ➤ Special Education Teachers, Kindergarten and Elementary School (25-2052.00)
- ➤ Special Education Teachers, Middle School (25-2053.00)
- ➤ Special Education Teachers, Secondary School (25-2054.00)

Teacher Assistants

- **2014 Median Pay** .... $24,430 per year
- **Typical Entry-Level Education** ....Some college, no degree
- **Work Experience in a Related Occupation**.............. None
- **On-the-job Training** .... None
- **Number of Jobs, 2014** 1,234,100
- **Job Outlook, 2014–24** .... 6% (As fast as average)
- **Employment Change, 2014–24** 78,600

What Teacher Assistants Do

Teacher assistants work under a teacher's supervision to give students additional attention and instruction.

Duties. Teacher assistants typically do the following:

- Reinforce lessons presented by teachers by reviewing material with students one-on-one or in small groups
- Enforce school and class rules to help teach students proper behavior
- Help teachers with recordkeeping, such as tracking attendance and calculating grades
- Help teachers prepare for lessons by getting materials ready or setting up equipment, such as computers
- Supervise students in class, between classes, during lunch and recess, and on field trips

Teacher assistants also are called *teacher aides, instructional aides, paraprofessionals, education assistants*, and *paraeducators*.

Teacher assistants work with or under the guidance of a licensed teacher. Generally, teachers introduce new material to students while teacher assistants help reinforce the lessons by working with individual students or small groups of students. For example, after the teacher presents a lesson, a teacher assistant may help a small group of students as they try to master the material.

Teachers may seek feedback from assistants to monitor students' progress. Some teachers and teacher assistants meet regularly to

Teacher assistants support and assist children in learning class material, using the teacher's lesson plans.

discuss lesson plans and student development. Teacher assistants sometimes help teachers by grading tests and checking homework.

Some teacher assistants work only with special education students. Some of these students attend regular classes, and teacher assistants help them understand the material and adapt the information to their learning style. Teacher assistants may work with students who have more severe disabilities in separate classrooms. They help these students with basic needs, such as eating or personal hygiene. With young adults, they may help students with disabilities learn skills necessary for them to find a job or live independently after graduation.

Some teacher assistants work in specific locations in the school. For example, some work in computer laboratories, teaching students how to use computers and helping them use software. Others work as recess or lunchroom attendants, supervising students during these times of the day.

Although most teacher assistants work in elementary, middle, and high schools, others work in preschools and childcare centers. Often, one or two assistants work with a lead teacher to provide the individual attention that young children need. They help with educational activities. They also supervise the children at play and help with feeding and other basic care.

Work Environment

Teacher assistants held about 1.2 million jobs in 2014. They work in both private and public elementary, middle, and high schools. They also work in preschools, at childcare centers, at community centers, and for religious organizations.

In 2014, about 77 percent of teacher assistants were employed by elementary and secondary schools and 9 percent were employed by child day care services.

Teacher assistants may spend some time outside, when students are at recess or getting on and off the bus. Those who work with special education students may need to lift the students at certain times.

Work Schedules. About 2 in 5 teacher assistants worked part time in 2014. Some ride the bus with students before and after school. Although many do not work during the summer, some work in year-round schools or help teachers in summer school.

Education/Training

Teacher assistants typically need to have completed at least 2 years of college coursework.

Education. Most school districts require applicants to have completed at least 2 years of college coursework or have earned an associate's degree. Teacher assistants in schools that have a Title 1 program (a federal program for schools with a large proportion of students from low-income households) must have at least a 2-year degree, 2 years of college, or pass a state or local assessment.

Associate's degree programs for teacher assistants prepare the participants to develop educational materials, observe students, and understand the role of teachers and teaching assistants in the classroom.

Most states require instructional aides who work with special-needs students to pass a skills-based test.

Important Qualities

Communication skills. Teacher assistants need to discuss students' progress with teachers and parents, so they need to be able to communicate well.

Interpersonal skills. Teacher assistants interact with a variety of people, including teachers, students, parents, and administrators. They need to develop good working relationships with the people they work with.

Median Annual Wages, May 2014

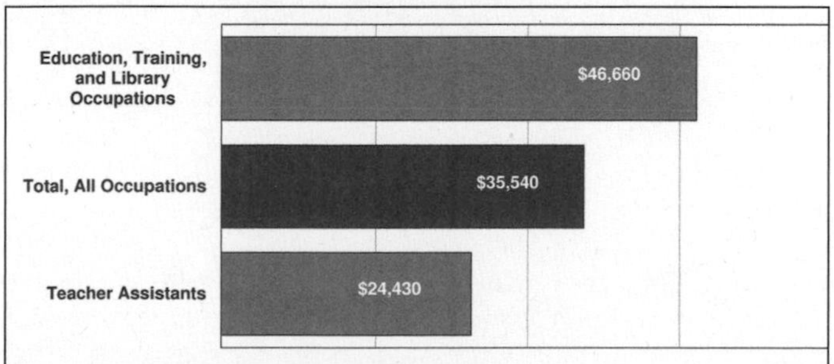

Note: All Occupations includes all occupations in the U.S. Economy.
Source: U.S. Bureau of Labor Statistics, Occupational Employment Statistics

Percent Change in Employment, Projected 2014–2024

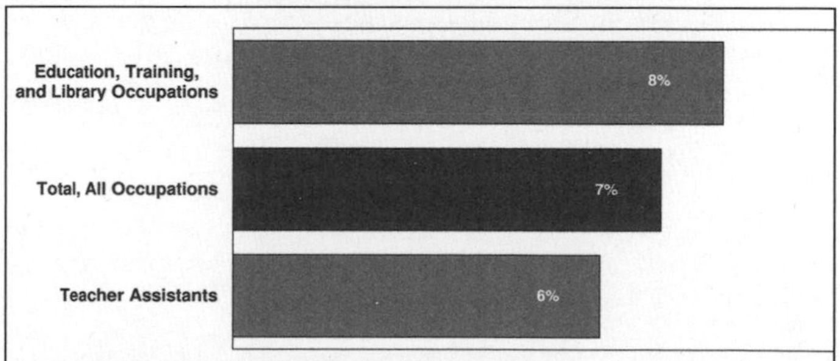

Note: All Occupations includes all occupations in the U.S. Economy.
Source: U.S. Bureau of Labor Statistics, Office of Occupational Statistics and Employment Projections

Employment Projections Data for Teacher Assistants

Occupational Title	SOC Code	Employment, 2014	Projected Employment, 2024	Change, 2014–2024	
				Percent	Numeric
Teacher assistants	25-9041	1,234,100	1,312,800	6	78,600

Source: U.S. Bureau of Labor Statistics, Employment Projections Program

Similar Occupations. This table shows a list of occupations with job duties that are similar to those of teacher assistants.

Occupations	Entry-level Education	2014 Median Pay	Projected Job Growth	Average Annual Openings
Career and Technical Education Teachers	Bachelor's degree	$51,830	4%	1,020
Childcare Workers	High school diploma or equivalent	$19,730	5%	6,930
High School Teachers	Bachelor's degree	$56,310	6%	5,590
Kindergarten and Elementary School Teachers	Bachelor's degree	$53,760	6%	8,780
Library Technicians and Assistants	See Education/Training	$27,420	5%	1,120
Middle School Teachers	Bachelor's degree	$54,940	6%	3,680
Occupational Therapy Assistants and Aides	See Education/Training	$52,300	40%	1,680
Preschool Teachers	Associate's degree	$28,120	7%	2,960
Special Education Teachers	Bachelor's degree	$55,980	6%	2,810

Patience. Working with students of different abilities and backgrounds can be difficult. Teacher assistants must be patient with students who struggle with material.

Resourcefulness. To reinforce lessons, teacher assistants must explain information to students in a way that meets each student's learning style.

Pay

The median annual wage for teacher assistants was $24,430 in May 2014. The median wage is the wage at which half the workers in an occupation earned more than that amount and half earned less. The lowest 10 percent earned less than $17,510, and the highest 10 percent earned more than $37,270.

About 2 in 5 teacher assistants worked part time in 2014. Some monitor students on school buses before and after school. Although many do not work during the summer, some work in year-round schools or assist teachers in summer school.

Union Membership. Compared with workers in all occupations, teacher assistants had a higher percentage of workers who belonged to a union in 2014.

Job Outlook

Employment of teacher assistants is projected to grow 6 percent from 2014 to 2024, about as fast as the average for all occupations. Student enrollment is expected to increase from 2014 to 2024. The increase in the number of students will affect the average classroom size, possibly spurring demand for teacher assistants. In addition, there will be continued demand for special education services and, in turn, demand for teacher assistants who work with these students.

Teacher assistants' positions are more of a supplementary position, as opposed to teachers, who hold a primary position. Therefore, teacher assistants' employment opportunities may be limited because school districts are more likely to eliminate teacher assistant positions rather than teacher positions when there are budget cuts.

Job Prospects. In addition to job openings due to employment growth, numerous openings will arise as assistants leave the occupation and must be replaced. Because of the education requirements and low pay, many workers transfer to other occupations or leave the labor force to take care of family responsibilities, to return to school, or for other reasons.

Contacts for More Information

For more information about teacher assistants, visit

- National Education Association (www.nea.org)
- American Federation of Teachers (www.aft.org)
- National Resource Center for Paraeducators (www.nrcpara.org)

O*NET

- Teacher Assistants (25-9041.00)

Entertainment and Sports

Actors

- **2014 Median Pay** .... $19.82 per hour
- **Typical Entry-Level Education** .... Some college, no degree
- **Work Experience in a Related Occupation** .... None
- **On-the-job Training** .... Long-term on-the-job training
- **Number of Jobs, 2014** 69,400
- **Job Outlook, 2014–24** .... 10% (Faster than average)
- **Employment Change, 2014–24** 6,600

What Actors Do

Actors express ideas and portray characters in theater, film, television, and other performing arts media. They interpret a writer's script to entertain or inform an audience.

Duties. Actors typically do the following:

- Read scripts and meet with agents and other professionals before accepting a role
- Audition in front of directors, producers, and casting directors
- Research their character's personal traits and circumstances to portray the characters more authentically to an audience
- Memorize their lines
- Rehearse their lines and performance, including on stage or in front of the camera, with other actors
- Discuss their role with the director, producer, and other actors to improve the overall performance of the show
- Perform the role, following the director's directions

Most actors struggle to find steady work, and few achieve recognition as stars. Some work as "extras"—actors who have no lines to deliver but are included in scenes to give a more realistic setting. Some actors do voiceover or narration work for animated features, audiobooks, or other electronic media.

In some stage or film productions, actors sing, dance, or play a musical instrument. For some roles, an actor must learn a new skill, such as horseback riding or stage fighting.

Most actors have long periods of unemployment between roles and often hold other jobs in order to make a living. Some actors teach acting classes as a second job.

Work Environment

Actors held about 69,400 jobs in 2014. They work in various settings, including production studios, theaters, theme parks, or on location. About 1 out of 5 actors were self-employed in 2014.

Work assignments are usually short, ranging from 1 day to a few months, and actors often hold another job in order to make a living. They are frequently under the stress of having to find their next job. Some actors in touring companies may have employment for several years.

Actors may perform in unpleasant conditions, such as in outdoors in bad weather or while wearing an uncomfortable costume or makeup.

Work Schedules. Work hours for actors are extensive and irregular. Early morning, evening, weekend, and holiday work is common. About 1 out of 3 actors worked part time in 2014. Few actors work full time, and many have variable schedules. Those who work in theater may travel with a touring show across the country. Film and television actors may also travel to work on location.

Education/Training

Many actors enhance their skills through formal dramatic education, and long-term training is common.

Education. Formal education in drama is a common entry route for actors. Many who specialize in theater have bachelor's degrees, but a degree is not required.

Although some people succeed in acting without getting a formal education, most actors acquire some formal preparation through a theater company's acting conservatory or a university drama or theater arts program. Students can take college classes in drama or filmmaking to prepare for a career as an actor. Classes in dance or music may help as well.

Actors who do not have a college degree may take acting or film classes to learn their craft. Community colleges, acting conservatories, and private film schools typically offer these classes. Many theater companies also have education programs.

Important Qualities

Creativity. Actors interpret their characters' feelings and motives in order to portray the characters in the most compelling way.

Memorization skills. Actors memorize many lines before filming begins or a show opens. Television actors often appear on camera with little time to memorize scripts, and scripts frequently may be revised or even written just moments before filming.

Persistence. They must be able to accept rejection and keep going.

Physical stamina. Actors should be in good enough physical condition to endure the heat from stage or studio lights and the weight of heavy costumes or makeup. They may work many hours, including acting in more than one performance a day, and they must do so without getting overly tired.

Reading skills. Actors must read scripts and be able to interpret how a writer has developed their character.

Speaking skills. Actors—particularly stage actors—must be able to say their lines clearly, project their voice, and pronounce words so that audiences understand them.

Actors spend a lot of time rehearsing their lines.

Median Hourly Wages, May 2014

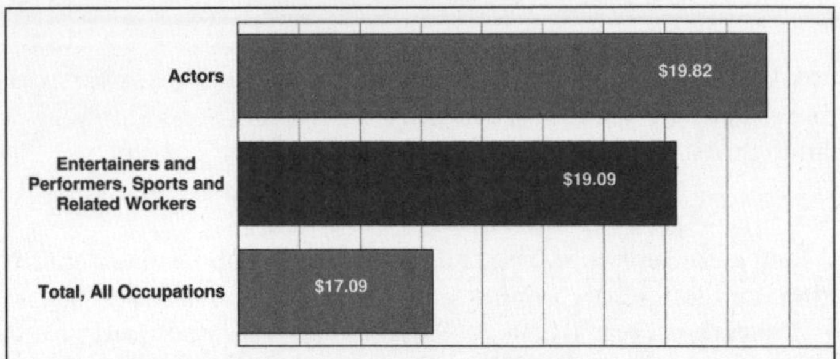

Note: All Occupations includes all occupations in the U.S. Economy.
Source: U.S. Bureau of Labor Statistics, Occupational Employment Statistics

Percent Change in Employment, Projected 2014–2024

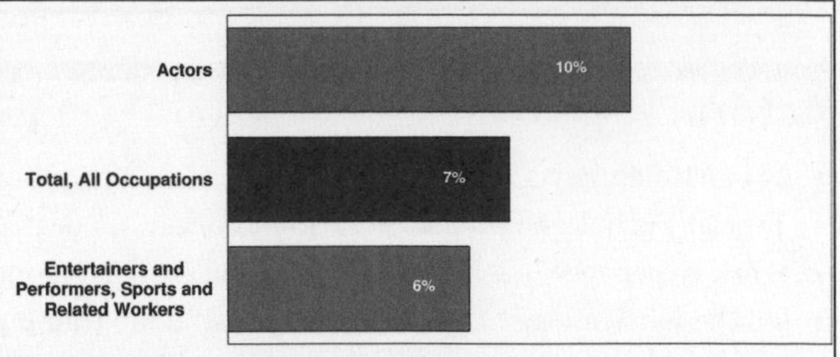

Note: All Occupations includes all occupations in the U.S. Economy.
Source: U.S. Bureau of Labor Statistics, Office of Occupational Statistics and Employment Projections

In addition to these qualities, actors usually must be physically coordinated to perform predetermined, sometimes complex movements with other actors, such as dancing or stage fighting, in order to complete a scene.

Training. It takes many years of practice to develop the skills needed to be successful as an actor, and actors never truly finish training. They work to improve their acting skills throughout their career. Many actors continue to train through workshops, rehearsals, or mentoring by a drama coach.

Every role is different, and an actor may need to learn something new for each one. For example, a role may require learning how to sing or dance, or an actor may have to learn to speak with an accent or to play a musical instrument or sport.

Many aspiring actors begin by participating in school plays or local theater productions. In television and film, actors usually start out in smaller roles or independent movies and work their way up to bigger productions.

Advancement. As an actor's reputation grows, he or she may work on bigger projects or in more prestigious venues. Some actors become producers and directors.

Pay

The median hourly wage for actors was $19.82 in May 2014. The median wage is the wage at which half the workers in an occupation earned more than that amount and half earned less. The lowest 10 percent earned less than $9.00, and the highest 10 percent earned more than $90.00.

Union Membership. Compared with workers in all occupations, actors had a higher percentage of workers who belonged to a union in 2014. Many film and television actors join the Screen Actors Guild-American Federation of Television and Radio Artists (SAG-AFTRA), whereas many stage actors join the Actors' Equity Association. Union membership can help set work rules and with benefits, and assist actors to receive bigger parts for more pay. Union dues can be expensive; however, for actors who are beginning their careers.

Job Outlook

Employment of actors is projected to grow 10 percent from 2014 to 2024, faster than the average for all occupations. Job growth in the

Employment Projections Data for Actors

Occupational Title	SOC Code	Employment, 2014	Projected Employment, 2024	Change, 2014–2024 Percent	Change, 2014–2024 Numeric
Actors	27-2011	69,400	76,100	10	6,600

Source: U.S. Bureau of Labor Statistics, Employment Projections Program

Similar Occupations. This table shows a list of occupations with job duties that are similar to those of actors.

Occupations	Entry-level Education	2014 Median Pay	Projected Job Growth	Average Annual Openings
Announcers	See Education/Training	$29,010	-11%	-580
Dancers and Choreographers	See Education/Training	The annual wage is not available.	5%	110
Film and Video Editors and Camera Operators	Bachelor's degree	$52,470	11%	640
Multimedia Artists and Animators	Bachelor's degree	$63,630	6%	390
Musicians and Singers	No formal educational credential	The annual wage is not available.	3%	600
Producers and Directors	Bachelor's degree	$69,100	9%	1,110

motion picture industry will stem from continued strong demand for new movies and television shows.

Production companies are experimenting with new content delivery methods, such as video on demand and online television, which may lead to more work for actors in the future. However, these delivery methods are still in their early stages, and it remains to be seen how successful they will be.

Actors who work in performing arts companies are expected to see slower job growth than those in film. Many small and medium-size theaters have difficulty getting funding. As a result, the number of performances is expected to decline. Large theaters, with their more stable sources of funding and more well-known plays and musicals, should provide more opportunities.

Job Prospects. Actors face intense competition for jobs. Most roles, no matter how minor, have many actors auditioning for them. For stage roles, actors with a bachelor's degree in theater may have a better chance than those without one.

Contacts for More Information

For more information about actors, visit

- ➤ Actors' Equity Association (www.actorsequity.org)
- ➤ National Endowment for the Arts (www.nea.gov)
- ➤ SAG-AFTRA (www.sagaftra.org)

O*NET

- ➤ Actors (27-2011.00)

Athletes and Sports Competitors

- **2014 Median Pay** .... $43,350 per year
- **Typical Entry-Level Education** .... No formal educational credential
- **Work Experience in a Related Occupation**.............. None
- **On-the-job Training** .... Long-term on-the-job training
- **Number of Jobs, 2014** 13,700
- **Job Outlook, 2014–24** .... 6% (As fast as average)
- **Employment Change, 2014–24** 800

What Athletes and Sports Competitors Do

Athletes and sports competitors participate in organized, officiated sporting events to entertain spectators.

Duties. Athletes and sports competitors typically do the following:

- Practice to develop and improve their skills
- Maintain their sports equipment in good condition
- Train, exercise, and follow special diets to stay in the best physical condition
- Take instructions from coaches and other sports staff during games regarding strategy and tactics
- Follow the rules of the sport during competitions and games
- Assess their individual and team performance after each event and identify their strengths and weaknesses

Many people dream of becoming a paid professional athlete. Few people, however, beat the odds and make a full-time living from professional athletics. And when they do, professional athletes often have short careers with little job security.

When playing a game, athletes and sports competitors must understand the game strategies while following the rules and regulations of the sport. The events in which athletes compete include team sports, such as baseball, softball, hockey, and soccer, and individual sports, such as golf, tennis, swimming, and skiing. The level of play varies greatly. Some athletes may compete in regional competitions, while other athletes compete in national or international events.

Athletes and sports competitors practice under the direction of coaches, sports instructors, or athletic trainers.

Being an athlete involves more than competing in athletic events. Athletes spend most days practicing skills and improving teamwork under the guidance of a coach or a sports instructor. They review videotapes to critique and improve their own performances and techniques. Athletes must also study their opponents' tendencies and weaknesses so as to gain a competitive advantage.

Some athletes work regularly with fitness trainers and instructors to gain muscle and stamina and to prevent injury. Because of the physical demands required by many sports, career-ending injuries are always a risk. Even minor injuries may put a player at risk of replacement.

Because competition at all levels is extremely intense and job security is always in question, many athletes train throughout the year to maintain or improve their form and technique and remain in peak physical condition. Very little downtime from the sport exists at the professional level.

Work Environment

Athletes and sports competitors held about 13,700 jobs in 2014. More than half were employed in the spectator sports industry.

Athletes and sports competitors who participate in outdoor competitions may be exposed to all weather conditions of the season in which they play their sport. Additionally, many athletes must travel to sporting events, which may include long bus rides or plane trips, and, in some cases, international travel.

Work Schedules. Athletes and sports competitors often work irregular hours, including evenings, weekends, and holidays. During the sports season, they usually work more than 40 hours a week for several months as they practice, train, travel, and compete in events.

Injuries and Illnesses. Athletes who play a contact sport, such as football or hockey, are highly susceptible to injuries. Because of this, many athletes wear pads, gloves, goggles, helmets, and other protective gear to protect against injury.

Median Annual Wages, May 2014

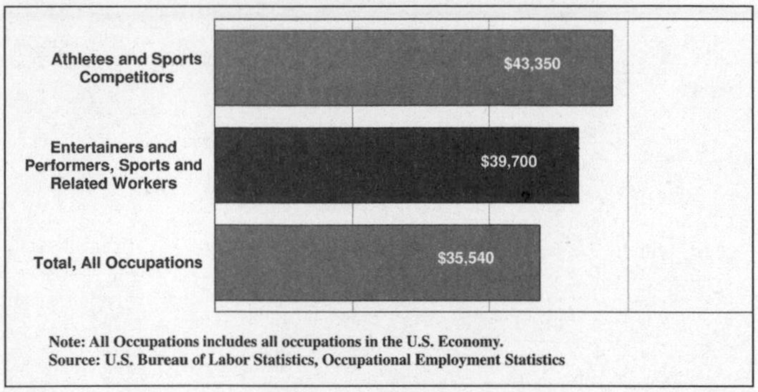

Percent Change in Employment, Projected 2014–2024

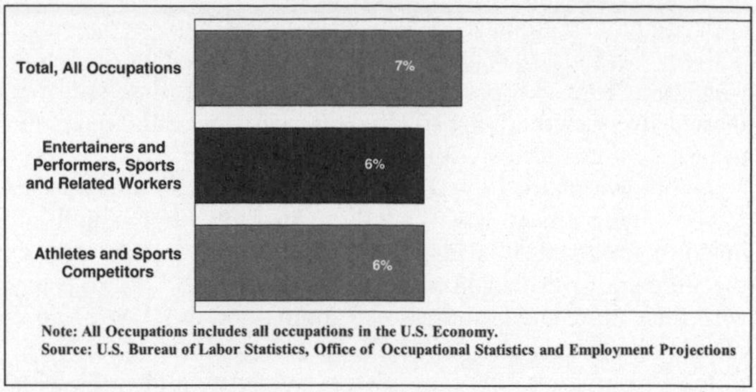

Education/Training

No formal educational credential is required to become an athlete or sports competitor. Athletes must have superior athletic talent and immense knowledge of their sport, which they usually get through years of experience at lower levels of competition.

Education. Although athletes and sports competitors typically have at least a high school diploma or equivalent, no formal educational credential is required to enter the occupation. They must have extensive knowledge of the way the sport is played, especially its rules, regulations, and strategies.

Other Experience. Athletes typically learn the rules of the game and develop their skills by playing the sport at lower levels of competition. For most sports, athletes compete in high school and collegiate athletics or on club teams. In addition, athletes may improve their skills by taking private or group lessons or attending sports camps.

Training. It typically takes many years of practice and experience to become an athlete or sports competitor.

Licenses, Certifications, and Registrations. Some sports and localities require athletes and sports competitors to be licensed or certified to practice. For example, racecar drivers need to be licensed to compete in the various races. The governing body of the sport may revoke licenses and suspend participants who do not meet the required performance or training. In addition, athletes may have their licenses or certification suspended for inappropriate activity.

Advancement. Turning professional is often the biggest advancement that an aspiring athlete can make in his or her career. They often begin to compete immediately, although some may spend more time on the bench (as a reserve) to gain experience. In some sports, such as baseball, athletes may begin their professional career on a minor league team before moving up to the major leagues. Professional athletes generally advance in their sport by displaying superior performance and receiving accolades, and in turn they earn a higher salary. Others may receive endorsements from companies and brands.

Important Qualities

Athleticism. Nearly all athletes and sports competitors must possess superior athletic ability to be able to compete successfully against opponents.

Concentration. Athletes and sports competitors must be extremely focused when competing and block out distractions from fans and opponents. The difference between winning and losing can often be a result of a momentary lapse in concentration.

Decision-making skills. Athletes and sports competitors often must make split-second decisions. Football quarterbacks, for example, usually only have seconds to decide whether to pass the football or not.

Dedication. Athletes and sports competitors must practice regularly to develop their skills and improve or maintain their physical conditioning. It often takes years to become successful, so athletes must be dedicated to their sport.

Hand-eye coordination. For many sports, including tennis and baseball, the need to gauge and strike a fast-moving ball is highly dependent on the athlete's hand-eye coordination.

Stamina. Endurance can benefit athletes and sports competitors, particularly those athletes who participate in long-lasting sports competitions, such as marathons.

Teamwork. Because many athletes compete in a team sport, such as hockey or soccer, the ability to work with teammates as a cohesive unit is important for success.

Many professional athletes are also required to pass drug tests.

Pay

The median annual wage for athletes and sports competitors was $43,350 in May 2014. The median wage is the wage at which half the workers in an occupation earned more than that amount and half earned less. The lowest 10 percent earned less than $20,190, and the highest 10 percent earned more than $187,200.

Job Outlook

Employment of athletes and sports competitors is projected to grow 6 percent from 2014 to 2024, about as fast as the average

Employment Projections Data for Athletes and Sports Competitors

Occupational Title	SOC Code	Employment, 2014	Projected Employment, 2024	Change, 2014–2024 Percent	Change, 2014–2024 Numeric
Athletes and sports competitors	27-2021	13,700	14,500	6	800

Source: U.S. Bureau of Labor Statistics, Employment Projections Program

Similar Occupations. This table shows a list of occupations with job duties that are similar to those of athletes and sports competitors.

Occupations	Entry-level Education	2014 Median Pay	Projected Job Growth	Average Annual Openings
Coaches and Scouts	Bachelor's degree	$30,640	6%	1,480
Fitness Trainers and Instructors	High school diploma or equivalent	$34,980	8%	2,340
Recreation Workers	High school diploma or equivalent	$22,620	10%	3,890
Umpires, Referees, and Other Sports Officials	High school diploma or equivalent	$24,090	5%	100

for all occupations. Growth will be primarily due to population growth and increasing public interest in professional sports.

Growth and geographic shifts in population may lead to an increase in the number of professional sports teams. Some professional sports leagues may expand to new cities in the United States, creating new teams and new job opportunities for those looking to become professional athletes.

However, expansion is rare in professional sports leagues. Creating new teams is very costly and risky, requiring strong support from fans and both local and state government. When leagues do expand, they typically only create one or two teams at a time. Conversely, some teams and sports leagues may disband altogether because of a lack of interest in the sport.

Instead, some teams simply relocate to another city that has a greater interest in the sport and a larger fan base. In this case no new jobs for athletes would be created.

Job Prospects. Competition for professional athlete jobs will continue to be extremely intense. Very few high school or college athletes become professional athletes. In a major sport, such as basketball, only about 1 in 3,000 high school athletes make it to the professional level.

Most professional athletes can deliver peak performances for only a short time. Careers last only a few years because of debilitating injuries or retirements. Yearly replacement needs for these jobs is high and may create some job opportunities.

However, the talented young men and women who dream of becoming sports superstars greatly outnumber the number of openings.

Contacts for More Information

For more information about team and individual sports, visit

- National Collegiate Athletic Association (www.ncaa.org)
- National Council of Youth Sports (www.ncys.org)
- National Federation of State High School Associations (www.nfhs.org)

For more information related to individual sports, refer to the organization that represents the sport.

O*NET

- Athletes and Sports Competitors (27-2021.00)

Coaches and Scouts

- **2014 Median Pay** .... $30,640 per year
- **Typical Entry-Level Education** .... Bachelor's degree
- **Work Experience in a Related Occupation**.............. None
- **On-the-job Training** .... None
- **Number of Jobs, 2014** 250,600
- **Job Outlook, 2014–24**................. 6% (As fast as average)
- **Employment Change, 2014–24** 14,800

What Coaches and Scouts Do

Coaches teach amateur and professional athletes the skills they need to succeed at their sport. Scouts look for new players, evaluating their skills and likelihood for success at the college, amateur, or professional level. Many coaches are also involved in scouting potential athletes.

Duties. Coaches typically do the following:

- Plan, organize, and conduct practice sessions
- Analyze the strengths and weaknesses of individual athletes and opposing teams
- Plan strategies and choose team members for each game
- Provide direction, encouragement, and motivation to prepare athletes for games
- Call plays and make decisions about strategy and player substitutions during games
- Plan and direct physical conditioning programs that enable athletes to achieve maximum performance
- Instruct athletes on proper techniques, game strategies, sportsmanship, and the rules of the sport
- Keep records of athletes' and opponents' performance
- Identify and recruit potential athletes
- Arrange for and offer incentives to prospective players

Coaches teach professional and amateur athletes the fundamental skills of individual and team sports. They hold training and practice sessions to improve the athletes' form, technique, skills, and stamina. Along with refining athletes' individual skills, coaches are also responsible for instilling in their players the importance of good sportsmanship, a competitive spirit, and teamwork.

Many coaches evaluate their opponents to determine game strategies and to establish specific plays to practice. During competition, coaches call specific plays intended to surprise or overpower the opponent, and they may substitute players for optimum team chemistry and success.

Many high school coaches are primarily academic teachers or other school administrators who supplement their income by coaching part time.

Some people who teach the fundamental skills of individual and teams sports may be known as *sports instructors* rather than coaches. Like coaches, sports instructors hold practice sessions, assign specific drills, and correct athletes' techniques. They may spend their time working one-on-one with athletes, designing customized training programs for each individual. Sports instructors may specialize in teaching athletes the skills of an individual sport, such as tennis, golf, or karate. Some sports instructors, such as pitching instructors in baseball, may teach individual athletes involved in team sports.

However, many sports instructors work with people who simply have an interest in learning a new sport rather than athletes competing in events. For example, a skiing instructor may give individual or group lessons to those interested in learning how to ski.

Scouts typically do the following:

- Read newspapers and other news sources to find athletes to consider
- Attend games, view videotapes of the athletes' performances, and study statistics about the athletes to determine talent and potential
- Talk to the athlete and the coaches to see if the athlete has what it takes to succeed
- Report to the coach, manager, or owner of the team for which he or she is scouting
- Arrange for and offer incentives to prospective players

Scouts evaluate the skills of both amateur and professional athletes. Scouts seek out top athletic candidates for colleges or professional teams and evaluate their likelihood of success at a higher competitive level.

Work Environment

Coaches and scouts held about 250,600 jobs in 2014. The industries that employed the most coaches and scouts were as follows:

Elementary and secondary schools; state, local, and private	24%
Arts, entertainment, and recreation	20
Colleges, universities, and professional schools; state, local, and private	20

About 1 in 10 were self-employed in 2014.

Some scouts may work for organizations that work directly with high school athletes. These scouts collect information on the athlete and help promote him or her to potential colleges.

At the college level, scouts typically work for scouting organizations or as self-employed scouts to help colleges recruit the best high school athletes.

Scouts at the professional level are typically employed by the team or organization directly.

Those people who coach and scout for outdoor sports may be exposed to all weather conditions of the season. In addition, they must travel often to attend sporting events. This is particularly true for those in professional sports.

Work Schedules. Coaches and scouts often work irregular hours, including evenings, weekends, and holidays. Professional or college coaches usually work more than 40 hours a week for several months during the sport's season, if not most of the year. Many high school coaches work part time and may have other jobs aside from coaching.

Education/Training

Coaches and scouts typically need a bachelor's degree. They must also have extensive knowledge of the sport. Coaches typically gain this knowledge through their own experiences playing the sport at some level. Although previous playing experience may be beneficial, it is not required for most scouting jobs.

Education. College and professional coaches must usually have a bachelor's degree. This degree can typically be in any subject. However, some coaches may decide to study exercise and sports science, physiology, kinesiology, nutrition and fitness, physical education, and sports medicine.

High schools typically hire teachers or administrators at the school for most coaching jobs. If no suitable teacher is found, schools hire a qualified candidate from outside the school. For more information on education requirements for teachers, see the profile on high school teachers.

Scouts must also typically have a bachelor's degree. Some scouts decide to get a degree in business, marketing, sales, or sports management.

Other Experience. College and professional coaching jobs also typically require experience playing the sport at some level.

Scouting jobs typically do not require experience playing a sport at the college or professional level, but it can be beneficial. Employers look for applicants with a passion for sports and an ability to spot young players who have exceptional athletic ability and skills.

Licenses, Certifications, and Registrations. Most state high school athletic associations require coaches to be certified or at least complete mandatory education courses.

Certification often requires coaches to be a minimum age (at least 18 years old) and be trained in cardiopulmonary resuscitation (CPR) and first aid. Some states also require coaches to attend classes related to sports safety and coaching fundamentals prior to becoming certified. For information of specific state coaching requirements, contact the state's high school athletic association or visit the National Association of State Boards of Education.

Although most public high school coaches need to meet these state requirements in order to become a coach, certification may not be required for coaching and sports instructor jobs in private schools.

Some schools may require coaches to have a teaching license and complete a background check.

Certification requirements for college coaching positions also vary.

Additional certification may be highly desirable or even required in order to become an instructor in scuba diving, tennis, golf, karate, or other individual sports. There are many certifying

Coaches organize amateur and professional athletes and teach them the fundamental skills of individual and team sports.

Median Annual Wages, May 2014

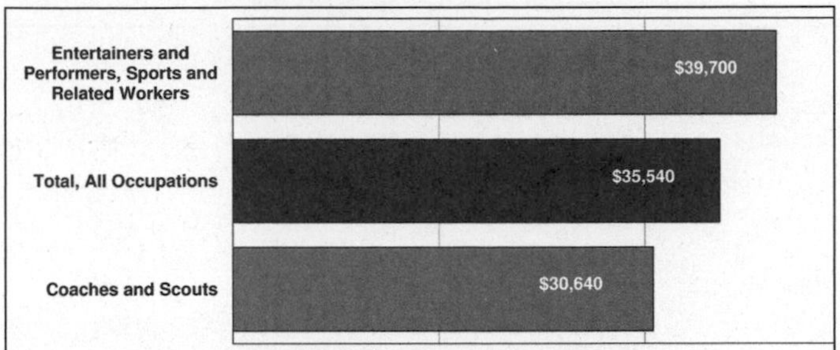

Note: All Occupations includes all occupations in the U.S. Economy.
Source: U.S. Bureau of Labor Statistics, Occupational Employment Statistics

Percent Change in Employment, Projected 2014–2024

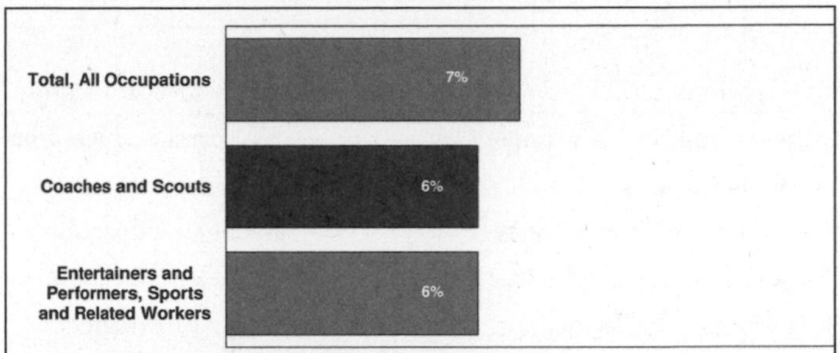

Note: All Occupations includes all occupations in the U.S. Economy.
Source: U.S. Bureau of Labor Statistics, Office of Occupational Statistics and Employment Projections

organizations specific to the various sports, and their requirements vary.

Part-time workers and those in smaller facilities or youth leagues are less likely to need formal education or training and may not need certification.

Advancement. To reach the ranks of professional coaches, a candidate usually needs years of coaching experience and a winning record at a college. Some coaches may not have previous coaching experience but are nevertheless hired at the professional level due to their success as an athlete in that sport.

Some college coaches begin their careers as graduate assistants or assistant coaches to gain the knowledge and experience needed to become a head coach. Large schools and colleges that compete at the highest levels require a head coach with substantial experience at another school or as an assistant coach.

Other college coaches may start out as high school coaches before moving up to the collegiate level.

Scouts may begin working as talent spotters in a particular area or region. They typically advance to become supervising scouts responsible for a whole territory or region.

Important Qualities

Communication skills. Because coaches instruct, organize, and motivate athletes, they must have excellent communication skills. They must effectively communicate proper techniques, strategies, and rules of the sport so every player on the team understands.

Decision-making skills. Coaches must choose the appropriate players to use at a given position at a given time during a game and know the proper time to utilize game-managing tools such as timeouts. Coaches and scouts also must be very selective when recruiting players from lower levels of athletics.

Dedication. Coaches must attend daily practices and assist their team and individual athletes in improving their skills and physical conditioning. Coaches must be dedicated to their sport, as it often takes years to become successful.

Interpersonal skills. Being able to relate to athletes helps coaches and scouts foster positive relationships with their current players and recruit potential players.

Leadership skills. Coaches must demonstrate good leadership skills to get the most out of athletes. They also must be able to motivate, develop, and direct young athletes.

Resourcefulness. Coaches must find a strategy and develop a game plan that yields the best chances for winning. Coaches often need to create original plays or formations that provide a competitive advantage and confuse opponents.

Pay

The median annual wage for coaches and scouts was $30,640 in May 2014. The median wage is the wage at which half the workers in an occupation earned more than that amount and half earned less. The lowest 10 percent earned less than $17,570, and the highest 10 percent earned more than $68,950.

In May 2014, the median annual wages for coaches and scouts in the top industries in which they worked were as follows:

Colleges, universities, and professional schools; state, local, and private	$42,500
Arts, entertainment, and recreation	32,580
Elementary and secondary schools; state, local, and private	25,320

Job Outlook

Employment of coaches and scouts is projected to grow 6 percent from 2014 to 2024, about as fast as the average for all occupations. Rising participation in high school and college sports should increase demand for coaches and scouts.

High school enrollment is projected to increase over the next decade, resulting in a rise in the number of student-athletes. As schools offer more athletic programs and more students participate in sports, the demand for coaches may increase.

Participation in college sports is also projected to increase over the next decade, particularly at smaller colleges and in women's sports. Many small, Division-III colleges are expanding their sports programs and adding new teams as a way to help promote the school and recruit potential students. However, new rules allowing an increase in scholarship payments to student-athletes

Employment Projections Data for Coaches and Scouts

Occupational Title	SOC Code	Employment, 2014	Projected Employment, 2024	Change, 2014–2024 Percent	Change, 2014–2024 Numeric
Coaches and scouts	27-2022	250,600	265,400	6	14,800

Source: U.S. Bureau of Labor Statistics, Employment Projections Program

Similar Occupations. This table shows a list of occupations with job duties that are similar to those of coaches and scouts.

Occupations	Entry-level Education	2014 Median Pay	Projected Job Growth	Average Annual Openings
Athletes and Sports Competitors	No formal educational credential	$43,350	6%	80
Athletic Trainers	Bachelor's degree	$43,370	21%	540
Dietitians and Nutritionists	Bachelor's degree	$56,950	16%	1,100
Fitness Trainers and Instructors	High school diploma or equivalent	$34,980	8%	2,340
High School Teachers	Bachelor's degree	$56,310	6%	5,590
Kindergarten and Elementary School Teachers	Bachelor's degree	$53,760	6%	8,780
Middle School Teachers	Bachelor's degree	$54,940	6%	3,680
Umpires, Referees, and Other Sports Officials	High school diploma or equivalent	$24,090	5%	100

may result in funding cuts to smaller collegiate sports programs and the accompanying coaching staffs.

The growing interest in college and professional sports will also increase demand for scouts. Colleges must attract the best athletes to remain competitive. Successful teams help colleges enhance their reputation, recruit future students, and raise donations from alumni. Colleges, therefore, will increasingly rely on scouts to recruit the best possible high school athletes. In addition, as college tuition increases and scholarships become more competitive, high school athletes will hire scouts directly, in an effort to increase their chances of receiving a college scholarship.

However, funding for athletic programs at schools often is cut first when budgets become tight. For example, some high schools within the same school district may combine their sports programs in an effort to cut costs. Still, the popularity of team sports often enables shortfalls to be offset with help from fundraisers, booster clubs, and parents.

Job Prospects. Strong competition is expected for higher paying jobs at the college level and will be even greater for jobs in professional sports.

Job prospects at the high school level should be good, but coaching jobs typically go to those teaching in the school. Those who have a degree or are state certified to teach academic subjects, therefore, should have the best prospects for getting coaching and instructor jobs at high schools. The need to replace the amount of high school coaches who change occupations or leave the labor force also will provide some jobs.

Coaches in girls' and women's sports may have better job opportunities due to a growing number of participants and leagues.

Competition is also likely to be strong for jobs as scouts, particularly for professional teams.

Contacts for More Information

For more information about coaching and scouting for team and individual sports, visit

➤ National Collegiate Scouting Association (www.ncsasports.org)
➤ National High School Coaches Association (www.nhsca.com)
➤ National Association of State Boards of Education (www.nasbe.org)

For more information related to individual sports, refer to the organization that represents the sport.

O*NET

➤ Coaches and Scouts (27-2022.00)

Dancers and Choreographers

- **2014 Median Pay** .... $16.87 per hour
- **Typical Entry-Level Education** .... See Education/Training
- **Work Experience in a Related Occupation** .... See Education/Training
- **On-the-job Training** .... Long-term on-the-job training
- **Number of Jobs, 2014** 20,100
- **Job Outlook, 2014–24** .... 5% (As fast as average)
- **Employment Change, 2014–24** 1,100

What Dancers and Choreographers Do

Dancers and choreographers use dance performances to express ideas and stories. There are many types of dance, such as ballet, tango, modern dance, tap, and jazz.

Duties. Dancers typically do the following:

- Audition for a part in a show or for a job within a dance company
- Learn complex dance movements that entertain an audience
- Rehearse several hours each day to prepare for their performance
- Study new and emerging types of dance
- Work closely with instructors, choreographers, or other dancers to interpret or modify their routines
- Attend promotional events, such as photography sessions, for the production in which they are appearing

Dancers spend years learning dances and perfecting their skills. They usually perform as part of a group and know a variety of dance styles, including ballet, musical theater, and modern dance. In addition to traditional performances in front of a live audience, many perform on TV, in videos on the Internet, and in music videos, where they also may sing or act. Many dancers perform in shows at casinos, theme parks, and on cruise ships.

Choreographers typically do the following:

- Put together moves in a sequence to create dances or interpretations of existing dances
- Choose the music that will accompany a dance routine
- Audition dancers for a role in a show or within a dance company

- Assist with costume design, lighting, and other artistic aspects of a show
- Teach complex dance movements
- Study new and emerging types of dance to design more creative dance routines
- Help with the administrative duties of a dance company, such as budgeting

Choreographers create original dances and develop new interpretations of existing dances. They work in theaters, dance companies, and movie studios. During rehearsals, they typically demonstrate dance moves, to instruct dancers in the proper technique. Many choreographers also perform the dance routines they create. Some choreographers work with performers who are not trained dancers. For example, the complex martial arts scenes performed by actors in movies are arranged by choreographers who specialize in martial arts.

Some dancers and choreographers hold other jobs between roles to make a living. Some people with dance backgrounds become dance teachers.

Work Environment

Dancers and choreographers held about 20,100 jobs in 2014. The industries that employed the most dancers and choreographers were as follows:

Educational services; state, local, and private	28%
Performing arts companies	24
Amusement, gambling, and recreation industries	9
Drinking places (alcoholic beverages)	9
Spectator sports	4

About half of dancers and choreographers worked in schools and performing arts companies in 2014. About 1 in 7 were self-employed.

Injuries and Illnesses. Dance takes a toll on a person's body, so on-the-job injuries for dancers are common. Many dancers stop performing by the time they reach their late thirties because of the physical demands of their work. Nonperforming dancers may continue to work as choreographers, directors, or dance teachers.

Work Schedules. Schedules for dancers and choreographers vary, depending on where they work. During tours, dancers and choreographers have long workdays, rehearsing most of the day and performing at night. Some work part time at casinos, on cruise ships, and at theme parks.

Choreographers who work in dance schools may have a standard workweek when they are instructing students. They also spend hours working independently to create new dance routines.

Dancers work closely with instructors, choreographers, or other dancers to interpret or modify their routines.

Education/Training

Education and training requirements vary with the type of dancer; however, all dancers need many years of formal training. Nearly all choreographers began their careers as dancers.

Education and Training. Many dancers begin training when they are young and continue to learn throughout their careers. Ballet dancers begin training the earliest, usually between the ages of 5 and 8 for girls and a few years later for boys. Their training becomes more serious as they enter their teens, and most ballet dancers begin their professional careers by the time they are 18.

Leading professional dance companies sometimes have intensive summer training programs from which they might select candidates for admission to their regular full-time training programs.

Modern dancers normally begin formal training while they are in high school. They attend after-school dance programs and summer training programs to prepare for their career or for a college dance program.

Some dancers and choreographers pursue postsecondary education. Many colleges and universities offer bachelor's and/or master's degrees in dance, typically through departments of theater or fine arts. In March 2015, there were about 85 dance programs accredited by the National Association of Schools of Dance. Most programs include coursework in a variety of dance styles, including modern, jazz, ballet, and hip-hop. Most entrants into college dance programs have previous formal training.

Some choreographers work as dance teachers. Teaching dance in a college, high school, or elementary school requires a college

Median Hourly Wages, May 2014

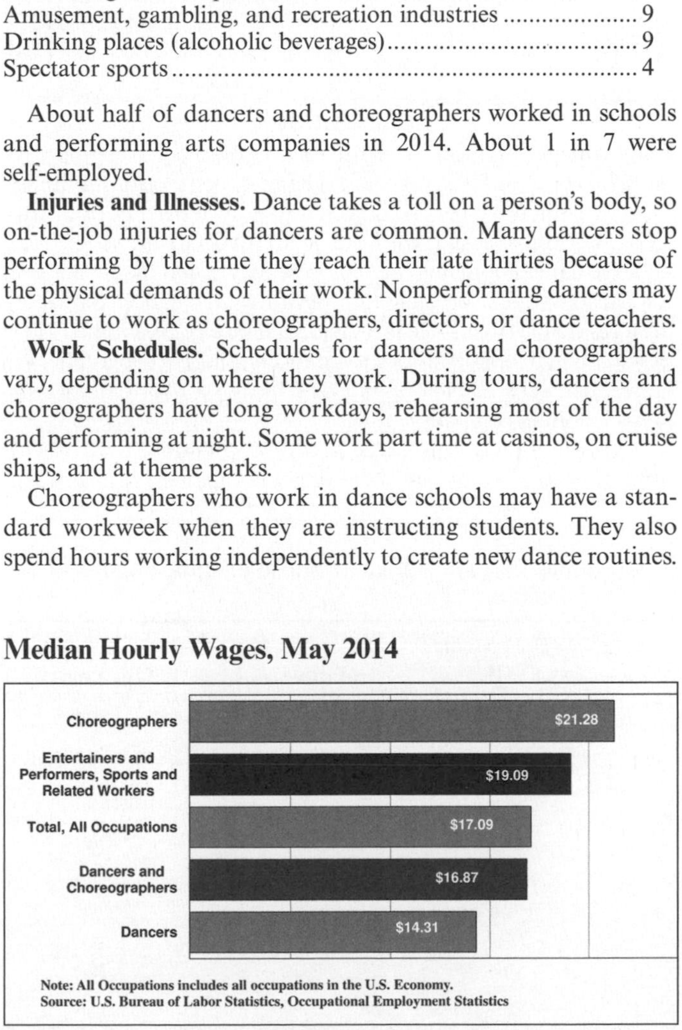

Percent Change in Employment, Projected 2014–2024

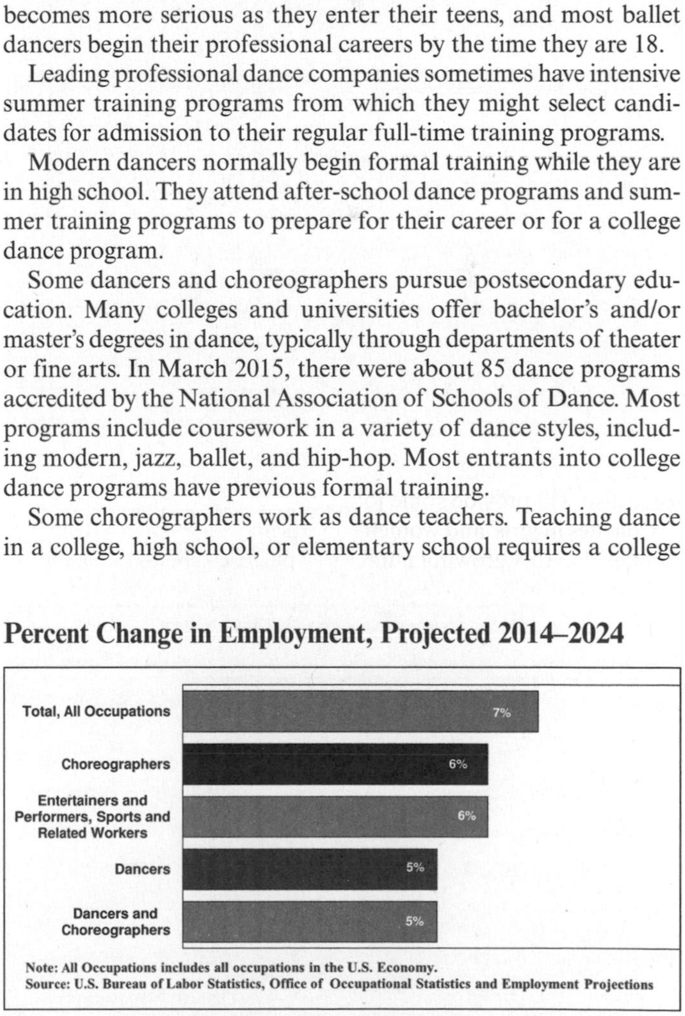

Employment Projections Data for Dancers and Choreographers

Occupational Title	SOC Code	Employment, 2014	Projected Employment, 2024	Change, 2014–2024	
				Percent	Numeric
Dancers and choreographers	27-2030	20,100	21,100	5	1,100
Dancers	27-2031	13,000	13,600	5	600
Choreographers	27-2032	7,100	7,500	6	400

Source: U.S. Bureau of Labor Statistics, Employment Projections Program

degree. Some dance studios and conservatories prefer instructors who have a degree but may accept previous work, in lieu of a degree.

Work Experience in a Related Occupation. Nearly all choreographers begin their careers as dancers. While working as dancers, they study different types of dance and learn how to choreograph routines.

Advancement. Some dancers take on more responsibility if they are promoted to dance captain in musical theater or a ballet master/ballet mistress in concert dance companies. They lead rehearsals or work with less-experienced dancers when the choreographer is not present.

Eventually, some dancers become choreographers. Dancers and choreographers may also become theater, film, or television producers and directors.

Important Qualities

Athleticism. Successful dancers must have excellent balance, physical strength, and physical dexterity, so they can move their bodies without falling or losing their sense of rhythm.

Creativity. Dancers need artistic ability and creativity to express ideas through movement. Choreographers also must have artistic ability and innovative ideas, to create new and interesting dance routines.

Interpersonal skills. Dancers and choreographers may find job opportunities by networking within their communities.

Leadership skills. Choreographers must be able to direct a group of dancers to perform the routines that they have created.

Persistence. Dancers must commit to years of intense practice. They need to be able to accept rejection after an audition and to continue to practice for future performances. Choreographers must keep studying and creating new routines.

Physical stamina. Dancers are often physically active for long periods, so they must be able to rehearse for many hours without getting tired.

Teamwork. Most dance routines involve a group, so dancers must be able to work together to be successful.

Pay

The median hourly wage for dancers was $14.31 in May 2014. The median wage is the wage at which half the workers in an occupation earned more than that amount and half earned less. The lowest 10 percent earned less than $8.52, and the highest 10 percent earned more than $34.44.

The median hourly wage for choreographers was $21.28 in May 2014. The lowest 10 percent earned less than $9.06, and the highest 10 percent earned more than $48.96.

In May 2014, the median hourly wages for dancers and choreographers in the top industries in which they worked were as follows:

Educational services; state, local, and private	$19.84
Performing arts companies	19.62
Amusement, gambling, and recreation industries	12.56
Spectator sports	12.26
Drinking places (alcoholic beverages)	11.18

Job Outlook

Employment of dancers is projected to grow 5 percent from 2014 to 2024, about as fast as the average for all occupations. Employment of choreographers is projected to grow 6 percent from 2014 to 2024, about as fast as the average for all occupations.

Large dance companies are not expected to add many jobs over the decade, so dancers may find positions in smaller companies, or in companies that stage professional dance competitions. There may be better opportunities for dancers and choreographers in large cities, such as New York and Chicago, or for dancers who join a traveling company.

A growing interest in dance and in pop culture may provide opportunities in fields outside of dance companies, such as TV or

Similar Occupations. This table shows a list of occupations with job duties that are similar to those of dancers and choreographers.

Occupations	Entry-level Education	2014 Median Pay	Projected Job Growth	Average Annual Openings
Actors	Some college, no degree	The annual wage is not available.	10%	660
Art Directors	Bachelor's degree	$85,610	2%	180
Music Directors and Composers	Bachelor's degree	$48,180	3%	260
Musicians and Singers	No formal educational credential	The annual wage is not available.	3%	600
Postsecondary Teachers	See Education/Training	$70,790	13%	17,700
Producers and Directors	Bachelor's degree	$69,100	9%	1,110

movies, casinos, theme parks, or as judges in dance competitions. Many dancers and choreographers, nonetheless, struggle to find opportunities to express themselves; dance companies rely on word-of-mouth, grants, and public funding. However, public funding and grants for dance performances can be highly competitive.

The growing interest in dance in pop culture is expected to lead more people to enroll in dance schools, and growing enrollment should create more jobs for choreographers and dancers who provide lessons.

Job Prospects. Dancers and choreographers face intense competition, and the number of applicants is expected to vastly exceed the number of job openings.

Dancers who attend schools or conservatories associated with a dance company may have a better chance of finding work at that company than other dancers.

Contacts for More Information

For more information about dancers and choreographers, visit

- Dance USA (www.danceusa.org)
- National Endowment for the Arts (www.nea.gov)
- National Association of Schools of Dance (http://nasd.arts-accredit.org)
- USA Dance (http://usadance.org)

O*NET

- Dancers (27-2031.00)
- Choreographers (27-2032.00)

Music Directors and Composers

- **2014 Median Pay** .... $48,180 per year $23.16 per hour
- **Typical Entry-Level Education** .... Bachelor's degree
- **Work Experience in a Related Occupation** .... Less than 5 years
- **On-the-job Training** .... None
- **Number of Jobs, 2014** 82,100
- **Job Outlook, 2014–24** .... 3% (Slower than average)
- **Employment Change, 2014–24** 2,600

What Music Directors and Composers Do

Music directors, also called *conductors*, lead orchestras and other musical groups during performances and recording sessions.

Duties. Music directors typically do the following:

- Select musical arrangements and compositions to be performed for live audiences or recordings
- Prepare for performances by reviewing and interpreting musical scores
- Direct rehearsals to prepare for performances and recordings
- Choose guest performers and soloists
- Audition new performers or assist section leaders with auditions
- Practice conducting to improve their technique
- Meet with potential donors and attend fundraisers

Music directors lead orchestras, choirs, and other musical groups. They ensure that the musicians play with one coherent sound, balancing the melody, timing, rhythm, and volume. They also give feedback to musicians and section leaders so that they can achieve the sound and style they want for the piece.

Most music directors and composers work for religious organizations and schools.

Music directors may work with a variety of orchestras and musical groups, including church choirs, youth orchestras, and high school or college bands, choirs, or orchestras. Some work with orchestras that accompany dance and opera companies.

Composers typically do the following:

- Write original music that orchestras, bands, and other musical groups perform
- Arrange existing music into new compositions
- Write lyrics for music or work with a lyricist
- Meet with companies, orchestras, or other musical groups that are interested in commissioning a piece of music
- Study and listen to music of various styles for inspiration
- Work with musicians to record their music

Composers write music for a variety of musical groups and users. Some work in a particular style of music, such as classical or jazz. They also may write for musicals, operas, or other types of theatrical productions.

Some composers write scores for movies or television; others write jingles for commercials. Many songwriters focus on composing music for audiences of popular music.

Some composers use instruments to help them as they write music. Others use software that allows them to hear a piece without musicians.

Some music directors and composers give private music lessons to children and adults. Others work as music teachers in elementary, middle, or high schools. For more information, see the profiles on kindergarten and elementary school teachers, middle school teachers, and high school teachers.

For more information about careers in music, see the profile on musicians and singers.

Median Annual Wages, May 2014

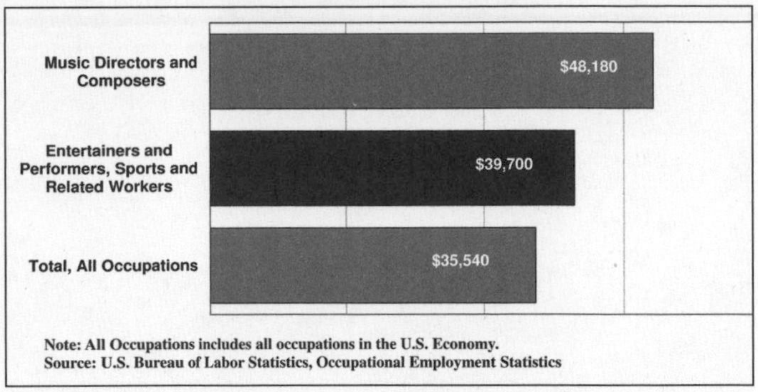

Percent Change in Employment, Projected 2014–2024

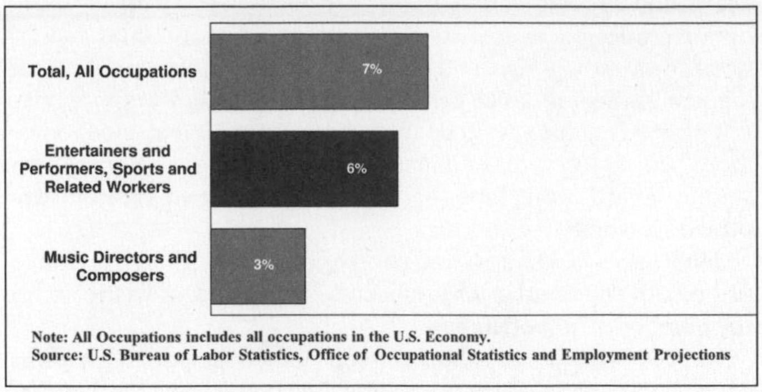

Work Environment

Music directors and composers held about 82,100 jobs in 2014. The industries that employed the most music directors and composers were as follows:

Religious, grantmaking, civic, professional, and similar organizations	52%
Elementary and secondary schools; state, local, and private	15
Performing arts companies	3

Music directors and composers work for religious organizations and in schools. Music directors also work in concert halls and recording studios. They may spend a lot of time traveling to different performances. Composers can work in offices, recording studios, or their own homes. About 1 out of 4 were self-employed in 2014.

Jobs for music directors and composers are found all over the country. However, many jobs are located in cities in which entertainment activities are concentrated, such as New York, Los Angeles, Nashville, and Chicago.

Work Schedules. Rehearsals and recording sessions are commonly held during business hours, but performances take place most often on nights and weekends. Because music writing is done primarily independently, composers may be able to set their own schedules.

Education/Training

Educational and training requirements for music directors and composers vary, although most positions require related work experience. A conductor for a symphony orchestra typically needs a master's degree; a choir director may need a bachelor's degree. There are no formal educational requirements for those interested in writing popular music.

Education. Employers generally prefer candidates with a master's degree in music theory, music composition, or conducting for positions as a conductor or classical composer.

Applicants to postsecondary programs in music typically are required to submit recordings, audition in person, or both. These programs teach students about music history and styles, as well as educate them in composing and conducting techniques. Information on degree programs is available from the National Association of Schools of Music (http://nasm.arts-accredit.org/).

A bachelor's degree typically is required for those who want to work as a choir director.

There are no specific educational requirements for those interested in writing popular music. These composers usually find employment by submitting recordings of their compositions to bands, singers, record companies, and movie studios. Composers may promote themselves through personal websites, social media, or online video or audio of their musical work.

Important Qualities

Discipline. Talent is not enough for most music directors and composers to find employment in this field. They must constantly practice and seek to improve their technique and style.

Interpersonal skills. Music directors and composers need to work with agents, musicians, and recording studios. Being friendly, respectful, and open to criticism as well as praise, while enjoying being with others, can help music directors and composers work well with a variety of people.

Leadership. Music directors and composers must guide musicians and singers by preparing musical arrangements and helping them achieve the best possible sound.

Musical talent. To become a music director or composer, one must have musical talent.

Perseverance. Music directors and composers need determination and perseverance to continue submitting their compositions after receiving rejections. Also, reviewing auditions can be frustrating because it may take many different auditions to find the best musicians.

Promotional skills. Music directors and composers need to promote their performances through local communities, word of mouth, and social media platforms. Good self-promotional skills are helpful in building a fan base and getting more work opportunities.

Training. Music directors and composers typically begin their musical training at a young age by learning to play an instrument or singing, and perhaps performing as a musician or singer. Music

Employment Projections Data for Music Directors and Composers

Occupational Title	SOC Code	Employment, 2014	Projected Employment, 2024	Change, 2014–2024 Percent	Change, 2014–2024 Numeric
Music directors and composers	27-2041	82,100	84,700	3	2,600

Source: U.S. Bureau of Labor Statistics, Employment Projections Program

Similar Occupations. This table shows a list of occupations with job duties that are similar to those of music directors and composers.

Occupations	Entry-level Education	2014 Median Pay	Projected Job Growth	Average Annual Openings
Actors	Some college, no degree	The annual wage is not available.	10%	660
Dancers and Choreographers	See Education/Training	The annual wage is not available.	5%	110
High School Teachers	Bachelor's degree	$56,310	6%	5,590
Kindergarten and Elementary School Teachers	Bachelor's degree	$53,760	6%	8,780
Middle School Teachers	Bachelor's degree	$54,940	6%	3,680
Musicians and Singers	No formal educational credential	The annual wage is not available.	3%	600
Postsecondary Teachers	See Education/Training	$70,790	13%	17,700
Producers and Directors	Bachelor's degree	$69,100	9%	1,110
Writers and Authors	Bachelor's degree	$58,850	2%	310

directors and composers who are interested in classical music may seek additional training through music camps and fellowships. These programs provide participants with classes, lessons, and performance opportunities.

Work Experience in a Related Occupation. Music directors and composers often work as musicians or singers in a group, a choir, or an orchestra before they take on a leadership role. They use this time to master their instrument and gain an understanding of how the group functions.

Pay

The median annual wage for music directors and composers was $48,180 in May 2014. The median wage is the wage at which half the workers in an occupation earned more than that amount and half earned less. The lowest 10 percent earned less than $21,610, and the highest 10 percent earned more than $91,860.

In May 2014, the median annual wages for music directors and composers in the top industries in which they worked were as follows:

Performing arts companies $56,870
Elementary and secondary schools; state, local, and private 49,460
Religious, grantmaking, civic, professional, and similar organizations 39,770

Job Outlook

Employment of music directors and composers is projected to grow 3 percent from 2014 to 2024, slower than the average for all occupations.

The number of people attending musical performances, such as symphonies and concerts, and theatrical performances, such as ballets and musical theater, is expected to increase moderately. Music directors will be needed to lead orchestras for concerts and musical theater performances. They also will conduct the music that accompanies ballet troupes and opera companies.

In addition, there will likely be a need for composers to write original music and arrange known works for performances. Composers will be needed as well to write film scores and music for television and commercials.

However, growth is expected to be limited because orchestras, opera companies, and other musical groups can have difficulty getting funds. Some music groups are nonprofit organizations that rely on donations and corporate sponsorships, in addition to ticket sales, to fund their work. These organizations often have difficulty finding enough money to cover their expenses. In addition, growth may be limited for music directors who work for public schools because state and local governments continue to struggle with school budgets.

Job Prospects. Despite expected growth, tough competition for jobs is anticipated because of the large number of people interested in entering this field. In particular, there will be considerable competition for full-time music director and composer positions. Candidates with exceptional musical talent and dedication should have the best opportunities.

Music directors and composers may experience periods without work. During these times, they may work in other occupations, give music lessons, attend auditions, or write music.

Contacts for More Information

For information about music degree programs, visit

➤ National Association of Schools of Music (http://nasm.arts-accredit.org)

For more information about careers in music, visit

➤ Future of Music Coalition (http://futureofmusic.org)

O*NET

➤ Music Directors and Composers (27-2041.00)
➤ Music Directors (27-2041.01)
➤ Music Composers and Arrangers (27-2041.04)

Musicians and Singers

- **2014 Median Pay** .... $24.16 per hour
- **Typical Entry-Level Education** .... No formal educational credential
- **Work Experience in a Related Occupation**.............. None
- **On-the-job Training** .... Long-term on-the-job training
- **Number of Jobs, 2014** 173,300
- **Job Outlook, 2014–24**............. 3% (Slower than average)
- **Employment Change, 2014–24** 6,000

What Musicians and Singers Do

Musicians and singers play instruments or sing for live audiences and in recording studios. They perform in a variety of styles, such as classical, jazz, opera, hip-hop, and rock.

Duties. Musicians and singers typically do the following:

- Perform music for live audiences and recordings
- Audition for positions in orchestras, choruses, bands, and other types of music groups
- Practice playing instruments or singing to improve their technique
- Rehearse to prepare for performances
- Find locations for performances or concerts
- Travel, sometimes great distances, to performance venues
- Promote their careers by maintaining a website or social media presence or doing photo shoots and interviews

Musicians play one or more instruments. To make themselves more marketable, many musicians become proficient in multiple musical instruments or styles.

Musicians play in bands, orchestras, or small groups. Those in bands may play at weddings, private parties, clubs, or bars while they try to build enough fans to get a recording contract or representation by an agent. Some musicians work as part of a large group of musicians who must work and practice together, such as an orchestra. A few musicians become section leaders, who may be responsible for assigning parts to other musicians or for leading rehearsals.

Other musicians are session musicians, who specialize in playing backup for a singer or band leader during recording sessions and live performances.

Singers perform vocal music in a variety of styles. Some specialize in a particular vocal style, such as opera or jazz; others perform in a variety of musical genres. Singers, particularly those who specialize in opera or classical music, may perform in different languages, such as French or Italian. Opera singers act out a story by singing instead of speaking the dialogue. Some singers become background singers, providing vocals to harmonize or support a lead singer.

In some cases, musicians and singers write their own music to record and perform. For more information about careers in songwriting, see the profile on music directors and composers.

Some musicians and singers give private music lessons to children and adults. Others with a background in music may teach music in public and private schools, but they typically need a bachelor's degree and a teaching license. For more information, see the profiles on kindergarten and elementary school teachers, middle school teachers, and high school teachers.

Work Environment

Musicians and singers held about 173,300 jobs in 2014. The industries that employed the most musicians and singers were as follows:

Religious, grantmaking, civic, professional, and similar organizations	44%
Performing arts, spectator sports, and related industries	13
Educational services; state, local, and private	2

Musicians and singers perform in settings such as concert halls, arenas, and clubs. In 2014, about 2 out of 5 musicians and singers were self-employed. Most of the rest worked for religious organizations and performing arts companies.

Musicians and singers who give recitals or perform in nightclubs travel frequently and may tour nationally or internationally. Some spend time in recording studios. There are many jobs in cities that have a high concentration of entertainment activities, such as New York, Los Angeles, Chicago, and Nashville.

Work Schedules. Rehearsals and recording sessions are commonly held during business hours, but live performances are most often at night and on weekends.

Many musicians and singers find only part-time or intermittent work, and may have long periods of unemployment between jobs. The stress of constantly looking for work leads many to accept permanent full-time jobs in other occupations while working part time as a musician or singer.

Education/Training

There are no postsecondary education requirements for musicians or singers interested in performing popular music. However, many performers of classical music and opera have at least a bachelor's degree.

Education. Performers of popular music do not need formal educational credentials. Many musicians and singers of classical music and opera have a bachelor's degree in music theory or performance. To be accepted into one of these programs, applicants are typically required to submit recordings or audition in person, and sometimes, must do both.

Undergraduate music programs teach students about music history and styles, and teach methods for improving their instrumental and vocal technique and musical expression. Undergraduate voice programs also teach courses in diction, which help students perform opera in foreign languages.

Musicians face keen competition, especially for full-time jobs.

Median Hourly Wages, May 2014

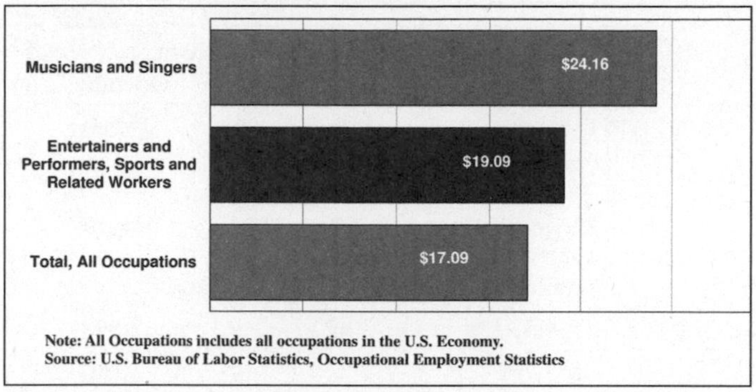

Percent Change in Employment, Projected 2014–2024

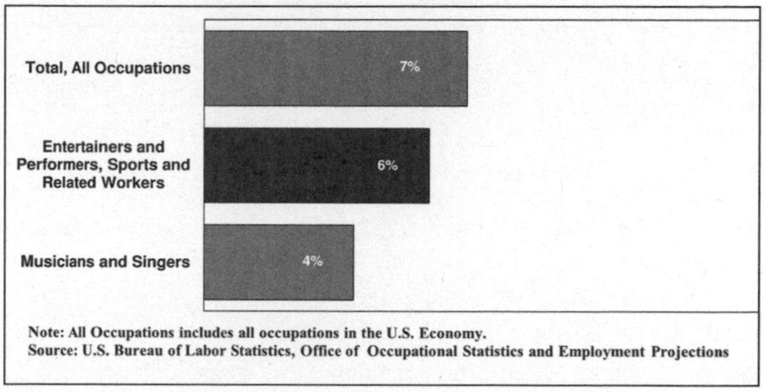

Some musicians and singers choose to continue their education by pursuing a master's degree in fine arts or music.

Training. Musicians and singers need extensive and prolonged training and practice to acquire the skills and knowledge necessary to interpret music at a professional level. They typically begin singing or learning to play an instrument by taking lessons and classes when they are at a young age. In addition, they must practice often to develop their talent and technique.

Musicians and singers interested in performing classical music may seek additional training through music camps and fellowships. These programs provide participants with classes, lessons, and performance opportunities.

Important Qualities

Dedication. Auditioning for jobs can be a frustrating process because it may take many different auditions to get hired. Musicians and singers need determination and dedication to continue to audition after receiving many rejections.

Discipline. Talent is not enough for most musicians and singers to find employment in this field. They must constantly practice and rehearse to improve their technique, style, and performances.

Interpersonal skills. Musicians and singers need to work well with a variety of people, such as agents, music producers, conductors, and other musicians. Good people skills are helpful in building good working relationships.

Musical talent. Professional musicians or singers must have superior musical abilities.

Physical stamina. Musicians and singers who play in concerts or in nightclubs and those who tour must be able to endure frequent travel and irregular performance schedules.

Promotional skills. Musicians and singers need to promote their performances through local communities, word of mouth, and social media. Good self-promotional skills are helpful in building a fan base.

Advancement. As with other occupations in which people perform, advancement for musicians and singers means becoming better known, finding work more easily, and earning more money for each performance. Successful musicians and singers often rely on agents or managers to find them jobs, negotiate contracts, and develop their careers.

Pay

The median hourly wage for musicians and singers was $24.16 in May 2014. The median wage is the wage at which half the workers in an occupation earned more than that amount and half earned less. The lowest 10 percent earned less than $8.98, and the highest 10 percent earned more than $66.11.

In May 2014, the median hourly wages for musicians and singers in the top industries in which they worked were as follows:

Performing arts, spectator sports, and related industries	$27.29
Educational services; state, local, and private	21.49
Religious, grantmaking, civic, professional, and similar organizations	19.24

Job Outlook

Employment of musicians and singers is projected to grow 3 percent from 2014 to 2024, slower than the average for all occupations. Growth will be attributed to increases in demand for musical performances.

Digital downloads and streaming platforms make it easier for fans to listen to recordings and view performances. Easier access to recordings gives musicians more publicity and grows interest in their work, and concertgoers may become interested in seeing them perform live. Moreover, some musicians and singers license their music for use in advertisements or other commercial purposes, which creates more exposure and additional revenue opportunities.

There may be some additional demand for musicians to serve as session musicians and backup artists for recordings and to go on tour. Singers may be needed to sing backup and to make recordings for commercials, films, and television.

However, employment growth will likely be limited in orchestras, opera companies, and other musical groups because they can have difficulty getting funding. Some musicians and singers work for nonprofit organizations that rely on donations, government funding, and corporate sponsorships in addition to ticket sales to

Employment Projections Data for Musicians and Singers

Occupational Title	SOC Code	Employment, 2014	Projected Employment, 2024	Change, 2014–2024 Percent	Change, 2014–2024 Numeric
Musicians and singers	27-2042	173,300	179,300	3	6,000

Source: U.S. Bureau of Labor Statistics, Employment Projections Program

Similar Occupations. This table shows a list of occupations with job duties that are similar to those of musicians and singers.

Occupations	Entry-level Education	2014 Median Pay	Projected Job Growth	Average Annual Openings
Actors	Some college, no degree	The annual wage is not available.	10%	660
Dancers and Choreographers	See Education/Training	The annual wage is not available.	5%	110
High School Teachers	Bachelor's degree	$56,310	6%	5,590
Kindergarten and Elementary School Teachers	Bachelor's degree	$53,760	6%	8,780
Middle School Teachers	Bachelor's degree	$54,940	6%	3,680
Music Directors and Composers	Bachelor's degree	$48,180	3%	260
Postsecondary Teachers	See Education/Training	$70,790	13%	17,700
Producers and Directors	Bachelor's degree	$69,100	9%	1,110

fund their work. During economic downturns, these organizations may have trouble finding enough funding to cover their expenses.

Job Prospects. There will be tough competition for jobs because of the large number of people who are interested in becoming musicians and singers. Many musicians and singers experience periods of unemployment, and there will likely be considerable competition for full-time positions.

Musicians and singers with exceptional musical talent and dedication should have the best opportunities.

Contacts for More Information

For more information about music careers and compensation, visit

➤ Future of Music Coalition (http://futureofmusic.org)

For more information about music degree programs, visit

➤ National Association of Schools of Music (http://nasm.arts-accredit.org)

O*NET

➤ Musicians and Singers (27-2042.00)
➤ Singers (27-2042.01)
➤ Musicians, Instrumental (27-2042.02)

Producers and Directors

- **2014 Median Pay** .... $69,100 per year $33.22 per hour
- **Typical Entry-Level Education** .... Bachelor's degree
- **Work Experience in a Related Occupation** .... Less than 5 years
- **On-the-job Training** .... None
- **Number of Jobs, 2014** 122,600
- **Job Outlook, 2014–24** .... 9% (Faster than average)
- **Employment Change, 2014–24** 11,100

What Producers and Directors Do

Producers and directors create motion pictures, television shows, live theater, commercials, and other performing arts productions. They interpret a writer's script to entertain or inform an audience.

Duties. Producers and directors typically do the following:

- Select scripts or topics for a film, show, commercial, or play
- Audition and select cast members and the film or stage crew
- Approve the design and financial aspects of a production
- Oversee the production process, including performances, lighting, and choreography
- Oversee the postproduction process, including editing, special effects, music selection, and a performance's overall tone
- Ensure that a project stays on schedule and within budget
- Promote finished works or productions through interviews, advertisements, and film festivals

Large productions often have *associate*, *assistant*, and *line producers* who share responsibilities. For example, on a large movie set an *executive producer* is in charge of the entire production, and a line producer runs the day-to-day operations. A TV show may employ several assistant producers to whom the head or executive producer gives certain duties, such as supervising the costume and makeup team.

Similarly, large productions usually employ several *assistant directors*, who help the director with tasks such as making set changes or notifying the performers when it is their time to go onstage. The specific responsibilities of assistant producers or directors vary with the size and type of production they work on.

Producers make the business and financial decisions for a motion picture, TV show, commercial, or stage production. They raise money for the project and hire the director and crew. The crew may include set and costume designers, film and video editors, a musical director, a choreographer, and other workers. Some producers may assist in the selection of cast members. Producers set the budget and approve any major changes to the project. They make sure that the production is completed on time, and they are ultimately responsible for the final product.

Directors are responsible for the creative decisions of a production. They select cast members, conduct rehearsals, and direct the work of the cast and crew. During rehearsals, they work with the actors to help them more accurately portray their characters. For nonfiction video, such as documentaries or live broadcasts, directors choose topics or subjects to film. They investigate the topic and may interview relevant participants or experts on camera. Directors also work with cinematographers and other crew members to ensure the final product matches the overall vision.

Directors work with set designers, costume designers, location scouts, and art directors to build a project's set. During a film's postproduction phase, they work closely with film editors and music supervisors to make sure that the final product comes out the way the producer and director envisioned. Stage directors, unlike television or film directors who document their product with cameras, make sure the cast and crew give a consistently strong live performance. For more information, see the profiles on actors, writers and authors, film and video editors and camera operators, dancers and choreographers, and multimedia artists and animators.

Although directors are in charge of the creative aspects of a show, they ultimately answer to producers. Some directors also share producing duties for their own films.

Work Environment

Producers and directors held about 122,600 jobs in 2014. The industries that employed the most producers and directors were as follows:

Motion picture and video industries	26%
Radio and television broadcasting	20
Performing arts, spectator sports, and related industries	8
Advertising, public relations, and related services	6
Cable and other subscription programming	3

Producers and directors work under a lot of pressure, and many are under constant stress to finish their work on time. Work assignments may be short, ranging from 1 day to a few months. They sometimes must work in unpleasant conditions, such as bad weather.

About 1 of 5 producers and directors were self-employed in 2014.

Work Schedules. Work hours for producers and directors can be long and irregular. Evening, weekend, and holiday work is common. About 1 out of 3 worked more than 40 hours per week in 2014. Many producers and directors do not work a standard workweek because their schedules may change with each assignment or project. Theater directors and producers may travel with a touring show across the country, while those in film and television may work on location (a site away from the studio, where all or part of the filming occurs).

Education/Training

Most producers and directors have a bachelor's degree and several years of work experience in an occupation related to motion picture, TV, or theater production, such as an actor, film and video editor, or cinematographer.

Producers and directors often work long, irregular hours.

Education. Producers and directors usually have a bachelor's degree. Many students study film or cinema at colleges and universities. In these programs, students learn about film history, editing, screenwriting, cinematography, and the filmmaking process. Others major in writing, acting, journalism, or communication. Some producers earn a degree in business, arts management, or nonprofit management.

Many stage directors complete a degree in theater and some go on to receive a Master of Fine Arts (MFA) degree. Classes may include directing, playwriting, set design, and acting. As of May 2015, the National Association of Schools of Theatre accredited more than 180 programs in theater arts.

Work Experience in a Related Occupation. Producers and directors might start out working in a theatrical management office as a business or company manager. In television or film, they might start out as an assistant or another low-profile studio job.

Median Annual Wages, May 2014

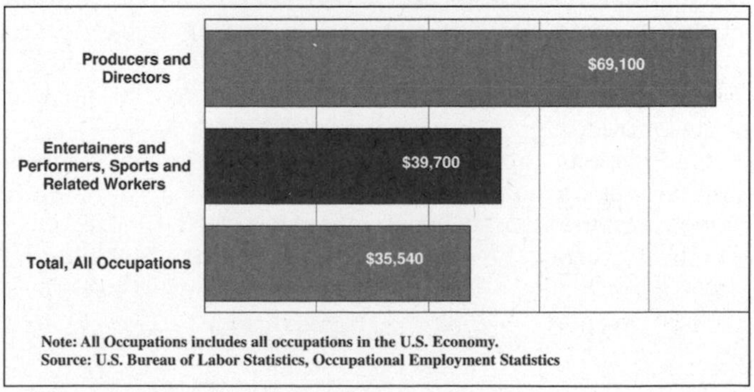

Percent Change in Employment, Projected 2014–2024

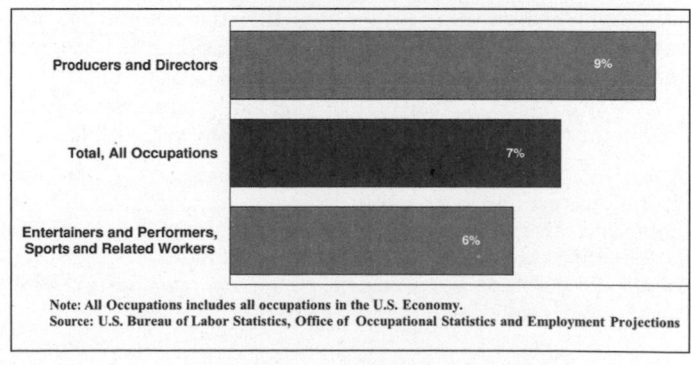

Employment Projections Data for Producers and Directors

Occupational Title	SOC Code	Employment, 2014	Projected Employment, 2024	Change, 2014–2024 Percent	Change, 2014–2024 Numeric
Producers and directors	27-2012	122,600	133,800	9	11,100

Source: U.S. Bureau of Labor Statistics, Employment Projections Program

Similar Occupations. This table shows a list of occupations with job duties that are similar to those of producers and directors.

Occupations	Entry-level Education	2014 Median Pay	Projected Job Growth	Average Annual Openings
Actors	Some college, no degree	The annual wage is not available.	10%	660
Art Directors	Bachelor's degree	$85,610	2%	180
Dancers and Choreographers	See Education/Training	The annual wage is not available.	5%	110
Film and Video Editors and Camera Operators	Bachelor's degree	$52,470	11%	640
Multimedia Artists and Animators	Bachelor's degree	$63,630	6%	390
Top Executives	Bachelor's degree	$102,750	6%	14,700
Writers and Authors	Bachelor's degree	$58,850	2%	310

Advancement. As a producer's or director's reputation grows, he or she may work on larger projects that attract more attention or publicity.

Important Qualities

Communication skills. Producers and directors must coordinate the work of many different people to finish a production on time and within budget.

Creativity. Because a script can be interpreted in different ways, directors must decide how they want to interpret it and then how to represent the script's ideas on the screen or stage.

Leadership skills. A director instructs actors and helps them portray their characters in a believable manner. They also supervise the crew, who are responsible for the behind the scenes work.

Time-management skills. Producers must find and hire the best director and crew for the production. They make sure that all involved do their jobs effectively, keeping within a production schedule and a budget.

Pay

The median annual wage for producers and directors was $69,100 in May 2014. The median wage is the wage at which half the workers in an occupation earned more than that amount and half earned less. The lowest 10 percent earned less than $31,380, and the highest 10 percent earned more than $187,200.

In May 2014, the median annual wages for producers and directors in the top industries in which they worked were as follows:

Advertising, public relations, and related services	$90,690
Motion picture and video industries	77,330
Cable and other subscription programming	66,790
Performing arts, spectator sports, and related industries	60,110
Radio and television broadcasting	57,280

Some producers and directors earn a percentage of ticket sales. A few of the most successful producers and directors have extraordinarily high earnings, but most do not.

Job Outlook

Employment of producers and directors is projected to grow 9 percent from 2014 to 2024, faster than the average for all occupations. Some job growth in the motion picture and video industry is expected to stem from strong demand from the public for more movies and television shows, as well as an increased demand from foreign audiences for U.S.-produced films. Also, consumer demand for reality shows on television is expected to increase, so more producers and directors will be needed to create and oversee editing of these programs.

In addition, production companies are experimenting with new content delivery methods, such as watching TV on mobile devices and online, which may lead to more work opportunities for producers and directors in the future. These delivery methods are still in their early stages, however, and their potential for success is not entirely known.

Theater producers and directors who work in small- and medium-sized theaters may see slower job growth because many of those theaters have difficulty finding funding as fewer tickets are sold. Large theaters in big cities, such as New York and Los Angeles, which usually have more stable sources of funding, should provide more opportunities.

Job Prospects. Producers and directors face intense competition for jobs because there are many more people who want to work in this field than there are jobs available. In film, directors who have experience on film sets should have the best job prospects. Producers who have good business skills will likely have the best prospects.

Contacts for More Information

For more information about producers and directors, visit
- Directors Guild of America (www.dga.org)
- Producers Guild of America (www.producersguild.org)
- National Association of Schools of Theater (http://nast.arts-accredit.org)
- National Endowment for the Arts (www.nea.gov)

O*NET

- Producers and Directors (27-2012.00)
- Producers (27-2012.01)
- Directors—Stage, Motion Pictures, Television, and Radio (27-2012.02)
- Program Directors (27-2012.03)
- Talent Directors (27-2012.04)

Umpires, Referees, and Other Sports Officials

- **2014 Median Pay** .... $24,090 per year
- **Typical Entry-Level Education** .... High school diploma or equivalent
- **Work Experience in a Related Occupation**.............. None
- **On-the-job Training** .... Moderate-term on-the-job training
- **Number of Jobs, 2014** 19,800
- **Job Outlook, 2014–24** .... 5% (As fast as average)
- **Employment Change, 2014–24** 1,000

What Umpires, Referees, and Other Sports Officials Do

Umpires, referees, and other sports officials preside over competitive athletic or sporting events to help maintain standards of play. They detect infractions and decide penalties according to the rules of the game.

Duties. Umpires, referees, and other sports officials typically do the following:

- Officiate at sporting events, games, and competitions
- Judge performances in sporting competitions to determine a winner
- Inspect sports equipment and examine all participants to ensure safety
- Keep track of event times, starting or stopping play when necessary
- Signal participants and other officials when infractions occur or to regulate play or competition
- Settle claims of infractions or complaints by participants
- Enforce the rules of the game and assess penalties when necessary

While officiating at sporting events, umpires, referees, and other sports officials must anticipate play and position themselves where they can best see the action, assess the situation, and determine any violations of the rules.

Sports officials typically rely on their judgment to rule on infractions and penalties. Officials in some sports may use video replay to help make the correct call.

Some sports officials, such as boxing referees, may work independently. Others, such as baseball or softball umpires, work in groups. Each official working in a group may have different responsibilities. For example, in baseball, one umpire is responsible for signaling balls and strikes while others are responsible for signaling fair and foul balls out in the field.

Regardless of the sport, the job is highly stressful because officials often must make split-second rulings. These rulings sometimes result in strong disagreement expressed by players, coaches, and spectators.

Many umpires, referees, and other sports officials are primarily employed in other occupations and supplement their income by officiating part time.

Work Environment

Umpires, referees, and other sports officials held about 19,800 jobs in 2014. The industries that employed the most umpires, referees, and other sports officials were as follows:

State and local government, excluding education and hospitals	30%
Amusement, gambling, and recreation industries	23
Educational services; state, local, and private	13
Performing arts, spectator sports, and related industries	11
Civic, social, professional, and similar organizations	10

Umpires, referees, and other sports officials work indoors and outdoors. Officials working outdoors will be exposed to all types of weather conditions. Some workers must travel on long bus rides to sporting events. Others, especially officials in professional sports, travel by air.

Some sports require officials to run, sprint, or jog for an extended period of time.

Because sports officials must observe play and often make split-second rulings, the work can be filled with pressure. Strong disagreements and criticism from athletes, coaches, and fans can result in additional stress.

Work Schedules. Umpires, referees, and other sports officials often work irregular hours, including evenings, weekends, and holidays. Many work part time.

Umpires and referees keep track of event times, starting or stopping play when necessary.

Median Annual Wages, May 2014

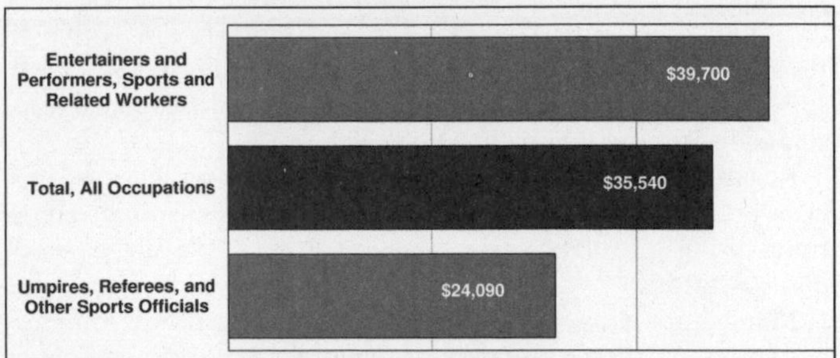

Note: All Occupations includes all occupations in the U.S. Economy.
Source: U.S. Bureau of Labor Statistics, Occupational Employment Statistics

Percent Change in Employment, Projected 2014–2024

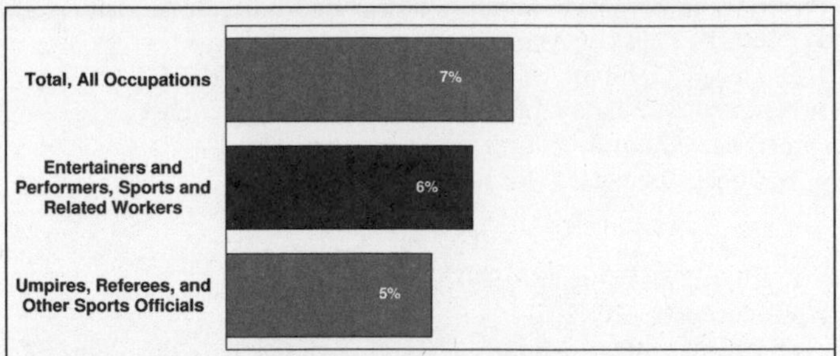

Note: All Occupations includes all occupations in the U.S. Economy.
Source: U.S. Bureau of Labor Statistics, Office of Occupational Statistics and Employment Projections

Education/Training

Educational requirements vary by state and are sometimes determined by the local sports association. Although some states have no formal education requirements, other states require umpires, referees, and other sports officials to have a high school diploma. Training requirements also vary by state and the level and type of sport. All sports, however, require extensive knowledge of the rules of the game.

Education and Training. Each state and sport association has its own education requirements for umpires, referees, and other sports officials. Some states do not require formal education, while others require sports officials to have a high school diploma.

For more information on educational requirements by state, refer to the specific state athletic or activity association.

Umpires, referees, and other sports officials may be required to attend training sessions and seminars before, during, and after the season. These sessions allow officials to learn about rule changes, review and evaluate their own performances, and improve their officiating.

Licenses, Certifications, and Registrations. To officiate at high school athletic events, umpires, referees, and other officials must typically register with the state or local agency that oversees high school athletics. They also typically need to pass an exam on the rules of the particular game. Some states and associations may require applicants to attend umpiring or refereeing classes before taking the exam or joining an association.

Some local associations may require officials to attend monthly association meetings.

Other associations require officials to attend annual training workshops before renewing their officiating license.

For more information on licensing and certification requirements, visit your state's high school athletic association website or the National Association of Sports Officials.

Advancement. Most new umpires, referees, and other sports officials begin by officiating youth or freshmen high school sports. After a few years, they may advance to the junior varsity or varsity levels. Those who wish to advance to the collegiate level must typically officiate at the varsity high school level for many years.

For some umpires, referees, and other sports officials, working in professional sports is the biggest advancement. Some officials may advance through the high school and collegiate levels to reach the professional level. Some sports, such as baseball, have their own professional training schools that prepare aspiring umpires and officials for a career at the minor and major league levels. In this system, umpires begin their professional career officiating in the minor leagues and typically need 7 to 10 years of experience before moving up into the major leagues.

Standards for umpires and other officials become more stringent as the level of competition advances.

Other Experience. Umpires, referees, and other sports official must have immense knowledge of the rules of the game they are officiating. Many officials gain the knowledge of the game by attending training sessions or camps that teach the important rules and regulations of the sport.

Some officials may also have gained this knowledge through years of playing the sport at some level. However, previous playing experience is not a requirement to become an umpire, referee, or other sports officials.

Important Qualities

Communication skills. Umpires, referees, and other sports officials must have good communication skills because they inform athletes on the rules of the game and settle disputes between competing players. Some sports officials also must communicate violations and infractions to opposing team players, coaches, and spectators.

Decision-making skills. Umpires, referees, and other sports officials must observe play, assess various situations, and often make split-second decisions.

Good vision. Umpires, referees, and other sports officials must have good vision to view infractions and determine any violations during play. In some sports, such as diving or gymnastics, sports officials must also be able to clearly observe an athlete's form for imperfections.

Stamina. Many umpires, referees, and other sports officials are required to stand, walk, run, or squat for long periods during games and events.

Employment Projections Data for Umpires, Referees, and Other Sports Officials

Occupational Title	SOC Code	Employment, 2014	Projected Employment, 2024	Change, 2014–2024	
				Percent	Numeric
Umpires, referees, and other sports officials	27-2023	19,800	20,700	5	1,000

Source: U.S. Bureau of Labor Statistics, Employment Projections Program

Similar Occupations. This table shows a list of occupations with job duties that are similar to those of umpires, referees, and other sports officials.

Occupations	Entry-level Education	2014 Median Pay	Projected Job Growth	Average Annual Openings
Athletes and Sports Competitors	No formal educational credential	$43,350	6%	80
Coaches and Scouts	Bachelor's degree	$30,640	6%	1,480

Teamwork. Because many umpires, referees, and other sports officials work in teams to officiate a game, the ability to cooperate and come to a mutual decision is essential.

Pay

The median annual wage for umpires, referees, and other sports officials was $24,090 in May 2014. The median wage is the wage at which half the workers in an occupation earned more than that amount and half earned less. The lowest 10 percent earned less than $17,500, and the highest 10 percent earned more than $57,340.

In May 2014, the median annual wages for umpires, referees, and other sports officials in the top industries in which they worked were as follows:

Performing arts, spectator sports, and related industries	$27,050
State and local government, excluding education and hospitals	26,500
Amusement, gambling, and recreation industries	23,580
Civic, social, professional, and similar organizations	23,420
Educational services; state, local, and private	20,130

Most umpires, referees, and other sports officials, however, are paid on a per-game basis. Pay typically rises as the level of competition increases.

Job Outlook

Employment of umpires, referees, and other sports officials is projected to grow 5 percent from 2014 to 2024, about as fast as the average for all occupations. Demand for umpires, referees, and other sports officials is projected to grow as population growth increases the overall number of people participating in organized sports.

High school enrollment is projected to increase over the next decade, which could result in a rise in the number of student-athletes. As schools offer more athletic programs and more students participate in sports, the demand for umpires, referees, and other sports officials may increase.

However, funding for athletic programs often is cut first when budgets become tight. Still, the popularity of interscholastic sports sometimes enables shortfalls to be offset with assistance from fundraisers, booster clubs, and parents.

Participation in college sports is also projected to increase over the next decade, particularly at smaller colleges and in women's sports. Many small, Division III colleges are expanding their sports programs and adding new teams to help promote the school and recruit students.

However, new rules allowing an increase in the scholarship payments to student-athletes may result in funding cuts to smaller collegiate sports programs. This could negatively affect the employment of umpires, referees, and officials if enough programs are eliminated.

Job Prospects. Overall job prospects for umpires, referees, and other sports officials are expected to be good at the youth and high school levels. Those with prior officiating experience will have the best job opportunities.

However, competition is expected to be very strong for the college and professional levels. Many people are attracted to working in sports, and the collegiate and professional levels typically have few job openings and low turnover.

Contacts for More Information

For more information about umpires, referees, and other sports officials, visit

➤ National Association of Sports Officials (www.naso.org)

For more information on umpires, referees, and other sports officials, refer to the organization that represents the sport and the locality.

O*NET

➤ Umpires, Referees, and Other Sports Officials (27-2023.00)

Farming, Fishing, and Forestry

Agricultural Workers

- **2014 Median Pay** .... $19,330 per year
  $9.30 per hour
- **Typical Entry-Level Education** .... See Education/Training
- **Work Experience in a Related Occupation**.............. None
- **On-the-job Training** ....Short-term on-the-job training
- **Number of Jobs, 2014** 761,700
- **Job Outlook, 2014–24**............................... -6% (Decline)
- **Employment Change, 2014–24** .... -47,500

What Agricultural Workers Do

Agricultural workers maintain the quality of farms, crops, and livestock by operating machinery and doing physical labor under the supervision of farmers, ranchers, and other agricultural managers.

Duties. Agricultural workers typically do the following:

- Harvest and inspect crops by hand
- Irrigate farm soil and maintain ditches or pipes and pumps
- Operate and service farm machinery and tools
- Spray fertilizer or pesticide solutions to control insects, fungi, and weeds
- Move shrubs, plants, and trees with wheelbarrows or tractors
- Feed livestock and clean and disinfect their pens, cages, yards, and hutches
- Examine animals to detect symptoms of illnesses or injuries
- Use brands, tags, or tattoos to mark livestock in order to identify ownership and grade
- Herd livestock to pastures for grazing or to scales, trucks, or other enclosures
- Administer vaccines to protect animals from diseases

The following are examples of types of agricultural workers:

Crop, nursery, and greenhouse farmworkers and laborers perform numerous tasks related to growing and harvesting grains, fruits, vegetables, nuts, and other crops. They plant, seed, prune, irrigate, and harvest crops, and pack and load them for shipment.

Farmworkers also apply pesticides, herbicides, and fertilizers to crops. They repair fences and some farm equipment.

Nursery and greenhouse workers prepare land or greenhouse beds for growing horticultural products such as trees, plants, flowers, and sod. They also plant, water, prune, weed, and spray the plants. They may cut, roll, and stack sod; stake trees; tie, wrap, and pack plants to fill orders; and dig up or move field-grown shrubs and trees.

Farm and ranch animal farmworkers care for live animals, including cattle, sheep, pigs, goats, horses, poultry, finfish, shellfish, and bees. These animals usually are raised to supply meat, fur, skins, feathers, eggs, milk, or honey.

These farmworkers may feed, herd, brand, weigh, and load animals. They also keep records on animals; examine animals to detect diseases and injuries; and administer medications, vaccinations, or insecticides.

Many workers clean and maintain animal housing areas every day. On dairy farms, animal farmworkers operate milking machines.

Agricultural equipment operators use a variety of farm equipment to plow and sow seeds, as well as maintain and harvest crops. They may use tractors, fertilizer spreaders, balers, combines, threshers, and trucks. These workers also operate machines such as conveyor belts, loading machines, separators, cleaners, and dryers. Workers may make adjustments and minor repairs to equipment.

Animal breeders use their knowledge of genetics and animal science to select and breed animals that will produce offspring with desired traits and characteristics. For example, they breed chickens that lay more eggs, pigs that produce leaner meat, and sheep with more desirable wool. Other animal breeders breed and raise cats, dogs, and other household pets.

To know which animals to breed and when to breed them, animal breeders keep detailed records. Breeders note animals' health, size, and weight, as well as the amount and quality of the product they produce. Animal breeders also track the traits of animals' offspring.

Work Environment

Agricultural workers held about 761,700 jobs in 2014.

They usually work outdoors in all kinds of weather. Animal breeders consult with farmers, ranchers, and other agricultural managers about their livestock.

A nursery worker waters flowers in a greenhouse.

Median Annual Wages, May 2014

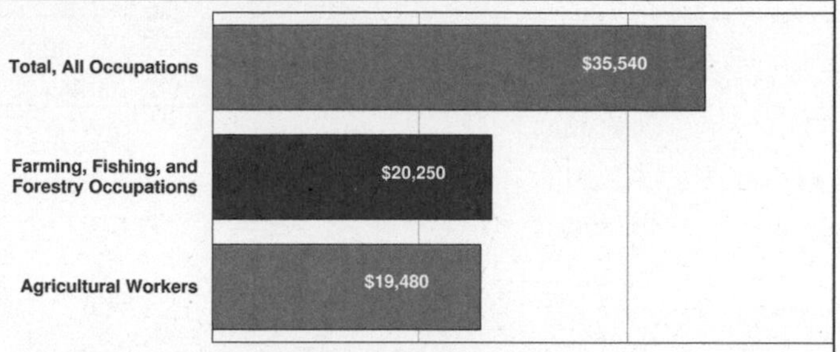

Note: All Occupations includes all occupations in the U.S. Economy.
Source: U.S. Bureau of Labor Statistics, Occupational Employment Statistics

Percent Change in Employment, Projected 2014–2024

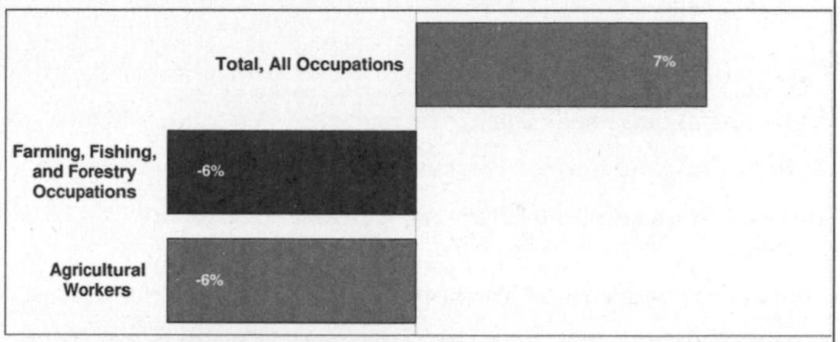

Note: All Occupations includes all occupations in the U.S. Economy.
Source: U.S. Bureau of Labor Statistics, Office of Occupational Statistics and Employment Projections

Agricultural workers' work can be difficult. To harvest fruits and vegetables by hand, workers frequently bend and crouch. They also lift and carry crops and tools that may be heavy.

Injuries and Illnesses. Agricultural work can be dangerous. Agricultural workers risk exposure to pesticides sprayed on crops or plants. Exposure can be minimal, however, if workers follow appropriate safety procedures. Tractors and other farm machinery can cause serious injuries, so workers must be constantly alert. Agricultural workers who work directly with animals risk being bitten or kicked.

Work Schedules. Some agricultural workers, called *migrant farmworkers*, move from location to location as crops ripen. Their unsettled lifestyles and periods of unemployment between jobs can cause stress.

Many agricultural workers have seasonal work schedules. Seasonal workers typically work longer periods during planting or harvesting times or when animals must be sheltered and fed.

Education/Training

Agricultural workers typically receive on-the-job training. A high school diploma is not needed for most jobs as an agricultural worker; however, a high school diploma typically is needed for animal breeders.

Education and Training. Most agricultural workers do not need a high school diploma; however, animal breeders typically need a high school diploma. Some jobs as an animal breeder may require some postsecondary education.

Agricultural workers typically receive some short-term on-the-job training. Employers instruct them on how to use simple farming tools and more complex machinery while following appropriate safety procedures. More experienced workers also are expected to perform routine maintenance on the tools they use.

Important Qualities

Dexterity. Agricultural workers need excellent hand-eye coordination to harvest crops and operate farm machinery.

Listening skills. Agricultural workers need to work well with others. Because they take instructions from farmers and other agricultural managers, effective listening is critical.

Physical stamina. Agricultural workers need to be able to perform laborious tasks repeatedly.

Physical strength. Agricultural workers must be strong enough to lift heavy objects, including tools and crops.

Mechanical skills. Agricultural workers must be able to operate complex farm machinery. They also occasionally do routine maintenance on the machinery.

Work Experience in a Related Occupation. Animal breeders sometimes need previous work experience interacting with livestock. Ranch workers may transition into animal breeding after they become more familiar with animals and learn how to handle them.

Advancement. Agricultural workers may advance to crew leader or other supervisory positions. The ability to speak both English and Spanish is helpful for agricultural supervisors.

Some agricultural workers aspire to become farmers, ranchers, or agricultural managers or to own their own farms and ranches. Knowledge of produce and livestock may provide an excellent background for becoming buyers or purchasing agents of farm products. Those who earn a college degree in agricultural science could become agricultural or food scientists.

Pay

The median annual wage for agricultural workers was $19,330 in May 2014. The median wage is the wage at which half the workers in an occupation earned more than that amount and half earned

Employment Projections Data for Agricultural Workers

Occupational Title	SOC Code	Employment, 2014	Projected Employment, 2024	Change, 2014–2024 Percent	Change, 2014–2024 Numeric
Agricultural workers	—	761,700	714,200	-6	-47,500
Animal breeders	45-2021	7,000	6,900	-2	-100
Agricultural equipment operators	45-2091	57,800	60,900	5	3,100
Farmworkers and laborers, crop, nursery, and greenhouse	45-2092	470,200	427,300	-9	-42,900
Farmworkers, farm, ranch, and aquacultural animals	45-2093	216,100	209,100	-3	-7,000
Agricultural workers, all other	45-2099	10,600	10,000	-6	-600

Source: U.S. Bureau of Labor Statistics, Employment Projections Program

Similar Occupations. This table shows a list of occupations with job duties that are similar to those of agricultural workers.

Occupations	Entry-level Education	2014 Median Pay	Projected Job Growth	Average Annual Openings
Agricultural and Food Science Technicians	Associate's degree	$35,140	5%	160
Animal Care and Service Workers	High school diploma or equivalent	$20,610	11%	2,570
Farmers, Ranchers, and Other Agricultural Managers	High school diploma or equivalent	$68,050	-2%	-1,810
Forest and Conservation Workers	High school diploma or equivalent	$27,160	4%	60
Grounds Maintenance Workers	See Education/Training	$24,810	6%	7,760

less. The lowest 10 percent earned less than $17,290, and the highest 10 percent earned more than $31,040.

Median annual wages for agricultural workers in May 2014 were as follows:

Animal breeders $40,000
Agricultural workers, all other 27,380
Agricultural equipment operators 26,910
Farmworkers, farm, ranch, and aquacultural animals 22,930
Farmworkers and laborers, crop, nursery, and greenhouse 19,060

Job Outlook

Employment of agricultural workers is projected to decline 6 percent from 2014 to 2024. Agricultural workers should have good job prospects overall.

Despite international demand for crops and other agricultural products, fewer agricultural workers may be needed as these establishments continue to consolidate. In addition, technological advancements in farm equipment are raising output per farmworker, a factor that also could affect employment for agricultural workers.

Still, agricultural workers may find opportunities at smaller farms that sell their products directly to consumers through venues such as farmers' markets. These direct-to-consumer farms have grown in popularity, and farmers may hire agricultural workers as an alternative to expensive machinery.

Job Prospects. Job prospects for agricultural workers—especially agricultural equipment operators and crop, greenhouse, and nursery farmworkers—should be strong because workers frequently leave the occupation due to the intense physical nature of the work.

Prospects will be best for those who can speak both English and Spanish.

Contacts for More Information

For more information about agricultural workers, visit

➤ Association of Farmworker Opportunity Programs (http://afop.org)

For more information about agriculture policy and farm advocacy, visit

➤ Center for Rural Affairs (www.cfra.org)

For more information about federal programs, such as the Beginning Farmer and Rancher Competitive Grants Program, visit

➤ National Institute of Food and Agriculture, U.S. Department of Agriculture (www.csrees.usda.gov)

➤ New Farmers, U.S. Department of Agriculture (www.usda.gov/newfarmers)

For more general information about farming in the United States, visit

➤ Farm Service Agency, U.S. Department of Agriculture (www.fsa.usda.gov/FSA)

O*NET

➤ Animal Breeders (45-2021.00)
➤ Agricultural Equipment Operators (45-2091.00)
➤ Farmworkers and Laborers, Crop, Nursery, and Greenhouse (45-2092.00)
➤ Nursery Workers (45-2092.01)
➤ Farmworkers and Laborers, Crop (45-2092.02)
➤ Farmworkers, Farm, Ranch, and Aquacultural Animals (45-2093.00)
➤ Agricultural Workers, All Other (45-2099.00)

Fishing and Hunting Workers

- **2014 Median Pay** .... $32,530 per year $15.64 per hour
- **Typical Entry-Level Education** ..... No formal educational credential
- **Work Experience in a Related Occupation** .... None
- **On-the-job Training** .... See Education/Training
- **Number of Jobs, 2014** 28,400
- **Job Outlook, 2014–24** .... -1% (Little or no change)
- **Employment Change, 2014–24** .... -200

What Fishing and Hunting Workers Do

Fishing and hunting workers catch and trap various types of animal life. The fish and wild animals they catch are for human food, animal feed, bait, and other uses.

Duties. Fishers and related fishing workers typically do the following:

- Locate fish with the use of fish-finding equipment
- Direct fishing operations and supervise the crew of fishing vessels
- Steer vessels and operate navigational instruments
- Maintain engines, fishing gear, and other onboard equipment by making minor repairs
- Sort, pack, and store the catch in holds with ice and other freezing methods
- Measure fish to ensure that they are of legal size
- Return undesirable or illegal catches to the water
- Guide nets, traps, and lines onto vessels by hand or with hoisting equipment
- Signal other workers to move, hoist, and position loads of the catch

Hunters and trappers typically do the following:

- Locate wild animals with the use of animal-finding equipment
- Catch wild animals with weapons, such as rifles or bows, or with traps like snares
- Sort, pack, and store the catch with ice and other freezing methods
- Follow hunting regulations, which vary by state and always include a safety component
- Sell what they catch for food and decorative purposes

To plot a ship's course, fishing boat captains use electronic navigational equipment, including global positioning systems (GPSs), as well as compasses and charts. They also use radar and sonar to avoid obstacles above and below the water and to find fish.

Some fishers work in deep water on large fishing boats that are equipped for long stays at sea. Some process the catch on board and prepare the fish for sale.

Other fishers work in shallow water on small boats that often have a crew of only one or two. They might put nets across the mouths of rivers or inlets; use pots and traps to catch fish or shellfish, such as lobsters and crabs; or use dredges to gather other shellfish, such as oysters and scallops.

A small portion of commercial fishing requires diving with diving suits or scuba gear. These divers use spears to catch fish and nets to gather shellfish, sea urchins, abalone, and sponges.

Some fishers harvest marine vegetation rather than fish. They use rakes and hoes to gather Irish moss and kelp.

Fishers work in commercial fishing, which does not include recreational fishing. For more information on workers on boats that handle fishing charters, see the profile on water transportation workers.

Aquaculture—raising and harvesting fish and other aquatic life under controlled conditions in ponds or confined bodies of water—is a different field. For more information, see the profile on farmers, ranchers, and agricultural managers.

The *fishing boat captain* plans and oversees the fishing operation, the fish to be sought, and the location of the best fishing grounds, as well as the method of capture, duration of the trip, and sale of the catch. They also record daily activities in the ship's log. Increasingly, they are using the Internet to bypass processors and sell their fish directly to consumers, grocery stores, and restaurants.

Fishers that specialize in catching certain species include *crabbers* and *lobster catchers*.

Hunters and trappers locate wild animals with GPS instruments, compasses, charts, and whistles. They then catch and kill them with weapons or traps. Hunters and trappers sell the wild animals they catch, either for food or decorative purposes.

Work Environment

Fishing and hunting workers held about 28,400 jobs in 2014. Approximately 3 out of 5 fishers and hunting workers were self-employed in 2014. Fishing and hunting operations are conducted under various environmental conditions, depending on the geographic region, body of water or land, and kinds of animals sought. Storms, fog, and wind may hamper fishing vessels or cause them to suspend fishing operations and return to port.

Although fishing gear has improved and operations have become more mechanized, netting and processing fish are nonetheless strenuous activities. Newer vessels have improved living quarters and amenities, but crews still experience the aggravations of confined quarters and the absence of family.

Injuries and Illnesses. Commercial fishing and hunting can be dangerous and can lead to workplace injuries or fatalities. Fishing and hunting workers often work under hazardous conditions. Transportation to a hospital or doctor is often not readily available for these workers since they be out at sea or in a remote area.

Most fatalities that happen to fishers and related fishing workers are from drowning. The crew must guard against the danger of injury from malfunctioning fishing gear, entanglement in fishing nets and gear, slippery decks, ice formation, or large waves washing over the deck. Malfunctioning navigation and communication equipment and other factors may lead to collisions, shipwrecks, or other dangerous situations, such as vessels becoming caught in storms. For more information on injuries and fatalities of fishers and fishing related works, read the *Beyond the Numbers* article, "Facts of the catch: occupational injuries, illnesses, and fatalities to fishing workers, 2003–2009." Hunters and trappers have fewer injuries and fatalities than fishers, and most of them are accidents related to the weapons and traps they use. Hunters and trappers minimize injury by wearing the appropriate gear, and following detailed safety procedures. Specific safety guidelines vary by state.

Work Schedules. Fishing and hunting workers endure strenuous outdoor work and long hours. Commercial fishing trips may require workers to be away from their home port for several weeks or months.

Education/Training

Fishing and hunting workers usually learn on the job. A formal educational credential is not required.

Education. A formal educational credential is not required for one to become fishing or hunting worker. However, fishers may improve their chances of getting a job by enrolling in a 2-year vocational–technical program. Some community colleges and universities offer fishery technology and related programs that include courses in seamanship, vessel operations, marine safety, navigation, vessel repair, and fishing gear technology. These programs are typically located near coastal areas and include hands-on experience.

Training. Most fishing and hunting workers learn on the job. They first learn how to sort and clean the animals they catch. Fishers would go on to learn to operate the boat and fishing equipment.

A fisher tends to his equipment on his fishing boat.

Median Annual Wages, May 2014

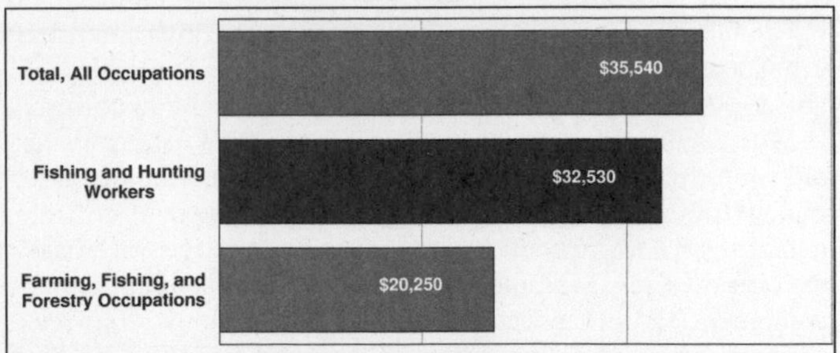

Note: All Occupations includes all occupations in the U.S. Economy.
Source: U.S. Bureau of Labor Statistics, Occupational Employment Statistics

Percent Change in Employment, Projected 2014–2024

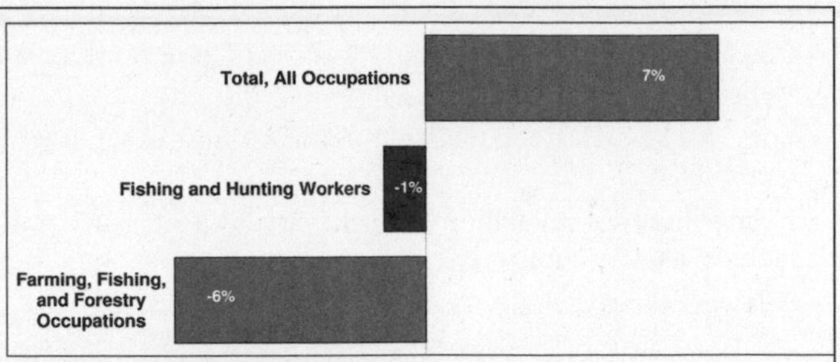

Note: All Occupations includes all occupations in the U.S. Economy.
Source: U.S. Bureau of Labor Statistics, Office of Occupational Statistics and Employment Projections

Many prospective fishers start by finding work through family or friends, or simply by walking around the docks and asking for employment. Aspiring fishers also can look online for employment. Some larger trawlers and processing ships are run by big fishing companies with human resources departments to which new workers can apply. Operators of large commercial fishing vessels must complete a training course approved by the U.S. Coast Guard.

Important Qualities

Critical-thinking skills. Fishing and hunting workers must reach conclusions through sound reasoning and judgment. They determine how to improve their catch and must react appropriately to weather conditions.

Detail oriented. Fishing and hunting workers must be precise and accurate when measuring the quality of their catch or prey. They must also pay attention to detail when working with various fishing gear so as to guard against injury.

Listening skills. Because they take instructions from captains and other crew members or hunters, fishing and hunting workers need to communicate well with others. Therefore, effective listening is critical to these workers.

Machine operation skills. Fishing and hunting workers must be able to operate, and perform routine maintenance on, complex fishing and navigation machinery, as well as weapons and traps.

Physical stamina. Fishing and hunting workers need endurance. They must be able to work long hours, often under strenuous conditions.

Physical strength. Fishing and hunting workers must use physical strength, along with hand dexterity and coordination, to perform difficult tasks repeatedly.

Licenses, Certifications, and Registrations. Captains of fishing boats and hunters and trappers must be licensed.

Crew members on certain fish-processing vessels may need a merchant mariner's document. The U.S. Coast Guard issues these documents, as well as licenses, to people who meet specific health, physical, and academic requirements.

States set licensing requirements for boats operating in state waters, defined as inland waters and waters within 3 miles of the coast.

Fishers need a permit to fish in almost any water. Permits are distributed by states for state waters and by regional fishing councils for federal waters. The permits specify the fishing season, the type and amount of fish that may be caught, and, sometimes, the type of permissible fishing gear.

Hunters and trappers need a license from states to hunt in any land or forest. Licenses specify the hunting season, the type and amount of wild animals that may be caught, and the type of weapons or traps that can be used.

Advancement. Experienced, reliable fishing boat deckhands can become boatswains, then second mates, first mates, and, finally, captains. Those who are interested in ship engineering may gain experience with maintaining and repairing ship engines to become licensed chief engineers on large commercial boats. In doing so, they must meet the Coast Guard's licensing requirements as well. For more information, see the profile on water transportation workers.

Almost all captains are self-employed, and most eventually own, or partially own, one or more fishing boats. Most hunters and trappers are also self-employed.

Pay

Many fishers are seasonal workers, and those jobs are usually filled by students and by people from other occupations who are available for seasonal work, such as teachers. For example, employment of fishers in Alaska increases significantly during the summer months, which constitute the salmon season. During these times, fishers can expect to work long hours. Additionally, states may allow hunters and trappers to hunt or trap only during certain times of the year depending on the type of wild animals sought.

Job Outlook

Employment of fishing and hunting workers is projected is projected to show little or no change from 2014 to 2024. Fishing and hunting workers depend on the ability of fish stocks and wild

Employment Projections Data for Fishing and Hunting Workers

Occupational Title	SOC Code	Employment, 2014	Projected Employment, 2024	Change, 2014–2024	
				Percent	Numeric
Fishing and hunting workers	—	28,400	28,200	-1	-200

Source: U.S. Bureau of Labor Statistics, Employment Projections Program

Similar Occupations. This table shows a list of occupations with job duties that are similar to those of fishing and hunting workers.

Occupations	Entry-level Education	2014 Median Pay	Projected Job Growth	Average Annual Openings
Water Transportation Workers	See Education/Training	$53,130	9%	720

animals to reproduce and grow. Government regulation, such as catch limits and quotas, can affect the number of fish stocks and the supply of animals available for fishing and hunting.

In order to conserve the fish population in the coming years, the need for setting catch limits has risen. Governmental efforts to replenish stocks are getting some positive results, which could lead to increased fish stocks in the future. The U.S. government sets catch limits for every species it manages. One way the government regulates fisheries is through catch shares, a type of quota that dictates how many fish each fisher may catch and keep. However, depending on the quantity allowed or the type of fish that is caught, purchasing additional quotas can be expensive and may therefore have a negative impact on fishing employment. Similarly, reliance on farm-raised livestock will lessen the demand for meat that is caught in the wild, reducing demand for hunters and trappers.

Although improvements in fishing gear and vessel design have increased fish hauls, rising seafood imports are affecting fishing income and causing some fishers to leave the industry. However, because competition from imported seafood tends to be concentrated in specific species, some regions are more affected than others.

Job Prospects. Most job openings will result from the need to replace fishing and hunting workers who leave the occupation. Many workers leave because of the strenuous and hazardous nature of the job and the lack of a steady year-round income. The best prospects should be with large fishing operations and for seasonal employment.

Contacts for More Information

For more information about licensing of fishing boat captains and about requirements for merchant mariner documentation, visit

➤ National Maritime Center, U.S. Coast Guard Headquarters (www.uscg.mil/nmc)

For more information about hunting licenses, visit

➤ Where to Hunt (www.wheretohunt.org)

For more information about injuries and safety issues, visit

➤ Centers for Disease Control and Prevention (CDC) (www.cdc.gov/niosh/topics/fishing)

Related BLS Article

Beyond the Numbers: "Facts of the catch: occupational injuries, illnesses, and fatalities to fishing workers, 2003–2009," (http://tinyurl.com/zhcvjdn)

O*NET

➤ Fishers and Related Fishing Workers (45-3011.00)

➤ Hunters and Trappers (45-3021.00)

Forest and Conservation Workers

- **2014 Median Pay** .... $27,160 per year; $13.06 per hour
- **Typical Entry-Level Education** .... High school diploma or equivalent
- **Work Experience in a Related Occupation** .... None
- **On-the-job Training** .... Moderate-term on-the-job training
- **Number of Jobs, 2014** 14,000
- **Job Outlook, 2014–24** .... 4% (Slower than average)
- **Employment Change, 2014–24** 600

What Forest and Conservation Workers Do

Forest and conservation workers measure and improve the quality of forests. Under the supervision of foresters and forest and conservation technicians, they develop, maintain, and protect forests.

Duties. Forest and conservation workers typically do the following:

- Plant seedlings to reforest land
- Clear away brush and debris from trails, roadsides, and camping areas
- Count and measure trees during tree-measuring efforts
- Select or cut trees according to markings, sizes, types, or grades
- Spray trees with insecticides and fungicides to kill insects and protect the trees from disease
- Identify and remove diseased or undesirable trees
- Inject vegetation with insecticides and herbicides
- Help prevent and suppress forest fires
- Check equipment to ensure that it is operating properly

Forest and conservation workers are supervised by foresters and forest and conservation technicians, who direct their work and evaluate their progress.

Forest and conservation workers perform basic tasks to maintain and improve the quality of the forest. They use digging and planting tools to plant seedlings and power saws to cut down diseased trees.

Some forest workers work on tree farms or orchards, where they plant, cultivate, and harvest many different kinds of trees. Their duties vary with the type of farm and may include planting seedlings or spraying to control weed growth and insects.

Some forest and conservation workers work in forest nurseries, where they sort through tree seedlings, discarding the ones that do not meet standards. Others use hand tools or their hands to gather woodland products, such as decorative greenery, tree cones, bark, moss, and other wild plant life. Some may tap trees to make syrup or chemicals.

Forest and conservation workers strive to promote growth of individual trees and entire forests.

Forest and conservation workers who are employed by or under contract with state and local governments may clear brush and debris from trails, roads, roadsides, and camping areas. They may clean kitchens and restrooms at recreational facilities and campgrounds.

Workers with a fire protection background help to suppress forest fires. For example, they may construct firebreaks, which are gaps in vegetation that can help slow down or stop the progress of a fire. In addition, they may work with technicians to determine how quickly fires spread and how successful fire suppression activities were. For example, workers help count how many trees will be affected by a fire. They also sometimes respond to forest emergencies.

Work Environment

Forest and conservation workers held about 14,000 jobs in 2014. The industries that employed the most forest and conservation workers were as follows:

State government, excluding education and hospitals	23%
Local government, excluding education and hospitals	14
Social advocacy organizations	3
Logging	3

Forest and conversation workers typically work for state and local governments or on privately owned forest lands or nurseries. Governments also employ forest and conservation workers on a contract basis.

Forest and conservation workers work mainly in the western and southeastern areas of the United States, where there are many national and state forests, and on private forests and parks.

Forest and conversation workers work outdoors, sometimes in remote locations and in all types of weather. However, the increased use of machines has reduced some of the discomfort of working in bad weather and has made tasks much safer. Workers also use proper safety measures and equipment, such as hardhats, protective eyewear, and safety clothing.

Most of these jobs are physically demanding. Forest and conservation workers may have to walk long distances through densely wooded areas and carry their equipment with them.

Injuries and Illnesses. Forest and conversation workers whose primary duties involve fire suppression must take safety precautions because the work can be dangerous. Workers must follow prescribed safety procedures and wear proper safety gear.

Work Schedules. Many forest and conservation workers are employed full time and work regular hours. Seasonal employees may be expected to work longer hours and at night. Responding to an emergency may require workers to work additional hours and at any time of day.

Education/Training

Most workers get on-the-job training.

Education. Forest and conservation workers typically need a high school diploma and a valid driver's license before they begin working. Some vocational and technical schools and community colleges offer courses leading to a 2-year technical degree in forestry. The programs typically offer courses in forest management technology, wildlife management, conservation, or timber harvesting. Programs that include field trips to watch and

Median Annual Wages, May 2014

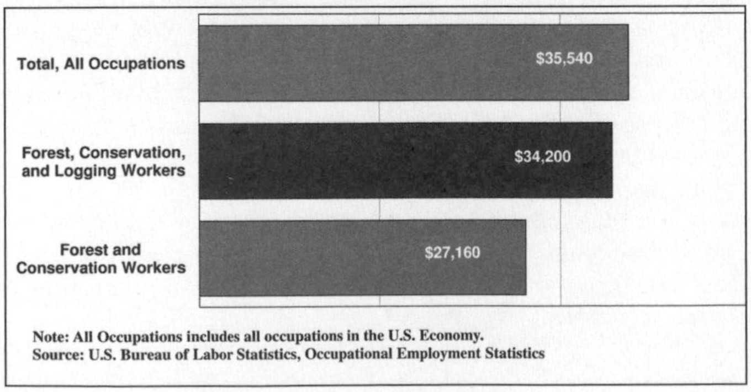

Percent Change in Employment, Projected 2014–2024

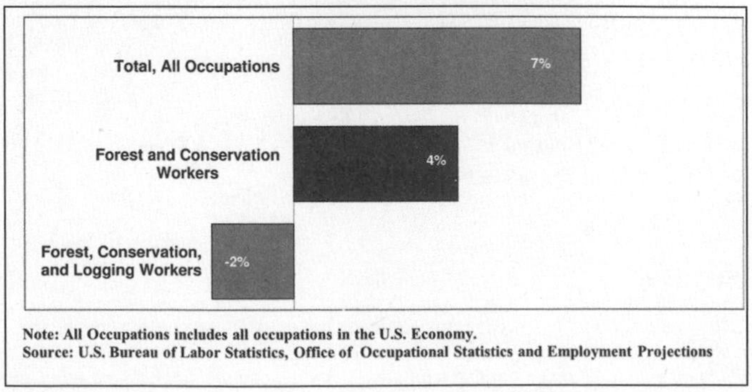

Employment Projections Data for Forest and Conservation Workers

Occupational Title	SOC Code	Employment, 2014	Projected Employment, 2024	Change, 2014–2024	
				Percent	Numeric
Forest and conservation workers	45-4011	14,000	14,600	4	600

Source: U.S. Bureau of Labor Statistics, Employment Projections Program

Similar Occupations. This table shows a list of occupations with job duties that are similar to those of forest and conservation workers.

Occupations	Entry-level Education	2014 Median Pay	Projected Job Growth	Average Annual Openings
Agricultural Workers	See Education/Training	$19,330	-6%	-4,750
Conservation Scientists and Foresters	Bachelor's degree	$60,360	7%	270
Firefighters	Postsecondary nondegree award	$45,970	5%	1,740
Grounds Maintenance Workers	See Education/Training	$24,810	6%	7,760
Logging Workers	High school diploma or equivalent	$35,160	-4%	-200

participate in forestry activities provide particularly good background knowledge.

Training. Entry-level forest and conservation workers generally get on-the-job training as they help more experienced workers. They do routine labor-intensive tasks, such as planting or thinning trees. When the opportunity arises, they learn from experienced technicians and foresters who do more complex tasks, such as gathering data. Workers also learn safety procedures, including how to operate equipment safely and how to maintain safety gear.

In addition, some states require that crews and individuals receive training, and sometimes a license, in the use of commercial pesticides. For more information, consult states' Departments of Agriculture.

Important Qualities

Communication skills. Forest and conservation workers must convey information effectively to technicians and other workers.

Decision-making skills. Forest and conservation workers must make quick, intelligent decisions, especially when they face dangerous conditions.

Detail oriented. Forest and conservation workers must watch gauges, dials, or other indicators to determine whether equipment and tools are working properly. Workers must follow safety procedures with precision.

Listening skills. Forest and conservation workers must give full attention to what their superiors are saying. They must understand the instructions they are given before performing tasks.

Physical stamina. Forest and conservation workers plant trees and repeatedly perform a variety of physical tasks. They also must be able to walk long distances through densely wooded areas and carry heavy equipment with them.

Advancement. To advance their careers and become forest and conservation technicians or foresters, forest and conservation workers usually need an associate's or bachelor's degree in forestry or a related field.

Pay

The median annual wage for forest and conservation workers was $27,160 in May 2014. The median wage is the wage at which half the workers in an occupation earned more than that amount and half earned less. The lowest 10 percent earned less than $16,800, and the highest 10 percent earned more than $46,390.

In May 2014, the median annual wages for forest and conservation workers in the top industries in which they worked were as follows:

Logging	$32,650
Local government, excluding education and hospitals	30,160
Social advocacy organizations	23,090
State government, excluding education and hospitals	22,060

Job Outlook

Employment of forest and conservation workers is projected to grow 4 percent from 2014 to 2024, slower than the average for all occupations. On the one hand, heightened demand for U.S. timber and wood pellets may help to increase demand for these workers. On the other hand, new technologies, such as remote sensing, allow fewer workers to perform certain tasks such as tree counts and tree identifications.

There is likely to be an increase in wildfires caused by unpredictable climate conditions and overgrown vegetation on forest lands, which would in turn increase the fire suppression activities of forest and conservation workers. Most employment growth for forest and conservation workers is likely to be in state-owned forest lands. As more people continue to build homes in western forests, there will be greater need for workers to protect those areas from fire dangers.

Job Prospects. Job prospects will be best for workers who have a background in fire suppression activities. Workers who follow standard safety procedures, remain physically fit, and work well in teams will have the best opportunities.

Contacts for More Information

For information about forestry careers and schools offering education in forestry, visit

- Society of American Foresters (www.safnet.org)

For information about careers in forestry, particularly conservation forestry and land management, visit

- Forest Stewards Guild (www.forestguild.org)
- U.S. Forest Service (www.fs.fed.us)

➤ National Association of State Departments of Agriculture (www.nasda.org/9383/States.aspx)

O*NET

➤ Forest and Conservation Workers (45-4011.00)

Logging Workers

- **2014 Median Pay** .... $35,160 per year $16.90 per hour
- **Typical Entry-Level Education** .... High school diploma or equivalent
- **Work Experience in a Related Occupation** .... None
- **On-the-job Training** .... Moderate-term on-the-job training
- **Number of Jobs, 2014** 53,700
- **Job Outlook, 2014–24** .... -4% (Decline)
- **Employment Change, 2014–24** .... -2,000

What Logging Workers Do

Logging workers harvest thousands of acres of forests each year. The timber they harvest provides the raw material for countless consumer and industrial products.

Duties. Logging workers typically do the following:

- Cut down trees
- Fasten cables around logs to be dragged by tractors
- Operate machinery that drag logs to the landing or deck area
- Separate logs by species and type of wood and load them onto trucks
- Drive and maneuver feller-buncher tree harvesters to shear trees and cut logs into desired lengths
- Grade logs according to characteristics such as knot size and straightness
- Inspect equipment for safety, and perform necessary basic maintenance tasks, before using the equipment

The cutting and logging of timber is done by a logging crew. The following are examples of types of logging workers:

Fallers cut down trees with hand-held power chain saws.

Buckers work alongside fallers, trimming the tops and branches of felled trees and bucking (cutting) the logs into specific lengths.

Tree climbers use special equipment to scale tall trees and remove their limbs. They carry heavy tools and safety gear as they climb the trees, and are kept safe by a harness attached to a rope.

A logging worker cuts a log into smaller lengths.

Choke setters fasten steel cables or chains, known as chokers, around logs to be skidded (dragged) by tractors or forwarded by the cable-yarding system to the landing or deck area, where the logs are separated by species and type of product.

Rigging slingers and chasers set up and dismantle the cables and guy wires of the yarding system.

Log sorters, markers, movers, and chippers sort, mark, and move logs on the basis of their species, size, and ownership. They also tend machines that chip up logs.

Logging equipment operators use tree harvesters to fell trees, shear off tree limbs, and cut trees into desired lengths. They drive tractors and operate self-propelled machines called skidders or forwarders, which drag or transport logs to a loading area.

Log graders and scalers inspect logs for defects and measure the logs to determine their volume. They estimate the value of logs or pulpwood. These workers often use hand-held data collection devices into which they enter data about trees.

A logging crew might consist of the following members:

- One or two tree fallers or one or two logging equipment operators with a tree harvester to cut down trees
- One bucker to cut logs
- Two choke setters with tractors to drag felled trees to the loading deck
- One logging equipment operator to delimb, cut logs to length, and load the logs onto trucks

Median Annual Wages, May 2014

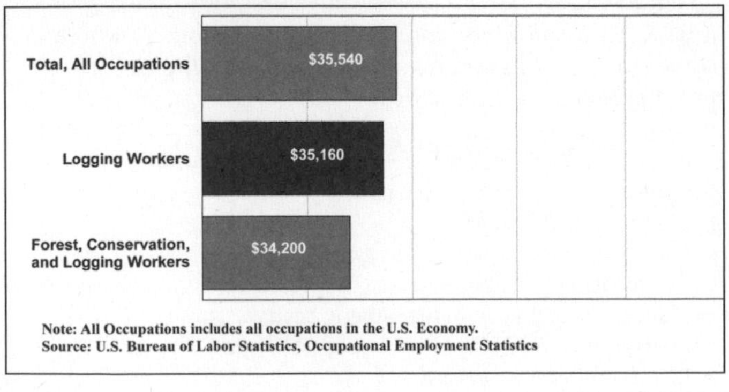

Percent Change in Employment, Projected 2014–2024

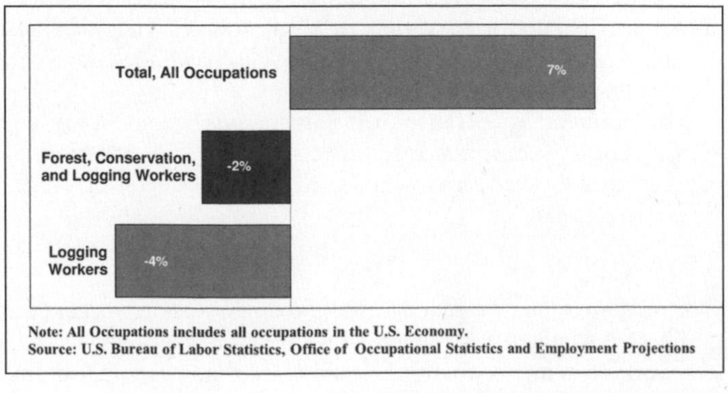

Employment Projections Data for Logging Workers

Occupational Title	SOC Code	Employment, 2014	Projected Employment, 2024	Change, 2014–2024	
				Percent	Numeric
Logging workers	45-4020	53,700	51,700	-4	-2,000
Fallers	45-4021	8,200	6,800	-17	-1,400
Logging equipment operators	45-4022	37,300	37,100	0	-100
Log graders and scalers	45-4023	3,700	3,700	-2	-100
Logging workers, all other	45-4029	4,500	4,100	-7	-300

Source: U.S. Bureau of Labor Statistics, Employment Projections Program

Work Environment

Logging workers held about 53,700 jobs in 2014. About 1 out of 4 were self-employed.

Logging is physically demanding and can be dangerous. Workers spend all their time outdoors, sometimes in poor weather and often in isolated areas. The increased use of enclosed machines has decreased some of the discomforts caused by bad weather and has generally made logging much safer.

Most logging work involves lifting, climbing, and other strenuous activities, although machinery has eliminated some heavy labor. Falling branches, vines, and rough terrain are constant hazards, as are dangers associated with felling trees and handling logs.

Chain saws and other power equipment can be dangerous; therefore, workers must be careful and must use proper safety measures and equipment, such as hardhats, safety clothing, protective-hearing devices, and boots.

Injuries and Illnesses. Despite the industry's strong emphasis on safety, logging workers have a high rate of fatal occupational injuries. Most fatalities occur through contact with a machine or an object, such as a log.

Work Schedules. Workers sometimes commute long distances between their homes and logging sites. In more densely populated states, commuting distances are shorter. Logging work is often seasonal, and workers can find more employment opportunities during the warmer months because snow and cold weather adversely affect working conditions.

Education/Training

They get on-the-job training to become familiar with forest environments and to learn how to operate logging machinery.

Education. A high school diploma is enough for most logging worker jobs. Some vocational or technical schools and community colleges offer associate's degrees or certificates in forest technology. This additional education may help workers get a job. Programs may include field trips to observe or participate in logging activities.

A few community colleges offer education programs for equipment operators.

Training. Many states have training programs for loggers. Although specific coursework may vary by state, programs usually include technical instruction or field training in a number of areas, including best management practices, environmental compliance, and reforestation.

Safety training is a vital part of logging workers' instruction. Many state forestry or logging associations provide training sessions for logging equipment operators, whose jobs require more technical skill than other logging positions. Sessions take place in the field, where trainees have the opportunity to practice various logging techniques and use particular equipment.

Logging companies and trade associations offer training programs for workers who operate large, expensive machinery and equipment. The training program often culminates with a state-recognized safety certification from the logging company.

Important Qualities

Communication skills. Logging workers must communicate with other crew members so that they can cut and delimb trees efficiently and safely.

Decision-making skills. Logging workers must make quick, intelligent decisions when hazards arise.

Detail oriented. Logging workers must watch gauges, dials, and other indicators to determine whether their equipment and tools are working properly.

Physical stamina. Logging workers need to be able to perform laborious tasks repeatedly.

Physical strength. Logging workers must be able to handle heavy equipment.

Pay

The median annual wage for logging workers was $35,160 in May 2014. The median wage is the wage at which half the workers in an occupation earned more than that amount and half earned less. The lowest 10 percent earned less than $22,370, and the highest 10 percent earned more than $52,340.

Median annual wages for logging workers in May 2014 were as follows:

Logging workers, all other	$35,460
Log graders and scalers	35,430
Logging equipment operators	35,190
Fallers	34,490

Similar Occupations. This table shows a list of occupations with job duties that are similar to those of logging workers.

Occupations	Entry-level Education	2014 Median Pay	Projected Job Growth	Average Annual Openings
Conservation Scientists and Foresters	Bachelor's degree	$60,360	7%	270
Construction Equipment Operators	High school diploma or equivalent	$42,900	10%	4,320
Forest and Conservation Workers	High school diploma or equivalent	$27,160	4%	60

Job Outlook

Employment of logging workers is projected to decline 4 percent from 2014 to 2024. However, there will be a need to replace workers who retire or leave the occupation permanently.

Domestic timber producers continue to face competition from foreign producers.

In addition, efforts to conserve federal forest lands have yielded policies that limit the logging industry's ability to cultivate raw forest material. However, federal legislation designed to prevent destructive wildfires by thinning susceptible forests may result in some additional jobs.

Ongoing mechanization within the logging industry will spur demand for logging equipment operators because they will be increasingly needed to operate equipment. Mechanization of logging operations and improvements in logging equipment have increased productivity and made logging work safer, resulting in less demand for logging workers who work by hand. However, some fallers will continue to be needed to fell trees on slopes that cannot be accessed by large machinery.

During prolonged periods of inactivity, some workers may stay on the job to maintain or repair logging machinery and equipment while others receive unemployment benefits, seek work elsewhere, or retire.

Job Prospects. Job opportunities should be good because of the need to replace older workers who leave the occupation for retirement or for other jobs that are less physically demanding.

Employment of logging workers can be unsteady because changes in the level of construction, particularly residential construction, can cause short-term slowdowns in logging activities.

Contacts for More Information

For information about timber-cutting and logging careers and links to state associations, visit

➤ Forest Resources Association, Inc. (www.forestresources.org)

O*NET

➤ Fallers (45-4021.00)

➤ Logging Equipment Operators (45-4022.00)

➤ Log Graders and Scalers (45-4023.00)

➤ Logging Workers, All Other (45-4029.00)

Food Preparation and Serving

Bartenders

- **2014 Median Pay** .... $19,050 per year
  $9.16 per hour
- **Typical Entry-Level Education** ..... No formal educational credential
- **Work Experience in a Related Occupation** .... None
- **On-the-job Training** ....Short-term on-the-job training
- **Number of Jobs, 2014** 580,900
- **Job Outlook, 2014–24** .... 10% (Faster than average)
- **Employment Change, 2014–24** 60,100

What Bartenders Do

Bartenders mix drinks and serve them directly to customers or through wait staff.

Duties. Bartenders typically do the following:

- Greet customers, give them menus, and inform them about daily specials
- Take drink orders from customers
- Pour and serve wine, beer, and other drinks and beverages
- Mix drinks according to recipes
- Check identification of customers to ensure that they are of legal drinking age
- Clean bars, tables, and work areas
- Collect payments from customers and return change
- Manage bar operation and order and maintain liquor and bar supplies

Bartenders fill drink orders either directly from customers at the bar or through waiters and waitresses who place drink orders for dining room customers. Bartenders must know a wide range of drink recipes and be able to mix drinks correctly and quickly. When measuring and pouring beverages they must avoid spillage or over pouring. They also must work well with waiters and waitresses and other kitchen staff to ensure that customers receive prompt service.

Some establishments, especially busy establishments with many customers, use equipment that automatically measures and pours drinks at the push of a button. Bartenders who use this equipment, however, still must become familiar with the ingredients for special drink requests and be able to work quickly to handle numerous drink orders.

Bartenders in some establishments also use carbonated beverage dispensers, cocktail shakers, commercial strainers, trigger sprayers, and ice shaver machines.

In addition to mixing and serving drinks, bartenders stock and prepare garnishes for drinks and maintain an adequate supply of ice, glasses, and other bar supplies. They also wash glassware and utensils and serve food to customers who eat at the bar. Bartenders are usually responsible for ordering and maintaining an inventory of liquor, mixers, and other bar supplies.

Some bartenders run their own bar or catering business. In addition to their standard bartending duties, these owners also are responsible for hiring, training, and supervising their staff; budgeting for and ordering supplies; and setting prices.

Work Environment

Bartenders held about 580,900 jobs in 2014.

The industries that employed the most bartenders in 2014 were as follows:

Restaurants and other eating places	46%
Drinking places (alcoholic beverages)	29
Civic and social organizations	8
Traveler accommodation	7

Bartenders work at restaurants, bars, clubs, hotels, and other food service and drinking establishments. Although bartenders typically work indoors, some bartenders work outdoors at pool or beach bars or at catered events.

During busy hours, bartenders are under pressure to serve customers quickly and efficiently, while ensuring that no alcohol is served to minors or overly intoxicated customers.

Bartenders perform repetitive tasks, and sometimes they lift heavy kegs of beer and cases of liquor. In addition, the work can be stressful, particularly when they deal with intoxicated customers to whom they must deny service.

Because bartenders often are on the front lines of customer service in bars and restaurants, a neat appearance is important. Those who work in upscale restaurants and bars may be required to wear uniforms, including ties or aprons, which may be provided by their employers.

Work Schedules. Bartenders often work late evenings, weekends, and holidays. About 4 in 10 worked part time in 2014.

Bartenders who run their own establishments often work many hours managing all business aspects to ensure bills and salaries are paid, supplies are ordered, and the business is profitable.

Education/Training

Most bartenders learn their skills through short-term on-the-job training usually lasting a few weeks. No formal education is required.

Bartenders spend most of their work time on their feet.

Median Hourly Wages, May 2014

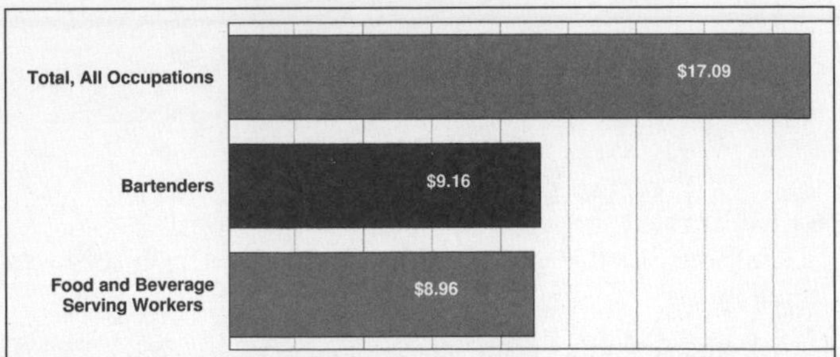

Note: All Occupations includes all occupations in the U.S. Economy.
Source: U.S. Bureau of Labor Statistics, Occupational Employment Statistics

Percent Change in Employment, Projected 2014–2024

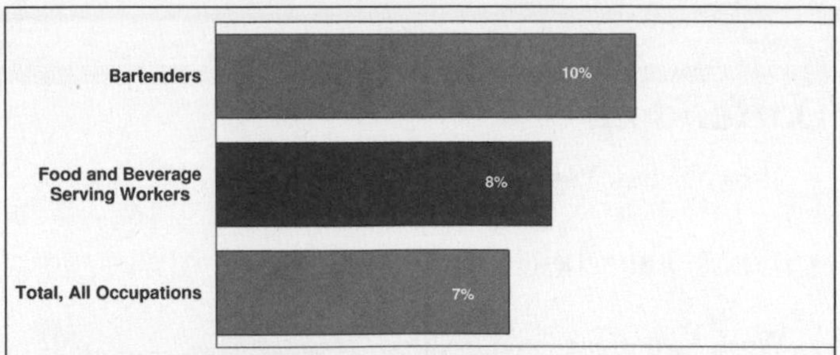

Note: All Occupations includes all occupations in the U.S. Economy.
Source: U.S. Bureau of Labor Statistics, Office of Occupational Statistics and Employment Projections

Many bartenders are promoted from other jobs at the establishments in which they work. Bartenders at upscale establishments usually have attended bartending classes or have previous work experience.

Although most states require workers who serve alcoholic beverages to be at least 18 years old, most bartenders are 25 or older. Bartenders must be familiar with state and local laws concerning the sale of alcoholic beverages.

Education. No formal education is required to become a bartender. However, some aspiring bartenders acquire their skills by attending a school for bartending or by attending bartending classes at a vocational or technical school. These programs often include instruction on state and local laws and regulations concerning the sale of alcohol, cocktail recipes, proper attire and conduct, and stocking a bar. The length of each program varies, but most courses last a few weeks. Some schools help their graduates find jobs.

Training. Most bartenders receive on-the-job training, usually lasting a few weeks, under the guidance of an experienced bartender. Training focuses on cocktail recipes, bar-setup procedures, and customer service, including how to handle unruly customers and other challenging situations. In food service establishments where bartenders serve food, the training may cover teamwork and proper food-handling procedures.

Some employers teach bartending skills to new workers by providing self-study programs, online programs, videos, and instructional booklets that explain service skills. Such programs communicate the philosophy of the establishment, help new bartenders build rapport with other staff, and instill a desire to work as a team.

Work Experience in a Related Occupation. Some bartenders qualify through related work experience. They may start as bartender helpers and progress into full-fledged bartenders as they learn basic mixing procedures and recipes. Some bartenders also may start as waiters and waitresses.

Advancement. Advancement for bartenders is usually limited to finding a job in a busier or more upscale restaurant or bar where prospects for earning tips are better. Some bartenders advance to supervisory jobs, such as dining room supervisor, maitre d', assistant manager, and restaurant general manager. A few bartenders open their own bars.

Important Qualities

Communication skills. Bartenders must listen carefully to their customers' orders, explain drink and food items, and make menu recommendations. They also should be able to converse with customers on a variety of subjects and create a friendly and welcoming environment.

Customer-service skills. Bartenders must have good customer-service skills to ensure repeat business.

Decision-making skills. Bartenders must be able to make good decisions. For example, they should be able to detect intoxicated and underage customers and deny service to those individuals.

Interpersonal skills. Bartenders should be able to tell a joke and laugh with a customer to build rapport.

Physical stamina. Bartenders spend hours on their feet preparing drinks and serving customers.

Physical strength. Bartenders should be able to lift and carry heavy cases of liquor, beer, and other bar supplies, which often weigh up to 50 pounds.

Pay

The median hourly wage for bartenders was $9.16 in May 2014. The median wage is the wage at which half the workers in an occupation earned more than that amount and half earned less. The lowest 10 percent earned less than $7.98, and the highest 10 percent earned more than $16.79.

Bartenders' earnings often come from a combination of hourly wages and tips from customers. Earnings vary greatly, depending on the type of establishment. For example, in some popular and busy restaurants, bars, and casinos, bartenders make more in tips than in wages.

Tipped employees earn at least the federal minimum wage ($7.25 per hour, as of July 24, 2009), which may be paid as a combination of direct wages and tips, depending on the state. Direct wages may be as low as $2.13 per hour according to the Fair Labor Standards Act (FLSA).

According to the FLSA, tipped employees are those who regularly receive more than $30 a month in tips. The Wage and Hour Division of the U.S. Department of Labor maintains a website with minimum wages for tipped employees, by state, although

Employment Projections Data for Bartenders

Occupational Title	SOC Code	Employment, 2014	Projected Employment, 2024	Change, 2014–2024 Percent	Change, 2014–2024 Numeric
Bartenders	35-3011	580,900	640,900	10	60,100

Source: U.S. Bureau of Labor Statistics, Employment Projections Program

Similar Occupations. This table shows a list of occupations with job duties that are similar to those of bartenders.

Occupations	Entry-level Education	2014 Median Pay	Projected Job Growth	Average Annual Openings
Cashiers	No formal educational credential	$19,060	2%	6,700
Flight Attendants	High school diploma or equivalent	$42,290	2%	220
Food and Beverage Serving and Related Workers	No formal educational credential	$18,550	10%	45,180
Food Preparation Workers	No formal educational credential	$19,560	6%	5,480
Waiters and Waitresses	No formal educational credential	$18,730	3%	6,890

some localities have enacted minimum wages higher than their state requires.

Job Outlook

Employment of bartenders is projected to grow 10 percent from 2014 to 2024, faster than the average for all occupations.

Population and income growth are expected to result in greater demand for food, drinks, and entertainment at a variety of food service and drinking places. In response, many new bars, taverns, clubs, and restaurants are expected to open and existing establishments are expected to expand to meet demand, resulting in more bartenders to serve drinks to customers.

Some hotels and motels are restructuring their food and alcohol service, thus moderating employment growth of bartenders in these industries. However, other restaurants are expected to open or expand their food and bar services in hotels to meet travelers' demand for food and drinks.

Job Prospects. Job opportunities are expected to be very good because of the need to replace the many workers who leave the occupation each year.

Strong competition is expected for bartending jobs in popular restaurants and fine-dining establishments, where tips are highest. Those who have graduated from bartending schools and those with previous work experience and excellent customer-service skills should have the best job prospects.

Contacts for More Information

For more information about bartenders, visit

➤ National Restaurant Association (www.restaurant.org)

O*NET

➤ Bartenders (35-3011.00)

Chefs and Head Cooks

- **2014 Median Pay** .... $41,610 per year $20.01 per hour
- **Typical Entry-Level Education** .... High school diploma or equivalent
- **Work Experience in a Related Occupation**............ 5 years or more
- **On-the-job Training** .... None
- **Number of Jobs, 2014** 127,500
- **Job Outlook, 2014–24**............... 9% (Faster than average)
- **Employment Change, 2014–24** 11,300

What Chefs and Head Cooks Do

Chefs and head cooks oversee the daily food preparation at restaurants and other places where food is served. They direct kitchen staff and handle any food-related concerns.

Duties. Chefs and head cooks typically do the following:

- Check the freshness of food and ingredients
- Supervise and coordinate activities of cooks and other food preparation workers
- Develop recipes and determine how to present dishes
- Plan menus and ensure the quality of meals
- Inspect supplies, equipment, and work areas for cleanliness and functionality
- Hire, train, and supervise cooks and other food preparation workers
- Order and maintain an inventory of food and supplies
- Monitor sanitation practices and follow kitchen safety standards

Chefs and head cooks use a variety of kitchen and cooking equipment, including step-in coolers, high-quality knives, meat slicers, and grinders. They also have access to large quantities of meats, spices, and produce. Some chefs use scheduling and purchasing software to help them in their administrative tasks.

Chefs who run their own restaurant or catering business are often busy with kitchen and office work. Some chefs use social

Chefs, head cooks, and food preparation and serving supervisors work long hours preparing ingredients before cooking.

Median Annual Wages, May 2014

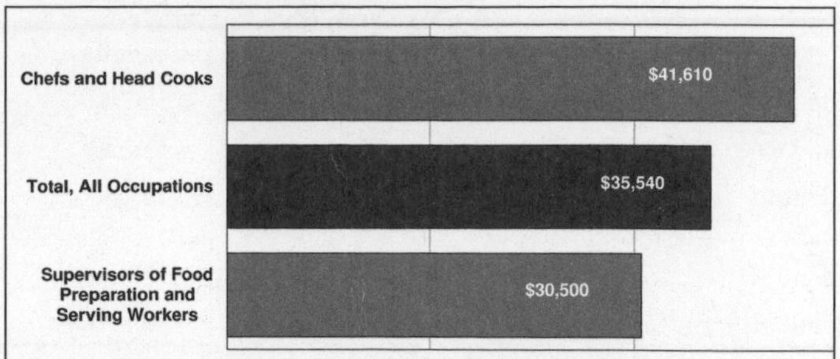

Note: All Occupations includes all occupations in the U.S. Economy.
Source: U.S. Bureau of Labor Statistics, Occupational Employment Statistics

Percent Change in Employment, Projected 2014–2024

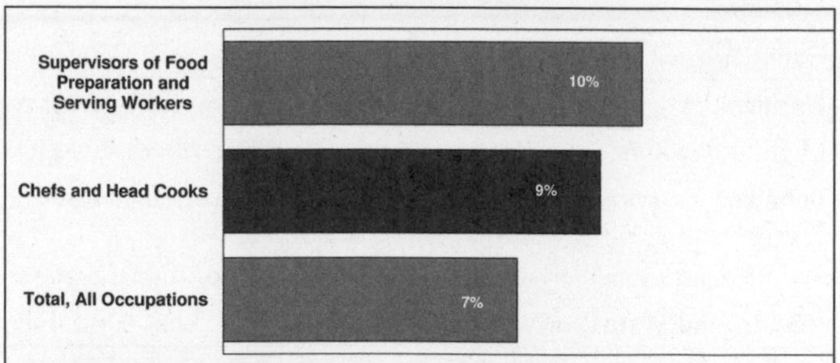

Note: All Occupations includes all occupations in the U.S. Economy.
Source: U.S. Bureau of Labor Statistics, Office of Occupational Statistics and Employment Projections

media to promote their business by advertising new menu items or addressing customer reviews.

The following are examples of types of chefs and head cooks:

Executive chefs, head cooks, and chefs de cuisine are responsible primarily for overseeing the operation of a kitchen. They coordinate the work of sous chefs and other cooks, who prepare most of the meals. Executive chefs also have many duties beyond the kitchen. They design the menu, review food and beverage purchases, and often train cooks and other food preparation workers. Some executive chefs primarily handle administrative tasks and may spend less time in the kitchen.

Sous chefs are a kitchen's second-in-command. They supervise the restaurant's cooks, prepare meals, and report results to the head chefs. In the absence of the head chef, sous chefs run the kitchen.

Private household chefs typically work full time for one client, such as a corporate executive, university president, or diplomat, who regularly entertains as part of his or her official duties.

Work Environment

Chefs and head cooks held about 127,500 jobs in 2014. The industries that employed the most chefs and head cooks were as follows:

Restaurants and other eating places	52%
Special food services	11
Traveler accommodation	10

Chefs and head cooks work in restaurants, hotels, private households, and other food service facilities, all of which must be kept clean and sanitary. Chefs and head cooks usually stand for long periods and work in a fast-paced environment.

About 1 in 20 chefs and head cooks were self-employed in 2014. Because some self-employed chefs run their own restaurant or catering business, their work can be more stressful. For example, outside the kitchen, they often spend many hours managing all aspects of the business to ensure that bills and salaries are paid and that the business is profitable.

Injuries and Illnesses. Kitchens are usually crowded and filled with dangerous objects and areas, such as hot ovens and slippery floors. As a result, chefs and head cooks have a higher rate of injuries and illnesses than the national average. The most common hazards include slips, falls, cuts, and burns and are seldom serious. To reduce these risks, workers often wear long-sleeve shirts and nonslip shoes.

Work Schedules. Most chefs and head cooks work full time, including early mornings, late evenings, weekends, and holidays. Many chefs and head cooks work more than 40 hours a week because they oversee the delivery of food supplies early in the day and use the afternoon to prepare special menu items.

Education/Training

Most chefs and head cooks learn their skills through work experience. Others receive training at a community college, technical school, culinary arts school, or 4-year college. A small number learn through apprenticeship programs or in the Armed Forces.

Education. Although postsecondary education is not required for chefs and head cooks, many attend programs at community colleges, technical schools, culinary arts schools, and 4-year colleges. Candidates are typically required to have a high school diploma or equivalent to enter these programs.

Students in culinary programs spend most of their time in kitchens, practicing their cooking skills. Programs cover all aspects of kitchen work, including menu planning, food sanitation procedures, and purchasing and inventory methods. Most training programs also require students to gain experience in a commercial kitchen through an internship or apprenticeship program.

Work Experience in a Related Occupation. Most chefs and head cooks start working in other positions, such as line cooks, learning cooking skills from the chefs they work for. Many spend years working in kitchens before gaining enough experience to be promoted to chef or head cook positions.

Training. Some chefs and head cooks train on the job, where they learn the same skills as in a formal education program. Some train in mentorship programs, where they work under the direction of an experienced chef. Executive chefs, head cooks, and sous chefs who work in upscale restaurants often have many years of training and experience.

Some chefs and head cooks learn through apprenticeship programs sponsored by professional culinary institutes, industry

Employment Projections Data for Chefs and Head Cooks

Occupational Title	SOC Code	Employment, 2014	Projected Employment, 2024	Change, 2014–2024	
				Percent	Numeric
Chefs and head cooks	35-1011	127,500	138,800	9	11,300

Source: U.S. Bureau of Labor Statistics, Employment Projections Program

Similar Occupations. This table shows a list of occupations with job duties that are similar to those of chefs and head cooks.

Occupations	Entry-level Education	2014 Median Pay	Projected Job Growth	Average Annual Openings
Bakers	No formal educational credential	$23,600	7%	1,300
Cooks	See Education/Training	$21,120	4%	9,700
Food and Beverage Serving and Related Workers	No formal educational credential	$18,550	10%	45,180
Food Preparation Workers	No formal educational credential	$19,560	6%	5,480
Food Service Managers	High school diploma or equivalent	$48,560	5%	1,570

associations, or trade unions in coordination with the U.S. Department of Labor. Apprenticeship programs generally last 2 years and combine instructions and on-the-job training. Apprentices must complete at least 1,000 hours of both instructions and paid on-the-job training. Courses typically cover food sanitation and safety, basic knife skills, and equipment operation. Apprentices spend the rest of their training learning practical skills in a commercial kitchen under a chef's supervision.

The American Culinary Federation accredits more than 200 academic training programs at postsecondary schools and sponsors apprenticeships around the country. The basic qualifications required for entering an apprenticeship program are as follows:

- Minimum age of 17
- High school education or equivalent
- Passing grade in substance abuse screening

Some chefs and head cooks receive formal training in the Armed Forces or from individual hotel or restaurant chains.

Licenses, Certifications, and Registrations. Although not required, certification can show competence and lead to advancement and higher pay. The American Culinary Federation certifies personal chefs, in addition to various levels of chefs, such as certified sous chefs or certified executive chefs. Certification standards are based primarily on work-related experience and formal training. Minimum work experience for certification can range from 6 months to 5 years, depending on the level of certification.

Important Qualities

Business skills. Executive chefs and chefs who run their own restaurant need to understand the restaurant business. They should know how to budget for supplies, set prices, and manage workers so that the restaurant is profitable.

Communication skills. Chefs must communicate their instructions clearly and effectively to staff so that customers' orders are prepared correctly.

Creativity. Chefs and head cooks need to be creative in order to develop and prepare interesting and innovative recipes. They should be able to use various ingredients to create appealing meals for their customers.

Dexterity. Chefs and head cooks need excellent manual dexterity, including proper knife techniques for cutting, chopping, and dicing.

Leadership skills. Chefs and head cooks must have the ability to motivate kitchen staff and develop constructive and cooperative working relationships with them.

Physical stamina. Chefs and head cooks often work long shifts and sometimes spend entire evenings on their feet, overseeing the preparation and serving of meals.

Sense of taste and smell. Chefs and head cooks must have a keen sense of taste and smell in order to inspect food quality and to design meals that their customers enjoy.

Time-management skills. Chefs and head cooks must efficiently manage their time and the time of their staff. They ensure that meals are prepared correctly and that customers are served on time, especially during busy hours.

Pay

The median annual wage for chefs and head cooks was $41,610 in May 2014. The median wage is the wage at which half the workers in an occupation earned more than that amount and half earned less. The lowest 10 percent earned less than $23,140, and the highest 10 percent earned more than $73,720.

In May 2014, the median annual wages for chefs and head cooks in the top industries in which they worked were as follows:

Traveler accommodation	$48,140
Special food services	43,660
Restaurants and other eating places	38,330

The level of pay for chefs and head cooks varies greatly by region and employer. Pay is usually highest in upscale restaurants and hotels, where many executive chefs work, as well as in major metropolitan and resort areas.

About 1 in 20 chefs and head cooks were self-employed in 2014. Some self-employed chefs run their own restaurant or catering business.

Job Outlook

Employment of chefs and head cooks is projected to grow 9 percent from 2014 to 2024, faster than the average for all occupations.

Population and income growth will result in greater demand for high-quality dishes at a variety of dining venues. As a result, more restaurants and other dining places are expected to open to satisfy consumer desire for dining out.

In addition, consumers increasingly are preferring healthier meals and faster service. This trend will contribute to the growth of fast-casual restaurants, representing a segment within limited-service restaurants where consumers pay for food before eating. Many of these new establishments will require more chefs and head cooks.

Consumers also are continuing to demand healthier meals made from scratch in restaurants, in cafeterias, in grocery stores, and by catering services. To ensure high-quality dishes, these establishments are increasingly hiring experienced chefs to oversee food preparation.

Job Prospects. Job opportunities should be best for chefs and head cooks with several years of work experience. The majority of job openings will result from the need to replace workers who leave the occupation. The fast pace, time demands, and high energy levels required for these jobs often lead to a high rate of turnover.

There will be strong competition for jobs at upscale restaurants, hotels, and casinos, where the pay is typically highest. Workers with a combination of business skills, previous work experience, and culinary creativity should have the best job prospects.

Contacts for More Information

For more information about chefs, including a directory of 2-year and 4-year colleges that offer courses or training programs, visit

- American Culinary Federation (www.acfchefs.org)
- National Restaurant Association (www.restaurant.org)

For information about becoming a private chef, visit

- American Personal & Private Chef Association (www.personalchef.com)

Related BLS Article

For more information about chefs, see *Career Outlook*: "Interview with a Chef" (http://tinyurl.com/gu83sb5)

O*NET

- Chefs and Head Cooks (35-1011.00)

Cooks

- **2014 Median Pay** .... $21,120 per year $10.16 per hour
- **Typical Entry-Level Education** .... See Education/Training
- **Work Experience in a Related Occupation**... See Education/Training
- **On-the-job Training** .... See Education/Training
- **Number of Jobs, 2014** 2,290,800
- **Job Outlook, 2014–24** .... 4% (Slower than average)
- **Employment Change, 2014–24** 97,000

What Cooks Do

Cooks prepare, season, and cook a wide range of foods, which may include soups, salads, entrees, and desserts.

Duties. Cooks typically do the following:

- Ensure the freshness of food and ingredients
- Weigh, measure, and mix ingredients according to recipes
- Bake, grill, or fry meats, fish, vegetables, and other foods
- Boil and steam meats, fish, vegetables, and other foods
- Arrange, garnish, and sometimes serve food
- Clean work areas, equipment, utensils, and dishes
- Cook, handle, and store food or ingredients

Cooks usually work under the direction of chefs, head cooks, or food service managers. Large restaurants and food service establishments often have multiple menus and large kitchen staffs. Teams of restaurant cooks, sometimes called *assistant cooks* or *line cooks*, work at assigned stations equipped with the necessary types of stoves, grills, pans, and ingredients.

Job titles often reflect the principal ingredient cooks prepare or the type of cooking they do—*vegetable cook*, *fry cook*, or *grill cook*, for example.

Cooks use a variety of kitchen equipment, including broilers, grills, slicers, grinders, and blenders.

The responsibilities of cooks vary depending on where they work, the size of the facility, and the level of service offered. However, in all establishments, they follow established sanitation procedures when handling food. For example, they store food and ingredients at the correct temperatures to prevent bacterial growth.

The following are examples of types of cooks:

Restaurant cooks prepare a wide selection of dishes and cook most orders individually. Some restaurant cooks may order supplies, set menu prices, and plan the daily menu.

Fast-food cooks prepare a limited selection of menu items in fast-food restaurants. They cook and package food, such as hamburgers and fried chicken, to be kept warm until served. For more information on workers who prepare and serve items in fast-food restaurants, see the profiles on food preparation workers and food and beverage serving and related workers.

Institution and cafeteria cooks work in the kitchens of schools, cafeterias, businesses, hospitals, and other institutions. For each meal, they prepare a large quantity of a limited number of entrees, vegetables, and desserts, according to preset menus. These cooks usually prepare meals in advance and seldom take special orders.

Short-order cooks prepare foods in restaurants and coffee shops that emphasize fast service and quick food preparation. They usually prepare sandwiches, fry eggs, and cook french fries, often working on several orders at the same time.

Private household cooks, sometimes called *personal chefs*, plan and prepare meals in private homes, according to the client's tastes and dietary needs. They order groceries and supplies, clean the kitchen, and wash dishes and utensils. They also may cater parties, holiday meals, luncheons, and other social events. Private household cooks typically work for one full-time client, although some are self-employed or employed by an agency, regularly making meals for multiple clients.

Work Environment

Cooks held about 2.3 million jobs in 2014. The industries that employed the most cooks in 2014 were as follows:

Restaurants and other eating places	69%
Health care and social assistance	7
Elementary and secondary schools; state, local, and private	5

Cooks work in restaurants, schools, hospitals, hotels, and other establishments where food is prepared and served. They often prepare only part of a dish and coordinate with other cooks and kitchen workers to complete meals on time. Some work in private homes.

Cooks stand for long periods and work under pressure in a fast-paced environment. Although most cooks work indoors in kitchens, some may work outdoors at food stands, at catered events, or in mobile food trucks.

Injuries and Illnesses. Kitchens are usually crowded and filled with potential dangers, such as hot ovens or slippery floors. Institution and cafeteria cooks, in particular, have a higher rate of injuries and illnesses than the national average. The most common hazards are slips, falls, cuts, and burns, but the injuries are seldom serious. To reduce the risks, cooks wear long-sleeve shirts, gloves, aprons, and nonslip shoes.

Work Schedules. Most cooks work full time. Work shifts often include early mornings, late evenings, weekends, and holidays. Schedules for cooks in school cafeterias and some institutional cafeterias are usually more regular. Cooks working in schools may work just during the school year, typically for 9 or 10 months. Similarly, some resort establishments offer seasonal employment only.

Cooks and food preparation workers must perform their duties quickly to keep up with food orders.

Education/Training

Most cooks learn their skills through on-the-job training and work-related experience. Although no formal education is required, some restaurant cooks and private household cooks attend culinary schools. Others attend vocational or apprenticeship programs.

Education. Vocational cooking schools, professional culinary institutes, and some colleges offer culinary programs for aspiring cooks. These programs generally last from a few months to 2 years and may offer courses in advanced cooking techniques, international cuisines, and various cooking styles. To enter these programs, candidates may be required to have a high school diploma or equivalent. Depending on the type and length of the program, graduates generally qualify for entry-level positions as a restaurant cook.

Training. Most cooks learn their skills through on-the-job training, usually lasting a few weeks. Trainees generally first learn kitchen basics and workplace safety and then learn how to handle and cook food.

Some cooks learn through an apprenticeship program. Professional culinary institutes, industry associations, and trade unions may sponsor such programs for cooks. Typical apprenticeships last 1 year and combine technical training and work experience. Apprentices complete courses in food sanitation and safety, basic knife skills, and equipment operation. They also learn practical cooking skills under the supervision of an experienced chef.

The American Culinary Federation accredits more than 200 academic training programs and sponsors apprenticeships through these programs around the country. The basic qualifications for entering an apprenticeship program are as follows:

- Minimum age of 17
- High school education or equivalent
- Pass substance abuse screening

Some hotels, a number of restaurants, and the Armed Forces have their own training programs.

Work Experience in a Related Occupation. Many cooks learn their skills through work-related experience. They typically start as a kitchen helper or food preparation worker, learning basic cooking skills before they advance to assistant cook or line cook positions. Some learn by working under the guidance of a more experienced cook.

Advancement. The American Culinary Federation certifies chefs, personal chefs, pastry chefs, and culinary administrators, among others. For cooks seeking advancement to higher level chef positions, certification can show accomplishment and lead to higher paying positions.

Advancement opportunities for cooks often depend on training, work experience, and the ability to prepare more complex dishes. Those who learn new cooking skills and who handle greater responsibility, such as supervising kitchen staff in the absence of a chef, often advance. Some cooks may train or supervise kitchen staff, and some may become head cooks, chefs, or food service managers.

Important Qualities

Comprehension. Cooks need to understand orders and follow recipes to prepare dishes correctly.

Customer-service skills. Restaurant and short-order cooks must be able to interact effectively with customers and handle special requests.

Median Hourly Wages, May 2014

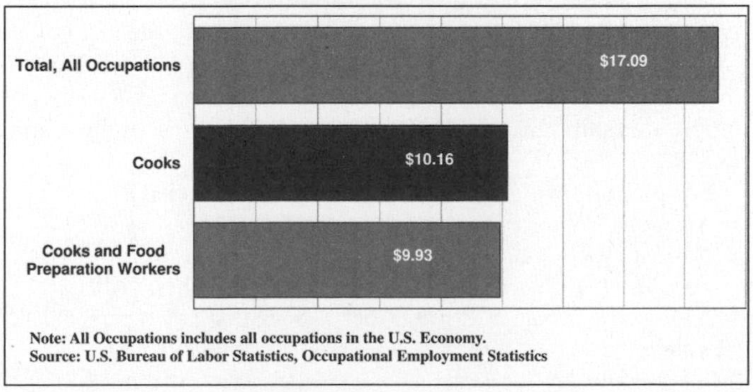

Percent Change in Employment, Projected 2014–2024

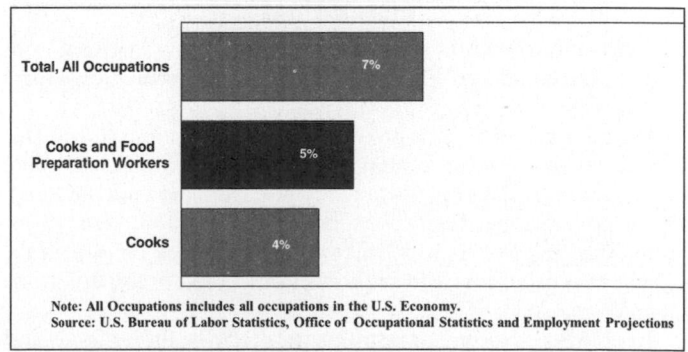

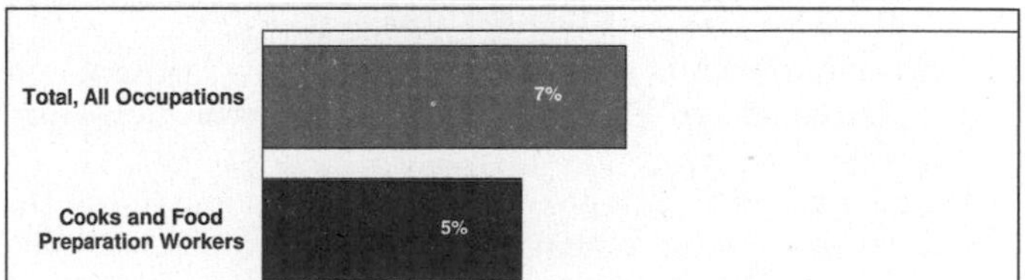

Employment Projections Data for Cooks

Occupational Title	SOC Code	Employment, 2014	Projected Employment, 2024	Change, 2014–2024 Percent	Change, 2014–2024 Numeric
Cooks	35-2010	2,290,800	2,387,800	4	97,000
Cooks, fast food	35-2011	524,400	444,000	-15	-80,400
Cooks, institution and cafeteria	35-2012	417,600	443,900	6	26,300
Cooks, private household	35-2013	35,900	36,200	1	200
Cooks, restaurant	35-2014	1,109,700	1,268,700	14	158,900
Cooks, short order	35-2015	181,600	172,300	-5	-9,300
Cooks, all other	35-2019	21,500	22,800	6	1,300

Source: U.S. Bureau of Labor Statistics, Employment Projections Program

Similar Occupations. This table shows a list of occupations with job duties that are similar to those of cooks.

Occupations	Entry-level Education	2014 Median Pay	Projected Job Growth	Average Annual Openings
Bakers	No formal educational credential	$23,600	7%	1,300
Chefs and Head Cooks	High school diploma or equivalent	$41,610	9%	1,130
Food and Beverage Serving and Related Workers	No formal educational credential	$18,550	10%	45,180
Food Preparation Workers	No formal educational credential	$19,560	6%	5,480
Food Service Managers	High school diploma or equivalent	$48,560	5%	1,570

Dexterity. Cooks should have excellent hand-eye coordination. For example, they need to use proper knife techniques for cutting, chopping, and dicing.

Physical stamina. Cooks spend a lot of time standing in one place, cooking food over hot stoves, and cleaning work areas.

Sense of taste and smell. Cooks must have a keen sense of taste and smell to prepare meals that customers enjoy.

Pay

The median hourly wage for cooks was $10.16 in May 2014. The median wage is the wage at which half the workers in an occupation earned more than that amount and half earned less. The lowest 10 percent earned less than $8.09, and the highest 10 percent earned more than $14.82.

Median hourly wages for cooks in May 2014 were as follows:

Cooks, all other	$12.01
Cooks, institution and cafeteria	11.27
Cooks, private household	11.03
Cooks, restaurant	10.81
Cooks, short order	9.71
Cooks, fast food	8.91

Job Outlook

Overall employment of cooks is projected to grow 4 percent from 2014 to 2024, slower than the average for all occupations. Individual growth rates will vary by specialty.

Population and income growth are expected to result in greater consumer demand for food at a variety of dining places. People will continue to eat out, buy takeout meals, or have food delivered. In response to increased consumer demand, more restaurants, cafeterias, and catering services will open and serve more meals. These establishments will require more cooks to prepare meals for customers.

In addition, consumers continue to prefer healthier foods and faster service in restaurants, grocery stores, and other dining venues. To prepare high quality meals at these places, many managers and chefs will require more experienced cooks, such as restaurant cooks, over short-order cooks.

Employment growth of fast food cooks will be limited as these establishments choose to hire other workers such as food preparation and serving workers, who can prepare and also serve food to customers.

Institution and cafeteria cooks are primarily employed in schools, nursing care facilities, government offices, and hospitals. Some of these facilities contract out their food service to food service operators, also known as food service companies. These companies will hire more institution and cafeteria cooks to prepare food in these establishments.

Job Prospects. Overall job opportunities are expected to be very good as a result of employment growth and the need to replace workers who leave the occupation. Cooks with previous training and related work experience will have the best job prospects.

Those who can prepare more complex dishes will have the best job opportunities at restaurant chains, upscale restaurants, and hotels.

Contacts for More Information

For information about culinary apprenticeship programs registered with the U.S. Department of Labor, contact the local office of your state employment service agency, or check the U.S. Department of Labor's ApprenticeshipUSA program (www.dol.gov/apprenticeship/jquery1445866707949=302) online or by phone at 877-872-5627.

For more information about cooking careers, visit

- American Culinary Federation (www.acfchefs.org)
- National Restaurant Association (www.restaurant.org)

For information about becoming a personal chef, visit

- American Personal & Private Chef Association (www.personalchef.com)

O*NET

- Cooks, Fast Food (35-2011.00)
- Cooks, Institution and Cafeteria (35-2012.00)
- Cooks, Private Household (35-2013.00)
- Cooks, Restaurant (35-2014.00)
- Cooks, Short Order (35-2015.00)
- Cooks, All Other (35-2019.00)

Food and Beverage Serving and Related Workers

- **2014 Median Pay** .... $18,550 per year $8.92 per hour
- **Typical Entry-Level Education** .... No formal educational credential
- **Work Experience in a Related Occupation**.............. None
- **On-the-job Training** .... See Education/Training
- **Number of Jobs, 2014** 4,731,800
- **Job Outlook, 2014–24**............ 10% (Faster than average)
- **Employment Change, 2014–24** 451,800

What Food and Beverage Serving and Related Workers Do

Food and beverage serving and related workers perform a variety of customer service, food preparation, and cleaning duties in restaurants, cafeterias, and other eating and drinking establishments.

Duties. Food and beverage serving and related workers typically do the following:

- Greet customers and answer their questions about menu items and specials
- Take food or drink orders from customers
- Prepare food and drink orders, such as sandwiches, salads, and coffee
- Relay customers' orders to other kitchen staff
- Serve food and drinks to customers at a counter, at a stand, or in a hotel room
- Clean assigned work areas, dining tables, or serving counters
- Replenish and stock service stations, cabinets, and tables
- Set tables or prepare food trays for new customers

Food and beverage serving and related workers are the front line of customer service in restaurants, cafeterias, and other food service establishments. Depending on the establishment, they take customers' food and drink orders and serve food and beverages.

Most work as part of a team, helping coworkers to improve workflow and customer service. The job titles of food and beverage serving and related workers vary with where they work and what they do.

The following are examples of types of food and beverage serving and related workers:

Combined food preparation and serving workers, including fast food, are employed primarily by fast-food restaurants. They take food and beverage orders, prepare or retrieve items when ready, fill cups with beverages, and accept customers' payments. They also heat food items and make salads and sandwiches.

Counter attendants take orders and serve food over a counter in snack bars, cafeterias, movie theaters, and coffee shops. They fill cups with coffee, soda, and other beverages, and may prepare fountain specialties, such as milkshakes and ice cream sundaes. Counter attendants take carryout orders from diners and wrap or place items in containers. They clean counters, prepare itemized bills, and accept customers' payments.

Food servers, nonrestaurant, serve food to customers outside of a restaurant environment. Many deliver room service meals in hotels or meals to hospital rooms. Some act as carhops, bringing orders to customers in parked cars.

Dining room and cafeteria attendants and bartender helpers—sometimes collectively referred to as *bus staff*—help waiters, waitresses, and bartenders by cleaning and setting tables, removing dirty dishes, and keeping serving areas stocked with supplies. They also may help waiters and waitresses by bringing meals out of the kitchen, distributing dishes to diners, filling water glasses, and delivering condiments. *Cafeteria attendants* stock serving tables with food trays, dishes, and silverware. They sometimes carry trays to dining tables for customers. *Bartender helpers* keep bar equipment clean and glasses washed.

Hosts and hostesses greet customers and manage reservation and waiting lists. They may direct customers to coatrooms, restrooms, or a waiting area until their table is ready. Hosts and hostesses assign guests to tables suitable for the size of their group, escort patrons to their seats, and provide menus. They also take reservations over the phone, arrange parties, and help with other customers' requests.

Work Environment

Food and beverage serving and related workers held about 4.7 million jobs in 2014. About 73 percent worked in restaurants, including full-service and fast-food restaurants in 2014.

Employment in the detailed occupations of the food and beverage serving and related workers group in 2014 was as follows:

Combined food preparation and serving workers, including fast food	3,159,700
Counter attendants, cafeteria, food concession, and coffee shop	481,200
Dining room and cafeteria attendants and bartender helpers	415,300
Hosts and hostesses, restaurant, lounge, and coffee shop	376,400
Food servers, nonrestaurant	253,100
Food preparation and serving related workers, all other	46,100

Food and beverage serving workers assist diners at cafeterias.

Median Hourly Wages, May 2014

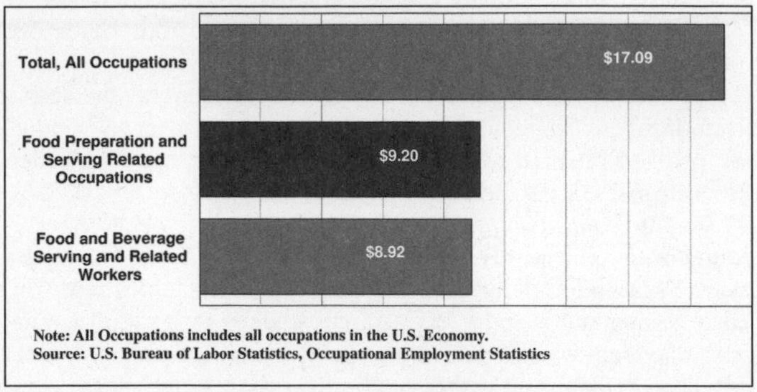

Percent Change in Employment, Projected 2014–2024

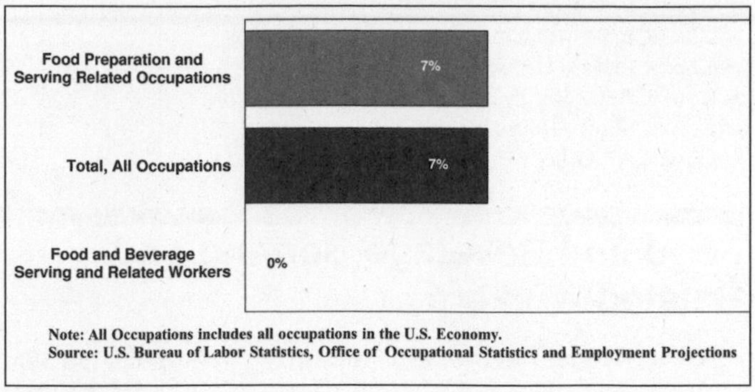

Food and beverage serving and related workers are on their feet most of the time and often carry heavy trays of food, dishes, and glassware. During busy dining periods, they are under pressure to serve customers quickly and efficiently.

Injuries and Illnesses. Food preparation and serving areas in restaurants often have potential safety hazards, such as hot ovens and slippery floors. As a result, counter attendants, food servers, dining room and cafeteria attendants, and bartender helpers have a higher rate of injuries and illnesses than the national average. Common hazards include slips, cuts, and burns, but the injuries are seldom serious. To reduce these risks, workers often wear gloves, aprons, or nonslip shoes.

Work Schedules. Many food and beverage serving and related workers were employed part time in 2014. For example, about 1 in 2 combined food preparation and serving workers, including fast food, the largest occupation in this profile, worked part time in 2014. Because food service and drinking establishments typically have extended dining hours, early morning, late evening, weekend, and holidays work is common. Those who work in school cafeterias have more regular hours and may work only during the school year, usually 9 to 10 months.

In addition, business hours in restaurants allow for flexible schedules that appeal to many teenagers, who can gain work experience. Compared with all other occupations, a much larger proportion of food and beverage serving and related workers were 16 to 19 years old in 2014.

Education/Training

Most food and beverage service jobs are entry-level jobs and do not require a high school diploma. The majority of workers receive short-term on-the-job training.

Most states require workers, such as nonrestaurant servers, who serve alcoholic beverages to be 18 years of age or older.

Education. There are no formal education requirements for becoming a food and beverage serving worker.

Training. Most workers learn their skills through short-term on-the-job training, usually lasting several weeks. Training includes basic customer service, kitchen safety, safe food-handling procedures, and good sanitation habits.

Some employers, particularly those in fast-food restaurants, teach new workers with the use of self-study programs, online programs, audiovisual presentations, or instructional booklets that explain food preparation and service procedures. However, most food and beverage serving and related workers learn their skills by watching and working with more experienced workers.

Some full-service restaurants provide new dining room employees with classroom training sessions that alternate with periods of on-the-job work experience. The training communicates the operating philosophy of the restaurant, helps new employees establish a personal rapport with other staff, teaches employees formal serving techniques, and instills a desire in the staff to work as a team.

Some nonrestaurant servers and bartender helpers who work in establishments where alcohol is served may need training on state and local laws concerning the sale of alcoholic beverages. Some states, counties, and cities mandate such training, which typically lasts a few hours and can be taken online or in-house.

Employment Projections Data for Food and Beverage Serving and Related Workers

Occupational Title	SOC Code	Employment, 2014	Projected Employment, 2024	Change, 2014–2024 Percent	Change, 2014–2024 Numeric
Food and beverage serving and related workers	—	4,731,800	5,183,600	10	451,800
Combined food preparation and serving workers, including fast food	35-3021	3,159,700	3,503,200	11	343,500
Counter attendants, cafeteria, food concession, and coffee shop	35-3022	481,200	510,000	6	28,900
Food servers, nonrestaurant	35-3041	253,100	287,000	13	33,800
Dining room and cafeteria attendants and bartender helpers	35-9011	415,300	440,700	6	25,400
Hosts and hostesses, restaurant, lounge, and coffee shop	35-9031	376,400	393,200	4	16,700
Food preparation and serving related workers, all other	35-9099	46,100	49,600	8	3,500

Source: U.S. Bureau of Labor Statistics, Employment Projections Program

Similar Occupations. This table shows a list of occupations with job duties that are similar to those of food and beverage serving and related workers.

Occupations	Entry-level Education	2014 Median Pay	Projected Job Growth	Average Annual Openings
Bartenders	No formal educational credential	$19,050	10%	6,010
Cashiers	No formal educational credential	$19,060	2%	6,700
Cooks	See Education/Training	$21,120	4%	9,700
Flight Attendants	High school diploma or equivalent	$42,290	2%	220
Food Preparation Workers	No formal educational credential	$19,560	6%	5,480
Retail Sales Workers	No formal educational credential	$21,670	7%	33,100
Waiters and Waitresses	No formal educational credential	$18,730	3%	6,890

Advancement. Advancement opportunities are limited to those who remain on the job for a long time. However, some dining room and cafeteria attendants and bartender helpers may advance to waiter, waitress, or bartender positions as they learn the basics of serving food or preparing drinks.

Important Qualities

Communication skills. Food and beverage serving and related workers must listen carefully to their customers' orders and relay them correctly to the kitchen staff so that the orders are prepared to the customers' request.

Customer-service skills. Food service establishments rely on good food and customer service to keep customers and succeed in a competitive industry. As a result, workers should be courteous and be able to attend to customers' requests.

Physical stamina. Food and beverage serving and related workers spend most of their worktime standing, carrying heavy trays, cleaning work areas, and attending to customers' needs.

Pay

The median hourly wage for food and beverage serving and related workers was $8.92 in May 2014. The median wage is the wage at which half the workers in an occupation earned more than that amount and half earned less. The lowest 10 percent earned less than $7.87, and the highest 10 percent earned more than $11.89.

Median hourly wages for food and beverage serving and related workers in May 2014 were as follows:

Food preparation and serving related workers, all other	$9.86
Food servers, nonrestaurant	9.57
Dining room and cafeteria attendants and bartender helpers	9.02
Counter attendants, cafeteria, food concession, and coffee shop	9.01
Hosts and hostesses, restaurant, lounge, and coffee shop	9.00
Combined food preparation and serving workers, including fast food	8.85

Job Outlook

Overall employment of food and beverage serving and related workers is projected to grow 10 percent from 2014 to 2024, faster than the average for all occupations. Employment growth, however, will vary by occupation (see Employment Projections table for details).

As a growing population continues to dine out, purchase takeout meals, or have food delivered, more restaurants, particularly fast-food and casual dining restaurants, are expected to open. In response, more food and beverage serving workers, including fast-food workers, will be required to serve customers.

In addition, nontraditional food service operations, such as those inside grocery stores and cafeterias in hospitals and residential care facilities, will serve more prepared meals. Because these workers are essential to the operation of a food-serving establishment, they will continue to be in demand.

Job Prospects. Job opportunities for food and beverage serving and related workers will be excellent because many workers leave the occupation each year, resulting in a large number of job openings.

Workers with related work experience and excellent customer-service skills should have the best job opportunities at upscale restaurants. Still, those seeking positions at these establishments will face strong competition because the prospect of higher tips attracts many applicants.

Contacts for More Information

For more information on food and beverage serving careers, visit

➤ National Restaurant Association (www.restaurant.org)

O*NET

➤ Combined Food Preparation and Serving Workers, Including Fast Food (35-3021.00)

➤ Counter Attendants, Cafeteria, Food Concession, and Coffee Shop (35-3022.00)

➤ Baristas (35-3022.01)

➤ Food Servers, Nonrestaurant (35-3041.00)

➤ Dining Room and Cafeteria Attendants and Bartender Helpers (35-9011.00)

➤ Hosts and Hostesses, Restaurant, Lounge, and Coffee Shop (35-9031.00)

➤ Food Preparation and Serving Related Workers, All Other (35-9099.00)

Food Preparation Workers

- **2014 Median Pay** .... $19,560 per year, $9.40 per hour
- **Typical Entry-Level Education** .... No formal educational credential
- **Work Experience in a Related Occupation** .... None
- **On-the-job Training** .... Short-term on-the-job training
- **Number of Jobs, 2014** 873,900
- **Job Outlook, 2014–24** .... 6% (As fast as average)
- **Employment Change, 2014–24** 54,800

What Food Preparation Workers Do

Food preparation workers perform many routine tasks under the direction of cooks, chefs, or food service managers. Food preparation workers prepare cold foods, slice meat, peel and cut vegetables, brew coffee or tea, and perform many other food service tasks.

Duties. Food preparation workers typically do the following:

- Clean and sanitize work areas, equipment, utensils, and dishes
- Weigh or measure ingredients, such as meats and liquids
- Prepare fruit and vegetables for cooking
- Cut meats, poultry, and seafood and prepare them for cooking
- Mix ingredients for salads
- Store food in designated containers and storage areas to prevent spoilage
- Take and record the temperature of food and food storage areas
- Place food trays over food warmers for immediate service

Food preparation workers perform routine, repetitive tasks under the direction of cooks, chefs, or food service managers. To help cooks and other kitchen staff, they prepare ingredients for dishes by slicing and dicing vegetables and by making salads and cold food items. Other common duties include keeping salad bars and buffet tables stocked and clean.

Food preparation workers retrieve pots and pans, clean and store kitchen equipment, and unload and store food supplies. When needed, they retrieve food and equipment for cooks and chefs. In some kitchens, food preparation workers use a variety of commercial kitchen equipment, such as commercial dishwashers, blenders, slicers, or grinders.

In restaurants, workers stock and use soda machines, coffeemakers, and espresso machines to prepare beverages for customers. In fast-food restaurants, food preparation workers may take customer orders and process payments.

Work Environment

Food preparation workers held about 873,900 jobs in 2014. The industries that employed the most food preparation workers were as follows:

Restaurants and other eating places	49%
Grocery stores	16
Special food services	6
Elementary and secondary schools; state, local, and private	5

Food preparation workers are employed in restaurants, hotels, and other places where food is served, such as grocery stores, schools, hospitals, and cafeterias.

Food preparation workers wash and cut up fresh ingredients.

The work is often strenuous. Food preparation workers may stand for hours at a time while cleaning or preparing ingredients. Some may be required to lift and carry heavy pots or unload heavy food supplies.

The fast-paced environment in kitchens can be hectic and stressful, especially during peak dining hours. Therefore, food preparation workers must work well with cooks and other kitchen staff so that dishes are prepared properly and on time.

Injuries and Illnesses. Food preparation areas in kitchens often have potential safety hazards, such as hot ovens and slippery floors. As a result, food preparation workers have a higher rate of injuries and illnesses than the national average. The most common hazards include slips, falls, cuts, and burns, but these injuries are seldom serious. To reduce risks, workers often wear gloves, aprons, and nonslip shoes.

Work Schedules. About 1 in 2 food preparation workers were employed part time in 2014. Because many restaurants are open extended hours, working early mornings, late evenings, weekends, or holidays is common. Those who work in school cafeterias may have hours that are more regular and may work only during the school year, usually for 9 or 10 months. Some resorts offer seasonal employment.

Education/Training

Food preparation workers typically learn their skills through on-the-job training. No formal education or previous work experience is required.

Median Hourly Wages, May 2014

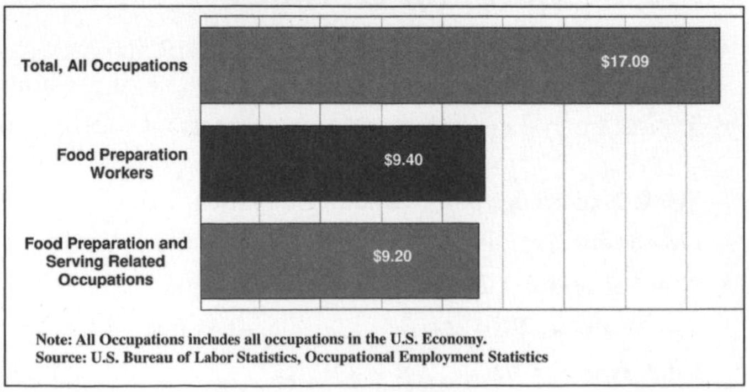

Percent Change in Employment, Projected 2014–2024

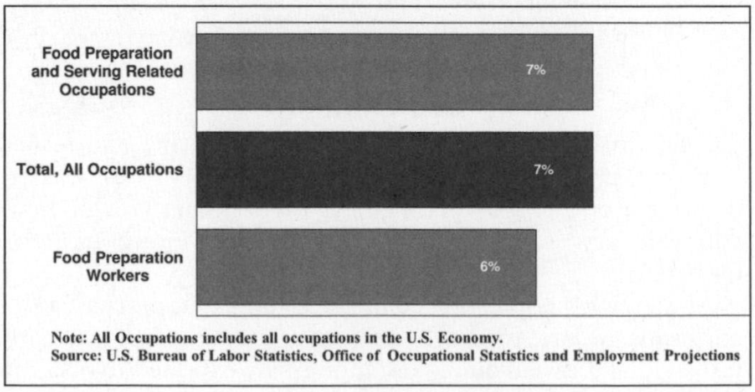

Employment Projections Data for Food Preparation Workers

Occupational Title	SOC Code	Employment, 2014	Projected Employment, 2024	Change, 2014–2024 Percent	Change, 2014–2024 Numeric
Food preparation workers	35-2021	873,900	928,800	6	54,800

Source: U.S. Bureau of Labor Statistics, Employment Projections Program

Similar Occupations. This table shows a list of occupations with job duties that are similar to those of food preparation workers.

Occupations	Entry-level Education	2014 Median Pay	Projected Job Growth	Average Annual Openings
Bakers	No formal educational credential	$23,600	7%	1,300
Butchers	No formal educational credential	$28,660	5%	700
Chefs and Head Cooks	High school diploma or equivalent	$41,610	9%	1,130
Cooks	See Education/Training	$21,120	4%	9,700
Food and Beverage Serving and Related Workers	No formal educational credential	$18,550	10%	45,180

Education. There are no formal education requirements for becoming a food preparation worker.

Training. Most food preparation workers learn their skills through short-term on-the-job training, usually lasting several weeks. Trainees typically start by working under the supervision of an experienced worker, who teaches them basic kitchen duties. Training also may include basic sanitation and workplace safety regulations, as well as instructions on how to handle and prepare food.

Important Qualities

Dexterity. Food preparation workers chop vegetables, cut meat, and perform many other tasks with sharp knives. They must have the ability to work quickly and safely with sharp objects.

Listening skills. Food preparation workers must understand customers' orders and follow directions from cooks, chefs, or food service managers.

Physical stamina. Food preparation workers stand on their feet for long periods while they prepare food, clean work areas, or lift heavy pots from the stove.

Physical strength. Food preparation workers should be strong enough to lift and carry heavy food supply boxes, which often can weigh up to 50 pounds.

Advancement. Advancement opportunities for food preparation workers depend on their training and work experience. Many food preparation workers advance to assistant or line cook positions as they learn basic cooking skills.

Pay

The median hourly wage for food preparation workers was $9.40 in May 2014. The median wage is the wage at which half the workers in an occupation earned more than that amount and half earned less. The lowest 10 percent earned less than $8.04, and the highest 10 percent earned more than $14.09.

In May 2014, the median hourly wages for food preparation workers in the top industries in which they worked were as follows:

Elementary and secondary schools; state, local, and private	$11.35
Special food services	10.04
Grocery stores	9.77
Restaurants and other eating places	9.17

Pay for food preparation workers varies by employer and region. Pay is usually highest for workers in elementary and secondary schools and in major metropolitan and resort areas.

Job Outlook

Employment of food preparation workers is projected to grow 6 percent from 2014 to 2024, about as fast as the average for all occupations.

Population and income growth are expected to result in greater consumer demand for food at a variety of dining places, including restaurants and grocery stores. In response, more restaurants and food establishments are expected to open. Many of these establishments, including nursing and residential care facilities, will require food preparation workers to wash and cut ingredients, clean work areas, and store and retrieve supplies. In addition, consumers continue to prefer fresh meals made from scratch, and chefs and cooks in various food service venues will require the assistance of food preparation workers to prepare these more labor-intensive meals.

Some restaurants and cafeterias customize their food orders from wholesalers and distributors in an effort to lower costs. For example, they may order pre-washed, -cut, or -seasoned ingredients, such as meat or vegetables. Employment growth of food preparation workers will be moderate at these dining establishments.

Job Prospects. Job opportunities for food preparation workers should be very good because of the need to replace workers who leave the occupation each year.

Jobseekers with related work experience should find opportunities at upscale restaurants. However, individuals seeking full-time positions at these restaurants will face strong competition because the number of job applicants often exceeds the number of job openings.

Contacts for More Information

For more information about job opportunities, contact local employers and local offices of the state employment service.

For more information about food preparation workers, visit

➤ National Restaurant Association (www.restaurant.org)

O*NET

➤ Food Preparation Workers (35-2021.00)

Waiters and Waitresses

- **2014 Median Pay** .... $18,730 per year $9.01 per hour
- **Typical Entry-Level Education** .... No formal educational credential
- **Work Experience in a Related Occupation** .... None
- **On-the-job Training** .... Short-term on-the-job training
- **Number of Jobs, 2014** 2,465,100
- **Job Outlook, 2014–24** .... 3% (Slower than average)
- **Employment Change, 2014–24** 68,900

Waitresses bring food from the kitchen and sometimes refill customers' drinks.

What Waiters and Waitresses Do

Waiters and waitresses take orders and serve food and beverages to customers in dining establishments.

Duties. Waiters and waitresses typically do the following:

- Greet customers, present menus, and explain daily specials to customers
- Answer questions related to the menu
- Take food and beverage orders from customers
- Relay food and beverage orders to the kitchen staff
- Prepare drinks and food garnishes
- Carry trays of food or drinks from the kitchen to the dining tables
- Remove dirty dishes and glasses, and clean tables after customers finish meals
- Prepare itemized checks and take payments from customers
- Set up dining areas, refill condiments, and stock service areas

Waiters and waitresses, also called *servers*, are responsible for ensuring that customers have a satisfying dining experience. The specific duties of servers vary with the establishment in which they work.

In casual-dining restaurants that offer simple menu items, such as salads, soups, and sandwiches, servers provide fast, efficient, and courteous service. In fine-dining restaurants, where more complicated meals are prepared and are often served over several courses, waiters and waitresses emphasize personal, attentive treatment at a more leisurely pace. For example, they may suggest a beverage choice such as a wine recommendation with certain foods.

Waiters and waitresses may meet with managers and chefs before each shift to discuss the menu or specials, review ingredients for potential food allergies, or talk about any food safety concerns. They also discuss coordination between the kitchen and the dining room and review any customer service issues from the previous day or shift.

In establishments where alcohol is served, waiters and waitresses verify the age of customers and ensure that they meet legal requirements for the purchase of alcohol.

Work Environment

Waiters and waitresses held about 2.5 million jobs in 2014. About 78 percent worked in full-service restaurants—establishments that provide food service to customers who are served while seated and pay after eating.

Waiters and waitresses are on their feet most of the time and often carry heavy trays of food, dishes, and drinks. The work can be hectic and fast-paced. During busy dining periods, they are under pressure to serve customers quickly and efficiently. They must be able to work well as a team with kitchen staff to ensure that customers receive prompt service.

Because waiters and waitresses are the front line of customer service in food service and drinking establishments, appearance is important. Those who work in fine-dining and upscale restaurants may be required to wear uniforms, including ties or aprons, which are typically provided by their employer.

Work Schedules. About 1 in 2 waiters and waitresses worked part time in 2014. Many work early mornings, late evenings, weekends, and holidays. This is especially true for those who work in

Median Hourly Wages, May 2014

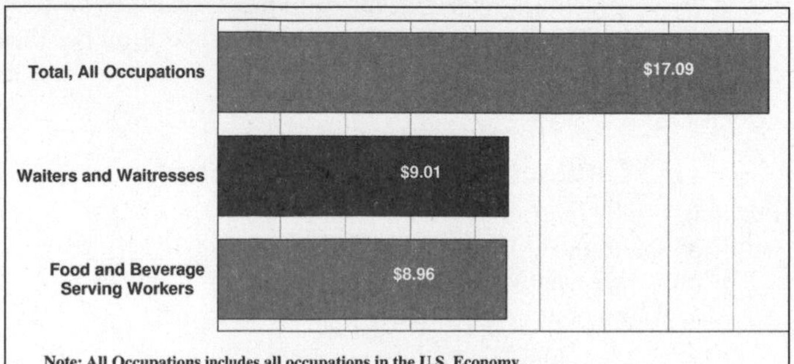

Note: All Occupations includes all occupations in the U.S. Economy.
Source: U.S. Bureau of Labor Statistics, Occupational Employment Statistics

Percent Change in Employment, Projected 2014–2024

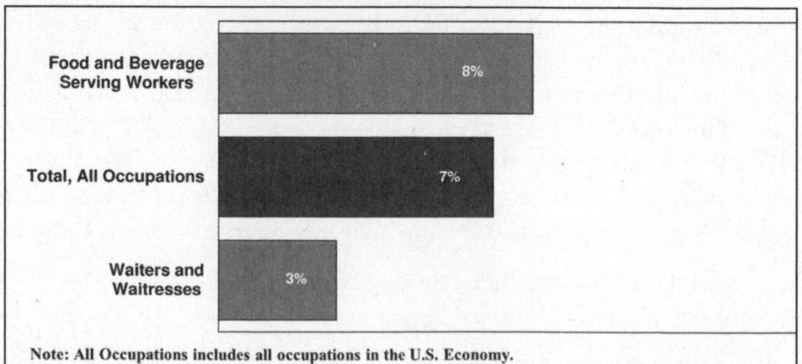

Note: All Occupations includes all occupations in the U.S. Economy.
Source: U.S. Bureau of Labor Statistics, Office of Occupational Statistics and Employment Projections

Employment Projections Data for Waiters and Waitresses

Occupational Title	SOC Code	Employment, 2014	Projected Employment, 2024	Change, 2014–2024 Percent	Change, 2014–2024 Numeric
Waiters and waitresses	35-3031	2,465,100	2,534,000	3	68,900

Source: U.S. Bureau of Labor Statistics, Employment Projections Program

full-service restaurants, which employed about 78 percent of all waiters and waitresses in 2014.

In resorts that offer seasonal employment, waiters and waitresses might work for only a few months each year.

Education/Training

Most waiter and waitress jobs are entry level, and workers learn through short-term on-the-job training. No formal education or previous work experience is required to enter the occupation.

Most states require workers who serve alcoholic beverages to be at least 18 years of age, but some states require servers to be older. Waiters and waitresses who serve alcohol must be familiar with state and local laws concerning the sale of alcoholic beverages.

Education. No formal education is required to become a waiter or waitress.

Training. Most waiters and waitresses learn their skills through short-term on-the-job training, usually lasting a few weeks. Trainees typically work with an experienced waiter or waitress, who teaches them basic serving techniques.

Some full-service restaurants provide new employees with some form of classroom training that alternates with periods of on-the-job work experience. These training programs communicate the operating philosophy of the restaurant, help new servers establish a rapport with other staff, teach serving techniques, and instill a desire to work as a team. They also discuss customer service situations and the proper ways to handle unpleasant circumstances or unruly customers.

Training for waiters and waitresses in establishments that serve alcohol typically involves learning state and local laws concerning the sale of alcoholic beverages. Some states, counties, and cities mandate the training, which typically lasts a few hours and can be taken online or in-house.

Important Qualities

Communication skills. Waiters and waitresses must listen carefully to customers' specific requests, ask questions, and relay the information to the kitchen staff, so that orders are prepared to the customers' satisfaction.

Customer-service skills. Waiters and waitresses spend most of their work time serving customers. They should be friendly and polite and be able to develop a rapport with customers.

Detail oriented. Waiters and waitresses must record customers' orders accurately. They need be able to recall the details of each order and match the food or drink orders to the correct customers.

Interpersonal skills. Waiters and waitresses should be courteous, tactful, and attentive as they deal with customers in all circumstances to resolve any issues that arise.

Physical stamina. Waiters and waitresses spend hours on their feet carrying heavy trays, dishes, and drinks.

Pay

The median hourly wage for waiters and waitresses was $9.01 in May 2014. The median wage is the wage at which half the workers in an occupation earned more than that amount and half earned less. The lowest 10 percent earned less than $7.92, and the highest 10 percent earned more than $15.35.

Many waiters and waitresses get their earnings from a combination of hourly wages and customer tips. Earnings vary greatly with the type of establishment and locality. For example, tips are generally much higher in upscale restaurants in major metropolitan areas and resorts.

Tipped employees earn at least the federal minimum wage ($7.25 per hour, as of July 24, 2009), which may be paid as a combination of direct wages and tips, depending on the state. Direct wages may be as low as $2.13 per hour according to the Fair Labor Standards Act (FLSA).

According to the FLSA, tipped employees are those who regularly receive more than $30 a month in tips. The Wage and Hour Division of the U.S. Department of Labor maintains a website with minimum wages for tipped employees, by state, although some localities have enacted minimum wages higher than their state requires.

Many employers provide meals and furnish uniforms, but some may deduct the cost from wages.

About 1 in 2 waiters and waitresses worked part time in 2014. Many work early mornings, late evenings, weekends, and holidays. This is especially true for those who work in full-service

Similar Occupations. This table shows a list of occupations with job duties that are similar to those of waiters and waitresses.

Occupations	Entry-level Education	2014 Median Pay	Projected Job Growth	Average Annual Openings
Bartenders	No formal educational credential	$19,050	10%	6,010
Cashiers	No formal educational credential	$19,060	2%	6,700
Flight Attendants	High school diploma or equivalent	$42,290	2%	220
Food and Beverage Serving and Related Workers	No formal educational credential	$18,550	10%	45,180
Retail Sales Workers	No formal educational credential	$21,670	7%	33,100

restaurants, which employed about 78 percent of all waiters and waitresses in 2014.

In resorts that offer seasonal employment, waiters and waitresses might be employed for only a few months each year.

Job Outlook

Employment of waiters and waitresses is projected to grow 3 percent from 2014 to 2024, slower than the average for all occupations.

As the population grows and more people dine out, new restaurants are expected to open. Many establishments, particularly full-service restaurants, will continue to use waiters and waitresses to serve food and beverages and provide customer service.

Technology-driven payment and ordering systems increasingly are being used in some food service establishments, including some restaurants. In these places, waiters and waitresses may mostly serve food or drinks, because customers can order and pay for food using electronic devices, such as tabletop tablets, phones, or other devices.

Job Prospects. Job opportunities for waiters and waitresses are expected to be very good, primarily because of the large number of workers who leave the occupation each year.

Candidates with previous work experience and excellent customer-service skills will have the best job opportunities in upscale restaurants. Strong competition at these establishments is expected, as potential earnings from tips are greater than at other restaurants and the number of job applicants usually exceeds the number of job openings.

Contacts for More Information

For more information on careers as a waiter or waitress, visit

➤ National Restaurant Association (www.restaurant.org)

O*NET

➤ Waiters and Waitresses (35-3031.00)

Healthcare

Athletic Trainers

- **2014 Median Pay** .... $43,370 per year
- **Typical Entry-Level Education** .... Bachelor's degree
- **Work Experience in a Related Occupation** .... None
- **On-the-job Training** .... None
- **Number of Jobs, 2014** 25,400
- **Job Outlook, 2014–24** .... 21% (Much faster than average)
- **Employment Change, 2014–24** 5,400

What Athletic Trainers Do

Athletic trainers specialize in preventing, diagnosing, and treating muscle and bone injuries and illnesses.

Duties. Athletic trainers typically do the following:

- Apply protective or injury-preventive devices, such as tape, bandages, and braces
- Recognize and evaluate injuries
- Provide first aid or emergency care
- Develop and carry out rehabilitation programs for injured athletes
- Plan and implement comprehensive programs to prevent injury and illness among athletes
- Perform administrative tasks, such as keeping records and writing reports on injuries and treatment programs

Athletic trainers work with people of all ages and all skill levels, from young children to soldiers and professional athletes. Athletic trainers are usually one of the first healthcare providers on the scene when injuries occur. They work under the direction of a licensed physician and with other healthcare providers, often discussing specific injuries and treatment options or evaluating and treating patients, as directed by a physician. Some athletic trainers meet with a team physician or consulting physician regularly.

An athletic trainer's administrative responsibilities may include regular meetings with an athletic director or another administrative officer to deal with budgets, purchasing, policy implementation, and other business-related issues. Athletic trainers plan athletic programs that are compliant with federal and state regulations, such as laws related to athlete concussions.

Athletic trainers should not be confused with fitness trainers and instructors, including personal trainers.

Work Environment

Athletic trainers held about 25,400 jobs in 2014. The industries that employed the most athletic trainers were as follows:

Educational services; state, local, and private	37%
Ambulatory healthcare services	26
Hospitals; state, local, and private	13
Fitness and recreational sports centers	11
Spectator sports	5

Many athletic trainers work in educational settings, such as colleges, universities, elementary schools, and secondary schools. Others work in hospitals, fitness centers, or physicians' offices, or for professional sports teams. Some athletic trainers work with military, with law enforcement, or with performing artists.

Athletic trainers may spend their time working outdoors on sports fields in all types of weather.

Work Schedules. Most athletic trainers work full time. Athletic trainers who work with teams during sporting events may work evenings or weekends and travel often.

Education/Training

Athletic trainers need at least a bachelor's degree. Nearly all states require athletic trainers to have a license or certification; requirements vary by state.

Education. Athletic trainers need at least a bachelor's degree from an accredited college or university. Master's degree programs are also common. Degree programs have classroom and clinical components, including science and health-related courses, such as biology, anatomy, physiology, and nutrition.

The Commission on Accreditation of Athletic Training Education (CAATE) accredits athletic trainer programs, including postprofessional and residency athletic trainer programs.

High school students interested in postsecondary athletic training programs should take courses in anatomy, physiology, and physics.

Important Qualities

Compassion. Athletic trainers work with athletes and patients who may be in considerable pain or discomfort. The trainers must be sympathetic while providing treatments.

Decision-making skills. Athletic trainers must be able to make informed clinical decisions that could affect the health or livelihood of patients.

Detail oriented. Athletic trainers must record patients' progress accurately and ensure that they are receiving the appropriate treatments or practicing the correct fitness regimen.

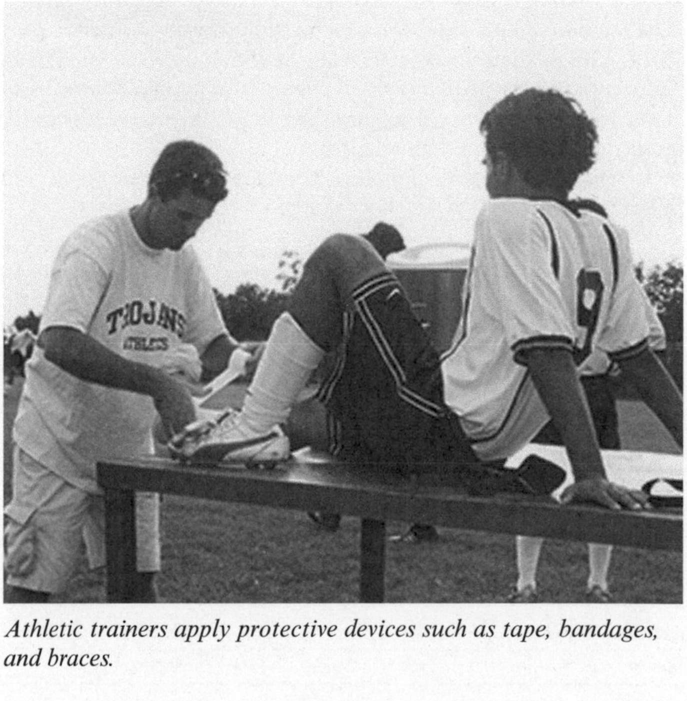

Athletic trainers apply protective devices such as tape, bandages, and braces.

Median Annual Wages, May 2014

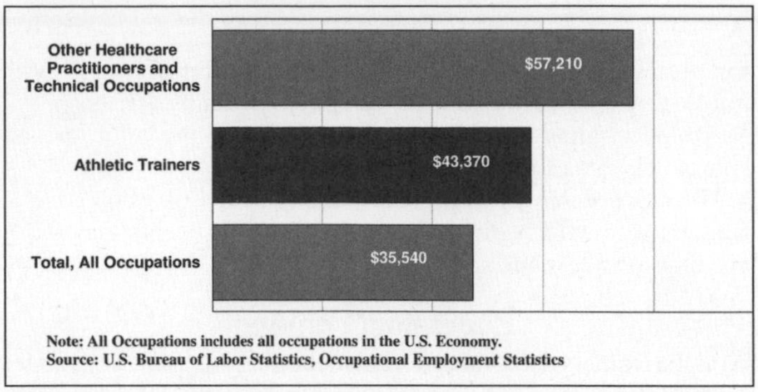

Percent Change in Employment, Projected 2014–2024

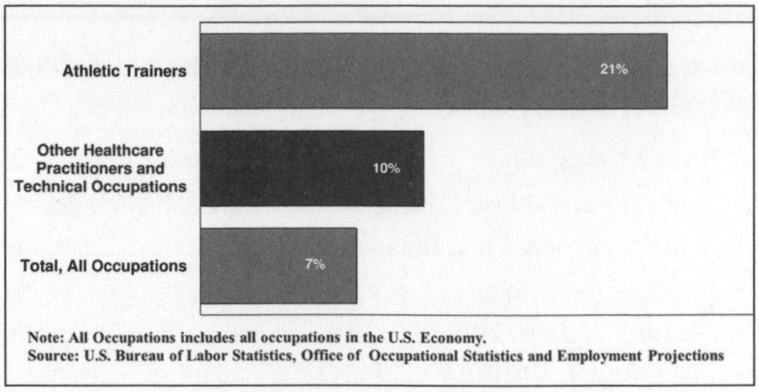

Interpersonal skills. Athletic trainers must have strong interpersonal skills in order to manage difficult situations. They must communicate well with others, including physicians, patients, athletes, coaches, and parents.

Licenses, Certifications, and Registrations. Nearly all states require athletic trainers to be licensed or certified; requirements vary by state. For specific requirements, contact the particular state's licensing or credentialing board or athletic trainer association.

The Board of Certification for the Athletic Trainer (BOC) offers the standard certification examination that most states use for licensing athletic trainers. Certification requires graduating from a CAATE-accredited program and completing the BOC exam. To maintain certification, athletic trainers must adhere to the BOC Standards of Practice and Disciplinary Process and take continuing education courses.

Advancement. Assistant athletic trainers may become head athletic trainers, athletic directors, or physician, hospital, or clinic practice administrators. In any of these positions, they will assume a management role. Athletic trainers working in colleges and universities may pursue an advanced degree to increase their advancement opportunities.

Pay

The median annual wage for athletic trainers was $43,370 in May 2014. The median wage is the wage at which half the workers in an occupation earned more than that amount and half earned less. The lowest 10 percent earned less than $27,610, and the highest 10 percent earned more than $67,070.

In May 2014, the median annual wages for athletic trainers in the top industries in which they worked were as follows:

Educational services; state, local, and private	$46,240
Hospitals; state, local, and private	44,610
Spectator sports	41,960
Ambulatory healthcare services	41,250
Fitness and recreational sports centers	40,010

Job Outlook

Employment of athletic trainers is projected to grow 21 percent from 2014 to 2024, much faster than the average for all occupations. As people become more aware of sports-related injuries at a young age, demand for athletic trainers is expected to increase.

Recent research reveals that the effects of concussions are particularly severe and long lasting for child athletes. Although concussions are dangerous at any age, children's brains are still developing and are at risk for permanent complications. Some states require public secondary schools to employ athletic trainers as part of their sports programs. Because athletic trainers are usually onsite with athletes and are often the first responders when injuries occur, the demand for trainers in schools should continue to increase.

In addition, advances and more sophisticated treatments in injury prevention and detection are projected to increase the demand for athletic trainers. Growth in an increasingly active middle-aged and elderly population will likely lead to an increased incidence of athletic-related injuries, such as sprains. Sports programs at all ages and for all experience levels will continue to create demand for athletic trainers.

Insurance and workers' compensation costs have become a concern for many employers and insurance companies, especially in areas where employees are often injured on the job. For example, military bases hire athletic trainers to help train and rehabilitate injured military personnel. These trainers also create programs aimed at keeping injury rates down. Depending on the state, some insurance companies recognize athletic trainers as healthcare providers and reimburse the cost of an athletic trainer's services.

Job Prospects. Job prospects will be best for candidates with a degree from a bachelor's or master's degree program that is accredited by the Commission on Accreditation of Athletic Training Education (CAATE) and for those who have certification from the Board of Certification for the Athletic Trainer (BOC).

Contacts for More Information

For more information about athletic trainers, visit

➤ National Athletic Trainers' Association (www.nata.org)

Employment Projections Data for Athletic Trainers

Occupational Title	SOC Code	Employment, 2014	Projected Employment, 2024	Change, 2014–2024 Percent	Change, 2014–2024 Numeric
Athletic trainers	29-9091	25,400	30,800	21	5,400

Source: U.S. Bureau of Labor Statistics, Employment Projections Program

Similar Occupations. This table shows a list of occupations with job duties that are similar to those of athletic trainers.

Occupations	Entry-level Education	2014 Median Pay	Projected Job Growth	Average Annual Openings
Chiropractors	Doctoral or professional degree	$66,720	17%	790
EMTs and Paramedics	Postsecondary nondegree award	$31,700	24%	5,850
Exercise Physiologists	Bachelor's degree	$46,270	11%	150
Massage Therapists	Postsecondary nondegree award	$37,180	22%	3,650
Occupational Therapists	Master's degree	$78,810	27%	3,040
Physical Therapists	Doctoral or professional degree	$82,390	34%	7,180
Physician Assistants	Master's degree	$95,820	30%	2,870
Recreational Therapists	Bachelor's degree	$44,000	12%	220
Respiratory Therapists	Associate's degree	$56,730	12%	1,490

For more information about accredited athletic training programs, visit

➤ Commission on Accreditation of Athletic Training Education (http://caate.net)

For more information about certification and state regulatory requirements for athletic trainers, visit

➤ Board of Certification for the Athletic Trainer (www.bocatc.org/index.php)

O*NET

➤ Athletic Trainers (29-9091.00)

Audiologists

- **2014 Median Pay** .... $73,060 per year $35.13 per hour
- **Typical Entry-Level Education** .... Doctoral or professional degree
- **Work Experience in a Related Occupation**.............. None
- **On-the-job Training** .... None
- **Number of Jobs, 2014** 13,200
- **Job Outlook, 2014–24**.... 29% (Much faster than average)
- **Employment Change, 2014–24** 3,800

What Audiologists Do

Audiologists diagnose, manage, and treat a patient's hearing, balance, or related ear problems.

Duties. Audiologists typically do the following:

- Examine patients who have hearing, balance, or related ear problems
- Assess the results of the examination and diagnose problems
- Determine and administer treatment to meet patients' goals
- Provide treatment for tinnitus, a condition that causes ringing in the ear
- Fit and dispense hearing aids
- Counsel patients and their families on ways to listen and communicate, such as by lip reading or through technology
- Evaluate patients regularly to check on hearing and balance and to continue or change the treatment plan
- Record patient progress
- Research the causes and treatment of hearing and balance disorders
- Educate patients on ways to prevent hearing loss

Audiologists use audiometers, computers, and other devices to test patients' hearing ability and balance. They work to determine the extent of hearing damage and identify the underlying cause. Audiologists measure the loudness at which a person begins to hear sounds and the person's ability to distinguish between sounds and understand speech.

Before determining treatment options, audiologists evaluate psychological information to measure the impact of hearing loss on a patient. Treatment may include cleaning wax out of ear canals, fitting and checking hearing aids, or fitting the patient with cochlear implants to improve hearing. Cochlear implants are tiny devices that are placed under the skin near the ear and deliver electrical impulses directly to the auditory nerve in the brain. This allows a person with certain types of deafness to be able to hear.

Audiologists also counsel patients on other ways to cope with profound hearing loss, such as by learning to lip read or by using technology.

Audiologists can help a patient suffering from vertigo or other balance problems. They work with patients and provide them

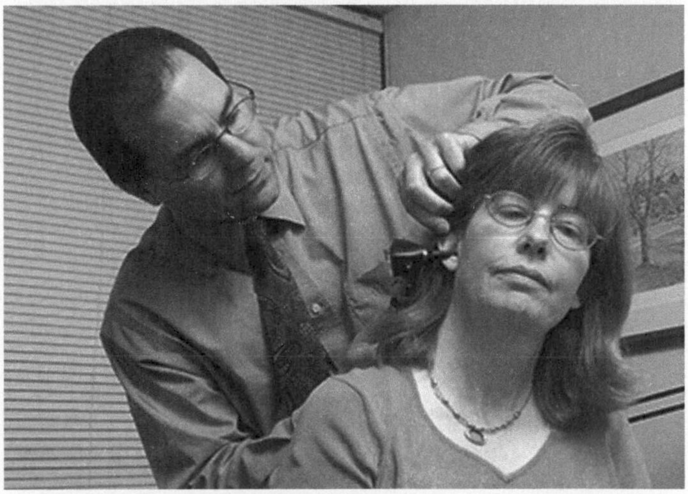

Audiologists examine individuals and identify symptoms of hearing loss and other auditory, balance, and related sensory and neural problems.

Median Annual Wages, May 2014

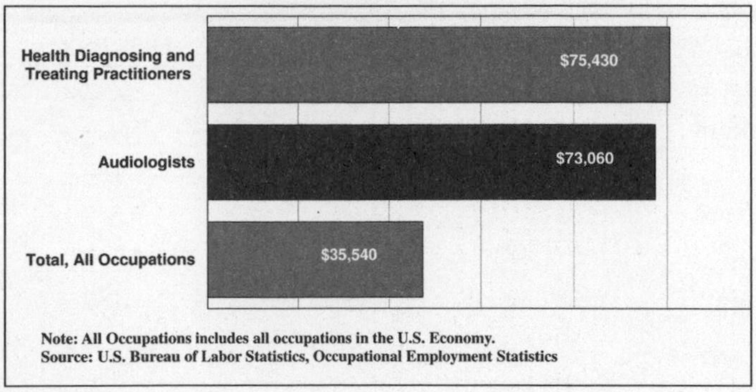

Percent Change in Employment, Projected 2014–2024

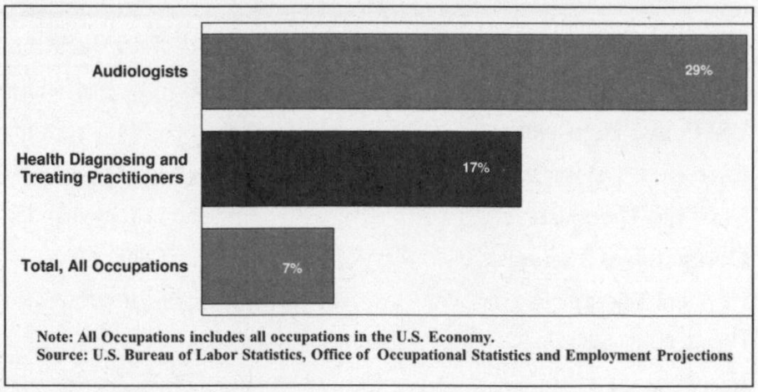

with exercises involving head movement or positioning that might relieve some of their symptoms.

Some audiologists specialize in working with the elderly or with children. Others educate the public on hearing loss prevention. Audiologists may design products to help protect the hearing of workers on the job. Audiologists who are self-employed hire employees, keep records, order equipment and supplies, and complete other tasks related to running a business.

Work Environment

Audiologists held about 13,200 jobs in 2014. The industries that employed the most audiologists were as follows:

Offices of other health practitioners	25%
Offices of physicians	25
Hospitals; state, local, and private	14
Educational services; state, local, and private	12
Health and personal care stores	11

Most audiologists work in healthcare facilities, such as hospitals, physicians' offices, and audiology clinics. Some work in schools or for school districts and travel between facilities. Others work in health and personal care stores. Audiologists work closely with registered nurses, audiology assistants (a type of medical assistant), and other healthcare workers.

Work Schedules. Most audiologists worked full time in 2014, although about 1 out of 3 worked part time. Some work weekends and evenings to meet patients' needs. Those who work on a contract basis may spend time traveling between facilities. For example, an audiologist who is contracted by a school system may have to travel between different schools to provide services.

Education/Training

Audiologists need a doctoral degree and must be licensed in all states. Requirements for licensure vary by state.

Education. The doctoral degree in audiology (Au.D.) is a graduate program that typically takes 4 years to complete. A bachelor's degree in any field is needed to enter one of these programs.

Graduate coursework includes anatomy, physiology, physics, genetics, normal and abnormal communication development, diagnosis and treatment, pharmacology, and ethics. Programs also include supervised clinical practice. Graduation from a program accredited by the Council on Academic Accreditation is required to get a license in most states.

Licenses, Certifications, and Registrations. Requirements vary by state. For specific requirements, contact your state's licensing board for audiologists.

Audiologists can earn the Certificate of Clinical Competence in Audiology (CCC-A), offered by the American Speech-Language-Hearing Association. They also may be credentialed through the American Board of Audiology. Certification can be earned by graduating from an accredited doctoral program and passing a standardized exam. Certification may be required by some states or employers. Some states may allow certification in place of some education or training requirements needed for licensure.

Important Qualities

Communication skills. Audiologists need to communicate test results, diagnoses, and proposed treatments, so patients clearly understand the situation and options. They also may need to work on teams with other healthcare providers and education specialists regarding patient care.

Compassion. Audiologists work with patients who may be frustrated or emotional because of their hearing or balance problems. Audiologists should be empathetic and supportive of patients and their families.

Critical-thinking skills. Audiologists must concentrate when testing a patient's hearing and be able to analyze each patient's situation, to offer the best treatment. They must also be able to provide alternative plans when patients do not respond to initial treatment.

Patience. Audiologists must work with patients who may need a lot of time and special attention.

Problem-solving skills. Audiologists must figure out the causes of problems with hearing and balance and determine the appropriate treatment or treatments to address them.

Pay

The median annual wage for audiologists was $73,060 in May 2014. The median wage is the wage at which half the workers in an occupation earned more than that amount and half earned less. The lowest 10 percent earned less than $47,580, and the highest 10 percent earned more than $110,960.

In May 2014, the median annual wages for audiologists in the top industries in which they worked were as follows:

Hospitals; state, local, and private	$78,070
Offices of other health practitioners	73,350
Offices of physicians	72,100
Educational services; state, local, and private	70,840
Health and personal care stores	69,670

Job Outlook

Employment of audiologists is projected to grow 29 percent from 2014 to 2024, much faster than the average for all occupations. However, because it is a small occupation, the fast growth will result in only 3,800 new jobs over the 10-year period.

An aging baby-boom population and growing life expectancies will continue to increase the demand for most healthcare services. Hearing loss and balance disorders become more prevalent as

Employment Projections Data for Audiologists

Occupational Title	SOC Code	Employment, 2014	Projected Employment, 2024	Change, 2014–2024 Percent	Change, 2014–2024 Numeric
Audiologists	29-1181	13,200	16,900	29	3,800

Source: U.S. Bureau of Labor Statistics, Employment Projections Program

Similar Occupations. This table shows a list of occupations with job duties that are similar to those of audiologists.

Occupations	Entry-level Education	2014 Median Pay	Projected Job Growth	Average Annual Openings
Optometrists	Doctoral or professional degree	$101,410	27%	1,100
Physical Therapists	Doctoral or professional degree	$82,390	34%	7,180
Physicians and Surgeons	Doctoral or professional degree	This wage is equal to or greater than $187,200.	14%	9,930
Psychologists	See Education/Training	$70,700	19%	3,250
Speech-Language Pathologists	Master's degree	$71,550	21%	2,890

people age, so the aging population is likely to increase demand for audiologists.

The early identification and diagnosis of hearing disorders in infants also may spur employment growth. Advances in hearing aid design, such as smaller size and the reduction of feedback, may make such devices more appealing as a means to minimize the effects of hearing loss. This may lead to more demand for audiologists.

Job Prospects. Demand may be greater in areas with large numbers of retirees, so audiologists who are willing to relocate may have the best job prospects.

Contacts for More Information

For information on state-specific licensing requirements, contact the state's licensing board.

For more information about audiologists, including requirements for certification and state licensure, visit

- ➤ American Speech-Language-Hearing Association (ASHA) (www.asha.org)
- ➤ American Board of Audiology (www.boardofaudiology.org)
- ➤ American Academy of Audiology (www.audiology.org)

O*NET

- ➤ Audiologists (29-1181.00)

Chiropractors

- **2014 Median Pay** .... $66,720 per year $32.08 per hour
- **Typical Entry-Level Education** .... Doctoral or professional degree
- **Work Experience in a Related Occupation** .... None
- **On-the-job Training** .... None
- **Number of Jobs, 2014** 45,200
- **Job Outlook, 2014–24** ...... 17% (Much faster than average)
- **Employment Change, 2014–24** 7,900

What Chiropractors Do

Chiropractors care for patients with health problems of the neuromusculoskeletal system, which includes nerves, bones, muscles, ligaments, and tendons. They use spinal adjustments and manipulation, and other techniques to manage patients' health concerns, such as back and neck pain.

Duties. Chiropractors typically do the following:

- Assess a patient's medical condition by reviewing their medical history, listening to the patient's concerns, and performing a physical examination
- Analyze the patient's posture, spine, and reflexes
- Conduct tests, including evaluating a patient's posture and taking X-rays
- Provide neuromusculoskeletal therapy, which involves adjusting a patient's spinal column and other joints by hand
- Give additional treatments, such as applying heat or cold to a patient's injured areas
- Advise patients on health and lifestyle issues, such as exercise, nutrition, and sleep habits
- Refer patients to other healthcare professionals, if needed

Chiropractors focus on patients' overall health. Chiropractors believe that misalignments of the spinal joints interfere with a person's neuromuscular system and can result in lower resistance to disease, as well as other conditions of poor health.

Some chiropractors use procedures such as massage therapy, rehabilitative exercise, and ultrasound in addition to spinal adjustments and manipulation. They also may apply supports, such as braces or shoe inserts, to treat patients and relieve pain.

In addition to operating a general chiropractic practice, some chiropractors concentrate in areas such as sports, neurology, orthopedics, pediatrics, or nutrition, among others. Chiropractors in private practice are responsible for marketing their businesses, hiring staff, and keeping records.

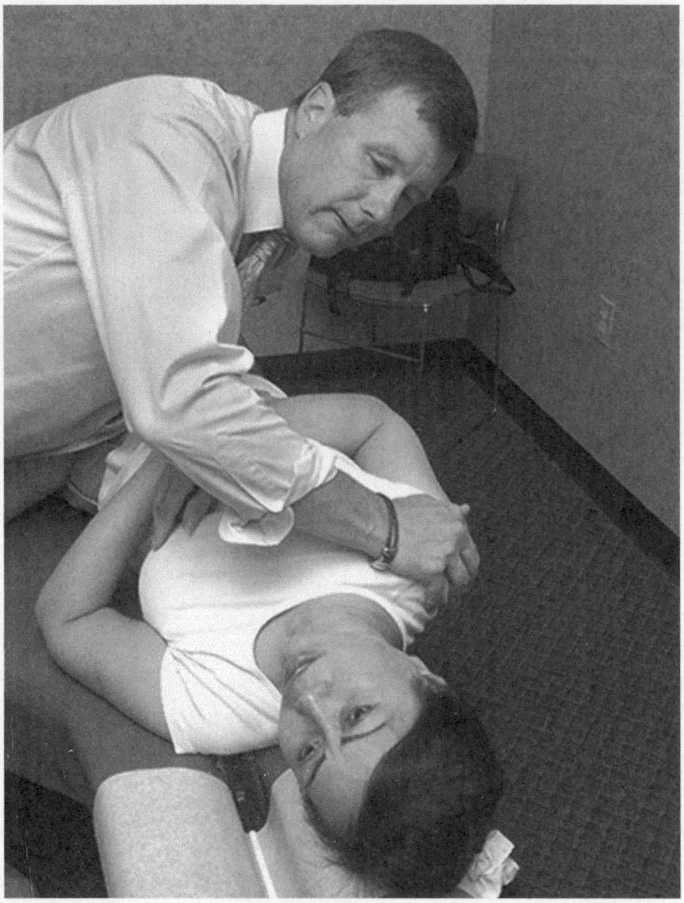

Chiropractors analyze the patient's posture and spine and may manually adjust the spinal column.

Work Environment

Chiropractors held about 45,200 jobs in 2014. Most chiropractors work in a solo or group practice. About 1 in 3 were self-employed in 2014. A small number work in hospitals or physicians' offices.

Chiropractors typically work in office settings. They may be on their feet for long periods when examining and treating patients.

Work Schedules. Although most chiropractors worked full time, about 1 in 4 worked part time in 2014. Chiropractors may work in the evenings or on weekends to accommodate working patients. Self-employed chiropractors set their own hours.

Education/Training

Chiropractors must earn a Doctor of Chiropractic (D.C.) degree and a state license. Doctor of Chiropractic programs typically take 4 years to complete and require at least 3 years of undergraduate college education for admission.

Education. Prospective chiropractors are required to have a Doctor of Chiropractic (D.C.) degree—a postgraduate professional degree that typically takes 4 years to complete. In 2014, there were 15 Doctor of Chiropractic programs on 18 campuses accredited by The Council on Chiropractic Education.

Admission to D.C. programs requires at least 90 semester hours of undergraduate education, with courses in the liberal arts and sciences, such as physics, chemistry, and biology. However, many students earn a bachelor's degree before applying to a chiropractic program.

Chiropractic education consists of classroom work in anatomy, physiology, biology, and similar subjects. Chiropractic students also get supervised clinical experience, in which they train in spinal assessment, spinal adjustment techniques, and diagnosis. D.C. programs also may include classroom work in business management and billing and finance.

Some chiropractors complete postgraduate programs offered by associations leading to diplomate credentials. These programs provide additional training in specialty areas, such as orthopedics and pediatrics, and classes are taken at chiropractic colleges. Others may choose to earn a master's degree in a related topic, such as nutrition or sports rehabilitation. Some D.C. programs offer a dual-degree option, in which students may earn a master's degree in a second topic while completing their D.C.

Licenses, Certifications, and Registrations. All states and the District of Columbia require chiropractors to be licensed. Although specific requirements vary by state, all jurisdictions require the completion of an accredited Doctor of Chiropractic (D.C.) program. Some states require chiropractors to have a bachelor's degree.

In addition, all jurisdictions require passing the National Board of Chiropractic Examiners exam, which includes basic and clinical sciences, clinical case studies, and a practical exam. Many jurisdictions also require applicants to pass state-specific law exams, called jurisprudence exams. All states require continuing education to maintain a chiropractic license. Check with your state's board of chiropractic examiners or health department for more specific information on licensure.

Important Qualities

Decision-making skills. Chiropractors must determine the best course of action when treating a patient. They must also decide when to refer patients to other healthcare professionals.

Median Annual Wages, May 2014

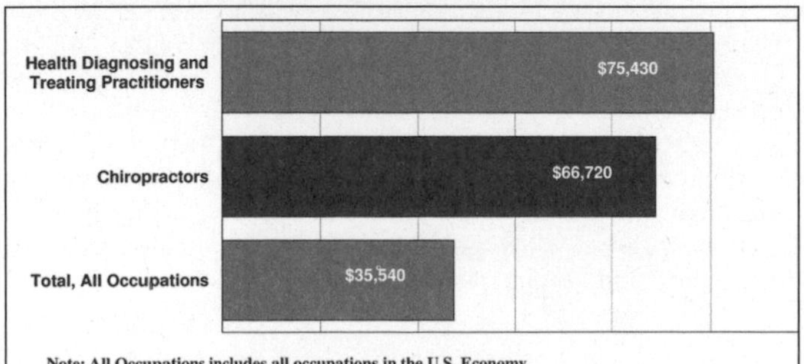

Note: All Occupations includes all occupations in the U.S. Economy.
Source: U.S. Bureau of Labor Statistics, Occupational Employment Statistics

Percent Change in Employment, Projected 2014–2024

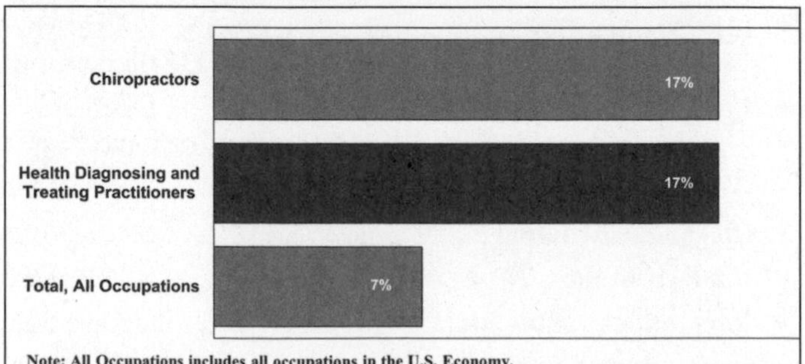

Note: All Occupations includes all occupations in the U.S. Economy.
Source: U.S. Bureau of Labor Statistics, Office of Occupational Statistics and Employment Projections

Employment Projections Data for Chiropractors

Occupational Title	SOC Code	Employment, 2014	Projected Employment, 2024	Change, 2014–2024 Percent	Change, 2014–2024 Numeric
Chiropractors	29-1011	45,200	53,100	17	7,900

Source: U.S. Bureau of Labor Statistics, Employment Projections Program

Similar Occupations. This table shows a list of occupations with job duties that are similar to those of chiropractors.

Occupations	Entry-level Education	2014 Median Pay	Projected Job Growth	Average Annual Openings
Athletic Trainers	Bachelor's degree	$43,370	21%	540
Exercise Physiologists	Bachelor's degree	$46,270	11%	150
Massage Therapists	Postsecondary nondegree award	$37,180	22%	3,650
Occupational Therapists	Master's degree	$78,810	27%	3,040
Physical Therapists	Doctoral or professional degree	$82,390	34%	7,180
Physicians and Surgeons	Doctoral or professional degree	This wage is equal to or greater than $187,200.	14%	9,930
Podiatrists	Doctoral or professional degree	$120,700	14%	140

Detail oriented. Chiropractors must be observant and pay attention to details so that they can make proper diagnoses and avoid mistakes that could harm patients.

Dexterity. Because they use their hands to perform manual adjustments to the spine and other joints, chiropractors should have good coordination to perform therapy effectively.

Empathy. Chiropractors often care for people who are in pain. They must be understanding and sympathetic to their patients' problems and needs.

Interpersonal skills. Chiropractors must be personable in order to keep clients coming to their practice. Also, because chiropractors frequently touch patients in performing therapy, they should be able to put their patients at ease.

Pay

The median annual wage for chiropractors was $66,720 in May 2014. The median wage is the wage at which half the workers in an occupation earned more than that amount and half earned less. The lowest 10 percent earned less than $31,440, and the highest 10 percent earned more than $143,760.

Chiropractors tend to earn significantly less early in their careers and then earn more as they build a client base and become owners of, or partners in, a practice.

Job Outlook

Employment of chiropractors is projected to grow 17 percent from 2014 to 2024, much faster than the average for all occupations. People across all age groups are increasingly becoming interested in alternative or complementary healthcare. Chiropractic care is appealing to patients because chiropractors use nonsurgical methods of treatment and do not prescribe drugs.

Chiropractic treatment of the back, neck, limbs, and involved joints has become more accepted as a result of research and changing attitudes about additional approaches to healthcare. As a result, chiropractors are increasingly working with other healthcare workers, such as physicians and physical therapists, through referrals and complementary care.

The aging of the large baby-boom generation will lead to new opportunities for chiropractors. Older adults are more likely to have neuromusculoskeletal and joint problems and they are seeking treatment for these conditions more often as they lead longer, more active lives.

Demand for chiropractic treatment is related to the ability of patients to pay, either directly or through health insurance. Although most insurance plans now cover chiropractic services, the extent of such coverage varies among plans. However, the number of individuals who have access to health insurance is expected to continue to increase because of federal health insurance reform.

Contacts for More Information

For information on a career as a chiropractor, visit

- American Chiropractic Association (www.acatoday.org)
- International Chiropractors Association (www.chiropractic.org)
- StudentDC (www.studentdc.com)

For a list of chiropractic programs and institutions, as well as for general information on chiropractic education, visit

- Association of Chiropractic Colleges (www.chirocolleges.org)
- The Council on Chiropractic Education (www.cce-usa.org)

For information on state education and licensure requirements, visit

- Federation of Chiropractic Licensing Boards (www.fclb.org)

For information about licensing exams, visit

- National Board of Chiropractic Examiners (www.nbce.org)

O*NET

- Chiropractors (29-1011.00)

Dental Assistants

- **2014 Median Pay** .... $35,390 per year $17.02 per hour
- **Typical Entry-Level Education** .... Postsecondary nondegree award
- **Work Experience in a Related Occupation** .... None
- **On-the-job Training** .... None
- **Number of Jobs, 2014** 318,800
- **Job Outlook, 2014–24** ...... 18% (Much faster than average)
- **Employment Change, 2014–24** 58,600

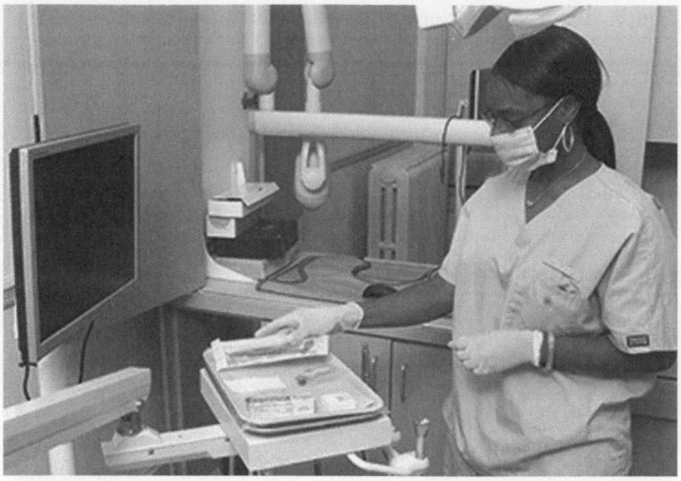

Dental assistants sterilize and disinfect instruments and equipment.

What Dental Assistants Do

Dental assistants perform many tasks, ranging from patient care and taking X-rays to recordkeeping and scheduling appointments. Their duties vary by state and by the dentists' offices where they work.

Duties. Dental assistants typically do the following:

- Ensure that patients are comfortable in the dental chair
- Prepare patients and the work area for treatments and procedures
- Sterilize dental instruments
- Help dentists by handing them instruments during procedures
- Keep patients' mouths dry by using suction hoses and other equipment
- Instruct patients in proper oral hygiene
- Process X-rays and complete lab tasks, under the direction of a dentist
- Keep records of dental treatments
- Schedule patient appointments
- Work with patients on billing and payment

Assistants who perform lab tasks, such as taking impressions of a patient's teeth, work under the direction of a dentist. They may prepare materials for dental impressions or to create temporary crowns.

All dental assistants complete certain tasks, such as helping dentists with procedures and keeping patient records. Dental assistants are allowed to perform the following procedures in some states:

- Coronal polishing
- Sealant application
- Fluoride application
- Topical anesthetic application

Coronal polishing, which means removing soft deposits such as plaque, gives teeth a cleaner appearance. In sealant application, a dental assistant paints a thin, plastic substance over teeth that seals out food particles and acid-producing bacteria to keep teeth from developing cavities. Fluoride application, in which fluoride is put directly on the teeth, is another anticavity measure. Some dental assistants may be qualified to apply topical anesthetic to an area of a patient's mouth, temporarily numbing the area to help prepare a patient for procedures.

Each state regulates the scope of practice for dental assistants. Visit www.danb.org/en/Meet-State-Requirements.aspx.

Work Environment

Dental assistants held about 318,800 jobs in 2014. Almost all dental assistants work in dentists' offices. Dental assistants work under the supervision of dentists and work closely with dental hygienists in their day-to-day activities.

Dental assistants wear safety glasses, surgical masks, protective clothing, and gloves to protect themselves and patients from infectious diseases. They also must follow safety procedures to minimize risks associated with X-ray machines.

Work Schedules. Most dental assistants work full time. However, nearly 1 in 3 assistants worked part-time in 2014. Some may work evenings or weekends.

Median Annual Wages, May 2014

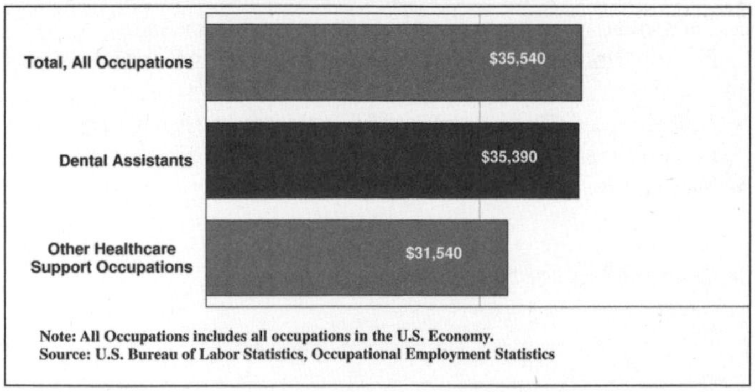

Percent Change in Employment, Projected 2014–2024

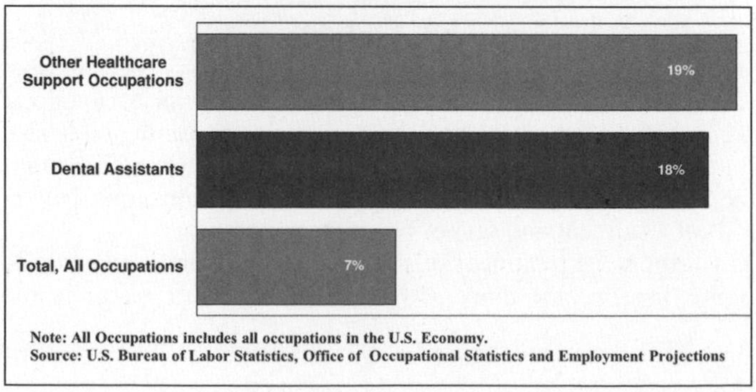

Employment Projections Data for Dental Assistants

Occupational Title	SOC Code	Employment, 2014	Projected Employment, 2024	Change, 2014–2024 Percent	Change, 2014–2024 Numeric
Dental assistants	31-9091	318,800	377,400	18	58,600

Source: U.S. Bureau of Labor Statistics, Employment Projections Program

Education/Training

There are several possible paths to becoming a dental assistant. Some states require assistants to graduate from an accredited program and pass an exam. In other states, there are no formal educational requirements.

Education. Some states require dental assistants to graduate from an accredited program and pass an exam. Most programs are offered by community colleges, although they also may be offered by vocational or technical schools. Most programs take about 1 year to complete and lead to a certificate or diploma. Programs that last 2 years are less common and lead to an associate's degree. The Commission on Dental Accreditation (CODA), part of the American Dental Association, accredited nearly 300 dental assisting training programs in 2015.

Accredited programs include classroom and laboratory work in which students learn about teeth, gums, jaws, and other areas that dentists work on and the instruments that dentists use. These programs also include supervised practical experience.

High school students interested in a career as a dental assistant should take courses in biology, chemistry, and anatomy.

Training. Dental assistants who do not have formal education in dental assisting may learn their duties through on-the-job training. A dental assistant or dentist in the office teaches the new assistant dental terminology, the names of the instruments, how to complete daily tasks, how to interact with patients, and other activities necessary to help keep the dental office running smoothly.

Important Qualities

Detail oriented. Dental assistants must follow specific rules and protocols, such as infection control procedures, when helping dentists treat patients. Assistants also must be aware of what tasks they are allowed to complete in the state where they work.

Dexterity. Dental assistants must be good at working with their hands. They generally work in tight quarters on a small part of the body, using very precise tools and instruments.

Interpersonal skills. Dental assistants must work closely with dentists and patients. Sometimes, patients are in extreme pain and/or mental stress, so the assistant should be sensitive to their emotions.

Listening skills. Dental assistants should be able to listen to patients and other healthcare workers. They need to follow directions from a dentist or dental hygienist, so they can help treat patients and do tasks, such as taking an X-ray.

Organizational skills. Dental assistants should have excellent organizational skills. They should have the correct tools in place for a dentist or dental hygienist to use when treating a patient.

Licenses, Certifications, and Registrations. Some states require dental assistants to be licensed, registered, or certified. In other states, there are no formal requirements to become an entry-level dental assistant.

States that allow assistants to perform expanded duties, such as coronal polishing, require that they be licensed, registered, or hold certifications from the Dental Assisting National Board (DANB). To earn certification from DANB, applicants must pass an exam. The educational requirements for DANB certification are that dental assistants must either have graduated from an accredited program or have a high school diploma and complete the required amount of work experience. Applicants also must have current certification in CPR (cardiopulmonary resuscitation).

In addition, many states require assistants to meet specific education or training requirements in order to work with radiography (X-ray) equipment. Requirements vary by state. Contact state boards of dentistry for specific requirements.

Pay

The median annual wage for dental assistants was $35,390 in May 2014. The median wage is the wage at which half the workers in an occupation earned more than that amount and half earned less. The lowest 10 percent earned less than $24,580, and the highest 10 percent earned more than $49,540.

Job Outlook

Employment of dental assistants is projected to grow 18 percent from 2014 to 2024, much faster than the average for all occupations. Ongoing research linking oral health and general health will likely continue to increase the demand for preventive dental services. Dentists will continue to hire more dental assistants to complete routine tasks, allowing the dentist to see more patients in

Similar Occupations. This table shows a list of occupations with job duties that are similar to those of dental assistants.

Occupations	Entry-level Education	2014 Median Pay	Projected Job Growth	Average Annual Openings
Dental Hygienists	Associate's degree	$71,520	19%	3,740
Medical Assistants	Postsecondary nondegree award	$29,960	23%	13,890
Nursing Assistants and Orderlies	See Education/Training	$25,090	17%	26,780
Occupational Therapy Assistants and Aides	See Education/Training	$52,300	40%	1,680
Pharmacy Technicians	High school diploma or equivalent	$29,810	9%	3,470
Physical Therapist Assistants and Aides	See Education/Training	$41,640	40%	5,140
Surgical Technologists	Postsecondary nondegree award	$43,350	15%	1,470

their practice and to spend their time on more complex procedures. As dental practices grow, more dental assistants will be needed.

As the large baby-boom population ages, and as people keep more of their original teeth than did previous generations, the need to maintain and treat teeth will continue to increase the need for dental care.

In addition, the number of individuals who have access to health insurance is expected to continue to increase because of federal health insurance reform. People with new or expanded dental insurance coverage will be more likely to visit a dentist than in the past. This will increase the demand for all dental services, including those performed by dental assistants.

Job Prospects. Overall, job opportunities for dental assistants are expected to be good. Dental assistants with advanced certification or training will likely have the best job prospects.

Contacts for More Information

For more information about becoming a dental assistant and for a list of accredited dental assistant programs, visit

➤ Commission on Dental Accreditation, American Dental Association (www.ada.org/117.aspx)

For more information about becoming a Certified Dental Assistant and for a list of state boards of dentistry, visit

➤ Dental Assisting National Board, Inc. (www.danb.org)

O*NET

➤ Dental Assistants (31-9091.00)

Dental Hygienists

- **2014 Median Pay** .... $71,520 per year $34.38 per hour
- **Typical Entry-Level Education** .... Associate's degree
- **Work Experience in a Related Occupation** .... None
- **On-the-job Training** .... None
- **Number of Jobs, 2014** 200,500
- **Job Outlook, 2014–24** ...... 19% (Much faster than average)
- **Employment Change, 2014–24** 37,400

What Dental Hygienists Do

Dental hygienists clean teeth, examine patients for signs of oral diseases such as gingivitis, and provide other preventive dental care. They also educate patients on ways to improve and maintain good oral health.

Duties. Dental hygienists typically do the following:

- Remove tartar, stains, and plaque from teeth
- Apply sealants and fluorides to help protect teeth
- Take and develop dental X-rays
- Assess patients' oral health and report findings to dentists
- Document patient care and treatment plans
- Educate patients about oral hygiene techniques, such as how to brush and floss correctly

Dental hygienists use many types of tools to do their job. They clean and polish teeth with hand, power, and ultrasonic tools. In some cases, they use lasers. Hygienists remove stains with an air-polishing device, which sprays a combination of air, water, and baking soda. They polish teeth with a powered tool that works like an automatic toothbrush. Hygienists use X-ray machines to take pictures to check for tooth or jaw problems.

Dental hygienists help patients develop and maintain good oral health. For example, they may explain the relationship between diet and oral health. They also may give advice to patients on how to select toothbrushes and other oral-care devices.

The tasks hygienists may perform, and the extent that they must be supervised by a dentist, varies by state and by the setting in which the dental hygienist works. Some states allow hygienists to independently diagnosis health problems and provide some treatments, such as application of fluorides and sealants.

Work Environment

Dental hygienists held about 200,500 jobs in 2014. Almost all dental hygienists worked in dentists' offices in 2014. A small number of hygienists worked in other settings, including offices of physicians, outpatient clinics, and schools. Dental hygienists work closely with dentists.

Dental hygienists wear safety glasses, surgical masks, and gloves to protect themselves and patients from infectious diseases. When taking X-rays, they follow strict procedures to protect themselves and patients from radiation.

Work Schedules. About half of dental hygienists worked part time in 2014. Dentists often hire hygienists to work only a few days a week, so some hygienists work for more than one dentist.

Education/Training

Dental hygienists need an associate's degree in dental hygiene. Programs typically take 3 years to complete. All states require dental hygienists to be licensed; requirements vary by state.

Education. Dental hygienists typically need an associate's degree in dental hygiene. Bachelor's degrees in dental hygiene are also available, but are less common. A bachelor's or master's degree usually is required for research, teaching, or clinical practice in public or school health programs.

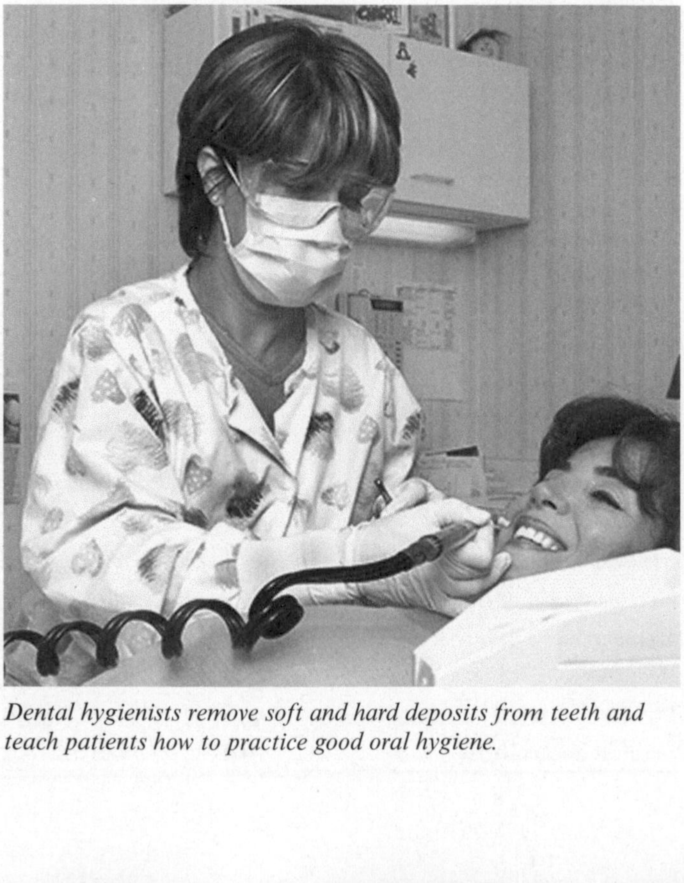

Dental hygienists remove soft and hard deposits from teeth and teach patients how to practice good oral hygiene.

Median Annual Wages, May 2014

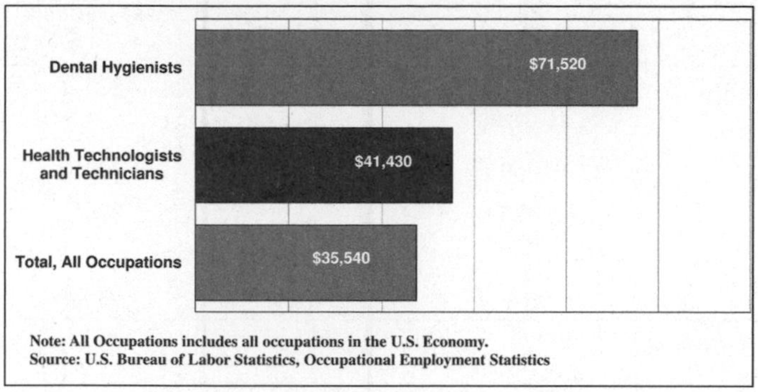

Note: All Occupations includes all occupations in the U.S. Economy.
Source: U.S. Bureau of Labor Statistics, Occupational Employment Statistics

Percent Change in Employment, Projected 2014–2024

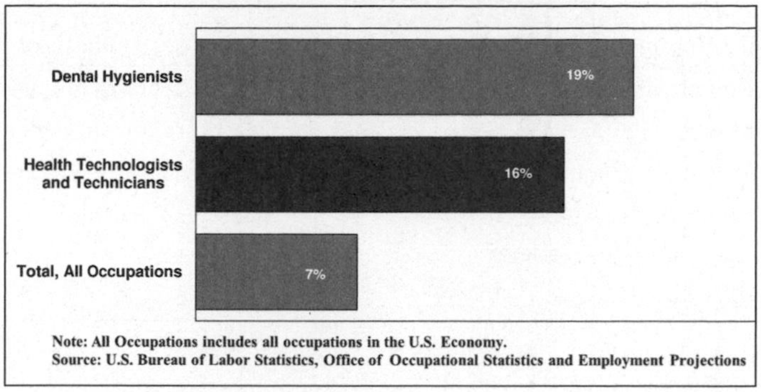

Note: All Occupations includes all occupations in the U.S. Economy.
Source: U.S. Bureau of Labor Statistics, Office of Occupational Statistics and Employment Projections

Dental hygiene programs are commonly found in community colleges, technical schools, and universities. In 2015, the Commission on Dental Accreditation, part of the American Dental Association, accredited more than 300 dental hygiene programs.

Programs typically take 3 years to complete, and offer laboratory, clinical, and classroom instruction. Areas of study include anatomy, physiology, nutrition, radiography, pathology, medical ethics, head and neck anatomy, patient management, and periodontics, which is the study of gum disease.

High school students interested in becoming dental hygienists should take courses in biology, chemistry, and math. Most dental hygiene programs also require applicants to have completed at least 1 year of college. Specific entrance requirements vary by school.

Important Qualities

Critical thinking. Dental hygienists must use critical thinking skills in order to assess and evaluate patients.

Compassion. Some patients are in extreme pain or have fears about undergoing dental treatment, and the hygienist must be sensitive to their emotions.

Detail oriented. Dental hygienists must follow specific rules and protocols to help dentists diagnose and treat a patient. Depending on the state in which they work and/or the treatment provided, dental hygienists may work without the direct supervision of a dentist.

Dexterity. Dental hygienists must be good at working with their hands. They generally work in tight quarters on a small part of the body, requiring fine motor skills using very precise tools and instruments.

Interpersonal skills. Dental hygienists must work closely with dentists and patients.

Licenses, Certifications, and Registrations. Every state requires dental hygienists to be licensed; requirements vary by state. In most states, a degree from an accredited dental hygiene program and passing grades on written and clinical examinations is required for licensure. To maintain licensure, hygienists must complete continuing education requirements. For specific requirements, contact your state's medical or health board.

Many jobs also require cardiopulmonary resuscitation (CPR) certification.

Pay

The median annual wage for dental hygienists was $71,520 in May 2014. The median wage is the wage at which half the workers in an occupation earned more than that amount and half earned less. The lowest 10 percent earned less than $49,190, and the highest 10 percent earned more than $97,390.

Some dental hygienists receive benefits, such as vacation, sick leave, and contributions to their retirement fund. However, benefits vary by employer and may be available only to full-time workers.

About half of dental hygienists worked part time in 2014. Dentists often hire hygienists to work only a few days a week, so some hygienists work for more than one dentist.

Job Outlook

Employment of dental hygienists is projected to grow 19 percent from 2014 to 2024, much faster than the average for all occupations. Ongoing research linking oral health and general health will continue to spur the demand for preventive dental services.

The demand for dental services will increase as the population ages, cosmetic dental services become increasingly popular, and access to health insurance continues to grow.

As the large baby-boom population ages and people retain more of their original teeth than previous generations did, the need to maintain and treat these teeth will continue to drive demand for dental care.

Cosmetic dental services, such as teeth-whitening treatments, have become increasingly popular. This trend is expected to continue as new technologies allow for less invasive, faster procedures.

The number of individuals who have access to health insurance is expected to continue to increase because of federal health insurance reform. People with new or expanded dental insurance coverage will be more likely to visit an oral healthcare provider than in the past. As a result, the demand for all dental services, including those performed by hygienists, will increase.

Employment Projections Data for Dental Hygienists

Occupational Title	SOC Code	Employment, 2014	Projected Employment, 2024	Change, 2014–2024	
				Percent	Numeric
Dental hygienists	29-2021	200,500	237,900	19	37,400

Source: U.S. Bureau of Labor Statistics, Employment Projections Program

Similar Occupations. This table shows a list of occupations with job duties that are similar to those of dental hygienists.

Occupations	Entry-level Education	2014 Median Pay	Projected Job Growth	Average Annual Openings
Dental Assistants	Postsecondary nondegree award	$35,390	18%	5,860
Dentists	Doctoral or professional degree	$154,640	18%	2,670
Medical Assistants	Postsecondary nondegree award	$29,960	23%	13,890
Physician Assistants	Master's degree	$95,820	30%	2,870
Radiation Therapists	Associate's degree	$80,090	14%	230
Registered Nurses	Bachelor's degree	$66,640	16%	43,930

Job Prospects. Although the demand for dental services is growing, the number of new graduates from dental hygiene programs also has increased, resulting in more competition for jobs. Candidates can expect very strong competition for most full-time hygienist positions. Job seekers with previous work experience should have the best job opportunities. In addition, new dental hygiene-based workforce models are emerging and may provide additional opportunities for dental hygienists.

Contacts for More Information

For information about educational requirements and available accredited programs for dental hygienists, visit

➤ American Dental Hygienists' Association (www.adha.org)

For information about accredited programs and educational requirements, visit

➤ Commission on Dental Accreditation, American Dental Association (www.ada.org/en/coda)

The State Board of Dental Examiners in each state can provide information on licensing requirements.

O*NET

➤ Dental Hygienists (29-2021.00)

Dentists

- **2014 Median Pay** .... $154,640 per year $74.34 per hour
- **Typical Entry-Level Education** .... Doctoral or professional degree
- **Work Experience in a Related Occupation** .... None
- **On-the-job Training** .... See Education/Training
- **Number of Jobs, 2014** 151,500
- **Job Outlook, 2014–24** ...... 18% (Much faster than average)
- **Employment Change, 2014–24** 26,700

What Dentists Do

Dentists diagnose and treat problems with patients' teeth, gums, and related parts of the mouth. They provide advice and instruction on taking care of the teeth and gums and on diet choices that affect oral health.

Duties. Dentists typically do the following:

- Remove decay from teeth and fill cavities
- Repair cracked or fractured teeth and remove teeth
- Place sealants or whitening agents on teeth
- Administer anesthetics to keep patients from feeling pain during procedures
- Prescribe antibiotics or other medications
- Examine X-rays of teeth, gums, the jaw, and nearby areas in order to diagnose problems
- Make models and measurements for dental appliances, such as dentures, to fit patients
- Teach patients about diets, flossing, the use of fluoride, and other aspects of dental care

Dentists use a variety of equipment, including X-ray machines, drills, mouth mirrors, probes, forceps, brushes, and scalpels. They also use lasers, digital scanners, and other computer technologies, such as digital dentistry.

In addition, dentists in private practice oversee a variety of administrative tasks, including bookkeeping and buying equipment and supplies. They employ and supervise dental hygienists, dental assistants, dental laboratory technicians, and receptionists.

Most dentists are general practitioners and handle a variety of dental needs. Other dentists practice in 1 of 9 specialty areas:

Dental public health specialists promote good dental health and the prevention of dental diseases in specific communities.

Endodontists perform root-canal therapy, by which they remove the nerves and blood supply from injured or infected teeth.

Oral and maxillofacial radiologists diagnose diseases in the head and neck through the use of imaging technologies.

Oral and maxillofacial surgeons operate on the mouth, jaws, teeth, gums, neck, and head, performing procedures such as surgically repairing a cleft lip and palate or removing impacted teeth.

Oral pathologists diagnose conditions in the mouth, such as bumps or ulcers, and oral diseases, such as cancer.

Orthodontists straighten teeth by applying pressure to the teeth with braces or other appliances.

Pediatric dentists focus on dentistry for children and special-needs patients.

Periodontists treat the gums and bone supporting the teeth.

Prosthodontists replace missing teeth with permanent fixtures, such as crowns and bridges, or with removable fixtures, such as dentures.

Work Environment

Dentists held about 151,500 jobs in 2014. Some dentists own their own businesses and work alone or with a small staff. Other dentists have partners in their practice, and some work for more established dentists as associate dentists. In 2014, about 1 out of 4 dentists were self-employed.

Dentists usually work in dentists' offices. They wear masks, gloves, and safety glasses to protect themselves and their patients from infectious diseases.

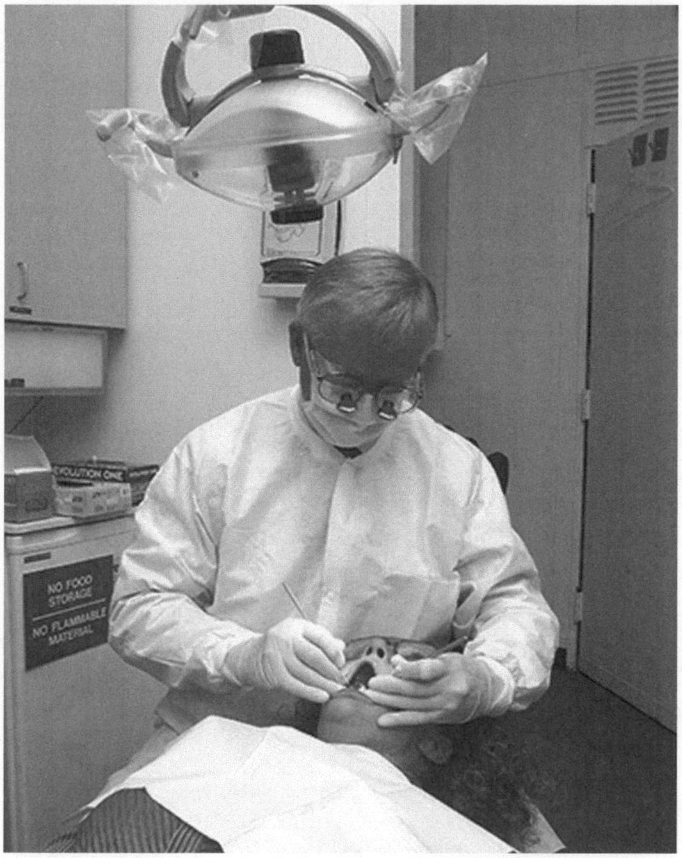

Dentists remove tooth decay, fill cavities, and repair fractured teeth.

Work Schedules. Most dentists work full time. Some work evenings and weekends to meet their patients' needs. The number of hours worked varies greatly among dentists.

Education/Training

Dentists must be licensed in the state(s) in which they work. Licensure requirements vary by state, although candidates usually must graduate from an accredited dental school and pass written and practical exams.

Education. All dental schools require applicants to have completed certain science courses, such as biology and chemistry, before entering dental school. Students typically need at least a bachelor's degree to enter most dental programs, although no specific major is required. However, majoring in a science, such as biology, might increase one's chances of being accepted. Requirements vary by school.

College undergraduates who plan on applying to dental school usually must take the Dental Admission Test (DAT) during their junior year. Admission to dental school can be competitive. Dental schools use these tests along with other factors, such as grade point average, interviews, and recommendations, to admit students into their programs.

Dental school programs typically include coursework in subjects such as local anesthesia, anatomy, periodontics (the study of oral disease and health), and radiology. All programs at dental schools include clinical experience in which students work directly with patients under the supervision of a licensed dentist.

Completion of a dental program results in one of three degrees: Doctor of Dental Surgery (DDS), Doctor of Dental Medicine (DDM), and Doctor of Medical Dentistry (DMD). In 2015, the Commission on Dental Accreditation, part of the American Dental Association, accredited more than 60 dental school programs.

High school students who want to become dentists should take courses in chemistry, physics, biology, anatomy, and math.

Training. All nine dental specialties require dentists to complete additional training before practicing that specialty. This training is usually a 2- to 4-year residency in a program related to their specialty. General dentists do not require any additional training after dental school.

Dentists who want to teach or do research full time usually spend an additional 2 to 5 years in advanced dental training. Many practicing dentists also teach part time, including supervising students in dental school clinics.

Licenses, Certifications, and Registrations. Dentists must be licensed in the state(s) in which they work. All states require dentists to be licensed; requirements vary by state. Most states require a dentist to have a degree from an accredited dental school and to pass the written and practical National Board Dental Examinations.

In addition, a dentist who wants to practice in one of the nine specialties must have a license in that specialty. Licensure requires the completion of a residency after dental school and, in some cases, the completion of a special state exam.

Important Qualities

Communication skills. Dentists must have excellent communication skills. They must be able to communicate effectively with patients, dental hygienists, dental assistants, and receptionists.

Detail oriented. Dentists must be detail oriented so that patients receive appropriate treatments and medications. They also must pay attention to the shape and color of teeth and to the space

Median Annual Wages, May 2014

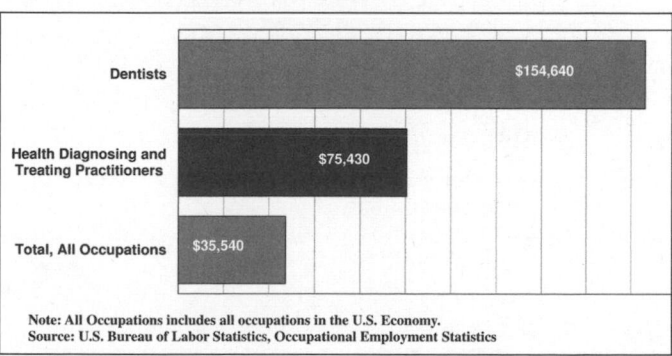

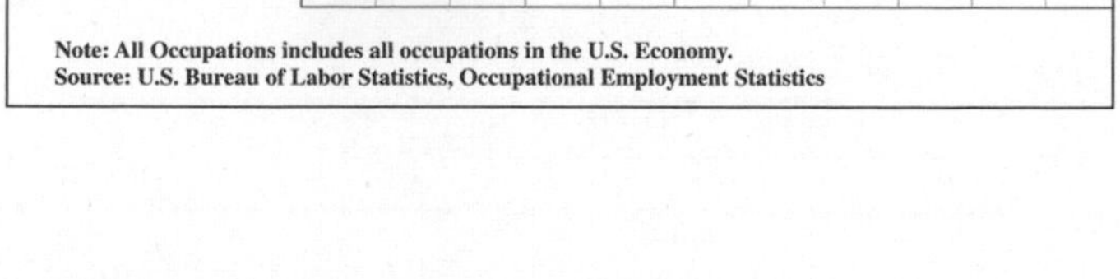

Percent Change in Employment, Projected 2014–2024

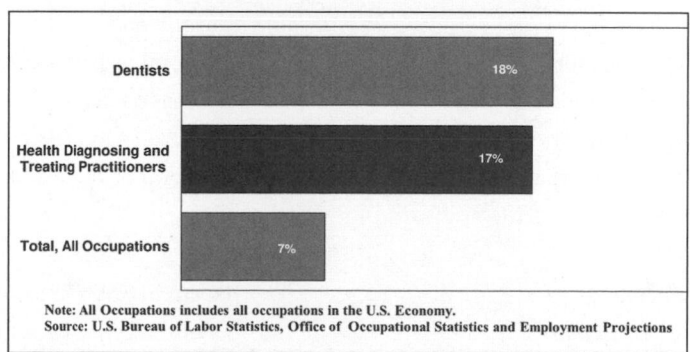

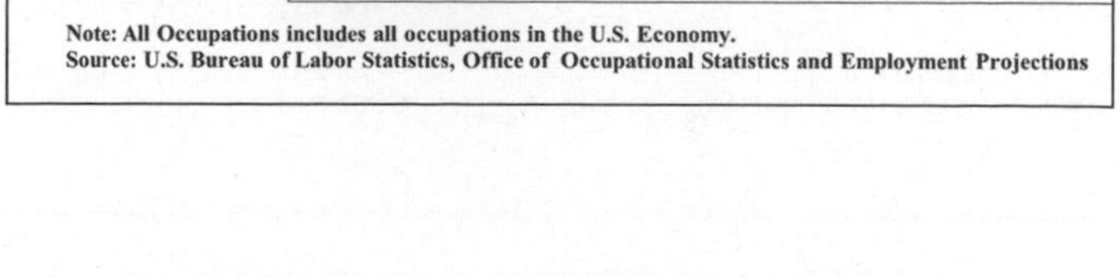

Employment Projections Data for Dentists

Occupational Title	SOC Code	Employment, 2014	Projected Employment, 2024	Change, 2014–2024 Percent	Change, 2014–2024 Numeric
Dentists	29-1020	151,500	178,200	18	26,700
Dentists, general	29-1021	129,000	152,300	18	23,300
Oral and maxillofacial surgeons	29-1022	6,800	8,000	18	1,200
Orthodontists	29-1023	8,200	9,700	18	1,500
Prosthodontists	29-1024	800	1,000	18	100
Dentists, all other specialists	29-1029	6,700	7,300	9	600

Source: U.S. Bureau of Labor Statistics, Employment Projections Program

between them. For example, they may need to closely match a false tooth with a patient's other teeth.

Dexterity. Dentists must be good at working with their hands. They work with tools in a limited area.

Leadership skills. Most dentists work in their own practice. This requires them to manage and lead a staff.

Organizational skills. Strong organizational skills, including the ability to keep accurate records of patient care, are critical in both medical and business settings.

Patience. Dentists may work for long periods of time with patients who need special attention. Children and patients with a fear of dental work may require a lot of patience.

Physical stamina. Dentists should be comfortable performing physical tasks, such as bending over patients for long periods.

Problem-solving skills. Dentists need strong problem-solving skills. They must evaluate patients' symptoms and choose the appropriate treatments.

Pay

The median annual wage for dentists was $154,640 in May 2014. The median wage is the wage at which half the workers in an occupation earned more than that amount and half earned less. The lowest 10 percent earned less than $70,220, and the highest 10 percent earned more than $187,200.

Median annual wages for dentists in May 2014 were as follows:

Oral and maxillofacial surgeons	$187,200 or more
Orthodontists	187,200 or more
Dentists, all other specialists	170,110
Dentists, general	149,540
Prosthodontists	100,280

Earnings vary with the dentist's location, number of hours worked, specialty, and number of years in practice.

Job Outlook

Employment of dentists is projected to grow 18 percent from 2014 to 2024, much faster than the average for all occupations. Demand for dental services will increase as the population ages, cosmetic dental services become increasingly popular, and access to health insurance continues to grow.

Many members of the growing and aging baby-boom generation will need dental work. Because each generation is more likely to keep their teeth than past generations, more dental care will be needed in the years to come. In addition, there will be increased demand for complicated dental work, including dental implants or bridges. The risk of oral cancer increases significantly with age, and complications can require both cosmetic and functional dental reconstruction.

Cosmetic dental services, such as teeth-whitening treatments, are becoming increasingly popular. This trend is expected to continue as new technologies allow for less invasive, faster procedures.

Dentists will continue to see an increase in public demand for their services as studies continue to link oral health to overall health. They will need to provide care and instruction aimed at promoting good oral hygiene, rather than just providing treatments such as fillings.

Dentists are likely to hire more hygienists and dental assistants to handle routine services. Productivity increases derived from new technology, such as digital dentistry and radiography, should allow dentists to reduce the time needed to see each patient. As a result, dentists will be able to expand their practices and see more patients.

Whether patients seek care is dependent largely on their insurance coverage. The number of individuals who have access to health insurance is expected to continue to increase because of federal health insurance reform. People with new or expanded dental insurance coverage will be more likely to visit a dentist than in the past.

Similar Occupations. This table shows a list of occupations with job duties that are similar to those of dentists.

Occupations	Entry-level Education	2014 Median Pay	Projected Job Growth	Average Annual Openings
Chiropractors	Doctoral or professional degree	$66,720	17%	790
Dental Hygienists	Associate's degree	$71,520	19%	3,740
Optometrists	Doctoral or professional degree	$101,410	27%	1,100
Physicians and Surgeons	Doctoral or professional degree	This wage is equal to or greater than $187,200.	14%	9,930
Podiatrists	Doctoral or professional degree	$120,700	14%	140
Veterinarians	Doctoral or professional degree	$87,590	9%	690

Job Prospects. Job prospects for dentists are expected to be good. There are still areas of the country where patients need dental care but have little access to it. Job prospects will be especially good for dentists who are willing to work in these areas.

In addition, many dentists are expected to retire in the next decade and replacement workers will be needed to fill those positions.

Contacts for More Information

For more information about dentists, including information on accredited dental schools and state boards of dental examiners, visit

- ➤ American Dental Association, Commission on Dental Accreditation (www.ada.org/en/coda)

For information on admission to dental schools, visit

- ➤ American Dental Education Association (www.adea.org)

For more information on general dentistry or on a specific dental specialty, visit

- ➤ Academy of General Dentistry (www.agd.org)
- ➤ American Association of Oral and Maxillofacial Surgeons (www.aaoms.org)
- ➤ American Academy of Pediatric Dentistry (www.aapd.org)
- ➤ American Academy of Periodontology (www.perio.org)
- ➤ American College of Prosthodontists (www.gotoapro.org)
- ➤ American Association of Endodontists (www.aae.org)
- ➤ American Academy of Oral and Maxillofacial Radiology (www.aaomr.org)
- ➤ American Association of Public Health Dentistry (www.aaphd.org)

O*NET

- ➤ Dentists, General (29-1021.00)
- ➤ Oral and Maxillofacial Surgeons (29-1022.00)
- ➤ Orthodontists (29-1023.00)
- ➤ Prosthodontists (29-1024.00)
- ➤ Dentists, All Other Specialists (29-1029.00)

Diagnostic Medical Sonographers and Cardiovascular Technologists and Technicians, Including Vascular Technologists

- **2014 Median Pay** .... $62,540 per year $30.07 per hour
- **Typical Entry-Level Education** .... Associate's degree
- **Work Experience in a Related Occupation** .... None
- **On-the-job Training** .... None
- **Number of Jobs, 2014** 112,700
- **Job Outlook, 2014–24** ...... 24% (Much faster than average)
- **Employment Change, 2014–24** 27,600

What Diagnostic Imaging Workers Do

Diagnostic medical sonographers and cardiovascular technologists and technicians, including vascular technologists, operate special imaging equipment to create images or conduct tests. The images and test results help physicians assess and diagnose medical conditions. Some technologists assist physicians and surgeons during surgical procedures.

Duties. Diagnostic imaging workers typically do the following:

- Prepare patients for procedures by taking a patient's medical history and answering any questions about the procedure
- Prepare and maintain diagnostic imaging equipment
- Operate equipment to obtain diagnostic images or to conduct tests
- Review images or test results to check for quality and adequate coverage of the areas needed for diagnoses
- Recognize the difference between normal and abnormal images and other diagnostic information
- Analyze diagnostic information to provide a summary of findings for physicians
- Record findings and keep track of patients' records

Diagnostic medical sonographers specialize in creating images of the body's organs and tissues. The images are known as sonograms (or ultrasounds). Sonograms are often the first imaging test performed when disease is suspected. Diagnostic medical sonographers may work closely with physicians or surgeons before, during, and after procedures. The following are examples of types of diagnostic medical sonographers:

- *Abdominal sonographers* specialize in imaging a patient's abdominal cavity and nearby organs, such as the kidney, liver, gallbladder, pancreas, or spleen. Abdominal sonographers may assist with biopsies or other examinations requiring ultrasound guidance.
- *Breast sonographers* specialize in imaging a patient's breast tissues. Sonography can confirm the presence of cysts and tumors that may have been detected by the patient, physician, or a mammogram. Breast sonographers work closely with physicians and assist with procedures that track tumors and help to provide information for making decisions about the best treatment options for breast cancer patients.
- *Musculoskeletal sonographers* specialize in imaging muscles, ligaments, tendons, and joints. These sonographers may assist with ultrasound guidance for injections, or during surgical procedures, that deliver medication or treatment directly to affected tissues.
- *Pediatric sonographers* specialize in imaging child and infant patients. Many of the medical conditions they image are associated with premature births or birth defects. Pediatric sonographers may work closely with pediatricians and other caregivers.
- *Obstetric and gynecologic sonographers* specialize in imaging the female reproductive system. Many pregnant women receive sonograms to track the baby's growth and health. Obstetrical sonographers work closely with physicians in detecting congenital birth defects.

Diagnostic sonography uses high-frequency sound waves to produce images of the inside of the body. The sonographer uses an instrument called an ultrasound transducer on the parts of the patient's body that are being examined. The transducer emits pulses of sound that bounce back, causing echoes. The echoes are then sent to the ultrasound machine, which processes them and displays them as images used by physicians for diagnosis.

Cardiovascular technologists and technicians create images, conduct tests, or assist with surgical procedures involving the heart. The following are examples of types of cardiovascular technologists and technicians:

- *Cardiac sonographers (echocardiographers)* specialize in imaging a patient's heart and use ultrasound equipment to examine the heart's chambers, valves, and vessels. The images are known as echocardiograms. The echocardiogram procedure may be done while the patient is either resting or after being physically active. Cardiac sonographers also may take echocardiograms of fetal hearts so that physicians can diagnose cardiac conditions during pregnancy. Cardiac sonographers work closely with physicians or surgeons before, during, and after procedures.

- *Cardiovascular invasive specialists or cardiac catheterization technologists,* also known as cardiovascular technologists, monitor patients' heart rates and help physicians in diagnosing and treating problems with patients' hearts. They assist with cardiac catheterization, which involves threading a catheter through a patient's artery to the heart. They also prepare and monitor patients during open-heart surgery and during the insertion of pacemakers and stents. Technologists prepare patients for procedures by shaving and cleansing the area where the catheter will be inserted and administering topical anesthesia. During the procedure, they monitor the patient's blood pressure and heart rate.
- *Cardiographic or electrocardiogram (EKG) technicians* specialize in electrocardiogram (EKG) testing. EKG machines monitor the heart's performance through electrodes attached to a patient's chest, arms, and legs. The tests can be done while the patient is at rest or while the patient is physically active. For a stress test, the patient walks on a treadmill and the technician gradually increases the speed to observe the effect of increased exertion.

Vascular technologists (vascular sonographers) are closely related to cardiovascular technologists and their duties are similar to those of diagnostic medical sonographers. Vascular technologists create images of blood vessels and collect data that help physicians diagnose disorders affecting blood flow.

Vascular technologists often measure a patient's blood pressure and the volume of blood in their arms, legs, fingers, and toes to evaluate blood flow and identify blocked arteries. They complete noninvasive procedures using specialized ultrasound instruments or blood pressure cuffs to record information, such as the blood flow in arteries and veins, blood pressure (blood volume), oxygen saturation, and the presence of blood clots in the body. Vascular technologists may work closely with physicians or surgeons before, during, and after procedures.

Work Environment

Diagnostic imaging workers held about 112,700 jobs in 2014. The industries that employed the most diagnostic medical sonographers and cardiovascular technologists and technicians, including vascular technologists were as follows:

Hospitals; state, local, and private	68%
Offices of physicians	20
Medical and diagnostic laboratories	7

These workers complete most of their work at diagnostic imaging machines in dimly lit rooms, but they also may perform procedures at patients' bedsides. Diagnostic imaging workers may be on their feet for long periods and may need to lift or turn patients who are disabled.

Work Schedules. Most diagnostic imaging workers work full time. Some may work evenings, weekends, or overnight because they work in facilities that are always open.

Education/Training

Diagnostic imaging workers need formal education, such as an associate's degree or a postsecondary certificate. Many employers also require professional certification.

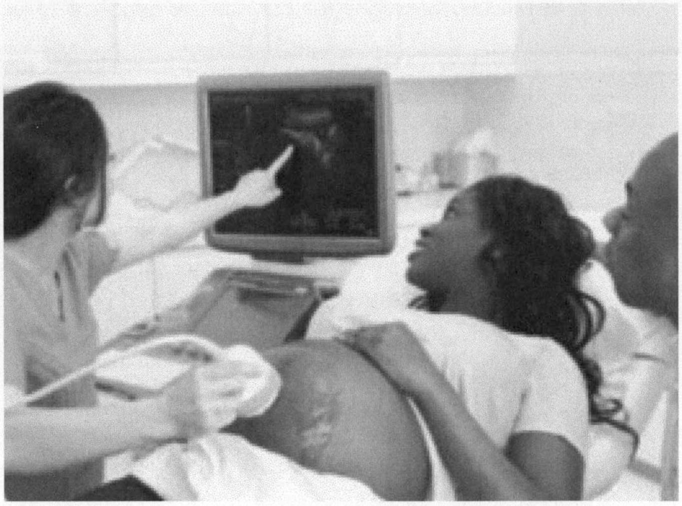

Diagnostic medical sonographers operate special equipment to create images.

Education. Colleges and universities offer both associate's and bachelor's degree programs in sonography and in cardiovascular and vascular technology. One-year certificate programs also are available from colleges or hospitals.

Employers typically prefer graduates of programs accredited by the Commission on Accreditation of Allied Health Education Programs (CAAHEP).

Sonography, cardiovascular, and vascular education programs usually include courses in anatomy, medical terminology, and applied sciences. Most sonography programs are divided into the specialized fields that correspond to the relevant certification exams, such as abdominal sonography or breast sonography. Cardiovascular and vascular programs include coursework in either invasive or noninvasive cardiovascular or vascular technology procedures. In addition to classroom study, most programs also include a clinical component in which students earn credit while working under a more experienced technologist in a hospital, physician's office, or imaging laboratory.

High school students who are interested in diagnostic medical sonography, cardiovascular technology, or vascular technology should take courses in anatomy, physiology, physics, and math.

Licenses, Certifications, and Registrations. Most employers prefer to hire diagnostic imaging workers with professional certification. Many insurance providers and Medicare pay for procedures only if a certified sonographer, technologist, or technician performed the work. Certification is available from the American Registry for Diagnostic Medical Sonographers and Cardiovascular Credentialing International.

Diagnostic imaging workers can earn certification by graduating from an accredited program and passing an exam. Most of the certifications are for specialties in diagnostic imaging; for example, a sonographer can earn a certification in abdominal sonography. Most diagnostic imaging workers have at least one certification, but many earn multiple certifications.

In addition, many employers prefer to hire candidates who have a Basic Life Support certification, which shows they are trained to provide CPR.

Few states require diagnostic medical sonographers to be licensed. Professional certification is typically required for licensure; other requirements vary by state. Contact state medical boards for more information.

Median Annual Wages, May 2014

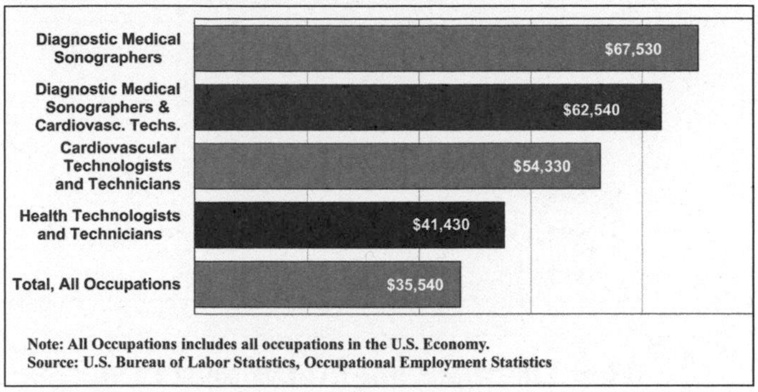

Percent Change in Employment, Projected 2014–2024

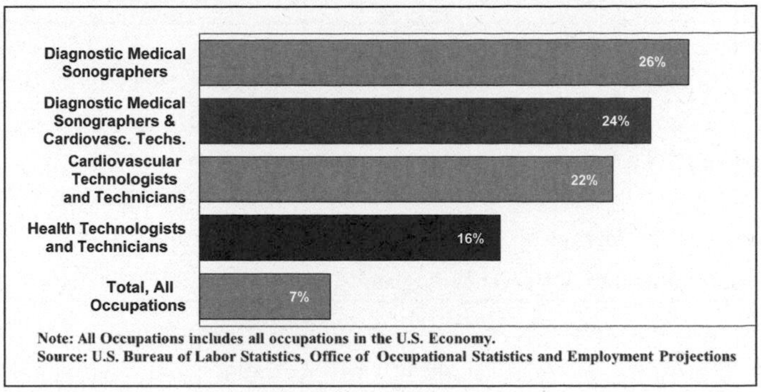

Important Qualities

Detail oriented. Diagnostic imaging workers must follow precise instructions to obtain the images needed to diagnose and treat patients. They must also pay attention to the screen while scanning a patient's body because the cues that contrast healthy areas with unhealthy ones may be subtle.

Hand-eye coordination. To get quality images, diagnostic imaging workers must be able to accurately move equipment on the patient's body in response to what they see on the screen.

Interpersonal skills. Diagnostic imaging workers must work closely with patients. Sometimes patients are in extreme pain or mental stress, and they must get cooperation from the patient to create usable images.

Physical stamina. Diagnostic imaging workers are on their feet for long periods and must be able to lift and move patients who need assistance.

Technical skills. Diagnostic imaging workers must understand how to operate complex machinery and computerized instruments.

Pay

The median annual wage for cardiovascular technologists and technicians was $54,330 in May 2014. The median wage is the wage at which half the workers in an occupation earned more than that amount and half earned less. The lowest 10 percent earned less than $28,110, and the highest 10 percent earned more than $84,940.

The median annual wage for diagnostic medical sonographers was $67,530 in May 2014. The lowest 10 percent earned less than $46,930, and the highest 10 percent earned more than $93,850.

In May 2014, the median annual wages for diagnostic imaging workers in the top industries in which they worked were as follows:

Medical and diagnostic laboratories	$65,460
Offices of physicians	64,590
Hospitals; state, local, and private	61,490

Job Outlook

Employment of diagnostic medical sonographers is projected to grow 26 percent from 2014 to 2024, much faster than the average for all occupations. Employment of cardiovascular technologists and technicians, including vascular technologists, is projected to grow 22 percent from 2014 to 2024, much faster than the average for all occupations.

As imaging technology evolves, medical facilities will continue to use ultrasound to replace more invasive, costly procedures. Ultrasound is often less expensive than other imaging technologies and is often used as a first-line tool for diagnosis. Third-party payers encourage the use of these noninvasive measures over invasive ones in order to save on costs. Diagnostic medical sonographers, cardiovascular technologists and technicians, and vascular technologists will continue to be needed in healthcare settings to provide an alternative to imaging techniques that involve radiation.

As the large baby-boom population ages, the need to diagnose medical conditions—such as blood clots and heart disease—will likely increase. Imaging technology is a tool used in making these diagnoses.

Additionally, the number of individuals who have access to health insurance is expected to continue to increase because of federal health insurance reform. Diagnostic imaging workers will continue to be needed to use and maintain the equipment needed for diagnosis and treatment.

Job Prospects. Diagnostic imaging personnel who are certified are expected to have the best job opportunities. Job opportunities increase when diagnostic imaging personnel are certified in more than one specialty.

Contacts for More Information

For more information about diagnostic medical sonographers, visit

➤ Society of Diagnostic Medical Sonography (www.sdms.org)

Employment Projections Data for Diagnostic Medical Sonographers and Cardiovascular Technologists and Technicians, Including Vascular Technologists

Occupational Title	SOC Code	Employment, 2014	Projected Employment, 2024	Change, 2014–2024 Percent	Change, 2014–2024 Numeric
Diagnostic medical sonographers and cardiovascular technologists and technicians, including vascular technologists	—	112,700	140,200	24	27,600
Cardiovascular technologists and technicians	29-2031	52,000	63,500	22	11,500
Diagnostic medical sonographers	29-2032	60,700	76,700	26	16,000

Source: U.S. Bureau of Labor Statistics, Employment Projections Program

Similar Occupations. This table shows a list of occupations with job duties that are similar to those of diagnostic imaging workers.

Occupations	Entry-level Education	2014 Median Pay	Projected Job Growth	Average Annual Openings
Medical and Clinical Laboratory Technologists and Technicians	See Education/Training	$49,310	16%	5,210
Nuclear Medicine Technologists	Associate's degree	$72,100	2%	30
Radiation Therapists	Associate's degree	$80,090	14%	230
Radiologic and MRI Technologists	Associate's degree	$57,370	9%	2,070

For more information about cardiovascular technologists and technicians, including vascular technologists, visit

➤ Alliance of Cardiovascular Professionals (www.acp-online.org)
➤ American Society of Echocardiography (www.asecho.org/)
➤ Society for Vascular Ultrasound (www.svunet.org)

For more information about registration and certification, visit

➤ American Registry of Radiologic Technologists (www.arrt.org)
➤ Cardiovascular Credentialing International (www.cci-online.org)
➤ American Registry for Diagnostic Medical Sonography (www.ardms.org)

For a current list of accredited education programs in diagnostic medical sonography and cardiovascular technology, including vascular technology, visit

➤ Commission on Accreditation of Allied Health Education Programs (www.caahep.org/Find-An-Accredited-Program)
➤ Society for Vascular Ultrasound (www.svunet.org)

For more information about diagnostic medical sonographers, visit

➤ Society of Diagnostic Medical Sonography (www.sdms.org)

For more information about cardiovascular technologists and technicians, including vascular technologists, visit

➤ Alliance of Cardiovascular Professionals (www.acp-online.org)
➤ American Society of Echocardiography (www.asecho.org/)
➤ Society for Vascular Ultrasound (www.svunet.org)

For more information about registration and certification, visit

➤ American Registry of Radiologic Technologists (www.arrt.org)
➤ Cardiovascular Credentialing International (www.cci-online.org)
➤ American Registry for Diagnostic Medical Sonography (www.ardms.org)

For a current list of accredited education programs in diagnostic medical sonography and cardiovascular technology, including vascular technology, visit

➤ Commission on Accreditation of Allied Health Education Programs (www.caahep.org/Find-An-Accredited-Program/)
➤ Society for Vascular Ultrasound (www.svunet.org)

O*NET

➤ Cardiovascular Technologists and Technicians (29-2031.00)
➤ Diagnostic Medical Sonographers (29-2032.00)

Dietitians and Nutritionists

- **2014 Median Pay** .... $56,950 per year; $27.38 per hour
- **Typical Entry-Level Education** .... Bachelor's degree
- **Work Experience in a Related Occupation** .... None
- **On-the-job Training** .... Internship/residency
- **Number of Jobs, 2014** 66,700
- **Job Outlook, 2014–24** .... 16% (Much faster than average)
- **Employment Change, 2014–24** 11,000

What Dietitians and Nutritionists Do

Dietitians and nutritionists are experts in the use of food and nutrition to promote health and manage disease. They advise people on what to eat in order to lead a healthy lifestyle or achieve a specific health-related goal.

Duties. Dietitians and nutritionists typically do the following:

- Assess patients' and clients' nutritional and health needs
- Counsel patients on nutrition issues and healthy eating habits
- Develop meal plans, taking both cost and clients' preferences into account
- Evaluate the effects of meal plans and change the plans as needed
- Promote better health by speaking to groups about diet, nutrition, and the relationship between good eating habits and preventing or managing specific diseases
- Keep up with or contribute to the latest food and nutritional science research
- Write reports to document patients' progress

Dietitians and nutritionists evaluate the health of their clients. Based on their findings, dietitians and nutritionists advise clients on which foods to eat—and which to avoid—to improve their health.

Many dietitians and nutritionists provide customized information for specific individuals. For example, a dietitian or nutritionist might teach a client with diabetes how to plan meals to balance the client's blood sugar. Others work with groups of people who have similar needs. For example, a dietitian or nutritionist might plan a diet with healthy fat and limited sugar to help clients who are at risk for heart disease. They may work with other healthcare professionals to coordinate patient care.

Dietitians and nutritionists who are self-employed may meet with patients, or they may work as consultants for a variety of organizations. They may need to spend time on marketing and other business-related tasks, such as scheduling appointments, keeping records, and preparing educational programs or informational materials for clients.

Although many dietitians and nutritionists do similar tasks, there are several specialties within the occupations. The following are examples of types of dietitians and nutritionists:

Clinical dietitians and clinical nutritionists provide medical nutrition therapy. They work in hospitals, long-term care facilities, clinics, private practice, and other institutions. They create nutritional programs based on the health needs of patients or residents and counsel patients on how to improve their health through nutrition. Clinical dietitians and clinical nutritionists may further specialize, such as by working only with patients with kidney diseases or those with diabetes.

Dietitians counsel individuals and groups on nutritional practices designed to prevent disease and promote health.

Community dietitians and community nutritionists develop programs and counsel the public on topics related to food, health, and nutrition. They often work with specific groups of people, such as adolescents or the elderly. They work in public health clinics, government and nonprofit agencies, health maintenance organizations (HMOs), and other settings.

Management dietitians plan food programs. They work in food service settings such as cafeterias, hospitals, prisons, and schools. They may be responsible for buying food and for carrying out other business-related tasks, such as budgeting. Management dietitians may oversee kitchen staff or other dietitians.

Work Environment

Dietitians and nutritionists held about 66,700 jobs in 2014. The industries that employed the most dietitians and nutritionists were as follows:

Hospitals; state, local, and private	30%
Government	14
Nursing and residential care facilities	10
Outpatient care centers	8
Accommodation and food services	5

Dietitians also may work in physicians' offices or in schools.

Work Schedules. Most dietitians and nutritionists worked full time in 2014, although about 1 out of 4 worked part time. They may work evenings and weekends to meet with clients who are unavailable at other times.

Education/Training

Most dietitians and nutritionists have a bachelor's degree and have completed supervised training through an internship. Many states require dietitians and nutritionists to be licensed.

Education. Most dietitians and nutritionists have a bachelor's degree in dietetics, foods and nutrition, clinical nutrition, public health nutrition, or a related area. Dietitians also may study food service systems management. Programs include courses in nutrition, psychology, chemistry, and biology.

Many dietitians and nutritionists have advanced degrees.

Training. Dietitians and nutritionists typically receive several hundred hours of supervised training, usually in the form of an internship following graduation from college. Some dietetics schools offer coordinated programs in dietetics that allow students to complete supervised training as part of their undergraduate or graduate-level coursework.

Licenses, Certifications, and Registrations. Most states require dietitians and nutritionists to be licensed in order to practice. Other states require only state registration or certification to use certain titles, and a few states have no regulations for this occupation.

The requirements for state licensure and state certification vary by state, but most include having a bachelor's degree in food and nutrition or a related area, completing supervised practice, and passing an exam.

Many dietitians choose to earn the Registered Dietitian Nutritionist (RDN) credential. Although the RDN is not always required, the qualifications are often the same as those necessary for becoming a licensed dietitian in states that require a license. Many employers prefer or require the RDN, which is administered by the Commission on Dietetic Registration, the credentialing agency for the Academy of Nutrition and Dietetics.

The RDN requires dietitian nutritionists to complete a minimum of a bachelor's degree and a Dietetic Internship (DI), which consists of at least 1,200 hours of supervised experience. Students may complete both criteria at once through a coordinated program, or they may finish their required coursework before applying for an internship. These programs are accredited by the Accreditation Council for Education in Nutrition and Dietetics (ACEND), part of the Academy of Nutrition and Dietetics. In order to maintain the RDN credential, dietitians and nutritionists who have earned it must complete 75 continuing professional education credits every 5 years.

Median Annual Wages, May 2014

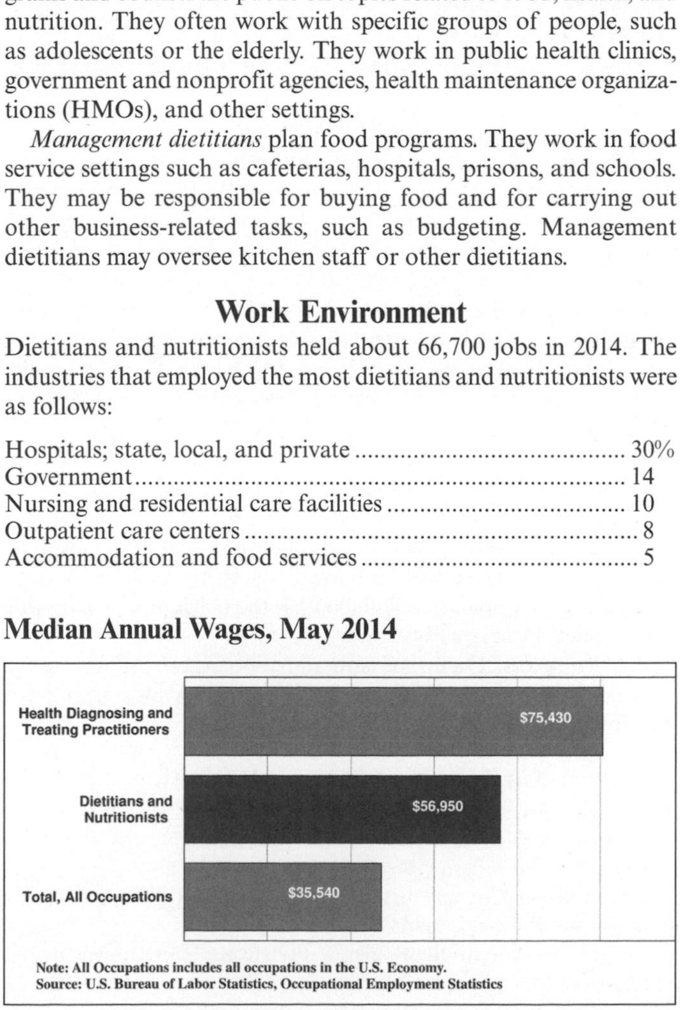

Percent Change in Employment, Projected 2014–2024

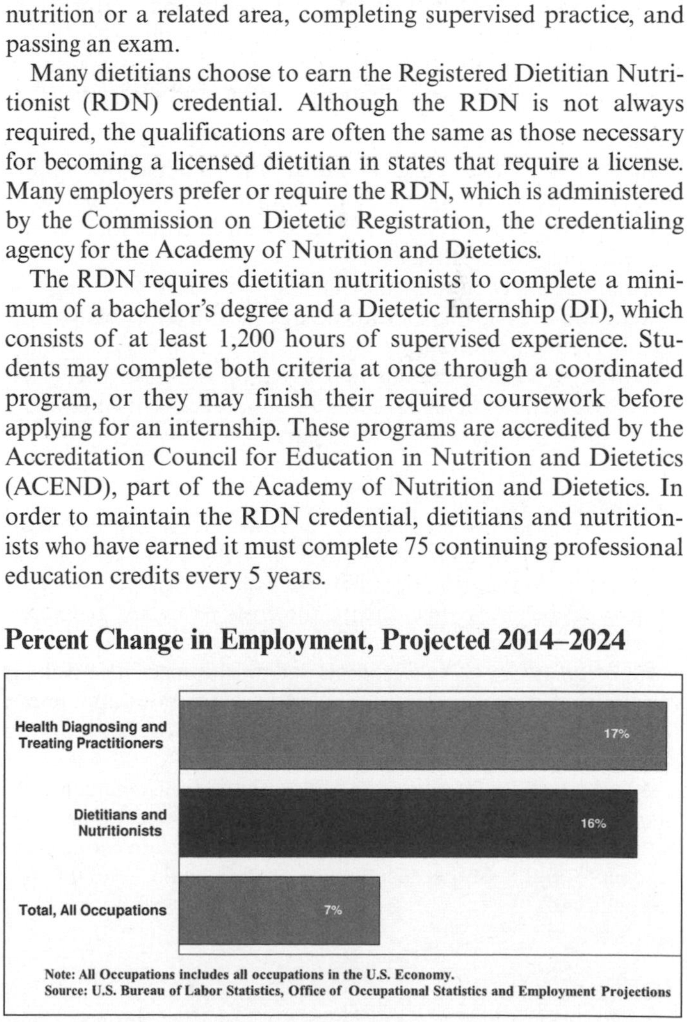

Employment Projections Data for Dietitians and Nutritionists

Occupational Title	SOC Code	Employment, 2014	Projected Employment, 2024	Change, 2014–2024	
				Percent	Numeric
Dietitians and nutritionists	29-1031	66,700	77,600	16	11,000

Source: U.S. Bureau of Labor Statistics, Employment Projections Program

Similar Occupations. This table shows a list of occupations with job duties that are similar to those of dietitians and nutritionists.

Occupations	Entry-level Education	2014 Median Pay	Projected Job Growth	Average Annual Openings
Health Educators and Community Health Workers	See Education/Training	$42,450	13%	1,560
Registered Nurses	Bachelor's degree	$66,640	16%	43,930
Rehabilitation Counselors	Master's degree	$34,380	9%	1,080

Nutritionists may earn the Certified Nutrition Specialist (CNS) credential to show an advanced level of knowledge. The CNS credential is accepted in several states for licensure purposes. To qualify for the credential, applicants must have a master's or doctoral degree, complete 1,000 hours of experience, and pass an exam. The credential is administered by the Board for Certification of Nutrition Specialists.

Dietitians and nutritionists may seek additional certifications in an area of specialty. The Commission on Dietetic Registration offers specialty certifications in oncology nutrition, renal nutrition, gerontological nutrition, pediatric nutrition, and sports dietetics.

Important Qualities

Analytical skills. Dietitians and nutritionists must keep up to date with the latest food and nutrition research. They should be able to interpret scientific studies and translate nutrition science into practical eating advice.

Compassion. Dietitians and nutritionists must be caring and empathetic when helping clients address health and dietary issues and any related emotions.

Listening skills. Dietitians and nutritionists must listen carefully to understand clients' goals and concerns. They may work with other healthcare workers as part of a team to improve the health of a patient, and they need to listen to team members when constructing eating plans.

Organizational skills. Because there are many aspects to the work of dietitians and nutritionists, they should be able to stay organized. Management dietitians, for example, must consider the nutritional needs of their clients, the costs of meals, and access to food.

Problem-solving skills. Dietitians and nutritionists must evaluate the health status of patients and determine the most appropriate food choices for a client to improve his or her overall health or manage a disease.

Speaking skills. Dietitians and nutritionists must explain complicated topics in a way that people with less technical knowledge can understand. They must be able to clearly explain eating plans to clients and to other healthcare professionals involved in a patient's care.

Pay

The median annual wage for dietitians and nutritionists was $56,950 in May 2014. The median wage is the wage at which half the workers in an occupation earned more than that amount and half earned less. The lowest 10 percent earned less than $35,040, and the highest 10 percent earned more than $79,840.

In May 2014, the median annual wages for dietitians and nutritionists in the top industries in which they worked were as follows:

Outpatient care centers	$61,210
Hospitals; state, local, and private	57,510
Nursing and residential care facilities	56,510
Government	55,270
Accommodation and food services	54,970

Job Outlook

Employment of dietitians and nutritionists is projected to grow 16 percent from 2014 to 2024, much faster than the average for all occupations. In recent years, interest in the role of food and nutrition in promoting health and wellness has increased, particularly as a part of preventative healthcare in medical settings.

According to the Centers for Disease Control, more than one-third of U.S. adults are obese. Many diseases, such as diabetes and kidney disease, are associated with obesity. The importance of diet in preventing and treating illnesses is now well known. More dietitians and nutritionists will be needed to provide care for people with these conditions. In addition, there will be demand for dietitians in grocery stores to help consumers make healthy food choices.

As the baby-boom generation grows older and looks for ways to stay healthy, there will be more demand for dietetic services. Also, an aging population will increase the need for dietitians and nutritionists in nursing homes.

Job Prospects. Dietitians and nutritionists who have earned advanced degrees or certification in a specialty area may enjoy better job prospects.

Contacts for More Information

For more information about dietitians and nutritionists, visit

- Academy of Nutrition and Dietetics (www.eatright.org)

For a list of academic programs, visit

- Accreditation Council for Education in Nutrition and Dietetics (www.eatrightacend.org/ACEND)

For information on the Registered Dietitian Nutritionist (RDN) exam and other specialty credentials, visit

- Commission on Dietetic Registration (www.cdrnet.org)

For information on the Certified Nutrition Specialist (CNS) exam and credential, visit

➤ Board for Certification of Nutrition Specialists (http://cbns.org)

O*NET

➤ Dietitians and Nutritionists (29-1031.00)

EMTs and Paramedics

- **2014 Median Pay** .... $31,700 per year $15.24 per hour
- **Typical Entry-Level Education** .... Postsecondary nondegree award
- **Work Experience in a Related Occupation**.............. None
- **On-the-job Training** .... None
- **Number of Jobs, 2014** 241,200
- **Job Outlook, 2014–24**......24% (Much faster than average)
- **Employment Change, 2014–24** 58,500

What EMTs and Paramedics Do

Emergency medical technicians (EMTs) and paramedics care for the sick or injured in emergency medical settings. People's lives often depend on the quick reaction and competent care provided by these workers. EMTs and paramedics respond to emergency calls, performing medical services and transporting patients to medical facilities.

A 911 operator sends EMTs and paramedics to the scene of an emergency, where they often work with police and firefighters.

Duties. EMTs and paramedics typically do the following:

- Respond to 911 calls for emergency medical assistance, such as cardiopulmonary resuscitation (CPR) or bandaging a wound
- Assess a patient's condition and determine a course of treatment
- Provide first-aid treatment or life support care to sick or injured patients
- Transport patients safely in an ambulance
- Transfer patients to the emergency department of a hospital or other healthcare facility
- Report their observations and treatment to physicians, nurses, or other healthcare facility staff
- Document medical care given to patients
- Inventory, replace, and clean supplies and equipment after use

When transporting a patient in an ambulance, one EMT or paramedic may drive the ambulance while another monitors the patient's vital signs and gives additional care. Some paramedics work as part of a helicopter's or an airplane's flight crew to transport critically ill or injured patients to a hospital.

EMTs and paramedics also transport patients from one medical facility to another. Some patients may need to be transferred to a hospital that specializes in treating their particular injury or illness or to a facility that provides long-term care, such as a nursing home.

If a patient has a contagious disease, EMTs and paramedics decontaminate the interior of the ambulance and may need to report the case to the proper authorities.

The specific responsibilities of EMTs and paramedics depend on their level of certification and the state they work in. The National Registry of Emergency Medical Technicians (NREMT) provides national certification of EMTs and paramedics at three levels: EMT, Advanced EMT, and Paramedic. Some states, however, have their own certification programs and use similar titles.

An *EMT*, also known as an *EMT-Basic*, cares for patients at the scene of an incident and while taking patients by ambulance to a hospital. An EMT has the skills to assess a patient's condition and to manage respiratory, cardiac, and trauma emergencies.

An *Advanced EMT*, also known as an *EMT-Intermediate*, has completed the requirements for the EMT level, as well as instruction in more advanced medical procedures, such as administering intravenous fluids and some medications.

Paramedics provide more extensive prehospital care than do EMTs. In addition to doing the tasks of EMTs, paramedics can give medications orally and intravenously, interpret electrocardiograms (EKGs)—which monitor heart function—and use other monitors and complex equipment.

The specific tasks or procedures EMTs and paramedics are allowed to perform at any level vary by state.

Work Environment

EMTs and paramedics held about 241,200 jobs in 2014. The industries that employed the most EMTs and paramedics were as follows:

Ambulance services	48%
Local government, excluding education and hospitals	29
Hospitals; state, local, and private	16

The above percentages exclude volunteer EMTs and paramedics who do not receive pay.

EMTs and paramedics work both indoors and outdoors, in all types of weather. Their work is physically strenuous and can be stressful, sometimes involving life-or-death situations.

Volunteer EMTs and paramedics share many of the same duties as paid EMTs and paramedics. They volunteer for fire departments, providers of emergency medical services, or hospitals. They may respond to only a few calls per month.

Injuries and Illnesses. EMTs and paramedics are required to do considerable kneeling, bending, and lifting while caring for and moving patients. They may be exposed to contagious diseases

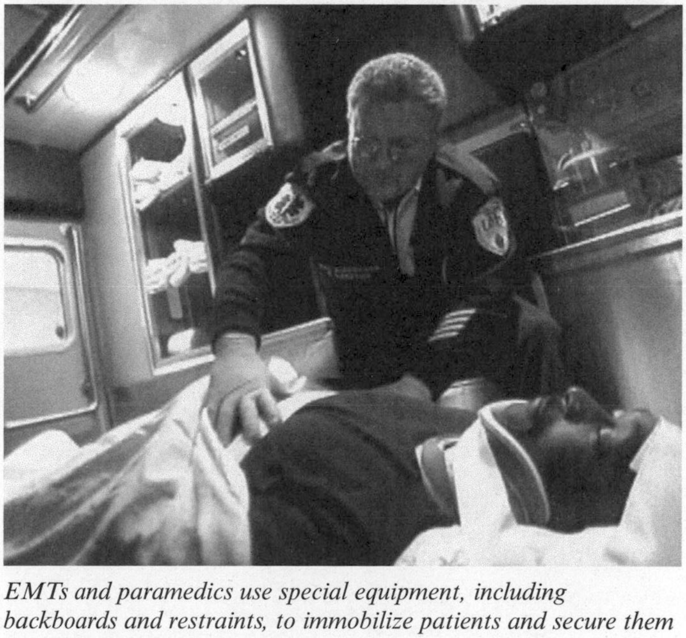

EMTs and paramedics use special equipment, including backboards and restraints, to immobilize patients and secure them in the ambulance for transport.

Median Annual Wages, May 2014

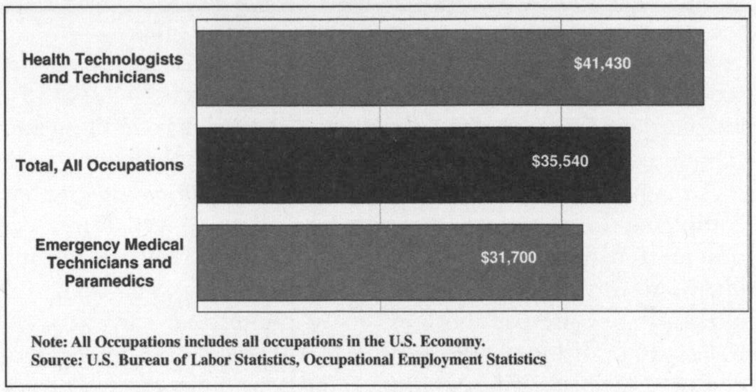

Percent Change in Employment, Projected 2014–2024

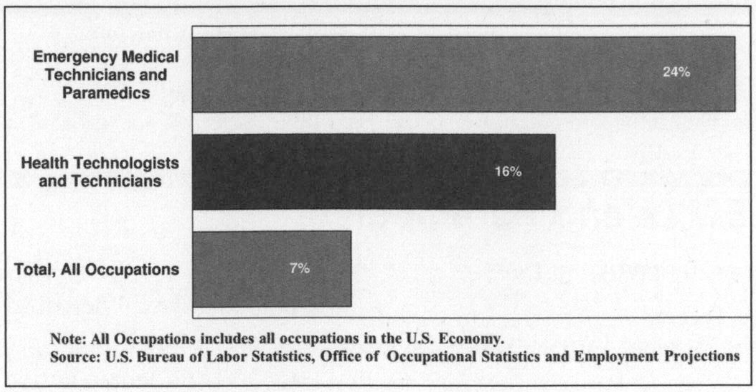

and viruses, such as hepatitis B and HIV. Sometimes they can be injured by combative patients. These risks can be reduced by following proper safety procedures, such as waiting for police to clear an area in violent situations or wearing gloves while working with a patient.

Work Schedules. Most paid EMTs and paramedics work full time. About 1 in 3 worked more than 40 hours per week in 2014. Because EMTs and paramedics must be available to work in emergencies, they may work overnight and on weekends. Some EMTs and paramedics work shifts in 12- or 24-hour increments. Volunteer EMTs and paramedics have variable work schedules. For example, they may work only a few days per week.

Education/Training

Emergency medical technicians (EMTs) and paramedics must complete a postsecondary educational program. All states require EMTs and paramedics to be licensed; requirements vary by state.

Education. Both a high school diploma or equivalent and cardiopulmonary resuscitation (CPR) certification typically are required for entry into postsecondary educational programs in emergency medical technology. Most of these programs are nondegree award programs that can be completed in less than 1 year; others last up to 2 years. Paramedics, however, may need an associate's degree. Programs in emergency medical technology are offered by technical institutes, community colleges, and facilities that specialize in emergency care training.

The Commission on Accreditation of Allied Health Education Programs offers a list of accredited programs for EMTs and paramedics, by state.

Programs at the EMT level include instruction in assessing patients' conditions, dealing with trauma and cardiac emergencies, clearing obstructed airways, using field equipment, and handling emergencies. Formal courses include about 150 hours of specialized instruction, and some instruction may take place in a hospital or ambulance setting.

Programs at the Advanced EMT level typically require about 400 hours of instruction. At this level, candidates learn EMT-level skills as well as more advanced ones, such as using complex airway devices, intravenous fluids, and some medications.

Paramedics have the most advanced level of education. They must complete EMT and Advanced EMT levels of instruction, along with courses in advanced medical skills. Community colleges and technical schools may offer these programs, which require about 1,200 hours of instruction and may lead to an associate's degree. Paramedics' broader scope of practice may include stitching wounds or administering intravenous medications.

High school students interested in becoming EMTs or paramedics should take courses in anatomy and physiology.

Licenses, Certifications, and Registrations. The National Registry of Emergency Medical Technicians (NREMT) certifies EMTs and paramedics. All levels of NREMT certification require completing a certified education program and passing the national exam. The national exam has both written and practical parts.

All states require EMTs and paramedics to be licensed; requirements vary by state. In most states, an individual who has NREMT certification qualifies for licensure; in others, passing an equivalent state exam is required. Usually, an applicant must be over the age of 18. Many states require background checks and may not give a license to an applicant who has a criminal history.

Although some emergency medical services hire separate drivers, most EMTs and paramedics take a course requiring about 8 hours of instruction before they can drive an ambulance.

Important Qualities

Compassion. EMTs and paramedics must be able to provide emotional support to patients in an emergency, especially patients who are in life-threatening situations or extreme mental distress.

Interpersonal skills. EMTs and paramedics usually work on teams and must be able to coordinate their activities closely with others in stressful situations.

Listening skills. EMTs and paramedics need to listen to patients to determine the extent of their injuries or illnesses.

Physical strength. EMTs and paramedics need to be physically fit. Their job requires a lot of bending, lifting, and kneeling.

Problem-solving skills. EMTs and paramedics must evaluate patients' symptoms and administer appropriate treatments.

Employment Projections Data for EMTs and Paramedics

Occupational Title	SOC Code	Employment, 2014	Projected Employment, 2024	Change, 2014–2024 Percent	Change, 2014–2024 Numeric
Emergency medical technicians and paramedics	29-2041	241,200	299,600	24	58,500

Source: U.S. Bureau of Labor Statistics, Employment Projections Program

Similar Occupations. This table shows a list of occupations with job duties that are similar to those of EMTs and paramedics.

Occupations	Entry-level Education	2014 Median Pay	Projected Job Growth	Average Annual Openings
Firefighters	Postsecondary nondegree award	$45,970	5%	1,740
Physician Assistants	Master's degree	$95,820	30%	2,870
Police and Detectives	See Education/Training	$58,630	4%	3,310
Registered Nurses	Bachelor's degree	$66,640	16%	43,930

Speaking skills. EMTs and paramedics need to clearly explain procedures to patients, give orders, and relay information to others.

Pay

The median annual wage for EMTs and paramedics was $31,700 in May 2014. The median wage is the wage at which half the workers in an occupation earned more than that amount and half earned less. The lowest 10 percent earned less than $20,690, and the highest 10 percent earned more than $54,690.

In May 2014, the median annual wages for EMTs and paramedics in the top industries in which they worked were as follows:

Local government, excluding education and hospitals....... $34,740
Hospitals; state, local, and private 34,290
Ambulance services.. 29,460

Job Outlook

Employment of emergency medical technicians (EMTs) and paramedics is projected to grow 24 percent from 2014 to 2024, much faster than the average for all occupations. Emergencies, such as car crashes, natural disasters, and acts of violence, will continue to create demand for EMTs and paramedics. Demand for part-time, volunteer EMTs and paramedics in rural areas and smaller metropolitan areas will also continue.

Growth in the middle-aged and elderly population will lead to an increase in age-related health emergencies, such as heart attacks and strokes. This increase, in turn, will create greater demand for EMT and paramedic services. An increase in the number of specialized medical facilities will require more EMTs and paramedics to transfer patients with specific conditions to these facilities for treatment.

Contacts for More Information

For more information about emergency medical technicians and paramedics, visit

- National Association of Emergency Medical Technicians (www.naemt.org)
- National Highway Traffic Safety Administration, Office of Emergency Medical Services (www.ems.gov)
- National Registry of Emergency Medical Technicians (www.nremt.org)

For information about educational programs, visit

- Commission on Accreditation of Allied Health Education Programs (www.caahep.org/default.aspx)

O*NET

- Emergency Medical Technicians and Paramedics (29-2041.00)

Exercise Physiologists

- **2014 Median Pay** .... $46,270 per year $22.25 per hour
- **Typical Entry-Level Education** .... Bachelor's degree
- **Work Experience in a Related Occupation**............... None
- **On-the-job Training** .... None
- **Number of Jobs, 2014** 14,500
- **Job Outlook, 2014–24**............ 11% (Faster than average)
- **Employment Change, 2014–24** 1,500

What Exercise Physiologists Do

Exercise physiologists develop fitness and exercise programs that help patients recover from chronic diseases and improve cardiovascular function, body composition, and flexibility.

Duties. Exercise physiologists typically do the following:

- Analyze a patient's medical history to determine the best possible exercise and fitness regimen for the patient
- Perform fitness and stress tests with medical equipment and analyze the resulting patient data
- Measure blood pressure, oxygen usage, heart rhythm, and other key patient health indicators
- Develop exercise programs to improve patient health
- Supervise clinical tests to ensure patient safety

Exercise physiologists, sometimes called kinesiotherapists, work to improve overall patient health. Many of their patients suffer from health problems such as cardiovascular disease or pulmonary

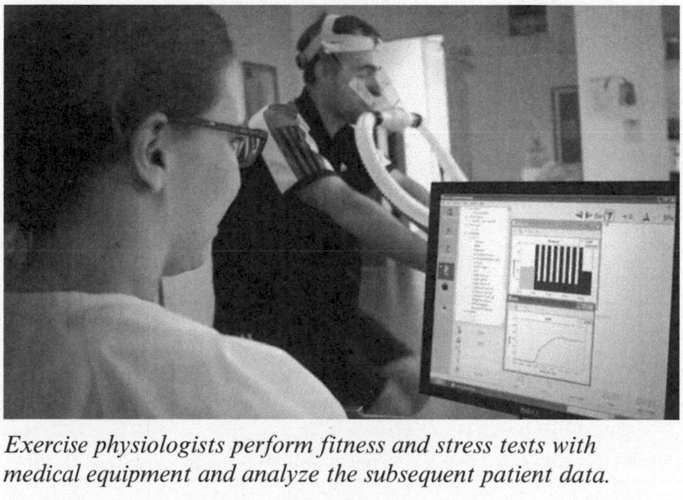

Exercise physiologists perform fitness and stress tests with medical equipment and analyze the subsequent patient data.

Median Annual Wages, May 2014

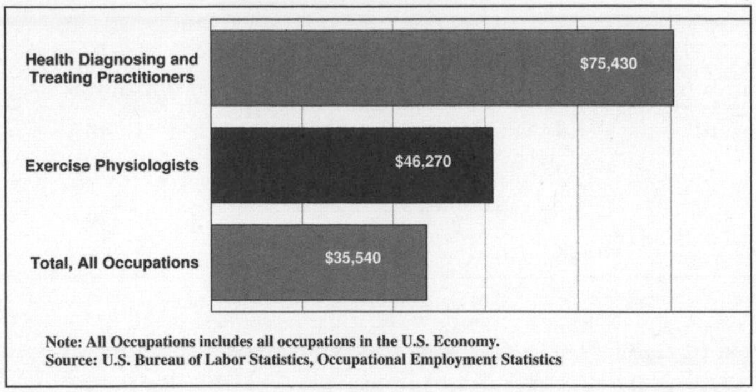

Percent Change in Employment, Projected 2014–2024

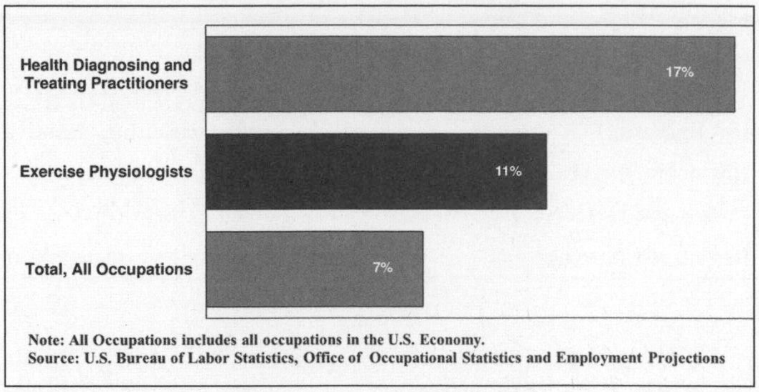

(lung) disease. Exercise physiologists provide health education and exercise plans to improve key health indicators.

Some physiologists work closely with primary care physicians, who may prescribe exercise regiments for their patients and refer them to exercise physiologists. The physiologists then work with patients to develop individualized treatment plans that will help the patients meet their health and fitness goals.

Exercise physiologists should not be confused with fitness trainers and instructors (including personal trainers) or athletic trainers.

Work Environment

Exercise physiologists held about 14,500 jobs in 2014. The industries that employed the most exercise physiologists were as follows:

Hospitals; state, local, and private	27%
Ambulatory healthcare services	10
Federal government	3
Individual and family services	2

About half of exercise physiologists were self-employed in 2014.

Work Schedules. Most exercise physiologists work full time.

Education/Training

Degree programs include science and health-related courses, such as biology, anatomy, kinesiology, and nutrition, as well as clinical work.

Education. Master's degree programs also are common. Both degree programs include courses in science and health-related subjects, such as biology, anatomy, kinesiology, and nutrition, as well as clinical work. In 2015, there were about 50 exercise programs accredited by the Commission on Accreditation of Allied Health Education Programs (CAAHEP).

High school students interested in postsecondary exercise physiology programs should take courses in anatomy, physiology, and physics.

Licenses, Certifications, and Registrations. Louisiana is the only state that requires exercise physiologists to be licensed, although many states have pending legislation to create formal licensure requirements.

The American Society of Exercise Physiologists (ASEP) offers the Exercise Physiologist Certified (EPC) certification, which physiologists can use to demonstrate their qualifications. Certification requires graduation with a relevant bachelor's degree and coursework, completing the ASEP exam, and taking continuing education courses every 5 years.

The American College of Sports Medicine (ACSM) also offers certifications for exercise physiologists: the Certified Clinical Exercise Physiologist (CEP) credential for candidates with a bachelor's degree and the Registered Clinical Exercise Physiologist® (RCEP) for candidates with a master's degree. Candidates also must have at least 400 or 600 hours of supervised clinical experience for the CEP and RCEP credential, respectively, and pass an exam.

Important Qualities

Compassion. Exercise physiologists work with patients who may be in considerable pain or discomfort. Therefore, they must be sympathetic while providing treatments and developing individualized exercise programs for the patients.

Decision-making skills. Exercise physiologists must be able to make informed clinical decisions because those decisions could affect the health or livelihood of patients.

Detail oriented. Exercise physiologists must be able to record detailed, accurate information about their patients' conditions and about any progress the patients make. For example, they must ensure that patients are completing the appropriate stress tests or practicing the correct fitness regimen.

Interpersonal skills. Exercise physiologists must have strong interpersonal skills and be able to manage difficult situations. They must be able to communicate well with others, including physicians, patients, and patients' families.

Pay

The median annual wage for exercise physiologists was $46,270 in May 2014. The median wage is the wage at which half the workers in an occupation earned more than that amount and half earned

Employment Projections Data for Exercise Physiologists

Occupational Title	SOC Code	Employment, 2014	Projected Employment, 2024	Change, 2014–2024 Percent	Change, 2014–2024 Numeric
Exercise physiologists	29-1128	14,500	16,000	11	1,500

Source: U.S. Bureau of Labor Statistics, Employment Projections Program

Similar Occupations. This table shows a list of occupations with job duties that are similar to those of exercise physiologists.

Occupations	Entry-level Education	2014 Median Pay	Projected Job Growth	Average Annual Openings
Athletic Trainers	Bachelor's degree	$43,370	21%	540
Nuclear Medicine Technologists	Associate's degree	$72,100	2%	30
Occupational Therapists	Master's degree	$78,810	27%	3,040
Physical Therapists	Doctoral or professional degree	$82,390	34%	7,180
Physician Assistants	Master's degree	$95,820	30%	2,870
Recreational Therapists	Bachelor's degree	$44,000	12%	220
Respiratory Therapists	Associate's degree	$56,730	12%	1,490

less. The lowest 10 percent earned less than $30,700, and the highest 10 percent earned more than $73,010.

In May 2014, the median annual wages for exercise physiologists in the top industries in which they worked were as follows:

Federal government $69,580
Individual and family services.......... 50,130
Hospitals; state, local, and private 46,650
Ambulatory healthcare services 42,450

Job Outlook

Employment of exercise physiologists is projected to grow 11 percent from 2014 to 2024, faster than the average for all occupations. Demand may rise as hospitals emphasize exercise and preventive care as part of their treatment and long-term rehabilitation from chronic diseases, such as cardiovascular and pulmonary diseases.

However, because this is a small occupation in terms of employment, competition for available positions is expected to remain high. Additionally, because licensure for exercise physiologists is not common, there are few recognized standards of practice for these workers.

Contacts for More Information

For more information about exercise physiologists and certifications, visit

- ➤ American Society of Exercise Physiologists (www.asep.org)
- ➤ American College of Sports Medicine (www.acsm.org)
- ➤ Committee on Accreditation for the Exercise Sciences (www.coaes.org/home.html)
- ➤ Clinical Exercise Physiology Association (http://tinyurl.com/6v53bc2)

O*NET

- ➤ Exercise Physiologists (29-1128.00)

Genetic Counselors

- **2014 Median Pay** .... $67,500 per year
  $32.45 per hour
- **Typical Entry-Level Education** .... Master's degree
- **Work Experience in a Related Occupation**.......... None
- **On-the-job Training** .... None
- **Number of Jobs, 2014** 2,400
- **Job Outlook, 2014–24**......29% (Much faster than average)
- **Employment Change, 2014–24** 700

What Genetic Counselors Do

Genetic counselors assess individual or family risk for a variety of inherited conditions, such as genetic disorders and birth defects. They provide information and support to other healthcare providers, or to individuals and families concerned with the risk of inherited conditions.

Duties. Genetic counselors typically do the following:

- Interview patients to obtain comprehensive individual family and medical histories
- Evaluate genetic information to identify patients or families at risk for specific genetic risks
- Write detailed consultation reports to provide information on complex genetic concepts for patients or referring physicians
- Discuss testing options and the associated risks, benefits, and limitations with patients and families
- Counsel patients and family members by providing information, education, or reassurance regarding genetic risks and inherited conditions
- Participate in professional organizations or conferences to keep abreast of developments in genetics and genomics

Genetic counselors identify specific genetic disorders or risks through the study of genetics. A genetic disorder or syndrome is inherited. For parents who are expecting children, counselors

Genetic counselors explain the chances of a genetic condition occurring or recurring within a family.

use genetics to predict whether a baby is likely to have hereditary disorders, such as Down syndrome and cystic fibrosis, among others. Genetic counselors also assess the risk for an adult to develop diseases with a genetic component, such as certain forms of cancer.

Counselors identify these conditions by studying patients' genes through DNA testing. Medical laboratory technologists perform lab tests, which genetic counselors then evaluate and use for counseling patients and their families. They share this information with other health professionals, such as physicians. For more information, see the profiles on medical and clinical laboratory technologists and technicians and physicians and surgeons.

According to a 2014 survey from the National Society of Genetic Counselors, approximately three-fourths of genetic counselors work in traditional areas of genetic counseling: prenatal, cancer, and pediatric. The survey noted that the number of specialized fields for genetic counselors has increased. More genetic counselors are specializing in fields such as cardiovascular health, genomic medicine, neurogenetics, and psychiatry.

Work Environment

Genetic counselors held about 2,400 jobs in 2014. The industries that employed the most genetic counselors were as follows:

Hospitals; state, local, and private	39%
Offices of physicians	20
Colleges, universities, and professional schools; state, local, and private	12

Genetic counselors work with families, patients, and other medical professionals.

Work Schedules. Most genetic counselors work full time and have a standard work schedule.

Education/Training

Genetic counselors typically need a master's degree in genetic counseling or genetics, and board certification.

Education. The typical entry route for genetic counselor's is a master's degree in genetic counseling or genetics.

Coursework in genetic counseling includes public health, epidemiology, psychology, and developmental biology. Classes emphasize genetics, public health, and patient empathy. Students also must complete clinical rotations, during which they work directly with patients and clients. Clinical rotations provide supervised experience for students, allowing them to work in different work environments, such as prenatal diagnostic centers, pediatric hospitals, or cancer centers.

In 2014, there were 31 master's degree programs in the United States that were accredited by the Accreditation Council for Genetic Counseling.

Licenses, Certifications, and Registrations. The American Board of Genetic Counseling provides certification for genetic counselors. To become certified, a student must complete an accredited master's degree program and pass an exam. Counselors must complete continuing education courses to maintain their board certification.

As of 2015, 20 states required genetic counselors to be licensed, and other states have pending legislation for licensure. Certification is typically needed to get a license. For specific licensing requirements, contact the state's medical board.

Important Qualities

Compassion. Patients may seek advice on family care or serious illnesses.

Critical-thinking skills. Genetic counselors analyze laboratory findings to determine how best to advise a patient or family. They use their applied knowledge of genetics to assess inherited risks properly.

Decision-making skills. Genetic counselors must use their expertise and experience to determine how to share their findings properly with patients.

Speaking skills. Genetic counselors must be able to simplify complex findings so that their patients understand them.

Pay

The median annual wage for genetic counselors was $67,500 in May 2014. The median wage is the wage at which half the workers in an occupation earned more than that amount and half earned less. The lowest 10 percent earned less than $43,950, and the highest 10 percent earned more than $99,980.

In May 2014, the median annual wages for genetic counselors in the top industries in which they worked were as follows:

Hospitals; state, local, and private	$66,410
Offices of physicians	65,180
Colleges, universities, and professional schools; state, local, and private	59,340

Job Outlook

Employment of genetic counselors is projected to grow 29 percent from 2014 to 2024, much faster than the average for all occupations. However, because it is a small occupation, the growth will result in only about 700 new jobs over the 10-year period.

Ongoing technological innovations, including lab tests and developments in genomics, are giving counselors the opportunities to conduct more types of analyses. Cancer genomics, for example, can determine a patient's risk for specific types of cancer. The number and types of tests that genetic counselors can administer

Median Annual Wages, May 2014

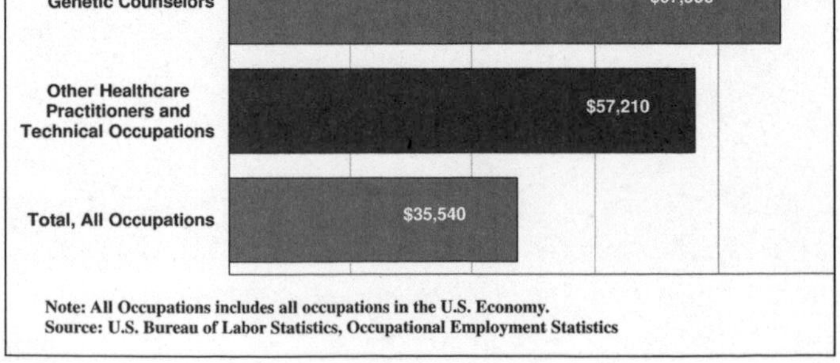

Note: All Occupations includes all occupations in the U.S. Economy.
Source: U.S. Bureau of Labor Statistics, Occupational Employment Statistics

Percent Change in Employment, Projected 2014–2024

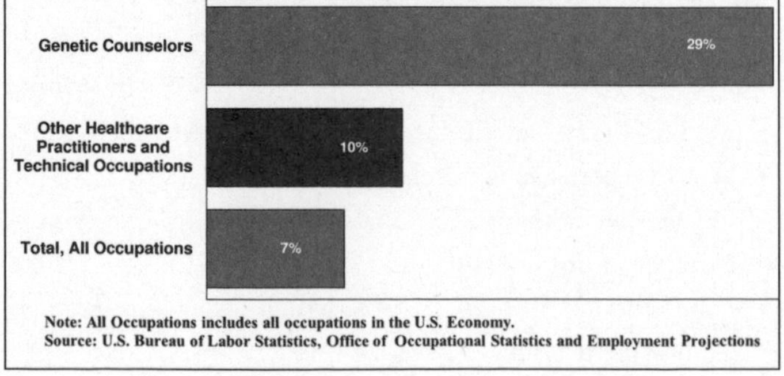

Note: All Occupations includes all occupations in the U.S. Economy.
Source: U.S. Bureau of Labor Statistics, Office of Occupational Statistics and Employment Projections

Employment Projections Data for Genetic Counselors

Occupational Title	SOC Code	Employment, 2014	Projected Employment, 2024	Change, 2014–2024 Percent	Change, 2014–2024 Numeric
Genetic counselors	29-9092	2,400	3,100	29	700

Source: U.S. Bureau of Labor Statistics, Employment Projections Program

Similar Occupations. This table shows a list of occupations with job duties that are similar to those of genetic counselors.

Occupations	Entry-level Education	2014 Median Pay	Projected Job Growth	Average Annual Openings
Epidemiologists	Master's degree	$67,420	6%	40
Health Educators and Community Health Workers	See Education/Training	$42,450	13%	1,560
Medical Scientists	Doctoral or professional degree	$79,930	8%	900
Mental Health Counselors and Marriage and Family Therapists	Master's degree	$42,250	19%	3,140
Physicians and Surgeons	Doctoral or professional degree	This wage is equal to or greater than $187,200.	14%	9,930

and evaluate has increased over the past few years. Similarly, many types of genetic tests are covered by health insurance providers.

Job Prospects. Genetic counselors who graduate from an accredited program and pass the board certification exam can generally expect the most favorable job prospects. Ongoing innovations in genetic testing are likely to create demand for certified genetic counselors.

Contacts for More Information

For more information about genetic counselors, certification, and schools offering education in genetic counseling, visit

➤ American Board of Genetic Counseling (http://tinyurl.com/kxchcct)

For more information about genetic counseling career requirements and developments in genetics, including licensure, visit

➤ National Society of Genetic Counselors (www.nsgc.org)

For more information about accreditation and schools offering education in genetic counseling, visit

➤ Accreditation Council for Genetic Counseling (www.gceducation.org/Pages/default.aspx)

O*NET

➤ Genetic Counselors (29-9092.00)

Home Health Aides

- **2014 Median Pay** .... $21,380 per year $10.28 per hour
- **Typical Entry-Level Education** .... No formal educational credential
- **Work Experience in a Related Occupation**.............. None
- **On-the-job Training** ....Short-term on-the-job training
- **Number of Jobs, 2014** 913,500
- **Job Outlook, 2014–24**......38% (Much faster than average)
- **Employment Change, 2014–24** 348,400

What Home Health Aides Do

Home health aides help people with disabilities, chronic illness, or cognitive impairment with activities of daily living. They often help older adults who need assistance. In some states, home health aides may be able to give a client medication or check the client's vital signs under the direction of a nurse or other healthcare practitioner.

Duties. Home health aides typically do the following:

- Assist clients in their daily personal tasks, such as bathing or dressing
- Provide basic health-related services according to a client's needs, such as checking vital signs or administering prescribed medication at scheduled times
- Do light housekeeping, such as laundry, washing dishes, and vacuuming in a client's home

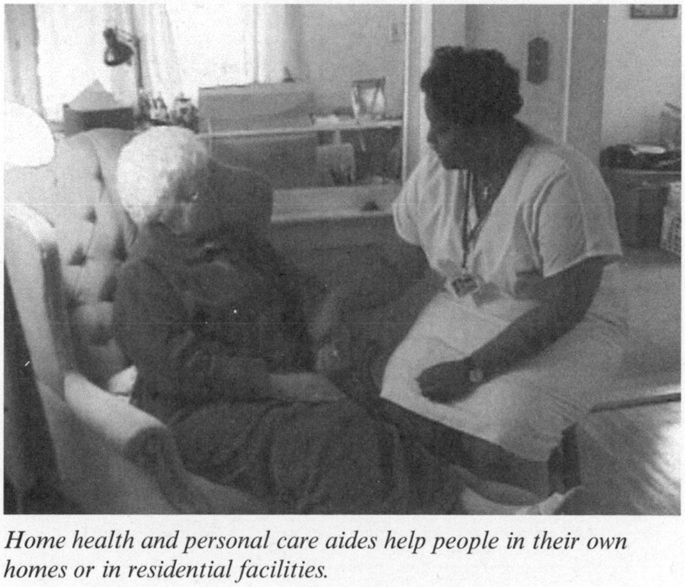

Home health and personal care aides help people in their own homes or in residential facilities.

Median Annual Wages, May 2014

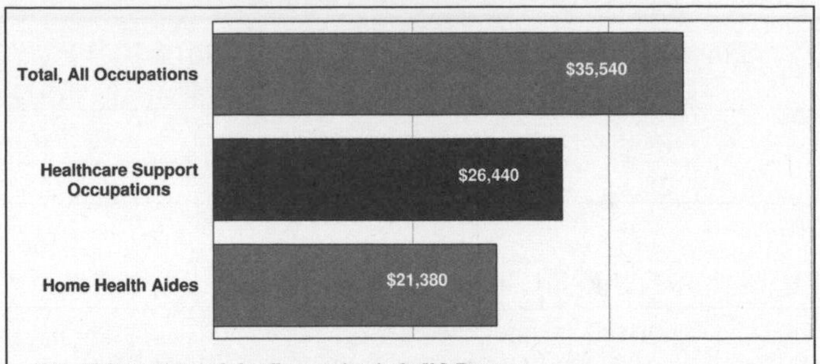

Note: All Occupations includes all occupations in the U.S. Economy.
Source: U.S. Bureau of Labor Statistics, Occupational Employment Statistics

Percent Change in Employment, Projected 2014–2024

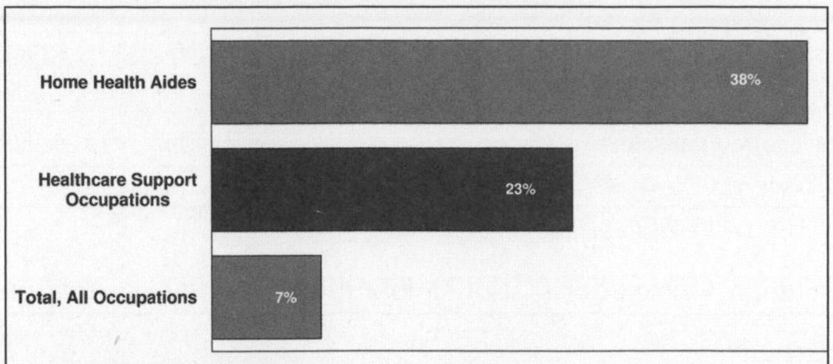

Note: All Occupations includes all occupations in the U.S. Economy.
Source: U.S. Bureau of Labor Statistics, Office of Occupational Statistics and Employment Projections

- Help to organize a client's schedule and plan appointments
- Arrange transportation to doctors' offices or for other kinds of outings
- Shop for groceries and prepare meals to meet a client's dietary specifications
- Help to keep clients engaged in their social networks and communities

Home health aides, unlike personal care aides, typically work for certified home health or hospice agencies that receive government funding and therefore must comply with regulations. They work under the direct supervision of medical professionals, usually nurses. These aides keep records of services performed and of clients' conditions and progress. They report changes in clients' conditions to supervisors or case managers. Home health aides also work with therapists and other medical staff.

Depending on their clients' needs, home health aides may provide some basic health-related services, such as checking a client's pulse, temperature, and respiration rate. They may also help with simple prescribed exercises and or with giving medications. Occasionally, they change bandages or dressings, give massages, care for skin, or help with braces and artificial limbs. With special training, experienced home health aides also may help with medical equipment such as ventilators, which help clients breathe.

Work Environment

Home health aides held about 913,500 jobs in 2014. The industries that employed the most home health aides were as follows:

Home healthcare services	38%
Services for the elderly and persons with disabilities	24
Residential intellectual and developmental disability, mental health, and substance abuse facilities	11
Continuing care retirement communities and assisted living facilities for the elderly	10

Most work in a client's home; others work in small group homes or larger care communities. Some home health aides go to the same home every day or week for months or even years. Some visit four or five clients in the same day, while others work only with one client all day. They may work with other aides in shifts so that the client always has an aide. They help people in hospices and day services programs, and also help people with disabilities go to work and stay engaged in their communities.

Work Schedules. Most home health aides worked full time in 2014. They may be required to work evening and weekend hours to attend to their clients' needs.

Injuries and Illnesses. Work as a home health aide can be physically and emotionally demanding. Aides must guard against back injury because they often move clients into and out of bed or help them to stand or walk.

In addition, home health aides frequently work with clients who have cognitive impairments or mental health issues and who may display difficult or violent behaviors. Aides also face hazards from minor infections and exposure to communicable diseases, but can lessen their chance of infection by following proper procedures.

Education/Training

There is no formal education requirement for home health aides, but most aides have at least a high school diploma. Home health aides who work for certified home health or hospice agencies must complete formal training and pass a standardized test.

Education. Although a high school diploma or equivalent is not generally required, most home health aides have one before entering the occupation. Some formal education programs may be available from community colleges or vocational schools.

Licenses, Certifications, and Registrations. Home health aides who work for agencies that receive reimbursement from Medicare or Medicaid must get a minimum level of training and pass a competency evaluation to be certified. Training typically includes learning about personal hygiene, reading and recording vital signs, infection control, and basic nutrition. Aides may take a competency exam to become certified without taking any training.

Additional requirements for certification vary by state. In some states, the only requirement for employment is on-the-job training, which employers generally provide. Other states require formal training, which is available from community colleges, vocational schools, elder care programs, and home healthcare agencies. In addition, states may conduct background checks on prospective

Employment Projections Data for Home Health Aides

Occupational Title	SOC Code	Employment, 2014	Projected Employment, 2024	Change, 2014–2024 Percent	Change, 2014–2024 Numeric
Home health aides	31-1011	913,500	1,261,900	38	348,400

Source: U.S. Bureau of Labor Statistics, Employment Projections Program

Similar Occupations. This table shows a list of occupations with job duties that are similar to those of home health aides.

Occupations	Entry-level Education	2014 Median Pay	Projected Job Growth	Average Annual Openings
Childcare Workers	High school diploma or equivalent	$19,730	5%	6,930
Licensed Practical and Licensed Vocational Nurses	Postsecondary nondegree award	$42,490	16%	11,730
Medical Assistants	Postsecondary nondegree award	$29,960	23%	13,890
Nursing Assistants and Orderlies	See Education/Training	$25,090	17%	26,780
Occupational Therapy Assistants and Aides	See Education/Training	$52,300	40%	1,680
Personal Care Aides	No formal educational credential	$20,440	26%	45,810
Physical Therapist Assistants and Aides	See Education/Training	$41,640	40%	5,140
Registered Nurses	Bachelor's degree	$66,640	16%	43,930
Social and Human Service Assistants	High school diploma or equivalent	$29,790	11%	4,420

aides. For specific state requirements, contact the state's health board.

In addition, many home health aides may be required to obtain CPR certification.

Training. Home health aides may be trained in housekeeping tasks, such as cooking for clients who have special dietary needs. Aides learn basic safety techniques, including how to respond in an emergency. Specific training may be needed for certification if state certification is required.

In addition, clients have their own preferences, and aides may need time to become comfortable working with them.

Important Qualities

Detail oriented. Home health aides must adhere to specific rules and protocols to help take care of clients. Aides must carefully follow instructions from healthcare professionals, such as how to care for a client's wound or how to identify changes in a client's condition.

Integrity. Home health aides should make clients feel comfortable when they tend to personal activities, such as helping a client bathe. In addition, home health aides must be dependable and trustworthy so that clients and their families can rely on them.

Interpersonal skills. Home health aides must work closely with their clients. Sometimes, clients are in extreme pain or distress, and aides must be sensitive to their emotions. Aides must be compassionate, and they must enjoy helping people.

Physical stamina. Home health aides should be comfortable performing physical tasks. They might need to lift or turn clients.

Pay

The median annual wage for home health aides was $21,380 in May 2014. The median wage is the wage at which half the workers in an occupation earned more than that amount and half earned less. The lowest 10 percent earned less than $17,040, and the highest 10 percent earned more than $29,560.

In May 2014, the median annual wages for home health aides in the top industries in which they worked were as follows:

Continuing care retirement communities and assisted living facilities for the elderly	$21,660
Residential intellectual and developmental disability, mental health, and substance abuse facilities	21,590
Home healthcare services	21,160
Services for the elderly and persons with disabilities	20,880

Job Outlook

Employment of home health aides is projected to grow 38 percent from 2014 to 2024, much faster than the average for all occupations.

As the baby-boom population ages and the elderly population grows, the demand for home health aides to provide assistance will continue to increase. The older population often has health problems and will need help with daily activities.

Elderly clients and people with disabilities are increasingly relying on home care as a less expensive alternative to nursing homes or hospitals. Clients who need help with everyday tasks and household chores, rather than medical care, can reduce their medical expenses by returning to their homes.

Another factor that will likely lead to an increase in the demand for home care is that most clients prefer to be cared for in their homes, where they are most comfortable. Studies have found that home care is often more effective than care in a nursing home or hospital.

Job Prospects. Job prospects for home health aides are excellent. This occupation is large and is projected to add many jobs. In addition, the low pay and high emotional demands may cause many workers to leave this occupation, and they will have to be replaced.

Contacts for More Information

For more information about home health aides, including voluntary credentials for aides, visit

➤ National Association for Home Care & Hospice (www.nahc.org)

O*NET

➤ Home Health Aides (31-1011.00)

Licensed Practical and Licensed Vocational Nurses

- **2014 Median Pay** .... $42,490 per year $20.43 per hour
- **Typical Entry-Level Education** .... Postsecondary nondegree award
- **Work Experience in a Related Occupation** .... None
- **On-the-job Training** .... None
- **Number of Jobs, 2014** 719,900
- **Job Outlook, 2014–24** .... 16% (Much faster than average)
- **Employment Change, 2014–24** 117,300

What Licensed Practical and Licensed Vocational Nurses Do

Licensed practical nurses (LPNs) and licensed vocational nurses (LVNs) provide basic medical care. They work under the direction of registered nurses and doctors.

Duties. Licensed practical and licensed vocational nurses typically do the following:

- Monitor patients' health—for example, by checking their blood pressure
- Administer basic patient care, including changing bandages and inserting catheters
- Provide for the basic comfort of patients, such as helping them bathe or dress
- Discuss the care they are providing with patients and listen to their concerns
- Report patients' status and concerns to registered nurses and doctors
- Keep records on patients' health

Duties of LPNs and LVNs vary, depending on their work setting and the state in which they work. For example, they may reinforce teaching done by registered nurses regarding how family members should care for a relative; help to deliver, care for, and feed infants; collect samples for testing and do routine laboratory tests; or feed patients who need help eating.

LPNs and LVNs may be limited to doing certain tasks, depending on the state where they work. For example, in some states, LPNs with proper training can give medication or start intravenous (IV) drips, but in other states LPNs cannot perform these tasks. State regulations also govern the extent to which LPNs and LVNs must be directly supervised. For example, an LPN may provide certain forms of care only with instructions from a registered nurse.

In some states, experienced licensed practical and licensed vocational nurses oversee and direct other LPNs or LVNs and unlicensed medical staff.

Work Environment

Licensed practical and licensed vocational nurses held about 719,900 jobs in 2014. The industries that employed the most licensed practical and licensed vocational nurses were as follows:

Nursing and residential care facilities	38%
Hospitals; state, local, and private	17
Offices of physicians	13
Home healthcare services	11
Government	7

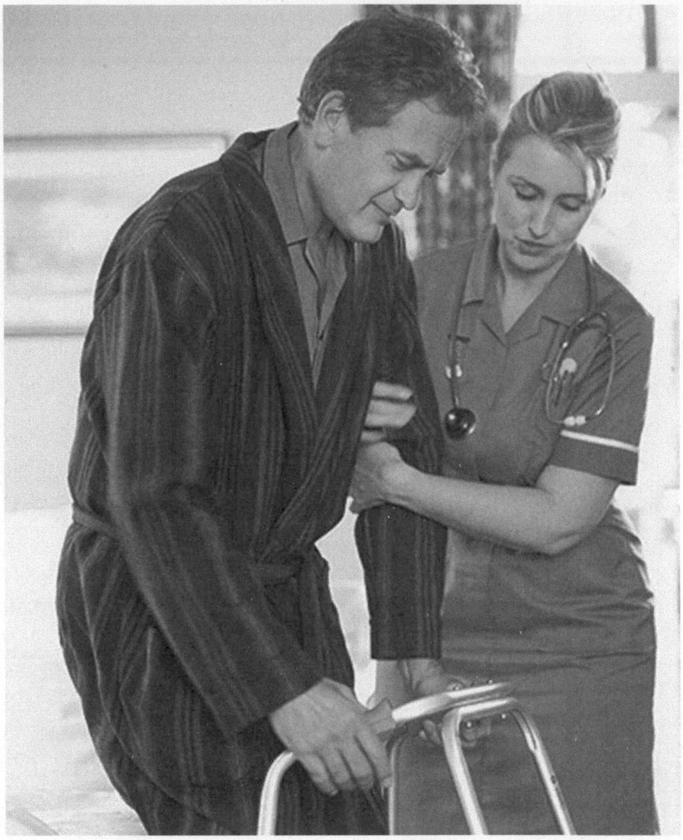

Licensed practical nurses may assist patients with bathing, dressing, standing, and walking.

Nurses must often be on their feet for much of the day and may have to lift patients who have trouble moving in bed, standing, or walking. These duties can be stressful, as can dealing with ill and injured people.

Work Schedules. Most licensed practical and licensed vocational nurses work full time, although about 1 in 5 worked part time in 2014. Many LPNs and LVNs work shifts during nights, weekends, or holidays, because patients need medical care at all hours. They may be required to work shifts of longer than 8 hours.

Education/Training

Becoming a licensed practical or licensed vocational nurse (LPN or LVN) requires completing an approved educational program. LPNs and LVNs also must have a license.

Education. LPNs and LVNs must complete an approved educational program. These programs award a certificate or diploma

Median Annual Wages, May 2014

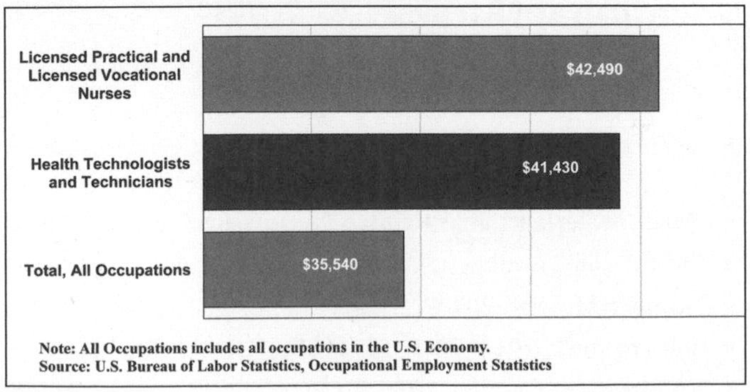

Percent Change in Employment, Projected 2014–2024

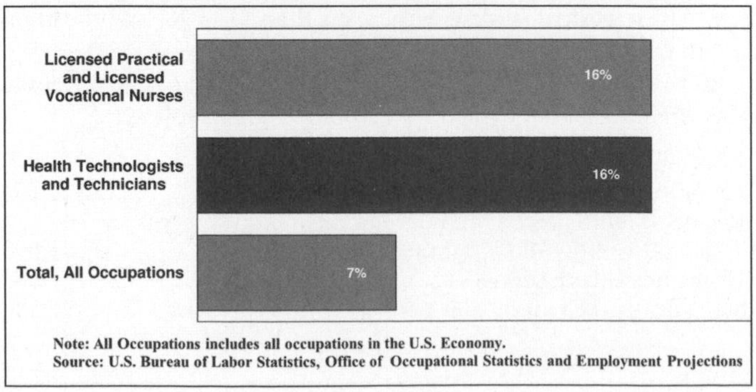

Employment Projections Data for Licensed Practical and Licensed Vocational Nurses

Occupational Title	SOC Code	Employment, 2014	Projected Employment, 2024	Change, 2014–2024 Percent	Change, 2014–2024 Numeric
Licensed practical and licensed vocational nurses	29-2061	719,900	837,200	16	117,300

Source: U.S. Bureau of Labor Statistics, Employment Projections Program

and typically take about 1 year to complete, but may take longer. They are commonly found in technical schools and community colleges, although some programs may be available in high schools or hospitals.

Practical nursing programs combine classroom learning in subjects such as nursing, biology, and pharmacology. All programs also include supervised clinical experience.

Contact state boards of nursing for lists of approved programs.

Licenses, Certifications, and Registrations. After completing a state-approved educational program, prospective LPNs and LVNs can take the National Council Licensure Examination (NCLEX-PN). In all states, they must pass the exam to get a license and work as an LPN or LVN. For more information on the NCLEX-PN examination and a list of state boards of nursing, visit the National Council of State Boards of Nursing.

LPNs and LVNs may choose to become certified through professional associations in areas such as gerontology and IV therapy. Certifications show that an LPN or LVN has an advanced level of knowledge about a specific subject.

In addition, employers may prefer to hire candidates who are trained to provide cardiopulmonary resuscitation (CPR).

Important Qualities

Compassion. Licensed practical and licensed vocational nurses must be empathetic and caring toward the people they serve.

Detail oriented. LPNs and LVNs need to be responsible and detail oriented, because they must make sure that patients get the correct care at the right time.

Interpersonal skills. Interacting with patients and other healthcare providers is a big part of their jobs, so LPNs and LVNs need good interpersonal skills.

Patience. Dealing with sick and injured people may be stressful. LPNs and LVNs should be patient, so they can cope with any stress that stems from providing care to these patients.

Physical stamina. LPNs and LVNs should be comfortable performing physical tasks, such as bending over patients for a long time.

Speaking skills. It is important that LPNs and LVNs be able to communicate effectively. For example, they may need to relay information about a patient's current condition to a registered nurse.

Advancement. With experience, licensed practical and licensed vocational nurses may advance to supervisory positions. Some LPNs and LVNs advance to other healthcare occupations. For example, an LPN may complete a LPN to RN education program to become a registered nurse.

Pay

The median annual wage for licensed practical and licensed vocational nurses was $42,490 in May 2014. The median wage is the wage at which half the workers in an occupation earned more than that amount and half earned less. The lowest 10 percent earned less than $31,640, and the highest 10 percent earned more than $58,710.

In May 2014, the median annual wages for licensed practical and licensed vocational nurses in the top industries in which they worked were as follows:

Nursing and residential care facilities	$43,700
Home healthcare services	43,670
Government	43,480
Hospitals; state, local, and private	41,400
Offices of physicians	38,150

Job Outlook

Employment of licensed practical and licensed vocational nurses is projected to grow 16 percent from 2014 to 2024, much faster than the average for all occupations.

As the baby-boom population ages, the overall need for healthcare services is expected to increase. LPNs and LVNs will be needed in residential care facilities and in home health environments to care for older patients.

A number of chronic conditions, such as diabetes and obesity, have become more prevalent in recent years. LPNs and LVNs will be needed to assist and care for patients with chronic conditions in skilled nursing and other extended care facilities. In addition, many procedures that once could be done only in hospitals are now being done outside of hospitals, creating demand in other settings, such as outpatient care centers.

Similar Occupations. This table shows a list of occupations with job duties that are similar to those of licensed practical and licensed vocational nurses.

Occupations	Entry-level Education	2014 Median Pay	Projected Job Growth	Average Annual Openings
Nursing Assistants and Orderlies	See Education/Training	$25,090	17%	26,780
Occupational Therapy Assistants and Aides	See Education/Training	$52,300	40%	1,680
Physical Therapist Assistants and Aides	See Education/Training	$41,640	40%	5,140
Psychiatric Technicians and Aides	See Education/Training	$28,470	5%	760
Registered Nurses	Bachelor's degree	$66,640	16%	43,930
Surgical Technologists	Postsecondary nondegree award	$43,350	15%	1,470

The number of individuals who have access to health insurance is expected to continue to increase because of federal health insurance reform. LPNs will be needed, particularly in ambulatory care settings, to care for the newly insured who seek primary and preventative care services.

Job Prospects. High emotional and physical demands may cause workers to leave the occupation, creating potential job openings. Job prospects should be favorable for LPNs and LVNs who are willing to work in rural and medically underserved areas.

Contacts for More Information

For more information about licensed practical or licensed vocational nurses, visit

➤ National Federation of Licensed Practical Nurses (www.nflpn.org)

For more information about the National Council Licensure Examination (NCLEX-PN) and a list of individual state boards of nursing, visit

➤ National Council of State Boards of Nursing (www.ncsbn.org/index.htm)

O*NET

➤ Licensed Practical and Licensed Vocational Nurses (29-2061.00)

Massage Therapists

- **2014 Median Pay** .... $37,180 per year $17.88 per hour
- **Typical Entry-Level Education** .... Postsecondary nondegree award
- **Work Experience in a Related Occupation** .... None
- **On-the-job Training** .... None
- **Number of Jobs, 2014** 168,800
- **Job Outlook, 2014–24** ...... 22% (Much faster than average)
- **Employment Change, 2014–24** 36,500

What Massage Therapists Do

Massage therapists treat clients by using touch to manipulate the muscles and other soft tissues of the body. With their touch, therapists relieve pain, help heal injuries, improve circulation, relieve stress, increase relaxation, and aid in the general wellness of clients.

Duties. Massage therapists typically do the following:

- Talk with clients about their symptoms, medical history, and desired results
- Evaluate clients to locate painful or tense areas of the body
- Manipulate muscles and other soft tissues of the body
- Provide clients with guidance on stretching, strengthening, overall relaxation, and how to improve their posture
- Document clients' conditions and progress

Massage therapists use touch to treat clients' injuries and to promote the clients' general wellness. They use their hands, fingers, forearms, elbows, and sometimes feet to knead muscles and soft tissues of the body.

Massage therapists may use lotions and oils, and massage tables or chairs, when treating a client. A massage can be as short as 5–10 minutes or could last more than an hour.

Therapists talk with clients about what they hope to achieve through massage. Massage therapists may suggest personalized treatment plans for their clients, including information about additional relaxation techniques to practice between sessions.

Massage therapists can specialize in many different types of massage or modalities. Swedish massage, deep-tissue massage, and sports massage are just a few of the many modalities of massage therapy. Most massage therapists specialize in several modalities, which require different techniques.

The type of massage given typically depends on the client's needs and physical condition. For example, therapists may use a special technique for elderly clients that they would not use for athletes. Some forms of massage are given solely to one type of client; for example, prenatal massage is given only to pregnant women.

Massage therapists who are self-employed may need to do business-related tasks such as marketing, booking appointments, and maintaining financial records. They may also have to buy supplies and do laundry.

Work Environment

Massage therapists held about 168,800 jobs in 2014. About half of massage therapists were self-employed in 2014.

Massage therapists work in an array of settings, such as spas, franchised clinics, physicians' offices, hotels, and fitness centers. Some massage therapists also travel to clients' homes or offices to give a massage. Others work out of their own homes. Many massage therapists, especially those who are self-employed, provide their own table or chair, sheets, pillows, and body lotions or oils.

A massage therapist's working conditions depend heavily on the venue in which the massage is performed and on what the client wants. For example, when giving a massage to help clients relax, massage therapists generally work in dimly lit settings and use candles, incense, and calm, soothing music. In contrast, a massage meant to help rehabilitate a client with an injury may be conducted in a well-lit setting with several other people receiving treatment in the same room.

Injuries and Illnesses. Because giving a massage is physically demanding, massage therapists can injure themselves if they do not use the proper techniques. Repetitive-motion problems and fatigue from standing for extended periods are most common.

Therapists can limit these risks by using good body mechanics, spacing sessions properly, exercising, and, in many cases, receiving a massage themselves regularly.

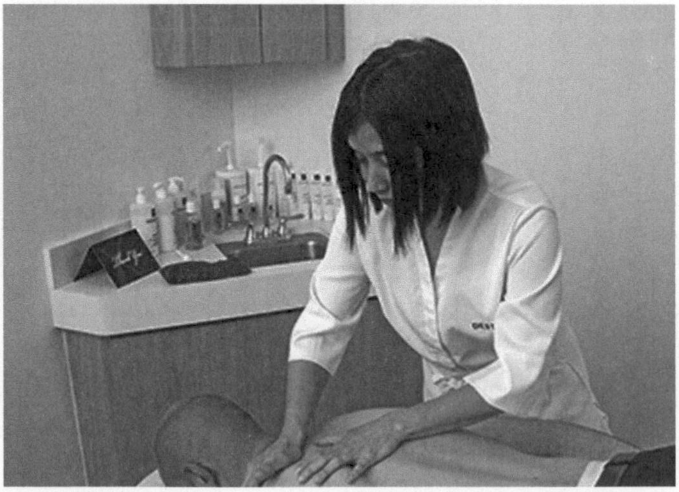

Massage therapists apply pressure to relieve stress and promote health.

Median Annual Wages, May 2014

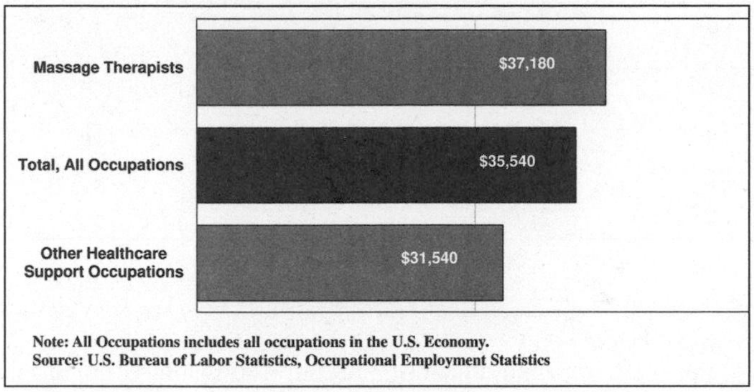

Percent Change in Employment, Projected 2014–2024

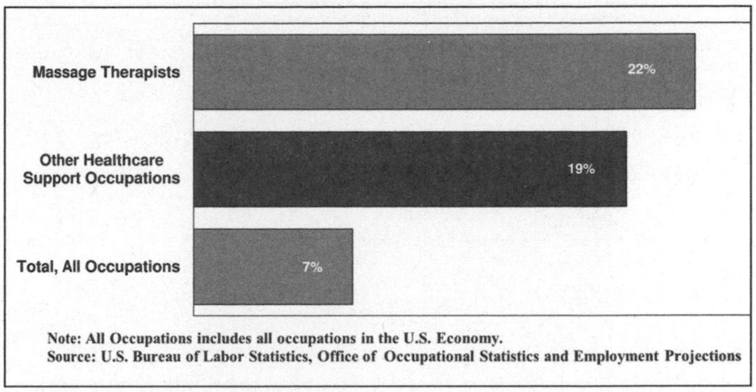

Work Schedules. About half of massage therapists worked part time in 2014.

Because therapists work by appointment in most cases, their schedules and the number of hours worked each week vary considerably. Moreover, because of the strength and endurance needed to give a massage, many therapists cannot perform massage services 8 hours per day, 5 days per week.

In addition to giving massages, therapists, especially those who are self-employed, may spend time recording clients' notes, marketing, booking clients, washing linens, and conducting other general business tasks.

Education/Training

Massage therapists typically complete a postsecondary education program of 500 or more hours of study and experience, although standards and requirements vary greatly by state or other jurisdiction. Most states regulate massage therapy and require massage therapists to have a license or certification.

Education. Education requirements for massage therapists vary greatly by state or locality. Education programs are typically found in private or public postsecondary institutions. Most programs require at least 500 hours of study for their completion; some programs require 1,000 or more hours.

A high school diploma or equivalent is usually required for admission to a massage therapy program. Programs generally include both classroom study and hands-on practice of massage techniques. Programs cover subjects such as anatomy; physiology, which is the study of organs and tissues; kinesiology, which is the study of motion and body mechanics; pathology, which is the study of disease; business management; and ethics.

Programs may concentrate on certain modalities, or specialties, of massage. Several programs also offer job placement services and continuing education. Both full-time and part-time programs are available.

Licenses, Certifications, and Registrations. In 2014, 45 states and the District of Columbia regulated massage therapy. Although not all states license massage therapy, they may have regulations at the local level.

In states with massage therapy regulations, workers must get a license or certification before practicing massage. State regulations typically require graduation from an approved massage therapy program and passing an exam.

The exam may be a state-specific exam or the Massage and Bodywork Licensing Examination (MBLEx) licensure exam, offered by the Federation of State Massage Therapy Boards.

Therapists also may need to pass a background check, have liability insurance, and be certified in cardiopulmonary resuscitation (CPR). Many states require massage therapists to complete continuing education credits and to renew their license periodically. Those wishing to practice massage therapy should look into legal requirements for the state and locality in which they intend to practice.

Important Qualities

Communication skills. Massage therapists need to listen carefully to clients in order to understand what they want to achieve through massage sessions.

Decision-making skills. Massage therapists must evaluate each client's needs and recommend the best treatment on the basis of that person's needs.

Empathy. Massage therapists must give clients a positive experience, which requires building trust between therapist and client. Making clients feel comfortable is necessary for therapists to expand their client base.

Integrity. Massage therapists often have access to client information such as medical histories. Therefore, they must be trustworthy and protect the privacy of their clients.

Physical stamina. Massage therapists may give several treatments during a workday and have to stay on their feet throughout massage appointments.

Physical strength and dexterity. Massage therapists must be strong and able to exert pressure through a variety of movements of the arms and hands when manipulating a client's muscles.

Time-management skills. Massage therapists must tailor an appointment to a client's specific needs. Therapists must use their appointment time wisely to help each client accomplish his or her goals.

Employment Projections Data for Massage Therapists

Occupational Title	SOC Code	Employment, 2014	Projected Employment, 2024	Change, 2014–2024 Percent	Change, 2014–2024 Numeric
Massage therapists	31-9011	168,800	205,200	22	36,500

Source: U.S. Bureau of Labor Statistics, Employment Projections Program

Similar Occupations. This table shows a list of occupations with job duties that are similar to those of massage therapists.

Occupations	Entry-level Education	2014 Median Pay	Projected Job Growth	Average Annual Openings
Athletic Trainers	Bachelor's degree	$43,370	21%	540
Exercise Physiologists	Bachelor's degree	$46,270	11%	150
Physical Therapist Assistants and Aides	See Education/Training	$41,640	40%	5,140
Physical Therapists	Doctoral or professional degree	$82,390	34%	7,180

Pay

The median annual wage for massage therapists was $37,180 in May 2014. The median wage is the wage at which half the workers in an occupation earned more than that amount and half earned less. The lowest 10 percent earned less than $18,460, and the highest 10 percent earned more than $71,950.

Most massage therapists earn a combination of wages and tips.

Job Outlook

Employment of massage therapists is projected to grow 22 percent from 2014 to 2024, much faster than the average for all occupations. Continued growth in the demand for massage services will lead to new openings for massage therapists.

As an increasing number of states adopt licensing requirements and standards for therapists, the practice of massage is likely to be respected and accepted by more people as a way to treat pain and to improve overall wellness.

Similarly, as more healthcare providers understand the benefits of massage, demand will likely increase as these services become part of treatment plans. However, demand in healthcare settings will be tempered by limited insurance coverage for massage services.

Massage also offers specific benefits to particular groups of people whose continued demand for massage services will lead to overall growth for the occupation. For example, many sports teams hire massage therapists to help their athletes rehabilitate from injuries and to relieve or manage pain.

The number of massage clinic franchises has increased in recent years. Many franchised clinics offer more affordable massages than those provided at spas and resorts, making massage services available to a wider range of customers.

However, demand for massage services may be limited by the overall state of the economy. During tough economic times, both the number of people who seek massage therapy and the frequency of their massages may decline.

Job Prospects. In states that regulate massage therapy, opportunities should be available to those who complete formal programs and pass a professionally recognized exam. However, new massage therapists should expect that it can take time build a client base.

Because referrals are an important source of work for massage therapists, marketing and networking may help increase the number of job opportunities. Joining a professional association also can help build strong contacts and further increase the likelihood of steady work. In addition, massage therapists may be able to attract a wider variety of clients by completing education programs in multiple modalities.

Contacts for More Information

For more information about careers in massage therapy, visit

➤ Associated Bodywork & Massage Professionals (www.abmp.com)

➤ American Massage Therapy Association (www.amtamassage.org/index.html)

➤ National Certification Board for Therapeutic Massage & Bodywork (www.ncbtmb.org)

For more information about national testing and national certification, visit

➤ Federation of State Massage Therapy Boards (www.fsmtb.org)

For more information about accredited massage therapy programs, visit

➤ Commission on Massage Therapy Accreditation (http://comta.org)

O*NET

➤ Massage Therapists (31-9011.00)

Medical and Clinical Laboratory Technologists and Technicians

- **2014 Median Pay** .... $49,310 per year
  $23.71 per hour
- **Typical Entry-Level Education** .... See Education/Training
- **Work Experience in a Related Occupation**.............. None
- **On-the-job Training** .... None
- **Number of Jobs, 2014** 328,200
- **Job Outlook, 2014–24**..... 16% (Much faster than average)
- **Employment Change, 2014–24** 52,100

What Medical and Clinical Laboratory Technologists and Technicians Do

Medical laboratory technologists (commonly known as *medical laboratory scientists*) and medical laboratory technicians collect samples and perform tests to analyze body fluids, tissue, and other substances.

Duties. Medical laboratory technologists and technicians typically do the following:

- Analyze body fluids, such as blood, urine, and tissue samples, and record normal or abnormal findings
- Study blood samples for use in transfusions by identifying the number of cells, the cell morphology or the blood group, blood type, and compatibility with other blood types
- Operate sophisticated laboratory equipment, such as microscopes and cell counters
- Use automated equipment and computerized instruments capable of performing a number of tests at the same time
- Log data from medical tests and enter results into a patient's medical record
- Discuss results and findings of laboratory tests and procedures with physicians
- Supervise or train medical laboratory technicians

Both technicians and technologists perform tests and procedures that physicians and surgeons or other healthcare personnel order. However, technologists perform more complex tests and laboratory procedures than technicians do. For example, technologists may prepare specimens and perform detailed manual tests, whereas technicians perform routine tests that may be more automated. Medical laboratory technicians usually work under the general supervision of medical laboratory technologists or laboratory managers.

Technologists in small laboratories perform many types of tests; in large laboratories, they sometimes specialize. The following are examples of types of specialized medical laboratory technologists:

Blood bank technologists, or *immunohematology technologists*, collect blood, classify it by type, and prepare blood and its components for transfusions.

Clinical chemistry technologists prepare specimens and analyze the chemical and hormonal contents of body fluids.

Cytotechnologists prepare slides of body cells and examine these cells with a microscope for abnormalities that may signal the beginning of a cancerous growth.

Immunology technologists examine elements of the human immune system and its response to foreign bodies.

Microbiology technologists examine and identify bacteria and other microorganisms.

Molecular biology technologists perform complex protein and nucleic acid tests on cell samples.

Like technologists, medical laboratory technicians may work in several areas of the laboratory or specialize in one particular area. For example, histotechnicians cut and stain tissue specimens for pathologists, who are doctors who study the cause and development of diseases at a microscopic level.

Technologists and technicians often specialize after they have worked in a particular area for a long time or have received advanced education or training in that area.

Work Environment

Medical laboratory technologists held about 164,800 jobs in 2014. The industries that employed the most medical laboratory technologists in 2014 were as follows:

Hospitals; state, local, and private	58%
Medical and diagnostic laboratories	17
Offices of physicians	8
Colleges, universities, and professional schools; state, local, and private	5

Medical laboratory technicians held about 163,400 jobs in 2014. The industries that employed the most medical laboratory technicians in 2014 were as follows:

Hospitals; state, local, and private	44%
Medical and diagnostic laboratories	19
Offices of physicians	12
Colleges, universities, and professional schools; state, local, and private	5

Medical laboratory personnel are trained to work with infectious specimens or with materials that are caustic or produce fumes. When they follow proper methods to control infection and sterilize equipment, the risk decreases. They wear protective masks, gloves, and goggles for their safety.

Technologists and technicians can be on their feet for long periods, and they may need to lift or turn disabled patients to collect samples.

Work Schedules. Most medical laboratory technologists and technicians work full time. Technologists and technicians who work in facilities that operate around the clock, such as hospitals and some independent laboratories, may work evening, weekend, or overnight hours.

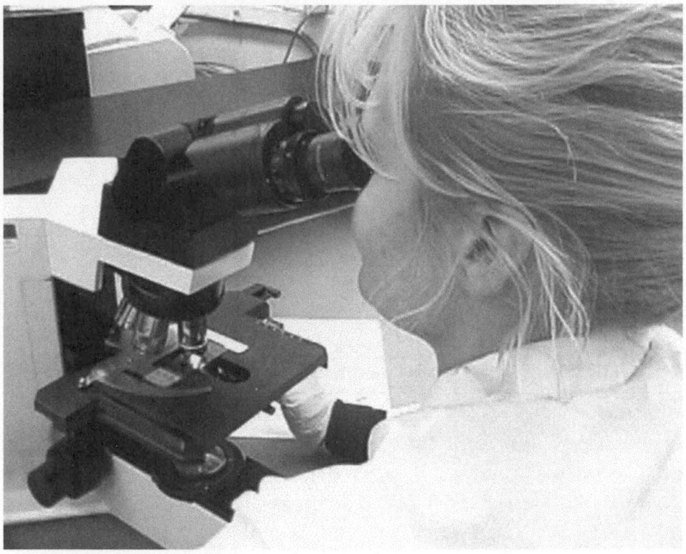

Clinical laboratory personnel examine and test body fluids and cells.

Education/Training

Technicians usually need an associate's degree or a postsecondary certificate. Some states require technologists and technicians to be licensed.

Education. An entry-level job for technologists usually requires a bachelor's degree in medical technology or life sciences.

A bachelor's degree program in medical laboratory technology, also known as a medical laboratory scientist degree, includes courses in chemistry, biology, microbiology, math, and statistics. Coursework emphasizes laboratory skills, including safety procedures and lab management.

The courses may be offered through a university or hospital-based program that students attend during their senior year of college. College graduates who major in other sciences and meet a program's prerequisites, such as having completed required courses in biology and chemistry or maintaining a certain GPA, also may apply to a medical laboratory science program.

Medical laboratory technicians often complete an associate's degree program in clinical laboratory science. A limited number of 1-year certificate programs are available from hospitals, and admission requirements vary. The Armed Forces and vocational or technical schools also may offer certificate programs for medical laboratory technicians. Technician coursework addresses the theoretical and practical aspects of each of the major laboratory disciplines.

High school students who are interested in pursuing a career in the medical laboratory sciences should take classes in chemistry, biology, and math.

Licenses, Certifications, and Registrations. Some states require laboratory personnel to be licensed. Requirements vary by state and specialty. For specific requirements, contact state departments of health, state boards of occupational licensing, or visit The American Society for Clinical Laboratory Science.

Certification of medical laboratory technologists and technicians is required for licensure in some states. Although certification is not required to enter the occupation in all cases, employers typically prefer to hire certified technologists and technicians.

Median Annual Wages, May 2014

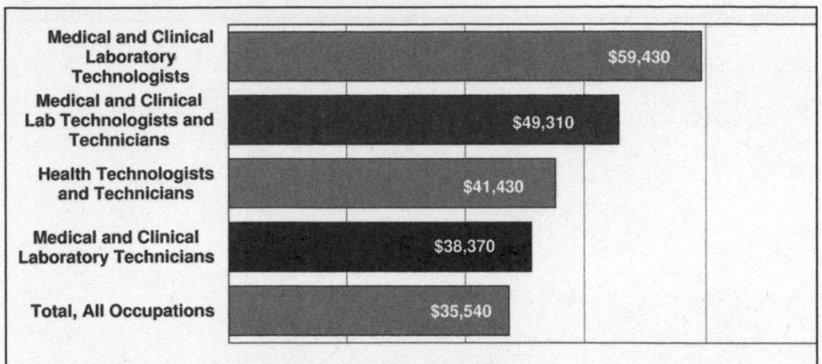

Note: All Occupations includes all occupations in the U.S. Economy.
Source: U.S. Bureau of Labor Statistics, Occupational Employment Statistics

Percent Change in Employment, Projected 2014–2024

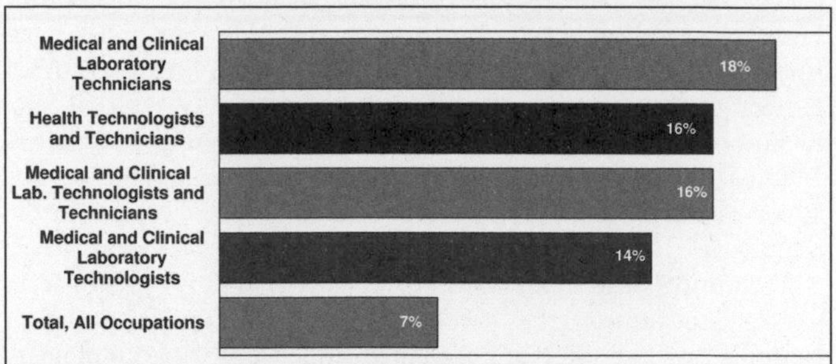

Note: All Occupations includes all occupations in the U.S. Economy.
Source: U.S. Bureau of Labor Statistics, Office of Occupational Statistics and Employment Projections

Medical laboratory technologists and technicians can obtain a general certification as a medical laboratory technologist or technician, respectively, or a certification in a specialty, such as cytotechnology or medical biology. Most credentialing institutions require that technologists complete an accredited education program in order to qualify to sit for an exam. For more credentialing information, visit the National Accrediting Agency for Clinical Laboratory Sciences.

Important Qualities

Ability to use technology. Medical laboratory technologists and technicians must understand how to operate complex machinery.

Detail oriented. Medical laboratory technologists and technicians must follow exact instructions in order to perform tests or procedures correctly.

Dexterity. Medical laboratory technologists and technicians need to be skilled with their hands. They work closely with needles and precise laboratory instruments and must handle these tools effectively.

Physical stamina. Medical laboratory technologists and technicians may work on their feet for long periods while collecting samples. They may need to lift or turn disabled patients to collect samples for testing.

Advancement. After additional education, work experience, or certification, technologists and technicians may specialize in one of many areas of laboratory science, such as immunology, histotechnology, or clinical chemistry. Some medical laboratory technicians advance to technologist positions after gaining experience and additional education.

Pay

The median annual wage for medical and clinical laboratory technologists was $59,430 in May 2014. The median wage is the wage at which half the workers in an occupation earned more than that amount and half earned less. The lowest 10 percent earned less than $40,640, and the highest 10 percent earned more than $82,180.

The median annual wage for medical and clinical laboratory technicians was $38,370 in May 2014. The lowest 10 percent earned less than $25,500, and the highest 10 percent earned more than $59,750.

In May 2014, the median annual wages for medical laboratory technologists in the top industries in which they worked were as follows:

Hospitals; state, local, and private	$59,530
Medical and diagnostic laboratories	59,310
Offices of physicians	55,590
Colleges, universities, and professional schools—state, local, and private	53,610

In May 2014, the median annual wages for medical laboratory technicians in the top industries in which they worked were as follows:

Hospitals; state, local, and private	$39,050
Offices of physicians	38,570
Colleges, universities, and professional schools—state, local, and private	38,000
Medical and diagnostic laboratories	37,360

Job Outlook

Employment of medical laboratory technologists is projected to grow 14 percent from 2014 to 2024, much faster the average for all occupations. Employment of medical laboratory technicians is projected to grow 18 percent from 2014 to 2024, much faster than the average for all occupations.

An increase in the aging population is expected to lead to a greater need to diagnose medical conditions, such as cancer or type 2 diabetes, through laboratory procedures. Prenatal testing for various types of genetic conditions also is increasingly common. Medical laboratory technologists and technicians will be in demand to use and maintain the equipment needed for diagnosis and treatment.

The number of individuals who have access to health insurance is expected to continue to increase because of federal health

Employment Projections Data for Medical and Clinical Laboratory Technologists and Technicians

Occupational Title	SOC Code	Employment, 2014	Projected Employment, 2024	Change, 2014–2024 Percent	Change, 2014–2024 Numeric
Clinical laboratory technologists and technicians	29-2010	328,200	380,300	16	52,100
Medical and clinical laboratory technologists	29-2011	164,800	187,900	14	23,100
Medical and clinical laboratory technicians	29-2012	163,400	192,400	18	29,000

Source: U.S. Bureau of Labor Statistics, Employment Projections Program

Similar Occupations. This table shows a list of occupations with job duties that are similar to those of medical and clinical laboratory technologists and technicians.

Occupations	Entry-level Education	2014 Median Pay	Projected Job Growth	Average Annual Openings
Biological Technicians	Bachelor's degree	$41,290	5%	410
Chemical Technicians	Associate's degree	$44,180	2%	120
Chemists and Materials Scientists	Bachelor's degree	$74,720	3%	260
Veterinary Technologists and Technicians	Associate's degree	$31,070	19%	1,790

insurance reform. As a result, demand for the services of laboratory personnel may grow as more patients who were previously uninsured, or found treatment to be cost-prohibitive, seek laboratory tests.

Job Prospects. Job prospects will be best for medical and clinical laboratory technologists and technicians who complete an accredited education program and earn professional certification.

Contacts for More Information

For more information about medical laboratory technologists and technicians, visit

➤ The American Society for Clinical Laboratory Science (www.ascls.org)
➤ American Society of Cytopathology (www.cytopathology.org)

For a list of accredited and approved educational programs for medical laboratory personnel, visit

➤ National Accrediting Agency for Clinical Laboratory Sciences (www.naacls.org)

For information on certification, visit

➤ American Association of Bioanalysts (www.aab.org)
➤ American Medical Technologists (www.amt1.com)
➤ American Society for Clinical Pathology (www.ascp.org)

O*NET

➤ Medical and Clinical Laboratory Technologists (29-2011.00)
➤ Cytogenetic Technologists (29-2011.01)
➤ Cytotechnologists (29-2011.02)
➤ Histotechnologists and Histologic Technicians (29-2011.03)
➤ Medical and Clinical Laboratory Technicians (29-2012.00)

Medical Assistants

- **2014 Median Pay** .... $29,960 per year $14.41 per hour
- **Typical Entry-Level Education** .... Postsecondary nondegree award
- **Work Experience in a Related Occupation**.............. None
- **On-the-job Training** .... None
- **Number of Jobs, 2014** 591,300
- **Job Outlook, 2014–24**.... 23% (Much faster than average)
- **Employment Change, 2014–24** 138,900

What Medical Assistants Do

Medical assistants complete administrative and clinical tasks in the offices of physicians, hospitals, and other healthcare facilities. Their duties vary with the location, specialty, and size of the practice.

Duties. Medical assistants typically do the following:

- Record patient history and personal information
- Measure vital signs, such as blood pressure
- Help the physician with patient examinations
- Give patients injections or medications as directed by the physician and as permitted by state law
- Schedule patient appointments
- Prepare blood samples for laboratory tests
- Enter patient information into medical records

Medical assistants take and record patients' personal information. They must be able to keep that information confidential and discuss it only with other medical personnel who are involved in treating the patient.

Electronic health records (EHRs) are changing some medical assistants' jobs. More and more physicians are adopting EHRs, moving all their patient information from paper to electronic records. Assistants need to learn the EHR software that their office uses.

Medical assistants should not be confused with physician assistants, who examine, diagnose, and treat patients under a physician's supervision.

In larger practices or hospitals, medical assistants may specialize in either administrative or clinical work.

Administrative medical assistants often fill out insurance forms or code patients' medical information. They often answer telephones and schedule patient appointments.

Clinical medical assistants have different duties, depending on the state where they work. They may do basic laboratory tests, dispose of contaminated supplies, and sterilize medical instruments. They may have additional responsibilities, such as instructing patients about medication or special diets, preparing patients for X-rays, removing stitches, drawing blood, or changing dressings.

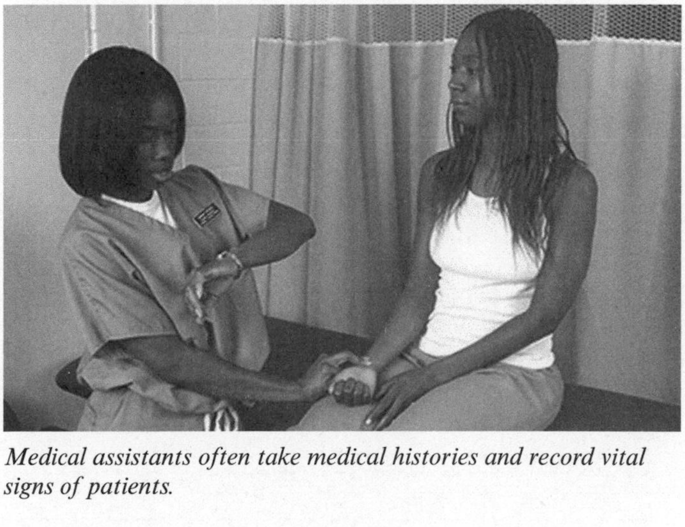

Medical assistants often take medical histories and record vital signs of patients.

Some medical assistants specialize according to the type of medical office where they work. The following are examples of specialized medical assistants:

Ophthalmic medical assistants and optometric assistants help ophthalmologists and optometrists, respectively, provide eye care. They show patients how to insert, remove, and care for contact lenses. Ophthalmic medical assistants also may help an ophthalmologist in surgery.

Podiatric medical assistants work closely with podiatrists (foot doctors). They may make castings of feet, expose and develop X-rays, and help podiatrists in surgery.

Work Environment

Medical assistants held about 591,300 jobs in 2014. The industries that employed the most medical assistants were as follows:

Offices of physicians	59%
Hospitals; state, local, and private	15
Offices of other health practitioners	10
Outpatient care centers	7

Most of these assistants work in physicians' offices, hospitals, outpatient clinics, and other healthcare facilities. In 2014, more than half of all medical assistants worked in physicians' offices.

Work Schedules. Most medical assistants work full time. Some work evenings, weekends, or holidays to cover shifts in medical facilities that are always open.

Education/Training

Most medical assistants have postsecondary education such as a certificate. Others enter the occupation with a high school diploma and learn through on-the-job training.

Education. Medical assistants typically graduate from postsecondary education programs. Although there are no formal educational requirements for becoming a medical assistant in most states, employers may prefer to hire assistants who have completed these programs.

Programs for medical assisting are available from community colleges, vocational schools, technical schools, and universities and take about 1 year to complete. These programs usually lead to a certificate or diploma. Some community colleges offer 2-year programs that lead to an associate's degree. All programs have classroom and laboratory portions that include lessons in anatomy and medical terminology.

Some medical assistants have a high school diploma or equivalent and learn their duties on the job. High school students interested in a career as a medical assistant should take courses in biology, chemistry, and anatomy.

Important Qualities

Analytical skills. Medical assistants must be able to understand and follow medical charts and diagnoses. They may be required to code a patient's medical records for billing purposes.

Detail oriented. Medical assistants need to be precise when taking vital signs or recording patient information. Physicians and insurance companies rely on accurate records.

Interpersonal skills. Medical assistants need to be able to discuss patient information with other medical personnel, such as physicians. They often interact with patients who may be in pain or in distress, so they need to be able to act in a calm and professional manner.

Technical skills. Medical assistants should be able to use basic clinical instruments so they can take a patient's vital signs, such as heart rate and blood pressure.

Training. Medical assistants who do not have postsecondary education learn their skills through on-the-job training. Physicians or other medical assistants may teach a new assistant medical terminology, the names of the instruments, how to do daily tasks, how to interact with patients, and other tasks that help keep an office running smoothly. Medical assistants also learn how to code both paper and electronic health records (EHRs) and how to record patient information. It can take several months for an assistant to complete training, depending on the facility.

Licenses, Certifications, and Registrations. Medical assistants are not required to be certified in most states. However, employers prefer to hire certified assistants.

Several organizations offer certification. An applicant must pass an exam and have taken one of several routes to be eligible for each certification. These routes include graduation from an accredited program and work experience, among others. In most cases, an applicant must be at least 18 years old before applying for certification.

The National Commission for Certifying Agencies, part of the Institute for Credentialing Excellence, accredits five certifications for medical assistants:

- Certified Medical Assistant (CMA) from the American Association of Medical Assistants
- Registered Medical Assistant (RMA) from American Medical Technologists
- National Certified Medical Assistant (NCMA) from the National Center for Competency Testing
- Certified Clinical Medical Assistant (CCMA) from the National Healthcareer Association
- Certified Medical Administrative Assistant (CMAA) from the National Healthcareer Association

Median Annual Wages, May 2014

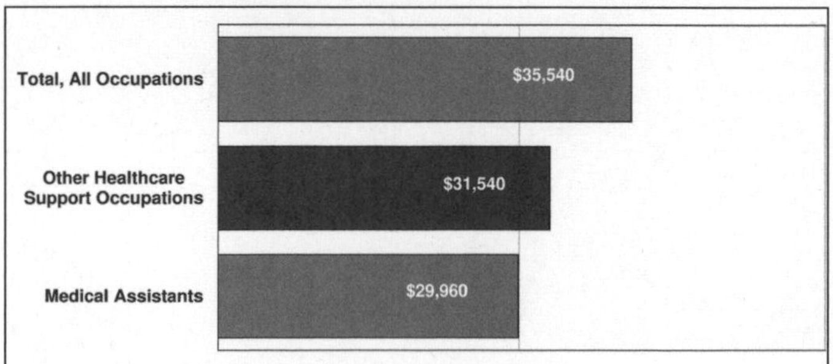

Note: All Occupations includes all occupations in the U.S. Economy.
Source: U.S. Bureau of Labor Statistics, Occupational Employment Statistics

Percent Change in Employment, Projected 2014–2024

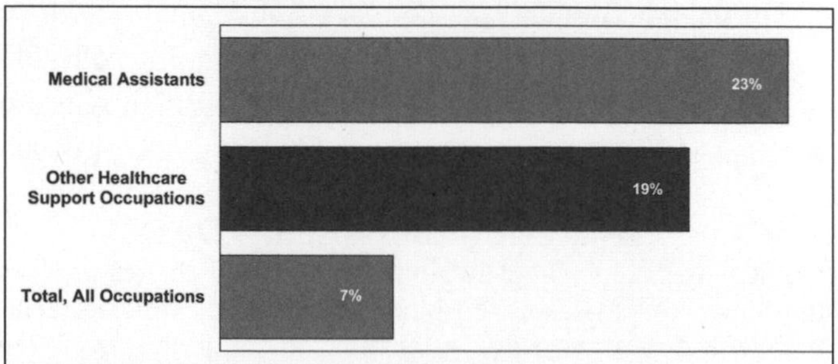

Note: All Occupations includes all occupations in the U.S. Economy.
Source: U.S. Bureau of Labor Statistics, Office of Occupational Statistics and Employment Projections

Employment Projections Data for Medical Assistants

Occupational Title	SOC Code	Employment, 2014	Projected Employment, 2024	Change, 2014–2024 Percent	Change, 2014–2024 Numeric
Medical assistants	31-9092	591,300	730,200	23	138,900

Source: U.S. Bureau of Labor Statistics, Employment Projections Program

Similar Occupations. This table shows a list of occupations with job duties that are similar to those of medical assistants.

Occupations	Entry-level Education	2014 Median Pay	Projected Job Growth	Average Annual Openings
Dental Assistants	Postsecondary nondegree award	$35,390	18%	5,860
Dental Hygienists	Associate's degree	$71,520	19%	3,740
Licensed Practical and Licensed Vocational Nurses	Postsecondary nondegree award	$42,490	16%	11,730
Medical Records and Health Information Technicians	Postsecondary nondegree award	$35,900	15%	2,900
Nursing Assistants and Orderlies	See Education/Training	$25,090	17%	26,780
Occupational Therapy Assistants and Aides	See Education/Training	$52,300	40%	1,680
Pharmacy Technicians	High school diploma or equivalent	$29,810	9%	3,470
Physical Therapist Assistants and Aides	See Education/Training	$41,640	40%	5,140

Some states may require assistants to graduate from an accredited program, pass an exam, or both, in order to practice. Contact the state board of medicine for more information.

Pay

The median annual wage for medical assistants was $29,960 in May 2014. The median wage is the wage at which half the workers in an occupation earned more than that amount and half earned less. The lowest 10 percent earned less than $21,540, and the highest 10 percent earned more than $42,760.

In May 2014, the median annual wages for medical assistants in the top industries in which they worked were as follows:

Outpatient care centers	$31,100
Hospitals; state, local, and private	31,050
Offices of physicians	30,160
Offices of other health practitioners	27,250

Job Outlook

Employment of medical assistants is projected to grow 23 percent from 2014 to 2024, much faster than the average for all occupations. The growth of the aging baby-boom population will continue to increase demand for preventive medical services, which are often provided by physicians. As their practices expand, physicians will hire more assistants to perform routine administrative and clinical duties, allowing the physicians to see more patients.

An increasing number of group practices, clinics, and other healthcare facilities need support workers, particularly medical assistants, to complete both administrative and clinical duties. Medical assistants work mostly in primary care, a steadily growing sector of the healthcare industry. In addition, the number of individuals who have access to health insurance is expected to continue to increase because of federal health insurance reform, increasing patient access to medical care.

Job Prospects. Medical assistants who earn certification and have familiarity with EHRs may have better job prospects.

Contacts for More Information

For more information about becoming a medical assistant, including information on certification, visit

➤ American Association of Medical Assistants (www.aama-ntl.org)
➤ American Medical Technologists (www.americanmedtech.org/default.aspx)
➤ National Center for Competency Testing (www.ncctinc.com)
➤ National Healthcareer Association (www.nhanow.com)
➤ Institute for Credentialing Excellence (www.credentialingexcellence.org)
➤ American Optometric Association (www.aoa.org)
➤ American Society of Podiatric Medical Assistants (www.aspma.org)
➤ Joint Commission on Allied Health Personnel in Ophthalmology (www.jcahpo.org)

For lists of accredited educational programs in medical assisting, visit

➤ Commission on Accreditation of Allied Health Education Programs (www.caahep.org)
➤ Accrediting Bureau of Health Education Schools (http://tinyurl.com/qh9cdf9)
➤ Medical Assistant Schools Directory (www.medicalassistantschools.com)

O*NET

➤ Medical Assistants (31-9092.00)

Medical Records and Health Information Technicians

- **2014 Median Pay** .... $35,900 per year, $17.26 per hour
- **Typical Entry-Level Education** .... Postsecondary nondegree award
- **Work Experience in a Related Occupation** .... None
- **On-the-job Training** .... None

- **Number of Jobs, 2014** 188,600
- **Job Outlook, 2014–24**...... 15% (Much faster than average)
- **Employment Change, 2014–24** 29,000

What Medical Records and Health Information Technicians Do

Medical records and health information technicians, commonly referred to as *health information technicians*, organize and manage health information data by ensuring that it maintains its quality, accuracy, accessibility, and security in both paper files and electronic systems. They use various classification systems to code and categorize patient information for insurance reimbursement purposes, for databases and registries, and to maintain patients' medical and treatment histories.

Duties. Health information technicians typically do the following:

- Review patients' records for timeliness, completeness, accuracy, and appropriateness of data
- Organize and maintain data for clinical databases and registries
- Track patient outcomes for quality assessment
- Use classification software to assign clinical codes for reimbursement and data analysis
- Electronically record data for collection, storage, analysis, retrieval, and reporting
- Maintain confidentiality of patients' records

Health information technicians document patients' health information, including their medical history, symptoms, examination and test results, treatments, and other information about healthcare services that are provided to patients. Their duties vary by employer and by the size of the facility in which they work.

Although health information technicians do not provide direct patient care, they work regularly with registered nurses and other healthcare professionals. They meet with these workers to clarify diagnoses or to get additional information to make sure that records are complete and accurate.

The increasing adaptation and use of electronic health records (EHRs) will continue to change the job responsibilities of health information technicians. Technicians will need to be familiar with, or be able to learn, EHR computer software, follow EHR security and privacy practices, and analyze electronic data to improve healthcare information, as more healthcare providers and hospitals adopt EHR systems.

Some medical records and health information technicians specialize in coding medical information for insurance purposes.

Health information technicians can specialize in many aspects of health information. Some work as *medical coders*, sometimes called *coding specialists*, or as *cancer registrars*.

Medical coders typically do the following:

- Review patient information for preexisting conditions, such as diabetes
- Assign appropriate diagnoses and procedure codes for patient care, population health statistics, and billing purposes
- Work as a liaison between the health clinician and billing offices

Cancer registrars typically do the following:

- Review patients' records and pathology reports to verify completeness and accuracy
- Assign classification codes to represent the diagnosis and treatment of cancers and benign tumors
- Conduct annual follow-ups to track treatment, survival, and recovery
- Compile and analyze cancer patient information for research purposes
- Maintain facility, regional, and national databases of cancer patients

Work Environment

Medical records and health information technicians held about 188,600 jobs in 2014. The industries that employed the most medical records and health information technicians were as follows:

Median Annual Wages, May 2014

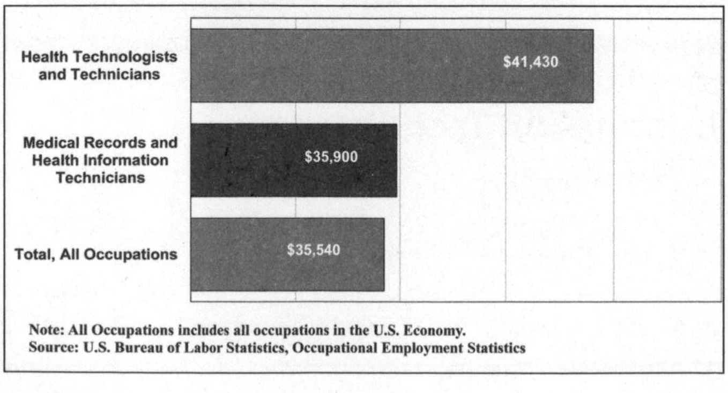

Percent Change in Employment, Projected 2014–2024

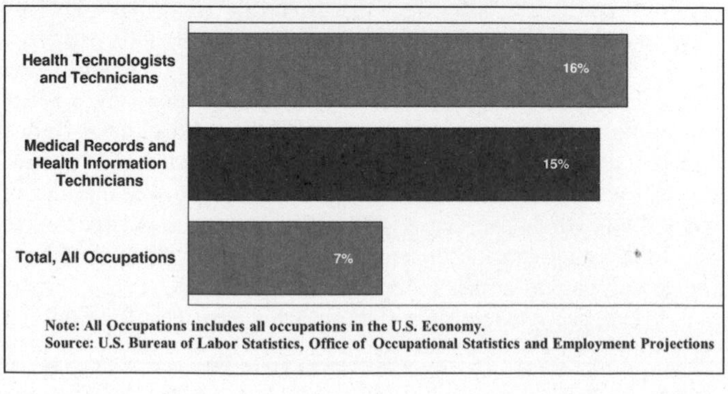

Hospitals; state, local, and private	38%
Offices of physicians	21
Nursing care facilities (skilled nursing facilities)	7
Administrative and support services	6
Professional, scientific, and technical services	5

More than half worked in hospitals or physicians' offices in 2014, and most others worked in various healthcare settings. Technicians typically work in offices and may spend many hours in front of computer monitors. Some technicians may work from home.

Work Schedules. Most health information technicians work full time. In healthcare facilities that are always open, such as hospitals, technicians may work evening or overnight shifts.

Education/Training

Health information technicians typically need a postsecondary certificate to enter the occupation, although some may need an associate's degree. Certification is often required.

Education. Postsecondary certificate and associate's degree programs in health information technology typically include courses in medical terminology, anatomy and physiology, health data requirements and standards, classification and coding systems, healthcare reimbursement methods, healthcare statistics, and computer systems. Applicants to health information technology programs may increase their chances of admission by taking high school courses in health, computer science, math, and biology.

A high school diploma or equivalent and previous experience in a healthcare setting are enough to qualify for some positions, but most jobs for health information technicians require postsecondary education.

Important Qualities

Analytical skills. Health information technicians must be able to understand and follow medical records and diagnoses, and then decide how best to code them in a patient's medical records.

Detail oriented. Health information technicians must be accurate when recording and coding patient information.

Integrity. Health information technicians work with patient data that are required, by law, to be kept confidential. They must exercise caution and a strong sense of ethics when working with this information in order to protect patient confidentiality.

Interpersonal skills. Health information technicians need to be able to discuss patient information, discrepancies, and data requirements with other professionals such as physicians and finance personnel.

Technical skills. Health information technicians must be able to use coding and classification software and the electronic health record (EHR) system that their healthcare organization or physician practice has adopted.

Licenses, Certifications, and Registrations. Most employers prefer to hire health information technicians who have certification, or they may expect applicants to earn certification shortly after being hired. A health information technician can earn certification from several organizations. Certifications include the Registered Health Information Technician (RHIT) and the Certified Tumor Registrar (CTR), among others.

Some organizations base certification on passing an exam. Others require graduation from an accredited program. Many coding certifications also require coding experience in a work setting. Once certified, technicians typically must renew their certification regularly and take continuing education courses.

A few states and facilities require cancer registrars to be licensed. Licensure requires the completion of a formal education program and the Certified Tumor Registrar (CTR) certification.

Advancement. Health information technicians may advance to other health information positions by receiving additional education and certifications. Technicians may be able to advance to a position as a medical or health services manager after completing a bachelor's or master's degree program and taking the required certification courses. Requirements vary by facility.

Pay

The median annual wage for medical records and health information technicians was $35,900 in May 2014. The median wage is the wage at which half the workers in an occupation earned more than that amount and half earned less. The lowest 10 percent earned less than $23,340, and the highest 10 percent earned more than $59,160.

In May 2014, the median annual wages for medical records and health information technicians in the top industries in which they worked were as follows:

Professional, scientific, and technical services	$39,410
Hospitals; state, local, and private	38,090
Nursing care facilities (skilled nursing facilities)	35,260
Administrative and support services	34,760
Offices of physicians	31,060

Job Outlook

Employment of health information technicians is projected to grow 15 percent from 2014 to 2024, much faster than the average for all occupations.

An aging population will require more medical services, and health information technicians will be needed to organize and manage the older generations' health information data. Moreover, the number of individuals who have access to health insurance is expected to continue to increase because of federal health insurance reform.

This will mean more claims for reimbursement from insurance companies.

Additional records, coupled with widespread use of electronic health records (EHRs) by all types of healthcare providers, will lead to an increased need for technicians to organize and manage the associated information in all areas of the healthcare industry.

Cancer registrars are expected to continue to be in high demand. As the population ages, there will likely be more types of special

Employment Projections Data for Medical Records and Health Information Technicians

Occupational Title	SOC Code	Employment, 2014	Projected Employment, 2024	Change, 2014–2024 Percent	Change, 2014–2024 Numeric
Medical records and health information technicians	29-2071	188,600	217,600	15	29,000

Source: U.S. Bureau of Labor Statistics, Employment Projections Program

Similar Occupations. This table shows a list of occupations with job duties that are similar to those of medical records and health information technicians.

Occupations	Entry-level Education	2014 Median Pay	Projected Job Growth	Average Annual Openings
Information Clerks	See Education/Training	$31,500	2%	2,580
Medical and Health Services Managers	Bachelor's degree	$92,810	17%	5,630
Medical Transcriptionists	Postsecondary nondegree award	$34,750	-3%	-220

purpose registries because many illnesses are detected and treated later in life.

Job Prospects. Prospects will be best for those with a certification in health information, such as the Registered Health Information Technician (RHIT) or the Certified Tumor Registrar (CTR). As EHR systems continue to become more common, health information technicians with computer skills will be needed to use them.

Contacts for More Information

For more information about health information technicians, including details about certification, visit

- American Health Information Management Association (www.ahima.org)
- American Academy of Professional Coders (www.aapc.com)
- Professional Association of Healthcare Coding Specialists (www.pahcs.org)
- National Healthcareer Association (www.nhanow.com/home.aspx)

For more information about medical coding and billing, visit

- Medical Billing & Coding (www.medbillingcodingonline.org)

For more information about cancer registrars, visit

- National Cancer Registrars Association (www.ncra-usa.org/i4a/pages/index.cfm?pageid=1)

For a list of accredited training programs, visit

- Commission on Accreditation for Health Informatics and Information Management Education (www.cahiim.org)

O*NET

- Medical Records and Health Information Technicians (29-2071.00)

Medical Transcriptionists

- **2014 Median Pay** .... $34,750 per year, $16.71 per hour
- **Typical Entry-Level Education** .... Postsecondary nondegree award
- **Work Experience in a Related Occupation** .... None
- **On-the-job Training** .... None
- **Number of Jobs, 2014** 70,000
- **Job Outlook, 2014–24** .... -3% (Decline)
- **Employment Change, 2014–24** .... -2,200

What Medical Transcriptionists Do

Medical transcriptionists, sometimes referred to as *healthcare documentation specialists*, listen to voice recordings that physicians and other healthcare workers make and convert them into written reports. They also may review and edit medical documents created using speech recognition technology. Transcriptionists interpret medical terminology and abbreviations in preparing patients' medical histories, discharge summaries, and other documents.

Duties. Medical transcriptionists typically do the following:

- Listen to the recorded dictation of a doctor or other healthcare worker
- Transcribe and interpret the dictation into diagnostic test results, operative reports, referral letters, and other documents
- Review and edit drafts prepared by speech recognition software, making sure that the transcription is correct, complete, and consistent in style
- Translate medical abbreviations and jargon into the appropriate long form
- Identify inconsistencies, errors, and missing information within a report that could compromise patient care
- Follow up with the healthcare provider to ensure the accuracy of the reports
- Submit health records for physicians to approve
- Follow patient confidentiality guidelines and legal documentation requirements
- Enter medical reports into electronic health records (EHR) systems
- Perform quality improvement audits

Traditionally, medical transcriptionists used audio playback equipment or software that is connected to their computer. However, technological advances have changed the way medical transcription is done. In the past, medical transcriptionists would listen to an entire dictation to produce a transcribed report. While many transcriptionists still perform these traditional transcription services, others are taking on additional roles. Today, many medical documents are prepared with the use of speech recognition technology, in which specialized software automatically prepares an initial draft of a report. The transcriptionist then reviews the draft for accuracy, identifying any errors and editing the report, when necessary. They use word-processing and other specialized software, as well as medical reference materials, as needed.

To do their work, medical transcriptionists must become familiar with medical terminology, anatomy and physiology, diagnostic procedures, pharmacology, and treatment assessments. Their ability to understand what the healthcare worker has recorded, correctly transcribe that information, and identify any inaccuracies in the transcript is critical to reducing the chance that patients will get ineffective or even harmful treatments.

Transcriptionists may need to be familiar with EHR systems. They may create templates, help develop documentation policies, and train physicians on how to use EHR systems.

Medical transcriptionists who work in doctors' offices may have other duties, such as answering phones and greeting patients.

Work Environment

Medical transcriptionists held about 70,000 jobs in 2014. The industries that employed the most medical transcriptionists were as follows:

Medical transcriptionists listen to recorded dictation from physicians and other healthcare workers.

Hospitals; state, local, and private	32%
Offices of physicians	23
Administrative and support services	21
Medical and diagnostic laboratories	3
Management of companies and enterprises	2

Most medical transcriptionists work for hospitals or in physicians' offices. Some work for companies that provide transcription services to healthcare establishments, and others are self-employed.

Many transcriptionists work from home offices, receiving dictation and submitting drafts electronically.

Work Schedules. Most medical transcriptionists work full time, although about one-fourth worked part time in 2014. Medical transcriptionists who work from home may work outside typical business hours and may have some flexibility in determining their schedules.

Education/Training

Medical transcriptionists typically need postsecondary education. Prospective medical transcriptionists must have an understanding of medical terminology, anatomy and physiology, grammar, and word-processing software.

Education. Employers prefer to hire transcriptionists who have completed postsecondary education in medical transcription, which is offered by vocational schools, community colleges, and distance-learning programs. Medical transcription programs are typically 1-year certificate programs, although there are also associate's degree programs.

Programs normally include coursework in anatomy, medical terminology, risk management, legal issues relating to healthcare documentation, and English grammar and punctuation. Many of these programs include supervised on-the-job experience. Some transcriptionists, especially those already familiar with medical terminology from previous experience as a nurse or medical secretary, become proficient through refresher courses and training.

Licenses, Certifications, and Registrations. Although certification is not required, some medical transcriptionists choose to become certified. The Association for Healthcare Documentation Integrity offers the Registered Healthcare Documentation Specialist (RHDS) and the Certified Healthcare Documentation Specialist (CHDS) certifications. Both certifications require passing an exam and periodic retesting or continuing education.

The RHDS certification, formerly known as the Registered Medical Transcriptionist (RMT), is for recent graduates with less than 2 years of experience and who work in a single specialty environment, such as a clinic or a doctor's office.

The CHDS certification, formerly known as the Certified Medical Transcriptionist (CMT), is for transcriptionists who have at least 2 years of experience and those who handle dictation in several medical specialties.

Important Qualities

Computer skills. Medical transcriptionists must be comfortable using computers and word-processing software, because those tools are an essential part of their jobs. Transcriptionists also may need to know how to operate electronic health records (EHR) systems.

Critical-thinking skills. Transcriptionists must be able to assess medical reports and spot any inaccuracies and inconsistencies in finished drafts. They must also be able to think critically when doing research to find the information that they need and to ensure that sources are both accurate and reliable.

Listening skills. Transcriptionists must listen carefully to dictation from physicians. They must be able to hear and interpret the intended meaning of the medical report.

Time-management skills. Because dictation must be done quickly, medical transcriptionists must be comfortable working under short deadlines.

Writing skills. Medical transcriptionists need a good understanding of the English language and grammar.

Pay

The median annual wage for medical transcriptionists was $34,750 in May 2014. The median wage is the wage at which half the

Median Annual Wages, May 2014

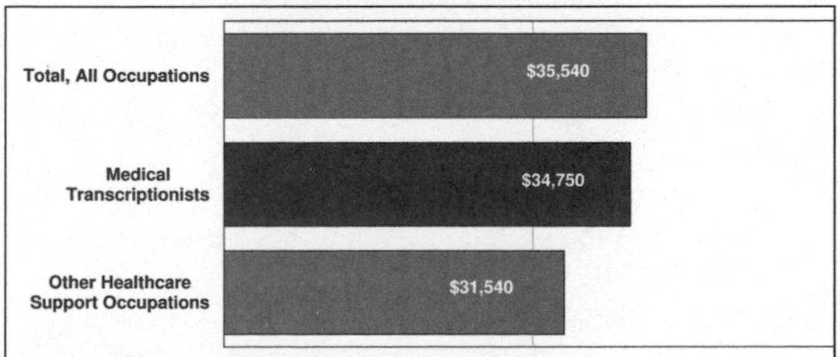

Note: All Occupations includes all occupations in the U.S. Economy.
Source: U.S. Bureau of Labor Statistics, Occupational Employment Statistics

Percent Change in Employment, Projected 2014–2024

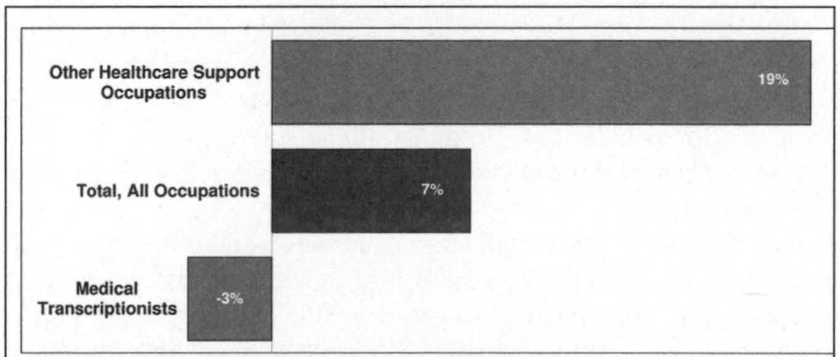

Note: All Occupations includes all occupations in the U.S. Economy.
Source: U.S. Bureau of Labor Statistics, Office of Occupational Statistics and Employment Projections

Employment Projections Data for Medical Transcriptionists

Occupational Title	SOC Code	Employment, 2014	Projected Employment, 2024	Change, 2014–2024	
				Percent	Numeric
Medical transcriptionists	31-9094	70,000	67,800	-3	-2,200

Source: U.S. Bureau of Labor Statistics, Employment Projections Program

Similar Occupations. This table shows a list of occupations with job duties that are similar to those of medical transcriptionists.

Occupations	Entry-level Education	2014 Median Pay	Projected Job Growth	Average Annual Openings
Court Reporters	Postsecondary nondegree award	$49,860	2%	30
Information Clerks	See Education/Training	$31,500	2%	2,580
Medical Assistants	Postsecondary nondegree award	$29,960	23%	13,890
Medical Records and Health Information Technicians	Postsecondary nondegree award	$35,900	15%	2,900
Receptionists	High school diploma or equivalent	$26,760	10%	9,780
Secretaries and Administrative Assistants	High school diploma or equivalent	$35,970	3%	11,880

workers in an occupation earned more than that amount and half earned less. The lowest 10 percent earned less than $22,220, and the highest 10 percent earned more than $49,290.

In May 2014, the median annual wages for medical transcriptionists in the top industries in which they worked were as follows:

Medical and diagnostic laboratories	$38,340
Hospitals; state, local, and private	36,480
Management of companies and enterprises	35,460
Offices of physicians	34,890
Administrative and support services	30,340

Some medical transcriptionists are paid based on the volume of transcription they produce. Others are paid an hourly rate or an annual salary.

Job Outlook

Employment of medical transcriptionists is projected to decline 3 percent from 2014 to 2024. Technological advances have changed the way medical transcription is done. Fewer transcriptionists are projected to be needed as speech recognition software and other technological advances make transcriptionists more productive.

The number of individuals who have access to health insurance is expected to continue to increase because of federal health insurance reform. The increasing volume of healthcare services will result in a growing number of medical tests and procedures, all of which will require transcription.

However, technological advances such as speech recognition software allow transcriptions to be prepared using fewer medical transcriptionists. And as healthcare providers seek to cut costs, some have hired transcription services to do transcriptions rather than do them in house. Some of those services are being contracted out to other countries, which hampers employment growth domestically.

Job Prospects. Prospects should be better for transcriptionists with formal education and for those with experience in electronic health records (EHR) management, training, and quality assessment. Job opportunities will stem from transcriptionists who retire over the next decade, creating opportunities for new transcriptionists.

Contacts for More Information

For more information about medical transcriptionists and for a list of accredited medical transcription programs, visit

➤ Association for Healthcare Documentation Integrity (www.ahdionline.org)

O*NET

➤ Medical Transcriptionists (31-9094.00)

Nuclear Medicine Technologists

- **2014 Median Pay** .... $72,100 per year, $34.66 per hour
- **Typical Entry-Level Education** .... Associate's degree
- **Work Experience in a Related Occupation** .... None
- **On-the-job Training** .... None
- **Number of Jobs, 2014** 20,700
- **Job Outlook, 2014–24** .... 2% (Slower than average)
- **Employment Change, 2014–24** 300

What Nuclear Medicine Technologists Do

Nuclear medicine technologists operate equipment that creates images of areas of a patient's body. They prepare radioactive drugs and administer them to patients. The radioactive drugs cause abnormal areas of the body to appear different from normal areas in the images.

Duties. Nuclear medicine technologists typically do the following:

- Explain imaging procedures to the patient and answer questions
- Follow safety procedures to protect themselves and the patient from unnecessary radiation exposure
- Examine machines to ensure that they are working properly
- Prepare radioactive drugs and administer them to the patient
- Monitor the patient to check for unusual reactions to the drugs

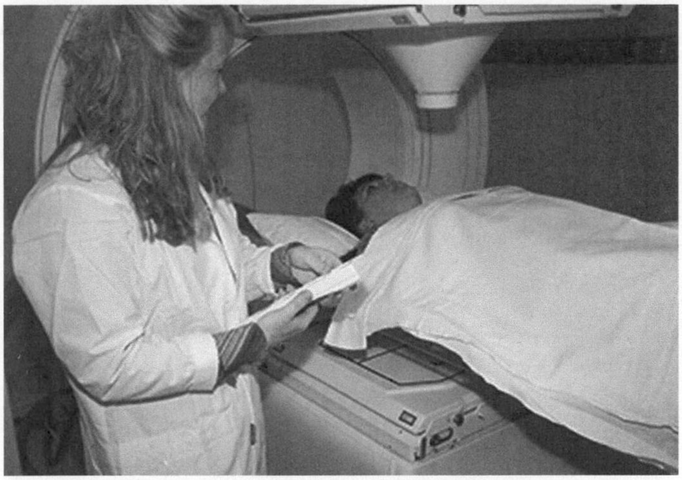

Nuclear medicine technologists operate complicated equipment that requires mechanical ability and manual dexterity.

- Operate equipment that creates images of areas in the body, such as images of organs
- Keep detailed records of procedures
- Follow radiation disposal and safety procedures

Radioactive drugs, known as radiopharmaceuticals, give off radiation, allowing special scanners to monitor tissue and organ functions. Abnormal areas show higher-than-expected or lower-than-expected concentrations of radioactivity. Physicians and surgeons then interpret the images to help diagnose the patient's condition. For example, tumors can be seen in organs during a scan because of their concentration of the radioactive drugs.

After graduation from an accredited program, a technologist can choose to specialize in positron emission tomography (PET) or nuclear cardiology. PET uses a machine that creates a three-dimensional image of a part of the body, such as the brain. Nuclear cardiology uses radioactive drugs to obtain images of the heart. Patients may exercise during the imaging process while the technologist creates images of the heart and blood flow.

Work Environment

Nuclear medicine technologists held about 20,700 jobs in 2014. The industries that employed the most nuclear medicine technologists were as follows:

Hospitals; state, local, and private	69%
Offices of physicians	20
Medical and diagnostic laboratories	6
Outpatient care centers	2

Technologists are on their feet for long periods and may need to lift or turn patients who are disabled.

Work Schedules. Most nuclear medicine technologists work full time. Some nuclear medicine technologists work evenings, weekends, or overnight because imaging is sometimes needed in emergencies.

Injuries and Illnesses. Although radiation hazards exist in this occupation, they are minimized by the use of gloves and other shielding devices. Nuclear medicine technologists wear badges that measure radiation levels in the radiation area. Instruments monitor their radiation exposure and detailed records are kept on how much radiation they get over their lifetime. When preparing radioactive drugs, technologists use safety procedures to minimize radiation exposure to patients, other healthcare workers, and themselves.

Like other healthcare workers, nuclear medicine technologists may be exposed to infectious diseases.

Education/Training

Nuclear medicine technologists typically need an associate's degree from an accredited nuclear medicine technology program. Technologists must be licensed in about one half of the states; requirements vary by state.

Education. Nuclear medicine technologists typically need an associate's degree in nuclear medicine technology. Bachelor's degrees are also common. Some technologists become qualified by completing an associate's or a bachelor's degree program in a related health field, such as radiologic technology or nursing, and then completing a 12-month certificate program in nuclear medicine technology.

Nuclear medicine technology programs often include courses in human anatomy and physiology, physics, chemistry, radioactive drugs, and computer science. In addition, these programs include clinical experience—practice under the supervision of a certified nuclear medicine technologist and a physician or surgeon who specializes in nuclear medicine.

The Joint Review Committee on Educational Programs in Nuclear Medicine Technology accredits nuclear medicine programs. Graduating from an accredited program may be required for licensure or by an employer.

High school students who are interested in nuclear medicine technology should take courses in math and science, such as biology, chemistry, anatomy, and physics.

Licenses, Certifications, and Registrations. As of 2015, about half of all states required nuclear medicine technologists to be

Median Annual Wages, May 2014

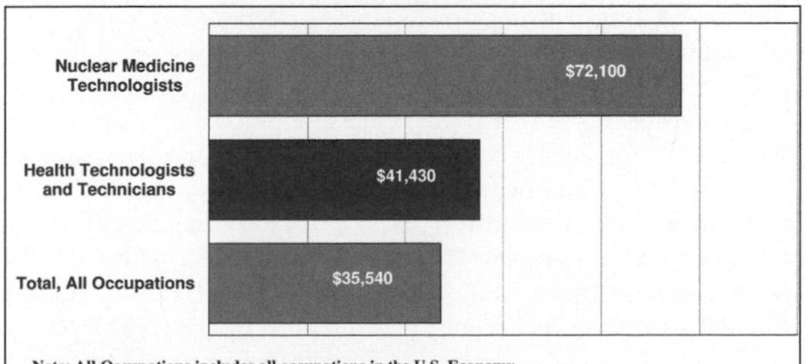

Note: All Occupations includes all occupations in the U.S. Economy.
Source: U.S. Bureau of Labor Statistics, Occupational Employment Statistics

Percent Change in Employment, Projected 2014–2024

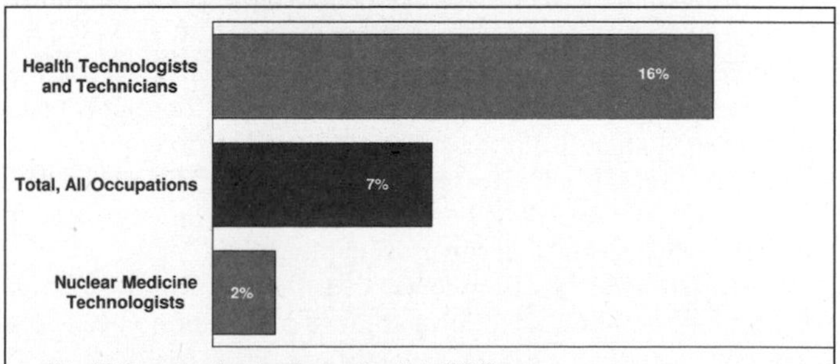

Note: All Occupations includes all occupations in the U.S. Economy.
Source: U.S. Bureau of Labor Statistics, Office of Occupational Statistics and Employment Projections

Employment Projections Data for Nuclear Medicine Technologists

Occupational Title	SOC Code	Employment, 2014	Projected Employment, 2024	Change, 2014–2024	
				Percent	Numeric
Nuclear medicine technologists	29-2033	20,700	21,000	2	300

Source: U.S. Bureau of Labor Statistics, Employment Projections Program

Similar Occupations. This table shows a list of occupations with job duties that are similar to those of nuclear medicine technologists.

Occupations	Entry-level Education	2014 Median Pay	Projected Job Growth	Average Annual Openings
Diagnostic Medical Sonographers and Cardiovascular Technologists and Technicians, Including Vascular Technologists	Associate's degree	$62,540	24%	2,760
Medical and Clinical Laboratory Technologists and Technicians	See Education/Training	$49,310	16%	5,210
Radiation Therapists	Associate's degree	$80,090	14%	230
Radiologic and MRI Technologists	Associate's degree	$57,370	9%	2,070

licensed. Requirements vary by state. For specific requirements, contact the state's health board.

Most nuclear medicine technologists become certified. Although certification is not required for a license, it fulfills most of the requirements for state licensure.

Some employers require certification, regardless of state regulations. Certification usually involves graduating from an accredited nuclear medicine technology program. Certification is available from the American Registry of Radiologic Technologists (ARRT) and the Nuclear Medicine Technology Certification Board (NMTCB).

In addition to receiving general certification, technologists can earn specialty certifications that show their proficiency in specific procedures or on certain equipment. A technologist can earn certification in positron emission tomography (PET), nuclear cardiology (NCT), or computed tomography (CT). The NMTCB offers NCT, PET, and CT certification exams.

Important Qualities

Ability to use technology. Nuclear medicine technologists work with computers and large pieces of technological equipment and must be comfortable operating them.

Analytical skills. Nuclear medicine technologists must understand anatomy, physiology, and other sciences and be able to calculate accurate dosages.

Compassion. Nuclear medicine technologists must be able to reassure and calm patients who are under physical and emotional stress.

Detail oriented. Nuclear medicine technologists must follow exact instructions to make sure that the correct dosage is given and that the patient is not overexposed to radiation.

Interpersonal skills. Nuclear medicine technologists interact with patients and often work as part of a team. They must be able to follow instructions from a supervising physician.

Physical stamina. Nuclear medicine technologists must stand for long periods and be able to lift and move patients who need help.

Pay

The median annual wage for nuclear medicine technologists was $72,100 in May 2014. The median wage is the wage at which half the workers in an occupation earned more than that amount and half earned less. The lowest 10 percent earned less than $52,080, and the highest 10 percent earned more than $96,570.

In May 2014, the median annual wages for nuclear medicine technologists in the top industries in which they worked were as follows:

Outpatient care centers	$75,330
Offices of physicians	74,390
Hospitals; state, local, and private	71,780
Medical and diagnostic laboratories	69,070

Job Outlook

Employment of nuclear medicine technologists is projected to grow 2 percent from 2014 to 2024, slower than the average for all occupations.

An aging population may lead to the need for nuclear medicine technologists who can provide imaging to patients with certain medical conditions, such as heart disease. Moreover, the number of individuals who have access to health insurance is expected to continue to increase because of federal health insurance reform. This reform may increase the demand for medical imaging services, including those provided by nuclear medicine technologists.

However, employment growth may be tempered as many medical facilities and third-party payers encourage the use of less costly, noninvasive imaging technologies, such as ultrasound.

Job Prospects. Nuclear medicine technologists can improve their job prospects by completing a bachelor's degree from an accredited program or earning a specialty certification, such as in positron emission tomography (PET), nuclear cardiology (NCT), or computed tomography (CT). Certification is available from the American Registry of Radiologic Technologists (ARRT) and the Nuclear Medicine Technology Certification Board (NMTCB).

Contacts for More Information

For more information about nuclear medicine technologists, visit

➤ Society of Nuclear Medicine and Molecular Imaging (www.snmmi.org)

For a list of accredited programs in nuclear medicine technology, visit

➤ Joint Review Committee on Educational Programs in Nuclear Medicine Technology (www.jrcnmt.org)

For more information about certification for nuclear medicine technologists, visit

➤ Nuclear Medicine Technology Certification Board (www.nmtcb.org/root/default.php)

➤ American Registry of Radiologic Technologists (www.arrt.org)

O*NET

➤ Nuclear Medicine Technologists (29-2033.00)

Nurse Anesthetists, Nurse Midwives, and Nurse Practitioners

- **2014 Median Pay** .... $102,670 per year
  $49.36 per hour
- **Typical Entry-Level Education** ....Master's degree
- **Work Experience in a Related Occupation**.............. None
- **On-the-job Training** .... None
- **Number of Jobs, 2014** 170,400
- **Job Outlook, 2014–24**.... 31% (Much faster than average)
- **Employment Change, 2014–24** 53,400

What Nurse Anesthetists, Nurse Midwives, and Nurse Practitioners Do

Nurse anesthetists, nurse midwives, and nurse practitioners, also referred to as *advanced practice registered nurses (APRNs)*, coordinate patient care and may provide primary and specialty healthcare. The scope of practice varies from state to state.

Duties. Advanced practice registered nurses typically do the following:

- Take and record patients' medical histories and symptoms
- Perform physical exams and observe patients
- Create plans for patients' care or contribute to existing plans
- Perform and order diagnostic tests
- Operate and monitor medical equipment
- Diagnose various health problems
- Analyze test results or changes in a patient's condition, and alter treatment plans, as needed
- Give patients medicines and treatments
- Evaluate a patient's response to medicines and treatments
- Consult with doctors and other healthcare professionals, as needed
- Counsel and teach patients and their families how to stay healthy or manage their illnesses or injuries
- Conduct research

APRNs work independently or in collaboration with physicians. In most states, they can prescribe medications, order medical tests, and diagnose health problems. They may provide primary and preventive care and may specialize in care for certain groups of people, such as children, pregnant women, or patients with mental health disorders.

Some APRN duties are the same as those for registered nurses, including gathering information about a patient's condition and taking action to treat or manage the patient's health. However, APRNs are trained to perform many additional functions, including ordering and evaluating test results, referring patients to specialists, and diagnosing and treating ailments. APRNs focus on patient-centered care, which means understanding a patient's concerns and lifestyle before choosing a course of action.

APRNs also may conduct research or teach staff about new policies or procedures. Others may provide consultation services based on a specific field of knowledge, such as oncology, which is the study of cancer.

The following are types of APRNs:

Nurse anesthetists (CRNAs) provide anesthesia and related care before, during, and after surgical, therapeutic, diagnostic, and obstetrical procedures. They also provide pain management and some emergency services. Before a procedure begins, nurse anesthetists discuss with a patient any medications the patient is taking as well as any allergies or illnesses the patient may have, so that anesthesia can be safely administered. Nurse anesthetists then give a patient general anesthesia to put the patient to sleep so they feel no pain during surgery or administer a regional or local anesthesia to numb an area of the body. They remain with the patient throughout a procedure to monitor vital signs and adjust the anesthesia as necessary.

Nurse midwives (CNMs) provide care to women, including gynecological exams, family planning services, and prenatal care. They deliver babies; manage emergency situations during labor, such as hemorrhaging; repair lacerations; and may provide surgical assistance to physicians during cesarean births. They may act as primary care providers for women and newborns. Nurse midwives also provide wellness care, educating their patients on how to lead healthy lives by discussing topics such as nutrition and disease prevention. Nurse midwives also provide care to their patients' partners for sexual or reproductive health issues.

Nurse practitioners (NPs) serve as primary and specialty care providers, delivering advanced nursing services to patients and their families. NPs assess patients, determine the best way to improve or manage a patient's health, and discuss ways to integrate health promotion strategies into a patient's life. They typically care

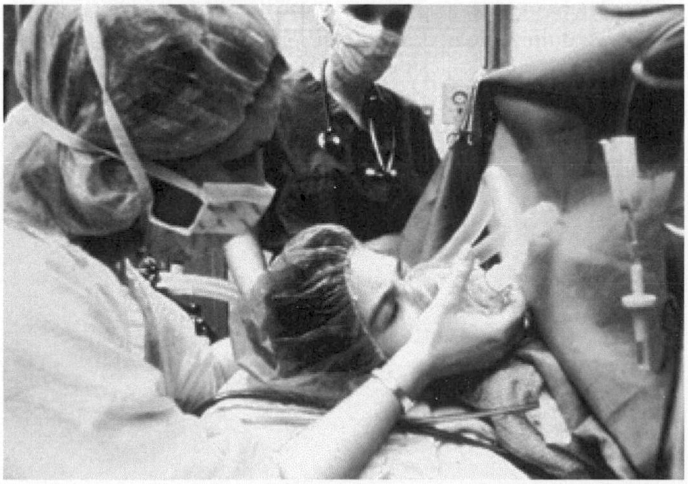

Nurse anesthetists administer every type of anesthetic, working in collaboration with other healthcare professionals.

for a certain population of people. For instance, NPs may work in adult and geriatric health, pediatric health, or psychiatric and mental health.

Although the scope of their duties varies some by state, many nurse practitioners work independently, prescribe medications, and order laboratory tests. All nurse practitioners consult with physicians and other health professionals when needed.

See the profile on registered nurses for more information on *clinical nurse specialists* (CNSs), also considered to be a type of APRN.

Work Environment

Nurse anesthetists, nurse midwives, and nurse practitioners held about 170,400 jobs in 2014. The industries that employed the most nurse anesthetists, nurse midwives, and nurse practitioners were as follows:

Offices of physicians	48%
Hospitals; state, local, and private	28
Outpatient care centers	7
Educational services; state, local, and private	3
Offices of other health practitioners	3

Advanced practice registered nurses (APRNs) work in a variety of settings including physicians' offices, hospitals, schools, and clinics. Nurse midwives also work in birthing centers. Some APRNs may treat patients in their patients' homes.

APRNs may also travel long distances to help care for patients in places where there are not enough healthcare workers.

Injuries and Illnesses. APRN work can be both physically and emotionally demanding. Some APRNs spend much of their day on their feet. They are vulnerable to back injuries because they must lift and move patients. APRN work can also be stressful because they make critical decisions that affect a patient's health.

Because of the environments in which they work, APRNs may come in close contact with infectious diseases. Therefore, they must follow strict, standardized guidelines to guard against diseases and other dangers, such as accidental needle sticks or patient outbursts.

Work Schedules. APRNs working in physicians' offices or schools typically work during normal business hours. Those working in hospitals and various other healthcare facilities may work in shifts to provide round-the-clock patient care. They may work nights, weekends, and holidays. Some APRNs, especially those who work in critical care or those who deliver babies, also may be required to be on call.

Most APRNs work full time.

Education/Training

Nurse anesthetists, nurse midwives, and nurse practitioners, also referred to as advanced practice registered nurses (APRNs), must earn at least a master's degree in one of the specialty roles. APRNs must also be licensed registered nurses in their state and pass a national certification exam.

Education. Nurse anesthetists, nurse midwives, and nurse practitioners must earn a master's degree from an accredited program. These programs include both classroom education and clinical experience. Courses in anatomy, physiology, and pharmacology are common as well as coursework specific to the chosen APRN role.

An APRN must have a registered nursing (RN) license before pursuing education in one of the advanced practice roles, and a strong background in science is helpful.

Most APRN programs prefer candidates who have a bachelor's degree in nursing. However, some schools offer bridge programs for registered nurses with an associate's degree or diploma in nursing. Graduate-level programs are also available for individuals who did not obtain a bachelor's degree in nursing but in a related health science field. These programs prepare the student for the RN licensure exam in addition to the APRN curriculum

Although a master's degree is the most common form of entry-level education, many APRNs choose to earn a Doctor of Nursing Practice (DNP) or a Ph.D. The specific educational requirements and qualifications for each of the roles are available on professional organizations' websites.

Nurse anesthetists must have 1 year of clinical experience as a prerequisite for admission to an accredited nurse anesthetist program. Candidates typically have experience working as a registered nurse in an acute care or critical care setting.

Licenses, Certifications, and Registrations. Most states recognize all of the APRN roles. In states that recognize some or all of the roles, APRNs must have a registered nursing license, complete an accredited graduate-level program, and pass a national certification exam. Each state's board of nursing can provide details.

The Consensus Model for APRN Regulation, a document developed by a wide variety of professional nursing organizations, including the National Council of State Boards of Nursing, aims to standardize APRN requirements. The model recommends that all APRNs complete a graduate degree from an accredited program; be a licensed registered nurse; pass a national certification exam; and earn a second license specific to one of the APRN roles and to a certain group of patients.

Certification is required in the vast majority of states to use an APRN title. Certification is used to show proficiency in an APRN role and is often a requirement for state licensure.

Median Annual Wages, May 2014

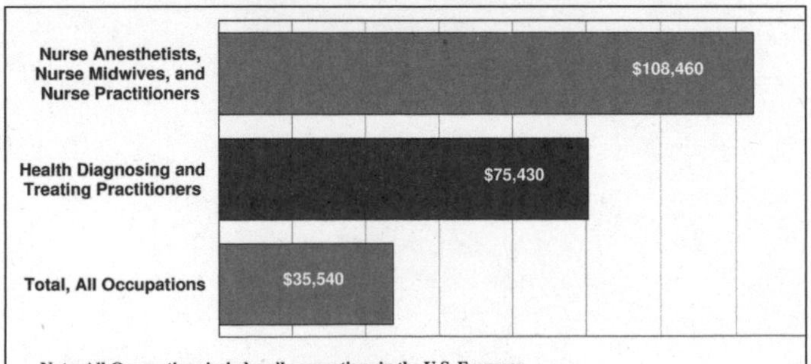

Note: All Occupations includes all occupations in the U.S. Economy.
Source: U.S. Bureau of Labor Statistics, Occupational Employment Statistics

Percent Change in Employment, Projected 2014–2024

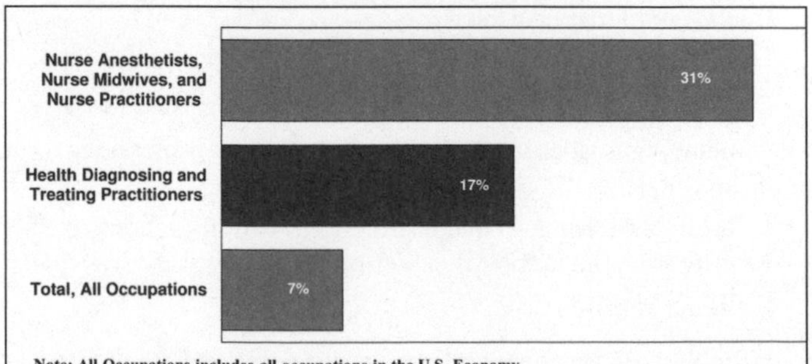

Note: All Occupations includes all occupations in the U.S. Economy.
Source: U.S. Bureau of Labor Statistics, Office of Occupational Statistics and Employment Projections

Employment Projections Data for Nurse Anesthetists, Nurse Midwives, and Nurse Practitioners

Occupational Title	SOC Code	Employment, 2014	Projected Employment, 2024	Change, 2014–2024	
				Percent	Numeric
Nurse anesthetists, nurse midwives, and nurse practitioners	—	170,400	223,800	31	53,400
Nurse anesthetists	29-1151	38,200	45,600	19	7,400
Nurse midwives	29-1161	5,300	6,600	25	1,300
Nurse practitioners	29-1171	126,900	171,700	35	44,700

Source: U.S. Bureau of Labor Statistics, Employment Projections Program

The National Board of Certification and Recertification for Nurse Anesthetists (NBCRNA) offers the National Certification Examination (NCE). Certified registered nurse anesthetists (CRNAs) must recertify every 2 years, which includes 40 hours of continuing education.

The American Midwifery Certification Board offers the Certified Nurse-Midwife (CNM). Individuals with this designation must recertify every 5 years.

There are a number of certification exams for nurse practitioners because of the large number of populations NPs may work with and the number of specialty areas in which they may practice. Certifications are available from a number of professional organizations, including the American Nurses Credentialing Center and the Pediatric Nursing Certification Board.

Important Qualities

Communication skills. Advanced practice registered nurses must be able to communicate with patients and other healthcare professionals to ensure that the appropriate course of action is understood.

Critical-thinking skills. APRNs must be able to assess changes in a patient's health, quickly determine the most appropriate course of action, and decide if a consultation with another healthcare professional is needed.

Compassion. Nurses should be caring and sympathetic when treating patients who are in pain or who are experiencing emotional distress.

Detail oriented. APRNs must be responsible and detail-oriented because they provide various treatments and medications that affect the health of their patients. During an evaluation, they must pick up on even the smallest changes in a patient's condition.

Interpersonal skills. Advanced practice registered nurses must work with patients and families as well as with other healthcare providers and staff within the organizations where they provide care. They should work as part of a team to determine and execute the best possible healthcare options for the patients they treat.

Leadership skills. Advanced practice registered nurses often work in positions of seniority. They must effectively lead and sometimes manage other nurses on staff when providing patient care.

Resourcefulness. APRNs must know where to find the answers that they need in a timely fashion.

Advancement. Because the APRN designation is in itself an advancement of one's career, many APRNs choose to remain in this role for the duration of their career. Some APRNs may take on managerial or administrative roles, while others go into academia. APRNs who earn a doctoral degree may conduct independent research or work in an interprofessional research team.

Pay

The median annual wage for nurse anesthetists, nurse midwives, and nurse practitioners was $102,670 in May 2014. The median wage is the wage at which half the workers in an occupation earned more than that amount and half earned less. The lowest 10 percent earned less than $71,240, and the highest 10 percent earned more than $168,000.

Median annual wages for nurse anesthetists, nurse midwives, and nurse practitioners in May 2014 were as follows:

Nurse anesthetists	$153,780
Nurse midwives	96,970
Nurse practitioners	95,350

Job Outlook

Employment of nurse anesthetists, nurse midwives, and nurse practitioners is projected to grow 31 percent from 2014 to 2024, much faster than the average for all occupations. Growth will occur because of an increase in the demand for healthcare services. Several factors will contribute to this demand, including a large number of newly insured patients resulting from healthcare legislation, an increased emphasis on preventive care, and the large, aging baby-boom population.

The number of individuals who have access to health insurance is expected to continue to increase because of federal health insurance reform. Advanced practice registered nurses (APRNs) can perform many of the same services as physicians. APRNs will be needed to provide preventive and primary care, particularly in offices of physicians, clinics, and other ambulatory care settings.

APRNs will also be needed to care for the aging baby-boom generation. As baby boomers age, they will experience ailments and complex conditions that require medical care. APRNs will be needed to keep these patients healthy and to treat the growing number of patients with chronic and acute conditions.

As states change their laws governing APRN practice authority, APRNs are being allowed to perform more services. They are also becoming more widely recognized by the public as a source for primary healthcare.

Job Prospects. Overall, job opportunities for advanced practice registered nurses are likely to be excellent. APRNs will be in high demand, particularly in medically underserved areas such as inner cities and rural areas. Job opportunities may exist from attrition.

Contacts for More Information

For information about nurse anesthetists, including a list of accredited programs, visit

➤ American Association of Nurse Anesthetists (www.aana.com/Pages/default.aspx)

For information about nurse midwives, including a list of accredited programs, visit

➤ American College of Nurse-Midwives (www.midwife.org)

Similar Occupations. This table shows a list of occupations with job duties that are similar to those of nurse anesthetists, nurse midwives, and nurse practitioners.

Occupations	Entry-level Education	2014 Median Pay	Projected Job Growth	Average Annual Openings
Audiologists	Doctoral or professional degree	$73,060	29%	380
Occupational Therapists	Master's degree	$78,810	27%	3,040
Physical Therapists	Doctoral or professional degree	$82,390	34%	7,180
Physician Assistants	Master's degree	$95,820	30%	2,870
Physicians and Surgeons	Doctoral or professional degree	This wage is equal to or greater than $187,200.	14%	9,930
Registered Nurses	Bachelor's degree	$66,640	16%	43,930
Speech-Language Pathologists	Master's degree	$71,550	21%	2,890

For information about nurse practitioners, including a list of accredited programs, visit

➤ American Association of Nurse Practitioners (www.aanp.org/)

For more information about registered nurses, including credentialing, visit

➤ American Nurses Association (http://nursingworld.org)

For more information about nursing education and being a registered nurse, visit

➤ National League for Nursing (www.nln.org)

For information about undergraduate and graduate nursing education, nursing career options, and financial aid, visit

➤ American Association of Colleges of Nursing (www.aacn.nche.edu)

For information about the Consensus Model and for a list of the states' Boards of Nursing, visit

➤ National Council of State Boards of Nursing (www.ncsbn.org/index.htm)

For information about certification, visit

➤ National Board of Certification and Recertification for Nurse Anesthetists (www.nbcrna.com/Pages/default.aspx)

➤ American Midwifery Certification Board (www.amcbmidwife.org)

➤ American Nurses Credentialing Center (http://nursecredentialing.org)

➤ Pediatric Nursing Certification Board (www.pncb.org/ptistore/control/exams/index)

O*NET

➤ Nurse Anesthetists (29-1151.00)

➤ Nurse Midwives (29-1161.00)

➤ Nurse Practitioners (29-1171.00)

Nursing Assistants and Orderlies

- **2014 Median Pay** .... $25,090 per year $12.06 per hour
- **Typical Entry-Level Education** .... See Education/Training
- **Work Experience in a Related Occupation** .... None
- **On-the-job Training** .... See Education/Training
- **Number of Jobs, 2014** 1,545,200
- **Job Outlook, 2014–24** .... 17% (Much faster than average)
- **Employment Change, 2014–24** 267,800

What Nursing Assistants and Orderlies Do

Nursing assistants, sometimes called *nursing aides*, help provide basic care for patients in hospitals and residents of long-term care facilities, such as nursing homes. Orderlies transport patients and clean treatment areas.

Duties. Nursing assistants provide basic care and help with activities of daily living. They typically do the following:

- Clean and bathe patients or residents
- Help patients use the toilet and dress
- Turn, reposition, and transfer patients between beds and wheelchairs
- Listen to and record patients' health concerns and report that information to nurses
- Measure patients' vital signs, such as blood pressure and temperature
- Serve meals and help patients eat

Some nursing assistants also may dispense medication, depending on their training level and the state in which they work.

In nursing homes and residential care facilities, assistants are often the principal caregivers. They have more contact with residents than other members of the staff. Because some residents stay in a nursing home for months or years, assistants may develop close relationships with their residents.

Orderlies typically do the following:

- Assist patients with moving about the facility, such as pushing wheelchairs
- Clean equipment and facilities
- Change linens
- Stock supplies

Nursing assistants and orderlies work as part of a healthcare team under the supervision of licensed practical or licensed vocational nurses and registered nurses.

Work Environment

Nursing assistants held about 1.5 million jobs in 2014. Orderlies held about 53,000 jobs in 2014.

The industries that employed the most nursing assistants in 2014 were as follows:

Nursing care facilities (skilled nursing facilities)	41%
Hospitals; state, local, and private	25

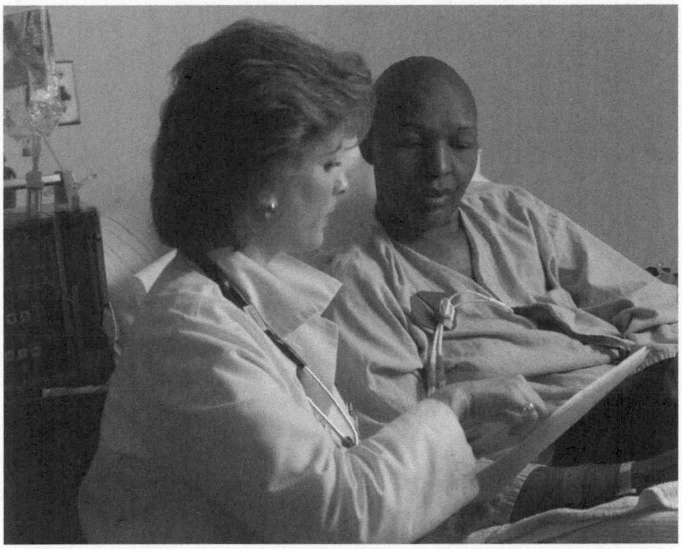

Nursing aides should be personable and enjoy helping people.

Continuing care retirement communities and assisted living facilities for the elderly 11
Home healthcare services 5
Government 4

The industries that employed the most orderlies in 2014 were as follows:

Hospitals; state, local, and private 70%
Nursing care facilities (skilled nursing facilities) 11
Ambulatory healthcare services 6
Government 4
Continuing care retirement communities and assisted living facilities for the elderly 3

The work of nursing assistants and orderlies can be strenuous. They spend much of their time on their feet as they take care of many patients or residents.

Injuries and Illnesses. Because they frequently lift people and do other physically demanding tasks, nursing assistants and orderlies have a higher rate of injuries and illnesses than the national average. They are typically trained in how to properly lift and move patients, which can reduce the risk of injuries.

Work Schedules. Most nursing assistants and orderlies work full time. Because nursing homes and hospitals provide care at all hours, nursing assistants and orderlies may need to work nights, weekends, and holidays.

Education/Training

Nursing assistants must complete a state-approved education program and must pass their state's competency exam. Orderlies generally have at least a high school diploma.

Education and Training. Nursing assistants must complete a state-approved education program in which they learn the basic principles of nursing and complete supervised clinical work. These programs are found in high schools, community colleges, vocational and technical schools, hospitals, and nursing homes.

In addition, nursing assistants typically complete a brief period of on-the-job training to learn about their specific employer's policies and procedures.

Orderlies typically have at least a high school diploma and receive a short period of on-the-job training.

Licenses, Certifications, and Registrations. After completing a state-approved education program, nursing assistants take a competency exam. Passing this exam allows them to use state-specific titles. In some states, a nursing assistant or aide is called a Certified Nursing Assistant (CNA), but titles vary from state to state.

Nursing assistants who have passed the competency exam are placed on a state registry. Nursing assistants must be on the state registry to work in a nursing home.

Some states have other requirements as well, such as continuing education and a criminal background check. Check with state boards of nursing or health for more information.

In some states, nursing assistants can earn additional credentials, such as becoming a Certified Medication Assistant (CMA). As a CMA, they can give medications.

Orderlies do not need a license; however, many jobs require a Basic Life Support (BLS) certification, which shows they are trained to provide cardiopulmonary resuscitation (CPR).

Important Qualities

Communication skills. Nursing assistants and orderlies must be able to communicate effectively to address patients' or residents' concerns. They also need to relay important information to other healthcare workers.

Compassion. Nursing assistants and orderlies assist and care for the sick, injured, and elderly. Doing so requires a compassionate and empathetic attitude.

Patience. The routine tasks of cleaning, feeding, and bathing patients or residents can be stressful. Nursing assistants and orderlies must have patience in order to complete these tasks.

Physical stamina. Nursing assistants and orderlies spend much of their time on their feet. They should be comfortable performing physical tasks, such as lifting or moving patients.

Median Annual Wages, May 2014

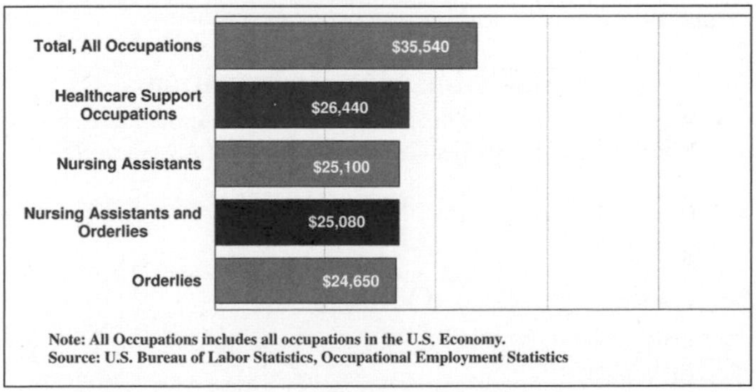

Percent Change in Employment, Projected 2014–2024

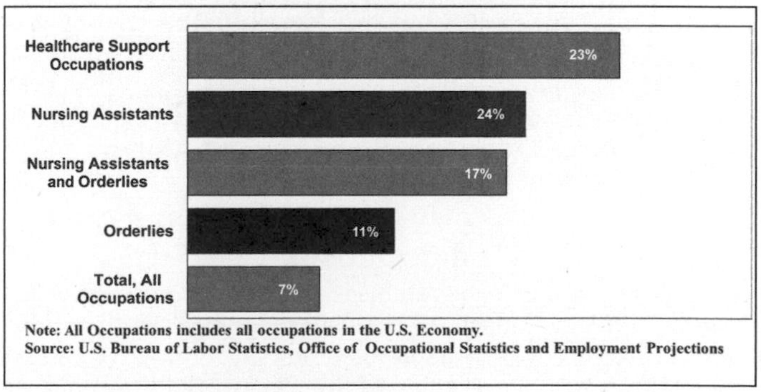

Employment Projections Data for Nursing Assistants and Orderlies

Occupational Title	SOC Code	Employment, 2014	Projected Employment, 2024	Change, 2014–2024	
				Percent	Numeric
Nursing assistants and orderlies	—	1,545,200	1,813,000	17	267,800
Nursing assistants	31-1014	1,492,100	1,754,100	18	262,000
Orderlies	31-1015	53,000	58,800	11	5,800

Source: U.S. Bureau of Labor Statistics, Employment Projections Program

Similar Occupations. This table shows a list of occupations with job duties that are similar to those of nursing assistants and orderlies.

Occupations	Entry-level Education	2014 Median Pay	Projected Job Growth	Average Annual Openings
Home Health Aides	No formal educational credential	$21,380	38%	34,840
Licensed Practical and Licensed Vocational Nurses	Postsecondary nondegree award	$42,490	16%	11,730
Medical Assistants	Postsecondary nondegree award	$29,960	23%	13,890
Occupational Therapy Assistants and Aides	See Education/Training	$52,300	40%	1,680
Personal Care Aides	No formal educational credential	$20,440	26%	45,810
Physical Therapist Assistants and Aides	See Education/Training	$41,640	40%	5,140
Psychiatric Technicians and Aides	See Education/Training	$28,470	5%	760
Registered Nurses	Bachelor's degree	$66,640	16%	43,930

Pay

The median annual wage for nursing assistants was $25,100 in May 2014. The median wage is the wage at which half the workers in an occupation earned more than that amount and half earned less. The lowest 10 percent earned less than $18,790, and the highest 10 percent earned more than $36,170.

The median annual wage for orderlies was $24,650 in May 2014. The lowest 10 percent earned less than $18,110, and the highest 10 percent earned more than $37,710.

In May 2014, the median annual wages for nursing assistants in the top industries in which they worked were as follows:

Government	$30,200
Hospitals; state, local, and private	27,360
Nursing care facilities (skilled nursing facilities)	24,120
Continuing care retirement communities and assisted living facilities for the elderly	23,650
Home healthcare services	23,080

In May 2014, the median annual wages for orderlies in the top industries in which they worked were as follows:

Government	$29,260
Ambulatory healthcare services	26,040
Hospitals; state, local, and private	25,000
Nursing care facilities (skilled nursing facilities)	21,250
Continuing care retirement communities and assisted living facilities for the elderly	20,500

Job Outlook

Employment of nursing assistants is projected to grow 18 percent from 2014 to 2024, much faster than the average for all occupations. Employment of orderlies is projected to grow 11 percent from 2014 to 2024, faster than the average for all occupations.

As the baby-boom population ages, many nursing assistants and orderlies will be needed to assist and care for elderly patients in long-term care facilities, such as nursing homes. Older people are more likely than younger people to experience dementia, as well as chronic diseases such as heart disease and diabetes. More nursing assistants will be needed to care for patients with these conditions.

Demand for nursing assistants may be constrained by the fact that many nursing homes rely on government funding. Cuts to programs, such as Medicare and Medicaid, may affect patients' ability to pay for nursing home care. In addition, patient preferences and shifts in federal and state funding are increasing the demand for home and community-based long-term care, which should lead to increased opportunities for nursing assistants working in home health and community rehabilitation services.

Job Prospects. Job prospects for nursing assistants who have completed a state-approved education program and passed their state's competency exam should be good, particularly in home healthcare services and community-based care settings. The low pay and high emotional and physical demands cause many workers to leave the occupation, and they will have to be replaced. This creates opportunities for job seekers.

Contacts for More Information

For more information about nursing assistants and orderlies, visit

- National Association of Health Care Assistants (http://nahcacareforce.org)
- National Network of Career Nursing Assistants (www.cna-network.org)

O*NET

- Nursing Assistants (31-1014.00)
- Orderlies (31-1015.00)

Occupational Health and Safety Specialists

- **2014 Median Pay** .... $69,210 per year
  $33.27 per hour
- **Typical Entry-Level Education** .... Bachelor's degree
- **Work Experience in a Related Occupation** .... None
- **On-the-job Training** .... None
- **Number of Jobs, 2014** 70,300
- **Job Outlook, 2014–24** .... 4% (Slower than average)
- **Employment Change, 2014–24** 2,800

What Occupational Health and Safety Specialists Do

Occupational health and safety specialists analyze many types of work environments and work procedures. Specialists inspect workplaces for adherence to regulations on safety, health, and the environment. They also design programs to prevent disease or injury to workers and damage to the environment.

Duties. Occupational health and safety specialists typically do the following:

- Identify hazards in the workplace
- Collect samples of potentially toxic materials for analysis
- Inspect and evaluate workplace environments, equipment, and practices for compliance with corporate and government health and safety standards and regulations
- Design and implement workplace processes and procedures that help protect workers from hazardous work conditions
- Investigate accidents and incidents to identify their causes and to determine how they might be prevented
- Conduct training on a variety of topics, such as emergency preparedness

Occupational health and safety specialists examine the workplace for environmental or physical factors that could affect employee health, safety, comfort, and performance. They may examine factors such as lighting, equipment, materials, and ventilation. Specialists seek to increase worker productivity by reducing absenteeism and equipment downtime. They also seek to save money by lowering insurance premiums and workers' compensation payments and by preventing government fines.

Some specialists develop and conduct employee safety and training programs. These programs cover a range of topics, such as how to use safety equipment correctly and how to respond in an emergency.

In addition to protecting workers, specialists work to prevent harm to property, the environment, and the public by inspecting workplaces for chemical, physical, radiological, and biological hazards. Specialists who work for governments conduct safety inspections and can impose fines.

Occupational health and safety specialists work with engineers and physicians to control or fix hazardous conditions or equipment. They also work closely with occupational health and safety technicians to collect and analyze data in the workplace.

The tasks of occupational health and safety specialists vary by industry, workplace, and types of hazards affecting employees. The following are examples of types of occupational health and safety specialists:

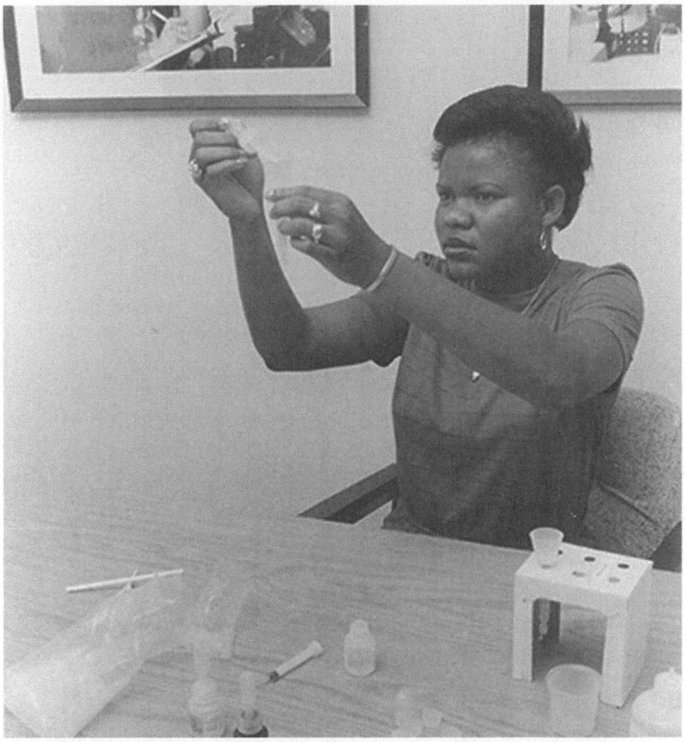

Occupational health and safety specialists may conduct inspections and inform an organization's managers of areas not in compliance with state and federal laws and employer policies.

Ergonomists consider the design of industrial, office, and other equipment to maximize workers' comfort, safety, and productivity.

Industrial or occupational hygienists identify workplace health hazards, such as lead, asbestos, noise, pesticides, and communicable diseases.

Work Environment

Occupational health and safety specialists held about 70,300 jobs in 2014. The industries that employed the most occupational health and safety specialists were as follows:

State and local government, excluding education and hospitals	18%
Manufacturing	16
Federal government, excluding postal service	11
Professional, scientific, and technical services	10
Construction	7

About 29 percent of occupational health and safety specialists worked for federal, state, and local governments in 2014. In the federal government, specialists are employed by various agencies, including the Centers for Disease Control and Prevention's National Institute for Occupational Safety and Health (NIOSH) and the Occupational Safety and Health Administration (OSHA). Most large government agencies employ specialists to protect agency employees. In addition to working for governments, occupational health and safety specialists worked in management, scientific, and technical consulting services; education services; hospitals; and manufacturing.

Occupational health and safety specialists work in a variety of settings, such as offices, factories, and mines. Their jobs often involve considerable fieldwork and travel. They may be exposed to strenuous, dangerous, or stressful conditions. Specialists use gloves, helmets, respirators, and other personal protective and safety equipment to minimize the risk of illness and injury.

Median Annual Wages, May 2014

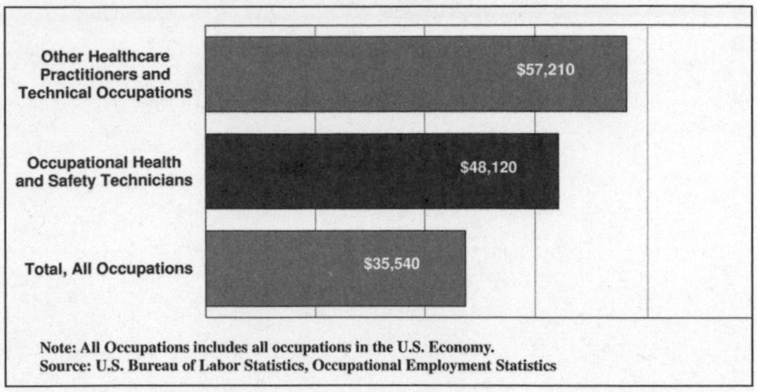

Percent Change in Employment, Projected 2014–2024

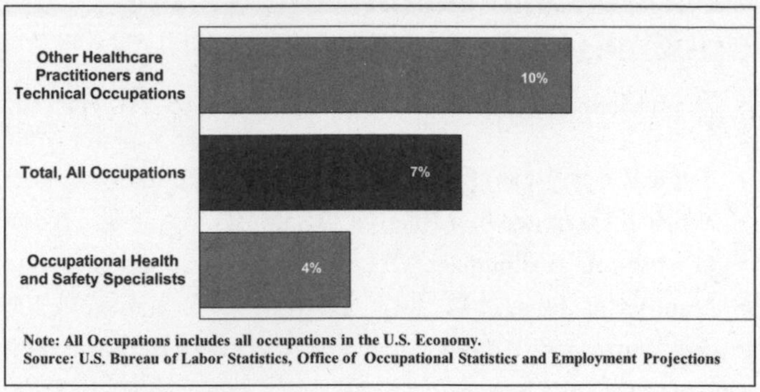

Work Schedules. Most occupational health and safety specialists work full time. Some specialists may work weekends or irregular hours in emergencies.

Education/Training

Occupational health and safety specialists typically need a bachelor's degree in occupational health and safety or in a related scientific or technical field.

Education. Occupational health and safety specialists typically need a bachelor's degree in occupational health and safety or in a related scientific or technical field, such as engineering, biology, or chemistry. For some positions, a master's degree in industrial hygiene, health physics, or a related subject is required.

Typical courses include radiation science, hazardous material management and control, risk communications, and respiratory protection. These courses may vary with the specialty in which a student wants to work. For example, courses in health physics focus on topics that differ from those in industrial hygiene.

High school students interested in becoming occupational health and safety specialists should take courses in English, math, chemistry, biology, and physics.

Important Qualities

Ability to use technology. Occupational health and safety specialists must be able to use advanced technology. They often work with complex testing equipment.

Communication skills. Occupational health and safety specialists must be able to communicate safety instructions and concerns to employees and managers. They need to be able to work with technicians to collect and test samples of possible hazards, such as dust or vapors, in the workplace.

Detail oriented. Occupational health and safety specialists need to understand and follow safety standards and complex government regulations.

Physical stamina. Occupational health and safety specialists must be able to stand for long periods and be able to travel regularly. Some specialists work in environments that can be uncomfortable, such as tunnels or mines.

Problem-solving skills. Occupational health and safety specialists must be able to solve problems in order to design and implement workplace processes and procedures that help protect workers from hazardous work conditions.

Licenses, Certifications, and Registrations. Although certification is voluntary, many employers encourage it. Certification is available through several organizations, depending on the field in which the specialists work. Specialists must have graduated from an accredited educational program and have work experience to be eligible to take most certification exams. To keep their certification, specialists usually are required to complete periodic continuing education.

Pay

The median annual wage for occupational health and safety specialists was $69,210 in May 2014. The median wage is the wage at which half the workers in an occupation earned more than that amount and half earned less. The lowest 10 percent earned less than $40,760, and the highest 10 percent earned more than $101,000.

In May 2014, the median annual wages for occupational health and safety specialists in the top industries in which they worked were as follows:

Federal government, excluding postal service	$76,620
Manufacturing	70,390
Professional, scientific, and technical services	70,210
Construction	65,190
State and local government, excluding education and hospitals	59,600

Job Outlook

Employment of occupational health and safety specialists is projected to grow 4 percent from 2014 to 2024, slower than the average for all occupations.

Specialists will be needed to work in a wide variety of industries to ensure that employers are adhering to both existing and new regulations. In addition, technological advances will allow for the

Employment Projections Data for Occupational Health and Safety Specialists

Occupational Title	SOC Code	Employment, 2014	Projected Employment, 2024	Change, 2014–2024	
				Percent	Numeric
Occupational health and safety specialists	29-9011	70,300	73,100	4	2,800

Source: U.S. Bureau of Labor Statistics, Employment Projections Program

Similar Occupations. This table shows a list of occupations with job duties that are similar to those of occupational health and safety specialists.

Occupations	Entry-level Education	2014 Median Pay	Projected Job Growth	Average Annual Openings
Construction and Building Inspectors	High school diploma or equivalent	$56,040	8%	810
Environmental Scientists and Specialists	Bachelor's degree	$66,250	11%	1,020
Fire Inspectors	See Education/Training	$54,020	6%	90
Health and Safety Engineers	Bachelor's degree	$81,830	6%	160
Occupational Health and Safety Technicians	High school diploma or equivalent	$48,120	9%	140

use of new machinery, and specialists will be needed to create the machinery, as well as procedures to ensure its safe use.

In addition, specialists will be necessary because insurance costs and workers' compensation costs have become a concern for many employers and insurance companies. An aging population is remaining in the workforce longer than past generations did, and older workers usually have a greater proportion of workers' compensation claims.

Job Prospects. Despite slower-than-average employment growth, job opportunities for individuals with advanced degrees are expected to be good. Candidates with certification may enjoy more job opportunities. In addition, a large number of currently practicing occupational health and safety specialists are expected to retire over the coming decade, creating opportunities for new specialists.

Contacts for More Information

For more information about credentialing in industrial hygiene, visit

➤ American Board of Industrial Hygiene (www.abih.org)

For more information about occupations in safety, a list of safety and related academic programs, and credentialing, visit

➤ Board of Certified Safety Professionals (www.bcsp.org)

For more information about occupational health and safety, visit

➤ U.S. Department of Labor, Occupational Safety and Health Administration (OSHA) (www.osha.gov)

➤ Centers for Disease Control and Prevention, National Institute for Occupational Safety and Health (NIOSH) (www.cdc.gov/niosh)

To find job openings for occupational health and safety positions in the federal government, visit

➤ USAJOBS (www.usajobs.gov)

O*NET

➤ Occupational Health and Safety Specialists (29-9011.00)

Occupational Health and Safety Technicians

- **2014 Median Pay** .... $48,120 per year $23.14 per hour
- **Typical Entry-Level Education** .... High school diploma or equivalent
- **Work Experience in a Related Occupation** .... None
- **On-the-job Training** .... Moderate-term on-the-job training
- **Number of Jobs, 2014** 15,100
- **Job Outlook, 2014–24** .... 9% (Faster than average)
- **Employment Change, 2014–24** 1,400

What Occupational Health and Safety Technicians Do

Occupational health and safety technicians collect data on the health and safety conditions of the workplace. Technicians work with occupational health and safety specialists in conducting tests and measuring hazards to help prevent harm to workers, property, the environment, and the general public.

Duties. Occupational health and safety technicians typically do the following:

- Inspect, test, and evaluate workplace environments, equipment, and practices to ensure that they follow safety standards and government regulations
- Collect samples of potentially toxic materials
- Work with occupational health and safety specialists to fix hazardous conditions or equipment
- Evaluate programs on workplace health and safety
- Educate employers and workers about workplace safety
- Demonstrate the correct use of safety equipment

Occupational health and safety technicians prepare and calibrate scientific equipment.

- Investigate incidents and accidents to identify what caused them and how they might be prevented

Technicians conduct tests and collect samples and measurements as part of workplace inspections. For example, they may collect and handle samples of dust, mold, gases, vapors, or other hazardous materials. They conduct both routine and special inspections that an occupational health and safety specialist orders.

Technicians inspect workplace environments and practices. They may examine machinery and equipment, such as scaffolding and lifting devices, to be sure that they meet appropriate safety regulations. Technicians may check to make sure that workers are using required protective gear, such as masks and hardhats. Technicians also check to ensure that hazardous materials are stored correctly.

In addition to working to maintain employee health and safety, technicians work with specialists to increase worker productivity by reducing absences and equipment downtime. These actions save companies money by lowering insurance premiums and workers' compensation payments, preventing government fines, and improving productivity and product quality.

Although all occupational health and safety technicians work to maintain the health of workers and the environment, their responsibilities vary by the type of industry and workplace they work in and the hazards that might affect the employees. For example, a technician may test the levels of dangerous gases at a waste-processing plant or may inspect the lighting and ventilation in an office setting. Both of these inspections are focused on maintaining the health of the workers and the environment.

The following are examples of types of occupational health and safety technicians:

Health physics technicians work in places that use radiation and radioactive material. Their goal is to protect people and the environment from hazardous radiation exposure.

Industrial or occupational hygiene technicians examine the workplace for health hazards, such as exposure to lead, asbestos, pesticides, or contagious diseases.

Mine examiners inspect mines for proper airflow and potential health hazards, such as the buildup of methane or other harmful gases.

Work Environment

Occupational health and safety technicians held about 15,100 jobs in 2014. The industries that employed the most occupational health and safety technicians were as follows:

Government	18%
Manufacturing	16
Management, scientific, and technical consulting services	10
Hospitals; state, local, and private	7
Support activities for mining	6

Occupational health and safety technicians work in a variety of settings, including offices, factories, and mines. Most private companies either employ their own occupational health and safety workers or contract with firms that provide such services.

Their jobs often involve considerable fieldwork and travel. In addition, occupational health and safety technicians may be exposed to strenuous, dangerous, or stressful conditions. Injuries are minimized by the use of gloves, helmets, and other safety equipment.

Work Schedules. Most occupational health and safety technicians work full time. Some technicians may work weekends or irregular hours in emergencies.

Education/Training

Occupational health and safety technicians typically enter the occupation through one of two paths. Some technicians learn through on-the-job training; others enter with postsecondary education, such as an associate's degree or certificate.

Education. Employers typically require technicians to have at least a high school diploma. High school students interested in this occupation should complete courses in English, mathematics, chemistry, biology, and physics.

Some employers prefer to hire technicians who have earned an associate's degree or certificate from a community college or vocational school. These programs typically take 2 years or less. They include courses in respiratory protection, hazard communication, and material-handling and storage procedures.

Postsecondary programs include instruction on standard laws and procedures; however, some on-the-job training usually is required to familiarize the technician with specific work environments.

Training. Technicians usually receive on-the-job training. They learn about specific laws and inspection procedures, and learn to conduct tests and recognize hazards. The length of training varies with the employee's level of experience, education, and industry in which he or she works.

Some technicians enter the occupation through a combination of related work experience and training. They may take on health and safety tasks at the company where they are employed. For example, an employee may volunteer to complete annual workstation inspections for an office in which he or she already works.

Licenses, Certifications, and Registrations. Certification is not required for someone to become an occupational health and safety technician; however, many employers encourage it.

To apply for certification, technicians must have earned a high school diploma, possess related on-the-job experience, and pass

Median Annual Wages, May 2014

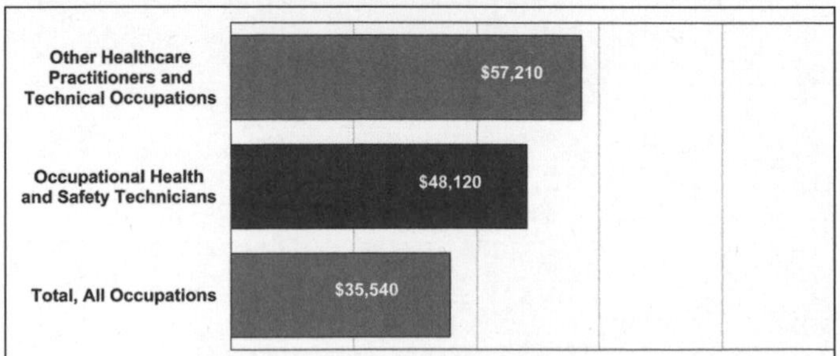

Note: All Occupations includes all occupations in the U.S. Economy.
Source: U.S. Bureau of Labor Statistics, Occupational Employment Statistics

Percent Change in Employment, Projected 2014–2024

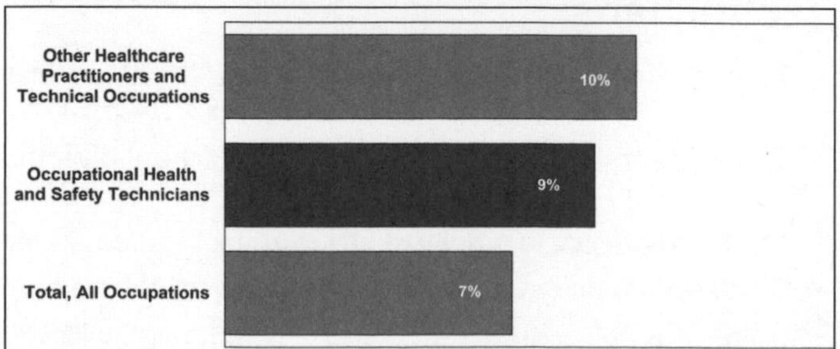

Note: All Occupations includes all occupations in the U.S. Economy.
Source: U.S. Bureau of Labor Statistics, Office of Occupational Statistics and Employment Projections

Employment Projections Data for Occupational Health and Safety Technicians

Occupational Title	SOC Code	Employment, 2014	Projected Employment, 2024	Change, 2014–2024	
				Percent	Numeric
Occupational health and safety technicians	29-9012	15,100	16,500	9	1,400

Source: U.S. Bureau of Labor Statistics, Employment Projections Program

Similar Occupations. This table shows a list of occupations with job duties that are similar to those of occupational health and safety technicians.

Occupations	Entry-level Education	2014 Median Pay	Projected Job Growth	Average Annual Openings
Construction and Building Inspectors	High school diploma or equivalent	$56,040	8%	810
Environmental Science and Protection Technicians	Associate's degree	$42,190	9%	340
Fire Inspectors	See Education/Training	$54,020	6%	90
Occupational Health and Safety Specialists	Bachelor's degree	$69,210	4%	280

a standardized health and safety exam. The Board of Certified Safety Professionals (BCSP) offers the following certifications at the technician level:

- The Construction Health and Safety Technician (CHST) Certification requires the applicant to have specific education or experience in construction safety. These technicians protect workers on construction sites from injury or illness.
- The Occupational Health and Safety Technologist (OHST) Certification is designed for workers who perform occupational health and safety tasks full or part time as part of their job duties.

Important Qualities

Ability to use technology. Occupational health and safety technicians often work with computers and complex testing equipment.

Communication skills. Occupational health and safety technicians must be able to work with specialists to collect and test samples of possible hazards, such as dust or vapors, in the workplace.

Detail oriented. Occupational health and safety technicians must be able to understand and follow safety standards and complex government regulations.

Physical stamina. Occupational health and safety technicians must be able to stay on their feet for long periods and travel on a regular basis.

Problem-solving skills. Occupational health and safety technicians must be able to solve problems in order to assist specialists in protecting workers from hazardous work conditions.

Advancement. Occupational health and safety technicians can become occupational health and safety specialists by earning a bachelor's degree or advanced degree.

Pay

The median annual wage for occupational health and safety technicians was $48,120 in May 2014. The median wage is the wage at which half the workers in an occupation earned more than that amount and half earned less. The lowest 10 percent earned less than $29,840, and the highest 10 percent earned more than $77,010.

In May 2014, the median annual wages for occupational health and safety technicians in the top industries in which they worked were as follows:

Support activities for mining	$54,610
Government	48,210
Manufacturing	46,570
Management, scientific, and technical consulting services	43,750
Hospitals; state, local, and private	42,230

Job Outlook

Employment of occupational health and safety technicians is projected to grow 9 percent from 2014 to 2024, faster than the average for all occupations. Technicians will be needed to conduct tests, measure hazards, and ensure that employers are adhering to existing and new safety and health regulations.

In addition, technological advances will allow for the use of new machinery, and technicians will be needed to conduct inspections and evaluate usage of the machinery with regard to worker health and safety.

Insurance and workers' compensation costs have become a concern for many employers and insurance companies. Because older workers usually have a greater incidence of workers' compensation claims, these costs can become higher with an aging population remaining in the workforce longer. Occupational health and safety technicians will be needed to work with occupational health and safety specialists in maintaining safety for all workers.

Although most occupational health and safety technicians work under the supervision of specialists, technicians can complete many routine tasks with little or no supervision. As a result, some employers may operate with more technicians because they are more cost effective than specialists.

Job Prospects. Applicants for jobs as occupational health and safety technicians with knowledge or a background in the sciences and experience in more than one area of health and safety or certification will have the best prospects.

Contacts for More Information

For more information about occupational health and safety technicians, visit

➤ Center for Disease Control and Prevention, National Institute for Occupational Safety and Health (NIOSH) (www.cdc.gov/niosh)

➤ U.S. Department of Labor, Occupational Safety and Health Administration (OSHA) (www.osha.gov)

For information on industrial or occupational hygiene, visit

➤ American Industrial Hygiene Association (AIHA) (www.aiha.org/Pages/default.aspx)

For more information on careers in safety and a list of safety and related academic programs, visit

➤ Board of Certified Safety Professionals (BCSP) (www.bcsp.org)

Information about jobs in state and local governments and in private industry is available from state employment service offices.

O*NET

➤ Occupational Health and Safety Technicians (29-9012.00)

Occupational Therapists

- **2014 Median Pay** .... $78,810 per year
  $37.89 per hour
- **Typical Entry-Level Education** ....Master's degree
- **Work Experience in a Related Occupation**.............. None
- **On-the-job Training** .... None
- **Number of Jobs, 2014** 114,600
- **Job Outlook, 2014–24**......27% (Much faster than average)
- **Employment Change, 2014–24** 30,400

What Occupational Therapists Do

Occupational therapists treat injured, ill, or disabled patients through the therapeutic use of everyday activities. They help these patients develop, recover, and improve the skills needed for daily living and working.

Duties. Occupational therapists typically do the following:

- Review patients' medical history, ask the patients questions, and observe them doing tasks
- Evaluate a patient's condition and needs
- Develop a treatment plan for patients, identifying specific goals and the types of activities that will be used to help the patient work toward those goals
- Help people with various disabilities with different tasks, such as teaching a stroke victim how to get dressed
- Demonstrate exercises—for example, stretching the joints for arthritis relief—that can help relieve pain in people with chronic conditions
- Evaluate a patient's home or workplace and, on the basis of the patient's health needs, identify potential improvements, such as labeling kitchen cabinets for an older person with poor memory
- Educate a patient's family and employer about how to accommodate and care for the patient
- Recommend special equipment, such as wheelchairs and eating aids, and instruct patients on how to use that equipment
- Assess and record patients' activities and progress for patient evaluations, for billing, and for reporting to physicians and other healthcare providers

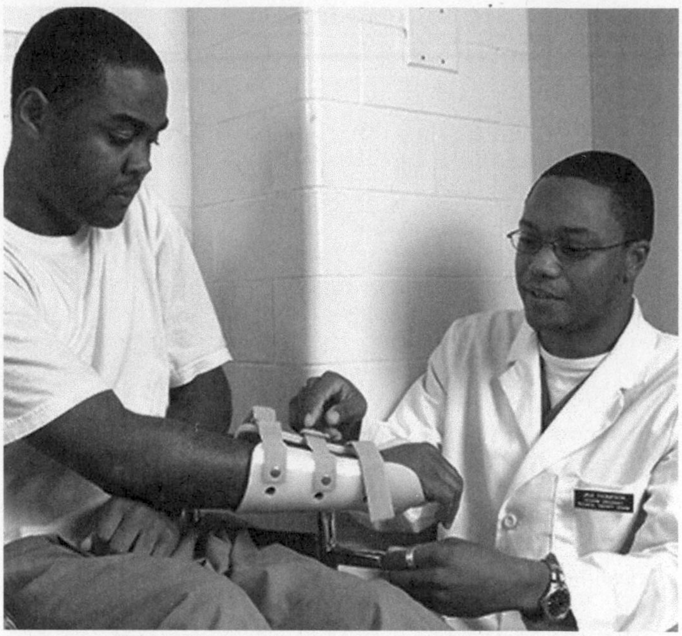

Occupational therapists help patients learn to perform all types of activities, from using a computer to caring for daily needs such as dressing, cooking, and eating.

Patients with permanent disabilities, such as cerebral palsy, often need help performing daily tasks. Therapists show patients how to use appropriate adaptive equipment, such as leg braces, wheelchairs, and eating aids. These devices help patients perform a number of daily tasks, allowing them to function more independently.

Some occupational therapists work with children in educational settings. They evaluate disabled children's abilities, modify classroom equipment to accommodate children with certain disabilities, and help children participate in school activities. Therapists also may provide early intervention therapy to infants and toddlers who have, or are at risk of having, developmental delays.

Therapists who work with the elderly help their patients lead more independent and active lives. They assess patients' abilities and environment and make recommendations to improve the patients' everyday lives. For example, therapists may identify potential fall hazards in a patient's home and recommend their removal.

In some cases, occupational therapists help patients create functional work environments. They evaluate the workspace, recommend modifications, and meet with the patient's employer to collaborate on changes to the patient's work environment or schedule.

Occupational therapists also may work in mental health settings, where they help patients who suffer from developmental disabilities, mental illness, or emotional problems. Therapists teach these patients skills such as managing time, budgeting, using public transportation, and doing household chores in order to help them cope with, and engage in, daily life activities. In addition, therapists may work with individuals who have problems with drug abuse, alcoholism, depression, or other disorders. They may also work with people who have been through a traumatic event, such as a car accident.

Some occupational therapists, such as those employed in hospitals, work as part of a healthcare team along with doctors, registered nurses, and other types of therapists. They may work with patients who have chronic conditions, such as diabetes, or

Median Annual Wages, May 2014

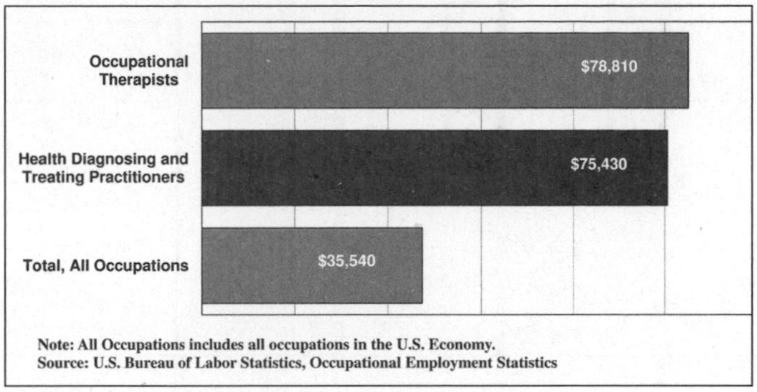

Percent Change in Employment, Projected 2014–2024

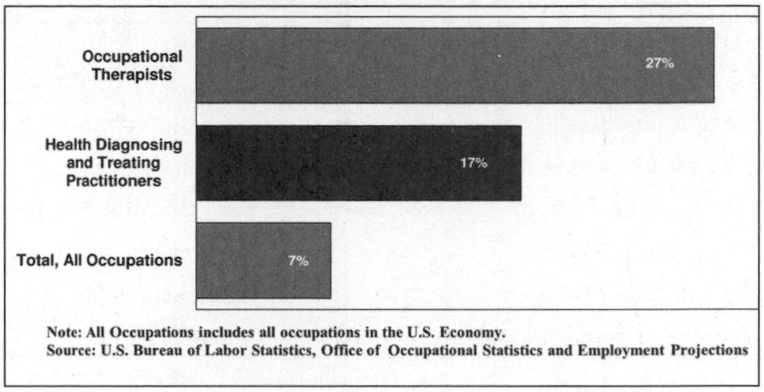

help rehabilitate a patient recovering from hip replacement surgery. Occupational therapists also oversee the work of occupational therapy assistants and aides.

Work Environment

Occupational therapists held about 114,600 jobs in 2014. The industries that employed the most occupational therapists were as follows:

Hospitals; state, local, and private	27%
Offices of physical, occupational and speech therapists, and audiologists	24
Elementary and secondary schools; state, local, and private	12
Nursing care facilities (skilled nursing facilities)	9
Home healthcare services	9

Therapists may spend a lot of time on their feet while working with patients. They also may be required to lift and move patients or heavy equipment. Many work in multiple facilities and have to travel from one job to another.

Work Schedules. Most occupational therapists worked full time in 2014. About 1 out of 4 worked part time. They may work nights or weekends, as needed, to accommodate patients' schedules.

Education/Training

Occupational therapists need at least a master's degree in occupational therapy; some therapists have a doctoral degree. Occupational therapists also must be licensed.

Education. Most occupational therapists enter the occupation with a master's degree in occupational therapy. In 2014, there were nearly 200 occupational therapy programs accredited by the Accreditation Council for Occupational Therapy Education, part of the American Occupational Therapy Association.

Admission to graduate programs in occupational therapy generally requires a bachelor's degree and specific coursework, including biology and physiology. Many programs also require applicants to have volunteered or worked in an occupational therapy setting.

Master's programs usually take 2 to 3 years to complete; doctoral programs take about 3 years. Some schools offer a dual-degree program in which the student earns a bachelor's degree and a master's degree in 5 years. Part-time programs that offer courses on nights and weekends are also available.

Both master's and doctoral programs require at least 24 weeks of supervised fieldwork, in which prospective occupational therapists gain clinical work experience.

Licenses, Certifications, and Registrations. All states require occupational therapists to be licensed. Licensing requirements vary by state, but all require candidates to pass the national examination administered by the National Board for Certification in Occupational Therapy (NBCOT). To sit for the NBCOT exam, candidates must have earned a degree from an accredited educational program and completed all fieldwork requirements.

Therapists must pass the NBCOT exam to use the title "Occupational Therapist, Registered" (OTR). They must also take continuing education classes to maintain certification.

The American Occupational Therapy Association also offers a number of board and specialty certifications for therapists who want to demonstrate their advanced or specialized knowledge in areas of practice, such as pediatrics, mental health, or low vision.

Important Qualities

Communication skills. Occupational therapists must be able to listen attentively to what patients tell them and must be able to explain what they want their patients to do.

Compassion. Occupational therapists are usually drawn to the profession by a desire to help people and improve their daily lives. Therapists must be sensitive to a patient's needs and concerns, especially when assisting the patient with his or her personal activities.

Flexibility. Occupational therapists must be flexible when treating patients. Because not every type of therapy will work for each patient, therapists may need to be creative when determining the treatment plans and adaptive devices that best suit each patient's needs.

Interpersonal skills. Because occupational therapists spend their time teaching and explaining therapies to patients, they should be able to earn the trust and respect of those patients and their families.

Employment Projections Data for Occupational Therapists

Occupational Title	SOC Code	Employment, 2014	Projected Employment, 2024	Change, 2014–2024 Percent	Change, 2014–2024 Numeric
Occupational therapists	29-1122	114,600	145,100	27	30,400

Source: U.S. Bureau of Labor Statistics, Employment Projections Program

Similar Occupations. This table shows a list of occupations with job duties that are similar to those of occupational therapists.

Occupations	Entry-level Education	2014 Median Pay	Projected Job Growth	Average Annual Openings
Athletic Trainers	Bachelor's degree	$43,370	21%	540
Exercise Physiologists	Bachelor's degree	$46,270	11%	150
Occupational Therapy Assistants and Aides	See Education/Training	$52,300	40%	1,680
Physical Therapists	Doctoral or professional degree	$82,390	34%	7,180
Recreational Therapists	Bachelor's degree	$44,000	12%	220
Speech-Language Pathologists	Master's degree	$71,550	21%	2,890

Patience. Dealing with injuries, illnesses, and disabilities is frustrating for many people. Occupational therapists should be patient in order to provide quality care to the people they serve.

Writing skills. When communicating in writing with other members of the patient's medical team, occupational therapists must be able to explain clearly the treatment plan for the patient and any progress made by the patient.

Pay

The median annual wage for occupational therapists was $78,810 in May 2014. The median wage is the wage at which half the workers in an occupation earned more than that amount and half earned less. The lowest 10 percent earned less than $52,670, and the highest 10 percent earned more than $112,950.

In May 2014, the median annual wages for occupational therapists in the top industries in which they worked were as follows:

Nursing care facilities (skilled nursing facilities)	$86,690
Home healthcare services	86,010
Offices of physical, occupational and speech therapists, and audiologists	82,230
Hospitals; state, local, and private	78,400
Elementary and secondary schools; state, local, and private	68,250

Job Outlook

Employment of occupational therapists is projected to grow 27 percent from 2014 to 2024, much faster than the average for all occupations. Occupational therapy will continue to be an important part of treatment for people with various illnesses and disabilities, such as Alzheimer's disease, cerebral palsy, autism, or the loss of a limb.

The need for occupational therapists is expected to increase as the large baby-boom generation ages and people remain active later in life. Occupational therapists can help senior citizens maintain their independence by recommending home modifications and strategies that make daily activities easier. Therapists also play a large role in the treatment of many conditions and ailments commonly associated with aging, such as arthritis and stroke.

Occupational therapists also will be needed in a variety of healthcare settings to treat patients with chronic conditions, such as diabetes. Patients will continue to seek noninvasive outpatient treatment for long-term disabilities and illnesses, either in their homes or in residential care environments. These patients may need occupational therapy to become more independent in and to perform a variety of daily tasks.

Demand for occupational therapy services also will stem from patients with autism spectrum disorder. More therapists will be needed in schools to assist children with autism in improving their social skills and accomplishing a variety of daily tasks. Demand for occupational therapy services is related to the ability of patients to pay, either directly or through health insurance. The number of individuals who have access to health insurance is expected to continue to increase because of federal health insurance reform. Both rehabilitation and habilitation services are included among essential health benefits to be covered by insurers; however, coverage may vary by state.

Job Prospects. Job opportunities should be good for licensed occupational therapists in all settings, particularly acute hospital, rehabilitation, and orthopedic settings, because the elderly receive most of their treatment in these settings. Occupational therapists with specialized knowledge in a treatment area also will have better job prospects.

Contacts for More Information

For more information about occupational therapists, visit

- American Occupational Therapy Association, Inc. (www.aota.org)

For more information about the certification exam for Occupational Therapist, Registered, visit

- National Board for Certification in Occupational Therapy (www.nbcot.org)

For information regarding the requirements for practice as an occupational therapist in schools, contact state occupational therapy regulatory agencies.

O*NET

- Occupational Therapists (29-1122.00)
- Low Vision Therapists, Orientation and Mobility Specialists, and Vision Rehabilitation Therapists (29-1122.01)

Occupational Therapy Assistants and Aides

- **2014 Median Pay** ..... $52,300 per year; $25.14 per hour
- **Typical Entry-Level Education** ..... See Education/Training
- **Work Experience in a Related Occupation** ..... None
- **On-the-job Training** ..... See Education/Training
- **Number of Jobs, 2014** 41,900
- **Job Outlook, 2014–24** ..... 40% (Much faster than average)
- **Employment Change, 2014–24** 16,800

What Occupational Therapy Assistants and Aides Do

Occupational therapy assistants and aides help patients develop, recover, and improve the skills needed for daily living and working. Occupational therapy assistants are directly involved in providing therapy to patients; occupational therapy aides typically perform support activities. Both assistants and aides work under the direction of occupational therapists.

Duties. Occupational therapy assistants typically do the following:

- Help patients do therapeutic activities, such as stretches and other exercises
- Lead children who have developmental disabilities in play activities that promote coordination and socialization
- Encourage patients to complete activities and tasks
- Teach patients how to use special equipment—for example, showing a patient with Parkinson's disease how to use devices that make eating easier
- Record patients' progress, report to occupational therapists, and do other administrative tasks

Occupational therapy aides typically do the following:

- Prepare treatment areas, such as setting up therapy equipment
- Transport patients
- Clean treatment areas and equipment
- Help patients with billing and insurance forms
- Perform clerical tasks, including scheduling appointments and answering telephones

Occupational therapy assistants collaborate with occupational therapists to develop and carry out a treatment plan for each patient. Activities described in plans range from teaching the proper way for patients to move from a bed into a wheelchair to advising patients on the best way to stretch their muscles. For example, an occupational therapy assistant might work with injured workers to help them get back into the workforce by teaching them how to work around lost motor skills. Occupational therapy assistants also may work with people who have learning disabilities, teaching them skills that allow them to be more independent.

Occupational therapy assistants teach patients how to use special equipment, such as wheelchairs.

Assistants monitor activities to make sure that patients are doing them correctly. They record the patient's progress and provide feedback to the occupational therapist so that the therapist can change the treatment plan if the patient is not getting the desired results.

Occupational therapy aides typically prepare materials and assemble equipment used during treatment. They may assist patients with moving to and from treatment areas. After a therapy session, aides clean the treatment area, put away equipment, and gather laundry.

Occupational therapy aides also fill out insurance forms and other paperwork and are responsible for a range of clerical tasks, such as scheduling appointments, answering the telephone, and monitoring inventory levels.

Work Environment

Occupational therapy assistants held about 33,000 jobs in 2014. Occupational therapy aides held about 8,800 jobs in 2014.

The industries that employed the most occupational therapy assistants in 2014 were as follows:

Offices of physical, occupational and speech therapists, and audiologists	40%
Nursing care facilities (skilled nursing facilities)	18
Hospitals; state, local, and private	17
Home healthcare services	6
Educational services; state, local, and private	5

The industries that employed the most occupational therapy aides in 2014 were as follows:

Offices of physical, occupational and speech therapists, and audiologists	36%
Hospitals; state, local, and private	28
Nursing care facilities (skilled nursing facilities)	15
Social assistance	6
Educational services; state, local, and private	4

Occupational therapy assistants and aides work primarily in occupational therapists' offices, hospitals, and nursing care facilities.

Occupational therapy assistants and aides spend much of their time on their feet, setting up equipment and, in the case of assistants, working with patients. Constant kneeling and stooping are part of the job, as is the need to sometimes lift patients.

Work Schedules. Most occupational therapy assistants and aides work full time. Occupational therapy assistants and aides may work during evenings or on weekends to accommodate patients' schedules.

Education/Training

Occupational therapy assistants need an associate's degree from an accredited occupational therapy assistant program. They also must be licensed in most states. Occupational therapy aides typically have a high school diploma or equivalent.

Education and Training. Occupational therapy assistants typically need an associate's degree from an accredited program. Occupational therapy assistant programs are commonly found in community colleges and technical schools. In 2014, there were more than 200 occupational therapy assistant programs accredited by the Accreditation Council for Occupational Therapy Education, a branch of the American Occupational Therapy Association.

Median Annual Wages, May 2014

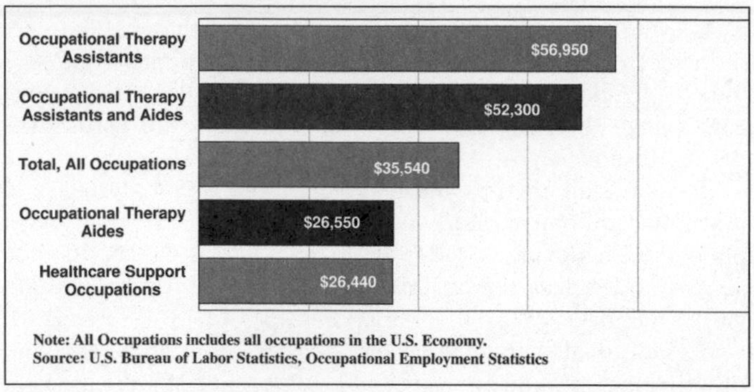

Percent Change in Employment, Projected 2014–2024

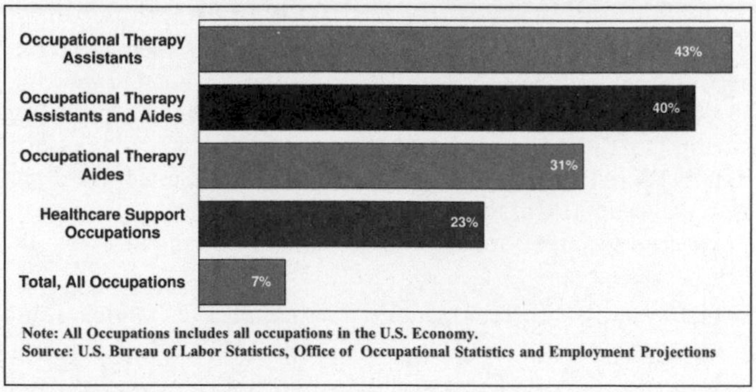

These programs generally require 2 years of full-time study and include instruction in subjects such as psychology, biology, and pediatric health. In addition to taking coursework, occupational therapy assistants must complete at least 16 weeks of fieldwork to gain hands-on work experience.

People interested in becoming an occupational therapy assistant should take high school courses in biology and health education. They also can increase their chances of getting into a community college or technical school program by doing volunteer work in a healthcare setting, such as a nursing care facility, an occupational therapist's office, or a physical therapist's office.

Occupational therapy aides typically have a high school diploma or equivalent. They are trained on the job under the supervision of more experienced assistants or aides. Training can last from several days to a few weeks and covers a number of topics, including the setting up of therapy equipment and infection control procedures, among others. Previous work experience in healthcare, as well as certifications in cardiopulmonary resuscitation (CPR) and basic life support (BLS), may be helpful in getting a job.

Important Qualities

Compassion. Occupational therapy assistants and aides frequently work with patients who struggle with many of life's basic activities. As a result, they should be compassionate and have the ability to encourage others.

Detail oriented. Occupational therapy assistants and aides must be able to quickly and accurately follow the instructions, both written and spoken, of an occupational therapist. In addition, aides must pay attention to detail when performing clerical tasks, such as helping a patient fill out an insurance form.

Flexibility. Assistants must be flexible when treating patients. Because not every type of therapy will work for each patient, assistants may need to be creative when working with occupational therapists to determine the best type of therapy to use for achieving a patient's goals.

Interpersonal skills. Occupational therapy assistants and aides spend much of their time interacting with patients and therefore should be friendly and courteous. They also should be able to communicate clearly with patients and with patients' families to the extent of their training.

Physical strength. Assistants and aides need to have a moderate degree of strength because of the physical exertion required to assist patients. Constant kneeling, stooping, and standing for long periods also are part of the job.

Licenses, Certifications, and Registrations. Nearly all states require occupational therapy assistants to be licensed or registered. Licensure typically requires the completion of an accredited occupational therapy assistant education program, completion of all fieldwork requirements, and passing the National Board for Certification in Occupational Therapy (NBCOT) exam. Some states have additional requirements.

Occupational therapy assistants must pass the NBCOT exam to use the title "Certified Occupational Therapy Assistant" (COTA). They must also take continuing education classes to maintain their certification.

The American Occupational Therapy Association also offers a number of specialty certifications for occupational therapy assistants who want to demonstrate their specialized level of knowledge, skills, and abilities in specialized areas of practice such as low vision or feeding, eating and swallowing.

Occupational therapy aides are not regulated.

Advancement. Some occupational therapy assistants and aides advance by gaining additional education and becoming occupational therapists. A small number of occupational therapist "bridge" education programs are designed to qualify occupational therapy assistants to advance and become therapists.

Pay

The median annual wage for occupational therapy assistants was $56,950 in May 2014. The median wage is the wage at which half the workers in an occupation earned more than that amount and half earned less. The lowest 10 percent earned less than $36,420, and the highest 10 percent earned more than $76,790.

The median annual wage for occupational therapy aides was $26,550 in May 2014. The lowest 10 percent earned less than $18,330, and the highest 10 percent earned more than $44,240.

Employment Projections Data for Occupational Therapy Assistants and Aides

Occupational Title	SOC Code	Employment, 2014	Projected Employment, 2024	Change, 2014–2024	
				Percent	Numeric
Occupational therapy assistants and aides	31-2010	41,900	58,700	40	16,800
Occupational therapy assistants	31-2011	33,000	47,100	43	14,100
Occupational therapy aides	31-2012	8,800	11,600	31	2,700

Source: U.S. Bureau of Labor Statistics, Employment Projections Program

Similar Occupations. This table shows a list of occupations with job duties that are similar to those of occupational therapy assistants and aides.

Occupations	Entry-level Education	2014 Median Pay	Projected Job Growth	Average Annual Openings
Dental Assistants	Postsecondary nondegree award	$35,390	18%	5,860
Medical Assistants	Postsecondary nondegree award	$29,960	23%	13,890
Occupational Therapists	Master's degree	$78,810	27%	3,040
Pharmacy Technicians	High school diploma or equivalent	$29,810	9%	3,470
Physical Therapist Assistants and Aides	See Education/Training	$41,640	40%	5,140

In May 2014, the median annual wages for occupational therapy assistants in the top industries in which they worked were as follows:

Home healthcare services.. $63,480
Nursing care facilities (skilled nursing facilities).................. 61,440
Offices of physical, occupational and speech therapists, and audiologists.. 58,970
Hospitals; state, local, and private....................................... 51,120
Educational services; state, local, and private...................... 45,030

In May 2014, the median annual wages for occupational therapy aides in the top industries in which they worked were as follows:

Educational services; state, local, and private.................... $29,830
Nursing care facilities (skilled nursing facilities).................. 28,830
Hospitals; state, local, and private....................................... 28,640
Social assistance.. 27,110
Offices of physical, occupational and speech therapists, and audiologists.. 21,820

Job Outlook

Employment of occupational therapy assistants is projected to grow 43 percent from 2014 to 2024, much faster than the average for all occupations.

Employment of occupational therapy aides is projected to grow 31 percent from 2014 to 2024, much faster than the average for all occupations. However, because it is a small occupation, the fast growth will result in only about 2,700 new jobs over the 10-year period.

Demand for occupational therapy is likely to grow over the coming decade in response to the health needs of the aging baby-boom generation and a growing elderly population. Older adults are more prone than younger people to conditions and ailments such as arthritis and stroke. These conditions can affect one's ability to perform a variety of everyday activities. Occupational therapy assistants and aides will be needed to help occupational therapists in caring for these patients. Occupational therapy will also continue to be used to treat children and young adults with developmental disabilities, such as autism.

In addition, demand for occupational therapy assistants is likely to stem from healthcare providers (especially long-term care facilities, such as nursing homes) employing more assistants to reduce the cost of occupational therapy services. After the therapist has evaluated a patient and designed a treatment plan, the occupational therapy assistant can provide many aspects of the treatment that the therapist prescribed.

Demand for occupational therapy services is related to the ability of patients to pay, either directly or through health insurance. The number of individuals who have access to health insurance is expected to continue to increase because of federal health insurance reform. Both rehabilitation and habilitation services are included among essential health benefits to be covered by insurers; however, coverage may vary by state. Occupational therapy assistants and aides will be needed to help therapists treat additional patients and to ensure that treatment facility operations run smoothly.

Job Prospects. Occupational therapy assistants and aides with experience working in an occupational therapy office or other healthcare setting should have the best job opportunities. However, occupational therapy aides may face strong competition from the large pool of qualified people, because requirements for entry are low.

Contacts for More Information

For more information about occupational therapy assistants or aides, visit

➤ American Occupational Therapy Association, Inc. (www.aota.org)

For more information about certification for occupational therapy assistants, visit

➤ National Board for Certification in Occupational Therapy (www.nbcot.org)

O*NET

➤ Occupational Therapy Assistants (31-2011.00)

➤ Occupational Therapy Aides (31-2012.00)

Opticians, Dispensing

- **2014 Median Pay** .... $34,280 per year $16.48 per hour
- **Typical Entry-Level Education**........ High school diploma or equivalent
- **Work Experience in a Related Occupation**............... None
- **On-the-job Training** .... Long-term on-the-job training
- **Number of Jobs, 2014** 75,200
- **Job Outlook, 2014–24**...... 24% (Much faster than average)
- **Employment Change, 2014–24** 17,800

What Opticians, Dispensing Do

Dispensing opticians help fit eyeglasses and contact lenses, following prescriptions from ophthalmologists and optometrists. They also help customers decide which eyeglass frames or contact lenses to buy.

Duties. Opticians typically do the following:

- Receive customers' prescriptions for eyeglasses or contact lenses
- Measure customers' eyes and faces, such as the distance between their pupils

Median Annual Wages, May 2014

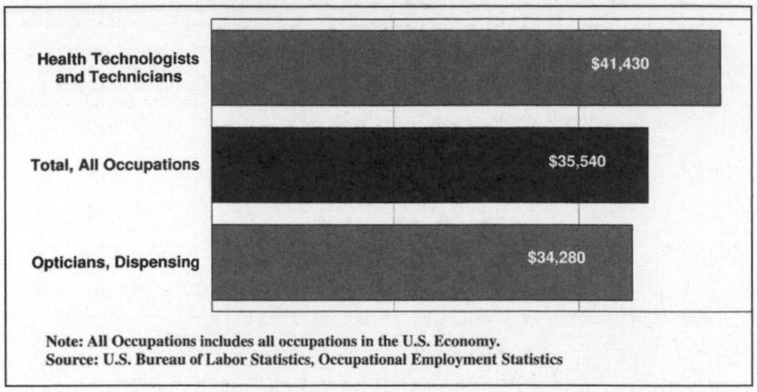

Percent Change in Employment, Projected 2014–2024

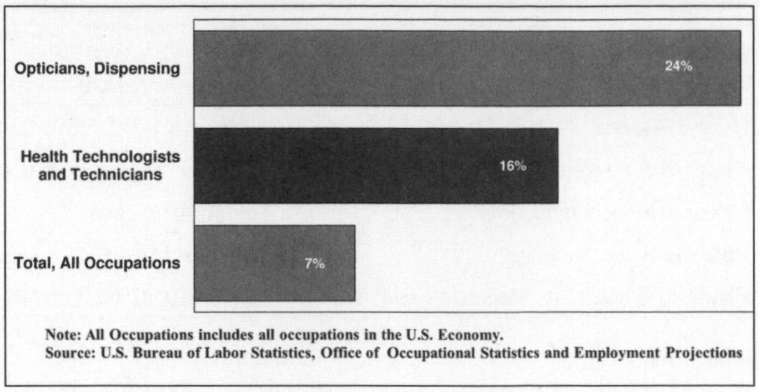

- Help customers choose eyeglass frames and lens treatments, such as eyewear for occupational use or sports, tints or anti-reflective coatings, based on their vision needs and style preferences
- Create work orders for ophthalmic laboratory technicians, providing information about the lenses needed
- Adjust eyewear to ensure a good fit
- Repair or replace broken eyeglass frames
- Educate customers about eyewear—for example, show them how to care for their contact lenses
- Perform business tasks, such as maintaining sales records, keeping track of customers' prescriptions, and ordering and maintaining inventory

Opticians who work in small shops or prepare custom orders may cut lenses and insert them into frames—tasks usually performed by ophthalmic laboratory technicians. For more information, see the profile on dental and ophthalmic laboratory technicians and medical appliance technicians.

Work Environment

Dispensing opticians held about 75,200 jobs in 2014. The industries that employed the most dispensing opticians were as follows:

Offices of optometrists	38%
Health and personal care stores	31
Offices of physicians	10
Department stores	3

About half of opticians worked in offices of optometrists or offices of physicians in 2014. Other opticians worked in stores that sell eyeglasses, contact lenses, visual aids, and other optical goods. These stores may be stand-alone businesses or parts of larger retail establishments, such as department stores.

Opticians who work as part of a group optometry or medical practice work with optometrists and ophthalmologists to provide eye-related medical care to patients. For more information on ophthalmologists, see the profile on physicians and surgeons.

Work Schedules. Opticians who work in large retail establishments, such as department stores, may have to work evenings and weekends. Most opticians work full time, although part-time opportunities also are available.

Education/Training

Opticians typically have a high school diploma or equivalent and receive some form of on-the-job training. Some opticians enter the occupation with an associate's degree or a certificate from a community college or technical school. About half of the states require opticians to be licensed.

Education and Training. Opticians typically have a high school diploma or equivalent and learn job skills through on-the-job training. Training includes technical instruction in which, for example, a new optician measures a customer's eyes or adjusts frames under the supervision of an experienced optician. Trainees also learn sales and office management practices. Some opticians complete an apprenticeship, which typically takes at least 2 years.

Other opticians complete a postsecondary education program at a community college or technical school. These programs award a 2-year associate's degree or a 1-year certificate. As of 2015, the Commission on Opticianry Accreditation accredited 22 programs in 14 states.

Education programs typically include both classroom instruction and clinical experience. Coursework includes classes in optics, eye physiology, math, and business management, among other topics. Students also do supervised clinical work that gives them hands-on experience working as opticians and learning optical math, optical physics, and the use of precision measuring instruments. Some programs have distance-learning options.

The National Academy of Opticianry offers the Ophthalmic Career Progression Program (OCPP), a program designed for individuals who are already working in the field. The OCPP offers opticians another way to prepare for licensure exams or certifications.

Licenses, Certifications, and Registrations. About half of the states require opticians to be licensed. Licensure usually requires completing formal education through an approved program or completing an apprenticeship. In addition, opticians must pass

Employment Projections Data for Opticians, Dispensing

Occupational Title	SOC Code	Employment, 2014	Projected Employment, 2024	Change, 2014–2024 Percent	Change, 2014–2024 Numeric
Opticians, dispensing	29-2081	75,200	93,000	24	17,800

Source: U.S. Bureau of Labor Statistics, Employment Projections Program

Similar Occupations. This table shows a list of occupations with job duties that are similar to those of dispensing opticians.

Occupations	Entry-level Education	2014 Median Pay	Projected Job Growth	Average Annual Openings
Dental and Ophthalmic Laboratory Technicians and Medical Appliance Technicians	High school diploma or equivalent	$33,430	10%	870
Jewelers and Precious Stone and Metal Workers	High school diploma or equivalent	$36,870	-11%	-450
Optometrists	Doctoral or professional degree	$101,410	27%	1,100
Orthotists and Prosthetists	Master's degree	$64,040	23%	190

one or more exams to be licensed. The opticianry licensing board in each state can supply information on licensing requirements.

Opticians may choose to become certified in eyeglass dispensing or contact lens dispensing or both. Certification requires passing exams from the American Board of Opticianry (ABO) and National Contact Lens Examiners (NCLE). Nearly all state licensing boards use the ABO and NCLE exams as the basis for state licensing. Some states also require opticians to pass state-specific practical exams.

In most states that require licensure, opticians must renew their license every 1 to 3 years and must complete continuing education requirements.

Important Qualities

Business skills. Opticians are often responsible for the business aspects of running an optical store. They should be comfortable making decisions and have some knowledge of sales and inventory management.

Communication skills. Opticians must be able to listen closely to what customers want. They must be able to clearly explain options and instructions for care in ways that customers understand.

Customer service skills. Because some opticians work in stores, they must answer questions and know about the products they sell. They interact with customers on a very personal level, fitting eyeglasses or contact lenses. To succeed, they must be friendly, courteous, patient, and helpful to customers.

Decision-making skills. Opticians must determine what adjustments need to be made to eyeglasses and contact lenses. They must decide which materials and styles are most appropriate for each customer on the basis of their preferences and lifestyle.

Dexterity. Opticians frequently use special tools to make final adjustments and repairs to eyeglasses. They must have good hand-eye coordination to do that work quickly and accurately.

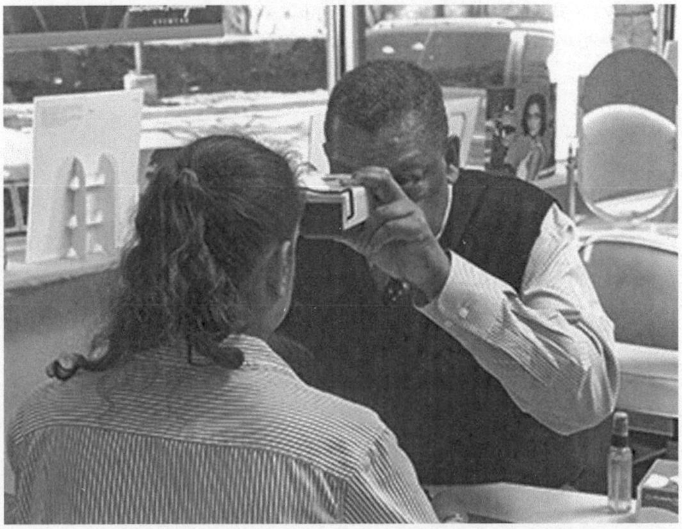

Dispensing opticians deal directly with the public, so they should be tactful, pleasant, and communicate well.

Pay

The median annual wage for dispensing opticians was $34,280 in May 2014. The median wage is the wage at which half the workers in an occupation earned more than that amount and half earned less. The lowest 10 percent earned less than $21,510, and the highest 10 percent earned more than $55,160.

In May 2014, the median annual wages for dispensing opticians in the top industries in which they worked were as follows:

Offices of physicians	$37,630
Health and personal care stores	37,330
Offices of optometrists	32,580
Department stores	27,590

Job Outlook

Employment of opticians is projected to grow 24 percent from 2014 to 2024, much faster than the average for all occupations.

The growth in the older population is anticipated to lead to greater demand for eye care services. Because people usually have eye problems more frequently as they age, the need for opticians is likely to grow with the increase in the number of older people.

Increasing rates of chronic diseases such as diabetes may also increase demand for opticianry services because some chronic diseases cause vision problems. Additional opticians will be needed to fill prescriptions for corrective eyewear for individuals with conditions that damage their eyesight.

A growing proportion of opticians are expected to find employment in group medical practices. Optometrists and ophthalmologists are increasingly offering glasses and contact lenses to their patients as a way to expand their businesses, leading to a greater need for opticians in those settings.

However, employment growth is expected to be constrained by increases in productivity that will allow a given number of opticians to serve more customers.

Job Prospects. Having an associate's degree from an accredited program and ABO and NCLE certifications may improve an applicant's job prospects.

Contacts for More Information

For more information about dispensing opticians, including certifications and a list of state licensing boards for opticians, visit

➤ American Board of Opticianry and National Contact Lens Examiners (www.abo-ncle.org)

For a list of accredited programs, visit

➤ Commission on Opticianry Accreditation (www.coaccreditation.com)

For more information about optician education, visit

➤ National Federation of Opticianry Schools (www.nfos.org)

➤ National Academy of Opticianry (www.nao.org)

O*NET

➤ Opticians, Dispensing (29-2081.00)

Optometrists

- **2014 Median Pay** .... $101,410 per year $48.76 per hour
- **Typical Entry-Level Education** .... Doctoral or professional degree
- **Work Experience in a Related Occupation** .... None
- **On-the-job Training** .... None
- **Number of Jobs, 2014** 40,600
- **Job Outlook, 2014–24**..... 27% (Much faster than average)
- **Employment Change, 2014–24** 11,000

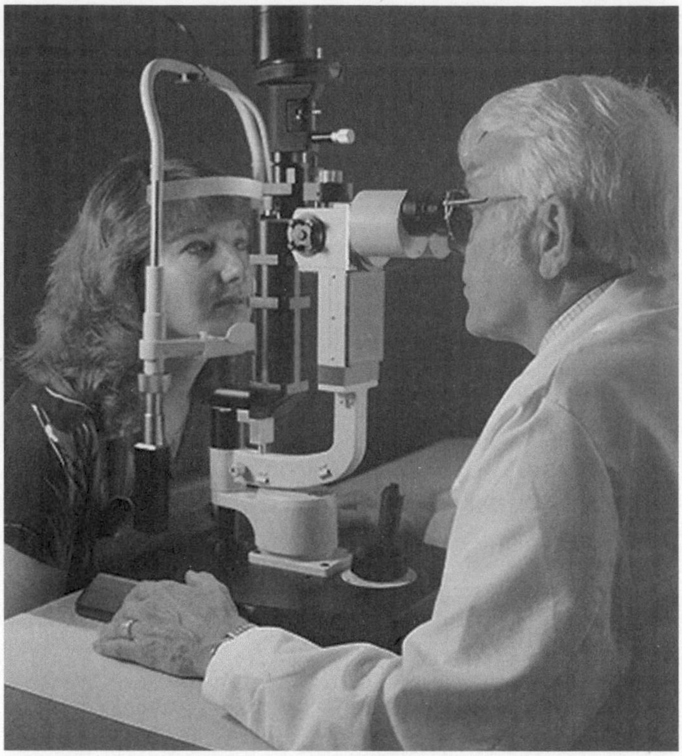

The Doctor of Optometry degree requires the completion of a 4-year program at an accredited optometry school.

What Optometrists Do

Optometrists examine the eyes and other parts of the visual system. They also diagnose and treat visual problems and manage diseases, injuries, and other disorders of the eyes. They prescribe eyeglasses or contact lenses as needed.

Duties. Optometrists typically do the following:

- Perform vision tests and analyze results
- Diagnose sight problems, such as nearsightedness or farsightedness, and eye diseases, such as glaucoma
- Prescribe eyeglasses, contact lenses, and other visual aids, and if state law permits, medications
- Perform minor surgical procedures to correct or treat visual or eye health issues
- Provide treatments such as vision therapy or low-vision rehabilitation
- Provide pre- and postoperative care to patients undergoing eye surgery—for example, examining a patient's eyes the day after surgery
- Evaluate patients for the presence of other diseases and conditions, such as diabetes or hypertension, and refer patients to other healthcare providers as needed
- Promote eye and general health by counseling patients

Some optometrists spend much of their time providing specialized care, particularly if they are working in a group practice with other optometrists or physicians. For example, some optometrists mostly treat patients with only partial sight, a condition known as low vision. Others may focus on treating infants and children.

Optometrists promote eye health and counsel patients on how general health can affect eyesight. For example, they may counsel patients on how smoking cessation or weight loss can reduce vision problems.

Many optometrists own their practice and those who do may spend more time on general business activities, such as hiring employees, ordering supplies, and marketing their business.

Median Annual Wages, May 2014

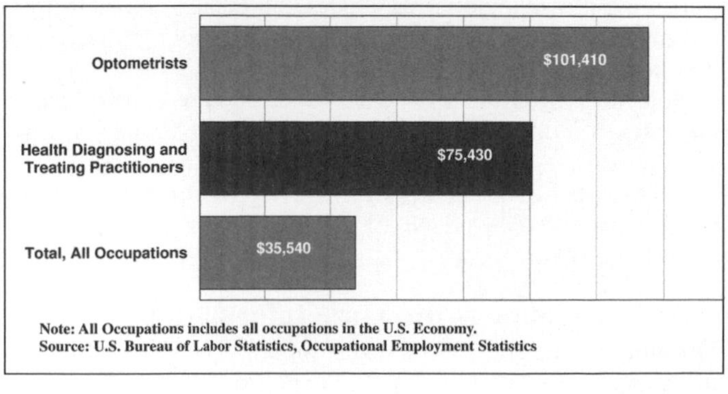

Percent Change in Employment, Projected 2014–2024

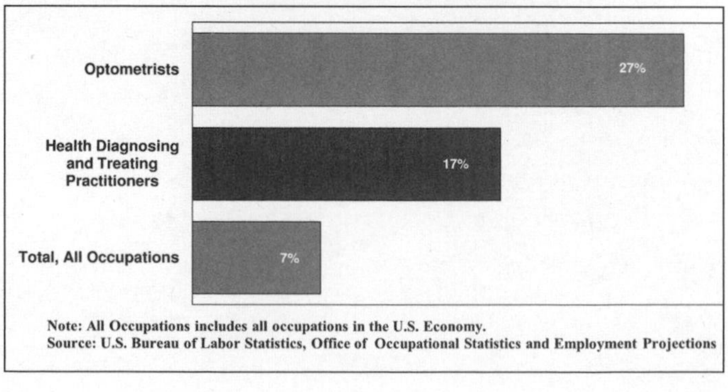

Employment Projections Data for Optometrists

Occupational Title	SOC Code	Employment, 2014	Projected Employment, 2024	Change, 2014–2024	
				Percent	Numeric
Optometrists	29-1041	40,600	51,600	27	11,000

Source: U.S. Bureau of Labor Statistics, Employment Projections Program

Optometrists also may work as postsecondary teachers, do research in optometry colleges, or work as consultants in the eye care industry.

Optometrists should not be confused with ophthalmologists or dispensing opticians. Ophthalmologists are physicians who perform eye surgery and treat eye diseases in addition to performing eye exams and prescribing eyeglasses and contact lenses. For more information on ophthalmologists, see the physicians and surgeons profile. Dispensing opticians fit and adjust eyeglasses and, in some states, fill contact lens prescriptions that an optometrist or ophthalmologist has written.

Work Environment

Optometrists held about 40,600 jobs in 2014. About 49 percent of optometrists worked in stand-alone offices of optometry. Optometrists may also work in doctors' offices and optical goods stores. About 1 in 6 optometrists were self-employed in 2014.

Work Schedules. Most optometrists work full time. Some work evenings and weekends to accommodate patients' needs.

Education/Training

Optometrists must complete a Doctor of Optometry (O.D.) degree program and obtain a license to practice in a particular state. O.D. programs take 4 years to complete, and most students have a bachelor's degree before entering such a program.

Education. Optometrists need an O.D. degree. In 2015, there were 23 accredited O.D. programs in the United States, one of which was in Puerto Rico.

Applicants to O.D. programs must have completed at least 3 years of postsecondary education. Required courses include those in biology or zoology, chemistry, physics, English, and math. Most students have a bachelor's degree with a pre-medical or biological sciences emphasis before enrolling in an O.D. program.

Applicants to O.D. programs must also take the Optometry Admission Test (OAT), a computerized exam that tests applicants in four subject areas: science, reading comprehension, physics, and quantitative reasoning.

O.D. programs take 4 years to complete. They combine classroom learning and supervised clinical experience. Coursework includes anatomy, physiology, biochemistry, optics, visual science, and the diagnosis and treatment of diseases and disorders of the visual system.

After finishing an O.D. degree, some optometrists complete a 1-year residency program to get advanced clinical training in the area in which they wish to specialize. Areas of specialization for residency programs include family practice, low vision rehabilitation, pediatric or geriatric optometry, and ocular disease, among others.

Licenses, Certifications, and Registrations. All states require optometrists to be licensed. To get a license, a prospective optometrist must have an O.D. degree from an accredited optometry school and must complete all sections of the National Board of Examiners in Optometry exam.

Some states require individuals to pass an additional clinical exam or an exam on laws relating to optometry. All states require optometrists to take continuing education classes and to renew their license periodically. The board of optometry in each state can provide information on licensing requirements.

Optometrists who wish to demonstrate an advanced level of knowledge may choose to become certified by the American Board of Optometry.

Important Qualities

Decision-making skills. Optometrists must be able to evaluate the results of a variety of diagnostic tests and decide on the best course of treatment for a patient.

Detail oriented. Optometrists must ensure that patients receive appropriate treatment and medications and that prescriptions are accurate. They must also monitor and record various pieces of information related to patient care.

Interpersonal skills. Because they spend much of their time examining patients, optometrists must be able to help their patients feel at ease. Optometrists also must be able to communicate well with other healthcare professionals.

Similar Occupations. This table shows a list of occupations with job duties that are similar to those of optometrists.

Occupations	Entry-level Education	2014 Median Pay	Projected Job Growth	Average Annual Openings
Chiropractors	Doctoral or professional degree	$66,720	17%	790
Dentists	Doctoral or professional degree	$154,640	18%	2,670
Opticians, Dispensing	High school diploma or equivalent	$34,280	24%	1,780
Physicians and Surgeons	Doctoral or professional degree	This wage is equal to or greater than $187,200.	14%	9,930
Podiatrists	Doctoral or professional degree	$120,700	14%	140
Veterinarians	Doctoral or professional degree	$87,590	9%	690

Speaking skills. Optometrists must be able to clearly explain eye care instructions to their patients, as well as answer patients' questions.

Pay

The median annual wage for optometrists was $101,410 in May 2014. The median wage is the wage at which half the workers in an occupation earned more than that amount and half earned less. The lowest 10 percent earned less than $52,270, and the highest 10 percent earned more than $187,200.

Job Outlook

Employment of optometrists is projected to grow 27 percent from 2014 to 2024, much faster than the average for all occupations.

Because vision problems tend to occur more frequently later in life, an aging population will require more optometrists. As people age, they become more susceptible to conditions that impair vision, such as cataracts and macular degeneration.

The number of people with chronic diseases, such as diabetes, has grown in recent years. Diabetes has been linked to increased rates of several eye conditions, including diabetic retinopathy, a condition that affects the blood vessels in the eye and may lead to loss of vision. More optometrists will be needed to monitor, treat, and refer individuals with chronic conditions stemming from diabetes.

In addition, nearly all health plans cover medical eye care and many cover preventive eye exams. Furthermore, the number of individuals, particularly children, who have access to vision or eye care insurance is expected to continue to increase because of federal health insurance reform. More optometrists will be needed to provide services to more patients.

Job Prospects. Because the number of optometrists is limited by the number of accredited optometry schools, licensed optometrists should expect good job prospects. Like admission to professional degree programs in other fields, admission to optometry programs is highly competitive.

Students who choose to complete a residency program gain additional experience that may improve their job prospects. Certification from the American Board of Optometry may also be viewed favorably by employers.

In addition, a large number of currently practicing optometrists are expected to retire over the coming decade, creating opportunities for new optometrists.

Contacts for More Information

For more information about optometry, visit

➤ American Optometric Association (www.aoa.org)

For more information about optometrists, including a list of accredited optometric programs, visit

➤ Association of Schools and Colleges of Optometry (www.opted.org)

For information on specific admission requirements and sources of financial aid, contact the admissions officers of individual optometry schools.

For more information about the national board exam, visit

➤ National Boards of Examiners in Optometry (www.optometry.org)

For more information about certification, visit

➤ American Board of Optometry (www.americanboardofoptometry.org)

O*NET

➤ Optometrists (29-1041.00)

Orthotists and Prosthetists

- **2014 Median Pay** .... $64,040 per year
$30.79 per hour
- **Typical Entry-Level Education** .... Master's degree
- **Work Experience in a Related Occupation** .... None
- **On-the-job Training** .... Internship/residency
- **Number of Jobs, 2014** 8,300
- **Job Outlook, 2014–24** .... 23% (Much faster than average)
- **Employment Change, 2014–24** 1,900

What Orthotists and Prosthetists Do

Orthotists and prosthetists design and fabricate medical supportive devices and measure and fit patients for them. These devices include artificial limbs (arms, hands, legs, and feet), braces, and other medical or surgical devices.

Duties. Orthotists and prosthetists typically do the following:

- Evaluate and interview patients to determine their needs
- Take measurements or impressions of the part of a patient's body that will be fitted with a brace or artificial limb
- Design and fabricate orthopedic and prosthetic devices based on physicians' prescriptions
- Select materials to be used for the orthotic or prosthetic device
- Instruct patients in how to use and care for their devices
- Adjust, repair, or replace prosthetic and orthotic devices
- Document care in patients' records

Orthotists and prosthetists may work in both orthotics and prosthetics, or they may choose to specialize in one area. Orthotists are

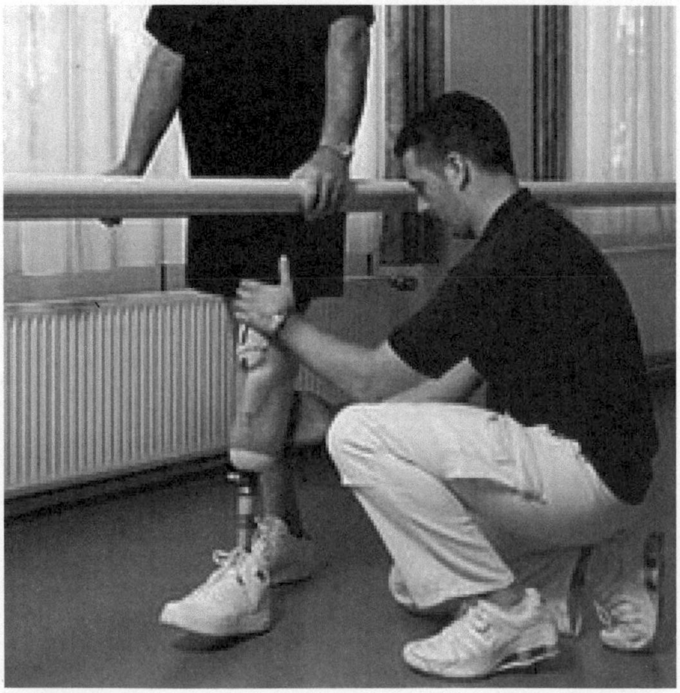

O&P professionals can work on both orthotics and prosthetics or may choose to specialize in one or the other.

Median Annual Wages, May 2014

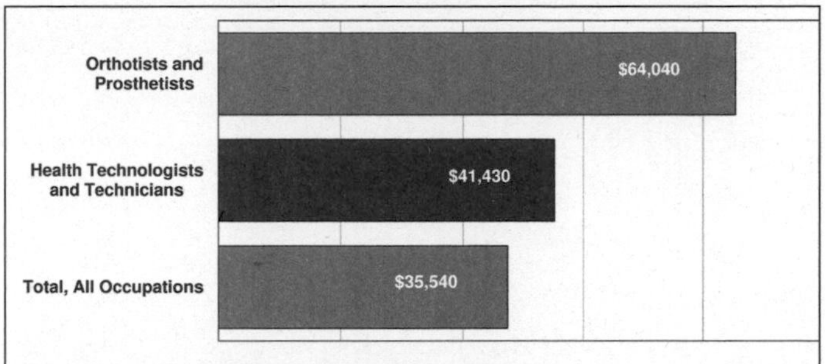

Note: All Occupations includes all occupations in the U.S. Economy.
Source: U.S. Bureau of Labor Statistics, Occupational Employment Statistics

Percent Change in Employment, Projected 2014–2024

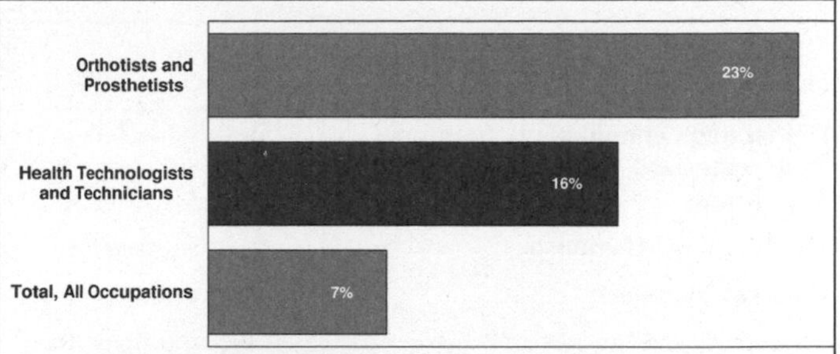

Note: All Occupations includes all occupations in the U.S. Economy.
Source: U.S. Bureau of Labor Statistics, Office of Occupational Statistics and Employment Projections

specifically trained to work with medical supportive devices, such as spinal or knee braces. Prosthetists are specifically trained to work with prostheses, such as artificial limbs and other body parts.

Some orthotists and prosthetists construct devices for their patients. Others supervise the construction of the orthotic or prosthetic devices by medical appliance technicians.

Work Environment

Orthotists and prosthetists held about 8,300 jobs in 2014. The industries that employed the most orthotists and prosthetists were as follows:

Medical equipment and supplies manufacturing	31%
Health and personal care stores	21
Ambulatory healthcare services	18
Hospitals; state, local, and private	11
Federal government, excluding postal service	8

Orthotists and prosthetists who fabricate orthotics and prosthetics may be exposed to health or safety hazards when handling certain materials, but there is little risk of injury if workers follow proper procedures, such as wearing goggles, gloves, and masks.

Work Schedules. Most orthotists and prosthetists work full time.

Education/Training

Orthotists and prosthetists need a master's degree and certification. Both orthotists and prosthetists must complete a residency before they can be certified.

Education. All orthotists and prosthetists must complete a master's degree in orthotics and prosthetics. These programs include courses in upper and lower extremity orthotics and prosthetics, spinal orthotics, and plastics and other materials used for fabrication. In addition, orthotics and prosthetics programs have a clinical component in which the student works under the direction of an orthotist or prosthetist.

Master's programs usually take 2 years to complete. Prospective students seeking a master's degree can have a bachelor's degree in any discipline if they have fulfilled prerequisite courses in science and math. Requirements vary by program.

In 2015, there were 13 orthotics and prosthetics programs accredited by the Commission on Accreditation of Allied Health Education Program (CAAHEP).

Training. Following graduation from a master's degree program, candidates must complete a residency that has been accredited by the National Commission on Orthotic and Prosthetic Education (NCOPE). Candidates typically complete a 1-year residency program in either orthotics or prosthetics. Individuals who want to become certified in both orthotics and prosthetics need to complete 1 year of residency training for each specialty or, less commonly, an 18-month residency in both orthotics and prosthetics.

Licenses, Certifications, and Registrations. Some states require orthotists and prosthetists to be licensed. States that license orthotists and prosthetists often require certification in order for them to practice, although requirements vary by state. Many orthotists and prosthetists become certified regardless of state requirements, because certification demonstrates competence.

The American Board for Certification in Orthotics, Prosthetics & Pedorthics (ABC) and the Board of Certification/Accreditation (BOC) offer certifications for orthotists and prosthetists. To earn certification, a candidate must complete a CAAHEP-accredited master's program, an NCOPE-accredited residency program, and pass a series of three exams.

Important Qualities

Communication skills. Orthotists and prosthetists must be able to communicate effectively with the technicians who often fabricate the medical devices. They must also be able to explain to patients how to use and care for the devices.

Detail oriented. Orthotists and prosthetists must be precise when recording measurements to ensure that devices are fabricated and fit properly.

Leadership skills. Orthotists and prosthetists who work in their own offices must be effective leaders. They must be able to manage a staff of other professionals in their office.

Patience. Orthotists and prosthetists may work for long periods with patients who need special attention.

Physical dexterity. Orthotists and prosthetists must be good at working with their hands. They may fabricate orthotics or prosthetics with intricate mechanical parts.

Employment Projections Data for Orthotists and Prosthetists

Occupational Title	SOC Code	Employment, 2014	Projected Employment, 2024	Change, 2014–2024 Percent	Change, 2014–2024 Numeric
Orthotists and prosthetists	29-2091	8,300	10,100	23	1,900

Source: U.S. Bureau of Labor Statistics, Employment Projections Program

Similar Occupations. This table shows a list of occupations with job duties that are similar to those of orthotists and prosthetists.

Occupations	Entry-level Education	2014 Median Pay	Projected Job Growth	Average Annual Openings
Dental and Ophthalmic Laboratory Technicians and Medical Appliance Technicians	High school diploma or equivalent	$33,430	10%	870
Occupational Therapists	Master's degree	$78,810	27%	3,040
Physical Therapists	Doctoral or professional degree	$82,390	34%	7,180
Physicians and Surgeons	Doctoral or professional degree	This wage is equal to or greater than $187,200.	14%	9,930
Respiratory Therapists	Associate's degree	$56,730	12%	1,490

Physical stamina. Orthotists and prosthetists should be comfortable performing physical tasks, such as working with shop equipment and hand tools. They may spend a lot of time bending over or crouching to examine or measure patients.

Problem-solving skills. Orthotists and prosthetists must evaluate their patients' situations and often look for creative solutions to their rehabilitation needs.

Pay

The median annual wage for orthotists and prosthetists was $64,040 in May 2014. The median wage is the wage at which half the workers in an occupation earned more than that amount and half earned less. The lowest 10 percent earned less than $35,240, and the highest 10 percent earned more than $110,690.

In May 2014, the median annual wages for orthotists and prosthetists in the top industries in which they worked were as follows:

Medical equipment and supplies manufacturing	$71,040
Health and personal care stores	68,890
Federal government, excluding postal service	65,720
Ambulatory healthcare services	59,340
Hospitals; state, local, and private	56,530

The wages for orthotists and prosthetists vary substantially depending on the industries they work in.

Job Outlook

Employment of orthotists and prosthetists is projected to grow 23 percent from 2014 to 2024, much faster than the average for all occupations. However, because it is a small occupation, the fast growth will result in only about 1,900 new jobs over the 10-year period.

The large aging baby-boom population will create a need for orthotists and prosthetists, because both diabetes and cardiovascular disease, which are two leading causes of limb loss, are more common among older people. In addition, older people will continue to need other devices designed and fitted by orthotists and prosthetists, such as braces and orthopedic footwear.

Advances in technology are allowing more people to survive traumatic events. Patients with traumatic injuries, such as some veterans, will continue to need orthotists and prosthetists to create devices that allow the patients to regain or improve mobility and functionality.

Moreover, the number of individuals who have access to health insurance is expected to continue to increase because of federal health insurance reform. Patients who were previously uninsured or found treatment to be cost prohibitive may opt for new or replacement devices, such as braces or artificial limbs.

Job Prospects. Job prospects should be best for orthotists and prosthetists with professional certification. Although it is not required in all states, certification shows a specific level of educational knowledge and training that employers may prefer.

Contacts for More Information

For more information about orthotists and prosthetists, visit

➤ American Academy of Orthotists & Prosthetists (www.oandp.org)

For a list of accredited programs for orthotists and prosthetists, visit

➤ Commission on Accreditation of Allied Health Education Programs (www.caahep.org)

For a list of accredited residency programs for orthotists and prosthetists, visit

➤ National Commission on Orthotic and Prosthetic Education (www.ncope.org)

For more information about certification for orthotists and prosthetists, visit

➤ American Board for Certification in Orthotics, Prosthetics & Pedorthics (www.abcop.org/Pages/default.aspx)

➤ Board of Certification/Accreditation (www.bocusa.org)

O*NET

➤ Orthotists and Prosthetists (29-2091.00)

Personal Care Aides

- **2014 Median Pay** .... $20,440 per year; $9.83 per hour
- **Typical Entry-Level Education** .... No formal educational credential
- **Work Experience in a Related Occupation** .... None
- **On-the-job Training** .... Short-term on-the-job training
- **Number of Jobs, 2014** 1,768,400
- **Job Outlook, 2014–24** .... 26% (Much faster than average)
- **Employment Change, 2014–24** 458,100

Personal care aides may prepare and serve meals for those who have difficulty doing so for themselves.

What Personal Care Aides Do

Personal care aides help clients with self-care and everyday tasks. They also provide social supports and assistance that enable clients to participate in their communities.

Duties. Personal care aides typically do the following:

- Care for and assist clients with cognitive impairments, such as Alzheimer's or mental illness
- Engage clients by talking to or playing games with them, or by taking them for walks
- Help clients with hygiene-related tasks, such as bathing, brushing teeth, and going to the bathroom
- Transfer clients to and from a bed or a wheelchair
- Complete housekeeping tasks, such as changing bed linens, washing dishes, and cleaning living areas
- Help prepare and plan meals
- Assist with organizing a client's schedule and schedule appointments
- Arrange transportation to and from doctors' offices or the store
- Help clients pay bills or manage money
- Shop for personal items and groceries
- Assist clients in going to work and participating in their communities

Personal care aides—also called *caregivers* and *personal attendants*—help clients with self-care and daily activities. Personal care aides perform tasks that are similar to those of home health aides. However, personal care aides cannot provide any medical services, whereas home health aides may provide basic medical services.

Direct support professionals work with people who have developmental or intellectual disabilities. They may help create a behavior plan and teach self-care skills, such as doing laundry or cooking meals. They may also provide other personal assistance services.

Work Environment

Personal care aides held about 1.8 million jobs in 2014. The industries that employed the most personal care aides were as follows:

Services for the elderly and persons with disabilities	43%
Home healthcare services	17
Residential intellectual and developmental disability, mental health, and substance abuse facilities	9
Continuing care retirement communities and assisted living facilities for the elderly	6
Vocational rehabilitation services	3

Some are hired directly by the client or the client's family, but many are employed by organizations or agencies that provide in-home services or support.

Some aides work in many facilities or homes during the day, whereas others may work with a single client. Personal care aides may help people in hospice and day service programs or may help people with disabilities go to work and stay engaged in their communities.

Work Schedules. Most personal care aides worked full time in 2014, although 2 out of 5 worked part time. They may be required to work evening and weekend hours to attend to their clients' needs.

Injuries and Illnesses. Personal care aides have a higher rate of injuries and illnesses than the national average. Work as an aide can be physically and emotionally demanding. Aides may become injured when lifting clients or transferring them into and out of beds or wheelchairs. Aides often work with clients who have mental health issues or cognitive impairments and who may become difficult or violent at times. There are also dangers when working with clients who have communicable diseases or infections. Personal care aides can guard against many injuries and illnesses by following proper procedures.

Education/Training

There are no formal education requirements for personal care aides, but most aides have a high school diploma.

Median Annual Wages, May 2014

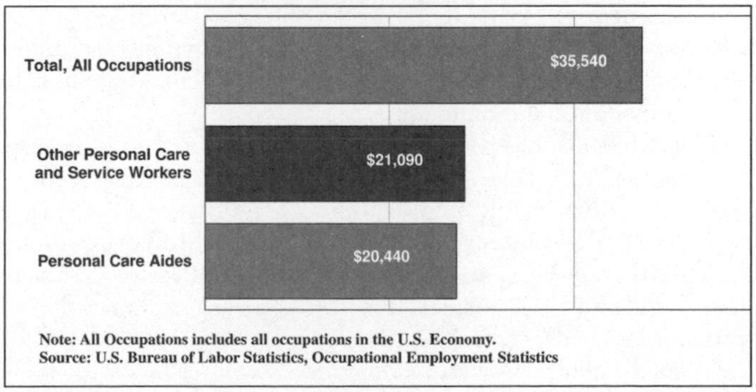

Percent Change in Employment, Projected 2014–2024

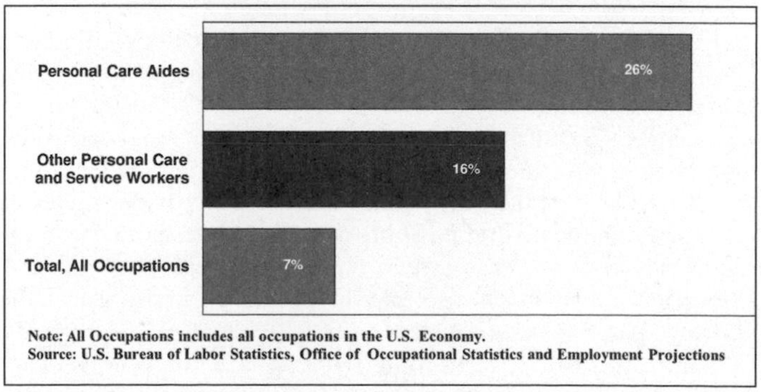

Employment Projections Data for Personal Care Aides

Occupational Title	SOC Code	Employment, 2014	Projected Employment, 2024	Change, 2014–2024 Percent	Change, 2014–2024 Numeric
Personal care aides	39-9021	1,768,400	2,226,500	26	458,100

Source: U.S. Bureau of Labor Statistics, Employment Projections Program

Similar Occupations. This table shows a list of occupations with job duties that are similar to those of personal care aides.

Occupations	Entry-level Education	2014 Median Pay	Projected Job Growth	Average Annual Openings
Childcare Workers	High school diploma or equivalent	$19,730	5%	6,930
Home Health Aides	No formal educational credential	$21,380	38%	34,840
Licensed Practical and Licensed Vocational Nurses	Postsecondary nondegree award	$42,490	16%	11,730
Medical Assistants	Postsecondary nondegree award	$29,960	23%	13,890
Nursing Assistants and Orderlies	See Education/Training	$25,090	17%	26,780
Occupational Therapy Assistants and Aides	See Education/Training	$52,300	40%	1,680
Physical Therapist Assistants and Aides	See Education/Training	$41,640	40%	5,140
Social and Human Service Assistants	High school diploma or equivalent	$29,790	11%	4,420

Education. Although there are no formal education requirements for personal care aides, employers may prefer candidates with a high school diploma.

Training. Aides may be trained on the job by registered nurses, other personal care aides, or their direct employer. They are trained in specific tasks, such as how to work with a client who has a cognitive impairment and how to assist a client in preparing meals.

Most employers require aides to have training or certification in first aid and cardiopulmonary resuscitation (CPR).

Important Qualities

Detail oriented. Personal care aides must follow specific rules and protocols to help take care of clients. They must pay close attention to a client's medical condition, quickly noting any changes that may require assistance from medical personnel.

Integrity. Personal care aides should make clients feel comfortable when the aides tend to personal activities, such as helping a client bathe. In addition, personal care aides must be dependable and trustworthy so that clients and their families can rely on them.

Interpersonal skills. Sometimes clients are in extreme pain or distress, and aides must be sensitive to their emotions. Aides must be compassionate, and they must enjoy helping people.

Physical stamina. Personal care aides should be comfortable performing physical tasks. They often need to lift or turn clients who have a disability.

Licenses, Certifications, and Registrations. Personal care aides may be required to complete a formal training program depending on the state where they work, and state laws vary widely in terms of the requirements that must be met. Some states and organizations may conduct background checks on prospective aides. A competency evaluation also may be required to ensure that the aide can perform certain tasks.

There are no federal training requirements for personal care aides. For specific state requirements, contact the state's health board.

Pay

The median annual wage for personal care aides was $20,440 in May 2014. The median wage is the wage at which half the workers in an occupation earned more than that amount and half earned less. The lowest 10 percent earned less than $16,580, and the highest 10 percent earned more than $27,910.

In May 2014, the median annual wages for personal care aides in the top industries in which they worked were as follows:

Residential intellectual and developmental disability, mental health, and substance abuse facilities	$21,590
Vocational rehabilitation services	21,100
Continuing care retirement communities and assisted living facilities for the elderly	21,040
Services for the elderly and persons with disabilities	20,660
Home healthcare services	18,670

Job Outlook

Employment of personal care aides is projected to grow 26 percent from 2014 to 2024, much faster than the average for all occupations.

As the baby-boom population ages, there will be an increase in the number of clients requiring assistance. As clients age, they often develop health or mobility problems and require assistance with daily tasks. The demand for the services that personal care aides provide will continue to rise.

Elderly clients and people with disabilities who do not require medical care are increasingly choosing home care instead of entering nursing homes or hospitals. Home care is often a less expensive and more comfortable experience for the client. Moreover, studies have found that home care is frequently more effective than care in a nursing home or hospital. Because personal care aides do not provide any medical services, they are a less expensive option for families or clients who seek someone to help clients with daily activities or perform light household chores.

Job Prospects. Job prospects for personal care aides are expected to be excellent. The occupation is large and is projected to grow quickly, adding many jobs. In addition, the low pay and high emotional demands cause many workers to leave the occupation, and they will have to be replaced.

Contacts for More Information

For more information about personal care aides, visit
➤ Paraprofessional Healthcare Institute (http://phinational.org)

O*NET

➤ Personal Care Aides (39-9021.00)

Pharmacists

- **2014 Median Pay** .... $120,950 per year
  $58.15 per hour
- **Typical Entry-Level Education** .... Doctoral or professional degree
- **Work Experience in a Related Occupation** .... None
- **On-the-job Training** .... None
- **Number of Jobs, 2014** 297,100
- **Job Outlook, 2014–24** .... 3% (Slower than average)
- **Employment Change, 2014–24** 9,100

What Pharmacists Do

Pharmacists dispense prescription medications to patients and offer expertise in the safe use of prescriptions. They also may conduct health and wellness screenings, provide immunizations, oversee the medications given to patients, and provide advice on healthy lifestyles.

Duties. Pharmacists typically do the following:

- Fill prescriptions, verifying instructions from physicians on the proper amounts of medication to give to patients
- Check whether prescriptions will interact negatively with other drugs that a patient is taking or any medical conditions the patient has
- Instruct patients on how and when to take a prescribed medicine and inform them about potential side effects they may experience from taking the medicine
- Give flu shots and, in most states, other vaccinations
- Advise patients about general health topics, such as diet, exercise, and managing stress, and on other issues, such as what equipment or supplies would be best to treat a health problem
- Complete insurance forms and work with insurance companies to ensure that patients get the medicines they need
- Oversee the work of pharmacy technicians and pharmacists in training (interns)
- Keep records and do other administrative tasks
- Teach other healthcare practitioners about proper medication therapies for patients

Some pharmacists who own their pharmacy or manage a chain pharmacy spend time on business activities, such as inventory management. Pharmacists also must take continuing education courses throughout their career to keep up with the latest advances in pharmacological science.

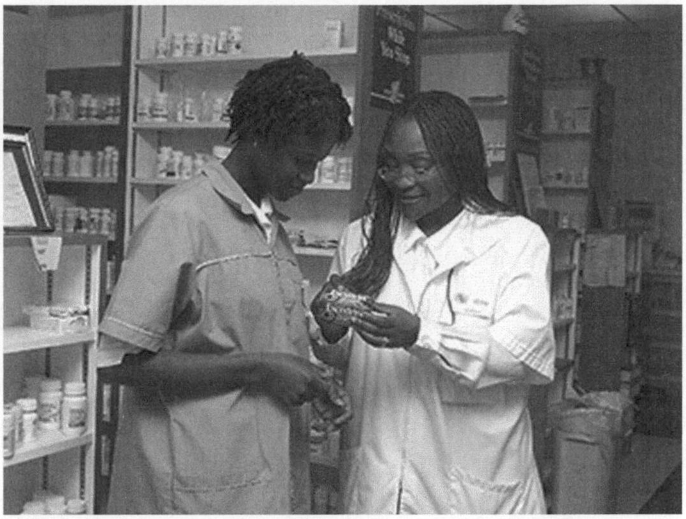

Pharmacists provide prescription medications to patients in hospitals, grocery stores, and a variety of other settings.

With most drugs, pharmacists use standard dosages from pharmaceutical companies. However, some pharmacists create customized medications by mixing ingredients themselves, a process known as compounding.

The following are examples of types of pharmacists:

Community pharmacists work in retail stores such as chain drug stores or independently owned pharmacies. They dispense medications to patients and answer any questions that patients may have about prescriptions, over-the-counter medications, or any health concerns that the patient may have. They also may provide some primary care services such as giving flu shots.

Clinical pharmacists work in hospitals, clinics, and other healthcare settings. They spend little time dispensing prescriptions. Instead, they are involved in direct patient care. Clinical pharmacists may go on rounds in a hospital with a physician or healthcare team. They recommend medications to give to patients and oversee the dosage and timing of the delivery of those medications. They also may conduct some medical tests and offer advice to patients. For example, pharmacists working in a diabetes clinic may counsel patients on how and when to take medications, suggest healthy food choices, and monitor patients' blood sugar.

Consultant pharmacists advise healthcare facilities or insurance providers on patient medication use or improving pharmacy services. They also may give advice directly to patients, such as helping seniors manage their prescriptions.

Pharmaceutical industry pharmacists work in areas such as marketing, sales, or research and development. They may design or conduct clinical drug trials and help to develop new drugs. They may also help to establish safety regulations and ensure quality control for drugs.

Some pharmacists work as college professors. They may teach pharmacy students or conduct research. For more information, see the profile on postsecondary teachers.

Work Environment

Pharmacists held about 297,100 jobs in 2014. The industries that employed the most pharmacists were as follows:

Pharmacies and drug stores	42%
General medical and surgical hospitals; private	19
Grocery stores	8
Department stores	4

Median Annual Wages, May 2014

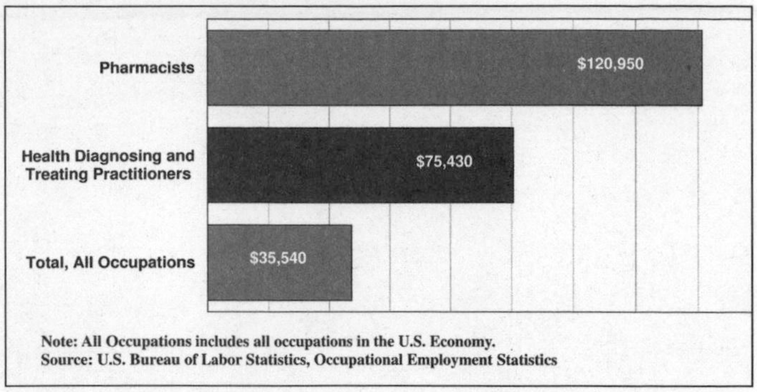

Percent Change in Employment, Projected 2014–2024

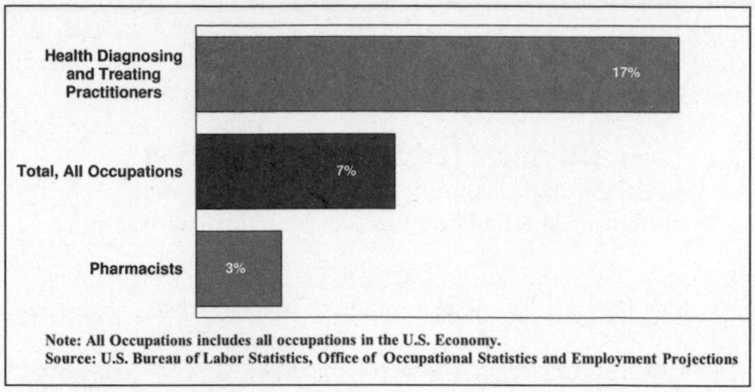

Pharmacists work in pharmacies, including those in grocery and drug stores. They also work in hospitals and other healthcare facilities. Some pharmacists work for the government and the military. In most settings, they spend much of the workday on their feet.

Work Schedules. Most pharmacists work full time, although about 1 in 5 worked part time in 2014. Because many pharmacies are open at all hours, some pharmacists work nights and weekends.

Education/Training

Pharmacists must have a Doctor of Pharmacy (Pharm.D.) degree from an accredited pharmacy program. They must also be licensed, which requires passing licensure and law exams.

Education. Prospective pharmacists are required to have a Doctor of Pharmacy (Pharm.D.) degree, a postgraduate professional degree. In July 2014, there were 130 Doctor of Pharmacy programs fully accredited by the Accreditation Council for Pharmacy Education (ACPE).

Admissions requirements vary by program; however, all Doctor of Pharmacy programs require applicants to take postsecondary courses such as chemistry, biology, and anatomy. Most programs require at least 2 years of undergraduate study, although some require a bachelor's degree. Most programs also require applicants to take the Pharmacy College Admissions Test (PCAT).

Pharm.D. programs usually take 4 years to finish, although some programs offer a 3-year option. Some schools admit high school graduates into a 6-year program. A Pharm.D. program includes courses in chemistry, pharmacology, and medical ethics. Students also complete supervised work experiences, sometimes referred to as internships, in different settings such as hospitals and retail pharmacies.

Some pharmacists who own their own pharmacy may choose to get a master's degree in business administration (MBA) in addition to their Doctor of Pharmacy degree. Others may get a degree in public health.

Training. Following graduation from a Pharm.D. program, pharmacists seeking an advanced position, such as a clinical pharmacy or research job, may need to complete a 1- to 2-year residency. Pharmacists who choose to complete the 2-year residency option receive additional training in a specialty area such as internal medicine or geriatric care.

Licenses, Certifications, and Registrations. All states license pharmacists. After they finish the Pharm.D. program, prospective pharmacists must pass two exams to get a license. The North American Pharmacist Licensure Exam (NAPLEX) tests pharmacy skills and knowledge. The Multistate Pharmacy Jurisprudence Exam (MPJE) or a state-specific test on pharmacy law is also required. Applicants also must complete a number of hours as an intern, which varies by state.

Pharmacists who administer vaccinations and immunizations need to be certified in most states. States typically use the American Pharmacists Association's Pharmacy-Based Immunization Delivery program as a qualification for certification.

Pharmacists also may choose to earn a certification to show their advanced level of knowledge in a certain area. For instance, a pharmacist may become a Certified Diabetes Educator, a qualification offered by the National Certification Board for Diabetes Educators, or earn certification in a specialty area, such as nutrition or oncology, from the Board of Pharmacy Specialties. Certifications from both organizations require varying degrees of work experience, as well as passing an exam and paying a fee.

Important Qualities

Analytical skills. Pharmacists must provide safe medications efficiently. To do this, they must be able to evaluate a patient's needs and the prescriber's orders, and have extensive knowledge of the effects and appropriate circumstances for giving out a specific medication.

Communication skills. Pharmacists frequently offer advice to patients. They might need to explain how to take a medicine, for example, and what its side effects are. They also need to offer clear direction to pharmacy technicians and interns.

Computer skills. Pharmacists need computer skills to use any electronic health record (EHR) systems that their organization has adopted.

Detail oriented. Pharmacists are responsible for ensuring the accuracy of the prescriptions they fill. They must be able to find the information that they need to make decisions about what

Employment Projections Data for Pharmacists

Occupational Title	SOC Code	Employment, 2014	Projected Employment, 2024	Change, 2014–2024 Percent	Change, 2014–2024 Numeric
Pharmacists	29-1051	297,100	306,200	3	9,100

Source: U.S. Bureau of Labor Statistics, Employment Projections Program

Similar Occupations. This table shows a list of occupations with job duties that are similar to those of pharmacists.

Occupations	Entry-level Education	2014 Median Pay	Projected Job Growth	Average Annual Openings
Biochemists and Biophysicists	Doctoral or professional degree	$84,940	8%	280
Medical Scientists	Doctoral or professional degree	$79,930	8%	900
Pharmacy Technicians	High school diploma or equivalent	$29,810	9%	3,470
Physicians and Surgeons	Doctoral or professional degree	This wage is equal to or greater than $187,200.	14%	9,930
Registered Nurses	Bachelor's degree	$66,640	16%	43,930

medications are appropriate for each patient, because improper use of medication can pose serious health risks.

Managerial skills. Pharmacists—particularly those who run a retail pharmacy—must have good managerial skills, including the ability to manage inventory and oversee a staff.

Pay

The median annual wage for pharmacists was $120,950 in May 2014. The median wage is the wage at which half the workers in an occupation earned more than that amount and half earned less. The lowest 10 percent earned less than $89,320, and the highest 10 percent earned more than $150,550.

In May 2014, the median annual wages for pharmacists in the top industries in which they worked were as follows:

Department stores $126,310
Grocery stores.. 121,740
Pharmacies and drug stores 121,190
General medical and surgical hospitals; private 118,980

Job Outlook

Employment of pharmacists is projected to grow 3 percent from 2014 to 2024, slower than the average for all occupations. Several factors are likely to contribute to this increase.

Demand is projected to increase for pharmacists in a variety of healthcare settings, including hospitals and clinics. These facilities will need more pharmacists to oversee the medications given to patients and to provide patient care, performing tasks such as testing a patient's blood sugar or cholesterol.

The large baby-boom generation is aging, and older people typically use more prescription medicines than younger people. Higher rates of chronic diseases such as diabetes among all age groups will also lead to demand for prescription medications. In addition, scientific advances will lead to new drug products.

The number of individuals who have access to health insurance is expected to continue to increase because of federal health insurance reform. As more people have access to insurance coverage, more pharmacists will be needed to fill their prescriptions and to consult with patients about their medications.

Employment of pharmacists in traditional retail settings is projected to decline slightly as mail order and online pharmacy sales increase.

Job Prospects. The number of pharmacy schools has grown in recent years, creating more pharmacy school graduates and therefore more competition for jobs. Students who choose to complete a residency program gain additional experience that may improve their job prospects. Certification from the Board of Pharmacy Specialties or as a Certified Diabetes Educator also may be viewed favorably by employers.

Contacts for More Information

For more information about pharmacists, visit

- American Society of Health-System Pharmacists (www.ashp.org)
- National Association of Chain Drug Stores (www.nacds.org)
- American Pharmacists Association (www.pharmacist.com)
- American College of Clinical Pharmacy (www.accp.com)

For information on pharmacy as a career, preprofessional and professional requirements, programs offered by colleges of pharmacy, and student financial aid, visit

- American Association of Colleges of Pharmacy (www.aacp.org/Pages/Default.aspx)

For more information about accredited Doctor of Pharmacy programs, visit

- Accreditation Council for Pharmacy Education (www.acpe-accredit.org)

For more information about certification options, visit

- Board of Pharmacy Specialties (www.bpsweb.org)
- National Certification Board for Diabetes Educators (www.ncbde.org)

O*NET

- Pharmacists (29-1051.00)

Pharmacy Technicians

- **2014 Median Pay** .... $29,810 per year
  $14.33 per hour
- **Typical Entry-Level Education** .... High school diploma or equivalent
- **Work Experience in a Related Occupation**.............. None
- **On-the-job Training** .... Moderate-term on-the-job training
- **Number of Jobs, 2014** 372,500
- **Job Outlook, 2014–24** .... 9% (Faster than average)
- **Employment Change, 2014–24** 34,700

What Pharmacy Technicians Do

Pharmacy technicians help pharmacists dispense prescription medication to customers or health professionals. They work in retail pharmacies and hospitals.

Duties. Pharmacy technicians typically do the following:

Pharmacy technicians fill prescriptions and check inventory.

- Collect information needed to fill a prescription from customers or health professionals
- Measure amounts of medication for prescriptions
- Package and label prescriptions
- Organize inventory and alert pharmacists to any shortages of medications or supplies
- Accept payment for prescriptions and process insurance claims
- Enter customer or patient information, including any prescriptions taken, into a computer system
- Answer phone calls from customers
- Arrange for customers to speak with pharmacists if customers have questions about medications or health matters

Pharmacy technicians work under the supervision of pharmacists, who must review prescriptions before they are given to patients. In most states, technicians can compound or mix some medications and call physicians for prescription refill authorizations. Technicians also may need to operate automated dispensing equipment when filling prescription orders.

Pharmacy technicians working in hospitals and other medical facilities prepare a greater variety of medications, such as intravenous medications. They may make rounds in the hospital, giving medications to patients.

Work Environment

Pharmacy technicians held about 372,500 jobs in 2014. The industries that employed the most pharmacy technicians were as follows:

Pharmacies and drug stores	52%
General medical and surgical hospitals; private	13
Other general merchandise stores	7
Grocery stores	7
Department stores	4

Pharmacy technicians work primarily in pharmacies, including those found in grocery and drug stores. Some technicians work in hospitals or other healthcare facilities. Pharmacy technicians spend most of the workday on their feet.

Work Schedules. Most pharmacy technicians work full time. Pharmacies may be open at all hours. Therefore, pharmacy technicians may have to work nights or weekends.

Education/Training

Becoming a pharmacy technician usually requires earning a high school diploma or the equivalent. Pharmacy technicians typically learn through on-the-job training, or they may complete a postsecondary education program. Most states regulate pharmacy technicians, which is a process that may require passing an exam or completing a formal education or training program.

Education and Training. Many pharmacy technicians learn how to perform their duties through on-the-job training. These programs vary in length and subject matter according to the employer's requirements.

Other pharmacy technicians enter the occupation after completing postsecondary education programs in pharmacy technology. These programs are usually offered by vocational schools or community colleges. Most programs award a certificate after 1 year or less, although some programs last longer and lead to an associate's degree. They cover a variety of subjects, such as arithmetic used in pharmacies, recordkeeping, ways of dispensing medications, and pharmacy law and ethics. Technicians also learn the names, uses, and doses of medications. Most programs also include clinical experience opportunities, in which students gain hands-on experience in a pharmacy.

The American Society of Health-System Pharmacists (ASHP) accredits pharmacy technician programs that include at least 600 hours of instruction over a minimum of 15 weeks. In 2015, there were 286 fully accredited programs, including a few in retail drugstore chains.

Licenses, Certifications, and Registrations. Most states regulate pharmacy technicians in some way. Consult state Boards of Pharmacy for particular regulations. Requirements for pharmacy technicians in the states that regulate them typically include some or all of the following:

- High school diploma or GED
- Formal education or training program

Median Annual Wages, May 2014

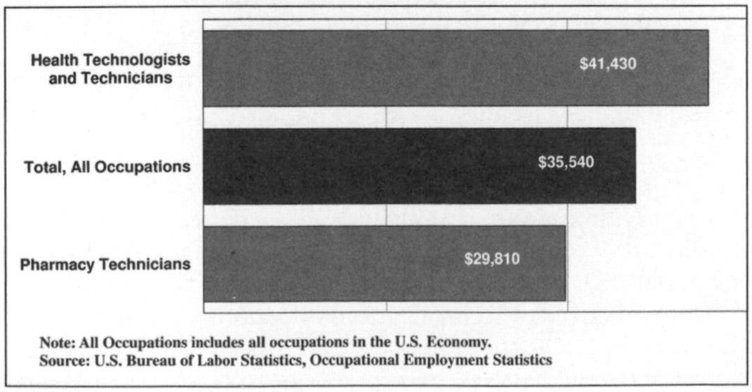

Percent Change in Employment, Projected 2014–2024

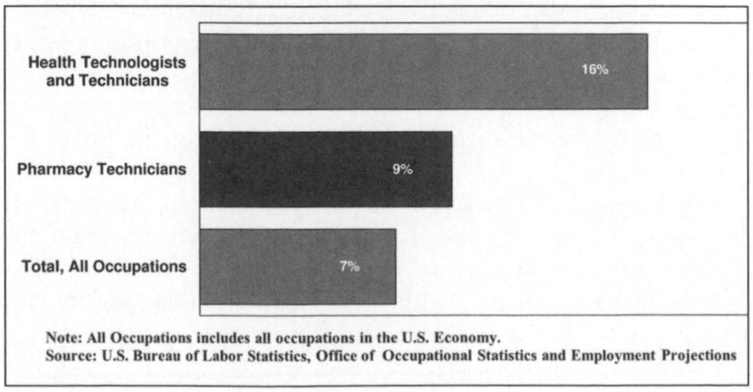

Employment Projections Data for Pharmacy Technicians

Occupational Title	SOC Code	Employment, 2014	Projected Employment, 2024	Change, 2014–2024 Percent	Change, 2014–2024 Numeric
Pharmacy technicians	29-2052	372,500	407,200	9	34,700

Source: U.S. Bureau of Labor Statistics, Employment Projections Program

Similar Occupations. This table shows a list of occupations with job duties that are similar to those of pharmacy technicians.

Occupations	Entry-level Education	2014 Median Pay	Projected Job Growth	Average Annual Openings
Dental Assistants	Postsecondary nondegree award	$35,390	18%	5,860
Medical Assistants	Postsecondary nondegree award	$29,960	23%	13,890
Medical Records and Health Information Technicians	Postsecondary nondegree award	$35,900	15%	2,900
Medical Transcriptionists	Postsecondary nondegree award	$34,750	-3%	-220
Pharmacists	Doctoral or professional degree	$120,950	3%	910

- Exam
- Fees
- Continuing education
- Criminal background check

Some states and employers require pharmacy technicians to be certified. Even where it is not required, certification may make it easier to get a job. Many employers will pay for their pharmacy technicians to take the certification exam.

Two organizations offer certification. The Pharmacy Technician Certification Board (PTCB) certification requires a high school diploma and the passing of an exam. Applicants for the National Healthcareer Association (NHA) certification must be at least 18 years old, have a high school diploma, and have completed a training program or have 1 year of work experience. Technicians must recertify every 2 years by completing 20 hours of continuing education courses.

Important Qualities

Customer-service skills. Pharmacy technicians spend much of their time interacting with customers, so being helpful and polite is required of pharmacy technicians in a retail setting.

Detail oriented. Serious health problems can result from mistakes in filling prescriptions. Although the pharmacist is responsible for ensuring the safety of all medications dispensed, pharmacy technicians should pay attention to detail so that complications are avoided.

Listening skills. Pharmacy technicians must communicate clearly with pharmacists and doctors when taking prescription orders. When speaking with customers, technicians must listen carefully to understand customers' needs and determine if they need to speak with a pharmacist.

Math skills. Pharmacy technicians need to have an understanding of the math concepts used in pharmacies when counting pills and compounding medications.

Organizational skills. Working as a pharmacy technician involves balancing a variety of responsibilities. Pharmacy technicians need good organizational skills to complete the work delegated by pharmacists while at the same time providing service to customers or patients.

Pay

The median annual wage for pharmacy technicians was $29,810 in May 2014. The median wage is the wage at which half the workers in an occupation earned more than that amount and half earned less. The lowest 10 percent earned less than $20,730, and the highest 10 percent earned more than $43,900.

In May 2014, the median annual wages for pharmacy technicians in the top industries in which they worked were as follows:

General medical and surgical hospitals; private	$34,640
Grocery stores	28,550
Other general merchandise stores	28,400
Department stores	28,150
Pharmacies and drug stores	28,080

Job Outlook

Employment of pharmacy technicians is projected to grow 9 percent from 2014 to 2024, faster than the average for all occupations. Several factors will lead to increased demand for prescription medications.

The population is aging, and older people typically use more prescription medicines than younger people. Higher rates of chronic diseases such as diabetes among all age groups also will lead to increased demand for prescription medications. Advances in pharmaceutical research will allow for more prescription medications to be used to fight diseases.

The number of individuals who have health insurance is expected to continue to increase because of federal health insurance reform. As more people have access to insurance coverage, more pharmacy technicians will be needed to handle their prescriptions.

In addition, pharmacy technicians may be needed to take on a greater role in pharmacy operations because pharmacists are increasingly performing more patient care activities such as giving flu shots. Technicians will need to perform tasks such as collecting patient information, preparing more types of medications, and verifying the work of other technicians, tasks formerly done by pharmacists.

Contacts for More Information

For more information about accredited pharmacy technician programs, visit

➤ American Society of Health-System Pharmacists (www.ashp.org)

For more information about state licensure laws, contact individual state Boards of Pharmacy, or visit

➤ National Association of Boards of Pharmacy (www.nabp.net)

For more information about certification, visit

➤ Pharmacy Technician Certification Board (www.ptcb.org)

➤ National Healthcareer Association (www.nhanow.com/home.aspx)

O*NET

➤ Pharmacy Technicians (29-2052.00)

Phlebotomists

- **2014 Median Pay** .... $30,670 per year $14.74 per hour
- **Typical Entry-Level Education** .... Postsecondary nondegree award
- **Work Experience in a Related Occupation**.............. None
- **On-the-job Training** .... None
- **Number of Jobs, 2014** 112,700
- **Job Outlook, 2014–24**......25% (Much faster than average)
- **Employment Change, 2014–24** 28,100

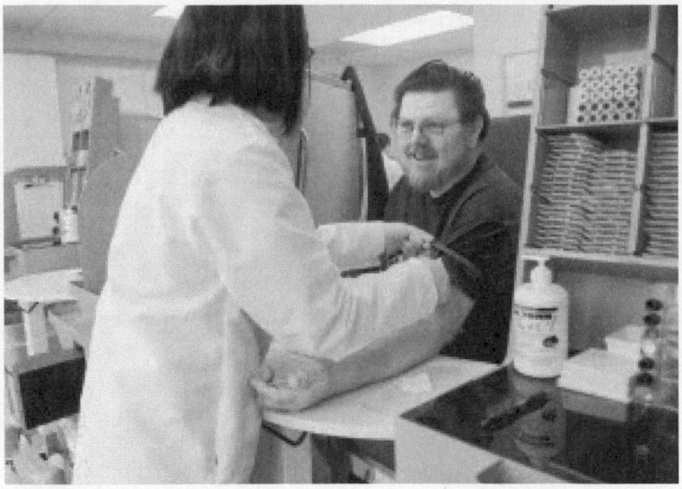

Phlebotomists draw blood for tests, transfusions, donations, or research.

What Phlebotomists Do

Phlebotomists draw blood for tests, transfusions, research, or blood donations. Some of them explain their work to patients and provide assistance if patients have adverse reactions after their blood is drawn.

Duties. Phlebotomists typically do the following:

- Draw blood from patients and blood donors
- Talk with patients and donors to help them feel less nervous about having their blood drawn
- Verify a patient's or donor's identity to ensure proper labeling of the blood
- Label the drawn blood for testing or processing
- Enter patient information into a database
- Assemble and maintain medical instruments such as needles, test tubes, and blood vials

Phlebotomists primarily draw blood, which is then used for different kinds of medical laboratory testing. In medical and diagnostic laboratories, patient interaction is often only with the phlebotomist. Because all blood samples look the same, phlebotomists must identify and label the sample they have drawn and enter it into a database. Some phlebotomists draw blood for other purposes, such as at blood drives where people donate blood. In order to avoid causing infection or other complications, phlebotomists must keep their work area and instruments clean and sanitary.

Work Environment

Phlebotomists held about 112,700 jobs in 2014. The industries that employed the most phlebotomists were as follows:

Hospitals; state, local, and private	38%
Medical and diagnostic laboratories	28
Other ambulatory healthcare services	18
Offices of physicians	9

Phlebotomists work mainly in hospitals, medical and diagnostic laboratories, blood donor centers, and doctors' offices. Phlebotomists who collect blood donations sometimes travel to different offices and sites in order to set up mobile donation centers.

Work Schedules. Most phlebotomists work full time. Some phlebotomists, particularly those who work in hospitals and labs, may need to work nights, weekends, and holidays.

Median Annual Wages, May 2014

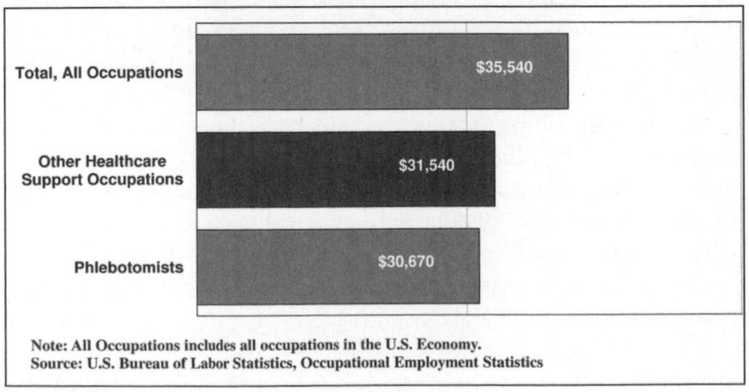

Percent Change in Employment, Projected 2014–2024

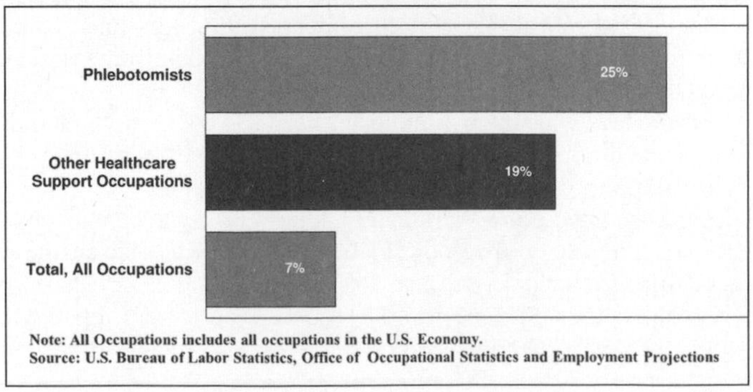

Employment Projections Data for Phlebotomists

Occupational Title	SOC Code	Employment, 2014	Projected Employment, 2024	Change, 2014–2024 Percent	Change, 2014–2024 Numeric
Phlebotomists	31-9097	112,700	140,800	25	28,100

Source: U.S. Bureau of Labor Statistics, Employment Projections Program

Similar Occupations. This table shows a list of occupations with job duties that are similar to those of phlebotomists.

Occupations	Entry-level Education	2014 Median Pay	Projected Job Growth	Average Annual Openings
Dental Assistants	Postsecondary nondegree award	$35,390	18%	5,860
Medical and Clinical Laboratory Technologists and Technicians	See Education/Training	$49,310	16%	5,210
Medical Assistants	Postsecondary nondegree award	$29,960	23%	13,890
Medical Records and Health Information Technicians	Postsecondary nondegree award	$35,900	15%	2,900
Medical Transcriptionists	Postsecondary nondegree award	$34,750	-3%	-220
Veterinary Assistants and Laboratory Animal Caretakers	High school diploma or equivalent	$23,790	9%	660
Veterinary Technologists and Technicians	Associate's degree	$31,070	19%	1,790

Education/Training

Phlebotomists typically enter the occupation with a postsecondary nondegree award from a phlebotomy program. Almost all employers look for phlebotomists who have earned professional certification.

Education and Training. Phlebotomists typically enter the occupation with a postsecondary nondegree award from a phlebotomy program. Programs are available from community colleges, vocational schools, or technical schools. These programs usually take less than 1 year to complete and lead to a certificate or diploma. Programs have classroom sessions and laboratory work and include instruction in anatomy, physiology, and medical terminology. Phlebotomists also learn specific procedures on how to identify, label, and track blood samples.

Many phlebotomists enter the occupation with a high school diploma and are trained to be a phlebotomist on the job.

Licenses, Certifications, and Registrations. Almost all employers prefer to hire phlebotomists who have earned professional certification.

Several organizations offer certifications for phlebotomists. The National Center for Competency Testing (NCCT), National Healthcareer Association (NHA), the American Society for Clinical Pathology (ASCP), and the American Medical Technologists (AMT) offer Phlebotomy Technician certifications.

Candidates for certification typically need some classroom education, as well as some clinical experience. Certification testing usually includes a written exam and may include practical components, such as drawing blood. Requirements vary by certifying organization. California, Louisiana, Nevada, and Washington require their phlebotomists to be certified.

Important Qualities

Compassion. Some patients or clients are afraid of having their blood drawn, so phlebotomists should be caring in performing their duties.

Detail oriented. Phlebotomists must draw the correct vials of blood for the tests ordered, track vials of blood, and enter data into a database. Attention to detail is necessary; otherwise, the specimens may be misplaced or lost, or a patient may be injured.

Dexterity. Phlebotomists work with their hands, and they must be able to use their equipment efficiently and properly.

Hand-eye coordination. Phlebotomists draw blood from many patients, and they must perform their duties successfully on the first attempt, or their patients will experience discomfort.

Pay

The median annual wage for phlebotomists was $30,670 in May 2014. The median wage is the wage at which half the workers in an occupation earned more than that amount and half earned less. The lowest 10 percent earned less than $22,150, and the highest 10 percent earned more than $43,800.

In May 2014, the median annual wages for phlebotomists in the top industries in which they worked were as follows:

Medical and diagnostic laboratories	$32,240
Other ambulatory healthcare services	30,080
Offices of physicians	30,020
Hospitals; state, local, and private	29,820

Job Outlook

Employment of phlebotomists is projected to grow 25 percent from 2014 to 2024, much faster than the average for all occupations. Hospitals, diagnostic laboratories, blood donor centers, and other locations will need phlebotomists to perform bloodwork.

Blood analysis remains an essential function in medical laboratories and hospitals. Demand for phlebotomists will remain high as doctors and other healthcare professionals require bloodwork for analysis and diagnosis.

The number of individuals who have access to health insurance is expected to continue to increase because of federal health insurance reform. There will be greater demand for blood tests and other bloodwork-related services, increasing the need for phlebotomists.

Job Prospects. Job prospects are greatest for phlebotomists who receive certification from one of several reputable organizations, such as the National Center for Competency Testing (NCCT), National Healthcareer Association (NHA), the American Society for Clinical Pathology (ASCP), or the American Medical Technologists (AMT).

Contacts for More Information

For more information about phlebotomy and how to receive a phlebotomy certificate, visit

- Center for Phlebotomy Education (www.phlebotomy.com)
- American Medical Technologists (AMT) (http://americanmedtech.org/Home.aspx)
- National Health Career Association (www.nhanow.com/home.aspx)
- National Center for Competency Testing (www.ncctinc.com)
- American Society for Clinical Pathology (www.ascp.org)

O*NET

- Phlebotomists (31-9097.00)

Physical Therapist Assistants and Aides

- **2014 Median Pay** .... $41,640 per year $20.02 per hour
- **Typical Entry-Level Education** .... See Education/Training
- **Work Experience in a Related Occupation** .... None
- **On-the-job Training** .... See Education/Training
- **Number of Jobs, 2014** 128,700
- **Job Outlook, 2014–24** ...... 40% (Much faster than average)
- **Employment Change, 2014–24** 51,400

What Physical Therapist Assistants and Aides Do

Physical therapist assistants, sometimes called *PTAs*, and physical therapist aides work under the direction and supervision of physical therapists. They help patients who are recovering from injuries and illnesses regain movement and manage pain. Physical therapist assistants are involved in the direct care of patients. Physical therapist aides often do tasks that are indirectly related to patient care, such as cleaning and setting up the treatment area, moving patients, and performing clerical duties.

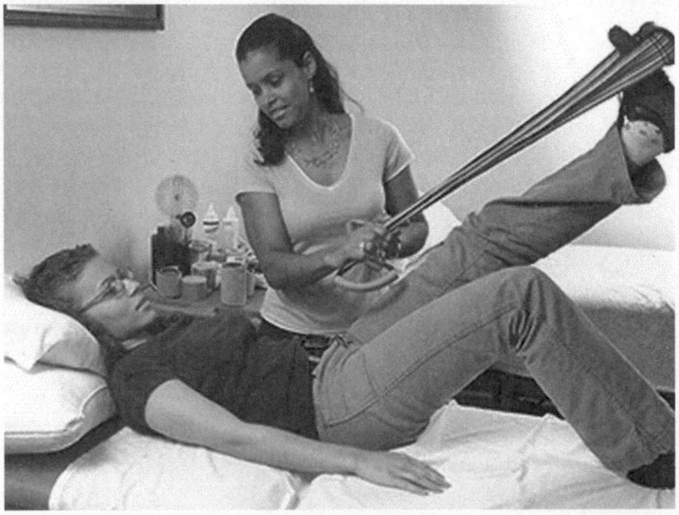

Physical therapist assistants and aides provide treatment that improves patient mobility, relieves pain, and prevents or lessens physical disabilities, under the direction of physical therapists.

Duties. Physical therapist assistants typically do the following:

- Observe patients before, during, and after therapy, noting patient status and reporting it to a physical therapist
- Help patients do specific exercises as part of the plan of care
- Treat patients using a variety of techniques, such as massage and stretching
- Use devices and equipment, such as walkers, to help patients
- Educate a patient and family members about what to do after treatment

Physical therapist aides typically do the following:

- Clean treatment areas and set up therapy equipment
- Wash linens
- Help patients move to or from a therapy area
- Do clerical tasks, such as answering phones and scheduling patients

Physical therapist assistants help physical therapists provide care to patients. Under the direction and supervision of physical therapists, they treat patients through exercise, massage, gait and balance training, and other therapeutic interventions. Physical therapist assistants record patients' progress and report the results of each treatment to the physical therapist.

Physical therapist aides work under the direct supervision of a physical therapist or physical therapist assistant. They usually are responsible for keeping the treatment area clean and organized, and preparing for each patient's therapy. They also help patients who need assistance moving to or from a treatment area. In addition, aides do a variety of clerical tasks, such as ordering supplies, scheduling treatment sessions, and filling out insurance forms. The types of tasks that physical therapist aides are allowed to perform vary by state. Contact your state licensing board for more information.

Work Environment

Physical therapist assistants held about 78,700 jobs in 2014. Physical therapist aides held about 50,000 jobs in 2014.

The industries that employed the most physical therapist assistants in 2014 were as follows:

Offices of physical, occupational and speech therapists, and audiologists	43%
Hospitals; state, local, and private	23
Nursing care facilities (skilled nursing facilities)	11
Home healthcare services	9
Offices of physicians	5

The industries that employed the most physical therapist aides in 2014 were as follows:

Offices of physical, occupational and speech therapists, and audiologists	55%
Hospitals; state, local, and private	21
Offices of physicians	8
Nursing care facilities (skilled nursing facilities)	6
Government	3

Physical therapist assistants and aides are frequently on their feet and moving as they set up equipment and help and treat patients. Because they must often lift and move patients, they are

Median Annual Wages, May 2014

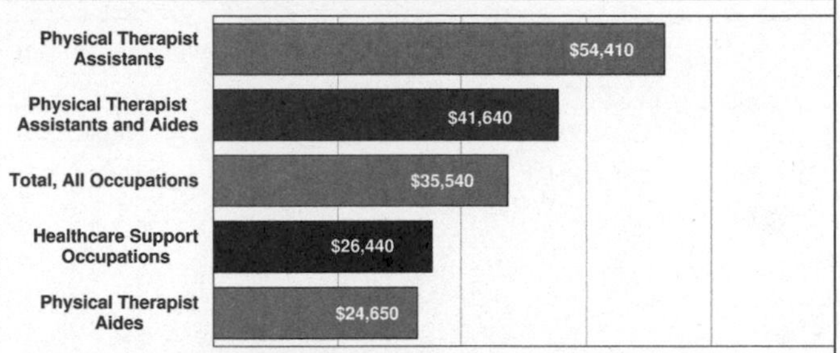

Note: All Occupations includes all occupations in the U.S. Economy.
Source: U.S. Bureau of Labor Statistics, Occupational Employment Statistics

Percent Change in Employment, Projected 2014–2024

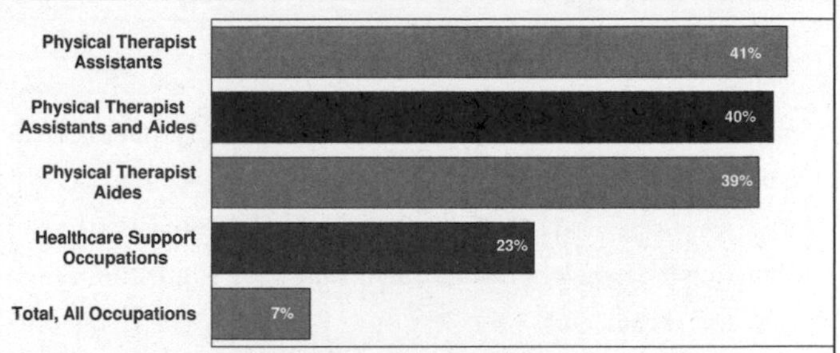

Note: All Occupations includes all occupations in the U.S. Economy.
Source: U.S. Bureau of Labor Statistics, Office of Occupational Statistics and Employment Projections

vulnerable to back injuries. Assistants and aides can limit these risks by using proper techniques when they assist patients.

Work Schedules. Most physical therapist assistants and aides work full time. Some night and weekend work may be required as many physical therapy offices and clinics have extended hours to accommodate patients' schedules.

Education/Training

Physical therapist assistants entering the profession need an associate's degree from an accredited program. All states require physical therapist assistants to be licensed or certified. Physical therapist aides usually have a high school diploma and receive on-the-job training.

Education and Training. All states require physical therapist assistants to have an associate's degree from an accredited physical therapist assistant program. There were more than 300 associate's degree programs for physical therapist assistants accredited by the Commission on Accreditation in Physical Therapy Education in 2015.

Programs typically last about 2 years. Classroom study includes courses in algebra, English, anatomy, physiology, and psychology. Assistants also gain hands-on experience during supervised clinical work. They may earn certifications in cardiopulmonary resuscitation (CPR) and other first-aid skills.

Physical therapist aides typically have a high school diploma or the equivalent. They usually gain clinical experience through on-the-job training that can last from about a week to a month. Employers often prefer to hire applicants with computer skills.

Licenses, Certifications, and Registrations. All states require physical therapist assistants to be licensed or certified. Licensure typically requires graduation from an accredited physical therapist assistant program and passing the National Physical Therapy Exam for physical therapist assistants administered by the Federation of State Boards of Physical Therapy. Some states require that applicants pass additional state-administered exams, undergo a criminal background check, and be at least 18 years old. Physical therapist assistants also may need to take continuing education courses to keep their license. Check with your state board for specific licensing requirements.

Physical therapist aides are not required to be licensed.

Important Qualities

Compassion. Physical therapist assistants and aides should enjoy helping people. They work with people who are in pain, and they must have empathy to help their patients.

Detail oriented. Like other healthcare professionals, physical therapist assistants and aides should be organized and have a keen eye for detail. They must keep accurate records and follow written and verbal instructions carefully to ensure quality care.

Dexterity. Physical therapist assistants should be comfortable using their hands to provide manual therapy and therapeutic exercises. Aides should also be comfortable working with their hands to set up equipment and prepare treatment areas.

Interpersonal skills. Physical therapist assistants and aides spend much of their time interacting with clients, their families, and other healthcare practitioners; and therefore should be courteous and friendly.

Physical stamina. Physical therapist assistants and aides are frequently on their feet and moving as they work with their patients. They must often kneel, stoop, bend, and stand for long periods. They should enjoy physical activity.

Pay

The median annual wage for physical therapist assistants was $54,410 in May 2014. The median wage is the wage at which half the workers in an occupation earned more than that amount and half earned less. The lowest 10 percent earned less than $31,840, and the highest 10 percent earned more than $75,530.

The median annual wage for physical therapist aides was $24,650 in May 2014. The lowest 10 percent earned less than $18,370, and the highest 10 percent earned more than $36,830.

Employment Projections Data for Physical Therapist Assistants and Aides

Occupational Title	SOC Code	Employment, 2014	Projected Employment, 2024	Change, 2014–2024 Percent	Change, 2014–2024 Numeric
Physical therapist assistants and aides	31-2020	128,700	180,200	40	51,400
Physical therapist assistants	31-2021	78,700	110,700	41	31,900
Physical therapist aides	31-2022	50,000	69,500	39	19,500

Source: U.S. Bureau of Labor Statistics, Employment Projections Program

Similar Occupations. This table shows a list of occupations with job duties that are similar to those of physical therapist assistants and aides.

Occupations	Entry-level Education	2014 Median Pay	Projected Job Growth	Average Annual Openings
Dental Assistants	Postsecondary nondegree award	$35,390	18%	5,860
Medical Assistants	Postsecondary nondegree award	$29,960	23%	13,890
Nursing Assistants and Orderlies	See Education/Training	$25,090	17%	26,780
Occupational Therapy Assistants and Aides	See Education/Training	$52,300	40%	1,680
Pharmacy Technicians	High school diploma or equivalent	$29,810	9%	3,470
Physical Therapists	Doctoral or professional degree	$82,390	34%	7,180
Psychiatric Technicians and Aides	See Education/Training	$28,470	5%	760

In May 2014, the median annual wages for physical therapist assistants in the top industries in which they worked were as follows:

Nursing care facilities (skilled nursing facilities)............... $62,280
Home healthcare services.. 59,890
Offices of physical, occupational and speech therapists, and audiologists... 53,130
Hospitals; state, local, and private...................................... 51,870
Offices of physicians.. 51,790

In May 2014, the median annual wages for physical therapist aides in the top industries in which they worked were as follows:

Nursing care facilities (skilled nursing facilities)............... $27,860
Hospitals; state, local, and private...................................... 27,060
Offices of physicians.. 26,230
Government... 25,080
Offices of physical, occupational and speech therapists, and audiologists... 23,390

Job Outlook

Employment of physical therapist assistants is projected to grow 41 percent from 2014 to 2024, much faster than the average for all occupations. Employment of physical therapist aides is projected to grow 39 percent from 2014 to 2024, much faster than the average for all occupations.

Demand for physical therapy services is expected to increase in response to the health needs of an aging population, particularly the large baby-boom generation. This group is staying more active later in life than previous generations. However, many baby boomers also are entering the prime age for heart attacks and strokes, increasing the demand for cardiac and physical rehabilitation. Older people also are particularly vulnerable to a number of chronic and debilitating conditions that require therapeutic services. These patients often need additional help in their treatment, making the roles of physical therapist assistants and aides vital.

In addition, a number of chronic conditions, such as diabetes and obesity, have become more prevalent in recent years. More physical therapist assistants and aides will be needed to manage the effects of such conditions and help patients maintain their mobility.

Medical and technological developments should permit an increased percentage of trauma victims and newborns with birth defects to survive, creating added demand for therapy and rehabilitative services. In addition, the number of individuals who have access to health insurance is expected to continue to increase because of federal health insurance reform.

Physical therapists are expected to increasingly use physical therapist assistants, particularly in long-term care environments, in order to reduce the cost of physical therapy services. Once the physical therapist has evaluated a patient and designed a plan of care, the assistant can provide many parts of the treatment, as directed by the therapist.

Job Prospects. Opportunities for physical therapist assistants are expected to be very good. Physical therapist assistants will be needed to help physical therapists care for and manage more patients. However, physical therapist aides may face strong competition from the large pool of qualified people since requirements for entry are low.

Job opportunities should be particularly good in settings where the elderly are most often treated, such as skilled-nursing homes, home health, and outpatient orthopedic facilities. Job prospects should be especially favorable in rural areas, as many physical therapists cluster in highly populated urban and suburban areas.

Contacts for More Information

For more information about physical therapist assistants, visit

➤ American Physical Therapy Association (www.apta.org)

For a list of schools offering accredited programs, visit

➤ Commission on Accreditation in Physical Therapy Education (www.capteonline.org/home.aspx)

For more information about state licensing requirements and about the National Physical Therapy Exam, visit

➤ Federation of State Boards of Physical Therapy (www.fsbpt.org)

O*NET

➤ Physical Therapist Assistants (31-2021.00)

➤ Physical Therapist Aides (31-2022.00)

Physical Therapists

- **2014 Median Pay**................................ $82,390 per year $39.61 per hour
- **Typical Entry-Level Education**..................... Doctoral or professional degree
- **Work Experience in a Related Occupation**.............. None
- **On-the-job Training**... None
- **Number of Jobs, 2014**.. 210,900
- **Job Outlook, 2014–24**.... 34% (Much faster than average)
- **Employment Change, 2014–24**............................. 71,800

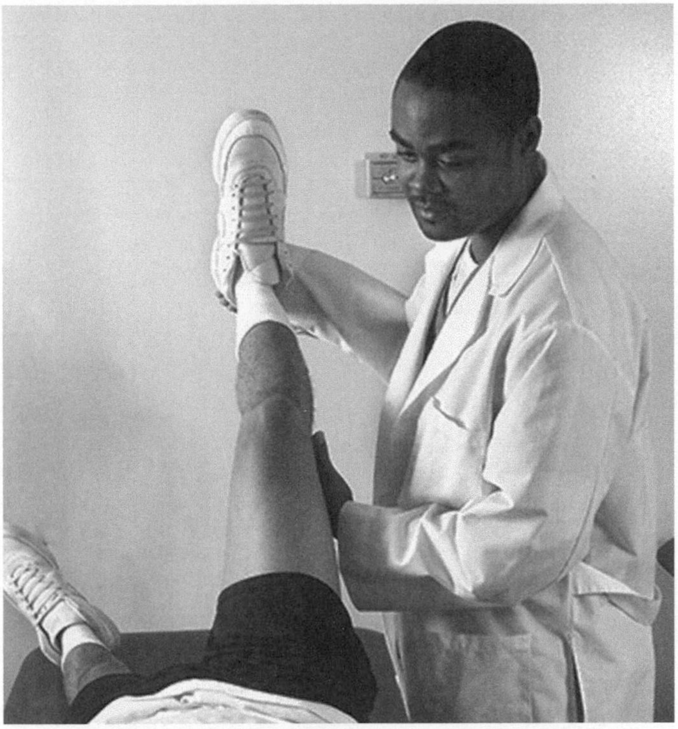

Physical therapists may practice in hospitals, clinics, private offices, private homes, or schools.

What Physical Therapists Do

Physical therapists, sometimes called *PTs*, help injured or ill people improve their movement and manage their pain. These therapists are often an important part of rehabilitation, treatment, and prevention of patients with chronic conditions, illnesses, or injuries.

Duties. Physical therapists typically do the following:

- Review patients' medical history and any referrals or notes from doctors, surgeons, or other healthcare workers
- Diagnose patients' functions and movements by observing them stand or walk and by listening to their concerns, among other methods
- Develop individualized plans of care for patients, outlining the patients' goals and the expected outcomes of the plans
- Use exercises, stretching maneuvers, hands-on therapy, and equipment to ease patients' pain, help them increase their mobility, prevent further pain or injury, and facilitate health and wellness
- Evaluate and record a patient's progress, modifying a plan of care and trying new treatments as needed
- Educate patients and their families about what to expect from the recovery process and how best to cope with challenges throughout the process

Physical therapists provide care to people of all ages who have functional problems resulting from back and neck injuries; sprains, strains, and fractures; arthritis; amputations; neurological disorders, such as stroke or cerebral palsy; injuries related to work and sports; and other conditions.

Physical therapists are educated to use a variety of different techniques to care for their patients. These techniques include exercises; training in functional movement, which includes the use of equipment such as canes, crutches, wheelchairs, and walkers; and special movements of joints, muscles, and other soft tissue to improve movement and decrease pain.

The work of physical therapists varies by type of patient. For example, a patient working to recover mobility lost after a stroke needs different care from a patient who is recovering from a sports injury. Some physical therapists specialize in one type of care, such as orthopedics or geriatrics. Many physical therapists also help patients to maintain or improve mobility by developing fitness and wellness programs to encourage healthier and more active lifestyles.

Physical therapists work as part of a healthcare team, overseeing the work of physical therapist assistants and aides and consulting with physicians and surgeons and other specialists.

Work Environment

Physical therapists held about 210,900 jobs in 2014. The industries that employed the most physical therapists were as follows:

Offices of physical, occupational and speech therapists, and audiologists	34%
Hospitals; state, local, and private	27
Home healthcare services	12
Nursing and residential care facilities	7
Offices of physicians	5

Physical therapists spend much of their time on their feet, working with patients. Because they must often lift and move patients, they are vulnerable to back injuries. Therapists can limit these risks by using proper body mechanics and lifting techniques when assisting patients.

Work Schedules. Most physical therapists work full time. About 1 in 5 worked part time in 2014. Although most therapists work during normal business hours, some may work evenings or weekends.

Median Annual Wages, May 2014

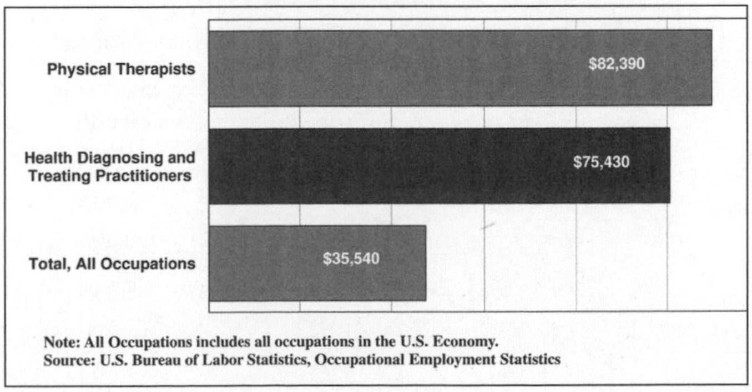

Percent Change in Employment, Projected 2014–2024

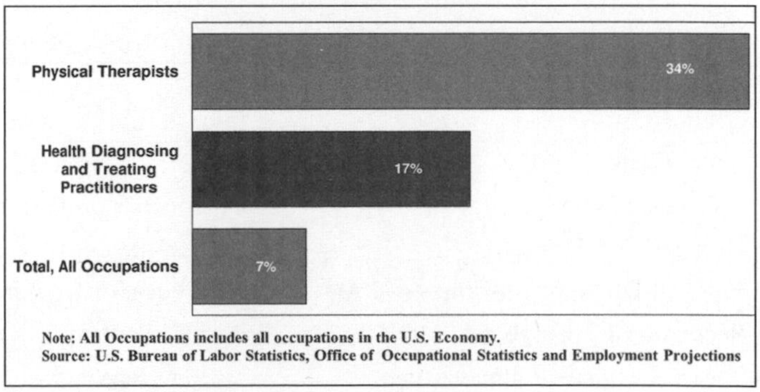

Employment Projections Data for Physical Therapists

Occupational Title	SOC Code	Employment, 2014	Projected Employment, 2024	Change, 2014–2024 Percent	Change, 2014–2024 Numeric
Physical therapists	29-1123	210,900	282,700	34	71,800

Source: U.S. Bureau of Labor Statistics, Employment Projections Program

Education/Training

Physical therapists need a Doctor of Physical Therapy (DPT) degree. All states require physical therapists to be licensed.

Education. In 2015, there were more than 200 programs for physical therapists accredited by the Commission on Accreditation in Physical Therapy Education (CAPTE). All programs offer a Doctor of Physical Therapy (DPT) degree.

DPT programs typically last 3 years. Most programs require a bachelor's degree for admission as well as specific educational prerequisites, such as classes in anatomy, physiology, biology, chemistry, and physics. Some programs admit college freshmen into 6- or 7-year programs that allow students to graduate with both a bachelor's degree and a DPT. Most DPT programs require applicants to apply through the Physical Therapist Centralized Application Service (PTCAS).

Physical therapist programs often include courses in biomechanics, anatomy, physiology, neuroscience, and pharmacology. Physical therapist students also complete at least 30 weeks of clinical work, during which they gain supervised experience in areas such as acute care and orthopedic care.

Physical therapists may apply to and complete a clinical residency program after graduation. Residencies typically last about 1 year and provide additional training and experience in specialty areas of care. Therapists who have completed a residency program may choose to specialize further by completing a fellowship in an advanced clinical area.

Licenses, Certifications, and Registrations. All states require physical therapists to be licensed. Licensing requirements vary by state but all include passing the National Physical Therapy Examination administered by the Federation of State Boards of Physical Therapy. Several states also require a law exam and a criminal background check. Continuing education is typically required for physical therapists to keep their license. Check with state boards for specific licensing requirements.

After gaining work experience, some physical therapists choose to become a board-certified specialist. The American Board of Physical Therapy Specialties offers certification in 8 clinical specialty areas, including orthopedics, sports, and geriatric physical therapy. Board specialist certification requires passing an exam and at least 2,000 hours of clinical work or completion of an American Physical Therapy Association (APTA)-accredited residency program in the specialty area.

Important Qualities

Compassion. Physical therapists are often drawn to the profession in part by a desire to help people. They work with people who are in pain and must have empathy for their patients.

Detail oriented. Like other healthcare providers, physical therapists should have strong analytic and observational skills to diagnose a patient's problem, evaluate treatments, and provide safe, effective care.

Dexterity. Physical therapists must use their hands to provide manual therapy and therapeutic exercises. They should feel comfortable massaging and otherwise physically assisting patients.

Interpersonal skills. Because physical therapists spend a lot of time interacting with patients, they should enjoy working with people. They must be able to clearly explain treatment programs, motivate patients, and listen to patients' concerns to provide effective therapy.

Physical stamina. Physical therapists spend much of their time on their feet, moving as they demonstrate proper techniques and help patients perform exercises. They should enjoy physical activity.

Resourcefulness. Physical therapists customize treatment plans for patients. They must be flexible and able to adapt plans of care to meet the needs of each patient.

Pay

The median annual wage for physical therapists was $82,390 in May 2014. The median wage is the wage at which half the workers in an occupation earned more than that amount and half earned less. The lowest 10 percent earned less than $56,800, and the highest 10 percent earned more than $116,090.

In May 2014, the median annual wages for physical therapists in the top industries in which they worked were as follows:

Home healthcare services	$89,310
Nursing and residential care facilities	88,930
Hospitals; state, local, and private	83,380
Offices of physicians	81,630
Offices of physical, occupational and speech therapists, and audiologists	79,130

Similar Occupations. This table shows a list of occupations with job duties that are similar to those of physical therapists.

Occupations	Entry-level Education	2014 Median Pay	Projected Job Growth	Average Annual Openings
Audiologists	Doctoral or professional degree	$73,060	29%	380
Chiropractors	Doctoral or professional degree	$66,720	17%	790
Occupational Therapists	Master's degree	$78,810	27%	3,040
Physical Therapist Assistants and Aides	See Education/Training	$41,640	40%	5,140
Recreational Therapists	Bachelor's degree	$44,000	12%	220
Speech-Language Pathologists	Master's degree	$71,550	21%	2,890

Job Outlook

Employment of physical therapists is projected to grow 34 percent from 2014 to 2024, much faster than the average for all occupations.

Demand for physical therapy services will come in part from the large number of aging baby boomers, who are staying more active later in life than their counterparts of previous generations. Older people are more likely to experience heart attacks, strokes, and mobility-related injuries that require physical therapy for rehabilitation.

In addition, a number of chronic conditions, such as diabetes and obesity, have become more prevalent in recent years. More physical therapists will be needed to help these patients maintain their mobility and manage the effects of chronic conditions.

Advances in medical technology have increased the use of outpatient surgery to treat a variety of injuries and illnesses. Medical and technological developments also are expected to permit a greater percentage of trauma victims and newborns with birth defects to survive, creating additional demand for rehabilitative care. Physical therapists will continue to play an important role in helping these patients recover more quickly from surgery.

Furthermore, the number of individuals who have access to health insurance is expected to continue to increase because of federal health insurance reform. Physical therapists will be needed to assist patients with rehabilitation and treatment of any chronic conditions or injuries.

Job Prospects. Job opportunities are expected to be good for licensed physical therapists in all settings. Job prospects should be particularly good in acute-care hospitals, skilled-nursing facilities, and orthopedic settings, where the elderly are most often treated. Job prospects should be especially favorable in rural areas because many physical therapists live in highly populated urban and suburban areas.

Contacts for More Information

For more information about physical therapists, visit

➤ American Physical Therapy Association (www.apta.org)

For more information about accredited physical therapy programs, visit

➤ Commission on Accreditation in Physical Therapy Education (www.capteonline.org/home.aspx)

For more information about state licensing requirements and about the National Physical Therapy Exam, visit

➤ Federation of State Boards of Physical Therapy (www.fsbpt.org)

For more information about certification, visit

➤ American Board of Physical Therapy Specialties (www.abpts.org/home.aspx)

For more information about how to apply to DPT programs, visit

➤ Physical Therapist Centralized Application Service (PTCAS) (www.ptcas.org/home.aspx)

O*NET

➤ Physical Therapists (29-1123.00)

Physician Assistants

- **2014 Median Pay** .... $95,820 per year
  $46.07 per hour
- **Typical Entry-Level Education** .... Master's degree
- **Work Experience in a Related Occupation** .... None

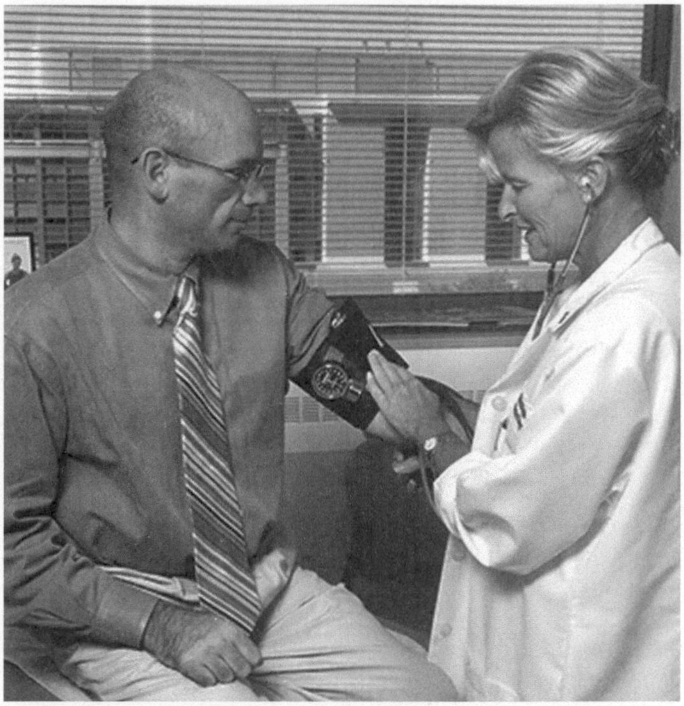

Physician assistants are formally trained to provide diagnostic, therapeutic, and preventive healthcare services, under the supervision of a physician.

- **On-the-job Training** .... None
- **Number of Jobs, 2014** 94,400
- **Job Outlook, 2014–24** .... 30% (Much faster than average)
- **Employment Change, 2014–24** 28,700

What Physician Assistants Do

Physician assistants, also known as *PAs*, practice medicine on teams with physicians, surgeons, and other healthcare workers. They examine, diagnose, and treat patients.

Duties. Physician assistants typically do the following:

- Take or review patients' medical histories
- Examine patients
- Order and interpret diagnostic tests, such as X-rays or blood tests
- Diagnose a patient's injury or illness
- Give treatment, such as setting broken bones and immunizing patients
- Educate and counsel patients and their families—for example, answering questions about how to care for a child with asthma
- Prescribe medicine
- Assess and record a patient's progress
- Research the latest treatments to ensure the quality of patient care
- Conduct or participate in outreach programs; talking to groups about managing diseases and promoting wellness

Physician assistants work on teams with physicians or surgeons and other healthcare workers. Their specific duties and the extent to which they must be supervised by physicians or surgeons differ from state to state.

Median Annual Wages, May 2014

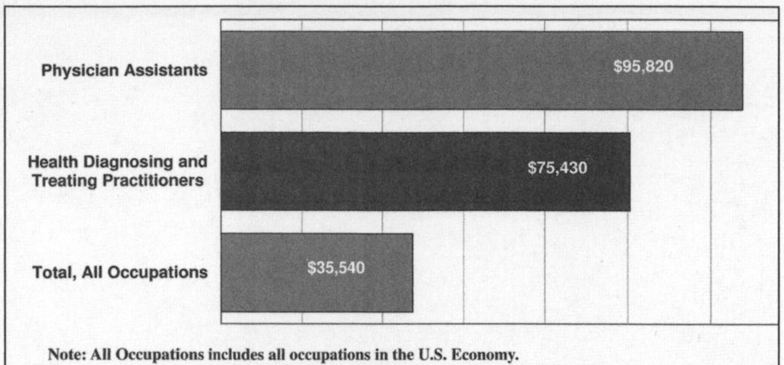

Note: All Occupations includes all occupations in the U.S. Economy.
Source: U.S. Bureau of Labor Statistics, Occupational Employment Statistics

Percent Change in Employment, Projected 2014–2024

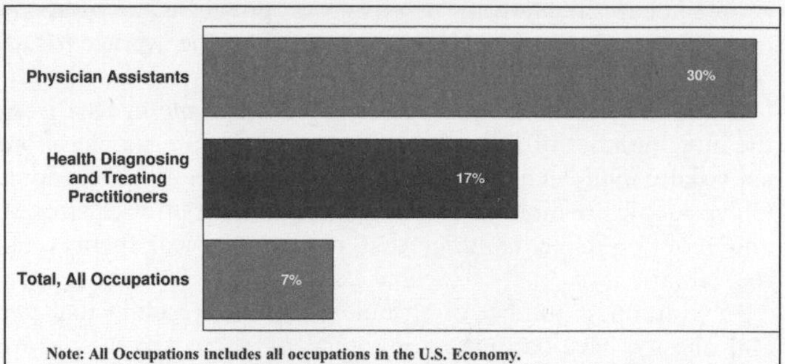

Note: All Occupations includes all occupations in the U.S. Economy.
Source: U.S. Bureau of Labor Statistics, Office of Occupational Statistics and Employment Projections

Physician assistants work in all areas of medicine, including primary care and family medicine, emergency medicine, surgery, and psychiatry. The work of physician assistants depends in large part on their specialty or the type of medical practice where they work. For example, a physician assistant working in surgery may close incisions and provide care before, during, and after the operation. A physician assistant working in pediatrics may examine a child and give routine vaccinations.

In some areas, especially rural and medically underserved communities, physician assistants may be the primary care providers at clinics where a physician is present only 1 or 2 days per week. In these locations, physician assistants collaborate with the physician as needed and as required by law.

Some physician assistants make house calls or visit nursing homes to treat patients.

Physician assistants are different from medical assistants. Medical assistants do routine clinical and clerical tasks and they do not practice medicine.

Work Environment

Physician assistants held about 94,400 jobs in 2014. The industries that employed the most physician assistants were as follows:

Offices of physicians	57%
Hospitals; state, local, and private	22
Outpatient care centers	7
Government	3
Educational services; state, local, and private	3

Physician assistant work can be both physically and emotionally demanding. Physician assistants spend much of their time on their feet, making rounds and evaluating patients. Physician assistants who work in operating rooms often stand for extended periods.

Work Schedules. Most physician assistants work full time. About 1 out of 5 worked part time in 2014. In hospitals, physician assistants may work nights, weekends, or holidays. They may also be on call, meaning that they must be ready to respond to a work request with little notice.

Education/Training

Physician assistants typically need a master's degree from an accredited educational program. Earning that degree usually takes at least 2 years of full-time postgraduate study. All states require physician assistants to be licensed.

Education. Most applicants to physician assistant education programs already have a bachelor's degree and some healthcare-related work experience. Although admissions requirements vary from program to program, most programs require 2 to 4 years of undergraduate coursework with a focus in science. Many applicants already have experience as registered nurses or as EMTs and paramedics before they apply to a physician assistant program.

Physician assistant education programs usually take at least 2 years of full-time study. About 200 education programs were accredited by the Accreditation Review Commission on Education for the Physician Assistant, Inc. (ARC-PA) in 2014. Almost all of these accredited programs offer a master's degree.

Physician assistant education includes classroom and laboratory instruction in subjects such as pathology, human anatomy, physiology, clinical medicine, pharmacology, physical diagnosis, and medical ethics. The programs also include supervised clinical training in several areas, including family medicine, internal medicine, emergency medicine, and pediatrics.

Sometimes students serve in one or more clinical rotations in these areas under the supervision of a physician who is looking to hire a physician assistant. In this way, clinical rotations may lead to permanent employment.

Licenses, Certifications, and Registrations. All states and the District of Columbia require physician assistants to be licensed. To become licensed, candidates must pass the Physician Assistant National Certifying Examination (PANCE) from the National Commission on Certification of Physician Assistants (NCCPA). A physician assistant who passes the exam may use the credential "Physician Assistant-Certified (PA-C)."

To keep their certification, physician assistants must complete 100 hours of continuing education every 2 years. The recertification exam is required every 10 years.

Employment Projections Data for Physician Assistants

Occupational Title	SOC Code	Employment, 2014	Projected Employment, 2024	Change, 2014–2024 Percent	Change, 2014–2024 Numeric
Physician assistants	29-1071	94,400	123,200	30	28,700

Source: U.S. Bureau of Labor Statistics, Employment Projections Program

Similar Occupations. This table shows a list of occupations with job duties that are similar to those of physician assistants.

Occupations	Entry-level Education	2014 Median Pay	Projected Job Growth	Average Annual Openings
Nurse Anesthetists, Nurse Midwives, and Nurse Practitioners	Master's degree	$102,670	31%	5,340
Occupational Therapists	Master's degree	$78,810	27%	3,040
Physical Therapists	Doctoral or professional degree	$82,390	34%	7,180
Physicians and Surgeons	Doctoral or professional degree	This wage is equal to or greater than $187,200.	14%	9,930
Registered Nurses	Bachelor's degree	$66,640	16%	43,930
Speech-Language Pathologists	Master's degree	$71,550	21%	2,890

In addition, state licensure laws require physician assistants to hold an agreement with a supervising physician. Although the physician does not need to be onsite at all times, collaboration between physicians and physician assistants is required for practice.

Important Qualities

Compassion. Physician assistants deal with patients who are sick or injured and may be in extreme pain or distress. They must be able to treat patients and their families with compassion and understanding.

Detail oriented. Physician assistants should be observant and have a strong ability to focus when evaluating and treating patients.

Emotional stability. Physician assistants, particularly those working in surgery or emergency medicine, should be able to work well under pressure. They must remain calm in stressful situations in order to provide quality care.

Problem-solving skills. Physician assistants need to evaluate patients' symptoms and administer the appropriate treatments. They must be diligent when investigating complicated medical issues so that they can determine the best course of treatment for each patient.

Advancement. Some physician assistants pursue additional education in a specialty. Postgraduate educational programs are available in areas such as emergency medicine and psychiatry. To enter one of these programs, a physician assistant must be a graduate of an accredited program and be certified by the NCCPA.

As they gain greater clinical knowledge and experience, physician assistants can earn new responsibilities and higher wages. For example, experienced physician assistants may supervise other staff and physician assistant students or they may become an executive leader of a healthcare organization.

Pay

The median annual wage for physician assistants was $95,820 in May 2014. The median wage is the wage at which half the workers in an occupation earned more than that amount and half earned less. The lowest 10 percent earned less than $64,100, and the highest 10 percent earned more than $134,720.

In May 2014, the median annual wages for physician assistants in the top industries in which they worked were as follows:

Outpatient care centers	$100,750
Hospitals; state, local, and private	99,360
Offices of physicians	94,670
Educational services; state, local, and private	91,740
Government	90,340

Job Outlook

Employment of physician assistants is projected to grow 30 percent from 2014 to 2024, much faster than the average for all occupations.

Demand for healthcare services will increase because of the growing and aging population. More people means more need for healthcare providers, and baby boomers will require more medical attention as they age. An increase in several chronic diseases, such as diabetes, will drive the need for physician assistants to provide preventive care and treat those who are sick. Furthermore, the number of individuals who have access to health insurance is expected to increase because of federal health insurance reform.

Physician assistants, who can perform many of the same services as doctors, are expected to have a larger role in giving routine care because they are more cost effective than physicians. As more physicians retire or enter specialty areas of medicine, more physician assistants are expected to take on the role of primary care provider.

The role of physician assistants is expected to expand as states continue to allow them to perform more procedures; as team-based models of care become more widely used; and as insurance companies expand their coverage of physician assistant services.

Job Prospects. Good job prospects are expected, particularly for physician assistants working in rural and medically underserved areas, as well as physician assistants working in primary care.

Contacts for More Information

For more information about physician assistants, visit

- American Academy of Physician Assistants (www.aapa.org)

For a list of accredited physician assistant programs, visit

- Physician Assistant Education Association (www.paeaonline.org)
- Accreditation Review Commission on Education for the Physician Assistant, Inc. (ARC-PA) (www.arc-pa.org)

For information about certification requirements, visit

- National Commission on Certification of Physician Assistants (www.nccpa.net)

O*NET

- Physician Assistants (29-1071.00)
- Anesthesiologist Assistants (29-1071.01)

Physicians and Surgeons

- **2014 Median Pay** .... This wage is equal to or greater than $187,200 per year or $90.00 per hour.

- **Typical Entry-Level Education** .... Doctoral or professional degree
- **Work Experience in a Related Occupation** .... None
- **On-the-job Training** .... Internship/residency
- **Number of Jobs, 2014** 708,300
- **Job Outlook, 2014–24** ..... 14% (Much faster than average)
- **Employment Change, 2014–24** 99,300

What Physicians and Surgeons Do

Physicians and surgeons diagnose and treat injuries or illnesses. Physicians examine patients; take medical histories; prescribe medications; and order, perform, and interpret diagnostic tests. They often counsel patients on diet, hygiene, and preventive healthcare. Surgeons operate on patients to treat injuries, such as broken bones; diseases, such as cancerous tumors; and deformities, such as cleft palates.

There are two types of physicians, with corresponding degrees: M.D. (Medical Doctor) and D.O. (Doctor of Osteopathic Medicine). Both use the same methods of treatment, including drugs and surgery, but D.O.s place additional emphasis on the body's musculoskeletal system, preventive medicine, and holistic (whole-person) patient care. D.O.s are most likely to be primary care physicians, although they can be found in all specialties.

Duties. Physicians and surgeons typically do the following:

- Take a patient's medical history
- Update charts and patient information to show current findings and treatments
- Order tests for nurses or other healthcare staff to perform
- Review test results to identify any abnormal findings
- Recommend and design a plan of treatment
- Address concerns or answer questions that patients have about their health and well-being
- Help patients take care of their health by discussing topics such as proper nutrition and hygiene

Physicians and surgeons work in one or more specialties. The following are examples of types of physicians and surgeons:

Anesthesiologists focus on the care of surgical patients and on pain relief. They administer drugs (anesthetics) that reduce or eliminate the sensation of pain during an operation or another medical procedure. During surgery, they are responsible for adjusting the amount of anesthetic as needed and monitoring the patient's heart rate, body temperature, blood pressure, and breathing. They also work outside of the operating room, providing pain relief in the intensive care unit, during labor and delivery of babies, and for patients who suffer from chronic pain. Anesthesiologists work with other physicians and surgeons to decide on treatments and procedures before, during, and after surgery.

Family and general physicians assess and treat a range of conditions that occur in everyday life. These conditions include anything from sinus and respiratory infections to broken bones. Family and general physicians typically have regular, long-term patients.

General internists diagnose and provide nonsurgical treatment for a range of problems that affect internal organ systems such as the stomach, kidneys, liver, and digestive tract. Internists use a variety of diagnostic techniques to treat patients through medication or hospitalization. They work mostly with adult patients.

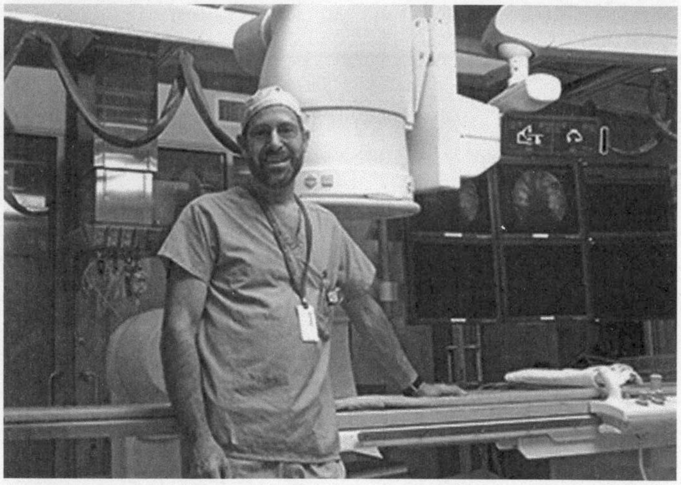

Physicians examine patients, obtain medical histories, and order, perform, and interpret diagnostic tests.

General pediatricians provide care for infants, children, teenagers, and young adults. They specialize in diagnosing and treating problems specific to younger people. Most pediatricians treat common illnesses, minor injuries, and infectious diseases, and administer vaccinations. Some pediatricians specialize in pediatric surgery or serious medical conditions that commonly affect younger patients, such as autoimmune disorders or chronic ailments.

Obstetricians and gynecologists (OB/GYNs) provide care related to pregnancy, childbirth, and the female reproductive system. They treat and counsel women throughout their pregnancy and deliver babies. They also diagnose and treat health issues specific to women, such as breast cancer, cervical cancer, hormonal disorders, and symptoms related to menopause.

Psychiatrists are primary mental health physicians. They diagnose and treat mental illnesses through a combination of personal counseling (psychotherapy), psychoanalysis, hospitalization, and medication. Psychotherapy involves regular discussions with patients about their problems. The psychiatrist helps them find solutions through changes in their behavioral patterns, explorations of their past experiences, or group and family therapy sessions. Psychoanalysis involves long-term psychotherapy and counseling for patients. Psychiatrists may prescribe medications to correct chemical imbalances that cause some mental illnesses.

Surgeons treat injuries, diseases, and deformities through operations. Using a variety of instruments, a surgeon corrects physical deformities, repairs bone and tissue after injuries, or performs preventive or elective surgeries on patients. Although a large number perform general surgery, many surgeons choose to specialize in a specific area. Specialties include orthopedic surgery (the treatment of the musculoskeletal system), neurological surgery (treatment of the brain and nervous system), cardiovascular surgery, and plastic or reconstructive surgery. Like other physicians, surgeons examine patients, perform and interpret diagnostic tests, and counsel patients on preventive healthcare. Some specialist physicians also perform surgery.

Physicians and surgeons may work in a number of other medical and surgical specialties and subspecialties. The following specialists are some of the most common examples:

- Allergists (specialists in diagnosing and treating hay fever or other allergies)
- Cardiologists (heart specialists)
- Dermatologists (skin specialists)

- Gastroenterologists (digestive system specialists)
- Ophthalmologists (eye specialists)
- Pathologists (specialists who study body tissue to see if it is normal or abnormal)
- Radiologists (specialists who review and interpret X-rays and other images and deliver radiation treatments for cancer and other illnesses)

Physicians work daily with other healthcare staff, such as registered nurses, other physicians, medical assistants, and medical records and health information technicians.

Work Environment

Physicians and surgeons held about 708,300 jobs in 2014. Many physicians work in private offices or clinics, often with a small staff of nurses and administrative personnel. Some practice independently or with a small group of other doctors. About 1 out of 10 physicians was self-employed in 2014.

Increasingly, physicians are working in group practices, healthcare organizations, or hospitals, where they share a large number of patients with other doctors. The group setting allows them more time off and lets them coordinate care for their patients, but it gives them less independence than solo practitioners have.

Surgeons and anesthesiologists usually work in sterile environments while performing surgery and may stand for long periods.

Work Schedules. Most physicians and surgeons work full time. Many physicians and surgeons work long, irregular, and overnight hours. Physicians and surgeons may travel between their offices and hospitals to care for their patients. While on call, a physician may need to address a patient's concerns over the phone or make an emergency visit to a hospital or nursing home.

Education/Training

Physicians and surgeons have demanding education and training requirements. Almost all physicians complete at least 4 years of undergraduate school, 4 years of medical school, and, depending on their specialty, 3 to 7 years in internship and residency programs.

Education. Most applicants to medical school have at least a bachelor's degree, and many have advanced degrees. Although no specific major is required, all students must complete undergraduate work in biology, chemistry, physics, math, and English. Students also take courses in the humanities and social sciences. In addition, some students volunteer at local hospitals or clinics to gain experience in a healthcare setting.

Medical schools are highly competitive. Most applicants must submit transcripts, scores from the Medical College Admission Test (MCAT), and letters of recommendation. Schools also consider an applicant's personality, leadership qualities, and participation in extracurricular activities. Most schools require applicants to interview with members of the admissions committee.

A few medical schools offer combined undergraduate and medical school programs that last 6 or 7 years.

Students spend most of the first 2 years of medical school in laboratories and classrooms, taking courses such as anatomy, biochemistry, pharmacology, psychology, medical ethics, and the laws governing medicine. They also gain practical skills, learning to take medical histories, examine patients, and diagnose illnesses.

During their last 2 years, medical students work with patients under the supervision of experienced physicians in hospitals and clinics. Through rotations in internal medicine, family practice, obstetrics and gynecology, pediatrics, psychiatry, and surgery, they gain experience in diagnosing and treating illnesses in a variety of areas.

Important Qualities

Communication skills. Physicians and surgeons need to be excellent communicators. They must be able to communicate effectively with their patients and other healthcare support staff.

Compassion. Physicians and surgeons deal with patients who are sick or injured and may be in extreme pain or distress. Physicians and surgeons must be able to treat patients and their families with compassion and understanding.

Detail oriented. Physicians and surgeons must ensure that patients are receiving appropriate treatment and medications. They must also monitor and record various pieces of information related to patient care.

Dexterity. Physicians and surgeons must be good at working with their hands. They may work with very precise and sometimes sharp tools, and mistakes can have serious consequences.

Leadership skills. Physicians who work in their own practice need to be effective leaders. They must be able to manage a staff of other professionals to run their practice.

Organizational skills. Some physicians own their own practice. Strong organizational skills, including good recordkeeping, are critical in both medical and business settings.

Patience. Physicians and surgeons may work for long periods with patients who need special attention. Persons who fear medical treatment may require more patience.

Physical stamina. Physicians and surgeons should be comfortable performing physical tasks, such as lifting or turning disabled patients. Surgeons may spend a great deal of time bending over patients during surgery.

Median Annual Wages, May 2014

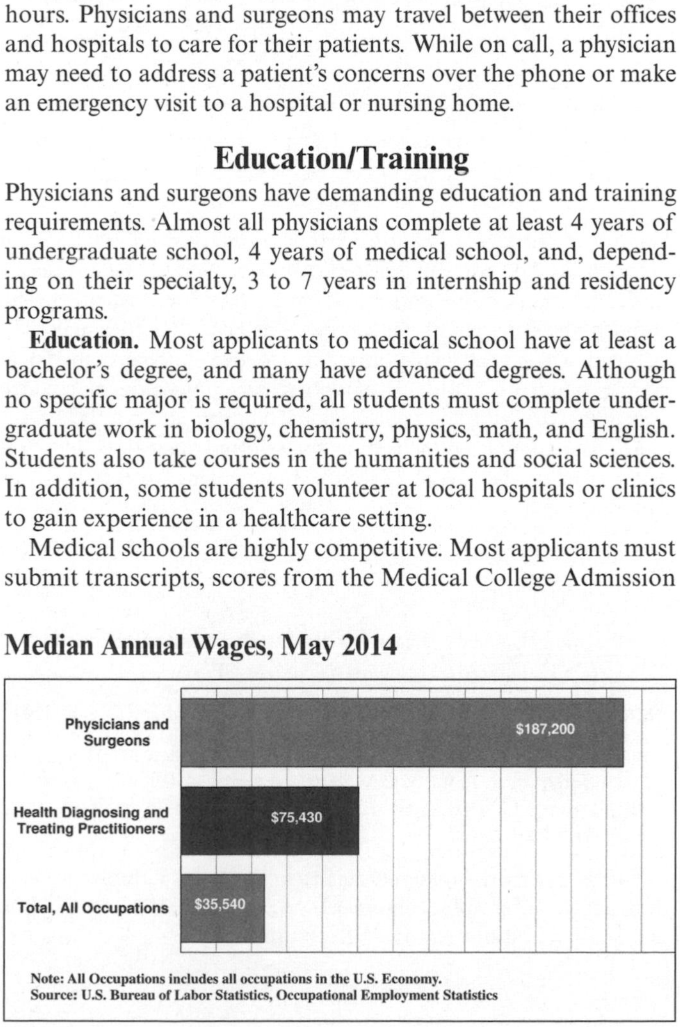

Note: All Occupations includes all occupations in the U.S. Economy.
Source: U.S. Bureau of Labor Statistics, Occupational Employment Statistics

Percent Change in Employment, Projected 2014–2024

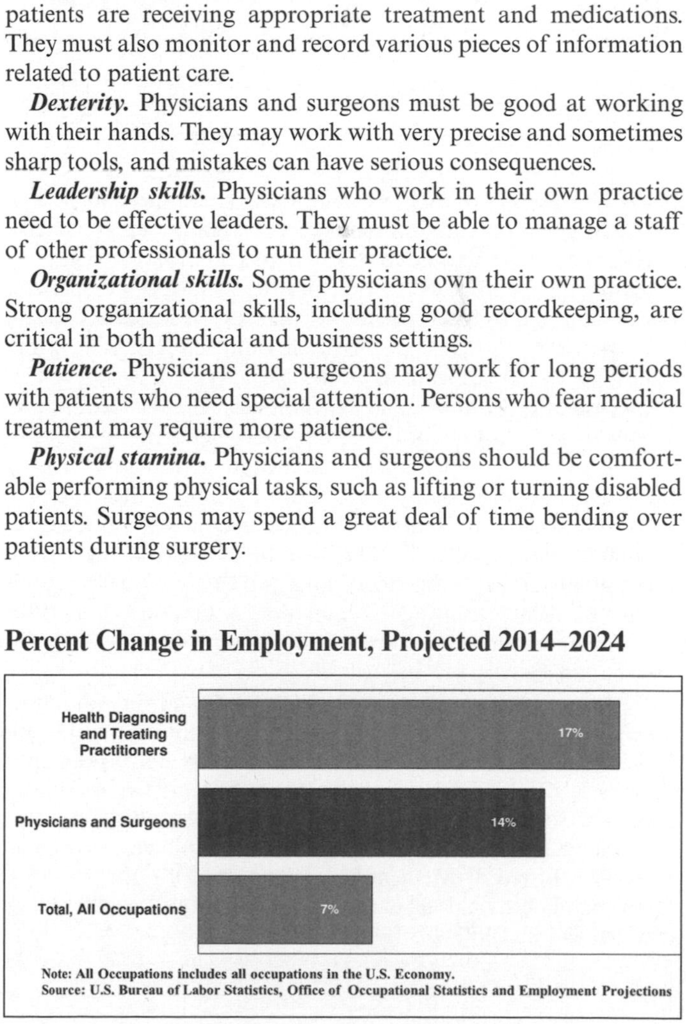

Note: All Occupations includes all occupations in the U.S. Economy.
Source: U.S. Bureau of Labor Statistics, Office of Occupational Statistics and Employment Projections

Employment Projections Data for Physicians and Surgeons

Occupational Title	SOC Code	Employment, 2014	Projected Employment, 2024	Change, 2014–2024 Percent	Change, 2014–2024 Numeric
Physicians and surgeons	29-1060	708,300	807,600	14	99,300
Anesthesiologists	29-1061	33,700	40,800	21	7,100
Family and general practitioners	29-1062	139,800	154,100	10	14,300
Internists, general	29-1063	54,300	59,400	9	5,100
Obstetricians and gynecologists	29-1064	24,400	28,700	18	4,300
Pediatricians, general	29-1065	34,800	38,400	10	3,600
Psychiatrists	29-1066	28,200	32,400	15	4,200
Surgeons	29-1067	46,000	55,100	20	9,100
Physicians and surgeons, all other	29-1069	347,200	398,800	15	51,700

Source: U.S. Bureau of Labor Statistics, Employment Projections Program

Similar Occupations. This table shows a list of occupations with job duties that are similar to those of physicians and surgeons.

Occupations	Entry-level Education	2014 Median Pay	Projected Job Growth	Average Annual Openings
Chiropractors	Doctoral or professional degree	$66,720	17%	790
Dentists	Doctoral or professional degree	$154,640	18%	2,670
Nurse Anesthetists, Nurse Midwives, and Nurse Practitioners	Master's degree	$102,670	31%	5,340
Optometrists	Doctoral or professional degree	$101,410	27%	1,100
Physician Assistants	Master's degree	$95,820	30%	2,870
Podiatrists	Doctoral or professional degree	$120,700	14%	140
Registered Nurses	Bachelor's degree	$66,640	16%	43,930
Veterinarians	Doctoral or professional degree	$87,590	9%	690

Problem-solving skills. Physicians and surgeons need to evaluate patients' symptoms and administer the appropriate treatments. They need to do this quickly if a patient's life is threatened.

Training. After medical school, almost all graduates enter a residency program in their specialty of interest. A residency usually takes place in a hospital and varies in duration, generally lasting from 3 to 7 years, depending on the specialty.

Licenses, Certifications, and Registrations. All states require physicians and surgeons to be licensed; requirements vary by state. To qualify for a license, candidates must graduate from an accredited medical school and complete residency training in their specialty.

All physicians and surgeons also must pass a standardized national licensure exam. M.D.s take the U.S. Medical Licensing Examination (USMLE). D.O.s take the Comprehensive Osteopathic Medical Licensing Examination (COMLEX-USA). For specific state information about licensing, contact your state's medical board.

Certification is not required for physicians and surgeons; however, it may increase their employment opportunities. M.D.s and D.O.s seeking board certification in a specialty may spend up to 7 years in residency training; the length of time varies with the specialty. To become board certified, candidates must complete a residency program and pass a specialty certification exam from the American Board of Medical Specialties (ABMS), the American Osteopathic Association (AOA), or the American Board of Physician Specialties (ABPS).

Pay

Wages for physicians and surgeons are among the highest of all occupations. According to the Medical Group Management Association's Physician Compensation and Production Survey, median total compensation for physicians varies with their type of practice. In 2014, physicians practicing primary care received total median annual compensation of $241,273 and physicians practicing in medical specialties received total median annual compensation of $411,852.

Median annual compensation for selected specialties in 2014, as reported by the Medical Group Management Association, was as follows:

Anesthesiology	$443,859
General surgery	395,456
Obstetrics/gynecology	317,496
Psychiatry	245,673
Internal Medicine	238,227
Pediatrics	226,408
Family Medicine (without Obstetrics)	221,419

Source: MGMA DataDive™ Provider Compensation 2015. Used with permission from MGMA, 104 Inverness Terrace East, Englewood, Colorado 80112. 877.275.6462. www.mgma.com. Copyright 2015.

Earnings vary with the physician's or surgeon's number of years in practice, geographic region of practice, hours worked, skill, personality, and professional reputation.

Job Outlook

Employment of physicians and surgeons is projected to grow 14 percent from 2014 to 2024, much faster than the average for all occupations. The growing and aging population is expected to drive overall growth in the demand for physician services as consumers continue to seek high levels of care that uses the latest technologies, diagnostic tests, and therapies.

Although the demand for physicians and surgeons is expected to continue, some factors will likely temper growth. New technologies will allow physicians to treat more patients in the same amount of time, thereby reducing the number of physicians who would be needed to complete the same tasks. In addition, physician assistants and nurse practitioners can do many of the routine duties of physicians and may be used to reduce costs at hospitals and doctor's offices.

Demand for physicians' services is sensitive to changes in healthcare reimbursement policies. Consumers may seek fewer physician services if changes to health coverage result in higher out-of-pocket costs for them. However, the number of individuals who have access to health insurance is expected to continue to increase because of federal health insurance reform. Such access will in turn increase demand for the services of physicians and surgeons.

Job Prospects. Job prospects should be good for physicians who are willing to practice in rural and low-income areas, because these areas tend to have difficulty attracting physicians. Job prospects also should be good for physicians in specialties dealing with health issues that largely affect aging baby boomers. For example, physicians specializing in cardiology and radiology will be needed because the risks for heart disease and cancer increase as people age.

Contacts for More Information

For more information about physicians and surgeons, visit

- American Medical Association (www.ama-assn.org)
- American Osteopathic Association (www.osteopathic.org)

For more information about various medical specialties, visit

- American Academy of Family Physicians (www.aafp.org/online/en/home.html)
- American Board of Medical Specialties (www.abms.org)
- American Board of Physician Specialties (www.abpsus.org)
- American Congress of Obstetricians and Gynecologists (www.acog.org)
- American College of Surgeons (www.facs.org)

For a list of medical schools and residency programs, as well as for general information on premedical education, financial aid, and medicine as a career, visit

- Association of American Medical Colleges (www.aamc.org)
- American Association of Colleges of Osteopathic Medicine (www.aacom.org/Pages/default.aspx)

For information about licensing, visit

- Federation of State Medical Boards (www.fsmb.org)

O*NET

- Anesthesiologists (29-1061.00)
- Family and General Practitioners (29-1062.00)
- Internists, General (29-1063.00)
- Obstetricians and Gynecologists (29-1064.00)
- Pediatricians, General (29-1065.00)
- Psychiatrists (29-1066.00)
- Surgeons (29-1067.00)
- Physicians and Surgeons, All Other (29-1069.00)
- Allergists and Immunologists (29-1069.01)
- Dermatologists (29-1069.02)
- Hospitalists (29-1069.03)
- Neurologists (29-1069.04)
- Nuclear Medicine Physicians (29-1069.05)
- Ophthalmologists (29-1069.06)
- Pathologists (29-1069.07)
- Physical Medicine and Rehabilitation Physicians (29-1069.08)
- Preventive Medicine Physicians (29-1069.09)
- Radiologists (29-1069.10)
- Sports Medicine Physicians (29-1069.11)
- Urologists (29-1069.12)

Podiatrists

- **2014 Median Pay** .... $120,700 per year $58.03 per hour
- **Typical Entry-Level Education** .... Doctoral or professional degree
- **Work Experience in a Related Occupation** .... None
- **On-the-job Training** .... Internship/residency
- **Number of Jobs, 2014** 9,600
- **Job Outlook, 2014–24** ...... 14% (Much faster than average)
- **Employment Change, 2014–24** 1,400

What Podiatrists Do

Podiatrists provide medical and surgical care for people with foot, ankle, and lower leg problems. They diagnose illnesses, treat injuries, and perform surgery involving the lower extremities.

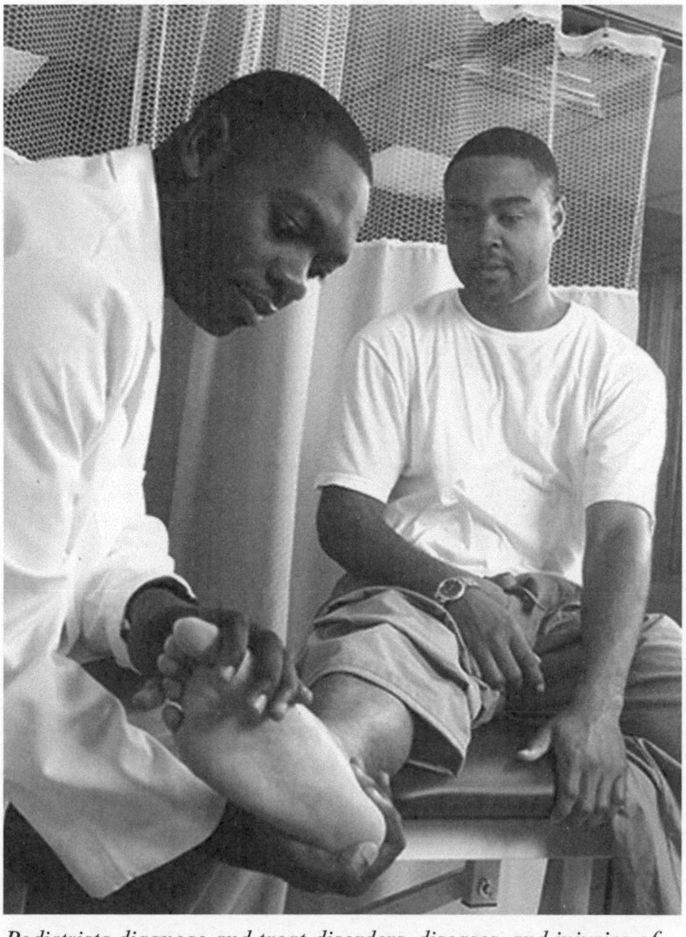

Podiatrists diagnose and treat disorders, diseases, and injuries of the foot and lower leg.

Median Annual Wages, May 2014

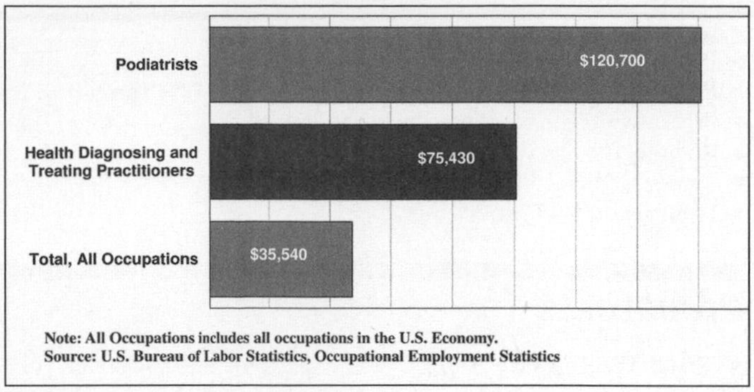

Percent Change in Employment, Projected 2014–2024

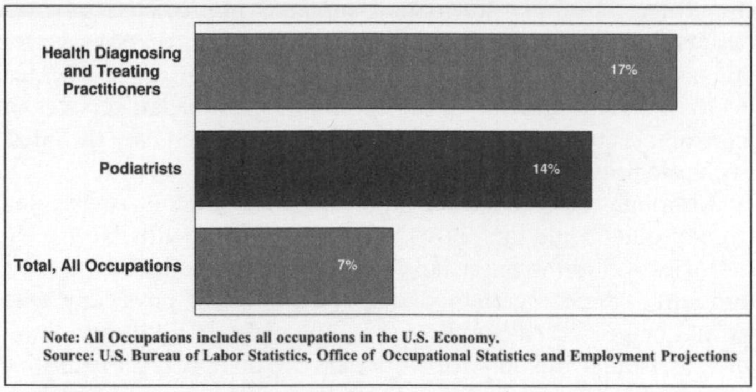

Duties. Podiatrists typically do the following:

- Assess the condition of a patient's feet, ankles, or lower legs by reviewing his or her medical history, listening to the patient's concerns, and performing a physical examination
- Diagnose foot, ankle, and lower leg problems through physical exams, X-rays, medical laboratory tests, and other methods
- Provide treatment for foot, ankle, and lower leg ailments, such as prescribing special shoe inserts (orthotics) to improve a patient's mobility
- Perform foot and ankle surgeries, such as removing bone spurs, fracture repairs, and correcting other foot and ankle deformities
- Advise and instruct patients on foot and ankle care and on general wellness techniques
- Prescribe medications
- Coordinate patient care with other physicians
- Refer patients to other physicians or specialists if they detect larger health problems, such as diabetes
- Conduct research, read journals, and attend conferences to keep up with advances in podiatric medicine and surgery

Podiatrists treat a variety of foot and ankle ailments, including calluses, ingrown toenails, heel spurs, arthritis, congenital foot and ankle deformities, and arch problems. They also treat foot and leg problems associated with diabetes and other diseases. Some podiatrists spend most of their time performing advanced surgery, such as foot and ankle reconstruction. Others may choose a specialty such as sports medicine or pediatrics.

Podiatrists who own their practice may spend time on business-related activities, such as hiring employees and managing inventory.

Work Environment

Podiatrists held about 9,600 jobs in 2014.

Most podiatrists work in offices of podiatry, either on their own or with other podiatrists. Some work in group practices with other physicians or specialists. Others work in private and public hospitals and outpatient care centers. Podiatrists may work closely with physicians and surgeons, registered nurses, and medical assistants.

Work Schedules. Most podiatrists work full time. Podiatrists' offices may be open in the evenings or on weekends to accommodate patients. In hospitals, podiatrists may have to work occasional nights or weekends, or may be on call.

Education/Training

Podiatrists must earn a Doctor of Podiatric Medicine (DPM) degree and complete a 3-year residency program. Every state requires podiatrists to be licensed.

Education. Podiatrists must have a Doctor of Podiatric Medicine (DPM) degree from an accredited college of podiatric medicine. A DPM degree program takes 4 years to complete. In 2014, there were 9 colleges of podiatric medicine accredited by the Council on Podiatric Medical Education.

Admission to podiatric medicine programs requires at least 3 years of undergraduate education, including specific courses in laboratory sciences such as biology, chemistry, and physics, as well as general coursework in subjects such as English. In practice, nearly all prospective podiatrists earn a bachelor's degree before attending a college of podiatric medicine. Admission to DPM programs usually requires taking the Medical College Admission Test (MCAT).

Courses for a Doctor of Podiatric Medicine degree are similar to those for other medical degrees. They include anatomy, physiology, pharmacology, and pathology among other subjects. During their last 2 years, podiatric medical students gain supervised experience by completing clinical rotations.

Training. After earning a DPM, podiatrists must apply to and complete a 3-year podiatric medical and surgical residency (PMSR) program. Residency programs take place in hospitals

Employment Projections Data for Podiatrists

Occupational Title	SOC Code	Employment, 2014	Projected Employment, 2024	Change, 2014–2024	
				Percent	Numeric
Podiatrists	29-1081	9,600	11,000	14	1,400

Source: U.S. Bureau of Labor Statistics, Employment Projections Program

Similar Occupations. This table shows a list of occupations with job duties that are similar to those of podiatrists.

Occupations	Entry-level Education	2014 Median Pay	Projected Job Growth	Average Annual Openings
Chiropractors	Doctoral or professional degree	$66,720	17%	790
Dentists	Doctoral or professional degree	$154,640	18%	2,670
Occupational Therapists	Master's degree	$78,810	27%	3,040
Optometrists	Doctoral or professional degree	$101,410	27%	1,100
Orthotists and Prosthetists	Master's degree	$64,040	23%	190
Physical Therapists	Doctoral or professional degree	$82,390	34%	7,180
Physicians and Surgeons	Doctoral or professional degree	This wage is equal to or greater than $187,200.	14%	9,930

and provide both medical and surgical experience. They may do additional training in specific fellowship areas, such as sports medicine or pediatrics.

Licenses, Certifications, and Registrations. Podiatrists in every state must be licensed. Podiatrists must pay a fee and pass the American Podiatric Medical Licensing Exam (APMLE), offered by the National Board of Podiatric Medical Examiners. Some states also require podiatrists to take a state-specific exam.

Many podiatrists choose to become board certified. Certification generally requires a combination of work experience and passing an exam from the American Board of Foot and Ankle Surgery, the American Board of Podiatric Medicine, or the American Board of Multiple Specialties in Podiatry.

Important Qualities

Compassion. Since podiatrists provide care for patients who may be in pain, they must be able to treat patients with compassion and understanding.

Critical-thinking skills. Podiatrists must have a sharp, analytical mind to correctly diagnose a patient and determine the best course of treatment.

Detail oriented. To provide safe, effective healthcare, a podiatrist should be detail oriented. For example, a podiatrist must pay attention to a patient's medical history as well as current conditions when diagnosing a problem.

Interpersonal skills. Because podiatrists spend much of their time interacting with patients, they should be able to listen well and communicate effectively. For example, they should be able to tell a patient who is slated to undergo surgery what to expect and calm his or her fears.

Pay

The median annual wage for podiatrists was $120,700 in May 2014. The median wage is the wage at which half the workers in an occupation earned more than that amount and half earned less. The lowest 10 percent earned less than $50,430, and the highest 10 percent earned more than $187,200.

Job Outlook

Employment of podiatrists is projected to grow 14 percent from 2014 to 2024, much faster than the average for all occupations. However, because it is a small occupation, the fast growth will result in only about 1,400 new jobs over the 10-year period.

As the U.S. population both ages and increases, the number of people expected to have mobility and foot-related problems will rise. Growing rates of chronic conditions, such as diabetes and obesity, also may limit mobility of those with these conditions, and lead to problems such as poor circulation in the feet and lower extremities. More podiatrists will be needed to provide care for these patients.

Job Prospects. Job prospects for trained podiatrists should be good given that there are a limited number of colleges of podiatry. In addition, the retirement of currently practicing podiatrists in the coming years is expected to increase the number of job openings for podiatrists.

Contacts for More Information

For more information about podiatrists, visit

- American Podiatric Medical Association (www.apma.org)

For information on colleges of podiatric medicine and their entrance requirements, curricula, and student financial aid, visit

- American Association of Colleges of Podiatric Medicine (www.aacpm.org)

For a list of accredited podiatric programs and residency programs, visit

- Council on Podiatric Medical Education (www.cpme.org)

For more information about the podiatric licensing exam, visit

- American Podiatric Medical Licensing Association (http://apmle.com)

For more information about board certification, visit

- American Board of Foot and Ankle Surgery (www.abfas.org)
- American Board of Podiatric Medicine (www.abpmed.org)
- American Board of Multiple Specialties in Podiatry (www.abmsp.org)

O*NET

- Podiatrists (29-1081.00)

Psychiatric Technicians and Aides

- **2014 Median Pay** .... $28,470 per year $13.69 per hour
- **Typical Entry-Level Education** .... See Education/Training
- **Work Experience in a Related Occupation** .... See Education/Training
- **On-the-job Training** .... Short-term on-the-job training
- **Number of Jobs, 2014** 145,200
- **Job Outlook, 2014–24** .... 5% (As fast as average)
- **Employment Change, 2014–24** 7,600

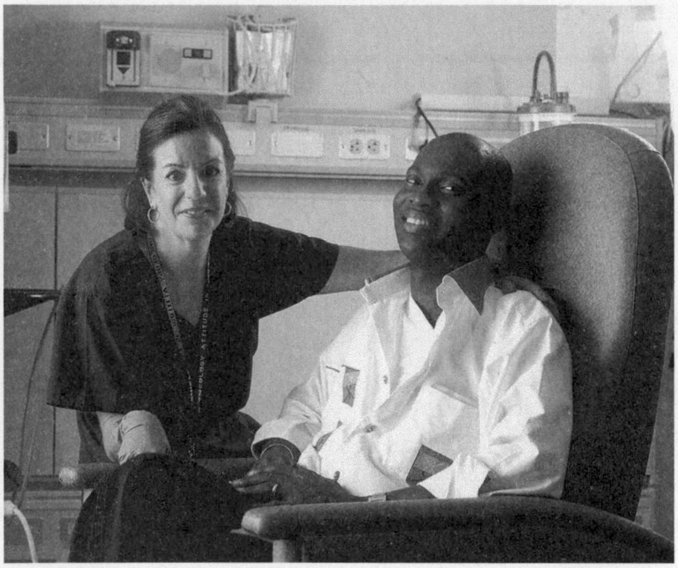

Psychiatric technicians and aides work in psychiatric hospitals, residential mental health facilities, and related healthcare settings, like drug or alcohol treatment centers.

What Psychiatric Technicians and Aides Do

Psychiatric technicians and aides care for people who have mental illness and developmental disabilities. Technicians typically provide therapeutic care and monitor their patients' conditions. Aides help patients in their daily activities and ensure a safe, clean environment.

Duties. Psychiatric technicians, sometimes called mental health technicians, typically do the following:

- Observe patients' behavior, listen to their concerns, and record their condition
- Lead patients in therapeutic and recreational activities
- Give medications and other treatments to patients, following instructions from doctors and other medical professionals
- Help with admitting and discharging patients
- Monitor patients' vital signs, such as their blood pressure
- Help patients with activities of daily living, including eating and bathing
- Restrain patients who may become physically violent

Psychiatric aides typically do the following:

- Monitor patients' behavior and location in a mental healthcare facility
- Help patients with their daily living activities, such as bathing and dressing
- Serve meals and help patients eat
- Keep facilities clean by doing tasks such as changing bed linens
- Participate in group activities, such as playing sports and going on field trips
- Help transport patients within a hospital or residential care facility
- Restrain patients who may become physically violent

Many psychiatric technicians and aides work with patients who are severely developmentally disabled and need intensive care. Others work with patients undergoing rehabilitation for drug and alcohol addiction. The work of psychiatric technicians and aides varies with the types of patients they work with.

Psychiatric technicians and aides work as part of a medical team under the direction of physicians and with other team members, who may include psychiatrists, psychologists, psychiatric nurses, social workers, counselors, and therapists. For more information on the counselors and therapists they may work with, see the profiles on substance abuse and behavioral disorder counselors, rehabilitation counselors, and mental health counselors and marriage and family therapists.

Because they have such close contact with patients, psychiatric technicians and aides can have a great deal of influence on patients' outlook and treatment.

Work Environment

Psychiatric technicians held about 67,900 jobs in 2014. Psychiatric aides held about 77,300 jobs in 2014.

The industries that employed the most psychiatric technicians in 2014 were as follows:

Psychiatric and substance abuse hospitals; state, local, and private	40%
State government, excluding education and hospitals	21
General medical and surgical hospitals; state, local, and private	15
Residential mental health and substance abuse facilities	6
Outpatient mental health and substance abuse centers	3

The industries that employed the most psychiatric aides in 2014 were as follows:

Psychiatric and substance abuse hospitals; state, local, and private	38%
State government, excluding education and hospitals	27
Residential intellectual and developmental disability facilities	9

Median Annual Wages, May 2014

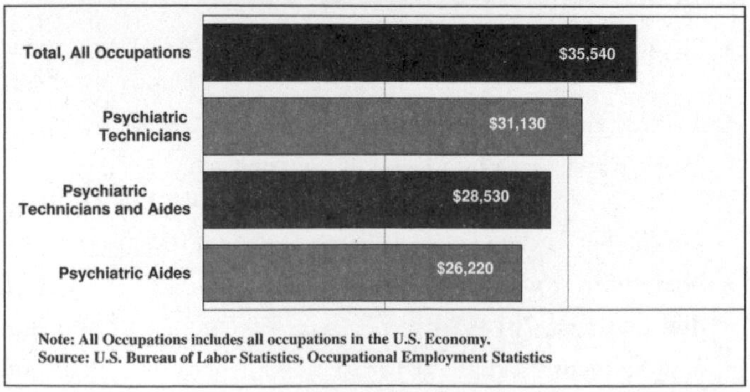

Percent Change in Employment, Projected 2014–2024

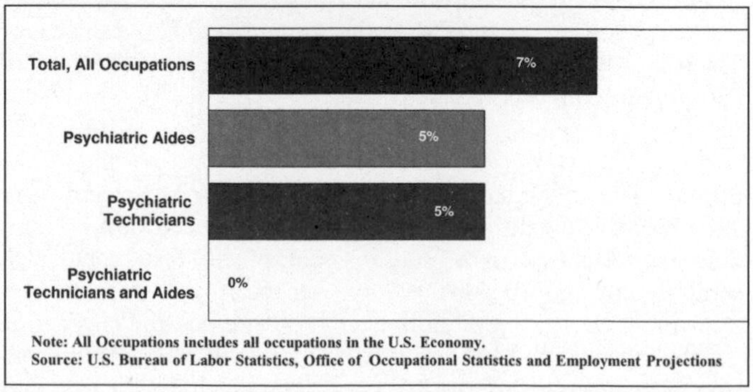

Employment Projections Data for Psychiatric Technicians and Aides

Occupational Title	SOC Code	Employment, 2014	Projected Employment, 2024	Change, 2014–2024 Percent	Change, 2014–2024 Numeric
Psychiatric technicians and aides	—	145,200	152,800	5	7,600
Psychiatric technicians	29-2053	67,900	71,400	5	3,500
Psychiatric aides	31-1013	77,300	81,400	5	4,100

Source: U.S. Bureau of Labor Statistics, Employment Projections Program

Residential mental health and substance abuse facilities........... 7
General medical and surgical hospitals; private........................ 4

Psychiatric technicians and aides may spend much of their shift on their feet. Some of the work that psychiatric aides do may be unpleasant. They may care for patients whose illnesses make them disoriented, uncooperative, or violent.

Injuries and Illnesses. Because their work requires many physically demanding tasks, such as lifting patients, psychiatric technicians and aides have high injury and illness rates.

Work Schedules. Psychiatric technicians and aides may work full time or part time. Because hospitals and residential facilities are open at all hours, many psychiatric technicians and aides work nights, weekends, and holidays.

Education/Training

Psychiatric technicians typically need postsecondary education, and aides need at least a high school diploma. Both technicians and aides get on-the-job training.

Education. Psychiatric technicians typically have a postsecondary certificate. Often, they have experience as a nursing assistant or a licensed practical nurse and have completed postsecondary education in nursing.

Some psychiatric technicians also may have a postsecondary certificate or associate's degree in psychiatric or mental health technology. These programs are offered by community colleges and technical schools and include courses in biology, psychology, and counseling. Psychiatric technician programs may include supervised work experience or cooperative programs, in which students gain academic credit for structured work experience.

Psychiatric aides typically need a high school diploma.

Training. Psychiatric technicians and aides usually have a short period of on-the-job training before they can work without direct supervision.

Training may include working with patients while under the close supervision of an experienced technician or aide. Technicians and aides also may attend workshops, lectures, or in-service training.

Work Experience in a Related Occupation. Psychiatric technicians typically need clinical experience, which can be gained by working in occupations such as nursing assistant or licensed practical nurse.

Important Qualities

Compassion. Because psychiatric technicians and aides spend much of their time interacting with patients, they should be caring and want to help people.

Interpersonal skills. Psychiatric technicians and aides often provide ongoing care for patients, so they should be able to develop a rapport with them. Gaining such rapport makes psychiatric technicians and aides better able to treat their patients and evaluate their condition.

Observational skills. Technicians must watch patients closely and be sensitive to any changes in behavior. For their safety and that of their patients, they must recognize signs of discomfort or trouble among patients.

Patience. Working with the mentally ill can be emotionally challenging. Psychiatric technicians and aides must be able to stay calm in stressful situations.

Physical stamina. Psychiatric technicians and aides must be able to lift, move, and sometimes restrain patients. They must also be able to spend much of their time on their feet.

Licenses, Certifications, and Registrations. Most states do not license psychiatric technicians. California is one of the larger states

Similar Occupations. This table shows a list of occupations with job duties that are similar to those of psychiatric technicians and aides.

Occupations	Entry-level Education	2014 Median Pay	Projected Job Growth	Average Annual Openings
Childcare Workers	High school diploma or equivalent	$19,730	5%	6,930
Home Health Aides	No formal educational credential	$21,380	38%	34,840
Licensed Practical and Licensed Vocational Nurses	Postsecondary nondegree award	$42,490	16%	11,730
Medical Assistants	Postsecondary nondegree award	$29,960	23%	13,890
Nursing Assistants and Orderlies	See Education/Training	$25,090	17%	26,780
Occupational Therapy Assistants and Aides	See Education/Training	$52,300	40%	1,680
Personal Care Aides	No formal educational credential	$20,440	26%	45,810
Registered Nurses	Bachelor's degree	$66,640	16%	43,930
Social and Human Service Assistants	High school diploma or equivalent	$29,790	11%	4,420

that does. For those states that license them, technicians usually are required to complete an accredited education program, pass an exam, and pay a fee to be licensed.

Psychiatric aides are not required to be licensed.

The American Association of Psychiatric Technicians offers four levels of certification for psychiatric technicians. The certifications allow technicians to show a high level of professional competency. Requirements vary by certification.

Pay

The median annual wage for psychiatric technicians was $31,130 in May 2014. The median wage is the wage at which half the workers in an occupation earned more than that amount and half earned less. The lowest 10 percent earned less than $20,990, and the highest 10 percent earned more than $57,280.

The median annual wage for psychiatric aides was $26,220 in May 2014. The lowest 10 percent earned less than $18,760, and the highest 10 percent earned more than $42,310.

In May 2014, the median annual wages for psychiatric technicians in the top industries in which they worked were as follows:

State government, excluding education and hospitals	$35,200
Psychiatric and substance abuse hospitals; state, local, and private	31,460
General medical and surgical hospitals; state, local, and private	31,400
Residential mental health and substance abuse facilities	26,060
Outpatient mental health and substance abuse centers	22,400

In May 2014, the median annual wages for psychiatric aides in the top industries in which they worked were as follows:

General medical and surgical hospitals; private	$29,660
Psychiatric and substance abuse hospitals; state, local, and private	28,180
State government, excluding education and hospitals	26,100
Residential mental health and substance abuse facilities	24,220
Residential intellectual and developmental disability facilities	21,610

Job Outlook

Employment of psychiatric technicians and aides is projected to grow 5 percent from 2014 to 2024, about as fast as the average for all occupations.

Cognitive mental disorders, such as Alzheimer's disease and dementia, are more likely to occur among older persons. As the nation's population ages and people live longer, demand for psychiatric technicians and aides in residential facilities is expected to rise so that these workers can care for patients affected by such disorders. Psychiatric technicians and aides also will be needed in correctional facilities, to care for the aging prisoner population.

More psychiatric technicians and aides will be needed in residential treatment facilities and in outpatient care centers to care for patients with developmental disabilities, mental illness, and substance abuse problems. There is a long-term trend toward treating psychiatric patients in community-based settings rather than in hospitals. These settings allow patients greater independence, and they are often more cost effective.

The number of individuals who have access to health insurance is expected to continue to increase because of federal health insurance reform. Such reform will expand coverage of mental health disorders to millions of people, and more technicians and aides will be needed to provide mental health services for them.

Contacts for More Information

For more information about psychiatric technicians and aides, visit

➤ American Association of Psychiatric Technicians (www.psychtechs.org)

O*NET

➤ Psychiatric Technicians (29-2053.00)

➤ Psychiatric Aides (31-1013.00)

Radiation Therapists

- **2014 Median Pay** .... $80,090 per year $38.51 per hour
- **Typical Entry-Level Education** .... Associate's degree
- **Work Experience in a Related Occupation** .... None
- **On-the-job Training** .... None
- **Number of Jobs, 2014** 16,600
- **Job Outlook, 2014–24** .... 14% (Much faster than average)
- **Employment Change, 2014–24** 2,300

What Radiation Therapists Do

Radiation therapists treat cancer and other diseases in patients by administering radiation treatments.

Duties. Radiation therapists typically do the following:

- Explain treatment plans to the patient and answer questions about treatment
- Follow safety procedures to protect the patient and themselves from overexposure to radiation
- Examine machines to make sure they are safe and working properly
- X-ray the patient to determine the exact location of the area requiring treatment
- Check computer programs to make sure the machine will give the correct dose of radiation to the appropriate area of the patient's body
- Operate the machine to treat the patient with radiation
- Monitor the patient to check for unusual reactions to the treatment
- Keep detailed records of treatment

Radiation therapists work in hospitals, offices of physicians, and outpatient centers.

Median Annual Wages, May 2014

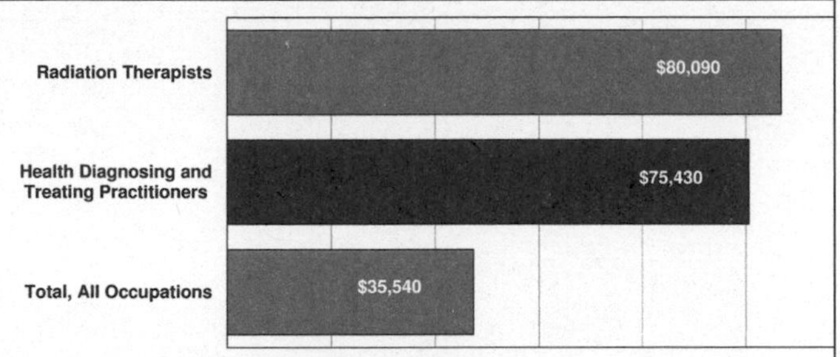

Note: All Occupations includes all occupations in the U.S. Economy.
Source: U.S. Bureau of Labor Statistics, Occupational Employment Statistics

Percent Change in Employment, Projected 2014–2024

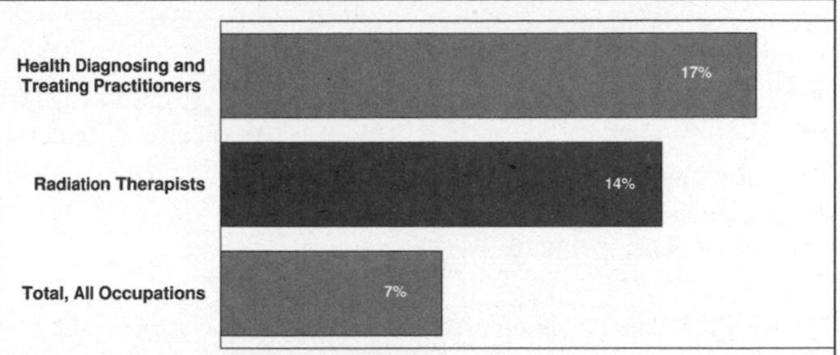

Note: All Occupations includes all occupations in the U.S. Economy.
Source: U.S. Bureau of Labor Statistics, Office of Occupational Statistics and Employment Projections

Radiation therapists operate machines called linear accelerators, which are used to deliver radiation therapy. These machines direct high-energy X-rays at specific cancer cells in a patient's body, shrinking or removing them.

They often work with the following specialists:

- Radiation oncologists, physicians who specialize in radiation therapy
- Oncology nurses, registered nurses who specialize in caring for patients with cancer
- Medical physicists, physicists who help in the planning of radiation treatments and the development of better and safer radiation therapies

Work Environment

Radiation therapists held about 16,600 jobs in 2014. Most therapists work in hospitals, offices of physicians, and outpatient centers.

Radiation therapists are on their feet for long periods and may need to lift or turn disabled patients. Because they work with radiation and radioactive material, radiation therapists must follow safety procedures to make sure that they are not exposed to a potentially harmful amount of radiation. These procedures usually require therapists to stand in a different room while the patient undergoes radiation procedures.

Work Schedules. Most radiation therapists work full time. Radiation therapists keep a regular work schedule because radiation therapy procedures are usually planned in advance.

Education/Training

Most radiation therapists complete programs that lead to an associate's degree or bachelor's degree in radiation therapy. Radiation therapists must be licensed or certified in most states. Requirements vary by state, but often include passing a national certification exam.

Education. Employers usually prefer to hire applicants who have an associate's degree or a bachelor's degree in radiation therapy. However, candidates may qualify for some positions by completing a 12-month certificate program.

Radiation therapy programs include courses in radiation therapy procedures and the scientific theories behind them. These programs often include experience in a clinical setting and courses in human anatomy and physiology, physics, algebra, computer science, and research methodology. In 2014, there were about 120 accredited educational programs recognized by the American Registry of Radiologic Technologists.

Important Qualities

Detail oriented. Radiation therapists must follow exact instructions and input exact measurements to make sure the patient is exposed to the correct amount of radiation.

Interpersonal skills. Radiation therapists work closely with patients. It is important that therapists be comfortable interacting with people who may be going through physical and emotional stress.

Physical stamina. Radiation therapists must be able to be on their feet for long periods and be able to lift and move patients who need assistance.

Technical skills. Radiation therapists work with computers and large pieces of technological equipment, so they must be comfortable operating those devices.

Licenses, Certifications, and Registrations. In most states, radiation therapists must be licensed or certified. Requirements vary by state, but typically include graduation from an accredited radiation therapy program and American Registry of Radiologic Technologists (ARRT) certification.

To become ARRT certified, an applicant must complete an accredited radiation therapy program, adhere to ARRT ethical standards, and pass the ARRT certification exam. The exam covers radiation protection and quality assurance, clinical concepts in radiation oncology, treatment planning, treatment delivery, and patient care and education. A list of accredited programs is available from ARRT.

Many jobs also require cardiopulmonary resuscitation (CPR) or basic life support (BLS) certification.

Employment Projections Data for Radiation Therapists

Occupational Title	SOC Code	Employment, 2014	Projected Employment, 2024	Change, 2014–2024 Percent	Change, 2014–2024 Numeric
Radiation therapists	29-1124	16,600	18,900	14	2,300

Source: U.S. Bureau of Labor Statistics, Employment Projections Program

Similar Occupations. This table shows a list of occupations with job duties that are similar to those of radiation therapists.

Occupations	Entry-level Education	2014 Median Pay	Projected Job Growth	Average Annual Openings
Dental Hygienists	Associate's degree	$71,520	19%	3,740
Diagnostic Medical Sonographers and Cardiovascular Technologists and Technicians, Including Vascular Technologists	Associate's degree	$62,540	24%	2,760
Nuclear Medicine Technologists	Associate's degree	$72,100	2%	30
Nursing Assistants and Orderlies	See Education/Training	$25,090	17%	26,780
Radiologic and MRI Technologists	Associate's degree	$57,370	9%	2,070
Registered Nurses	Bachelor's degree	$66,640	16%	43,930

Advancement. With additional education and certification, therapists can become medical dosimetrists. Dosimetrists are responsible for calculating the correct dose of radiation that is used in the treatment of cancer patients.

Pay

The median annual wage for radiation therapists was $80,090 in May 2014. The median wage is the wage at which half the workers in an occupation earned more than that amount and half earned less. The lowest 10 percent earned less than $53,590, and the highest 10 percent earned more than $118,180.

Job Outlook

Employment of radiation therapists is projected to grow 14 percent from 2014 to 2024, much faster than the average for all occupations. However, because it is a small occupation, the fast growth will result in only about 2,300 new jobs over the 10-year period.

The risk of cancer increases as people age, so an aging population may increase demand for radiation therapists. Continued advancements in the detection of cancer and the development of more sophisticated treatment techniques may also lead to greater demand for radiation therapy.

Job Prospects. Candidates can expect very strong competition for most radiation therapist positions. Jobseekers with prior work experience should have the best job opportunities.

Contacts for More Information

For more information about radiation therapists, visit

➤ The American Registry of Radiologic Technologists (www.arrt.org)

➤ American Society of Radiologic Technologists (www.asrt.org)

For information about becoming a medical dosimetrist, visit

➤ American Association of Medical Dosimetrists (http://tinyurl.com/hq7t3yz)

O*NET

➤ Radiation Therapists (29-1124.00)

Radiologic and MRI Technologists

- **2014 Median Pay** .... $57,370 per year $27.58 per hour
- **Typical Entry-Level Education** .... Associate's degree
- **Work Experience in a Related Occupation** .... See Education/Training
- **On-the-job Training** .... None
- **Number of Jobs, 2014** 230,600
- **Job Outlook, 2014–24** .... 9% (Faster than average)
- **Employment Change, 2014–24** 20,700

What Radiologic and MRI Technologists Do

Radiologic technologists, also known as *radiographers*, perform diagnostic imaging examinations, such as X-rays, on patients. MRI technologists operate magnetic resonance imaging (MRI) scanners to create diagnostic images.

Duties. Radiologic and MRI technologists typically do the following:

- Adjust and maintain imaging equipment
- Precisely follow orders from physicians on what areas of the body to image
- Prepare patients for procedures, including taking a medical history and answering questions about the procedure
- Protect the patient by shielding exposed areas that do not need to be imaged
- Position the patient and the equipment in order to get the correct image
- Operate the computerized equipment to take the images
- Work with physicians to evaluate the images and to determine whether additional images need to be taken
- Keep detailed patient records

Healthcare professionals use many types of equipment to diagnose patients. Some radiologic technologists prepare a mixture for the patient to drink that allows soft tissue to be viewed on the images that the radiologist reviews.

Radiologic technologists might also specialize in mammography. *Mammographers* use low-dose X-ray systems to produce images of the breast. Technologists may be certified in multiple specialties.

MRI technologists specialize in magnetic resonance imaging scanners. They inject patients with contrast dyes so that the images will show up on the scanner. The scanners use magnetic fields in combination with the contrast agent to produce images that a physician can use to diagnose medical problems.

Healthcare professionals who specialize in other diagnostic equipment include nuclear medicine technologists and diagnostic medical sonographers, and cardiovascular technologists and technicians, including vascular technologists.

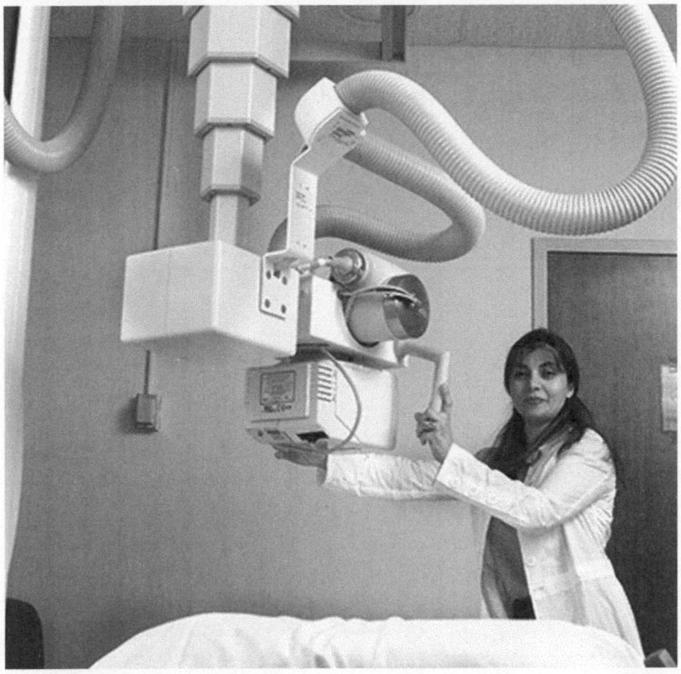

Radiologic technologists perform diagnostic imaging examinations on patients.

Work Environment

Radiologic technologists held about 197,000 jobs in 2014. MRI technologists held about 33,600 jobs in 2014.

The industries that employed the most radiologic technologists in 2014 were as follows:

Hospitals; state, local, and private	59%
Offices of physicians	21
Medical and diagnostic laboratories	8
Outpatient care centers	4

The industries that employed the most MRI technologists in 2014 were as follows:

Hospitals; state, local, and private	59%
Medical and diagnostic laboratories	20
Offices of physicians	14

Radiologic and MRI technologists work in healthcare facilities. Technologists are often on their feet for long periods and may need to lift or turn patients who are disabled.

Injuries and Illnesses. Like other healthcare workers, radiologic and MRI technologists may be exposed to infectious diseases. In addition, because radiologic and MRI technologists work with imaging equipment that uses radiation, they must wear badges that measure radiation levels in the radiation area. Detailed records are kept on their cumulative lifetime dose. Although radiation hazards exist in this occupation, they are minimized by the use of protective lead aprons, gloves, and other shielding devices, and by badges that monitor exposure to radiation.

Work Schedules. Most radiologic and MRI technologists work full time. Because imaging is sometimes needed in emergency situations, some technologists work evenings, weekends, or overnight.

Education/Training

Radiologic and MRI technologists typically need an associate's degree. Many MRI technologists start out as radiologic technologists and specialize later in their career. Technologists must be licensed or certified in most states; requirements vary by state.

Education. An associate's degree is the most common educational requirement for radiologic and MRI technologists. There also are postsecondary education programs that lead to graduate certificates or bachelor's degrees. Education programs typically include both classroom study and clinical work. Coursework includes anatomy, pathology, patient care, radiation physics and protection, and image evaluation.

The Joint Review Committee on Education in Radiologic Technology (JRCERT) accredits programs in radiography. Completing an accredited program is required for licensure in some states.

High school students who are interested in radiologic or MRI technology should take courses that focus on math and science, such as anatomy, biology, chemistry, physiology, and physics.

Work Experience in a Related Occupation. MRI technologists typically have less than 5 years of work experience as radiologic technologists.

Licenses, Certifications, and Registrations. Radiologic and MRI technologists must be licensed or certified in most states; requirements vary by state. To become licensed, technologists must graduate from an accredited program and must pass a certification exam from the state or from the American Registry of Radiologic Technologists (ARRT).

Many MRI technologists first are licensed or certified radiologic technologists who have the required amount of work experience in magnetic resonance imaging to meet the certification standard. Beginning in 2016, MRI technologists must complete a set number of documented imaging examinations and 16 hours of formal education to be certified. Those who do not have experience as a radiologic technologist must first complete a formal education program before taking the certification exam. MRI certification is available from the ARRT and is accepted by most states for licensure.

For specific state requirements, contact the state's health board.

Median Annual Wages, May 2014

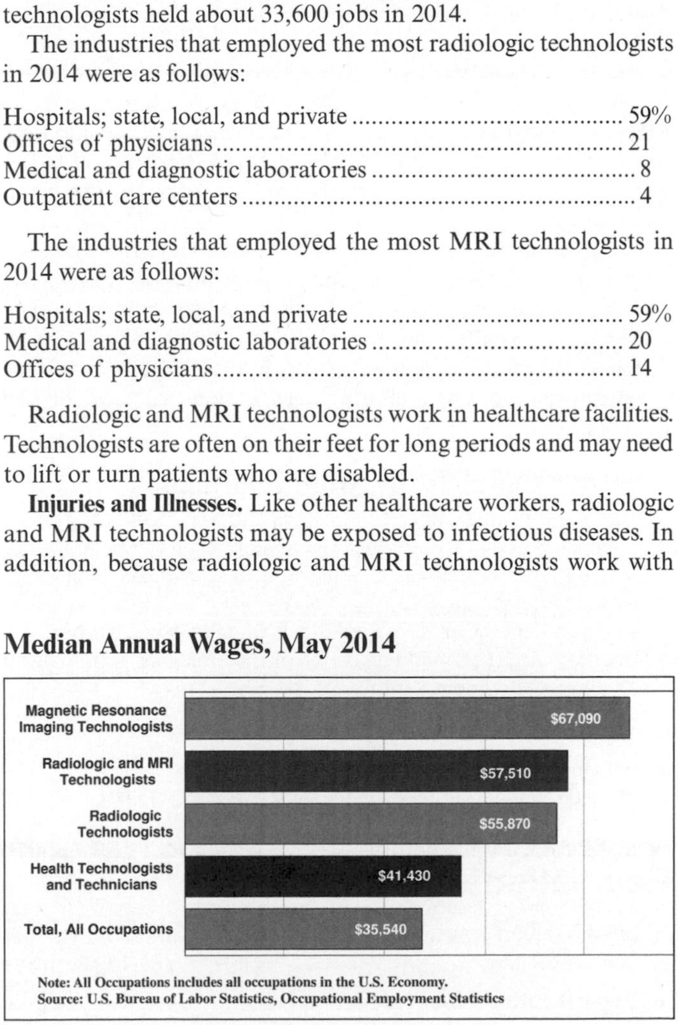

Percent Change in Employment, Projected 2014–2024

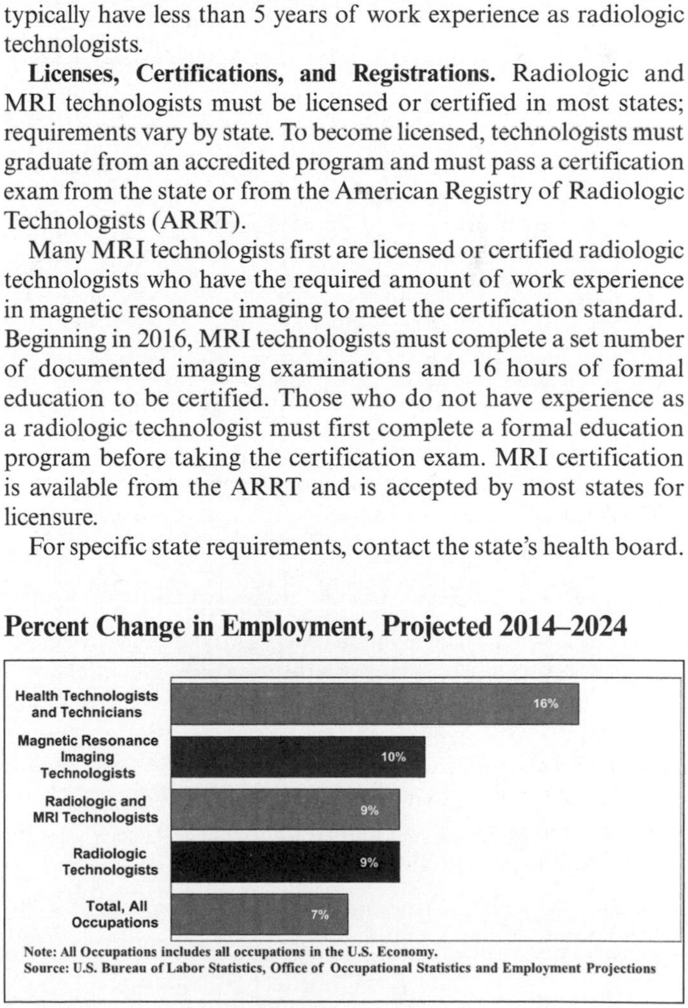

Employment Projections Data for Radiologic and MRI Technologists

Occupational Title	SOC Code	Employment, 2014	Projected Employment, 2024	Change, 2014–2024 Percent	Change, 2014–2024 Numeric
Radiologic and MRI technologists	—	230,600	251,200	9	20,700
Radiologic technologists	29-2034	197,000	214,200	9	17,200
Magnetic resonance imaging technologists	29-2035	33,600	37,100	10	3,500

Source: U.S. Bureau of Labor Statistics, Employment Projections Program

Similar Occupations. This table shows a list of occupations with job duties that are similar to those of radiologic and MRI technologists.

Occupations	Entry-level Education	2014 Median Pay	Projected Job Growth	Average Annual Openings
Diagnostic Medical Sonographers and Cardiovascular Technologists and Technicians, Including Vascular Technologists	Associate's degree	$62,540	24%	2,760
Nuclear Medicine Technologists	Associate's degree	$72,100	2%	30
Radiation Therapists	Associate's degree	$80,090	14%	230

Important Qualities

Detail oriented. Radiologic and MRI technologists must follow exact instructions to get the images needed for diagnoses.

Interpersonal skills. Radiologic and MRI technologists work closely with patients who may be in extreme pain or mentally stressed. Technologists must be able to put the patient at ease to get usable images.

Math skills. Radiologic and MRI technologists may need to calculate and mix the right doses of chemicals used in imaging procedures.

Physical stamina. Radiologic and MRI technologists often work on their feet for long periods during their shift and they must be able to lift and move patients who need assistance.

Technical skills. Radiologic and MRI technologists must understand how to operate complex machinery.

Pay

The median annual wage for radiologic technologists was $55,870 in May 2014. The median wage is the wage at which half the workers in an occupation earned more than that amount and half earned less. The lowest 10 percent earned less than $37,610, and the highest 10 percent earned more than $80,080.

The median annual wage for magnetic resonance imaging technologists was $67,090 in May 2014. The lowest 10 percent earned less than $46,310, and the highest 10 percent earned more than $92,220.

In May 2014, the median annual wages for radiologic technologists in the top industries in which they worked were as follows:

Medical and diagnostic laboratories	$56,980
Hospitals; state, local, and private	56,900
Outpatient care centers	55,750
Offices of physicians	50,990

In May 2014, the median annual wages for MRI technologists in the top industries in which they worked were as follows:

Medical and diagnostic laboratories	$68,200
Offices of physicians	67,620
Hospitals; state, local, and private	66,290

Job Outlook

Employment of radiologic technologists is projected to grow 9 percent from 2014 to 2024, faster than the average for all occupations. Employment of MRI technologists is projected to grow 10 percent from 2014 to 2024, faster than the average for all occupations.

As the population grows older, there will be an increase in medical conditions, such as cancer and Alzheimer's disease, which require imaging as a tool for making diagnoses. Radiologic and MRI technologists will be needed to take the images. In addition, the number of individuals who have access to health insurance is expected to continue to increase because of federal health insurance reform.

However, employment growth of radiologic and MRI technologists may be tempered, as many medical facilities and third-party payers encourage the use of less-costly, noninvasive imaging technologies, such as ultrasound.

Job Prospects. Technologists who graduate from accredited programs and those with multiple certifications will have the best job prospects.

Contacts for More Information

For more information about radiologic and MRI technology, visit

- American Society of Radiologic Technologists (www.asrt.org)
- Joint Review Committee on Education in Radiologic Technology (www.jrcert.org)
- American Registry of Radiologic Technologists (www.arrt.org)
- American Registry of Magnetic Resonance Imaging Technologists (www.armrit.org/index.shtml)

O*NET

- Radiologic Technologists (29-2034.00)
- Magnetic Resonance Imaging Technologists (29-2035.00)

Recreational Therapists

- **2014 Median Pay** .... $44,000 per year
$21.15 per hour
- **Typical Entry-Level Education** .... Bachelor's degree

- **Work Experience in a Related Occupation**.............. None
- **On-the-job Training** .... None
- **Number of Jobs, 2014** 18,600
- **Job Outlook, 2014–24**............ 12% (Faster than average)
- **Employment Change, 2014–24** 2,200

What Recreational Therapists Do

Recreational therapists plan, direct, and coordinate recreation-based treatment programs for people with disabilities, injuries, or illnesses. These therapists use a variety of modalities, including arts and crafts; drama, music, and dance; sports and games; aquatics; and community outings to help maintain or improve a patient's physical, social, and emotional well-being.

Duties. Recreational therapists typically do the following:

- Assess patients' needs through observations, medical records, tests, and discussions with other healthcare professionals, patients' families, and patients
- Create treatment plans and programs that meet patients' needs and interests
- Plan and implement interventions to prevent harm to a patient
- Engage patients in therapeutic activities, such as exercise, games, and community outings
- Help patients learn social skills needed to become or remain independent
- Teach patients about ways to cope with stress, anxiety, or depression
- Record and analyze a patient's progress
- Evaluate interventions for effectiveness

Recreational therapists help people reduce depression, stress, and anxiety; recover basic physical and mental abilities; build confidence; and socialize effectively.

They use activities, such as arts and crafts, dance, or sports, to help their patients. For example, a recreational therapist can help a patient who is paralyzed on one side of the body by teaching them to adapt activities, like casting a fishing rod or swinging a golf club, by using their functional side.

Therapists often treat specific groups of patients, such as children with cancer. Therapists may use activities such as kayaking or a ropes course to teach patients to stay active and to form social relationships.

Recreational therapists help people with disabilities integrate into the community by teaching them how to use community resources and recreational activities. For example, therapists may teach a patient who uses a wheelchair how to use public transportation.

Recreational therapists observe and document a patient's participation, reaction, and progress.

Therapists may also provide interventions for patients who need help developing social and coping skills. For example, a therapist may use a therapy dog to help patients manage their depression or anxiety.

Therapists may work with physicians or surgeons, registered nurses, psychologists, social workers, physical therapists, teachers, or occupational therapists. Recreational therapists are different from recreation workers, who organize recreational activities primarily for enjoyment.

Work Environment

Recreational therapists held about 18,600 jobs in 2014. The industries that employed the most recreational therapists were as follows:

Hospitals; state, local, and private	35%
Nursing care facilities (skilled nursing facilities)	20
Government	19
Ambulatory healthcare services	8
Continuing care retirement communities and assisted living facilities for the elderly	6

Median Annual Wages, May 2014

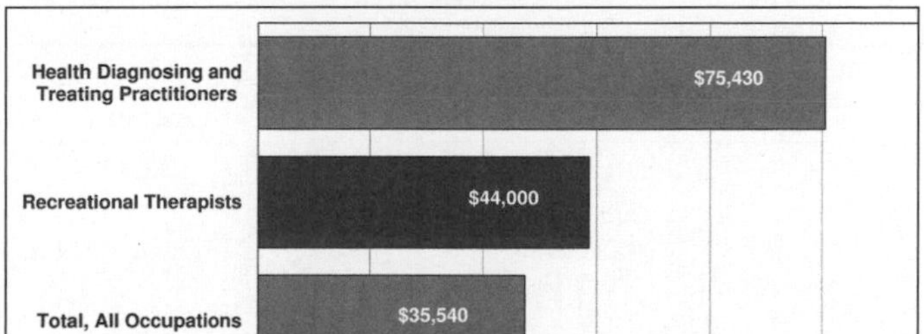

Percent Change in Employment, Projected 2014–2024

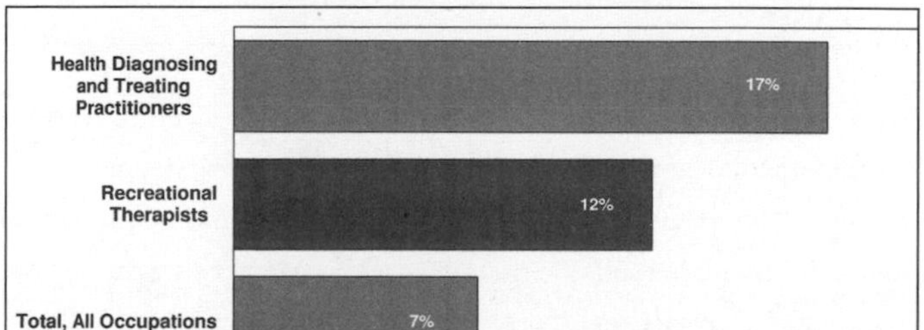

Employment Projections Data for Recreational Therapists

Occupational Title	SOC Code	Employment, 2014	Projected Employment, 2024	Change, 2014–2024 Percent	Change, 2014–2024 Numeric
Recreational therapists	29-1125	18,600	20,900	12	2,200

Source: U.S. Bureau of Labor Statistics, Employment Projections Program

Recreational therapists work in a variety of settings. Therapists often work in hospitals or nursing and residential care facilities. They also work in places such as substance abuse centers, outpatient rehabilitation centers, special education departments, and parks and recreation departments.

They may use offices for planning or other administrative activities, such as patient assessment, but may travel when working with patients. Therapy may be provided in a clinical setting or out in a community. For example, therapists may take their patients to fields and parks for sports and other outdoor activities.

Some therapists may spend a lot of time on their feet actively working with patients. Recreational therapists may also need to physically assist patients or lift heavy objects such as wheelchairs.

Work Schedules. Most recreational therapists work full time, although about 1 in 4 worked part time in 2014. Some recreational therapists work evenings and weekends to meet the needs of their patients.

Education/Training

Recreational therapists typically need a bachelor's degree. Many employers require therapists to be certified by the National Council for Therapeutic Recreation Certification (NCTRC).

Education. The typical entry route for recreational therapists is a bachelor's degree, usually in recreational therapy or a related field such as recreation and leisure studies.

Recreational therapy programs include courses in assessment, human anatomy, medical and psychiatric terminology, characteristics of illnesses and disabilities, and the use of assistive devices and technology. Bachelor's degree programs usually include an internship.

Licenses, Certifications, and Registrations. Most employers, particularly those in hospitals and other clinical settings, prefer to hire certified recreational therapists. The NCTRC offers the Certified Therapeutic Recreation Specialist (CTRS) credential. Candidates may qualify for certification through one of two pathways. The first option requires a bachelor's degree in recreational therapy, which includes the completion of a supervised internship of at least 560 hours, and passing an exam. The second option also requires passing an exam, but allows candidates with a bachelor's degree in an unrelated subject to qualify with a combination of education and work experience. Therapists must take continuing education classes to maintain certification.

NCTRC also offers specialty certification in five areas of practice: behavioral health, community inclusion services, developmental disabilities, geriatrics, and physical medicine/rehabilitation. Therapists also may earn certificates from other organizations to show proficiency in specific therapy techniques, such as aquatic therapy or aromatherapy.

As of 2014, only New Hampshire, North Carolina, Oklahoma, and Utah required recreational therapists to obtain a license. Requirements vary by state. For specific requirements, contact the state's medical board.

Important Qualities

Compassion. Recreational therapists should be kind and empathetic when providing support to patients and their families. They may deal with patients who are in pain or under emotional stress.

Leadership skills. Recreational therapists must be able to plan, develop, and implement intervention programs in an effective manner. They must be engaging and able to motivate patients to participate in a variety of therapeutic activities.

Listening skills. Recreational therapists must listen carefully to a patient's problems and concerns. They can then determine an appropriate course of treatment for that patient.

Patience. Recreational therapists may work with some patients who require more time and special attention than others.

Resourcefulness. Recreational therapists customize treatment plans for patients. They must be both creative and flexible when adapting activities or programs to each patient's needs.

Speaking skills. Recreational therapists need to communicate well with their patients. They must give clear directions during activities or instructions on healthy coping techniques.

Pay

The median annual wage for recreational therapists was $44,000 in May 2014. The median wage is the wage at which half the workers in an occupation earned more than that amount and half earned less. The lowest 10 percent earned less than $27,150, and the highest 10 percent earned more than $69,230.

Similar Occupations. This table shows a list of occupations with job duties that are similar to those of recreational therapists.

Occupations	Entry-level Education	2014 Median Pay	Projected Job Growth	Average Annual Openings
Occupational Therapists	Master's degree	$78,810	27%	3,040
Physical Therapists	Doctoral or professional degree	$82,390	34%	7,180
Rehabilitation Counselors	Master's degree	$34,380	9%	1,080
School and Career Counselors	Master's degree	$53,370	8%	2,250
Special Education Teachers	Bachelor's degree	$55,980	6%	2,810
Speech-Language Pathologists	Master's degree	$71,550	21%	2,890

In May 2014, the median annual wages for recreational therapists in the top industries in which they worked were as follows:

Government	$52,770
Hospitals; state, local, and private	46,690
Ambulatory healthcare services	41,400
Nursing care facilities (skilled nursing facilities)	38,960
Continuing care retirement communities and assisted living facilities for the elderly	37,740

Job Outlook

Employment of recreational therapists is projected to grow 12 percent from 2014 to 2024, faster than the average for all occupations.

As the U.S. population ages, more people will need recreational therapists to help treat age-related injuries and illnesses. Older people are more likely to suffer from stroke, Alzheimer's disease, and mobility-related injuries that may benefit from recreational therapy. Growth is expected in nursing care facilities, adult daycare programs, and other settings that care for geriatric patients.

Therapists will also be needed to help healthy seniors remain social and active in their communities. Recreational therapy services can help the aging population to maintain their independence later in life. For example, recreational therapists can help older people prevent falls by teaching them modified yoga exercises that improve balance and strength. Patients' preferences for aging at home, combined with shorter hospital stays, will shift treatment to outpatient and community-based settings rather than more costly hospital settings.

In addition, the number of people with chronic conditions, such as diabetes and obesity, is growing. Recreational therapists will be needed to help patients maintain their mobility, to teach patients about managing their conditions, and to help patients adjust recreational activities to meet any physical limitations. Therapists will be needed also to plan and lead programs designed to maintain overall wellness through participation in activities such as camps, day trips, and sports.

Recreational therapists will increasingly be utilized also in helping veterans manage service-related conditions such as post-traumatic stress disorder (PTSD) or injuries such as the loss of a limb. Recreational therapists can lead activities that help to reintegrate veterans into their communities and help them to adjust to any physical, social, or cognitive limitations.

Job Prospects. Job prospects will be best for recreational therapists with both a bachelor's degree and certification. Therapists who specialize in working with the elderly or who earn certification in geriatric therapy may have the best job prospects. In addition, demand may be greater in highly populated areas, so recreational therapists who are willing to relocate may have the best job prospects.

Contacts for More Information

For information and materials on careers and academic programs in recreational therapy, visit

➤ American Therapeutic Recreation Association (www.atra-online.com)

For more information about certification, visit

➤ National Council for Therapeutic Recreation Certification (http://nctrc.org)

O*NET

➤ Recreational Therapists (29-1125.00)
➤ Art Therapists (29-1125.01)
➤ Music Therapists (29-1125.02)

Registered Nurses

- **2014 Median Pay** .... $66,640 per year / $32.04 per hour
- **Typical Entry-Level Education** .... Bachelor's degree
- **Work Experience in a Related Occupation** .... None
- **On-the-job Training** .... None
- **Number of Jobs, 2014** 2,751,000
- **Job Outlook, 2014–24** ...... 16% (Much faster than average)
- **Employment Change, 2014–24** 439,300

What Registered Nurses Do

Registered nurses (RNs) provide and coordinate patient care, educate patients and the public about various health conditions, and provide advice and emotional support to patients and their family members.

Duties. Registered nurses typically do the following:

- Record patients' medical histories and symptoms
- Administer patients' medicines and treatments
- Set up plans for patients' care or contribute to existing plans
- Observe patients and record the observations
- Consult and collaborate with doctors and other healthcare professionals
- Operate and monitor medical equipment
- Help perform diagnostic tests and analyze the results
- Teach patients and their families how to manage illnesses or injuries
- Explain what to do at home after treatment

Most registered nurses work as part of a team with physicians and other healthcare specialists. Some registered nurses oversee licensed practical nurses, nursing assistants, and home health aides.

Registered nurses' duties and titles often depend on where they work and the patients they work with. For example, an oncology nurse may work with cancer patients or a geriatric nurse may work

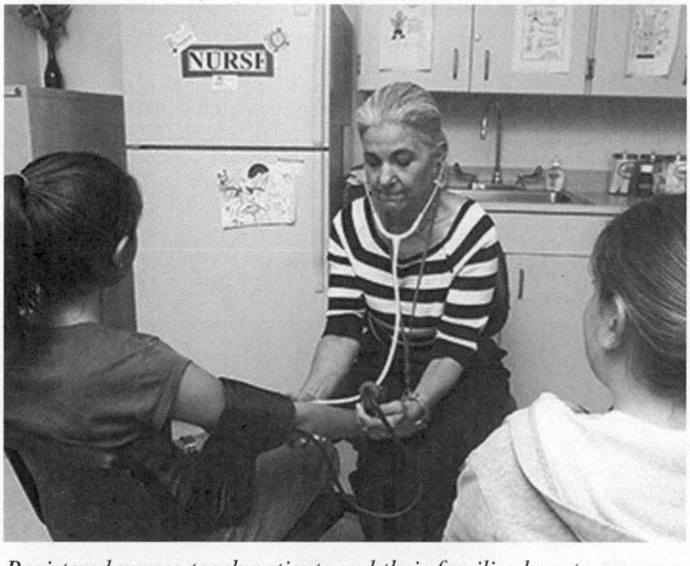

Registered nurses teach patients and their families how to manage their illness or injury.

with elderly patients. Some registered nurses combine one or more areas of practice. For example, a pediatric oncology nurse works with children and teens who have cancer.

Many possibilities for working with specific patient groups exist. The following list includes just a few examples:

Addiction nurses care for patients who need help to overcome addictions to alcohol, drugs, and other substances.

Cardiovascular nurses care for patients with heart disease and people who have had heart surgery.

Critical care nurses work in intensive-care units in hospitals, providing care to patients with serious, complex, and acute illnesses and injuries that need very close monitoring and treatment.

Genetics nurses provide screening, counseling, and treatment for patients with genetic disorders, such as cystic fibrosis.

Neonatology nurses take care of newborn babies.

Nephrology nurses care for patients who have kidney-related health issues stemming from diabetes, high blood pressure, substance abuse, or other causes.

Rehabilitation nurses care for patients with temporary or permanent disabilities.

Registered nurses may work to promote public health, by educating people on warning signs and symptoms of disease or managing chronic health conditions. They may also run health screenings, immunization clinics, blood drives, or other community outreach programs. Other nurses staff the health clinics in schools.

Some nurses do not work directly with patients, but they must still have an active registered nurse license. For example, they may work as nurse educators, healthcare consultants, public policy advisors, researchers, hospital administrators, salespeople for pharmaceutical and medical supply companies, or as medical writers and editors.

Clinical nurse specialists (CNSs) are a type of advanced practice registered nurse (APRN). They provide direct patient care in one of many nursing specialties, such as psychiatric-mental health or pediatrics. CNSs also provide indirect care, by working with other nurses and various other staff to improve the quality of care that patients receive. They often serve in leadership roles and may educate and advise other nursing staff. CNSs also may conduct research and may advocate for certain policies.

Work Environment

Registered nurses held about 2.8 million jobs in 2014. The industries that employed the most registered nurses were as follows:

Hospitals; state, local, and private	61%
Nursing and residential care facilities	7
Offices of physicians	7
Home healthcare services	6
Government	6

Registered nurses are the largest healthcare occupation. They work in hospitals, physicians' offices, home healthcare services, and nursing care facilities. Others work in schools or outpatient clinics, or serve in the military. Home health and public health nurses travel to patients' homes, schools, community centers, and other sites.

Some nurses move frequently, traveling in the United States and throughout the world to help care for patients in places where there are not enough healthcare workers.

Injuries and Illnesses. Registered nurses may spend a lot of time walking, bending, stretching, and standing. They are vulnerable to back injuries, because they often must lift and move patients.

In addition, the work of registered nurses may put them in close contact with people who have infectious diseases, and they frequently come in contact with potentially harmful and hazardous drugs and other substances. Therefore, registered nurses must follow strict, standardized guidelines to guard against diseases and other dangers, such as radiation, accidental needle sticks, or the chemicals used to create a sterile and clean environment.

Work Schedules. Because patients in hospitals and nursing care facilities need round-the-clock care, nurses in these settings usually work in shifts, covering all 24 hours. They may work nights, weekends, and holidays. They also may be on call.

Nurses who work in offices, schools, and other places that do not provide 24-hour care are more likely to work regular business hours.

In 2014, about 1 out of 6 registered nurses worked part time.

Education/Training

Registered nurses usually take one of three education paths: a Bachelor of Science degree in nursing (BSN), an associate's degree in nursing (ADN), or a diploma from an approved nursing program. Registered nurses also must be licensed.

Education. In all nursing education programs, students take courses in anatomy, physiology, microbiology, chemistry, nutrition, psychology, and other social and behavioral sciences, as well as in liberal arts. BSN programs typically take 4 years to complete; ADN and diploma programs usually take 2 to 3 years to complete. All programs include supervised clinical experience.

Bachelor's degree programs usually include additional education in the physical and social sciences, communication, leadership, and critical thinking. These programs also offer more clinical experience in nonhospital settings. A bachelor's degree or higher is often necessary for administrative positions, research, consulting, and teaching.

Generally, licensed graduates of any of the three types of education programs (bachelor's, associate's, or diploma) qualify for entry-level positions as a staff nurse. However,

Median Annual Wages, May 2014

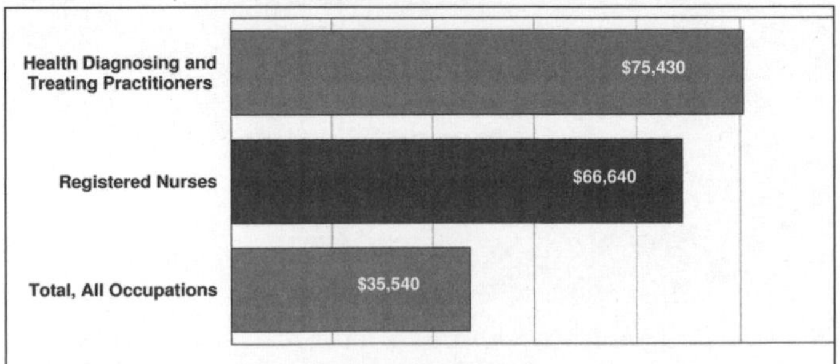

Note: All Occupations includes all occupations in the U.S. Economy.
Source: U.S. Bureau of Labor Statistics, Occupational Employment Statistics

Percent Change in Employment, Projected 2014–2024

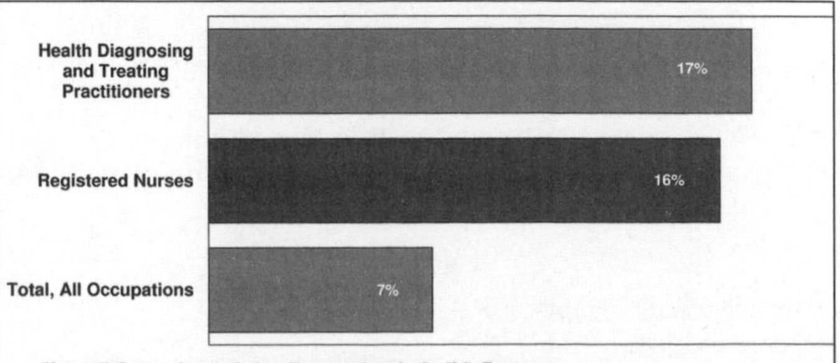

Note: All Occupations includes all occupations in the U.S. Economy.
Source: U.S. Bureau of Labor Statistics, Office of Occupational Statistics and Employment Projections

employers—particularly those in hospitals—may require a bachelor's degree.

Many registered nurses with an ADN or diploma choose to go back to school to earn a bachelor's degree through an RN-to-BSN program. There are also master's degree programs in nursing, combined bachelor's and master's programs, and accelerated programs for those who wish to enter the nursing profession and already hold a bachelor's degree in another field. Some employers offer tuition reimbursement.

Clinical nurse specialists (CNSs) must earn a master's degree in nursing and typically already have 1 or more years of work experience as an RN or in a related field. CNSs who conduct research typically need a doctoral degree.

Licenses, Certifications, and Registrations. In all states, the District of Columbia, and U.S. territories, registered nurses must have a nursing license. To become licensed, nurses must graduate from an approved nursing program and pass the National Council Licensure Examination (NCLEX-RN).

Other requirements for licensing vary by state. Each state's board of nursing can give details. For more information on the NCLEX-RN and a list of state boards of nursing, visit the National Council of State Boards of Nursing.

Nurses may become certified through professional associations in specific areas, such as ambulatory care, gerontology, and pediatrics, among others. Although certification is usually voluntary, it demonstrates adherence to a higher standard, and some employers require it.

CNSs must satisfy additional state licensing requirements, such as earning specialty certifications. Contact state boards of nursing for specific requirements.

Important Qualities

Critical-thinking skills. Registered nurses must be able to assess changes in the health status of patients, including determining when to take corrective action and when to make referrals.

Communication skills. Registered nurses must be able to communicate effectively with patients in order to understand their concerns and assess their health conditions. Nurses need to explain instructions, such as how to take medication, clearly. They must be able to work in teams with other health professionals and communicate the patients' needs.

Compassion. Registered nurses should be caring and empathetic when caring for patients.

Detail oriented. Registered nurses must be responsible and detail oriented because they must make sure that patients get the correct treatments and medicines at the right time.

Emotional stability. Registered nurses need emotional resilience and the ability to manage their emotions to cope with human suffering, emergencies, and other stresses.

Organizational skills. Nurses often work with multiple patients with various health needs. Organizational skills are critical to ensure that each patient is given appropriate care.

Physical stamina. Nurses should be comfortable performing physical tasks, such as moving patients. They may be on their feet for most of their shift.

Advancement. Most registered nurses begin as staff nurses in hospitals or community health settings. With experience, good performance, and continuous education, they can move to other settings or be promoted to positions with more responsibility.

In management, nurses can advance from assistant clinical nurse manager, charge nurse, or head nurse to more senior-level administrative roles, such as assistant director or director of nursing, vice president of nursing, or chief nursing officer. Increasingly, management-level nursing positions are requiring a graduate degree in nursing or health services administration. Administrative positions require leadership, communication skills, negotiation skills, and good judgment.

Some nurses move into the business side of healthcare. Their nursing expertise and experience on a healthcare team equip them to manage ambulatory, acute, home-based, and chronic care businesses. Employers—including hospitals, insurance companies, pharmaceutical manufacturers, and managed care organizations, among others—need registered nurses for jobs in health planning and development, marketing, consulting, policy development, and quality assurance.

Some RNs choose to become nurse anesthetists, nurse midwives, or nurse practitioners, which, along with clinical nurse specialists, are types of advanced practice registered nurses (APRNs). APRNs may provide primary and specialty care, and in many states they may prescribe medications.

Other nurses work as postsecondary teachers in colleges and universities.

Pay

The median annual wage for registered nurses was $66,640 in May 2014. The median wage is the wage at which half the workers in an occupation earned more than that amount and half earned less. The lowest 10 percent earned less than $45,880, and the highest 10 percent earned more than $98,880.

In May 2014, the median annual wages for registered nurses in the top industries in which they worked were as follows:

Government	$70,540
Hospitals; state, local, and private	68,490
Home healthcare services	63,810
Nursing and residential care facilities	59,840
Offices of physicians	59,550

Employers may offer flexible work schedules, childcare, educational benefits, and bonuses.

Job Outlook

Employment of registered nurses is projected to grow 16 percent from 2014 to 2024, much faster than the average for all occupations. Growth will occur for a number of reasons.

Demand for healthcare services will increase because of the aging population, given that older people typically have more medical problems than younger people. Nurses also will be needed to educate and care for patients with various chronic conditions, such as arthritis, dementia, diabetes, and obesity.

Employment Projections Data for Registered Nurses

Occupational Title	SOC Code	Employment, 2014	Projected Employment, 2024	Change, 2014–2024	
				Percent	Numeric
Registered nurses	29-1141	2,751,000	3,190,300	16	439,300

Source: U.S. Bureau of Labor Statistics, Employment Projections Program

Similar Occupations. This table shows a list of occupations with job duties that are similar to those of registered nurses.

Occupations	Entry-level Education	2014 Median Pay	Projected Job Growth	Average Annual Openings
Dental Hygienists	Associate's degree	$71,520	19%	3,740
Diagnostic Medical Sonographers and Cardiovascular Technologists and Technicians, Including Vascular Technologists	Associate's degree	$62,540	24%	2,760
EMTs and Paramedics	Postsecondary nondegree award	$31,700	24%	5,850
Licensed Practical and Licensed Vocational Nurses	Postsecondary nondegree award	$42,490	16%	11,730
Nurse Anesthetists, Nurse Midwives, and Nurse Practitioners	Master's degree	$102,670	31%	5,340
Physician Assistants	Master's degree	$95,820	30%	2,870
Social Workers	See Education/Training	$45,500	12%	7,480

In addition, the number of individuals who have access to health insurance is expected to continue to increase because of federal health insurance reform. People who previously were uninsured or found treatment to be cost prohibitive will obtain health insurance and have access to primary and preventive care services. More nurses will be needed to care for these patients in offices of physicians, clinics, and other ambulatory care settings.

The financial pressure on hospitals to discharge patients as soon as possible may result in more people being admitted to long-term care facilities and outpatient care centers, and greater need for healthcare at home. Job growth is expected in facilities that provide long-term rehabilitation for stroke and head injury patients, and in facilities that treat people with Alzheimer's disease. In addition, because many older people prefer to be treated at home or in residential care facilities, registered nurses will be in demand in those settings.

Growth also is expected to be faster than average in outpatient care centers, where patients do not stay overnight, such as those which provide same-day chemotherapy, rehabilitation, and surgery. In addition, an increased number of procedures, as well as more sophisticated procedures previously done only in hospitals, are being performed in ambulatory care settings and physicians' offices.

Job Prospects. Overall, job opportunities for registered nurses are expected to be good. However, the supply of new nurses entering the labor market has increased in recent years. This increase has resulted in competition for jobs in some areas of the country. Generally, registered nurses with a Bachelor of Science degree in nursing (BSN) will have better job prospects than those without one. Employers also may prefer candidates who have some related work experience.

Job opportunities should be good because of the need to replace workers who retire over the coming decade and because of the growing number of people with access to healthcare services.

Contacts for More Information

For more information about registered nurses, including credentialing, visit

➤ American Nurses Association (www.nursingworld.org)

For more information about nursing education and being a registered nurse, visit

➤ American Society of Registered Nurses (www.asrn.org)
➤ Johnson & Johnson, Discover Nursing (www.discovernursing.com)
➤ National League for Nursing (www.nln.org)
➤ National Student Nurses Association (www.nsna.org)

For more information about undergraduate and graduate nursing education, nursing career options, and financial aid, visit

➤ American Association of Colleges of Nursing (www.aacn.nche.edu)

For more information about RN-to-BSN programs, visit

➤ RN to BSN Online (www.rntobsnonline.com)

For more information about the National Council Licensure Examination (NCLEX-RN) and a list of individual state boards of nursing, visit

➤ National Council of State Boards of Nursing (www.ncsbn.org/index.htm)

For more information about clinical nurse specialists, including a list of accredited programs, visit

➤ National Association of Clinical Nurse Specialists (www.nacns.org)

O*NET

➤ Registered Nurses (29-1141.00)
➤ Acute Care Nurses (29-1141.01)
➤ Advanced Practice Psychiatric Nurses (29-1141.02)
➤ Critical Care Nurses (29-1141.03)
➤ Clinical Nurse Specialists (29-1141.04)

Respiratory Therapists

- **2014 Median Pay** .... $56,730 per year; $27.27 per hour
- **Typical Entry-Level Education** .... Associate's degree
- **Work Experience in a Related Occupation** .... None
- **On-the-job Training** .... None
- **Number of Jobs, 2014** 120,700
- **Job Outlook, 2014–24** .... 12% (Faster than average)
- **Employment Change, 2014–24** 14,900

What Respiratory Therapists Do

Respiratory therapists care for patients who have trouble breathing—for example, from a chronic respiratory disease, such as asthma or emphysema. Their patients range from premature infants with undeveloped lungs to elderly patients who have diseased lungs. They also provide emergency care to patients suffering from heart attacks, drowning, or shock.

Duties. Respiratory therapists typically do the following:

- Interview and examine patients with breathing or cardiopulmonary disorders
- Consult with physicians to develop patient treatment plans
- Perform diagnostic tests, such as measuring lung capacity
- Treat patients by using a variety of methods, including chest physiotherapy and aerosol medications
- Monitor and record patients' progress
- Teach patients how to use treatments and equipment, such as ventilators

Respiratory therapists use various tests to evaluate patients. For example, therapists test lung capacity by having patients breathe into an instrument that measures the volume and flow of oxygen when they inhale and exhale. Respiratory therapists also may take blood samples and use a blood gas analyzer to test oxygen and carbon dioxide levels.

Respiratory therapists perform chest physiotherapy on patients to remove mucus from their lungs and make it easier for them to breathe. Removing mucus is necessary for patients suffering from lung diseases, such as cystic fibrosis, and involves the therapist vibrating the patient's rib cage, often by tapping the patient's chest and encouraging him or her to cough.

Respiratory therapists may connect patients who cannot breathe on their own to ventilators that deliver oxygen to the lungs. Therapists insert a tube in the patient's windpipe (trachea) and connect the tube to ventilator equipment. They set up and monitor the equipment to ensure that the patient is receiving the correct amount of oxygen at the correct rate.

Respiratory therapists who work in home care teach patients and their families to use ventilators and other life-support systems in their homes. During these visits, they may inspect and clean equipment, check the home for environmental hazards, and ensure that patients know how to use their medications. Therapists also make emergency home visits when necessary.

In some hospitals, respiratory therapists are involved in related areas, such as diagnosing breathing problems for people with sleep apnea and counseling people on how to stop smoking.

Work Environment

Respiratory therapists held about 120,700 jobs in 2014. Most—about 4 out of 5—respiratory therapists work in hospitals. Others work in nursing care facilities and physicians' offices. Respiratory therapists are on their feet for long periods and may need to lift or turn disabled patients. Therapists work closely with registered nurses, physicians and surgeons, and medical assistants.

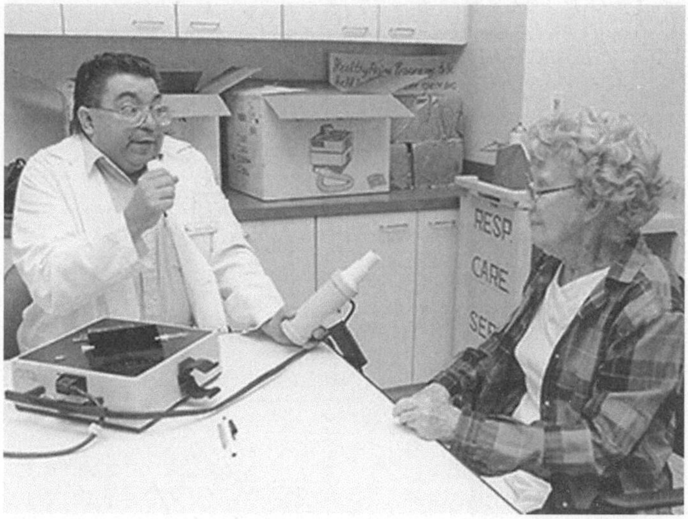

Respiratory therapists interview patients, perform limited physical examinations, and conduct diagnostic tests.

Work Schedules. Most respiratory therapists work full time. Because they may work in medical facilities, such as hospitals that are always open, some may work evening, night, or weekend hours.

Education/Training

Respiratory therapists are licensed in all states except Alaska; requirements vary by state.

Education. Respiratory therapists need at least an associate's degree, but employers may prefer applicants who have a bachelor's degree. Educational programs are offered by colleges and universities, vocational–technical institutes, and the Armed Forces. Completion of a program that is accredited by the Commission on Accreditation for Respiratory Care may be required for licensure.

Respiratory therapy programs typically include courses in human anatomy and physiology, chemistry, physics, microbiology, pharmacology, and math. Other courses deal with therapeutic and diagnostic procedures and tests, equipment, patient assessment, and cardiopulmonary resuscitation (CPR). In addition to coursework, programs have clinical components that allow therapists to gain supervised, practical experience in treating patients.

High school students interested in applying to respiratory therapy programs should take courses in health, biology, math, chemistry, and physics.

Licenses, Certifications, and Registrations. Respiratory therapists are licensed in all states except Alaska, although requirements vary by state. Licensure requirements in most states include

Median Annual Wages, May 2014

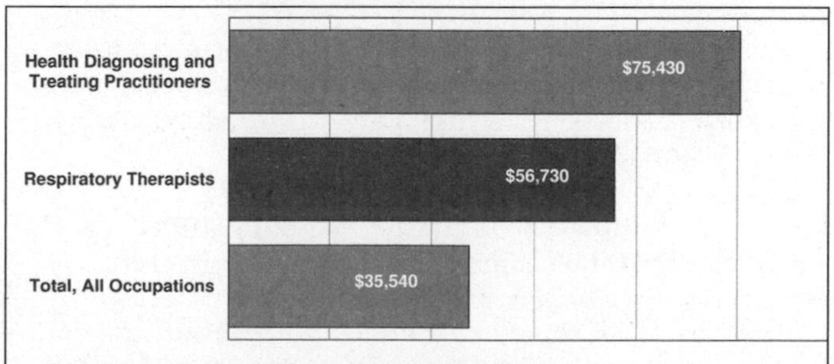

Note: All Occupations includes all occupations in the U.S. Economy.
Source: U.S. Bureau of Labor Statistics, Occupational Employment Statistics

Percent Change in Employment, Projected 2014–2024

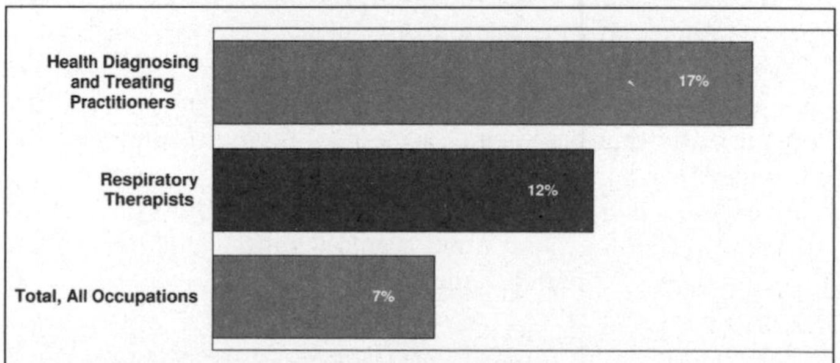

Note: All Occupations includes all occupations in the U.S. Economy.
Source: U.S. Bureau of Labor Statistics, Office of Occupational Statistics and Employment Projections

Employment Projections Data for Respiratory Therapists

Occupational Title	SOC Code	Employment, 2014	Projected Employment, 2024	Change, 2014–2024	
				Percent	Numeric
Respiratory therapists	29-1126	120,700	135,500	12	14,900

Source: U.S. Bureau of Labor Statistics, Employment Projections Program

Similar Occupations. This table shows a list of occupations with job duties that are similar to those of respiratory therapists.

Occupations	Entry-level Education	2014 Median Pay	Projected Job Growth	Average Annual Openings
Athletic Trainers	Bachelor's degree	$43,370	21%	540
Exercise Physiologists	Bachelor's degree	$46,270	11%	150
Occupational Therapists	Master's degree	$78,810	27%	3,040
Physical Therapists	Doctoral or professional degree	$82,390	34%	7,180
Radiation Therapists	Associate's degree	$80,090	14%	230
Registered Nurses	Bachelor's degree	$66,640	16%	43,930
Speech-Language Pathologists	Master's degree	$71,550	21%	2,890

passing a state or professional certification exam. For specific state requirements, contact the state's health board.

The National Board for Respiratory Care (NBRC) is the main certifying body for respiratory therapists. The Board offers two levels of certification: Certified Respiratory Therapist (CRT) and Registered Respiratory Therapist (RRT).

CRT is the first-level certification. Applicants must have earned an associate's degree from an accredited respiratory therapy program, or completed the equivalent coursework in a bachelor's degree program, and pass an exam.

The second-level certification is RRT certification. Applicants must already have CRT certification, meet other education or experience requirements, and pass an exam.

Important Qualities

Compassion. Respiratory therapists should be able to provide emotional support to patients undergoing treatment and be sympathetic to their needs.

Detail oriented. Respiratory therapists must be detail oriented to ensure that patients are receiving the appropriate treatments and medications in a timely manner. They must also monitor and record various pieces of information related to patient care.

Interpersonal skills. Respiratory therapists interact with patients and often work as part of a team. They must be able to follow instructions from a supervising physician.

Patience. Respiratory therapists may work for long periods with patients who need special attention.

Problem-solving skills. Respiratory therapists need strong problem-solving skills. They must evaluate patients' symptoms, consult with other healthcare professionals, and recommend and administer the appropriate treatments.

Science and math skills. Respiratory therapists must understand anatomy, physiology, and other sciences and be able to calculate the right dose of a patient's medicine.

Pay

The median annual wage for respiratory therapists was $56,730 in May 2014. The median wage is the wage at which half the workers in an occupation earned more than that amount and half earned less. The lowest 10 percent earned less than $41,380, and the highest 10 percent earned more than $78,230.

Job Outlook

Employment of respiratory therapists is projected to grow 12 percent from 2014 to 2024, faster than the average for all occupations. Growth in the middle-aged and elderly population will lead to an increased incidence of respiratory conditions such as pneumonia, chronic obstructive pulmonary disease (COPD), and other disorders that can permanently damage the lungs or restrict lung function. The aging population will in turn lead to an increased demand for respiratory therapy services and treatments, mostly in hospitals.

In addition, a growing emphasis on reducing readmissions in hospitals may result in more demand for respiratory therapists in nursing homes and in doctors' offices. Furthermore, the number of individuals who have access to health insurance is expected to continue to increase because of federal health insurance reform.

Advances in preventing and detecting disease, improved medications, and more sophisticated treatments will also increase the demand for respiratory therapists. Other conditions affecting the general population, such as respiratory problems due to smoking and air pollution, along with respiratory emergencies, will continue to create demand for respiratory therapists.

Job Prospects. Job prospects will be best for therapists willing to travel to look for job opportunities. Some areas will be saturated with workers, while other areas (more often, rural areas) will be in need of respiratory therapists' services.

Contacts for More Information

For more information about respiratory therapists, visit

➤ American Association for Respiratory Care (www.aarc.org)

For a list of accredited educational programs for respiratory care practitioners, visit

➤ Commission on Accreditation for Respiratory Care (www.coarc.com)

For a list of state licensing agencies, as well as information on gaining credentials in respiratory care, visit

➤ The National Board for Respiratory Care, Inc. (www.nbrc.org/Pages/default.aspx)

O*NET

➤ Respiratory Therapists (29-1126.00)

Speech-Language Pathologists

- **2014 Median Pay** .... $71,550 per year
$34.40 per hour
- **Typical Entry-Level Education** .... Master's degree
- **Work Experience in a Related Occupation** .... None
- **On-the-job Training** .... None
- **Number of Jobs, 2014** 135,400
- **Job Outlook, 2014–24** .... 21% (Much faster than average)
- **Employment Change, 2014–24** 28,900

What Speech-Language Pathologists Do

Speech-language pathologists (sometimes called *speech therapists*) assess, diagnose, treat, and help to prevent communication and swallowing disorders in patients. Speech, language, and swallowing disorders result from a variety of causes, such as a stroke, brain injury, hearing loss, developmental delay, Parkinson's disease, a cleft palate, or autism.

Duties. Speech-language pathologists typically do the following:

- Evaluate patients' levels of speech, language, or swallowing difficulty
- Identify treatment options
- Create and carry out an individualized treatment plan that addresses patients' specific functional needs
- Teach patients how to make sounds and improve their voices
- Work with patients to develop and strengthen the muscles used to swallow
- Counsel patients and families on how to cope with communication and swallowing disorders

Speech-language pathologists work with patients who have problems with speech and language, including related cognitive or social communication problems. Their patients may be unable to speak at all, or they may speak with difficulty or have rhythm and fluency problems, such as stuttering. Speech-language pathologists may work with people who are unable to understand language or with those who have voice disorders, such as inappropriate pitch or a harsh voice.

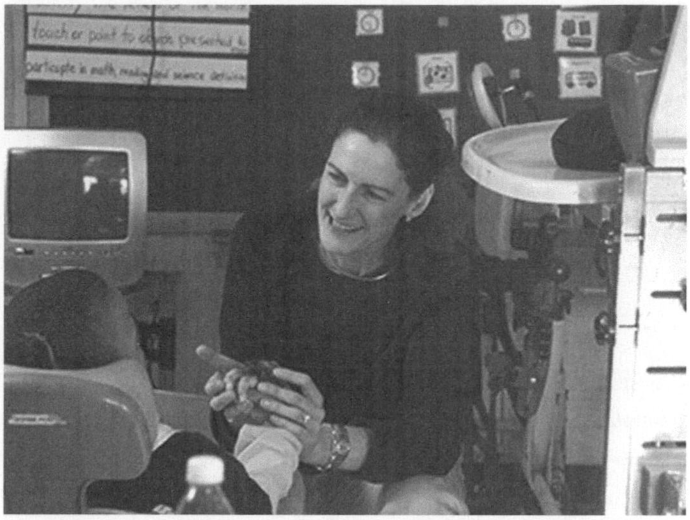

Speech-language pathologists usually work at desks or tables in clean comfortable surroundings.

Speech-language pathologists also must complete administrative tasks, including keeping accurate records. They record their initial patient evaluations and diagnoses, track treatment progress, and note any changes in a patient's condition or treatment plan.

Some speech-language pathologists specialize in working with specific age groups, such as children or the elderly. Others focus on treatment programs for specific communication or swallowing problems, such as those resulting from strokes or a cleft palate.

In medical facilities, speech-language pathologists work with physicians and surgeons, social workers, psychologists, and other healthcare workers. In schools, they work with teachers, other school personnel, and parents to develop and carry out individual or group programs, provide counseling, and support classroom activities. For more information on teachers, see the profiles on preschool teachers, kindergarten and elementary school teachers, middle school teachers, high school teachers, and special education teachers.

Work Environment

Speech-language pathologists held about 135,400 jobs in 2014. The industries that employed the most speech-language pathologists were as follows:

Educational services; state, local, and private	44%
Offices of physical, occupational and speech therapists, and audiologists	19

Median Annual Wages, May 2014

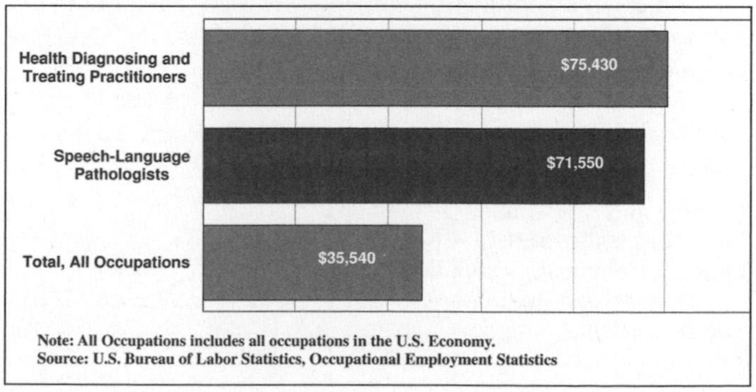

Percent Change in Employment, Projected 2014–2024

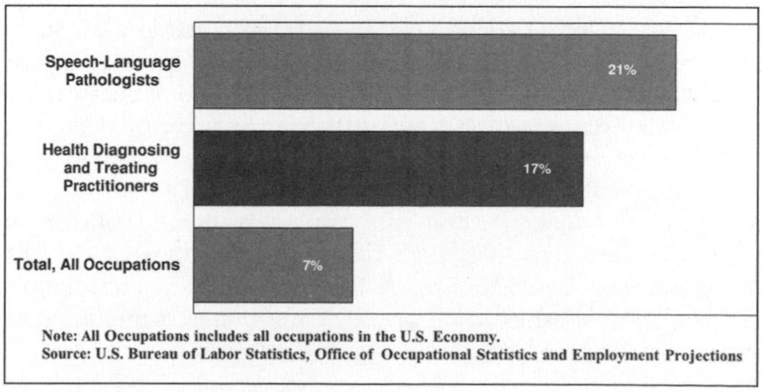

Employment Projections Data for Speech-Language Pathologists

Occupational Title	SOC Code	Employment, 2014	Projected Employment, 2024	Change, 2014–2024 Percent	Change, 2014–2024 Numeric
Speech-language pathologists	29-1127	135,400	164,300	21	28,900

Source: U.S. Bureau of Labor Statistics, Employment Projections Program

Similar Occupations. This table shows a list of occupations with job duties that are similar to those of speech-language pathologists.

Occupations	Entry-level Education	2014 Median Pay	Projected Job Growth	Average Annual Openings
Audiologists	Doctoral or professional degree	$73,060	29%	380
Occupational Therapists	Master's degree	$78,810	27%	3,040
Physical Therapists	Doctoral or professional degree	$82,390	34%	7,180
Psychologists	See Education/Training	$70,700	19%	3,250
Recreational Therapists	Bachelor's degree	$44,000	12%	220

Hospitals; state, local, and private 13%
Nursing and residential care facilities 5
Social assistance 4

About 2 out of 5 speech-language pathologists worked in schools in 2014. Most others worked in healthcare facilities, such as hospitals.

Work Schedules. Most speech-language pathologists work full time. About 1 out of 4 worked part time in 2014. Some speech language pathologists, such as those working for schools, may need to travel between different schools or facilities.

Education/Training

Speech-language pathologists typically need at least a master's degree. They must be licensed in most states; requirements vary by state.

Education. Speech-language pathologists typically enter the occupation after getting at least a master's degree. Although master's programs do not require a particular undergraduate degree for admission, certain courses must be taken before entering a program. Required courses vary by institution.

Graduate programs often include courses in speech and language development, age-specific speech disorders, alternative communication methods, and swallowing disorders. These programs also include supervised clinical experience.

The Council on Academic Accreditation (CAA), part of the American Speech-Language-Hearing Association, accredits education programs in speech-language pathology. Graduation from an accredited program is required for certification and, often, for state licensure.

Licenses, Certifications, and Registrations. Almost all states require speech-language pathologists to be licensed. A license requires at least a master's degree and supervised clinical experience. Many states require graduation from an accredited master's program to get a license. For specific requirements, contact your state's medical or health licensure board.

Speech-language pathologists can earn the Certificate of Clinical Competence in Speech-Language Pathology (CCC-SLP), offered by the American Speech-Language-Hearing Association. Certification satisfies some or all of the requirements for state licensure and may be required by some employers.

Speech-language pathologists who work in schools may need a specific teaching certification. For specific requirements, contact your state's department of education or the private institution in which you are interested.

Important Qualities

Analytical skills. Speech-language pathologists must select the most appropriate diagnostic tools and analyze the results to arrive at an accurate diagnosis and develop an appropriate treatment plan.

Communication skills. Speech-language pathologists need to communicate test results, diagnoses, and proposed treatments in a way that patients and their families can understand.

Compassion. Speech-language pathologists work with people who are often frustrated by their difficulties. Speech-language pathologists must be able to support emotionally demanding patients and their families.

Critical-thinking skills. Speech-language pathologists must be able to adjust their treatment plans as needed, finding alternative ways to help their patients.

Detail oriented. Speech-language pathologists must take detailed notes on patient progress and treatment.

Listening skills. Speech-language pathologists must listen to a patient's symptoms and concerns to decide on the appropriate course of treatment.

Pay

The median annual wage for speech-language pathologists was $71,550 in May 2014. The median wage is the wage at which half the workers in an occupation earned more than that amount and half earned less. The lowest 10 percent earned less than $44,940, and the highest 10 percent earned more than $111,000.

In May 2014, the median annual wages for speech-language pathologists in the top industries in which they worked were as follows:

Nursing and residential care facilities $88,920
Hospitals; state, local, and private 77,660
Offices of physical, occupational and speech therapists, and audiologists 77,500
Social assistance 67,240
Educational services; state, local, and private 63,440

Union Membership. Compared with workers in all occupations, speech-language pathologists had a higher percentage of workers who belonged to a union in 2014.

Job Outlook

Employment of speech-language pathologists is projected to grow 21 percent from 2014 to 2024, much faster than the average for all occupations.

As the large baby-boom population grows older, there will be more instances of health conditions, such as strokes and hearing loss that cause speech or language impairments. Speech-language pathologists will be needed to treat the increased number of speech and language disorders in the older population.

Increased awareness of speech and language disorders, such as stuttering, in younger children should lead to a need for more speech-language pathologists who specialize in treating that age group. Also, an increasing number of pathologists will be needed to work with children with autism to improve their ability to communicate and socialize effectively.

In addition, medical advances are improving the survival rate of premature infants and victims of trauma and strokes, many of whom need help from speech-language pathologists.

Job Prospects. Overall job opportunities for speech-language pathologists are expected to be good. Generally, speech-language pathologists who are willing to relocate will have the best job opportunities.

Contacts for More Information

For more information about speech-language pathologists, a description of the Certificate of Clinical Competence in Speech-Language Pathology (CCC-SLP) credential, and a list of accredited graduate programs in speech-language pathology, visit

➤ American Speech-Language-Hearing Association (www.asha.org)

State licensing boards have information about licensure requirements. State departments of education can provide information about certification requirements for those who want to work in public schools.

O*NET

➤ Speech-Language Pathologists (29-1127.00)

Surgical Technologists

- **2014 Median Pay** .... $43,350 per year $20.84 per hour
- **Typical Entry-Level Education** .... Postsecondary nondegree award
- **Work Experience in a Related Occupation** .... None
- **On-the-job Training** .... None
- **Number of Jobs, 2014** 99,800
- **Job Outlook, 2014–24** ...... 15% (Much faster than average)
- **Employment Change, 2014–24** 14,700

What Surgical Technologists Do

Surgical technologists, also called *operating room technicians*, assist in surgical operations. They prepare operating rooms, arrange equipment, and help doctors during surgeries.

Duties. Surgical technologists typically do the following:

- Prepare operating rooms for surgery
- Sterilize equipment and make sure that there are adequate supplies for surgery
- Ready patients for surgery, such as by washing and disinfecting incision sites
- Help surgeons during surgery by passing them instruments and other sterile supplies
- Count supplies, such as sponges and instruments
- Maintain a sterile environment

Surgical technologists work as members of a healthcare team alongside physicians and surgeons, registered nurses, and other healthcare workers.

Before an operation, surgical technologists prepare the operating room by setting up surgical instruments and equipment. They also prepare patients for surgery by washing and disinfecting incision sites, positioning the patients on the operating table, covering them with sterile drapes, and taking them to and from the operating room. Surgical technologists prepare sterile solutions and medications used in surgery and check that all surgical equipment is working properly. They help the surgical team put on sterile gowns and gloves.

During an operation, surgical technologists pass instruments and supplies to surgeons and first assistants. They also hold retractors, hold internal organs in place during the procedure, or set up robotic surgical equipment. Technologists also may handle specimens taken for laboratory analysis.

Once the operation is complete, surgical technologists may apply bandages and other dressings to the incision site. They may also help transfer patients to recovery rooms and restock operating rooms after a procedure.

Surgical first assistants have a hands-on role, directly assisting surgeons during a procedure. For instance, they may help to suction the incision site or suture a wound.

Work Environment

Surgical technologists held about 99,800 jobs in 2014. About 70 percent of surgical technologists worked in hospitals in 2014. Some work in outpatient care centers or in offices of physicians who perform outpatient surgery.

Surgical technologists wear scrubs (special sterile clothing) while they are in the operating room. Their work may be physically

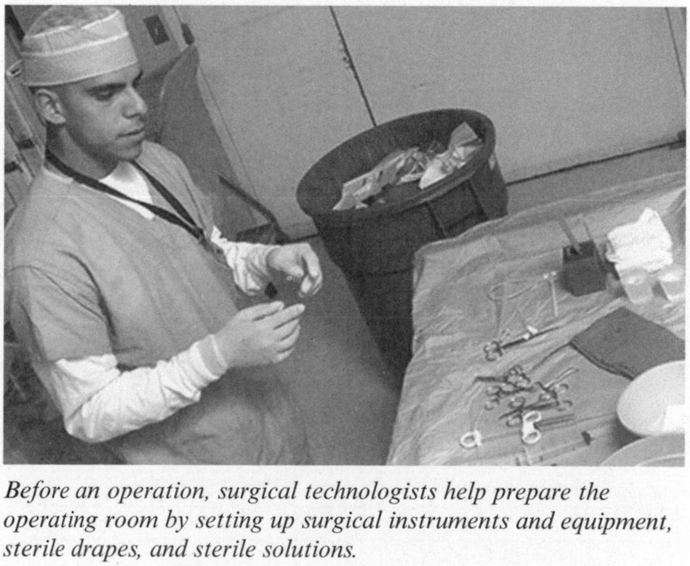

Before an operation, surgical technologists help prepare the operating room by setting up surgical instruments and equipment, sterile drapes, and sterile solutions.

Median Annual Wages, May 2014

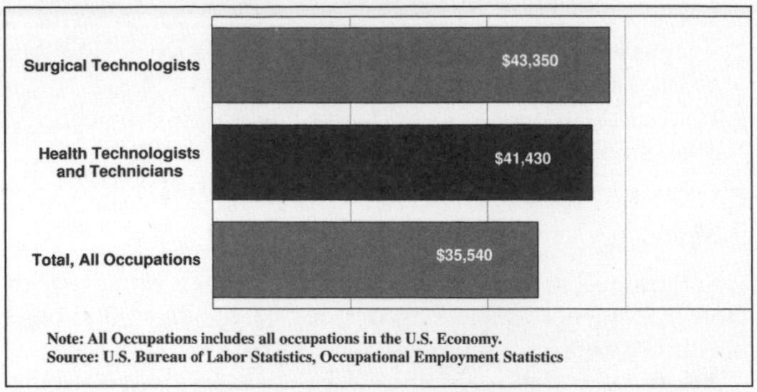

Percent Change in Employment, Projected 2014–2024

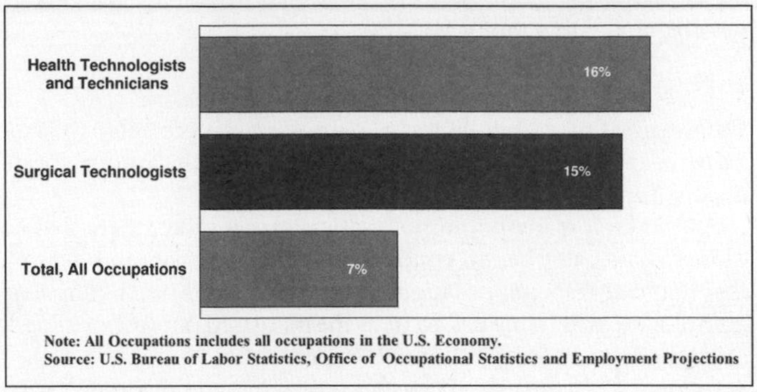

demanding, requiring them to be on their feet for long periods. Surgical technologists also may need to help move patients or lift heavy trays of medical supplies. At times, they may be exposed to communicable diseases and unpleasant sights, odors, and materials.

Work Schedules. Most surgical technologists work full time. Surgical technologists employed in hospitals may work or be on call during nights, weekends, and holidays. They may also be required to work shifts lasting longer than 8 hours.

Education/Training

Surgical technologists typically need a postsecondary certificate or an associate's degree. Certification can be beneficial in finding a job. A small number of states regulate surgical technologists.

Education. Surgical technologists typically need postsecondary education. Many community colleges and vocational schools, as well as some universities and hospitals, have accredited programs in surgical technology. Programs range in length from several months to 2 years, and they grant a diploma, certificate, or associate's degree upon completion. Admission typically requires a high school diploma or the equivalent.

Surgical technology education includes courses in anatomy, biology, medical terminology, pharmacology, and other topics. Surgical technologists are trained in the care and safety of patients, sterilization techniques, how to set up technical or robotic equipment, and preventing and controlling infections. In addition to classroom study, students also work in supervised clinical settings to gain hands-on experience.

First surgical assistants may complete a formal education program in surgical assisting. Others may work as a surgical technologist and receive additional on-the-job training before becoming a first assistant.

Important Qualities

Detail oriented. Surgical technologists must pay close attention to their work at all times. For example, they need to provide the correct sterile equipment for surgeons during an operation.

Dexterity. Surgical technologists should be comfortable working with their hands. They must be able to provide needed equipment quickly.

Integrity. Because they are trusted to provide sterile supplies and quality patient care during surgical procedures, surgical technologists must have integrity.

Physical stamina. Surgical technologists should be comfortable standing for extended periods.

Stress-management skills. Working in an operating room can be stressful. Surgical technologists should be able to work well under pressure while providing a high level of care.

Licenses, Certifications, and Registrations. Certification can be beneficial in finding a job. Surgical technologists may earn certification through credentialing organizations.

Certification through The National Board of Surgical Technology and Surgical Assisting allows the use of the title "Certified Surgical Technologist (CST)." Certification typically requires completing an accredited formal education program or military training program and passing an exam.

Certification through the National Center for Competency Testing allows the use of the title "Tech in Surgery-Certified (NCCT)." Applicants may qualify through formal education, military training, work experience, or other eligibility paths. All require documenting critical skills and passing an exam.

Both certifications require surgical technologists to complete continuing education to maintain their certification.

In addition, many jobs require technologists to become certified in CPR or basic life support, or both.

A small number of states have regulations governing the work of surgical technologists or surgical assistants, or both.

The National Board of Surgical Technology and Surgical Assisting, the National Commission for the Certification of Surgical Assistants, and the American Board of Surgical Assistants offer certification for surgical first assistants.

Advancement. Surgical technologists may choose to advance to other healthcare occupations, such as registered nurse. Technologists may also choose to become a postsecondary teacher of health specialties.

Employment Projections Data for Surgical Technologists

Occupational Title	SOC Code	Employment, 2014	Projected Employment, 2024	Change, 2014–2024	
				Percent	Numeric
Surgical technologists	29-2055	99,800	114,500	15	14,700

Source: U.S. Bureau of Labor Statistics, Employment Projections Program

Similar Occupations. This table shows a list of occupations with job duties that are similar to those of surgical technologists.

Occupations	Entry-level Education	2014 Median Pay	Projected Job Growth	Average Annual Openings
Dental Assistants	Postsecondary nondegree award	$35,390	18%	5,860
Licensed Practical and Licensed Vocational Nurses	Postsecondary nondegree award	$42,490	16%	11,730
Medical and Clinical Laboratory Technologists and Technicians	See Education/Training	$49,310	16%	5,210
Medical Assistants	Postsecondary nondegree award	$29,960	23%	13,890

Pay

The median annual wage for surgical technologists was $43,350 in May 2014. The median wage is the wage at which half the workers in an occupation earned more than that amount and half earned less. The lowest 10 percent earned less than $30,780, and the highest 10 percent earned more than $62,170.

Job Outlook

Employment of surgical technologists is projected to grow 15 percent from 2014 to 2024, much faster than the average for all occupations. Several factors will lead to demand for surgical technologists.

Advances in medical technology have made surgery safer, and more operations are being done to treat a variety of illnesses and injuries. In addition, the number of individuals who have access to health insurance is expected to continue to increase because of federal health insurance reform, which should in turn lead to increased demand for surgical services.

The aging of the large baby-boom generation also is expected to increase the need for surgical technologists, because older people usually require more operations. Moreover, as these individuals age, they may be more willing than those in previous generations to seek medical treatment to improve their quality of life. For example, an individual may decide to have a knee replacement operation in order to maintain an active lifestyle.

Job Prospects. Job prospects should be best for surgical technologists who have completed an accredited education program and hold a certification.

Contacts for More Information

For more information about surgical technologists, visit

- ➤ Association of Surgical Technologists (www.ast.org)

For information about certification, visit

- ➤ The National Board of Surgical Technology and Surgical Assisting (http://nbstsa.org)
- ➤ National Center for Competency Testing (www.ncctinc.com)
- ➤ National Commission for the Certification of Surgical Assistants (http://csaexam.com)
- ➤ American Board of Surgical Assistants (www.absa.net)

O*NET

- ➤ Surgical Technologists (29-2055.00)

Veterinarians

- **2014 Median Pay** .... $87,590 per year $42.11 per hour
- **Typical Entry-Level Education** .... Doctoral or professional degree
- **Work Experience in a Related Occupation** .... None
- **On-the-job Training** .... None
- **Number of Jobs, 2014** 78,300
- **Job Outlook, 2014–24** .... 9% (Faster than average)
- **Employment Change, 2014–24** 6,900

What Veterinarians Do

Veterinarians care for the health of animals and work to improve public health. They diagnose, treat, and research medical conditions and diseases of pets, livestock, and other animals.

Duties. Veterinarians typically do the following:

- Examine animals to diagnose their health problems
- Treat and dress wounds
- Perform surgery on animals
- Test for and vaccinate against diseases
- Operate medical equipment, such as X-ray machines
- Advise animal owners about general care, medical conditions, and treatments
- Prescribe medication
- Euthanize animals

Veterinarians treat the injuries and illnesses of pets and other animals with a variety of medical equipment, including surgical tools and X-ray and ultrasound machines. They provide treatment

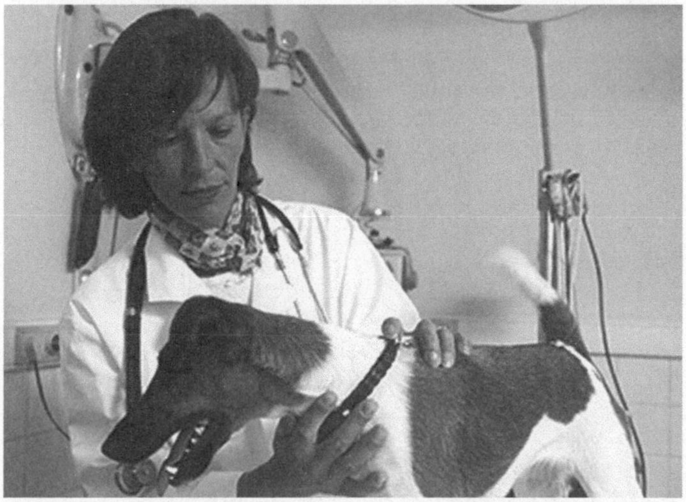

Employment opportunities for veterinarians are expected to be very good, but competition for admission to veterinary school is keen.

Median Annual Wages, May 2014

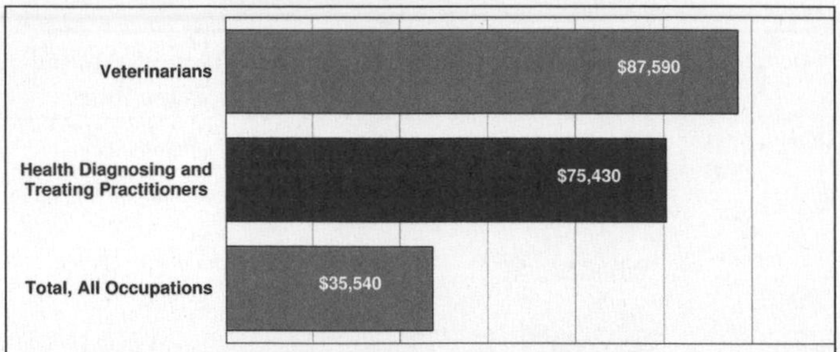

Note: All Occupations includes all occupations in the U.S. Economy.
Source: U.S. Bureau of Labor Statistics, Occupational Employment Statistics

Percent Change in Employment, Projected 2014–2024

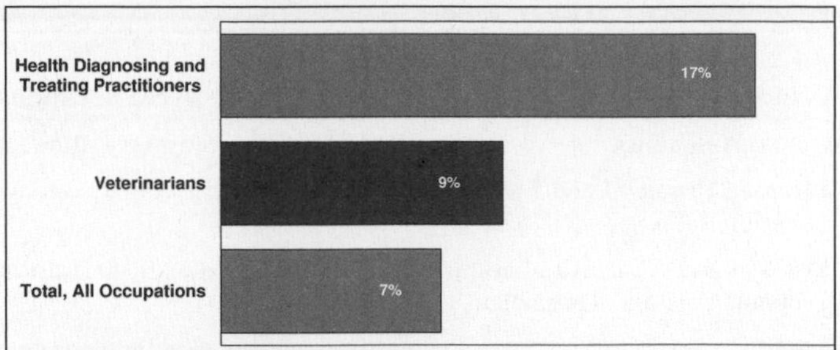

Note: All Occupations includes all occupations in the U.S. Economy.
Source: U.S. Bureau of Labor Statistics, Office of Occupational Statistics and Employment Projections

for animals that is similar to the services a physician provides to treat humans.

The following are examples of types of veterinarians:

Companion animal veterinarians treat pets and generally work in private clinics and hospitals. According to the American Veterinary Medical Association, more than 75 percent of veterinarians who work in private clinical practice treat pets. They most often care for cats and dogs, but also treat other pets, such as birds, ferrets, and rabbits. These veterinarians diagnose and provide treatment for animal health problems, consult with owners of animals about preventive healthcare, and carry out medical and surgical procedures, such as vaccinations, dental work, and setting fractures.

Equine veterinarians work with horses. In 2014, about 6 percent of private practice veterinarians diagnosed and treated horses.

Food animal veterinarians work with farm animals such as pigs, cattle, and sheep, which are raised to be food sources. In 2014, about 7 percent of private practice veterinarians treated food animals. They spend much of their time at farms and ranches treating illnesses and injuries and testing for and vaccinating against disease. They may advise owners or managers about feeding, housing, and general health practices.

Food safety and inspection veterinarians inspect and test livestock and animal products for major animal diseases, provide vaccines to treat animals, enhance animal welfare, conduct research to improve animal health, and enforce government food safety regulations. They design and administer animal and public health programs for the prevention and control of diseases transmissible among animals and between animals and people.

Research veterinarians work in laboratories, conducting clinical research on human and animal health problems. These veterinarians may perform tests on animals to identify the effects of drug therapies, or they may test new surgical techniques. They may also research how to prevent, control, and eliminate food- and animal-borne illnesses and diseases.

Some veterinarians become postsecondary teachers at colleges and universities.

Work Environment

Veterinarians held about 78,300 jobs in 2014, of which about 74 percent were in the veterinary services industry. Others held positions in federal, state, or local government; animal production, and in colleges and universities. About 1 in 6 veterinarians were self-employed in 2016.

Most veterinarians work in private clinics and hospitals. Others travel to farms, work in laboratories or classrooms, or work for the government.

Veterinarians who treat horses or food animals travel between their offices and farms and ranches. They work outdoors in all kinds of weather and may have to perform surgery, often in remote locations.

Veterinarians who work in food safety and inspection travel to farms, slaughterhouses, and food-processing plants to inspect the health of animals and ensure that safety protocols are being followed by the facility.

Veterinarians who conduct research work primarily in offices and laboratories. They spend much of their time dealing with people, rather than animals.

The work can be emotionally stressful, as veterinarians deal with sick animals and the animals' anxious owners. Also, the workplace can be noisy, as animals make noise when sick or being handled. Working on farms and ranches, in slaughterhouses, or with wildlife can also be physically demanding.

Injuries and Illnesses. When working with animals that are frightened or in pain, veterinarians risk being bitten, kicked, and scratched. In addition, veterinarians working with diseased animals risk being infected by the disease.

Work Schedules. Veterinarians often work additional hours. Some work nights or weekends, and they may have to respond to emergencies outside of scheduled work hours.

Education/Training

Veterinarians must have a Doctor of Veterinary Medicine degree from an accredited veterinary college and a state license.

Education. Veterinarians must complete a Doctor of Veterinary Medicine (D.V.M. or V.M.D.) degree at an accredited college of veterinary medicine. There are currently 30 colleges with accredited programs in the United States. A veterinary medicine program generally takes 4 years to complete and includes classroom, laboratory, and clinical components.

Although not required, most applicants to veterinary school have a bachelor's degree. Veterinary medical colleges typically require applicants to have taken many science classes, including biology, chemistry, anatomy, physiology, zoology, microbiology, and animal science. Most programs also require math, humanities, and social science courses.

Admission to veterinary programs is competitive, and less than half of all applicants were accepted in 2014.

In veterinary medicine programs, students take courses on animal anatomy and physiology, as well as disease prevention, diagnosis, and treatment. Most programs include 3 years of classroom, laboratory, and clinical work. Students typically spend the final year of the 4-year program doing clinical rotations in a veterinary medical center or hospital.

Employment Projections Data for Veterinarians

Occupational Title	SOC Code	Employment, 2014	Projected Employment, 2024	Change, 2014–2024 Percent	Change, 2014–2024 Numeric
Veterinarians	29-1131	78,300	85,200	9	6,900

Source: U.S. Bureau of Labor Statistics, Employment Projections Program

Similar Occupations. This table shows a list of occupations with job duties that are similar to those of veterinarians.

Occupations	Entry-level Education	2014 Median Pay	Projected Job Growth	Average Annual Openings
Agricultural and Food Scientists	Bachelor's degree	$60,690	5%	190
Animal Care and Service Workers	High school diploma or equivalent	$20,610	11%	2,570
Medical Scientists	Doctoral or professional degree	$79,930	8%	900
Physicians and Surgeons	Doctoral or professional degree	This wage is equal to or greater than $187,200.	14%	9,930
Veterinary Assistants and Laboratory Animal Caretakers	High school diploma or equivalent	$23,790	9%	660
Veterinary Technologists and Technicians	Associate's degree	$31,070	19%	1,790
Zoologists and Wildlife Biologists	Bachelor's degree	$58,270	4%	80

Licenses, Certifications, and Registrations. Veterinarians must be licensed in order to practice in the United States. Licensing requirements vary by state, but all states require prospective veterinarians to complete an accredited veterinary program and to pass the North American Veterinary Licensing Examination. Veterinarians working for the state or federal government may not be required to have a state license, because each agency has different requirements.

Most states not only require the national exam but also have a state exam that covers state laws and regulations. Few states accept licenses from other states, so veterinarians who want to be licensed in another state usually must take that state's exam.

The American Veterinary Medical Association offers certification in 40 specialties, such as surgery, microbiology, and internal medicine. Although certification is not required for veterinarians, it can show exceptional skill and expertise in a particular field. To sit for a specialty certification exam, veterinarians must have a certain number of years of experience in the field, complete additional education, and complete a residency program, typically lasting 3 to 4 years. Requirements vary by specialty.

Other Experience. Some veterinary medical colleges weigh experience heavily during the admissions process. Formal experience, such as previous work with veterinarians or scientists in clinics, agribusiness, research, or some area of health science, is particularly advantageous. Less formal experience, such as working with animals on a farm, at a stable, or in an animal shelter, can also be helpful.

Although graduates of a veterinary program can begin practicing once they receive their license, some veterinarians pursue further education and training. Some new veterinary graduates enter internship or residency programs to gain specialized experience.

Important Qualities

Compassion. Veterinarians must be compassionate when working with animals and their owners. They must treat animals with kindness and respect, and must be sensitive when dealing with the animal owners.

Communication skills. Strong communication skills are essential for veterinarians, who must be able to discuss their recommendations and explain treatment options to animal owners and give instructions to their staff.

Decision-making skills. Veterinarians must decide the correct method for treating the injuries and illnesses of animals. For instance, deciding to euthanize a sick animal can be difficult.

Management skills. Management skills are important for veterinarians who manage private clinics or laboratories, or direct teams of technicians or inspectors. In these settings, they are responsible for providing direction, delegating work, and overseeing daily operations.

Manual dexterity. Manual dexterity is important for veterinarians, because they must control their hand movements and be precise when treating injuries and performing surgery.

Problem-solving skills. Veterinarians need strong problem-solving skills because they must figure out what is ailing animals. Those who test animals to determine the effects of drug therapies also need excellent diagnostic skills.

Pay

The median annual wage for veterinarians was $87,590 in May 2014. The median wage is the wage at which half the workers in an occupation earned more than that amount and half earned less. The lowest 10 percent earned less than $52,530, and the highest 10 percent earned more than $157,390.

Job Outlook

Employment of veterinarians is projected to grow 9 percent from 2014 to 2024, faster than the average for all occupations. Veterinarians will continue to be needed to diagnose and treat animals.

Veterinary medicine has advanced considerably. Veterinarians are able to offer more services today that are comparable to healthcare for humans, including more complicated procedures like cancer treatments and kidney transplants.

There also will be employment growth in areas such as food and animal safety, where organizations work to prevent foodborne contaminations and diseases in animals; public health, where organizations work to protect the health of an entire population; and disease control. Veterinarians will continue to be needed to inspect the food supply and to ensure animal and human health.

Job Prospects. Candidates can expect competition for most veterinarian positions. Job seekers with a specialization and prior work experience should have the best job opportunities.

The number of new graduates from veterinary schools has increased to roughly 3,000 per year, resulting in greater competition for jobs than in recent years. Additionally, most veterinary graduates are attracted to companion animal care, so there will be fewer job opportunities in that field.

Job opportunities in farm animal care will be better, because fewer veterinarians compete to work on large animals. Also, there will be some job opportunities available in the federal government in food safety, animal health, and public health. Job opportunities will also become available as veterinarians retire opening up positions for new veterinarians.

Veterinary schools also train veterinarians for positions in other fields, such as public health, disease control, corporate sales, and population studies. With potentially fewer opportunities in companion animal care, many graduating veterinarians will likely have better job prospects in these areas.

Contacts for More Information

For more information about careers in veterinary medicine, a list of U.S. schools and colleges of veterinary medicine, and information on accreditation policies, visit

➤ American Veterinary Medical Association (www.avma.org)

For more information about veterinary education, visit

➤ Association of American Veterinary Medical Colleges (www.aavmc.org)

For information about veterinarian positions with the federal government, visit

➤ USAJOBS (www.usajobs.gov)

O*NET

➤ Veterinarians (29-1131.00)

Veterinary Assistants and Laboratory Animal Caretakers

- **2014 Median Pay** .... $23,790 per year
$11.44 per hour
- **Typical Entry-Level Education** .... High school diploma or equivalent
- **Work Experience in a Related Occupation** .... None
- **On-the-job Training** .... Short-term on-the-job training
- **Number of Jobs, 2014** 73,400
- **Job Outlook, 2014–24** .... 9% (Faster than average)
- **Employment Change, 2014–24** 6,600

What Veterinary Assistants and Laboratory Animal Caretakers Do

Veterinary assistants and laboratory animal caretakers look after animals in laboratories, animal hospitals, and clinics. They care for the animals by performing routine tasks under the supervision of scientists, veterinarians, and veterinary technologists and technicians.

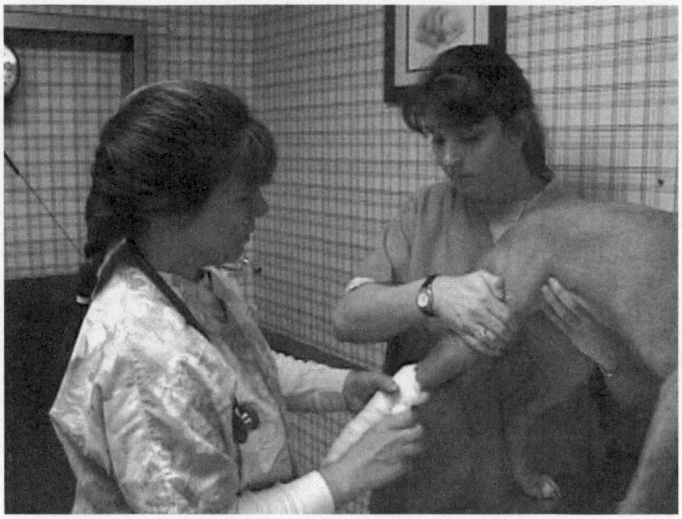

Veterinary assistants work under the supervision of a veterinarian.

Duties. Veterinary assistants and laboratory animal caretakers typically do the following:

- Feed, bathe, and exercise animals
- Clean and disinfect cages, kennels, and examination and operating rooms
- Restrain animals during examination and laboratory procedures
- Maintain and sterilize surgical instruments and equipment
- Monitor and care for animals after surgery
- Help provide emergency first aid to sick and injured animals
- Give medication or immunizations that veterinarians prescribe
- Assist in the collection of blood, urine, and tissue samples

Veterinary assistants and laboratory animal caretakers are responsible for many daily tasks, such as feeding, weighing, and taking the temperature of animals. Other duties may include giving medication, cleaning cages, and providing nursing care before and after surgery and other medical procedures.

Veterinary assistants and laboratory animal caretakers play a large role in helping veterinarians and animal scientists with surgery and other minor procedures. They may prepare equipment and pass surgical instruments and materials to veterinarians during surgery. They also move animals and restrain them during testing and other procedures.

Veterinary assistants typically work in clinics and animal hospitals, helping veterinarians and veterinary technologists and technicians treat injuries and illnesses of animals.

Laboratory animal caretakers work in laboratories under the supervision of a veterinarian, scientist, veterinary technician, or veterinary technologist. Their daily tasks include feeding animals, cleaning kennels, and monitoring the animals.

Work Environment

Veterinary assistants and laboratory animal caretakers held about 73,400 jobs in 2014. Eighty-five percent were employed in the veterinary services industry, which includes private clinics and animal hospitals. Most others were employed in colleges, universities, and research facilities.

The work of veterinary assistants and laboratory animal caretakers may be physically and emotionally demanding. Workers

Median Annual Wages, May 2014

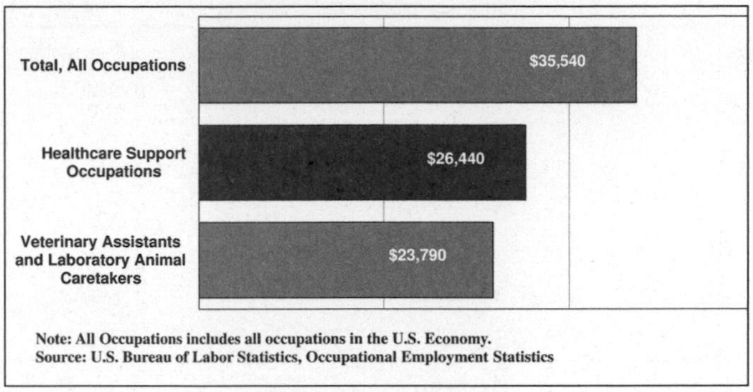

Percent Change in Employment, Projected 2014–2024

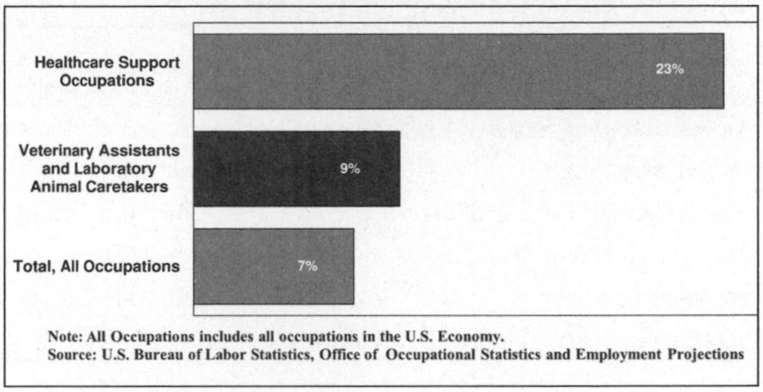

may handle sick or abused animals and may assist in euthanizing animals.

Injuries and Illnesses. Veterinary assistants and laboratory animal caretakers have a higher rate of injuries and illnesses than the national average. When working with scared and aggressive animals, workers may be bitten, scratched, or kicked. A worker also may be injured while holding, bathing, or restraining an animal.

Work Schedules. About 1 in 3 veterinary assistants and laboratory animal caretakers worked part time in 2014. Many clinics and laboratories operate 24 hours a day, so veterinary assistants and laboratory animal caretakers may be required to work nights, weekends, and holidays.

Education/Training

Most veterinary assistants and laboratory animal caretakers have a high school diploma and learn the occupation on the job. Experience working with animals can be helpful for job seekers.

Education. Most workers entering the occupation have a high school diploma or its equivalent.

Training. Most veterinary assistants and laboratory animal caretakers are trained on the job, but some employers prefer candidates who already have experience working with animals.

Licenses, Certifications, and Registrations. Although certification is not mandatory, it allows workers to demonstrate competency in animal husbandry, health and welfare, and facility administration. Employers may prefer to hire candidates who have certification, and it may be required for advancement.

The National Association of Veterinary Technicians in America (NAVTA) offers the Approved Veterinary Assistant (AVA) designation for veterinary assistants. To qualify for the designation, candidates must graduate from a NAVTA-approved program and pass an exam.

Laboratory animal caretakers can become certified through the American Association for Laboratory Animal Science (AALAS). AALAS offers three levels of certification: Assistant Laboratory Animal Technician (ALAT), Laboratory Animal Technician (LAT), and Laboratory Animal Technologist (LATG). For AALAS certification, candidates must have experience working in a laboratory animal facility and pass an exam.

Important Qualities

Communication skills. Veterinary assistants and laboratory animal caretakers often communicate with pet owners, veterinarians, veterinary technologists and technicians, and other assistants. Good communication skills are especially important when dealing with an emergency, such as an ill or injured animal needing immediate attention.

Detail oriented. Veterinary assistants and laboratory animal caretakers must follow strict instructions. For example, workers must be precise when sterilizing surgical equipment, monitoring animals, and giving medication.

Dexterity. Veterinary assistants and laboratory animal caretakers must handle animals and use medical instruments and laboratory equipment with care.

Empathy. Veterinary assistants and laboratory animal caretakers must treat animals with kindness and be empathetic to both the animals and their owners.

Physical strength. Veterinary assistants and laboratory animal caretakers must be able to handle, move, and restrain animals.

Pay

The median annual wage for veterinary assistants and laboratory animal caretakers was $23,790 in May 2014. The median wage is the wage at which half the workers in an occupation earned more than that amount and half earned less. The lowest 10 percent earned less than $17,500, and the highest 10 percent earned more than $36,200.

Job Outlook

Employment of veterinary assistants and laboratory animal caretakers is projected to grow 9 percent from 2014 to 2024, faster than the average for all occupations. Veterinary assistants and laboratory animal caretakers will be needed to assist veterinarians and other veterinary care staff.

Although some establishments are replacing veterinary assistant positions with veterinary technicians and technologists, growth of

Employment Projections Data for Veterinary Assistants and Laboratory Animal Caretakers

Occupational Title	SOC Code	Employment, 2014	Projected Employment, 2024	Change, 2014–2024 Percent	Change, 2014–2024 Numeric
Veterinary assistants and laboratory animal caretakers	31-9096	73,400	80,000	9	6,600

Source: U.S. Bureau of Labor Statistics, Employment Projections Program

Similar Occupations. This table shows a list of occupations with job duties that are similar to those of veterinary assistants and laboratory animal caretakers.

Occupations	Entry-level Education	2014 Median Pay	Projected Job Growth	Average Annual Openings
Animal Care and Service Workers	High school diploma or equivalent	$20,610	11%	2,570
Dental Assistants	Postsecondary nondegree award	$35,390	18%	5,860
Nursing Assistants and Orderlies	See Education/Training	$25,090	17%	26,780
Surgical Technologists	Postsecondary nondegree award	$43,350	15%	1,470
Veterinarians	Doctoral or professional degree	$87,590	9%	690
Veterinary Technologists and Technicians	Associate's degree	$31,070	19%	1,790

the pet care industry means that the number of veterinary assistant positions should continue to increase.

Demand for laboratory animal caretakers is expected to grow in areas such as public health, where organizations work to protect the health of an entire population; food and animal safety, where organizations work to prevent foodborne contaminations and diseases in animals; national disease control; and biomedical research on human health problems.

Job Prospects. Overall job opportunities for veterinary assistants and laboratory animal caretakers are expected to be very good. Veterinary assistants experience a high rate of job turnover, so many positions will become available from workers who leave the occupation each year.

Contacts for More Information

For more information about certification as a laboratory animal caretaker, visit

➤ American Association for Laboratory Animal Science (www.aalas.org)

For more information about certification as a veterinary assistant, visit

➤ National Association of Veterinary Technicians in America (www.navta.net)

For more information about becoming a veterinary assistant, including career opportunities, visit

➤ American Animal Hospital Association (www.aaha.org)

O*NET

➤ Veterinary Assistants and Laboratory Animal Caretakers (31-9096.00)

Veterinary Technologists and Technicians

- **2014 Median Pay** .... $31,070 per year $14.94 per hour
- **Typical Entry-Level Education** .... Associate's degree
- **Work Experience in a Related Occupation** .... None
- **On-the-job Training** .... None
- **Number of Jobs, 2014** 95,600
- **Job Outlook, 2014–24** ...... 19% (Much faster than average)
- **Employment Change, 2014–24** 17,900

What Veterinary Technologists and Technicians Do

Veterinary technologists and technicians perform medical tests under the supervision of a licensed veterinarian to assist in diagnosing the injuries and illnesses of animals.

Duties. Veterinary technologists and technicians typically do the following:

- Observe the behavior and condition of animals
- Provide nursing care or emergency first aid to recovering or injured animals
- Bathe animals, clip nails or claws, and brush or cut animals' hair
- Restrain animals during exams or procedures
- Administer anesthesia to animals, and monitor their responses
- Collect laboratory samples, such as blood, urine, or tissue, for testing
- Perform laboratory tests, such as urinalyses and blood counts
- Take and develop X-rays
- Prepare animals and instruments for surgery
- Administer medications, vaccines, and treatments prescribed by a veterinarian
- Collect and record patients' case histories

Veterinarians rely on technologists and technicians to conduct a variety of clinical and laboratory procedures, including postoperative care, dental care, and specialized nursing care.

Veterinary technologists and technicians who work in research-related jobs do similar work. For example, they are responsible for making sure that animals are handled carefully and treated humanely. They also help veterinarians or scientists on research projects in areas such as biomedical research, disaster preparedness, and food safety.

Veterinary technologists and technicians most often work with small-animal practitioners who care for cats and dogs, but they may also perform a variety of tasks involving mice, rats, sheep, pigs, cattle, birds, or other animals.

Veterinary technologists and technicians can specialize in a particular discipline. Specialties include dentistry, anesthesia, emergency and critical care, and zoological medicine.

Veterinary technologists usually have a 4-year bachelor's degree in veterinary technology. Although some technologists work in private clinical practices, many work in more advanced research-related jobs, usually under the guidance of a scientist or veterinarian. Working primarily in a laboratory setting, they may administer medications; prepare tissue samples for examination; or record information on an animal's genealogy, weight, diet, and signs of pain.

Veterinary technicians usually have a 2-year associate's degree in a veterinary technology program. They generally work in private clinical practices under the guidance of a licensed veterinarian. Technicians may perform laboratory tests, such as a urinalysis, and help veterinarians conduct a variety of other diagnostic tests. Although some of their work is done in a laboratory setting, many technicians also talk with animal owners. For example, they explain a pet's condition or how to administer medication prescribed by a veterinarian.

Work Environment

Veterinary technologists and technicians held about 95,600 jobs in 2014, of which 91 percent were in the veterinary services industry.

They also may work in laboratories, colleges and universities, and rescue leagues.

Their jobs may be physically or emotionally demanding. For example, they may witness abused animals or may need to help euthanize sick, injured, or unwanted animals.

Injuries and Illnesses. Veterinary technologists and technicians have a higher rate of injuries and illnesses than the national average. When working with scared or aggressive animals, they may be bitten, scratched, or kicked. Injuries may happen while the technologist or technician is holding, cleaning, or restraining an animal.

Work Schedules. Many clinics and laboratories are staffed 24 hours a day, so veterinary technologists and technicians may have to work evenings, weekends, or holidays. Many technicians have variable schedules.

Education/Training

There are primarily two levels of education for entry into this occupation: a 4-year program for veterinary technologists and a 2-year program for veterinary technicians.

Education. Veterinary technologists and technicians must complete a postsecondary program in veterinary technology. In 2015, there were 231 veterinary technology programs accredited by the American Veterinary Medical Association (AVMA). Most of these programs offer a 2-year associate's degree for veterinary technicians. Twenty-three colleges offer a 4-year bachelor's degree in veterinary technology. Nine schools offer coursework through distance learning.

People interested in becoming a veterinary technologist or technician should take high school classes in biology and other sciences, as well as math.

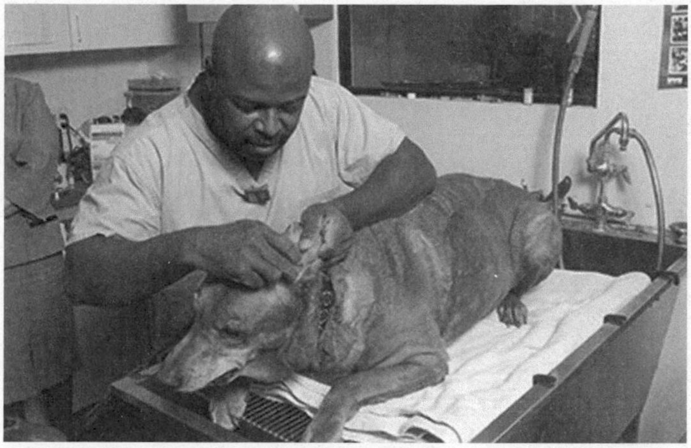

Veterinary technologists and technicians often assist veterinarians by conducting tests.

Licenses, Certifications, and Registrations. Although each state regulates veterinary technologists and technicians differently, most candidates must pass a credentialing exam. Most states require technologists and technicians to pass the Veterinary Technician National Examination (VTNE), offered by the American Association of Veterinary State Boards.

For technologists seeking work in a research facility, the American Association for Laboratory Animal Science (AALAS) offers the following certifications for technicians and technologists: Laboratory Animal Technician (LAT) and Laboratory Animal Technologist (LATG).

Although certification is not mandatory, workers at each level can show competency in animal husbandry, health and welfare, and facility administration and management to prospective employers. To become certified, candidates must have work experience in a laboratory animal facility and pass the AALAS examination.

Important Qualities

Communication skills. Veterinary technologists and technicians spend a substantial amount of their time communicating with supervisors, animal owners, and other staff. In addition, a growing number of technicians counsel pet owners on animal behavior and nutrition.

Compassion. Veterinary technologists and technicians must treat animals with kindness and must be sensitive when dealing with the owners of sick pets.

Detail oriented. Veterinary technologists and technicians must pay attention to detail. They must be precise when

Median Annual Wages, May 2014

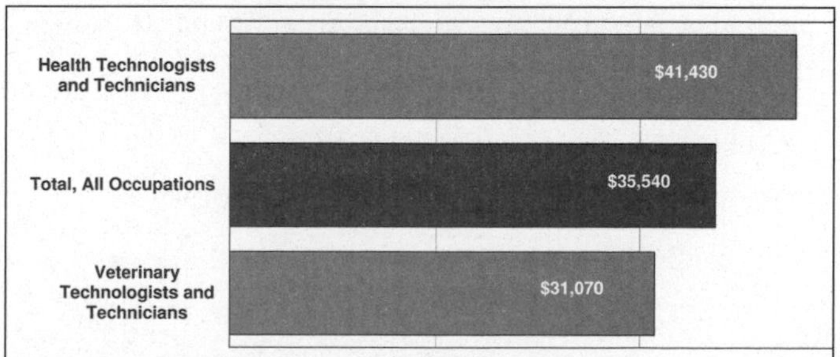

Note: All Occupations includes all occupations in the U.S. Economy.
Source: U.S. Bureau of Labor Statistics, Occupational Employment Statistics

Percent Change in Employment, Projected 2014–2024

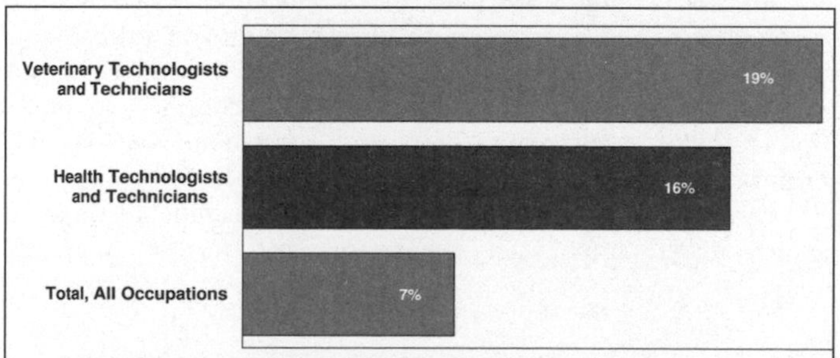

Note: All Occupations includes all occupations in the U.S. Economy.
Source: U.S. Bureau of Labor Statistics, Office of Occupational Statistics and Employment Projections

Employment Projections Data for Veterinary Technologists and Technicians

Occupational Title	SOC Code	Employment, 2014	Projected Employment, 2024	Change, 2014–2024 Percent	Change, 2014–2024 Numeric
Veterinary technologists and technicians	29-2056	95,600	113,600	19	17,900

Source: U.S. Bureau of Labor Statistics, Employment Projections Program

Similar Occupations. This table shows a list of occupations with job duties that are similar to those of veterinary technologists and technicians.

Occupations	Entry-level Education	2014 Median Pay	Projected Job Growth	Average Annual Openings
Animal Care and Service Workers	High school diploma or equivalent	$20,610	11%	2,570
Medical and Clinical Laboratory Technologists and Technicians	See Education/Training	$49,310	16%	5,210
Radiologic and MRI Technologists	Associate's degree	$57,370	9%	2,070
Surgical Technologists	Postsecondary nondegree award	$43,350	15%	1,470
Veterinarians	Doctoral or professional degree	$87,590	9%	690
Veterinary Assistants and Laboratory Animal Caretakers	High school diploma or equivalent	$23,790	9%	660

recording information, performing diagnostic tests, and administering medication.

Manual dexterity. Veterinary technologists and technicians must handle animals, medical instruments, and laboratory equipment with care. They do intricate tasks, such as dental work, giving anesthesia, and taking X-rays, which require a steady hand.

Problem-solving skills. Veterinary technologists and technicians need strong problem-solving skills in order to identify injuries and illnesses and offer the appropriate treatment.

Pay

The median annual wage for veterinary technologists and technicians was $31,070 in May 2014. The median wage is the wage at which half the workers in an occupation earned more than that amount and half earned less. The lowest 10 percent earned less than $21,390, and the highest 10 percent earned more than $45,710.

Veterinary technologists and technicians working in research positions often earn more than those in other fields.

Job Outlook

Employment of veterinary technologists and technicians is projected to grow 19 percent from 2014 to 2024, much faster than the average for all occupations.

Clinics and animal hospitals are increasingly using veterinary technologists and technicians to provide more general care and perform more laboratory work, allowing them to operate more efficiently. Furthermore, veterinarians will continue to prefer higher skilled veterinary technologists and technicians over veterinary assistants for more complex work.

There will also be demand for veterinary technicians in areas such food and animal safety, where organizations work to prevent foodborne contaminations and diseases in animals; public health, where organizations work to protect the health of an entire population; disease control; and biomedical research on human health problems.

Job Prospects. Overall job opportunities for veterinary technologists and technicians are expected to be good, particularly in rural areas. However, the number of veterinary technology programs has grown rapidly in recent years, so the number of new graduates vying for jobs over the coming decade should result in greater competition than in the past. The need to replace workers who leave the occupation each year also will result in job openings.

Contacts for More Information

For information about careers in veterinary medicine and a listing of AVMA-accredited veterinary technology programs, visit

➤ American Veterinary Medical Association (www.avma.org)

For more information about becoming a veterinary technician or technologist, visit

➤ National Association of Veterinary Technicians in America (www.navta.net)

For information about certification as a laboratory animal technician or technologist, visit

➤ American Association for Laboratory Animal Science (www.aalas.org)

For information about the Veterinary Technician National Examination (VTNE), visit

➤ American Association of Veterinary State Boards (www.aavsb.org)

O*NET

➤ Veterinary Technologists and Technicians (29-2056.00)

Aircraft and Avionics Equipment Mechanics and Technicians

- **2014 Median Pay** .... $56,980 per year
$27.40 per hour
- **Typical Entry-Level Education** .... See Education/Training
- **Work Experience in a Related Occupation** .... None
- **On-the-job Training** .... None
- **Number of Jobs, 2014** 137,300
- **Job Outlook, 2014–24** .... 1% (Little or no change)
- **Employment Change, 2014–24** 1,600

What Aircraft and Avionics Equipment Mechanics and Technicians Do

Aircraft and avionics equipment mechanics and technicians repair and perform scheduled maintenance on aircraft. They also perform aircraft inspections as required by the Federal Aviation Administration (FAA).

Duties. Aircraft mechanics typically do the following:

- Diagnose mechanical or electrical problems
- Repair wings, brakes, electrical systems, and other aircraft components
- Replace defective parts, using hand tools or power tools
- Examine replacement aircraft parts for defects
- Read maintenance manuals to identify repair procedures
- Test aircraft parts with gauges and other diagnostic equipment
- Inspect completed work to ensure that it meets performance standards
- Keep records of maintenance and repair work

Avionics technicians typically do the following:

- Test electronic instruments, using circuit testers, oscilloscopes, and voltmeters
- Interpret flight test data to diagnose malfunctions and performance problems
- Assemble components, such as electrical controls and junction boxes, and install software
- Install instrument panels, using hand tools, power tools, and soldering irons
- Repair or replace malfunctioning components
- Keep records of maintenance and repair work

Airplanes are highly complex machines that require reliable parts and service to fly safely. To keep an airplane in operating condition, aircraft and avionics equipment mechanics and technicians perform scheduled maintenance, make repairs, and complete inspections. They must follow detailed federal regulations set by the FAA that dictate maintenance schedules for different operations.

Many mechanics are generalists and work on many different types of aircraft, such as jets, piston-driven airplanes, and helicopters. Others specialize in one section, such as the engine, hydraulic system, or electrical system, of a particular type of aircraft. In independent repair shops, mechanics usually inspect and repair many types of aircraft.

Most mechanics who work on civilian aircraft have either one or both of the FAA's Airframe and Powerplant (A&P) certificates. Mechanics who have these certificates are authorized to work on most parts of the aircraft, excluding flight instruments and major work on propellers. Maintaining a plane's electronic flight instruments is typically the job of specialized avionics technicians.

The following are examples of types of aircraft and avionics equipment mechanics and technicians:

Airframe and Powerplant (A&P) mechanics are certified generalist mechanics who can independently perform many maintenance and alteration tasks on aircraft. A&P mechanics repair and maintain most parts of an aircraft, including the engines, landing gear, brakes, and air-conditioning system. Some specialized activities require additional experience and certification.

Maintenance schedules for aircraft may be based on hours flown, days since the last inspection, trips flown, or a combination of these factors. Maintenance also may need to be done at other times to address specific issues recognized by mechanics or manufacturers.

Mechanics use precision instruments to measure wear and identify defects. They may use X-rays or magnetic or ultrasonic inspection equipment to discover cracks that cannot be seen on a plane's exterior. They check for corrosion, distortion, and cracks in the aircraft's main body, wings, and tail. They then repair the metal, fabric, wood, or composite materials that make up the airframe and skin.

After completing all repairs, mechanics must test the equipment to ensure that it works properly. Aircraft equipped with digital monitoring systems can provide mechanics with valuable diagnostic information from electronic consoles. Mechanics also must keep records of all maintenance that they do on an aircraft.

The A&P ratings generally are considered the initial and most basic ratings needed for a worker to be a professional mechanic. Many additional certifications and specializations can be gained

Avionics technicians are responsible for repairing an aircraft's electronics systems.

to enable mechanics to perform additional duties. Some of these specializations are as follows:

Avionics technicians are specialists who repair and maintain a plane's electronic instruments, such as radio communication devices and equipment, radar systems, and navigation aids. As the use of digital technology increases, more time is spent maintaining computer systems. The ability to repair and maintain many avionics and flight instrument systems is granted through the Airframe rating, but other licenses or certifications may be needed.

Designated airworthiness representatives (DARs) examine, inspect, and test aircraft for airworthiness. They issue airworthiness certificates, which aircraft must have to fly. There are two types of DARs: manufacturing DARs and maintenance DARs.

Inspection authorized (IA) mechanics are mechanics who have both Airframe and Powerplant certification and may perform inspections on aircraft and return them to service. IA mechanics are able to do a wider variety of maintenance and alterations than any other type of maintenance personnel. They can do comprehensive annual inspections or return aircraft to service after a major repair.

Repairmen certificate holders may or may not have the A&P certificate or other certificates. Repairmen certificates are issued by certified repair stations to aviation maintenance personnel, and the certificates allow them to do specific duties. Repairmen certificates are valid only while the mechanic works at the issuing repair center and are not transferable to other employers.

Work Environment

Aircraft mechanics and avionics technicians held about 137,300 jobs in 2014. The majority worked for private companies and about 14 percent worked for the federal government. Approximately 87 percent were aircraft mechanics and the rest were avionics technicians.

The industries that employed the most aircraft mechanics and service technicians in 2014 were as follows:

Support activities for air transportation	28%
Scheduled air transportation	22
Aerospace product and parts manufacturing	15
Federal government, excluding postal service	15
Nonscheduled air transportation	5

The industries that employed the most avionics technicians in 2014 were as follows:

Aerospace product and parts manufacturing	30%
Support activities for air transportation	30
Federal government, excluding postal service	11
Scheduled air transportation	8
Employment services	4

Mechanics and technicians work in hangars, in repair stations, or on airfields. They must meet strict deadlines while maintaining safety standards.

Most mechanics and technicians work near major airports. Mechanics may work outside on the airfield, or in climate-controlled shops and hangars. Civilian mechanics employed by the U.S. Armed Forces work on military installations.

Injuries and Illnesses. Aircraft and avionics equipment mechanics and technicians experience rates of injuries and illnesses that are higher than the national average.

Mechanics and technicians often lift heavy objects, handle dangerous chemicals, or operate large power tools. They may work on scaffolds or ladders, and noise and vibrations are common, especially when engines are being tested. However, mechanics take precautions against injury, such as wearing ear protection and brightly colored vests to ensure that they are seen when working around large aircraft.

Work Schedules. Mechanics and technicians usually work full time on rotating 8-hour shifts. Overtime and weekend work are common. Day shifts usually are reserved for mechanics with the most seniority. General aviation mechanics and technicians typically have more flexible schedules than those working for airlines.

Education/Training

Many aircraft and avionics equipment mechanics and technicians learn their trade at an FAA-approved aviation maintenance technician school. Others enter with a high school education or equivalent and are trained on the job. Some workers enter the occupation after getting training in the military. Aircraft mechanics and avionics technicians typically are certified by the FAA. See Title 14 of the Code of Federal Regulations (14 CFR) part 65, subparts D and E, for the most current requirements for becoming a certified mechanic.

Education and Training. Aircraft mechanics and service technicians often enter the occupation after attending a Part 147 FAA-approved aviation maintenance technician school. These schools award a certificate of completion that the FAA recognizes as an alternative to the experience requirements stated in regulations. The schools also grant holders the right to take the relevant FAA exams.

Some aircraft mechanics and service technicians enter the occupation with a high school diploma or equivalent and receive on-the-job training to learn their skills and to be able to pass the FAA exams. Other workers enter the occupation after getting training in the military. Aviation maintenance personnel who are not certified by the FAA work under supervision until they have enough experience and knowledge and become certified.

Avionics technicians typically earn an associate's degree before entering the occupation. Aircraft controls, systems, and flight

Median Annual Wages, May 2014

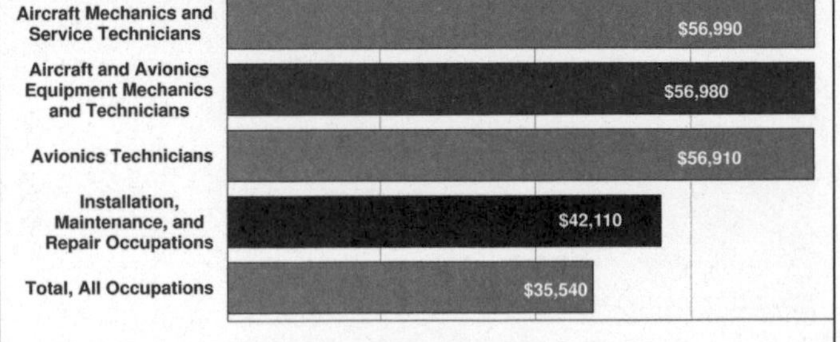

Note: All Occupations includes all occupations in the U.S. Economy.
Source: U.S. Bureau of Labor Statistics, Occupational Employment Statistics

Percent Change in Employment, Projected 2014–2024

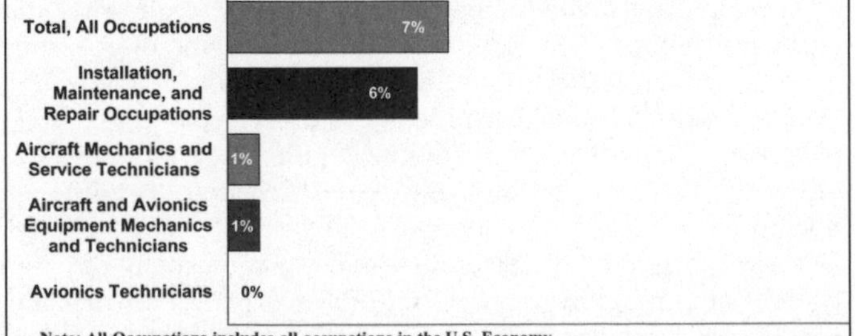

Note: All Occupations includes all occupations in the U.S. Economy.
Source: U.S. Bureau of Labor Statistics, Office of Occupational Statistics and Employment Projections

Employment Projections Data for Aircraft and Avionics Equipment Mechanics and Technicians

Occupational Title	SOC Code	Employment, 2014	Projected Employment, 2024	Change, 2014–2024	
				Percent	Numeric
Aircraft and avionics equipment mechanics and technicians	—	137,300	138,900	1	1,600
Avionics technicians	49-2091	17,400	17,500	0	100
Aircraft mechanics and service technicians	49-3011	119,900	121,500	1	1,600

Source: U.S. Bureau of Labor Statistics, Employment Projections Program

instruments have become increasingly digital and computerized. Maintenance workers who have the proper background in aviation flight instruments or computer repair are needed to maintain these complex systems.

Licenses, Certifications, and Registrations. Although aircraft and avionics equipment mechanics and technicians are not required to get licenses or certifications, most do, because these credentials often improve a mechanic's wages and chances for employment. The FAA requires that aircraft maintenance be done either by a certified mechanic with the appropriate ratings or authorizations or under the supervision of such a mechanic.

The FAA offers separate certifications for bodywork (Airframe mechanics, or "A") and engine work (Powerplant mechanics, or "P"), but employers may prefer to hire mechanics who have both Airframe and Powerplant (A&P) ratings. The A&P ratings generally certify that aviation mechanics meet basic knowledge and ability standards.

Mechanics must be at least 18 years of age, be fluent in English, and have 30 months of experience to qualify for either the A or the P rating or both (the A&P rating). If only one rating is sought by the mechanic, 18 months' experience is required to take either the Airframe or the Powerplant exam. However, completion of a program at a Part 147 FAA-approved aviation maintenance technician school can substitute for the experience requirement and shorten the time requirements for becoming eligible to take the FAA exams.

Applicants must pass written, oral, and practical exams that demonstrate the required skills. Candidates must pass all the tests within a timeframe of 2 years.

To keep their certification, mechanics must have completed relevant repair or maintenance work within the previous 24 months. To fulfill this requirement, mechanics may take classes from their employer, a school, or an aircraft manufacturer.

Avionics technicians typically are certified through a repair station for the specific work being done, or else they hold the Airframe rating to work on an aircraft's electronic and flight instrument systems. An Aircraft Electronics Technician (AET) certification is available through the National Center for Aerospace & Transportation Technologies (NCATT). It certifies that aviation mechanics have a basic level of knowledge in the subject area, but it is not required by the FAA for any specific tasks. Avionics technicians who work on communications equipment may need to have the proper radiotelephone operator certification issued by the Federal Communications Commission (FCC).

Other licenses and certifications are available to mechanics who wish to increase their skill set or advance their careers. The Inspection Authorization (IA) is available to mechanics who have had their A&P ratings for at least 3 years and meet other requirements. These mechanics are able to sign off on many major repairs and alterations. Mechanics can get numerous other certifications, such as Repairmen of light-sport aircraft and Designated Airworthiness Representative (DAR).

Important Qualities

Strength and agility. Mechanics and technicians may need to carry or move heavy equipment or aircraft parts. They may need to climb on airplanes, balance, and reach without falling.

Detail oriented. Mechanics and technicians need to adjust airplane parts to exact specifications. For example, they often use precision tools to tighten wheel bolts to an exact tension.

Dexterity. Mechanics and technicians must possess dexterity to coordinate the movement of their fingers and hands in order to grasp, manipulate, or assemble parts.

Observational skills. Mechanics and technicians must recognize engine noises, read gauges, and collect other information to determine whether an aircraft's systems are working properly.

Troubleshooting skills. Mechanics and technicians diagnose complex problems, and they need to evaluate options to correct those problems.

Work Experience in a Related Occupation. Avionics technicians may begin their careers as aircraft mechanics and service technicians. As aircraft mechanics and service technicians gain experience, they may study independently, attend formal classes, or otherwise choose to pursue additional certifications that grant privileges to work on specialized flight instruments. Eventually, they may become dedicated avionics technicians who work exclusively on flight instruments.

Advancement. As aircraft mechanics gain experience, they may advance to lead mechanic, lead inspector, or shop supervisor. Opportunities are best for those who have an inspection authorization (IA). Many specialist certifications are available that allow mechanics to do a wider variety of repairs and alterations.

Mechanics with broad experience in maintenance and repair might become inspectors or examiners for the FAA.

Additional business and management training may help aircraft and avionics equipment mechanics and technicians open their own maintenance facility.

Pay

The median annual wage for avionics technicians was $56,910 in May 2014. The median wage is the wage at which half the workers in an occupation earned more than that amount and half earned less. The lowest 10 percent earned less than $35,260, and the highest 10 percent earned more than $85,320.

The median annual wage for aircraft mechanics and service technicians was $56,990 in May 2014. The lowest 10 percent earned less than $34,940, and the highest 10 percent earned more than $86,930.

In May 2014, the median annual wages for aircraft mechanics and service technicians in the top industries in which they worked were as follows:

Scheduled air transportation	$64,620
Aerospace product and parts manufacturing	60,360
Nonscheduled air transportation	59,590

Similar Occupations. This table shows a list of occupations with job duties that are similar to those of aircraft and avionics equipment mechanics and technicians.

Occupations	Entry-level Education	2014 Median Pay	Projected Job Growth	Average Annual Openings
Aerospace Engineering and Operations Technicians	Associate's degree	$63,780	4%	40
Automotive Body and Glass Repairers	High school diploma or equivalent	$39,260	9%	1,530
Automotive Service Technicians and Mechanics	Postsecondary nondegree award	$37,120	5%	3,910
Electrical and Electronics Engineering Technicians	Associate's degree	$59,820	-2%	-280
Electrical and Electronics Installers and Repairers	Postsecondary nondegree award	$53,900	-4%	-540
Electricians	High school diploma or equivalent	$51,110	14%	8,590
Electro-mechanical Technicians	Associate's degree	$53,070	1%	10
Heavy Vehicle and Mobile Equipment Service Technicians	High school diploma or equivalent	$45,930	5%	1,010
Mechanical Engineering Technicians	Associate's degree	$53,530	2%	90
Network and Computer Systems Administrators	Bachelor's degree	$75,790	8%	3,020

Federal government, excluding postal service $56,260
Support activities for air transportation 50,530

In May 2014, the median annual wages for avionics technicians in the top industries in which they worked were as follows:

Scheduled air transportation.. $74,330
Aerospace product and parts manufacturing...................... 62,200
Federal government, excluding postal service...................... 55,000
Support activities for air transportation 52,350
Employment services 45,350

Union Membership. Compared with workers in all occupations, aircraft and avionics equipment mechanics and technicians had a higher percentage of workers who belonged to a union in 2014.

Job Outlook

Employment of aircraft and avionics equipment mechanics and technicians is projected to show little or no change from 2014 to 2024.

Air traffic is expected to increase gradually over the coming decade. However, new aircraft generally are expected to require less maintenance than older aircraft. Airlines may continue to outsource maintenance work to specialized maintenance and repair shops both domestically and abroad. Increased specialization will allow maintenance facilities to use their resources more efficiently and therefore limit growth in the number of aircraft and avionics equipment mechanics and technicians.

Job Prospects. Competition for aircraft and avionics equipment mechanic and technician jobs varies with the type of job sought. In general, job opportunities will be best for mechanics who hold an A&P certificate and have knowledge about the most cutting-edge technologies and composite materials. Familiarity with computers and digital systems will help provide the best opportunities.

Contacts for More Information

For more information about aircraft and avionics equipment mechanics and technicians, visit

➤ Aircraft Mechanics Fraternal Association (www.amfanational.org)
➤ Aviation Maintenance Magazine (www.avm-mag.com)
➤ Federal Aviation Administration (www.faa.gov)
➤ National Business Aviation Association (www.nbaa.org)
➤ National Center for Aerospace & Transportation Technologies (www.ncatt.org)
➤ Professional Aviation Maintenance Association (http://pama.org)

O*NET

➤ Avionics Technicians (49-2091.00)
➤ Aircraft Mechanics and Service Technicians (49-3011.00)

Automotive Body and Glass Repairers

- **2014 Median Pay** .... $39,260 per year, $18.87 per hour
- **Typical Entry-Level Education** .... High school diploma or equivalent
- **Work Experience in a Related Occupation**.............. None
- **On-the-job Training** .... See Education/Training
- **Number of Jobs, 2014** 169,100
- **Job Outlook, 2014–24** .... 9% (Faster than average)
- **Employment Change, 2014–24** 15,300

What Automotive Body and Glass Repairers Do

Automotive body and glass repairers restore, refinish, and replace vehicle bodies and frames, windshields, and window glass.

Duties. Automotive body repairers typically do the following:

- Review damage reports, prepare cost estimates, and plan work
- Inspect cars for structural damage
- Remove damaged body parts, including bumpers, fenders, hoods, grilles, and trim
- Realign car frames and chassis to repair structural damage
- Hammer out or patch dents, dimples, and other minor body damage

- Fit, attach, and weld replacement parts into place
- Sand, buff, and prime refurbished and repaired surfaces
- Apply new finish to restored body parts

Automotive glass installers and repairers typically do the following:

- Examine damaged windshields and assess reparability
- Clean damaged areas and prepare the surfaces for repair
- Stabilize chips and cracks with clear resin
- Remove glass that cannot be repaired
- Check windshield frames for rust
- Clean windshield frames and prepare them for installation
- Apply urethane sealant to the windshield frames
- Install replacement glass
- Replace any parts removed prior to repairs

Automotive body and glass repairers can repair most damage from vehicle collisions and make vehicles look and drive like new. Repairs may be minor, such as replacing a cracked windshield, or major, such as replacing an entire door panel. After a major collision, the underlying frame of a car can become weakened or compromised. Body repairers restore the structural integrity of car frames to manufacturer specifications.

Body repairers use many tools for their work. They use pneumatic tools and plasma cutters to remove damaged parts, such as bumpers and door panels. They also often use heavy-duty hydraulic jacks and hammers for major structural repairs, such as aligning the body. For some work, they use common hand tools, such as metal files, pliers, wrenches, hammers, and screwdrivers.

In some cases, body repairers complete an entire job by themselves. In other cases, especially in large shops, they use an assembly line approach in which they work as a team with each individual performing a specialized task.

Although body repairers sometimes prime and paint repaired parts, painting and coating workers generally perform these tasks.

Glass installers and repairers often travel to the customer's location and perform their work in the field. They commonly use specialized tools such as vacuum pumps to fill windshield cracks and chips with a stabilizing resin. When windshields are badly damaged, they use knives to remove the damaged windshield, and then they secure the new windshield using a special urethane adhesive.

Automotive body and glass repairers must carefully restore cars to given specifications following an accident.

Work Environment

Automotive body and glass repairers held about 169,100 jobs in 2014. About 66 percent worked in automotive repair and maintenance shops and 17 percent worked for automobile dealers. About 1 in 10 automotive body and glass repairers were self-employed in 2014.

Body repairers typically work indoors in body shops, which are often noisy. Most shops are well ventilated, so that dust and paint fumes can be dispersed. Glass installers and repairers often travel to the customer's location to repair damaged windshields and window glass.

Automotive body and glass repairers sometimes work in awkward and cramped positions, and their work can be physically demanding.

Injuries and Illnesses. Automotive body repairers have one of the highest rates of injuries and illnesses of all occupations. These workers commonly suffer minor injuries, such as cuts, burns, and scrapes. Following safety procedures helps to avoid serious accidents.

Work Schedules. Most automotive body and glass repairers work full time. When shops have to complete a backlog of work, overtime is common. This often includes working evenings and weekends.

Education/Training

Most employers prefer to hire automotive body and glass repairers who have completed a formal training program in automotive body or glass repair. Still, many new body and glass repairers begin work without formal training. Industry certification is increasingly important.

Education. High school, trade and technical school, and community college programs in collision repair combine hands-on practice and technical instruction. Topics usually include electronics, repair cost estimation, and welding, all of which provide a strong educational foundation for a career as a body repairer. Although not required, postsecondary education often provides the best preparation.

Trade and technical school programs typically award certificates after 6 months to 1 year of study. Some community colleges offer 2-year programs in collision repair. Many of these schools also offer certificates for individual courses, so students can take classes part time or as needed.

Licenses, Certifications, and Registrations. Although not required, certification is recommended because it shows competence and usually brings higher pay. In some instances it is required for advancement beyond entry-level work.

Certification from the National Institute for Automotive Service Excellence (ASE) is a standard credential for body repairers. In addition, many vehicle and paint manufacturers have product certification programs that train body repairers in specific technologies and repair methods.

A few states require a license to perform automotive glass installation and repair. Check with your state for more information.

Training. New workers typically begin their on-the-job training by helping an experienced body repairer with basic tasks, such as fixing minor dents. As they gain experience, they move on to more complex work, such as aligning car frames. Some body repairers may become trained in as little as 1 year, but they generally need 2 or 3 years of hands-on training to become fully independent body repairers.

Median Annual Wages, May 2014

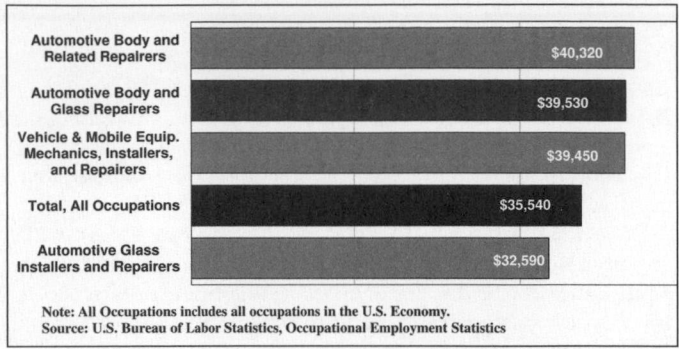

Note: All Occupations includes all occupations in the U.S. Economy.
Source: U.S. Bureau of Labor Statistics, Occupational Employment Statistics

Percent Change in Employment, Projected 2014–2024

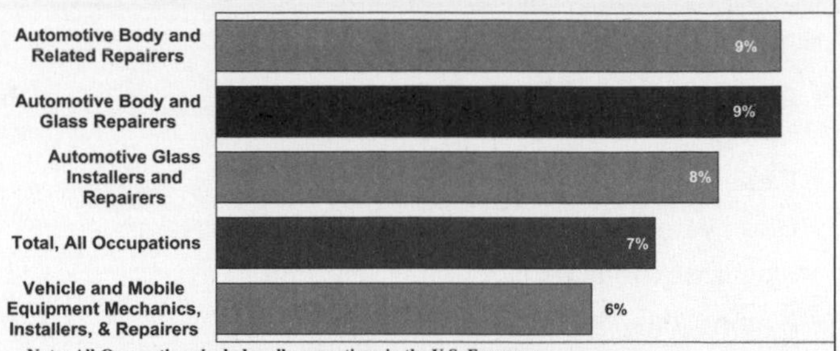

Note: All Occupations includes all occupations in the U.S. Economy.
Source: U.S. Bureau of Labor Statistics, Office of Occupational Statistics and Employment Projections

Basic automotive glass installation and repair can be learned in as little as 6 months, but becoming fully independent can take up to a year of training.

Formally educated workers often require significantly less on-the-job training and typically advance to independent work more quickly than those who do not have the same level of education.

Throughout their careers, body repairers need to continue their education and training to keep up with rapidly changing automotive technology. Body repairers are expected to develop their skills by reading technical manuals and by attending classes and seminars. Many employers regularly send workers to advanced training programs, such as those offered by the Inter-Industry Conference on Auto Collision Repair (I-CAR).

Advancement. Automotive body and glass repairers earn more money as they gain experience, and some may advance into management positions within body shops, especially those workers with 2- or 4-year degrees.

Important Qualities

Critical-thinking skills. Automotive body and glass repairers must be able to evaluate vehicle damage and determine necessary repair strategies. In some cases, they must decide if a vehicle is "totaled," or too damaged to justify the cost of repair.

Customer-service skills. Automotive body and glass repairers must discuss auto body and glass problems, along with options to fix them, with customers. Workers must be courteous, good listeners, and ready to answer customers' questions.

Detail oriented. Automotive body and glass repairers must pay close attention to detail. Restoring a damaged auto body or windshield to its original state requires workers to have a keen eye for even the smallest imperfection.

Dexterity. Many body repairers' tasks, such as removing door panels, hammering out dents, and using hand tools to install parts, require a steady hand and good hand-eye coordination.

Mechanical skills. Body repairers must know which diagnostic, hydraulic, pneumatic, and other power equipment and tools are appropriate for certain procedures and repairs. They must know how to apply the correct techniques and methods necessary to repair modern automobiles.

Physical strength. Automotive body and glass repairers must sometimes lift heavy parts, such as door panels and windshields.

Time-management skills. Automotive body and glass repairers must be timely in their repairs. For many people, their automobile is their primary mode of transportation.

Pay

The median annual wage for automotive body and related repairers was $40,320 in May 2014. The median wage is the wage at which half the workers in an occupation earned more than that amount and half earned less. The lowest 10 percent earned less than $24,640, and the highest 10 percent earned more than $68,590.

The median annual wage for automotive glass installers and repairers was $32,590 in May 2014. The lowest 10 percent earned less than $20,330, and the highest 10 percent earned more than $48,840.

The majority of repair shops and auto dealers pay automotive body and glass repairers on an incentive basis. In addition to receiving a guaranteed base salary, employers pay workers a set amount for completing various tasks. Their earnings depend on both the amount of work assigned and how fast they complete it.

Trainees typically earn between 30 percent and 60 percent of experienced workers' pay. They are paid by the hour until they are competent enough to be paid on an incentive basis.

Job Outlook

Employment of automotive body and glass repairers is projected to grow 9 percent from 2014 to 2024, faster than the average for all occupations.

While the frequency of accidents has declined in recent decades, an increase in the number of vehicles on the road should bolster demand for automotive body and glass repair over the next decade. In some cases, demand may fluctuate throughout the year due to the seasonality of inclement weather in some regions. The need

Employment Projections Data for Automotive Body and Glass Repairers

Occupational Title	SOC Code	Employment, 2014	Projected Employment, 2024	Change, 2014–2024 Percent	Change, 2014–2024 Numeric
Automotive body and glass repairers	—	169,100	184,300	9	15,300
Automotive body and related repairers	49-3021	149,700	163,500	9	13,700
Automotive glass installers and repairers	49-3022	19,300	20,800	8	1,500

Source: U.S. Bureau of Labor Statistics, Employment Projections Program

Similar Occupations. This table shows a list of occupations with job duties that are similar to those of automotive body and glass repairers.

Occupations	Entry-level Education	2014 Median Pay	Projected Job Growth	Average Annual Openings
Automotive Service Technicians and Mechanics	Postsecondary nondegree award	$37,120	5%	3,910
Diesel Service Technicians and Mechanics	High school diploma or equivalent	$43,630	12%	3,160
Glaziers	High school diploma or equivalent	$38,410	4%	190
Heavy Vehicle and Mobile Equipment Service Technicians	High school diploma or equivalent	$45,930	5%	1,010
Painting and Coating Workers	See Education/Training	$33,740	1%	210

for repair may be greater during the winter months in areas with snow and ice, for example, because these conditions increase the chance of accidents.

The adoption of advanced safety features, such as automatic braking for collision avoidance and more durable automotive glass, may reduce future demand for automotive body and glass repair work, but this technology will take time to become commonplace.

Job Prospects. Job opportunities are projected to be very good for automotive body and glass repairers. The best opportunities in automotive body repair will be available to those with industry certification and formal training in automotive body repair and refinishing, and in collision repair. Those without any training or experience will face strong competition for jobs.

The need to replace experienced automotive body and glass repairers who retire, change occupations, or stop working for other reasons will also provide many job opportunities.

Contacts for More Information

For more information about careers in automotive body and glass repair, visit

- ➤ Accrediting Commission of Career Schools and Colleges (www.accsc.org)
- ➤ Inter-Industry Conference on Auto Collision Repair (http://i-car.com)
- ➤ National Automotive Technicians Education Foundation (www.natef.org)
- ➤ National Glass Association (www.glass.org)
- ➤ National Institute for Automotive Service Excellence (www.ase.com)
- ➤ Society of Collision Repair Specialists (www.scrs.com)

O*NET

- ➤ Automotive Body and Related Repairers (49-3021.00)
- ➤ Automotive Glass Installers and Repairers (49-3022.00)

Automotive Service Technicians and Mechanics

- **2014 Median Pay** .... $37,120 per year $17.84 per hour
- **Typical Entry-Level Education** .... Postsecondary nondegree award
- **Work Experience in a Related Occupation** .... None
- **On-the-job Training** .... Short-term on-the-job training
- **Number of Jobs, 2014** 739,900
- **Job Outlook, 2014–24** .... 5% (As fast as average)
- **Employment Change, 2014–24** 39,100

What Automotive Service Technicians and Mechanics Do

Automotive service technicians and mechanics, often called *service technicians* or service techs, inspect, maintain, and repair cars and light trucks.

Duties. Automotive service technicians and mechanics typically do the following:

- Identify problems, often by using computerized diagnostic equipment
- Plan work procedures, using charts, technical manuals, and experience
- Test parts and systems to ensure that they work properly
- Follow checklists to ensure that all critical parts are examined
- Perform basic care and maintenance, including changing oil, checking fluid levels, and rotating tires
- Repair or replace worn parts, such as brake pads, wheel bearings, and sensors
- Perform repairs to manufacturer and customer specifications
- Explain automotive problems and repairs to clients

Although service technicians work on traditional mechanical systems, such as engines, transmissions, and drive belts, they must also be familiar with a growing number of electronic systems. Braking, transmission, and steering systems, for example, are controlled primarily by computers and electronic components.

Other integrated electronic systems, such as accident-avoidance sensors, are becoming common as well. In addition, a growing number of technicians are required to work on vehicles that consume alternative fuels, such as ethanol and electricity.

Service technicians use many different tools, including computerized diagnostic tools and power tools such as pneumatic wrenches, lathes, welding torches, and jacks and hoists. These tools usually are owned by their employers.

Service technicians also use many common hand tools, such as wrenches, pliers, and sockets and ratchets. Service technicians generally own these tools themselves. In fact, experienced workers often have thousands of dollars invested in their personal tool collection. For example, some invest in their own set of pneumatic tools—such as impact wrenches—powered by compressed air.

The following are examples of types of service technicians:

Automotive air-conditioning technicians install and repair air-conditioners and parts, such as compressors, condensers, and controls. These workers must be trained and certified in handling refrigerants.

Brake technicians diagnose brake system problems, adjust brakes, replace brake rotors and pads, and make other repairs on brake systems. Some technicians specialize in both brake and front-end work. (See "Front-end technicians.")

Drivability technicians, also known as *diagnostic technicians*, use their extensive knowledge of engine management and fuel, electrical, ignition, and emissions systems to diagnose issues that prevent engines from performing efficiently. They often use the onboard diagnostic system of a car and electronic testing equipment such as scan tools and multimeters to find the malfunction.

Front-end technicians diagnose ride, handling, and tire wear problems. To correct these problems, they frequently use special alignment equipment and wheel-balancing machines.

Transmission technicians and rebuilders work on gear trains, couplings, hydraulic pumps, and other parts of transmissions. An extensive knowledge of computer controls and the ability to diagnose electrical and hydraulic problems are needed to work on these complex components.

For information about technicians who work on large trucks and buses, see the profile on diesel service technicians and mechanics.

For information about technicians who work on farm equipment, construction vehicles, and railcars, see the profile on heavy vehicle and mobile equipment service technicians.

For information about technicians who repair and service motorcycles, motorboats, and small all-terrain vehicles, see the profile on small engine mechanics.

Work Environment

Automotive service technicians and mechanics held about 739,900 jobs in 2014. The industries that employed the most automotive service technicians and mechanics were as follows:

Automobile dealers	30%
Automotive mechanical and electrical repair and maintenance	28
Automotive parts, accessories, and tire stores	9

About 1 in 10 automotive service technicians and mechanics were self-employed in 2014.

Service technicians stand for most of the day, and they typically work in well-ventilated and well-lit repair shops. Although technicians often identify and fix automotive problems with computers, they commonly work with greasy parts and tools, sometimes in uncomfortable positions.

Automotive service technicians and mechanics perform routine vehicle maintenance as well as major repairs.

Work Schedules. Most service technicians work full time, and many work evenings or weekends. Overtime is common.

Injuries and Illnesses. Automotive service technicians and mechanics have one of the highest rates of injuries and illnesses of all occupations. Service technicians must frequently work with heavy parts and tools. As a result, workplace injuries, such as small cuts, sprains, and bruises, are common.

Education/Training

Employers prefer that automotive service technicians and mechanics complete a formal training program at a postsecondary institution. Industry certification is usually required once the person is employed.

Education. High school courses in automotive repair, electronics, computers, and mathematics provide a good background for prospective service technicians. However, high school graduates typically need further training to become fully qualified.

Completing a vocational or other postsecondary education program in automotive service technology is considered the best preparation for entry-level positions. Programs usually last 6

Median Annual Wages, May 2014

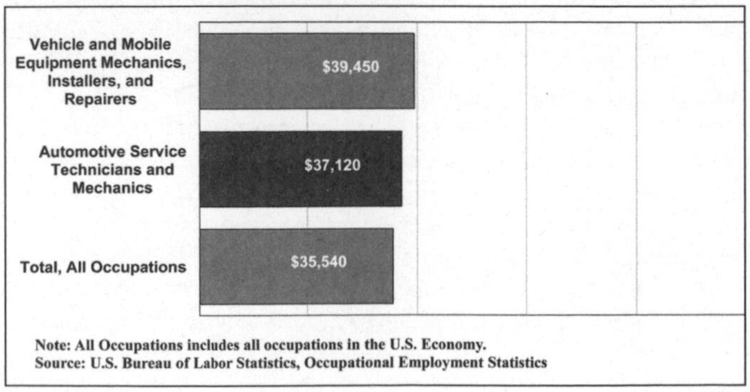

Percent Change in Employment, Projected 2014–2024

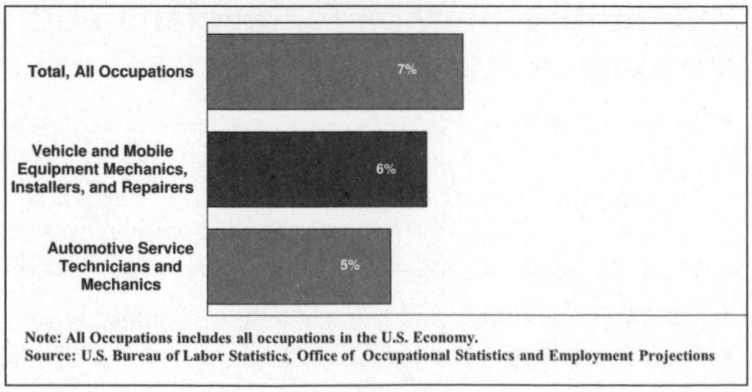

months to a year and provide intensive career preparation through classroom instruction and hands-on practice. Short-term certificate programs in a particular subject, such as brake maintenance or engine performance, are also available.

Some service technicians get an associate's degree. Courses usually include mathematics, electronics, and automotive repair. Some programs add classes in customer service and other necessary skills.

Various automobile manufacturers and dealers sponsor associate's degree programs. Students in these programs typically spend alternating periods attending classes full time and working full time in service shops under the guidance of an experienced technician.

Training. Service technicians who have graduated from postsecondary programs in automotive service technology generally require little on-the-job training.

Those who have not completed postsecondary education, however, generally start as trainee technicians, technicians' helpers, or lubrication workers. They gradually acquire more knowledge and experience by working with experienced mechanics and technicians.

Licenses, Certifications, and Registrations. The U.S. Environmental Protection Agency (EPA) requires all technicians who buy or work with refrigerants to be certified in proper refrigerant handling. No formal test preparation is required, but many trade schools, unions, and employer associations offer training programs designed for the EPA exam.

Certification from the National Institute for Automotive Service Excellence (ASE) is the standard credential for service technicians. Certification demonstrates competence and usually brings higher pay. Many employers require their service technicians to become certified.

ASE certification is available in nine different automobile specialty areas: automatic transmission/transaxle, brakes, light vehicle diesel engines, electrical/electronic systems, engine performance, engine repair, heating and air-conditioning, manual drive train and axles, and suspension and steering.

To become certified, technicians must have at least 2 years of experience (or relevant schooling and 1 year of experience) and pass an exam. Technicians who achieve certification in all of the foregoing areas (light vehicle diesel engine certification is not required) may earn ASE Master Technician status.

Important Qualities

Customer-service skills. Service technicians must discuss automotive problems—along with options to fix them—with their customers. Because workers may depend on repeat clients for business, they must be courteous, good listeners, and ready to answer customers' questions.

Detail oriented. Service technicians must be aware of small details when inspecting or repairing vehicle systems, because mechanical and electronic malfunctions are often due to misalignments or other easy-to-miss causes.

Dexterity. Service technicians perform many tasks that require steady hands and good hand-eye coordination, such as assembling or attaching components and subassemblies.

Mechanical skills. Service technicians must be familiar with engine components and systems and know how they interact with each other. They often must take apart major parts for repairs and be able to put them back together properly.

Organizational skills. Service technicians must keep workspaces clean and organized in order to maintain safety and ensure accountability of parts.

Physical strength. Service technicians must sometimes lift and maneuver heavy parts such as engines and body panels.

Troubleshooting skills. Service technicians must be able to use diagnostic equipment on engine systems and components in order to identify and fix problems in increasingly complicated mechanical and electronic systems. They must be familiar with electronic control systems and the appropriate tools needed to fix and maintain them.

Pay

The median annual wage for automotive service technicians and mechanics was $37,120 in May 2014. The median wage is the wage at which half the workers in an occupation earned more than that amount and half earned less. The lowest 10 percent earned less than $20,800, and the highest 10 percent earned more than $62,280.

In May 2014, the median annual wages for automotive service technicians and mechanics in the top industries in which they worked were as follows:

Automobile dealers	$41,980
Automotive mechanical and electrical repair and maintenance	34,750
Automotive parts, accessories, and tire stores	31,550

Many experienced technicians working for automobile dealers and independent repair shops receive a commission related to the labor cost charged to the customer. Under this system, which is commonly known as "flat rate" or "flag rate," weekly earnings depend on the amount of work completed. Some repair shops may pay technicians on an hourly basis instead.

Job Outlook

Employment of automotive service technicians and mechanics is projected to grow 5 percent from 2014 to 2024, about as fast as the average for all occupations.

The number of vehicles in use continues to rise, and more entry-level service technicians will be needed to perform basic maintenance and repair, such as replacing brake pads and changing oil. New technologies, however, such as electric vehicles, may limit future demand for automotive service technicians and mechanics because they will be more reliable and thus require less maintenance and repair.

Employment Projections Data for Automotive Service Technicians and Mechanics

Occupational Title	SOC Code	Employment, 2014	Projected Employment, 2024	Change, 2014–2024 Percent	Change, 2014–2024 Numeric
Automotive service technicians and mechanics	49-3023	739,900	779,000	5	39,100

Source: U.S. Bureau of Labor Statistics, Employment Projections Program

Similar Occupations. This table shows a list of occupations with job duties that are similar to those of automotive service technicians and mechanics.

Occupations	Entry-level Education	2014 Median Pay	Projected Job Growth	Average Annual Openings
Automotive Body and Glass Repairers	High school diploma or equivalent	$39,260	9%	1,530
Diesel Service Technicians and Mechanics	High school diploma or equivalent	$43,630	12%	3,160
Heavy Vehicle and Mobile Equipment Service Technicians	High school diploma or equivalent	$45,930	5%	1,010
Small Engine Mechanics	See Education/Training	$34,130	4%	320

Job Prospects. With some employers reporting difficulty finding workers with the right skills and education, job opportunities for qualified applicants should be very good, whether they obtained their knowledge through education or experience. Of these workers, those who have completed formal postsecondary training programs or achieved ASE certification should enjoy the best job prospects.

Those without formal automotive training or certification are likely to face strong competition for entry-level jobs.

Many job openings will be in automobile dealerships and independent repair shops, where most service technicians currently work.

Contacts for More Information

For more details about work opportunities, contact local automobile dealers and repair shops or local offices of the state employment service. The state employment service also may have information about training programs.

For information about careers, education, and training programs, visit

- Automotive Youth Educational Systems (www.ayes.org)
- National Automotive Technicians Education Foundation (www.natef.org)

For information about certification, visit

- National Institute for Automotive Service Excellence (www.ase.com)

O*NET

- Automotive Service Technicians and Mechanics (49-3023.00)
- Automotive Master Mechanics (49-3023.01)
- Automotive Specialty Technicians (49-3023.02)

Diesel Service Technicians and Mechanics

- **2014 Median Pay** .... $43,630 per year, $20.98 per hour
- **Typical Entry-Level Education** .... High school diploma or equivalent
- **Work Experience in a Related Occupation** .... None
- **On-the-job Training** .... Long-term on-the-job training
- **Number of Jobs, 2014** 263,900
- **Job Outlook, 2014–24** .... 12% (Faster than average)
- **Employment Change, 2014–24** 31,600

What Diesel Service Technicians and Mechanics Do

Diesel service technicians and mechanics inspect, repair, or overhaul buses and trucks, or maintain and repair any type of diesel engine.

Duties. Diesel service technicians and mechanics typically do the following:

- Consult with customers and read work orders to determine work required
- Plan work procedures, using technical charts and manuals
- Inspect brake systems, steering mechanisms, transmissions, engines, and other parts of vehicles
- Follow checklists to ensure that all critical parts are examined
- Read and interpret diagnostic test results to identify mechanical problems
- Repair or replace malfunctioning components, parts, and other mechanical or electrical equipment
- Perform basic care and maintenance, including changing oil, checking fluid levels, and rotating tires
- Test-drive vehicles to ensure that they run smoothly

Because of their efficiency and durability, diesel engines have become the standard in powering trucks and buses. Other heavy vehicles and mobile equipment, including bulldozers and cranes, are also powered by diesel engines, as are many commercial boats, and some passenger vehicles and pickups.

Diesel technicians handle many kinds of repairs. They may work on a vehicle's electrical system, make major engine repairs, or retrofit exhaust systems with emission control systems to comply with pollution regulations.

Diesel engine maintenance and repair is becoming more complex as engines and other components use more electronic systems to control their operation. For example, fuel injection and engine timing systems rely heavily on microprocessors to maximize fuel efficiency and minimize harmful emissions. In most shops, workers often use hand-held or laptop computers to diagnose problems and adjust engine functions.

In addition to using computerized diagnostic equipment, diesel technicians use a variety of power and machine tools, such as pneumatic wrenches, lathes, grinding machines, and welding equipment. Hand tools, including pliers, sockets and ratchets, and screwdrivers, are commonly used.

Employers typically provide expensive power tools and computerized equipment, but workers generally acquire their own hand tools over time.

For more information on technicians and mechanics who work primarily on automobiles, see the profile on automotive service technicians and mechanics.

For more information on technicians and mechanics who work primarily on farm equipment, construction vehicles, and rail cars, see the profile on heavy vehicle and mobile equipment service technicians.

For more information on technicians and mechanics who work primarily on motorboats, motorcycles, and small all-terrain vehicles, see the profile on small engine mechanics.

Diesel service technicians and mechanics repair large trucks to keep them running smoothly.

Work Environment

Diesel service technicians and mechanics held about 263,900 jobs in 2014. The industries that employed the most diesel service technicians and mechanics were as follows:

Truck transportation	19%
Wholesale trade	15
State and local government, excluding education and hospitals	10
Automotive repair and maintenance	8

Diesel technicians usually work in well-ventilated and sometimes noisy repair shops. They occasionally repair vehicles on roadsides or at worksites.

Injuries and Illnesses. Diesel service technicians and mechanics have one of the highest rates of injuries and illnesses of all occupations. Diesel technicians often lift heavy parts and tools, handle greasy or dirty equipment, and work in uncomfortable positions. Sprains and cuts are common among diesel technicians. Workers will need to follow some safety precautions when in the workplace.

Work Schedules. Most diesel technicians work full time. Overtime is common, as many repair shops extend their service hours during evenings and weekends. In addition, some truck and bus repair shops provide 24-hour maintenance and repair services.

Education/Training

Most diesel technicians learn informally on the job after a high school education, but employers increasingly prefer applicants who have completed postsecondary training programs in diesel engine repair. Although not required, industry certification can demonstrate a diesel technician's competence and experience.

Education. Most employers require a high school diploma or equivalent. High school or postsecondary courses in automotive repair, electronics, and mathematics provide a strong educational background for a career as a diesel technician.

An increasing number of employers look for workers with postsecondary training in diesel engine repair. Many community colleges and trade and vocational schools offer certificate or degree programs in diesel engine repair.

Programs mix classroom instruction with hands-on training, including the basics of diesel technology, repair techniques and equipment, and practical exercises. Students also learn how to interpret technical manuals and electronic diagnostic reports.

Training. Diesel technicians who begin working without any postsecondary education are trained extensively on the job. Trainees are assigned basic tasks, such as cleaning parts, checking fuel and oil levels, and driving vehicles in and out of the shop.

After they learn routine maintenance and repair tasks and demonstrate competence, trainees move on to more complicated subjects such as vehicle diagnostics. This process can take from 3 to 4 years, at which point a trainee is usually considered a journey-level diesel technician.

Over the course of their careers, diesel technicians must learn to use new techniques and equipment. Employers often send experienced technicians to special training classes conducted by manufacturers and vendors to learn about the latest diesel technology.

Licenses, Certifications, and Registrations. Certification from the National Institute for Automotive Service Excellence (ASE) is the standard credential for diesel and other automotive service technicians and mechanics. Although not required, this certification demonstrates a diesel technician's competence and experience to potential employers and clients, and often brings higher pay.

Diesel technicians may be certified in specific repair areas, such as drive trains, electronic systems, or preventative maintenance and

Median Annual Wages, May 2014

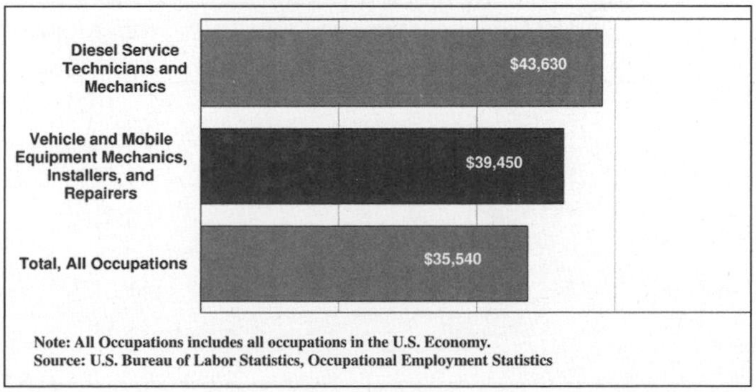

Percent Change in Employment, Projected 2014–2024

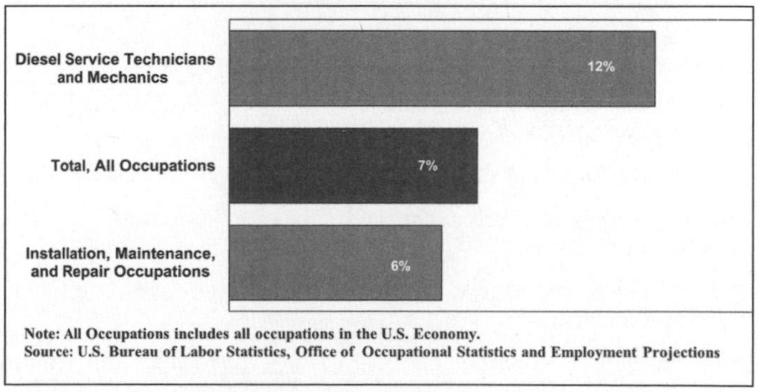

Employment Projections Data for Diesel Service Technicians and Mechanics

Occupational Title	SOC Code	Employment, 2014	Projected Employment, 2024	Change, 2014–2024	
				Percent	Numeric
Bus and truck mechanics and diesel engine specialists	49-3031	263,900	295,500	12	31,600

Source: U.S. Bureau of Labor Statistics, Employment Projections Program

inspection. To earn certification, technicians must have 2 years of work experience and pass one or more ASE exams. To remain certified, diesel technicians must pass a recertification exam every 5 years.

Many diesel technicians are required to have a commercial driver's license so they may test-drive buses and large trucks.

Important Qualities

Customer-service skills. Diesel technicians frequently discuss automotive problems and necessary repairs with their customers. They must be courteous, good listeners, and ready to answer customers' questions.

Detail oriented. Diesel technicians must be aware of small details when inspecting or repairing engines and components, because mechanical and electronic malfunctions are often due to misalignments and other easy-to-miss causes.

Dexterity. Mechanics need a steady hand and good hand-eye coordination for many tasks, such as disassembling engine parts, connecting or attaching components, or using hand tools.

Mechanical skills. Diesel technicians must be familiar with engine components and systems and know how they interact with each other. They often disassemble major parts for repairs, and they must be able to put them back together properly.

Organizational skills. Diesel technicians must keep workspaces clean and organized in order to maintain safety and ensure accountability for parts.

Strength. Diesel technicians often lift heavy parts and tools, such as exhaust system components and pneumatic wrenches.

Troubleshooting skills. Diesel technicians must be able to use diagnostic equipment on engine systems and components in order to identify and fix problems in increasingly complicated mechanical and electronic systems. They must be familiar with electronic control systems and the appropriate tools needed to fix and maintain them.

Pay

The median annual wage for diesel service technicians and mechanics was $43,630 in May 2014. The median wage is the wage at which half the workers in an occupation earned more than that amount and half earned less. The lowest 10 percent earned less than $28,130, and the highest 10 percent earned more than $65,350.

In May 2014, the median annual wages for diesel service technicians and mechanics in the top industries in which they worked were as follows:

State and local government, excluding education and hospitals	$50,680
Wholesale trade	44,610
Automotive repair and maintenance	40,630
Truck transportation	39,800

Many diesel technicians, especially those employed by truck fleet dealers and repair shops, receive a commission in addition to their base salary.

Job Outlook

Employment of diesel service technicians and mechanics is projected to grow 12 percent from 2014 to 2024, faster than the average for all occupations.

As more freight is shipped across the country, additional diesel-powered trucks will be needed to carry freight where trains and pipelines are not available or economical. Additionally, diesel cars and light trucks are becoming more popular, and more diesel technicians will be needed to maintain and repair these vehicles.

Job Prospects. Workers who have completed formal postsecondary education and have strong technical skills should have the best job opportunities, followed by graduates of accredited high school automotive programs.

Workers without formal training often require more supervision and on-the-job instruction than others. These untrained workers will face strong competition for jobs because training is an expensive and time-consuming process for employers.

Contacts for More Information

For more information about careers and education for diesel service technicians and mechanics, visit

➤ Association of Diesel Specialists (www.diesel.org)

Similar Occupations. This table shows a list of occupations with job duties that are similar to those of diesel service technicians and mechanics.

Occupations	Entry-level Education	2014 Median Pay	Projected Job Growth	Average Annual Openings
Aircraft and Avionics Equipment Mechanics and Technicians	See Education/Training	$56,980	1%	160
Automotive Body and Glass Repairers	High school diploma or equivalent	$39,260	9%	1,530
Automotive Service Technicians and Mechanics	Postsecondary nondegree award	$37,120	5%	3,910
Heavy Vehicle and Mobile Equipment Service Technicians	High school diploma or equivalent	$45,930	5%	1,010
Small Engine Mechanics	See Education/Training	$34,130	4%	320

- National Automotive Technicians Education Foundation (www.natef.org)
- Automotive Youth Educational Systems (www.ayes.org)

For more information about certification, visit

- National Institute for Automotive Service Excellence (www.ase.com)

O*NET

- Bus and Truck Mechanics and Diesel Engine Specialists (49-3031.00)

Electrical and Electronics Installers and Repairers

- **2014 Median Pay** .... $53,900 per year $25.91 per hour
- **Typical Entry-Level Education** .... Postsecondary nondegree award
- **Work Experience in a Related Occupation** .... None
- **On-the-job Training** .... See Education/Training
- **Number of Jobs, 2014** 136,100
- **Job Outlook, 2014–24** .... -4% (Decline)
- **Employment Change, 2014–24** .... -5,400

What Electrical and Electronics Installers and Repairers Do

Electrical and electronics installers and repairers install or repair a variety of electrical equipment in telecommunications, transportation, utilities, and other industries.

Duties. Electrical and electronics installers and repairers typically do the following:

- Prepare cost estimates for clients
- Refer to service guides, schematics, and manufacturer specifications
- Repair or replace defective parts, such as motors, fuses, or gaskets
- Reassemble and test equipment after repairs
- Maintain records of parts used, labor time, and final charges

Modern manufacturing plants and transportation systems use a large amount of electrical and electronics equipment, from assembly line motors to sonar systems. Electrical and electronics installers and repairers fix and maintain these complex pieces of equipment.

Because automated electronic control systems are becoming more complex, repairers use software programs and testing equipment to diagnose malfunctions. Among their diagnostic tools are multimeters—which measure voltage, current, and resistance—and advanced multimeters, which measure the capacitance, inductance, and current gain of transistors.

Repairers also use signal generators, which provide test signals, and oscilloscopes, which display signals graphically. In addition, repairers often use hand tools such as pliers, screwdrivers, and wrenches to replace faulty parts and adjust equipment.

The following are examples of types of electrical and electronics installers and repairers:

Commercial and industrial electrical and electronics equipment repairers adjust, test, repair, or install electronic equipment, such as industrial controls, transmitters, and antennas.

Electrical and electronics installers and repairers of transportation equipment install, adjust, or maintain mobile communication equipment, including sound, sonar, security, navigation, and surveillance systems on trains, watercraft, or other vehicles.

Powerhouse, substation, and relay electrical and electronics repairers inspect, test, maintain, or repair electrical equipment used in generating stations, substations, and in-service relays. These workers also may be known as *powerhouse electricians, relay technicians,* or *power transformer repairers.*

Electric motor, power tool, and related repairers—such as *armature winders, generator mechanics,* and *electric golf cart repairers*—specialize in installing, maintaining, and repairing electric motors, wiring, or switches.

Electronic equipment installers and repairers of motor vehicles install, diagnose, and repair sound, security, and navigation equipment in motor vehicles. These installers and repairers work with a range of complex electronic equipment, including digital audio and video players, navigation systems, and passive and active security systems.

Electrical and electronics installers and repairers may also specialize, according to how and where they work:

Field technicians often travel to factories or a customer's site to repair broken down equipment. Because repairing components is a complex activity, workers usually remove and replace defective units, such as circuit boards, instead of fixing them. Defective units are discarded or returned to the manufacturer or a specialized shop for repair.

Bench technicians work in repair shops in factories and service centers, fixing components that cannot be repaired on a factory floor. These workers also locate and repair circuit defects, such as poorly soldered joints, blown fuses, or malfunctioning transistors.

Work Environment

Electrical and electronics installers and repairers held about 136,100 jobs in 2014.

Employment in the detailed occupations that make up this group in 2014 was distributed as follows:

Electrical and electronics repairers, commercial and industrial equipment 67,800

Motor vehicle electronic equipment installers and repairers normally work indoors in well-ventilated and well-lighted repair shops.

Median Annual Wages, May 2014

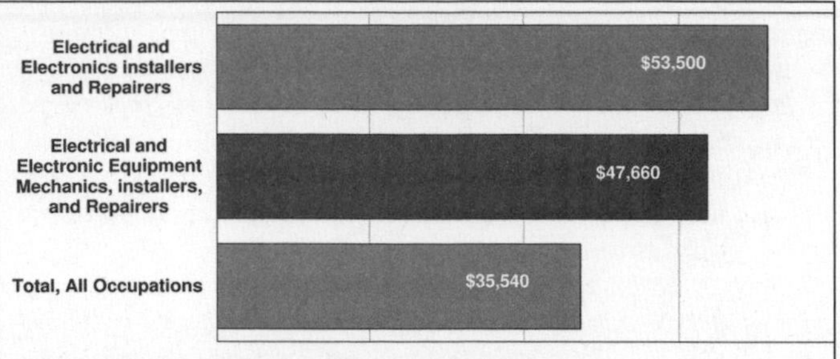

Note: All Occupations includes all occupations in the U.S. Economy.
Source: U.S. Bureau of Labor Statistics, Occupational Employment Statistics

Percent Change in Employment, Projected 2014–2024

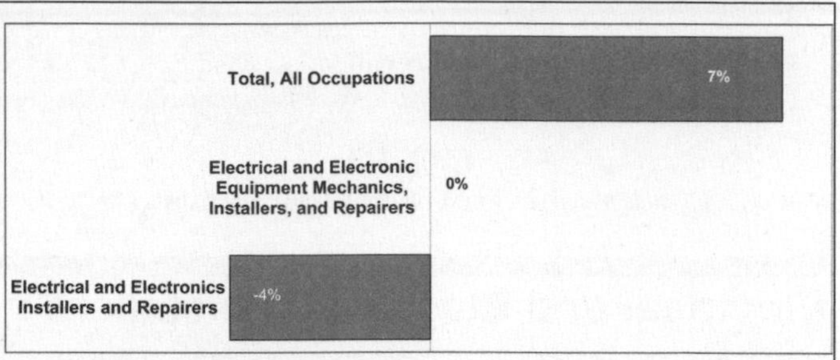

Note: All Occupations includes all occupations in the U.S. Economy.
Source: U.S. Bureau of Labor Statistics, Office of Occupational Statistics and Employment Projections

Electrical and electronics repairers, powerhouse, substation, and relay	22,700
Electric motor, power tool, and related repairers	19,300
Electrical and electronics installers and repairers, transportation equipment	14,800
Electronic equipment installers and repairers, motor vehicles	11,500

Some electrical and electronics installers and repairers work in factories, which can be noisy and sometimes warm. Bench technicians work primarily in repair shops, which are quiet and well lit. Motor vehicle electronic equipment installers and repairers normally work in repair shops or in electronics stores.

Installers and repairers may have to lift heavy equipment and work in awkward positions. They spend most of their day walking, standing, or kneeling.

Work Schedules. The vast majority of electrical and electronics installers and repairers work full time.

Education/Training

Most electrical and electronics installers and repairers need specialized courses at a technical college prior to employment. Gaining certification is common and can be useful in getting a job.

Education. Electrical and electronics installers and repairers must understand electrical equipment and electronics. As a result, employers often prefer applicants who have taken courses in electronics at a community college or technical school. Courses usually cover AC and DC electronics, electronic devices, and microcontrollers. It is important for prospects to choose schools that include hands-on training in order to gain practical experience.

Training. In addition to technical education, workers usually receive training on specific types of equipment. This may involve manufacturer-specific training in order for repairers to perform warranty work.

Entry-level repairers usually begin by working with experienced technicians who provide technical guidance and work independently after developing their skills.

Licenses, Certifications, and Registrations. While certification is not required, a number of organizations offer certification which can be useful in getting a job. A number of organizations offer certification. For example, the Electronics Technicians Association International (ETA International) offers more than 50 certification programs in numerous electronics specialties for various levels of competency. The International Society of Certified Electronics Technicians (ISCET) also offers certification for several levels of competence. The ISCET focuses on a broad range of topics, including basic electronics, electronic systems, and appliance service. To become certified, applicants must meet prerequisites and pass a comprehensive exam.

Important Qualities

Color vision. Workers must be able to identify the color-coded components that are often used in electronic equipment.

Communication skills. Field technicians work closely with customers, so they must listen to and understand customers' descriptions of problems and explain solutions in a simple, clear manner.

Physical stamina. Some workers must stand at their station for their full shift, which can be tiring.

Physical strength. Workers may need to lift heavy parts during the repair process. Some components weigh over 50 pounds.

Technical skills. Workers use a variety of mechanical and diagnostic tools to install or repair equipment.

Troubleshooting skills. Workers must be able to identify problems with equipment and systems and make the necessary repairs.

Pay

The median annual wage for electrical and electronics installers and repairers was $53,900 in May 2014. The median wage is the wage at which half the workers in an occupation earned more than that amount and half earned less. The lowest 10 percent earned less than $29,580, and the highest 10 percent earned more than $79,110.

Median annual wages for electrical and electronics installers and repairers in May 2014 were as follows:

Electrical and electronics repairers, powerhouse, substation, and relay	$71,400
Electrical and electronics installers and repairers, transportation equipment	56,000
Electrical and electronics repairers, commercial and industrial equipment	54,640
Electric motor, power tool, and related repairers	39,220
Electronic equipment installers and repairers, motor vehicles	31,020

Job Outlook

Overall employment of electrical and electronics installers and repairers is projected to decline 4 percent from 2014 to 2024. Growth rates will vary by occupation.

Employment of motor vehicle electronic equipment installers and repairers, which represents less than 10 percent of this profile's 2014 employment, is projected to decline 50 percent from 2014 to 2024. Motor vehicle manufacturers continue to install more and higher quality sound, security, entertainment, and navigation systems in new vehicles. These new electronic systems require less maintenance and will limit installation of aftermarket products.

Employment of powerhouse, substation, and relay electrical and electronics installers and repairers is projected to decline 5 percent from 2014 to 2024. Although the installation of new,

Employment Projections Data for Electrical and Electronics Installers and Repairers

Occupational Title	SOC Code	Employment, 2014	Projected Employment, 2024	Change, 2014–2024 Percent	Change, 2014–2024 Numeric
Electrical and electronics installers and repairers	—	136,100	130,700	-4	-5,400
Electric motor, power tool, and related repairers	49-2092	19,300	20,000	4	700
Electrical and electronics installers and repairers, transportation equipment	49-2093	14,800	15,400	4	700
Electrical and electronics repairers, commercial and industrial equipment	49-2094	67,800	67,800	0	100
Electrical and electronics repairers, powerhouse, substation, and relay	49-2095	22,700	21,700	-5	-1,000
Electronic equipment installers and repairers, motor vehicles	49-2096	11,500	5,800	-50	-5,800

Source: U.S. Bureau of Labor Statistics, Employment Projections Program

Similar Occupations. This table shows a list of occupations with job duties that are similar to those of electrical and electronics installers and repairers.

Occupations	Entry-level Education	2014 Median Pay	Projected Job Growth	Average Annual Openings
Aircraft and Avionics Equipment Mechanics and Technicians	See Education/Training	$56,980	1%	160
Broadcast and Sound Engineering Technicians	See Education/Training	$41,350	7%	770
Electricians	High school diploma or equivalent	$51,110	14%	8,590
Elevator Installers and Repairers	High school diploma or equivalent	$78,620	13%	270
General Maintenance and Repair Workers	High school diploma or equivalent	$36,170	6%	8,350
Telecommunications Equipment Installers and Repairers	Postsecondary nondegree award	$55,190	-4%	-780

energy-efficient technologies will likely spur demand for some new workers, privatization in the utilities industries should improve productivity and more than offset any employment gains.

Employment of electric motor, power tool, and related repairers is projected to grow 4 percent from 2014 to 2024, slower than the average for all occupations. Improvements in electrical and electronic equipment design, as well as the increased use of disposable tool parts, will result in slow employment growth.

Employment of electrical and electronics installers and repairers of transportation equipment is projected to grow 4 percent from 2014 to 2024, slower than the average for all occupations. Increasing employment in the rail transportation industry—the largest employing segment of these specialists—drives most of the employment growth.

Employment of electrical and electronics installers and repairers of commercial and industrial equipment, which represents about half of this profile's 2014 employment, is projected to show little or no change from 2014 to 2024. As competition increases, businesses strive to lower costs by increasing and improving automation. Equipment that needs service and repair would generally increase the demand for electrical workers, but improved reliability of equipment is expected to offset that demand and temper overall employment growth.

Job Prospects. Overall job opportunities should be excellent for qualified workers with technical education—including an associate's degree in electronics—along with certification.

The best job opportunities should be for commercial and industrial equipment installers and repairers as the need to replace retiring workers should result in many job openings. Conversely, few opportunities will be available for motor vehicle equipment installers and repairers as the amount of aftermarket installations continues to decline.

Contacts for More Information

For information about electrical and electronics installers and repairers, including careers and certification, visit

- Electronics Technicians Association International (www.eta-i.org)
- International Society of Certified Electronics Technicians (www.iscet.org)

O*NET

- Electric Motor, Power Tool, and Related Repairers (49-2092.00)
- Electrical and Electronics Installers and Repairers, Transportation Equipment (49-2093.00)
- Electrical and Electronics Repairers, Commercial and Industrial Equipment (49-2094.00)
- Electrical and Electronics Repairers, Powerhouse, Substation, and Relay (49-2095.00)
- Electronic Equipment Installers and Repairers, Motor Vehicles (49-2096.00)

General Maintenance and Repair Workers

- **2014 Median Pay** .... $36,170 per year
$17.39 per hour
- **Typical Entry-Level Education** .... High school diploma or equivalent
- **Work Experience in a Related Occupation** .... None
- **On-the-job Training** .... Long-term on-the-job training
- **Number of Jobs, 2014** 1,374,700
- **Job Outlook, 2014–24** .... 6% (As fast as average)
- **Employment Change, 2014–24** 83,500

What General Maintenance and Repair Workers Do

General maintenance and repair workers fix and maintain machines, mechanical equipment, and buildings. They paint, repair flooring, and work on plumbing, electrical, and air-conditioning and heating systems.

Duties. General maintenance and repair workers typically do the following:

- Maintain and repair machines, mechanical equipment, and buildings
- Fix or replace faulty electrical switches, outlets, and circuit breakers
- Inspect and diagnose problems and figure out the best way to correct them
- Perform routine preventive maintenance to ensure that machines continue to run smoothly
- Assemble and set up machinery or equipment
- Plan repair work using blueprints or diagrams
- Do general cleaning and upkeep of buildings and properties
- Order supplies from catalogs and storerooms
- Meet with clients to estimate repairs and costs
- Keep detailed records of their work

General maintenance and repair workers are hired for maintenance and repair tasks that are not complex enough to need the specialized training of a licensed tradesperson, such as a plumber or electrician.

These workers are also responsible for recognizing when a job is above their skill level and requires the expertise of an electrician; a carpenter; a heating, air-conditioning, and refrigeration mechanic or installer; or a plumber, pipefitter, or steamfitter.

General maintenance and repair workers may fix plaster or drywall. They may fix or paint roofs, windows, doors, floors, woodwork, and other parts of buildings.

They also maintain and repair specialized equipment and machinery in cafeterias, laundries, hospitals, stores, offices, and factories.

General maintenance and repair workers get supplies and repair parts from distributors or storerooms to fix problems. They use common hand and power tools, such as screwdrivers, saws, drills, wrenches, and hammers to fix, replace, or repair equipment and parts of buildings.

Work Environment

General maintenance and repair workers held about 1.4 million jobs in 2014. The industries that employed the most general maintenance and repair workers were as follows:

Real estate and rental and leasing	20%
Manufacturing	14
State and local government, excluding education and hospitals	10
Healthcare and social assistance	8
Educational services; state, local, and private	8

General maintenance and repair workers often carry out many different tasks in a single day at any number of locations. They may work inside a single building, such as a hotel or hospital, or be responsible for the maintenance of many buildings, such as those in an apartment complex or on a college campus.

General maintenance and repair workers may have to stand for long periods or lift heavy objects. These workers may work in uncomfortably hot or cold environments, in uncomfortable or cramped positions, or on ladders. The work involves a lot of walking, climbing, and reaching.

Injuries and Illnesses. General maintenance workers have one of the highest rates of injuries and illnesses of all occupations. Workers risk electrical shocks, falls, cuts, and bruises.

Work Schedules. Most general maintenance workers work full time, including evenings or weekends. Some are on call for emergency repairs.

Education/Training

Jobs in this field typically do not require any formal education beyond high school. General maintenance and repair workers often learn their skills on the job. They start by doing simple tasks and watching and learning from skilled maintenance workers.

Education. Many maintenance and repair workers learn some basic skills in high school shop or technical education classes, postsecondary trade or vocational schools, or community colleges.

Courses in mechanical drawing, electricity, woodworking, blueprint reading, mathematics, and computers are useful. Maintenance and repair workers often do work that involves electrical,

General maintenance and repair workers often carry out many different tasks in a single day, at any number of locations.

Median Annual Wages, May 2014

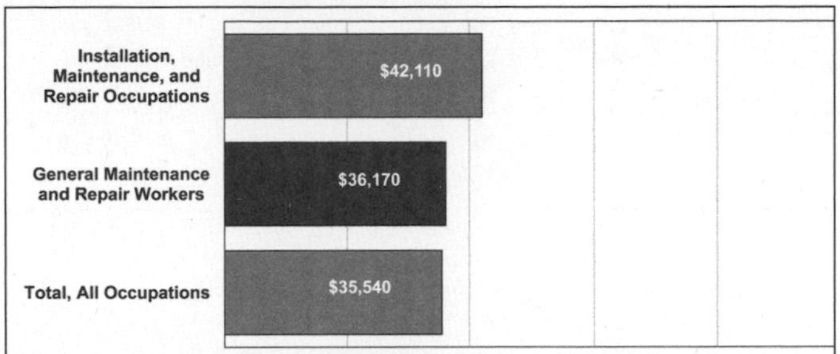

Note: All Occupations includes all occupations in the U.S. Economy.
Source: U.S. Bureau of Labor Statistics, Occupational Employment Statistics

Percent Change in Employment, Projected 2014–2024

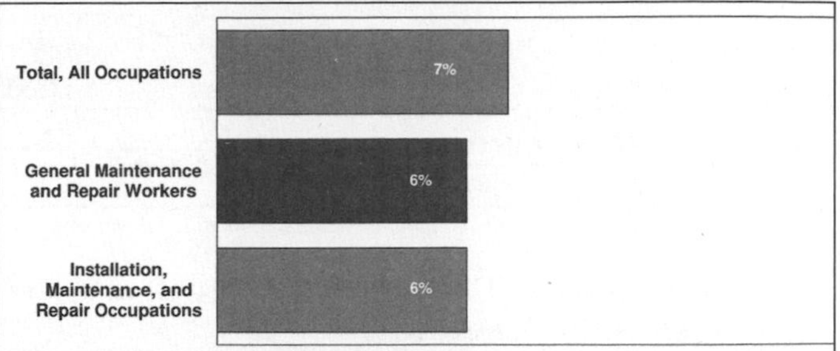

Note: All Occupations includes all occupations in the U.S. Economy.
Source: U.S. Bureau of Labor Statistics, Office of Occupational Statistics and Employment Projections

plumbing, heating, and air-conditioning systems or painting and roofing tasks. Workers need a good working knowledge of many repair and maintenance tasks.

Practical training, available at many adult education centers and community colleges, is another option for workers to learn tasks such as drywall repair and basic plumbing.

Training. General maintenance and repair workers usually start by watching and learning from skilled maintenance workers. They begin by doing simple tasks, such as fixing leaky faucets and replacing lightbulbs. After gaining experience, general maintenance and repair workers move on to more difficult tasks, such as overhauling machinery or building walls.

Some general maintenance and repair workers learn their skills by assisting other types of repair or construction workers, including machinery repairers, carpenters, or electricians.

Licenses, Certifications, and Registrations. Licensing requirements vary by state and locality. For more complex tasks, workers may need to be licensed in a particular specialty, such as electrical or plumbing work.

Advancement. Some maintenance and repair workers decide to train in one specific craft and become craftworkers, such as electricians, heating and air-conditioning mechanics, or plumbers.

Other maintenance workers eventually open their own repair or contracting business. However, those who want to become a project manager or own their own business may need some postsecondary education or a degree in construction management. For more information, see the profile on construction managers.

Within small organizations, promotion opportunities may be limited.

Important Qualities

Customer-service skills. These workers interact with customers on a regular basis. They need to be friendly and able to address customers' questions.

Dexterity. Many repair and maintenance tasks, such as repairing small devices, connecting or attaching components, and using hand tools, require a steady hand and good hand-eye coordination.

Troubleshooting skills. Workers find, diagnose, and repair problems. They perform tests to figure out the cause of problems before fixing equipment.

Pay

The median annual wage for general maintenance and repair workers was $36,170 in May 2014. The median wage is the wage at which half the workers in an occupation earned more than that amount and half earned less. The lowest 10 percent earned less than $21,370, and the highest 10 percent earned more than $59,170.

In May 2014, the median annual wages for general maintenance and repair workers in the top industries in which they worked were as follows:

Manufacturing	$42,620
State and local government, excluding education and hospitals	38,020
Educational services; state, local, and private	37,770
Healthcare and social assistance	35,280
Real estate and rental and leasing	32,860

Job Outlook

Employment of general maintenance and repair workers is projected to grow 6 percent from 2014 to 2024, about as fast as the average for all occupations.

Employment will increase as the real estate market continues to improve. Increasing home prices and sales may drive demand for remodeling and maintenance work. In addition, maintenance and repair workers will continue to be needed to upgrade and renovate older homes and the large inventory of foreclosed and distressed properties caused by the most recent recession.

Demographic changes also may affect the demand for general maintenance and repair workers. Because homeowners typically prefer to remain in their homes as they age, demand may increase for workers as the large baby-boom generation nears retirement. These older homeowners will invest in projects and renovations to accommodate their future living needs and allow them to remain in their homes following retirement.

The large millennial generation will also be entering the prime working-age and household-forming age cohort over the next decade. Although this generation has delayed home ownership because of financial and debt obligations, it is projected that many will enter the housing market over the next 10 years.

In addition to single-family homes, maintenance and repair work is also needed for other types of properties. Due to the aging of many types of buildings, maintenance and repair workers will be needed to work on rental units and commercial and public buildings.

Many general maintenance and repair workers are employed in industries related to real estate, so employment opportunities may be sensitive to fluctuations in the economy. Some workers may experience periods of unemployment when the overall level of construction and real estate development falls. However, maintenance and repairs continue during economic downturns as people opt to repair, rather than replace, equipment.

Job Prospects. Employment growth and the need to replace workers who leave the occupation each year will likely result in good job prospects. Many job openings are expected as experienced workers retire.

Employment Projections Data for General Maintenance and Repair Workers

Occupational Title	SOC Code	Employment, 2014	Projected Employment, 2024	Change, 2014–2024 Percent	Change, 2014–2024 Numeric
Maintenance and repair workers, general	49-9071	1,374,700	1,458,100	6	83,500

Source: U.S. Bureau of Labor Statistics, Employment Projections Program

Similar Occupations. This table shows a list of occupations with job duties that are similar to those of general maintenance and repair workers.

Occupations	Entry-level Education	2014 Median Pay	Projected Job Growth	Average Annual Openings
Boilermakers	High school diploma or equivalent	$59,860	9%	150
Carpenters	High school diploma or equivalent	$40,820	6%	6,040
Construction Managers	Bachelor's degree	$85,630	5%	1,780
Electrical and Electronics Installers and Repairers	Postsecondary nondegree award	$53,900	-4%	-540
Electricians	High school diploma or equivalent	$51,110	14%	8,590
Heating, Air Conditioning, and Refrigeration Mechanics and Installers	Postsecondary nondegree award	$44,630	14%	3,960
Plumbers, Pipefitters, and Steamfitters	High school diploma or equivalent	$50,660	12%	4,910

In addition, because many workers left the construction and maintenance industry during the most recent recession, overall job prospects for general maintenance and repair workers should be good over the coming decade as construction, maintenance, and remodeling activity continues to rebound.

Those with experience in repair- or maintenance-related fields should continue to have the best job prospects.

Contacts for More Information

For more information, visit

➤ United Handyman Association (http://theuha.net)

O*NET

➤ Maintenance and Repair Workers, General (49-9071.00)

Heating, Air Conditioning, and Refrigeration Mechanics and Installers

- **2014 Median Pay** .... $44,630 per year
  $21.46 per hour
- **Typical Entry-Level Education** .... Postsecondary nondegree award
- **Work Experience in a Related Occupation**............... None
- **On-the-job Training** .... Long-term on-the-job training
- **Number of Jobs, 2014** 292,000
- **Job Outlook, 2014–24**.... 14% (Much faster than average)
- **Employment Change, 2014–24** 39,600

What Heating, Air Conditioning, and Refrigeration Mechanics and Installers Do

Heating, air conditioning, and refrigeration mechanics and installers—often called *HVACR technicians*—work on heating, ventilation, cooling, and refrigeration systems that control the temperature and air quality in buildings.

Duties. Heating, air conditioning, and refrigeration mechanics and installers typically do the following:

- Use blueprints or design specifications to install or repair HVACR systems
- Connect systems to fuel and water supply lines, air ducts, and other components
- Install electrical wiring and controls and test for their proper operation
- Inspect and maintain customers' HVACR systems
- Test individual components to determine necessary repairs
- Repair or replace worn or defective parts
- Determine HVACR systems' energy use and make recommendations to improve their efficiency

Heating and air conditioning systems control the temperature, humidity, and overall air quality in homes, businesses, and other buildings. By providing a climate-controlled environment, refrigeration systems make it possible to store and transport food, medicine, and other perishable items.

Although HVACR technicians are trained to install, maintain, and repair heating, air conditioning, and refrigeration systems, many focus their work on installation, maintenance, or repair. Some technicians specialize in one or more specific aspects of HVACR, such as radiant heating systems, solar panels, testing and balancing, or commercial refrigeration.

When installing or repairing air conditioning and refrigeration systems, technicians must follow government regulations regarding

A heating, air conditioning, and refrigeration mechanic works on a thermostat for a heating and air-conditioning system.

the conservation, recovery, and recycling of refrigerants. The regulations include those concerning the proper handling and disposal of fluids and pressurized gases.

Some HVACR technicians sell service contracts to their clients, providing periodic maintenance of heating and cooling systems. The service usually includes inspecting the system, cleaning ducts, replacing filters, and checking refrigerant levels.

Other workers sometimes help install or repair cooling and heating systems. For example, on a large air conditioning installation job, especially one in which workers are covered by union contracts, ductwork may be installed by sheet metal workers, electrical work by electricians, and pipework by plumbers, pipefitters, and steamfitters. Boiler systems sometimes are installed by a boilermaker. In addition, home appliance repairers usually service window air conditioners and household refrigerators.

HVACR technicians use many different tools. For example, they often use screwdrivers, wrenches, pipe cutters, and other basic hand tools when installing systems. Technicians also use more sophisticated tools, such as carbon monoxide testers, voltmeters, combustion analyzers, and acetylene torches, to test or install system components.

Work Environment

Heating, air conditioning, and refrigeration mechanics and installers held about 292,000 jobs in 2014, of which 63 percent were in the plumbing, heating, and air conditioning contractors industry. About 1 in 10 were self-employed in 2014.

HVACR technicians work mostly in homes, schools, stores, hospitals, office buildings, or factories. Some technicians are assigned to specific jobsites at the beginning of each day. Others travel to several different locations, making service calls.

Although most technicians work indoors, some may have to work on outdoor heat exchangers, even in bad weather. Technicians often work in awkward or cramped spaces, and some work in buildings that are uncomfortable because the air conditioning or heating system is not working properly.

Injuries and Illnesses. HVACR technicians have one of the highest rates of injuries and illnesses of all occupations. Potential hazards include electrical shock, burns, muscle strains, and injuries from handling heavy equipment.

Appropriate safety equipment is necessary in handling refrigerants, because they are hazardous and contact can cause skin damage, frostbite, or blindness. When working in tight spaces, inhalation of refrigerants is also a risk. Several refrigerants are highly flammable and require additional care.

Work Schedules. The vast majority of HVACR technicians work full time, with occasional evening or weekend shifts. During peak heating and cooling seasons, they often work overtime or irregular hours. Although most technicians are employed by construction contractors, about 1 in 10 are self-employed workers who have the ability to set their own schedules.

Technicians who service refrigeration, heating, and air conditioning equipment generally have stable employment throughout the year, particularly because a growing number of manufacturers and contractors now provide or even require year-round service contracts.

Education/Training

Because HVACR systems have become increasingly complex, employers generally prefer applicants with postsecondary education or those who have completed an apprenticeship. Some states and localities require technicians to be licensed. Workers may need to pass a background check prior to being hired.

Education. A growing number of HVACR technicians receive postsecondary instruction from technical and trade schools or community colleges that offer programs in heating, air conditioning, and refrigeration. These programs generally last from 6 months to 2 years and lead to a certificate or an associate's degree. To keep program costs lower, many schools are combining online lectures with in-class lab work.

High school students interested in becoming an HVACR technician should take courses in vocational education, math, and physics. Knowledge of plumbing or electrical work and a basic understanding of electronics is also helpful.

Training. Some HVACR technicians learn their trade exclusively on the job, although this practice is becoming much less common. Those who do usually begin by assisting experienced technicians with basic tasks, such as insulating refrigerant lines or cleaning furnaces. In time, they move on to more difficult tasks, including cutting and soldering pipes or checking electrical circuits.

Some technicians receive their training through an apprenticeship. Apprenticeship programs usually last 3 to 5 years. Each year, apprentices must have at least 2,000 hours of on-the-job training and a minimum of 144 hours of related technical education. Over the course of the apprenticeship, technicians learn safety practices, blueprint reading, and how to use tools. They also learn about the numerous systems that heat and cool buildings. To enter an apprenticeship program, a trainee must meet the following requirements:

- Be at least 18 years old
- Have a high school diploma or equivalent
- Pass a basic math test
- Pass a substance abuse screening
- Have a valid driver's license

Apprenticeship programs frequently are run by joint committees representing local chapters of various organizations, including the following:

- Air Conditioning Contractors of America, Inc.
- Associated Builders and Contractors

Median Annual Wages, May 2014

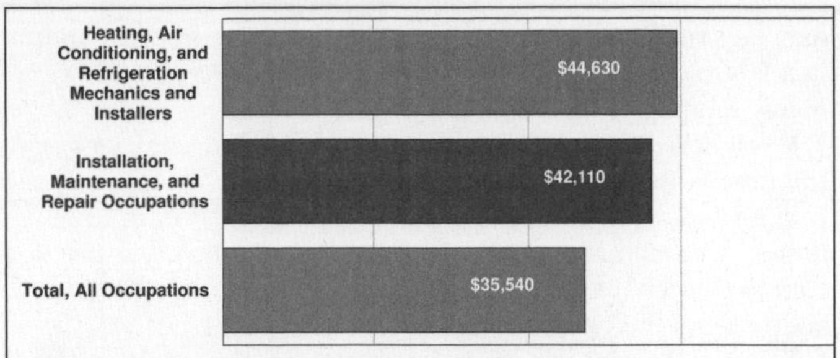

Note: All Occupations includes all occupations in the U.S. Economy.
Source: U.S. Bureau of Labor Statistics, Occupational Employment Statistics

Percent Change in Employment, Projected 2014–2024

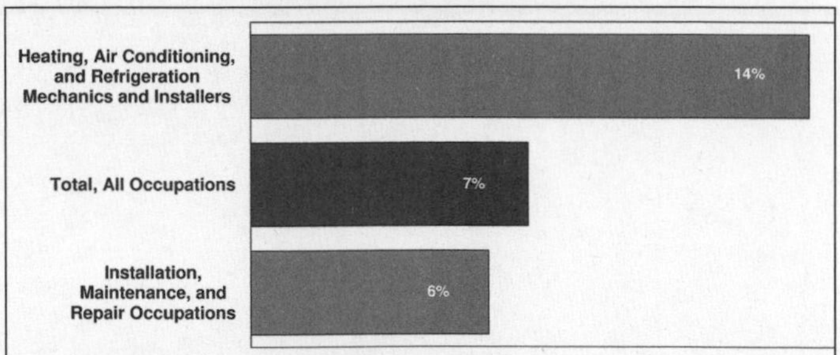

Note: All Occupations includes all occupations in the U.S. Economy.
Source: U.S. Bureau of Labor Statistics, Office of Occupational Statistics and Employment Projections

- Mechanical Contractors Association of America
- Home Builders Institute
- Plumbing-Heating-Cooling Contractors Association
- SMART, the International Association of Sheet Metal, Air, Rail and Transportation Workers
- United Association Union of Plumbers, Fitters, Welders, and Service Techs

Licenses, Certifications, and Registrations. The U.S. Environmental Protection Agency (EPA) requires all technicians who buy, handle, or work with refrigerants to be certified in proper refrigerant handling. To become certified, technicians must pass a written exam specific to one of three specializations: Type I—small appliances; Type II—high-pressure refrigerants; and Type III—low-pressure refrigerants. Many trade schools, unions, and employer associations offer training programs designed to prepare students for the EPA exam.

Whether having learned the occupation through postsecondary education or through other means, HVACR technicians may take several different tests that measure their abilities. These tests require different levels of experience. Technicians with relevant coursework and less than 2 years of experience may take the entry-level certification exams. These exams test basic competency in residential heating and cooling, light commercial heating and cooling, and commercial refrigeration. Technicians can take the exams at technical and trade schools.

HVACR technicians who have at least 1 year of installation experience and 2 years of maintenance and repair experience can take a number of specialized exams. These exams certify their competency in working with specific types of equipment, such as oil-burning furnaces or compressed-refrigerant cooling systems. Many organizations offer certifying exams. For example, North American Technician Excellence offers the Industry Competency Exam; HVAC Excellence offers a Secondary Employment Ready Exam, a Secondary Heating, Electrical, Air Conditioning Technology exam, and a Heating, Electrical, Air Conditioning Technology Plus exam; the National Occupational Competency Testing Institute offers a basic test and an advanced test in conjunction with the Home Builders Institute; the Refrigerating Engineers and Technicians Association offers the entry-level Certified Assistant Refrigeration Operator and Certified Industrial Refrigeration Operator certifications; and the Refrigeration Service Engineers Society (RSES) offers EPA certification and specialized-knowledge certificates.

Certifications can be helpful because they show that the technician has specific competencies. Some employers actively seek out industry-certified HVACR technicians.

Some states and localities require HVACR technicians to be licensed. Although specific licensing requirements vary, all candidates must pass an exam.

Important Qualities

Customer-service skills. HVACR technicians often work in customers' homes or business offices, so it is important that they be friendly, polite, and punctual. Repair technicians sometimes must deal with unhappy customers whose heating or air conditioning is not working.

Detail oriented. HVACR technicians must carefully maintain records of all work performed. The records must include the nature of the work performed and the time it took, as well as list specific parts and equipment that were used.

Math skills. HVACR technicians need to calculate the correct load requirements to ensure that the HVACR equipment properly heats or cools the space required.

Mechanical skills. HVACR technicians install and work on complicated climate-control systems, so they must understand the HVAC components and be able to properly assemble, disassemble, and, if needed, program them.

Physical stamina. HVACR technicians may spend many hours walking and standing. The constant physical activity can be tiring.

Physical strength. HVACR technicians may have to lift and support heavy equipment and components, often without help.

Time-management skills. HVACR technicians frequently have a set number of daily maintenance calls. They should be able to keep a schedule and complete all necessary repairs or tasks.

Employment Projections Data for Heating, Air Conditioning, and Refrigeration Mechanics and Installers

Occupational Title	SOC Code	Employment, 2014	Projected Employment, 2024	Change, 2014–2024 Percent	Change, 2014–2024 Numeric
Heating, air conditioning, and refrigeration mechanics and installers	49-9021	292,000	331,600	14	39,600

Source: U.S. Bureau of Labor Statistics, Employment Projections Program

Similar Occupations. This table shows a list of occupations with job duties that are similar to those of heating, air conditioning, and refrigeration mechanics and installers.

Occupations	Entry-level Education	2014 Median Pay	Projected Job Growth	Average Annual Openings
Boilermakers	High school diploma or equivalent	$59,860	9%	150
Electricians	High school diploma or equivalent	$51,110	14%	8,590
Plumbers, Pipefitters, and Steamfitters	High school diploma or equivalent	$50,660	12%	4,910
Sheet Metal Workers	High school diploma or equivalent	$45,070	7%	940
Solar Photovoltaic Installers	High school diploma or equivalent	$40,020	24%	140

Troubleshooting skills. HVACR technicians must be able to identify problems on malfunctioning heating, air conditioning, and refrigeration systems and then determine the best way to repair them.

Because HVACR workers often work in and around people's homes, they may need to pass a background check before being hired.

Pay

The median annual wage for heating, air conditioning, and refrigeration mechanics and installers was $44,630 in May 2014. The median wage is the wage at which half the workers in an occupation earned more than that amount and half earned less. The lowest 10 percent earned less than $27,630, and the highest 10 percent earned more than $70,820.

Apprentices usually earn about half of the wage paid to experienced workers. As they learn to do more, their pay increases.

Job Outlook

Employment of heating, air conditioning, and refrigeration mechanics and installers is projected to grow 14 percent from 2014 to 2024, much faster than the average for all occupations.

Commercial and residential building construction will drive employment growth. The growing number of sophisticated climate-control systems is also expected to increase demand for qualified HVACR technicians.

Repair and replacement of HVACR systems is a large part of what technicians do. Climate-control systems generally need replacement after 10 to 15 years. The growing emphasis on energy efficiency and pollution reduction is likely to increase the demand for HVACR technicians as climate-control systems are retrofitted, upgraded, or replaced entirely. In addition, regulations prohibiting the discharge and production of older types of refrigerant pollutants will result in the need to modify or replace many existing air conditioning systems.

Job Prospects. Job opportunities for HVACR technicians are expected to be excellent, particularly for those who have completed training at an accredited technical school or through an apprenticeship. Candidates familiar with computer tablets and electronics, as well as those who have developed troubleshooting skills, will have the best job opportunities as employers continue to have difficulty finding qualified technicians to install, maintain, and repair complex new systems.

Technicians who specialize in new installation work may experience periods of unemployment when the level of new construction activity declines. Maintenance and repair work, however, usually remains relatively stable. Business owners and homeowners depend on their climate-control or refrigeration systems year round and must keep them in good working order, regardless of economic conditions.

Contacts for More Information

For details about apprenticeships or other work opportunities, contact the offices of the state employment service, the state apprenticeship agency, local contractors, or local union–management HVACR apprenticeship committees. Apprenticeship information is available from the U.S. Department of Labor's ApprenticeshipUSA program (www.dol.gov/apprenticeship) online or by phone at 877-872-5627.

For more information about career opportunities, training, and certification, visit

- Air Conditioning Contractors of America, Inc. (www.acca.org)
- Air-Conditioning, Heating, and Refrigeration Institute (www.ahrinet.org)
- Associated Builders and Contractors (www.abc.org)
- Carbon Monoxide Safety Association (http://cosafety.org/Default.aspx)
- Green Mechanical Council (www.greenmech.org)
- Home Builders Institute (www.hbi.org)
- HVAC Excellence (www.hvacexcellence.org)
- Mechanical Contractors Association of America (www.mcaa.org)
- National Occupational Competency Testing Institute (www.nocti.org)
- NCCER (www.nccer.org)
- North American Technician Excellence (www.natex.org)
- Plumbing-Heating-Cooling Contractors Association (www.phccweb.org)
- Radiant Professionals Alliance (www.radiantpanelassociation.org)
- Refrigerating Engineers and Technicians Association (http://reta.com)
- Refrigeration Service Engineers Society (RSES) (www.rses.org)
- International Association of Sheet Metal, Air, Rail and Transportation Workers (SMART) (http://smart-union.org)
- United Association Union of Plumbers, Fitters, Welders, and Service Techs (www.ua.org)

O*NET

- Heating, Air Conditioning, and Refrigeration Mechanics and Installers (49-9021.00)
- Heating and Air Conditioning Mechanics and Installers (49-9021.01)
- Refrigeration Mechanics and Installers (49-9021.02)

Heavy Vehicle and Mobile Equipment Service Technicians

- **2014 Median Pay** .... $45,930 per year
  $22.08 per hour
- **Typical Entry-Level Education** .... High school diploma or equivalent
- **Work Experience in a Related Occupation** .... None
- **On-the-job Training** .... Long-term on-the-job training
- **Number of Jobs, 2014** 186,500
- **Job Outlook, 2014–24** .... 5% (As fast as average)
- **Employment Change, 2014–24** 10,100

What Heavy Vehicle and Mobile Equipment Service Technicians Do

Heavy vehicle and mobile equipment service technicians, also called *mechanics*, inspect, maintain, and repair vehicles and machinery used in construction, farming, rail transportation, and other industries.

Duties. Heavy vehicle and mobile equipment service technicians typically do the following:

- Consult equipment operating manuals, blueprints, and drawings
- Perform scheduled maintenance, such as cleaning and lubricating parts
- Diagnose and identify malfunctions, using computerized tools and equipment
- Inspect, repair, and replace defective or worn parts, such as bearings, pistons, and gears
- Overhaul and test major components, such as engines, hydraulics, and electrical systems
- Disassemble and reassemble heavy equipment and components
- Travel to worksites to repair large equipment, such as cranes
- Maintain logs of equipment condition and work performed

Heavy vehicles and mobile equipment are critical to many industrial activities, including construction and railroad transportation. Various types of equipment, such as tractors, cranes, and bulldozers, are used to haul materials, till land, lift beams, and dig earth to pave the way for development and construction.

Heavy vehicle and mobile equipment service technicians repair and maintain engines, hydraulic systems, transmissions, and electrical systems of agricultural, industrial, construction, and rail equipment. They ensure the performance and safety of fuel lines, brakes, and other systems.

Service technicians use diagnostic computers and equipment to identify problems and make adjustments or repairs. For example, they may use an oscilloscope to observe the signals produced by electronic components. Service technicians also use many different power and machine tools, including pneumatic wrenches, lathes, and welding equipment. A pneumatic tool, such as an impact wrench, is an air tool powered by compressed air.

Service technicians also use many different hand tools, such as screwdrivers, pliers, and wrenches, to work on small parts and in hard-to-reach areas. They generally purchase these tools over the course of their careers, often investing thousands of dollars in their inventory.

After identifying malfunctioning equipment, service technicians repair, replace, and recalibrate components such as hydraulic pumps and spark plugs. This may involve disassembling and reassembling major equipment or making adjustments through an onboard computer program.

Farm equipment mechanics and service technicians service and repair farm equipment, such as tractors and harvesters. They also work on smaller consumer-grade lawn and garden tractors. Most work for dealer repair shops, where farmers increasingly send their equipment for maintenance.

Mobile heavy equipment mechanics repair and maintain construction and surface mining equipment, such as bulldozers, cranes, graders, and excavators. Most work for governments, equipment rental and leasing shops, and large construction and mining companies.

Rail car repairers specialize in servicing railroad locomotives, subway cars, and other rolling stock. They usually work for railroad, public and private transit companies, and rail car manufacturers.

For information about technicians and mechanics who work primarily on automobiles, see the profile on automotive service technicians and mechanics.

For information about technicians and mechanics who work primarily on large trucks and buses, see the profile on diesel service technicians and mechanics.

For information about technicians and mechanics who primarily work on motorboats, motorcycles, and small all-terrain vehicles, see the profile on small engine mechanics.

Work Environment

Heavy vehicle and mobile equipment service technicians held about 186,500 jobs in 2014. Most service technicians worked for private companies.

About 60 percent of farm equipment mechanics and service technicians worked for farm and garden machinery and equipment merchant wholesalers, and about 13 percent worked in crop production in 2014.

About 26 percent of mobile heavy equipment mechanics worked for machinery, equipment, and supplies merchant wholesalers, and another 19 percent worked in construction in 2014. About 14

Heavy vehicle and mobile equipment service technicians and mechanics often work on hydraulic equipment, performing needed repairs.

Median Annual Wages, May 2014

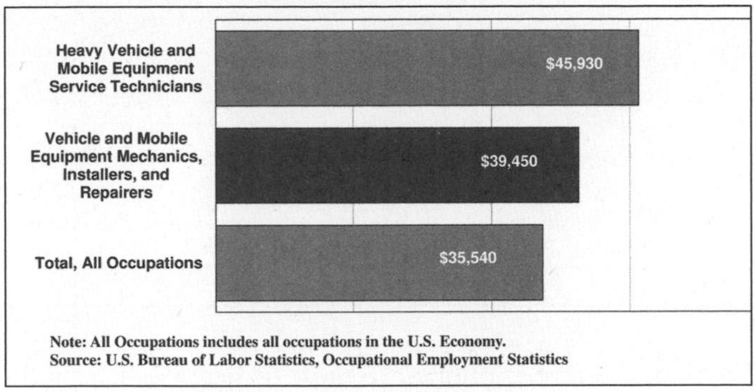

Percent Change in Employment, Projected 2014–2024

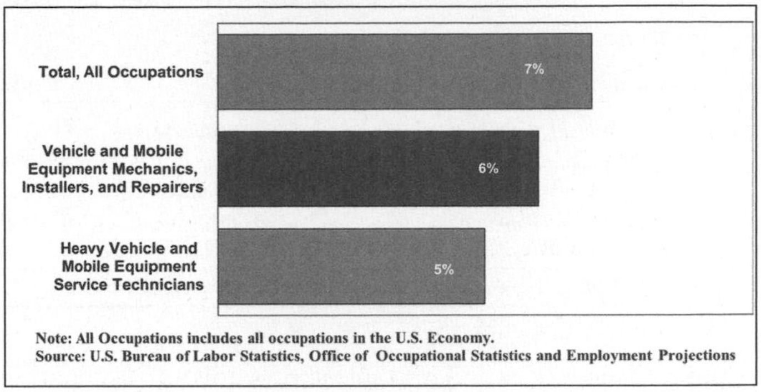

percent worked in government, and about 9 percent were employed in mining, quarrying, and oil and gas extraction.

Most rail car repairers—about 84 percent—worked in transportation and warehousing, which includes rail transportation and support activities for rail transportation in 2014.

Although many service technicians work indoors in repair shops, some service technicians travel to worksites to make repairs because it is often too expensive to transport heavy or mobile equipment to a shop. Generally, more experienced service technicians specialize in field service. These workers drive trucks that are specially equipped with replacement parts and tools, and they spend considerable time outdoors and often drive long distances.

Heavy vehicle and mobile equipment service technicians often lift heavy parts and tools, handle greasy and dirty equipment, and stand or lie in awkward positions.

Work Schedules. Most heavy vehicle and mobile equipment service technicians work full time, and many work evenings or weekends. Overtime is common.

Farm equipment mechanics' work varies by time of the year. During busy planting and harvesting seasons, for example, mechanics often work six or seven 12-hour days per week. In the slower winter months; however, they may work less than full time.

Education/Training

Most heavy vehicle and mobile equipment service technicians have a high school diploma or equivalent. Because vehicle and equipment technology is increasingly sophisticated and computerized, some employers prefer to hire service technicians who have completed a formal training program at a postsecondary institution.

Education. Most heavy vehicle and mobile equipment service technicians have a high school diploma or equivalent. High school courses in automotive repair, electronics, physics, and welding provide a strong foundation for a service technician's career. However, high school graduates often need further training to become fully qualified.

Completing a vocational or other postsecondary training program in diesel technology or heavy equipment mechanics is increasingly considered the best preparation for some entry-level positions. Offered by vocational schools and community colleges, these programs cover the basics of diagnostic techniques, electronics, and other related subjects. Most programs last 1 to 2 years and lead to certificates of completion. Other programs, which lead to associate's degrees, generally take 2 years to complete.

Training. Entry-level workers with no formal background in heavy vehicle repair often receive a few months of on-the-job training before they begin performing routine service tasks and making minor repairs. Trainees advance to more complex work as they show competence, and usually become fully qualified after 3 to 4 years of work.

Service technicians who have completed a postsecondary training program in diesel technology or heavy equipment mechanics require less training.

Many employers send new service technicians to training sessions conducted by equipment manufacturers. Training sessions may focus on particular components and technologies or types of equipment.

Licenses, Certifications, and Registrations. Some manufacturers offer certification in specific repair methods or equipment. Although not required, certification can demonstrate a service technician's competence and usually commands higher pay.

Important Qualities

Dexterity. Heavy vehicle and mobile equipment service technicians must perform many tasks, such as disassembling engine parts, connecting or attaching components, and using hand tools, with a steady hand and good hand-eye coordination.

Mechanical skills. Heavy vehicle and mobile equipment service technicians must be familiar with engine components and systems and know how they interact with each other. They must often disassemble major parts for repairs and be able to reassemble them.

Organizational skills. Heavy vehicle and mobile equipment service technicians must maintain accurate service records and parts inventories.

Physical strength. Heavy vehicle and mobile equipment service technicians must be able to lift and move heavy equipment, tools, and parts without risking injury.

Troubleshooting skills. Heavy vehicle and mobile equipment service technicians must be familiar with diagnostic equipment, which can help find the source of malfunctions when they are difficult to identify.

Pay

The median annual wage for heavy vehicle and mobile equipment service technicians was $45,930 in May 2014. The median wage is the wage at which half the workers in an occupation earned more than that amount and half earned less. The lowest 10 percent earned less than $28,890, and the highest 10 percent earned more than $67,070.

Median annual wages for heavy vehicle and mobile equipment service technicians in May 2014 were as follows:

Rail car repairers	$54,020
Mobile heavy equipment mechanics, except engines	47,580
Farm equipment mechanics and service technicians	36,150

Employment Projections Data for Heavy Vehicle and Mobile Equipment Service Technicians

Occupational Title	SOC Code	Employment, 2014	Projected Employment, 2024	Change, 2014–2024 Percent	Change, 2014–2024 Numeric
Heavy vehicle and mobile equipment service technicians and mechanics	49-3040	186,500	196,500	5	10,100
Farm equipment mechanics and service technicians	49-3041	40,300	43,200	7	2,900
Mobile heavy equipment mechanics, except engines	49-3042	124,700	131,300	5	6,600
Rail car repairers	49-3043	21,500	22,000	3	600

Source: U.S. Bureau of Labor Statistics, Employment Projections Program

Similar Occupations. This table shows a list of occupations with job duties that are similar to those of heavy vehicle and mobile equipment service technicians.

Occupations	Entry-level Education	2014 Median Pay	Projected Job Growth	Average Annual Openings
Aircraft and Avionics Equipment Mechanics and Technicians	See Education/Training	$56,980	1%	160
Automotive Service Technicians and Mechanics	Postsecondary nondegree award	$37,120	5%	3,910
Diesel Service Technicians and Mechanics	High school diploma or equivalent	$43,630	12%	3,160
Industrial Machinery Mechanics, Machinery Maintenance Workers, and Millwrights	High school diploma or equivalent	$47,450	16%	7,340
Small Engine Mechanics	See Education/Training	$34,130	4%	320

Job Outlook

Employment of heavy vehicle and mobile equipment service technicians is projected to grow 5 percent from 2014 to 2024, about as fast as the average for all occupations.

As the stock of heavy vehicles and mobile equipment continues to increase, more service technicians will be needed to maintain them. Growth rates will vary by specialty.

Employment of farm equipment mechanics and service technicians is projected to grow 7 percent, about as fast as the average for all occupations. Demand for farm equipment repairers will be driven primarily by the need for agricultural products to feed a growing population. Demand for other products, such as biofuels, will also increase repairer employment.

Employment of mobile heavy equipment mechanics is projected to grow 5 percent, about as fast as the average for all occupations. Population and business growth will result in the construction of more houses, office buildings, roads, bridges, and other structures, creating a steady demand for mobile heavy equipment mechanics.

Employment of rail car repairers is projected to grow 3 percent, slower than the average for all occupations. Rail car repairers will continue to be needed to repair rail cars used for freight shipping and transportation, as well as public transportation.

Job Prospects. Most job opportunities will come from the need to replace workers who retire or leave the occupation. Those who have completed formal postsecondary training programs should enjoy the best job prospects. Those without formal training or certification are likely to face strong competition for entry-level jobs.

The majority of job openings are expected to be in sectors that sell, rent, or lease heavy vehicles and mobile equipment, where a large proportion of service technicians are employed.

The construction and mining industries, which use large numbers of heavy equipment, are sensitive to fluctuations in the economy. As a result, job opportunities for service technicians in these sectors will vary with overall economic conditions.

Job opportunities for farm equipment mechanics are seasonal, and are generally best during warmer months.

Contacts for More Information

For more details about job openings for heavy vehicle and mobile equipment service technicians, consult local heavy and mobile equipment dealers and distributors, construction contractors, and government agencies. Local offices of the state employment service also may have information on job openings and training programs.

For more information about careers and training programs, visit

- Associated Equipment Distributors (www.aedcareers.com)
- National Automotive Technicians Education Foundation (www.natef.org)
- National Institute for Automotive Service Excellence (www.ase.com/Home.aspx)

O*NET

- Farm Equipment Mechanics and Service Technicians (49-3041.00)
- Mobile Heavy Equipment Mechanics, Except Engines (49-3042.00)
- Rail Car Repairers (49-3043.00)

Industrial Machinery Mechanics, Machinery Maintenance Workers, and Millwrights

- **2014 Median Pay** .... $47,450 per year
  $22.82 per hour
- **Typical Entry-Level Education** .... High school diploma or equivalent

- **Work Experience in a Related Occupation**.............. None
- **On-the-job Training** .... See Education/Training
- **Number of Jobs, 2014** 464,400
- **Job Outlook, 2014–24**.... 16% (Much faster than average)
- **Employment Change, 2014–24** 73,400

What Industrial Machinery Mechanics, Machinery Maintenance Workers, and Millwrights Do

Industrial machinery mechanics and machinery maintenance workers maintain and repair factory equipment and other industrial machinery, such as conveying systems, production machinery, and packaging equipment.Millwrights install, dismantle, repair, reassemble, and move machinery in factories, power plants, and construction sites.

Duties. Industrial machinery mechanics typically do the following:

- Read technical manuals to understand equipment and controls
- Disassemble machinery and equipment when there is a problem
- Repair or replace broken or malfunctioning components
- Perform tests and run initial batches to make sure that the machine is running smoothly
- Adjust and calibrate equipment and machinery to optimal specifications

Machinery maintenance workers typically do the following:

- Detect minor problems by performing basic diagnostic tests
- Clean and lubricate equipment or machinery
- Check the performance of machinery
- Test malfunctioning machinery to determine whether major repairs are needed
- Adjust equipment and reset or calibrate sensors and controls

Millwrights typically do the following:

- Install or repair machinery and equipment
- Adjust and align machine parts
- Replace defective parts of machinery as needed
- Take apart existing machinery to clear floor space for new machinery
- Move machinery and equipment

Industrial machinery mechanics, also called *maintenance machinists*, keep machines in good working order. To do this task, they must be able to detect and correct errors before the machine or the products it produces are damaged. Industrial machinery mechanics use technical manuals, their understanding of industrial equipment, and careful observation to determine the cause of a problem. For example, after hearing a vibration from a machine, they must decide whether it is the result of worn belts, weak motor bearings, or some other problem. These mechanics often need years of training and experience to be able to diagnose all of the problems they find in their work. They may use computerized diagnostic systems and vibration analysis techniques to help figure out the source of problems. Examples of machines they may work with are robotic welding arms, automobile assembly line conveyor belts, and hydraulic lifts.

After diagnosing a problem, the industrial machinery mechanic may take the equipment apart to repair or replace the necessary

Industrial machinery mechanics and maintenance workers adjust and calibrate equipment.

parts. Mechanics use their knowledge of electronics and computer programming to repair sophisticated equipment. Once a repair is made, mechanics test a machine to ensure that it is running smoothly. Industrial machinery mechanics also do preventive maintenance.

In addition to working with hand tools, mechanics commonly use lathes, grinders, or drill presses. Many also are required to weld.

Machinery maintenance workers do basic maintenance and repairs on machines. They clean and lubricate machinery, perform basic diagnostic tests, check the performance of the machine, and test damaged machine parts to determine whether major repairs are necessary.

Machinery maintenance workers must follow machine specifications and adhere to maintenance schedules. They perform minor repairs, generally leaving major repairs to machinery mechanics.

All maintenance workers use a variety of tools to do repairs and preventive maintenance. For example, they may use a screwdriver or socket wrenches to adjust a motor's alignment, or they might use a hoist to lift a heavy printing press off the ground.

Millwrights install, maintain, and disassemble industrial machines. Putting together a machine can take a few days or several weeks.

Millwrights perform repairs that include replacing worn or defective parts of machines. Millwrights also may be involved in taking apart the entire machine, a common situation when a manufacturing plant needs to clear floor space for new machinery. In taking apart a machine, each part of the machine must be carefully disassembled, categorized, and packaged.

Millwrights use a variety of hand tools, such as hammers and levels, as well as equipment for welding, brazing, and cutting. They also use measuring tools, such as micrometers, measuring tapes, lasers, and other precision-measuring devices. On large projects, they commonly use cranes and trucks. When millwrights and managers determine the best place for a machine, millwrights use forklifts, hoists, winches, cranes, and other equipment to bring the parts to the desired location.

Work Environment

Industrial machinery mechanics, machinery maintenance workers, and millwrights held about 464,400 jobs in 2014. The industries

Median Annual Wages, May 2014

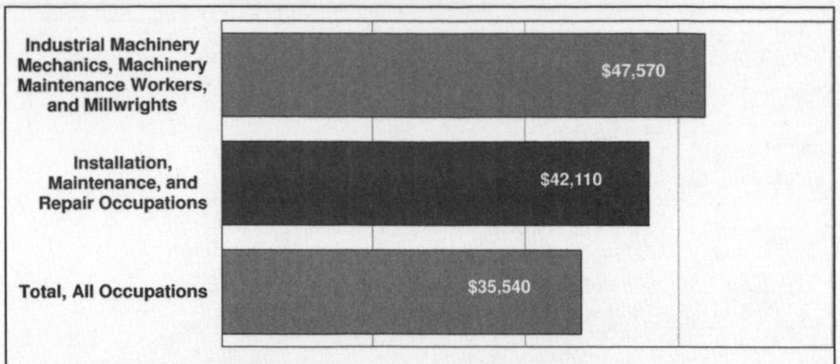

Note: All Occupations includes all occupations in the U.S. Economy.
Source: U.S. Bureau of Labor Statistics, Occupational Employment Statistics

Percent Change in Employment, Projected 2014–2024

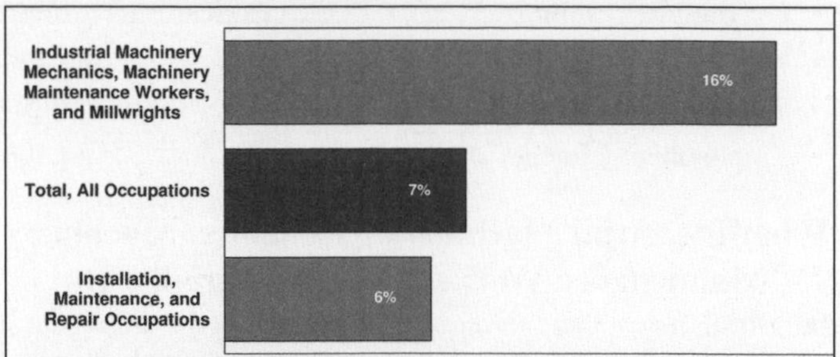

Note: All Occupations includes all occupations in the U.S. Economy.
Source: U.S. Bureau of Labor Statistics, Office of Occupational Statistics and Employment Projections

that employed the most industrial machinery mechanics, machinery maintenance workers, and millwrights were as follows:

Manufacturing	54%
Wholesale trade	9
Commercial and industrial machinery and equipment (except automotive and electronic) repair and maintenance	9

Most worked in factories, refineries, food-processing facilities, or power plants, or at construction sites.

Injuries and Illnesses. Industrial machinery mechanics and machinery maintenance workers have higher rates of injuries and illnesses than the national average. To avoid injuries, workers must follow safety precautions and use protective equipment, such as hardhats, safety glasses, steel-toed shoes, gloves, and earplugs.

Work Schedules. Most industrial machinery mechanics and machinery maintenance workers are employed full time during regular business hours. However, mechanics may be on call and work night or weekend shifts. Overtime is common, particularly for mechanics.

Millwrights are typically employed on a contract basis and frequently spend only a few days or weeks at a single site—as long as it takes them to assemble or disassemble an industrial machine. As a result, workers often have variable schedules and may experience downtime between jobs.

Education/Training

Industrial machinery mechanics, machinery maintenance workers, and millwrights typically need a high school diploma. However, industrial machinery mechanics need a year or more of training after high school, whereas machinery maintenance workers typically receive on-the-job training that lasts a few months to a year.

Most millwrights go through an apprenticeship program that lasts about 4 years. Programs are usually a combination of technical instruction and on-the-job training. Others learn their trade through a 2-year associate's degree program in industrial maintenance.

Education. Employers of industrial machinery mechanics, machinery maintenance workers, and millwrights generally require them to have at least a high school diploma or equivalent. Employers prefer to hire workers who have taken high school or postsecondary courses in mechanical drawing, mathematics, blueprint reading, computer programming, and electronics. Some mechanics and millwrights complete a 2-year associate's degree program in industrial maintenance.

Training. Industrial machinery mechanics and machinery maintenance workers learn how to perform routine tasks, such as setting up, cleaning, lubricating, and starting machinery. They may also be instructed in subjects such as shop mathematics, blueprint reading, proper hand tools use, welding, electronics, and computer programming. This training may be offered on the job by professional trainers hired by the employer or by representatives of equipment manufacturers.

Most millwrights learn their trade through a 3- or 4-year apprenticeship. For each year of the program, apprentices must have at least 144 hours of relevant technical instruction and 2,000 hours of paid on-the-job training. On the job, apprentices learn to set up, clean, lubricate, repair, and start machinery. During technical instruction, they are taught welding, mathematics, how to read blueprints, how to use electronic and pneumatic devices, and how to use grease and fluid properly. Many also receive computer training.

After completing an apprenticeship program, millwrights are considered fully qualified and can usually perform tasks with less guidance.

Employers, local unions, contractor associations, and the state labor department often sponsor apprenticeship programs. The basic qualifications for entering an apprenticeship program are as follows:

- Minimum age of 18
- High school diploma or equivalent
- Physically able to do the work

Employment Projections Data for Industrial Machinery Mechanics, Machinery Maintenance Workers, and Millwrights

Occupational Title	SOC Code	Employment, 2014	Projected Employment, 2024	Change, 2014–2024 Percent	Change, 2014–2024 Numeric
Industrial machinery mechanics, machinery maintenance workers, and millwrights	—	464,400	537,800	16	73,400
Industrial machinery mechanics	49-9041	332,200	391,900	18	59,700
Maintenance workers, machinery	49-9043	91,200	98,700	8	7,400
Millwrights	49-9044	40,900	47,100	15	6,200

Source: U.S. Bureau of Labor Statistics, Employment Projections Program

Similar Occupations. This table shows a list of occupations with job duties that are similar to those of industrial machinery mechanics, machinery maintenance workers, and millwrights.

Occupations	Entry-level Education	2014 Median Pay	Projected Job Growth	Average Annual Openings
Electrical and Electronics Engineers	Bachelor's degree	$93,260	0%	-10
Electricians	High school diploma or equivalent	$51,110	14%	8,590
General Maintenance and Repair Workers	High school diploma or equivalent	$36,170	6%	8,350
Machinists and Tool and Die Makers	High school diploma or equivalent	$41,510	6%	2,900
Plumbers, Pipefitters, and Steamfitters	High school diploma or equivalent	$50,660	12%	4,910
Welders, Cutters, Solderers, and Brazers	High school diploma or equivalent	$37,420	4%	1,440

Important Qualities

Manual dexterity. When handling very small parts, workers must have a steady hand and good hand-eye coordination.

Mechanical skills. Industrial machinery mechanics, machinery maintenance workers, and millwrights use technical manuals and sophisticated diagnostic equipment to figure out why machines are not working. Workers must be able to reassemble large, complex machines after finishing a repair.

Troubleshooting skills. Industrial machinery mechanics, machinery maintenance workers, and millwrights must observe, diagnose, and fix problems that a machine may be having.

Pay

The median annual wage for industrial machinery mechanics, machinery maintenance workers, and millwrights was $47,450 in May 2014. The median wage is the wage at which half the workers in an occupation earned more than that amount and half earned less. The lowest 10 percent earned less than $30,130, and the highest 10 percent earned more than $72,400.

Median annual wages for industrial machinery mechanics, machinery maintenance workers, and millwrights in May 2014 were as follows:

Millwrights	$50,460
Industrial machinery mechanics	48,630
Maintenance workers, machinery	42,640

Job Outlook

Employment of industrial machinery mechanics, machinery maintenance workers, and millwrights is projected to grow 16 percent from 2014 to 2024, much faster than the average for all occupations. Employment growth will vary by occupation.

Employment of industrial machinery mechanics is projected to grow 18 percent from 2014 to 2024, much faster than the average for all occupations. The increased adoption of sophisticated manufacturing machinery will require more mechanics to keep machines in good working order.

Employment of machinery maintenance workers is projected to grow 8 percent from 2014 to 2024, about as fast as the average for all occupations. Increased automation, including the use of many computer-controlled machines in factories and manufacturing plants, should raise the demand for machinery maintenance workers in order to keep the machines operating well.

Employment of millwrights is projected to grow 15 percent from 2014 to 2024, much faster than the average for all occupations. The increased use of machinery in manufacturing will require millwrights to install and disassemble this equipment, as well as perform some repair work on it.

Job Prospects. Overall, applicants with a broad range of skills in machine repair are expected to have good job prospects as older workers retire or otherwise leave the occupation.

Those who complete apprenticeships and educational programs designed for industrial machinery repair should have the best job prospects.

Contacts for More Information

For information about industrial machinery mechanics and machinery maintenance workers, visit

- National Association of Manufacturers (www.nam.org)
- Society for Maintenance & Reliability Professionals (http://tinyurl.com/hl7nkhs)

For information about millwrights and the precision-machined products industry, training, and apprenticeships, visit

- Precision Machined Products Association (www.pmpa.org)

For further information on apprenticeship programs, write to the Apprenticeship Council of your state's labor department or to local firms that employ machinery mechanics and repairers. Apprenticeship information is also available from the U.S. Department of Labor's ApprenticeshipUSA program (www.dol.gov/apprenticeship) online or by phone at 877-872-5627.

O*NET

- Industrial Machinery Mechanics (49-9041.00)
- Maintenance Workers, Machinery (49-9043.00)
- Millwrights (49-9044.00)

Line Installers and Repairers

- **2014 Median Pay** .... $61,740 per year, $29.68 per hour
- **Typical Entry-Level Education** .... High school diploma or equivalent
- **Work Experience in a Related Occupation** .... None
- **On-the-job Training** .... Long-term on-the-job training
- **Number of Jobs, 2014** 236,600
- **Job Outlook, 2014–24** .... 6% (As fast as average)
- **Employment Change, 2014–24** 13,700

What Line Installers and Repairers Do

Line installers and repairers, also known as *line workers*, install or repair electrical power systems and telecommunications cables, including fiber optics.

Duties. Electrical power-line installers and repairers typically do the following:

- Install, maintain, or repair the power lines that move electricity
- Identify defective devices, voltage regulators, transformers, and switches
- Inspect and test power lines and auxiliary equipment
- String power lines between poles, towers, and buildings
- Climb poles and transmission towers and use truck-mounted buckets to get to equipment
- Operate power equipment when installing and repairing poles, towers, and lines
- Drive work vehicles to job sites
- Follow safety standards and procedures

Telecommunications line installers and repairers typically do the following:

- Install, maintain, or repair telecommunications equipment
- Inspect or test lines or cables
- Lay underground cable, including fiber optic lines, directly in trenches
- Pull cables in underground conduit
- Install aerial cables, including over lakes or across rivers
- Operate power equipment when installing and repairing poles, towers, and lines
- Drive work vehicles to job sites
- Set up service for customers

A complex network of physical power lines and cables provides consumers with electricity, landline telephone communication, cable television, and Internet access. Line installers and repairers, also known as *line workers*, are responsible for installing and maintaining these networks.

Line installers and repairers can specialize in different areas depending on the type of network and industry in which they work:

Electrical power-line installers and repairers install and maintain the power grid—the network of power lines that moves electricity from generating plants to customers. They routinely work with high-voltage electricity, which requires extreme caution. The electrical current can range from hundreds of thousands of volts for long-distance transmission lines that make up the power grid to less than 10,000 volts for distribution lines that supply electricity to homes and businesses.

Line workers who maintain the interstate power grid work in crews that travel to locations throughout a large region to service transmission lines and towers. Workers employed by local utilities work mainly with lower voltage distribution lines, maintaining equipment such as transformers, voltage regulators, and switches. They also may work on traffic lights and street lights.

Telecommunications line installers and repairers install and maintain the lines and cables used by network communications companies. Depending on the service provided—local and long-distance telephone, cable television, or Internet—telecommunications companies use different types of cables, including fiber-optic cables. Unlike metallic cables that carry electricity, fiber-optic cables are made of glass and transmit signals using light. Working with fiber optics requires special skills, such as the ability to splice and terminate optical cables. Additionally, workers use specialized equipment to test and troubleshoot cables and networking equipment.

Most line installers need several years of on-the-job training.

Because these systems are complicated, many line workers also specialize by duty:

Line installers install new cable. They may work for construction contractors, utilities, or telecommunications companies. Workers generally start a new job by digging underground trenches or erecting utility poles and towers to carry the wires and cables. They use a variety of construction equipment, including digger derricks, which are trucks equipped with augers and cranes used to dig holes in the ground and set poles in place. Line installers also use trenchers, cable plows, and directional bore machines, which are used to cut openings in the earth to lay underground cables. Once the poles, towers, tunnels, or trenches are ready, workers install the new cable.

Line repairers are employed by utilities and telecommunications companies that maintain existing power and telecommunications lines. Maintenance needs may be identified in a variety of ways, including remote monitoring, aerial inspections, and by customer reports of service outages. Line repairers often must replace aging or outdated equipment, so many of these workers have installation duties in addition to their repair duties.

When a problem is reported, line repairers must identify the cause and fix it. This usually involves diagnostic testing using specialized equipment and repair work. To work on poles, line installers usually use bucket trucks to raise themselves to the top of the structure, although all line workers must be adept at climbing poles and towers when necessary. Workers use special safety equipment to keep them from falling when climbing utility poles and towers.

Storms and other natural disasters can cause extensive damage to power lines. When power is lost, line repairers must work quickly to restore service to customers.

Work Environment

Line installers and repairers held about 236,600 jobs in 2014. The industries that employed the most line installers and repairers were as follows:

Wired telecommunications carriers	26%
Electric power generation, transmission and distribution	24
Utility system construction	20

Electrical contractors and other wiring installation contractors...12
Local government, excluding education and hospitals.............7

The work of line installers and repairers can be physically demanding. Line installers must be comfortable working at great heights and in confined spaces. Despite the help of bucket trucks, all line workers must be able to climb utility poles and transmission towers and balance while working on them.

Their work often requires that they drive utility vehicles, travel long distances, and work outdoors.

Line installers and repairers often must work under challenging weather conditions, such as in snow, wind, rain, and extreme heat and cold, in order to keep electricity flowing.

Injuries and Illnesses. Line workers encounter serious hazards on their jobs and must follow safety procedures to minimize danger. For example, workers must wear safety equipment when entering underground manholes and test for the presence of gas before going underground.

Specifically, electric power-line workers have hazardous jobs. A worker can be electrocuted if he or she comes in contact with a live cable on a high-voltage power line. When workers engage live wires, they use electrically insulated protective devices and tools to minimize their risk.

Power lines are typically higher than telephone lines, increasing the risk of severe injury from a fall. To prevent injuries, line installers use fall-protection equipment when working on poles or towers. Safety procedures and training have significantly reduced the danger for line workers. However, the occupation is still among the most dangerous. As a result, telecommunications and electrical line workers have a rate of injuries and illnesses that is higher than the national average.

Work Schedules. Although most work full time during regular business hours, some line installers and repairers must work evenings and weekends. In emergencies or after storms and other natural disasters, workers may have to work long hours for several days in a row.

Education/Training

A high school diploma or equivalent is typically required for entry-level positions, but most line installers and repairers need technical instruction and long-term on-the-job training to become proficient. Apprenticeships are also common.

Education. Most companies require line installers and repairers to have a high school diploma or equivalent. Employers prefer candidates with basic knowledge of algebra and trigonometry. In addition, technical knowledge of electricity or electronics obtained through military service, vocational programs, or community colleges can also be helpful.

Many community colleges offer programs in telecommunications, electronics, or electricity. Some programs work with local companies to offer 1-year certificates that emphasize hands-on field work.

More advanced 2-year associate's degree programs provide students with a broad knowledge of the technology used in telecommunications and electrical utilities. These programs offer courses in electricity, electronics, fiber optics, and microwave transmission.

Training. Electrical line installers and repairers often must complete apprenticeships or other employer training programs. These programs, which can last up to 3 years, combine on-the-job training with technical instruction and are sometimes administered jointly by the employer and the union representing the workers. For example, the Electrical Training Alliance offers apprenticeship programs in four specialty areas. The basic qualifications to enter an apprenticeship program are as follows:

- Minimum age of 18
- High school education or equivalent
- One year of algebra
- Qualifying score on an aptitude test
- Pass substance abuse screening

Line installers and repairers who work for telecommunications companies typically receive several years of on-the-job training. They also may be encouraged to attend training from equipment manufacturers, schools, unions, or industry training organizations.

Licenses, Certifications, and Registrations. Although not mandatory, certification for line installers and repairers is also available from several associations. For example, the Electrical Training ALLIANCE offers certification for line installers and repairers in several specialty areas.

In addition, The Fiber Optic Association (FOA) offers two levels of fiber optic certification for telecommunications line installers and repairers.

Workers who drive heavy company vehicles usually need a commercial driver's license.

Advancement. Entry-level line workers generally begin with an apprenticeship, which includes both classroom training and hands-on work experience. As they learn additional skills from more experienced workers, they may advance to more complex tasks. In time, experienced line workers advance to more sophisticated maintenance and repair positions in which they are responsible for increasingly large portions of the network.

After 3 to 4 years of working, qualified line workers reach the journey level. A journey-level line worker is no longer considered an apprentice and can perform most tasks without supervision. Journey-level line workers also may qualify for positions at other

Median Annual Wages, May 2014

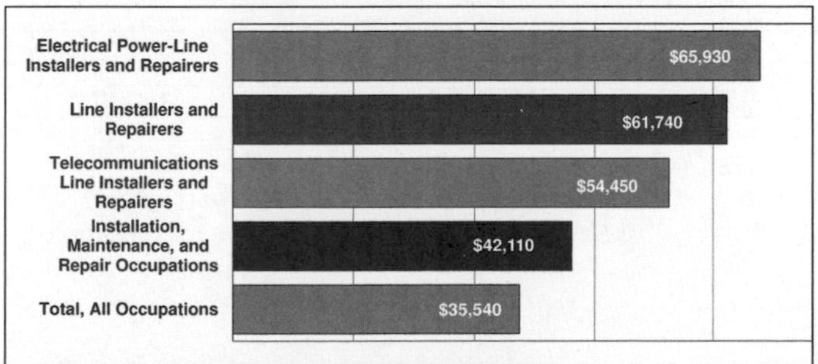

Note: All Occupations includes all occupations in the U.S. Economy.
Source: U.S. Bureau of Labor Statistics, Occupational Employment Statistics

Percent Change in Employment, Projected 2014–2024

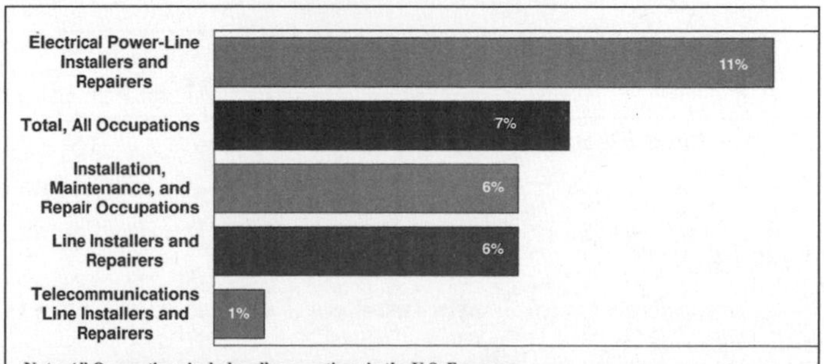

Note: All Occupations includes all occupations in the U.S. Economy.
Source: U.S. Bureau of Labor Statistics, Office of Occupational Statistics and Employment Projections

Employment Projections Data for Line Installers and Repairers

Occupational Title	SOC Code	Employment, 2014	Projected Employment, 2024	Change, 2014–2024 Percent	Change, 2014–2024 Numeric
Line installers and repairers	49-9050	236,600	250,300	6	13,700
Electrical power-line installers and repairers	49-9051	118,600	131,600	11	13,000
Telecommunications line installers and repairers	49-9052	118,000	118,700	1	700

Source: U.S. Bureau of Labor Statistics, Employment Projections Program

companies. Workers with many years of experience may become first-line supervisors or trainers.

Important Qualities

Color vision. Workers who handle electrical wires and cables must be able to distinguish colors because the wires and cables are often color coded.

Mechanical skills. Line installers and repairers must have the knowledge and skills to repair or replace complex electrical and telecommunications lines and equipment.

Physical stamina. Line installers and repairers often must climb poles and work at great heights with heavy tools and equipment. Therefore, installers and repairers should be able to work for long periods without tiring easily.

Physical strength. Line installers and repairers must be strong enough to lift heavy tools, cables, and equipment on a regular basis.

Teamwork. Because workers often rely on their fellow crew members for their safety, teamwork is critical.

Technical skills. Line installers use sophisticated diagnostic equipment on circuit breakers, switches, and transformers. They must be familiar with electrical systems and the appropriate tools needed to fix and maintain them.

Troubleshooting skills. Line installers and repairers must be able to diagnose problems in increasingly complex electrical systems and telecommunication lines.

Pay

The median annual wage for electrical power-line installers and repairers was $65,930 in May 2014. The median wage is the wage at which half the workers in an occupation earned more than that amount and half earned less. The lowest 10 percent earned less than $36,090, and the highest 10 percent earned more than $94,030.

The median annual wage for telecommunications line installers and repairers was $54,450 in May 2014. The lowest 10 percent earned less than $28,530, and the highest 10 percent earned more than $81,160.

In May 2014, the median annual wages for line installers and repairers in the top industries in which they worked were as follows:

Electric power generation, transmission and distribution	$69,250
Wired telecommunications carriers	65,440
Local government, excluding education and hospitals	61,930
Utility system construction	49,020
Electrical contractors and other wiring installation contractors	45,210

Union Membership. Compared with workers in all occupations, line installers and repairers had a higher percentage of workers who belonged to a union in 2014.

Job Outlook

Employment of line installers and repairers is projected to grow 6 percent from 2014 to 2024, about as fast as the average for all occupations. Employment growth will vary by specialty.

Employment of telecommunications line installers and repairers is projected to show little or no change from 2014 to 2024. As the population grows and customers increasingly demand enhanced connectivity, installers will continue to build out and provide newer and faster telephone, cable, and Internet services. However, growth may be limited because many households already have access to high speed Internet.

Employment of electrical power-line installers and repairers is projected to grow 11 percent from 2014 to 2024, faster than the average for all occupations. Employment growth will be largely due to the growing population and expansion of cities. With each new housing development or office park, new electric power lines are installed and will require maintenance. In addition, the interstate power grid will continue to grow in complexity to ensure reliability.

Job Prospects. Good job opportunities are expected overall. Highly skilled workers with apprenticeship training or a 2-year associate's degree in telecommunications, electronics, or electricity should have the best job opportunities.

Similar Occupations. This table shows a list of occupations with job duties that are similar to those of line installers and repairers.

Occupations	Entry-level Education	2014 Median Pay	Projected Job Growth	Average Annual Openings
Electrical and Electronics Engineers	Bachelor's degree	$93,260	0%	-10
Electricians	High school diploma or equivalent	$51,110	14%	8,590
Power Plant Operators, Distributors, and Dispatchers	High school diploma or equivalent	$72,910	-6%	-330
Telecommunications Equipment Installers and Repairers	Postsecondary nondegree award	$55,190	-4%	-780

Employment opportunities should be particularly good for electrical power-line installers and repairers, as workers in this field retire or leave the occupation for another job.

Contacts for More Information

For information about apprenticeships or job opportunities for line installers and repairers, contact local electrical contractors, a local chapter of the International Brotherhood of Electrical Workers, a local joint union–management apprenticeship committee, or the nearest office of your state employment service or apprenticeship agency. Apprenticeship information is available from the U.S. Department of Labor's toll-free help line, 1 (877) 872-5627 or the Employment and Training Administration (www.doleta.gov/OA/eta_default.cfm).

For more information about line installers and repairers, visit

- ➤ American Public Power Association (www.publicpower.org)
- ➤ Center for Energy Workforce Development (www.cewd.org/roadmap)
- ➤ Telecommunications Industry Association (www.tiaonline.org)

For information about certification, visit

- ➤ The Fiber Optic Association (www.thefoa.org)
- ➤ Electrical Training ALLIANCE (www.electricaltrainingalliance.org)

O*NET

- ➤ Electrical Power-Line Installers and Repairers (49-9051.00)
- ➤ Telecommunications Line Installers and Repairers (49-9052.00)

Medical Equipment Repairers

- **2014 Median Pay** .... $45,660 per year $21.95 per hour
- **Typical Entry-Level Education** .... Associate's degree
- **Work Experience in a Related Occupation** .... None
- **On-the-job Training** .... Moderate-term on-the-job training
- **Number of Jobs, 2014** 48,000
- **Job Outlook, 2014–24** .... 6% (As fast as average)
- **Employment Change, 2014–24** 2,900

What Medical Equipment Repairers Do

Medical equipment repairers install, maintain, and repair patient care equipment.

Duties. Medical equipment repairers typically do the following:

- Install medical equipment
- Test and calibrate parts and equipment
- Repair and replace parts
- Perform preventive maintenance and service
- Keep records of maintenance and repairs
- Review technical manuals and regularly attend training sessions
- Explain and demonstrate how to operate medical equipment
- Manage replacement of medical equipment

Medical equipment repairers, also known as *biomedical equipment technicians (BMET)*, repair a wide range of electronic, electromechanical, and hydraulic equipment used in hospitals and health practitioners' offices. They may work on patient monitors, defibrillators, ventilators, anesthesia machines, and other life-supporting equipment. They also may work on medical imaging equipment (X-rays, CAT scanners, and ultrasound equipment),

Medical equipment repairers often test and calibrate equipment.

voice-controlled operating tables, and electric wheelchairs. In addition, they repair medical equipment that dentists and eye doctors' use.

If a machine has problems or is not functioning to its potential, repairers first diagnose the problem. They then adjust the mechanical, electronic, or hydraulic parts or modify the software in order to recalibrate the equipment and fix the issue.

To do their work, medical equipment repairers use a variety of tools. Most use hand tools, such as screwdrivers, wrenches, and soldering irons. Others use electronic tools, such as multimeters (an electronic measuring device that combines several measures) and computers. Much of the equipment that they maintain and repair use specialized test-equipment software. Repairers use this software to calibrate the machines.

Many doctors, particularly specialty practitioners, rely on complex medical devices to run tests and diagnose patients, and they must be confident that the readings are accurate. Therefore, medical equipment repairers sometimes perform routine scheduled maintenance to ensure that sophisticated equipment, such as X-ray machines and CAT scanners, are in good working order. For less complicated equipment, such as electric hospital beds, workers make repairs as needed.

In a hospital setting, medical equipment repairers must be comfortable working around patients because repairs occasionally must take place while equipment is being used. When this is the case, the repairer must take great care to ensure that their work activities do not disturb patients.

Although some medical equipment repairers are trained to fix a variety of equipment, others specialize in repairing one or a small number of machines.

Work Environment

Medical equipment repairers held about 48,000 jobs in 2014. The industries that employed the most medical equipment repairers were as follows:

Professional and commercial equipment and supplies merchant wholesalers	27%
Electronic and precision equipment repair and maintenance	19
Hospitals; state, local, and private	13
Ambulatory healthcare services	8
Health and personal care stores	4

About 1 in 7 medical equipment repairers were self-employed in 2014.

Medical equipment repairers work for wholesale suppliers and at hospitals, electronic repair and maintenance shops, and health and personal care stores. Because repairing vital medical equipment is urgent, the work can be stressful.

Medical equipment repairers who work as contractors often have to travel—sometimes long distances—to perform needed repairs. Repairers often must work in a patient-caring environment, which has the potential to expose them to diseases and other health risks.

Work Schedules. Although medical equipment repairers usually work during the day, they are sometimes expected to be on call, including evenings and weekends. Most work full time, but some repairers have variable schedules.

Education/Training

Employers generally prefer candidates who have an associate's degree in biomedical technology or engineering. Depending on the area of specialization, repairers may need a bachelor's degree, especially for advancement.

Education. Education requirements for medical equipment repairers vary, depending on a worker's experience and area of specialization. However, the most common education is an associate's degree in biomedical equipment technology or engineering. Those who repair less-complicated equipment, such as hospital beds and electric wheelchairs, may learn entirely through on-the-job training, sometimes lasting up to 1 year. Repairers who work on more sophisticated equipment, such as CAT scanners and defibrillators, may need a bachelor's degree.

Training. New workers generally observe and help experienced repairers for 3 to 6 months to start. As they learn, workers gradually become more independent while still under supervision.

Each piece of equipment is different, so medical equipment repairers must learn each one separately. In some cases, this requires studying a machine's technical specifications and operating manual. Medical device manufacturers also may provide technical training.

Medical equipment technology is rapidly evolving, and new devices are frequently introduced. Repairers must continually update their skills and knowledge of new technologies and equipment through seminars and self-study. The original equipment manufacturers (OEMs) may also offer training.

Licenses, Certifications, and Registrations. Although not mandatory, certification can demonstrate competence and professionalism, making candidates more attractive to employers. It can also increase a repairer's opportunities for advancement. Most manufacturers and employers, particularly those in hospitals, often pay for their in-house medical repairers to become certified.

Some associations offer certifications for medical equipment repairers. For example, the Association for the Advancement of Medical Instrumentation (AAMI) offers certification in three specialty areas—Certified Biomedical Equipment Technician (CBET), Certified Radiology Equipment Specialists (CRES), and Certified Laboratory Equipment Specialist (CLES).

Important Qualities

Communication skills. Medical equipment repairers must effectively communicate technical information by telephone, in writing, and in person when speaking to clients, supervisors, and co-workers.

Dexterity. Many tasks, such as connecting or attaching parts and using hand tools, require a steady hand and good hand-eye coordination.

Mechanical skills. Medical equipment repairers must be familiar with medical components and systems and how they interact. Often, repairers must disassemble and reassemble major parts for repair.

Physical stamina. Standing, crouching, and bending in awkward positions are common when making repairs to equipment. Therefore, workers should be physically fit.

Technical skills. Technicians use sophisticated diagnostic tools when working on complex medical equipment. They must be familiar with both the equipment's internal parts and the appropriate tools needed to fix them.

Time-management skills. Because repairing vital medical equipment is urgent, workers must make good use of their time and perform repairs quickly.

Median Annual Wages, May 2014

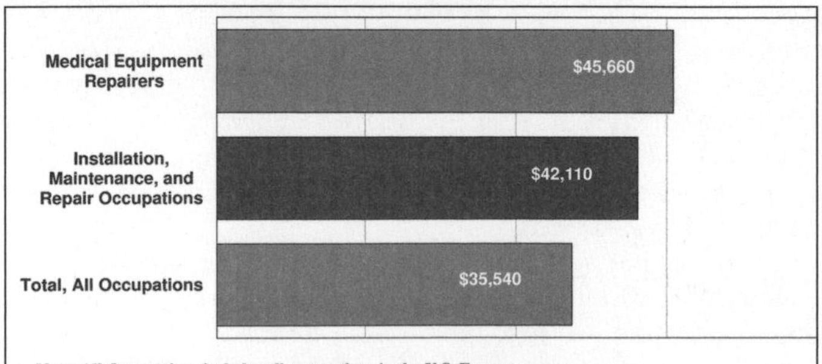

Note: All Occupations includes all occupations in the U.S. Economy.
Source: U.S. Bureau of Labor Statistics, Occupational Employment Statistics

Percent Change in Employment, Projected 2014–2024

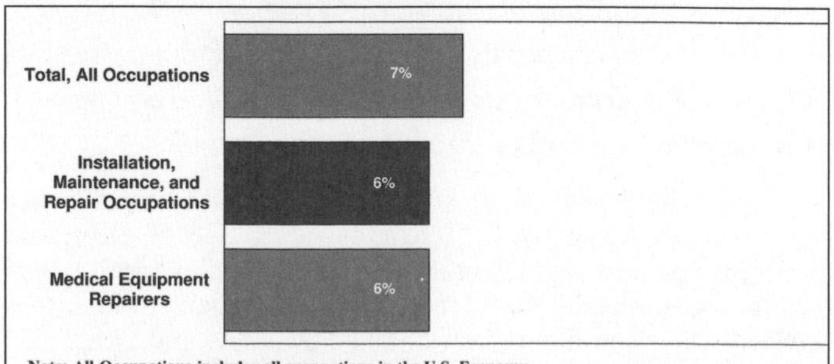

Note: All Occupations includes all occupations in the U.S. Economy.
Source: U.S. Bureau of Labor Statistics, Office of Occupational Statistics and Employment Projections

Employment Projections Data for Medical Equipment Repairers

Occupational Title	SOC Code	Employment, 2014	Projected Employment, 2024	Change, 2014–2024 Percent	Change, 2014–2024 Numeric
Medical equipment repairers	49-9062	48,000	50,900	6	2,900

Source: U.S. Bureau of Labor Statistics, Employment Projections Program

Similar Occupations. This table shows a list of occupations with job duties that are similar to those of medical equipment repairers.

Occupations	Entry-level Education	2014 Median Pay	Projected Job Growth	Average Annual Openings
Aircraft and Avionics Equipment Mechanics and Technicians	See Education/Training	$56,980	1%	160
General Maintenance and Repair Workers	High school diploma or equivalent	$36,170	6%	8,350
Industrial Machinery Mechanics, Machinery Maintenance Workers, and Millwrights	High school diploma or equivalent	$47,450	16%	7,340
Medical and Clinical Laboratory Technologists and Technicians	See Education/Training	$49,310	16%	5,210

Troubleshooting skills. As medical equipment becomes more intricate, problems become more difficult to identify. Therefore, repairers must be able to find and solve problems that are not immediately apparent.

Pay

The median annual wage for medical equipment repairers was $45,660 in May 2014. The median wage is the wage at which half the workers in an occupation earned more than that amount and half earned less. The lowest 10 percent earned less than $27,660, and the highest 10 percent earned more than $74,750.

In May 2014, the median annual wages for medical equipment repairers in the top industries in which they worked were as follows:

Hospitals; state, local, and private $51,390
Electronic and precision equipment repair and maintenance 47,000
Professional and commercial equipment and supplies merchant wholesalers 46,680
Ambulatory healthcare services 42,470
Health and personal care stores 35,380

Job Outlook

Employment of medical equipment repairers is projected to grow 6 percent from 2014 to 2024, about as fast as the average for all occupations. Employment growth will stem from both greater demand for healthcare services and the increasing types and complexity of the equipment these workers maintain and repair.

A significant factor in the greater demand for healthcare services is the aging population. As people age, they usually need more medical care. With the expected increase in the number of older adults and with people living longer, health professionals are prescribing more medical tests that use new, complex equipment.

Changes in technology are bringing hospitals and health professionals additional and more complex medical equipment. More medical equipment repairers should be needed to maintain and repair CAT scans, electrocardiograms, magnetic resonance imaging, ultrasounds, X-ray machines, and other new equipment. They also will be needed to maintain and repair the sophisticated machines that private practitioners and technicians use to diagnose and treat problems with eyes, teeth, and other parts of the body. Some repairers will be needed to maintain and repair less complex health equipment, such as electric beds and wheelchairs.

Job Prospects. A combination of rapid employment growth and the need to replace workers who leave the occupation each year will result in excellent job opportunities over the coming decade.

Candidates who have an associate's degree in biomedical equipment technology or engineering should have the best job prospects. Job opportunities should be even better for those who are willing to relocate, because often there are relatively few qualified applicants in rural areas.

Contacts for More Information

For more information about medical equipment repairers, including a listing of schools offering related programs of study and information about certification, visit

- Association for the Advancement of Medical Instrumentation (www.aami.org)
- Federation of Medical Equipment Support Associations (www.fmesa.org)
- Medical Equipment & Technology Association (www.mymeta.org)

O*NET

- Medical Equipment Repairers (49-9062.00)

Small Engine Mechanics

- **2014 Median Pay** .... $34,130 per year
$16.41 per hour
- **Typical Entry-Level Education** .... See Education/Training
- **Work Experience in a Related Occupation** .... None
- **On-the-job Training** .... See Education/Training
- **Number of Jobs, 2014** 71,700
- **Job Outlook, 2014–24** .... 4% (Slower than average)
- **Employment Change, 2014–24** 3,200

Motorcycle mechanics use hand tools to make needed adjustments and repairs.

What Small Engine Mechanics Do

Small engine mechanics inspect, service, and repair motorized power equipment. Mechanics often specialize in one type of equipment, such as motorcycles, motorboats, or outdoor power equipment.

Duties. Small engine mechanics typically do the following:

- Discuss equipment issues, maintenance plans, and work performed with customers
- Perform routine engine maintenance, such as lubricating parts and replacing spark plugs
- Test and inspect engines for malfunctioning parts
- Adjust components according to specifications
- Repair or replace worn, defective, or broken parts
- Reassemble and reinstall components and engines following repairs
- Keep records of inspections, test results, work performed, and parts used

Small engine mechanics work on power equipment ranging from snowmobiles to chainsaws. When equipment breaks down, mechanics use many strategies to diagnose the source and the extent of the problem. Small engine mechanics identify mechanical, electrical, and fuel system problems and make necessary repairs.

Mechanics' tasks vary in complexity and difficulty. Maintenance inspections and repairs, for example, involve minor adjustments or the replacement of a single part. On the other hand, piston calibration and spark plug replacement may require taking an engine apart completely. Some mechanics use computerized equipment to tune racing motorcycles and motorboats.

Mechanics use a variety of hand tools, including screwdrivers, wrenches, and pliers, for many common tasks. Some mechanics may also use compression gauges, ammeters, and voltmeters to test engine performance. For more complicated procedures, they commonly use pneumatic tools, which are powered by compressed air, or diagnostic equipment.

Although employers usually provide the more expensive tools and testing equipment, mechanics usually own their own hand tools. Some mechanics have thousands of dollars invested in their tool collections.

Motorboat mechanics and service technicians maintain and repair the mechanical and electrical components of boat engines. Most of their work, whether on small outboard engines or large diesel-powered inboard motors, is performed at docks and marinas where the repair shop is located. Motorboat mechanics may also work on propellers, steering mechanisms, marine plumbing, and other boat equipment.

Motorcycle mechanics specialize in working on motorcycles, scooters, mopeds, dirt bikes, and all-terrain vehicles. They service engines, transmissions, brakes, and ignition systems and make minor body repairs, among other tasks. Most work for dealerships, servicing and repairing specific makes and models.

Outdoor power equipment and other small engine mechanics service and repair outdoor power equipment, such as lawnmowers, edge trimmers, garden tractors, and portable generators. Some mechanics may work on snow blowers and snowmobiles, but this work is highly seasonal and regional.

For information about technicians and mechanics who work primarily on automobiles, see the profile on automotive service technicians and mechanics.

For information about technicians who work primarily on large trucks and buses, see the profile on diesel service technicians and mechanics.

For information about technicians and mechanics who work primarily on farm equipment, construction vehicles, and rail cars, see the profile on heavy vehicle and mobile equipment service technicians.

Work Environment

Small engine mechanics held about 71,700 jobs in 2014. Many of these workers—about 33 percent—were employed by other motor vehicle dealers, including motorcycle, boat, and other motor vehicle dealers. About 13 percent worked in lawn and garden equipment and supplies stores, and another 10 percent worked in personal and household goods repair and maintenance. About 1 in 10 were self-employed.

Small engine mechanics generally work in well-ventilated but noisy repair shops. They sometimes make onsite repair calls, which may require working in poor weather conditions. When repairing onboard engines, motorboat mechanics may work in cramped and uncomfortable positions.

Work Schedules. Most small engine mechanics work full time, although seasonal work hours often fluctuate.

Most mechanics are busiest during the spring and summer, when demand for work on equipment from lawnmowers to motorboats is the highest. During the peak seasons, some mechanics work many overtime hours. In contrast, some may only work part time during the winter, when demand for small engine work is lowest.

Many employers try to keep work more consistent by scheduling major repair work, such as engine rebuilds, during the off-season.

Education/Training

Small engine mechanics typically enter the occupation with a high school diploma or postsecondary nondegree award and learn their trade through on-the-job training. As motorized power equipment becomes more sophisticated, employers increasingly prefer to hire mechanics who have completed postsecondary education programs.

Education. Motorboat and outdoor power equipment mechanics typically begin work with a high school diploma and learn on the job, although some of them seek postsecondary education.

Median Annual Wages, May 2014

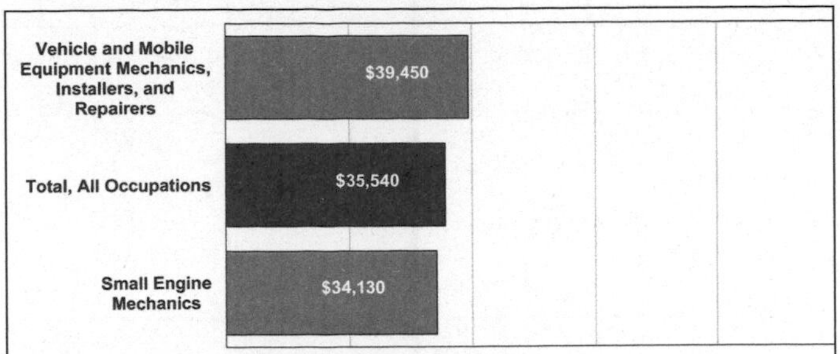

Note: All Occupations includes all occupations in the U.S. Economy.
Source: U.S. Bureau of Labor Statistics, Occupational Employment Statistics

Percent Change in Employment, Projected 2014–2024

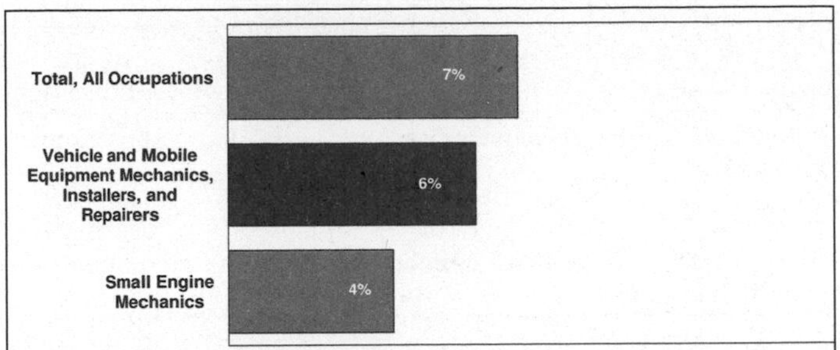

Note: All Occupations includes all occupations in the U.S. Economy.
Source: U.S. Bureau of Labor Statistics, Office of Occupational Statistics and Employment Projections

High school or vocational school courses in small engine repair and automobile mechanics are often beneficial.

Motorcycle mechanics typically complete postsecondary education programs in motorcycle repair, and employers prefer to hire these workers because they usually require significantly less on-the-job training.

Training. Trainees work closely with experienced mechanics while learning basic tasks, such as replacing spark plugs or disassembling engine components. As they gain experience, trainees move on to more difficult tasks, such as advanced computerized diagnosis and engine overhauls. Achieving competency may take anywhere from several months to 3 years, depending on a mechanic's specialization and ability.

Because of the increased complexity of boat and motorcycle engines, motorcycle and motorboat mechanics who do not complete postsecondary education often need more on-the-job training than outdoor power equipment mechanics.

Employers frequently send mechanics to training courses run by motorcycle, motorboat, and outdoor power equipment manufacturers and dealers, which teach mechanics the most up-to-date technology and techniques. Often, these courses are a prerequisite to performing warranty and manufacturer-specific work.

Licenses, Certifications, and Registrations. Many motorboat and motorcycle manufacturers offer certification specific to their own models, and certification from the Equipment & Engine Training Council is the recognized industry credential for outdoor power equipment mechanics. Although not required, certification can demonstrate a mechanic's competence and usually brings higher pay.

Motorcycle mechanics usually need a driver's license with a motorcycle endorsement.

Important Qualities

Customer-service skills. Small engine mechanics frequently discuss problems and necessary repairs with their customers. They must be courteous, good listeners, and ready to answer customers' questions.

Detail oriented. Small engine mechanics must be aware of small details when inspecting or repairing engines and components, because mechanical and electronic malfunctions are often due to misalignments and other easy-to-miss causes.

Dexterity. Small engine mechanics need a steady hand and good hand-eye coordination for many tasks, such as disassembling engine parts, connecting or attaching components, and using hand tools.

Mechanical skills. Small engine mechanics must be familiar with engine components and systems and know how they interact with each other. They often disassemble major parts for repairs, and they must be able to put them back together properly.

Organizational skills. Small engine mechanics keep workspaces clean and organized in order to maintain safety and ensure accountability for parts.

Troubleshooting skills. Small engine mechanics must be able to use diagnostic equipment on engine systems and components in order to identify and fix problems. They must be familiar with electronic control systems and the appropriate tools needed to fix and maintain them.

Pay

The median annual wage for small engine mechanics was $34,130 in May 2014. The median wage is the wage at which half the workers in an occupation earned more than that amount and half earned less. The lowest 10 percent earned less than $21,110, and the highest 10 percent earned more than $53,760.

Median annual wages for small engine mechanics in May 2014 were as follows:

Motorboat mechanics and service technicians	$37,340
Motorcycle mechanics	34,010
Outdoor power equipment and other small engine mechanics	32,120

Employment Projections Data for Small Engine Mechanics

Occupational Title	SOC Code	Employment, 2014	Projected Employment, 2024	Change, 2014–2024 Percent	Change, 2014–2024 Numeric
Small engine mechanics	49-3050	71,700	74,900	4	3,200
Motorboat mechanics and service technicians	49-3051	22,500	23,100	3	600
Motorcycle mechanics	49-3052	17,000	18,000	6	1,000
Outdoor power equipment and other small engine mechanics	49-3053	32,300	33,800	5	1,500

Source: U.S. Bureau of Labor Statistics, Employment Projections Program

Similar Occupations. This table shows a list of occupations with job duties that are similar to those of small engine mechanics.

Occupations	Entry-level Education	2014 Median Pay	Projected Job Growth	Average Annual Openings
Automotive Service Technicians and Mechanics	Postsecondary nondegree award	$37,120	5%	3,910
Diesel Service Technicians and Mechanics	High school diploma or equivalent	$43,630	12%	3,160
Heavy Vehicle and Mobile Equipment Service Technicians	High school diploma or equivalent	$45,930	5%	1,010

Job Outlook

Employment of small engine mechanics is projected to grow 4 percent from 2014 to 2024, slower than the average for all occupations. Growth rates will vary by specialty.

Since the number of registered motorcycles has increased steadily in recent years, there will continue to be a need for motorcycle repair services. As a result, employment of motorcycle mechanics is projected to grow 6 percent over the next 10 years, about as fast as the average for all occupations.

Because boat engines and engines and parts for outdoor power equipment have become more sophisticated and efficient, there will continue to be demand for repair services as people are less able to repair and service their own equipment. Employment of motorboat mechanics and service technicians is projected to grow 3 percent, slower than the average, while employment of outdoor power equipment and all other small engine mechanics is projected to grow 5 percent, about as fast as the average for all occupations.

Job Prospects. Job opportunities are expected to be best for candidates with postsecondary education. Those without postsecondary education can expect to face strong competition for jobs.

Contacts for More Information

For more information on motorboat mechanics and training programs, visit

➤ Association of Marine Technicians (www.am-tech.org)

For more information on outdoor power equipment and other small engine mechanics and training programs, visit

➤ Equipment & Engine Training Council (www.eetc.org)

To learn about job opportunities for small engine mechanics, contact local motorcycle, motorboat, and lawn and garden equipment dealers; boatyards; and marinas. Local offices of the state employment service also may have information about employment and training opportunities.

O*NET

➤ Motorboat Mechanics and Service Technicians (49-3051.00)

➤ Motorcycle Mechanics (49-3052.00)

➤ Outdoor Power Equipment and Other Small Engine Mechanics (49-3053.00)

Telecommunications Equipment Installers and Repairers

- **2014 Median Pay** .... $55,190 per year $26.53 per hour
- **Typical Entry-Level Education** .... Postsecondary nondegree award
- **Work Experience in a Related Occupation**.............. None
- **On-the-job Training**....... Moderate-term on-the-job training
- **Number of Jobs, 2014** 218,600
- **Job Outlook, 2014–24**............................... -4% (Decline)
- **Employment Change, 2014–24** .... -7,800

What Telecommunications Equipment Installers and Repairers Do

Telecommunications equipment installers and repairers, also known as *telecom technicians*, set up and maintain devices or equipment that carry communications signals, connect to telephone lines, and access the Internet.

Duties. Telecommunications equipment installers and repairers typically do the following:

- Install communications equipment in offices, private homes, and buildings that are under construction
- Set up, rearrange, and replace routing and dialing equipment
- Inspect and service equipment, wiring, and phone jacks
- Repair or replace faulty, damaged, and malfunctioning equipment
- Test repaired, newly installed, and updated equipment to ensure that it works properly
- Adjust or calibrate equipment settings to improve its performance
- Keep records of maintenance, repairs, and installations
- Demonstrate and explain the use of equipment to customers

Telephone, computer, and cable telecommunications systems rely on equipment to process and transmit vast amounts of data. Telecommunications equipment installers and repairers install and service this equipment.

These workers use many different tools to inspect equipment and diagnose problems. For instance, to locate distortions in signals, they may employ spectrum analyzers and polarity probes. They also commonly use hand tools, including screwdrivers and pliers, to take equipment apart and repair it.

Many telecom technicians also work with computers, specialized hardware, and other diagnostic equipment. They follow manufacturers' instructions or technical manuals to install or update software and programs for devices.

Telecommunications equipment installers and repairers who work at a client's location must track hours worked, parts used, and costs incurred. Workers who set up and maintain lines outdoors are classified as line installers and repairers.

The specific tasks of telecom technicians vary depending on their specialization and where they work.

Telecommunications equipment installers and repairers often use computers to diagnose problems with telecommunications switching equipment.

The following are examples of types of telecommunications equipment installers and repairers:

Central office technicians set up and maintain switches, routers, fiber optic cables, and other equipment at switching hubs, called central offices. These hubs send, process, and amplify data from thousands of telephone, Internet, and cable connections. Telecom technicians receive alerts on equipment malfunctions from auto-monitoring switches and are able to correct the problems remotely.

Headend technicians perform similar work to central office technicians, but work at distribution centers for cable and television companies, called headends. Headends are control centers in which technicians monitor signals for cable network companies that provide cable television and modem services to subscribers in the local area.

PBX installers and repairers set up and service private branch exchange (PBX) switchboards. This equipment relays incoming, outgoing, and interoffice telephone calls and may process Internet access and telephone communications, such as Voice over Internet Protocol (VoIP) technology.

PBX installers and repairers connect telecom equipment to communications cables. They test and repair the connections to ensure that adequate power is available and communication links work properly. They install and repair frames, supports, power systems, alarms, and telephone sets. Because switches and switchboards are computerized, PBX installers also install software or program the equipment.

Station installers and repairers—sometimes known as *home installers and repairers*—set up and repair telecommunications equipment in customers' homes and businesses. For example, they set up modems to install telephone, Internet, and cable television services.

When customers have problems, station repairers test the customer's lines to determine if the problem is inside the building or outside. If the problem is inside, they try to repair it. If the problem is outside, they refer the problem to line repairers.

Work Environment

Telecommunications equipment installers and repairers held about 218,600 jobs in 2014. The industries that employed the most telecommunications equipment installers and repairers were as follows:

Wired telecommunications carriers	61%
Specialty trade contractors	12
Cable and other subscription programming	4
Wireless telecommunications carriers (except satellite)	4

Some telecom technicians generally work in central offices or electronic service centers. They frequently travel to installation and repair sites, such as homes and offices. Equipment installation may require climbing on rooftops and into attics, and climbing ladders and telephone poles.

Telecom technicians occasionally work in cramped, awkward positions where they often stoop, crouch, crawl, or reach high to do their work. Sometimes they must lift or move heavy equipment and parts. They also may work on equipment while it is powered, so they need to take necessary precautions.

Injuries and Illnesses. Telecom technicians have a higher rate of injuries and illnesses than the national average. Common injuries include minor falls and electrical shocks.

To reduce risk of injury, workers wear hardhats and harnesses when working on ladders or on elevated equipment. To prevent electrical shocks, technicians also may lock off power to equipment under repair.

Work Schedules. Most telecom technicians work full time.

Some businesses offer 24-hour repair services. Telecom technicians in these companies work shifts, including evenings, holidays, and weekends. Some are on call around the clock in case of emergencies.

Education/Training

Telecommunications equipment installers and repairers typically need postsecondary education in electronics, telecommunications, or computer technology and receive on-the-job training. Industry certification is required for some positions.

Median Annual Wages, May 2014

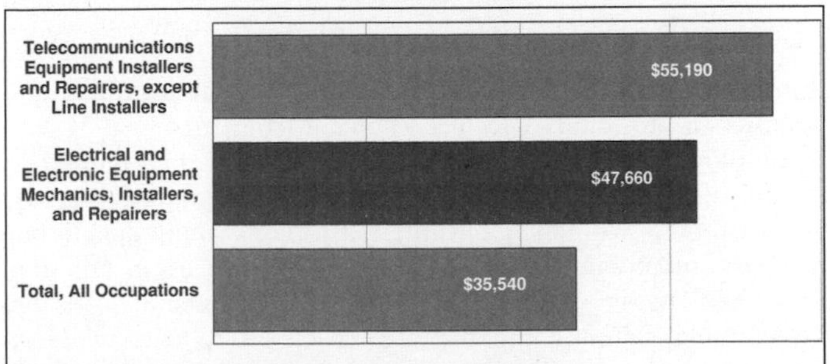

Note: All Occupations includes all occupations in the U.S. Economy.
Source: U.S. Bureau of Labor Statistics, Occupational Employment Statistics

Percent Change in Employment, Projected 2014–2024

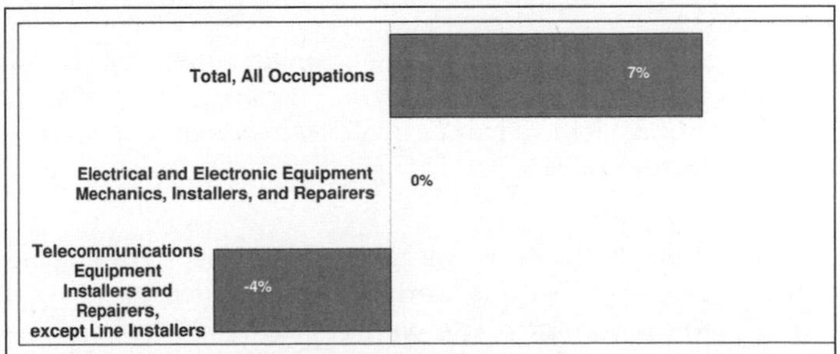

Note: All Occupations includes all occupations in the U.S. Economy.
Source: U.S. Bureau of Labor Statistics, Office of Occupational Statistics and Employment Projections

Employment Projections Data for Telecommunications Equipment Installers and Repairers

Occupational Title	SOC Code	Employment, 2014	Projected Employment, 2024	Change, 2014–2024 Percent	Change, 2014–2024 Numeric
Telecommunications equipment installers and repairers, except line installers	49-2022	218,600	210,800	-4	-7,800

Source: U.S. Bureau of Labor Statistics, Employment Projections Program

Similar Occupations. This table shows a list of occupations with job duties that are similar to those of telecommunications equipment installers and repairers.

Occupations	Entry-level Education	2014 Median Pay	Projected Job Growth	Average Annual Openings
Broadcast and Sound Engineering Technicians	See Education/Training	$41,350	7%	770
Line Installers and Repairers	High school diploma or equivalent	$61,740	6%	1,370

Education. Postsecondary education in electronics, telecommunications, or computers is typically needed for telecom technicians.

Technical instruction in basic electronics, telecommunications, and computer science offered in community colleges and technical schools may be particularly helpful. Most programs lead to a certificate or an associate's degree in electronics repair, computer science, or related subjects.

Some employers prefer to hire candidates with an associate's degree, particularly for positions such as central office technicians, headend technicians, and those working with commercial communications systems.

Training. Once hired, telecom technicians receive on-the-job training, typically lasting a few months. Training involves a combination of classroom instruction and hands-on work with an experienced technician. In these settings, workers learn the equipment's internal parts and the tools needed for repair. Technicians who have completed postsecondary education often require less on-the-job instruction than those who have not.

Some companies may send new employees to training sessions to learn about equipment, procedures, and technologies offered by equipment manufacturers or industry organizations.

Because technology in this field constantly changes, telecom technicians must continue learning about new equipment over the course of their careers.

Licenses, Certifications, and Registrations. Some technicians must be certified to perform certain tasks or to work on specific equipment. Certification requirements vary by employer and specialization.

Organizations, such as the Society of Cable Telecommunications Engineers, offer certifications for telecom technicians. Some manufacturers also provide certifications for working with specific equipment.

Advancement. Advancement opportunities often depend on previous work experience and training. Repairers with extensive knowledge of equipment may be qualified to become manufacturing sales representatives.

Important Qualities

Color vision. Telecom technicians must be able to distinguish different colors because they work with color-coded wires.

Customer-service skills. Telecom technicians who work in customers' homes and offices should be friendly and polite. They must be able to teach people how to maintain and operate communications equipment.

Dexterity. Telecom technicians' tasks, such as repairing small devices, connecting components, and using hand tools, require a steady hand and good hand-eye coordination.

Mechanical skills. Telecom technicians must be familiar with the devices they install and repair, their internal parts, and the appropriate tools needed to use, install, or fix them. They must also be able to understand manufacturers' instructions when installing or repairing equipment.

Troubleshooting skills. Telecom technicians must be able to troubleshoot and devise solutions to problems that are not immediately apparent.

Pay

The median annual wage for telecommunications equipment installers and repairers was $55,190 in May 2014. The median wage is the wage at which half the workers in an occupation earned more than that amount and half earned less. The lowest 10 percent earned less than $30,610, and the highest 10 percent earned more than $77,200.

In May 2014, the median annual wages for telecommunications equipment installers and repairers in the top industries in which they worked were as follows:

Wired telecommunications carriers	$58,660
Wireless telecommunications carriers (except satellite)	58,440
Cable and other subscription programming	49,910
Specialty trade contractors	44,210

Some businesses offer 24-hour repair services. Telecom technicians in these companies work shifts, including evenings, holidays, and weekends. Some are on call around the clock in case of emergencies.

Job Outlook

Employment of telecommunications equipment installers and repairers is projected to decline 4 percent from 2014 to 2024.

Employment is declining in the telecommunications industries, specifically in wired telecommunications carriers, which employs most of these workers. Consumers are increasingly demanding wireless and mobile services, which often require less installation, instead of landline-based services. This shift in demand means that telecommunications companies are expected to require fewer telecommunications equipment installers. In addition, as equipment is becoming sturdier and requiring fewer repairs, employment of telecommunications equipment installers and repairers may decline further.

Job Prospects. Some job opportunities should come from the need to replace workers who leave the occupation. Although job opportunities will vary by specialty, those with an associate degree and strong customer-service skills should have the best job prospects.

Technologies such as mobile video streaming and broadband Internet require high data transfer rates in telecommunications systems. Central office, PBX installers, and headend technicians will be needed to service and upgrade switches and routers to handle increased usage and volume, resulting in very good job opportunities.

Contacts for More Information

For information about career, training, and certification opportunities for telecommunications equipment installers and repairers, visit

- Communications Workers of America (www.cwa-union.org)
- International Brotherhood of Electrical Workers (www.ibew.org)
- National Coalition for Telecommunications Education and Learning (www.nactel.org)
- Society of Cable Telecommunications Engineers (www.scte.org/default.aspx)
- Telecommunications Industry Association (www.tiaonline.org)

O*NET

- Telecommunications Equipment Installers and Repairers, Except Line Installers (49-2022.00)

Wind Turbine Technicians

- **2014 Median Pay** .... $48,800 per year
  $23.46 per hour
- **Typical Entry-Level Education** .... Some college, no degree
- **Work Experience in a Related Occupation** .... None
- **On-the-job Training** .... Long-term on-the-job training
- **Number of Jobs, 2014** 4,400
- **Job Outlook, 2014–24** .... 108% (Much faster than average)
- **Employment Change, 2014–24** 4,800

What Wind Turbine Technicians Do

Wind turbine service technicians, also known as *windtechs*, install, maintain, and repair wind turbines.

Duties. Wind turbine service technicians typically do the following:

- Inspect the exterior and physical integrity of towers
- Climb towers to inspect or repair wind turbine equipment
- Perform routine maintenance on wind turbines
- Test and troubleshoot electrical, mechanical, and hydraulic components and systems
- Replace worn or malfunctioning components
- Collect turbine data for testing or research and analysis
- Service underground transmission systems, wind field substations, or fiber optic sensing and control systems

Wind turbines are large mechanical devices that convert wind energy into electricity. They are located in areas where there is consistent wind. The turbine is made up of three major components: a tower, three blades, and a nacelle, which is composed of an outer case, generator, gearbox, and brakes. Wind turbine service technicians install and repair the various components of these structures.

Although some windtechs are involved in building new wind turbines, most of their work is in maintaining them, particularly the nacelles, which contain the equipment that generates electricity.

Maintenance schedules are largely determined by a turbine's hours in operation, but can also vary by manufacturer. Turbines are monitored electronically from a central office, 24 hours a day. When a problem is detected, windtechs travel to the worksite and make the repairs. Most manufacturers recommend annual maintenance, which includes inspecting components and lubricating parts. For turbines that operate year round, routine maintenance may occur one to three times a year.

Windtechs use safety harnesses and a variety of hand and power tools to do their work. They also use computers to diagnose electrical malfunctions. Most turbine monitoring equipment is located in the nacelle, which can be accessed both on- and offsite.

Work Environment

Wind turbine technicians held about 4,400 jobs in 2014. The industries that employed the most wind turbine technicians were as follows:

Electric power generation, transmission and distribution	24%
Commercial and industrial machinery and equipment (except automotive and electronic) repair and maintenance	23
Utility system construction	23

Windtechs generally work outdoors, often at great heights and with a partner. For example, when repairing blades, windtechs rappel—or descend by sliding down a rope—from the nacelle to the section of the blade that needs servicing. To reach the mechanical equipment, workers must climb ladders—sometimes more than 260 feet tall—while wearing a fall protection harness and carrying tools. When maintaining mechanical systems, windtechs work in the confined space of the nacelle.

Because many wind farms are located away from urban areas, windtechs often are their own first responders in the event of an accident.

For major service or repairs, additional windtechs and other specialists, such as electricians, may be needed to complete the job quickly.

Because they work at high elevations, wind turbine technicians must wear proper equipment to stay safe on the job.

Median Annual Wages, May 2014

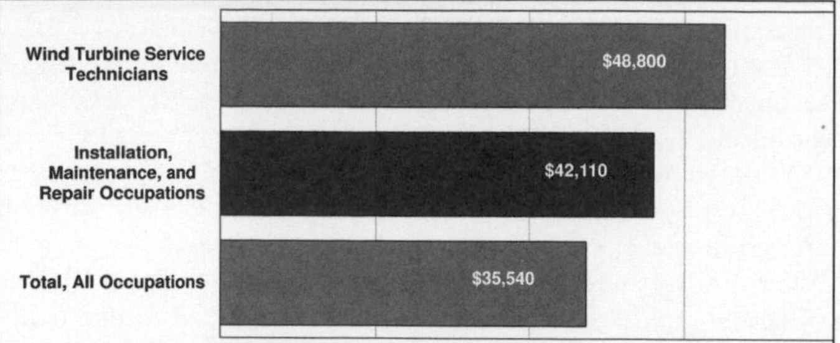

Note: All Occupations includes all occupations in the U.S. Economy.
Source: U.S. Bureau of Labor Statistics, Occupational Employment Statistics

Percent Change in Employment, Projected 2014–2024

Note: All Occupations includes all occupations in the U.S. Economy.
Source: U.S. Bureau of Labor Statistics, Office of Occupational Statistics and Employment Projections

Work Schedules. Although the majority of windtechs work full time, they may also be on call to handle emergencies during evenings and weekends.

When a wind turbine is not functioning, technicians must find the problem and make the necessary repairs as quickly as possible.

Windtechs often travel to rural areas, where many wind farms are located.

Education/Training

Most wind turbine service technicians, also known as windtechs, learn their trade by attending a technical school. They are also trained by their employer after hiring.

Education. Most windtechs learn their trade by attending technical schools. Many workers complete their coursework, although strong demand leads some employers to hire windtech interns before they graduate. Associate's degree programs for wind turbine service technicians usually take 2 years and are offered at technical schools and community colleges.

Many technical schools have onsite wind turbines that students can work on as part of their studies. In addition to lab coursework, other areas of focus that reflect the various skill sets needed to do the job include the following:

- High angle rescue, safety, first aid, and CPR training
- Electrical maintenance
- Hydraulic maintenance
- Braking systems
- Mechanical systems, including blade inspection and maintenance
- Computers and programmable logic control systems

Training. In addition to associate's degree coursework, windtechs typically receive more than 12 months of on-the-job training related to the specific wind turbines they will maintain and service. Part of this training is manufacturer training. Other training may include an internship with a wind turbine servicing contractor.

Some windtechs are former electricians. Regardless of experience, all candidates must complete wind turbine training in addition to any other construction training they may already have. For example, the International Brotherhood of Electrical Workers offers intensive courses that provide wind turbine training specifically for journey electricians.

Other windtechs learn their trade through an apprenticeship. For each year of the program, apprentices must have at least 144 hours of related technical instruction and 2,000 hours of paid on-the-job training. With prior experience or training, the time spent in apprenticeship may be reduced. Apprenticeships focus on safety, first aid, and CPR training; electrical, hydraulic, and mechanical systems maintenance; braking systems; and computers and programmable logic control systems.

Unions and individual contractors offer apprenticeship programs. The basic qualifications for workers to enter an apprenticeship program are the following:

- Minimum age of 18
- High school diploma or equivalent
- Physically and mentally able to do the job
- One year of high school or equivalent algebra with at least a grade of "C"

Licenses, Certifications, and Registrations. Although not mandatory, certification can demonstrate a basic level of knowledge and professionalism. The Electronics Technicians Association, International offers certification for those who install small wind towers, such as backyard turbines.

Important Qualities

Detail oriented. Windtechs must maintain records of all of the services that are performed. Turbine maintenance requires precise measurements, a strict order of operations, and numerous safety procedures.

Mechanical skills. Windtechs must understand and be able to maintain and repair all mechanical, hydraulic, braking, and electrical systems of a turbine.

Physical stamina. Windtechs must be able to climb to the tops of turbines, often with tools and equipment. Some tower ladders may be 260 feet high or taller.

Physical strength. Windtechs must lift heavy equipment, parts, and tools, some of which weigh in excess of 45 pounds.

Employment Projections Data for Wind Turbine Technicians

Occupational Title	SOC Code	Employment, 2014	Projected Employment, 2024	Change, 2014–2024 Percent	Numeric
Wind turbine service technicians	49-9081	4,400	9,200	108	4,800

Source: U.S. Bureau of Labor Statistics, Employment Projections Program

Similar Occupations. This table shows a list of occupations with job duties that are similar to those of wind turbine technicians.

Occupations	Entry-level Education	2014 Median Pay	Projected Job Growth	Average Annual Openings
Electrical and Electronics Installers and Repairers	Postsecondary nondegree award	$53,900	-4%	-540
Electricians	High school diploma or equivalent	$51,110	14%	8,590
Elevator Installers and Repairers	High school diploma or equivalent	$78,620	13%	270
Heating, Air Conditioning, and Refrigeration Mechanics and Installers	Postsecondary nondegree award	$44,630	14%	3,960
Industrial Machinery Mechanics, Machinery Maintenance Workers, and Millwrights	High school diploma or equivalent	$47,450	16%	7,340
Plumbers, Pipefitters, and Steamfitters	High school diploma or equivalent	$50,660	12%	4,910

Troubleshooting skills. Windtechs must diagnose and repair problems. When a turbine performs abnormally, technicians must determine the cause and make the necessary repairs.

Unafraid of heights and confined spaces. Windtechs repair turbines that are often at least 260 feet high, and they must work in confined spaces in order to access mechanical components of the turbine.

Pay

The median annual wage for wind turbine technicians was $48,800 in May 2014. The median wage is the wage at which half the workers in an occupation earned more than that amount and half earned less. The lowest 10 percent earned less than $36,350, and the highest 10 percent earned more than $70,770.

In May 2014, the median annual wages for wind turbine technicians in the top industries in which they worked were as follows:

Electric power generation, transmission and distribution $53,470
Commercial and industrial machinery and equipment (except automotive and electronic) repair and maintenance 49,000
Utility system construction 45,500

Apprentices' wages start at 60 percent of a fully trained windtech's wages. Apprentices receive pay increases as they learn to do more.

Job Outlook

Employment of wind turbine service technicians, also known as *windtechs*, is projected to grow 108 percent from 2014 to 2024, much faster than the average for all occupations. However, because it is a small occupation, the fast growth will result in only about 4,800 new jobs over the 10-year period.

Development of taller towers with larger blades has reduced the cost of wind power generation, making it more competitive with coal, natural gas, and other forms of power generation. As additional wind turbines are erected, more windtechs will be needed to install and maintain turbines.

The most consistent winds are found offshore, and several offshore wind projects are currently being explored. If approved and developed, many more technicians will be needed.

Job Prospects. Job prospects for qualified windtechs are expected to be excellent. The number of wind turbines being installed is increasing, which should result in continuing demand for windtechs. There is also a shortage of qualified workers in some areas. Because many people prefer not to work in confined spaces or at great heights, competition for jobs is lessened.

Job opportunities vary by individual state. Wind farms are generally more prevalent in the Great Plains, the Midwest, and along coasts, and windtechs will likely find more job opportunities in these areas.

Contacts for More Information

For details about apprenticeships or other work opportunities in this trade, contact the offices of the state employment service, the state apprenticeship agency, local electrical contractors or firms that employ windtechs, or local union–management apprenticeship committees. Apprenticeship information is available from the U.S. Department of Labor's ApprenticeshipUSA program (www.dol.gov/apprenticeship) online or by phone at 877-872-5627.

For more information about union apprenticeship and training programs for electricians, visit

- International Brotherhood of Electrical Workers (www.ibew.org)

For more information about other educational opportunities and certification, visit

- American Wind Energy Association (http://awea.org)
- Electronics Technicians Association, International (www.eta-i.org)

O*NET

- Wind Turbine Service Technicians (49-9081.00)

Legal

Arbitrators, Mediators, and Conciliators

- **2014 Median Pay** ..... $57,180 per year, $27.49 per hour
- **Typical Entry-Level Education** ..... Bachelor's degree
- **Work Experience in a Related Occupation** ..... Less than 5 years
- **On-the-job Training** ..... Moderate-term on-the-job training
- **Number of Jobs, 2014** 8,400
- **Job Outlook, 2014–24** ..... 9% (Faster than average)
- **Employment Change, 2014–24** 800

What Arbitrators, Mediators, and Conciliators Do

Arbitrators, mediators, and conciliators facilitate negotiation and dialogue between disputing parties to help resolve conflicts outside of the court system.

Duties. Arbitrators, mediators, and conciliators typically do the following:

- Facilitate communication between disputants to guide parties toward mutual agreement
- Clarify issues, concerns, needs, and interests of all parties involved
- Conduct initial meetings with disputants to outline the arbitration process
- Settle procedural matters such as fees, or determine details such as witness numbers and time requirements
- Set up appointments for parties to meet for mediation or arbitration
- Interview claimants, agents, or witnesses to obtain information about disputed issues
- Prepare settlement agreements for disputants to sign
- Apply relevant laws, regulations, policies, or precedents to reach conclusions
- Evaluate information from documents such as claim applications, birth or death certificates, and physician or employer records

Arbitrators, mediators, and conciliators help opposing parties settle disputes outside of court. They hold private, confidential hearings, which are less formal than a court trial.

Arbitrators are usually attorneys, business professionals, or retired judges with expertise in a particular field. As impartial third parties, they hear and decide disputes between opposing parties. Arbitrators may work alone or in a panel with other arbitrators. In some cases, arbitrators may decide procedural issues, such as what evidence may be submitted and when hearings will be held.

Arbitration may be required by law for some claims and disputes. When it is not thus required, the parties in dispute sometimes voluntarily agree to arbitration rather than proceed with litigation or a trial. In some cases, parties may appeal the arbitrator's decision.

Mediators are neutral parties who help people resolve their disputes. However, unlike arbitrators, they do not make decisions. Rather, mediators help facilitate discussion and guide the parties toward a mutually acceptable agreement. If the opposing sides cannot reach a settlement with the mediator's help, they are free to pursue other options.

Conciliators are similar to mediators. Their role is to help guide opposing sides to a settlement. However, they typically meet with the parties separately. The opposing sides must decide in advance if they will be bound by the conciliator's recommendations. The conciliator typically has no authority to seek evidence or call witnesses, nor do they usually write decisions or make awards.

Work Environment

Arbitrators, mediators, and conciliators held about 8,400 jobs in 2014. The industries that employed the most arbitrators, mediators, and conciliators were as follows:

Legal services	19%
Local government, excluding education and hospitals	15
State government, excluding education and hospitals	15
Religious, grantmaking, civic, professional, and similar organizations	5
Finance and insurance	4

They may travel to a neutral site chosen for negotiations.

Work Schedules. Most arbitrators, mediators, and conciliators work full time. However, some may work part time and also may have other occupations or careers.

Education/Training

Arbitrators, mediators, and conciliators learn their skills through a combination of education, training, and work experience.

Education. Education is one part of becoming an arbitrator, mediator, or conciliator. Some colleges and universities offer certificate programs, 2-year master's degrees, or doctoral degree programs in dispute or conflict resolution. However, few candidates receive a degree specific to the field of arbitration, mediation, or

Arbitrators, mediators, and conciliators resolve disputes and facilitate negotiations between parties.

Median Annual Wages, May 2014

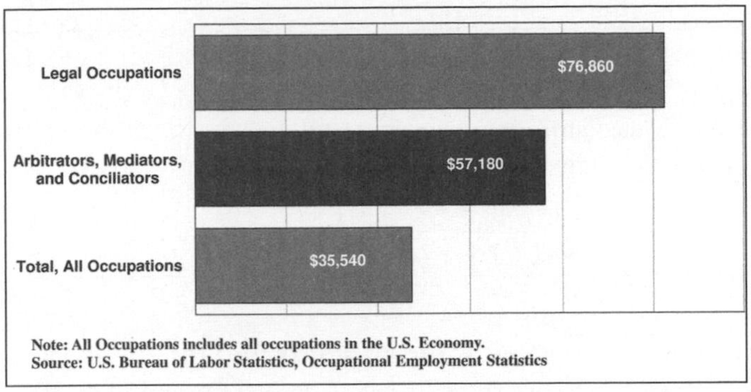

Percent Change in Employment, Projected 2014–2024

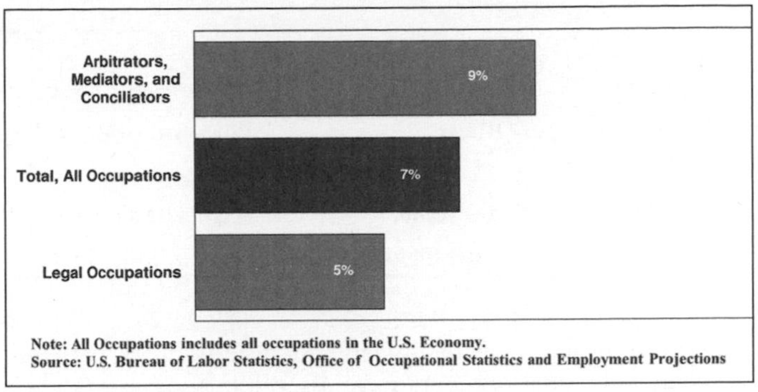

conflict resolution. Instead, applicants may use these programs to supplement their existing educational degree and work experience in other fields.

Rather, many positions require an educational degree appropriate to the applicant's field of expertise, and a bachelor's degree is often sufficient. Many other positions, however, require applicants to have a law degree, a master's in business administration, or some other advanced degree.

Work Experience in a Related Occupation. Arbitrators, mediators, and conciliators are usually lawyers, retired judges, or business professionals with expertise in a particular field, such as construction or insurance. They need to have knowledge of that industry and be able to relate well to people from different cultures and backgrounds.

Training. Although there are no state requirements for mediators working in private settings, mediators typically must meet specific training or experience standards to practice in state-funded or court-appointed mediation cases. Qualifications and standards vary by state or by court. However, most states require mediators to complete 20 to 40 hours of training courses. Some states require additional hours of training in a specialty area.

Some states also require mediators to work under the supervision of an experienced mediator for a certain number of cases before becoming qualified.

Training for arbitrators, mediators, and conciliators is available through independent mediation programs, national and local mediation membership organizations, and postsecondary schools. Training is also available by volunteering at a community mediation center.

Licenses, Certifications, and Registrations. There is no national license for arbitrators, mediators, and conciliators. However, as with training requirements, some states require arbitrators and mediators to become certified to work on certain types of cases. State requirements vary widely.

Some states require licenses appropriate to the applicant's field of expertise. For example, some courts may require applicants to be licensed attorneys or certified public accountants.

Important Qualities

Critical-thinking skills. Arbitrators, mediators, and conciliators must apply rules of law. They must remain neutral and not let their own personal assumptions interfere with the proceedings.

Decision-making skills. Arbitrators, mediators, and conciliators must be able to weigh facts, apply the law or rules, and make a decision relatively quickly.

Interpersonal skills. Arbitrators, mediators, and conciliators deal with disputing parties and must be able to facilitate discussion in a calm and respectful way.

Listening skills. Arbitrators, mediators, and conciliators must pay close attention to what is being said in order for them to evaluate information.

Reading skills. Arbitrators, mediators, and conciliators must be able to evaluate and distinguish important facts from large amounts of complex information.

Writing skills. Arbitrators, mediators, and conciliators write recommendations or decisions relating to appeals or disputes. They must be able to write their decisions clearly so that all sides understand the decision.

Pay

The median annual wage for arbitrators, mediators, and conciliators was $57,180 in May 2014. The median wage is the wage at which half the workers in an occupation earned more than that amount and half earned less. The lowest 10 percent earned less than $33,200, and the highest 10 percent earned more than $121,050.

In May 2014, the median annual wages for arbitrators, mediators, and conciliators in the top industries in which they worked were as follows:

Finance and insurance	$67,860
Local government, excluding education and hospitals	61,340
State government, excluding education and hospitals	59,720
Religious, grantmaking, civic, professional, and similar organizations	56,010
Legal services	55,720

Employment Projections Data for Arbitrators, Mediators, and Conciliators

Occupational Title	SOC Code	Employment, 2014	Projected Employment, 2024	Change, 2014–2024 Percent	Change, 2014–2024 Numeric
Arbitrators, mediators, and conciliators	23-1022	8,400	9,200	9	800

Source: U.S. Bureau of Labor Statistics, Employment Projections Program

Similar Occupations. This table shows a list of occupations with job duties that are similar to those of arbitrators, mediators, and conciliators.

Occupations	Entry-level Education	2014 Median Pay	Projected Job Growth	Average Annual Openings
Judges and Hearing Officers	Doctoral or professional degree	$102,380	-1%	-40
Lawyers	Doctoral or professional degree	$114,970	6%	4,380
Paralegals and Legal Assistants	Associate's degree	$48,350	8%	2,120
Private Detectives and Investigators	High school diploma or equivalent	$44,570	5%	180

Some arbitrators, mediators, and conciliators work part time and may have other occupations or careers.

Job Outlook

Employment of arbitrators, mediators, and conciliators is projected to grow 9 percent from 2014 to 2024, faster than the average for all occupations. However, because it is a small occupation, the fast growth will result in only about 800 new jobs over the 10-year period.

Arbitration and other alternative dispute resolution methods often are seen as faster and less expensive than trials and litigation. In addition, many contracts, including employment, customer, and real estate contracts, include clauses requiring complaints and disputes to be decided through mediation or arbitration.

However, many arbitrators, mediators, and conciliators work for state or local governments, and budgetary constraints may limit employment growth. Also, in some cases or industries, litigation is unavoidable or its benefits are preferred over the benefits gained in other types of conflict resolution.

Job Prospects. Because arbitrators, mediators, and conciliators deal extensively with legal issues and disputes, those with a law degree should have better job prospects. In addition, lawyers with expertise or experience in one or more particular legal areas, such as environmental, health, or corporate law, should have the best job prospects.

Contacts for More Information

For more information about arbitrators, mediators, and conciliators, visit

➤ American Arbitration Association (http://tinyurl.com/z8m8qa9)
➤ Association for Conflict Resolution (http://tinyurl.com/hhk8qb2)
➤ Mediation Training Institute International (www.mediationworks.com)

O*NET

➤ Arbitrators, Mediators, and Conciliators (23-1022.00)

Court Reporters

- **2014 Median Pay** .... $49,860 per year $23.97 per hour
- **Typical Entry-Level Education** .... Postsecondary nondegree award
- **Work Experience in a Related Occupation** .... None
- **On-the-job Training** .... Short-term on-the-job training
- **Number of Jobs, 2014** 20,800
- **Job Outlook, 2014–24** .... 2% (Slower than average)
- **Employment Change, 2014–24** 300

What Court Reporters Do

Court reporters create word-for-word transcriptions at trials, depositions, administrative hearings, and other legal proceedings. Some court reporters provide captioning for television and real-time translation for deaf or hard-of-hearing people at public events, in business meetings, and in classrooms.

Duties. Court reporters typically do the following:

- Attend depositions, hearings, proceedings, and other events that require written transcripts
- Capture spoken dialogue with specialized equipment, including stenography machines, video and audio recording devices, and covered microphones
- Report speakers' identification, gestures, and actions
- Read or play back all or a portion of the proceedings upon request from the judge
- Ask speakers to clarify inaudible or unclear statements or testimony
- Review the notes they have taken regarding the names of speakers and any technical terminology they used
- Edit transcripts for typographical errors
- Provide copies of transcripts and recordings to the courts, counsels, and parties involved
- Transcribe television or movie dialogue onto screens to help deaf or hard-of-hearing viewers
- Provide real-time translation in classes and other public forums in which deaf or hard-of-hearing students and other individuals are participating

Court reporters create word-for-word transcripts of speeches, conversations, legal proceedings, meetings, or other events.

Court reporters play a critical role in legal proceedings, which require an exact record of what was said. They are responsible for producing a complete, accurate, and secure legal transcript of courtroom proceedings, witnesses' testimonies, and depositions.

Court reporters in the legal setting also help judges and attorneys by capturing, organizing, and producing the official record of the proceedings. The official record allows users to efficiently search for important information contained in the transcript. Court reporters also index and catalog exhibits used during court proceedings.

Some court reporters, however, do not work in the legal setting or in courtrooms. These reporters primarily serve people who are deaf or hard-of-hearing by transcribing speech to text as the speech occurs.

The following are examples of types of court reporters who do not work in the legal setting:

Broadcast captioners are court reporters who provide captions for television programs (called closed captions). These reporters transcribe dialogue onto television monitors to help deaf or hard-of-hearing viewers or others viewing television programs in public places. Some broadcast captioners may translate dialogue in real time during broadcasts; others may caption during the postproduction of a program.

Communication Access Real-Time Translation (CART) providers are court reporters who work primarily with deaf or hard-of-hearing people in a variety of settings. They assist clients during board meetings, doctor's appointments, or any other events in which real-time translation is needed. For example, CART providers may caption the dialogue of high school and college classes and provide an immediate transcript to students who are hard-of-hearing or who are learning English as a second language.

Although some court reporters may accompany their clients to events, many broadcast captioners and CART providers work remotely. An Internet or phone connection allows them to hear and type without having to be in the room.

Court reporters who work with deaf or hard-of-hearing people turn speech into text. For information on workers who help deaf or hard-of-hearing people through sign language, cued speech, or other spoken or gestural means, see the profile on interpreters and translators.

Court reporters may use different methods for recording speech, such as stenotype machine recording, steno mask recording, and electronic recording.

Court reporters use stenotype machines to record dialogue as it is spoken. Stenotype machines work like keyboards, but create words through key combinations rather than single characters, allowing court reporters to keep up with fast-moving dialogue. Court reporters who use stenotype machines are known as *stenographers*.

Key combinations entered on a stenotype machine are recorded in a computer program. The program uses computer-assisted transcription to translate the key combinations into the words and phrases they represent, creating real-time, readable text. The court reporter then reviews the text for accuracy and corrects spelling and grammatical errors.

Voice writers record everything that is said by judges, witnesses, attorneys, and others in a court proceeding, and prepare written transcripts.

Court reporters also may use steno masks to transcribe speech. Court reporters who use steno masks speak directly into a covered microphone, recording dialogue and reporting gestures and actions. Because the microphone is covered, others cannot hear what the reporter is saying. The recording is sometimes converted by computerized voice-recognition software into a transcript that the court reporter reviews for accuracy, spelling, and grammar.

For both stenotype machine recording and steno mask recording, court reporters must create, maintain, and continuously update an online dictionary that the computer software uses to transcribe the key presses or voice recordings into text. For example, court reporters may put in the names of people involved in a court case or the specific words or specialized, technical jargon that are typically used in that type of legal proceeding.

Court reporters also may use digital recorders in their job. Digital recording creates an audio or video record rather than a written transcript. Court reporters who use digital recorders operate and monitor the recording equipment. They also take notes to identify the speakers and provide context for the recording. In some cases, court reporters use the audio recording to create a written transcript.

Work Environment

Court reporters held about 20,800 jobs in 2014. The industries that employed the most court reporters were as follows:

Local government, excluding education and hospitals	34%
State government, excluding education and hospitals	32
Business support services	24

Many court reporters work for state or local government in courts or legislatures. Many also work as freelance reporters and are hired by law firms or corporations for pretrial depositions and other events on an as-needed basis.

Many court reporters must travel to various courthouses or offices in different locations. However, some broadcast captioners and Communication Access Real-Time Translation (CART) providers work remotely from either their home or a central office.

Because of the speed and accuracy required to capture a verbatim record and the time-sensitive nature of legal proceedings, some court reporting positions may be stressful.

Work Schedules. Court reporters who work in a court setting typically work full time recording events and preparing transcripts. Freelance reporters have more flexibility in setting their work schedules.

Education/Training

Many community colleges and technical institutes offer postsecondary certificate programs for court reporters. Many states require court reporters who work in legal settings to be licensed by a state or certified by a professional association.

Education. Many court reporters receive formal training at community colleges or technical institutes, which have different programs that lead to either a certificate or an associate's degree in court reporting. Either degree will qualify applicants for many entry-level positions. Certification programs prepare students to pass the licensing exams and typing-speed tests required by most states and employers.

Most court reporting programs include courses in English grammar and phonetics, legal procedures, and legal terminology.

Students also practice preparing transcripts to improve the speed and accuracy of their work.

Some schools also offer training in the use of different transcription machines, such as stenotype machines or steno masks.

Graduating from a court reporting program can take between 2 and 5 years.

Licenses, Certifications, and Registrations. Many states require court reporters who work in legal settings to be licensed or certified by a professional association. Licensing requirements vary by state and by method of court reporting.

The National Court Reporters Association (NCRA) offers certification for court reporters, broadcast captioners, and Communication Access Real-Time Translation (CART) providers. Currently, 22 states accept or use the Registered Professional Reporter (RPR) certification in place of a state certification or licensing exam.

Digital and voice reporters may obtain certification through the American Association of Electronic Reporters and Transcribers (AAERT), which offers the Certified Electronic Reporter (CER) and Certified Electronic Transcriber (CET) designations.

Voice reporters may also obtain certification through the National Verbatim Reporters Association (NVRA). As with the RPR designation, some states with certification or licensing requirements will accept the NVRA designation in place of the state license.

Certification through the NCRA, AAERT, and NVRA all require the successful completion of a written test, as well as a skills test in which applicants must type, record, or transcribe a minimum number of words per minute with a high level of accuracy.

In addition, all associations require court reporters to obtain a certain amount of continuing education credits in order to renew their certification.

For more information on certification, exam, and continuing education requirements, visit the specific association's website. State licensing and continuing education requirements can be found by visiting the state association's or state judicial agency's website.

Training. After completing their formal program, court reporters must undergo a few weeks of on-the-job training. This typically includes additional skills training as well as training on the more technical terminology that may be used during complex medical or legal proceedings.

Important Qualities

Concentration. Court reporters must be able to concentrate for long periods. They must remain focused on the dialogue they are recording, even in the presence of auditory distractions.

Detail oriented. Court reporters must be able to produce error-free work, because they create transcripts that serve as legal records.

Listening skills. Court reporters must give their full attention to speakers and capture every word that is said.

Writing skills. Court reporters need a good command of grammar, vocabulary, and punctuation.

Pay

The median annual wage for court reporters was $49,860 in May 2014. The median wage is the wage at which half the workers in an occupation earned more than that amount and half earned less. The lowest 10 percent earned less than $26,670, and the highest 10 percent earned more than $94,140.

In May 2014, the median annual wages for court reporters in the top industries in which they worked were as follows:

Local government, excluding education and hospitals	$54,940
State government, excluding education and hospitals	51,890
Business support services	41,680

Freelance court reporters are paid for their time, but can also sell their transcripts per page for an additional profit.

Job Outlook

Employment of court reporters is projected to grow 2 percent from 2014 to 2024, slower than the average for all occupations. Demand for court reporters will be influenced by new federal regulations requiring an expanded use of captioning for television, the Internet, and other technologies.

Reporters will increasingly be needed for captioning outside of legal proceedings. All new television programming will continue to need closed captioning. In addition, new federal regulations have expanded captioning requirements and set quality and accuracy standards for both live and prerecorded programs. Networks will likely increase their use of broadcast captioners in order to comply with these new federal regulations.

Growth of the elderly population also will increase demand for court reporters who are Communication Access Real-Time Translation (CART) providers or who can accompany their clients to doctor's appointments, town hall meetings, and religious services. In addition, movie theaters and sports stadiums will provide closed captioning for deaf or hard-of-hearing customers.

Employment growth, however, may be somewhat limited because of budgetary constraints in state and local governments. Although local and state revenue and spending have increased since the end of the recession, continued budget uncertainty and other spending obligations may lead to only modest growth in government hiring.

The increased use of digital audio recording technology also may hinder employment growth. Some states already have replaced stenographic court reporters with this technology; other states are

Median Annual Wages, May 2014

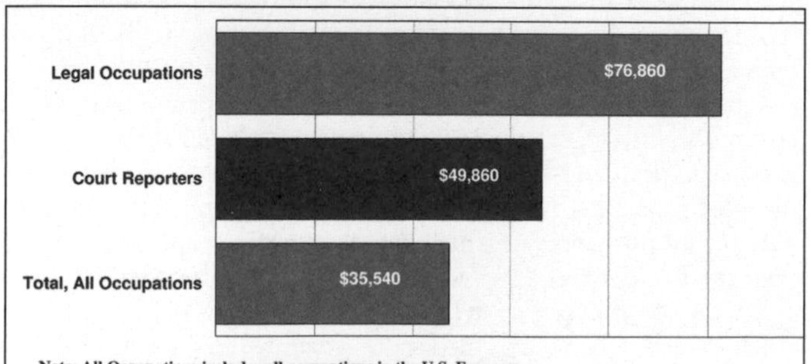

Note: All Occupations includes all occupations in the U.S. Economy.
Source: U.S. Bureau of Labor Statistics, Occupational Employment Statistics

Percent Change in Employment, Projected 2014–2024

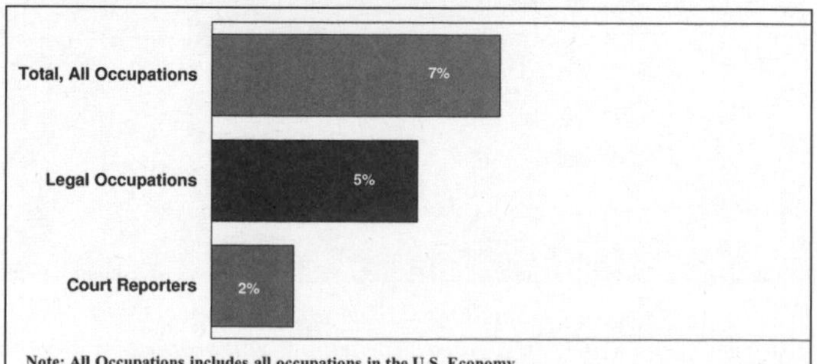

Note: All Occupations includes all occupations in the U.S. Economy.
Source: U.S. Bureau of Labor Statistics, Office of Occupational Statistics and Employment Projections

Employment Projections Data for Court Reporters

Occupational Title	SOC Code	Employment, 2014	Projected Employment, 2024	Change, 2014–2024 Percent	Change, 2014–2024 Numeric
Court reporters	23-2091	20,800	21,100	2	300

Source: U.S. Bureau of Labor Statistics, Employment Projections Program

Similar Occupations. This table shows a list of occupations with job duties that are similar to those of court reporters.

Occupations	Entry-level Education	2014 Median Pay	Projected Job Growth	Average Annual Openings
Interpreters and Translators	Bachelor's degree	$43,590	29%	1,750
Medical Transcriptionists	Postsecondary nondegree award	$34,750	-3%	-220

currently assessing the reliability, accuracy, and costs associated with installing and maintaining digital audio and video equipment and software.

However, even with the increased use of digital recorders, electronic reporters should still be needed to monitor the courtroom equipment and to transcribe, verify, and supervise the production of transcripts after proceedings have been recorded.

Job Prospects. Job prospects for graduates of court reporting programs are expected to be very good. Court reporters with experience and training in CART and real-time captioning will have the best job prospects.

Contacts for More Information

For more information on becoming a court reporter, including information on training programs and certification as a Registered Professional Reporter, visit

➤ National Court Reporters Association (www.ncra.org)

For more information on certification and legal resources, as well as becoming an electronic or digital reporter, visit

➤ American Association of Electronic Reporters and Transcribers (www.aaert.org)

For more information on voice writing and certification, visit

➤ National Verbatim Reporters Association (www.nvra.org)

O*NET

➤ Court Reporters (23-2091.00)

Judges and Hearing Officers

- **2014 Median Pay** .... $102,380 per year $49.22 per hour
- **Typical Entry-Level Education** .... Doctoral or professional degree
- **Work Experience in a Related Occupation**............ 5 years or more
- **On-the-job Training** ....Short-term on-the-job training
- **Number of Jobs, 2014** 44,800
- **Job Outlook, 2014–24** ....-1% (Little or no change)
- **Employment Change, 2014–24** .... -400

What Judges and Hearing Officers Do

Judges and hearing officers apply the law by overseeing the legal process in courts. They also conduct pretrial hearings, resolve administrative disputes, facilitate negotiations between opposing parties, and issue legal decisions.

Duties. Judges and hearing officers typically do the following:

- Research legal issues
- Read and evaluate information from documents, such as motions, claim applications, and records
- Preside over hearings and listen to and read arguments by opposing parties
- Determine if the information presented supports the charge, claim, or dispute
- Decide if the procedure is being conducted according to the rules and law
- Apply laws or precedents to reach judgments and to resolve disputes between parties
- Write opinions, decisions, and instructions regarding cases, claims, and disputes

Judges decide cases when the law does not require a jury trial or when the parties waive their right to a jury.

Median Annual Wages, May 2014

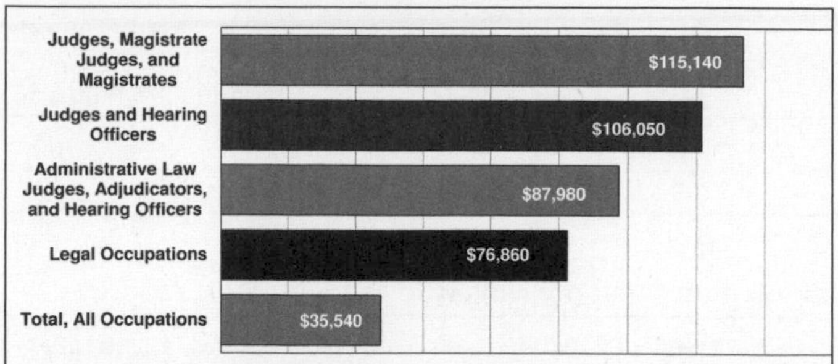

Note: All Occupations includes all occupations in the U.S. Economy.
Source: U.S. Bureau of Labor Statistics, Occupational Employment Statistics

Percent Change in Employment, Projected 2014–2024

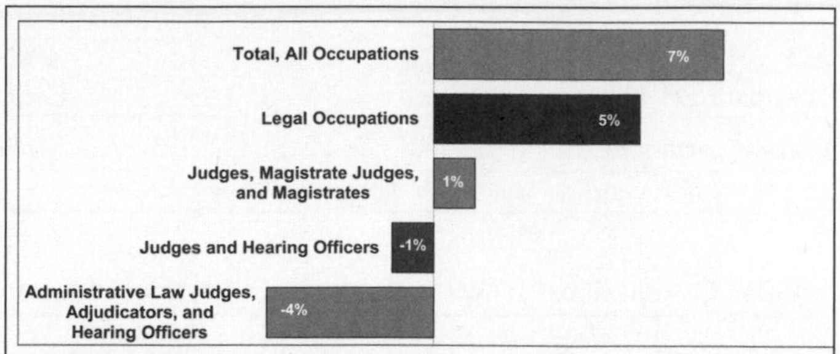

Note: All Occupations includes all occupations in the U.S. Economy.
Source: U.S. Bureau of Labor Statistics, Office of Occupational Statistics and Employment Projections

Judges commonly preside over trials and hearings of cases regarding nearly every aspect of society, from individual traffic offenses to issues concerning the rights of large corporations. Judges listen to arguments and determine if the evidence presented deserves a trial. In criminal cases, judges may decide that people charged with crimes should be held in jail until the trial, or they may set conditions for their release. They also approve search warrants and arrest warrants.

Judges interpret the law to determine how a trial will proceed, which is particularly important when unusual circumstances arise for which standard procedures have not been established. They ensure that hearings and trials are conducted fairly and that the legal rights of all involved parties are protected.

In trials in which juries are selected to decide the case, judges instruct jurors on applicable laws and direct them to consider the facts from the evidence. For other trials, judges decide the case. A judge who determines guilt in criminal cases may impose a sentence or penalty on the guilty party. In civil cases, the judge may award relief, such as compensation for damages, to the parties who win lawsuits.

Judges use various forms of technology, such as electronic databases and software, to manage cases and to prepare for trials. In some cases, a judge may manage the court's administrative and clerical staff.

The following are examples of types of judges and hearing officers:

Judges, magistrate judges, and magistrates preside over trials and hearings. They typically work in local, state, and federal courts.

In local and state court systems, they have a variety of titles, such as *municipal court judge, county court judge*, and *justice of the peace*. Traffic violations, misdemeanors, small-claims cases, and pretrial hearings make up the bulk of these judges' work.

In federal and state court systems, *district court judges* and *general trial court judges* have authority over any case in their system. *Appellate court judges* rule on a small number of cases, by reviewing decisions of the lower courts and lawyers' written and oral arguments.

Administrative law judges, adjudicators, and hearing officers usually work for local, state, and federal government agencies. They decide many issues, such as whether a person is eligible for workers' compensation benefits or whether employment discrimination occurred.

Work Environment

Judges and hearing officers held about 44,800 jobs in 2014. The industries that employed the most judges and hearing officers were as follows:

State government, excluding education and hospitals	49%
Local government, excluding education and hospitals	42
Federal government	9

Judges and hearing officers do most of their work in offices and courtrooms. Their jobs can be demanding, because they must sit in the same position in the court or hearing room for long periods and give undivided attention to the process.

Some judges and hearing officers may be required to travel to different counties and courthouses throughout their state.

Work Schedules. Most judges and hearing officers work full time, but some may work additional hours to prepare for hearings.

Some courthouses have evening and weekend hours. In addition, judges have to be on call during nights or weekends to issue emergency orders, such as search warrants and restraining orders.

Education/Training

Judges and hearing officers typically must have a law degree and work experience as a lawyer.

Education. Although there may be a few positions available for those with a bachelor's degree, a law degree typically is required for most jobs as a local, state, or federal judge or hearing officer.

In addition to earning a law degree, federal administrative law judges must pass a competitive exam from the U.S. Office of Personnel Management.

Earning a law degree usually takes 7 years of full-time study after high school: 4 years of undergraduate study, followed by 3 years of law school. Law degree programs include courses such as constitutional law, contracts, property law, civil procedure, and legal writing. For more information on how to become a lawyer, see the profile on lawyers.

Most judges and magistrates must be appointed or elected into their positions, a procedure that often takes political support. Many local and state judges are appointed to serve fixed renewable terms, ranging from 4 to 14 years. A few judges, such as appellate court judges, are appointed for life. Judicial nominating commissions screen candidates for judgeships in many states and for some federal judgeships. Some local and state judges are elected to a specific term in an election process.

For specific state information, including information on the number of judgeships by state, term lengths, and requirements for qualification, visit the National Center for State Courts.

Work Experience in a Related Occupation. Most judges and hearing officers learn their skills through years of experience as practicing lawyers. Some states allow those who are not lawyers to hold limited-jurisdiction judgeships, but opportunities are better for those with law experience.

Training. All states have some type of orientation for newly elected or appointed judges. The Federal Judicial Center, American Bar Association, National Judicial College, and National Center for State Courts provide judicial education and training for judges and other judicial branch personnel.

Employment Projections Data for Judges and Hearing Officers

Occupational Title	SOC Code	Employment, 2014	Projected Employment, 2024	Change, 2014–2024 Percent	Change, 2014–2024 Numeric
Judges and hearing officers	—	44,800	44,400	-1	-400
Administrative law judges, adjudicators, and hearing officers	23-1021	15,000	14,500	-4	-500
Judges, magistrate judges, and magistrates	23-1023	29,700	29,900	1	200

Source: U.S. Bureau of Labor Statistics, Employment Projections Program

More than half of all states, as well as Puerto Rico, require judges to take continuing education courses while serving on the bench. General and continuing education courses usually last from a few days to 3 weeks.

Licenses, Certifications, and Registrations. Most judges and hearing officers are required to have a law license. In addition, they typically must maintain their law license and good standing with their state bar association while working as a judge or hearing officer.

Advancement. Advancement for some judicial workers means moving to courts with a broader jurisdiction. Advancement for various hearing officers includes taking on more complex cases, practicing law, and becoming district court judges.

Important Qualities

Critical-thinking skills. Judges and hearing officers must apply rules of law. They cannot let their own personal assumptions interfere with the proceedings. For example, they must base their decisions on specific meanings of the law when evaluating and deciding whether a person is a threat to others and must be sent to jail.

Decision-making skills. Judges and hearing officers must be able to weigh the facts, to apply the law and rules, and to make a decision relatively quickly.

Listening skills. Judges and hearing officers evaluate information, so they must pay close attention to what is being said.

Reading skills. Judges and hearing officers must be able to distinguish important facts from large amounts of sometimes complex information and then evaluate the facts objectively.

Writing skills. Judges and hearing officers write recommendations and decisions on appeals and disputes. They must be able to write their decisions clearly so that all sides understand the decision.

Pay

The median annual wage for administrative law judges, adjudicators, and hearing officers was $87,980 in May 2014. The median wage is the wage at which half the workers in an occupation earned more than that amount and half earned less. The lowest 10 percent earned less than $41,510, and the highest 10 percent earned more than $156,750.

The median annual wage for judges, magistrate judges, and magistrates was $115,140 in May 2014. The lowest 10 percent earned less than $31,480, and the highest 10 percent earned more than $178,920.

In May 2014, the median annual wages for judges and hearing officers in the top industries in which they worked were as follows:

Federal government	$128,890
State government, excluding education and hospitals	111,900
Local government, excluding education and hospitals	77,150

Job Outlook

Employment of judges and hearing officers is projected to show little or no change from 2014 to 2024.

The number of federal and state judgeships is projected to remain steady because nearly every new position for a judge must be authorized and approved by a legislature.

However, budgetary constraints in federal, state, and local governments are expected to limit the ability of these governments to fill vacant positions or authorize new ones. Furthermore, budgetary concerns may limit the employment growth of hearing officers and administrative law judges working for local, state, and federal government agencies, despite the continued need for these workers to settle disputes.

In addition, the desire of parties to resolve disputes through mediation or arbitration, rather than litigation and trials, may adversely affect the demand for judges and hearing officers.

Job Prospects. The prestige associated with becoming a judge will ensure continued competition for these positions. Most job openings will arise as a result of judges and hearing officers leaving the occupation because of retirement, to teach, or because their elected term is over.

Contacts for More Information

For more information about state courts and judgeships, visit

➤ National Center for State Courts (www.ncsc.org)

For more information about federal judges, visit

➤ Administrative Office of the United States Courts (www.uscourts.gov/Home.aspx)

Similar Occupations. This table shows a list of occupations with job duties that are similar to those of judges and hearing officers.

Occupations	Entry-level Education	2014 Median Pay	Projected Job Growth	Average Annual Openings
Arbitrators, Mediators, and Conciliators	Bachelor's degree	$57,180	9%	80
Lawyers	Doctoral or professional degree	$114,970	6%	4,380
Paralegals and Legal Assistants	Associate's degree	$48,350	8%	2,120
Private Detectives and Investigators	High school diploma or equivalent	$44,570	5%	180

For more information about judicial education and training for judges and other judicial branch personnel, visit
- Federal Judicial Center (www.fjc.gov)
- American Bar Association (www.americanbar.org)
- The National Judicial College (www.judges.org)

O*NET
- Administrative Law Judges, Adjudicators, and Hearing Officers (23-1021.00)
- Judges, Magistrate Judges, and Magistrates (23-1023.00)

Lawyers

- **2014 Median Pay** .... $114,970 per year $55.27 per hour
- **Typical Entry-Level Education** .... Doctoral or professional degree
- **Work Experience in a Related Occupation** .... None
- **On-the-job Training** .... None
- **Number of Jobs, 2014** 778,700
- **Job Outlook, 2014–24** .... 6% (As fast as average)
- **Employment Change, 2014–24** 43,800

What Lawyers Do

Lawyers advise and represent individuals, businesses, and government agencies on legal issues and disputes.

Duties. Lawyers typically do the following:
- Advise and represent clients in courts, before government agencies, and in private legal matters
- Communicate with their clients, colleagues, judges, and others involved in the case
- Conduct research and analysis of legal problems
- Interpret laws, rulings, and regulations for individuals and businesses
- Present facts in writing and verbally to their clients or others and argue on behalf of their clients
- Prepare and file legal documents, such as lawsuits, appeals, wills, contracts, and deeds

Lawyers, also called *attorneys*, act as both advocates and advisors.

As advocates, they represent one of the parties in criminal or civil trials by presenting evidence and arguing in support of their client.

As advisors, lawyers counsel their clients about their legal rights and obligations and suggest courses of action in business and personal matters. All attorneys research the intent of laws and judicial decisions and apply the laws to the specific circumstances that their clients face.

Lawyers often oversee the work of support staff, such as paralegals and legal assistants.

Lawyers may have different titles and different duties, depending on where they work.

While working in a law firm, lawyers, sometimes called *associates*, perform legal work for individuals or businesses. Some attorneys who work at law firms, such as *criminal law attorneys* or *defense attorneys*, represent and defend the accused.

Attorneys also work for federal, state, and local governments. *Prosecutors* typically work for the government to file a lawsuit, or charge, against an individual or corporation accused of violating the law. Some may also work as *public defense attorneys* and represent individuals who could not afford to hire their own private attorney.

Others may work as *government counsels* for administrative bodies of government and executive or legislative branches. They write and interpret laws and regulations and set up procedures to enforce them. Government counsels also write legal reviews on agencies' decisions. They argue civil and criminal cases on behalf of the government.

Corporate counsels, also called *in-house counsels*, are lawyers who work for corporations. They advise a corporation's executives about legal issues related to the corporation's business activities. These issues may involve patents, government regulations, contracts with other companies, property interests, taxes, or collective-bargaining agreements with unions.

Legal aid lawyers work for private, nonprofit organizations that work to help disadvantaged people. They generally handle civil cases, such as those about leases, job discrimination, and wage disputes, rather than criminal cases.

In addition to working in different industries, lawyers often specialize in a particular area. The following are just some examples of the different types of lawyers that specialize in specific legal areas:

Environmental lawyers deal with issues and regulations that are related to the environment. They may represent advocacy groups, waste disposal companies, and government agencies to make sure they comply with the relevant laws.

Tax lawyers handle a variety of tax-related issues for individuals and corporations. Tax lawyers may help clients navigate complex tax regulations, so that they pay the appropriate tax on items such as income, profits, or property. For example, they may advise a corporation on how much tax it needs to pay from profits made in different states to comply with the Internal Revenue Service (IRS) rules.

Trial lawyers spend most of their time outside the courtroom conducting research, interviewing clients and witnesses, and handling other details in preparation for a trial.

Intellectual property lawyers deal with the laws related to inventions, patents, trademarks, and creative works, such as music, books, and movies. An intellectual property lawyer may advise a client about whether it is okay to use published material in the client's forthcoming book.

Family lawyers handle a variety of legal issues that pertain to the family. They may advise clients regarding divorce, child custody, and adoption proceedings.

Securities lawyers work on legal issues arising from the buying and selling of stocks, ensuring that all disclosure requirements are met. They may advise corporations that are interested in listing in the stock exchange through an initial public offering (IPO) or in buying shares in another corporation.

Litigation lawyers handle all lawsuits and disputes between parties. These could be disputes over contracts, personal injuries, or real estate and property. Litigation lawyers may specialize in a certain area, such as personal injury law, or may be a general lawyer for all types of disputes and lawsuits.

Some attorneys become teachers in law schools. For more information on law school professors, see the profile on postsecondary teachers.

Work Environment

Lawyers held about 778,700 jobs in 2014. The industries that employed the most lawyers were as follows:

Legal services	48%
Local government, excluding education and hospitals	7
State government, excluding education and hospitals	5
Federal government	5
Finance and insurance	3

About 1 in 5 lawyers were self-employed in 2014.

Lawyers work mostly in offices. However, some travel to attend meetings with clients at various locations, such as homes, hospitals, or prisons. Others travel to appear before courts. Lawyers may face heavy pressure during work, for example during trials or when trying to meet deadlines.

Work Schedules. The majority of lawyers work full time, and many work more than the usual 40 hours per week. Lawyers who are in private practice or those who work in large firms often work additional hours, conducting research and preparing and reviewing documents.

Education/Training

All lawyers must have a law degree and must also typically pass a state's written bar examination.

Education. Becoming a lawyer usually takes 7 years of full-time study after high school—4 years of undergraduate study, followed by 3 years of law school. Most states and jurisdictions require lawyers to complete a juris doctor (J.D.) degree from a law school accredited by the American Bar Association (ABA). ABA accreditation signifies that the law school—particularly its curricula and faculty—meets certain standards.

A bachelor's degree is required for entry into most law schools, and courses in English, public speaking, government, history, economics, and mathematics are useful.

Almost all law schools, particularly those approved by the ABA, require applicants to take the Law School Admission Test (LSAT). This test measures applicants' aptitude for the study of law.

A J.D. degree program includes courses such as constitutional law, contracts, property law, civil procedure, and legal writing. Law students may choose specialized courses in areas such as tax, labor, and corporate law.

Licenses. Prospective lawyers take licensing exams called "bar exams." When lawyers receive the license to practice law, they are "admitted to the bar."

To practice law in any state, a person must be admitted to the state's bar under rules established by the jurisdiction's highest court. The requirements vary by individual states and jurisdictions. For more details on individual state and jurisdiction requirements, visit the National Conference of Bar Examiners.

Most states require that applicants graduate from an ABA-accredited law school, pass one or more written bar exams, and be found by an admitting board to have the character to represent and advise others. Prior felony convictions, academic misconduct, or a history of substance abuse are just some factors that may disqualify an applicant from being admitted to the bar.

Lawyers who want to practice in more than one state often must take the bar exam in each state.

After graduation, lawyers must keep informed about legal developments that affect their practices. Almost all states require lawyers to participate in continuing legal education either every year or every 3 years.

Many law schools and state and local bar associations provide continuing legal education courses that help lawyers stay current with recent developments. Courses vary by state and generally cover a subject within the practice of law, such as legal ethics, taxes and tax fraud, and healthcare. Some states allow lawyers to take their continuing education credits through online courses.

Advancement. Newly hired attorneys usually start as associates and work with more experienced lawyers. After several years, some lawyers may be admitted to partnership of their firm, which means they become partial owners of the firm.

After gaining a few years of work experience, some lawyers go into practice for themselves or move to the legal department of a large corporation. Very few in-house attorneys are hired directly out of law school.

A small number of experienced lawyers are nominated or elected to judgeships. Other lawyers may become full-time law school faculty and administrators. For more information about judges and law school faculty, see the profile on judges and hearing officers and the profile on postsecondary teachers.

Other Experience. Law students often gain practical experience by participating in school-sponsored legal clinics, in a school's moot court competitions, in practice trials under the supervision of experienced lawyers and judges, and through research and writing on legal issues for a school's law journals.

Part-time jobs or summer internships in law firms, government agencies, and corporate legal departments also provide valuable experience. Some smaller firms, government agencies, and public interest organizations may hire students as summer associate interns after they have completed their first year at law school. Many larger firms' summer internship programs are only eligible to law students who have completed their second year. These experiences can help law students decide what kind of legal work they want to focus on in their careers, and these internships may lead directly to a job after graduation.

Important Qualities

Analytical skills. Lawyers help their clients resolve problems and issues. As a result, they must be able to analyze large amounts of information, determine relevant facts, and propose viable solutions.

Interpersonal skills. Lawyers must win the respect and confidence of their clients by building a trusting relationship, so that clients feel comfortable enough to share personal information related to their case.

Median Annual Wages, May 2014

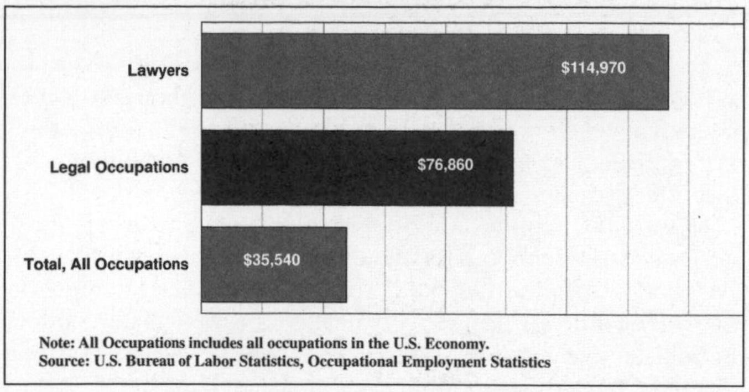

Percent Change in Employment, Projected 2014–2024

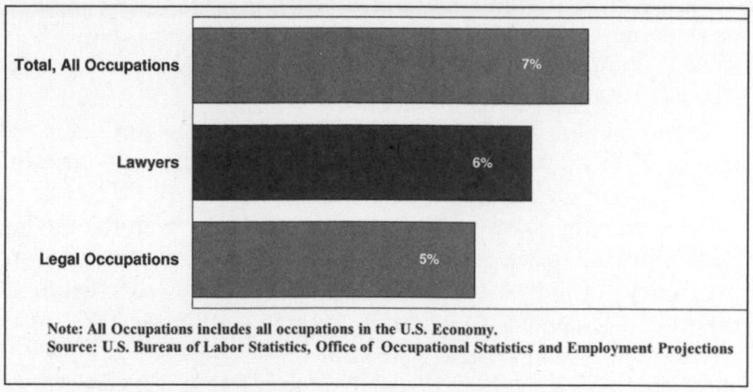

Problem-solving skills. Lawyers must separate their emotions and prejudice from their clients' problems and objectively evaluate the matter. Therefore, good problem-solving skills are important for lawyers, to prepare the best defense and recommendation.

Research skills. Preparing legal advice or representation for a client commonly requires substantial research. All lawyers need to be able to find what applicable laws and regulations apply to a specific matter.

Speaking skills. Clients hire lawyers to speak on their behalf. Lawyers must be able to clearly present and explain their case to arbitrators, mediators, opposing parties, judges, or juries.

Writing skills. Lawyers need to be precise and specific when preparing documents, such as wills, trusts, and powers of attorney.

Pay

The median annual wage for lawyers was $114,970 in May 2014. The median wage is the wage at which half the workers in an occupation earned more than that amount and half earned less. The lowest 10 percent earned less than $55,400, and the highest 10 percent earned more than $187,200.

In May 2014, the median annual wages for lawyers in the top industries in which they worked were as follows:

Finance and insurance	$140,630
Federal government	137,500
Legal services	117,080
Local government, excluding education and hospitals	90,350
State government, excluding education and hospitals	81,050

Salaries of experienced lawyers vary widely according to the type, size, and location of their employer. Lawyers who own their own practices usually earn less than those who are partners in law firms.

Job Outlook

Employment of lawyers is projected to grow 6 percent from 2014 to 2024, about as fast as the average for all occupations. Demand for legal work is expected to continue as individuals, businesses, and all levels of government require legal services in many areas.

Despite this need for legal services, more price competition over the next decade may lead law firms to rethink their project staffing to reduce costs to clients. Clients are expected to cut back on legal expenses by demanding less expensive rates and scrutinizing invoices. Work that was previously assigned to lawyers, such as document review, may now be given to paralegals and legal assistants. Some routine legal work may also be outsourced to other lower-cost legal providers located overseas.

While law firms will continue to be the largest employers of lawyers, many large corporations are increasing their in-house legal departments to cut costs. For many companies, the high cost of hiring outside counsel lawyers and their support staff makes it more economical to shift work to their in-house legal department. This will lead to an increase in the demand of lawyers in a variety of settings, such as financial and insurance firms, consulting firms, and healthcare providers.

The federal government is likely to continue to need lawyers to prosecute or defend civil cases on behalf of the United States, prosecute criminal cases brought by the federal government, and collect money owed to the federal government. However, budgetary constraints at all levels of government, especially federal, will likely moderate employment growth.

Job Prospects. Competition for jobs should continue to be strong because more students are graduating from law school each year than there are jobs available. Some recent law school graduates who have been unable to find permanent positions are turning to the growing number of temporary staffing firms that place attorneys in short-term jobs. This service allows companies to hire lawyers as needed and permits beginning lawyers to develop practical skills.

Because of the strong competition, a law school graduate's willingness to relocate and his or her work experience are becoming more important. However, to be licensed in another state, a lawyer may have to take an additional state bar examination.

Contacts for More Information

For more information about law schools and a career in law, visit

➤ American Bar Association (www.americanbar.org)

Employment Projections Data for Lawyers

Occupational Title	SOC Code	Employment, 2014	Projected Employment, 2024	Change, 2014–2024 Percent	Change, 2014–2024 Numeric
Lawyers	23-1011	778,700	822,500	6	43,800

Source: U.S. Bureau of Labor Statistics, Employment Projections Program

Similar Occupations. This table shows a list of occupations with job duties that are similar to those of lawyers.

Occupations	Entry-level Education	2014 Median Pay	Projected Job Growth	Average Annual Openings
Arbitrators, Mediators, and Conciliators	Bachelor's degree	$57,180	9%	80
Judges and Hearing Officers	Doctoral or professional degree	$102,380	-1%	-40
Paralegals and Legal Assistants	Associate's degree	$48,350	8%	2,120
Postsecondary Teachers	See Education/Training	$70,790	13%	17,700

➤ National Association for Law Placement (www.nalp.org)

For more information about the Law School Admission Test (LSAT) and the law school application process, visit

➤ Law School Admission Council (www.lsac.org)

For a list of state and jurisdiction admission bar offices, visit

➤ National Conference of Bar Examiners (www.ncbex.org)

The requirements for admission to the bar in a particular state or other jurisdiction may be obtained at the state capital, from the clerk of the state Supreme Court, or from the administrator of the State Board of Bar Examiners.

O*NET

➤ Lawyers (23-1011.00)

Paralegals and Legal Assistants

- **2014 Median Pay** .... $48,350 per year
  $23.24 per hour
- **Typical Entry-Level Education** .... Associate's degree
- **Work Experience in a Related Occupation** .... None
- **On-the-job Training** .... None
- **Number of Jobs, 2014** 279,500
- **Job Outlook, 2014–24** .... 8% (As fast as average)
- **Employment Change, 2014–24** 21,200

What Paralegals and Legal Assistants Do

Paralegals and legal assistants do a variety of tasks to support lawyers, including maintaining and organizing files, conducting legal research, and drafting documents.

Duties. Paralegals and legal assistants typically do the following:

- Investigate and gather the facts of a case
- Conduct research on relevant laws, regulations, and legal articles
- Organize and maintain documents in paper or electronic filing systems
- Gather and arrange evidence and other legal documents for attorney review and case preparation
- Write or summarize reports to help lawyers prepare for trials
- Draft correspondence and legal documents, such as contracts and mortgages
- Get affidavits and other formal statements that may be used as evidence in court
- Help lawyers during trials by handling exhibits, taking notes, or reviewing trial transcripts
- File exhibits, briefs, appeals and other legal documents with the court or opposing counsel
- Call clients, witnesses, lawyers, and outside vendors to schedule interviews, meetings, and depositions

Paralegals and legal assistants help lawyers prepare for hearings, trials, and corporate meetings.

Paralegals use technology and computer software for managing and organizing the increasing amount of documents and data collected during a case. Many paralegals use computer software to catalog documents, and to review documents for specific keywords or subjects. Because of these responsibilities, paralegals must be familiar with electronic database management and be current on the latest software used for electronic discovery. Electronic discovery refers to all electronic materials obtained by the parties during the litigation or investigation. These materials may be emails, data, documents, accounting databases, and websites.

Paralegals' specific duties often vary depending on the area of law in which they work.

Corporate paralegals, for example, often help lawyers prepare employee contracts, shareholder agreements, stock-option plans, and companies' annual financial reports. Corporate paralegals may monitor and review government regulations to ensure that the corporation is aware of new legal requirements.

Litigation paralegals maintain documents received from clients, conduct research for lawyers, retrieve and organize evidence for use at depositions and trials, and draft settlement agreements. Some litigation paralegals may also help coordinate the logistics of attending a trial, including reserving office space, transporting exhibits and documents to the courtroom, and setting up computers and other equipment.

Paralegals may also specialize in other legal areas, such as personal injury, criminal law, employee benefits, intellectual property, bankruptcy, immigration, family law, and real estate.

Specific job duties may also vary by the size of the law firm.

In litigation involving many supporting documents, paralegals usually use computer databases to retrieve, organize, and index various materials.

In small firms, paralegals' duties tend to vary more. In addition to reviewing and organizing documents, paralegals may prepare written reports that help lawyers determine how to handle their cases. If lawyers decide to file lawsuits on behalf of clients, paralegals may help draft documents to be filed with the court.

In large organizations, paralegals may work on a particular phase of a case, rather than handling a case from beginning to end. For example, paralegals may only review legal material for internal use, maintain reference files, conduct research for lawyers, or collect and organize evidence for hearings. After gaining experience, a paralegal may become responsible for more complicated tasks.

Paralegals and legal assistants often work in teams with attorneys, fellow paralegals, and other legal support staff.

Unlike the work of other administrative and legal support staff employed in a law firm, the paralegal's work is billed to the client.

Paralegals may have frequent interactions with clients and third-party vendors. In addition, experienced paralegals may assume supervisory responsibilities, such as overseeing team projects or delegating work to other paralegals.

Work Environment

Paralegals and legal assistants held about 279,500 jobs in 2014. The industries that employed the most paralegals and legal assistants were as follows:

Legal services	72%
Local government, excluding education and hospitals	6
Federal government	5
State government, excluding education and hospitals	4
Finance and insurance	3

Paralegals do most of their work in offices. Occasionally, they may travel to gather information, collect and review documents, accompany attorneys to depositions or trials, and do other tasks.

Some of the work can be fast-paced, and paralegals must be able to work on multiple projects under tight deadlines.

Work Schedules. Most paralegals and legal assistants work full time. Some may have to work more than 40 hours per week in order to meet deadlines.

Education/Training

Most paralegals and legal assistants have an associate's degree in paralegal studies, or a bachelor's degree in another field and a certificate in paralegal studies.

Education. There are several paths a person can take to become a paralegal. Candidates can enroll in a community college paralegal program to earn an associate's degree. However, many employers prefer, or even require, applicants to have a bachelor's degree.

Because only a small number of schools offer bachelor's and master's degrees in paralegal studies, applicants typically have a bachelor's degree in another subject and earn a certificate in paralegal studies.

Associate's and bachelor's degree programs in paralegal studies usually offer paralegal training courses in legal research, legal writing, and the legal applications of computers, along with courses in other academic subjects, such as corporate law and international law. Most certificate programs provide intensive paralegal training for people who already hold college degrees.

Employers sometimes hire college graduates with no legal experience or legal education and train them on the job. In these cases, the new employee may have experience in a technical field that is useful to law firms, such tax preparation, nursing, or criminal justice.

Other Experience. In many cases, employers prefer candidates who have at least 1 year of experience in a law firm or other office setting. In addition, a technical understanding of a specific legal specialty can be helpful. For example, a personal-injury law firm may desire a paralegal with a background in nursing or health administration.

Work experience in a law firm or other office setting is particularly important for people who do not have formal paralegal training.

Many paralegal training programs offer an internship, in which students gain practical experience by working for several months in a private law firm, the office of a public defender or attorney general, a corporate legal department, a legal aid organization, or a government agency. Internship experience helps students improve their technical skills and can enhance their employment prospects.

Certifications

Although not required, some employers may prefer to hire applicants who have completed a paralegal certification program. Many national and local paralegal organizations offer voluntary paralegal certifications to students able to pass an exam. Other organizations offer voluntary paralegal certifications for paralegals who meet certain experience and education criteria. For more information about paralegal certifications, see the Contacts for More Information section.

Important Qualities

Communication skills. Paralegals must be able to document and present their research and related information to their supervising attorney.

Computer skills. Paralegals need to be familiar with using computers for legal research and litigation support. They also use computer programs for organizing and maintaining important documents.

Median Annual Wages, May 2014

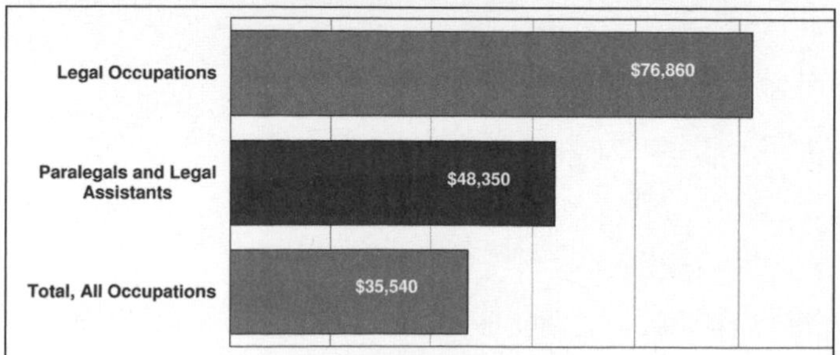

Note: All Occupations includes all occupations in the U.S. Economy.
Source: U.S. Bureau of Labor Statistics, Occupational Employment Statistics

Percent Change in Employment, Projected 2014–2024

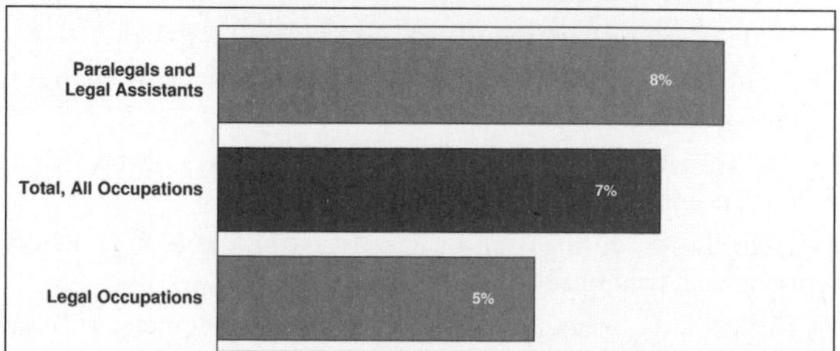

Note: All Occupations includes all occupations in the U.S. Economy.
Source: U.S. Bureau of Labor Statistics, Office of Occupational Statistics and Employment Projections

Employment Projections Data for Paralegals and Legal Assistants

Occupational Title	SOC Code	Employment, 2014	Projected Employment, 2024	Change, 2014–2024 Percent	Numeric
Paralegals and legal assistants	23-2011	279,500	300,800	8	21,200

Source: U.S. Bureau of Labor Statistics, Employment Projections Program

Similar Occupations. This table shows a list of occupations with job duties that are similar to those of paralegals and legal assistants.

Occupations	Entry-level Education	2014 Median Pay	Projected Job Growth	Average Annual Openings
Claims Adjusters, Appraisers, Examiners, and Investigators	See Education/Training	$62,300	3%	960
Lawyers	Doctoral or professional degree	$114,970	6%	4,380
Occupational Health and Safety Specialists	Bachelor's degree	$69,210	4%	280
Occupational Health and Safety Technicians	High school diploma or equivalent	$48,120	9%	140
Secretaries and Administrative Assistants	High school diploma or equivalent	$35,970	3%	11,880

Interpersonal skills. Paralegals spend most of their time working with clients and other professionals and must be able to develop good relationships. They must make clients feel comfortable sharing personal information related to their cases.

Organizational skills. Paralegals may be responsible for many cases at one time. They must adapt quickly to changing deadlines.

Research skills. Paralegals need good research and investigative skills to conduct legal research.

Pay

The median annual wage for paralegals and legal assistants was $48,350 in May 2014. The median wage is the wage at which half the workers in an occupation earned more than that amount and half earned less. The lowest 10 percent earned less than $30,280, and the highest 10 percent earned more than $77,830.

In May 2014, the median annual wages for paralegals and legal assistants in the top industries in which they worked were as follows:

Federal government	$63,420
Finance and insurance	57,250
Local government, excluding education and hospitals	49,320
Legal services	46,280
State government, excluding education and hospitals	44,340

Job Outlook

Employment of paralegals and legal assistants is projected to grow 8 percent from 2014 to 2024, about as fast as the average for all occupations.

As law firms try to increase the efficiency of legal services and reduce their costs, they are expected to hire more paralegals and legal assistants. In these cases, paralegals and legal assistants can take on a "hybrid" role within the firm, performing not only traditional paralegal duties but also some of the tasks previously assigned to legal secretaries or other legal support workers.

Law firms also are attempting to reduce billing costs as clients push for less expensive legal services. Due to their lower billing rates to clients, paralegals can be a less costly alternative to lawyers despite performing a wide variety of tasks once done by entry-level lawyers. This should cause an increase in demand for paralegals and legal assistants.

Although law firms will continue to be the largest employers of paralegals, many large corporations are increasing their in-house legal departments to cut costs. For many companies, the high cost of outside counsel makes it more economical to have an in-house legal department. This will lead to an increase in the demand for legal workers in a variety of settings, such as finance and insurance firms, consulting firms, and healthcare providers.

However, demand for paralegals within certain practice areas is dependent upon the overall health of the economy. During periods of slow economic growth, law firms' workloads may decrease as clients become less likely to engage in litigation, mergers, or other types of activity requiring legal expertise. When work is slow, lawyers will have less work to delegate to paralegals. This may make a firm less likely to keep some paralegals on staff or to hire new ones until the workload increases.

Job Prospects. This occupation attracts many applicants, and competition for jobs will be strong. Experienced, formally trained paralegals with strong computer and database management skills should have the best job prospects. In addition, many firms will prefer paralegals with experience and specialization in high-demand practice areas.

Contacts for More Information

For more information on the Certified Legal Assistant certification, schools that offer training programs in a specific State, and standards and guidelines for paralegals, visit

- NALA – The National Association of Legal Assistants (www.nala.org)

For information on the Professional Paralegal certification, visit

- NALS – The Association for Legal Professionals (www.nals.org)

For information on the Paralegal Advanced Competency Exam, paralegal careers, and paralegal training programs visit

- National Federation of Paralegal Associations (www.paralegals.org)

O*NET

- Paralegals and Legal Assistants (23-2011.00)

Life, Physical, and Social Science

Agricultural and Food Science Technicians

- **2014 Median Pay** .... $35,140 per year; $16.89 per hour
- **Typical Entry-Level Education** .... Associate's degree
- **Work Experience in a Related Occupation** .... None
- **On-the-job Training** .... Moderate-term on-the-job training
- **Number of Jobs, 2014** 33,000
- **Job Outlook, 2014–24** .... 5% (As fast as average)
- **Employment Change, 2014–24** 1,600

What Agricultural and Food Science Technicians Do

Agricultural and food science technicians assist agricultural and food scientists by performing duties such as measuring and analyzing the quality of food and agricultural products. Duties range from typical agricultural labor with added recordkeeping duties to laboratory testing with significant amounts of office work, depending on the particular field the technician works in.

Duties. Specific duties of these technicians vary with their specialty.

Agricultural science technicians typically do the following:

- Follow protocols to collect, prepare, analyze, and properly store crop or animal samples
- Operate farm equipment and maintain agricultural production areas to conform to scientific testing parameters
- Examine animal and crop specimens to determine the presence of diseases or other problems
- Measure ingredients used in animal feed and other inputs
- Prepare and operate laboratory testing equipment
- Compile and analyze test results
- Prepare charts, presentations, and reports describing test results

Food science technicians typically do the following:

- Collect and prepare samples in accordance with established procedures
- Test food, food additives, and food containers to ensure that they comply with established safety standards
- Help food scientists with food research, development, and quality control
- Analyze chemical properties of food to determine ingredients and formulas
- Compile and analyze test results
- Prepare charts, presentations, and reports describing test results
- Prepare and maintain quantities of chemicals needed to perform laboratory tests
- Maintain a safe, sterile laboratory environment

Agricultural and food science technicians work in offices, laboratories, and processing plants.

Agricultural and food science technicians often specialize by subject area. Some popular subjects are animal health, farm machinery, fertilizers, agricultural chemicals, and processing technology. Duties can vary considerably with the specialization, because work settings may vary.

Agricultural science technicians who work in private industry typically focus on increasing the productivity of crops and animals. These workers may keep detailed records, collect samples for analyses, ensure that samples meet proper safety and quality standards, and test crops and animals for disease or to otherwise confirm the results of scientific experiments.

Food science technicians who work in private industry typically evaluate food and crops while investigating new production or processing techniques. They also ensure that products will be fit for distribution or are produced as efficiently as expected. Many food science technicians spend time inspecting foodstuffs, chemicals, and additives to determine whether they are safe and have the proper combination of ingredients.

Work Environment

Agricultural and food science technicians held about 33,000 jobs in 2014.

The industries that employed the most agricultural and food science technicians in 2014 were as follows:

Food manufacturing	19%
Colleges, universities, and professional schools; state	17
Animal production and aquaculture	12
Crop production	11
Support activities for agriculture and forestry	8

Technicians work in a variety of settings, including laboratories, processing plants, farms and ranches, greenhouses, and offices. Technicians who work in processing plants and agricultural work settings may face noise from processing and farming machinery, extreme temperatures, and odors from chemicals or animals.

Work Schedules. Agricultural and food science technicians typically work full time and have standard work schedules. Some of these technicians work longer hours, have variable schedules, or travel extensively.

Education/Training

Agricultural and food science technicians typically need an associate's degree in biology, chemistry, crop or animal science, or a related field. Many positions require a bachelor's degree. For those positions requiring only a high school diploma, technicians typically need to have previous work experience. Technicians often receive on-the-job training that may cover topics such as production techniques, personal hygiene, and sanitation procedures.

Education. Students interested in this occupation should take as many high school science and math classes as possible. A solid background in applied chemistry, biology, physics, math, and statistics is important. Knowledge of how to use spreadsheets and databases also may be necessary.

Agricultural and food science technicians typically need an associate's degree in biology, chemistry, crop or animal science, or a related field from an accredited college or university. Many agricultural and food science technician positions require a bachelor's degree. While in college, prospective technicians learn through a combination of technical instruction and hands-on experiences, such as internships.

Some agricultural and food science technicians successfully enter the occupation with a high school diploma but typically need related work experience and on-the-job training that may last a year or more.

A background in the biological or chemical sciences is important for most agricultural and food science technicians. Students may find it helpful to take courses in biology, chemistry, plant or animal science, and agricultural engineering as part of their programs. Many schools offer internships, cooperative-education, and other programs designed to provide hands-on experience and enhance employment prospects.

Training. Agricultural and food science technicians typically undergo on-the-job training. Various federal government regulations outline the types of training needed for technicians, which varies according to the work environment and specific job requirements. Training may cover topics such as production techniques, personal hygiene, and sanitation procedures.

Important Qualities

Analytical skills. Agricultural and food science technicians must conduct a variety of observations and on-site measurements, all of which require precision and accuracy.

Communication skills. Agricultural and food science technicians must be able to understand and give clear instructions, keep detailed records, and, occasionally, write reports.

Critical-thinking skills. Agricultural and food science technicians reach conclusions through sound reasoning and judgment. They determine how to improve food quality and must test products for a variety of safety standards.

Interpersonal skills. Agricultural and food science technicians need to work well with others. They may supervise agricultural and food science workers and receive instruction from scientists or specialists, so effective communication is critical.

Physical stamina. Agricultural and food science technicians who work in manufacturing or agricultural settings may need to stand for long periods, lift objects, and generally perform physical labor.

Work Experience in a Related Occupation. Workers who enter the occupation with only a high school diploma often must have years of experience in a related occupation during which they develop their knowledge of agriculture or manufacturing processes. For more information, see the profiles on food and tobacco processing workers and agricultural workers.

Pay

The median annual wage for agricultural and food science technicians was $35,140 in May 2014. The median wage is the wage at which half the workers in an occupation earned more than that amount and half earned less. The lowest 10 percent earned less than $22,380, and the highest 10 percent earned more than $55,170.

Job Outlook

Employment of agricultural and food science technicians is projected to grow 5 percent from 2014 to 2024, about as fast as the average for all occupations. Advances in technology and scientific knowledge related to food production will require greater control of the production and processing activities, increasing demand for these workers. Continued population growth will drive the need to make production and processing methods more efficient. Greater awareness and enforcement of food safety regulations will expand inspection requirements, increasing the need for agricultural and food science technicians as producers and manufacturers seek ways to improve the quality of their products.

Contacts for More Information

For more information about agricultural and soil science occupations, including certification, visit

- American Society of Agronomy (www.agronomy.org)
- Soil Science Society of America (www.soils.org)

For more information about food and animal science occupations, including certifications, visit

- American Registry of Professional Animal Scientists (www.arpas.org)

Median Annual Wages, May 2014

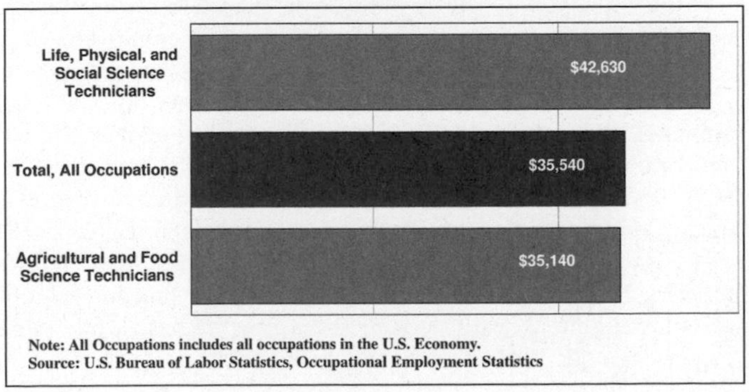

Percent Change in Employment, Projected 2014–2024

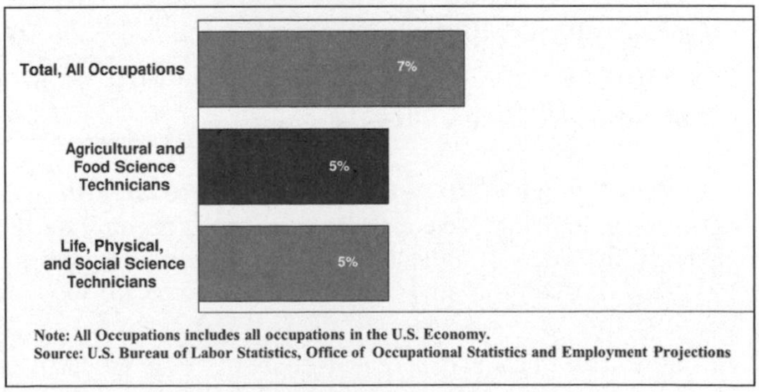

Employment Projections Data for Agricultural and Food Science Technicians

Occupational Title	SOC Code	Employment, 2014	Projected Employment, 2024	Change, 2014–2024 Percent	Change, 2014–2024 Numeric
Agricultural and food science technicians	19-4011	33,000	34,700	5	1,600

Source: U.S. Bureau of Labor Statistics, Employment Projections Program

Similar Occupations. This table shows a list of occupations with job duties that are similar to those of agricultural and food science technicians.

Occupations	Entry-level Education	2014 Median Pay	Projected Job Growth	Average Annual Openings
Agricultural and Food Scientists	Bachelor's degree	$60,690	5%	190
Agricultural Engineers	Bachelor's degree	$71,730	4%	10
Agricultural Workers	See Education/Training	$19,330	-6%	-4,750
Animal Care and Service Workers	High school diploma or equivalent	$20,610	11%	2,570
Biological Technicians	Bachelor's degree	$41,290	5%	410
Chemical Technicians	Associate's degree	$44,180	2%	120
Conservation Scientists and Foresters	Bachelor's degree	$60,360	7%	270
Farmers, Ranchers, and Other Agricultural Managers	High school diploma or equivalent	$68,050	-2%	-1,810
Food and Tobacco Processing Workers	See Education/Training	$26,230	2%	330
Microbiologists	Bachelor's degree	$67,790	4%	80

- American Society of Animal Science (www.asas.org)
- Institute of Food Technologists (www.ift.org)

For information from related governmental agencies, visit

- U.S. Department of Agriculture (www.usda.gov/wps/portal/usda/usdahome)
- U.S. Food and Drug Administration (www.fda.gov)
- Smithsonian Institute (http://forces.si.edu/soils/index.html)

O*NET

- Agricultural and Food Science Technicians (19-4011.00)
- Agricultural Technicians (19-4011.01)
- Food Science Technicians (19-4011.02)

Agricultural and Food Scientists

- **2014 Median Pay** .... $60,690 per year $29.18 per hour
- **Typical Entry-Level Education** .... Bachelor's degree
- **Work Experience in a Related Occupation** .... None
- **On-the-job Training** .... None
- **Number of Jobs, 2014** 36,100
- **Job Outlook, 2014–24** .... 5% (As fast as average)
- **Employment Change, 2014–24** 1,900

What Agricultural and Food Scientists Do

Agricultural and food scientists research ways to improve the efficiency and safety of agricultural establishments and products.

Duties. Agricultural and food scientists typically do the following:

- Conduct research and experiments to improve the productivity and sustainability of field crops and farm animals
- Create new food products and develop new and better ways to process, package, and deliver them
- Study the composition of soil as it relates to plant growth, and research ways to improve it
- Communicate research findings to the scientific community, food producers, and the public
- Travel between facilities to oversee the implementation of new projects

Agricultural and food scientists play an important role in maintaining and expanding the nation's food supply. Many work in basic or applied research and development. Basic research seeks to understand the biological and chemical processes by which crops and livestock grow. Applied research uses the knowledge gained to discover ways to improve the quality, quantity, and safety of agricultural products.

Many agricultural and food scientists work with little supervision, forming their own hypotheses and developing their research methods. In addition, they often lead teams of technicians or students who help in their research. Agricultural and food scientists who are employed in private industry may need to travel between different sites to perform various duties for their employers.

The following are types of agricultural and food scientists:

Animal scientists typically conduct research on domestic farm animals. With a focus on food production, they explore animal genetics, nutrition, reproduction, diseases, growth, and development. They work to develop efficient ways to produce and process meat, poultry, eggs, and milk. Animal scientists may crossbreed animals to make them more productive or improve other characteristics. They advise farmers on how to upgrade housing for animals, lower animal death rates, increase growth rates, or otherwise increase the quality and efficiency of livestock.

Food scientists and technologists use chemistry, biology, and other sciences to study the basic elements of food. They analyze the nutritional content of food, discover new food sources, and research ways to make processed foods safe and healthy. Food technologists generally work in product development, applying findings from food science research to develop new or better ways of selecting, preserving, processing, packaging, and distributing food. Some food scientists use nanotechnology—problem-solving techniques that work on an atomic scale—to develop sensors that can detect contaminants in food. Other food scientists enforce government regulations, inspecting food-processing areas to ensure that they are sanitary and meet waste management standards.

Soil scientists examine the composition of soil, how it affects plant or crop growth, and how alternative soil treatments affect crop productivity. They develop methods of conserving and managing soil that farmers and forestry companies can use. Because soil science is closely related to environmental science, people trained in soil science also work to ensure environmental quality and effective land use.

Plant scientists work to improve crop yields and advise food and crop developers about techniques that could enhance production. They may develop ways to control pests and weeds.

Agricultural and food scientists in private industry commonly work for food production companies, farms, and processing plants. They typically improve inspection standards or overall food quality. They spend their time in a laboratory, where they do tests and experiments, or in the field, where they take samples or assess overall conditions. Other agricultural and food scientists work for pharmaceutical companies, where they use biotechnology processes to develop drugs or other medical products. Some look for ways to process agricultural products into fuels, such as ethanol produced from corn.

At universities, agricultural and food scientists do research and investigate new methods of improving animal or soil health, nutrition, and other facets of food quality. They also write grants to organizations, such as the United States Department of Agriculture (USDA) or the National Institutes of Health (NIH), to get funding for their research. For more information on professors who teach agricultural and food science at universities, see the profile on postsecondary teachers.

In the federal government, agricultural and food scientists conduct research on animal safety and on methods of improving food and crop production. They spend most of their time conducting clinical trials or developing experiments on animal and plant subjects. Agricultural and food scientists eventually present their findings in peer-reviewed journals or other publications.

Work Environment

Agricultural and food scientists held about 36,100 jobs in 2014.

Agricultural and food scientists work in various industries, including colleges and universities, manufacturing, and in scientific research and development. The work of agricultural and food scientists takes place in laboratories, in offices, and in the field. They spend most of their time studying data and reports in a laboratory or an office. Fieldwork includes visits to farms or processing plants.

When visiting a food or animal production facility, agricultural and food scientists must follow biosecurity measures, wear suitable clothing, and tolerate the environment associated with food production processes. This environment may include noise associated with large production machinery, cold temperatures associated with food production or storage, and close proximity to animal byproducts.

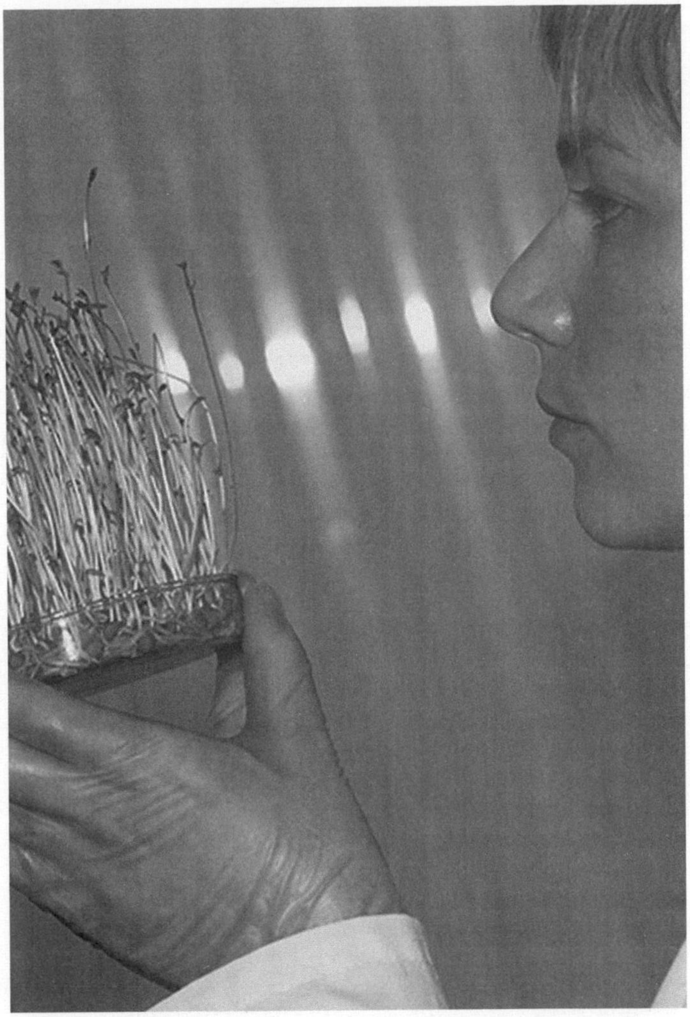

Some agricultural and food scientists conduct experiments on new varieties of crops.

The industries that employed the most animal scientists in 2014 were as follows:

Colleges, universities, and professional schools; state	31%
Research and development in the physical, engineering, and life sciences	17
Support activities for agriculture and forestry	15
Colleges, universities, and professional schools; private	9
Management, scientific, and technical consulting services	6

The industries that employed the most food scientists and technologists in 2014 were as follows:

Food manufacturing	45%
Research and development in the physical, engineering, and life sciences	13
Management of companies and enterprises	10
Colleges, universities, and professional schools; state	6
Testing laboratories	3

The industries that employed the most soil and plant scientists in 2014 were as follows:

Research and development in the physical, engineering, and life sciences	18%
Colleges, universities, and professional schools; state	17
Management, scientific, and technical consulting services	13
Merchant wholesalers, nondurable goods	11
Federal government, excluding postal service	8

Median Annual Wages, May 2014

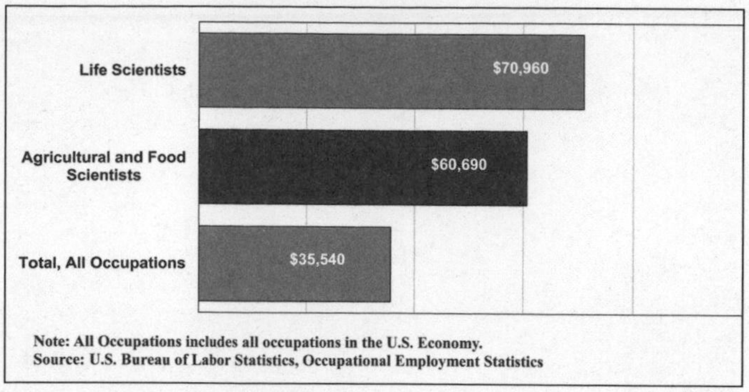

Percent Change in Employment, Projected 2014–2024

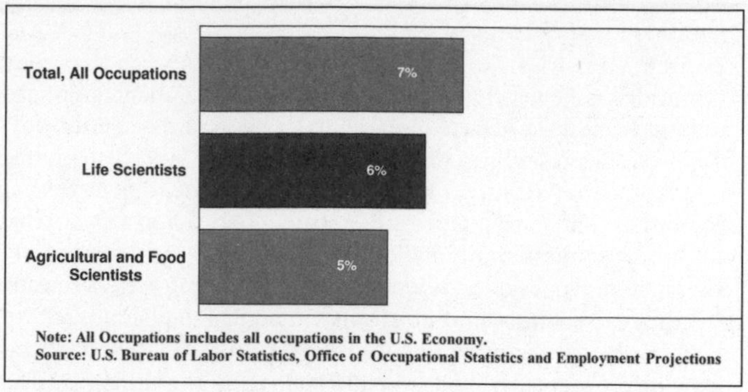

Work Schedules. Agricultural and food scientists typically work full time and have standard schedules. Certain positions may require travel. The amount of travel can vary widely.

Education/Training

Agricultural and food scientists need at least a bachelor's degree from an accredited postsecondary institution, although many earn more advanced degrees. Some animal scientists earn a Doctor of Veterinary Medicine (DVM).

Education. Every state has at least one land-grant college that offers agricultural science degrees. Many other colleges and universities also offer agricultural science degrees or related courses. Degrees in related sciences, such as biology, chemistry, and physics, or in a related engineering specialty also may qualify people for many agricultural science jobs.

Undergraduate coursework for food scientists and technologists and for soil and plant scientists typically includes biology, chemistry, botany, and plant conservation. Students preparing to be food scientists take courses such as food chemistry, food analysis, food microbiology, food engineering, and food-processing operations. Students preparing to be soil and plant scientists take courses in plant pathology, soil chemistry, entomology (the study of insects), plant physiology, and biochemistry.

Undergraduate students in the agricultural and food sciences typically gain a strong foundation in their specialty, with an emphasis on teamwork through internships and research opportunities. Students also are encouraged to take humanities courses, which can help them develop good communication skills, and computer courses, which can familiarize them with common programs and databases.

Many people with bachelor's degrees in agricultural sciences find work in related jobs rather than becoming an agricultural or food scientist. For example, a bachelor's degree in agricultural science is a useful background for farming, ranching, agricultural inspection, farm credit institutions, or companies that make or sell feed, fertilizer, seed, or farm equipment. Combined with coursework in business, agricultural and food science could be a good background for managerial jobs in farm-related or ranch-related businesses. For more information, see the profile on farmers, ranchers, and other agricultural managers.

Many students with bachelor's degrees in application-focused food sciences or agricultural sciences earn advanced degrees in applied topics such as nutrition or dietetics. Students who major in a more basic field, such as biology or chemistry, may be better suited for getting their Ph.D. and doing research within the agricultural and food sciences. During graduate school, there is additional emphasis on lab work and original research, in which prospective animal scientists have the opportunity to do experiments and sometimes supervise undergraduates.

Advanced research topics include genetics, animal reproduction, and biotechnology, among others. Advanced coursework also emphasizes statistical analysis and experiment design, which are important as Ph.D. candidates begin their research.

Some agricultural and food scientists receive a Doctor of Veterinary Medicine. Like Ph.D. candidates in animal science, a prospective veterinarian must first have a bachelor's degree before getting into veterinary school.

Important Qualities

Communication skills. Communication skills are critical for agricultural and food scientists. They must be able to explain their studies: what they were trying to learn, the methods they used, what they found, and what they think the implications of their findings are. They must also be able to communicate well when working with others, including technicians and student assistants.

Critical-thinking skills. Agricultural and food scientists must use their expertise to determine the best way to answer a specific research question.

Data-analysis skills. Agricultural and food scientists, like other researchers, collect data using a variety of methods, including quantitative surveys. They must then apply standard data analysis techniques to understand the data and get the answers to the questions they are studying.

Employment Projections Data for Agricultural and Food Scientists

Occupational Title	SOC Code	Employment, 2014	Projected Employment, 2024	Change, 2014–2024 Percent	Change, 2014–2024 Numeric
Agricultural and food scientists	19-1010	36,100	38,000	5	1,900
Animal scientists	19-1011	2,900	3,200	7	200
Food scientists and technologists	19-1012	15,400	16,000	3	500
Soil and plant scientists	19-1013	17,700	18,900	7	1,200

Source: U.S. Bureau of Labor Statistics, Employment Projections Program

Similar Occupations. This table shows a list of occupations with job duties that are similar to those of agricultural and food scientists.

Occupations	Entry-level Education	2014 Median Pay	Projected Job Growth	Average Annual Openings
Agricultural and Food Science Technicians	Associate's degree	$35,140	5%	160
Biochemists and Biophysicists	Doctoral or professional degree	$84,940	8%	280
Biological Technicians	Bachelor's degree	$41,290	5%	410
Chemical Technicians	Associate's degree	$44,180	2%	120
Conservation Scientists and Foresters	Bachelor's degree	$60,360	7%	270
Environmental Scientists and Specialists	Bachelor's degree	$66,250	11%	1,020
Farmers, Ranchers, and Other Agricultural Managers	High school diploma or equivalent	$68,050	-2%	-1,810
Microbiologists	Bachelor's degree	$67,790	4%	80
Veterinarians	Doctoral or professional degree	$87,590	9%	690
Zoologists and Wildlife Biologists	Bachelor's degree	$58,270	4%	80

Math skills. Agricultural and food scientists, like many other scientists, must have a sound grasp of mathematical concepts.

Observation skills. Agricultural and food scientists conduct experiments that require precise observation of samples and other data. Any mistake could lead to inconclusive or inaccurate results.

Licenses, Certifications, and Registrations. Some states require soil scientists to be licensed to practice. Licensing requirements vary by state, but generally include holding a bachelor's degree with a certain number of credit hours in soil science, working under a licensed scientist for a certain number of years, and passing an examination.

Otherwise, certifications are generally not required for agriculture and food scientists, but they can be useful in advancing one's career. Agricultural and food scientists can get certifications from organizations such as the American Society of Agronomy, the American Registry of Professional Animal Scientists (ARPAS), the Institute of Food Technologists (IFT), or the Soil Science Society of America (SSSA), and others. These certifications recognize expertise in agricultural and food science, and enhance the status of those who are certified.

Qualification for certification is generally based on education, previous professional experience, and passing a comprehensive exam. Scientists may need to take continuing education courses to keep their certification, and they must follow the organization's code of ethics.

Other Experience. Internships are highly recommended for prospective food scientists and technologists. Many entry-level jobs in this occupation are related to food manufacturing, and firsthand experience can be highly valued in that environment.

Pay

The median annual wage for agricultural and food scientists was $60,690 in May 2014. The median wage is the wage at which half the workers in an occupation earned more than that amount and half earned less. The lowest 10 percent earned less than $35,670, and the highest 10 percent earned more than $106,080.

Median annual wages for agricultural and food scientists in May 2014 were as follows:

Food scientists and technologists	$61,480
Animal scientists	61,110
Soil and plant scientists	59,920

Job Outlook

Employment of agricultural and food scientists is projected to grow 5 percent from 2014 to 2024, about as fast as the average for all occupations.

Employment of agricultural and food scientists is projected to grow as research into agricultural production methods and techniques continues. Pressures such as population growth, increased demand for water resources, combating pests and pathogens, changes in climate and weather patterns, and additional demand for agriculture products, such as biofuels, will continue to spur improvements in agricultural efficiency and sustainability.

Animal scientists will be needed to investigate and improve the diets, living conditions, and even genetic makeup of livestock. Food scientists and technologists will work to improve food-processing techniques, ensuring that products are safe, waste is limited, and food is shipped efficiently and safely. Soil and plant scientists will continue to try to understand and map soil composition. They will investigate ways to improve soils and will continue to selectively breed crops to resist pests and disease, improve taste, or to find uses for byproducts.

Job Prospects. A number of job vacancies will arise because many scientists are expected to retire within the next 10 years.

Contacts for More Information

For more information about food and animal scientists, including certifications, visit

- American Society of Agronomy (www.agronomy.org)
- American Society of Animal Science (www.asas.org)
- American Registry of Professional Animal Scientists (www.arpas.org)
- Institute of Food Technologists (www.ift.org)

For more information about agricultural and soil scientists, including certifications, visit

- Soil Science Society of America (www.soils.org)

For information from related governmental agencies, visit

- U.S. Food and Drug Administration (www.fda.gov)
- Smithsonian Institute (http://forces.si.edu/soils/index.html)
- U.S. Department of Agriculture (www.usda.gov/wps/portal/usda/usdahome)

O*NET

- Animal Scientists (19-1011.00)
- Food Scientists and Technologists (19-1012.00)
- Soil and Plant Scientists (19-1013.00)

Anthropologists and Archeologists

- **2014 Median Pay** .... $59,280 per year
  $28.50 per hour
- **Typical Entry-Level Education** .... Master's degree
- **Work Experience in a Related Occupation** .... None
- **On-the-job Training** .... None
- **Number of Jobs, 2014** 7,700
- **Job Outlook, 2014–24** .... 4% (Slower than average)
- **Employment Change, 2014–24** 300

What Anthropologists and Archeologists Do

Anthropologists and archeologists study the origin, development, and behavior of humans. They examine the cultures, languages, archeological remains, and physical characteristics of people in various parts of the world.

Duties. Anthropologists and archeologists typically do the following:

- Plan research projects to answer questions and test hypotheses about human behavior and the interaction between humans within a culture, between different cultures, and between nature and culture
- Develop data collection methods tailored to a particular region, specialty, or project
- Collect information from observations, interviews, and documents
- Record and manage records of observations taken in the field
- Analyze data, laboratory samples, and other sources of information to uncover patterns about human life, culture, and origins
- Prepare reports and present research findings
- Advise organizations on the cultural impact of policies, programs, and products

By drawing and building on knowledge from the humanities and the social, physical, and biological sciences, anthropologists and archeologists examine the ways of life, languages, archeological remains, and physical characteristics of people in various parts of the world. They also examine the customs, values, and social patterns of different cultures.

Many anthropologists and archeologists use sophisticated tools and technologies in their work. Although the equipment used varies by task and specialty, it often includes excavation and measurement tools, laboratory and recording equipment, statistical and database software, and geographic information systems (GIS). Technology is integral to modern research and fieldwork and the use of new technologies is rapidly expanding in the field.

Archeologists examine, recover, and preserve evidence of human activity from past cultures. They analyze human remains and artifacts, such as tools, pottery, cave paintings, and ruins of buildings. They connect their findings with information about past environments to learn about the history, customs, and living habits of people in earlier eras.

Archeologists also manage and protect archeological sites. Some work in national parks or at historical sites, providing site protection and educating the public. Others assess building sites to ensure that construction plans comply with federal regulations on site preservation. Archeologists often specialize in a particular geographic area, period, or object of study, such as animal remains or underwater sites.

Some anthropologists study the social and cultural consequences of current human issues, such as overpopulation, natural disasters, warfare, and poverty; others study the prehistory and the evolution of humans.

A growing number of anthropologists perform market research for businesses by studying the demand for products by a particular culture or social group. Using their anthropological background and a variety of techniques—including interviews, surveys, and observations—they may collect data on how a product is used by specific demographic groups.

The following are examples of types of anthropologists:

Biological anthropologists, also known as *physical anthropologists*, research the evolution and development of the human species. They look for early evidence of human life, analyze genetics, study primates, and examine the biological variations in humans. They analyze how culture and biology influence each other. Some may examine human remains found at archeological sites to understand population demographics or to identify factors—such as nutrition and disease—that affected these populations. Others may work as forensic anthropologists in medical or legal settings, identifying and analyzing skeletal remains and genetic material.

Cultural anthropologists study the customs, cultures, and social lives of groups. They investigate social practices and processes in settings that range from remote, unindustrialized villages to modern urban centers. Cultural anthropologists often spend time living in the societies they study and collect information through observations, interviews, and surveys.

Linguistic anthropologists study how humans communicate and how language shapes social life. They investigate nonverbal communication, the structure and development of languages, and differences among languages. They also examine the role of language in different cultures, how social and cultural factors affect language, and how language affects a person's experiences. Many linguistic anthropologists study non-European languages, which they learn directly from native speakers.

Archeologists mark archeological sites carefully so they can record exactly where they have found human artifacts.

Work Environment

Anthropologists and archeologists held about 7,700 jobs in 2014. The industries that employed the most anthropologists and archeologists were as follows:

Research and development in the social sciences and humanities	28%
Management, scientific, and technical consulting services	23
Federal government, excluding postal service	19
State and local government, excluding education and hospitals	8
Engineering services	7

Anthropologists and archeologists worked in research organizations, government, and consulting firms among other types of organizations. The work of anthropologists varies according to the specific job. Although most anthropologists work in an office, some analyze samples in laboratories or work in the field.

Archeologists often work for cultural resource management (CRM) firms. CRM firms identify, assess, and preserve archeological sites and ensure that developers and builders comply with regulations regarding archeological sites. Archeologists also work in museums, at historical sites, and for government agencies, such as the U.S. Department of the Interior's National Park Service.

Anthropologists and archeologists often do fieldwork, either in the United States or in foreign countries. Fieldwork may involve learning foreign languages, living in remote areas, and examining and excavating archeological sites. Fieldwork usually requires travel for extended periods—about 4 to 8 weeks per year. They often will have to return to the field for several years to complete their research.

Fieldwork may require travel to remote areas or international locations, where anthropologists and archeologists must live with the people they study to learn about their culture. The work can involve rugged living conditions and strenuous physical exertion. While in the field, anthropologists and archeologists often work many hours to meet research deadlines. They may also work with limited funding for their projects.

Work Schedules. Most anthropologists and archeologists work full time during regular business hours. When doing fieldwork, anthropologists and archeologists may be required to travel and work many and irregular hours, including evenings and weekends.

Education/Training

Anthropologists and archeologists need a master's degree or Ph.D. in anthropology or archeology. Experience doing fieldwork in either discipline is also important. Bachelor's degree holders may find work as assistants or fieldworkers.

Education. Most anthropologists and archeologists qualify for available positions with a master's degree in anthropology or archeology. The typical master's degree program takes 2 years to complete and includes field or laboratory research.

Anthropology and archeology students typically conduct field research during their graduate programs, often working abroad or in community-based research. Many students also attend archeological field schools, which teach students how to excavate historical and archeological sites and how to record and interpret their findings and data.

Although a master's degree is enough for many positions, a Ph.D. may be needed for jobs that require leadership skills and advanced technical knowledge. Anthropologists and archeologists typically need a Ph.D. to work internationally in order to comply with the requirements of foreign governments. A Ph.D. takes several years of study beyond a master's degree. Ph.D. students must also complete a doctoral dissertation, which typically includes between 18 and 30 months of field research.

Those with a bachelor's degree in anthropology or archeology and work experience gained through an internship or field school can work as field or laboratory technicians or research assistants. However, anthropologists and archeologists need a master's degree to advance beyond entry-level positions.

Many people with a Ph.D. in anthropology or archeology become professors or museum curators. For more information, see the profiles on postsecondary teachers, and archivists, curators, and museum workers.

Other Experience. Graduates of anthropology and archeology programs usually need work experience in their respective fields and training in quantitative and qualitative research methods. Many students gain experience through field training or internships with museums, historical societies, or nonprofit organizations.

Important Qualities

Analytical skills. Anthropologists and archeologists must possess knowledge of scientific methods and data, which are often used in their research.

Critical-thinking skills. Anthropologists and archeologists must be able to draw conclusions from observations, laboratory experiments, and other methods of research.

Communication skills. Anthropologists and archeologists often have to present their research and findings to their peers and to general audiences.

Investigative skills. Anthropologists and archeologists must seek and explore all facts relevant to their research. They must be able to combine various sources of information to try to solve problems and to answer research questions.

Median Annual Wages, May 2014

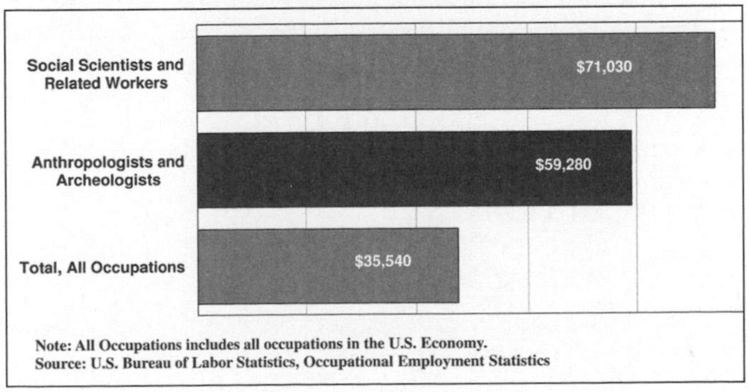

Percent Change in Employment, Projected 2014–2024

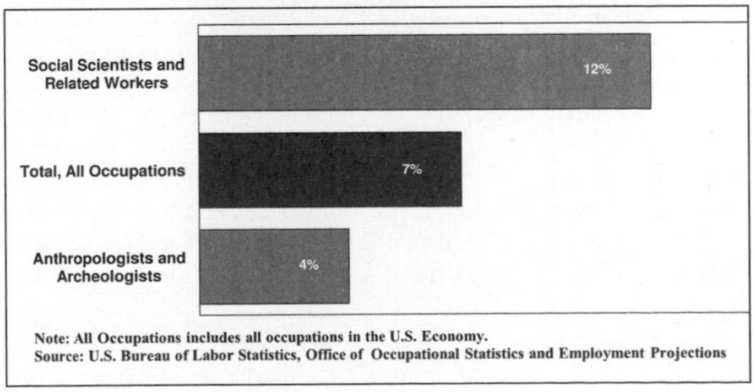

Employment Projections Data for Anthropologists and Archeologists

Occupational Title	SOC Code	Employment, 2014	Projected Employment, 2024	Change, 2014–2024 Percent	Change, 2014–2024 Numeric
Anthropologists and archeologists	19-3091	7,700	8,000	4	300

Source: U.S. Bureau of Labor Statistics, Employment Projections Program

Similar Occupations. This table shows a list of occupations with job duties that are similar to those of anthropologists and archeologists.

Occupations	Entry-level Education	2014 Median Pay	Projected Job Growth	Average Annual Openings
Archivists, Curators, and Museum Workers	See Education/Training	$46,300	7%	210
Economists	Master's degree	$95,710	6%	120
Geographers	Bachelor's degree	$76,420	-2%	0
Historians	Master's degree	$55,870	2%	10
Postsecondary Teachers	See Education/Training	$70,790	13%	17,700
Psychologists	See Education/Training	$70,700	19%	3,250
Sociologists	Master's degree	$72,810	-1%	0
Survey Researchers	Master's degree	$49,760	12%	190

Writing skills. Anthropologists and archeologists need strong writing skills because they often write reports detailing their research findings and publish results in scholarly journals and public interest publications.

Pay

The median annual wage for anthropologists and archeologists was $59,280 in May 2014. The median wage is the wage at which half the workers in an occupation earned more than that amount and half earned less. The lowest 10 percent earned less than $34,580, and the highest 10 percent earned more than $93,650.

In May 2014, the median annual wages for anthropologists and archeologists in the top industries in which they worked were as follows:

Federal government, excluding postal service	$74,120
State and local government, excluding education and hospitals	55,710
Research and development in the social sciences and humanities	55,070
Management, scientific, and technical consulting services	54,780
Engineering services	54,300

Job Outlook

Employment of anthropologists and archeologists is projected to grow 4 percent from 2014 to 2024, slower than the average for all occupations. These workers will be needed to study human life, history, and culture, and to apply that knowledge to current issues.

Corporations will continue to use anthropological research to gain a better understanding of consumer demand within specific cultures or social groups. Anthropologists and archeologists will also be needed to analyze markets, allowing businesses to serve their clients better or to target new customers or demographic groups.

Archeologists will be needed to monitor construction projects, ensuring that builders comply with federal regulations on the preservation and handling of archeological and historical artifacts.

Because anthropological and archeological research may be dependent on research funding, federal budgetary decisions can affect the rate of employment growth in research.

Job Prospects. Overall, prospective anthropologists and archeologists will likely face strong competition for jobs because of the small number of positions relative to applicants. Job prospects will be best for candidates with a Ph.D., extensive anthropological or archeological fieldwork experience, and experience in quantitative and qualitative research methods.

Job opportunities for anthropologists are expected to continue to grow in businesses and consulting firms. Archeologists should have the best job prospects in cultural resource management (CRM) firms.

Contacts for More Information

For more information about careers in anthropology and archeology, visit

- American Anthropological Association (www.aaanet.org)

For more information about careers in archeology, visit

- Archaeological Institute of America (www.archaeological.org)
- Society for American Archaeology (www.saa.org)

For more information about physical anthropologists, visit

- American Association of Physical Anthropologists (www.physanth.org)

O*NET

- Anthropologists and Archeologists (19-3091.00)
- Anthropologists (19-3091.01)
- Archeologists (19-3091.02)

Atmospheric Scientists, Including Meteorologists

- **2014 Median Pay** .... $87,980 per year
  $42.30 per hour
- **Typical Entry-Level Education** .... Bachelor's degree
- **Work Experience in a Related Occupation** .... None
- **On-the-job Training** .... None
- **Number of Jobs, 2014** 11,800
- **Job Outlook, 2014–24** .... 9% (Faster than average)
- **Employment Change, 2014–24** 1,100

What Atmospheric Scientists, Including Meteorologists Do

Atmospheric scientists study the weather and climate, and how those conditions affect human activity and Earth in general. They may develop forecasts, collect and compile data from the field, assist in the development of new data collection instruments, or advise clients on risks or opportunities caused by weather events and climate change.

Duties. Atmospheric scientists typically do the following:

- Measure temperature, atmospheric pressure, humidity, wind speed, dew point, and other properties of the atmosphere
- Use computer models that analyze data about the atmosphere (also called meteorological data)
- Write computer programs to support their modeling efforts
- Generate weather graphics for users
- Report current weather conditions
- Prepare long- and short-term weather forecasts by using computers, mathematical models, satellites, radar, and local station data
- Plan, organize, and participate in outreach programs aimed at educating the public about weather
- Issue warnings to protect life and property when threatened by severe weather, such as hurricanes, tornadoes, and flash floods
- Produce forecasts for transportation activities, including aviation, boating and shipping, and road transportation

Atmospheric scientists use highly developed instruments and computer programs to do their jobs. For example, they use weather balloons, radar systems, and satellites to monitor the weather and collect data. The data they collect and analyze are critical to understanding air pollution, drought, changes in the ozone layer, long-term changes in the climate, and other issues. Atmospheric scientists also use graphics software to illustrate their forecasts and reports in order to advise their clients or the public.

Many atmospheric scientists work with other geoscientists or even social scientists to help solve problems in areas such as commerce, energy, transportation, agriculture, and the environment. For example, some atmospheric scientists work on teams with engineers and geologists to find the best locations for new wind farms, which are groups of wind turbines used to generate electricity. Others work closely with hydrologists and politicians to study the impact climate change may have on water supplies and to manage water resources.

The following are examples of types of atmospheric scientists:

Atmospheric chemists study atmospheric components, reactions, measurement techniques, and processes. They study climates and gases, chemical reactions that occur in clouds, and ultraviolet radiation.

Atmospheric scientists monitor current weather conditions and make weather forecasts.

Atmospheric physicists and dynamists study the physical movements and interactions that occur in the atmosphere. They may study how terrain affects weather and causes turbulence, how solar phenomena affect satellite communications and navigation, or they may study the causes and effects of lightning.

Broadcast meteorologists give forecasts to the general public through television, radio, and the Internet. They use graphics software to develop maps and charts that explain their forecasts. Not all weather broadcasters seen on television are meteorologists or atmospheric scientists. For more information on broadcasters who do not have specific training in meteorology, but present weather conditions and forecasts, see the profile on reporters, correspondents, and broadcast news analysts.

Climatologists study historical weather patterns to interpret long-term weather patterns or shifts in climate by using primarily statistical methods. Global climate change is the main area of study for climatologists. Paleoclimatology is a specialization within this field. Climatologists who specialize in paleoclimatology may take samples from icebergs and other sources to gather data on the atmosphere that cover very long periods of time.

Climate scientists work on the theoretical foundations and the modeling of climate change. The nature of this work requires the use of complex mathematical models to try to forecast many months, and sometimes longer, into the future. Their studies can be used to design buildings, plan heating and cooling systems, and aid in efficient land use and agricultural production.

Forensic meteorologists use historical weather data to reconstruct the weather conditions for a specific location and time. They investigate what role weather played in unusual events such as traffic accidents and fires. Forensic meteorologists may be called as experts to testify in court.

Research meteorologists develop new methods of data collection, observation, and forecasting. They also conduct studies to improve basic understandings of climate, weather, and other aspects of the atmosphere. For example, some research meteorologists study severe weather patterns, such as hurricanes and tornadoes, to understand why cyclones form and to develop better ways of predicting them. Others focus on environmental problems, such as air pollution. Research meteorologists often work with scientists in other fields. For example, they may work with computer scientists to develop new forecasting software or with oceanographers to study interactions between the ocean and the atmosphere. They may also work with engineers to develop new instruments so that they can collect the data they need.

Weather forecasters use computer and mathematical models to produce weather reports and short-term forecasts that can range from a few minutes to more than a week. They develop forecasts for the general public and for specific customers such as airports, farmers, utilities, insurance companies, and other businesses. For example, they may provide forecasts to power suppliers so that the suppliers can plan for events, such as heat waves, which would cause a change in electricity demand. They also issue advanced warnings for potentially severe weather such as blizzards and hurricanes. Some forecasters prepare long-range outlooks to predict whether temperatures and precipitation levels will be above or below average in a particular month or season. These workers become familiar with general weather patterns, atmospheric predictability, precipitation, and forecasting techniques.

Some people with an atmospheric science background may become professors or teachers. For more information, see the profile on postsecondary teachers.

Work Environment

Atmospheric scientists, including meteorologists held about 11,800 jobs in 2014. The industries that employed the most atmospheric scientists, including meteorologists were as follows:

Professional, scientific, and technical services	40%
Federal government	26
Colleges, universities, and professional schools; state, local, and private	20
Television broadcasting	6

In the federal government, most atmospheric scientists work as weather forecasters with the National Weather Service of the National Oceanic and Atmospheric Administration (NOAA) in weather stations throughout the United States—at airports, in or near cities, and in isolated and remote areas. In smaller stations, they often work alone; in larger ones, they work as part of a team. In addition, hundreds of members of the Armed Forces are involved in atmospheric science.

Atmospheric scientists involved in professional, scientific, and technical services or research often work in offices and laboratories. Some may travel frequently to collect data in the field and to observe weather events, such as tornadoes, up close. They also observe actual weather conditions from the ground or from an aircraft. These scientists may also create small replicas of weather phenomena, in an off-site setting such as a warehouse, for study of the actual phenomena.

Broadcast meteorologists present their reports to the general public from television and radio studios. They also may broadcast from outdoor locations to tell audiences about current weather conditions.

Atmospheric scientists who work in private industry may have to travel to meet with clients or to gather information in the field. For example, forensic meteorologists may need to collect information from the scene of an accident as part of their investigation.

Work Schedules. Most atmospheric scientists work full time. Weather conditions can change quickly, so weather forecasters need to continuously monitor conditions. Many, especially entry-level staff at field stations, work rotating shifts to cover all 24 hours in a day. For this reason, they work nights, weekends, and holidays to provide the most current weather information. In addition, they work extended hours during severe weather, such as hurricanes. Other atmospheric scientists have a standard workweek, although researchers may work nights and weekends on particular projects.

Education/Training

Atmospheric scientists need a bachelor's degree in meteorology or a closely related earth sciences field for most positions. For research positions, atmospheric scientists need a master's degree at minimum, but usually will need a Ph.D.

Education. Atmospheric scientists typically need a bachelor's degree, either in atmospheric science or a related scientific field that specifically studies atmospheric qualities and phenomena. Bachelor's degrees in physics, chemistry, or geology are usually adequate, alternative preparation for those who wish to enter the atmospheric sciences. Many schools offer atmospheric science courses through other departments, such as physics and geosciences. Prospective meteorologists usually take courses outside of the typical atmospheric sciences field.

Course requirements, in addition to courses in meteorology and atmospheric science, usually include advanced courses in physics and mathematics. Classes in computer programming are important because many atmospheric scientists have to write and edit the computer software programs that produce forecasts. Coursework in communications is also becoming important as organizations are increasing their efforts to make their data accessible to the public and to educate their communities and the nation. And because of recent advancements in technology, a class in remote sensing of the environment, by radar or satellite, may be required.

Courses should be taken in subjects that are relevant to their desired area of specialization. For example, those who wish to become broadcast meteorologists for radio or television stations may take courses in speech, journalism, or related fields.

Median Annual Wages, May 2014

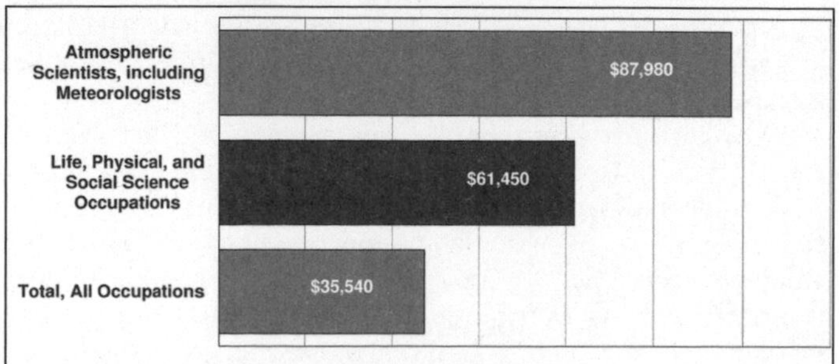

Note: All Occupations includes all occupations in the U.S. Economy.
Source: U.S. Bureau of Labor Statistics, Occupational Employment Statistics

Percent Change in Employment, Projected 2014–2024

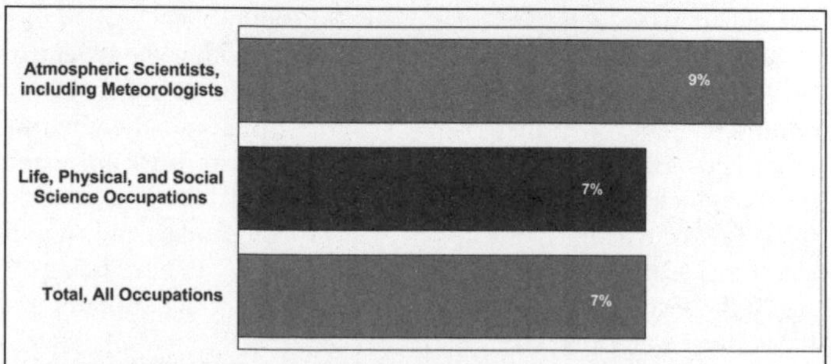

Note: All Occupations includes all occupations in the U.S. Economy.
Source: U.S. Bureau of Labor Statistics, Office of Occupational Statistics and Employment Projections

Employment Projections Data for Atmospheric Scientists, Including Meteorologists

Occupational Title	SOC Code	Employment, 2014	Projected Employment, 2024	Change, 2014–2024 Percent	Numeric
Atmospheric and space scientists	19-2021	11,800	12,900	9	1,100

Source: U.S. Bureau of Labor Statistics, Employment Projections Program

Atmospheric scientists who work in research must at least have a master's degree, but will usually need a Ph.D. in atmospheric science or a related field. Most graduate programs do not require prospective students to have a bachelor's degree in atmospheric science; a bachelor's degree in mathematics, physics, or engineering is excellent preparation for graduate study in atmospheric science. In addition to advanced meteorological coursework, graduate students take courses in other disciplines, such as oceanography and geophysics.

Important Qualities

Analytical skills. Atmospheric scientists must be able to focus for many hours, working with computer models and massive amounts of data to prepare analyses on their findings.

Communication skills. Atmospheric scientists need to be able to write and speak clearly so that their knowledge about the weather can be used effectively by communities and individuals.

Critical-thinking skills. Atmospheric scientists need to be able to analyze the results of their computer models and forecasts to determine the most likely outcome.

Math skills. Atmospheric scientists use calculus, statistics, and other advanced topics in mathematics to develop models used to forecast the weather. They also use mathematical calculations to study the relationship between properties of the atmosphere, such as how changes in air pressure may affect air temperature.

Training. Atmospheric scientists and meteorologists who find employment in the National Weather Service will need to take 200 hours of on-the-job training per year for the first 2 years of employment.

Advancement. Although it is not necessary for entry, a master's degree in atmospheric science can greatly enhance employment opportunities, pay, and advancement potential for meteorologists in government and private industry. A master's degree in business administration (MBA) may be useful for meteorologists interested in working in private industry as consultants who help firms make important business decisions on the basis of their forecasts.

Pay

The median annual wage for atmospheric scientists, including meteorologists was $87,980 in May 2014. The median wage is the wage at which half the workers in an occupation earned more than that amount and half earned less. The lowest 10 percent earned less than $50,030, and the highest 10 percent earned more than $128,670.

In May 2014, the median annual wages for atmospheric scientists, including meteorologists in the top industries in which they worked were as follows:

Federal government	$99,090
Television broadcasting	84,860
Professional, scientific, and technical services	82,610
Colleges, universities, and professional schools; state, local, and private	71,900

Job Outlook

Employment of atmospheric scientists is projected to grow 9 percent from 2014 to 2024, faster than the average for all occupations.

New computer models have vastly improved the accuracy of forecasts and allowed atmospheric scientists to tailor forecasts to specific purposes. This should maintain, and perhaps increase, the need for atmospheric scientists working in private industry as businesses demand more specialized weather information.

Businesses increasingly rely on just-in-time delivery to avoid the expenses incurred by traditional inventory management methods. Severe weather can interrupt ground or air transportation and delay inventory delivery. Businesses have begun to maintain forecasting teams around the clock to advise delivery personnel, helping them stay on schedule. In addition, severe weather patterns have become widely recognized, and industries have become increasingly concerned about their impact, which will create demand for work in atmospheric science.

As utility companies continue to adopt wind and solar power, they must depend more heavily on weather forecasting to arrange for buying and selling power. This should lead to increased reliance on atmospheric scientists to help utilities know when they can sell their excess power, and when they will need to buy.

Job Prospects. Prospective atmospheric scientists should expect continued competition because the number of graduates from meteorology programs is expected to exceed the number of job openings requiring only a bachelor's degree. Workers with a graduate degree should have better prospects than those whose highest level of education is a bachelor's degree. Prospective atmospheric scientists with knowledge of advanced mathematics also will have better job prospects because of the highly quantitative nature of much of this occupation's work.

Competition may be strong for research positions at colleges and universities because of the limited number of positions available. Few opportunities are expected in federal government because atmospheric scientists will be hired only to replace workers who retire or leave for other reasons. Budget constraints are also expected to limit hiring by federal agencies such as the National Weather Service. The best job prospects for meteorologists are expected to be in private industry.

The National Weather Service and the University Corporation for Atmospheric Research (UCAR) sponsor an online training program called COMET. The training, for both novice and fully trained atmospheric scientists, helps participants to stay current with the latest science and technology. Training is offered in a series of self-paced lessons, which are combined into courses. Certificates of completion are awarded for both lessons and courses. Completing such coursework may help prospective atmospheric scientists to have better job prospects.

Contacts for More Information

For more information about atmospheric scientists, including a list of colleges and universities offering atmospheric science programs, visit

➤ American Meteorological Society (www.ametsoc.org)

Similar Occupations. This table shows a list of occupations with job duties that are similar to those of atmospheric scientists, including meteorologists.

Occupations	Entry-level Education	2014 Median Pay	Projected Job Growth	Average Annual Openings
Chemists and Materials Scientists	Bachelor's degree	$74,720	3%	260
Computer Programmers	Bachelor's degree	$77,550	-8%	-2,650
Environmental Engineers	Bachelor's degree	$83,360	12%	680
Environmental Scientists and Specialists	Bachelor's degree	$66,250	11%	1,020
Geoscientists	Bachelor's degree	$89,910	10%	380
Hydrologists	Bachelor's degree	$78,370	7%	50
Mathematicians	Master's degree	$103,720	21%	70
Physicists and Astronomers	Doctoral or professional degree	$109,290	7%	150
Postsecondary Teachers	See Education/Training	$70,790	13%	17,700

➤ National Weather Association (www.nwas.org/links/career_info.php)

For a broad range of information concerning atmospheric scientists within the geosciences perspective, visit

➤ American Geosciences Institute (www.americangeosciences.org)

For more information about atmospheric science careers in research, visit

➤ University Corporation for Atmospheric Research (UCAR) (http://www2.ucar.edu)

For more information about federal government education requirements for atmospheric science positions, visit

➤ U.S. Office of Personnel Management (http://tinyurl.com/5nbjpg)

For more information about the COMET training program, visit

➤ MetEd (www.meted.ucar.edu/training_detail.php)

To find job openings for atmospheric scientists in the federal government, visit

➤ USAJOBS (www.usajobs.gov)

For information about federal government atmospheric science careers in the National Weather Service and other agencies within the National Oceanic and Atmospheric Administration, visit

➤ National Oceanic and Atmospheric Administration (www.noaa.gov)

O*NET

➤ Atmospheric and Space Scientists (19-2021.00)

Biochemists and Biophysicists

- **2014 Median Pay** .... $84,940 per year $40.84 per hour
- **Typical Entry-Level Education** .... Doctoral or professional degree
- **Work Experience in a Related Occupation** .... None
- **On-the-job Training** .... None
- **Number of Jobs, 2014** 34,100
- **Job Outlook, 2014–24** .... 8% (As fast as average)
- **Employment Change, 2014–24** 2,800

What Biochemists and Biophysicists Do

Biochemists and biophysicists study the chemical and physical principles of living things and of biological processes, such as cell development, growth, heredity, and disease.

Duties. Biochemists and biophysicists typically do the following:

- Plan and conduct complex projects in basic and applied research
- Manage laboratory teams and monitor the quality of their work
- Isolate, analyze, and synthesize proteins, fats, DNA, and other molecules
- Research the effects of substances such as drugs, hormones, and nutrients on tissues and biological processes
- Keep up with current knowledge by reviewing the findings of other researchers and by attending conferences
- Prepare technical reports, research papers, and recommendations based on their research findings
- Present research findings to scientists, engineers, and other colleagues

Biochemists and biophysicists use advanced technologies, such as lasers and fluorescent microscopes, to conduct scientific experiments and analysis. They also use X-rays and computer modeling software to determine the three-dimensional structures of proteins and other molecules. Biochemists and biophysicists involved in biotechnology research use chemical enzymes to synthesize recombinant DNA.

Biochemists and biophysicists work in basic and applied research. Basic research is conducted without any immediately known application; the goal is to expand human knowledge. Applied research is directed toward solving a particular problem.

Biochemists involved in basic research may study the molecular mechanisms by which cells feed, divide, and grow. Others study the evolution of plants and animals, to understand how genetic traits are carried through successive generations.

Biophysicists may conduct basic research to learn how nerve cells communicate or how proteins work. Biochemists and biophysicists who conduct basic research typically must submit written grant proposals to colleges and universities, private foundations, and the federal government to get the money they need for their research.

Biochemists and biophysicists who conduct applied research attempt to develop products and processes that improve people's lives. For example, in medicine, biochemists and biophysicists develop tests used to detect infections, genetic disorders, and other diseases. They also develop new drugs and medications, such as those used to treat cancer or Alzheimer's disease.

Applied research in biochemistry and biophysics has many uses outside of medicine. In agriculture, biochemists and biophysicists research ways to genetically engineer crops so that they will be resistant to drought, disease, insects, and other afflictions. Biochemists and biophysicists also investigate alternative fuels, such as biofuels—renewable energy sources from plants. In addition, they develop ways to protect the environment and clean up pollution.

Many people with a biochemistry background become professors and teachers. For more information, see the profile on postsecondary teachers.

Work Environment

Biochemists and biophysicists held about 34,100 jobs in 2014. The industries that employed the most biochemists and biophysicists were as follows:

Research and development in the physical, engineering, and life sciences	47%
Colleges, universities, and professional schools; state, local, and private	16
Pharmaceutical and medicine manufacturing	14
Management of companies and enterprises	3
Basic chemical manufacturing	2

Biochemists and biophysicists typically work in laboratories and offices, to conduct experiments and analyze the results. Those who work with dangerous organisms or toxic substances in the laboratory must follow safety procedures to avoid contamination.

Most biochemists and biophysicists work on teams. Research projects are often interdisciplinary, and biochemists and biophysicists frequently work with experts in other fields, such as physics, chemistry, computer science, and engineering. Those working in biological research generate large amounts of data. They collaborate with specialists called *bioinformaticians*, who use their knowledge of statistics, mathematics, engineering, and computer science to mine datasets for correlations that might explain biological phenomena.

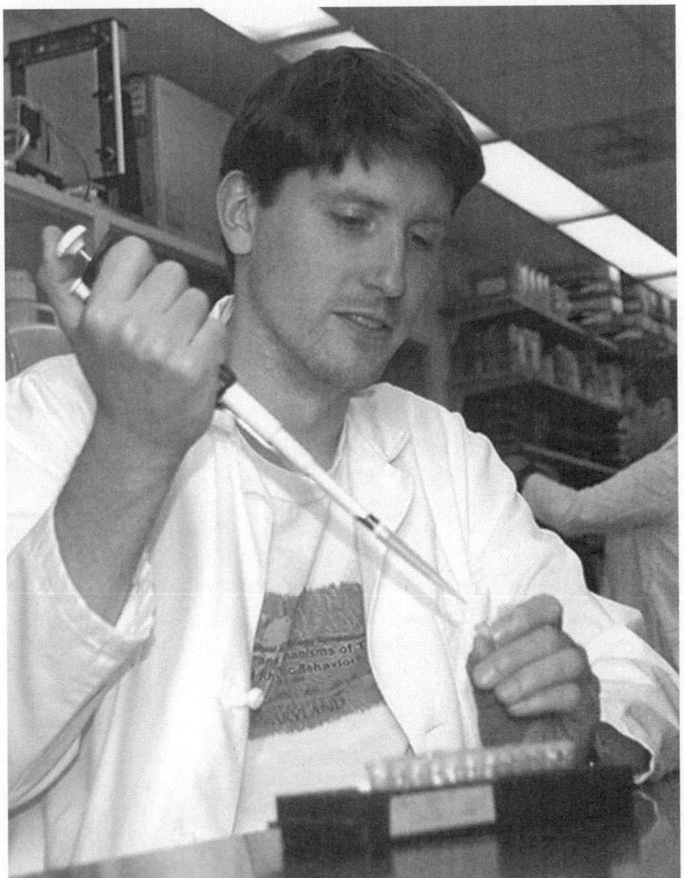

Biochemists and biophysicists conduct research in college or university, private industry, and government laboratories.

Some biotech companies need researchers to help sell their products. These products often rely on very complex technologies, and having an expert explain them to potential customers might be necessary. This role for researchers may be more common in smaller companies, where workers often fulfill multiple roles, such as working in research and in sales. Working in sales may require a substantial amount of travel. For more information on sales representatives, see the profile on wholesale and manufacturing sales representatives.

Work Schedules. Most biochemists and biophysicists work full time and keep regular hours. They may occasionally have to work additional hours to meet project deadlines or to perform time-sensitive laboratory experiments.

Education/Training

Most Ph.D. holders begin their careers in temporary postdoctoral research positions. Bachelor's and master's degree holders are qualified for some entry-level positions in biochemistry and biophysics.

Education. Most Ph.D. holders in biochemistry and biophysics have bachelor's degrees in biochemistry or a related field, such as biology, chemistry, physics, or engineering. High school students can prepare for college by taking classes related to the natural and physical sciences, as well as math and computer science.

Students in bachelor's degree programs in biochemistry or a related field typically take courses in mathematics, physics, and computer science in addition to courses in the biological and chemical sciences. Courses in mathematics and computer science are important for biochemists and biophysicists, who must be able to do complex data analysis. Most bachelor's degree programs include required laboratory coursework. Additional laboratory coursework is excellent preparation for graduate school or for getting an entry-level position in industry. Students can gain valuable laboratory experience by working for a university's laboratories. Occasionally, they can also gain such experience through internships with prospective employers, such as pharmaceutical and medicine manufacturers.

Ph.D. programs typically include advanced coursework in topics such as toxicology, genetics, and proteomics (the study of proteins). Several graduate programs include courses in bioinformatics, which involves using computers to study and analyze large amounts of biological data. Graduate students also spend a lot of time conducting laboratory research. Study at the master's level is generally considered good preparation for those interested in doing hands-on laboratory work. Ph.D.-level studies provide additional training in the planning and execution of research projects.

Training. Most biochemistry and biophysics Ph.D. holders begin their careers in temporary postdoctoral research positions. During their postdoctoral appointments, they work with experienced scientists as they continue to learn about their specialties or develop a broader understanding of related areas of research.

Postdoctoral positions frequently offer the opportunity to publish research findings. A solid record of published research is essential to getting a permanent college or university faculty position.

Important Qualities

Analytical skills. Biochemists and biophysicists must be able to conduct scientific experiments and analyses with accuracy and precision.

Median Annual Wages, May 2014

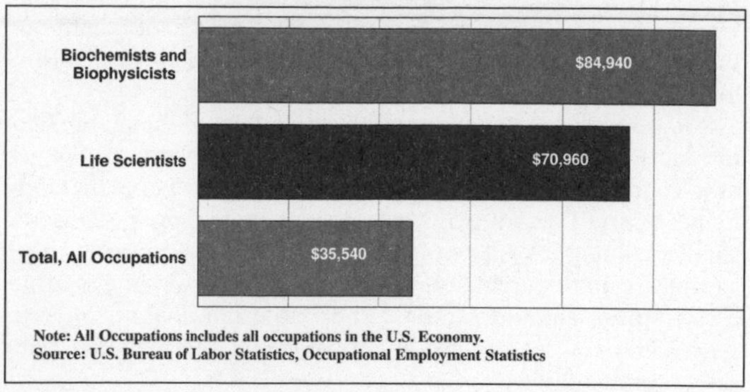

Percent Change in Employment, Projected 2014–2024

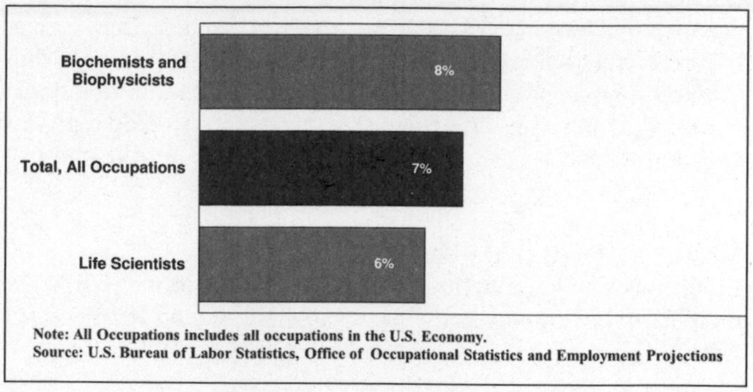

Communication skills. Biochemists and biophysicists have to write and publish reports and research papers, give presentations of their findings, and communicate with team members.

Critical-thinking skills. Biochemists and biophysicists draw conclusions from experimental results through sound reasoning and judgment.

Interpersonal skills. Biochemists and biophysicists typically work on interdisciplinary research teams and need to work well with others toward a common goal. Many serve as team leaders and must be able to motivate and direct other team members.

Math skills. Biochemists and biophysicists use complex equations and formulas regularly in their work; they also need a broad understanding of mathematics, including calculus and statistics.

Perseverance. Biochemists and biophysicists need to be thorough in their research and in their approach to problems. Scientific research involves substantial trial and error, and biochemists and biophysicists must not become discouraged in their work.

Problem-solving skills. Biochemists and biophysicists use scientific experiments and analysis to find solutions to complex scientific problems.

Time-management skills. Biochemists and biophysicists usually need to meet deadlines when conducting research. They must be able to manage time and prioritize tasks efficiently while maintaining their quality of work.

Advancement. Some biochemists and biophysicists become natural sciences managers. Those who pursue management careers spend much of their time on administrative tasks, such as preparing budgets and schedules.

Pay

The median annual wage for biochemists and biophysicists was $84,940 in May 2014. The median wage is the wage at which half the workers in an occupation earned more than that amount and half earned less. The lowest 10 percent earned less than $44,220, and the highest 10 percent earned more than $149,130.

In May 2014, the median annual wages for biochemists and biophysicists in the top industries in which they worked were as follows:

Management of companies and enterprises	$114,180
Research and development in the physical, engineering, and life sciences	89,420
Pharmaceutical and medicine manufacturing	87,360
Basic chemical manufacturing	73,020
Colleges, universities, and professional schools; state, local, and private	55,570

Job Outlook

Employment of biochemists and biophysicists is projected to grow 8 percent from 2014 to 2024, about as fast as the average for all occupations. More biochemists and biophysicists are expected to be needed to do basic research that increases scientific knowledge and to research and develop biological products and processes that improve people's lives. However, budgetary concerns may limit researchers' access to funding for basic research.

The large baby-boom population is aging, and that, along with the demand for lifesaving new drugs and procedures to cure and to prevent disease, likely will drive demand for biochemists and biophysicists involved in biomedical research. For example, biochemists will be needed to conduct genetic research and to develop new medicines and treatments that are used to fight genetic disorders and diseases such as cancer. They will also be needed to develop new tests used to detect diseases and other illnesses. Currently, it is the smaller pharmaceutical companies, rather than the large companies, that tend to do biomedical research. This state of affairs helps the larger companies avoid risks and costs.

Areas of research and development in biotechnology other than health also are expected to provide employment growth for biochemists and biophysicists. Greater demand for clean energy should increase the need for biochemists who research and develop alternative energy sources, such as biofuels. A growing population and rising food prices are expected to fuel the development of genetically engineered crops and livestock that provide greater yields and require fewer resources. Efforts to discover new and improved ways to clean up and preserve the environment will increase demand for biochemists and biophysicists as well.

Employment Projections Data for Biochemists and Biophysicists

Occupational Title	SOC Code	Employment, 2014	Projected Employment, 2024	Change, 2014–2024 Percent	Change, 2014–2024 Numeric
Biochemists and biophysicists	19-1021	34,100	36,900	8	2,800

Source: U.S. Bureau of Labor Statistics, Employment Projections Program

Similar Occupations. This table shows a list of occupations with job duties that are similar to those of biochemists and biophysicists.

Occupations	Entry-level Education	2014 Median Pay	Projected Job Growth	Average Annual Openings
Agricultural and Food Scientists	Bachelor's degree	$60,690	5%	190
Biological Technicians	Bachelor's degree	$41,290	5%	410
Biomedical Engineers	Bachelor's degree	$86,950	23%	510
Chemists and Materials Scientists	Bachelor's degree	$74,720	3%	260
Epidemiologists	Master's degree	$67,420	6%	40
Medical Scientists	Doctoral or professional degree	$79,930	8%	900
Microbiologists	Bachelor's degree	$67,790	4%	80
Natural Sciences Managers	Bachelor's degree	$120,050	3%	180
Physicians and Surgeons	Doctoral or professional degree	This wage is equal to or greater than $187,200.	14%	9,930
Physicists and Astronomers	Doctoral or professional degree	$109,290	7%	150
Postsecondary Teachers	See Education/Training	$70,790	13%	17,700
Zoologists and Wildlife Biologists	Bachelor's degree	$58,270	4%	80

Job Prospects. Biochemists and biophysicists involved in basic research should expect strong competition for permanent research and faculty positions at colleges and universities. Biochemists and biophysicists with postdoctoral experience who have had research articles published in scientific journals should have the best prospects for these positions. Many biochemists and biophysicists work through multiple postdoctoral appointments before getting a permanent position in academia.

A large portion of basic research in biochemistry and biophysics is dependent on funding from the federal government through the National Institutes of Health and the National Science Foundation. Therefore, federal budgetary decisions will have a large impact on job prospects in basic research from year to year. Typically, there is strong competition among biochemists and biophysicists for research funding.

Most applied research projects that involve biochemists and biophysicists require the expertise of scientists in multiple fields, such as microbiology, medicine, and chemistry. Biochemists and biophysicists who have a broad understanding of molecular biology and its relationship to other disciplines should have the best job opportunities.

Those who gain laboratory experience through coursework or employment during their undergraduate studies will be the best prepared and have the best chances of gaining employment or entering graduate-level programs.

Contacts for More Information

For more information about biochemists, visit

- American Chemical Society (www.acs.org/content/acs/en.html)
- American Chemical Society Division of Biological Chemistry (www.divbiolchem.org)
- American Society for Biochemistry and Molecular Biology (www.asbmb.org)

For more information about biophysicists, visit

- Biophysical Society (www.biophysics.org)

For general information about careers in biological sciences, visit

- American Institute of Biological Sciences (www.aibs.org/home/index.html)
- Federation of American Societies for Experimental Biology (www.faseb.org)

O*NET

- Biochemists and Biophysicists (19-1021.00)

Biological Technicians

- **2014 Median Pay** .... $41,290 per year $19.85 per hour
- **Typical Entry-Level Education** .... Bachelor's degree
- **Work Experience in a Related Occupation** .... None
- **On-the-job Training** .... None
- **Number of Jobs, 2014** 79,300
- **Job Outlook, 2014–24** .... 5% (As fast as average)
- **Employment Change, 2014–24** 4,100

What Biological Technicians Do

Biological technicians help biological and medical scientists conduct laboratory tests and experiments.

Duties. Biological technicians typically do the following:

- Set up, maintain, and clean laboratory instruments and equipment, such as microscopes, scales, and test tubes
- Gather and prepare biological samples, such as blood, food, and bacteria cultures, for laboratory analysis
- Conduct biological tests and experiments
- Document their work, including procedures, observations, and results
- Analyze experimental data and interpret results
- Write reports that summarize their findings

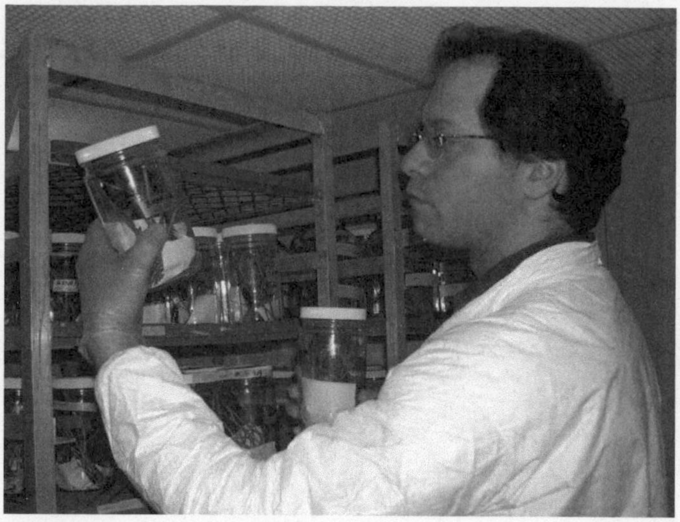

Most biological technicians work in laboratories.

Most biological technicians work on teams. Biological technicians typically are responsible for doing scientific tests, experiments, and analyses under the supervision of biologists or other scientists who direct and evaluate their work. Biological technicians use traditional laboratory instruments, advanced robotics, and automated equipment to conduct experiments. They use specialized computer software to collect, analyze, and model experimental data. Some biological technicians collect samples in the field, so they may need certain skills, such as the ability to hike long distances over sometimes rugged terrain to collect water samples.

Biological technicians work in many research areas. They may assist medical researchers by helping to develop new medicines and treatments used to prevent, treat, or cure diseases.

Biological technicians working in a microbiological context, sometimes referred to as *laboratory assistants*, typically study living microbes and perform techniques specific to microbiology, such as growing cultures in petri dishes or staining specimens to aid in their identification.

Technicians working in biotechnology apply the knowledge and techniques they have gained from basic research to product development.

Biological technicians also may work in private industry and assist in the study of a wide range of topics concerning mining and industrial production. They may test samples in environmental impact studies, or monitor production processes to help ensure that products are not contaminated.

Biological technicians working for the U.S. Department of Agriculture or other government agencies may perform biological testing to support agricultural research and wildlife and resource management goals.

Work Environment

Biological technicians held about 79,300 jobs in 2014. The industries that employed the most biological technicians were as follows:

Research and development in the physical, engineering, and life sciences	26%
Colleges, universities, and professional schools; state	16
Federal government, excluding postal service	12
Colleges, universities, and professional schools; private	10
Chemical manufacturing	9

Biological technicians typically work in laboratories and offices, where they conduct experiments and analyze the results under the supervision of biological scientists and medical scientists. Some biological technicians who do fieldwork may be exposed to weather events and wildlife, such as mosquitoes.

Biological technicians must follow strict procedures to avoid contaminating the experiment, themselves, or the environment. Some experiments may involve dangerous organisms or toxic substances.

Biological technicians work together on teams under the direction of biologists or other scientists.

Work Schedules. Most biological technicians work full time and keep regular hours.

Education/Training

Biological technicians typically need a bachelor's degree in biology or a closely related field. It is important for prospective biological technicians to gain laboratory experience while they are in school.

Education. Biological technicians typically need a bachelor's degree in biology or a closely related field. Most colleges and universities offer bachelor's degree programs in the biological sciences.

Biological science programs usually include courses in general biology, as well as in specific subfields such as ecology, microbiology, and physiology. In addition to taking courses in biology, students must study chemistry, mathematics, and physics. Computer science courses are helpful for learning how to model and simulate biological processes and for learning how to operate some laboratory equipment.

Laboratory experience is important for prospective biological technicians, so students should take biology courses that emphasize laboratory work.

Median Annual Wages, May 2014

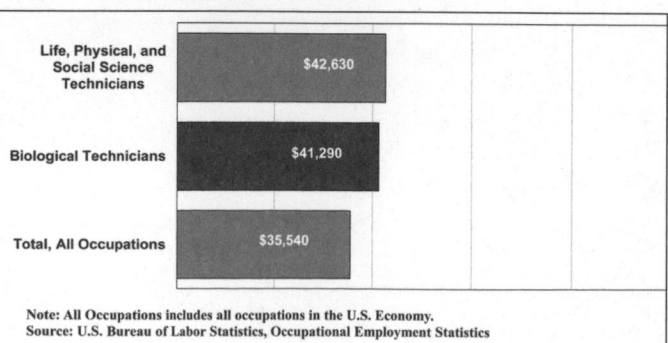

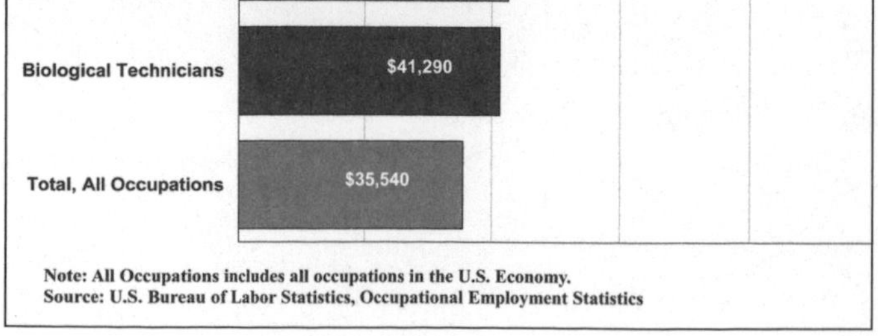

Percent Change in Employment, Projected 2014–2024

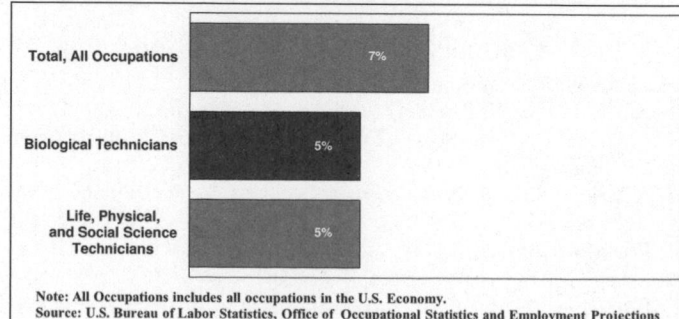

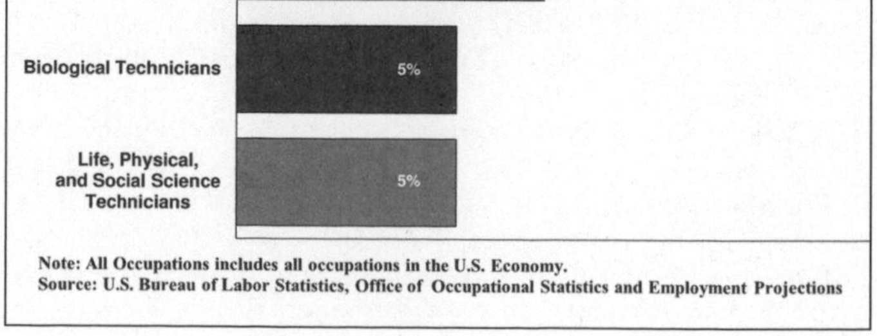

Employment Projections Data for Biological Technicians

Occupational Title	SOC Code	Employment, 2014	Projected Employment, 2024	Change, 2014–2024 Percent	Change, 2014–2024 Numeric
Biological technicians	19-4021	79,300	83,500	5	4,100

Source: U.S. Bureau of Labor Statistics, Employment Projections Program

Similar Occupations. This table shows a list of occupations with job duties that are similar to those of biological technicians.

Occupations	Entry-level Education	2014 Median Pay	Projected Job Growth	Average Annual Openings
Agricultural and Food Science Technicians	Associate's degree	$35,140	5%	160
Biochemists and Biophysicists	Doctoral or professional degree	$84,940	8%	280
Chemical Technicians	Associate's degree	$44,180	2%	120
Environmental Science and Protection Technicians	Associate's degree	$42,190	9%	340
Epidemiologists	Master's degree	$67,420	6%	40
Forensic Science Technicians	Bachelor's degree	$55,360	27%	380
Geoscientists	Bachelor's degree	$89,910	10%	380
Medical and Clinical Laboratory Technologists and Technicians	See Education/Training	$49,310	16%	5,210
Medical Scientists	Doctoral or professional degree	$79,930	8%	900
Microbiologists	Bachelor's degree	$67,790	4%	80
Zoologists and Wildlife Biologists	Bachelor's degree	$58,270	4%	80

Important Qualities

Analytical skills. Biological technicians need to conduct scientific experiments and analyses with accuracy and precision.

Communication skills. Biological technicians must understand and follow the instructions of their managing scientists. They also need to be able to communicate their processes and findings clearly in written reports.

Critical-thinking skills. Biological technicians draw conclusions from experimental results through sound reasoning and judgment.

Observational skills. Biological technicians must constantly monitor their experiments. They need to keep a complete, accurate record of their work, including the conditions under which the experiment was carried out, the procedures they followed, and the results they obtained.

Technical skills. Biological technicians need to set up and operate sophisticated equipment and instruments. They also may need to adjust equipment to ensure that experiments are conducted properly.

Other Experience. Prospective biological technicians should have laboratory experience. In addition to coursework, students may gain laboratory experience during summer internships with prospective employers, such as pharmaceutical and medicine manufacturers, or in university laboratories.

Advancement. Biological technicians may advance to scientist positions, such as microbiologist, after a few years of experience working as a technician or after earning a master's degree or Ph.D. Gaining more experience and higher levels of education often allows biological technicians to move into positions such as natural sciences managers or postsecondary teachers.

Pay

The median annual wage for biological technicians was $41,290 in May 2014. The median wage is the wage at which half the workers in an occupation earned more than that amount and half earned less. The lowest 10 percent earned less than $26,300, and the highest 10 percent earned more than $67,920.

In May 2014, the median annual wages for biological technicians in the top industries in which they worked were as follows:

Chemical manufacturing	$47,280
Research and development in the physical, engineering, and life sciences	44,410
Colleges, universities, and professional schools; private	42,510
Colleges, universities, and professional schools; state	38,920
Federal government, excluding postal service	36,440

Job Outlook

Employment of biological technicians is projected to grow 5 percent from 2014 to 2024, about as fast as the average for all occupations. Greater demand for biotechnology research is expected to increase the need for these workers.

Biotechnology research plays a key role in scientific advancements that improve people's quality of life. Biological technicians will be needed to help scientists develop new treatments for diseases, such as cancer and Alzheimer's disease.

In agriculture, biotechnology research will be used to create genetically engineered crops that provide greater yields and require less pesticide and fertilizer. Efforts to discover new and improved ways to clean and preserve the environment also will continue to add to job growth. In addition, biological technicians will be needed to help develop alternative sources of energy, such as biofuels and better sources of renewable biomass.

Job Prospects. Applicants who have laboratory experience, either through coursework or through previous work experience, should have the best opportunities.

Contacts for More Information

For more information on career opportunities in the biological sciences, visit

➤ American Institute of Biological Sciences (www.aibs.org)
➤ American Society for Cell Biology (www.ascb.org)
➤ American Society for Microbiology (www.asm.org)
➤ Federation of American Societies for Experimental Biology (www.faseb.org)

To find job openings for biological technicians in the federal government, visit

➤ USAJOBS (www.usajobs.gov)

O*NET

➤ Biological Technicians (19-4021.00)

Chemical Technicians

- **2014 Median Pay** .... $44,180 per year; $21.24 per hour
- **Typical Entry-Level Education** .... Associate's degree
- **Work Experience in a Related Occupation** .... None
- **On-the-job Training** .... Moderate-term on-the-job training
- **Number of Jobs, 2014** 66,500
- **Job Outlook, 2014–24** .... 2% (Slower than average)
- **Employment Change, 2014–24** 1,200

What Chemical Technicians Do

Chemical technicians use laboratory instruments and techniques to help chemists and chemical engineers research, develop, produce, and test chemical products and processes.

Duties. Chemical technicians typically do the following:

- Monitor chemical processes and test the quality of products to make sure that they meet standards and specifications
- Set up and maintain laboratory instruments and equipment
- Troubleshoot production problems or malfunctioning instruments
- Prepare chemical solutions
- Conduct chemical and physical experiments, tests, and analyses for a variety of purposes, including research and development
- Compile and interpret results of tests and analyses
- Prepare technical reports, graphs, and charts, and give presentations that summarize their results

Most chemical technicians work on teams. Typically, they are led by chemists or chemical engineers who direct their work and evaluate their results. For example, some chemical technicians help chemists and other scientists develop new medicines. Others help chemical engineers develop more efficient production processes.

Chemical technicians' duties and titles often depend on where they work. The following are the two main types of chemical technicians:

Laboratory technicians typically help scientists conduct experiments and analyses. Often, they prepare chemical solutions, test products for quality and performance, and analyze compounds produced through complex chemical processes. Chemical laboratory technicians may analyze samples of air and water to monitor pollution levels. Laboratory technicians usually set up and maintain laboratory equipment and instruments.

Processing technicians monitor the quality of products and processes at chemical manufacturing facilities. For example, they adjust processing equipment to improve production efficiency and output. They also collect samples from production batches, which then are tested for impurities and other defects. In addition, processing technicians test product packaging to make sure that it is well designed, will hold up well, and will have a limited impact on the environment.

Work Environment

Chemical technicians held about 66,500 jobs in 2014. The industries that employed the most chemical technicians were as follows:

Testing laboratories	21%
Research and development in the physical, engineering, and life sciences	10
Pharmaceutical and medicine manufacturing	9
Basic chemical manufacturing	8
Colleges, universities, and professional schools; state, local, and private	5

Chemical technicians typically work in laboratories or in industrial facilities such as chemical and pharmaceutical manufacturing plants.

Injuries and Illnesses. Chemical technicians can be exposed to health or safety hazards when handling certain chemicals and plant equipment, but there is little risk if proper procedures are followed.

Work Schedules. Most technicians work full time. Occasionally, they may have to work additional hours to meet project deadlines or troubleshoot problems with manufacturing processes. Some may work irregular hours to monitor laboratory experiments or plant operations.

Education/Training

Chemical technicians need an associate's degree or 2 years of postsecondary education for most jobs. Most chemical technicians also receive on-the-job training.

Science technicians monitor experiments and record the results.

Median Annual Wages, May 2014

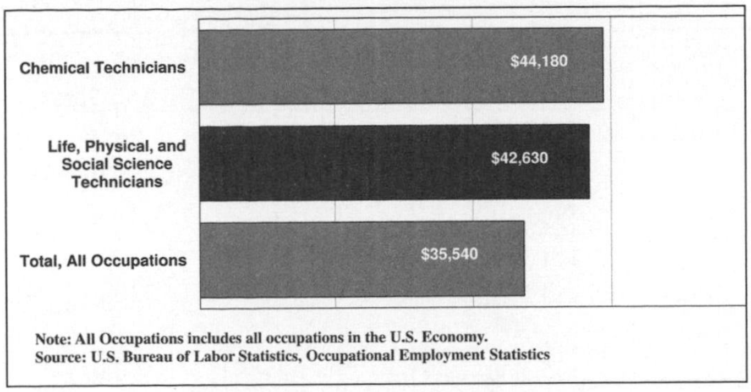

Education. For most jobs, chemical technicians need an associate's degree in applied science or chemical technology or 2 years of postsecondary education.

Many technical and community colleges offer programs in applied sciences or chemical technology. Students typically take classes in mathematics, physics, and biology, in addition to chemistry courses. Coursework in statistics and computer science is also useful, because technicians routinely do data analysis and modeling.

One of the most important aspects of any degree program is laboratory time. Laboratory coursework provides students with hands-on experience in conducting experiments and using various instruments and techniques properly. Many schools also offer internships and cooperative-education programs that help students gain employment experience while attending school.

Important Qualities

Ability to use technology. Chemical technicians must be able to set up and operate sophisticated equipment and instruments. They also may need to adjust the equipment to ensure that experiments and processes are running properly and safely.

Analytical skills. Chemical technicians must be able to conduct scientific experiments with accuracy and precision.

Communication skills. Chemical technicians must explain their work to scientists and engineers, and to workers who may not have a technical background. They often write reports to communicate their results.

Critical-thinking skills. Chemical technicians reach their conclusions through sound reasoning and judgment.

Interpersonal skills. Chemical technicians must be able to work well with others as part of a team because they often work with scientists, engineers, and other technicians.

Observation skills. Chemical technicians must carefully monitor chemical experiments and processes. They must keep complete records of their work, including conditions, procedures, and results.

Time-management skills. Chemical technicians often work on multiple tasks and projects at the same time and must be able to prioritize their assignments.

Percent Change in Employment, Projected 2014–2024

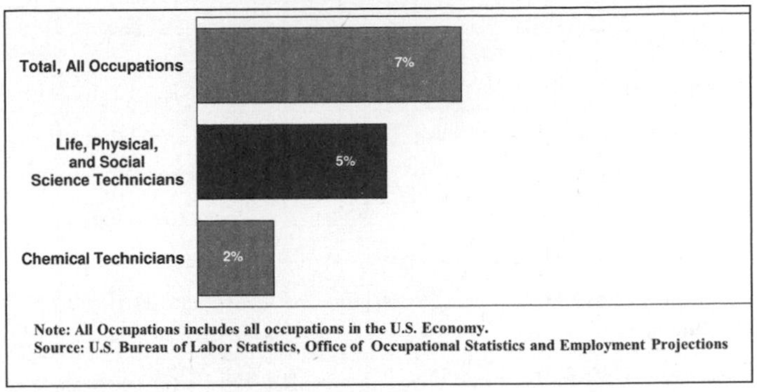

Training. Most chemical technicians receive on-the-job training. Typically, experienced technicians teach new employees proper methods and procedures for conducting experiments and operating equipment. The length of training varies with the new employee's level of experience and education and the industry the worker is employed in.

Advancement. Technicians who have a bachelor's degree may advance to positions as chemical engineers or chemists. For more information, see the profiles on chemical engineers and chemists and materials scientists.

Pay

The median annual wage for chemical technicians was $44,180 in May 2014. The median wage is the wage at which half the workers in an occupation earned more than that amount and half earned less. The lowest 10 percent earned less than $27,100, and the highest 10 percent earned more than $73,160.

In May 2014, the median annual wages for chemical technicians in the top industries in which they worked were as follows:

Basic chemical manufacturing	$50,180
Research and development in the physical, engineering, and life sciences	47,930
Pharmaceutical and medicine manufacturing	45,270
Colleges, universities, and professional schools; state, local, and private	41,660
Testing laboratories	37,200

Job Outlook

Employment of chemical technicians is projected to grow 2 percent from 2014 to 2024, slower than the average for all occupations. Declines in the employment of chemical technicians are projected in all chemical manufacturing industries, including pharmaceutical manufacturing. However, the development of cheaper energy and sources of raw materials, such as shale gas, is expected to spur some chemical manufacturing activity to return to the United States. Their return should generate demand for these workers in the next decade.

Employment Projections Data for Chemical Technicians

Occupational Title	SOC Code	Employment, 2014	Projected Employment, 2024	Change, 2014–2024 Percent	Change, 2014–2024 Numeric
Chemical technicians	19-4031	66,500	67,700	2	1,200

Source: U.S. Bureau of Labor Statistics, Employment Projections Program

Similar Occupations. This table shows a list of occupations with job duties that are similar to those of chemical technicians.

Occupations	Entry-level Education	2014 Median Pay	Projected Job Growth	Average Annual Openings
Agricultural and Food Science Technicians	Associate's degree	$35,140	5%	160
Biological Technicians	Bachelor's degree	$41,290	5%	410
Chemical Engineers	Bachelor's degree	$96,940	2%	60
Chemists and Materials Scientists	Bachelor's degree	$74,720	3%	260
Environmental Science and Protection Technicians	Associate's degree	$42,190	9%	340
Forensic Science Technicians	Bachelor's degree	$55,360	27%	380
Geological and Petroleum Technicians	Associate's degree	$54,810	12%	190
Medical and Clinical Laboratory Technologists and Technicians	See Education/Training	$49,310	16%	5,210
Nuclear Technicians	Associate's degree	$74,690	-5%	-30

Chemical technicians will continue to be in demand in scientific research and development (R&D) and to monitor the quality of chemical products and processes. Greater interest in environmental issues, such as pollution control, clean energy, and sustainability, are expected to increase the demand for chemistry R&D. Many chemical and pharmaceutical manufacturers are expected to outsource their scientific R&D and testing operations to professional, scientific, and technical services firms that specialize in these services.

Job Prospects. As the instrumentation and techniques used in research, development, and production become more complex, employers will seek job candidates with highly developed technical skills. Job opportunities are expected to be best for graduates of applied science technology programs who are well trained in the latest technology and sophisticated equipment used in laboratories or production facilities.

Contacts for More Information

For more information about chemical technicians, visit

➤ American Chemical Society (www.acs.org/content/acs/en.html)

➤ American Chemistry Council (www.americanchemistry.com)

O*NET

➤ Chemical Technicians (19-4031.00)

Chemists and Materials Scientists

- **2014 Median Pay** .... $74,720 per year
  $35.92 per hour
- **Typical Entry-Level Education** .... Bachelor's degree
- **Work Experience in a Related Occupation** .... None
- **On-the-job Training** .... None
- **Number of Jobs, 2014** 98,400
- **Job Outlook, 2014–24** .... 3% (Slower than average)
- **Employment Change, 2014–24** 2,600

What Chemists and Materials Scientists Do

Chemists and materials scientists study substances at the atomic and molecular levels and the ways in which the substances interact with one another. They use their knowledge to develop new and improved products and to test the quality of manufactured goods.

Duties. Chemists and materials scientists typically do the following:

- Plan and carry out complex research projects, such as the development of new products and testing methods
- Direct technicians and other workers in testing and analyzing components and the physical properties of materials
- Instruct scientists and technicians on proper chemical processing and testing procedures, including ingredients, mixing times, and operating temperatures
- Prepare solutions, compounds, and reagents used in laboratory procedures
- Analyze substances to determine their composition and concentration of elements
- Conduct tests on materials and other substances to ensure that safety and quality standards are met
- Write technical reports that detail methods and findings
- Present research findings to scientists, engineers, and other colleagues

Some chemists and materials scientists work in basic research. Others work in applied research. In basic research, chemists investigate the properties, composition, and structure of matter. They also experiment with combinations of elements and the ways in which they interact. In applied research, chemists investigate possible new products and ways to improve existing ones. Chemistry research has led to the discovery and development of new and improved drugs, plastics, and cleaners, as well as thousands of other products.

Materials scientists study the structures and chemical properties of various materials in order to develop new products or enhance existing ones. They determine ways to strengthen or combine materials, or develop new materials, for use in a variety of products. Applications of materials science include inventing or improving ceramics, metallic alloys, and superconducting materials.

Chemists and materials scientists use computers and a wide variety of sophisticated laboratory instrumentation for modeling, simulation, and experimental analysis. For example, some chemists use three-dimensional computer modeling software to study the structure and properties of complex molecules.

Chemists and materials scientists develop new uses for substances and materials.

The number of scientific research projects that involve multiple disciplines is increasing, and it is common for chemists and materials scientists to work on teams with other scientists, such as biologists, physicists, computer specialists, and engineers. For example, in pharmaceutical research, chemists may work with biologists to develop new drugs and with engineers to design ways to mass-produce the new drugs. For more information, see the profiles on biochemists and biophysicists, microbiologists, zoologists and wildlife biologists, physicists and astronomers, computer and information technology occupations, and engineering occupations.

Chemists often specialize in a particular branch of the field. The following are examples of types of chemists:

Analytical chemists determine the structure, composition, and nature of substances by examining and identifying their various elements or compounds. They also study the relationships and interactions among the parts of compounds. Some analytical chemists specialize in developing new methods of analysis and new techniques for carrying out their work. Their research has a wide range of applications, including food safety, pharmaceuticals, and pollution control.

Inorganic chemists study the structure, properties, and reactions of molecules that do not contain carbon, such as metals. They work to understand the behavior and the characteristics of inorganic substances. Inorganic chemists figure out how these materials, such as ceramics and superconductors, can be modified, separated, or used in products.

Medicinal chemists research and develop chemical compounds that can be used as pharmaceutical drugs. They work on teams with other scientists and engineers to create and test new drug products. They also help develop new and improved manufacturing processes to produce new drugs on a large scale effectively.

Organic chemists study the structure, properties, and reactions of molecules that contain carbon. They also design and make new organic substances that have unique properties and applications. These compounds in turn, have been used to develop many commercial products, such as pharmaceutical drugs and plastics.

Physical chemists study the fundamental characteristics of how matter behaves on a molecular and atomic level and how chemical reactions occur. On the basis of their analyses, physical chemists may develop new theories, such as how complex structures are formed. Physical chemists often work closely with materials scientists, to research and develop potential uses for new materials.

Theoretical chemists investigate theoretical methods that can predict the outcomes of chemical experiments. Theoretical chemistry encompasses a variety of specializations itself, although most specializations incorporate advanced computation and programming. Some examples of theoretical chemists are computational chemists, mathematical chemists, and chemical informaticians.

Materials scientists tend to specialize by the material they work with most often. A few examples of materials in which these scientists specialize are ceramics, glasses, metals, nanomaterials (extremely small substances), polymers, and semiconductors.

A growing number of chemists work in interdisciplinary fields, such as biochemistry and geochemistry. For more information, see the profiles on biochemists and biophysicists and geoscientists.

Many people with a chemistry background become professors or teachers. For more information, see the profiles on high school teachers and postsecondary teachers.

Work Environment

Chemists and materials scientists held about 98,400 jobs in 2014; about 91,100 were chemist jobs and 7,300 were held by materials scientists.

The industries that employed the most chemists in 2014 were as follows:

Research and development in the physical, engineering, and life sciences	18%
Pharmaceutical and medicine manufacturing	16
Testing laboratories	10
Federal government, excluding postal service	7
Basic chemical manufacturing	5

Most materials scientists work in manufacturing and in scientific research and development. The industries that employed the most materials scientists in 2014 were as follows:

Research and development in the physical, engineering, and life sciences	27%
Colleges, universities, and professional schools; state, local, and private	9
Basic chemical manufacturing	6
Pharmaceutical and medicine manufacturing	5
Management of companies and enterprises	5

Chemists and materials scientists typically work in laboratories and offices, where they conduct experiments and analyze their results. In addition to working in laboratories, materials scientists work with engineers and processing specialists in industrial manufacturing facilities. Some chemists also work in these facilities and usually are responsible for monitoring the environmental conditions at the plant. Chemists and materials scientists who work for manufacturing companies may have to travel occasionally, especially if their company has multiple facilities. Others may work outdoors to collect samples and conduct onsite analysis of air, soil, or water.

Median Annual Wages, May 2014

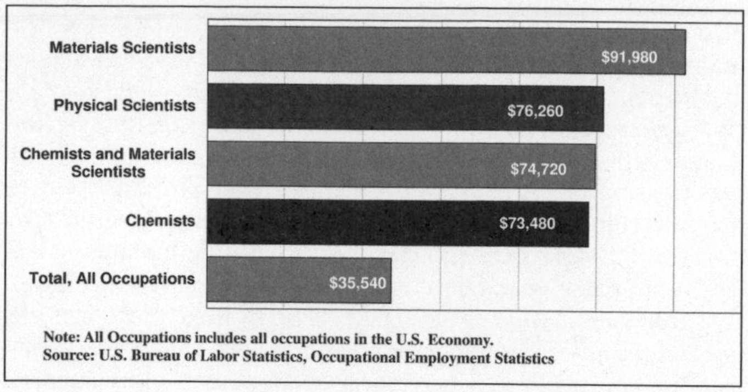

Percent Change in Employment, Projected 2014–2024

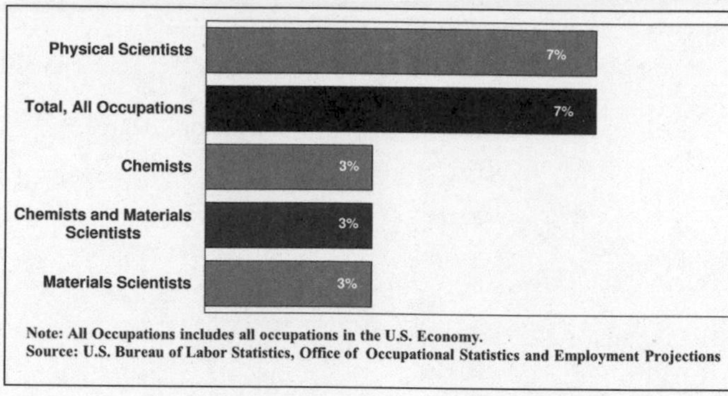

Chemists and materials scientists typically work on research teams. They need to be able to work well with others toward a common goal. Many serve in a leadership capacity and need to be able to motivate and direct other team members.

Injuries and Illnesses. Chemists and materials scientists may be exposed to health or safety hazards when handling certain chemicals, but there is little risk if they follow proper procedures, such as wearing protective clothing when handling hazardous chemicals.

Work Schedules. Chemists and materials scientists typically work full time and keep regular hours. Occasionally, they may have to work additional hours to meet project deadlines or perform time-sensitive laboratory experiments during off-hours.

Education/Training

Chemists and materials scientists need at least a bachelor's degree in chemistry or a related field. However, a master's degree or Ph.D. is required for many research jobs.

Education. A bachelor's degree in chemistry or in a related field is needed for entry-level chemist or materials scientist jobs. Although some materials scientists hold a degree in materials science, most have a degree in chemistry, physics, or engineering. Many jobs require a master's degree or a Ph.D. and also may require significant levels of work experience. Chemists and materials scientists with a Ph.D. and postdoctoral experience typically lead basic- or applied-research teams.

Many colleges and universities offer degree programs in chemistry that are approved by the American Chemical Society. There are few programs specifically in materials science, but the number of programs is gradually increasing. Some colleges offer materials science as a specialization within their chemistry programs, and some engineering schools offer degrees in the joint field of materials science and engineering. High school students can prepare for college coursework by taking chemistry, math, and computer science classes.

Undergraduate chemistry majors typically are required to take courses in analytical, organic, inorganic, and physical chemistry. In addition to chemistry coursework, they take classes in mathematics, biological sciences, and physics. Computer science courses are essential, because chemists and materials scientists need computer skills to perform modeling and simulation tasks, manage and manipulate databases, and operate computerized laboratory equipment.

Laboratory experience, either at a college or university, or through internships, fellowships, or work-study programs in industry, is also useful.

Graduate students studying chemistry commonly specialize in a subfield, such as analytical chemistry or inorganic chemistry. For example, those interested in doing research in the pharmaceutical industry usually develop a strong background in medicinal or organic chemistry.

Important Qualities

Analytical skills. Chemists and materials scientists carry out scientific experiments and studies. They must be precise and accurate in their analyses, because errors could invalidate their research.

Communication skills. Chemists and materials scientists need to communicate with team members and other scientists. They must be able to read and write technical reports and give presentations.

Critical-thinking skills. Chemists and materials scientists carefully evaluate their own work and the work of others. They must determine if results and conclusions are based on sound science.

Interpersonal skills. Chemists and materials scientists typically work on interdisciplinary research teams and need to work well with others toward a common goal. Many serve as team leaders and must be able to motivate and direct other team members.

Math skills. Chemists and materials scientists regularly use complex mathematical equations and formulas, and they need a broad understanding of mathematics, including calculus, algebra, and statistics.

Organizational skills. Chemists and materials scientists need to document processes carefully in order to conform to regulations and industry procedures. Disorganization in the workplace can lead to legal problems, damage to equipment, and chemical spills.

Employment Projections Data for Chemists and Materials Scientists

Occupational Title	SOC Code	Employment, 2014	Projected Employment, 2024	Change, 2014–2024	
				Percent	Numeric
Chemists and materials scientists	—	98,400	101,000	3	2,600
Chemists	19-2031	91,100	93,500	3	2,400
Materials scientists	19-2032	7,300	7,500	3	200

Source: U.S. Bureau of Labor Statistics, Employment Projections Program

Similar Occupations. This table shows a list of occupations with job duties that are similar to those of chemists and materials scientists.

Occupations	Entry-level Education	2014 Median Pay	Projected Job Growth	Average Annual Openings
Agricultural and Food Scientists	Bachelor's degree	$60,690	5%	190
Biochemists and Biophysicists	Doctoral or professional degree	$84,940	8%	280
Chemical Engineers	Bachelor's degree	$96,940	2%	60
Environmental Scientists and Specialists	Bachelor's degree	$66,250	11%	1,020
Geoscientists	Bachelor's degree	$89,910	10%	380
High School Teachers	Bachelor's degree	$56,310	6%	5,590
Materials Engineers	Bachelor's degree	$87,690	1%	30
Natural Sciences Managers	Bachelor's degree	$120,050	3%	180
Physicists and Astronomers	Doctoral or professional degree	$109,290	7%	150
Postsecondary Teachers	See Education/Training	$70,790	13%	17,700

Perseverance. Scientific research involves substantial trial and error, and chemists and materials scientists must not become discouraged in their work.

Problem-solving skills. Chemists and materials scientists research and develop new and improved chemical products, processes, and materials. This work requires a great deal of trial and error on the part of chemists and materials scientists before a unique solution is found.

Time-management skills. Chemists and materials scientists usually need to meet deadlines when conducting research. They must be able to manage time and prioritize tasks efficiently while maintaining their quality of work.

Advancement. Chemists typically receive greater responsibility and independence in their work as they gain experience. Greater responsibility also is gained through further education. Ph.D. chemists usually lead research teams and have control over the direction and content of projects, but even Ph.D. holders have room to advance as they gain experience. As chemists become more proficient in managing research projects, they may take on larger, more complicated, and more expensive projects.

Some chemists and materials scientists become natural sciences managers.

Pay

The median annual wage for chemists was $73,480 in May 2014. The median wage is the wage at which half the workers in an occupation earned more than that amount and half earned less. The lowest 10 percent earned less than $41,560, and the highest 10 percent earned more than $126,220.

The median annual wage for materials scientists was $91,980 in May 2014. The lowest 10 percent earned less than $47,860, and the highest 10 percent earned more than $143,960.

In May 2014, the median annual wages for chemists in the top industries in which they worked were as follows:

Federal government, excluding postal service $103,380
Research and development in the physical, engineering, and life sciences 85,460
Pharmaceutical and medicine manufacturing 73,130
Basic chemical manufacturing 69,350
Testing laboratories... 55,800

In May 2014, the median annual wages for materials scientists in the top industries in which they worked scientists were as follows:

Basic chemical manufacturing $114,960
Research and development in the physical, engineering, and life sciences.. 95,660
Management of companies and enterprises......................... 90,280
Pharmaceutical and medicine manufacturing...................... 79,120
Colleges, universities, and professional schools; state, local, and private.. 57,150

Job Outlook

Employment of chemists and materials scientists is projected to grow 3 percent from 2014 to 2024, slower than the average for all occupations. Many chemists and materials scientists are employed in manufacturing industries that are projected to decline.

Employment of chemists is projected to grow 3 percent as they continue to be needed in scientific research and development (R&D) and to monitor the quality of products and processes.

Employment of materials scientists is projected to grow 3 percent as demand increases for cheaper, safer, and better quality materials for a variety of purposes, such as electronics, energy, and transportation.

Chemists research and solve a wide range of problems and are employed in a similarly wide range of industries. About a third of all chemists are employed in chemical manufacturing industries; the remainder work at colleges and universities, in government, and for independent testing and research laboratories. Some chemical manufacturing industries, such as pharmaceutical manufacturing, increasingly may be outsourcing their R&D activities, rather than doing the research in-house. This outsourcing strategy is likely to cause faster growth in the employment of chemists in small, independent research-and-development firms than in the more traditional large manufacturers. However, as the economy improves and the expansion in domestic natural gas production lowers the cost of energy and raw inputs, manufacturers may have less of an incentive than they had in the past to outsource their R&D activities.

Environmental research will offer many new opportunities for chemists and materials scientists. For example, chemical manufacturing industries will continue to develop technologies and processes that reduce pollution and improve energy efficiency at manufacturing facilities. Chemists also will continue to be needed to monitor pollution levels at manufacturing facilities and to ensure compliance with local, state, and federal environmental regulations.

Job Prospects. In addition to job openings resulting from employment growth, some job openings will result from the need to replace chemists and materials scientists who retire or otherwise leave the occupations.

Chemists and materials scientists with advanced degrees, particularly those with a Ph.D. and work experience, are expected to have better opportunities. Large pharmaceutical and biotechnology firms provide openings for these workers at research laboratories, and many others work in colleges and universities. Furthermore, chemists with advanced degrees will continue to fill most senior research and upper-management positions. For more information, see the profile on natural sciences managers.

Contacts for More Information

For information on career opportunities, earnings, and education for chemists and materials scientists, visit

➤ American Chemical Society (www.acs.org/content/acs/en.html)
➤ American Chemistry Council (www.americanchemistry.com/default.aspx)
➤ ASM International (www.asminternational.org)
➤ Materials Research Society (www.mrs.org/home)
➤ National Resource Center for Materials Technology Education (http://materialseducation.org)

For more information about certified degree programs in chemistry, visit

➤ American Chemical Society Committee on Professional Training (http://tinyurl.com/hu7eyu2)

To find job openings for chemists and scientists in the federal government, visit

➤ USAJOBS (www.usajobs.gov)

O*NET

➤ Chemists (19-2031.00)
➤ Materials Scientists (19-2032.00)

Conservation Scientists and Foresters

- **2014 Median Pay** .... $60,360 per year $29.02 per hour
- **Typical Entry-Level Education** .... Bachelor's degree
- **Work Experience in a Related Occupation** .... None
- **On-the-job Training** .... None
- **Number of Jobs, 2014** 36,500
- **Job Outlook, 2014–24** .... 7% (As fast as average)
- **Employment Change, 2014–24** 2,700

What Conservation Scientists and Foresters Do

Conservation scientists and foresters manage the overall land quality of forests, parks, rangelands, and other natural resources.

Duties. Conservation scientists typically do the following:

- Oversee forestry and conservation activities to ensure compliance with government regulations and habitat protection
- Negotiate terms and conditions for forest harvesting and land-use contracts
- Establish plans for managing forest lands and resources
- Monitor forest-cleared lands to ensure that they are suitable for future use
- Work with private landowners, governments, farmers, and others to improve land for forestry purposes, while at the same time protecting the environment

Foresters typically do the following:

- Supervise activities of forest and conservation workers and technicians
- Choose and prepare sites for new trees, using controlled burning, bulldozers, or herbicides to clear land
- Monitor the regeneration of forests
- Direct and participate in forest fire suppression
- Determine ways to remove timber with minimum environmental damage

Conservation scientists manage, improve, and protect the country's natural resources. They work with private landowners and federal, state, and local governments to find ways to use and improve the land while safeguarding the environment. Conservation scientists advise farmers, ranchers, and other agricultural managers on how they can improve their land for agricultural purposes and to control erosion.

Foresters have a wide range of duties, and their responsibilities vary with their employer. Some primary duties of foresters are drawing up plans to regenerate forested lands, monitoring the progress of those lands, and supervising tree harvests. Another duty of a forester is devising plans to keep forests free from disease, harmful insects, and damaging wildfires. Many foresters supervise forest and conservation workers and technicians, directing their work and evaluating their progress.

Conservation scientists and foresters evaluate data on forest and soil quality, assessing damage to trees and forest lands caused by fires and logging activities. In addition, they lead activities, such as suppressing fires and planting seedlings. Fire suppression activities include measuring how quickly fires will spread and how successfully the planned suppression activities turn out.

Conservation scientists and foresters use their skills to determine a fire's impact on a region's environment. Communication with firefighters and other forest workers is an important component of fire suppression and controlled burn activities because the information that conservation scientists and foresters provide can determine how firefighters work.

Conservation scientists and foresters use a number of tools to perform their jobs. They use clinometers to measure the heights of trees, diameter tapes to measure a tree's circumference, and increment borers and bark gauges to measure the growth of trees so that timber volumes can be computed and growth rates estimated.

In addition, conservation scientists and foresters often use remote sensing (aerial photographs and other imagery taken from airplanes and satellites) and geographic information systems (GIS) data to map large forest or range areas and to detect widespread trends of forest and land use. They make extensive use of handheld computers and global positioning systems (GPSs) to study these maps.

The following are examples of types of conservation scientists:

Conservation land managers work for land trusts or other conservation organizations to protect the wildlife habitat, biodiversity, scenic value, and other unique attributes of preserves and conservation lands.

Range managers, also called *range conservationists*, protect rangelands to maximize their use without damaging the environment. Rangelands contain many natural resources and cover

Conservation scientists and foresters often work outdoors.

hundreds of millions of acres in the United States, mainly in the western states and Alaska.

Range managers may inventory soils, plants, and animals; develop resource management plans; help to restore degraded ecosystems; or help manage a ranch. They also maintain soil stability and vegetation for uses such as wildlife habitats and outdoor recreation. Like foresters, they work to prevent and reduce wildfires and invasive animal species.

Soil and water conservationists give technical help to people who are concerned with the conservation of soil, water, and related natural resources. For private landowners, they develop programs to make the most productive use of land without damaging it. They also help landowners with issues such as dealing with erosion. They help private landowners and governments by advising on water quality, preserving water supplies, preventing groundwater contamination, and conserving water.

The following are examples of types of foresters:

Procurement foresters buy timber by contacting local forest owners and negotiating a sale. This activity typically involves taking inventory on the type, amount, and location of all standing timber on the property. Procurement foresters then appraise the timber's worth, negotiate its purchase, and draw up a contract. The forester then subcontracts with loggers or pulpwood cutters to remove the trees and to help lay out roads to get to the timber.

Urban foresters live and work in larger cities and manage urban trees. They are concerned with quality-of-life issues, including air quality, shade, and storm water runoff.

Conservation education foresters train teachers and students about issues facing forest lands.

Work Environment

Conservation scientists and foresters held about 36,500 jobs in 2014.

The industries that employed the most conservation scientists in 2014 were as follows:

Federal government, excluding postal service	34%
State government, excluding education and hospitals	24
Local government, excluding education and hospitals	17
Social advocacy organizations	10

The industries that employed the most foresters in 2014 were as follows:

Support activities for agriculture and forestry	22%
State government, excluding education and hospitals	21
Forestry	14
Federal government, excluding postal service	9
Local government, excluding education and hospitals	9

Conservation scientists and foresters work for governments (federal, state, or local), on privately owned lands, or for social advocacy organizations. In the western and southwestern United States, they usually work for the federal government because of the number of national parks in that part of the country. In the eastern United States, they often work for private landowners. Social advocacy organizations employ foresters and conservation scientists in working with lawmakers on behalf of sustainable land use and other issues facing forest land. These organizations are concerned with the long-term impact of carbon emissions on forests worldwide.

Conservation scientists and foresters typically work in offices, in laboratories, and outdoors, sometimes doing fieldwork in remote locations. When visiting or working near logging operations or wood yards, they wear a hardhat and other protective gear.

The work can be physically demanding. Some conservation scientists and foresters work outdoors in all types of weather. They may need to walk long distances through dense woods and underbrush to carry out their work. Insect bites, poisonous plants, and other natural hazards present some risk.

In an isolated location, a forester or conservation scientist may work alone, measuring tree densities and regeneration or performing other outdoor activities. Other foresters work closely with the public, educating them about the forest or the proper use of recreational sites.

Fire suppression activities are an important aspect of their duties, which involve prevention as well as emergency responses. Therefore, their work has occasional risk.

Work Schedules. Most conservation scientists and foresters work full time and have a standard work schedule. Responding

Median Annual Wages, May 2014

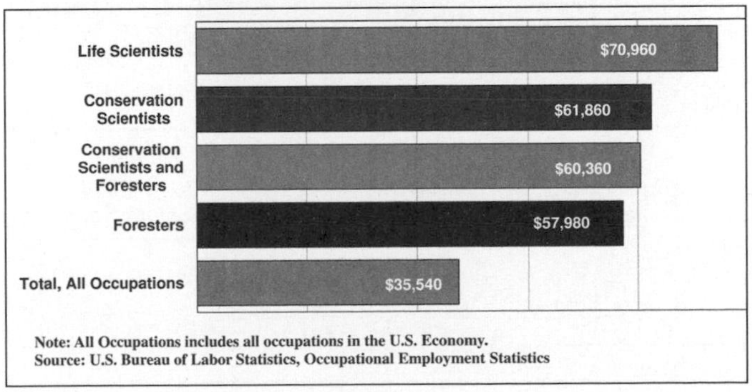

Percent Change in Employment, Projected 2014–2024

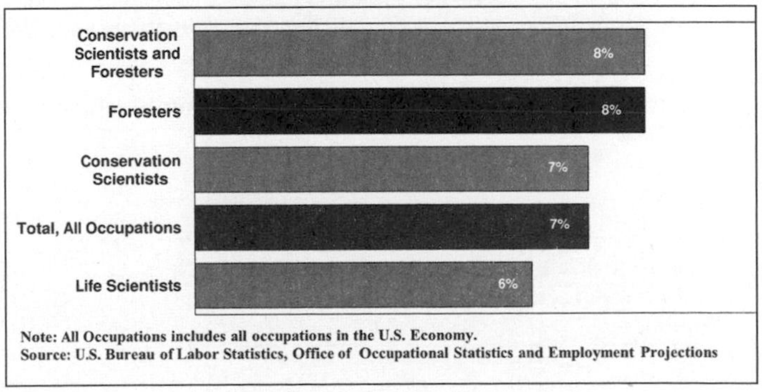

to emergencies or fires may require them to work more than 40 hours per week.

Education/Training

Employers seek applicants who have degrees from programs that are accredited by the Society of American Foresters or other organizations.

Education. Conservation scientists and foresters typically need a bachelor's degree in forestry or a related field, such as agricultural science, rangeland management, or environmental science. Although graduate work is not generally required, some conservation scientists and foresters get a master's degree or Ph.D.

Bachelor's degree programs are designed to prepare conservation scientists and foresters for their career or a graduate degree. Alongside practical skills, theory and education are important parts of these programs.

Bachelor's and advanced degree programs in forestry and related fields typically include courses in ecology, biology, and forest resource measurement. Scientists and foresters also typically have a background in a geographic information systems (GIS) technology, remote sensing, and other forms of computer modeling.

In 2015, there were nearly 50 bachelor's and master's degree programs in forestry, urban forestry, and natural resources and ecosystem management accredited by the Society of American Foresters.

Important Qualities

Analytical skills. Conservation scientists and foresters must evaluate the results of a variety of field tests and experiments, all of which require precision and accuracy. They use sophisticated computer modeling to prepare their analyses.

Critical-thinking skills. Conservation scientists and foresters reach conclusions through sound reasoning and judgment. They determine how to improve forest conditions, and they must react appropriately to fires.

Decision-making skills. Conservation scientists and foresters must use their expertise and experience to determine whether their findings will have an impact on soil, forest lands, and the spread of fires.

Management skills. Conservation scientists and foresters need to work well with the forest and conservation workers and technicians they supervise, so effective communication is critical.

Physical stamina. Conservation scientists and foresters often walk long distances in steep and wooded areas. They work in all kinds of weather, including extreme heat and cold.

Speaking skills. Conservation scientists and foresters must give clear instructions to forest and conservation workers and technicians, who typically do the labor necessary for proper forest maintenance. They also need to communicate clearly with landowners and, in some cases, the general public.

Licenses, Certifications, and Registrations. As of 2015, 15 states have some type of credentialing process for foresters, typically required or voluntary registration. Conservation workers do not need a license.

Although it is not required, conservation scientists and foresters may choose to earn certification because it shows a high level of professional competency.

The Society of American Foresters (SAF) offers certification to foresters. Candidates must have at least a bachelor's degree from an SAF-accredited program or from a forestry program that is substantially equivalent. The candidate also must have qualifying professional experience and pass an exam.

The Society for Range Management offers professional certification in rangeland management or as a range management consultant. To be certified, candidates must hold a bachelor's degree in range management or a related field, have 5 years of full-time related work experience, and pass an exam.

Advancement. Many conservation scientists and foresters advance to take on managerial duties. They also may conduct research or work on policy issues, often after getting an advanced degree. Foresters in management usually leave fieldwork behind, spending more of their time in an office, working with teams to develop management plans and supervising others.

Soil conservationists usually begin working within one district and may advance to a state, regional, or national level. Soil conservationists also can transfer to occupations such as farm or ranch management advisor or land appraiser.

Pay

The median annual wage for conservation scientists was $61,860 in May 2014. The median wage is the wage at which half the workers in an occupation earned more than that amount and half earned less. The lowest 10 percent earned less than $38,000, and the highest 10 percent earned more than $92,400.

The median annual wage for foresters was $57,980 in May 2014. The lowest 10 percent earned less than $37,680, and the highest 10 percent earned more than $85,750.

Job Outlook

Employment of conservation scientists and foresters is projected to grow 7 percent from 2014 to 2024, about as fast as the average for all occupations.

Most employment growth is expected to be in state and local government-owned forest lands, particularly in the western United States. In recent years, the prevention and suppression of wildfires has become the primary concern for government agencies managing forests and rangelands. Governments are likely to hire more foresters as the number of forest fires increases and more people live on or near forest lands. Both the development of previously unused lands and changing weather conditions have contributed to increasingly devastating and costly fires.

In addition, heightened demand for American timber and wood pellets is likely to help increase the overall job prospects for

Employment Projections Data for Conservation Scientists and Foresters

Occupational Title	SOC Code	Employment, 2014	Projected Employment, 2024	Change, 2014–2024 Percent	Change, 2014–2024 Numeric
Conservation scientists and foresters	19-1030	36,500	39,300	7	2,700
Conservation scientists	19-1031	21,100	22,500	7	1,400
Foresters	19-1032	15,500	16,800	8	1,300

Source: U.S. Bureau of Labor Statistics, Employment Projections Program

Similar Occupations. This table shows a list of occupations with job duties that are similar to those of conservation scientists and foresters.

Occupations	Entry-level Education	2014 Median Pay	Projected Job Growth	Average Annual Openings
Agricultural and Food Scientists	Bachelor's degree	$60,690	5%	190
Environmental Science and Protection Technicians	Associate's degree	$42,190	9%	340
Firefighters	Postsecondary nondegree award	$45,970	5%	1,740
Forest and Conservation Workers	High school diploma or equivalent	$27,160	4%	60
Zoologists and Wildlife Biologists	Bachelor's degree	$58,270	4%	80

conservation scientists and foresters. Jobs in private forests especially are likely to grow alongside demand for timber and pellets.

Job Prospects. Increases in funding and the need to replace retiring workers should create opportunities for foresters and range managers. Restoring lands affected by fires also will be a major task, particularly in the southwestern and western states, where fires are most common. Job prospects will likely be best for conservation scientists and foresters who have a strong understanding of geographic information systems (GIS) technology, remote sensing, and other software tools.

Contacts for More Information

For more information about conservation scientists and foresters, including schools offering education in forestry, visit

➤ Society of American Foresters (www.safnet.org)

For information about careers in forestry, particularly conservation forestry and land management, visit

➤ Forest Guild (www.forestguild.org)
➤ Society for Range Management (www.rangelands.org)
➤ US Forest Service (www.fs.fed.us)

O*NET

➤ Conservation Scientists (19-1031.00)
➤ Soil and Water Conservationists (19-1031.01)
➤ Range Managers (19-1031.02)
➤ Park Naturalists (19-1031.03)
➤ Foresters (19-1032.00)

Economists

- **2014 Median Pay** .... $95,710 per year, $46.02 per hour
- **Typical Entry-Level Education** ....Master's degree
- **Work Experience in a Related Occupation**.............. None
- **On-the-job Training** .... None
- **Number of Jobs, 2014** 21,500
- **Job Outlook, 2014–24**................. 6% (As fast as average)
- **Employment Change, 2014–24** 1,200

What Economists Do

Economists study the production and distribution of resources, goods, and services by collecting and analyzing data, researching trends, and evaluating economic issues.

Duties. Economists typically do the following:

- Research and analyze economic issues
- Conduct surveys and collect data
- Analyze data using mathematical models and statistical techniques
- Prepare reports, tables, and charts and present research results
- Interpret and forecast market trends
- Advise businesses, governments, and individuals on economic topics
- Design policies or make recommendations for solving economic problems
- Write articles for publication in academic journals and other media sources

Economists apply economic analysis to issues within a variety of fields, such as education, health, development, and the environment. Some economists study the cost of products, healthcare, or energy. Others examine employment levels, business cycles, exchange rates, taxes, inflation, or interest rates.

Economists often study historical trends and use them to make forecasts. They research and analyze data using a variety of software programs, including spreadsheets, statistical analysis, and database management programs. They sometimes give a presentation of their research to various audiences.

Many economists work in federal, state, and local government. Federal government economists collect and analyze data about the U.S. economy, including employment, prices, productivity, and wages, among other types of data. They also project spending needs and inform policymakers on the economic impact of laws and regulations.

Preparing reports on the results of economic research is an important part of an economist's job.

Economists working for corporations help them understand how the economy will affect their business. Specifically, economists may analyze issues such as consumer demand and sales to help a company maximize its profits.

Economists also work for research firms and think tanks, where they study and analyze a variety of economic issues. Their analyses and forecasts are frequently published in newspapers and journal articles.

Some economists work for companies with major international operations and for international organizations such as the World Bank, International Monetary Fund, and United Nations.

Many economists become postsecondary teachers.

The following are examples of types of economists:

Behavioral economists study the effects of psychological and social factors on the economic decision making of an individual. They research how these factors lead to and affect the outcome of an economic decision.

Econometricians develop models and use mathematical analyses to test economic relationships. They use techniques such as calculus, game theory, and regression analysis to explain economic facts or trends in all areas of economics.

Financial economists analyze savings, investments, and risk. They also study financial markets and financial institutions.

Industrial organization economists study how companies within an industry are organized and how they compete. They also examine how antitrust laws, which regulate attempts by companies to restrict competition, affect markets.

International economists study international trade and the impact of tariffs and trade restrictions. They also examine global financial markets and exchange rates.

Labor economists study the supply of workers and the demand for labor by employers. They research employment levels and how wages are set. They also analyze the effects of labor-related policies, such as minimum wage laws, and institutions, such as unions.

Macroeconomists and *monetary economists* examine the economy as a whole. They may research trends related to unemployment, inflation, and economic growth. They also study fiscal and monetary policies, which examine the effects of money supply and interest rates on the economy.

Microeconomists analyze supply and demand decisions of individuals and firms. For example, they may determine the quantity of products consumers will demand at a particular price.

Public finance economists analyze the role of government in the economy. Specifically, they may analyze the effects of tax cuts, budget deficits, and welfare policies.

Work Environment

Economists held about 21,500 jobs in 2014. The industries that employed the most economists were as follows:

Federal government, excluding postal service	21%
Management, scientific, and technical consulting services	18
Scientific research and development services	15
State and local government, excluding education and hospitals	15
Finance and insurance	5

Economists typically work independently in an office. However, many economists collaborate with other economists and statisticians, sometimes working on teams. Some economists work from home, and others may be required to travel as part of their job or to attend conferences.

Some economists combine a full-time job in universities or businesses with part-time consulting work.

Work Schedules. Most economists work full time. Some work under pressure of deadlines and tight schedules that may require overtime hours. About 1 out of 4 economists worked more than 40 hours per week in 2014.

Education/Training

Most economists need a master's degree or Ph.D. However, some entry-level jobs—primarily in government—are available for workers with a bachelor's degree.

Education. A master's degree or Ph.D. is required for most economist jobs. Positions in business, research, or international organizations often require a combination of graduate education and work experience.

Students can pursue an advanced degree in economics with a bachelor's degree in a number of fields, but a strong background in mathematics is essential. A Ph.D. in economics may require several years of study after earning a bachelor's degree, including completion of detailed research in a specialty field.

Candidates with a bachelor's degree may qualify for some entry-level economist positions, including jobs with the federal government. An advanced degree is sometimes required for advancement to higher level positions.

Most students who complete a bachelor's degree in economics find jobs outside the economics profession as research assistants, financial analysts, market research analysts, and similar positions in business, finance, and consulting.

Other Experience. Aspiring economists can gain valuable experience from internships that involve gathering and analyzing data, researching economic issues and trends, and writing reports on their findings. In addition, related experience, such as working in business or finance, can be advantageous.

Median Annual Wages, May 2014

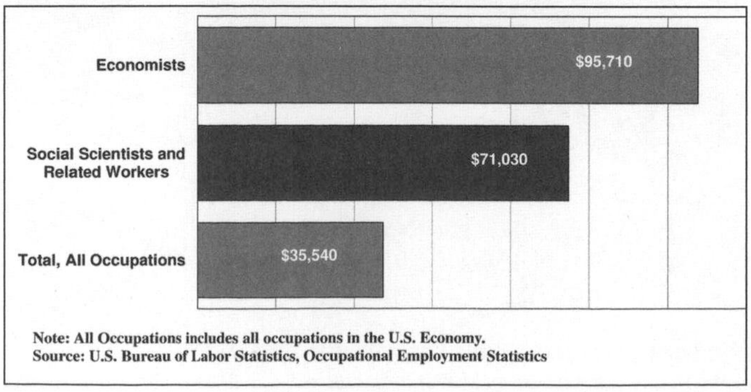

Note: All Occupations includes all occupations in the U.S. Economy.
Source: U.S. Bureau of Labor Statistics, Occupational Employment Statistics

Percent Change in Employment, Projected 2014–2024

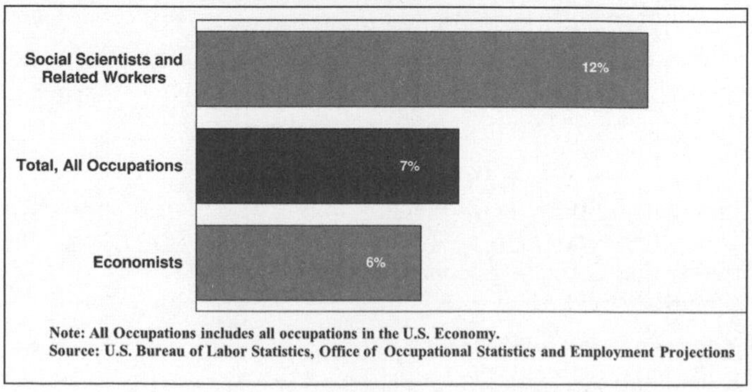

Note: All Occupations includes all occupations in the U.S. Economy.
Source: U.S. Bureau of Labor Statistics, Office of Occupational Statistics and Employment Projections

Employment Projections Data for Economists

Occupational Title	SOC Code	Employment, 2014	Projected Employment, 2024	Change, 2014–2024 Percent	Change, 2014–2024 Numeric
Economists	19-3011	21,500	22,700	6	1,200

Source: U.S. Bureau of Labor Statistics, Employment Projections Program

Similar Occupations. This table shows a list of occupations with job duties that are similar to those of economists.

Occupations	Entry-level Education	2014 Median Pay	Projected Job Growth	Average Annual Openings
Actuaries	Bachelor's degree	$96,700	18%	440
Budget Analysts	Bachelor's degree	$71,220	3%	150
Financial Analysts	Bachelor's degree	$78,620	12%	3,230
Market Research Analysts	Bachelor's degree	$61,290	19%	9,230
Mathematicians	Master's degree	$103,720	21%	70
Operations Research Analysts	Bachelor's degree	$76,660	30%	2,760
Political Scientists	Master's degree	$104,920	-2%	-10
Postsecondary Teachers	See Education/Training	$70,790	13%	17,700
Statisticians	Master's degree	$79,990	34%	1,010
Survey Researchers	Master's degree	$49,760	12%	190

Important Qualities

Analytical skills. Economists must be able to review data, observe patterns, and draw logical conclusions. For example, some economists analyze historical employment trends to make future projections on jobs.

Communication skills. Economists must be able to explain their work to others. They may give presentations, explain reports, or advise clients on economic issues. They may collaborate with colleagues and sometimes must explain economic concepts to those without a background in economics.

Critical-thinking skills. Economists must be able to use logic and reasoning to solve complex problems. For instance, they might identify how economic trends may affect an organization.

Detail oriented. Economists must pay attention to details. Precise data analysis is necessary to ensure accuracy in their findings.

Math skills. Economists use the principles of statistics, calculus, and other advanced topics in mathematics in their economic analyses.

Writing skills. Economists must be able to present their findings clearly. Many economists prepare reports for colleagues or clients; others write for publication in journals or for news media.

Pay

The median annual wage for economists was $95,710 in May 2014. The median wage is the wage at which half the workers in an occupation earned more than that amount and half earned less. The lowest 10 percent earned less than $50,440, and the highest 10 percent earned more than $170,780.

In May 2014, the median annual wages for economists in the top industries in which they worked were as follows:

Finance and insurance	$113,060
Federal government, excluding postal service	110,240
Management, scientific, and technical consulting services	97,960
Scientific research and development services	92,490
State and local government, excluding education and hospitals	65,380

Job Outlook

Employment of economists is projected to grow 6 percent from 2014 to 2024, about as fast as the average for all occupations.

Businesses and organizations across many industries are increasingly relying on economic analysis and quantitative methods to analyze and forecast business, sales, and other economic trends. Demand for economists should grow as a result of the increasing complexity of the global economy, additional financial regulations, and a more competitive business environment. As a result, demand for economists should be highest in private industry, especially in management, scientific, and professional consulting services.

However, employment in the federal government—the largest employer of economists—is projected to decline over the next ten years due to anticipated reductions in federal spending.

Job Prospects. In general, job opportunities should be good. Candidates with a master's degree or Ph.D., strong quantitative and analytical skills—particularly with large datasets—and related work experience will have the best prospects.

Applicants with a bachelor's degree may face very strong competition for jobs. As a result, bachelor's degree holders will likely find jobs outside the economist occupation, working instead as research assistants, financial analysts, market analysts, and in similar positions in business, finance, and consulting.

Contacts for More Information

For more information about economists, visit

➤ American Economic Association (www.aeaweb.org)

For information about careers in business economics, visit

➤ National Association for Business Economics (www.nabe.com)

For information on federal government education requirements for economist positions, visit

➤ U.S. Office of Personnel Management (http://tinyurl.com/odplxe4)

To find job openings for economists in the federal government, visit

➤ USAJOBS (www.usajobs.gov)

O*NET

➤ Economists (19-3011.00)
➤ Environmental Economists (19-3011.01)

Environmental Science and Protection Technicians

- **2014 Median Pay** .... $42,190 per year
  $20.29 per hour
- **Typical Entry-Level Education** .... Associate's degree
- **Work Experience in a Related Occupation** .... None
- **On-the-job Training** .... None
- **Number of Jobs, 2014** 36,200
- **Job Outlook, 2014–24** .... 9% (Faster than average)
- **Employment Change, 2014–24** 3,400

What Environmental Science and Protection Technicians Do

Environmental science and protection technicians monitor the environment and investigate sources of pollution and contamination, including those affecting public health. In addition, they work to ensure that environmental violations are prevented.

Duties. Environmental science and protection technicians typically do the following:

- Inspect establishments, including public places and businesses, to ensure that there are no environmental, health, or safety hazards
- Set up and maintain equipment used to monitor pollution levels, such as remote sensors that measure emissions from smokestacks
- Collect samples of air, soil, water, and other materials for laboratory analysis
- Clearly label, track, and ensure the integrity of samples being transported to the laboratory
- Use equipment such as microscopes to evaluate and analyze samples for the presence of pollutants or other contaminants
- Prepare charts and reports that summarize test results
- Discuss test results and analyses with clients
- Verify compliance with regulations to help prevent pollution

Many environmental science and protection technicians work under the supervision of environmental scientists and specialists, who direct the technicians' work and evaluate their results. In addition, they often work on teams with scientists, engineers, and technicians in other fields to solve complex problems related to environmental degradation and public health. For example, they may work on teams with geoscientists and hydrologists to manage the cleanup of contaminated soils and groundwater around an abandoned bomb manufacturing site.

Most environmental science and protection technicians work for state or local governments, testing laboratories, or consulting firms.

In **state and local governments**, environmental science and protection technicians spend a lot of time inspecting businesses and public places, and investigating complaints related to air quality, water quality, and food safety. Sometimes they may be involved with enforcement of environmental regulations. They may help protect the environment and people's health by performing environmental impact studies of new construction or by evaluating the environmental health of sites that may contaminate the environment, such as abandoned industrial sites.

Environmental science and protection technicians work in testing laboratories collecting and tracking samples, and performing tests that are often similar to what is done by chemical technicians, biological technicians, or microbiologists. However, the work done by environmental science and protection technicians focuses on topics that are directly related to the environment and how it affects human health.

In **consulting firms**, environmental science and protection technicians help clients monitor and manage the environment and comply with regulations. For example, they help businesses develop cleanup plans for contaminated sites, and they recommend ways to reduce, control, or eliminate pollution. Also, environmental science and protection technicians conduct feasibility studies for, and monitor the environmental impact of new construction projects.

Environmental science and protection technicians typically specialize in either laboratory testing or in fieldwork and sample collection. However, it is common for laboratory technicians to occasionally collect samples from the field, and for fieldworkers to do some work in a laboratory.

Work Environment

Environmental science and protection technicians held about 36,200 jobs in 2014. The industries that employed the most environmental science and protection technicians were as follows:

Management, scientific, and technical consulting services	26%
Local government, excluding education and hospitals	18
Testing laboratories	12
State government, excluding education and hospitals	8
Engineering services	6

Environmental science and protection technicians work in laboratories, offices, and the field. Fieldwork offers a variety of settings. For example, a technician may investigate an abandoned manufacturing plant, or work outdoors testing the water quality of lakes and rivers. They may work near streams and rivers, monitoring the levels of pollution caused by runoff from cities and landfills, or they may have to use the crawl spaces under a house in

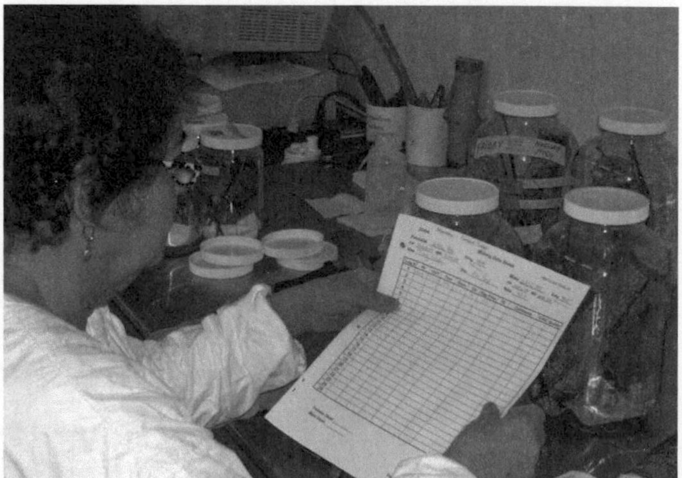

The work of environmental science and protection technicians is often divided between the outdoors and the laboratory.

Median Annual Wages, May 2014

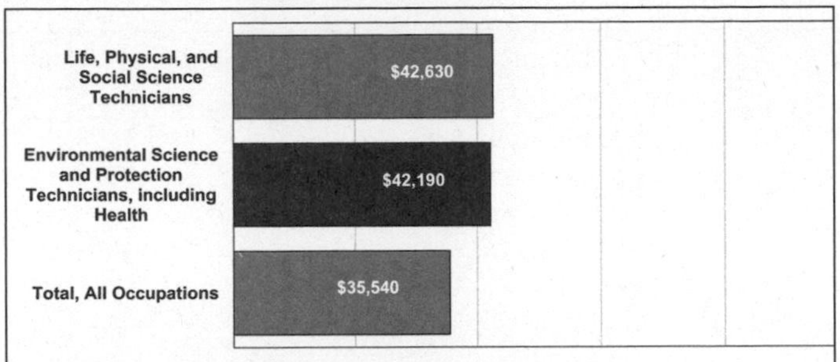

Note: All Occupations includes all occupations in the U.S. Economy.
Source: U.S. Bureau of Labor Statistics, Occupational Employment Statistics

Percent Change in Employment, Projected 2014–2024

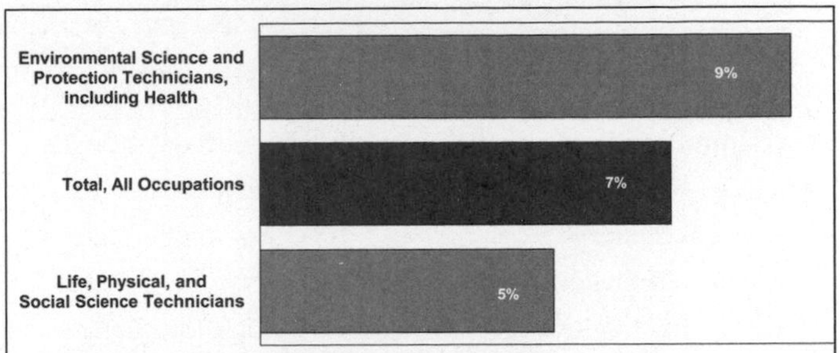

Note: All Occupations includes all occupations in the U.S. Economy.
Source: U.S. Bureau of Labor Statistics, Office of Occupational Statistics and Employment Projections

order to neutralize natural health risks such as radon. While working outdoors, they may be exposed to adverse weather conditions.

In the field, environmental science and protection technicians spend most of their time on their feet, which can be physically demanding. They also may need to carry and set up testing equipment, which can involve some heavy lifting and frequent bending and crouching.

Work Schedules. Environmental science and protection technicians typically work full time. They may work outdoors in all types of weather. They may also need to travel to meet with clients or to perform fieldwork. This may occasionally require technicians to work long or irregular hours.

Education/Training

Environmental science and protection technicians typically need an associate's degree or 2 years of postsecondary education, although some positions may require a bachelor's degree.

Education. Environmental science and protection technicians typically need an associate's degree in environmental science, environmental health, public health, or a related degree. Because of the wide range of tasks, environments, and industries in which these technicians work, there are jobs that do not require postsecondary education and others that require a bachelor's degree.

A background in natural sciences is important for environmental science and protection technicians. Students should take courses in chemistry, biology, geology, and physics. Coursework in mathematics, statistics, and computer science also is useful because technicians routinely do data analysis and modeling.

Many schools offer internships and cooperative-education programs, which help students gain valuable experience while attending school. Internships and cooperative-education experience can enhance the students' employment prospects.

Many technical and community colleges offer programs in environmental studies or a related technology, such as remote sensing or geographic information systems (GISs). Associate's degree programs at community colleges traditionally are designed to easily transfer to bachelor's degree programs at public colleges and universities.

Important Qualities

Analytical skills. Environmental science and protection technicians must be able to carry out a wide range of laboratory and field tests, and their results must be accurate and precise.

Communication skills. Environmental science and protection technicians must have good listening and writing skills, because they must follow precise directions for sample collection and communicate their results effectively in their written reports. They also may need to discuss their results with colleagues, clients, and sometimes public audiences.

Critical-thinking skills. Environmental science and protection technicians reach their conclusions through sound reasoning and judgment. They have to be able to determine the best way to address environmental hazards.

Interpersonal skills. Environmental science and protection technicians need to be able to work well and collaborate with others, because they often work with scientists and other technicians.

Licenses, Certifications, and Registrations. In some states, environmental science and protection technicians need a license to do certain types of environmental and health inspections. For example, some states require licensing for technicians who test buildings for radon. Licensure requirements vary by state but typically include certain levels of education and experience and a passing score on an exam.

Pay

The median annual wage for environmental science and protection technicians was $42,190 in May 2014. The median wage is the wage at which half the workers in an occupation earned more than that amount and half earned less. The lowest 10 percent earned less than $26,660, and the highest 10 percent earned more than $71,240.

In May 2014, the median annual wages for environmental science and protection technicians in the top industries in which they worked were as follows:

Local government, excluding education and hospitals....... $45,590
Engineering services.. 43,390
Management, scientific, and technical
consulting services.. 40,550

Employment Projections Data for Environmental Science and Protection Technicians

Occupational Title	SOC Code	Employment, 2014	Projected Employment, 2024	Change, 2014–2024 Percent	Change, 2014–2024 Numeric
Environmental science and protection technicians, including health	19-4091	36,200	39,600	9	3,400

Source: U.S. Bureau of Labor Statistics, Employment Projections Program

Similar Occupations. This table shows a list of occupations with job duties that are similar to those of environmental science and protection technicians.

Occupations	Entry-level Education	2014 Median Pay	Projected Job Growth	Average Annual Openings
Agricultural and Food Science Technicians	Associate's degree	$35,140	5%	160
Biological Technicians	Bachelor's degree	$41,290	5%	410
Chemical Technicians	Associate's degree	$44,180	2%	120
Environmental Engineering Technicians	Associate's degree	$48,170	10%	190
Environmental Engineers	Bachelor's degree	$83,360	12%	680
Environmental Scientists and Specialists	Bachelor's degree	$66,250	11%	1,020
Forensic Science Technicians	Bachelor's degree	$55,360	27%	380
Geoscientists	Bachelor's degree	$89,910	10%	380
Hydrologists	Bachelor's degree	$78,370	7%	50
Medical and Clinical Laboratory Technologists and Technicians	See Education/Training	$49,310	16%	5,210
Occupational Health and Safety Specialists	Bachelor's degree	$69,210	4%	280
Occupational Health and Safety Technicians	High school diploma or equivalent	$48,120	9%	140
Veterinary Technologists and Technicians	Associate's degree	$31,070	19%	1,790

State government, excluding education and hospitals........ $40,070
Testing laboratories... 36,840

Job Outlook

Employment of environmental science and protection technicians is projected to grow 9 percent from 2014 to 2024, faster than the average for all occupations. Heightened public interest in the hazards facing the environment, such as fracking, as well as the increasing demands placed on the environment by population growth, is expected to spur demand for environmental science and protection technicians.

Most employment growth for environmental science and protection technicians is projected to be in the industry of management, scientific, and technical consulting services. More businesses and governments are expected to use these firms in the future to help them monitor and manage the environment and comply with regulations.

Job Prospects. Environmental science and protection technicians should have good opportunities for employment. In addition to openings due to growth, many job openings are expected to be created by those who retire or leave the occupation for other reasons. Job candidates with an associate's degree and laboratory experience should have the best opportunities.

Contacts for More Information

For more information about environmental health technicians and related occupations, visit

➤ National Environmental Health Association (www.neha.org)

For more information about training, visit

➤ UCAR (www.ucp.ucar.edu/educators-and-students)

For more information specific to radon technicians, visit

➤ National Radon Safety Board (www.nrsb.org)

O*NET

➤ Environmental Science and Protection Technicians, Including Health (19-4091.00)

Environmental Scientists and Specialists

- **2014 Median Pay** .... $66,250 per year
  $31.85 per hour
- **Typical Entry-Level Education** ....Bachelor's degree
- **Work Experience in a Related Occupation**.............. None
- **On-the-job Training** .... None
- **Number of Jobs, 2014** 94,600
- **Job Outlook, 2014–24**............ 11% (Faster than average)
- **Employment Change, 2014–24** 10,200

What Environmental Scientists and Specialists Do

Environmental scientists and specialists use their knowledge of the natural sciences to protect the environment and human health. They may clean up polluted areas, advise policymakers, or work with industry to reduce waste.

Duties. Environmental scientists and specialists typically do the following:

- Determine data collection methods for research projects, investigations, and surveys
- Collect and compile environmental data from samples of air, soil, water, food, and other materials for scientific analysis
- Analyze samples, surveys, and other information to identify and assess threats to the environment
- Develop plans to prevent, control, or fix environmental problems, such as land or water pollution
- Provide information and guidance to government officials, businesses, and the general public on possible environmental hazards and health risks
- Prepare technical reports and presentations that explain their research and findings

Environmental scientists and specialists analyze environmental problems and develop solutions. For example, many environmental scientists and specialists work to reclaim lands and waters that have been contaminated by pollution. Others assess the risks that new construction projects pose to the environment and make recommendations to governments and businesses on how to minimize the environmental impact of these projects. Environmental scientists and specialists may do research and provide advice on manufacturing practices, such as advising against the use of chemicals that are known to harm the environment.

The federal government and many state and local governments have regulations to ensure that there is clean air to breathe, safe water to drink, and no hazardous materials in the soil. The regulations also place limits on development, particularly near sensitive ecosystems such as wetlands. Environmental scientists and specialists who work for governments ensure that the regulations are followed. Other environmental scientists and specialists work for consulting firms that help companies comply with regulations and policies.

Some environmental scientists and specialists focus on environmental regulations that are designed to protect people's health, while others focus on regulations designed to minimize society's impact on the ecosystem. The following are examples of types of specialists:

Climate change analysts study effects on ecosystems caused by the changing climate. They may do outreach education activities and grant writing typical of scientists.

Environmental health specialists study how environmental factors impact human health. They investigate potential environmental health risks. For example, they may investigate and address issues arising from soil and water contamination caused by nuclear weapons manufacturing. They also educate the public about potential health risks present in the environment.

Environmental restoration planners assess polluted sites and determine the cost and activities necessary to clean up the area.

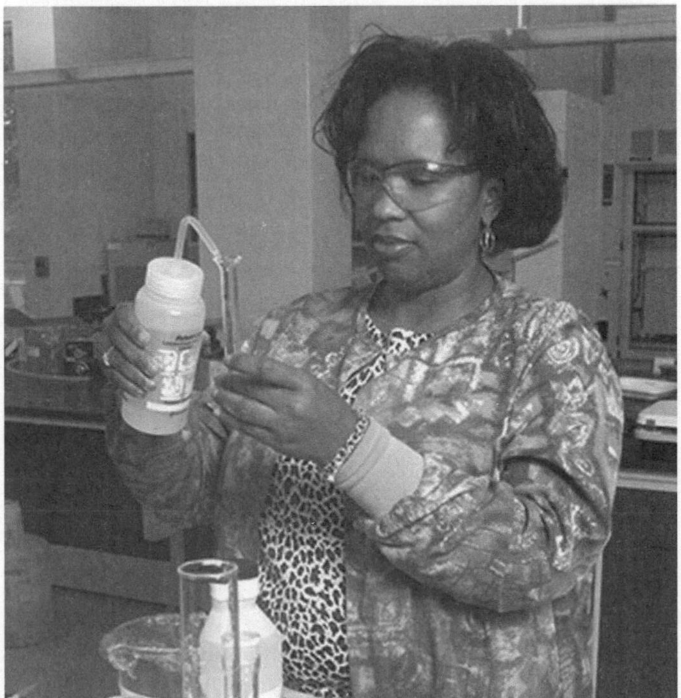

Environmental scientists research methods to reduce hazards that affect the environment or public health.

Industrial ecologists work with industry to increase the efficiency of their operations and thereby limit the impacts these activities have on the environment. They analyze costs and benefits of various programs, as well as their impacts on ecosystems.

Other environmental scientists and specialists perform work and receive training similar to that of other physical or life scientists, but they focus on environmental issues. Environmental chemists are an example.

Environmental chemists study the effects that various chemicals have on ecosystems. For example, they look at how acids affect plants, animals, and people. Some areas in which they work include waste management and the remediation of contaminated soils, water, and air.

Many people with backgrounds in environmental science become postsecondary teachers or high school teachers.

Work Environment

Environmental scientists and specialists held about 94,600 jobs in 2014. The industries that employed the most environmental scientists and specialists were as follows:

Management, scientific, and technical consulting services	23%
State government, excluding education and hospitals	22
Local government, excluding education and hospitals	13
Engineering services	10
Federal government, excluding postal service	6

Environmental scientists and specialists work in offices and laboratories. Some may spend time in the field gathering data and monitoring environmental conditions firsthand, but this work is much more likely to be done by environmental science and protection technicians. Fieldwork can be physically demanding, and environmental scientists and specialists may work in all types of weather. Environmental scientists and specialists may have to travel to meet with clients or present research at conferences.

Work Schedules. Most environmental scientists and specialists work full time. They may have to work more than 40 hours a week when working in the field.

Education/Training

For most jobs, environmental scientists and specialists need at least a bachelor's degree in a natural science.

Education. For most entry-level jobs, environmental scientists and specialists must have a bachelor's degree in environmental science or a science-related field, such as biology, chemistry, physics, geosciences, or engineering. However, a master's degree may be needed for advancement. Environmental scientists and specialists who have a doctoral degree make up a small percentage of the occupation, and this level of training is typically needed only for the relatively few postsecondary teaching and basic research positions.

A bachelor's degree in environmental science offers a broad approach to the natural sciences. Students typically take courses in biology, chemistry, geology, and physics. Students often take specialized courses in hydrology or waste management as part of their degree as well. Classes in environmental policy and regulation are also beneficial. Students who want to reach the Ph.D. level and have a career in academia or as an environmental scientist doing basic research may find it advantageous to major in a more specific natural science such as chemistry, biology, physics, or geology, rather than a broader environmental science degree.

Students should look for classes and internships that include work in computer modeling, data analysis, and geographic information systems. Students with experience in these programs will be

Median Annual Wages, May 2014

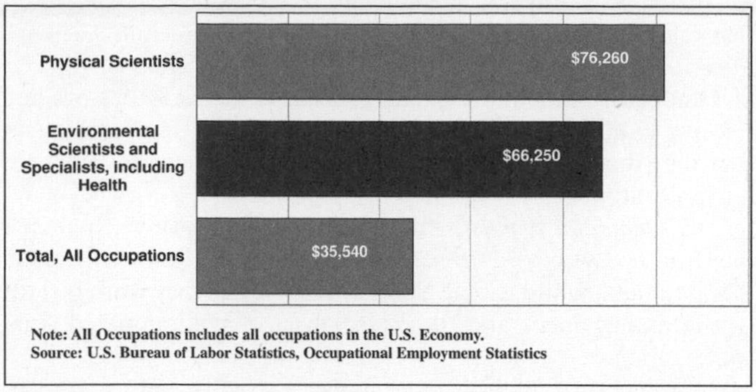

Percent Change in Employment, Projected 2014–2024

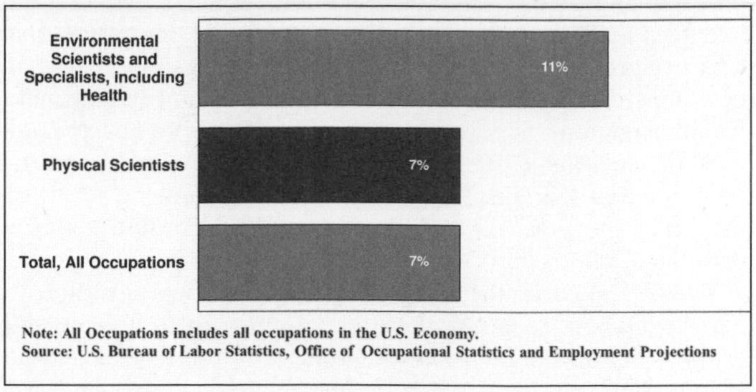

the best prepared to enter the job market. The University Consortium of Atmospheric Research (UCAR) offers several programs to help students broaden their understanding of environmental sciences.

Important Qualities

Analytical skills. Environmental scientists and specialists base their conclusions on careful analysis of scientific data. They must consider all possible methods and solutions in their analyses.

Communication skills. Environmental scientists and specialists may need to present and explain their findings to audiences of varying backgrounds and to write technical reports.

Interpersonal skills. Environmental scientists and specialists typically work on teams with scientists, engineers, and technicians. Team members must be able to work together effectively to achieve their goals.

Problem-solving skills. Environmental scientists and specialists try to find the best possible solution to problems that affect the environment and people's health.

Self-discipline. Environmental scientists and specialists may spend a lot of time working alone. They need to be able to stay motivated and get their work done without supervision.

Advancement. Environmental scientists and specialists often begin their careers as field analysts, research assistants, or technicians in laboratories and offices. As they gain experience, they earn more responsibilities and autonomy, and may supervise the work of technicians or other scientists. Eventually, they may be promoted to project leader, program manager, or other management or research position.

Other environmental scientists and specialists go on to work as researchers or faculty at colleges and universities.

Licenses, Certifications, and Registrations. Environmental scientists and specialists can become Certified Hazardous Materials Managers through the Institute of Hazardous Materials Management. This certification, which must be renewed every 5 years, shows that an environmental scientist or specialist is staying current with developments relevant to this occupation's work.

Work Experience in a Related Occupation. Some environmental scientists and specialists begin their careers as scientists in related occupations, such as hydrology or engineering, and then move into the more interdisciplinary field of environmental science.

Pay

The median annual wage for environmental scientists and specialists was $66,250 in May 2014. The median wage is the wage at which half the workers in an occupation earned more than that amount and half earned less. The lowest 10 percent earned less than $39,730, and the highest 10 percent earned more than $114,990.

In May 2014, the median annual wages for environmental scientists and specialists in the top industries in which they worked were as follows:

Federal government, excluding postal service	$97,000
Engineering services	68,240
Management, scientific, and technical consulting services	68,060
Local government, excluding education and hospitals	61,270
State government, excluding education and hospitals	59,010

Job Outlook

Employment of environmental scientists and specialists is projected to grow 11 percent from 2014 to 2024, faster than the average for all occupations. Heightened public interest in the hazards facing the environment, as well as the increasing demands placed on the environment by population growth, is projected to spur demand for environmental scientists and specialists.

Most employment growth for environmental scientists and specialists is projected to be in private consulting firms that help clients monitor and manage environmental concerns and comply with regulations. However, many jobs will remain concentrated in state and local levels of government and closely related industries.

More businesses are expected to consult with environmental scientists and specialists in the future to help them minimize the impact their operations have on the environment. For example, environmental consultants help businesses to develop practices that minimize waste, prevent pollution, and conserve resources. Other environmental scientists and specialists are expected to be

Employment Projections Data for Environmental Scientists and Specialists

Occupational Title	SOC Code	Employment, 2014	Projected Employment, 2024	Change, 2014–2024 Percent	Change, 2014–2024 Numeric
Environmental scientists and specialists, including health	19-2041	94,600	104,800	11	10,200

Source: U.S. Bureau of Labor Statistics, Employment Projections Program

Similar Occupations. This table shows a list of occupations with job duties that are similar to those of environmental scientists and specialists.

Occupations	Entry-level Education	2014 Median Pay	Projected Job Growth	Average Annual Openings
Agricultural and Food Scientists	Bachelor's degree	$60,690	5%	190
Anthropologists and Archeologists	Master's degree	$59,280	4%	30
Atmospheric Scientists, Including Meteorologists	Bachelor's degree	$87,980	9%	110
Biochemists and Biophysicists	Doctoral or professional degree	$84,940	8%	280
Chemists and Materials Scientists	Bachelor's degree	$74,720	3%	260
Conservation Scientists and Foresters	Bachelor's degree	$60,360	7%	270
Environmental Engineers	Bachelor's degree	$83,360	12%	680
Environmental Science and Protection Technicians	Associate's degree	$42,190	9%	340
Epidemiologists	Master's degree	$67,420	6%	40
Geoscientists	Bachelor's degree	$89,910	10%	380
Hydrologists	Bachelor's degree	$78,370	7%	50
Microbiologists	Bachelor's degree	$67,790	4%	80
Natural Sciences Managers	Bachelor's degree	$120,050	3%	180
Occupational Health and Safety Specialists	Bachelor's degree	$69,210	4%	280
Postsecondary Teachers	See Education/Training	$70,790	13%	17,700
Zoologists and Wildlife Biologists	Bachelor's degree	$58,270	4%	80

needed to help planners develop and construct buildings, utilities, and transportation systems that protect natural resources and limit damage to the land.

Job Prospects. Environmental scientists and specialists should have good job opportunities. In addition to growth, many job openings will be created by scientists who retire, advance to management positions, or change careers.

Contacts for More Information

For more information about environmental scientists and specialists, including training, visit

- American Geosciences Institute (www.americangeosciences.org)
- UCAR (www.ucp.ucar.edu/educators-and-students)

For more information about certification as a Certified Hazardous Materials Manager, visit

- Institute of Hazardous Materials Management (www.ihmm.org/certificants/chmm)

For information about environmental health specialists and related occupations, visit

- National Environmental Health Association (www.neha.org/index.shtml)

O*NET

- Environmental Scientists and Specialists, Including Health (19-2041.00)
- Climate Change Analysts (19-2041.01)
- Environmental Restoration Planners (19-2041.02)
- Industrial Ecologists (19-2041.03)

Epidemiologists

- **2014 Median Pay** .... $67,420 per year
  $32.41 per hour
- **Typical Entry-Level Education** ....Master's degree
- **Work Experience in a Related Occupation**.............. None
- **On-the-job Training** .... None
- **Number of Jobs, 2014** 5,800
- **Job Outlook, 2014–24**................. 6% (As fast as average)
- **Employment Change, 2014–24** 400

What Epidemiologists Do

Epidemiologists are public health professionals who investigate patterns and causes of disease and injury in humans. They seek to reduce the risk and occurrence of negative health outcomes through research, community education and health policy.

Duties. Epidemiologists typically do the following:

- Plan and direct studies of public health problems to find ways to prevent and to treat them if they arise
- Collect and analyze data—through observations, interviews, and surveys, and by using samples of blood or other bodily fluids—to find the causes of diseases or other health problems
- Communicate their findings to health practitioners, policymakers, and the public
- Manage public health programs by planning programs, monitoring their progress, analyzing data, and seeking ways to improve the programs in order to improve public health outcomes
- Supervise professional, technical, and clerical personnel

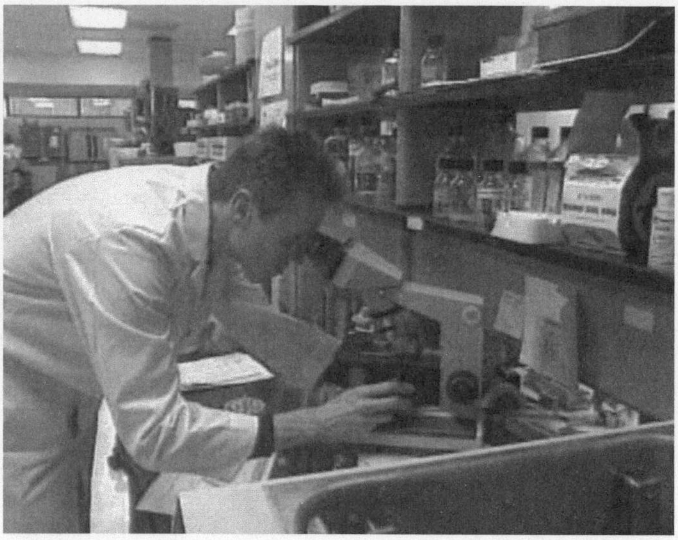

Epidemiologists need at least a master's degree from an accredited postsecondary institution.

Epidemiologists collect and analyze data to investigate health issues. For example, an epidemiologist might collect and analyze demographic data to determine who is at the highest risk for a particular disease. They also may research and investigate the trends in populations of survivors of certain diseases, such as cancer, so that effective treatments can be identified and repeated across the population.

Epidemiologists typically work either in applied public health or in research. Applied epidemiologists work for state and local governments, addressing public health problems directly. They often are involved with education outreach and survey efforts in communities. Research epidemiologists typically work for universities or in affiliation with federal agencies, such as the Centers for Disease Control and Prevention (CDC) or the National Institutes of Health (NIH).

Epidemiologists who work in private industry commonly conduct research for health insurance companies or pharmaceutical companies. Those in nonprofit companies often do public health advocacy work. Epidemiologists involved in research are rarely advocates, because scientific research is expected to be unbiased.

Epidemiologists typically specialize in one or more of the following public health areas:

- Infectious diseases
- Public health preparedness and emergency response
- Maternal and child health
- Chronic diseases
- Environmental health
- Injury
- Occupational health
- Behavioral epidemiology
- Oral health

For more information on occupations that concentrate on the biological workings of disease or the effects of disease on individuals, see the profiles for biochemists and biophysicists, medical scientists, microbiologists, and physicians and surgeons.

Work Environment

Epidemiologists held about 5,800 jobs in 2014. The industries that employed the most epidemiologists were as follows:

State government, excluding education and hospitals	31%
Local government, excluding education and hospitals	22
General medical and surgical hospitals; private	12
Research and development in the physical, engineering, and life sciences	10
Colleges, universities, and professional schools; state, local, and private	10

Epidemiologists typically work in offices and laboratories at health departments for state and local governments, in hospitals, and at colleges and universities. Work environments can vary widely, however, because of the diverse nature of epidemiological specializations. Epidemiologists also may work in the field, where they support emergency actions, or in clinical settings.

Most epidemiologists spend their time studying data and reports in an office setting. Work in laboratories and the field tends to be delegated to specialized scientists and other technical staff. In state and local government public health departments, epidemiologists may be more active in the community and may need to travel to support community education efforts or to administer studies and surveys.

Because modern science has greatly reduced the amount of infectious disease in developed countries, infectious disease epidemiologists are more likely to travel to remote areas and developing nations in order to carry out their studies. Epidemiologists have minimal risk when they work in laboratories or in the field, because they have received appropriate training and take extensive precautions before interacting with samples or patients.

Work Schedules. Most epidemiologists work full time and have a standard work schedule. Occasionally, epidemiologists may have to work long or irregular hours in order to complete fieldwork or tend to duties during public health emergencies.

Median Annual Wages, May 2014

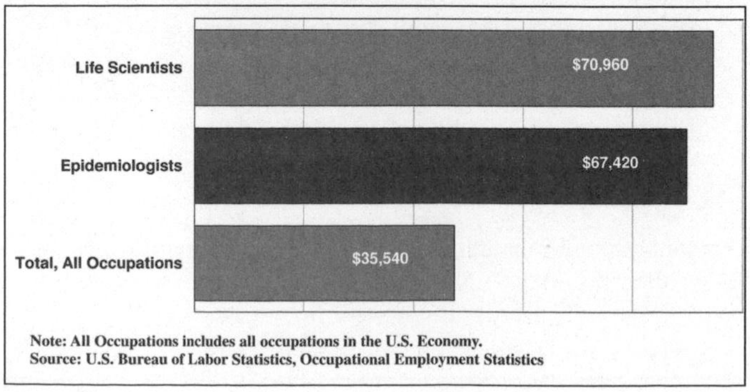

Percent Change in Employment, Projected 2014–2024

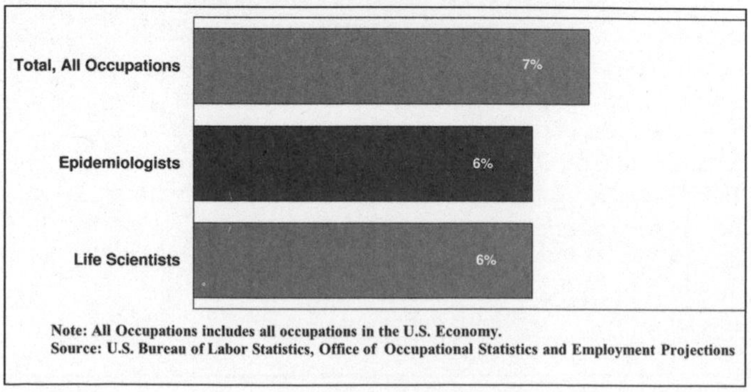

Employment Projections Data for Epidemiologists

Occupational Title	SOC Code	Employment, 2014	Projected Employment, 2024	Change, 2014–2024	
				Percent	Numeric
Epidemiologists	19-1041	5,800	6,100	6	400

Source: U.S. Bureau of Labor Statistics, Employment Projections Program

Similar Occupations. This table shows a list of occupations with job duties that are similar to those of epidemiologists.

Occupations	Entry-level Education	2014 Median Pay	Projected Job Growth	Average Annual Openings
Anthropologists and Archeologists	Master's degree	$59,280	4%	30
Environmental Scientists and Specialists	Bachelor's degree	$66,250	11%	1,020
Geographers	Bachelor's degree	$76,420	-2%	0
Health Educators and Community Health Workers	See Education/Training	$42,450	13%	1,560
Medical Scientists	Doctoral or professional degree	$79,930	8%	900
Microbiologists	Bachelor's degree	$67,790	4%	80
Physicians and Surgeons	Doctoral or professional degree	This wage is equal to or greater than $187,200.	14%	9,930
Political Scientists	Master's degree	$104,920	-2%	-10
Registered Nurses	Bachelor's degree	$66,640	16%	43,930
Survey Researchers	Master's degree	$49,760	12%	190

Education/Training

Epidemiologists need at least a master's degree from an accredited college or university. Most epidemiologists have a master's degree in public health (MPH) or a related field, and some have completed a doctoral degree in epidemiology or medicine.

Education. Epidemiologists typically need at least a master's degree from an accredited college or university. A master's degree in public health with an emphasis in epidemiology is most common, but epidemiologists can earn degrees in a wide range of related fields and specializations. Epidemiologists who direct research projects—including those who work as postsecondary teachers in colleges and universities—have a Ph.D. or medical degree in their chosen field.

Coursework in epidemiology includes classes in public health, biological and physical sciences, and math and statistics. Classes emphasize statistical methods, causal analysis, and survey design. Advanced courses emphasize multiple regression, medical informatics, reviews of previous biomedical research, comparisons of healthcare systems, and practical applications of data.

Many master's degree programs in public health, as well as other programs that are specific to epidemiology, require students to complete an internship or practicum that typically ranges from a semester to a year.

Some epidemiologists have both a degree in epidemiology and a medical degree. These scientists often work in clinical capacities. In medical school, students spend most of their first 2 years in laboratories and classrooms, taking courses such as anatomy, biochemistry, physiology, pharmacology, psychology, microbiology, and pathology. Medical students also have the option to choose electives such as medical ethics and medical laws. They also learn to take medical histories, examine patients, and diagnose illnesses.

Important Qualities

Communication skills. Epidemiologists must use their speaking and writing skills to inform the public and community leaders about public health risks. Clear communication also is required for an epidemiologist to work effectively with other health professionals.

Critical-thinking skills. Epidemiologists analyze data to determine how best to respond to a public health problem or an urgent health-related emergency.

Detail oriented. Epidemiologists must be precise and accurate in moving from observation and interview to conclusions.

Math and statistical skills. Epidemiologists may need advanced math and statistical skills in designing and administering studies and surveys. Skill in using large databases and statistical computer programs may also be important.

Teaching skills. Epidemiologists may be involved in community outreach activities that educate the public about health risks and healthy living.

Pay

The median annual wage for epidemiologists was $67,420 in May 2014. The median wage is the wage at which half the workers in an occupation earned more than that amount and half earned less. The lowest 10 percent earned less than $43,530, and the highest 10 percent earned more than $112,360.

In May 2014, the median annual wages for epidemiologists in the top industries in which they worked were as follows:

Research and development in the physical, engineering, and life sciences	$89,360
General medical and surgical hospitals; private	79,750

Colleges, universities, and professional schools; state, local, and private... $64,650
Local government, excluding education and hospitals......... 63,600
State government, excluding education and hospitals.......... 63,200

Job Outlook

Employment of epidemiologists is projected to grow 6 percent from 2014 to 2024, about as fast as the average for all occupations. Continued improvements in medical recordkeeping will further improve epidemiologists' ability to track health outcomes, demographic data, and other useful data. Improvements in statistical and mapping software will improve analysis and make epidemiological data more useful thereby requiring the expertise of epidemiologists.

Demand for epidemiologists is expected to be strong in state and local governments over the next 10 years, but uncertain budgetary conditions are likely to moderate growth. Greater requirements for hospitals to track health outcomes and local population health concerns may increase the need for epidemiologists in hospitals.

Job Prospects. Interest in public health and epidemiology has risen over the past decade. The number of master's degree programs in public health specializing in epidemiology, as well as the number of graduates from these programs, has increased. Some entrants are finding strong competition for jobs, but applicants who are willing to work in any of the various specialties found in this occupation, rather than those tied to one specialty, rarely have trouble finding work. Because epidemiology is a diverse field, opportunities can generally be found if one takes a broad view.

Contacts for More Information

For more information about epidemiologists, visit

➤ Council of State and Territorial Epidemiologists (www.cste.org)
➤ The Society for Healthcare Epidemiology of America (www.shea-online.org)

For more information about epidemiology careers in the federal government, visit

➤ Centers for Disease Control and Prevention (http://jobs.cdc.gov)
➤ National Institutes of Health (www.nih.gov)

For public health-related information, visit

➤ American Public Health Association (www.apha.org)
➤ National Academy for State Health Policy (www.nashp.org)
➤ Public Health Foundation (www.phf.org/Pages/default.aspx)

O*NET

➤ Epidemiologists (19-1041.00)

Forensic Science Technicians

- **2014 Median Pay** .... $55,360 per year
  $26.61 per hour
- **Typical Entry-Level Education** .... Bachelor's degree
- **Work Experience in a Related Occupation** .... None
- **On-the-job Training** .... Moderate-term on-the-job training
- **Number of Jobs, 2014** 14,400
- **Job Outlook, 2014–24** .... 27% (Much faster than average)
- **Employment Change, 2014–24** 3,800

What Forensic Science Technicians Do

Forensic science technicians aid criminal investigations by collecting and analyzing evidence. Many technicians specialize in either crime scene investigation or laboratory analysis. Most forensic science technicians spend some time writing reports.

Duties. At crime scenes, forensic science technicians typically do the following:

- Analyze crime scenes to determine what and how evidence should be collected
- Take photographs of the crime scene and evidence
- Make sketches of the crime scene
- Record observations and findings, such as the location and position of evidence
- Collect evidence, including weapons, fingerprints, and bodily fluids
- Catalog and preserve evidence for transfer to crime labs

In laboratories, forensic science technicians typically do the following:

- Perform chemical, biological, and microscopic analyses on evidence taken from crime scenes
- Explore possible links between suspects and criminal activity, using the results of DNA or other scientific analyses
- Examine digital media for pertinent information
- Consult with experts in specialized fields, such as toxicology (the study of poisons and their effect on the body) and odontology (a branch of forensic medicine that concentrates on teeth)
- Reconstruct crime scenes

Forensic science technicians may be generalists who perform many or all of the duties listed above or they may specialize in certain techniques and sciences. Generalist forensic science technicians, sometimes called *criminalists* or *crime scene investigators*, collect evidence at the scene of a crime and perform scientific and technical analysis in laboratories or offices.

Forensic science technicians who work primarily in laboratories may specialize in the natural sciences or engineering. These workers, such as *forensic pathologists* and *latent print examiners*, typically use chemicals and laboratory equipment such as microscopes when analyzing evidence. They also may use computers to examine fingerprints, DNA, and other evidence collected at crime scenes. They often work to match evidence to people or other known elements, such as vehicles or weapons. Most forensic science technicians who perform laboratory analysis specialize in a specific type of evidence, such as DNA or ballistics.

Some forensic science technicians, called *forensic computer examiners* or *digital forensics analysts*, specialize in computer-based crimes. They collect and analyze data to uncover and prosecute electronic fraud, scams, and identity theft. The abundance of digital data helps them solve crimes in the physical world as well. Computer forensics technicians must adhere to the same strict standards of evidence gathering found in general forensic science because legal cases depend on the integrity of evidence.

All forensic science technicians prepare written reports that detail their findings and investigative methods. They must be able to explain their reports to lawyers, detectives, and other law enforcement officials. In addition, forensic science technicians may be called to testify in court about their findings and methods.

Forensic science technicians work at crime scenes and in laboratories.

Work Environment

Forensic science technicians held about 14,400 jobs in 2014. About 88 percent forensic science technicians work in state and local government in the following workplaces:

- Police departments and offices
- Crime laboratories
- Morgues
- Medical examiner/coroner offices

Forensic science technicians may have to work outside in all types of weather, spend many hours in laboratories and offices, or do some combination of both. They often work in groups or teams with specialists and other law enforcement personnel. Many specialist forensic science technicians work only in laboratories.

Crime scene investigators travel throughout their jurisdictions, which may be cities, counties, or states. Crimes can happen anywhere, so crime scene investigators and criminalists, especially at the state level, may experience a considerable amount of travel.

Crime scene investigators regularly see the results of violent crime.

Work Schedules. Most laboratory forensic science technicians work full time during standard hours. Crime scene investigators may work staggered day, evening, or night shifts and may have to work overtime because they must always be available to collect or analyze evidence. Technicians working in laboratories usually work a standard workweek, although they may have to be on call outside of normal business hours if they are needed to work immediately on a case. Small police departments may have to rely on part-time forensic science technicians.

Education/Training

Forensic science technicians typically need at least a bachelor's degree in a natural science, such as chemistry or biology, or in forensic science. On-the-job training is usually required both for those who investigate crime scenes and for those who work in labs.

Education. Forensic science technicians typically need at least a bachelor's degree in a natural science, such as chemistry or biology, or in forensic science. Forensic science programs may specialize in a specific area of study, such as toxicology, pathology, or DNA. Students who attend general natural science programs should make an effort to take classes related to forensic science. A list of schools that offer degrees in forensic science is available from the American Academy of Forensic Sciences. Many of those who seek to become forensic science technicians will have an undergraduate degree in the natural sciences and a master's degree in forensic science.

Many crime scene investigators are sworn police officers and have met educational requirements necessary for admittance into a police academy. Applicants for nonuniformed crime scene investigator jobs should have a bachelor's degree in either forensic science, with a strong basic science background, or the natural sciences, but some agencies hire applicants with a high school diploma and years of related work experience. For more information on police officers, see the profile on police and detectives.

Training. Forensic science technicians receive on-the-job training before they are ready to work on cases independently.

Newly hired crime scene investigators typically assist experienced investigators. New investigators often learn proper procedures and methods for collecting and documenting evidence while working under supervision.

Median Annual Wages, May 2014

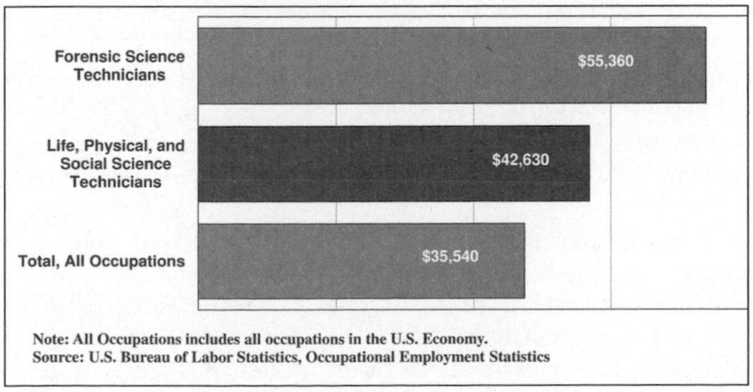

Percent Change in Employment, Projected 2014–2024

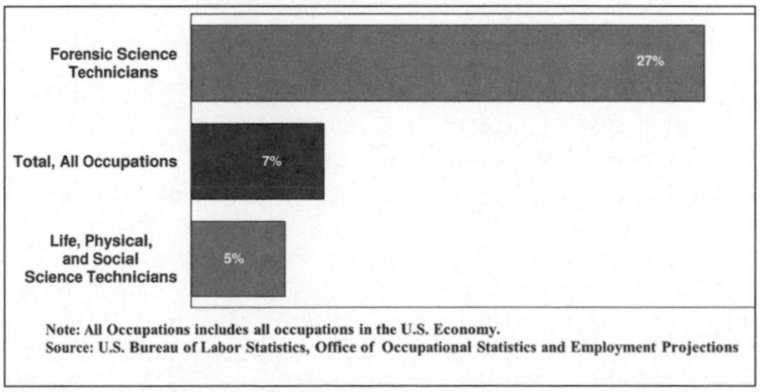

Employment Projections Data for Forensic Science Technicians

Occupational Title	SOC Code	Employment, 2014	Projected Employment, 2024	Change, 2014–2024	
				Percent	Numeric
Forensic science technicians	19-4092	14,400	18,200	27	3,800

Source: U.S. Bureau of Labor Statistics, Employment Projections Program

Similar Occupations. This table shows a list of occupations with job duties that are similar to those of forensic science technicians.

Occupations	Entry-level Education	2014 Median Pay	Projected Job Growth	Average Annual Openings
Biochemists and Biophysicists	Doctoral or professional degree	$84,940	8%	280
Biological Technicians	Bachelor's degree	$41,290	5%	410
Chemical Technicians	Associate's degree	$44,180	2%	120
Chemists and Materials Scientists	Bachelor's degree	$74,720	3%	260
Environmental Science and Protection Technicians	Associate's degree	$42,190	9%	340
Epidemiologists	Master's degree	$67,420	6%	40
Fire Inspectors	See Education/Training	$54,020	6%	90
Hazardous Materials Removal Workers	High school diploma or equivalent	$38,520	7%	330
Medical and Clinical Laboratory Technologists and Technicians	See Education/Training	$49,310	16%	5,210
Medical Scientists	Doctoral or professional degree	$79,930	8%	900
Police and Detectives	See Education/Training	$58,630	4%	3,310
Private Detectives and Investigators	High school diploma or equivalent	$44,570	5%	180

Forensic science technicians learn laboratory specialties on the job. The length of this training varies by specialty. Technicians may need to pass a proficiency exam or otherwise be approved by a laboratory or accrediting body before they are allowed to perform independent casework or testify in court.

Throughout their careers, forensic science technicians need to keep up with advances in technology and science that improve the collection or analysis of evidence.

Licenses, Certifications, and Registrations. A range of licenses and certifications is available to help credential, and aid in the professional development of, many types of forensic science technicians. Certifications and licenses are not typically necessary for entry into the occupation. Credentials can vary widely because standards and regulations vary considerably from one jurisdiction to another.

Important Qualities

Communication skills. Forensic science technicians write reports and testify in court. They often work with other law enforcement officials and specialists.

Composure. Forensic science technicians must maintain their objectivity and professionalism, even while viewing the results of violence and destruction.

Critical-thinking skills. Forensic science technicians use their best judgment when matching physical evidence, such as fingerprints and DNA, to suspects.

Detail oriented. Forensic science technicians must be able to notice small changes in mundane objects to be good at collecting and analyzing evidence.

Math and science skills. Forensic science technicians need a solid understanding of statistics and natural sciences to be able to analyze evidence at a crime scene.

Physical stamina. Forensic science technicians may need to spend much of their day at a crime scene either standing or kneeling.

Problem-solving skills. Forensic science technicians use scientific tests and methods to help law enforcement officials solve crimes.

Pay

The median annual wage for forensic science technicians was $55,360 in May 2014. The median wage is the wage at which half the workers in an occupation earned more than that amount and half earned less. The lowest 10 percent earned less than $33,610, and the highest 10 percent earned more than $91,400.

Job Outlook

Employment of forensic science technicians is projected to grow 27 percent from 2014 to 2024, much faster than the average for all occupations. However, because it is a small occupation, the fast growth will result in only about 3,800 new jobs over the 10-year period.

Scientific and technological advances are expected to increase the availability, reliability, and usefulness of objective forensic information used as evidence in trials. As a result, forensic science technicians will be able to provide even greater value than before. Popular media have increased the awareness of forensic evidence among potential jurors, and there is now an expectation that forensic evidence should contribute to many trials. More forensic science technicians will be needed to provide timely forensics information to law enforcement agencies and courts.

However, federal, state, and local budgets will have a large effect on the number of jobs that exist for forensic science technicians. Larger police departments will be more able to staff full-time forensic science technicians, but they, too, may face budget constraints.

Job Prospects. Competition for jobs may be strong because of the substantial interest in forensic science and crime scene investigation that has been generated by popular media. Applicants who have both a bachelor's degree in a natural science and a master's degree in forensic science should have the best opportunities.

Contacts for More Information

For more information about forensic science technicians and related specialists, visit

- American Academy of Forensic Sciences (www.aafs.org)
- American Board of Criminalistics (www.criminalistics.com)
- American Board of Medicolegal Death Investigators (www.abmdi .org)
- Association of Firearm and Tool Mark Examiners (www.afte.org)
- International Crime Scene Investigators Association (www.icsia.org)

O*NET

- Forensic Science Technicians (19-4092.00)

Geographers

- **2014 Median Pay** .... $76,420 per year $36.74 per hour
- **Typical Entry-Level Education** .... Bachelor's degree
- **Work Experience in a Related Occupation** .... None
- **On-the-job Training** .... None
- **Number of Jobs, 2014** 1,400
- **Job Outlook, 2014–24** .... -2% (Decline)
- **Employment Change, 2014–24** 0

What Geographers Do

Geographers study Earth and its land, features, and inhabitants. They also examine phenomena such as political or cultural structures and study the physical and human geographic characteristics of regions ranging in scale from local to global.

Duties. Geographers typically do the following:

- Gather geographic data through field observations, maps, photographs, satellite imagery, and censuses
- Conduct research, using methods such as surveys, interviews, and focus groups
- Create and modify maps, graphs, diagrams, or other visual representations of geographic data
- Analyze the geographic distribution of physical and cultural characteristics and occurrences
- Use geographic information systems (GIS) to collect, analyze, and display geographic data
- Write reports and present research findings
- Assist, advise, or lead others in using GIS and geographic data
- Combine geographic data with data pertaining to a particular specialty, such as economics, the environment, health, or politics

Geographers use several technologies in their work, such as GIS, remote sensing, and global positioning systems (GPS). Geographers use GIS to find relationships and trends in geographic data. These systems allow geographers to present data visually as maps, reports, and charts. For example, geographers can overlay aerial or satellite images with GIS data, such as population density in a given region, and create computerized maps. They then use the maps to guide governments, businesses, and the general public on a variety of issues, such as developing marketing strategies; planning homes, roads, and landfills; and responding to disasters.

Many people who study geography and who use GIS in their work are employed as surveyors, cartographers and photogrammetrists, surveying and mapping technicians, urban and regional planners, and geoscientists.

The following are examples of types of geographers:

Physical geographers examine the physical aspects of a region and how those aspects relate to humans. They study features of the natural environment, such as landforms, climates, soils, natural hazards, water, and plants. For example, physical geographers may map where a natural resource occurs in a country or study the implications of proposed economic development on the surrounding natural environment.

Human geographers analyze the organization of human activity and its relationships with the physical environment. Human geographers often combine issues from other disciplines into their research, which may include economic, social, or political topics. In their research, some human geographers rely primarily on statistical techniques and others rely on nonstatistical sources, such as field observations and interviews.

Human geographers are often further classified by their area of specialty:

- *Cultural geographers* examine the relationship between geography and culture, studying how features such as religion, language, and ethnicity relate to location.
- *Economic geographers* study economic activities and the distribution of resources. They may research subjects such as regional employment and the location of industries.
- *Environmental geographers* research the impact humans have on the environment and how human activities affect natural processes. They combine aspects of both physical and human

Geographers use maps and global positioning systems in their work.

Median Annual Wages, May 2014

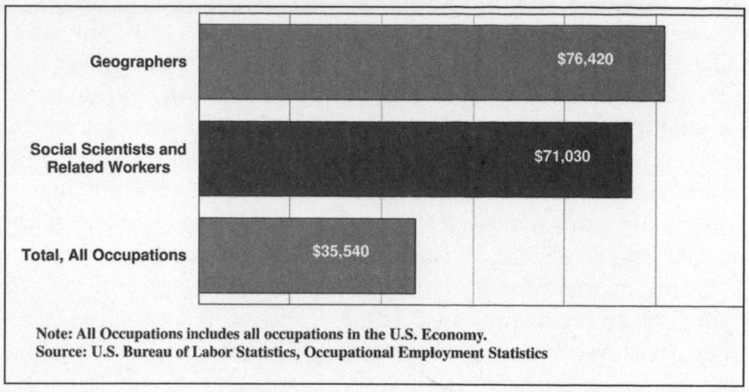

Percent Change in Employment, Projected 2014–2024

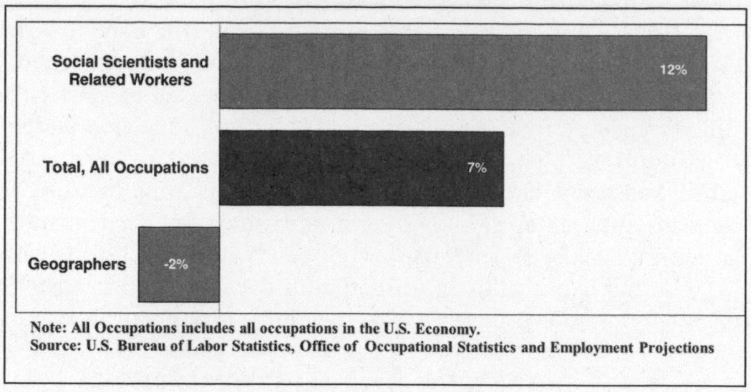

geography and commonly study issues such as climate change, desertification, and deforestation.

- *Medical geographers* investigate the distribution of health issues, healthcare, and disease. For example, a medical geographer may examine the incidence of disease in a certain region.
- *Political geographers* study the relationship between geography and political structures and processes.
- *Regional geographers* focus on the geographic factors in a particular region that ranges in size from a neighborhood to an entire continent.
- *Urban geographers* study cities and metropolitan areas. They may examine how certain geographic factors, such as climate, affect population density in cities.

Geographers often work on projects with people in related fields. For example, economic geographers may work with urban planners, civil engineers, legislators, and real estate professionals to determine the best location for new public transportation infrastructure.

Some people with a geography degree become postsecondary teachers.

Work Environment

Geographers held about 1,400 jobs in 2014. The industries that employed the most geographers were as follows:

Federal government, excluding postal service	58%
Engineering services	10
State and local government, excluding education and hospitals	8
Junior colleges, colleges, universities, and professional schools; state, local, and private	8

Many geographers do fieldwork to gather information and data. For example, geographers often make site visits to observe geographic features, such as the landscape and environment. Some geographers travel to the region they are studying, and sometimes that means working in foreign countries and remote locations.

Work Schedules. Most geographers work full time during standard business hours.

Education/Training

Geographers need a bachelor's degree for most entry-level positions and for positions within the federal government. Work experience and a master's degree are typically required for more advanced positions.

Education. Geographers with a bachelor's degree qualify for most entry-level jobs and for positions with the federal government. Geographers outside of the federal government may need a master's degree in geography or in geographic information systems (GIS). Some positions allow candidates to substitute work experience or GIS proficiency for an advanced degree. Top research positions usually require a Ph.D. or a master's degree and several years of relevant work experience.

Most geography programs include courses in both physical and human geography, statistics or math, remote sensing, and GIS. In addition, courses in a specialized area of expertise are becoming increasingly important because the geography field is broad and interdisciplinary. For example, business, economics, or real estate courses are becoming increasingly important for geographers working in private industry.

Positions for geography professors require a Ph.D. For more information, see the profile on postsecondary teachers.

Other Experience. Students and new graduates often gain experience through internships. This type of practical experience allows students to develop new skills, explore their interests, and become familiar with the industry. Internships can be useful for job seekers, because some employers prefer workers who have practical experience.

Licenses, Certifications, and Registrations. Although certification is not required, most positions require geographers to be proficient in GIS, and certification can demonstrate a level of professional expertise. The GIS Certification Institute offers the GIS professional (GISP) certification for geographers. Candidates may qualify for certification through a combination of education, professional experience, and contributions to the profession, such as publications or participation in conferences. The American Society for Photogrammetry and Remote Sensing also offers certification in GIS. Candidates may qualify for certification with 3 years of experience in GIS, four references, and the completion of a written exam.

Employment Projections Data for Geographers

Occupational Title	SOC Code	Employment, 2014	Projected Employment, 2024	Change, 2014–2024 Percent	Change, 2014–2024 Numeric
Geographers	19-3092	1,400	1,400	-2	0

Source: U.S. Bureau of Labor Statistics, Employment Projections Program

Similar Occupations. This table shows a list of occupations with job duties that are similar to those of geographers.

Occupations	Entry-level Education	2014 Median Pay	Projected Job Growth	Average Annual Openings
Anthropologists and Archeologists	Master's degree	$59,280	4%	30
Cartographers and Photogrammetrists	Bachelor's degree	$60,930	29%	360
Economists	Master's degree	$95,710	6%	120
Geoscientists	Bachelor's degree	$89,910	10%	380
Market Research Analysts	Bachelor's degree	$61,290	19%	9,230
Political Scientists	Master's degree	$104,920	-2%	-10
Postsecondary Teachers	See Education/Training	$70,790	13%	17,700
Sociologists	Master's degree	$72,810	-1%	0
Surveying and Mapping Technicians	High school diploma or equivalent	$40,770	-8%	-430
Surveyors	Bachelor's degree	$57,050	-2%	-90
Urban and Regional Planners	Master's degree	$66,940	6%	240

Important Qualities

Analytical skills. Geographers commonly analyze information and spatial data from a variety of sources, such as maps, photographs, and censuses. They must then be able to draw conclusions from their analyses of different sets of data.

Communication skills. Geographers must be able to communicate with coworkers; present, explain, and defend their research; and work well on teams.

Computer skills. Geographers must be proficient in GIS programming and database management and should be comfortable creating and manipulating digital images in the software.

Critical-thinking skills. Geographers need critical-thinking skills when doing research because they must choose the appropriate data, methods, and scale of analysis for projects. For example, after reviewing a set of population data, they may determine the implications of a particular development plan.

Writing skills. Geographers often write reports or articles detailing their research findings. They also may need to write proposals so that they can receive funding for their research or projects.

Pay

The median annual wage for geographers was $76,420 in May 2014. The median wage is the wage at which half the workers in an occupation earned more than that amount and half earned less. The lowest 10 percent earned less than $43,480, and the highest 10 percent earned more than $104,670.

In May 2014, the median annual wages for geographers in the top industries in which they worked were as follows:

Federal government, excluding postal service	$83,180
Engineering services	65,080
State and local government, excluding education and hospitals	63,040
Junior colleges, colleges, universities, and professional schools; state, local, and private	41,750

Job Outlook

Employment of geographers is projected to decline 2 percent from 2014 to 2024.

More than half of all geographers are employed in the federal government. Governments and businesses rely on geographers to research topics such as natural hazards, the use of resources, and climate change. However, efforts to cut spending are expected to result in a decline in federal government employment, adversely impacting employment of geographers.

Job Prospects. Job seekers can expect strong competition for jobs because of the small size of the occupation. Those with master's degrees, specialized subject matter expertise, and experience working with geographic technologies, such as geographic information systems (GIS), should have the best job prospects. Workers who have used geographic technologies to complete projects and solve problems within their specialized subfields should have better job opportunities.

Many workers with a background in geography find geography-related jobs, but most of these positions do not have the title of geographer. Some of these occupations are surveyors, cartographers and photogrammetrists, surveying and mapping technicians, urban and regional planners, and geoscientists.

Contacts for More Information

For more information about geographers, visit

➤ Association of American Geographers (www.aag.org)

For more information about geographic information systems (GIS) certification, visit

➤ GIS Certification Institute (www.gisci.org)

For information about federal government education requirements for geographer positions, visit

➤ U.S. Office of Personnel Management (www.opm.gov)

To find job openings for geographers in the federal government, visit

➤ USAJOBS (www.usajobs.gov)

O*NET

➤ Geographers (19-3092.00)

Geological and Petroleum Technicians

- **2014 Median Pay** .... $54,810 per year / $26.35 per hour
- **Typical Entry-Level Education** .... Associate's degree
- **Work Experience in a Related Occupation** .... None
- **On-the-job Training** .... Moderate-term on-the-job training

- **Number of Jobs, 2014** 16,500
- **Job Outlook, 2014–24** .... 12% (Faster than average)
- **Employment Change, 2014–24** 1,900

What Geological and Petroleum Technicians Do

Geological and petroleum technicians provide support to scientists and engineers in exploring and extracting natural resources, such as minerals, oil, and natural gas.

Duties. Geological and petroleum technicians typically do the following:

- Install and maintain laboratory and field equipment
- Gather samples such as rock, mud, and soil in the field and prepare samples for laboratory analysis
- Conduct scientific tests on samples to determine their content and characteristics
- Record data from tests and compile information from reports, computer databases, and other sources
- Prepare reports and maps that can be used to define geological characteristics of areas that may have valuable resources
- Monitor well exploration activities and record data such as well temperatures and pressures
- Document their investigations and compare actual productivity with their estimates

Geological and petroleum technicians tend to specialize in either fieldwork and laboratory work, or working in offices where they analyze data. However, many technicians have duties that overlap into multiple areas.

In the field, geological and petroleum technicians use sophisticated equipment such as seismic instruments to gather geological data. They also use tools to collect rock samples and other materials for scientific analysis. In laboratories, these technicians analyze the samples for evidence of hydrocarbons, useful metals, or precious gemstones.

Geological and petroleum technicians use computers to analyze data from samples collected in the field and from previous research. They use geographic information system (GIS) software to map geological data; the software creates a visual representation and makes the data easier to understand. The results of their analysis may explain a new site's potential for further exploration and development or may focus on monitoring the current and future productivity of an existing site.

Geological and petroleum technicians work on geological prospecting and surveying teams under the supervision of scientists and engineers, who evaluate the work for accuracy and make final decisions about current and potential production sites. Geologic and petroleum technicians might work with scientists and technicians in other fields as well. For example, geological and petroleum technicians might work with environmental scientists and technicians to monitor the environmental impact of drilling and other activities.

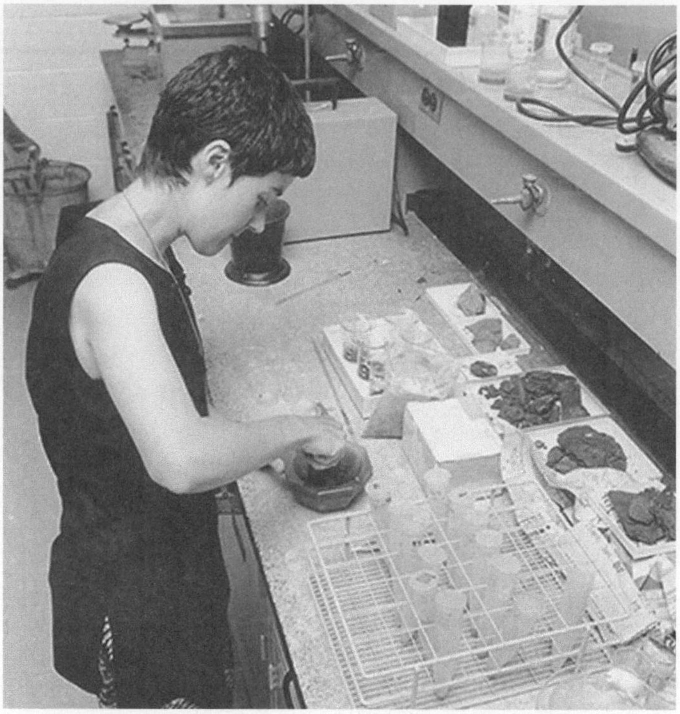

Geological and petroleum technicians help identify and map locations that are suitable for oil and gas wells.

Work Environment

Geological and petroleum technicians held about 16,500 jobs in 2014. The industries that employed the most geological and petroleum technicians were as follows:

Support activities for mining	32%
Oil and gas extraction	23
Engineering services	10
Testing laboratories	6
Management, scientific, and technical consulting services	4

Geological and petroleum technicians spend most of their time in the field and in laboratories, or analyzing data in offices. In addition, technicians may need to stay on location in the field for days or weeks to collect data and monitor equipment. Geological and petroleum technicians who work in offices spend most of

Median Annual Wages, May 2014

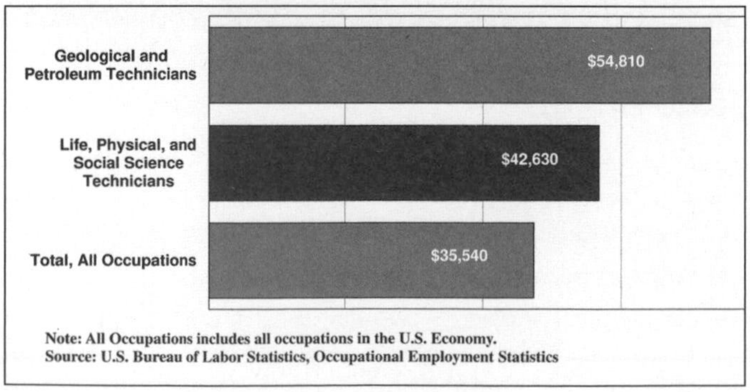

Percent Change in Employment, Projected 2014–2024

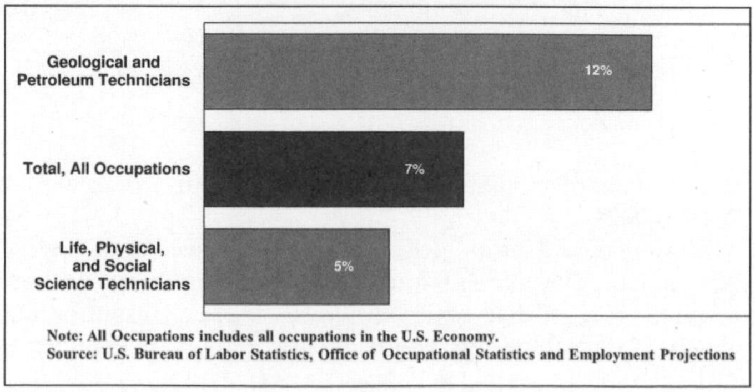

Employment Projections Data for Geological and Petroleum Technicians

Occupational Title	SOC Code	Employment, 2014	Projected Employment, 2024	Change, 2014–2024 Percent	Change, 2014–2024 Numeric
Geological and petroleum technicians	19-4041	16,500	18,500	12	1,900

Source: U.S. Bureau of Labor Statistics, Employment Projections Program

their time working on computers—organizing and analyzing data, writing reports, and producing maps.

Work Schedules. Most geological and petroleum technicians work full time. Technicians generally work a standard schedule in laboratories and offices, but hours spent in the field may be long or irregular.

Education/Training

Geological and petroleum technicians typically need an associate's degree or 2 years of postsecondary training in applied science or science-related technology. Some jobs may require a bachelor's degree. Geological and petroleum technicians also receive on-the-job training.

Education. Although some entry-level positions require only a high school diploma, most employers prefer applicants who have at least an associate's degree or 2 years of postsecondary training in applied science or a science-related technology. Geological and petroleum technician jobs that are data intensive or otherwise highly technical may require at least a bachelor's degree.

Many community colleges and technical institutes offer programs in the geosciences, petroleum, mining, or a related technology, such as geographic information systems (GIS). Community colleges offer associate's degree programs designed to provide an easy transition to bachelor's degree programs at colleges and universities; such programs can be useful for future career advancement.

Regardless of the program, most students take classes in geology, mathematics, computer science, chemistry, and physics. Many schools also offer internships and cooperative-education programs that help students gain experience while attending school.

Important Qualities

Analytical skills. Geological and petroleum technicians examine data, using a variety of complex techniques, including laboratory experimentation and computer modeling.

Communication skills. Geological and petroleum technicians explain their methods and findings through oral and written reports to scientists, engineers, managers, and other technicians.

Critical-thinking skills. Geological and petroleum technicians must use their best judgment when interpreting scientific data and determining what is relevant to their work.

Interpersonal skills. Geological and petroleum technicians need to be able to work well with others and as part of a team.

Physical stamina. To do fieldwork, geological and petroleum technicians need to be in good physical shape in order to hike to remote locations while carrying testing and sampling equipment.

Training. Most geological and petroleum technicians receive on-the-job training under the supervision of technicians who have more experience. During training, new technicians gain hands-on experience using field and laboratory equipment, as well as computer programs such as modeling and mapping software. The length of training can vary with the technician's previous experience and education and with the specifics of the job.

Pay

The median annual wage for geological and petroleum technicians was $54,810 in May 2014. The median wage is the wage at which half the workers in an occupation earned more than that amount and half earned less. The lowest 10 percent earned less than $26,690, and the highest 10 percent earned more than $94,750.

In May 2014, the median annual wages for geological and petroleum technicians in the top industries in which they worked were as follows:

Oil and gas extraction	$67,160
Management, scientific, and technical consulting services	59,440
Support activities for mining	54,430
Engineering services	45,900
Testing laboratories	43,030

Job Outlook

Employment of geological and petroleum technicians is projected to grow 12 percent from 2014 to 2024, faster than the average for all occupations. Strong demand for natural gas is expected to increase demand for geological exploration and extraction in the future.

Similar Occupations. This table shows a list of occupations with job duties that are similar to those of geological and petroleum technicians.

Occupations	Entry-level Education	2014 Median Pay	Projected Job Growth	Average Annual Openings
Cartographers and Photogrammetrists	Bachelor's degree	$60,930	29%	360
Civil Engineering Technicians	Associate's degree	$48,340	5%	350
Civil Engineers	Bachelor's degree	$82,050	8%	2,360
Geoscientists	Bachelor's degree	$89,910	10%	380
Hydrologists	Bachelor's degree	$78,370	7%	50
Petroleum Engineers	Bachelor's degree	$130,050	10%	340
Surveying and Mapping Technicians	High school diploma or equivalent	$40,770	-8%	-430

Because geological and petroleum technicians sometimes are involved in ongoing production processes, such as monitoring a well's productivity, more of these workers will be needed as production increases. Demand for exploration of resources such as coal, metals, and other mined goods generally is expected to continue as it has historically or even to increase over the projection period. This growth will be due to the growing world population and number of industrialized countries.

Job Prospects. The best job prospects will be for those technicians who have hands-on training, through an internship or co-op program, and technical skills in computer programs such as geographic information systems (GIS).

Contacts for More Information

For more information about careers in geology, visit

➤ American Geosciences Institute (www.americangeosciences.org)

For more information about careers in oil and gas exploration, visit

➤ American Association of Petroleum Geologists (www.aapg.org)

➤ Society of Petroleum Engineers (www.spe.org/index.php)

For more information about careers in coal and mineral extraction, visit

➤ National Mining Association (www.nma.org)

O*NET

➤ Geological and Petroleum Technicians (19-4041.00)

➤ Geophysical Data Technicians (19-4041.01)

➤ Geological Sample Test Technicians (19-4041.02)

Geoscientists

- **2014 Median Pay** .... $89,910 per year
$43.22 per hour
- **Typical Entry-Level Education** .... Bachelor's degree
- **Work Experience in a Related Occupation** .... None
- **On-the-job Training** .... None
- **Number of Jobs, 2014** 36,400
- **Job Outlook, 2014–24** .... 10% (Faster than average)
- **Employment Change, 2014–24** 3,800

What Geoscientists Do

Geoscientists study the physical aspects of Earth, such as its composition, structure, and processes, to learn about its past, present, and future.

Duties. Geoscientists typically do the following:

- Plan and carry out field studies, in which they visit locations to collect samples and conduct surveys
- Analyze aerial photographs, well logs (detailed records of geologic formations found during drilling), rock samples, and other data sources to locate deposits of natural resources and estimate their size
- Conduct laboratory tests on samples collected in the field
- Make geologic maps and charts
- Prepare written scientific reports
- Present their findings to clients, colleagues, and other interested parties
- Review reports and research done by other scientists

Geoscientists use a wide variety of tools, both simple and complex. During a typical day in the field, they may use a hammer and chisel to collect rock samples and then use ground-penetrating radar equipment to search for oil or minerals. In laboratories, they may use X-rays and electron microscopes to determine the chemical and physical composition of rock samples. They may also use remote sensing equipment to collect data, as well as geographic information systems (GIS) and modeling software to analyze the data collected.

Geoscientists often supervise the work of technicians and coordinate work with other scientists, both in the field and in the lab.

Many geoscientists are involved in the search for and development of natural resources, such as petroleum. Others work in environmental protection and preservation, and are involved in projects to clean up and reclaim land. Some specialize in a particular aspect of Earth, such as its oceans.

The following are examples of types of geoscientists:

Engineering geologists apply geologic principles to civil and environmental engineering. They offer advice on major construction projects and help with other projects, such as environmental cleanup and reducing natural hazards.

Geologists study the materials, processes, and history of Earth. They investigate how rocks were formed and what has happened to them since their formation. There are subgroups of geologists as well, such as *stratigraphers*, who study stratified rock, and mineralogists, who study the structure and composition of minerals.

Geochemists use physical and organic chemistry to study the composition of elements found in groundwater, such as water from wells or aquifers, and of earth materials, such as rocks and sediment.

Geophysicists use the principles of physics to learn about Earth's surface and interior. They also study the properties of Earth's magnetic, electric, and gravitational fields.

Oceanographers study the motion and circulation of ocean waters; the physical and chemical properties of the oceans; and how these properties affect coastal areas, climate, and weather.

Paleontologists study fossils found in geological formations in order to trace the evolution of plant and animal life and the geologic history of Earth.

Petroleum geologists explore Earth for oil and gas deposits. They analyze geological information to identify sites that should be explored. They collect rock and sediment samples from sites through drilling and other methods and test the samples for the presence of oil and gas. They also estimate the size of oil and gas deposits and work to develop sites to extract oil and gas.

Seismologists study earthquakes and related phenomena, such as tsunamis. They use seismographs and other instruments to collect data on these events.

For a more extensive list of geoscientist specialties, visit the American Geosciences Institute.

People with a geoscience background may become postsecondary teachers.

Work Environment

Geoscientists held about 36,400 jobs in 2014. The industries that employed the most geoscientists were as follows:

Oil and gas extraction	22%
Engineering services	17
Management, scientific, and technical consulting services	15
State government, excluding education and hospitals	8
Colleges, universities, and professional schools; state, local, and private	7

Geoscientists study Earth, often looking for natural resources.

About 1 in 5 worked in the mining, quarrying, and oil and gas extraction industry in 2014. Also, about 3 out of 10 geoscientists were employed in Texas in 2014, because of the prominence of those activities in that state. Workers in natural resource extraction fields usually work as part of a team, with other scientists and engineers. For example, they may work closely with petroleum engineers to find and develop new sources of oil and natural gas.

Most geoscientists split their time among working in the field, in laboratories, and in offices. Fieldwork can take geoscientists to remote locations all over the world. For example, oceanographers may spend months at sea on a research ship, and researchers studying advanced topics may need to collaborate with top scientists around the world. Extensive travel and long periods away from home can be physically and psychologically demanding.

The search for natural resources often takes geoscientists involved in exploration to remote areas and foreign countries. When in the field, geoscientists may work in both warm and cold climates, in all types of weather. They may have to travel by helicopter or in vehicles with four-wheel drive and cover large areas on foot. Having outdoor skills, such as camping and boat-handling skills, may be useful.

Work Schedules. Most geoscientists work full time. They may work additional or irregular hours when doing fieldwork. Geoscientists travel frequently to meet with clients and to conduct fieldwork.

Education/Training

Geoscientists typically need at least a bachelor's degree for most entry-level positions. In several states, geoscientists may need a license to offer their services to the public.

Education. Geoscientists need at least a bachelor's degree for most entry-level positions. However, some workers begin their careers as geoscientists with a master's degree. A Ph.D. is necessary for most basic research and college teaching positions.

A degree in geoscience is preferred by employers, although a degree in physics, chemistry, biology, mathematics, engineering, or computer science usually is accepted if it includes coursework in geology.

Most geoscience programs include geology courses in mineralogy, petrology, and structural geology, which are important for all geoscientists. In addition to classes in geology, most programs require students to take courses in other physical sciences, mathematics, engineering, and computer science. Some programs include training on specific software packages that will be useful to those seeking a career as a geoscientist.

Computer knowledge is essential for geoscientists. Students who have experience with computer modeling, data analysis, and digital mapping will be the most prepared to enter the job market.

Many employers seek applicants who have gained field and laboratory experience while pursuing a degree. Summer field camp programs offer students the opportunity to work closely with professors and apply their classroom knowledge in the field. Students can gain valuable experience in data collection and geologic mapping.

Important Qualities

Communication skills. Geoscientists write reports and research papers. They must be able to present their findings clearly to clients or professionals who do not have a background in geoscience.

Critical-thinking skills. Geoscientists base their findings on sound observation and careful evaluation of data.

Interpersonal skills. Most geoscientists work as part of a team with engineers, technicians, and other scientists.

Outdoor skills. Geoscientists may spend significant amounts of time outdoors. Familiarity with camping skills, general comfort being outside for long periods, and specific skills such as boat handling or even being able to pilot an aircraft could prove useful for geoscientists.

Physical stamina. Geoscientists may need to hike to remote locations while carrying testing and sampling equipment when they conduct fieldwork.

Problem-solving skills. Geoscientists work on complex projects filled with challenges. Evaluating statistical data and other forms of information in order to make judgments and inform the actions of other workers requires a special ability to perceive and address problems.

Licenses, Certifications, and Registrations. Some states require geoscientists to obtain a license to practice. Requirements vary

Median Annual Wages, May 2014

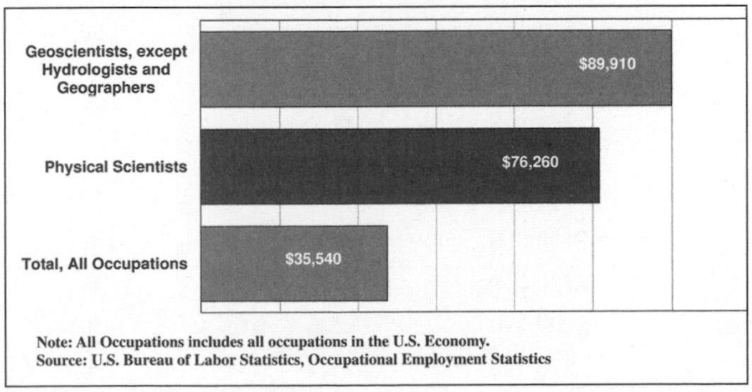

Percent Change in Employment, Projected 2014–2024

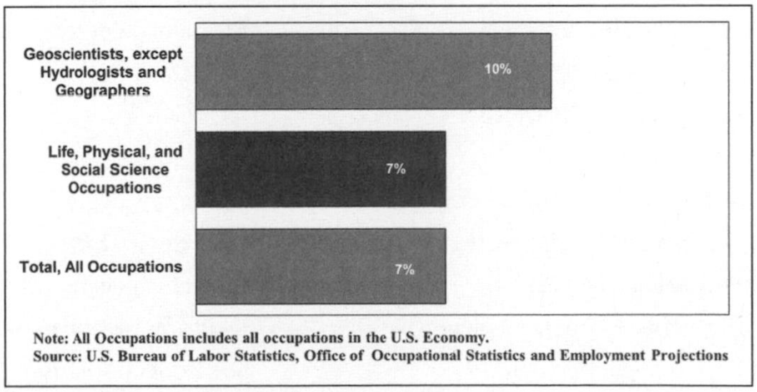

Employment Projections Data for Geoscientists

Occupational Title	SOC Code	Employment, 2014	Projected Employment, 2024	Change, 2014–2024 Percent	Change, 2014–2024 Numeric
Geoscientists, except hydrologists and geographers	19-2042	36,400	40,200	10	3,800

Source: U.S. Bureau of Labor Statistics, Employment Projections Program

by state but typically include minimum education and experience requirements and a passing score on an exam.

Pay

The median annual wage for geoscientists was $89,910 in May 2014. The median wage is the wage at which half the workers in an occupation earned more than that amount and half earned less. The lowest 10 percent earned less than $46,400, and the highest 10 percent earned more than $187,200.

In May 2014, the median annual wages for geoscientists in the top industries in which they worked were as follows:

Oil and gas extraction	$135,380
Engineering services	78,300
Colleges, universities, and professional schools; state, local, and private	78,140
Management, scientific, and technical consulting services	74,100
State government, excluding education and hospitals	63,130

Job Outlook

Employment of geoscientists is projected to grow 10 percent from 2014 to 2024, faster than the average for all occupations. The need for energy, environmental protection, and responsible land and resource management is projected to spur demand for geoscientists.

Horizontal drilling and hydraulic fracturing are examples of new technologies that are expected to increase demand for geoscientists. These technologies allow for the extraction of previously inaccessible oil and gas resources, and geoscientists will be needed to study the effects such technologies have on the surrounding areas. As oil prices increase in the future, even more technologies will likely be introduced that expand the ability to reach untapped oil reserves or introduce alternative ways to provide energy for the expanding population.

Geoscientists will be needed to help plan the construction of wind farms, geothermal power plants, and solar power plants. Alternative energies, such as wind energy, geothermal energy, and solar energy, can use large areas of land and affect wildlife and other natural processes. In addition, only certain areas are suitable for harvesting these energies. For example, geothermal energy plants must be located near sufficient hot ground water, and one task for geoscientists would be studying maps and charts to decide if the site is suitable.

An expanding population and the corresponding increased use of space and resources may create a continued need for geoscientists.

Job Prospects. Job opportunities should be excellent for geoscientists, particularly those with a master's degree. In addition to job growth, a number of job openings are expected as geoscientists leave the workforce through retirement and for other reasons.

Geoscientists with a doctoral degree will likely face competition for positions in academia and research.

Computer knowledge is essential for geoscientists. Students who have experience with computer modeling, data analysis, and digital mapping will be the most prepared to enter the job market.

Fewer opportunities are expected in state and federal governments than in the past. Budget constraints are likely to limit hiring by state governments and federal agencies, such as the U.S.

Similar Occupations. This table shows a list of occupations with job duties that are similar to those of geoscientists.

Occupations	Entry-level Education	2014 Median Pay	Projected Job Growth	Average Annual Openings
Agricultural and Food Scientists	Bachelor's degree	$60,690	5%	190
Anthropologists and Archeologists	Master's degree	$59,280	4%	30
Atmospheric Scientists, Including Meteorologists	Bachelor's degree	$87,980	9%	110
Chemists and Materials Scientists	Bachelor's degree	$74,720	3%	260
Civil Engineers	Bachelor's degree	$82,050	8%	2,360
Environmental Engineers	Bachelor's degree	$83,360	12%	680
Environmental Scientists and Specialists	Bachelor's degree	$66,250	11%	1,020
Geological and Petroleum Technicians	Associate's degree	$54,810	12%	190
Hydrologists	Bachelor's degree	$78,370	7%	50
Mining and Geological Engineers	Bachelor's degree	$90,160	6%	50
Natural Sciences Managers	Bachelor's degree	$120,050	3%	180
Petroleum Engineers	Bachelor's degree	$130,050	10%	340
Physicists and Astronomers	Doctoral or professional degree	$109,290	7%	150
Postsecondary Teachers	See Education/Training	$70,790	13%	17,700

Geological Survey. In addition, more of the work traditionally done by government agencies is expected to be contracted out to consulting firms in the future. Most opportunities for geoscientists are expected to be related to resource extraction—in particular, gas and oil exploration and extraction operations.

Contacts for More Information

For more information about geoscientists, visit

- American Geosciences Institute (www.agiweb.org)
- Geological Society of America (www.geosociety.org)
- IUGS (http://iugs.org/index.php?page=publications)
- U.S. National Committee for Geological Sciences (http://tinyurl.com/j7gvvhc)

For information about petroleum geologists, visit

- American Association of Petroleum Geologists (www.aapg.org)

For more information about licensure for geologists, visit

- American Institute of Professional Geologists (www.aipg.org/Licensure/stateregboards.htm)

To find job openings for geoscientists in the federal government, visit

- USAJOBS (www.usajobs.gov)

For information on federal government education requirements for geoscience positions, visit

- U.S. Office of Personnel Management (http://tinyurl.com/hhtd28f)

O*NET

- Geoscientists, Except Hydrologists and Geographers (19-2042.00)

Historians

- **2014 Median Pay** .... $55,870 per year
  $26.86 per hour
- **Typical Entry-Level Education** ....Master's degree
- **Work Experience in a Related Occupation**.............. None
- **On-the-job Training** .... None
- **Number of Jobs, 2014** 3,500
- **Job Outlook, 2014–24**............. 2% (Slower than average)
- **Employment Change, 2014–24** 100

What Historians Do

Historians research, analyze, interpret, and present the past by studying historical documents and sources.

Duties. Historians typically do the following:

- Gather historical data from various sources, including archives, books, and artifacts
- Analyze and interpret historical information to determine its authenticity and significance
- Trace historical developments in a particular field
- Engage with the public through educational programs and presentations
- Archive or preserve materials and artifacts in museums, visitor centers, and historic sites
- Provide advice or guidance on historical topics and preservation issues
- Write reports, articles, and books on findings and theories

Historians conduct research and analysis for governments, businesses, nonprofits, historical associations, and other organizations. They use a variety of sources in their work, including government

Historians may spend much of their time researching and writing reports.

and institutional records, newspapers, photographs, interviews, films, and unpublished manuscripts, such as personal diaries, letters, and other primary documents. They also may process, catalog, and archive these documents and artifacts.

Many historians present and interpret history in order to inform or build upon public knowledge of past events. They often trace and build a historical profile of a particular person, area, idea, organization, or event. Once their research is complete, they present their findings through articles, books, reports, exhibits, websites, and educational programs.

In government, some historians conduct research to provide historical context for current policy issues. For example, they may research the history of Social Security as background for a new bill or upcoming funding debate. Many write about the history of a particular government agency, activity, or program, such as a military operation or the space program.

In historical associations, historians preserve artifacts and explain the historical significance of a wide variety of subjects, such as historic buildings, religious groups, and battlegrounds.

Historians who work for businesses may examine historical evidence for legal cases and regulatory matters.

Many people with an educational background in history become high school teachers or postsecondary teachers.

Work Environment

Historians held about 3,500 jobs in 2014. The industries that employed the most historians were as follows:

State and local government, excluding education and hospitals	39%
Federal government, excluding postal service	22
Professional, scientific, and technical services	21

Historians also worked in museums, archives, historical societies, research organizations, and nonprofits. Some worked as consultants for these organizations while being employed by consulting firms, and some worked as independent consultants.

Work Schedules. Most historians work full time during regular business hours. Some work independently and are able to set their own schedules. Historians who work in museums or other institutions open to the public may work evenings or weekends. Some historians may travel to collect artifacts, conduct interviews, or visit an area to better understand its culture and environment.

Median Annual Wages, May 2014

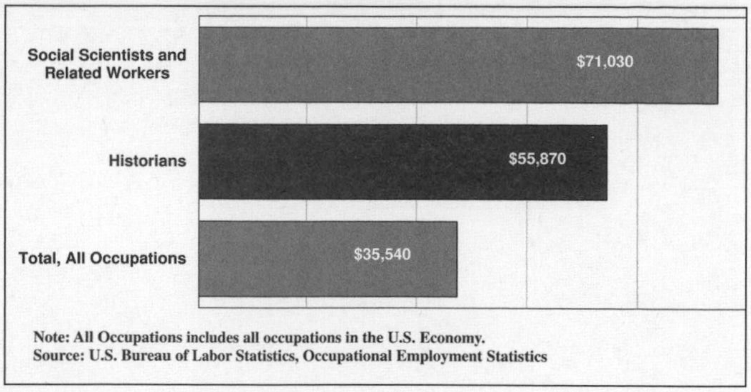

Percent Change in Employment, Projected 2014–2024

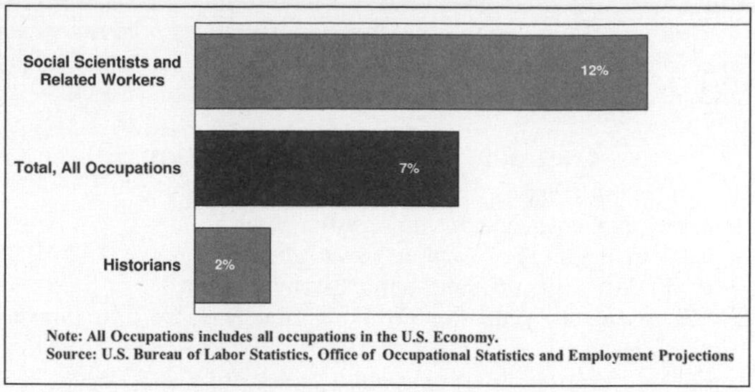

Education/Training

Although most historian positions require a master's degree, some research positions require a doctoral degree. Candidates with a bachelor's degree may qualify for some entry-level positions, but most will not be traditional historian jobs.

Education. Historians need a master's degree or Ph.D. for most positions. Many historians have a master's degree in history or public history. Others complete degrees in related fields, such as museum studies, historical preservation, or archival management.

In addition to coursework, most master's programs in public history and similar fields require an internship as part of the curriculum. Internships offer an opportunity for students to learn practical skills, such as handling and preserving artifacts and creating exhibits. They also give students an opportunity to apply their academic knowledge in a hands-on setting.

Research positions within the federal government and positions in academia typically require a Ph.D. Students in history Ph.D. programs usually concentrate in a specific area of history. Possible specializations include a particular country or region, period, or field, such as social, political, or cultural history.

Candidates with a bachelor's degree in history may qualify for entry-level positions at museums, historical associations, or other small organizations. However, most bachelor's degree holders usually work outside of traditional historian jobs—for example, jobs in education, communications, law, business, publishing, or journalism.

Many people with an educational background in history become high school teachers or postsecondary teachers.

Important Qualities

Analytical skills. Historians must be able to examine various types of historical resources and draw logical conclusions based on their findings.

Communication skills. Historians must communicate effectively when collaborating with colleagues and when presenting their research to the public.

Problem-solving skills. Historians try to answer questions about the past. They may investigate something unknown about a past idea, event, or person; decipher historical information; or identify how the past has affected the present.

Research skills. Historians must be able to examine and process information from a large number of historical resources, including documents, images, and material artifacts.

Writing skills. Writing skills are essential for historians as they often present their findings in reports, articles, and books.

Pay

The median annual wage for historians was $55,870 in May 2014. The median wage is the wage at which half the workers in an occupation earned more than that amount and half earned less. The lowest 10 percent earned less than $27,550, and the highest 10 percent earned more than $101,640.

In May 2014, the median annual wages for historians in the top industries in which they worked were as follows:

Federal government, excluding postal service	$89,980
Professional, scientific, and technical services	56,870
State and local government, excluding education and hospitals	39,130

Job Outlook

Employment of historians is projected to grow 2 percent from 2014 to 2024, slower than the average for all occupations.

Employment in the federal government, where more than 1 out of 5 historians worked in 2014, is expected to decline slightly over the coming decade, due to expected reductions in federal spending.

Historians who are employed in settings outside of the federal government, such as historical societies and historical consulting firms, are expected to see some job growth. However, many of these organizations that employ historians depend on donations or public funding. Thus, employment growth from 2014 to 2024 will depend largely on the amount of funding available.

Job Prospects. Historians may face very strong competition for most jobs. Because of the popularity of history degree programs, applicants are expected to outnumber positions available. Those with a master's degree or Ph.D. should have the best job opportunities.

Practical skills or hands-on work experience in a specialized field such as collections, fundraising, or exhibit design also may be beneficial. Job seekers may gain this experience through internships, related work experience, or volunteering. Positions are often available at local museums, historical societies, government agencies, or nonprofit and other organizations.

Because historians have broad training and education in writing, analytical research, and critical thinking, they can apply their skills to many different occupations—for example, as writers and authors, editors, postsecondary teachers, high school teachers, or policy analysts.

Also, there are many history-related jobs that do not have the title of historian. Workers with a background in history often look for closely related jobs, working as archivists, curators, and museum workers, social science or humanities researchers, and cultural resource managers.

Contacts for More Information

For more information about historians, visit

- American Association for State and Local History (www.aaslh.org)
- American Historical Association (www.historians.org)

Employment Projections Data for Historians

Occupational Title	SOC Code	Employment, 2014	Projected Employment, 2024	Change, 2014–2024 Percent	Change, 2014–2024 Numeric
Historians	19-3093	3,500	3,500	2	100

Source: U.S. Bureau of Labor Statistics, Employment Projections Program

Similar Occupations. This table shows a list of occupations with job duties that are similar to those of historians.

Occupations	Entry-level Education	2014 Median Pay	Projected Job Growth	Average Annual Openings
Anthropologists and Archeologists	Master's degree	$59,280	4%	30
Archivists, Curators, and Museum Workers	See Education/Training	$46,300	7%	210
Economists	Master's degree	$95,710	6%	120
Editors	Bachelor's degree	$54,890	-5%	-620
Geographers	Bachelor's degree	$76,420	-2%	0
High School Teachers	Bachelor's degree	$56,310	6%	5,590
Political Scientists	Master's degree	$104,920	-2%	-10
Postsecondary Teachers	See Education/Training	$70,790	13%	17,700
Sociologists	Master's degree	$72,810	-1%	0
Writers and Authors	Bachelor's degree	$58,850	2%	310

➤ National Council on Public History (http://ncph.org)
➤ Organization of American Historians (www.oah.org)

To find job openings for historians in the federal government, visit

➤ USAJOBS (www.usajobs.gov)

O*NET

➤ Historians (19-3093.00)

Hydrologists

- **2014 Median Pay** .... $78,370 per year $37.68 per hour
- **Typical Entry-Level Education** .... Bachelor's degree
- **Work Experience in a Related Occupation** .... None
- **On-the-job Training** .... None
- **Number of Jobs, 2014** 7,000
- **Job Outlook, 2014–24** .... 7% (As fast as average)
- **Employment Change, 2014–24** 500

What Hydrologists Do

Hydrologists study how water moves across and through Earth's crust. They study how rain, snow, and other forms of precipitation impact river flows or groundwater levels, and how surface water and groundwater evaporate back into the atmosphere or eventually reach the oceans. Hydrologists analyze how water influences the surrounding environment and how changes to the environment influence the quality and quantity of water. They use their expertise to solve problems concerning water quality and availability.

Duties. Hydrologists typically do the following:

- Measure the properties of bodies of water, such as volume and stream flow
- Collect water and soil samples to test for certain properties, such as the pH or pollution levels
- Analyze data on the environmental impacts of pollution, erosion, drought, and other problems
- Research ways to minimize the negative impacts of erosion, sedimentation, or pollution on the environment
- Use computer models to forecast future water supplies, the spread of pollution, floods, and other events
- Evaluate the feasibility of water-related projects, such as hydroelectric power plants, irrigation systems, and wastewater treatment facilities
- Prepare written reports and presentations of their findings

Hydrologists may use remote sensing equipment to collect data. They, or technicians whom they supervise, usually install and maintain this equipment. Hydrologists also use sophisticated computer programs to analyze the data collected. Computer models are often developed by hydrologists to help them understand complex datasets. Hydrologists also use geographic information systems (GIS) and global positioning system (GPS) equipment to do their jobs.

Hydrologists work closely with engineers, scientists, and public officials to study and manage the water supply. For example, they work with policymakers to develop water conservation plans and with biologists to monitor wildlife in order to allow for their water needs.

Most hydrologists specialize in a particular water source or a certain aspect of the water cycle, such as the evaporation of water from lakes and streams. The following are examples of types of hydrologists:

Groundwater hydrologists study the water below Earth's surface. Most groundwater hydrologists focus on the cleanup of groundwater contaminated by spilled chemicals at a factory, an airport, or a gas station. Some groundwater hydrologists focus on water

Hydrologists often perform laboratory tests on water samples that were collected in the field.

supply and decide the best locations for wells and the amount of water available for pumping. These hydrologists often give advice about the best places to build waste disposal sites to ensure that groundwater is not contaminated.

Surface water hydrologists study water from aboveground sources such as streams, lakes, and snowpacks. They may predict future water levels by tracking usage and precipitation data to help reservoir managers decide when to release or store water. They also produce flood forecasts and help develop flood management plans.

Work done by hydrologists can sometimes include topics typically associated with atmospheric scientists, including meteorologists. Scientists with an education in hydrology who concentrate their efforts in the area of water quality are environmental scientists and specialists. Some people with a hydrology background become high school teachers or postsecondary teachers.

Work Environment

Hydrologists held about 7,000 jobs in 2014. The industries that employed the most hydrologists were as follows:

Federal government, excluding postal service	28%
Management, scientific, and technical consulting services	22
Engineering services	17
State government, excluding education and hospitals	17
Local government, excluding education and hospitals	9

Hydrologists work in offices and in the field. In offices, hydrologists spend much their time using computers to analyze data and model their findings. In the field, hydrologists may have to wade into lakes and streams to collect samples or to read and inspect monitoring equipment. Hydrologists also need to write reports detailing the status of surface water and groundwater in specific regions. Many jobs require significant travel. Jobs in the private sector may require international travel.

Work Schedules. Most hydrologists work full time. However, the length of daily shifts may vary when hydrologists work in the field.

Education/Training

Hydrologists need at least a bachelor's degree for entry-level positions; however, some workers begin their careers with a master's degree.

Education. Hydrologists need at least a bachelor's degree, and some begin their careers with a master's degree. Applicants for advanced research and university faculty positions typically need a Ph.D.

Few universities offer undergraduate degrees in hydrology; instead, most universities offer hydrology concentrations in their geosciences, engineering, or earth science programs. Students interested in becoming hydrologists need extensive coursework in math, statistics, and physical, computer, and life sciences. Hydrologists may find it helpful to have a background in economics, environmental law, and other government policy related topics. Knowledge of these areas may help hydrologists communicate with and understand the goals of policymakers and other government workers.

Important Qualities

Analytical skills. Hydrologists need to analyze data collected in the field and examine the results of laboratory tests.

Communication skills. Hydrologists prepare detailed reports that document their research methods and findings. They may have to present their findings to people who do not have a technical background, such as government officials or the general public.

Critical-thinking skills. Hydrologists assess the potential risks to the water supply by pollution, floods, droughts, and other threats. They develop water management plans to handle these threats.

Interpersonal skills. Most hydrologists work as part of a diverse team with engineers, technicians, and other scientists.

Physical stamina. When they are in the field, hydrologists may need to hike to remote locations while carrying testing and sampling equipment.

Pay

The median annual wage for hydrologists was $78,370 in May 2014. The median wage is the wage at which half the workers in an occupation earned more than that amount and half earned less.

Median Annual Wages, May 2014

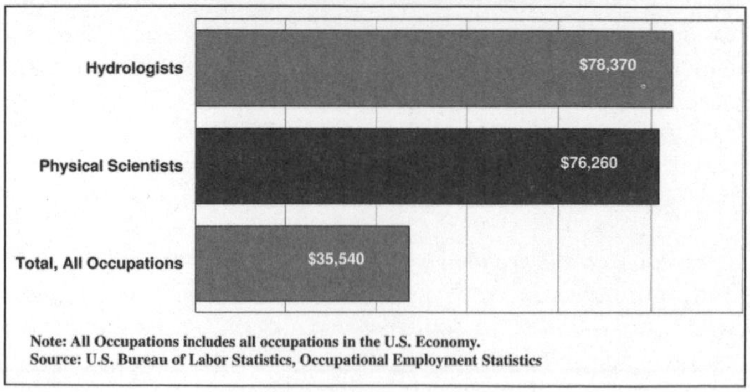

Percent Change in Employment, Projected 2014–2024

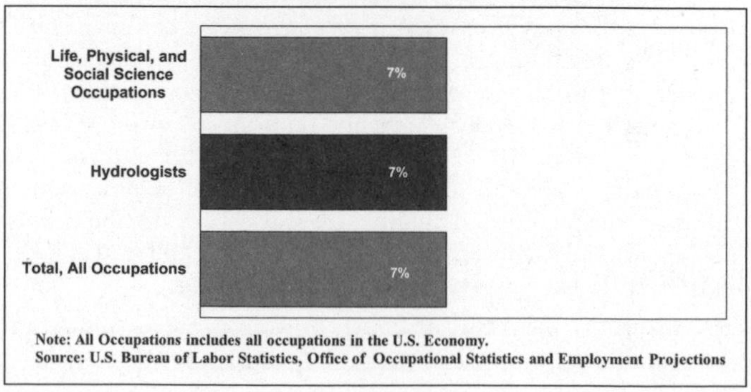

Employment Projections Data for Hydrologists

Occupational Title	SOC Code	Employment, 2014	Projected Employment, 2024	Change, 2014–2024 Percent	Change, 2014–2024 Numeric
Hydrologists	19-2043	7,000	7,500	7	500

Source: U.S. Bureau of Labor Statistics, Employment Projections Program

Similar Occupations. This table shows a list of occupations with job duties that are similar to those of hydrologists.

Occupations	Entry-level Education	2014 Median Pay	Projected Job Growth	Average Annual Openings
Atmospheric Scientists, Including Meteorologists	Bachelor's degree	$87,980	9%	110
Civil Engineers	Bachelor's degree	$82,050	8%	2,360
Conservation Scientists and Foresters	Bachelor's degree	$60,360	7%	270
Environmental Engineers	Bachelor's degree	$83,360	12%	680
Environmental Science and Protection Technicians	Associate's degree	$42,190	9%	340
Environmental Scientists and Specialists	Bachelor's degree	$66,250	11%	1,020
Geoscientists	Bachelor's degree	$89,910	10%	380
Landscape Architects	Bachelor's degree	$64,570	5%	120
Postsecondary Teachers	See Education/Training	$70,790	13%	17,700
Surveyors	Bachelor's degree	$57,050	-2%	-90
Urban and Regional Planners	Master's degree	$66,940	6%	240

The lowest 10 percent earned less than $50,090, and the highest 10 percent earned more than $117,190.

In May 2014, the median annual wages for hydrologists in the top industries in which they worked were as follows:

Engineering services	$87,610
Federal government, excluding postal service	85,390
Management, scientific, and technical consulting services	82,200
Local government, excluding education and hospitals	69,960
State government, excluding education and hospitals	62,840

Job Outlook

Employment of hydrologists is projected to grow 7 percent from 2014 to 2024, about as fast as the average for all occupations. Demand for the services of hydrologists will stem from increases in human activities such as mining, construction, and hydraulic fracturing. Environmental concerns, especially global climate change and the possibility of sea-level rise in addition to local concerns such as flooding and drought, are likely to increase demand for hydrologists in the future.

Managing the nation's water resources will be critical as the population grows and increased human activity changes the natural water cycle. Population expansion into areas that were previously uninhabited may increase the risk of flooding, and new communities may encounter water availability issues. These issues will all need the understanding and knowledge that hydrologists have to find sustainable solutions. However, as governments are the main consumers of hydrologic information, budget constraints will limit growth.

More hydrologists will be necessary to assess the threats that global climate change poses to local, state, and national water supplies. For example, changes in climate affect the severity and frequency of droughts and floods. Hydrologists are critical to developing comprehensive water management plans that address these and other problems linked to climate change.

Contacts for More Information

For more information about hydrology and the work of hydrologists in the federal government, visit

- U.S. Geological Survey (www.usgs.gov)

For information on federal government requirements for hydrology positions, visit

- U.S. Office of Personnel Management (http://tinyurl.com/hybkrpx)

To find job openings for hydrologists in the federal government, visit

- USAJOBS (www.usajobs.gov)

For more information about careers in hydrology, visit

- American Geophysical Union (http://sites.agu.org)
- American Geosciences Institute (www.agiweb.org)
- American Institute of Hydrology (www.aihydrology.org)
- American Water Resources Association (www.awra.org)

For information from universities about research in the water sciences, visit

- Consortium of Universities for the Advancement of Hydrologic Science, INC. (CUAHSI) (www.cuahsi.org)

For informal education and training in hydrology and other geoscience topics, visit

- MetEd (www.meted.ucar.edu/index.php)

O*NET

- Hydrologists (19-2043.00)

Medical Scientists

- **2014 Median Pay** .... $79,930 per year $38.43 per hour
- **Typical Entry-Level Education** .... Doctoral or professional degree
- **Work Experience in a Related Occupation** .... None
- **On-the-job Training** .... None
- **Number of Jobs, 2014** 107,900
- **Job Outlook, 2014–24** .... 8% (As fast as average)
- **Employment Change, 2014–24** 9,000

What Medical Scientists Do

Medical scientists conduct research aimed at improving overall human health. They often use clinical trials and other investigative methods to reach their findings.

Duties. Medical scientists typically do the following:

- Design and conduct studies that investigate both human diseases and methods to prevent and treat them
- Prepare and analyze medical samples and data to investigate causes and treatment of toxicity, pathogens, or chronic diseases
- Standardize drug potency, doses, and methods to allow for the mass manufacturing and distribution of drugs and medicinal compounds
- Create and test medical devices
- Develop programs that improve health outcomes, in partnership with health departments, industry personnel, and physicians
- Write research grant proposals and apply for funding from government agencies and private funding sources
- Follow procedures to avoid contamination and maintain safety

Many medical scientists form hypotheses and develop experiments, with little supervision. They often lead teams of technicians, and sometimes students, who perform support tasks. For example, a medical scientist working in a university laboratory may have undergraduate assistants take measurements and make observations for the scientist's research.

Medical scientists study the causes of diseases and other health problems. For example, a medical scientist who does cancer research might put together a combination of drugs that could slow the cancer's progress. A clinical trial may be done to test the drugs. A medical scientist may work with licensed physicians to test the new combination on patients who are willing to participate in the study.

In a clinical trial, patients agree to help determine if a particular drug, a combination of drugs, or some other medical intervention works. Without knowing which group they are in, patients in a drug-related clinical trial receive either the trial drug or a placebo—a pill or injection that looks like the trial drug but does not actually contain the drug.

Medical scientists analyze the data from all the patients in the clinical trial, to see how the trial drug performed. They compare the results with those obtained from the control group that took the placebo, and they analyze the attributes of the participants. After they complete their analysis, medical scientists may write about and publish their findings.

Medical scientists do research both to develop new treatments and to try to prevent health problems. For example, they may study the link between smoking and lung cancer or between diet and diabetes.

Medical scientists who work in private industry usually have to research the topics that benefit their company the most, rather than investigate their own interests. Although they may not have the pressure of writing grant proposals to get money for their research, they may have to explain their research plans to nonscientist managers or executives.

Medical scientists usually specialize in an area of research. The following are examples of types of medical scientists:

Cancer researchers research the causes of cancers, as well as ways to prevent and cure cancers. They may specialize in one or more types of cancer.

Clinical and medical informaticians develop new ways to use large datasets. They look for explanations of health outcomes through the statistical analysis of data.

Clinical pharmacologists research, develop, and test current and new drugs. They investigate the full effects that drugs have on human health. Their interests may range from understanding specific molecules to the effects that drugs have on large populations.

Gerontologists study the changes that people go through as they get older. Medical scientists who specialize in this field seek to understand the biology of aging and investigate ways to improve the quality of our later years.

Immunochemists investigate the reactions and effects that various chemicals and drugs have on the human immune system.

Neuroscientists study the brain and nervous system.

Research histologists have a specific skill set that is used to study human tissue. They investigate how tissue grows, heals, and dies, and may investigate grafting techniques that can help people who have experienced serious injury.

Medical scientists work in offices and laboratories.

Serologists research fluids found in the human body, such as blood and saliva. Applied serologists often work in forensic science. For more information on forensic science, see the profile on forensic science technicians.

Toxicologists research the harmful effects of drugs, household chemicals, and other potentially poisonous substances. They seek to ensure the safety of drugs, radiation, and other treatments by investigating safe dosage limits.

Work Environment

Medical scientists held about 107,900 jobs in 2014. The industries that employed the most medical scientists were as follows:

Research and development in the physical, engineering, and life sciences	34%
Colleges, universities, and professional schools; state, local, and private	27
Hospitals; state, local, and private	15
Pharmaceutical and medicine manufacturing	6
Medical and diagnostic laboratories	4

They spend most of their time studying data and reports. Medical scientists sometimes work with dangerous biological samples and chemicals, but they take precautions that ensure a safe environment.

Work Schedules. Most medical scientists work full time.

Education/Training

Medical scientists typically have a Ph.D., usually in biology or a related life science. Some medical scientists get a medical degree instead of a Ph.D., but prefer doing research to practicing as a physician.

Education. Students planning careers as medical scientists typically pursue a bachelor's degree in biology, chemistry, or a related field. Undergraduate students benefit from taking a broad range of classes, including life sciences, physical sciences, and math. Students also typically take courses that develop communication and writing skills, because they must learn to write grants effectively and publish research findings.

After students have completed their undergraduate studies, they typically enter Ph.D. programs. Dual-degree programs are available that pair a Ph.D. with a range of specialized medical degrees. A few degree programs that are commonly paired with Ph.D. studies are Medical Doctor (M.D.), Doctor of Dental Surgery (D.D.S.), Doctor of Dental Medicine (D.M.D.), and Doctor of Osteopathic Medicine (D.O.). Whereas Ph.D. studies focus on research methods, such as project design and data interpretation, students in dual-degree programs learn both the clinical skills needed to be a physician and the research skills needed to be a scientist.

Graduate programs emphasize both laboratory work and original research. These programs offer prospective medical scientists the opportunity to develop their experiments and, sometimes, to supervise undergraduates. Ph.D. programs culminate in a thesis that the candidate presents before a committee of professors. Students may specialize in a particular field, such as gerontology, neurology, or cancer.

Those who go to medical school spend most of the first 2 years in labs and classrooms, taking courses such as anatomy, biochemistry, physiology, pharmacology, psychology, microbiology, pathology, medical ethics, and medical law. They also learn how to record medical histories, examine patients, and diagnose illnesses. They may be required to participate in residency programs, meeting the same requirements that physicians and surgeons have to fulfill.

Medical scientists often continue their education with postdoctoral work. Postdoctoral work provides additional and more independent lab experience, including experience in specific processes and techniques such as gene splicing, which is transferable to other research projects.

Licenses, Certifications, and Registrations. Medical scientists primarily conduct research and typically do not need licenses or certifications. However, those who administer drugs, gene therapy, or otherwise practice medicine on patients in clinical trials or a private practice need a license to practice as a physician.

Important Qualities

Communication skills. Communication is critical, because medical scientists must be able to explain their conclusions. In addition, medical scientists write grant proposals, because grants often are required to fund their research.

Critical-thinking skills. Medical scientists must use their expertise to determine the best method for solving a specific research question.

Data-analysis skills. Medical scientists use statistical techniques, so that they can properly quantify and analyze health research questions.

Decision-making skills. Medical scientists must determine what research questions to ask, how best to investigate the questions, and what data will best answer the questions.

Observation skills. Medical scientists conduct experiments that require precise observation of samples and other health data. Any mistake could lead to inconclusive or misleading results.

Pay

The median annual wage for medical scientists was $79,930 in May 2014. The median wage is the wage at which half the workers in an occupation earned more than that amount and half earned less. The lowest 10 percent earned less than $43,150, and the highest 10 percent earned more than $148,210.

Median Annual Wages, May 2014

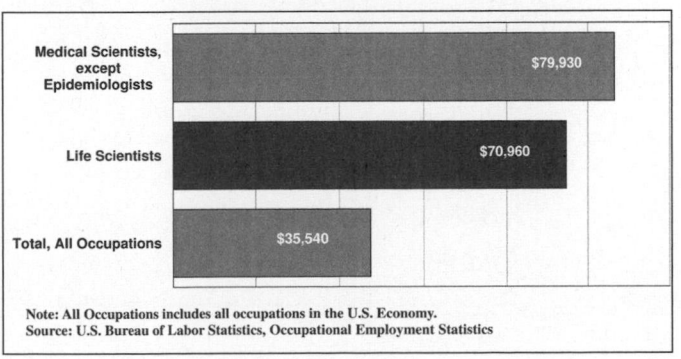

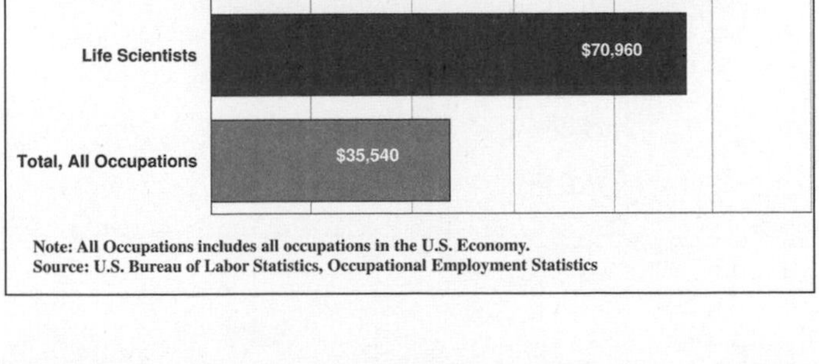

Note: All Occupations includes all occupations in the U.S. Economy.
Source: U.S. Bureau of Labor Statistics, Occupational Employment Statistics

Percent Change in Employment, Projected 2014–2024

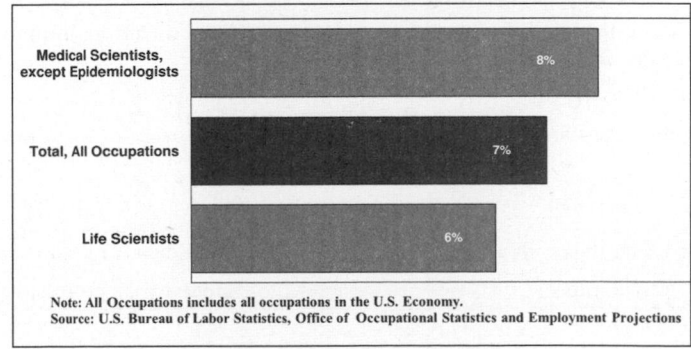

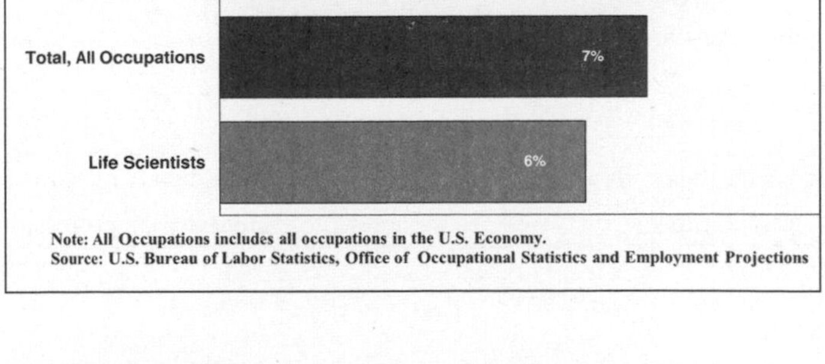

Note: All Occupations includes all occupations in the U.S. Economy.
Source: U.S. Bureau of Labor Statistics, Office of Occupational Statistics and Employment Projections

Employment Projections Data for Medical Scientists

Occupational Title	SOC Code	Employment, 2014	Projected Employment, 2024	Change, 2014–2024 Percent	Change, 2014–2024 Numeric
Medical scientists, except epidemiologists	19-1042	107,900	116,800	8	9,000

Source: U.S. Bureau of Labor Statistics, Employment Projections Program

In May 2014, the median annual wages for medical scientists in the top industries in which they worked were as follows:

Pharmaceutical and medicine manufacturing	$102,400
Research and development in the physical, engineering, and life sciences	92,770
Medical and diagnostic laboratories	82,700
Hospitals; state, local, and private	73,590
Colleges, universities, and professional schools; state, local, and private	58,140

Job Outlook

Employment of medical scientists is projected to grow 8 percent from 2014 to 2024, about as fast as the average for all occupations. A larger and aging population, increased rates of several chronic conditions, and a growing reliance on pharmaceuticals are all factors that are expected to increase demand for medical scientists. In addition, a greater understanding of biological processes and new discoveries should open frontiers in research that are expected to require the services of medical scientists.

Medical scientists will be needed for research related to treating diseases such as AIDS, Alzheimer's disease, and cancer. Research into treatment problems, such as resistance to antibiotics, also should spur growth. In addition, a higher population density and the increasing frequency of international travel may facilitate the spread of existing diseases and possibly give rise to new ones. Medical scientists will continue to be needed because they contribute to the development of treatments and medicines that improve human health.

The federal government is a major source of funding for medical research. Going forward, the level of federal funding will continue to affect competition for winning and renewing research grants.

Contacts for More Information

For more information about research specialties and opportunities within specialized fields for medical scientists, visit

- American Association for Cancer Research (www.aacr.org/Pages/Home.aspx)
- American Society for Biochemistry and Molecular Biology (www.asbmb.org)
- American Society for Clinical Pharmacology and Therapeutics (www.ascpt.org)
- American Society for Pharmacology and Experimental Therapeutics (www.aspet.org)
- Gerontological Society of America (www.geron.org)
- Society for Neuroscience (www.sfn.org)
- Society of Toxicology (www.toxicology.org)

O*NET

- Medical Scientists, Except Epidemiologists (19-1042.00)

Microbiologists

- **2014 Median Pay** .... $67,790 per year; $32.59 per hour
- **Typical Entry-Level Education** .... Bachelor's degree
- **Work Experience in a Related Occupation** .... None
- **On-the-job Training** .... None
- **Number of Jobs, 2014** 22,400
- **Job Outlook, 2014–24** .... 4% (Slower than average)
- **Employment Change, 2014–24** 800

Similar Occupations. This table shows a list of occupations with job duties that are similar to those of medical scientists.

Occupations	Entry-level Education	2014 Median Pay	Projected Job Growth	Average Annual Openings
Agricultural and Food Scientists	Bachelor's degree	$60,690	5%	190
Biochemists and Biophysicists	Doctoral or professional degree	$84,940	8%	280
Epidemiologists	Master's degree	$67,420	6%	40
Health Educators and Community Health Workers	See Education/Training	$42,450	13%	1,560
Medical and Clinical Laboratory Technologists and Technicians	See Education/Training	$49,310	16%	5,210
Microbiologists	Bachelor's degree	$67,790	4%	80
Physicians and Surgeons	Doctoral or professional degree	This wage is equal to or greater than $187,200.	14%	9,930
Postsecondary Teachers	See Education/Training	$70,790	13%	17,700
Veterinarians	Doctoral or professional degree	$87,590	9%	690

What Microbiologists Do

Microbiologists study microorganisms such as bacteria, viruses, algae, fungi, and some types of parasites. They try to understand how these organisms live, grow, and interact with their environments.

Duties. Microbiologists typically do the following:

- Plan and conduct complex research projects, such as improving sterilization procedures or developing new drugs to combat infectious diseases
- Perform laboratory services that are used in the diagnosis and treatment of illnesses
- Supervise the work of biological technicians and other workers and evaluate the accuracy of their results
- Isolate and maintain cultures of bacteria or other microorganisms for study
- Identify and classify microorganisms found in specimens collected from humans, plants, animals, or the environment
- Monitor the effect of microorganisms on plants, animals, other microorganisms, or the environment
- Keep up with current knowledge by reviewing the findings of other researchers and by attending conferences
- Prepare technical reports, publish research papers, and make recommendations based on their research findings
- Present research findings to scientists, nonscientist executives, engineers, other colleagues, and the public

Many microbiologists work in research and development conducting basic research or applied research. The aim of basic research is to increase scientific knowledge. An example is growing strains of bacteria in various conditions to learn how they react to those conditions. Other microbiologists conduct applied research and develop new products to solve particular problems. For example, microbiologists may develop genetically engineered crops, better biofuels, or new vaccines.

Microbiologists use computers and a wide variety of sophisticated laboratory instruments to do their experiments. Electron microscopes are used to study bacteria, and advanced computer software is used to analyze the growth of microorganisms found in samples.

It is increasingly common for microbiologists to work on teams with technicians and scientists in other fields, because many scientific research projects involve multiple disciplines. Microbiologists may work with medical scientists or biochemists while researching new drugs, or they may work in medical diagnostic laboratories alongside physicians and nurses to help prevent, treat, and cure diseases. For more information, see the profiles on biochemists and biophysicists, physicians and surgeons, and registered nurses.

The following are examples of types of microbiologists:

Bacteriologists study the growth, development, and other properties of bacteria, including the positive and negative effects that bacteria have on plants, animals, and humans.

Clinical microbiologists perform a wide range of clinical laboratory tests on specimens collected from plants, humans, and animals to aid in detection of disease. Clinical and medical microbiologists whose work involves directly researching human health may be classified as medical scientists.

Environmental microbiologists study the ways in which microorganisms interact with the environment. They may study the use of microbes to clean up areas contaminated by heavy metals or study how microbes could aid crop growth.

Industrial microbiologists study and solve problems related to industrial production processes. They may examine microbial growth found in the pipes of a chemical factory, monitor the impact industrial waste has on the local ecosystem, or oversee the microbial activities used in cheese production to ensure quality.

Mycologists study the properties of fungi such as yeast and mold, as well as the ways fungi can be used (for example, in food or the environment) to benefit society.

Parasitologists study the life cycle of parasites, the parasite-host relationship, and how parasites adapt to different environments. They may investigate the outbreak and control of parasitic diseases such as malaria.

Public health microbiologists examine specimens in order to track, control, and prevent communicable diseases and other health hazards. They typically provide laboratory services for local health departments and community health programs.

Virologists study the structure, development, and other properties of viruses and any effects viruses have on infected organisms.

Many people with a microbiology background become high school teachers or postsecondary teachers.

Work Environment

Microbiologists held about 22,400 jobs in 2014. The industries that employed the most microbiologists were as follows:

Research and development in the physical, engineering, and life sciences	24%
Pharmaceutical and medicine manufacturing	21
Federal government, excluding postal service	12
Colleges, universities, and professional schools; state	9
State government, excluding education and hospitals	7

They typically work in laboratories and offices, where they conduct experiments and analyze the results. Microbiologists who work with dangerous organisms must follow strict safety procedures to avoid contamination. Some microbiologists may conduct onsite visits or collect samples from lakes, streams, and oceans, and, as a result, may travel occasionally and spend some time outside.

Basic researchers who work in academia usually choose the focus of their research and run their own laboratories. Applied researchers who work for companies study the products that the company will sell or suggest modifications to the production process so that the company can become more efficient. Basic researchers often need to fund their research by winning grants.

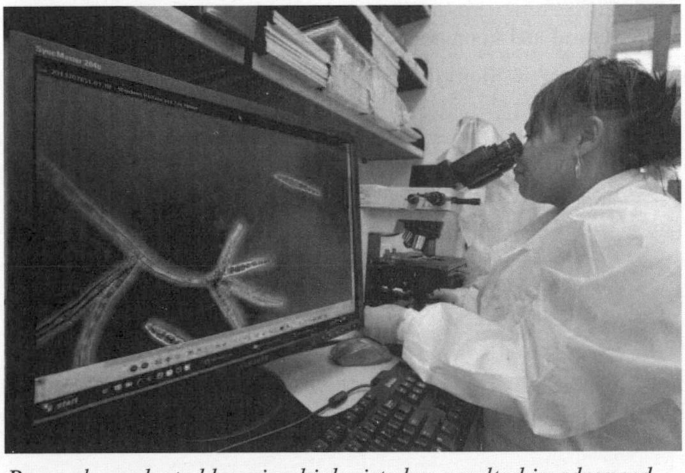

Research conducted by microbiologists has resulted in advanced treatments for many diseases.

Median Annual Wages, May 2014

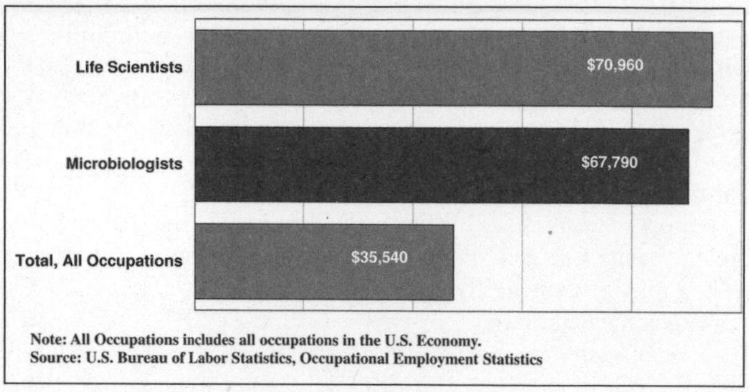

Percent Change in Employment, Projected 2014–2024

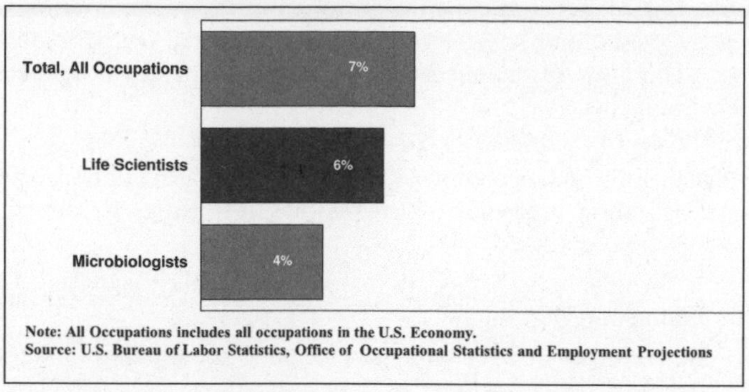

These grants often put pressure on researchers to meet deadlines and other specifications. Research grants are generally awarded through a competitive selection process.

Work Schedules. Most microbiologists work full time and keep regular hours.

Education/Training

A bachelor's degree in microbiology or a closely related field is needed for entry-level microbiologist jobs. A Ph.D. is needed to carry out independent research and to work in universities.

Education. Microbiologists need at least a bachelor's degree in microbiology or a closely related field such as biochemistry or cell biology. Many colleges and universities offer degree programs in biological sciences, including microbiology.

Most microbiology majors take core courses in microbial genetics and microbial physiology and elective classes such as environmental microbiology and virology. Students also must take classes in other sciences, such as biochemistry, chemistry, and physics, because it is important for microbiologists to have a broad understanding of the sciences. Courses in statistics, mathematics, and computer science are important for microbiologists because they must be able to do complex data analysis.

It is important for prospective microbiologists to have laboratory experience before entering the workforce. Most undergraduate microbiology programs include a mandatory laboratory requirement, but additional laboratory coursework is recommended. Students also can gain valuable laboratory experience through internships with prospective employers such as drug manufacturers.

Microbiologists typically need a Ph.D. to carry out independent research and work in colleges and universities. Graduate students studying microbiology commonly specialize in a subfield such as bacteriology or immunology. Ph.D. programs usually include class work, laboratory research, and completing a thesis or dissertation.

Training. Many microbiology Ph.D. holders begin their careers in temporary postdoctoral research positions. During their postdoctoral appointment, they work with experienced scientists as they continue to learn about their specialties and develop a broader understanding of related areas of research.

Postdoctoral positions typically offer the opportunity to publish research findings. A solid record of published research is essential to getting a permanent college or university faculty position.

Important Qualities

Communication skills. Microbiologists should be able to effectively communicate their research processes and findings so that knowledge may be applied correctly.

Detail oriented. Microbiologists must be able to conduct scientific experiments and analyses with accuracy and precision.

Interpersonal skills. Microbiologists typically work on research teams and thus must work well with others toward a common goal. Many also lead research teams and must be able to motivate and direct other team members.

Logical-thinking skills. Microbiologists draw conclusions from experimental results through sound reasoning and judgment.

Math skills. Microbiologists regularly use complex mathematical equations and formulas in their work. Therefore, they need a broad understanding of mathematics, including calculus and statistics.

Observation skills. Microbiologists must constantly monitor their experiments. They need to keep a complete, accurate record of their work, noting conditions, procedures, and results.

Perseverance. Microbiological research involves substantial trial and error, and microbiologists must not become discouraged in their work.

Problem-solving skills. Microbiologists use scientific experiments and analysis to find solutions to complex scientific problems.

Time-management skills. Microbiologists usually need to meet deadlines when conducting research and laboratory tests. They must be able to manage time and prioritize tasks efficiently while maintaining their quality of work.

Advancement. Microbiologists typically receive greater responsibility and independence in their work as they gain experience. They also gain greater responsibility through certification and higher education. Ph.D. microbiologists usually lead research teams and control the direction and content of projects.

Some microbiologists move into managerial positions, often as natural sciences managers. Those who pursue management careers

Employment Projections Data for Microbiologists

Occupational Title	SOC Code	Employment, 2014	Projected Employment, 2024	Change, 2014–2024	
				Percent	Numeric
Microbiologists............	19-1022	22,400	23,200	4	800

Source: U.S. Bureau of Labor Statistics, Employment Projections Program

Similar Occupations. This table shows a list of occupations with job duties that are similar to those of microbiologists.

Occupations	Entry-level Education	2014 Median Pay	Projected Job Growth	Average Annual Openings
Agricultural and Food Scientists	Bachelor's degree	$60,690	5%	190
Biochemists and Biophysicists	Doctoral or professional degree	$84,940	8%	280
Biological Technicians	Bachelor's degree	$41,290	5%	410
Chemical Technicians	Associate's degree	$44,180	2%	120
Epidemiologists	Master's degree	$67,420	6%	40
Medical and Clinical Laboratory Technologists and Technicians	See Education/Training	$49,310	16%	5,210
Medical Scientists	Doctoral or professional degree	$79,930	8%	900
Natural Sciences Managers	Bachelor's degree	$120,050	3%	180
Physicians and Surgeons	Doctoral or professional degree	This wage is equal to or greater than $187,200.	14%	9,930
Postsecondary Teachers	See Education/Training	$70,790	13%	17,700
Zoologists and Wildlife Biologists	Bachelor's degree	$58,270	4%	80

spend much of their time on administrative tasks such as preparing budgets and schedules.

Licenses, Certifications, and Registrations. Certifications are available for clinical microbiologists and for those who specialize in the fields of food safety and quality and pharmaceuticals and medical devices. They may help workers gain employment in the occupation or advance to new positions of responsibility. Certifications are not mandatory for the majority of work done by microbiologists.

Pay

The median annual wage for microbiologists was $67,790 in May 2014. The median wage is the wage at which half the workers in an occupation earned more than that amount and half earned less. The lowest 10 percent earned less than $38,830, and the highest 10 percent earned more than $125,000.

In May 2014, the median annual wages for microbiologists in the top industries in which they worked were as follows:

Federal government, excluding postal service	$98,300
Research and development in the physical, engineering, and life sciences	69,410
Pharmaceutical and medicine manufacturing	67,460
State government, excluding education and hospitals	53,300
Colleges, universities, and professional schools; state	49,590

Job Outlook

Employment of microbiologists is projected to grow 4 percent from 2014 to 2024, slower than the average for all occupations. More microbiologists will be needed to contribute to basic research and solve problems encountered in industrial production processes. However, employment of microbiologists is projected to decline in the federal government.

The development of new medicines and treatments is expected to increase the demand for microbiologists in pharmaceutical and biotechnology research. Microbiologists will be needed to research and develop new medicines and treatments, such as vaccines and antibiotics that are used to fight infectious diseases. In addition, microbiologists will be needed to help pharmaceutical and biotechnology companies develop biological drugs that are produced with the aid of microorganisms.

Aside from improving health, other areas of research and development in biotechnology are expected to provide employment growth for microbiologists. Many companies, from food producers to chemical companies, will need microbiologists to ensure product quality and production efficiency. Increasing demand for clean energy should drive the need for microbiologists who research and develop alternative energy sources such as biofuels and biomass. In agriculture, more microbiologists will be needed to help develop genetically engineered crops that provide greater yields and require less pesticide and fertilizer. Finally, efforts to discover new and improved ways to preserve the environment and safeguard the public's health also will increase demand for microbiologists.

Job Prospects. Microbiology is a thriving field that should provide good prospects for qualified workers. Most of the applied research projects that microbiologists are involved in require the expertise of scientists in multiple fields such as biophysics, chemistry, and medicine. Microbiologists with some familiarity of other disciplines should have the best opportunities.

Much of basic research depends on funding from the federal government through the National Institutes of Health, the National Science Foundation, and private venture capitalists. Federal budgetary decisions and venture capital availability will affect job prospects in basic research from year to year. There is strong competition among microbiologists for research funding. However, many opportunities for microbiologists are likely to be available.

Contacts for More Information

For more information about microbiologists, visit

- American Society for Microbiology (www.asm.org)
- Society for Industrial Microbiology and Biotechnology (www.simbhq.org)

To find job openings for microbiologists in the federal government, visit

- USAJOBS (www.usajobs.gov)

For general information about careers and specialties in biological sciences, visit

- American Institute of Biological Sciences (www.aibs.org/home/index.html)
- American Society for Cell Biology (http://ascb.org)
- Federation of American Societies for Experimental Biology (www.faseb.org)

For information about microbiologists' tools and activities, visit

- The Virtual Urchin (http://virtualurchin.stanford.edu)

For more information about microbiological topics, visit

- Microbiological Garden (http://tinyurl.com/zq64uju)
- The Tree of Life Web Project (www.tolweb.org/tree/phylogeny.html)

O*NET

- Microbiologists (19-1022.00)

Nuclear Technicians

- **2014 Median Pay** .... $74,690 per year $35.91 per hour
- **Typical Entry-Level Education** .... Associate's degree
- **Work Experience in a Related Occupation** .... None
- **On-the-job Training** .... Moderate-term on-the-job training
- **Number of Jobs, 2014** 6,800
- **Job Outlook, 2014–24** .... -5% (Decline)
- **Employment Change, 2014–24** .... -300

What Nuclear Technicians Do

Nuclear technicians typically work in nuclear energy production or assist physicists, engineers, and other professionals in nuclear research. They operate special equipment used in these activities and monitor the levels of radiation that are produced.

Duties. Nuclear technicians typically do the following:

- Monitor the performance of equipment used in nuclear experiments and power generation
- Measure the levels and types of radiation produced by nuclear experiments, power generation, and other activities
- Collect samples of air, water, and soil, and test for radioactive contamination
- Instruct personnel on radiation safety procedures and warn them of hazardous conditions
- Operate and maintain radiation monitoring equipment

Job duties and titles of nuclear technicians often depend on where they work and what purpose the facility serves. Most nuclear technicians work in nuclear power plants, where they ensure that reactors and other equipment are operated safely and efficiently. The following are types of nuclear technicians who work in the power generation industry:

Operating technicians monitor the performance of systems in nuclear power plants. They measure levels of radiation and other contaminants in water systems. The levels they find could indicate a leak or could decrease the efficiency of the turbines in the power plants. They measure efficiency and ensure safety by making calculations based on factors such as temperature, pressure, and radiation intensity. Operating technicians must make adjustments and repairs to maintain or improve the performance of reactors and other equipment.

Radiation protection technicians monitor levels of radiation contamination to protect personnel in nuclear power facilities and the surrounding environment. They use radiation detectors to measure levels in and around facilities, and they use dosimeters to measure the levels present in people and objects. With the data collected, they map radiation levels throughout the plant and the surrounding environment. From their findings, they recommend radioactive decontamination plans and safety procedures for personnel. They also monitor worker activity from a control room and alert personnel who may be entering a dangerous area or working in an unsafe way.

Nuclear technicians also work in waste management and treatment facilities, where they monitor the disposal, recycling, and storage of nuclear waste. They perform duties similar to those of radiation protection technicians at nuclear power plants.

Some nuclear technicians work in laboratories. They help nuclear physicists, nuclear engineers, and other scientists conduct research and develop new types of nuclear reactors, fuels, medicines, and other technologies. They use equipment such as radiation detectors, spectrometers (utilized to measure gamma ray and X-ray radiation), and particle accelerators to conduct experiments and gather data. They also may use remote-controlled equipment to manipulate radioactive materials or materials exposed to radiation.

Work Environment

Nuclear technicians held about 6,800 jobs in 2014. The industries that employed the most nuclear technicians were as follows:

Electric power generation, transmission and distribution	62%
Manufacturing	8
Management, scientific, and technical consulting services	3
Engineering services	3
Research and development in the physical, engineering, and life sciences	3

In nuclear power plants, nuclear technicians typically work in offices and control rooms where they use computers and other equipment to monitor and help operate nuclear reactors. Nuclear technicians also need to measure radiation levels onsite, requiring them to visit several areas in and around the plant throughout the workday. This task may sometimes require them to work outside, regardless of weather conditions. Working around nuclear reactors may involve exposure to high temperatures. Nuclear technicians who conduct scientific tests for scientists and engineers typically work in laboratories.

Nuclear technicians must take precautions when working with or around nuclear materials. They often have to wear protective

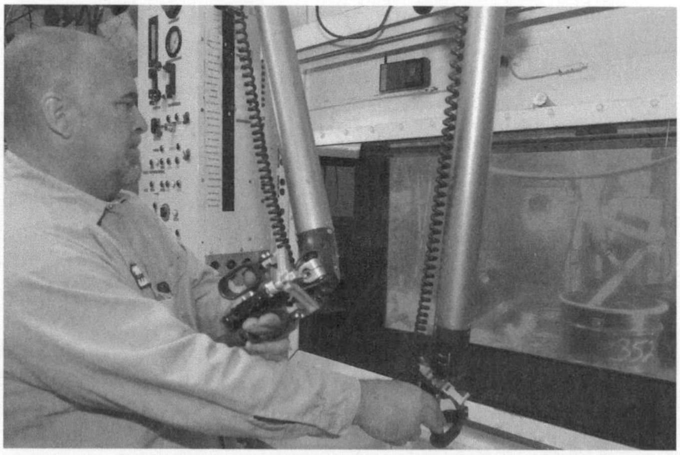

Nuclear technicians may use robotic arms and hands when working with nuclear materials.

gear and special badges that indicate whether they have been exposed to radiation. Protective gear may include hardhats, hearing and eye protection, plastic suits, and respirators.

Work Schedules. Most nuclear technicians work full time. In power plants, which operate 24 hours a day, technicians may work variable schedules that include nights, holidays, and weekends. Occasionally, plants stop operations for maintenance and upgrades. Workers may need to work overtime during these periods. In laboratories, technicians typically work during normal business hours.

Education/Training

Nuclear technicians typically need an associate's degree in nuclear science or a nuclear-related technology. Some may have gained equivalent experience from serving in the military. Nuclear technicians also go through extensive on-the-job training. For safety and security reasons, nuclear technicians usually must undergo a background check and receive some type of security clearance after they are hired.

Education. Nuclear technicians typically need an associate's degree, or they may have equivalent experience from serving in the military—specifically, the U.S. Navy. Many community colleges and technical institutes offer associate's degree programs in nuclear science, nuclear technology, or related fields. Students study nuclear energy, radiation, and the equipment and components used in nuclear power plants and laboratories. Other coursework includes mathematics, physics, and chemistry.

Training. In nuclear power plants, nuclear technicians start out as trainees under the supervision of more experienced technicians. During their training, they are taught the proper ways to use operating and monitoring equipment. They are also taught safety procedures, regulations, and plant policies. Workers who do not have the appropriate associate's degree or its equivalent usually havc a substantial period of onsite technical training provided by their employer before they begin full duties and a normal training schedule.

Training varies with the technician's previous experience and education. Most training programs last between 6 months and 2 years. Nuclear technicians go through additional training and education throughout their careers to keep up with advances in nuclear science and technology.

Licenses, Certifications, and Registrations. The Nuclear Energy Institute offers a certificate through its Nuclear Uniform Curriculum Program. The American Society for Nondestructive Testing offers Industrial Radiography and Radiation Safety Personnel certification. The National Registry of Radiation Protection Technologists offers certification as a Registered Radiation Protection Technologist.

Important Qualities

Communication skills. Nuclear technicians receive complex instructions from scientists and engineers that they must follow exactly. They have to be able to ask questions to clarify anything they do not understand. Nuclear technicians must be able to explain their work to scientists, engineers, and reactor operators. They must also instruct others on safety procedures and warn them of hazardous conditions. Many of the daily procedures and work processes must be thoroughly documented because of the risky nature of the work.

Computer skills. Nuclear technicians must be able to use computers for plant operations and for normal office work, such as documenting their activities.

Critical-thinking skills. Nuclear technicians must carefully evaluate all available information before deciding on a course of action. For example, radiation protection technicians must evaluate data from radiation detectors to determine if areas are safe and must develop decontamination plans if they are not safe.

Interpersonal skills. Nuclear technicians must be comfortable having open and honest discussions with supervisors because clear communication is very important to maintaining a high level of safety.

Math skills. Nuclear technicians use scientific and mathematical formulas to analyze experimental and production data, such as reaction rates and radiation exposures.

Mechanical skills. Nuclear technicians need to have strong mechanical aptitude. Nuclear power facilities are complex, and workers need to understand how the facilities work in order to make adjustments and repairs to equipment and to maintain a safe working environment. Employers hiring nuclear technicians in nuclear power plants often conduct mechanical aptitude tests as part of the hiring process.

Monitoring skills. Nuclear technicians must be able to assess data from sensors, gauges, and other instruments to make sure that equipment and experiments are functioning properly and that radiation levels are controlled.

Advancement. With additional training and experience, technicians may become nuclear power reactor operators at nuclear power plants. Technicians can become nuclear engineers by earning a bachelor's degree in nuclear engineering. Nuclear physicists need a Ph.D. in physics. For more information, see the profiles on power plant operators, distributors, and dispatchers; nuclear engineers; and physicists and astronomers.

Pay

The median annual wage for nuclear technicians was $74,690 in May 2014. The median wage is the wage at which half the workers in an occupation earned more than that amount and half earned

Median Annual Wages, May 2014

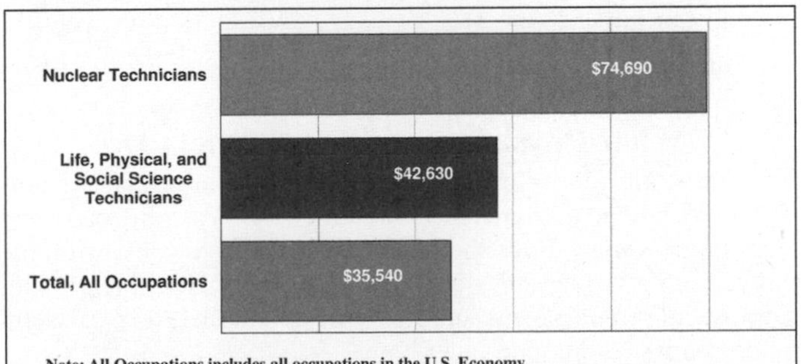

Note: All Occupations includes all occupations in the U.S. Economy.
Source: U.S. Bureau of Labor Statistics, Occupational Employment Statistics

Percent Change in Employment, Projected 2014–2024

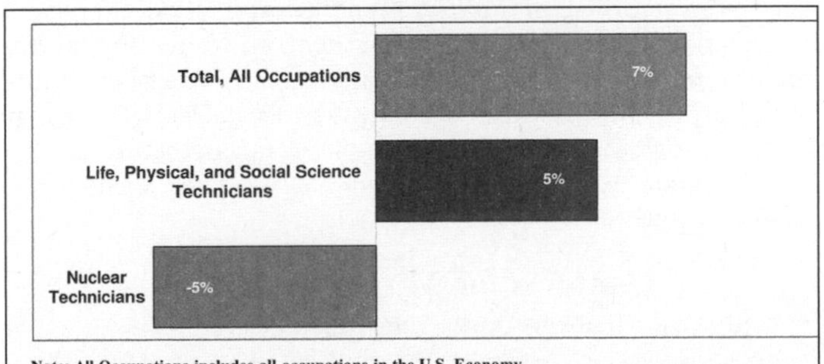

Note: All Occupations includes all occupations in the U.S. Economy.
Source: U.S. Bureau of Labor Statistics, Office of Occupational Statistics and Employment Projections

Employment Projections Data for Nuclear Technicians

Occupational Title	SOC Code	Employment, 2014	Projected Employment, 2024	Change, 2014–2024	
				Percent	Numeric
Nuclear technicians	19-4051	6,800	6,400	-5	-300

Source: U.S. Bureau of Labor Statistics, Employment Projections Program

Similar Occupations. This table shows a list of occupations with job duties that are similar to those of nuclear technicians.

Occupations	Entry-level Education	2014 Median Pay	Projected Job Growth	Average Annual Openings
Chemical Technicians	Associate's degree	$44,180	2%	120
Hazardous Materials Removal Workers	High school diploma or equivalent	$38,520	7%	330
Mechanical Engineering Technicians	Associate's degree	$53,530	2%	90
Nuclear Engineers	Bachelor's degree	$100,470	-4%	-70
Nuclear Medicine Technologists	Associate's degree	$72,100	2%	30
Occupational Health and Safety Technicians	High school diploma or equivalent	$48,120	9%	140
Physicists and Astronomers	Doctoral or professional degree	$109,290	7%	150
Power Plant Operators, Distributors, and Dispatchers	High school diploma or equivalent	$72,910	-6%	-330

less. The lowest 10 percent earned less than $46,430, and the highest 10 percent earned more than $102,400.

In May 2014, the median annual wages for nuclear technicians in the top industries in which they worked were as follows:

Management, scientific, and technical consulting services	$84,520
Electric power generation, transmission and distribution	76,210
Research and development in the physical, engineering, and life sciences	69,670
Manufacturing	60,280
Engineering services	59,910

Job Outlook

Employment of nuclear technicians is projected to decline 5 percent from 2014 to 2024.

Technicians will be needed to help maintain and upgrade the existing stock of nuclear power plants. However, traditional forms of power generation are becoming more productive due to increased automation, which will contribute to the decline. In addition, increasing pressure from alternative forms of power generation, such as solar arrays and wind turbines will impact employment growth in traditional energy production.

Technicians are expected to be in demand to develop nuclear medical technology, enforce waste management safety standards, and work in defense-related areas such as nuclear security. In addition, environmental remediation of infrastructure at now defunct nuclear facilities will create the need for spending on cleanup projects.

Contacts for More Information

For more information about nuclear technicians, visit

➤ Center for Energy Workforce Development (www.cewd.org)

➤ Get Into Energy (www.getintoenergy.com)

➤ Nuclear Energy Institute (www.nei.org)

For information about certification, visit

➤ American Society for Nondestructive Testing (http://asnt.org/MajorSiteSections/Certification)

➤ National Registry of Radiation Protection Technologists (www.nrrpt.org)

O*NET

➤ Nuclear Technicians (19-4051.00)

➤ Nuclear Equipment Operation Technicians (19-4051.01)

➤ Nuclear Monitoring Technicians (19-4051.02)

Physicists and Astronomers

- **2014 Median Pay** .... $109,290 per year; $52.54 per hour
- **Typical Entry-Level Education** .... Doctoral or professional degree
- **Work Experience in a Related Occupation** .... None
- **On-the-job Training** .... None
- **Number of Jobs, 2014** 20,000
- **Job Outlook, 2014–24** .... 7% (As fast as average)
- **Employment Change, 2014–24** 1,500

What Physicists and Astronomers Do

Physicists and astronomers study the ways in which various forms of matter and energy interact. Theoretical physicists and astronomers may study the nature of time or the origin of the universe. Some physicists design and perform experiments with sophisticated equipment such as particle accelerators, electron microscopes, and lasers.

Duties. Physicists and astronomers typically do the following:

- Develop scientific theories and models that attempt to explain the properties of the natural world, such as the force of gravity or the formation of atoms
- Plan and conduct scientific experiments and studies to test theories and discover properties of matter and energy
- Write proposals and apply for research grants
- Do complex mathematical calculations to analyze physical and astronomical data, such as data that may indicate the existence of planets in distant solar systems
- Design new scientific equipment, such as telescopes and lasers
- Develop computer software to analyze and model data
- Write scientific papers that may be published in scholarly journals
- Present research findings at scientific conferences and lectures

Physicists explore the fundamental properties and laws that govern space, time, energy, and matter. Some physicists study theoretical areas, such as the fundamental properties of atoms and molecules and the evolution of the universe. Others design and perform experiments with sophisticated equipment such as particle accelerators, electron microscopes, and lasers. Many apply their knowledge of physics to practical areas, such as developing advanced materials and medical equipment.

Astronomers study planets, stars, galaxies, and other celestial bodies. They use ground-based equipment, such as radio and optical telescopes, and space-based equipment, such as the Hubble Space Telescope. Some astronomers focus their research on objects in our solar system, such as the sun or planets. Others study distant stars, galaxies, and phenomena such as neutron stars and black holes, and some monitor space debris that could interfere with satellite operations.

Many physicists and astronomers work in basic research with the aim of increasing scientific knowledge. These researchers may attempt to develop theories that better explain what gravity is or how the universe works or was formed. Other physicists and astronomers work in applied research. They use the knowledge gained from basic research to affect new developments in areas such as energy, electronics, communications, navigation, and medical technology. For example, because of the work of physicists, lasers are used in surgery and microwave ovens are used in most kitchens.

Astronomers and physicists typically work on research teams together with engineers, technicians, and other scientists. Some senior astronomers and physicists may be responsible for assigning tasks to other team members and monitoring their progress. They may also be responsible for finding funding for their projects and therefore may need to write applications for research grants.

Although all of physics involves the same fundamental principles, physicists generally specialize in one of many subfields. The following are examples of types of physicists:

Astrophysicists study the physics of the universe. "Astrophysics" is a term that is often used interchangeably with "astronomy."

Atomic, molecular, and optical physicists study atoms, simple molecules, electrons, and light, as well as the interactions among them. Some look for ways to control the states of individual atoms, because such control might allow for further miniaturization or might contribute toward the development of new materials or computer technology.

Condensed matter physicists study the physical properties of condensed phases of matter, such as liquids and solids. They study phenomena ranging from superconductivity to liquid crystals.

Research jobs for physicists and astronomers usually require a Ph.D.

Medical physicists work in healthcare and use their knowledge of physics to develop new medical technologies and radiation-based treatments. For example, some develop better and safer radiation therapies for cancer patients. Others may develop more accurate imaging technologies that use various forms of radiant energy, such as magnetic resonance imaging (MRI) and ultrasound imaging.

Particle and nuclear physicists study the properties of atomic and subatomic particles, such as quarks, electrons, and nuclei, and the forces that cause their interactions.

Plasma physicists study plasmas, which are considered a distinct state of matter and occur naturally in stars and interplanetary space and artificially in neon signs and plasma screen televisions. Many plasma physicists study ways to create fusion reactors that might be a future source of energy.

Unlike physicists, astronomers cannot experiment on their subjects, because they are so far away that they cannot be touched or interacted with. Therefore, astronomers generally make observations or work on theory. Observational astronomers observe celestial objects and collect data on them. Theoretical astronomers analyze, model, and theorize about systems and how they work and evolve. Some astronomers specialize further into other subfields. The following are examples of types of astronomers who specialize by the objects and phenomena they study:

Cosmologists and *extragalactic astronomers* study the entire universe. They study the history, the creation and evolution, and the possible futures of the universe and its galaxies. These scientists have recently developed several theories important to the study of physics and astronomy, including string, dark-matter, and dark-energy theories.

Galactic, planetary, solar, and stellar astronomers study different phenomena that take place in the universe, specializing in certain parts of it. For example, solar astronomers study the sun, while stellar astronomers study other stars and associated phenomena.

High-energy astrophysicists collect and analyze X-rays, gamma rays, and other forms of high-energy rays that can help locate and study black holes or neutron stars.

Observational astronomers and *optical astronomers* use optical telescopes to study their subjects.

Radio astronomers use radio telescopes to analyze the radio spectrum for data about their subjects.

Growing numbers of physicists work in interdisciplinary fields, such as biophysics, chemical physics, and geophysics. For more information, see the profiles on biochemists and biophysicists and geoscientists.

Many people with a physics or astronomy background become professors or teachers. For more information, see the profiles on high school teachers and postsecondary teachers.

Work Environment

Physicists held about 18,100 jobs, and astronomers held about 1,900 jobs, in 2014. The industries that employed the most physicists in 2014 were as follows:

Scientific research and development services	27%
Colleges, universities, and professional schools; state, local, and private	21
Federal government, excluding postal service	18
Hospitals; state, local, and private	7
Management, scientific, and technical consulting services	6

The industries that employed the most astronomers in 2014 were as follows:

Colleges, universities, and professional schools; state, local, and private	39%
Scientific research and development services	30
Federal government, excluding postal service	26

The National Aeronautics and Space Administration (NASA) and the U.S. Department of Defense have traditionally been two of the largest employers of physicists and astronomers in the federal government. The scientific research-and-development industry includes both private and federally funded national laboratories, such as the Fermi National Accelerator Laboratory in Illinois and the Goddard Institute in Maryland.

Physics research is usually done in small- or medium-sized laboratories. However, experiments in some areas of physics, such as nuclear and high-energy physics, may require extremely large and expensive equipment, such as particle accelerators and nuclear reactors. Although physics research may require extensive experimentation in laboratories, physicists still spend much of their time in offices, planning, analyzing, fundraising, and reporting on research.

Most astronomers work in offices and may visit observatories a few times a year. An observatory is a building that houses ground-based telescopes used to gather data and make observations. Some astronomers work full time in observatories.

Increasingly, observations are being done remotely via the Internet without the need for travel to an observatory. Observational astronomers rarely look through a telescope with their eyes, but instead use computers and sophisticated telescopes that can detect radiation other than visible light, such as gamma rays or radio waves. Rather than making direct observations, theoretical astronomers typically use the data from observational astronomers to develop their theories.

Some physicists and astronomers work away from home temporarily at national or international facilities that have unique equipment, such as particle accelerators and gamma ray telescopes. They also frequently travel to meetings to present research results, discuss ideas with colleagues, and learn more about new developments in their field.

Work Schedules. Most physicists and astronomers work full time. Astronomers may need to work at night, because radiation from the sun tends to interfere less with observations made during nighttime hours. Most astronomers typically visit observatories only a few times per year and therefore keep normal office hours.

Education/Training

Physicists and astronomers typically need a Ph.D. for jobs in research and academia. However, physicist jobs in the federal government typically require a bachelor's degree in physics. After receiving a Ph.D. in physics or astronomy, many researchers seeking careers in academia begin in temporary postdoctoral research positions.

Education. A Ph.D. in physics, astronomy, or a related field is needed for jobs in research or academia or for independent research positions in industry.

Graduate students usually concentrate in a subfield of physics or astronomy, such as condensed matter physics or cosmology. In addition to taking courses in physics or astronomy, Ph.D. students need to take courses in mathematics, such as calculus, linear algebra, and statistics. Computer science classes also are essential, because physicists and astronomers often develop specialized computer programs that are used to gather, analyze, and model data.

Those with a master's degree in physics may qualify for jobs in applied research and development for manufacturing and healthcare companies. Many master's degree programs specialize in preparing students for physics-related research-and-development positions that do not require a Ph.D.

Most physics and astronomy graduate students have bachelor's degrees in physics or a related field. Because astronomers need a strong background in physics, a bachelor's degree in physics is often considered good preparation for Ph.D. programs in astronomy, although an undergraduate degree in astronomy may be preferred by some universities. Undergraduate physics programs provide a broad background in the natural sciences and mathematics. Typical courses include classical and quantum mechanics, thermodynamics, optics, and electromagnetism.

Those with only a bachelor's degree in physics usually are qualified to work as technicians and research assistants in related fields, such as engineering and computer science. Those with a bachelor's degree in astronomy also may qualify to work as an assistant at an observatory. Students who do not want to continue their studies to the doctorate level may want to take courses in instrument building and computer science.

Some master's degree and bachelor's degree holders find work in the federal government. Others may become science teachers in middle schools and high schools. For more information, see the profiles on middle school teachers and high school teachers.

Training. Many physics and astronomy Ph.D. holders who seek employment as full-time researchers begin their careers in a temporary postdoctoral research position, which typically lasts 2 to 3 years. During their postdoctoral appointment, they work with experienced scientists and continue to learn about their specialties or develop a broader understanding of related areas of research. Senior scientists may carefully supervise their initial work, but as these postdoctoral workers gain experience, they usually do more complex tasks and have greater independence in their work.

Important Qualities

Analytical skills. Physicists and astronomers need to be able to think logically to carry out scientific experiments and studies. They must be precise and accurate in their analyses because errors could invalidate their research. They must also be able to find and use funding effectively.

Communication skills. Physicists and astronomers present their research at scientific conferences, to the public, or to government and business leaders. Physicists and astronomers write technical reports that may be published in scientific journals. They also write proposals for research funding.

Median Annual Wages, May 2014

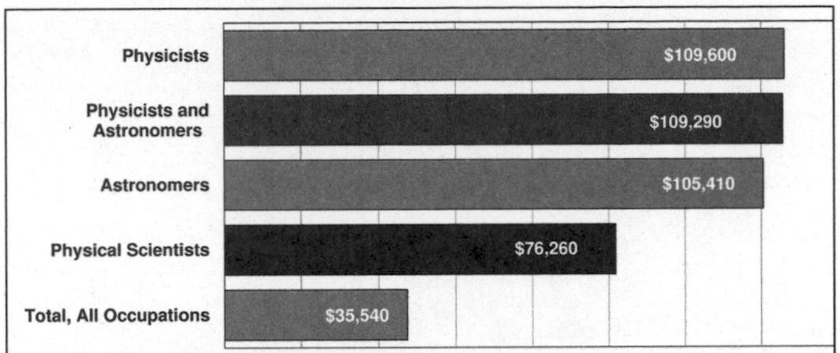

Note: All Occupations includes all occupations in the U.S. Economy.
Source: U.S. Bureau of Labor Statistics, Occupational Employment Statistics

Percent Change in Employment, Projected 2014–2024

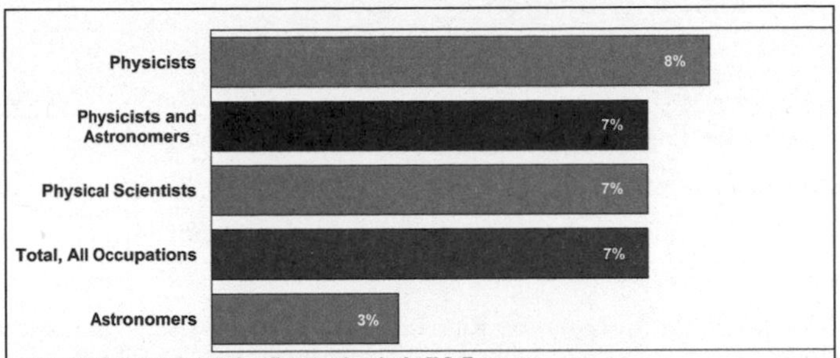

Note: All Occupations includes all occupations in the U.S. Economy.
Source: U.S. Bureau of Labor Statistics, Office of Occupational Statistics and Employment Projections

Concentration. Physicists and astronomers analyze large datasets to try to discern patterns that will yield information. This work often requires the ability to focus for hours over the course of many days.

Critical-thinking skills. Physicists and astronomers must carefully evaluate their own work and the work of others. They must determine whether results and conclusions are accurate and based on sound science.

Curiosity. Physicists and astronomers work in fields that are always on the cutting edge of technology. They must be very keen to learn continuously throughout their career. In-depth knowledge must be gained on a wide range of technical subjects, from computer programming to particle colliders.

Interpersonal skills. Physicists and astronomers must collaborate extensively with others in both academic and industrial research contexts. They need to be able to work well with others toward a common goal. Interpersonal skills also should help researchers secure funding for their projects.

Math skills. Physicists and astronomers perform complex calculations involving calculus, geometry, algebra, and other areas of mathematics. They must be able to express their research in mathematical terms.

Problem-solving skills. Physicists and astronomers use scientific observation and analysis, as well as creative thinking, to solve complex scientific problems.

Self-discipline. Physicists and astronomers spend a lot of time working alone and need to be able to stay motivated in their work.

Licenses, Certifications, and Registrations. Some positions with the federal government, such as those involving nuclear energy and other sensitive research areas, may require applicants to be U.S. citizens and hold a security clearance.

Advancement. With experience, physicists and astronomers may gain greater independence in their work, as well as larger research budgets. Those in university positions may also gain tenure with more experience. Some physicists and astronomers move into managerial positions, typically as a natural sciences manager, and spend a large part of their time preparing budgets and schedules. Physicists and astronomers need a Ph.D. for most management positions. For more information, see the profile on natural sciences managers.

Physics as a discipline seeks to describe the physical universe at a deep and detailed level but is not limited to a specific body of knowledge. Rather, it is characterized as a broad set of problem-solving skills and strategies based on scientific principles that can be applied in many contexts. Employers requiring someone who can understand complex, often mathematically sophisticated problems and devise effective solutions to them often hire physicists for other types of jobs.

Pay

The median annual wage for astronomers was $105,410 in May 2014. The median wage is the wage at which half the workers in an occupation earned more than that amount and half earned less. The lowest 10 percent earned less than $52,160, and the highest 10 percent earned more than $162,630.

The median annual wage for physicists was $109,600 in May 2014. The lowest 10 percent earned less than $54,930, and the highest 10 percent earned more than $184,650.

In May 2014, the median annual wages for physicists in the top industries in which they worked were as follows:

Hospitals; state, local, and private	$162,870
Management, scientific, and technical consulting services	119,130
Scientific research and development services	117,110
Federal government, excluding postal service	112,320
Colleges, universities, and professional schools; state, local, and private	65,720

In May 2014, the median annual wages for astronomers in the top industries in which they worked were as follows:

Federal government, excluding postal service	$141,660
Scientific research and development services	113,340
Colleges, universities, and professional schools; state, local, and private	71,760

Employment Projections Data for Physicists and Astronomers

Occupational Title	SOC Code	Employment, 2014	Projected Employment, 2024	Change, 2014–2024 Percent	Change, 2014–2024 Numeric
Astronomers and physicists	19-2010	20,000	21,400	7	1,500
Astronomers	19-2011	1,900	1,900	3	100
Physicists	19-2012	18,100	19,500	8	1,400

Source: U.S. Bureau of Labor Statistics, Employment Projections Program

Similar Occupations. This table shows a list of occupations with job duties that are similar to those of physicists and astronomers.

Occupations	Entry-level Education	2014 Median Pay	Projected Job Growth	Average Annual Openings
Aerospace Engineers	Bachelor's degree	$105,380	-2%	-160
Biochemists and Biophysicists	Doctoral or professional degree	$84,940	8%	280
Chemists and Materials Scientists	Bachelor's degree	$74,720	3%	260
Civil Engineers	Bachelor's degree	$82,050	8%	2,360
Computer and Information Research Scientists	Doctoral or professional degree	$108,360	11%	270
Computer Hardware Engineers	Bachelor's degree	$108,430	3%	240
Electrical and Electronics Engineers	Bachelor's degree	$93,260	0%	-10
Geoscientists	Bachelor's degree	$89,910	10%	380
Mathematicians	Master's degree	$103,720	21%	70
Mechanical Engineers	Bachelor's degree	$83,060	5%	1,460
Nuclear Engineers	Bachelor's degree	$100,470	-4%	-70
Postsecondary Teachers	See Education/Training	$70,790	13%	17,700

Job Outlook

Employment of physicists and astronomers is projected to grow 7 percent from 2014 to 2024, about as fast as the average for all occupations.

Growth in the federal government's spending for research in physics and astronomy is expected to be more or less flat, but it should continue to drive the need for physicists and astronomers, especially at colleges, universities, and national laboratories.

Federal spending is the primary source of physics- and astronomy-related research funds, especially for basic research. Additional federal funding for energy and for advanced manufacturing research is expected to continue to drive the need for physicists.

People with a physics background will continue to be in demand in medicine, information technology, communications technology, semiconductor technology, and other applied research-and-development fields.

Job Prospects. Competition for permanent research appointments, such as those at colleges and universities, is expected to be strong. Increasingly, those with a Ph.D. may need to work through multiple postdoctoral appointments before finding a permanent position. In addition, the number of research proposals submitted for funding has been growing faster than the amount of funds available, causing more competition for research grants.

Despite competition for traditional research jobs, prospects should be good for physicists in applied research, development, and related technical fields. Graduates with any academic degree in physics or astronomy, from a bachelor's degree to a doctorate, will find their knowledge of science and mathematics useful for entry into many other occupations. Database management skills also are beneficial, because of the large datasets these professionals work with.

A large part of physics and astronomy research depends on federal funds, so federal budgets have a substantial impact on job prospects from year to year, especially for astronomers, who are more likely than physicists to depend on federal funding for their work.

Contacts for More Information

For more information about astronomy careers and for a listing of colleges and universities offering astronomy programs, visit

➤ American Astronomical Society (http://aas.org)

For a listing of colleges and universities offering physics programs, visit

➤ Physics Careers Resource (www.compadre.org/careers)

For more information about physics careers and education, visit

➤ American Institute of Physics (www.aip.org)

➤ American Physical Society (www.aps.org)

To find job openings for physicists and astronomers in the federal government, visit

➤ USAJOBS (www.usajobs.gov)

O*NET

➤ Astronomers (19-2011.00)

➤ Physicists (19-2012.00)

Political Scientists

- **2014 Median Pay** .... $104,920 per year $50.44 per hour
- **Typical Entry-Level Education** ....Master's degree
- **Work Experience in a Related Occupation**............... None
- **On-the-job Training** .... None
- **Number of Jobs, 2014** 6,200
- **Job Outlook, 2014–24**................................ -2% (Decline)
- **Employment Change, 2014–24** .... -100

What Political Scientists Do

Political scientists study the origin, development, and operation of political systems. They research political ideas and analyze governments, policies, political trends, and related issues.

Duties. Political scientists typically do the following:

- Research political subjects, such as the U.S. political system, relations between the United States and foreign countries, and political ideologies
- Collect and analyze data from sources, such as public opinion surveys and election results

- Develop theories, using qualitative sources, such as historical documents
- Test theories, using quantitative methods, such as statistical analysis
- Evaluate the effects of policies and laws on government, businesses, and people
- Monitor current events, policy decisions, and other issues relevant to their work
- Forecast political, economic, and social trends
- Present research results by writing reports, giving presentations, and publishing articles

Political scientists usually conduct research within one of four primary subfields: national politics, comparative politics, international relations, or political theory.

Often, political scientists use qualitative methods in their research, gathering information from numerous sources. For example, they may use historical documents to analyze past government structures and policies. Political scientists also rely heavily on quantitative methods to develop and research theories. For example, they may analyze data to see whether a relationship exists between a certain political system and a particular outcome. Political scientists study topics such as U.S. political parties, how political structures differ among countries, globalization, and the history of political thought.

Political scientists also work as *policy analysts*, perhaps working for organizations that have a stake in policy, such as government, labor, and political organizations. They evaluate current policies and events using public opinion surveys, economic data, and election results. From these sources, they can learn the expected impact of new policies.

Political scientists often research the effects of government policies on a particular region or population, both domestically and internationally. As a result, they provide information and analysis that help in planning, developing, or carrying out policies.

Many people with a political science background become postsecondary teachers and high school teachers.

Work Environment

Political scientists held about 6,200 jobs in 2014. The industries that employed the most political scientists were as follows:

Federal government, excluding postal service	55%
Professional, scientific, and technical services	23
Educational services; state, local, and private	9

Work Schedules. Political scientists typically work full time in an office. They may work additional hours to finish reports and meet deadlines.

Political scientists sometimes work with teams of research assistants.

Education/Training

Political scientists need a master's degree or Ph.D. in political science, public administration, or a related field.

Education. Most political scientists need to complete either a master's or Ph.D. program. To be admitted to a graduate program, applicants should complete undergraduate courses in political science, writing, and statistics. Applicants also benefit from having related work or internship experience.

Political scientists often complete a master of public administration (MPA), master of public policy (MPP), or master of public affairs degree. These programs usually combine several disciplines, and students can choose to concentrate in a specific area of interest. Most offer core courses in research methods, policy formation, program evaluation, and statistics. Some colleges and universities also offer master's degrees in political science, international relations, or other applied political science specialties.

Some political scientists also complete a Ph.D. program, which requires several years of coursework followed by independent research for a dissertation. Most Ph.D. candidates choose to specialize in one of four primary subfields of political science: national politics, comparative politics, international relations, or political theory.

Political scientists who teach at colleges and universities need a Ph.D. Graduates with a master's degree in political science sometimes become postsecondary teachers and high school teachers.

Jobseekers with a bachelor's degree in political science usually qualify for entry-level positions in a related field, such as assistants or research assistants for research organizations, political campaigns, or nonprofit organization. They may also qualify for some

Median Annual Wages, May 2014

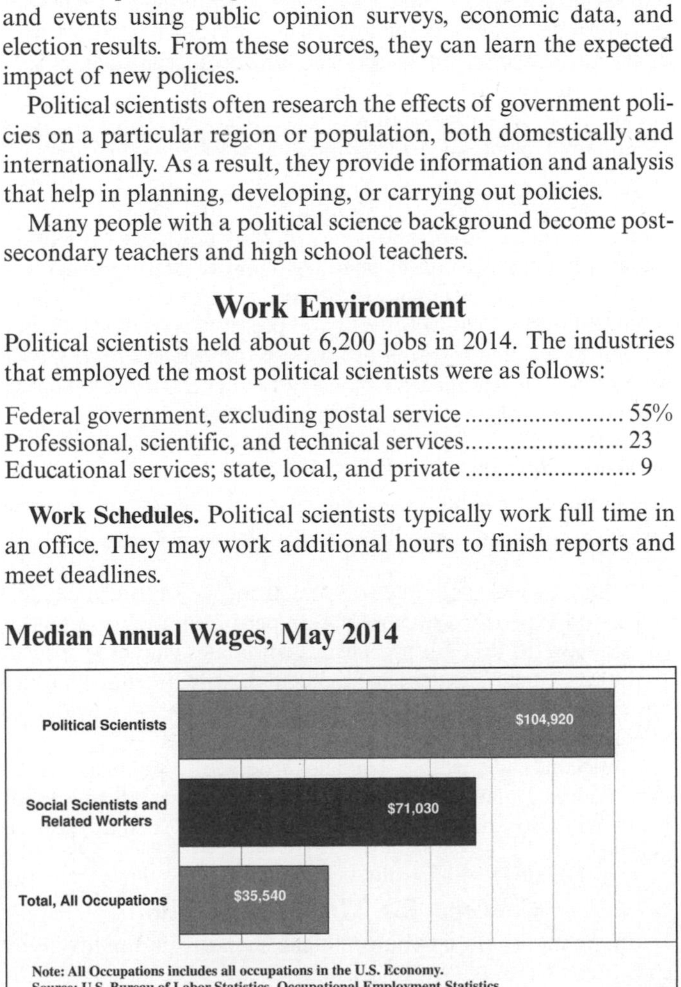

Percent Change in Employment, Projected 2014–2024

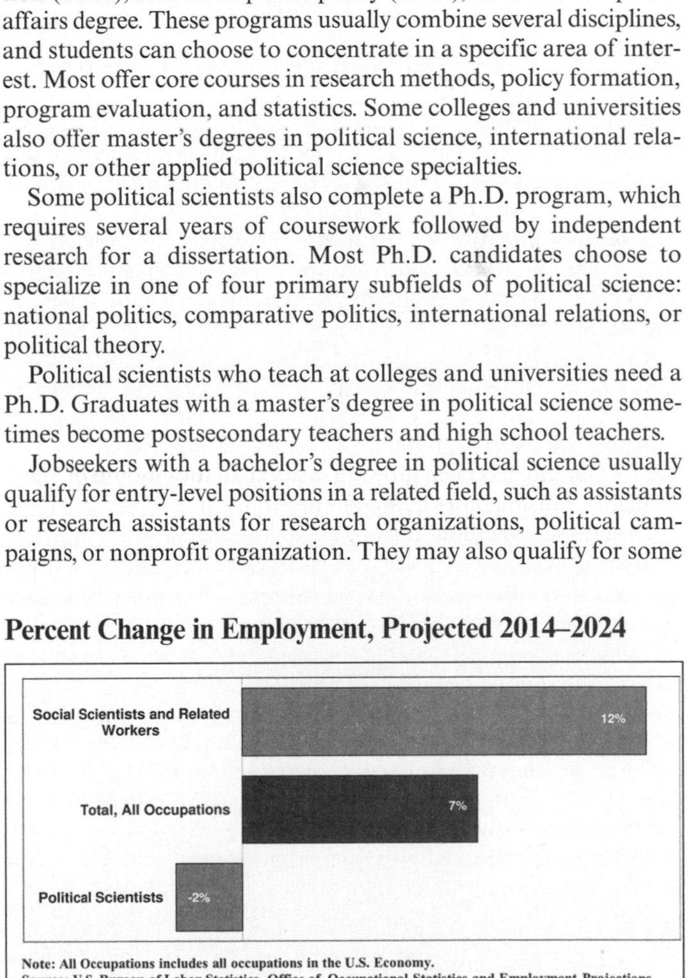

Employment Projections Data for Political Scientists

Occupational Title	SOC Code	Employment, 2014	Projected Employment, 2024	Change, 2014–2024 Percent	Change, 2014–2024 Numeric
Political scientists	19-3094	6,200	6,000	-2	-100

Source: U.S. Bureau of Labor Statistics, Employment Projections Program

Similar Occupations. This table shows a list of occupations with job duties that are similar to those of political scientists.

Occupations	Entry-level Education	2014 Median Pay	Projected Job Growth	Average Annual Openings
Anthropologists and Archeologists	Master's degree	$59,280	4%	30
Economists	Master's degree	$95,710	6%	120
Market Research Analysts	Bachelor's degree	$61,290	19%	9,230
Postsecondary Teachers	See Education/Training	$70,790	13%	17,700
Sociologists	Master's degree	$72,810	-1%	0
Survey Researchers	Master's degree	$49,760	12%	190
Urban and Regional Planners	Master's degree	$66,940	6%	240

government positions. Others go into fields outside of politics and policymaking, such as business or law.

Other Experience. Job seekers who have earned a bachelor's degree can benefit from internships or volunteer work when looking for entry-level positions in political science or a related field. Internships can give students a chance to apply their academic knowledge in a professional setting and to develop the analytic, research, and writing skills needed for the field.

Important Qualities

Analytical skills. Political scientists often use qualitative and quantitative research methods. They rely on their analytical skills when they collect, evaluate, and interpret data.

Communication skills. Political scientists often collaborate with other researchers when writing reports or giving presentations. They must communicate their findings to a wide variety of audiences.

Critical-thinking skills. Political scientists must be able to examine and process available information and draw logical conclusions from their findings.

Intellectual curiosity. Political scientists must continually explore new ideas and information to produce original papers and research. They must stay current on political subjects and come up with new ways to think about and address issues.

Writing skills. Writing skills are essential for political scientists, because they often write research papers. They must be able to convey their research results clearly.

Pay

The median annual wage for political scientists was $104,920 in May 2014. The median wage is the wage at which half the workers in an occupation earned more than that amount and half earned less. The lowest 10 percent earned less than $52,150, and the highest 10 percent earned more than $153,960.

In May 2014, the median annual wages for political scientists in the top industries in which they worked were as follows:

Federal government, excluding postal service	$116,910
Professional, scientific, and technical services	94,500
Educational services; state, local, and private	57,060

Job Outlook

Employment of political scientists is projected to decline 2 percent from 2014 to 2024.

More than half of all political scientists are employed by the federal government. Political scientists will continue to be needed in government to assess the impact of government policies, such as the efficiencies of public services, effects of departmental cuts, and advantages of proposed improvements. However, efforts to cut spending are expected to result in a decline in federal government employment, adversely impacting employment of political scientists.

Political organizations, lobbying firms, and many nonprofit, labor, and social organizations rely on the knowledge of political scientists to manage complicated legal and regulatory issues and policies. Political scientists will be needed at research and policy organizations to focus specifically on politics and political theory. Organizations that research or advocate for specific causes, such as immigration, healthcare, or the environment, also need political scientists to analyze policies relating to their field.

Job Prospects. Political scientists should face strong competition for most jobs. The small number of positions, combined with the popularity of political science programs in colleges and universities, means that there will likely be many qualified candidates for relatively few positions.

Candidates with a graduate degree, strong writing and analytical skills, and experience researching or performing policy analysis should have the best job prospects. Candidates who have specialized knowledge or experience in their field of interest will also have better job opportunities. Internships or volunteer work also may be helpful.

Some candidates with a bachelor's degree in political science may find entry-level jobs as assistants and research assistants. Many will also find positions in other in fields, such as business and law.

Contacts for More Information

For more information about political scientists and political science careers, visit

➤ American Political Science Association (www.apsanet.org)

- American Association of Political Consultants (www.theaapc.org)

For more information about college programs in public affairs and administration, visit

- Network of Schools of Public Policy, Affairs, and Administration (www.naspaa.org)

O*NET

- Political Scientists (19-3094.00)

Psychologists

- **2014 Median Pay** .... $70,700 per year $33.99 per hour
- **Typical Entry-Level Education** .... See Education/Training
- **Work Experience in a Related Occupation** .... None
- **On-the-job Training** .... Internship/residency
- **Number of Jobs, 2014** 173,900
- **Job Outlook, 2014–24** .... 19% (Much faster than average)
- **Employment Change, 2014–24** 32,500

What Psychologists Do

Psychologists study cognitive, emotional, and social processes and behavior by observing, interpreting, and recording how people relate to one another and their environments.

Duties. Psychologists typically do the following:

- Conduct scientific studies of behavior and brain function
- Collect information through observations, interviews, surveys, and other methods
- Identify psychological, emotional, behavioral, or organizational issues and diagnose disorders, using information obtained from their research
- Research and identify behavioral or emotional patterns
- Test for patterns that will help them better understand and predict behavior
- Discuss the treatment of problems with their clients
- Write articles, research papers, and reports to share findings and educate others

Psychologists seek to understand and explain thoughts, emotions, feelings, and behavior. Psychologists use techniques such as observation, assessment, and experimentation to develop theories about the beliefs and feelings that influence a person.

Psychologists often gather information and evaluate behavior through controlled laboratory experiments, psychoanalysis, or psychotherapy. They also may administer personality, performance, aptitude, or intelligence tests. They look for patterns of behavior or relationships between events, and use this information when testing theories in their research or treating patients.

The following are examples of types of psychologists:

Clinical psychologists assess, diagnose, and treat mental, emotional, and behavioral disorders. Clinical psychologists help people deal with problems ranging from short-term personal issues to severe, chronic conditions.

Clinical psychologists are trained to use a variety of approaches to help individuals. Although strategies generally differ by specialty, clinical psychologists often interview patients, give diagnostic tests, and provide individual, family, or group psychotherapy. They also design behavior modification programs and help patients implement their particular program.

Some clinical psychologists focus on certain populations, such as children or the elderly, or certain specialties, such as the following:

- *Health psychologists* study how psychological and behavioral factors interact with health and illness. They educate both patients and medical staff on psychological issues and promote healthy-living strategies. They also investigate and develop programs to address common health-related behaviors, such as smoking, poor diet, and sedentary behavior.
- *Neuropsychologists* study the effects of brain injuries, brain disease, developmental disorders, or mental health conditions on behavior and thinking. They test patients affected by known or suspected brain conditions to determine impacts on thinking and to direct patients' treatment.

Clinical psychologists often consult with other health professionals regarding the best treatment for patients, especially treatment that includes medication. Currently, Illinois, Louisiana, and New Mexico allow clinical psychologists to prescribe medication to patients. Most states, however, do not allow psychologists to prescribe medication for treatment.

Counseling psychologists help patients deal with and understand problems, including issues at home, at the workplace, or in their community. Through counseling, they work with patients to identify their strengths or resources they can use to manage problems. For information on other counseling occupations, see the profiles on mental health counselors and marriage and family therapists, substance abuse and behavioral disorder counselors, and social workers.

Developmental psychologists study the psychological progress and development that take place throughout life. Many developmental psychologists focus on children and adolescents, but they also may study aging and problems facing older adults.

Forensic psychologists use psychological principles in the legal and criminal justice system to help judges, attorneys, and other legal specialists understand the psychological aspects of

Psychologists who deal directly with patients must be emotionally stable, mature, sensitive, and have strong communication skills.

a particular case. They often testify in court as expert witnesses. They typically specialize in family, civil, or criminal case work.

Industrial-organizational psychologists apply psychology to the workplace by using psychological principles and research methods to solve problems and improve the quality of work life. They study issues such as workplace productivity, management or employee working styles, and employee morale. They also work with management on matters such as policy planning, employee screening or training, and organizational development.

School psychologists apply psychological principles and techniques to education and developmental disorders. They may address student learning and behavioral problems; design and implement performance plans, and evaluate performances; and counsel students and families. They also may consult with other school-based professionals to suggest improvements to teaching, learning, and administrative strategies.

Social psychologists study how people's mindsets and behavior are shaped by social interactions. They examine both individual and group interactions and may investigate ways to improve interactions.

Some psychologists become postsecondary teachers or high school teachers.

Work Environment

Psychologists held about 173,900 jobs in 2014. The industries that employed the most psychologists were as follows:

Elementary and secondary schools; state, local, and private	25%
Government	10
Offices of mental health practitioners (except physicians)	9
Hospitals; state, local, and private	6
Individual and family services	5

Nearly 1 in 3 psychologists were self-employed in 2014.

Some psychologists work alone, doing independent research, consulting with clients, or counseling patients. Others work as part of a healthcare team, collaborating with physicians, social workers, and others to treat illness and promote overall wellness.

Many clinical and counseling psychologists work in private practice. Others work in outpatient clinics, hospitals, rehabilitation facilities, and community and mental health centers.

Industrial-organizational psychologists work in business settings or human resources offices. They may also work in federal or state agencies, consulting firms, or private research organizations.

Most research psychologists work in colleges and universities, government agencies, or private research organizations.

Most school psychologists work in public schools, ranging from elementary school through college. They also work in private schools, universities, hospitals, clinics, community treatment centers, and independent practice.

Work Schedules. Psychologists in private practice often set their own hours, and many work part time as independent consultants. They may work evenings or weekends to accommodate clients. Those employed in hospitals or other healthcare facilities may also have evening or weekend shifts. Most psychologists in clinics, government, industry, or schools work full-time schedules during regular business hours.

Education/Training

Although psychologists typically need a doctoral degree in psychology, a master's degree is sufficient for some positions. Psychologists in independent practice also need a license.

Education. Most clinical, counseling, and research psychologists need a doctoral degree. Students can complete a Ph.D. in psychology or a Doctor of Psychology (Psy.D.) degree. A Ph.D. in psychology is a research degree that is obtained after taking a comprehensive exam and writing a dissertation based on original research. Ph.D. programs typically include courses on statistics and experimental procedures. The Psy.D. is a clinical degree and is often based on practical work and examinations rather than a dissertation. In clinical, counseling, school, or health service settings, students usually complete a 1-year internship as part of the doctoral program.

School psychologists need an advanced degree and certification or licensure to work. The advanced degree is most commonly the education specialist degree (Ed.S.), which typically requires a minimum of 60 graduate semester credit hours and a 1,200-hour supervised internship. Some school psychologists may have a doctoral degree in school psychology or a master's degree. School psychologists' programs include coursework in both education and psychology because their work addresses education and mental health components of students' development.

Graduates with a master's degree in psychology can work as industrial-organizational psychologists. When working under the supervision of a doctoral psychologist, master's graduates can also work as psychological assistants in clinical, counseling, or research settings. Master's degree programs typically include courses in industrial-organizational psychology, statistics, and research design.

Most master's degree programs do not require an undergraduate major in psychology, but do require coursework in introductory psychology, experimental psychology, and statistics. Some doctoral degree programs require applicants to have a master's degree in psychology; others will accept applicants with a bachelor's degree and a major in psychology.

Most graduates with a bachelor's degree in psychology find work in other fields such as business administration, sales, or education.

Licenses, Certifications, and Registrations. In most states, practicing psychology or using the title of "psychologist" requires licensure. In all states and the District of Columbia, psychologists who practice independently must be licensed where they work.

Licensing laws vary by state and type of position. Most clinical and counseling psychologists need a doctorate in psychology, an internship, at least 1 to 2 years of supervised professional experience, and to pass the Examination for Professional Practice in Psychology. Information on specific state requirements can be obtained from the Association of State and Provincial Psychology Boards. In many states, licensed psychologists must complete continuing education courses to keep their licenses.

The American Board of Professional Psychology awards specialty certification in 15 areas of psychology, such as clinical health, couple and family, or rehabilitation. The American Board of Professional Neuropsychology offers certification in neuropsychology. Board certification can demonstrate professional expertise in a specialty area. Certification is not required for most psychologists, but some hospitals and clinics do require certification. In those cases, candidates must have a doctoral degree in psychology, state license or certification, and any additional criteria of the specialty field.

Training. Prospective practicing psychologists must have pre- or postdoctoral supervised experience, including an internship. Internships allow students to gain experience in an applied setting. Candidates must complete an internship before they can qualify

Median Annual Wages, May 2014

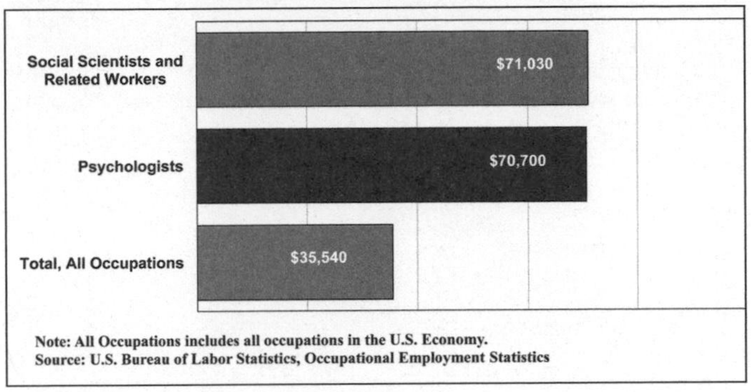

Percent Change in Employment, Projected 2014–2024

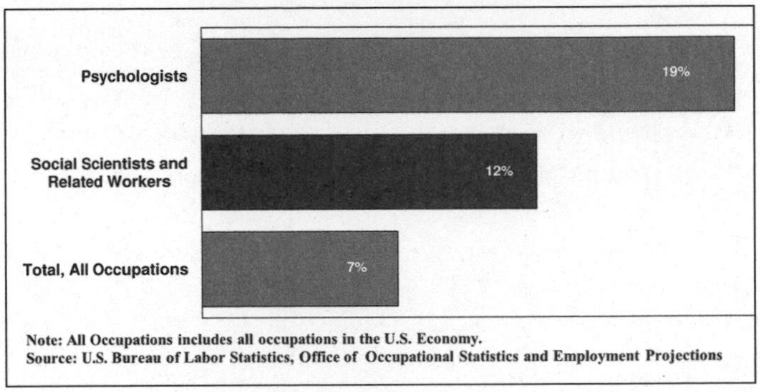

for state licensure. The required number of hours of the internship varies by state.

Important Qualities

Analytical skills. Psychologists must be able to examine the information they collect and draw logical conclusions from it.

Communication skills. Psychologists must have strong communication skills because they spend much of their time listening to and speaking with patients.

Observational skills. Psychologists study attitude and behavior. They must be able to watch people and understand the possible meanings of facial expressions, body positions, actions, and interactions.

Patience. Psychologists must be able to demonstrate patience, because conducting research or treating patients may take a long time.

People skills. Psychologists study and help people. They must be able to work well with clients, patients, and other professionals.

Problem-solving skills. Psychologists need problem-solving skills to design research, evaluate programs, and find treatments or solutions for mental and behavioral problems.

Trustworthiness. Psychologists must keep patients' problems in confidence, and patients must be able to trust psychologists' expertise in treating sensitive problems.

Pay

The median annual wage for psychologists was $70,700 in May 2014. The median wage is the wage at which half the workers in an occupation earned more than that amount and half earned less. The lowest 10 percent earned less than $40,240, and the highest 10 percent earned more than $114,290.

Median annual wages for psychologists in May 2014 were as follows:

Psychologists, all other	$92,110
Industrial-organizational psychologists	76,950
Clinical, counseling, and school psychologists	68,900

Job Outlook

Overall employment of psychologists is projected to grow 19 percent from 2014 to 2024, much faster than the average for all occupations. Employment growth will vary by occupation.

Employment of clinical, counseling, and school psychologists is projected to grow 20 percent from 2014 to 2024, much faster than the average for all occupations. Greater demand for psychological services in schools, hospitals, mental health centers, and social services agencies should drive employment growth.

Demand for clinical and counseling psychologists will increase as people continue to turn to psychologists for help with their problems. Psychologists will also be needed to provide services to an aging population, helping people deal with the mental and physical changes that happen as they grow older. Psychological services are also needed for veterans suffering from war trauma, for survivors of other trauma, and for individuals with autism.

Employment of school psychologists will continue to grow because of the raised awareness of the connection between mental health and learning and the need for mental health services in schools. School psychologists will be needed to work with students, particularly those with special needs, learning disabilities, and behavioral issues. Schools rely on school psychologists to assess and counsel students. In addition, school psychologists will be needed to study how factors both in school and outside of school affect learning, which teachers and administrators can use to improve education. However, opportunities may be limited, because employment of school psychologists in public schools and universities is contingent on state and local budgets.

Employment of industrial-organizational psychologists is projected to grow 19 percent from 2014 to 2024, much faster than the average for all occupations. However, because it is a small occupation, the fast growth will result in only about 400 new jobs over the 10-year period. Organizations will continue to use industrial-organizational psychologists to help select and keep employees, increase organizational productivity and efficiency, and improve office morale.

Employment Projections Data for Psychologists

Occupational Title	SOC Code	Employment, 2014	Projected Employment, 2024	Change, 2014–2024 Percent	Change, 2014–2024 Numeric
Psychologists	19-3030	173,900	206,400	19	32,500
Clinical, counseling, and school psychologists	19-3031	155,300	185,900	20	30,500
Industrial-organizational psychologists	19-3032	2,000	2,300	19	400
Psychologists, all other	19-3039	16,600	18,300	10	1,600

Source: U.S. Bureau of Labor Statistics, Employment Projections Program

Similar Occupations. This table shows a list of occupations with job duties that are similar to those of psychologists.

Occupations	Entry-level Education	2014 Median Pay	Projected Job Growth	Average Annual Openings
Anthropologists and Archeologists	Master's degree	$59,280	4%	30
Market Research Analysts	Bachelor's degree	$61,290	19%	9,230
Mental Health Counselors and Marriage and Family Therapists	Master's degree	$42,250	19%	3,140
Physicians and Surgeons	Doctoral or professional degree	This wage is equal to or greater than $187,200.	14%	9,930
Postsecondary Teachers	See Education/Training	$70,790	13%	17,700
School and Career Counselors	Master's degree	$53,370	8%	2,250
Social Workers	See Education/Training	$45,500	12%	7,480
Sociologists	Master's degree	$72,810	-1%	0
Special Education Teachers	Bachelor's degree	$55,980	6%	2,810
Substance Abuse and Behavioral Disorder Counselors	Bachelor's degree	$39,270	22%	2,120
Survey Researchers	Master's degree	$49,760	12%	190

Job Prospects. Competition for jobs for psychologists will vary by specialty and level of education obtained. Industrial-organizational psychologists are expected to face competition for positions because of the large number of qualified applicants. Industrial-organizational psychologists with extensive training in quantitative research methods may have a competitive edge.

Overall, candidates with a doctoral or education specialist degree and postdoctoral work experience will have the best job opportunities in clinical, counseling, or school psychology positions. Candidates with a master's degree will face competition for most positions, and many of them will find jobs with alternative titles, as nearly all states restrict the use of the title "psychologist" to Ph.D. or Psy.D. degree holders.

Most graduates with a bachelor's degree in psychology find work in other fields such as business administration, sales, or education. However, they may be able to find work in the field of psychology as assistants to psychologists.

Contacts for More Information

For more information about careers in all fields of psychology, visit

➤ American Psychological Association (www.apa.org)

For more information about careers for school psychologists, visit

➤ National Association of School Psychologists (www.nasponline.org)

For more information about state licensing requirements, visit

➤ Association of State and Provincial Psychology Boards (www.asppb.net)

For more information about psychology specialty certifications, visit

➤ American Board of Professional Psychology (www.abpp.org)

For more information about industrial-organizational psychologists, visit

➤ Society for Industrial and Organizational Psychology (www.siop.org)

For more information about careers and certification in neuropsychology, visit

➤ American Board of Professional Neuropsychology (http://abn-board.com)

O*NET

➤ Clinical, Counseling, and School Psychologists (19-3031.00)
➤ School Psychologists (19-3031.01)
➤ Clinical Psychologists (19-3031.02)
➤ Counseling Psychologists (19-3031.03)
➤ Industrial-Organizational Psychologists (19-3032.00)
➤ Psychologists, All Other (19-3039.00)
➤ Neuropsychologists and Clinical Neuropsychologists (19-3039.01)

Sociologists

- **2014 Median Pay** .... $72,810 per year
  $35.01 per hour
- **Typical Entry-Level Education** ....Master's degree
- **Work Experience in a Related Occupation**.............. None
- **On-the-job Training** .... None
- **Number of Jobs, 2014** 2,600
- **Job Outlook, 2014–24**...............-1% (Little or no change)
- **Employment Change, 2014–24** 0

What Sociologists Do

Sociologists study society and social behavior by examining the groups, cultures, organizations, social institutions, and processes that develop when people interact and work together.

Duties. Sociologists typically do the following:

- Design research projects to test theories about social issues
- Collect data through surveys, observations, interviews, and other sources
- Analyze and draw conclusions from data
- Prepare reports, articles, or presentations detailing their research findings
- Collaborate with and advise other social scientists, policymakers, or other groups on research findings and sociological issues

Sociologists often read and write research articles or reports.

Sociologists study human behavior, interaction, and organization within the context of larger social, political, and economic forces. They observe the activity of social, religious, political, and economic groups, organizations, and institutions. They examine the effect of social influences, including organizations and institutions, on different individuals and groups. They also trace the origin and growth of these groups and interactions. For example, they may research the impact of a new law or policy on a specific demographic.

Sociologists often use both quantitative and qualitative methods when conducting research, and they frequently use statistical analysis programs during the research process.

Administrators, educators, lawmakers, and social workers use sociological research to solve social problems and formulate public policy. Sociologists specialize in a wide range of social topics, including the following:

- Health
- Crime
- Education
- Racial and ethnic relations
- Families
- Population
- Gender
- Poverty
- Aging

Sociologists who specialize in crime may be called *criminologists* or *penologists*. These workers apply their sociological knowledge to conduct research and analyze penal systems and populations and to study the causes and effects of crime.

Many people with a sociology background become postsecondary teachers and high school teachers. Most others, particularly those with a bachelor's degree in sociology, often find work in related jobs outside the sociologist profession as policy analysts, demographers, survey researchers, and statisticians.

Work Environment

Sociologists held about 2,600 jobs in 2014. The industries that employed the most sociologists were as follows:

Research and development in the social sciences and humanities	43%
Educational services; state, local, and private	27
State and local government, excluding education and hospitals	15

Sociologists typically work in an office. They may work outside of an office setting when conducting research through interviews or observations or presenting research results.

Work Schedules. Most sociologists work full time during regular business hours.

Education/Training

Most sociology jobs require a master's degree or Ph.D. Many bachelor's degree holders find positions in related fields, such as social services, education, or public policy.

Education. Sociologists typically need a master's degree or Ph.D. There are two types of sociology master's degree programs: traditional programs and applied, clinical, and professional programs. Traditional programs prepare students to enter a Ph.D. program. Applied, clinical, and professional programs prepare students to enter the workplace, teaching them the necessary analytical skills to perform sociological research in a professional setting.

Many students who complete a Ph.D. in sociology become postsecondary teachers. Other Ph.D. graduates often become research sociologists for nonprofits, businesses, and governments.

Courses in research methods and statistics are important for both master's and Ph.D. candidates. Many programs also offer opportunities to gain experience through internships or by preparing reports for clients.

Although some graduates with a bachelor's degree find work as sociology research assistants, most find positions in other fields. Sociology is a broad field of study with diverse application. Graduates with a bachelor's degree in sociology are often able to apply

Median Annual Wages, May 2014

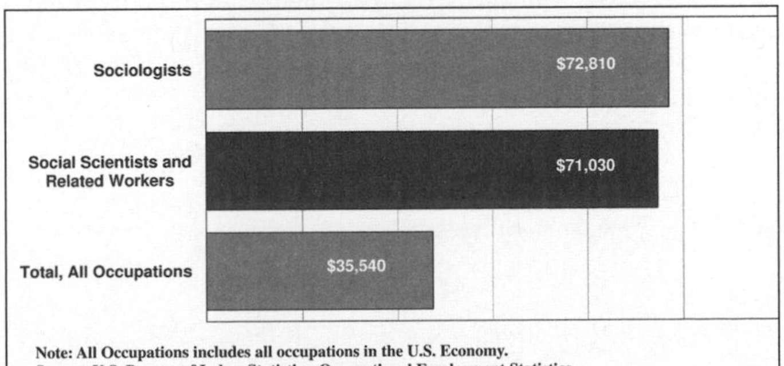

Note: All Occupations includes all occupations in the U.S. Economy.
Source: U.S. Bureau of Labor Statistics, Occupational Employment Statistics

Percent Change in Employment, Projected 2014–2024

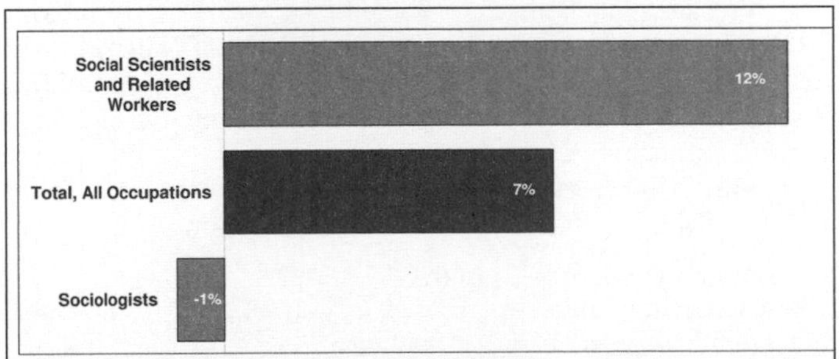

Note: All Occupations includes all occupations in the U.S. Economy.
Source: U.S. Bureau of Labor Statistics, Office of Occupational Statistics and Employment Projections

Employment Projections Data for Sociologists

Occupational Title	SOC Code	Employment, 2014	Projected Employment, 2024	Change, 2014–2024	
				Percent	Numeric
Sociologists	19-3041	2,600	2,500	-1	0

Source: U.S. Bureau of Labor Statistics, Employment Projections Program

Similar Occupations. This table shows a list of occupations with job duties that are similar to those of sociologists.

Occupations	Entry-level Education	2014 Median Pay	Projected Job Growth	Average Annual Openings
Anthropologists and Archeologists	Master's degree	$59,280	4%	30
Economists	Master's degree	$95,710	6%	120
Political Scientists	Master's degree	$104,920	-2%	-10
Postsecondary Teachers	See Education/Training	$70,790	13%	17,700
Psychologists	See Education/Training	$70,700	19%	3,250
Social Workers	See Education/Training	$45,500	12%	7,480
Statisticians	Master's degree	$79,990	34%	1,010
Survey Researchers	Master's degree	$49,760	12%	190
Urban and Regional Planners	Master's degree	$66,940	6%	240

their knowledge to many different industries, including social services, human resources, and government.

Other Experience. Candidates with a bachelor's degree may benefit from internships or volunteer work when looking for entry-level positions in sociology or a related field. These types of opportunities give students a chance to apply their academic knowledge in a professional setting and develop skills needed for the field.

Important Qualities

Analytical skills. Sociologists must be able to carefully analyze data and other information, often using statistical methods to test their theories.

Communication skills. Sociologists need strong communication skills when they conduct interviews, collaborate with colleagues, and present research results.

Critical-thinking skills. Sociologists must be able to think critically when doing research. They must design research projects and collect, process, and analyze information to draw logical conclusions about society and about various groups of people.

Writing skills. Sociologists frequently write reports detailing their findings.

Pay

The median annual wage for sociologists was $72,810 in May 2014. The median wage is the wage at which half the workers in an occupation earned more than that amount and half earned less. The lowest 10 percent earned less than $39,580, and the highest 10 percent earned more than $127,890.

In May 2014, the median annual wages for sociologists in the top industries in which they worked were as follows:

Research and development in the social sciences and humanities	$79,820
State and local government, excluding education and hospitals	68,710
Educational services; state, local, and private	55,140

Job Outlook

Employment of sociologists is projected to show little or no change from 2014 to 2024.

Nearly half of all sociologists are employed in social science research organizations, where sociologists are needed to research society and human interactions. However, this social science research is largely dependent on federal funding and grants, which have been increasingly difficult to obtain at historical levels. Employment growth in this industry is projected to decline from 2014 to 2024, as a result of this tightening of federal spending.

Sociologists will also be needed to apply sociological research to other disciplines as well. For example, sociologists may collaborate with researchers in other social sciences, such as economists, psychologists, and survey researchers, to study how social structures or groups influence policy decisions about health, education, politics, criminal justice, business, or economics.

Job Prospects. Candidates with a Ph.D., strong statistical and research skills, and a background in applied sociology will have the best job prospects. However, Ph.D. holders can expect to face very strong competition for sociologist positions because sociology is a popular field of study with a relatively small number of positions.

Many bachelor's and master's degree holders will find positions in related fields, such as social services, education, healthcare, public policy, or other areas. Although these fields require the skills and concepts that sociologists learn as part of their education, workers should face less competition for positions not specifically labeled as "sociologists."

Contacts for More Information

For more information about careers in sociology, visit

➤ American Sociological Association (www.asanet.org)

O*NET

➤ Sociologists (19-3041.00)

Survey Researchers

- **2014 Median Pay** .... $49,760 per year
$23.92 per hour
- **Typical Entry-Level Education** ....Master's degree
- **Work Experience in a Related Occupation**.............. None
- **On-the-job Training** .... None
- **Number of Jobs, 2014** 16,700
- **Job Outlook, 2014–24**............ 12% (Faster than average)
- **Employment Change, 2014–24** 1,900

What Survey Researchers Do

Survey researchers design surveys and analyze data. Surveys are used to collect factual data, such as employment and salary information, or to ask questions in order to understand people's opinions, preferences, beliefs, or desires.

Duties. Survey researchers typically do the following:

- Conduct background research on survey topics
- Plan and design surveys and determine appropriate survey methods
- Test surveys to make sure that people will understand the questions being asked
- Coordinate the work of survey interviewers and data collectors
- Account for and solve problems caused by nonrespondents or other sampling issues
- Analyze data using statistical software and techniques
- Summarize survey data using tables, graphs, and fact sheets
- Evaluate surveys, methods, and performance to improve future surveys

Survey researchers design and conduct surveys for different research purposes. Surveys for scientific research cover various fields, including government, health, social sciences, and education. For example, a survey researcher may try to capture information about the prevalence of drug use or disease.

Some survey researchers design public opinion surveys, which are intended to gather information about the attitudes and opinions of society or of a certain group. Surveys can cover a wide variety of topics, including politics, culture, the economy, or health.

Other survey researchers design marketing surveys which examine products or services that consumers want, need, or prefer. Researchers who collect and analyze market research data are known as market research analysts.

Survey researchers may conduct surveys in many different formats, such as interviews, questionnaires, and focus groups (in-person, small group sessions with a facilitator). They use different methods to collect data, including the Internet, mail, and telephone and in-person interviews.

Some researchers use surveys to solicit the opinions of an entire population, such as the decennial census, and others use them to target a smaller group, such as a specific demographic group, residents of a particular state, or members of a political party.

Researchers survey a sample of the population and use statistics to make sure the sample accurately represents the target population group. Researchers use a variety of statistical techniques and analytical software to plan surveys, adjust for errors in the data, and analyze the results.

Survey researchers sometimes supervise interviewers who collect the survey data through in-person interviews or by telephone.

Work Environment

Survey researchers held about 16,700 jobs in 2014. The industries that employed the most survey researchers were as follows:

Other professional, scientific, and technical services	49%
Scientific research and development services	15
Educational services; state, local, and private	9
Management, scientific, and technical consulting services	7
Religious, grantmaking, civic, professional, and similar organizations	6

They work in research firms, polling organizations, nonprofits, corporations, colleges and universities, and government agencies.

Survey researchers who conduct interviews have frequent contact with the public. Some may work outside the office, traveling to meet with clients or conducting in-person interviews and focus group sessions. When designing surveys and analyzing data, they usually work alone in an office setting, though some work on teams with other researchers.

Work Schedules. Most survey researchers work full time during regular business hours. They may sometimes work for extended periods to meet project deadlines.

Education/Training

Many research positions require a master's degree or Ph.D., though a bachelor's degree may be sufficient for some entry-level positions. In addition, employers generally prefer candidates who have previous experience performing research, using statistics, and analyzing data.

Education. Many research positions require a master's degree or Ph.D. Survey researchers can have a master's degree in a variety of fields, including marketing or survey research, statistics, and the social sciences.

A bachelor's degree is sufficient for some entry-level positions. To prepare to enter this occupation, students should take courses in research methods, survey methodology, and statistics. Many also may benefit from taking business courses, such as marketing and consumer behavior, and social science courses, such as psychology, sociology, and economics.

Other Experience. Prospective survey researchers can gain experience through internships or fellowships. Many businesses,

Survey researchers use data from surveys to measure consumer preferences.

Median Annual Wages, May 2014

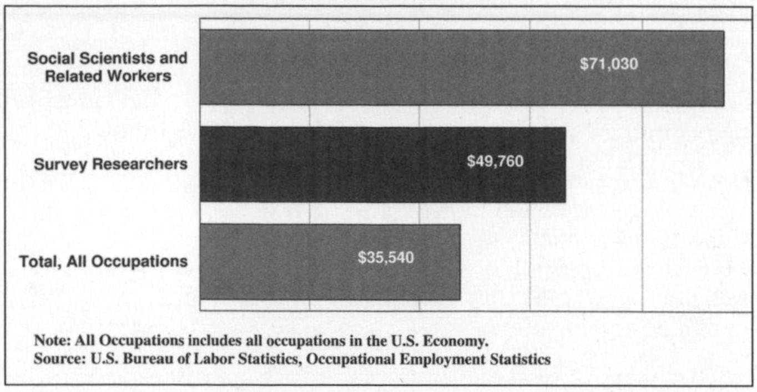

Percent Change in Employment, Projected 2014–2024

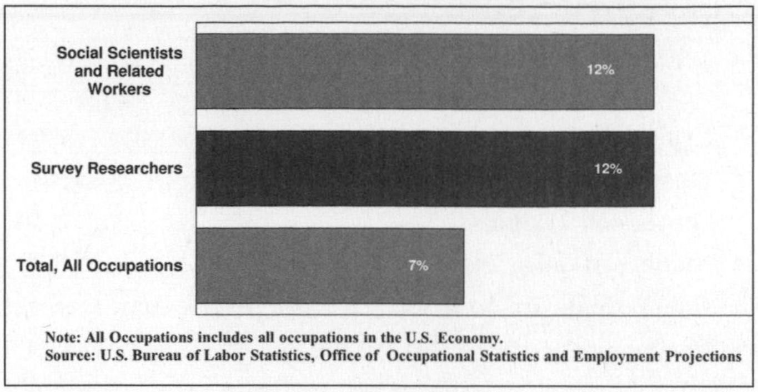

research and polling firms, and marketing companies offer internships for college students or recent graduates who want to work in market and survey research.

Licenses, Certifications, and Registrations. Survey researchers are not required by law to be licensed or certified. Although not mandatory, certification can show a level of professional competence.

The Marketing Research Association offers the Professional Researcher Certification for survey researchers. To qualify, candidates must have at least 3 years of experience working in opinion and marketing research, pass an exam, and be a member of a professional organization. Researchers must complete continuing education courses and apply for renewal every 2 years to maintain their certification.

Important Qualities

Analytical skills. Survey researchers must be able to apply statistical techniques to large amounts of data and interpret the results correctly. They also should be proficient in the statistical software used to analyze data.

Communication skills. Survey researchers need strong communication skills when conducting surveys and interpreting and presenting results to clients.

Critical-thinking skills. Survey researchers must design or choose a survey and survey method that best captures the information needed. They must also be able to look at the data and draw reasonable conclusions from the results of the survey.

Detail oriented. Survey researchers must pay attention to details, because survey results depend on collecting, analyzing, and reporting the data accurately.

Problem-solving skills. Survey researchers need problem-solving skills when identifying survey design issues, adjusting survey questions, and interpreting survey results.

Pay

The median annual wage for survey researchers was $49,760 in May 2014. The median wage is the wage at which half the workers in an occupation earned more than that amount and half earned less. The lowest 10 percent earned less than $19,000, and the highest 10 percent earned more than $95,070.

In May 2014, the median annual wages for survey researchers in the top industries in which they worked were as follows:

Scientific research and development services	$63,160
Educational services; state, local, and private	55,240
Religious, grantmaking, civic, professional, and similar organizations	54,250
Management, scientific, and technical consulting services	51,280
Other professional, scientific, and technical services	40,380

Job Outlook

Employment of survey researchers is projected to grow 12 percent from 2014 to 2024, faster than the average for all occupations.

Organizations in all industries rely on data and information acquired through research, and survey researchers play an important role in the research process. Governments, the media, nonprofits, and other organizations will continue to use public opinion research to learn about citizens' thoughts and perspectives. They use this information to understand groups of people; measure a program's effectiveness; or gauge support for people, policies, and actions. For example, public opinion research may help governments make decisions on transit systems, social programs, and numerous other issues.

Survey researchers are also expected to be needed to design surveys for businesses. In an increasingly competitive economy, firms will continue to use market and consumer research surveys to help make business decisions, improve their products or services, and compete in the market. Many of these researcher jobs will be in consulting firms.

Research is an evolving field. Companies regularly adopt new research methods and new data sources which may increase productivity. For example, collecting information from social media sites and data mining—finding trends in large sets of existing data—are expected to reduce the need for some traditional survey methods, such as telephone and in-person interviews. Employment growth may be tempered by these changing research methods.

Job Prospects. Job opportunities should be best for those with an advanced degree in market or survey research, statistics, or the social sciences. Job seekers with strong statistical and analytical skills and research experience should have good job prospects. Because of the relatively small number of survey researcher positions, bachelor's degree holders will likely face strong competition from more qualified candidates.

Contacts for More Information

For more information about careers in survey research, visit

- American Association for Public Opinion Research (www.aapor.org)
- Council of American Survey Research Organizations (www.casro.org)
- Marketing Research Association (www.marketingresearch.org)

O*NET

- Survey Researchers (19-3022.00)

Employment Projections Data for Survey Researchers

Occupational Title	SOC Code	Employment, 2014	Projected Employment, 2024	Change, 2014–2024 Percent	Change, 2014–2024 Numeric
Survey researchers	19-3022	16,700	18,700	12	1,900

Source: U.S. Bureau of Labor Statistics, Employment Projections Program

Similar Occupations. This table shows a list of occupations with job duties that are similar to those of survey researchers.

Occupations	Entry-level Education	2014 Median Pay	Projected Job Growth	Average Annual Openings
Advertising Sales Agents	High school diploma or equivalent	$47,890	-3%	-450
Advertising, Promotions, and Marketing Managers	Bachelor's degree	$123,450	9%	1,970
Economists	Master's degree	$95,710	6%	120
Market Research Analysts	Bachelor's degree	$61,290	19%	9,230
Operations Research Analysts	Bachelor's degree	$76,660	30%	2,760
Political Scientists	Master's degree	$104,920	-2%	-10
Psychologists	See Education/Training	$70,700	19%	3,250
Sociologists	Master's degree	$72,810	-1%	0
Statisticians	Master's degree	$79,990	34%	1,010

Urban and Regional Planners

- **2014 Median Pay** .... $66,940 per year
  $32.18 per hour
- **Typical Entry-Level Education** .... Master's degree
- **Work Experience in a Related Occupation** .... None
- **On-the-job Training** .... None
- **Number of Jobs, 2014** 38,000
- **Job Outlook, 2014–24** .... 6% (As fast as average)
- **Employment Change, 2014–24** 2,400

What Urban and Regional Planners Do

Urban and regional planners develop land use plans and programs that help create communities, accommodate population growth, and revitalize physical facilities in towns, cities, counties, and metropolitan areas.

Duties. Urban and regional planners typically do the following:

- Meet with public officials, developers, and the public regarding development plans and land use
- Administer government plans or policies affecting land use, the environment, zoning, historic buildings, public utilities, community facilities, housing, community design, and transportation
- Gather and analyze market research data, censuses, and economic and environmental studies
- Conduct field investigations to analyze factors affecting community development and decline, including land use
- Review site plans submitted by developers
- Assess the feasibility of proposals and identify needed changes
- Recommend whether proposals should be approved or denied
- Present projects to communities, planning officials, and planning commissions
- Stay current on zoning or building codes, environmental regulations, and other legal issues

Urban and regional planners identify community needs and develop short- and long-term solutions to develop and revitalize communities and areas. For example, planners examine ideas for proposed facilities, such as schools, to ensure that these facilities will meet the needs of a changing population.

As an area grows or changes, planners help communities manage the related economic, social, and environmental issues, such as planning a new park, sheltering the homeless, and making the region more attractive to businesses.

Some planners work on broad, community-wide projects; others focus on specific issues. Ultimately, planners advocate the best use of a community's land and resources for residential, commercial, industrial, educational, and recreational purposes.

When beginning a project, planners work with public officials, community members, and other groups to identify community issues and goals. Using research and data analysis, and collaborating with interest groups, they formulate strategies to address issues and to meet goals.

Planners also may help carry out community plans by overseeing projects and organizing the work of the groups involved. Projects may range from a policy recommendation for a specific initiative to a long-term, comprehensive area plan.

Urban and regional planners use a variety of tools and technology in their work, including geographic information systems (GIS) that analyze and manipulate data. GIS is used to integrate data with digital maps. For example, planners use GIS to overlay a land map with population density indicators. They also use statistical software, visualization and presentation programs, financial spreadsheets, and other database and software programs.

Urban and regional planners develop plans to use land for the growth and revitalization of communities.

The following are examples of types of urban and regional planners:

Land use and code enforcement planners are concerned with the way land is used and whether development plans comply with codes, which are the standards and laws of a jurisdiction. These planners work to carry out effective planning and zoning policies and ordinances. For example, a planner may develop a policy to encourage development in an underutilized location and to discourage development in an environmentally sensitive area.

Transportation planners develop transportation plans and programs for an area. They identify transportation needs and issues, assess the impact of transportation services or systems, and anticipate and address future transportation patterns. For example, as growth outside the city creates more jobs, the need for public transportation to get workers to those jobs increases. Transportation planners develop and model possible solutions and explain the possibilities to planning boards and the public.

Environmental and natural resources planners attempt to mitigate the harmful effects of development on the environment. They may focus on conserving resources, preventing destruction of ecosystems, or cleaning polluted areas.

Economic development planners focus on the economic activities of an area. They may work to expand or diversify commercial activity, attract businesses, create jobs, or build housing.

Urban design planners strive to make building architecture, streets, and public spaces look and function in accordance with an area's development and design goals. They combine planning with aspects of architecture and landscape architecture. Urban design planners focus on issues such as city layout, street design, and building and landscape patterns.

Work Environment

Urban and regional planners held about 38,000 jobs in 2014. The industries that employed the most urban and regional planners were as follows:

Local government, excluding education and hospitals	66%
Architectural, engineering, and related services	13
State government, excluding education and hospitals	10
Management, scientific, and technical consulting services	5

Planners work throughout the country in all municipality sizes, but most work in large metropolitan areas.

Planners often collaborate with public officials, engineers, architects, lawyers, and developers.

Urban and regional planners often travel to sites to inspect the proposed changes and their impact on land conditions, the environment, and use.

Work Schedules. Most urban and regional planners work full time during normal business hours, but some also work evenings or weekends to attend meetings with officials, planning commissions, and neighborhood groups. In 2014, about 1 in 5 planners worked more than 40 hours per week.

Education/Training

Urban and regional planners need a master's degree from an accredited planning program to qualify for most positions.

Education. Most urban and regional planners have a master's degree from an accredited urban or regional planning program. In 2015, there were 72 programs accredited by the Planning Accreditation Board that offered a master's degree in planning.

Many master's programs accept students with a wide range of undergraduate backgrounds. However, many candidates who enter master's degree programs have a bachelor's degree in economics, geography, political science, or environmental design.

Median Annual Wages, May 2014

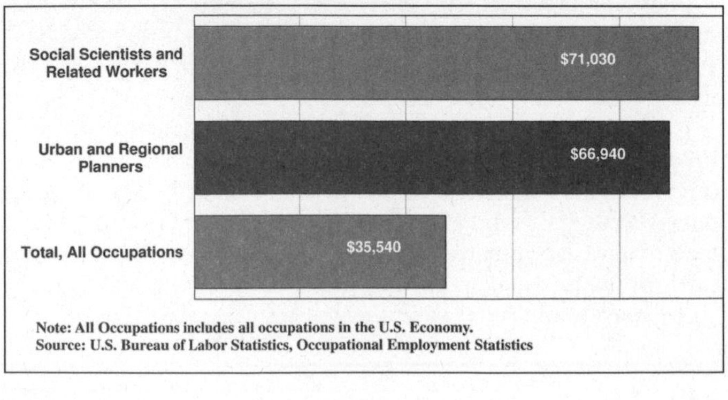

Percent Change in Employment, Projected 2014–2024

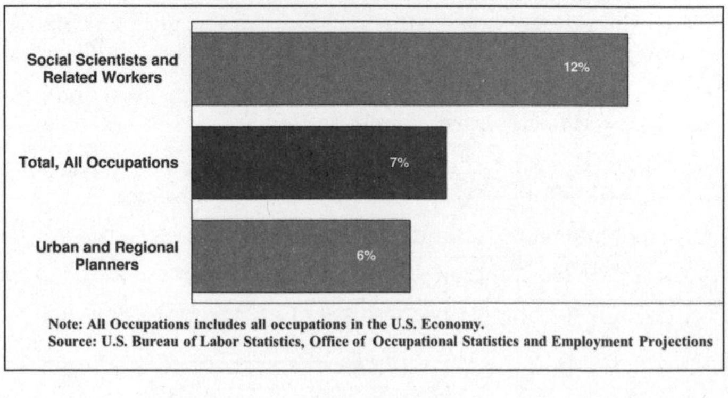

Most master's programs include spending considerable time in seminars, workshops, and laboratory courses, in which students learn to analyze and solve planning problems. Although most master's programs have a similar core curriculum, they often differ in the courses they offer and the issues on which they focus. For example, programs located in agricultural states may focus on rural planning, and programs located in an area with high population density may focus on urban revitalization.

Some planners have a background in a related field, such as public administration, architecture, or landscape architecture.

Aspiring planners with a bachelor's degree can qualify for a small number of jobs as assistant or junior planners. There are currently 15 accredited bachelor's degree programs in planning. Candidates with a bachelor's degree typically need work experience in planning, public policy, or a related field.

Other Experience. Although not necessary for all positions, some entry-level positions require 1 to 2 years of work experience in a related field, such as architecture, public policy, or economic development. Many students gain experience through real-world planning projects or part-time internships while enrolled in a master's planning program. Others enroll in full-time internships after completing their degree.

Licenses, Certifications, and Registrations. As of 2015, New Jersey was the only state that required urban and regional planners to be licensed, although Michigan required registration to use the title "community planner." More information can be requested from the regulatory boards of New Jersey and Michigan.

The American Institute of Certified Planners (AICP) offers the professional AICP Certification for planners. To become certified, candidates must meet certain education and experience requirements and pass an exam. Certification must be maintained every 2 years. Although certification is not required for all planning positions, some organizations prefer to hire certified planners.

Important Qualities

Analytical skills. Urban and regional planners analyze information and data from a variety of sources, such as market research studies, censuses, and environmental impact studies. They use statistical techniques and technologies such as geographic information systems (GIS) in their analyses to determine the significance of the data.

Communication skills. Urban and regional planners must be able to communicate clearly and effectively because they often give presentations and meet with a wide variety of audiences, including public officials, interest groups, and community members.

Decision-making skills. Urban and regional planners must weigh all possible planning options and combine analysis, creativity, and realism to choose the appropriate action or plan.

Management skills. Urban and regional planners must be able to manage projects, which may include overseeing tasks, planning assignments, and making decisions.

Writing skills. Urban and regional planners need strong writing skills because they often prepare research reports, write grant proposals, and correspond with colleagues and stakeholders.

Pay

The median annual wage for urban and regional planners was $66,940 in May 2014. The median wage is the wage at which half the workers in an occupation earned more than that amount and half earned less. The lowest 10 percent earned less than $42,220, and the highest 10 percent earned more than $99,560.

In May 2014, the median annual wages for urban and regional planners in the top industries in which they worked were as follows:

Architectural, engineering, and related services	$72,490
Local government, excluding education and hospitals	65,730
State government, excluding education and hospitals	65,380
Management, scientific, and technical consulting services	60,760

Job Outlook

Employment of urban and regional planners is projected to grow 6 percent from 2014 to 2024, about as fast as the average for all occupations. Demographic and environmental changes will drive employment growth for planners.

Within cities, urban planners will be needed to develop revitalization projects and address issues associated with population growth, environmental degradation, and resource scarcity. Similarly, suburban areas and municipalities will need planners to address the challenges associated with population changes, including housing needs and transportation systems.

Planners will also be needed as new and existing communities require extensive development and improved infrastructure, including housing, roads, sewer systems, parks, and schools.

However, local and state government budgets may affect the employment of planners in government, because development projects are contingent on available funds.

Job Prospects. Job opportunities for planners often depend on economic conditions. When municipalities and developers have funds for development projects, planners are in higher demand. However, planners often face strong competition for jobs in an economic downturn when there is less funding for development work. Planners who are willing to relocate for work will have more job opportunities.

Contacts for More Information

For more information about careers in urban and regional planning, visit

➤ American Planning Association (www.planning.org)

For more information about certification in urban and regional planning, visit

➤ American Institute of Certified Planners (www.planning.org/aicp)

For more information about New Jersey licensure in planning, visit

➤ New Jersey State Board of Professional Planners (www.njconsumeraffairs.gov/plan/Pages/default.aspx)

For more information about accredited urban and regional planning programs, visit

➤ Planning Accreditation Board (www.planningaccreditationboard.org)

Employment Projections Data for Urban and Regional Planners

Occupational Title	SOC Code	Employment, 2014	Projected Employment, 2024	Change, 2014–2024 Percent	Change, 2014–2024 Numeric
Urban and regional planners	19-3051	38,000	40,400	6	2,400

Source: U.S. Bureau of Labor Statistics, Employment Projections Program

Similar Occupations. This table shows a list of occupations with job duties that are similar to those of urban and regional planners.

Occupations	Entry-level Education	2014 Median Pay	Projected Job Growth	Average Annual Openings
Architects	Bachelor's degree	$74,520	7%	780
Cartographers and Photogrammetrists	Bachelor's degree	$60,930	29%	360
Civil Engineers	Bachelor's degree	$82,050	8%	2,360
Economists	Master's degree	$95,710	6%	120
Geographers	Bachelor's degree	$76,420	-2%	0
Landscape Architects	Bachelor's degree	$64,570	5%	120
Market Research Analysts	Bachelor's degree	$61,290	19%	9,230
Survey Researchers	Master's degree	$49,760	12%	190
Surveyors	Bachelor's degree	$57,050	-2%	-90

O*NET

➤ Urban and Regional Planners (19-3051.00)

Zoologists and Wildlife Biologists

- **2014 Median Pay** .... $58,270 per year
  $28.02 per hour
- **Typical Entry-Level Education** .... Bachelor's degree
- **Work Experience in a Related Occupation** .... None
- **On-the-job Training** .... None
- **Number of Jobs, 2014** 21,300
- **Job Outlook, 2014–24** .... 4% (Slower than average)
- **Employment Change, 2014–24** 800

What Zoologists and Wildlife Biologists Do

Zoologists and wildlife biologists study animals and other wildlife and how they interact with their ecosystems. They study the physical characteristics of animals, animal behaviors, and the impacts humans have on wildlife and natural habitats.

Duties. Zoologists and wildlife biologists typically do the following:

- Develop and conduct experimental studies with animals in controlled or natural surroundings
- Collect biological data and specimens for analysis
- Study the characteristics of animals, such as their interactions with other species, reproduction, population dynamics, diseases, and movement patterns
- Analyze the influence that human activity has on wildlife and their natural habitats
- Research, initiate, and maintain ways of improving breeding programs that support healthy game animals, endangered species, or other wild populations of land or aquatic life
- Estimate, monitor, and manage wildlife populations and invasive plants and animals
- Write research papers, reports, and scholarly articles that explain their findings
- Give presentations on research findings to academics and the general public
- Develop conservation plans and make recommendations on wildlife conservation and management issues to policymakers and the general public

Zoologists and wildlife biologists perform a variety of scientific tests and experiments. For example, they take blood samples from animals to assess their levels of nutrition, check animals for disease and parasites, and tag animals in order to track them. Although the roles and abilities of zoologists and wildlife biologists often overlap, zoologists typically conduct scientific investigations and basic research on particular types of animals, such as birds or amphibians, whereas wildlife biologists are more likely to study specific ecosystems or animal populations, such as a particular at-risk species. Wildlife biologists also do applied work, such as that involving the conservation and management of wildlife populations.

Zoologists and wildlife biologists use geographic information systems (GIS), modeling software, and other computer programs to estimate wildlife populations and track the movements of animals. They also use these computer programs to forecast the spread of invasive species or diseases, project changes in the availability of habitat, and assess other potential threats to wildlife.

Zoologists and wildlife biologists conduct research for a variety of purposes. For example, many zoologists and wildlife biologists work to increase our knowledge and understanding of wildlife species. Traditionally, many wildlife biologists researched ways to encourage abundant game animal populations in order to increase recreational hunting and tourism. Today, many also work with public officials in conservation efforts that protect species from threats and help animal populations return to and remain at sustainable levels.

Most zoologists and wildlife biologists work on research teams with other scientists and technicians. For example, zoologists and wildlife biologists may work with environmental scientists and hydrologists to monitor water pollution and its effects on fish populations.

Zoologists generally specialize first in either vertebrates or invertebrates and then in specific species. Following are some examples of specialization by species:

- *Cetologists* study marine mammals, such as whales and dolphins.
- *Entomologists* study insects, such as beetles and butterflies.

- *Herpetologists* study reptiles and amphibians, such as snakes and frogs.
- *Ichthyologists* study wild fish, such as sharks and lungfish.
- *Mammalogists* study mammals, such as monkeys and bears.
- *Ornithologists* study birds, such as hawks and penguins.
- *Teuthologists* study cephalopods, such as octopuses and cuttlefish.

Some zoologists and wildlife biologists specialize in studying wildlife according to the type of water or land where the wildlife lives. The following are examples of those who specialize by habitat:

- *Limnologists* study organisms that live in freshwater.
- *Marine biologists* study organisms that live in saltwater.
- *Terrestrial biologists* study organisms that live on land, including plants and microbes.

Other zoologists and wildlife biologists are identified by the aspects of zoology and wildlife biology they study, such as evolution and animal behavior. Following are some examples:

- *Botanists* study plants, including their growth, diseases, and structures. Agronomists study the particular plant science concerning crop production. For more information on agronomists, see the profile on agricultural and food scientists.
- *Ecologists* study ecosystems, which include all relationships between organisms and the surrounding environments.
- *Evolutionary biologists* study the origins of species and the changes in their inherited characteristics over generations.

Many people with a zoology and wildlife biology background become high school teachers or college or university professors. For more information, see the profiles on high school teachers and postsecondary teachers.

Work Environment

Zoologists and wildlife biologists held about 21,300 jobs in 2014. The industries that employed the most zoologists and wildlife biologists were as follows:

State government, excluding education and hospitals	33%
Federal government, excluding postal service	21
Management, scientific, and technical consulting services	10
Research and development in the physical, engineering, and life sciences	8
Colleges, universities, and professional schools; state	7

They work in offices, laboratories, and outdoors. Depending on their job and interests, they may spend considerable time in the field gathering data and studying animals in their natural habitats. Other zoologists and wildlife biologists may spend very little time in the field.

Zoologists and wildlife biologists may study animals in the field or in captivity.

For example, marine biologists may spend months at sea on a research ship. Other zoologists and wildlife biologists may spend significant amounts of time in deserts or remote mountainous and woodland regions. The ability to travel and study nature firsthand is often viewed as a benefit of working in these occupations, but few modern amenities may be available to those who travel in remote areas.

Fieldwork can be physically demanding, and zoologists and wildlife biologists work in both warm and cold climates and in all types of weather. For example, marine biologists may need to spend significant amounts of time in cold water and on ships, which may cause seasickness. In all environments, working as a zoologist or wildlife biologist can be emotionally demanding because interpersonal contact may be limited.

Work Schedules. Most zoologists and wildlife biologists work full time. They may work long or irregular hours, especially when doing fieldwork. Zoologists and wildlife biologists who work with nocturnal animals may need to work at night at least some of the time.

Education/Training

Zoologists and wildlife biologists need a bachelor's degree for entry-level positions; a master's degree is often needed for higher

Median Annual Wages, May 2014

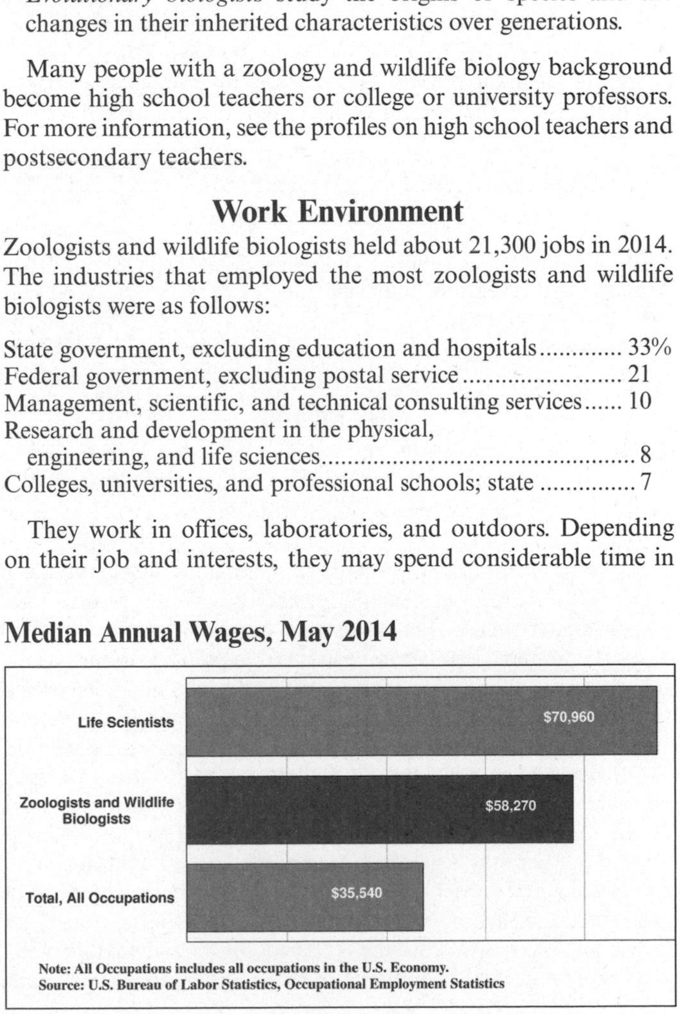

Percent Change in Employment, Projected 2014–2024

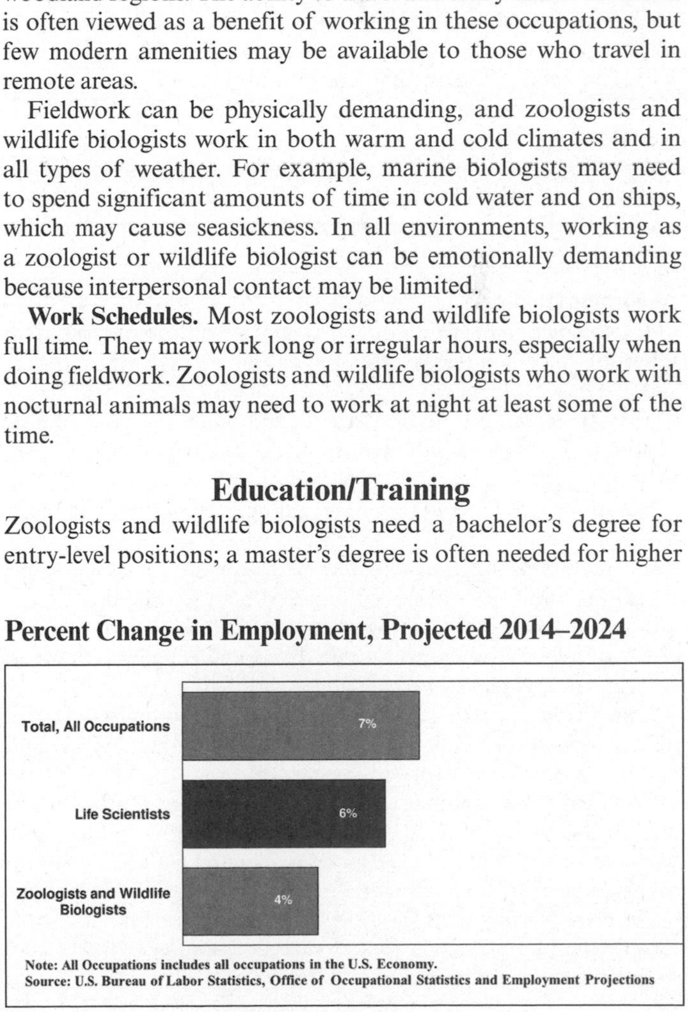

Employment Projections Data for Zoologists and Wildlife Biologists

Occupational Title	SOC Code	Employment, 2014	Projected Employment, 2024	Change, 2014–2024	
				Percent	Numeric
Zoologists and wildlife biologists	19-1023	21,300	22,200	4	800

Source: U.S. Bureau of Labor Statistics, Employment Projections Program

level investigative or scientific work. A Ph.D. is necessary to lead independent research and for most university research positions.

Education. Zoologists and wildlife biologists need at least a bachelor's degree. Many schools offer bachelor's degree programs in zoology and wildlife biology or in a closely related field, such as ecology. An undergraduate degree in biology with coursework in zoology and wildlife biology also is good preparation for a career as a zoologist or wildlife biologist.

Zoologists and wildlife biologists typically need at least a master's degree for higher level investigative or scientific work. A Ph.D. is necessary for the majority of independent research positions and for university research positions. Most Ph.D.-level researchers need to be familiar with computer programming and statistical software.

Students typically take zoology and wildlife biology courses in ecology, anatomy, wildlife management, and cellular biology. They also take courses that focus on a particular group of animals, such as herpetology (reptiles and amphibians) or ornithology (birds). Courses in botany, chemistry, and physics are important because zoologists and wildlife biologists must have a well-rounded scientific background. Wildlife biology programs may focus on applied techniques in habitat analysis and conservation. Students also should take courses in mathematics and statistics, given that zoologists and wildlife biologists must be able to do complex data analysis.

Knowledge of computer science is important because zoologists and wildlife biologists frequently use advanced computer software, such as geographic information systems (GIS) and modeling software, to do their work.

Important Qualities

Communication skills. Zoologists and wildlife biologists write scientific papers and give talks to the public, policymakers, and academics.

Critical-thinking skills. Zoologists and wildlife biologists need sound reasoning and judgment to draw conclusions from experimental results and scientific observations.

Emotional stamina and stability. Zoologists and wildlife biologists may need to endure long periods with little human contact. As with other occupations that deal with animals, emotional stability is important in working with injured or sick animals.

Interpersonal skills. Zoologists and wildlife biologists typically work on teams. They must be able to work effectively with others to achieve their goals or to negotiate conflicting goals.

Observation skills. Zoologists and wildlife biologists must be able to notice slight changes in an animal's characteristics, such as changes in its behavior or appearance.

Outdoor skills. Zoologists and wildlife biologists may need to chop firewood, swim in cold water, navigate rough terrain in poor weather, or perform other activities associated with life in remote areas.

Problem-solving skills. Zoologists and wildlife biologists try to find the best possible solutions to threats that affect wildlife, such as disease and habitat loss.

Other Experience. Some zoologists and wildlife biologists may need to have well-rounded outdoor skills. They may need to be able to drive a tractor, use a generator, or provide for themselves in remote locations.

Many zoology and wildlife biology students gain practical experience through internships, volunteer work, or some other type of employment during college or soon after graduation.

Advancement. Zoologists and wildlife biologists typically receive greater responsibility and independence in their work as they gain experience. More education also can lead to greater responsibility. Zoologists and wildlife biologists with a Ph.D. usually lead independent research and control the direction and content of projects. In addition, they may be responsible for finding much of their own funding.

Pay

The median annual wage for zoologists and wildlife biologists was $58,270 in May 2014. The median wage is the wage at which half the workers in an occupation earned more than that amount and half earned less. The lowest 10 percent earned less than $38,080, and the highest 10 percent earned more than $96,720.

In May 2014, the median annual wages for zoologists and wildlife biologists in the top industries in which they worked were as follows:

Federal government, excluding postal service	$74,110
Research and development in the physical, engineering, and life sciences	59,950
Colleges, universities, and professional schools; state	59,180
Management, scientific, and technical consulting services	55,130
State government, excluding education and hospitals	52,690

Job Outlook

Employment of zoologists and wildlife biologists is projected to grow 4 percent from 2014 to 2024, slower than the average for all occupations. More zoologists and wildlife biologists will be needed to study the impact of human population growth on wildlife and their natural habitats. However, because most funding comes from governmental agencies, demand for zoologists and wildlife biologists will be limited by budgetary constraints.

As the human population grows and expands into new areas, it will expose wildlife to threats such as disease, invasive species, and habitat loss. Increased human activity can cause problems such as pollution and climate change, which endanger wildlife. Zoologists and wildlife biologists will be needed to study and gain an understanding of the impact of these factors. Many states will continue to employ zoologists and wildlife biologists to manage animal populations for tourism purposes, such as hunting game, sightseeing, and conservation. Changes in climate patterns can be detrimental to the migration habits of animals, and increased sea levels can destroy wetlands; therefore, zoologists and wildlife biologists will be needed to research, develop, and carry out wildlife

Similar Occupations. This table shows a list of occupations with job duties that are similar to those of zoologists and wildlife biologists.

Occupations	Entry-level Education	2014 Median Pay	Projected Job Growth	Average Annual Openings
Agricultural and Food Scientists	Bachelor's degree	$60,690	5%	190
Animal Care and Service Workers	High school diploma or equivalent	$20,610	11%	2,570
Biochemists and Biophysicists	Doctoral or professional degree	$84,940	8%	280
Biological Technicians	Bachelor's degree	$41,290	5%	410
Conservation Scientists and Foresters	Bachelor's degree	$60,360	7%	270
Environmental Scientists and Specialists	Bachelor's degree	$66,250	11%	1,020
Microbiologists	Bachelor's degree	$67,790	4%	80
Postsecondary Teachers	See Education/Training	$70,790	13%	17,700
Veterinarians	Doctoral or professional degree	$87,590	9%	690

management and conservation plans that combat these threats and protect our natural resources.

Job Prospects. Zoologists and wildlife biologists may face strong competition when looking for employment. Applicants with practical experience gained through internships, summer jobs, or volunteer work done before, or shortly after graduation should have better chances at finding employment.

Contacts for More Information

For more information about zoologists and wildlife biologists, visit

- The Wildlife Society (www.wildlife.org)
- Association of Zoos and Aquariums (www.aza.org)
- American Society of Ichthyologists and Herpetologists (www.asih.org)
- American Society of Mammalogists (www.mammalsociety.org)
- Ornithological Societies of North America (www.osnabirds.org)
- Zoological Association of America (http://zaa.org)

For more information about issues in zoology and wildlife biology, visit

- U.S. Fish and Wildlife Service (www.fws.gov)
- U.S. Geological Survey (http://education.usgs.gov/index.html)
- National Park Service (www.nature.nps.gov/index.cfm)

For more information about careers in botany, visit

- Botanical Society of America (www.botany.org/bsa/careers)

For more information about careers in ecology, visit

- Ecological Society of America (www.esa.org/esa)

For information on federal government education requirements for zoologists and wildlife biologists, visit

- U.S. Office of Personnel Management (http://tinyurl.com/onrkvnh)

To find job openings for zoologists and wildlife biologists in the federal government, visit

- USAJOBS (www.usajobs.gov)

Related BLS Article

For information on working as an ornithologist (a type of zoologist), see the Career Outlook article "You're a What? Ornithologist" (www.bls.gov/careeroutlook/2013/summer/yawhat.pdf).

O*NET

- Zoologists and Wildlife Biologists (19-1023.00)

Management

Administrative Services Managers

- **2014 Median Pay** .... $83,790 per year
$40.28 per hour
- **Typical Entry-Level Education** .... Bachelor's degree
- **Work Experience in a Related Occupation** .... Less than 5 years
- **On-the-Job Training** .... None
- **Number of Jobs 2014** 287,300
- **Job Outlook, 2014–24** .... 8% (As fast as average)
- **Employment Change, 2014–24** 23,500

What Administrative Services Managers Do

Administrative services managers plan, direct, and coordinate supportive services of an organization. Their specific responsibilities vary, but administrative service managers typically maintain facilities and supervise activities that include recordkeeping, mail distribution, and office upkeep. In a small organization, they may direct all support services and may be called the *business office manager*. Large organizations may have several layers of administrative managers who specialize in different areas.

Duties. Administrative services managers typically do the following:

- Buy, store, and distribute supplies
- Supervise clerical and administrative personnel
- Set goals and deadlines for their department
- Develop, manage, and monitor records
- Recommend changes to policies or procedures in order to improve operations, such as changing what supplies are kept or how to improve recordkeeping
- Plan budgets for contracts, equipment, and supplies
- Monitor the facility to ensure that it remains safe, secure, and well maintained
- Oversee the maintenance and repair of machinery, equipment, and electrical and mechanical systems
- Ensure that facilities meet environmental, health, and security standards and comply with government regulations

An organization may have several managers who oversee activities that meet the needs of multiple departments, such as mail, printing and copying, recordkeeping, security, building maintenance, and recycling.

The work of administrative services managers can make a difference in employees' productivity and satisfaction. For example, an administrative services manager might be responsible for making sure that the organization has the supplies and services it needs. In addition, an administrative services manager who is responsible for coordinating space allocation might take into account employee morale and available funds when determining the best way to arrange a given physical space.

Administrative services managers also ensure that the organization honors its contracts and follows government regulations and safety standards.

Administrative services managers may examine energy consumption patterns, technology usage, and office equipment. For example, managers may recommend buying new or different equipment or supplies in order to lower energy costs or improve indoor air quality.

Administrative services managers also plan for maintenance and the future replacement of equipment, such as computers. A timely replacement of equipment can help save money for the organization, because eventually the cost of upgrading and maintaining equipment becomes higher than the cost of buying new equipment.

The following are examples of types of administrative services managers:

Contract administrators handle buying, storing, and distributing equipment and supplies. They also oversee getting rid of surplus or unclaimed property.

Facility managers oversee buildings, grounds, equipment, and supplies. Their duties fall into several categories, including overseeing operations and maintenance, planning and managing projects, and dealing with environmental factors.

Facility managers may oversee renovation projects to improve efficiency or ensure that facilities meet government regulations and environmental, health, and security standards. For example, they may influence building renovation projects by recommending energy-saving alternatives or efficiencies that reduce waste. In addition, facility managers continually monitor the facility to ensure that it remains safe, secure, and well maintained. Facility managers also are responsible for directing staff, including maintenance, grounds, and custodial workers.

Administrative services managers review plans and contracts to ensure smooth implementation.

Median Annual Wages, May 2014

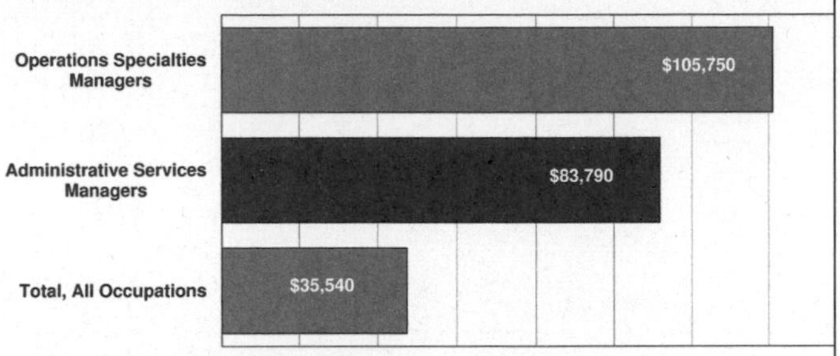

Note: All Occupations includes all occupations in the U.S. Economy.
Source: U.S. Bureau of Labor Statistics, Occupational Employment Statistics

Percent Change in Employment, Projected 2014–2024

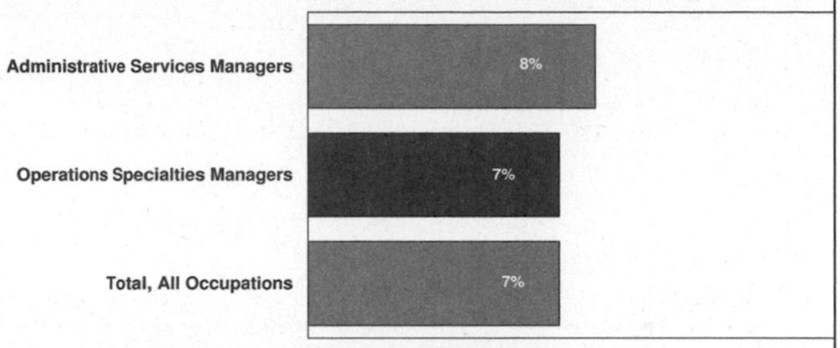

Note: All Occupations includes all occupations in the U.S. Economy.
Source: U.S. Bureau of Labor Statistics, Office of Occupational Statistics and Employment Projections

Records and information managers develop, monitor, and manage an organization's records. They provide information to executive management, and they ensure that employees throughout the organization follow information and records management guidelines. They may direct the operations of on-site or off-site records facilities. They should be familiar with the technology that is used to manage both physical and electronic records. Records and information managers also work closely with an organization's attorneys, technology, and business operations personnel.

Work Environment

Administrative services managers held about 287,300 jobs in 2014. The industries that employed the most administrative services managers were as follows:

Educational services; state, local, and private	14%
Healthcare and social assistance	13
State and local government, excluding education and hospitals	11
Professional, scientific, and technical services	9
Finance and insurance	8

They sometimes make site visits around the building, go outdoors to supervise groundskeeping activities, or inspect other facilities under their management.

Work Schedules. Most administrative services managers worked full time in 2014. About 1 in 4 worked more than 40 hours per week. Facility managers often are on call to address a variety of problems that can arise in a facility during nonworking hours.

Education/Training

Educational requirements vary by the type of organization and the work performed. Administrative services managers must have related work experience.

Education. A bachelor's degree is typically required for someone to become an administrative services manager. However, some jobseekers may be able to enter the occupation with a high school diploma. Those with a bachelor's degree typically study business, engineering, facility management, or information management.

Licenses, Certifications, and Registrations. The International Facility Management Association offers a competency-based professional certification program for administrative services managers. Completing this program may give prospective job candidates an advantage. The program has two levels: the Facilities Management Professional (FMP) certification and the Certified Facility Manager (CFM) certification. People entering the profession can get the FMP as a steppingstone to the CFM. For the CFM, applicants must meet certain educational and experience requirements. The CFM must be renewed every 3 years by completing continuing education and professional development requirements.

For records and information managers, the Institute of Certified Records Managers offers the Certified Records Manager (CRM) certification. For those specializing in information governance, ARMA International offers the Information Governance Professional (IGP) certification.

Work Experience in a Related Occupation. Administrative services managers must have related work experience reflecting managerial and leadership abilities. For example, contract administrators need experience in purchasing and sales, as well as knowledge of the variety of supplies, machinery, and equipment that their organization uses. Managers who are concerned with supply, inventory, and distribution should be experienced in receiving, warehousing, packaging, shipping, transportation, and related operations.

Advancement. Advancement of facility managers is based on the practices and size of individual organizations. Some facility managers transfer among departments within an organization or work their way up from technical positions. Others advance through a progression of facility management positions that offer additional responsibilities. Advancement is easier in large organizations that employ several levels and types of administrative services managers.

A master's degree in business administration or a related field can enhance a manager's opportunities to advance to a higher level position, such as director of administrative services. Some experienced managers may join or establish a management consulting firm to provide administrative management services to other organizations on a contract basis.

Employment Projections Data for Administrative Services Managers

Occupational Title	SOC Code	Employment, 2014	Projected Employment, 2024	Change, 2014–2024 Percent	Change, 2014–2024 Numeric
Administrative services managers	11-3011	287,300	310,800	8	23,500

Source: U.S. Bureau of Labor Statistics, Employment Projections Program

Similar Occupations. This table shows a list of occupations with job duties that are similar to those of administrative services managers.

Occupations	Entry-level Education	2014 Median Pay	Projected Job Growth	Average Annual Openings
Buyers and Purchasing Agents	Bachelor's degree	$58,520	2%	720
Cost Estimators	Bachelor's degree	$60,050	9%	1,870
Property, Real Estate, and Community Association Managers	High school diploma or equivalent	$54,270	8%	2,530
Top Executives	Bachelor's degree	$102,750	6%	14,700

Important Qualities

Analytical skills. Administrative services managers must be able to review an organization's procedures and find ways to improve efficiency.

Communication skills. Much of an administrative services manager's time is spent working with other people. Therefore, communication is a key quality.

Detail oriented. Administrative services managers must pay attention to details. This quality is necessary across a range of tasks, from ensuring that the organization complies with building codes to managing the process of buying equipment.

Leadership skills. In managing workers and coordinating administrative duties, administrative services managers must be able to motivate employees and deal with issues that may arise.

Pay

The median annual wage for administrative services managers was $83,790 in May 2014. The median wage is the wage at which half the workers in an occupation earned more than that amount and half earned less. The lowest 10 percent earned less than $45,590, and the highest 10 percent earned more than $149,180.

In May 2014, the median annual wages for administrative services managers in the top industries in which they worked were as follows:

Finance and insurance $95,720
Professional, scientific, and technical services 94,040
State and local government, excluding education and hospitals 81,900
Educational services; state, local, and private 80,180
Healthcare and social assistance 78,180

Job Outlook

Employment of administrative services managers is projected to grow 8 percent from 2014 to 2024, about as fast as the average for all occupations. Administrative tasks, including facility management and records and information management, will remain important in a wide range of industries.

A greater focus on the environmental impact and energy efficiency of buildings will keep facility managers in demand. Improving energy efficiency can reduce costs and often is required by regulation. For example, building codes typically ensure that buildings meet environmental standards. Facility managers will be needed to oversee these improvements, in areas from heating and air-conditioning systems to roofing. In addition, facility managers will be needed to plan for natural disasters, ensuring that any damage to a building will be minimal and that the organization can get back to work quickly.

Technology also is expected to affect the work of facility managers in upcoming years. "Smart building" technology will provide facility managers with timely and detailed information, such as equipment failure alerts and reminders to perform maintenance. This information will allow facility managers to complete their work more efficiently and may reduce the total number of managers needed to perform these tasks.

Contract administrators also are expected to be in demand as organizations contract out many services, such as food services, janitorial services, grounds maintenance, and equipment repair.

Records and information managers also are expected to see employment growth. Demand is expected to be particularly strong for those working in "information governance," which includes the privacy and legal aspects of records management. As new technologies such as cloud computing and mobile devices continue to be introduced, records and information managers will have a critical role in helping organizations address the impact of the new technology on the organization's records and information management practices.

Job Prospects. Applicants will likely face strong competition for the limited number of higher level administrative services management jobs. However, an increase in the expected number of retirements in upcoming years should produce more job openings. In addition, competition should be less intense for lower level management jobs. Job prospects also are expected to be better for those who can manage a wide range of responsibilities than for those who specialize in particular functions.

Contacts for More Information

For more information about facility management, as well as the Certified Facility Manager designation, visit

➤ International Facility Management Association (www.ifma.org)

For more information about records and information management, visit

➤ ARMA International (www.arma.org)
➤ Institute of Certified Records Managers (www.icrm.org)

O*NET

➤ Administrative Services Managers (11-3011.00)

Advertising, Promotions, and Marketing Managers

- **2014 Median Pay** .... $123,450 per year; $59.35 per hour
- **Typical Entry-Level Education** .... Bachelor's degree
- **Work Experience in a Related Occupation** .... See Education/Training
- **On-the-job Training** .... None
- **Number of Jobs, 2014** 225,200
- **Job Outlook, 2014–24** .... 9% (Faster than average)
- **Employment Change, 2014–24** 19,700

What Advertising, Promotions, and Marketing Managers Do

Advertising, promotions, and marketing managers plan programs to generate interest in products or services. They work with art directors, sales agents, and financial staff members.

Duties. Advertising, promotions, and marketing managers typically do the following:

- Work with department heads or staff to discuss topics such as budgets and contracts, marketing plans, and the selection of advertising media
- Plan promotional campaigns such as contests, coupons, or giveaways
- Plan advertising campaigns, including which media to advertise in, such as radio, television, print, online media, and billboards
- Negotiate advertising contracts
- Evaluate the look and feel of websites used in campaigns or layouts, which are sketches or plans for an advertisement
- Initiate market research studies and analyze their findings to understand customer and market opportunities for businesses
- Develop pricing strategies for products or services marketed to the target customers of a firm
- Meet with clients to provide marketing or technical advice
- Direct the hiring of advertising, promotions, and marketing staff and oversee their daily activities

Advertising managers create interest among potential buyers of a product or service. They do this for a department, for an entire organization, or on a project basis (referred to as an account). Advertising managers work in advertising agencies that put together advertising campaigns for clients, in media firms that sell advertising space or time, and in organizations that advertise heavily.

Advertising managers work with sales staff and others to generate ideas for an advertising campaign. They oversee the staff that develops the advertising. They work with the finance department to prepare a budget and cost estimates for the campaign.

Often, advertising managers serve as liaisons between the client and the advertising or promotion agency that develops and places the ads. In larger organizations with extensive advertising departments, different advertising managers may oversee in-house accounts and creative and media services departments.

In addition, some advertising managers specialize in a particular field or type of advertising. For example, *media directors* determine the way in which an advertising campaign reaches customers. They can use any or all of various media, including radio, television, newspapers, magazines, the Internet, and outdoor signs.

Advertising managers known as *account executives* manage clients' accounts, but they are not responsible for developing or supervising the creation or presentation of advertising. That task becomes the work of the creative services department.

Promotions managers direct programs that combine advertising with purchasing incentives to increase sales. Often, the programs use direct mail, inserts in newspapers, Internet advertisements, in-store displays, product endorsements, or special events to target customers. Purchasing incentives may include discounts, samples, gifts, rebates, coupons, sweepstakes, or contests.

Marketing managers estimate the demand for products and services that an organization and its competitors offer. They identify potential markets for the organization's products.

Advertising, promotions, and marketing managers often serve as liaisons between the firm requiring the advertising and an advertising or promotion agency that develops and places the ads.

Marketing managers also develop pricing strategies to help organizations maximize their profits and market share while ensuring that the organizations' customers are satisfied. They work with sales, public relations, and product development staff.

For example, a marketing manager may monitor trends that indicate the need for a new product or service. Then he or she oversees the development of that product or service. For more information on sales or public relations, see the profiles on sales managers, public relations and fundraising managers, public relations specialists, and market research analysts.

Work Environment

Advertising and promotions managers held about 31,000 jobs in 2014. The industries that employed the most advertising and promotions managers in 2014 were as follows:

Advertising, public relations, and related services	31%
Information	17
Retail trade	9
Management of companies and enterprises	8
Wholesale trade	6

Marketing managers held about 194,300 jobs in 2014. The industries that employed the most marketing managers in 2014 were as follows:

Professional, scientific, and technical services	21%
Management of companies and enterprises	17
Manufacturing	12
Finance and insurance	10
Wholesale trade	9

Median Annual Wages, May 2014

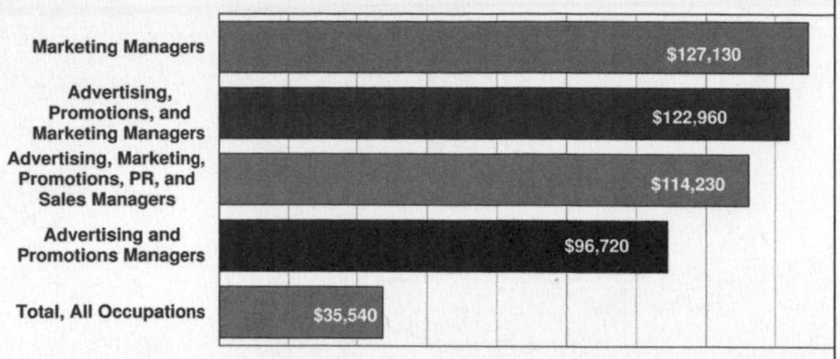

Note: All Occupations includes all occupations in the U.S. Economy.
Source: U.S. Bureau of Labor Statistics, Occupational Employment Statistics

Percent Change in Employment, Projected 2014–2024

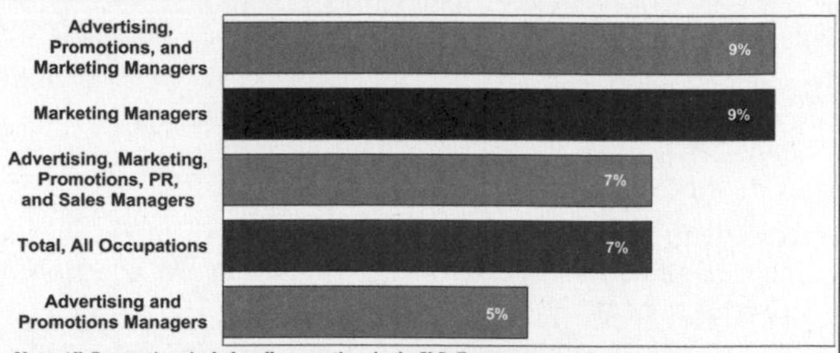

Note: All Occupations includes all occupations in the U.S. Economy.
Source: U.S. Bureau of Labor Statistics, Office of Occupational Statistics and Employment Projections

Because the work of advertising, promotions, and marketing managers directly affects a firm's revenue, people in these occupations typically work closely with top executives. The jobs of advertising, promotions, and marketing managers are usually stressful, particularly near deadlines. They may travel to meet with clients or media representatives.

Work Schedules. Most advertising, promotions, and marketing managers work full time. About 2 in 5 advertising and promotions managers worked more than 40 hours per week in 2014.

Education/Training

A bachelor's degree is required for most advertising, promotions, and marketing management positions. These managers typically have work experience in advertising, marketing, promotions, or sales.

Education. A bachelor's degree is required for most advertising, promotions, and marketing management positions. For advertising management positions, some employers prefer a bachelor's degree in advertising or journalism. A relevant course of study might include classes in marketing, consumer behavior, market research, sales, communication methods and technology, visual arts, art history, and photography.

Most marketing managers need a bachelor's degree. Courses in business law, management, economics, finance, computer science, mathematics, and statistics are advantageous. For example, courses in computer science are helpful in developing an approach to maximize online traffic, by utilizing online search results, because maximizing such traffic is critical for digital advertisements and promotions. In addition, completing an internship while in school can be useful.

Work Experience in a Related Occupation. Advertising, promotional, and marketing managers typically have work experience in advertising, marketing, promotions, or sales. For example, many managers are former sales representatives; buyers or purchasing agents; or public relations specialists.

Important Qualities

Analytical skills. Advertising, promotions, and marketing managers must be able to analyze industry trends to determine the most promising strategies for their organization.

Communication skills. Managers must be able to communicate effectively with a broad-based team made up of other managers or staff members during the advertising, promotions, and marketing process. They must also be able to communicate persuasively with the public.

Creativity. Advertising, promotions, and marketing managers must be able to generate new and imaginative ideas.

Decision-making skills. Managers often must choose between competing advertising and marketing strategies put forward by staff.

Interpersonal skills. These managers must deal with a range of people in different roles, both inside and outside the organization.

Organizational skills. Advertising, promotions, and marketing managers must manage their time and budget efficiently while directing and motivating staff members.

Pay

The median annual wage for advertising and promotions managers was $96,720 in May 2014. The median wage is the wage at which half the workers in an occupation earned more than that amount and half earned less. The lowest 10 percent earned less than $45,060, and the highest 10 percent earned more than $187,200.

The median annual wage for marketing managers was $127,130 in May 2014. The lowest 10 percent earned less than $65,980, and the highest 10 percent earned more than $187,200.

Job Outlook

Employment of advertising and promotions managers is projected to grow 5 percent from 2014 to 2024, about as fast as the average for all occupations.

Employment of marketing managers is projected to grow 9 percent from 2014 to 2024, faster than the average for all occupations.

Employment Projections Data for Advertising, Promotions, and Marketing Managers

Occupational Title	SOC Code	Employment, 2014	Projected Employment, 2024	Change, 2014–2024 Percent	Change, 2014–2024 Numeric
Advertising, promotions, and marketing managers	—	225,200	244,900	9	19,700
Advertising and promotions managers	11-2011	31,000	32,400	5	1,500
Marketing managers	11-2021	194,300	212,500	9	18,200

Source: U.S. Bureau of Labor Statistics, Employment Projections Program

Similar Occupations. This table shows a list of occupations with job duties that are similar to those of advertising, promotions, and marketing managers.

Occupations	Entry-level Education	2014 Median Pay	Projected Job Growth	Average Annual Openings
Advertising Sales Agents	High school diploma or equivalent	$47,890	-3%	-450
Art Directors	Bachelor's degree	$85,610	2%	180
Editors	Bachelor's degree	$54,890	-5%	-620
Financial Managers	Bachelor's degree	$115,320	7%	3,770
Graphic Designers	Bachelor's degree	$45,900	1%	360
Market Research Analysts	Bachelor's degree	$61,290	19%	9,230
Public Relations and Fundraising Managers	Bachelor's degree	$101,510	7%	470
Public Relations Specialists	Bachelor's degree	$55,680	6%	1,490
Sales Managers	Bachelor's degree	$110,660	5%	1,900

Advertising, promotional, and marketing campaigns are expected to continue being essential as organizations seek to maintain and expand their market share. Advertising and promotions managers will be needed to plan, direct, and coordinate advertising and promotional campaigns, as well as to introduce new products into the marketplace.

Newspaper publishers, one of the top-employing industries of advertising and promotions managers, is projected to decline over the projection period. The continued rise of electronic media will result in decreasing demand for print newspapers. However, advertising and promotions managers are expected to see employment growth in other areas, in which they will be needed to manage digital media campaigns, which often target customers through the use of websites, social media, or live chats.

Through the Internet, advertising campaigns can reach a target audience across many platforms. This greater reach can increase the scale of the campaigns that advertising and promotions managers oversee. With better advertising management software, advertising and promotions managers can control these campaigns more easily, increasing their productivity, and thereby limiting the potential employment growth.

Because marketing managers and their departments are important to an organization's revenue, marketing managers are less likely to be let go than other types of managers. Marketing managers will continue to be in demand as organizations seek to market their products to specific customers and localities.

Job Prospects. Advertising, promotions, and marketing manager positions are highly desirable and are often sought by other managers and experienced professionals. As a result, strong competition is expected for these occupations. With Internet-based advertising becoming more important, advertising managers who can navigate the digital world should have the best prospects.

Contacts for More Information

For more information about advertising managers, visit

➤ American Association of Advertising Agencies (www.aaaa.org)

O*NET

➤ Advertising and Promotions Managers (11-2011.00)
➤ Green Marketers (11-2011.01)
➤ Marketing Managers (11-2021.00)

Architectural and Engineering Managers

- **2014 Median Pay** .... $130,620 per year $62.80 per hour
- **Typical Entry-Level Education** .... Bachelor's degree
- **Work Experience in a Related Occupation** .... 5 years or more
- **On-the-job Training** .... None
- **Number of Jobs, 2014** 182,100
- **Job Outlook, 2014–24** .... 2% (Slower than average)
- **Employment Change, 2014–24** 3,700

What Architectural and Engineering Managers Do

Architectural and engineering managers plan, direct, and coordinate activities in architectural and engineering companies.

Duties. Architectural and engineering managers typically do the following:

- Make detailed plans for the development of new products and designs
- Determine staff, training, and equipment needs
- Propose budgets for projects and programs
- Hire and supervise staff
- Lead research and development projects to produce new products, processes, or designs
- Check the technical accuracy of their staff's work
- Ensure the soundness of methods their staff uses
- Coordinate work with other staff and managers

Architectural and engineering managers use their knowledge of architecture or engineering to oversee a variety of activities. They may direct and coordinate production, operations, quality assurance, testing, or maintenance at manufacturing sites, industrial plants, engineering services firms, and research and development laboratories.

Architectural and engineering managers are responsible for developing the overall concept of a new product or for solving the technical problems that prevent the completion of a project. To

In addition to technical knowledge, architectural and engineering managers need administrative and communication skills.

accomplish this, they must determine technical goals and produce detailed plans.

Architectural and engineering managers spend a great deal of time coordinating the activities of their staff with the activities of other staff or organizations. They often confer with other managers, including those in finance, production, and marketing, as well as with contractors and equipment and materials suppliers.

In addition, architectural and engineering managers must know how to prepare budgets, hire staff, and supervise employees. They propose budgets for projects and programs and determine staff, training, and equipment needs. These managers must also hire people and assign them specific parts of each project to carry out. Architectural and engineering managers supervise the work of their employees, set schedules, and create administrative procedures.

Work Environment

Architectural and engineering managers held about 182,100 jobs in 2014. The industries that employed the most architectural and engineering managers were as follows:

Manufacturing	36%
Architectural, engineering, and related services	25
Government	10
Management of companies and enterprises	5
Scientific research and development services	5

Most architectural and engineering managers work in offices, although some may also work in laboratories and industrial production plants or at construction sites.

Work Schedules. Most architectural and engineering managers work full time, and about half worked more than 40 hours a week in 2014. These managers are often under considerable pressure to meet deadlines and budgets.

Education/Training

Architectural and engineering managers typically need at least a bachelor's degree and considerable work experience as an architect or engineer.

Education. Most architectural and engineering managers have at least a bachelor's degree in an engineering specialty or a professional degree in architecture.

Many also gain business management skills by completing a master's degree in engineering management (MEM or MsEM) or technology management (MSTM) or a master's degree in business administration (MBA). Some workers earn their master's degree before advancing to management positions, and others earn it while they work as a manager. Employers will sometimes pay for such education. Typically, those who prefer to manage in technical areas pursue an MsEM or MSTM and those interested in more general management skills earn an MBA.

Engineering management programs usually include classes in accounting, engineering economics, financial management, industrial and human resources management, and quality control.

Technology management programs typically provide instruction in production and operations management, project management, computer applications, quality control, safety and health issues, statistics, and general management principles.

Work Experience in a Related Occupation. Managers advance to their positions after years of employment as an architect or engineer. They usually have experience working on difficult or complex projects, developing designs, solving problems, and making decisions. Before moving up to a management position, they also typically gain experience leading engineering teams.

Important Qualities

Analytical skills. Architectural and engineering managers must evaluate information carefully and solve complex problems.

Communication skills. Architectural and engineering managers oversee staff and work together with other levels of management. They must communicate orders effectively and lead teams to meet goals.

Detail oriented. Architectural and engineering managers must pay attention to detail. Their duties require an understanding of complex systems since a minor error can cause major problems.

Median Annual Wages, May 2014

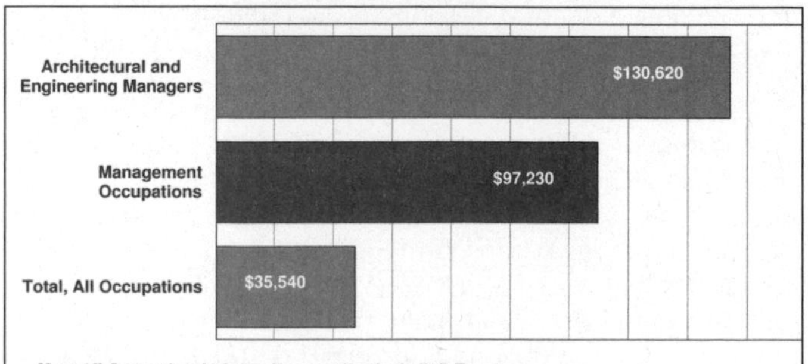

Note: All Occupations includes all occupations in the U.S. Economy.
Source: U.S. Bureau of Labor Statistics, Occupational Employment Statistics

Percent Change in Employment, Projected 2014–2024

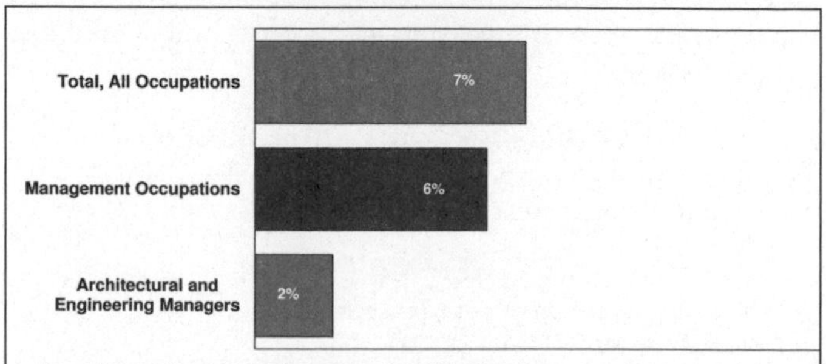

Note: All Occupations includes all occupations in the U.S. Economy.
Source: U.S. Bureau of Labor Statistics, Office of Occupational Statistics and Employment Projections

Employment Projections Data for Architectural and Engineering Managers

Occupational Title	SOC Code	Employment, 2014	Projected Employment, 2024	Change, 2014–2024	
				Percent	Numeric
Architectural and engineering managers...............................	11-9041	182,100	185,800	2	3,700

Source: U.S. Bureau of Labor Statistics, Employment Projections Program

Math skills. Architectural and engineering managers use calculus and other advanced mathematics to develop new products and processes.

Organizational skills. Architectural and engineering managers keep track of many workers, schedules, and budgets simultaneously.

Pay

The median annual wage for architectural and engineering managers was $130,620 in May 2014. The median wage is the wage at which half the workers in an occupation earned more than that amount and half earned less. The lowest 10 percent earned less than $83,580, and the highest 10 percent earned more than $187,200.

In May 2014, the median annual wages for architectural and engineering managers in the top industries in which they worked were as follows:

Scientific research and development services	$154,040
Management of companies and enterprises.......................	134,840
Manufacturing...	130,690
Architectural, engineering, and related services	128,350
Government..	122,590

In addition, architectural and engineering managers, especially those at higher levels, often receive more benefits—such as expense accounts and bonuses—than workers who are not managers.

Job Outlook

Employment of architectural and engineering managers is projected to grow 2 percent from 2014 to 2024, slower than the average for all occupations. Employment growth will largely reflect the growth of the industries in which these managers are employed.

For example, employment of architectural and engineering managers in the engineering services industry is projected to grow 12 percent from 2014 to 2024, adding the most new architectural and engineering manager jobs. Engineering services is composed of consulting firms that provide services to many different industries. Civil engineering services—the construction of large buildings, roads, and other infrastructure projects—are the most common services this industry provides. Demand for these services is expected to be high as the nation's aging infrastructure needs repair and expansion. Mechanical and electrical engineering services are also commonly done by this industry, and these services will continue to be needed for many different projects.

However, employment in manufacturing—the largest industry employing architectural and engineering managers—is projected

Similar Occupations. This table shows a list of occupations with job duties that are similar to those of architectural and engineering managers.

Occupations	Entry-level Education	2014 Median Pay	Projected Job Growth	Average Annual Openings
Aerospace Engineers	Bachelor's degree	$105,380	-2%	-160
Agricultural Engineers	Bachelor's degree	$71,730	4%	10
Architects	Bachelor's degree	$74,520	7%	780
Biomedical Engineers	Bachelor's degree	$86,950	23%	510
Chemical Engineers	Bachelor's degree	$96,940	2%	60
Civil Engineers	Bachelor's degree	$82,050	8%	2,360
Construction Managers	Bachelor's degree	$85,630	5%	1,780
Electrical and Electronics Engineers	Bachelor's degree	$93,260	0%	-10
Environmental Engineers	Bachelor's degree	$83,360	12%	680
Health and Safety Engineers	Bachelor's degree	$81,830	6%	160
Industrial Engineers	Bachelor's degree	$81,490	1%	210
Industrial Production Managers	Bachelor's degree	$92,470	-4%	-630
Materials Engineers	Bachelor's degree	$87,690	1%	30
Mechanical Engineers	Bachelor's degree	$83,060	5%	1,460
Natural Sciences Managers	Bachelor's degree	$120,050	3%	180
Nuclear Engineers	Bachelor's degree	$100,470	-4%	-70
Petroleum Engineers	Bachelor's degree	$130,050	10%	340

to decline 7 percent from 2014 to 2024, impeding overall growth of the occupation.

Job Prospects. Because these jobs are highly desirable, candidates can expect very strong competition for openings.

Those with technical knowledge, strong communication skills, and years of related work experience, especially working on complex projects, will likely be in the best position to become managers.

In addition, because architectural and engineering managers are involved in the financial, production, and marketing activities of their firm, business management skills can be beneficial for those seeking management positions.

Contacts for More Information

For information on architecture and engineering management programs, visit

➤ American Institute of Architects (www.aia.org)

➤ ABET (www.abet.org)

➤ Association of Technology, Management, and Applied Engineering (http://atmae.org)

O*NET

➤ Architectural and Engineering Managers (11-9041.00)

➤ Biofuels/Biodiesel Technology and Product Development Managers (11-9041.01)

Compensation and Benefits Managers

- **2014 Median Pay** .... $108,070 per year, $51.96 per hour
- **Typical Entry-Level Education** .... Bachelor's degree
- **Work Experience in a Related Occupation** .... 5 years or more
- **On-the-job Training** .... None
- **Number of Jobs, 2014** 16,900
- **Job Outlook, 2014–24** .... 6% (As fast as average)
- **Employment Change, 2014–24** 1,100

What Compensation and Benefits Managers Do

Compensation managers plan, develop, and oversee programs to determine how much an organization pays its employees and how employees are paid. Benefits managers plan, direct, and coordinate retirement plans, health insurance, and other benefits that an organization offers its employees.

Duties. Compensation and benefits managers typically do the following:

- Set the organization's pay structure and benefits offerings
- Determine competitive wage rates and develop or modify compensation plans
- Evaluate employee benefits policies to assess whether they are current, competitive, and legal
- Choose and manage outside partners, such as benefits vendors, insurance brokers, and investment managers
- Coordinate and supervise the work activities of specialists and support staff
- Oversee the distribution of pay and benefits information to the organization's employees
- Ensure that pay and benefits plans comply with federal and state regulations
- Prepare a program budget and keep operations within budget

Although some managers administer both the compensation and benefits programs in an organization, other managers—particularly at large organizations—often specialize and oversee one or the other. All managers, however, routinely meet with senior staff, managers of other human resources departments, and the financial officers of their organization. They provide expertise and make recommendations on compensation and benefits policies, programs, and plans.

In addition to their administrative responsibilities, compensation and benefits managers also have technical and analytical duties. For example, they may perform complex data analysis to determine the best pay and benefits plans for an organization. They may also monitor trends affecting pay and benefits and assess how their organization can improve its practices or policies. Using a variety of analytical, database, and presentation software, managers draw conclusions, present their findings, and make recommendations to other managers in the organization.

Compensation managers are responsible for managing an organization's pay structure. They monitor market conditions and government regulations to ensure their pay rates are current and competitive. They analyze data on wages and salaries, and they evaluate how their organization's pay structure compares with that of other companies. Compensation managers use this information to maintain or develop pay scales for an organization.

Some also design pay-for-performance plans, which include guidelines for bonuses and incentive pay. They also may help determine commission rates and other incentives for sales staff.

Benefits managers administer a company's employee benefits program, which includes retirement plans, leave policies, wellness programs, and insurance policies such as health, life, and disability. They select benefits vendors and manage enrollment, renewal, and delivery of benefits to the organization's employees. They must frequently monitor government regulations and market trends to ensure that their programs are current, competitive, and legal.

Compensation and benefits managers explain company procedures and benefits to new employees.

Median Annual Wages, May 2014

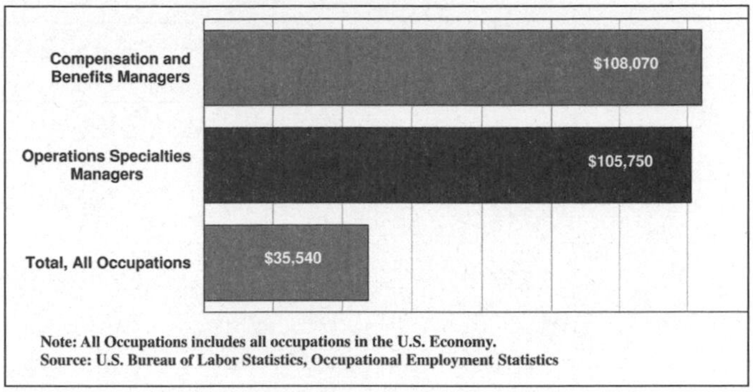

Percent Change in Employment, Projected 2014–2024

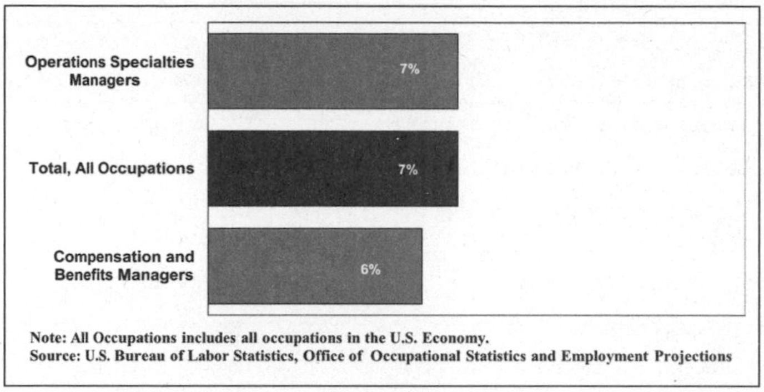

Work Environment

Compensation and benefits managers held about 16,900 jobs in 2014 and work in nearly every industry. Most of these managers work in offices.

Work Schedules. Most compensation and benefits managers work full time. About 1 in 3 worked more than 40 hours per week in 2014. They may work more hours during peak times to meet deadlines, especially during the benefits enrollment period of their organization.

Education/Training

Candidates need a combination of education and related work experience to become a compensation and benefits manager.

Education. Compensation and benefits managers need at least a bachelor's degree for most positions, and some jobs require a master's degree. Because not all undergraduate programs offer a degree in human resources, managers often have a bachelor's degree in business administration, business management, finance, or a related field.

Some employers prefer to hire managers who have a master's degree, particularly one with a concentration in human resources management, finance, or business administration (MBA).

Work Experience in a Related Occupation. Related work experience is essential for compensation and benefits managers. Managers often specialize in either compensation or benefits, depending on the type of experience they gain in previous jobs. For example, compensation and benefits managers often start out as compensation, benefits, and job analysis specialists. Work experience in other human resource fields, finance, or management is also helpful for getting a job as a compensation and benefits manager.

Licenses, Certifications, and Registrations. Although compensation and benefits managers are not legally required to be certified, certification can show expertise and credibility. Many employers prefer to hire certified candidates, and some positions may require certification.

Certification programs for management positions often require several years of related work experience to qualify for the certifying exam. Many professional associations for human resources workers offer certifications. Some associations, including the International Foundation of Employee Benefit Plans and WorldatWork, offer certification programs that specialize in compensation and benefits. Others, including the HR Certification Institute, offer general human resources credentials.

Important Qualities

Analytical skills. Compensation and benefits managers must analyze data on salaries and the cost of benefits, and assess and devise programs that best fit an organization and its employees.

Business acumen. Compensation and benefits managers must manage a budget, build a case for their recommendations, and understand how compensation and benefits plans affect the company's finances.

Communication skills. Compensation and benefits managers must direct staff, give presentations, and work with colleagues. For example, they may present the advantages of a certain pay scale to management and address any concerns.

Decision-making skills. Compensation and benefits managers must weigh the strengths and weaknesses of different pay structures and benefits plans and choose the best options for an organization.

Leadership skills. Compensation and benefits managers must coordinate the work activities of their staff and properly administer compensation and benefits programs, ensuring work is completed accurately and on schedule.

Writing skills. Compensation and benefits managers must prepare clearly written informational materials on compensation and benefits plans for an organization's employees. They must also clearly convey recommendations in written reports.

Pay

The median annual wage for compensation and benefits managers was $108,070 in May 2014. The median wage is the wage at which half the workers in an occupation earned more than that amount and half earned less. The lowest 10 percent earned less than $58,370, and the highest 10 percent earned more than $187,200.

Employment Projections Data for Compensation and Benefits Managers

Occupational Title	SOC Code	Employment, 2014	Projected Employment, 2024	Change, 2014–2024 Percent	Change, 2014–2024 Numeric
Compensation and benefits managers....................................	11-3111	16,900	18,000	6	1,100

Source: U.S. Bureau of Labor Statistics, Employment Projections Program

Similar Occupations. This table shows a list of occupations with job duties that are similar to those of compensation and benefits managers.

Occupations	Entry-level Education	2014 Median Pay	Projected Job Growth	Average Annual Openings
Administrative Services Managers	Bachelor's degree	$83,790	8%	2,350
Buyers and Purchasing Agents	Bachelor's degree	$58,520	2%	720
Compensation, Benefits, and Job Analysis Specialists	Bachelor's degree	$60,600	4%	340
Financial Managers	Bachelor's degree	$115,320	7%	3,770
Human Resources Managers	Bachelor's degree	$102,780	9%	1,080
Human Resources Specialists	Bachelor's degree	$57,420	5%	2,200
Top Executives	Bachelor's degree	$102,750	6%	14,700
Training and Development Managers	Bachelor's degree	$101,930	7%	230
Training and Development Specialists	Bachelor's degree	$57,340	7%	1,890

Job Outlook

Employment of compensation and benefits managers is projected to grow 6 percent from 2014 to 2024, about as fast as the average for all occupations.

As organizations focus on reducing compensation and benefits costs, many have established increasingly complex plans that include, for example, pay-for-performance strategies and health and wellness programs. Organizations will need managers to evaluate and direct these compensation and benefits policies and plans.

Due to healthcare reform and rising healthcare costs, organizations will need the expertise of benefits managers when choosing, updating, and administering their benefits policies. Similarly, compensation managers will be needed to analyze compensation policies and design competitive compensation packages.

Many organizations increasingly contract out a portion of their compensation and benefits functions to human resources consulting firms in order to reduce costs and gain access to technical expertise. For example, to reduce administrative costs, organizations commonly use an outside vendor for processing payroll and insurance claims. These consulting firms are able to automate tasks and operate call centers to handle employee questions, thereby reducing the need for compensation and benefits managers.

Job Prospects. Job seekers can expect very strong competition for available jobs because compensation and benefits manager positions typically offer high pay, and job openings often attract many qualified applicants. Those who have a master's degree, certification, and extensive experience working with compensation or benefits plans should have the best job opportunities.

Contacts for More Information

For more information about compensation and benefits managers, including certification, visit

➤ International Foundation of Employee Benefit Plans (www.ifebp.org)

➤ WorldatWork (www.worldatwork.org)

For more information about human resources careers, visit

➤ Society for Human Resource Management (www.shrm.org)

For more information about human resources certifications, visit

➤ HR Certification Institute (www.hrci.org)

O*NET

➤ Compensation and Benefits Managers (11-3111.00)

Computer and Information Systems Managers

- **2014 Median Pay** .... $127,640 per year $61.37 per hour
- **Typical Entry-Level Education** .... Bachelor's degree
- **Work Experience in a Related Occupation** .... 5 years or more
- **On-the-job Training** .... None
- **Number of Jobs, 2014** 348,500
- **Job Outlook, 2014–24** .... 15% (Much faster than average)
- **Employment Change, 2014–24** 53,700

What Computer and Information Systems Managers Do

Computer and information systems managers, often called information technology (IT) managers or IT project managers, plan, coordinate, and direct computer-related activities in an organization. They help determine the information technology goals of an organization and are responsible for implementing computer systems to meet those goals.

Duties. Computer and information systems managers typically do the following:

- Analyze their organization's computer needs and recommend possible upgrades for top executives to consider
- Plan and direct the installation and maintenance of computer hardware and software
- Ensure the security of an organization's network and electronic documents
- Assess the costs and benefits of new projects and justify funding on projects to top executives
- Learn about new technology and look for ways to upgrade their organization's computer systems
- Determine short- and long-term personnel needs for their department
- Plan and direct the work of other IT professionals, including computer systems analysts, software developers, information security analysts, and computer support specialists

- Negotiate with vendors to get the highest level of service for their organization's technology

Few managers carry out all of these duties. There are various types of computer and information systems managers, and the specific duties of each are determined by the size and structure of the firm. Smaller firms may not employ every type of manager.

The following are examples of types of computer and information systems managers:

Chief information officers (CIOs) are responsible for the overall technology strategy of their organizations. They help determine the technology or information goals of an organization and then oversee implementation of technology to meet those goals.

CIOs may focus on a specific area, such as electronic data processing or information systems, but CIOs tend to focus more on long-term or big picture issues. At small organizations a CIO has more direct control over the IT department, and at larger organizations other managers under the CIO may handle the day-to-day activities of the IT department.

CIOs who do not have technical expertise and who focus solely on a company's business aspects are included in a separate profile on top executives.

Chief technology officers (CTOs) evaluate new technology and determine how it can help their organization. When both CIOs and CTOs are present, the CTO usually has more technical expertise.

The CTO is responsible for designing and recommending the appropriate technology solutions to support the policies and directives issued by the CIO. CTOs also work with different departments to implement the organization's technology plans.

The CTO usually reports directly to the CIO and may be responsible for overseeing the development of new technologies or other research and development activities. When a company does not have a CIO, the CTO determines the overall technology strategy for the firm and presents it to top executives.

IT directors, including management information systems (MIS) directors, are in charge of their organizations' information technology (IT) departments, and they directly supervise other employees. IT directors help to determine the business requirements for IT systems, and they implement the policies that have been chosen by top executives. IT directors often have a direct role in hiring members of the IT department. It is their job to ensure the availability of data and network services by coordinating IT activities. IT directors also oversee the financial aspects of their department, such as budgeting.

IT security managers oversee their organizations' network and data security. They work with top executives to plan security policies and promote a culture of information security throughout the organization. They develop programs to keep employees aware

Computer and information systems managers oversee a variety of workers, including systems analysts, support specialists, and software engineers.

of security threats. These managers must keep up to date on IT security measures. They also supervise investigations if there is a security violation.

Work Environment

Computer and information systems managers held about 348,500 jobs in 2014. The industries that employed the most computer and information systems managers were as follows:

Computer systems design and related services	20%
Finance and insurance	12
Information	11
Management of companies and enterprises	10
Manufacturing	9

As network speeds increase, telecommuting is becoming more common. Although few managers can work remotely, many have to supervise employees who work from home.

Work Schedules. Most computer and information systems managers work full time. If problems arise, managers must work overtime to come up with solutions. In 2014, about 2 in 5 worked more than 40 hours per week.

Education/Training

Typically, a bachelor's degree in computer or information science, plus related work experience, is required. Many computer and information systems managers also have a graduate degree.

Median Annual Wages, May 2014

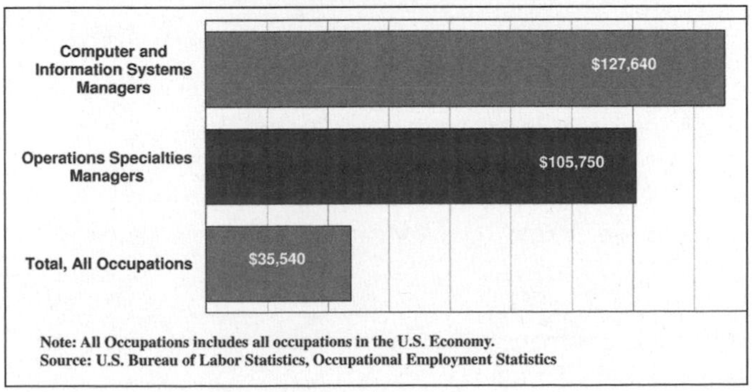

Percent Change in Employment, Projected 2014–2024

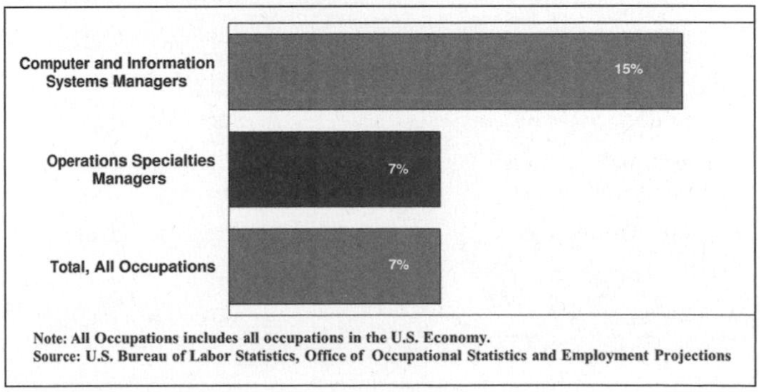

Employment Projections Data for Computer and Information Systems Managers

Occupational Title	SOC Code	Employment, 2014	Projected Employment, 2024	Change, 2014–2024	
				Percent	Numeric
Computer and information systems managers	11-3021	348,500	402,200	15	53,700

Source: U.S. Bureau of Labor Statistics, Employment Projections Program

Education. Computer and information systems managers normally must have a bachelor's degree in a computer- or information science–related field. Such a degree usually takes 4 years to complete and includes courses in computer programming, software development, and mathematics. Management information systems (MIS) programs usually include business classes as well as computer-related ones.

Many organizations require their computer and information systems managers to have a graduate degree as well. A Master of Business Administration (MBA) is common and takes 2 years beyond the undergraduate level to complete. Many people pursuing an MBA take classes while working, an option that can increase the time required to complete that degree.

Work Experience in a Related Occupation. Most jobs for computer and information systems managers require several years of experience in a related information technology (IT) job. Lower level management positions may require only a few years of experience. Directors are more likely to need 5 to 10 years of related work experience. A chief technology officer (CTO), who oversees the technology plan for a large organization, may need more than 15 years of experience in the IT field before being considered for a job.

The number of years of experience required varies with the organization. Generally, smaller or newer companies do not require as much experience as larger or more established ones.

Computer systems are used throughout the economy, and IT employees may gain experience in a variety of industries. However, an applicant's work experience should be in the same industry they are applying to work in. For example, an IT security manager should have previously worked in information security. A hospital IT director should have experience in the healthcare field.

Advancement. Most computer and information systems managers start out as lower level managers and advance to higher positions within the IT department. IT directors or project managers can advance to become CTOs. A CTO or other manager who is especially business minded can advance to become a chief information officer (CIO), the person in charge of all IT-related decisions in an organization. CIOs can advance to become top executives in an organization.

Important Qualities

Analytical skills. IT managers must be able to analyze problems and consider and select the best ways to solve them.

Business skills. IT managers must develop and implement strategic plans to reach the goals of their organizations.

Communication skills. IT managers must be able to explain their work to top executives and give clear instructions to their subordinates.

Decision-making skills. Some IT managers must make important decisions about how to allocate resources in order to reach their organizations' goals.

Leadership skills. IT managers must be able to lead and motivate IT teams or departments so that workers are efficient and effective.

Organizational skills. Some IT managers must coordinate the work of several different IT departments to make the organization run efficiently.

Pay

The median annual wage for computer and information systems managers was $127,640 in May 2014. The median wage is the wage at which half the workers in an occupation earned more than

Similar Occupations. This table shows a list of occupations with job duties that are similar to those of computer and information systems managers.

Occupations	Entry-level Education	2014 Median Pay	Projected Job Growth	Average Annual Openings
Computer and Information Research Scientists	Doctoral or professional degree	$108,360	11%	270
Computer Hardware Engineers	Bachelor's degree	$108,430	3%	240
Computer Network Architects	Bachelor's degree	$98,430	9%	1,270
Computer Programmers	Bachelor's degree	$77,550	-8%	-2,650
Computer Systems Analysts	Bachelor's degree	$82,710	21%	11,860
Database Administrators	Bachelor's degree	$80,280	11%	1,340
Information Security Analysts	Bachelor's degree	$88,890	18%	1,480
Network and Computer Systems Administrators	Bachelor's degree	$75,790	8%	3,020
Software Developers	Bachelor's degree	$97,990	17%	18,660
Top Executives	Bachelor's degree	$102,750	6%	14,700
Web Developers	Associate's degree	$63,490	27%	3,950

that amount and half earned less. The lowest 10 percent earned less than $78,470, and the highest 10 percent earned more than $187,200.

In May 2014, the median annual wages for computer and information systems managers in the top industries in which they worked were as follows:

Information	$143,680
Computer systems design and related services	135,190
Finance and insurance	132,580
Manufacturing	130,970
Management of companies and enterprises	130,790

Job Outlook

Employment of computer and information systems managers is projected to grow 15 percent from 2014 to 2024, much faster than the average for all occupations.

Demand for computer and information systems managers will grow as firms increasingly expand their operations to digital platforms. Computer and information systems managers will be responsible for implementing these goals.

Employment growth will result from the need to bolster cybersecurity in computer and information systems used by businesses. Industries such as retail trade will work to implement more robust security policies as cyber threats increase.

A number of jobs in this occupation are expected to be created in the healthcare industry, which is aggressively implementing information technology. This industry is expected to greatly increase information technology (IT) use, resulting in job growth. In the insurance carriers industry, employment of IT managers is projected to grow 26 percent.

An increase in the popularity of cloud computing may result in firms outsourcing services from on-premise IT departments to cloud-computing companies. This will shift IT services from IT departments in noncomputer industries, such as financial firms or schools, to firms engaged in computer systems design and related services.

Job Prospects. Prospects should be favorable in this occupation because older computer and information systems managers will retire over the decade. Many companies note that it is difficult to find qualified applicants for positions.

Because innovation is fast paced in IT, opportunities should be best for those who have extensive work experience and knowledge of the newest technology.

Contacts for More Information

For more information about computer careers, visit

➤ Association for Computing Machinery (www.acm.org)
➤ CompTIA (www.techamerica.org)
➤ Computing Research Association (www.cra.org)
➤ IEEE Computer Society (www.computer.org)

For more information about opportunities for women pursuing information technology careers, visit

➤ National Center for Women & Information Technology (www.ncwit.org)

O*NET

➤ Computer and Information Systems Managers (11-3021.00)

Construction Managers

- **2014 Median Pay** .... $85,630 per year
  $41.17 per hour
- **Typical Entry-Level Education** .... Bachelor's degree
- **Work Experience in a Related Occupation** .... None
- **On-the-Job Training** ...... Moderate-term on-the-job training
- **Number of Jobs 2014** 373,200
- **Job Outlook, 2014–24** .... 5% (As fast as average)
- **Employment Change, 2014–24** 17,800

What Construction Managers Do

Construction managers plan, coordinate, budget, and supervise construction projects from start to finish.

Duties. Construction managers typically do the following:

- Prepare cost estimates, budgets, and work timetables
- Interpret and explain contracts and technical information to other professionals
- Report work progress and budget matters to clients
- Collaborate with architects, engineers, and other construction specialists
- Select subcontractors and schedule and coordinate their activities
- Respond to work delays, emergencies, and other problems
- Comply with legal requirements, building and safety codes, and other regulations

Construction managers direct and monitor the progress of construction activities, occasionally through construction supervisors or other construction managers.

Construction managers, often called *general contractors* or *project managers*, coordinate and supervise a wide variety of projects, including the building of all types of public, residential, commercial, and industrial structures, as well as roads, memorials, and bridges. Either a general contractor or a construction manager will oversee the construction phase of a project, although a construction manager may also consult with the client during the design phase to help refine construction plans and control costs.

Construction managers oversee specialized contractors and other personnel. They schedule and coordinate all construction processes so that projects meet design specifications. They ensure that projects are completed on time and within budget. Some managers may be responsible for several projects at once—for example, the construction of multiple apartment buildings.

Construction managers work closely with other building specialists, such as architects, civil engineers, and a variety of trade workers, including stonemasons, electricians, and carpenters. Projects may require specialists in everything from structural steel and painting to landscaping, paving roads, and excavating sites. Depending on the project, construction managers may interact with lawyers and local government officials. For example, when working on city-owned property or municipal buildings, managers sometimes confer with city inspectors to ensure that all regulations are met.

For projects too large to be managed by one person, such as office buildings and industrial complexes, a top-level construction manager hires other construction managers to be in charge of different aspects of the project. For example, each construction manager would oversee a specific phase of the project, such as structural foundation, plumbing, or electrical work, and choose subcontractors to complete it. The top-level construction manager would then collaborate and coordinate with the other construction managers.

To maximize efficiency and productivity, construction managers often perform the tasks of a cost estimator. They use specialized cost-estimating and planning software to allocate time and money in order to complete their projects. Many managers also use software to plan the best way to get materials to the building site.

Work Environment

Construction managers held about 373,200 jobs in 2014. The industries that employed the most construction managers were as follows:

Specialty trade contractors	18%
Nonresidential building construction	15
Residential building construction	9
Heavy and civil engineering construction	7

About 4 in 10 construction managers were self-employed in 2014.

Many construction managers have a main office, but they spend most of their time working out of a field office at the construction site, where they monitor the project and make daily decisions about construction activities. For those managing multiple projects, frequent travel between sites is required.

Work Schedules. Most construction managers work full time. However, the need to meet deadlines and to respond to delays and emergencies often requires construction managers to work many hours. Many managers may also be on call 24 hours a day.

Education/Training

Large construction firms increasingly prefer candidates with both construction experience and a bachelor's degree in a construction-related field. While some individuals with a high school diploma and many years of experience in a construction trade may be hired as construction managers, these individuals are typically qualified to become self-employed general contractors.

Education. It is becoming increasingly important for construction managers to have a bachelor's degree in construction science, construction management, architecture, or engineering. As construction processes become more complex, employers are placing greater importance on specialized education.

More than 100 colleges and universities offer accredited bachelor's degree programs in construction science, building science, or construction engineering. These programs include courses in project control and management, design, construction methods and materials, cost estimation, building codes and standards, and contract administration. Courses in mathematics and statistics are also relevant.

More than fifty 2-year colleges offer construction management or construction technology programs. An associate's degree combined with work experience is typical for managers who supervise smaller projects.

A few universities offer master's degree programs in construction management.

Those with a high school diploma and several years of relevant work experience may qualify to become a construction manager, although most are qualified to become self-employed general contractors.

Training. New construction managers are typically hired as assistants and work under the guidance of an experienced manager. This training period may last several months to several years, depending on the firm.

Work Experience in a Related Occupation. If the typical education is not obtained, practical construction experience is important

Median Annual Wages, May 2014

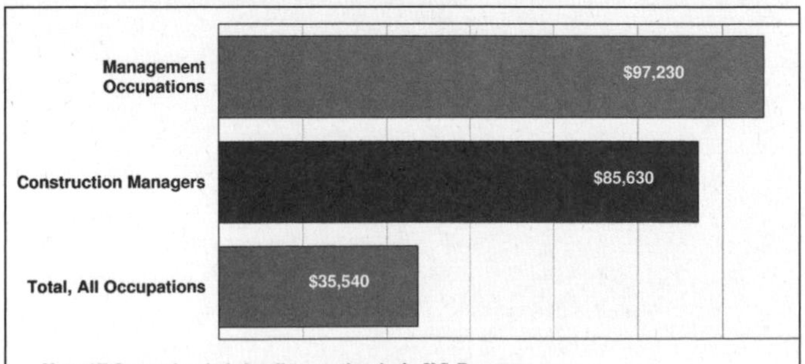

Note: All Occupations includes all occupations in the U.S. Economy.
Source: U.S. Bureau of Labor Statistics, Occupational Employment Statistics

Percent Change in Employment, Projected 2014–2024

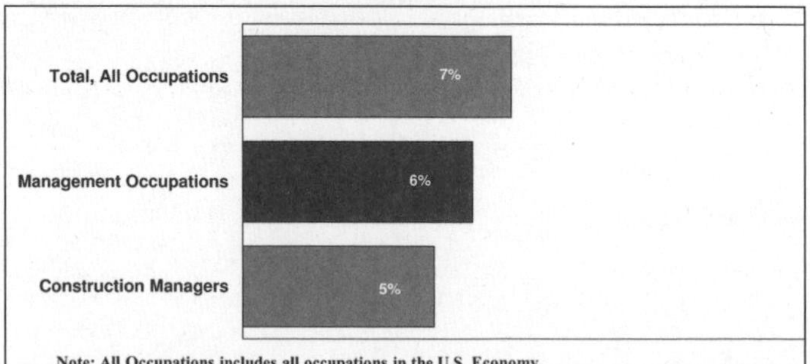

Note: All Occupations includes all occupations in the U.S. Economy.
Source: U.S. Bureau of Labor Statistics, Office of Occupational Statistics and Employment Projections

Employment Projections Data for Construction Managers

Occupational Title	SOC Code	Employment, 2014	Projected Employment, 2024	Change, 2014–2024	
				Percent	Numeric
Construction managers	11-9021	373,200	391,100	5	17,800

Source: U.S. Bureau of Labor Statistics, Employment Projections Program

for jobseekers, because it reduces the need for initial on-the-job training. Internships, cooperative education programs, and previous work in the construction industry can provide that experience. Some construction managers become qualified solely through extensive construction experience, spending many years in carpentry, masonry, or other construction specialties.

Licenses, Certifications, and Registrations. Although not required, certification is becoming increasingly important for construction managers. Certification is valuable because it can demonstrate knowledge and experience.

The Construction Management Association of America awards the Certified Construction Manager (CCM) designation to workers who have the required experience and who pass a technical exam. It is recommended that applicants for this certification complete a self-study course that covers the professional role of a construction manager, legal issues, the allocation of risk, and other topics related to construction management.

The American Institute of Constructors awards the Associate Constructor (AC) and Certified Professional Constructor (CPC) designations to candidates who meet its requirements and pass the appropriate construction exams.

Some states require licensure for construction managers. For more information, contact your state licensing board.

Important Qualities

Analytical skills. Most managers plan a project strategy, handle unexpected issues and delays, and solve problems that arise over the course of the project. In addition, many managers use cost-estimating and planning software to determine costs and the materials and time required to complete projects.

Business skills. Construction managers address budget matters and coordinate and supervise workers. Choosing competent staff and establishing good working relationships with them is critical.

Customer-service skills. Construction managers are in constant contact with owners, inspectors, and the public. They must form good working relationships with these people and ensure their needs are met.

Decision-making skills. Construction managers choose personnel and subcontractors for specific tasks and jobs. Often, these choices must be made quickly to meet deadlines and budgets.

Initiative. Self-employed construction managers generate their business opportunities and must be proactive in finding new clients. They often market their services and bid on jobs, and they must also learn to perform special home improvement projects, such as installing mosaic glass tiles, sanding wood floors, and insulating homes.

Leadership skills. Managers must effectively delegate tasks to construction workers, subcontractors, and other lower level managers.

Speaking skills. Managers must give clear orders, explain complex information to construction workers and clients, and discuss technical details with other building specialists, such as architects. Self-employed construction managers must get their own projects, so the need to sell their services to potential clients is critical.

Technical skills. Managers must know construction methods and technologies, and must be able to interpret contracts and technical drawings.

Time-management skills. Construction managers must meet deadlines. They ensure that construction phases are completed on time so that the next phase can begin as scheduled. For instance, a building's foundation cannot be constructed until the land is completely excavated.

Writing skills. Construction managers must write proposals, plans, and budgets, as well as document the progress of the work for clients and others involved in the building process.

Pay

The median annual wage for construction managers was $85,630 in May 2014. The median wage is the wage at which half the workers in an occupation earned more than that amount and half earned less. The lowest 10 percent earned less than $50,990, and the highest 10 percent earned more than $150,250.

In May 2014, the median annual wages for construction managers in the top industries in which they worked were as follows:

Heavy and civil engineering construction	$88,320
Nonresidential building construction	88,120
Specialty trade contractors	81,800
Residential building construction	74,880

Some salaried construction managers may also earn bonuses and overtime pay. About 4 in 10 construction managers were self-employed in 2014, and their earnings are highly dependent on the amount of business they generate.

Job Outlook

Employment of construction managers is projected to grow 5 percent from 2014 to 2024, about as fast as the average for all occupations.

Construction managers will be needed as overall construction activity expands. Population and business growth will result in the construction of new residences, office buildings, retail outlets, hospitals, schools, restaurants, and other structures over the coming decade. Also, the need to improve portions of the national infrastructure will spur employment growth as roads, bridges, and sewer pipe systems are upgraded or replaced.

In addition, a growing emphasis on retrofitting buildings to make them more energy efficient should create jobs for general contractors, who are more likely to manage the renovation and upgrading of buildings than oversee new large-scale construction projects.

To ensure that projects are completed on time and under budget, firms are increasingly focusing on hiring construction managers. Furthermore, construction processes and building technology are becoming more complex, requiring greater oversight and spurring demand for specialized management personnel.

Job Prospects. Job opportunities for qualified construction managers are expected to be good. Specifically, those with a bachelor's degree in construction science, construction management, or civil

Similar Occupations. This table shows a list of occupations with job duties that are similar to those of construction managers.

Occupations	Entry-level Education	2014 Median Pay	Projected Job Growth	Average Annual Openings
Architects	Bachelor's degree	$74,520	7%	780
Architectural and Engineering Managers	Bachelor's degree	$130,620	2%	370
Civil Engineers	Bachelor's degree	$82,050	8%	2,360
Cost Estimators	Bachelor's degree	$60,050	9%	1,870
Landscape Architects	Bachelor's degree	$64,570	5%	120

engineering, coupled with construction experience, will have the best job prospects.

Although employment growth will provide many new jobs, a substantial number of construction managers are expected to retire over the next decade, resulting in additional job openings.

Employment of construction managers, like that of many other construction workers, is sensitive to fluctuations in the economy. On the one hand, workers in the construction industry may experience periods of unemployment when the overall level of construction falls. On the other hand, peak periods of building activity may produce abundant job opportunities for construction managers.

Contacts for More Information

For information about construction manager certification, visit

➤ American Institute of Constructors (www.professionalconstructor.org)

For more information about construction management and construction manager certification, visit

➤ Construction Management Association of America (http://cmaanet.org)

For information on accredited construction science and management educational programs, visit

➤ ABET (www.abet.org)

➤ American Council for Construction Education (www.acce-hq.org)

➤ NCCER (www.nccer.org)

O*NET

➤ Construction Managers (11-9021.00)

Elementary, Middle, and High School Principals

- **2014 Median Pay** .... $89,540 per year
- **Typical Entry-Level Education** .... Master's degree
- **Work Experience in a Related Occupation** .... 5 years or more
- **On-the-job Training** .... None
- **Number of Jobs, 2014** 240,000
- **Job Outlook, 2014–24** .... 6% (As fast as average)
- **Employment Change, 2014–24** 14,000

What Elementary, Middle, and High School Principals Do

Elementary, middle, and high school principals manage all school operations, including daily school activities. They coordinate curricula, oversee teachers and other school staff, and provide a safe and productive learning environment for students.

Duties. Elementary, middle, and high school principals typically do the following:

- Manage school activities and staff, including teachers and support personnel
- Establish and oversee class schedules
- Develop, implement, and maintain curriculum standards
- Counsel and discipline students
- Observe teachers and classroom activities
- Assist teachers in managing students' behavior
- Evaluate teachers' performance
- Meet with parents and teachers to discuss students' progress and behavior
- Assess and prepare reports on test scores and other student achievement data
- Organize professional development programs and workshops for staff
- Manage the school's budget, order school supplies, and schedule maintenance
- Establish and coordinate security procedures for students, staff, and visitors

Elementary, middle, and high school principals manage the overall operation of schools, including building maintenance and cafeteria services. They set and oversee academic goals and ensure that teachers have the necessary equipment and resources. In public schools, principals also implement standards and programs set by the school district, state, and/or federal regulations. They evaluate and prepare reports on their school's performance based on these standards by assessing student achievement and teacher performance. Principals may establish and oversee additional programs in their school, such as counseling, special education programs, and before- and after-school childcare programs.

Principals serve as the public face of their school. They meet with superintendents, legislators, and members of the community to request or explain funding for their schools. They also address the concerns of parents and members of the community.

The duties of principals vary by the size of the school and district. In larger schools and districts, principals have additional resources and staff to help them achieve goals. For example, large school districts often have instructional coordinators who help with data analysis and with teachers' professional development. Principals also may have staff who oversee the hiring process of all school personnel, including teachers, custodians, and cafeteria workers. Principals in small school districts may need to assume these and other duties themselves.

Many schools have assistant principals who help principals with school administration. Principals typically assign specific

Elementary, middle, and high school principals provide leadership to teachers and other members of school staff and manage the day-to-day operations of schools.

administrative duties to their assistant principals. In some school districts, assistant principals are hired to handle a specific subject area, such as literacy or math. Assistants may be assigned to handle student safety, provide student academic counseling, or enforce disciplinary or attendance rules. They may also coordinate buses or supervise building and grounds maintenance.

Work Environment

Elementary, middle, and high school principals held about 240,000 jobs in 2014.

Principals work in public or private elementary, middle, or high schools. Some work in public magnet or charter schools. Others work in private religious schools.

Elementary, middle, and high school principals hold leadership positions with significant responsibility. Working with students may be rewarding. However, coordinating and interacting with faculty, parents, students, community members, and state and local policymakers can be demanding. Principals' work can sometimes be stressful because they are accountable for schools meeting state and federal standards for student performance and teacher qualification.

Work Schedules. Principals typically work full time. They may work evenings or weekends to meet with parents and other members of the community and to attend school functions, such as concerts and athletic events.

Many principals work year round and do not have summers off, even if students are not in school. During the summer, principals prepare for the upcoming school year, schedule building maintenance, order school supplies, and hire teachers and other staff.

Education/Training

Most schools require elementary, middle, and high school principals to have a master's degree in education administration or leadership. Most principals also have work experience as teachers.

Education. Principals typically need a master's degree in education leadership or education administration. These master's degree programs prepare future principals to manage staff, prepare and manage budgets, set goals, and work with parents and the community. To enter the master's degree programs, candidates typically need a bachelor's degree in education, school counseling, or a related field.

Work Experience in a Related Occupation. Principals typically need several years of work experience as a teacher. For more information on how to become a teacher, see the profiles on kindergarten and elementary school teachers, middle school teachers, and high school teachers.

Licenses, Certifications, and Registrations. Most states require public school principals to be licensed as school administrators. Licensure requirements vary by state, but most require a master's degree. Some states have alternative programs for candidates who do not have a master's degree in education administration or leadership. Most states also require candidates to pass an exam and a background check.

Principals in private schools are not required to have a state-issued license.

Advancement. An assistant principal can advance to become a principal. Some principals advance to become superintendents, which may require completion of additional education. Others become instructional coordinators.

Important Qualities

Communication skills. Principals must communicate effectively with students, teachers, and parents. For example, when dealing with student disciplinary or academic issues, they consult with and listen to parents and teachers to understand the problem.

Critical-thinking skills. Principals analyze student test results and testing procedures to determine if improvements are needed. They must assess the available options and choose the best means to help students achieve better results.

Decision-making skills. Because principals are responsible for students, staff members, and the overall operation of the school, they consider many factors when making decisions.

Median Annual Wages, May 2014

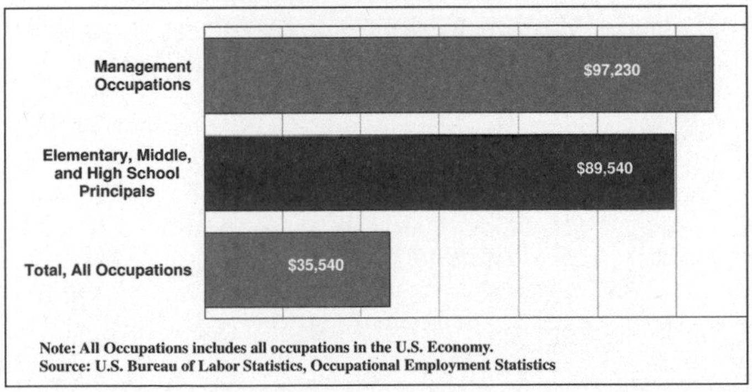

Percent Change in Employment, Projected 2014–2024

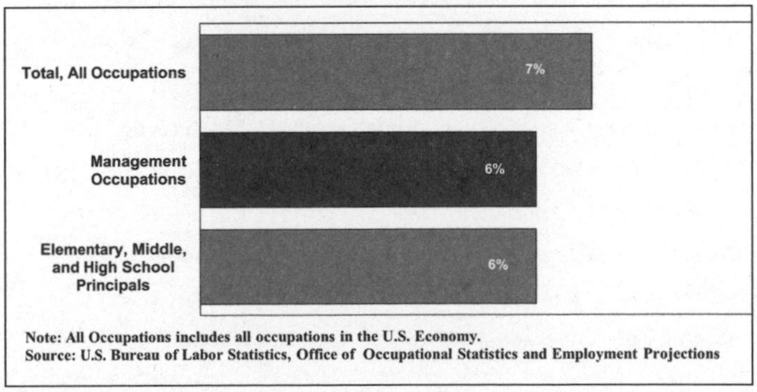

Employment Projections Data for Elementary, Middle, and High School Principals

Occupational Title	SOC Code	Employment, 2014	Projected Employment, 2024	Change, 2014–2024 Percent	Change, 2014–2024 Numeric
Education administrators, elementary and secondary school	11-9032	240,000	254,000	6	14,000

Source: U.S. Bureau of Labor Statistics, Employment Projections Program

Interpersonal skills. Because principals work with teachers, parents, and superintendents, they must be able to develop positive working relationships with them.

Leadership skills. Principals set educational goals and establish policies and procedures for the school. They need to be able to motivate teachers and other staff to achieve set goals.

Problem-solving skills. Teachers, students, and other staff members report problems to the principal. Principals need to be able to analyze problems, and develop and implement appropriate solutions.

Pay

The median annual wage for elementary, middle, and high school principals was $89,540 in May 2014. The median wage is the wage at which half the workers in an occupation earned more than that amount and half earned less. The lowest 10 percent earned less than $59,250, and the highest 10 percent earned more than $129,300.

Job Outlook

Employment of elementary, middle, and high school principals is projected to grow 6 percent from 2014 to 2024, about as fast as the average for all occupations. Employment growth will be driven by increases in school enrollments.

From 2014 to 2024, the number of students enrolled in schools is projected to increase. Some additional schools may open to accommodate these students, resulting in a need for more assistant principals and principals.

Despite expected increases in enrollment, employment growth of school principals will depend on state and local budgets. Budget constraints may delay the building or opening of new schools. In addition, some school districts may consolidate and close some schools within their districts, thereby limiting employment growth.

Job Prospects. Job prospects will be best for candidates with a master's degree and with teaching experience. As the large baby-boom generation retires, there may be better opportunities for candidates to advance into the principal occupation. Additional vacancies may stem from individuals who choose to leave the position due to heavy workloads and high job-related stress.

However, job opportunities will vary by region of the country. The population and student enrollments have grown faster in the South and West in recent years. Job opportunities for principals may be better in those parts of the country.

Contacts for More Information

For more information on elementary, middle, and high school principals, visit

- National Association of Elementary School Principals (http://naesp.org)
- National Association of Secondary School Principals (www.nassp.org)

O*NET

- Education Administrators, Elementary and Secondary School (11-9032.00)

Similar Occupations. This table shows a list of occupations with job duties that are similar to those of elementary, middle, and high school principals.

Occupations	Entry-level Education	2014 Median Pay	Projected Job Growth	Average Annual Openings
Career and Technical Education Teachers	Bachelor's degree	$51,830	4%	1,020
High School Teachers	Bachelor's degree	$56,310	6%	5,590
Instructional Coordinators	Master's degree	$61,550	7%	1,050
Kindergarten and Elementary School Teachers	Bachelor's degree	$53,760	6%	8,780
Librarians	Master's degree	$56,170	2%	270
Middle School Teachers	Bachelor's degree	$54,940	6%	3,680
Postsecondary Education Administrators	Master's degree	$88,390	9%	1,520
Postsecondary Teachers	See Education/Training	$70,790	13%	17,700
Preschool and Childcare Center Directors	Bachelor's degree	$45,260	7%	420
Preschool Teachers	Associate's degree	$28,120	7%	2,960
School and Career Counselors	Master's degree	$53,370	8%	2,250
Special Education Teachers	Bachelor's degree	$55,980	6%	2,810
Teacher Assistants	Some college, no degree	$24,430	6%	7,860

Emergency Management Directors

- **2014 Median Pay** .... $64,360 per year $30.94 per hour
- **Typical Entry-Level Education** .... Bachelor's degree
- **Work Experience in a Related Occupation**............ 5 years or more
- **On-the-Job Training** .... None
- **Number of Jobs 2014** 10,500
- **Job Outlook, 2014–24** .... 6% (As fast as average)
- **Employment Change, 2014–24** 700

What Emergency Management Directors Do

Emergency management directors prepare plans and procedures for responding to natural disasters and other emergencies. They also help lead the response during and after emergencies, often in coordination with public safety officials, elected officials, nonprofit organizations, and government agencies.

Duties. Emergency management directors typically do the following:

- Assess hazards and prepare plans to respond to emergencies and disasters in order to minimize risk to people and property
- Meet with public safety officials, private companies, and the general public to get recommendations regarding emergency response plans
- Organize emergency response training programs and exercises for staff, volunteers, and other responders
- Coordinate the sharing of resources and equipment within the community and across communities to assist in responding to an emergency
- Prepare and analyze damage assessments following disasters or emergencies
- Review emergency plans of individual organizations, such as medical facilities, to ensure their adequacy
- Apply for federal funding for emergency management planning, responses and recovery and report on the use of funds allocated
- Review local emergency operations plans and revise them if necessary
- Maintain facilities used during emergency operations

Emergency management directors are responsible for planning and leading the responses to natural disasters and other emergencies. Directors work with government agencies, nonprofits, private companies, and the general public to develop effective plans that minimize damage and disruptions during an emergency.

To develop emergency response plans, directors typically research "best practices" from around the country and from other emergency management agencies. Directors also must prepare plans and procedures that meet local, state, and federal regulations.

Directors must analyze the resources, equipment, and staff available to respond to emergencies. If resources or equipment are lacking, directors must either revise their plans or obtain the needed resources from another community or state. Many directors coordinate with fire, emergency medical service, police departments, and public works agencies in other communities to locate and share equipment during an emergency. Directors must be in contact with other agencies to collect and share information regarding the scope of the emergency, the potential costs, and the resources or staff needed.

After plans are developed, emergency management directors typically ensure that individuals and groups become familiar with the emergency procedures. Directors often use social media to disseminate plans and warnings to the general public.

Emergency management directors run training courses and disaster exercises for staff, volunteers, and local agencies to ensure an effective and coordinated response to an emergency. Directors also may visit schools, hospitals, or other community groups to update everyone on the emergency plans.

During an emergency, directors typically maintain a command center at which personnel monitor and manage the emergency operations. Directors help lead the response, making adjustments to or prioritizing certain actions if necessary. These actions may include ordering evacuations, conducting rescue missions, or opening up public shelters for those displaced by the disaster. Emergency management directors also may need to conduct press conferences or other outreach activities to keep the public informed about the emergency.

Following an emergency, directors must assess the damage to their community and must coordinate getting assistance and supplies into the community if necessary. Directors may need to request state or federal assistance to help execute their emergency response plan and provide support to affected citizens, organizations, and communities. Directors may also revise their plans and procedures to prepare for future emergencies or disasters.

Emergency management directors working for hospitals, universities, or private companies may be called *business continuity managers*. Similar to their counterparts in local and state government, business continuity managers prepare plans and procedures to help businesses maintain operations and minimize losses during and after an emergency.

Work Environment

Emergency management directors held about 10,500 jobs in 2014. The industries that employed the most emergency management directors were as follows:

Local government, excluding education and hospitals	52%
State government, excluding education and hospitals	12
Hospitals; state, local, and private	9
Professional, scientific, and technical services	6

Emergency management directors sometimes need to coordinate their activities with federal authorities.

Median Annual Wages, May 2014

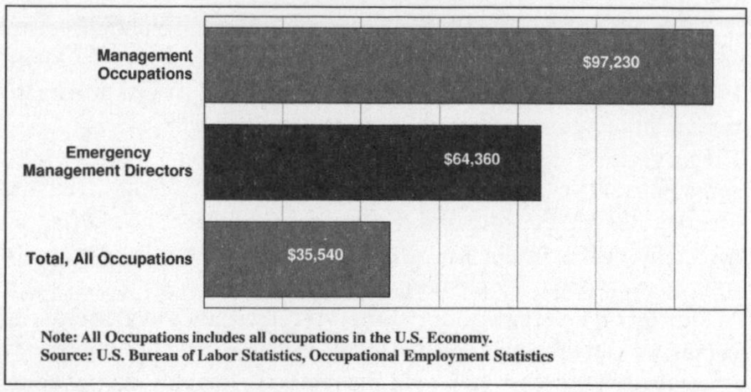

Percent Change in Employment, Projected 2014–2024

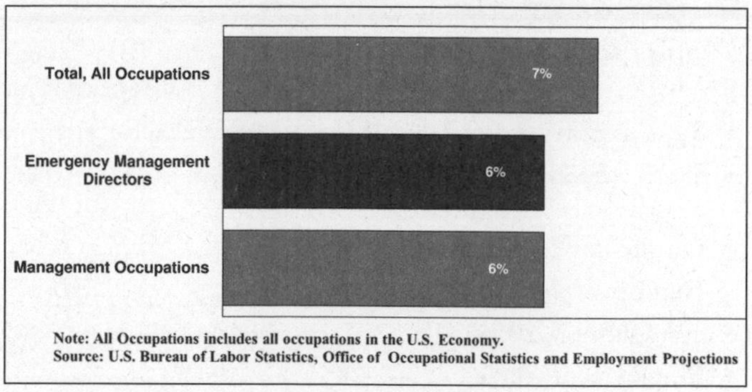

Colleges, universities, and professional schools; state, local, and private.. 4%

Although most emergency management directors work in an office, they typically travel to meet with various government agencies, community groups, and private companies.

Many directors work in stressful situations during disasters and emergencies.

Work Schedules. Most emergency management directors work full time. In addition, most are on call at all times and may need to work overtime to respond to emergencies and to support emergency management operations. Others may work evenings and weekends to meet with various community groups in preparing their emergency response plans.

Education/Training

Emergency management directors typically need a bachelor's degree, as well as multiple years of work experience in emergency response, disaster planning, or public administration.

Education. Emergency management directors typically need a bachelor's degree in business or public administration, accounting, finance, emergency management, or public health. Some directors working in the private sector in the area of business continuity management may need to have a degree in computer science, information systems administration, or another information technology (IT) field.

Some smaller municipalities or local governments may hire applicants who have just a high school diploma. However, these applicants usually need extensive work experience in emergency management if they are to be hired.

Work Experience in a Related Occupation. Applicants typically need multiple years of work experience, often with the military, law enforcement, fire safety, or in another emergency management field, before they can be hired as an emergency management director. Previous work experience in these areas enables applicants to make difficult decisions in stressful and time-sensitive situations. Such experience also prepares one to work with various agencies to ensure that proper resources are used to respond to emergencies.

For more information, see the profiles on police and detectives, firefighters, police, fire, and ambulance dispatchers, and EMTs and paramedics.

Licenses, Certifications, and Registrations. Some states require directors to obtain certification within a certain timeframe after being hired in the position.

Many agencies and states offer voluntary certificate programs to help emergency management directors obtain additional skills. Some employers may prefer or even require a Certified Emergency Manager® (CEM®), Certified Business Continuity Professional (CBCP), or equivalent designation. Emergency management directors can attain the CEM designation through the International Association of Emergency Managers (IAEM); the certification must be renewed every 5 years. The CBCP designation is given by the Disaster Recovery Institute International (DRI) and must be renewed every 2 years.

Both associations require applicants to complete a certain number of continuing education courses prior to recertification.

Important Qualities

Communication skills. Emergency management directors must write out and communicate their emergency preparedness plans to all levels of government, as well as to the public.

Critical-thinking skills. Emergency management directors must anticipate hazards and problems that may arise from an emergency in order to respond effectively.

Decision-making skills. Emergency management directors must make timely decisions, often in stressful situations. They must also identify the strengths and weaknesses of all solutions and approaches, as well as the costs and benefits of each action.

Interpersonal skills. Emergency management directors must work with other government agencies, law enforcement and fire officials, and the general public to coordinate emergency responses.

Leadership skills. To ensure effective responses to emergencies, emergency management directors need to organize and train a variety of people.

Employment Projections Data for Emergency Management Directors

Occupational Title	SOC Code	Employment, 2014	Projected Employment, 2024	Change, 2014–2024 Percent	Change, 2014–2024 Numeric
Emergency management directors..	11-9161	10,500	11,200	6	700

Source: U.S. Bureau of Labor Statistics, Employment Projections Program

Similar Occupations. This table shows a list of occupations with job duties that are similar to those of emergency management directors.

Occupations	Entry-level Education	2014 Median Pay	Projected Job Growth	Average Annual Openings
Budget Analysts	Bachelor's degree	$71,220	3%	150
EMTs and Paramedics	Postsecondary nondegree award	$31,700	24%	5,850
Firefighters	Postsecondary nondegree award	$45,970	5%	1,740
Management Analysts	Bachelor's degree	$80,880	14%	10,340
Police and Detectives	See Education/Training	$58,630	4%	3,310
Top Executives	Bachelor's degree	$102,750	6%	14,700

Pay

The median annual wage for emergency management directors was $64,360 in May 2014. The median wage is the wage at which half the workers in an occupation earned more than that amount and half earned less. The lowest 10 percent earned less than $33,370, and the highest 10 percent earned more than $116,900.

In May 2014, the median annual wages for emergency management directors in the top industries in which they worked were as follows:

Colleges, universities, and professional schools; state, local, and private $84,640
Professional, scientific, and technical services 77,720
Hospitals; state, local, and private 75,420
Local government, excluding education and hospitals 58,020
State government, excluding education and hospitals 54,820

Job Outlook

Employment of emergency management directors is projected to grow 6 percent from 2014 to 2024, about as fast as the average for all occupations.

Every geographic region has the potential for weather-related emergencies such as flooding, droughts, hurricanes, and tornadoes. Increasing urbanization and continued population growth in coastal regions may increase the number of people who are vulnerable to these emergencies. Emergency management directors will be needed to develop response plans to protect more people and property, and to limit the damage from emergencies and disasters.

Employment is projected to increase as both local and state governments place a greater emphasis on preparing for natural and human-made emergencies and seek to minimize the risks of being underprepared to deal with such emergencies. Employment growth, however, may be somewhat limited because of budgetary constraints in state and local governments. Although local and state revenue and spending have increased since the end of the recession, continued budget uncertainty and other spending obligations may lead to only modest growth in government hiring.

In addition, some local and state governments rely on federal financial assistance to fund their emergency management agencies. Yet similar budgetary problems at the federal level may lead to continued cutbacks in funding and grants to local and state agencies, further limiting the hiring of emergency management personnel. Some smaller counties may not hire full-time, stand-alone emergency management directors, choosing instead to shift the job responsibilities to the fire chief, police chief, or other government employees.

Employment, therefore, is likely to grow fastest in private companies. Emergency management directors will be needed to help businesses and organizations continue to provide essential products and services during and after emergencies. However, as in state and local government, some smaller companies, hospitals, or college campuses may not have a stand-alone director. Instead, an information technology (IT) director, a registered nurse, or a public safety officer may handle the emergency management duties.

Job Prospects. Competition for jobs is expected to be strong. Emergency management directors are a relatively small occupation, and only modest increases in state and local government budgets mean that new job openings are likely to be limited.

However, retirements over the next decade may provide some opportunities for those interested in entering the occupation. Applicants with extensive work experience in an emergency management role will have the best job prospects.

Contacts for More Information

For more information on emergency management directors, visit

- National Emergency Management Association (www.nemaweb.org)
- International Association of Emergency Managers (www.iaem.com)

O*NET

- Emergency Management Directors (11-9161.00)

Farmers, Ranchers, and Other Agricultural Managers

- **2014 Median Pay** .... $68,050 per year $32.72 per hour
- **Typical Entry-Level Education** .... High school diploma or equivalent
- **Work Experience in a Related Occupation** .... 5 years or more
- **On-the-job Training** .... None
- **Number of Jobs, 2014** 929,800
- **Job Outlook, 2014–24** .... -2% (Decline)
- **Employment Change, 2014–24** .... -18,100

What Farmers, Ranchers, and Other Agricultural Managers Do

Farmers, ranchers, and other agricultural managers operate establishments that produce crops, livestock, and dairy products.

Duties. Farmers, ranchers, and other agricultural managers typically do the following:

- Supervise all steps of the crop production and ranging process, including planting, fertilizing, harvesting, and herding
- Determine how to raise crops or livestock by evaluating factors such as market conditions, disease, soil conditions, and the availability of federal programs
- Select and purchase supplies, such as seed, fertilizers, and farm machinery
- Ensure that farm machinery is maintained and repaired
- Adapt their duties to the seasons, weather conditions, or a crop's growing cycle
- Maintain farm facilities, such as water pipes, hoses, fences, and animal shelters
- Serve as the sales agent for livestock, crops, and dairy products
- Record financial, tax, production, and employee information

Farmers, ranchers, and other agricultural managers produce enough crops and livestock to meet the needs of the United States and still have more left over for export.

Farmers, ranchers, and other agricultural managers monitor the constantly changing prices for their products. They use different strategies to protect themselves from unpredictable changes in the markets. For example, farmers carefully plan the combination of crops that they grow, so if the price of one crop drops, they will have enough income from another crop to make up for the loss. Farmers and ranchers also track disease and weather conditions closely, because disease and bad weather may have a negative impact on crop yields or animal health. When farmers and ranchers plan ahead, they may be able to store their crops or keep their livestock to take advantage of higher prices later in the year.

Most farm output goes to food-processing companies. However, some farmers now choose to sell their goods directly to consumers through farmers' markets or use cooperatives to reduce their financial risk and to gain a larger share of the final price of their goods. In community-supported agriculture (CSA), cooperatives sell shares of a harvest to consumers before the planting season in order to ensure a market for the farm's produce.

Farmers, ranchers, and other agricultural managers also negotiate with banks and other credit lenders to get financing, because they must buy seed, livestock, and equipment before they have products to sell.

Farmers and ranchers own and operate mainly family-owned farms. They also may lease land from a landowner and operate it as a working farm.

The size of the farm or range determines which tasks farmers and ranchers handle. Those who operate small farms or ranges usually do all tasks, including harvesting and inspecting the land, growing crops, and raising animals. In addition, they keep records, service machinery, and maintain buildings.

Some farmers work primarily with crops and vegetables, whereas other farmers and ranchers handle livestock.

By contrast, farmers and ranchers who operate large farms have employees—including agricultural workers—who help with physical work. Some employees of large farms are in nonfarm occupations, working as truck drivers, sales representatives, bookkeepers, or information technology specialists.

Farmers and ranchers track technological improvements in animal breeding and seeds, choosing new products that might increase output. Many livestock and dairy farmers monitor and attend to the health of their herds, tasks that may include assisting in births.

Agricultural managers take care of the day-to-day operation of one or more farms, ranches, nurseries, timber tracts, greenhouses, and other agricultural establishments for corporations, farmers, and owners who do not live and work on their farm or ranch.

Agricultural managers usually do not do production activities themselves. Instead, they hire and supervise farm and livestock workers to do most daily production tasks.

Managers may determine budgets. They may decide how to store and transport crops. They oversee the proper maintenance of equipment and property.

The following are examples of types of farmers, ranchers, and other agricultural managers:

Crop farmers and managers—those who grow grain, fruits and vegetables, and other crops—are responsible for all steps of plant growth. After a harvest, they make sure that the crops are properly packaged and stored.

Median Annual Wages, May 2014

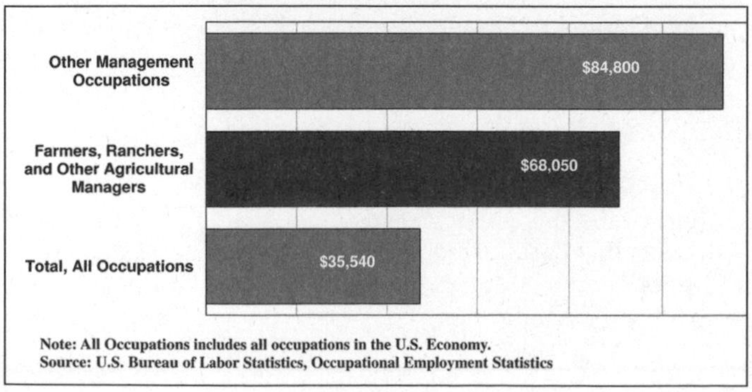

Percent Change in Employment, Projected 2014–2024

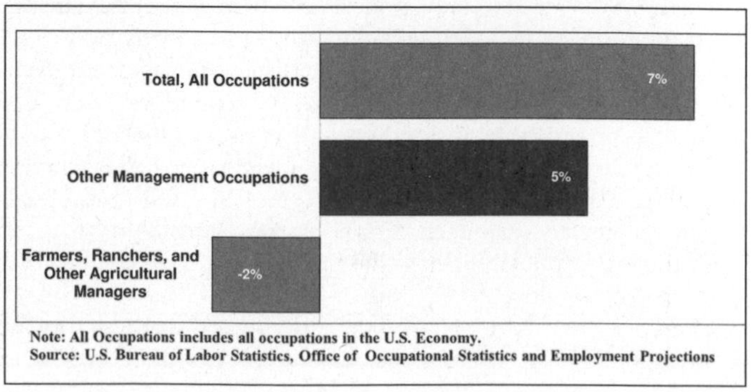

Livestock, dairy, and poultry farmers, ranchers, and managers feed and care for animals. They keep livestock in barns, pens, and other farm buildings. These workers also oversee the breeding and marketing of the animals in their care.

Horticultural specialty farmers and managers oversee the production of fruits, vegetables, flowers, and plants (including turf) used for landscaping. They also grow grapes, berries, and nuts used in making wine.

Aquaculture farmers and managers raise fish and shellfish in ponds, floating net pens, raceways, and recirculating systems. They stock, feed, protect, and maintain aquatic life used for food and for recreational fishing.

Work Environment

Farmers, ranchers, and other agricultural managers held about 929,800 jobs in 2014. About 7 in 10 were self-employed. The rest were wage and salary workers.

Farmers, ranchers, and other agricultural managers typically work outdoors and may spend some time in offices. They sometimes do strenuous physical work.

Some farmers work primarily with crops and vegetables. Other farmers and ranchers handle livestock.

Injuries and Illnesses. The work environment for farmers, ranchers, and other agricultural managers can be hazardous. Tractors, tools, and other farm machinery can cause serious injury, so workers must be alert on the job. They must operate equipment and handle chemicals properly to avoid accidents and safeguard the surrounding environment.

Work Schedules. Most farmers, ranchers, and other agricultural managers work full time. Farm work can be seasonal and the number of hours worked may change according to the season. Farmers and farm managers on crop farms usually work from sunrise to sunset during the planting and harvesting seasons. During the rest of the year, they plan the next season's crops, market their output, and repair and maintain machinery. About one-third worked more than 40 hours per week in 2014.

On livestock-producing farms and ranches, work goes on throughout the year. Animals must be fed and cared for every day.

On very large farms, farmers and farm managers spend time meeting with farm supervisors. Managers who oversee several farms may divide their time between traveling to meet farmers and landowners and staying in their offices to plan farm operations.

Education/Training

Farmers, ranchers, and other agricultural managers usually have at least a high school diploma and typically gain skills through work experience.

Education. Farmers, ranchers, and other agricultural managers usually have at least a high school diploma. As farm and land management has grown more complex and costly, farmers, ranchers, and other agricultural managers have increasingly needed postsecondary education, such as an associate's degree or a bachelor's degree in agriculture or a related field.

There are a number of government programs that help new farmers get an education in farming. All state university systems have at least one land-grant college or university with a school of agriculture. Common programs of study include business (with a concentration in agriculture), plant breeding, farm management, agronomy, dairy science, and agricultural economics.

Work Experience in a Related Occupation. Prospective farmers, ranchers, and agricultural managers typically work and gain experience under more experienced farmers. Some of them may grow up on a family farm and learn that way. The amount of experience that is needed varies with the complexity of the work and the size of the farm. Those with postsecondary education in agriculture may not need previous work experience. Universities and various forms of government assistance give prospective farmers alternatives to working on a farm or growing up on one.

Important Qualities

Analytical skills. Farmers, ranchers, and other agricultural managers must monitor and assess the quality of their land or livestock. These tasks require precision and accuracy.

Critical-thinking skills. Farmers, ranchers, and other agricultural managers make tough decisions through sound reasoning and judgment. They determine how to improve their harvest and livestock, all the while reacting appropriately to external factors.

Interpersonal skills. Farmers, ranchers, and other agricultural managers supervise laborers and other workers, so effective communication is critical.

Mechanical skills. Farmers, ranchers, and other agricultural managers must be able to operate complex machinery and occasionally perform routine maintenance.

Physical strength. Farmers, ranchers, and other agricultural managers—particularly those who work on small farms—must be able to perform physically strenuous, repetitive tasks, such as lifting heavy objects and bending at the waist.

Training. Those without postsecondary education take a longer time to learn the more complex aspects of farming. A small number of farms offer apprenticeships to help young people learn the practical skills of farming and ranching. Government projects, such as the Beginning Farmer and Rancher Development Program, provide a way for people without any farm training to be paired with experienced farmers, learning through internships or apprentice programs.

Licenses, Certifications, and Registrations. To show competency in farm management, agricultural managers may choose to become certified. The American Society of Farm Managers and Rural Appraisers (ASFMRA) offers the Accredited Farm Manager accreditation to ASFMRA members who have 4 years of work experience and a bachelor's degree. A complete list of requirements, including consultant course work and exams, is available from ASFMRA.

Employment Projections Data for Farmers, Ranchers, and Other Agricultural Managers

Occupational Title	SOC Code	Employment, 2014	Projected Employment, 2024	Change, 2014–2024 Percent	Change, 2014–2024 Numeric
Farmers, ranchers, and other agricultural managers	11-9013	929,800	911,700	-2	-18,100

Source: U.S. Bureau of Labor Statistics, Employment Projections Program

Similar Occupations. This table shows a list of occupations with job duties that are similar to those of farmers, ranchers, and other agricultural managers.

Occupations	Entry-level Education	2014 Median Pay	Projected Job Growth	Average Annual Openings
Agricultural and Food Science Technicians	Associate's degree	$35,140	5%	160
Agricultural and Food Scientists	Bachelor's degree	$60,690	5%	190
Agricultural Workers	See Education/Training	$19,330	-6%	-4,750
Buyers and Purchasing Agents	Bachelor's degree	$58,520	2%	720

Pay

The median annual wage for farmers, ranchers, and other agricultural managers was $68,050 in May 2014. The median wage is the wage at which half the workers in an occupation earned more than that amount and half earned less. The lowest 10 percent earned less than $34,170, and the highest 10 percent earned more than $121,690.

Incomes of farmers and ranchers vary from year to year because prices of farm products fluctuate with weather conditions and other factors. In addition to earning income from their farm business, farmers can receive government subsidies or other payments that add to their income and reduce some of the risk of farming.

Also, more farmers, especially operators of small farms, are relying more on off-farm sources of income, such as community-supported agriculture (CSA) programs.

Job Outlook

Employment of farmers, ranchers, and other agricultural managers is projected to decline 2 percent from 2014 to 2024. The continuing ability of the agricultural sector to produce more with fewer workers will cause some farmers to go out of business.

As land, machinery, seed, and chemicals become more expensive, only well-capitalized farmers and corporations will be able to buy many of the farms that become available. These larger, more productive farms are better able to withstand the adverse effects of climate and price fluctuations on farm output and income.

Still, several initiatives, such as the Beginning Farmer and Rancher Development Program and the various farm loan programs, are designed to help farmers and ranchers acquire land and operating capital. These programs may help to offset the market pressures that farmers and ranchers face.

In contrast, agricultural managers should have more opportunities. Owners of large tracts of land, who often do not live on the property they own, increasingly will seek the expertise of agricultural managers to run their farms and ranches as businesses.

Job Prospects. Despite the expected continued consolidation of farmland and the projected decline in overall employment of this occupation, job prospects will be good for an increasing number of small-scale farmers who have developed successful market niches that involve personalized, direct contact with their customers. Many are finding opportunities in organic food production. Others use farmers' markets that cater directly to urban and suburban consumers, allowing the farmers to capture a greater share of consumers' food dollars.

Some small-scale farmers may improve their job prospects by participating in collectively owned marketing cooperatives that process and sell their products. Other farmers participate in community-supported agriculture (CSA) cooperatives that allow consumers to buy a share of the farmer's harvest directly.

Contacts for More Information

For more information about agriculture policy and farm advocacy, visit

- Center for Rural Affairs (www.cfra.org)

For more information about federal resources for agriculture, visit the following websites at the U.S. Department of Agriculture:

- New Farmers (www.usda.gov/newfarmers)
- Beginning Farmer and Rancher Development Program (http://tinyurl.com/h2yfqdr)
- Farm Service Agency (www.fsa.usda.gov/FSA)
- Know Your Farmer, Know Your Food (http://tinyurl.com/2eux6k8)

For more information on farm manager certification, visit

- American Society of Farm Managers and Rural Appraisers (www.asfmra.org)

O*NET

- Farmers, Ranchers, and Other Agricultural Managers (11-9013.00)
- Nursery and Greenhouse Managers (11-9013.01)
- Farm and Ranch Managers (11-9013.02)
- Aquacultural Managers (11-9013.03)

Financial Managers

- **2014 Median Pay** .... $115,320 per year $55.44 per hour
- **Typical Entry-Level Education** .... Bachelor's degree
- **Work Experience in a Related Occupation** .... 5 years or more
- **On-the-job Training** .... None
- **Number of Jobs, 2014** 555,900
- **Job Outlook, 2014–24** .... 7% (As fast as average)
- **Employment Change, 2014–24** 37,700

What Financial Managers Do

Financial managers are responsible for the financial health of an organization. They produce financial reports, direct investment activities, and develop strategies and plans for the long-term financial goals of their organization.

Duties. Financial managers typically do the following:

- Prepare financial statements, business activity reports, and forecasts
- Monitor financial details to ensure that legal requirements are met
- Supervise employees who do financial reporting and budgeting
- Review company financial reports and seek ways to reduce costs
- Analyze market trends to maximize profits and find expansion opportunities
- Help management make financial decisions

Financial managers oversee the preparation of financial reports and investment activities.

The role of the financial manager, particularly in business, is changing in response to technological advances that have substantially reduced the amount of time it takes to produce financial reports. Financial managers' main responsibility used to be monitoring a company's finances, but they now do more data analysis and advise senior managers on ways to maximize profits. They often work on teams, acting as business advisors to top executives.

Financial managers also do tasks that are specific to their organization or industry. For example, government financial managers must be experts on government appropriations and budgeting processes, and healthcare financial managers must know about topics in healthcare finance. Moreover, financial managers must be knowledgeable about special tax laws and regulations that affect their industry.

The following are examples of types of financial managers:

Chief financial officers (CFOs) are accountable for the accuracy of a company's or organization's financial reporting, especially among publicly traded companies. As head of a company's entire financial department, they manage the lower level financial managers. They oversee the company's financial goals, objectives, and budgets.

Controllers direct the preparation of financial reports that summarize and forecast the organization's financial position, such as income statements, balance sheets, and analyses of future earnings or expenses. Controllers also are in charge of preparing special reports required by governmental agencies that regulate businesses. Often, controllers oversee the accounting, audit, and budget departments of their organization.

Treasurers and *finance officers* direct their organization's budgets to meet its financial goals. They oversee the investment of funds and carry out strategies to raise capital (such as issuing stocks or bonds) to support the firm's expansion. They also develop financial plans for mergers (two companies joining together) and acquisitions (one company buying another).

Credit managers oversee their firm's credit business. They set credit-rating criteria, determine credit ceilings, and monitor the collections of past-due accounts.

Cash managers monitor and control the flow of cash that comes in and goes out of the company to meet the company's business and investment needs. For example, they must project cash flow (amounts coming in and going out) to determine whether the company will have a shortage or surplus of cash.

Risk managers control financial risk by using strategies to limit or offset the probability of a financial loss or a company's exposure to financial uncertainty. Among the risks they try to limit are those that stem from currency or commodity price changes.

Insurance managers decide how best to limit a company's losses by obtaining insurance against risks, such as the need to make disability payments for an employee who gets hurt on the job or the costs imposed by a lawsuit against the company.

Work Environment

Financial managers held about 555,900 jobs in 2014. The industries that employed the most financial managers were as follows:

Finance and insurance	29%
Management of companies and enterprises	12
Professional, scientific, and technical services	11
Manufacturing	8
Government	8

Median Annual Wages, May 2014

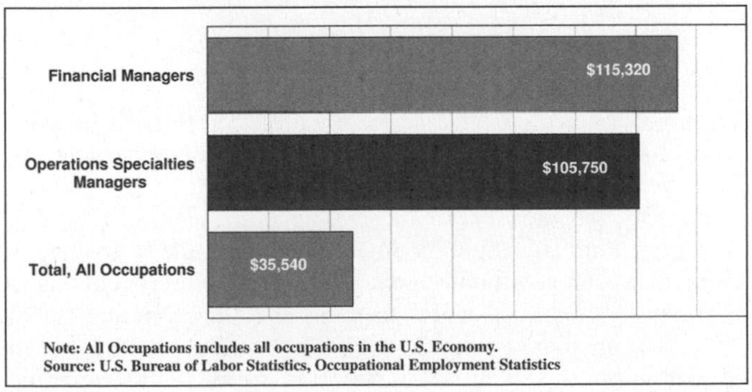

Percent Change in Employment, Projected 2014–2024

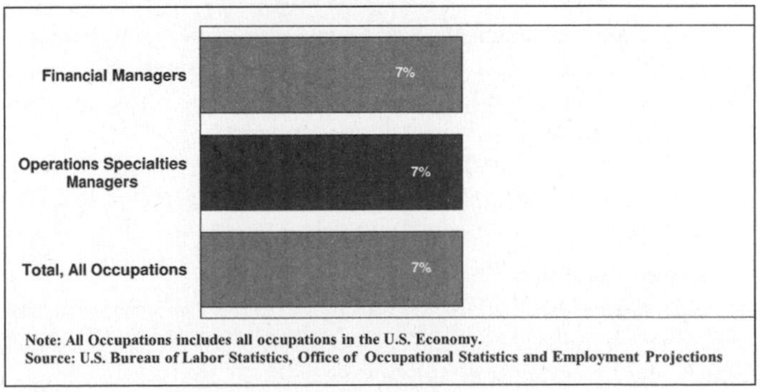

Employment Projections Data for Financial Managers

Occupational Title	SOC Code	Employment, 2014	Projected Employment, 2024	Change, 2014–2024	
				Percent	Numeric
Financial managers	11-3031	555,900	593,500	7	37,700

Source: U.S. Bureau of Labor Statistics, Employment Projections Program

Similar Occupations. This table shows a list of occupations with job duties that are similar to those of financial managers.

Occupations	Entry-level Education	2014 Median Pay	Projected Job Growth	Average Annual Openings
Accountants and Auditors	Bachelor's degree	$65,940	11%	14,240
Budget Analysts	Bachelor's degree	$71,220	3%	150
Financial Analysts	Bachelor's degree	$78,620	12%	3,230
Insurance Sales Agents	High school diploma or equivalent	$47,860	9%	4,350
Insurance Underwriters	Bachelor's degree	$64,220	-11%	-1,170
Loan Officers	Bachelor's degree	$62,620	8%	2,450
Personal Financial Advisors	Bachelor's degree	$81,060	30%	7,390

Financial managers work closely with top executives and with departments that develop the data financial managers need.

Work Schedules. Most financial managers work full time, and about 1 in 3 worked more than 40 hours per week in 2014.

Education/Training

Financial managers typically have a bachelor's degree and 5 years or more of experience in another business or financial occupation, such as an accountant, securities sales agent, or financial analyst.

Education. A bachelor's degree in finance, accounting, economics, or business administration is often the minimum education needed for financial managers. However, many employers now seek candidates with a master's degree, preferably in business administration, finance, or economics. These academic programs help students develop analytical skills and learn financial analysis methods and software.

Licenses, Certifications, and Registrations. Professional certification is not required, but some financial managers still get it to demonstrate a level of competence. The CFA Institute confers the Chartered Financial Analyst (CFA) certification to investment professionals who have at least a bachelor's degree, 4 years of work experience, and pass three exams. The Association for Financial Professionals confers the Certified Treasury Professional credential to those who pass an exam and have a minimum of 2 years of relevant experience.

Work Experience in a Related Occupation. Financial managers usually have experience in another business or financial occupation. For example, they may have worked as a loan officer, accountant, securities sales agent, or financial analyst.

In some cases, companies provide formal management training programs to help prepare highly motivated and skilled financial workers to become financial managers.

Important Qualities

Analytical skills. Financial managers increasingly are assisting executives in making decisions that affect their organization, a task which requires analytical ability.

Communication skills. Excellent communication skills are essential because financial managers must explain and justify complex financial transactions.

Detail oriented. In preparing and analyzing reports such as balance sheets and income statements, financial managers must be precise and attentive to their work in order to avoid errors.

Math skills. Financial managers must be skilled in math, including algebra. An understanding of international finance and complex financial documents also is important.

Organizational skills. Financial managers deal with a range of information and documents and so they must stay organized to do their jobs effectively.

Pay

The median annual wage for financial managers was $115,320 in May 2014. The median wage is the wage at which half the workers in an occupation earned more than that amount and half earned less. The lowest 10 percent earned less than $62,480, and the highest 10 percent earned more than $187,200.

In May 2014, the median annual wages for financial managers in the top industries in which they worked were as follows:

Professional, scientific, and technical services	$139,380
Management of companies and enterprises	133,200
Manufacturing	114,350
Finance and insurance	110,310
Government	104,720

Job Outlook

Employment of financial managers is projected to grow 7 percent from 2014 to 2024, about as fast as the average for all occupations. However, growth will vary by industry.

Services provided by financial managers, such as planning, directing, and coordinating investments, are likely to stay in demand as the economy grows. The United States remains an international financial center, meaning that the economic growth of countries around the world will likely contribute to employment growth in the U.S. financial industry. In recent years, companies have been accumulating more cash on their balance sheets, particularly among those with operations in foreign countries. As globalization continues, this trend is likely to persist. This should lead to demand for financial managers, as companies will be in need of cash management expertise.

The depository credit intermediation industry, which includes commercial banking and savings institutions, employs a large percentage of financial managers. As bank customers increasingly conduct transactions online, the number of bank branches is expected to decline, which should limit employment growth in this sector. However, employment declines here are expected to mainly affect clerical occupations, such as tellers, rather than financial managers. From 2014 to 2024, employment of financial managers is projected to grow 6 percent in this industry.

Job Prospects. As with other managerial occupations, jobseekers are likely to face competition because there are more applicants than job openings. Candidates with expertise in accounting and finance—particularly those with a master's degree or certification—should enjoy the best job prospects. An understanding of international finance and complex financial documents is important.

Contacts for More Information

For more information about financial managers, including certification, visit

➤ Financial Management Association International (www.fma.org)

For information about careers in financial and treasury management and the Certified Treasury Professional program, visit

➤ Association for Financial Professionals (www.afponline.org)

For information about the Chartered Financial Analyst program, visit

➤ CFA Institute (www.cfainstitute.org)

O*NET

➤ Financial Managers (11-3031.00)

➤ Treasurers and Controllers (11-3031.01)

➤ Financial Managers, Branch or Department (11-3031.02)

Food Service Managers

- **2014 Median Pay** .... $48,560 per year $23.34 per hour
- **Typical Entry-Level Education** .... High school diploma or equivalent
- **Work Experience in a Related Occupation** .... Less than 5 years
- **On-the-job Training** .... None
- **Number of Jobs, 2014** 305,000
- **Job Outlook, 2014–24** .... 5% (As fast as average)
- **Employment Change, 2014–24** 15,700

What Food Service Managers Do

Food service managers are responsible for the daily operation of restaurants and other establishments that prepare and serve food and beverages. They direct staff to ensure that customers are satisfied with their dining experience, and they manage the business to ensure that it is profitable.

Duties. Food service managers typically do the following:

- Hire, train, oversee, and sometimes fire employees
- Order food and beverages, equipment, and supplies

Food service managers ensure that food is in adequate supply and stored at the appropriate temperature.

- Oversee food preparation, portion sizes, and the overall presentation of food
- Inspect supplies, equipment, and work areas
- Ensure that employees comply with health and food safety standards
- Address complaints regarding food quality or service
- Schedule staff hours and assign duties
- Manage budgets and payroll records
- Establish standards for personnel performance and customer service

Managers coordinate activities of the kitchen and dining room staff to ensure that customers are served properly and in a timely manner. They oversee orders in the kitchen, and, if needed, they work with the chef to remedy any delays in service.

Food service managers are responsible for all functions of the business related to employees. For example, most managers interview, hire, train, oversee, appraise, discipline, and sometimes fire employees. Managers also schedule work hours, making sure that enough workers are present to cover each shift. During busy periods, they may expedite service by helping to serve customers, processing payments, or cleaning tables.

Managers also arrange for cleaning and maintenance services for the equipment and facility in order to comply with health and sanitary regulations. For example, they may arrange for trash removal, pest control, and heavy cleaning when the dining room and kitchen are not in use.

Most managers perform a variety of administrative tasks, such as managing employee records and preparing the payroll. They

Median Annual Wages, May 2014

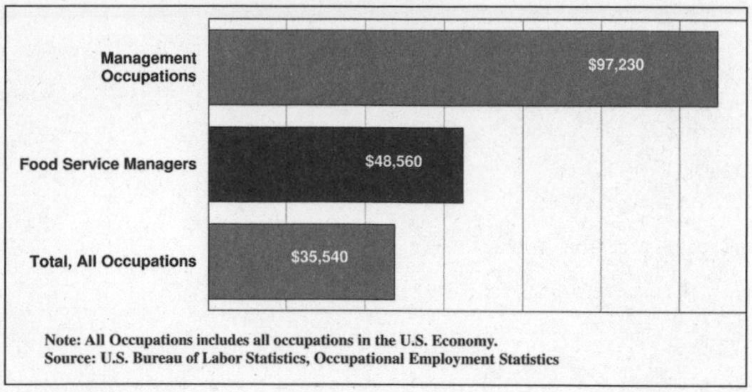

Percent Change in Employment, Projected 2014–2024

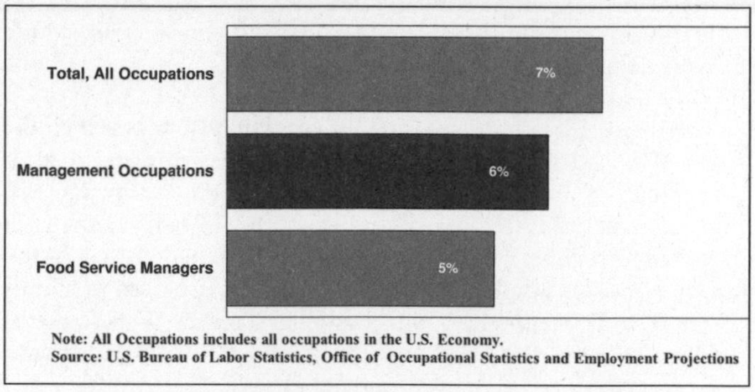

also may review or complete paperwork related to licensing, taxes and wages, and unemployment compensation. Although they sometimes assign these tasks to an assistant manager or bookkeeper, most managers are responsible for the accuracy of business records.

Some managers add up the cash and charge slips and secure them in a safe place. They also may check that ovens, grills, and other equipment are properly cleaned and secured, and that the establishment is locked at the close of business.

Those who manage their own business often deal with suppliers and arrange for the delivery of food and beverages and other supplies.

Full-service restaurants (those with table service) may have a management team that includes a general manager, one or more assistant managers, and an executive chef.

Work Environment

Food service managers held about 305,000 jobs in 2014.They typically work in restaurants, including fine-dining and fast-food chains and franchises. Others work in hotels, catering, and other establishments, such as cafeterias in schools, hospitals, or offices. In 2014, about 1 in 3 food service managers were self-employed.

Many food service managers work long shifts, and the job is often hectic. Dealing with dissatisfied customers can sometimes be stressful.

Work Schedules. Most food service managers work full time. Managers at fine-dining and fast-food restaurants often work long shifts, and some work more than 40 hours per week. Managers of institutional food service facilities in schools, factories, or office buildings usually work traditional business hours. Those who oversee multiple locations of a chain or franchise may be called in on short notice, including evenings, weekends, and holidays.

Education/Training

Most applicants qualify with a high school diploma and several years of work experience in the food service industry as a cook, waiter or waitress, or counter attendant. Some applicants have received additional training at a community college, technical or vocational school, culinary school, or 4-year college.

Education. Although a bachelor's degree is not required, some postsecondary education is increasingly preferred for many manager positions, especially at upscale restaurants and hotels. Some food service companies, hotels, and restaurant chains recruit management trainees from college hospitality or food service management programs. These programs may require the participants to work in internships and to have real-life food industry-related experiences in order to graduate.

Many colleges and universities offer bachelor's degree programs in restaurant and hospitality management or institutional food service management. In addition, numerous community colleges, technical institutes, and other institutions offer programs in the field that lead to an associate's degree. Some culinary schools offer programs in restaurant management with courses designed for those who want to start and run their own restaurant.

Most programs provide instruction in nutrition, sanitation, and food preparation, as well as courses in accounting, business law, and management. Some programs combine classroom and practical study with internships.

Work Experience in a Related Occupation. Most food service managers start working in industry-related jobs, such as cooks, waiters and waitresses, or hosts and hostesses. They often spend years working under the direction of an experienced worker, learning the necessary skills before they are promoted to manager positions.

Training. Managers who work for restaurant chains and food service management companies may be required to complete programs that combine classroom instruction and on-the-job training. Topics may include food preparation, sanitation, security, company policies, personnel management, and recordkeeping.

Licenses, Certifications, and Registrations. Although certification is not required, managers may obtain the Food Protection Managers Certification (FPMC) by passing a food safety exam. The American National Standards Institute accredits institutions that offer the FPMC.

In addition, the National Restaurant Association Educational Foundation awards the Foodservice Management Professional (FMP) designation, a voluntary certification to managers who meet the following criteria:

Employment Projections Data for Food Service Managers

Occupational Title	SOC Code	Employment, 2014	Projected Employment, 2024	Change, 2014–2024 Percent	Change, 2014–2024 Numeric
Food service managers	11-9051	305,000	320,700	5	15,700

Source: U.S. Bureau of Labor Statistics, Employment Projections Program

Similar Occupations. This table shows a list of occupations with job duties that are similar to those of food service managers.

Occupations	Entry-level Education	2014 Median Pay	Projected Job Growth	Average Annual Openings
Bartenders	No formal educational credential	$19,050	10%	6,010
Chefs and Head Cooks	High school diploma or equivalent	$41,610	9%	1,130
Lodging Managers	High school diploma or equivalent	$47,680	8%	370
Sales Managers	Bachelor's degree	$110,660	5%	1,900
Waiters and Waitresses	No formal educational credential	$18,730	3%	6,890

- Have supervisory experience in food service
- Have specialized training in food safety
- Pass a multiple-choice exam

The certification attests to professional competence, particularly for managers who learned their skills on the job.

Important Qualities

Business skills. Food service managers, especially those who run their own restaurant, must understand all aspects of the restaurant business. They should know how to budget for supplies, set prices, and manage workers to ensure that the restaurant is profitable.

Communication skills. Food service managers must give clear orders to staff and be able to communicate effectively with employees and customers.

Customer-service skills. Food service managers must be courteous and attentive when dealing with patrons. Satisfying customers' dining needs is critical to business success and ensures customer loyalty.

Detail oriented. Managers deal with many different types of activities. They ensure that there is enough food to serve to customers, they maintain financial records, and they ensure that the food meets health and safety standards.

Leadership skills. Managers must establish good working relationships to maintain a productive work environment. Carrying out this task may involve motivating workers and leading by example.

Organizational skills. Food service managers keep track of many different schedules, budgets, and staff. Their job becomes more complex as the size of the restaurant or food service facility increases.

Physical stamina. Managers, especially those who run their own restaurant, often work long shifts and sometimes spend entire evenings on their feet helping to serve customers.

Problem-solving skills. Managers need to be able to resolve personnel issues and customer-related problems.

Pay

The median annual wage for food service managers was $48,560 in May 2014. The median wage is the wage at which half the workers in an occupation earned more than that amount and half earned less. The lowest 10 percent earned less than $29,920, and the highest 10 percent earned more than $82,360.

Job Outlook

Employment of food service managers is projected to grow 5 percent from 2014 to 2024, about as fast as the average for all occupations.

Population and income growth are expected to result in greater demand for food at a variety of dining establishments. People will continue to dine out, purchase takeout meals, or have food delivered to their homes or workplaces. In response to increased consumer demand, more restaurants, cafeterias, and catering services are expected to open and serve more meals. Many of these establishments will require food service managers to oversee food preparation and service.

As a cost-saving measure, some companies may hire only one manager to oversee multiple restaurant or cafeteria locations or use first-line supervisors to perform the work usually done by managers. Consequently, some of these establishments may require fewer food service managers.

Job Prospects. Job opportunities should be best for food service managers with several years of work experience in a restaurant or food service establishment. Most job openings will result from the need to replace managers who leave the occupation.

Job seekers with a combination of work experience in food service and a bachelor's degree in hospitality, restaurant, or food service management should have an edge when competing for jobs at upscale hotels and restaurants.

Contacts for More Information

For more information about the Food Protection Manager Certification, visit

➤ American National Standards Institute (http://tinyurl.com/njroj2c)

For more information about food service managers, including a directory of college programs in food service, visit

➤ National Restaurant Association (www.restaurant.org)

For more information about food service managers and certification as a Foodservice Management Professional, visit

➤ National Restaurant Association Educational Foundation (www.nraef.org)

For general information about food service managers, visit

➤ Society for Hospitality and Foodservice Management (www.sfm-online.org)

O*NET

➤ Food Service Managers (11-9051.00)

Human Resources Managers

- **2014 Median Pay** .... $102,780 per year $49.41 per hour
- **Typical Entry-Level Education** .... Bachelor's degree
- **Work Experience in a Related Occupation** .... 5 years or more
- **On-the-job Training** .... None
- **Number of Jobs, 2014** 122,500
- **Job Outlook, 2014–24** .... 9% (Faster than average)
- **Employment Change, 2014–24** 10,800

What Human Resources Managers Do

Human resources managers plan, direct, and coordinate the administrative functions of an organization. They oversee the recruiting, interviewing, and hiring of new staff; consult with top executives on strategic planning; and serve as a link between an organization's management and its employees.

Duties. Human resources managers typically do the following:

- Plan and coordinate an organization's workforce to best use employees' talents
- Link an organization's management with its employees
- Plan and oversee employee benefit programs
- Serve as a consultant with other managers advising them on human resource issues, such as equal employment opportunity and sexual harassment
- Coordinate and supervise the work of specialists and support staff
- Oversee an organization's recruitment, interview, selection, and hiring processes
- Handle staffing issues, such as mediating disputes and directing disciplinary procedures

Every organization wants to attract, motivate, and keep qualified employees and match them to jobs for which they are well suited. Human resources managers accomplish this by directing the administrative functions of human resource departments. Their work involves overseeing employee relations, regulatory compliance, and employee-related services such as payroll, training, and benefits. They supervise the department's specialists and support staff and ensure that tasks are completed accurately and on time.

Human resources managers also consult with top executives regarding the organization's strategic planning. They identify ways to maximize the value of the organization's employees and ensure that they are used as efficiently as possible. For example, they might assess worker productivity and recommend changes to the organization's structure to help it meet budgetary goals.

Some human resources managers oversee all aspects of an organization's human resources department, including the compensation and benefits or training and development programs. In many larger organizations, these programs are directed by specialized managers, such as compensation and benefits managers and training and development managers.

The following are examples of types of human resources managers:

Labor relations directors, also called *employee relations managers*, oversee employment policies in union and nonunion settings. They draw up, negotiate, and administer labor contracts that cover issues such as grievances, wages, benefits, and union and management practices. They also handle labor complaints between employees and management and coordinate grievance procedures.

Payroll managers supervise the operations of an organization's payroll department. They ensure that all aspects of payroll are processed correctly and on time. They administer payroll procedures, prepare reports for the accounting department, and resolve any payroll problems or discrepancies.

Recruiting managers, sometimes called *staffing managers*, oversee the recruiting and hiring responsibilities of the human resources department. They often supervise a team of recruiters, and some take on recruiting duties when trying to fill high-level positions. They must develop a recruiting strategy that helps them meet the staffing needs of their organization and effectively compete for the best employees.

Human resources managers oversee an organization's recruitment, interview, selection, and hiring processes.

Work Environment

Human resources managers held about 122,500 jobs in 2014. The industries that employed the most human resources managers were as follows:

Management of companies and enterprises	15%
Manufacturing	14
Professional, scientific, and technical services	12
Government	10
Healthcare and social assistance	10

Human resources managers work in offices. Some managers, especially those working for organizations that have offices nationwide, must travel to visit other branches as well as to attend professional meetings or to recruit employees.

Work Schedules. Most human resources managers work full time during regular business hours.

About 1 in 3 human resources managers worked more than 40 hours per week in 2014.

Education/Training

Candidates need a combination of education and several years of related work experience to become a human resources manager. Although a bachelor's degree is sufficient for most positions, some jobs require a master's degree. Candidates should have strong interpersonal skills.

Education. Human resources managers usually need a bachelor's degree. There are bachelor's degree programs in human resources. Alternatively, candidates may complete a bachelor's degree in another field, such as finance, business management, education, or information technology. Courses in subjects such as conflict management or industrial psychology may be helpful.

Some higher-level jobs require a master's degree in human resources, labor relations, or business administration (MBA).

Work Experience in a Related Occupation. To demonstrate abilities in organizing, directing, and leading others, related work experience is essential for human resources managers. Some managers start out as human resources specialists or labor relations specialists. Others gain management experience in a variety of fields.

Median Annual Wages, May 2014

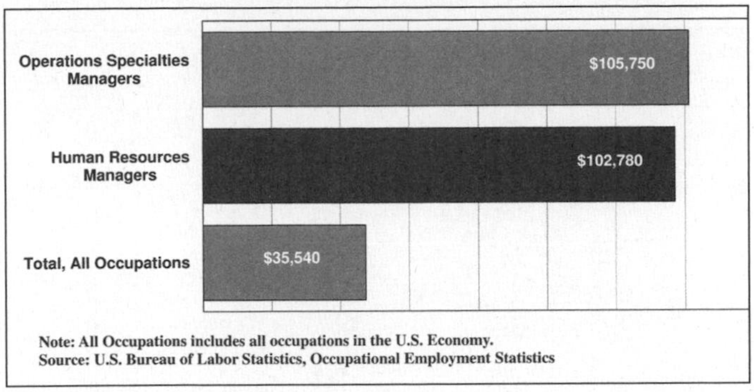

Percent Change in Employment, Projected 2014–2024

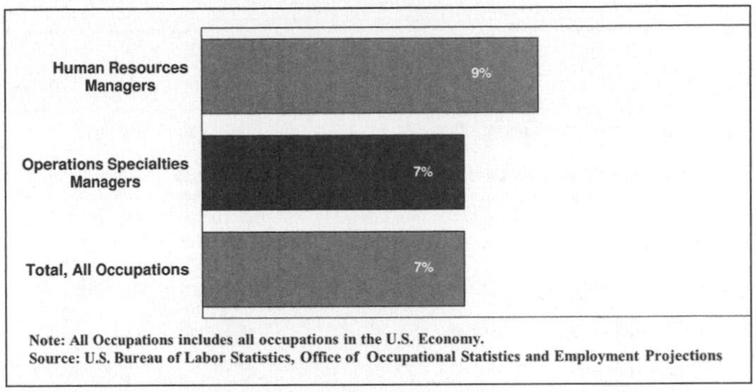

Management positions typically require an understanding of human resources programs, such as compensation and benefits plans; human resources software; and federal, state, and local employment laws.

Licenses, Certifications, and Registrations. Although certification is voluntary, it can show professional expertise and credibility and may enhance advancement opportunities. Many employers prefer to hire certified candidates, and some positions may require certification. The Society for Human Resource Management, Human Resource Certification Institute, WorldatWork, and the International Foundation of Employee Benefit Plans are among many professional associations that offer a variety of certification programs.

Important Qualities

Decision-making skills. Human resources managers must be able to balance the strengths and weaknesses of different options and decide the best course of action. Many of their decisions have a significant impact on workers or operations, such as deciding whether to hire an employee.

Interpersonal skills. Human resources managers need strong interpersonal skills because they regularly interact with people. They often collaborate on teams and must develop positive working relationships with their colleagues.

Leadership skills. Human resources managers must be able to direct a staff and oversee the operations of their department. They must coordinate work activities and ensure that workers in the department complete their duties and fulfill their responsibilities.

Organizational skills. Organizational skills are essential for human resources managers. They must be able to prioritize tasks and manage several projects at once.

Speaking skills. Human resources managers rely on strong speaking skills to give presentations and direct their staff. They must clearly communicate information and instructions to their staff and other employees.

Pay

The median annual wage for human resources managers was $102,780 in May 2014. The median wage is the wage at which half the workers in an occupation earned more than that amount and half earned less. The lowest 10 percent earned less than $60,440, and the highest 10 percent earned more than $183,590.

In May 2014, the median annual wages for human resources managers in the top industries in which they worked were as follows:

Professional, scientific, and technical services	$116,740
Management of companies and enterprises	115,520
Manufacturing	99,440
Government	94,560
Healthcare and social assistance	87,610

Job Outlook

Employment of human resources managers is projected to grow 9 percent from 2014 to 2024, faster than the average for all occupations.

Employment growth largely depends on the performance and growth of individual companies. As new companies form and organizations expand their operations, they will need more human resources managers to oversee and administer their programs.

Human resources managers will also be needed to ensure that firms adhere to changing and complex employment laws regarding occupational safety and health, equal employment opportunity, healthcare, wages, and retirement plans. For example, adoption of the Affordable Care Act may spur the need for more human resources managers, who can help to ensure that company policies are in compliance with regulations.

Job Prospects. Although job opportunities are expected to vary based on the staffing needs of individual companies, strong competition can be expected for most positions.

Job opportunities should be good in the management of companies and enterprises industry as organizations continue to use outside firms to assist with some of their human resources functions.

Candidates with certification or a master's degree—particularly those with a concentration in human resources management—should have the best job prospects.

Employment Projections Data for Human Resources Managers

Occupational Title	SOC Code	Employment, 2014	Projected Employment, 2024	Change, 2014–2024	
				Percent	Numeric
Human resources managers	11-3121	122,500	133,300	9	10,800

Source: U.S. Bureau of Labor Statistics, Employment Projections Program

Similar Occupations. This table shows a list of occupations with job duties that are similar to those of human resources managers.

Occupations	Entry-level Education	2014 Median Pay	Projected Job Growth	Average Annual Openings
Administrative Services Managers	Bachelor's degree	$83,790	8%	2,350
Compensation and Benefits Managers	Bachelor's degree	$108,070	6%	110
Compensation, Benefits, and Job Analysis Specialists	Bachelor's degree	$60,600	4%	340
Human Resources Specialists	Bachelor's degree	$57,420	5%	2,200
Labor Relations Specialists	Bachelor's degree	$56,950	-8%	-640
Top Executives	Bachelor's degree	$102,750	6%	14,700
Training and Development Managers	Bachelor's degree	$101,930	7%	230
Training and Development Specialists	Bachelor's degree	$57,340	7%	1,890

Those with a solid background and work experience in human resources programs, policies, and employment law should also have better job opportunities.

Contacts for More Information

For more information about human resources managers, including certification, visit

➤ Society for Human Resource Management (www.shrm.org/Pages/default.aspx)

➤ Human Resource Certification Institute (www.hrci.org)

For information about careers and certification in employee compensation and benefits, visit

➤ International Foundation of Employee Benefit Plans (www.ifebp.org)

➤ WorldatWork (www.worldatwork.org/waw/home/html/home.jsp)

For information about careers in employee training and development and certification, visit

➤ American Society for Training and Development (www.astd.org)

➤ International Society for Performance Improvement (www.ispi.org)

O*NET

➤ Human Resources Managers (11-3121.00)

Industrial Production Managers

- **2014 Median Pay** .... $92,470 per year $44.46 per hour
- **Typical Entry-Level Education** .... Bachelor's degree
- **Work Experience in a Related Occupation**............ 5 years or more
- **On-the-job Training** .... None
- **Number of Jobs, 2014** 173,400
- **Job Outlook, 2014–24** .... -4% (Decline)
- **Employment Change, 2014–24** .... -6,300

What Industrial Production Managers Do

Industrial production managers oversee the daily operations of manufacturing and related plants. They coordinate, plan, and direct the activities used to create a wide range of goods, such as cars, computer equipment, or paper products.

Duties. Industrial production managers typically do the following:

- Decide how best to use a plant's workers and equipment to meet production goals
- Ensure that production stays on schedule and within budget
- Hire, train, and evaluate workers
- Analyze production data
- Write production reports
- Monitor a plant's workers to ensure they meet performance and safety requirements

Industrial production managers oversee all stages of the production process.

- Streamline the production process
- Determine whether new machines are needed or whether overtime work is necessary
- Fix any production problems

Industrial production managers, also called *plant managers*, may oversee an entire manufacturing plant or a specific area of production.

Industrial production managers are responsible for carrying out quality control programs to make sure the finished product meets a specific level of quality. Often called *quality control systems managers*, these managers use programs to help identify defects in products, identify the cause of the defect, and solve the problem creating it. For example, a manager may determine that a defect is being caused by parts from an outside supplier. The manager can then work with the supplier to improve the quality of the parts.

Industrial production managers work closely with managers from other departments as well. For example, the procurement (buying) department orders the supplies that the production department uses. A breakdown in communication between these two departments can cause production slowdowns. Industrial production managers also communicate with other managers and departments, such as sales, warehousing, and research and design.

Work Environment

Industrial production managers held about 173,400 jobs in 2014. The industries that employed the most industrial production managers were as follows:

Fabricated metal product manufacturing	11%
Transportation equipment manufacturing	10
Machinery manufacturing	8
Chemical manufacturing	8
Food manufacturing	7

Industrial production managers split their time between the production area and a nearby office. When they are working in the production area, they may need to wear protective equipment such as a helmet or safety goggles.

Work Schedules. Most industrial production managers work full time, and almost half worked more than 40 hours per week in 2014. In some facilities, managers work night or weekend shifts and must be on call to deal with emergencies at any time.

Education/Training

Industrial production managers typically need a bachelor's degree and several years of related work experience.

Education. Employers prefer managers have at least a bachelor's degree. While the degree may be in any field, many industrial production managers have a bachelor's degree in business administration or industrial engineering. Sometimes, production workers with many years of experience take management classes and become a production manager. At large plants, where managers have more oversight responsibilities, employers may look for managers who have a Master of Business Administration (MBA) or a graduate degree in industrial management.

Work Experience in a Related Occupation. Many industrial production managers begin as production workers and move up through the ranks. They usually advance to a first-line supervisory position before eventually being selected for management. Most earn a college degree in business management or take company-sponsored classes to increase their chances of a promotion.

Production managers who join a firm immediately after graduating from college sometimes work as first-line supervisors before beginning their jobs as production managers.

Some managers begin working at a company directly after college or graduate school. They may spend their first few months in training programs, becoming familiar with the production process, company policies, and safety regulations. In large companies, many also spend short periods of time working in other departments, such as purchasing or accounting, to learn more about the company.

Important Qualities

Interpersonal skills. Industrial production managers must have excellent communication skills so they can work with managers from other departments, as well as with the company's senior-level management.

Leadership skills. To keep the production process running smoothly, industrial production managers must motivate and direct the employees they manage.

Problem-solving skills. Production managers must be able to identify problems immediately and solve them. For example, if a product has a defect, the manager determines whether it is a one-time problem or the result of the production process.

Time-management skills. To meet production deadlines, managers must carefully manage their employees' time as well as their own.

Licenses, Certifications, and Registrations. While not required, industrial production managers can earn certifications that show a higher level of competency in quality or management systems. The Association for Operations Management offers a Certified in Production and Inventory Management (CPIM) credential. The American Society for Quality offers credentials in quality control. Both certifications require specific amounts of work experience before applying for the credential, so they are generally not earned before entering the occupation.

Median Annual Wages, May 2014

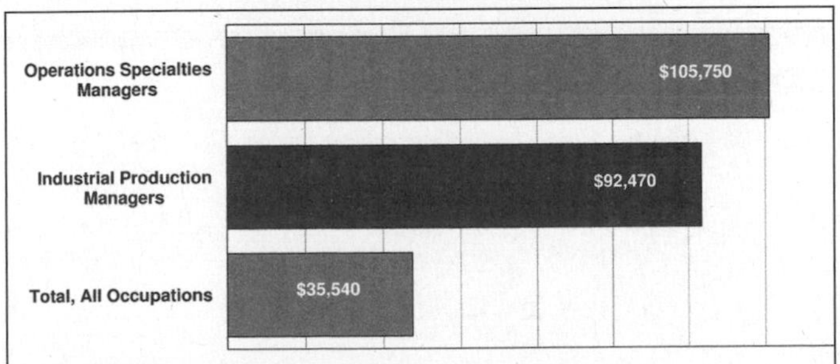

Note: All Occupations includes all occupations in the U.S. Economy.
Source: U.S. Bureau of Labor Statistics, Occupational Employment Statistics

Percent Change in Employment, Projected 2014–2024

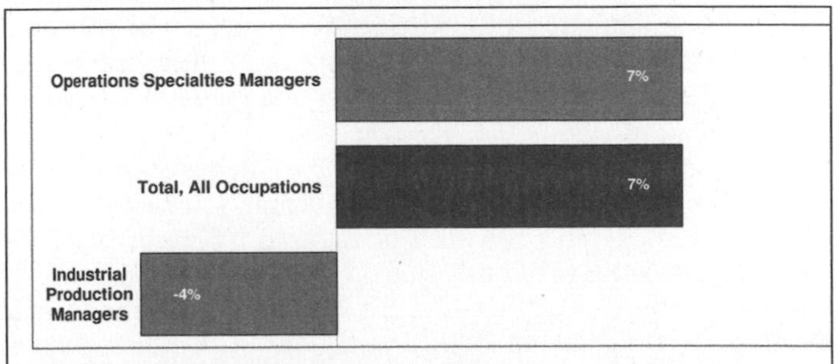

Note: All Occupations includes all occupations in the U.S. Economy.
Source: U.S. Bureau of Labor Statistics, Office of Occupational Statistics and Employment Projections

Employment Projections Data for Industrial Production Managers

Occupational Title	SOC Code	Employment, 2014	Projected Employment, 2024	Change, 2014–2024 Percent	Change, 2014–2024 Numeric
Industrial production managers	11-3051	173,400	167,000	-4	-6,300

Source: U.S. Bureau of Labor Statistics, Employment Projections Program

Similar Occupations. This table shows a list of occupations with job duties that are similar to those of industrial production managers.

Occupations	Entry-level Education	2014 Median Pay	Projected Job Growth	Average Annual Openings
Advertising, Promotions, and Marketing Managers	Bachelor's degree	$123,450	9%	1,970
Construction Managers	Bachelor's degree	$85,630	5%	1,780
Health and Safety Engineers	Bachelor's degree	$81,830	6%	160
Industrial Engineers	Bachelor's degree	$81,490	1%	210
Management Analysts	Bachelor's degree	$80,880	14%	10,340
Mechanical Engineers	Bachelor's degree	$83,060	5%	1,460
Operations Research Analysts	Bachelor's degree	$76,660	30%	2,760
Sales Managers	Bachelor's degree	$110,660	5%	1,900
Top Executives	Bachelor's degree	$102,750	6%	14,700

Pay

The median annual wage for industrial production managers was $92,470 in May 2014. The median wage is the wage at which half the workers in an occupation earned more than that amount and half earned less. The lowest 10 percent earned less than $56,290, and the highest 10 percent earned more than $158,170.

In May 2014, the median annual wages for industrial production managers in the top industries in which they worked were as follows:

Chemical manufacturing	$100,320
Transportation equipment manufacturing	96,740
Machinery manufacturing	91,420
Food manufacturing	85,000
Fabricated metal product manufacturing	84,360

Job Outlook

Employment of industrial production managers is projected to decline 4 percent from 2014 to 2024. Most of these managers are employed in various manufacturing industries, which may see a decrease in overall employment due to increased productivity. In the past, employment of industrial production managers was less affected by productivity gains, since these managers were responsible for coordinating work activities with the goal of increased productivity. However, as facilities adapt to this new, leaner production model, employment of workers and managers should be equally affected by productivity increases.

Some manufacturing jobs are at risk of being outsourced to other countries with lower wages, dampening some employment growth. However, this risk may be reduced by recent trends of "reshoring," where previously outsourced personnel and services are being brought back to the United States. In addition, some firms are moving jobs to lower cost regions of the United States rather than foreign countries in a trend referred to as "domestic sourcing."

Job Prospects. Applicants will likely face strong competition for positions, but those who have several years of experience and a bachelor's degree in industrial management or business administration should have the best prospects.

Contacts for More Information

For more information about careers in production management and certification, visit

- Association for Operations Management (APICS) (www.apics.org)

For more information about quality management and certification, visit

- American Society for Quality (http://asq.org/index.aspx)

For general information about manufacturing careers, visit

- National Association of Manufacturers (www.nam.org)

O*NET

- Industrial Production Managers (11-3051.00)
- Quality Control Systems Managers (11-3051.01)
- Geothermal Production Managers (11-3051.02)
- Biofuels Production Managers (11-3051.03)
- Biomass Power Plant Managers (11-3051.04)
- Methane/Landfill Gas Collection System Operators (11-3051.05)
- Hydroelectric Production Managers (11-3051.06)

Lodging Managers

- **2014 Median Pay** .... $47,680 per year, $22.93 per hour
- **Typical Entry-Level Education** .... High school diploma or equivalent
- **Work Experience in a Related Occupation** .... Less than 5 years
- **On-the-job Training** .... None

- **Number of Jobs, 2014** 48,400
- **Job Outlook, 2014–24** .... 8% (As fast as average)
- **Employment Change, 2014–24** 3,700

What Lodging Managers Do

Lodging managers ensure that guests on vacation or business travel have a pleasant experience at a hotel, motel, or other types of establishment with accommodations. Lodging managers also ensure that the establishment is run efficiently and profitably.

Duties. Lodging managers typically do the following:

- Inspect guest rooms, public areas, and grounds for cleanliness and appearance
- Ensure that company standards for guest services, décor, and housekeeping are met
- Answer questions from guests about hotel policies and services
- Keep track of how much money the hotel or lodging facility is making
- Interview, hire, train, and sometimes fire staff members
- Monitor staff performance to ensure that guests are happy and that the hotel is well run
- Coordinate front-office activities of hotels or motels and resolve problems
- Set room rates and budgets, approve expenditures, and allocate funds to various departments

A comfortable room, good food, and a helpful staff can make being away from home an enjoyable experience for guests on vacation or business travel. Lodging managers occasionally greet and register guests. They also try to make sure that guests have a good experience.

Lodging establishments vary in size, from independently owned bed-and-breakfasts to motels with just a few rooms or to hotels that can hold more than 1,000 guests. Services can vary by providing a room, granting access to a swimming pool, offering a free breakfast, having a full-service restaurant, having a lobby, operating a casino, and hosting conventions.

Many lodging managers use online social media for marketing purposes.

The following are examples of types of lodging managers:

General managers oversee all lodging operations at a property. At large hotels with several departments and multiple layers of management, the general manager and several assistant managers coordinate the activities of separate departments. These departments may include housekeeping, human resources, administration, marketing and sales, purchasing, security, maintenance, recreational facilities, and other activities. For more information, see the profiles on human resources managers; public relations and fundraising managers; financial managers; advertising, promotions, and marketing managers; and food service managers.

Revenue managers work in financial management, monitoring room sales and reservations, overseeing accounting and cash-flow matters at the hotel, projecting occupancy levels, and deciding which rooms to discount and when to offer special rates.

Front-office managers coordinate reservations and room assignments and train and direct the hotel's front-desk staff. They ensure that guests are treated courteously, that complaints and problems are resolved, and that requests for special services are carried out. Most front-office managers are also responsible for adjusting bills.

Convention service managers coordinate the activities of various departments, to accommodate meetings, conventions, and special events. They meet with representatives of groups to plan the number of conference rooms to be reserved, design the configuration of the meeting space, and determine what other services the groups will need, such as catering or audiovisual requirements. During a meeting or event, they resolve unexpected problems and ensure that hotel operations meet a group's expectations.

Work Environment

Lodging managers held about 48,400 jobs in 2014. More than half were employed in the traveler accommodation industry, which includes hotels and motels.

Most of the remainder worked in other lodging establishments, such as recreational vehicle (RV) and recreational camps, youth hostels, inns, boardinghouses, bed-and-breakfasts, casinos, and resorts. About 1 in 3 were self-employed.

The pressures of coordinating a wide range of activities, turning a profit for investors, and dealing with dissatisfied guests can be stressful.

Work Schedules. Most lodging managers are employed full time. Because hotels are open around the clock, working evenings, weekends, and holidays is common. Some managers must be on call 24 hours a day, particularly if they reside at the lodging establishment.

Education/Training

Many applicants can qualify as a lodging manager by having a high school diploma and several years of experience working in a hotel. However, most large, full-service hotels require applicants to have a bachelor's degree. Hotels that provide fewer services generally accept applicants who have an associate's degree or certificate in hotel management or operations.

Education. Currently, some states and the District of Columbia offer high school academic training for prospective lodging managers.

Most full-service hotel chains hire candidates with a bachelor's degree in hospitality or hotel management. Hotel management programs typically include instruction in hotel administration, accounting, marketing and sales, housekeeping, food service management and catering, and hotel maintenance and engineering. Systems training is also an integral part of many degree programs, because hotels use hospitality-specific software in reservations, billing, and housekeeping management. The Accreditation

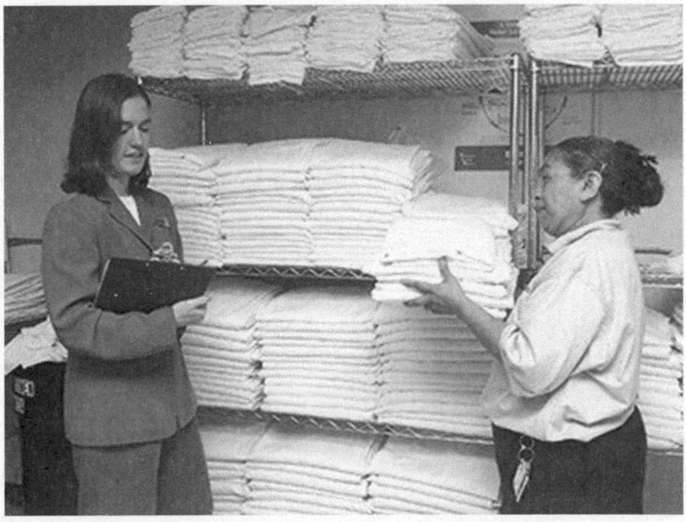

Lodging managers may oversee individual departments, such as housekeeping.

Median Annual Wages, May 2014

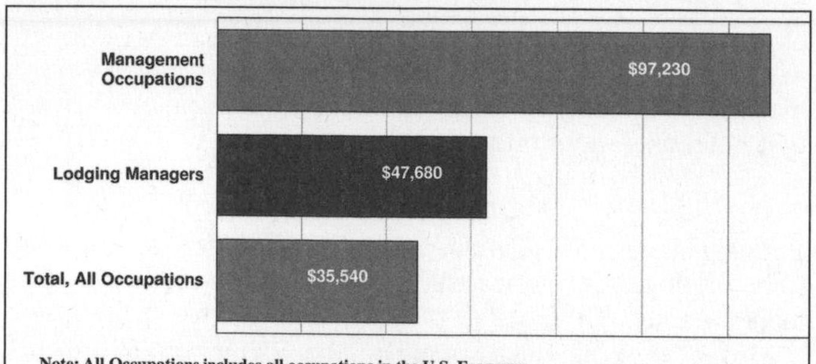

Note: All Occupations includes all occupations in the U.S. Economy.
Source: U.S. Bureau of Labor Statistics, Occupational Employment Statistics

Percent Change in Employment, Projected 2014–2024

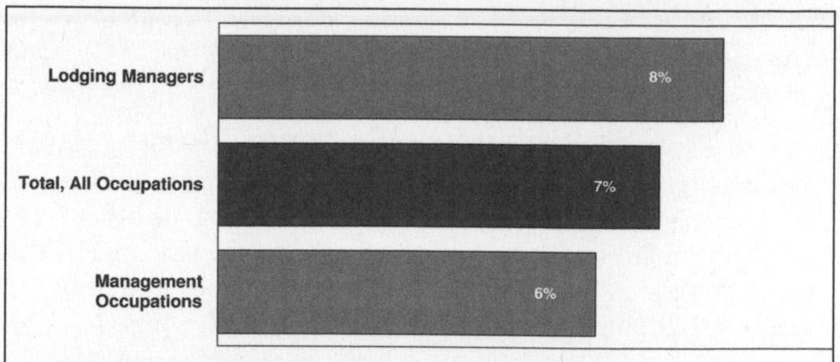

Note: All Occupations includes all occupations in the U.S. Economy.
Source: U.S. Bureau of Labor Statistics, Office of Occupational Statistics and Employment Projections

Commission for Programs in Hospitality Administration accredits about 60 hospitality management programs.

At hotels that provide fewer services, candidates with an associate's degree or certificate in hotel, restaurant, or hospitality management may qualify for a job as a lodging manager.

Also, many technical institutes and vocational and trade schools offer courses that are recognized by the hospitality industry that may help in getting a job.

Work Experience in a Related Occupation. Hotel employees who do not have hospitality management training, but who show leadership potential and have several years of related work experience, may qualify for assistant manager positions.

Licenses, Certifications, and Registrations. Aspiring high school students can enroll in the Hospitality and Tourism Management Program (HTMP) offered by the American Hotel & Lodging Educational Institute (AHLEI). The HTMP is a 2-year program that teaches management principles and leads to professional certification, the Certified Hospitality & Tourism Management Professional. College students and working professionals can also obtain the Certification in Hotel Industry Analytics (CHIA) through AHLEI.

Advancement. Large hotel chains may offer better opportunities than small, independently owned hotels for advancing from assistant manager to manager or from managing one hotel to being a regional manager. However, these opportunities usually involve relocating to another city or state.

Important Qualities

Business skills. Lodging managers address budget matters and coordinate and supervise workers. Operating a profitable hotel is important—as is the need to motivate and direct the work of employees.

Customer-service skills. Lodging managers must have excellent customer-service skills when dealing with guests. Satisfying guests' needs is critical to a hotel's success and helps to ensure customer loyalty.

Interpersonal skills. Lodging managers need strong interpersonal skills because they interact regularly with many different people. They must be effective communicators and must have positive interactions with guests and hotel staff, even in stressful situations.

Leadership skills. Lodging managers must establish good working relationships to ensure a productive work environment. This objective may involve motivating personnel, resolving conflicts, and listening to complaints or criticism from guests.

Listening skills. Lodging managers should have excellent listening skills. Listening to the needs of guests allows managers to take the appropriate course of action, ensuring guests' satisfaction. Listening to the needs of workers helps managers keep good working relationships with the staff.

Organizational skills. Lodging managers keep track of many different schedules, budgets, and people at once. This task becomes more complex as the size of the hotel increases.

Problem-solving skills. The ability to resolve personnel issues and guest-related dissatisfaction is critical to the work of lodging managers. As a result, they should be creative and practical when confronted with problems.

Pay

The median annual wage for lodging managers was $47,680 in May 2014. The median wage is the wage at which half the workers in an occupation earned more than that amount and half earned less. The lowest 10 percent earned less than $28,630, and the highest 10 percent earned more than $94,780.

Job Outlook

Employment of lodging managers is projected to grow 8 percent from 2014 to 2024, about as fast as the average for all occupations.

Expected growth in tourism, travel, and higher occupancy levels will contribute to the need for managers. However, as the lodging industry transitions toward more limited-service hotels and fewer full-service properties that have separate departments to manage—such as in-house restaurants and laundry—employment growth will be limited.

Some lodging places continue to streamline operations to cut expenses. Chain hotels, for instance, may choose to assign a single manager to oversee multiple properties within a local geographic

Employment Projections Data for Lodging Managers

Occupational Title	SOC Code	Employment, 2014	Projected Employment, 2024	Change, 2014–2024 Percent	Change, 2014–2024 Numeric
Lodging managers	11-9081	48,400	52,100	8	3,700

Source: U.S. Bureau of Labor Statistics, Employment Projections Program

Similar Occupations. This table shows a list of occupations with job duties that are similar to those of lodging managers.

Occupations	Entry-level Education	2014 Median Pay	Projected Job Growth	Average Annual Openings
Food Service Managers	High school diploma or equivalent	$48,560	5%	1,570
Gaming Services Workers	High school diploma or equivalent	$19,940	1%	100
Human Resources Managers	Bachelor's degree	$102,780	9%	1,080
Property, Real Estate, and Community Association Managers	High school diploma or equivalent	$54,270	8%	2,530
Sales Managers	Bachelor's degree	$110,660	5%	1,900

area. Still, some large full-service hotels, including casinos, resorts, and convention hotels that provide a wide range of services to a larger customer base, will continue to generate jobs for experienced managers.

Job Prospects. Those seeking jobs at hotels with the highest level of guest services are expected to face strong competition, as these positions are highly sought after by people trained in hospitality management or administration.

Applicants with a bachelor's degree in hospitality or hotel management are expected to have the best job opportunities, particularly at upscale and luxury hotels.

Contacts for More Information

For information about career, professional development, and training programs, visit

➤ American Hotel & Lodging Educational Institute (www.ahlei.org)

For information about schools and educational programs in hotel and restaurant management, including correspondence courses, visit

➤ Accreditation Commission for Programs in Hospitality Administration (www.acpha-cahm.org/accredited-programs)

➤ International Council on Hotel, Restaurant, and Institutional Education (www.chrie.org)

For information about lodging news operations, visit

➤ Hotel News Now (www.hotelnewsnow.com)

O*NET

➤ Lodging Managers (11-9081.00)

Medical and Health Services Managers

- **2014 Median Pay** .... $92,810 per year $44.62 per hour
- **Typical Entry-Level Education** .... Bachelor's degree
- **Work Experience in a Related Occupation** .... Less than 5 years
- **On-the-job Training** .... None
- **Number of Jobs, 2014** 333,000
- **Job Outlook, 2014–24** .... 17% (Much faster than average)
- **Employment Change, 2014–24** 56,300

What Medical and Health Services Managers Do

Medical and health services managers, also called *healthcare executives* or *healthcare administrators*, plan, direct, and coordinate medical and health services. They may manage an entire facility, a specific clinical area or department, or a medical practice for a group of physicians. Medical and health services managers must adapt to changes in healthcare laws, regulations, and technology.

Duties. Medical and health services managers typically do the following:

- Work to improve efficiency and quality in delivering healthcare services
- Develop departmental goals and objectives
- Ensure that the facility in which they work is up to date on and compliant with new laws and regulations
- Recruit, train, and supervise staff
- Manage the finances of the facility, such as patient fees and billing
- Create work schedules
- Prepare and monitor budgets and spending to ensure departments operate within allocated funds
- Represent the facility at investor meetings or on governing boards
- Keep and organize records of the facility's services, such as the number of inpatient beds used
- Communicate with members of the medical staff and department heads

Medical and health services managers work closely with physicians and surgeons, registered nurses, medical and clinical laboratory technologists and technicians, and other healthcare workers. Others may interact with patients or insurance agents.

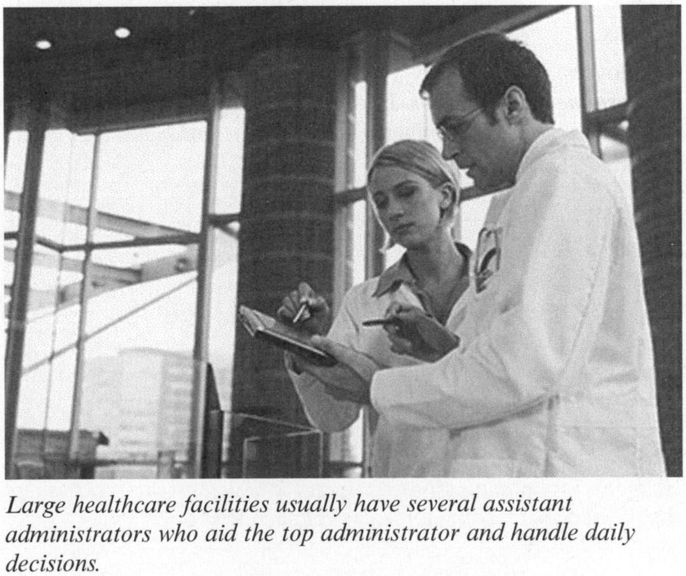

Large healthcare facilities usually have several assistant administrators who aid the top administrator and handle daily decisions.

Median Annual Wages, May 2014

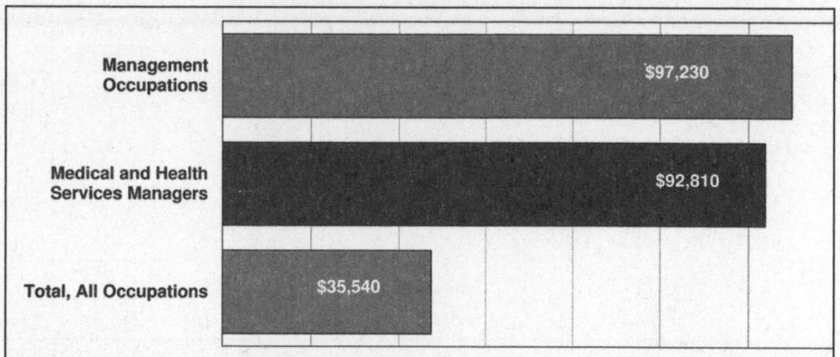

Note: All Occupations includes all occupations in the U.S. Economy.
Source: U.S. Bureau of Labor Statistics, Occupational Employment Statistics

Percent Change in Employment, Projected 2014–2024

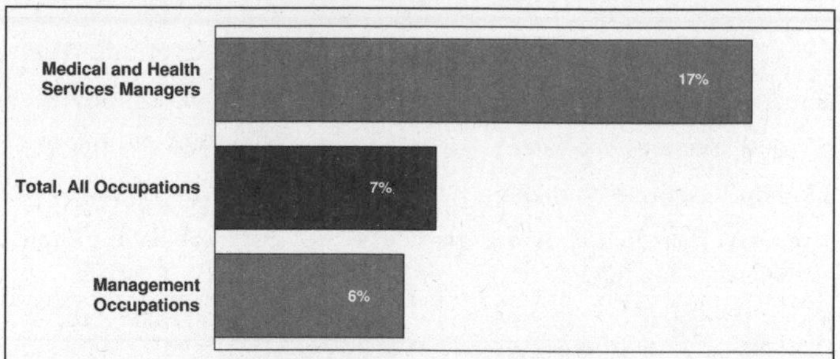

Note: All Occupations includes all occupations in the U.S. Economy.
Source: U.S. Bureau of Labor Statistics, Office of Occupational Statistics and Employment Projections

Medical and health services managers' titles depend on the facility or area of expertise in which they work. The following are examples of types of medical and health services managers:

Nursing home administrators manage staff, admissions, finances, and care of the building, as well as care of the residents in nursing homes. All states require licensure for nursing home administrators; licensing requirements vary by state.

Clinical managers oversee a specific department, such as nursing, surgery, or physical therapy, and have responsibilities based on that specialty. Clinical managers set and carry out policies, goals, and procedures for their departments; evaluate the quality of the staff's work; and develop reports and budgets.

Health information managers are responsible for the maintenance and security of all patient records and data. They must stay up to date with evolving information technology, current or proposed laws about health information systems, and trends in managing large amounts of complex data. Health information managers must ensure that databases are complete, accurate, and accessible only to authorized personnel. They also may supervise the work of medical records and health information technicians.

Assistant administrators work under the top administrator in larger facilities and often handle daily decisions. Assistants might direct activities in clinical areas, such as nursing, surgery, therapy, medical records, or health information. They also handle administrative tasks, such as ensuring that their department has the necessary supplies and that equipment is operational and up to date.

Work Environment

Medical and health services managers held about 333,000 jobs in 2014. The industries that employed the most medical and health services managers were as follows:

Hospitals; state, local, and private	37%
Nursing and residential care facilities	10
Offices of physicians	10
Government	9
Home healthcare services	6

Most medical and health services managers work in offices in healthcare facilities, including hospitals and nursing homes, and group medical practices.

Work Schedules. Most medical and health services managers work full time. About 1 in 3 managers worked more than 40 hours per week in 2014. Work during evenings or weekends may be required in healthcare settings that are open at all hours, such as hospitals and nursing homes. Medical and health services managers may need to be on call in case emergencies arise.

Education/Training

Most medical and health services managers have at least a bachelor's degree before entering the field. However, master's degrees are common and sometimes preferred by employers. Educational requirements vary by facility.

Education. Medical and health services managers typically need at least a bachelor's degree to enter the occupation. However, master's degrees are common and sometimes preferred by employers. Graduate programs often last between 2 and 3 years and may include up to 1 year of supervised administrative experience in a hospital or healthcare consulting setting.

Prospective medical and health services managers typically have a degree in health administration, health management, nursing, public health administration, or business administration. Degrees that focus on both management and healthcare combine business-related courses with courses in medical terminology, hospital organization, and health information systems. For example, a degree in health administration or health information management often includes courses in health services management, accounting and budgeting, human resources administration, strategic planning, law and ethics, health economics, and health information systems.

Work Experience in a Related Occupation. Many employers require prospective medical and health services managers to have some work experience in either an administrative or a clinical role in a hospital or other healthcare facility. For example, nursing home administrators usually have years of experience working as a registered nurse.

Others may begin their careers as medical records and health information technicians, administrative assistants, or financial clerks within a healthcare office.

Important Qualities

Analytical skills. Medical and health services managers must understand and follow current regulations and adapt to new laws.

Communication skills. These managers must effectively communicate policies and procedures with other health professionals and ensure their staff's compliance with new laws and regulations.

Detail oriented. Medical and health services managers must pay attention to detail. They might be required to organize and maintain scheduling and billing information for very large facilities, such as hospitals.

Interpersonal skills. Medical and health services managers discuss staffing problems and patient information with other professionals, such as physicians and health insurance representatives.

Leadership skills. These managers are often responsible for finding creative solutions to staffing or other administrative problems. They must hire, train, motivate, and lead staff.

Employment Projections Data for Medical and Health Services Managers

Occupational Title	SOC Code	Employment, 2014	Projected Employment, 2024	Change, 2014–2024 Percent	Change, 2014–2024 Numeric
Medical and health services managers	11-9111	333,000	389,300	17	56,300

Source: U.S. Bureau of Labor Statistics, Employment Projections Program

Technical skills. Medical and health services managers must stay up to date with advances in healthcare technology and data analytics. For example, they may need to use coding and classification software and electronic health record (EHR) systems as their facility adopts these technologies.

Licenses, Certifications, and Registrations. All states require licensure for nursing home administrators; requirements vary by state. In most states, these administrators must have a bachelor's degree, complete a state-approved training program, and pass a national licensing exam. Some states also require applicants to pass a state-specific exam; others may require applicants to have previous work experience in a healthcare facility. Some states also require licensure for administrators in assisted-living facilities. For information on specific state-by-state licensure requirements, visit the National Association of Long Term Care Administrator Boards.

A license is typically not required in other areas of medical and health services management. However, some positions may require applicants to have a registered nurse or social worker license.

Although certification is not required, some managers choose to become certified. Certification is available in many areas of practice. For example, the Professional Association of Health Care Office Management offers certification in medical management, the American Health Information Management Association offers health information management certification, and the American College of Health Care Administrators offers the Certified Nursing Home Administrator and Certified Assisted Living Administrator distinctions.

Advancement. Medical and health services managers advance by moving into higher paying positions with more responsibility. Some health information managers, for example, can advance to become responsible for the entire hospital's information systems. Other managers may advance to top executive positions within the organization.

Pay

The median annual wage for medical and health services managers was $92,810 in May 2014. The median wage is the wage at which half the workers in an occupation earned more than that amount and half earned less. The lowest 10 percent earned less than $55,890, and the highest 10 percent earned more than $161,150.

In May 2014, the median annual wages for medical and health services managers in the top industries in which they worked were as follows:

Hospitals; state, local, and private	$99,930
Government	98,310
Offices of physicians	86,050
Home healthcare services	81,940
Nursing and residential care facilities	76,730

Job Outlook

Employment of medical and health services managers is projected to grow 17 percent from 2014 to 2024, much faster than the average for all occupations. As the large baby-boom population ages and people remain active later in life, the healthcare industry as a whole should see an increase in the demand for medical services.

This increased demand should create greater needs for physicians and other healthcare workers, medical procedures, and healthcare facilities, and therefore greater needs for managers who organize and manage medical information and healthcare staff. There should be increased demand for nursing care facility administrators as baby boomers age.

Employment is projected to grow in offices of health practitioners. Many services previously provided in hospitals will shift to these settings, especially as medical technologies improve. Demand in medical group practice management is projected to grow as medical group practices become larger and more complex.

In addition, widespread use of electronic health records (EHRs) will continue to create demand for managers with knowledge of health information technology (IT) and informatics systems. Medical and health services managers will be needed to organize, manage, and integrate these records across areas of the healthcare industry.

Job Prospects. Job prospects for medical and health services managers are likely to be favorable. In addition to rising employment demand, the need to replace managers who retire over the next decade will result in some openings. Candidates with a master's degree in health administration or a related field, as well as knowledge of healthcare IT systems, will likely have the best prospects.

Similar Occupations. This table shows a list of occupations with job duties that are similar to those of medical and health services managers.

Occupations	Entry-level Education	2014 Median Pay	Projected Job Growth	Average Annual Openings
Human Resources Managers	Bachelor's degree	$102,780	9%	1,080
Insurance Underwriters	Bachelor's degree	$64,220	-11%	-1,170
Social and Community Service Managers	Bachelor's degree	$62,740	10%	1,320

Contacts for More Information

For more information about medical and healthcare management, visit

➤ Professional Association of Health Care Office Management (www.pahcom.com)
➤ American Health Information Management Association (www.ahima.org)
➤ American College of Health Care Administrators (www.achca.org)

For more information about academic programs in this field, visit

➤ Association of University Programs in Health Administration (www.aupha.org)
➤ Commission on Accreditation of Healthcare Management Education (www.cahme.org)

For information about career opportunities in healthcare management, visit

➤ American College of Healthcare Executives (www.ache.org)

For information about career opportunities in medical group practices and ambulatory care management, visit

➤ Medical Group Management Association (www.mgma.com)

For more information about licensure and training requirements for nursing home and assisted-living facility administrators, visit

➤ National Association of Long Term Care Administrator Boards (www.nabweb.org)

O*NET

➤ Medical and Health Services Managers (11-9111.00)

Natural Sciences Managers

- **2014 Median Pay** .... $120,050 per year $57.71 per hour
- **Typical Entry-Level Education** ....Bachelor's degree
- **Work Experience in a Related Occupation** .... 5 years or more
- **On-the-Job Training** .... None
- **Number of Jobs 2014** 55,100
- **Job Outlook, 2014–24** .... 3% (Slower than average)
- **Employment Change, 2014–24** 1,800

What Natural Sciences Managers Do

Natural sciences managers supervise the work of scientists, including chemists, physicists, and biologists. They direct activities related to research and development, and coordinate activities such as testing, quality control, and production.

Duties. Natural sciences managers typically do the following:

- Work with top executives to develop goals and strategies for researchers and developers
- Budget resources for projects and programs by determining staffing, training, and equipment needs
- Hire, supervise, and evaluate scientists, technicians, and other staff members
- Review staff members' methodology and the accuracy of their research results
- Ensure that laboratories are stocked with equipment and supplies
- Monitor the progress of projects, review research performed, and draft operational reports
- Provide technical assistance to scientists, technicians, and support staff
- Establish and follow administrative procedures, policies, and standards
- Communicate project proposals, research findings, and the status of projects to clients and top management

Natural sciences managers direct scientific research activities and direct and coordinate product development projects and production activities. The duties of natural sciences managers vary with the field of science (for example, biology or chemistry) or the industry they work in. Research projects may be aimed at improving manufacturing processes, advancing basic scientific knowledge, or developing new products.

Some natural sciences managers are former scientists and, after becoming managers, may continue to conduct their own research as well as oversee the work of others. These managers are sometimes called *working managers* and usually have smaller staffs, allowing them to do research in addition to carrying out their administrative duties.

Managers who are responsible for larger staffs may not have time to contribute to research and may spend all their time performing administrative duties.

Laboratory managers need to ensure that laboratories are fully supplied so that scientists can run their tests and experiments. Some specialize in the management of laboratory animals.

During all stages of a project, natural sciences managers coordinate the activities of their unit with those of other units or organizations. They work with higher levels of management; with financial, production, and marketing specialists; and with suppliers of equipment and materials.

Work Environment

Natural sciences managers held about 55,100 jobs in 2014. The industries that employed the most natural sciences managers were as follows:

Research and development in the physical, engineering, and life sciences	28%
Federal government, excluding postal service	19
Pharmaceutical and medicine manufacturing	9
Management of companies and enterprises	7
State government, excluding education and hospitals	6

Natural sciences managers prepare budgets for projects and programs and determine staff, training, and equipment needs.

Median Annual Wages, May 2014

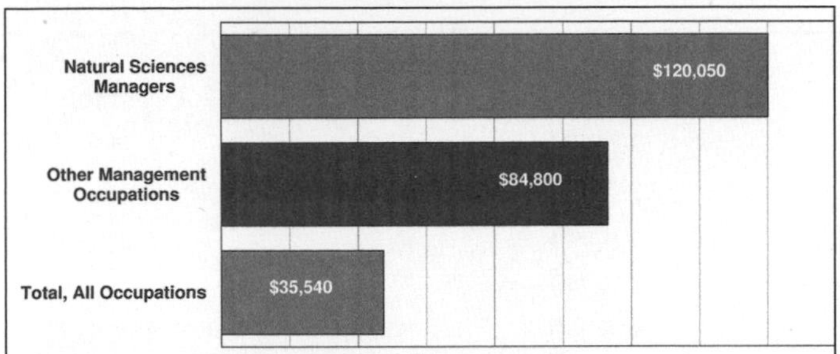

Note: All Occupations includes all occupations in the U.S. Economy.
Source: U.S. Bureau of Labor Statistics, Occupational Employment Statistics

Percent Change in Employment, Projected 2014–2024

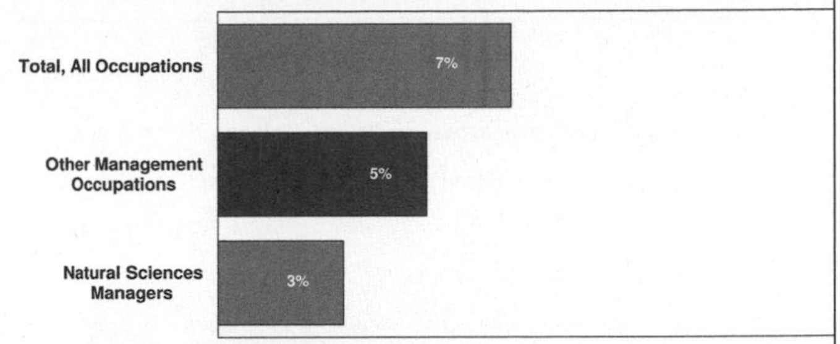

Note: All Occupations includes all occupations in the U.S. Economy.
Source: U.S. Bureau of Labor Statistics, Office of Occupational Statistics and Employment Projections

Although natural sciences managers work in many industries, about 1 in 4 of natural sciences managers were employed by federal and state governments in 2014. Many others worked in industries and businesses that rely on public funding through research grants or on other types of public and private funding.

Most of the time, they work in offices, but they also may spend time in laboratories. Like managers in other fields, natural sciences managers may spend a large portion of their time using computers and talking to other members of their organization.

Natural sciences managers have different requirements based on the size of their staff. Working managers who have research responsibilities and smaller staffs may need to work in laboratories or in the field. Managers with larger staffs spend their time primarily in an administrative role and expend little time doing research or working in the field or in laboratories. Field and laboratory work may require traveling, sometimes to remote locations.

Work Schedules. Almost all natural sciences managers work full time. About 2 out of 5 worked more than 40 hours per week in 2014.

Education/Training

Natural sciences managers usually advance to management positions after years of employment as scientists. Natural sciences managers typically have a bachelor's degree, master's degree, or Ph.D. in a scientific discipline or a related field, such as engineering. Some managers may find it helpful to have an advanced management degree—for example, a Professional Science Master's (PSM) degree, a Master of Business Administration (MBA), or a Master of Public Administration (MPA).

Education. Natural sciences managers typically begin their careers as scientists; therefore, most have a bachelor's degree, master's degree, or Ph.D. in a scientific discipline or a closely related field, such as engineering. Scientific and technical knowledge is essential for managers because they must be able to understand the work of their subordinates and provide technical assistance when needed.

Natural sciences managers who are interested in acquiring postsecondary education in management should be able to find master's degree or Ph.D. programs in a natural science that incorporate business management courses. A relatively new type of degree, called the Professional Science Master's (PSM), blends advanced training in a particular science field with business skills, such as communications and program management, and policy. Those interested in acquiring general management skills may pursue a Master of Business Administration (MBA) or a Master of Public Administration (MPA). Some natural sciences managers will have studied psychology or some other management-related field to enter this occupation.

Sciences managers must continually upgrade their knowledge because of the rapid growth of scientific developments.

Work Experience in a Related Occupation. Natural sciences managers usually advance to management positions after years of employment as scientists. While employed as scientists, they typically are given more responsibility and independence in their work as they gain experience. Eventually, they may lead research teams and have control over the direction and content of projects before being promoted to an administrative position.

Licenses, Certifications, and Registrations. Although certification is not typically required to become a natural sciences manager, many relevant certifications are available. These certifications range from those related to specific scientific areas of study or practice, such as laboratory animal management, to general management topics, such as project management, and are useful to natural sciences managers regardless of the organization being managed.

Important Qualities

Communication skills. Natural sciences managers must be able to communicate clearly to a variety of audiences, such as scientists, policymakers, and the public. Both written and oral communication are important.

Critical-thinking skills. Natural sciences managers must carefully evaluate the work of others. They must determine if their staff's methods and results are based on sound science.

Interpersonal skills. Natural sciences managers lead research teams and therefore need to work well with others in order to reach common goals. Managers routinely deal with conflict, which they must be able to turn into positive outcomes for their organization.

Employment Projections Data for Natural Sciences Managers

Occupational Title	SOC Code	Employment, 2014	Projected Employment, 2024	Change, 2014–2024 Percent	Change, 2014–2024 Numeric
Natural sciences managers	11-9121	55,100	56,900	3	1,800

Source: U.S. Bureau of Labor Statistics, Employment Projections Program

Similar Occupations. This table shows a list of occupations with job duties that are similar to those of natural sciences managers.

Occupations	Entry-level Education	2014 Median Pay	Projected Job Growth	Average Annual Openings
Agricultural and Food Scientists	Bachelor's degree	$60,690	5%	190
Architectural and Engineering Managers	Bachelor's degree	$130,620	2%	370
Biochemists and Biophysicists	Doctoral or professional degree	$84,940	8%	280
Chemists and Materials Scientists	Bachelor's degree	$74,720	3%	260
Environmental Scientists and Specialists	Bachelor's degree	$66,250	11%	1,020
Geoscientists	Bachelor's degree	$89,910	10%	380
Medical Scientists	Doctoral or professional degree	$79,930	8%	900
Physicists and Astronomers	Doctoral or professional degree	$109,290	7%	150
Postsecondary Teachers	See Education/Training	$70,790	13%	17,700

Leadership skills. Natural sciences managers must be able to organize, direct, and motivate others. They need to identify the strengths and weaknesses of their workers and create an environment in which the workers can succeed.

Problem-solving skills. Natural sciences managers use scientific observation and analysis to find solutions to complex technical questions.

Time-management skills. Natural sciences managers must be able to do multiple administrative, supervisory, and technical tasks while ensuring that projects remain on schedule.

Pay

The median annual wage for natural sciences managers was $120,050 in May 2014. The median wage is the wage at which half the workers in an occupation earned more than that amount and half earned less. The lowest 10 percent earned less than $70,020, and the highest 10 percent earned more than $187,200.

In May 2014, the median annual wages for natural sciences managers in the top industries in which they worked were as follows:

Management of companies and enterprises	$156,230
Research and development in the physical, engineering, and life sciences	149,850
Pharmaceutical and medicine manufacturing	122,820
Federal government, excluding postal service	109,390
State government, excluding education and hospitals	75,110

Job Outlook

Employment of natural sciences managers is projected to grow 3 percent from 2014 to 2024, slower than the average for all occupations. Employment growth should be affected by many of the same factors that affect employment growth for the scientists whom these managers supervise. However, job growth for managers is expected to be somewhat slower than that for scientists, because managers tend to be flexible in the number of workers they are able to manage. In addition, research and development activities are increasingly being outsourced to specialized scientific research services firms. This outsourcing will lead to some consolidation of management.

Job Prospects. In addition to job openings resulting from employment growth, openings will arise from the need to replace managers who retire or move into other occupations.

Competition for jobs in this occupation is expected to be strong because of its typically higher salaries, greater control over some types of projects, and better access to resources. Experiences can vary widely with the variety of industries and organizations these managers work in. Private industry, government, and colleges and universities will have different goals. Prospective managers should take these differences into consideration when applying for positions.

Contacts for More Information

For more information about Professional Science Master's programs, visit

➤ Professional Science Master's (www.sciencemasters.com)

➤ National Professional Science Master's Association (www.npsma.org)

For general information about science careers and news, including articles on natural science management, visit

➤ American Association for the Advancement of Science (www.aaas.org)

To find job openings for natural sciences managers in the federal government, visit

➤ USAJOBS (www.usajobs.gov)

O*NET

➤ Natural Sciences Managers (11-9121.00)

➤ Clinical Research Coordinators (11-9121.01)

➤ Water Resource Specialists (11-9121.02)

Postsecondary Education Administrators

- **2014 Median Pay** .... $88,390 per year, $42.49 per hour
- **Typical Entry-Level Education** .... Master's degree
- **Work Experience in a Related Occupation** .... Less than 5 years
- **On-the-Job Training** .... None
- **Number of Jobs 2014** 175,100
- **Job Outlook, 2014–24** .... 9% (Faster than average)
- **Employment Change, 2014–24** 15,200

What Postsecondary Education Administrators Do

Postsecondary education administrators oversee student services, academics, and faculty research at colleges and universities. Their

Postsecondary education administrators need to build good relationships with colleagues, students, and parents.

job duties vary depending on the area of the college they manage, such as admissions, the office of the registrar, or student affairs.

Duties. Postsecondary education administrators who work in *admissions* decide whether potential students should be admitted to the school. They typically do the following:

- Determine how many students to admit to the school
- Meet with prospective students and encourage them to apply
- Review applications to determine if each potential student should be admitted
- Analyze data about applicants and admitted students
- Prepare promotional materials about the school

Many admissions counselors are assigned a region of the country and travel to that region to speak to high school counselors and students.

Admissions officers often work with the financial aid department, which helps students determine whether they are able to afford tuition and creates packages of federal and institutional financial aid, if necessary.

Postsecondary education administrators who work in the *registrar's office*, sometimes called *registrars*, maintain student and course records. They typically do the following:

- Schedule and register students for classes
- Schedule space and times for classes
- Ensure that students meet graduation requirements
- Plan commencement ceremonies
- Prepare transcripts and diplomas for students
- Produce data about students and classes
- Maintain the academic records of the institution

Registrars have different duties throughout the school year. Before students register for classes, registrars must prepare schedules and course offerings. During registration and for the beginning of the semester, they help students sign up for, drop, and add courses. Toward the end of the semester, they plan graduation and ensure that students meet the requirements to graduate. Registrars need computer skills to create and maintain databases.

Postsecondary education administrators who work in *student affairs* are responsible for a variety of cocurricular school functions, such as student athletics and activities. They typically do the following:

- Advise students on topics such as housing issues, personal problems, or academics
- Communicate with parents or guardians
- Create, support, and assess nonacademic programs for students
- Schedule programs and services, such as athletic events or recreational activities

Postsecondary education administrators in student affairs can specialize in student activities, housing and residential life, or multicultural affairs. In student activities, they plan events and advise student clubs and organizations. In housing and residential life, they assign students rooms and roommates, ensure that residential facilities are well maintained, and train student workers, such as residential advisers. Education administrators who specialize in multicultural affairs plan events to celebrate different cultures and diverse backgrounds. Sometimes, they manage multicultural centers on campus.

Postsecondary education administrators can be *provosts* or *academic deans*. Provosts, also called *chief academic officers*, help college presidents develop academic policies, participate in making faculty appointments and tenure decisions, and manage budgets. Academic deans direct and coordinate the activities of the individual colleges or schools. For example, in a large university, a dean may oversee the law school.

Education administrators' duties depend on the size of their college or university. Small schools often have smaller staffs who take on many different responsibilities, but larger schools may have different offices for each of these functions. For example, at a small college, the Office of Student Life may oversee student athletics and other activities, whereas a large university may have an Athletics Department.

Median Annual Wages, May 2014

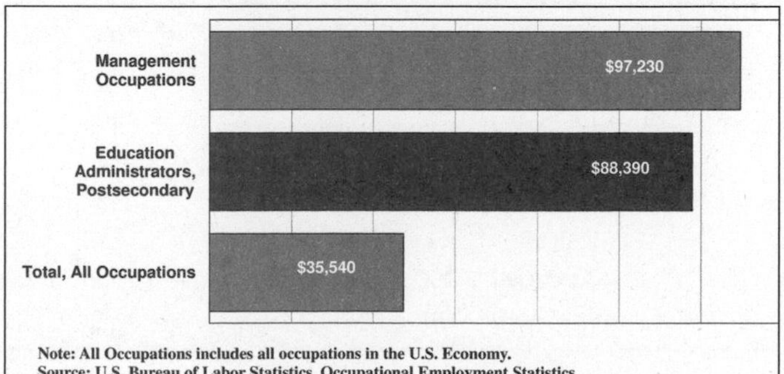

Percent Change in Employment, Projected 2014–2024

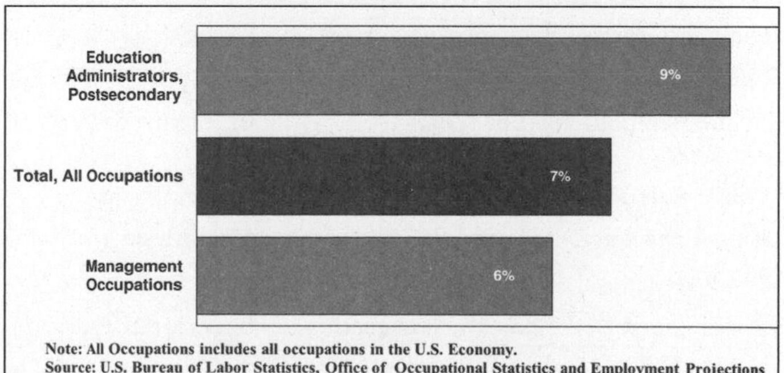

Employment Projections Data for Postsecondary Education Administrators

Occupational Title	SOC Code	Employment, 2014	Projected Employment, 2024	Change, 2014–2024 Percent	Change, 2014–2024 Numeric
Education administrators, postsecondary	11-9033	175,100	190,300	9	15,200

Source: U.S. Bureau of Labor Statistics, Employment Projections Program

Work Environment

Postsecondary education administrators held about 175,100 jobs in 2014. Some work for public schools, and others work for private schools.

In 2014, about 75 percent of postsecondary education administrators worked for colleges, universities, and professional schools. About 15 percent worked for junior colleges in 2014.

Work Schedules. Postsecondary education administrators generally work full time. Most work year-round, but some administrators may reduce their hours during the summer.

Education/Training

Although a bachelor's degree may be acceptable for some entry-level positions, a master's or higher degree is often required. Employers often want candidates who have experience working in the field, particularly for occupations such as registrars and academic deans.

Education. Educational requirements vary for different positions. A bachelor's degree may be sufficient, but a master's degree or Ph.D. is generally required. Degrees can be in a variety of disciplines, such as social work, accounting, or marketing.

Provosts and deans often must have a Ph.D. Some provosts and deans begin their career as professors and later move into administration. These administrators have doctorates in the field in which they taught. Other provosts and deans have a Ph.D. in higher education or a related field.

Work Experience in a Related Occupation. Employers typically prefer to hire candidates who have several years of experience in a college administrative setting. Some postsecondary education administrators work in the registrar's office or as a resident assistant while in college to gain the necessary experience. For other positions, such as those in admissions and student affairs, experience may or may not be necessary.

Important Qualities

Computer skills. Postsecondary education administrators often need to be adept at working with computers so they can create and maintain databases and use computer programs to manage student and school records.

Interpersonal skills. Those in admissions and student affairs need to be outgoing so they can encourage prospective students to apply to the school and existing students to participate in cocurricular activities.

Organizational skills. Administrators need to be organized so they can manage records, prioritize tasks, and coordinate the activities with their staff.

Problem-solving skills. Administrators often need to respond to difficult situations, develop creative solutions to problems, and react calmly when problems arise.

Advancement. Education administrators with advanced degrees can be promoted to higher level positions within their department or the college. Some become college presidents, an occupation which is discussed in the profile on top executives.

Pay

The median annual wage for postsecondary education administrators was $88,390 in May 2014. The median wage is the wage at which half the workers in an occupation earned more than that amount and half earned less. The lowest 10 percent earned less than $50,240, and the highest 10 percent earned more than $174,000.

In May 2014, the median annual wage in colleges, universities, and professional schools, the industry that employed the most postsecondary education administrators, was $91,160. The median annual wage in junior colleges, the second largest industry, was $82,930.

As part of their employee benefits plan, many colleges and universities allow full-time employees to attend classes for a discount or for free.

Similar Occupations. This table shows a list of occupations with job duties that are similar to those of postsecondary education administrators.

Occupations	Entry-level Education	2014 Median Pay	Projected Job Growth	Average Annual Openings
Administrative Services Managers	Bachelor's degree	$83,790	8%	2,350
Human Resources Managers	Bachelor's degree	$102,780	9%	1,080
Postsecondary Teachers	See Education/Training	$70,790	13%	17,700
Public Relations and Fundraising Managers	Bachelor's degree	$101,510	7%	470
Public Relations Specialists	Bachelor's degree	$55,680	6%	1,490
School and Career Counselors	Master's degree	$53,370	8%	2,250
Top Executives	Bachelor's degree	$102,750	6%	14,700
Training and Development Managers	Bachelor's degree	$101,930	7%	230

Job Outlook

Employment of postsecondary education administrators is projected to grow 9 percent from 2014 to 2024, faster than the average for all occupations. Expected growth is due to increases in enrollments.

People will continue to seek postsecondary education to accomplish their career goals. As more people enter colleges and universities, more postsecondary education administrators will be needed to serve the needs of these additional students.

Additional admissions officers will be needed to process students' applications. More registrars will be needed to register students for classes and ensure that they meet graduation requirements. More student affairs workers will be needed to make housing assignments and plan events for students.

Despite expected increases in enrollment, employment growth in public colleges and universities will depend on state and local government budgets. When state and local governments reduce budgets for higher education, postsecondary institutions may lay off employees, including administrators. As a result, employment growth may be somewhat limited by state and local government budget constraints.

Enrollment is expected to decrease in online colleges and universities. As a result, there will be less demand for postsecondary education administrators in these types of schools.

Job Prospects. Job prospects will be best for candidates who have experience working in higher education and for those with a master's degree.

Contacts for More Information

For more information about registrars or admissions counselors, visit

➤ American Association of Collegiate Registrars and Admissions Officers (www.aacrao.org)

For more information about education administrators specializing in student affairs, visit

➤ NASPA: Student Affairs Administrators in Higher Education (http://naspa.org)

O*NET

➤ Education Administrators, Postsecondary (11-9033.00)

Preschool and Childcare Center Directors

- **2014 Median Pay** .... $45,260 per year $21.76 per hour
- **Typical Entry-Level Education** .... Bachelor's degree
- **Work Experience in a Related Occupation** .... Less than 5 years
- **On-the-job Training** .... None
- **Number of Jobs, 2014** 64,000
- **Job Outlook, 2014–24** .... 7% (As fast as average)
- **Employment Change, 2014–24** 4,200

What Preschool and Childcare Center Directors Do

Preschool and childcare center directors supervise and lead staffs, oversee daily activities, design curriculums, and prepare budgets. They are responsible for all aspects of their program.

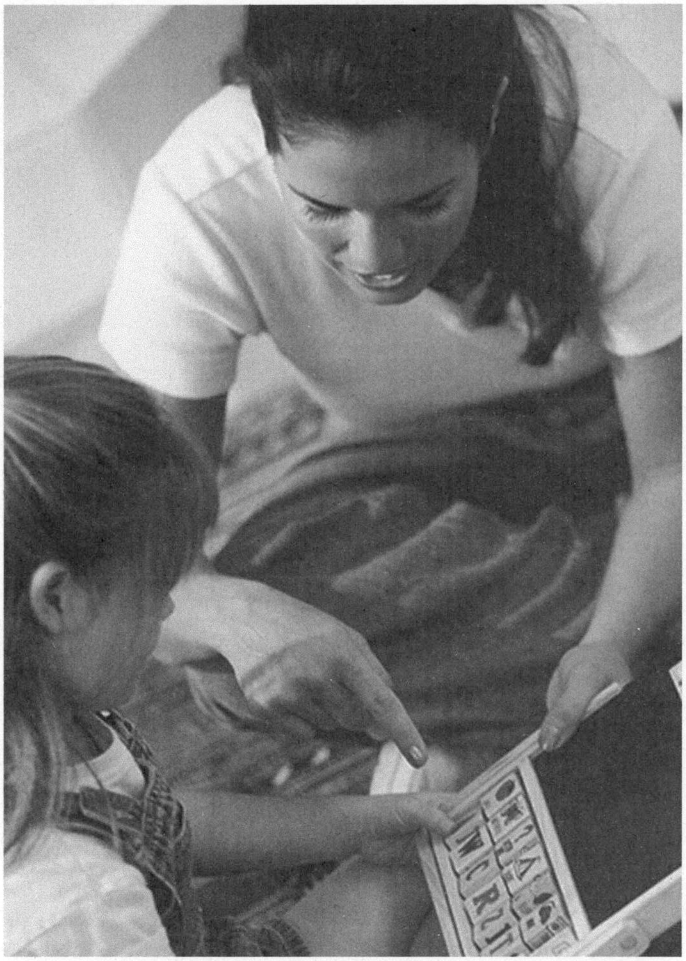

Preschool and childcare center directors assist staff with caring for and teaching children.

Duties. Preschool and childcare center directors typically do the following:

- Supervise preschool teachers and childcare workers
- Hire and train new staff members
- Provide training and professional development opportunities for staff
- Establish policies and communicate them to staff and parents
- Develop educational programs and standards
- Ensure instructional excellence
- Assist staff in resolving conflicts between children
- Aid staff in communicating with parents
- Meet with parents and staff to discuss students' progress
- Prepare budgets and allocate program funds
- Ensure facilities are maintained and cleaned according to state regulations

Some preschools and childcare centers are independently owned and operated. In these facilities, directors must follow the instructions and guidelines of the owner. Sometimes, directors own the facilities, so they decide how to operate them.

Other preschools and childcare centers are part of a national chain or franchise. The director of a chain or franchise also must ensure that the facility meets its parent organization's standards and regulations.

Median Annual Wages, May 2014

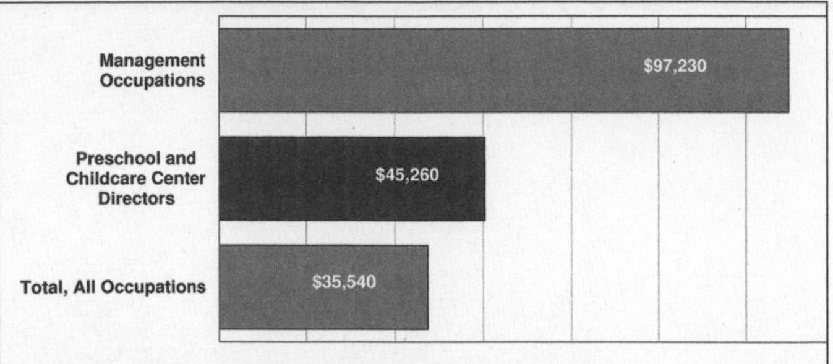

Note: All Occupations includes all occupations in the U.S. Economy.
Source: U.S. Bureau of Labor Statistics, Occupational Employment Statistics

Percent Change in Employment, Projected 2014–2024

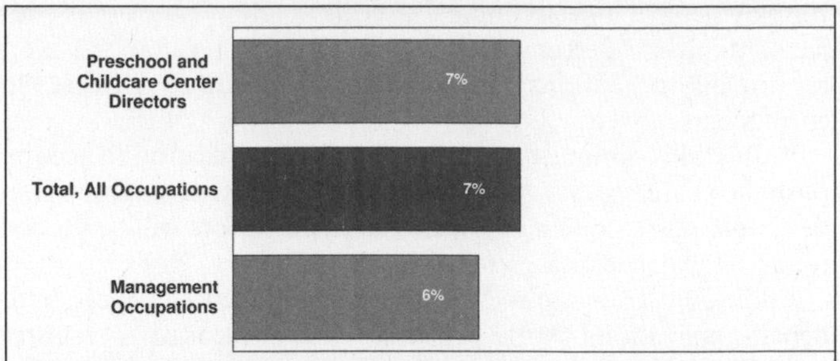

Note: All Occupations includes all occupations in the U.S. Economy.
Source: U.S. Bureau of Labor Statistics, Office of Occupational Statistics and Employment Projections

In addition, some preschools and childcare centers, such as Head Start programs, receive state and federal funding. Directors of these schools and centers must ensure that their programs, staff, and facilities meet state and federal guidelines. For example, they must ensure that the staff meets the educational requirements set by the Department of Health and Human Services.

Work Environment

Preschool and childcare center directors held about 64,000 jobs in 2014. The industries that employed the most preschool and childcare center directors were as follows:

Child day care services	51%
Religious, grantmaking, civic, professional, and similar organizations	18
Elementary and secondary schools; state, local, and private	12
Individual and family services	4

Although preschool and childcare center directors work in schools and childcare centers, they spend most of their day in an office. They also visit classrooms to check on students, speak to preschool teachers or childcare workers, and meet with parents.

Many preschool and childcare center directors find working in an early childhood educational environment rewarding, but they also have significant responsibilities. Coordinating and interacting with staff, parents, and children can be fast paced and stimulating, but can be stressful as well.

Work Schedules. Preschool and childcare center directors generally work full time. Some work more than 40 hours per week. When childcare centers are open, a director must always be on staff, so directors and assistant directors stagger their schedules to ensure that someone is always available.

Education/Training

A college degree and experience in early childhood education is typically required to become a preschool and childcare center director. Some states or employers require preschool and childcare center directors to have a nationally recognized credential, such as the Child Development Associate (CDA).

Education. Most states require preschool and childcare center directors to have at least an associate's or bachelor's degree in early childhood education. These degree programs teach students about child development, provide strategies for teaching young children, and discuss how to observe and document children's progress. Employers may prefer candidates who have a degree, or at least some postsecondary coursework, in early childhood education.

Work Experience in a Related Occupation. Most states require preschool and childcare center directors to have experience in early childhood education. The amount of experience required varies by state.

Licenses, Certifications, and Registrations. Many states require childcare centers, including those in private homes, to be licensed. To qualify for licensure, staff must pass a background check, have a complete record of immunizations, and meet a minimum training requirement. Some states require staff to have certifications in cardiopulmonary resuscitation (CPR) and first aid.

Some states and employers require preschool and childcare center directors to have a nationally recognized credential. Most often, states require the CDA credential offered by the Council for Professional Recognition. Obtaining the CDA credential requires coursework, experience in the field, and being observed while working with children. The credential is valid for 3 years and requires renewal.

Some states recognize the Certified Childcare Professional (CCP) designation offered by the National Early Childhood Program Accreditation. Some of the requirements for obtaining the CCP are that the candidate must be at least 18 years old, have a high school diploma, have experience in the field, take courses in early childhood education, and pass an exam. The CCP accreditation requires renewal every 2 years through the CCP maintenance process.

Important Qualities

Business skills. Preschool and childcare center directors manage childcare centers and need to be able to operate the business effectively.

Communication skills. Preschool and childcare center directors need to inform parents and staff about the progress of the

Employment Projections Data for Preschool and Childcare Center Directors

Occupational Title	SOC Code	Employment, 2014	Projected Employment, 2024	Change, 2014–2024 Percent	Change, 2014–2024 Numeric
Education administrators, preschool and childcare center/program	11-9031	64,000	68,200	7	4,200

Source: U.S. Bureau of Labor Statistics, Employment Projections Program

Similar Occupations. This table shows a list of occupations with job duties that are similar to those of preschool and childcare center directors.

Occupations	Entry-level Education	2014 Median Pay	Projected Job Growth	Average Annual Openings
Childcare Workers	High school diploma or equivalent	$19,730	5%	6,930
High School Teachers	Bachelor's degree	$56,310	6%	5,590
Kindergarten and Elementary School Teachers	Bachelor's degree	$53,760	6%	8,780
Middle School Teachers	Bachelor's degree	$54,940	6%	3,680
Preschool Teachers	Associate's degree	$28,120	7%	2,960
Special Education Teachers	Bachelor's degree	$55,980	6%	2,810
Teacher Assistants	Some college, no degree	$24,430	6%	7,860

children. They need good writing and speaking skills to convey this information successfully.

Interpersonal skills. Preschool and childcare center directors must be able to develop good relationships with parents, children, and staff.

Leadership skills. Preschool and childcare center directors supervise staff, so they need good leadership skills to inspire staff to work diligently. They also must enforce rules and regulations.

Organizational skills. Directors need to maintain clear records about children and staff. In addition, they must be able to multitask when several people or situations require their attention.

Pay

The median annual wage for preschool and childcare center directors was $45,260 in May 2014. The median wage is the wage at which half the workers in an occupation earned more than that amount and half earned less. The lowest 10 percent earned less than $28,520, and the highest 10 percent earned more than $87,120.

In May 2014, the median annual wages for preschool and childcare center directors in the top industries in which they worked were as follows:

Elementary and secondary schools; state, local, and private	$68,970
Individual and family services	49,540
Religious, grantmaking, civic, professional, and similar organizations	45,280
Child day care services	41,980

Job Outlook

Employment of preschool and childcare center directors is projected to grow 7 percent from 2014 to 2024, about as fast as the average for all occupations.

The number of children who are of preschool age is expected to increase, although their share of the overall population should remain constant. As a result, a greater number of working parents will continue to need help caring for their children.

In addition, a continued focus on the importance of early childhood education—specifically preschool—should increase demand for childcare centers. Early childhood education is widely recognized as important for a child's intellectual and emotional development.

However, the increasing cost of childcare and the increasing number of stay-at-home parents may reduce demand in the child daycare services industry.

Job Prospects. Overall job opportunities for preschool and childcare center directors are expected to be favorable. Workers with formal postsecondary education, such as an associate's or bachelor's degree, should have better job prospects than those with only a high school diploma. Those with a bachelor's degree should have the best prospects.

Contacts for More Information

For more information on childcare centers, visit

➤ Child Care Aware (http://childcareaware.org)

For information about early childhood education, visit

➤ National Association for the Education of Young Children (www.naeyc.org)

For more information about professional credentials, visit

➤ Council for Professional Recognition (www.cdacouncil.org)

➤ National Early Childhood Program Accreditation (www.necpa.net)

O*NET

➤ Education Administrators, Preschool and Childcare Center/Program (11-9031.00)

Property, Real Estate, and Community Association Managers

- **2014 Median Pay** .... $54,270 per year $26.09 per hour
- **Typical Entry-Level Education** .... High school diploma or equivalent
- **Work Experience in a Related Occupation**......... Less than 5 years
- **On-the-job Training** .... None
- **Number of Jobs, 2014** 313,800
- **Job Outlook, 2014–24** .... 8% (As fast as average)
- **Employment Change, 2014–24** 25,300

What Property, Real Estate, and Community Association Managers Do

Property, real estate, and community association managers take care of the many aspects of residential, commercial, or industrial properties. They make sure the property is well maintained, has a nice appearance, operates smoothly, and preserves its resale value.

Duties. Property, real estate, and community association managers typically do the following:

- Meet with prospective renters and show them properties
- Discuss the lease and explain the terms of occupancy or ownership
- Collect monthly fees from tenants or individual owners
- Inspect all building facilities, including the grounds and equipment
- Arrange for new equipment or repairs as needed
- Pay bills or delegate bill payment for such expenditures as taxes, insurance, payroll, and maintenance
- Contract for trash removal, maintenance, landscaping, security, and other services
- Investigate and settle complaints, disturbances, and violations
- Keep records of rental activity and owner requests
- Prepare budgets and financial reports
- Comply with anti-discrimination laws when renting or advertising, such as the Americans with Disabilities Act, the Federal Fair Housing Amendment Act, and local fair housing laws

When owners of homes, apartments, office buildings, or retail or industrial properties lack the time or expertise needed for the day-to-day management of their real estate properties, they often hire a property or real estate manager or a community association manager. Managers are employed either directly by the owner or indirectly through a contract with a property management firm.

The following are examples of types of property, real estate, and community association managers:

Property and real estate managers oversee the operation of income-producing commercial or residential properties and ensure that real estate investments achieve their expected revenues. They handle the financial operations of the property, making certain that rent is collected and that mortgages, taxes, insurance premiums, payroll, and maintenance bills are paid on time. They may oversee financial statements, and periodically report to the owners on the status of the property, occupancy rates, expiration dates of leases, and other matters. When vacancies occur, property managers may advertise the property or hire a leasing agent to find a tenant. They may also suggest to the owners what rent to charge.

Community association managers work on behalf of homeowner or community associations to manage the communal property and services of condominiums, cooperatives, and planned communities. Usually hired by a volunteer board of directors of the association, they manage the daily affairs and supervise the maintenance of property and facilities that the homeowners use jointly through the association. Like property managers, community association managers collect monthly fees, prepare financial statements and budgets, negotiate with contractors, and help to resolve complaints. Community association managers also help homeowners and non-owner residents comply with association rules and regulations.

Onsite property managers are responsible for the day-to-day operation of a single property, such as an apartment complex, an office building, or a shopping center. To ensure that the property is well maintained, onsite managers routinely inspect the grounds, facilities, and equipment to determine whether maintenance or repairs are needed. They meet with current tenants to handle requests for repairs or to resolve complaints. They also meet with prospective tenants to show vacant apartments or office space. In addition, onsite managers enforce the terms of rental or lease contracts along with an association's governing rules. They make sure that tenants pay their rent on time, follow restrictions on

When vacancies occur, property, real estate, and community association managers may advertise the property or hire a leasing agent to find a tenant.

parking or pets, and follow the correct procedures when the lease is up. Other important duties of onsite managers include keeping accurate, up-to-date records of income and expenditures from property operations and submitting regular expense reports to the senior-level property manager or the owner(s).

Real estate asset managers plan and direct the purchase, sale, and development of real estate properties on behalf of businesses and investors. They focus on long-term strategic financial planning, rather than on the day-to-day operations of the property. In deciding to acquire property, real estate asset managers consider several factors, such as property values, taxes, zoning, population growth, transportation, and traffic volume and patterns. Once a site is selected, they negotiate contracts to buy or lease the property on the most favorable terms. Real estate asset managers review their company's real estate holdings periodically and identify properties that are no longer financially profitable. They then negotiate the sale of the properties or arrange for the end of leases.

Work Environment

Property, real estate, and community association managers held about 313,800 jobs in 2014. The industries that employed the most property, real estate, and community association managers were as follows:

Activities related to real estate	23%
Lessors of real estate	16
Offices of real estate agents and brokers	3
Civic, social, professional, and similar organizations	3

About 2 in 5 property, real estate, and community association managers were self-employed.

Most property, real estate, and community association managers work out of an office. However, many managers spend much of their time away from their desks. Onsite managers, in particular, may spend a large part of their workday visiting the building engineer, showing apartments, dealing with owners and board members, checking on the janitorial and maintenance staff, or investigating problems reported by residents. Real estate asset managers may spend time away from home while traveling to company real estate holdings or searching for properties to buy.

Managing properties or community associations, or selling and leasing real estate can sometimes be stressful.

Work Schedules. Property, real estate, and community association managers often must attend evening meetings with residents, property owners, community association board members, or civic groups. As a result, long workdays are common. Some apartment managers are required to live in the apartment complexes where they work, so that they are available to respond to emergencies even when they are off duty.

Most property, real estate, and community association managers work full time. However, about 1 in 5 worked part time in 2014.

Education/Training

Although many employers prefer to hire college graduates, a high school diploma or equivalent is enough for some jobs. Some managers receive vocational training. Other managers must have a real estate license.

Education. Many employers prefer to hire college graduates for property management positions, particularly for offsite positions dealing with a property's finances or contract management. Employers also prefer to hire college graduates to manage residential and commercial properties. A bachelor's or master's degree in business administration, accounting, finance, real estate, or public administration is preferred for commercial management positions. Managers of commercial properties and those dealing with a property's finances and contract management increasingly are finding that they need a bachelor's or master's degree in business administration, accounting, finance, or real estate management, especially if they do not have much practical experience.

Work Experience in a Related Occupation. Experience in real estate sales is a good background for onsite managers because real estate salespeople also show commercial properties to prospective tenants or buyers.

Licenses, Certifications, and Registrations. Real estate managers who buy or sell property must have a real estate license in the state in which they practice. In a few states, property and community association managers must also have a real estate license. Managers of public housing subsidized by the federal government must hold certifications.

Property, real estate, and community association managers working in Alaska, California, Colorado, Connecticut, Florida, Georgia, Illinois, Nevada, Virginia, and the District of Columbia are required to obtain professional credentials or licensure. Requirements vary by state, but many managers working in states without requirements still obtain designations to show competence and professionalism. BOMI International, the Community Associations Institute, the Institute of Real Estate Management, the National Association of Residential Property Managers, and the Community Association Managers International Certification Board all offer various designations, certifications, and professional development courses. Most states require recertification every 2 years.

In addition, employers may require managers to attend formal training programs from various professional and trade real estate associations. Employers send managers to these programs to develop their management skills and expand their knowledge of specialized fields, such as how to operate and maintain mechanical systems in buildings, how to improve property values, insurance and risk management, personnel management, business and real estate law, community association risks and liabilities, tenant relations, communications, accounting and financial concepts, and reserve funding. Managers also participate in these programs to prepare themselves for positions of greater responsibility in property management. With related job experience, completing these programs and receiving a satisfactory score on a written exam can lead to certification or the formal award of a professional designation by the sponsoring association.

Advancement. Many people begin property management careers as assistant managers, working closely with a property manager. In time, many assistants advance to property manager positions.

Some people start as onsite managers of apartment buildings, office complexes, or community associations. As they gain experience, they may advance to positions of greater responsibility. Those who excel as onsite managers often transfer to assistant offsite property manager positions, in which they gain experience handling a broad range of property management responsibilities.

The responsibilities and pay of property, real estate, and community association managers increase as these workers manage more and larger properties. Property managers are often responsible for several properties at a time. Some experienced managers open their own property management firms.

Important Qualities

Customer-service skills. Property, real estate, and community association managers must provide excellent customer service to keep existing clients and expand their business with new ones.

Interpersonal skills. Because property, real estate, and community association managers interact with people every day, they must have excellent interpersonal skills.

Listening skills. Property, real estate, and community association managers must listen to and understand residents and property owners in order to meet their needs.

Median Annual Wages, May 2014

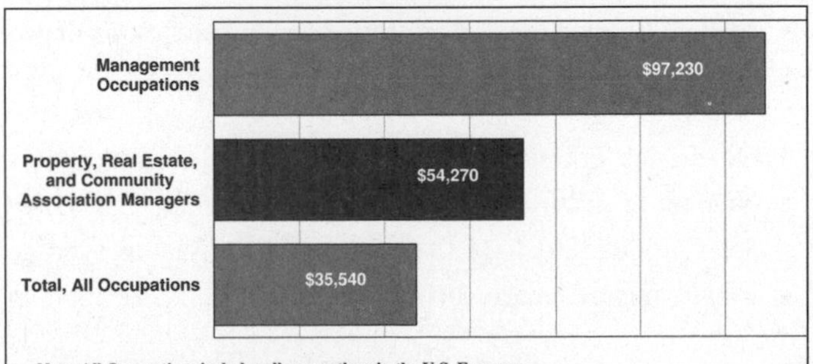

Note: All Occupations includes all occupations in the U.S. Economy.
Source: U.S. Bureau of Labor Statistics, Occupational Employment Statistics

Percent Change in Employment, Projected 2014–2024

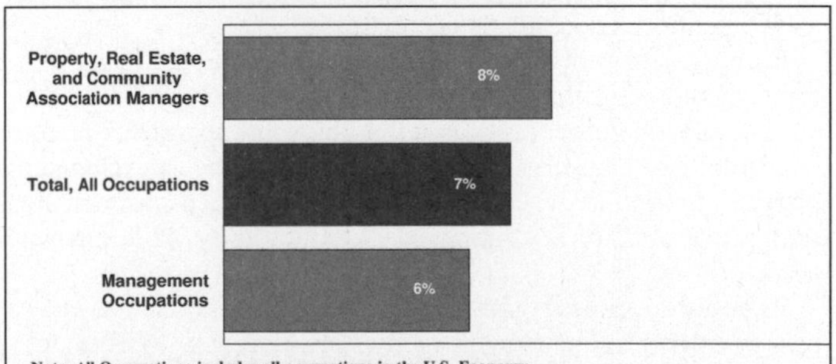

Note: All Occupations includes all occupations in the U.S. Economy.
Source: U.S. Bureau of Labor Statistics, Office of Occupational Statistics and Employment Projections

Employment Projections Data for Property, Real Estate, and Community Association Managers

Occupational Title	SOC Code	Employment, 2014	Projected Employment, 2024	Change, 2014–2024 Percent	Change, 2014–2024 Numeric
Property, real estate, and community association managers	11-9141	313,800	339,100	8	25,300

Source: U.S. Bureau of Labor Statistics, Employment Projections Program

Similar Occupations. This table shows a list of occupations with job duties that are similar to those of property, real estate, and community association managers.

Occupations	Entry-level Education	2014 Median Pay	Projected Job Growth	Average Annual Openings
Administrative Services Managers	Bachelor's degree	$83,790	8%	2,350
Food Service Managers	High school diploma or equivalent	$48,560	5%	1,570
Lodging Managers	High school diploma or equivalent	$47,680	8%	370
Real Estate Brokers and Sales Agents	High school diploma or equivalent	$43,430	3%	1,090

Organizational skills. Property, real estate, and community association managers must be able to plan, coordinate, and direct multiple contractors at the same time, often for multiple properties.

Problem-solving skills. Property, real estate, and community association managers must be able to mediate disputes or legal issues between residents, homeowners, or board members.

Speaking skills. Property, real estate, and community association managers must understand leasing or rental contracts and must be able to clearly explain the materials and answer questions raised by a resident or group of board members.

Pay

The median annual wage for property, real estate, and community association managers was $54,270 in May 2014. The median wage is the wage at which half the workers in an occupation earned more than that amount and half earned less. The lowest 10 percent earned less than $28,240, and the highest 10 percent earned more than $117,130.

In May 2014, the median annual wages for property, real estate, and community association managers in the top industries in which they worked were as follows:

Civic, social, professional, and similar organizations	$52,400
Activities related to real estate	51,750
Offices of real estate agents and brokers	51,650
Lessors of real estate	51,080

Job Outlook

Employment of property, real estate, and community association managers is projected to grow 8 percent from 2014 to 2024, about as fast as the average for all occupations.

Employment growth will result from more people living in the types of buildings that property management companies operate, such as apartment buildings, condominiums, cooperatives, planned communities, and senior housing. Increasingly, new developments provide community services and have jointly owned common areas that are professionally managed by community or homeowner associations.

In addition, property owners are becoming increasingly aware that property management firms help make properties more profitable and improve the resale value of homes and commercial property.

Job Prospects. Job opportunities should be best for those with a bachelor's degree in business administration, real estate, or a related field and for those with professional certification.

Because of the projected increase in the elderly population, particularly good job opportunities are expected for those with experience managing retirement centers, age-restricted communities, and healthcare facilities.

Contacts for More Information

For information about professional designation and certification programs for property, real estate, and community association managers, visit

- BOMI International (www.bomi.org)
- Community Associations Institute (www.caionline.org)
- Community Association Managers International Certification Board (www.camicb.org)
- Institute of Real Estate Management (www.irem.org)
- National Association of Residential Property Managers (www.narpm.org)

O*NET

- Property, Real Estate, and Community Association Managers (11-9141.00)

Public Relations and Fundraising Managers

- **2014 Median Pay** .... $101,510 per year; $48.80 per hour
- **Typical Entry-Level Education** .... Bachelor's degree
- **Work Experience in a Related Occupation** .... 5 years or more
- **On-the-job Training** .... None
- **Number of Jobs, 2014** 65,800
- **Job Outlook, 2014–24** .... 7% (As fast as average)
- **Employment Change, 2014–24** 4,700

What Public Relations and Fundraising Managers Do

Public relations managers plan and direct the creation of material that will maintain or enhance the public image of their employer or client. Fundraising managers coordinate campaigns that bring in donations for their organization.

Duties. Public relations managers typically do the following:

- Write press releases and prepare information for the media
- Identify main client groups and audiences and determine the best way to reach them
- Designate an appropriate spokesperson or information source for media inquiries
- Help clients communicate effectively with the public
- Develop their organization's or client's corporate image and identity
- Assist and inform an organization's executives and spokespeople
- Devise advertising and promotion programs
- Assign, supervise, and review the activities of staff

Fundraising managers typically do the following:

- Manage progress towards achieving an organization's fundraising goals
- Develop and carry out fundraising strategies
- Identify and contact potential donors
- Create and plan different events that can generate donations
- Meet face-to-face with highly important donors
- Apply for grants
- Assign, supervise, and review the activities of staff

Public relations managers review press releases and sponsor corporate events to help maintain and improve the image of their organization or client.

Public relations managers help to clarify their organization's point of view to its main audience through media releases and interviews. They observe social, economic, and political trends that might ultimately affect their organization, and they recommend ways to enhance the firm's image based on those trends. For example, in response to a growing concern about the environment, the public relations manager for an oil company may create a campaign to publicize its efforts to develop cleaner fuels.

In large organizations, public relations managers often supervise a staff of public relations specialists. They also work with advertising, promotions, and marketing managers to ensure that advertising campaigns are compatible with the image the company or client is trying to portray. For example, if a firm decides to emphasize its appeal to a certain group, such as young people, the public relations manager needs to make sure that current advertisements are well received by that group.

In addition, public relations managers may handle internal communications, such as company newsletters, and may help financial managers produce an organization's reports. They may also draft speeches, arrange interviews, and maintain other forms of public contact to help the organization's top executives.

Public relations managers must be able to work well with many types of specialists to report the facts accurately. In some cases, the information they write has legal consequences. As a result, they must work with the company's or client's lawyers to be sure that the information they release is both legally accurate and clear to the public.

Fundraising managers oversee campaigns and events intended to bring in donations for their organization. Many organizations that employ fundraisers rely heavily on the donations they gather in order to run their operations.

Fundraising managers usually decide which fundraising techniques are necessary in a certain situation. Common techniques may include annual campaigns, capital campaigns, planned giving, or major gifts. In addition, social media has created a new avenue for fundraising managers to connect with more potential donors and to spread their organization's message.

Those who work on annual campaigns focus heavily on contacting donors who have given in the past, and request that they give again. Finding new contacts for future donations is also a component of a successful annual campaign.

Capital campaigns are different; they are generally used to raise money over a shorter time period and for a specific project, such as the construction of a new building at a university.

Fundraisers who spend most of their time on planned giving must have specialized training in taxes regarding gifts of stocks, bonds, charitable annuities, and real estate bequests in a will. Major gifts are a feature of many different campaigns and are generally requested in person given the large value of the potential donation.

Work Environment

Public relations and fundraising managers held about 65,800 jobs in 2014. The industries that employed the most public relations and fundraising managers were as follows:

Religious, grantmaking, civic, professional, and similar organizations	24%
Educational services; state, local, and private	19
Professional, scientific, and technical services	13
Management of companies and enterprises	9
State and local government, excluding education and hospitals	6

Public relations and fundraising managers usually work in offices during regular business hours. However, many must travel to deliver speeches and attend meetings and community activities.

They work in high-stress environments, often managing and organizing several events at the same time.

Public relations managers and specialists work in fairly high-stress environments, often managing and organizing several events at the same time.

Median Annual Wages, May 2014

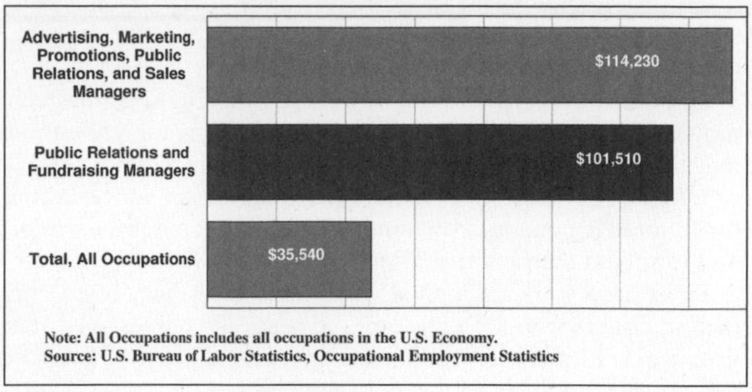

Percent Change in Employment, Projected 2014–2024

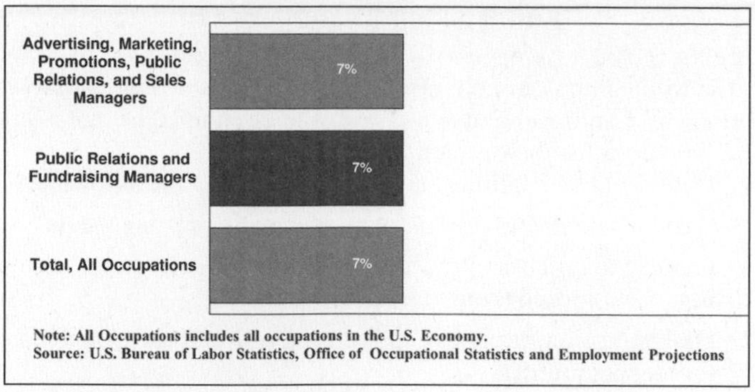

Work Schedules. Most public relations and fundraising managers work full time, which often includes long hours. About 1 in 3 managers worked more than 40 hours per week in 2014.

Education/Training

Public relations and fundraising managers need at least a bachelor's degree, and some positions may require a master's degree. Many years of related work experience are also necessary.

Education. For public relations and fundraising management positions, a bachelor's degree in public relations, communications, English, fundraising, or journalism is generally required. However, some employers prefer a master's degree, particularly in public relations, journalism, fundraising, or nonprofit management.

Courses in advertising, business administration, public affairs, public speaking, and creative and technical writing can be helpful.

Licenses, Certifications, and Registrations. Although not mandatory, public relations managers can get certified through the Public Relations Society of America. Candidates qualify based on years of experience and must pass an exam to become certified.

The International Association of Business Communicators offers a credential to demonstrate a level of knowledge and expertise.

The Certified Fund Raising Executive program, offered by CFRE International, is voluntary, but fundraisers who pursue certification demonstrate a level of professional competency to prospective employers. Candidates are required to have 5 years of work experience in fundraising and have 80 hours of continuing education through conference attendance and classroom instruction to qualify. Fundraisers must apply for renewal every 3 years to keep their certification valid.

Work Experience in a Related Occupation. Public relations and fundraising managers must have several years of experience in a related or entry-level position, such as a public relations specialist or fundraiser.

Lower level management positions may require only a few years of experience, whereas directors are more likely to need 5 to 10 years of related work experience.

Important Qualities

Communication skills. Managers deal with the public regularly; therefore, they must be friendly enough to build rapport and receive cooperation from their media contacts and donors.

Leadership skills. Public relations and fundraising managers often lead large teams of specialists or fundraisers and must be able to guide their activities.

Organizational skills. Public relations and fundraising managers are often in charge of running several events at the same time, requiring superior organizational skills.

Problem-solving skills. Managers sometimes must explain how the company or client is handling sensitive issues. They must use good judgment in what they report and how they report it.

Speaking skills. Public relations and fundraising managers regularly speak on behalf of their organization. When doing so, they must be able to explain the organization's position clearly.

Writing skills. Managers must be able to write well-organized and clear press releases and speeches. They must be able to grasp the key messages they want to get across and write them succinctly in order to keep the attention of busy readers or listeners.

Pay

The median annual wage for public relations and fundraising managers was $101,510 in May 2014. The median wage is the wage at which half the workers in an occupation earned more than that amount and half earned less. The lowest 10 percent earned less than $55,420, and the highest 10 percent earned more than $187,200.

In May 2014, the median annual wages for public relations and fundraising managers in the top industries in which they worked were as follows:

Professional, scientific, and technical services	$130,040
Management of companies and enterprises	117,410
Educational services; state, local, and private	95,280
Religious, grantmaking, civic, professional, and similar organizations	93,900
State and local government, excluding education and hospitals	84,340

Employment Projections Data for Public Relations and Fundraising Managers

Occupational Title	SOC Code	Employment, 2014	Projected Employment, 2024	Change, 2014–2024 Percent	Change, 2014–2024 Numeric
Public relations and fundraising managers	11-2031	65,800	70,500	7	4,700

Source: U.S. Bureau of Labor Statistics, Employment Projections Program

Similar Occupations. This table shows a list of occupations with job duties that are similar to those of public relations and fundraising managers.

Occupations	Entry-level Education	2014 Median Pay	Projected Job Growth	Average Annual Openings
Advertising Sales Agents	High school diploma or equivalent	$47,890	-3%	-450
Advertising, Promotions, and Marketing Managers	Bachelor's degree	$123,450	9%	1,970
Market Research Analysts	Bachelor's degree	$61,290	19%	9,230
Multimedia Artists and Animators	Bachelor's degree	$63,630	6%	390
Public Relations Specialists	Bachelor's degree	$55,680	6%	1,490

Job Outlook

Employment of public relations and fundraising managers is projected to grow 7 percent from 2014 to 2024, about as fast as the average for all occupations.

As online social media increases the speed at which news travels, public relations managers will be needed to address good and bad news for their organization or client.

Organizations continue to emphasize community outreach and customer relations as a way to enhance their reputation and visibility. Public opinion can change quickly, particularly as news spreads rapidly through the Internet. Consequently, public relations managers will be needed to coordinate and help respond to news developments in order to maintain their organization's reputation.

Fundraising managers are expected to become increasingly important for organizations (such as colleges and universities) that depend heavily on donations. More nonprofit organizations are focusing on cultivating an online presence and are increasingly using social media for fundraising activities.

Job Prospects. Competition for public relations and fundraising manager jobs is expected to be very strong.

Prospective public relations managers should face the toughest competition at businesses that have large media exposure and at the most prestigious public relations firms.

Job prospects for fundraising managers should be best for those with a master's degree in philanthropic studies or fundraising. These degree programs lead to experience in the industry, giving graduates an advantage over those who do not have such experience.

Contacts for More Information

For more information about public relations and fundraising managers, including professional certification in public relations, visit

➤ CFRE International (www.cfre.org)
➤ Public Relations Society of America (www.prsa.org)
➤ International Association of Business Communicators (www.iabc.com)

O*NET

➤ Public Relations and Fundraising Managers (11-2031.00)

Sales Managers

- **2014 Median Pay** .... $110,660 per year $53.20 per hour
- **Typical Entry-Level Education** .... Bachelor's degree
- **Work Experience in a Related Occupation** .... Less than 5 years
- **On-the-job Training** .... None
- **Number of Jobs, 2014** 376,300
- **Job Outlook, 2014–24** .... 5% (As fast as average)
- **Employment Change, 2014–24** 19,000

What Sales Managers Do

Sales managers direct organizations' sales teams. They set sales goals, analyze data, and develop training programs for organizations' sales representatives.

Duties. Sales managers typically do the following:

- Resolve customer complaints regarding sales and service
- Prepare budgets and approve expenditures
- Monitor customer preferences to determine the focus of sales efforts
- Analyze sales statistics
- Project sales and determine the profitability of products and services
- Determine discount rates or special pricing plans
- Develop plans to acquire new customers or clients through direct sales techniques, cold calling, and business-to-business marketing visits
- Assign sales territories and set sales quotas
- Plan and coordinate training programs for sales staff

Sales managers' responsibilities vary with the size of their organizations. However, most sales managers direct the distribution of goods and services by assigning sales territories, setting sales goals, and establishing training programs for the organization's sales representatives.

Some sales managers recruit, hire, and train new members of the sales staff. For more information about sales workers, see the profiles on retail sales workers and wholesale and manufacturing sales representatives.

Sales managers advise sales representatives on ways to improve their sales performance. In large multiproduct organizations, they oversee regional and local sales managers and their staffs.

Sales managers also stay in contact with dealers and distributors. They analyze sales statistics generated from their staff to determine the sales potential and inventory requirements of products and stores and to monitor customers' preferences.

Sales managers work closely with managers from other departments in the organization. For example, the marketing department identifies new customers that the sales department can target. The relationship between these two departments is critical to helping an organization expand its client base. Sales managers also work closely with research and design departments because they

Most sales managers have a bachelor's degree and previous work experience as a sales representative.

know customers' preferences, and with warehousing departments because they know inventory needs.

The following are examples of types of sales managers:

Business to business (B2B) sales managers oversee sales from one business to another. These managers may work for a manufacturer selling to a wholesaler, or a wholesaler selling to a retailer. Examples of these workers include sales managers overseeing sales of software to business firms, and sales managers overseeing wholesale food sales to grocery stores.

Business to consumer (B2C) sales managers oversee direct sales between businesses and individual consumers. These managers typically work in retail settings. Examples of these workers include sales managers of automobile dealerships and department stores.

Work Environment

Sales managers held about 376,300 jobs in 2014. The industries that employed the most sales managers were as follows:

Retail trade	20%
Wholesale trade	20
Manufacturing	12
Finance and insurance	9
Professional, scientific, and technical services	8

Sales managers have a lot of responsibility, and the position can be stressful. Many sales managers travel to national, regional, and local offices and to dealers' and distributors' offices.

Work Schedules. Most sales managers work full time. They often must work additional hours including some evenings and weekends.

Education/Training

Most sales managers have a bachelor's degree and work experience as a sales representative.

Education. Most sales managers have a bachelor's degree, although some have a master's degree. Educational requirements are less strict for job candidates who have significant work experience. Courses in business law, management, economics, accounting, finance, mathematics, marketing, and statistics are advantageous.

Work Experience in a Related Occupation. Work experience is typically required for someone to become a sales manager. The preferred duration varies, but employers usually seek candidates who have at least 1 to 5 years of experience in sales.

Sales managers typically enter the occupation from other sales and related occupations, such as sales representatives or purchasing agents. In small organizations, the number of sales manager positions often is limited, so advancement for sales workers usually comes slowly. In large organizations, promotion may occur more quickly.

Important Qualities

Analytical skills. Sales managers must collect and interpret complex data to target the most promising geographic areas and demographic groups, and determine the most effective sales strategies.

Communication skills. Sales managers need to work with colleagues and customers, so they must be able to communicate clearly.

Customer-service skills. When helping to make a sale, sales managers must listen and respond to the customer's needs.

Leadership skills. Sales managers must be able to evaluate how their sales staff performs and must develop strategies for meeting sales goals.

Pay

The median annual wage for sales managers was $110,660 in May 2014. The median wage is the wage at which half the workers in an occupation earned more than that amount and half earned less. The lowest 10 percent earned less than $53,620, and the highest 10 percent earned more than $187,200.

In May 2014, the median annual wages for sales managers in the top industries in which they worked were as follows:

Finance and insurance	$143,190
Professional, scientific, and technical services	141,400
Wholesale trade	116,260

Median Annual Wages, May 2014

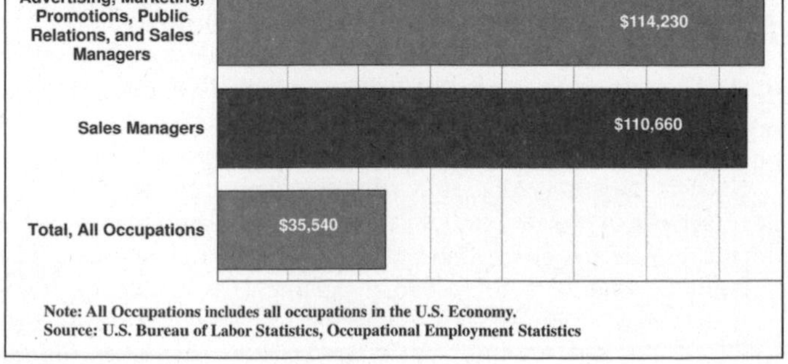

Percent Change in Employment, Projected 2014–2024

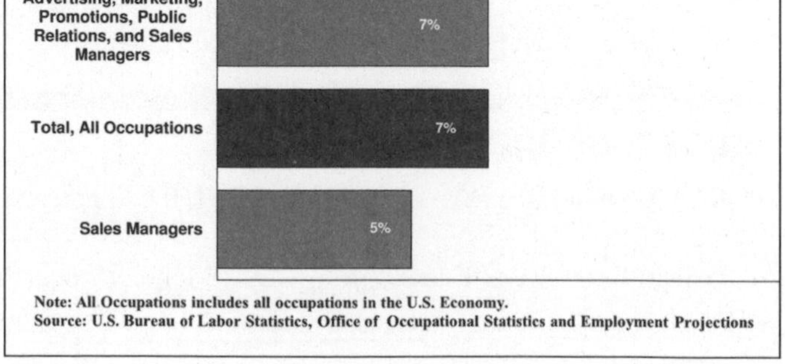

Employment Projections Data for Sales Managers

Occupational Title	SOC Code	Employment, 2014	Projected Employment, 2024	Change, 2014–2024	
				Percent	Numeric
Sales managers	11-2022	376,300	395,300	5	19,000

Source: U.S. Bureau of Labor Statistics, Employment Projections Program

Similar Occupations. This table shows a list of occupations with job duties that are similar to those of sales managers.

Occupations	Entry-level Education	2014 Median Pay	Projected Job Growth	Average Annual Openings
Advertising Sales Agents	High school diploma or equivalent	$47,890	-3%	-450
Advertising, Promotions, and Marketing Managers	Bachelor's degree	$123,450	9%	1,970
Buyers and Purchasing Agents	Bachelor's degree	$58,520	2%	720
Market Research Analysts	Bachelor's degree	$61,290	19%	9,230
Public Relations and Fundraising Managers	Bachelor's degree	$101,510	7%	470
Public Relations Specialists	Bachelor's degree	$55,680	6%	1,490
Retail Sales Workers	No formal educational credential	$21,670	7%	33,100
Sales Engineers	Bachelor's degree	$96,340	7%	490
Wholesale and Manufacturing Sales Representatives	See Education/Training	$58,380	7%	11,720

Manufacturing 114,870
Retail trade 78,440

Compensation methods for sales managers vary significantly with the type of organization and the product sold. Most employers use a combination of salary and commissions or salary plus bonuses. Commissions usually are a percentage of the value of sales, whereas bonuses may depend on individual performance, on the performance of all sales workers in the group or district, or on the organization's performance.

Job Outlook

Employment of sales managers is projected to grow 5 percent from 2014 to 2024, about as fast as the average for all occupations. Employment growth of these managers will depend primarily on growth or contraction in the industries that employ them.

An effective sales team remains crucial for profitability. As the economy grows, organizations will focus on generating new sales and will look to their sales strategy as a way to increase competitiveness.

Growth is expected to be stronger for sales managers in business-to-business sales than in business-to-consumer sales, because the rise of online shopping will reduce the need for sales calls to individual consumers.

Sales workers are some of the most important personnel in an organization. Therefore, sales managers are less likely to be let go than other types of managers, except in the case of organizations that are merging and consolidating.

Offshoring of these workers is also unlikely. Although domestic companies may hire some sales managers in foreign countries, those workers will function largely to support expansion into foreign markets rather than to replace domestic sales managers.

Job Prospects. Strong competition is expected because other managers and highly experienced professionals often seek these jobs.

Contacts for More Information

For more information about sales managers, visit

➤ Sales Management Association (http://salesmanagement.org)

O*NET

➤ Sales Managers (11-2022.00)

Social and Community Service Managers

- **2014 Median Pay** .... $62,740 per year
  $30.16 per hour
- **Typical Entry-Level Education** .... Bachelor's degree
- **Work Experience in a Related Occupation** .... 5 years or more
- **On-the-Job Training** .... None
- **Number of Jobs 2014** 138,500
- **Job Outlook, 2014–24** .... 10% (Faster than average)
- **Employment Change, 2014–24** 13,200

What Social and Community Service Managers Do

Social and community service managers coordinate and supervise social service programs and community organizations. They manage staff who provide social services to the public.

Duties. Social and community service managers typically do the following:

- Work with members of the community and other stakeholders to identify necessary programs and services

Social and community service managers meet with members of the community and funders to discuss their programs.

- Oversee administrative aspects of programs to meet the objectives of the stakeholders
- Establish methods to gather information about the impact of their programs
- Analyze data to determine the effectiveness of programs
- Suggest and implement improvements to programs and services
- Develop and manage budgets for programs and organizations
- Plan and manage outreach activities to advocate for increased awareness of programs
- Write proposals for social services funding

Social and community service managers work for a variety of social and human service organizations. Some of these organizations focus on working with a particular demographic, such as children, people who are homeless, older adults, or veterans. Other such organizations focus on helping people with particular challenges, such as mental health needs, the presence of chronic hunger, and long-term unemployment.

Social and community service managers are often expected to show that their programs and services are effective. They collect statistics and other information to evaluate the impact that programs have in their community or on their target audience. They are usually required to report this information to administrators or funders. They may also use evaluations to identify areas that need improvement for programs to be more effective, such as providing mentorship and assessments for their staff.

Although the specific job duties of social and community service managers may vary with the size of the organization, most managers must recruit, hire, and train new staff members. They also supervise staff, such as social workers, who provide services directly to clients.

In large agencies, social and community service managers tend to have specialized duties. They may be responsible for running only one program in an organization and reporting to the agency's upper management. They usually do not design programs but instead supervise and implement programs set up by administrators, elected officials, or other stakeholders.

In small organizations, social and community managers often have many roles. They represent the organization to the public through speaking engagements or in community-wide committees; they oversee programs and execute their implementations; they spend time on administrative tasks, such as managing budgets; and they also help with raising funds and meeting with potential donors.

Work Environment

Social and community service managers held about 138,500 jobs in 2014. The industries that employed the most social and community service managers were as follows:

Individual and family services	27%
State and local government, excluding education and hospitals	18
Religious, grantmaking, civic, professional, and similar organizations	14
Nursing and residential care facilities	11
Community and vocational rehabilitation services	9

They work for nonprofit organizations, private for-profit social service companies, and government agencies.

Work Schedules. Social and community service managers typically work full time. They may work extended hours to meet deadlines or when preparing new programs; about one-quarter worked more than 40 hours per week in 2014.

Education/Training

Social and community service managers need at least a bachelor's degree and some work experience. However, many employers prefer candidates who have a master's degree.

Education. A bachelor's degree in social work, urban studies, public or business administration, public health, or a related field is the minimum requirement for most social and community service manager jobs. Many employers prefer candidates with a master's degree. Coursework in statistics, program management, and policy analysis is considered helpful.

Median Annual Wages, May 2014

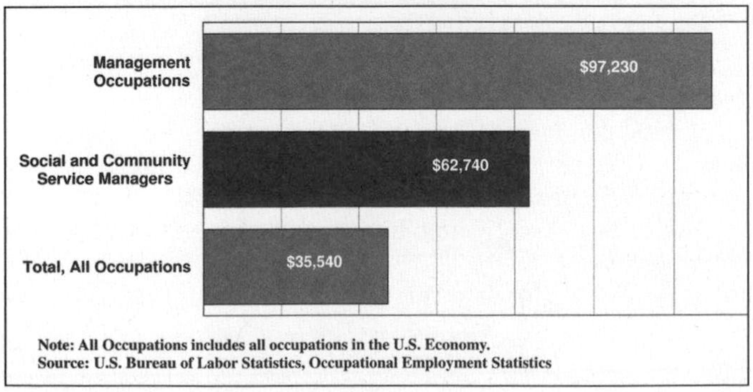

Percent Change in Employment, Projected 2014–2024

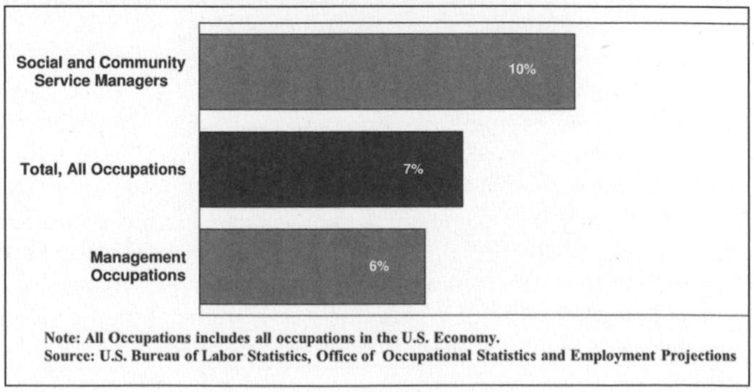

Employment Projections Data for Social and Community Service Managers

Occupational Title	SOC Code	Employment, 2014	Projected Employment, 2024	Change, 2014–2024 Percent	Change, 2014–2024 Numeric
Social and community service managers	11-9151	138,500	151,700	10	13,200

Source: U.S. Bureau of Labor Statistics, Employment Projections Program

Similar Occupations. This table shows a list of occupations with job duties that are similar to those of social and community service managers.

Occupations	Entry-level Education	2014 Median Pay	Projected Job Growth	Average Annual Openings
Health Educators and Community Health Workers	See Education/Training	$42,450	13%	1,560
Mental Health Counselors and Marriage and Family Therapists	Master's degree	$42,250	19%	3,140
Probation Officers and Correctional Treatment Specialists	Bachelor's degree	$49,060	4%	330
Rehabilitation Counselors	Master's degree	$34,380	9%	1,080
School and Career Counselors	Master's degree	$53,370	8%	2,250
Social and Human Service Assistants	High school diploma or equivalent	$29,790	11%	4,420
Social Workers	See Education/Training	$45,500	12%	7,480
Substance Abuse and Behavioral Disorder Counselors	Bachelor's degree	$39,270	22%	2,120

Work Experience in a Related Occupation. Work experience often is needed for someone to become a social and community service manager, and is essential for those wishing to enter the occupation with a bachelor's degree. Lower-level management positions may require only a few years of experience, although social and community service directors typically have much more experience. Candidates can get this experience by working as a social worker or in a similar occupation.

Important Qualities

Analytical skills. Social and community service managers need to understand and evaluate data in order to provide strategic guidance to their organization. They must be able to monitor and evaluate current programs as well as determine new initiatives.

Communication skills. Social and community service managers must be able to speak and write clearly so that others can understand them. Working with the community and employees requires effective communication. Public speaking experience is also helpful because social and community service managers often participate in community outreach.

Interpersonal skills. Social and community service managers should have good interpersonal skills. When speaking with members of their staff or members of the community, they must be tactful and able to explain and discuss all matters related to services that are needed.

Managerial skills. Social and community service managers spend much of their time administering budgets and responding to a wide variety of issues.

Problem-solving skills. Social and community service managers must be able to address client, staff, and agency-related issues as they occur.

Time-management skills. Social and community service managers must prioritize and handle numerous tasks for multiple customers, often in a short timeframe.

Pay

The median annual wage for social and community service managers was $62,740 in May 2014. The median wage is the wage at which half the workers in an occupation earned more than that amount and half earned less. The lowest 10 percent earned less than $38,260, and the highest 10 percent earned more than $104,540.

In May 2014, the median annual wages for social and community service managers in the top industries in which they worked were as follows:

State and local government, excluding education and hospitals	$71,850
Religious, grantmaking, civic, professional, and similar organizations	64,320
Individual and family services	58,480
Nursing and residential care facilities	57,070
Community and vocational rehabilitation services	56,600

Job Outlook

Employment of social and community service managers is projected to grow 10 percent from 2014 to 2024, faster than the average for all occupations.

Much of the job growth in this occupation is the result of an increasingly aging population. An increase in the number of older adults will result in a need for more social services, such as adult daycare and meal delivery. Social and community service managers, who administer programs that provide these services, will likely be needed to meet this increased demand. Employment of social and community service managers is expected to increase the most in industries serving the elderly, such as services for the elderly and persons with disabilities.

In addition, employment growth is projected as more people seek treatment for their addictions and as illegal drug offenders are increasingly sent to treatment programs rather than to jail. As a result, managers who direct treatment programs will be needed.

Although this occupation is projected to have employment growth, gains could be limited by budget cuts in state and local governments. Social and human services rely heavily on government funding, and if funding decreases, services may not grow fast enough to meet demand.

Contacts for More Information

For more information about social and community service managers, visit

- Network for Social Work Management (http://socialworkmanager.org)
- Council on Social Work Education (www.cswe.org)
- National Association of Social Workers (www.socialworkers.org)

O*NET

- Social and Community Service Managers (11-9151.00)

Top Executives

- **2014 Median Pay** .... $102,750 per year $49.40 per hour
- **Typical Entry-Level Education** .... Bachelor's degree
- **Work Experience in a Related Occupation** .... 5 years or more
- **On-the-job Training** .... None
- **Number of Jobs, 2014** 2,467,500
- **Job Outlook, 2014–24** .... 6% (As fast as average)
- **Employment Change, 2014–24** 147,000

What Top Executives Do

Top executives devise strategies and policies to ensure that an organization meets its goals. They plan, direct, and coordinate operational activities of companies and organizations.

Duties. Top executives typically do the following:

- Establish and carry out departmental or organizational goals, policies, and procedures
- Direct and oversee an organization's financial and budgetary activities
- Manage general activities related to making products and providing services
- Consult with other executives, staff, and board members about general operations
- Negotiate or approve contracts and agreements
- Appoint department heads and managers
- Analyze financial statements, sales reports, and other performance indicators
- Identify places to cut costs and to improve performance, policies, and programs

The responsibilities of top executives largely depend on an organization's size. For example, an owner or manager of a small organization, such as an independent retail store, often is responsible for purchasing, hiring, training, quality control, and day-to-day supervisory duties. In large organizations, however, top executives typically focus more on formulating policies and strategic planning, while general and operations managers direct day-to-day operations.

The following are examples of types of top executives working in the private sector:

Chief executive officers (CEOs), who are also known by titles such as *executive director*, *managing director*, or *president*, provide overall direction for companies and organizations. CEOs manage company operations, formulate and implement policies, and ensure goals are met. They collaborate with and direct the work of other top executives and typically report to a board of directors.

Chief operating officers (COOs) oversee other executives who direct the activities of various departments, such as human resources and sales. They also carry out the organization's guidelines on a day-to-day basis.

General and operations managers oversee operations that are too diverse and general to be classified into one area of management or administration. Responsibilities may include formulating policies, managing daily operations, and planning the use of materials and human resources. They make staff schedules, assign work, and ensure that projects are completed. In some organizations, the tasks of chief executive officers may overlap with those of general and operations managers.

The following are examples of types of top executives working in the public sector:

Mayors, along with *governors, city managers*, and *county administrators*, are chief executive officers of governments. They typically oversee budgets, programs, and the use of resources. Mayors and governors must be elected to office, whereas managers and administrators are typically appointed.

Most educational systems, regardless of whether they are public or private school systems, also employ executive officers. The following are examples of top executives working in the elementary, secondary, and postsecondary educational school systems:

School superintendents and *college* or *university presidents* are chief executive officers of school districts and postsecondary

Top executives need highly developed management skills and the ability to communicate clearly and persuasively.

Median Annual Wages, May 2014

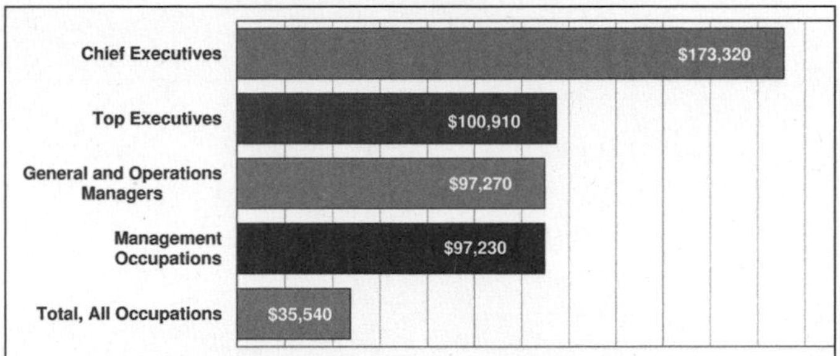

Note: All Occupations includes all occupations in the U.S. Economy.
Source: U.S. Bureau of Labor Statistics, Occupational Employment Statistics

Percent Change in Employment, Projected 2014–2024

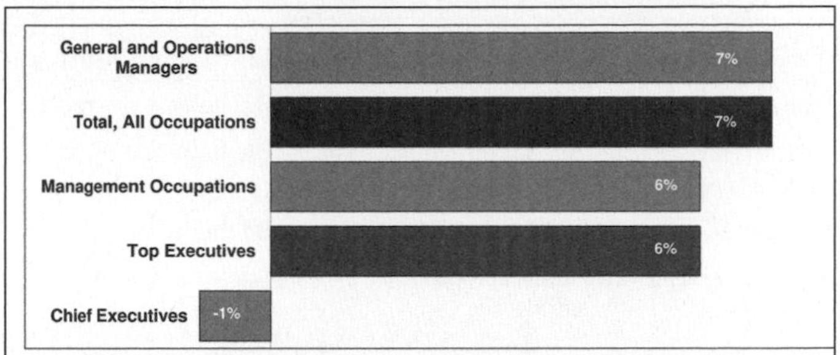

Note: All Occupations includes all occupations in the U.S. Economy.
Source: U.S. Bureau of Labor Statistics, Office of Occupational Statistics and Employment Projections

schools. They manage issues such as student achievement, budgets and resources, general operations, and relations with government agencies and other stakeholders.

Work Environment

Top executives held about 2.5 million jobs in 2014. General and operations managers held about 2.1 million of these jobs while chief executives held about 343,400 jobs.

Top executives work in nearly every industry. They work for both large and small businesses, ranging from companies in which they are the sole employee to firms with thousands of employees.

Top executives of large organizations typically have large offices and numerous support staff. However, the work of top executives is often stressful because they are under intense pressure to succeed. Executives in charge of poorly performing organizations or departments may find their jobs in jeopardy.

Top executives frequently travel to attend meetings and conferences or to visit their company's local, regional, national, and international offices.

Work Schedules. Top executives often work many hours, including evenings and weekends. In 2014, about half worked more than 40 hours per week.

Education/Training

Although education and training requirements vary widely by position and industry, many top executives have at least a bachelor's degree and a considerable amount of work experience.

Education. Many top executives have a bachelor's or master's degree in business administration or in an area related to their field of work. Top executives in the public sector often have a degree in business administration, public administration, law, or the liberal arts. Top executives of large corporations often have a master's degree in business administration (MBA).

College presidents and school superintendents are typically required to have a master's degree, although a doctorate is often preferred.

Although many mayors, governors, or other public sector executives have at least a bachelor's degree, these positions typically do not have any specific education requirements.

Work Experience in a Related Occupation. Many top executives advance within their own firm, moving up from lower level managerial or supervisory positions. However, other companies may prefer to hire qualified candidates from outside their organization. Top executives who are promoted from lower level positions may be able to substitute experience for education to move up in the company. For example, in industries such as retail trade or transportation, workers without a college degree may work their way up to higher levels within the company to become executives or general managers.

Chief executives typically need extensive managerial experience. Executives are also expected to have experience in the organization's area of specialty. Most general and operations managers hired from outside an organization need lower-level supervisory or management experience in a related field.

Some general managers advance to higher-level managerial or executive positions. Company training programs, executive development programs, and certification can often benefit managers or executives hoping to advance.

Important Qualities

Communication skills. Top executives must be able to communicate clearly and persuasively. They must effectively discuss issues and negotiate with others, direct subordinates, and explain their policies and decisions to those within and outside the organization.

Decision-making skills. Top executives need decision-making skills when setting policies and managing an organization. They must assess different options and choose the best course of action, often daily.

Leadership skills. Top executives must be able to lead an organization successfully by coordinating policies, people, and resources.

Management skills. Top executives must shape and direct the operations of an organization. For example, they must manage business plans, employees, and budgets.

Employment Projections Data for Top Executives

Occupational Title	SOC Code	Employment, 2014	Projected Employment, 2024	Change, 2014–2024 Percent	Change, 2014–2024 Numeric
Top executives	—	2,525,900	2,672,500	6	146,600
Chief executives	11-1011	343,400	339,400	-1	-4,100
General and operations managers	11-1021	2,124,100	2,275,200	7	151,100

Source: U.S. Bureau of Labor Statistics, Employment Projections Program

Similar Occupations. This table shows a list of occupations with job duties that are similar to those of top executives.

Occupations	Entry-level Education	2014 Median Pay	Projected Job Growth	Average Annual Openings
Administrative Services Managers	Bachelor's degree	$83,790	8%	2,350
Advertising, Promotions, and Marketing Managers	Bachelor's degree	$123,450	9%	1,970
Architectural and Engineering Managers	Bachelor's degree	$130,620	2%	370
Computer and Information Systems Managers	Bachelor's degree	$127,640	15%	5,370
Construction Managers	Bachelor's degree	$85,630	5%	1,780
Financial Managers	Bachelor's degree	$115,320	7%	3,770
Human Resources Managers	Bachelor's degree	$102,780	9%	1,080
Industrial Production Managers	Bachelor's degree	$92,470	-4%	-630
Medical and Health Services Managers	Bachelor's degree	$92,810	17%	5,630
Sales Managers	Bachelor's degree	$110,660	5%	1,900

Problem-solving skills. Top executives need to identify and resolve issues within an organization. They must be able to recognize shortcomings and effectively carry out solutions.

Time-management skills. Top executives do many tasks at the same time, typically under their own direction, to ensure that their work gets done and that they meet their goals.

Pay

The median annual wage for chief executives was $173,320 in May 2014. The median wage is the wage at which half the workers in an occupation earned more than that amount and half earned less. The lowest 10 percent earned less than $72,750, and the highest 10 percent earned more than $187,200.

The median annual wage for general and operations managers was $97,270 in May 2014. The lowest 10 percent earned less than $45,130, and the highest 10 percent earned more than $187,200.

Because the responsibilities of general and operations managers vary significantly among industries, earnings also tend to vary considerably.

Top executives are among the highest paid workers in the United States. However, salary levels can vary substantially. For example, a top manager in a large corporation can earn significantly more than the mayor of a small town.

In addition to salaries, total compensation for corporate executives often includes stock options and other performance bonuses. They also may enjoy benefits, such as access to expense allowances, use of company-owned aircraft and cars, club memberships, and company-paid insurance premiums. Nonprofit and government executives usually receive fewer of these types of benefits.

Job Outlook

Employment of top executives is projected to grow 6 percent from 2014 to 2024, about as fast as the average for all occupations. Employment growth will vary widely by industry and is largely dependent on the rate of industry growth.

Top executives are essential for running companies and organizations and their work is central to the success of a company.

Generally, employment growth will be driven by the formation of new organizations and expansion of existing ones, which will require more managers and executives to direct these operations.

However, the rate of new firm creation has slowed over the past few years, with economic activity and employment becoming increasingly concentrated in larger, more mature companies. Younger Americans who came of age during the Great Recession are characterized by an aversion to financial risk. As they reach the peak age of entrepreneurship over the next decade, new firm creation may continue to slow. This may negatively affect the demand for chief executives.

Job Prospects. Top executives are expected to face very strong competition for jobs. The high pay and prestige associated with these positions attract many qualified applicants.

For chief executives, those with an advanced degree and extensive managerial experience will have the best job prospects.

For general and operations managers, education requirements vary by industry, but candidates who can demonstrate strong leadership abilities and experience getting positive results will have better job opportunities.

Contacts for More Information

For more information about top executives, including educational programs, visit

- American Management Association (www.amanet.org)
- National Management Association (http://nma1.org)

For more information about executive financial management careers, visit

- Financial Executives International (www.financialexecutives.org/KenticoCMS/home.aspx)
- Financial Management Association International (www.fma.org)

For information about management skills development, including the Certified Manager (CM) credential, visit

- Institute of Certified Professional Managers (www.icpm.biz)

O*NET

- Chief Executives (11-1011.00)
- Chief Sustainability Officers (11-1011.03)
- General and Operations Managers (11-1021.00)

Training and Development Managers

- **2014 Median Pay** .... $101,930 per year $49.01 per hour
- **Typical Entry-Level Education** .... Bachelor's degree
- **Work Experience in a Related Occupation** .... 5 years or more

- **On-the-job Training** .... None
- **Number of Jobs, 2014** 32,900
- **Job Outlook, 2014–24** .... 7% (As fast as average)
- **Employment Change, 2014–24** 2,300

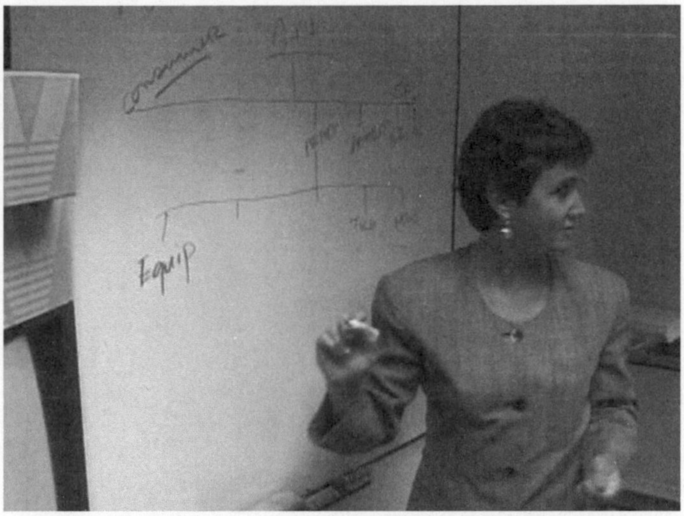

Training and development managers often give presentations.

What Training and Development Managers Do

Training and development managers plan, direct, and coordinate programs to enhance the knowledge and skills of an organization's employees. They also oversee a staff of training and development specialists.

Duties. Training and development managers typically do the following:

- Assess employees' needs for training
- Align training with the organization's strategic goals
- Create and manage a training budget, ensuring that operations are within budget
- Develop and implement training programs that make the best use of available resources
- Update training programs to ensure that they are current
- Oversee the creation of educational materials, such as online learning modules
- Review training materials from a variety of vendors and select materials with appropriate content
- Teach training methods and skills to instructors and supervisors
- Evaluate the effectiveness of training programs and instructors

Companies want to promote a more productive and knowledgeable workforce to stay competitive in business. Providing opportunity for development is a selling point for recruiting high-quality employees, and it helps retain employees who can contribute to business growth. Training and development managers work to align training and development with an organization's goals.

Training and development managers oversee training programs, staff, and budgets. They are responsible for organizing training programs, including creating or selecting course content and materials. Training often takes place in classrooms or training facilities. Increasingly, training is in the form of a video, self-guided instructional manual, or online application and delivered through a computer, tablet, or other hand-held electronic device. Training may also be collaborative, with employees informally connecting with experts, mentors, and colleagues, often through social media or other online mediums. Managers must ensure that training methods, content, software, systems, and equipment are appropriate and meaningful.

Training and development managers typically supervise a staff of training and development specialists, such as instructional designers, program developers, and instructors. Managers teach training methods to specialists who, in turn, instruct the organization's employees—both new and experienced. Managers direct the daily activities of specialists and evaluate their effectiveness. Although most managers primarily oversee specialists and training and development program operations, some—particularly those in smaller companies—also may conduct training courses.

To enhance employees' skills and an organization's overall quality of work, training and development managers often confer with managers of each department to identify its training needs. They may work with top executives and financial officers to identify and match training priorities with overall business goals. They also prepare training budgets and ensure that expenses stay within budget.

Work Environment

Training and development managers held about 32,900 jobs in 2014. The industries that employed the most training and development managers were as follows:

Management of companies and enterprises	16%
Finance and insurance	12
Professional, scientific, and technical services	12
Educational services; state, local, and private	10
Healthcare and social assistance	8

Training and development managers typically work in offices. Some travel between a main office and regional offices or training

Median Annual Wages, May 2014

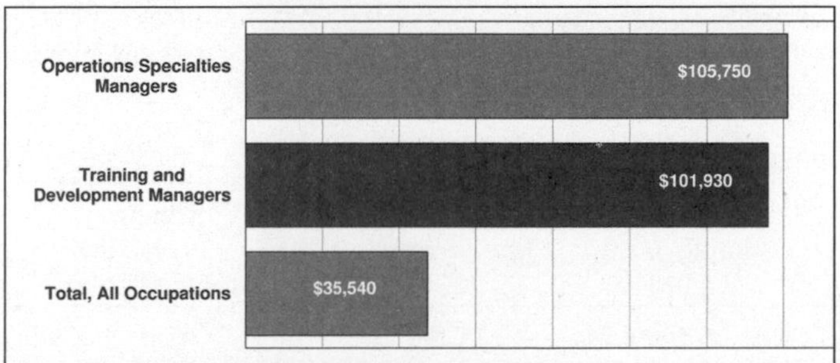

Note: All Occupations includes all occupations in the U.S. Economy.
Source: U.S. Bureau of Labor Statistics, Occupational Employment Statistics

Percent Change in Employment, Projected 2014–2024

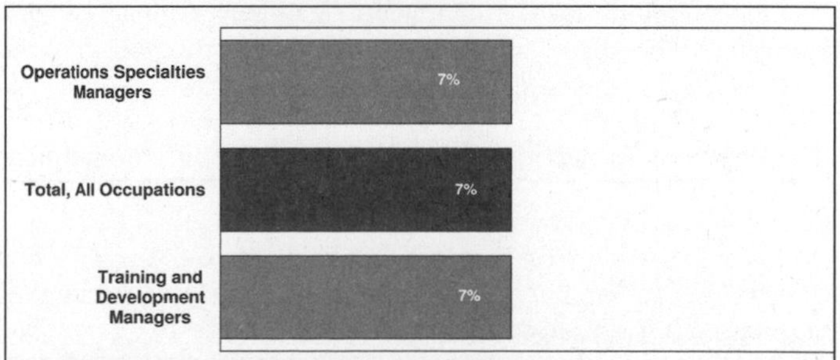

Note: All Occupations includes all occupations in the U.S. Economy.
Source: U.S. Bureau of Labor Statistics, Office of Occupational Statistics and Employment Projections

facilities. They spend much of their time working with people and overseeing training activities.

Work Schedules. Most training and development managers work full time during regular business hours. However, training and development managers do work overtime more than the average worker; about half worked more than 40 hours per week in 2014.

Education/Training

Candidates need a combination of education and related work experience to become a training and development manager. Although training and development managers need a bachelor's degree for many positions, some jobs require a master's degree.

Education. Training and development managers need a bachelor's degree for many positions, and some jobs require a master's degree. They can have a variety of educational backgrounds, but they often have a bachelor's degree in human resources, business administration, or a related field.

Many employers prefer or require training and development managers to have a master's degree, usually with a concentration in training and development, human resources management, organizational development, or business administration.

Training and development managers also may benefit from studying instructional design, behavioral psychology, or educational psychology. In addition, as technology continues to play a larger role in training and development, a growing number of organizations seek candidates who have a background in information technology or computer science.

Work Experience in a Related Occupation. Related work experience is essential for training and development managers. Many positions require work experience in training and development or another human resources field, management, or teaching. For example, many training and development managers start out as training and development specialists. Some employers also prefer experience in the industry in which the company operates. Increasingly, employers are looking for workers with experience in information technology as organizations introduce more e-learning and technology-based tools.

Licenses, Certifications, and Registrations. Although training and development managers are not legally required to be certified, certification can show professional expertise and credibility. Many employers prefer to hire certified candidates, and some positions may require certification.

Many professional associations for human resources professionals offer classes to enhance the skills of their members. Some associations, including the Association for Talent Development and International Society for Performance Improvement, specialize in training and development and offer certification programs.

Important Qualities

Communication skills. Training and development managers must clearly communicate information and facilitate learning by diverse audiences. They also must be able to effectively convey instructions to their staff.

Critical-thinking skills. Training and development managers use critical-thinking skills when assessing classes, materials, and programs. They must identify the training needs of an organization and recognize where changes and improvements can be made.

Decision-making skills. Training and development managers must select or create the best training programs to meet the needs of the organization. For example, they must review available training methods and materials and choose those that best fit each program.

Interpersonal skills. Training and development managers need strong interpersonal skills because delivering training programs requires collaborating with staff, trainees, subject matter experts, and the organization's leaders. They also accomplish much of their work through teams.

Leadership skills. Managers are often in charge of a staff and are responsible for many programs. They must be able to organize, motivate, and instruct those working under them.

Pay

The median annual wage for training and development managers was $101,930 in May 2014. The median wage is the wage at which half the workers in an occupation earned more than that amount and half earned less. The lowest 10 percent earned less than $57,920, and the highest 10 percent earned more than $178,360.

In May 2014, the median annual wages for training and development managers in the top industries in which they worked were as follows:

Professional, scientific, and technical services	$113,780
Management of companies and enterprises	108,480
Finance and insurance	103,350
Healthcare and social assistance	98,030
Educational services; state, local, and private	95,360

Job Outlook

Employment of training and development managers is projected to grow 7 percent from 2014 to 2024, about as fast as the average for all occupations. In many occupations, employees are required to take continuing education and skill development courses throughout their careers, creating demand for workers who develop and provide training materials.

Innovations in training methods and learning technology are expected to continue throughout the next decade, particularly for organizations with remote workers. Organizations increasingly use social media, visual simulations, mobile learning, and social networks in their training programs. As social media and collaborative learning become more common, training and development managers will need to modify training programs, allocate budgets, and integrate these features into training programs and curricula.

In addition, as companies seek to reduce costs, training and development managers may be required to structure programs to enlist available experts, take advantage of existing resources, and facilitate positive relationships among staff. Training and development

Employment Projections Data for Training and Development Managers

Occupational Title	SOC Code	Employment, 2014	Projected Employment, 2024	Change, 2014–2024	
				Percent	Numeric
Training and development managers	11-3131	32,900	35,200	7	2,300

Source: U.S. Bureau of Labor Statistics, Employment Projections Program

Similar Occupations. This table shows a list of occupations with job duties that are similar to those of training and development managers.

Occupations	Entry-level Education	2014 Median Pay	Projected Job Growth	Average Annual Openings
Career and Technical Education Teachers	Bachelor's degree	$51,830	4%	1,020
Compensation and Benefits Managers	Bachelor's degree	$108,070	6%	110
Compensation, Benefits, and Job Analysis Specialists	Bachelor's degree	$60,600	4%	340
Human Resources Managers	Bachelor's degree	$102,780	9%	1,080
Human Resources Specialists	Bachelor's degree	$57,420	5%	2,200
Instructional Coordinators	Master's degree	$61,550	7%	1,050
Postsecondary Education Administrators	Master's degree	$88,390	9%	1,520
Psychologists	See Education/Training	$70,700	19%	3,250
School and Career Counselors	Master's degree	$53,370	8%	2,250
Top Executives	Bachelor's degree	$102,750	6%	14,700
Training and Development Specialists	Bachelor's degree	$57,340	7%	1,890

managers may use informal collaborative learning and social media to engage and train employees in the most cost effective way.

Job Prospects. Overall, job prospects should be very good, particularly in industries with a lot of regulation, like finance and insurance. Job openings will stem from the need to replace workers who retire or otherwise leave the occupation.

Contacts for More Information

For more information about training and development managers, visit

- Association for Talent Development (www.td.org)
- International Society for Performance Improvement (www.isp.org)

For information about human resources management careers and certification, visit

- Society for Human Resource Management (www.shrm.org)

O*NET

- Training and Development Managers (11-3131.00)

Math

Actuaries

- **2014 Median Pay** .... $96,700 per year
  $46.49 per hour
- **Typical Entry-Level Education** .... Bachelor's degree
- **Work Experience in a Related Occupation**.............. None
- **On-the-job Training** .... Long-term on-the-job training
- **Number of Jobs, 2014** 24,600
- **Job Outlook, 2014–24** .... 18% (Much faster than average)
- **Employment Change, 2014–24** 4,400

What Actuaries Do

Actuaries analyze the financial costs of risk and uncertainty. They use mathematics, statistics, and financial theory to assess the risk that an event will occur, and they help businesses and clients develop policies that minimize the cost of that risk. Actuaries' work is essential to the insurance industry.

Duties. Actuaries typically do the following:

- Compile statistical data and other information for further analysis
- Estimate the probability and likely economic cost of an event such as death, sickness, an accident, or a natural disaster
- Design, test, and administer insurance policies, investments, pension plans, and other business strategies to minimize risk and maximize profitability
- Produce charts, tables, and reports that explain calculations and proposals
- Explain their findings and proposals to company executives, government officials, shareholders, and clients

Most actuarial work is done with computers. Actuaries use database software to compile information. They use advanced statistics and modeling software to forecast the probability of an event occurring, the potential costs of the event if it does occur, and whether the insurance company has enough money to pay future claims.

Actuaries typically work on teams that often include managers and professionals in other fields, such as accounting, underwriting, and finance. For example, some actuaries work with accountants and financial analysts to set the price for security offerings or with market research analysts to forecast demand for new products.

Most actuaries work at insurance companies, where they help design policies and determine the premiums that should be charged for each policy. They must ensure that the premiums are profitable yet competitive with other insurance companies.

Actuaries in the insurance industry typically specialize in a specific field of insurance, such as one of the following:

Health insurance actuaries help develop long-term care and health insurance policies by predicting expected costs of providing care under the terms of an insurance contract. Their predictions are based on numerous factors, including family history, geographic location, and occupation.

Life insurance actuaries help develop annuity and life insurance policies for individuals and groups by estimating, on the basis of risk factors such as age, gender, and tobacco use, how long someone is expected to live.

Property and casualty insurance actuaries help develop insurance policies that insure policyholders against property loss and liability resulting from accidents, natural disasters, fires, and other events. They calculate the expected number of claims resulting from automobile accidents, which varies with the insured person's age, sex, driving history, type of car, and other factors.

Some actuaries apply their expertise to financial matters outside of the insurance industry. For example, they develop investment strategies that manage risks and maximize returns for companies or individuals.

Pension and retirement benefits actuaries design, test, and evaluate company pension plans to determine if the expected funds available in the future will be enough to ensure payment of future benefits. They must report the results of their evaluations to the federal government. Pension actuaries also help businesses develop other types of retirement plans, such as 401(k)s and healthcare plans for retirees. In addition, they provide retirement planning advice to individuals.

Enterprise risk actuaries identify any risks, including economic, financial, and geopolitical risks that may affect a company's short-term or long-term objectives. They help top executives determine how much risk the business is willing to take, and they develop strategies to respond to these issues.

Actuaries also work in the public sector. In the federal government, actuaries may evaluate proposed changes to Social Security or Medicare or conduct economic and demographic studies to project future benefit obligations. At the state level, actuaries may examine and regulate the rates charged by insurance companies.

Some actuaries are considered consultants and provide advice to clients on a contract basis. Many consulting actuaries audit the work of internal actuaries at insurance companies or handle actuarial duties for insurance companies that are not large enough to keep their own actuaries on staff.

Actuaries need a strong background in mathematics.

Work Environment

Actuaries held about 24,600 jobs in 2014. The industries that employed the most actuaries were as follows:

Finance and insurance	71%
Professional, scientific, and technical services	15
Management of companies and enterprises	9
Government	4

Actuaries typically work in an office setting. However, actuaries who work for consulting firms may need to travel to meet with clients.

Work Schedules. Most actuaries work full time, and about 1 in 4 worked more than 40 hours per week in 2014.

Education/Training

Actuaries need a bachelor's degree, typically in mathematics, actuarial science, statistics, or some other analytical field. Students must complete coursework in economics, applied statistics, and corporate finance, and must pass a series of exams to become certified professionals.

Education. Actuaries must have a strong background in mathematics, statistics, and business. Typically, an actuary has an undergraduate degree in mathematics, actuarial science, statistics, or some other analytical field.

To become certified professionals, students must complete coursework in economics, applied statistics, and corporate finance.

Students also should take classes outside of mathematics and business to prepare them for a career as an actuary. Coursework in computer science, especially programming languages, and the ability to use and develop spreadsheets, databases, and statistical analysis tools, are valuable. Classes in writing and public speaking will improve students' ability to communicate in the business world.

Licenses, Certification, and Registrations. Two professional societies—the Casualty Actuarial Society (CAS) and the Society of Actuaries (SOA)—sponsor programs leading to full professional status. The CAS and SOA offer two levels of certification: associate and fellow.

The CAS certifies actuaries who work in the property and casualty field, which includes automobile, homeowners, medical malpractice, and workers' compensation insurance.

The SOA certifies actuaries who work in life insurance, health insurance, retirement benefits, investments, and finance.

The main requirement for associate certification in each society is the completion of exams. The SOA requires that candidates pass five exams for associate (ASA) certification. The CAS requires that candidates pass seven exams for associate (ACAS) certification.

Many employers expect students to have passed at least one of the initial actuary exams needed for professional certification before graduation.

In addition, both CAS and SOA require that candidates take seminars on professionalism. Both societies have mandatory e-learning courses for candidates.

It typically takes 4 to 6 years for an actuary to get an ACAS or an ASA certification because each exam requires hundreds of hours of study and months of preparation.

After becoming associates, actuaries typically take another 2 to 3 years to earn fellowship status.

The SOA offers fellowship certification in five separate tracks: life and annuities, group and health benefits, retirement benefits, investments, and finance/enterprise risk management. Unlike the SOA, the CAS does not offer specialized study tracks for fellowship certification.

Both the CAS and the SOA have a continuing education requirement. Most actuaries meet this requirement by attending training seminars that are sponsored by their employers or the societies.

Pension actuaries typically must be licensed by the U.S. Department of Labor and U.S. Department of the Treasury's Joint Board for the Enrollment of Actuaries. Applicants must meet certain experience requirements and pass two exams administered through the SOA to qualify for enrollment.

Other Experience. Because there are different types of practice areas, including health, life, pension, and casualty, internships may be helpful for students deciding on which actuarial track to pursue.

Training. Most entry-level actuaries start out as trainees. They are typically on teams with more experienced actuaries who serve as mentors. At first, they perform basic tasks, such as compiling data, but as they gain more experience, they may conduct research and write reports. Beginning actuaries may spend time working in other departments, such as marketing, underwriting, and product development, to learn all aspects of the company's work and how actuarial work applies to them.

Most employers support their actuaries throughout the certification process. For example, employers typically pay the cost of exams and study materials. Many firms provide paid time to study and encourage their employees to set up study groups. Employees usually receive raises or bonuses for each exam that they pass.

Advancement. Advancement depends largely on job performance and the number of actuarial exams passed. For example, actuaries who achieve fellowship status often supervise the work of other actuaries and provide advice to senior management. Actuaries with a broad knowledge of risk management and how it applies to business can rise to executive positions in their companies, such as chief risk officer or chief financial officer.

Median Annual Wages, May 2014

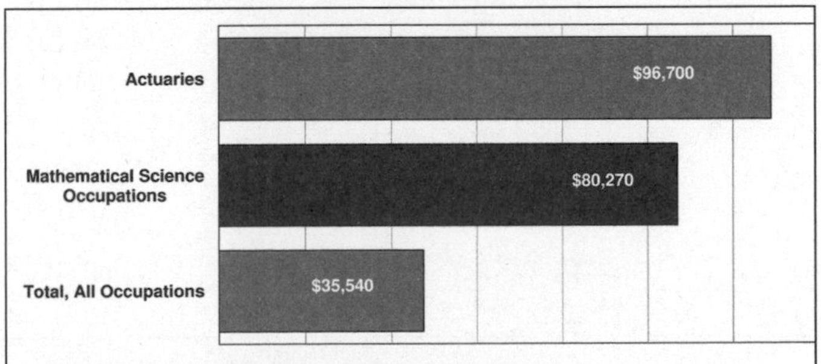

Note: All Occupations includes all occupations in the U.S. Economy.
Source: U.S. Bureau of Labor Statistics, Occupational Employment Statistics

Percent Change in Employment, Projected 2014–2024

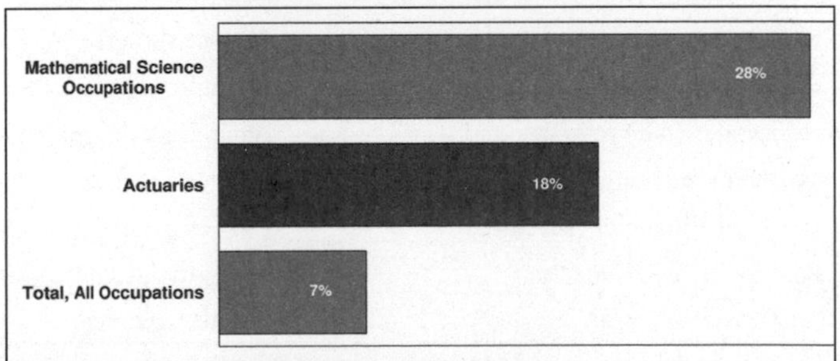

Note: All Occupations includes all occupations in the U.S. Economy.
Source: U.S. Bureau of Labor Statistics, Office of Occupational Statistics and Employment Projections

Employment Projections Data for Actuaries

Occupational Title	SOC Code	Employment, 2014	Projected Employment, 2024	Change, 2014–2024	
				Percent	Numeric
Actuaries	15-2011	24,600	29,000	18	4,400

Source: U.S. Bureau of Labor Statistics, Employment Projections Program

Important Qualities

Analytical skills. Actuaries use analytical skills to identify patterns and trends in complex sets of data to determine the factors that have an effect on certain types of events.

Communication skills. Actuaries must be able to explain complex technical matters to those without an actuarial background. They must also communicate clearly through the reports and memos that describe their work and recommendations.

Computer skills. Actuaries must know programming languages and be able to use and develop spreadsheets, databases, and statistical analysis tools.

Interpersonal skills. Actuaries serve as leaders and members of teams, so they must be able to listen to other people's opinions and suggestions before reaching a conclusion.

Math skills. Actuaries quantify risk by using the principles of calculus, statistics, and probability.

Problem-solving skills. Actuaries identify risks and develop ways for businesses to manage those risks.

Pay

The median annual wage for actuaries was $96,700 in May 2014. The median wage is the wage at which half the workers in an occupation earned more than that amount and half earned less. The lowest 10 percent earned less than $58,080, and the highest 10 percent earned more than $180,680.

In May 2014, the median annual wages for actuaries in the top industries in which they worked were as follows:

Finance and insurance	$98,310
Professional, scientific, and technical services	96,880
Government	94,710
Management of companies and enterprises	89,630

Job Outlook

Employment of actuaries is projected to grow 18 percent from 2014 to 2024, much faster than the average for all occupations. However, because it is a small occupation, the fast growth will result in only about 4,400 new jobs over the 10-year period.

Actuaries will be needed to develop, price, and evaluate a variety of insurance products and calculate the costs of new risks.

More actuaries will also be needed to help companies manage their own risk, a practice known as enterprise risk management. Actuaries will help companies avoid, manage, and respond to any potential financial risks across all areas of their business operations. This analysis helps companies adjust their business or investment strategies to achieve economic returns and respond to new financial regulations and requirements.

Insurance companies will need actuaries to analyze the large amount of information, such as medical or property data, collected from consumers. The increase in available data will allow insurance companies to better develop new products, set competitive prices, predict consumer behavior, and make more accurate projections of future risks and costs.

In addition, health insurance companies will require more actuaries to help evaluate the effects of changing healthcare regulations and guidelines, expand into new insurance markets, and offer products to new customers. However, consolidation among health insurance companies and providers may limit growth in this area.

Job Prospects. Job opportunities should be somewhat favorable for applicants interested in an actuarial career. However, competition may grow, because the number of students sitting for actuarial exams has increased in the past few years. Students who have passed at least two actuarial exams and have had an internship while in college should have the best job prospects for entry-level positions.

Similar Occupations. This table shows a list of occupations with job duties that are similar to those of actuaries.

Occupations	Entry-level Education	2014 Median Pay	Projected Job Growth	Average Annual Openings
Accountants and Auditors	Bachelor's degree	$65,940	11%	14,240
Budget Analysts	Bachelor's degree	$71,220	3%	150
Cost Estimators	Bachelor's degree	$60,050	9%	1,870
Economists	Master's degree	$95,710	6%	120
Financial Analysts	Bachelor's degree	$78,620	12%	3,230
Insurance Underwriters	Bachelor's degree	$64,220	-11%	-1,170
Mathematicians	Master's degree	$103,720	21%	70
Personal Financial Advisors	Bachelor's degree	$81,060	30%	7,390
Postsecondary Teachers	See Education/Training	$70,790	13%	17,700
Statisticians	Master's degree	$79,990	34%	1,010

Contacts for More Information

For more information about actuaries, visit
- American Academy of Actuaries (www.actuary.org)

For more information about actuaries in property and casualty insurance, visit
- Casualty Actuarial Society (www.casact.org)

For more information about actuaries in life and health insurance, retirement benefits, investments, and finance/enterprise risk management, visit
- Society of Actuaries (www.soa.org/member)

For more information about how to become an actuary, visit
- Be an Actuary (www.beanactuary.org)

For more information about pension actuaries, visit
- American Society of Pension Professionals and Actuaries (www.asppa.org)

O*NET

- Actuaries (15-2011.00)

Mathematicians

- **2014 Median Pay** .... $103,720 per year
  $49.86 per hour
- **Typical Entry-Level Education** .... Master's degree
- **Work Experience in a Related Occupation** .... None
- **On-the-Job Training** .... None
- **Number of Jobs 2014** 3,500
- **Job Outlook, 2014–24** .... 21% (Much faster than average)
- **Employment Change, 2014–24** 700

What Mathematicians Do

Mathematicians conduct research to develop and understand mathematical principles. They also analyze data and apply mathematical techniques to help solve real-world problems.

Duties. Mathematicians typically do the following:

- Develop new mathematical rules, theories, and concepts in areas such as algebra and geometry
- Use mathematical formulas and models to prove or disprove theories
- Apply mathematical theories and techniques to solve practical problems in business, engineering, the sciences, and other fields
- Develop mathematical or statistical models to analyze data
- Interpret data and report conclusions drawn from their analyses
- Use data analysis to support and improve business decisions
- Read professional journals, talk with other mathematicians, and attend professional conferences to maintain their knowledge of current trends

Some mathematicians apply theories and techniques, such as mathematical modeling, to solve practical problems. These mathematicians, sometimes known as *applied mathematicians*, typically work with individuals in other occupations to solve these problems. For example, they may work with chemists, materials scientists, and chemical engineers to analyze the effectiveness of new drugs. Other applied mathematicians may work with industrial designers to study the aerodynamic characteristics of new automobiles.

Applied mathematicians use math to solve practical problems.

Other mathematicians may study theoretical or abstract concepts in mathematics. Sometimes called *theoretical mathematicians*, they identify, research, and resolve unexplained issues in mathematics. They are concerned primarily with exploring new areas and relationships of mathematical theories to increase knowledge and understanding about the field.

Despite the differences between applied and theoretical mathematics, these areas frequently overlap. Many mathematicians, particularly those in government or private industry, will use both applied and theoretical knowledge in their job duties.

However, most people with a degree in mathematics or who develop mathematical theories and models are not formally known as mathematicians. Instead, they work in related fields and professions. In the computer systems design and related services industries, for example, they may be known as computer programmers or systems analysts. In finance, they may be known as quantitative analysts or statisticians. Other industries may refer to them as data scientists.

Computer and information research scientists, physicists and astronomers, economists, actuaries, operations research analysts, engineers, and many other occupations also use mathematics extensively.

Some people with a mathematics background become middle school or high school math teachers.

Many people with a Ph.D. in mathematics, particularly theoretical mathematics, work as postsecondary teachers in education institutions. They usually have a mix of teaching and research responsibilities. Some may conduct individual research or collaborate with other professors or mathematicians. Collaborators may work together at the same institution or from different locations.

Work Environment

Mathematicians held about 3,500 jobs in 2014. The industries that employed the most mathematicians were as follows:

Federal government	30%
Scientific research and development services	16
Colleges, universities, and professional schools; state, local, and private	13
Finance and insurance	7
Manufacturing	5

Mathematicians typically work in offices. They also may work on teams with engineers, scientists, and other occupations.

Work Schedules. Most mathematicians work full time. Deadlines and last-minute requests for data or analysis may require overtime.

Median Annual Wages, May 2014

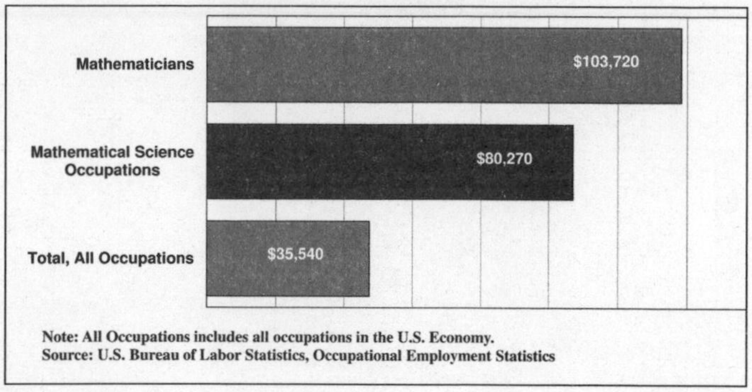

Percent Change in Employment, Projected 2014–2024

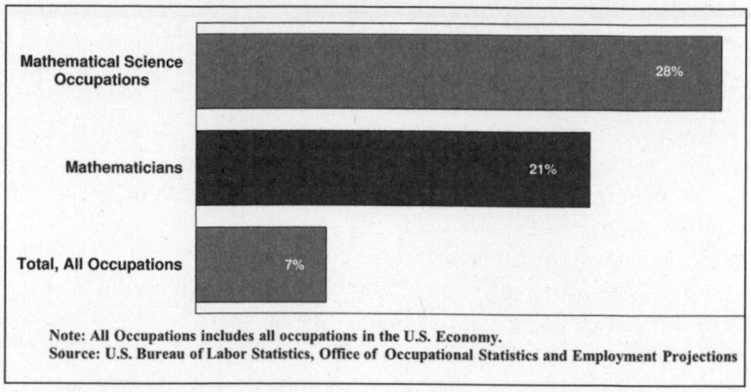

In addition, mathematicians may have to travel to attend seminars and conferences.

Education/Training

Mathematicians typically need at least a master's degree in mathematics. However, some positions are available for those with a bachelor's degree.

Education. In private industry, mathematicians typically need an advanced degree, either a master's degree or a doctorate. For jobs with the federal government, candidates need at least a bachelor's degree in mathematics or significant coursework in mathematics.

Most colleges and universities offer a bachelor's degree in mathematics. Courses usually include calculus, differential equations, and linear and abstract algebra. Many colleges and universities advise or require mathematics students to take courses in a related field, such as computer science, engineering, physics, or statistics. Because mathematicians often work with data analysis software, computer programming courses may be particularly beneficial for students.

Many universities offer master's and doctoral degrees in theoretical or applied mathematics. Many students who get a doctoral degree work as professors of mathematics in a college or university.

Also, holders of bachelor's degrees who meet state certification requirements may become middle school or high school mathematics teachers.

Students who are interested in becoming mathematicians should take as many math courses as possible in high school.

Important Qualities

Analytical skills. Mathematicians use mathematical techniques and models to analyze large amounts of data. They must determine the appropriate software packages and understand computer programming languages to design and develop new techniques and models. They must also be precise and accurate in their analysis.

Communication skills. Mathematicians must interact with, and propose solutions to, people who may not have extensive knowledge of mathematics.

Math skills. Mathematicians use statistics, calculus, and linear algebra to develop their models and analyses.

Problem-solving skills. Mathematicians must devise new solutions to problems encountered by scientists or engineers.

Pay

The median annual wage for mathematicians was $103,720 in May 2014. The median wage is the wage at which half the workers in an occupation earned more than that amount and half earned less. The lowest 10 percent earned less than $54,830, and the highest 10 percent earned more than $157,090.

In May 2014, the median annual wages for mathematicians in the top industries in which they worked were as follows:

Manufacturing	$121,670
Scientific research and development services	115,480
Federal government	107,440
Finance and insurance	89,810
Colleges, universities, and professional schools; state, local, and private	57,300

Job Outlook

Employment of mathematicians is projected to grow 21 percent from 2014 to 2024, much faster than the average for all occupations. However, because it is a small occupation, the fast growth will result in only about 700 new jobs over the 10-year period.

The amount of digitally stored data will increase over the next decade as more people and companies conduct business online and use social media, smartphones, and other mobile devices. As a result, businesses will increasingly need mathematicians to analyze the large amount of information and data collected. Analyses will help companies improve their business processes, design and develop new products, and even advertise products to potential customers.

Mathematicians also will be needed to help information security analysts create data-security systems to protect confidential information of individuals and businesses.

Job Prospects. Because the occupation is small and there are relatively few mathematician positions, strong competition for jobs is expected. Despite the strong competition for formal mathematician positions, many candidates with a background in advanced

Employment Projections Data for Mathematicians

Occupational Title	SOC Code	Employment, 2014	Projected Employment, 2024	Change, 2014–2024 Percent	Change, 2014–2024 Numeric
Mathematicians	15-2021	3,500	4,200	21	700

Source: U.S. Bureau of Labor Statistics, Employment Projections Program

Similar Occupations. This table shows a list of occupations with job duties that are similar to those of mathematicians.

Occupations	Entry-level Education	2014 Median Pay	Projected Job Growth	Average Annual Openings
Actuaries	Bachelor's degree	$96,700	18%	440
Computer Programmers	Bachelor's degree	$77,550	-8%	-2,650
Computer Systems Analysts	Bachelor's degree	$82,710	21%	11,860
Database Administrators	Bachelor's degree	$80,280	11%	1,340
Financial Analysts	Bachelor's degree	$78,620	12%	3,230
Market Research Analysts	Bachelor's degree	$61,290	19%	9,230
Nuclear Engineers	Bachelor's degree	$100,470	-4%	-70
Operations Research Analysts	Bachelor's degree	$76,660	30%	2,760
Physicists and Astronomers	Doctoral or professional degree	$109,290	7%	150
Postsecondary Teachers	See Education/Training	$70,790	13%	17,700
Statisticians	Master's degree	$79,990	34%	1,010
Survey Researchers	Master's degree	$49,760	12%	190

mathematical techniques and modeling will find good job opportunities in other, closely related fields.

Those with a graduate degree in mathematics, very strong quantitative and data analysis skills, and a background in a related discipline, such as business, computer science, or statistics, should have the best job prospects. Computer programming skills also are important to many employers.

Contacts for More Information

For more information about mathematicians, including training, especially for doctoral-level employment, visit

➤ American Mathematical Society (www.ams.org)

For specific information on careers in applied mathematics, visit

➤ Society for Industrial and Applied Mathematics (www.siam.org)

For information on federal government requirements for mathematician positions, visit

➤ U.S. Office of Personnel Management (www.opm.gov)

To find job openings for mathematicians in the federal government, visit

➤ USAJOBS (www.usajobs.gov)

O*NET

➤ Mathematicians (15-2021.00)

Operations Research Analysts

- **2014 Median Pay** .... $76,660 per year $36.86 per hour
- **Typical Entry-Level Education** .... Bachelor's degree
- **Work Experience in a Related Occupation** .... None
- **On-the-Job Training** .... None
- **Number of Jobs 2014** 91,300
- **Job Outlook, 2014–24** .... 30% (Much faster than average)
- **Employment Change, 2014–24** 27,600

What Operations Research Analysts Do

Operations research analysts use advanced mathematical and analytical methods to help organizations solve problems and make better decisions.

Duties. Operations research analysts typically do the following:

- Identify and solve real-world problems in areas such as business, logistics, healthcare, or other fields
- Collect and organize information from a variety of sources, such as computer databases, sales histories, and customer feedback
- Gather input from workers involved in all aspects of a problem or from others who have specialized knowledge, so that they can help solve the problem
- Examine information to figure out what is relevant to a problem and what methods might be used to analyze it
- Use statistical analysis, simulations, predictive modeling, or other methods to analyze information and develop practical solutions to business problems
- Advise managers and other decision makers on the impacts of various courses of action to take in order to address a problem
- Write memos, reports, and other documents explaining their findings and recommendations for managers, executives, and other officials

Operations research analysts can advance by becoming technical specialists or supervisors on more complicated projects.

Operations research analysts are involved in all aspects of an organization. They help managers decide how to allocate resources, develop production schedules, manage the supply chain, and set prices. For example, they may help decide how to organize products in supermarkets or help companies figure out the most effective way to ship and distribute products.

Analysts must first identify and understand the problem to be solved or the processes to be improved. Analysts typically collect relevant data from the field and interview clients or managers involved in the business processes being examined. Analysts show the implications of pursuing different actions and may assist in achieving a consensus on how to proceed.

Operations research analysts use sophisticated computer software, such as databases and statistical programs, and modeling packages, to analyze and solve problems. Analysts use these mathematical programs to simulate current and future events and evaluate alternative courses of action. Analysts break down problems into their various parts and analyze the effect that different changes and circumstances would have on each of these parts. For example, to help an airline schedule flights and decide what to charge for tickets, analysts may take into account the cities that have to be connected, the amount of fuel required to fly those routes, the expected number of passengers, pilots' schedules, maintenance costs, and fuel prices.

There is no one way to solve a problem, and analysts must weigh the costs and benefits of alternative solutions or approaches in their recommendations to managers.

Because problems are complex and often require expertise from many disciplines, most analysts work on teams. Once a manager reaches a final decision, these teams may work with others in the organization to ensure that the plan arrived at is successful.

Work Environment

Operations research analysts held about 91,300 jobs in 2014. The industries that employed the most operations research analysts were as follows:

Finance and insurance	26%
Professional, scientific, and technical services	23
Manufacturing	11
Management of companies and enterprises	9
Federal government	6

Most operations research analysts in the federal government work for the Department of Defense, which also employs a large number of analysts through private consulting firms.

Operations research analysts spend most of their time in offices. Some may spend time in the field to gather information and observe business processes directly. Analysts may also travel to work with clients and company executives and to attend conferences.

Because problems are complex and often require expertise from many disciplines, most analysts work on teams. Once a manager reaches a final decision, these teams may work with others in the organization to ensure that the plan arrived at is successful. Because they work on projects that are of immediate interest to top managers, operations research analysts often are under pressure to meet deadlines.

Work Schedules. Almost all operations research analysts work full time. About 1 in 6 worked more than 40 hours per week in 2014.

Education/Training

Although applicants may need a master's degree for most operations research positions, a bachelor's degree is enough for some entry-level positions. Because few schools offer bachelor's and advanced degree programs in operations research, analysts typically have degrees in other, related fields.

Education. Although some employers prefer to hire applicants with a master's degree, many entry-level positions are available for those with a bachelor's degree. Although some schools offer bachelor's and advanced degree programs in operations research, some analysts have degrees in other technical or quantitative fields, such as engineering, computer science, analytics, or mathematics.

Because operations research is based on quantitative analysis, students need extensive coursework in mathematics. Courses include statistics, calculus, and linear algebra. Coursework in computer science is important because analysts rely on advanced statistical and database software to analyze and model data. Courses in other areas, such as engineering, economics, and political science, are useful because operations research is a multidisciplinary field with a wide variety of applications.

Continuing education is important for operations research analysts. Keeping up with advances in technology, software tools, and improved analytical methods is vital.

Other Experience. Many operations research analysts who work with the military are veterans of the U.S. Armed Forces.

Some positions may require applicants to undergo a background check in order to attain a security clearance.

Important Qualities

Analytical skills. Operations research analysts use a wide range of methods, such as forecasting, data mining, and statistical analysis, to examine and interpret data. They must determine the appropriate software packages and understand computer programming languages to design and develop new techniques and models.

Communication skills. Operations research analysts often present their data and conclusions to managers and other executives.

Median Annual Wages, May 2014

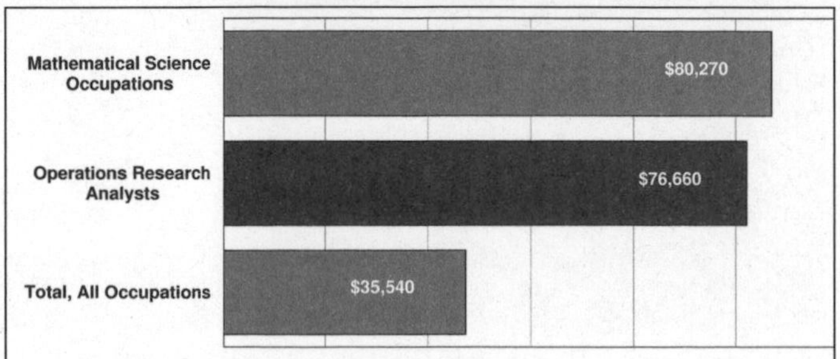

Note: All Occupations includes all occupations in the U.S. Economy.
Source: U.S. Bureau of Labor Statistics, Occupational Employment Statistics

Percent Change in Employment, Projected 2014–2024

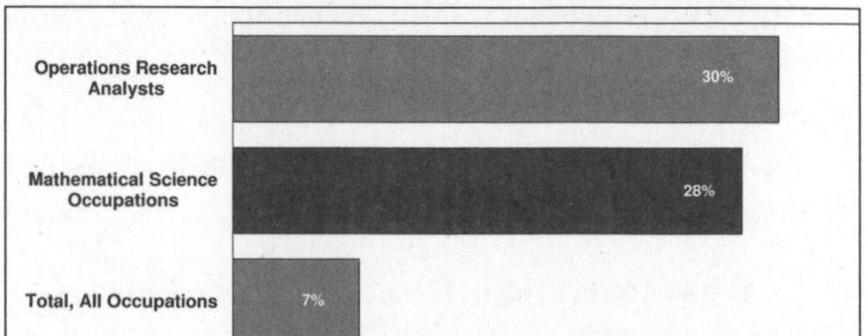

Note: All Occupations includes all occupations in the U.S. Economy.
Source: U.S. Bureau of Labor Statistics, Office of Occupational Statistics and Employment Projections

Employment Projections Data for Operations Research Analysts

Occupational Title	SOC Code	Employment, 2014	Projected Employment, 2024	Change, 2014–2024 Percent	Change, 2014–2024 Numeric
Operations research analysts	15-2031	91,300	118,900	30	27,600

Source: U.S. Bureau of Labor Statistics, Employment Projections Program

Similar Occupations. This table shows a list of occupations with job duties that are similar to those of operations research analysts.

Occupations	Entry-level Education	2014 Median Pay	Projected Job Growth	Average Annual Openings
Economists	Master's degree	$95,710	6%	120
Industrial Engineers	Bachelor's degree	$81,490	1%	210
Logisticians	Bachelor's degree	$73,870	2%	250
Management Analysts	Bachelor's degree	$80,880	14%	10,340
Market Research Analysts	Bachelor's degree	$61,290	19%	9,230
Mathematicians	Master's degree	$103,720	21%	70
Software Developers	Bachelor's degree	$97,990	17%	18,660
Statisticians	Master's degree	$79,990	34%	1,010

They also need to communicate technical information to people without a technical background.

Critical-thinking skills. Operations research analysts must be able to figure out what information is relevant to their work. They also must be able to evaluate the costs and benefits of alternative solutions before making a recommendation.

Interpersonal skills. Operations research analysts typically work on teams. They also need to be able to convince managers and top executives to accept their recommendations.

Math skills. The models and methods used by operations research analysts are rooted in statistics, calculus, linear algebra, and other advanced mathematical disciplines.

Problem-solving skills. Operations research analysts need to be able to diagnose problems on the basis of information given to them by others. They then analyze relevant information to solve the problems.

Writing skills. Operations research analysts write memos, reports, and other documents explaining their findings and recommendations.

Pay

The median annual wage for operations research analysts was $76,660 in May 2014. The median wage is the wage at which half the workers in an occupation earned more than that amount and half earned less. The lowest 10 percent earned less than $42,810, and the highest 10 percent earned more than $132,220.

In May 2014, the median annual wages for operations research analysts in the top industries in which they worked were as follows:

Federal government	$107,440
Manufacturing	87,030
Professional, scientific, and technical services	82,540
Management of companies and enterprises	78,380
Finance and insurance	71,810

Job Outlook

Employment of operations research analysts is projected to grow 30 percent from 2014 to 2024, much faster than the average for all occupations. As technology advances and companies seek efficiency and cost savings, demand for operations research analysis should continue to grow. In addition, increasing demand should occur for analysts in the field of analytics in order to improve business planning and decision making.

Operations research analysts will continue to be needed to provide support for the Armed Forces and to assist in the development and implementation of policies and programs in other areas of government.

Technological advances have made it faster and easier for organizations to get data. In addition, improvements in analytical software have made operations research more affordable and more applicable to a wider range of areas. More companies are expected to employ operations research analysts to help them turn data into valuable information that managers can use in order to make better decisions in all aspects of their business. For example, operations research analysts will be needed to help businesses improve their manufacturing operations and logistics.

Job Prospects. Opportunities should be better for those who have a master's or Ph.D. degree in operations research, management science, or a related field. Applicants with business experience in addition to strong analytical skills will also likely have the best job prospects.

Contacts for More Information

For more information about operations research analysts, visit

- Institute for Operations Research and the Management Sciences (www.informs.org)
- Military Operations Research Society (www.mors.org)

For information about analytics and analytics certification, visit

- Certified Analytics Professionals (www.certifiedanalytics.org/index.php)

O*NET

- Operations Research Analysts (15-2031.00)

Statisticians

- **2014 Median Pay** .... $79,990 per year
  $38.46 per hour
- **Typical Entry-Level Education** .... Master's degree
- **Work Experience in a Related Occupation** .... None
- **On-the-job Training** .... None
- **Number of Jobs, 2014** 30,000
- **Job Outlook, 2014–24** .... 34% (Much faster than average)
- **Employment Change, 2014–24** 10,100

Advanced computer programs have led to jobs for statisticians in many industries.

What Statisticians Do

Statisticians use statistical methods to collect and analyze data and to help solve real-world problems in business, engineering, healthcare, or other fields.

Duties. Statisticians typically do the following:

- Decide what data are needed to answer specific questions or problems
- Determine methods for finding or collecting data
- Design surveys, experiments, or opinion polls to collect data
- Collect data or train others to do so
- Analyze and interpret data
- Report conclusions from their analyses

Statisticians design surveys, questionnaires, experiments, and opinion polls to collect the data they need. Surveys may be mailed, conducted over the phone, collected online, or gathered through some other means.

Some surveys, such as the U.S. census, include data from nearly everyone. For most surveys and opinion polls, however, statisticians use sampling to collect data from some people in a particular group. Statisticians determine the type and size of the sample to be surveyed or polled.

Statisticians use specialized statistical software to analyze data. In their analyses, statisticians identify trends and relationships within the data. They also conduct tests to find out the data's validity and to account for high survey nonresponse rates or sampling error. Some statisticians may help create new software to analyze data more accurately and efficiently.

Statisticians present the findings from their analyses and discuss the data's limitations to prevent inaccurate conclusions from being drawn. They may present written reports, tables, charts, and graphs to other team members and to clients. Statisticians also recommend how to improve the design of future surveys or experiments.

Statisticians work in many fields, such as education, marketing, psychology, sports, or any other field that requires the collection and analysis of data. In particular, government, healthcare, and research and development companies employ many statisticians.

Government. Statisticians working in government develop and analyze surveys that collect a variety of data, including unemployment rates, wages, and other estimates pertaining to jobs and workers. Other statisticians help to figure out the average level of pesticides in drinking water, the number of endangered species living in a particular area, or the number of people who have a certain disease.

Some statisticians employed by the federal government are known as mathematical statisticians.

Median Annual Wages, May 2014

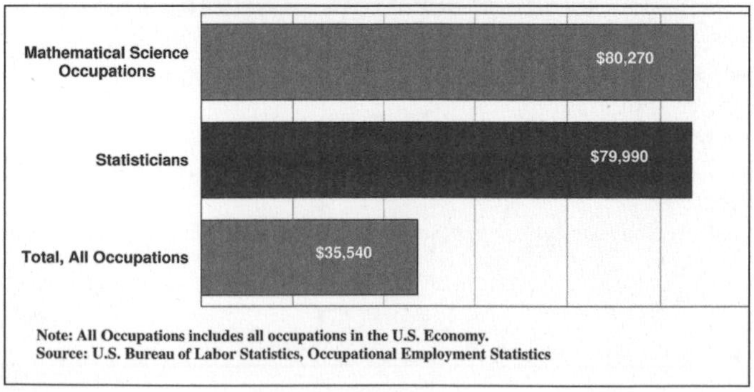

Percent Change in Employment, Projected 2014–2024

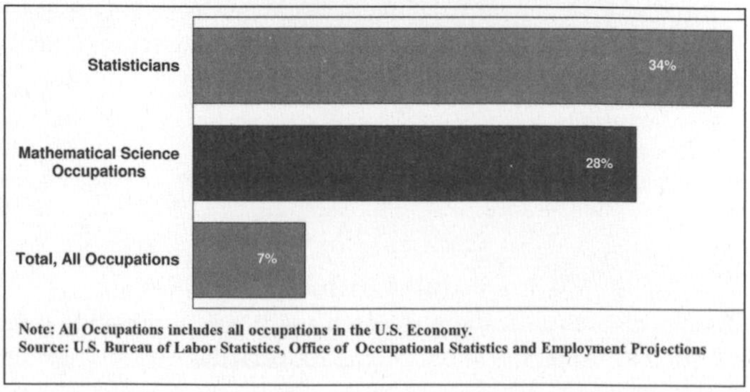

Healthcare. Statisticians known as biostatisticians or biometricians work in pharmaceutical companies, public health agencies, or hospitals. They may design studies to test whether drugs successfully treat diseases or medical conditions. They may also help identify the sources of outbreaks of illnesses in humans and animals.

Research and development. Statisticians design experiments for product testing and development. For instance, they may help design experiments to see how car engines perform when exposed to extreme weather conditions. Statisticians may also help develop marketing strategies and prices for consumer goods.

Statisticians often collaborate with other occupations in the design and conduct of the research.

Some people with a degree in statistics or who collect and analyze statistical data may not be formally known as statisticians. Instead, they may work in related fields and professions. In some industries, for example, they may be known as quantitative analysts, market research analysts, data analysts, or data scientists.

Work Environment

Statisticians held about 30,000 jobs in 2014. The industries that employed the most statisticians were as follows:

Federal government	15%
Scientific research and development services	14
Finance and insurance	13
Colleges, universities, and professional schools; state, local, and private	9
Management, scientific, and technical consulting services	7

Federal statisticians are commonly employed at the U.S. Census Bureau, Bureau of Economic Analysis, National Agricultural Statistics Service, or Bureau of Labor Statistics.

Statisticians often work in teams with other professionals. For example, in pharmaceutical companies, statisticians may work with scientists to test drugs for government approval. In insurance companies, they may work with actuaries to calculate the risks of insuring different events.

Statisticians may travel occasionally to meet with team members, set up surveys and research projects, or oversee the collection of data.

Work Schedules. Statisticians typically work full time.

Education/Training

Mathematicians typically need at least a master's degree in mathematics. However, a bachelor's degree is sufficient for some entry-level jobs. Research and academic jobs generally require a Ph.D.

Education. Statisticians typically need at least a master's degree, although some entry-level jobs are available for those with a bachelor's degree. Most statisticians have degrees in mathematics, economics, computer science, or another quantitative field. A bachelor's degree in statistics typically includes courses in linear algebra, calculus, experimental design, survey methodology, probability, and statistical theory.

Many colleges and universities advise students to take courses in a related field, such as computer science, engineering, physics, or mathematics. These courses can help prepare students to work in a variety of industries. Coursework in engineering or physical science, for example, may be useful for statisticians working in manufacturing on quality or productivity improvement. A background in biology, chemistry, or health sciences is useful for work testing pharmaceutical or agricultural products.

Because statisticians often work with data analysis software, computer programming courses may be particularly beneficial for students.

Important Qualities

Analytical skills. Statisticians use statistical techniques and models to analyze large amounts of data. They must determine the appropriate software packages and understand computer programming languages to design and develop new techniques and models. They must also be precise and accurate in their analyses.

Communication skills. Statisticians often work with, and propose solutions to, people who do not have extensive knowledge of mathematics or statistics. They must be able to present statistical information and ideas so that others will understand.

Math skills. Statisticians use statistics, calculus, and linear algebra to develop their models and analyses.

Problem-solving skills. Statisticians must develop techniques to overcome problems in data collection and analysis, such as high nonresponse rates, so that they can draw meaningful conclusions.

Pay

The median annual wage for statisticians was $79,990 in May 2014. The median wage is the wage at which half the workers in an occupation earned more than that amount and half earned less. The lowest 10 percent earned less than $43,840, and the highest 10 percent earned more than $129,830.

In May 2014, the median annual wages for statisticians in the top industries in which they worked were as follows:

Federal government	$98,320
Scientific research and development services	90,390
Finance and insurance	77,740
Management, scientific, and technical consulting services	69,550
Colleges, universities, and professional schools; state, local, and private	68,350

Job Outlook

Employment of statisticians is projected to grow 34 percent from 2014 to 2024, much faster than the average for all occupations. Growth is expected to result from more widespread use of statistical analysis to make informed business, healthcare, and policy decisions. In addition, the large increase in available data from the Internet will open up new areas for analysis.

A substantial amount of data is generated from Internet searching and the use of social media, smartphones, and other mobile devices. Businesses, particularly those in the retail, finance, and insurance industries, will increasingly need statisticians to organize, analyze, and sort through the data for commercial reasons.

Employment Projections Data for Statisticians

Occupational Title	SOC Code	Employment, 2014	Projected Employment, 2024	Change, 2014–2024	
				Percent	Numeric
Statisticians	15-2041	30,000	40,100	34	10,100

Source: U.S. Bureau of Labor Statistics, Employment Projections Program

Similar Occupations. This table shows a list of occupations with job duties that are similar to those of statisticians.

Occupations	Entry-level Education	2014 Median Pay	Projected Job Growth	Average Annual Openings
Actuaries	Bachelor's degree	$96,700	18%	440
Computer Systems Analysts	Bachelor's degree	$82,710	21%	11,860
Economists	Master's degree	$95,710	6%	120
Financial Analysts	Bachelor's degree	$78,620	12%	3,230
Market Research Analysts	Bachelor's degree	$61,290	19%	9,230
Mathematicians	Master's degree	$103,720	21%	70
Operations Research Analysts	Bachelor's degree	$76,660	30%	2,760
Survey Researchers	Master's degree	$49,760	12%	190

Analyses will help companies improve their business processes, design and develop new products, and advertise products to potential customers.

In addition, statisticians will be needed in the pharmaceutical industry. The aging of the U.S. population will encourage pharmaceutical companies to develop new treatments and medical technologies. Biostatisticians will be needed to conduct the research and clinical trials necessary for companies to obtain approval for their products from the Food and Drug Administration.

The occupation will also see growth in research and development in the physical, engineering, and life sciences, fields in which statisticians' skills in designing tests and assessing results are highly useful.

Job Prospects. Job prospects for statisticians are projected to be very good. An increasing number of jobs over the next decade will require high levels of statistical knowledge. Job opportunities are expected to be favorable for those with very strong quantitative and data analysis skills. Computer programming skills will remain important to many employers.

Graduates with a master's degree in statistics and a strong background in a related discipline, such as finance, biology, engineering, or computer science, are projected to have the best prospects of finding jobs in their field of study.

Contacts for More Information

For more information about statisticians, visit

➤ American Statistical Association (www.amstat.org)

For more information on doctoral-level careers and training in mathematics, a field closely related to statistics, visit

➤ American Mathematical Society (www.ams.org)

For information on job openings for statisticians or mathematical statisticians in the federal government, visit

➤ USAJOBS (www.usajobs.gov)

O*NET

➤ Statisticians (15-2041.00)

➤ Biostatisticians (15-2041.01)

➤ Clinical Data Managers (15-2041.02)

Media and Communication

Announcers

- **2014 Median Pay** .... $29,010 per year
  $13.95 per hour
- **Typical Entry-Level Education** .... See Education/Training
- **Work Experience in a Related Occupation** .... None
- **On-the-job Training** .... Short-term on-the-job training
- **Number of Jobs, 2014** 52,500
- **Job Outlook, 2014–24** .... -11% (Decline)
- **Employment Change, 2014–24** .... -5,800

What Announcers Do

Announcers present music, news, and sports and may provide commentary or interview guests about these other important topics. Some act as masters of ceremonies (emcees) or disc jockeys (DJs) at weddings, parties, or clubs.

Duties. Radio and television announcers typically do the following:

- Present music, news, sports, the weather, the time, and commercials
- Interview guests and moderate panels or discussions on their shows
- Announce station programming information, such as program schedules, station breaks for commercials, or public service information
- Research topics for comment and discussion during shows
- Read prepared scripts on radio or television shows
- Comment on important news stories
- Provide commentary for the audience during sporting events, at parades, and on other occasions
- Select program content
- Make promotional appearances at public or private events

Radio and television announcers present music or the news and comment on important current events. Announcers are expected to be up to date with current events or a specific field, such as politics or sports, so that they can comment on these issues during their programs. They may research and prepare information on current topics before appearing on air. In addition, announcers schedule guests on their shows and work with producers to develop other creative content.

The following are examples of types of radio and television announcers:

Disc jockeys, or *DJs*, broadcast music for radio stations. They typically specialize in one kind of music genre and announce selections as they air them. While on air, DJs comment on the music being broadcast as well as on weather and traffic conditions. They may take requests from listeners, interview guests, or manage listener contests.

Talk show hosts may work in radio or television and specialize in a certain area of interest, such as politics, personal finance, sports, or health. They contribute to the preparation of program content, interview guests, and discuss issues with viewers, listeners, or the studio audience.

Podcasters record shows that can be downloaded for listening through a computer or mobile device. Like traditional talk radio, podcasts typically focus on a specific subject, such as sports, politics, or movies. Podcasters may also interview guests and experts on the specific program topic. However, podcasts are different from traditional radio broadcasts. Podcasts are prerecorded so audiences can download and listen to these shows at any time. Listeners can also subscribe to a podcast to have new episodes automatically downloaded to their computer or mobile devices.

Radio and television announcers also may be responsible for other aspects of television or radio broadcasting. They may operate studio equipment, sell commercial time to advertisers, or produce advertisements and other recorded material. At many radio stations, announcers do much of the work traditionally done by editors and broadcast technicians, such as broadcasting program schedules, commercials, and public service announcements.

Many radio and television announcers increasingly maintain a presence on social media sites. Establishing a presence allows them to promote their stations and better engage with their audiences, especially through listener feedback, music requests, or program contests. Announcers also make promotional appearances at charity functions or other community events.

Many radio stations now require DJs to update station websites with show schedules, interviews, or photos.

Public address system and other announcers typically do the following:

- Meet with event directors to review schedules and obtain other event details

Radio announcers who broadcast music often are called disc jockeys, or DJs.

- Present information or announcements, such as train schedules or security precautions
- Introduce upcoming acts and guide the audience through the entertainment
- Provide commentary for a live audience during sporting, performing arts, or other events
- Make promotional appearances at public or private events

A public address system announcer's role is to enhance the performance and entertain and inform the audience. They may prepare their own scripts or improvise lines in their speeches.

The specific duties of public address system announcers will vary greatly depending on where these announcers work. For example, a ringmaster at a circus directs the audience's attention to the appropriate act.

Train announcers are responsible for reading prepared scripts containing details and data related to train schedules and safety procedures. Their job is to provide information rather than entertainment.

Public address system announcers for a sports team may have to present starting lineups (official lists of players who will participate in an event), read advertisements, and announce players as they enter and exit a game.

The following are examples of types of public address system and other announcers:

Party DJs are hired to provide music and commentary at an event, such as a wedding, a birthday party, or a corporate party. Many DJs use digital files or portable media devices.

Emcees host planned events. They introduce speakers or performers to the audience. They may tell jokes or provide commentary to transition from one speaker to the next.

Work Environment

Announcers held about 52,500 jobs in 2014. The industries that employed the most announcers were as follows:

Radio broadcasting	47%
Television broadcasting	7
Performing arts, spectator sports, and related industries	6
Food services and drinking places	6

Radio and television announcers held about 42,300 jobs in 2014. About 1 in 4 radio and television announcers were self-employed in 2014.

Public address system and other announcers held about 10,200 jobs in 2014. About 1 in 4 public address system and other announcers were percent were self-employed in 2014.

Radio and television announcers usually work in well-lit, air-conditioned, soundproof studios. Some radio DJs can produce and record their shows while working from home.

The pressure of deadlines and tight work schedules can be stressful.

Work Schedules. Although most announcers work full time, many work part time.

Many radio and television stations are on air 24 hours a day. Some announcers present early morning shows, when most people are getting ready for work or commuting. Others do late-night programs. Some announcers have to work weekends or on holidays.

The shifts, however, are not as varied as in the past. More stations are recording shows during the day, eliminating the need to have an announcer work overnight hours.

Education/Training

Educational requirements for announcers vary. Radio and television announcers typically need a bachelor's degree in journalism, broadcasting, or communications, along with work experience gained from internships or working at their college radio or television station. Public address announcers typically need a high school diploma. Both occupations will typically need some short-term on-the-job training.

Education. Although public address announcers do not need any formal education beyond a high school diploma, radio and television announcers should have a bachelor's degree to be competitive for entry-level positions. Radio and television announcers typically need a bachelor's degree in programs such as communications, broadcasting, or journalism.

College broadcasting programs offer courses, such as voice and diction, to help students improve their vocal qualities. In addition, these programs prepare students to work with the computer and audio equipment and software used at radio and television studios.

Training. Public address system and other announcers typically need short-term on-the-job training upon being hired. This training allows these announcers to become familiar with the equipment they will be using during sporting and entertainment events. For sports public address announcers, training also may include basic rules and information for the sports they are covering.

Radio and television announcers may also need some short-term on-the-job training to learn to operate the audio and production equipment. Many employers, however, expect applicants to have some basic skills prior to employment. Applicants typically gain these skills from their college degree program, work on the college radio or television station, or previous internships.

Advancement. Because radio and television stations in smaller markets have smaller staff, advancement within the same small-market station is unlikely. Rather, many radio and television announcers advance by relocating to a station in a larger market.

Announcers typically need a few years at a small-market station to work out the "kinks" of their on-air personalities. During that time, they learn to sound more comfortable and credible as an on-air talent and become more conversational with their cohosts and guests. Therefore, time and experience allow applicants to advance to positions in larger markets, which offer higher pay and more responsibility and challenges.

When making hiring decisions, large-market stations rely on announcers' personalities and past performance. Radio and television announcers need to have proven that they can attract, engage, and keep a sizeable audience.

Many stations also rely on radio and television announcers to do other tasks, such as creating and updating a social media presence on social networking sites, making promotional appearances on behalf of the station, or even selling commercial time to advertisers. Therefore, an applicant needs to have demonstrated versatility and flexibility at the smaller-market station.

Important Qualities

Computer skills. Announcers, especially those seeking careers in radio or television, should have good computer skills and be able to use computers, editing equipment, and other broadcast-related devices.

Interpersonal skills. Radio and television announcers must be able to interview guests and answer phone calls on air. Party disc jockeys (DJs) and emcees should be comfortable working with clients to plan entertainment options.

Median Annual Wages, May 2014

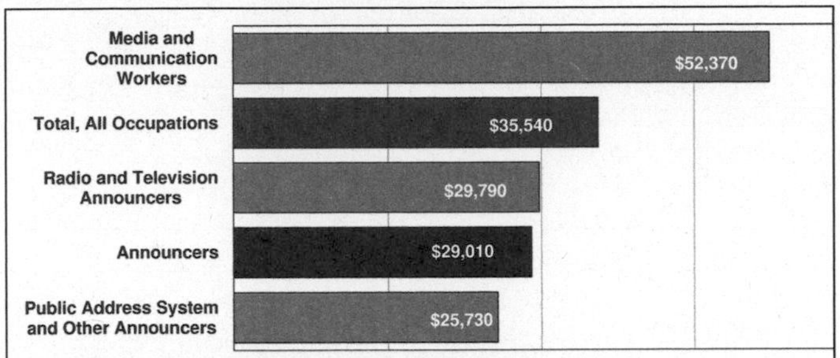

Note: All Occupations includes all occupations in the U.S. Economy.
Source: U.S. Bureau of Labor Statistics, Occupational Employment Statistics

Percent Change in Employment, Projected 2014–2024

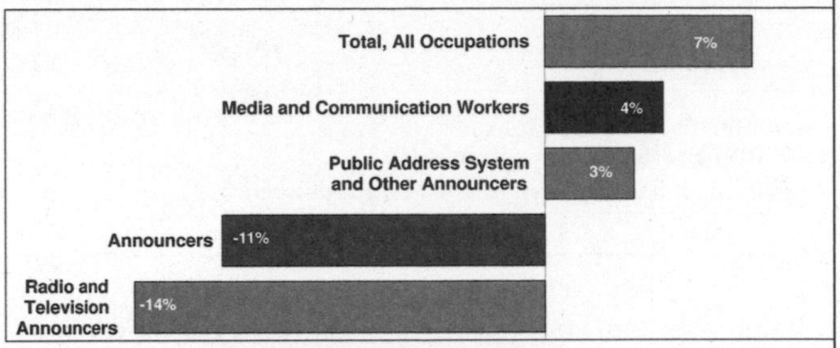

Note: All Occupations includes all occupations in the U.S. Economy.
Source: U.S. Bureau of Labor Statistics, Office of Occupational Statistics and Employment Projections

Persistence. Entry into this occupation is very competitive, and many auditions may be needed for an opportunity to work on the air. Many entry-level announcers must be willing to work for a small station and be flexible to move to a small market to secure their first job.

Research skills. Announcers must research the important topics of the day in order to be knowledgeable enough to comment on them during their program.

Speaking skills. Announcers must have a pleasant and well-controlled voice, good timing, and excellent pronunciation.

Writing skills. Announcers need strong writing skills because they normally write their own material.

Pay

The median annual wage for radio and television announcers was $29,790 in May 2014. The median wage is the wage at which half the workers in an occupation earned more than that amount and half earned less. The lowest 10 percent earned less than $17,610, and the highest 10 percent earned more than $80,000.

The median annual wage for public address system and other announcers was $25,730 in May 2014. The lowest 10 percent earned less than $17,180, and the highest 10 percent earned more than $63,820.

In May 2014, the median annual wages for announcers in the top industries in which they worked were as follows:

Performing arts, spectator sports, and related industries	$38,940
Television broadcasting	37,840
Radio broadcasting	27,660
Food services and drinking places	24,190

In general, announcers working in larger markets earn more than those working in smaller markets.

Job Outlook

Employment of announcers is projected to decline 11 percent from 2014 to 2024.

Employment of radio and television announcers is projected to decline 14 percent from 2014 to 2024. Employment of public address system and other announcers is projected to grow 3 percent from 2014 to 2024, slower than the average for all occupations.

Continuing consolidation of radio and television stations will limit the employment growth for radio and television announcers. Many stations have consolidated and centralized their programming functions, including on-air announcing positions.

Consolidation among broadcasting companies also may contribute to increasing use of syndicated programming and programs originating outside a station's viewing or listening area. Radio stations can use voice tracking, also called "cyber jockeying," to prerecord their segments rather than air them live. A radio announcer, therefore, can record many segments for use at a later date or even on another radio station in another media market.

This technique allows stations to use fewer employees, while still appearing to air live shows, and it can be more cost effective than airing live or local programming. However, it has eliminated most late-night shifts and allowed multiple stations to use material from the same announcer.

In addition, over-the-air radio broadcasts will continue to face competition from an increasing number of online and satellite radio stations. More listeners, particularly younger listeners, are tuning into these stations, which can be personalized and play nonstop music based on a listener's preferences. The growing popularity of these online stations may reduce the amount of time audiences spend listening to traditional radio broadcasts, in turn decreasing the demand for radio DJs.

However, Internet radio may positively influence employment growth. Startup costs for Internet radio stations are relatively lower than the costs for land-based radio. These stations can be used to create niche programming or target a specific demographic or listening audience and provide new opportunities for announcers.

In addition, the growing number of national news and satellite stations may increase the demand for local radio and television programs. Listeners want local programs with news and information that are more relevant to their communities instead of nationalized content. Therefore, to distinguish themselves from other stations or other media formats, stations may add local elements to their broadcasts.

Demand for public address system announcers will remain stable. These announcers will continue to present important information to customers or provide entertainment for special events.

Job Prospects. Strong competition is expected for jobs as a radio or television announcer. Many of the openings will be due to people leaving jobs and the need to replace workers who move out of smaller markets or out of the radio or television fields entirely.

Applicants need to be persistent and flexible because many entry-level positions will require moving to a smaller market city. Small radio and television stations are more inclined to hire beginners, but the pay is low.

Those with a formal education in journalism, broadcasting, or mass communications and with hands-on work experience at a radio or television network will have the best job prospects.

In addition, because announcers may be responsible for gathering video or audio for their programs or for updating and maintaining the station's website, multimedia and computer skills are beneficial.

Employment Projections Data for Announcers

Occupational Title	SOC Code	Employment, 2014	Projected Employment, 2024	Change, 2014–2024 Percent	Change, 2014–2024 Numeric
Announcers	27-3010	52,500	46,700	-11	-5,800
Radio and television announcers	27-3011	42,300	36,300	-14	-6,100
Public address system and other announcers	27-3012	10,200	10,500	3	300

Source: U.S. Bureau of Labor Statistics, Employment Projections Program

Similar Occupations. This table shows a list of occupations with job duties that are similar to those of announcers.

Occupations	Entry-level Education	2014 Median Pay	Projected Job Growth	Average Annual Openings
Actors	Some college, no degree	The annual wage is not available.	10%	660
Broadcast and Sound Engineering Technicians	See Education/Training	$41,350	7%	770
Musicians and Singers	No formal educational credential	The annual wage is not available.	3%	600
Producers and Directors	Bachelor's degree	$69,100	9%	1,110
Reporters, Correspondents, and Broadcast News Analysts	Bachelor's degree	$37,200	-9%	-480
Writers and Authors	Bachelor's degree	$58,850	2%	310

Contacts for More Information

For more information about the broadcasting industry, in which many announcers are employed, visit

➤ National Association of Broadcasters (www.nab.org)

For more information on sports public address announcers, visit

➤ National Association of Sports Public Address Announcers (www.naspaa.net)

O*NET

➤ Radio and Television Announcers (27-3011.00)

➤ Public Address System and Other Announcers (27-3012.00)

Broadcast and Sound Engineering Technicians

- **2014 Median Pay** .... $41,350 per year; $19.88 per hour
- **Typical Entry-Level Education** .... See Education/Training
- **Work Experience in a Related Occupation** .... None
- **On-the-Job Training** .... Short-term on-the-job training
- **Number of Jobs 2014** 117,200
- **Job Outlook, 2014–24** .... 7% (As fast as average)
- **Employment Change, 2014–24** 7,700

What Broadcast and Sound Engineering Technicians Do

Broadcast and sound engineering technicians set up, operate, and maintain the electrical equipment for radio programs, television broadcasts, concerts, sound recordings, and movies.

Duties. Broadcast and sound engineering technicians typically do the following:

- Operate, monitor, and adjust audio, video, lighting, and broadcast equipment to ensure consistent quality
- Set up and take down equipment for events and live performances
- Record speech, music, and other sounds on recording equipment or computers, sometimes using complex software
- Synchronize sounds and dialogue with action taking place on television or in movie productions
- Convert video and audio records to digital formats for editing on computers
- Install audio, video, and lighting equipment in hotels, offices, and schools
- Report any problems that arise with complex equipment and make routine repairs
- Keep records of recordings and equipment used

These workers may be called broadcast or sound engineering *technicians, operators*, or *engineers*. At smaller radio and television stations, broadcast and sound technicians may do many jobs. At larger stations, they are likely to do more specialized work, although their job assignments may vary from day to day. They set up and operate audio and video equipment, and the kind of equipment they use may depend on the particular type of technician or industry.

Broadcast and sound engineering technicians share many of the same responsibilities, but their duties may vary with their specific area of focus.

Audio and video equipment technicians set up and operate audio and video equipment. They also connect wires and cables and set up and operate sound and mixing boards and related electronic equipment.

Audio and video equipment technicians work with microphones, speakers, video screens, projectors, video monitors, and recording equipment. The equipment they operate is used for meetings, concerts, sports events, conventions, and news conferences. In addition, they may operate equipment at conferences and at presentations for businesses and universities.

Audio and video equipment technicians may also set up and operate custom lighting systems. They frequently work directly with clients and must provide solutions to problems in a simple, clear manner.

Broadcast technicians set up, operate, and maintain equipment that regulates the signal strength, clarity, and ranges of sounds and colors for radio or television broadcasts. They operate transmitters to broadcast radio or television programs and use computer programs to edit audio and video recordings.

Sound engineering technicians operate computers and equipment that record, synchronize, mix, or reproduce music, voices, or sound effects in recording studios, sporting arenas, theater productions, or movie and video productions. They record audio performances or events and may combine tracks that were recorded separately to create a multilayered final product. Sound engineering technicians operate transmitters to broadcast radio or television programs and use computers to program the equipment and edit audio recordings.

The following are examples of types of broadcast and sound engineering technicians:

Recording engineers operate and maintain video- and sound-recording equipment. These engineers work with computers, computer networks, and software to produce special effects for radio, television, or movies.

Sound mixers, or *rerecording mixers*, produce soundtracks for movies or television programs. They rerecord songs or compositions that already have been commercially released. After filming or recording is complete, these workers often dub the final product by adding or removing sounds.

Broadcast technicians set up, operate, and maintain electrical equipment.

Field technicians set up and operate portable equipment outside the studio—for example, for television news coverage. Because this coverage requires so much electronic equipment and the technology is changing so rapidly, many technicians are assigned exclusively to news coverage teams.

Chief engineers, transmission engineers, and *broadcast field supervisors* oversee other technicians and maintain broadcasting equipment.

Work Environment

Broadcast and sound engineering technicians held about 117,200 jobs in 2014. The industries that employed the most broadcast and sound engineering technicians were as follows:

Radio and television broadcasting	22%
Motion picture, video, and sound recording industries	15
Arts, entertainment, and recreation	11

Broadcast and sound engineering technicians typically work indoors in radio, television, movie, or recording studios. However, some work outdoors in all types of conditions in order to broadcast news and other programming on location. Audio and video technicians also set up systems in offices, arenas, hotels, schools, government agencies, hospitals, and homes.

Technicians doing maintenance may climb poles or antenna towers; those setting up equipment may do heavy lifting.

About 1 in 10 broadcast and sound engineering technicians were self-employed in 2014.

Work Schedules. Technicians typically work full time. Some may occasionally work overtime to meet broadcast deadlines or set up for live events. Evening, weekend, and holiday work is common because most stations are on the air 24 hours a day.

Technicians who work on motion pictures may be on a tight schedule and may work additional hours to meet contract deadlines with movie studios.

Education/Training

Broadcast and sound engineering technicians typically need postsecondary education. Depending on the work they do, it could either be a postsecondary nondegree award or an associate's degree.

Education. Audio and video equipment technicians, as well as sound engineering technicians, typically need a postsecondary nondegree award or certificate, whereas broadcast technicians typically need an associate's degree. However, in some cases workers in any of these occupations may need only a high school diploma to be eligible for entry-level positions.

Postsecondary nondegree programs for audio and video equipment technicians and sound engineering technicians may take several months to a year to complete. The programs include hands-on experience with the equipment used in many entry-level positions.

Broadcast technicians typically need an associate's degree. In addition to courses in math and science, coursework for prospective broadcast technicians should emphasize practical skills such as video editing and production management.

Prospective broadcast and sound engineering technicians should complete high school courses in math, physics, and electronics. They must have excellent computer skills to be successful.

Training. Because technology is constantly improving, technicians often enroll in continuing education courses and they receive on-the-job training to become skilled in new equipment and hardware. On-the-job training includes topics such as setting up cables or automation systems, testing electrical equipment,

Median Annual Wages, May 2014

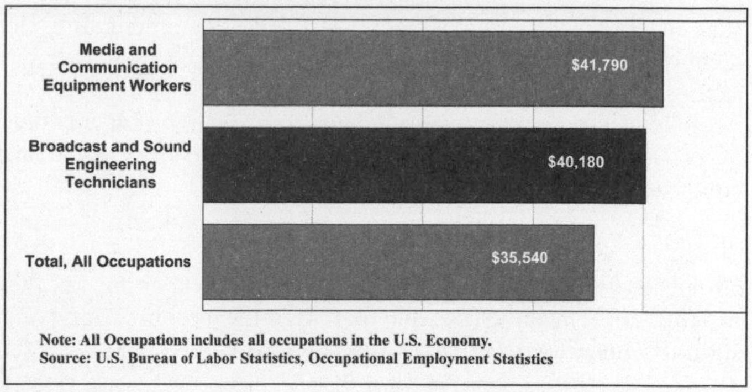

Percent Change in Employment, Projected 2014–2024

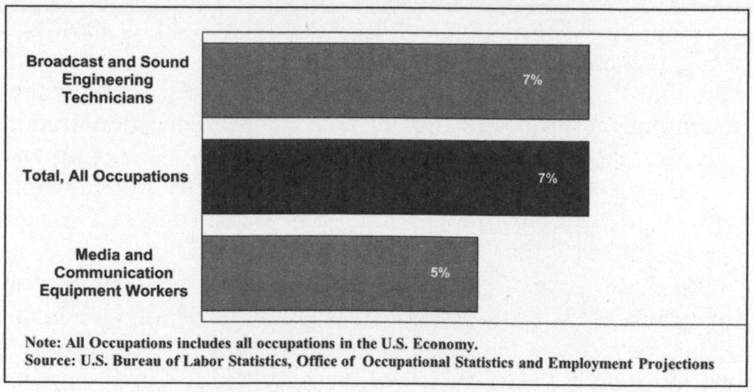

learning the codes and standards of the industry, and following safety procedures.

Training for new hires can be accomplished in a variety of ways, depending on the types of products and services the employer provides. Although some apprenticeship programs do exist, more frequently a new technician will accompany a more experienced technician to get the training and skills necessary for advancement.

Licenses, Certifications, and Registrations. Although not required by most employers, earning voluntary certification will offer advantages in getting a job as a broadcast or sound engineering technician. Certification tells employers that the technician meets certain industry standards and has kept up to date with new technologies.

For example, the Society of Broadcast Engineers offers eight broadcast engineering certifications, two operator certifications, and two broadcast networking certifications. All of them require passing an exam. Similarly, InfoComm International offers an audiovisual Certified Technology Specialist credential.

Other Experience. Practical experience working in a high school or college audiovisual department also can help prepare someone to be an audio and video equipment technician.

Advancement. Although many broadcast and sound engineering technicians work first in small markets or at small stations in big markets, after they gain the necessary experience and skills they often transfer to larger, better-paying radio or television stations. Few large stations hire someone without previous experience, and they value more specialized skills.

Experienced workers with strong technical skills can become supervisory technicians or chief engineers. To become chief engineer at large television stations, technicians typically need a bachelor's degree in engineering or computer science.

Important Qualities

Communication skills. Technicians need to communicate with supervisors and coworkers to ensure that clients' needs are met and that equipment is set up properly before broadcasts, live performances, and presentations.

Computer skills. Technicians use computer systems to program equipment and edit audio and video recordings.

Manual dexterity. Some technicians set up audio and visual equipment and cables, a job that requires a steady hand and good hand-eye coordination. Others adjust small knobs, dials, and sliders during radio and television broadcasts and live performances.

Problem-solving skills. Technicians need to recognize equipment problems and propose possible solutions to them. Employers typically desire applicants with a variety of skills, such as setting up equipment, maintaining the equipment, and troubleshooting and solving any problems that arise.

Pay

The median annual wage for broadcast and sound engineering technicians was $41,350 in May 2014. The median wage is the wage at which half the workers in an occupation earned more than that amount and half earned less. The lowest 10 percent earned less than $20,610, and the highest 10 percent earned more than $78,510.

Median annual wages for broadcast and sound engineering technicians in May 2014 were as follows:

Sound engineering technicians	$49,870
Audio and video equipment technicians	41,780
Broadcast technicians	36,560

In May 2014, the median annual wages for broadcast and sound engineering technicians in the top industries in which they worked were as follows:

Motion picture, video, and sound recording industries	$48,000
Arts, entertainment, and recreation	42,260
Radio and television broadcasting	34,260

Technicians working in major cities typically earn more than those working in smaller locations.

Employment Projections Data for Broadcast and Sound Engineering Technicians

Occupational Title	SOC Code	Employment, 2014	Projected Employment, 2024	Change, 2014–2024 Percent	Change, 2014–2024 Numeric
Broadcast and sound engineering technicians	—	117,200	124,900	7	7,700
Audio and video equipment technicians	27-4011	70,900	79,400	12	8,400
Broadcast technicians	27-4012	30,100	28,200	-6	-2,000
Sound engineering technicians	27-4014	16,100	17,400	8	1,200

Source: U.S. Bureau of Labor Statistics, Employment Projections Program

Similar Occupations. This table shows a list of occupations with job duties that are similar to those of broadcast and sound engineering technicians.

Occupations	Entry-level Education	2014 Median Pay	Projected Job Growth	Average Annual Openings
Computer Support Specialists	See Education/Training	$50,380	12%	8,880
Electrical and Electronics Engineering Technicians	Associate's degree	$59,820	-2%	-280
Electrical and Electronics Installers and Repairers	Postsecondary nondegree award	$53,900	-4%	-540
Film and Video Editors and Camera Operators	Bachelor's degree	$52,470	11%	640

Job Outlook

Employment of broadcast and sound engineering technicians is projected to grow 7 percent from 2014 to 2024, about as fast as the average for all occupations. Growth is expected to stem from businesses, schools, and radio and television stations seeking new equipment to improve their audio and video capabilities.

Employment of audio and visual equipment technicians is projected to grow 12 percent from 2014 to 2024, faster than the average for all occupations. More audio and video technicians should be needed to set up new equipment or upgrade and maintain old, complex systems for a variety of organizations.

More companies are increasing their video budgets so they can use video conferencing to reduce travel costs and communicate worldwide with other offices and clients. An increase in the use of digital signs for schools, hospitals, and hotels also will lead to higher demand for audio and video equipment technicians.

In addition, schools and universities are seeking to improve their audio and video capabilities to attract and keep the best students. They are building classrooms with interactive whiteboards and video equipment so teachers can give more interactive multimedia presentations and record their lectures.

Employment of broadcast technicians is projected to decline 6 percent from 2014 to 2024. More television stations are consolidating the broadcasting duties of multiple local stations into one single site in a term referred to in the industry as "central casting." This trend may continue to reduce the overall number of broadcast technicians.

Employment of sound engineering technicians is projected to grow 8 percent from 2014 to 2024, about as fast as the average for all occupations. The television and motion picture industry will continue to need technicians to improve the sound quality of shows and movies. Television and motion picture companies are installing the latest technologies, such as digital or three-dimensional screens, in movie and home theaters and are converting existing theaters to new formats.

Job Prospects. Competition for jobs will be strong. This occupation attracts many applicants who are interested in working with the latest technology and electronic equipment. Many applicants also are attracted to working in the radio and television industry.

Those looking for work in this industry will have the most job opportunities in smaller markets or stations. Those with hands-on experience with complex electronics and software or with work experience at a radio or television station will have the best job prospects. In addition, technicians should be versatile, because they set up, operate, and maintain equipment.

An associate's or bachelor's degree in broadcast technology, broadcast production, computer networking, or a related field also will improve job prospects for applicants.

Contacts for More Information

For more career information and links to employment resources, visit

- National Association of Broadcasters (www.nab.org)

For more information about certification and links to employment information, visit

- Society of Broadcast Engineers (www.sbe.org)

For more information on certification and career information for audio and video equipment technicians, visit

- InfoComm International (http://tinyurl.com/ywubys)
- National Systems Contractors Association (www.nsca.org)

O*NET

- Audio and Video Equipment Technicians (27-4011.00)
- Broadcast Technicians (27-4012.00)
- Sound Engineering Technicians (27-4014.00)

Editors

- **2014 Median Pay** .... $54,890 per year $26.39 per hour
- **Typical Entry-Level Education** .... Bachelor's degree
- **Work Experience in a Related Occupation** .... Less than 5 years
- **On-the-job Training** .... None
- **Number of Jobs, 2014** 117,200
- **Job Outlook, 2014–24** .... -5% (Decline)
- **Employment Change, 2014–24** .... -6,200

What Editors Do

Editors plan, review, and revise content for publication.

Duties. Editors typically do the following:

- Read content and correct spelling, punctuation, and grammatical errors
- Rewrite text to make it easier for readers to understand
- Verify facts using standard reference sources
- Evaluate submissions from writers to decide what to publish
- Work with writers to help their ideas and stories succeed
- Develop story and content ideas according to the publication's style and editorial policy
- Allocate space for the text, photos, and illustrations that make up a story
- Approve final versions submitted by staff

Editors plan, coordinate, and revise material for publication in books, newspapers, magazines, or websites. Editors review story ideas and decide what material will appeal most to readers. During the review process, editors offer comments to improve the product, and suggest titles and headlines. In smaller organizations, a single editor may perform all of the editorial duties or share them with only a few other people.

The following are examples of types of editors:

Copy editors review text for errors in grammar, punctuation, and spelling and check for readability, style, and agreement with editorial policy. They suggest revisions, such as changing words and rearranging sentences and paragraphs to improve clarity or accuracy. They also may carry out research, confirm sources for writers, and verify facts, dates, and statistics. In addition, they may arrange page layouts of articles, photographs, and advertising.

Publication assistants who work for book-publishing houses may read and evaluate manuscripts submitted by freelance writers, proofread uncorrected drafts, and answer questions about published material. Assistants on small newspapers or in smaller media markets may compile articles available from wire services or the Internet, answer phones, and proofread articles.

Assistant editors are responsible for a particular subject, such as local news, international news, feature stories, or sports. Most assistant editors work for newspaper publishers, television broadcasters, magazines, book publishers, or advertising and public relations firms.

Executive editors oversee assistant editors and generally have the final say about what stories are published and how they are covered. Executive editors typically hire writers, reporters, and other employees. They also plan budgets and negotiate contracts with freelance writers, who are sometimes called "stringers" in the news industry. Although many executive editors work for newspaper publishers, some work for television broadcasters, magazines, or advertising and public relations firms.

Managing editors typically work for magazines, newspaper publishers, and television broadcasters, and are responsible for the daily operations of a news department.

Work Environment

Editors held about 117,200 jobs in 2014. The industries that employed the most editors were as follows:

Newspaper, periodical, book, and directory publishers	44%
Professional, scientific, and technical services	8
Religious, grantmaking, civic, professional, and similar organizations	8
Educational services; state, local, and private	5

Editors check a writer's sources and facts for accuracy.

Although most editors work in offices, a growing number now work remotely from home. They often use desktop or electronic publishing software, scanners, and other electronic communications equipment to produce their material.

Jobs are somewhat concentrated in major media and entertainment markets—Boston, Chicago, Los Angeles, New York, and Washington, DC—but improved communications and Internet capabilities are allowing editors to work from a greater variety of locations.

Overseeing and coordinating multiple writing projects simultaneously is common among editors and may lead to stress, fatigue, or other chronic problems.

Freelance editors face the added pressures of finding work on an ongoing basis and continually adjusting to new work environments.

Work Schedules. Most editors work full time, and their schedules are generally determined by production deadlines and the type of editorial position. Editors typically work in busy offices and have to deal with production deadline pressures and the stresses of ensuring that the information they publish is accurate. As a result, editors often work many hours, especially at those times leading up to a publication deadline. These work hours can be even more

Median Annual Wages, May 2014

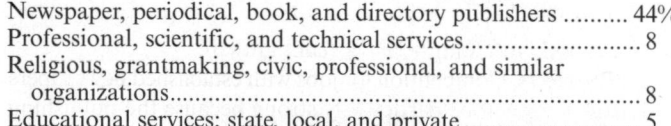

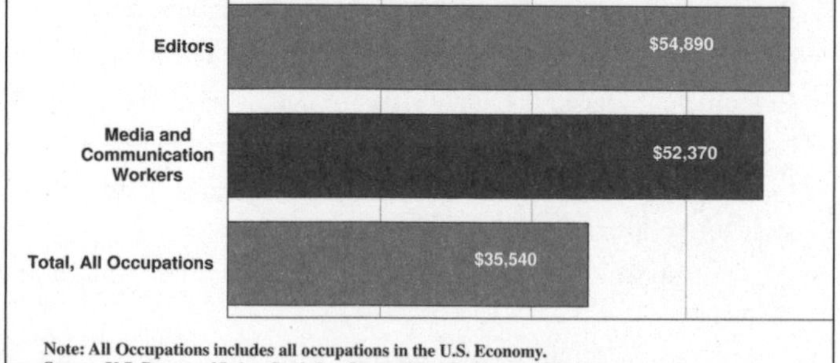

Percent Change in Employment, Projected 2014–2024

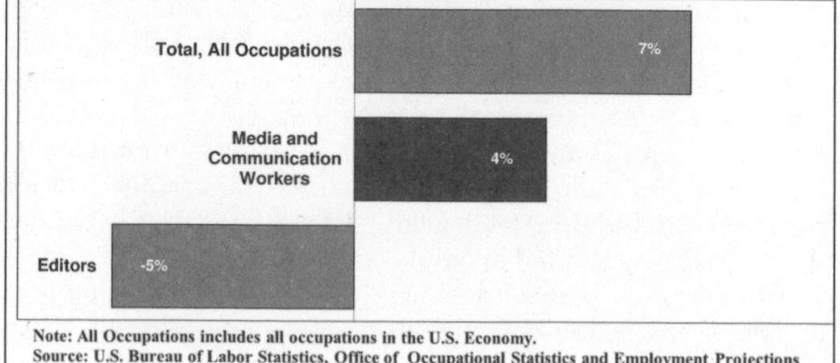

Employment Projections Data for Editors

Occupational Title	SOC Code	Employment, 2014	Projected Employment, 2024	Change, 2014–2024 Percent	Change, 2014–2024 Numeric
Editors	27-3041	117,200	111,000	-5	-6,200

Source: U.S. Bureau of Labor Statistics, Employment Projections Program

frequent when an editor is working on digital material for the Internet or for a live broadcast.

Education/Training

A bachelor's degree in communications, journalism, or English, combined with previous writing and proofreading experience, is typically required to be an editor.

Education. Employers generally prefer candidates with a bachelor's degree in communications, journalism, or English. They also prefer candidates with mass- or cross-media experience.

Those with other backgrounds who can show strong writing skills also may find jobs as editors. Editors who deal with specific subject matter may need previous related work experience. For example, fashion editors may need expertise in fashion that they gain through formal training or work experience.

Work Experience in a Related Occupation. Many editors start off as editorial assistants, writers, or reporters.

Those who are particularly skilled at identifying good stories, recognizing writing talent, and interacting with writers may be interested in editing jobs.

Other Experience. Editors also can gain experience by working on high school and college newspapers, and for magazines, radio and television stations, advertising and publishing companies, or nonprofit organizations. Magazines and newspapers also have internships for students. For example, the American Society of Magazine Editors offers a Magazine Internship Program to qualified full-time students in their junior or senior year of college. Interns may write stories, conduct research and interviews, and gain general publishing experience.

The ability to use computers is necessary for editors to stay in touch with writers and other editors and to work on the increasingly important digital media or online side of a publication. Familiarity with electronic publishing, graphics, web design, and multimedia production is also important, because more content is being offered online.

Advancement. Some editors hold management positions and must make decisions related to running a business. For them, advancement generally means moving up to publications with larger circulation or greater prestige. Copy editors may move into original writing or substantive editing positions, or become freelancers.

Important Qualities

Creativity. Editors must be creative, curious, and knowledgeable in a broad range of topics. Some editors must regularly come up with interesting story ideas and attention-grabbing headlines.

Detail oriented. One of an editor's main tasks is to make sure that material is error free and matches the style of a publication.

Good judgment. Editors must decide if certain stories are ethical or if there is enough evidence to report them.

Interpersonal skills. In working with writers, editors must have tact and the ability to guide and encourage them in their work.

Writing skills. Editors must ensure that all written content has correct grammar, punctuation, and syntax. Editors must be able to write clearly and logically.

Pay

The median annual wage for editors was $54,890 in May 2014. The median wage is the wage at which half the workers in an occupation earned more than that amount and half earned less. The lowest 10 percent earned less than $28,980, and the highest 10 percent earned more than $109,940.

In May 2014, the median annual wages for editors in the top industries in which they worked were as follows:

Religious, grantmaking, civic, professional, and similar organizations	$58,770
Professional, scientific, and technical services	57,020
Educational services; state, local, and private	54,790
Newspaper, periodical, book, and directory publishers	53,320

Job Outlook

Employment of editors is projected to decline 5 percent from 2014 to 2024 as print media continues to face strong pressure from online publications.

Despite some job growth for editors in online media, the number of traditional editing jobs in print newspapers and magazines is declining and will temper employment growth.

Job Prospects. Competition for jobs with established newspapers and magazines will be particularly strong because the publishing industry is projected to decline in employment. Editors who have adapted to online media and are comfortable writing for and working with a variety of electronic and digital tools will have an advantage in finding work. Although the way in which people

Similar Occupations. This table shows a list of occupations with job duties that are similar to those of editors.

Occupations	Entry-level Education	2014 Median Pay	Projected Job Growth	Average Annual Openings
Announcers	See Education/Training	$29,010	-11%	-580
Reporters, Correspondents, and Broadcast News Analysts	Bachelor's degree	$37,200	-9%	-480
Technical Writers	Bachelor's degree	$69,030	10%	530
Writers and Authors	Bachelor's degree	$58,850	2%	310

consume media is changing, editors will continue to add value by reviewing and revising drafts and keeping the style and voice of a publication consistent.

Contacts for More Information

For more information about editors, visit

- American Copy Editors Society (www.copydesk.org/?homepage=1)
- American Society of Magazine Editors (www.magazine.org/asme)
- Association of Alternative Newsmedia (www.altweeklies.com)
- Radio and Television Digital News Association (www.rtdna.org)

O*NET

- Editors (27-3041.00)

Film and Video Editors and Camera Operators

- **2014 Median Pay** .... $52,470 per year $25.23 per hour
- **Typical Entry-Level Education** .... Bachelor's degree
- **Work Experience in a Related Occupation** .... None
- **On-the-job Training** .... None
- **Number of Jobs, 2014** 58,900
- **Job Outlook, 2014–24** .... 11% (Faster than average)
- **Employment Change, 2014–24** 6,400

What Film and Video Editors and Camera Operators Do

Film and video editors and camera operators manipulate images that entertain or inform an audience. Camera operators capture a wide range of material for TV shows, motion pictures, music videos, documentaries, or news and sporting events. Editors take footage shot by camera operators and organize it into a final product. They collaborate with producers and directors to create the final production.

Duties. Film and video editors and camera operators typically do the following:

- Shoot and record television programs, motion pictures, music videos, documentaries, or news and sporting events
- Organize digital footage with video editing software
- Collaborate with a director to determine the overall vision of the production
- Discuss filming and editing techniques with a director to improve a scene
- Select the appropriate equipment, such as the type of lens or lighting
- Shoot or edit a scene based on the director's vision

Many camera operators have one or more assistants working under their supervision. The assistants set up the camera equipment and may be responsible for its storage and care. They also help the operator determine the best shooting angle and make sure that the camera stays in focus.

Likewise, editors often have one or more assistants. The assistants support the editor by keeping track of each shot in a database or loading digital video into an editing bay. Assistants also may do some of the editing tasks.

The increased use of digital filming has changed the work of a large number of editors and camera operators. Many operators prefer using digital cameras because these smaller, more inexpensive instruments give them more flexibility in shooting angles. Digital cameras also have changed the job of some camera assistants: instead of loading film or choosing lenses, they download digital images or choose a type of software program to use with the camera.

Nearly all editing work is done on a computer, and editors often are trained in a specific type of editing software.

The following are examples of types of camera operators:

Studio camera operators work in a broadcast studio and videotape their subjects from a fixed position. There may be one or several cameras in use at a time. Operators normally follow directions that give the order of the shots. They often have time to practice camera movements before shooting begins. If they are shooting a live event, they must be able to make adjustments at a moment's notice and follow the instructions of the show's director.

Cinematographers film motion pictures. They usually have a team of camera operators and assistants working under them. They determine the angles and types of equipment that will best capture a shot. They also adjust the lighting in a shot, because that is an important part of how the image looks.

Cinematographers may use stationary cameras that shoot whatever passes in front of them, or they may use a camera mounted on a track and move around the action. Some cinematographers sit on cranes to film an action scene; others carry the camera on their shoulder while they move around the action.

Some cinematographers specialize in filming cartoons or special effects.

Videographers film or videotape private ceremonies or special events, such as weddings. They also may work with companies and make corporate documentaries on a variety of topics. Some videographers post their work on video-sharing websites for prospective clients. Most videographers edit their own material.

Many videographers run their own business or do freelance work. They may submit bids, write contracts, and get permission to shoot on locations that may not be open to the public. They also get copyright protection for their work and keep financial records.

Many editors and camera operators, particularly videographers, put their creative work online. If it becomes popular, they gain more recognition, which can lead to future employment or freelance opportunities.

Most video editing is done digitally.

Median Annual Wages, May 2014

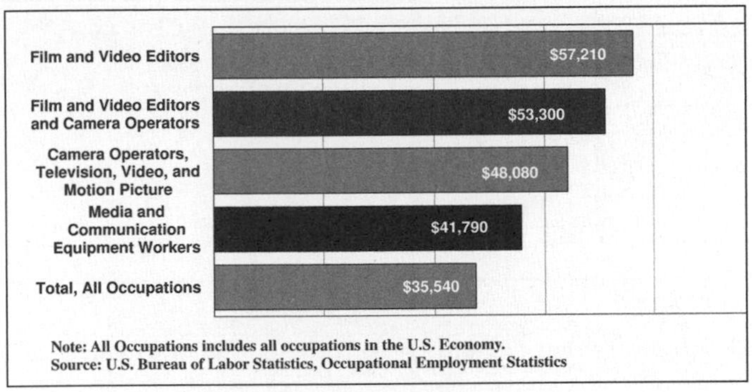

Percent Change in Employment, Projected 2014–2024

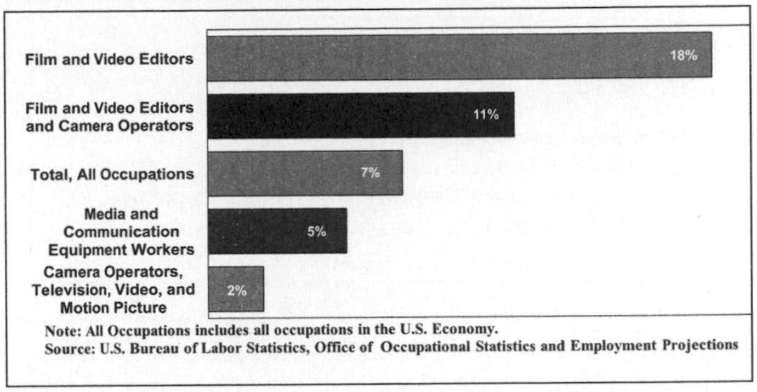

Work Environment

Film and video editors and camera operators typically work in studios or in office settings. Camera operators and videographers often shoot raw footage on location.

Film and video editors held about 33,500 jobs in 2014. About 48 percent were employed by motion picture and video industries and 8 percent worked in television broadcasting. About 3 out of 10 film and video editors were self-employed in 2014.

Camera operators held about 25,400 jobs in 2014. About 28 percent worked in motion picture and video industries, and 22 percent worked in radio and television broadcasting. About 3 out of 10 camera operators were self-employed in 2014.

Film and video editors work in editing rooms by themselves, or with producers and directors, for many hours at a time. Cinematographers and operators who film movies or TV shows may film on location and be away from home for months at a time. Operators who travel must usually carry heavy equipment to their shooting locations.

Some camera operators work in uncomfortable or even dangerous conditions, such as severe weather, military conflicts, and natural disasters. They may have to stand for long periods waiting for an event to take place. They may carry heavy equipment while on shooting assignment.

Work Schedules. Work hours vary with the type of operator or editor, although most work full time. Those who work in broadcasting may put in additional hours to meet a deadline. Those who work in the motion picture industry may have long, irregular hours while filming, but go through a period of looking for work once a film is complete and before they are hired for their next job.

Education/Training

Film and video editors and camera operators typically need a bachelor's degree in a field related to film or broadcasting.

Education. Many colleges offer courses in cinematography or video-editing software. Coursework involves a mix of film theory with practical training.

Film and video editors and camera operators must have an understanding of digital cameras and editing software because both are now used on film sets.

Training. Editors may complete a brief period of on-the-job training. Some employers may offer new employees training in the type of specialized editing software they use. Most editors eventually specialize in one type of software, but beginners should be familiar with as many types as possible.

Licenses, Certifications, and Registrations. Certification is a way for editors to demonstrate competence in various types of editing software. To earn certification, video editors must pass a comprehensive exam. Candidates can prepare for the exam on their own, through online tutorials, or through classroom instruction.

Important Qualities

Communication skills. Film and video editors and camera operators must communicate with other members of a production team, including producers and directors, to ensure that the project goes smoothly.

Computer skills. Film and video editors must use sophisticated editing software.

Creativity. Film and video editors and camera operators should be able to imagine what the result of their filming or editing will look like to an audience.

Detail oriented. Editors look at every frame of film and decide what should be kept and what should be cut in order to maintain the best content.

Hand-eye coordination. Camera operators need to be able to move about the action while holding a camera steady.

Physical stamina. Camera operators may need to carry heavy equipment for long periods of time, particularly when they are filming on location.

Visual skills. Film and video editors and camera operators must be able to see clearly what they are filming or editing in the postproduction process.

Pay

The median annual wage for camera operators, television, video, and motion picture was $48,080 in May 2014. The median wage is the wage at which half the workers in an occupation earned more than that amount and half earned less. The lowest 10 percent earned less than $23,620, and the highest 10 percent earned more than $95,160.

The median annual wage for film and video editors was $57,210 in May 2014. The lowest 10 percent earned less than $25,520, and the highest 10 percent earned more than $145,620.

Job Outlook

Employment of film and video editors is projected to grow 18 percent from 2014 to 2024, much faster than the average for all occupations. Employment of camera operators is projected to grow 2 percent from 2014 to 2024, slower than the average for all occupations.

Production companies and video freelancers are working with new content delivery methods, such as mobile and online TV, which may lead to more work for editors and camera operators.

In broadcasting, the consolidation of roles, such as field reporters who edit their own work, and the increasing reliance on

Employment Projections Data for Film and Video Editors and Camera Operators

Occupational Title	SOC Code	Employment, 2014	Projected Employment, 2024	Change, 2014–2024	
				Percent	Numeric
Television, video, and motion picture camera operators and editors	27-4030	58,900	65,300	11	6,400
Camera operators, television, video, and motion picture	27-4031	25,400	25,900	2	500
Film and video editors	27-4032	33,500	39,400	18	5,900

Source: U.S. Bureau of Labor Statistics, Employment Projections Program

Similar Occupations. This table shows a list of occupations with job duties that are similar to those of film and video editors and camera operators.

Occupations	Entry-level Education	2014 Median Pay	Projected Job Growth	Average Annual Openings
Broadcast and Sound Engineering Technicians	See Education/Training	$41,350	7%	770
Editors	Bachelor's degree	$54,890	-5%	-620
Multimedia Artists and Animators	Bachelor's degree	$63,630	6%	390
Photographers	High school diploma or equivalent	$30,490	3%	390
Producers and Directors	Bachelor's degree	$69,100	9%	1,110
Reporters, Correspondents, and Broadcast News Analysts	Bachelor's degree	$37,200	-9%	-480

amateur film footage, may lead to fewer jobs for editors and camera operators at TV stations. However, more editors are expected to be needed in the motion picture industry because of an increase in special effects and overall available content.

Job Prospects. Most job openings are projected to be in entertainment hubs such as New York, Atlanta, and Los Angeles because specialized editing workers are in demand there. Still, film and video editors and camera operators will face strong competition for jobs. Those with more experience at a TV station or on a film set should have the best prospects. Video editors can also improve their prospects by developing skills with different types of specialized editing software.

Contacts for More Information

For more information about film and video editors and camera operators, visit

➤ Motion Picture Editors Guild (www.editorsguild.com)

O*NET

➤ Camera Operators, Television, Video, and Motion Picture (27-4031.00)

➤ Film and Video Editors (27-4032.00)

Interpreters and Translators

- **2014 Median Pay** .... $43,590 per year
  $20.96 per hour
- **Typical Entry-Level Education** .... Bachelor's degree
- **Work Experience in a Related Occupation** .... None
- **On-the-job Training** .... Short-term on-the-job training
- **Number of Jobs, 2014** 61,000
- **Job Outlook, 2014–24** .... 29% (Much faster than average)
- **Employment Change, 2014–24** 17,500

What Interpreters and Translators Do

Interpreters and translators convert information from one language into another language. Interpreters work in spoken or sign language; translators work in written language.

Duties. Interpreters and translators typically do the following:

- Convert concepts in the source language to equivalent concepts in the target language
- Compile information and technical terms into glossaries and terminology databases to be used in translations
- Speak, read, and write fluently in at least two languages, one of which is English
- Relay the style and tone of the original language
- Render spoken messages accurately, quickly, and clearly

Interpreters and translators aid communication by converting messages or text from one language into another language. Although some people do both, interpreting and translating are different professions: interpreters work with spoken communication, and translators work with written communication.

Interpreters convert information from one spoken language into another—or, in the case of sign language interpreters, between spoken language and sign language. The goal of an interpreter is to have people hear the interpretation as if it were the original language. Interpreters usually must be fluent speakers or signers of both languages, because they communicate back and forth among people who do not share a common language.

There are three common modes of interpreting: simultaneous, consecutive, and whispered.

- **Simultaneous.** Simultaneous interpreters cannot begin interpreting until the general meaning of the sentence is understood. Simultaneous interpreting requires interpreters to listen or watch and speak or sign at the same time someone is speaking or signing. It requires a high level of concentration. For that reason, simultaneous interpreters usually work in pairs, each interpreting for about 20 to 30 minutes and then resting while the other interprets. Simultaneous interpreters are often familiar with the subject matter, so they can anticipate the end of the speaker's sentences.

- **Consecutive**. Consecutive interpreting begins only after the speaker has said or signed a group of words or sentences. Consecutive interpreters may take notes while listening to or watching the speakers before presenting their interpretation. Note taking is an essential part of consecutive interpreting.
- **Whispered**. Interpreters in this mode sit very close to the listeners and provide a simultaneous interpretation in a quiet voice.

Translators convert written materials from one language into another language. The goal of a translator is to have people read the translation as if it were the original written material. To do that, the translator must be able to write in a way that maintains or duplicates the structure and style of the original text while keeping the ideas and facts of the original material accurate. Translators must properly transmit any cultural references, including slang, and other expressions that do not translate literally.

Translators must read the original language fluently. They usually translate into their native language.

Nearly all translation work is done on a computer, and translators receive and submit most assignments electronically. Translations often go through several revisions before becoming final.

Translation usually is done with computer-assisted translation (CAT) tools, in which a computer database of previously translated sentences or segments (called a "translation memory") may be used to translate new text. CAT tools allow translators to work more efficiently and consistently.

Interpretation and translation services are needed in virtually all subject areas. Although some interpreters and translators do not specialize in any particular field or industry, many focus on one or more areas of expertise.

The following are examples of types of interpreters and translators:

Community interpreters work in community-based environments, providing vital language interpretation one-on-one or in small-group settings. Community interpreters often are needed at parent-teacher conferences, immigration courts, motor vehicle administrations, social security offices, business meetings, new-home purchases, and many other community settings.

Conference interpreters work at conferences that have non-English-speaking attendees. The work is often in the field of international business or diplomacy, although conference interpreters can interpret for any organization that works with speakers of foreign languages. Employers generally prefer more experienced interpreters who have the ability to convert from at least two languages into one native language—for example, the ability to interpret from Spanish and French into English. For some positions, such as those with the United Nations, this qualification is required.

Conference interpreters often do simultaneous interpreting. Attendees at a conference who do not understand the language of the speaker wear earphones tuned to the interpreter who speaks the language they want to hear. The interpreter listens to a bit of the speaker's talk and then translates that bit. Simultaneous interpreters must be able to listen to the speaker's next bit of talk while translating the previous bit.

Health or medical interpreters and translators typically work in healthcare settings and help patients communicate with doctors, nurses, technicians, and other medical staff. Interpreters and translators must have knowledge of medical terminology and of common medical terms in both languages.

Interpreters and translators must have a thorough understanding of various languages.

Health or medical interpreters must be sensitive to patients' personal circumstances, as well as maintain confidentiality and ethical standards. Interpretation is frequently provided remotely, either by video relay or over the phone.

Health or medical translators often do not have the same level of personal interaction with patients and providers that interpreters do. They translate primarily informational brochures, materials that patients must read and sign, website information, and patients' records from one language into another.

Liaison or escort interpreters accompany either U.S. visitors abroad or foreign visitors in the United States who have limited English proficiency. Interpreting in both formal and informal settings, these specialists ensure that the visitors can communicate during their stay. Frequent travel is common for liaison or escort interpreters.

Legal or judicial interpreters and translators typically work in courts and other legal settings. At hearings, arraignments, depositions, and trials, they help people who have limited English proficiency. Accordingly, they must understand legal terminology. Many court interpreters must sometimes read documents aloud in a language other than that in which they were written, a task known as sight translation. Legal or judiciary interpreters and translators must have a strong understanding of legal terminology and the legal process in all of the languages in which they are working.

Literary translators convert journal articles, books, poetry, and short stories from one language into another language. They work to keep the tone, style, and meaning of the author's work. Whenever possible, literary translators work closely with authors to capture the intended meaning, as well as the literary and cultural characteristics, of the original publication.

Localizers adapt text and graphics used in a product or service from one language into another language, a task known as localization. Localization specialists work to make it appear as though the product originated in the country where it will be sold. They must not only know both languages, but also understand the technical information they are working with and the culture of the people who will be using the product or service. Localizers make extensive use of computer and web-based localization tools and generally work in teams.

Localization may include adapting websites, software, marketing materials, user documentation, and various other publications. Usually, these adaptations are related to products and services in information technology, manufacturing, and other business sectors.

Localization may be helped by computer-assisted translation, which helps improve translation efficiency and ensures consistent terminology.

Sign language interpreters facilitate communication between people who are deaf or hard of hearing and people who can hear. Sign language interpreters must be fluent in English and in American Sign Language (ASL), which combines signing, finger spelling, and specific body language. ASL is a separate language from English and has its own grammar.

Some interpreters specialize in other forms of interpreting for people who are deaf or hard of hearing.

Some people who are deaf or hard of hearing are able to lip-read English instead of signing in ASL. Interpreters who work with these people do "oral interpretation," mouthing speech silently and very carefully so that their lips can be read easily. They also may use facial expressions and gestures to help the lip-reader understand.

Other modes of interpreting include cued speech, which uses hand shapes placed near the mouth to give lip-readers more information; signing exact English; and tactile signing, which is interpreting for people who are blind as well as deaf by making hand signs into the deaf and blind person's hand.

Trilingual interpreters facilitate communication among an English speaker, a speaker of another language, and an ASL user. They must have the versatility, adaptability, and cultural understanding necessary to interpret in all three languages without changing the fundamental meaning of the message.

Work Environment

Interpreters and translators held about 61,000 jobs in 2014. The industries that employed the most interpreters and translators were as follows:

Professional, scientific, and technical services	29%
Educational services; state, local, and private	26
Healthcare and social assistance	16
Government	7

About 1 in 5 were self-employed in 2014.

Interpreters work in settings such as schools, hospitals, courtrooms, and conference centers. They must sometimes travel to conferences. Simultaneous interpreting can be stressful, because the interpreter must keep up with the speaker, who may not know to slow down when an interpreter is present. Interpreters work in pairs when assignments are longer than 20–30 minutes long to prevent mental fatigue.

Translators typically work from home. They receive and submit their work electronically, and must sometimes deal with the pressure of deadlines and tight schedules. Some translators are employees at translation companies or individual organizations.

Work Schedules. Self-employed interpreters and translators often have variable work schedules, which may include periods of limited work and periods of long, irregular hours. Most interpreters and translators work full time during regular business hours.

Education/Training

Although interpreters and translators typically need at least a bachelor's degree, the most important requirement is that they be fluent in at least two languages (English and at least one other language). Many complete job-specific training programs. It is not necessary for interpreters and translators to have been raised in two languages to succeed in these jobs, but many grew up communicating in the languages in which they use for work.

Education. The educational backgrounds of interpreters and translators vary widely, but it is essential that they be fluent in English and at least one other language.

High school students interested in becoming an interpreter or translator should take a broad range of courses that focus on English writing and comprehension, foreign languages, and computer proficiency. Other helpful pursuits for prospects include spending time in a foreign country, engaging in direct contact with foreign cultures, and reading extensively on a variety of subjects in English and at least one other language. Through community organizations, students interested in sign language interpreting may take introductory classes in American Sign Language (ASL) and seek out volunteer opportunities to work with people who are deaf or hard of hearing.

Beyond high school, people interested in becoming interpreters or translators have numerous educational options. Although many jobs require a bachelor's degree, majoring in a language is not always necessary. Rather, an educational background in a particular field of study can provide a natural area of subject-matter expertise.

Training. Interpreters and translators generally need specialized training on how to do their work. Formal programs in interpreting and translating are available at colleges and universities nationwide and through nonuniversity training programs, conferences, and courses.

Many people who work as interpreters or translators in more technical areas—such as software localization, engineering, or finance—have a master's degree. Those working in the community as court or medical interpreters or translators are more likely to complete job-specific training programs or certificates.

Licenses, Certifications, and Registrations. There is currently no universal certification required of interpreters and translators beyond passing the required court interpreting exams offered by most states. However, workers can take a variety of tests that show proficiency. For example, the American Translators Association provides certification in 27 language combinations involving English.

Federal courts provide judiciary certification for Spanish, Navajo, and Haitian Creole interpreters, and many states offer their own certifications or licenses for these languages.

The National Association of the Deaf and the Registry of Interpreters for the Deaf jointly offer certification for general sign language interpreters. In addition, the registry offers specialty tests in legal interpreting, speech reading, and deaf-to-deaf interpreting—which includes interpreting among deaf speakers of different native languages and from ASL to tactile signing.

The U.S. Department of State has a three-test series for prospective interpreters—one test in simple consecutive interpreting (for escort work), another in simultaneous interpreting (for court work), and a third in conference-level interpreting (for international conferences)—as well as a test for prospective translators. These tests are not considered a credential, but their completion indicates that a person has significant skill in the occupation.

The International Association of Conference Interpreters offers information for conference interpreters.

The Certification Commission for Healthcare Interpreters offers two types of certifications for healthcare interpreters: Associate Healthcare Interpreter, for interpreters of languages other than Spanish, Arabic, and Mandarin; and Certified Healthcare Interpreter, for interpreters of Spanish, Arabic, and Mandarin.

Median Annual Wages, May 2014

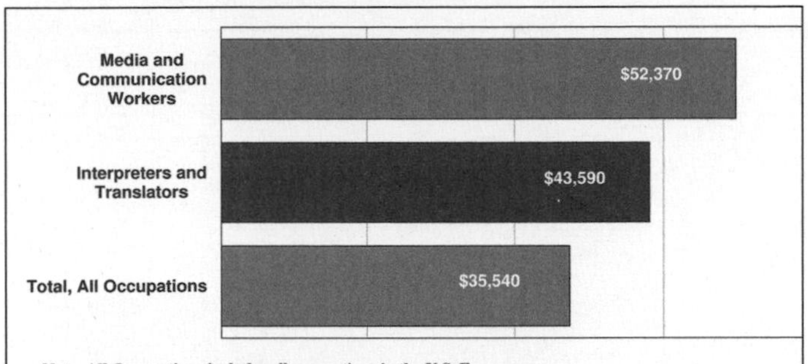

Note: All Occupations includes all occupations in the U.S. Economy.
Source: U.S. Bureau of Labor Statistics, Occupational Employment Statistics

Percent Change in Employment, Projected 2014–2024

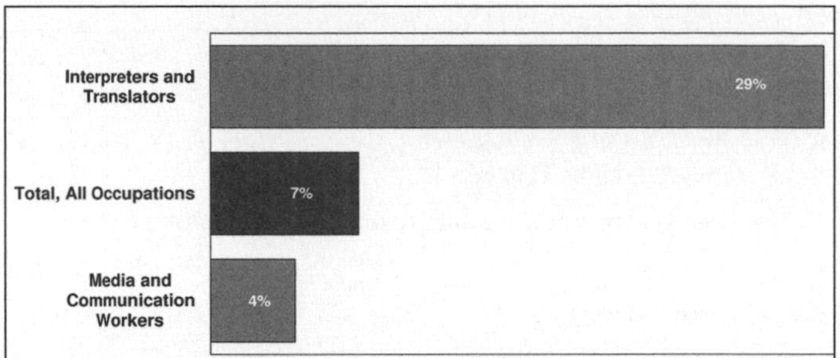

Note: All Occupations includes all occupations in the U.S. Economy.
Source: U.S. Bureau of Labor Statistics, Office of Occupational Statistics and Employment Projections

The National Board of Certification for Medical Interpreters offers certification for medical interpreters of Spanish.

Other Experience. A good way for translators to learn firsthand about the occupation is to start working in-house for a translation company. Doing informal or volunteer work is an excellent way for people seeking interpreter or translator jobs to gain experience.

Volunteer opportunities for interpreters are available through community organizations, hospitals, and sporting events, such as marathons, that involve international competitors.

Paid or unpaid internships are other ways that interpreters and translators can gain experience. Escort interpreting may offer an opportunity for inexperienced candidates to work alongside a more experienced interpreter. Interpreters also may find it easier to begin working in industries with particularly high demand for language services, such as court or medical interpreting.

Whatever path of entry new interpreters and translators pursue, they should develop mentoring relationships with experienced workers in the field to build their skills and confidence and to establish and expand a network of contacts. Mentoring may be formal, such as that received through a professional association, or informal, such as that engaged in with a coworker or an acquaintance who has experience as an interpreter or translator. Both the American Translators Association and the Registry of Interpreters for the Deaf offer formal mentoring programs.

Advancement. After interpreters and translators have enough experience, they can move up to more difficult assignments, seek certification, and obtain editorial responsibility. They can also manage or start their own business.

Many self-employed interpreters and translators start their own business by first establishing themselves in their field. They may submit resumes and samples to different translation and interpreting companies and work for companies that match their skills with a job. Many then get work on the basis of their reputation or through referrals from existing clients.

Important Qualities

Business skills. Self-employed and freelance interpreters and translators need general business skills to manage their finances and careers successfully. They must set prices for their work, bill customers, keep records, and market their services in order to build their client base.

Concentration. Interpreters and translators must have the ability to concentrate while others are speaking or moving around them.

Cultural sensitivity. Interpreters and translators must be sensitive to cultural differences and expectations among the people whom they are helping to communicate. Successful interpreting and translating is a matter not only of knowing the words in different languages but also of understanding people's cultures.

Dexterity. Sign language interpreters must be able to make quick and coordinated hand, finger, and arm movements when interpreting.

Interpersonal skills. Interpreters and translators, particularly those who are self-employed, must be able to get along with those who hire or use their services in order to retain clients and attract new business.

Listening skills. Interpreters must listen carefully when interpreting for audiences to ensure that they hear and interpret correctly.

Reading skills. Translators must be able to read in all of the languages in which they are working.

Speaking skills. Interpreters and translators must speak clearly in all of the languages in which they are working.

Writing skills. Translators must be able to write clearly and effectively in all of the languages in which they are working.

Pay

The median annual wage for interpreters and translators was $43,590 in May 2014. The median wage is the wage at which half the workers in an occupation earned more than that amount and half earned less. The lowest 10 percent earned less than $22,240, and the highest 10 percent earned more than $80,650.

In May 2014, the median annual wages for interpreters and translators in the top industries in which they worked were as follows:

Government	$52,480
Professional, scientific, and technical services	48,640
Educational services; state, local, and private	41,640
Healthcare and social assistance	40,720

Employment Projections Data for Interpreters and Translators

Occupational Title	SOC Code	Employment, 2014	Projected Employment, 2024	Change, 2014–2024 Percent	Change, 2014–2024 Numeric
Interpreters and translators	27-3091	61,000	78,500	29	17,500

Source: U.S. Bureau of Labor Statistics, Employment Projections Program

Similar Occupations. This table shows a list of occupations with job duties that are similar to those of interpreters and translators.

Occupations	Entry-level Education	2014 Median Pay	Projected Job Growth	Average Annual Openings
Adult Literacy and High School Equivalency Diploma Teachers	Bachelor's degree	$49,590	7%	550
Career and Technical Education Teachers	Bachelor's degree	$51,830	4%	1,020
Court Reporters	Postsecondary nondegree award	$49,860	2%	30
High School Teachers	Bachelor's degree	$56,310	6%	5,590
Kindergarten and Elementary School Teachers	Bachelor's degree	$53,760	6%	8,780
Medical Transcriptionists	Postsecondary nondegree award	$34,750	-3%	-220
Middle School Teachers	Bachelor's degree	$54,940	6%	3,680
Postsecondary Teachers	See Education/Training	$70,790	13%	17,700
Special Education Teachers	Bachelor's degree	$55,980	6%	2,810
Technical Writers	Bachelor's degree	$69,030	10%	530
Writers and Authors	Bachelor's degree	$58,850	2%	310

Wages depend on the language, specialty, skill, experience, education, and certification of the interpreter or translator, as well as on the type of employer. Wages of interpreters and translators vary widely. Interpreters and translators who know languages that are in high demand or that relatively few people can translate often earn higher wages. Those who perform services requiring a high level of skill, such as conference interpreters, also receive higher pay.

Self-employed interpreters usually charge per hour. Half-day or full-day rates are also common.

Job Outlook

Employment of interpreters and translators is projected to grow 29 percent from 2014 to 2024, much faster than the average for all occupations. Employment growth reflects increasing globalization and a more diverse U.S. population, which is expected to require more interpreters and translators.

Demand will likely remain strong for translators of frequently translated languages, such as French, German, Portuguese, Russian, and Spanish. Demand also should be strong for translators of Arabic and other Middle Eastern languages and for the principal Asian languages: Chinese, Hindi, Japanese, and Korean.

Demand for American Sign Language interpreters is expected to grow rapidly, driven by the increasing use of video relay services, which allow people to conduct online video calls and use a sign language interpreter.

In addition, growing international trade and broadening global ties should require more interpreters and translators. The ongoing need for military and national security interpreters and translators should result in more jobs as well. Emerging markets in Asia and Africa are expected to increase the need for translation and interpreting in languages spoken on those continents.

Computers have made the work of translators and localization specialists more efficient. However, these jobs cannot be entirely automated, because computers cannot yet produce work comparable to the work that human translators do in most cases.

Job Prospects. Job prospects should be best for those who have at least a bachelor's degree and for those who have professional certification. Those with a master's degree in interpreting and/or translation also should have an advantage.

In addition, urban areas—especially Washington, DC; New York; San Francisco; and Los Angeles—should continue to provide the largest numbers of jobs, especially for interpreters.

Job prospects for interpreters and translators should also vary by specialty and language. For example, interpreters and translators of Spanish should have good job prospects because of expected increases in the population of Spanish speakers in the United States. Similarly, job opportunities should be plentiful for interpreters and translators specializing in healthcare and law, because of the critical need for all parties to fully understand the information communicated in those fields.

In addition, there should be many job opportunities for specialists in localization, driven by the globalization of business and the expansion of the Internet.

Interpreters for the deaf will continue to have favorable employment prospects because there are relatively few people with the needed skills.

Contacts for More Information

For more information about interpreters, visit

- Discover Interpreting (www.discoverinterpreting.com)

For more information about interpreter and literary translator specialties, including professional certification, visit

- American Translators Association (www.atanet.org)
- Certification Commission for Healthcare Interpreters (www.cchicertification.org)
- International Association of Conference Interpreters (http://aiic.net)
- National Association of Judiciary Interpreters and Translators (www.najit.org)
- National Board of Certification for Medical Interpreters (www.certifiedmedicalinterpreters.org)
- National Council on Interpreting in Health Care (www.ncihc.org)
- Registry of Interpreters for the Deaf (www.rid.org)

For more information about testing to become a federal contract interpreter or translator, visit

- U.S. State Department (www.state.gov/m/a/ols/c56573.htm)

O*NET

- Interpreters and Translators (27-3091.00)

Photographers

- **2014 Median Pay** .... $30,490 per year
  $14.66 per hour
- **Typical Entry-Level Education** .... High school diploma or equivalent
- **Work Experience in a Related Occupation** .... None
- **On-the-job Training** .... Long-term on-the-job training
- **Number of Jobs, 2014** 124,900
- **Job Outlook, 2014–24** .... 3% (Slower than average)
- **Employment Change, 2014–24** 3,900

What Photographers Do

Photographers use their technical expertise, creativity, and composition skills to produce and preserve images that tell a story or record an event.

Duties. Photographers typically do the following:

- Market and advertise services to attract clients
- Analyze and plan the composition of photographs
- Use various photographic techniques and lighting equipment
- Capture subjects in commercial-quality photographs
- Enhance the subject's appearance with natural or artificial light
- Use photo-enhancing software
- Maintain a digital portfolio to demonstrate their work

Today, most photographers use digital cameras instead of the traditional film cameras. Digital cameras capture images electronically, so the photographer can edit the image on a computer. Images can be stored on portable memory devices, such as compact disks, memory cards, and flash drives. Once the raw image has been transferred to a computer, photographers can use processing software to crop or modify the image and enhance it through color correction and other specialized effects. Photographers who edit their own pictures use computers, high-quality printers, and editing software. For information on workers who specialize in developing and processing photographic images from film or digital media, see photographic process workers and processing machine operators included in Occupations Not Covered in Detail.

Photographers who work for commercial clients often will present finalized photographs in a digital format to the client. Wedding and portrait photographers, who serve primarily noncommercial clients, frequently also provide framing services and present the photographs they capture in albums.

Many wedding and portrait photographers are self-employed. Photographers who own and operate their own business have additional responsibilities. They must advertise, schedule appointments, set and adjust equipment, purchase supplies, keep records, bill customers, pay bills, and—if they have employees—hire, train, and direct their workers.

In addition, some photographers teach photography classes or conduct workshops in schools or in their own studios.

The following are examples of types of photographers:

Portrait photographers take pictures of individuals or groups of people and usually work in their own studios. Photographers who specialize in weddings, religious ceremonies, or school photographs may work on location.

Commercial and industrial photographers take pictures of various subjects, such as buildings, models, merchandise, artifacts, and landscapes. These photographs, which frequently are taken on location, are used for a variety of purposes, including magazine covers and images to supplement analyses of engineering projects.

Aerial photographers travel in planes or helicopters to capture photographs of buildings and landscapes. They often use cameras with gyrostabilizers to counteract the movement of the aircraft and ensure high-quality images.

Scientific photographers focus on the accurate visual representation of subjects and therefore limit the use of image manipulation software to clarify an image. Scientific photographs record scientific or medical data or phenomena. Scientific photographers typically use microscopes to photograph subjects.

News photographers, also called *photojournalists*, photograph people, places, and events for newspapers, journals, magazines, or television. In addition to taking still photos, photojournalists often work with digital video.

Fine arts photographers sell their photographs as artwork. In addition to having technical knowledge of subjects such as lighting and the use of lenses, fine arts photographers need artistic talent and creativity. Most use traditional film instead of digital cameras.

University photographers serve as general photographers for academic institutions. They may be required to take portraits, document events, or take photographs for press releases. University photographers are found primarily in larger academic institutions, because smaller institutions often contract with freelancers to do their photography work.

Work Environment

Photographers held about 124,900 jobs in 2014. In 2014, about 3 in 5 photographers were self-employed.

Portrait photographers take pictures of individuals or groups of people and often work out of their own studios.

Median Hourly Wages, May 2014

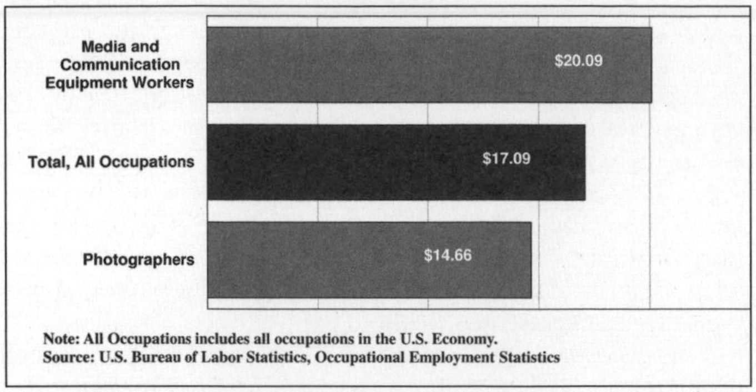

Percent Change in Employment, Projected 2014–2024

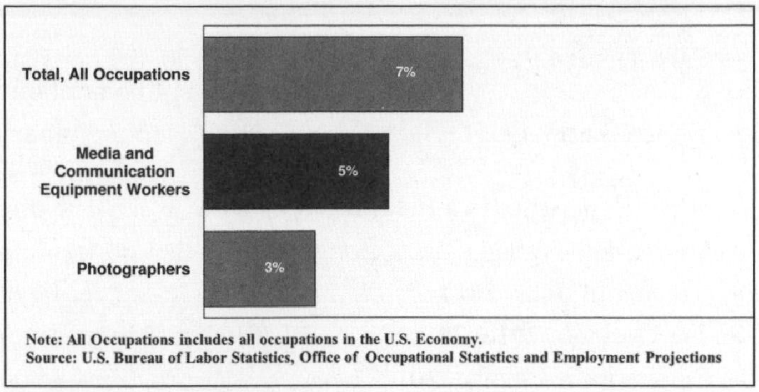

The work environment for photographers varies considerably with their specialty.

Portrait photographers may work in studios, but they also often travel to take photographs at a client's location, such as a school, a company office, or a private home.

News photographers and commercial photographers may travel locally or internationally. News photographers often work long, irregular hours in uncomfortable or even dangerous surroundings and must be available to work on short notice. For example, a news photographer may be sent to a war zone to capture images.

Aerial photographers often work in planes or helicopters.

Work Schedules. About 3 in 10 photographers worked part time in 2014. Hours often are flexible so that photographers can meet with current and potential clients or visit the sites where they will work. Demand for certain types of photographers may fluctuate with the season. For example, the demand for wedding photographers typically increases in the spring and summer.

Education/Training

Although postsecondary education is not required for portrait photographers, many take classes because employers usually seek applicants with a "good eye" and creativity, as well as a good technical understanding of photography. Photojournalists and industrial and scientific photographers often need a bachelor's degree.

Education. Although postsecondary education is not required for most photographers, many take classes or earn a bachelor's degree in a related field because such an education can improve their skills and employment prospects.

Many universities, community and junior colleges, vocational–technical institutes, and private trade and technical schools offer classes in photography. Basic courses in photography cover equipment, processes, and techniques. Art schools may offer useful training in photographic design and composition.

Entry-level positions in photojournalism or in industrial or scientific photography generally require a college degree in photography or in a field related to the industry in which the photographer seeks employment. For example, classes in biology, medicine, or chemistry may be useful for scientific photographers.

Business, marketing, and accounting classes can be helpful for self-employed photographers.

Training. Photographers have a talent or natural ability for taking good photos, and this talent is typically cultivated over years of practice. For many artists, including photographers, developing a portfolio—a collection of an artist's work that demonstrates his or her styles and abilities—is essential. A portfolio is necessary because art directors, clients, and others often want to look at one when deciding whether to hire or contract with the photographer.

Photographers often start working as an assistant to a professional photographer. This work provides an opportunity to gain experience, build the photographers' portfolios, and gain exposure to prospective clients.

Important Qualities

Artistic ability. Photographers capture their subjects in images, and they must be able to evaluate the artistic quality of a photograph. Photographers need a "good eye"—the ability to use colors, shadows, shades, light, and distance to compose good photographs.

Business skills. Photographers must be able to plan marketing strategies, reach out to prospective clients, and anticipate seasonal employment.

Computer skills. Most photographers do their own postproduction work and must be familiar with photo-editing software. They also use computers to maintain a digital portfolio.

Customer-service skills. Photographers must be able to understand the needs of their clients and propose solutions to any problems that arise.

Detail oriented. Photographers who do their own postproduction work must be careful not to overlook details and must be thorough when editing photographs. In addition, photographers accumulate many photographs and must maintain them in an orderly fashion.

Interpersonal skills. Photographers often photograph people. They must communicate effectively to achieve a certain composition in a photograph.

Employment Projections Data for Photographers

Occupational Title	SOC Code	Employment, 2014	Projected Employment, 2024	Change, 2014–2024 Percent	Change, 2014–2024 Numeric
Photographers	27-4021	124,900	128,800	3	3,900

Source: U.S. Bureau of Labor Statistics, Employment Projections Program

Similar Occupations. This table shows a list of occupations with job duties that are similar to those of photographers.

Occupations	Entry-level Education	2014 Median Pay	Projected Job Growth	Average Annual Openings
Architects	Bachelor's degree	$74,520	7%	780
Craft and Fine Artists	See Education/Training	$44,400	2%	90
Desktop Publishers	Associate's degree	$38,200	-21%	-310
Fashion Designers	Bachelor's degree	$64,030	3%	70
Film and Video Editors and Camera Operators	Bachelor's degree	$52,470	11%	640
Graphic Designers	Bachelor's degree	$45,900	1%	360
Industrial Designers	Bachelor's degree	$64,620	2%	80
Reporters, Correspondents, and Broadcast News Analysts	Bachelor's degree	$37,200	-9%	-480

Pay

The median hourly wage for photographers was $14.66 in May 2014. The median wage is the wage at which half the workers in an occupation earned more than that amount and half earned less. The lowest 10 percent earned less than $8.71, and the highest 10 percent earned more than $33.14.

Job Outlook

Employment of photographers is projected to grow 3 percent from 2014 to 2024, slower than the average for all occupations. Overall growth will be limited because of the decreasing cost of digital cameras and the increasing number of amateur photographers and hobbyists. In addition, stock photographic services available online give individuals and businesses access to stock photographs for a fee or subscription, possibly dampening demand for photographers.

Employment of self-employed photographers is projected to grow 9 percent from 2014 to 2024. Demand for portrait photographers will continue as people continue to want new portraits. In addition, corporations will continue to require the services of commercial photographers to develop compelling advertisements to sell products.

Declines in the newspaper industry will reduce demand for news photographers to provide still images for print. Employment of photographers in newspaper publishing is projected to decline 41 percent from 2014 to 2024.

Job Prospects. Photographers will face strong competition for most jobs. Because of reduced barriers to entry, there will be many qualified candidates for relatively few positions.

In addition, salaried jobs may be more difficult to obtain as companies increasingly contract with freelancers rather than hire their own photographers. Job prospects will be best for candidates who are multitalented and possess related skills, such as editing pictures and capturing digital video.

Contacts for More Information

For more information about careers in photography, visit

➤ American Society of Media Photographers (http://asmp.org)

For more information about university photographers, visit

➤ University Photographers' Association of America (www.upaa.org)

O*NET

➤ Photographers (27-4021.00)

Public Relations Specialists

- **2014 Median Pay** .... $55,680 per year
  $26.77 per hour
- **Typical Entry-Level Education** .... Bachelor's degree
- **Work Experience in a Related Occupation** .... None
- **On-the-job Training** .... None
- **Number of Jobs, 2014** 240,700
- **Job Outlook, 2014–24** .... 6% (As fast as average)
- **Employment Change, 2014–24** 14,900

What Public Relations Specialists Do

Public relations specialists create and maintain a favorable public image for the organization they represent. They design media releases to shape public perception of their organization and to increase awareness of its work and goals.

Duties. Public relations specialists typically do the following:

- Write press releases and prepare information for the media
- Respond to information requests from the media
- Help clients communicate effectively with the public
- Help maintain their organization's corporate image and identity
- Draft speeches and arrange interviews for an organization's top executives
- Evaluate advertising and promotion programs to determine whether they are compatible with their organization's public relations efforts
- Evaluate public opinion of clients through social media

Public relations specialists, also called *communications specialists* and *media specialists*, handle an organization's communication with the public, including consumers, investors, reporters, and other media specialists. In government, public relations specialists may be called *press secretaries*. In this setting, workers keep the public informed about the activities of government officials and agencies.

Public relations specialists draft press releases and contact people in the media who might print or broadcast their material. Many radio or television special reports, newspaper stories, and magazine articles start at the desks of public relations specialists. For example, a press release might describe a public issue, such as health, energy, or the environment, and what an organization does concerning that issue.

Press releases are increasingly being sent through the Internet and social media, in addition to publication through traditional media outlets. Public relations specialists are often in charge of monitoring and responding to social media questions and concerns.

Public relations specialists are different from advertisers in that they get their stories covered by media instead of purchasing ad space in publications and on television.

Work Environment

Public relations specialists held about 240,700 jobs in 2014. The industries that employed the most public relations specialists were as follows:

Religious, grantmaking, civic, professional, and similar organizations	22%
Professional, scientific, and technical services	21
Educational services; state, local, and private	12
Healthcare and social assistance	7
State and local government, excluding education and hospitals	7

Public relations specialists usually work in offices, but they also deliver speeches, attend meetings and community activities, and occasionally travel.

Work Schedules. Most public relations specialists work full time during regular business hours. Long workdays are common, as is overtime.

Education/Training

Public relations specialists typically need a bachelor's degree. Employers prefer candidates who have studied public relations, journalism, communications, English, or business.

Education. Public relations specialists typically need a bachelor's degree in public relations, journalism, communications, English, or business. Through such programs, students produce a portfolio of work that demonstrates their ability to prospective employers.

Training. Entry-level workers typically begin by maintaining files of material about an organization's activities, skimming and retaining relevant media articles, and assembling information for speeches and pamphlets. After gaining experience, public relations specialists begin to write news releases, speeches, articles for publication, or carry out public relations programs.

Other Experience. Internships at public relations firms or in the public relations departments of other businesses can be helpful in getting a job as a public relations specialist.

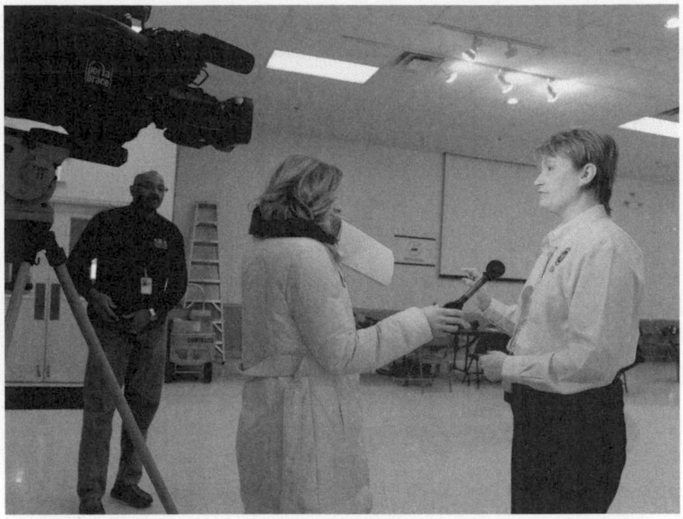

Public relations specialists handle an organization's communication with the public, including consumers, investors, and media outlets.

Some employers prefer candidates who have experience communicating with others through a school newspaper or a leadership position in school or in their community.

Important Qualities

Interpersonal skills. Public relations specialists deal with the public and the media regularly; therefore, they must be open and friendly to maintain a favorable image for their organization.

Organizational skills. Public relations specialists are often in charge of managing several events at the same time, requiring superior organizational skills.

Problem-solving skills. Public relations specialists sometimes must explain how a company or client is handling sensitive issues. They must use good judgment in what they report and how they report it.

Speaking skills. Public relations specialists regularly speak on behalf of their organization. When doing so, they must be able to clearly explain the organization's position.

Writing skills. Public relations specialists must be able to write well-organized and clear press releases and speeches. They must be able to grasp the key messages they want to get across and write them in a short, succinct way to get the attention of busy readers or listeners.

Median Annual Wages, May 2014

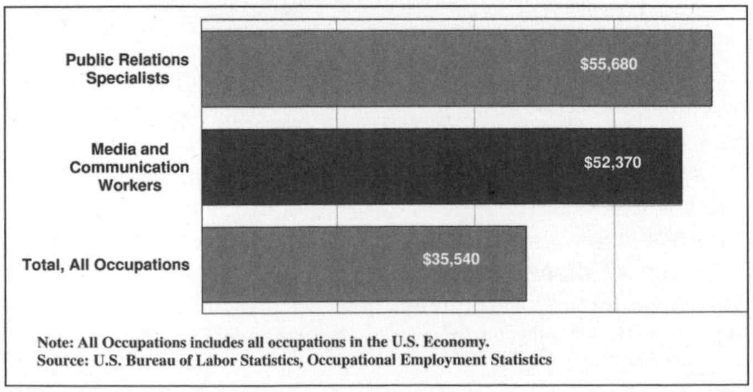

Percent Change in Employment, Projected 2014–2024

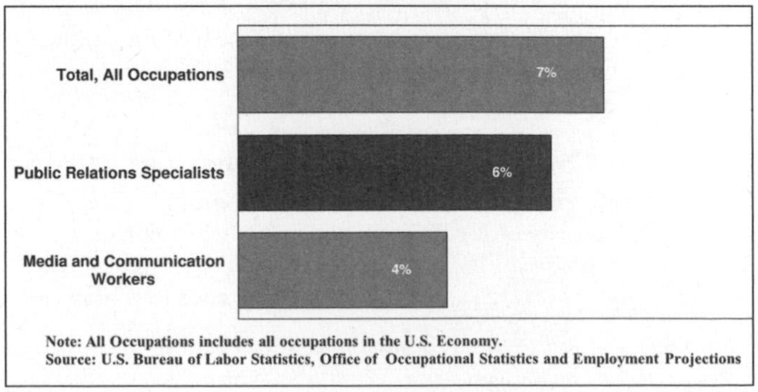

Employment Projections Data for Public Relations Specialists

Occupational Title	SOC Code	Employment, 2014	Projected Employment, 2024	Change, 2014–2024	
				Percent	Numeric
Public relations specialists	27-3031	240,700	255,600	6	14,900

Source: U.S. Bureau of Labor Statistics, Employment Projections Program

Similar Occupations. This table shows a list of occupations with job duties that are similar to those of public relations specialists.

Occupations	Entry-level Education	2014 Median Pay	Projected Job Growth	Average Annual Openings
Advertising Sales Agents	High school diploma or equivalent	$47,890	-3%	-450
Advertising, Promotions, and Marketing Managers	Bachelor's degree	$123,450	9%	1,970
Editors	Bachelor's degree	$54,890	-5%	-620
Market Research Analysts	Bachelor's degree	$61,290	19%	9,230
Meeting, Convention, and Event Planners	Bachelor's degree	$46,490	10%	990
Multimedia Artists and Animators	Bachelor's degree	$63,630	6%	390
Public Relations and Fundraising Managers	Bachelor's degree	$101,510	7%	470
Wholesale and Manufacturing Sales Representatives	See Education/Training	$58,380	7%	11,720
Writers and Authors	Bachelor's degree	$58,850	2%	310

Pay

The median annual wage for public relations specialists was $55,680 in May 2014. The median wage is the wage at which half the workers in an occupation earned more than that amount and half earned less. The lowest 10 percent earned less than $31,190, and the highest 10 percent earned more than $105,720.

In May 2014, the median annual wages for public relations specialists in the top industries in which they worked were as follows:

Professional, scientific, and technical services.................... $59,250
State and local government, excluding education and hospitals.................... 54,640
Religious, grantmaking, civic, professional, and similar organizations.................... 53,920
Educational services; state, local, and private.................... 51,140
Healthcare and social assistance.................... 49,700

Job Outlook

Employment of public relations specialists is projected to grow 6 percent from 2014 to 2024, about as fast as the average for all occupations.

Organizations will continue to emphasize community outreach and customer relations as a way to maintain and enhance their reputation and visibility. Public opinion can change quickly, particularly because both good and bad news spreads rapidly through the Internet. Consequently, public relations specialists will be needed to respond to news developments and maintain their organization's reputation.

The growing use of social media also is expected to increase employment for public relations specialists. These media outlets will create more work for public relations specialists as they try to appeal to consumers and the general public in new ways. Public relations specialists will be needed to help their clients use these new types of social media effectively.

Job Prospects. Because many college graduates apply for the limited amount of public relations positions each year, candidates can expect strong competition for jobs.

Candidates can expect particularly strong competition at advertising firms, organizations with large media exposure, and at prestigious public relations firms.

Contacts for More Information

For more information about public relations managers, including professional certification in public relations, visit

- Public Relations Society of America (www.prsa.org)
- Public Relations Student Society of America (http://prssa.org)
- International Association of Business Communicators (www.iabc.com)

O*NET

- Public Relations Specialists (27-3031.00)

Reporters, Correspondents, and Broadcast News Analysts

- **2014 Median Pay** .... $37,200 per year, $17.88 per hour
- **Typical Entry-Level Education** .... Bachelor's degree
- **Work Experience in a Related Occupation** .... None
- **On-the-job Training** .... None
- **Number of Jobs, 2014** 54,400
- **Job Outlook, 2014–24** .... -9% (Decline)
- **Employment Change, 2014–24** .... -4,800

What Reporters, Correspondents, and Broadcast News Analysts Do

Reporters, correspondents, and broadcast news analysts inform the public about news and events happening internationally, nationally, and locally. They report the news for newspapers, magazines, websites, television, and radio.

Duties. Reporters, correspondents, and broadcast news analysts typically do the following:

- Research topics and stories that an editor or news director has assigned to them
- Interview people who have information, analysis, or opinions about a story or article
- Write articles for newspapers, blogs, and magazines and write scripts to be read on television or radio
- Review articles for accuracy and proper style and grammar
- Develop relationships with experts and contacts who provide tips and leads on stories
- Analyze and interpret information to increase their audiences' understanding of the news
- Update stories as new information becomes available

Reporters and correspondents, also called *journalists*, often work for a particular type of media organization, such as a television or radio station, newspaper, or website.

Those who work in television and radio set up and conduct interviews, which can be broadcast live or recorded for future broadcasts. These workers are often responsible for editing interviews and other recordings to create a cohesive story and for writing and recording voiceovers that provide the audience with the facts of the story. They may create multiple versions of the same story for different broadcasts or different media platforms.

Most television and radio shows have hosts, also called *anchors*, who report the news and introduce stories from reporters.

Journalists for print media conduct interviews and write articles to be used in newspapers, magazines, and online publications. Because most newspapers and magazines have print and online versions, reporters typically produce content for both versions. Doing so often requires staying up to date with new developments of a story so that the online editions can be updated with the most current information.

Some journalists may convey stories through both broadcast and print media, as well as help manage the organization's web content. For example, television stations often have a website, and a reporter may post a blog or an article for the website. Similarly, a reporter working for newspapers or magazines may create videos or podcasts that people access online.

Stations are increasingly relying on multimedia journalists to publish content on a variety of platforms, including radio and television stations, websites, and mobile devices. Multimedia journalists typically record, report, write, and edit their own stories. They also gather the audio, video, or graphics that accompany their stories.

Reporters and correspondents may need to maintain a presence on social media networking sites. Many use social media to cover live events, provide additional information for readers and viewers, promote their stations and newscasts, and engage better with their audiences.

Some journalists, particularly those in large cities or large news organizations, cover a particular topic, such as sports, medicine, or politics. Journalists who work in small cities, towns, or organizations may need to cover a wider range of subjects.

Some reporters live in other countries and cover international news.

Some reporters—particularly those who work for print news—are self-employed and take freelance assignments from news organizations. Freelance assignments are given to writers on an as-needed basis. Because freelance reporters are paid for the individual story, they work with many organizations and often spend some of their time marketing their stories and looking for their next assignment.

Some people with a background as a reporter or correspondent work as postsecondary teachers and teach journalism or communications at colleges and universities.

Broadcast news analysts are another type of media occupation. Broadcast news analysts are often called upon to provide their opinion, rather than reporting, on a particular news story. They may appear on television, radio, or in print and offer their opinion to viewers, listeners, or readers. However, most broadcast news analysts come from fields outside of journalism and have expertise in a particularly subject—for example, politics, business, or medicine—and are hired on a contract basis to provide their opinion of the subjects being discussed. Becoming a broadcast news analyst is typically not a career path for new journalists.

Work Environment

Reporters and correspondents held about 49,300 jobs in 2014. Broadcast news analysts held about 5,100 jobs.

Most reporters and correspondents work for newspaper publishers or in radio or television broadcasting. About 1 in 6 were self-employed in 2014.

Reporters and correspondents spend a lot of time in the field, conducting interviews and investigating stories. Many reporters

Television reporters often compose stories and report "live" from the scene.

Median Annual Wages, May 2014

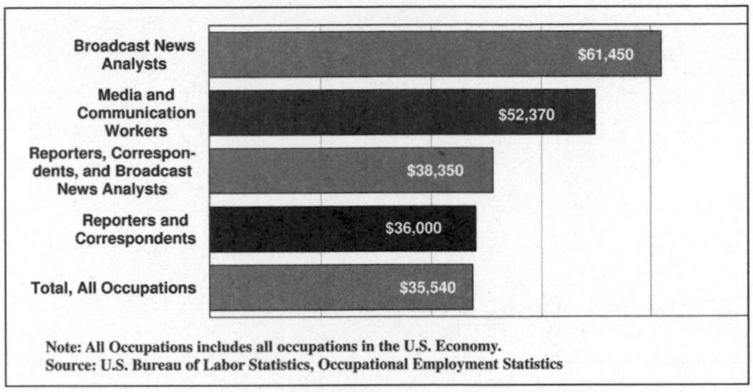

Percent Change in Employment, Projected 2014–2024

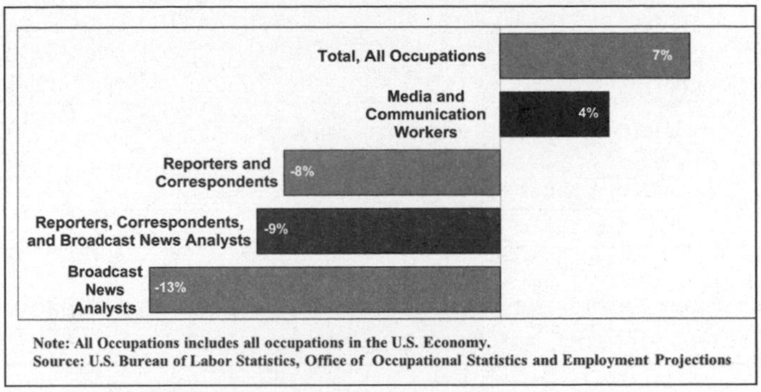

spend little to no time in an office. They travel to be on location for events or to meet contacts and file stories remotely.

Reporters and correspondents covering international news often live in other countries.

Working on stories about natural disasters or wars can put reporters in dangerous situations. In addition, reporters may often face pressure or stress when trying to meet a deadline or cover breaking news.

Reporters may also collaborate with editors, photographers, videographers, and other journalists when working on a story.

Work Schedules. Most reporters, correspondents, and broadcast news analysts work full time. The work is often fast paced, with constant demands to meet deadlines and to be the first reporter to publish a news story on a subject. Reporters may need to work additional hours or change their work schedules in order to follow breaking news. Because news can happen at any time of the day, journalists may need to work nights and weekends.

Education/Training

Employers generally prefer to hire reporters and correspondents who have a bachelor's degree in journalism or communications along with an internship or work experience from a college radio or television station or a newspaper.

Education. Most employers prefer workers who have a bachelor's degree in journalism or communications. However, some employers may hire applicants who have a degree in a related subject, such as English or political science, and relevant work experience.

Bachelor's degree programs in journalism and communications include classes in journalistic ethics and techniques for researching stories and conducting interviews. Some programs may require students to take liberal arts classes, such as English, history, economics, and political science, so that students are prepared to cover stories on a wide range of subjects.

Some journalism students may benefit from classes in multimedia design, coding, and programming. Because content is increasingly being delivered on television, websites, and mobile devices, reporters need to know how to develop stories with video, audio, data, and graphics.

Some schools offer graduate programs in journalism and communications. These programs prepare students who have a bachelor's degree in another field to become journalists.

Other Experience. Employers generally require workers to have experience gained through internships or by working on school newspapers. While attending college, many students seek multiple internships with different news organizations. These internships allow students the opportunities to work on stories and put together a portfolio of their best writing samples or on-air appearances.

Advancement. After gaining more work experience, reporters and correspondents can advance by moving from news organizations in small cities or towns to news organizations in large cities. Larger markets offer job opportunities with higher pay and more responsibility and challenges. Reporters and correspondents also may become editors or news directors.

Important Qualities

Communication skills. Journalists must be able to report the news both verbally and in writing. Strong writing skills are important for journalists in all kinds of media.

Computer skills. Journalists should be able to use editing equipment and other broadcast-related devices.

Interpersonal skills. To develop contacts and conduct interviews, reporters need to build good relationships with many people. They also need to work well with other journalists, editors, and news directors.

Objectivity. Journalists need to report the facts of the news without inserting their opinion or bias into the story.

Persistence. Sometimes, getting the facts of a story is difficult, particularly when those involved refuse to be interviewed or provide comment. Journalists need to be persistent in their pursuit of the story.

Stamina. The work of journalists is often fast paced and exhausting. Reporters must be able to keep up with the additional hours of work.

Pay

The median annual wage for broadcast news analysts was $61,450 in May 2014. The median wage is the wage at which half the workers in an occupation earned more than that amount and half earned less. The lowest 10 percent earned less than $28,210, and the highest 10 percent earned more than $182,470.

The median annual wage for reporters and correspondents was $36,000 in May 2014. The lowest 10 percent earned less than $21,090, and the highest 10 percent earned more than $81,940.

Job Outlook

Employment of reporters, correspondents, and broadcast news analysts is projected to decline 9 percent from 2014 to 2024. Employment of reporters and correspondents is projected to decline 8 percent, while employment of broadcast news analysts is projected to decline 13 percent from 2014 to 2024. Declining advertising revenue in radio, newspapers, and television will negatively impact the employment growth for these occupations.

Employment Projections Data for Reporters, Correspondents, and Broadcast News Analysts

Occupational Title	SOC Code	Employment, 2014	Projected Employment, 2024	Change, 2014–2024 Percent	Change, 2014–2024 Numeric
News analysts, reporters and correspondents	27-3020	54,400	49,600	-9	-4,800
Broadcast news analysts	27-3021	5,100	4,500	-13	-600
Reporters and correspondents	27-3022	49,300	45,100	-8	-4,200

Source: U.S. Bureau of Labor Statistics, Employment Projections Program

Similar Occupations. This table shows a list of occupations with job duties that are similar to those of reporters, correspondents, and broadcast news analysts.

Occupations	Entry-level Education	2014 Median Pay	Projected Job Growth	Average Annual Openings
Announcers	See Education/Training	$29,010	-11%	-580
Atmospheric Scientists, Including Meteorologists	Bachelor's degree	$87,980	9%	110
Broadcast and Sound Engineering Technicians	See Education/Training	$41,350	7%	770
Editors	Bachelor's degree	$54,890	-5%	-620
Film and Video Editors and Camera Operators	Bachelor's degree	$52,470	11%	640
Photographers	High school diploma or equivalent	$30,490	3%	390
Postsecondary Teachers	See Education/Training	$70,790	13%	17,700
Public Relations and Fundraising Managers	Bachelor's degree	$101,510	7%	470
Public Relations Specialists	Bachelor's degree	$55,680	6%	1,490
Technical Writers	Bachelor's degree	$69,030	10%	530
Writers and Authors	Bachelor's degree	$58,850	2%	310

Readership and circulation of newspapers are expected to continue to decline over the next decade. In addition, television and radio stations are increasingly publishing content online and on mobile devices. As a result, news organizations may have more difficulty selling traditional forms of advertising, which is often their primary source of revenue.

Declining revenue will force news organizations to downsize and employ fewer journalists. Increasing demand for online news may offset some of the downsizing. However, because online and mobile ad revenue is typically less than print revenue, the growth in digital advertising may not offset the decline in print advertising, circulation, and readership.

News organizations also continue to consolidate and increasingly are sharing resources, staff, and content with other media outlets. For example, reporters are able to gather and report on news for multiple media stations owned by the same corporation, while television stations reuse news and material already gathered by other stations and reporters. As consolidations, mergers, and news sharing continue, the demand for journalists may decrease.

Following a merger or content-sharing agreements, some news agencies may reduce the number of reporters and correspondents on staff. However, in some instances, consolidations may help limit the loss of jobs. Mergers may allow financially troubled newspapers, radio stations, and television stations to keep staff because of increased funding and resources from the larger organization.

Job Prospects. Reporters, correspondents, and broadcast news analysts are expected to face strong competition for jobs, because of the large number of workers who are interested in entering the field and the projected employment declines in both occupations. Those with experience in the field—experience often gained through internships or by working for school newspapers, television stations, or radio stations—should have the best job prospects.

Multimedia journalism experience, including recording and editing pieces, should also improve job prospects. Because stations are increasingly publishing content on multiple media platforms, particularly the web, employers may prefer applicants who have experience in website design and coding.

In addition, opportunities will likely be better in small local newspapers or television and radio stations.

Competition will be particularly strong in large metropolitan areas, at national newspapers with higher circulation figures, and at network television stations.

Contacts for More Information

For more information about broadcast news analysts, visit

➤ National Association of Broadcasters (www.nab.org)

➤ Radio Television Digital News Association (www.rtdna.org)

For more information about careers in journalism and about internships, visit

➤ Dow Jones News Fund (www.newsfund.org)

➤ Society of Professional Journalists (www.spj.org)

O*NET

➤ Broadcast News Analysts (27-3021.00)

➤ Reporters and Correspondents (27-3022.00)

Technical Writers

- **2014 Median Pay** .... $69,030 per year
$33.19 per hour
- **Typical Entry-Level Education** .... Bachelor's degree
- **Work Experience in a Related Occupation**......... Less than 5 years
- **On-the-job Training** .... Short-term on-the-job training
- **Number of Jobs, 2014** 52,000
- **Job Outlook, 2014–24** .... 10% (Faster than average)
- **Employment Change, 2014–24** 5,300

What Technical Writers Do

Technical writers, also called *technical communicators*, prepare instruction manuals, how-to guides, journal articles, and other supporting documents to communicate complex and technical information more easily. They also develop, gather, and disseminate technical information through an organization's communications channels.

Duties. Technical writers typically do the following:

- Determine the needs of users of technical documentation
- Study product samples and talk with product designers and developers
- Work with technical staff to make products easier to use and thus require fewer instructions
- Organize and write supporting content for products
- Use photographs, drawings, diagrams, animation, and charts that increase users' understanding
- Select appropriate medium for message or audience, such as manuals or online videos
- Standardize content across platforms and media
- Gather user feedback to update and improve content
- Revise content as new issues arise

Technical writers create paper-based and digital operating instructions, how-to manuals, assembly instructions, and "frequently asked questions" pages to help technical support staff, consumers, and other users within a company or an industry. After a product is released, technical writers also may work with product liability specialists and customer-service managers to improve the end-user experience through product design changes.

Technical writers often work with computer hardware engineers, scientists, computer support specialists, and software developers to manage the flow of information among project workgroups during development and testing. Therefore, technical writers must be able to understand complex information and communicate the information to people with diverse professional backgrounds.

Applying their knowledge of the user of the product, technical writers may serve as part of a team conducting usability studies to help improve the design of a product that is in the prototype stage. Technical writers may conduct research on their topics through personal observation, library and Internet research, and discussions with technical specialists.

Technical writers are also responsible for managing the consistency of technical content and its use across business departments including product development, manufacturing, marketing, and customer relations.

Technical writers use computer and communications technologies extensively, which allows them to work from home or wherever their work takes them.

Some technical writers help write grant proposals for research scientists and institutions.

Increasingly, technical information is being delivered online and through social media. Technical writers are using the interactive technologies of the web and social media to blend text, graphics, multidimensional images, sound, and video.

Work Environment

Technical writers held about 52,000 jobs in 2014. The industries that employed the most technical writers were as follows:

Professional, scientific, and technical services	38%
Manufacturing	15
Information	12
Administrative and support services	8

Most technical writers work in offices. They routinely work with engineers and other technology experts to manage the flow of information throughout an organization.

Although most technical writers are employed directly by the companies that use their services, some work on a freelance basis and are paid per assignment. Either they are self-employed, or they work for a technical consulting firm and are given specific short-term or recurring assignments, such as writing about a new product or coordinating the work and communication among different offices to keep a project on track.

Technical writing jobs are usually concentrated in locations, such as California and Texas, with information technology or scientific and technical research companies.

Work Schedules. Technical writers may be expected to work evenings and weekends to coordinate with those in other time zones or to meet deadlines. Most work full time.

Education/Training

A college degree is usually required for a position as a technical writer. In addition, experience with a technical subject, such as computer science, web design, or engineering, is important.

Education. Employers generally prefer candidates with a bachelor's degree in journalism, English, or communications. Many technical writing jobs require both a degree and knowledge in a specialized field, such as engineering, computer science, or medicine. Web design experience also is helpful because of the growing use of online technical documentation.

Median Annual Wages, May 2014

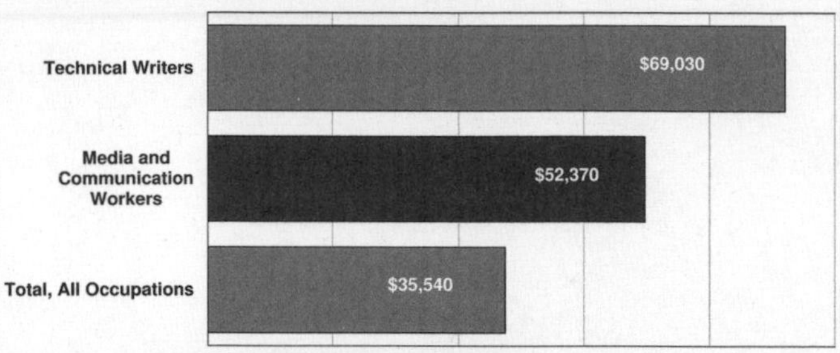

Note: All Occupations includes all occupations in the U.S. Economy.
Source: U.S. Bureau of Labor Statistics, Occupational Employment Statistics

Percent Change in Employment, Projected 2014–2024

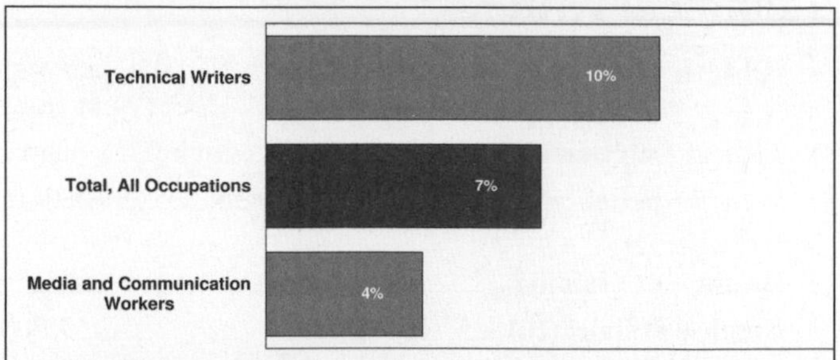

Note: All Occupations includes all occupations in the U.S. Economy.
Source: U.S. Bureau of Labor Statistics, Office of Occupational Statistics and Employment Projections

Work Experience in a Related Occupation. Some technical writers begin their careers as specialists or research assistants in a technical field. They eventually develop technical communication skills and assume primary responsibilities for technical writing. In small firms, beginning technical writers may work on projects right away; in larger companies with more standard procedures, beginners may observe experienced technical writers and interact with specialists before being assigned projects.

Training. Many technical writers need short-term on-the-job training to adapt to a different style of writing.

Licenses, Certifications, and Registrations. Some associations, including the Society for Technical Communication, offer certification for technical writers. In addition, the American Medical Writers Association offers extensive continuing education programs and certificates in medical writing. These certificates are available to professionals in the medical and allied scientific communication fields.

Although not mandatory, certification can demonstrate competence and professionalism, making candidates more attractive to employers. It can also increase a technical writer's opportunities for advancement.

Advancement. Prospects for advancement generally include working on more complex projects and leading or training junior staff. Some technical writers become self-employed and produce work on a freelance basis.

Important Qualities

Communication skills. Technical writers must be able to take complex, technical information and translate it for colleagues and consumers who have nontechnical backgrounds.

Detail oriented. Technical writers create detailed instructions for others to follow. As a result, they must be detailed and precise at every step so that the instructions can be useful.

Imagination. Technical writers must be able to think about a procedure or product in the way a person without technical experience would think about it.

Teamwork. Technical writers must be able to work well with others. They are almost always part of a team: with other writers; with designers, editors, and illustrators; and with the technical people whose information they are explaining.

Technical skills. Technical writers must be able to understand highly complex information. Many technical writers need a background in engineering or computer science in order to do this.

Writing skills. Technical communicators must have excellent writing skills to be able to explain technical information clearly.

Pay

The median annual wage for technical writers was $69,030 in May 2014. The median wage is the wage at which half the workers in an occupation earned more than that amount and half earned less. The lowest 10 percent earned less than $41,450, and the highest 10 percent earned more than $108,460.

In May 2014, the median annual wages for technical writers in the top industries in which they worked were as follows:

Professional, scientific, and technical services	$71,040
Administrative and support services	69,750
Information	69,150
Manufacturing	68,100

Job Outlook

Employment of technical writers is projected to grow 10 percent from 2014 to 2024, faster than the average for all occupations.

The continuing expansion of scientific and technical products and growth in web-based product support will drive employment demand for technical writers. Growth and change in the high-technology and electronics industries will result in a greater need for those who can write instruction manuals and communicate information clearly to users.

Professional, scientific, and technical services firms are expected to continue to grow rapidly and should be a good source of new jobs even as the occupation finds acceptance in a broader range of industries.

Job Prospects. Job opportunities, especially for applicants with technical skills, are expected to be good. The growing reliance on technologically sophisticated products in the home and the workplace and the increasing complexity of medical and scientific

Employment Projections Data for Technical Writers

Occupational Title	SOC Code	Employment, 2014	Projected Employment, 2024	Change, 2014–2024	
				Percent	Numeric
Technical writers	27-3042	52,000	57,300	10	5,300

Source: U.S. Bureau of Labor Statistics, Employment Projections Program

Similar Occupations. This table shows a list of occupations with job duties that are similar to those of technical writers.

Occupations	Entry-level Education	2014 Median Pay	Projected Job Growth	Average Annual Openings
Computer Hardware Engineers	Bachelor's degree	$108,430	3%	240
Computer Programmers	Bachelor's degree	$77,550	-8%	-2,650
Editors	Bachelor's degree	$54,890	-5%	-620
Interpreters and Translators	Bachelor's degree	$43,590	29%	1,750
Public Relations and Fundraising Managers	Bachelor's degree	$101,510	7%	470
Public Relations Specialists	Bachelor's degree	$55,680	6%	1,490
Writers and Authors	Bachelor's degree	$58,850	2%	310

information needed for daily living will create many new job opportunities for technical writers.

In addition, the need to replace workers who retire over the coming decade will result in some job openings. However, there will be competition among freelance technical writers.

Contacts for More Information

For more information about technical writers, visit

- American Medical Writers Association (www.amwa.org)
- National Association of Science Writers (www.nasw.org)
- Society for Technical Communication (www.stc.org)

O*NET

- Technical Writers (27-3042.00)

Writers and Authors

- **2014 Median Pay** .... $58,850 per year $28.30 per hour
- **Typical Entry-Level Education** .... Bachelor's degree
- **Work Experience in a Related Occupation** .... None
- **On-the-job Training** .. Moderate-term on-the-job training
- **Number of Jobs, 2014** 136,500
- **Job Outlook, 2014–24** .... 2% (Slower than average)
- **Employment Change, 2014–24** 3,100

What Writers and Authors Do

Writers and authors develop written content for advertisements, books, magazines, movie and television scripts, songs, blogs, or other types of media.

Duties. Writers and authors typically do the following:

- Choose subject matter that interests readers
- Write fiction or nonfiction through scripts, novels, biographies, and more
- Conduct research to obtain factual information and authentic detail
- Write advertising copy for newspapers, magazines, broadcasts, and the Internet
- Present drafts to editors and clients for feedback
- Work with editors and clients to shape the material so it can be published

Writers and authors develop written material—namely, stories and advertisements—for books, magazines, and online publications.

Writers must establish their credibility with editors and readers through strong research and the use of appropriate sources and citations. Writers and authors select the material they want to use and then convey the information to readers. With help from editors, they may revise or rewrite sections, searching for the best organization and the most appropriate phrasing.

An increasing number of writers are *freelance writers*—that is, they are self-employed and sell their written content to book and magazine publishers; news organizations; advertising agencies; and movie, theater, and television producers. Many freelance writers are hired to complete specific short-term or recurring assignments, such as writing a newspaper column, contributing to a series of articles in a magazine, or producing an organization's newsletter.

An increasing number of writers are producing material that is published directly online, in videos and on blogs.

The following are examples of types of writers and authors:

Copywriters prepare advertisements to promote the sale of a good or service. They often work with a client to produce written content, such as advertising themes, jingles, and slogans.

Biographers write a thorough account of a person's life. They gather information from interviews and research about the person to accurately portray important events in that person's life.

Writers and authors work in an office or wherever they have a computer.

Bloggers write posts to a web log (shortened to "blog") that usually pertain to any topic or a specific field, such as fashion, news, or sports.

Generalists write about any topic of interest, unlike writers who usually specialize in a given field.

Novelists write books of fiction, creating characters and plots that may be imaginary or based on real events.

Songwriters compose music and lyrics for songs. They may write and perform their own songs or sell their work to a music publisher. They sometimes work with a client to produce advertising themes, jingles, and slogans, and they may be involved in marketing the product or service.

Playwrights write scripts for theatrical productions. They come up with a concept, write lines for actors to say, produce stage direction for actors to follow, and suggest ideas for theatrical set design.

Screenwriters create scripts for movies and television. They may produce original stories, characters, and dialogue, or turn a book into a movie or television script. Some may produce content for radio broadcasts and other types of performance.

Journalists write articles and reports on current events. For more information, see the profile on reporters, correspondents, and broadcast news analysts.

Work Environment

Writers and authors held about 136,500 jobs in 2014. The industries that employed the most writers and authors were as follows:

Information	10%
Professional, scientific, and technical services	8
Religious, grantmaking, civic, professional, and similar organizations	4
Arts, entertainment, and recreation	3

In 2014, about two-thirds of writers and authors were self-employed.

Writers and authors work in an office, at home, or wherever else they have access to a computer.

Jobs are somewhat concentrated in major media and entertainment markets—Los Angeles, New York, and Washington, DC—but improved communications and Internet capabilities allow writers and authors to work from almost anywhere. Many prefer to work outside these cities and travel regularly to meet with publishers and clients and to perform research or conduct in-person interviews.

Work Schedules. About 1 in 4 writers and authors worked part time in 2014. Some writers keep regular office hours, either to stay in contact with sources and editors or to set up a writing routine, but many writers set their own hours.

Freelance writers are paid per assignment; therefore, they work any number of hours necessary to meet a deadline. As a result, they must be willing to work evenings and weekends to produce something acceptable to an editor or client. Although many freelance writers enjoy running their own business and working flexible hours, most routinely face the pressures of juggling multiple projects or continually looking for new work.

Education/Training

A college degree in English, journalism, or communications is generally required for a salaried position as a writer or author. Experience can be gained through internships, but any form of writing that improves skill, such as blogging, is beneficial. Excellent writing skills are essential.

Education. A bachelor's degree is typically needed for a full-time job as a writer. Because writing skills are essential in this occupation, many employers prefer candidates with a degree in English, journalism, or communications.

Other Experience. Writers can obtain job experience by working for high school and college newspapers, magazines, radio and television stations, advertising and publishing companies, or nonprofit organizations. College theater and music programs offer playwrights and songwriters an opportunity to have their work performed. Many magazines and newspapers also have internships for students. Interns may write stories, conduct research and interviews, and gain general publishing experience.

Employers also increasingly prefer new applicants to have the ability to code and program web pages or manipulate data to create a visual story using tables, charts, and maps.

In addition, anyone with Internet access can start a blog and gain writing experience. Some of this writing may lead to paid assignments regardless of education, because the quality of writing, the unique perspective, and the size of the potential audience are the greatest determinants of success for a piece of writing. Online publications require knowledge of computer software and editing tools that are used to combine text with graphics, audio, video, and animation.

Writers or authors can come from a variety of backgrounds and experiences as long as they demonstrate strong writing skills.

Training. Writers and authors may need to gain some writing experience through on-the-job training with more experienced writers and editors before their work is ready for publication.

Writers who want to write about a particular topic may need formal training or experience related to that topic.

Because many writers today prepare material directly for the Internet, knowing graphic design, page layout, and multimedia software can be advantageous.

Median Annual Wages, May 2014

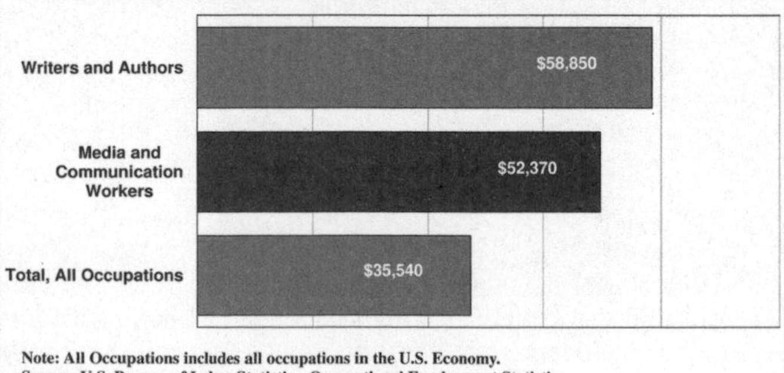

Note: All Occupations includes all occupations in the U.S. Economy.
Source: U.S. Bureau of Labor Statistics, Occupational Employment Statistics

Percent Change in Employment, Projected 2014–2024

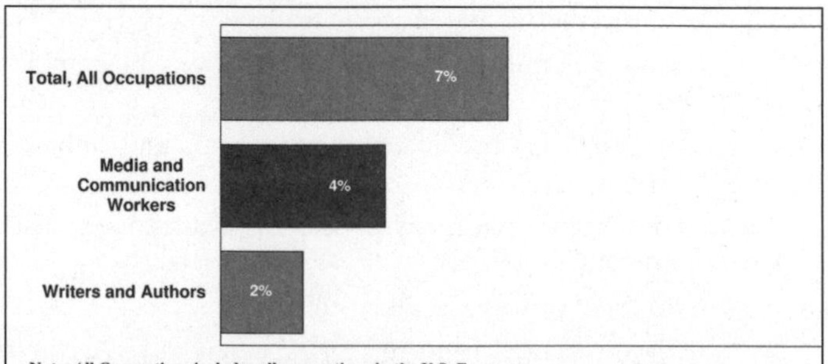

Note: All Occupations includes all occupations in the U.S. Economy.
Source: U.S. Bureau of Labor Statistics, Office of Occupational Statistics and Employment Projections

Employment Projections Data for Writers and Authors

Occupational Title	SOC Code	Employment, 2014	Projected Employment, 2024	Change, 2014–2024 Percent	Change, 2014–2024 Numeric
Writers and authors	27-3043	136,500	139,700	2	3,100

Source: U.S. Bureau of Labor Statistics, Employment Projections Program

Similar Occupations. This table shows a list of occupations with job duties that are similar to those of writers and authors.

Occupations	Entry-level Education	2014 Median Pay	Projected Job Growth	Average Annual Openings
Announcers	See Education/Training	$29,010	-11%	-580
Editors	Bachelor's degree	$54,890	-5%	-620
Public Relations and Fundraising Managers	Bachelor's degree	$101,510	7%	470
Public Relations Specialists	Bachelor's degree	$55,680	6%	1,490
Reporters, Correspondents, and Broadcast News Analysts	Bachelor's degree	$37,200	-9%	-480
Technical Writers	Bachelor's degree	$69,030	10%	530

Licenses, Certifications, and Registrations. Some associations offer certifications for writers and authors. Certification can demonstrate competence and professionalism, making candidates more attractive to employers. For example, the American Grant Writers' Association (AGWA) offers the Certified Grant Writer® credential.

Certification can also increase opportunities for advancement.

Advancement. Beginning writers and authors can get a start and put their name on work immediately by writing for smaller businesses, local newspapers, advertising agencies, and nonprofit organizations. However, opportunities for advancement within these organizations may be limited because they usually do not have enough regular work.

Writers and authors can advance their careers further by building a reputation, taking on more complex writing assignments, and getting published in more prestigious markets and publications. Having published work that has been well received and maintaining a track record of meeting deadlines are important for advancement.

Many editors begin work as writers. Those who are particularly skilled at identifying stories, correcting writing style, and interacting with writers may be interested in editing jobs.

Important Qualities

Adaptability. Writers and authors need to be able to adapt to newer software platforms and programs, including various Content Management Systems (CMS).

Creativity. Writers and authors must be able to develop new and interesting plots, characters, or ideas so they can come up with new stories.

Critical-thinking skills. Writers and authors must have dual expertise in thinking through or understanding new concepts, and conveying it through writing.

Determination. Writers and authors sometimes work on projects that take years to complete. Freelance writers who are paid per assignment must demonstrate perseverance and personal drive to meet deadlines.

Persuasion. Writers, especially those in advertising, must be able to persuade others to feel a certain way about a good or service.

Social perceptiveness. Writers and authors must understand how readers react to certain ideas in order to connect with their audience.

Writing skills. Writers and authors must be able to write clearly and effectively in order to convey feeling and emotion and communicate with readers.

Pay

The median annual wage for writers and authors was $58,850 in May 2014. The median wage is the wage at which half the workers in an occupation earned more than that amount and half earned less. The lowest 10 percent earned less than $28,640, and the highest 10 percent earned more than $114,820.

In May 2014, the median annual wages for writers and authors in the top industries in which they worked were as follows:

Professional, scientific, and technical services	$63,770
Arts, entertainment, and recreation	60,700
Religious, grantmaking, civic, professional, and similar organizations	57,240
Information	54,770

Freelance writers earn income from their articles, books, and, less commonly, television and movie scripts. Although most freelance writers work on individual projects for multiple publishers, many support themselves with income derived from other sources. Freelancers generally have to provide for their own health insurance and pension, unless they receive coverage from another job.

Job Outlook

Employment of writers and authors is projected to grow 2 percent from 2014 to 2024, slower than the average for all occupations.

Despite slower than average employment growth, online publications and services are growing in number and sophistication, spurring demand for writers and authors with web and multimedia experience.

Some experienced writers should find work in the public relations departments of corporations and nonprofit organizations. Others will likely find freelance work for newspaper, magazine, or journal publishers, and some will write books.

Job Prospects. Strong competition is expected for most job openings, given that many people are attracted to this occupation. Competition for jobs with established newspapers and magazines will be particularly strong because employment in the publishing industry is projected to decline.

Writers and authors who have adapted to online media and are comfortable writing for and working with a variety of electronic and digital tools should have an advantage in finding work. The declining costs of self-publishing and the growing popularity of electronic books will allow many freelance writers to have their work published.

Contacts for More Information

For more information about writers and authors, visit

- American Grant Writers' Association, Inc. (www.agwa.us)
- American Society of Journalists and Authors (www.asja.org)
- Association of Writers & Writing Programs (www.awpwriter.org)
- National Association of Science Writers (www.nasw.org)
- Society of Professional Journalists (www.spj.org)
- Writers Guild of America, East (www.wgaeast.org)

O*NET

- Writers and Authors (27-3043.00)
- Copy Writers (27-3043.04)
- Poets, Lyricists and Creative Writers (27-3043.05)

Military Careers

What People in the Military Do

Members of the U.S. military service maintain the U.S. national defense. While some service members work in occupations specific to the military, such as fighter pilots or infantrymen, many work in occupations that also exist in the civilian workplace, such as nurses, doctors, and lawyers. Members serve in the Army, Navy, Air Force, Marine Corps, or Coast Guard, or in the Reserve components of these branches, and in the Air National Guard and Army National Guard. (The Coast Guard, which is included in this profile, is part of the Department of Homeland Security.)

Duties. The military distinguishes between enlisted and officer careers. Enlisted personnel make up about 82 percent of the Armed Forces and carry out military operations. The remaining 18 percent are officers—military leaders who manage operations and enlisted personnel. About 8 percent of officers are warrant officers, a type of officers who are technical and tactical experts in a specific area; for example, Army aviators make up one group of warrant officers.

Enlisted personnel typically do the following:

- Participate in, or support, military operations, such as combat or training operations, or humanitarian or disaster relief
- Operate, maintain, and repair equipment
- Perform technical and support activities
- Supervise junior enlisted personnel

Officers typically do the following:

- Plan, organize, and lead troops and activities in military operations
- Manage enlisted personnel
- Operate and command aircraft, ships, or armored vehicles
- Provide medical, legal, engineering, and other services to military personnel

Types of Enlisted Personnel

The following are examples of types of occupations for enlisted personnel:

Administrative personnel maintain information on personnel, equipment, funds, and other military-related activities. They work in support areas, such as finance, accounting, legal affairs, maintenance, supply, and transportation.

Combat specialty personnel train and work in combat units, such as the infantry, artillery, or Special Forces. For example, infantry specialists conduct ground combat operations, armored vehicle specialists operate battle tanks, and seamanship specialists maintain ships. Combat specialty personnel may maneuver against enemy forces and fire artillery, guns, mortars, or missiles to neutralize them. They may also operate various types of combat vehicles, such as amphibious assault vehicles, tanks, or small boats. Members of elite Special Forces teams are trained to perform specialized missions anywhere in the world on a moment's notice.

Construction personnel build or repair buildings, airfields, bridges, and other structures. They may also operate heavy equipment, such as bulldozers or cranes. They work with engineers and other building specialists as part of military construction teams. Some construction personnel specialize in an area such as plumbing, electrical wiring, or water purification.

Electronic and electrical equipment repair personnel maintain and repair electronic equipment used by the military. Repairers specialize in an area such as aircraft electrical systems, computers, optical equipment, communications, or weapons systems. For example, weapons electronic maintenance technicians maintain and repair electronic components and systems that help locate targets and help aim and fire weapons.

Engineering, science, and technical personnel perform a variety of tasks, such as operating technical equipment, solving problems, and collecting and interpreting information. They perform technical tasks in information technology, environmental health and safety, or intelligence:

- *Environmental health and safety specialists* inspect military facilities and food supplies to ensure that they are safe for use and consumption.
- *Information technology specialists* manage and maintain computer and network systems.
- *Intelligence specialists* gather information and prepare reports for military planning and operations.

Healthcare personnel provide medical services to military personnel and their family members. They may work as part of a patient-service team with doctors, nurses, or other healthcare professionals. Some specialize in providing emergency medical treatment in combat or remote areas. Others specialize in laboratory testing of tissue and blood samples; maintaining pharmacy supplies or patients' records; assisting with dental procedures; operating diagnostic tools, such as X-ray and ultrasound machines; or other healthcare tasks.

Human resources development personnel recruit qualified people into the military, place them in suitable occupations, and provide training programs:

- *Personnel specialists* maintain information about military personnel and their training, job assignments, promotions, and health.
- *Recruiting specialists* provide information about military careers; explain pay, benefits, and military life; and recruit individuals into the military.
- *Training specialists and instructors* teach military personnel how to perform their jobs.

Machine operator and repair personnel operate industrial equipment and machinery to make and repair parts for a variety of equipment and structures. They may operate engines, nuclear reactors, or water pumps, usually performing a specific job. Welders and metalworkers, for example, work with various types of metals to repair or form the structural parts of ships, buildings, or equipment. Survival equipment specialists inspect, maintain, and repair survival equipment, such as parachutes and aircraft life-support equipment.

Media and public affairs personnel prepare and present information about military activities to the military and the public. They take photographs, make video programs, present news and music programs, or conduct interviews.

Protective service personnel enforce military laws and regulations and provide emergency responses to disasters:

Firefighters prevent and extinguish fires in buildings, on aircraft, and aboard ships.

Table 1. Active duty enlisted personnel by broad occupational group and branch of military, and Coast Guard, May 2015

Occupational Group — Enlisted	Army	Air Force	Coast Guard	Marine Corps	Navy	Total enlisted personnel in each occupational group
Administrative	6,140	14,046	1,507	12,018	18,635	52,346
Combat Specialty	109,625	677	649	39,350	8,388	158,689
Construction	15,313	5,195	—	6,252	3,987	30,747
Electronic and Electrical Equipment Repair	31,051	29,310	4,341	16,822	48,236	129,760
Engineering, Science, and Technical	43,567	49,162	1,256	26,917	39,611	160,513
Healthcare	29,986	15,441	707	—	25,345	71,479
Human Resource Development	16,558	7,720	1	2,214	3,941	30,434
Machine Operator and Production	4,107	6,063	1,688	2,539	8,542	22,939
Media and Public Affairs	6,646	7,095	136	2,439	3,859	20,175
Protective Service	1,802	32,573	2,720	6,096	12,011	75,202
Support Service	9,901	4,981	1,145	2,263	8,129	26,419
Transportation and Material Handling	48,096	27,840	9,879	23,213	37,709	146,737
Vehicle and Machinery Mechanic	45,344	41,555	5,532	21,511	47,353	161,295
Non-occupation or unspecified coded personnel	2,984	5,038	1,439	1,161	2,555	13,177
Total enlisted personnel for each military branch and Coast Guard	391,120	246,696	31,000	162,795	268,301	1,099,912

Source: U.S. Department of Defense, Defense Manpower Data Center

Military police responsibilities include controlling traffic, preventing crime, and responding to emergencies.

Other law enforcement and security specialists investigate crimes committed on military property and guard inmates in military correctional facilities.

Support service personnel provide services that support the morale and well-being of military personnel and their families:

Food service specialists prepare food in dining halls, hospitals, and ships.

Religious program specialists assist chaplains with religious services, religious education programs, and related administrative duties.

Transportation and material-handling personnel transport military personnel and cargo. Most personnel within this occupational group are classified according to the mode of transportation, such as aircraft, motor vehicle, or ship:

- *Aircrew members* operate equipment on aircraft.
- *Cargo specialists* load and unload military supplies, using forklifts and cranes.
- *Quartermasters and boat operators* navigate and pilot many types of small watercraft, including tugboats, gunboats, and barges.
- *Vehicle drivers* operate various military vehicles, including fuel or water tank trucks.

Vehicle and machinery mechanical personnel conduct preventive and corrective maintenance on aircraft, automotive and heavy equipment, and powerhouse station equipment. These workers specialize by the type of equipment that they maintain:

- *Aircraft mechanics* inspect and service various types of aircraft.
- *Automotive and heavy-equipment mechanics* maintain and repair vehicles, such as Humvees, trucks, tanks, and other combat vehicles. They also repair bulldozers and other construction equipment.
- *Heating and cooling mechanics* install and repair air-conditioning, refrigeration, and heating equipment.
- *Marine engine mechanics* repair and maintain engines on ships, boats, and other watercraft.
- *Powerhouse mechanics* install, maintain, and repair electrical and mechanical equipment in power-generating stations.

Types of Officers

The following are examples of types of officers:

Combat specialty officers plan and direct military operations, oversee combat activities, and serve as combat leaders. They may be in charge of tanks and other armored assault vehicles, artillery systems, special operations, or infantry units. This group also includes naval surface warfare and submarine warfare officers, combat pilots, and aircrews.

Engineering, science, and technical officers' responsibilities depend on their area of expertise. They work in scientific and professional occupations, such as atmospheric scientists, meteorologists, physical scientists, biological scientists, social scientists, attorneys, and other types of scientists or professionals. For example, meteorologists in the military may study the weather to assist in planning flight paths for aircraft.

Executive, administrative, and managerial officers manage administrative functions in the Armed Forces, such as human resources management, training, personnel, information, police, or other support services. Officers who oversee military bands are included in this category.

Healthcare officers provide medical services to military personnel in order to maintain or improve their health and physical readiness. Officers such as physicians, physician assistants, nurses, and dentists examine, diagnose, and treat patients. Other healthcare officers provide therapy, rehabilitative treatment, and additional healthcare for patients:

- *Dentists* treat diseases, disorders, and injuries of the mouth.
- *Nurses* provide and coordinate patient care in military hospitals and clinics.
- *Optometrists* treat vision problems and prescribe glasses, contact lenses, or medications.
- *Pharmacists* purchase, store, and dispense drugs and medicines.
- *Physical therapists* and *occupational therapists* plan and administer therapy to help patients adjust to injuries, regain independence, and return to work.
- *Physicians, surgeons*, and *physician assistants* examine patients, diagnose injuries and illnesses, and provide treatment to military personnel and their families.

- *Psychologists* provide mental healthcare and may also conduct research on behavior and emotions.

Human resource development officers manage recruitment, placement, and training programs in the military:

- *Personnel managers* direct and oversee military personnel functions, such as job assignments, staff promotions, and career counseling.
- *Recruiting managers* direct and oversee recruiting personnel and recruiting activities.
- *Training and education directors* identify training needs and develop and manage educational programs.

Media and public affairs officers oversee the development, production, and presentation of information or events for the military and the public. They manage the production of videos and television and radio broadcasts that are used for training, news, and entertainment. Some plan, develop, and direct the activities of military bands. Public affairs officers respond to public inquiries about military activities and prepare news releases.

Protective service officers are responsible for the safety and protection of individuals and property on military bases and vessels. Emergency management officers plan and prepare for all types of disasters. They develop warning, evacuation, and response procedures in preparation for disasters. Law enforcement and security officers enforce all applicable laws on military bases and oversee investigations of crimes.

Support services officers manage military activities in key functional areas, such as logistics, transportation, and supply. They may oversee the transportation and distribution of materials by ground vehicles, aircraft, or ships. They also direct food service facilities and other support activities. Purchasing and contracting managers negotiate and monitor contracts for equipment, supplies, and services that the military buys from the private sector.

Transportation officers manage and perform activities related to the safe transport of military personnel and equipment by air and water. They operate and command an aircraft or a ship:

- Navigators use radar, radio, and other navigation equipment to determine their position and plan their route of travel.
- Pilots in the military fly various types of military airplanes and helicopters to carry troops and equipment.

Skills learned in military training often can be carried over to civilian jobs.

- Ships' engineers direct engineering departments, including engine operations, maintenance, and power generation, aboard ships.

Work Environment

In May 2015, more than 2.3 million people served in the Armed Forces. More than 1.3 million were on active duty, including the following subtotals:

Army	487,037
Navy	322,928
Air Force	307,845
Marines	183,787

In addition, about 1 million people served in the Reserves in these branches and in the Air National Guard and Army National Guard. About 39,452 people served in the Coast Guard, which is part of the Department of Homeland Security in May 2015.

The specific work environments and conditions pertaining to military occupations depend on the occupational specialty, unit, branch of service, and other factors. Most active-duty military personnel live and work on or near military bases and facilities

Table 2. Active duty officer personnel by broad occupational group and branch of military, and Coast Guard, May 2015

Occupational Group — Officer	Army	Air Force	Coast Guard	Marine Corps	Navy	Total enlisted personnel in each occupational group
Combat Specialty	22,865	3,799	65	4,388	6,402	37,519
Engineering, Science, and Technical	24,353	15,227	215	4,261	10,631	54,687
Executive, Administrative, and Managerial	13,763	6,716	220	2,516	7,105	30,320
Healthcare	12,052	9,046	0		6,805	27,903
Human Resource Development	2,933	1,588	154	706	3,587	8,968
Media and Public Affairs	326	300	16	190	264	1,096
Protective Service	3,215	1,010	70	409	1,053	5,757
Support Service	1,705	746	12	42	966	3,471
Transportation	12,550	18,543	586	6,048	10,724	48,451
Non-occupation or unspecified coded personnel	2,155	4,174	7,114	2,432	7,090	22,965
Total officer personnel for each military branch and Coast Guard	95,917	61,149	8,452	20,992	54,627	241,137

Source: U.S. Department of Defense, Defense Manpower Data Center

throughout the United States and the world. These bases and facilities usually offer housing and amenities, such as stores and recreation centers.

Service members move regularly for training or job assignments, with most rotations lasting 2 to 4 years. Some are deployed internationally to defend U.S. national interests.

Military members must be both physically and mentally fit, and ready to participate in, or support, combat missions that may be difficult and dangerous and involve long periods away from family. Some personnel, however, are rarely deployed near combat areas.

Table 3 shows officers, warrant officers, and enlisted ranks, by grade and branch of service, who served on active duty in May 2015.

Injuries. Members of the military are often placed in dangerous situations with the risk of serious injury or death. Members deployed to combat zones or those who work in dangerous areas, such as the flight deck of an aircraft carrier, face a higher risk of injury or death.

Work Schedules. Military personnel on active duty typically work full time. However, hours vary with the person's occupational specialty, rank, and branch of service, as well as with the needs of the military. Personnel must be prepared to work additional hours to fulfill missions.

How to Become a Member of the Armed Forces

After basic training, military members attend additional training at technical schools that prepare them for a particular military occupational specialty.

To join the military, applicants must meet age, education, aptitude, physical, and character requirements. These requirements vary by branch of service and for officers and enlisted members.

Although entry requirements for each service vary, certain qualifications for enlistment are common to all branches:

- Minimum of 17 years of age
- U.S. citizenship or permanent resident status
- Pass a background investigation
- Never convicted of a felony
- Able to pass a drug test

Applicants who are 17 years old must have the consent of a parent or legal guardian before entering the military.

Age limits for entering active-duty service are as follows:

- in the Army, the maximum age is 35
- in the Navy, the maximum age is 34
- in the Marine Corps, the maximum age is 29
- in the Air Force, the maximum age is 39
- in the Coast Guard, the maximum age is 27

All applicants must meet certain physical requirements for height, weight, vision, and overall health. Officers must be U.S. citizens. Officers and some enlisted members must be able to obtain a security clearance. Candidates interested in becoming officers through training in the federal service academies must be unmarried and without dependents.

Service members are assigned an occupational specialty based on their aptitude, previous training, and the needs of their branch of service. All members must sign a contract and commit to a minimum term of service.

A recruiter can help a prospective service member determine whether he or she qualifies for enlistment or as an officer. A recruiter can also explain the various enlistment options and describe the military occupational specialties.

Women are eligible to enter most military specialties. They may become mechanics, missile maintenance technicians, heavy-equipment operators, and fighter pilots, or they may enter into medical care, administrative support, and intelligence specialties. Generally, women are excluded only from occupations involving direct exposure to combat. However, all services have plans to integrate and open these occupations to women in the near future.

Become an enlisted member. Prospective recruits who wish to enlist must take a placement exam called the Armed Forces Vocational Aptitude Battery (ASVAB), which is used to determine an applicant's suitability for military occupational specialties.

A recruiter can schedule applicants to take the ASVAB without any obligation to join the military. Many high schools offer the exam as a way for students to explore the possibility of a military career. The selection for a certain job specialty is based on ASVAB test results, the physical requirements for the job, and the needs of the service.

Applicants who decide to join the military must pass the physical examination before signing an enlistment contract. The contract involves a number of enlistment options, such as the length of active-duty or reserve-duty time, the length and kind of job training, and the amount of bonuses that may be earned, if any. Most active-duty programs have first-term enlistments of 4 years, although there are some 2-, 3-, and 6-year programs.

All branches of the Armed Services offer a delayed-entry program allowing candidates to postpone entry to active duty for up to 14 months after enlisting. High school students can enlist during their senior year and enter service after graduation. Others may delay entry because their desired job training is not immediately available or because they need time to arrange their personal affairs.

Become an officer. To become an officer, candidates typically need to have at least a bachelor's degree, be a U.S. citizen, pass a background check, and meet physical and age requirements. Candidates for officer positions do not need to take the ASVAB. Some achieve officer candidacy by completing a degree and training through the federal service academies (Army, Navy, Air Force, Coast Guard, and Merchant Marine) or through the Reserve Officers' Training Corps (ROTC) programs offered at many colleges and universities.

Education. All branches of the Armed Forces require their members to be high school graduates or have equivalent credentials. Officers usually need a bachelor's degree. Some officers entering the service may need to have education beyond a bachelor's degree. For example, officers entering as military lawyers need a law degree.

Those who want to become an officer have several options to meet the education requirements, including the aforementioned federal service academies (Army, Navy, Air Force, Coast Guard, and Merchant Marine), the Reserve Officers' Training Corps (ROTC) programs, Officer Candidate School (OCS), and other programs.

Important Qualities

Mental preparedness. Members of the Armed Forces must be mentally fit and able to handle stressful situations that can occur during military operations.

Physical fitness. Members of the Armed Forces must be physically fit to participate in, or support, combat missions that may be difficult or dangerous.

Table 3. Military rank and employment for Activity Duty Personnel, May 2015

Grade	Army	Navy	Air Force	Marine Corps	Coast Guard	Active Duty Personnel (including Coast Guard)
Commissioned Officers:						
O-10	General	Admiral	General	General	Admiral	37
O-9	Lieutenant General	Vice Admiral	Lieutenant General	Lieutenant General	Vice Admiral	144
O-8	Major General	Rear Admiral (Upper Half)	Major General	Major General	Rear Admiral (Upper Half)	306
O-7	Brigadier General	Rear Admiral (Lower Half)	Brigadier General	Brigadier General	Rear Admiral (Lower Half)	401
O-6	Colonel	Captain	Colonel	Colonel	Captain	11,411
O-5	Lieutenant Colonel	Commander	Lieutenant Colonel	Lieutenant Colonel	Commander	27,877
O-4	Major	Lieutenant Commander	Major	Major	Lieutenant Commander	43,421
O-3	Captain	Lieutenant	Captain	Captain	Lieutenant	77,012
O-2	1st Lieutenant	Lieutenant Junior Grade	1st Lieutenant	1st Lieutenant	Lieutenant Junior Grade	29,514
O-1	2nd Lieutenant	Ensign	2nd Lieutenant	2nd Lieutenant	Ensign	23,504
Warrant Officers:						
W-5	Chief Warrant Officer 5	Chief Warrant Officer 5	—	Chief Warrant Officer 5		821
W-4	Chief Warrant Officer 4	Chief Warrant Officer 4	—	Chief Warrant Officer 4	Chief Warrant Officer 4	2,828
W-3	Chief Warrant Officer 3	Chief Warrant Officer 3	—	Chief Warrant Officer 3	Chief Warrant Officer 3	5,457
W-2	Chief Warrant Officer 2	Chief Warrant Officer 2	—	Chief Warrant Officer 2	Chief Warrant Officer 2	7,561
W-1	Warrant Officer 1		—	Warrant Officer 1		2,391
Enlisted Personnel:						
E-9	Sergeant Major	Master Chief Petty Officer	Chief Master Sergeant	Sergeant Major/ Master Gunnery Sergeant	Master Chief Petty Officer	10,012
E-8	First Sergeant/ Master Sergeant	Senior Chief Petty Officer	Senior Master Sergeant	First Sergeant/ Master Sergeant	Senior Chief Petty Officer	26,629
E-7	Sergeant First Class	Chief Petty Officer	Master Sergeant	Gunnery Sergeant	Chief Petty Officer	90,148
E-6	Staff Sergeant	Petty Officer First Class	Technical Sergeant	Staff Sergeant	Petty Officer First Class	158,306
E-5	Sergeant	Petty Officer Second Class	Staff Sergeant	Sergeant	Petty Officer Second Class	221,513
E-4	Corporal/Specialist	Petty Officer Third Class	Senior Airman	Corporal	Petty Officer Third Class	267,554
E-3	Private First Class	Seaman	Airman First Class	Lance Corporal	Seaman	191,160
E-2	Private	Seaman Apprentice	Airman	Private First Class	Seaman Apprentice	63,207
E-1	Private	Seaman Recruit	Airman Basic	Private	Seaman Recruit	40,383

Source: U.S. Department of Defense, Defense Manpower Data Center

Readiness. Members of the Armed Forces must be ready and able to report for military assignments on short notice.

Training. Training for enlisted personnel. Newly enlisted members of the Armed Forces undergo initial-entry training, better known as basic training or boot camp. Basic training includes courses in military skills and protocols and lasts 7 to 13 weeks, including a week of orientation and introduction to military life. Basic training also includes weapons training, team building, and rigorous physical exercise designed to improve strength and endurance.

Following basic training, enlisted members attend technical schools for additional training that prepares them for a particular military occupational specialty. This formal training period generally lasts from 10 to 20 weeks. Training for certain occupations—nuclear power plant operator, for example—may take as long as a year. In addition to getting classroom instruction, military members receive on-the-job training at their first duty assignment.

Training for warrant officers. All services except the U.S. Air Force have warrant officer programs. Selection to attend Warrant Officer Candidate School is highly competitive and is restricted to those who meet rank and length-of-service requirements. The only exception is the selection process for Army aviator warrant officers, a process that has no requirement of previous military service. Training may last several weeks.

Training for officers. Officer training in the Armed Forces is provided through the federal service academies (Army, Navy, Air Force, Coast Guard, and Merchant Marine), the Reserve Officers' Training Corps (ROTC) program, Officer Candidate School (OCS) or Officer Training School (OTS), the National Guard (State Officer Candidate School programs), and the Uniformed Services University of the Health Sciences.

Training for officers in the federal service academies. The federal service academies provide a Bachelor of Science (B.S.) degree. Midshipmen and cadets receive free room and board, free tuition, free medical and dental care, and a monthly allowance. Graduates receive regular or reserve commissions and typically have a 5-year active-duty obligation, which may be longer for some specialties, such as medicine or aviation.

Service academy cadet or midshipman candidates must be nominated by an authorized source, usually a member of Congress. In addition, nominees must submit their academic record, college aptitude test scores, and recommendations from teachers or other school officials. They must also pass a medical examination. Academies make appointments from the list of eligible nominees. Appointments to the Coast Guard Academy, however, are based on merit and do not require a nomination.

Training for officers in ROTC programs. Participants in ROTC programs take regular college courses along with 3 to 5 hours of military instruction per week. After graduation, they may serve as officers on active duty or in the Reserves or National Guard. In the last 2 years of an ROTC program, students receive a monthly allowance while attending school, as well as additional pay for summer training. ROTC scholarships for 2, 3, and 4 years of school are available on a competitive basis.

Training for officers through OCS or OTS. College graduates can earn a commission in the Armed Forces through OCS or OTS training programs in the Army, Navy, Air Force, Marine Corps, Coast Guard, Air National Guard, and Army National Guard. These programs consist of several weeks of academic, physical, and leadership training. Those who complete the programs as officers must usually complete their service obligation on active duty.

Training for officers through the Uniformed Services University of Health Sciences. Personnel with training in certain health occupations may qualify for direct appointment as officers. For those studying health professions, financial assistance and internship opportunities are available from the military in return for specified periods of military service. Prospective medical students can apply to the Uniformed Services University of the Health Sciences, which offers a salary and free tuition in a program leading to a Doctor of Medicine (M.D.) degree. In return, graduates must serve for at least 7 years in either the military or the U.S. Public Health Service.

Training for officers through direct appointments. Direct appointments also are available for those qualified to serve in other specialty areas, such as the Judge Advocate General's Corps for those in the legal field or the Chaplain Corps for those in religious ministry. All prospective officers who enter the service through a direct appointment attend several weeks of military-related training that typically includes courses in military orientation, academic subjects, and officer leadership and tactics. This program usually lasts a few months.

Licenses, Certifications, and Registrations. Depending on the occupational specialty, members of the military may need to have and maintain civilian licenses or certifications. For example, officers serving as lawyers, also known as judge advocates, may need to have and maintain their state bar licenses to enter and remain in the U.S. military. Air traffic controllers, dental assistants, medical laboratory technicians, and many others also need to have civilian occupation equivalent licenses or certifications.

Advancement. Each branch of the military has different criteria for determining the promotion of personnel. Criteria for promotion may include time in service and in grade, job performance, a fitness report, and passing scores on written exams. Enlisted personnel can be promoted to higher ranks, which may include serving in a supervisory position and being in charge of junior enlisted members.

Each military service may have other advancement opportunities for its enlisted personnel. For example, enlisted personnel may become warrant officers if they complete a bachelor's degree, have several years of experience in higher enlisted positions, and meet age and physical requirements. The Army offers a direct enlistment option to become a warrant officer aviator.

Officers can also be promoted to higher ranks, which may include the command of a military unit of both enlisted members and officers, or being in charge of an entire military base.

Pay

Basic pay is based on rank and time in service. The pay structure for military personnel is shown in Table 4. Pay bands are the same for all branches. Members of the Armed Forces may receive additional pay based on their job assignment or qualifications. For example, they receive additional pay for foreign, hazardous, submarine, or flight duty, or for being medical or dental officers. Retirement pay is generally available after 20 years of service.

In addition to receiving basic pay, members of the military are either housed free of charge on base or they receive a housing allowance.

Members who serve for a certain number of years may receive other benefits. These benefits may include educational benefits through the Montgomery GI Bill, which pays for a portion of educational costs at accredited institutions; medical care at military or the U.S. Department of Veterans Affairs hospitals; and guaranteed home loans.

Military personnel on active duty typically work full time. However, hours vary with the person's occupational specialty, rank, and branch of service, as well as with the needs of the military. Personnel must be prepared to work additional hours to fulfill missions.

Job Outlook

The total number of active-duty and reserve personnel serving in the Armed Forces is expected to remain roughly the same through 2024.

The goal of the Armed Forces is to maintain a force sufficient to deter, fight, and overcome various threats or conflicts in multiple regions at the same time. Emerging conflicts and threatening global events, however, could lead to restructuring and a demand for a larger force. Consequently, the nation is expected to maintain

Table 4. Monthly pay by military rank and years of service, January 2015, (O-officers, W-warrant officers, E-enlisted members)

Pay Grade	Years of Service											
	2 or less	Over 2	Over 3	Over 4	Over 6	Over 8	Over 10	Over 12	Over 14	Over 16	Over 18	Over 20
O-10												$16,072.20
O-9												14,056.80
O-8	9,946.20	10,272.00	10,488.30	10,548.60	10,818.60	11,269.20	11,373.90	11,802.00	11,924.70	12,293.40	12,827.10	13,319.10
O-7	8,264.40	8,648.40	8,826.00	8,967.30	9,222.90	9,475.80	9,767.70	10,059.00	10,351.20	11,269.20	12,043.80	12,043.80
O-6	6,186.60	6,796.80	7,242.90	7,242.90	7,270.50	7,582.20	7,623.30	7,623.30	8,056.50	8,822.40	9,272.10	9,721.50
O-5	5,157.60	5,810.10	6,212.10	6,288.00	6,539.10	6,689.10	7,019.10	7,261.50	7,574.70	8,053.80	8,281.20	8,506.50
O-4	4,449.90	5,151.30	5,495.10	5,571.60	5,890.50	6,232.80	6,659.10	6,990.60	7,221.00	7,353.60	7,430.10	7,430.10
O-3	3,912.60	4,435.20	4,787.10	5,219.40	5,469.60	5,744.10	5,921.10	6,213.00	6,365.40	6,365.40	6,365.40	6,365.40
O-2	3,380.70	3,850.20	4,434.30	4,584.00	4,678.50	4,678.50	4,678.50	4,678.50	4,678.50	4,678.50	4,678.50	4,678.50
O-1	2,934.30	3,054.30	3,692.10	3,692.10	3,692.10	3,692.10	3,692.10	3,692.10	3,692.10	3,692.10	3,692.10	3,692.10
W-5												7,189.50
W-4	4,043.40	4,349.70	4,474.20	4,597.20	4,808.70	5,018.10	5,229.90	5,548.80	5,828.10	6,094.20	6,311.70	6,523.80
W-3	3,692.40	3,846.30	4,004.10	4,056.00	4,221.30	4,546.80	4,885.50	5,045.10	5,229.60	5,419.80	5,761.50	5,992.50
W-2	3,267.30	3,576.30	3,671.70	3,736.80	3,948.90	4,278.30	4,441.50	4,602.00	4,798.50	4,951.80	5,091.00	5,257.50
W-1	2,868.30	3,176.70	3,259.80	3,435.00	3,642.60	3,948.30	4,091.10	4,290.30	4,486.80	4,641.30	4,783.20	4,956.00
E-9							4,885.20	4,995.90	5,135.40	5,299.20	5,465.10	5,730.30
E-8						3,999.00	4,175.70	4,285.20	4,416.60	4,558.80	4,815.30	4,945.20
E-7	2,780.10	3,034.20	3,150.30	3,304.20	3,424.50	3,630.90	3,747.00	3,953.40	4,125.00	4,242.30	4,367.10	4,415.40
E-6	2,404.50	2,645.70	2,762.40	2,876.10	2,994.60	3,261.00	3,364.80	3,565.80	3,627.30	3,672.00	3,724.20	3,724.20
E-5	2,202.90	2,350.80	2,464.50	2,580.60	2,761.80	2,951.40	3,107.10	3,125.70	3,125.70	3,125.70	3,125.70	3,125.70
E-4	2,019.60	2,122.80	2,238.00	2,351.40	2,451.60	2,451.60	2,451.60	2,451.60	2,451.60	2,451.60	2,451.60	2,451.60
E-3	1,823.40	1,938.00	2,055.30	2,055.30	2,055.30	2,055.30	2,055.30	2,055.30	2,055.30	2,055.30	2,055.30	2,055.30
E-2	1,734.00	1,734.00	1,734.00	1,734.00	1,734.00	1,734.00	1,734.00	1,734.00	1,734.00	1,734.00	1,734.00	1,734.00
E-1	1,546.80											

Source: U.S. Department of Defense, Defense Finance and Accounting Services

adequate personnel in the Reserve, Army National Guard, and Air National Guard.

Job Prospects. Opportunities should be very good for qualified individuals in all branches of the Armed Forces through 2024. All services have needs to fill entry-level and professional positions as current members of the Armed Forces move up through the ranks, leave the service, or retire.

All services of the Armed Forces establish recruiting goals for each year to replace those who complete their military service commitment, leave the service, or retire. For example, about 240,000 personnel were recruited in the Armed Forces active and reserve components in 2014. The military has been an all-volunteer force since the end of the draft in 1973.

When the economy is thriving and civilian employment opportunities are generally more favorable, it is more difficult for the military to meet its recruitment quotas. It is also more difficult to meet these goals during times of war, when recruitment goals typically rise. During economic downturns, candidates for military service may face competition.

Contacts for More Information

Each of the military services publishes handbooks, fact sheets, and pamphlets describing its entrance requirements, its training opportunities, and other aspects of military careers. These publications are available at all recruiting stations; at most state employment service offices; and in high schools, colleges, and public libraries.

For more information on the individual services, visit

- U.S. Air Force (www.airforce.com)
- Air National Guard (www.ang.af.mil)
- U.S. Army (www.goarmy.com)
- Army National Guard (arng.ng.mil/SitePages/Home.aspx)
- U.S. Coast Guard (www.uscg.mil)
- U.S. Marine Corps (www.marines.com)
- U.S. Navy (www.navy.com)

In addition, the Defense Manpower Data Center, an agency of the Department of Defense, maintains a website that provides information and resources for parents, educators, and young adults who are curious about joining military service. To see the information, visit

- Today's Military (www.todaysmilitary.com)

For more information about military testing, visit

- ASVAB (http://official-asvab.com/index.htm)

Similar Occupations

The military employs people in numerous occupational specialties, many of which are similar to civilian occupations. To match military occupations with similar civilian occupations, O*Net OnLine offers the Military Crosswalk Search tool (www.onetonline.org/crosswalk/MOC).

Bill and Account Collectors

- **2014 Median Pay** .... $33,700 per year $16.20 per hour
- **Typical Entry-Level Education** .... High school diploma or equivalent
- **Work Experience in a Related Occupation**.............. None
- **On-the-Job Training**....Moderate-term on-the-job training
- **Number of Jobs 2014** 350,400
- **Job Outlook, 2014–24** .... -6% (Decline)
- **Employment Change, 2014–24** .... -19,600

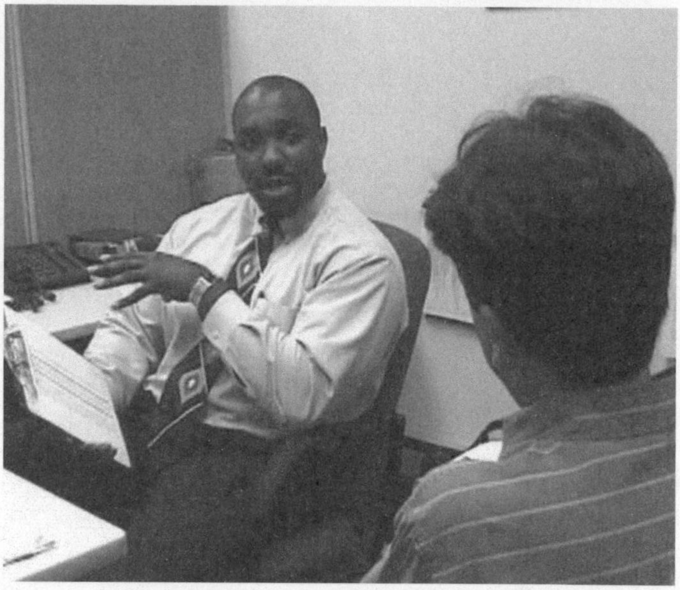

Bill and account collectors must have good communication and people skills as their work requires daily interactions with customers.

What Bill and Account Collectors Do

Bill and account collectors try to recover payment on overdue bills. They negotiate repayment plans with debtors and help them find solutions to make paying their overdue bills easier.

Duties. Bill and account collectors typically do the following:

- Find consumers and businesses who have overdue bills
- Track down consumers who have an out-of-date address by using the Internet, post office, credit bureaus, or neighbors—a process called "skip tracing"
- Inform debtors that they have an overdue bill and try to negotiate a payment
- Explain the terms of sale or contract with the debtor, when necessary
- Learn the reasons for the overdue bills, which can help with the negotiations
- Offer credit advice or refer a consumer to a debt counselor, when appropriate

Bill and account collectors generally contact debtors by phone, although sometimes they do so by mail. They use computer systems to update contact information and record past collection attempts with a particular debtor. Keeping these records can help collectors with future negotiations.

The main job of bill and account collectors is finding a solution that is acceptable to the debtor and maximizes payment to the creditor. Listening to the debtor and paying attention to his or her concerns can help the collector negotiate a solution.

After the collector and debtor agree on a repayment plan, the collector continually checks to ensure that the debtor pays on time. If the debtor does not pay, the collector submits a statement to the creditor, who can take legal action. In extreme cases, this legal action may include taking back goods or disconnecting service.

Collectors must follow federal and state laws that govern debt collection. These laws require that collectors make sure they are talking with the debtor before announcing that the purpose of the call is to collect a debt. A collector also must give a statement, called "mini-Miranda," which informs the account holder that they are speaking with a bill or debt collector.

Although many collectors work for third-party collection agencies, some work in-house for the original creditor, such as a credit-card company or a healthcare provider. The day-to-day activities of in-house collectors are generally the same as those of other collectors.

Collectors usually have goals they are expected to meet. Typically, these include calls per hour and success rates.

Median Annual Wages, May 2014

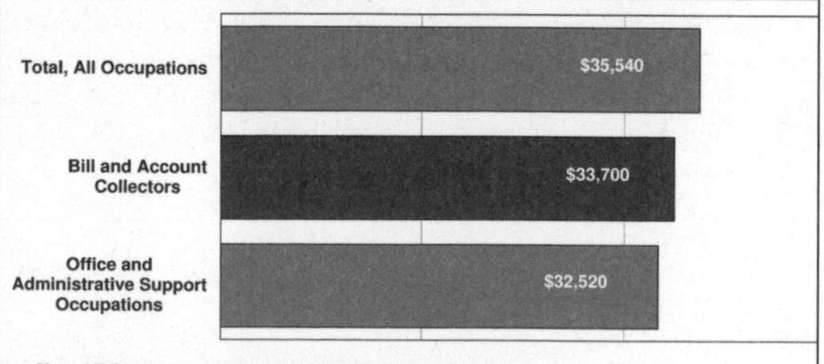

Note: All Occupations includes all occupations in the U.S. Economy.
Source: U.S. Bureau of Labor Statistics, Occupational Employment Statistics

Percent Change in Employment, Projected 2014–2024

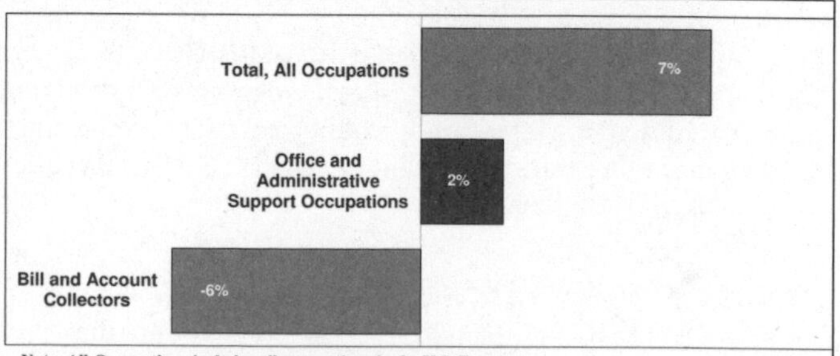

Note: All Occupations includes all occupations in the U.S. Economy.
Source: U.S. Bureau of Labor Statistics, Office of Occupational Statistics and Employment Projections

Employment Projections Data for Bill and Account Collectors

Occupational Title	SOC Code	Employment, 2014	Projected Employment, 2024	Change, 2014–2024 Percent	Change, 2014–2024 Numeric
Bill and account collectors	43-3011	350,400	330,900	-6	-19,600

Source: U.S. Bureau of Labor Statistics, Employment Projections Program

Work Environment

Bill and account collectors held about 350,400 jobs in 2014. The industries that employed the most bill and account collectors were as follows:

Business support services	27%
Credit intermediation and related activities	19
Healthcare and social assistance	14
Professional, scientific, and technical services	7
Management of companies and enterprises	5

Many collectors work in a call center for a third-party collection agency rather than the original creditor. Whichever industry the collectors work in, most of their time is spent on the phone tracking down or negotiating with debtors. They also spend time on the computer, updating information and recording the results of their calls.

Collectors' work can be stressful because many people become angry and confrontational when pressed about their debts. Collectors often face resistance while trying to do their job duties. Successful collectors must face regular rejection and still be ready to make the next call in a polite and positive voice. Fortunately, some consumers appreciate help in resolving their outstanding debts and can be quite grateful.

Work Schedules. Most bill and account collectors work full time. Some collectors work flexible schedules, often calling people on weekends or during the evenings as they learn the best times to call.

Education/Training

Collectors usually must have a high school diploma. They commonly receive a few months of on-the-job training.

Education. Most bill and account collectors are required to have a high school diploma, although some employers prefer applicants who have taken some college courses. Communication, accounting, and basic computer courses are examples of classes that are helpful for entering this occupation.

Training. Collectors usually get 1 to 3 months of on-the-job training after being hired. Training includes learning the company's policies and computer software and learning the laws for debt collection in the Fair Debt Collection Practices Act, as well as their state's debt-collection regulations. Collectors also may be trained in negotiation techniques.

Important Qualities

Listening skills. Collectors must pay attention to what debtors say when trying to negotiate a repayment plan. Learning the particular situation of the debtors and how they fell into debt can help collectors suggest solutions.

Negotiating skills. The main aspects of a collector's job are reconciling the differences between two parties (the debtor and the creditor) and offering a solution that is acceptable to both parties.

Speaking skills. Collectors must be able to speak to debtors to explain their choices and ensure that they fully understand what is being said.

Pay

The median annual wage for bill and account collectors was $33,700 in May 2014. The median wage is the wage at which half the workers in an occupation earned more than that amount and half earned less. The lowest 10 percent earned less than $22,240, and the highest 10 percent earned more than $51,120.

In May 2014, the median annual wages for bill and account collectors in the top industries in which they worked were as follows:

Management of companies and enterprises	$35,700
Professional, scientific, and technical services	35,600
Healthcare and social assistance	35,080
Credit intermediation and related activities	34,900
Business support services	29,190

Job Outlook

Employment of bill and account collectors is projected to decline 6 percent from 2014 to 2024.

The collection industry has experienced consolidation in recent years, as larger agencies have increased market share, and smaller agencies have declined. This has decreased employment, as overlapping positions have been eliminated. Further industry consolidation should continue to limit employment growth for collectors.

In addition, the increasing efficiency of collectors is expected to slow employment growth for this occupation. New software and

Similar Occupations. This table shows a list of occupations with job duties that are similar to those of bill and account collectors.

Occupations	Entry-level Education	2014 Median Pay	Projected Job Growth	Average Annual Openings
Bookkeeping, Accounting, and Auditing Clerks	Some college, no degree	$36,430	-8%	-14,870
Customer Service Representatives	High school diploma or equivalent	$31,200	10%	25,290
Financial Clerks	High school diploma or equivalent	$36,260	6%	8,930
Information Clerks	See Education/Training	$31,500	2%	2,580
Loan Officers	Bachelor's degree	$62,620	8%	2,450

automated calling systems should increase productivity and allow collectors to handle more accounts.

Although some collection jobs will likely be sent to other countries where wages are lower, creditors should continue to hire some collectors in the United States.

Job Prospects. Job prospects are likely to be excellent for this occupation. Workers frequently leave the occupation, which leads to numerous job openings.

Unlike many other occupations, collections jobs usually remain stable during economic downturns. When the economy weakens, many consumers and businesses fall behind on their financial obligations, increasing the amount of debt to be collected. However, the success rate of collectors decreases because fewer people can afford to pay their debts.

Contacts for More Information

For more information about bill and account collectors, visit

➤ ACA International, the Association of Credit and Collections Professionals (www.acainternational.org)

O*NET

➤ Bill and Account Collectors (43-3011.00)

Bookkeeping, Accounting, and Auditing Clerks

- **2014 Median Pay** .... $36,430 per year $17.51 per hour
- **Typical Entry-Level Education** .... Some college, no degree
- **Work Experience in a Related Occupation** .... None
- **On-the-job Training** .... Moderate-term on-the-job training
- **Number of Jobs, 2014** 1,760,300
- **Job Outlook, 2014–24** .... -8% (Decline)
- **Employment Change, 2014–24** .... -148,700

What Bookkeeping, Accounting, and Auditing Clerks Do

Bookkeeping, accounting, and auditing clerks produce financial records for organizations. They record financial transactions, update statements, and check financial records for accuracy.

Duties. Bookkeeping, accounting, and auditing clerks typically do the following:

- Use bookkeeping software, online spreadsheets, and databases
- Enter (post) financial transactions into the appropriate computer software
- Receive and record cash, checks, and vouchers
- Put costs (debits) and income (credits) into the software, assigning each to an appropriate account
- Produce reports, such as balance sheets (costs compared with income), income statements, and totals by account
- Check for accuracy in figures, postings, and reports
- Reconcile or note and report any differences they find in the records

The records that bookkeeping, accounting, and auditing clerks work with include expenditures (money spent), receipts (money that comes in), accounts payable (bills to be paid), accounts receivable (invoices, or what other people owe the organization), and profit and loss (a report that shows the organization's financial health).

Workers in this occupation have a wide range of tasks. Some are full-charge bookkeeping clerks who maintain an entire organization's books. Others are accounting clerks who handle specific tasks.

These clerks use basic mathematics (adding, subtracting) throughout the day.

Bookkeeping, accounting, and auditing clerks use specialized computer accounting software, spreadsheets, and databases to enter information from receipts or bills. They must be comfortable using computers to record and calculate data.

The widespread use of computers also has enabled bookkeeping, accounting, and auditing clerks to take on additional responsibilities, such as payroll, billing, purchasing (buying), and keeping track of overdue bills. Many of these functions require clerks to communicate with clients.

Bookkeeping clerks, also known as *bookkeepers*, often are responsible for some or all of an organization's accounts, known as the general ledger. They record all transactions and post debits (costs) and credits (income).

They also produce financial statements and other reports for supervisors and managers. Bookkeepers prepare bank deposits by compiling data from cashiers, verifying receipts, and sending cash, checks, or other forms of payment to the bank.

In addition, they may handle payroll, make purchases, prepare invoices, and keep track of overdue accounts.

Accounting clerks typically work for larger companies and have more specialized tasks. Their titles, such as accounts payable clerk or accounts receivable clerk, often reflect the type of accounting they do.

The responsibilities of accounting clerks frequently vary by level of experience. Entry-level accounting clerks may post details of transactions (including date, type, and amount), add up accounts, and determine interest charges. They also may monitor loans and accounts to ensure that payments are up to date.

More advanced accounting clerks may add and balance billing vouchers, ensure that account data are complete and accurate, and code documents according to an organization's procedures.

Bookkeeping, accounting, and auditing clerks handle financial records for many small businesses.

Auditing clerks check figures, postings, and documents to ensure that they are mathematically accurate and properly coded. They also correct or note errors for accountants or other workers to fix.

Work Environment

Bookkeeping, accounting, and auditing clerks held about 1.8 million jobs in 2014. The industries that employed the most bookkeeping, accounting, and auditing clerks were as follows:

Professional, scientific, and technical services	12%
Retail trade	9
Wholesale trade	7
Healthcare and social assistance	7
Finance and insurance	7

The professional, scientific, and technical services industry includes the accounting, tax preparation, bookkeeping, and payroll services sub-industry.

Bookkeeping, accounting, and auditing clerks work in offices. Bookkeepers who work for multiple firms may visit their clients' places of business. They often work alone, but sometimes they collaborate with accountants, managers, and auditing clerks from other departments.

Work Schedules. Many bookkeeping, accounting, and auditing clerks work full time. About 1 in 4 worked part time in 2014. They may work additional hours to meet deadlines at the end of the fiscal year, during tax time, or when monthly or yearly accounting audits are done. Those who work in hotels, restaurants, and stores may put in overtime during peak holiday and vacation seasons.

Education/Training

Most bookkeeping, accounting, and auditing clerks need some postsecondary education and also learn some of their skills on the job. They must have basic math and computer skills, including knowledge of spreadsheets and bookkeeping software.

Education. Employers generally require bookkeeping, accounting, and auditing clerks to have some postsecondary education, particularly coursework in accounting. However, some candidates can be hired with just a high school diploma.

Training. Bookkeeping, accounting, and auditing clerks usually get on-the-job training. Under the guidance of a supervisor or another experienced employee, new clerks learn how to do their tasks, including double-entry bookkeeping. In double-entry bookkeeping, each transaction is entered twice, once as a debit (cost) and once as a credit (income), to ensure that all accounts are balanced.

Some formal classroom training also may be necessary, such as training in specialized computer software. This on-the-job training typically takes around 6 months.

Licenses, Certifications, and Registrations. Some bookkeeping, accounting, and auditing clerks become certified. For those who do not have postsecondary education, certification is a particularly useful way to gain expertise in the field. The Certified Bookkeeper (CB) designation, awarded by the American Institute of Professional Bookkeepers, shows that those who have earned it have the skills and knowledge needed to carry out all bookkeeping tasks, including overseeing payroll and balancing accounts, according to accepted accounting procedures.

For certification, candidates must have at least 2 years of full-time bookkeeping experience or equivalent part-time work, pass a four-part exam, and adhere to a code of ethics.

The National Association of Certified Public Bookkeepers also offers certification. The Uniform Bookkeeper Certification Examination is an online test with 50 multiple-choice questions. Test takers must answer 75 percent of the questions correctly to pass the exam.

Advancement. With appropriate experience and education, some bookkeeping, accounting, and auditing clerks may become accountants or auditors.

Important Qualities

Computer skills. Bookkeeping, accounting, and auditing clerks need to be comfortable using computer spreadsheets and bookkeeping software.

Detail oriented. These clerks are responsible for producing accurate financial records. They must pay attention to detail in order to avoid making errors and recognize errors that others have made.

Integrity. Bookkeeping, accounting, and auditing clerks have control of an organization's financial documentation, which they must use properly and keep confidential. It is vital that they keep records transparent and guard against misappropriating an organization's funds.

Math skills. Bookkeeping, accounting, and auditing clerks deal with numbers daily and should be comfortable with basic arithmetic.

Pay

The median annual wage for bookkeeping, accounting, and auditing clerks was $36,430 in May 2014. The median wage is the wage at which half the workers in an occupation earned more than that amount and half earned less. The lowest 10 percent earned less than $22,480, and the highest 10 percent earned more than $56,470.

In May 2014, the median annual wages for bookkeeping, accounting, and auditing clerks in the top industries in which they worked were as follows:

Professional, scientific, and technical services	$37,890

Median Annual Wages, May 2014

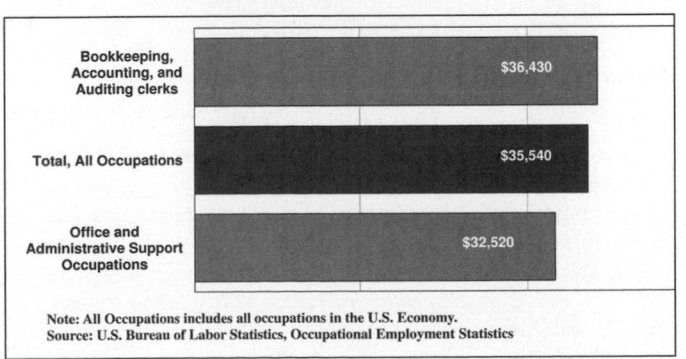

Note: All Occupations includes all occupations in the U.S. Economy.
Source: U.S. Bureau of Labor Statistics, Occupational Employment Statistics

Percent Change in Employment, Projected 2014–2024

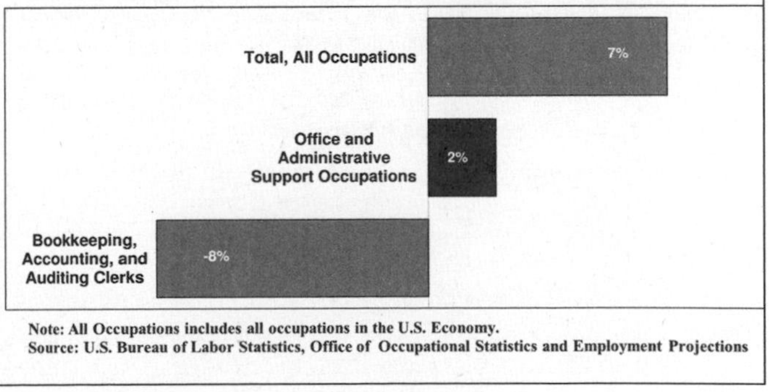

Note: All Occupations includes all occupations in the U.S. Economy.
Source: U.S. Bureau of Labor Statistics, Office of Occupational Statistics and Employment Projections

Employment Projections Data for Bookkeeping, Accounting, and Auditing Clerks

Occupational Title	SOC Code	Employment, 2014	Projected Employment, 2024	Change, 2014–2024 Percent	Change, 2014–2024 Numeric
Bookkeeping, accounting, and auditing clerks	43-3031	1,760,300	1,611,500	-8	-148,700

Source: U.S. Bureau of Labor Statistics, Employment Projections Program

Similar Occupations. This table shows a list of occupations with job duties that are similar to those of bookkeeping, accounting, and auditing clerks.

Occupations	Entry-level Education	2014 Median Pay	Projected Job Growth	Average Annual Openings
Accountants and Auditors	Bachelor's degree	$65,940	11%	14,240
Budget Analysts	Bachelor's degree	$71,220	3%	150
Cost Estimators	Bachelor's degree	$60,050	9%	1,870
Financial Clerks	High school diploma or equivalent	$36,260	6%	8,930
Loan Officers	Bachelor's degree	$62,620	8%	2,450
Tax Examiners and Collectors, and Revenue Agents	Bachelor's degree	$51,120	-6%	-420

Finance and insurance $37,450
Wholesale trade 36,840
Healthcare and social assistance 36,130
Retail trade 31,980

Job Outlook

Employment of bookkeeping, accounting, and auditing clerks is projected to decline 8 percent from 2014 to 2024.

Technological change is expected to reduce demand for these workers. Software improvements, such as cloud computing, have automated many of the tasks performed by bookkeepers. As a result, bookkeepers will increasingly be hired on a contract basis through third-party bookkeeping firms, rather than being held on staff.

Demand for bookkeeping is tied particularly to the growth of small businesses, which tend to hire bookkeepers rather than accountants due to their relatively lower cost. Therefore, economic growth should create some openings for bookkeepers to keep these organizations' financial records.

Job Prospects. Because bookkeeping, accounting, and auditing clerks make up a large occupation, there will be a large number of job openings from workers leaving the occupation. Thus, opportunities to enter the occupation should be plentiful.

Contacts for More Information

For more information about bookkeeping, accounting, and auditing clerks, visit

➤ American Institute of Professional Bookkeepers (www.aipb.org)
➤ National Association of Certified Public Bookkeepers (www.nacpb.org)

O*NET

➤ Bookkeeping, Accounting, and Auditing Clerks (43-3031.00)

Customer Service Representatives

- **2014 Median Pay** .... $31,200 per year, $15.00 per hour
- **Typical Entry-Level Education** .... High school diploma or equivalent
- **Work Experience in a Related Occupation** .... None
- **On-the-job Training** .... Short-term on-the-job training
- **Number of Jobs, 2014** 2,581,800
- **Job Outlook, 2014–24** .... 10% (Faster than average)
- **Employment Change, 2014–24** 252,900

What Customer Service Representatives Do

Customer service representatives interact with customers to handle complaints, process orders, and provide information about an organization's products and services.

Duties. Customer service representatives typically do the following:

- Listen to customers' questions and concerns, and provide answers or responses
- Provide information about products and services
- Take orders, calculate charges, and process billing or payments
- Review or make changes to customer accounts
- Handle returns or complaints
- Record details of customer contacts and actions taken
- Refer customers to supervisors or more experienced employees

Customer service representatives answer questions or requests from customers or the public. They typically provide services by phone, but some also interact with customers face to face, by email, or live chat.

The specific duties of customer service representatives vary by industry. For example, representatives who work in banks may answer customers' questions about their accounts. Representatives

Good communication and problem-solving skills are essential for customer service representatives.

who work for utility and communication companies may help customers with service problems, such as outages. Those who work in retail stores often handle returns, process refunds, and help customers locate items. Some representatives make changes to customers' accounts, such as updating addresses or canceling orders. Although selling is not their main job, some representatives may help generate sales while providing information about a product or service.

Customer service representatives typically use a telephone, computer, and other office equipment. For example, representatives who work in call centers answer phone calls and use computers to review and select standard responses from a list of options. Those employed in retail stores use registers to process returns or orders.

Work Environment

Customer service representatives held about 2.6 million jobs in 2014. The industries that employed the most customer service representatives were as follows:

Administrative and support services	18%
Retail trade	12
Insurance carriers and related activities	12
Monetary authorities, credit intermediation, and related activities	9

Customer service representatives are employed in nearly every industry. Many work in telephone call centers, credit and insurance agencies, banks, and retail stores.

Representatives usually work in an office setting, sharing a large room with other employees. As a result, the work area can be crowded and noisy. Some workers may be under pressure to answer a designated number of calls while supervisors monitor them for quality assurance. In addition, the work can sometimes be stressful when they interact with dissatisfied customers.

In retail stores, representatives may spend hours on their feet assisting customers in person.

Work Schedules. Although most customer service representatives work full time, about 1 in 5 worked part time in 2014.

Positions in call centers may require early morning or late night shifts because some are open 24 hours a day. Weekend or holiday work is also common.

In retail stores, customer service representatives are often needed to work during busy times, such as evenings, weekends, and holidays. Some companies hire additional workers during the holiday season when more customers are expected.

Education/Training

Customer service representatives typically need a high school diploma and receive on-the-job training to learn the specific skills needed for the job. They should be good at communicating and interacting with people and have some experience using computers.

Education. Customer service representatives typically need a high school diploma.

Training. Customer service representatives usually receive short-term on-the-job training, lasting 2 to 3 weeks. Those who work in finance and insurance may need several months of training to learn more complicated financial regulations.

General customer-service training may focus on procedures for answering questions, information about a company's products and services, and computer and telephone use. Trainees often work under the guidance of an experienced worker for the first few weeks of employment.

In certain industries, such as finance and insurance, customer service representatives must remain current with changing regulations.

Licenses, Certifications, and Registrations. Customer service representatives who provide information about finance and insurance may need a state license. Although licensing requirements vary by state, they usually include passing a written exam. Some employers and organizations may provide training for these exams.

Important Qualities

Communication skills. Customer service representatives must be able to provide information in writing, by phone, or in person so that customers can understand them.

Median Hourly Wages, May 2014

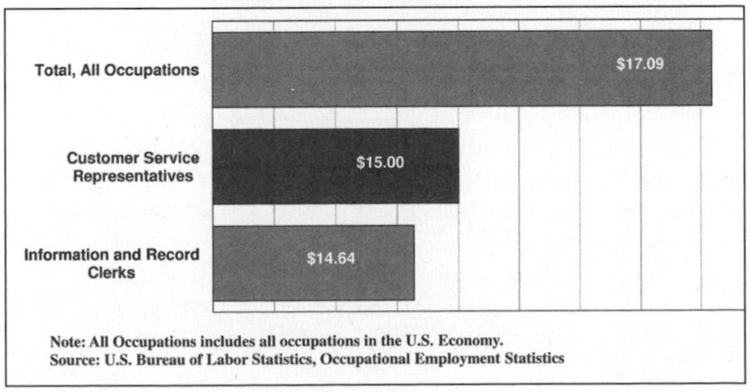

Percent Change in Employment, Projected 2014–2024

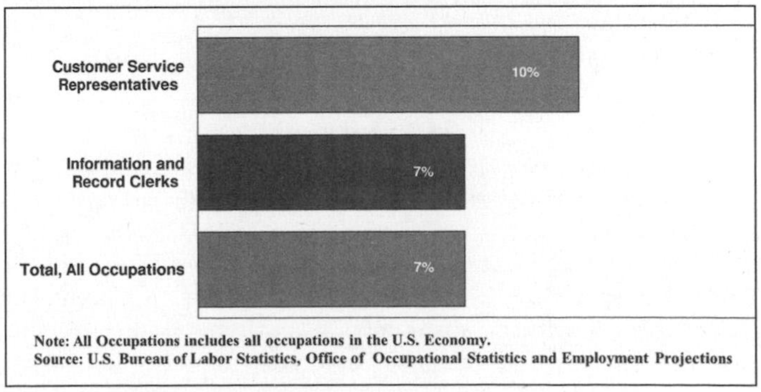

Employment Projections Data for Customer Service Representatives

Occupational Title	SOC Code	Employment, 2014	Projected Employment, 2024	Change, 2014–2024 Percent	Change, 2014–2024 Numeric
Customer service representatives	43-4051	2,581,800	2,834,800	10	252,900

Source: U.S. Bureau of Labor Statistics, Employment Projections Program

Similar Occupations. This table shows a list of occupations with job duties that are similar to those of customer service representatives.

Occupations	Entry-level Education	2014 Median Pay	Projected Job Growth	Average Annual Openings
Cashiers	No formal educational credential	$19,060	2%	6,700
Computer Support Specialists	See Education/Training	$50,380	12%	8,880
Financial Clerks	High school diploma or equivalent	$36,260	6%	8,930
Information Clerks	See Education/Training	$31,500	2%	2,580
Insurance Sales Agents	High school diploma or equivalent	$47,860	9%	4,350
Receptionists	High school diploma or equivalent	$26,760	10%	9,780
Retail Sales Workers	No formal educational credential	$21,670	7%	33,100
Tellers	High school diploma or equivalent	$25,760	-8%	-4,000
Wholesale and Manufacturing Sales Representatives	See Education/Training	$58,380	7%	11,720

Customer-service skills. Representatives help companies retain customers by answering their questions and complaints in a helpful and professional manner.

Interpersonal skills. Representatives should be able to create positive interactions with customers.

Listening skills. Representatives must listen carefully and understand a customer's situation in order to assist them.

Patience. Representatives should be patient and polite, especially when interacting with dissatisfied customers.

Problem-solving skills. Representatives must determine solutions to a customer's problem. By resolving issues effectively, representatives contribute to customer loyalty and retention.

Pay

The median hourly wage for customer service representatives was $15.00 in May 2014. The median wage is the wage at which half the workers in an occupation earned more than that amount and half earned less. The lowest 10 percent earned less than $9.55, and the highest 10 percent earned more than $24.82.

In May 2014, the median hourly wages for customer service representatives in the top industries in which they worked were as follows:

Insurance carriers and related activities	$16.69
Monetary authorities, credit intermediation, and related activities	15.57
Administrative and support services	12.94
Retail trade	11.82

Job Outlook

Employment of customer service representatives is projected to grow 10 percent from 2014 to 2024, faster than the average for all occupations.

Overall employment growth should result from growing industries that specialize in handling customer service. Specifically, telephone call centers, also known as customer contact centers, are expected to add the most new jobs for customer service representatives. Employment of representatives in these centers is projected to grow 39 percent from 2014 to 2024. Some businesses are increasingly contracting out their customer service operations to telephone call centers because they provide consolidated sales and customer service functions.

Employment growth of customer service representatives in all other industries will be driven by growth of those industries, as well as consumers' demand for products and services that require customer support. Some companies will continue to use in-house service centers to differentiate themselves from competitors, particularly for inquiries that are more complex, such as refunding accounts or confirming insurance coverage.

However, some companies are increasingly using Internet self-service or interactive voice-response systems that enable customers to resolve simple problems, such as changing addresses or reviewing account billing, without speaking to a representative.

In addition, some businesses are expected to move customer service functions to other countries in order to cut costs, a practice known as offshoring. However, demand for customer service representatives in the United States should continue as companies adjust to consumers' preference for U.S.-based customer support.

Job Prospects. Job prospects for customer service representatives are expected to be good because of the need to replace workers who leave the occupation.

Contacts for More Information

For more information about customer service representatives, visit

➤ International Customer Management Institute (www.icmi.com)

For more information about training and certification in the insurance industry, visit

➤ National Alliance for Insurance Research and Education (www.scic.com)

O*NET

➤ Customer Service Representatives (43-4051.00)

➤ Patient Representatives (43-4051.03)

Desktop Publishers

- **2014 Median Pay** .... $38,200 per year
  $18.37 per hour
- **Typical Entry-Level Education** .... Associate's degree
- **Work Experience in a Related Occupation**.............. None
- **On-the-job Training** .... Short-term on-the-job training
- **Number of Jobs, 2014** 14,800
- **Job Outlook, 2014–24** .... -21% (Decline)
- **Employment Change, 2014–24** .... -3,100

Desktop publishers format text, data, photographs, and other graphics into documents that are to be printed.

What Desktop Publishers Do

Desktop publishers use computer software to design page layouts for newspapers, books, brochures, and other items that are printed or published online.

Duties. Desktop publishers typically do the following:

- Review text, graphics, or other materials created by writers and designers
- Edit graphics, such as photographs or illustrations
- Import text and graphics into publishing software
- Integrate images and text to create cohesive pages
- Adjust text properties, such as size, column width, and spacing
- Revise layouts and make corrections as necessary
- Submit or upload final files for printing or online publishing

Desktop publishers use publishing software to create page layouts for print or electronic publication. They may edit text by correcting its spelling, punctuation, and grammar.

Desktop publishers often work with other design, media, or marketing workers, including writers, editors, and graphic designers. For example, they work with graphic designers to come up with images that complement the text and fit the available space.

Work Environment

Desktop publishers held about 14,800 jobs in 2014. The industries that employed the most desktop publishers were as follows:

Newspaper, periodical, book, and directory publishers	31%
Printing and related support activities	14
Professional, scientific, and technical services	12

About one-third of desktop publishers worked in publishing industries. Others worked for companies in industries that produce their own published materials, such as in professional, scientific, and technical services.

Work Schedules. Many desktop publishers work full time, and they may need to work additional hours to meet publication deadlines. Some may work various shifts, such as morning, evening, or night.

Education/Training

Desktop publishers usually need an associate's degree, and they also receive short-term on-the-job training, lasting about 1 month.

Education. Desktop publishers usually need an associate's degree, often in graphic design, graphic arts, or graphic communications. Community colleges and technical schools offer desktop-publishing courses, which teach students how to create electronic page layouts and format text and graphics with the use of desktop-publishing software.

Training. Desktop publishers typically receive short-term on-the-job training lasting about 1 month. They learn by working closely with more experienced workers or by taking classes that teach them how to use desktop-publishing software. Workers often need to continue training because publishing software changes over time.

Important Qualities

Artistic ability. Desktop publishers must have a good eye for how graphics and text will look, so that they can create pages that are visually appealing and legible.

Median Annual Wages, May 2014

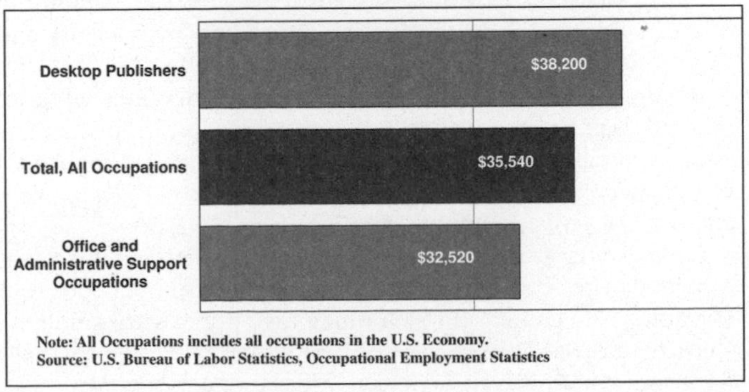

Percent Change in Employment, Projected 2014–2024

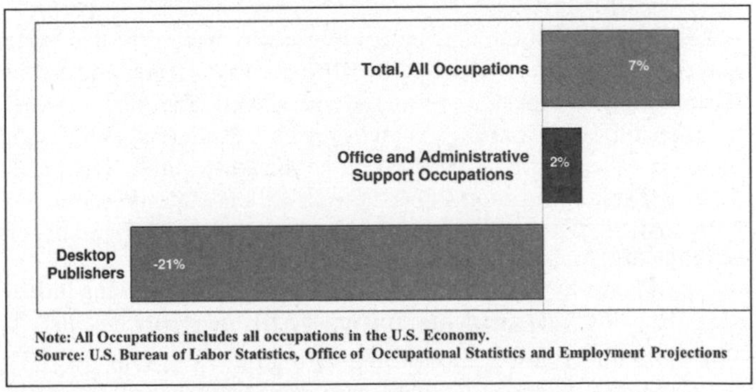

Employment Projections Data for Desktop Publishers

Occupational Title	SOC Code	Employment, 2014	Projected Employment, 2024	Change, 2014–2024	
				Percent	Numeric
Desktop publishers	43-9031	14,800	11,700	-21	-3,100

Source: U.S. Bureau of Labor Statistics, Employment Projections Program

Similar Occupations. This table shows a list of occupations with job duties that are similar to those of desktop publishers.

Occupations	Entry-level Education	2014 Median Pay	Projected Job Growth	Average Annual Openings
Editors	Bachelor's degree	$54,890	-5%	-620
Film and Video Editors and Camera Operators	Bachelor's degree	$52,470	11%	640
Graphic Designers	Bachelor's degree	$45,900	1%	360
Multimedia Artists and Animators	Bachelor's degree	$63,630	6%	390
Technical Writers	Bachelor's degree	$69,030	10%	530

Communication skills. Desktop publishers must be able to collaborate with others, such as writers, editors, and graphic designers, and communicate ideas effectively.

Detail oriented. Desktop publishers must pay attention to details such as margins, font sizes, and the overall appearance and accuracy of their work.

Organizational skills. Desktop publishers often work under strict deadlines and must be good at scheduling and prioritizing tasks in order to have documents ready in time for publication.

Other Experience. Many employers prefer to hire workers who have experience preparing layouts and using desktop-publishing software. Students may gain experience by working on a publication for a school or other organization.

Pay

The median annual wage for desktop publishers was $38,200 in May 2014. The median wage is the wage at which half the workers in an occupation earned more than that amount and half earned less. The lowest 10 percent earned less than $20,780, and the highest 10 percent earned more than $65,650.

In May 2014, the median annual wages for desktop publishers in the top industries in which they worked were as follows:

Professional, scientific, and technical services	$43,520
Printing and related support activities	38,340
Newspaper, periodical, book, and directory publishers	34,080

Job Outlook

Employment of desktop publishers is projected to decline 21 percent from 2014 to 2024.

Desktop publishing is commonly used to design printed materials, such as advertisements, brochures, newsletters, and forms. Companies are expected to hire fewer desktop publishers, however, as other types of workers—such as graphic designers, web designers, and editors—increasingly perform desktop-publishing tasks.

As organizations increasingly publish their materials electronically instead of printing them, employment of desktop publishers may decline further.

Contacts for More Information

For more information about the printing industry, visit

➤ Printing Industries of America (www.printing.org)

O*NET

➤ Desktop Publishers (43-9031.00)

Financial Clerks

- **2014 Median Pay** .... $36,260 per year, $17.44 per hour
- **Typical Entry-Level Education** .... High school diploma or equivalent
- **Work Experience in a Related Occupation** .... None
- **On-the-job Training** .... See Education/Training
- **Number of Jobs, 2014** 1,426,500
- **Job Outlook, 2014–24** .... 6% (As fast as average)
- **Employment Change, 2014–24** 89,300

What Financial Clerks Do

Financial clerks do administrative work for many types of organizations. They keep records, help customers, and carry out financial transactions.

Duties. Financial clerks typically do the following:

- Keep and update financial records
- Compute bills and charges
- Offer customer assistance
- Carry out financial transactions

Financial clerks give administrative and clerical support in financial settings. Their specific job duties vary by specialty and by setting.

Billing and posting clerks calculate charges, develop bills, and prepare them to be mailed to customers. They review documents such as purchase orders, sales tickets, charge slips, and hospital records to compute fees or charges due. They also contact customers to get or give account information.

Gaming cage workers work in casinos and other gaming establishments. The "cage" in which they work is the central depository for money and gaming chips. Gaming cage workers sell gambling chips, tokens, or tickets to patrons. They count funds and reconcile daily summaries of transactions in order to balance books.

Payroll and timekeeping clerks compile and post employee time and payroll data. They verify and record attendance, hours worked, and pay adjustments. They ensure that employees are paid on time and that their paychecks are accurate.

Procurement clerks compile requests for materials, prepare purchase orders, keep track of purchases and supplies, and handle questions about orders. They respond to questions from customers and suppliers about the status of orders. They handle requests to change or cancel orders. They make sure that purchases arrive on schedule and that the items meet the purchaser's specifications.

Brokerage clerks help with tasks associated with securities such as stocks, bonds, commodities, and other kinds of investments. Their duties include writing orders for stock purchases and sales, computing transfer taxes, verifying stock transactions, accepting and delivering securities, distributing dividends, and keeping records of daily transactions and holdings.

Credit authorizers, checkers, and clerks review the credit history, and get the information needed to determine the creditworthiness, of individuals or businesses applying for credit. Credit authorizers evaluate customers' computerized credit records and payment histories to decide, based on predetermined standards, whether to approve new credit. Credit checkers call or write credit departments of business and service establishments to get information about applicants' credit standing.

Loan interviewers, also called *loan processors* or *loan clerks*, interview applicants and others to get and verify personal and financial information needed to complete loan applications. They also prepare the documents that go to the appraiser and are issued at the closing of a loan.

New accounts clerks interview people who want to open accounts in financial institutions. They explain the account services available to prospective customers and help them fill out applications. They also investigate and correct errors in accounts.

Insurance claims and policy processing clerks process applications for insurance policies. They also handle customers' requests to change or cancel their existing policies. Their duties include interviewing clients and reviewing insurance applications to ensure that all questions have been answered. They also notify insurance agents and accounting departments of policy cancellations or changes.

Work Environment

Financial clerks held about 1.4 million jobs in 2014. The industries that employed the most financial clerks were as follows:

Insurance carriers and related activities	20%
Credit intermediation and related activities	18
Healthcare and social assistance	17
Professional, scientific, and technical services	7

Financial clerks work in a variety of office settings, including bank branches, medical offices, and government agencies.

Work Schedules. Most financial clerks work full time.

Education/Training

A high school diploma or equivalent is typically required for most financial clerk jobs. These workers usually learn their duties through on-the-job training.

Education. Financial clerks typically need a high school diploma or equivalent to enter the occupation. Employers of brokerage

Median Annual Wages, May 2014

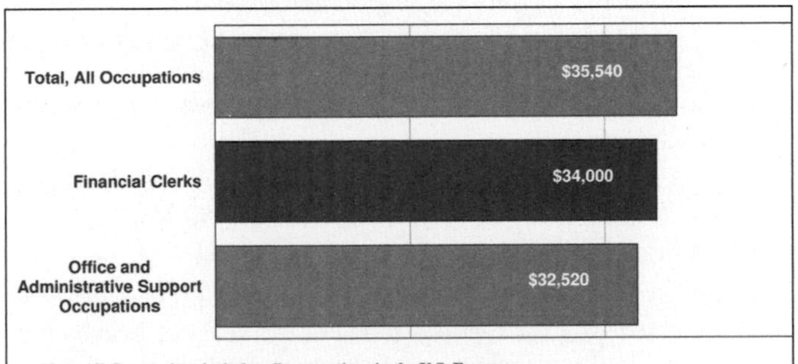

Note: All Occupations includes all occupations in the U.S. Economy.
Source: U.S. Bureau of Labor Statistics, Occupational Employment Statistics

Percent Change in Employment, Projected 2014–2024

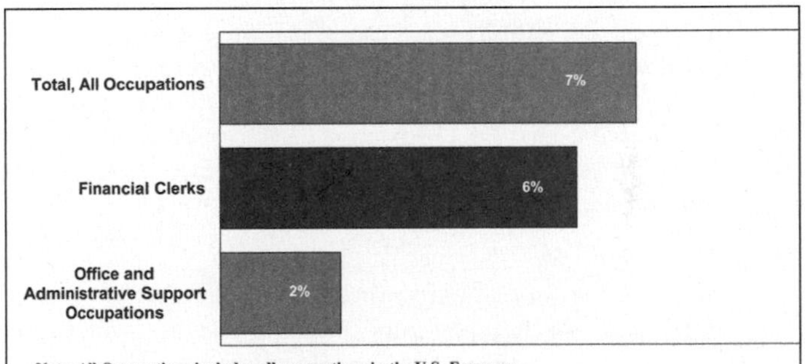

Note: All Occupations includes all occupations in the U.S. Economy.
Source: U.S. Bureau of Labor Statistics, Office of Occupational Statistics and Employment Projections

Employment Projections Data for Financial Clerks

Occupational Title	SOC Code	Employment, 2014	Projected Employment, 2024	Change, 2014–2024 Percent	Change, 2014–2024 Numeric
Financial clerks	—	1,426,500	1,515,900	6	89,300
Billing and posting clerks	43-3021	514,600	581,100	13	66,500
Gaming cage workers	43-3041	11,300	11,900	5	600
Payroll and timekeeping clerks	43-3051	172,800	166,900	-3	-5,900
Procurement clerks	43-3061	72,300	66,300	-8	-6,000
Brokerage clerks	43-4011	57,200	62,400	9	5,200
Credit authorizers, checkers, and clerks	43-4041	46,100	43,300	-6	-2,800
Loan interviewers and clerks	43-4131	213,800	232,300	9	18,500
New accounts clerks	43-4141	52,900	48,600	-8	-4,300
Insurance claims and policy processing clerks	43-9041	285,400	303,100	6	17,700

Source: U.S. Bureau of Labor Statistics, Employment Projections Program

Gaming cage workers exchange tickets and chips for money.

clerks may prefer candidates who have taken some college courses in business or economics and, in some cases, require a 2- or 4-year college degree.

Training. Most financial clerks learn how to do their job duties through on-the-job training. Some formal technical training also may be necessary; for example, gaming cage workers may need training in specific gaming regulations and procedures.

Advancement. Financial clerks can advance to related occupations in finance. For example, a loan interviewer or clerk can become a loan officer, and a brokerage clerk can become a securities, commodities, or financial services sales agent, after obtaining the required education and license.

Important Qualities

Communication skills. Financial clerks should have good communication skills so that they can explain policies and procedures to colleagues and customers.

Math skills. The job duties of financial clerks, including calculating charges and checking credit scores, require basic math skills.

Organizational skills. Strong organizational skills are important for financial clerks because they must be able to find files quickly and efficiently.

Pay

The median annual wage for financial clerks was $36,260 in May 2014. The median wage is the wage at which half the workers in an occupation earned more than that amount and half earned less. The lowest 10 percent earned less than $24,820, and the highest 10 percent earned more than $54,720.

Median annual wages for financial clerks in May 2014 were as follows:

Brokerage clerks	$47,520
Procurement clerks	39,930
Payroll and timekeeping clerks	39,700
Loan interviewers and clerks	36,880
Insurance claims and policy processing clerks	36,740
Credit authorizers, checkers, and clerks	34,550
Billing and posting clerks	34,410
New accounts clerks	34,000
Gaming cage workers	25,810

Job Outlook

Employment of financial clerks is projected to grow 6 percent from 2014 to 2024, about as fast as the average for all occupations. Projected employment change will vary by specialty as follows:

- Employment of billing and posting clerks is projected to grow 13 percent. Job growth is anticipated to be particularly strong for those in medical billing because increased demand for healthcare services will require more of these workers.
- Employment of loan interviewers and clerks is projected to grow 9 percent. Tighter lending standards and regulations will create demand for workers whose job is to verify the accuracy of loan applications. However, the use of online loan applications will somewhat reduce the need for these workers to conduct in-person interviews.
- Employment of brokerage clerks is projected to grow 9 percent. The automation of securities transactions will lead to slower growth for these workers.
- Employment of insurance claims and policy processing clerks is projected to grow 6 percent. These workers are heavily concentrated in the insurance industry; therefore, their job growth will be determined mainly by the performance of the insurance industry as a whole.

Similar Occupations. This table shows a list of occupations with job duties that are similar to those of financial clerks.

Occupations	Entry-level Education	2014 Median Pay	Projected Job Growth	Average Annual Openings
Bill and Account Collectors	High school diploma or equivalent	$33,700	-6%	-1,960
Bookkeeping, Accounting, and Auditing Clerks	Some college, no degree	$36,430	-8%	-14,870
Gaming Services Workers	High school diploma or equivalent	$19,940	1%	100
Information Clerks	See Education/Training	$31,500	2%	2,580
Medical Records and Health Information Technicians	Postsecondary nondegree award	$35,900	15%	2,900
Secretaries and Administrative Assistants	High school diploma or equivalent	$35,970	3%	11,880
Tellers	High school diploma or equivalent	$25,760	-8%	-4,000

- Employment of gaming cage workers is projected to grow 5 percent. Employment may grow as more state-owned casinos open and the private gaming industry expands.
- Employment of payroll and timekeeping clerks is projected to decline 3 percent. The automation of this work and the use of computer software that allows employees to update and record their own payroll and timekeeping information will reduce demand for these workers.
- Employment of credit authorizers, checkers, and clerks is projected to decline 6 percent. The availability of online credit reports will reduce the need for these workers.
- Employment of procurement clerks is projected to decline 8 percent. The need for procurement clerks may be limited because of the increasing use of the Internet to place orders, a situation which means that fewer procurement clerks will be required to handle the same number of orders.
- Employment of new accounts clerks is projected to decline 8 percent. There is less of a need for these workers because many customers can now open accounts online.

Job Prospects. Job prospects for financial clerks are likely to be favorable, because many workers are expected to leave this occupation. Employers will need to hire new workers to replace those leaving the occupation.

Contacts for More Information

For more information about financial clerks, visit

➤ American Bankers Association (www.aba.com)
➤ Mortgage Bankers Association (www.mba.org)

O*NET

➤ Billing and Posting Clerks (43-3021.00)
➤ Statement Clerks (43-3021.01)
➤ Billing, Cost, and Rate Clerks (43-3021.02)
➤ Gaming Cage Workers (43-3041.00)
➤ Payroll and Timekeeping Clerks (43-3051.00)
➤ Procurement Clerks (43-3061.00)
➤ Brokerage Clerks (43-4011.00)
➤ Credit Authorizers, Checkers, and Clerks (43-4041.00)
➤ Credit Authorizers (43-4041.01)
➤ Credit Checkers (43-4041.02)
➤ Loan Interviewers and Clerks (43-4131.00)
➤ New Accounts Clerks (43-4141.00)
➤ Insurance Claims and Policy Processing Clerks (43-9041.00)
➤ Insurance Claims Clerks (43-9041.01)
➤ Insurance Policy Processing Clerks (43-9041.02)

General Office Clerks

- **2014 Median Pay** .... $28,670 per year
$13.78 per hour
- **Typical Entry-Level Education** .... High school diploma or equivalent
- **Work Experience in a Related Occupation** .... None
- **On-the-job Training** .... Short-term on-the-job training
- **Number of Jobs, 2014** 3,062,500
- **Job Outlook, 2014–24** .... 3% (Slower than average)
- **Employment Change, 2014–24** 95,800

What General Office Clerks Do

General office clerks perform a variety of clerical tasks, including answering telephones, typing documents, and filing records.

Duties. General office clerks typically do the following:

- Answer and transfer telephone calls or take messages
- Sort and deliver incoming mail and send outgoing mail
- Schedule appointments and receive customers or visitors
- Provide general information to staff, clients, or the public
- Type, format, or edit routine memos or other reports
- Copy, file, and update paper and electronic documents
- Prepare and process bills and other office documents
- Collect information and perform data entry

Rather than performing a single specialized task, general office clerks have responsibilities that often change daily with the current needs of the employer.

Some clerks file documents or answer phones; others enter data into computers or perform other tasks using software applications. They also frequently use photocopiers, scanners, fax machines, and other office equipment.

The specific duties assigned to clerks will depend on the type of office in which they work. For example, a general office clerk at a college or university processes application materials and answers questions from prospective students. A clerk at a hospital files and retrieves medical records.

Work Environment

General office clerks held about 3.1 million jobs in 2014. The industries that employed the most general office clerks were as follows:

General office clerks operate photocopiers, fax machines, and other office equipment.

Median Hourly Wages, May 2014

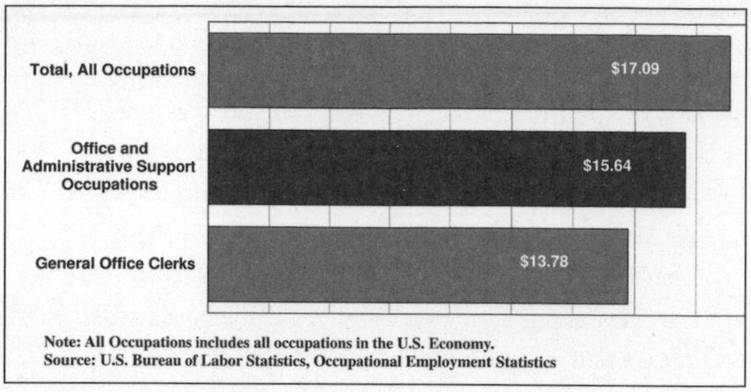

Percent Change in Employment, Projected 2014–2024

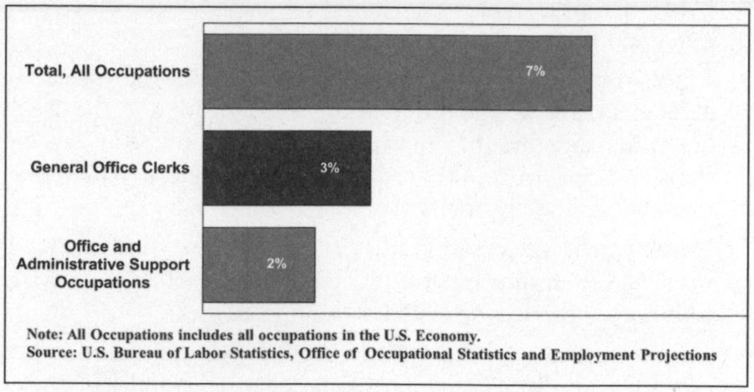

Healthcare and social assistance	12%
Educational services; state, local, and private	12
Administrative and support services	10
Government	9

General office clerks usually work in office settings.

Work Schedules. Many general office clerks work full time. About 1 in 4 clerks worked part time in 2014.

Education/Training

General office clerks typically need a high school diploma or equivalent and learn their skills on the job.

Education. Courses in using computer applications, such as word processing and spreadsheet software, may be particularly helpful.

Training. General office clerks usually learn their skills while on the job. Their training typically lasts up to 1 month and may include instructions on office procedures, proper phone etiquette, and the use of office equipment.

Advancement. General office clerks may advance to other administrative positions with more responsibility, such as executive secretaries and executive administrative assistants.

Advancement opportunities often depend on work experience and the knowledge of computer applications, such as word processing and spreadsheet software.

Important Qualities

Customer-service skills. Clerks often provide general information to company staff, customers, or the public. They should be courteous and prompt with their responses.

Detail oriented. Clerks perform many clerical tasks, such as preparing bills that require attention to detail.

Organizational skills. Office clerks file and retrieve records. They need to keep records organized to be able to access them quickly and efficiently.

Pay

The median hourly wage for general office clerks was $13.78 in May 2014. The median wage is the wage at which half the workers in an occupation earned more than that amount and half earned less. The lowest 10 percent earned less than $8.79, and the highest 10 percent earned more than $22.54.

In May 2014, the median hourly wages for general office clerks in the top industries in which they worked were as follows:

Government	$15.67
Healthcare and social assistance	13.95
Educational services; state, local, and private	13.58
Administrative and support services	12.82

Job Outlook

Employment of general office clerks is projected to grow 3 percent from 2014 to 2024, slower than the average for all occupations. Employment growth will vary by industry.

For example, healthcare facilities are expected to require more workers to handle administrative tasks related to billing and insurance processing as more people have access to health insurance and medical services. Additionally, further demand for clerical support in these facilities is expected as more baby boomers become eligible for Social Security and Medicare. Conversely, employment of general office clerks in government is projected to decline, as other workers are increasingly performing tasks that general office clerks used to do.

Some tasks of office clerks have been affected by technology. For example, many organizations maintain electronic documents or use automated phone systems, reducing the need for some general office clerks.

Job Prospects. Job prospects are expected to be good because of the need to replace workers who leave the occupation. Candidates who have a combination of work experience and knowledge of computer applications should have the best job prospects.

Contacts for More Information

For more information about administrative occupations, visit

➤ International Association of Administrative Professionals (www.iaap-hq.org)

O*NET

➤ Office Clerks, General (43-9061.00)

Employment Projections Data for General Office Clerks

Occupational Title	SOC Code	Employment, 2014	Projected Employment, 2024	Change, 2014–2024 Percent	Change, 2014–2024 Numeric
Office clerks, general	43-9061	3,062,500	3,158,200	3	95,800

Source: U.S. Bureau of Labor Statistics, Employment Projections Program

Similar Occupations. This table shows a list of occupations with job duties that are similar to those of general office clerks.

Occupations	Entry-level Education	2014 Median Pay	Projected Job Growth	Average Annual Openings
Bookkeeping, Accounting, and Auditing Clerks	Some college, no degree	$36,430	-8%	-14,870
Customer Service Representatives	High school diploma or equivalent	$31,200	10%	25,290
Information Clerks	See Education/Training	$31,500	2%	2,580
Material Recording Clerks	See Education/Training	$25,810	3%	8,470
Receptionists	High school diploma or equivalent	$26,760	10%	9,780
Secretaries and Administrative Assistants	High school diploma or equivalent	$35,970	3%	11,880

Information Clerks

- **2014 Median Pay** .... $31,500 per year
  $15.14 per hour
- **Typical Entry-Level Education** .... See Education/Training
- **Work Experience in a Related Occupation**.............. None
- **On-the-job Training** .... See Education/Training
- **Number of Jobs, 2014** 1,545,000
- **Job Outlook, 2014–24** .... 2% (Slower than average)
- **Employment Change, 2014–24** 25,800

What Information Clerks Do

Information clerks perform routine clerical duties such as maintaining records, collecting data, and providing information to customers.

Duties. Information clerks typically do the following:

- Prepare routine reports, claims, bills, or orders
- Collect and record data from customers, staff, and the public
- Answer questions from customers and the public about products or services
- File and maintain paper or electronic records

Information clerks perform routine office support functions in an organization, business, or government. They use telephones, computers, and other office equipment such as scanners and fax machines.

Correspondence clerks respond to inquiries from the public or customers. They prepare standard responses to requests for merchandise, damage claims, delinquent accounts, incorrect billings, or complaints about unsatisfactory services. They also may review the organization's records and type response letters for their supervisors to sign.

Court clerks organize and maintain court records. They prepare the calendar of cases, also known as the docket, and inform attorneys and witnesses about court appearances. Court clerks also receive, file, and forward court documents.

Eligibility interviewers conduct interviews both in person and over the phone to determine if applicants qualify for government assistance and benefits. They answer applicants' questions about programs and may refer them to other agencies for assistance.

File clerks maintain electronic or paper records. They enter and retrieve data, organize records, and file documents. In organizations with electronic filing systems, file clerks scan and upload documents.

Hotel, motel, and resort desk clerks, also called *front desk clerks*, provide customer service to guests at the establishment's front desk. They check guests in and out, assign rooms, and process payments. They also keep occupancy records; take, confirm, or change room reservations; and provide information on the hotel's policies and services. In addition, front desk clerks answer phone calls, take and deliver messages for guests, and handle guests' requests and complaints. For example, when guests report problems in their rooms, clerks coordinate with maintenance staff to resolve the issue.

Human resources assistants provide administrative support to human resources managers. They maintain personnel records on employees, including their addresses, employment history, and performance evaluations. They may post information about job openings and compile candidates' resumes for review.

Interviewers conduct interviews over the phone, in person, through mail, or online. They use the information to complete forms, applications, or questionnaires for market research surveys, census forms, and medical histories. Interviewers typically follow set procedures and questionnaires to obtain specific information.

License clerks process applications for licenses and permits, administer tests, and collect application fees. They determine if applicants are qualified to receive particular licenses or if additional documentation needs to be submitted. They also maintain records of applications received and licenses issued.

Hotel, motel, and resort desk clerks provide customer service to hotel guests and other customers often at the hotel's front desk.

Median Annual Wages, May 2014

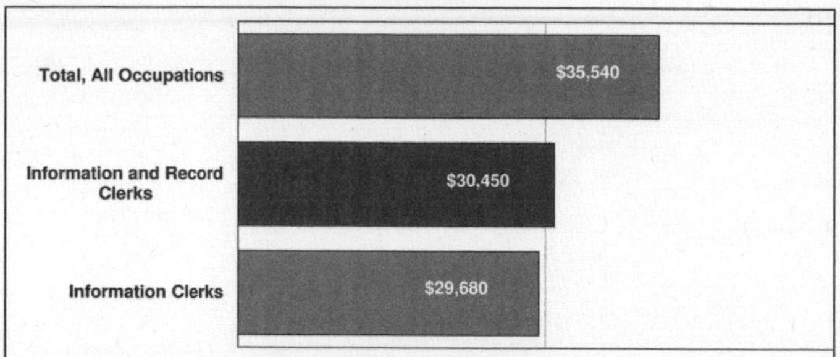

Note: All Occupations includes all occupations in the U.S. Economy.
Source: U.S. Bureau of Labor Statistics, Occupational Employment Statistics

Percent Change in Employment, Projected 2014–2024

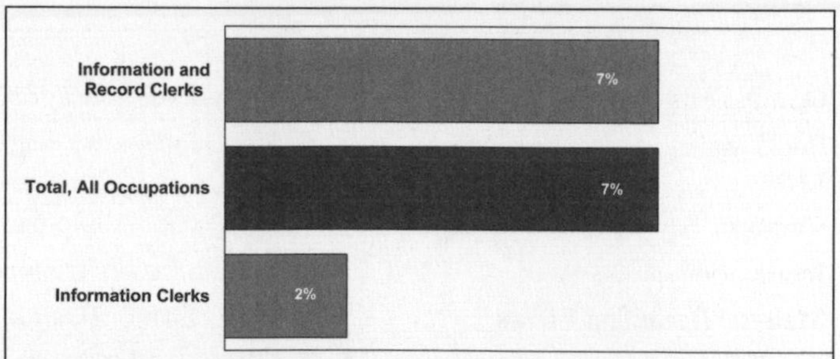

Note: All Occupations includes all occupations in the U.S. Economy.
Source: U.S. Bureau of Labor Statistics, Office of Occupational Statistics and Employment Projections

Municipal clerks provide administrative support for town or city governments by maintaining government records. They record, maintain, and distribute minutes of town and city council meetings to local officials and staff and help prepare for elections. They also may answer requests for information from local, state, and federal officials and the public.

Order clerks receive orders from customers and process payments. For example, they may enter customer information, such as addresses and payment methods, into the order entry system. They also answer questions about prices and shipping.

Reservation and transportation ticket agents and travel clerks take and confirm passengers' reservations for hotels and transportation. They also sell and issue tickets and answer questions about itineraries, rates, and package tours. Ticket agents who work at airports and railroads also check bags and issue boarding passes to passengers.

Work Environment

Information clerks held about 1.5 million jobs in 2014 and were employed in nearly every industry. However, employment was mostly concentrated in government agencies, hotels, and healthcare facilities.

Although most clerks work in an office setting, interviewers may travel to applicants' locations to interview them.

The work of information clerks who provide customer service can be stressful, particularly when dealing with dissatisfied customers.

Reservation and transportation ticket agents at airports or shipping counters lift and maneuver heavy luggage or packages, sometimes weighing up to 100 pounds.

Work Schedules. Most information clerks work full time. However, part-time work is common for hotel clerks, file clerks, and interviewers.

Clerks in lodging and transportation establishments that are open around the clock may work evenings, weekends, and holidays.

Injuries and Illnesses. Reservation and transportation ticket agents have a higher rate of injuries and illnesses than the national average. The most common injuries are muscle strains from lifting heavy suitcases.

Education/Training

Information clerks typically need a high school diploma and learn their skills on the job. Employers may prefer to hire candidates with some college education or an associate's degree, depending on the occupation.

Education. Candidates typically need a high school diploma for most positions. However, employers may prefer to hire candidates with some college education or an associate's degree. This is particularly true for eligibility interviewers, human resources assistants, and municipal clerks. Courses in social sciences, as well as word processing and spreadsheet applications, are particularly helpful.

Training. Most information clerks receive short-term on-the-job training, usually lasting a few weeks. Training typically covers clerical procedures and the use of computer applications. Those employed in government receive training that may last several

Employment Projections Data for Information Clerks

Occupational Title	SOC Code	Employment, 2014	Projected Employment, 2024	Change, 2014–2024	
				Percent	Numeric
Information clerks	—	1,545,000	1,570,800	2	25,800
Correspondence clerks	43-4021	8,400	7,200	-15	-1,200
Court, municipal, and license clerks	43-4031	140,800	147,100	4	6,300
Eligibility interviewers, government programs	43-4061	129,900	132,000	2	2,100
File clerks	43-4071	159,000	150,100	-6	-8,900
Hotel, motel, and resort desk clerks	43-4081	243,200	265,100	9	21,900
Interviewers, except eligibility and loan	43-4111	198,000	208,300	5	10,400
Order clerks	43-4151	195,900	194,300	-1	-1,500
Human resources assistants, except payroll and timekeeping	43-4161	140,600	134,800	-4	-5,800
Reservation and transportation ticket agents and travel clerks	43-4181	140,800	138,800	-1	-2,000
Information and record clerks, all other	43-4199	188,500	193,000	2	4,600

Source: U.S. Bureau of Labor Statistics, Employment Projections Program

Similar Occupations. This table shows a list of occupations with job duties that are similar to those of information clerks.

Occupations	Entry-level Education	2014 Median Pay	Projected Job Growth	Average Annual Openings
Bookkeeping, Accounting, and Auditing Clerks	Some college, no degree	$36,430	-8%	-14,870
Customer Service Representatives	High school diploma or equivalent	$31,200	10%	25,290
Financial Clerks	High school diploma or equivalent	$36,260	6%	8,930
General Office Clerks	High school diploma or equivalent	$28,670	3%	9,580
Human Resources Specialists	Bachelor's degree	$57,420	5%	2,200
Labor Relations Specialists	Bachelor's degree	$56,950	-8%	-640
Lodging Managers	High school diploma or equivalent	$47,680	8%	370
Material Recording Clerks	See Education/Training	$25,810	3%	8,470
Receptionists	High school diploma or equivalent	$26,760	10%	9,780

months and include learning about various government programs and regulations.

Advancement. Some information clerks may advance to other administrative positions with more responsibilities, such as office supervisor or office manager. With completion of a bachelor's degree, some human resources assistants may become human resources specialists.

Important Qualities

Communication skills. Information clerks must be able to explain policies and procedures clearly to customers and the public.

Integrity. Information clerks, particularly human resources assistants, have access to confidential information. They must be trusted to adhere to the applicable confidentiality and privacy rules governing the dissemination of this information.

Interpersonal skills. Information clerks who work with the public and customers must understand and communicate information effectively in order to establish positive relationships.

Organizational skills. Information clerks must be able to retrieve files and other important information quickly and efficiently.

Pay

The median annual wage for information clerks was $31,500 in May 2014. The median wage is the wage at which half the workers in an occupation earned more than that amount and half earned less. The lowest 10 percent earned less than $18,890, and the highest 10 percent earned more than $49,980.

Median annual wages for information clerks in May 2014 were as follows:

Eligibility interviewers, government programs	$42,200
Human resources assistants, except payroll and timekeeping	38,040
Information and record clerks, all other	37,700
Correspondence clerks	35,460
Court, municipal, and license clerks	35,460
Reservation and transportation ticket agents and travel clerks	33,510
Order clerks	31,180
Interviewers, except eligibility and loan	30,790
File clerks	27,580
Hotel, motel, and resort desk clerks	20,610

Job Outlook

Employment of information clerks is projected to grow 2 percent from 2014 to 2024, slower than the average for all occupations. Employment growth of information clerks will vary by occupation (see Employment Projections table).

Increased travel is expected to result in the demand for new hotels and other lodging establishments. Because customer service and hospitality are not easily automated, clerks will continue to provide services to guests in hotels.

As more baby boomers become eligible for Social Security and Medicare, demand for clerical support to handle eligibility requests will also increase. In addition, the number of individuals who have access to health insurance is expected to continue to increase because of federal health insurance reform, resulting in a greater need for office staff in healthcare facilities.

Despite the continued demand for information clerks, however, overall employment growth is expected to be limited as organizations and businesses consolidate their administrative functions. For example, businesses increasingly use online applications for benefits and employment, thereby streamlining the process and requiring fewer workers.

Furthermore, increased use of online ordering and reservations systems and self-service ticketing kiosks will result in the need for fewer clerks to process orders and maintain files. In some businesses, including medical offices, receptionists and other workers are increasingly performing tasks that used to be done by clerks.

Job Prospects. Overall job prospects should be good because of the need to replace workers who leave the occupation each year. Job opportunities are expected to be best in hotels and other lodging establishments.

Contacts for More Information

For more information about hotel, motel and resort desk clerks, visit

- American Hotel & Lodging Association (www.ahla.com)

For more information about human resources assistants, visit

- Society for Human Resource Management (www.shrm.org)

O*NET

- Correspondence Clerks (43-4021.00)
- Court, Municipal, and License Clerks (43-4031.00)
- Court Clerks (43-4031.01)
- Municipal Clerks (43-4031.02)
- License Clerks (43-4031.03)
- Eligibility Interviewers, Government Programs (43-4061.00)
- File Clerks (43-4071.00)
- Hotel, Motel, and Resort Desk Clerks (43-4081.00)
- Interviewers, Except Eligibility and Loan (43-4111.00)

- Order Clerks (43-4151.00)
- Human Resources Assistants, Except Payroll and Timekeeping (43-4161.00)
- Reservation and Transportation Ticket Agents and Travel Clerks (43-4181.00)
- Information and Record Clerks, All Other (43-4199.00)

Material Recording Clerks

- **2014 Median Pay** .... $25,810 per year $12.41 per hour
- **Typical Entry-Level Education**.... See Education/Training
- **Work Experience in a Related Occupation**.............. None
- **On-the-job Training** .... See Education/Training
- **Number of Jobs, 2014** 2,924,300
- **Job Outlook, 2014–24**............. 3% (Slower than average)
- **Employment Change, 2014–24** 84,700

What Material Recording Clerks Do

Material recording clerks track product information in order to keep businesses and supply chains on schedule. They ensure proper scheduling, recordkeeping, and inventory control.

Duties. Material recording clerks typically do the following:

- Keep records of items shipped, received, or transferred to another location
- Compile reports on various aspects of changes in production or inventory
- Find, sort, or move goods between different parts of the business
- Check inventory records for accuracy

Material recording clerks use computers, tablets, or hand-held devices to keep track of inventory. Sensors and tags enable these computers to automatically detect when and where products are moved, allowing clerks to keep updated reports without manually counting items.

Production, planning, and expediting clerks manage the flow of information, work, and materials within or among offices in a business. They compile reports on the progress of work and on any production problems that arise. These clerks set workers' schedules, estimate costs, keep track of materials, and write special orders for new materials. They perform general office tasks, such as entering data or distributing mail. Expediting clerks maintain contact with vendors to ensure that supplies and equipment are shipped on time.

Shipping, receiving, and traffic clerks keep track of and record outgoing and incoming shipments. Clerks may scan barcodes with hand-held devices or use radio frequency identification (RFID) scanners to keep track of inventory. They check if shipment orders were correctly processed in their company's computer system. They also compute freight costs and prepare invoices. Some clerks move goods from the warehouse to the loading dock.

Stock clerks and order fillers receive, unpack, and track merchandise. Stock clerks move products from a warehouse to store shelves. They keep a record of items that enter or leave the stockroom and inspect for damaged goods. These clerks also use hand-held scanners to keep track of merchandise. Order fillers retrieve customer orders and prepare them to be shipped.

Material and product inspecting clerks weigh, measure, check, sample, and keep records on materials, supplies, and equipment that enters a warehouse. They verify the quantity and quality of items they are assigned to examine, checking for defects and recording what they find. They use scales, counting devices, and calculators. Some workers decide what to do about a defective product, such as to scrap it or send it back to the factory to be repaired. Some clerks also prepare reports, such as reports about warehouse inventory levels.

Work Environment

Material recording clerks held about 2.9 million jobs in 2014.

Stock clerks and order fillers held about 1.9 million jobs in 2014. About 69 percent worked in retail trade, such as grocery and other general merchandise stores, and about 11 percent worked in wholesale trade.

Shipping, receiving, and traffic clerks held about 670,200 jobs in 2014. About 28 percent worked in manufacturing, and about 24 percent worked in wholesale trade.

Production, planning, and expediting clerks held about 304,600 jobs in 2014. About 36 percent worked in manufacturing, and about 9 percent worked in professional, scientific, and technical services.

Material and product inspecting clerks held about 71,300 jobs in 2014. About 20 percent worked in administrative and support services, and about 18 percent worked in manufacturing.

Shipping, receiving, and traffic clerks; production, planning, and expediting clerks; and material and product inspector clerks usually work in an office inside a warehouse or manufacturing plant.

Although shipping clerks and material inspecting clerks prepare reports in an office, they also spend time in the warehouse, where they sometimes handle packages or automatic equipment such as conveyor systems.

Stock clerks and order fillers usually work in retail settings and sometimes help customers. They move items from the back room to the store's shelves, a job that can involve frequent bending and lifting.

Work Schedules. Production, planning, and expediting clerks; shipping, receiving, and traffic clerks; and material and product inspecting clerks usually work full time. Some clerks work nights and weekends or holidays when large shipments arrive.

About 1 in 3 of stock clerks and order fillers worked part time in 2014. Evening and weekend work is common because they work when retail stores are open. They sometimes work overnight shifts when large shipments arrive or when it is time to take inventory.

Shipping clerks weigh orders for shipment.

Median Annual Wages, May 2014

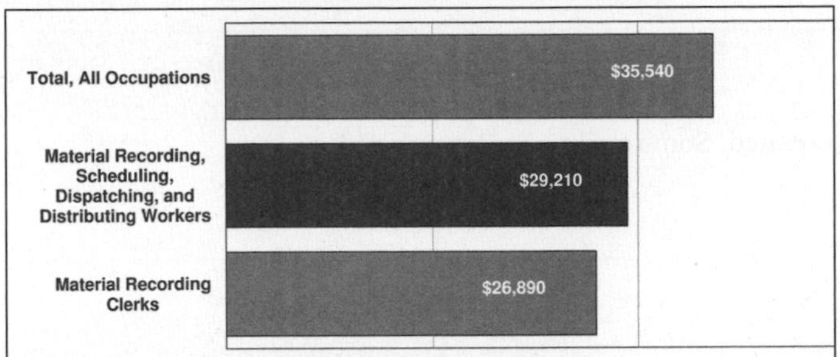

Note: All Occupations includes all occupations in the U.S. Economy.
Source: U.S. Bureau of Labor Statistics, Occupational Employment Statistics

Percent Change in Employment, Projected 2014–2024

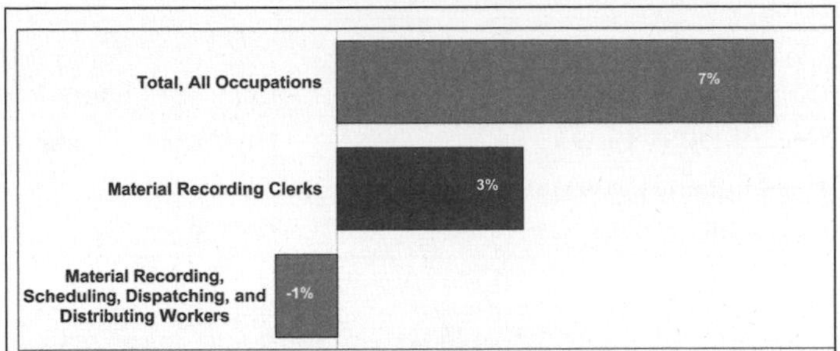

Note: All Occupations includes all occupations in the U.S. Economy.
Source: U.S. Bureau of Labor Statistics, Office of Occupational Statistics and Employment Projections

Education/Training

Material recording clerks usually need to have a high school diploma and are trained on the job. There are no formal education requirements for stock clerks and order fillers.

Education. Production, planning, and expediting clerks; shipping, receiving, and traffic clerks; and material and product inspecting clerks need a high school diploma or equivalent.

Production, planning, and expediting clerks need to have basic knowledge of computer applications such as spreadsheet software.

There are no formal education requirements for stock clerks and order fillers.

Training. Material recording clerks usually learn to do their work on the job. Training for most material recording clerks may last less than a month. Production, planning, and expediting clerks' training can take several months.

Typically, a supervisor or more experienced worker trains new clerks.

Material recording clerks first learn to count stock and mark inventory and then move onto more difficult tasks, such as recordkeeping. Production clerks need to learn how their company operates before they can write production and work schedules.

Advancement. With additional training or education, material recording clerks may advance to other positions within their firm, such as purchasing agent. Clerks in retail establishments can move into the sales department.

Important Qualities

Communication skills. Production, planning, and expediting clerks are frequently in contact with suppliers, vendors, and production managers and need to be able to communicate the firm's scheduling needs effectively.

Customer-service skills. Stock clerks sometimes interact with customers in retail stores and may have to get the item the customer is looking for from the storeroom.

Detail oriented. Material and product inspecting clerks check items for defects, some of which are small and difficult to spot.

Math skills. Some material recording clerks use math to calculate shipping costs or take measurements.

Pay

The median annual wage for material recording clerks was $25,810 in May 2014. The median wage is the wage at which half the workers in an occupation earned more than that amount and half earned less. The lowest 10 percent earned less than $17,680, and the highest 10 percent earned more than $46,700.

Median annual wages for material recording clerks in May 2014 were as follows:

Production, planning, and expediting clerks	$45,670
Shipping, receiving, and traffic clerks	29,930
Weighers, measurers, checkers, and samplers, recordkeeping	28,570
Stock clerks and order fillers	22,850

Job Outlook

Employment of material recording clerks is projected to grow 3 percent from 2014 to 2024, slower than the average for all occupations. Employment growth will vary by occupation (see Employment Projections table).

Although the increase in the use of radio frequency identification (RFID) tags should allow stock clerks to more quickly locate an item or count inventory in some retail stores, stocking shelves and filling orders will still require these workers.

In warehouses, both RFID tags and increased use of other technology, such as hand-held devices that read barcodes automatically, will affect shipping, receiving, and traffic clerks because these technologies should make it easier to keep track of material. The use of these technologies is expected to allow fewer clerks to do the same amount of work.

Employment Projections Data for Material Recording Clerks

Occupational Title	SOC Code	Employment, 2014	Projected Employment, 2024	Change, 2014–2024 Percent	Change, 2014–2024 Numeric
Material recording clerks	—	2,924,300	3,008,900	3	84,700
Production, planning, and expediting clerks	43-5061	304,600	310,900	2	6,300
Shipping, receiving, and traffic clerks	43-5071	670,200	655,700	-2	-14,500
Stock clerks and order fillers	43-5081	1,878,100	1,971,100	5	92,900
Weighers, measurers, checkers, and samplers, recordkeeping	43-5111	71,300	71,200	0	-100

Source: U.S. Bureau of Labor Statistics, Employment Projections Program

Similar Occupations. This table shows a list of occupations with job duties that are similar to those of material recording clerks.

Occupations	Entry-level Education	2014 Median Pay	Projected Job Growth	Average Annual Openings
General Office Clerks	High school diploma or equivalent	$28,670	3%	9,580
Hand Laborers and Material Movers	No formal educational credential	$23,560	5%	17,550
Information Clerks	See Education/Training	$31,500	2%	2,580

Technologies, such as barcodes, electronic and optical readers, and RFID tags, are expected to increase accuracy in shipping, thereby reducing the number of times a product needs to be weighed, checked, or measured. This reduction is expected to limit employment of material and product inspecting clerks.

Production, planning, and expediting clerks plan and schedule production and shipment processes, functions that remain difficult to substitute with technology.

Job Prospects. Job opportunities for material recording clerks will be very good because of the need to replace workers who leave these occupations. The increase in the use of RFID and other technologies will enable clerks who have experience using them to have better job prospects.

Contacts for More Information

For more information about material recording clerks, visit

- MHI (www.mhi.org)
- Warehousing Education and Research Council (www.werc.org)

O*NET

- Production, Planning, and Expediting Clerks (43-5061.00)
- Shipping, Receiving, and Traffic Clerks (43-5071.00)
- Stock Clerks and Order Fillers (43-5081.00)
- Stock Clerks, Sales Floor (43-5081.01)
- Marking Clerks (43-5081.02)
- Stock Clerks—Stockroom, Warehouse, or Storage Yard (43-5081.03)
- Order Fillers, Wholesale and Retail Sales (43-5081.04)
- Weighers, Measurers, Checkers, and Samplers, Recordkeeping (43-5111.00)

Police, Fire, and Ambulance Dispatchers

- **2014 Median Pay** .... $37,410 per year, $17.99 per hour
- **Typical Entry-Level Education** .... High school diploma or equivalent
- **Work Experience in a Related Occupation** .... None
- **On-the-job Training** .. Moderate-term on-the-job training
- **Number of Jobs, 2014** 102,000
- **Job Outlook, 2014–24** .... -3% (Decline)
- **Employment Change, 2014–24** .... -3,000

What Police, Fire, and Ambulance Dispatchers Do

Police, fire, and ambulance dispatchers, also called *public safety telecommunicators*, answer emergency and nonemergency calls.

Duties. Police, fire, and ambulance dispatchers typically do the following:

- Answer 9-1-1 emergency telephone and alarm system calls
- Determine the type of emergency and its location and decide the appropriate response on the basis of agency procedures
- Relay information to the appropriate first-responder agency
- Coordinate the dispatch of emergency response personnel to accident scenes
- Give basic over-the-phone medical instructions before emergency personnel arrive
- Provide advice to callers about how they may best stay safe while waiting for assistance
- Monitor and track the status of police, fire, and ambulance units
- Synchronize responses with other area communication centers
- Keep detailed records of calls

Dispatchers answer calls from people who need help from police, firefighters, emergency services, or a combination of the three. They take emergency, nonemergency, and alarm system calls.

Dispatchers must stay calm while collecting vital information from callers to determine the severity of a situation and the location of those who need help. They then communicate this information to the appropriate first-responder agencies.

Dispatchers keep detailed records of the calls that they answer. They use computers to log important facts, such as the nature of the incident and the caller's name and location. Most computer systems detect the location of cell phones and landline phones automatically.

Some dispatchers also use crime databases, maps, and weather reports to best prepare first responders for the situations they will encounter. Other dispatchers monitor alarm systems, alerting law enforcement or fire personnel when a crime or fire occurs. In some situations, dispatchers must work with people in other jurisdictions to share information and transfer calls.

Dispatchers often must instruct callers on what to do before responders arrive. Many dispatchers are trained to offer medical help over the phone. For example, they might help the caller to provide first aid at the scene until emergency medical services arrive.

Work Environment

Police, fire, and ambulance dispatchers held about 102,000 jobs in 2014.

About 81 percent of dispatchers worked for local governments in 2014, with the majority employed by law enforcement agencies and fire departments. Some dispatchers work for state governments or for private companies.

Dispatchers work in communication centers, often called public safety answering points (PSAPs).

Work as a dispatcher can be stressful. Dispatchers often work long shifts, take many calls, and deal with troubling situations. Some calls require them to assist people who are in life-threatening situations, and the pressure to respond quickly and calmly can be demanding.

Police, fire, and ambulance dispatchers work in a communication center, often called a public safety answering point (PSAP).

Work Schedules. Most dispatchers work 8- to 12-hour shifts, but some agencies require even longer ones. Overtime is common in this occupation.

Because emergencies can happen at any time, dispatchers are required to work some shifts during evenings, weekends, and holidays.

Education/Training

Most police, fire, and ambulance dispatchers have a high school diploma. Many states require dispatchers to have training and certification.

In addition, candidates must pass a written exam and a typing test. In some instances, applicants may need to pass a background check, lie detector and drug tests, and tests for hearing and vision.

Most states require dispatchers to be U.S. citizens, and some jobs require a driver's license. Experience using computers and in customer service can be helpful. The ability to speak Spanish is also desirable in this occupation.

Education. Most dispatchers are required to have a high school diploma.

Training. Training requirements vary by state. The Association of Public-Safety Communications Officials (APCO International) provides a list of states requiring training and certification.

Some states require 40 or more hours of initial training, and some require continuing education every 2 to 3 years. Other states do not mandate any specific training, leaving individual localities and agencies to structure their own requirements and conduct their own courses.

Some agencies have their own programs for certifying dispatchers; others use training from a professional association. The Association of Public-Safety Communications Officials (APCO International), the National Emergency Number Association (NENA), and the International Academies of Emergency Dispatch (IAED) have established a number of recommended standards and best practices that agencies often use as a guideline for their own training programs.

Training is usually conducted in a classroom and on the job, and is often followed by a probationary period of about 1 year. However, the period may vary by agency, as there is no national standard governing training or probation.

Training covers a wide variety of topics, such as local geography, agency protocols, and standard procedures. Dispatchers are also taught how to use specialized equipment, such as two-way radios and computer-aided dispatch software. Computer systems that dispatchers use consist of several monitors that display call information, maps, relevant criminal history, and video, depending on the location of the incident. Dispatchers often receive specialized training to prepare for high-risk incidents, such as child abductions and suicidal callers.

Licenses, Certifications, and Registrations. The Association of Public-Safety Communications Officials (APCO) provides a list of states requiring training and certification. One certification is the Emergency Medical Dispatcher (EMD) certification, which enables dispatchers to give medical assistance over the phone.

Dispatchers may choose to pursue additional certifications, such as the National Emergency Number Association's Emergency Number Professional (ENP) certification or APCO's Registered Public-Safety Leader (RPL) certification, which demonstrate their leadership skills and knowledge of the profession.

Advancement. Dispatchers can become senior dispatchers or supervisors before advancing to administrative positions, in which they may focus on a specific area, such as training, or on policy and procedures.

Training and certifications, such as emergency medical technician (EMT) training, can aid those looking to advance. Additional education and related work experience may be helpful in advancing to management-level positions.

Important Qualities

Ability to multitask. Dispatchers must stay calm in order to simultaneously answer calls, collect vital information, coordinate responders, use mapping software and camera feeds, and assist callers.

Median Annual Wages, May 2014

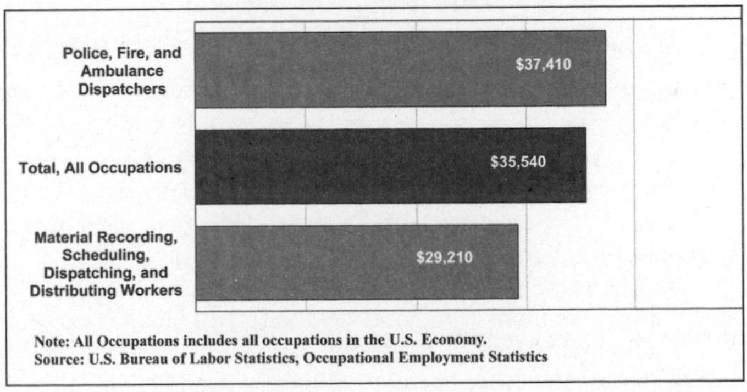

Note: All Occupations includes all occupations in the U.S. Economy.
Source: U.S. Bureau of Labor Statistics, Occupational Employment Statistics

Percent Change in Employment, Projected 2014–2024

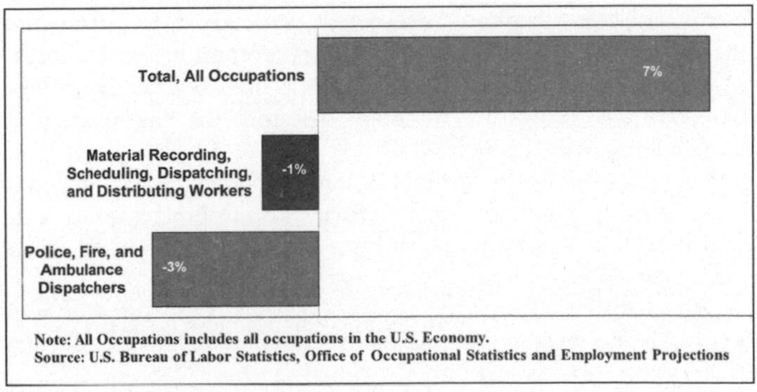

Note: All Occupations includes all occupations in the U.S. Economy.
Source: U.S. Bureau of Labor Statistics, Office of Occupational Statistics and Employment Projections

Employment Projections Data for Police, Fire, and Ambulance Dispatchers

Occupational Title	SOC Code	Employment, 2014	Projected Employment, 2024	Change, 2014–2024 Percent	Change, 2014–2024 Numeric
Police, fire, and ambulance dispatchers	43-5031	102,000	99,000	-3	-3,000

Source: U.S. Bureau of Labor Statistics, Employment Projections Program

Similar Occupations. This table shows a list of occupations with job duties that are similar to those of police, fire, and ambulance dispatchers.

Occupations	Entry-level Education	2014 Median Pay	Projected Job Growth	Average Annual Openings
Air Traffic Controllers	Associate's degree	$122,340	-9%	-210
Customer Service Representatives	High school diploma or equivalent	$31,200	10%	25,290
EMTs and Paramedics	Postsecondary nondegree award	$31,700	24%	5,850

Communication skills. Dispatchers work with law enforcement, emergency response teams, and civilians. They must be able to communicate the nature of an emergency effectively and coordinate the appropriate response.

Decision-making skills. Dispatchers must be able to choose between tasks that are competing for their attention. They must be able to quickly determine the appropriate action when people call for help.

Empathy. Dispatchers must be willing and able to help callers who have a wide range of needs. They must be calm, polite, and sympathetic, while also collecting relevant information quickly.

Listening skills. Dispatchers must listen carefully to collect relevant details, even though some callers might have trouble speaking because of anxiety or stress.

Pay

The median annual wage for police, fire, and ambulance dispatchers was $37,410 in May 2014. The median wage is the wage at which half the workers in an occupation earned more than that amount and half earned less. The lowest 10 percent earned less than $23,790, and the highest 10 percent earned more than $58,870.

Most dispatchers work 8- to 12-hour shifts, but some agencies require even longer ones. Overtime is common in this occupation.

Because emergencies can happen at any time, dispatchers are required to work some shifts on evenings, weekends, and holidays.

Job Outlook

Employment of police, fire, and ambulance dispatchers is projected to decline 3 percent from 2014 to 2024.

Although the prevalence of cell phones has increased the number of calls that dispatchers receive, advanced 9-1-1 systems have increased the efficiency of emergency communication centers, allowing them to serve broader regions than before. Consolidation of these centers is expected to reduce the employment of dispatchers.

Local and state governments employ most police, fire, and ambulance dispatchers. Therefore, any future budget constraints will likely further limit the number of dispatchers hired in the coming decade.

Job Prospects. Overall job prospects should be favorable because the work of a dispatcher remains stressful and demanding, leading some applicants to seek other types of work.

The majority of positions will come from the need to replace the large number of dispatchers expected to transfer to other occupations or leave the labor force.

Those with good communication skills and experience using computers should have the best job prospects.

Contacts for More Information

For more information about police, fire, and ambulance dispatcher training and certification, visit

- Association of Public-Safety Communications Officials (www.apco911.org)
- International Academies of Emergency Dispatch (www.emergencydispatch.org)
- National Emergency Number Association (www.nena.org)
- U.S. Department of Transportation's National 911 Program (http://911.gov)

O*NET

- Police, Fire, and Ambulance Dispatchers (43-5031.00)

Postal Service Workers

- **2014 Median Pay** .... $54,720 per year; $26.31 per hour
- **Typical Entry-Level Education** .... High school diploma or equivalent
- **Work Experience in a Related Occupation** .... None
- **On-the-job Training** .... Short-term on-the-job training
- **Number of Jobs, 2014** 484,600
- **Job Outlook, 2014–24** .... -28% (Decline)
- **Employment Change, 2014–24** .... -136,000

What Postal Service Workers Do

Postal service workers sell postal products and collect, sort, and deliver mail.

Duties. Postal service workers typically do the following:

- Collect letters and parcels
- Sort incoming letters and parcels
- Sell stamps and other postal products

- Get customer signatures for registered, certified, and insured mail
- Operate various types of postal equipment
- Distribute incoming mail from postal trucks

Postal service workers receive and process mail for delivery to homes, businesses, and post office boxes. Workers are classified based on the type of work they perform.

The following are examples of types of Postal Service workers:

Postal service mail carriers deliver mail to homes and businesses in cities, towns, and rural areas. Most travel established routes, delivering and collecting mail. Carriers cover their routes by foot, vehicle, or a combination of both. Some mail carriers collect money for postage due. Others, particularly in rural areas, sell postal products, such as stamps and money orders. All carriers must be able to answer customers' questions about postal regulations and services and, upon request, provide change-of-address cards and other postal forms.

Postal service clerks sell stamps, money orders, postal stationery, mailing envelopes, and boxes in post offices throughout the country. These workers register, certify, and insure mail, calculate and collect postage, and answer questions about other postal matters. They also may help sort mail.

Postal service mail sorters, processors, and processing machine operators prepare incoming and outgoing mail for distribution at post offices and mail processing centers. They load and unload postal trucks and move mail around processing centers. They also operate and adjust mail processing and sorting machinery.

Postal Service mail carriers receive good benefits.

Work Environment

Postal service workers held about 484,600 jobs in 2014. They all worked in the federal government.

Employment in the detailed occupations that make up postal service workers was distributed as follows:

Postal service mail carriers	297,400
Postal service mail sorters, processors, and processing machine operators	117,600
Postal service clerks	69,600

Postal service clerks and mail sorters, processors, and processing machine operators work indoors, typically in a post office. Mail carriers mostly work outdoors, delivering mail in all kinds of weather. Although carriers face many natural hazards, such as extreme temperatures and wet and icy roads and sidewalks, the work is not especially dangerous. However, repetitive stress injuries from lifting and bending may occur.

Work Schedules. Most postal service workers are employed full time. However, overtime is sometimes required, particularly during the holiday season. Because mail is delivered 6 days a week, many postal service workers must work on Saturdays.

Education/Training

A high school diploma or equivalent is required to become a postal service worker. All applicants for these jobs must take a written exam.

Education. Although there is no specific postsecondary education requirement to become a postal service worker, all applicants must have a good command of English.

Postal service mail carriers must be at least 18 years old. They must be U.S. citizens or have permanent resident-alien status. Males must have registered with the Selective Service when they reached age 18.

All applicants must pass a written exam that measures speed and accuracy at checking names and numbers and the ability to memorize mail distribution procedures. Job seekers should contact the post office or mail processing center where they want to work to find out when exams are given.

Median Annual Wages, May 2014

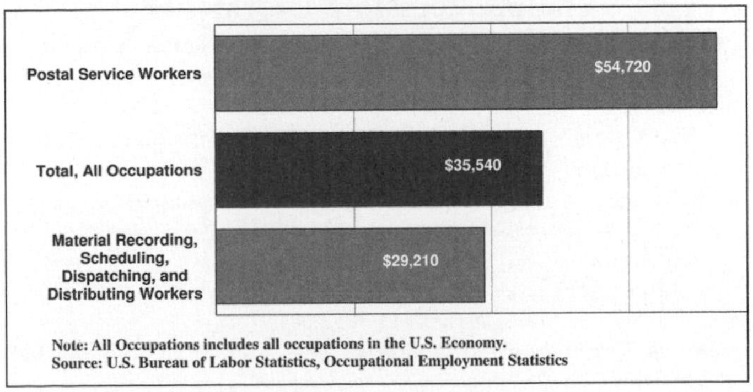

Percent Change in Employment, Projected 2014–2024

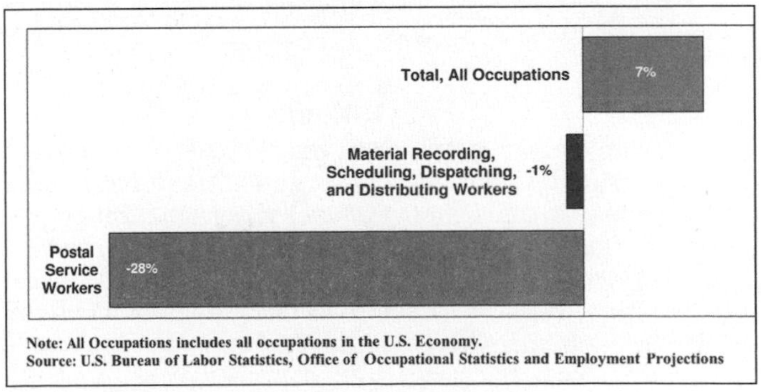

Employment Projections Data for Postal Service Workers

Occupational Title	SOC Code	Employment, 2014	Projected Employment, 2024	Change, 2014–2024 Percent	Change, 2014–2024 Numeric
Postal service workers	43-5050	484,600	348,600	-28	-136,000
Postal service clerks	43-5051	69,600	51,300	-26	-18,300
Postal service mail carriers	43-5052	297,400	219,400	-26	-78,100
Postal service mail sorters, processors, and processing machine operators	43-5053	117,600	78,000	-34	-39,700

Source: U.S. Bureau of Labor Statistics, Employment Projections Program

Similar Occupations. This table shows a list of occupations with job duties that are similar to those of postal service workers.

Occupations	Entry-level Education	2014 Median Pay	Projected Job Growth	Average Annual Openings
Delivery Truck Drivers and Driver/Sales Workers	High school diploma or equivalent	$27,490	4%	4,810
Retail Sales Workers	No formal educational credential	$21,670	7%	33,100

When accepted, applicants must undergo a criminal background check and pass a physical exam and a drug test. Applicants also may be asked to show that they can lift and handle heavy mail sacks. Mail carriers who drive at work must have a safe driving record, and applicants must receive a passing grade on a road test.

Training. Newly hired postal service workers receive short-term on-the-job training, usually lasting less than 1 month. Those who have a mail route may initially work alongside an experienced carrier.

Important Qualities

Customer-service skills. Postal service workers, particularly clerks, regularly interact with customers. As a result, they must be courteous and tactful and provide good client service.

Physical stamina. Postal service workers, particularly carriers, must be able to stand or walk for long periods.

Physical strength. Postal service workers must be able to lift heavy mail bags and parcels without injuring themselves.

Pay

The median annual wage for postal service workers was $54,720 in May 2014. The median wage is the wage at which half the workers in an occupation earned more than that amount and half earned less. The lowest 10 percent earned less than $31,840, and thc highest 10 percent earned more than $57,510.

Median annual wages for postal service workers in May 2014 were as follows:

Postal service mail carriers	$57,200
Postal service clerks	55,590
Postal service mail sorters, processors, and processing machine operators	54,520

Job Outlook

Overall employment of postal service workers is projected to decline 28 percent from 2014 to 2024. Automated sorting systems, cluster mailboxes, and tight budgets will adversely affect employment. Employment declines, however, will vary by specialty.

Employment of postal service clerks is projected to decline 26 percent from 2014 to 2024. Employment may be adversely affected by the decline in First-Class Mail volume due to increasing use of automated bill pay and email.

Employment of postal service mail carriers is projected to decline 26 percent from 2014 to 2024. Employment may be adversely affected by the use of automated "delivery point sequencing" systems that sort letter mail directly. This reduces the amount of time that carriers spend sorting, allowing them to spend more time on the streets delivering mail.

The amount of time carriers save on sorting letter mail and flat mail will allow them to increase the size of their routes, which should reduce the need to hire more carriers. In addition, the postal service is moving toward more centralized mail delivery, such as the use of cluster mailboxes, to cut down on the number of door-to-door deliveries.

However, the post office is playing a greater role in the delivery of goods purchased online. An increase in the number of deliverable packages as a result of e-commerce may slow the rate of employment decline for carriers.

Employment of postal service mail sorters, processors, and processing machine operators is projected to decline 34 percent from 2014 to 2024. The postal service will likely need fewer workers because new mail sorting technology can read text and automatically sort, forward, and process mail. The greater use of online services to pay bills and the increased use of email should also reduce the need for sorting and processing workers.

Job Prospects. Despite declining employment, the need to replace workers who retire will result in some job openings. However, very strong competition can be expected as the number of applicants typically exceeds the number of available positions.

Contacts for More Information

For more information about postal service workers, including job requirements, entrance examinations, and employment opportunities, visit

- United States Postal Service (http://about.usps.com/careers/welcome.htm)
- National Association of Letter Carriers (www.nalc.org)

O*NET

- Postal Service Clerks (43-5051.00)
- Postal Service Mail Carriers (43-5052.00)
- Postal Service Mail Sorters, Processors, and Processing Machine Operators (43-5053.00)

Receptionists

- **2014 Median Pay** .... $26,760 per year $12.87 per hour
- **Typical Entry-Level Education** .... High school diploma or equivalent
- **Work Experience in a Related Occupation** .... None
- **On-the-job Training** .... Short-term on-the-job training
- **Number of Jobs, 2014** 1,028,600
- **Job Outlook, 2014–24** .... 10% (Faster than average)
- **Employment Change, 2014–24** 97,800

What Receptionists Do

Receptionists perform administrative tasks, such as answering phones, receiving visitors, and providing general information about their organization to the public and customers.

Duties. Receptionists typically do the following:

- Answer telephone calls and take messages or forward calls
- Schedule and confirm appointments and maintain calendars
- Greet and welcome customers, clients, and other visitors
- Check visitors in and direct or escort them to specific destinations
- Inform other employees of visitors' arrivals or cancellations
- Enter customer data and send correspondence
- Copy, file, and maintain paper or electronic documents
- Handle incoming and outgoing mail and email

Receptionists are often the first employee of an organization to have contact with a customer or client. They are responsible for making a good first impression for the organization, which can affect the organization's success.

The specific responsibilities of receptionists vary depending on where they work. Receptionists in hospitals and doctors' offices may collect patients' personal information and direct patients to the waiting room. Some may handle billing and insurance payments.

In beauty or hair salons, they schedule appointments, direct clients to the hairstylist, and may serve as cashiers.

In factories, large corporations, and government offices, receptionists also may provide a security function. For example, they control access, provide visitor passes, and arrange to take visitors to the proper office.

When they are not busy with callers or visitors, receptionists perform other office tasks, such as processing documents or entering data.

Receptionists answer telephones, route and screen calls, greet visitors, respond to inquiries from the public, and provide information about the organization.

Receptionists use telephones, computers, and other office equipment such as scanners and fax machines.

Work Environment

Receptionists held about 1 million jobs in 2014. The industries that employed the most receptionists were as follows:

Offices of physicians	19%
Offices of dentists	7
Offices of other health practitioners	6
Personal care services	6
Veterinary services	5

Although receptionists are employed in nearly every industry, many work in healthcare, veterinary, and personal care services, including physicians' and dentists' offices, veterinary offices, and hair salons.

Receptionists usually work in an area that is visible and easily accessible to the public and other employees, such as the front desk of a lobby or waiting room.

Some receptionists may face stressful situations, as they answer numerous phone calls and sometimes deal with difficult callers.

Work Schedules. Although most receptionists work during regular business hours, about 3 in 10 worked part time in 2014. Some receptionists, such as those who work in hospitals and nursing homes, may work evenings and weekends.

Median Hourly Wages, May 2014

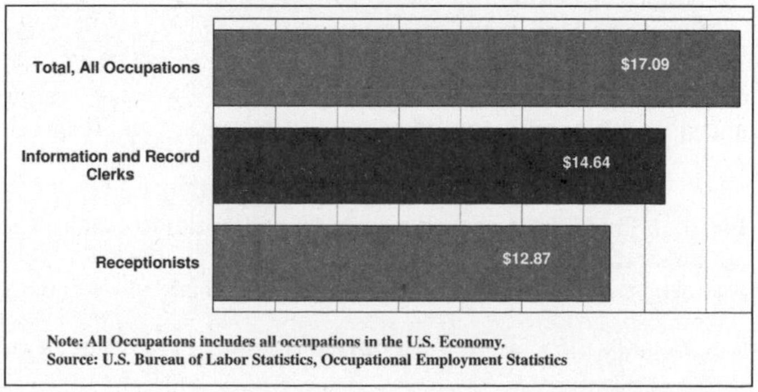

Percent Change in Employment, Projected 2014–2024

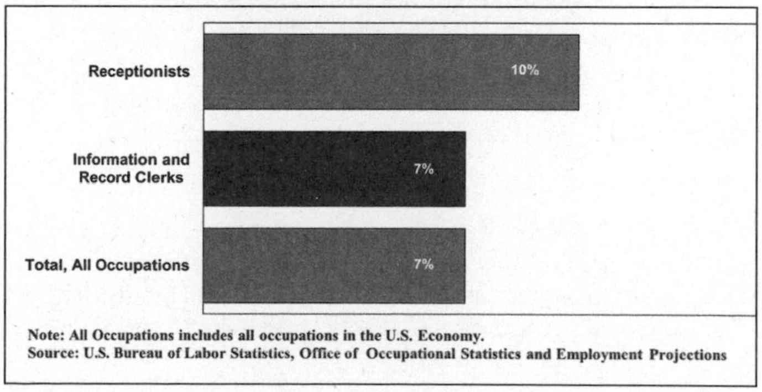

Employment Projections Data for Receptionists

Occupational Title	SOC Code	Employment, 2014	Projected Employment, 2024	Change, 2014–2024	
				Percent	Numeric
Receptionists and information clerks	43-4171	1,028,600	1,126,300	10	97,800

Source: U.S. Bureau of Labor Statistics, Employment Projections Program

Similar Occupations. This table shows a list of occupations with job duties that are similar to those of receptionists.

Occupations	Entry-level Education	2014 Median Pay	Projected Job Growth	Average Annual Openings
Customer Service Representatives	High school diploma or equivalent	$31,200	10%	25,290
General Office Clerks	High school diploma or equivalent	$28,670	3%	9,580
Information Clerks	See Education/Training	$31,500	2%	2,580
Secretaries and Administrative Assistants	High school diploma or equivalent	$35,970	3%	11,880
Tellers	High school diploma or equivalent	$25,760	-8%	-4,000

Education/Training

Although hiring requirements vary by industry and employer, receptionists typically need a high school diploma and good communication skills.

Education. Receptionists typically need a high school diploma or equivalent, and employers may prefer to hire candidates who have experience with certain computer software applications. Courses in word processing and spreadsheet applications can be particularly helpful.

Training. Most receptionists receive short-term on-the-job training, usually lasting a few days to a week. Training typically covers procedures for visitors, and for telephone and computer use. Medical and legal offices also may instruct new employees on privacy rules related to patient and client information.

Advancement. Receptionists may advance to other administrative positions with more responsibilities, such as secretaries and administrative assistants. Advancement opportunities often depend on the employee's experience in using computer applications, such as word processing and spreadsheet applications.

Important Qualities

Communication skills. Receptionists must speak and write clearly so that others may understand them.

Customer-service skills. Receptionists represent an organization. As a result, they should be courteous, professional, and helpful toward the public and customers.

Integrity. Receptionists may handle client and patient data, especially in medical and legal offices. They must be trustworthy and protect their clients' privacy.

Interpersonal skills. Receptionists should be comfortable interacting with people, even in stressful situations.

Organizational skills. Receptionists take messages, schedule appointments, and maintain employee files. They need good organizational skills to manage their diverse responsibilities.

Pay

The median hourly wage for receptionists was $12.87 in May 2014. The median wage is the wage at which half the workers in an occupation earned more than that amount and half earned less. The lowest 10 percent earned less than $8.94, and the highest 10 percent earned more than $18.55.

In May 2014, the median hourly wages for receptionists in the top industries in which they worked were as follows:

Offices of dentists	$15.17
Offices of physicians	13.50
Offices of other health practitioners	12.44
Veterinary services	12.30
Personal care services	10.30

Job Outlook

Employment of receptionists is projected to grow 10 percent from 2014 to 2024, faster than the average for all occupations.

Growing healthcare industries are projected to lead demand for receptionists, particularly in the offices of physicians, other healthcare practitioners, and dentists. The number of individuals who have access to health insurance is expected to continue to increase because of federal health insurance reform. Coupled with demand for medical services from an aging population, this should result in a strong outlook for receptionists in the healthcare industries. Additionally, some receptionists' tasks, such as checking patients in and coordinating patient care, are not easily automated.

Employment growth of receptionists in most other industries is expected to be slower as organizations continue to automate or consolidate administrative functions, such as by using computer software or websites to interact with the public or customers. In addition, organizations will continue to use technology, such as automated phone and online systems, further reducing the need for receptionists.

Job Prospects. Overall job prospects should be very good, with the best job opportunities in the healthcare industries.

Many job openings will stem from the need to replace workers who leave the occupation. Those with related work experience and experience in using computer applications, such as word processing and spreadsheet applications, should have the best job prospects.

Contacts for More Information

For more information about training for receptionists and other administrative careers, visit

➤ American Society of Administrative Professionals (www.asaporg.com)

➤ Association of Executive and Administrative Professionals (www.theaeap.com)

- International Association of Administrative Professionals (www.iaap-hq.org)

O*NET

- Receptionists and Information Clerks (43-4171.00)

Secretaries and Administrative Assistants

- **2014 Median Pay** .... $35,970 per year $17.30 per hour
- **Typical Entry-Level Education** .... High school diploma or equivalent
- **Work Experience in a Related Occupation** .... See Education/Training
- **On-the-job Training** .... See Education/Training
- **Number of Jobs, 2014** 3,976,800
- **Job Outlook, 2014–24** .... 3% (Slower than average)
- **Employment Change, 2014–24** 118,800

What Secretaries and Administrative Assistants Do

Secretaries and administrative assistants perform routine clerical and administrative duties. They organize files, prepare documents, schedule appointments, and support other staff.

Duties. Secretaries and administrative assistants typically do the following:

- Answer telephones and take messages or transfer calls
- Schedule appointments and update event calendars
- Arrange staff meetings
- Handle incoming and outgoing mail and faxes
- Prepare memos, invoices, or other reports
- Edit documents
- Maintain databases and filing systems, whether electronic or paper
- Perform basic bookkeeping

Secretaries and administrative assistants perform a variety of clerical and administrative duties that are necessary to run an organization efficiently. They use computer software to create spreadsheets; manage databases; and prepare presentations, reports, and documents. They also may negotiate with vendors, buy supplies, and manage stockrooms or corporate libraries. Secretaries and administrative assistants also use videoconferencing, fax machines, and other office equipment. Specific job duties vary by experience, job title, and specialty.

Executive secretaries and executive administrative assistants provide high-level administrative support for an office and for top executives of an organization. They often handle more complex responsibilities, such as reviewing incoming documents, conducting research, and preparing reports. Some also supervise clerical staff.

Legal secretaries perform work requiring knowledge of legal terminology and procedures. They prepare legal documents, such as summonses, complaints, motions, and subpoenas under the supervision of an attorney or a paralegal. They also review legal journals and help with legal research—for example, by verifying quotes and citations in legal briefs.

Secretaries and administrative assistants often use computers to create spreadsheets, compose correspondence, manage databases, and create presentations and reports.

Medical secretaries transcribe dictation and prepare reports or articles for physicians or medical scientists. They also take simple medical histories of patients, arrange for patients to be hospitalized, or process insurance payments. Medical secretaries need to be familiar with medical terminology and codes, medical records, and hospital or laboratory procedures.

Secretaries and administrative assistants, except legal, medical, and executive is the largest subcategory of secretaries and administrative assistants. They handle an office's administrative activities in almost every sector of the economy, including schools, government, and private corporations. For example, secretaries in schools are often responsible for handling most of the communications among parents, students, the community, teachers, and school administrators. They schedule appointments, receive visitors, and keep track of students' records.

Work Environment

Secretaries and administrative assistants held about 4 million jobs in 2014 and worked in nearly every industry.

Many secretaries and administrative assistants work in schools, hospitals, governments, and legal and medical offices.

Employment in the detailed occupations of the secretaries and administrative assistants group in 2014 was distributed as follows:

Secretaries and administrative assistants, except legal, medical, and executive	2,457,000
Executive secretaries and executive administrative assistants	776,600
Medical secretaries	527,600
Legal secretaries	215,500

Most secretaries and administrative assistants work in an office setting. Some administrative assistants, who are also known as virtual assistants, typically work out of their own homes.

Work Schedules. Most secretaries and administrative assistants work full time.

Education/Training

High school graduates who have experience using computer software applications, such as word processing and spreadsheets, usually qualify for entry-level positions. Although most secretaries learn their job in several weeks, many legal and medical secretaries

Median Annual Wages, May 2014

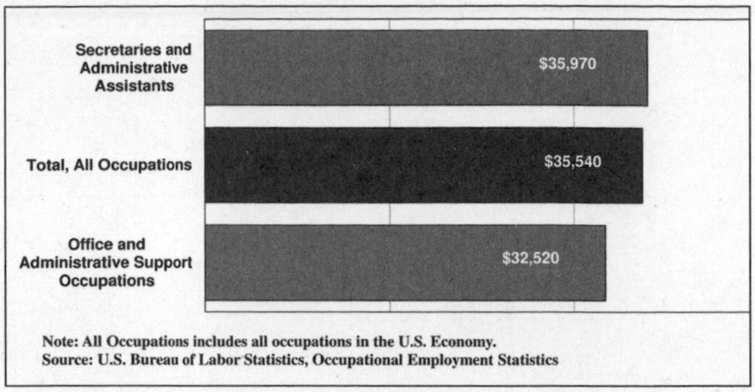

Percent Change in Employment, Projected 2014–2024

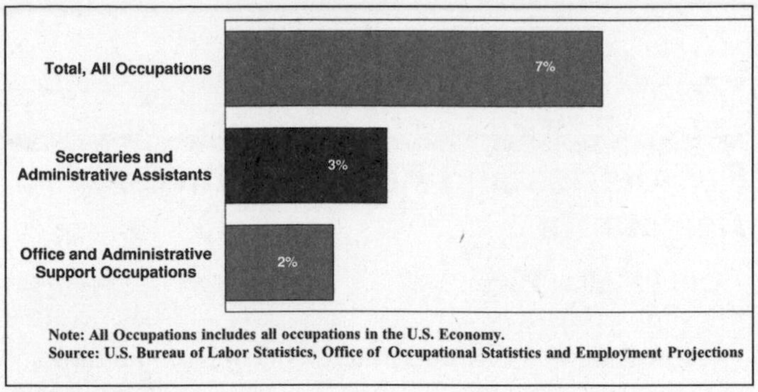

require additional training to learn industry-specific terminology. Executive secretaries usually need several years of related work experience.

Education. High school graduates can take courses in word processing and office procedures at technical schools or community colleges. Some temporary placement agencies also provide training in word processing, spreadsheet, and database software.

Some medical and legal secretaries learn industry-specific terminology and practices by attending courses offered at community colleges or technical schools. For executive secretary positions, employers increasingly prefer to hire those who have taken some college courses or have a bachelor's degree.

Training. Secretaries and administrative assistants typically learn their skills through short-term on-the-job training, usually lasting a few weeks. During this time they learn about administrative procedures, including how to prepare documents. Medical and legal secretaries' training may last several months as they learn industry-specific terminology and practices.

Work Experience in a Related Occupation. Executive secretaries can gain experience by working in administrative positions that have less challenging responsibilities. Many secretaries and administrative assistants advance to higher-level administrative positions.

Licenses, Certifications, and Registrations. Although not required, certification can demonstrate competency to employers.

The International Association of Administrative Professionals offers the Certified Administrative Professional (CAP) certification. Candidates must have a minimum of 2 to 4 years of administrative work experience, depending on their level of education, and pass an examination.

Legal secretaries have several certification options. For example, those with 1 year of general office experience, or who have completed an approved training course, can acquire the Accredited Legal Professional (ALP) certification through a testing process administered by NALS (previously known as National Association of Legal Secretaries). NALS also offers the Professional Legal Secretary (PLS) certification, considered to be an advanced certification for legal support professionals.

The Certified Legal Secretary Specialist (CLSS) certification is conferred by Legal Secretaries International in areas such as intellectual property, criminal law, civil litigation, probate, and business law. Candidates typically need to have 5 years of legal experience and pass an examination to become certified.

Advancement. Secretaries and administrative assistants generally advance to other administrative positions with more responsibilities, such as office supervisor, office manager, or executive secretary.

With additional training, many legal secretaries become paralegals or legal assistants.

Important Qualities

Integrity. Many secretaries and administrative assistants are trusted to handle sensitive information. For example, medical secretaries collect patient data that is required, by law, to be kept confidential in order to protect patient privacy.

Interpersonal skills. Secretaries and administrative assistants interact with clients, customers, or staff. They should communicate effectively and be courteous when interacting with others to create a positive work environment and client experience.

Organizational skills. Secretaries and administrative assistants keep files, folders, and schedules in proper order so an office can run efficiently.

Writing skills. Secretaries and administrative assistants write memos and emails when communicating with managers, employees, and customers. Therefore, they must have good grammar, ensure accuracy, and maintain a professional tone.

Employment Projections Data for Secretaries and Administrative Assistants

Occupational Title	SOC Code	Employment, 2014	Projected Employment, 2024	Change, 2014–2024 Percent	Numeric
Secretaries and administrative assistants	43-6000	3,976,800	4,095,600	3	118,800
Executive secretaries and executive administrative assistants	43-6011	776,600	732,000	-6	-44,600
Legal secretaries	43-6012	215,500	206,700	-4	-8,900
Medical secretaries	43-6013	527,600	635,800	21	108,200
Secretaries and administrative assistants, except legal, medical, and executive	43-6014	2,457,000	2,521,100	3	64,000

Source: U.S. Bureau of Labor Statistics, Employment Projections Program

Similar Occupations. This table shows a list of occupations with job duties that are similar to those of secretaries and administrative assistants.

Occupations	Entry-level Education	2014 Median Pay	Projected Job Growth	Average Annual Openings
Bookkeeping, Accounting, and Auditing Clerks	Some college, no degree	$36,430	-8%	-14,870
Court Reporters	Postsecondary nondegree award	$49,860	2%	30
General Office Clerks	High school diploma or equivalent	$28,670	3%	9,580
Information Clerks	See Education/Training	$31,500	2%	2,580
Medical Records and Health Information Technicians	Postsecondary nondegree award	$35,900	15%	2,900
Medical Transcriptionists	Postsecondary nondegree award	$34,750	-3%	-220
Paralegals and Legal Assistants	Associate's degree	$48,350	8%	2,120
Receptionists	High school diploma or equivalent	$26,760	10%	9,780

Pay

The median annual wage for secretaries and administrative assistants was $35,970 in May 2014. The median wage is the wage at which half the workers in an occupation earned more than that amount and half earned less. The lowest 10 percent earned less than $22,170, and the highest 10 percent earned more than $59,560.

Median annual wages for secretaries and administrative assistants in May 2014 were as follows:

Executive secretaries and executive administrative assistants $51,270
Legal secretaries 42,770
Secretaries and administrative assistants, except legal, medical, and executive 33,240
Medical secretaries 32,240

Job Outlook

Overall employment of secretaries and administrative assistants is projected to grow 3 percent from 2014 to 2024, slower than the average for all occupations.

Employment of secretaries, except legal, medical, and executive, the largest occupation in this profile by far, is projected to grow 3 percent from 2014 to 2024, slower than the average for all occupations. In some organizations, technology is expected to substitute some functions that secretaries used to do and enable other staff to prepare their own documents without the assistance of secretaries.

Employment of medical secretaries is projected to grow 21 percent from 2014 to 2024, much faster than the average for all occupations. Employment of medical secretaries will depend on growth of the healthcare industry. The number of individuals who have access to health insurance is expected to continue to increase because of federal health insurance reform. In addition, aging baby boomers will demand more medical services as they become eligible for Social Security and Medicare. As a result of these effects, medical secretaries will be needed to handle administrative tasks related to billing and insurance processing.

Employment of executive secretaries and administrative assistants is projected to decline 6 percent from 2014 to 2024. This is largely because many executive secretaries and executive administrative assistants can support more than one manager in an organization. In addition, many managers now perform work that was previously done by their executive secretaries. For example, they often type their own correspondence or schedule their own travel and meetings.

Employment of legal secretaries, the smallest occupation in this profile, is projected to decline 4 percent from 2014 to 2024. In legal firms, paralegals and legal assistants use technologies that enable them to perform work previously done by legal secretaries, such as preparing and filing documents.

Job Prospects. Many job openings are expected to come from the need to replace secretaries and administrative assistants who leave the occupation.

Those with a combination of related work experience and experience using computer software applications to perform word processing and create spreadsheets should have the best job prospects.

Contacts for More Information

For more information about careers in secretarial and administrative work, visit

- Association of Executive and Administrative Professionals (www.theaeap.com)
- International Association of Administrative Professionals (www.iaap-hq.org)

For more information about legal secretaries and administrative assistants, visit

- Legal Secretaries International Inc (www.legalsecretaries.org)
- NALS (www.nals.org)

For more information about virtual assistants, visit

- International Virtual Assistants Association (www.ivaa.org)

O*NET

- Executive Secretaries and Executive Administrative Assistants (43-6011.00)
- Legal Secretaries (43-6012.00)
- Medical Secretaries (43-6013.00)
- Secretaries and Administrative Assistants, Except Legal, Medical, and Executive (43-6014.00)

Tellers

- **2014 Median Pay** .... $25,760 per year
$12.38 per hour
- **Typical Entry-Level Education** .... High school diploma or equivalent
- **Work Experience in a Related Occupation**.............. None

Tellers work in bank branches and assist customers with simple financial transactions.

- **On-the-job Training** .... Short-term on-the-job training
- **Number of Jobs, 2014** 520,500
- **Job Outlook, 2014–24** .... -8% (Decline)
- **Employment Change, 2014–24** .... -40,000

What Tellers Do

Tellers are responsible for accurately processing routine transactions at a bank. These transactions include cashing checks, depositing money, and collecting loan payments.

Duties. Tellers typically do the following:

- Count the cash in their drawer at the start of their shift
- Accept checks, cash, and other forms of payment from customers
- Answer questions from customers about their accounts
- Prepare specialized types of funds, such as traveler's checks, savings bonds, and money orders
- Exchange dollars for foreign currency
- Order bank cards and checks for customers
- Record all transactions electronically throughout their shift
- Count the cash in their drawer at the end of their shift and make sure the amounts balance

Tellers are responsible for the safe and accurate handling of the money they process. When cashing a check, they must verify the customer's identity and make sure that the account has enough money to cover the transaction. When counting cash, tellers must be careful not to make errors. If a customer is interested in financial products or services, such as certificates of deposits (CDs) and loans, tellers explain the products and services offered by the bank and refer the customer to the appropriate personnel.

In most banks, tellers record account changes using computers that give them easy access to the customer's financial information. Tellers also can use this information when recommending a new product or service.

Head tellers manage teller operations. Besides doing the same tasks as those done by other tellers, they perform some managerial duties, such as setting work schedules or helping less experienced tellers. Because of their experience, head tellers may deal with difficult customer problems, such as errors in customer accounts. Head tellers also go to the vault (where larger amounts of money are kept) and ensure that other tellers have enough cash to cover their shift.

Work Environment

Tellers held about 520,500 jobs in 2014. About 91 percent worked in the depository credit intermediation industry, which includes commercial bank branches.

Work Schedules. Although most tellers worked full time, about 1 in 4 worked part time in 2014.

Education/Training

Most tellers have a high school diploma and receive about 1 month of on-the-job training. Some banks do background checks before hiring a new teller.

Education. Tellers usually need a high school diploma or equivalent. Some tellers may take some college courses, but a degree is rarely required for a job applicant to be hired.

Training. New tellers usually receive brief on-the-job training, typically lasting about 1 month. Normally, a head teller or another experienced teller trains them. During this training, tellers learn how to balance cash drawers and verify signatures. They also learn the computer software that their bank uses and the financial products and services the bank offers.

Advancement. Experienced tellers can advance within their bank. They can become head tellers or move to other supervisory positions. Some tellers can advance to other occupations, such as loan officer. They can also move to sales positions.

Important Qualities

Customer-service skills. Tellers spend their day interacting with bank customers. They must be friendly, helpful, and patient. They must be able to understand customer needs and explain service options to their customers.

Median Annual Wages, May 2014

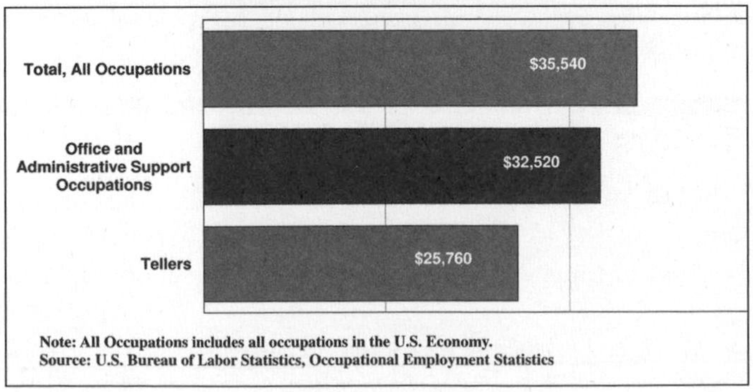

Percent Change in Employment, Projected 2014–2024

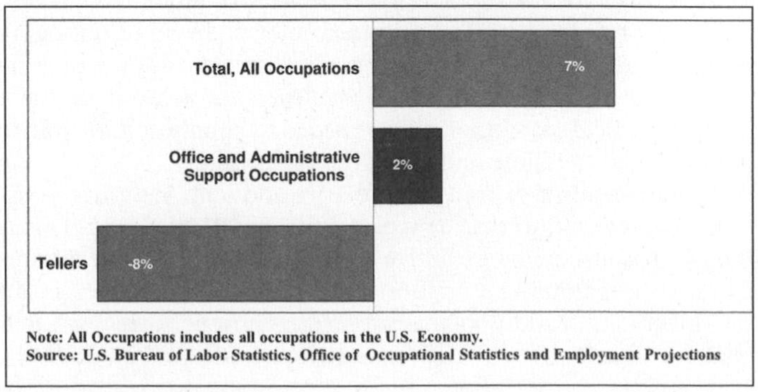

Employment Projections Data for Tellers

Occupational Title	SOC Code	Employment, 2014	Projected Employment, 2024	Change, 2014–2024	
				Percent	Numeric
Tellers	43-3071	520,500	480,500	-8	-40,000

Source: U.S. Bureau of Labor Statistics, Employment Projections Program

Similar Occupations. This table shows a list of occupations with job duties that are similar to those of tellers.

Occupations	Entry-level Education	2014 Median Pay	Projected Job Growth	Average Annual Openings
Bookkeeping, Accounting, and Auditing Clerks	Some college, no degree	$36,430	-8%	-14,870
Cashiers	No formal educational credential	$19,060	2%	6,700
Customer Service Representatives	High school diploma or equivalent	$31,200	10%	25,290
Information Clerks	See Education/Training	$31,500	2%	2,580
Loan Officers	Bachelor's degree	$62,620	8%	2,450
Receptionists	High school diploma or equivalent	$26,760	10%	9,780

Detail oriented. Tellers must be sure not to make errors when dealing with customers' money.

Math skills. Because they count and handle large amounts of money, tellers must be good at arithmetic.

Pay

The median annual wage for tellers was $25,760 in May 2014. The median wage is the wage at which half the workers in an occupation earned more than that amount and half earned less. The lowest 10 percent earned less than $20,070, and the highest 10 percent earned more than $35,950.

Job Outlook

Employment of tellers is projected to decline 8 percent from 2014 to 2024.

Historically, job growth for tellers was driven by the expansion of bank branches, where most tellers work. However, the number of bank branches has been in decline because of industry consolidation and technological change.

The rise of online and mobile banking allows customers to handle many transactions traditionally performed by tellers, such as depositing checks. As more people use these tools, fewer bank customers will visit the teller window. This will result in decreased demand for tellers. Some banks also are developing systems that allow customers to interact with tellers through webcams at ATMs. This technology will allow tellers to service a greater number of customers from one location, reducing the number of tellers needed for each bank.

Job Prospects. Job prospects for tellers should be favorable because many workers leave this occupation.

Contacts for More Information

For general information about the banking industry, visit

➤ American Bankers Association (www.aba.com)

O*NET

➤ Tellers (43-3071.00)

Personal Care and Service

Animal Care and Service Workers

- **2014 Median Pay** .... $20,610 per year
  $9.91 per hour
- **Typical Entry-Level Education** .... High school diploma or equivalent
- **Work Experience in a Related Occupation** .... None
- **On-the-job Training** .... See Education/Training
- **Number of Jobs, 2014** 241,600
- **Job Outlook, 2014–24** .... 11% (Faster than average)
- **Employment Change, 2014–24** 25,700

What Animal Care and Service Workers Do

Animal care and service workers provide care for animals. They feed, groom, bathe, and exercise pets and other nonfarm animals. Job tasks vary by position and place of work.

Duties. Animal care and service workers typically do the following:

- Give food and water to animals
- Clean equipment and the living spaces of animals
- Monitor animals and record details of their diet, physical condition, and behavior
- Examine animals for signs of illness or injury
- Exercise animals
- Bathe animals, trim nails, clip hair, and attend to other grooming needs
- Train animals to obey or to behave in a specific manner

Animal care and service workers train, feed, groom, and exercise animals. They also clean, disinfect, and repair animal cages. They play with the animals, provide companionship, and observe behavioral changes that could indicate illness or injury.

Boarding kennels, pet stores, animal shelters, rescue leagues, veterinary hospitals and clinics, stables, aquariums and natural aquatic habitats, zoological parks, and many laboratories house animals and employ animal care and service workers.

Nonfarm animal caretakers typically work with cats and dogs in animal shelters or rescue leagues. All caretakers attend to the basic needs of animals, but experienced caretakers may have more responsibilities, such as helping to vaccinate or euthanize animals under the direction of a veterinarian. Caretakers also may have administrative duties, such as keeping records, answering questions from the public, educating visitors about pet health, and screening people who want to adopt an animal.

Animal trainers train animals for obedience, performance, riding, security, or assisting people with disabilities. They familiarize animals with human voices and contact, and they teach animals to respond to commands. Most animal trainers work with dogs and horses, but some work with marine mammals, such as dolphins. Trainers teach a variety of skills. For example, some may train dogs to guide people with disabilities; others teach animals to cooperate with veterinarians or train animals for a competition or show.

Groomers specialize in maintaining a pet's appearance. Kennels, veterinary clinics, or pet supply stores employ groomers, where they groom mostly dogs, but some cats, too. In addition to cutting, trimming, and styling pets' fur, groomers clip nails, clean ears, and bathe pets. Groomers also schedule appointments, sell products to pet owners, and identify problems that may require veterinary attention.

Groomers may operate their own business, work in a grooming salon, or run their own mobile grooming service that travels to clients' homes. Demand for mobile grooming services is growing because these services are convenient for pet owners, allowing the pet to stay in its familiar environment.

Grooms care for horses. Grooms work at stables and are responsible for feeding, grooming, and exercising horses. They saddle and unsaddle horses, give them rubdowns, and cool them off after a ride. In addition, grooms clean stalls, polish saddles, and organize the tack room where they keep harnesses, saddles, and bridles. They also take care of food and supplies for the horses. Experienced grooms sometimes help train horses.

Keepers care for animals in zoos. They plan diets, feed, and monitor the eating patterns of animals. They also clean the animals' enclosures, monitor their behavior, and watch for signs of illness or injury. Depending on the size of the zoo, they may work with one species or multiple species of animals. Keepers may help raise young animals, and they often spend time answering questions from the public.

Kennel attendants care for pets while their owners are working or traveling. Basic attendant duties include cleaning cages and dog runs, and feeding, exercising, and playing with animals. Experienced attendants also may provide basic healthcare, bathe animals, and attend to other basic grooming needs.

Pet sitters look after animals while their owner is away. Most pet sitters feed, walk, and play with pets daily. They go to the pet owner's home, allowing the pet to stay in its familiar surroundings and follow its routine. More experienced pet sitters also may bathe, groom, or train pets. Pet sitters typically watch over dogs, but some also take care of cats and other pets.

Work Environment

Animal care and service workers held about 241,600 jobs in 2014. About 85 percent of these workers were nonfarm animal caretakers, and 15 percent were animal trainers.

Animal care and service workers are employed in a variety of settings. Many work at kennels; others work at zoos, stables, animal shelters, pet stores, veterinary clinics, and aquariums. Mobile groomers and pet sitters typically travel to customers' homes. Caretakers of show and sports animals must travel to competitions. Nearly 1 in 4 animal care and service workers were self-employed in 2014.

Although most animal care and service workers consider the work enjoyable and rewarding, they may face unpleasant and emotionally distressing situations at times. For example, those who work in shelters may observe abused, injured, or sick animals. Some caretakers may have to help veterinarians euthanize injured or unwanted animals. In addition, a lot the work involves physical tasks, such as moving and cleaning cages, lifting bags of food, and exercising animals.

Injuries and Illnesses. Nonfarm animal caretakers have a higher rate of injuries and illnesses than the national average. Caretakers may be bitten, scratched, or kicked when working with scared or

Animal caretakers who specialize in grooming or maintaining a pet's appearance are called groomers.

aggressive animals. Injuries may also happen while the caretaker is holding, cleaning, or restraining an animal.

Work Schedules. Animals need care around the clock, so many facilities, such as kennels, zoos, animal shelters, and stables operate 24 hours a day. Therefore, caretakers often work irregular hours including evenings, weekends, and holidays. About 1 in 4 animal trainers and about 1 in 3 animal caretakers worked part time in 2014. Self-employed workers often set their own schedule.

Education/Training

Most animal care and service workers have a high school diploma and learn the occupation on the job. Many employers prefer to hire people who have experience with animals.

Education. Most animal care and service worker positions require at least a high school diploma or equivalent.

Although pet groomers typically learn by working under the guidance of an experienced groomer, they can also attend grooming schools. The length of each program varies with the school and the number of advanced skills taught.

Most zoos require keepers to have a bachelor's degree in biology, animal science, or a related field.

Animal trainers usually need a high school diploma or equivalent, although some positions may require a bachelor's degree. For example, marine mammal trainers usually need a bachelor's degree in marine biology, animal science, biology, or a related field.

Dog trainers and horse trainers typically qualify by taking courses at community colleges or vocational and private training schools.

Training. Most animal care and service workers learn through on-the-job training. They begin by performing basic tasks and work up to positions that require more responsibility and experience.

Some animal care and service workers may receive training before they enter their position. For example, caretakers in shelters can attend training programs through the Humane Society of the United States and the American Humane Association. Pet groomers often learn their trade by training under the guidance of an experienced groomer.

Licenses, Certifications, and Registrations. Although not required by law, certifications may help workers establish their credentials and enhance their skills. For example, several professional associations and hundreds of private vocational and state-approved trade schools offer certification for dog trainers.

The National Dog Groomers Association of America offers certification for master status as a groomer. Both the National Association of Professional Pet Sitters and Pet Sitters International offer a home-study certification program for pet sitters. Marine mammal trainers should be certified in scuba-diving.

For self-employed workers, many states require animal care and service workers to have a business license.

Other Experience. For many caretaker positions, it helps to have experience working with animals. Nearly all animal trainer and zookeeper positions require candidates to have experience with animals. Volunteering and internships at zoos and aquariums are excellent ways to gain experience in working with animals.

Important Qualities

Compassion. Animal care and service workers must be compassionate when dealing with animals and their owners. They should like animals and must treat them with kindness.

Customer-service skills. Animal care and service workers should understand pet owners' needs so they can provide services that leave the owners satisfied. Some workers may need to deal with distraught pet owners. For example, caretakers working in animal shelters may need to reassure owners looking for a lost pet.

Detail oriented. Animal care and service workers must be detail oriented because they are often responsible for keeping animals on a strict diet, maintaining records, and monitoring changes in animals' behavior.

Median Annual Wages, May 2014

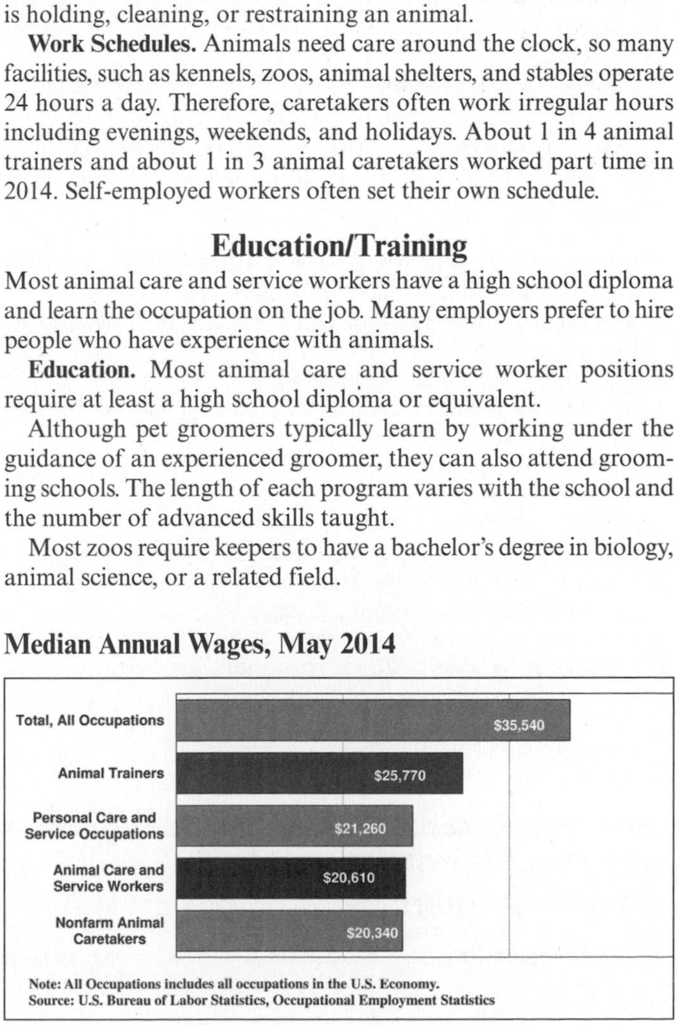

Percent Change in Employment, Projected 2014–2024

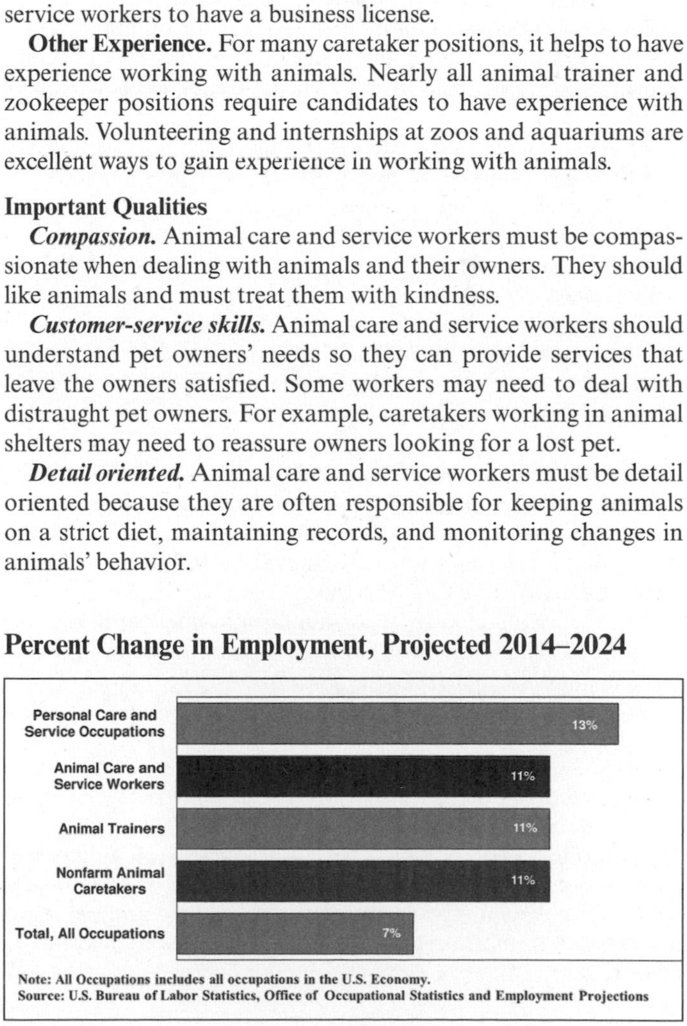

Employment Projections Data for Animal Care and Service Workers

Occupational Title	SOC Code	Employment, 2014	Projected Employment, 2024	Change, 2014–2024	
				Percent	Numeric
Animal care and service workers	—	241,600	267,300	11	25,700
Animal trainers	39-2011	36,800	40,900	11	4,100
Nonfarm animal caretakers	39-2021	204,800	226,400	11	21,600

Source: U.S. Bureau of Labor Statistics, Employment Projections Program

Similar Occupations. This table shows a list of occupations with job duties that are similar to those of animal care and service workers.

Occupations	Entry-level Education	2014 Median Pay	Projected Job Growth	Average Annual Openings
Agricultural Workers	See Education/Training	$19,330	-6%	-4,750
Farmers, Ranchers, and Other Agricultural Managers	High school diploma or equivalent	$68,050	-2%	-1,810
Veterinarians	Doctoral or professional degree	$87,590	9%	690
Veterinary Assistants and Laboratory Animal Caretakers	High school diploma or equivalent	$23,790	9%	660
Veterinary Technologists and Technicians	Associate's degree	$31,070	19%	1,790

Patience. Animal caretakers and all animal trainers need to be patient when training or working with animals that do not respond to commands.

Physical stamina. Stamina is important for animal care and service workers because their work often involves kneeling, crawling, bending, and lifting heavy supplies, such as bags of food.

Problem-solving skills. Animal trainers must be able to assess whether the animals are responding to teaching methods and identify which methods are most successful.

Reliability. In order to meet the customer's needs, animal care and service workers need to care for animals in a scheduled and timely manner.

Trustworthiness. Pet sitters must demonstrate that they can be trusted when caring for animals and properties while the owner is away.

Pay

The median annual wage for animal trainers was $25,770 in May 2014. The median wage is the wage at which half the workers in an occupation earned more than that amount and half earned less. The lowest 10 percent earned less than $17,650, and the highest 10 percent earned more than $57,160.

The median annual wage for nonfarm animal caretakers was $20,340 in May 2014. The lowest 10 percent earned less than $16,750, and the highest 10 percent earned more than $33,880.

Job Outlook

Overall employment of animal care and service workers is projected to grow 11 percent from 2014 to 2024, faster than the average for all occupations.

As more households own pets, employment of animal care and service workers in the pet services industry will continue to grow. Employment in kennels, grooming shops, and pet stores is projected to increase to keep up with the growing demand for animal care.

Job Prospects. Job opportunities are projected to be very good for most positions. Employment growth and high job turnover are expected to result in many openings for dog trainers, groomers, pet sitters, kennel attendants, and caretakers in shelters and rescue leagues.

However, jobseekers will face very strong competition for positions as marine mammal trainers, horse trainers, and zookeepers. The relatively few positions and the popularity of the occupations should result in far more applicants than available positions.

Contacts for More Information

For more information about pet groomers, visit

- National Dog Groomers Association of America, Inc. (www.nationaldoggroomers.com)
- Petgroomer.com (http://petgroomer.com)

For more information about pet sitters, including certification information, visit

- National Association of Professional Pet Sitters (www.petsitters.org)
- Pet Sitters International (www.petsit.com)

For more information about animal trainers, visit

- Association of Professional Dog Trainers (www.apdt.com)
- International Marine Animal Trainers' Association (www.imata.org)

For more information about keepers, visit

- Association of Zoos & Aquariums (www.aza.org)
- American Association of Zoo Keepers (http://aazk.org)

O*NET

- Animal Trainers (39-2011.00)
- Nonfarm Animal Caretakers (39-2021.00)

Barbers, Hairdressers, and Cosmetologists

- **2014 Median Pay** .... $23,200 per year
  $11.15 per hour

- **Typical Entry-Level Education** .... Postsecondary nondegree award
- **Work Experience in a Related Occupation** .... None
- **On-the-job Training** .... None
- **Number of Jobs, 2014** 656,400
- **Job Outlook, 2014–24** .... 10% (Faster than average)
- **Employment Change, 2014–24** 64,400

What Barbers, Hairdressers, and Cosmetologists Do

Barbers, hairdressers, and cosmetologists provide haircutting, hairstyling, and a range of other beauty services.

Duties. Barbers, hairdressers, and cosmetologists typically do the following:

- Inspect and analyze hair, skin, and scalp to recommend treatment
- Discuss hairstyle options
- Wash, color, lighten, and condition hair
- Chemically change hair textures
- Cut, dry, and style hair
- Receive payments from clients
- Clean and disinfect all tools and work areas

Barbers, hairdressers, and cosmetologists provide hair and beauty services to enhance clients' appearance. Those who operate their own barbershop or salon have managerial duties that may include hiring, supervising, and firing workers, as well as keeping business and inventory records, ordering supplies, and arranging for advertising.

Barbers cut, trim, shampoo, and style hair, mostly for male clients. They also may fit hairpieces, perform facials, and offer facial shaving. Depending on the state in which they work, some barbers are licensed to color, bleach, and highlight hair and to offer permanent-wave services. Common tools include combs, scissors, straight razors, and clippers.

Hairdressers, or *hairstylists*, offer a wide range of hair services, such as shampooing, cutting, coloring, and styling. They often advise clients, both male and female, on how to care for their hair at home. They also keep records of products and services provided to clients, such as hair color, shampoo, conditioner, and hair treatment used. Tools include hairbrushes, scissors, blow dryers, and curling irons.

Cosmetologists provide scalp and facial treatments and makeup analysis. Some also clean and style wigs and hairpieces. In addition, most cosmetologists actively recommend professional hair care products or salon hair care products.

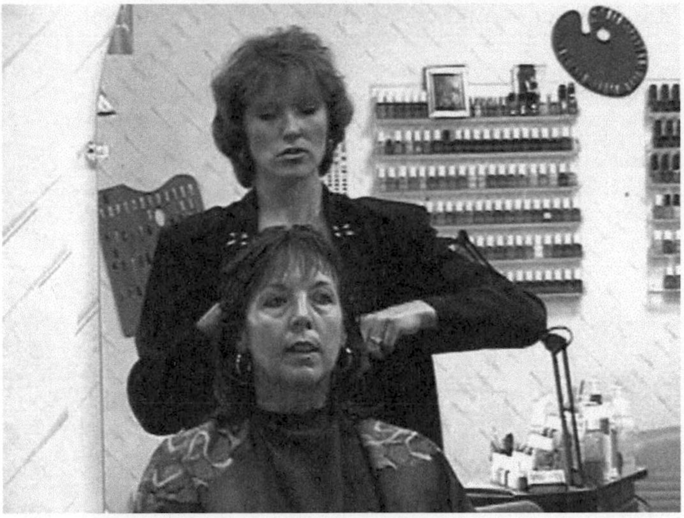

Barbers, hairdressers, and cosmetologists wash, color, and dry hair.

Work Environment

Barbers, hairdressers, and cosmetologists held about 656,400 jobs in 2014. Nearly half were self-employed.

Employment in the detailed occupations that make up barbers, hairdressers, and cosmetologists was distributed as follows:

Hairdressers, hairstylists, and cosmetologists	597,200
Barbers	59,200

Barbers, hairdressers, and cosmetologists work mostly in a barbershop or salon, although some work in a spa, hotel, or resort. Some lease booth space from a salon owner. Some manage salons or open their own shop after several years of experience.

Barbers, hairdressers, and cosmetologists usually work in pleasant surroundings with good lighting. Physical stamina is important, because they are on their feet for most of their shift. Prolonged exposure to some chemicals may cause skin irritation, so they often wear protective clothing, such as disposable gloves or aprons.

Work Schedules. Many barbers, hairdressers, and cosmetologists work full time, however part-time positions are also common. Those who run their own barbershop or salon may have long hours. Work schedules often include evenings and weekend—the times when barbershops and beauty salons are busiest. Those who are self-employed usually determine their own schedules.

Median Hourly Wages, May 2014

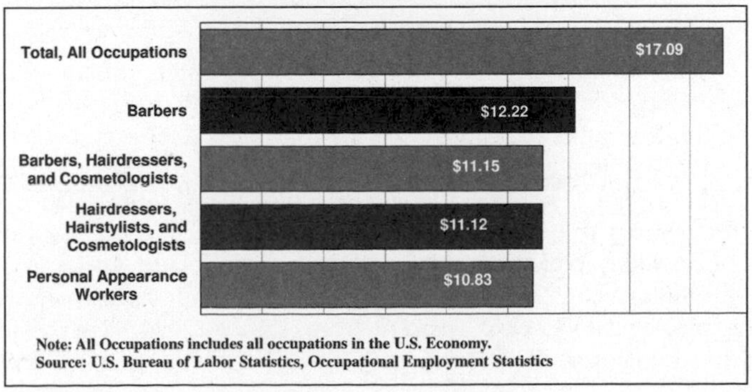

Percent Change in Employment, Projected 2014–2024

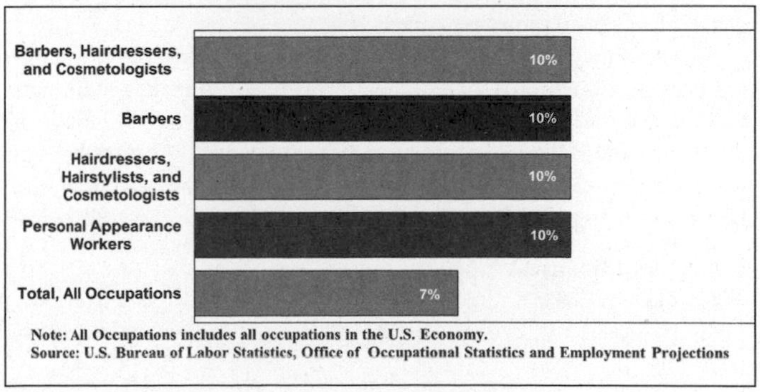

Employment Projections Data for Barbers, Hairdressers, and Cosmetologists

Occupational Title	SOC Code	Employment, 2014	Projected Employment, 2024	Change, 2014–2024 Percent	Change, 2014–2024 Numeric
Barbers, hairdressers, hairstylists and cosmetologists	39-5010	656,400	720,700	10	64,400
Barbers	39-5011	59,200	65,100	10	6,000
Hairdressers, hairstylists, and cosmetologists	39-5012	597,200	655,600	10	58,400

Source: U.S. Bureau of Labor Statistics, Employment Projections Program

Similar Occupations. This table shows a list of occupations with job duties that are similar to those of barbers, hairdressers, and cosmetologists.

Occupations	Entry-level Education	2014 Median Pay	Projected Job Growth	Average Annual Openings
Manicurists and Pedicurists	Postsecondary nondegree award	$19,620	10%	1,170
Skincare Specialists	Postsecondary nondegree award	$29,050	12%	660

Education/Training

All states require barbers, hairdressers, and cosmetologists to be licensed. To qualify for a license, candidates are required to graduate from a state-approved cosmetology program.

Education. A high school diploma or equivalent is required for some positions. In addition, every state requires that barbers, hairdressers, and cosmetologists complete a program in a state-licensed barber or cosmetology school. Programs in hairstyling, skin care, and other personal appearance services are available in postsecondary vocational schools.

Full-time programs in barbering and cosmetology usually last at least 9 months and may lead to an associate's degree. Most of these workers take advanced courses in hairstyling or in other personal appearance services to keep up with the latest trends. Those who want to open their own business also may take courses in sales and marketing.

Licenses, Certifications, and Registrations. Barbers, hairdressers, and cosmetologists must obtain a license in order to work. Qualifications for a license vary by state, but generally, a person must fulfill the following criteria:

- Reached a minimum age of 16
- Received a high school diploma or equivalent
- Graduated from a state-licensed barber or cosmetology school

After graduating from a state-approved training program, students take a state licensing exam that includes a written test and, in some cases, a practical test of styling skills or an oral exam.

In many states, cosmetology training may be credited toward a barbering license and vice versa, and a few states combine the two licenses. A fee usually is required to apply for a license, and periodic renewals may be necessary.

Some states have reciprocity agreements that allow licensed barbers and cosmetologists to get a license in another state without needing additional formal training or state board testing, but such agreements are not common. Consequently, people who want to work in a particular state should review the laws of that state before entering a training program.

Important Qualities

Creativity. Barbers, hairdressers, and cosmetologists must keep up with the latest trends and be ready to try new hairstyles for their clients.

Customer-service skills. Workers must be pleasant, friendly, and able to interact with customers in order to retain clients.

Listening skills. Barbers, hairdressers, and cosmetologists should be good listeners. They must listen carefully to what the client wants in order to make sure that the client is happy with the result.

Physical stamina. Barbers, hairdressers, and cosmetologists must be able to stand on their feet for long periods.

Tidiness. Workers must keep a neat personal appearance and keep their work area clean and sanitary. This requirement is necessary for the health and safety of their clients and for making clients comfortable enough so that they will want to return.

Time-management skills. Time-management skills are important in scheduling appointments and providing services. For example, routine haircuts do not require the precise timing of some other services, such as applying neutralizer after a permanent wave. Clients who receive timely hair care are more likely to return.

Pay

The median hourly wage for barbers was $12.22 in May 2014. The median wage is the wage at which half the workers in an occupation earned more than that amount and half earned less. The lowest 10 percent earned less than $8.39, and the highest 10 percent earned more than $21.94.

The median hourly wage for hairdressers, hairstylists, and cosmetologists was $11.12 in May 2014. The lowest 10 percent earned less than $8.25, and the highest 10 percent earned more than $22.04.

Barbers, hairdressers, and cosmetologists may receive tips from customers. High-quality work and customer service usually contribute to greater tip totals.

Job Outlook

Overall employment of barbers, hairdressers, and cosmetologists is projected to grow 10 percent from 2014 to 2024, faster than the average for all occupations.

Employment of barbers is projected to grow 10 percent from 2014 to 2024, faster than the average for all occupations. The need for barbers will stem primarily from an increasing population, which will lead to greater demand for basic hair care services.

Employment of hairdressers, hairstylists, and cosmetologists is projected to grow 10 percent from 2014 to 2024, faster than the average for all occupations. Demand for hair coloring, hair straightening, and other advanced hair treatments has risen in recent years, a trend that is expected to continue over the coming decade.

Job Prospects. Overall job opportunities are expected to be good. A large number of job openings will stem from the need to replace workers who transfer to other occupations, retire, or leave the occupation for other reasons. However, workers should expect strong competition for jobs and clients at higher paying salons, of which there are relatively few and for which applicants must compete with a large pool of experienced hairdressers and cosmetologists.

Contacts for More Information

For more information about barbers, hairdressers, and cosmetologists, including training, visit

- American Association of Cosmetology Schools (www.beautyschools.org)
- National Association of Barber Boards of America (www.nationalbarberboards.com)

For information about state licensing, practice exams, and other professional links, visit

- National-Interstate Council of State Boards of Cosmetology (www.nictesting.org)
- Professional Beauty Association (www.probeauty.org)

O*NET

- Barbers (39-5011.00)
- Hairdressers, Hairstylists, and Cosmetologists (39-5012.00)

Childcare Workers

- **2014 Median Pay** .... $19,730 per year $9.48 per hour
- **Typical Entry-Level Education** .... High school diploma or equivalent
- **Work Experience in a Related Occupation**.............. None
- **On-the-job Training** ....Short-term on-the-job training
- **Number of Jobs, 2014** 1,260,600
- **Job Outlook, 2014–24** .... 5% (As fast as average)
- **Employment Change, 2014–24** 69,300

What Childcare Workers Do

Childcare workers provide care for children when parents and other family members are unavailable. They attend to children's basic needs, such as bathing and feeding. In addition, some help children prepare for kindergarten or help older children with homework.

Duties. Childcare workers typically do the following:

- Supervise and monitor the safety of children in their care
- Prepare and organize mealtimes and snacks for children
- Help children keep good hygiene
- Change the diapers of infants and toddlers
- Organize activities or implement a curriculum that allows children to learn about the world and explore their interests
- Develop schedules and routines to ensure that children have enough physical activity, rest, and playtime
- Watch for signs of emotional or developmental problems in children and bring the problems to the attention of their parents
- Keep records of children's progress, routines, and interests

Childcare workers read and play with babies and toddlers to introduce basic concepts, such as manners. For example, they teach young children how to share and take turns by playing games with other children.

Childcare workers often help preschool-age children prepare for kindergarten. Young children learn from playing, solving problems, questioning, and experimenting. Childcare workers use play and other instructional techniques to help children's development. For example, they use storytelling and rhyming games to teach language and vocabulary. They may help improve children's social skills by having them work together to build something in a sandbox. Childcare workers may teach math by having children count when building with blocks. They also involve the children in creative activities, such as art, dance, and music.

Childcare workers can also watch school-age children before and after school. They often help these children with homework and may take them to afterschool activities, such as sports practices and club meetings.

During the summer, when children are out of school, childcare workers may watch older children as well as younger ones for the entire day while the parents are at work.

The following are examples of types of childcare workers:

Childcare center workers work in teams in childcare centers that offer programs such as Head Start and Early Head Start. They often work with preschool teachers and teacher assistants to teach children through a structured curriculum. They prepare daily and long-term schedules of activities to stimulate and educate the children in their care. They also monitor and keep records of the children's progress.

Family childcare providers care for children in the providers' own homes during traditional working hours. They need to ensure that their homes and all staff they employ meet the regulations for family childcare providers.

In addition, family childcare providers perform tasks related to running their business. For example, they write contracts that set rates of pay, when payment can be expected, and the number of hours children can be in care. Furthermore, they establish policies about issues including whether sick children can be in their care, who can pick children up, and how behavioral issues will be dealt

Childcare workers nurture, teach, and care for children who have not yet entered kindergarten and older children before and after school.

with. Family childcare providers frequently spend some of their time marketing their services to prospective families.

Nannies work in the homes of the children they care for and the parents who employ them. Most often, they work full time for one family. They may be responsible for driving children to school, appointments, or afterschool activities. Some live in the homes of the families that employ them.

Babysitters, like nannies, work in the homes of the children in their care. However, they work for many families instead of just one. In addition, they generally do not work full time, but rather take care of the children on occasional nights and weekends when parents have other obligations.

Work Environment

Childcare workers held about 1.3 million jobs in 2014. The industries that employed the most childcare workers were as follows:

Child day care services	24%
Elementary and secondary schools; state, local, and private	10
Religious, grantmaking, civic, professional, and similar organizations	8

They are employed in childcare centers, preschools, public schools, and private homes.

Family childcare workers care for children in their own homes. They may convert a portion of their living space into a dedicated space for the children. Nannies and babysitters usually work in their employers' homes. In 2014, a little over one-quarter of childcare workers were self-employed.

Many states limit the number of children that each staff member is responsible for by regulating the ratio of staff to children. The ratios vary with the age of the children. Childcare workers are responsible for a relatively few number of babies and toddlers. However, workers can be responsible for greater numbers of older children.

Work Schedules. Although most childcare workers worked full time, about 2 in 5 worked part time in 2014.

Childcare workers' schedules vary widely. Childcare centers usually are open year round, with long hours so that parents can drop off and pick up their children before and after work. Some centers employ full-time and part-time staff with staggered shifts to cover the entire day.

Family childcare providers may work long or unusual hours to fit parents' work schedules. In some cases, these childcare providers may offer evening and overnight care to meet the needs of families. After the children go home, childcare providers often have more responsibilities, such as shopping for food or supplies, doing accounting, keeping records, and cleaning.

Nannies may work either full or part time. Full-time nannies may work more than 40 hours a week to give parents enough time to commute to and from work.

Education/Training

Education and training requirements vary by setting, state, and employer. They range from no formal education to a certification in early childhood education.

Education. Childcare workers must meet education and training requirements, which vary by state. Some states require these workers to have a high school diploma, but many states do not have any education requirements for entry-level positions. However, workers with postsecondary education or an early childhood education credential may be qualified for higher level positions.

Employers often prefer to hire workers with at least a high school diploma and, in some cases, some postsecondary education in early childhood education.

Workers in Head Start programs must at least be enrolled in a program in which they will earn a postsecondary degree in early childhood education or a child development credential.

States do not regulate educational requirements for nannies. However, some employers may prefer to hire workers with at least some formal instruction in childhood education or a related field, particularly when they will be hired as full-time nannies.

Licenses, Certifications, and Registrations. Many states require childcare centers, including those in private homes, to be licensed. To qualify for licensure, staff must pass a background check, have a complete record of immunizations, and meet a minimum training requirement. Some states require staff to have certifications in CPR and first aid.

Some states and employers require childcare workers to have a nationally recognized credential. Most often, states require the Child Development Associate (CDA) credential offered by the Council for Professional Recognition. Obtaining the CDA credential requires coursework, experience in the field, and a period during which the applicant is observed while working with children. The CDA credential is valid for 3 years and requires renewal.

Some states recognize the Certified Childcare Professional (CCP) designation offered by the National Early Childhood Program Accreditation. Some of the requirements needed to obtain the CCP are that the candidate must be at least 18 years old, have a high school diploma, have experience in the field, take courses in early childhood education, and pass an exam. The CCP accreditation requires renewal every 2 years through the CCP maintenance process.

The National Association for Family Child Care (NAFCC) offers a nationally recognized accreditation for family childcare providers. This accreditation requires training and experience in

Median Hourly Wages, May 2014

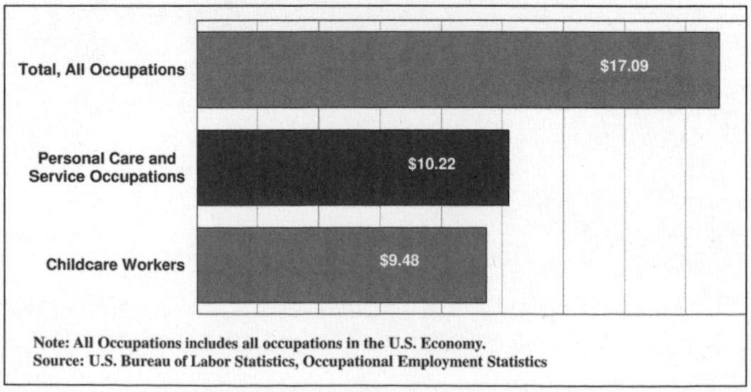

Percent Change in Employment, Projected 2014–2024

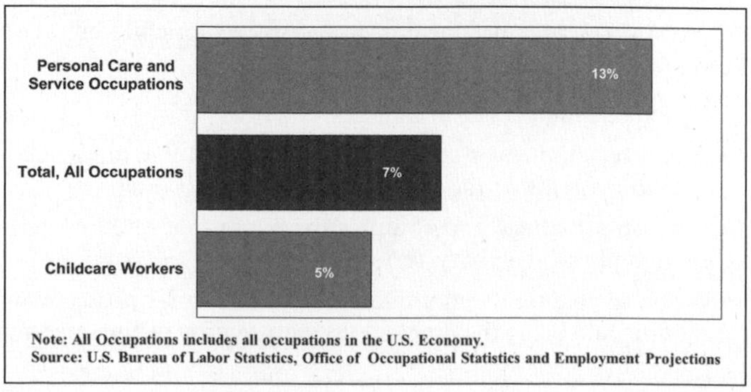

Employment Projections Data for Childcare Workers

Occupational Title	SOC Code	Employment, 2014	Projected Employment, 2024	Change, 2014–2024 Percent	Change, 2014–2024 Numeric
Childcare workers	39-9011	1,260,600	1,329,900	5	69,300

Source: U.S. Bureau of Labor Statistics, Employment Projections Program

Similar Occupations. This table shows a list of occupations with job duties that are similar to those of childcare workers.

Occupations	Entry-level Education	2014 Median Pay	Projected Job Growth	Average Annual Openings
Kindergarten and Elementary School Teachers	Bachelor's degree	$53,760	6%	8,780
Preschool and Childcare Center Directors	Bachelor's degree	$45,260	7%	420
Preschool Teachers	Associate's degree	$28,120	7%	2,960
Special Education Teachers	Bachelor's degree	$55,980	6%	2,810
Teacher Assistants	Some college, no degree	$24,430	6%	7,860

the field, as well as a period during which the applicant is observed while working with children.

Training. Many states and employers require providers to complete some training before beginning work. Also, many states require staff in childcare centers to complete a minimum number of hours of training annually. Training may include information about basic care of babies, such as how to warm a bottle, and customer-service skills.

Important Qualities

Communication skills. Childcare workers must be able to talk with parents and colleagues about the progress of the children in their care. They need good speaking skills to provide this information effectively and good listening skills to understand parents' instructions.

Decision-making skills. Good judgment is necessary for childcare workers so they can respond to emergencies or difficult situations.

Instructional skills. Childcare workers need to be able to explain things in terms young children can understand.

Interpersonal skills. Childcare workers need to work well with people to develop good relationships with parents, children, and colleagues.

Patience. Working with children can be frustrating, so childcare workers need to be able to respond to overwhelming and difficult situations calmly.

Physical stamina. Working with children can be physically taxing, so childcare workers should have a lot of energy.

Pay

The median hourly wage for childcare workers was $9.48 in May 2014. The median wage is the wage at which half the workers in an occupation earned more than that amount and half earned less. The lowest 10 percent earned less than $7.97, and the highest 10 percent earned more than $14.46.

In May 2014, the median hourly wages for childcare workers in the top industries in which they worked were as follows:

Elementary and secondary schools; state, local, and private	$11.01
Religious, grantmaking, civic, professional, and similar organizations	9.20
Child day care services	9.16

Pay varies with the worker's education and work setting. Those in formal childcare settings and those with more education usually earn higher wages. Pay for self-employed workers is based on the number of hours they work and the number and ages of the children in their care.

Job Outlook

Employment of childcare workers is projected to grow 5 percent from 2014 to 2024, about as fast as the average for all occupations.

Parents will continue to need assistance during working hours to care for their children. Early childhood education has also become widely recognized as important for children's development. This should increase demand for childcare workers.

However, the increasing cost of childcare and growth in the number of stay-at-home parents may reduce demand for childcare workers.

Job Prospects. Overall job opportunities for childcare workers are expected to be favorable. Workers with formal education should have the best job prospects. However, even those without formal education who are interested in the occupation should have little trouble finding employment because of the need to replace workers who leave the occupation.

Contacts for More Information

For more information about becoming a childcare provider, visit

- Child Care Aware (http://childcareaware.org)

For more information about working as a nanny, visit

- International Nanny Association (www.nanny.org)

For more information about family childcare providers, visit

- National Association for Family Child Care (www.nafcc.org)

For more information about early childhood education, visit

- National Association for the Education of Young Children (www.naeyc.org)

For more information about professional credentials, visit

- Council for Professional Recognition (www.cdacouncil.org)
- National Early Childhood Program Accreditation (www.necpa.net)

O*NET

- Childcare Workers (39-9011.00)
- Nannies (39-9011.01)

Fitness Trainers and Instructors

- **2014 Median Pay** .... $34,980 per year
$16.82 per hour
- **Typical Entry-Level Education** .... High school diploma or equivalent
- **Work Experience in a Related Occupation** .... None
- **On-the-job Training** .... Short-term on-the-job training
- **Number of Jobs, 2014** 279,100
- **Job Outlook, 2014–24** .... 8% (As fast as average)
- **Employment Change, 2014–24** 23,400

What Fitness Trainers and Instructors Do

Fitness trainers and instructors lead, instruct, and motivate individuals or groups in exercise activities, including cardiovascular exercises (exercises for the heart and blood circulation), strength training, and stretching. They work with people of all ages and skill levels.

Duties. Fitness trainers and instructors typically do the following:

- Demonstrate how to perform various exercises and routines
- Watch clients do exercises
- Demonstrate or explain correct exercise techniques to minimize injuries and improve fitness
- Provide alternative exercises during workouts or classes for different levels of fitness and skill
- Monitor clients' progress and adapt programs as needed
- Explain and enforce safety rules and regulations on sports, recreational activities, and the use of exercise equipment
- Give clients information or resources about nutrition, weight control, and lifestyle issues
- Give emergency first aid if needed

Both *group fitness instructors* and *specialized fitness instructors* plan or choreograph their own classes. Classes may include cardiovascular exercises, such as aerobics or dance; strength training, such as lifting weights; or both. Instructors choose music that is appropriate for their exercise class and create a routine or a set of moves for participants to follow. Some may teach prechoreographed routines that were originally created by fitness companies or other organizations.

Personal fitness trainers design and carry out workout routines specific to the needs of their clients. They may work with individual clients or teach group classes. In larger facilities, personal trainers often sell their training sessions to gym members. They start by evaluating their clients' current fitness level, personal goals, and skills. Then, they develop personalized training programs for their clients to follow, and they monitor the clients' progress.

Fitness trainers and instructors in smaller facilities often do a variety of tasks in addition to their fitness duties, such as tending the front desk, signing up new members, giving tours of the facility, or supervising the weight-training and cardiovascular equipment areas. Fitness trainers and instructors also may promote their facilities and instruction by various means, such as through social media, by writing newsletters or blog articles, or by creating posters and flyers.

Gyms and other types of health clubs offer many different activities for clients. However, trainers and instructors frequently specialize in only a few areas. The following are examples of types of fitness trainers and instructors:

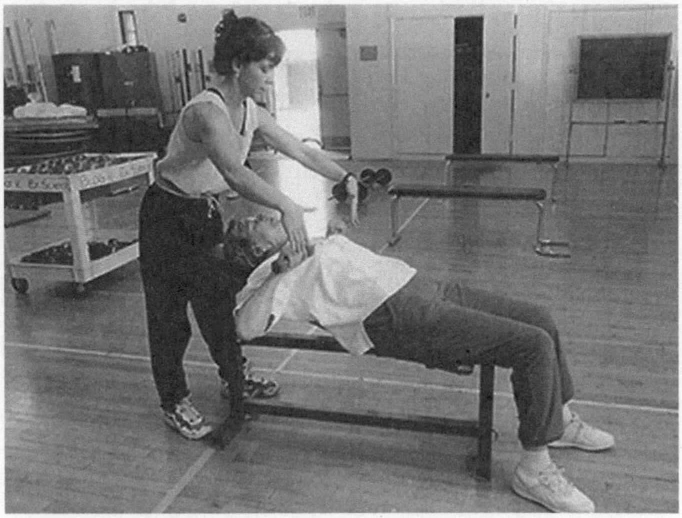

Personal trainers work one-on-one or with two or three clients, either in a gym or in the client's home.

Personal fitness trainers work with an individual client or a small group. They may train in a gym or in the clients' homes. Personal fitness trainers assess the clients' level of physical fitness and help them set and reach their fitness goals.

Group fitness instructors organize and lead group exercise classes, which can include aerobic exercises, stretching, or muscle conditioning. Some classes are set to music. In these classes, instructors may select the music and choreograph an exercise sequence.

Specialized fitness instructors teach popular conditioning methods, such as Pilates or yoga. In these classes, instructors show the different moves and positions of the particular method. They also watch students and correct those who are doing the exercises improperly.

Fitness directors oversee the fitness-related aspects of a gym or other type of health club. They often handle administrative duties, such as scheduling personal training sessions for clients and creating workout incentive programs. They may select and order fitness equipment for their facility.

Work Environment

Fitness trainers and instructors held about 279,100 jobs in 2014. The industries that employed the most fitness trainers and instructors were as follows:

Fitness and recreational sports centers	58%
Civic and social organizations	12
Educational services; state, local, and private	5
Government	4
Healthcare and social assistance	4

Fitness trainers and instructors work in facilities such as health clubs, fitness or recreation centers, gyms, and yoga and Pilates studios. These may be stand-alone centers or centers maintained by other types of establishments for their employees or for members of civic and social organizations. Some work in client's homes.

About 1 out of 10 fitness trainers and instructors were self-employed in 2014.

Work Schedules. Fitness trainers and instructors may work nights, weekends, or holidays. Some travel to different gyms or to clients' homes to teach classes or conduct personal training sessions. Some group fitness instructors and personal fitness trainers

Median Annual Wages, May 2014

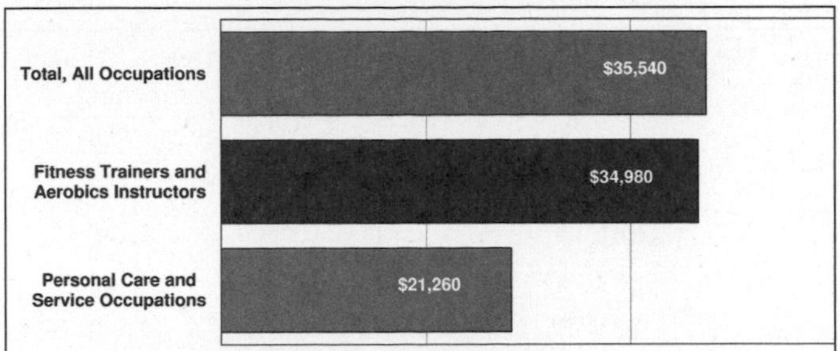

Note: All Occupations includes all occupations in the U.S. Economy.
Source: U.S. Bureau of Labor Statistics, Occupational Employment Statistics

Percent Change in Employment, Projected 2014–2024

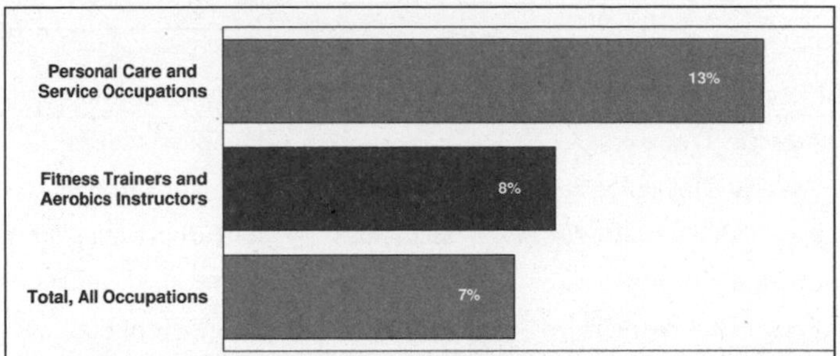

Note: All Occupations includes all occupations in the U.S. Economy.
Source: U.S. Bureau of Labor Statistics, Office of Occupational Statistics and Employment Projections

work other full-time jobs and teach fitness classes or conduct personal training sessions during evenings or weekends.

Education/Training

The education and training required for fitness trainers and instructors varies by type of specialty, and employers often hire those with certification. Personal fitness trainers, group fitness instructors, and specialized fitness instructors each need different preparation. Requirements also vary by facility.

Education. Almost all trainers and instructors have at least a high school diploma before entering the occupation. An increasing number of employers are requiring fitness workers, particularly personal trainers, to have an associate's or bachelor's degree related to a health or fitness field, such as exercise science, kinesiology, or physical education. Programs often include courses in nutrition, exercise techniques, biology, anatomy, and group fitness. Personal trainers also learn how to develop fitness programs for clients of all ages.

Licenses, Certifications, and Registrations. Employers prefer to hire fitness trainers and instructors who are certified. Many personal trainers must be certified before they begin working with clients or with members of a gym or other type of health club. Group fitness instructors can begin work without certification, but employers often encourage or require them to become certified. Most specialized fitness instructors receive certification for their preferred type of training, such as yoga or Pilates.

Many organizations offer certification. The National Commission for Certifying Agencies (NCCA), part of the Institute for Credentialing Excellence, lists certifying organizations that are accredited.

All certification exams have a written part, and some also have a practical part. The exams measure the candidate's knowledge of human physiology, understanding of proper exercise techniques, and ability to assess clients' fitness levels and develop appropriate exercise programs. Many certifying organizations offer study materials to prepare for the exam, including books, webinars, other audio and visual materials, and exam preparation workshops and seminars.

Advanced certification requires an associate's or bachelor's degree in an exercise-related subject that includes more-specialized instruction, such as training athletes, working with people who are injured or ill, or advising clients on general health. For more information, see the profiles on athletic trainers and exercise physiologists.

Most trainers or instructors need certification in cardiopulmonary resuscitation (CPR) and automated external defibrillators before applying for certification in physical fitness.

Training. After becoming a certified personal trainer, new trainers typically work alongside an experienced trainer before they are allowed to train clients alone.

Training for specialized fitness instructors can vary greatly. For example, the duration of programs for yoga instructors can range from a few days to more than 2 years. The Yoga Alliance offers several credentials that require a minimum of between 200 and 500 hours, with a specified number of hours in techniques, teaching methods, anatomy, physiology, philosophy, and other areas.

Important Qualities

Customer-service skills. Many fitness trainers and instructors must sell their services, motivating clients to hire them as personal trainers or to sign up for the classes they lead. Fitness trainers and instructors must therefore be polite, friendly, and encouraging to maintain relationships with their clients.

Communication skills. Fitness trainers and instructors must be able to clearly explain or demonstrate exercises to clients.

Listening skills. Fitness trainers and instructors must be able to listen carefully to what clients tell them in order to determine the clients' fitness levels and desired fitness goals.

Motivational skills. Getting fit and staying fit takes a lot of work for many clients. To keep clients coming back for more classes or to continue personal training, fitness trainers and instructors must keep their clients motivated.

Physical fitness. Fitness trainers and instructors need to be physically fit because their job requires a considerable amount of exercise. Group instructors often participate in classes, and personal trainers often need to demonstrate exercises to their clients.

Employment Projections Data for Fitness Trainers and Instructors

Occupational Title	SOC Code	Employment, 2014	Projected Employment, 2024	Change, 2014–2024 Percent	Change, 2014–2024 Numeric
Fitness trainers and aerobics instructors	39-9031	279,100	302,500	8	23,400

Source: U.S. Bureau of Labor Statistics, Employment Projections Program

Similar Occupations. This table shows a list of occupations with job duties that are similar to those of fitness trainers and instructors.

Occupations	Entry-level Education	2014 Median Pay	Projected Job Growth	Average Annual Openings
Athletic Trainers	Bachelor's degree	$43,370	21%	540
Exercise Physiologists	Bachelor's degree	$46,270	11%	150
Physical Therapist Assistants and Aides	See Education/Training	$41,640	40%	5,140
Physical Therapists	Doctoral or professional degree	$82,390	34%	7,180
Recreation Workers	High school diploma or equivalent	$22,620	10%	3,890
Recreational Therapists	Bachelor's degree	$44,000	12%	220

Problem-solving skills. Fitness trainers and instructors must evaluate each client's level of fitness and create an appropriate fitness plan to meet the client's individual needs.

Advancement. Fitness trainers and instructors who are interested in management positions should get a bachelor's degree in exercise science, physical education, kinesiology, or a related subject. Experience often is required in order for a trainer or instructor to advance to a management position in a health club or fitness center. Many organizations prefer a master's degree for certain positions.

Personal trainers may eventually advance to a head trainer position and become responsible for hiring and overseeing the personal training staff or for bringing in new personal training clients. Head trainers also are responsible for procuring athletic equipment, such as weights or fitness machines. Some fitness trainers and instructors go into business for themselves and open their own fitness centers.

Pay

The median annual wage for fitness trainers and instructors was $34,980 in May 2014. The median wage is the wage at which half the workers in an occupation earned more than that amount and half earned less. The lowest 10 percent earned less than $18,110, and the highest 10 percent earned more than $67,560.

In May 2014, the median annual wages for fitness trainers and instructors in the top industries in which they worked were as follows:

Fitness and recreational sports centers	$36,420
Healthcare and social assistance	35,260
Educational services; state, local, and private	32,190
Government	31,800
Civic and social organizations	30,700

Fitness trainers and instructors may work nights, weekends, or holidays. Some travel to different gyms or to clients' homes to teach classes or conduct personal training sessions. Some group fitness instructors and personal fitness trainers work other full-time jobs and teach fitness classes or conduct personal training sessions during evenings or weekends.

Job Outlook

Employment of fitness trainers and instructors is projected to grow 8 percent from 2014 to 2024, about as fast as the average for all occupations.

As businesses, government, and insurance organizations continue to recognize the benefits of health and fitness programs for their employees, incentives to join gyms or other types of health clubs are expected to increase the need for fitness trainers and instructors. For example, some organizations may open their own exercise facilities onsite to promote employee wellness.

Other employment growth will come from the continuing emphasis on exercise to combat obesity and encourage healthier lifestyles for people of all ages. In particular, the baby-boom generation should continue to remain active to help prevent injuries and illnesses associated with aging.

Participation in yoga and Pilates is expected to continue to increase, driven partly by older adults who want low-impact forms of exercise and relief from arthritis and other ailments.

Job Prospects. Job prospects should be best for workers with professional certification or increased levels of formal education in health or fitness.

Contacts for More Information

For more information about fitness careers and about health and fitness programs in universities and other institutions, visit

➤ American College of Sports Medicine (www.acsm.org)

➤ National Strength and Conditioning Association (www.nsca.com)

For information about certifications for personal trainers and group fitness instructors, visit

➤ American Council on Exercise (www.acefitness.org)

➤ National Academy of Sports Medicine (www.nasm.org)

➤ National Federation of Professional Trainers (www.NFPT.com)

National Commission for Certifying Agencies (part of the Institute for Credentialing Excellence) (www.credentialingexcellence.org/ncca)

➤ US Registry of Exercise Professionals (www.usreps.org/Pages/default.aspx)

For information about health clubs and sports clubs, visit

➤ International Health, Racquet, & Sportsclub Association (www.ihrsa.org)

For information about yoga teacher certification and a list of registered schools, visit

➤ Yoga Alliance (www.yogaalliance.org)

O*NET

➤ Fitness Trainers and Aerobics Instructors (39-9031.00)

Funeral Service Workers

- **2014 Median Pay** .... $52,520 per year
$25.25 per hour
- **Typical Entry-Level Education** .... Associate's degree
- **Work Experience in a Related Occupation** .... See Education/Training
- **On-the-job Training** .... See Education/Training

- **Number of Jobs, 2014** 60,400
- **Job Outlook, 2014–24** .... 5% (As fast as average)
- **Employment Change, 2014–24** 3,100

What Funeral Service Workers Do

Funeral service workers organize and manage the details of a funeral.

Duties. Funeral service workers typically do the following:

- Offer counsel and comfort to families and friends of the deceased
- Arrange for removal of the deceased's body
- Prepare the remains (body)
- File death certificates and other legal documents
- Train junior staff

Funeral service workers help to determine the locations, dates, and times of visitations (wakes), funerals or memorial services, burials, and cremations. They handle other details as well, such as helping the family decide whether the body should be buried, entombed, or cremated. This decision is critical because funeral practices vary among cultures and religions.

Most funeral service workers attend to the administrative aspects pertaining to the person's death, including submitting papers to state officials to receive a death certificate. They also may help resolve insurance claims, apply for funeral benefits, or notify the Social Security Administration or the U.S. Veterans Administration of the death.

A growing number of funeral service workers work with clients who wish to plan their own funerals in advance to ensure that their needs are met.

Funeral service workers also may help individuals adapt to changes in their lives following a death by providing information on support groups.

The following are examples of types of funeral service workers:

Funeral service managers oversee the general operations of a funeral home business. They perform a wide variety of duties, such as planning and allocating the resources of the funeral home, managing staff, and handling marketing and public relations.

Morticians, undertakers, and funeral directors plan the details of a funeral. They often prepare obituary notices and arrange for pallbearers and clergy services. If a burial is chosen, they schedule the opening and closing of a grave with a representative of the cemetery. If cremation is chosen, they coordinate the process with the crematory. They also prepare the sites of all services and provide transportation for the deceased and mourners. In addition, they arrange the shipment of bodies out of state or out of country for final disposition.

Funeral service workers handle the details of funerals.

Finally, these workers handle administrative duties. For example, they often must apply for the transfer of any pensions, insurance policies, or annuities on behalf of survivors.

Most morticians, undertakers, and funeral directors embalm bodies. Embalming is a cosmetic and temporary preservative process through which the body is prepared for a viewing by family and friends of the deceased.

Work Environment

Funeral service workers held about 60,400 jobs in 2014. Approximately 54 percent worked in the death care services industry. About half of all funeral service workers were self-employed in 2014.

Funeral services traditionally take place in a house of worship, in a funeral home, or at a gravesite or crematory. However, some families prefer holding the service in their home or in a social center.

Funeral service managers work mostly in a funeral home office.

Morticians, undertakers, and funeral directors work mostly in funeral homes that have a merchandise display room and, sometimes, a chapel. Some also may operate a crematory or cemetery, which may be on the premises. The mood can be quiet and somber, and the work is often stressful, because workers must arrange the various details of a funeral within 24 to 72 hours of death. In addition, they may be responsible for managing multiple funerals on the same day.

Although workers sometimes may come into contact with bodies that have contagious diseases, the work is not dangerous if proper safety and health regulations are followed. Those working in crematories are exposed to high temperatures and must wear protective clothing.

Work Schedules. Most funeral service workers are employed full time. They are often on call and long workdays are common, including evenings and weekends.

Education/Training

An associate's degree in funeral service or mortuary science is the typical education requirement for funeral service workers. With the exception of funeral service managers, all workers must be licensed in Washington, DC, and every state in which they work, except Colorado which offers a voluntary certification program.

Education. An associate's degree in mortuary science is the typical education requirement for all funeral service workers. Courses taken usually include those covering the topics of ethics, grief counseling, funeral service, and business law. All accredited programs also include courses in embalming and restorative techniques. States have their own education requirements, and state licensing laws vary. Most employers require applicants to be 21 years old; have 2 years of formal education; serve a 1-year internship before, during, or after attending a mortuary college; and pass a state licensing exam after graduation.

In some states, licensure for funeral directors and embalmers is separate.

The American Board of Funeral Service Education (ABFSE) accredits 58 funeral service and mortuary science programs, most of which are 2-year associate's degree programs offered at community colleges. Some programs offer a bachelor's degree.

Median Annual Wages, May 2014

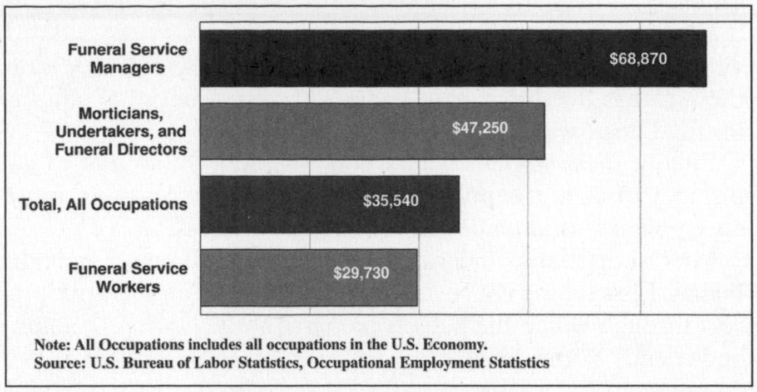

Percent Change in Employment, Projected 2014–2024

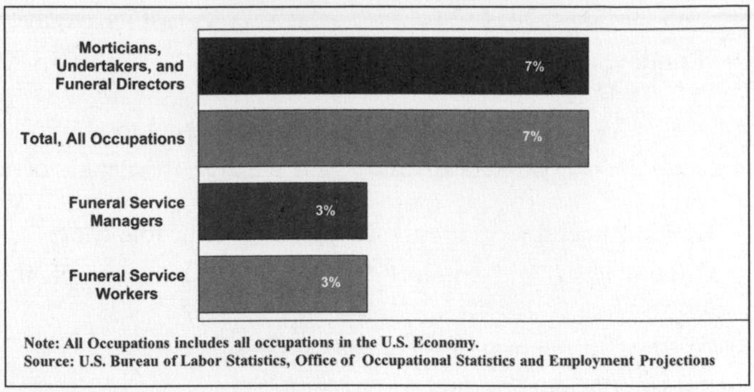

Although an associate's degree is usually adequate, some employers prefer applicants to have a bachelor's degree.

High school students can prepare to become a funeral service worker by taking courses in biology, chemistry, and business, and by participating in public speaking.

Part-time or summer jobs in funeral homes also provide valuable experience.

Training. Morticians, undertakers, and funeral directors must complete hands-on training, usually lasting 1 to 3 years, under the direction of a licensed funeral director or manager. The internship may be completed before, during, or after completing a 2-year funeral service or mortuary science program and passing a national board exam. Internships provide practical experience in all aspects of the funeral service.

Licenses, Certifications, and Registrations. With the exception of funeral service managers, all workers must be licensed in Washington, DC, and every state in which they work, except Colorado which offers a voluntary certification program. Although licensing laws and examinations vary by state, most applicants must meet the following criteria:

- Be 21 years old
- Complete 2 years in an ABFSE funeral service or mortuary science program, and pass a national board exam
- Serve an internship lasting 1 to 3 years

Applicants must then pass a state licensing exam. Working in multiple states will require multiple licenses. For specific requirements, applicants should contact each applicable state licensing board.

Most states require funeral directors and embalmers to receive continuing education credits annually to keep their licenses.

The International Cemetery, Cremation and Funeral Association (ICCFA) and the National Funeral Directors Association (NFDA) offer crematory certification designations. A growing number of states are requiring certification for those who will perform cremations. For specific requirements, applicants should contact their state board.

Other Experience. Workers increasingly are being required to have some office management experience, particularly for funeral service managers who run their own funeral home business.

Important Qualities

Business skills. Knowledge of financial statements and the ability to run a funeral home efficiently and profitably are important for funeral directors and managers.

Compassion. Death is a delicate and emotional matter. Funeral service workers must be able to treat clients with care and sympathy in their time of loss.

Interpersonal skills. Funeral service workers should have good interpersonal skills. When speaking with families, for instance, they must be tactful and able to explain and discuss all matters about services provided.

Time-management skills. Funeral service workers must be able to handle numerous tasks for multiple customers, often over a short timeframe.

Pay

The median annual wage for funeral service managers was $68,870 in May 2014. The median wage is the wage at which half the workers in an occupation earned more than that amount and half earned less. The lowest 10 percent earned less than $38,850, and the highest 10 percent earned more than $137,410.

The median annual wage for morticians, undertakers, and funeral directors was $47,250 in May 2014. The lowest 10 percent earned less than $25,910, and the highest 10 percent earned more than $83,520.

Job Outlook

Overall employment of funeral service workers is projected to grow 5 percent from 2014 to 2024, about as fast as the average for all occupations.

Employment of morticians, undertakers, and funeral directors is projected to grow 7 percent from 2014 to 2024, about as fast as the average for all occupations. Demand for funeral service workers will stem from deaths in the aging population.

Employment Projections Data for Funeral Service Workers

Occupational Title	SOC Code	Employment, 2014	Projected Employment, 2024	Change, 2014–2024	
				Percent	Numeric
Funeral service workers	—	71,000	72,400	2	1,400
Funeral service managers	11-9061	29,300	30,300	3	1,000
Morticians, undertakers, and funeral directors	39-4031	31,100	33,200	7	2,100

Source: U.S. Bureau of Labor Statistics, Employment Projections Program

Similar Occupations. This table shows a list of occupations with job duties that are similar to those of funeral service workers.

Occupations	Entry-level Education	2014 Median Pay	Projected Job Growth	Average Annual Openings
Administrative Services Managers	Bachelor's degree	$83,790	8%	2,350
Advertising, Promotions, and Marketing Managers	Bachelor's degree	$123,450	9%	1,970
Human Resources Managers	Bachelor's degree	$102,780	9%	1,080
Physicians and Surgeons	Doctoral or professional degree	This wage is equal to or greater than $187,200.	14%	9,930
Psychologists	See Education/Training	$70,700	19%	3,250
Social Workers	See Education/Training	$45,500	12%	7,480

These workers increasingly are performing day-to-day routine tasks, including many administrative duties, such as filling out paperwork and securing death certificates. In addition, as a growing number of baby boomers prearrange their end-of-life services, these workers, through their services, will offer people a stress-free understanding that their final wishes will be met.

Employment of funeral service managers is projected to grow 3 percent from 2014 to 2024, slower than the average for all occupations. Despite growth of the death care industry, fewer managers will be needed as morticians, undertakers, and funeral directors increasingly handle the day-to-day activities at a funeral home.

Job Prospects. Job prospects for funeral service workers are expected to be good overall. Opportunities should be particularly favorable for those who are licensed as both a funeral director and an embalmer, for those willing to relocate, and for certified crematory operators.

Some job openings should result from the need to replace workers who retire or leave the occupation each year.

Contacts for More Information

For more information about funeral service workers, including accredited mortuary science programs, visit

➤ National Funeral Directors Association (http://nfda.org)

For scholarships and educational programs in funeral service and mortuary science, visit

➤ American Board of Funeral Service Education (www.abfse.org)

➤ National Funeral Directors & Morticians Association, Inc. (www.nfdma.com)

For information about crematories, visit

➤ Cremation Association of North America (www.cremationassociation.org)

➤ International Cemetery, Cremation and Funeral Association (www.iccfa.com)

Candidates should contact their state board for specific licensing requirements.

O*NET

➤ Funeral Service Managers (11-9061.00)

➤ Morticians, Undertakers, and Funeral Directors (39-4031.00)

Gaming Services Workers

- **2014 Median Pay** .... $19,940 per year $9.59 per hour
- **Typical Entry-Level Education** .... High school diploma or equivalent
- **Work Experience in a Related Occupation** .... See Education/Training
- **On-the-job Training** .... See Education/Training
- **Number of Jobs, 2014** 131,900
- **Job Outlook, 2014–24** .... 1% (Little or no change)
- **Employment Change, 2014–24** 1,000

What Gaming Services Workers Do

Gaming services workers serve customers in gambling establishments, such as casinos or racetracks. Some workers tend slot machines or deal cards. Others take bets or pay out winnings. Still others supervise or manage gaming workers and operations.

Duties. Gaming services workers typically do the following:

- Interact with customers and ensure that they have a pleasant experience
- Monitor customers for violations of gaming regulations or casino policies
- Inform their supervisor or a security employee of any irregularities they observe
- Enforce safety rules and report hazards
- Explain how to play the games to customers

Gaming managers and supervisors direct and oversee the gaming operations and personnel in their assigned area. Supervisors circulate among the tables to make sure that everything is running smoothly and that all areas are properly staffed. Gaming managers and supervisors typically do the following:

- Keep an eye on customers and employees to ensure compliance with all gaming and casino rules
- Communicate with other departments if security or customer-service issues arise
- Address customers' complaints about service
- Explain house operating rules, such as betting limits, if customers do not understand them

- Ensure payouts are correct
- Schedule when and where employees in their section will work
- Interview, hire, and train new employees

Slot supervisors oversee the activities of the slot department. The job duties of this occupation have changed significantly, as slot machines have become more automated in recent years. Because most casinos use video slot machines that give out tickets instead of cash and thus require very little oversight, workers in this occupation spend most of their time providing customer service to slot players. Slot supervisors typically do the following:

- Watch over the slot section and ensure that players are satisfied with the games
- Refill machines with tickets or money when they run out
- Pay large jackpots
- Reset cash slot machines after a payout
- Respond to and resolve customer complaints
- Interview, hire, and train new employees

Gaming dealers operate table games such as craps, blackjack, and roulette. They stand or sit behind tables while serving customers. Dealers control the pace and action of the game. They announce each player's move to the rest of the table and let players know when it is their turn. Most dealers are often required to work at least two games, usually blackjack or craps. Gaming dealers typically do the following:

- Give out cards and provide dice or other equipment to customers
- Determine winners, calculate and pay off winning bets, and collect on losing bets
- Continually inspect cards or dice
- Inform players of the rules of the game
- Keep track of the amount of money that customers have already bet
- Exchange paper money for gaming chips

Gaming and sports book writers and runners handle bets on sporting events and take and record bets for customers. Sports book writers and runners also verify tickets and pay out winning tickets. In addition, they help run games such as bingo and keno.

Many gaming dealers specialize in one type of game.

Some gaming runners collect winning tickets from customers in a casino. Gaming and sports book writers and runners typically do the following:

- Scan tickets and calculate winnings
- Operate the equipment that randomly selects bingo or keno numbers
- Announce bingo or keno numbers when they are selected
- Oversee the cash that comes in (on bets) and goes out (on winnings) during their shift

Education/Training

Most gaming jobs require a high school diploma or equivalent. Some casinos may require gaming managers to have a college degree. In addition, all gaming services workers must have excellent customer-service skills.

Education. Gaming dealers, gaming supervisors, sports book writers and runners, and slot supervisors typically need a high school diploma or equivalent. Educational requirements for gaming managers, however, differ by casino. Although some casinos may only require a high school diploma or equivalent, others require gaming managers to have a college degree. Those who choose to pursue a degree may study hotel management, hospitality, or accounting in addition to taking formal management classes.

Training. Individual casinos or other gaming establishments have their own training requirements. New gaming dealers may be sent to gaming school for a few weeks to learn a casino game, such as blackjack or craps. These schools teach the rules and procedures of the game, as well as state and local laws and regulations related to the game.

Although gaming school is primarily for new employees, some experienced dealers have to go to gaming school if they want to be trained in a new casino game.

Completing gaming school before being hired may increase a prospective dealer's chances of being hired, but it does not guarantee a job. Casinos usually audition prospective dealers for open positions to assess their personal qualities.

Gaming and sports book writers and runners usually do not have to go to gaming school. They can be trained by the casino in less than 1 month. The casino teaches them state and local laws and regulations related to the game, as well the particulars of their job, such as keno calling.

Licenses, Certifications, and Registrations. Gaming services workers must be licensed by a state regulatory agency, such as a state casino control board or gaming commission. Licensing requirements for supervisory or managerial positions may differ from those for gaming dealers, gaming and sports book writers and runners, and all other gaming workers. However, all applicants for a license must provide photo identification and pay a fee. They must also typically pass an extensive background check and drug test. Failure to pass the background check may prevent candidates from getting a job or a gaming license.

Age requirements also vary by state. For specific licensing requirements, visit the state's gaming commission website.

Work Experience in a Related Occupation. Gaming and slot supervisors and gaming managers usually have several years of experience working in a casino. Gaming supervisors often have experience as a dealer or in the customer outreach department of the casino. Slot supervisors usually have experience as a slot technician or slot attendant. Some also may have worked in entry-level marketing or customer-service positions.

Median Annual Wages, May 2014

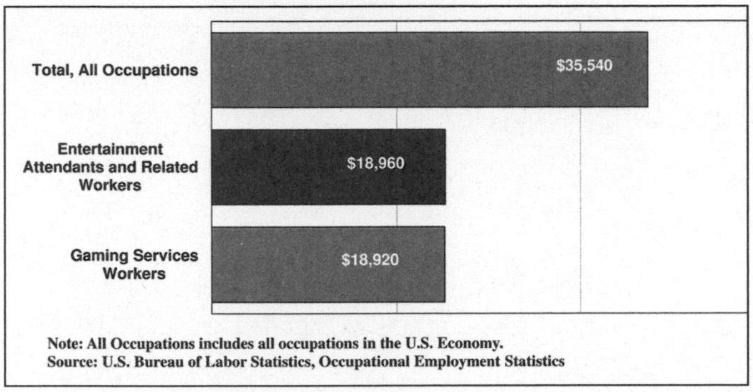

Percent Change in Employment, Projected 2014–2024

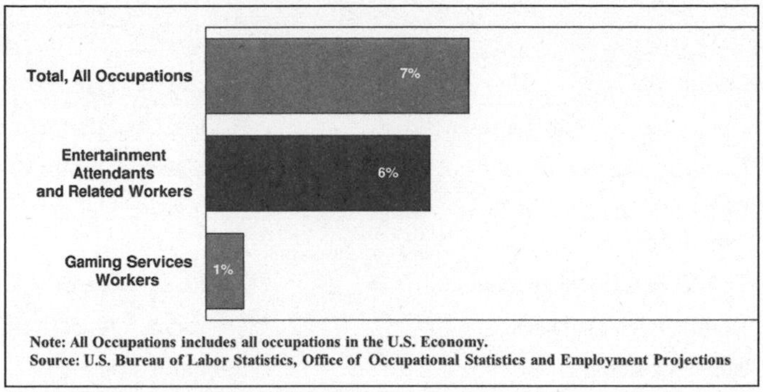

Advancement. Gaming managers are often promoted from positions as slot or gaming supervisors. They also may be moved from a management job in another part of the resort, such as hospitality, after learning about casino operations through an internship or on-the-job training.

Gaming dealers can advance to gaming supervisors and eventually managers. A slot supervisor can also advance to gaming manager.

Important Qualities

Communication skills. Gaming services workers must be able to explain the rules of the game to customers and answer any questions they have. Simple misunderstandings can cost a customer a lot of money and damage the reputation of the casino.

Customer-service skills. All gaming jobs involve a lot of interaction with customers. The success or failure of a casino depends on how customers view the casino, making customer service important for all gaming services occupations.

Leadership skills. Gaming managers and supervisors oversee other gaming services workers and must be able to guide them in doing their jobs and developing their skills.

Math skills. Because they deal with large amounts of money, many casino workers must be good at math.

Organizational skills. Gaming managers and supervisors must be well organized to handle administrative and other tasks required in overseeing gaming services workers.

Patience. All gaming services workers have to be able to keep their composure when they handle a customer who becomes upset or breaks a rule. They also must be patient in dealing with equipment failure or malfunction.

Pay

The median annual wage for gaming services workers was $19,940 in May 2014. The median wage is the wage at which half the workers in an occupation earned more than that amount and half earned less. The lowest 10 percent earned less than $16,880, and the highest 10 percent earned more than $53,870.

Median annual wages for gaming services workers in May 2014 were as follows:

Gaming managers	$67,310
Gaming supervisors	49,420
Slot supervisors	33,270
Gaming service workers, all other	24,240
Gaming and sports book writers and runners	22,560
Gaming dealers	18,560

Job Outlook

Employment of gaming services workers is projected to show little or no change from 2014 to 2024.

Employment will be driven by the increasing popularity of gambling establishments. Additional states currently without commercial gaming establishments may allow new casinos to be built over the next decade in an effort to bring in more tax revenue.

However, the risk of oversaturation may force some states to scale back their plans to build new casinos. As more states approve the expansion in the number of gaming establishments, the competition for customers will increase. Those establishments that fail to keep or attract customers may be forced to close, thereby negating some of the jobs created from new casinos.

In addition, the share of casino revenue attributed to gaming has been steadily falling over the past few years. This trend is likely to persist as younger customers are typically spend an increasingly larger share of their money on other forms of entertainment rather than gaming.

Furthermore, the legalization of online gambling in some states may draw some customers away from traditional brick-and-mortar casinos.

Employment Projections Data for Gaming Services Workers

Occupational Title	SOC Code	Employment, 2014	Projected Employment, 2024	Change, 2014–2024 Percent	Numeric
Gaming services workers	—	131,900	132,900	1	1,000
Gaming managers	11-9071	3,800	3,800	-1	0
Gaming supervisors	39-1011	27,800	28,000	1	200
Slot supervisors	39-1012	7,100	6,900	-3	-200
Gaming dealers	39-3011	68,500	68,900	1	400
Gaming and sports book writers and runners	39-3012	11,500	11,900	3	400
Gaming service workers, all other	39-3019	13,200	13,400	2	200

Source: U.S. Bureau of Labor Statistics, Employment Projections Program

Similar Occupations. This table shows a list of occupations with job duties that are similar to those of gaming services workers.

Occupations	Entry-level Education	2014 Median Pay	Projected Job Growth	Average Annual Openings
Customer Service Representatives	High school diploma or equivalent	$31,200	10%	25,290
Lodging Managers	High school diploma or equivalent	$47,680	8%	370
Public Relations and Fundraising Managers	Bachelor's degree	$101,510	7%	470
Public Relations Specialists	Bachelor's degree	$55,680	6%	1,490
Retail Sales Workers	No formal educational credential	$21,670	7%	33,100
Sales Managers	Bachelor's degree	$110,660	5%	1,900
Security Guards and Gaming Surveillance Officers	High school diploma or equivalent	$24,470	5%	5,500

Employment of slot supervisors is projected to decline 3 percent from 2014 to 2024. Younger gaming customers typically prefer more interactive table games compared with slot machines. As a result, some casinos may swap out their slots to make room for more table games.

Job Prospects. Although jobs are expected to open as workers leave the occupation, strong competition is expected for jobs at casinos. Those with work experience in customer service at a hotel or resort should have better job prospects because of the importance of customer service in casinos.

Those already with a gaming license and knowledge and training in different casino games will have the best job prospects.

Contacts for More Information

For more information about gaming services workers, visit
- American Gaming Association (www.americangaming.org)
- Casino Careers (www.casinocareers.com)

O*NET

- Gaming Managers (11-9071.00)
- Gaming Supervisors (39-1011.00)
- Slot Supervisors (39-1012.00)
- Gaming Dealers (39-3011.00)
- Gaming and Sports Book Writers and Runners (39-3012.00)
- Gaming Service Workers, All Other (39-3019.00)

Manicurists and Pedicurists

- **2014 Median Pay** ..... $19,620 per year, $9.43 per hour
- **Typical Entry-Level Education** ..... Postsecondary nondegree award
- **Work Experience in a Related Occupation** ..... None
- **On-the-job Training** ..... None
- **Number of Jobs, 2014** 113,600
- **Job Outlook, 2014–24** ..... 10% (Faster than average)
- **Employment Change, 2014–24** 11,700

What Manicurists and Pedicurists Do

Manicurists and pedicurists clean, shape, and beautify fingernails and toenails.

Duties. Manicurists and pedicurists typically do the following:

- Discuss nail treatments and services available
- Remove nail polish
- Clean, trim, and file nails
- Reduce calluses and rough skin
- Massage and moisturize hands (for a manicure) and feet (for a pedicure)
- Polish or buff nails
- Advise clients about nail and skin care for hands and feet
- Promote and sell nail and skin care products
- Clean and disinfect their work area and tools

Manicurists and pedicurists work exclusively on the hands and feet, providing treatments to groom fingernails and toenails. A typical treatment involves soaking the clients' hands or feet to soften the skin in order to remove dead skin cells. Manicurists and pedicurists apply lotion to the hands and feet to moisturize the skin. They also may shape and apply polish to artificial fingernails.

Manicurists and pedicurists use a variety of tools, including nail clippers, nail files, and specialized cuticle tools. They must be focused while they perform their duties, because most of the tools they use are sharp. Keeping their tools clean and sanitary is important.

Nail technicians work in salons and provide various services including manicures.

Median Hourly Wages, May 2014

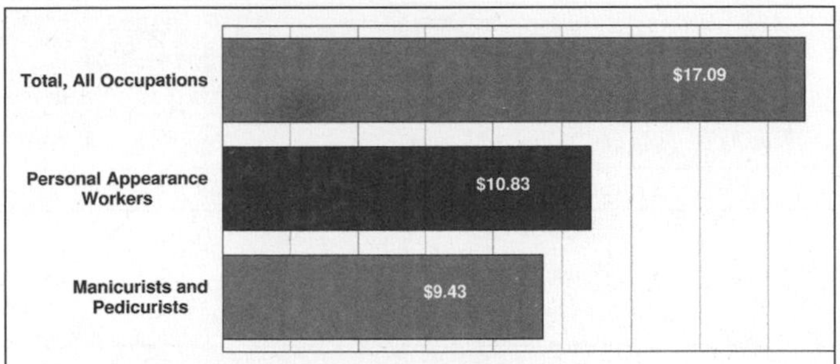

Note: All Occupations includes all occupations in the U.S. Economy.
Source: U.S. Bureau of Labor Statistics, Occupational Employment Statistics

Percent Change in Employment, Projected 2014–2024

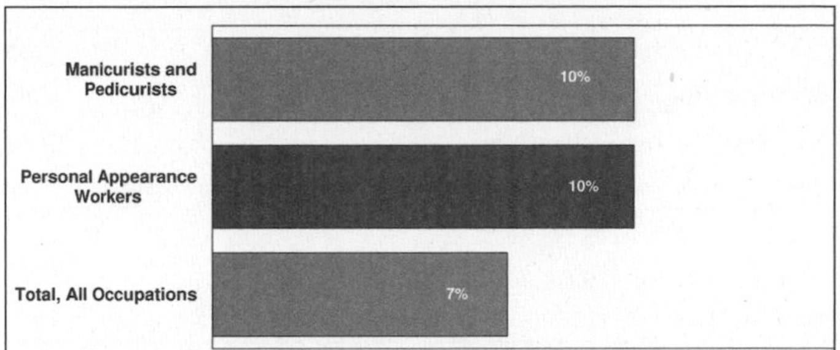

Note: All Occupations includes all occupations in the U.S. Economy.
Source: U.S. Bureau of Labor Statistics, Office of Occupational Statistics and Employment Projections

Some manicurists and pedicurists operate their own nail salon business. They manage the daily decision-making tasks, such as keeping inventory records and ordering supplies. They also hire and supervise workers and sell nail care products, such as nail polish and hand or foot cream, to clients. A small, but growing, number of workers make house calls. Their mobile manicure and pedicure services are popular because clients consider them convenient.

Work Environment

Manicurists and pedicurists held about 113,600 jobs in 2014, of which 68 percent were in the personal care services industry. About 3 in 10 were self-employed, many running their own nail salon business.

Manicurists and pedicurists usually work in a nail salon, spa, or hair salon. The job involves a lot of sitting. Those who own a mobile grooming company must travel to their clients' homes.

Manicurists and pedicurists use chemicals when working on fingernails and toenails, so they often wear protective clothing, including protective gloves and masks.

Work Schedules. Although most manicurists and pedicurists work full time, many have variable schedules and work part time. Their schedules often are determined by the type of establishment. For example, a full-service salon may require manicurists and pedicurists to work an 8-hour day. A boutique hair salon, however, may require fewer work hours on a part-time basis. Longer work days are not unusual for self-employed workers. Weekends and evenings tend to be the busiest times for manicurists and pedicurists.

Education/Training

Manicurists and pedicurists must complete a state-approved cosmetology or nail technician program and then pass a state exam for licensure, which all states except Connecticut require.

Education. Manicurists and pedicurists must complete a state-approved cosmetology or nail technician program. Currently, there are hundreds of programs nationwide.

Licenses, Certifications, and Registrations. State licensing requirements vary. However, applicants need to be at least 16 years old and have a high school diploma or the equivalent. After completing a state-approved cosmetology or nail technician program, manicurists and pedicurists must take a written exam and a practical exam to get a license through their state board. Mobile manicure and pedicure services require a separate license.

The National–Interstate Council of State Boards of Cosmetology provides information on state examinations for licensing, with sample questions. The Professional Beauty Association and the American Association of Cosmetology Schools also provide information on state examinations, as well as offering other professional links.

Important Qualities

Business skills. Manicurists and pedicurist who run their own nail salon must understand general business principles. For example, they should be skilled at administrative tasks, such as accounting and personnel management, and be able to manage a salon efficiently and profitably.

Creativity. The ability to neatly finish small, intricate designs is important, as is the ability to suggest nail designs and match them to individual tastes.

Customer-service skills. Good listening and interpersonal skills are important in working with clients. Also, meeting the needs of clients, including interacting with them while doing a manicure or pedicure, encourages repeat business.

Dexterity. A steady hand is essential in achieving a creative and precise nail design. In addition, because manicurists and pedicurists often use sharp tools, they must have good finger dexterity.

Pay

The median hourly wage for manicurists and pedicurists was $9.43 in May 2014. The median wage is the wage at which half the workers in an occupation earned more than that amount and half earned less. The lowest 10 percent earned less than $8.27, and the highest 10 percent earned more than $15.43.

Job Outlook

Employment of manicurists and pedicurists is projected to grow 10 percent from 2014 to 2024, faster than the average for all occupations.

The increase in employment reflects demand for new nail services being offered, such as mini-sessions (quick manicures at a low cost) and mobile manicures and pedicures (house calls).

The desire among young women and a growing number of men to lead a healthier lifestyle through better grooming and wellness also should result in higher employment for manicurists and pedicurists.

Considered a low-cost luxury service, manicures and pedicures will continue to be in demand by individuals at all income levels.

Job Prospects. Job opportunities should be very good overall. The growing number of nail salons and the need to replace workers who leave the occupation each year will result in many job openings.

Contacts for More Information

For information about training and cosmetology schools, visit

- American Association of Cosmetology Schools (www.beautyschools.org)

Employment Projections Data for Manicurists and Pedicurists

Occupational Title	SOC Code	Employment, 2014	Projected Employment, 2024	Change, 2014–2024	
				Percent	Numeric
Manicurists and pedicurists	39-5092	113,600	125,300	10	11,700

Source: U.S. Bureau of Labor Statistics, Employment Projections Program

Similar Occupations. This table shows a list of occupations with job duties that are similar to those of manicurists and pedicurists.

Occupations	Entry-level Education	2014 Median Pay	Projected Job Growth	Average Annual Openings
Barbers, Hairdressers, and Cosmetologists	Postsecondary nondegree award	$23,200	10%	6,440
Skincare Specialists	Postsecondary nondegree award	$29,050	12%	660

➤ International Pedicure Association (www.pedicureassociation.org)

For information about state licensing, practice exams, and other professional links, visit

➤ National–Interstate Council of State Boards of Cosmetology (www.nictesting.org)

➤ Professional Beauty Association (www.probeauty.org/links)

O*NET

➤ Manicurists and Pedicurists (39-5092.00)

Recreation Workers

- **2014 Median Pay** .... $22,620 per year $10.88 per hour
- **Typical Entry-Level Education** .... High school diploma or equivalent
- **Work Experience in a Related Occupation** .... None
- **On-the-job Training** ....Short-term on-the-job training
- **Number of Jobs, 2014** 379,300
- **Job Outlook, 2014–24** .... 10% (Faster than average)
- **Employment Change, 2014–24** 38,900

What Recreation Workers Do

Recreation workers design and lead recreational and leisure activities for groups in volunteer agencies or recreation facilities, such as playgrounds, parks, camps, aquatic centers, and senior centers. They may lead activities such as arts and crafts, dance, sports, adventure programs, music, and camping.

Duties. Recreation workers typically do the following:

- Plan, organize, and lead activities for groups or recreation centers
- Explain the rules of activities and instruct participants at a variety of skill levels
- Enforce safety rules to prevent injury
- Modify activities to suit the needs of specific groups, such as seniors
- Administer basic first aid if needed
- Organize and set up the equipment that is used in recreational activities

The specific responsibilities of recreation workers vary greatly with their job title, their level of training, and the state they work in. The following are examples of types of recreation workers:

Activity specialists provide instruction and coaching primarily in one activity, such as dance, swimming, or tennis. These workers may work in camps, aquatic centers, or anywhere else where there is interest in a single activity.

Recreation leaders are responsible for a recreation program's daily operation. They primarily organize and direct participants, schedule the use of facilities, set up and keep records of equipment use, and ensure that recreation facilities and equipment are used and maintained properly. They may lead classes and provide instruction in a recreational activity, such as kayaking or golf.

Camp counselors work directly with youths in residential (overnight) or day camps. They often lead and instruct children and teenagers in a variety of outdoor activities, such as swimming, hiking, horseback riding, or nature study. Counselors also provide guidance and supervise daily living and socialization. Some counselors may specialize in a specific activity, such as archery, boating, music, drama, or gymnastics.

Work Environment

Recreation workers held about 379,300 jobs in 2014. The industries that employed the most recreation workers were as follows:

Local government, excluding education and hospitals	30%
Nursing and residential care facilities	15
Religious, grantmaking, civic, professional, and similar organizations	14
Arts, entertainment, and recreation	11
Social assistance	9

Many workers spend much of their time outdoors. Recreation directors and supervisors, however, typically spend most of their time in an office, planning programs and special events.

All recreation workers risk injury while participating in physical activities.

Work Schedules. Many recreation workers, such as camp counselors or activity specialists, work weekends or part time or irregular hours, or may be seasonally employed. Seasonal workers may work as few as 90 days or as long as 9 months during a season, depending on where they are employed and the type of activity they lead. For example, in areas of the United States that have warm winters, outdoor swimming pools may employ related recreation workers for a majority of the year. In other areas of the country, they may work only during the summer.

Education/Training

Education and training requirements for recreation workers vary with the type of job, but workers typically need at least a high school diploma or the equivalent and receive on-the-job training.

Education and Training. Recreation workers typically need at least a high school diploma or the equivalent. Many receive on-the-job training that typically lasts less than a month.

Entry-level educational requirements vary with the type of position. For example, an activity leader position working with the elderly will have different requirements than a position as a summer camp counselor working with children.

Some positions may require a bachelor's degree or college coursework. In 2014, the Council on Accreditation of Parks, Recreation, Tourism, and Related Professions, a branch of the National Recreation and Park Association (NRPA), accredited 80 bachelor's degree programs in recreation or leisure studies. A bachelor's degree in other subjects, such as liberal arts or public administration, may also qualify applicants for some positions.

Important Qualities

Communication skills. Recreation workers must be able to communicate well. They often work with large groups of people and need to give clear instructions, motivate participants, and maintain order and safety.

Flexibility. Recreation workers must be flexible when planning activities. They must be able to adapt plans to suit changing environmental conditions and participants' needs.

Leadership skills. Recreation workers should be able to lead both large and small groups. They often lead activities for people of all ages and abilities.

Physical strength. Recreation workers need to be physically fit. Their job may require a considerable amount of movement because they often demonstrate activities while explaining them.

Problem-solving skills. Recreation workers need strong problem-solving skills. They must be able to create and reinvent activities and programs for all types of participants.

For recreation workers who generally work part time, such as camp counselors and activity specialists, certain qualities may be more important than education. These qualities include a worker's experience leading activities, the ability to work well with children or the elderly, and the ability to ensure the safety of participants.

Licenses, Certifications, and Registrations. The NRPA offers four certifications for recreation workers:

- Certified Parks and Recreation Professional (CPRP)
- Certified Parks and Recreation Executive (CPRE)
- Aquatic Facility Operator (AFO)
- Certified Playground Safety Inspector (CPSI)

Many recreation workers spend most of their time outdoors in various weather conditions.

Applicants may qualify for certification with different combinations of education and work experience. They also must take continuing education classes to maintain their certification.

The American Camp Association offers four certificates for various levels of camp staff, from Entry-Level Staff Certificate to Camp Director Certificate. Individuals who complete online courses may show their advanced level of knowledge of core competencies.

Some recreation jobs require other kinds of certification. For example, a lifesaving certificate is often required for teaching or coaching water-related activities. These certifications are available from organizations such as the YMCA or the American Red Cross. Specific requirements vary by job and employer.

Median Annual Wages, May 2014

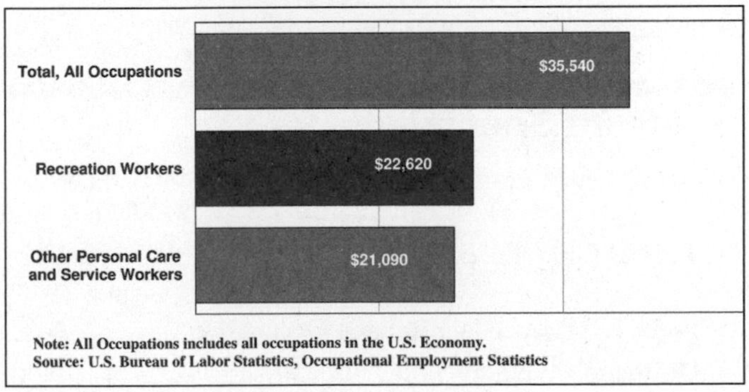

Percent Change in Employment, Projected 2014–2024

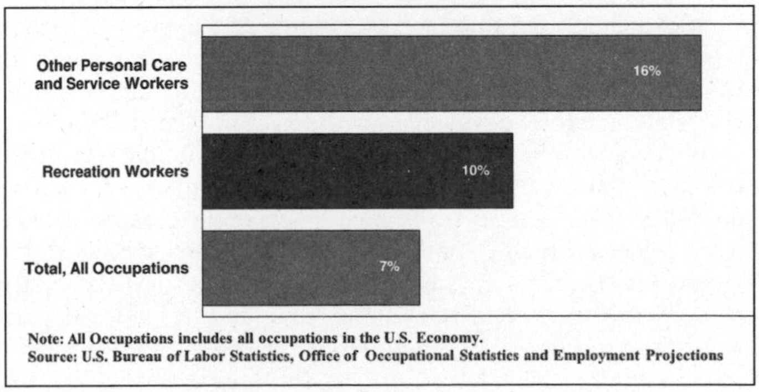

Employment Projections Data for Recreation Workers

Occupational Title	SOC Code	Employment, 2014	Projected Employment, 2024	Change, 2014–2024 Percent	Change, 2014–2024 Numeric
Recreation workers	39-9032	379,300	418,300	10	38,900

Source: U.S. Bureau of Labor Statistics, Employment Projections Program

Similar Occupations. This table shows a list of occupations with job duties that are similar to those of recreation workers.

Occupations	Entry-level Education	2014 Median Pay	Projected Job Growth	Average Annual Openings
Athletic Trainers	Bachelor's degree	$43,370	21%	540
Exercise Physiologists	Bachelor's degree	$46,270	11%	150
Fitness Trainers and Instructors	High school diploma or equivalent	$34,980	8%	2,340
Meeting, Convention, and Event Planners	Bachelor's degree	$46,490	10%	990
Probation Officers and Correctional Treatment Specialists	Bachelor's degree	$49,060	4%	330
Psychologists	See Education/Training	$70,700	19%	3,250
Recreational Therapists	Bachelor's degree	$44,000	12%	220
Rehabilitation Counselors	Master's degree	$34,380	9%	1,080
School and Career Counselors	Master's degree	$53,370	8%	2,250
Social Workers	See Education/Training	$45,500	12%	7,480

Advancement. As workers gain experience, they may be promoted to positions with greater responsibilities. Recreation workers with experience and managerial skills may advance to supervisory or managerial positions. Eventually, they may become directors of a recreation department or may start their own recreation company.

Pay

The median annual wage for recreation workers was $22,620 in May 2014. The median wage is the wage at which half the workers in an occupation earned more than that amount and half earned less. The lowest 10 percent earned less than $17,190, and the highest 10 percent earned more than $39,230.

In May 2014, the median annual wages for recreation workers in the top industries in which they worked were as follows:

Nursing and residential care facilities	$24,840
Social assistance	22,930
Local government, excluding education and hospitals	22,650
Religious, grantmaking, civic, professional, and similar organizations	20,930
Arts, entertainment, and recreation	19,700

Job Outlook

Employment of recreation workers is projected to grow 10 percent from 2014 to 2024, faster than the average for all occupations. In response to growing rates of childhood obesity, a number of federal, state, and local campaigns have been established to encourage young people to be physically active. As more emphasis is placed on the importance of exercise, more recreation workers will be needed to work in local government parks and recreation departments, fitness centers, sports centers, and camps specializing in younger participants. Additional recreation workers will be needed to work for fitness centers as some parks and recreation departments seek to cut costs by contracting out the services of activity specialists, especially those in fitness, from these centers.

In addition, as the baby-boom generation grows older, there will be more demand for recreation workers to work with older clients in social assistance organizations and in nursing and residential care facilities.

Job Prospects. Job prospects will be best for those seeking part-time, seasonal, or temporary recreation jobs. Because workers in these jobs tend to be students or young people, they must be replaced when they leave for school or jobs in other occupations, thus creating many job openings.

Workers with higher levels of formal education related to recreation should have better prospects at getting year-round full-time positions. Volunteer experience, part-time work during school, and a summer job also are viewed favorably for both full- and part-time positions.

Contacts for More Information

For information on careers, certification, and academic programs in parks and recreation, visit

➤ National Recreation and Park Association (www.nrpa.org)

For information about a career as a camp counselor, visit

➤ American Camp Association (www.acacamps.org)

O*NET

➤ Recreation Workers (39-9032.00)

Skincare Specialists

- **2014 Median Pay** .... $29,050 per year, $13.97 per hour
- **Typical Entry-Level Education** .... Postsecondary nondegree award
- **Work Experience in a Related Occupation** .... None
- **On-the-job Training** .... None

- **Number of Jobs, 2014** 55,000
- **Job Outlook, 2014–24**............ 12% (Faster than average)
- **Employment Change, 2014–24** 6,600

What Skincare Specialists Do

Skincare specialists cleanse and beautify the face and body to enhance a person's appearance.

Duties. Skincare specialists typically do the following:

- Evaluate clients' skin condition and appearance
- Discuss available treatments and determine which products will improve clients' skin quality
- Remove unwanted hair, using wax, laser, or other approved treatments
- Clean the skin before applying makeup
- Recommend skin care products, such as cleansers, lotions, or creams
- Teach and advise clients on how to apply makeup, and how to take care of their skin
- Refer clients to another skincare specialist, such as a dermatologist, for serious skin problems
- Disinfect equipment and clean work areas

Skincare specialists give facials, full-body treatments, and head and neck massages to improve the health and appearance of the skin. Some may provide other skin care treatments, such as peels, masks, and scrubs, to remove dead or dry skin.

In addition to working with clients, skincare specialists create daily skincare routines based on skin analysis and help clients understand which skincare products will work best for them. A growing number of specialists actively sell skincare products, such as cleansers, lotions, and creams.

Those who operate their own salons have managerial duties that include hiring, firing, and supervising workers, as well as keeping business and inventory records, ordering supplies, and arranging for advertising.

Work Environment

Skincare specialists held about 55,000 jobs in 2014. The industries that employed the most skincare specialists were as follows:

Personal care services	49%
Offices of physicians	7
Health and personal care stores	5
Other amusement and recreation industries	3

About 3 in 10 skincare specialists were self-employed in 2014.

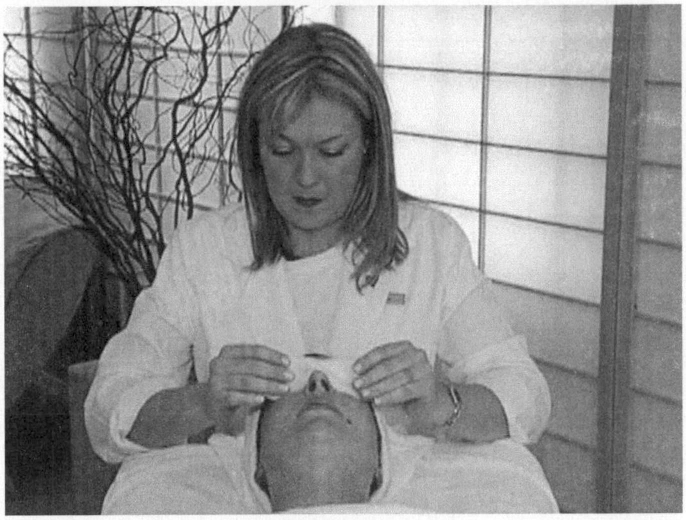

Skincare specialists cleanse and beautify a client's face and body.

Skincare specialists usually work in salons and beauty and health spas. Some also work in medical offices. These workers may have to stand for extended periods of time.

Because skincare specialists must evaluate the condition of the skin, good lighting and clean surroundings are important. Protective clothing and good ventilation also may be necessary, because skincare specialists often use chemicals on the face and body.

Work Schedules. Skincare specialists typically work full time, with many working evenings and weekends. Working more than 40 hours a week is common, especially for self-employed workers.

Education/Training

Skincare specialists must complete a state-approved cosmetology or esthetician program and then pass a state exam for licensure, which all states except Connecticut require.

Education. Skincare specialists usually take a state-approved cosmetology or esthetician program. Although some high schools offer vocational training, most people receive their training from a postsecondary vocational school. The Associated Skin Care Professionals, the largest organization devoted to these workers, offers a State Regulation Guide, which includes the number of prerequisite hours required to complete a cosmetology program.

Training. Newly hired specialists sometimes receive on-the-job training, especially if their jobs require working with chemicals. Those who are employed in a medical environment also may receive on-the-job training, often working alongside an experienced skincare specialist.

Median Hourly Wages, May 2014

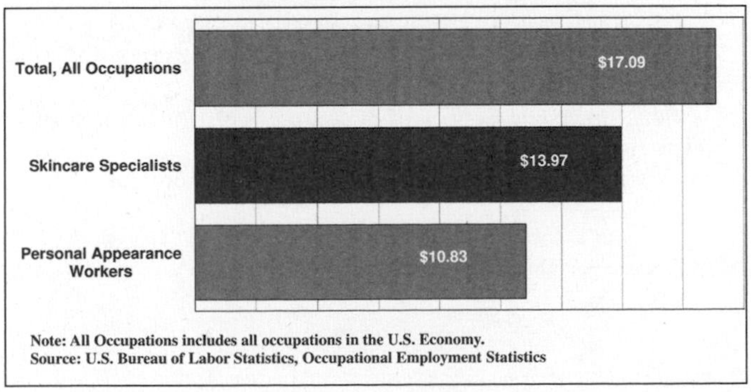

Percent Change in Employment, Projected 2014–2024

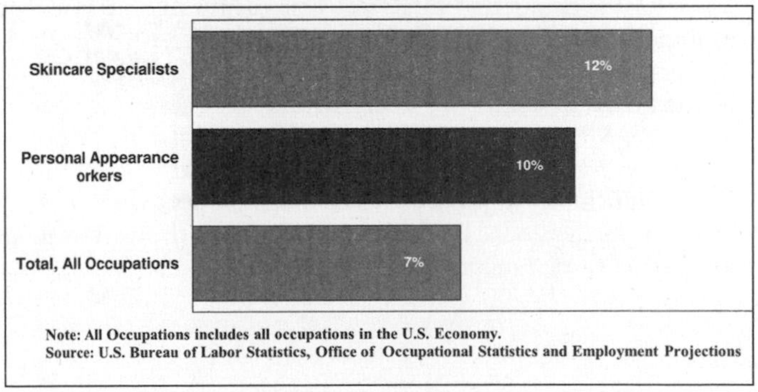

Employment Projections Data for Skincare Specialists

Occupational Title	SOC Code	Employment, 2014	Projected Employment, 2024	Change, 2014–2024 Percent	Change, 2014–2024 Numeric
Skincare specialists	39-5094	55,000	61,600	12	6,600

Source: U.S. Bureau of Labor Statistics, Employment Projections Program

Similar Occupations. This table shows a list of occupations with job duties that are similar to those of skincare specialists.

Occupations	Entry-level Education	2014 Median Pay	Projected Job Growth	Average Annual Openings
Barbers, Hairdressers, and Cosmetologists	Postsecondary nondegree award	$23,200	10%	6,440
Manicurists and Pedicurists	Postsecondary nondegree award	$19,620	10%	1,170
Massage Therapists	Postsecondary nondegree award	$37,180	22%	3,650

Licenses, Certifications, and Registrations. After completing an approved cosmetology or esthetician program, skincare specialists take a written and practical exam to get a state license. Licensing requirements vary by state, so those interested should contact their state board.

The National-Interstate Council of State Boards of Cosmetology provides contact information on state examinations for licensing, with sample exam questions. The Professional Beauty Association and the American Association of Cosmetology Schools also provide information on state examinations, as well as offering other professional links.

Many states offer continuing education seminars and programs designed to keep skincare specialists current on new techniques and products. Post-licensing training is also available through manufacturers, associations, and at trade shows.

Important Qualities

Business skills. Skincare specialists who run their own salon must understand general business principles. For example, they should be skilled at administrative tasks, such as accounting and personnel management, and be able to manage a salon efficiently and profitably.

Customer-service skills. Skincare specialists should be friendly and courteous to their clients. Repeat business is important, particularly for self-employed workers.

Initiative. Self-employed skincare specialists generate their own business opportunities and must be proactive in finding new clients.

Physical stamina. Skincare specialists must be able to spend most of their day standing and massaging clients' faces and bodies.

Tidiness. Workers must keep a neat personal appearance and keep their work area clean and sanitary. This requirement is necessary for the health and safety of their clients and increases the likelihood that clients will return.

Time-management skills. Time-management skills are important in scheduling appointments and providing services.

Pay

The median hourly wage for skincare specialists was $13.97 in May 2014. The median wage is the wage at which half the workers in an occupation earned more than that amount and half earned less. The lowest 10 percent earned less than $8.50, and the highest 10 percent earned more than $28.31.

In May 2014, the median hourly wages for skincare specialists in the top industries in which they worked were as follows:

Offices of physicians	$17.82
Other amusement and recreation industries	17.18
Personal care services	13.45
Health and personal care stores	11.63

Job Outlook

Employment of skincare specialists is projected to grow 12 percent from 2014 to 2024, faster than the average for all occupations.

The increase in employment reflects demand for new services being offered, such as mini-sessions (quick facials at a lower cost) and mobile facials (making house calls). In addition, the desire among many women and a growing number of men to reduce the effects of aging and to lead a healthier lifestyle through better grooming, including skin treatments for relaxation and well-being, should result in employment growth.

Job Prospects. Job opportunities should be good because of the growing number of beauty salons and spas. Those with related work experience should have the best job opportunities.

Contacts for More Information

For more information about skincare specialists, visit

- Aesthetics International Association (www.aestheticsassociation.com)
- Associated Skin Care Professionals (www.ascpskincare.com)

For information about cosmetology schools, visit

- American Association of Cosmetology Schools (www.beautyschools.org)

For information about the spa industry, visit

- International Spa Association (www.experienceispa.com)

For information about state licensing, practice exams, and other professional links, visit

- National-Interstate Council of State Boards of Cosmetology (www.nictesting.org)
- Professional Beauty Association (www.probeauty.org/links)

O*NET

- Skincare Specialists (39-5094.00)

Production

Assemblers and Fabricators

- **2014 Median Pay** .... $29,280 per year
  $14.08 per hour
- **Typical Entry-Level Education** .... High school diploma or equivalent
- **Work Experience in a Related Occupation** .... None
- **On-the-job Training** .... Moderate-term on-the-job training
- **Number of Jobs, 2014** 1,834,000
- **Job Outlook, 2014–24** ....-1% (Little or no change)
- **Employment Change, 2014–24** .... -9,700

What Assemblers and Fabricators Do

Assemblers and fabricators assemble finished products and the parts that go into them. They use tools, machines, and their hands to make engines, computers, aircraft, ships, boats, toys, electronic devices, control panels, and more.

Duties. Assemblers and fabricators typically do the following:

- Read and understand schematics and blueprints
- Use hand tools or machines to assemble parts
- Conduct quality control checks
- Work closely with designers and engineers in product development

Assemblers and fabricators have an important role in the manufacturing process. They assemble both finished products and the pieces that go into them. The products encompass a full range of manufactured goods, including aircraft, toys, household appliances, automobiles, computers, and electronic devices.

Changes in technology have transformed the manufacturing and assembly process. Modern manufacturing systems use robots, computers, programmable motion-control devices, and various sensing technologies. These technological changes affect the way in which goods are made and the jobs of those who make them. Advanced assemblers must be able to work with these new technologies and use them to manufacture goods.

The job of an assembler or fabricator requires a range of knowledge and skills. Skilled assemblers putting together complex machines, for example, read detailed schematics that show how to assemble the machine. After determining how parts should connect, they use hand or power tools to trim, shim, cut, and make other adjustments to fit components together. Once the parts are properly aligned, they connect them with bolts and screws or weld or solder pieces together.

Quality control is important throughout the assembly process, so assemblers look for faulty components and mistakes in the assembly process. They help fix problems before defective products are made.

Manufacturing techniques are moving away from traditional assembly line systems toward lean manufacturing systems, which use teams of workers to produce entire products or components. Lean manufacturing has changed the nature of the assemblers' duties.

It has become more common to involve assemblers and fabricators in product development. Designers and engineers consult manufacturing workers during the design stage to improve product reliability and manufacturing efficiency. Some experienced assemblers work with designers and engineers to build prototypes or test products.

Although most assemblers and fabricators are classified as team assemblers, others specialize in producing one type of product or perform the same or similar tasks throughout the assembly process.

The following are examples of types of assemblers and fabricators:

Aircraft structure, surfaces, rigging, and systems assemblers fit, fasten, and install parts of airplanes, space vehicles, or missiles, such as the wings, fuselage, landing gear, rigging and control equipment, and heating and ventilating systems.

Coil winders, tapers, and finishers wind wire coils of electrical components used in a variety of electric and electronic products, including resistors, transformers, generators, and electric motors.

Electrical and electronic equipment assemblers build products such as electric motors, computers, electronic control devices, and sensing equipment. Automated systems have been put in place because many small electronic parts are too small or fragile for human assembly. Much of the remaining work of electrical and electronic assemblers is done by hand during the small-scale production of electronic devices used in all types of aircraft, military

Assemblers test circuits in electronic devices.

systems, and medical equipment. Production by hand requires these workers to use devices such as soldering irons.

Electromechanical equipment assemblers assemble and modify electromechanical devices such as household appliances, computed tomography scanners, or vending machines. The workers use a variety of tools, such as rulers, rivet guns, and soldering irons.

Engine and machine assemblers construct, assemble, and rebuild engines, turbines, and machines used in automobiles, construction and mining equipment, and power generators.

Structural metal fabricators and fitters cut, align, and fit together structural metal parts and may help weld or rivet the parts together.

Fiberglass laminators and fabricators laminate layers of fiberglass on molds to form boat decks and hulls, bodies for golf carts, automobiles, and other products.

Team assemblers work on an assembly line, but they rotate through different tasks, rather than specializing in a single task. The team may decide how the work is assigned and how different tasks are done. Some aspects of lean production, such as rotating tasks and seeking worker input on improving the assembly process, are common to all assembly and fabrication occupations.

Timing device assemblers, adjusters, and calibrators do precision assembling or adjusting of timing devices within very narrow tolerances.

Work Environment

Assemblers and fabricators held about 1.8 million jobs in 2014; most of these jobs were in manufacturing industries.

Employment in the detailed occupations that make up assemblers and fabricators was distributed as follows:

Team assemblers	1,144,200
Assemblers and fabricators, all other	240,700
Electrical and electronic equipment assemblers	207,200
Structural metal fabricators and fitters	79,200
Electromechanical equipment assemblers	47,200
Aircraft structure, surfaces, rigging, and systems assemblers	40,600
Engine and other machine assemblers	39,000
Fiberglass laminators and fabricators	19,200
Coil winders, tapers, and finishers	14,900
Timing device assemblers and adjusters	1,700

Most assemblers and fabricators work in manufacturing plants, and working conditions vary by plant and by industry. Many physically difficult tasks have been automated or made easier through the use of power tools, such as tightening massive bolts or moving heavy parts into position. Assembly work, however, may still involve long periods of standing, sitting, or working on ladders, such as in the shipbuilding industry.

Injuries and Illnesses. Some assemblers may come into contact with potentially harmful chemicals or fumes, but ventilation systems normally minimize any harmful effects. Other assemblers may come in contact with oil and grease, and their work areas may be noisy. Fiberglass laminators and fabricators are exposed to fiberglass, which may irritate the skin. Therefore, fiberglass workers must wear gloves and long sleeves and must use respirators for safety.

Work Schedules. Most assemblers and fabricators are employed full time, sometimes working evenings and weekends.

Education/Training

The education level and qualifications needed to enter these jobs vary depending on the industry and employer. Although a high school diploma is enough for most jobs, experience and additional training is needed for more advanced assembly work.

Education. Most employers require a high school diploma or the equivalent for assembler and fabricator positions.

Training. Workers usually receive on-the-job training, sometimes including employer-sponsored technical instruction.

Some employers may require specialized training or an associate's degree for the most skilled assembly and fabrication jobs. For example, jobs with electrical, electronic, and aircraft and motor vehicle products manufacturers typically require more formal education through technical schools. Apprenticeship programs are also available.

Licenses, Certifications, and Registrations. The Fabricators & Manufacturers Association, International (FMA) offers the Precision Sheet Metal Operator Certification (PSMO) and the Precision Press Brake Certification (PPB). Although not required, becoming certified can demonstrate competence and professionalism. It also may help a candidate advance in the profession.

In addition, many employers that hire electrical and electronic assembly workers, especially those in the aerospace and defense industries, require certifications in soldering.

Important Qualities

Color vision. Assemblers and fabricators who make electrical and electronic products must be able to distinguish different colors because the wires they work with often are color coded.

Dexterity. Assemblers and fabricators should have a steady hand and good hand-eye coordination, as they must grasp, manipulate, or assemble parts and components that are often very small.

Math skills. Assemblers and fabricators must know basic math and must be able to use computers, as the manufacturing process continues to advance technologically.

Mechanical skills. Modern production systems require assemblers and fabricators to be able to use programmable motion-control devices, computers, and robots on the factory floor.

Median Annual Wages, May 2014

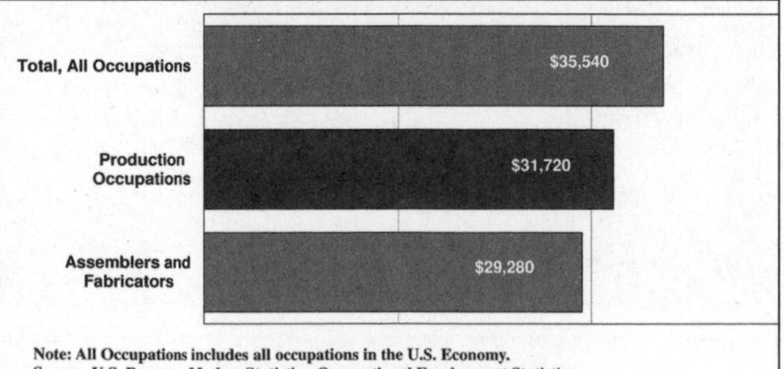

Note: All Occupations includes all occupations in the U.S. Economy.
Source: U.S. Bureau of Labor Statistics, Occupational Employment Statistics

Percent Change in Employment, Projected 2014–2024

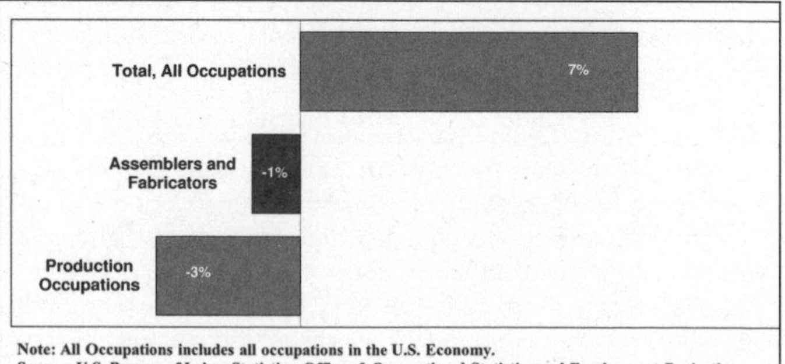

Note: All Occupations includes all occupations in the U.S. Economy.
Source: U.S. Bureau of Labor Statistics, Office of Occupational Statistics and Employment Projections

Employment Projections Data for Assemblers and Fabricators

Occupational Title	SOC Code	Employment, 2014	Projected Employment, 2024	Change, 2014–2024 Percent	Change, 2014–2024 Numeric
Assemblers and fabricators	—	1,834,000	1,824,300	-1	-9,700
Aircraft structure, surfaces, rigging, and systems assemblers	51-2011	40,600	38,600	-5	-2,000
Coil winders, tapers, and finishers	51-2021	14,900	14,100	-6	-900
Electrical and electronic equipment assemblers	51-2022	207,200	197,000	-5	-10,200
Electromechanical equipment assemblers	51-2023	47,200	44,700	-5	-2,500
Engine and other machine assemblers	51-2031	39,000	39,000	0	0
Structural metal fabricators and fitters	51-2041	79,200	80,800	2	1,600
Fiberglass laminators and fabricators	51-2091	19,200	18,600	-3	-600
Team assemblers	51-2092	1,144,200	1,137,700	-1	-6,500
Timing device assemblers and adjusters	51-2093	1,700	1,600	-2	0
Assemblers and fabricators, all other	51-2099	240,700	252,200	5	11,500

Source: U.S. Bureau of Labor Statistics, Employment Projections Program

Physical stamina. Assemblers and fabricators must be able to stand for long periods and perform repetitious work.

Physical strength. Assemblers and fabricators must be strong enough to lift heavy components or pieces of machinery. Some assemblers, such as those in the aerospace industry, must frequently bend or climb ladders when assembling parts.

Technical skills. Assemblers and fabricators must be able to understand technical manuals, blueprints, and schematics for a wide range of products and machines to properly manufacture the final product.

Pay

The median annual wage for assemblers and fabricators was $29,280 in May 2014. The median wage is the wage at which half the workers in an occupation earned more than that amount and half earned less. The lowest 10 percent earned less than $18,820, and the highest 10 percent earned more than $49,470.

Median annual wages for assemblers and fabricators in May 2014 were as follows:

Aircraft structure, surfaces, rigging, and systems assemblers	$48,340
Engine and other machine assemblers	38,310
Structural metal fabricators and fitters	36,570
Coil winders, tapers, and finishers	32,980
Electromechanical equipment assemblers	32,760
Timing device assemblers and adjusters	30,060
Electrical and electronic equipment assemblers	29,910
Fiberglass laminators and fabricators	28,950
Team assemblers	28,370
Assemblers and fabricators, all other	26,380

Job Outlook

Employment of assemblers and fabricators is projected to show little or no change from 2014 to 2024.

Within the manufacturing sector, employment of assemblers and fabricators will be determined largely by the growth or decline in the production of certain manufactured goods. In general, overall employment is not expected to grow as fast as all other occupations because many manufacturing sectors are expected to become more efficient and able to produce more with fewer workers.

However, some individual industries are projected to have more jobs than others. The administrative and support services industry is projected to gain jobs over the decade as demand for temporary help services experiences growth. Thus, the need for assemblers for temporary employment is expected to grow. In most other manufacturing industries, improved processes, tools, and, in some cases, automation will reduce job growth. Automation will replace workers in operations with a large volume of simple, repetitive work.

However, automation is not expected to have a large effect on the assembly of products that are low in volume or very complicated. Intricate product manufacturing and complicated techniques often cannot be automated.

The use of team production techniques has been one factor in the continuing productivity growth of the manufacturing sector, boosting output and improving the quality of goods.

Some U.S. manufacturers have sent their assembly functions to countries where labor costs are lower. Decisions by U.S. corporations to move manufacturing to other nations may limit employment growth for assemblers in some industries.

The largest increase in the number of assemblers and fabricators is projected to be in the employment services industry, which

Similar Occupations. This table shows a list of occupations with job duties that are similar to those of assemblers and fabricators.

Occupations	Entry-level Education	2014 Median Pay	Projected Job Growth	Average Annual Openings
Industrial Machinery Mechanics, Machinery Maintenance Workers, and Millwrights	High school diploma or equivalent	$47,450	16%	7,340
Metal and Plastic Machine Workers	High school diploma or equivalent	$33,550	-13%	-13,390
Welders, Cutters, Solderers, and Brazers	High school diploma or equivalent	$37,420	4%	1,440

supplies temporary workers to various industries. Temporary workers are gaining importance in the manufacturing sector and other sectors, as companies facing cost pressures strive for a more flexible workforce to meet fluctuations in the market.

Job Prospects. Qualified applicants, including those with technical vocational training and certification, are likely to have the best job opportunities in the manufacturing sector, particularly in growing, high-technology industries, such as aerospace and electro-medical devices.

Many job openings are expected to result from the need to replace workers who leave or retire from this large occupation.

Contacts for More Information

For more information about assemblers and fabricators, including certification, training, and professional development, visit

➤ Fabricators & Manufacturers Association, International (http://fmanet.org)

For information about careers in manufacturing, visit

➤ Nuts, Bolts & Thingamajigs (www.nutsandboltsfoundation.org)

For information about certifications in electronics soldering, visit:

➤ Association Connecting Electronics Industries (www.ipc.org)

O*NET

➤ Aircraft Structure, Surfaces, Rigging, and Systems Assemblers (51-2011.00)
➤ Coil Winders, Tapers, and Finishers (51-2021.00)
➤ Electrical and Electronic Equipment Assemblers (51-2022.00)
➤ Electromechanical Equipment Assemblers (51-2023.00)
➤ Engine and Other Machine Assemblers (51-2031.00)
➤ Structural Metal Fabricators and Fitters (51-2041.00)
➤ Fiberglass Laminators and Fabricators (51-2091.00)
➤ Team Assemblers (51-2092.00)
➤ Timing Device Assemblers and Adjusters (51-2093.00)
➤ Assemblers and Fabricators, All Other (51-2099.00)

Bakers

- **2014 Median Pay** .... $23,600 per year $11.35 per hour
- **Typical Entry-Level Education** ..... No formal educational credential
- **Work Experience in a Related Occupation** .... None
- **On-the-job Training** ....Long-term on-the-job training
- **Number of Jobs, 2014** 185,300
- **Job Outlook, 2014–24** .... 7% (As fast as average)
- **Employment Change, 2014–24** 13,000

What Bakers Do

Bakers mix ingredients according to recipes to make breads, pastries, and other baked goods.

Duties. Bakers typically do the following:

- Check the quality of baking ingredients
- Prepare equipment for baking
- Measure and weigh flour and other ingredients
- Combine measured ingredients in mixers or blenders
- Knead, roll, cut, and shape dough
- Place dough into pans, into molds, or onto baking sheets
- Set oven temperatures
- Place items into ovens or onto grills
- Observe color and state of products being baked
- Apply glazes, icings, or other toppings

Bakers produce various types and quantities of breads, pastries, and other baked goods sold by grocers, wholesalers, restaurants, and institutional food services. Some bakers create new recipes.

The following are examples of types of bakers:

Commercial bakers work in manufacturing facilities that produce breads, pastries, and other baked products. In these facilities, bakers use high-volume mixing machines, ovens, and other equipment, which may be automated, to mass-produce standardized baked goods. They carefully follow instructions for production schedules and recipes.

Retail bakers work primarily in grocery stores and specialty shops, including bakeries. In these settings, they produce smaller quantities of baked goods for people to eat in the shop or for sale as specialty baked goods. Retail bakers may take orders from customers, prepare baked products to order, and occasionally serve customers. Although the quantities prepared and sold in these stores are often small, they usually come in a wide variety of flavors and sizes. Most retail bakers are also responsible for cleaning their work area and equipment and unloading supplies.

Some retail bakers own bakery shops or other types of businesses where they make and sell breads, pastries, pies, and other baked goods. In addition to preparing the baked goods and overseeing the entire baking process, they are also responsible for hiring, training, and supervising their staff. They must budget for and order supplies, set prices, and decide how much to produce each day.

Work Environment

Bakers held about 185,300 jobs in 2014. The industries that employed the most bakers were as follows:

Bakeries and tortilla manufacturing	28%
Grocery stores	26
Restaurants and other eating places	16

About 1 in 20 bakers were self-employed in 2014.

The work can be stressful because bakers follow time-sensitive baking procedures and often work under strict deadlines. For example, bakers must follow daily production schedules to bake products in sufficient quantities while maintaining consistent quality. In manufacturing facilities, they often work with other production workers, such as helpers and maintenance staff, so that equipment is cleaned and ready.

Bakers are exposed to high temperatures when working around hot ovens. They stand for hours at a time while observing the baking process, making the dough, or cleaning the baking equipment.

Bakers who run their own business often spend additional hours managing all aspects of the business to ensure bills and salaries are paid, supplies are ordered, and the business is profitable.

Injuries and Illnesses. Bakeries, especially large manufacturing facilities, are filled with potential dangers such as hot ovens, mixing machines, and dough cutters. As a result, bakers have a higher rate of injuries and illnesses than the national average.

Although their work is generally safe, bakers may endure back strains caused by lifting or moving heavy bags of flour or other products. Other common risks include cuts, scrapes, and burns. To reduce these risks, bakers often wear back supports, aprons, and gloves.

Work Schedules. About 3 in 10 bakers worked part time in 2014.

Bakers prepare various types of baked goods and apply icing.

Grocery stores and restaurants, which employed about 40 percent of bakers in 2014, sell freshly baked goods throughout the day. As a result, bakers are often scheduled to work shifts during early mornings, late evenings, weekends, and holidays.

Bakers who work in commercial bakeries that bake continuously may have to work late evenings and weekends. Bakers who run their own businesses often spend additional hours managing all aspects of the business to ensure bills and salaries are paid, supplies are ordered, and the business is profitable.

Education/Training

Long-term on-the-job training is the most common path to gain the skills necessary to become a baker. Some bakers start their careers through an apprenticeship program or by attending a technical or culinary school. No formal education is required.

Education. Although there are no formal education requirements to become a baker, some candidates attend a technical or culinary school. Programs generally last from 1 to 2 years and cover nutrition, food safety, and basic math. To enter these programs, candidates may be required to have a high school diploma or equivalent.

Training. Most bakers learn their skills through long-term on-the-job training, typically lasting 1 to 3 years. Some employers may provide apprenticeship programs for aspiring bakers. Bakers in specialty bakery shops and grocery stores often start as apprentices or trainees and learn the basics of baking, icing, and decorating. They usually study topics such as nutrition, sanitation procedures, and basic baking. Some participate in correspondence study and may work toward a certificate in baking.

In manufacturing facilities, commercial bakers learn how to operate and maintain the industrial mixing and blending equipment that is used to produce baked goods. They also learn how to combine ingredients and how temperature and humidity affect ingredients and the baking process.

Other Experience. Some bakers learn their skills through work experience related to baking. For example, they may start as a baker's assistant and progress into a full-fledged baker as they learn baking techniques.

Licenses, Certifications, and Registrations. Certification is voluntary and shows that a baker has the skills and knowledge to work at a retail baking establishment.

The Retail Bakers of America offers certification in four levels of competence, with a focus on several topics, including baking sanitation, management, retail sales, and staff training. Those who wish to become certified must satisfy a combination of education and experience requirements before taking an exam.

The education and experience requirements vary by the level of certification desired. For example, a Certified Journey Baker requires no education but must have at least 1 year of work experience. A Certified Baker must have 4 years of work experience and 30 hours of sanitation coursework; a Certified Master Baker must have 8 years of work experience, 30 hours of sanitation coursework, and 30 hours of professional development education.

Important Qualities

Detail oriented. Bakers must closely monitor their products in the oven to keep them from burning. They also should have an eye for detail because many pastries and cakes require intricate decorations.

Math skills. Bakers must possess basic math skills, especially knowledge of fractions, in order to precisely mix recipes, weigh ingredients, or adjust mixes.

Physical stamina. Bakers stand on their feet for extended periods while they prepare dough, monitor baking, or package baked goods.

Physical strength. Bakers should be able to lift and carry heavy bags of flour and other ingredients, which may weigh up to 50 pounds.

Pay

The median annual wage for bakers was $23,600 in May 2014. The median wage is the wage at which half the workers in an occupation earned more than that amount and half earned less. The lowest 10 percent earned less than $17,570, and the highest 10 percent earned more than $37,580.

Median Annual Wages, May 2014

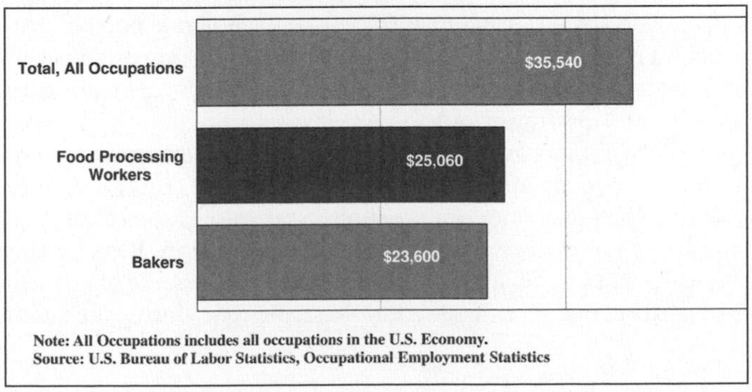

Percent Change in Employment, Projected 2014–2024

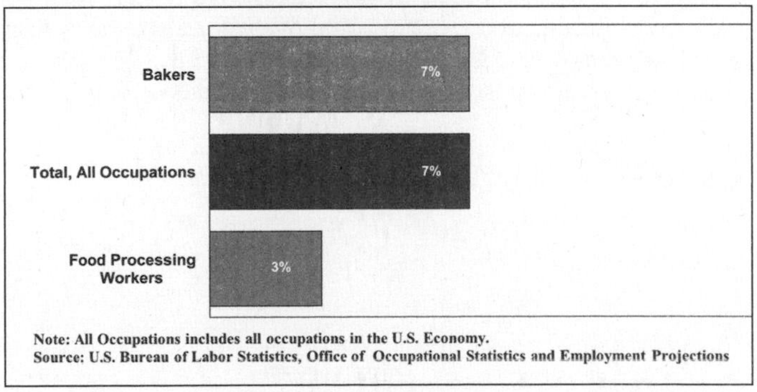

Employment Projections Data for Bakers

Occupational Title	SOC Code	Employment, 2014	Projected Employment, 2024	Change, 2014–2024 Percent	Change, 2014–2024 Numeric
Bakers	51-3011	185,300	198,300	7	13,000

Source: U.S. Bureau of Labor Statistics, Employment Projections Program

Similar Occupations. This table shows a list of occupations with job duties that are similar to those of bakers.

Occupations	Entry-level Education	2014 Median Pay	Projected Job Growth	Average Annual Openings
Chefs and Head Cooks	High school diploma or equivalent	$41,610	9%	1,130
Cooks	See Education/Training	$21,120	4%	9,700
Food and Tobacco Processing Workers	See Education/Training	$26,230	2%	330
Food Preparation Workers	No formal educational credential	$19,560	6%	5,480

In May 2014, the median annual wages for bakers in the top industries in which they worked were as follows:

Grocery stores.. $23,800
Bakeries and tortilla manufacturing 23,520
Restaurants and other eating places.................. 22,730

About 3 in 10 bakers worked part time in 2014.

Grocery stores and restaurants, which employed about 40 percent of all bakers in 2014, sell freshly baked goods throughout the day. As a result, bakers are often scheduled to work shifts during early mornings, late evenings, weekends, and holidays.

Bakers who work in commercial bakeries that bake continuously may have to work late evenings and weekends.

Job Outlook

Employment of bakers is projected to grow 7 percent from 2014 to 2024, about as fast as the average for all occupations.

Population and income growth are expected to result in greater demand for specialty baked goods, such as cupcakes, pies, and cakes, from grocery stores, retail bakeries, and restaurants.

However, employment of bakers is projected to decline in food manufacturing as these facilities increasingly use automated machines and equipment to mass-produce baked goods.

Job Prospects. Job opportunities will be very good because of the need to replace workers who leave the occupation every year. Bakers with years of experience, particularly in preparing specialty baked products, should have the best job opportunities.

Contacts for More Information

For information about job opportunities, contact local employers and local offices of the state employment service.

For information about certification or training programs, visit

➤ AIB International (www.aibonline.org)
➤ Retail Bakers of America (www.retailbakersofamerica.org)

O*NET

➤ Bakers (51-3011.00)

Butchers

- **2014 Median Pay** .... $28,660 per year
  $13.78 per hour
- **Typical Entry-Level Education**...... No formal educational credential
- **Work Experience in a Related Occupation**.............. None
- **On-the-job Training** .... Long-term on-the-job training
- **Number of Jobs, 2014** 139,000
- **Job Outlook, 2014–24**................. 5% (As fast as average)
- **Employment Change, 2014–24** 7,000

What Butchers Do

Butchers cut, trim, and package meat for retail sale.

Duties. Butchers typically do the following:

- Sharpen and adjust knives and cutting equipment
- Receive, inspect, and store meat upon delivery
- Cut, bone, or grind pieces of meat
- Weigh, wrap, and display meat or meat products
- Cut or prepare meats to specification or customers' orders
- Store meats in refrigerators or freezers at the required temperature
- Keep inventory of meat and order meat supplies
- Clean equipment and work areas to maintain health and sanitation standards

Butchers cut and trim meat from larger, wholesale portions into steaks, chops, roasts, and other cuts. They then prepare meat for sale by performing various duties, such as weighing meat, wrapping it, and putting it out for display. In retail stores, they also wait on customers and prepare special cuts of meat upon request.

Butchers in meat processing plants are also known as *meat cutters*. They may have a more limited range of duties than those working in a grocery store or specialty meat shop. Because they typically work on an assembly line, those in processing plants usually perform one specific function—a single cut—during their shift.

Butchers use tools such as knives, grinders, or meat saws. They must follow sanitation standards while working and when cleaning equipment, countertops, and working areas in order to prevent meat contamination.

Some butchers run their own retail store. In these settings, they usually track inventory, order supplies, and perform other recordkeeping duties.

Work Environment

Butchers held about 139,000 jobs in 2014. The industries that employed the most butchers were as follows:

Grocery stores	73%
Specialty food stores	8
Animal slaughtering and processing	7

The work can be physically demanding, particularly for those who make repetitive cuts in processing plants. Butchers typically stand while cutting meat and must often lift and move heavy carcasses or boxes of meat supplies.

Because meat must be kept at cool temperatures, butchers commonly work in cold rooms—typically around 40 degrees Fahrenheit—for extended periods.

Butchers must keep their hands and working areas clean to prevent contamination, and those working in retail settings must remain presentable for customers.

Injuries and Illnesses. Butchers use tools that can be dangerous, such as sharp knives and meat saws, and work in areas with slippery floors and surfaces. To reduce the risk of cuts and falls, workers wear protective clothing, such as cut-resistant gloves, heavy aprons, and nonslip footwear.

Work Schedules. Most butchers work full time. Butchers who work in grocery or retail stores may work early mornings, late evenings, weekends, and holidays. Workers in animal slaughtering and processing facilities may work shifts that start in the early morning or in the afternoon or evening.

Butchers who run their own meat shops often work many hours.

Education/Training

Most butchers learn their skills through on-the-job training lasting more than a year. No formal education is required.

Education. There are no formal education requirements to become a butcher.

Training. Butchers typically learn their skills on the job and the length of training varies considerably. Training for simple cutting may take only a few weeks. However, more complicated cutting tasks generally require training that may last from several months to more than a year.

Butchers cut steaks and chops and shape and tie roasts.

Training for entry-level workers often begins by learning less difficult tasks, such as making simple cuts, removing bones, or dividing wholesale cuts into retail portions. Under the guidance of more experienced workers, trainees learn the proper use and care of tools and equipment. For example, they learn how to sharpen their knives and clean working areas and equipment.

Trainees also may learn how to shape, roll, and tie roasts, prepare sausage, and cure meat. Those employed in retail stores are usually taught basic business operations, such as inventory control, meat buying, and recordkeeping. Employees also receive training in food safety to minimize the risk of foodborne pathogens in meats.

Butchers who follow religious dietary guidelines for food preparation may be required to undergo more specialized training and certification before becoming endorsed by a religious organization to prepare meat.

Important Qualities

Concentration. Butchers must pay close attention to what they are doing in order to avoid injury and wasting meat.

Customer-service skills. Butchers who work in retail stores should be courteous, be able to answer customers' questions, and fill orders to customers' satisfaction.

Dexterity. Butchers use sharp knives and meat cutting equipment as part of their duties. Therefore, they must have good hand control in order to make proper cuts of meat that are the right size.

Physical stamina. Butchers spend hours on their feet while cutting, packaging, or storing meat.

Median Annual Wages, May 2014

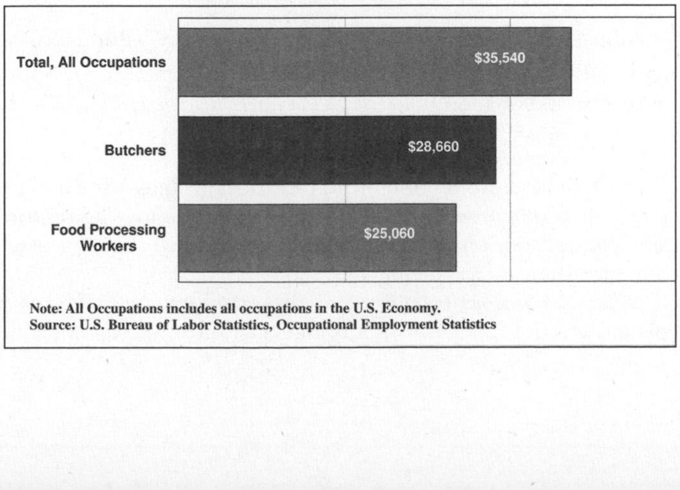

Percent Change in Employment, Projected 2014–2024

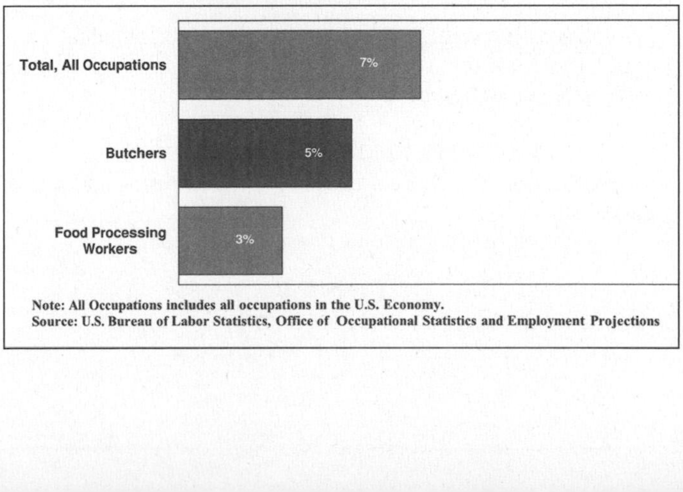

Employment Projections Data for Butchers

Occupational Title	SOC Code	Employment, 2014	Projected Employment, 2024	Change, 2014–2024 Percent	Change, 2014–2024 Numeric
Butchers and meat cutters	51-3021	139,000	146,000	5	7,000

Source: U.S. Bureau of Labor Statistics, Employment Projections Program

Similar Occupations. This table shows a list of occupations with job duties that are similar to those of butchers.

Occupations	Entry-level Education	2014 Median Pay	Projected Job Growth	Average Annual Openings
Chefs and Head Cooks	High school diploma or equivalent	$41,610	9%	1,130
Food and Tobacco Processing Workers	See Education/Training	$26,230	2%	330

Physical strength. Butchers should be strong enough to lift and carry heavy boxes of meat, which may weigh more than 50 pounds.

Pay

The median annual wage for butchers was $28,660 in May 2014. The median wage is the wage at which half the workers in an occupation earned more than that amount and half earned less. The lowest 10 percent earned less than $18,670, and the highest 10 percent earned more than $45,920.

In May 2014, the median annual wages for butchers in the top industries in which they worked were as follows:

Grocery stores.. $28,700
Specialty food stores.. 26,990
Animal slaughtering and processing.................................. 26,920

Job Outlook

Employment of butchers is projected to grow 5 percent from 2014 to 2024, about as fast as the average for all occupations.

The popularity of various meat products such as sausages, cured meats, and specialty cuts is expected to drive employment growth of butchers in retail stores, such as grocery and specialty food stores.

However, meat processing plants continue to consolidate animal slaughtering and meat processing by preparing and packaging meat products in one place. As a result, employment of butchers in these facilities is projected to decline, since fewer workers may be needed to cut, trim, and package meats in these settings.

Job Prospects. Many butcher and meat cutter jobs, particularly those in processing plants, are physically demanding, with difficult working conditions. As a result, job opportunities are expected to be good because of the need to replace workers who leave the occupation each year.

Workers with several years of work experience, including training in various meat cutting techniques, should have the best job prospects as retail butchers.

Contacts for More Information

For information about the meat processing industry and related trends, visit

➤ North American Meat Institute (www.meatami.com)

O*NET

➤ Butchers and Meat Cutters (51-3021.00)

Dental and Ophthalmic Laboratory Technicians and Medical Appliance Technicians

- **2014 Median Pay** .... $33,430 per year $16.07 per hour
- **Typical Entry-Level Education** .... High school diploma or equivalent
- **Work Experience in a Related Occupation**.............. None
- **On-the-job Training** .... See Education/Training
- **Number of Jobs, 2014** 83,500
- **Job Outlook, 2014–24**............ 10% (Faster than average)
- **Employment Change, 2014–24** 8,700

What Dental and Ophthalmic Laboratory Technicians and Medical Appliance Technicians Do

Dental and ophthalmic laboratory technicians and medical appliance technicians construct, fit, or repair appliances and devices, including dentures, eyeglasses, and prosthetics.

Duties. Dental and ophthalmic laboratory technicians and medical appliance technicians typically do the following:

- Follow detailed work orders and prescriptions
- Determine which materials and tools will be needed
- Bend, form, and shape fabric or material
- Polish and shape appliances and devices, using hand or power tools
- Adjust appliances or devices to allow for a more natural look or to improve function
- Inspect the final product for quality and accuracy
- Repair damaged appliances and devices

In small laboratories and offices, technicians may handle every phase of production. In larger ones, technicians may be responsible for only one phase of production, such as polishing, measuring, or testing.

Dental laboratory technicians use impressions, or molds, of a patient's teeth to create crowns, bridges, dentures, and other dental

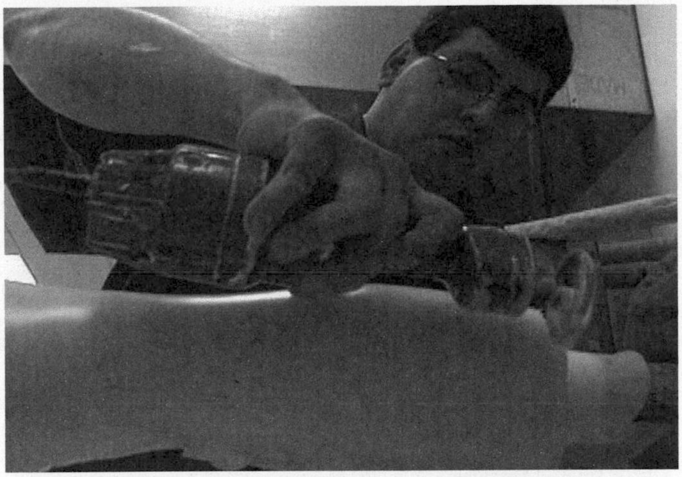

Orthotic and prosthetic technicians take prescriptions from orthotists and prosthetists to create medical appliances.

appliances. They work closely with dentists, but have limited contact with patients.

Dental laboratory technicians work with small hand tools, such as files and polishers. They work with many different materials, including wax, plastic, and porcelain, to make prosthetic appliances. In some cases, technicians use computer programs to create appliances or to get impressions sent from a dentist's office.

Dental laboratory technicians can specialize in one of six areas: orthodontic appliances, crowns and bridges, complete dentures, partial dentures, implants, or ceramics. Technicians may have different job titles, depending on their specialty. For example, technicians who make porcelain and acrylic restorations, such as veneers and bridges, are called *dental ceramists*.

Ophthalmic laboratory technicians make prescription eyeglasses and contact lenses. They are also commonly known as *manufacturing opticians*, *optical mechanics*, or *optical goods workers*.

Although they make some lenses by hand, ophthalmic laboratory technicians often use automated equipment. Some technicians manufacture lenses for optical instruments, such as telescopes and binoculars. Ophthalmic laboratory technicians should not be confused with dispensing opticians, who work with customers to select eyewear and may prepare work orders for ophthalmic laboratory technicians.

Medical appliance technicians construct, fit, and repair medical supportive devices, including arch supports, facial parts, and foot and leg braces.

Medical appliance technicians use many different types of materials, such as metal, plastic, and leather, to create a variety of medical devices for patients who need them because of a birth defect, an accident, disease, amputation, or the effects of aging. For example, some medical appliance technicians make hearing aids.

Orthotic and prosthetic technicians are medical appliance technicians who create orthoses (braces, supports, and other devices) and prostheses (replacement limbs and facial parts). These technicians work closely with orthotists or prosthetists.

Work Environment

Dental and ophthalmic laboratory technicians and medical appliance technicians held about 83,500 jobs in 2014. The industries that employed the most dental and ophthalmic laboratory technicians and medical appliance technicians were as follows:

Medical equipment and supplies manufacturing	54%
Ambulatory healthcare services	14
Health and personal care stores	11

Dental and ophthalmic laboratory technicians and medical appliance technicians typically work in clean, well-lit, and well-ventilated laboratories. Most laboratories are small and employ only a few workers. Some laboratories, however, have as many as several hundred employees. Other technicians work in health and personal care stores or in healthcare facilities.

Technicians may be exposed to health and safety hazards when they handle certain materials, but there is little risk if they follow proper procedures, such as wearing goggles, gloves, or masks. They may spend a great deal of time standing or bending.

Work Schedules. Most dental and ophthalmic laboratory technicians and medical appliance technicians work full time.

Education/Training

Dental or ophthalmic laboratory technicians or medical appliance technicians typically need a high school diploma or equivalent and receive on-the-job training.

Education. Ophthalmic laboratory technicians and medical appliance technicians typically need at least a high school diploma or equivalent. There are some postsecondary programs available at community colleges or technical or vocational schools in dental laboratory technology and ophthalmic laboratory technology, but these are not common. High school students interested in becoming dental or ophthalmic laboratory technicians or medical appliance technicians should take courses in science, math, computer programming, and art.

Training. Most dental and ophthalmic laboratory technicians and medical appliance technicians learn their skills through on-the-job training. They usually begin as helpers in a laboratory and learn more advanced skills as they gain experience. For example, dental laboratory technicians may begin by pouring plaster into an impression to make a model. As they become more experienced,

Median Annual Wages, May 2014

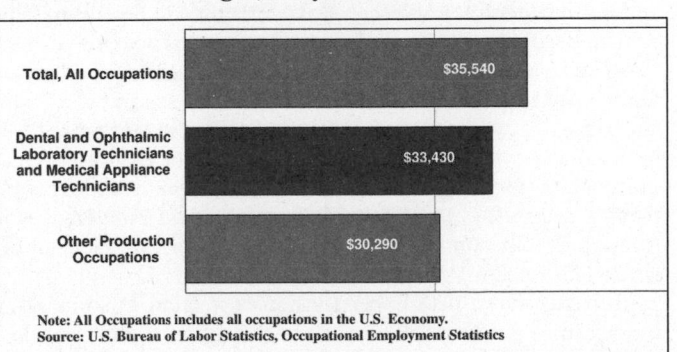

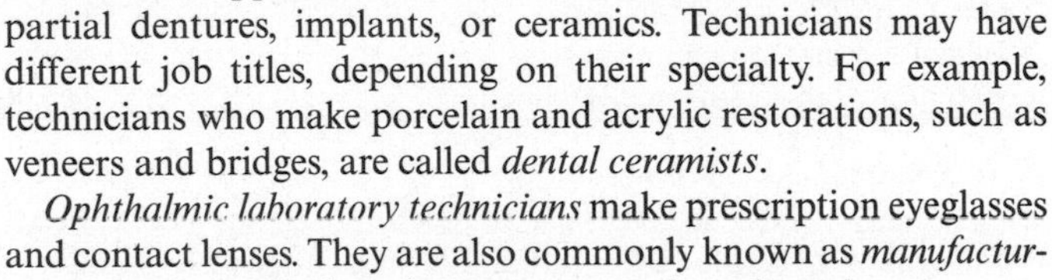

Note: All Occupations includes all occupations in the U.S. Economy.
Source: U.S. Bureau of Labor Statistics, Occupational Employment Statistics

Percent Change in Employment, Projected 2014–2024

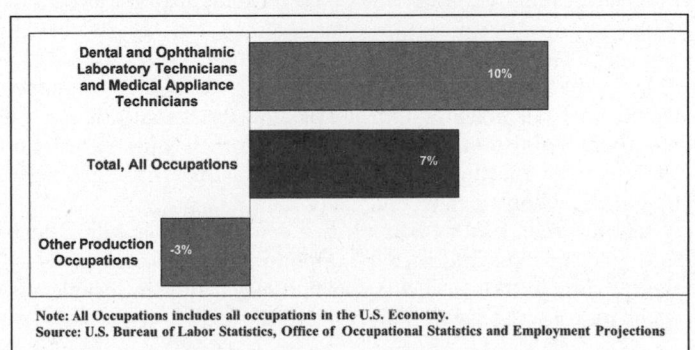

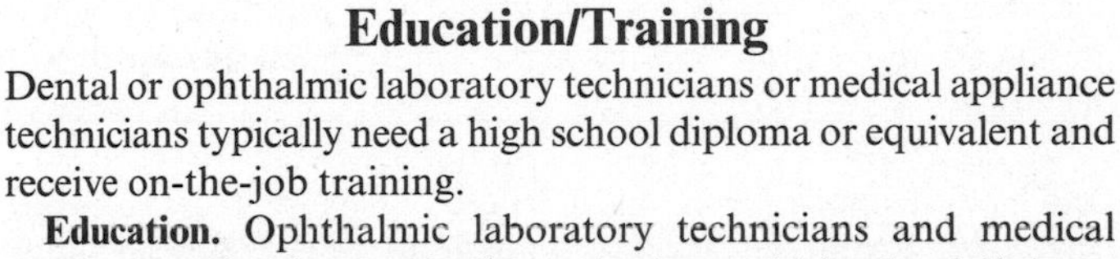

Note: All Occupations includes all occupations in the U.S. Economy.
Source: U.S. Bureau of Labor Statistics, Office of Occupational Statistics and Employment Projections

Employment Projections Data for Dental and Ophthalmic Laboratory Technicians and Medical Appliance Technicians

Occupational Title	SOC Code	Employment, 2014	Projected Employment, 2024	Change, 2014–2024	
				Percent	Numeric
Dental and ophthalmic laboratory technicians and medical appliance technicians	—	83,500	92,200	10	8,700
Dental laboratory technicians	51-9081	38,700	42,900	11	4,200
Medical appliance technicians	51-9082	14,600	16,100	11	1,600
Ophthalmic laboratory technicians	51-9083	30,200	33,200	10	3,000

Source: U.S. Bureau of Labor Statistics, Employment Projections Program

they may progress to more complex tasks, such as making porcelain crowns and bridges. Because all laboratories are different, the length of training varies.

Important Qualities

Detail oriented. Dental and ophthalmic laboratory technicians and medical appliance technicians must pay attention to detail. Technicians must follow work orders and prescriptions accurately and precisely. In addition, they need to be able to recognize and correct any imperfections in their work.

Dexterity. Dental and ophthalmic laboratory technicians and medical appliance technicians must work well with their hands because they use precise laboratory instruments.

Interpersonal skills. Dental and ophthalmic laboratory technicians and medical appliance technicians need to be able to work effectively with others because they may be part of a team of technicians working on a single project. In addition, they need good communication skills to ensure safety when they work with hazardous materials.

Technical skills. Dental and ophthalmic laboratory technicians and medical appliance technicians need to have an in depth knowledge of how different tools and materials work. They also must understand how to operate complex machinery. Some procedures are automated, so technicians must know how to operate and change the programs that run the machinery.

Licenses, Certifications, and Registrations. Certification is not required for dental and ophthalmic laboratory technicians or medical appliance technicians. However, technicians may choose to earn specialty certifications because they show professional competence in a specialized field.

The National Board for Certification in Dental Laboratory Technology (NBC) offers certification as a Certified Dental Technician (CDT). Certification is available in six specialty areas: orthodontic appliances, crowns and bridges, complete dentures, partial dentures, implants, and ceramics.

To qualify for the CDT, technicians must have at least 5 years of on-the-job training or experience in dental technology or have graduated from an accredited dental laboratory technician program. Candidates also must pass 3 exams within a period of 4 years.

The American Board for Certification in Orthotics, Prosthetics & Pedorthics (ABCOP) offers certification for medical appliance technicians. Technicians are eligible for the certification exam after completing an accredited program or if they have 2 years of experience as a technician under the direct supervision of a certified medical appliance technician.

Advancement. In large laboratories, dental and ophthalmic laboratory technicians and medical appliance technicians may work their way up to a supervisory level and may train new technicians. Some may go on to own their own laboratory.

Medical appliance technicians can advance to become orthotists or prosthetists after completing additional formal education. These practitioners work with patients who need braces, prostheses, or related devices.

Pay

The median annual wage for dental and ophthalmic laboratory technicians and medical appliance technicians was $33,430 in May 2014. The median wage is the wage at which half the workers in an occupation earned more than that amount and half earned less. The lowest 10 percent earned less than $20,980, and the highest 10 percent earned more than $57,520.

Median annual wages for dental and ophthalmic laboratory technicians and medical appliance technicians in May 2014 were as follows:

Dental laboratory technicians	$36,830
Medical appliance technicians	35,580
Ophthalmic laboratory technicians	28,890

Job Outlook

Employment of dental and ophthalmic laboratory technicians and medical appliance technicians is projected to grow 10 percent from 2014 to 2024, faster than the average for all occupations.

As cosmetic prosthetics, such as veneers and crowns, become less expensive, demand for these appliances will likely increase. Accidents and poor oral health, which can cause damage and loss of teeth, will continue to create a need for dental laboratory technician services.

On the one hand, because the risk of oral cancer increases significantly with age, an aging population will increase demand for dental appliances, given that complications can require both cosmetic and functional dental reconstruction.

On the other hand, because baby boomers and their children visited the dentist more than previous generations did, received fluoride treatments, and received more dental health education, they are more likely to retain their teeth than previous generations were. These factors will likely lead to a decrease in the number of full and partial dentures and other prosthetics used to replace missing teeth and will temper demand for the technicians who make them.

An aging baby-boomer population is projected to create a need for medical appliance technicians because diabetes and cardiovascular disease, two leading causes of loss of limbs, are more likely to occur as people age. The demand for orthotic devices, such as braces and orthopedic footwear, will increase because older people tend to need these supportive devices. In addition, advances in technology may spur demand for prostheses that allow for more natural movement.

Moreover, most people need vision correction at some point in their lives. As the population continues to grow and age, more

Similar Occupations. This table shows a list of occupations with job duties that are similar to those of dental and ophthalmic laboratory technicians and medical appliance technicians.

Occupations	Entry-level Education	2014 Median Pay	Projected Job Growth	Average Annual Openings
Dentists	Doctoral or professional degree	$154,640	18%	2,670
Medical Equipment Repairers	Associate's degree	$45,660	6%	290
Opticians, Dispensing	High school diploma or equivalent	$34,280	24%	1,780
Optometrists	Doctoral or professional degree	$101,410	27%	1,100
Orthotists and Prosthetists	Master's degree	$64,040	23%	190

people will need more vision aids, such as glasses and contact lenses, and this need will increase demand for ophthalmic laboratory technicians.

Contacts for More Information

For a list of accredited programs in dental laboratory technology, visit

➤ Commission on Dental Accreditation, American Dental Association (www.ada.org/en/coda)

For information about requirements for certification of dental laboratory technicians, visit

➤ National Board for Certification in Dental Laboratory Technology (http://nbccert.org/homepage.cfm)

For information about career opportunities in commercial dental laboratories, visit

➤ National Association of Dental Laboratories (http://nadl.org/home-page.cfm)

For a list of ophthalmic laboratories, visit

➤ The Vision Council (www.thevisioncouncil.org)

For a list of accredited programs for medical appliance technicians, visit

➤ American Academy of Orthotists & Prosthetists (www.oandp.org)

➤ National Commission on Orthotic and Prosthetic Education (www.ncope.org)

For information on requirements for certification of medical appliance technicians, visit

➤ American Board for Certification in Orthotics, Prosthetics & Pedorthics (www.abcop.org/Pages/default.aspx)

O*NET

➤ Dental Laboratory Technicians (51-9081.00)

➤ Medical Appliance Technicians (51-9082.00)

➤ Ophthalmic Laboratory Technicians (51-9083.00)

Food and Tobacco Processing Workers

- **2014 Median Pay** .... $26,230 per year $12.61 per hour
- **Typical Entry-Level Education** .... See Education/Training
- **Work Experience in a Related Occupation**.............. None
- **On-the-job Training**...Moderate-term on-the-job training
- **Number of Jobs, 2014** 223,000
- **Job Outlook, 2014–24** .... 2% (Slower than average)
- **Employment Change, 2014–24** 3,300

What Food and Tobacco Processing Workers Do

Food and tobacco processing workers operate equipment that mixes, cooks, or processes ingredients used in the manufacturing of food and tobacco products.

Duties. Food and tobacco processing workers typically do the following:

- Set up, start, or load food or tobacco processing equipment
- Check, weigh, and mix ingredients according to recipes
- Set and control temperatures, flow rates, and pressures of machinery
- Monitor and adjust ingredient mixes during production processes
- Observe and regulate equipment gauges and controls
- Report equipment malfunctions to team leaders or maintenance staff
- Clean workspaces and equipment in accordance with health and safety standards
- Check final products to ensure quality

Food and tobacco processing workers often have different duties depending on the type of machinery they use or goods they process.

Food and tobacco roasting, baking, and drying machine operators and tenders operate machines that produce roasted, baked, or dried food or tobacco products. For example, *dryers of fruits and vegetables* operate machines that produce raisins, prunes, or other dehydrated foods. *Tobacco roasters* tend machines that cure tobacco for wholesale distribution to cigarette manufacturers and other makers of tobacco products. Others, such as *coffee roasters*, follow recipes and tend machines to produce standard or specialty coffees.

Food batchmakers typically work in facilities that produce baked goods, pasta, and tortillas. Workers mix ingredients to make dough, load and unload ovens, operate pasta extruders, and perform tasks specific to large-scale commercial baking. Some workers are identified by the type of food they produce. For example, those who prepare cheese are known as *cheese makers* and those who make candy are known as *candy makers*.

Food cooking machine operators and tenders operate or tend cooking equipment to prepare food products. For example, workers who preserve and can fruits and vegetables usually operate equipment to cook and preserve their products.

Potato and corn chip manufacturing workers operate baking and frying equipment. Sugar and confectionary manufacturers use equipment that blends, heats, coats, and packages candies, chocolates, or other sweets.

Other workers operate machines that mix spices, mill grains, or extract oil from seeds.

Food processing workers cut meat into smaller sizes and wrap them for sale.

Work Environment

Food and tobacco processing workers held about 223,000 jobs in 2014 and mostly worked in food manufacturing facilities.

The industries that employed the most food and tobacco processing workers in 2014 were as follows:

Bakeries and tortilla manufacturing	16%
Animal slaughtering and processing	15
Other food manufacturing	13
Fruit and vegetable preserving and specialty food manufacturing	11
Dairy product manufacturing	9

Food manufacturing facilities are typically large, open floor areas with loud machinery, requiring workers to wear ear protection to guard against noise. Workers are frequently exposed to high temperatures when working around cooking machinery. Some work in cold environments for long periods with goods that need to be refrigerated or frozen.

Depending on the type of food or tobacco being processed, workers may be required to wear masks, hair nets, or gloves to protect the product from possible contamination.

Workers usually stand for the majority of their shifts while tending machines or observing the production process. Loading, unloading, or cleaning equipment may require lifting, bending, and reaching.

Workers on assembly lines must be able to keep up with the line speed while maintaining product quality.

Injuries and Illnesses. Working around hot liquids or machinery that cuts or presses can be dangerous. The most common hazards are slips, falls, or cuts. To reduce the risks of injuries, workers are required to wear protective clothing and nonslip shoes.

Work Schedules. Most food and tobacco processing workers are employed full time. Because of varying production schedules, working early morning, evening, or night shifts is common in many manufacturing facilities.

Some food processing facilities are seasonal and open only a few months a year. During this period, facilities may operate 24 hours a day and require workers to work one of the various shifts.

Education/Training

There are no formal education requirements for some food and tobacco processing workers. However, food batchmakers and food cooking machine operators typically need a high school diploma or equivalent. Food and tobacco processing workers learn their skills through on-the-job training.

Education. A high school diploma or equivalent is the usual entry route for food batchmakers and food cooking machine operators.

Because workers often adjust the quantity of ingredients that go into a mix, basic math and reading skills are considered helpful.

Training. Food and tobacco processing workers learn on the job. Training may last from a few weeks to a few months. During training, workers learn health and safety rules related to the type of food or tobacco that they process. Training also involves learning how to operate specific equipment, following safety procedures, and reporting equipment malfunctions.

Experienced workers typically show trainees how to properly use and care for equipment.

Important Qualities

Coordination. Food and tobacco processing workers must be quick and have good hand-eye coordination to keep up with the assembly line.

Detail oriented. Workers must be able to detect small changes in they quality or quantity of food products. They must also closely follow health and safety standards to avoid food contamination and injury.

Physical stamina. Workers stand on their feet for long periods as they tend machines and monitor the production process.

Median Annual Wages, May 2014

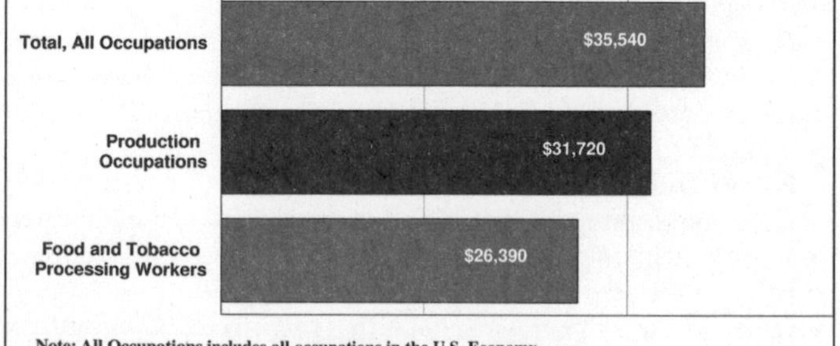

Note: All Occupations includes all occupations in the U.S. Economy.
Source: U.S. Bureau of Labor Statistics, Occupational Employment Statistics

Percent Change in Employment, Projected 2014–2024

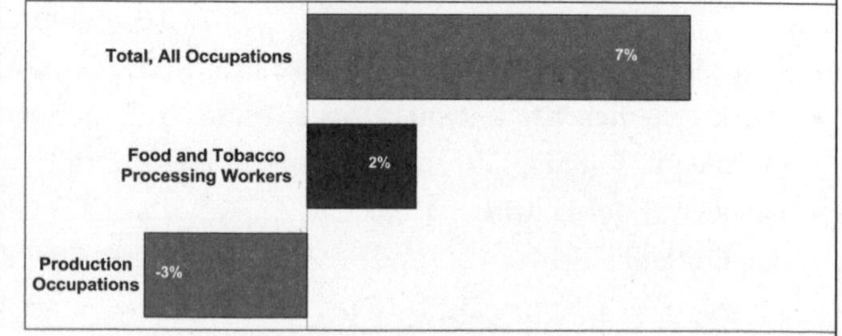

Note: All Occupations includes all occupations in the U.S. Economy.
Source: U.S. Bureau of Labor Statistics, Office of Occupational Statistics and Employment Projections

Employment Projections Data for Food and Tobacco Processing Workers

Occupational Title	SOC Code	Employment, 2014	Projected Employment, 2024	Change, 2014–2024 Percent	Numeric
Food and tobacco processing workers	—	223,000	226,300	2	3,300
Food and tobacco roasting, baking, and drying machine operators and tenders	51-3091	18,500	18,700	1	100
Food batchmakers	51-3092	122,500	122,000	0	-500
Food cooking machine operators and tenders	51-3093	37,500	38,000	1	500
Food processing workers, all other	51-3099	44,400	47,700	7	3,300

Source: U.S. Bureau of Labor Statistics, Employment Projections Program

Similar Occupations. This table shows a list of occupations with job duties that are similar to those of food and tobacco processing workers.

Occupations	Entry-level Education	2014 Median Pay	Projected Job Growth	Average Annual Openings
Bakers	No formal educational credential	$23,600	7%	1,300
Cooks	See Education/Training	$21,120	4%	9,700
Food Preparation Workers	No formal educational credential	$19,560	6%	5,480
Metal and Plastic Machine Workers	High school diploma or equivalent	$33,550	-13%	-13,390

Physical strength. Food and tobacco processing workers should be strong enough to lift or move heavy boxes of ingredients, which often can weigh up to 50 pounds.

Pay

The median annual wage for food and tobacco processing workers was $26,230 in May 2014. The median wage is the wage at which half the workers in an occupation earned more than that amount and half earned less. The lowest 10 percent earned less than $18,030, and the highest 10 percent earned more than $42,680.

Median annual wages for food and tobacco processing workers in May 2014 were as follows:

Food and tobacco roasting, baking, and drying machine operators and tenders $27,680
Food cooking machine operators and tenders 27,590
Food batchmakers 26,770
Food processing workers, all other 23,780

Job Outlook

Employment of food and tobacco processing workers is projected to grow 2 percent from 2014 to 2024, slower than the average for all occupations.

Population growth and continuing consumer preference for convenience foods are expected to drive employment of these workers, particularly in retail trade establishments, such as grocery or specialty food stores.

Food manufacturing companies increasingly are using automation to raise productivity. For example, they use equipment that automatically weighs and mixes ingredients, requiring fewer processing workers. As these companies further consolidate their facilities and streamline production processes, they will need fewer workers to operate machines.

Job Prospects. The need to replace food and tobacco processing workers who leave the occupation should result in many job openings each year. Those with related work experience in manufacturing will have the best job opportunities.

The food processing industry continues to consolidate. As a result, job prospects should be best in large food processing facilities, which are commonly located in rural areas or near smaller cities.

Contacts for More Information

For more information about line workers and food safety, visit

- U.S. Department of Agriculture Food Safety and Inspection Service (www.fsis.usda.gov)
- U.S. Food and Drug Administration (www.fda.gov)

For more information about the food industry, visit

- Food Engineering (www.foodengineeringmag.com)
- Grocery Manufacturers Association (www.gmaonline.org)

O*NET

- Food and Tobacco Roasting, Baking, and Drying Machine Operators and Tenders (51-3091.00)
- Food Batchmakers (51-3092.00)
- Food Cooking Machine Operators and Tenders (51-3093.00)
- Food Processing Workers, All Other (51-3099.00)

Jewelers and Precious Stone and Metal Workers

- **2014 Median Pay** .... $36,870 per year $17.73 per hour
- **Typical Entry-Level Education** .... High school diploma or equivalent
- **Work Experience in a Related Occupation** .... None
- **On-the-job Training** .... Long-term on-the-job training
- **Number of Jobs, 2014** 39,800
- **Job Outlook, 2014–24** .... -11% (Decline)
- **Employment Change, 2014–24** .... -4,500

What Jewelers and Precious Stone and Metal Workers Do

Jewelers and precious stone and metal workers design, manufacture, and sell jewelry. They also adjust, repair, and appraise gems and jewelry.

Duties. Jewelers and precious stone and metal workers typically do the following:

- Create jewelry from precious metals and stones
- Examine and grade diamonds and other gems
- Clean and polish jewelry using polishing wheels and chemical baths
- Repair jewelry by replacing broken clasps, altering ring sizes, or resetting stones
- Smooth joints and rough spots and polish smoothed areas
- Compute the costs of labor and material for new pieces and repairs
- Model new pieces with carved wax or computer-aided design, and then cast them in metal
- Shape metal to hold the gems in pieces of jewelry
- Solder pieces together and insert stones

Technology is helping to produce high-quality jewelry at a reduced cost and in less time than traditional methods allow. For example, lasers are often used for cutting and improving the quality of stones, for intricate engraving or design work, and for inscribing personal messages on jewelry. Jewelers also use lasers to weld metals together without seams or blemishes, improving the quality and appearance of jewelry.

Some manufacturing firms use computer-aided design and computer-aided manufacturing (CAD/CAM) to make product design easier and to automate some steps. With CAD, jewelers can create a model of a piece of jewelry on a computer and then view the effect of changing different aspects—for example, the design, the stone, or the setting—before cutting a stone or taking other costly steps. With CAM, they can then create a mold of the piece, which makes producing many copies easy.

Some jewelers also use CAD software to design custom jewelry. They let the customer review the design on a computer and see the effect of changes, so that the customer is satisfied before committing to the expense of a customized piece of jewelry.

The following are examples of types of jewelers and precious stone and metal workers:

Precious metal workers expertly manipulate gold, silver, and other metals. They use pliers and other hand tools to shape and manipulate metal. Some may mix alloy ingredients according to metallurgical properties.

Gemologists analyze, describe, and certify the quality and characteristics of gemstones. After using microscopes, computerized tools, and other grading instruments to examine gemstones or finished pieces of jewelry, they write reports certifying that the items are of a particular quality. Most gemologists have completed the Graduate Gemologist program through the Gemological Institute of America.

Jewelry appraisers carefully examine jewelry to determine its value and then write appraisal documents. They determine value by researching the jewelry market and by using reference books, auction catalogs, price lists, and the Internet. They may work for jewelry stores, appraisal firms, auction houses, pawnbrokers, or insurance companies. Many gemologists also become appraisers.

Jewelers need a high degree of skill and must pay attention to detail.

Bench jewelers usually work for jewelry retailers, doing tasks ranging from simple jewelry cleaning and repair to making molds and pieces from scratch.

Work Environment

Jewelers and precious stone and metal workers held about 39,800 jobs in 2014. The industries that employed the most jewelers and precious stone and metal workers were as follows:

Clothing and clothing accessories stores	27%
Jewelry and silverware manufacturing	16
Merchant wholesalers, durable goods	10

About 4 in 10 were self-employed in 2014. Some work from home and sell their products at trade and craft shows on weekends. Online sales are also a growing source of sales for jewelers.

Most wage and salary workers in this occupation are employed in jewelry stores, repair shops, and manufacturing plants.

Jewelers and precious stone and metal workers spend much of their time at a workbench, although computers are also becoming an increasingly important tool in the jewelry industry as computer-aided design (CAD) can save workers time and resources. Many tools, such as jeweler's torches and lasers, must be handled carefully to avoid injury. Polishing processes such as chemical baths also must be performed in a safe manner.

In retail stores, jewelers may talk with customers about repairs, perform custom design work, and sell items to customers. Because many of their materials are valuable, jewelers must follow security procedures, including making use of burglar alarms and, in larger jewelry stores, working in the presence of security guards.

Work Schedules. Jewelers and precious stone and metal workers have varied work schedules. Self-employed workers often decide their own hours, and many work weekends, showing and selling their products at trade and craft shows. Retail store workers might also work nonstandard hours because they must be available when customers are not working, such as on holidays and weekends. About 1 in 4 worked part time in 2014.

Median Annual Wages, May 2014

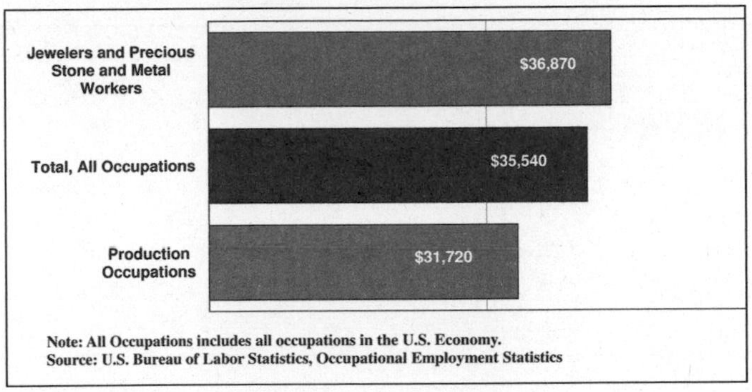

Percent Change in Employment, Projected 2014–2024

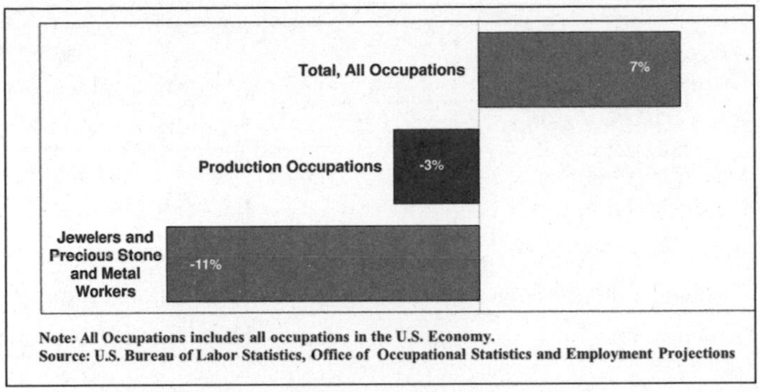

Education/Training

Jewelers and precious stone and metal workers can enter the occupation on the basis of their education, which is typically earning a high school diploma, or receive on-the-job training, or a combination of the two.

Education. Although most jewelers and precious stone and metal workers have a high school diploma, many trade schools offer courses for workers who seek additional education. Course topics can include introduction to gems and metals, resizing, repair, and computer-aided design (CAD). Programs vary from 6 months to 1 year, and many teach students how to design, cast, set, and polish jewelry and gems, as well as how to use and care for a jeweler's tools and equipment. Graduates of these programs may be more attractive to employers because they require less on-the-job training. Many gemologists graduate from the Gemological Institute of America. Trade programs usually require applicants to have a high school diploma or equivalent.

Training. Some jewelers learn on the job. For example, in jewelry manufacturing plants, workers develop their skills through on-the-job training. The length of training required to become proficient depends on the difficulty of the specialty. Training usually focuses on casting, setting stones, making models, or engraving.

Other Experience. Some workers gain their skills through related work experience. This may include working alongside a bench jeweler or gemologist while performing the duties of a salesperson in a retail jewelry store. Time spent in a store with a bench jeweler or gemologist can provide valuable experience.

Advancement. In manufacturing, some jewelers advance to supervisory jobs, such as master jeweler or head jeweler. Jewelers who work in jewelry stores or repair shops may become managers.

Important Qualities

Artistic ability. Jewelers must have the ability to create designs that are unique and beautiful.

Detail oriented. Jewelers and precious stone and metal workers must pay attention to large and small details on the pieces they make.

Dexterity. Jewelers and precious stone and metal workers must precisely move their fingers and tools in order to grasp, manipulate, and assemble very small objects.

Fashion sense. Jewelry designers must know what is stylish and attractive and presently in demand by consumers.

Interpersonal skills. Jewelers and precious stone and metal workers interact with customers, whether they sell products in stores or at craft shows.

Near vision. Jewelers and precious stone and metal workers need the ability to see details at close range (within a few feet of the observer).

Visualization skills. Jewelers and precious stone and metal workers must imagine how something might look after its shape is altered or when its parts are rearranged.

Pay

The median annual wage for jewelers and precious stone and metal workers was $36,870 in May 2014. The median wage is the wage at which half the workers in an occupation earned more than that amount and half earned less. The lowest 10 percent earned less than $21,130, and the highest 10 percent earned more than $61,720.

In May 2014, the median annual wages for jewelers and precious stone and metal workers in the top industries in which they worked were as follows:

Clothing and clothing accessories stores	$40,220
Merchant wholesalers, durable goods	33,320
Jewelry and silverware manufacturing	32,630

Jewelers who work in retail stores may earn commissions for jewelry sold.

Job Outlook

Employment of jewelers and precious stone and metal workers is projected to decline 11 percent from 2014 to 2024. Employment of these workers is expected to decline because most jewelry is now manufactured outside of the United States. Additionally, traditional jewelry stores may continue to lose some of their customers to nontraditional sellers, such as department stores, and this shift is also likely to result in declined employment levels for jewelers and precious stone and metal workers.

Employment Projections Data for Jewelers and Precious Stone and Metal Workers

Occupational Title	SOC Code	Employment, 2014	Projected Employment, 2024	Change, 2014–2024 Percent	Change, 2014–2024 Numeric
Jewelers and precious stone and metal workers	51-9071	39,800	35,300	-11	-4,500

Source: U.S. Bureau of Labor Statistics, Employment Projections Program

Similar Occupations. This table shows a list of occupations with job duties that are similar to those of jewelers and precious stone and metal workers.

Occupations	Entry-level Education	2014 Median Pay	Projected Job Growth	Average Annual Openings
Craft and Fine Artists	See Education/Training	$44,400	2%	90
Fashion Designers	Bachelor's degree	$64,030	3%	70
Industrial Designers	Bachelor's degree	$64,620	2%	80
Retail Sales Workers	No formal educational credential	$21,670	7%	33,100
Welders, Cutters, Solderers, and Brazers	High school diploma or equivalent	$37,420	4%	1,440
Woodworkers	High school diploma or equivalent	$28,900	-1%	-140

Job Prospects. Job opportunities should be available for bench jewelers who are skilled at design or repair. Some jewelers will be needed to replace those who retire or who leave the occupation for other reasons. As jewelers retire, shops lose expertise and knowledge that is difficult and costly to replace.

Job opportunities in jewelry stores and repair shops should be best for those who have graduated from a trade school or training program and have related work experience.

Strong competition is expected for mass manufacturing jobs and for jewelry designers who wish to create their own jewelry lines. Although demand for customized and boutique jewelry is strong, it is often difficult for independent designers to establish themselves in the market. Experience with computer-aided design (CAD) makes creating custom pieces of jewelry easier.

During economic downturns, demand for jewelry products and jewelers usually decreases. However, demand for repair workers should remain strong even during economic slowdowns because maintaining and repairing jewelry is cheaper than buying new jewelry.

Contacts for More Information

For more information about jewelers, precious stone and metal workers, and gemologists, including job opportunities and training programs, visit

➤ Gemological Institute of America Inc. (www.gia.edu)
➤ Jewelers of America (www.jewelers.org)
➤ Manufacturing Jewelers & Suppliers of America (www.mjsa.org)

O*NET

➤ Jewelers and Precious Stone and Metal Workers (51-9071.00)
➤ Jewelers (51-9071.01)
➤ Gem and Diamond Workers (51-9071.06)
➤ Precious Metal Workers (51-9071.07)

Machinists and Tool and Die Makers

- **2014 Median Pay** .... $41,510 per year
$19.96 per hour
- **Typical Entry-Level Education** .... High school diploma or equivalent
- **Work Experience in a Related Occupation**.............. None
- **On-the-job Training** .... Long-term on-the-job training
- **Number of Jobs, 2014** 477,500
- **Job Outlook, 2014–24** .... 6% (As fast as average)
- **Employment Change, 2014–24** 29,000

What Machinists and Tool and Die Makers Do

Machinists and tool and die makers set up and operate a variety of computer-controlled and mechanically controlled machine tools to produce precision metal parts, instruments, and tools.

Duties. Machinists typically do the following:

- Work from blueprints, sketches, or computer-aided design (CAD) and computer-aided manufacturing (CAM) files
- Set up, operate, and disassemble manual, automatic, and computer-numeric-controlled (CNC) machine tools
- Align, secure, and adjust cutting tools and workpieces
- Monitor the feed and speed of machines
- Turn, mill, drill, shape, and grind machine parts to specifications
- Measure, examine, and test completed products for defects
- Smooth the surfaces of parts or products
- Present finished workpieces to customers and make modifications if needed

Tool and die makers typically do the following:

- Read blueprints, sketches, specifications, or CAD and CAM files for making tools and dies
- Compute and verify dimensions, sizes, shapes, and tolerances of workpieces
- Set up, operate, and disassemble conventional, manual, and CNC machine tools
- File, grind, and adjust parts so that they fit together properly
- Test completed tools and dies to ensure that they meet specifications
- Smooth and polish the surfaces of tools and dies

Machinists use machine tools, such as lathes, milling machines, and grinders, to produce precision metal parts. Many machinists must be able to use both manual and CNC machinery. CNC machines control the cutting tool speed and do all necessary cuts to create a part. The machinist determines the cutting path, the speed of the cut, and the feed rate by programming instructions into the CNC machine.

Although workers may produce large quantities of one part, precision machinists often produce small batches or one-of-a-kind items. The parts that machinists make range from simple steel bolts to titanium bone screws for orthopedic implants. Hydraulic parts, antilock brakes, and automobile pistons are other widely known products that machinists make.

Some machinists repair or make new parts for existing machinery. After an industrial machinery mechanic discovers a broken part in a machine, a machinist remanufactures the part. The

Machinists remove and replace worn-out machine tools.

machinist refers to blueprints and performs the same machining operations that were used to create the original part in order to create the replacement.

Because the technology of machining is changing rapidly, workers must learn to operate a wide range of machines. Some newer manufacturing processes use lasers, water jets, and electrified wires to cut the workpiece. Although some of the computer controls are similar to those of other machine tools, machinists must understand the unique capabilities and features of different machines. As engineers create new types of machine tools, machinists must learn new machining properties and techniques.

Toolmakers craft precision tools that are used to cut, shape, and form metal and other materials. They also produce jigs and fixtures—devices that hold metal while it is bored, stamped, or drilled—and gauges and other measuring devices.

Die makers construct metal forms, called dies, that are used to shape metal in stamping and forging operations. They also make metal molds for die casting and for molding plastics, ceramics, and composite materials.

Many tool and die makers use CAD to develop products and parts. Designs are entered into computer programs that produce blueprints for the required tools and dies. Computer-numeric control programmers, found in the metal and plastic machine workers profile, convert CAD designs into CAM programs that contain instructions for a sequence of cutting tool operations. Once these programs are developed, CNC machines follow the set of instructions contained in the program to produce the part. Machinists normally operate CNC machines, but tool and die makers often are trained to both operate CNC machines and write CNC programs and thus may do either task.

Work Environment

Machinists and tool and die makers held about 477,500 jobs in 2014. Machinists held about 399,700 jobs in 2014. Tool and die makers held about 77,800 jobs in 2014. The vast majority worked in manufacturing, including machine shops, toolrooms, and factories.

The industries that employed the most machinists and tool and die makers in 2014 were as follows:

Fabricated metal product manufacturing	31%
Machinery manufacturing	20
Transportation equipment manufacturing	14

Injuries and Illnesses. Although the work of machinists and tool and die makers is not inherently dangerous, working around machine tools presents hazards, and workers must follow precautions. For example, workers must wear protective equipment, such as safety glasses, to shield against bits of flying metal, earplugs to dampen the noise produced by machinery, and masks to limit their exposure to fumes.

Work Schedules. Although many machinists and tool and die makers work full time during regular business hours, some work on evenings and weekends because facilities may operate around the clock. Overtime is also common.

Education/Training

There are many different ways to become a machinist or tool and die maker. Machinists train in apprenticeship programs, vocational schools, or community or technical colleges, or on the job. To become a fully trained tool and die maker takes several years of technical instruction and on-the-job training. Good math and problem-solving skills, in addition to familiarity with computer software, are important. A high school diploma or equivalent is necessary.

Education. In high school, students should take math courses, especially trigonometry and geometry. They also should take courses in blueprint reading, metalworking, and drafting, if available.

Some advanced positions, such as those in the aircraft manufacturing industry, require the use of advanced applied calculus and physics. The increasing use of computer-controlled machinery requires machinists and tool and die makers to have experience using computers before entering a training program.

Some community colleges and technical schools have 2-year programs that train students to become machinists or tool and die makers. These programs usually teach design and blueprint reading, how to use a variety of welding and cutting tools, and the programming and function of computer numerically controlled (CNC) machines.

Training. There are multiple ways for workers to gain competency in the job as a tool or die maker. One common way is through long-term on-the-job training, which lasts 1 year or longer.

Apprenticeship programs, typically sponsored by a manufacturer, provide another way to become a machinist or tool and die maker, but they are often hard to get into. Apprentices usually have a high school diploma or equivalent, and most have taken algebra and trigonometry classes.

Apprenticeship programs often consist of paid shop training and related technical instruction lasting several years. The technical instruction typically is provided in cooperation with local community colleges and vocational–technical schools.

Apprentices usually work 40 hours per week and receive technical instruction during evenings. Trainees often begin as machine operators and gradually take on more difficult assignments. Machinists and tool and die makers must be experienced in using computers to work with CAD/CAM technology, CNC machine tools, and computerized measuring machines. Some machinists become tool and die makers.

A number of machinists and tool and die makers receive their technical training from community and technical colleges. Employees may learn this way while being employed by a manufacturer that supports the employee's training goals and provides needed on-the-job training as well.

Even after completing a formal training program, tool and die makers still need years of experience to become highly skilled.

Median Annual Wages, May 2014

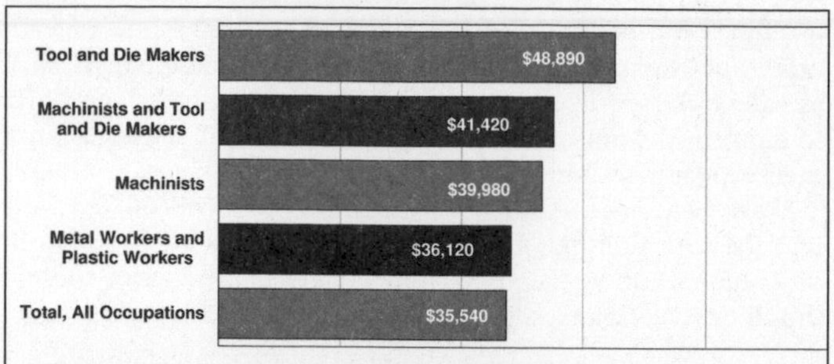

Note: All Occupations includes all occupations in the U.S. Economy.
Source: U.S. Bureau of Labor Statistics, Occupational Employment Statistics

Percent Change in Employment, Projected 2014–2024

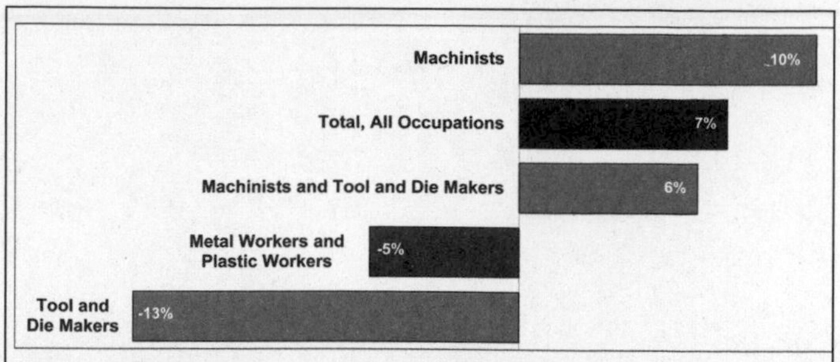

Note: All Occupations includes all occupations in the U.S. Economy.
Source: U.S. Bureau of Labor Statistics, Office of Occupational Statistics and Employment Projections

Licenses, Certifications, and Registrations. To boost the skill level of machinists and tool and die makers and to create a more uniform standard of competency, a number of training facilities and colleges offer certification programs. The Skills Certification System, for example, is an industry-driven program that aims to align education pathways with career pathways. In addition, journey-level certification is available from state apprenticeship boards after completing an apprenticeship.

Completing a recognized certification program provides machinists and tool and die makers with better job opportunities and helps employers judge the abilities of new hires.

Important Qualities

Analytical skills. Machinists and tool and die makers must understand highly technical blueprints, models, and specifications so that they can craft precision tools and metal parts.

Manual dexterity. The work of machinists and tool and die makers must be highly accurate. For example, machining parts may demand accuracy to within .0001 of an inch, a level of accuracy that requires workers' concentration and dexterity.

Math skills and computer application experience. Workers must have good math skills and be experienced using computers to work with CAD/CAM technology, CNC machine tools, and computerized measuring machines.

Mechanical skills. Machinists and tool and die makers must operate milling machines, lathes, grinders, laser and water cutting machines, wire electrical discharge machines, and other machine tools. They may also use a variety of hand tools and power tools.

Physical stamina. The ability to endure extended periods of standing and performing repetitious movements is important for machinists and tool and die makers.

Technical skills. Machinists and tool and die makers must understand computerized measuring machines and metalworking processes, such as stock removal, chip control, and heat treating and plating.

Pay

The median annual wage for machinists was $39,980 in May 2014. The median wage is the wage at which half the workers in an occupation earned more than that amount and half earned less. The lowest 10 percent earned less than $24,620, and the highest 10 percent earned more than $60,740.

The median annual wage for tool and die makers was $48,890 in May 2014. The lowest 10 percent earned less than $31,310, and the highest 10 percent earned more than $72,120.

The pay of apprentices is tied to their skill level. As they gain more skills and reach specific levels of performance and experience, their pay increases.

Job Outlook

Overall employment of machinists and tool and die makers is projected to grow 6 percent from 2014 to 2024, about as fast as the average for all occupations. Employment growth will vary by specialty.

Employment of machinists is projected to grow 10 percent from 2014 to 2024, faster than the average for all occupations. Despite improvements in technologies, such as computer numerically controlled (CNC) machine tools, autoloaders, high-speed machining, and lights-out manufacturing, machinists will still be required to set up, monitor, and maintain these automated systems.

In addition, employers will continue to need machinists, who have a wide range of skills and are capable of using modern production techniques in a machine shop. As manufacturers invest in new equipment, modify production techniques, and implement product design changes more rapidly, they will continue to rely heavily on experienced machinists.

Employment of tool and die makers is projected to decline 13 percent from 2014 to 2024. Foreign competition in manufacturing and advances in automation, including CNC machine tools and computer-aided design (CAD), should reduce employment of tool and die makers.

Job Prospects. Job opportunities for machinists and tool and die makers should be very good, as employers continue to value the wide-ranging skills of these workers. Also, many young people

Employment Projections Data for Machinists and Tool and Die Makers

Occupational Title	SOC Code	Employment, 2014	Projected Employment, 2024	Change, 2014–2024 Percent	Change, 2014–2024 Numeric
Machinists and tool and die makers	—	477,500	506,600	6	29,000
Machinists	51-4041	399,700	438,900	10	39,200
Tool and die makers	51-4111	77,800	67,700	-13	-10,100

Source: U.S. Bureau of Labor Statistics, Employment Projections Program

Similar Occupations. This table shows a list of occupations with job duties that are similar to those of machinists and tool and die makers.

Occupations	Entry-level Education	2014 Median Pay	Projected Job Growth	Average Annual Openings
Industrial Machinery Mechanics, Machinery Maintenance Workers, and Millwrights	High school diploma or equivalent	$47,450	16%	7,340
Metal and Plastic Machine Workers	High school diploma or equivalent	$33,550	-13%	-13,390
Welders, Cutters, Solderers, and Brazers	High school diploma or equivalent	$37,420	4%	1,440

with the education and skills needed to become machinists and tool and die makers prefer to attend college or may not wish to enter production occupations. Therefore, the number of workers learning to be machinists and tool and die makers is expected to be smaller than the number of job openings arising each year from the need to replace experienced machinists who retire or leave the occupation for other reasons.

Contacts for More Information

For more information about machinists and tool and die makers, including training and certification, visit

- ➤ Fabricators & Manufacturers Association, International (FMA) (www.fmanet.org)
- ➤ National Institute for Metalworking Skills (NIMS) (www.nims-skills.org)

For information about manufacturing careers, including machinery and tool and die makers, visit

- ➤ American Mold Builders Association (AMBA) (www.amba.org)
- ➤ Association for Manufacturing Technology (AMT) (www.amtonline.org)
- ➤ National Tooling and Machining Association (NTMA) (www.ntma.org)
- ➤ Precision Machined Products Association (PMPA) (www.pmpa.org)
- ➤ Precision Metalforming Association (PMA) (www.pma.org/home)

O*NET

- ➤ Machinists (51-4041.00)
- ➤ Tool and Die Makers (51-4111.00)

Metal and Plastic Machine Workers

- **2014 Median Pay** .... $33,550 per year $16.13 per hour
- **Typical Entry-Level Education** .... High school diploma or equivalent
- **Work Experience in a Related Occupation** .... None
- **On-the-job Training** .... See Education/Training
- **Number of Jobs, 2014** 1,048,700
- **Job Outlook, 2014–24** ....-13% (Decline)
- **Employment Change, 2014–24** ....-133,900

What Metal and Plastic Machine Workers Do

Metal and plastic machine workers set up and operate machines that cut, shape, and form metal and plastic materials or pieces.

Duties. Metal and plastic machine workers typically do the following:

- Set up machines according to blueprints
- Monitor machines for unusual sound or vibration
- Insert material into machines, manually or with a hoist
- Operate metal or plastic molding, casting, or coremaking machines
- Adjust machine settings for temperature, cycle times, and speed and feed rates
- Remove finished products and smooth rough edges and imperfections
- Test and compare finished workpieces to specifications
- Remove and replace dull cutting tools
- Document production numbers in a computer database

Consumer products are made with many metal and plastic parts. These parts are produced by machines that are operated by metal and plastic machine workers. In general, these workers are separated into two groups: those who set up machines for operation and those who operate machines during production. However, many workers perform both tasks.

Although many workers both set up and operate machines, some specialize in one of the following job types:

Machine setters, or setup workers, prepare the machines before production, perform test runs, and, if necessary, adjust and make minor repairs to the machinery before and during operation.

If, for example, the cutting tool inside a machine becomes dull after extended use, it is common for a setter to remove the tool, use a grinder or file to sharpen it, and reinstall it into the machine. New tools are produced by tool and die makers.

After installing the tools into a machine, setup workers often produce the initial batch of goods, inspect the products, and turn the machine over to an operator.

Machine operators and tenders monitor the machinery during operation.

After a setter prepares a machine for production, an operator observes the machine and the products it makes. Operators may have to load the machine with materials for production or adjust the machine's speeds during production. They must periodically inspect the parts a machine produces. If they detect a minor problem, operators may fix it themselves. If the repair is more serious, they may have an industrial machinery mechanic fix it.

Setters, operators, and tenders are usually identified by the type of machine they work with. Job duties generally vary with the size of the manufacturer and the type of machine being operated. Although some workers specialize in one or two types of machinery, many are trained to set up or operate a variety of machines. Machine operators are often able to control multiple machines at the same time because of increased automation.

In addition, new production techniques, such as team-oriented "lean" manufacturing, require machine operators to rotate between different machines. Rotating assignments results in more varied work but also requires workers to have a wide range of skills.

Computer-controlled machine tool operators operate computer-controlled machines or robots to perform functions on metal or plastic workpieces.

Computer numerically controlled machine tool programmers develop computer programs to control the machining or processing of metal or plastic parts by automatic machine tools, equipment, or systems.

Extruding and drawing machine setters, operators, and tenders set up or operate machines to extrude (pull out) thermoplastic or metal materials in the form of tubes, rods, hoses, wire, bars, or structural shapes.

Forging machine setters, operators, and tenders set up or operate machines that shape or form metal or plastic parts.

Rolling machine setters, operators, and tenders set up or operate machines to roll steel or plastic or to flatten, temper, or reduce the thickness of materials.

Cutting, punching, and press machine setters, operators, and tenders set up or operate machines to saw, cut, shear, notch, bend, or straighten metal or plastic materials.

Drilling and boring machine tool setters, operators, and tenders set up or operate drilling machines to drill, bore, mill, or countersink metal or plastic workpieces.

Grinding, lapping, polishing, and buffing machine tool setters, operators, and tenders set up or operate grinding and related tools that remove excess material from surfaces, sharpen edges or corners, or buff or polish metal or plastic workpieces.

Lathe and turning machine tool setters, operators, and tenders set up or operate lathe and turning machines to turn, bore, thread, or form metal or plastic materials, such as wire or rod.

Milling and planing machine setters, operators, and tenders set up or operate milling or planing machines to shape, groove, or profile metal or plastic workpieces.

Metal-refining furnace operators and tenders operate or tend furnaces, such as gas, oil, coal, electric-arc or electric induction, open-hearth, and oxygen furnaces. These furnaces may be used to melt and refine metal before casting or to produce specified types of steel.

Machine operators stop production when faulty parts are produced.

Pourers and casters operate hand-controlled mechanisms to pour and regulate the flow of molten metal into molds to produce castings or ingots.

Model makers set up and operate machines, such as milling and engraving machines to make working models of metal or plastic objects.

Patternmakers lay out, machine, fit, and assemble castings and parts to metal or plastic foundry patterns and core molds.

Foundry mold and coremakers make or form wax or sand cores or molds used in the production of metal castings in foundries.

Molding, coremaking, and casting machine setters, operators, and tenders set up or operate metal or plastic molding, casting, or coremaking machines to mold or cast metal or thermoplastic parts or products.

Multiple machine tool setters, operators, and tenders set up or operate more than one type of cutting or forming machine tool or robot.

Welding, soldering, and brazing machine setters, operators, and tenders (including workers who operate laser cutters or laser-beam machines) set up or operate welding, soldering, or brazing machines or robots that weld, braze, solder, or heat treat metal products, components, or assemblies.

Heat treating equipment setters, operators, and tenders set up or operate heating equipment, such as heat treating furnaces, flame-hardening machines, induction machines, soaking pits, or vacuum equipment, to temper, harden, anneal, or heat-treat metal or plastic objects.

Plating and coating machine setters, operators, and tenders set up or operate plating or coating machines to coat metal or plastic products with zinc, copper, nickel, or some other metal to protect or decorate surfaces (includes electrolytic processes).

Work Environment

Metal and plastic machine workers held about 1 million jobs in 2014. Nearly all worked in manufacturing industries.

Employment in the detailed occupations that make up this group was distributed as follows in 2014:

Cutting, punching, and press machine setters, operators, and tenders, metal and plastic	192,200
Computer-controlled machine tool operators, metal and plastic	148,800
Molding, coremaking, and casting machine setters, operators, and tenders, metal and plastic	129,500
Multiple machine tool setters, operators, and tenders, metal and plastic	99,800
Extruding and drawing machine setters, operators, and tenders, metal and plastic	73,400
Grinding, lapping, polishing, and buffing machine tool setters, operators, and tenders, metal and plastic	71,400
Welding, soldering, and brazing machine setters, operators, and tenders	59,500
Lathe and turning machine tool setters, operators, and tenders, metal and plastic	42,900
Plating and coating machine setters, operators, and tenders, metal and plastic	36,100
Rolling machine setters, operators, and tenders, metal and plastic	33,700
Computer numerically controlled machine tool programmers, metal and plastic	25,100
Milling and planing machine setters, operators, and tenders, metal and plastic	22,400
Forging machine setters, operators, and tenders, metal and plastic	21,600

Heat treating equipment setters, operators, and tenders, metal and plastic....21,300
Metal-refining furnace operators and tenders....21,200
Drilling and boring machine tool setters, operators, and tenders, metal and plastic....17,800
Foundry mold and coremakers....12,000
Pourers and casters, metal....9,800
Model makers, metal and plastic....6,200
Patternmakers, metal and plastic....3,800

Metal and plastic machine workers are employed mostly in factories.

These workers often operate powerful, high-speed machines that can be dangerous, so they must observe safety rules. Operators usually wear protective equipment, such as safety glasses, earplugs, and steel-toed boots to protect them from flying particles of metal or plastic, machine noise, and heavy objects, respectively.

Other required safety equipment varies by work setting and machine. For example, respirators are common for those in the plastics industry who work near materials that emit dangerous fumes or dust.

Work Schedules. Most metal and plastic machine workers are employed full time. Overtime is common, and because many manufacturers run their machinery for extended periods, evening and weekend work is also common.

Education/Training

A few months of on-the-job training is enough for most workers to learn basic machine operations, but 1 year or more is required to become proficient. Computer-controlled machine workers may need more training.

Education. Employers prefer metal and plastic machine workers who have a high school diploma. Prospective workers can improve their employment opportunities by completing high school courses in computer programming and vocational technology, and by gaining a working knowledge of the properties of metals and plastics. Having a sturdy math background, including taking courses in algebra, geometry, trigonometry, and basic statistics, is also useful.

Some community colleges and other schools offer courses and certificate programs in operating metal and plastics machines.

Training. Machine operator trainees usually begin by watching and helping experienced workers on the job. Under supervision, they may start by supplying materials, starting and stopping the machines, or by removing finished products. Then they advance to more difficult tasks that operators perform, such as adjusting feed speeds, changing cutting tools, and inspecting a finished product for defects. Eventually, some develop the skills and experience to set up machines and help newer operators.

The complexity of the equipment usually determines the time required to become an operator. Some operators and tenders learn basic machine operations and functions in a few months, but other workers, such as computer-controlled machine tool operators, may need a year or more to become proficient.

Some employers prefer to hire workers who either have completed or are enrolled in a training program.

As the manufacturing process continues to utilize more computerized machinery, knowledge of computer-aided design (CAD), computer-aided manufacturing (CAM), and computer numerically controlled (CNC) machines can be helpful.

Licenses, Certifications, and Registrations. Certification can show competence and professionalism and can be helpful for advancement. The National Institute for Metalworking Skills (NIMS) offers certification in numerous metalworking specializations.

Advancement. Advancement usually includes higher pay and more responsibilities. With experience and expertise, workers can become trainees for more advanced positions. It is common for machine operators to move into setup or machinery maintenance positions. Setup workers may become industrial machinery mechanics and maintenance workers, or machinists or tool and die makers.

Experienced workers with good communication and analytical skills may move into supervisory positions.

Important Qualities

Computer skills. Metal and plastic machine workers must often be able to use programmable devices, computers, and robots on the factory floor.

Dexterity. Metal and plastic machine workers who work in metal and plastic machined goods manufacturing use precise hand movements to make the necessary shapes, cuts, and edges that designs require.

Mechanical skills. Metal and plastic machine workers set up and operate machinery. They must be comfortable working with machines and have a good understanding of how the machines and all their parts work.

Physical stamina. Metal and plastic machine workers must be able to stand for long periods and perform repetitive work.

Physical strength. Metal and plastic machine workers must be strong enough to guide and load heavy and bulky parts and materials into machines.

Pay

The median annual wage for metal and plastic machine workers was $33,550 in May 2014. The median wage is the wage at which half the workers in an occupation earned more than that amount

Median Annual Wages, May 2014

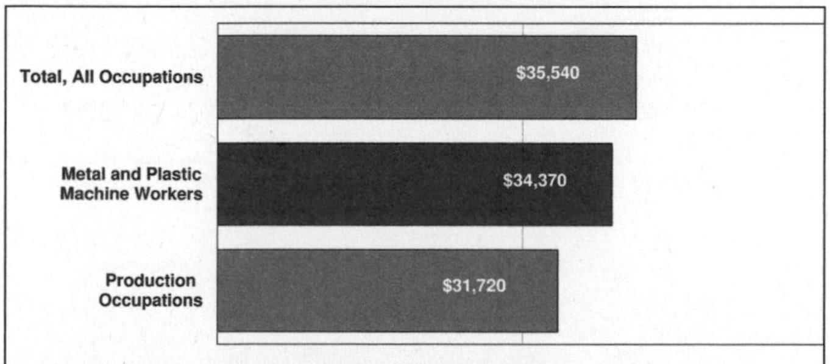

Note: All Occupations includes all occupations in the U.S. Economy.
Source: U.S. Bureau of Labor Statistics, Occupational Employment Statistics

Percent Change in Employment, Projected 2014–2024

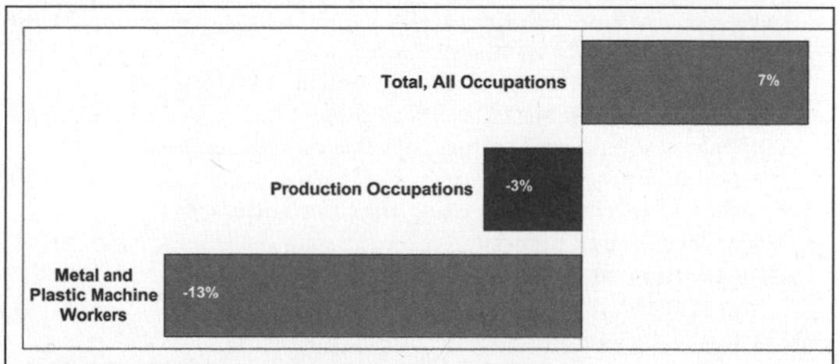

Note: All Occupations includes all occupations in the U.S. Economy.
Source: U.S. Bureau of Labor Statistics, Office of Occupational Statistics and Employment Projections

and half earned less. The lowest 10 percent earned less than $21,400, and the highest 10 percent earned more than $51,720.

Median annual wages for metal and plastic machine workers in May 2014 were as follows:

Computer numerically controlled machine tool programmers, metal and plastic $47,500
Model makers, metal and plastic 46,180
Patternmakers, metal and plastic 41,390
Metal-refining furnace operators and tenders 41,140
Rolling machine setters, operators, and tenders, metal and plastic 39,900
Milling and planing machine setters, operators, and tenders, metal and plastic 37,100
Computer-controlled machine tool operators, metal and plastic 36,440
Lathe and turning machine tool setters, operators, and tenders, metal and plastic 36,260
Heat treating equipment setters, operators, and tenders, metal and plastic 35,320
Welding, soldering, and brazing machine setters, operators, and tenders 35,180
Drilling and boring machine tool setters, operators, and tenders, metal and plastic 34,500
Multiple machine tool setters, operators, and tenders, metal and plastic 34,140
Forging machine setters, operators, and tenders, metal and plastic 33,710
Grinding, lapping, polishing, and buffing machine tool setters, operators, and tenders, metal and plastic 32,660
Extruding and drawing machine setters, operators, and tenders, metal and plastic 32,610
Pourers and casters, metal 32,410
Foundry mold and coremakers 31,340
Cutting, punching, and press machine setters, operators, and tenders, metal and plastic 30,680
Plating and coating machine setters, operators, and tenders, metal and plastic 30,210
Molding, coremaking, and casting machine setters, operators, and tenders, metal and plastic 28,810

Job Outlook

Employment of metal and plastic machine workers is projected to decline 13 percent from 2014 to 2024. Employment declines stem from advances in technology and foreign competition.

One of the most important factors influencing employment of these occupations is the use of labor-saving machinery. Many

Employment Projections Data for Metal and Plastic Machine Workers

Occupational Title	SOC Code	Employment, 2014	Projected Employment, 2024	Change, 2014–2024	
				Percent	Numeric
Metal and plastic machine workers	—	1,048,700	914,700	-13	-133,900
Computer-controlled machine tool operators, metal and plastic	51-4011	148,800	174,800	17	26,000
Computer numerically controlled machine tool programmers, metal and plastic	51-4012	25,100	29,900	19	4,800
Extruding and drawing machine setters, operators, and tenders, metal and plastic	51-4021	73,400	55,500	-24	-17,900
Forging machine setters, operators, and tenders, metal and plastic	51-4022	21,600	17,000	-21	-4,600
Rolling machine setters, operators, and tenders, metal and plastic	51-4023	33,700	29,100	-14	-4,600
Cutting, punching, and press machine setters, operators, and tenders, metal and plastic	51-4031	192,200	152,700	-21	-39,500
Drilling and boring machine tool setters, operators, and tenders, metal and plastic	51-4032	17,800	14,100	-21	-3,700
Grinding, lapping, polishing, and buffing machine tool setters, operators, and tenders, metal and plastic	51-4033	71,400	55,800	-22	-15,700
Lathe and turning machine tool setters, operators, and tenders, metal and plastic	51-4034	42,900	34,300	-20	-8,600
Milling and planing machine setters, operators, and tenders, metal and plastic	51-4035	22,400	17,800	-21	-4,600
Metal-refining furnace operators and tenders	51-4051	21,200	20,200	-5	-1,000
Pourers and casters, metal	51-4052	9,800	7,200	-27	-2,600
Model makers, metal and plastic	51-4061	6,200	4,900	-22	-1,300
Patternmakers, metal and plastic	51-4062	3,800	2,900	-23	-900
Foundry mold and coremakers	51-4071	12,000	8,700	-28	-3,300
Molding, coremaking, and casting machine setters, operators, and tenders, metal and plastic	51-4072	129,500	97,200	-25	-32,300
Multiple machine tool setters, operators, and tenders, metal and plastic	51-4081	99,800	97,300	-2	-2,500
Welding, soldering, and brazing machine setters, operators, and tenders	51-4122	59,500	48,800	-18	-10,700
Heat treating equipment setters, operators, and tenders, metal and plastic	51-4191	21,300	17,200	-20	-4,200
Plating and coating machine setters, operators, and tenders, metal and plastic	51-4193	36,100	29,400	-18	-6,700

Source: U.S. Bureau of Labor Statistics, Employment Projections Program

Similar Occupations. This table shows a list of occupations with job duties that are similar to those of metal and plastic machine workers.

Occupations	Entry-level Education	2014 Median Pay	Projected Job Growth	Average Annual Openings
Assemblers and Fabricators	High school diploma or equivalent	$29,280	-1%	-970
Computer Programmers	Bachelor's degree	$77,550	-8%	-2,650
Industrial Machinery Mechanics, Machinery Maintenance Workers, and Millwrights	High school diploma or equivalent	$47,450	16%	7,340
Machinists and Tool and Die Makers	High school diploma or equivalent	$41,510	6%	2,900
Painting and Coating Workers	See Education/Training	$33,740	1%	210

firms are adopting technologies such as computer numerically controlled (CNC) machine tools and robots to improve quality and lower production costs. The switch to CNC machinery requires computer programmers instead of machine setters, operators, and tenders. Therefore, demand for manual machine tool operators and tenders is likely to be reduced by these new technologies, and conversely, demand for CNC machine programmers is expected to be strong.

The demand for metal and plastic machine workers is also affected by the demand for the parts they produce. Both the plastic and metal manufacturing industries face foreign competition that limits the orders for parts produced in this country. Some U.S. manufacturers have sent their production to foreign countries, reducing jobs for machine setters and operators. However, some companies are bringing jobs back to the United States from overseas, and this is expected to continue over the coming decade.

Job Prospects. Workers who are able to operate CNC machines are expected to have the best job prospects. Workers who have an extensive background in machine operations, industry certifications, and good knowledge of the properties of metals and plastics should also have good job opportunities.

A high number of job openings should be created by the need to replace workers who leave these occupations.

Contacts for More Information

For more information about metal and plastic machine workers, including training and certification, visit

- Fabricators & Manufacturers Association, International (FMA) (www.fmanet.org)
- National Institute for Metalworking Skills (NIMS) (www.nims-skills.org)

For information about manufacturing careers, machinery, and equipment, visit

- Association for Manufacturing Technology (AMT) (www.amtonline.org)
- National Tooling and Machining Association (NTMA) (www.ntma.org)
- Precision Machined Products Association (PMPA) (www.pmpa.org)
- Precision Metalforming Association (PMA) (www.pma.org/home)

O*NET

- Computer-Controlled Machine Tool Operators, Metal and Plastic (51-4011.00)
- Computer Numerically Controlled Machine Tool Programmers, Metal and Plastic (51-4012.00)
- Extruding and Drawing Machine Setters, Operators, and Tenders, Metal and Plastic (51-4021.00)
- Forging Machine Setters, Operators, and Tenders, Metal and Plastic (51-4022.00)
- Rolling Machine Setters, Operators, and Tenders, Metal and Plastic (51-4023.00)
- Cutting, Punching, and Press Machine Setters, Operators, and Tenders, Metal and Plastic (51-4031.00)
- Drilling and Boring Machine Tool Setters, Operators, and Tenders, Metal and Plastic (51-4032.00)
- Grinding, Lapping, Polishing, and Buffing Machine Tool Setters, Operators, and Tenders, Metal and Plastic (51-4033.00)
- Lathe and Turning Machine Tool Setters, Operators, and Tenders, Metal and Plastic (51-4034.00)
- Milling and Planing Machine Setters, Operators, and Tenders, Metal and Plastic (51-4035.00)
- Metal-Refining Furnace Operators and Tenders (51-4051.00)
- Pourers and Casters, Metal (51-4052.00)
- Model Makers, Metal and Plastic (51-4061.00)
- Patternmakers, Metal and Plastic (51-4062.00)
- Foundry Mold and Coremakers (51-4071.00)
- Molding, Coremaking, and Casting Machine Setters, Operators, and Tenders, Metal and Plastic (51-4072.00)
- Multiple Machine Tool Setters, Operators, and Tenders, Metal and Plastic (51-4081.00)
- Welding, Soldering, and Brazing Machine Setters, Operators, and Tenders (51-4122.00)
- Heat Treating Equipment Setters, Operators, and Tenders, Metal and Plastic (51-4191.00)
- Plating and Coating Machine Setters, Operators, and Tenders, Metal and Plastic (51-4193.00)

Painting and Coating Workers

- **2014 Median Pay** .... $33,740 per year
  $16.22 per hour
- **Typical Entry-Level Education**.... See Education/Training
- **Work Experience in a Related Occupation**.............. None
- **On-the-job Training**...Moderate-term on-the-job training
- **Number of Jobs, 2014** 169,500
- **Job Outlook, 2014–24**................1% (Little or no change)
- **Employment Change, 2014–24** 2,100

What Painting and Coating Workers Do

Painting and coating workers often use machines to paint and coat a wide range of products, including cars, jewelry, and ceramics.

Duties. Painting and coating workers typically do the following:

- Set up and operate machines that paint or coat products
- Select the paint or coating needed for the job

- Clean and prepare products to be painted or coated
- Determine the required flow of paint and the quality of the coating
- Apply paint or coating
- Clean and maintain tools, equipment, and work areas

Millions of items ranging from cars to furniture are coated by paint, varnish, rustproofing, or other types of liquid applications. Painting or coating is used to make a product more attractive or protect it from the elements. The paint finish on an automobile, for example, makes the vehicle more attractive and provides protection from corrosion.

Before workers begin to apply the paint or other coating, they often need to prepare the surface by sanding or cleaning it carefully to prevent dust from becoming trapped under the paint. Masking is frequently required and involves carefully covering portions of the product with tape and paper.

After the product is prepared, workers may use a number of techniques to apply the paint or coating. A common technique is dipping an item in a large vat of paint or some other coating. Spraying products with paint or another coating is also common. Many factories use automated painting systems.

The following are examples of types of painting and coating workers:

Coating, painting, and spraying machine setters, operators, and tenders position the spray guns, set the nozzles, and synchronize the action of the guns with the speed of the conveyor carrying products through the machine. During the process, these workers program the machine, tend the equipment, watch gauges on the control panel, and check products to ensure that they are being painted evenly. The operator may use a manual spray gun to touch up flaws.

Dippers use power hoists to immerse products in vats of paint, liquid plastic, or other solutions. This technique is commonly used for small parts of electronic equipment, such as cell phones.

Painting, coating, and decorating workers apply coatings to furniture, glass, pottery, toys, books, and other products. Paper is often coated to give it a gloss. Silver, tin, and copper solutions are frequently sprayed onto glass to make mirrors.

Spraying machine operators use spray guns to coat metal, wood, ceramic, fabric, and paper products with paint and other coating solutions.

Transportation equipment painters are the best known group of painting and coating workers. There are three major specialties:

- Transportation equipment workers, or *automotive painters*, usually refinish old or damaged cars, trucks, and buses in automotive repair and paint shops by applying paint by hand with a spray gun. Those who work in repair shops are among the most competent manual spray operators: they perform intricate, detailed work and mix paints to match the original color—a task that is especially difficult if the color has faded. Painting an old car is similar to painting other metal objects.
- Transportation equipment painters work on new cars and oversee several automated steps. A modern car is first dipped in an anticorrosion bath, then coated with colored paint, and finally painted with several coats of clear paint to prevent damage to the colored paint.
- Other transportation equipment painters either paint equipment that is too large to paint automatically—such as ships or giant construction equipment—or do touchup work to fix flaws in the paint that are caused by damage either during assembly or during the automated painting process.

Automotive painters wear ventilators to ensure safety.

Work Environment

Painting and coating workers held about 169,500 jobs in 2014. Employment in the detailed occupations that make up painting and coating workers in 2014 was distributed as follows:

Coating, painting, and spraying machine setters, operators, and tenders	97,700
Painters, transportation equipment	54,300
Painting, coating, and decorating workers	17,500

Painting and coating is usually done in specially ventilated areas. Nonetheless, workers must wear masks or respirators that cover their nose and mouth.

Coating workers often stand for long periods. When using a spray gun, they may have to bend, stoop, or crouch in uncomfortable positions to reach different parts of the products.

Injuries and Illnesses. Both transportation equipment painters and painting, coating, and decorating workers have higher rates of injuries and illnesses than the national average. Hazards include muscle strains and exposure to toxic materials. More sophisticated paint booths and fresh-air ventilation systems are increasingly being installed in factories to provide a safer work environment.

Work Schedules. The vast majority of painting and coating workers are employed full time. Automotive painters in repair shops often work overtime, depending on the number of vehicles that need painting.

Education/Training

Most painting and coating workers learn on the job after earning a high school diploma or equivalent. Training for new workers usually lasts from a few days to several months.

Education. Painting and coating workers in the manufacturing sector usually must have a high school diploma or equivalent. Employers outside of manufacturing sometimes hire workers without a high school diploma.

Taking high school courses in automotive painting is recommended.

Median Annual Wages, May 2014

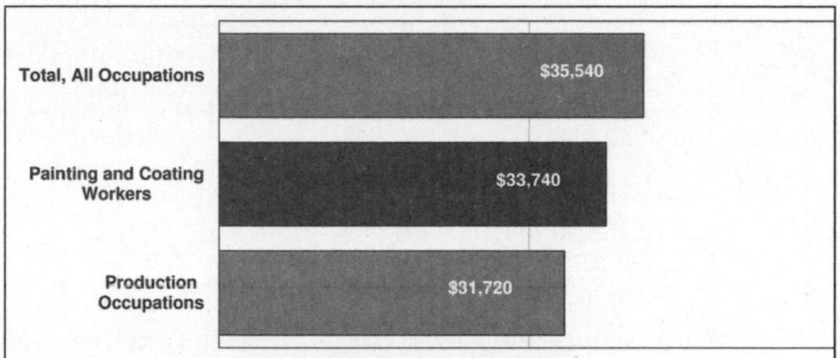

Note: All Occupations includes all occupations in the U.S. Economy.
Source: U.S. Bureau of Labor Statistics, Occupational Employment Statistics

Percent Change in Employment, Projected 2014–2024

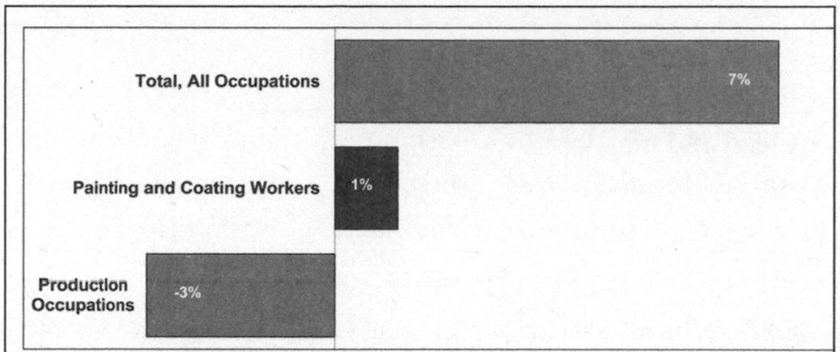

Note: All Occupations includes all occupations in the U.S. Economy.
Source: U.S. Bureau of Labor Statistics, Office of Occupational Statistics and Employment Projections

Some automotive painters attend a technical or vocational school where they receive hands-on training and learn the intricacies of mixing and applying different types of paint.

Training. Most entry-level workers receive on-the-job training that may last from a few days to a few months.

Workers who operate computer-controlled equipment may require additional training in computer programming.

Manufacturing transportation equipment painters typically learn to paint on the job.

Licenses, Certifications, and Registrations. Voluntary certification by the National Institute for Automotive Service Excellence (ASE) is recognized as the standard of achievement for automotive painters. To obtain certification, painters must pass a written exam and have at least 2 years of experience in the field. Recertification is required every 5 years. Few painting and coating workers other than automobile painters obtain certification.

ASE-approved training in refinishing taken while one is enrolled in high school, a trade or vocational school, or a community college may substitute for up to 1 year of work experience. To keep the certification, painters must retake the exam at least every 5 years.

Important Qualities

Artistic ability. Some workers make elaborate or decorative designs. For example, some automotive painters specialize in making custom designs for vehicles.

Color vision. Workers must be able to blend new paint colors in order to match existing colors on a surface.

Mechanical skills. Workers must be able to operate and maintain sprayers that apply paints and coatings.

Physical stamina. Some workers must stand at their station for extended periods. Continuous standing or activity can be tiring.

Physical strength. Workers may need to lift heavy objects. Some products that are painted or coated may weigh over 50 pounds.

Pay

The median annual wage for painting and coating workers was $33,740 in May 2014. The median wage is the wage at which half the workers in an occupation earned more than that amount and half earned less. The lowest 10 percent earned less than $21,280, and the highest 10 percent earned more than $56,050.

Median annual wages for painting and coating workers in May 2014 were as follows:

Painters, transportation equipment	$40,770
Coating, painting, and spraying machine setters, operators, and tenders	31,460
Painting, coating, and decorating workers	28,750

Job Outlook

Employment of painting and coating workers is projected to show little or no change from 2014 to 2024. Employment growth will vary by occupation and industry.

Employment of coating, painting, and spraying machine setters, operators, and tenders—the largest occupation in this profile—is projected to show little or no change from 2014 to 2024. Although many consumer, commercial, and industrial products require painting or coating and thus will provide job opportunities for these workers, productivity gains are expected to offset any employment growth.

Employment of transportation equipment painters is projected to grow 6 percent from 2014 to 2024, about as fast as the average for all occupations. The majority of new jobs will be driven by the need for painters in repair shops.

Employment of painting, coating, and decorating workers is projected to decline 2 percent from 2014 to 2024. Increased automation in most manufacturing facilities will reduce job opportunities for these workers.

Employment Projections Data for Painting and Coating Workers

Occupational Title	SOC Code	Employment, 2014	Projected Employment, 2024	Change, 2014–2024 Percent	Change, 2014–2024 Numeric
Painting and coating workers	—	169,500	171,700	1	2,100
Coating, painting, and spraying machine setters, operators, and tenders	51-9121	97,700	97,000	-1	-700
Painters, transportation equipment	51-9122	54,300	57,500	6	3,200
Painting, coating, and decorating workers	51-9123	17,500	17,200	-2	-300

Source: U.S. Bureau of Labor Statistics, Employment Projections Program

Similar Occupations. This table shows a list of occupations with job duties that are similar to those of painting and coating workers.

Occupations	Entry-level Education	2014 Median Pay	Projected Job Growth	Average Annual Openings
Automotive Body and Glass Repairers	High school diploma or equivalent	$39,260	9%	1,530
Metal and Plastic Machine Workers	High school diploma or equivalent	$33,550	-13%	-13,390
Painters, Construction and Maintenance	No formal educational credential	$35,950	7%	2,650

Job Prospects. As with many manufacturing jobs, employers often report difficulty finding qualified workers. Therefore, job opportunities should be very good for those with painting experience.

Many job openings should result from the need to replace workers who leave the occupation and from increased specialization in manufacturing.

Contacts for More Information

For more information about job opportunities for painting and coating workers, visit

- Local manufacturers
- Automotive body repair shops
- Motor vehicle dealers
- Vocational schools
- Local unions representing painting and coating workers
- Local offices of state employment services

For a directory of certified automotive painting programs, visit

- National Automotive Technician Education Foundation (http://tinyurl.com/cus4ljt)
- National Institute for Automotive Service Excellence (http://tinyurl.com/z3b3yyw)

O*NET

- Coating, Painting, and Spraying Machine Setters, Operators, and Tenders (51-9121.00)
- Painters, Transportation Equipment (51-9122.00)
- Painting, Coating, and Decorating Workers (51-9123.00)

Power Plant Operators, Distributors, and Dispatchers

- **2014 Median Pay** .... $72,910 per year $35.05 per hour
- **Typical Entry-Level Education** .... High school diploma or equivalent
- **Work Experience in a Related Occupation** .... None
- **On-the-job Training** .... Long-term on-the-job training
- **Number of Jobs, 2014** 60,000
- **Job Outlook, 2014–24** .... -6% (Decline)
- **Employment Change, 2014–24** .... -3,300

What Power Plant Operators, Distributors, and Dispatchers Do

Power plant operators, distributors, and dispatchers control the systems that generate and distribute electric power.

Duties. Power plant operators, distributors, and dispatchers typically do the following:

- Control power-generating equipment, which may use any one type of fuel, such as coal, nuclear fuel, or natural gas
- Read charts, meters, and gauges to monitor voltage and electricity flows
- Check equipment and indicators to detect evidence of operating problems
- Adjust controls to regulate the flow of power
- Start or stop generators, turbines, and other equipment as necessary

Electricity is one of our nation's most vital resources. Power plant operators, distributors, and dispatchers control power plants and the flow of electricity from plants to substations, which distribute electricity to businesses, homes, and factories. Electricity is generated from many sources, including coal, gas, nuclear energy, hydroelectric energy (from water sources), and wind and solar power.

Nuclear power reactor operators control nuclear reactors. They adjust control rods, which affect how much electricity a reactor generates. They monitor reactors, turbines, generators, and cooling systems, adjusting controls as necessary. Operators also start and stop equipment and record the data produced. They may need to respond to abnormalities, determine the causes, and take corrective action.

Power distributors and dispatchers, also known as *systems operators*, control the flow of electricity as it travels from generating stations to substations and users. In exercising such control, operators monitor and operate current converters, voltage transformers, and circuit breakers over a network of transmission and distribution lines. They prepare and issue switching orders to route electrical currents around areas that need maintenance or repair. They must detect and respond to emergencies, such as transformer or transmission line failures, which can cause cascading power outages over the network of transmission and distribution lines they control. They may work with plant operators to troubleshoot electricity generation issues.

Power plant operators control, operate, and maintain machinery to generate electricity. They use control boards to distribute power among generators and regulate the output of several generators. They monitor instruments to maintain voltage and electricity flows from the plant to meet consumer demand for electricity—demand that fluctuates throughout the day.

Work Environment

Power plant operators, distributors, and dispatchers held about 60,000 jobs in 2014.

In 2014, most power plant operators, distributors, and dispatchers worked in the electric power generation, transmission, and distribution industry. About 8 in 10 nuclear power plant operators and about 7 in 10 power plant operators worked in this industry.

Power distributors and dispatchers are less concentrated in the electric power generation, transmission, and distribution industry, in which only about half worked.

Operators, distributors, and dispatchers who work in control rooms generally sit or stand at a control station. The work is not physically strenuous, but it does require constant attention. Workers also may do rounds, checking equipment and doing other work outside the control room. Transmission stations and substations where distributors and dispatchers work are typically in locations that are separate from the location of the generating station where power plant operators work.

Because power transmission is both vitally important and sensitive to attack, security is a major concern for utility companies. Nuclear power plants and transmission stations have especially high security, and employees work in secure environments.

Work Schedules. Because electricity is provided around the clock, operators, distributors, and dispatchers usually work rotating 8- or 12-hour shifts. As a result, all operators share the less desirable shifts. Work on rotating shifts can be stressful and tiring because of the constant changes in living and sleeping patterns.

Education/Training

Power plant operators, distributors, and dispatchers need extensive on-the-job training, which may include a combination of classroom and hands-on training. Nuclear power reactor operators also need a license. Many jobs require a background check, and workers are subject to drug and alcohol screenings.

Many companies require prospective workers to take the Power Plant Maintenance and Plant Operator exams from the Edison Electrical Institute to see if they have the right aptitudes for this work. These tests measure reading comprehension, understanding of mechanical concepts, spatial ability, and mathematical ability.

Education. Power plant operators, distributors, and dispatchers need at least a high school diploma. However, employers may prefer workers who have a college or vocational school degree.

Employers generally look for people with strong math and science backgrounds for these highly technical jobs. Understanding electricity and math, especially algebra and trigonometry, is important.

Training. Power plant operators and dispatchers undergo rigorous, long-term on-the-job training and technical instruction. Several years of onsite training and experience are necessary for a worker to become fully qualified. Even fully qualified operators and dispatchers must take regular training courses to keep their skills up to date.

Nuclear power reactor operators usually start working as equipment operators or auxiliary operators, helping more experienced workers operate and maintain the equipment while learning the basics of how to operate the power plant.

Power plant operators use computers to report unusual incidents, malfunctioning equipment, or maintenance performed during their shifts.

Along with this extensive on-the-job training, nuclear power plant operators typically receive formal technical training to prepare for the license exam from the U.S. Nuclear Regulatory Commission (NRC). Once licensed, operators are authorized to control equipment that affects the power of the reactor in a nuclear power plant. Operators continue frequent onsite training, which familiarizes them with new monitoring systems that provide operators better real-time information regarding the plant.

Licenses, Certifications, and Registrations. Nuclear power reactor operators must be licensed through the NRC. To become licensed, operators must meet training and experience requirements, pass a medical exam, and pass the NRC licensing exam. To keep their license, operators must pass a plant-operating exam each year, pass a medical exam every 2 years, and apply for renewal of their license every 6 years. Licenses cannot be transferred between plants, so an operator must get a new license to operate in another facility.

Power plant operators who do not work at a nuclear power reactor may be licensed as engineers or firefighters by state licensing boards. Requirements vary by state and depend on the specific job functions that the operator performs.

Power distributors and dispatchers who are in positions in which they could affect the power grid must be certified through the

Median Annual Wages, May 2014

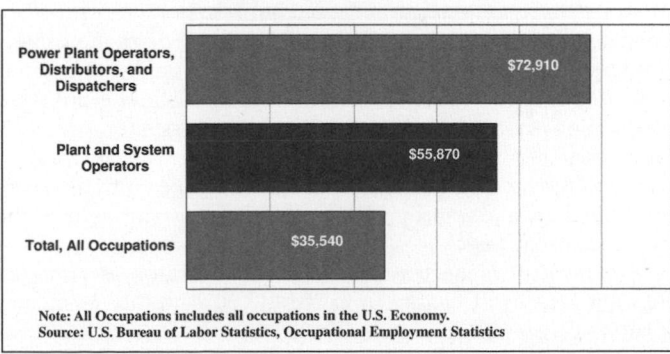

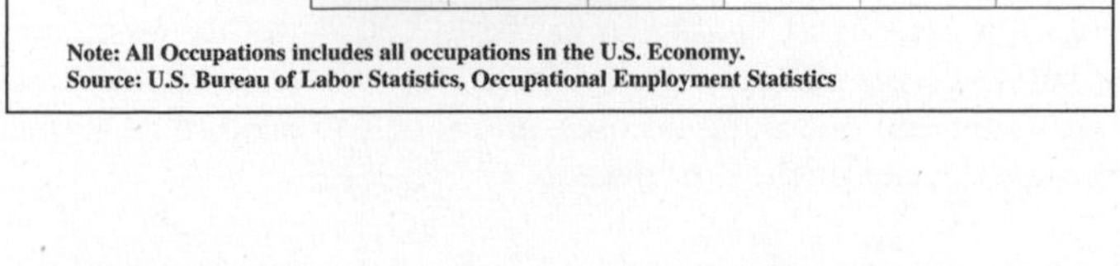

Percent Change in Employment, Projected 2014–2024

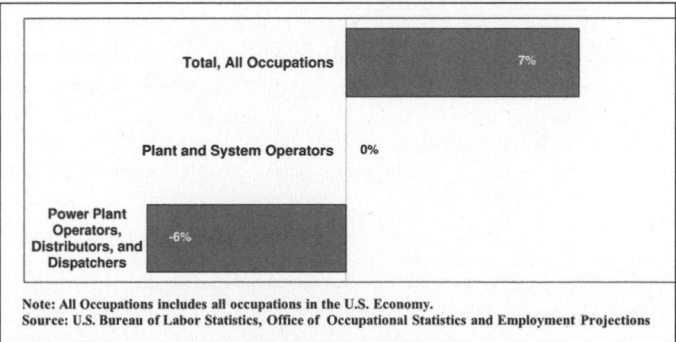

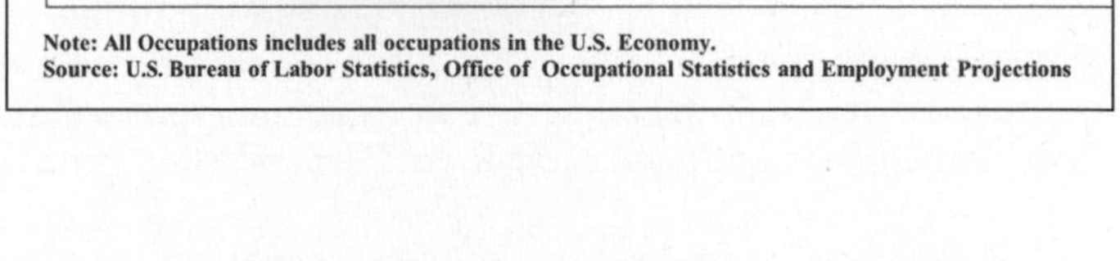

Employment Projections Data for Power Plant Operators, Distributors, and Dispatchers

Occupational Title	SOC Code	Employment, 2014	Projected Employment, 2024	Change, 2014–2024 Percent	Change, 2014–2024 Numeric
Power plant operators, distributors, and dispatchers	51-8010	60,000	56,700	-6	-3,300
Nuclear power reactor operators	51-8011	7,500	7,400	-1	-100
Power distributors and dispatchers	51-8012	11,400	10,800	-5	-600
Power plant operators	51-8013	41,100	38,400	-7	-2,700

Source: U.S. Bureau of Labor Statistics, Employment Projections Program

Similar Occupations. This table shows a list of occupations with job duties that are similar to those of power plant operators, distributors, and dispatchers.

Occupations	Entry-level Education	2014 Median Pay	Projected Job Growth	Average Annual Openings
Construction Equipment Operators	High school diploma or equivalent	$42,900	10%	4,320
Electrical and Electronics Installers and Repairers	Postsecondary nondegree award	$53,900	-4%	-540
Electricians	High school diploma or equivalent	$51,110	14%	8,590
Line Installers and Repairers	High school diploma or equivalent	$61,740	6%	1,370
Stationary Engineers and Boiler Operators	High school diploma or equivalent	$56,330	1%	60
Water and Wastewater Treatment Plant and System Operators	High school diploma or equivalent	$44,100	6%	700

North American Electric Reliability Corporation's System Operator Certification Program. With sufficient training and experience, workers can become shift supervisors, trainers, or consultants.

Nuclear power plant operators begin working in nuclear power plants, typically as nonlicensed operators. After in-plant training and passing the NRC licensing exam, they become licensed reactor operators. Licensed operators can then advance to senior reactor operators, who supervise the operation of all controls in the control room. Senior reactor operators also may become plant managers or licensed operator instructors.

Important Qualities

Concentration skills. Power plant operators, distributors, and dispatchers must be careful, attentive, and persistent. They must be able to concentrate on a task, such as monitoring the temperature of reactors over a certain length of time without being distracted.

Detail oriented. Power plant operators, distributors, and dispatchers must monitor complex controls and intricate machinery to ensure that everything is operating properly.

Dexterity. Power plant operators, distributors, and dispatchers must use precise and repeated motions when working in a control room.

Mechanical skills. Power plant operators, distributors, and dispatchers must know how to work with machines and use tools. They must be familiar with how to operate, repair, and maintain equipment.

Problem-solving skills. Power plant operators, distributors, and dispatchers must find and quickly solve problems that arise with equipment or controls.

Pay

The median annual wage for power plant operators, distributors, and dispatchers was $72,910 in May 2014. The median wage is the wage at which half the workers in an occupation earned more than that amount and half earned less. The lowest 10 percent earned less than $47,460, and the highest 10 percent earned more than $97,300.

Median annual wages for power plant operators, distributors, and dispatchers in May 2014 were as follows:

Nuclear power reactor operators	$82,500
Power distributors and dispatchers	78,240
Power plant operators	70,070

Job Outlook

Employment of power plant operators, distributors, and dispatchers is projected to decline 6 percent from 2014 to 2024. Electricity usage is expected to grow more slowly because of advances in technology and increased energy efficiency. These developments will in turn dampen employment growth for the occupation.

Employment growth will vary by specialty. Employment of power plant operators in nonnuclear power plants is projected to decline 7 percent from 2014 to 2024. As old power plants close, they will be replaced with new plants that produce electricity more efficiently and, in many cases, have higher electricity-generating capacities. These new plants will have modernized control rooms that are more automated and that provide workers with more information. As a result, workers will be able to work more effectively, perhaps limiting the number of new job opportunities.

Employment of power distributors and dispatchers is projected to decline 5 percent from 2014 to 2024. Although some distributors and dispatchers will be needed to manage an increasingly complex electrical grid, employment growth will be tempered by advances in technology and smart grid projects that automate some of the work of dispatchers.

Employment of nuclear power reactor operators is projected to show little or no change from 2014 to 2024. Although no new plants have opened since the 1990s, new sites have applied for construction and operating licenses, and they will need to be staffed before the end of the next decade.

Job Prospects. Job prospects should be better for those with related training and good mechanical skills. Many people will seek these high-paying jobs, so prospects will be best for those with strong technical and mechanical skills.

Contacts for More Information

For more information about power plant operators, nuclear power reactor operators, and power plant distributors and dispatchers, visit

- American Public Power Association (www.publicpower.org)
- Center for Energy Workforce Development (www.cewd.org)
- International Brotherhood of Electrical Workers (www.ibew.org)

For more information on nuclear power reactor operators, including licensing, visit

- U.S. Nuclear Regulatory Commission (www.nrc.gov)
- Nuclear Energy Institute (www.nei.org)

For information on certification for power distributors and dispatchers, visit

- North American Electric Reliability Corporation (www.nerc.com)

O*NET

- Nuclear Power Reactor Operators (51-8011.00)
- Power Distributors and Dispatchers (51-8012.00)
- Power Plant Operators (51-8013.00)

Quality Control Inspectors

- **2014 Median Pay** .... $35,330 per year $16.99 per hour
- **Typical Entry-Level Education** .... High school diploma or equivalent
- **Work Experience in a Related Occupation** .... None
- **On-the-job Training**...Moderate-term on-the-job training
- **Number of Jobs, 2014** 496,600
- **Job Outlook, 2014–24** .... 0% (Little or no change)
- **Employment Change, 2014–24** .... -1,100

What Quality Control Inspectors Do

Quality control inspectors examine products and materials for defects or deviations from specifications.

Duties. Quality control inspectors typically do the following:

- Read blueprints and specifications
- Monitor operations to ensure that they meet production standards
- Recommend adjustments to the assembly or production process
- Inspect, test, or measure materials or products being produced
- Measure products with rulers, calipers, gauges, or micrometers
- Accept or reject finished items
- Remove all products and materials that fail to meet specifications
- Discuss inspection results with those responsible for products
- Report inspection and test data

Quality control inspectors ensure, for example, that the food or medicine you take will not make you sick, that your car will run properly, and that your pants will not split the first time you wear them. These workers monitor quality standards for nearly all manufactured products, including foods, textiles, clothing, glassware, motor vehicles, electronic components, computers, and structural steel. Specific job duties vary across the wide range of industries in which these inspectors work.

Quality control workers rely on many tools to do their jobs. Although some still use hand-held measurement devices, such as calipers and alignment gauges, workers more commonly operate electronic inspection equipment, such as coordinate-measuring machines (CMMs). Inspectors testing electrical devices may use voltmeters, ammeters, and ohmmeters to test potential difference, current flow, and resistance, respectively.

Quality control workers record the results of their inspections through test reports. When they find defects, inspectors notify supervisors and help to analyze and correct production problems.

In some firms, the inspection process is completely automated, with advanced vision inspection systems installed at one or several points in the production process. Inspectors in these firms monitor the equipment, review output, and conduct random product checks.

The following are examples of types of quality control inspectors:

Inspectors mark, tag, or note problems. They may reject defective items outright, send them for repair, or fix minor problems themselves. If the product is acceptable, the inspector certifies it. Inspectors may further specialize in the following jobs:

- *Materials inspectors* check products by sight, sound, or feel to locate imperfections such as cuts, scratches, missing pieces, or crooked seams.
- *Mechanical inspectors* generally verify that parts fit, move correctly, and are properly lubricated. They may check the pressure of gases and the level of liquids, test the flow of electricity, and conduct test runs to ensure that machines run properly.

Samplers test or inspect a sample for malfunctions or defects during a batch or production run.

Sorters separate goods according to length, size, fabric type, or color.

Testers repeatedly test existing products or prototypes under real-world conditions. Through these tests, manufacturers determine how long a product will last, what parts will break down first, and how to improve durability.

Weighers weigh quantities of materials for use in production.

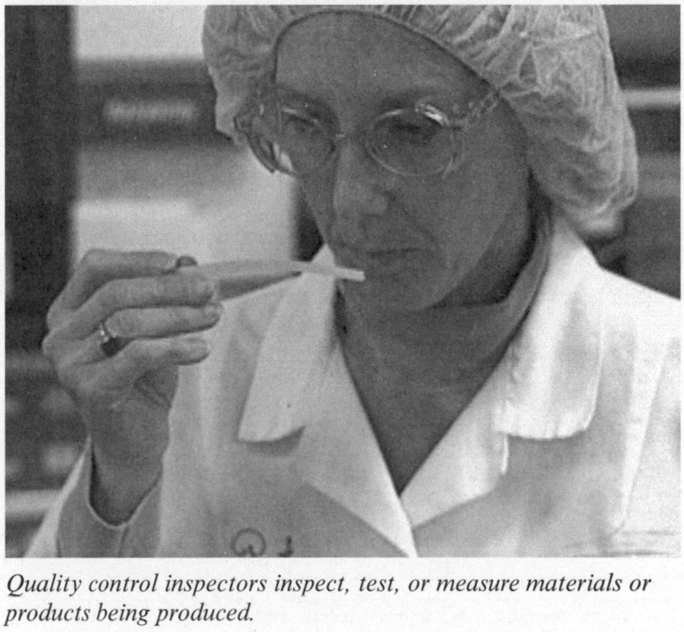

Quality control inspectors inspect, test, or measure materials or products being produced.

Median Hourly Wages, May 2014

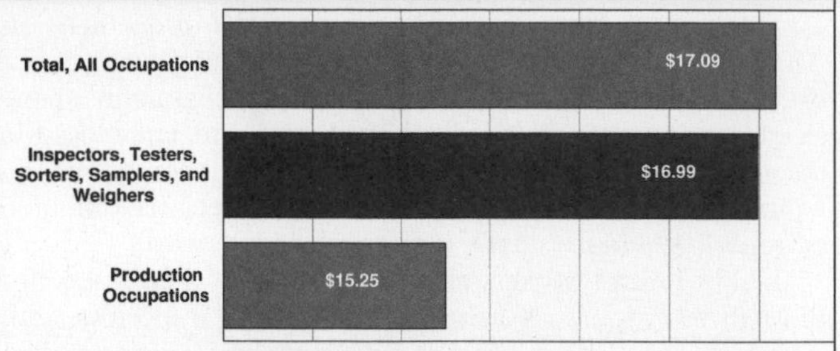

Note: All Occupations includes all occupations in the U.S. Economy.
Source: U.S. Bureau of Labor Statistics, Occupational Employment Statistics

Percent Change in Employment, Projected 2014–2024

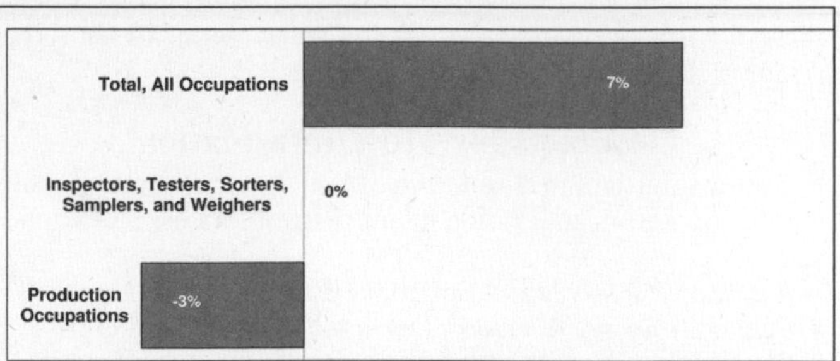

Note: All Occupations includes all occupations in the U.S. Economy.
Source: U.S. Bureau of Labor Statistics, Office of Occupational Statistics and Employment Projections

Work Environment

Quality control inspectors held about 496,600 jobs in 2014. The industries that employed the most quality control inspectors were as follows:

Manufacturing	66%
Professional, scientific, and technical services	9
Administrative and support services	8
Wholesale trade	5

Work environments vary by industry and establishment size; some inspectors examine similar products for an entire shift, others examine a variety of items.

In manufacturing, it is common for most inspectors to remain at a single workstation. Inspectors in some industries may be on their feet all day and may have to lift heavy items. In other industries, workers may sit during their shift and read electronic printouts of data.

Workers in heavy-manufacturing plants may be exposed to the noise and grime of machinery. In other plants, inspectors work in clean, air-conditioned environments suitable for testing products.

Injuries and Illnesses. Some quality control inspectors may be exposed to airborne particles, which may irritate the eyes and skin. As a result, workers typically wear protective eyewear, ear plugs, and appropriate clothing.

Work Schedules. Although most quality control inspectors work full time during regular business hours, some inspectors work evenings or weekends. Shift assignments generally are based on seniority. Overtime may be required to meet production deadlines.

Education/Training

Most quality control inspectors need a high school diploma and receive on-the-job training that typically lasts as little as 1 month or up to 1 year.

Education and Training. Education and training requirements vary with the responsibilities of the quality control worker. For inspectors who do simple pass/fail tests of products, a high school diploma and some in-house training are generally enough. Workers usually receive on-the-job training that typically lasts for as little as 1 month or up to 1 year.

Candidates for inspector jobs can improve their chances of finding work by studying industrial trades in high school or in a postsecondary vocational program. Laboratory work in the natural or biological sciences also may improve a person's analytical skills and increase their chances of finding work in medical or pharmaceutical labs, where many of these workers are employed.

Training for new inspectors may cover the use of special meters, gauges, computers, and other instruments; quality control techniques such as Six Sigma; blueprint reading; safety; and reporting requirements. Some postsecondary training programs exist, but many employers prefer to train inspectors on the job.

As manufacturers use more automated techniques that require less inspection by hand, workers in this occupation increasingly must know how to operate and program more sophisticated equipment and utilize software applications. Because these operations require additional skills, higher education may be necessary. To address this need, some colleges are offering associate's degrees in fields such as quality control management.

Licenses, Certifications, and Registrations. The American Society for Quality (ASQ) offers various certifications, including a designation for Certified Quality Inspector (CQI), and numerous sources of information and various levels of Six Sigma certifications. Certification can demonstrate competence and professionalism, making candidates more attractive to employers. It can also increase opportunities for advancement. Requirements for certification generally include a certain number of years of experience in the field and passing an exam.

Important Qualities

Dexterity. Quality control inspectors should be able to quickly remove sample parts or products during the manufacturing process.

Math skills. Knowledge of basic math and computer skills are important because measuring, calibrating, and calculating specifications are major parts of quality control testing.

Mechanical skills. Quality control inspectors must be able to use specialized tools and machinery when testing products.

Physical stamina. Quality control inspectors must be able to stand for long periods on the job.

Employment Projections Data for Quality Control Inspectors

Occupational Title	SOC Code	Employment, 2014	Projected Employment, 2024	Change, 2014–2024 Percent	Change, 2014–2024 Numeric
Inspectors, testers, sorters, samplers, and weighers	51-9061	496,600	495,500	0	-1,100

Source: U.S. Bureau of Labor Statistics, Employment Projections Program

Similar Occupations. This table shows a list of occupations with job duties that are similar to those of quality control inspectors.

Occupations	Entry-level Education	2014 Median Pay	Projected Job Growth	Average Annual Openings
Construction and Building Inspectors	High school diploma or equivalent	$56,040	8%	810
Fire Inspectors	See Education/Training	$54,020	6%	90

Physical strength. Because workers sometimes lift heavy objects, inspectors should be in good physical condition.

Technical skills. Quality control inspectors must understand blueprints, technical documents, and manuals which help ensure that products and parts meet quality standards.

Pay

The median hourly wage for quality control inspectors was $16.99 in May 2014. The median wage is the wage at which half the workers in an occupation earned more than that amount and half earned less. The lowest 10 percent earned less than $10.01, and the highest 10 percent earned more than $29.06.

In May 2014, the median hourly wages for quality control inspectors in the top industries in which they worked were as follows:

Professional, scientific, and technical services....................$17.89
Manufacturing...17.30
Wholesale trade...16.05
Administrative and support services...................................12.63

Job Outlook

Employment of quality control inspectors is projected to show little or no change from 2014 to 2024.

Many manufacturers have invested in automated inspection equipment to improve quality and productivity. Continued improvements in technology allow manufacturers to automate inspection tasks, increasing workers' productivity and reducing the demand for inspectors.

Manufacturers increasingly are integrating quality control into the production process. Many inspection duties are being reassigned from specialized inspectors to fabrication and assembly workers, who monitor quality at every stage of production. In addition, the growing use of statistical process control results in smarter inspections. Using this system, manufacturers survey the sources and incidence of defects so that they can focus their efforts on reducing the number of defective products. These factors are expected to result in less demand for quality control inspectors.

Despite technological advances in quality control in many industries, automation is not always a substitute for inspecting by hand. Personal inspections will continue to be needed for products that require testing taste, smell, texture, appearance, complexity of fabric, or performance of the product. Automation will likely become more important for inspecting elements related to size, such as length, width, or thickness.

Job Prospects. Good job opportunities are expected to arise over the coming decade as quality control inspectors retire or leave the occupation for other reasons.

Those with advanced skills, such as improvement certifications for Lean and Six Sigma, and related work experience should qualify for many of these quality control inspector positions.

Contacts for More Information

For more information about quality control inspectors, including certification, visit

➤ American Society for Quality (ASQ) (http://asq.org/index.aspx)

For more information about quality control training, visit

➤ International Society of Automation (ISA) www.isa.org)
➤ Quality Assurance Association (QAA) (www.qualityassurance association.org)
➤ Society of Quality Assurance (SQA) (www.sqa.org)

O*NET

➤ Inspectors, Testers, Sorters, Samplers, and Weighers (51-9061.00)

Stationary Engineers and Boiler Operators

- **2014 Median Pay**.................................$56,330 per year
  $27.08 per hour
- **Typical Entry-Level Education**........High school diploma or equivalent
- **Work Experience in a Related Occupation**..............None
- **On-the-job Training**.........Long-term on-the-job training
- **Number of Jobs, 2014**..39,100
- **Job Outlook, 2014–24**...............1% (Little or no change)
- **Employment Change, 2014–24**................................600

What Stationary Engineers and Boiler Operators Do

Stationary engineers and boiler operators control stationary engines, boilers, or other mechanical equipment to provide utilities for buildings or for industrial purposes.

Duties. Stationary engineers and boiler operators typically do the following:

- Operate engines, boilers, and auxiliary equipment
- Read gauges, meters, and charts to track boiler operations
- Monitor boiler water, chemical, and fuel levels
- Activate valves to change the amount of water, air, and fuel in boilers
- Fire coal furnaces or feed boilers, using gas feeds or oil pumps
- Inspect equipment to ensure that it is operating efficiently
- Check safety devices routinely
- Record data and keep logs of operation, maintenance, and safety activity

Most large office buildings, malls, warehouses, and other commercial facilities have extensive heating, ventilation, and air-conditioning systems that maintain comfortable temperatures all year long. Industrial plants often have additional facilities to

Stationary engineers and boiler operators control and maintain equipment that is used to generate heat or electricity.

provide electrical power, steam, or other services. Stationary engineers and boiler operators control and maintain these systems, which include boilers, air-conditioning and refrigeration equipment, turbines, generators, pumps, and compressors.

Stationary engineers and boiler operators start up, regulate, repair, and shut down equipment. They monitor meters, gauges, and computerized controls to ensure that equipment operates safely and within established limits. They use sophisticated electrical and electronic test equipment to service, troubleshoot, repair, and monitor heating, cooling, and ventilation systems.

Stationary engineers and boiler operators also perform routine maintenance. They may completely overhaul or replace defective valves, gaskets, or bearings. In addition, stationary engineers and boiler operators lubricate moving parts, replace filters, and remove soot and corrosion that can make a boiler less efficient.

Work Environment

Stationary engineers and boiler operators held about 39,100 jobs in 2014. The industries that employed the most stationary engineers and boiler operators were as follows:

Manufacturing	27%
State and local government, excluding education and hospitals	17
Junior colleges, colleges, universities, and professional schools; state, local, and private	12
General medical and surgical hospitals; private	12
Real estate	5

They were employed in a variety of industries. Because most stationary engineers and boiler operators work in large commercial or industrial buildings, the majority of jobs were in manufacturing, government, educational services, and hospitals.

In a large building or industrial plant, a senior stationary engineer or boiler operator may be in charge of all mechanical systems in the building and may supervise a team of assistant stationary engineers, assistant boiler tenders, and other operators or mechanics.

In small buildings, there may be only one stationary engineer or boiler operator who operates and maintains all of the systems.

Some stationary engineers and boiler operators are exposed to high temperatures, dust, dirt, and loud noise from the equipment. Maintenance duties may require contact with oil, grease, and smoke.

Workers spend much of their time on their feet. They also may have to crawl inside boilers and work while crouched, or kneel to inspect, clean, or repair equipment.

Injuries and Illnesses. Stationary engineers and boiler operators work around hazardous machinery. They must follow procedures to guard against burns, electric shock, noise, dangerous moving parts, and exposure to hazardous materials.

Work Schedules. Most stationary engineers and boiler operators work full time during regular business hours. In facilities that operate around the clock, engineers and operators usually work one of three 8-hour shifts on a rotating basis. Because buildings such as hospitals are open 365 days a year and depend on the steam generated by boilers and other machines, many of these workers must work weekends and holidays.

Education/Training

Stationary engineers and boiler operators need at least a high school diploma and are trained on the job by more experienced engineers and operators. Many employers require stationary engineers and boiler operators to demonstrate competency through licenses or company-specific exams before they are allowed to operate equipment without supervision.

Education. Stationary engineers and boiler operators need at least a high school diploma. Students should take courses in math, science, and mechanical and technical subjects.

With the growing complexity of the work, vocational school or college courses may benefit workers trying to advance in the occupation.

Training. Stationary engineers and boiler operators typically learn their work through long-term on-the-job training under the supervision of an experienced engineer or operator. Trainees are assigned basic tasks, such as monitoring the

Median Annual Wages, May 2014

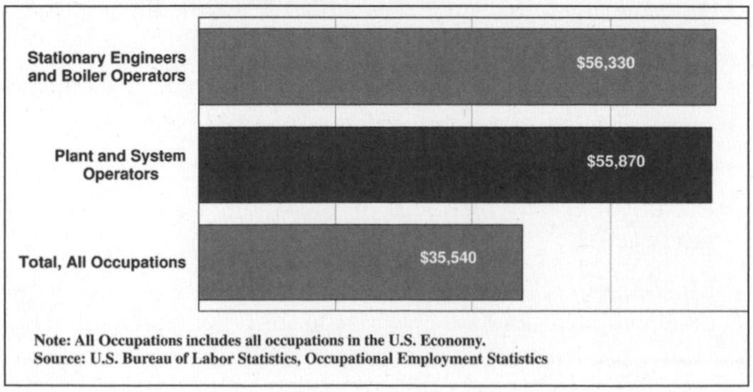

Percent Change in Employment, Projected 2014–2024

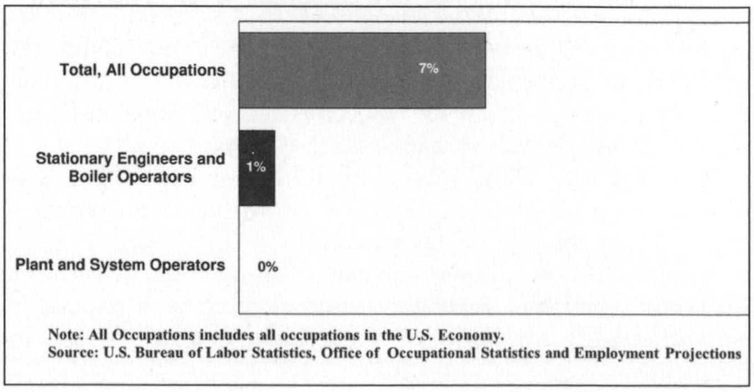

temperatures and pressures in the heating and cooling systems and low-pressure boilers. After they demonstrate competence in basic tasks, trainees move on to more complicated tasks, such as the repair of cracks or ruptured tubes for high-pressure boilers.

Some stationary engineers and boiler operators complete apprenticeship programs sponsored by the International Union of Operating Engineers. Apprenticeships usually last 4 years, include 8,000 hours of on-the-job training, and require 600 hours of technical instruction. Apprentices learn about operating and maintaining equipment; using controls and balancing heating, ventilation, and air conditioning (HVAC) systems; safety; electricity; and air quality. Employers may prefer to hire these workers because they usually require considerably less on-the-job training. However, because of the limited number of apprenticeship programs, employers often have difficulty finding workers who have completed one.

Experienced stationary engineers and boiler operators update their skills regularly through training, especially when new equipment is introduced or when regulations change.

Licenses, Certifications, and Registrations. Some state and local governments require licensure for stationary engineers and boiler operators. These governments typically have several classes of stationary engineer and boiler operator licenses. Each class specifies the type and size of equipment the engineer is permitted to operate without supervision. Many employers require stationary engineers and boiler operators to demonstrate competency through licenses or company-specific exams before they are allowed to operate the equipment without supervision.

A top-level engineer or operator is qualified to run a large facility, supervise others, and operate equipment of all types and capacities. Engineers and operators with licenses below this level are limited in the types or capacities of equipment they may operate without supervision.

Applicants for licensure usually must be at least 18 years of age, meet experience requirements, and pass a written exam. In some cases, employers may require that workers be licensed before starting the job. A stationary engineer or boiler operator who moves from one state or city to another may have to pass an examination for a new license because of regional differences in licensing requirements.

Advancement. Generally, stationary engineers and boiler operators can advance as they become qualified to operate larger, more powerful, and more varied equipment by obtaining higher class licenses. In jurisdictions where licenses are not required, workers usually advance by taking company-administered exams, ensuring a level of knowledge needed to operate different types of boilers safely.

Important Qualities

Detail oriented. Stationary engineers and boiler operators monitor intricate machinery, gauges, and meters to ensure that everything is operating properly.

Dexterity. Stationary engineers and boiler operators must use precise motions to control or repair machines. They grasp tools and use their hands to perform many tasks.

Mechanical skills. Stationary engineers and boiler operators must know how to use tools and work with machines. They must be able to repair, maintain, and operate equipment.

Problem-solving skills. Stationary engineers and boiler operators must figure out how things work and quickly solve problems that arise with equipment or controls.

Pay

The median annual wage for stationary engineers and boiler operators was $56,330 in May 2014. The median wage is the wage at which half the workers in an occupation earned more than that amount and half earned less. The lowest 10 percent earned less than $35,110, and the highest 10 percent earned more than $85,670.

In May 2014, the median annual wages for stationary engineers and boiler operators in the top industries in which they worked were as follows:

Real estate	$65,280
State and local government, excluding education and hospitals	62,370
General medical and surgical hospitals; private	58,160
Junior colleges, colleges, universities, and professional schools; state, local, and private	53,350
Manufacturing	50,650

Union Membership. Compared with workers in all occupations, stationary engineers and boiler operators had a higher percentage of workers who belonged to a union in 2014.

Job Outlook

Employment of stationary engineers and boiler operators is projected to show little or no change from 2014 to 2024. Employment in manufacturing industries is projected to decline over the projection period, contributing to the slow growth for stationary engineers.

Although this occupation is spread across many industries, it is concentrated in those which require large commercial and industrial buildings. As a result, most employment gains will come from growth in these industries.

Faster employment growth is expected in education and healthcare services as more buildings are built to accommodate a growing population in need of these services. Stationary engineers and boiler operators are especially important in buildings that operate around the clock and need precise temperature control, such as hospitals.

Job Prospects. Job prospects for stationary engineers and boiler operators should be excellent as older workers in the occupation retire.

Job opportunities should be best for those with apprenticeship training. Although apprenticeship programs have a competitive

Employment Projections Data for Stationary Engineers and Boiler Operators

Occupational Title	SOC Code	Employment, 2014	Projected Employment, 2024	Change, 2014–2024 Percent	Change, 2014–2024 Numeric
Stationary engineers and boiler operators	51-8021	39,100	39,700	1	600

Source: U.S. Bureau of Labor Statistics, Employment Projections Program

Similar Occupations. This table shows a list of occupations with job duties that are similar to those of stationary engineers and boiler operators.

Occupations	Entry-level Education	2014 Median Pay	Projected Job Growth	Average Annual Openings
Boilermakers	High school diploma or equivalent	$59,860	9%	150
General Maintenance and Repair Workers	High school diploma or equivalent	$36,170	6%	8,350
Heating, Air Conditioning, and Refrigeration Mechanics and Installers	Postsecondary nondegree award	$44,630	14%	3,960
Industrial Machinery Mechanics, Machinery Maintenance Workers, and Millwrights	High school diploma or equivalent	$47,450	16%	7,340
Power Plant Operators, Distributors, and Dispatchers	High school diploma or equivalent	$72,910	-6%	-330
Water and Wastewater Treatment Plant and System Operators	High school diploma or equivalent	$44,100	6%	700

application process, they are the most reliable path of entry into the occupation.

Contacts for More Information

For information about apprenticeships, vocational training, and job opportunities, visit

➤ State employment service offices
➤ Local chapters of the International Union of Operating Engineers (www.iuoe.org)
➤ Vocational schools
➤ State and local licensing agencies

Information about apprenticeships is also available from the U.S. Department of Labor's toll-free help line, (877) 872-5627; or the Employment and Training Administration (www.doleta.gov/OA/eta_default.cfm).

For more information about training or becoming a stationary engineer or boiler operator, visit

➤ National Association of Power Engineers, Inc. (www.powerengineers.com)

O*NET

➤ Stationary Engineers and Boiler Operators (51-8021.00)

Water and Wastewater Treatment Plant and System Operators

- **2014 Median Pay** .... $44,100 per year
  $21.20 per hour
- **Typical Entry-Level Education** .... High school diploma or equivalent
- **Work Experience in a Related Occupation** .... None
- **On-the-job Training** .... Long-term on-the-job training
- **Number of Jobs, 2014** 117,000
- **Job Outlook, 2014–24** .... 6% (As fast as average)
- **Employment Change, 2014–24** 7,000

What Water and Wastewater Treatment Plant and System Operators Do

Water and wastewater treatment plant and system operators manage a system of machines, often through the use of control boards, to transfer or treat water or wastewater.

Duties. Water and wastewater treatment plant and system operators typically do the following:

- Add chemicals, such as ammonia or chlorine, to disinfect water or other liquids
- Inspect equipment on a regular basis
- Monitor operating conditions, meters, and gauges
- Collect and test water and sewage samples
- Record meter and gauge readings and operational data
- Operate equipment to purify and clarify water or to process or dispose of sewage
- Clean and maintain equipment, tanks, filter beds, and other work areas
- Follow U.S. Environmental Protection Agency (EPA) regulations
- Ensure safety standards are met

It takes a lot of work to get water from natural sources—reservoirs, streams, and groundwater—into people's taps. Similarly, it is a complicated process to convert the wastewater from drains and sewers into a form that is safe to release into the environment.

The specific duties of plant operators depend on the type and size of the plant. In a small plant, one operator may be responsible

Water and wastewater treatment plant and system operators read meters and gauges to make sure that plant equipment is working properly.

for maintaining all of the systems. In large plants, multiple operators work the same shifts and are more specialized in their duties, often relying on computerized systems to help them monitor plant processes.

Water treatment plant and system operators work in water treatment plants. Fresh water is pumped from wells, rivers, streams, or reservoirs to water treatment plants, where it is treated and distributed to customers. Water treatment plant and system operators run the equipment, control the processes, and monitor the plants that treat water to make it safe to drink.

Wastewater treatment plant and system operators do similar work to remove pollutants from domestic and industrial waste. Used water, also known as wastewater, travels through sewer pipes to treatment plants where it is treated and either returned to streams, rivers, and oceans, or used for irrigation.

Work Environment

Water and wastewater treatment plant and system operators held about 117,000 jobs in 2014, of which 78 percent were in local government. About 11 percent worked for water, sewage, and other systems utilities.

Injuries and Illnesses. Water and wastewater treatment plant and system operators work both indoors and outdoors. They may be exposed to noise from machinery and are often exposed to unpleasant odors. Operators' work is physically demanding and usually is performed in locations that are unclean or difficult to access.

They must pay close attention to safety procedures because of hazardous conditions, such as slippery walkways, the presence of dangerous gases, and malfunctioning equipment. As a result, workers experience an occupational injury and illness rate that is much higher than the average for all occupations.

Operators are trained in emergency management procedures and use safety equipment to protect their health, as well as that of the public.

Work Schedules. Most water and waste treatment plant and system operators work full time. Plants operate 24 hours a day, 7 days a week. In small plants, operators are likely to work during the day and be on call nights and weekends. In medium- and large-size plants that require constant monitoring, operators work in shifts to control the plant at all hours.

Occasionally, operators must work during emergencies. For example, weather conditions may cause large amounts of stormwater or wastewater to flow into sewers, exceeding a plant's capacity. Emergencies may also be caused by malfunctions within a plant, such as chemical leaks or oxygen deficiencies.

Education/Training

Water and wastewater treatment plant and system operators typically need a high school diploma and a license to work. They also typically undergo on-the-job training.

Education. Water and wastewater treatment plant and system operators need a high school diploma or equivalent to become operators. Employers may prefer applicants who have completed a certificate or an associate's degree program in a related field such as environmental science or wastewater treatment technology, as it reduces the amount of training a worker will need. These programs are generally offered at community colleges, technical schools, and trade associations.

Training. Water and wastewater treatment plant and system operators need long-term on-the-job training to become fully qualified. Trainees usually start as attendants or operators-in-training and learn their skills on the job under the direction of an experienced operator. The trainees learn by observing and doing routine tasks, such as recording meter readings, taking samples of wastewater and sludge, and performing simple maintenance and repair work on plant equipment.

Larger treatment plants usually combine this on-the-job training with formal classroom or self-paced study programs. As plants get larger and more complicated, operators need more skills before they are allowed to work without supervision.

Licenses, Certifications, and Registrations. Water and wastewater treatment plant and system operators must be licensed by the state in which they work. Requirements and standards vary widely depending on the state.

State licenses typically have multiple levels, which indicate the operator's experience and training. Although some states will honor licenses from other states, operators who move from one state to another may need to take a new set of exams to become licensed in their new state.

Advancement. Most states have multiple levels of licenses for water and wastewater treatment plant and system operators. Each increase in license level allows the operator to control a larger plant and more complicated processes without supervision.

At the largest plants, operators who have the highest license level work as shift supervisors and may be in charge of large teams of operators.

Important Qualities

Analytical skills. Water and wastewater treatment plant and system operators must conduct tests and inspections on water or wastewater and evaluate the results.

Detail oriented. Water and wastewater treatment plant and system operators must monitor machinery, gauges, dials, and controls to ensure everything is operating properly. Because tap water

Median Annual Wages, May 2014

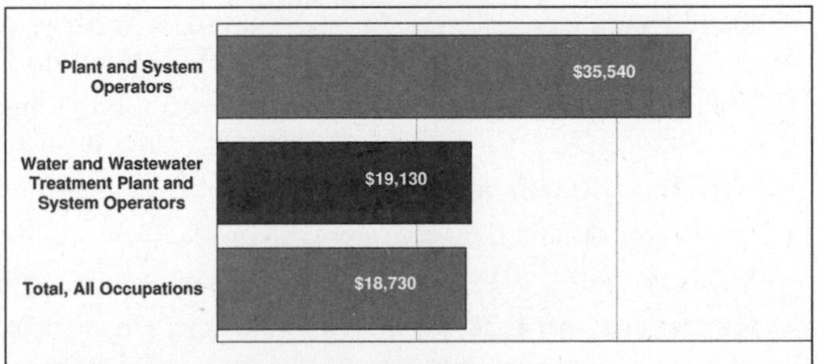

Note: All Occupations includes all occupations in the U.S. Economy.
Source: U.S. Bureau of Labor Statistics, Occupational Employment Statistics

Percent Change in Employment, Projected 2014–2024

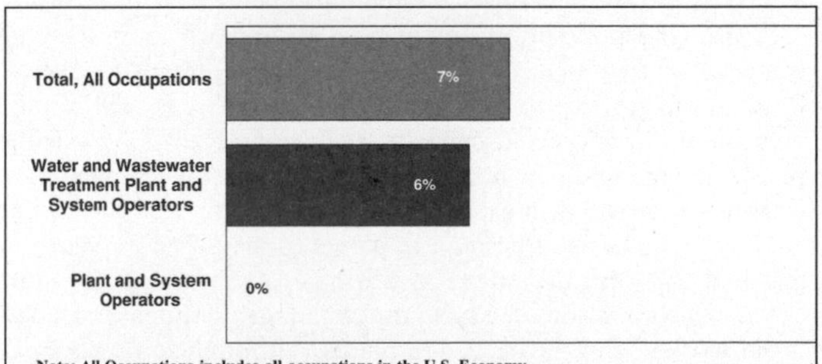

Note: All Occupations includes all occupations in the U.S. Economy.
Source: U.S. Bureau of Labor Statistics, Office of Occupational Statistics and Employment Projections

Employment Projections Data for Water and Wastewater Treatment Plant and System Operators

Occupational Title	SOC Code	Employment, 2014	Projected Employment, 2024	Change, 2014–2024 Percent	Change, 2014–2024 Numeric
Water and wastewater treatment plant and system operators	51-8031	117,000	124,000	6	7,000

Source: U.S. Bureau of Labor Statistics, Employment Projections Program

Similar Occupations. This table shows a list of occupations with job duties that are similar to those of water and wastewater treatment plant and system operators.

Occupations	Entry-level Education	2014 Median Pay	Projected Job Growth	Average Annual Openings
Construction Equipment Operators	High school diploma or equivalent	$42,900	10%	4,320
General Maintenance and Repair Workers	High school diploma or equivalent	$36,170	6%	8,350
Hydrologists	Bachelor's degree	$78,370	7%	50
Power Plant Operators, Distributors, and Dispatchers	High school diploma or equivalent	$72,910	-6%	-330
Stationary Engineers and Boiler Operators	High school diploma or equivalent	$56,330	1%	60

and wastewater are highly regulated by the U.S. Environmental Protection Agency, operators must be careful and thorough in completing these tasks.

Math skills. Water and wastewater treatment plant and system operators must have the ability to apply data to formulas that determine treatment requirements, flow levels, and concentration levels.

Mechanical skills. Water and wastewater treatment plant and system operators must know how to work with machines and use tools. They must be familiar with how to operate, repair, and maintain equipment.

Pay

The median annual wage for water and wastewater treatment plant and system operators was $44,100 in May 2014. The median wage is the wage at which half the workers in an occupation earned more than that amount and half earned less. The lowest 10 percent earned less than $26,640, and the highest 10 percent earned more than $70,270.

Union Membership. Compared with workers in all occupations, water and wastewater treatment plant and system operators had a higher percentage of workers who belonged to a union in 2014.

Job Outlook

Employment of water and wastewater treatment plant and system operators is projected to grow 6 percent from 2014 to 2024, about as fast as the average for all occupations.

A growing population and increased demand for water and wastewater treatment services will drive employment growth. Population growth, particularly in suburban areas, will require new plants or increased capacity at current plants. As existing plants expand and new plants are built to meet this demand, new operator jobs will be created.

New regulations often require plants to install new systems or features that operators need to control. As plants become more advanced with automated systems to manage treatment processes, fewer workers may be needed in plants. Although some work can be automated, plants will still need skilled workers to operate increasingly complex controls and water and wastewater systems.

Job Prospects. Job prospects for water and wastewater treatment plant and system operators should be excellent. Positions of older water and wastewater treatment plant and system operators who retire will need to be filled. Job prospects will be best for those with training or education in water or wastewater systems and good mechanical skills.

Contacts for More Information

For information on employment opportunities, contact state or local water pollution control agencies, state water and wastewater operator associations, state environmental training centers, or local offices of the state employment service.

For information related to a career as a water or wastewater treatment plant and system operator, visit

➤ American Water Works Association (www.awwa.org)
➤ The National Rural Water Association (www.nrwa.org)
➤ Water Environment Federation (www.wef.org)
➤ Work for Water (www.workforwater.org)

O*NET

➤ Water and Wastewater Treatment Plant and System Operators (51-8031.00)

Welders, Cutters, Solderers, and Brazers

- **2014 Median Pay** .... $37,420 per year $17.99 per hour
- **Typical Entry-Level Education** .... High school diploma or equivalent
- **Work Experience in a Related Occupation** .... None
- **On-the-job Training**...Moderate-term on-the-job training
- **Number of Jobs, 2014** 397,900
- **Job Outlook, 2014–24** .... 4% (Slower than average)
- **Employment Change, 2014–24** 14,400

What Welders, Cutters, Solderers, and Brazers Do

Welders, cutters, solderers, and brazers use hand-held or remotely controlled equipment to join or cut metal parts. They also fill holes, indentations, or seams of metal products.

Duties. Welders, cutters, solderers, and brazers typically do the following:

- Study blueprints, sketches, or specifications
- Calculate dimensions to be welded
- Inspect structures or materials to be welded
- Ignite torches or start power supplies
- Monitor the welding process to avoid overheating
- Maintain equipment and machinery

Welding is the most common way of permanently joining metal parts. In this process, heat is applied to metal pieces, melting and fusing them to form a permanent bond. Because of its strength, welding is used in shipbuilding, automobile manufacturing and repair, aerospace applications, and thousands of other manufacturing activities. Welding also is used to join steel beams in the construction of buildings, bridges, and other structures and to join pipes in pipelines, power plants, and refineries.

Welders work in a wide variety of industries, from car racing to manufacturing. The work that welders do and the equipment they use vary with the industry. Arc welding, the most common type of welding today, uses electrical currents to create heat and bond metals together—but there are more than 100 different processes that a welder can use. The type of weld normally is determined by the types of metals being joined and the conditions under which the welding is to take place.

Cutters use heat to cut and trim metal objects to specific dimensions. The work of *arc, plasma,* and *oxy-gas cutters* is closely related to that of welders. However, instead of joining metals, cutters use the heat from an electric arc, a stream of ionized gas called plasma, or burning gases to cut and trim metal objects to specific dimensions. Cutters also dismantle large objects, such as ships, railroad cars, automobiles, buildings, and aircraft. Some operate and monitor cutting machines similar to those used by welding machine operators.

Solderers and *brazers* also use heat to join two or more metal objects together. Soldering and brazing are similar, except that the temperature used to melt the filler metal is lower in soldering. Soldering uses metals with a melting point below 840 degrees Fahrenheit. Brazing uses metals with a higher melting point.

Soldering and brazing workers use molten metal to join two pieces of metal. However, the metal added during the soldering or brazing process has a melting point lower than that of the piece, so only the added metal is melted, not the piece. Therefore, these processes normally do not create distortions or weaknesses in the piece, as can occur with welding.

Soldering commonly is used to make electrical and electronic circuit boards, such as computer chips. Soldering workers tend to work with small pieces that must be positioned precisely.

Brazing often is used to connect cast iron and thinner metals that the higher temperatures of welding would warp. Brazing also can be used to apply coatings to parts in order to reduce wear and protect against corrosion.

Work Environment

Welders, cutters, solderers, and brazers held about 397,900 jobs in 2014. The industries that employed the most welders, cutters, solderers, and brazers were as follows:

Welders inspect the placement of parts before bonding metals.

Manufacturing	60%
Specialty trade contractors	6
Repair and maintenance	5
Merchant wholesalers, durable goods	4

Welders and cutters may work outdoors, often in inclement weather, or indoors, sometimes in a confined area designed to contain sparks and glare. When working outdoors, they may work on a scaffold or platform high off the ground.

In addition, they may have to lift heavy objects and work in awkward positions while bending, stooping, or standing to work overhead.

Injuries and Illnesses. Welders, cutters, solderers, and brazers are often exposed to a number of hazards, including very hot materials and the intense light created by the arc. They wear safety shoes, heat-resistant gloves, goggles, masks with protective lenses, and other equipment to prevent burns and eye injuries and to protect them from falling objects.

The Occupational Safety & Health Administration requires that welders work in safely ventilated areas in order to avoid danger from inhaling gases and fine particles that can result from welding processes. Because of these hazards, welding, cutting, soldering, and brazing workers have a rate of injuries and illnesses that is higher than the national average. However, they can minimize injuries if they follow safety procedures.

Work Schedules. Most welders, cutters, solderers, and brazers work full time, and overtime is common. Many manufacturing firms have two or three 8- to 12-hour shifts each day, allowing the firm to continue production around the clock if needed. As a

Median Annual Wages, May 2014

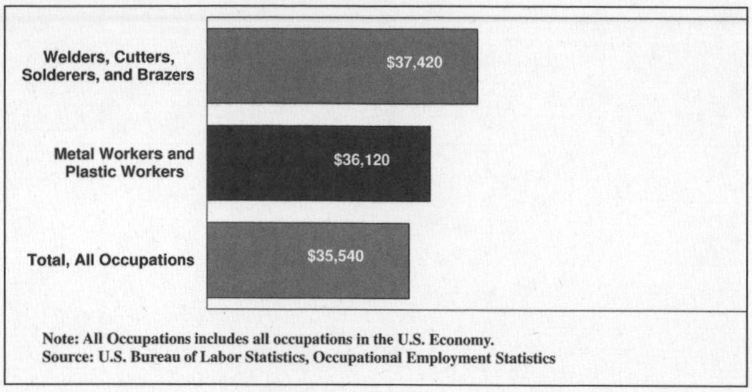

Percent Change in Employment, Projected 2014–2024

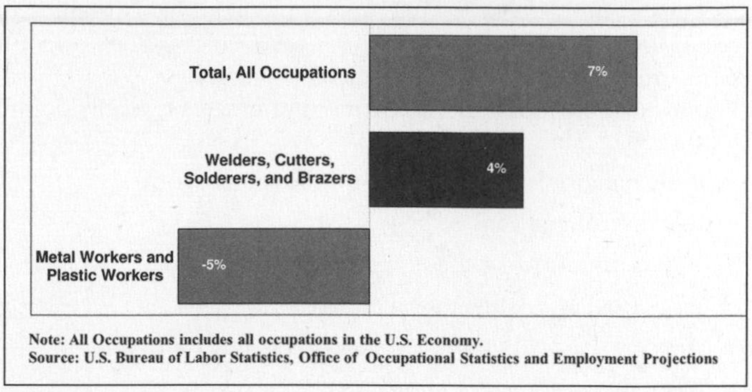

result, welders, cutters, solderers, and brazers may work evenings and weekends.

Education/Training

A high school diploma or equivalent combined with technical and on-the-job training is typically required to become a welder, cutter, solderer, or brazer.

Education & Training. A high school diploma or equivalent combined with technical and on-the-job training is typically required to become a welder, cutter, solderer, or brazer. High school technical education courses and postsecondary institutions, such as vocational–technical institutes, community colleges, and private welding, soldering, and brazing schools offer formal technical training. In addition, the U.S. Armed Forces operate welding and soldering schools.

Courses in blueprint reading, shop mathematics, mechanical drawing, physics, chemistry, and metallurgy are helpful.

An understanding of electricity also is helpful, and knowledge of computers is gaining importance as welding, soldering, and brazing machine operators become more responsible for programming robots and other computer-controlled machines.

Although numerous employers are willing to hire inexperienced entry-level workers and train them on the job, many prefer to hire workers who have been through training or credentialing programs. Even entry-level workers with formal technical training still receive several months of on-the-job training.

Licenses, Certifications, and Registrations. Courses leading to certification are offered at many welding schools. For example, the American Welding Society offers the Certified Welder and Certified Welding Fabricator designations.

Some welding positions require general certification in welding or certification in specific skills, such as Certified Welding Inspector or Certified Robotic Arc Welding.

The Institute for Printed Circuits offers certification and training in soldering. In industries such as aerospace and defense, which need highly skilled workers, many employers require these certifications. Certification can show mastery of lead-free soldering techniques, which are important to many employers.

Some employers pay the cost of training and testing for employees.

Important Qualities

Detail oriented. Welders, cutters, solderers, and brazers perform precision work, often with straight edges and minimal flaws. The ability to see details and characteristics of the joint and detect changes in molten metal flows requires good eyesight and attention to detail.

Manual dexterity. Welders, cutters, solderers, and brazers must have a steady hand to hold a torch in one place. Workers must also have good hand-eye coordination.

Physical stamina. The ability to endure long periods of standing or repetitious movements is important for welders, cutters, solderers, and brazers.

Physical strength. Welders, cutters, solderers, and brazers must be in good physical condition. They often must lift heavy pieces of metal and move welding or cutting equipment, and sometimes bend, stoop, or reach while working.

Spatial-orientation skills. Welders, cutters, solderers, and brazers must be able to read, understand, and interpret two- and three-dimensional diagrams in order to fit metal products correctly.

Technical skills. Welders, cutters, solderers, and brazers must be able to operate manual or semiautomatic welding equipment to fuse metal segments.

Pay

The median annual wage for welders, cutters, solderers, and brazers was $37,420 in May 2014. The median wage is the wage at which half the workers in an occupation earned more than that amount and half earned less. The lowest 10 percent earned less than $25,510, and the highest 10 percent earned more than $58,590.

In May 2014, the median annual wages for welders, cutters, solderers, and brazers in the top industries in which they worked were as follows:

Specialty trade contractors	$39,300
Repair and maintenance	36,850
Manufacturing	36,400
Merchant wholesalers, durable goods	35,510

Employment Projections Data for Welders, Cutters, Solderers, and Brazers

Occupational Title	SOC Code	Employment, 2014	Projected Employment, 2024	Change, 2014–2024 Percent	Change, 2014–2024 Numeric
Welders, cutters, solderers, and brazers	51-4121	397,900	412,300	4	14,400

Source: U.S. Bureau of Labor Statistics, Employment Projections Program

Similar Occupations. This table shows a list of occupations with job duties that are similar to those of welders, cutters, solderers, and brazers.

Occupations	Entry-level Education	2014 Median Pay	Projected Job Growth	Average Annual Openings
Assemblers and Fabricators	High school diploma or equivalent	$29,280	-1%	-970
Boilermakers	High school diploma or equivalent	$59,860	9%	150
Jewelers and Precious Stone and Metal Workers	High school diploma or equivalent	$36,870	-11%	-450
Machinists and Tool and Die Makers	High school diploma or equivalent	$41,510	6%	2,900
Metal and Plastic Machine Workers	High school diploma or equivalent	$33,550	-13%	-13,390
Plumbers, Pipefitters, and Steamfitters	High school diploma or equivalent	$50,660	12%	4,910
Sheet Metal Workers	High school diploma or equivalent	$45,070	7%	940

Wages for welders, cutters, solderers, and brazers vary with the worker's experience and skill level, the industry, and the size of the company.

Job Outlook

Employment of welders, cutters, solderers, and brazers is projected to grow 4 percent from 2014 to 2024, slower than the average for all occupations.

Employment growth reflects the need for welders in manufacturing because of the importance and versatility of welding as a manufacturing process. The basic skills of welding are similar across industries, so welders can easily shift from one industry to another, depending on where they are needed most. For example, welders who are laid off in the automotive manufacturing industry may be able to find work in the oil and gas industry.

The nation's aging infrastructure will require the expertise of welders, cutters, solderers, and brazers to help rebuild bridges, highways, and buildings. The construction of new power generation facilities and, specifically, pipelines transporting natural gas and oil will also result in new jobs.

Job Prospects. Overall job prospects will vary with the worker's skill level. Job prospects should be good for welders trained in the latest technologies. However, welders who do not have up-to-date training may face strong competition for jobs.

For all welders, job prospects should be better for those willing to relocate.

Contacts for More Information

For more information about welders, cutters, solderers, and brazers, visit

- American Welding Society (www.aws.org)
- Fabricators & Manufacturers Association, International (http://fmanet.org)
- Institute for Printed Circuits (www.ipc.org)
- Precision Machined Products Association (www.pmpa.org)

O*NET

- Welders, Cutters, Solderers, and Brazers (51-4121.00)
- Welders, Cutters, and Welder Fitters (51-4121.06)
- Solderers and Brazers (51-4121.07)

Woodworkers

- **2014 Median Pay** .... $28,900 per year $13.90 per hour
- **Typical Entry-Level Education** .... High school diploma or equivalent
- **Work Experience in a Related Occupation**.............. None
- **On-the-job Training** .... See Education/Training
- **Number of Jobs, 2014** 237,200
- **Job Outlook, 2014–24** ....-1% (Little or no change)
- **Employment Change, 2014–24** .... -1,400

What Woodworkers Do

Woodworkers manufacture a variety of products such as cabinets and furniture, using wood, veneers, and laminates. They often combine and incorporate different materials into wood.

Duties. Woodworkers typically do the following:

- Understand detailed architectural drawings, schematics, shop drawings, and blueprints
- Prepare and set up machines and tooling for woodwork manufacturing
- Lift wood pieces onto machines, either by hand or with hoists
- Operate woodworking machines, including saws and milling and sanding machines
- Listen for unusual sounds or detect excessive vibration in machinery
- Ensure that products meet industry standards and project specifications, making adjustments as necessary
- Select and adjust the proper cutting, milling, boring, and sanding tools for completing a job
- Use hand tools to trim pieces or assemble products

Despite the abundance of plastics, metals, and other materials, wood products continue to be an important part of our daily lives. Woodworkers make wood products from lumber and synthetic wood materials. Many of these products, including most furniture, kitchen cabinets, and musical instruments, are mass produced. Other products are custom made from architectural designs and drawings.

Although the term "woodworker" may evoke the image of a craftsman who uses hand tools to build ornate furniture, the modern woodworking trade is highly technical and relies on advanced equipment and highly skilled operators. Workers use automated machinery, such as computerized numerical control (CNC) machines, to do much of the work with great accuracy.

Even specialized artisans generally use CNC machines and a variety of power tools in their work. Much of the work is done in a high-production assembly line facility, but there is also some work that is customized and does not lend itself to being made on an assembly line.

Woodworkers set up, operate, and tend all types of woodworking machines, such as saws, milling machines, drill presses, lathes, shapers, routers, sanders, planers, and wood-fastening machines. Operators set up the equipment, cut and shape wooden parts, and verify dimensions, using a template, caliper, and rule. After the parts are machined, woodworkers add fasteners and adhesives and connect the parts to form an assembled unit. They also install hardware, such as pulls and drawer slides, and fit specialty products for glass, metal trims, electrical components, and stone. Finally, workers then sand, stain, and, if necessary, coat the wood product with a sealer or topcoats, such as a lacquer or varnish.

Many of these tasks are handled by different workers with specialized training.

The following are examples of types of woodworkers:

Cabinetmakers and *bench carpenters* cut, shape, assemble, and make parts for wood products. They often design and create sets of cabinets that are customized for particular spaces. In some cases, their duties begin with designing a set of cabinets to specifications and end with installing the cabinets.

Furniture finishers shape, finish, and refinish damaged and worn furniture. They may work with antiques and must judge how to preserve and repair them. They also do the staining, sealing, and top coating at the end of the process of making wooden products.

Wood sawing machine setters, operators, and tenders specialize in operating specific pieces of woodworking machinery. They often operate CNC machines.

Woodworkers set up equipment, verify dimensions, and cut and shape wooden parts.

Woodworking machine setters, operators, and tenders, except sawing, operate woodworking machines, such as drill presses, lathes, routers, sanders, and planers.

Work Environment

Woodworkers held about 237,200 jobs in 2014. The industries that employed the most woodworkers were as follows:

Other wood product manufacturing	23%
Wood kitchen cabinet and countertop manufacturing	21
Household and institutional furniture manufacturing	11
Sawmills and wood preservation	10
Office furniture (including fixtures) manufacturing	10

Although many smaller shops employ a few workers, production factories can have as many as 2,000 employees.

Working conditions vary with the specific job duties. At times, workers have to handle heavy, bulky materials and may encounter noise and dust. As a result, they regularly wear hearing protection devices, safety glasses, and respirators or masks.

Injuries and Illnesses. Woodworkers are exposed to hazards such as harmful dust, chemicals, or fumes, and must often wear a respirator or mask. Others may be exposed to excessive noise and must wear hearing protection devices.

Most injuries involve sprains, back pain, carpal tunnel syndrome, and hernia. These injuries or illnesses come from excessive amounts of awkward bending, reaching, twisting, and overexertion or repetition.

Work Schedules. Most woodworkers work full time during regular business hours.

Education/Training

A high school diploma is typically required to become a woodworker. Although some entry-level jobs can be learned in less than 1 year, becoming fully proficient generally takes at least 3 years of on-the-job training. The ability to use computer-controlled machinery is becoming increasingly important.

Education. Because of the growing sophistication of machinery, many employers are seeking applicants who have a high school diploma or the equivalent. People seeking woodworking jobs can enhance their employment prospects by completing high school and getting training in computer applications and math.

Some woodworkers obtain their skills by taking courses at technical schools or community colleges. Others attend universities that offer training in wood technology, furniture manufacturing, wood engineering, and production management. These programs prepare students for jobs in production, supervision, engineering, and management, and are becoming increasingly important as woodworking technology advances.

Training. Education is helpful, but woodworkers are trained primarily on the job, where they learn skills from experienced workers. Beginning workers are given basic tasks, such as placing a piece of wood through a machine and stacking the finished product at the end of the process.

As they gain experience, new woodworkers perform more complex tasks with less supervision. In about 1 year, they learn basic machine operations and job tasks. Becoming a skilled woodworker often takes 3 or more years. Skilled workers can read blueprints, set up machines, and plan work sequences.

Licenses, Certifications, and Registrations. Although not required, becoming certified can demonstrate competence and professionalism. It also may help a candidate advance in the profession. The Architectural Woodwork Institute (AWI) publishes product standards for the industry, and offers training programs

Median Hourly Wages, May 2014

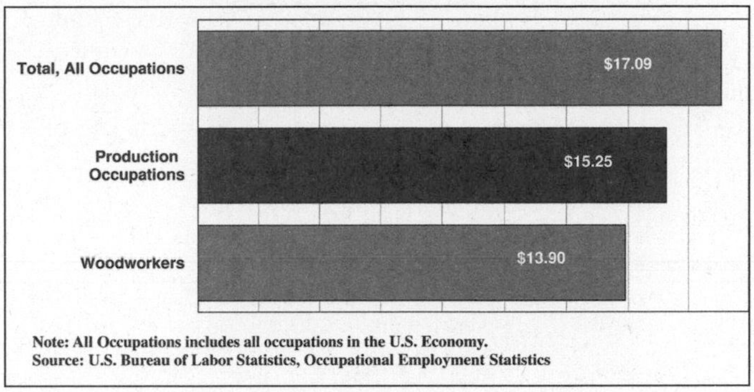

Percent Change in Employment, Projected 2014–2024

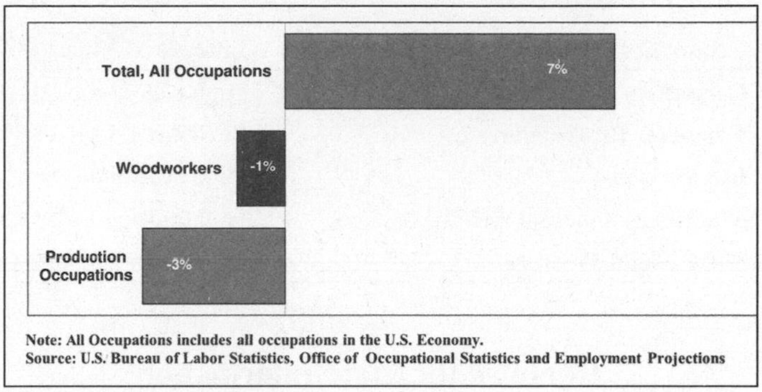

for mid-management positions. The Woodwork Career Alliance of North America offers a national certificate program, with five progressive credentials, which adds a level of credibility to the work of woodworkers.

Important Qualities

Detail oriented. Woodworkers must pay attention to details in order to meet specifications and to keep themselves safe.

Dexterity. Woodworkers must make precise cuts with a variety of hand tools and power tools, so they need a steady hand and good hand-eye coordination.

Math skills. Knowledge of basic math and computer skills are important, particularly for those who work in manufacturing, in which technology continues to advance. Woodworkers need to understand basic geometry to visualize how the wood pieces will fit together to fabricate a three-dimensional object, such as a cabinet or piece of furniture.

Mechanical skills. The use of hand tools such as screwdrivers and wrenches, is required to set up, adjust, and calibrate machines. Modern technology systems require woodworkers to be able to use computers and other programmable devices.

Physical stamina. The ability to endure long periods of standing and repetitious movements is crucial for woodworkers, who often stand all day performing many of the same functions.

Physical strength. Woodworkers must be strong enough to lift bulky and heavy pieces of wood.

Technical skills. Woodworkers must be able to understand and interpret design drawings and technical manuals for a range of products and machines.

Pay

The median hourly wage for woodworkers was $13.90 in May 2014. The median wage is the wage at which half the workers in an occupation earned more than that amount and half earned less. The lowest 10 percent earned less than $9.26, and the highest 10 percent earned more than $21.76.

Median hourly wages for woodworkers in May 2014 were as follows:

Cabinetmakers and bench carpenters	$15.18
Furniture finishers	13.85
Woodworking machine setters, operators, and tenders, except sawing	13.20
Sawing machine setters, operators, and tenders, wood	13.00

Job Outlook

Employment of woodworkers is projected to show little or no change from 2014 to 2024.

Employment growth will stem from greater demand for domestic wood products. In particular, the continuing need to repair and renovate residential and commercial properties will likely require more woodworkers.

However, automation and a greater emphasis on computerized numerical controlled machines should limit the employment growth of some woodworkers in the wood product manufacturing industries.

Employment growth is expected to be good for woodworkers who specialize in items used in renovation, such as moldings, cabinets, stairs, and windows. Firms that focus on custom woodwork should be able to compete against imports without the need to outsource jobs to other countries.

Job Prospects. Woodworkers who know how to create and carry out custom designs on a computer should have the best job opportunities in manufacturing industries.

Those who can demonstrate leadership, problem-solving, and advanced math skills should also have the best job prospects.

Some job openings will result from the need to replace those who retire or leave the occupation for another job.

Employment Projections Data for Woodworkers

Occupational Title	SOC Code	Employment, 2014	Projected Employment, 2024	Change, 2014–2024 Percent	Change, 2014–2024 Numeric
Woodworkers	—	254,600	253,100	-1	-1,500
Cabinetmakers and bench carpenters	51-7011	98,100	99,300	1	1,300
Furniture finishers	51-7021	17,100	16,700	-2	-400
Sawing machine setters, operators, and tenders, wood	51-7041	50,000	49,500	-1	-500
Woodworking machine setters, operators, and tenders, except sawing	51-7042	72,100	70,400	-2	-1,700

Source: U.S. Bureau of Labor Statistics, Employment Projections Program

Similar Occupations. This table shows a list of occupations with job duties that are similar to those of woodworkers.

Occupations	Entry-level Education	2014 Median Pay	Projected Job Growth	Average Annual Openings
Carpenters	High school diploma or equivalent	$40,820	6%	6,040
Computer Programmers	Bachelor's degree	$77,550	-8%	-2,650
Ironworkers	High school diploma or equivalent	$48,520	9%	710
Machinists and Tool and Die Makers	High school diploma or equivalent	$41,510	6%	2,900
Sheet Metal Workers	High school diploma or equivalent	$45,070	7%	940

Contacts for More Information

For more information about woodworkers, visit

- Architectural Woodwork Institute (http://awinet.org)
- Association for Manufacturing Technology (www.amtonline.org)
- Fabricators & Manufacturers Association, International (http://fmanet.org)
- National Tooling and Machining Association (www.ntma.org)
- Woodwork Career Alliance of North America (www.woodworkcareer.org)
- Woodworking Machinery Industry Association (www.wmia.org)

O*NET

- Cabinetmakers and Bench Carpenters (51-7011.00)
- Furniture Finishers (51-7021.00)
- Sawing Machine Setters, Operators, and Tenders, Wood (51-7041.00)
- Woodworking Machine Setters, Operators, and Tenders, Except Sawing (51-7042.00)

Protective Service

Correctional Officers and Bailiffs

- **2014 Median Pay** .... $39,700 per year
  $19.08 per hour
- **Typical Entry-Level Education**........ High school diploma or equivalent
- **Work Experience in a Related Occupation**.............. None
- **On-the-job Training**...Moderate-term on-the-job training
- **Number of Jobs, 2014** 474,800
- **Job Outlook, 2014–24**............. 4% (Slower than average)
- **Employment Change, 2014–24** 17,900

What Correctional Officers and Bailiffs Do

Correctional officers are responsible for overseeing individuals who have been arrested and are awaiting trial or who have been sentenced to serve time in jail or prison. Bailiffs, also known as *marshals* or *court officers*, are law enforcement officers who maintain safety and order in courtrooms. Their duties, which vary by location, include enforcing courtroom rules, assisting judges, guarding juries, delivering court documents, and providing general security for courthouses.

Duties. Correctional officers typically do the following:

- Enforce rules and keep order within jails or prisons
- Supervise activities of inmates
- Aid in rehabilitation and counseling of prisoners
- Inspect facilities to ensure that they meet security and safety standards
- Search inmates for contraband items
- Report on inmate conduct

Inside the prison or jail, correctional officers enforce rules and regulations. They maintain security by preventing disturbances, assaults, and escapes. They must also ensure the whereabouts of all inmates at all times.

On any given day, officers search inmates for contraband, such as weapons and drugs, settle disputes between inmates, and enforce discipline. Officers enforce regulations through effective communication and the use of progressive sanctions, which involve punishments such as loss of privileges. Sanctions are progressive in that they start out small for a lesser offense but become more severe for more serious offenses. In addition, officers may aid inmates in their rehabilitation by scheduling work assignments, counseling, and educational opportunities.

Correctional officers inspect facilities periodically. They check cells and other areas for unsanitary conditions, contraband, signs of a security breach (such as tampering with window bars and doors), and any other evidence of violations of the rules. Officers also inspect mail and visitors for prohibited items. They write reports and fill out daily logs detailing inmate behavior and anything else of note that occurred during their shift.

Correctional officers may have to restrain inmates in handcuffs and leg irons to escort them safely to and from cells and to see authorized visitors. Officers also escort prisoners between the institution where they are held and courtrooms, medical facilities, and other destinations.

Correctional officers must report any inmate who violates the rules. If a crime is committed within their institution or an inmate escapes, they help law enforcement authorities investigate and search for the escapee.

Because prisoners typically stay longer in state and federal prisons than in county jails, correctional officers in prisons get to know the people in their charge.

Correctional officers have no law enforcement responsibilities outside their place of work.

Work Environment

Correctional officers and bailiffs held about 474,800 jobs in 2014. Correctional officers and jailers held about 457,600 jobs in 2014. Bailiffs held about 17,300 jobs in 2014. About 95 percent of correctional officers and bailiffs worked for federal, state, and local governments. The remainder were employed by private companies that provide correctional services to prisons and jails.

Correctional officers may work indoors or outdoors. Some correctional institutions are modern and temperature controlled, but others are old, overcrowded, hot, and noisy.

Correctional officers may be required to stand for long periods. Bailiffs generally work in courtrooms.

Injuries and Illnesses. Working in a correctional institution can be stressful and dangerous. Every year, correctional officers are injured in confrontations with inmates and some are exposed to contagious diseases. As a result, correctional officers have one of the highest rates of injuries and illnesses of all occupations. Bailiffs work with prisoners, who may become violent.

The job demands that officers be alert and ready to react throughout their entire shift. As a result, some officers experience anxiety.

Work Schedules. Correctional officers usually work 8 hours per day, 5 days per week, on rotating shifts. Because jail and prison security must be provided around the clock, officers work all hours of the day and night, weekends and holidays. Some correctional facilities have longer shifts and more days off between scheduled

Correctional officers inspect mail and visitors for prohibited items.

Median Annual Wages, May 2014

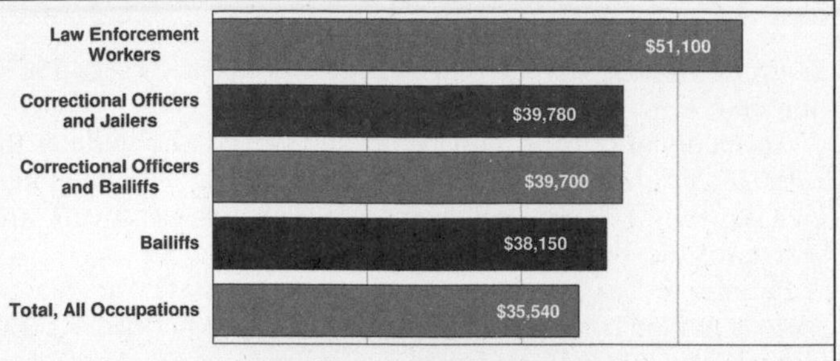

Note: All Occupations includes all occupations in the U.S. Economy.
Source: U.S. Bureau of Labor Statistics, Occupational Employment Statistics

Percent Change in Employment, Projected 2014–2024

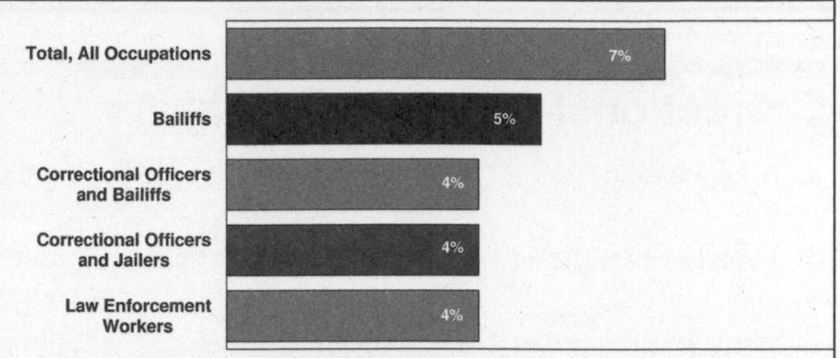

Note: All Occupations includes all occupations in the U.S. Economy.
Source: U.S. Bureau of Labor Statistics, Office of Occupational Statistics and Employment Projections

workweeks. Many officers are required to work overtime. Bailiffs' hours are determined by when court is in session.

Education/Training

Correctional officers go through a training academy and then are assigned to a facility for on-the-job training. Although qualifications vary by state and agency, all agencies require a high school diploma. Bailiff positions also require a high school diploma. Federal agencies may also require some college education or previous work experience.

Correctional officers must be U.S. citizens or permanent residents, and must have no felony convictions. Many agencies establish a minimum age for correctional officers, which is typically between 18 and 21 years of age. New applicants for federal corrections positions must be appointed before they are 37 years old.

Education. Correctional officers must have at least a high school diploma or equivalent. Some state and local corrections agencies require some college credits. Law enforcement or military experience may be substituted for this requirement.

For employment in federal prisons, the Federal Bureau of Prisons requires entry-level correctional officers to have at least a bachelor's degree; 3 years of full-time experience in a field providing counseling, assistance, or supervision to individuals; or a combination of the two.

Training. Federal, state, and some local departments of corrections, as well as some private corrections companies, provide training for correctional officers based on guidelines established by the American Correctional Association (ACA). Some states have regional training academies that are available to local agencies. Academy trainees receive instruction in a number of subjects, including self-defense, institutional policies, regulations, operations, and custody and security procedures. Although most correctional officers do not carry firearms when on duty, they may receive training in the use of firearms.

After formal academy instruction, state and local correctional agencies provide on-the-job training, including training on legal restrictions and interpersonal relations. Trainees typically receive several weeks or months of training under the supervision of an experienced officer. However, on-the-job training varies widely from agency to agency.

New federal correctional officers must undergo 200 hours of formal training within the first year of employment, including 120 hours of specialized training at the Federal Bureau of Prisons residential training center. Experienced officers receive annual in-service training to keep up to date on new developments and procedures.

Correctional officers who are members of prison tactical response teams are trained to respond to disturbances, riots, hostage situations, and other dangerous circumstances. Team members practice disarming prisoners, wielding weapons, and using other tactics to maintain the safety of inmates and officers alike.

Bailiffs must undergo training in court procedures and the proper way to place someone under arrest, and they may also learn how to use a firearm.

Other Experience. Military experience is viewed as excellent preparation for becoming a correctional officer.

Advancement. Qualified officers may advance to the position of correctional sergeant. Sergeants are responsible for maintaining security and directing the activities of other officers. Qualified officers may also be promoted to supervisory or administrative positions, including warden. Officers sometimes transfer to related jobs, such as probation officers and correctional treatment specialists.

Important Qualities

Good judgment. Correctional officers and bailiffs must use both their training and common sense to quickly determine the best course of action and to take the necessary steps to achieve a desired outcome.

Interpersonal skills. Correctional officers and bailiffs must be able to interact and communicate effectively with inmates and others to maintain order in correctional facilities and courtrooms.

Negotiating skills. Correctional officers must be able to assist others in resolving differences in order to avoid conflict.

Employment Projections Data for Correctional Officers and Bailiffs

Occupational Title	SOC Code	Employment, 2014	Projected Employment, 2024	Change, 2014–2024 Percent	Change, 2014–2024 Numeric
Bailiffs, correctional officers, and jailers	33-3010	474,800	492,800	4	17,900
Bailiffs	33-3011	17,300	18,100	5	800
Correctional officers and jailers	33-3012	457,600	474,700	4	17,100

Source: U.S. Bureau of Labor Statistics, Employment Projections Program

Similar Occupations. This table shows a list of occupations with job duties that are similar to those of correctional officers and bailiffs.

Occupations	Entry-level Education	2014 Median Pay	Projected Job Growth	Average Annual Openings
Police and Detectives	See Education/Training	$58,630	4%	3,310
Probation Officers and Correctional Treatment Specialists	Bachelor's degree	$49,060	4%	330
Security Guards and Gaming Surveillance Officers	High school diploma or equivalent	$24,470	5%	5,500

Physical strength. Correctional officers and bailiffs must have the strength to physically subdue inmates or others.

Self-discipline. Correctional officers must control their emotions when confronted with hostile situations.

Pay

The median annual wage for bailiffs was $38,150 in May 2014. The median wage is the wage at which half the workers in an occupation earned more than that amount and half earned less. The lowest 10 percent earned less than $20,630, and the highest 10 percent earned more than $70,970.

The median annual wage for correctional officers and jailers was $39,780 in May 2014. The lowest 10 percent earned less than $27,280, and the highest 10 percent earned more than $72,790.

In addition to receiving typical benefits, correctional officers employed in the public sector usually are provided with uniforms or with a clothing allowance to buy their own uniforms. Many departments offer retirement benefits, although benefits vary.

Union Membership. Compared with workers in all occupations, correctional officers had a higher percentage of workers who belonged to a union in 2014.

Job Outlook

Employment of correctional officers and bailiffs is projected to grow 4 percent from 2014 to 2024, slower than the average for all occupations.

Correctional officers will continue to be needed to watch over the U.S. prison population. Most states are projecting that they will have more prisoners in the future. However, changes to criminal laws can have a large effect on how many people are arrested and incarcerated each year.

Faced with high costs for keeping people in prison, many state governments have moved toward laws requiring shorter prison terms and alternatives to prison. While keeping the public safe, community-based programs designed to rehabilitate prisoners and limit their risk of repeated offenses may also reduce prisoner counts.

Bailiffs will continue to be needed to keep order in courtrooms.

Job Prospects. Job prospects should be good as some local and state corrections agencies experience high job turnover. The need to replace correctional officers who retire, transfer to other occupations, or leave the labor force—coupled with rising employment demand—should generate job openings.

Contacts for More Information

For more information about correctional officers, visit

➤ American Correctional Association (www.aca.org)

➤ American Jail Association (www.aja.org)

For information about career opportunities for correctional officers at the federal level, visit

➤ Federal Bureau of Prisons (www.bop.gov)

For information about federal government requirements for correctional officers position, visit

➤ U.S. Office of Personnel Management (http://tinyurl.com/c98gp6e)

To find job openings for correctional officers, visit

➤ USAJOBS (www.usajobs.gov)

O*NET

➤ Bailiffs (33-3011.00)

➤ Correctional Officers and Jailers (33-3012.00)

Fire Inspectors

- **2014 Median Pay** .... $54,020 per year $25.97 per hour
- **Typical Entry-Level Education** .... See Education/Training
- **Work Experience in a Related Occupation** .... See Education/Training
- **On-the-job Training** ... Moderate-term on-the-job training
- **Number of Jobs, 2014** 14,100
- **Job Outlook, 2014–24** .... 6% (As fast as average)
- **Employment Change, 2014–24** 900

What Fire Inspectors Do

Fire inspectors examine buildings to detect fire hazards and ensure that federal, state, and local fire codes are met. Fire investigators determine the origin and cause of fires and explosions.

Duties. Fire inspectors typically do the following:

- Search for fire hazards
- Ensure that buildings comply with fire codes
- Test fire alarms, sprinklers, and other fire protection equipment
- Inspect gasoline storage tanks and air compressors
- Review emergency evacuation plans
- Conduct follow-up visits to make sure that infractions do not recur
- Review building plans with developers
- Conduct fire and safety education programs
- Maintain fire inspection files that may be used in a court of law
- Administer burn permits and monitor controlled burns

Fire investigators typically do the following:

- Collect and analyze evidence from scenes of fires and explosions
- Interview witnesses
- Reconstruct the scene of a fire or arson

- Send evidence to laboratories to be tested for fingerprints or accelerants
- Analyze information with chemists, engineers, and attorneys
- Document evidence by taking photographs and creating diagrams
- Determine the origin and cause of a fire
- Keep detailed records and protect evidence for use in a court of law
- Testify in civil and criminal legal proceedings
- Exercise police powers, such as the power of arrest, and carry a weapon

Forest fire inspectors and prevention specialists assess fire hazards in both public and residential areas. They look for fire code infractions and for conditions that pose a wildfire risk. They also recommend ways to reduce fire hazards. During patrols, they enforce fire regulations and report fire conditions to their central command center.

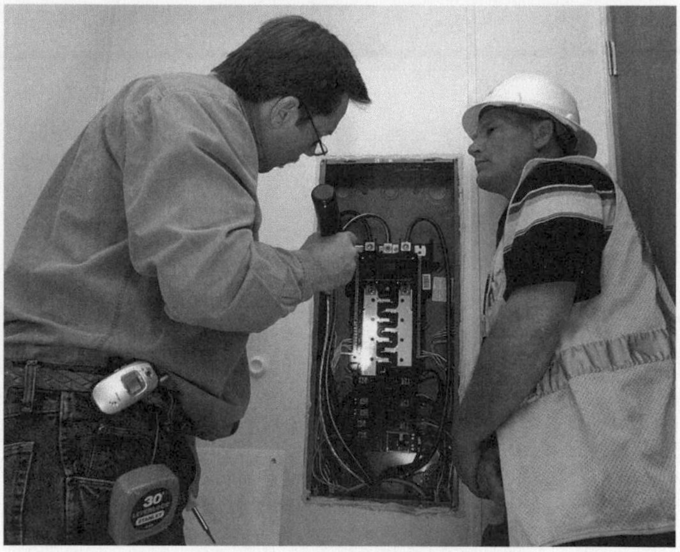

Fire inspectors ensure that buildings comply with fire codes.

Work Environment

Fire inspectors held about 14,100 jobs in 2014. Fire inspectors and investigators held about 12,400 of those jobs, while forest fire inspectors and prevention specialists held the remaining 1,700 jobs. About 88 percent of all fire inspectors worked for state and local governments in 2014. A few also worked for insurance companies or attorneys' offices.

Fire inspectors work both in offices and in the field. In the field, inspectors examine public buildings, such as museums, and multifamily residential buildings, such as high-rise condominiums. They may also visit and inspect other structures, such as arenas and industrial plants. Investigators must visit the scene where a fire has occurred. They may be exposed to poor ventilation, smoke, fumes, and other hazardous agents.

Forest fire inspectors and prevention specialists check on outdoor installations and open land to assess the risk of fire in those places.

Injuries and Illnesses. Fire inspectors and investigators have a higher rate of injuries and illnesses than the national average. For example, it can be very dangerous to walk on unstable, fire-damaged structures. Also, inhaling fumes from a fire can result in adverse health issues.

When working in the field, inspectors and investigators often must wear protective clothing, such as boots, gloves, and a helmet.

Work Schedules. Fire inspectors typically work during regular business hours, but investigators often work evenings, weekends, and holidays because they must be ready to respond when fires happen.

Education/Training

Fire inspectors and investigators typically have previous work experience as a firefighter or police officer, where many have completed a postsecondary educational program for emergency medical technicians (EMTs). Forest fire inspectors and prevention specialists typically enter the occupation with a high school diploma or equivalent.

Workers attend training academies and receive on-the-job training in inspection and investigation.

Fire inspectors and investigators usually must pass a background check, which may include a drug test. Most employers also require inspectors and investigators to have a valid driver's license, and investigators usually need to be U.S. citizens because of their police powers.

Education. Because fire inspectors and investigators typically have previous work experience as a firefighter or police officer, many have completed a postsecondary educational program for emergency medical technicians (EMTs). Some employers prefer candidates with a 2- or 4-year degree in fire science, engineering, or chemistry. For those candidates interested in becoming forest fire inspectors and prevention specialists, a high school education is typically required.

Work Experience in a Related Occupation. Most fire inspectors and investigators are required to have work experience in a related occupation, such as firefighters or police officers. Some fire departments or law enforcement agencies require investigators to have a certain number of years within the organization or to be a

Median Annual Wages, May 2014

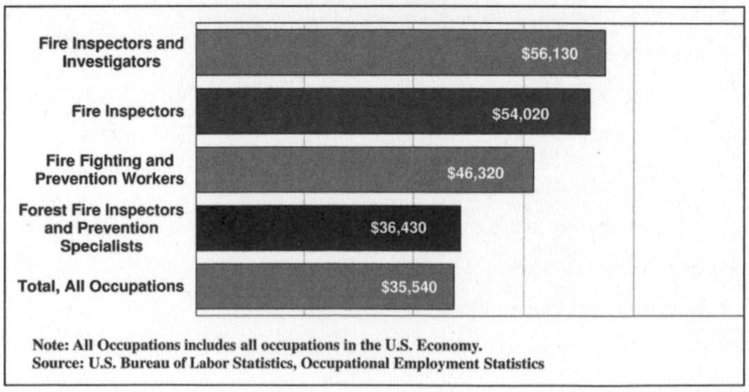

Percent Change in Employment, Projected 2014–2024

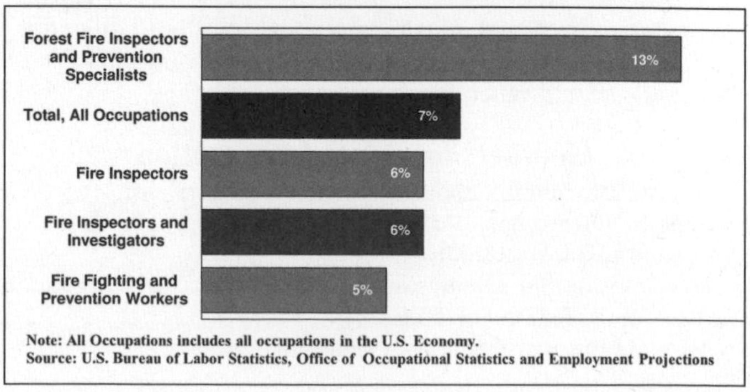

certain rank, such as lieutenant or captain, before they are eligible for promotion to an inspector or investigator position. Forest fire inspectors and prevention specialists also may need experience working in the fire service before being hired.

Training. Training requirements vary by state, but programs usually include instruction in a classroom setting in addition to on-the-job training.

Classroom training often takes place at a fire or police academy over the course of several months. A variety of topics are covered, including guidelines for conducting an inspection or investigation, legal codes, courtroom procedures, protocols for handling hazardous and explosive materials, and the proper use of equipment.

In most agencies, after inspectors and investigators have finished their classroom training, they also receive on-the-job training, during which they work with a more experienced officer.

Employers, such as the Bureau of Alcohol, Tobacco, Firearms and Explosives (ATF) and the Federal Bureau of Investigation (FBI), and organizations, such as the National Fire Academy and the International Association of Arson Investigators, offer training programs in fire investigation.

Licenses, Certifications, and Registrations. Many states have certification exams that cover standards established by the National Fire Protection Association. Many states require additional training for inspectors and investigators each year in order for them to maintain their certification.

The National Fire Protection Association also offers several certifications, such as Certified Fire Inspector and Certified Fire Protection Specialist, for fire inspectors. Some jobs in the private sector require that job candidates already have these certifications.

In addition, fire investigators may choose to pursue certification from a nationally recognized professional association, such as the Certified Fire Investigator (CFI) certification from the International Association of Arson Investigators (IAAI) or the Certified Fire and Explosion Investigator (CFEI) certification from the National Association of Fire Investigators (NAFI). The Bureau of Alcohol, Tobacco, Firearms and Explosives (ATF) also offers a CFI certification, although the program is available only to ATF employees. The process of obtaining certification can teach new skills and demonstrate competency.

Fire investigators who work for private companies may have to obtain a private investigator license from their state.

Important Qualities

Communication skills. Fire inspectors must clearly explain fire code violations to building and property managers. They must carefully interview witnesses as part of their fact-finding mission.

Critical-thinking skills. Fire inspectors must be able to recognize code violations and recommend a way to fix the problem. They must be able to analyze evidence from a fire and come to a reasonable conclusion.

Detail oriented. Fire inspectors must notice details when inspecting a site for code violations or investigating the cause of a fire.

Integrity. Fire inspectors must be consistent in the methods they use to enforce fire codes. They must be unbiased when conducting their research and when testifying as an expert witness in court.

Physical strength. Fire inspectors may have to move debris at the site of a fire in order to get a more accurate understanding of the scene.

Pay

The median annual wage for fire inspectors and investigators was $56,130 in May 2014. The median wage is the wage at which half the workers in an occupation earned more than that amount and half earned less. The lowest 10 percent earned less than $34,010, and the highest 10 percent earned more than $90,330.

The median annual wage for forest fire inspectors and prevention specialists was $36,430 in May 2014. The lowest 10 percent earned less than $24,550, and the highest 10 percent earned more than $74,050.

Job Outlook

Employment of fire inspectors is projected to grow 6 percent from 2014 to 2024, about as fast as the average for all occupations. Employment growth will vary by specialty.

Employment of fire inspectors and investigators is projected to grow 5 percent from 2014 to 2024, about as fast as the average for all occupations. Fire inspectors will be needed to assess potential fire hazards in newly constructed residential, commercial, public, and other buildings in the coming decade. Fire inspectors will also be needed to ensure that existing buildings meet updated and revised federal, state, and local fire codes each year. Although the number of structural fires occurring across the country has been falling for some time, fire investigators will still be needed to determine the cause of fires and explosions.

Employment of forest fire inspectors and prevention specialists is projected to grow 13 percent from 2014 to 2024, faster than the average for all occupations. Forest fire inspectors and prevention specialists are expected to be needed to help prevent and control the increasingly destructive wildfires that the United States has been experiencing.

Job Prospects. Job seekers should expect strong competition for the number of available positions. Many job openings will come from the need to replace workers who leave the occupation.

Those who have previous work experience in fire suppression, have completed some fire science education, or have training related to criminal investigation should have the best job prospects.

Contacts for More Information

For more information about federal fire investigator jobs, visit

➤ Bureau of Alcohol, Tobacco, Firearms and Explosives (www.atf.gov)

➤ Federal Bureau of Investigation (www.fbi.gov)

Employment Projections Data for Fire Inspectors

Occupational Title	SOC Code	Employment, 2014	Projected Employment, 2024	Change, 2014–2024	
				Percent	Numeric
Fire inspectors	33-2020	14,100	15,000	6	900
Fire inspectors and investigators	33-2021	12,400	13,100	5	700
Forest fire inspectors and prevention specialists	33-2022	1,700	2,000	13	200

Source: U.S. Bureau of Labor Statistics, Employment Projections Program

Similar Occupations. This table shows a list of occupations with job duties that are similar to those of fire inspectors.

Occupations	Entry-level Education	2014 Median Pay	Projected Job Growth	Average Annual Openings
Firefighters	Postsecondary nondegree award	$45,970	5%	1,740
Police and Detectives	See Education/Training	$58,630	4%	3,310
Private Detectives and Investigators	High school diploma or equivalent	$44,570	5%	180

For more information about fire inspectors' and investigators' training, visit

➤ National Fire Academy (www.usfa.dhs.gov/nfa)

For information about standards for fire inspectors and investigators, visit

➤ National Fire Protection Association (www.nfpa.org)

For information about certifications, visit

➤ International Association of Arson Investigators (www.firearson.com)

➤ National Association of Fire Investigators (www.nafi.org)

O*NET

➤ Fire Inspectors and Investigators (33-2021.00)

➤ Fire Inspectors (33-2021.01)

➤ Fire Investigators (33-2021.02)

➤ Forest Fire Inspectors and Prevention Specialists (33-2022.00)

Firefighters

- **2014 Median Pay** .... $45,970 per year $22.10 per hour
- **Typical Entry-Level Education** .... Postsecondary nondegree award
- **Work Experience in a Related Occupation**.............. None
- **On-the-job Training** .... Long-term on-the-job training
- **Number of Jobs, 2014** 327,300
- **Job Outlook, 2014–24**................. 5% (As fast as average)
- **Employment Change, 2014–24** 17,400

What Firefighters Do

Firefighters control and put out fires, and respond to emergency situations where life, property, or the environment is at risk.

Duties. Firefighters typically do the following:

- Drive fire trucks and other emergency vehicles
- Put out fires using water hoses, fire extinguishers, and water pumps
- Find and rescue victims in burning buildings or in other emergency situations
- Treat sick or injured people
- Prepare written reports on emergency incidents
- Clean and maintain equipment
- Conduct drills and physical fitness training
- Provide public education on fire safety

When responding to an emergency, firefighters are responsible for connecting hoses to hydrants, operating the pumps that power the hoses, climbing ladders, and using other tools to break through debris. Firefighters also enter burning buildings to extinguish fires and rescue individuals. Many firefighters are responsible for providing medical attention. Two out of three calls to firefighters are for medical emergencies, not fires, according to the National Fire Protection Association.

Firefighters' duties may change several times while they are at the scene of an emergency. In some cases they remain at disaster scenes for days, for example, rescuing trapped survivors and assisting with medical treatment.

When firefighters are not responding to an emergency, they are on call at a fire station. During this time, they regularly inspect equipment and perform practice drills. They also eat and sleep and remain on call, as their shifts usually last 24 hours.

Some firefighters also work in hazardous materials units and are specially trained to control and clean up hazardous materials, such as oil spills and chemical accidents. They work with hazardous materials removal workers in these cases.

Wildland firefighters are specially trained firefighters. They use heavy equipment and water hoses to control forest fires. They also frequently create fire lines—a swath of cut-down trees and dug-up grass in the path of a fire—to deprive a fire of fuel. They will also use prescribed fires to burn potential fire fuel under controlled conditions. Some wildland firefighters, known as *smoke jumpers*, parachute from airplanes to reach otherwise inaccessible areas.

Work Environment

Firefighters held about 327,300 jobs in 2014. The vast majority—about 91 percent—worked for local governments. Most of the remainder worked for federal and state governments. A few worked at airports, chemical plants, and other industrial sites.

These employment numbers exclude volunteer firefighters. There are approximately twice as many volunteer firefighters as there are paid career firefighters.

Volunteer firefighters share the same duties as paid firefighters and account for the majority of firefighters in many areas.

Firefighters help protect the public by responding to fires and a variety of other emergencies.

According to the National Fire Protection Association, about 69 percent of fire departments were staffed entirely by volunteer firefighters in 2013.

When not on the scene of an emergency, firefighters work at fire stations, where they sleep, eat, and remain on call. When an alarm sounds, firefighters respond, regardless of the weather or time of day.

Injuries and Illnesses. Firefighters have one of the highest rates of injuries and illnesses of all occupations. They often encounter dangerous situations, including collapsing floors and walls, traffic accidents, and overexposure to flames and smoke. As a result, workers must wear protective gear to help lower these risks. Often, the protective gear can be very heavy and hot.

Work Schedules. Firefighters typically work long and varied hours. Most firefighters work 24-hour shifts on duty and are off the following 48 or 72 hours. Some firefighters work 10/14 shifts, which means 10 hours working and 14 hours off. When combating forest and wildland fires, firefighters may work for extended periods. For example, the 2003 California Fire Siege took weeks of constant effort by California wildland firefighters to stop.

Education/Training

Firefighters typically need a high school diploma and training in emergency medical services. Prospective firefighters must pass written and physical tests, complete a series of interviews, go through training at a fire academy, and hold an emergency medical technician (EMT) certification.

Applicants for firefighter jobs typically must be at least 18 years old and have a valid driver's license. They must also pass a medical exam and drug screening to be hired. After being hired, firefighters may be subject to random drug tests and will also need to complete routine physical fitness assessments.

Education. The entry-level education needed to become a firefighter is a high school diploma or equivalent. However, some classwork beyond high school, such as airway management and trauma care, is usually needed to obtain the emergency medical technician (EMT) basic certification. EMT requirements vary by city and state.

Training. Entry-level firefighters receive a few months of training at fire academies run by the fire department or by the state. Through classroom instruction and practical training, recruits study fire-fighting and fire-prevention techniques, local building codes, and emergency medical procedures. They also learn how to fight fires with standard equipment, including axes, chain saws, fire extinguishers, and ladders. After attending a fire academy, firefighters must usually complete a probationary period.

Some fire departments have accredited apprenticeship programs that last up to 4 years. These programs combine technical instruction with on-the-job training under the supervision of experienced firefighters.

In addition to participating in training programs conducted by local or state fire departments and agencies, some firefighters attend federal training sessions sponsored by the National Fire Academy. These training sessions cover topics including anti-arson techniques, disaster preparedness, hazardous materials control, and public fire safety and education.

Licenses, Certifications, and Registrations. Usually, firefighters must be certified as emergency medical technicians at the EMT-Basic level. In addition, some fire departments require firefighters to be certified as an EMT-Paramedic. The National Registry of Emergency Medical Technicians (NREMT) certifies EMTs and paramedics. Both levels of NREMT certification require completing a training or education program and passing the national exam. The national exam has both a written part and a practical part. EMTs and paramedics may work with firefighters at the scenes of accidents.

Some states have mandatory or voluntary firefighter training and certification programs.

The National Fire Academy also offers an Executive Fire Officer certification. To be eligible, firefighters must have a bachelor's degree.

Other Experience. Working as a volunteer firefighter may help in getting a job as a career firefighter.

Advancement. Firefighters can be promoted to engineer, then to lieutenant, captain, battalion chief, assistant chief, deputy chief, and, finally, chief. For promotion to positions beyond battalion chief, many fire departments now require applicants to have a bachelor's degree, preferably in fire science, public administration, or a related field. Some firefighters eventually become fire inspectors or investigators after gaining enough experience.

Important Qualities

Communication skills. Firefighters must be able to communicate conditions at an emergency scene to other firefighters and to emergency-response crews.

Courage. Firefighters' daily job duties involve dangerous situations, such as entering a burning building.

Decision-making skills. Firefighters must be able to make quick and smart decisions in an emergency. The ability to make good decisions under pressure could potentially save someone's life.

Physical stamina. Firefighters may have to stay at disaster scenes for long periods of time to rescue and treat victims. Fighting fires requires prolonged use of strength and endurance.

Physical strength. Firefighters must be strong enough to carry heavy equipment and move debris at an emergency site. They must also be able to carry victims who are injured or cannot walk.

Median Annual Wages, May 2014

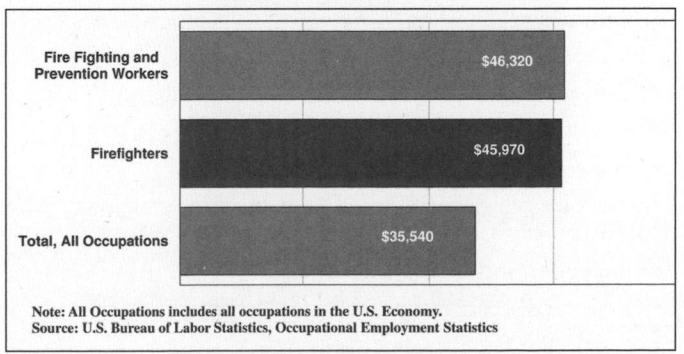

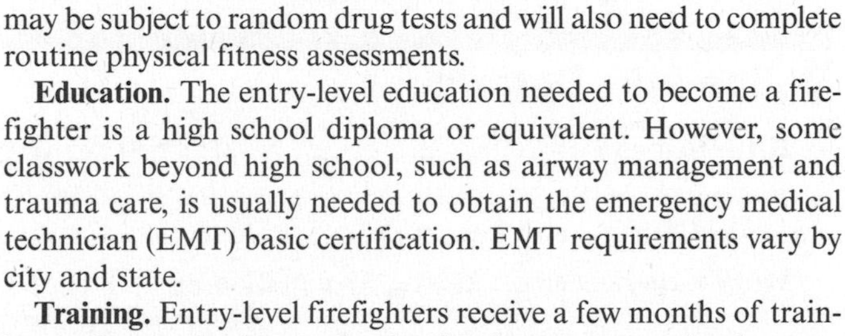

Note: All Occupations includes all occupations in the U.S. Economy.
Source: U.S. Bureau of Labor Statistics, Occupational Employment Statistics

Percent Change in Employment, Projected 2014–2024

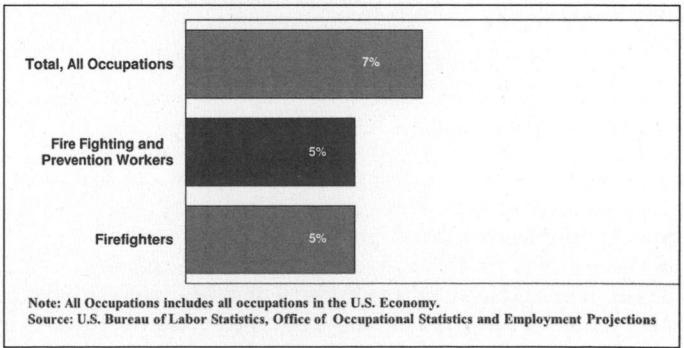

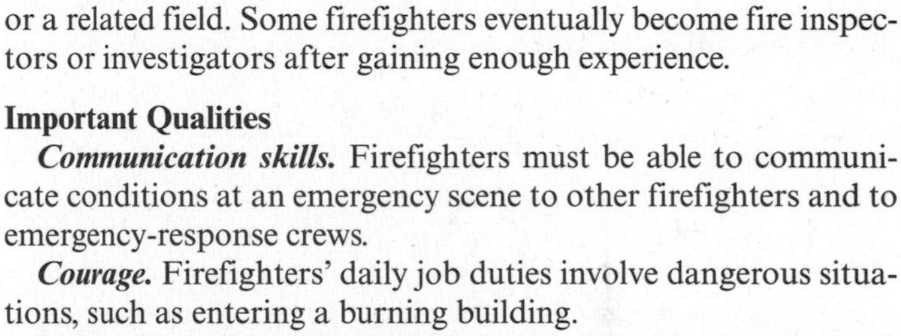

Note: All Occupations includes all occupations in the U.S. Economy.
Source: U.S. Bureau of Labor Statistics, Office of Occupational Statistics and Employment Projections

Employment Projections Data for Firefighters

Occupational Title	SOC Code	Employment, 2014	Projected Employment, 2024	Change, 2014–2024 Percent	Change, 2014–2024 Numeric
Firefighters	33-2011	327,300	344,700	5	17,400

Source: U.S. Bureau of Labor Statistics, Employment Projections Program

Similar Occupations. This table shows a list of occupations with job duties that are similar to those of firefighters.

Occupations	Entry-level Education	2014 Median Pay	Projected Job Growth	Average Annual Openings
Correctional Officers and Bailiffs	High school diploma or equivalent	$39,700	4%	1,790
EMTs and Paramedics	Postsecondary nondegree award	$31,700	24%	5,850
Fire Inspectors	See Education/Training	$54,020	6%	90
Police and Detectives	See Education/Training	$58,630	4%	3,310
Security Guards and Gaming Surveillance Officers	High school diploma or equivalent	$24,470	5%	5,500

Pay

The median annual wage for firefighters was $45,970 in May 2014. The median wage is the wage at which half the workers in an occupation earned more than that amount and half earned less. The lowest 10 percent earned less than $22,130, and the highest 10 percent earned more than $81,450.

Union Membership. Most firefighters belonged to a union in 2014. The largest organizer of firefighters is the International Association of Fire Fighters.

Job Outlook

Employment of firefighters is projected to grow 5 percent from 2014 to 2024, about as fast as the average for all occupations.

Improved building materials and building codes have resulted in a long-term decrease in fires and fire fatalities, but firefighters will still be needed to respond to fires. Fires can spread rapidly so controlling them quickly is very important. Wildland firefighters will still be needed to combat active fires and manage the environment to reduce the impact of fires. Firefighters will also continue to respond to medical emergencies.

Job Prospects. Prospective firefighters will likely face strong competition for jobs. Many people are attracted to the job's challenges and the opportunity for public service. Additionally, many people are attracted to the career because its education requirement is a high school diploma. As a result, a department may receive hundreds of applicants for a single position.

Physically fit applicants with high test scores, some postsecondary firefighter education, and paramedic training should have the best job prospects.

Contacts for More Information

For information about a career as a firefighter, contact your local fire department or visit

- ➤ International Association of Fire Fighters (www.iaff.org)
- ➤ International Association of Women in Fire & Emergency Services (www.i-women.org)
- ➤ U.S. Fire Administration (www.usfa.fema.gov)
- ➤ National Fire Protection Association (www.nfpa.org)

For information about professional qualifications and a list of colleges and universities offering 2- or 4-year degree programs in fire science and fire prevention, visit

- ➤ National Fire Academy, U.S. Fire Administration (www.usfa.fema.gov/nfa)

O*NET

- ➤ Firefighters (33-2011.00)
- ➤ Municipal Firefighters (33-2011.01)
- ➤ Forest Firefighters (33-2011.02)

Police and Detectives

- **2014 Median Pay** .... $58,630 per year $28.19 per hour
- **Typical Entry-Level Education** .... See Education/Training
- **Work Experience in a Related Occupation**..................See Education/Training
- **On-the-job Training**...Moderate-term on-the-job training
- **Number of Jobs, 2014** 806,400
- **Job Outlook, 2014–24** .... 4% (Slower than average)
- **Employment Change, 2014–24** 33,100

What Police and Detectives Do

Police officers protect lives and property. Detectives and criminal investigators, who are sometimes called *agents* or *special agents*, gather facts and collect evidence of possible crimes.

Duties. Police officers, detectives, and criminal investigators typically do the following:

- Enforce laws
- Respond to emergency and nonemergency calls
- Patrol assigned areas
- Conduct traffic stops and issue citations
- Search for vehicle records and warrants using computers in the field
- Obtain warrants and arrest suspects
- Collect and secure evidence from crime scenes
- Observe the activities of suspects

- Write detailed reports and fill out forms
- Prepare cases and testify in court

Police officers pursue and apprehend people who break the law. They then warn, cite, or arrest them. Most police officers patrol their jurisdictions and investigate suspicious activity. They also respond to calls, issue traffic tickets, and give first aid to accident victims.

Detectives perform investigative duties, such as gathering facts and collecting evidence.

The daily activities of police and detectives vary with their occupational specialty, such as canine units and special weapons and tactics (SWAT). Job duties differ at the local, state, or federal level. Duties differ among federal agencies because they enforce different aspects of the law. Regardless of job duties or location, police officers and detectives at all levels must write reports and keep detailed records that will be needed if they testify in court. Most carry law enforcement tools, such as radios, handcuffs, and guns.

State and Local Law Enforcement

Uniformed police officers have general law enforcement duties. They wear uniforms that allow the public to easily recognize them as police officers. They have regular patrols and also respond to emergency and nonemergency calls. During patrols, officers look for any signs of criminal activity and may conduct searches and arrest suspected criminals.

Some police officers work only on a specific type of crime, such as narcotics. Officers, especially those working in large departments, may work in special units, such as horseback, motorcycle, canine corps, and special weapons and tactics (SWAT). Typically, officers must work as patrol officers for a certain number of years before they may be appointed to a special unit.

Some agencies, such as public college and university police forces, public school police, and transit police, have special geographic and enforcement responsibilities.

State police officers, sometimes called *state troopers* or *highway patrol officers*, have many of the same duties as other police officers, but they may spend more time enforcing traffic laws and issuing traffic citations. State police officers have authority to work anywhere in the state and are frequently called on to help other law enforcement agencies, especially those in rural areas or small towns.

Transit and railroad police patrol railroad yards and transit stations. They protect property, employees, and passengers from crimes such as thefts and robberies. They remove trespassers from railroad and transit properties and check IDs of people who try to enter secure areas.

Sheriffs and deputy sheriffs enforce the law on the county level. Sheriffs' departments tend to be relatively small. Sheriffs are usually elected by the public and do the same work as a local or county police chief. Some sheriffs' departments do the same work as officers in urban police departments. Others mainly operate the county jails and provide services in local courts. Police and sheriffs' deputies who provide security in city and county courts are sometimes called bailiffs.

Detectives and criminal investigators are uniformed or plainclothes investigators who gather facts and collect evidence for criminal cases. They conduct interviews, examine records, observe the activities of suspects, and participate in raids and arrests. Detectives usually specialize in investigating one type of crime, such as homicide or fraud. Detectives are typically assigned cases on a rotating basis and work on them until an arrest and trial are completed or until the case is dropped.

The daily activities of police and detectives vary with their occupational specialty.

Fish and game wardens enforce fishing, hunting, and boating laws. They patrol fishing and hunting areas, conduct search and rescue operations, investigate complaints and accidents, and educate the public about laws pertaining to the outdoors. Federal fish and game wardens are often referred to as Federal Wildlife Officers.

Federal Law Enforcement

Federal law enforcement officials carry out many of the same duties that other police officers do, and they also have jurisdiction over the entire country. Many federal agents are highly specialized. The following are examples of federal agencies in which officers and agents enforce particular types of laws.

- Federal Bureau of Investigation (FBI) agents are the federal government's principal investigators, responsible for enforcing more than 200 categories of federal statutes and conducting sensitive national security investigations.
- Drug Enforcement Administration (DEA) agents enforce laws and regulations relating to illegal drugs.
- United States Secret Service uniformed officers protect the President, the Vice President, their immediate families, and other public officials. Other Secret Service agents investigate financial crimes.
- Federal Air Marshals provide air security by guarding against attacks targeting U.S. aircraft, passengers, and crews.
- U.S. Border Patrol agents protect the U.S. land and sea boundaries.

See the Contacts for More Information section for additional information about federal law enforcement agencies.

Work Environment

Police and detectives held about 806,400 jobs in 2014. Most police and detectives work for local governments and some work for state governments or the federal government.

Police and detective work can be physically demanding, stressful, and dangerous. Officers must be alert and ready to react throughout their entire shift. Officers regularly work at crime and accident scenes and deal with the death and suffering that they encounter there. Although a career in law enforcement may be stressful, many officers find it rewarding to help members of their communities.

Median Annual Wages, May 2014

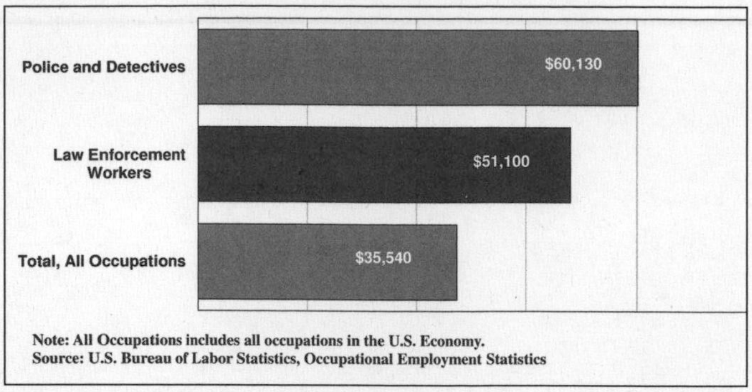

Percent Change in Employment, Projected 2014–2024

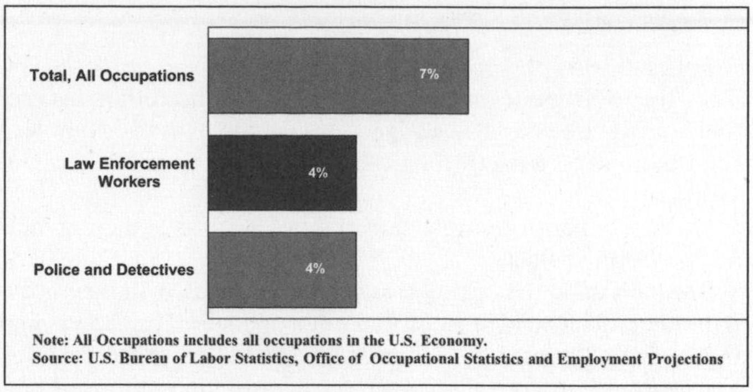

The jobs of some federal agents, such as U.S. Secret Service and DEA special agents, require extensive travel, often on short notice. These agents may relocate a number of times over the course of their careers. Some special agents, such as U.S. Border Patrol agents, may work outdoors in rugged terrain and in all kinds of weather.

Injuries and Illnesses. Police and sheriff's patrol officers have one of the highest rates of injuries and illnesses of all occupations. They may face physical injuries during conflicts with criminals and motor-vehicle pursuits or when exposed to other high-risk situations or diseases. Transit and railroad police also have a high rate of injuries and illnesses.

Work Schedules. Uniformed officers, detectives, agents, and wardens usually work full time. Paid overtime is common. Shift work is necessary because the public must be protected at all times.

Education/Training

Education requirements range from a high school diploma to a college degree. Most police and detectives must graduate from their agency's training academy before completing a period of on-the-job training. Candidates must be U.S. citizens, usually at least 21 years old, and able to meet rigorous physical and personal qualification standards. A felony conviction or drug use may disqualify a candidate.

Education. Police and detective applicants must have at least a high school diploma or equivalent, although many federal agencies and some police departments require some college coursework or a college degree. Many community colleges, 4-year colleges, and universities offer programs in law enforcement and criminal justice, and agencies may offer financial assistance to officers who pursue these, or related, degrees. Knowledge of a foreign language is an asset in many federal agencies and geographical regions.

Fish and game wardens applying for federal jobs with the U.S. Fish & Wildlife Service typically need a college degree; and those applying to work for a state's natural resources department often need a high school diploma or some college study in a related field, such as biology or natural resources management.

Federal agencies typically require a bachelor's degree. For example, FBI and DEA special agent applicants are often college graduates.

State and local agencies encourage applicants to continue their education after high school, by taking courses and training related to law enforcement. Many applicants for entry-level police jobs have taken some college classes, and a significant number are college graduates. Many community colleges, 4-year colleges, and universities offer programs in law enforcement and criminal justice. Many agencies offer financial assistance to officers who pursue these or related degrees.

Training. Candidates for appointment usually attend a training academy before becoming an officer. Training includes classroom instruction in state and local laws and constitutional law, civil rights, and police ethics. Recruits also receive training and supervised experience in areas such as patrol, traffic control, firearm use, self-defense, first aid, and emergency response.

Federal law enforcement agents undergo extensive training, usually at the U.S. Marine Corps base in Quantico, Virginia, or at a Federal Law Enforcement Training Center.

Work Experience in a Related Occupation. Detectives normally begin their careers as police officers before being promoted to detective.

FBI special agent applicants typically must have at least 3 years of professional work experience in areas ranging from computer science to accounting.

Other Experience. Some police departments have cadet programs for people interested in a career in law enforcement who do not yet meet age requirements for becoming an officer. These cadets do clerical work and attend classes until they reach the minimum age requirement and can apply for a position with the regular force. Military or police experience may be considered beneficial for potential cadets.

Employment Projections Data for Police and Detectives

Occupational Title	SOC Code	Employment, 2014	Projected Employment, 2024	Change, 2014–2024 Percent	Change, 2014–2024 Numeric
Police and detectives	—	806,400	839,500	4	33,100
Detectives and criminal investigators	33-3021	116,700	115,300	-1	-1,400
Fish and game wardens	33-3031	6,200	6,300	2	100
Police and sheriff's patrol officers	33-3051	680,000	714,200	5	34,200
Transit and railroad police	33-3052	3,600	3,700	4	100

Source: U.S. Bureau of Labor Statistics, Employment Projections Program

Similar Occupations. This table shows a list of occupations with job duties that are similar to those of police and detectives.

Occupations	Entry-level Education	2014 Median Pay	Projected Job Growth	Average Annual Openings
Correctional Officers and Bailiffs	High school diploma or equivalent	$39,700	4%	1,790
EMTs and Paramedics	Postsecondary nondegree award	$31,700	24%	5,850
Firefighters	Postsecondary nondegree award	$45,970	5%	1,740
Private Detectives and Investigators	High school diploma or equivalent	$44,570	5%	180
Probation Officers and Correctional Treatment Specialists	Bachelor's degree	$49,060	4%	330
Security Guards and Gaming Surveillance Officers	High school diploma or equivalent	$24,470	5%	5,500

Cadet candidates must be U.S. citizens, usually be at least 21 years old, have a driver's license, and meet specific physical qualifications. Applicants may have to pass physical exams of vision, hearing, strength, and agility, as well as written exams. Previous work or military experience is often seen as a plus. Candidates typically go through a series of interviews and may be asked to take lie detector and drug tests. A felony conviction may disqualify a candidate.

Advancement. Police officers usually become eligible for promotion after a probationary period. Promotions to corporal, sergeant, lieutenant, and captain usually are made according to a candidate's position on a promotion list, as determined by scores on a written examination and on-the-job performance. In large departments, promotion may enable an officer to become a detective or to specialize in one type of police work, such as working with juveniles.

Important Qualities

Communication skills. Police, detectives, and fish and game wardens must be able to speak with people when gathering facts about a crime and to express details about a given incident in writing.

Empathy. Police officers need to understand the perspectives of a wide variety of people in their jurisdiction and have a willingness to help the public.

Good judgment. Police and detectives must be able to determine the best way to solve a wide array of problems quickly.

Leadership skills. Police officers must be comfortable with being a highly visible member of their community, as the public looks to them for assistance in emergency situations.

Perceptiveness. Officers, detectives, and fish and game wardens must be able to anticipate a person's reactions and understand why people act a certain way.

Physical stamina. Officers and detectives must be in good physical shape, both to pass required tests for entry into the field, and to keep up with the daily rigors of the job.

Physical strength. Police officers must be strong enough to physically apprehend offenders.

Pay

The median annual wage for police and detectives was $58,630 in May 2014. The median wage is the wage at which half the workers in an occupation earned more than that amount and half earned less. The lowest 10 percent earned less than $33,760, and the highest 10 percent earned more than $96,760.

Median annual wages for police and detectives in May 2014 were as follows:

Detectives and criminal investigators	$79,870
Police and sheriff's patrol officers	56,810
Transit and railroad police	51,690
Fish and game wardens	50,880

Job Outlook

Employment of police and detectives is projected to grow 4 percent from 2014 to 2024, slower than the average for all occupations.

While a continued desire for public safety is expected to result in a need for more officers, demand for employment is expected to vary depending on location, driven largely by local and state budgets. Even with crime rates falling in the last few years, demand for police services to maintain and improve public safety is expected to continue.

Job Prospects. Overall job prospects are expected to be good. Applicants with a bachelor's degree and law enforcement or military experience, especially investigative experience, as well as those who speak more than one language, should have the best job opportunities.

Because the level of government spending determines the level of employment for police and detectives, the number of job opportunities can vary from year to year and from place to place.

Contacts for More Information

For general information about sheriffs, visit
- National Sheriffs' Association (www.sheriffs.org)

For information about chiefs of police, visit
- International Association of Chiefs of Police (www.theiacp.org)

For more information about careers in state and local law enforcement, visit
- Bureau of Justice Assistance (www.bja.gov)
- International Association of Chiefs of Police (www.theiacp.org)

For more information about federal law enforcement, visit
- Bureau of Alcohol, Tobacco, Firearms and Explosives (www.atf.gov)
- Drug Enforcement Administration (www.dea.gov)
- Federal Bureau of Investigation (www.fbi.gov)
- U.S. Customs and Border Protection (www.cbp.gov)
- U.S. Department of Homeland Security (www.dhs.gov)
- U.S. Marshals Service (www.usmarshals.gov)
- United States Secret Service (www.secretservice.gov)
- U.S. Fish & Wildlife Service (www.fws.gov)

O*NET

- Detectives and Criminal Investigators (33-3021.00)
- Police Detectives (33-3021.01)
- Police Identification and Records Officers (33-3021.02)
- Criminal Investigators and Special Agents (33-3021.03)
- Immigration and Customs Inspectors (33-3021.05)
- Intelligence Analysts (33-3021.06)
- Fish and Game Wardens (33-3031.00)

- ➤ Police and Sheriff's Patrol Officers (33-3051.00)
- ➤ Police Patrol Officers (33-3051.01)
- ➤ Sheriffs and Deputy Sheriffs (33-3051.03)
- ➤ Transit and Railroad Police (33-3052.00)

Private Detectives and Investigators

- **2014 Median Pay** .... $44,570 per year $21.43 per hour
- **Typical Entry-Level Education** .... High school diploma or equivalent
- **Work Experience in a Related Occupation** .... Less than 5 years
- **On-the-job Training**...Moderate-term on-the-job training
- **Number of Jobs, 2014** 34,900
- **Job Outlook, 2014–24** .... 5% (As fast as average)
- **Employment Change, 2014–24** 1,800

Private detectives and investigators may use many methods to determine the facts in a case.

What Private Detectives and Investigators Do

Private detectives and investigators search for information about legal, financial, and personal matters. They offer many services, such as verifying people's backgrounds and statements, finding missing persons, and investigating computer crimes.

Duties. Private detectives and investigators typically do the following:

- Interview people to gather information
- Search public or court records to uncover clues
- Conduct surveillance
- Collect evidence to present in court or to a client
- Verify employment and income
- Check for civil judgments and criminal history
- Investigate computer crimes and information theft

Private detectives and investigators offer many services for individuals, attorneys, and businesses. Examples are performing background checks, investigating employees for possible theft from a company, proving or disproving infidelity in a divorce case, and helping to locate a missing person.

Private detectives and investigators use a variety of tools when researching the facts in a case. Much of their work is done with a computer, allowing them to obtain information such as telephone numbers, details about social networks, descriptions of online activities, and records of a person's prior arrests. They make phone calls to verify facts and interview people when conducting a background investigation.

Investigators may go undercover to observe people and to obtain information.

Detectives also conduct surveillance when investigating a case. They may watch locations, such as a person's home or office, often from a hidden position. Using cameras and binoculars, detectives gather information on people of interest.

Detectives and investigators must be mindful of the law when conducting investigations. Because they lack police authority, their work must be done with the same authority as a private citizen. As a result, they must have a good understanding of federal, state, and local laws, such as privacy laws, and other legal issues affecting their work. Otherwise, evidence they collect may not be usable in court and they could face prosecution.

The following are examples of types of private detectives and investigators:

Computer forensics investigators specialize in recovering, analyzing, and presenting information from computers to be used as evidence. Many focus on recovering deleted emails and documents.

Legal investigators help prepare criminal defenses, verify facts in civil lawsuits, locate witnesses, and serve legal documents. They often work for lawyers and law firms.

Corporate investigators conduct internal and external investigations for corporations. Internally, they may investigate drug use in the workplace or ensure that expense accounts are not abused. Externally, they may try to identify and stop criminal schemes, such as fraudulent billing by a supplier.

Financial investigators may be hired to collect financial information on individuals and companies attempting to make large financial transactions. These investigators are often certified public accountants (CPAs) who work closely with investment bankers and other accountants. Investigators might search for assets to recover damages awarded by a court in fraud and theft cases.

Work Environment

Private detectives and investigators held about 34,900 jobs in 2014. The industries that employed the most private detectives and investigators were as follows:

Investigation, guard, and armored car services	30%
Government	7
Finance and insurance	6
Retail trade	6

Nearly 1 in 4 private detectives and investigators were self-employed in 2014.

Private detectives and investigators work in many environments, depending on the case. Some spend more time in offices, performing computer searches and making phone calls. Others spend more time in the field, conducting interviews or performing surveillance.

Although investigators often work alone, some work with others while conducting surveillance or carrying out large, complicated assignments.

Some of the work can involve confrontation, and some situations may call for the investigator to be armed. In most cases, however, a weapon is not necessary because private detectives and investigators' purpose is to gather information, not to enforce laws or apprehend criminals.

Private detectives and investigators may have to work with demanding, and sometimes distraught, clients.

Work Schedules. Private detectives and investigators often work irregular hours because they conduct surveillance and contact people outside of normal work hours. They may work early mornings, evenings, weekends, and holidays.

In addition, they may have to work outdoors or from a vehicle, in all kinds of weather, depending on what the subject of the investigation is doing.

Education/Training

Private detectives and investigators typically need several years of work experience in law enforcement or the military. Workers must also have a high school diploma, and the vast majority of states require private detectives and investigators to have a license.

Education. Education requirements vary greatly with the job, but most jobs require a high school diploma. Some, though, may require a 2- or 4-year degree in a field such as criminal justice or police science.

Corporate investigators typically need a bachelor's degree. Often, coursework in finance, accounting, and business is preferred. Because many financial investigators have an accounting background, they typically have a bachelor's degree in accounting or a related field and may be certified public accountants (CPAs).

Computer forensics investigators often need a bachelor's degree in computer science or criminal justice. Some colleges and universities now offer certificate programs in computer forensics, and others offer a bachelor's or a master's degree.

Training. Most private detectives and investigators learn through on-the-job experience, often lasting several years.

Although new investigators must learn how to gather information, additional training depends on the type of firm that hires them. For instance, at an insurance company, a new investigator will learn on the job how to recognize insurance fraud. Corporate investigators hired by large companies may receive formal training in business practices, management structure, and various finance-related topics.

Because computer forensics specialists need to both use computers and possess investigative skills, extensive training may be required. Many learn their trade while working for a law enforcement agency for several years. At work, they are taught how to gather evidence and spot computer-related crimes.

Continuing education is important for computer forensics investigators because they work with changing technologies. Investigators must learn the latest methods of fraud detection and new software programs. Many accomplish this task by attending conferences and courses offered by software vendors and professional associations.

Work Experience in a Related Occupation. Private detectives and investigators typically must have previous work experience, usually in law enforcement, the military, or federal intelligence. Those in such jobs, who are frequently able to retire after 20 or 25 years of service, may become private detectives or investigators in a second career.

Other private detectives and investigators previously may have worked for insurance or collections companies, as paralegals, in finance, or in accounting.

Licenses, Certifications, and Registrations. The vast majority of states require private detectives and investigators to have a license. Requirements vary with the state. Professional Investigator Magazine has links to each state's licensing requirements. Because laws often change, jobseekers should verify the licensing laws related to private investigators with the state and locality in which they want to work.

In most states, detectives and investigators who carry handguns must meet additional requirements.

Although there are no licenses specific to computer forensics investigators, some states require them to be licensed private investigators. Even in states and localities where they are not required to be licensed, having a private investigator license is useful because it allows computer forensics investigators to perform related investigative work.

Candidates may also obtain certification, although it is not required for employment. Still, becoming certified through professional organizations can demonstrate competence and may help candidates advance in their careers.

For investigators who specialize in negligence or criminal defense investigation, the National Association of Legal Investigators offers the Certified Legal Investigator certification. For investigators who specialize in security, ASIS International offers the Professional Certified Investigator certification.

Important Qualities

Communication skills. Private detectives and investigators must listen carefully and ask appropriate questions when interviewing a person of interest.

Decision-making skills. Private detectives and investigators must be able to think on their feet and make quick decisions, based on the limited information that they have at a given time.

Inquisitiveness. Private detectives and investigators must want to ask questions and search for the truth.

Patience. Private detectives and investigators may have to spend long periods conducting surveillance while waiting for an event to occur. Investigations may take a long time, and they may not provide a resolution quickly—or at all.

Median Annual Wages, May 2014

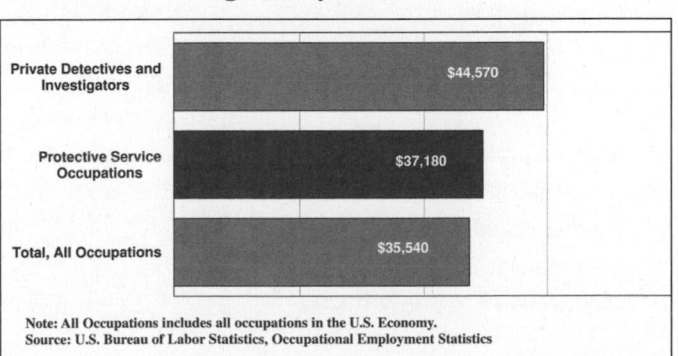

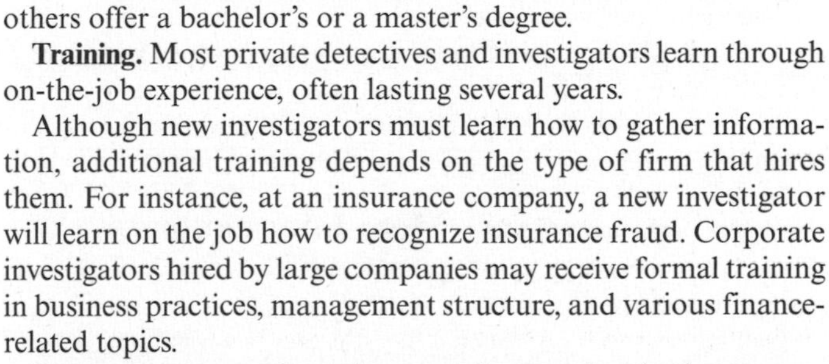

Note: All Occupations includes all occupations in the U.S. Economy.
Source: U.S. Bureau of Labor Statistics, Occupational Employment Statistics

Percent Change in Employment, Projected 2014–2024

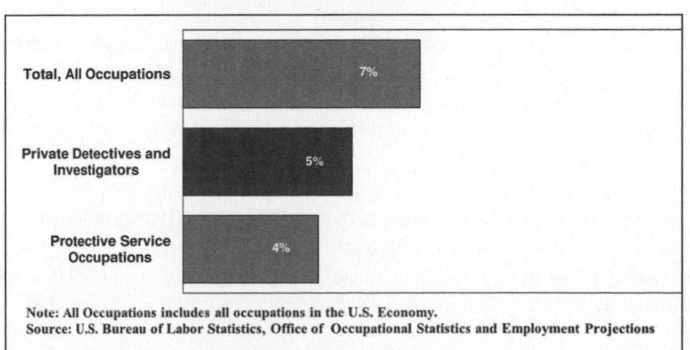

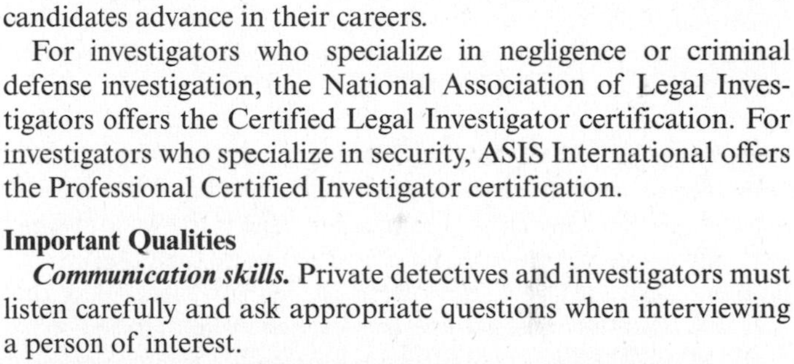

Note: All Occupations includes all occupations in the U.S. Economy.
Source: U.S. Bureau of Labor Statistics, Office of Occupational Statistics and Employment Projections

Employment Projections Data for Private Detectives and Investigators

Occupational Title	SOC Code	Employment, 2014	Projected Employment, 2024	Change, 2014–2024 Percent	Change, 2014–2024 Numeric
Private detectives and investigators	33-9021	34,900	36,700	5	1,800

Source: U.S. Bureau of Labor Statistics, Employment Projections Program

Similar Occupations. This table shows a list of occupations with job duties that are similar to those of private detectives and investigators.

Occupations	Entry-level Education	2014 Median Pay	Projected Job Growth	Average Annual Openings
Accountants and Auditors	Bachelor's degree	$65,940	11%	14,240
Bill and Account Collectors	High school diploma or equivalent	$33,700	-6%	-1,960
Claims Adjusters, Appraisers, Examiners, and Investigators	See Education/Training	$62,300	3%	960
Financial Analysts	Bachelor's degree	$78,620	12%	3,230
Financial Examiners	Bachelor's degree	$76,310	10%	370
Personal Financial Advisors	Bachelor's degree	$81,060	30%	7,390
Police and Detectives	See Education/Training	$58,630	4%	3,310
Security Guards and Gaming Surveillance Officers	High school diploma or equivalent	$24,470	5%	5,500

Resourcefulness. Private detectives and investigators must work persistently with whatever leads they have, no matter how limited, to determine the next step toward their goal. They sometimes need to anticipate what a person of interest will do next.

Pay

The median annual wage for private detectives and investigators was $44,570 in May 2014. The median wage is the wage at which half the workers in an occupation earned more than that amount and half earned less. The lowest 10 percent earned less than $27,000, and the highest 10 percent earned more than $85,560.

In May 2014, the median annual wages for private detectives and investigators in the top industries in which they worked were as follows:

Finance and insurance	$52,090
Government	45,150
Investigation, guard, and armored car services	43,400
Retail trade	32,630

Job Outlook

Employment of private detectives and investigators is projected to grow 5 percent from 2014 to 2024, about as fast as the average for all occupations.

Technological advances have led to an increase in cybercrimes, such as identity theft, credit card fraud, and spamming. Internet scams, as well as other types of financial and insurance fraud, create demand for investigative services, particularly by the legal services industry.

Background checks will continue to be a source of work for many investigators, because both employers and personal contacts wish to verify a person's credibility.

Job Prospects. Strong competition for jobs can be expected because private detective and investigator careers attract many qualified people, including relatively young retirees from law enforcement and the military.

The best job opportunities will be for entry-level positions in detective agencies. Candidates with related work experience, as well as those with strong interviewing skills and familiarity with computers, may find more job opportunities than others.

Contacts for More Information

For more information about private detectives and investigators, including information on certification, visit

➤ National Association of Legal Investigators (www.nalionline.org)
➤ ASIS International (www.asisonline.org)

For information about state licensing requirements, visit

➤ Professional Investigator Magazine (www.pimagazine.com/links/pi-license-requirements)

O*NET

➤ Private Detectives and Investigators (33-9021.00)

Security Guards and Gaming Surveillance Officers

- **2014 Median Pay** .... $24,470 per year, $11.76 per hour
- **Typical Entry-Level Education** .... High school diploma or equivalent
- **Work Experience in a Related Occupation** .... None
- **On-the-job Training** .... Short-term on-the-job training
- **Number of Jobs, 2014** 1,102,500
- **Job Outlook, 2014–24** .... 5% (As fast as average)
- **Employment Change, 2014–24** 55,000

Guards assigned to static security positions usually stay at one location for a specified length of time.

What Security Guards and Gaming Surveillance Officers Do

Security guards and gaming surveillance officers patrol and protect property against theft, vandalism, terrorism, and illegal activity.

Duties. Security guards and gaming surveillance officers typically do the following:

- Protect and enforce laws on an employer's property
- Monitor alarms and closed-circuit TV (CCTV) cameras
- Control access for employees and visitors
- Conduct security checks over a specified area
- Write reports on what they observed while on duty
- Serve as witnesses for court testimony
- Detain violators

Security guards, also called *security officers*, protect property, enforce rules on the property, and deter criminal activity. Some guards are assigned a stationary position from which they monitor alarms or surveillance cameras. Other guards are assigned a patrol area where they conduct security checks.

Gaming surveillance officers and gaming investigators act as security agents for casinos. Using audio and video equipment in an observation room, they watch casino operations for suspicious activities, such as cheating and theft, and monitor compliance with rules, regulations, and laws. They maintain and organize recordings from security cameras, which are sometimes used as evidence in police investigations.

Guards and officers must remain alert, looking out for anything unusual. In an emergency, they are required to call for assistance from police, fire, or ambulance services. Some security guards are armed.

A security guard's responsibilities vary from one employer to another. In retail stores, guards protect people, records, merchandise, money, and equipment. They may work with undercover store detectives to prevent theft by customers and employees, detain shoplifting suspects until the police arrive, and patrol parking lots.

In office buildings, banks, hotels, and hospitals, guards maintain order and protect the organization's customers, staff, and property.

Guards who work in museums and art galleries protect paintings and exhibits by watching people and inspecting the contents of patrons' handbags.

In factories, government buildings, and military bases, security guards protect workers and equipment and check the credentials of people and vehicles entering and leaving the premises.

Guards working in parks and at sports stadiums control crowds, supervise parking and seating, and direct traffic.

Security guards stationed at the entrances to bars and nightclubs keep underage people from entering, collect cover charges, and maintain order among customers.

Security guards working in schools and universities patrol the buildings and grounds, looking for suspicious activity.

Work Environment

Security guards and gaming surveillance officers held about 1.1 million jobs in 2014, of which nearly all were held by security guards.

Security guards work in a wide variety of places, including public buildings, stores, and office buildings. Gaming surveillance officers and investigators mostly work in gaming facilities operated by local governments. They are employed only in those states, and on those Indian reservations, where gambling is legal.

Security guards held nearly 1.1 million jobs in 2014. The industries that employed the most security guards in 2014 were as follows:

Investigation, guard, and armored car services	58%
Educational services; state, local, and private	6
Health care and social assistance	6

Gaming surveillance officers held about 7,000 jobs in 2014. The industries that employed the most gaming surveillance officers in 2014 were as follows:

Gambling industries (except casino hotels)	38%
Casino hotels	30
Local government, excluding education and hospitals	20

Most security guards spend considerable time on their feet, either at a single post or patrolling buildings and grounds. Some may sit for long periods behind a counter or in a guardhouse at the entrance to a gated facility or community.

Guards who work during the day may have a great deal of contact with other employees and the public.

Although the work can be routine, it can also be hazardous, particularly when an altercation occurs.

Most gaming surveillance officers sit behind a desk observing gamers on video surveillance equipment.

Injuries and Illnesses. Security guards have a higher rate of injuries and illnesses than the national average. Although the work is mostly routine, the work can also be dangerous. As a result, guards must always be alert for threats to themselves and the people and property they are protecting.

Work Schedules. Security guards and gaming surveillance officers usually work in shifts of 8 hours, or longer, with rotating schedules.

Education/Training

Most security guard jobs require a high school diploma. Gaming surveillance officers sometimes need experience with security and video surveillance. Most states require guards to be registered with the state, especially if they carry a firearm.

Median Annual Wages, May 2014

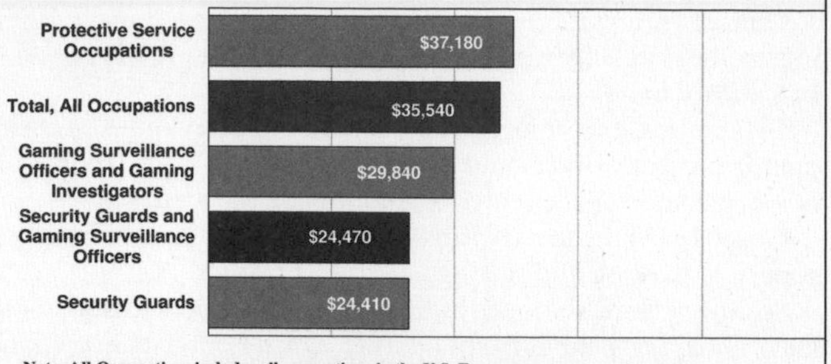

Note: All Occupations includes all occupations in the U.S. Economy.
Source: U.S. Bureau of Labor Statistics, Occupational Employment Statistics

Percent Change in Employment, Projected 2014–2024

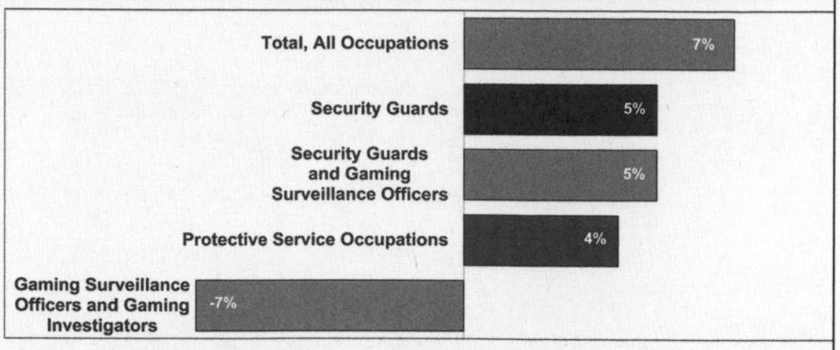

Note: All Occupations includes all occupations in the U.S. Economy.
Source: U.S. Bureau of Labor Statistics, Office of Occupational Statistics and Employment Projections

Education. Security guards generally need a high school diploma or equivalent, although some jobs may not have any education requirements. Gaming surveillance officers also need a high school diploma or equivalent and may need experience with video surveillance technology depending upon assignment.

Training. Although most employers provide instruction for newly hired guards, the amount of training they receive varies. Most guards, however, learn their job in a few weeks. During those few weeks, training from their employer typically covers emergency procedures, detention of suspected criminals, and proper communication.

Many states recommend that security guards receive approximately 8 hours of pre-assignment training, 8–16 hours of on-the-job training, and 8 hours of annual training. This may include training in protection, public relations, report writing, deterring crises, first aid, and other specialized training related to the guard's assignment.

Training is more rigorous for armed guards because they require weapons training. Armed guards may be tested periodically in the use of firearms.

For gaming surveillance officers and investigators, some employers prefer candidates with previous work experience in casinos or individuals with a background in law enforcement. Experience with video technology can also be helpful in using surveillance systems and software.

Drug testing may be required as a condition of employment and randomly during employment.

Licenses, Certifications, and Registrations. Although registration requirements vary by state, basic qualifications for candidates are as follows:

- Be at least 18 years old
- Pass a background check
- Complete training

Guards who carry weapons usually must be registered by the appropriate government authority. Armed guard positions have more stringent background checks and entry requirements than those of unarmed guards. Rigorous hiring and screening programs, including background, criminal record, and fingerprint checks, are required for armed guards in most states.

Some jobs may also require a driver's license.

Advancement. Some guards advance to supervisory or security manager positions. Those with experience or postsecondary education should have an advantage. Armed security guards have a greater potential for advancement and enjoy higher earnings.

Some guards with management skills open their own security guard business. Guards can also move to an organization that needs higher levels of security, which may result in more prestige or higher pay.

Important Qualities

Decision-making skills. Guards and officers must be able to quickly determine the best course of action when a dangerous situation arises.

Patience. Security guards and officers may need to spend long periods standing and observing their environment without distractions.

Observation skills. Guards and officers must be alert and aware of their surroundings, and be able to quickly recognize anything out of the ordinary.

Physical strength. Guards must be strong enough to apprehend offenders and to handle emergency situations.

Pay

The median annual wage for gaming surveillance officers and gaming investigators was $29,840 in May 2014. The median wage is the wage at which half the workers in an occupation earned more than that amount and half earned less. The lowest 10 percent earned less than $20,850, and the highest 10 percent earned more than $47,740.

The median annual wage for security guards was $24,410 in May 2014. The lowest 10 percent earned less than $17,720, and the highest 10 percent earned more than $44,200.

Employment Projections Data for Security Guards and Gaming Surveillance Officers

Occupational Title	SOC Code	Employment, 2014	Projected Employment, 2024	Change, 2014–2024 Percent	Change, 2014–2024 Numeric
Security guards and gaming surveillance officers	—	1,102,500	1,157,500	5	55,000
Gaming surveillance officers and gaming investigators	33-9031	7,000	6,600	-7	-500
Security guards	33-9032	1,095,400	1,150,900	5	55,500

Source: U.S. Bureau of Labor Statistics, Employment Projections Program

Similar Occupations. This table shows a list of occupations with job duties that are similar to those of security guards and gaming surveillance officers.

Occupations	Entry-level Education	2014 Median Pay	Projected Job Growth	Average Annual Openings
Correctional Officers and Bailiffs	High school diploma or equivalent	$39,700	4%	1,790
Gaming Services Workers	High school diploma or equivalent	$19,940	1%	100
Police and Detectives	See Education/Training	$58,630	4%	3,310
Private Detectives and Investigators	High school diploma or equivalent	$44,570	5%	180

Job Outlook

Overall employment of security guards and gaming surveillance officers is projected to grow 5 percent from 2014 to 2024, about as fast as the average for all occupations. Employment growth will vary by occupation.

Employment of security guards is projected to grow 5 percent from 2014 to 2024, about as fast as the average for all occupations. Security guards will continue to be needed to protect both people and property because of concerns about crime, vandalism, and terrorism.

Employment of gaming surveillance officers and investigators is projected to decline 7 percent from 2014 to 2024. Although states continue to legalize gambling and casinos continue to grow in number, advances in video surveillance and anti-cheating technology may limit the employment of gaming surveillance officers and investigators.

Job Prospects. Overall job opportunities are projected to be excellent, especially for security guards. The large size of the occupation and the number of workers who leave the occupation each year may result in many job openings. However, there will be more competition for higher paying positions that require more training and experience.

Candidates who have experience with video surveillance equipment should have the best job prospects in the gaming industry. Those with a background in law enforcement will also have an advantage.

Contacts for More Information

The *Handbook* does not have contacts for more information for this occupation.

O*NET

- Gaming Surveillance Officers and Gaming Investigators (33-9031.00)
- Security Guards (33-9032.00)

Advertising Sales Agents

- **2014 Median Pay** .... $47,890 per year
  $23.02 per hour
- **Typical Entry-Level Education** .... High school diploma or equivalent
- **Work Experience in a Related Occupation** .... None
- **On-the-job Training**...Moderate-term on-the-job training
- **Number of Jobs, 2014** 167,900
- **Job Outlook, 2014–24** .... -3% (Decline)
- **Employment Change, 2014–24** .... -4,500

Bringing in new clients is an important part of an advertising sales agent's job.

What Advertising Sales Agents Do

Advertising sales agents, also called *advertising sales representatives*, sell advertising space to businesses and individuals. They contact potential clients, make sales presentations, and maintain client accounts.

Duties. Advertising sales agents typically do the following:

- Locate and contact potential clients to offer their firm's advertising services
- Explain to clients how specific types of advertising will help promote their products or services in the most effective way
- Provide clients with estimates of the costs of advertising products or services
- Process all correspondence and paperwork related to accounts
- Prepare and deliver sales presentations to new and existing clients
- Inform clients of available options for advertising art, formats, or features and provide samples of previous work for other clients
- Deliver advertising or illustration proofs to clients for approval
- Prepare promotional plans, sales literature, media kits, and sales contracts
- Recommend appropriate sizes and formats for advertising

Advertising sales agents work outside the office occasionally, meeting with clients and prospective clients at their places of business. Some may make telephone sales calls as well—calling prospects, attempting to sell the media firm's advertising space or time, and arranging follow-up appointments with interested prospects.

A critical part of building relationships with clients is learning about their needs. Before the first meeting with a client, a sales agent gathers background information on the client's products, current clients, prospective clients, and the geographic area of the target market.

The sales agent then meets with the client to explain how specific types of advertising will help promote the client's products or services most effectively. If a client wishes to proceed, the advertising sales agent prepares and presents an advertising proposal to the client. The proposal may include an overview of the advertising medium to be used, sample advertisements, and cost estimates for the project.

Because of consolidation among media industries, agents are increasingly selling several types of ads in one package. For example, agents may sell ads that would be found in print editions, as well as online editions, of a particular publication, such as a newspaper.

In addition to maintaining sales and overseeing their accounts, advertising sales agents analyze sales statistics and prepare reports about clients' accounts. They keep up to date on industry trends by reading about both current and new products, and they monitor the sales, prices, and products of their competitors.

In many firms, the advertising sales agent drafts contracts, which specify the cost and the advertising work to be done. Agents also may continue to help the client, answering questions or addressing problems the client may have with the proposal.

In addition, sales agents may be responsible for developing sales tools, promotional plans, and media kits, all of which they use to help make a sale. In other cases, firms may have a marketing team that sales agents work with to develop these sales tools.

Work Environment

Advertising sales agents held about 167,900 jobs in 2014. The industries that employed the most advertising sales agents were as follows:

Advertising, public relations, and related services	36%
Newspaper publishers	14
Radio broadcasting	10
Television broadcasting	8
Other information services	4

Selling can be stressful because income and job security depend directly on agents' ability to keep and expand their client base.

Getting new accounts is an important part of the job, and agents may spend much of their time traveling to and visiting prospective advertisers and maintaining relationships with current clients.

Median Annual Wages, May 2014

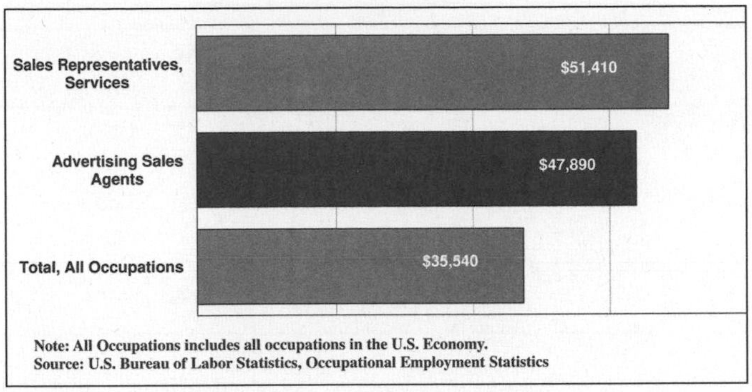

Percent Change in Employment, Projected 2014–2024

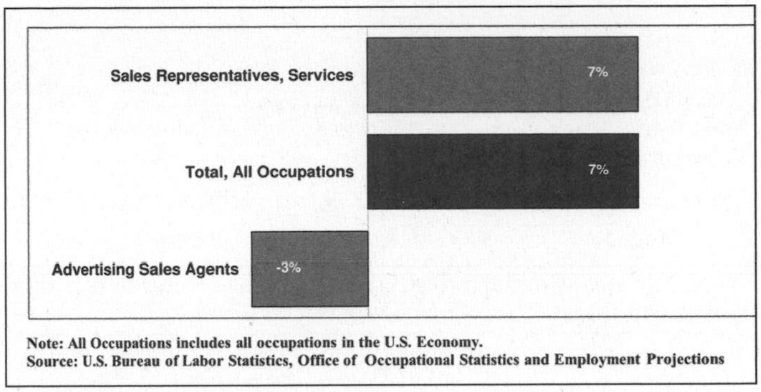

Sales agents also may work in their employer's offices and handle sales for walk-in clients or for those who call or email the firm to ask about advertising.

Work Schedules. Most advertising sales agents work full time. About 1 in 4 advertising sales agents worked more than 40 hours a week in 2014. Some work irregular hours and on weekends and holidays.

Education/Training

Although a high school diploma is typically enough education for an entry-level advertising sales position, some employers prefer applicants with a bachelor's degree. Proven sales success and communication skills are essential. Most training for advertising sales agents takes place on the job.

Education. Although a high school diploma is typically the minimum education requirement for an entry-level advertising sales position, a college degree is sometimes helpful. Publishing companies with large circulations and broadcasting stations with a large audience may prefer workers with at least a college degree. Courses in marketing, communications, business, and advertising are helpful. For those who have a proven record of successfully selling other products, educational requirements are not likely to be strict.

Training. Most training takes place on the job and can be either formal or informal. In the majority of cases, an experienced sales manager instructs a newly hired advertising sales agent who lacks sales experience. In this one-on-one environment, supervisors typically coach new hires and observe them as they make sales calls and contact clients. Supervisors then advise the new hires on ways to improve their interaction with clients. Employers may bring in consultants to lead formal training sessions when agents sell to a specialized market segment, such as automotive dealers or real estate professionals.

Advancement. Agents with proven leadership ability and a strong sales record may advance to supervisory and managerial positions, such as sales manager, account executive, and vice president of sales. Successful advertising sales agents may also advance to positions in other industries, such as corporate sales.

Important Qualities

Communication skills. Advertising sales agents must be persuasive during sales calls. In addition, they should listen to the client's desires and concerns, and recommend an appropriate advertising package.

Initiative. Advertising sales agents must actively seek new clients, keep in touch with current clients, and expand their client base, in order to meet sales quotas.

Organizational skills. Agents work with many clients, each of whom may be at a different stage in the sales process. Agents must be well organized to keep track of their clients and potential clients.

Self-confidence. Advertising sales agents should be confident when calling potential clients (making cold calls). Because potential clients are often unwilling to commit on a first call, agents frequently must continue making sales calls, even if rejected at first.

Pay

The median annual wage for advertising sales agents was $47,890 in May 2014. The median wage is the wage at which half the workers in an occupation earned more than that amount and half earned less. The lowest 10 percent earned less than $23,050, and the highest 10 percent earned more than $113,120.

In May 2014, the median annual wages for advertising sales agents in the top industries in which they worked were as follows:

Other information services	$56,960
Advertising, public relations, and related services	54,930
Television broadcasting	54,770
Radio broadcasting	41,590
Newspaper publishers	36,750

Performance-based pay, including bonuses and commissions, can make up a large portion of an advertising sales agent's earnings. Most employers pay some combination of salaries, commissions, and bonuses. Commissions usually are based on individual sales numbers. Bonuses may depend on individual performance, the performance of all sales workers in a group, or the performance of the entire firm.

Employment Projections Data for Advertising Sales Agents

Occupational Title	SOC Code	Employment, 2014	Projected Employment, 2024	Change, 2014–2024 Percent	Change, 2014–2024 Numeric
Advertising sales agents	41-3011	167,900	163,400	-3	-4,500

Source: U.S. Bureau of Labor Statistics, Employment Projections Program

Similar Occupations. This table shows a list of occupations with job duties that are similar to those of advertising sales agents.

Occupations	Entry-level Education	2014 Median Pay	Projected Job Growth	Average Annual Openings
Advertising, Promotions, and Marketing Managers	Bachelor's degree	$123,450	9%	1,970
Insurance Sales Agents	High school diploma or equivalent	$47,860	9%	4,350
Sales Managers	Bachelor's degree	$110,660	5%	1,900
Wholesale and Manufacturing Sales Representatives	See Education/Training	$58,380	7%	11,720

Job Outlook

Employment of advertising sales agents is projected to decline 3 percent from 2014 to 2024.

Media companies will continue to rely on advertising revenue for profitability, driving growth in the advertising industry as a whole. Employment growth of advertising sales agents will largely follow broader industry trends. For example, newspaper print advertising is expected to decline, but some of this decline will be offset by the sale of digital ads on newspaper websites. Therefore, although employment of advertising sales agents is projected to decline in the newspaper publishers industry, it is not projected to decline as fast as other occupations in that industry.

However, an increasing amount of advertising is expected to be concentrated in digital media, including online video ads, search engine ads, and other digital ads intended for cell phones or tablet-style computers. Digital advertising on the Internet allows companies to directly target potential consumers because websites usually are associated with the types of products that those consumers would like to buy. Digital advertising can be done without an advertising sales agent, possibly dampening growth for this occupation. For example, in some cases it can be done through a software application or search engine program. Therefore, an increase in digital advertising expenditures will not necessarily result in increased demand for advertising sales agents.

Job Prospects. Competition is expected to be strong for jobs as advertising sales agents. Applicants with experience in sales and those with a bachelor's degree should have the best opportunities.

Contacts for More Information

For information about advertising sales in the newspaper industry, visit

➤ Newspaper Association of America (www.naa.org)

For information about the radio advertising industry, visit

➤ Radio Advertising Bureau (www.rab.com)

O*NET

➤ Advertising Sales Agents (41-3011.00)

Cashiers

- **2014 Median Pay** .... $19,060 per year $9.16 per hour
- **Typical Entry-Level Education**......No formal educational credential
- **Work Experience in a Related Occupation**.............. None
- **On-the-job Training** ....Short-term on-the-job training
- **Number of Jobs, 2014** 3,424,200
- **Job Outlook, 2014–24**.............. 2% (Slower than average)
- **Employment Change, 2014–24** 67,000

What Cashiers Do

Cashiers process payments from customers purchasing goods and services.

Duties. Cashiers typically do the following:

- Greet customers
- Scan or register customers' purchases
- Accept payments from customers and give change and receipts
- Bag or wrap customers' purchases
- Process returns and exchanges of merchandise
- Answer customers' questions and provide information about store policies
- Help customers sign up for store rewards programs or credit cards
- Count the money in their register at the beginning and end of each shift

In some establishments, cashiers have to check the age of their customers when selling age-restricted products, such as alcohol and tobacco. Some cashiers may have duties not directly related to sales and customer service, such as mopping floors, taking out the trash, and other custodial tasks. Others may stock shelves or mark prices on items.

Cashiers must be friendly and courteous when interacting with customers.

Median Hourly Wages, May 2014

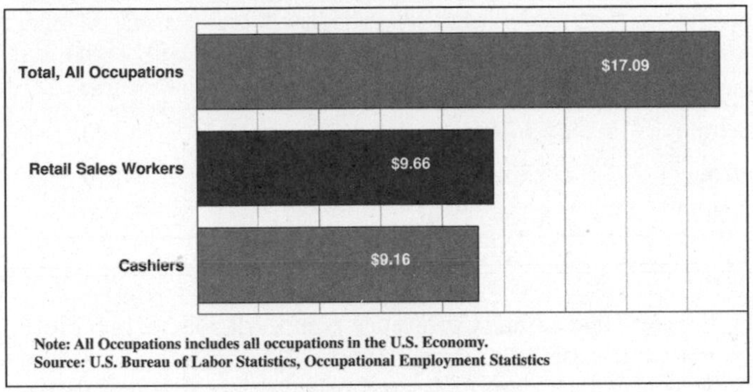

Percent Change in Employment, Projected 2014–2024

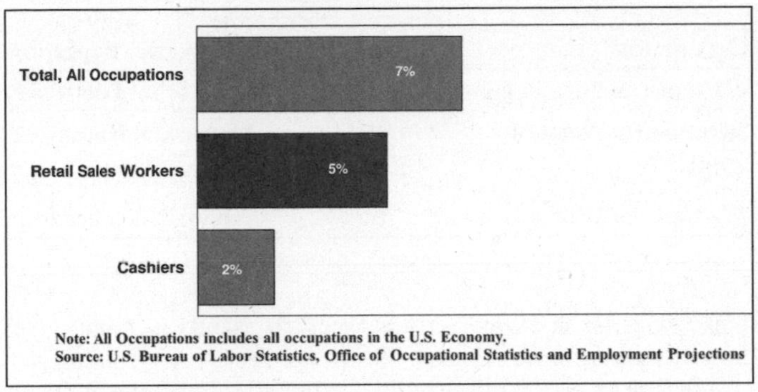

Cashiers use scanners, registers, or calculators to process payments and returns or exchanges of merchandise.

Work Environment

Cashiers held about 3.4 million jobs in 2014. The industries that employed the most cashiers were as follows:

Grocery stores	24%
Gasoline stations	17
Other general merchandise stores	12
Restaurants and other eating places	8
Department stores	6

Most cashiers work in retail establishments such as grocery stores, gasoline stations, and other general merchandise stores.

The work is often repetitive, and cashiers spend most of their time standing behind counters or checkout stands. Dealing with dissatisfied customers can be stressful.

Work Schedules. Cashiers' work hours vary by employer, and sometimes require them to work during weekends and holidays. Some cashiers employed in establishments that operate 24 hours a day, such as gasoline stations, work overnight shifts. Part-time work is common.

Employers may restrict the use of time off from Thanksgiving through early January because that is the busiest time of year for most retailers.

Education/Training

Cashiers are trained on the job. There are no formal education requirements to become a cashier.

Education. Although most jobs for cashiers have no specific education requirements, some employers may prefer applicants with a high school diploma or equivalent. Cashiers should have a basic knowledge of mathematics, because they need to be able to make change and count the money in their registers.

Training. Cashiers receive on-the-job training, which may last a few weeks. An experienced worker typically helps new cashiers learn how to operate equipment such as scanners or registers.

Advancement. Working as a cashier is often a steppingstone to other careers in retail. For example, with experience, cashiers may become customer service representatives, retail sales workers, or sales managers.

Important Qualities

Communication skills. Cashiers must pay attention to customers' questions and explain pricing.

Customer-service skills. Cashiers must be courteous and friendly when helping customers.

Dexterity. Cashiers use their hands to operate registers and scan purchases.

Integrity. Cashiers must calculate payments accurately and be trusted to process customers' financial information.

Patience. Cashiers must be able to remain calm when interacting with customers.

Physical stamina. Cashiers stand for long periods.

Pay

The median hourly wage for cashiers was $9.16 in May 2014. The median wage is the wage at which half the workers in an occupation earned more than that amount and half earned less. The lowest 10 percent earned less than $7.98, and the highest 10 percent earned more than $13.48.

In May 2014, the median hourly wages for cashiers in the top industries in which they worked were as follows:

Grocery stores	$9.27
Other general merchandise stores	9.18
Department stores	9.01
Gasoline stations	8.96
Restaurants and other eating places	8.90

Many beginning or inexperienced cashiers earn the federal minimum wage ($7.25 per hour as of July, 24, 2009), but many states set minimum wages higher than the federal minimum.

Job Outlook

Employment of cashiers is projected to grow 2 percent from 2014 to 2024, slower than the average for all occupations. While retail sales are expected to increase over the next decade, employment growth of cashiers should be limited due to advances in

Employment Projections Data for Cashiers

Occupational Title	SOC Code	Employment, 2014	Projected Employment, 2024	Change, 2014–2024 Percent	Change, 2014–2024 Numeric
Cashiers	41-2011	3,424,200	3,491,100	2	67,000

Source: U.S. Bureau of Labor Statistics, Employment Projections Program

Similar Occupations. This table shows a list of occupations with job duties that are similar to those of cashiers.

Occupations	Entry-level Education	2014 Median Pay	Projected Job Growth	Average Annual Openings
Customer Service Representatives	High school diploma or equivalent	$31,200	10%	25,290
Retail Sales Workers	No formal educational credential	$21,670	7%	33,100
Tellers	High school diploma or equivalent	$25,760	-8%	-4,000
Waiters and Waitresses	No formal educational credential	$18,730	3%	6,890

technology, such as self-service checkout stands in retail stores and increasing online sales.

Job Prospects. Job opportunities should be very good, primarily because of the need to replace the large number of workers who leave the occupation each year.

Historically, workers under the age of 25 have filled many of the openings for cashiers. In 2014, nearly half of all cashiers were 24 years old or younger.

Contacts for More Information

The *Handbook* does not have contacts for more information for this occupation.

O*NET

➤ Cashiers (41-2011.00)

Insurance Sales Agents

- **2014 Median Pay** .... $47,860 per year $23.01 per hour
- **Typical Entry-Level Education** .... High school diploma or equivalent
- **Work Experience in a Related Occupation** .... None
- **On-the-job Training**...Moderate-term on-the-job training
- **Number of Jobs, 2014** 466,100
- **Job Outlook, 2014–24** .... 9% (Faster than average)
- **Employment Change, 2014–24** 43,500

What Insurance Sales Agents Do

Insurance sales agents contact potential customers and sell one or more types of insurance. Insurance sales agents explain various insurance policies and help clients choose plans that suit them.

Duties. Insurance sales agents typically do the following:

- Call potential clients in order to expand their own customer base
- Interview prospective clients to get information about their financial resources and discuss existing coverage
- Explain the features of various policies
- Analyze clients' current insurance policies and suggest additions or other changes
- Customize insurance programs to suit individual clients
- Handle policy renewals
- Maintain electronic and paper records

Insurance sales agents commonly sell one or more types of insurance, such as property and casualty, life, health, and long-term care insurance.

Property and casualty insurance agents sell policies that protect people and businesses from financial loss resulting from automobile accidents, fire, theft, and other events that can damage property. For businesses, property and casualty insurance also covers workers' compensation claims, product liability claims, or medical malpractice claims.

Life insurance agents specialize in selling policies that pay beneficiaries when a policyholder dies. Life insurance agents also sell annuities that promise a retirement income.

Health and long-term care insurance agents sell policies that cover the costs of medical care and assisted-living services in old age. They also may sell dental insurance and short-term and long-term disability insurance.

Agents may specialize in any one of these products or function as generalists providing multiple products.

An increasing number of insurance sales agents offer their clients—especially those approaching retirement—comprehensive financial-planning services. Such services include retirement planning, estate planning, and help in setting up pension plans for businesses. In addition to offering insurance, these agents may become licensed to sell mutual funds, variable annuities, and other securities. This practice is most common with life insurance agents who already sell annuities, but many property and casualty agents also sell financial products. For more information on agents who sell financial products, see the profile on securities, commodities, and financial services sales agents.

Many agents spend a lot of time marketing their services and creating their own base of clients. They do this in a variety of ways, including making "cold" sales calls to people who are not current clients.

Potential clients often use comparison shopping tools online to learn about different policies and obtain information from insurance companies. Clients can either purchase a policy directly from the website or contact the company to speak with a sales agent.

Insurance agents also find new clients through referrals by current clients. Keeping clients happy so that they recommend the agent to others is a key to success for insurance sales agents.

Insurance agents may work for a single insurance company or an insurance brokerage.

Captive agents are insurance sales agents who work exclusively for one insurance company. They can only sell policies provided by the company that employs them.

Independent insurance agents work for insurance brokerages, selling the policies of several companies. They match insurance policies for their clients with the company that offers the best rate and coverage.

Work Environment

Insurance sales agents held about 466,100 jobs in 2014. About 82 percent of insurance sales agents worked in the insurance carriers and related activities industry, and about 1 in 7 were self-employed. Most worked for insurance agencies and brokerages, which sell the

An increasing number of insurance sales agents offer comprehensive financial planning services to their clients.

policies of several companies. Others worked directly for a single insurance carrier.

Most insurance sales agents work in offices, although some may spend time traveling to meet with clients. Their work environment varies with the type of company that employs them. Because some companies are small, agents may work alone or with only a few others.

Work Schedules. Insurance sales agents usually determine their own hours of work and often schedule evening and weekend appointments for the convenience of clients. Some sales agents meet with clients during business hours and then spend evenings doing paperwork and preparing presentations to prospective clients. Most agents work full time, and about 1 in 5 worked more than 40 hours per week in 2014.

Education/Training

Although most employers require agents to have a high school diploma, many agents have a bachelor's degree. Agents must be licensed in the states where they work.

Education. A high school diploma is the typical requirement for insurance sales agents, although a bachelor's degree can improve one's job prospects. Public-speaking classes can be useful in improving sales techniques, and often agents will have taken courses in business, finance, or economics. Business knowledge is also helpful for sales agents hoping to advance to a managerial position.

Training. Insurance sales agents learn many of their job duties on the job from other agents. Many employers have new agents shadow an experienced agent. This practice allows the new agent to learn how to conduct the company's business and to understand how the agency interacts with clients.

Employers also are increasingly placing greater emphasis on continuing professional education as the variety of financial products sold by insurance sales agents grows. Changes in tax laws, government benefits programs, and other state and federal regulations can affect the insurance needs of clients and the way in which agents conduct business. Agents can enhance their selling skills and broaden their knowledge of insurance and other financial services by taking courses at colleges and universities or by attending conferences and seminars sponsored by insurance organizations.

Licenses, Certifications, and Registrations. Insurance sales agents must have a license in the states where they work. Separate licenses are required for agents to sell life and health insurance and property and casualty insurance. In most states, licenses are issued only to applicants who complete specified courses and who pass state exams covering insurance fundamentals and state insurance laws. Most state licensing authorities also require agents to take continuing education courses focusing on insurance laws, consumer protection, ethics, and the technical details of various insurance policies.

As the demand for financial-planning services increases, many agents also choose to get licensed and certified to sell securities and other financial products. Licensing and certification requires substantial study time to pass an additional exam—either the Series 6 or Series 7 licensing exam, both of which are administered by the Financial Industry Regulatory Authority (FINRA). The Series 6 exam is for agents who want to sell only mutual funds and variable annuities. The Series 7 exam is the main FINRA series license, which qualifies agents as general securities sales representatives.

A number of organizations offer certifications that show an agent's expertise in insurance specialties. These certifications are

Median Annual Wages, May 2014

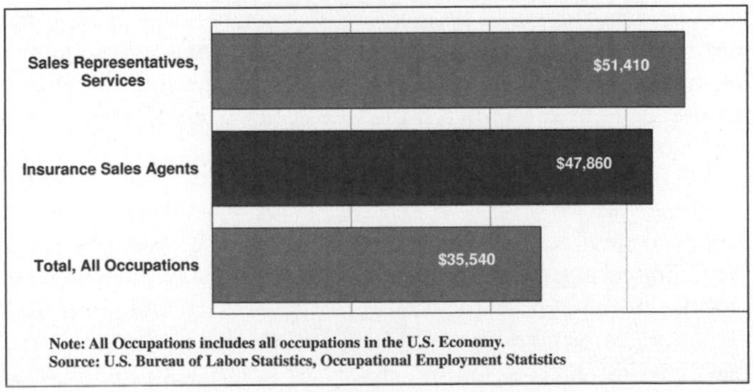

Percent Change in Employment, Projected 2014–2024

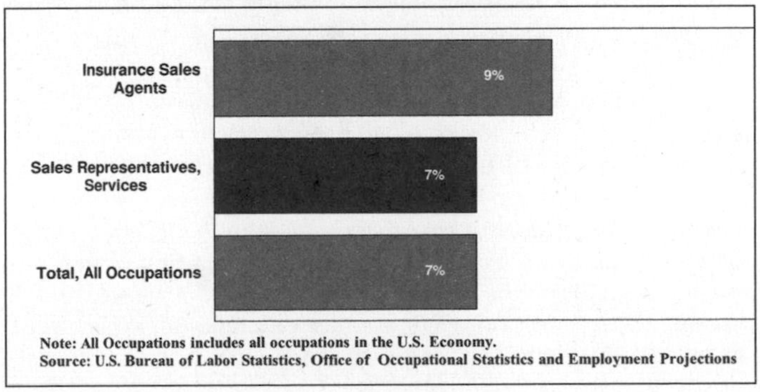

Employment Projections Data for Insurance Sales Agents

Occupational Title	SOC Code	Employment, 2014	Projected Employment, 2024	Change, 2014–2024	
				Percent	Numeric
Insurance sales agents..	41-3021	466,100	509,500	9	43,500

Source: U.S. Bureau of Labor Statistics, Employment Projections Program

Similar Occupations. This table shows a list of occupations with job duties that are similar to those of insurance sales agents.

Occupations	Entry-level Education	2014 Median Pay	Projected Job Growth	Average Annual Openings
Advertising Sales Agents	High school diploma or equivalent	$47,890	-3%	-450
Insurance Underwriters	Bachelor's degree	$64,220	-11%	-1,170
Personal Financial Advisors	Bachelor's degree	$81,060	30%	7,390
Real Estate Brokers and Sales Agents	High school diploma or equivalent	$43,430	3%	1,090
Sales Managers	Bachelor's degree	$110,660	5%	1,900
Securities, Commodities, and Financial Services Sales Agents	Bachelor's degree	$72,070	10%	3,250
Wholesale and Manufacturing Sales Representatives	See Education/Training	$58,380	7%	11,720

not required for employment, but they can give job candidates an advantage over other applicants. Certifications also can be a source of continuing education credit. For details on specific designations, contact The Institutes and The American College of Financial Services.

Important Qualities

Analytical skills. Insurance sales agents must evaluate the characteristics of each client to determine the appropriate insurance policy.

Communication skills. Insurance sales agents must be able to communicate effectively with customers by listening to their requests and suggesting suitable policies.

Initiative. Insurance sales agents need to actively seek out new customers to maintain a flow of commissions.

Self-confidence. Insurance sales agents should be confident when making "cold" calls (calls to prospective customers who have not been contacted before). They must speak clearly and persuasively and maintain their composure if rejected.

Pay

The median annual wage for insurance sales agents was $47,860 in May 2014. The median wage is the wage at which half the workers in an occupation earned more than that amount and half earned less. The lowest 10 percent earned less than $25,710, and the highest 10 percent earned more than $119,970.

Many independent agents are paid by commission only. Sales workers who are employees of an agency or an insurance carrier may be paid in one of three ways: salary only, salary plus commission, or salary plus bonus.

In general, commissions are the most common form of compensation, especially for experienced agents. The amount of the commission depends on the type and amount of insurance sold and on whether the transaction is a new policy or a renewal. When agents meet their sales goals or when an agency meets its profit goals, agents usually get bonuses. Some agents involved with financial planning receive a fee for their services rather than a commission.

Job Outlook

Employment of insurance sales agents is projected to grow 9 percent from 2014 to 2024, faster than the average for all occupations.

Because the profitability of insurance companies depends on a steady stream of new customers, the demand for insurance sales agents is expected to continue. Employment growth will likely be strongest for independent sales agents as insurance companies rely more on brokerages and less on captive agents as a way to control costs.

Many clients do their own Internet research and purchase insurance online. This practice somewhat reduces demand for insurance sales agents, because many purchases can then be made without their services. However, agents are still needed to interact with clients to help them understand their options and choose a policy that is right for them. Many people lack the time or expertise to study the different types of insurance to decide what they need. These clients will continue to rely on the advice from insurance sales agents.

Employment growth should be stronger for agents selling health and long-term care insurance. As the population ages over the next decade, demand will likely increase for packages that cover long-term care. The number of individuals who have access to health insurance will increase because of federal health insurance reform. Insurance companies will rely on sales agents to enroll people from this new customer base.

Job Prospects. College graduates who have sales ability, excellent customer-service skills, and expertise in a range of insurance and financial services products are likely to have the best prospects. Multilingual agents may have an advantage, because they can serve a wider customer base. In addition, insurance terminology is often technical, so agents who have a firm understanding of the relevant technical and legal terms also should be desirable to employers.

Many beginning agents fail to earn enough from commissions to meet their income goals. These agents eventually transfer to other careers. Many job openings are likely to result from the need to replace agents who leave the occupation or retire.

Agents may face some competition from traditional securities brokers and bankers who also sell insurance policies. Insurance sales agents will need to expand the products and services they offer as consolidation increases among insurance companies, banks, and brokerage firms and as demand increases from clients for more comprehensive financial planning.

Contacts for More Information

For more information about insurance sales agents, visit

- National Association of Professional Insurance Agents (www.pianet.org)
- Insurance Information Institute (www.iii.org)

For more information about insurance sales agents in the healthcare industry, visit

- National Association of Health Underwriters (www.nahu.org)

For more information about certifications, visit

- The Institutes (www.theinstitutes.org)
- The American College of Financial Services (www.theamericancollege.edu)

For more information about securities licensure, visit

- Financial Industry Regulatory Authority (FINRA) (www.finra.org)

Information about insurance sales agent licensure is available from state insurance department websites.

O*NET

- Insurance Sales Agents (41-3021.00)

Models

- **2014 Median Pay** .... $19,970 per year $9.60 per hour
- **Typical Entry-Level Education**......No formal educational credential
- **Work Experience in a Related Occupation**.............. None
- **On-the-job Training** .... None
- **Number of Jobs, 2014** 5,800
- **Job Outlook, 2014–24**................0% (Little or no change)
- **Employment Change, 2014–24** 0

What Models Do

Models pose for artists, photographers, or customers to help advertise a variety of products, including clothing, cosmetics, food, and appliances.

Duties. Models typically do the following:

- Display clothing and merchandise in print and online advertisements
- Promote products and services in television commercials
- Wear designers' clothing for runway fashion shows
- Represent companies and brands at conventions, trade shows, and other events
- Pose for photos, paintings, or sculptures
- Work closely with photographers, hair and clothing stylists, makeup artists, and clients to produce a desired look
- Create and maintain a portfolio of their work

Models appear in printed publications, at live modeling events, and on television to advertise and promote products and services.

- Travel to meet and interview with potential clients
- Conduct research on the product being promoted—for example, the designer or type of clothing fabric
- Answer questions from consumers about the products

Almost all models sign with modeling agencies. Agencies represent and promote a model to clients in return for a portion of the model's earnings. Models typically apply for a position with an agency by submitting their photographs through its website or by attending open casting calls and meeting with agents directly.

Models must research an agency before signing, in order to ensure that the agency has a good reputation in the modeling industry. For information on agencies, models should contact a local consumer affairs organization, such as the Better Business Bureau.

Some freelance models do not sign with agencies. Instead, they market themselves to potential clients and apply for modeling jobs directly. However, because most clients prefer to work with agents, it is difficult for new models to pursue a freelance career.

Models must put together and maintain up-to-date portfolios and composite cards. A portfolio is a collection of a model's previous work. A composite card contains the best photographs from a model's portfolio, along with his or her body measurements. Both portfolios and composite cards are typically taken to all casting calls and client auditions.

Because advertisers often need to target specific segments of the population, models may specialize in a certain area. For example, petite and plus-size fashions are modeled by women whose sizes are respectively smaller and larger than that worn by the typical model. Models who are disabled may be used to model fashions or products for consumers with disabilities. "Parts" models have a body part, such as a hand or foot, particularly well-suited to model products such as nail polish or shoes.

Models appear in different types of media to promote a product or service. Models advertise products and merchandise in magazine or newspaper advertisements, department store catalogs, or television commercials. Increasingly, models are appearing in online ads or on retail websites. Models also pose for sketch artists, painters, and sculptors.

Models often participate in photo shoots and pose for photographers to show off the features of clothing and other products.

Median Hourly Wages, May 2014

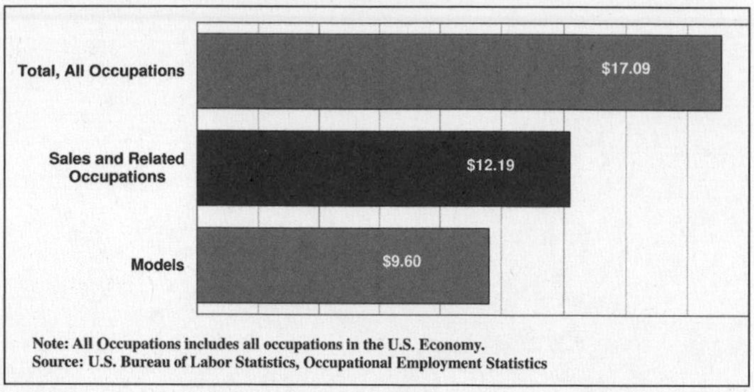

Percent Change in Employment, Projected 2014–2024

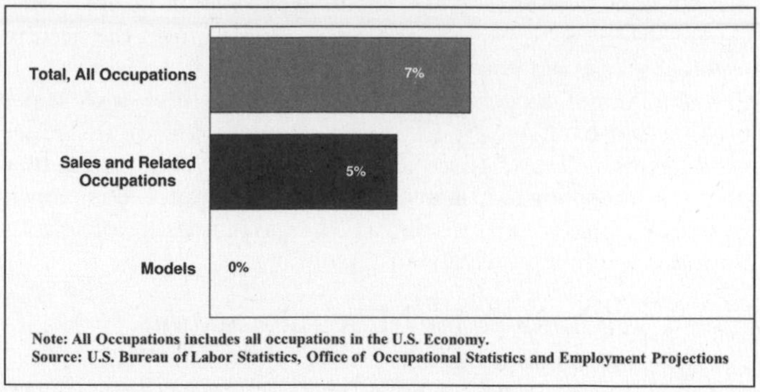

Models change their posture and facial expressions to capture the look the client wants. The photographer usually takes many pictures of the model in different poses and expressions during the photo shoot.

Models also display clothes and merchandise live in different situations. At fashion shows, models stand, turn, and walk to show off clothing to an audience of photographers, journalists, designers, and garment buyers. Other clients may require models to interact directly with customers. In retail establishments and department stores, models display clothing directly to shoppers and describe the features and prices of the merchandise. At trade shows or conventions, models show off a business' products and provide information to consumers. These models may work alongside demonstrators and product promoters to help advertise and sell merchandise.

Models often prepare for photo shoots or fashion shows by having their hair and makeup done by professionals in those industries. The hair stylists and makeup artists may touch up the model's hair and makeup and change the model's look throughout the event. However, models are sometimes responsible for applying their own makeup and bringing their own clothing.

Work Environment

Models held about 5,800 jobs in May 2014. Many models work for clothing stores. Other models work for educational services, including modeling schools.

Models work in a variety of conditions, from comfortable photography studios and runway fashion shows to outdoors in all weather conditions.

Models also may need to travel for photo shoots or to meet clients in different cities.

Work Schedules. Models' schedules can be demanding and stressful. Many models work part time and have unpredictable work schedules. They must be ready to work for a show or attend a photo shoot on short notice. The number of hours worked varies with the job. Many models experience periods of unemployment.

Education/Training

No formal education credential is required to become a model. Specific requirements depend on the client, with different jobs requiring different physical characteristics. However, most models must be within certain ranges for height, weight, and clothing size to meet the needs of fashion designers, photographers, and advertisers.

Education. There are no formal educational credentials required to become a model. Most modeling agencies allow applicants to email photos directly to the agency. The agency then contacts and interviews prospective models who are well liked. Many agencies also have "open calls," whereby aspiring models can walk into an agency during a specified time and meet directly with agents and clients.

Some aspiring models attend modeling schools that provide training in posing, walking, applying makeup, and other basic tasks. Although some models are discovered when agents scout for "fresh faces" at modeling schools, attending such schools does not necessarily lead to job opportunities.

Advancement. Models advance by working more regularly and being selected for assignments that offer higher pay. They may appear in magazines, print advertising campaigns, commercials, or runway shows that have higher profiles and provide more widespread exposure.

Because advancement depends on a model's previous work, maintaining a good portfolio of high-quality, up-to-date photographs is important in getting assignments.

A model's selection of an agency is also important for advancement: the better the reputation and skill of the agency, the more assignments a model is likely to get.

Important Qualities

Requirements may change slightly over time as perceptions of physical beauty change.

Discipline. A model's career depends on the person's maintaining his or her physical characteristics. Models must control their diet, exercise regularly, and get enough sleep to stay healthy and

Employment Projections Data for Models

Occupational Title	SOC Code	Employment, 2014	Projected Employment, 2024	Change, 2014–2024 Percent	Change, 2014–2024 Numeric
Models	41-9012	5,800	5,800	0	0

Source: U.S. Bureau of Labor Statistics, Employment Projections Program

Similar Occupations. This table shows a list of occupations with job duties that are similar to those of models.

Occupations	Entry-level Education	2014 Median Pay	Projected Job Growth	Average Annual Openings
Actors	Some college, no degree	The annual wage is not available.	10%	660
Barbers, Hairdressers, and Cosmetologists	Postsecondary nondegree award	$23,200	10%	6,440
Fashion Designers	Bachelor's degree	$64,030	3%	70
Photographers	High school diploma or equivalent	$30,490	3%	390

photogenic. Haircuts, pedicures, and manicures are necessary work-related expenses.

Interpersonal skills. Models must interact with a large number of people, such as agents, photographers, and customers. It is important to be polite, professional, prompt, and respectful.

Listening skills. Models must be able to take direction from photographers and clients during photo shoots and commercials.

Organizational skills. Models must be able to manage their portfolios and their work and travel schedules.

Persistence. Competition for jobs is strong, and most clients have specific needs for each job, so patience and persistence are essential.

Photogenic. Models spend most of their time being photographed. They must be comfortable in front of a camera in order for photographers to capture the desired look.

Style. Models must have a basic knowledge of hair styling, makeup, and clothing. For photographic and runway work, models must be able to move gracefully and confidently.

Pay

The median hourly wage for models was $9.60 in May 2014. The median wage is the wage at which half the workers in an occupation earned more than that amount and half earned less. The lowest 10 percent earned less than $8.13, and the highest 10 percent earned more than $23.86.

Job Outlook

Employment of models is projected to show little or no change from 2014 to 2024.

Rising retail sales, particularly online and e-commerce sales, will encourage businesses to increase their digital advertising and marketing budgets. Models will be needed for online publications, digital advertisements, and websites to reach out to these potential customers. Although models will still be needed to promote products in print advertisements and catalogs, businesses have begun shifting away from this traditional form of advertising.

Increasing consumer confidence and spending also may encourage businesses to introduce new advertising campaigns and product launches. These ventures will require models to promote and market products in stores, television commercials, and fashion shows.

However, less expensive digital and social media options are allowing companies to interact and build relationships with customers in new ways. Companies can now promote their products and brands directly to consumers. This direct promotion will lessen the need for professional models or large-scale advertising campaigns.

In addition, businesses may cut back on their advertising budgets during economic downturns, making them less likely to develop new advertising campaigns or hire models.

Job Prospects. Many people are drawn to this occupation because of its glamour and potential for fame. However, no education, training, or work experience is required to enter the occupation, so many applicants will be competing for very few job openings.

Although more jobs may be available in large cities such as New York and Los Angeles, competition for these jobs is expected to be very strong. Aspiring models may have the best job opportunities in smaller cities, working for smaller modeling agencies and local clients and businesses.

Age, weight, and height requirements are typically less rigid for models appearing in commercials and advertisements than for those looking to become runway or fashion models.

In addition, as the U.S. population becomes increasingly diverse and businesses become more globalized, demand for racially and ethnically diverse models will likely increase.

Contacts for More Information

For information about modeling schools and agencies in your area, contact a local consumer affairs organization, such as the Better Business Bureau (www.bbb.org).

O*NET

➤ Models (41-9012.00)

Real Estate Brokers and Sales Agents

- **2014 Median Pay** .... $43,430 per year $20.88 per hour
- **Typical Entry-Level Education** .... High school diploma or equivalent
- **Work Experience in a Related Occupation** .... See Education/Training
- **On-the-job Training** .... See Education/Training
- **Number of Jobs, 2014** 421,300
- **Job Outlook, 2014–24** .... 3% (Slower than average)
- **Employment Change, 2014–24** 10,900

What Real Estate Brokers and Sales Agents Do

Real estate brokers and sales agents help clients buy, sell, and rent properties. Although brokers and agents do similar work, brokers are licensed to manage their own real estate businesses. Sales agents must work with a real estate broker.

Duties. Real estate brokers and sales agents typically do the following:

- Solicit potential clients to buy, sell, and rent properties
- Advise clients on prices, mortgages, market conditions, and related information

- Compare properties to determine a competitive market price
- Generate lists of properties for sale, including details such as location and features
- Promote properties through advertisements, open houses, and listing services
- Take prospective buyers or renters to see properties
- Present purchase offers to sellers for consideration
- Mediate negotiations between buyer and seller
- Ensure that all terms of purchase contracts are met
- Prepare documents, such as loyalty contracts, purchase agreements, and deeds

Because of the complexity of buying or selling a home or commercial property, people often seek help from real estate brokers and sales agents.

Most real estate brokers and sales agents sell residential property. Others sell commercial property, and a small number sell industrial, agricultural, or other types of real estate.

Brokers and agents can represent either the buyer or the seller in a transaction. Buyers' brokers and agents meet with clients to understand what they are looking for in a property and how much they can afford. Sellers' brokers and agents meet with clients to help them decide how much to ask for and to convince them that the agent or broker can find them a qualified buyer.

Real estate brokers and sales agents must be knowledgeable about the real estate market in their area. To match properties to clients' needs, they should be familiar with local communities, including knowing the crime information and the proximity to schools and shopping. Brokers and agents also must stay current on financing options; government programs; types of available mortgages; and real estate, zoning, and fair housing laws.

Real estate brokers are licensed to manage their own businesses. As independent businesspeople, brokers often sell real estate owned by others. In addition to helping clients buy and sell properties, they may help rent or manage properties for a fee. Many operate a real estate office, handling business details and overseeing the work of sales agents.

Real estate sales agents must work with a broker. Sales agents often work for brokers on a contract basis, earning a portion of the commission from each property they sell.

Most real estate brokers and sales agents sell residential property.

Work Environment

Real estate brokers and sales agents held about 421,300 jobs in 2014. About half of all brokers and sales agents were self-employed in 2014. Most of the rest worked in the real estate industry in brokerage offices, leasing offices, and other real estate establishments.

Workplace size can range from a one-person business to a large firm with numerous branch offices. Many brokers have franchise agreements with national or regional real estate companies. Under this arrangement, the broker pays a fee to be affiliated with a widely known real estate organization.

Although some real estate brokers and sales agents work in a typical office environment, others are able to telecommute and work out of their homes. In both cases, however, real estate workers spend much of their time away from their desks, showing properties to customers, traveling to see properties for sale, and meeting with prospective clients.

Work Schedules. Many real estate brokers and sales agents work more than 40 hours per week. They often work evenings and weekends to accommodate clients' schedules. Many brokers and sales agents spend a significant amount of time networking and attending community events to meet potential clients. Although they frequently work irregular hours, many can set their own schedules.

Some brokers and sales agents work part time and may combine their real estate activities with other careers.

Education/Training

Real estate brokers and sales agents need at least a high school diploma. Both brokers and sales agents must be licensed. To become licensed, candidates typically must complete a number of real estate courses and pass a licensing exam.

Education. Real estate brokers and sales agents must have at least a high school diploma or equivalent. Although most brokers and agents must take state-accredited prelicensing courses to become licensed, some states may waive this requirement if the candidate has taken college courses in real estate.

As the real estate market becomes more competitive and complex, some employers are preferring to hire candidates with college courses or a college degree. Some community colleges, colleges, and universities offer courses in real estate. Some offer associate's and bachelor's degree programs in real estate, and many others offer certificate programs. Courses in finance, business administration, economics, and law also can be useful.

Brokers intending to open their own company often take business courses, such as marketing and accounting.

In addition to offering prelicensing courses, many real estate associations have courses and professional development programs for both beginners and experienced agents. These courses cover a variety of topics, such as real estate fundamentals, real estate law, and mortgage financing.

Licenses, Certifications, and Registrations. In all states and the District of Columbia, real estate brokers and sales agents must be licensed. Licensing requirements vary by state, but most have similar basic requirements:

Candidates must:

- Be 18 years old
- Complete a number of real estate courses
- Pass an exam

Some states have additional requirements, such as passing a background check. Licenses typically are not transferable among

Median Annual Wages, May 2014

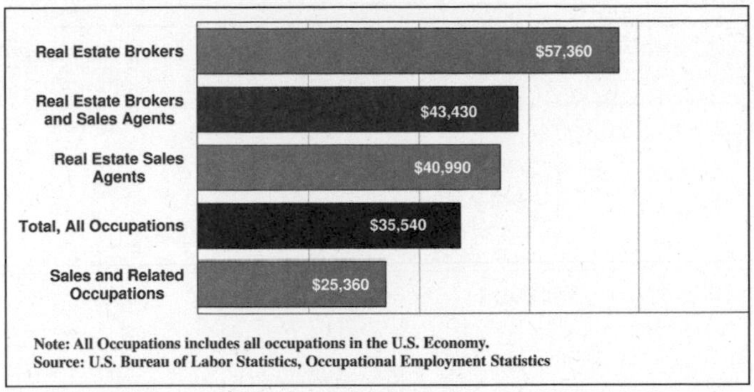

Percent Change in Employment, Projected 2014–2024

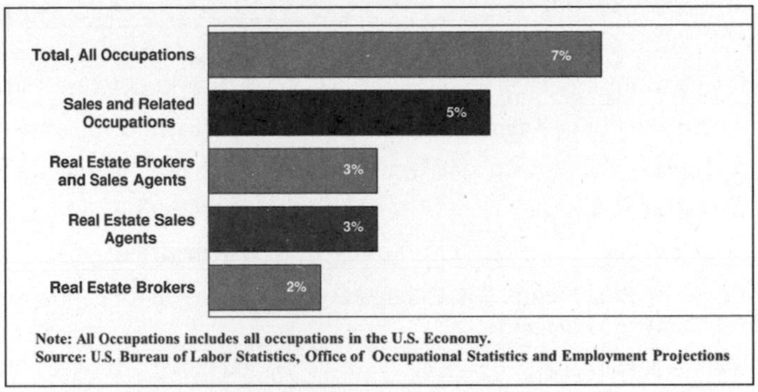

states. However, some states have reciprocity agreements and will accept licenses issued by some other states.

To obtain a broker's license, individuals generally need 1 to 3 years of experience as a licensed sales agent. They also must take additional formal training courses. In some states, a bachelor's degree may be substituted in place of some experience or training requirements.

State licenses typically must be renewed every 2 to 4 years. In most states, brokers and agents must complete continuing education courses to renew their license. To verify exact licensing requirements, prospective brokers and agents should contact the real estate licensing commission of the state in which they wish to work.

Work Experience in a Related Occupation. To get a broker's license in most states, real estate brokers must have experience working as a licensed real estate sales agent. Requirements vary by state, but most require 1 to 3 years of experience.

Training. Real estate sales agents improve their skills through practice and repetition. Because of the sales environment and the complexity of real estate deals, new agents typically observe and work closely with more senior agents. In addition, some of the larger real estate companies provide formal classroom training for new agents as a way to gain knowledge and experience, while others provide training to employees studying for their real estate licensing exam.

Advancement. Sales agents who earn their broker's license may open their own offices.

Important Qualities

Business skills. Because most brokers are self-employed, they must manage every aspect of their business. This task includes reaching out to prospective clients, handling their finances, and advertising their services.

Interpersonal skills. Strong interpersonal skills are essential for real estate brokers and sales agents, because they spend much of their time interacting with clients and customers. To attract and keep clients, they must be pleasant, enthusiastic, and trustworthy.

Organizational skills. Real estate brokers and sales agents must be able to work independently, managing their own time and organizing, planning, and prioritizing their work.

Problem-solving skills. Real estate brokers and sales agents need to be able to quickly (sometimes immediately) address concerns clients or potential customers may have with a property. They also mediate negotiations between seller and buyer.

Pay

The median annual wage for real estate brokers was $57,360 in May 2014. The median wage is the wage at which half the workers in an occupation earned more than that amount and half earned less. The lowest 10 percent earned less than $23,880, and the highest 10 percent earned more than $178,770.

The median annual wage for real estate sales agents was $40,990 in May 2014. The lowest 10 percent earned less than $21,540, and the highest 10 percent earned more than $105,270.

Brokers and sales agents earn most of their income from commissions on sales. The commission varies by the type of property and its value. Commissions often are divided among the buying agent, selling agent, brokers, and firms.

An agent's income, therefore, often depends on economic conditions, the agent's individual motivation, and the types of property available. Income usually increases as agents become better and more experienced at sales. Earnings can be irregular, especially for beginners, and agents sometimes go weeks or months without a sale. Some agents become active in community organizations and local real estate organizations to broaden their contacts and increase their sales.

Job Outlook

Employment of real estate brokers and sales agents is projected to grow 3 percent from 2014 to 2024, slower than the average for all occupations.

Because people are increasingly using real estate brokers and sales agents when purchasing homes, employment is projected to grow as the real estate market improves.

Employment Projections Data for Real Estate Brokers and Sales Agents

Occupational Title	SOC Code	Employment, 2014	Projected Employment, 2024	Change, 2014–2024 Percent	Change, 2014–2024 Numeric
Real estate brokers and sales agents	41-9020	421,300	432,100	3	10,900
Real estate brokers	41-9021	83,900	85,400	2	1,500
Real estate sales agents	41-9022	337,400	346,800	3	9,400

Source: U.S. Bureau of Labor Statistics, Employment Projections Program

Similar Occupations. This table shows a list of occupations with job duties that are similar to those of real estate brokers and sales agents.

Occupations	Entry-level Education	2014 Median Pay	Projected Job Growth	Average Annual Openings
Advertising Sales Agents	High school diploma or equivalent	$47,890	-3%	-450
Appraisers and Assessors of Real Estate	Bachelor's degree	$52,570	8%	680
Insurance Sales Agents	High school diploma or equivalent	$47,860	9%	4,350
Loan Officers	Bachelor's degree	$62,620	8%	2,450
Property, Real Estate, and Community Association Managers	High school diploma or equivalent	$54,270	8%	2,530
Sales Engineers	Bachelor's degree	$96,340	7%	490
Securities, Commodities, and Financial Services Sales Agents	Bachelor's degree	$72,070	10%	3,250
Wholesale and Manufacturing Sales Representatives	See Education/Training	$58,380	7%	11,720

Both financial and nonfinancial factors spur demand for home sales. Real estate is perceived as a good long-term investment, and many people want to own their homes.

Population growth also will continue to stimulate the need for new brokers and agents. The large millennial generation will be entering the prime working-age and household-forming age cohort over the next decade. Although this generation has delayed home ownership because of financial and debt considerations, it is projected that many will enter the housing market over the next 10 years.

In addition to being first-time home buyers, people will need brokers and agents when looking for a larger home, relocating for a new job, and other reasons.

An improving job market and rising consumer spending also will drive demand for brokers and agents to handle commercial, retail, and industrial real estate transactions.

However, the real estate market is sensitive to fluctuations in the economy, and employment of real estate brokers and agents will vary accordingly. In periods of economic growth or stability, employment should grow to accommodate people looking to buy homes and businesses looking to expand office or retail space. Alternatively, during periods of declining economic activity or rising interest rates, the amount of work for brokers and agents will slow and employment may decline.

Job Prospects. It is relatively easy to enter the occupation, but getting listings as a broker or an agent depends on the real estate market and overall economic conditions. As the economy expands and more people look to buy homes, job competition may increase as more people obtain their real estate license. In contrast, although the real estate market declines in an economic downturn, there also tend to be fewer active and licensed real estate agents.

New agents will face competition from well-established, more experienced brokers and agents. Because income is dependent on sales, beginners may have trouble sustaining themselves in the occupation during periods of slower activity.

Brokers should fare better because they generally have a large client base from years of experience as sales agents. Those with strong sales ability and extensive social and business connections in their communities should have the best chances for success.

Contacts for More Information

Information on licensing requirements for real estate brokers and sales agents is available from most local real estate organizations and from the state real estate commission or board.

For more information about opportunities in real estate, visit

➤ National Association of Real Estate Brokers (www.nareb.com)
➤ National Association of Realtors (www.realtor.org)

O*NET

➤ Real Estate Brokers (41-9021.00)
➤ Real Estate Sales Agents (41-9022.00)

Retail Sales Workers

- **2014 Median Pay** .... $21,670 per year $10.42 per hour
- **Typical Entry-Level Education**......No formal educational credential
- **Work Experience in a Related Occupation**.............. None
- **On-the-job Training** .... See Education/Training
- **Number of Jobs, 2014** 4,859,600
- **Job Outlook, 2014–24** .... 7% (As fast as average)
- **Employment Change, 2014–24** 331,000

What Retail Sales Workers Do

Retail sales workers include both those who sell retail merchandise, such as clothing, furniture, and cars, (called *retail salespersons*) and those who sell spare and replacement parts and equipment, especially car parts (called *parts salespersons*). Both types of workers help customers find the products they want and process customers' payments.

Duties. Retail sales workers typically do the following:

- Greet customers and offer them assistance
- Recommend merchandise based on customers' wants and needs
- Explain the use and benefit of merchandise to customers
- Answer customers' questions
- Show how merchandise works, if applicable

- Add up customers' total purchases and accept payment
- Inform customers about current sales, promotions, and policies about payments and exchanges

The following are examples of types of retail sales workers:

Retail salespersons work in stores where they sell goods, such as books, cars, clothing, cosmetics, electronics, furniture, lumber, plants, shoes, and many other types of merchandise.

In addition to helping customers find and select items to buy, many retail salespersons process the payment for the sale, which typically involves operating cash registers.

After taking payment for the purchases, retail salespersons may bag or package the purchases.

Depending on the hours they work, retail salespersons may have to open or close cash registers. This includes counting the money in the register and separating charge slips, coupons, and exchange vouchers. They may also make deposits at a cash office.

For information about other workers who receive and disburse money, see the profile on cashiers.

In addition, retail salespersons may help stock shelves or racks, arrange for mailing or delivery of purchases, mark price tags, take inventory, and prepare displays.

For some retail sales jobs, particularly those involving expensive and complex items, retail sales workers need special knowledge or skills. For example, those who sell cars must be able to explain the features of various models, manufacturers' specifications, different types of options on the car, financing available, and the details of associated warranties.

In addition, retail sales workers must recognize security risks and thefts and understand their organization's procedures for handling thefts—procedures that may include notifying security guards or calling police.

Parts salespersons sell spare and replacement parts and equipment, especially car parts. Most work in either automotive parts stores or automobile dealerships. They take customers' orders, inform customers of part availability and price, and take inventory.

Retail salespersons work in various settings, including clothing stores, automobile dealers, and electronics and appliance stores.

Work Environment

Retail sales workers held about 4.9 million jobs in 2014. The industries that employed the most retail sales workers were as follows:

Clothing and clothing accessories stores	20%
General merchandise stores	19
Motor vehicle and parts dealers	11
Building material and garden equipment and supplies dealers	10
Sporting goods, hobby, book, and music stores	7

Most retail sales work is performed in clean, well-lit stores. Workers often stand for long periods and may need permission from a supervisor to leave the sales floor. If they sell items such as cars, plants, or lumberyard materials, they may work outdoors.

Work Schedules. Many sales workers work evenings and weekends, particularly during holidays and other peak sales periods. Because the end-of-year holiday season is often the busiest time, many employers limit retail sales workers' use of vacation time between November and the beginning of January.

About 1 in 3 retail salespersons worked part time in 2014.

Education/Training

Typically, there are no formal education requirements for retail sales workers. Most receive on-the-job training, which usually lasts a few days to a few months.

Education. Although retail or parts sales positions usually have no formal education requirements, some employers prefer applicants who have a high school diploma or equivalent, especially employers who sell technical products or "big-ticket" items, such as electronics or cars.

Training. Most retail sales workers receive on-the-job training, which usually lasts a few days to a few months. In small stores, an experienced employee often trains newly hired workers. In large stores, training programs are more formal and usually conducted over several days.

During training sessions, topics often include customer service, security, the store's policies and procedures, and how to operate the cash register.

Median Hourly Wages, May 2014

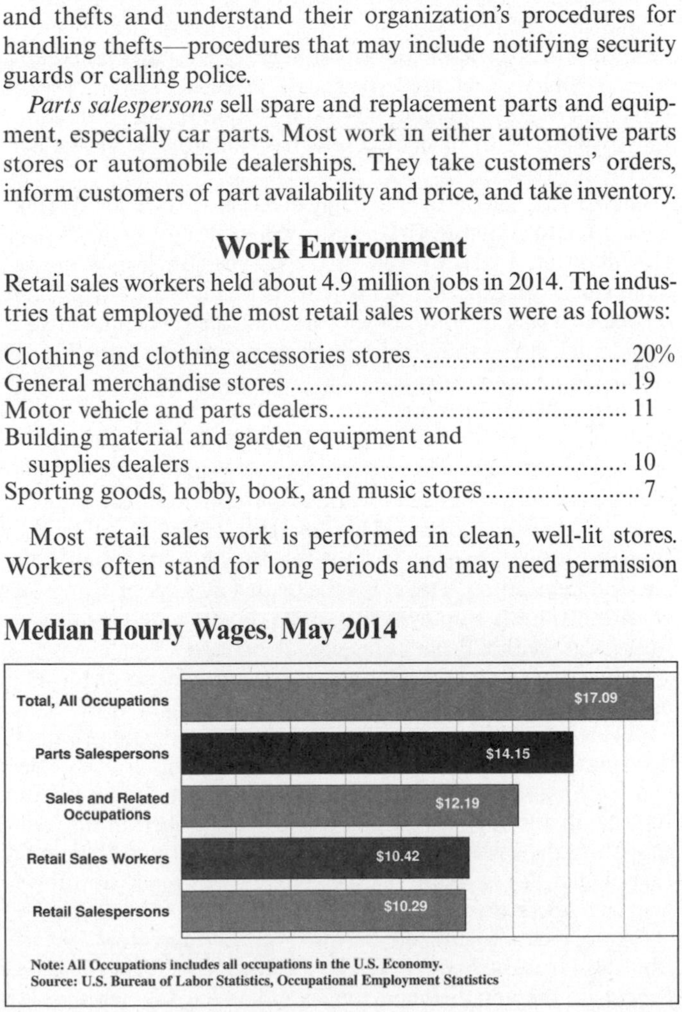

Percent Change in Employment, Projected 2014–2024

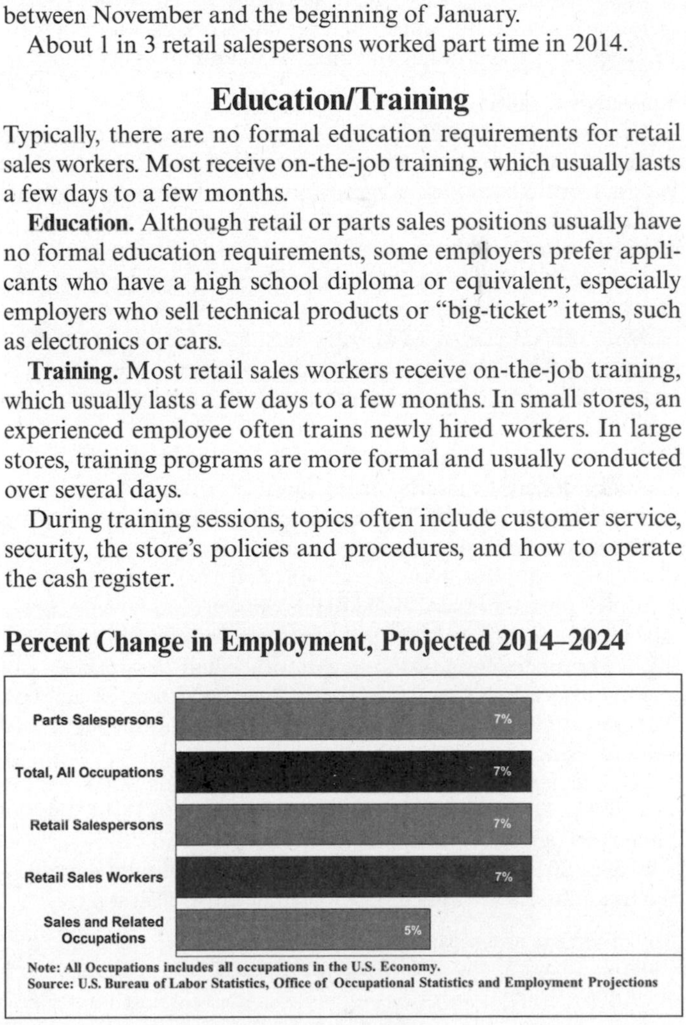

Employment Projections Data for Retail Sales Workers

Occupational Title	SOC Code	Employment, 2014	Projected Employment, 2024	Change, 2014–2024 Percent	Change, 2014–2024 Numeric
Retail sales workers	—	4,859,600	5,190,600	7	331,000
Parts salespersons	41-2022	234,700	251,500	7	16,800
Retail salespersons	41-2031	4,624,900	4,939,100	7	314,200

Source: U.S. Bureau of Labor Statistics, Employment Projections Program

Depending on the type of product they are selling, employees may be given additional specialized training. For example, salespersons working in cosmetics get instruction on the types of products the store offers and for whom the cosmetics would be most beneficial. Likewise, those who sell computers may be instructed on the technical differences between computer products.

Because providing exceptional service to customers is a priority for many employers, employees often get periodic training to update and refine their skills.

Advancement. Retail sales workers typically have opportunities to advance to supervisory or managerial positions. Some employers want candidates for managerial positions to have a college degree.

As sales workers gain experience and seniority, they often move into positions that have greater responsibility and may be given their choice of departments in which to work. This opportunity often means moving to positions with higher potential earnings and commissions. The highest earnings potential usually involves selling "big-ticket" items—such as cars, jewelry, furniture, and electronics. These positions often require workers with extensive knowledge of the product and an excellent talent for persuasion.

Important Qualities

Customer-service skills. Retail sales workers must be responsive to the wants and needs of customers. They should explain the product options available to customers and make appropriate recommendations.

Interpersonal skills. A friendly and outgoing personality is important for these workers because the job requires almost constant interaction with people.

Math skills. Retail sales workers must have the ability to calculate price totals, discounts, and change owed to customers.

Persistence. A large number of attempted sales may not be successful, so sales workers should not be discouraged easily. They must start each new sales attempt with a positive attitude.

Selling skills. Retail sales workers must be persuasive when interacting with customers. They must clearly and effectively explain the benefits of the merchandise.

Pay

The median hourly wage for parts salespersons was $14.15 in May 2014. The median wage is the wage at which half the workers in an occupation earned more than that amount and half earned less. The lowest 10 percent earned less than $8.90, and the highest 10 percent earned more than $24.40.

The median hourly wage for retail salespersons was $10.29 in May 2014. The lowest 10 percent earned less than $8.19, and the highest 10 percent earned more than $18.89.

In May 2014, the median hourly wages for retail sales workers in the top industries in which they worked were as follows:

Motor vehicle and parts dealers	$14.72
Building material and garden equipment and supplies dealers	12.15
Sporting goods, hobby, book, and music stores	9.61
General merchandise stores	9.56
Clothing and clothing accessories stores	9.39

Compensation systems vary by type of establishment and merchandise sold. Retail sales workers get hourly wages, commissions, or a combination of the two. Under a commission system, they get a percentage of the sales they make. This system offers sales workers the opportunity to increase their earnings considerably, but they may find that their earnings depend strongly on their ability to sell their product and on the ups and downs of the economy.

Many retail sales workers work evenings and weekends, particularly during holidays and other peak sales periods. Because the end-of-year holiday season is often the busiest time, many employers limit sales workers' use of vacation time between November and the beginning of January.

About 1 in 3 retail salespersons worked part time in 2014.

Job Outlook

Employment of retail sales workers is projected to grow 7 percent from 2014 to 2024, about as fast as the average for all occupations.

Employment of retail salespersons is projected to grow 7 percent from 2014 to 2024, about as fast as the average for all occupations. Employment of retail salespersons has traditionally grown with the overall economy.

Online sales have grown strongly in recent years, and this trend is expected to continue. Online sales will likely affect employment growth of retail sales workers in a few ways. "Brick-and-mortar" retail stores are expected to increase their emphasis on customer service as a way to compete with online sellers. Therefore, traditional retail stores should hire more sales workers to provide this service. In addition, cost pressure may drive retailers to ask their in-store staff to do more. This means they may want workers who can perform a broad range of job duties that include helping customers find items, operating a cash register, and re-stocking shelves. Because retail sales workers have this versatile range of functions, their usage should also increase. However, online sales strength is also expected to limit the growth of the number of physical retail stores. Therefore, the limited number of stores may constrain overall employment growth, even though retail sales workers use within these stores should increase.

Online sales are projected to affect specific segments of the retail industry to varying extents. For instance, book and media stores are likely to see the most severe declines due to online competition. However, other retail segments, such as automobile dealers and clothing stores, have experienced much less of an impact. In general, although consumers are increasing their online retail shopping, they will continue to do the majority of their retail shopping in stores. Retail salespersons will be needed in stores to help customers and complete sales.

Employment of parts salespersons is projected to grow 7 percent from 2014 to 2024, about as fast as the average for all occupations. People are keeping their cars longer and are buying new cars less

Similar Occupations. This table shows a list of occupations with job duties that are similar to those of retail sales workers.

Occupations	Entry-level Education	2014 Median Pay	Projected Job Growth	Average Annual Openings
Cashiers	No formal educational credential	$19,060	2%	6,700
Customer Service Representatives	High school diploma or equivalent	$31,200	10%	25,290
Information Clerks	See Education/Training	$31,500	2%	2,580
Insurance Sales Agents	High school diploma or equivalent	$47,860	9%	4,350
Real Estate Brokers and Sales Agents	High school diploma or equivalent	$43,430	3%	1,090
Sales Engineers	Bachelor's degree	$96,340	7%	490
Securities, Commodities, and Financial Services Sales Agents	Bachelor's degree	$72,070	10%	3,250
Wholesale and Manufacturing Sales Representatives	See Education/Training	$58,380	7%	11,720

often. Older cars need to be serviced more frequently, creating demand for car parts and parts salespersons. However, growth may be slowed by competition from online parts retailers.

Job Prospects. Many workers leave this occupation, which means there will be a large number of job openings. This should result in many employment opportunities for qualified workers.

Contacts for More Information

For information about the retail industry, visit

➤ National Retail Federation (http://nrf.com)

➤ Retail Industry Leaders Association (www.rila.org)

For information about training for a career in automobile sales, visit

➤ National Automobile Dealers Association (www.nada.org)

O*NET

➤ Parts Salespersons (41-2022.00)

➤ Retail Salespersons (41-2031.00)

Sales Engineers

- **2014 Median Pay** .... $96,340 per year $46.32 per hour
- **Typical Entry-Level Education** .... Bachelor's degree
- **Work Experience in a Related Occupation** .... None
- **On-the-job Training**...Moderate-term on-the-job training
- **Number of Jobs, 2014** 69,900
- **Job Outlook, 2014–24** .... 7% (As fast as average)
- **Employment Change, 2014–24** 4,900

What Sales Engineers Do

Sales engineers sell complex scientific and technological products or services to businesses. They must have extensive knowledge of the products' parts and functions and must understand the scientific processes that make these products work.

Duties. Sales engineers typically do the following:

- Prepare and deliver technical presentations explaining products or services to existing and prospective customers
- Confer with customers and engineers to assess equipment needs and to determine system requirements
- Collaborate with sales teams to understand customer requirements and provide sales support
- Secure and renew orders and arrange delivery
- Plan and modify products to meet customer needs
- Help clients solve problems with installed equipment
- Recommend improved materials or machinery to customers, showing how changes will lower costs or increase production
- Help in researching and developing new products

They use their technical skills to explain the benefits of their products or services to potential customers and to show how their products or services are better than their competitors'. Some sales engineers work for the companies that design and build technical products. Others work for independent sales firms.

Many of the duties of sales engineers are similar to those of other salespersons. They must interest the client in buying their products or services, negotiate a price, and complete the sale. To do this, sales engineers give technical presentations during which they explain the technical aspects of the product and how it will solve a specific customer problem.

Some sales engineers, however, team with salespersons who concentrate on marketing and selling the product, which lets the sales engineer concentrate on the technical aspects of the job. By

Sales engineers use scientific knowledge to help their customers choose the right technical products.

Median Annual Wages, May 2014

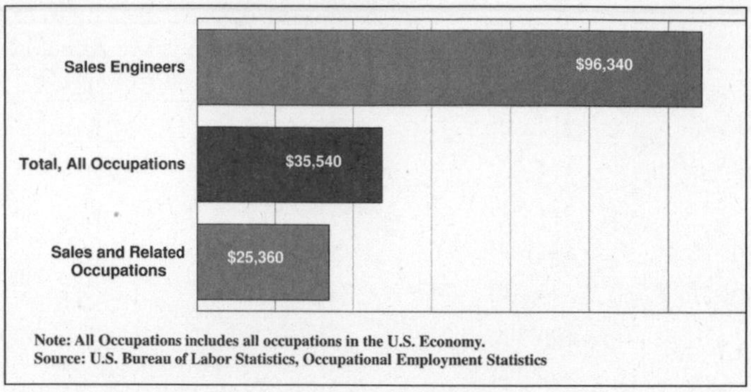

Percent Change in Employment, Projected 2014–2024

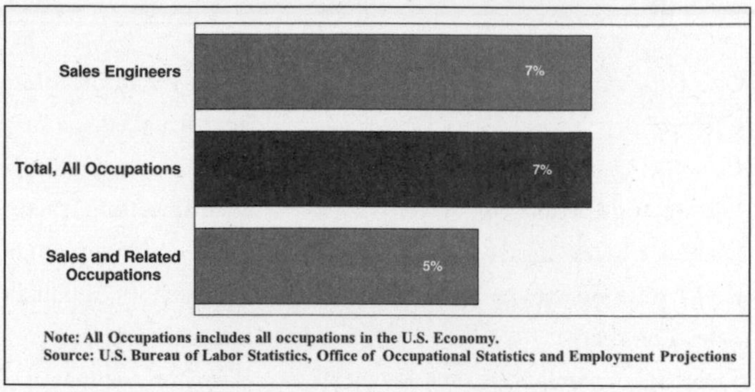

working as part of a sales team, each member is able to focus on his or her strengths and expertise. For more information on other sales occupations, see the profile on wholesale and manufacturing sales representatives.

In addition to giving technical presentations, sales engineers are increasingly doing other tasks related to sales, such as market research. They also may ask for technical requirements from customers and modify and adjust products to meet customers' specific needs. Some sales engineers work with research and development (R&D) departments to help identify and develop new products.

Work Environment

Sales engineers held about 69,900 jobs in 2014. The industries that employed the most sales engineers were as follows:

Merchant wholesalers, durable goods	24%
Manufacturing	21
Computer systems design and related services	18
Wholesale electronic markets and agents and brokers	10
Telecommunications	7

Because sales regions may cover several states, sales engineers may be away from home for several days or even weeks at a time. Other sales engineers cover a smaller region and spend only a few nights away from home. International travel to secure contracts with foreign clients is becoming more common.

Sales engineers may encounter stress because their income and job security often depend directly on their success in sales and customer service.

Work Schedules. Most sales engineers work full time, and about 1 in 3 worked more than 40 hours per week in 2014. Some may work additional and irregular hours to meet sales goals and client needs. However, many sales engineers can decide their own schedules.

Education/Training

A bachelor's degree is typically required to become a sales engineer. Successful sales engineers combine technical knowledge of the products or services they are selling with strong interpersonal skills.

Education. Sales engineers typically need a bachelor's degree in engineering or a related field. However, a worker without a degree, but with previous sales experience as well as technical experience or training, sometimes holds the title of sales engineer. Workers who have a degree in a science, such as chemistry, or in business with little or no previous sales experience, also may be called sales engineers.

University engineering programs generally require 4 years of study. They vary in content, but all programs include courses in math and the physical sciences. In addition, most programs require developing strong computer skills.

Most engineering programs require students to choose an area of specialization. The most common majors are electrical, mechanical, or civil engineering, but some engineering departments offer additional majors, such as chemical, biomedical, or computer hardware engineering. However, some undergraduate programs offer a general engineering curriculum; students then specialize in a particular area either on the job or in graduate school.

Training. New graduates with engineering degrees typically need sales experience and training before they can work independently as sales engineers. Training covers general sales techniques and may involve teaming with a sales mentor who is familiar with the employer's business practices, customers, procedures, and company culture. After the training period, sales engineers may continue to partner with someone who lacks technical skills yet excels in the art of sales.

It is important for sales engineers to continue their engineering and sales education throughout their careers. Much of their value to their employers depends on their knowledge of, and ability to sell, the latest technologies. Sales engineers in high-technology fields, such as information technology and advanced electronics, may find that their technical knowledge rapidly becomes obsolete, requiring frequent retraining.

Advancement. Promotions may include a higher commission rate, a larger sales territory, or elevation to the position of supervisor or sales manager.

Important Qualities

Interpersonal skills. Strong interpersonal skills are a valuable characteristic for sales engineers, both for building relationships

Employment Projections Data for Sales Engineers

Occupational Title	SOC Code	Employment, 2014	Projected Employment, 2024	Change, 2014–2024 Percent	Change, 2014–2024 Numeric
Sales engineers	41-9031	69,900	74,900	7	4,900

Source: U.S. Bureau of Labor Statistics, Employment Projections Program

Similar Occupations. This table shows a list of occupations with job duties that are similar to those of sales engineers.

Occupations	Entry-level Education	2014 Median Pay	Projected Job Growth	Average Annual Openings
Aerospace Engineers	Bachelor's degree	$105,380	-2%	-160
Buyers and Purchasing Agents	Bachelor's degree	$58,520	2%	720
Computer Hardware Engineers	Bachelor's degree	$108,430	3%	240
Electrical and Electronics Engineers	Bachelor's degree	$93,260	0%	-10
Industrial Engineers	Bachelor's degree	$81,490	1%	210
Insurance Sales Agents	High school diploma or equivalent	$47,860	9%	4,350
Mechanical Engineers	Bachelor's degree	$83,060	5%	1,460
Securities, Commodities, and Financial Services Sales Agents	Bachelor's degree	$72,070	10%	3,250
Wholesale and Manufacturing Sales Representatives	See Education/Training	$58,380	7%	11,720

with clients and effectively communicating with other members of the sales team.

Problem-solving skills. Sales engineers must be able to listen to the customer's desires and concerns, and then recommend solutions, possibly including customizing a product.

Self-confidence. Sales engineers should be confident and persuasive when making sales presentations.

Technological skills. Sales engineers must have extensive knowledge of the technologically sophisticated products they sell in order to explain their advantages and answer questions.

Pay

The median annual wage for sales engineers was $96,340 in May 2014. The median wage is the wage at which half the workers in an occupation earned more than that amount and half earned less. The lowest 10 percent earned less than $55,850, and the highest 10 percent earned more than $160,250.

In May 2014, the median annual wages for sales engineers in the top industries in which they worked were as follows:

Computer systems design and related services	$109,100
Telecommunications	108,450
Wholesale electronic markets and agents and brokers	92,980
Merchant wholesalers, durable goods	91,810
Manufacturing	85,930

How much a sales engineer earns varies significantly by the type of firm and the product sold. Most employers offer a combination of salary and commission payments or salary plus a bonus. Some sales engineers who work for independent sales companies earn only commissions. Commissions are usually based on the value of sales. Bonuses may depend on individual performance, on the performance of all workers in the group or district, or on the company's performance. Earnings from commissions and bonuses may vary from year to year depending on sales ability, the demand for the company's products or services, and the overall economy. In addition to their earnings, sales engineers who work for manufacturers are usually reimbursed for expenses such as transportation, meals, hotels, and customer entertainment.

Job Outlook

Employment of sales engineers is projected to grow 7 percent from 2014 to 2024, about as fast as the average for all occupations. As a wider range of technologically sophisticated products comes on the market, sales engineers will be in demand to help sell products or services related to these products.

Employment growth is likely to be strong for sales engineers selling computer software and hardware. Strong overall industry growth is expected in computer systems design and related services, which is the top employing industry of sales engineers. This will contribute to employment growth for the occupation. Employment of sales engineers in computer systems design and related services is projected to grow 21 percent from 2014 to 2024.

Growth is also expected to be strong in independent sales agencies (companies that sell on behalf of manufacturers without taking title to the goods being sold). As manufacturing companies outsource their sales staff as a way to control costs, employment in these independent agencies should increase.

Job Prospects. Successful sales engineers must have strong technical knowledge of the products they are selling, in addition to having interpersonal skills and the ability to persuade. Job prospects should be good for candidates with these abilities.

Contacts for More Information

For more information about careers in sales occupations, visit

- Manufacturers' Agents National Association (MANA) (www.manaonline.org)
- Manufacturers' Representatives Educational Research Foundation (MRERF) (http://mrerf.org)

O*NET

- Sales Engineers (41-9031.00)

Securities, Commodities, and Financial Services Sales Agents

- **2014 Median Pay** .... $72,070 per year, $34.65 per hour
- **Typical Entry-Level Education** .... Bachelor's degree
- **Work Experience in a Related Occupation** .... None
- **On-the-job Training** ... Moderate-term on-the-job training
- **Number of Jobs, 2014** 341,500
- **Job Outlook, 2014–24** .... 10% (Faster than average)
- **Employment Change, 2014–24** 32,500

What Securities, Commodities, and Financial Services Sales Agents Do

Securities, commodities, and financial services sales agents connect buyers and sellers in financial markets. They sell securities to individuals, advise companies in search of investors, and conduct trades.

Duties. Securities, commodities, and financial services sales agents typically do the following:

- Contact prospective clients to present information and explain available services
- Offer advice on the purchase or sale of particular securities
- Buy and sell securities, such as stocks and bonds
- Buy and sell commodities, such as corn, oil, and gold
- Monitor financial markets and the performance of individual securities
- Analyze company finances to provide recommendations for public offerings, mergers, and acquisitions
- Evaluate cost and revenue of agreements

Securities, commodities, and financial services sales agents deal with a wide range of products and clients. Agents spend much of the day interacting with people, whether selling stock to an individual or discussing the status of a merger deal with a company executive. The work is usually stressful because agents deal with large amounts of money and have time constraints.

A security or commodity can be traded in two ways: electronically or in an auction-style setting on the floor of an exchange market. Markets such as the National Association of Securities Dealers Automated Quotation system (NASDAQ) use vast computer networks rather than human traders to match buyers and sellers. Others, such as the New York Stock Exchange (NYSE), rely on floor brokers to complete transactions.

The following are examples of types of securities, commodities, and financial services sales agents:

Brokers sell securities and commodities directly to individual clients. They advise people on appropriate investments based on the client's needs and financial ability. The people they advise may have very different levels of expertise in financial matters.

Finding clients is a large part of a broker's job. They must create their own client base by calling from a list of potential clients. Some agents network by joining social groups, and others may rely on referrals from satisfied clients.

Investment bankers connect businesses that need money to finance their operations or expansion plans with investors who are interested in providing that funding. This process is called underwriting, and it is the main function of investment banks. The banks first sell their advisory services to help companies issue new stocks or bonds, and then the banks sell the issued securities to investors.

Some of the most important services that investment bankers provide are initial public offerings (IPOs), and mergers and acquisitions. An IPO is the process by which a company becomes open for public investment by issuing its first stock. Investment bankers must estimate how much the company is worth and ensure that it meets the legal requirements to become publicly traded.

Investment bankers also connect companies in mergers (when two companies join together) and acquisitions (when one company buys another). Investment bankers provide advice throughout the process to ensure that the transaction goes smoothly.

Investment banking sales agents and traders carry out buy-and-sell orders for stocks, bonds, and commodities from clients and make trades on behalf of the firm itself. Investment banks primarily employ these workers, although some work for commercial banks, hedge funds, and private equity groups. Because markets fluctuate so much, trading is a split-second decision-making process. Slight changes in the price of a trade can greatly affect its profitability, making the trader's decision extremely important.

People increasingly seek the advice and services of securities, commodities, and financial services sales agents to realize their financial goals.

Floor brokers work directly on the floor—a large room where trading is done—of a securities or commodities exchange. After a trader places an order for a security, floor brokers negotiate the price, make the sale, and forward the purchase price to the trader.

Financial services sales agents consult on a wide variety of banking, securities, insurance, and related services to individuals and businesses, often catering the services to meet the client's financial needs. They contact potential clients to explain their services, which may include the handling of checking accounts, loans, certificates of deposit, individual retirement accounts, credit cards, and estate and retirement planning.

Work Environment

Securities, commodities, and financial services sales agents held about 341,500 jobs in 2014. The industries that employed the most securities, commodities, and financial services sales agents were as follows:

Securities and commodity contracts intermediation and brokerage	35%
Depository credit intermediation	32
Other financial investment activities	11
Nondepository credit intermediation	5
Management of companies and enterprises	4

Most securities, commodities, and financial services sales agents work many hours under stressful conditions. The pace of work is fast, and managers are usually demanding of their workers, because both commissions and advancements are tied to sales.

Investment bankers travel extensively because they frequently work with companies in other countries.

Because computers can conduct trades faster than people can, electronic trading is quickly replacing verbal auction-style trades on exchange floors. The environment of the stock exchange is changing as a result, with more traders carrying out orders behind a desk and fewer working on the exchange floor.

A growing number of securities sales agents, employed mostly by discount or online brokerage firms, work in call-center environments. In these centers, hundreds of agents spend much of the day on the telephone taking orders from clients or offering help and information on their accounts.

Because most of the major investment banks are in New York City, employment of securities, commodities, and financial services sales agents is concentrated in that metropolitan area.

Work Schedules. Securities, commodities, and financial services sales agents usually work full time and more than 1 in 3 worked more than 40 hours per week in 2014. In addition, they may work evenings and weekends because many of their clients work during the day. Call centers often operate 24 hours a day, requiring agents to work in shifts.

Education/Training

A bachelor's degree is required for entry-level jobs, and a master's degree in business administration (MBA) is useful for advancement.

Education. Securities, commodities, and financial services sales agents generally must have a bachelor's degree to get an entry-level job. Studies in business, finance, accounting, or economics are important, especially for larger firms. Many firms hire summer interns before their last year of college, and those who are most successful are offered full-time jobs after they graduate.

Numerous agents eventually get a master's degree in business administration (MBA), which is often a requirement for high-level positions in the securities industry. Because the MBA exposes students to real-world business practices, it can be a major asset for jobseekers. Employers often reward MBA holders with higher level positions, better compensation, and large signing bonuses.

Training. Most employers provide intensive on-the-job training, teaching employees the specifics of the job, such as the products and services offered. Trainees in large firms may receive technical instruction in securities analysis and selling strategies. Firms often rotate their trainees among various departments to give them a broad understanding of the securities business.

Securities, commodities, and financial services sales agents must keep up with new products and services and other developments. They attend conferences and training seminars regularly.

Licenses, Certifications, and Registrations. Brokers and investment bankers must register as representatives of their firm with the Financial Industry Regulatory Authority (FINRA). To obtain the license, potential agents must pass a series of exams.

Many other licenses are available, each of which gives the holder the right to sell different investment products and services. Traders and some other sales representatives also need licenses, although these vary by firm and specialization. Financial services sales agents may need to be licensed, especially if they sell securities or insurance. Most firms offer training to help their employees pass the licensing exams.

Agents who are registered with FINRA must attend continuing education classes to keep their licenses. Courses consist of computer-based training on legal requirements or new financial products or services.

Although not always required, certification enhances professional standing and is recommended by employers. Brokers, investment bankers, and financial services sales agents can earn the Chartered Financial Analyst (CFA) certification, sponsored by the CFA Institute. To qualify for this certification, applicants need a bachelor's degree or 4 years of related work experience and must pass three exams, which require several hundred hours of independent study. Applicants also must have an international passport. Exams cover subjects in accounting, economics, securities analysis, financial markets and instruments, corporate finance, asset valuation, and portfolio management. Applicants can take the exams while they are getting the required work experience.

Advancement. Securities, commodities, and financial services sales agents usually advance to senior positions in a firm by accumulating a greater number of accounts. Although beginners often service the accounts of individual investors, they may eventually service large institutional accounts, such as those of banks and retirement funds.

After taking a series of tests, some brokers become portfolio managers and have greater authority to make investment decisions regarding an account. For more information on portfolio managers, see the profile on financial analysts.

Some experienced sales agents become branch office managers and supervise other sales agents while continuing to provide services for their own clients. A few agents advance to top management positions or become partners in their firms.

Many investment banks use an "up or out" policy, in which entry-level investment bankers are either promoted or terminated after 2 or 3 years. Investment banks use this policy to ensure that entry-level positions are not occupied long term, allowing the bank to bring in new workers.

Important Qualities

Analytical skills. To judge the profitability of potential deals, securities, commodities, and financial services sales agents must

Median Annual Wages, May 2014

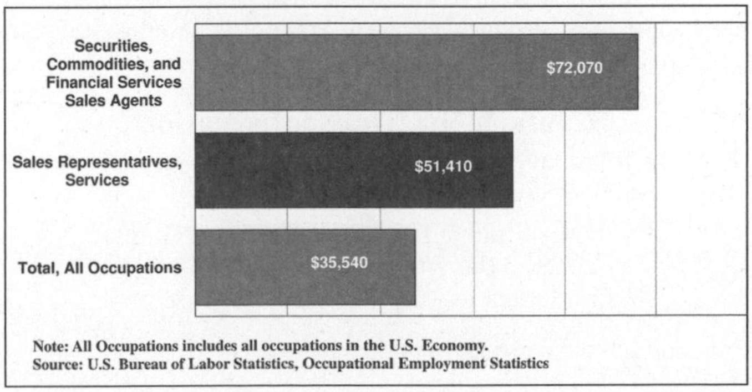

Percent Change in Employment, Projected 2014–2024

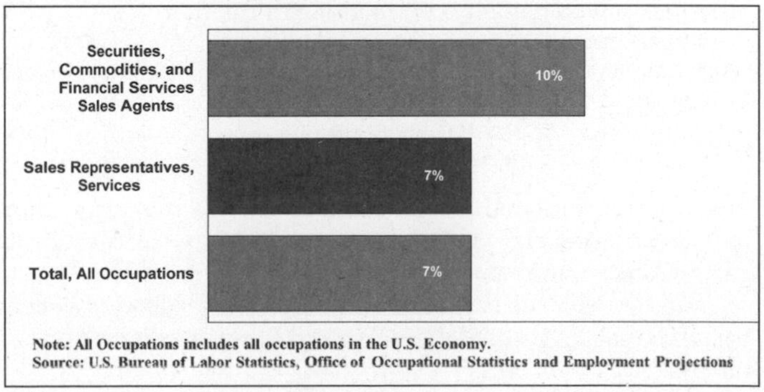

Employment Projections Data for Securities, Commodities, and Financial Services Sales Agents

Occupational Title	SOC Code	Employment, 2014	Projected Employment, 2024	Change, 2014–2024 Percent	Change, 2014–2024 Numeric
Securities, commodities, and financial services sales agents	41-3031	341,500	374,000	10	32,500

Source: U.S. Bureau of Labor Statistics, Employment Projections Program

Similar Occupations. This table shows a list of occupations with job duties that are similar to those of securities, commodities, and financial services sales agents.

Occupations	Entry-level Education	2014 Median Pay	Projected Job Growth	Average Annual Openings
Financial Analysts	Bachelor's degree	$78,620	12%	3,230
Financial Managers	Bachelor's degree	$115,320	7%	3,770
Insurance Sales Agents	High school diploma or equivalent	$47,860	9%	4,350
Personal Financial Advisors	Bachelor's degree	$81,060	30%	7,390
Real Estate Brokers and Sales Agents	High school diploma or equivalent	$43,430	3%	1,090

have strong analytical skills. This includes computer programming skills which they use to analyze financial products.

Customer-service skills. Securities, commodities, and financial services sales agents must be persuasive and make clients feel comfortable with the agent's recommendations.

Decision-making skills. Investment banking traders must make split-second decisions, with large sums of money at stake.

Detail oriented. Investment bankers must pay close attention to the details of initial public offerings and mergers and acquisitions because small changes can have large consequences.

Initiative. Securities, commodities, and financial services sales agents must create their own client base by making "cold" sales calls to people to whom they have not been referred and to people not expecting the call.

Math skills. Securities, commodities, and financial services sales agents need to be familiar with mathematical tools, including investment formulas.

Pay

The median annual wage for securities, commodities, and financial services sales agents was $72,070 in May 2014. The median wage is the wage at which half the workers in an occupation earned more than that amount and half earned less. The lowest 10 percent earned less than $32,170, and the highest 10 percent earned more than $187,200.

In May 2014, the median annual wages for securities, commodities, and financial services sales agents in the top industries in which they worked were as follows:

Securities and commodity contracts intermediation and brokerage	$112,550
Other financial investment activities	101,810
Management of companies and enterprises	80,820
Nondepository credit intermediation	57,860
Depository credit intermediation	42,950

Many securities and commodities brokers earn a commission based on the monetary value of the products they sell. Most firms pay brokers a minimum salary in addition to commissions.

Trainee brokers usually earn a salary until they develop a client base. The salary gradually decreases in favor of commissions as the broker gains clients.

Investment bankers in corporate finance and mergers and acquisitions generally earn a base salary with the opportunity to earn a substantial bonus. At higher levels, bonuses far exceed base salary.

Job Outlook

Employment of securities, commodities, and financial services sales agents is projected to grow 10 percent from 2014 to 2024, faster than the average for all occupations.

Services that investment bankers provide, such as helping with initial public offerings and mergers and acquisitions, will continue to be in demand as the economy grows. The United States remains an international financial center, meaning that the economic growth of countries around the world will contribute to employment growth in the American financial industry.

However, the financial services industry has experienced some consolidation in recent years, which has slowed employment growth for these workers. In addition, automated trading systems have reduced demand for securities traders.

Financial regulations, including restrictions on proprietary trading, have created a shift of employment among traders from investment banks to hedge funds; however, this shift should not affect overall employment growth for the occupation.

Job Prospects. The high pay associated with securities, commodities, and financial services sales agents draws many more applicants than there are openings. Therefore, competition for jobs is intense.

Certification and a graduate degree, such as a Chartered Financial Analyst (CFA) certification and a master's degree in business administration (MBA), can improve an applicant's prospects. For entry-level jobs, having an excellent grade-point average (GPA) in college is important.

Contacts for More Information

For more information about securities, commodities, and financial services sales agents, visit

➤ Global Academy of Finance and Management (www.gafm.com)

➤ Securities Industry and Financial Markets Association (SIFMA) (www.sifma.org)

For more information about licensing of securities, commodities, and financial services sales agents, visit

➤ Financial Industry Regulatory Authority (FINRA) (www.finra.org)

For more information about certification for securities, commodities, and financial services sales agents, visit

- ➤ CFA Institute (www.cfainstitute.org)

O*NET

- ➤ Securities, Commodities, and Financial Services Sales Agents (41-3031.00)
- ➤ Sales Agents, Securities and Commodities (41-3031.01)
- ➤ Sales Agents, Financial Services (41-3031.02)
- ➤ Securities and Commodities Traders (41-3031.03)

Travel Agents

- **2014 Median Pay** .... $34,800 per year $16.73 per hour
- **Typical Entry-Level Education** .... High school diploma or equivalent
- **Work Experience in a Related Occupation** .... None
- **On-the-job Training** ...Moderate-term on-the-job training
- **Number of Jobs, 2014** 74,100
- **Job Outlook, 2014–24** ....-12% (Decline)
- **Employment Change, 2014–24** .... -8,700

What Travel Agents Do

Travel agents sell transportation, lodging, and admission to entertainment activities to individuals and groups planning trips. They offer advice on destinations, plan trip itineraries, and make travel arrangements for clients.

Duties. Travel agents typically do the following:

- Arrange travel for business and vacation customers
- Determine customers' needs and preferences, such as schedules and costs
- Plan and arrange tour packages, excursions, and day trips
- Find fare and schedule information
- Calculate total travel costs
- Book reservations for travel, hotels, rental cars, and special events, such as tours and excursions
- Describe trips to clients and give details on required documents, such as passports and visas
- Give advice about local weather conditions, customs, and attractions
- Make alternative booking arrangements if changes arise before or during the trip

Travel agents sort through vast amounts of information to find the best possible trip arrangements for travelers. In addition, resorts and specialty groups use travel agents to promote vacation packages to their clients.

Travel agents also may visit destinations to get firsthand experience so that they can make recommendations to clients or colleagues. They may visit hotels, resorts, and restaurants to evaluate the comfort, cleanliness, and quality of the establishment. However, most of their time is spent talking with clients, promoting tours, and contacting airlines and hotels to make travel accommodations. Travel agents use a reservation system called a Global Distribution System (GDS) to access travel information and make reservations with travel suppliers such as airlines or hotels.

The following are examples of types of travel agents:

Leisure travel agents sell vacation packages to the general public. They are responsible for arranging trip itineraries based on clients' interests and budget. Leisure travel agents increasingly are focusing on a specific type of travel, such as adventure tours. Some may cater to a specific group of people, such as senior citizens or single people.

Corporate travel agents primarily make travel arrangements for businesses. They book travel accommodations for an organization's employees who are traveling to conduct business or attend conferences.

Work Environment

Travel agents held about 74,100 jobs in 2014.

They typically work in offices, but some work remotely because much of their time is spent on the phone and the computer. In some cases, busy offices or call centers may be noisy and crowded. Agents may face stress during travel emergencies or unanticipated schedule changes.

In 2014, 83 percent of all travel agents worked for the travel arrangement and reservation services industry, which includes those who work for travel agencies. In addition, about 1 in 10 travel agents were self-employed.

Work Schedules. Most travel agents work full time. Some work additional hours during peak travel times or when they must accommodate customers' schedule changes and last-minute needs.

Education/Training

A high school diploma typically is required for someone to become a travel agent. However, many employers prefer additional formal training. Good communication and computer skills are essential.

Education. Employers may prefer candidates who have taken classes related to the travel industry. Many community colleges,

Travel agents help clients plan personal and business trips.

Median Annual Wages, May 2014

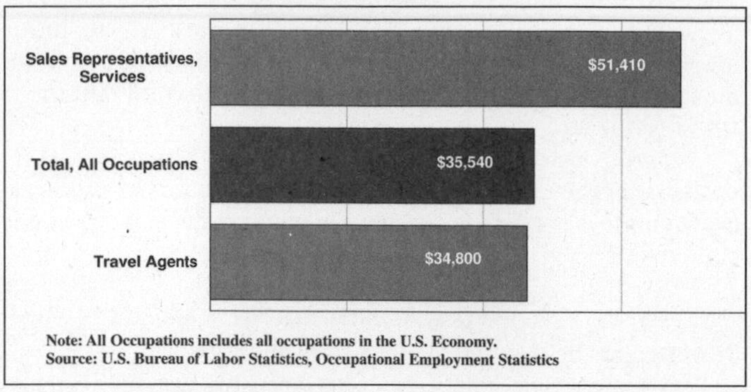

Percent Change in Employment, Projected 2014–2024

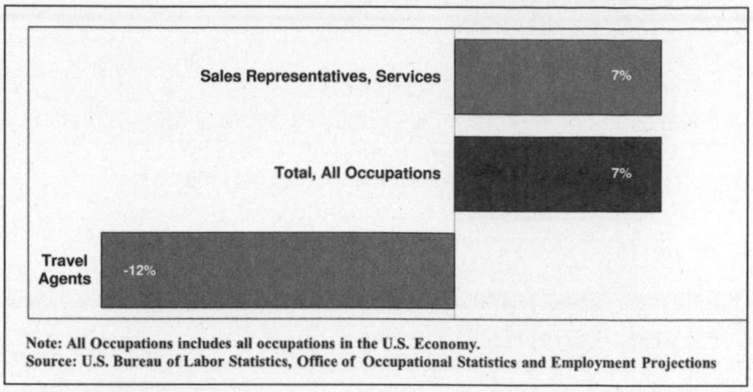

vocational schools, and industry associations offer technical training or continuing education classes in professional travel planning. Classes usually focus on reservations systems, marketing, and regulations regarding international travel. In addition, a few colleges offer degrees in travel and tourism.

Training. Employers in the travel industry always give some on-the-job training on the computer systems that are used in the industry. For example, a travel agent could be trained to work with a reservation system used by several airlines.

Licenses, Certifications, and Registrations. A good way to demonstrate competence for high school graduates with limited experience is to take the Travel Agent Proficiency (TAP) test. The test has no eligibility requirements and is administered by The Travel Institute.

The Travel Institute also provides training and professional certification opportunities for experienced travel agents. Different levels of certification are offered, depending on a travel agent's experience. Travel agents with limited experience can become a Certified Travel Associate (CTA) after completing a series of classes and exams. For those with at least 5 years of experience, the more highly advanced Certified Travel Counselor (CTC) certification can be achieved. Both the CTA and CTC require continuing education each year to maintain certification.

The International Air Transport Association (IATA) offers the Travel and Tourism Professional (TTP) designation, which requires varying degrees of experience depending on the achieved education level. The designation remains valid for 2 years and requires continuing education credits.

The Cruise Lines International Association (CLIA) offers three levels of certification: Accredited (ACC), Master (MCC), and Elite Cruise Counselor (ECC). Each level requires a certain amount of training and product knowledge.

Some states require agents to have a business license to sell travel services. Requirements among states vary greatly. Contact individual state licensing agencies for more information.

Other Experience. Some agencies prefer travel agents with firsthand experience visiting a country. These agencies especially prefer travel agents who specialize in specific destinations or particular types of travelers, such as groups with a special interest or corporate travelers.

Important Qualities

Adventurousness. Travel agencies that specialize in exotic destinations or particular types of travel, such as adventure travel or ecotourism, may prefer to hire travel agents who share these interests.

Communication skills. Travel agents must listen to customers, understand their travel needs, and offer appropriate travel advice and information.

Customer-service skills. When customers need to make last-minute changes in their travel arrangements, travel agents must be able to respond to questions and complaints in a friendly and professional manner.

Detail oriented. Travel agents must pay attention to details in order to ensure that the reservations they make match travelers' needs. They must make reservations at the correct dates, times, and locations to meet travelers' schedules.

Organizational skills. Travel agents often work on itineraries for many customers at once. Keeping client information in order and ensuring that bills and receipts are processed in a timely manner is essential.

Sales skills. Travel agents must be able to persuade clients to buy transportation, lodging, or tours. Sometimes they might need to persuade tour operators, airline staff, or others to take care of their clients' special needs. Earnings for many travel agents depend on commissions and service fees.

Pay

The median annual wage for travel agents was $34,800 in May 2014. The median wage is the wage at which half the workers in an occupation earned more than that amount and half earned less. The lowest 10 percent earned less than $19,680, and the highest 10 percent earned more than $59,070.

These wage data include money earned from commissions.

Job Outlook

Employment of travel agents is projected to decline 12 percent from 2014 to 2024.

Employment Projections Data for Travel Agents

Occupational Title	SOC Code	Employment, 2014	Projected Employment, 2024	Change, 2014–2024 Percent	Change, 2014–2024 Numeric
Travel agents	41-3041	74,100	65,400	-12	-8,700

Source: U.S. Bureau of Labor Statistics, Employment Projections Program

Similar Occupations. This table shows a list of occupations with job duties that are similar to those of travel agents.

Occupations	Entry-level Education	2014 Median Pay	Projected Job Growth	Average Annual Openings
Information Clerks	See Education/Training	$31,500	2%	2,580
Meeting, Convention, and Event Planners	Bachelor's degree	$46,490	10%	990
Secretaries and Administrative Assistants	High school diploma or equivalent	$35,970	3%	11,880

The ability of travelers to use the Internet to research vacations and book their own trips is expected to continue to suppress demand for travel agents. An increasing amount of travel is also expected to be booked on mobile devices.

However, the sheer number of travel and review websites can make travel planning a frustrating experience for some consumers. This may lead to an increasing number of people turning to travel agents to help filter through the options and give personal recommendations.

Job Prospects. Job prospects should be best for travel agents who specialize in specific destinations or particular types of travelers, such as groups with a special interest or corporate travelers.

Some job opportunities might result from a growing number of experienced travel agents reaching retirement age.

Contacts for More Information

For more information about training opportunities, visit

➤ American Society of Travel Agents (www.asta.org)
➤ Cruise Lines International Association (CLIA) (www.cruising.org)
➤ International Air Transport Association (IATA) (www.iata.org/Pages/default.aspx)

For more information about voluntary certification opportunities, visit

➤ The Travel Institute (www.thetravelinstitute.com)

O*NET

➤ Travel Agents (41-3041.00)

Wholesale and Manufacturing Sales Representatives

- **2014 Median Pay** .... $58,380 per year $28.07 per hour
- **Typical Entry-Level Education** .... See Education/Training
- **Work Experience in a Related Occupation** .... None
- **On-the-job Training**...Moderate-term on-the-job training
- **Number of Jobs, 2014** 1,800,900
- **Job Outlook, 2014–24** .... 7% (As fast as average)
- **Employment Change, 2014–24** 117,200

What Wholesale and Manufacturing Sales Representatives Do

Wholesale and manufacturing sales representatives sell goods for wholesalers or manufacturers to businesses, government agencies, and other organizations. They contact customers, explain product features, answer any questions that their customers may have, and negotiate prices.

Duties. Wholesale and manufacturing sales representatives typically do the following:

- Identify prospective customers by using business directories, following leads from existing clients, and attending trade shows and conferences
- Contact new and existing customers to discuss their needs and explain how specific products and services can meet these needs
- Help customers select products to meet customers' needs, product specifications, and regulations
- Emphasize product features that will meet customers' needs and exhibit product capabilities and limitations
- Answer customers' questions about prices, availability, and product uses
- Negotiate prices and terms of sale and service agreements
- Prepare sales contracts and submit orders for processing
- Collaborate with colleagues to exchange information, such as selling strategies and marketing information
- Follow up with customers to make sure they are satisfied with their purchases and to answer any questions or concerns

Wholesale and manufacturing sales representatives—sometimes called *manufacturers' representatives* or *manufacturers' agents*—generally work for manufacturers or wholesalers. Some work for a single organization, while others represent several companies and sell a range of products.

Rather than selling goods directly to consumers, wholesale and manufacturing sales representatives deal with businesses, government agencies, and other organizations. For more information about people who sell directly to consumers, see the profile on retail sales workers.

Some wholesale and manufacturing sales representatives deal with nonscientific products such as food, office supplies, and clothing. Other representatives specialize in technical and scientific products, ranging from agricultural and mechanical equipment to computer and pharmaceutical goods. For more information about people who specialize in sales of technical products and services, see the profile on sales engineers.

Wholesale and manufacturing sales representatives who lack expertise about a given product frequently team with a technical expert. In this arrangement, the technical expert—sometimes a sales engineer—attends the sales presentation to explain the product and answer questions or concerns. The sales representative makes the initial contact with customers, introduces the company's product, and obtains final agreement from the potential buyer.

By working with a technical expert, the representative is able to spend more time maintaining and soliciting accounts and less time needing to gain technical knowledge.

After the sale, representatives may make follow-up visits to ensure that equipment is functioning properly and may even help train customers' employees to operate and maintain new equipment.

Those selling consumer goods often suggest how and where merchandise should be displayed. When working with retailers,

Sales representatives may travel extensively to meet with clients.

they may help arrange promotional programs, store displays, and advertising.

In addition to selling products, wholesale and manufacturing sales representatives analyze sales statistics, prepare reports, and handle administrative duties such as filing expense accounts, scheduling appointments, and making travel plans.

Staying up to date on new products and the changing needs of customers is important. Sales representatives accomplish this in a variety of ways, including attending trade shows at which new products and technologies are showcased. They attend conferences and conventions to meet other sales representatives and clients and to discuss new product developments. They also read about new and existing products and monitor the sales, prices, and products of their competitors.

The following are examples of types of wholesale and manufacturing sales representatives:

Inside sales representatives work mostly in offices while making sales. Frequently, they are responsible for getting new clients by "cold calling" various organizations, which means they call potential customers who are not expecting to be contacted in order to establish an initial contact. They also take incoming calls from customers who are interested in their product, and process paperwork to complete the sale.

Outside sales representatives spend much of their time traveling to and visiting with current clients and prospective buyers. During a sales call, they discuss the client's needs and suggest how they can meet those needs with merchandise or services. They may show samples or catalogs that describe items their company provides, and they may inform customers about prices, availability, and ways in which their products can save money and boost productivity. Because many sales representatives sell several complementary products made by different manufacturers, they may take a broad approach to their customers' businesses. For example, sales representatives may help install new equipment and train employees in its use.

Work Environment

Wholesale and manufacturing sales representatives held about 1.8 million jobs in 2014. The industries that employed the most wholesale and manufacturing sales representatives were as follows:

Wholesale electronic markets and agents and brokers	17%
Manufacturing	14
Machinery, equipment, and supplies merchant wholesalers	7
Professional and commercial equipment and supplies merchant wholesalers	6
Grocery and related product wholesalers	5

Some wholesale and manufacturing sales representatives have large territories and travel considerably. Because a sales region may cover several states, representatives may be away from home for several days or weeks at a time. Sales representatives who cover a smaller region may not spend much time away from home.

Inside wholesale and manufacturing sales representatives spend a lot of their time on the phone, selling goods, taking orders, and resolving problems or complaints about the merchandise. They also use web technology, including chat, email, and video conferencing, to contact clients.

Workers in this occupation can be under considerable stress because their income and job security often depend directly on the amount of merchandise they sell, and their companies usually set goals or quotas that they are expected to meet.

Work Schedules. Most wholesale and manufacturing sales representatives work full time. Since sales calls take place during regular working hours, many do much of the planning and paperwork involved with sales in the evening and on weekends. Although the hours are often irregular, many sales representatives may determine their own schedules.

Education/Training

Educational requirements vary, depending on the type of product sold. If the products are not scientific or technical, a high school diploma is generally enough for entry into the occupation. If the products are scientific or technical, sales representatives typically need at least a bachelor's degree.

Education. A high school diploma is sufficient for many positions, primarily for selling products that are not technical or scientific. However, those selling scientific and technical products typically must have a bachelor's degree. Scientific and technical

Median Annual Wages, May 2014

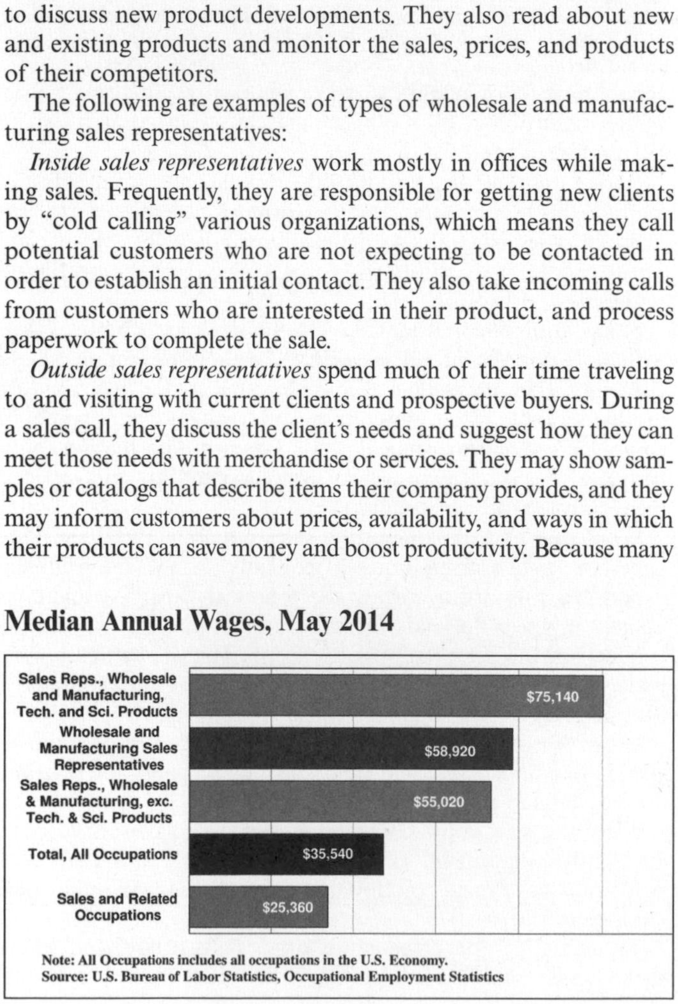

Percent Change in Employment, Projected 2014–2024

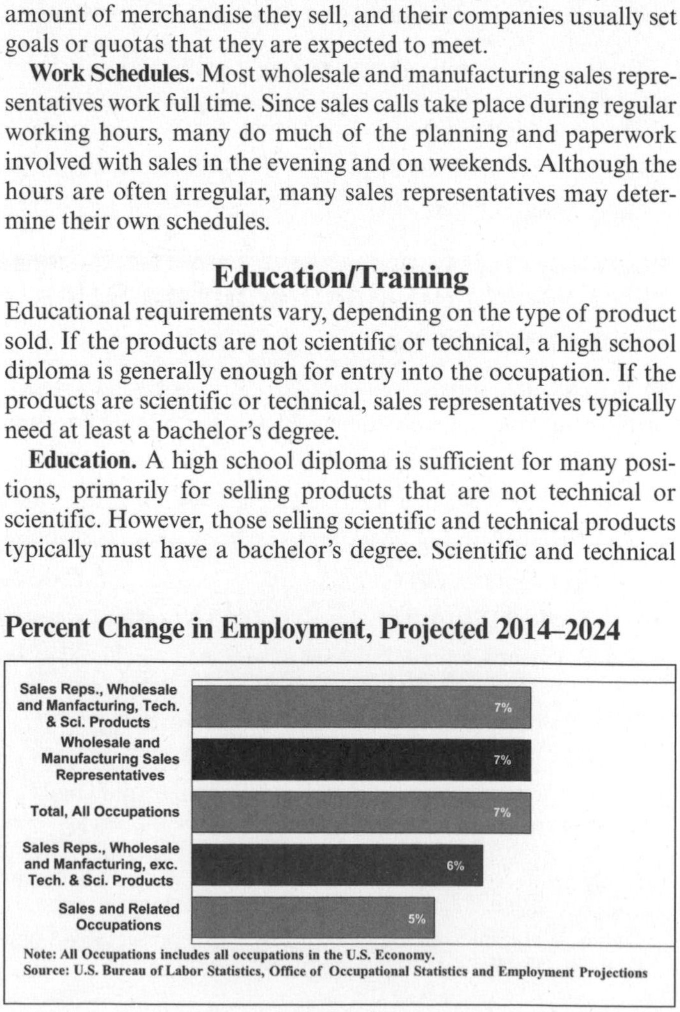

Employment Projections Data for Wholesale and Manufacturing Sales Representatives

Occupational Title	SOC Code	Employment, 2014	Projected Employment, 2024	Change, 2014–2024 Percent	Change, 2014–2024 Numeric
Sales representatives, wholesale and manufacturing	41-4000	1,800,900	1,918,200	7	117,200
Sales representatives, wholesale and manufacturing, technical and scientific products	41-4011	347,800	371,700	7	23,800
Sales representatives, wholesale and manufacturing, except technical and scientific products	41-4012	1,453,100	1,546,500	6	93,400

Source: U.S. Bureau of Labor Statistics, Employment Projections Program

products include pharmaceuticals, medical instruments, and industrial equipment. A degree in a field related to the product sold, such as chemistry, biology, or engineering, is often required.

Many sales representatives attend seminars in sales techniques or take courses in marketing, economics, communication, or even a foreign language to improve their ability to make sales.

Training. Many companies have formal training programs for beginning wholesale and manufacturing sales representatives that last up to 1 year. In some programs, trainees rotate among jobs in plants and offices to learn all phases of producing, installing, and distributing the product. In others, trainees receive formal technical instruction at the plant, followed by on-the-job training under the supervision of a field sales manager.

New employees may be trained by going along with experienced workers on their sales calls. As they gain familiarity with the firm's products and clients, the new workers gain more responsibility until they eventually get their own territory.

Licenses, Certifications, and Registrations. Many in this occupation have either the Certified Professional Manufacturers' Representative (CPMR) certification or the Certified Sales Professional (CSP) certification, both offered by the Manufacturers' Representatives Educational Research Foundation (MRERF). Certification typically involves completing formal technical training and passing an exam. In addition, the CPMR requires 10 hours of continuing education every year in order to maintain certification.

Other Experience. Although not required, sales experience can be helpful, particularly for nontechnical positions.

Advancement. Frequently, promotion takes the form of an assignment to a larger account or territory, where commissions are likely to be greater. Those who have good sales records and leadership ability may advance to higher level positions, such as sales supervisor, district manager, or vice president of sales. For more information on these positions, see the profile on sales managers.

Important Qualities

Customer-service skills. Sales representatives must be able to listen to the customer's needs and concerns before and after the sale.

Interpersonal skills. Sales representatives must be able to work well with many types of people. They must be able to build good relationships with clients and with other members of the sales team.

Self-confidence. Sales representatives must be confident and persuasive when making sales presentations. In addition, making a call to a potential customer who is not expecting to be contacted, or "cold calling," requires confidence and composure.

Stamina. Sales representatives are often on their feet for long periods of time and may carry heavy sample products.

Pay

The median annual wage for sales representatives, wholesale and manufacturing, technical and scientific products was $75,140 in May 2014. The median wage is the wage at which half the workers in an occupation earned more than that amount and half earned less. The lowest 10 percent earned less than $37,430, and the highest 10 percent earned more than $149,010.

The median annual wage for sales representatives, wholesale and manufacturing, except technical and scientific products was $55,020 in May 2014. The lowest 10 percent earned less than $26,790, and the highest 10 percent earned more than $116,230.

In May 2014, the median annual wages for wholesale and manufacturing sales representatives in the top industries in which they worked were as follows:

Similar Occupations. This table shows a list of occupations with job duties that are similar to those of wholesale and manufacturing sales representatives.

Occupations	Entry-level Education	2014 Median Pay	Projected Job Growth	Average Annual Openings
Advertising Sales Agents	High school diploma or equivalent	$47,890	-3%	-450
Buyers and Purchasing Agents	Bachelor's degree	$58,520	2%	720
Insurance Sales Agents	High school diploma or equivalent	$47,860	9%	4,350
Real Estate Brokers and Sales Agents	High school diploma or equivalent	$43,430	3%	1,090
Retail Sales Workers	No formal educational credential	$21,670	7%	33,100
Sales Engineers	Bachelor's degree	$96,340	7%	490
Securities, Commodities, and Financial Services Sales Agents	Bachelor's degree	$72,070	10%	3,250

Wholesale electronic markets and agents and brokers	$66,230
Professional and commercial equipment and supplies merchant wholesalers	62,130
Manufacturing	61,020
Machinery, equipment, and supplies merchant wholesalers	55,780
Grocery and related product wholesalers	52,970

Compensation methods for representatives vary significantly by the type of firm and the product sold. Most employers use a combination of salary and commissions or salary plus bonuses. Commissions are usually based on a percentage of sales. Bonuses may depend on individual performance, on the performance of all sales workers in the group or district, or on the company's performance.

Job Outlook

Employment of wholesale and manufacturing sales representatives is projected to grow 7 percent from 2014 to 2024, about as fast as the average for all occupations.

Employment growth for wholesale and manufacturing sales representatives will largely follow growth of the overall economy.

In addition to the total volume of sales, a wider range of products and technologies will lead to increased demand for sales representatives.

Because the work of sales representatives requires a lot of face-to-face interaction with potential buyers, this type of work is not likely to be outsourced to other countries.

Employment growth is expected to be strongest for sales representatives working at independent sales agencies. Companies are increasingly shifting their sales activities to independent agencies as a way to cut costs and boost revenue. These independent companies do not buy and hold the products they are selling. Instead, they operate on a fee or commission basis in representing the product manufacturer. Employment of sales representatives in this industry—wholesale electronic markets and agents and brokers—is projected to grow 26 percent from 2014 to 2024.

Job Prospects. Job opportunities should be best for those with previous sales experience. Though the large size of the occupation creates many job openings, the relatively high pay will also likely attract a large number of applicants.

Contacts for More Information

For more information about wholesale sales representatives, visit

- Manufacturers' Agents National Association (MANA) (www.manaonline.org)

For more information about certification, visit

- Manufacturers' Representatives Educational Research Foundation (MRERF) (http://mrerf.org)

O*NET

- Sales Representatives, Wholesale and Manufacturing, Technical and Scientific Products (41-4011.00)
- Solar Sales Representatives and Assessors (41-4011.07)
- Sales Representatives, Wholesale and Manufacturing, Except Technical and Scientific Products (41-4012.00)

Transportation and Material Moving

Air Traffic Controllers

- **2014 Median Pay** .... $122,340 per year
  $58.82 per hour
- **Typical Entry-Level Education** .... Associate's degree
- **Work Experience in a Related Occupation** .... None
- **On-the-job Training** .... Long-term on-the-job training
- **Number of Jobs, 2014** 24,500
- **Job Outlook, 2014–24** .... -9% (Decline)
- **Employment Change, 2014–24** .... -2,100

What Air Traffic Controllers Do

Air traffic controllers coordinate the movement of air traffic, to ensure that aircraft stay safe distances apart.

Duties. Air traffic controllers typically do the following:

- Issue landing and takeoff instructions to pilots
- Monitor and direct the movement of aircraft on the ground and in the air, using radar, computers, or visual references
- Control all ground traffic at airports, including baggage vehicles and airport workers
- Manage communications by transferring control of departing flights to other traffic control centers and accepting control of arriving flights
- Provide information to pilots, such as weather updates, runway closures, and other critical information
- Alert airport response staff, in the event of an aircraft emergency

Air traffic controllers' primary concern is safety, but they also must direct aircraft efficiently to minimize delays. They manage the flow of aircraft into and out of the airport airspace, guide pilots during takeoff and landing, and monitor aircraft as they travel through the skies.

Controllers usually manage multiple aircraft at the same time and must make quick decisions to ensure the safety of the aircraft. For example, a controller might direct one aircraft on its landing approach while providing another aircraft with weather information.

The following are examples of types of air traffic controllers:

Tower controllers direct the movement of vehicles on runways and taxiways. They check flight plans, give pilots clearance for takeoff or landing, and direct the movement of aircraft and other traffic on the runways and in other parts of the airport. Most work from control towers, watching the traffic they control.

Approach and departure controllers ensure that aircraft traveling within an airport's airspace maintain minimum separation for safety. They give clearances to enter controlled airspace and hand off control of aircraft to en route controllers. They use radar equipment to monitor flight paths and work in buildings known as Terminal Radar Approach Control Centers (TRACONs). They also provide information to pilots, such as weather conditions and other critical notices.

En route controllers monitor aircraft once they leave an airport's airspace. They work at air route traffic control centers located throughout the country, which typically are not located at airports.

Each center is assigned an airspace based on the geography and altitude of the area in which it is located. As an airplane approaches and flies through a center's airspace, en route controllers guide the airplane along its route. They may adjust the flight path of aircraft to avoid collisions and for safety in general.

As an airplane goes along its route, en route controllers hand the plane off to the next center, approach control, or tower along the path, as needed. En route controllers pay special attention to aircraft as they descend and get closer to the busier airspace around an airport. They turn the aircraft over to the airport's approach controllers when the aircraft is about 20 to 50 miles from the airport.

Some air traffic controllers work at the Air Traffic Control Systems Command Center. These controllers monitor traffic patterns within the entire national airspace. When they find a bottleneck, they provide instructions to other controllers, helping to prevent traffic jams. Their objective is to keep traffic levels manageable for the airport and for en route controllers.

Work Environment

Air traffic controllers held about 24,500 jobs in 2014. The majority of controllers worked for the Federal Aviation Administration (FAA).

Air traffic controllers work in control towers, approach control facilities, or en route centers. Many tower and approach/departure controllers work near large airports. En route controllers work in secure office buildings located across the country, which typically are not located at airports.

Approach/departure controllers often work in semi-dark rooms. The aircraft they control appear as points of light moving across their radar screens, and a well-lit room would make it difficult to see the screen properly.

Controllers must work rapidly and efficiently while maintaining total concentration. The mental stress of being responsible for the safety of aircraft and their passengers can be taxing. As a result, controllers tend to retire earlier than most workers: those with 20 years of experience are eligible to retire at age 50, while those

Competition for air traffic controller jobs is expected to remain high.

with 25 years of service may retire earlier than that. Controllers are required to retire at age 56.

Work Schedules. Most air traffic controllers work full time, and some work additional hours. Controllers may rotate shifts among day, evening, and night, because major control facilities operate continuously. Controllers also work weekend and holiday shifts. Less busy airports may have towers that do not operate on a 24-hour basis. Controllers at these airports have more normal work schedules.

Education/Training

To become an air traffic controller, an applicant must

- Be a U.S. citizen
- Have a bachelor's degree, or work experience, or a combination of education and experience totaling 3 years
- Pass medical and background checks
- Achieve a qualifying score on the Federal Aviation Administration (FAA) preemployment test, which includes a biographical assessment
- Pass the Air Traffic Standardized Aptitude Test (AT-SAT)
- Complete a training course at the FAA Academy (and start it before turning 31 years of age)

The AT-SAT is an 8-hour, computer-based exam. Some of the characteristics tested include arithmetic, prioritization, planning, tolerance for high intensity, decisiveness, visualization, problem solving, and movement detection.

Controllers also must pass a physical exam each year and a job performance exam twice per year. In addition, they must pass periodic drug screenings.

Education. The FAA sets guidelines for schools that offer a program called the Air Traffic Collegiate Training Initiative, or the AT-CTI program. AT-CTI schools offer 2- or 4-year degrees that are designed to prepare students for a career in air traffic control. The curriculum is not standardized, but courses focus on subjects that are fundamental to aviation. Topics include aviation weather, airspace, clearances, reading maps, federal regulations, and related topics.

Also known as a biodata test, the biographical assessment is a personality exam that looks at a candidate's response patterns in order to determine whether the person is a good fit for additional air traffic education. For more information, see the Office of Personnel Management (OPM) page on biodata tests. Applicants who pass both the AT-SAT and the biographical assessment are eligible to enroll in an intensive training course at the FAA Academy.

Air traffic controllers also may apply for positions through vacancy announcements made to the general public when such announcements are available. The announcements allow those with no special experience or education to apply to become air traffic controllers. These applicants generally must have completed a 4-year degree, have equivalent sequential work experience, or have some combination of the two. To improve their chances of passing the exam, applicants from the general public should try to educate themselves along the lines of the AT-CTI and AT-SAT standards.

Work Experience in a Related Occupation. Applicants with only a high school education will need to have years of sequential work experience or a combination of experience and education. Work experience includes work as a commercial pilot, navigator, or flight dispatcher. Other work experience that requires knowledge of aviation topics, such as weather and flight regulations, may be acceptable.

Candidates with previous air traffic control experience are automatically eligible to apply for air traffic controller positions. They do not need to take the FAA preemployment test. There can be specific job postings for those who already have experience working as an air traffic controller, such as through the military.

Training. Most newly hired air traffic controllers are trained at the FAA Academy, located in Oklahoma City, Oklahoma. The length of training varies with the position and the applicant's background. Applicants must be hired by their 31st birthday.

After graduating from the Academy, trainees are assigned to an air traffic control facility as developmental controllers, until they complete all requirements for becoming a certified air traffic controller. Developmental controllers begin their careers by supplying pilots with basic flight data and airport information. They then advance to positions within the control room that have more responsibility.

As the developmental controllers master various duties, they earn increases in pay and advance in their training. Those with previous controller experience may take less time to become fully certified.

Trainees who fail to complete the Academy or their on-the-job training within a specified time are usually dismissed.

There are opportunities for a controller to switch from an en route position to an airport position, although the transfer requires additional Academy training. Within both of these categories, controllers can transfer to jobs at different locations or advance to supervisory positions.

Licenses, Certifications, and Registrations. All air traffic controllers must hold an Air Traffic Control Tower Operator Certificate or be appropriately qualified and supervised as stated in Title 14 of the Code of Federal Regulations, Part 65. They must be at least 18 years old and fluent in English, and they must comply with all knowledge and skill requirements.

Median Annual Wages, May 2014

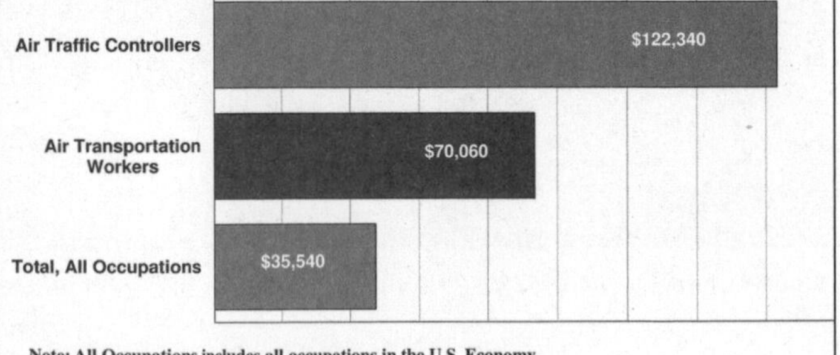

Note: All Occupations includes all occupations in the U.S. Economy.
Source: U.S. Bureau of Labor Statistics, Occupational Employment Statistics

Percent Change in Employment, Projected 2014–2024

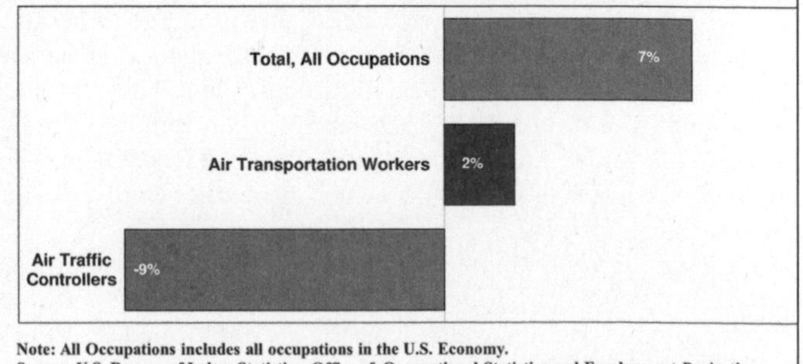

Note: All Occupations includes all occupations in the U.S. Economy.
Source: U.S. Bureau of Labor Statistics, Office of Occupational Statistics and Employment Projections

Employment Projections Data for Air Traffic Controllers

Occupational Title	SOC Code	Employment, 2014	Projected Employment, 2024	Change, 2014–2024 Percent	Change, 2014–2024 Numeric
Air traffic controllers	53-2021	24,500	22,400	-9	-2,100

Source: U.S. Bureau of Labor Statistics, Employment Projections Program

Similar Occupations. This table shows a list of occupations with job duties that are similar to those of air traffic controllers.

Occupations	Entry-level Education	2014 Median Pay	Projected Job Growth	Average Annual Openings
Aircraft and Avionics Equipment Mechanics and Technicians	See Education/Training	$56,980	1%	160
Airline and Commercial Pilots	See Education/Training	$103,390	5%	540
Cartographers and Photogrammetrists	Bachelor's degree	$60,930	29%	360
Police, Fire, and Ambulance Dispatchers	High school diploma or equivalent	$37,410	-3%	-300

Important Qualities

Communication skills. Air traffic controllers must be able to give clear, concise instructions, listen carefully to pilot's requests, and respond by speaking clearly.

Concentration skills. Controllers must be able to concentrate in a room where multiple conversations occur at once. For example, in a large airport tower, several controllers may be speaking with several pilots at the same time.

Decision-making skills. Controllers must make quick decisions. For example, when a pilot requests a change of altitude or heading to avoid poor weather, the controller must respond quickly so that the plane can operate safely.

Math skills. Controllers must be able to do arithmetic accurately and quickly. They often need to compute speeds, times, and distances, and they recommend heading and altitude changes.

Organizational skills. Controllers must be able to coordinate the actions of multiple flights. Controllers need to be able to prioritize tasks, because they may be required to guide several pilots at the same time.

Problem-solving skills. Controllers must be able to understand complex situations, such as the impact of changing weather patterns on a plane's flight path. Controllers must be able to review important information and provide pilots with appropriate solutions.

Pay

The median annual wage for air traffic controllers was $122,340 in May 2014. The median wage is the wage at which half the workers in an occupation earned more than that amount and half earned less. The lowest 10 percent earned less than $67,070, and the highest 10 percent earned more than $172,000.

The salaries for development controllers increase as they complete each new training phase. According to the FAA, the starting salary for more advanced controllers who have completed on-the-job training varies with the location of the facility, the complexity of the flight paths, and other factors. A full explanation of current starting wages can be found on the FAA Aviation Careers Page.

Union Membership. Compared with workers in all occupations, air traffic controllers had a higher percentage of workers who belonged to a union in 2014.

Job Outlook

Employment of air traffic controllers is projected to decline 9 percent from 2014 to 2024. Most employment opportunities will result from the need to replace workers who retire.

The Federal Aviation Administration (FAA) has not reduced, and does not expect to reduce, the overall number of controllers. Air traffic is likely to increase, and there will be employment opportunities because the FAA will need to replace retiring controllers. However, in the long term, the NextGen satellite-based system is expected to allow individual controllers to handle more air traffic.

Job Prospects. Job opportunities will be best for individuals with previous experience and those who are in their early twenties and can pass the FAA's biodata tests. Competition for air traffic controller jobs is expected to be very strong, with many people apply for a relatively small number of jobs. Those who are willing to live anywhere in the country will have an advantage.

Contacts for More Information

For more information about air traffic controllers, visit

➤ Federal Aviation Administration (www.faa.gov)

➤ National Air Traffic Controllers Association (www.natca.org)

For more information about biodata tests, visit

➤ U.S. Office of Personnel Management (http://tinyurl.com/hcrve2u)

O*NET

➤ Air Traffic Controllers (53-2021.00)

Airline and Commercial Pilots

- **2014 Median Pay** .... $103,390 per year
- **Typical Entry-Level Education** .... See Education/Training
- **Work Experience in a Related Occupation** .... See Education/Training
- **On-the-job Training** ... Moderate-term on-the-job training
- **Number of Jobs, 2014** 119,200
- **Job Outlook, 2014–24** .... 5% (As fast as average)
- **Employment Change, 2014–24** 5,400

Before every flight, pilots inspect the aircraft.

What Airline and Commercial Pilots Do

Airline and commercial pilots fly and navigate airplanes, helicopters, and other aircraft. Airline pilots fly for airlines that transport people and cargo on a fixed schedule. Commercial pilots fly aircraft for other purposes, such as charter flights, rescue operations, firefighting, aerial photography, and aerial application of agricultural materials.

Duties. Pilots typically do the following:

- Check the overall condition of the aircraft before and after every flight
- Ensure that the aircraft is balanced and below its weight limit
- Ensure that the fuel supply is adequate and that weather conditions are acceptable, and submit flight plans to air traffic control
- Communicate with air traffic control over the aircraft's radio system
- Operate and control aircraft along planned routes and during takeoffs and landings
- Monitor engines, fuel consumption, and other aircraft systems during flight
- Respond to changing conditions, such as weather events and emergencies (for example, an engine failure)
- Navigate the aircraft by using cockpit instruments and visual references

Many aircraft use two pilots. The captain or pilot in command, usually the most experienced pilot, supervises all other crew members and has primary responsibility for the flight. The copilot, often called the first officer or second in command, shares flight duties with the captain. Some older planes require a third pilot known as a flight engineer, who monitors instruments and operates controls. New technology has automated many of these tasks, and new aircraft do not require flight engineers.

Pilots must have good teamwork skills because they work closely with other pilots on the flight deck, as well as with air traffic controllers and flight dispatchers. They need to be able to coordinate actions and provide clear and honest feedback.

Pilots plan their flights carefully by making sure that the aircraft is operable and safe, that the cargo has been loaded correctly, and that weather conditions are acceptable. They file flight plans with air traffic control and may modify the plans in flight because of changing weather conditions or other factors.

Takeoff and landing can be the most difficult parts of a flight and require close coordination among the pilot, copilot, flight engineer, if present, and ground personnel. Once in the air, the captain and first officer usually alternate flying activities so that each can maintain their flying skills, as well as get rest. After landing, pilots must fill out records that document their flight and the status of the aircraft.

Many pilots will have some contact with passengers and customers. Charter and corporate pilots often will need to greet their passengers before embarking on the flight. Some airline pilots may have to help handle customer complaints.

Commercial pilots may have many more nonflight duties than airline pilots have. Commercial pilots may have to schedule flights, arrange for maintenance of the aircraft, and load luggage themselves. Agricultural pilots typically have to handle agricultural chemicals, such as pesticides, and may be involved in other agricultural practices in addition to flying. Flight instructors may need to spend time recruiting students or teaching ground school.

Pilots who routinely fly at low levels must constantly look for trees, bridges, power lines, transmission towers, and other dangerous obstacles. These obstacles present a common danger to agricultural pilots and air ambulance helicopter pilots, who frequently land on or near highways and accident sites that do not have improved landing strips.

The following are examples of types of pilots:

Airline pilots are commercial pilots who work primarily for airlines that transport passengers and cargo on a fixed schedule.

Corporate pilots fly for companies that own a fleet of planes to transport passengers such as company executives.

Commercial pilots are involved in unscheduled flight activities, such as aerial application, charter flights, aerial photography, and aerial tours.

Flight instructors are commercial pilots who use simulators and dual-controlled aircraft to teach students how to fly.

With proper training, airline pilots may also be deputized as federal law enforcement officers and be issued firearms to protect the cockpit.

Work Environment

Pilots held about 119,200 jobs in 2014.

About 64 percent worked as airline pilots, copilots, and flight engineers. The remainder worked as commercial pilots.

In 2014, most airline pilots, copilots, and flight engineers—about 87 percent—worked for scheduled air transportation providers, mainly the airlines.

The industries that employed the most commercial pilots in 2014 were as follows:

Nonscheduled air transportation	32%
Technical and trade schools; private	11
Support activities for air transportation	7
Ambulance services	7
Management of companies and enterprises	3

Pilots must learn to cope with several work-related hazards. For example, airline pilots assigned to long-distance routes may experience fatigue and jetlag. Weather and the condition of the aircraft also can pose unique hazards. In addition, flights can be long and flight decks are often sealed, so pilots must be able to work in small teams for long periods in close proximity to one another.

Commercial pilots face other types of job hazards. Many commercial pilot specialties, especially those which require a lot of low-altitude flying, can be dangerous. Aerial applicators, also known as crop dusters, may be exposed to toxic chemicals, typically use unimproved landing strips, and are at a higher risk of collision with power lines and birds than many other pilots are. Helicopter pilots involved in rescue operations regularly fly at low levels during bad weather or at night. These pilots also often land in areas surrounded by power lines and other obstacles, such as highways. In addition, pilots can be exposed to engine noise, but there is little risk of hearing impairment if proper hearing protection devices are used.

Although flying may not involve unusually high levels of physical effort, the high level of concentration required to fly an aircraft and the mental stress of being responsible for the safety of passengers can be fatiguing. Pilots must be alert and quick to react if something goes wrong, particularly during takeoff and landing. As a result, federal law requires pilots to retire at age 65.

Pilots work all over the country, but most are based near large airports.

Work Schedules. Federal regulations set maximum work hours and minimum requirements for rest between flights for most pilots. Airline pilots fly an average of 75 hours per month and work an additional 150 hours per month performing other duties. Pilots have variable work schedules that may include some days of intense work followed by some days off. Flight assignments are based on seniority. In general, that practice means that pilots who have worked at a company for a long time get preferred routes and schedules.

Airline pilots spend a considerable amount of time away from home because flight assignments often involve overnight layovers—sometimes up to several nights a week. When pilots are away from home, the airlines typically provide hotel accommodations, transportation to the airport, and an allowance for meals and other expenses.

Commercial pilots also have irregular schedules. They typically fly between 30 hours and 90 hours each month. Commercial pilots may have less free time than airline pilots because they frequently have more nonflight responsibilities than airline pilots have. Although most commercial pilots remain near their home overnight, they may still work nonstandard hours.

Education/Training

Most airline pilots begin their careers as commercial pilots. Commercial pilots typically need a high school diploma or equivalent. Airline pilots typically need a bachelor's degree. All pilots who are paid to fly must have at least a commercial pilot's license from the Federal Aviation Administration (FAA). In addition, airline pilots must have the Airline Transport Pilot (ATP) certificate. The ATP certificate, and instrument and multiengine ratings expand the privileges granted by the commercial pilot's license and may be required by certain employers.

Most pilots begin their flight training with independent instructors or through flight schools. Fixed base operators (FBO) usually provide a wide range of general aviation services, such as aircraft fueling, maintenance, and on-demand air transportation services, and they may also offer flight training. An FBO may manage a flight school or call its training department a school. Some flight schools are parts of 2- and 4-year colleges and universities.

Education and Training. Airline pilots typically need a bachelor's degree in any subject, along with a commercial pilot's license and an ATP certificate from the FAA. Airline pilots typically start their careers in flying as commercial pilots. Pilots usually accrue thousands of hours of flight experience to get a job with regional or major airlines.

The military traditionally has been an important source of experienced pilots because of the extensive training it provides. However, increased duty requirements have reduced the incentives for these pilots to transfer out of military aviation and into civilian aviation. Most military pilots who transfer to civilian aviation are able to transfer directly into the airlines rather than working in commercial aviation.

Commercial pilots must have a commercial pilot's license and typically need a high school diploma or the equivalent. Some employers have additional requirements. For example, agricultural pilots need to have an understanding of common agricultural practices, fertilizers, fungicides, herbicides, and pesticides. Flight instructors have to have special FAA-issued certificates and ratings, such as Certified Flight Instructor (CFI), CFI-Instrument (CFII), Multi-Engine Instructor (MEI), MEI-Instrument (MEII), and possibly others. Many additional requirements exist for other specialties. They range from being able to operate gliders and tow banners to being qualified to fly helicopters and airships.

Commercial pilots typically begin their flight training with independent FAA-certified flight instructors or at schools that offer flight training. The FAA certifies hundreds of civilian flight schools, which range from small FBOs to large state universities. Some colleges and universities offer pilot training as part of a 2- or 4-year aviation degree. Regardless of whether pilots attend flight schools or learn from independent instructors, all pilots need the FAA's commercial pilot license before they can be paid to fly. In addition, most commercial pilots need an instrument rating, typically to fly through clouds or other conditions that limit visibility. An instrument rating also is required to carry paying passengers more than 50 miles from the point of origin of their flight or at night.

Interviews for positions with major and regional airlines often reflect the FAA exams for pilot licenses, certificates, and instrument ratings, and can be intense. Airlines frequently will conduct their own psychological and aptitude tests in order to make sure

Median Annual Wages, May 2014

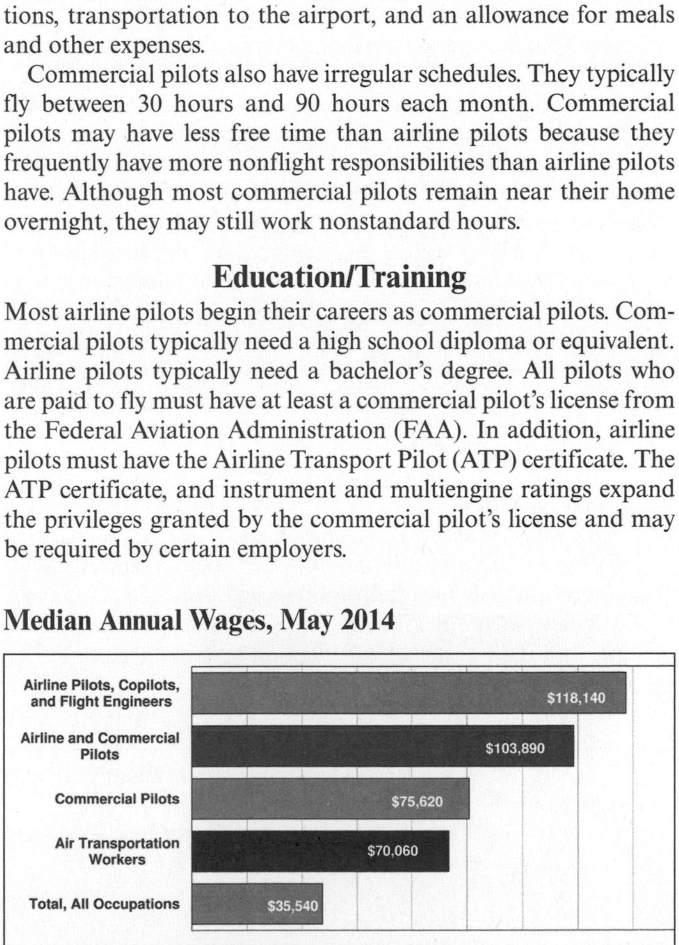

Note: All Occupations includes all occupations in the U.S. Economy.
Source: U.S. Bureau of Labor Statistics, Occupational Employment Statistics

Percent Change in Employment, Projected 2014–2024

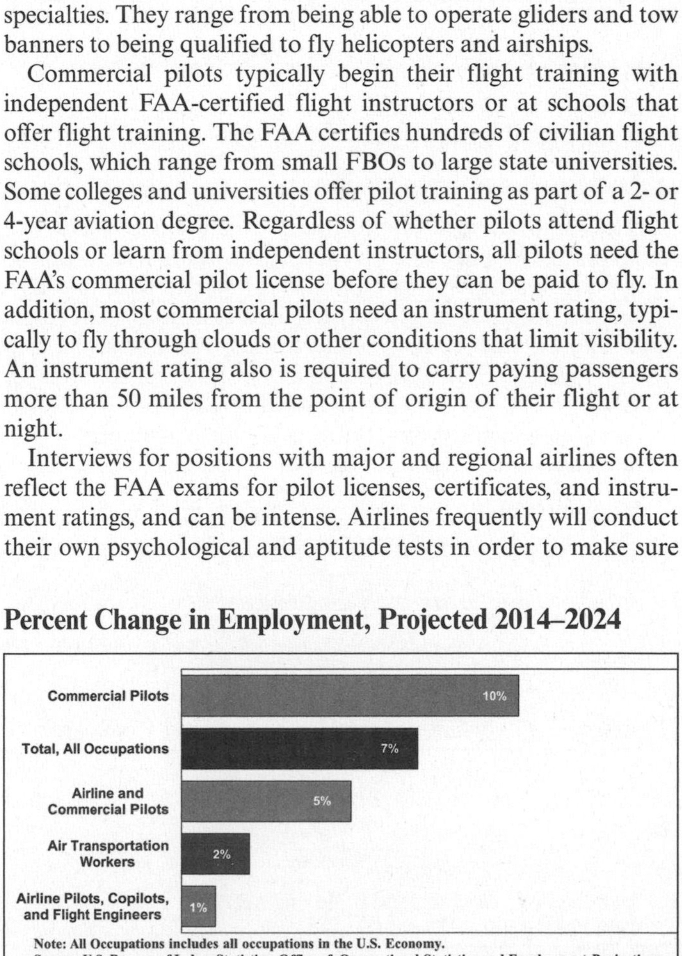

Note: All Occupations includes all occupations in the U.S. Economy.
Source: U.S. Bureau of Labor Statistics, Office of Occupational Statistics and Employment Projections

that their pilots are of good moral character and can make good decisions under pressure.

Airline and commercial pilots who are newly hired by airlines or on-demand air services companies must undergo moderate-term on-the-job training in accordance with Federal Aviation Regulations (FARs). This training usually includes 6–8 weeks of ground school and 25 hours of flight time. In addition, commercial pilots may need specific training based on the type of flying they are doing. For example, those who tow banners will likely need at least 200 hours in airplanes with conventional (tailwheel) landing gear. Further, various types of ratings for specific aircraft, such as the Boeing 737 or Cessna Citation, typically are acquired through employer-based training and generally are earned by pilots who have at least a commercial license.

Besides initial training and licensing requirements, all pilots must maintain their experience in performing certain maneuvers. This requirement means that pilots must perform specific maneuvers and procedures a given number of times within a specified amount of time. Furthermore, pilots must undergo periodic training and medical examinations, generally every year or every other year.

Work Experience in a Related Occupation. Airline pilots typically begin their careers as commercial pilots. Pilots usually accrue thousands of hours of flight experience as commercial pilots or in the military to get a job with regional or major airlines.

Licenses, Certifications, and Registrations. Those who are seeking a career as a professional pilot typically get their licenses and ratings in the following order:

- Student Pilot Certificate
- Private Pilot License
- Instrument Rating
- Commercial Pilot License
- Multi-Engine Rating
- Airline Transport Pilot Certificate

Each certificate and rating requires that pilots pass a written exam on the ground and a practical flying exam, usually called a check ride, in an appropriate aircraft. In addition to earning these licenses, many pilots get Certified Flight Instructor (CFI) rating after they get their commercial certificate. The CFI rating helps them build flight time and experience more quickly and at less personal expense. Current licensing regulations can be found in FARs.

Commercial pilot license. To qualify for a commercial pilot license, applicants must be at least 18 years old and meet certain flight-hour requirements. When student pilots first begin their training, they need to get a logbook and keep detailed records of their flight time. Also, their school may require them to log their ground instruction time. The logbook must be endorsed by the flight instructor in order for the student to be able to take the FAA knowledge and practical exams. For specific requirements, including details on the types and quantities of flight experience and knowledge requirements, see the FARs. Part 61 of Title 14 of the code of federal regulations (14 CFR part 61) covers the basic rules for the certification of pilots. Flight schools can train pilots in accordance with the rules from part 61 or the rules found in 14 CFR part 141.

In addition, applicants must pass the appropriate medical exam, meet all of the detailed flight experience and knowledge requirements, and pass a written exam and a practical flight exam in order to become commercially licensed. The physical exam confirms that the pilot's vision is correctable to 20/20 and that no physical handicaps exist that could impair the pilot's performance.

Commercial pilots must hold an instrument rating if they want to carry passengers for pay more than 50 miles from the point of origin of their flight or at night.

Instrument rating. Earning their instrument rating enables pilots to fly during periods of low visibility, also known as instrument meteorological conditions or IMC. They may qualify for this rating by having at least 40 hours of instrument flight experience and 50 hours of cross-country flight time as pilot in command and by meeting other requirements detailed in the FARs.

Airline transport pilot (ATP) certification. Beginning in 2013, all pilot crews of a scheduled commercial airliner must have ATP certificates. To earn the ATP certificate, applicants must be at least 23 years old, have a minimum of 1,500 hours of flight time, and pass written and practical flight exams. Furthermore, airline pilots usually maintain one or more aircraft-type ratings, which allow them to fly aircraft that require specific training, depending on the requirements of their particular airline. Some exceptions and alternative requirements are detailed in the FARs.

Pilots must pass periodic physical and practical flight examinations to be able to perform the duties granted by their certificate.

Other Experience. Minimum time requirements to get a certificate or rating may not be enough to get some jobs. To make up the gap between paying for training and flying for the major airlines, many commercial pilots begin their careers as flight instructors and on-demand charter pilots. These positions typically require less experience than airline jobs require. When pilots have built enough flying hours, they can apply to the airlines. Newly hired pilots at regional airlines typically have about 2,000 hours of flight experience. Newly hired pilots at major airlines typically have about 4,000 hours of flight experience. Many commercial piloting jobs have minimum requirements of around 500 hours. Numerous factors can affect this number, such as the type of flight time the pilot has.

Important Qualities

Communication skills. Pilots must speak clearly when conveying information to air traffic controllers and other crew members. They must also listen carefully for instructions.

Observational skills. Pilots must regularly watch over screens, gauges, and dials to make sure that all systems are in working

Employment Projections Data for Airline and Commercial Pilots

Occupational Title	SOC Code	Employment, 2014	Projected Employment, 2024	Change, 2014–2024 Percent	Change, 2014–2024 Numeric
Airline and commercial pilots	—	119,200	124,500	5	5,400
Airline pilots, copilots, and flight engineers	53-2011	75,700	76,500	1	800
Commercial pilots	53-2012	43,500	48,000	10	4,500

Source: U.S. Bureau of Labor Statistics, Employment Projections Program

Similar Occupations. This table shows a list of occupations with job duties that are similar to those of airline and commercial pilots.

Occupations	Entry-level Education	2014 Median Pay	Projected Job Growth	Average Annual Openings
Air Traffic Controllers	Associate's degree	$122,340	-9%	-210
Aircraft and Avionics Equipment Mechanics and Technicians	See Education/Training	$56,980	1%	160
Bus Drivers	High school diploma or equivalent	$30,220	6%	3,750
Construction Equipment Operators	High school diploma or equivalent	$42,900	10%	4,320
Delivery Truck Drivers and Driver/Sales Workers	High school diploma or equivalent	$27,490	4%	4,810
Flight Attendants	High school diploma or equivalent	$42,290	2%	220
Heavy and Tractor-trailer Truck Drivers	Postsecondary nondegree award	$39,520	5%	9,880
Material Moving Machine Operators	See Education/Training	$32,890	3%	1,950
Railroad Workers	High school diploma or equivalent	$53,670	-3%	-330
Taxi Drivers and Chauffeurs	No formal educational credential	$23,210	13%	3,060
Water Transportation Workers	See Education/Training	$53,130	9%	720

order. They also need to maintain situational awareness by looking for other aircraft or obstacles. Pilots must be able to see clearly, be able to judge the distance between objects, and possess good color vision.

Problem-solving skills. Pilots must be able to identify complex problems and figure out appropriate solutions. When a plane encounters turbulence, for example, pilots may assess the weather conditions and request a change in route or altitude from air traffic control.

Quick reaction time. Pilots must be able to respond quickly, and with good judgment, to any impending danger, because warning signals can appear with no notice.

Advancement. For airline pilots, advancement depends on a system of seniority outlined in collective bargaining contracts. Typically, after 1 to 5 years, flight engineers may advance to first officer positions and, after 5 to 15 years, first officers can become captains. In large companies, a captain could become a chief pilot or a director of aviation.

Pay

The median annual wage for airline pilots, copilots, and flight engineers was $118,140 in May 2014. The median wage is the wage at which half the workers in an occupation earned more than that amount and half earned less. The lowest 10 percent earned less than $64,780, and the highest 10 percent earned more than $187,200.

The median annual wage for commercial pilots was $75,620 in May 2014. The lowest 10 percent earned less than $35,250, and the highest 10 percent earned more than $141,210.

In May 2014, the median annual wages for commercial pilots in the top industries employing these pilots were as follows:

Management of companies and enterprises	$94,880
Nonscheduled air transportation	74,180
Support activities for air transportation	72,880
Technical and trade schools; private	70,940
Ambulance services	70,190

According to the Air Line Pilots Association, International, most airline pilots begin their careers earning about $20,000 per year. Wages increase each year until the pilot accumulates the experience and seniority needed to become a captain. The average captain at a regional airline earns about $55,000 per year, and the average captain at a major airline earns about $135,000 per year.

In addition, airline pilots receive an expense allowance, or "per diem," for every hour they are away from home, and they may earn extra pay for international flights. Airline pilots also are eligible for health insurance and retirement benefits, and their immediate families usually are entitled to free or reduced-fare flights.

Union Membership. Most airline and commercial pilots belonged to a union in 2014.

Job Outlook

Overall, employment of airline and commercial pilots is projected to grow 5 percent from 2014 to 2024, about as fast as the average for all occupations.

Employment of airline pilots, copilots, and flight engineers is projected to show little or no change from 2014 to 2024. It is likely that scheduled airlines will attempt to increase profitability over the next decade by increasing the average number of passengers in all of their aircraft. This goal will probably be achieved by eliminating routes with low demand and reducing the number of flights per day along more heavily used routes. These practices will ultimately lower the overall number of flights and lower the total number of pilot jobs.

Employment of commercial pilots is projected to grow 10 percent from 2014 to 2024, faster than the average for all occupations. Commercial pilots are projected to add jobs in various industries, including ambulance services and support activities for air transportation.

Job Prospects. Most job opportunities will arise from the need to replace pilots who leave the workforce. From 2014 to 2024, many pilots are expected to retire as they reach the required retirement age of 65.

Job prospects may be best with regional airlines, low-cost carriers, and nonscheduled aviation services because entry-level requirements are lower for regional and commercial jobs. There is typically less competition among applicants in these sectors than there is for major airlines.

Pilots seeking jobs at the major airlines will face strong competition because those firms tend to attract many more applicants than the number of job openings. Applicants also will have to compete with furloughed pilots for available jobs.

Pilots with the greatest number of flight hours usually have some advantage, but the type of time also matters a great deal. For example, pilots who have greater amounts of time in turbine engine-powered aircraft often have an advantage over those who do not. For this reason, military and experienced pilots will have an advantage over applicants whose flight time consists only of small piston-driven aircraft.

Contacts for More Information

For specific information about licensing requirements and other federal regulations regarding pilots and operators, visit

- ➤ Regulations concerning the certification of airmen and general flight rules (http://tinyurl.com/gqye3kl)
- ➤ Regulations concerning air carriers and operators for compensation or hire, and flight schools (http://tinyurl.com/zzs76j5)

For more information about pilots, visit

- ➤ Aircraft Owners and Pilots Association (www.aopa.org)
- ➤ Air Line Pilots Association, International (www.clearedtodream.org)
- ➤ Coalition of Airline Pilots Associations (www.capapilots.org)
- ➤ Federal Aviation Administration (www.faa.gov)
- ➤ Helicopter Association International (www.rotor.com)
- ➤ National Agricultural Aviation Association (www.agaviation.org)

O*NET

- ➤ Airline Pilots, Copilots, and Flight Engineers (53-2011.00)
- ➤ Commercial Pilots (53-2012.00)

Bus Drivers

- **2014 Median Pay** .... $30,220 per year $14.53 per hour
- **Typical Entry-Level Education** .... High school diploma or equivalent
- **Work Experience in a Related Occupation** .... None
- **On-the-job Training** .... See Education/Training
- **Number of Jobs, 2014** 665,000
- **Job Outlook, 2014–24** .... 6% (As fast as average)
- **Employment Change, 2014–24** 37,500

What Bus Drivers Do

Bus drivers transport people between various places—including, work, school, and shopping malls—and across state and national borders. Some drive regular routes, and others transport passengers on chartered trips or sightseeing tours. They drive a range of vehicles, from 15-passenger buses to 60-foot articulated buses (with two connected sections) that can carry more than 100 passengers.

Duties. Bus drivers typically do the following:

- Pick up and drop off passengers at designated locations
- Follow a planned route according to a time schedule
- Help disabled passengers get on and off the bus
- Obey traffic laws and state and federal transit regulations
- Follow procedures to ensure passenger safety
- Keep passengers informed of possible delays
- Perform basic maintenance (check the bus tires, lights, and oil)
- Keep the bus clean and presentable to the public

School bus drivers transport students to and from school and other activities. On school days, drivers pick up students in the morning and return them home in the afternoon. They also drive students to field trips, sporting events, and other activities. Between morning and afternoon trips, some drivers work at schools in other occupations, such as janitors, cafeteria workers, or mechanics. School bus drivers typically do the following:

- Ensure the safety of children getting on and off the bus
- Attend to the needs of children with disabilities
- Keep order and safety on the school bus
- Understand and enforce the school system's conduct rules
- Report disciplinary problems to the school district or parents

Local transit bus drivers follow a daily schedule while transporting people on regular routes along city or suburban streets. They stop frequently, often every few blocks and when a passenger requests a stop. Some large transit agencies may require bus drivers to submit traffic data for analysis. Local transit drivers typically do the following:

- Collect bus fares, sometimes making change for passengers
- Answer questions about schedules, routes, and transfer points
- Report accidents or other traffic disruptions to a central dispatcher

Intercity bus drivers transport passengers between cities or towns, sometimes crossing state lines. They usually pick up and drop off passengers at bus stations or curbside locations in downtown urban areas. Intercity drivers typically do the following:

- Ensure all passengers have a valid ticket to ride the bus
- Sell tickets to passengers when there are unsold seats available, if necessary
- Keep track of when passengers get on or off the bus
- Follow a central dispatcher's instruction when taking an alternate route
- Help passengers load or unload baggage

Charter bus drivers, sometimes called *motorcoach drivers*, transport passengers on chartered trips or sightseeing tours. Trip planners generally arrange their schedules and routes based on the convenience of the passengers, who are often on vacation. Motor coach drivers are sometimes away for long periods of time because they usually stay with the passengers for the length of the trip. Motor coach drivers typically do the following:

- Listen to and sometimes address passenger complaints
- Ensure the trip stays on schedule
- Help passengers load or unload baggage
- Account for all passengers before leaving a location
- Act as tour guides for passengers, if necessary

Work Environment

Bus drivers held about 665,000 jobs in 2014. Of those, about 75 percent were school bus drivers or special-client bus drivers.

School bus drivers or special-client bus drivers are usually employed by a school district or private transportation company that contracts with a district to provide bus service. Some school bus service is provided by a local government.

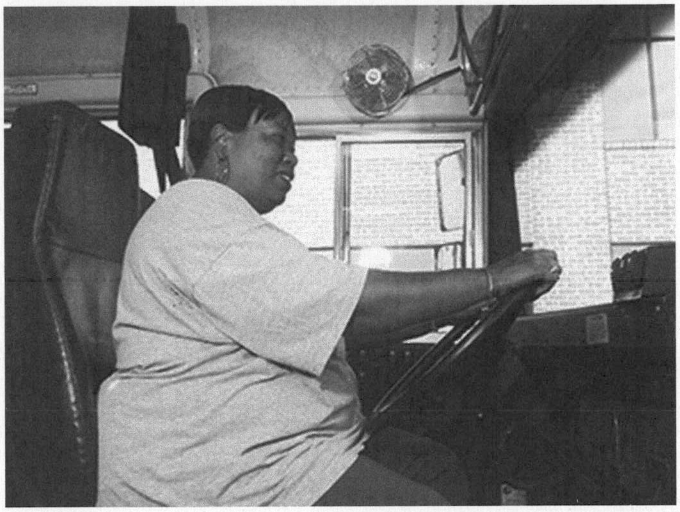

Bus drivers must be alert, especially in heavy traffic or in bad weather, to prevent accidents.

The industries that employed the most school bus drivers in 2014 were as follows:

Elementary and secondary schools; local	41%
School and employee bus transportation	30
Local government, excluding education and hospitals	12
Other transit and ground passenger transportation	6

Most transit bus drivers worked for local governments or urban transit systems, which are private companies that contract with a city or town to provide bus service. Most charter-bus drivers worked in the charter-bus industry, and intercity bus drivers typically work in the interurban and rural bus transportation industry.

The industries that employed the most transit and intercity bus drivers in 2014 were as follows:

Local government, excluding education and hospitals	48%
Urban transit systems	17
Charter bus industry	11
Interurban and rural bus transportation	6

Driving through heavy traffic or bad weather and dealing with unruly passengers can be stressful for bus drivers.

Injuries and Illnesses. Bus drivers, especially transit and intercity drivers, had a higher rate of work-related injuries and illnesses than the national average. Most injuries to bus drivers were due to highway accidents.

Work Schedules. School bus drivers work only when school is in session. Some make multiple runs if schools in their district each open and close at different times. Others make only two runs, one in the morning and one in the afternoon, so their work hours are limited.

Transit drivers may work weekends, late nights, and early mornings.

Motor coach drivers travel with their vacationing passengers. The trip schedule dictates a driver's hours. They may work all hours of the day, as well as weekends and holidays. Intercity bus drivers can spend some nights away because of long-distance routes. Other intercity bus drivers make a round trip and go home at the end of each shift.

Education/Training

Bus drivers must have a commercial driver's license (CDL). This can sometimes be earned during on-the-job training. A bus driver must possess a clean driving record and often may be required to pass a background check. They also must meet physical, hearing and vision requirements. In addition, bus drivers often need a high school diploma or the equivalent.

Education. Most employers prefer drivers to have a high school diploma or equivalent.

Training. Bus drivers typically go through 1 to 3 months of training. Part of the training is spent on a driving course, where drivers practice various maneuvers with a bus. They then begin to drive in light traffic and eventually make practice runs on the type of route that they expect to drive. New drivers make regularly scheduled trips with passengers and are accompanied by an experienced driver who gives helpful tips, answers questions, and evaluates the new driver's performance.

Some drivers' training is also spent in the classroom. They learn their company's rules and regulations, state and municipal traffic laws, and safe driving practices. Drivers also learn about schedules and bus routes, fares, and how to interact with passengers.

Licenses, Certifications, and Registrations. All bus drivers must have a commercial driver's license (CDL). Some new bus drivers can earn their CDL during on-the-job training. The qualifications for getting one vary by state but generally include passing both knowledge and driving tests. States have the right to not issue a license to someone who has had a CDL suspended by another state.

Drivers can get endorsements to a CDL that reflect their ability to drive a special type of vehicle. All bus drivers must have a passenger (P) endorsement, and school bus drivers must also have a school bus (S) endorsement. Getting the P and S endorsements requires additional knowledge and driving tests administered by a certified examiner.

Many states require all bus drivers to be 18 years of age or older and those who drive across state lines to be at least 21 years old.

Median Annual Wages, May 2014

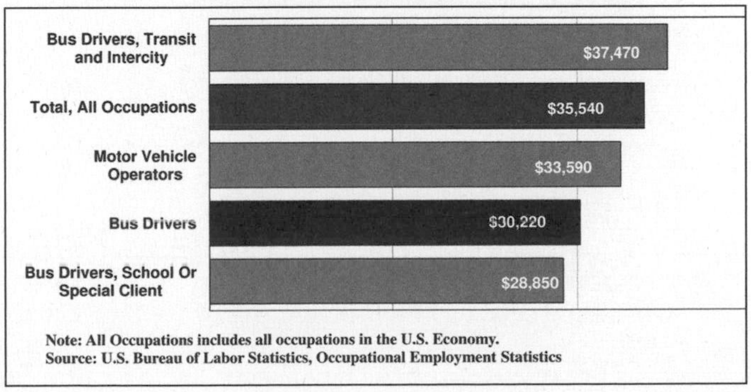

Percent Change in Employment, Projected 2014–2024

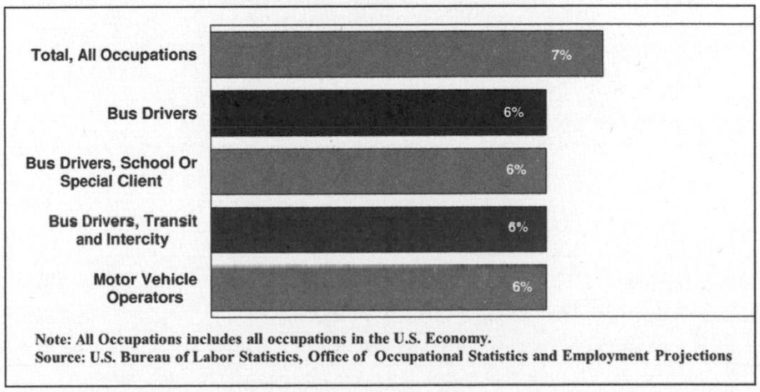

Federal regulations require interstate bus drivers to pass a physical exam and submit to random testing for drug or alcohol abuse while on duty. Most states impose similar regulations. Bus drivers can have their CDL suspended if they are convicted of a felony involving the use of a motor vehicle or of driving under the influence of alcohol or drugs. Other actions also can result in a suspension after multiple violations. A list of violations is available from the Federal Motor Carrier Safety Administration.

Most bus drivers are required to undergo background checks before they are hired.

Advancement. Opportunities for promotion are generally limited, but experienced drivers may become supervisors or dispatchers. Some veteran bus drivers become instructors of new bus drivers.

Important Qualities

Customer-service skills. Bus drivers regularly interact with passengers and must be courteous and helpful.

Hand-eye coordination. Driving a bus requires the controlled use of multiple limbs on the basis of what a person observes. Federal regulations require drivers to have normal use of their arms and legs.

Hearing ability. Bus drivers need good hearing. Federal regulations require the ability to hear a forced whisper in one ear at five feet (with or without the use of a hearing aid).

Patience. Because of possible traffic congestion and sometimes unruly passengers, bus drivers are put in stressful situations and must remain calm and continue to operate their bus.

Physical health. Federal and state regulations do not allow people to become bus drivers if they have a medical condition that may interfere with their operation of a bus, such as high blood pressure or epilepsy. A full list of medical reasons that keep someone from becoming a licensed bus driver is available from the Federal Motor Carrier Safety Administration.

Visual ability. Bus drivers must be able to pass vision tests. Federal regulations require at least 20/40 vision with a 70-degree field of vision in each eye and the ability to distinguish colors on a traffic light.

Pay

The median annual wage for bus drivers, transit and intercity was $37,470 in May 2014. The median wage is the wage at which half the workers in an occupation earned more than that amount and half earned less. The lowest 10 percent earned less than $21,390, and the highest 10 percent earned more than $61,570.

The median annual wage for bus drivers, school or special client was $28,850 in May 2014. The lowest 10 percent earned less than $17,880, and the highest 10 percent earned more than $44,610.

In May 2014, the median annual wages for school or special-client bus drivers in the top industries in which they worked were as follows:

Local government, excluding education and hospitals	$32,920
School and employee bus transportation	31,530
Elementary and secondary schools; local	27,270
Other transit and ground passenger transportation	26,290

In May 2014, the median annual wages for transit and intercity bus drivers in the top industries in which they worked were as follows:

Local government, excluding education and hospitals	$46,100
Interurban and rural bus transportation	35,840
Urban transit systems	35,150
Charter bus industry	27,760

Transit drivers may work weekends, late nights, and early mornings.

Union Membership. Compared with workers in all occupations, bus drivers had a higher percentage of workers who belonged to a union in 2014.

Job Outlook

Employment of bus drivers is projected to grow 6 percent from 2014 to 2024, about as fast as the average for all occupations.

Employment of school or special-client bus drivers is projected to grow 6 percent, largely because of an increase in the number of school-age children. However, growth will most likely occur for contracting services that provide school bus transport as more school districts outsource their transportation needs. In addition, the demand for special-needs transportation will continue to increase because of the aging population.

Employment of transit and intercity drivers (including charter buses) is projected to grow 6 percent. Some new Bus Rapid Transit (BRT) systems are opening throughout the country, which should create some employment opportunities. In addition, population movement toward large metropolitan areas will create more job opportunities for transit drivers.

Intercity bus travel that picks up passengers from curbside locations in urban downtowns should continue to grow. This form of travel is expected to remain popular due to the cheap fares and passenger conveniences such as Wi-Fi.

Job Prospects. Job opportunities for bus drivers should be favorable, especially for school bus drivers, as many drivers are expected to leave the occupation. Those willing to work part time or irregular shifts should have the best prospects. Prospects for motor coach and intercity drivers should also be favorable as the industry struggles to attract and retain qualified drivers.

Contacts for More Information

For more information about school bus drivers, visit

➤ National School Transportation Association (www.yellowbuses.org)

➤ National Association of State Directors of Pupil Transportation Services (www.nasdpts.org)

Employment Projections Data for Bus Drivers

Occupational Title	SOC Code	Employment, 2014	Projected Employment, 2024	Change, 2014–2024	
				Percent	Numeric
Bus drivers	53-3020	665,000	702,500	6	37,500
Bus drivers, transit and intercity	53-3021	167,800	177,600	6	9,800
Bus drivers, school or special client	53-3022	497,300	524,900	6	27,700

Source: U.S. Bureau of Labor Statistics, Employment Projections Program

Similar Occupations. This table shows a list of occupations with job duties that are similar to those of bus drivers.

Occupations	Entry-level Education	2014 Median Pay	Projected Job Growth	Average Annual Openings
Delivery Truck Drivers and Driver/Sales Workers	High school diploma or equivalent	$27,490	4%	4,810
Heavy and Tractor-trailer Truck Drivers	Postsecondary nondegree award	$39,520	5%	9,880
Railroad Workers	High school diploma or equivalent	$53,670	-3%	-330
Taxi Drivers and Chauffeurs	No formal educational credential	$23,210	13%	3,060
Water Transportation Workers	See Education/Training	$53,130	9%	720

For more information about transit bus drivers, visit

➤ American Public Transportation Association (www.apta.com/Pages/default.aspx)

For more information about motorcoach drivers, visit

➤ United Motorcoach Association (www.uma.org)

For more information on federal regulations for commercial vehicle drivers, visit

➤ Federal Motor Carrier Safety Administration (www.fmcsa.dot.gov)

O*NET

➤ Bus Drivers, Transit and Intercity (53-3021.00)

➤ Bus Drivers, School or Special Client (53-3022.00)

Delivery Truck Drivers and Driver/Sales Workers

- **2014 Median Pay** .... $27,490 per year $13.22 per hour
- **Typical Entry-Level Education** .... High school diploma or equivalent
- **Work Experience in a Related Occupation** .... None
- **On-the-job Training** .... Short-term on-the-job training
- **Number of Jobs, 2014** 1,330,000
- **Job Outlook, 2014–24** .... 4% (Slower than average)
- **Employment Change, 2014–24** 48,100

What Delivery Truck Drivers and Driver/Sales Workers Do

Delivery truck drivers and driver/sales workers pick up, transport, and drop off packages and light shipments within a small local region or urban area. They drive trucks with a 26,000-pound gross vehicle weight (GVW) capacity or less. Most of the time, they transport merchandise from a distribution center to businesses and households.

Duties. Delivery truck drivers and driver/sales workers typically do the following:

- Load and unload their cargo
- Communicate with costumers to determine pickup and delivery needs
- Report any incidents they encounter on the road to a dispatcher
- Follow all applicable traffic laws
- Report serious mechanical problems to the appropriate personnel
- Keep their truck and associated equipment clean and in good working order
- Accept payments for the shipment
- Handle paperwork, such as receipts or delivery confirmation notices

Most drivers generally receive instructions to go to a delivery location at a particular time, and it is up to them to determine the best route. Other drivers have a regular daily or weekly delivery schedule. All drivers must have a thorough understanding of an area's street grid and know which roads allow trucks and which do not.

Light truck drivers, often called *pickup and delivery* or *P&D drivers*, are the most common type of delivery driver. They drive small trucks or vans from distribution centers to delivery locations. Drivers make deliveries based on a set schedule. Some drivers stop at the distribution center once only, in the morning, and make many stops throughout the day. Others make multiple trips between the distribution center and delivery locations. Some drivers make deliveries from a retail location to customers.

Driver/sales workers are delivery drivers who have additional sales responsibilities. They recommend new products to businesses and solicit new customers. These drivers may have a regular delivery route and be responsible for adding new clients located along their route. For example, they may make regular deliveries to a hardware store and encourage the store's manager to offer a new type of product. Driver/sales workers also deliver goods, such as take-out food to consumers, and accept payment for those goods.

Work Environment

Light truck drivers or delivery services drivers held about 884,700 jobs in 2014.

Delivery drivers and driver/sales workers transport goods around an urban area or small region.

The industries that employed the most light truck or delivery service drivers in 2014 were as follows:

Retail trade	20%
Couriers and messengers	19
Wholesale trade	18

Driver/sales workers held about 445,300 jobs in 2014.

The industries that employed the most driver/sales workers in 2014 were as follows:

Restaurants and other eating places	35%
Wholesale trade	28
Retail trade	13

Delivery truck drivers and driver/sales workers have physically demanding jobs. When loading and unloading cargo, drivers do a lot of lifting, carrying, and walking. Driving in congested traffic or adhering to strict delivery timelines can also be stressful.

Injuries and Illnesses. Delivery truck drivers and driver/sales workers have a higher rate of injuries and illnesses than the national average. Injuries can result from workers lifting and moving heavy objects as well as automobile accidents.

Work Schedules. Most drivers work full time, and many work additional hours. Those who work on regular routes sometimes must begin work very early in the morning or work late at night. For example, a driver who delivers bread to a deli every day must be there before the deli opens. Drivers often work weekends and holidays.

Education/Training

Delivery truck drivers and driver/sales workers typically enter their occupations with a high school diploma or equivalent. However, some opportunities exist for those without a high school diploma. Workers undergo 1 month or less of on-the-job training. They must have a driver's license from the state in which they work and possess a clean driving record.

Education. Delivery truck drivers and driver/sales workers typically enter their occupations with a high school diploma or equivalent.

Training. Companies train new delivery truck drivers and driver/sales workers on the job. This may include driving training from a driver-mentor who rides along with a new employee to ensure that a new driver is able to operate a truck safely on crowded streets.

New drivers also have training to learn company policies about package drop-offs and returns, taking payment, and what to do with damaged goods.

Driver/sales workers must learn detailed information about the products they offer. Their company also may teach them proper sales techniques, such as how to approach potential new customers.

Licenses, Certifications, and Registrations. All delivery drivers need a driver's license.

Other Experience. Some delivery drivers begin as package loaders at warehouse facilities, especially if the driver works for a large company. For more information on package loaders, see the profile on hand laborers and material movers.

Important Qualities

Customer-service skills. When completing deliveries, drivers often interact with customers and should make a good impression to ensure repeat business.

Hand-eye coordination. When driving, delivery drivers need to observe their surroundings while simultaneously operating a complex machine.

Math skills. Because delivery truck drivers and driver/sales workers sometimes take payment, they must be able to count cash and make change quickly and accurately.

Patience. When driving through heavy traffic congestion, delivery drivers must remain calm and composed.

Sales skills. Driver/sales workers are expected to persuade customers to purchase new or different products from them.

Visual ability. To have a driver's license, delivery truck drivers and driver/sales workers must be able to pass a state vision test.

Pay

The median annual wage for driver/sales workers was $22,250 in May 2014. The median wage is the wage at which half the workers in an occupation earned more than that amount and half earned less. The lowest 10 percent earned less than $17,020, and the highest 10 percent earned more than $47,090.

The median annual wage for light truck or delivery services drivers was $29,570 in May 2014. The lowest 10 percent earned less than $18,460, and the highest 10 percent earned more than $60,710.

In May 2014, the median annual wages for driver/sales workers in the top industries in which they worked were as follows:

Wholesale trade	$29,590
Retail trade	25,340
Restaurants and other eating places	18,570

In May 2014, the median annual wages for light truck or delivery services drivers in the top industries in which they worked were as follows:

Couriers and messengers	$49,690
Wholesale trade	28,550
Retail trade	23,420

Median Annual Wages, May 2014

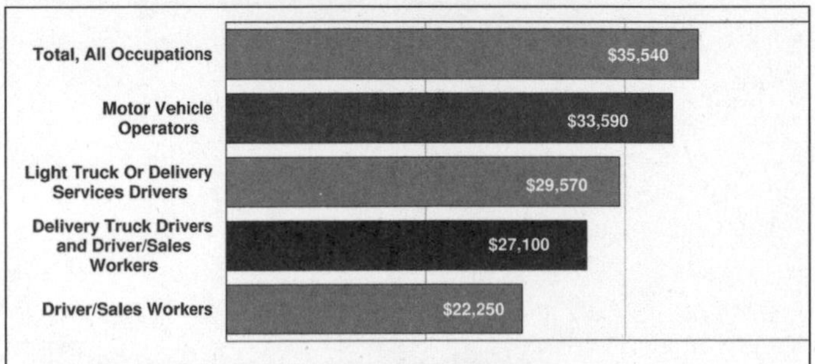

Note: All Occupations includes all occupations in the U.S. Economy.
Source: U.S. Bureau of Labor Statistics, Occupational Employment Statistics

Percent Change in Employment, Projected 2014–2024

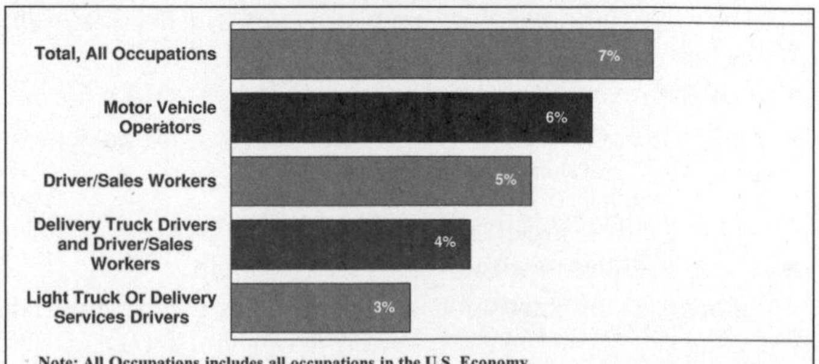

Note: All Occupations includes all occupations in the U.S. Economy.
Source: U.S. Bureau of Labor Statistics, Office of Occupational Statistics and Employment Projections

Employment Projections Data for Delivery Truck Drivers and Driver/Sales Workers

Occupational Title	SOC Code	Employment, 2014	Projected Employment, 2024	Change, 2014–2024	
				Percent	Numeric
Delivery truck drivers and driver/sales workers	—	1,330,000	1,378,100	4	48,100
Driver/sales workers	53-3031	445,300	466,100	5	20,800
Light truck or delivery services drivers	53-3033	884,700	911,900	3	27,300

Source: U.S. Bureau of Labor Statistics, Employment Projections Program

Similar Occupations. This table shows a list of occupations with job duties that are similar to those of delivery truck drivers and driver/sales workers.

Occupations	Entry-level Education	2014 Median Pay	Projected Job Growth	Average Annual Openings
Bus Drivers	High school diploma or equivalent	$30,220	6%	3,750
Hand Laborers and Material Movers	No formal educational credential	$23,560	5%	17,550
Heavy and Tractor-trailer Truck Drivers	Postsecondary nondegree award	$39,520	5%	9,880
Material Recording Clerks	See Education/Training	$25,810	3%	8,470
Postal Service Workers	High school diploma or equivalent	$54,720	-28%	-13,600
Railroad Workers	High school diploma or equivalent	$53,670	-3%	-330
Taxi Drivers and Chauffeurs	No formal educational credential	$23,210	13%	3,060
Water Transportation Workers	See Education/Training	$53,130	9%	720

Some drivers/sales workers, such as pizza delivery workers, receive tips in addition to hourly wages. Sales workers can also receive commissions from the products they sell.

Job Outlook

Employment of delivery truck drivers and drivers/sales workers is projected to grow 4 percent from 2014 to 2024, slower than the average for all occupations.

Employment of light truck or delivery services drivers is projected to grow 3 percent from 2014 to 2024, slower than the average for all occupations.

Continued e-commerce growth should increase demand for package delivery services, especially for the large and regional shipping companies. More light truck and delivery drivers will be needed to fulfill the growing number of e-commerce transactions.

However, improved routing through GPS technology can make existing light truck drivers more productive, which may limit the demand for additional drivers. With improved routing, drivers can be more efficient, navigating better in traffic and spending less time idling at each stop.

Employment of driver/sales workers is projected to grow 5 percent from 2014 to 2024, about as fast as the average for all occupations. As the number of restaurants that offer delivery services continues to expand, the demand for food delivery drivers should grow. Employment of driver/sales workers in the restaurants and other eating places industry is projected to grow 10 percent from 2014 to 2024.

Job Prospects. Job opportunities for delivery truck driver and driver/sales worker are expected to be competitive. Because these drivers do not have to spend long periods away from home, these jobs tend to be more desirable than long-haul trucking jobs. Job applicants with experience and a clean driving record, or who work for the company in another occupation, should have the best job prospects.

Contacts for More Information

For more information about truck drivers, including delivery truck drivers and driver/sales workers, visit

➤ American Trucking Associations (www.trucking.org)
➤ Professional Truck Driver Institute (www.ptdi.org)

O*NET

➤ Driver/Sales Workers (53-3031.00)
➤ Light Truck or Delivery Services Drivers (53-3033.00)

Flight Attendants

- **2014 Median Pay** .... $42,290 per year
- **Typical Entry-Level Education** .... High school diploma or equivalent
- **Work Experience in a Related Occupation**......... Less than 5 years
- **On-the-job Training**...Moderate-term on-the-job training
- **Number of Jobs, 2014** 97,900
- **Job Outlook, 2014–24** .... 2% (Slower than average)
- **Employment Change, 2014–24** 2,200

What Flight Attendants Do

Flight attendants provide routine services and respond to emergencies to ensure the safety and comfort of airline passengers.

Duties. Flight attendants typically do the following:

- Participate in preflight briefings with the pilots, to discuss cabin conditions and flight details
- Conduct preflight inspections of emergency equipment
- Demonstrate the use of safety equipment and emergency equipment

- Ensure that passengers have their seatbelts fastened when required and that all other safety requirements are met
- Serve, and sometimes sell, beverages, meals, or snacks
- Take care of passengers' needs, particularly those with special needs
- Reassure passengers during the flight, such as when the aircraft hits turbulence
- Administer and coordinate emergency medical care, as needed
- If an emergency arises, provide direction to passengers, including how to evacuate the aircraft

Airlines are required by law to provide flight attendants for the safety and security of passengers. The primary job of flight attendants is to keep passengers safe, ensuring that everyone follows security regulations and that the flight deck is secure. Flight attendants also try to make flights comfortable and stress free for passengers. At times, they may deal with passengers who display disruptive behavior.

About 1 hour before takeoff, the captain (pilot) may conduct a preflight briefing with flight attendants about relevant flight information, including the number of hours the flight will take, the route the plane will travel, and weather conditions. Flight attendants must ensure that emergency equipment is working, the cabin is clean, and there is an adequate supply of food and beverages on board. Flight attendants greet passengers as they board the aircraft, direct them to their seats, and provide assistance as needed.

Before the plane takes off, flight attendants demonstrate the proper use of safety equipment to all passengers, either in person or through a video recording. They also ensure that seatbelts are fastened, seats are locked in the upright position, and all carry-on items are properly stowed in accordance with federal law and company policy.

A flight attendant's most important responsibility, however, is to help passengers in the event of an emergency. This responsibility ranges from dealing with unruly passengers to performing first aid, fighting fires, protecting the flight deck, and directing evacuations. Flight attendants also answer questions about the flight, attend to passengers with special needs, and generally assist all passengers as needed.

Flight attendants spend a great deal of time away from home.

Before the plane lands, flight attendants once again ensure that seatbelts are fastened, seats are locked in the upright position, and all carry-on and galley items are properly stowed.

Before they leave the plane, flight attendants survey the condition of the cabin. They submit reports on any medical, safety, or security issues that may have occurred during the flight.

Work Environment

Flight attendants held about 97,900 jobs in 2014. Although most worked for scheduled airlines, a small number worked for corporations or chartered-flight companies.

Flight attendants work primarily in the cabin of passenger aircraft. Dealing directly with the public and standing for long periods can be stressful and tiring. Occasionally, flight attendants must deal with turbulence, which can make providing service more difficult and causes anxiety in some passengers. Although rare, dealing with emergencies and unruly customers also can be difficult and cause stress.

Flight attendants spend many nights away from home and often sleep in hotels or apartments shared by a group of flight attendants.

Injuries and Illnesses. Injuries may occur when overhead compartments are opened, during turbulence, when the attendant is pushing carts, or during aircraft emergencies. In addition, medical problems can arise from irregular sleep patterns, the stress of frequent travel, and exposure to ill passengers. As a result, flight attendants experience some work-related injuries and illnesses.

Work Schedules. Flight attendants usually have variable schedules. They often work nights, weekends, and holidays because airlines operate every day and have overnight flights. In most cases, a contract between the airline and the flight attendant union determines the total daily and monthly workable hours. A typical on-duty shift is usually about 12 to 14 hours per day. However, duty time can be increased for international flights. The Federal Aviation Administration (FAA) requires that flight attendants receive at least 9 consecutive hours of rest following any duty period before starting their next duty period.

Attendants usually fly 75 to 100 hours a month and generally spend another 50 hours a month on the ground, preparing flights, writing reports, and waiting for aircraft to arrive. They can spend several nights a week away from home. During this time, employers typically arrange hotel accommodations and a meal allowance.

An attendant's assignments of home base and route are based on seniority. New flight attendants must be flexible with their schedule and location. Almost all flight attendants start out working on call, also known as reserve status. Flight attendants on reserve usually live near their home airport, because they have to report to work on short notice.

As they earn more seniority, attendants gain more control over their schedules. For example, some senior flight attendants may choose to live outside their home base and commute to work. Others may choose to work only on regional flights. On small corporate airlines, flight attendants often work on an as-needed basis and must be able to adapt to changing schedules. About 1 in 4 flight attendants worked part time in 2014.

Education/Training

Flight attendants receive training from their employer and must be certified by the Federal Aviation Administration (FAA). Although

Median Annual Wages, May 2014

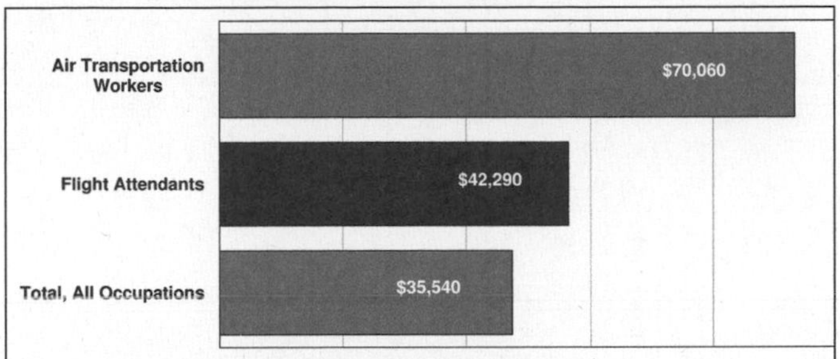

Note: All Occupations includes all occupations in the U.S. Economy.
Source: U.S. Bureau of Labor Statistics, Occupational Employment Statistics

Percent Change in Employment, Projected 2014–2024

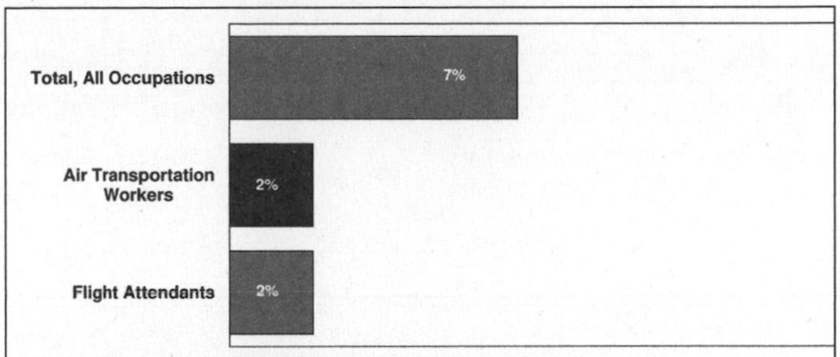

Note: All Occupations includes all occupations in the U.S. Economy.
Source: U.S. Bureau of Labor Statistics, Office of Occupational Statistics and Employment Projections

flight attendants must have at least a high school diploma or the equivalent, some airlines prefer to hire applicants who have taken some college courses. Prospective flight attendants typically need previous work experience in customer service.

Applicants must be at least 18 years old, be eligible to work in the United States, have a valid passport, and pass a background check and drug test. They must have vision that is correctable to at least 20/40 and often need to conform to height and weight requirements. Flight attendants also may have to pass a medical evaluation.

Education. A high school diploma is typically the minimum educational requirement for becoming a flight attendant. However, some airlines prefer to hire applicants who have taken some college courses.

Many employers prefer applicants with a degree in hospitality and tourism, public relations, business, social science, or communications. Those who work on international flights may have to be fluent in a foreign language. Some flight attendants attend flight attendant academies.

Work Experience in a Related Occupation. Flight attendants typically have 1 or 2 years of work experience in a service occupation before getting their first job as a flight attendant. This experience may include customer service positions in restaurants, hotels, or resorts. Experience in sales or in other positions that require close contact with the public and focus on service to customers also may help develop the skills needed to be a successful flight attendant.

Training. Once a flight attendant is hired, airlines provide their initial training, ranging from 3 to 6 weeks. The training usually takes place at the airline's flight training center and is required for FAA certification.

Trainees learn emergency procedures such as evacuating aircraft, operating emergency equipment, and administering first aid. They also receive specific instruction on flight regulations, company operations, and job duties.

Toward the end of the training, students go on practice flights. They must complete the training to keep a job with the airline. Once they have passed initial training, new flight attendants receive the FAA Certificate of Demonstrated Proficiency.

Licenses, Certifications, and Registrations. All flight attendants must be certified by the FAA. To become certified, flight attendants must complete their employer's initial training program and pass an exam. Flight attendants are certified for specific types of aircraft and must take new training for each type of aircraft on which they are to work, in addition to receiving recurrent training every year if they are to maintain their certification.

Advancement. After completing initial training, new flight attendants are typically placed on call, also known as reserve status. While on reserve status, attendants must be able to report to the airport on short notice to staff extra flights or fill in for absent crewmembers.

New attendants usually remain on reserve status for at least 1 year, but in some cities attendants may be on reserve for several years. After their stretch of time in this reserve period, flight attendants gain enough seniority to bid on monthly assignments. Assignments are based on seniority, and the most preferred routes go to the most experienced attendants.

Career advancement is based on seniority. Senior flight attendants exercise the most control over route assignments and schedules; therefore, they often can choose how much time to spend away from home. On international flights, senior attendants frequently oversee the work of other attendants. Senior attendants may be promoted to management positions in which they are responsible for recruiting, instructing, and scheduling.

Important Qualities

Attentiveness. Flight attendants must be aware of any security or safety risks during the flight. They also must be attentive to passengers' needs in order to ensure a pleasant travel experience.

Communication skills. Flight attendants should speak clearly, listen attentively, and interact comfortably with passengers and other crew members.

Customer-service skills. Flight attendants should have poise, tact, and resourcefulness to handle stressful situations and address passengers' needs.

Decision-making skills. Flight attendants must be able to act decisively in emergencies.

Employment Projections Data for Flight Attendants

Occupational Title	SOC Code	Employment, 2014	Projected Employment, 2024	Change, 2014–2024 Percent	Change, 2014–2024 Numeric
Flight attendants	53-2031	97,900	100,100	2	2,200

Source: U.S. Bureau of Labor Statistics, Employment Projections Program

Similar Occupations. This table shows a list of occupations with job duties that are similar to those of flight attendants.

Occupations	Entry-level Education	2014 Median Pay	Projected Job Growth	Average Annual Openings
Bartenders	No formal educational credential	$19,050	10%	6,010
Customer Service Representatives	High school diploma or equivalent	$31,200	10%	25,290
EMTs and Paramedics	Postsecondary nondegree award	$31,700	24%	5,850
Food and Beverage Serving and Related Workers	No formal educational credential	$18,550	10%	45,180
Retail Sales Workers	No formal educational credential	$21,670	7%	33,100
Waiters and Waitresses	No formal educational credential	$18,730	3%	6,890

Physical stamina. Flight attendants may need to lift baggage and stand and walk for long periods.

Flight attendants should present a professional appearance and not have visible tattoos, body piercings, or an unusual hairstyle or makeup.

Pay

The median annual wage for flight attendants was $42,290 in May 2014. The median wage is the wage at which half the workers in an occupation earned more than that amount and half earned less. The lowest 10 percent earned less than $28,820, and the highest 10 percent earned more than $72,560.

Flight attendants receive an allowance for meals and accommodations while working away from home. Although attendants are required to purchase an initial set of uniforms and luggage, the airlines usually pay for replacements and upkeep. Flight attendants generally are eligible for discounted airfare or free standby seats through their airline. Attendants often receive health and retirement benefits, and some airlines offer incentive pay for working holidays, nights, and weekends.

Union Membership. Most flight attendants belonged to a union in 2014.

Job Outlook

Employment of flight attendants is projected to grow 2 percent from 2014 to 2024, slower than the average for all occupations. In an effort to keep planes full, airlines are expected to slow the expansion of additional flights and new routes.

However, many airlines are replacing smaller regional aircraft with new, larger planes that can accommodate a greater number of passengers. This change may increase the number of flight attendants needed on some routes.

Job Prospects. Competition for jobs will remain strong because the occupation typically attracts many more applicants than there are job openings. When entry-level positions do become available, job prospects should be best for applicants with a college degree. Job opportunities may be slightly better at regional or low-cost airlines.

Most current job opportunities will come from the need to replace attendants who leave the workforce. Over the next decade, a number of flight attendants are expected to retire, creating opportunities for new workers.

Contacts for More Information

For more information about flight attendants, visit the career webpage of any airline company, contact its personnel department, or visit

➤ Association of Flight Attendants—CWA (www.afacwa.org)

➤ Association of Professional Flight Attendants (www.apfa.org)

➤ Federal Aviation Administration (www.faa.gov)

O*NET

➤ Flight Attendants (53-2031.00)

Hand Laborers and Material Movers

- **2014 Median Pay** .... $23,560 per year $11.33 per hour
- **Typical Entry-Level Education**......No formal educational credential
- **Work Experience in a Related Occupation**.............. None
- **On-the-job Training** ....Short-term on-the-job training
- **Number of Jobs, 2014** 3,719,300
- **Job Outlook, 2014–24** .... 5% (As fast as average)
- **Employment Change, 2014–24** 175,500

What Hand Laborers and Material Movers Do

Hand laborers and material movers manually move freight, stock, or other materials. Others feed or remove material to or from machines, clean vehicles, pick up unwanted household goods, and pack materials for moving.

Duties. Hand laborers and material movers typically do the following:

- Manually move material from one place to another
- Pack or wrap products by hand
- Keep a record of the material they move
- Signal machine operators who help move material
- Clean cars, equipment, and workplaces

In warehouses and wholesale and retail operations, hand laborers and material movers work closely with material moving machine operators and material recording clerks. Some workers are employed in manufacturing industries, where they load material onto conveyor belts or other machines.

Cleaners of vehicles and equipment wash automobiles and other vehicles, as well as storage tanks, pipelines, and related machinery. They use cleaning products, vacuums, hoses, and brushes. Most of these workers clean cars at a car wash, an automobile dealership, or a rental agency. Some clean industrial equipment at manufacturing firms. Some—for example, those who work at a car wash—interact with customers.

Hand laborers and freight, stock, and material movers move materials to and from storage and production areas, loading docks, delivery trucks, ships, and containers. Although their specific duties may vary, most of these movers, often called *pickers*, work in warehouses. Some workers retrieve products from storage and move them to loading areas. Other workers load and unload cargo from a truck. When moving a package, pickers keep track of the package number, sometimes with a hand-held scanner, to ensure proper delivery. Sometimes they open containers and sort the material.

Hand packers and packagers package a variety of materials by hand. They may label cartons, inspect items for defects, and keep records of items packed. Some of these workers pack materials for shipment and move them to a loading dock. Many hand packers are employed by grocery stores, where they bag groceries for customers at checkout.

Machine feeders and offbearers process materials by feeding them into equipment or by removing them from equipment. The equipment is generally operated by other workers, such as material moving machine operators. Machine feeders and offbearers help the operator if the machine becomes jammed or needs minor repairs. Machine feeders track the amount of material they process during a shift.

Refuse and recyclable material collectors gather garbage and recyclables from homes and businesses to transport to a dump, landfill, or recycling center. Many collectors lift garbage cans by hand and empty them into their truck. Some collectors drive the garbage or recycling truck along a scheduled route. When collecting materials from a dumpster, drivers use a hydraulic lift to empty the contents of the dumpster into their truck.

Work Environment

Hand laborers and material movers held about 3.7 million jobs in 2014.

Hand laborers and freight, stock, and material movers held about 2.4 million jobs in 2014. About 18 percent were employed in temporary help services, and about 8 percent worked in warehousing and storage in 2014.

Hand packers and packagers held about 695,400 jobs in 2014. About 21 percent were employed in grocery stores, and about 18 percent worked in temporary help services in 2014.

Cleaners of vehicles and equipment held about 346,900 jobs in 2014. About 38 percent were employed in the automotive repair and maintenance industry, and about 22 percent worked in the automobile dealers industry in 2014.

Refuse and recyclable material collectors held about 131,500 jobs in 2014. About 39 percent were employed in waste collection, and about 34 percent worked in local government in 2014.

Some material movers load and unload cargo from trucks.

Machine feeders and offbearers held about 104,200 jobs in 2014. About 64 percent were employed in manufacturing, and about 23 percent worked in warehousing and storage in 2014.

Hand laborers and material movers lift and carry heavy objects, and their work is usually repetitive and physically demanding. They bend, kneel, crouch, or crawl in awkward positions.

Injuries and Illnesses. Hand laborers and freight, stock, and material movers, and refuse and recyclable material collectors both have a higher rate of injuries and illnesses than the national average. Moving heavy objects around warehouses or onto trucks may lead to sprains, strains, and overexertion.

Work Schedules. Most hand laborers and material movers work full time. Almost 1 in 4 hand laborers and material movers worked part time in 2014.

Shifts longer than 8 hours are common, as is overtime. Because materials are shipped around the clock, some workers, especially those in warehousing, work overnight shifts.

Education/Training

Formal education is not usually required to become a hand laborer or material mover. Employers typically require only that applicants be physically able to perform the work.

Education. There are no formal education requirements to become a hand laborer or material mover.

Training. Most positions for hand laborers and material movers require less than 1 month of on-the-job training. Some workers need only a few days of training, and most training is done by a

Median Annual Wages, May 2014

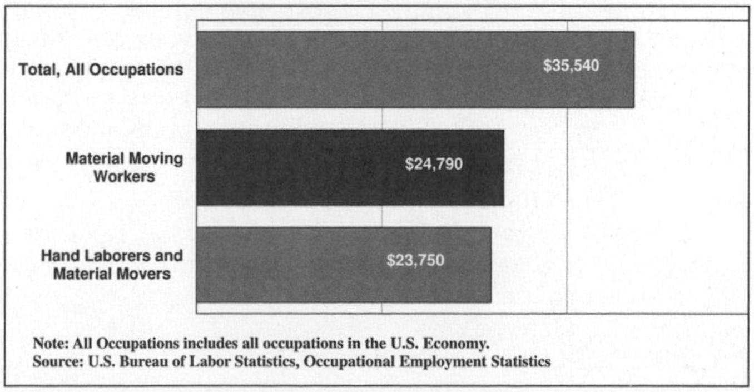

Percent Change in Employment, Projected 2014–2024

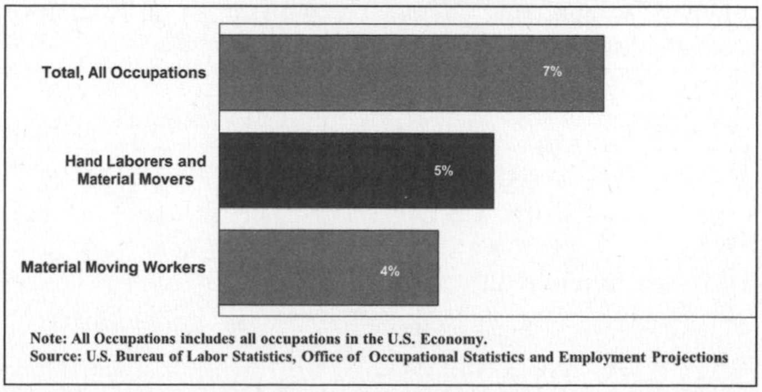

Employment Projections Data for Hand Laborers and Material Movers

Occupational Title	SOC Code	Employment, 2014	Projected Employment, 2024	Change, 2014–2024 Percent	Change, 2014–2024 Numeric
Hand laborers and material movers	—	3,719,300	3,894,800	5	175,500
Cleaners of vehicles and equipment	53-7061	346,900	380,000	10	33,100
Laborers and freight, stock, and material movers, hand	53-7062	2,441,300	2,566,400	5	125,100
Machine feeders and offbearers	53-7063	104,200	100,700	-3	-3,500
Packers and packagers, hand	53-7064	695,400	706,900	2	11,500
Refuse and recyclable material collectors	53-7081	131,500	140,900	7	9,400

Source: U.S. Bureau of Labor Statistics, Employment Projections Program

supervisor or a more experienced worker who decides when trainees are ready to work on their own.

Workers learn safety rules as part of their training. Many of these rules are standardized through the Occupational Safety & Health Administration (OSHA).

Licenses, Certifications, and Registrations. Refuse and recyclable material collectors who drive trucks that exceed a certain capacity—such as vehicles with the combined weight of the vehicle, passengers, and cargo exceeding 26,000 pounds—must have a commercial driver's license (CDL). Obtaining a CDL requires passing written, skill, and vision tests.

Important Qualities

Customer-service skills. Hand laborers and material movers who work with the public, such as grocery baggers or car wash attendants, must be pleasant and courteous to customers.

Hand-eye coordination. Most hand laborers and material movers use their arms and hands to manipulate objects or move objects into specific positions.

Listening skills. Hand laborers and material movers follow instructions that a supervisor gives them.

Physical stamina. Hand laborers and material movers need the endurance to perform strenuous tasks, such as moving or cleaning objects, throughout the day.

Physical strength. Some workers must be able to lift and carry heavy objects.

Pay

The median annual wage for hand laborers and material movers was $23,560 in May 2014. The median wage is the wage at which half the workers in an occupation earned more than that amount and half earned less. The lowest 10 percent earned less than $17,480, and the highest 10 percent earned more than $40,000.

Median annual wages for hand laborers and material movers in May 2014 were as follows:

Refuse and recyclable material collectors	$33,660
Machine feeders and offbearers	29,290
Laborers and freight, stock, and material movers, hand	24,430
Cleaners of vehicles and equipment	20,670
Packers and packagers, hand	20,330

Job Outlook

Overall employment of hand laborers and material movers is projected to grow 5 percent from 2014 to 2024, about as fast as the average for all occupations. Projected employment changes will vary by occupation.

Employment of cleaners of vehicles and equipment is projected to grow 10 percent from 2014 to 2024, faster than the average for all occupations. Demand for automotive repair and maintenance services, as well as a growing automobile dealers industry, are expected to drive employment growth of cleaners of vehicles and equipment.

Employment of refuse and recyclable material collectors is projected to grow 7 percent from 2014 to 2024, about as fast as the average for all occupations. Trash collection will likely continue to grow as the population grows, and collectors will be needed to remove trash.

Employment of hand laborers and freight, stock, and material movers is projected to grow 5 percent from 2014 to 2024, about as fast as the average for all occupations. Although some warehouses are installing equipment such as high-speed conveyors and sorting systems to increase efficiency, these workers will still be needed to move materials in nearly all sectors of the economy.

Employment of hand packers and packagers is projected to grow 2 percent from 2014 to 2024, slower than the average for all occupations. Grocery stores, which employ many hand packers and packagers, may employ fewer baggers as a growing number of cashiers bag

Similar Occupations. This table shows a list of occupations with job duties that are similar to those of hand laborers and material movers.

Occupations	Entry-level Education	2014 Median Pay	Projected Job Growth	Average Annual Openings
Construction Laborers and Helpers	See Education/Training	$30,190	13%	18,010
Delivery Truck Drivers and Driver/Sales Workers	High school diploma or equivalent	$27,490	4%	4,810
Heavy and Tractor-trailer Truck Drivers	Postsecondary nondegree award	$39,520	5%	9,880
Material Moving Machine Operators	See Education/Training	$32,890	3%	1,950
Water Transportation Workers	See Education/Training	$53,130	9%	720

groceries themselves. However, those employed in warehouses are expected to experience some employment gains as the industry grows.

Employment of machine feeders and offbearers is projected to decline 3 percent from 2014 to 2024. Many of these workers are employed in manufacturing industries, where some functions are automated, requiring fewer of these workers.

Job Prospects. Job prospects for hand laborers and material movers are expected to be very good. The need to replace workers who leave these occupations should create a large number of job openings.

Contacts for More Information

For more information about hand laborers and material movers, visit

- MHI (www.mhi.org)
- Warehousing Education and Research Council (www.werc.org)

O*NET

- Cleaners of Vehicles and Equipment (53-7061.00)
- Laborers and Freight, Stock, and Material Movers, Hand (53-7062.00)
- Machine Feeders and Offbearers (53-7063.00)
- Packers and Packagers, Hand (53-7064.00)
- Refuse and Recyclable Material Collectors (53-7081.00)

Heavy and Tractor-trailer Truck Drivers

- **2014 Median Pay** .... $39,520 per year
  $19.00 per hour
- **Typical Entry-Level Education** .... Postsecondary nondegree award
- **Work Experience in a Related Occupation**.............. None
- **On-the-job Training** ....Short-term on-the-job training
- **Number of Jobs, 2014** 1,797,700
- **Job Outlook, 2014–24** .... 5% (As fast as average)
- **Employment Change, 2014–24** 98,800

What Heavy and Tractor-trailer Truck Drivers Do

Heavy and tractor-trailer truck drivers transport goods from one location to another. Most tractor-trailer drivers are long-haul drivers and operate trucks with a gross vehicle weight (GVW) capacity of more than 26,000 pounds. These drivers deliver goods over intercity routes, sometimes spanning several states.

Duties. Heavy and tractor-trailer truck drivers typically do the following:

- Drive long distances
- Report to a dispatcher any incidents encountered on the road
- Follow all applicable traffic laws
- Inspect their trailers before and after the trip, and record any defects they find
- Maintain a log of their working hours, following all federal and state regulations
- Report serious mechanical problems to the appropriate personnel
- Keep their trucks and associated equipment clean and in good working order

Most heavy and tractor-trailer truck drivers' routes are assigned by a dispatcher, but some independent drivers still plan their own routes. They may use satellite tracking to help them plan.

A driver must know which roads allow trucks and which do not. Drivers also must plan legally required rest periods into their trip. Some drivers have one or two routes that they drive regularly, and others drivers take many different routes throughout the country. Also, some drivers have routes that include Mexico or Canada.

Companies sometimes use two drivers, known as teams, on long runs in order to minimize downtime. On these team runs, one driver sleeps in a berth behind the cab while the other drives.

Certain cargo requires drivers to adhere to additional safety regulations. Some heavy truck drivers who transport hazardous materials, such as chemical waste, must take special precautions when driving, and may carry specialized safety equipment in case of an accident. Other drivers, such as those carrying liquids, oversized loads, or cars, must follow rules that apply specifically to them.

Some long-haul truck drivers, called *owner–operators*, buy or lease trucks and go into business for themselves. In addition to their driving tasks, owner-operators also have business tasks, including finding and keeping clients and doing administrative work, such as accounting.

Work Environment

Heavy and tractor-trailer truck drivers held about 1.8 million jobs in 2014. The industries that employed the most heavy and tractor-trailer truck drivers were as follows:

General freight trucking	33%
Specialized freight trucking	13
Wholesale trade	11

Working as a long-haul truck driver is a major lifestyle choice because these drivers can be away from home for days or weeks at a time. They spend much of this time alone. Driving a truck can

Heavy truck and tractor-trailer drivers are often responsible for planning their own routes to their shipment destinations.

Median Annual Wages, May 2014

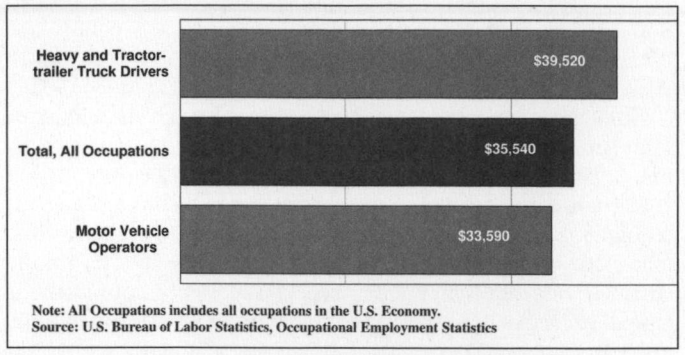

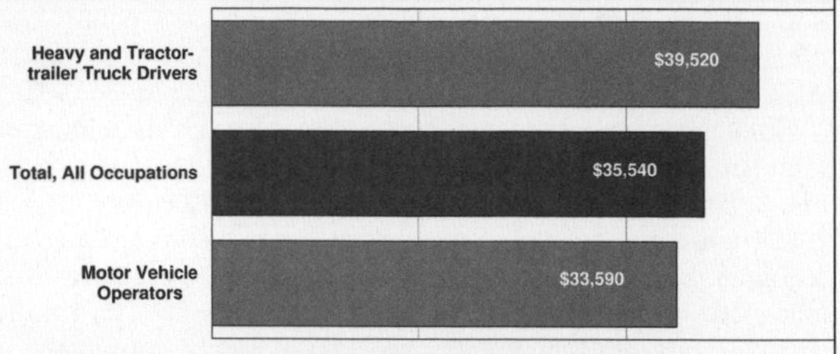

Note: All Occupations includes all occupations in the U.S. Economy.
Source: U.S. Bureau of Labor Statistics, Occupational Employment Statistics

Percent Change in Employment, Projected 2014–2024

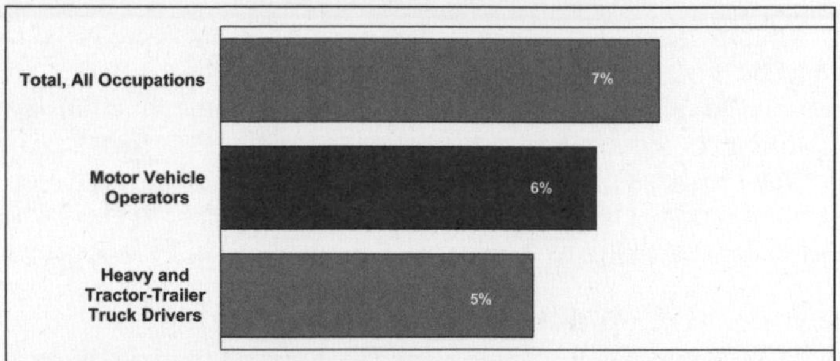

Note: All Occupations includes all occupations in the U.S. Economy.
Source: U.S. Bureau of Labor Statistics, Office of Occupational Statistics and Employment Projections

be a physically demanding job as well. Driving for many hours in a row can be tiring, and some drivers must load and unload cargo.

Injuries and Illnesses. Because of the potential for traffic accidents, heavy and tractor-trailer truck drivers have one of the highest rates of injuries and illnesses of all occupations.

Work Schedules. Most heavy tractor-trailer drivers work full time. The Federal Motor Carrier Safety Administration regulates the hours that a long-haul truck driver may work. Drivers may not work more than 14 straight hours, comprising up to 11 hours spent driving and the remaining time spent doing other work, such as unloading cargo. Between working periods, drivers must have at least 10 hours off duty. Drivers also are limited to driving no more than 60 hours within 7 days or 70 hours within 8 days; then drivers must take 34 hours off before starting another 7- or 8-day run. Drivers must record their hours in a logbook. Truck drivers often work nights, weekends, and holidays.

Education/Training

Heavy and tractor-trailer truck drivers usually have a high school diploma and attend a professional truck driving school. They must have a commercial driver's license (CDL).

Education. Most companies require their truck drivers to have a high school diploma or equivalent.

Many companies require drivers to attend professional truck driving schools, where they take training courses to learn how to maneuver large vehicles on highways or through crowded streets. During these classes, drivers also learn the federal laws and regulations governing interstate truck driving. Students attend either a private truck driving school or a program at a community college that lasts between 3 and 6 months.

Upon finishing their classes, drivers receive a certificate of completion.

The U.S. Department of Transportation is considering a requirement that mandates all newly hired interstate truck drivers to take a truck-driving course.

The Professional Truck Driver Institute (PTDI) certifies a small percentage of driver-training courses at truck driver training schools that meet both the industry standards and the U.S. Department of Transportation guidelines for training tractor-trailer drivers.

Licenses, Certifications, and Registrations. All long-haul truck drivers must have a commercial driver's license (CDL). Qualifications for obtaining a CDL vary by state but generally include passing both a knowledge test and a driving test. States have the right to refuse to issue a CDL to anyone who has had a CDL suspended by another state.

Drivers can get endorsements to their CDL that show their ability to drive a specialized type of vehicle. Truck drivers transporting hazardous materials (HAZMAT) must have a hazardous materials endorsement (H). Getting this endorsement requires passing an additional knowledge test and a background check.

Federal regulations require random testing of on-duty truck drivers for drug or alcohol abuse. In addition, truck drivers can have their CDL suspended if they are convicted of driving under the influence of alcohol or drugs or are convicted of a felony involving the use of a motor vehicle.

Other actions can result in a suspension after multiple violations. The Federal Motor Carrier Safety Administration website has a list of these violations. Additionally, some companies have stricter standards than what federal regulations require.

Training. After completing truck driving school and being hired by a company, drivers normally receive between 1 and 3 months of on-the-job training. During this time, they drive a truck with a more experienced mentor–driver in the passenger seat. This period of on-the-job training is given so that the new drivers will learn more about the specific type of truck they will drive and material they will transport.

Important Qualities

Hand-eye coordination. Drivers of heavy trucks and tractor-trailers must be able to coordinate their legs, hands, and eyes simultaneously so that they will react appropriately to the situation around them and drive the vehicle safely.

Hearing ability. Truck drivers need good hearing. Federal regulations require that a driver be able to hear a forced whisper in one ear at 5 feet (with or without the use of a hearing aid).

Employment Projections Data for Heavy and Tractor-trailer Truck Drivers

Occupational Title	SOC Code	Employment, 2014	Projected Employment, 2024	Change, 2014–2024	
				Percent	Numeric
Heavy and tractor-trailer truck drivers	53-3032	1,797,700	1,896,400	5	98,800

Source: U.S. Bureau of Labor Statistics, Employment Projections Program

Similar Occupations. This table shows a list of occupations with job duties that are similar to those of heavy and tractor-trailer truck drivers.

Occupations	Entry-level Education	2014 Median Pay	Projected Job Growth	Average Annual Openings
Bus Drivers	High school diploma or equivalent	$30,220	6%	3,750
Delivery Truck Drivers and Driver/Sales Workers	High school diploma or equivalent	$27,490	4%	4,810
Hand Laborers and Material Movers	No formal educational credential	$23,560	5%	17,550
Material Recording Clerks	See Education/Training	$25,810	3%	8,470
Railroad Workers	High school diploma or equivalent	$53,670	-3%	-330
Taxi Drivers and Chauffeurs	No formal educational credential	$23,210	13%	3,060
Water Transportation Workers	See Education/Training	$53,130	9%	720

Physical health. Federal regulations do not allow people to become truck drivers if they have a medical condition, such as high blood pressure or epilepsy, which may interfere with their ability to operate a truck. The Federal Motor Carrier Safety Administration website has a full list of medical conditions that disqualify someone from driving a long-haul truck.

Visual ability. Truck drivers must be able to pass vision tests. Federal regulations require a driver to have at least 20/40 vision with a 70-degree field of vision in each eye and the ability to distinguish the colors on a traffic light.

Pay

The median annual wage for heavy and tractor-trailer truck drivers was $39,520 in May 2014. The median wage is the wage at which half the workers in an occupation earned more than that amount and half earned less. The lowest 10 percent earned less than $25,740, and the highest 10 percent earned more than $61,150.

In May 2014, the median annual wages for heavy and tractor-trailer truck drivers in the top industries in which they worked were as follows:

General freight trucking	$41,690
Specialized freight trucking	40,100
Wholesale trade	38,950

Drivers of heavy trucks and tractor-trailers usually are paid by how many miles they have driven, plus bonuses. The per-mile rate varies from employer to employer and may depend on the type of cargo and the experience of the driver. Some long-distance drivers, especially owner–operators, are paid a share of the revenue from shipping.

Job Outlook

Employment of heavy and tractor-trailer truck drivers is projected to grow 5 percent from 2014 to 2024, about as fast as the average of all occupations.

The economy depends on truck drivers to transport freight and keep supply chains moving. As the demand for goods increases, more truck drivers will be needed. Trucks transport most of the freight in the United States, so, as households and businesses increase their spending, the trucking industry will grow.

The number of heavy trucks on the road has not reached prerecession levels, despite the increasing demand for freight transportation. To meet the demand, companies are starting to invest in new trucks that are more fuel efficient and easier to drive. For example, some new heavy trucks are equipped with automatic transmissions, blind-spot monitoring, and variable cruise control.

Demand for truck drivers is expected to remain strong in the oil and gas industries as more drivers are needed to transport materials to and from extraction sites.

Job Prospects. Job prospects for heavy and tractor-trailer truck drivers with the proper training and a clean driving record are projected to be very good. Because of truck drivers' difficult lifestyle and time spent away from home, many companies have trouble finding and retaining qualified long-haul drivers. In addition, many truck drivers are expected to retire in the coming years, creating even more job opportunities.

Contacts for More Information

For more information about truck drivers, visit

- American Trucking Associations (www.trucking.org)
- Federal Motor Carrier Safety Administration (www.fmcsa.dot.gov)

For more information about truck driving schools and programs, visit

- Commercial Vehicle Training Association (http://cvta.org)
- National Association of Publicly Funded Truck Driving Schools (http://napftds.org)
- Professional Truck Driver Institute (www.ptdi.org)

O*NET

- Heavy and Tractor-Trailer Truck Drivers (53-3032.00)

Material Moving Machine Operators

- **2014 Median Pay** .... $32,890 per year $15.81 per hour
- **Typical Entry-Level Education** .... See Education/Training
- **Work Experience in a Related Occupation** .... See Education/Training
- **On-the-job Training** .... See Education/Training
- **Number of Jobs, 2014** 679,900
- **Job Outlook, 2014–24** .... 3% (Slower than average)
- **Employment Change, 2014–24** 19,500

What Material Moving Machine Operators Do

Material moving machine operators use machinery to transport various objects. Some operators move construction materials around building sites or excavate earth from a mine. Others move goods around a warehouse or onto container ships.

Duties. Material moving machine operators typically do the following:

- Set up and inspect material moving equipment
- Control equipment with levers, wheels, or foot pedals
- Move material according to a plan or schedule
- Keep a record of the material they move and where they move it
- Make minor repairs to their equipment

In warehouses, most material moving machine operators use forklifts and conveyor belts. Wireless sensors and tags are increasingly used to keep track of merchandise, allowing operators to locate them faster. Some operators also check goods for damage. These operators usually work closely with hand laborers and material movers.

Many operators work for underground and surface mining companies. They help to dig or expose the mine, remove the earth and rock, and extract coal, ore, and other mined materials.

In construction, material moving machine operators remove earth to clear space for buildings. Some work on a building site for the entire length of the construction project. For example, certain material moving machine operators help to construct high-rise buildings by transporting materials to workers far above ground level.

All material moving machine operators are responsible for the safe operation of their equipment or vehicle.

Conveyor operators and tenders control conveyor systems that move materials on an automatic belt. They move materials to and from places such as storage areas, vehicles, and building sites. They monitor sensors on the conveyor to regulate the speed with which the conveyor belt moves. Operators may determine the route materials take along a conveyor based on shipping orders.

Crane and tower operators use tower and cable equipment to lift and move materials, machinery, or other heavy objects. From a control station, operators can extend and retract horizontal booms, rotate the superstructure, and lower and raise hooks attached to cables at the end of their crane or tower. Operators are usually guided by other workers on the ground using hand signals or voice signals through a radio. Most crane and tower operators work at construction sites or major ports, where they load and unload cargo. Some operators work in iron and steel mills.

Dredge operators excavate waterways. They operate equipment on the water to remove sand, gravel, or rock from harbors or lakes. Removing these materials helps to prevent erosion and maintain navigable waterways, and allows larger ships to use more ports. Dredging is also used to help restore wetlands and maintain beaches.

Excavating and loading machine and dragline operators use machines equipped with scoops or shovels. They dig sand, earth, or other materials and load them onto conveyors or into trucks for transport elsewhere. They may also move material within a confined area, such as a construction site. Operators typically receive instructions from workers on the ground through hand signals or radios. Most of these operators work in construction or mining industries.

Material moving machine operators use machinery to move goods around a warehouse or onto container ships.

Hoist and winch operators, also called *derrick operators*, control the movement of platforms, cables, and cages that transport workers or materials for industrial operations, such as constructing a high-rise building. Many of these operators raise platforms far above the ground. Operators regulate the speed of the equipment based on the needs of the workers. Many work in manufacturing, mining, and quarrying industries.

Industrial truck and tractor operators drive trucks and tractors that move materials around warehouses, storage yards, or worksites. These trucks, often called forklifts, have a lifting mechanism and forks, which make them useful for moving heavy and large objects. Some industrial truck and tractor operators drive tractors that pull trailers loaded with material around factories or storage areas.

Underground mining loading machine operators load coal, ore, and other rocks onto shuttles, mine cars, or conveyors for transport from a mine to the surface. They may use power shovels, hoisting engines equipped with scrapers or scoops, and automatic gathering arms that move materials onto a conveyor. Operators also drive their machines farther into the mine in order to gather more material.

Median Annual Wages, May 2014

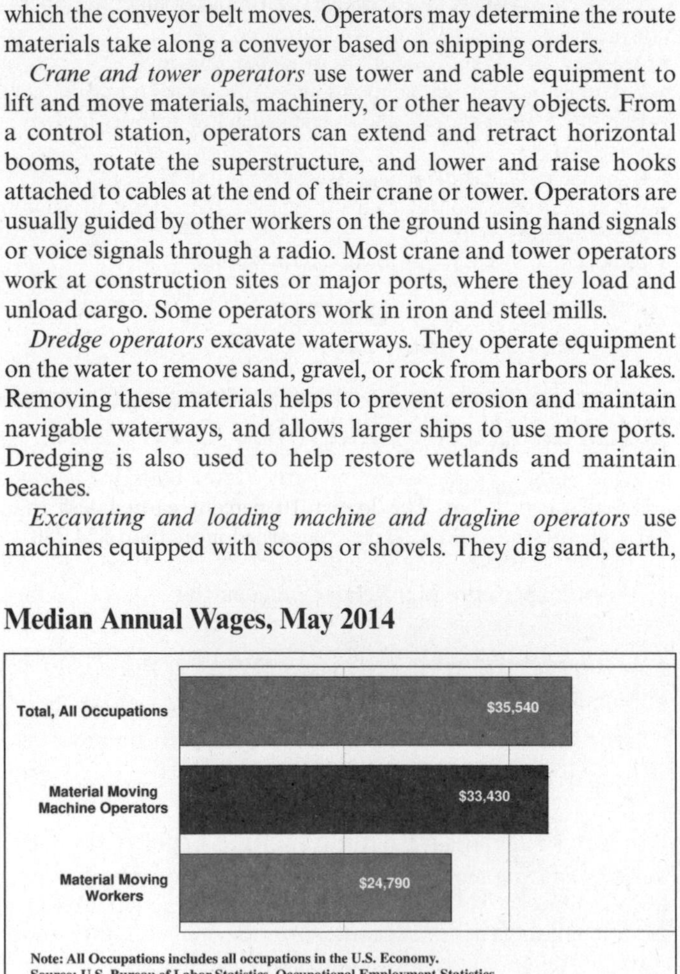

Percent Change in Employment, Projected 2014–2024

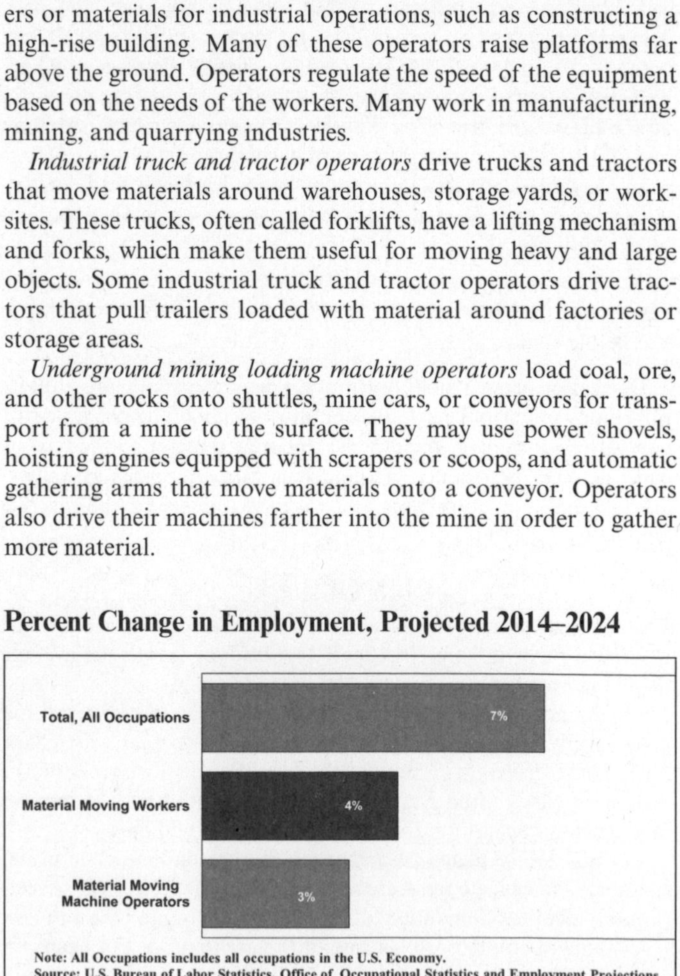

Work Environment

Material moving machine operators held about 679,900 jobs in 2014. They worked in a variety of industries, including manufacturing, transportation and warehousing, and wholesale trade. Some material moving machine operators worked in construction and mining.

Employment in the detailed occupations that make up this group in 2014 was distributed as follows:

Industrial truck and tractor operators	530,900
Excavating and loading machine and dragline operators	53,900
Crane and tower operators	45,500
Conveyor operators and tenders	39,700
Loading machine operators, underground mining	4,800
Hoist and winch operators	2,900
Dredge operators	2,200

Injuries and Illnesses. Some material moving machine operator jobs can be dangerous. For example, crane operators work outdoors at great heights in all types of weather.

Crane and tower operators, industrial truck and tractor operators, and excavating and loading machine and dragline operators, all have higher rates of injuries and illnesses than the national average.

Many workers wear gloves, hardhats, or respirators.

Work Schedules. Most material moving machine operators work full time, and overtime for them is common. Because materials are shipped around the clock, some operators—especially those in warehousing—work overnight shifts.

Education/Training

Education and training requirements vary by the occupation. Crane operators and excavating machine operators usually have several years of experience in related occupations, such as construction equipment operators or hoist or winch operators.

Education. Although no formal education is usually required, some companies prefer material moving machine operators to have a high school diploma. For crane operators, excavating machine operators, and dredge operators, however, a high school diploma or equivalent is typically required.

Training. Most material moving machine operators are trained on the job in less than a month. Some machines are more complex than others, such as cranes as compared with industrial trucks such as forklifts. Therefore, the amount of time spent in training will vary with the type of machine the operator is using. Learning to operate a forklift or an industrial truck in warehouses, for example, may take only a few days. Training to operate a crane for port operations may take several months. Most workers are trained by a supervisor or another experienced employee.

The International Union of Operating Engineers offers apprenticeship programs for heavy equipment operators, such as excavating machine operators or crane operators. Apprenticeships combine paid on-the-job training with technical instruction.

During their training, material moving machine operators learn a number of safety rules, many of which are standardized through the Occupational Safety & Health Administration (OSHA) and the Mine Safety and Health Administration (MSHA). Employers must certify that each operator has received the proper training. Operators who work with hazardous materials receive further specialized training.

Licenses, Certifications, and Registrations. A number of states and several cities require crane operators to be licensed. To get a license, operators typically must complete a skills test in which they show that they can control a crane. They also must pass a written exam that tests their knowledge of safety rules and procedures. Some crane operators and industrial truck and tractor operators may obtain certification, which includes passing a written exam.

Work Experience in a Related Occupation. Crane operators and excavating machine operators usually have several years of experience working as construction equipment operators or hoist and winch operators.

Important Qualities

Alertness. Material moving machine operators must be aware of their surroundings while operating machinery.

Hand-eye-foot coordination. Material moving machine operators should have steady hands and feet to guide and control heavy machinery precisely. They use hand controls to maneuver their machines through tight spaces, around large objects, and on uneven surfaces.

Mechanical skills. Material moving machine operators make minor adjustments to their machines and perform basic maintenance.

Visual ability. Material moving machine operators must be able to clearly see where they are driving or what they are moving. They must also watch for nearby workers, who may unknowingly be in their path.

Pay

The median annual wage for material moving machine operators was $32,890 in May 2014. The median wage is the wage at which half the workers in an occupation earned more than that amount and half earned less. The lowest 10 percent earned less than $21,460, and the highest 10 percent earned more than $54,280.

Employment Projections Data for Material Moving Machine Operators

Occupational Title	SOC Code	Employment, 2014	Projected Employment, 2024	Change, 2014–2024 Percent	Change, 2014–2024 Numeric
Material moving machine operators	—	679,900	699,400	3	19,500
Conveyor operators and tenders	53-7011	39,700	39,600	0	-100
Crane and tower operators	53-7021	45,500	49,000	8	3,400
Dredge operators	53-7031	2,200	2,300	9	200
Excavating and loading machine and dragline operators	53-7032	53,900	57,300	6	3,400
Loading machine operators, underground mining	53-7033	4,800	4,800	0	0
Hoist and winch operators	53-7041	2,900	2,900	2	0
Industrial truck and tractor operators	53-7051	530,900	543,500	2	12,600

Source: U.S. Bureau of Labor Statistics, Employment Projections Program

Similar Occupations. This table shows a list of occupations with job duties that are similar to those of material moving machine operators.

Occupations	Entry-level Education	2014 Median Pay	Projected Job Growth	Average Annual Openings
Construction Equipment Operators	High school diploma or equivalent	$42,900	10%	4,320
Delivery Truck Drivers and Driver/Sales Workers	High school diploma or equivalent	$27,490	4%	4,810
Hand Laborers and Material Movers	No formal educational credential	$23,560	5%	17,550
Heavy and Tractor-trailer Truck Drivers	Postsecondary nondegree award	$39,520	5%	9,880
Water Transportation Workers	See Education/Training	$53,130	9%	720

Median annual wages for material moving machine operators in May 2014 were as follows:

Crane and tower operators	$50,720
Loading machine operators, underground mining	50,290
Dredge operators	40,950
Excavating and loading machine and dragline operators	39,830
Hoist and winch operators	39,580
Industrial truck and tractor operators	31,340
Conveyor operators and tenders	31,220

Job Outlook

Employment of material moving machine operators is projected to grow 3 percent from 2014 to 2024, slower than the average for all occupations.

Employment of industrial truck and tractor operators is projected to grow 2 percent from 2014 to 2024. Employment of this occupation is concentrated in warehouse environments. Although the need for warehouses will grow as consumer spending increases, employment growth of these operators may be limited as more warehouses use equipment such as robotic pickers. This equipment increases the efficiency of operators, allowing warehouses to employ fewer of them.

Employment of excavating and loading machine and dragline operators is projected to grow 6 percent from 2014 to 2024. Many of these operators work in the construction industry, whose projected growth will drive job growth in this occupation.

Employment of crane and tower operators is projected to grow 8 percent from 2014 to 2024. As global shipping increases, more of these operators will be needed at ports to load and unload large cargo ships. However, increasing automation at ports may moderate growth. Employment of crane and tower operators also will be driven by growth in the construction industry, which employs many of these workers. Employment of crane operators is projected to grow 11 percent in construction.

Employment of conveyor operators and tenders is projected to show little or no change from 2014 to 2024. Employment growth will be limited as more warehouses use equipment such as high-speed conveyors, high-speed sorting systems, and robotic pickers. This equipment increases the efficiency of operators and tenders, allowing warehouses to employ fewer of them.

Employment of underground mining loading machine operators is projected to show little or no change from 2014 to 2024, largely due to an expected decline in coal mining, where many of these workers are employed.

Employment of hoist and winch operators is projected to grow 2 percent from 2014 to 2024. Similar to crane and tower operators, they will be needed at ports to help load and unload cargo, but employment growth for this occupation may be limited by port automation.

Employment of dredge operators is projected to grow 9 percent from 2014 to 2024. Demand for dredging of various water areas, including canals, lakes, rivers, and harbors, in order to improve the traffic on waterways and their recreational use, will drive employment growth of these workers.

Job Prospects. Job prospects are expected to be favorable. Many job openings should be created by the need to replace workers who leave these occupations.

Contacts for More Information

For more information about careers as a material moving machine operator, visit

- MHI (www.mhi.org)
- Warehousing Education and Research Council (www.werc.org)
- International Union of Operating Engineers (www.iuoe.org)
- National Commission for the Certification of Crane Operators (www.nccco.org)

O*NET

- Conveyor Operators and Tenders (53-7011.00)
- Crane and Tower Operators (53-7021.00)
- Dredge Operators (53-7031.00)
- Excavating and Loading Machine and Dragline Operators (53-7032.00)
- Loading Machine Operators, Underground Mining (53-7033.00)
- Hoist and Winch Operators (53-7041.00)
- Industrial Truck and Tractor Operators (53-7051.00)

Railroad Workers

- **2014 Median Pay** ..... $53,670 per year, $25.80 per hour
- **Typical Entry-Level Education** ..... High school diploma or equivalent
- **Work Experience in a Related Occupation** ..... See Education/Training
- **On-the-job Training** ... Moderate-term on-the-job training
- **Number of Jobs, 2014** 113,300
- **Job Outlook, 2014–24** ..... -3% (Decline)
- **Employment Change, 2014–24** ..... -3,300

What Railroad Workers Do

Workers in railroad occupations ensure that passenger and freight trains run on time and travel safely. Some workers drive trains,

Conductors are the head of the train's crew.

some coordinate the activities of the trains, and others operate signals and switches in the rail yard.

Duties. Railroad workers typically do the following:

- Check the mechanical condition of locomotives and make adjustments when necessary
- Document issues with a train that require further inspection
- Operate locomotive engines within or between stations

Freight trains move billions of tons of goods around the country to ports where they are shipped around the world. Passenger trains transport millions of passengers and commuters to destinations around the country. These railroad workers are essential to keeping freight and passenger trains running properly.

All workers in railroad occupations work together closely. Locomotive engineers travel with conductors and sometimes brake operators. Locomotive engineers and conductors are in constant contact and keep each other informed of any changes in the condition of the train.

Signal and switch operators communicate with both locomotive and rail yard engineers to make sure that trains end up at the correct destination. All occupations are in contact with dispatchers who give them directions on where to go and what to do.

Locomotive engineers drive freight or passenger trains between stations. They drive long-distance trains and commuter trains, but not subway trains. Most locomotive engineers drive diesel-electric engines, although some drive locomotives powered by battery or electricity.

Engineers must be aware of the goods their train is carrying because different types of freight require different types of driving, based on the conditions of the rails. For example, a train carrying hazardous material through a snowstorm is driven differently than a train carrying coal through a mountain region.

Locomotive engineers typically do the following:

- Monitor speed, air pressure, battery use, and other instruments to ensure that the locomotive runs smoothly
- Use a variety of controls, such as throttles and airbrakes, to operate the train
- Communicate with dispatchers over radios to get information about delays or changes in the schedule

Conductors travel on both freight and passenger trains. They coordinate activities of the train crew. On passenger trains, they ensure safety and comfort and make announcements to keep passengers informed. On freight trains they are responsible for overseeing the loading and unloading of cargo.

Conductors typically do the following:

- Check passengers' tickets
- Take payments from passengers who did not buy tickets in advance
- Announce stations and give other announcements as needed
- Help passengers to safety when needed
- Deal with unruly passengers when needed
- Oversee loading and unloading of cargo

Yardmasters do work similar to that of conductors, except that they do not travel on trains. They oversee and coordinate the activities of workers in the rail yard. They tell yard engineers where to move cars to fit the planned configuration or to load freight. Yardmasters ensure that trains are carrying the correct material before leaving the yard. Not all rail yards use yardmasters. In rail yards that do not have yardmasters, a conductor performs the duties of a yardmaster.

Yardmasters typically do the following:

- Review schedules, switching orders, and shipping records of freight trains
- Arrange for defective cars to be removed from a train for repairs
- Switch train traffic to a certain section of the line to allow other inbound and outbound trains to get around
- Break up or put together train cars according to a schedule

Rail yard engineers operate train engines within the rail yard. They move locomotives between tracks to keep the trains organized and on schedule. Some operate small locomotives called dinkeys. Sometimes, rail yard engineers are called *hostlers* and drive locomotives to and from maintenance shops or prepare them for the locomotive engineer. Some use remote locomotive technology to move freight cars within the rail yards.

Railroad brake, signal, or switch operators control equipment that keeps the trains running safely.

Brake operators help couple and uncouple train cars. Some travel with the train as part of the crew.

Signal operators install and maintain the signals along tracks and in the rail yard. Signals are important in preventing accidents because they allow increased communication between trains and dispatchers.

Switch operators control the track switches in rail yards. These switches allow trains to move between tracks and ensure trains are heading in the right direction.

Locomotive firers are sometimes part of a train crew and typically monitor tracks and train instruments. They look for equipment that is dragging, obstacles on the tracks, and other potential safety problems.

Few trains still use firers, because their work has been automated or is now done by a locomotive engineer or conductor.

Work Environment

Workers in railroad occupations held about 113,300 jobs in 2014.

Nearly all locomotive engineers; conductors and yardmasters; and brake, signal, and switch operators work in the rail transportation industry. Rail yard engineers work in rail transportation and support activities for rail transportation.

Median Annual Wages, May 2014

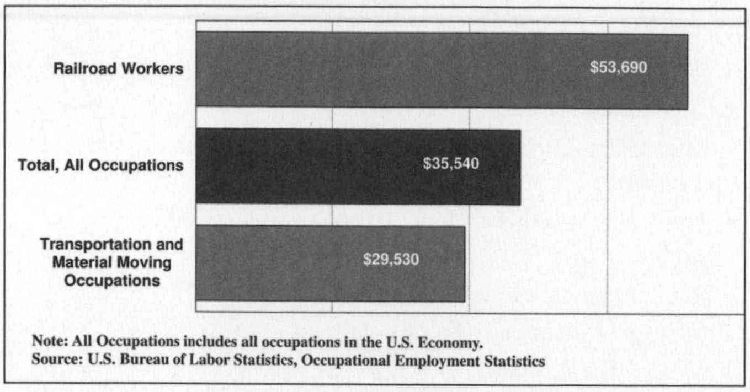

Percent Change in Employment, Projected 2014–2024

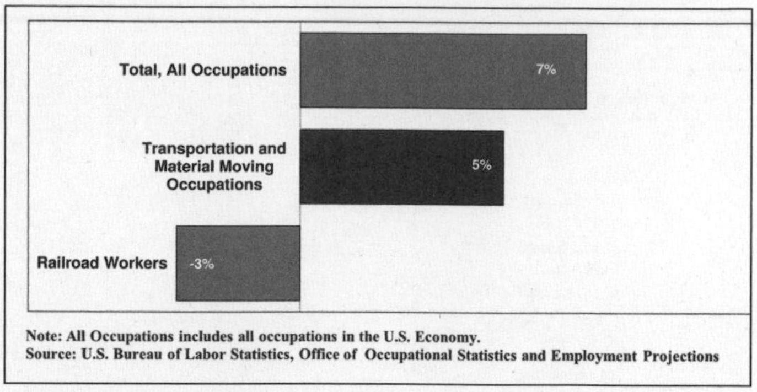

Rail yard engineers and brake, signal, and switch operators spend most of their time working outside, regardless of weather conditions.

Conductors on passenger trains generally work in cleaner, more comfortable conditions than conductors on freight trains. However, conductors on passenger trains sometimes must respond to upset or unruly passengers when a train is delayed.

Injuries and Illnesses. Rail yard engineers and conductors and yardmasters have a higher rate of injuries and illnesses than the national average. Rail yard workers must move heavy equipment around and climb up and down equipment, which can be dangerous.

Work Schedules. Trains are scheduled to operate 24 hours a day, 7 days a week, meaning that many railroad workers sometimes work nights, weekends, and holidays. Most rail employees work full time. Federal regulations require a minimum number of rest hours for train operators.

Locomotive engineers and conductors whose trains travel long routes can be away from home for long periods of time. Those who work on passenger trains with short routes generally have a more predictable schedule. Workers on some freight trains have irregular schedules.

For engineers, seniority (the number of years on the job) usually dictates who receives the most desired shifts. Some engineers, called extra board, are hired on a temporary basis and get an assignment only when a railroad needs an extra or substitute worker on a certain route.

Education/Training

Workers in railroad occupations generally need a high school diploma and several months of on-the-job training.

Education. Rail companies typically require a high school diploma or equivalent, especially for locomotive engineers and conductors.

Training. Locomotive engineers generally receive 2 to 3 months of on-the-job training before they can operate a train on their own. Typically, this training involves riding with an experienced engineer who teaches them the characteristics of that particular train route.

During training, an engineer learns the track length, where the switches are, and any unusual features of the track. An experienced engineer who switches to a new route also has to spend a few months in training to learn the route with an engineer who is familiar with it. In addition, railroad companies provide continuing education so that engineers can maintain their skills.

Most railroad companies have 1 to 3 months of on-the-job training for conductors and yardmasters. Amtrak (the passenger train company) and some of the larger freight railroad companies operate their own training programs. Smaller and regional railroads may send conductors to a central training facility or a community college.

Yardmasters may be sent to training programs or may be trained by an experienced yardmaster. They learn how to operate remote locomotive technology and how to manage railcars in the yard.

Conductors and yardmasters working for freight railroads also learn the proper procedures for loading and unloading different types of cargo. Conductors on passenger trains learn ticketing procedures and how to handle passengers.

Rail yard engineers and signal and switch operators also receive on-the-job training, generally through a company training program. This program may last a few weeks to a few months, depending on the company and the complexity of the job. The program may include some time in a classroom and some hands-on experience under the direction of an experienced employee.

Work Experience in a Related Occupation. Most locomotive engineers first work as conductors for several years.

Licenses, Certifications, and Registrations. Locomotive engineers must be certified by the Federal Railroad Administration (FRA). The certification, conducted by the railroad that employs

Employment Projections Data for Railroad Workers

Occupational Title	SOC Code	Employment, 2014	Projected Employment, 2024	Change, 2014–2024 Percent	Change, 2014–2024 Numeric
Railroad workers	—	113,300	110,000	-3	-3,300
Locomotive engineers	53-4011	40,400	39,500	-2	-900
Locomotive firers	53-4012	1,700	500	-70	-1,200
Rail yard engineers, dinkey operators, and hostlers	53-4013	4,000	4,100	1	100
Railroad brake, signal, and switch operators	53-4021	22,100	21,700	-2	-400
Railroad conductors and yardmasters	53-4031	45,100	44,300	-2	-900

Source: U.S. Bureau of Labor Statistics, Employment Projections Program

Similar Occupations. This table shows a list of occupations with job duties that are similar to those of railroad workers.

Occupations	Entry-level Education	2014 Median Pay	Projected Job Growth	Average Annual Openings
Bus Drivers	High school diploma or equivalent	$30,220	6%	3,750
Delivery Truck Drivers and Driver/Sales Workers	High school diploma or equivalent	$27,490	4%	4,810
Flight Attendants	High school diploma or equivalent	$42,290	2%	220
Heavy and Tractor-trailer Truck Drivers	Postsecondary nondegree award	$39,520	5%	9,880
Material Moving Machine Operators	See Education/Training	$32,890	3%	1,950
Taxi Drivers and Chauffeurs	No formal educational credential	$23,210	13%	3,060
Water Transportation Workers	See Education/Training	$53,130	9%	720

them, involves a written knowledge test, a skills test, and a supervisor determining that the engineer understands all physical aspects of the particular route on which he or she will be operating.

An experienced engineer who changes routes must be recertified for the new route. Even engineers who do not switch routes must be recertified every few years.

At the end of the certification process, the engineer must pass a vision and hearing test.

Conductors who operate on national, regional, or commuter railroads are also required to become certified. To receive certification, new conductors must pass a test that has been designed and administered by the railroad and approved by the FRA.

Advancement. Rail yard engineers, switch operators, and signal operators can advance to become conductors or yardmasters. Some conductors or yardmasters advance to become locomotive engineers.

Important Qualities

Communication skills. All rail employees have to be able to communicate effectively with other crewmembers and passengers to keep the trains on schedule.

Customer-service skills. Conductors on passenger trains ensure customers' comfort, make announcements, and answer any questions a passenger has. They must be courteous and patient. They may have to deal with unruly or upset passengers.

Decision-making skills. When operating a locomotive, engineers must plan ahead and make decisions minutes or even hours in advance.

Hand-eye coordination. Locomotive engineers have to operate various controls while staying aware of their surroundings.

Hearing ability. To show that they can hear warning signals and communicate with other employees, locomotive engineers have to pass a hearing test conducted by their rail company.

Leadership skills. On some trains, a conductor directs a crew. In rail yards, yardmasters oversee other workers.

Mechanical skills. All rail employees work with complex machines. Most have to be able to adjust equipment when it does not work properly. Some rail yard engineers spend most of their time fixing broken equipment or conducting daily mechanical inspections.

Physical strength. Some rail yard engineers have to lift heavy equipment.

Visual ability. To drive a train, locomotive engineers have to pass a vision test conducted by their rail company. Eyesight, peripheral vision, and color vision may be tested.

In addition, locomotive operators must be at least 21 years of age and pass a background test. They must also pass random drug and alcohol screenings over the course of their employment.

Pay

The median annual wage for railroad workers was $53,670 in May 2014. The median wage is the wage at which half the workers in an occupation earned more than that amount and half earned less. The lowest 10 percent earned less than $38,340, and the highest 10 percent earned more than $75,560.

Median annual wages for railroad workers in May 2014 were as follows:

Railroad conductors and yardmasters	$54,770
Locomotive engineers	54,500
Railroad brake, signal, and switch operators	52,360
Locomotive firers	46,740
Rail yard engineers, dinkey operators, and hostlers	43,880

Job Outlook

Employment of railroad workers is projected to decline 3 percent from 2014 to 2024.

Although demand for rail transportation may grow, an increase in productivity may hold back employment growth in rail occupations. Because building new tracks is expensive, freight companies have found other ways to increase capacity, such as double-stacking (stacking one railcar on top of another) or running longer trains.

However, an increase in intermodal freight—the shipment of goods through multiple transportation modes—may increase demand for railroad workers. In addition, the growing demand for crude oil transportation may result in the need for more railroad workers.

Employment of locomotive firers is projected to decline 70 percent from 2014 to 2024. Most railroads are phasing out this occupation, as their duties are typically performed by locomotive engineers and conductors.

Job Prospects. Job opportunities should be favorable for railroad workers. More railroad workers are nearing retirement than are workers in most occupations. When these workers begin to retire, many jobs should open up, except for locomotive firers, as railroad companies will continue to phase them out of the workforce.

Contacts for More Information

For more information about training programs and job opportunities in passenger rail, visit

- National Railroad Passenger Corporation (Amtrak) (www.amtrak.com)
- Association of American Railroads (AAR) (www.aar.org)

O*NET

- Locomotive Engineers (53-4011.00)
- Locomotive Firers (53-4012.00)
- Rail Yard Engineers, Dinkey Operators, and Hostlers (53-4013.00)
- Railroad Brake, Signal, and Switch Operators (53-4021.00)
- Railroad Conductors and Yardmasters (53-4031.00)

Taxi Drivers and Chauffeurs

- **2014 Median Pay** .... $23,210 per year $11.16 per hour
- **Typical Entry-Level Education**......No formal educational credential
- **Work Experience in a Related Occupation**.............. None
- **On-the-job Training** ....Short-term on-the-job training
- **Number of Jobs, 2014** 233,700
- **Job Outlook, 2014–24** .... 13% (Faster than average)
- **Employment Change, 2014–24** 30,600

What Taxi Drivers and Chauffeurs Do

Taxi drivers and chauffeurs drive people to and from the places they need to go, such as homes, workplaces, airports, and shopping centers. They must know their way around a city in order to take both residents and visitors to their destinations.

Duties. Taxi drivers and chauffeurs typically do the following:

- Drive taxicabs, limousines, company cars, or privately owned vehicles to transport passengers
- Pick up passengers and listen to where they want to go
- Help passengers load and unload their luggage
- Obey all traffic laws
- Collect fares, including allowed extra charges
- Check the car for problems and do basic maintenance
- Keep the inside and outside of their car clean
- Operate wheelchair lifts when needed
- Keep a record of miles traveled

Taxi drivers and chauffeurs must stay alert and monitor the conditions of the road. They have to take precautions to ensure their passengers' safety, especially in heavy traffic or bad weather. Taxi drivers and chauffeurs must also follow all vehicle-for-hire or livery regulations, such as where they can pick up passengers and how much they can charge.

Good drivers are familiar with the streets in the areas they serve. They choose the most efficient routes, considering the traffic at that time of day. They know where the most frequently requested destinations are, such as airports, train stations, convention centers, hotels, and other points of interest. They also know where to find fire and police stations and hospitals in case of an emergency.

Taxi drivers, also called *cab drivers* or *cabbies*, generally use a meter to determine the fare when a passenger requests a destination. Many customers request a cab by calling a central dispatcher who then tells the taxi driver the pickup location. Some drivers pick up passengers waiting in lines at cabstands or in the taxi line at airports, train stations, and hotels. In some large cities, cabbies drive around the streets looking for passengers, although this is not legal in all cities.

Ride-hailing drivers pick up passengers who request service through a smartphone app. The fare rate can fluctuate depending on demand; however, passengers are notified if the current fare rate is higher than usual. Passengers pay for the ride through a credit card that is linked to the app. Drivers use their own private vehicles and set their own hours.

Chauffeurs take passengers on prearranged trips. They operate limousines, vans, or private cars. They may work for hire for single trips or they may work for a person, a private business, or for a government agency. Customer service is important for chauffeurs, especially luxury car drivers. Some do the duties of executive assistants, acting as driver, secretary, and itinerary planner. Other chauffeurs drive large vans between airports or train stations and hotels.

Paratransit drivers transport people with special needs, such as the elderly or those with disabilities. They operate specially equipped vehicles designed to help people with a variety of needs in nonemergency situations. For example, their vehicles may be equipped with wheelchair lifts, and the driver helps a passenger with boarding.

Work Environment

Taxi drivers and chauffeurs held about 233,700 jobs in 2014. The industries that employed the most taxi drivers and chauffeurs were as follows:

Taxi and limousine service	21%
Healthcare and social assistance	15
Other transit and ground passenger transportation	10

About 1 in 5 taxi drivers and chauffeurs were self-employed. Some drivers may own their taxi and contract with a dispatch company that refers passengers and allows the driver to use their facilities for a fee. Other drivers lease a dispatch company's car as part of the fee. Drivers usually pay for their own expenses such as fuel.

Driving for long periods, especially in heavy traffic, can be stressful for taxi drivers and chauffeurs. In addition, they often have to pick up heavy luggage and packages.

Work Schedules. Work hours for taxi drivers and chauffeurs vary. About 1 in 5 worked part time in 2014. Evening and weekend

Job opportunities for taxi drivers and chauffeurs should be plentiful.

Median Annual Wages, May 2014

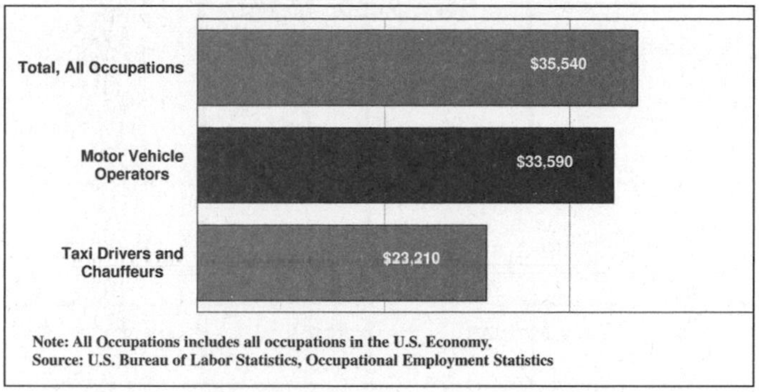

Percent Change in Employment, Projected 2014–2024

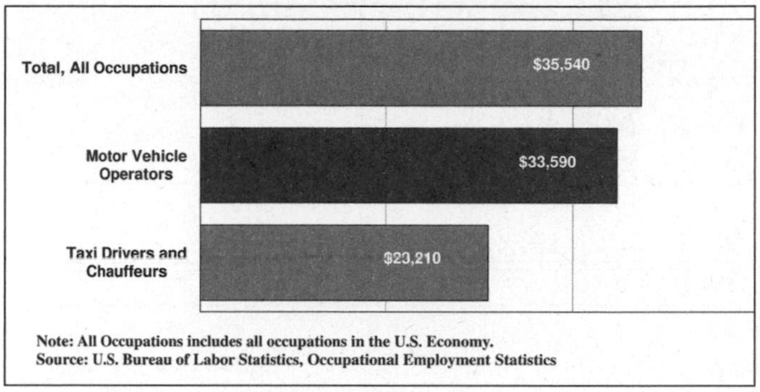

work is common. Some drivers work very late at night or early in the morning.

Taxi and ride-hailing drivers work with little or no supervision, and their work schedules are flexible. They can break for a meal or rest whenever they do not have a passenger.

Chauffeurs' work schedules are much more structured. The hours they work are based on the needs of their clients. Some chauffeurs are on call while they are not at work, so they must be ready to drive their client at a moment's notice.

Education/Training

Most taxi drivers and chauffeurs go through a brief training period. Many states and local municipalities require them to get a taxi or limousine license. Clean driving records and background checks are sometimes required. However, there usually is no formal educational requirement.

Education. No formal educational credential is typically required, although many taxi drivers and chauffeurs have a high school degree.

Training. Most taxi and limousine companies provide their new drivers with a short period of on-the-job training. This training usually takes from 1 day to 2 weeks, depending on the company and the location. Some municipalities require training by law.

Training typically covers local traffic laws, driver safety, and the local street layout. Taxi drivers also get training in operating the taximeter and communications equipment. Taxi drivers are trained in accordance with local regulations; in contrast, limousine chauffeurs usually are trained by their company, and customer service is emphasized. Ride-hailing drivers receive little to no training beyond how to work the electronic hailing app so they can pick up customers. Paratransit drivers receive special training in how to handle wheelchair lifts and other mechanical devices.

Licenses, Certifications, and Registrations. All taxi drivers and chauffeurs must have a regular automobile driver's license. States and local municipalities set other requirements; many require drivers to get a taxi or chauffeur's license. This normally requires passing a drug test and a written test about regulations and local geography.

The majority of states and municipalities do not have regulations pertaining to ride-hailing drivers because the service has just recently grown in popularity. A few cities have started to issue regulations and some have even ordered ride-hailing companies to cease and desist operations. Check with your local area for more information.

The Federal Motor Carrier Safety Administration requires that limousine drivers who transport at least 16 passengers at a time (including the driver) have a commercial driver's license (CDL) with a passenger (P) endorsement. To get these, a driver has to pass knowledge and driving skills tests.

Advancement. Taxi drivers and chauffeurs have limited advancement opportunities. Some taxi drivers start their own cab service by purchasing a taxi rather than leasing one through a dispatch company. For chauffeurs, advancement usually takes the form of driving more important clients and different types of cars. Some taxi drivers and chauffeurs can become a "lead driver," which means they train new drivers in addition to continuing to drive their own clients.

Important Qualities

Customer-service skills. Taxi drivers and chauffeurs regularly interact with their customers and have to represent their company positively and make sure passengers are satisfied with their ride. Because passengers rate ride-hailing drivers after each trip, excellent customer-service skills can lead to a favorable review.

Dependability. Customers rely on taxi drivers and chauffeurs to pick them up at the agreed-upon time so they get to their destinations when they need to be there.

Hand-eye coordination. Taxi drivers and chauffeurs have to be able to observe their surroundings and steer away from obstacles and dangerous drivers while operating a vehicle.

Initiative. Taxi drivers and chauffeurs usually work with little or no supervision, so they must be self-motivated and able to take initiative to earn a living.

Patience. Drivers must be calm and composed when driving through heavy traffic, congestion, or dealing with rude passengers.

Visual ability. Taxi drivers and chauffeurs must be able to pass a state-issued vision test in order to hold a driver's license.

Pay

The median annual wage for taxi drivers and chauffeurs was $23,210 in May 2014. The median wage is the wage at which half the workers in an occupation earned more than that amount and half earned less. The lowest 10 percent earned less than $17,470, and the highest 10 percent earned more than $37,470.

In May 2014, the median annual wages for taxi drivers and chauffeurs in the top industries in which they worked were as follows:

Taxi and limousine service	$23,810
Healthcare and social assistance	23,510
Other transit and ground passenger transportation	22,910

These wage data include money earned from tips. Taxi drivers and chauffeurs who provide good customer service are more likely to receive higher tips on each fare.

Employment Projections Data for Taxi Drivers and Chauffeurs

Occupational Title	SOC Code	Employment, 2014	Projected Employment, 2024	Change, 2014–2024	
				Percent	Numeric
Taxi drivers and chauffeurs	53-3041	233,700	264,400	13	30,600

Source: U.S. Bureau of Labor Statistics, Employment Projections Program

Similar Occupations. This table shows a list of occupations with job duties that are similar to those of taxi drivers and chauffeurs.

Occupations	Entry-level Education	2014 Median Pay	Projected Job Growth	Average Annual Openings
Automotive Service Technicians and Mechanics	Postsecondary nondegree award	$37,120	5%	3,910
Bus Drivers	High school diploma or equivalent	$30,220	6%	3,750
Delivery Truck Drivers and Driver/Sales Workers	High school diploma or equivalent	$27,490	4%	4,810
Heavy and Tractor-trailer Truck Drivers	Postsecondary nondegree award	$39,520	5%	9,880
Railroad Workers	High school diploma or equivalent	$53,670	-3%	-330
Water Transportation Workers	See Education/Training	$53,130	9%	720

Job Outlook

Employment of taxi drivers and chauffeurs is projected to grow 13 percent from 2014 to 2024, faster than the average for all occupations.

The innovation of ride-hailing services, which utilize electronic hailing through smartphone apps, should increase job growth. Specifically, the self-employed should see the most growth because ride-hailing companies classify drivers as independent contractors. Employment growth should result from ride-hailing services being introduced in more large- and medium-sized cities across the country.

Taxis and ride-hailing services generally operate in urban areas and complement public transit systems because people who regularly take a train or bus are more likely to use a taxi or ride-hailing service. Therefore, increasing demand for taxis and ride-hailing services should mostly occur in larger metropolitan areas.

Some employment growth for chauffeurs is expected because of an increasing amount of corporate travel. To be successful, most chauffeurs depend on clients who travel for business.

Job Prospects. Job prospects for taxi drivers and chauffeurs will likely be excellent. The occupation does not require any formal education and has low barriers to entry. Applicants with a clean driving record and flexible schedules should have the best chance of being hired. Most taxi drivers and chauffeurs work in metropolitan areas, and those areas that are experiencing fast economic growth should offer the most job opportunities.

Contacts for More Information

For more information about taxi drivers, chauffeurs, and paratransit drivers, visit

➤ Taxicab, Limousine, and Paratransit Association (www.tlpa.org)

For more information about limousine drivers, visit

➤ National Limousine Association (www.limo.org)

O*NET

➤ Taxi Drivers and Chauffeurs (53-3041.00)

Water Transportation Workers

- **2014 Median Pay** .... $53,130 per year
  $25.54 per hour
- **Typical Entry-Level Education** .... See Education/Training
- **Work Experience in a Related Occupation** .... See Education/Training
- **On-the-job Training** .... See Education/Training
- **Number of Jobs, 2014** 78,500
- **Job Outlook, 2014–24** .... 9% (Faster than average)
- **Employment Change, 2014–24** 7,200

What Water Transportation Workers Do

Water transportation workers operate and maintain vessels that take cargo and people over water. The vessels travel to and from foreign ports across the ocean and to domestic ports along the coasts, across the Great Lakes, and along the country's many inland waterways.

Duties. Water transportation workers typically do the following:

- Operate and maintain nonmilitary vessels
- Follow their vessel's strict chain of command
- Ensure the safety of all people and cargo on board

These workers, sometimes called *merchant mariners*, work on a variety of ships.

Some operate large deep-sea container ships to transport manufactured goods and refrigerated cargos around the world.

Others work on bulk carriers that move heavy commodities, such as coal or iron ore, across the oceans and over the Great Lakes.

Still others work on both large and small tankers that carry oil and other liquid products around the country and the world. Others work on supply ships that transport equipment and supplies to offshore oil and gas platforms.

Workers on tugboats help barges and other boats maneuver in small harbors and at sea.

Salvage vessels that offer emergency services also employ merchant mariners.

Cruise ships employ a large number of water transportation workers, and some merchant mariners work on ferries to transport passengers along shorter distances.

A typical deep-sea merchant ship, large coastal ship, or Great Lakes merchant ship employs a captain and a chief engineer, along with three mates, three assistant engineers, and a number of sailors and marine oilers. Smaller vessels that operate in harbors or rivers may have a smaller crew. The specific complement of mariners is dependent on U.S. Coast Guard regulations.

Also, there are other workers on ships, such as cooks, electricians, and mechanics. For more information, see the profiles on cooks, electricians, and general maintenance and repair workers.

Captains, sometimes called *masters*, have overall command of a vessel. They have the final responsibility for the safety of the crew, cargo, and passengers. Captains typically do the following:

- Supervise the work of the crew, including other officers
- Ensure that proper safety procedures are followed
- Prepare a maintenance and repair budget
- Oversee the loading and unloading of cargo or passengers
- Keep logs and other records that track the ship's movements and activities
- Interact with passengers on cruise ships

Mates, or *deck officers*, direct the operation of a vessel while the captain is off duty. Large ships have three officers, called first, second, and third mates. The first mate has the highest authority and takes command of the ship if the captain is incapacitated. Usually, the first mate is in charge of the cargo and/or passengers, the second mate is in charge of navigation, and the third mate is in charge of safety. On smaller vessels, there may be only one mate who handles all of the responsibilities. Deck officers typically do the following:

- Alternate watches with the captain and other officers
- Supervise and coordinate the activities of the deck crew
- Assist with docking the ship
- Monitor the ship's position, using charts and other navigational aides
- Determine the speed and direction of the vessel
- Inspect the cargo hold during loading, to ensure that the cargo is stowed according to specifications
- Make announcements to passengers when needed

Pilots guide ships in harbors, on rivers, and on other confined waterways. They are not part of a ship's crew but go aboard a ship to guide it through a particular waterway that they are familiar with. They work in places where a high degree of familiarity with local tides, currents, and hazards is needed. Some, called *harbor pilots*, work for ports and help many ships that come into the harbor during the day. When coming into a commercial port, a captain will often have to turn control of the vessel over to a pilot, who can safely guide it into the harbor. Pilots typically do the following:

- Board an unfamiliar ship from a small boat in the open water, often using a ladder
- Confer with a ship's captain about the vessel's destination and any special requirements it has

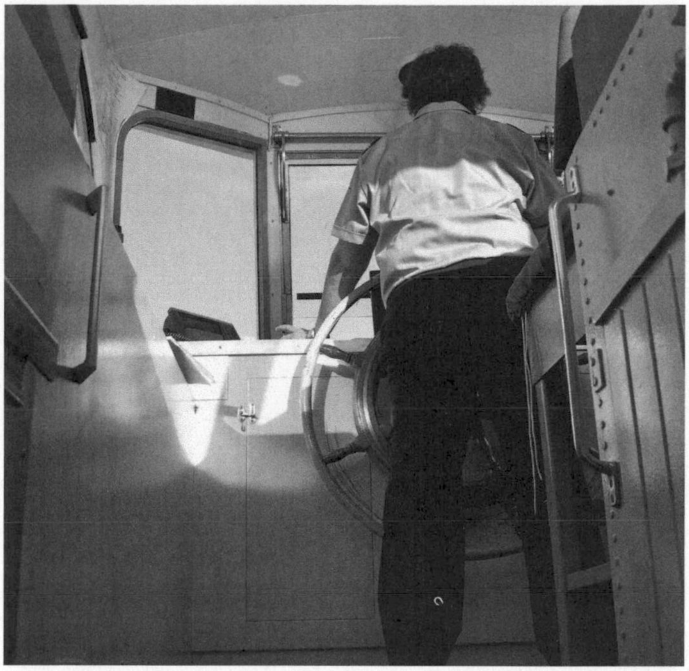

Sailors steer the ship and measure water depth in shallow water.

- Establish a positive working relationship with a vessel's captain and deck officers
- Receive mooring instructions from shore dispatchers

Sailors, or *deckhands*, operate and maintain the vessel and deck equipment. They make up the deck crew and keep all parts of a ship, other than areas related to the engine and motor, in good working order. New deckhands are called *ordinary seamen* and do the least complicated tasks. Experienced deckhands are called *able seamen* and usually make up most of a crew. Some large ships have a *boatswain,* who is the chief of the deck crew. Sailors typically do the following:

- Stand watch, looking for other vessels or obstructions in their ship's path and for navigational aids, such as buoys and lighthouses
- Steer the ship and measure water depth in shallow water
- Do routine maintenance, such as painting the deck and chipping away rust
- Keep the inside of the ship clean
- Handle lines when docking or departing
- Tie barges together when they are being towed
- Load and unload cargo
- Help passengers when needed

Ship engineers operate and maintain a vessel's propulsion system, which includes the engine, boilers, generators, pumps, and other machinery. Large vessels usually carry a *chief engineer*, who has command of the engine room and its crew, and a first, second, and third assistant engineer. The assistant engineer oversees the engine and related machinery when the chief engineer is off duty. Small ships might have only one engineer. Engineers typically do the following:

- Maintain the electrical, refrigeration, and ventilation systems of a ship
- Start the engine and regulate the vessel's speed, following the captain's orders

- Record information in an engineering log
- Keep an inventory of mechanical parts and supplies
- Do routine maintenance checks throughout the day
- Calculate refueling requirements

Marine oilers work in the engine room, helping the engineers keep the propulsion system in working order. They are the engine room equivalent of sailors. New oilers usually are called *wipers*, or *pumpmen*, on vessels handling liquid cargo. With experience, a wiper can become a Qualified Member of the Engine Department (QMED). Marine oilers typically do the following:

- Lubricate gears, shafts, bearings, and other parts of the engine or motor
- Read pressure and temperature gauges and record data
- Help engineers with repairs to machinery
- Connect hoses, operate pumps, and clean tanks
- Assist the deck crew with loading or unloading of cargo, if necessary

Motorboat operators run small, motor-driven boats that carry only a few passengers. They provide a variety of services, such as fishing charters, tours, and harbor patrols. Motorboat operators typically do the following:

- Check and change the oil and other fluids on their boat
- Pick up passengers and help them board the boat
- Act as a tour guide, if necessary

Work Environment

Water transportation workers held about 78,500 jobs in 2014. The industries that employed the most water transportation workers were as follows:

Support activities for water transportation	22%
Inland water transportation	21
Deep sea, coastal, and great lakes water transportation	19
Government	11
Scenic and sightseeing transportation, water	7

Water transportation workers usually work for long periods and can be exposed to all kinds of weather. Many people decide that life at sea is not for them because of difficult conditions onboard ships and long periods away from home.

However, companies try to provide pleasant living conditions aboard their vessels. Most vessels are now air conditioned and include comfortable living quarters. Many also include entertainment systems with satellite TV and Internet connections. Large ships usually have one or two full-time cooks as well.

Work Schedules. Workers on deep-sea ships can spend months at a time away from home.

Workers on supply ships have shorter trips, usually lasting for a few hours or days.

Tugboats and barges travel along the coasts and on inland waterways, and crews are usually away for 2 to 3 weeks at a time.

Those who work on the Great Lakes have longer trips, around 2 months, but often do not work in the winter, when the lakes freeze.

Crews on all vessels often work for long periods, 7 days a week, while aboard.

Ferry workers and motorboat operators usually are away only for a few hours at a time and return home each night. Many ferry and motorboat operators service ships for vacation destinations and have seasonal schedules.

Education/Training

Education and training requirements vary by the type of job. There are no educational requirements for entry-level sailors and oilers, but officers and engineers usually must have an endorsement certificate from the U.S. Coast Guard. Most water transportation jobs require the Transportation Worker Identification Credential (TWIC) from the Transportation Security Administration and a Merchant Marine Credential (MMC).

Education. Some deck officers, engineers, and pilots have a bachelor's degree from a merchant marine academy. The academy programs offer a bachelor's degree and a Merchant Marine Credential (MMC) with an endorsement as a third mate or third assistant engineer. Graduates of these programs also can choose to receive a commission as an ensign in the U.S. Naval Reserve, Merchant Marine Reserve, or U.S. Coast Guard Reserve.

Nonofficers, such as sailors or marine oilers, usually do not need a degree.

Training. Ordinary seamen, wipers, and other entry-level mariners get on-the-job training for 6 months to a year. The length of training depends on the size and type of ship and waterway they work on. For example, workers on deep-sea vessels need more complex training than those whose ships travel on a river.

Licenses, Certifications, and Registrations. All mariners working on ships with U.S. flags must have a Transportation Worker Identification Credential (TWIC) from the Transportation Security Administration. This credential states that a person is a U.S. citizen or permanent resident and has passed a security screening. The TWIC must be renewed every 5 years.

Mariners who work on ships traveling on the open ocean require the Standards of Training, Certification, and Watchkeeping (STWC) endorsement. Regional U.S. Coast Guard offices provide this training, and it includes topics such as first aid and lifeboat safety. The STWC training must be completed every 5 years.

Median Annual Wages, May 2014

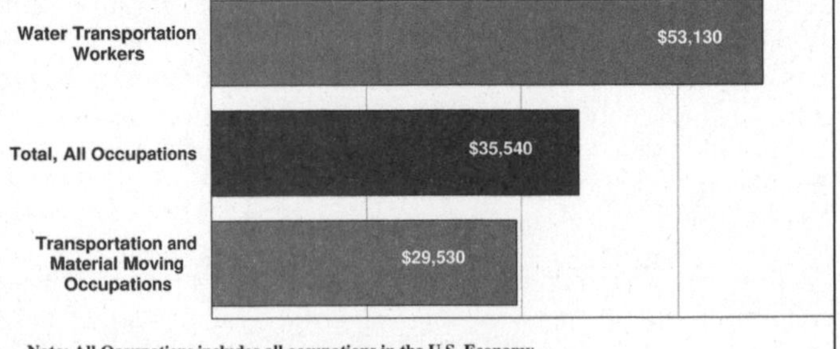

Note: All Occupations includes all occupations in the U.S. Economy.
Source: U.S. Bureau of Labor Statistics, Occupational Employment Statistics

Percent Change in Employment, Projected 2014–2024

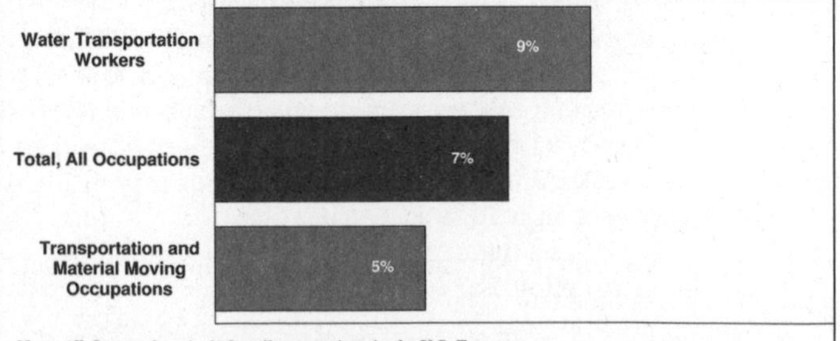

Note: All Occupations includes all occupations in the U.S. Economy.
Source: U.S. Bureau of Labor Statistics, Office of Occupational Statistics and Employment Projections

Employment Projections Data for Water Transportation Workers

Occupational Title	SOC Code	Employment, 2014	Projected Employment, 2024	Change, 2014–2024 Percent	Change, 2014–2024 Numeric
Water transportation workers	53-5000	78,500	85,700	9	7,200
Sailors and marine oilers	53-5011	28,300	30,900	9	2,600
Captains, mates, and pilots of water vessels	53-5021	35,100	38,700	10	3,600
Motorboat operators	53-5022	4,700	5,000	6	300
Ship engineers	53-5031	10,300	11,100	7	800

Source: U.S. Bureau of Labor Statistics, Employment Projections Program

Mariners who work on inland waterways and the Great Lakes are excluded from the STWC endorsement.

Most mariners also must have a Merchant Marine Credential (MMC), which they can apply for at a U.S. Coast Guard regional examination center. Entry-level employees, such as ordinary seamen or wipers, do not have to pass a written exam. However, some have to pass physical, hearing, and vision tests, and all must undergo a drug screening, to get their MMC. They also have to take a class on shipboard safety. The MMC must also be renewed every 5 years. More information on MMCs and endorsements is available from the U.S. Coast Guard National Maritime Center.

Pilots are licensed by the state in which they work. The U.S. Coast Guard licenses pilots on the Great Lakes. The requirements for these licenses vary, depending on where a pilot works.

Advancement. Crewmembers can apply for endorsements to their MMC that allow them to move into more advanced positions.

Wipers can get an endorsement to become a Qualified Member of the Engine Department (QMED) after 6 months of experience by passing a written test.

It takes 3 years of experience and the passing of a written test for an ordinary seaman to become an unlimited able seaman. However, several able seaman endorsements below the level of unlimited are available after 6 months to 1 year of experience, depending on the type of ship the seamen work on.

Able seamen can advance to become third mates after at least 3 years of experience in the deck department. This experience must be on a ship similar to the type they hope to serve on as an officer. They also must take several training courses and pass written and onboard exams to receive the third-mate endorsement on their MMC. The difficulty of these requirements increases with the complexity and size of the vessel. Similarly, QMEDs can receive an endorsement as a third assistant engineer after 3 years of experience in the engine room and upon completion of a number of training and testing requirements. Experience and testing requirements increase with the size and complexity of the ship.

Officers who graduate from a maritime academy receive an MMC with an endorsement of third mate or third assistant engineer, depending on which department they are trained in.

To move up each step of the occupation ladder, from third mate/third assistant engineer, to second mate, to first mate, and then to captain or chief engineer, requires 365 days of experience at the previous level. A second mate or second assistant engineer who wants to move to first mate/first assistant engineer also must complete a 12-week training course and pass an exam.

Work Experience in a Related Occupation. Many pilots have years of experience as a mate on a ship. The ship should be of the type they expect to pilot. For example, if they work at a deep-sea port, they should have experience on an oceangoing vessel.

Similarly, many motorboat operators must have several years of experience working on and driving a boat.

Important Qualities

Customer-service skills. Many motorboat operators interact with passengers and must ensure that the passengers have a pleasant experience.

Hand-eye coordination. Officers and pilots who steer ships have to operate various controls while staying aware of their surroundings.

Hearing ability. Mariners must pass a hearing test to get an MMC.

Manual dexterity. Crewmembers need good balance to maneuver through tight spaces and on wet or uneven surfaces.

Mechanical skills. Members of the engine department keep complex machines working properly.

Physical strength. Sailors on freight ships load and unload cargo. While away at sea, most workers have to do some heavy lifting.

Visual ability. Mariners must pass a vision test to get an MMC.

Pay

The median annual wage for water transportation workers was $53,130 in May 2014. The median wage is the wage at which half the workers in an occupation earned more than that amount and half earned less. The lowest 10 percent earned less than $25,690, and the highest 10 percent earned more than $110,630.

Median annual wages for water transportation workers in May 2014 were as follows:

Captains, mates, and pilots of water vessels	$72,340
Ship engineers	68,100
Sailors and marine oilers	39,100
Motorboat operators	37,120

Job Outlook

Employment of water transportation workers is projected to grow 9 percent from 2014 to 2024, faster than the average for all occupations.

Employment of sailors and marine oilers is projected to grow 9 percent from 2014 to 2024. Employment of captains, mates, and pilots of water vessels is projected to grow 10 percent. Employment of ship engineers is projected to grow 7 percent.

The rising demand for bulk commodities such as iron ore, grain, and petroleum should increase the need for these workers. Job growth is likely to be concentrated on inland rivers and the Great Lakes. As domestic oil production continues to increase, more oil tanker ships and barges may be called upon to deliver raw crude to refineries, which are typically located near waterways. In addition, the need to supply offshore oil platforms will contribute to some supply ship growth.

However, growth in domestic waterways freight may be limited because of strong competition from pipelines, railways, and trucks. Pipelines are the most efficient mode used to transport oil, and new systems are expected to be built to meet the growing demand. For

Similar Occupations. This table shows a list of occupations with job duties that are similar to those of water transportation workers.

Occupations	Entry-level Education	2014 Median Pay	Projected Job Growth	Average Annual Openings
Electrical and Electronics Installers and Repairers	Postsecondary nondegree award	$53,900	-4%	-540
Fishing and Hunting Workers	No formal educational credential	$32,530	-1%	-20
Heavy and Tractor-trailer Truck Drivers	Postsecondary nondegree award	$39,520	5%	9,880
Heavy Vehicle and Mobile Equipment Service Technicians	High school diploma or equivalent	$45,930	5%	1,010
Material Moving Machine Operators	See Education/Training	$32,890	3%	1,950
Plumbers, Pipefitters, and Steamfitters	High school diploma or equivalent	$50,660	12%	4,910
Railroad Workers	High school diploma or equivalent	$53,670	-3%	-330
Stationary Engineers and Boiler Operators	High school diploma or equivalent	$56,330	1%	60

other products, rail is a more direct route from the Midwest to a coastal port, which saves time and money.

Jobs in deep-sea shipping should remain stable because federal laws and subsidies ensure that there always will be a fleet of merchant ships with U.S. flags. Keeping a fleet of merchant ships is considered important for the nation's defense.

The popularity of river cruises as a type of vacation is growing. This trend may lead to more opportunities for workers on inland rivers such as the Mississippi or Ohio River. However, most ocean-going cruise ships go to international destinations, and these ships generally do not employ U.S. workers.

Employment of motorboat operators is projected to grow 6 percent from 2014 to 2024. Demand for these workers will be driven by growth in tourism and recreational activities, where they are primarily employed.

Job Prospects. Job prospects should be favorable for most water transportation workers. Many—especially sailors and marine oilers—leave these occupations, because recently hired workers often decide that they do not enjoy spending a lot of time away at sea.

High regulatory and security requirements may limit the number of applicants for all types of jobs.

Contacts for More Information

For more information about water transportation workers, including employment and training information, visit

➤ Maritime Administration, U.S. Department of Transportation (www.marad.dot.gov)

For more information about licensing requirements, visit

➤ U.S. Coast Guard (www.uscg.mil)

For information about jobs on barges, tugboats, and towboats traveling on inland and coastal waterways, visit

➤ The American Waterways Operators (www.americanwaterways.com)

➤ Lake Carriers' Association (www.lcaships.com)

➤ Passenger Vessel Association (www.passengervessel.com)

O*NET

➤ Sailors and Marine Oilers (53-5011.00)

➤ Captains, Mates, and Pilots of Water Vessels (53-5021.00)

➤ Ship and Boat Captains (53-5021.01)

➤ Mates—Ship, Boat, and Barge (53-5021.02)

➤ Pilots, Ship (53-5021.03)

➤ Motorboat Operators (53-5022.00)

➤ Ship Engineers (53-5031.00)

Data for Occupations Not Covered in Detail

Although hundreds of occupations are covered in detail in the *Occupational Outlook Handbook*, this chapter presents summary data on additional occupations for which employment projections are prepared but detailed occupational information is not developed. For each occupation, the Occupational Information Network (O*NET) code, the occupational definition, 2014 employment, the May 2014 median annual wage, the projected employment change and growth rate from 2014 to 2024, and education and training categories are presented.

Arts and Design Occupations

Merchandise Displayers and Window Trimmers

(O*NET 27-1026.00)

Plan and erect commercial displays, such as those in windows and interiors of retail stores and at trade exhibitions.

- **2014 employment:** 120,800
- **May 2014 median annual wage:** $26,590
- **Projected employment change, 2014–24:**
  - **Number of new jobs:** 3,300
  - **Growth rate:** 3 percent (slower than average)
- **Education and training:**
  - **Typical entry-level education:** High school diploma or equivalent
  - **Work experience in a related occupation:** None
  - **Typical on-the-job training:** Moderate-term on-the-job training

Set and Exhibit Designers

(O*NET 27-1027.00)

Design special exhibits and movie, television, and theater sets. May study scripts, confer with directors, and conduct research to determine appropriate architectural styles.

- **2014 employment:** 13,300
- **May 2014 median annual wage:** $49,810
- **Projected employment change, 2014–24:**
  - **Number of new jobs:** 900
  - **Growth rate:** 7 percent (about as fast as average)
- **Education and training:**
  - **Typical entry-level education:** Bachelor's degree
  - **Work experience in a related occupation:** None
  - **Typical on-the-job training:** None

Building and Grounds Cleaning Occupations

First-Line Supervisors of Housekeeping and Janitorial Workers

(O*NET 37-1011.00)

Directly supervise and coordinate work activities of cleaning personnel in hotels, hospitals, offices, and other establishments.

- **2014 employment:** 247,900
- **May 2014 median annual wage:** $36,270
- **Projected employment change, 2014–24:**
  - **Number of new jobs:** 14,900
  - **Growth rate:** 6 percent (about as fast as average)
- **Education and training:**
  - **Typical entry-level education:** High school diploma or equivalent
  - **Work experience in a related occupation:** Less than 5 years
  - **Typical on-the-job training:** None

First-Line Supervisors of Landscaping, Lawn Service, and Groundskeeping Workers

(O*NET 37-1012.00)

Directly supervise and coordinate activities of workers engaged in landscaping or groundskeeping activities. Work may involve reviewing contracts to determine service, machine, and workforce requirements; answering inquiries from potential customers regarding methods, materials, and price ranges; and preparing estimates according to labor, material, and machine costs.

- **2014 employment:** 178,000
- **May 2014 median annual wage:** $43,160
- **Projected employment change, 2014–24:**
  - **Number of new jobs:** 9,400
  - **Growth rate:** 5 percent (about as fast as average)
- **Education and training:**
  - **Typical entry-level education:** High school diploma or equivalent
  - **Work experience in a related occupation:** Less than 5 years
  - **Typical on-the-job training:** None

Maids and Housekeeping Cleaners

(O*NET 37-2012.00)

Perform any combination of light cleaning duties to maintain private households or commercial establishments, such as hotels and hospitals, in a clean and orderly manner. Duties may include making beds, replenishing linens, cleaning rooms and halls, and vacuuming.

- **2014 employment:** 1,457,700
- **May 2014 median annual wage:** $20,120
- **Projected employment change, 2014–24:**
  - **Number of new jobs:** 111,700
  - **Growth rate:** 8 percent (about as fast as average)
- **Education and training:**
  - **Typical entry-level education:** No formal educational credential
  - **Work experience in a related occupation:** None
  - **Typical on-the-job training:** Short-term on-the-job training

Business and Financial Occupations

Agents and Business Managers of Artists, Performers, and Athletes

(O*NET 13-1011.00)

Represent and promote artists, performers, and athletes in dealings with current or prospective employers. May handle contract negotiations and other business matters for clients.

- **2014 employment:** 19,700
- **May 2014 median annual wage:** $64,200
- **Projected employment change, 2014–24:**
  - **Number of new jobs:** 500
  - **Growth rate:** 3 percent (slower than average)
- **Education and training:**
  - **Typical entry-level education:** Bachelor's degree
  - **Work experience in a related occupation:** Less than 5 years
  - **Typical on-the-job training:** None

Compliance Officers

(O*NET 13-1041.00, 13-1041.01, 13-1041.02, 13-1041.03, 13-1041.04, 13-1041.06, and 13-1041.07)

Examine, evaluate, and investigate eligibility for or conformity with laws and regulations governing contract compliance of licenses and permits, and perform other compliance and enforcement inspection and analysis activities not classified elsewhere. Excludes "Financial Examiners" (13-2061), "Tax Examiners and Collectors, and Revenue Agents" (13-2081), "Occupational Health and Safety Specialists" (29-9011), "Occupational Health and Safety Technicians" (29-9012), "Transportation Security Screeners" (33-9093), "Agricultural Inspectors" (45-2011), "Construction and Building Inspectors" (47-4011), and "Transportation Inspectors" (53-6051).

- **2014 employment:** 260,300
- **May 2014 median annual wage:** $64,950
- **Projected employment change, 2014–24:**
  - **Number of new jobs:** 8,700
  - **Growth rate:** 3 percent (slower than average)
- **Education and training:**
  - **Typical entry-level education:** Bachelor's degree
  - **Work experience in a related occupation:** None
  - **Typical on-the-job training:** Moderate-term on-the-job training

Farm Labor Contractors

(O*NET 13-1074.00)

Recruit and hire seasonal or temporary agricultural laborers. May transport, house, and provide meals for workers.

- **2014 employment:** 100
- **May 2014 median annual wage:** $41,110
- **Projected employment change, 2014–24:**
  - **Number of new jobs:** 0
  - **Growth rate:** –9 percent (decline)
- **Education and training:**
  - **Typical entry-level education:** No formal educational credential
  - **Work experience in a related occupation:** Less than 5 years
  - **Typical on-the-job training:** Short-term on-the-job training

Credit Analysts

(O*NET 13-2041.00)

Analyze credit data and financial statements of individuals or firms to determine the degree of risk involved in extending credit or lending money. Prepare reports with credit information for use in decision making.

- **2014 employment:** 69,400
- **May 2014 median annual wage:** $67,020
- **Projected employment change, 2014–24:**
  - **Number of new jobs:** 4,200
  - **Growth rate:** 6 percent (about as fast as average)
- **Education and training:**
  - **Typical entry-level education:** Bachelor's degree
  - **Work experience in a related occupation:** None
  - **Typical on-the-job training:** None

Credit Counselors

(O*NET 13-2071.00 and 13-2071.01)

Advise and educate individuals or organizations on acquiring and managing debt. May provide guidance in determining the best type of loan and explaining loan requirements or restrictions. May help develop debt management plans, advise on credit issues, or provide budget, mortgage, and bankruptcy counseling.

- **2014 employment:** 32,600
- **May 2014 median annual wage:** $42,110
- **Projected employment change, 2014–24:**
  - **Number of new jobs:** 5,000
  - **Growth rate:** 15 percent (much faster than average)
- **Education and training:**
  - **Typical entry-level education:** Bachelor's degree
  - **Work experience in a related occupation:** None
  - **Typical on-the-job training:** Moderate-term on-the-job training

Tax Preparers

(O*NET 13-2082.00)

Prepare tax returns for individuals or small businesses. Excludes "Accountants and Auditors" (13-2011).

- **2014 employment:** 90,400
- **May 2014 median annual wage:** $35,990
- **Projected employment change, 2014–24:**
  - **Number of new jobs:** 1,400
  - **Growth rate:** 2 percent (slower than average)
- **Education and training:**
  - **Typical entry-level education:** High school diploma or equivalent
  - **Work experience in a related occupation:** None
  - **Typical on-the-job training:** Moderate-term on-the-job training

Community and Social Service Occupations

Clergy

(O*NET 21-2011.00)

Conduct religious worship and perform other spiritual functions associated with beliefs and practices of religious faiths or denominations. Provide spiritual and moral guidance and assistance to members.

- **2014 employment:** 244,200
- **May 2014 median annual wage:** $43,950
- **Projected employment change, 2014–24:**
  - **Number of new jobs:** 13,800
  - **Growth rate:** 6 percent (about as fast as average)
- **Education and training:**
  - **Typical entry-level education:** Bachelor's degree
  - **Work experience in a related occupation:** None
  - **Typical on-the-job training:** Moderate-term on-the-job training

Directors, Religious Activities and Education

(O*NET 21-2021.00)

Plan, direct, or coordinate programs designed to promote the religious education or activities of a denominational group. May provide counseling and guidance for marital, health, financial, and religious problems.

- **2014 employment:** 131,900
- **May 2014 median annual wage:** $38,480
- **Projected employment change, 2014–24:**
  - **Number of new jobs:** 5,700
  - **Growth rate:** 4 percent (slower than average)
- **Education and training:**
  - **Typical entry-level education:** Bachelor's degree
  - **Work experience in a related occupation:** Less than 5 years
  - **Typical on-the-job training:** None

Construction and Extraction Occupations

First-Line Supervisors of Construction Trades and Extraction Workers

(O*NET 47-1011.00 and 47-1011.03)

Directly supervise and coordinate activities of construction or extraction workers.

- **2014 employment:** 578,400
- **May 2014 median annual wage:** $60,990
- **Projected employment change, 2014–24:**
  - **Number of new jobs:** 57,700
  - **Growth rate:** 10 percent (faster than average)
- **Education and training:**
  - **Typical entry-level education:** High school diploma or equivalent
  - **Work experience in a related occupation:** 5 years or more
  - **Typical on-the-job training:** None

Paperhangers

(O*NET 47-2142.00)

Cover interior walls or ceilings of rooms with decorative wallpaper or fabric, or attach advertising posters on surfaces such as walls and billboards. May remove old materials or prepare surfaces to be papered.

- **2014 employment:** 6,400
- **May 2014 median annual wage:** $32,930
- **Projected employment change, 2014–24:**
  - **Number of new jobs:** 200
  - **Growth rate:** 2 percent (slower than average)
- **Education and training:**
  - **Typical entry-level education:** No formal educational credential
  - **Work experience in a related occupation:** None
  - **Typical on-the-job training:** Long-term on-the-job training

Pipelayers

(O*NET 47-2151.00)

Lay pipe for storm or sanitation sewers, drains, and water mains. Perform any combination of the following tasks: grade trenches or culverts, position pipes, or seal joints. Excludes "Welders, Cutters, Solderers, and Brazers" (51-4121).

- **2014 employment:** 45,700
- **May 2014 median annual wage:** $37,000
- **Projected employment change, 2014–24:**
  - **Number of new jobs:** 5,200
  - **Growth rate:** 11 percent (faster than average)
- **Education and training:**
  - **Typical entry-level education:** No formal educational credential
  - **Work experience in a related occupation:** None
  - **Typical on-the-job training:** Short-term on-the-job training

Plasterers and Stucco Masons

(O*NET 47-2161.00)

Apply interior or exterior plaster, cement, stucco, or similar materials. May also set ornamental plaster.

- **2014 employment:** 27,000
- **May 2014 median annual wage:** $37,550
- **Projected employment change, 2014–24:**
  - **Number of new jobs:** 1,900
  - **Growth rate:** 7 percent (about as fast as average)
- **Education and training:**
  - **Typical entry-level education:** No formal educational credential
  - **Work experience in a related occupation:** None
  - **Typical on-the-job training:** Long-term on-the-job training

Fence Erectors

(O*NET 47-4031.00)

Erect and repair fences, including gates, using hand and power tools.

- **2014 employment:** 24,400
- **May 2014 median annual wage:** $31,510
- **Projected employment change, 2014–24:**
  - **Number of new jobs:** 2,000
  - **Growth rate:** 8 percent (about as fast as average)
- **Education and training:**
  - **Typical entry-level education:** No formal educational credential
  - **Work experience in a related occupation:** None
  - **Typical on-the-job training:** Moderate-term on-the-job training

Highway Maintenance Workers

(O*NET 47-4051.00)

Maintain highways, municipal and rural roads, airport runways, and rights-of-way. Duties include patching broken or eroded pavement, repairing guard rails, highway markers, and snow fences. May also mow or clear brush from along roads or plow snow from roadways. Excludes "Tree Trimmers and Pruners" (37-3013).

- **2014 employment:** 151,300
- **May 2014 median annual wage:** $36,580

- **Projected employment change, 2014–24:**
  - **Number of new jobs:** 7,300
  - **Growth rate:** 5 percent (about as fast as average)
- **Education and training:**
  - **Typical entry-level education:** High school diploma or equivalent
  - **Work experience in a related occupation:** None
  - **Typical on-the-job training:** Moderate-term on-the-job training

Rail-Track Laying and Maintenance Equipment Operators

(O*NET 47-4061.00)

Lay, repair, and maintain track for standard or narrow-gauge railroad equipment used in regular railroad service or in plant yards, quarries, sand and gravel pits, and mines. Includes ballast cleaning machine operators and railroad bed tamping machine operators.

- **2014 employment:** 15,600
- **May 2014 median annual wage:** $51,840
- **Projected employment change, 2014–24:**
  - **Number of new jobs:** 1,500
  - **Growth rate:** 9 percent (faster than average)
- **Education and training:**
  - **Typical entry-level education:** High school diploma or equivalent
  - **Work experience in a related occupation:** None
  - **Typical on-the-job training:** Moderate-term on-the-job training

Septic Tank Servicers and Sewer Pipe Cleaners

(O*NET 47-4071.00)

Clean and repair septic tanks, sewer lines, or drains. May patch walls and partitions of tank, replace damaged drain tile, or repair breaks in underground piping.

- **2014 employment:** 24,700
- **May 2014 median annual wage:** $34,810
- **Projected employment change, 2014–24:**
  - **Number of new jobs:** 4,000
  - **Growth rate:** 16 percent (much faster than average)
- **Education and training:**
  - **Typical entry-level education:** No formal educational credential
  - **Work experience in a related occupation:** None
  - **Typical on-the-job training:** Moderate-term on-the-job training

Derrick Operators, Oil and Gas

(O*NET 47-5011.00)

Rig derrick equipment and operate pumps to circulate mud through drill holes.

- **2014 employment:** 21,700
- **May 2014 median annual wage:** $48,410
- **Projected employment change, 2014–24:**
  - **Number of new jobs:** 2,900
  - **Growth rate:** 13 percent (faster than average)
- **Education and training:**
  - **Typical entry-level education:** No formal educational credential
  - **Work experience in a related occupation:** None
  - **Typical on-the-job training:** Short-term on-the-job training

Rotary Drill Operators, Oil and Gas

(O*NET 47-5012.00)

Set up or operate a variety of drills to remove underground oil and gas, or remove core samples for testing during oil and gas exploration. Excludes "Earth Drillers, Except Oil and Gas" (47-5021).

- **2014 employment:** 27,700
- **May 2014 median annual wage:** $53,160
- **Projected employment change, 2014–24:**
  - **Number of new jobs:** 3,500
  - **Growth rate:** 13 percent (faster than average)
- **Education and training:**
  - **Typical entry-level education:** No formal educational credential
  - **Work experience in a related occupation:** None
  - **Typical on-the-job training:** Moderate-term on-the-job training

Service Unit Operators, Oil, Gas, and Mining

(O*NET 47-5013.00)

Operate equipment to increase oil flow from producing wells or to remove stuck pipe, casing, tools, or other obstructions from drilling wells. May also perform similar services in mining exploration operations. Includes fishing-tool technicians.

- **2014 employment:** 64,900
- **May 2014 median annual wage:** $44,970
- **Projected employment change, 2014–24:**
  - **Number of new jobs:** 4,700
  - **Growth rate:** 7 percent (about as fast as average)
- **Education and training:**
  - **Typical entry-level education:** No formal educational credential
  - **Work experience in a related occupation:** None
  - **Typical on-the-job training:** Moderate-term on-the-job training

Earth Drillers, Except Oil and Gas

(O*NET 47-5021.00)

Operate a variety of drills such as rotary, churn, and pneumatic to tap sub-surface water and salt deposits, to remove core samples during mineral exploration or soil testing, and to facilitate the use of explosives in mining or construction. May use explosives. Includes horizontal and earth-boring machine operators.

- **2014 employment:** 20,000
- **May 2014 median annual wage:** $43,540
- **Projected employment change, 2014–24:**
  - **Number of new jobs:** 2,700
  - **Growth rate:** 14 percent (much faster than average)
- **Education and training:**
  - **Typical entry-level education:** High school diploma or equivalent
  - **Work experience in a related occupation:** None
  - **Typical on-the-job training:** Moderate-term on-the-job training

Explosives Workers, Ordnance Handling Experts, and Blasters

(O*NET 47-5031.00)

Place and detonate explosives to demolish structures or to loosen, remove, or displace earth, rock, or other materials. May perform specialized handling, storage, and accounting procedures. Includes seismograph shooters. Excludes "Earth Drillers, Except Oil and Gas" (47-5021), who also may work with explosives.

- **2014 employment:** 8,100
- **May 2014 median annual wage:** $52,140
- **Projected employment change, 2014–24:**
  - **Number of new jobs:** 300
  - **Growth rate:** 4 percent (slower than average)
- **Education and training:**
  - **Typical entry-level education:** High school diploma or equivalent
  - **Work experience in a related occupation:** Less than 5 years
  - **Typical on-the-job training:** Long-term on-the-job training

Continuous Mining Machine Operators

(O*NET 47-5041.00)

Operate self-propelled mining machines that rip coal, metal and nonmetal ores, rock, stone, or sand from the mine face and load it onto conveyors or into shuttle cars in a continuous operation.

- **2014 employment:** 12,300
- **May 2014 median annual wage:** $48,440
- **Projected employment change, 2014–24:**
  - **Number of new jobs:** –600
  - **Growth rate:** –5 percent (decline)
- **Education and training:**
  - **Typical entry-level education:** No formal educational credential
  - **Work experience in a related occupation:** None
  - **Typical on-the-job training:** Moderate-term on-the-job training

Mine Cutting and Channeling Machine Operators

(O*NET 47-5042.00)

Operate machinery such as longwall shears, plows, and cutting machines to cut or channel along the faces or seams of coal mines, stone quarries, or other mining surfaces to facilitate blasting, separating, or removing minerals or materials from mines or from the Earth's surface. Includes shale planers.

- **2014 employment:** 7,400
- **May 2014 median annual wage:** $50,260
- **Projected employment change, 2014–24:**
  - **Number of new jobs:** –100
  - **Growth rate:** –2 percent (decline)
- **Education and training:**
  - **Typical entry-level education:** High school diploma or equivalent
  - **Work experience in a related occupation:** None
  - **Typical on-the-job training:** Moderate-term on-the-job training

Rock Splitters, Quarry

(O*NET 47-5051.00)

Separate blocks of rough dimension stone from quarry mass, using a jackhammer and wedges.

- **2014 employment:** 3,700
- **May 2014 median annual wage:** $33,240
- **Projected employment change, 2014–24:**
  - **Number of new jobs:** 300
  - **Growth rate:** 7 percent (about as fast as average)
- **Education and training:**
  - **Typical entry-level education:** No formal educational credential
  - **Work experience in a related occupation:** None
  - **Typical on-the-job training:** Short-term on-the-job training

Roof Bolters, Mining

(O*NET 47-5061.00)

Operate machinery to install roof support bolts in underground mines.

- **2014 employment:** 6,000
- **May 2014 median annual wage:** $54,860
- **Projected employment change, 2014–24:**
  - **Number of new jobs:** –600
  - **Growth rate:** –11 percent (decline)
- **Education and training:**
  - **Typical entry-level education:** High school diploma or equivalent
  - **Work experience in a related occupation:** None
  - **Typical on-the-job training:** Moderate-term on-the-job training

Roustabouts, Oil and Gas

(O*NET 47-5071.00)

Assemble or repair oil field equipment using hand and power tools. Perform other tasks as needed.

- **2014 employment:** 76,400
- **May 2014 median annual wage:** $35,780
- **Projected employment change, 2014–24:**
  - **Number of new jobs:** 6,300
  - **Growth rate:** 8 percent (about as fast as average)
- **Education and training:**
  - **Typical entry-level education:** No formal educational credential
  - **Work experience in a related occupation:** None
  - **Typical on-the-job training:** Moderate-term on-the-job training

Helpers—Extraction Workers

(O*NET 47-5081.00)

Help extraction craft workers, such as earth drillers, blasters and explosives workers, derrick operators, and mining machine operators, by performing duties requiring less skill. Duties include supplying equipment or cleaning work areas. Apprentice workers are classified with the appropriate skilled construction trade occupation (47-2011 through 47-2231).

- **2014 employment:** 25,800
- **May 2014 median annual wage:** $34,480
- **Projected employment change, 2014–24:**
  - **Number of new jobs:** 3,200
  - **Growth rate:** 13 percent (faster than average)
- **Education and training:**
  - **Typical entry-level education:** High school diploma or equivalent
  - **Work experience in a related occupation:** None
  - **Typical on-the-job training:** Moderate-term on-the-job training

Education Occupations

Graduate Teaching Assistants

(O*NET 25-1191.00)

Assist faculty or other instructional staff in postsecondary institutions by performing teaching or teaching-related duties, such as teaching lower level courses, developing teaching materials, preparing and giving examinations, and grading examinations or papers. Graduate teaching assistants must be enrolled in a graduate school program. Graduate assistants who primarily perform nonteaching duties, such as research, should be reported in the occupational category related to the work performed. Excludes "Teacher Assistants" (25-9041).

- **2014 employment:** 159,200
- **May 2014 median annual wage:** $31,570
- **Projected employment change, 2014-24:**
  - **Number of new jobs:** 9,900
  - **Growth rate:** 6 percent (about as fast as average)
- **Education and training:**
  - **Typical entry-level education:** Bachelor's degree
  - **Work experience in a related occupation:** None
  - **Typical on-the-job training:** None

Home Economics Teachers, Postsecondary

(O*NET 25-1192.00)

Teach courses in childcare, family relations, finance, nutrition, and related subjects pertaining to home management. Includes both teachers engaged primarily in teaching and those who do a combination of teaching and research.

- **2014 employment:** 4,300
- **May 2014 median annual wage:** $63,390
- **Projected employment change, 2014–24:**
  - **Number of new jobs:** –500
  - **Growth rate:** –12 percent (decline)
- **Education and training:**
  - **Typical entry-level education:** Master's degree
  - **Work experience in a related occupation:** None
  - **Typical on-the-job training:** None

Recreation and Fitness Studies Teachers, Postsecondary

(O*NET 25-1193.00)

Teach courses pertaining to recreation, leisure, and fitness studies, including exercise physiology and facilities management. Includes both teachers engaged primarily in teaching and those who do a combination of teaching and research.

- **2014 employment:** 22,100
- **May 2014 median annual wage:** $58,280
- **Projected employment change, 2014–24:**
  - **Number of new jobs:** 2,200
  - **Growth rate:** 10 percent (faster than average)
- **Education and training:**
  - **Typical entry-level education:** Doctoral or professional degree
  - **Work experience in a related occupation:** None
  - **Typical on-the-job training:** None

Self-Enrichment Education Teachers

(O*NET 25-3021.00)

Teach or instruct courses other than those which normally lead to an occupational objective or degree. Courses may include self-improvement, nonvocational, and nonacademic subjects. Teaching may or may not take place in a traditional educational institution. Excludes "Fitness Trainers and Aerobics Instructors" (39-9031). Flight instructors are included with "Aircraft Pilots and Flight Engineers" (53-2010).

- **2014 employment:** 348,700
- **May 2014 median annual wage:** $36,020
- **Projected employment change, 2014–24:**
  - **Number of new jobs:** 53,500
  - **Growth rate:** 15 percent (much faster than average)
- **Education and training:**
  - **Typical entry-level education:** High school diploma or equivalent
  - **Work experience in a related occupation:** Less than 5 years
  - **Typical on-the-job training:** None

Audio-Visual and Multimedia Collections Specialists

(O*NET 25-9011.00)

Prepare, plan, and operate multimedia teaching aids for use in education. May record, catalog, and file materials.

- **2014 employment:** 10,000
- **May 2014 median annual wage:** $44,070
- **Projected employment change, 2014–24:**
  - **Number of new jobs:** 800
  - **Growth rate:** 8 percent (about as fast as average)
- **Education and training:**
  - **Typical entry-level education:** Bachelor's degree
  - **Work experience in a related occupation:** Less than 5 years
  - **Typical on-the-job training:** None

Farm and Home Management Advisors

(O*NET 25-9021.00)

Advise, instruct, and assist individuals and families engaged in agriculture, agriculture-related processes, or home economics activities. Demonstrate procedures and apply research findings to solve problems; and instruct and train in product development, sales, and the use of machinery and equipment to promote general welfare. Includes county agricultural agents, feed and farm management advisors, home economists, and extension service advisors.

- **2014 employment:** 10,800
- **May 2014 median annual wage:** $46,520
- **Projected employment change, 2014–24:**
  - **Number of new jobs:** 1,200
  - **Growth rate:** 11 percent (faster than average)
- **Education and training:**
  - **Typical entry-level education:** Master's degree
  - **Work experience in a related occupation:** None
  - **Typical on-the-job training:** None

Farming, Fishing, and Forestry Occupations

First-Line Supervisors of Farming, Fishing, and Forestry Workers

(O*NET 45-1011.00, 45-1011.05, 45-1011.06, 45-1011.07, and 45-1011.08)

Directly supervise and coordinate the activities of agricultural, forestry, aquacultural, and related workers. Excludes "First-Line Supervisors of Landscaping, Lawn Service, and Groundskeeping Workers" (37-1012).

- **2014 employment:** 47,100
- **May 2014 median annual wage:** $44,880
- **Projected employment change, 2014–24:**
  - **Number of new jobs:** –3,900
  - **Growth rate:** –8 percent (decline)
- **Education and training:**
  - **Typical entry-level education:** High school diploma or equivalent
  - **Work experience in a related occupation:** Less than 5 years
  - **Typical on-the-job training:** None

Agricultural Inspectors

(O*NET 45-2011.00)

Inspect agricultural commodities, processing equipment, and facilities, and fish and logging operations, to ensure compliance with regulations and laws governing health, quality, and safety.

- **2014 employment:** 14,200
- **May 2014 median annual wage:** $43,090
- **Projected employment change, 2014–24:**
  - **Number of new jobs:** –100
  - **Growth rate:** –1 percent (little or no change)
- **Education and training:**
  - **Typical entry-level education:** Bachelor's degree
  - **Work experience in a related occupation:** None
  - **Typical on-the-job training:** Moderate-term on-the-job training

Graders and Sorters, Agricultural Products

(O*NET 45-2041.00)

Grade, sort, or classify unprocessed food and other agricultural products by size, weight, color, or condition. Excludes "Agricultural Inspectors" (45-2011).

- **2014 employment:** 53,000
- **May 2014 median annual wage:** $19,910
- **Projected employment change, 2014–24:**
  - **Number of new jobs:** –4,100
  - **Growth rate:** –8 percent (decline)
- **Education and training:**
  - **Typical entry-level education:** No formal educational credential
  - **Work experience in a related occupation:** None
  - **Typical on-the-job training:** Short-term on-the-job training

Food Preparation and Serving Occupations

First-Line Supervisors of Food Preparation and Serving Workers

(O*NET 35-1012.00)

Directly supervise and coordinate activities of workers who prepare and serve food.

- **2014 employment:** 890,100
- **May 2014 median annual wage:** $29,560
- **Projected employment change, 2014–24:**
  - **Number of new jobs:** 88,500
  - **Growth rate:** 10 percent (faster than average)
- **Education and training:**
  - **Typical entry-level education:** High school diploma or equivalent
  - **Work experience in a related occupation:** Less than 5 years
  - **Typical on-the-job training:** None

Dishwashers

(O*NET 35-9021.00)

Clean dishes, kitchen, food preparation equipment, or utensils.

- **2014 employment:** 507,400
- **May 2014 median annual wage:** $18,780
- **Projected employment change, 2014–24:**
  - **Number of new jobs:** –19,500
  - **Growth rate:** –4 percent (decline)
- **Education and training:**
  - **Typical entry-level education:** No formal educational credential
  - **Work experience in a related occupation:** None
  - **Typical on-the-job training:** Short-term on-the-job training

Healthcare Occupations

Dietetic Technicians

(O*NET 29-2051.00)

Assist in the provision of food service and nutritional programs under the supervision of a dietitian. May plan and produce meals based on established guidelines, teach principles of food and nutrition, or counsel individuals.

- **2014 employment:** 29,300
- **May 2014 median annual wage:** $25,780
- **Projected employment change, 2014–24:**
  - **Number of new jobs:** 3,900
  - **Growth rate:** 13 percent (faster than average)
- **Education and training:**
  - **Typical entry-level education:** Associate's degree
  - **Work experience in a related occupation:** None
  - **Typical on-the-job training:** None

Respiratory Therapy Technicians

(O*NET 29-2054.00)

Provide respiratory care under the direction of respiratory therapists and physicians.

- **2014 employment:** 10,700
- **May 2014 median annual wage:** $47,810
- **Projected employment change, 2014–24:**
  - **Number of new jobs:** –2,100
  - **Growth rate:** –19 percent (decline)
- **Education and training:**
  - **Typical entry-level education:** Associate's degree
  - **Work experience in a related occupation:** None
  - **Typical on-the-job training:** None

Ophthalmic Medical Technicians

(O*NET 29-2057.00)

Assist ophthalmologists by performing ophthalmic clinical functions. May administer eye exams, administer eye medications, and instruct the patient in the care and use of corrective lenses.

- **2014 employment:** 37,000

- **May 2014 median annual wage:** $35,230
- **Projected employment change, 2014–24:**
  - **Number of new jobs:** 9,100
  - **Growth rate:** 25 percent (much faster than average)
- **Education and training:**
  - **Typical entry-level education:** Postsecondary nondegree award
  - **Work experience in a related occupation:** None
  - **Typical on-the-job training:** None

Hearing Aid Specialists

(O*NET 29-2092.00)

Select and fit hearing aids for customers. Administer and interpret tests of hearing. Assess hearing instrument efficacy. Take ear impressions and prepare, design, and modify ear molds. Excludes "Audiologists" (29-1181).

- **2014 employment:** 5,900
- **May 2014 median annual wage:** $43,010
- **Projected employment change, 2014–24:**
  - **Number of new jobs:** 1,600
  - **Growth rate:** 27 percent (much faster than average)
- **Education and training:**
  - **Typical entry-level education:** High school diploma or equivalent
  - **Work experience in a related occupation:** None
  - **Typical on-the-job training:** None

Medical Equipment Preparers

(O*NET 31-9093.00)

Prepare, sterilize, install, or clean laboratory or healthcare equipment. May perform routine laboratory tasks and operate or inspect equipment.

- **2014 employment:** 52,000
- **May 2014 median annual wage:** $32,260
- **Projected employment change, 2014–24:**
  - **Number of new jobs:** 7,300
  - **Growth rate:** 14 percent (much faster than average)
- **Education and training:**
  - **Typical entry-level education:** High school diploma or equivalent
  - **Work experience in a related occupation:** None
  - **Typical on-the-job training:** Moderate-term on-the-job training

Pharmacy Aides

(O*NET 31-9095.00)

Record drugs delivered to the pharmacy, store incoming merchandise, and inform the supervisor of stock needs. May operate the cash register and accept prescriptions for filling.

- **2014 employment:** 41,500
- **May 2014 median annual wage:** $23,200
- **Projected employment change, 2014–24:**
  - **Number of new jobs:** 100
  - **Growth rate:** 0 percent (little or no change)
- **Education and training:**
  - **Typical entry-level education:** High school diploma or equivalent
  - **Work experience in a related occupation:** None
  - **Typical on-the-job training:** Short-term on-the-job training

Installation, Maintenance, and Repair Occupations

First-Line Supervisors of Mechanics, Installers, and Repairers

(O*NET 49-1011.00)

Directly supervise and coordinate the activities of mechanics, installers, and repairers. Excludes team or work leaders.

- **2014 employment:** 447,100
- **May 2014 median annual wage:** $62,150
- **Projected employment change, 2014–24:**
  - **Number of new jobs:** 24,300
  - **Growth rate:** 5 percent (about as fast as average)
- **Education and training:**
  - **Typical entry-level education:** High school diploma or equivalent
  - **Work experience in a related occupation:** Less than 5 years
  - **Typical on-the-job training:** None

Computer, Automated Teller, and Office Machine Repairers

(O*NET 49-2011.00)

Repair, adjust, or install computers, word processing systems, automated teller machines, and electronic office machines, such as duplicating and fax machines.

- **2014 employment:** 131,600
- **May 2014 median annual wage:** $36,560
- **Projected employment change, 2014–24:**
  - **Number of new jobs:** 3,200
  - **Growth rate:** 2 percent (slower than average)
- **Education and training:**
  - **Typical entry-level education:** Some college, no degree
  - **Work experience in a related occupation:** None
  - **Typical on-the-job training:** Short-term on-the-job training

Radio, Cellular, and Tower Equipment Installers and Repairs

(O*NET 49-2021.00 and 49-2021.01)

Repair, install or maintain mobile or stationary radio transmitting, broadcasting, and receiving equipment, and two-way radio communications systems used in cellular telecommunications, mobile broadband, ship-to-shore, and aircraft-to-ground communications, and radio equipment in service and emergency vehicles. May test and analyze network coverage.

- **2014 employment:** 13,600
- **May 2014 median annual wage:** $47,950
- **Projected employment change, 2014–24:**
  - **Number of new jobs:** 800
  - **Growth rate:** 6 percent (about as fast as average)
- **Education and training:**
  - **Typical entry-level education:** Associate's degree
  - **Work experience in a related occupation:** None
  - **Typical on-the-job training:** Moderate-term on-the-job training

Electronic Home Entertainment Equipment Installers and Repairers

(O*NET 49-2097.00)

Repair, adjust, or install audio or television receivers, stereo systems, camcorders, video systems, or other electronic home entertainment equipment.

- **2014 employment:** 29,600
- **May 2014 median annual wage:** $36,090
- **Projected employment change, 2014–24:**
  - **Number of new jobs:** 700
  - **Growth rate:** 2 percent (slower than average)
- **Education and training:**
  - **Typical entry-level education:** Postsecondary nondegree award
  - **Work experience in a related occupation:** None
  - **Typical on-the-job training:** Short-term on-the-job training

Security and Fire Alarm Systems Installers

(O*NET 49-2098.00)

Install, program, maintain, and repair security and fire alarm wiring and equipment. Ensure that work is in accordance with relevant codes. Excludes "Electricians" (47-2111), who do a broad range of electrical wiring.

- **2014 employment:** 64,000
- **May 2014 median annual wage:** $42,560
- **Projected employment change, 2014–24:**
  - **Number of new jobs:** 8,200
  - **Growth rate:** 13 percent (faster than average)
- **Education and training:**
  - **Typical entry-level education:** High school diploma or equivalent
  - **Work experience in a related occupation:** None
  - **Typical on-the-job training:** Moderate-term on-the-job training

Bicycle Repairers

(O*NET 49-3091.00)

Repair and service bicycles.

- **2014 employment:** 10,800
- **May 2014 median annual wage:** $26,370
- **Projected employment change, 2014–24:**
  - **Number of new jobs:** 2,300
  - **Growth rate:** 22 percent (much faster than average)
- **Education and training:**
  - **Typical entry-level education:** High school diploma or equivalent
  - **Work experience in a related occupation:** None
  - **Typical on-the-job training:** Moderate-term on-the-job training

Recreational Vehicle Service Technicians

(O*NET 49-3092.00)

Diagnose, inspect, adjust, repair, or overhaul recreational vehicles, including travel trailers. May specialize in maintaining gas, electrical, hydraulic, plumbing, or chassis/towing systems as well as in repairing generators, appliances, and interior components. Includes workers who perform customized van conversions. Excludes "Automotive Service Technicians and Mechanics" (49-3023) and "Bus and Truck Mechanics and Diesel Engine Specialists" (49-3031), who also work on recreation vehicles.

- **2014 employment:** 11,400
- **May 2014 median annual wage:** $35,630
- **Projected employment change, 2014–24:**
  - **Number of new jobs:** 400
  - **Growth rate:** 3 percent (slower than average)
- **Education and training:**
  - **Typical entry-level education:** High school diploma or equivalent
  - **Work experience in a related occupation:** None
  - **Typical on-the-job training:** Long-term on-the-job training

Tire Repairers and Changers

(O*NET 49-3093.00)

Repair and replace tires.

- **2014 employment:** 105,500
- **May 2014 median annual wage:** $23,730
- **Projected employment change, 2014–24:**
  - **Number of new jobs:** 4,300
  - **Growth rate:** 4 percent (slower than average)
- **Education and training:**
  - **Typical entry-level education:** High school diploma or equivalent
  - **Work experience in a related occupation:** None
  - **Typical on-the-job training:** Short-term on-the-job training

Mechanical Door Repairers

(O*NET 49-9011.00)

Install, service, or repair automatic door mechanisms and hydraulic doors. Includes garage door mechanics.

- **2014 employment:** 17,400
- **May 2014 median annual wage:** $37,080
- **Projected employment change, 2014–24:**
  - **Number of new jobs:** 1,900
  - **Growth rate:** 11 percent (faster than average)
- **Education and training:**
  - **Typical entry-level education:** High school diploma or equivalent
  - **Work experience in a related occupation:** None
  - **Typical on-the-job training:** Moderate-term on-the-job training

Control and Valve Installers and Repairers, Except Mechanical Door

(O*NET 49-9012.00)

Install, repair, and maintain mechanical regulating and controlling devices, such as electric meters, gas regulators, thermostats, safety and flow valves, and other mechanical governors.

- **2014 employment:** 42,400
- **May 2014 median annual wage:** $53,140
- **Projected employment change, 2014–24:**
  - **Number of new jobs:** 200
  - **Growth rate:** 0 percent (little or no change)
- **Education and training:**
  - **Typical entry-level education:** High school diploma or equivalent
  - **Work experience in a related occupation:** None
  - **Typical on-the-job training:** Moderate-term on-the-job training

Home Appliance Repairers

(O*NET 49-9031.00)

Repair, adjust, or install all types of electric or gas household appliances, such as refrigerators, washers, dryers, and ovens.

- **2014 employment:** 46,400
- **May 2014 median annual wage:** $35,410
- **Projected employment change, 2014–24:**
  - **Number of new jobs:** –1,600
  - **Growth rate:** –3 percent (decline)
- **Education and training:**
  - **Typical entry-level education:** High school diploma or equivalent
  - **Work experience in a related occupation:** None
  - **Typical on-the-job training:** Moderate-term on-the-job training

Refractory Materials Repairers, Except Brickmasons

(O*NET 49-9045.00)

Build or repair equipment such as furnaces, kilns, cupolas, boilers, converters, ladles, soaking pits, and ovens, using refractory materials.

- **2014 employment:** 1,800
- **May 2014 median annual wage:** $44,910
- **Projected employment change, 2014–24:**
  - **Number of new jobs:** 0
  - **Growth rate:** 1 percent (little or no change)
- **Education and training:**
  - **Typical entry-level education:** High school diploma or equivalent
  - **Work experience in a related occupation:** None
  - **Typical on-the-job training:** Moderate-term on-the-job training

Camera and Photographic Equipment Repairers

(O*NET 49-9061.00)

Repair and adjust cameras and photographic equipment, including commercial video and motion picture camera equipment.

- **2014 employment:** 3,700
- **May 2014 median annual wage:** $40,020
- **Projected employment change, 2014–24:**
  - **Number of new jobs:** 200
  - **Growth rate:** 5 percent (about as fast as average)
- **Education and training:**
  - **Typical entry-level education:** Associate's degree
  - **Work experience in a related occupation:** None
  - **Typical on-the-job training:** Long-term on-the-job training

Musical Instrument Repairers and Tuners

(O*NET 49-9063.00)

Repair percussion, stringed, reed, or wind instruments. May specialize in one area, such as piano tuning. Excludes "Electronic Home Entertainment Equipment Installers and Repairers" (49-2097), who repair electrical and electronic musical instruments.

- **2014 employment:** 8,600
- **May 2014 median annual wage:** $33,150
- **Projected employment change, 2014–24:**
  - **Number of new jobs:** 400
  - **Growth rate:** 4 percent (slower than average)
- **Education and training:**
  - **Typical entry-level education:** High school diploma or equivalent
  - **Work experience in a related occupation:** None
  - **Typical on-the-job training:** Apprenticeship

Watch Repairers

(O*NET 49-9064.00)

Repair, clean, and adjust mechanisms of timing instruments, such as watches and clocks. Includes watchmakers, watch technicians, and mechanical timepiece repairers.

- **2014 employment:** 2,700
- **May 2014 median annual wage:** $35,450
- **Projected employment change, 2014–24:**
  - **Number of new jobs:** –700
  - **Growth rate:** –26 percent (decline)
- **Education and training:**
  - **Typical entry-level education:** High school diploma or equivalent
  - **Work experience in a related occupation:** None
  - **Typical on-the-job training:** Long-term on-the-job training

Coin, Vending, and Amusement Machine Servicers and Repairers

(O*NET 49-9091.00)

Install, service, adjust, or repair coin, vending, or amusement machines including video games, jukeboxes, pinball machines, or slot machines.

- **2014 employment:** 34,900
- **May 2014 median annual wage:** $31,860
- **Projected employment change, 2014–24:**
  - **Number of new jobs:** –3,000
  - **Growth rate:** –9 percent (decline)
- **Education and training:**
  - **Typical entry-level education:** High school diploma or equivalent
  - **Work experience in a related occupation:** None
  - **Typical on-the-job training:** Short-term on-the-job training

Commercial Divers

(O*NET 49-9092.00)

Work below surface of waters, using scuba gear to inspect, repair, remove, or install equipment and structures. May use a variety of power and hand tools, such as drills, sledgehammers, torches, and welding equipment. May conduct tests or experiments, rig explosives, or photograph structures or marine life. Excludes "Fishers and Related Fishing Workers" (45-3011), "Athletes and Sports Competitors" (27-2021), and "Police and Sheriff's Patrol Officers" (33-3051).

- **2014 employment:** 4,400
- **May 2014 median annual wage:** $45,890
- **Projected employment change, 2014–24:**
  - **Number of new jobs:** 1,600
  - **Growth rate:** 37 percent (much faster than average)
- **Education and training:**
  - **Typical entry-level education:** Postsecondary nondegree award
  - **Work experience in a related occupation:** None
  - **Typical on-the-job training:** Moderate-term on-the-job training

Fabric Menders, Except Garment

(O*NET 49-9093.00)

Repair tears, holes, and other defects in fabrics, such as draperies, linens, parachutes, and tents.

- **2014 employment:** 800
- **May 2014 median annual wage:** $23,930
- **Projected employment change, 2014–24:**
  - **Number of new jobs:** –100
  - **Growth rate:** –13 percent (decline)
- **Education and training:**
  - **Typical entry-level education:** No formal educational credential
  - **Work experience in a related occupation:** None
  - **Typical on-the-job training:** Long-term on-the-job training

Locksmiths and Safe Repairers

(O*NET 49-9094.00)

Repair and open locks; make keys; change locks and safe combinations; and install and repair safes.

- **2014 employment:** 20,900
- **May 2014 median annual wage:** $38,600
- **Projected employment change, 2014–24:**
  - **Number of new jobs:** –3,100
  - **Growth rate:** –15 percent (decline)
- **Education and training:**
  - **Typical entry-level education:** High school diploma or equivalent
  - **Work experience in a related occupation:** None
  - **Typical on-the-job training:** Long-term on-the-job training

Manufactured Building and Mobile Home Installers

(O*NET 49-9095.00)

Move or install mobile homes or prefabricated buildings.

- **2014 employment:** 4,000
- **May 2014 median annual wage:** $29,600
- **Projected employment change, 2014–24:**
  - **Number of new jobs:** –1,200
  - **Growth rate:** –30 percent (decline)
- **Education and training:**
  - **Typical entry-level education:** High school diploma or equivalent
  - **Work experience in a related occupation:** None
  - **Typical on-the-job training:** Short-term on-the-job training

Riggers

(O*NET 49-9096.00)

Set up or repair rigging for construction projects, manufacturing plants, logging yards, ships and shipyards, or the entertainment industry.

- **2014 employment:** 20,800
- **May 2014 median annual wage:** $41,570
- **Projected employment change, 2014–24:**
  - **Number of new jobs:** 1,800
  - **Growth rate:** 9 percent (faster than average)
- **Education and training:**
  - **Typical entry-level education:** High school diploma or equivalent
  - **Work experience in a related occupation:** None
  - **Typical on-the-job training:** Short-term on-the-job training

Signal and Track Switch Repairers

(O*NET 49-9097.00)

Install, inspect, test, maintain, or repair electric gate crossings, signals, signal equipment, track switches, section lines, or intercommunications systems within a railroad system.

- **2014 employment:** 9,500
- **May 2014 median annual wage:** $60,640
- **Projected employment change, 2014–24:**
  - **Number of new jobs:** 0
  - **Growth rate:** 0 percent (little or no change)
- **Education and training:**
  - **Typical entry-level education:** High school diploma or equivalent
  - **Work experience in a related occupation:** None
  - **Typical on-the-job training:** Moderate-term on-the-job training

Helpers—Installation, Maintenance, and Repair Workers

(O*NET 49-9098.00)

Help installation, maintenance, and repair workers in maintenance, parts replacement, and repair of vehicles, industrial machinery, and electrical and electronic equipment. Perform duties such as furnishing tools, materials, and supplies to other workers; cleaning work area, machines, and tools; and holding materials or tools for other workers.

- **2014 employment:** 129,000
- **May 2014 median annual wage:** $25,390
- **Projected employment change, 2014–24:**
  - **Number of new jobs:** 12,200
  - **Growth rate:** 9 percent (faster than average)
- **Education and training:**
  - **Typical entry-level education:** High school diploma or equivalent
  - **Work experience in a related occupation:** None
  - **Typical on-the-job training:** Short-term on-the-job training

Legal Occupations

Judicial Law Clerks

(O*NET 23-1012.00)

Assist judges in court or by conducting research or preparing legal documents. Excludes "Lawyers" (23-1011) and "Paralegals and Legal Assistants" (23-2011).

- **2014 employment:** 12,400
- **May 2014 median annual wage:** $48,640
- **Projected employment change, 2014–24:**
  - **Number of new jobs:** –800
  - **Growth rate:** –6 percent (decline)
- **Education and training:**
  - **Typical entry-level education:** Doctoral or professional degree
  - **Work experience in a related occupation:** None
  - **Typical on-the-job training:** None

Title Examiners, Abstractors, and Searchers

(O*NET 23-2093.00)

Search real estate records, examine titles, or summarize pertinent legal or insurance documents or details for a variety of purposes. May compile lists of mortgages, contracts, and other instruments pertaining to titles by searching public and private records for law firms, real estate agencies, or title insurance companies.

- **2014 employment:** 71,100
- **May 2014 median annual wage:** $43,080
- **Projected employment change, 2014–24:**
  - **Number of new jobs:** –200
  - **Growth rate:** 0 percent (little or no change)
- **Education and training:**
  - **Typical entry-level education:** High school diploma or equivalent
  - **Work experience in a related occupation:** None
  - **Typical on-the-job training:** Short-term on-the-job training

Life, Physical, and Social Science Occupations

Social Science Research Assistants

(O*NET 19-4061.00 and 19-4061.01)

Assist social scientists in laboratory, survey, and other research. May help prepare findings for publication and assist in laboratory analysis, quality control, or data management. Excludes "Graduate Teaching Assistants" (25-1191).

- **2014 employment:** 32,000
- **May 2014 median annual wage:** $39,460
- **Projected employment change, 2014–24:**
  - **Number of new jobs:** 1,800
  - **Growth rate:** 6 percent (about as fast as average)
- **Education and training:**
  - **Typical entry-level education:** Bachelor's degree
  - **Work experience in a related occupation:** None
  - **Typical on-the-job training:** None

Forest and Conservation Technicians

(O*NET 19-4093.00)

Provide technical assistance regarding the conservation of soil, water, forests, or related natural resources. May compile data pertaining to size, content, condition, and other characteristics of forest tracts, under the direction of foresters; or train and lead forest workers in forest propagation, and fire prevention and suppression. May assist conservation scientists in managing, improving, and protecting rangelands and wildlife habitats. Excludes "Conservation Scientists" (19-1031) and "Foresters" (19-1032).

- **2014 employment:** 32,600
- **May 2014 median annual wage:** $35,260
- **Projected employment change, 2014–24:**
  - **Number of new jobs:** –1,900
  - **Growth rate:** –6 percent (decline)
- **Education and training:**
  - **Typical entry-level education:** Associate's degree
  - **Work experience in a related occupation:** None
  - **Typical on-the-job training:** None

Management Occupations

Legislators

(O*NET 11-1031.00)

Develop, introduce, or enact laws and statutes at the local, tribal, state, or federal level. Includes only workers in elected positions.

- **2014 employment:** 58,300
- **May 2014 median annual wage:** $20,180
- **Projected employment change, 2014–24:**
  - **Number of new jobs:** –400
  - **Growth rate:** –1 (little or no change)
- **Education and training:**
  - **Typical entry-level education:** Bachelor's degree
  - **Work experience in a related occupation:** Less than 5 years
  - **Typical on-the-job training:** None

Transportation, Storage, and Distribution Managers

(O*NET 11-3071.00, 11-3071.01, 11-3071.02, and 11-3071.03)

Plan, direct, or coordinate transportation, storage, or distribution activities in accordance with organizational policies and applicable government laws or regulations. Includes logistics managers.

- **2014 employment:** 111,600
- **May 2014 median annual wage:** $85,400
- **Projected employment change, 2014–24:**
  - **Number of new jobs:** 2,500
  - **Growth rate:** 2 percent (slower than average)
- **Education and training:**
  - **Typical entry-level education:** High school diploma or equivalent
  - **Work experience in a related occupation:** 5 years or more
  - **Typical on-the-job training:** None

Postmasters and Mail Superintendents

(O*NET 11-9131.00)

Plan, direct, or coordinate operational, administrative, management, and supportive services of a U.S. post office; or coordinate activities of workers engaged in postal and related work in an assigned post office.

- **2014 employment:** 17,300
- **May 2014 median annual wage:** $65,800
- **Projected employment change, 2014–24:**
  - **Number of new jobs:** –4,600
  - **Growth rate:** –26 percent (decline)
- **Education and training:**
  - **Typical entry-level education:** High school diploma or equivalent
  - **Work experience in a related occupation:** Less than 5 years
  - **Typical on-the-job training:** Moderate-term on-the-job training

Math Occupations

Mathematical Technicians

(O*NET 15-2091.00)

Apply standardized mathematical formulas, principles, and methodology to technological problems in engineering and physical sciences in relation to specific industrial and research objectives, processes, equipment, and products.

- **2014 employment:** 1,200
- **May 2014 median annual wage:** $54,140
- **Projected employment change, 2014–24:**
  - **Number of new jobs:** –200
  - **Growth rate:** –13 percent (decline)
- **Education and training:**
  - **Typical entry-level education:** Bachelor's degree
  - **Work experience in a related occupation:** None
  - **Typical on-the-job training:** None

Media and Communication Occupations

Radio Operators

(O*NET 27-4013.00)

Receive and transmit communications, using radiotelephone equipment in accordance with government regulations. May repair equipment. Excludes "Radio, Cellular, and Tower Equipment Installers and Repairers" (49-2021).

- **2014 employment:** 1,200
- **May 2014 median annual wage:** $46,380
- **Projected employment change, 2014–24:**
  - **Number of new jobs:** 0
  - **Growth rate:** –1 percent (little or no change)
- **Education and training:**
  - **Typical entry-level education:** High school diploma or equivalent
  - **Work experience in a related occupation:** None
  - **Typical on-the-job training:** Short-term on-the-job training

Office and Administrative Support Occupations

First-Line Supervisors of Office and Administrative Support Workers

(O*NET 43-1011.00)

Directly supervise and coordinate the activities of clerical and administrative support workers.

- **2014 employment:** 1,466,100
- **May 2014 median annual wage:** $50,780
- **Projected employment change, 2014–24:**
  - **Number of new jobs:** 121,200
  - **Growth rate:** 8 percent (about as fast as average)
- **Education and training:**
  - **Typical entry-level education:** High school diploma or equivalent
  - **Work experience in a related occupation:** Less than 5 years
  - **Typical on-the-job training:** None

Switchboard Operators, Including Answering Service

(O*NET 43-2011.00)

Operate telephone business systems equipment or switchboards to relay incoming, outgoing, and interoffice calls. May supply information to callers and record messages.

- **2014 employment:** 112,400
- **May 2014 median annual wage:** $26,550
- **Projected employment change, 2014–24:**
  - **Number of new jobs:** –37,000
  - **Growth rate:** –33 percent (decline)
- **Education and training:**
  - **Typical entry-level education:** High school diploma or equivalent
  - **Work experience in a related occupation:** None
  - **Typical on-the-job training:** Short-term on-the-job training

Telephone Operators

(O*NET 43-2021.00)

Provide information by accessing alphabetical, geographical, or other directories. Assist customers with special billing requests, such as charges to a third party and credits or refunds for incorrectly dialed numbers or bad connections. May handle emergency calls and assist children or people who have physical disabilities with making telephone calls.

- **2014 employment:** 13,100
- **May 2014 median annual wage:** $35,140
- **Projected employment change, 2014–24:**
  - **Number of new jobs:** –5,500
  - **Growth rate:** –42 percent (decline)
- **Education and training:**
  - **Typical entry-level education:** High school diploma or equivalent
  - **Work experience in a related occupation:** None
  - **Typical on-the-job training:** Short-term on-the-job training

Cargo and Freight Agents

(O*NET 43-5011.00)

Expedite and route movement of incoming and outgoing cargo and freight shipments in airline, train, and trucking terminals and shipping docks. Take orders from customers and arrange pickup of freight and cargo for delivery to loading platform. Prepare and examine bills of lading to determine shipping charges and tariffs.

- **2014 employment:** 78,800
- **May 2014 median annual wage:** $41,380
- **Projected employment change, 2014–24:**
  - **Number of new jobs:** 5,500
  - **Growth rate:** 7 percent (about as fast as average)
- **Education and training:**
  - **Typical entry-level education:** High school diploma or equivalent
  - **Work experience in a related occupation:** None
  - **Typical on-the-job training:** Short-term on-the-job training

Couriers and Messengers

(O*NET 43-5021.00)

Pick up and deliver messages, documents, packages, and other items between offices or departments within an establishment or directly to other business concerns, traveling by foot, bicycle, motorcycle, automobile, or public conveyance. Excludes "Light Truck or Delivery Services Drivers" (53-3033).

- **2014 employment:** 92,900
- **May 2014 median annual wage:** $26,640
- **Projected employment change, 2014–24:**
  - **Number of new jobs:** 4,800
  - **Growth rate:** 5 percent (about as fast as average)
- **Education and training:**
  - **Typical entry-level education:** High school diploma or equivalent
  - **Work experience in a related occupation:** None
  - **Typical on-the-job training:** Short-term on-the-job training

Dispatchers, Except Police, Fire, and Ambulance

(O*NET 43-5032.00)

Schedule and dispatch workers, work crews, equipment, or service vehicles for the conveyance of materials, freight, or passengers or for normal installation, service, or emergency repairs rendered outside the place of business. Duties may include using a radio, telephone, or computer to transmit assignments and compiling statistics and reports on work progress.

- **2014 employment:** 199,500
- **May 2014 median annual wage:** $36,690
- **Projected employment change, 2014–24:**
  - **Number of new jobs:** 8,800
  - **Growth rate:** 4 percent (slower than average)
- **Education and training:**
  - **Typical entry-level education:** High school diploma or equivalent
  - **Work experience in a related occupation:** None
  - **Typical on-the-job training:** Moderate-term on-the-job training

Meter Readers, Utilities

(O*NET 43-5041.00)

Read meters and record the consumption of electricity, gas, water, or steam.

- **2014 employment:** 37,400
- **May 2014 median annual wage:** $37,580
- **Projected employment change, 2014–24:**
  - **Number of new jobs:** –6,700
  - **Growth rate:** –18 percent (decline)
- **Education and training:**
  - **Typical entry-level education:** High school diploma or equivalent
  - **Work experience in a related occupation:** None
  - **Typical on-the-job training:** Short-term on-the-job training

Computer Operators

(O*NET 43-9011.00)

Monitor and control electronic computer and peripheral electronic data-processing equipment to process business, scientific, engineering, and other data according to operating instructions. Monitor and respond to operating and error messages. May enter commands at a computer terminal and set controls on the computer and peripheral devices. Excludes "Computer Occupations" (15-1100) and "Data Entry Keyers" (43-9021).

- **2014 employment:** 61,100
- **May 2014 median annual wage:** $39,590
- **Projected employment change, 2014–24:**
  - **Number of new jobs:** –11,600
  - **Growth rate:** –19 percent (decline)
- **Education and training:**
  - **Typical entry-level education:** High school diploma or equivalent
  - **Work experience in a related occupation:** None
  - **Typical on-the-job training:** Moderate-term on-the-job training

Data Entry Keyers

(O*NET 43-9021.00)

Operate a data entry device, such as a keyboard or photocomposing perforator. Duties may include verifying data and preparing materials for printing. Excludes "Word Processors and Typists" (43-9022).

- **2014 employment:** 216,800
- **May 2014 median annual wage:** $28,870
- **Projected employment change, 2014–24:**
  - **Number of new jobs:** –7,900
  - **Growth rate:** –4 percent (decline)
- **Education and training:**
  - **Typical entry-level education:** High school diploma or equivalent
  - **Work experience in a related occupation:** None
  - **Typical on-the-job training:** Moderate-term on-the-job training

Word Processors and Typists

(O*NET 43-9022.00)

Use a word processor, computer, or typewriter to type letters, reports, forms, or other material from rough draft, corrected copy, or voice recordings. May perform other clerical duties as assigned. Excludes "Data Entry Keyers" (43-9021), "Secretaries and Administrative Assistants" (43-6011 through 43-6014), "Court Reporters" (23-2091), and "Medical Transcriptionists" (31-9094).

- **2014 employment:** 90,700
- **May 2014 median annual wage:** $36,700
- **Projected employment change, 2014–24:**
  - **Number of new jobs:** –14,200
  - **Growth rate:** –16 percent (decline)
- **Education and training:**
  - **Typical entry-level education:** High school diploma or equivalent
  - **Work experience in a related occupation:** None
  - **Typical on-the-job training:** Short-term on-the-job training

Mail Clerks and Mail Machine Operators, Except Postal Service

(O*NET 43-9051.00)

Prepare incoming and outgoing mail for distribution. Use hand or mail-handling machines to time-stamp, open, read, sort, and route incoming mail; address, seal, stamp, fold, stuff, and affix postage to outgoing mail or packages. Duties also may include storing, filing, or archiving necessary records and completed forms.

- **2014 employment:** 104,900
- **May 2014 median annual wage:** $27,890
- **Projected employment change, 2014–24:**
  - **Number of new jobs:** –19,800
  - **Growth rate:** –19 percent (decline)

- **Education and training:**
  - **Typical entry-level education:** High school diploma or equivalent
  - **Work experience in a related occupation:** None
  - **Typical on-the-job training:** Short-term on-the-job training

Office Machine Operators, Except Computer

(O*NET 43-9071.00)

Operate one or more of a variety of office machines, such as photocopying, photographic, and duplicating machines. Excludes "Computer Operators" (43-9011), "Mail Clerks and Mail Machine Operators, Except Postal Service" (43-9051), and "Billing and Posting Clerks" (43-3021).

- **2014 employment:** 69,600
- **May 2014 median annual wage:** $28,510
- **Projected employment change, 2014–24:**
  - **Number of new jobs:** –11,500
  - **Growth rate:** –17 percent (decline)
- **Education and training:**
  - **Typical entry-level education:** High school diploma or equivalent
  - **Work experience in a related occupation:** None
  - **Typical on-the-job training:** Short-term on-the-job training

Proofreaders and Copy Markers

(O*NET 43-9081.00)

Read transcripts or proofread type to detect and correct any grammatical, typographical, or compositional errors. Excludes workers whose primary duty is editing copy. Includes proofreaders of Braille.

- **2014 employment:** 13,600
- **May 2014 median annual wage:** $34,980
- **Projected employment change, 2014–24:**
  - **Number of new jobs:** –300
  - **Growth rate:** –2 percent (decline)
- **Education and training:**
  - **Typical entry-level education:** Bachelor's degree
  - **Work experience in a related occupation:** None
  - **Typical on-the-job training:** None

Statistical Assistants

(O*NET 43-9111.00 and 43-9111.01)

Compile and compute data according to statistical formulas for use in statistical studies. May perform actuarial computations and compile charts and graphs for actuaries. Includes actuarial clerks.

- **2014 employment:** 16,600
- **May 2014 median annual wage:** $42,070
- **Projected employment change, 2014–24:**
  - **Number of new jobs:** –1,800
  - **Growth rate:** –11 percent (decline)
- **Education and training:**
  - **Typical entry-level education:** Bachelor's degree
  - **Work experience in a related occupation:** None
  - **Typical on-the-job training:** None

Personal Care and Service Occupations

First-Line Supervisors of Personal Service Workers

(O*NET 39-1021.00 and 39-1021.01)

Directly supervise and coordinate activities of personal service workers, such as flight attendants, hairdressers, or caddies.

- **2014 employment:** 255,800
- **May 2014 median annual wage:** $35,250
- **Projected employment change, 2014–24:**
  - **Number of new jobs:** 28,000
  - **Growth rate:** 11 percent (faster than average)
- **Education and training:**
  - **Typical entry-level education:** High school diploma or equivalent
  - **Work experience in a related occupation:** Less than 5 years
  - **Typical on-the-job training:** None

Motion Picture Projectionists

(O*NET 39-3021.00)

Set up and operate motion picture projection and related sound reproduction equipment.

- **2014 employment:** 6,700
- **May 2014 median annual wage:** $20,830
- **Projected employment change, 2014–24:**
  - **Number of new jobs:** –1,200
  - **Growth rate:** –18 percent (decline)
- **Education and training:**
  - **Typical entry-level education:** No formal educational credential
  - **Work experience in a related occupation:** None
  - **Typical on-the-job training:** Short-term on-the-job training

Ushers, Lobby Attendants, and Ticket Takers

(O*NET 39-3031.00)

Assist patrons at entertainment events by collecting admission tickets and passes from patrons, assisting in finding seats, searching for lost articles, and locating rest rooms and telephones.

- **2014 employment:** 113,900
- **May 2014 median annual wage:** $18,760
- **Projected employment change, 2014–24:**
  - **Number of new jobs:** 6,100
  - **Growth rate:** 5 percent (about as fast as average)
- **Education and training:**
  - **Typical entry-level education:** No formal educational credential
  - **Work experience in a related occupation:** None
  - **Typical on-the-job training:** Short-term on-the-job training

Amusement and Recreation Attendants

(O*NET 39-3091.00)

Perform a variety of duties at amusement or recreation facilities. May schedule the use of recreation facilities, maintain and provide equipment to participants in sporting events or recreational pursuits, or operate amusement concessions and rides.

- **2014 employment:** 288,600

- **May 2014 median annual wage:** $18,880
- **Projected employment change, 2014–24:**
  - **Number of new jobs:** 22,300
  - **Growth rate:** 8 percent (about as fast as average)
- **Education and training:**
  - **Typical entry-level education:** No formal educational credential
  - **Work experience in a related occupation:** None
  - **Typical on-the-job training:** Short-term on-the-job training

Costume Attendants

(O*NET 39-3092.00)

Select, fit, and take care of costumes for cast members, and aid entertainers. May assist with multiple costume changes during performances.

- **2014 employment:** 6,200
- **May 2014 median annual wage:** $41,670
- **Projected employment change, 2014–24:**
  - **Number of new jobs:** 500
  - **Growth rate:** 9 percent (faster than average)
- **Education and training:**
  - **Typical entry-level education:** High school diploma or equivalent
  - **Work experience in a related occupation:** None
  - **Typical on-the-job training:** Short-term on-the-job training

Locker Room, Coatroom, and Dressing Room Attendants

(O*NET 39-3093.00)

Provide personal items to patrons or customers in locker rooms, dressing rooms, or coatrooms.

- **2014 employment:** 18,600
- **May 2014 median annual wage:** $19,940
- **Projected employment change, 2014–24:**
  - **Number of new jobs:** 900
  - **Growth rate:** 5 percent (about as fast as average)
- **Education and training:**
  - **Typical entry-level education:** High school diploma or equivalent
  - **Work experience in a related occupation:** None
  - **Typical on-the-job training:** Short-term on-the-job training

Embalmers

(O*NET 39-4011.00)

Prepare dead bodies for interment in conformity with legal requirements.

- **2014 employment:** 3,800
- **May 2014 median annual wage:** $41,720
- **Projected employment change, 2014–24:**
  - **Number of new jobs:** –200
  - **Growth rate:** –6 percent (decline)
- **Education and training:**
  - **Typical entry-level education:** Postsecondary nondegree award
  - **Work experience in a related occupation:** None
  - **Typical on-the-job training:** Short-term on-the-job training

Funeral Attendants

(O*NET 39-4021.00)

Perform a variety of tasks during funerals, such as placing caskets in the parlor or chapel prior to services, arranging floral offerings or lights around caskets, directing or escorting mourners, closing caskets, and issuing and storing funeral equipment.

- **2014 employment:** 36,100
- **May 2014 median annual wage:** $23,080
- **Projected employment change, 2014–24:**
  - **Number of new jobs:** –400
  - **Growth rate:** –1 percent (little or no change)
- **Education and training:**
  - **Typical entry-level education:** High school diploma or equivalent
  - **Work experience in a related occupation:** None
  - **Typical on-the-job training:** Short-term on-the-job training

Makeup Artists, Theatrical and Performance

(O*NET 39-5091.00)

Apply makeup to performers to reflect the period, setting, and situation of their roles.

- **2014 employment:** 3,600
- **May 2014 median annual wage:** $44,310
- **Projected employment change, 2014–24:**
  - **Number of new jobs:** 700
  - **Growth rate:** 19 percent (much faster than average)
- **Education and training:**
  - **Typical entry-level education:** Postsecondary nondegree award
  - **Work experience in a related occupation:** None
  - **Typical on-the-job training:** None

Shampooers

(O*NET 39-5093.00)

Shampoo and rinse customers' hair.

- **2014 employment:** 23,800
- **May 2014 median annual wage:** $18,760
- **Projected employment change, 2014–24:**
  - **Number of new jobs:** 2,500
  - **Growth rate:** 10 percent (faster than average)
- **Education and training:**
  - **Typical entry-level education:** No formal educational credential
  - **Work experience in a related occupation:** None
  - **Typical on-the-job training:** Short-term on-the-job training

Baggage Porters and Bellhops

(O*NET 39-6011.00)

Handle baggage for travelers at transportation terminals or for guests at hotels or similar establishments.

- **2014 employment:** 43,600
- **May 2014 median annual wage:** $20,930
- **Projected employment change, 2014–24:**
  - **Number of new jobs:** 3,500
  - **Growth rate:** 8 percent (about as fast as average)
- **Education and training:**
  - **Typical entry-level education:** High school diploma or equivalent
  - **Work experience in a related occupation:** None
  - **Typical on-the-job training:** Short-term on-the-job training

Concierges

(O*NET 39-6012.00)

Assist patrons at hotel, apartment, or office building with personal services. May take messages, arrange or give advice on transportation, business services or entertainment, or monitor guest requests for housekeeping and maintenance.

- **2014 employment:** 31,200
- **May 2014 median annual wage:** $28,170
- **Projected employment change, 2014–24:**
  - **Number of new jobs:** 3,300
  - **Growth rate:** 10 percent (faster than average)
- **Education and training:**
  - **Typical entry-level education:** High school diploma or equivalent
  - **Work experience in a related occupation:** None
  - **Typical on-the-job training:** Moderate-term on-the-job training

Tour Guides and Escorts

(O*NET 39-7011.00)

Escort individuals or groups on sightseeing tours or through places of interest, such as industrial establishments, public buildings, and art galleries.

- **2014 employment:** 43,500
- **May 2014 median annual wage:** $23,930
- **Projected employment change, 2014–24:**
  - **Number of new jobs:** 2,200
  - **Growth rate:** 5 percent (about as fast as average)
- **Education and training:**
  - **Typical entry-level education:** High school diploma or equivalent
  - **Work experience in a related occupation:** None
  - **Typical on-the-job training:** Moderate-term on-the-job training

Travel Guides

(O*NET 39-7012.00)

Plan, organize, and conduct long-distance travel, tours, and expeditions for individuals and groups.

- **2014 employment:** 3,900
- **May 2014 median annual wage:** $35,100
- **Projected employment change, 2014–24:**
  - **Number of new jobs:** 0
  - **Growth rate:** 0 percent (little or no change)
- **Education and training:**
  - **Typical entry-level education:** High school diploma or equivalent
  - **Work experience in a related occupation:** None
  - **Typical on-the-job training:** Moderate-term on-the-job training

Residential Advisors

(O*NET 39-9041.00)

Coordinate activities in residential facilities in secondary school and college dormitories, group homes, or similar establishments. Order supplies and determine necessary maintenance, repairs, and furnishings. May maintain household records and assign rooms. May help residents solve problems or refer residents to counseling resources.

- **2014 employment:** 103,700
- **May 2014 median annual wage:** $24,340
- **Projected employment change, 2014–24:**
  - **Number of new jobs:** 14,100
  - **Growth rate:** 14 percent (much faster than average)
- **Education and training:**
  - **Typical entry-level education:** High school diploma or equivalent
  - **Work experience in a related occupation:** None
  - **Typical on-the-job training:** Short-term on-the-job training

Production Occupations

First-Line Supervisors of Production and Operating Workers

(O*NET 51-1011.00)

Directly supervise and coordinate the activities of production and operating workers, such as inspectors, precision workers, machine setters and operators, assemblers, fabricators, and plant and system operators. Excludes team or work leaders.

- **2014 employment:** 606,900
- **May 2014 median annual wage:** $55,520
- **Projected employment change, 2014–24:**
  - **Number of new jobs:** –18,700
  - **Growth rate:** –3 percent (decline)
- **Education and training:**
  - **Typical entry-level education:** High school diploma or equivalent
  - **Work experience in a related occupation:** Less than 5 years
  - **Typical on-the-job training:** None

Meat, Poultry, and Fish Cutters and Trimmers

(O*NET 51-3022.00)

Use hand or hand tools to perform routine cutting and trimming of meat, poultry, and seafood.

- **2014 employment:** 152,400
- **May 2014 median annual wage:** $23,350
- **Projected employment change, 2014–24:**
  - **Number of new jobs:** –200
  - **Growth rate:** 0 percent (little or no change)
- **Education and training:**
  - **Typical entry-level education:** No formal educational credential
  - **Work experience in a related occupation:** None
  - **Typical on-the-job training:** Short-term on-the-job training

Slaughterers and Meat Packers

(O*NET 51-3023.00)

Work in slaughtering, meat packing, or wholesale establishments performing precision functions involving the preparation of meat. Work may include specialized slaughtering tasks, cutting standard or premium cuts or meat for marketing, making sausage, or wrapping meats. Excludes "Meat, Poultry, and Fish Cutters, and Trimmers (51-3022), who perform routine meat cutting.

- **2014 employment:** 86,400
- **May 2014 median annual wage:** $25,560
- **Projected employment change, 2014–24:**
  - **Number of new jobs:** –500
  - **Growth rate:** –1 percent (little or no change)
- **Education and training:**
  - **Typical entry-level education:** No formal educational credential

- **Work experience in a related occupation:** None
- **Typical on-the-job training:** Short-term on-the-job training

Layout Workers, Metal and Plastic

(O*NET 51-4192.00)

Lay out reference points and dimensions on metal or plastic stock or workpieces, such as sheets, plates, tubes, structural shapes, castings, or machine parts, for further processing. Includes shipfitters.

- **2014 employment:** 13,400
- **May 2014 median annual wage:** $45,020
- **Projected employment change, 2014–24:**
  - **Number of new jobs:** –2,700
  - **Growth rate:** –20 percent (decline)
- **Education and training:**
  - **Typical entry-level education:** High school diploma or equivalent
  - **Work experience in a related occupation:** None
  - **Typical on-the-job training:** Moderate-term on-the-job training

Tool Grinders, Filers, and Sharpeners

(O*NET 51-4194.00)

Perform precision smoothing, sharpening, polishing, or grinding of metal objects.

- **2014 employment:** 11,500
- **May 2014 median annual wage:** $35,420
- **Projected employment change, 2014–24:**
  - **Number of new jobs:** –2,000
  - **Growth rate:** –18 percent (decline)
- **Education and training:**
  - **Typical entry-level education:** High school diploma or equivalent
  - **Work experience in a related occupation:** None
  - **Typical on-the-job training:** Moderate-term on-the-job training

Prepress Technicians and Workers

(O*NET 51-5111.00)

Format and proof text and images submitted by designers and clients into finished pages that can be printed. Includes digital and photo typesetting. May produce printing plates.

- **2014 employment:** 36,500
- **May 2014 median annual wage:** $37,200
- **Projected employment change, 2014–24:**
  - **Number of new jobs:** –9,000
  - **Growth rate:** –25 percent (decline)
- **Education and training:**
  - **Typical entry-level education:** Postsecondary nondegree award
  - **Work experience in a related occupation:** None
  - **Typical on-the-job training:** None

Printing Press Operators

(O*NET 51-5112.00)

Set up and operate digital, letterpress, lithographic, flexographic, gravure, or other printing machines. Includes short-run offset printing presses.

- **2014 employment:** 173,000
- **May 2014 median annual wage:** $35,100
- **Projected employment change, 2014–24:**
  - **Number of new jobs:** –21,600
  - **Growth rate:** –12 percent (decline)
- **Education and training:**
  - **Typical entry-level education:** High school diploma or equivalent
  - **Work experience in a related occupation:** None
  - **Typical on-the-job training:** Moderate-term on-the-job training

Print Binding and Finishing Workers

(O*NET 51-5113.00)

Bind books and other publications or finish printed products by hand or machine. May set up binding and finishing machines.

- **2014 employment:** 51,200
- **May 2014 median annual wage:** $29,500
- **Projected employment change, 2014–24:**
  - **Number of new jobs:** –7,000
  - **Growth rate:** –14 percent (decline)
- **Education and training:**
  - **Typical entry-level education:** High school diploma or equivalent
  - **Work experience in a related occupation:** None
  - **Typical on-the-job training:** Short-term on-the-job training

Laundry and Dry-Cleaning Workers

(O*NET 51-6011.00)

Operate or tend washing or dry-cleaning machines to wash or dry-clean industrial or household articles, such as cloth garments, suede, leather, furs, blankets, draperies, linens, rugs, and carpets. Includes spotters and dyers of these articles.

- **2014 employment:** 208,200
- **May 2014 median annual wage:** $20,320
- **Projected employment change, 2014–24:**
  - **Number of new jobs:** 3,700
  - **Growth rate:** 2 percent (slower than average)
- **Education and training:**
  - **Typical entry-level education:** No formal educational credential
  - **Work experience in a related occupation:** None
  - **Typical on-the-job training:** Short-term on-the-job training

Pressers, Textile, Garment, and Related Materials

(O*NET 51-6021.00)

Press or shape articles by hand or machine.

- **2014 employment:** 51,500
- **May 2014 median annual wage:** $20,150
- **Projected employment change, 2014–24:**
  - **Number of new jobs:** –3,400
  - **Growth rate:** –7 percent (decline)
- **Education and training:**
  - **Typical entry-level education:** No formal educational credential
  - **Work experience in a related occupation:** None
  - **Typical on-the-job training:** Short-term on-the-job training

Sewing Machine Operators

(O*NET 51-6031.00)

Operate or tend sewing machines to join, reinforce, decorate, or perform related sewing operations in the manufacture of garments or nongarment products.

- **2014 employment:** 153,900

- **May 2014 median annual wage:** $21,920
- **Projected employment change, 2014–24:**
  - **Number of new jobs:** –41,700
  - **Growth rate:** –27 percent (decline)
- **Education and training:**
  - **Typical entry-level education:** No formal educational credential
  - **Work experience in a related occupation:** None
  - **Typical on-the-job training:** Short-term on-the-job training

Shoe and Leather Workers and Repairers

(O*NET 51-6041.00)

Construct, decorate, or repair leather and leather-like products, such as luggage, shoes, and saddles.

- **2014 employment:** 9,700
- **May 2014 median annual wage:** $23,770
- **Projected employment change, 2014–24:**
  - **Number of new jobs:** –1,500
  - **Growth rate:** –15 percent (decline)
- **Education and training:**
  - **Typical entry-level education:** High school diploma or equivalent
  - **Work experience in a related occupation:** None
  - **Typical on-the-job training:** Moderate-term on-the-job training

Shoe Machine Operators and Tenders

(O*NET 51-6042.00)

Operate or tend a variety of machines to join, decorate, reinforce, or finish shoes and shoe parts.

- **2014 employment:** 3,500
- **May 2014 median annual wage:** $24,750
- **Projected employment change, 2014–24:**
  - **Number of new jobs:** –1,100
  - **Growth rate:** –31 percent (decline)
- **Education and training:**
  - **Typical entry-level education:** High school diploma or equivalent
  - **Work experience in a related occupation:** None
  - **Typical on-the-job training:** Short-term on-the-job training

Sewers, Hand

(O*NET 51-6051.00)

Sew, join, reinforce, or finish, usually with needle and thread, a variety of manufactured items. Includes weavers and stitchers. Excludes "Fabric Menders, Except Garment" (49-9093).

- **2014 employment:** 12,000
- **May 2014 median annual wage:** $23,630
- **Projected employment change, 2014–24:**
  - **Number of new jobs:** –1,200
  - **Growth rate:** –10 percent (decline)
- **Education and training:**
  - **Typical entry-level education:** No formal educational credential
  - **Work experience in a related occupation:** None
  - **Typical on-the-job training:** Moderate-term on-the-job training

Tailors, Dressmakers, and Custom Sewers

(O*NET 51-6052.00)

Design, make, alter, repair, or fit garments.

- **2014 employment:** 40,500
- **May 2014 median annual wage:** $26,460
- **Projected employment change, 2014–24:**
  - **Number of new jobs:** –3,400
  - **Growth rate:** –9 percent (decline)
- **Education and training:**
  - **Typical entry-level education:** No formal educational credential
  - **Work experience in a related occupation:** None
  - **Typical on-the-job training:** Moderate-term on-the-job training

Textile Bleaching and Dyeing Machine Operators and Tenders

(O*NET 51-6061.00)

Operate or tend machines to bleach, shrink, wash, dye, or finish textiles or synthetic or glass fibers.

- **2014 employment:** 11,700
- **May 2014 median annual wage:** $24,930
- **Projected employment change, 2014–24:**
  - **Number of new jobs:** –2,800
  - **Growth rate:** –24 percent (decline)
- **Education and training:**
  - **Typical entry-level education:** High school diploma or equivalent
  - **Work experience in a related occupation:** None
  - **Typical on-the-job training:** Short-term on-the-job training

Textile Cutting Machine Setters, Operators, and Tenders

(O*NET 51-6062.00)

Set up, operate, or tend machines that cut textiles.

- **2014 employment:** 14,300
- **May 2014 median annual wage:** $25,590
- **Projected employment change, 2014–24:**
  - **Number of new jobs:** –3,700
  - **Growth rate:** –26 percent (decline)
- **Education and training:**
  - **Typical entry-level education:** High school diploma or equivalent
  - **Work experience in a related occupation:** None
  - **Typical on-the-job training:** Moderate-term on-the-job training

Textile Knitting and Weaving Machine Setters, Operators, and Tenders

(O*NET 51-6063.00)

Set up, operate, or tend machines that knit, loop, weave, or draw in textiles. Excludes "Sewing Machine Operators" (51-6031).

- **2014 employment:** 27,900
- **May 2014 median annual wage:** $27,270
- **Projected employment change, 2014–24:**
  - **Number of new jobs:** –7,300
  - **Growth rate:** –26 percent (decline)
- **Education and training:**
  - **Typical entry-level education:** High school diploma or equivalent
  - **Work experience in a related occupation:** None
  - **Typical on-the-job training:** Short-term on-the-job training

Textile Winding, Twisting, and Drawing Out Machine Setters, Operators, and Tenders

(O*NET 51-6064.00)

Set up, operate, or tend machines that wind or twist textiles; or draw out and combine sliver, such as wool, hemp, or synthetic fibers. Includes slubber machine and drawing frame operators.

- **2014 employment:** 26,000
- **May 2014 median annual wage:** $26,250
- **Projected employment change, 2014–24:**
  - **Number of new jobs:** –5,600
  - **Growth rate:** –22 percent (decline)
- **Education and training:**
  - **Typical entry-level education:** High school diploma or equivalent
  - **Work experience in a related occupation:** None
  - **Typical on-the-job training:** Moderate-term on-the-job training

Extruding and Forming Machine Setters, Operators, and Tenders, Synthetic and Glass Fibers

(O*NET 51-6091.00)

Set up, operate, or tend machines that extrude and form continuous filaments from synthetic materials, such as liquid polymer, rayon, and fiberglass.

- **2014 employment:** 20,100
- **May 2014 median annual wage:** $32,970
- **Projected employment change, 2014–24:**
  - **Number of new jobs:** –2,800
  - **Growth rate:** –14 percent (decline)
- **Education and training:**
  - **Typical entry-level education:** High school diploma or equivalent
  - **Work experience in a related occupation:** None
  - **Typical on-the-job training:** Moderate-term on-the-job training

Fabric and Apparel Patternmakers

(O*NET 51-6092.00)

Draw and construct sets of precision master fabric patterns or layouts. May also mark and cut fabrics and apparel.

- **2014 employment:** 5,400
- **May 2014 median annual wage:** $41,310
- **Projected employment change, 2014–24:**
  - **Number of new jobs:** –1,400
  - **Growth rate:** –26 percent (decline)
- **Education and training:**
  - **Typical entry-level education:** High school diploma or equivalent
  - **Work experience in a related occupation:** None
  - **Typical on-the-job training:** Moderate-term on-the-job training

Upholsterers

(O*NET 51-6093.00)

Make, repair, or replace upholstery for household furniture or transportation vehicles.

- **2014 employment:** 42,200
- **May 2014 median annual wage:** $31,890
- **Projected employment change, 2014–24:**
  - **Number of new jobs:** –1,800
  - **Growth rate:** –4 percent (decline)
- **Education and training:**
  - **Typical entry-level education:** High school diploma or equivalent
  - **Work experience in a related occupation:** None
  - **Typical on-the-job training:** Moderate-term on-the-job training

Model Makers, Wood

(O*NET 51-7031.00)

Construct full-size and scale wooden precision models of products. Includes wood jig builders and loft workers.

- **2014 employment:** 2,600
- **May 2014 median annual wage:** $30,940
- **Projected employment change, 2014–24:**
  - **Number of new jobs:** 0
  - **Growth rate:** –1 percent (little or no change)
- **Education and training:**
  - **Typical entry-level education:** High school diploma or equivalent
  - **Work experience in a related occupation:** None
  - **Typical on-the-job training:** Moderate-term on-the-job training

Patternmakers, Wood

(O*NET 51-7032.00)

Plan, lay out, and construct wooden unit or sectional patterns used in forming sand molds for castings.

- **2014 employment:** 1,800
- **May 2014 median annual wage:** $37,980
- **Projected employment change, 2014–24:**
  - **Number of new jobs:** 0
  - **Growth rate:** 0 percent (little or no change)
- **Education and training:**
  - **Typical entry-level education:** High school diploma or equivalent
  - **Work experience in a related occupation:** None
  - **Typical on-the-job training:** Moderate-term on-the-job training

Chemical Plant and System Operators

(O*NET 51-8091.00)

Control or operate entire chemical processes or systems through the use of machines.

- **2014 employment:** 38,100
- **May 2014 median annual wage:** $55,900
- **Projected employment change, 2014–24:**
  - **Number of new jobs:** –3,500
  - **Growth rate:** –9 percent (decline)
- **Education and training:**
  - **Typical entry-level education:** High school diploma or equivalent
  - **Work experience in a related occupation:** None
  - **Typical on-the-job training:** Long-term on-the-job training

Gas Plant Operators

(O*NET 51-8092.00)

Distribute or process gas for utility companies and others by controlling compressors to maintain specified pressures on main pipelines.

- **2014 employment:** 16,700

- **May 2014 median annual wage:** $64,100
- **Projected employment change, 2014–24:**
  - **Number of new jobs:** –600
  - **Growth rate:** –3 percent (decline)
- **Education and training:**
  - **Typical entry-level education:** High school diploma or equivalent
  - **Work experience in a related occupation:** None
  - **Typical on-the-job training:** Long-term on-the-job training

Petroleum Pump System Operators, Refinery Operators, and Gaugers

(O*NET 51-8093.00)

Operate or control petroleum refining or processing units. May specialize in controlling manifold and pumping systems, gauging or testing oil in storage tanks, or regulating the flow of oil into pipelines.

- **2014 employment:** 42,400
- **May 2014 median annual wage:** $62,830
- **Projected employment change, 2014–24:**
  - **Number of new jobs:** 900
  - **Growth rate:** 2 percent (slower than average)
- **Education and training:**
  - **Typical entry-level education:** High school diploma or equivalent
  - **Work experience in a related occupation:** None
  - **Typical on-the-job training:** Long-term on-the-job training

Chemical Equipment Operators and Tenders

(O*NET 51-9011.00)

Operate or tend equipment to control chemical changes or reactions in the processing of industrial or consumer products. Equipment used includes devulcanizers, steam-jacketed kettles, and reactor vessels. Excludes "Chemical Plant and System Operators" (51-8091).

- **2014 employment:** 66,300
- **May 2014 median annual wage:** $48,090
- **Projected employment change, 2014–24:**
  - **Number of new jobs:** –5,500
  - **Growth rate:** –8 percent (decline)
- **Education and training:**
  - **Typical entry-level education:** High school diploma or equivalent
  - **Work experience in a related occupation:** None
  - **Typical on-the-job training:** Moderate-term on-the-job training

Separating, Filtering, Clarifying, Precipitating, and Still Machine Setters, Operators, and Tenders

(O*NET 51-9012.00)

Set up, operate, or tend continuous flow or vat-type equipment; filter presses; shaker screens; centrifuges; condenser tubes; precipitating, fermenting, or evaporating tanks; scrubbing towers; or batch stills. These machines extract, sort, or separate liquids, gases, or solids from other materials in order to recover a refined product. Includes dairy processing equipment operators. Excludes "Chemical Equipment Operators and Tenders" (51-9011).

- **2014 employment:** 43,800
- **May 2014 median annual wage:** $38,590
- **Projected employment change, 2014–24:**
  - **Number of new jobs:** –600
  - **Growth rate:**–1 percent (little or no change)
- **Education and training:**
  - **Typical entry-level education:** High school diploma or equivalent
  - **Work experience in a related occupation:** None
  - **Typical on-the-job training:** Moderate-term on-the-job training

Crushing, Grinding, and Polishing Machine Setters, Operators, and Tenders

(O*NET 51-9021.00)

Set up, operate, or tend machines to crush, grind, or polish materials, such as coal, glass, grain, stone, food, or rubber.

- **2014 employment:** 30,200
- **May 2014 median annual wage:** $33,070
- **Projected employment change, 2014–24:**
  - **Number of new jobs:** –2,300
  - **Growth rate:** –8 percent (decline)
- **Education and training:**
  - **Typical entry-level education:** High school diploma or equivalent
  - **Work experience in a related occupation:** None
  - **Typical on-the-job training:** Moderate-term on-the-job training

Grinding and Polishing Workers, Hand

(O*NET 51-9022.00)

Grind, sand, or polish, using hand tools or hand-held power tools, a variety of metal, wood, stone, clay, plastic, or glass objects. Includes chippers, buffers, and finishers.

- **2014 employment:** 29,900
- **May 2014 median annual wage:** $28,340
- **Projected employment change, 2014–24:**
  - **Number of new jobs:** –2,600
  - **Growth rate:** –9 percent (decline)
- **Education and training:**
  - **Typical entry-level education:** No formal educational credential
  - **Work experience in a related occupation:** None
  - **Typical on-the-job training:** Moderate-term on-the-job training

Mixing and Blending Machine Setters, Operators, and Tenders

(O*NET 51-9023.00)

Set up, operate, or tend machines that mix or blend materials, such as chemicals, tobacco, liquids, color pigments, or explosive ingredients. Excludes "Food Batchmakers" (51-3092).

- **2014 employment:** 125,100
- **May 2014 median annual wage:** $34,340
- **Projected employment change, 2014–24:**
  - **Number of new jobs:** –5,900
  - **Growth rate:** –5 percent (decline)
- **Education and training:**
  - **Typical entry-level education:** High school diploma or equivalent
  - **Work experience in a related occupation:** None
  - **Typical on-the-job training:** Moderate-term on-the-job training

Cutters and Trimmers, Hand

(O*NET 51-9031.00)

Use hand tools or hand-held power tools to cut and trim a variety of manufactured items, such as carpet, fabric, stone, glass, or rubber.

- **2014 employment:** 15,800
- **May 2014 median annual wage:** $25,920
- **Projected employment change, 2014–24:**
  - **Number of new jobs:** –2,800
  - **Growth rate:** –17 percent (decline)
- **Education and training:**
  - **Typical entry-level education:** No formal educational credential
  - **Work experience in a related occupation:** None
  - **Typical on-the-job training:** Short-term on-the-job training

Cutting and Slicing Machine Setters, Operators, and Tenders

(O*NET 51-9032.00)

Set up, operate, or tend machines that cut or slice materials, such as glass, stone, cork, rubber, tobacco, food, paper, or insulating material. Excludes "Woodworking Machine Setters, Operators, and Tenders" (51-7040), "Cutting, Punching, and Press Machine Setters, Operators, and Tenders, Metal and Plastic" (51-4031), and "Textile Cutting Machine Setters, Operators, and Tenders" (51-6062).

- **2014 employment:** 63,600
- **May 2014 median annual wage:** $32,040
- **Projected employment change, 2014–24:**
  - **Number of new jobs:** –5,200
  - **Growth rate:** –8 percent (decline)
- **Education and training:**
  - **Typical entry-level education:** High school diploma or equivalent
  - **Work experience in a related occupation:** None
  - **Typical on-the-job training:** Short-term on-the-job training

Extruding, Forming, Pressing, and Compacting Machine Setters, Operators, and Tenders

(O*NET 51-9041.00)

Set up, operate, or tend machines, such as glass forming machines, plodder machines, and tuber machines, to shape and form products, such as glassware, food, rubber, soap, brick, tile, clay, wax, tobacco, or cosmetics. Excludes "Paper Goods Machine Setters, Operators, and Tenders" (51-9196) and "Shoe Machine Operators and Tenders" (51-6042).

- **2014 employment:** 68,200
- **May 2014 median annual wage:** $32,100
- **Projected employment change, 2014–24:**
  - **Number of new jobs:** –9,200
  - **Growth rate:** –14 percent (decline)
- **Education and training:**
  - **Typical entry-level education:** High school diploma or equivalent
  - **Work experience in a related occupation:** None
  - **Typical on-the-job training:** Moderate-term on-the-job training

Furnace, Kiln, Oven, Drier, and Kettle Operators and Tenders

(O*NET 51-9051.00)

Operate or tend heating equipment other than basic metal, plastic, or food processing equipment. Includes activities, such as annealing glass, drying lumber, curing rubber, removing moisture from materials, and boiling soap.

- **2014 employment:** 20,900
- **May 2014 median annual wage:** $34,900
- **Projected employment change, 2014–24:**
  - **Number of new jobs:** –2,000
  - **Growth rate:** –10 percent (decline)
- **Education and training:**
  - **Typical entry-level education:** High school diploma or equivalent
  - **Work experience in a related occupation:** None
  - **Typical on-the-job training:** Moderate-term on-the-job training

Packaging and Filling Machine Operators and Tenders

(O*NET 51-9111.00)

Operate or tend machines that prepare industrial or consumer products for storage or shipment. Includes cannery workers who pack food products.

- **2014 employment:** 378,400
- **May 2014 median annual wage:** $26,410
- **Projected employment change, 2014–24:**
  - **Number of new jobs:** 3,800
  - **Growth rate:** 1 percent (little or no change)
- **Education and training:**
  - **Typical entry-level education:** High school diploma or equivalent
  - **Work experience in a related occupation:** None
  - **Typical on-the-job training:** Moderate-term on-the-job training

Semiconductor Processors

(O*NET 51-9141.00)

Perform any or all of the following functions in the manufacture of electronic semiconductors: load semiconductor material into furnace; saw formed ingots into segments; load individual segment into crystal growing chamber and monitor controls; locate crystal axis in ingot using x-ray equipment and saw ingots into wafers; and clean, polish, and load wafers into series of special purpose furnaces, chemical baths, and equipment used to form circuitry and change conductive properties.

- **2014 employment:** 25,300
- **May 2014 median annual wage:** $34,680
- **Projected employment change, 2014–24:**
  - **Number of new jobs:** –2,100
  - **Growth rate:** –8 percent (decline)
- **Education and training:**
  - **Typical entry-level education:** Associate's degree
  - **Work experience in a related occupation:** None
  - **Typical on-the-job training:** Moderate-term on-the-job training

Photographic Process Workers and Processing Machine Operators

(O*NET 51-9151.00)

Perform work to develop and process photographic images from film or from digital media. May perform precision tasks, such as editing photographic negatives and prints.

- **2014 employment:** 28,800
- **May 2014 median annual wage:** $24,600
- **Projected employment change, 2014–24:**
  - **Number of new jobs:** –9,500
  - **Growth rate:** –33 percent (decline)
- **Education and training:**
  - **Typical entry-level education:** High school diploma or equivalent
  - **Work experience in a related occupation:** None
  - **Typical on-the-job training:** Short-term on-the-job training

Adhesive Bonding Machine Operators and Tenders

(O*NET 51-9191.00)

Operate or tend bonding machines that use adhesives to join items for further processing or to form a completed product. Processes include joining veneer sheets into plywood; gluing paper; or joining rubber and rubberized fabric parts, plastic, simulated leather, or other materials. Excludes "Shoe Machine Operators and Tenders" (51-6042).

- **2014 employment:** 18,400
- **May 2014 median annual wage:** $31,340
- **Projected employment change, 2014–24:**
  - **Number of new jobs:** –1,200
  - **Growth rate:** –7 percent (decline)
- **Education and training:**
  - **Typical entry-level education:** High school diploma or equivalent
  - **Work experience in a related occupation:** None
  - **Typical on-the-job training:** Moderate-term on-the-job training

Cleaning, Washing, and Metal Pickling Equipment Operators and Tenders

(O*NET 51-9192.00)

Operate or tend machines that wash or clean products, such as barrels or kegs, glass items, tin plates, food, pulp, coal, plastic, or rubber, to remove impurities.

- **2014 employment:** 18,500
- **May 2014 median annual wage:** $26,910
- **Projected employment change, 2014–24:**
  - **Number of new jobs:** 100
  - **Growth rate:** 0 percent (little or no change)
- **Education and training:**
  - **Typical entry-level education:** No formal educational credential
  - **Work experience in a related occupation:** None
  - **Typical on-the-job training:** Moderate-term on-the-job training

Cooling and Freezing Equipment Operators and Tenders

(O*NET 51-9193.00)

Operate or tend equipment, such as cooling and freezing units, refrigerators, batch freezers, and freezing tunnels, to cool or freeze products, food, blood plasma, and chemicals.

- **2014 employment:** 8,800
- **May 2014 median annual wage:** $28,280
- **Projected employment change, 2014–24:**
  - **Number of new jobs:** –100
  - **Growth rate:** –1 percent (little or no change)
- **Education and training:**
  - **Typical entry-level education:** High school diploma or equivalent
  - **Work experience in a related occupation:** None
  - **Typical on-the-job training:** Moderate-term on-the-job training

Etchers and Engravers

(O*NET 51-9194.00)

Engrave or etch metal, wood, rubber, or other materials. Includes such workers as etcher-circuit processors, pantograph engravers, and silk-screen etchers. Photoengravers are included in "Prepress Technicians and Workers" (51-5111).

- **2014 employment:** 9,700
- **May 2014 median annual wage:** $29,250
- **Projected employment change, 2014–24:**
  - **Number of new jobs:** –300
  - **Growth rate:** –3 percent (decline)
- **Education and training:**
  - **Typical entry-level education:** High school diploma or equivalent
  - **Work experience in a related occupation:** None
  - **Typical on-the-job training:** Moderate-term on-the-job training

Molders, Shapers, and Casters, Except Metal and Plastic

(O*NET 51-9195.00, 51-9195.03, 51-9195.04, 51-9195.05, and 51-9195.07)

Mold, shape, form, cast, or carve products, such as food products, figurines, tile, pipes, and candles, consisting of clay, glass, plaster, concrete, stone, or combinations of materials.

- **2014 employment:** 41,400
- **May 2014 median annual wage:** $29,820
- **Projected employment change, 2014–24:**
  - **Number of new jobs:** –2,500
  - **Growth rate:** –6 percent (decline)
- **Education and training:**
  - **Typical entry-level education:** High school diploma or equivalent
  - **Work experience in a related occupation:** None
  - **Typical on-the-job training:** Long-term on-the-job training

Paper Goods Machine Setters, Operators, and Tenders

(O*NET 51-9196.00)

Set up, operate, or tend paper goods machines that perform a variety of functions, such as converting, sawing, corrugating, banding, wrapping, boxing, stitching, forming, or sealing paper or paperboard sheets into products.

- **2014 employment:** 91,900
- **May 2014 median annual wage:** $35,260
- **Projected employment change, 2014–24:**
  - **Number of new jobs:** –9,900
  - **Growth rate:** –11 percent (decline)
- **Education and training:**
  - **Typical entry-level education:** High school diploma or equivalent
  - **Work experience in a related occupation:** None
  - **Typical on-the-job training:** Moderate-term on-the-job training

Tire Builders

(O*NET 51-9197.00)

Operate machines to build tires.

- **2014 employment:** 18,100
- **May 2014 median annual wage:** $42,540
- **Projected employment change, 2014–24:**
  - **Number of new jobs:** –2,500
  - **Growth rate:** –14 percent (decline)
- **Education and training:**
  - **Typical entry-level education:** High school diploma or equivalent
  - **Work experience in a related occupation:** None
  - **Typical on-the-job training:** Moderate-term on-the-job training

Helpers—Production Workers

(O*NET 51-9198.00)

Help production workers by performing duties requiring less skill. Duties include supplying or holding materials or tools, and cleaning work areas and equipment. Apprentice workers are classified in the appropriate production occupations (51-0000).

- **2014 employment:** 419,200
- **May 2014 median annual wage:** $23,610
- **Projected employment change, 2014–24:**
  - **Number of new jobs:** –16,100
  - **Growth rate:** –4 percent (decline)
- **Education and training:**
  - **Typical entry-level education:** No formal educational credential
  - **Work experience in a related occupation:** None
  - **Typical on-the-job training:** Short-term on-the-job training

Protective Service Occupations

First-Line Supervisors of Correctional Officers

(O*NET 33-1011.00)

Directly supervise and coordinate activities of correctional officers and jailers.

- **2014 employment:** 47,600
- **May 2014 median annual wage:** $57,970
- **Projected employment change, 2014–24:**
  - **Number of new jobs:** 1,500
  - **Growth rate:** 3 percent (slower than average)
- **Education and training:**
  - **Typical entry-level education:** High school diploma or equivalent
  - **Work experience in a related occupation:** Less than 5 years
  - **Typical on-the-job training:** Moderate-term on-the-job training

First-Line Supervisors of Police and Detectives

(O*NET 33-1012.00)

Directly supervise and coordinate activities of members of the police force.

- **2014 employment:** 108,100
- **May 2014 median annual wage:** $80,930
- **Projected employment change, 2014–24:**
  - **Number of new jobs:** 4,500
  - **Growth rate:** 4 percent (slower than average)
- **Education and training:**
  - **Typical entry-level education:** High school diploma or equivalent
  - **Work experience in a related occupation:** Less than 5 years
  - **Typical on-the-job training:** Moderate-term on-the-job training

First-Line Supervisors of Fire Fighting and Prevention Workers

(O*NET 33-1021.00, 33-1021.01, and 33-1021.02)

Directly supervise and coordinate activities of workers engaged in firefighting and fire prevention and control.

- **2014 employment:** 63,500
- **May 2014 median annual wage:** $70,670
- **Projected employment change, 2014–24:**
  - **Number of new jobs:** 3,300
  - **Growth rate:** 5 percent (about as fast as average)
- **Education and training:**
  - **Typical entry-level education:** Postsecondary nondegree award
  - **Work experience in a related occupation:** Less than 5 years
  - **Typical on-the-job training:** Moderate-term on-the-job training

Parking Enforcement Workers

(O*NET 33-3041.00)

Patrol assigned areas, such as public parking lots or city streets, to issue tickets to overtime parking violators and illegally parked vehicles.

- **2014 employment:** 9,400
- **May 2014 median annual wage:** $36,570
- **Projected employment change, 2014–24:**
  - **Number of new jobs:** –2,000
  - **Growth rate:** –21 percent (decline)
- **Education and training:**
  - **Typical entry-level education:** High school diploma or equivalent
  - **Work experience in a related occupation:** None
  - **Typical on-the-job training:** Short-term on-the-job training

Animal Control Workers

(O*NET 33-9011.00)

Handle animals for the purpose of investigations of mistreatment, or control of abandoned, dangerous, or unattended animals.

- **2014 employment:** 15,000
- **May 2014 median annual wage:** $32,560
- **Projected employment change, 2014–24:**
  - **Number of new jobs:** 900
  - **Growth rate:** 6 percent (about as fast as average)
- **Education and training:**
  - **Typical entry-level education:** High school diploma or equivalent

- **Work experience in a related occupation:** None
- **Typical on-the-job training:** Moderate-term on-the-job training

Crossing Guards

(O*NET 33-9091.00)

Guide or control vehicular or pedestrian traffic at places such as streets, schools, railroad crossings, or construction sites.

- **2014 employment:** 69,800
- **May 2014 median annual wage:** $24,750
- **Projected employment change, 2014–24:**
  - **Number of new jobs:** 4,500
  - **Growth rate:** 6 percent (about as fast as average)
- **Education and training:**
  - **Typical entry-level education:** No formal educational credential
  - **Work experience in a related occupation:** None
  - **Typical on-the-job training:** Short-term on-the-job training

Lifeguards, Ski Patrol, and Other Recreational Protective Service Workers

(O*NET 33-9092.00)

Monitor recreational areas, such as pools, beaches, or ski slopes, to provide assistance and protection to participants.

- **2014 employment:** 141,300
- **May 2014 median annual wage:** $19,090
- **Projected employment change, 2014–24:**
  - **Number of new jobs:** 9,500
  - **Growth rate:** 7 percent (about as fast as average)
- **Education and training:**
  - **Typical entry-level education:** No formal educational credential
  - **Work experience in a related occupation:** None
  - **Typical on-the-job training:** Short-term on-the-job training

Transportation Security Screeners

(O*NET 33-9093.00)

Conduct screening of passengers, baggage, or cargo to ensure compliance with Transportation Security Administration (TSA) regulations. May operate basic security equipment, such as x-ray machines and hand wands, at screening checkpoints.

- **2014 employment:** 46,600
- **May 2014 median annual wage:** $38,090
- **Projected employment change, 2014–24:**
  - **Number of new jobs:** –4,200
  - **Growth rate:** –9 percent (decline)
- **Education and training:**
  - **Typical entry-level education:** High school diploma or equivalent
  - **Work experience in a related occupation:** None
  - **Typical on-the-job training:** Short-term on-the-job training

Sales Occupations

First-Line Supervisors of Retail Sales Workers

(O*NET 41-1011.00)

Directly supervise and coordinate activities of retail sales workers in an establishment or a department. Duties also may include management functions, such as purchasing, budgeting, accounting, and personnel work, in addition to supervisory duties.

- **2014 employment:** 1,537,800
- **May 2014 median annual wage:** $37,860
- **Projected employment change, 2014–24:**
  - **Number of new jobs:** 67,600
  - **Growth rate:** 4 percent (slower than average)
- **Education and training:**
  - **Typical entry-level education:** High school diploma or equivalent
  - **Work experience in a related occupation:** Less than 5 years
  - **Typical on-the-job training:** None

First-Line Supervisors of Non-Retail Sales Workers

(O*NET 41-1012.00)

Directly supervise and coordinate activities of sales workers other than retail sales workers. Duties also may include budgeting, accounting, and personnel work, in addition to supervisory duties..

- **2014 employment:** 430,700
- **May 2014 median annual wage:** $71,600
- **Projected employment change, 2014–24:**
  - **Number of new jobs:** 20,300
  - **Growth rate:** 5 percent (about as fast as average)
- **Education and training:**
  - **Typical entry-level education:** High school diploma or equivalent
  - **Work experience in a related occupation:** Less than 5 years
  - **Typical on-the-job training:** None

Gaming Change Persons and Booth Cashiers

(O*NET 41-2012.00)

Exchange coins, tokens, and chips for patrons' money. May issue payoffs and obtain customer's signature on receipt. May operate a booth in the slot machine area and count and audit money in drawers. Excludes "Cashiers" (41-2011).

- **2014 employment:** 13,300
- **May 2014 median annual wage:** $23,340
- **Projected employment change, 2014–24:**
  - **Number of new jobs:** –1,400
  - **Growth rate:** –11 percent (decline)
- **Education and training:**
  - **Typical entry-level education:** High school diploma or equivalent
  - **Work experience in a related occupation:** None
  - **Typical on-the-job training:** Short-term on-the-job training

Counter and Rental Clerks

(O*NET 41-2021.00)

Receive orders, generally in person, for repairs, rentals, and services. May describe available options, compute costs, and accept payment. Excludes "Counter Attendants, Cafeteria, Food Concession, and Coffee Shop" (35-3022), "Hotel, Motel, and Resort Desk Clerks" (43-4081), "Order Clerks" (43-4151), and "Reservation and Transportation Ticket Agents and Travel Clerks" (43-4181).

- **2014 employment:** 442,100
- **May 2014 median annual wage:** $23,860
- **Projected employment change, 2014–24:**
  - **Number of new jobs:** 16,300
  - **Growth rate:** 4 percent (slower than average)

- **Education and training:**
  - **Typical entry-level education:** No formal educational credential
  - **Work experience in a related occupation:** None
  - **Typical on-the-job training:** Short-term on-the-job training

Demonstrators and Product Promoters

(O*NET 41-9011.00)

Demonstrate merchandise and answer questions for the purpose of creating public interest in buying the product. May sell merchandise demonstrated.

- **2014 employment:** 93,000
- **May 2014 median annual wage:** $24,520
- **Projected employment change, 2014–24:**
  - **Number of new jobs:** 8,200
  - **Growth rate:** 9 percent (faster than average)
- **Education and training:**
  - **Typical entry-level education:** High school diploma or equivalent
  - **Work experience in a related occupation:** None
  - **Typical on-the-job training:** Short-term on-the-job training

Telemarketers

(O*NET 41-9041.00)

Solicit donations or orders for goods or services over the telephone.

- **2014 employment:** 237,900
- **May 2014 median annual wage:** $22,740
- **Projected employment change, 2014–24:**
  - **Number of new jobs:** –7,200
  - **Growth rate:** –3 percent (decline)
- **Education and training:**
  - **Typical entry-level education:** No formal educational credential
  - **Work experience in a related occupation:** None
  - **Typical on-the-job training:** Short-term on-the-job training

Door-to-Door Sales Workers, News and Street Vendors, and Related Workers

(O*NET 41-9091.00)

Sell goods or services door to door or on the street.

- **2014 employment:** 80,200
- **May 2014 median annual wage:** $21,530
- **Projected employment change, 2014–24:**
  - **Number of new jobs:** –1,100
  - **Growth rate:** –1 percent (little or no change)
- **Education and training:**
  - **Typical entry-level education:** No formal educational credential
  - **Work experience in a related occupation:** None
  - **Typical on-the-job training:** Short-term on-the-job training

Transportation and Material Moving Occupations

Aircraft Cargo Handling Supervisors

(O*NET 53-1011.00)

Supervise and coordinate the activities of ground crews in the loading, unloading, securing, and staging of aircraft cargo or baggage. May determine the quantity and orientation of cargo and compute aircraft center of gravity. May accompany aircraft as member of flight crew and monitor and handle cargo in flight, and assist and brief passengers on safety and emergency procedures. Includes loadmasters.

- **2014 employment:** 5,800
- **May 2014 median annual wage:** $47,760
- **Projected employment change, 2014–24:**
  - **Number of new jobs:** 0
  - **Growth rate:** 0 percent (little or no change)
- **Education and training:**
  - **Typical entry-level education:** High school diploma or equivalent
  - **Work experience in a related occupation:** Less than 5 years
  - **Typical on-the-job training:** None

First-Line Supervisors of Helpers, Laborers, and Material Movers, Hand

(O*NET 53-1021.00 and 53-1021.01)

Directly supervise and coordinate the activities of helpers, laborers, or material movers.

- **2014 employment:** 173,100
- **May 2014 median annual wage:** $46,690
- **Projected employment change, 2014–24:**
  - **Number of new jobs:** 3,800
  - **Growth rate:** 2 percent (slower than average)
- **Education and training:**
  - **Typical entry-level education:** High school diploma or equivalent
  - **Work experience in a related occupation:** Less than 5 years
  - **Typical on-the-job training:** None

First-Line Supervisors of Transportation and Material-Moving Machine and Vehicle Operators

(O*NET 53-1031.00)

Directly supervise and coordinate activities of transportation and material-moving machine and vehicle operators and helpers.

- **2014 employment:** 199,700
- **May 2014 median annual wage:** $54,930
- **Projected employment change, 2014–24:**
  - **Number of new jobs:** 5,900
  - **Growth rate:** 3 percent (slower than average)
- **Education and training:**
  - **Typical entry-level education:** High school diploma or equivalent
  - **Work experience in a related occupation:** Less than 5 years
  - **Typical on-the-job training:** None

Airfield Operations Specialists

(O*NET 53-2022.00)

Ensure the safe takeoff and landing of commercial and military aircraft. Duties include coordinating between air-traffic control and maintenance personnel; dispatching; using airfield landing and navigational aids; implementing airfield safety procedures; monitoring and maintaining flight records; and applying knowledge of weather information.

- **2014 employment:** 7,200
- **May 2014 median annual wage:** $49,180

- **Projected employment change, 2014–24:**
  - **Number of new jobs:** 300
  - **Growth rate:** 4 percent (slower than average)
- **Education and training:**
  - **Typical entry-level education:** High school diploma or equivalent
  - **Work experience in a related occupation:** None
  - **Typical on-the-job training:** Long-term on-the-job training

Ambulance Drivers and Attendants, Except Emergency Medical Technicians

(O*NET 53-3011.00)

Drive ambulance or assist ambulance driver in transporting sick, injured, or convalescent persons. Assist in lifting patients.

- **2014 employment:** 19,600
- **May 2014 median annual wage:** $24,080
- **Projected employment change, 2014–24:**
  - **Number of new jobs:** 6,500
  - **Growth rate:** 33 percent (much faster than average)
- **Education and training:**
  - **Typical entry-level education:** High school diploma or equivalent
  - **Work experience in a related occupation:** None
  - **Typical on-the-job training:** Moderate-term on-the-job training

Subway and Streetcar Operators

(O*NET 53-4041.00)

Operate subway or elevated suburban trains with no separate locomotive, or electric-powered streetcar, to transport passengers. May handle fares.

- **2014 employment:** 12,000
- **May 2014 median annual wage:** $62,130
- **Projected employment change, 2014–24:**
  - **Number of new jobs:** 600
  - **Growth rate:** 5 percent (about as fast as average)
- **Education and training:**
  - **Typical entry-level education:** High school diploma or equivalent
  - **Work experience in a related occupation:** None
  - **Typical on-the-job training:** Moderate-term on-the-job training

Bridge and Lock Tenders

(O*NET 53-6011.00)

Operate and tend bridges, canal locks, and lighthouses to permit marine passage on inland waterways, near shores, and at danger points in waterway passages. May supervise such operations. Includes drawbridge operators, lock operators, and slip bridge operators.

- **2014 employment:** 3,500
- **May 2014 median annual wage:** $48,120
- **Projected employment change, 2014–24:**
  - **Number of new jobs:** 0
  - **Growth rate:** –1 percent (little or no change)
- **Education and training:**
  - **Typical entry-level education:** High school diploma or equivalent
  - **Work experience in a related occupation:** None
  - **Typical on-the-job training:** Short-term on-the-job training

Parking Lot Attendants

(O*NET 53-6021.00)

Park vehicles or issue tickets for customers in a parking lot or garage. May collect a fee.

- **2014 employment:** 135,600
- **May 2014 median annual wage:** $19,800
- **Projected employment change, 2014–24:**
  - **Number of new jobs:** 5,800
  - **Growth rate:** 4 percent (slower than average)
- **Education and training:**
  - **Typical entry-level education:** No formal educational credential
  - **Work experience in a related occupation:** None
  - **Typical on-the-job training:** Short-term on-the-job training

Automotive and Watercraft Service Attendants

(O*NET 53-6031.00)

Service automobiles, buses, trucks, boats, and other automotive or marine vehicles with fuel, lubricants, and accessories. Collect payment for services and supplies. May lubricate the vehicle, change motor oil, install antifreeze, or replace lights or other accessories, such as windshield wiper blades or fan belts. May repair or replace tires.

- **2014 employment:** 105,800
- **May 2014 median annual wage:** $20,900
- **Projected employment change, 2014–24:**
  - **Number of new jobs:** 11,700
  - **Growth rate:** 11 percent (faster than average)
- **Education and training:**
  - **Typical entry-level education:** No formal educational credential
  - **Work experience in a related occupation:** None
  - **Typical on-the-job training:** Short-term on-the-job training

Traffic Technicians

(O*NET 53-6041.00)

Work under the direction of a traffic engineer to conduct field studies determining the volume and speed of traffic, the effectiveness of signals, the adequacy of lighting, and other factors that influence traffic conditions.

- **2014 employment:** 6,800
- **May 2014 median annual wage:** $43,430
- **Projected employment change, 2014–24:**
  - **Number of new jobs:** 400
  - **Growth rate:** 6 percent (about as fast as average)
- **Education and training:**
  - **Typical entry-level education:** High school diploma or equivalent
  - **Work experience in a related occupation:** None
  - **Typical on-the-job training:** Moderate-term on-the-job training

Transportation Inspectors

(O*NET 53-6051.00, 53-6051.01, 53-6051.07, and 53-6051.08)

Inspect equipment or goods in connection with the safe transport of cargo or people. Includes rail transportation inspectors, such as freight inspectors; rail inspectors; and other inspectors of transportation vehicles, not elsewhere classified. Excludes "Transportation Security Screeners" (33-9093).

- **2014 employment:** 26,400

- **May 2014 median annual wage:** $69,170
- **Projected employment change, 2014–24:**
  - **Number of new jobs:** 300
  - **Growth rate:** 1 percent (little or no change)
- **Education and training:**
  - **Typical entry-level education:** High school diploma or equivalent
  - **Work experience in a related occupation:** None
  - **Typical on-the-job training:** Moderate-term on-the-job training

Transportation Attendants, Except Flight Attendants

(O*NET 53-6061.00)

Provide services to ensure the safety and comfort of passengers aboard ships, buses, and trains or within the station or terminal. Perform duties such as greeting passengers, explaining the use of safety equipment, serving meals or beverages, and answering questions related to travel. Excludes "Baggage Porters and Bellhops" (39-6011).

- **2014 employment:** 16,500
- **May 2014 median annual wage:** $23,380
- **Projected employment change, 2014–24:**
  - **Number of new jobs:** 1,000
  - **Growth rate:** 6 percent (about as fast as average)
- **Education and training:**
  - **Typical entry-level education:** High school diploma or equivalent
  - **Work experience in a related occupation:** None
  - **Typical on-the-job training:** Short-term on-the-job training

Gas Compressor and Gas Pumping Station Operators

(O*NET 53-7071.00)

Operate steam, gas, electric motor, or internal combustion engine-driven compressors. Transmit, compress, or recover gases, such as butane, nitrogen, hydrogen, and natural gas.

- **2014 employment:** 5,100
- **May 2014 median annual wage:** $56,280
- **Projected employment change, 2014–24:**
  - **Number of new jobs:** 200
  - **Growth rate:** 3 percent (slower than average)
- **Education and training:**
  - **Typical entry-level education:** High school diploma or equivalent
  - **Work experience in a related occupation:** None
  - **Typical on-the-job training:** Moderate-term on-the-job training

Pump Operators, Except Wellhead Pumpers

(O*NET 53-7072.00)

Tend, control, or operate power-driven, stationary, or portable pumps and manifold systems to transfer gases, oil, other liquids, slurries, or powdered materials to and from various vessels and processes.

- **2014 employment:** 13,100
- **May 2014 median annual wage:** $43,500
- **Projected employment change, 2014–24:**
  - **Number of new jobs:** 1,100
  - **Growth rate:** 8 percent (about as fast as average)
- **Education and training:**
  - **Typical entry-level education:** High school diploma or equivalent
  - **Work experience in a related occupation:** None
  - **Typical on-the-job training:** Moderate-term on-the-job training

Wellhead Pumpers

(O*NET 53-7073.00)

Operate power pumps and auxiliary equipment to produce and maintain the flow of oil or gas from wells in oil fields.

- **2014 employment:** 13,900
- **May 2014 median annual wage:** $47,340
- **Projected employment change, 2014–24:**
  - **Number of new jobs:** 1,800
  - **Growth rate:** 13 percent (faster than average)
- **Education and training:**
  - **Typical entry-level education:** High school diploma or equivalent
  - **Work experience in a related occupation:** Less than 5 years
  - **Typical on-the-job training:** Moderate-term on-the-job training

Mine Shuttle Car Operators

(O*NET 53-7111.00)

Operate diesel or electric-powered shuttle cars in underground mines to transport materials from the working face to mine cars or conveyors.

- **2014 employment:** 2,700
- **May 2014 median annual wage:** $55,000
- **Projected employment change, 2014–24:**
  - **Number of new jobs:** –100
  - **Growth rate:** –2 percent (decline)
- **Education and training:**
  - **Typical entry-level education:** No formal educational credential
  - **Work experience in a related occupation:** None
  - **Typical on-the-job training:** Short-term on-the-job training

Tank Car, Truck, and Ship Loaders

(O*NET 53-7121.00)

Load and unload chemicals and bulk solids, such as coal, sand, and grain, into or from tank cars, trucks, or ships using material moving equipment. May perform a variety of other tasks relating to the shipment of products. May gauge or sample shipping tanks and test them for leaks.

- **2014 employment:** 13,000
- **May 2014 median annual wage:** $41,180
- **Projected employment change, 2014–24:**
  - **Number of new jobs:** 500
  - **Growth rate:** 4 percent (slower than average)
- **Education and training:**
  - **Typical entry-level education:** No formal educational credential
  - **Work experience in a related occupation:** None
  - **Typical on-the-job training:** Short-term on-the-job training

Occupational Information Network Coverage

The Occupational Information Network (O*NET), which replaced the Dictionary of Occupational Titles, is used by public employment service offices to classify and place jobseekers. The O*NET was developed by job analysts. The information on job duties, knowledge and skills, education and training, and other occupational characteristics comes directly from workers and employers. Information on O*NET is available from O*NET Project, U.S. Department of Labor/ETA, 200 Constitution Ave. NW, Room N-5637, Washington, DC 20210-0001. Internet: www.doleta.gov/programs/onet.

The O*NET reflects the 2010 Standard Occupational Classification (SOC) system. Presently with 845 detailed occupations, the SOC represents the federal government's most recent effort to analyze the occupational structure in the United States and to provide a universal occupational classification system. All federal agencies that collect occupational data adhere to the SOC. Information on the SOC, including its occupational structure, is available on the Internet: www.bls.gov/soc.

Occupational profiles in this 2016–2017 edition of the *Handbook* list the SOC codes that relate to, or match the definitions used in, the Bureau's Occupational Employment Statistics (OES) survey—the principal source of occupational employment data in the *Handbook*. The SOC codes are listed in each profile in one column of the Employment Projections data table. All related O*NET-SOC occupations also appear in the table below. The table is arranged by the O*NET-SOC code, followed by the O*NET-SOC title. The O*NET-SOC title provides a page reference to the corresponding *Handbook* profile or listing in the section called "Data for Occupations Not Covered in Detail."

O*NET-SOC Code	O*NET Title	Page
11-1011.00	Chief Executives	686
11-1011.03	Chief Sustainability Officers	686
11-1021.00	General and Operations Managers	686
11-1031.00	Legislators	924
11-2011.00	Advertising and Promotions Managers	630
11-2011.01	Green Marketers	630
11-2021.00	Marketing Managers	630
11-2022.00	Sales Managers	681
11-2031.00	Public Relations and Fundraising Managers	678
11-3011.00	Administrative Services Managers	628
11-3021.00	Computer and Information Systems Managers	638
11-3031.00	Financial Managers	652
11-3031.01	Treasurers and Controllers	652
11-3031.02	Financial Managers, Branch or Department	652
11-3051.00	Industrial Production Managers	660
11-3051.01	Quality Control Systems Managers	660
11-3051.02	Geothermal Production Managers	660
11-3051.03	Biofuels Production Managers	660
11-3051.04	Biomass Power Plant Managers	660
11-3051.05	Methane/Landfill Gas Collection System Operators	660
11-3051.06	Hydroelectric Production Managers	660
11-3061.00	Purchasing Managers	172
11-3071.00	Transportation, Storage, and Distribution Managers	924
11-3111.00	Compensation and Benefits Managers	636
11-3121.00	Human Resources Managers	657
11-3131.00	Training and Development Managers	688
11-9013.00	Farmers, Ranchers, and Other Agricultural Managers	649
11-9013.01	Nursery and Greenhouse Managers	649
11-9013.02	Farm and Ranch Managers	649
11-9013.03	Aquacultural Managers	649
11-9021.00	Construction Managers	641
11-9031.00	Education Administrators, Preschool and Childcare Center/Program	667
11-9032.00	Education Administrators, Elementary and Secondary School	644
11-9033.00	Education Administrators, Postsecondary	670
11-9041.00	Architectural and Engineering Managers	633
11-9041.01	Biofuels/Biodiesel Technology and Product Development Managers	633
11-9051.00	Food Service Managers	655
11-9061.00	Funeral Service Managers	780
11-9071.00	Gaming Managers	783
11-9081.00	Lodging Managers	662
11-9111.00	Medical and Health Services Managers	665
11-9121.00	Natural Sciences Managers	668
11-9121.01	Clinical Research Coordinators	668
11-9121.02	Water Resource Specialists	668
11-9131.00	Postmasters and Mail Superintendents	924
11-9141.00	Property, Real Estate, and Community Association Managers	675
11-9151.00	Social and Community Service Managers	683
11-9161.00	Emergency Management Directors	647
13-1011.00	Agents and Business Managers of Artists, Performers, and Athletes	913
13-1021.00	Buyers and Purchasing Agents, Farm Products	133
13-1022.00	Wholesale and Retail Buyers, Except Farm Products	133
13-1023.00	Purchasing Agents, Except Wholesale, Retail, and Farm Products	133
13-1031.00	Claims Adjusters, Examiners, and Investigators	136
13-1031.01	Claims Examiners, Property and Casualty Insurance	136
13-1031.02	Insurance Adjusters, Examiners, and Investigators	136
13-1032.00	Insurance Appraisers, Auto Damage	136
13-1041.00	Compliance Officers	914
13-1051.00	Cost Estimators	142
13-1071.00	Human Resources Specialists	151
13-1074.00	Farm Labor Contractors	914
13-1075.00	Labor Relations Specialists	156
13-1081.00	Logisticians	160
13-1081.01	Logistics Engineers	160
13-1081.02	Logistics Analysts	160
13-1111.00	Management Analysts	162
13-1121.00	Meeting, Convention, and Event Planners	167
13-1131.00	Fundraisers	149
13-1141.00	Compensation, Benefits, and Job Analysis Specialists	140
13-1151.00	Training and Development Specialists	178
13-1161.00	Market Research Analysts and Marketing Specialists	165
13-2011.00	Accountants and Auditors	125
13-2011.01	Accountants	125
13-2011.02	Auditors	125
13-2021.00	Appraisers and Assessors of Real Estate	128
13-2021.01	Assessors	128
13-2021.02	Appraisers, Real Estate	128
13-2031.00	Budget Analysts	131
13-2041.00	Credit Analysts	914
13-2051.00	Financial Analysts	144
13-2052.00	Personal Financial Advisors	170
13-2053.00	Insurance Underwriters	153
13-2061.00	Financial Examiners	147
13-2071.00	Credit Counselors	914
13-2072.00	Loan Officers	158
13-2081.00	Tax Examiners and Collectors, and Revenue Agents	175
13-2082.00	Tax Preparers	914
15-1111.00	Computer and Information Research Scientists	205
15-1121.00	Computer Systems Analysts	215
15-1121.01	Informatics Nurse Specialists	215
15-1122.00	Information Security Analysts	220
15-1131.00	Computer Programmers	209
15-1132.00	Software Developers, Applications	225
15-1133.00	Software Developers, Systems Software	225
15-1134.00	Web Developers	227
15-1141.00	Database Administrators	217
15-1142.00	Network and Computer Systems Administrators	222
15-1143.00	Computer Network Architects	207
15-1143.01	Telecommunications Engineering Specialists	207
15-1151.00	Computer User Support Specialists	212
15-1152.00	Computer Network Support Specialists	212
15-2011.00	Actuaries	692
15-2021.00	Mathematicians	695
15-2031.00	Operations Research Analysts	697
15-2041.00	Statisticians	700

Glossary

A

Annual: recurring, done, or performed every year; yearly

Applicant: a person who formally applies for a job

Apprenticeship: a formal relationship between a worker and sponsor that consists of a combination of on-the-job training and related occupation-specific instruction in which the worker learns the practical and theoretical aspects of an occupation; apprenticeship programs are sponsored by individual employers, joint employer-and-labor groups, and employee associations; apprenticeship programs usually provide at least 144 hours of occupation-specific technical instruction and 2,000 hours of on-the-job training per year over a 3- to 5-year period; examples of occupations that utilize apprenticeships include electricians and structural iron and steel workers

Associate's degree: degree awarded usually for at least 2 years of full-time academic study beyond high school

Average: the quantity calculated by adding a set of numbers and dividing the resulting sum by the quantity of numbers summed; see *Mean*

B

Baby-boom generation: individuals born between 1946 and 1964

Bachelor's degree: degree awarded usually for at least 4 years of full-time academic study beyond high school

Base year: year used as a reference point for comparison with later years; for example, 2014 is the base year for the 2014–2024 employment projections; employment in the base year is actual 2014 data, whereas employment in the target, or projection, year is projected

Business cycle: the periods of growth and decline in an economy; there are four stages in the cycle: expansion, when the economy grows; peak, the high point of an expansion; contraction, when the economy slows down; and trough, the low point of a contraction

C

Certification: award for demonstrating competency in a skill or set of skills, typically through the passage of an examination, work experience, training, or some combination thereof; certification is always voluntary; some certification programs may require a certain level of educational achievement for eligibility

Consolidation: the merger of two or more commercial interests or corporations

Current Population Survey (CPS): a national survey that samples 60,000 households on a monthly basis and collects information on labor force characteristics of the U.S. civilian noninstitutional population; the CPS is conducted by the Census Bureau for the Bureau of Labor Statistics

D

Demand for workers: total job openings resulting from employment growth and the need to replace workers who leave jobs

Doctoral or professional degree: degree awarded usually for at least 3 years of full-time academic work beyond a bachelor's degree; for example, some science and other occupations need a doctoral degree, and all lawyers, physicians, and dentists need a professional degree for employment

Domestic sourcing: moving jobs to lower cost regions of the United States instead of to other countries

Duties: the major tasks or activities that employees in an occupation usually perform

E

Earnings: pay or wages of a worker or group of workers for services performed during a specific period—for example, hourly, daily, weekly, or annually; see *Pay*, *Wages*

Education: levels of education typically needed for entry into an occupation are classified as follows:

- Less than high school
- High school diploma or equivalent
- Some college, no degree
- Associate's degree
- Bachelor's degree
- Master's degree
- Doctoral or professional degree

Employed: the situation of a person who has an agreement with an employer to work full time, part time, or on a contractual basis for that employer

Employment: the number of jobs in an occupation, including full-time, part-time, and self-employed

Employment growth/shrinkage: increase or decrease in the number of jobs

Entry level: the starting level for workers who are new to an occupation; different occupations may require different levels of education, training, or experience upon entry

F

Fieldwork: an investigation or search for material, data, etc., made in the field as opposed to the classroom, the laboratory, or official headquarters; for example, archeologists working at a dig site in the desert; historians or curators finding or collecting artifacts for museums; and environmental technicians collecting water samples from a pond, a stream, or an ocean

Fixed work schedules: schedules of employees who work the same hours on an ongoing basis—for example, 9 a.m.–5 p.m.

Flexible work schedules: schedules of employees who set their own hours within specified guidelines and with a fixed number of total hours

Full time: 35 hours or more per week, according to the Current Population Survey

G

GDP (gross domestic product): the market value of all final goods and services produced within a country in a given period; the most commonly used measure of the size of the overall economy; the Bureau of Economic Analysis (BEA) produces estimates of GDP

GED (General Educational Development): a credential signifying the completion of a program that is equivalent to a high school curriculum

Greater than full time: more than 40 hours per week

Growth rate: the percent change in the number of jobs added or lost in a U.S. occupation or industry over a given projection period; growth rate adjectives used in the *OOH* are defined by the following percent changes for the 2014–24 employment projections:

- Much faster than the average: 22 percent or more
- Faster than the average: 15 percent to 21 percent
- As fast as the average: 8 percent to 14 percent
- More slowly than the average: 3 percent to 7 percent
- Little or no change: -2 percent to 2 percent
- Decline: -3 percent or more

H

High school diploma or equivalent: award or credential that is equivalent to a high school diploma, such as a high school diploma itself or the General Educational Development (GED) credential

Household: all persons who occupy a housing unit such as an apartment or a single-family home

I

Important qualities: characteristics and personality traits that are likely needed for workers to be successful in given occupations

Industry: a group of establishments that produce similar products or provide similar services; see *North American Industry Classification System (NAICS)*

Injury and illness rate: ratio expressing the number of workers sustaining a wound, strain, or infection due to an incident or exposure at the workplace per 100 workers; the Occupational Safety and Health Administration (OSHA) considers an injury or illness to be work-related if an event or exposure in the work environment either caused or contributed to the resulting condition or significantly aggravated a preexisting condition; in general, an *OOH* profile will cite an injury and illness rate only if it is particularly high, compared with the rate for all other occupations

Internship: training under supervision in a professional setting, does not include internships that are suggested for advancement

J

Job: a specific instance of employment; a position of employment to be filled at an establishment; *see* Employment

Job openings: job openings occur when occupations grow, which creates new jobs, and when workers leave an occupation permanently, resulting in the need to replace them

Job outlook: a statement that conveys the projected rate of growth or decline in employment in an occupation over the next 10 years; also compares the projected growth rate with that projected for all other occupations; also see *Growth rate*

Job prospects: a qualitative measure of the competition for jobs that takes into consideration factors such as the growth or decline in numbers of jobs, the expected number of qualified workers, and/or the expected number of applicants; a comparison of the number of jobs with the number of potential workers and job seekers

K

L

Labor force: the sum of all persons 16 years and older in the civilian noninstitutional population who are either employed or unemployed but available for work and actively looking for work

Less than high school: the completion of any level of primary or secondary education that did not result in the awarding of a high school diploma or the equivalent

Licenses: permission granted by government agencies or other accrediting bodies that allows someone to work in a particular occupation or perform certain duties

Long-term on-the-job training: more than 12 months of on-the-job training, or alternatively, combined work experience and formal classroom instruction (not including apprenticeships) is needed for the worker to attain competency in the skills needed in the occupation

M

Master's degree: degree awarded usually for 1 or 2 years of full-time academic study beyond a bachelor's degree

Mean: the mathematical average of a set of numbers, calculated by adding the numbers and dividing the total by the number of numbers summed; see *Average*

Median: the middle number in an ordered list of numbers

Moderate-term on-the-job training: more than 1 month and up to 12 months of combined on-the-job experience and informal training is needed for the worker to attain competency in the skills needed in the occupation

N

North American Industry Classification System (NAICS): industry classification system used by federal statistical agencies in classifying business establishments for the purpose of collecting, analyzing, and publishing statistical data related to the U.S. economy

New job: an addition of a position to an establishment's payroll, usually as a result of economic expansion

Nonfixed work schedules: schedules of employees who work different hours on one job; often used to accommodate particular traits of individual workers or because the work required by the employers varies for each individual

Number of jobs: number of actual instances of employment according to the BLS National Employment Matrix; see www.bls.gov/emp/ep_projections_methods.htm for more information about the Matrix

Numeric change in employment: a projected change in the number of jobs in an occupation or industry

O

O*NET: an online research source that provides detailed descriptions of occupations for use by job seekers, workforce development and human resources professionals, students, and researchers; created for the U.S. Department of Labor, Employment and Training Administration, by the National Center for O*NET Development

On-the-job training: training or preparation that is typically needed, once employed in an occupation, to attain competency in the occupation; training is occupation-specific rather than job-specific; skills learned can be transferred to another job in the same occupation; examples of on-the-job training include:

- Apprenticeship
- Internship/Residency
- Long-term on-the-job training
- Moderate-term on-the-job training
- Short-term on-the-job training

Occupation: a craft, trade, profession, or other means of earning a living; a set of activities or tasks that employees are paid to perform and that together go by a certain name; employees who are in the same occupation perform essentially the same tasks, whether or not they work in the same industry

P

Pay: earnings or wages of a worker or a group of workers for services performed during a specific period—for example, hourly, daily, weekly, or annually; also see *Earnings*, *Wages*

Part time: less than 35 hours of work per week, according to the Current Population Survey

Percent: one part in a hundred—for example, 62 percent (also written 62%) means 62 parts out of 100

Percent change in employment: growth rates expressed as percentages

Percentile wage estimate: the value of a wage below which a certain percentage of workers fall

Personal consumption: total goods and services purchased by individuals in the U.S. economy; the amount of goods and services used or purchased by individuals or households in the U.S. economy; a key statistic in measuring or calculating overall GDP

Population: the total number of inhabitants of the United States, or the total number of observations under consideration in a statistical study

Postsecondary non-degree award: a certificate or other credential that is awarded by an educational institution upon completion of formal postsecondary schooling; the postsecondary non-degree certificate is different from certifications issued by professional organizations or certifying bodies; postsecondary non-degree award programs may last from just a few weeks to 2 years—examples of those who need postsecondary non-degree awards are nursing assistants, emergency medical technicians (EMT's) and paramedics, and hairstylists

Q

Qualifications: personality traits, education, training, work experience, or other qualities workers need to enter an occupation

R

Related occupations: occupations that have similar job duties; see *Similar occupations*

Replacement needs: the number of projected openings expected to result from workers who retire or permanently leave an occupation; replacement needs are calculated from monthly CPS data

Replacement rate: the rate at which workers permanently leave the occupations in which they are employed; large occupations that have high replacement rates need many workers to fill jobs that are vacated

Residency: training under supervision in a professional setting

Rotating work schedules: schedules that have a fixed number of hours and time off over a period of more than 1 week, but not a set weekly schedule

S

Salary: earnings of a worker or a group of workers for services performed during a specific period—for example, an hourly straight-time wage rate or, for workers not paid on an hourly basis, straight-time earnings divided by hours worked

Seasonal employment: employment that is not expected to last a full year, but that may reoccur; for example, many retail sales associates are hired only for the busy holiday season, and forest firefighters are more likely to be employed during the summer months, when vegetation is dryer

Self-employed: those who work for profit or fees in their own business, profession, trade, or farm; only the unincorporated self-employed are included in the self-employed category

Short-term on-the-job training: 1 month or less of on-the-job experience and informal training

Similar occupations: occupations that tend to share common daily tasks or require similar skills, rather than similar wages or education

SOC: the Standard Occupational Classification (SOC) system, which is used by all federal statistical agencies to classify workers into occupational categories for the purpose of collecting, calculating, or disseminating data

Some college, no degree: a high school diploma or equivalent, plus the completion of one or more postsecondary courses that did not result in a degree or award

Supply of workers: the number of people in the labor force; for most occupations, the supply of workers is smaller than the total number in the labor force because the supply is limited to those with particular education or training requirements

T

Training: see *On-the-job training*

U

Undergraduate degree: bachelor's degree or associate's degree

Union membership: the group of workers who join labor unions, hold union memberships, and enjoy benefits of the organized, coordinated efforts of the union to improve the work environment

V

Vocational school: a secondary school that teaches vocational trades, such as construction trades; vocational schools may or may not award degrees

W

Wages: earnings or pay of a worker or a group of workers for services performed during a specific period—for example, hourly, daily, weekly, or annually; also see *Earnings*, *Pay*

Work experience in a related occupation: the level of work experience in an occupation related to a given occupation; captures work experience that is commonly considered necessary by employers or is a commonly accepted substitute for other more formal types of training or education

Work schedules: the number of daily hours, weekly hours, and annual weeks that employees in an occupation are scheduled to, and do, work; short-term fluctuations and one-time events are not considered unless the change becomes permanent; types of work schedules include the following:

- Fixed work schedule
- Flexible work schedule
- Full time
- Greater than full time
- Nonfixed work schedule
- Part time
- Rotating work schedule

X, Y, Z

Index

B

C

D

E

F

G

H

I

J

K

L

M

N

O

P

Q

R

S

T

U

V

W

X

Y

Z